App. Alt.	OCT.—MAR. SUN Lower Limb	Upper Limb	APR.—SEPT. Lower Limb	Upper Limb	STARS PLANETS
° ′	′	′	′	′	′
0 00	−17·5	−49·8	−17·8	−49·6	−33·8
0 03	16·9	49·2	17·2	49·0	33·2
0 06	16·3	48·6	16·6	48·4	32·6
0 09	15·7	48·0	16·0	47·8	32·0
0 12	15·2	47·5	15·4	47·2	31·5
0 15	14·6	46·9	14·8	46·6	30·9
0 18	−14·1	−46·4	−14·3	−46·1	−30·4
0 21	13·5	45·8	13·8	45·6	29·8
0 24	13·0	45·3	13·3	45·1	29·3
0 27	12·5	44·8	12·8	44·6	28·8
0 30	12·0	44·3	12·3	44·1	28·3
0 33	11·6	43·9	11·8	43·6	27·9
0 36	−11·1	−43·4	−11·3	−43·1	−27·4
0 39	10·6	42·9	10·9	42·7	26·9
0 42	10·2	42·5	10·5	42·3	26·5
0 45	9·8	42·1	10·0	41·8	26·1
0 48	9·4	41·7	9·6	41·4	25·7
0 51	9·0	41·3	9·2	41·0	25·3
0 54	−8·6	−40·9	−8·8	−40·6	−24·9
0 57	8·2	40·5	8·4	40·2	24·5
1 00	7·8	40·1	8·0	39·8	24·1
1 03	7·4	39·7	7·7	39·5	23·7
1 06	7·1	39·4	7·3	39·1	23·4
1 09	6·7	39·0	7·0	38·8	23·0
1 12	−6·4	−38·7	−6·6	−38·4	−22·7
1 15	6·0	38·3	6·3	38·1	22·3
1 18	5·7	38·0	6·0	37·8	22·0
1 21	5·4	37·7	5·7	37·5	21·7
1 24	5·1	37·4	5·3	37·1	21·4
1 27	4·8	37·1	5·0	36·8	21·1
1 30	−4·5	−36·8	−4·7	−36·5	−20·8
1 35	4·0	36·3	4·3	36·1	20·3
1 40	3·6	35·9	3·8	35·6	19·9
1 45	3·1	35·4	3·4	35·2	19·4
1 50	2·7	35·0	2·9	34·7	19·0
1 55	2·3	34·6	2·5	34·3	18·6
2 00	−1·9	−34·2	−2·1	−33·9	−18·2
2 05	1·5	33·8	1·7	33·5	17·8
2 10	1·1	33·4	1·4	33·2	17·4
2 15	0·8	33·1	1·0	32·8	17·1
2 20	0·4	32·7	0·7	32·5	16·7
2 25	−0·1	32·4	−0·3	32·1	16·4
2 30	+0·2	−32·1	0·0	−31·8	−16·1
2 35	0·5	31·8	+0·3	31·5	15·8
2 40	0·8	31·5	0·6	31·2	15·4
2 45	1·1	31·2	0·9	30·9	15·2
2 50	1·4	30·9	1·2	30·6	14·9
2 55	1·7	30·6	1·4	30·4	14·6
3 00	+2·0	−30·3	+1·7	−30·1	−14·3
3 05	2·2	30·1	2·0	29·8	14·1
3 10	2·5	29·8	2·2	29·6	13·8
3 15	2·7	29·6	2·5	29·3	13·6
3 20	2·9	29·4	2·7	29·1	13·4
3 25	3·2	29·1	2·9	28·9	13·1
3 30	+3·4	−28·9	+3·1	−28·7	−12·9

App. Alt.	OCT.—MAR. SUN Lower Limb	Upper Limb	APR.—SEPT. Lower Limb	Upper Limb	STARS PLANETS
° ′	′	′	′	′	′
3 30	+3·4	−28·9	+3·1	−28·7	−12·9
3 35	3·6	28·7	3·3	28·5	12·7
3 40	3·8	28·5	3·6	28·2	12·5
3 45	4·0	28·3	3·8	28·0	12·3
3 50	4·2	28·1	4·0	27·8	12·1
3 55	4·4	27·9	4·1	27·7	11·9
4 00	+4·6	−27·7	+4·3	−27·5	−11·7
4 05	4·8	27·5	4·5	27·3	11·5
4 10	4·9	27·4	4·7	27·1	11·4
4 15	5·1	27·2	4·9	26·9	11·2
4 20	5·3	27·0	5·0	26·8	11·0
4 25	5·4	26·9	5·2	26·6	10·9
4 30	+5·6	−26·7	+5·3	−26·5	−10·7
4 35	5·7	26·6	5·5	26·3	10·6
4 40	5·9	26·4	5·6	26·2	10·4
4 45	6·0	26·3	5·8	26·0	10·3
4 50	6·2	26·1	5·9	25·9	10·1
4 55	6·3	26·0	6·1	25·7	10·0
5 00	+6·4	−25·9	+6·2	−25·6	−9·8
5 05	6·6	25·7	6·3	25·5	9·7
5 10	6·7	25·6	6·5	25·3	9·6
5 15	6·8	25·5	6·6	25·2	9·5
5 20	7·0	25·3	6·7	25·1	9·3
5 25	7·1	25·2	6·8	25·0	9·2
5 30	+7·2	−25·1	+6·9	−24·9	−9·1
5 35	7·3	25·0	7·1	24·7	9·0
5 40	7·4	24·9	7·2	24·6	8·9
5 45	7·5	24·8	7·3	24·5	8·8
5 50	7·6	24·7	7·4	24·4	8·7
5 55	7·7	24·6	7·5	24·3	8·6
6 00	+7·8	−24·5	+7·6	−24·2	−8·5
6 10	8·0	24·3	7·8	24·0	8·3
6 20	8·2	24·1	8·0	23·8	8·1
6 30	8·4	23·9	8·2	23·6	7·9
6 40	8·6	23·7	8·3	23·5	7·7
6 50	8·7	23·6	8·5	23·3	7·6
7 00	+8·9	−23·4	+8·7	−23·1	−7·4
7 10	9·1	23·2	8·8	23·0	7·2
7 20	9·2	23·1	9·0	22·8	7·1
7 30	9·3	23·0	9·1	22·7	6·9
7 40	9·5	22·8	9·2	22·6	6·8
7 50	9·6	22·7	9·4	22·4	6·7
8 00	+9·7	−22·6	+9·5	−22·3	−6·6
8 10	9·9	22·4	9·6	22·2	6·4
8 20	10·0	22·3	9·7	22·1	6·3
8 30	10·1	22·2	9·9	21·9	6·2
8 40	10·2	22·1	10·0	21·8	6·1
8 50	10·3	22·0	10·1	21·7	6·0
9 00	+10·4	−21·9	+10·2	−21·6	−5·9
9 10	10·5	21·8	10·3	21·5	5·8
9 20	10·6	21·7	10·4	21·4	5·7
9 30	10·7	21·6	10·5	21·3	5·6
9 40	10·8	21·5	10·6	21·2	5·5
9 50	10·9	21·4	10·6	21·2	5·4
10 00	+11·0	−21·3	+10·7	−21·1	−5·3

Additional corrections for temperature and pressure are given on the following page.

For bubble sextant observations ignore dip and use the star corrections for Sun, planets and stars.

ADDITIONAL REFRACTION CORRECTIONS FOR NON-STANDARD CONDITIONS

App. Alt.	A	B	C	D	E	F	G	H	J	K	L	M	N	P	App. Alt.
° ′	′	′	′	′	′	′	′	′	′	′	′	′	′	′	° ′
00 00	−7·3	−5·9	−4·6	−3·4	−2·2	−1·1	0·0	+1·0	+2·0	+3·0	+4·0	+4·9	+5·9	+6·9	00 00
00 30	5·5	4·5	3·5	2·6	1·7	0·8	0·0	0·8	1·6	2·3	3·1	3·8	4·5	5·3	00 30
01 00	4·4	3·5	2·8	2·0	1·3	0·7	0·0	0·6	1·2	1·8	2·4	3·0	3·6	4·2	01 00
01 30	3·5	2·9	2·2	1·7	1·1	0·5	0·0	0·5	1·0	1·5	2·0	2·5	2·9	3·4	01 30
02 00	2·9	2·4	1·9	1·4	0·9	0·4	0·0	0·4	0·8	1·3	1·7	2·0	2·4	2·8	02 00
02 30	−2·5	−2·0	−1·6	−1·2	−0·8	−0·4	0·0	+0·4	+0·7	+1·1	+1·4	+1·7	+2·1	+2·4	02 30
03 00	2·1	1·7	1·4	1·0	0·7	0·3	0·0	0·3	0·6	0·9	1·2	1·5	1·8	2·1	03 00
03 30	1·9	1·5	1·2	0·9	0·6	0·3	0·0	0·3	0·5	0·8	1·1	1·3	1·6	1·8	03 30
04 00	1·6	1·3	1·1	0·8	0·5	0·3	0·0	0·2	0·5	0·7	0·9	1·2	1·4	1·6	04 00
04 30	1·5	1·2	0·9	0·7	0·5	0·2.	0·0	0·2	0·4	0·6	0·8	1·0	1·3	1·5	04 30
05 00	−1·3	−1·1	−0·9	−0·6	−0·4	−0·2	0·0	+0·2	+0·4	+0·6	+0·8	+0·9	+1·1	+1·3	05 00
06	1·1	0·9	0·7	0·5	0·3	0·2	0·0	0·2	0·3	0·5	0·6	0·8	0·9	1·1	06
07	1·0	0·8	0·6	0·5	0·3	0·1	0·0	0·1	0·3	0·4	0·5	0·7	0·8	0·9	07
08	0·8	0·7	0·5	0·4	0·3	0·1	0·0	0·1	0·2	0·4	0·5	0·6	0·7	0·8	08
09	0·7	0·6	0·5	0·4	0·2	0·1	0·0	0·1	0·2	0·3	0·4	0·5	0·6	0·7	09
10 00	−0·7	−0·5	−0·4	−0·3	−0·2	−0·1	0·0	+0·1	+0·2	+0·3	+0·4	+0·5	+0·6	+0·7	10 00
12	0·6	0·5	0·4	0·3	0·2	0·1	0·0	0·1	0·2	0·2	0·3	0·4	0·5	0·5	12
14	0·5	0·4	0·3	0·2	0·1	0·1	0·0	0·1	0·1	0·2	0·3	0·3	0·4	0·5	14
16	0·4	0·3	0·3	0·2	0·1	0·1	0·0	0·1	0·1	0·2	0·2	0·3	0·3	0·4	16
18	0·4	0·3	0·2	0·2	0·1	−0·1	0·0	+0·1	0·1	0·2	0·2	0·3	0·3	0·4	18
20 00	−0·3	−0·3	−0·2	−0·2	−0·1	0·0	0·0	0·0	+0·1	+0·1	+0·2	+0·2	+0·3	+0·3	20 00
25	0·3	0·2	0·2	0·1	0·1	0·0	0·0	0·0	0·1	0·1	0·1	0·2	0·2	0·2	25
30	0·2	0·2	0·1	0·1	0·1	0·0	0·0	0·0	+0·1	0·1	0·1	0·1	0·2	0·2	30
35	0·2	0·1	0·1	0·1	−0·1	0·0	0·0	0·0	0·0	0·1	0·1	0·1	0·1	0·2	35
40	0·1	0·1	0·1	−0·1	0·0	0·0	0·0	0·0	0·0	+0·1	0·1	0·1	0·1	0·1	40
50 00	−0·1	−0·1	−0·1	0·0	0·0	0·0	0·0	0·0	0·0	0·0	+0·1	+0·1	+0·1	+0·1	50 00

The graph is entered with arguments temperature and pressure to find a zone letter; using as arguments this zone letter and apparent altitude (sextant altitude corrected for index error and dip), a correction is taken from the table. This correction is to be applied to the sextant altitude in addition to the corrections for standard conditions (for the Sun, stars and planets from page A2-A3 and for the Moon from pages xxxiv and xxxv).

THE

NAUTICAL

ALMANAC

FOR THE YEAR

2018

WASHINGTON:
Issued by the
Nautical Almanac Office
United States Naval Observatory
under the authority of the
Secretary of the Navy

TAUNTON:
Issued by
Her Majesty's
Nautical Almanac Office
United Kingdom
Hydrographic Office

U.S. GOVERNMENT PUBLISHING OFFICE
WASHINGTON: 2017

UNITED STATES

Washington: 2017

This is an official U.S. Government edition of this publication and is herein identified to certify its authenticity. Use of the 0-16 ISBN prefix is for U.S. Government Publishing Office Official Editions only. The Superintendent of Documents of the U.S. Government Publishing Office requests that any reprinted edition clearly be labeled as a copy of the authentic work with a new ISBN. See below for additional copyright information prior to reprinting.

UNITED KINGDOM

© *Crown Copyright 2017*

For sale by the Superintendent of Documents, U.S. Government Publishing Office Internet: bookstore.gpo.gov Phone: toll free (866) 512-1800; DC area (202) 512-1800 Fax: (202) 512-2104 Mail: 710 North Capitol Street NW, Washington, DC 20401

PREFACE

The British and American editions of *The Nautical Almanac*, which are identical in content, are produced jointly by H. M. Nautical Almanac Office, part of the United Kingdom Hydrographic Office, under the supervision of S. A. Bell and S. G. Nelmes, and by the Nautical Almanac Office, United States Naval Observatory, under the supervision of S. E. Urban and M. T. Stollberg, to the general requirements of the Royal Navy and of the United States Navy. The Almanac is printed separately in the United Kingdom and in the United States of America.

The data in this almanac, on written application, may be made available for reproduction. It can be made available in a form suitable for direct photographic reproduction, to the appropriate almanac-producing agency in any country; language changes in the headings of the ephemeral pages can be introduced, if desired, during reproduction. Under this arrangement, this almanac, with minor modifications and changes of language, has been adopted by a number of foreign countries.

This volume includes a section on Polar Phenomena. This gives graphs of the semiduration of sunlight, twilight and moonlight at high latitudes from which the times of rising and setting of the Sun and Moon and the times of civil twilight can be calculated. An explanation and examples are also given.

JOHN HUMPHREY
Chief Executive
UK Hydrographic Office
Admiralty Way, Taunton
Somerset, TA1 2DN
United Kingdom

MARC C. ECKARDT
Captain, U.S. Navy
Superintendent, U.S. Naval Observatory
3450 Massachusetts Avenue NW
Washington, D.C. 20392-5420
U.S.A.

December 2016

For sale by the Superintendent of Documents, U.S. Government Publishing Office
Internet: bookstore.gpo.gov   Phone: toll free (866) 512-1800;   DC area (202) 512-1800
Fax: (202) 512-2104 Mail: Stop IDCC, Washington, DC 20402-0001

ISBN 978-0-16-093741-5

RELIGIOUS CALENDARS

Epiphany	Jan. 6	Low Sunday	Apr. 8
Septuagesima Sunday	Jan. 28	Rogation Sunday	May 6
Quinquagesima Sunday	Feb. 11	Ascension Day—Holy Thursday	May 10
Ash Wednesday	Feb. 14	Whit Sunday—Pentecost	May 20
Quadragesima Sunday	Feb. 18	Trinity Sunday	May 27
Palm Sunday	Mar. 25	Corpus Christi	May 31
Good Friday	Mar. 30	First Sunday in Advent	Dec. 2
Easter Day	Apr. 1	Christmas Day (Tuesday)	Dec. 25
First Day of Passover (Pesach)	Mar. 31	Day of Atonement (Yom Kippur)	Sept. 19
Feast of Weeks (Shavuot)	May 20	First day of Tabernacles (Succoth)	Sept. 24
Jewish New Year 5779 (Rosh Hashanah)	Sept. 10		
Ramadân, First day of (tabular)	May 16	Islamic New Year (1440)	Sept. 12

The Jewish and Islamic dates above are tabular dates, which begin at sunset on the previous evening and end at sunset on the date tabulated. In practice, the dates of Islamic fasts and festivals are determined by an actual sighting of the appropriate new moon.

CIVIL CALENDAR—UNITED KINGDOM

Accession of Queen Elizabeth II	Feb. 6	The Queen's Official Birthday†	June 9
St David (Wales)	Mar. 1	Birthday of Prince Philip, Duke of	
Commonwealth Day	Mar. 12	Edinburgh	June 10
St Patrick (Ireland)	Mar. 17	Remembrance Sunday	Nov. 11
Birthday of Queen Elizabeth II	Apr. 21	Birthday of the Prince of Wales	Nov. 14
St George (England)	Apr. 23	St Andrew (Scotland)	Nov. 30
Coronation Day	June 2		

PUBLIC HOLIDAYS

England and Wales—Jan. 1†, Mar. 30, Apr. 2, May 7†, May 28, Aug. 27, Dec. 25, Dec. 26

Northern Ireland—Jan. 1†, Mar. 19†, Mar. 30, Apr. 2, May 7†, May 28, July 12†, Aug. 27, Dec. 25, Dec. 26

Scotland—Jan. 1, Jan. 2, Mar. 30, May 7, May 28†, Aug. 6, Dec. 25, Dec. 26†

CIVIL CALENDAR—UNITED STATES OF AMERICA

New Year's Day	Jan. 1	Labor Day	Sept. 3
Martin Luther King's Birthday	Jan. 15	Columbus Day	Oct. 8
Washington's Birthday	Feb. 19	General Election Day	Nov. 6
Memorial Day	May 28	Veterans Day	Nov. 11
Independence Day	July 4	Thanksgiving Day	Nov. 22

†Dates subject to confirmation

PHASES OF THE MOON

New Moon				First Quarter				Full Moon				Last Quarter			
	d	h	m		d	h	m		d	h	m		d	h	m
								Jan.	2	02	24	Jan.	8	22	25
Jan.	17	02	17	Jan.	24	22	20	Jan.	31	13	27	Feb.	7	15	54
Feb.	15	21	05	Feb.	23	08	09	Mar.	2	00	51	Mar.	9	11	20
Mar.	17	13	12	Mar.	24	15	35	Mar.	31	12	37	Apr.	8	07	18
Apr.	16	01	57	Apr.	22	21	46	Apr.	30	00	58	May	8	02	09
May	15	11	48	May	22	03	49	May	29	14	20	June	6	18	32
June	13	19	43	June	20	10	51	June	28	04	53	July	6	07	51
July	13	02	48	July	19	19	52	July	27	20	20	Aug.	4	18	18
Aug.	11	09	58	Aug.	18	07	49	Aug.	26	11	56	Sept.	3	02	37
Sept.	9	18	01	Sept.	16	23	15	Sept.	25	02	52	Oct.	2	09	45
Oct.	9	03	47	Oct.	16	18	02	Oct.	24	16	45	Oct.	31	16	40
Nov.	7	16	02	Nov.	15	14	54	Nov.	23	05	39	Nov.	30	00	19
Dec.	7	07	20	Dec.	15	11	49	Dec.	22	17	49	Dec.	29	09	34

DAYS OF THE WEEK AND DAYS OF THE YEAR

Day	JAN. Wk Yr	FEB. Wk Yr	MAR. Wk Yr	APR. Wk Yr	MAY Wk Yr	JUNE Wk Yr	JULY Wk Yr	AUG. Wk Yr	SEPT. Wk Yr	OCT. Wk Yr	NOV. Wk Yr	DEC. Wk Yr
1	M. 1	Th. 32	Th. 60	Su. 91	Tu. 121	F. 152	Su. 182	W. 213	Sa. 244	M. 274	Th. 305	Sa. 335
2	Tu. 2	F. 33	F. 61	M. 92	W. 122	Sa. 153	M. 183	Th. 214	Su. 245	Tu. 275	F. 306	Su. 336
3	W. 3	Sa. 34	Sa. 62	Tu. 93	Th. 123	Su. 154	Tu. 184	F. 215	M. 246	W. 276	Sa. 307	M. 337
4	Th. 4	Su. 35	Su. 63	W. 94	F. 124	M. 155	W. 185	Sa. 216	Tu. 247	Th. 277	Su. 308	Tu. 338
5	F. 5	M. 36	M. 64	Th. 95	Sa. 125	Tu. 156	Th. 186	Su. 217	W. 248	F. 278	M. 309	W. 339
6	Sa. 6	Tu. 37	Tu. 65	F. 96	Su. 126	W. 157	F. 187	M. 218	Th. 249	Sa. 279	Tu. 310	Th. 340
7	Su. 7	W. 38	W. 66	Sa. 97	M. 127	Th. 158	Sa. 188	Tu. 219	F. 250	Su. 280	W. 311	F. 341
8	M. 8	Th. 39	Th. 67	Su. 98	Tu. 128	F. 159	Su. 189	W. 220	Sa. 251	M. 281	Th. 312	Sa. 342
9	Tu. 9	F. 40	F. 68	M. 99	W. 129	Sa. 160	M. 190	Th. 221	Su. 252	Tu. 282	F. 313	Su. 343
10	W. 10	Sa. 41	Sa. 69	Tu. 100	Th. 130	Su. 161	Tu. 191	F. 222	M. 253	W. 283	Sa. 314	M. 344
11	Th. 11	Su. 42	Su. 70	W. 101	F. 131	M. 162	W. 192	Sa. 223	Tu. 254	Th. 284	Su. 315	Tu. 345
12	F. 12	M. 43	M. 71	Th. 102	Sa. 132	Tu. 163	Th. 193	Su. 224	W. 255	F. 285	M. 316	W. 346
13	Sa. 13	Tu. 44	Tu. 72	F. 103	Su. 133	W. 164	F. 194	M. 225	Th. 256	Sa. 286	Tu. 317	Th. 347
14	Su. 14	W. 45	W. 73	Sa. 104	M. 134	Th. 165	Sa. 195	Tu. 226	F. 257	Su. 287	W. 318	F. 348
15	M. 15	Th. 46	Th. 74	Su. 105	Tu. 135	F. 166	Su. 196	W. 227	Sa. 258	M. 288	Th. 319	Sa. 349
16	Tu. 16	F. 47	F. 75	M. 106	W. 136	Sa. 167	M. 197	Th. 228	Su. 259	Tu. 289	F. 320	Su. 350
17	W. 17	Sa. 48	Sa. 76	Tu. 107	Th. 137	Su. 168	Tu. 198	F. 229	M. 260	W. 290	Sa. 321	M. 351
18	Th. 18	Su. 49	Su. 77	W. 108	F. 138	M. 169	W. 199	Sa. 230	Tu. 261	Th. 291	Su. 322	Tu. 352
19	F. 19	M. 50	M. 78	Th. 109	Sa. 139	Tu. 170	Th. 200	Su. 231	W. 262	F. 292	M. 323	W. 353
20	Sa. 20	Tu. 51	Tu. 79	F. 110	Su. 140	W. 171	F. 201	M. 232	Th. 263	Sa. 293	Tu. 324	Th. 354
21	Su. 21	W. 52	W. 80	Sa. 111	M. 141	Th. 172	Sa. 202	Tu. 233	F. 264	Su. 294	W. 325	F. 355
22	M. 22	Th. 53	Th. 81	Su. 112	Tu. 142	F. 173	Su. 203	W. 234	Sa. 265	M. 295	Th. 326	Sa. 356
23	Tu. 23	F. 54	F. 82	M. 113	W. 143	Sa. 174	M. 204	Th. 235	Su. 266	Tu. 296	F. 327	Su. 357
24	W. 24	Sa. 55	Sa. 83	Tu. 114	Th. 144	Su. 175	Tu. 205	F. 236	M. 267	W. 297	Sa. 328	M. 358
25	Th. 25	Su. 56	Su. 84	W. 115	F. 145	M. 176	W. 206	Sa. 237	Tu. 268	Th. 298	Su. 329	Tu. 359
26	F. 26	M. 57	M. 85	Th. 116	Sa. 146	Tu. 177	Th. 207	Su. 238	W. 269	F. 299	M. 330	W. 360
27	Sa. 27	Tu. 58	Tu. 86	F. 117	Su. 147	W. 178	F. 208	M. 239	Th. 270	Sa. 300	Tu. 331	Th. 361
28	Su. 28	W. 59	W. 87	Sa. 118	M. 148	Th. 179	Sa. 209	Tu. 240	F. 271	Su. 301	W. 332	F. 362
29	M. 29		Th. 88	Su. 119	Tu. 149	F. 180	Su. 210	W. 241	Sa. 272	M. 302	Th. 333	Sa. 363
30	Tu. 30		F. 89	M. 120	W. 150	Sa. 181	M. 211	Th. 242	Su. 273	Tu. 303	F. 334	Su. 364
31	W. 31		Sa. 90		Th. 151		Tu. 212	F. 243		W. 304		M. 365

ECLIPSES

There are three eclipses of the Sun and two of the Moon.

1. *A total eclipse of the Moon*, January 31. The umbral eclipse begins at $11^h 48^m$ and ends at $15^h 12^m$. Totality lasts from $12^h 51^m$ to $14^h 08^m$. It is visible from North America except the eastern part, Oceania, Russia, Asia except the western part and northern Scandinavia.

2. *A partial eclipse of the Sun*, February 15. See map on page 6. The eclipse begins at $18^h 56^m$ and ends at $22^h 47^m$. The time of greatest eclipse is $20^h 51^m$, when 0.60 of the Sun's diameter is obscured.

3. *A partial eclipse of the Sun*, July 13. The eclipse begins at $01^h 48^m$ and ends at $04^h 14^m$. The time of greatest eclipse is $03^h 01^m$, when 0.34 of the Sun's diameter is obscured. It is visible from the tip of Wilkes Land in Antarctica, Tasmania and the southernmost part of South Australia.

4. *A total eclipse of the Moon*, July 27. The umbral eclipse begins at $18^h 24^m$ and ends at $22^h 19^m$. Totality lasts from $19^h 30^m$ to $21^h 14^m$. It is is visible from Antarctica, Australasia, central Asia, Africa, Scandinavia, Europe and the easternmost part of South America.

5. *A partial eclipse of the Sun*, August 11. See map on page 7. The eclipse begins at $08^h 02^m$ and ends at $11^h 31^m$. The time of greatest eclipse is $09^h 46^m$, when 0.74 of the Sun's diameter is obscured.

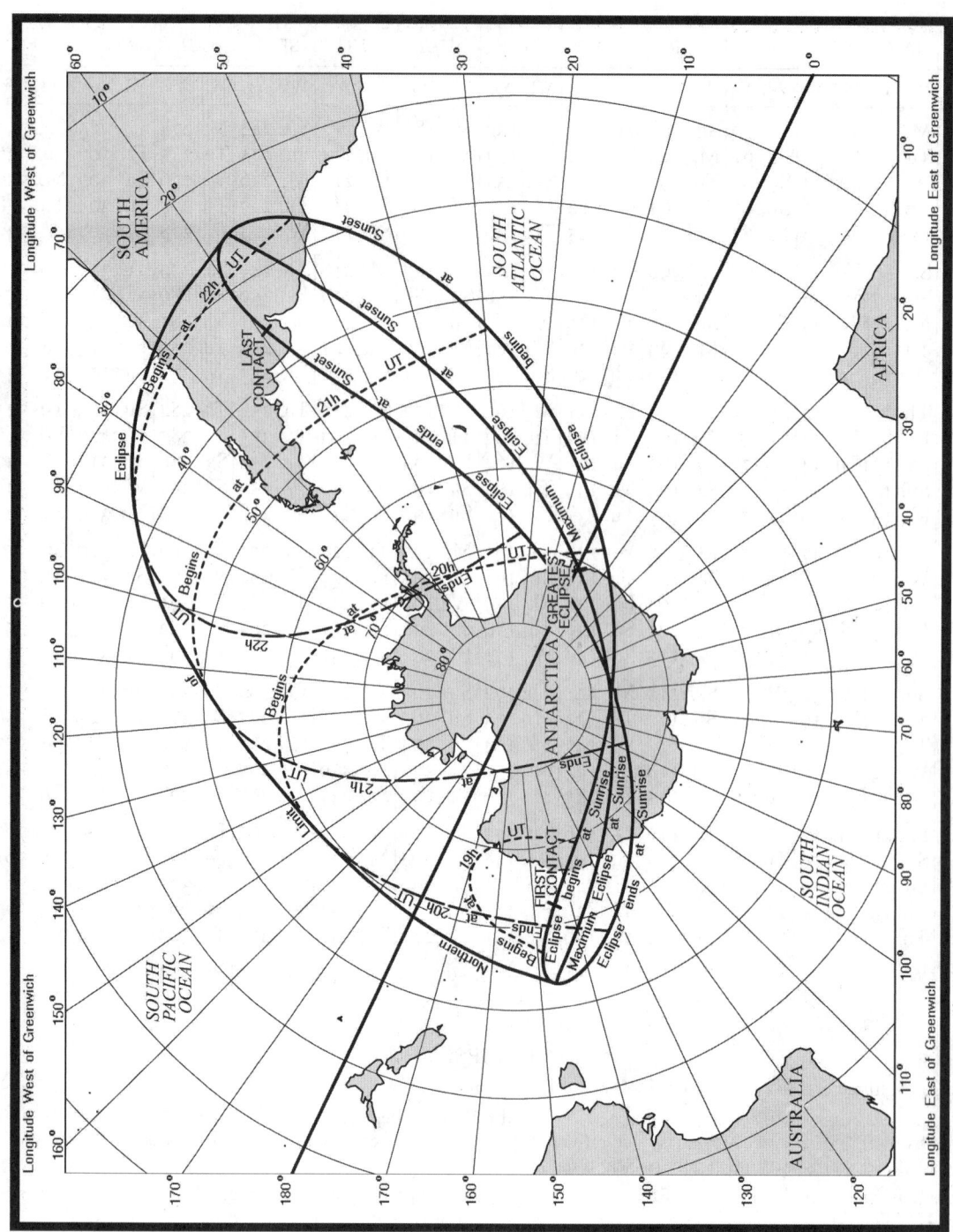

SOLAR ECLIPSE DIAGRAMS

The principal features shown on the above diagrams are: the paths of total and annular eclipses; the northern and southern limits of partial eclipse; the sunrise and sunset curves; dashed lines which show the times of beginning and end of partial eclipse at hourly intervals.

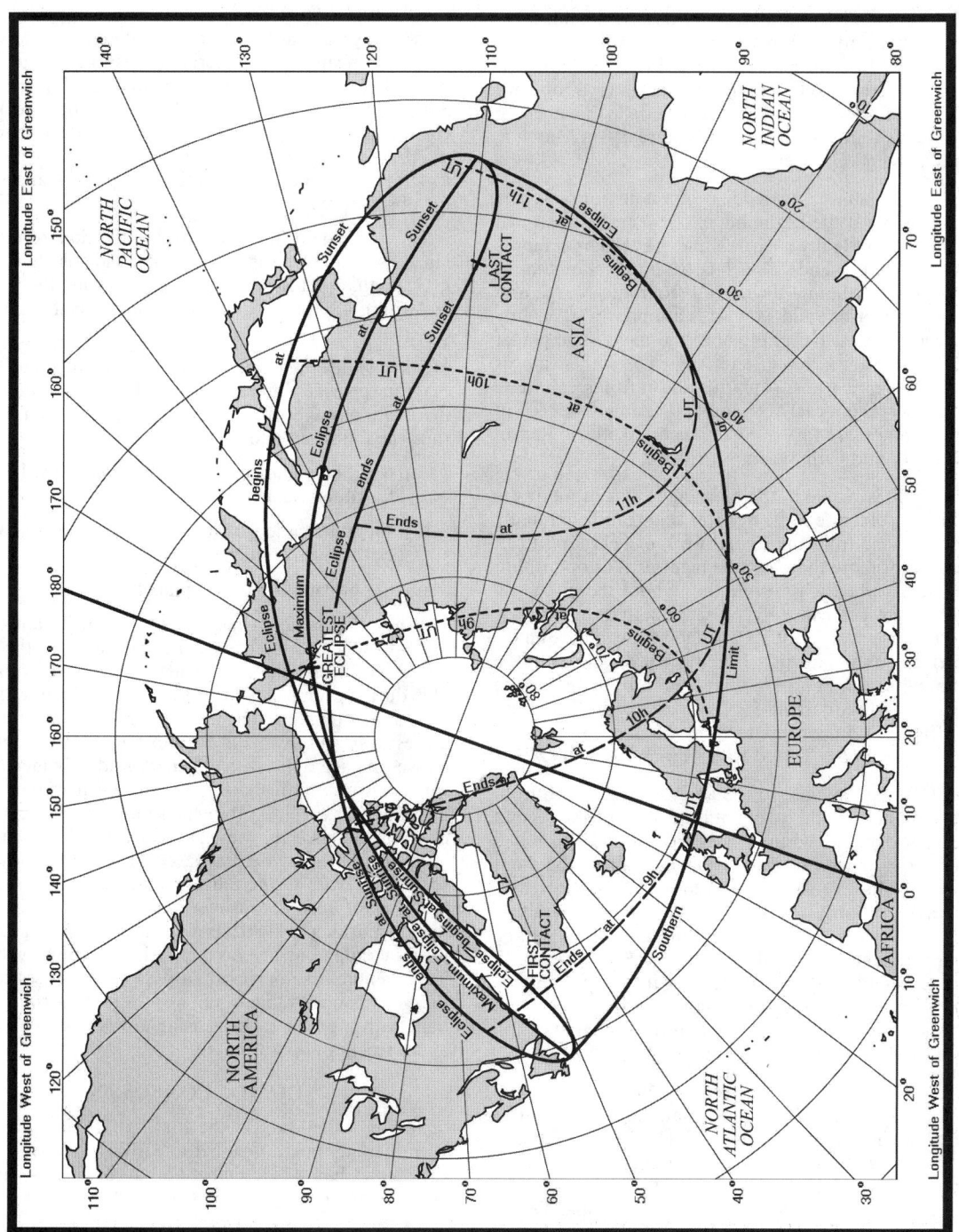

SOLAR ECLIPSE DIAGRAMS

Further details of the paths and times of central eclipse are given in
The Astronomical Almanac.

VISIBILITY OF PLANETS

VENUS is too close to the Sun for observation until the end of the third week of February when it appears as a brilliant object in the evening sky. In late October it again becomes too close to the Sun for observation until the start of November when it reappears in the morning sky. Venus is in conjunction with Mercury on March 5, March 18 and October 14.

MARS is visible as a reddish object in Libra in the morning sky at the beginning of the year. Its westward elongation gradually increases, and in February it moves through Scorpius and Ophiuchus (passing 5° N. of *Antares* on February 10), into Sagittarius from mid-March and Capricornus from mid-May. It is at opposition on July 27 when it is visible throughout the night. The planet returns to Sagittarius in late August and then moves through Capricornus, Aquarius and into Pisces in late December. From early December it can only be seen in the evening sky. Mars is in conjunction with Jupiter on January 7 and with Saturn on April 2.

JUPITER is visible in the morning sky in Libra at the beginning of the year. Its westward elongation gradually increases and from the second week of February it can be seen for more than half the night. It is at opposition on May 9 when it is visible throughout the night. By early August it can only be seen in the evening sky. From mid-November it becomes too close to the Sun for observation until in early December it reappears in the morning sky in Scorpius. It moves into Ophiuchus in mid-December (passing 5° N. of *Antares* on December 20). Jupiter is in conjunction with Mercury on October 30 and December 21 and with Mars on January 7.

SATURN is too close to the Sun for observation from the beginning of the year until the start of the second week of January when it rises just before sunrise in Sagittarius, in which constellation it remains throughout the year. Its westward elongation gradually increases and in early April it becomes visible for more than half the night. It is at opposition on June 27 when it can be seen throughout the night. From late September until mid-December it can only be seen in the evening sky and then becomes too close to the Sun for observation for the remainder of the year. Saturn is in conjunction with Mercury on January 13 and with Mars on April 2.

MERCURY can only be seen low in the east before sunrise, or low in the west after sunset (about the time of beginning or end of civil twilight). It is visible in the mornings between the following approximate dates: Jan. 1 (−0·3) to Feb. 4 (−0·7), Apr. 10 (+2·9) to May 29 (−1·3), Aug. 17 (+2·4) to Sept. 11 (−1·3) and Dec. 3 (+1·7) to Dec. 31 (−0·4); the planet is brighter at the end of each period. It is visible in the evenings between the following approximate dates: Feb. 28 (−1·4) to Mar. 25 (+2·3), June 14 (−1·3) to Aug. 1 (+2·9) and Oct. 4 (−0·7) to Nov. 21 (+1·5); the planet is brighter at the beginning of each period. The figures in parentheses are the magnitudes.

PLANET DIAGRAM

General Description. The diagram on the opposite page shows, in graphical form for any date during the year, the local mean time of meridian passage of the Sun, of the five planets Mercury, Venus, Mars, Jupiter, and Saturn, and of each 30° of SHA; intermediate lines corresponding to particular stars, may be drawn in by the user if desired. It is intended to provide a general picture of the availability of planets and stars for observation.

On each side of the line marking the time of meridian passage of the Sun a band, 45^m wide, is shaded to indicate that planets and most stars crossing the meridian within 45^m of the Sun are too close to the Sun for observation.

Method of use and interpretation. For any date, the diagram provides immediately the local mean times of meridian passage of the Sun, planets and stars, and thus the following information:

(a) whether a planet or star is too close to the Sun for observation;

(b) some indication of its position in the sky, especially during twilight;

(c) the proximity of other planets.

When the meridian passage of an outer planet occurs at midnight, the body is in opposition to the Sun and is visible all night; a planet may then be observable during both morning and evening twilights. As the time of meridian passage decreases, the body eventually ceases to be observable in the morning, but its altitude above the eastern horizon at sunset gradually increases; this continues until the body is on the meridian during evening twilight. From then onwards, the body is observable above the western horizon and its altitude at sunset gradually decreases; eventually the body becomes too close to the Sun for observation. When the body again becomes visible it is seen low in the east during morning twilight; its altitude at sunrise increases until meridian passage occurs during morning twilight. Then, as the time of meridian passage decreases to 0^h, the body is observable in the west during morning twilight with a gradually decreasing altitude, until it once again reaches opposition.

DO NOT CONFUSE

Jupiter with Mars in the first half of January and with Mercury in late October to early November and in the second half of December; on all occasions Jupiter is the brighter object.

Mercury with Saturn in mid-January when Mercury is the brighter object.

Mercury with Venus in late February to late March when Venus is the brighter object.

Mars with Saturn in late March to mid-April when Mars is the brighter object.

LOCAL MEAN TIME OF MERIDIAN PASSAGE

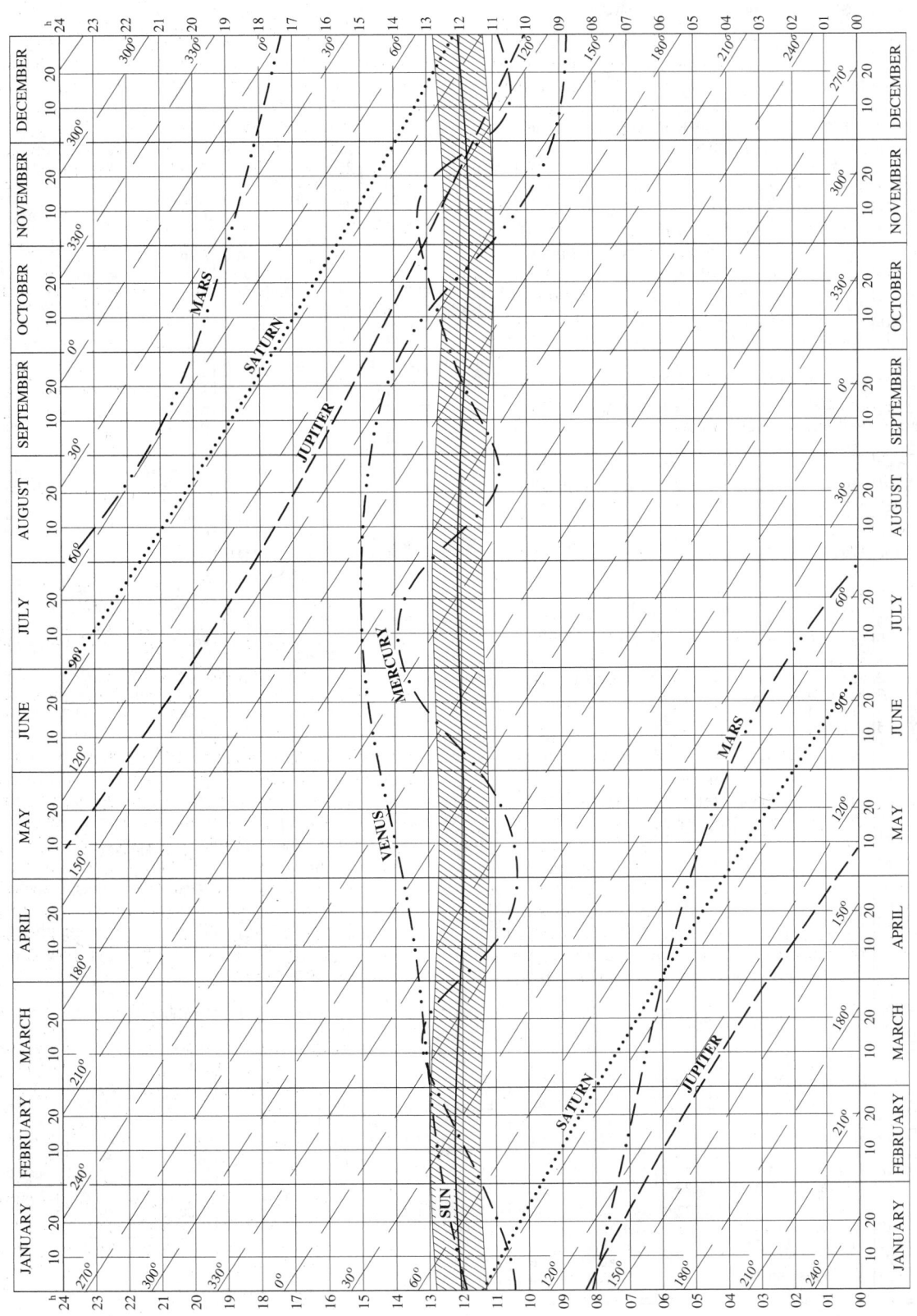

UT	ARIES GHA	VENUS −4.0 GHA	Dec	MARS +1.5 GHA	Dec	JUPITER −1.8 GHA	Dec	SATURN +0.5 GHA	Dec	STARS Name	SHA	Dec
1 00	100 35.8	181 17.1	S23 37.9	238 36.7	S15 13.7	235 49.0	S15 53.1	189 05.5	S22 31.9	Acamar	315 15.8	S40 14.3
01	115 38.2	196 16.2	37.7	253 37.6	14.2	250 51.0	53.2	204 07.6	31.9	Achernar	335 24.5	S57 09.2
02	130 40.7	211 15.2	37.6	268 38.5	14.7	265 53.0	53.3	219 09.8	31.9	Acrux	173 05.7	S63 11.5
03	145 43.2	226 14.2 ..	37.5	283 39.5 ..	15.1	280 55.1 ..	53.4	234 11.9 ..	31.9	Adhara	255 09.7	S29 00.0
04	160 45.6	241 13.3	37.4	298 40.4	15.6	295 57.1	53.5	249 14.1	31.9	Aldebaran	290 45.5	N16 32.5
05	175 48.1	256 12.3	37.3	313 41.3	16.1	310 59.2	53.6	264 16.2	31.9			
06	190 50.6	271 11.3	S23 37.2	328 42.2	S15 16.6	326 01.2	S15 53.8	279 18.4	S22 31.9	Alioth	166 18.1	N55 51.5
07	205 53.0	286 10.4	37.1	343 43.2	17.0	341 03.3	53.9	294 20.5	31.9	Alkaid	152 56.7	N49 13.3
08	220 55.5	301 09.4	36.9	358 44.1	17.5	356 05.3	54.0	309 22.7	31.9	Al Na'ir	27 40.3	S46 52.6
M 09	235 58.0	316 08.4 ..	36.8	13 45.0 ..	18.0	11 07.4 ..	54.1	324 24.8 ..	31.9	Alnilam	275 42.9	S 1 11.7
O 10	251 00.4	331 07.4	36.7	28 45.9	18.5	26 09.4	54.2	339 27.0	31.9	Alphard	217 52.8	S 8 44.3
N 11	266 02.9	346 06.5	36.6	43 46.9	18.9	41 11.4	54.3	354 29.1	31.8			
D 12	281 05.3	1 05.5	S23 36.5	58 47.8	S15 19.4	56 13.5	S15 54.4	9 31.2	S22 31.8	Alphecca	126 08.7	N26 39.3
A 13	296 07.8	16 04.5	36.3	73 48.7	19.9	71 15.5	54.6	24 33.4	31.8	Alpheratz	357 40.3	N29 11.4
Y 14	311 10.3	31 03.6	36.2	88 49.6	20.4	86 17.6	54.7	39 35.5	31.8	Altair	62 05.6	N 8 55.1
15	326 12.7	46 02.6 ..	36.1	103 50.6 ..	20.8	101 19.6 ..	54.8	54 37.7 ..	31.8	Ankaa	353 12.7	S42 12.8
16	341 15.2	61 01.6	36.0	118 51.5	21.3	116 21.7	54.9	69 39.8	31.8	Antares	112 22.8	S26 28.0
17	356 17.7	76 00.7	35.8	133 52.4	21.8	131 23.7	55.0	84 42.0	31.8			
18	11 20.1	90 59.7	S23 35.7	148 53.3	S15 22.3	146 25.8	S15 55.1	99 44.1	S22 31.8	Arcturus	145 53.1	N19 05.4
19	26 22.6	105 58.7	35.6	163 54.3	22.7	161 27.8	55.2	114 46.3	31.8	Atria	107 22.3	S69 03.2
20	41 25.1	120 57.8	35.4	178 55.2	23.2	176 29.8	55.4	129 48.4	31.8	Avior	234 16.1	S59 34.0
21	56 27.5	135 56.8 ..	35.3	193 56.1 ..	23.7	191 31.9 ..	55.5	144 50.6 ..	31.8	Bellatrix	278 28.4	N 6 21.7
22	71 30.0	150 55.8	35.2	208 57.0	24.1	206 33.9	55.6	159 52.7	31.8	Betelgeuse	270 57.6	N 7 24.4
23	86 32.5	165 54.9	35.0	223 58.0	24.6	221 36.0	55.7	174 54.9	31.8			
2 00	101 34.9	180 53.9	S23 34.9	238 58.9	S15 25.1	236 38.0	S15 55.8	189 57.0	S22 31.8	Canopus	263 54.2	S52 42.5
01	116 37.4	195 52.9	34.7	253 59.8	25.6	251 40.1	55.9	204 59.2	31.8	Capella	280 29.4	N46 00.8
02	131 39.8	210 52.0	34.6	269 00.7	26.0	266 42.1	56.0	220 01.3	31.8	Deneb	49 29.8	N45 20.9
03	146 42.3	225 51.0 ..	34.5	284 01.6 ..	26.5	281 44.2 ..	56.2	235 03.5 ..	31.8	Denebola	182 30.5	N14 28.2
04	161 44.8	240 50.0	34.3	299 02.6	27.0	296 46.2	56.3	250 05.6	31.8	Diphda	348 52.8	S17 53.5
05	176 47.2	255 49.1	34.2	314 03.5	27.4	311 48.3	56.4	265 07.8	31.8			
06	191 49.7	270 48.1	S23 34.0	329 04.4	S15 27.9	326 50.3	S15 56.5	280 09.9	S22 31.8	Dubhe	193 47.8	N61 39.0
07	206 52.2	285 47.2	33.9	344 05.3	28.4	341 52.4	56.6	295 12.1	31.8	Elnath	278 08.4	N28 37.2
08	221 54.6	300 46.2	33.7	359 06.3	28.9	356 54.4	56.7	310 14.2	31.8	Eltanin	90 45.3	N51 29.3
T 09	236 57.1	315 45.2 ..	33.6	14 07.2 ..	29.3	11 56.4 ..	56.8	325 16.3 ..	31.8	Enif	33 44.3	N 9 57.5
U 10	251 59.6	330 44.3	33.4	29 08.1	29.8	26 58.5	56.9	340 18.5	31.8	Fomalhaut	15 20.8	S29 31.8
E 11	267 02.0	345 43.3	33.3	44 09.0	30.3	42 00.5	57.1	355 20.6	31.8			
S 12	282 04.5	0 42.3	S23 33.1	59 09.9	S15 30.7	57 02.6	S15 57.2	10 22.8	S22 31.8	Gacrux	171 57.3	S57 12.5
D 13	297 07.0	15 41.4	33.0	74 10.9	31.2	72 04.6	57.3	25 24.9	31.8	Gienah	175 49.1	S17 38.3
A 14	312 09.4	30 40.4	32.8	89 11.8	31.7	87 06.7	57.4	40 27.1	31.8	Hadar	148 43.7	S60 27.1
Y 15	327 11.9	45 39.4 ..	32.7	104 12.7 ..	32.1	102 08.7 ..	57.5	55 29.2 ..	31.8	Hamal	327 57.1	N23 32.8
16	342 14.3	60 38.5	32.5	119 13.6	32.6	117 10.8	57.6	70 31.4	31.8	Kaus Aust.	83 40.2	S34 22.4
17	357 16.8	75 37.5	32.3	134 14.6	33.1	132 12.8	57.7	85 33.5	31.8			
18	12 19.3	90 36.5	S23 32.2	149 15.5	S15 33.6	147 14.9	S15 57.8	100 35.7	S22 31.8	Kochab	137 20.9	N74 04.8
19	27 21.7	105 35.6	32.0	164 16.4	34.0	162 16.9	58.0	115 37.8	31.8	Markab	13 35.4	N15 18.2
20	42 24.2	120 34.6	31.9	179 17.3	34.5	177 19.0	58.1	130 40.0	31.8	Menkar	314 11.6	N 4 09.4
21	57 26.7	135 33.7 ..	31.7	194 18.2 ..	35.0	192 21.0 ..	58.2	145 42.1 ..	31.8	Menkent	148 04.1	S36 27.2
22	72 29.1	150 32.7	31.5	209 19.2	35.4	207 23.1	58.3	160 44.3	31.8	Miaplacidus	221 38.1	S69 47.3
23	87 31.6	165 31.7	31.4	224 20.1	35.9	222 25.1	58.4	175 46.4	31.8			
3 00	102 34.1	180 30.8	S23 31.2	239 21.0	S15 36.4	237 27.2	S15 58.5	190 48.6	S22 31.8	Mirfak	308 35.5	N49 55.5
01	117 36.5	195 29.8	31.0	254 21.9	36.8	252 29.2	58.6	205 50.7	31.8	Nunki	75 54.9	S26 16.3
02	132 39.0	210 28.8	30.8	269 22.8	37.3	267 31.3	58.7	220 52.9	31.8	Peacock	53 15.0	S56 40.6
03	147 41.5	225 27.9 ..	30.7	284 23.8 ..	37.8	282 33.3 ..	58.9	235 55.0 ..	31.8	Pollux	243 23.6	N27 58.7
04	162 43.9	240 26.9	30.5	299 24.7	38.2	297 35.4	59.0	250 57.2	31.8	Procyon	244 56.2	N 5 10.5
05	177 46.4	255 26.0	30.3	314 25.6	38.7	312 37.4	59.1	265 59.3	31.8			
06	192 48.8	270 25.0	S23 30.1	329 26.5	S15 39.2	327 39.5	S15 59.2	281 01.5	S22 31.8	Rasalhague	96 03.9	N12 33.0
W 07	207 51.3	285 24.0	30.0	344 27.4	39.6	342 41.5	59.3	296 03.6	31.8	Regulus	207 40.0	N11 52.6
E 08	222 53.8	300 23.1	29.8	359 28.4	40.1	357 43.6	59.4	311 05.8	31.8	Rigel	281 08.8	S 8 11.1
D 09	237 56.2	315 22.1 ..	29.6	14 29.3 ..	40.6	12 45.6 ..	59.5	326 07.9 ..	31.8	Rigil Kent.	139 47.8	S60 54.1
N 10	252 58.7	330 21.1	29.4	29 30.2	41.0	27 47.7	59.6	341 10.1	31.8	Sabik	102 09.3	S15 44.6
E 11	268 01.2	345 20.2	29.2	44 31.1	41.5	42 49.7	59.8	356 12.2	31.8			
S 12	283 03.6	0 19.2	S23 29.1	59 32.0	S15 42.0	57 51.8	S15 59.9	11 14.4	S22 31.8	Schedar	349 36.9	N56 38.3
D 13	298 06.1	15 18.3	28.9	74 33.0	42.4	72 53.8	16 00.0	26 16.5	31.8	Shaula	96 18.1	S37 06.7
A 14	313 08.6	30 17.3	28.7	89 33.9	42.9	87 55.9	00.1	41 18.7	31.8	Sirius	258 30.7	S16 44.7
Y 15	328 11.0	45 16.3 ..	28.5	104 34.8 ..	43.3	102 57.9 ..	00.2	56 20.8 ..	31.8	Spica	158 28.1	S11 15.1
16	343 13.5	60 15.4	28.3	119 35.7	43.8	118 00.0	00.3	71 22.9	31.8	Suhail	222 49.8	S43 30.3
17	358 16.0	75 14.4	28.1	134 36.6	44.3	133 02.1	00.4	86 25.1	31.8			
18	13 18.4	90 13.5	S23 27.9	149 37.6	S15 44.7	148 04.1	S16 00.5	101 27.2	S22 31.8	Vega	80 37.3	N38 48.2
19	28 20.9	105 12.5	27.7	164 38.5	45.2	163 06.2	00.6	116 29.4	31.8	Zuben'ubi	137 02.2	S16 06.7
20	43 23.3	120 11.5	27.5	179 39.4	45.7	178 08.2	00.8	131 31.5	31.8		SHA	Mer. Pass.
21	58 25.8	135 10.6 ..	27.4	194 40.3 ..	46.1	193 10.3 ..	00.9	146 33.7 ..	31.8	Venus	79 19.0	11 57
22	73 28.3	150 09.6	27.2	209 41.2	46.6	208 12.3	01.0	161 35.8	31.8	Mars	137 24.0	8 04
23	88 30.7	165 08.7	27.0	224 42.2	47.1	223 14.4	01.1	176 38.0	31.8	Jupiter	135 03.1	8 12
Mer. Pass. 17 10.8		v −1.0	d 0.2	v 0.9	d 0.5	v 2.0	d 0.1	v 2.1	d 0.0	Saturn	88 22.1	11 19

UT	SUN GHA	SUN Dec	MOON GHA	v	MOON Dec	d	HP
d h	° ′	° ′	° ′	′	° ′	′	′
1 00	179 09.9	S23 01.1	16 05.7	3.2	N19 19.2	3.5	61.4
01	194 09.6	00.9	30 27.9	3.2	19 22.7	3.5	61.4
02	209 09.3	00.7	44 50.1	3.1	19 26.2	3.3	61.4
03	224 09.0	.. 00.5	59 12.2	3.1	19 29.5	3.1	61.4
04	239 08.7	00.3	73 34.3	3.1	19 32.6	3.0	61.4
05	254 08.4	23 00.1	87 56.4	3.0	19 35.6	2.8	61.4
06	269 08.1	S22 59.9	102 18.4	3.0	N19 38.4	2.7	61.4
07	284 07.8	59.7	116 40.4	2.9	19 41.1	2.5	61.4
M 08	299 07.6	59.5	131 02.3	2.9	19 43.6	2.4	61.4
O 09	314 07.3	.. 59.3	145 24.2	2.9	19 46.0	2.2	61.4
N 10	329 07.0	59.1	159 46.1	2.9	19 48.2	2.1	61.5
D 11	344 06.7	58.9	174 08.0	2.8	19 50.3	2.0	61.5
A 12	359 06.4	S22 58.7	188 29.8	2.8	N19 52.3	1.7	61.5
Y 13	14 06.1	58.5	202 51.6	2.8	19 54.0	1.7	61.5
14	29 05.8	58.3	217 13.4	2.7	19 55.7	1.4	61.5
15	44 05.5	.. 58.0	231 35.1	2.8	19 57.1	1.3	61.5
16	59 05.2	57.8	245 56.9	2.7	19 58.4	1.2	61.5
17	74 04.9	57.6	260 18.6	2.7	19 59.6	1.0	61.5
18	89 04.6	S22 57.4	274 40.3	2.7	N20 00.6	0.9	61.5
19	104 04.3	57.2	289 02.0	2.7	20 01.5	0.7	61.5
20	119 04.0	57.0	303 23.7	2.7	20 02.2	0.5	61.5
21	134 03.7	.. 56.8	317 45.4	2.7	20 02.7	0.4	61.5
22	149 03.5	56.5	332 07.1	2.6	20 03.1	0.2	61.5
23	164 03.2	56.3	346 28.7	2.7	20 03.3	0.1	61.5
2 00	179 02.9	S22 56.1	0 50.4	2.7	N20 03.4	0.1	61.5
01	194 02.6	55.9	15 12.1	2.7	20 03.3	0.2	61.5
02	209 02.3	55.7	29 33.8	2.6	20 03.1	0.4	61.5
03	224 02.0	.. 55.4	43 55.4	2.7	20 02.7	0.6	61.5
04	239 01.7	55.2	58 17.1	2.7	20 02.1	0.7	61.5
05	254 01.4	55.0	72 38.8	2.8	20 01.4	0.8	61.5
06	269 01.1	S22 54.8	87 00.6	2.7	N20 00.6	1.1	61.5
07	284 00.8	54.5	101 22.3	2.7	19 59.5	1.1	61.5
T 08	299 00.5	54.3	115 44.0	2.8	19 58.4	1.3	61.5
U 09	314 00.3	.. 54.1	130 05.8	2.8	19 57.1	1.5	61.5
E 10	329 00.0	53.9	144 27.6	2.8	19 55.6	1.7	61.5
S 11	343 59.7	53.6	158 49.4	2.8	19 53.9	1.7	61.4
D 12	358 59.4	S22 53.4	173 11.2	2.9	N19 52.2	2.0	61.4
A 13	13 59.1	53.2	187 33.1	2.9	19 50.2	2.1	61.4
Y 14	28 58.8	52.9	201 55.0	2.9	19 48.1	2.2	61.4
15	43 58.5	.. 52.7	216 16.9	3.0	19 45.9	2.4	61.4
16	58 58.2	52.5	230 38.9	3.0	19 43.5	2.5	61.4
17	73 57.9	52.2	245 00.9	3.0	19 41.0	2.7	61.4
18	88 57.7	S22 52.0	259 22.9	3.1	N19 38.3	2.9	61.4
19	103 57.4	51.8	273 45.0	3.1	19 35.4	2.9	61.4
20	118 57.1	51.5	288 07.1	3.2	19 32.5	3.2	61.3
21	133 56.8	.. 51.3	302 29.3	3.2	19 29.3	3.3	61.3
22	148 56.5	51.1	316 51.5	3.3	19 26.0	3.4	61.3
23	163 56.2	50.8	331 13.8	3.3	19 22.6	3.6	61.3
3 00	178 55.9	S22 50.6	345 36.1	3.3	N19 19.0	3.7	61.3
01	193 55.6	50.4	359 58.4	3.4	19 15.3	3.8	61.3
02	208 55.4	50.1	14 20.8	3.5	19 11.5	4.0	61.3
03	223 55.1	.. 49.9	28 43.3	3.5	19 07.5	4.2	61.2
04	238 54.8	49.6	43 05.8	3.6	19 03.3	4.3	61.2
05	253 54.5	49.4	57 28.4	3.7	18 59.0	4.4	61.2
06	268 54.2	S22 49.1	71 51.1	3.7	N18 54.6	4.5	61.2
W 07	283 53.9	48.9	86 13.8	3.7	18 50.1	4.7	61.2
E 08	298 53.6	48.7	100 36.5	3.9	18 45.4	4.9	61.1
D 09	313 53.3	.. 48.4	114 59.4	3.9	18 40.5	4.9	61.1
N 10	328 53.1	48.2	129 22.3	3.9	18 35.6	5.1	61.1
E 11	343 52.8	47.9	143 45.2	4.1	18 30.5	5.3	61.1
S 12	358 52.5	S22 47.7	158 08.3	4.1	N18 25.2	5.3	61.1
D 13	13 52.2	47.4	172 31.4	4.1	18 19.9	5.5	61.0
A 14	28 51.9	47.2	186 54.5	4.3	18 14.4	5.6	61.0
Y 15	43 51.6	.. 46.9	201 17.8	4.3	18 08.8	5.8	61.0
16	58 51.4	46.7	215 41.1	4.4	18 03.0	5.9	61.0
17	73 51.1	46.4	230 04.5	4.5	17 57.1	6.0	60.9
18	88 50.8	S22 46.2	244 28.0	4.5	N17 51.1	6.1	60.9
19	103 50.5	45.9	258 51.5	4.7	17 45.0	6.2	60.9
20	118 50.2	45.7	273 15.2	4.7	17 38.8	6.4	60.9
21	133 49.9	.. 45.4	287 38.9	4.8	17 32.4	6.5	60.8
22	148 49.6	45.1	302 02.7	4.9	17 25.9	6.6	60.8
23	163 49.4	44.9	316 26.6	4.9	N17 19.3	6.7	60.8
	SD 16.3	d 0.2	SD 16.7		16.7		16.6

Lat.	Twilight Naut.	Twilight Civil	Sunrise	Moonrise 1	2	3	4
°	h m	h m	h m	h m	h m	h m	h m
N 72	08 23	10 39	■■	□	□		16 57
N 70	08 04	09 48	■■	12 08	13 15	15 25	17 32
68	07 49	09 16	■■	13 19	14 26	16 06	17 56
66	07 37	08 52	10 26	13 56	15 03	16 34	18 15
64	07 26	08 34	09 48	14 22	15 29	16 55	18 30
62	07 17	08 18	09 22	14 43	15 49	17 12	18 43
60	07 09	08 05	09 02	15 00	16 06	17 26	18 54
N 58	07 02	07 54	08 45	15 14	16 20	17 38	19 03
56	06 55	07 44	08 31	15 26	16 32	17 49	19 11
54	06 50	07 35	08 19	15 37	16 43	17 58	19 18
52	06 44	07 27	08 08	15 46	16 52	18 06	19 25
50	06 39	07 20	07 58	15 55	17 00	18 14	19 31
45	06 28	07 05	07 38	16 13	17 18	18 29	19 43
N 40	06 18	06 52	07 22	16 27	17 33	18 42	19 54
35	06 09	06 40	07 08	16 40	17 45	18 53	20 02
30	06 00	06 30	06 56	16 51	17 56	19 03	20 10
20	05 44	06 11	06 35	17 10	18 14	19 19	20 23
N 10	05 28	05 55	06 17	17 26	18 30	19 34	20 35
0	05 12	05 38	06 00	17 41	18 45	19 47	20 46
S 10	04 53	05 20	05 43	17 57	19 00	20 01	20 57
20	04 31	05 00	05 25	18 13	19 16	20 15	21 08
30	04 03	04 36	05 03	18 32	19 35	20 31	21 21
35	03 44	04 21	04 50	18 43	19 45	20 41	21 29
40	03 22	04 03	04 36	18 56	19 58	20 52	21 38
45	02 52	03 41	04 18	19 11	20 12	21 04	21 48
S 50	02 09	03 12	03 56	19 29	20 30	21 20	22 00
52	01 43	02 58	03 46	19 38	20 38	21 27	22 05
54	01 03	02 41	03 34	19 48	20 48	21 35	22 12
56	////	02 19	03 20	19 59	20 58	21 44	22 19
58	////	01 52	03 04	20 11	21 10	21 54	22 26
S 60	////	01 09	02 45	20 26	21 24	22 05	22 35

Lat.	Sunset	Twilight Civil	Twilight Naut.	Moonset 1	2	3	4
°	h m	h m	h m	h m	h m	h m	h m
N 72	■■	13 29	15 46	□	□	□	12 20
N 70	■■	14 21	16 04	10 38	11 45	11 47	11 45
68	■■	14 53	16 19	09 27	10 34	11 05	11 19
66	13 42	15 16	16 32	08 50	09 57	10 37	10 59
64	14 20	15 35	16 42	08 24	09 31	10 15	10 43
62	14 46	15 50	16 51	08 03	09 10	09 57	10 30
60	15 07	16 03	16 59	07 47	08 53	09 43	10 18
N 58	15 23	16 14	17 06	07 33	08 39	09 30	10 08
56	15 37	16 24	17 13	07 21	08 27	09 19	10 00
54	15 50	16 33	17 19	07 10	08 16	09 10	09 52
52	16 00	16 41	17 24	07 01	08 07	09 01	09 45
50	16 10	16 48	17 29	06 53	07 58	08 54	09 38
45	16 30	17 04	17 41	06 35	07 40	08 37	09 25
N 40	16 46	17 17	17 51	06 20	07 26	08 24	09 14
35	17 00	17 28	18 00	06 08	07 13	08 12	09 04
30	17 12	17 38	18 08	05 57	07 02	08 02	08 55
20	17 33	17 57	18 24	05 39	06 43	07 45	08 41
N 10	17 51	18 14	18 40	05 23	06 27	07 29	08 28
0	18 08	18 30	18 56	05 08	06 12	07 15	08 16
S 10	18 25	18 48	19 15	04 53	05 56	07 01	08 03
20	18 43	19 08	19 37	04 37	05 40	06 45	07 50
30	19 05	19 32	20 05	04 18	05 21	06 27	07 35
35	19 17	19 47	20 23	04 08	05 10	06 17	07 26
40	19 32	20 05	20 47	03 55	04 57	06 05	07 16
45	19 50	20 27	21 15	03 41	04 42	05 51	07 04
S 50	20 11	20 55	21 58	03 23	04 24	05 34	06 50
52	20 22	21 10	22 24	03 15	04 15	05 26	06 43
54	20 34	21 27	23 02	03 05	04 05	05 16	06 35
56	20 47	21 48	////	02 55	03 54	05 06	06 27
58	21 03	22 15	////	02 43	03 41	04 55	06 17
S 60	21 23	22 56	////	02 29	03 27	04 41	06 06

Day	SUN Eqn. of Time 00h	SUN Eqn. of Time 12h	SUN Mer. Pass.	MOON Mer. Pass. Upper	MOON Mer. Pass. Lower	Age	Phase
d	m s	m s	h m	h m	h m	d	%
1	03 20	03 34	12 04	23 56	11 25	14	99
2	03 48	04 02	12 04	25 00	12 28	15	100
3	04 16	04 29	12 04	01 00	13 31	16	97

UT	ARIES	VENUS −4.0		MARS +1.4		JUPITER −1.8		SATURN +0.5		STARS		
d h	GHA	GHA	Dec	GHA	Dec	GHA	Dec	GHA	Dec	Name	SHA	Dec
4 00	103 33.2	180 07.7	S23 26.8	239 43.1	S15 47.5	238 16.4	S16 01.2	191 40.1	S22 31.8	Acamar	315 15.8	S40 14.3
01	118 35.7	195 06.7	26.6	254 44.0	48.0	253 18.5	01.3	206 42.3	31.8	Achernar	335 24.4	S57 09.2
02	133 38.1	210 05.8	26.4	269 44.9	48.4	268 20.5	01.4	221 44.4	31.8	Acrux	173 05.6	S63 11.6
03	148 40.6	225 04.8 ..	26.2	284 45.8 ..	48.9	283 22.6 ..	01.5	236 46.6 ..	31.8	Adhara	255 09.7	S29 00.0
04	163 43.1	240 03.9	26.0	299 46.8	49.4	298 24.6	01.6	251 48.7	31.8	Aldebaran	290 45.5	N16 32.5
05	178 45.5	255 02.9	25.7	314 47.7	49.8	313 26.7	01.8	266 50.9	31.8			
06	193 48.0	270 02.0	S23 25.5	329 48.6	S15 50.3	328 28.8	S16 01.9	281 53.0	S22 31.8	Alioth	166 18.1	N55 51.5
07	208 50.4	285 01.0	25.3	344 49.5	50.8	343 30.8	02.0	296 55.2	31.8	Alkaid	152 56.6	N49 13.3
T 08	223 52.9	300 00.0	25.1	359 50.4	51.2	358 32.9	02.1	311 57.3	31.8	Al Na'ir	27 40.3	S46 52.6
H 09	238 55.4	314 59.1 ..	24.9	14 51.3 ..	51.7	13 34.9 ..	02.2	326 59.5 ..	31.7	Alnilam	275 42.9	S 1 11.7
U 10	253 57.8	329 58.1	24.7	29 52.3	52.1	28 37.0	02.3	342 01.6	31.7	Alphard	217 52.8	S 8 44.3
R 11	269 00.3	344 57.2	24.5	44 53.2	52.6	43 39.0	02.4	357 03.8	31.7			
S 12	284 02.8	359 56.2	S23 24.3	59 54.1	S15 53.1	58 41.1	S16 02.5	12 05.9	S22 31.7	Alphecca	126 08.7	N26 39.3
D 13	299 05.2	14 55.3	24.1	74 55.0	53.5	73 43.1	02.6	27 08.1	31.7	Alpheratz	357 40.3	N29 11.4
A 14	314 07.7	29 54.3	23.8	89 55.9	54.0	88 45.2	02.7	42 10.2	31.7	Altair	62 05.6	N 8 55.1
Y 15	329 10.2	44 53.3 ..	23.6	104 56.8 ..	54.4	103 47.3 ..	02.9	57 12.4 ..	31.7	Ankaa	353 12.8	S42 12.8
16	344 12.6	59 52.4	23.4	119 57.8	54.9	118 49.3	03.0	72 14.5	31.7	Antares	112 22.8	S26 28.0
17	359 15.1	74 51.4	23.2	134 58.7	55.4	133 51.4	03.1	87 16.7	31.7			
18	14 17.6	89 50.5	S23 23.0	149 59.6	S15 55.8	148 53.4	S16 03.2	102 18.8	S22 31.7	Arcturus	145 53.1	N19 05.3
19	29 20.0	104 49.5	22.7	165 00.5	56.3	163 55.5	03.3	117 21.0	31.7	Atria	107 22.3	S69 03.2
20	44 22.5	119 48.6	22.5	180 01.4	56.7	178 57.5	03.4	132 23.1	31.7	Avior	234 16.1	S59 34.0
21	59 24.9	134 47.6 ..	22.3	195 02.4 ..	57.2	193 59.6 ..	03.5	147 25.3 ..	31.7	Bellatrix	278 28.4	N 6 21.7
22	74 27.4	149 46.7	22.1	210 03.3	57.7	209 01.7	03.6	162 27.4	31.7	Betelgeuse	270 57.6	N 7 24.4
23	89 29.9	164 45.7	21.8	225 04.2	58.1	224 03.7	03.7	177 29.6	31.7			
5 00	104 32.3	179 44.8	S23 21.6	240 05.1	S15 58.6	239 05.8	S16 03.8	192 31.7	S22 31.7	Canopus	263 54.2	S52 42.5
01	119 34.8	194 43.8	21.4	255 06.0	59.0	254 07.8	03.9	207 33.9	31.7	Capella	280 29.4	N46 00.8
02	134 37.3	209 42.8	21.1	270 06.9	15 59.5	269 09.9	04.1	222 36.0	31.7	Deneb	49 29.8	N45 20.9
03	149 39.7	224 41.9 ..	20.9	285 07.8	16 00.0	284 11.9 ..	04.2	237 38.2 ..	31.7	Denebola	182 30.4	N14 28.2
04	164 42.2	239 40.9	20.7	300 08.8	00.4	299 14.0	04.3	252 40.3	31.7	Diphda	348 52.8	S17 53.5
05	179 44.7	254 40.0	20.4	315 09.7	00.9	314 16.1	04.4	267 42.5	31.7			
06	194 47.1	269 39.0	S23 20.2	330 10.6	S16 01.3	329 18.1	S16 04.5	282 44.6	S22 31.7	Dubhe	193 47.7	N61 39.0
07	209 49.6	284 38.1	20.0	345 11.5	01.8	344 20.2	04.6	297 46.8	31.7	Elnath	278 08.4	N28 37.2
F 08	224 52.1	299 37.1	19.7	0 12.4	02.2	359 22.2	04.7	312 48.9	31.7	Eltanin	90 45.2	N51 29.3
R 09	239 54.5	314 36.2 ..	19.5	15 13.3 ..	02.7	14 24.3 ..	04.8	327 51.1 ..	31.7	Enif	33 44.3	N 9 57.5
I 10	254 57.0	329 35.2	19.2	30 14.3	03.2	29 26.4	04.9	342 53.2	31.7	Fomalhaut	15 20.8	S29 31.8
D 11	269 59.4	344 34.3	19.0	45 15.2	03.6	44 28.4	05.0	357 55.4	31.7			
A 12	285 01.9	359 33.3	S23 18.8	60 16.1	S16 04.1	59 30.5	S16 05.1	12 57.5	S22 31.7	Gacrux	171 57.3	S57 12.5
Y 13	300 04.4	14 32.4	18.5	75 17.0	04.5	74 32.5	05.3	27 59.7	31.7	Gienah	175 49.0	S17 38.4
14	315 06.8	29 31.4	18.3	90 17.9	05.0	89 34.6	05.4	43 01.8	31.7	Hadar	148 43.6	S60 27.1
15	330 09.3	44 30.5 ..	18.0	105 18.8 ..	05.4	104 36.7 ..	05.5	58 04.0 ..	31.7	Hamal	327 57.1	N23 32.8
16	345 11.8	59 29.5	17.8	120 19.8	05.9	119 38.7	05.6	73 06.1	31.7	Kaus Aust.	83 40.1	S34 22.4
17	0 14.2	74 28.6	17.5	135 20.7	06.3	134 40.8	05.7	88 08.3	31.7			
18	15 16.7	89 27.6	S23 17.3	150 21.6	S16 06.8	149 42.8	S16 05.8	103 10.4	S22 31.7	Kochab	137 20.8	N74 04.7
19	30 19.2	104 26.7	17.0	165 22.5	07.3	164 44.9	05.9	118 12.6	31.7	Markab	13 35.4	N15 18.2
20	45 21.6	119 25.7	16.8	180 23.4	07.7	179 47.0	06.0	133 14.7	31.7	Menkar	314 11.6	N 4 09.4
21	60 24.1	134 24.8 ..	16.5	195 24.3 ..	08.2	194 49.0 ..	06.1	148 16.9 ..	31.7	Menkent	148 04.0	S36 27.2
22	75 26.6	149 23.8	16.2	210 25.2	08.6	209 51.1	06.2	163 19.0	31.7	Miaplacidus	221 38.1	S69 47.3
23	90 29.0	164 22.9	16.0	225 26.2	09.1	224 53.1	06.3	178 21.2	31.7			
6 00	105 31.5	179 21.9	S23 15.7	240 27.1	S16 09.5	239 55.2	S16 06.4	193 23.3	S22 31.7	Mirfak	308 35.6	N49 55.5
01	120 33.9	194 21.0	15.5	255 28.0	10.0	254 57.3	06.5	208 25.5	31.7	Nunki	75 54.9	S26 16.3
02	135 36.4	209 20.0	15.2	270 28.9	10.4	269 59.3	06.7	223 27.6	31.7	Peacock	53 15.0	S56 40.6
03	150 38.9	224 19.1 ..	14.9	285 29.8 ..	10.9	285 01.4 ..	06.8	238 29.8 ..	31.7	Pollux	243 23.6	N27 58.7
04	165 41.3	239 18.1	14.7	300 30.7	11.3	300 03.5	06.9	253 31.9	31.7	Procyon	244 56.2	N 5 10.5
05	180 43.8	254 17.2	14.4	315 31.6	11.8	315 05.5	07.0	268 34.1	31.7			
06	195 46.3	269 16.2	S23 14.1	330 32.6	S16 12.2	330 07.6	S16 07.1	283 36.2	S22 31.7	Rasalhague	96 03.9	N12 33.0
07	210 48.7	284 15.3	13.9	345 33.5	12.7	345 09.6	07.2	298 38.4	31.7	Regulus	207 40.0	N11 52.6
S 08	225 51.2	299 14.3	13.6	0 34.4	13.1	0 11.7	07.3	313 40.5	31.6	Rigel	281 08.8	S 8 11.1
A 09	240 53.7	314 13.4 ..	13.3	15 35.3 ..	13.6	15 13.8 ..	07.4	328 42.7 ..	31.6	Rigil Kent.	139 47.8	S60 54.1
T 10	255 56.1	329 12.4	13.1	30 36.2	14.0	30 15.8	07.5	343 44.8	31.6	Sabik	102 09.3	S15 44.6
U 11	270 58.6	344 11.5	12.8	45 37.1	14.5	45 17.9	07.6	358 47.0	31.6			
R 12	286 01.0	359 10.5	S23 12.5	60 38.0	S16 15.0	60 20.0	S16 07.7	13 49.1	S22 31.6	Schedar	349 36.9	N56 38.3
D 13	301 03.5	14 09.6	12.2	75 38.9	15.4	75 22.0	07.8	28 51.3	31.6	Shaula	96 18.1	S37 06.7
A 14	316 06.0	29 08.7	12.0	90 39.9	15.9	90 24.1	07.9	43 53.4	31.6	Sirius	258 30.6	S16 44.7
Y 15	331 08.4	44 07.7 ..	11.7	105 40.8 ..	16.3	105 26.2 ..	08.0	58 55.6 ..	31.6	Spica	158 28.0	S11 15.1
16	346 10.9	59 06.8	11.4	120 41.7	16.8	120 28.2	08.1	73 57.7	31.6	Suhail	222 49.7	S43 30.3
17	1 13.4	74 05.8	11.1	135 42.6	17.2	135 30.3	08.3	88 59.9	31.6			
18	16 15.8	89 04.9	S23 10.9	150 43.5	S16 17.7	150 32.4	S16 08.4	104 02.0	S22 31.6	Vega	80 37.3	N38 48.1
19	31 18.3	104 03.9	10.6	165 44.4	18.1	165 34.4	08.5	119 04.2	31.6	Zuben'ubi	137 02.2	S16 06.8
20	46 20.8	119 03.0	10.3	180 45.3	18.6	180 36.5	08.6	134 06.3	31.6		SHA	Mer.Pass.
21	61 23.2	134 02.0 ..	10.0	195 46.2 ..	19.0	195 38.5 ..	08.7	149 08.5 ..	31.6		° '	h m
22	76 25.7	149 01.1	09.7	210 47.2	19.5	210 40.6	08.8	164 10.6	31.6	Venus	75 12.4	12 02
23	91 28.2	164 00.2	09.4	225 48.1	19.9	225 42.7	08.9	179 12.8	31.6	Mars	135 32.8	7 59
	h m									Jupiter	134 33.4	8 03
Mer. Pass. 16 59.1	v −1.0 d 0.2			v 0.9 d 0.5		v 2.1 d 0.1		v 2.2 d 0.0		Saturn	87 59.4	11 08

UT	SUN GHA	SUN Dec	MOON GHA	v	MOON Dec	d	HP
d h	° ′	° ′	° ′	′	° ′	′	′
4 00	178 49.1	S22 44.6	330 50.5	5.1	N17 12.6	6.8	60.8
01	193 48.8	44.4	345 14.6	5.1	17 05.8	7.0	60.7
02	208 48.5	44.1	359 38.7	5.2	16 58.8	7.0	60.7
03	223 48.2	.. 43.9	14 02.9	5.3	16 51.8	7.2	60.7
04	238 47.9	43.6	28 27.2	5.4	16 44.6	7.3	60.7
05	253 47.7	43.3	42 51.6	5.5	16 37.3	7.4	60.6
06	268 47.4	S22 43.1	57 16.1	5.6	N16 29.9	7.4	60.6
07	283 47.1	42.8	71 40.7	5.6	16 22.5	7.6	60.6
08	298 46.8	42.5	86 05.3	5.8	16 14.9	7.7	60.5
T 09	313 46.5	.. 42.3	100 30.1	5.8	16 07.2	7.8	60.5
H 10	328 46.3	42.0	114 54.9	6.0	15 59.4	7.9	60.5
U 11	343 46.0	41.8	129 19.9	6.0	15 51.5	8.0	60.4
R 12	358 45.7	S22 41.5	143 44.9	6.1	N15 43.5	8.1	60.4
S 13	13 45.4	41.2	158 10.0	6.2	15 35.4	8.2	60.4
D 14	28 45.1	41.0	172 35.2	6.3	15 27.2	8.3	60.3
A 15	43 44.8	.. 40.7	187 00.5	6.4	15 18.9	8.4	60.3
Y 16	58 44.6	40.4	201 25.9	6.5	15 10.5	8.4	60.3
17	73 44.3	40.1	215 51.4	6.6	15 02.1	8.6	60.2
18	88 44.0	S22 39.9	230 17.0	6.6	N14 53.5	8.6	60.2
19	103 43.7	39.6	244 42.6	6.8	14 44.9	8.8	60.2
20	118 43.4	39.3	259 08.4	6.8	14 36.1	8.8	60.1
21	133 43.2	.. 39.1	273 34.2	7.0	14 27.3	8.9	60.1
22	148 42.9	38.8	288 00.2	7.1	14 18.4	8.9	60.1
23	163 42.6	38.5	302 26.3	7.1	14 09.5	9.1	60.0
5 00	178 42.3	S22 38.2	316 52.4	7.2	N14 00.4	9.1	60.0
01	193 42.0	37.9	331 18.6	7.4	13 51.3	9.2	60.0
02	208 41.8	37.7	345 45.0	7.4	13 42.1	9.3	59.9
03	223 41.5	.. 37.4	0 11.4	7.5	13 32.8	9.4	59.9
04	238 41.2	37.1	14 37.9	7.6	13 23.4	9.4	59.8
05	253 40.9	36.8	29 04.5	7.7	13 14.0	9.5	59.8
06	268 40.6	S22 36.6	43 31.2	7.8	N13 04.5	9.6	59.8
07	283 40.4	36.3	57 58.0	7.9	12 54.9	9.6	59.7
F 08	298 40.1	36.0	72 24.9	8.0	12 45.3	9.7	59.7
R 09	313 39.8	.. 35.7	86 51.9	8.1	12 35.6	9.8	59.7
I 10	328 39.5	35.4	101 19.0	8.2	12 25.8	9.8	59.6
D 11	343 39.3	35.1	115 46.2	8.2	12 16.0	9.9	59.6
A 12	358 39.0	S22 34.9	130 13.4	8.4	N12 06.1	10.0	59.5
Y 13	13 38.7	34.6	144 40.8	8.4	11 56.1	10.0	59.5
14	28 38.4	34.3	159 08.2	8.6	11 46.1	10.0	59.5
15	43 38.2	.. 34.0	173 35.8	8.6	11 36.1	10.2	59.4
16	58 37.9	33.7	188 03.4	8.7	11 25.9	10.1	59.4
17	73 37.6	33.4	202 31.1	8.8	11 15.8	10.3	59.3
18	88 37.3	S22 33.1	216 58.9	8.9	N11 05.5	10.2	59.3
19	103 37.0	32.8	231 26.8	9.0	10 55.3	10.4	59.3
20	118 36.8	32.5	245 54.8	9.1	10 44.9	10.3	59.2
21	133 36.5	.. 32.2	260 22.9	9.1	10 34.6	10.5	59.2
22	148 36.2	32.0	274 51.0	9.3	10 24.1	10.4	59.2
23	163 35.9	31.7	289 19.3	9.3	10 13.7	10.5	59.1
6 00	178 35.7	S22 31.4	303 47.6	9.5	N10 03.2	10.6	59.1
01	193 35.4	31.1	318 16.1	9.5	9 52.6	10.6	59.0
02	208 35.1	30.8	332 44.6	9.6	9 42.0	10.6	59.0
03	223 34.8	.. 30.5	347 13.2	9.6	9 31.4	10.7	58.9
04	238 34.6	30.2	1 41.8	9.8	9 20.7	10.7	58.9
05	253 34.3	29.9	16 10.6	9.8	9 10.0	10.8	58.9
06	268 34.0	S22 29.6	30 39.4	10.0	N 8 59.2	10.8	58.8
07	283 33.8	29.3	45 08.4	10.0	8 48.4	10.8	58.8
S 08	298 33.5	29.0	59 37.4	10.1	8 37.6	10.8	58.7
A 09	313 33.2	.. 28.7	74 06.5	10.1	8 26.8	10.9	58.7
T 10	328 32.9	28.4	88 35.6	10.3	8 15.9	10.9	58.7
U 11	343 32.7	28.1	103 04.9	10.3	8 05.0	11.0	58.6
R 12	358 32.4	S22 27.8	117 34.2	10.4	N 7 54.0	10.9	58.6
D 13	13 32.1	27.5	132 03.6	10.5	7 43.1	11.0	58.5
A 14	28 31.8	27.2	146 33.1	10.6	7 32.1	11.0	58.5
Y 15	43 31.6	.. 26.9	161 02.7	10.6	7 21.1	11.1	58.5
16	58 31.3	26.5	175 32.3	10.7	7 10.0	11.1	58.4
17	73 31.0	26.2	190 02.0	10.8	6 59.0	11.1	58.4
18	88 30.8	S22 25.9	204 31.8	10.9	N 6 47.9	11.1	58.3
19	103 30.5	25.6	219 01.7	10.9	6 36.8	11.2	58.3
20	118 30.2	25.3	233 31.6	11.0	6 25.6	11.1	58.2
21	133 29.9	.. 25.0	248 01.6	11.0	6 14.5	11.2	58.2
22	148 29.7	24.7	262 31.6	11.2	6 03.3	11.1	58.2
23	163 29.4	24.4	277 01.8	11.2	N 5 52.2	11.2	58.1
	SD 16.3	d 0.3	SD 16.5		16.2		16.0

Lat.	Twilight Naut.	Civil	Sunrise	Moonrise 4	5	6	7
°	h m	h m	h m	h m	h m	h m	h m
N 72	08 19	10 30	■	16 57	19 12	21 12	23 03
N 70	08 01	09 43	■	17 32	19 30	21 21	23 05
68	07 47	09 12	11 29	17 56	19 45	21 28	23 07
66	07 35	08 49	10 20	18 15	19 57	21 35	23 08
64	07 25	08 31	09 45	18 30	20 07	21 40	23 09
62	07 16	08 17	09 19	18 43	20 15	21 44	23 10
60	07 08	08 04	09 00	18 54	20 22	21 48	23 11
N 58	07 01	07 53	08 43	19 03	20 28	21 51	23 11
56	06 55	07 43	08 30	19 11	20 34	21 54	23 12
54	06 49	07 35	08 18	19 18	20 39	21 57	23 12
52	06 44	07 27	08 07	19 25	20 43	22 00	23 13
50	06 39	07 20	07 58	19 31	20 47	22 02	23 13
45	06 28	07 05	07 38	19 43	20 56	22 07	23 14
N 40	06 18	06 52	07 22	19 54	21 03	22 11	23 15
35	06 09	06 41	07 09	20 02	21 10	22 14	23 16
30	06 01	06 30	06 57	20 10	21 15	22 17	23 16
20	05 45	06 12	06 36	20 23	21 25	22 22	23 17
N 10	05 30	05 56	06 18	20 35	21 33	22 27	23 19
0	05 13	05 39	06 02	20 46	21 41	22 31	23 20
S 10	04 55	05 22	05 45	20 57	21 48	22 36	23 20
20	04 33	05 02	05 27	21 08	21 56	22 40	23 22
30	04 05	04 38	05 05	21 21	22 06	22 46	23 23
35	03 47	04 23	04 53	21 29	22 11	22 49	23 23
40	03 25	04 06	04 38	21 38	22 17	22 52	23 24
45	02 56	03 44	04 21	21 48	22 24	22 56	23 25
S 50	02 14	03 16	04 00	22 00	22 33	23 01	23 26
52	01 49	03 02	03 49	22 05	22 37	23 03	23 27
54	01 13	02 45	03 38	22 12	22 41	23 05	23 27
56	////	02 25	03 24	22 19	22 46	23 08	23 28
58	////	01 58	03 09	22 26	22 51	23 11	23 28
S 60	////	01 19	02 50	22 35	22 57	23 14	23 29

Lat.	Sunset	Twilight Civil	Naut.	Moonset 4	5	6	7
°	h m	h m	h m	h m	h m	h m	h m
N 72	■	13 42	15 52	12 20	12 02	11 49	11 38
N 70	■	14 29	16 10	11 45	11 41	11 38	11 34
68	12 42	14 59	16 24	11 19	11 25	11 28	11 30
66	13 51	15 22	16 36	10 59	11 12	11 21	11 27
64	14 27	15 40	16 46	10 43	11 01	11 14	11 24
62	14 52	15 55	16 55	10 30	10 52	11 08	11 22
60	15 11	16 07	17 03	10 18	10 44	11 03	11 20
N 58	15 28	16 18	17 10	10 08	10 37	10 59	11 18
56	15 41	16 28	17 16	10 00	10 30	10 55	11 16
54	15 53	16 36	17 22	09 52	10 25	10 52	11 15
52	16 04	16 44	17 27	09 45	10 20	10 48	11 13
50	16 13	16 51	17 32	09 38	10 15	10 45	11 12
45	16 33	17 06	17 43	09 25	10 05	10 39	11 09
N 40	16 49	17 19	17 53	09 14	09 56	10 34	11 07
35	17 02	17 30	18 02	09 04	09 49	10 29	11 05
30	17 14	17 40	18 10	08 55	09 43	10 25	11 03
20	17 35	17 58	18 26	08 41	09 32	10 18	11 00
N 10	17 52	18 15	18 41	08 28	09 22	10 11	10 57
0	18 09	18 32	18 58	08 16	09 12	10 05	10 55
S 10	18 26	18 49	19 16	08 03	09 03	09 59	10 52
20	18 44	19 09	19 38	07 50	08 53	09 53	10 49
30	19 05	19 32	20 05	07 35	08 41	09 45	10 46
35	19 18	19 47	20 23	07 26	08 35	09 41	10 44
40	19 32	20 04	20 47	07 16	08 27	09 36	10 42
45	19 49	20 26	21 14	07 04	08 18	09 30	10 39
S 50	20 11	20 54	21 56	06 50	08 07	09 23	10 36
52	20 21	21 08	22 20	06 43	08 02	09 20	10 35
54	20 32	21 25	22 56	06 35	07 56	09 16	10 33
56	20 46	21 45	////	06 27	07 50	09 12	10 31
58	21 01	22 11	////	06 17	07 43	09 08	10 30
S 60	21 20	22 49	////	06 06	07 35	09 03	10 27

	SUN Eqn. of Time 00h	12h	Mer. Pass.	MOON Mer. Pass. Upper	Lower	Age	Phase
Day	m s	m s	h m	h m	h m	d	%
4	04 43	04 57	12 05	02 01	14 31	17	92
5	05 10	05 24	12 05	02 59	15 27	18	84
6	05 37	05 50	12 06	03 53	16 18	19	75

2018 JANUARY 7, 8, 9 (SUN., MON., TUES.)

UT	ARIES GHA	VENUS −4.0 GHA	Dec	MARS +1.4 GHA	Dec	JUPITER −1.8 GHA	Dec	SATURN +0.5 GHA	Dec	Name	SHA	Dec
d h	° ′	° ′	° ′	° ′	° ′	° ′	° ′	° ′	° ′		° ′	° ′
7 00	106 30.6	178 59.2	S23 09.1	240 49.0	S16 20.4	240 44.7	S16 09.0	194 14.9	S22 31.6	Acamar	315 15.8	S40 14.4
01	121 33.1	193 58.3	08.8	255 49.9	20.8	255 46.8	09.1	209 17.1	31.6	Achernar	335 24.5	S57 09.2
02	136 35.5	208 57.3	08.6	270 50.8	21.3	270 48.9	09.2	224 19.2	31.6	Acrux	173 05.6	S63 11.6
03	151 38.0	223 56.4 ..	08.3	285 51.7 ..	21.7	285 50.9 ..	09.3	239 21.4 ..	31.6	Adhara	255 09.7	S29 00.0
04	166 40.5	238 55.4	08.0	300 52.6	22.1	300 53.0	09.4	254 23.6	31.6	Aldebaran	290 45.5	N16 32.5
05	181 42.9	253 54.5	07.7	315 53.5	22.6	315 55.1	09.5	269 25.7	31.6			
06	196 45.4	268 53.6	S23 07.4	330 54.5	S16 23.0	330 57.1	S16 09.6	284 27.9	S22 31.6	Alioth	166 18.0	N55 51.5
07	211 47.9	283 52.6	07.1	345 55.4	23.5	345 59.2	09.7	299 30.0	31.6	Alkaid	152 56.6	N49 13.3
08	226 50.3	298 51.7	06.8	0 56.3	23.9	1 01.3	09.8	314 32.2	31.6	Al Na'ir	27 40.3	S46 52.6
09	241 52.8	313 50.7 ..	06.5	15 57.2 ..	24.4	16 03.3 ..	09.9	329 34.3 ..	31.6	Alnilam	275 42.9	S 1 11.7
10	256 55.3	328 49.8	06.2	30 58.1	24.8	31 05.4	10.1	344 36.5	31.6	Alphard	217 52.8	S 8 44.3
11	271 57.7	343 48.9	05.9	45 59.0	25.3	46 07.5	10.2	359 38.6	31.6			
12	287 00.2	358 47.9	S23 05.6	60 59.9	S16 25.7	61 09.6	S16 10.3	14 40.8	S22 31.6	Alphecca	126 08.6	N26 39.3
13	302 02.7	13 47.0	05.3	76 00.8	26.2	76 11.6	10.4	29 42.9	31.6	Alpheratz	357 40.4	N29 11.4
14	317 05.1	28 46.0	05.0	91 01.7	26.6	91 13.7	10.5	44 45.1	31.6	Altair	62 05.6	N 8 55.1
15	332 07.6	43 45.1 ..	04.7	106 02.6 ..	27.1	106 15.8 ..	10.6	59 47.2 ..	31.6	Ankaa	353 12.8	S42 12.8
16	347 10.0	58 44.2	04.3	121 03.6	27.5	121 17.8	10.7	74 49.4	31.6	Antares	112 22.8	S26 28.0
17	2 12.5	73 43.2	04.0	136 04.5	28.0	136 19.9	10.8	89 51.5	31.6			
18	17 15.0	88 42.3	S23 03.7	151 05.4	S16 28.4	151 22.0	S16 10.9	104 53.7	S22 31.6	Arcturus	145 53.0	N19 05.3
19	32 17.4	103 41.3	03.4	166 06.3	28.9	166 24.0	11.0	119 55.8	31.6	Atria	107 22.2	S69 03.2
20	47 19.9	118 40.4	03.1	181 07.2	29.3	181 26.1	11.1	134 58.0	31.6	Avior	234 16.1	S59 34.0
21	62 22.4	133 39.5 ..	02.8	196 08.1 ..	29.7	196 28.2 ..	11.2	150 00.1 ..	31.6	Bellatrix	278 28.4	N 6 21.7
22	77 24.8	148 38.5	02.5	211 09.0	30.2	211 30.2	11.3	165 02.3	31.5	Betelgeuse	270 57.6	N 7 24.4
23	92 27.3	163 37.6	02.1	226 09.9	30.6	226 32.3	11.4	180 04.4	31.5			
8 00	107 29.8	178 36.7	S23 01.8	241 10.8	S16 31.1	241 34.4	S16 11.5	195 06.6	S22 31.5	Canopus	263 54.2	S52 42.6
01	122 32.2	193 35.7	01.5	256 11.7	31.5	256 36.5	11.6	210 08.7	31.5	Capella	280 29.4	N46 00.8
02	137 34.7	208 34.8	01.2	271 12.7	32.0	271 38.5	11.7	225 10.9	31.5	Deneb	49 29.8	N45 20.8
03	152 37.1	223 33.8 ..	00.9	286 13.6 ..	32.4	286 40.6 ..	11.8	240 13.0 ..	31.5	Denebola	182 30.4	N14 28.2
04	167 39.6	238 32.9	00.5	301 14.5	32.9	301 42.7	11.9	255 15.2	31.5	Diphda	348 52.8	S17 53.5
05	182 42.1	253 32.0	23 00.2	316 15.4	33.3	316 44.7	12.0	270 17.3	31.5			
06	197 44.5	268 31.0	S22 59.9	331 16.3	S16 33.7	331 46.8	S16 12.1	285 19.5	S22 31.5	Dubhe	193 47.7	N61 39.0
07	212 47.0	283 30.1	59.6	346 17.2	34.2	346 48.9	12.2	300 21.7	31.5	Elnath	278 08.4	N28 37.2
08	227 49.5	298 29.2	59.2	1 18.1	34.6	1 51.0	12.4	315 23.8	31.5	Eltanin	90 45.2	N51 29.3
M 09	242 51.9	313 28.2 ..	58.9	16 19.0 ..	35.1	16 53.0 ..	12.5	330 26.0 ..	31.5	Enif	33 44.4	N 9 57.5
O 10	257 54.4	328 27.3	58.6	31 19.9	35.5	31 55.1	12.6	345 28.1	31.5	Fomalhaut	15 20.8	S29 31.8
N 11	272 56.9	343 26.4	58.2	46 20.8	35.9	46 57.2	12.7	0 30.3	31.5			
D 12	287 59.3	358 25.4	S22 57.9	61 21.7	S16 36.4	61 59.2	S16 12.8	15 32.4	S22 31.5	Gacrux	171 57.3	S57 12.5
A 13	303 01.8	13 24.5	57.6	76 22.7	36.8	77 01.3	12.9	30 34.6	31.5	Gienah	175 49.0	S17 38.4
Y 14	318 04.3	28 23.6	57.2	91 23.6	37.3	92 03.4	13.0	45 36.7	31.5	Hadar	148 43.6	S60 27.1
15	333 06.7	43 22.6 ..	56.9	106 24.5 ..	37.7	107 05.5 ..	13.1	60 38.9 ..	31.5	Hamal	327 57.1	N23 32.8
16	348 09.2	58 21.7	56.6	121 25.4	38.2	122 07.5	13.2	75 41.0	31.5	Kaus Aust.	83 40.1	S34 22.4
17	3 11.6	73 20.8	56.2	136 26.3	38.6	137 09.6	13.3	90 43.2	31.5			
18	18 14.1	88 19.8	S22 55.9	151 27.2	S16 39.0	152 11.7	S16 13.4	105 45.3	S22 31.5	Kochab	137 20.8	N74 04.7
19	33 16.6	103 18.9	55.5	166 28.1	39.5	167 13.8	13.5	120 47.5	31.5	Markab	13 35.4	N15 18.1
20	48 19.0	118 18.0	55.2	181 29.0	39.9	182 15.8	13.6	135 49.6	31.5	Menkar	314 11.6	N 4 09.4
21	63 21.5	133 17.0 ..	54.8	196 29.9 ..	40.4	197 17.9 ..	13.7	150 51.8 ..	31.5	Menkent	148 04.0	S36 27.2
22	78 24.0	148 16.1	54.5	211 30.8	40.8	212 20.0	13.8	165 53.9	31.5	Miaplacidus	221 38.1	S69 47.4
23	93 26.4	163 15.2	54.2	226 31.7	41.2	227 22.1	13.9	180 56.1	31.5			
9 00	108 28.9	178 14.3	S22 53.8	241 32.6	S16 41.7	242 24.1	S16 14.0	195 58.2	S22 31.5	Mirfak	308 35.6	N49 55.5
01	123 31.4	193 13.3	53.5	256 33.5	42.1	257 26.2	14.1	211 00.4	31.5	Nunki	75 54.9	S26 16.3
02	138 33.8	208 12.4	53.1	271 34.5	42.6	272 28.3	14.2	226 02.6	31.5	Peacock	53 15.0	S56 40.6
03	153 36.3	223 11.5 ..	52.8	286 35.4 ..	43.0	287 30.4 ..	14.3	241 04.7 ..	31.5	Pollux	243 23.6	N27 58.7
04	168 38.7	238 10.5	52.4	301 36.3	43.4	302 32.4	14.4	256 06.9	31.5	Procyon	244 56.2	N 5 10.5
05	183 41.2	253 09.6	52.0	316 37.2	43.9	317 34.5	14.5	271 09.0	31.5			
06	198 43.7	268 08.7	S22 51.7	331 38.1	S16 44.3	332 36.6	S16 14.6	286 11.2	S22 31.4	Rasalhague	96 03.9	N12 32.9
07	213 46.1	283 07.8	51.3	346 39.0	44.8	347 38.7	14.7	301 13.3	31.4	Regulus	207 40.0	N11 52.6
T 08	228 48.6	298 06.8	51.0	1 39.9	45.2	2 40.7	14.8	316 15.5	31.4	Rigel	281 08.8	S 8 11.1
U 09	243 51.1	313 05.9 ..	50.6	16 40.8 ..	45.6	17 42.8 ..	14.9	331 17.6 ..	31.4	Rigil Kent.	139 47.7	S60 54.1
E 10	258 53.5	328 05.0	50.3	31 41.7	46.1	32 44.9	15.0	346 19.8	31.4	Sabik	102 09.3	S15 44.6
S 11	273 56.0	343 04.0	49.9	46 42.6	46.5	47 47.0	15.1	1 21.9	31.4			
D 12	288 58.5	358 03.1	S22 49.5	61 43.5	S16 46.9	62 49.0	S16 15.2	16 24.1	S22 31.4	Schedar	349 37.0	N56 38.3
A 13	304 00.9	13 02.2	49.2	76 44.4	47.4	77 51.1	15.3	31 26.2	31.4	Shaula	96 18.1	S37 06.7
Y 14	319 03.4	28 01.3	48.8	91 45.3	47.8	92 53.2	15.4	46 28.4	31.4	Sirius	258 30.6	S16 44.7
15	334 05.9	43 00.3 ..	48.4	106 46.2 ..	48.3	107 55.3 ..	15.5	61 30.5 ..	31.4	Spica	158 28.0	S11 15.2
16	349 08.3	57 59.4	48.1	121 47.2	48.7	122 57.3	15.6	76 32.7	31.4	Suhail	222 49.7	S43 30.3
17	4 10.8	72 58.5	47.7	136 48.1	49.1	137 59.4	15.7	91 34.9	31.4			
18	19 13.2	87 57.6	S22 47.3	151 49.0	S16 49.6	153 01.5	S16 15.8	106 37.0	S22 31.4	Vega	80 37.3	N38 48.1
19	34 15.7	102 56.6	47.0	166 49.9	50.0	168 03.6	15.9	121 39.2	31.4	Zuben'ubi	137 02.1	S16 06.8
20	49 18.2	117 55.7	46.6	181 50.8	50.4	183 05.7	16.0	136 41.3	31.4		SHA	Mer. Pass.
21	64 20.6	132 54.8 ..	46.2	196 51.7 ..	50.9	198 07.7 ..	16.1	151 43.5 ..	31.4		° ′	h m
22	79 23.1	147 53.9	45.8	211 52.6	51.3	213 09.8	16.2	166 45.6	31.4	Venus	71 06.9	12 06
23	94 25.6	162 52.9	45.5	226 53.5	51.7	228 11.9	16.3	181 47.8	31.4	Mars	133 41.1	7 55
	h m									Jupiter	134 04.6	7 53
Mer. Pass. 16 47.3		v −0.9	d 0.3	v 0.9	d 0.4	v 2.1	d 0.1	v 2.2	d 0.0	Saturn	87 36.8	10 58

UT	SUN GHA	SUN Dec	MOON GHA	v	MOON Dec	d	HP
d h	° ′	° ′	° ′	′	° ′	′	′
7 00	178 29.1	S22 24.1	291 32.0	11.3	N 5 41.0	11.2	58.1
01	193 28.9	23.8	306 02.3	11.3	5 29.8	11.2	58.0
02	208 28.6	23.4	320 32.6	11.4	5 18.6	11.3	58.0
03	223 28.3	.. 23.1	335 03.0	11.5	5 07.3	11.2	58.0
04	238 28.0	22.8	349 33.5	11.5	4 56.1	11.2	57.9
05	253 27.8	22.5	4 04.0	11.7	4 44.9	11.3	57.9
S 06	268 27.5	S22 22.2	18 34.7	11.6	N 4 33.6	11.2	57.8
U 07	283 27.2	21.9	33 05.3	11.7	4 22.4	11.3	57.8
N 08	298 27.0	21.5	47 36.0	11.8	4 11.1	11.3	57.8
D 09	313 26.7	.. 21.2	62 06.8	11.9	3 59.8	11.2	57.7
A 10	328 26.4	20.9	76 37.7	11.9	3 48.6	11.3	57.7
Y 11	343 26.2	20.6	91 08.6	12.0	3 37.3	11.3	57.6
12	358 25.9	S22 20.2	105 39.6	12.0	N 3 26.0	11.3	57.6
13	13 25.6	19.9	120 10.6	12.1	3 14.7	11.3	57.6
14	28 25.4	19.6	134 41.7	12.1	3 03.4	11.2	57.5
15	43 25.1	.. 19.3	149 12.8	12.2	2 52.2	11.3	57.5
16	58 24.8	19.0	163 44.0	12.2	2 40.9	11.3	57.4
17	73 24.6	18.6	178 15.2	12.3	2 29.6	11.3	57.4
18	88 24.3	S22 18.3	192 46.5	12.4	N 2 18.3	11.2	57.4
19	103 24.0	18.0	207 17.9	12.4	2 07.1	11.3	57.3
20	118 23.8	17.6	221 49.3	12.4	1 55.8	11.2	57.3
21	133 23.5	.. 17.3	236 20.7	12.5	1 44.6	11.3	57.2
22	148 23.2	17.0	250 52.2	12.6	1 33.3	11.2	57.2
23	163 23.0	16.7	265 23.8	12.6	1 22.1	11.3	57.2
8 00	178 22.7	S22 16.3	279 55.4	12.6	N 1 10.8	11.2	57.1
01	193 22.4	16.0	294 27.0	12.7	0 59.6	11.2	57.1
02	208 22.2	15.7	308 58.7	12.7	0 48.4	11.2	57.1
03	223 21.9	.. 15.3	323 30.4	12.8	0 37.2	11.2	57.0
04	238 21.6	15.0	338 02.2	12.8	0 26.0	11.1	57.0
05	253 21.4	14.7	352 34.0	12.9	0 14.9	11.2	56.9
06	268 21.1	S22 14.3	7 05.9	12.9	N 0 03.7	11.1	56.9
07	283 20.8	14.0	21 37.8	12.9	S 0 07.4	11.2	56.9
08	298 20.6	13.6	36 09.7	13.0	0 18.6	11.1	56.8
M 09	313 20.3	.. 13.3	50 41.7	13.0	0 29.7	11.1	56.8
O 10	328 20.1	13.0	65 13.7	13.1	0 40.8	11.1	56.8
N 11	343 19.8	12.6	79 45.8	13.1	0 51.9	11.0	56.7
D 12	358 19.5	S22 12.3	94 17.9	13.1	S 1 02.9	11.1	56.7
A 13	13 19.3	11.9	108 50.0	13.2	1 14.0	11.0	56.6
Y 14	28 19.0	11.6	123 22.2	13.2	1 25.0	11.0	56.6
15	43 18.7	.. 11.3	137 54.4	13.2	1 36.0	11.0	56.6
16	58 18.5	10.9	152 26.6	13.2	1 47.0	10.9	56.5
17	73 18.2	10.6	166 58.8	13.3	1 57.9	11.0	56.5
18	88 18.0	S22 10.2	181 31.1	13.4	S 2 08.9	10.9	56.5
19	103 17.7	09.9	196 03.5	13.3	2 19.8	10.8	56.4
20	118 17.4	09.5	210 35.8	13.4	2 30.6	10.9	56.4
21	133 17.2	.. 09.2	225 08.2	13.4	2 41.5	10.8	56.4
22	148 16.9	08.8	239 40.6	13.4	2 52.3	10.9	56.3
23	163 16.7	08.5	254 13.0	13.5	3 03.2	10.7	56.3
9 00	178 16.4	S22 08.1	268 45.5	13.5	S 3 13.9	10.8	56.3
01	193 16.1	07.8	283 18.0	13.5	3 24.7	10.7	56.2
02	208 15.9	07.4	297 50.5	13.5	3 35.4	10.7	56.2
03	223 15.6	.. 07.1	312 23.0	13.6	3 46.1	10.7	56.2
04	238 15.4	06.7	326 55.6	13.6	3 56.8	10.6	56.1
05	253 15.1	06.4	341 28.2	13.6	4 07.4	10.6	56.1
06	268 14.8	S22 06.0	356 00.8	13.6	S 4 18.0	10.6	56.1
07	283 14.6	05.7	10 33.4	13.6	4 28.6	10.6	56.0
T 08	298 14.3	05.3	25 06.0	13.7	4 39.2	10.5	56.0
U 09	313 14.1	.. 05.0	39 38.7	13.6	4 49.7	10.4	56.0
E 10	328 13.8	04.6	54 11.3	13.7	5 00.1	10.5	55.9
S 11	343 13.5	04.2	68 44.0	13.7	5 10.6	10.5	55.9
D 12	358 13.3	S22 03.9	83 16.7	13.8	S 5 21.0	10.4	55.9
A 13	13 13.0	03.5	97 49.5	13.7	5 31.4	10.3	55.8
Y 14	28 12.8	03.2	112 22.2	13.8	5 41.7	10.3	55.8
15	43 12.5	.. 02.8	126 55.0	13.7	5 52.0	10.3	55.8
16	58 12.3	02.4	141 27.7	13.8	6 02.3	10.2	55.7
17	73 12.0	02.1	156 00.5	13.8	6 12.5	10.2	55.7
18	88 11.8	S22 01.7	170 33.3	13.8	S 6 22.7	10.2	55.7
19	103 11.4	01.4	185 06.1	13.8	6 32.9	10.1	55.7
20	118 11.2	01.0	199 38.9	13.8	6 43.0	10.0	55.6
21	133 11.0	.. 00.6	214 11.7	13.8	6 53.0	10.1	55.6
22	148 10.7	22 00.3	228 44.5	13.9	7 03.1	10.0	55.6
23	163 10.5	S21 59.9	243 17.4	13.8	S 7 13.1	9.9	55.5
	SD 16.3	d 0.3	SD 15.7	15.4			15.2

Lat.	Twilight Naut.	Twilight Civil	Sunrise	Moonrise 7	8	9	10
°	h m	h m	h m	h m	h m	h m	h m
N 72	08 15	10 19	■■	23 03	24 50	00 50	02 35
N 70	07 58	09 36	■■	23 05	24 45	00 45	02 22
68	07 44	09 07	11 09	23 07	24 41	00 41	02 13
66	07 32	08 46	10 13	23 08	24 37	00 37	02 04
64	07 23	08 28	09 40	23 09	24 35	00 35	01 58
62	07 14	08 14	09 16	23 10	24 32	00 32	01 52
60	07 07	08 02	08 57	23 11	24 30	00 30	01 47
N 58	07 00	07 51	08 41	23 11	24 28	00 28	01 42
56	06 54	07 42	08 28	23 12	24 26	00 26	01 38
54	06 48	07 34	08 16	23 12	24 25	00 25	01 35
52	06 43	07 26	08 06	23 13	24 23	00 23	01 32
50	06 38	07 19	07 57	23 13	24 22	00 22	01 29
45	06 28	07 04	07 38	23 14	24 19	00 19	01 22
N 40	06 18	06 52	07 22	23 15	24 17	00 17	01 17
35	06 09	06 41	07 09	23 16	24 15	00 15	01 13
30	06 01	06 31	06 57	23 16	24 13	00 13	01 09
20	05 46	06 13	06 37	23 18	24 11	00 11	01 02
N 10	05 31	05 57	06 19	23 19	24 08	00 08	00 56
0	05 15	05 41	06 03	23 20	24 06	00 06	00 51
S 10	04 57	05 24	05 46	23 20	24 03	00 03	00 45
20	04 35	05 04	05 28	23 22	24 01	00 01	00 39
30	04 08	04 41	05 08	23 23	23 58	24 33	00 33
35	03 50	04 26	04 55	23 23	23 56	24 29	00 29
40	03 28	04 09	04 41	23 24	23 55	24 25	00 25
45	03 00	03 48	04 24	23 25	23 53	24 20	00 20
S 50	02 19	03 20	04 03	23 26	23 50	24 14	00 14
52	01 56	03 06	03 53	23 27	23 49	24 11	00 11
54	01 22	02 50	03 42	23 27	23 48	24 08	00 08
56	////	02 31	03 29	23 28	23 46	24 05	00 05
58	////	02 08	03 14	23 28	23 45	24 02	00 02
S 60	////	01 30	02 56	23 29	23 43	23 58	24 13

Lat.	Sunset	Twilight Civil	Twilight Naut.	Moonset 7	8	9	10
°	h m	h m	h m	h m	h m	h m	h m
N 72	■■	13 55	15 59	11 38	11 29	11 19	11 08
N 70	■■	14 38	16 16	11 34	11 30	11 26	11 22
68	13 05	15 06	16 30	11 30	11 31	11 32	11 33
66	14 01	15 28	16 41	11 27	11 32	11 37	11 43
64	14 34	15 45	16 51	11 24	11 33	11 41	11 51
62	14 58	16 00	17 00	11 22	11 34	11 45	11 58
60	15 17	16 12	17 07	11 20	11 34	11 49	12 03
N 58	15 33	16 23	17 14	11 18	11 35	11 51	12 09
56	15 46	16 32	17 20	11 16	11 35	11 54	12 13
54	15 58	16 40	17 26	11 15	11 36	11 56	12 18
52	16 08	16 48	17 31	11 13	11 36	11 59	12 22
50	16 17	16 54	17 35	11 12	11 37	12 01	12 25
45	16 36	17 09	17 46	11 09	11 38	12 05	12 33
N 40	16 52	17 22	17 56	11 07	11 38	12 08	12 39
35	17 05	17 33	18 04	11 05	11 39	12 12	12 44
30	17 17	17 43	18 12	11 03	11 39	12 14	12 49
20	17 37	18 00	18 28	11 00	11 40	12 19	12 58
N 10	17 54	18 17	18 43	10 57	11 41	12 23	13 05
0	18 10	18 33	18 59	10 55	11 42	12 27	13 12
S 10	18 27	18 50	19 17	10 52	11 42	12 31	13 19
20	18 45	19 09	19 38	10 49	11 43	12 35	13 27
30	19 06	19 33	20 05	10 46	11 44	12 40	13 35
35	19 18	19 47	20 23	10 44	11 45	12 43	13 40
40	19 32	20 04	20 44	10 42	11 45	12 46	13 46
45	19 49	20 25	21 13	10 39	11 46	12 50	13 52
S 50	20 09	20 52	21 53	10 36	11 46	12 54	14 00
52	20 19	21 06	22 16	10 35	11 47	12 56	14 04
54	20 31	21 22	22 48	10 33	11 47	12 58	14 08
56	20 44	21 41	////	10 31	11 48	13 01	14 12
58	20 59	22 06	////	10 30	11 48	13 04	14 17
S 60	21 17	22 41	////	10 27	11 49	13 07	14 23

Day	SUN Eqn. of Time 00h	12h	Mer. Pass.	MOON Mer. Pass. Upper	Lower	Age	Phase
d	m s	m s	h m	h m	h m	d	%
7	06 03	06 16	12 06	04 43	17 07	20	65
8	06 29	06 41	12 07	05 31	17 54	21	55
9	06 54	07 06	12 07	06 16	18 39	22	44

UT	ARIES GHA	VENUS −4.0 GHA	Dec	MARS +1.4 GHA	Dec	JUPITER −1.9 GHA	Dec	SATURN +0.5 GHA	Dec	STARS Name	SHA	Dec
10 00	109 28.0	177 52.0	S22 45.1	241 54.4	S16 52.2	243 14.0	S16 16.4	196 49.9	S22 31.4	Acamar	315 15.8	S40 14.4
01	124 30.5	192 51.1	44.7	256 55.3	52.6	258 16.1	16.5	211 52.1	31.4	Achernar	335 24.5	S57 09.2
02	139 33.0	207 50.2	44.3	271 56.2	53.0	273 18.1	16.6	226 54.2	31.4	Acrux	173 05.5	S63 11.6
03	154 35.4	222 49.3 ..	43.9	286 57.1 ..	53.5	288 20.2 ..	16.7	241 56.4 ..	31.4	Adhara	255 09.7	S29 00.0
04	169 37.9	237 48.3	43.6	301 58.0	53.9	303 22.3	16.9	256 58.5	31.4	Aldebaran	290 45.5	N16 32.5
05	184 40.4	252 47.4	43.2	316 58.9	54.3	318 24.4	17.0	272 00.7	31.4			
W 06	199 42.8	267 46.5	S22 42.8	331 59.8	S16 54.8	333 26.5	S16 17.1	287 02.9	S22 31.4	Alioth	166 18.0	N55 51.5
E 07	214 45.3	282 45.6	42.4	347 00.7	55.2	348 28.5	17.2	302 05.0	31.4	Alkaid	152 56.6	N49 13.3
D 08	229 47.7	297 44.7	42.0	2 01.6	55.6	3 30.6	17.3	317 07.2	31.4	Al Na'ir	27 40.3	S46 52.6
N 09	244 50.2	312 43.7 ..	41.6	17 02.5 ..	56.1	18 32.7 ..	17.4	332 09.3 ..	31.4	Alnilam	275 42.9	S 1 11.7
E 10	259 52.7	327 42.8	41.2	32 03.4	56.5	33 34.8	17.5	347 11.5	31.4	Alphard	217 52.8	S 8 44.3
S 11	274 55.1	342 41.9	40.9	47 04.3	56.9	48 36.9	17.6	2 13.6	31.3			
D 12	289 57.6	357 41.0	S22 40.5	62 05.3	S16 57.4	63 38.9	S16 17.7	17 15.8	S22 31.3	Alphecca	126 08.6	N26 39.3
A 13	305 00.1	12 40.1	40.1	77 06.2	57.8	78 41.0	17.8	32 17.9	31.3	Alpheratz	357 40.4	N29 11.4
Y 14	320 02.5	27 39.1	39.7	92 07.1	58.2	93 43.1	17.9	47 20.1	31.3	Altair	62 05.6	N 8 55.1
15	335 05.0	42 38.2 ..	39.3	107 08.0 ..	58.7	108 45.2 ..	18.0	62 22.2 ..	31.3	Ankaa	353 12.8	S42 12.8
16	350 07.5	57 37.3	38.9	122 08.9	59.1	123 47.3	18.1	77 24.4	31.3	Antares	112 22.7	S26 28.0
17	5 09.9	72 36.4	38.5	137 09.8	16 59.5	138 49.4	18.2	92 26.6	31.3			
18	20 12.4	87 35.5	S22 38.1	152 10.7	S17 00.0	153 51.4	S16 18.3	107 28.7	S22 31.3	Arcturus	145 53.0	N19 05.3
19	35 14.8	102 34.6	37.7	167 11.6	00.4	168 53.5	18.4	122 30.9	31.3	Atria	107 22.2	S69 03.2
20	50 17.3	117 33.6	37.3	182 12.5	00.8	183 55.6	18.5	137 33.0	31.3	Avior	234 16.1	S59 34.1
21	65 19.8	132 32.7 ..	36.9	197 13.4 ..	01.3	198 57.7 ..	18.6	152 35.2 ..	31.3	Bellatrix	278 28.4	N 6 21.7
22	80 22.2	147 31.8	36.5	212 14.3	01.7	213 59.8	18.7	167 37.3	31.3	Betelgeuse	270 57.6	N 7 24.4
23	95 24.7	162 30.9	36.1	227 15.2	02.1	229 01.9	18.8	182 39.5	31.3			
11 00	110 27.2	177 30.0	S22 35.7	242 16.1	S17 02.5	244 03.9	S16 18.9	197 41.6	S22 31.3	Canopus	263 54.2	S52 42.6
01	125 29.6	192 29.1	35.3	257 17.0	03.0	259 06.0	19.0	212 43.8	31.3	Capella	280 29.4	N46 00.8
02	140 32.1	207 28.2	34.8	272 17.9	03.4	274 08.1	19.0	227 45.9	31.3	Deneb	49 29.8	N45 20.8
03	155 34.6	222 27.2 ..	34.4	287 18.8 ..	03.8	289 10.2 ..	19.1	242 48.1 ..	31.3	Denebola	182 30.4	N14 28.2
04	170 37.0	237 26.3	34.0	302 19.7	04.3	304 12.3	19.2	257 50.3	31.3	Diphda	348 52.9	S17 53.5
05	185 39.5	252 25.4	33.6	317 20.6	04.7	319 14.4	19.3	272 52.4	31.3			
T 06	200 42.0	267 24.5	S22 33.2	332 21.5	S17 05.1	334 16.4	S16 19.4	287 54.6	S22 31.3	Dubhe	193 47.6	N61 39.0
H 07	215 44.4	282 23.6	32.8	347 22.4	05.6	349 18.5	19.5	302 56.7	31.3	Elnath	278 08.4	N28 37.2
U 08	230 46.9	297 22.7	32.4	2 23.3	06.0	4 20.6	19.6	317 58.9	31.3	Eltanin	90 45.2	N51 29.2
R 09	245 49.3	312 21.8 ..	32.0	17 24.2 ..	06.4	19 22.7 ..	19.7	333 01.0 ..	31.3	Enif	33 44.4	N 9 57.5
S 10	260 51.8	327 20.9	31.5	32 25.1	06.8	34 24.8	19.8	348 03.2	31.3	Fomalhaut	15 20.8	S29 31.8
D 11	275 54.3	342 19.9	31.1	47 26.0	07.3	49 26.9	19.9	3 05.3	31.3			
A 12	290 56.7	357 19.0	S22 30.7	62 26.9	S17 07.7	64 29.0	S16 20.0	18 07.5	S22 31.3	Gacrux	171 57.2	S57 12.5
Y 13	305 59.2	12 18.1	30.3	77 27.8	08.1	79 31.0	20.1	33 09.7	31.2	Gienah	175 49.0	S17 38.4
14	321 01.7	27 17.2	29.9	92 28.7	08.5	94 33.1	20.2	48 11.8	31.2	Hadar	148 43.5	S60 27.2
15	336 04.1	42 16.3 ..	29.4	107 29.6 ..	09.0	109 35.2 ..	20.3	63 14.0 ..	31.2	Hamal	327 57.2	N23 32.8
16	351 06.6	57 15.4	29.0	122 30.5	09.4	124 37.3	20.4	78 16.1	31.2	Kaus Aust.	83 40.1	S34 22.4
17	6 09.1	72 14.5	28.6	137 31.4	09.8	139 39.4	20.5	93 18.3	31.2			
18	21 11.5	87 13.6	S22 28.1	152 32.3	S17 10.3	154 41.5	S16 20.6	108 20.4	S22 31.2	Kochab	137 20.7	N74 04.7
19	36 14.0	102 12.7	27.7	167 33.2	10.7	169 43.6	20.7	123 22.6	31.2	Markab	13 35.4	N15 18.1
20	51 16.5	117 11.8	27.3	182 34.1	11.1	184 45.6	20.8	138 24.7	31.2	Menkar	314 11.7	N 4 09.4
21	66 18.9	132 10.9 ..	26.9	197 35.0 ..	11.5	199 47.7 ..	20.9	153 26.9 ..	31.2	Menkent	148 04.0	S36 27.2
22	81 21.4	147 09.9	26.4	212 35.9	12.0	214 49.8	21.0	168 29.1	31.2	Miaplacidus	221 38.1	S69 47.4
23	96 23.8	162 09.0	26.0	227 36.8	12.4	229 51.9	21.1	183 31.2	31.2			
12 00	111 26.3	177 08.1	S22 25.6	242 37.8	S17 12.8	244 54.0	S16 21.2	198 33.4	S22 31.2	Mirfak	308 35.6	N49 55.5
01	126 28.8	192 07.2	25.1	257 38.7	13.2	259 56.1	21.3	213 35.5	31.2	Nunki	75 54.9	S26 16.3
02	141 31.2	207 06.3	24.7	272 39.6	13.7	274 58.2	21.4	228 37.7	31.2	Peacock	53 15.0	S56 40.6
03	156 33.7	222 05.4 ..	24.2	287 40.5 ..	14.1	290 00.3 ..	21.5	243 39.8 ..	31.2	Pollux	243 23.6	N27 58.7
04	171 36.2	237 04.5	23.8	302 41.4	14.5	305 02.4	21.6	258 42.0	31.2	Procyon	244 56.2	N 5 10.5
05	186 38.6	252 03.6	23.4	317 42.3	14.9	320 04.4	21.7	273 44.1	31.2			
F 06	201 41.1	267 02.7	S22 22.9	332 43.2	S17 15.3	335 06.5	S16 21.8	288 46.3	S22 31.2	Rasalhague	96 03.9	N12 32.9
R 07	216 43.6	282 01.8	22.5	347 44.1	15.8	350 08.6	21.9	303 48.5	31.2	Regulus	207 40.0	N11 52.6
I 08	231 46.0	297 00.9	22.0	2 45.0	16.2	5 10.7	22.0	318 50.6	31.2	Rigel	281 08.8	S 8 11.1
D 09	246 48.5	312 00.0 ..	21.6	17 45.9 ..	16.6	20 12.8 ..	22.1	333 52.8 ..	31.2	Rigil Kent.	139 47.7	S60 54.1
A 10	261 51.0	326 59.1	21.1	32 46.8	17.0	35 14.9	22.2	348 54.9	31.2	Sabik	102 09.3	S15 44.6
Y 11	276 53.4	341 58.2	20.7	47 47.7	17.5	50 17.0	22.3	3 57.1	31.2			
12	291 55.9	356 57.3	S22 20.2	62 48.6	S17 17.9	65 19.1	S16 22.4	18 59.2	S22 31.2	Schedar	349 37.0	N56 38.3
13	306 58.3	11 56.4	19.8	77 49.5	18.3	80 21.2	22.5	34 01.4	31.2	Shaula	96 18.1	S37 06.7
14	322 00.8	26 55.5	19.3	92 50.4	18.7	95 23.3	22.6	49 03.6	31.1	Sirius	258 30.6	S16 44.7
15	337 03.3	41 54.6 ..	18.9	107 51.3 ..	19.2	110 25.3 ..	22.7	64 05.7 ..	31.1	Spica	158 28.0	S11 15.2
16	352 05.7	56 53.7	18.4	122 52.2	19.6	125 27.4	22.8	79 07.9	31.1	Suhail	222 49.7	S43 30.3
17	7 08.2	71 52.8	18.0	137 53.1	20.0	140 29.5	22.9	94 10.0	31.1			
18	22 10.7	86 51.9	S22 17.5	152 54.0	S17 20.4	155 31.6	S16 23.0	109 12.2	S22 31.1	Vega	80 37.3	N38 48.1
19	37 13.1	101 51.0	17.1	167 54.9	20.8	170 33.7	23.1	124 14.3	31.1	Zuben'ubi	137 02.1	S16 06.8
20	52 15.6	116 50.1	16.6	182 55.8	21.3	185 35.8	23.2	139 16.5	31.1		SHA	Mer. Pass.
21	67 18.1	131 49.2 ..	16.1	197 56.7 ..	21.7	200 37.9 ..	23.3	154 18.7 ..	31.1		° ′	h m
22	82 20.5	146 48.3	15.7	212 57.6	22.1	215 40.0	23.3	169 20.8	31.1	Venus	67 02.8	12 11
23	97 23.0	161 47.4	15.2	227 58.5	22.5	230 42.1	23.4	184 23.0	31.1	Mars	131 48.9	7 50
	h m									Jupiter	133 36.8	7 43
Mer. Pass.	16 35.5	v −0.9	d 0.4	v 0.9	d 0.4	v 2.1	d 0.1	v 2.2	d 0.0	Saturn	87 14.5	10 48

UT	SUN GHA	SUN Dec	MOON GHA	v	MOON Dec	d	HP
d h	° ′	° ′	° ′	′	° ′	′	′
10 00	178 10.2	S21 59.5	257 50.2	13.9	S 7 23.0	9.9	55.5
01	193 10.0	59.2	272 23.1	13.8	7 32.9	9.9	55.5
02	208 09.7	58.8	286 55.9	13.9	7 42.8	9.8	55.5
03	223 09.5 ..	58.4	301 28.8	13.8	7 52.6	9.8	55.4
04	238 09.2	58.0	316 01.6	13.9	8 02.4	9.7	55.4
05	253 09.0	57.7	330 34.5	13.9	8 12.1	9.7	55.4
W 06	268 08.7	S21 57.3	345 07.4	13.9	S 8 21.8	9.6	55.4
E 07	283 08.4	56.9	359 40.3	13.8	8 31.4	9.6	55.3
D 08	298 08.2	56.6	14 13.1	13.9	8 41.0	9.6	55.3
N 09	313 07.9 ..	56.2	28 46.0	13.9	8 50.6	9.5	55.3
E 10	328 07.7	55.8	43 18.9	13.9	9 00.1	9.5	55.3
S 11	343 07.4	55.4	57 51.8	13.8	9 09.6	9.4	55.2
D 12	358 07.2	S21 55.1	72 24.6	13.9	S 9 19.0	9.3	55.2
A 13	13 06.9	54.7	86 57.5	13.9	9 28.3	9.3	55.2
Y 14	28 06.7	54.3	101 30.4	13.8	9 37.6	9.3	55.2
15	43 06.4 ..	53.9	116 03.2	13.9	9 46.9	9.2	55.1
16	58 06.2	53.5	130 36.1	13.8	9 56.1	9.2	55.1
17	73 05.9	53.2	145 09.0	13.8	10 05.3	9.1	55.1
18	88 05.7	S21 52.8	159 41.8	13.9	S10 14.4	9.0	55.1
19	103 05.4	52.4	174 14.7	13.8	10 23.4	9.0	55.0
20	118 05.2	52.0	188 47.5	13.9	10 32.4	9.0	55.0
21	133 04.9 ..	51.6	203 20.4	13.8	10 41.4	8.9	55.0
22	148 04.7	51.2	217 53.2	13.8	10 50.3	8.8	55.0
23	163 04.4	50.9	232 26.0	13.8	10 59.1	8.8	55.0
11 00	178 04.2	S21 50.5	246 58.8	13.9	S11 07.9	8.7	54.9
01	193 03.9	50.1	261 31.7	13.8	11 16.7	8.7	54.9
02	208 03.7	49.7	276 04.5	13.7	11 25.4	8.6	54.9
03	223 03.4 ..	49.3	290 37.2	13.8	11 34.0	8.6	54.9
04	238 03.2	48.9	305 10.0	13.8	11 42.6	8.5	54.8
05	253 02.9	48.5	319 42.8	13.8	11 51.1	8.4	54.8
T 06	268 02.7	S21 48.1	334 15.6	13.7	S11 59.5	8.4	54.8
H 07	283 02.4	47.8	348 48.3	13.7	12 07.9	8.4	54.8
U 08	298 02.2	47.4	3 21.0	13.8	12 16.3	8.2	54.7
R 09	313 02.0 ..	47.0	17 53.8	13.7	12 24.5	8.3	54.7
S 10	328 01.7	46.6	32 26.5	13.7	12 32.8	8.1	54.7
D 11	343 01.5	46.2	46 59.2	13.7	12 40.9	8.1	54.7
A 12	358 01.2	S21 45.8	61 31.9	13.6	S12 49.0	8.1	54.7
Y 13	13 01.0	45.4	76 04.5	13.7	12 57.1	8.0	54.7
14	28 00.7	45.0	90 37.2	13.6	13 05.1	7.9	54.7
15	43 00.5 ..	44.6	105 09.8	13.7	13 13.0	7.8	54.6
16	58 00.2	44.2	119 42.5	13.6	13 20.8	7.8	54.6
17	73 00.0	43.8	134 15.1	13.6	13 28.6	7.8	54.6
18	87 59.7	S21 43.4	148 47.7	13.6	S13 36.4	7.6	54.6
19	102 59.5	43.0	163 20.3	13.5	13 44.0	7.6	54.6
20	117 59.3	42.6	177 52.8	13.6	13 51.6	7.6	54.6
21	132 59.0 ..	42.2	192 25.4	13.5	13 59.2	7.5	54.5
22	147 58.8	41.8	206 57.9	13.5	14 06.7	7.4	54.5
23	162 58.5	41.4	221 30.4	13.5	14 14.1	7.3	54.5
12 00	177 58.3	S21 41.0	236 02.9	13.5	S14 21.4	7.3	54.5
01	192 58.0	40.6	250 35.4	13.5	14 28.7	7.2	54.5
02	207 57.8	40.2	265 07.9	13.4	14 35.9	7.1	54.5
03	222 57.6 ..	39.8	279 40.3	13.4	14 43.0	7.1	54.4
04	237 57.3	39.4	294 12.7	13.4	14 50.1	7.0	54.4
05	252 57.1	39.0	308 45.1	13.4	14 57.1	7.0	54.4
F 06	267 56.8	S21 38.6	323 17.5	13.4	S15 04.1	6.8	54.4
R 07	282 56.6	38.2	337 49.9	13.3	15 10.9	6.8	54.4
I 08	297 56.3	37.8	352 22.2	13.3	15 17.7	6.8	54.4
D 09	312 56.1 ..	37.4	6 54.5	13.3	15 24.5	6.6	54.4
A 10	327 55.9	36.9	21 26.8	13.3	15 31.1	6.6	54.3
Y 11	342 55.6	36.5	35 59.1	13.3	15 37.7	6.6	54.3
12	357 55.4	S21 36.1	50 31.4	13.2	S15 44.3	6.4	54.3
13	12 55.1	35.7	65 03.6	13.2	15 50.7	6.4	54.3
14	27 54.9	35.3	79 35.8	13.2	15 57.1	6.3	54.3
15	42 54.7 ..	34.9	94 08.0	13.2	16 03.4	6.2	54.3
16	57 54.4	34.5	108 40.2	13.2	16 09.6	6.2	54.3
17	72 54.2	34.0	123 12.4	13.1	16 15.8	6.1	54.3
18	87 54.0	S21 33.6	137 44.5	13.1	S16 21.9	6.0	54.2
19	102 53.7	33.2	152 16.6	13.1	16 27.9	5.9	54.2
20	117 53.5	32.8	166 48.7	13.1	16 33.8	5.9	54.2
21	132 53.2 ..	32.4	181 20.8	13.0	16 39.7	5.7	54.2
22	147 53.0	32.0	195 52.8	13.1	16 45.4	5.8	54.2
23	162 52.8	31.5	210 24.9	13.0	S16 51.2	5.6	54.2
	SD 16.3	d 0.4	SD 15.0		14.9		14.8

Lat.	Twilight Naut.	Twilight Civil	Sunrise	Moonrise 10	11	12	13
°	h m	h m	h m	h m	h m	h m	h m
N 72	08 09	10 08	■■■	02 35	04 21	06 14	08 41
N 70	07 53	09 29	■■■	02 22	04 00	05 38	07 19
68	07 40	09 02	10 53	02 13	03 43	05 13	06 40
66	07 29	08 41	10 05	02 04	03 30	04 53	06 14
64	07 20	08 25	09 34	01 58	03 19	04 38	05 53
62	07 12	08 11	09 11	01 52	03 09	04 25	05 37
60	07 05	07 59	08 53	01 47	03 02	04 14	05 23
N 58	06 58	07 49	08 38	01 42	02 55	04 04	05 11
56	06 52	07 40	08 25	01 38	02 48	03 56	05 01
54	06 47	07 32	08 14	01 35	02 43	03 49	04 52
52	06 42	07 25	08 04	01 32	02 38	03 42	04 44
50	06 37	07 18	07 55	01 29	02 34	03 36	04 37
45	06 27	07 04	07 37	01 22	02 24	03 24	04 22
N 40	06 18	06 51	07 21	01 17	02 16	03 13	04 09
35	06 09	06 41	07 08	01 13	02 09	03 04	03 59
30	06 01	06 31	06 57	01 09	02 03	02 57	03 49
20	05 47	06 14	06 37	01 02	01 53	02 43	03 33
N 10	05 32	05 58	06 20	00 56	01 44	02 31	03 19
0	05 16	05 42	06 04	00 51	01 35	02 20	03 06
S 10	04 58	05 25	05 48	00 45	01 27	02 10	02 53
20	04 37	05 06	05 30	00 39	01 18	01 58	02 40
30	04 11	04 43	05 10	00 33	01 08	01 45	02 24
35	03 53	04 29	04 58	00 29	01 02	01 37	02 15
40	03 32	04 12	04 44	00 25	00 56	01 29	02 05
45	03 04	03 52	04 28	00 20	00 48	01 19	01 53
S 50	02 25	03 25	04 07	00 14	00 39	01 07	01 38
52	02 03	03 12	03 58	00 11	00 35	01 01	01 31
54	01 32	02 56	03 47	00 08	00 30	00 55	01 23
56	00 31	02 37	03 34	00 05	00 25	00 48	01 15
58	////	02 13	03 19	00 02	00 20	00 41	01 06
S 60	////	01 41	03 02	24 13	00 13	00 32	00 55

Lat.	Sunset	Twilight Civil	Twilight Naut.	Moonset 10	11	12	13
°	h m	h m	h m	h m	h m	h m	h m
N 72	■■■	14 09	16 07	11 08	10 55	10 36	09 45
N 70	■■■	14 48	16 23	11 22	11 18	11 13	11 08
68	13 24	15 15	16 36	11 33	11 35	11 40	11 47
66	14 12	15 35	16 47	11 43	11 50	12 00	12 14
64	14 42	15 52	16 57	11 51	12 02	12 16	12 35
62	15 05	16 05	17 05	11 58	12 12	12 29	12 52
60	15 23	16 17	17 12	12 03	12 20	12 41	13 06
N 58	15 38	16 27	17 18	12 09	12 28	12 51	13 18
56	15 51	16 36	17 24	12 13	12 35	12 59	13 29
54	16 02	16 44	17 29	12 18	12 41	13 07	13 38
52	16 12	16 52	17 34	12 22	12 46	13 14	13 46
50	16 21	16 58	17 39	12 25	12 51	13 20	13 54
45	16 40	17 13	17 49	12 33	13 02	13 34	14 10
N 40	16 55	17 25	17 58	12 39	13 11	13 45	14 23
35	17 08	17 35	18 07	12 44	13 19	13 55	14 34
30	17 19	17 45	18 15	12 49	13 25	14 03	14 44
20	17 39	18 02	18 29	12 58	13 37	14 18	15 01
N 10	17 56	18 18	18 44	13 05	13 47	14 31	15 15
0	18 12	18 34	19 00	13 12	13 57	14 43	15 29
S 10	18 28	18 51	19 17	13 19	14 07	14 55	15 43
20	18 45	19 09	19 38	13 27	14 17	15 07	15 57
30	19 05	19 32	20 05	13 35	14 29	15 22	16 14
35	19 17	19 46	20 22	13 40	14 36	15 31	16 24
40	19 31	20 03	20 43	13 46	14 44	15 40	16 35
45	19 47	20 24	21 10	13 52	14 53	15 52	16 49
S 50	20 08	20 50	21 49	14 00	15 04	16 06	17 05
52	20 17	21 03	22 11	14 04	15 09	16 12	17 12
54	20 28	21 19	22 41	14 08	15 15	16 19	17 21
56	20 41	21 37	23 35	14 12	15 21	16 28	17 30
58	20 55	22 01	////	14 17	15 28	16 37	17 41
S 60	21 12	22 32	////	14 23	15 36	16 47	17 54

Day	SUN Eqn. of Time 00h	SUN Eqn. of Time 12h	SUN Mer. Pass.	MOON Mer. Pass. Upper	MOON Mer. Pass. Lower	Age	Phase
d	m s	m s	h m	h m	h m	d	%
10	07 19	07 31	12 08	07 01	19 24	23	35
11	07 43	07 55	12 08	07 46	20 09	24	26
12	08 06	08 18	12 08	08 31	20 54	25	18

UT	ARIES GHA	VENUS −4·0 GHA	Dec	MARS +1·4 GHA	Dec	JUPITER −1·9 GHA	Dec	SATURN +0·5 GHA	Dec	STARS Name	SHA	Dec
d h	° ′	° ′	° ′	° ′	° ′	° ′	° ′	° ′	° ′		° ′	° ′
13 00	112 25.4	176 46.5	S22 14.8	242 59.4	S17 22.9	245 44.2	S16 23.5	199 25.1	S22 31.1	Acamar	315 15.8	S40 14.4
01	127 27.9	191 45.6	14.3	258 00.3	23.4	260 46.3	23.6	214 27.3	31.1	Achernar	335 24.5	S57 09.2
02	142 30.4	206 44.7	13.8	273 01.2	23.8	275 48.4	23.7	229 29.4	31.1	Acrux	173 05.5	S63 11.6
03	157 32.8	221 43.8 ..	13.4	288 02.1 ..	24.2	290 50.5 ..	23.8	244 31.6 ..	31.1	Adhara	255 09.7	S29 00.0
04	172 35.3	236 42.9	12.9	303 02.9	24.6	305 52.6	23.9	259 33.8	31.1	Aldebaran	290 45.6	N16 32.5
05	187 37.8	251 42.0	12.4	318 03.8	25.0	320 54.6	24.0	274 35.9	31.1			
06	202 40.2	266 41.1	S22 12.0	333 04.7	S17 25.5	335 56.7	S16 24.1	289 38.1	S22 31.1	Alioth	166 18.0	N55 51.5
07	217 42.7	281 40.2	11.5	348 05.6	25.9	350 58.8	24.2	304 40.2	31.1	Alkaid	152 56.6	N49 13.2
S 08	232 45.2	296 39.3	11.0	3 06.5	26.3	6 00.9	24.3	319 42.4	31.1	Al Na'ir	27 40.3	S46 52.6
A 09	247 47.6	311 38.4 ..	10.5	18 07.4 ..	26.7	21 03.0 ..	24.4	334 44.5 ..	31.1	Alnilam	275 42.9	S 1 11.7
T 10	262 50.1	326 37.6	10.1	33 08.3	27.1	36 05.1	24.5	349 46.7	31.1	Alphard	217 52.7	S 8 44.3
U 11	277 52.6	341 36.7	09.6	48 09.2	27.5	51 07.2	24.6	4 48.9	31.1			
R 12	292 55.0	356 35.8	S22 09.1	63 10.1	S17 28.0	66 09.3	S16 24.7	19 51.0	S22 31.1	Alphecca	126 08.6	N26 39.3
D 13	307 57.5	11 34.9	08.6	78 11.0	28.4	81 11.4	24.8	34 53.2	31.0	Alpheratz	357 40.4	N29 11.4
A 14	322 59.9	26 34.0	08.2	93 11.9	28.8	96 13.5	24.9	49 55.3	31.0	Altair	62 05.6	N 8 55.0
Y 15	338 02.4	41 33.1 ..	07.7	108 12.8 ..	29.2	111 15.6 ..	25.0	64 57.5 ..	31.0	Ankaa	353 12.8	S42 12.8
16	353 04.9	56 32.2	07.2	123 13.7	29.6	126 17.7	25.1	79 59.6	31.0	Antares	112 22.7	S26 28.0
17	8 07.3	71 31.3	06.7	138 14.6	30.0	141 19.8	25.2	95 01.8	31.0			
18	23 09.8	86 30.4	S22 06.2	153 15.5	S17 30.5	156 21.9	S16 25.3	110 04.0	S22 31.0	Arcturus	145 53.0	N19 05.3
19	38 12.3	101 29.5	05.7	168 16.4	30.9	171 24.0	25.4	125 06.1	31.0	Atria	107 22.2	S69 03.2
20	53 14.7	116 28.6	05.3	183 17.3	31.3	186 26.1	25.4	140 08.3	31.0	Avior	234 16.1	S59 34.1
21	68 17.2	131 27.8 ..	04.8	198 18.2 ..	31.7	201 28.2 ..	25.5	155 10.4 ..	31.0	Bellatrix	278 28.4	N 6 21.7
22	83 19.7	146 26.9	04.3	213 19.1	32.1	216 30.3	25.6	170 12.6	31.0	Betelgeuse	270 57.6	N 7 24.4
23	98 22.1	161 26.0	03.8	228 20.0	32.5	231 32.4	25.7	185 14.8	31.0			
14 00	113 24.6	176 25.1	S22 03.3	243 20.9	S17 33.0	246 34.5	S16 25.8	200 16.9	S22 31.0	Canopus	263 54.2	S52 42.6
01	128 27.1	191 24.2	02.8	258 21.8	33.4	261 36.6	25.9	215 19.1	31.0	Capella	280 29.4	N46 00.8
02	143 29.5	206 23.3	02.3	273 22.7	33.8	276 38.7	26.0	230 21.2	31.0	Deneb	49 29.8	N45 20.8
03	158 32.0	221 22.4 ..	01.8	288 23.6 ..	34.2	291 40.8 ..	26.1	245 23.4 ..	31.0	Denebola	182 30.4	N14 28.2
04	173 34.4	236 21.5	01.3	303 24.5	34.6	306 42.9	26.2	260 25.5	31.0	Diphda	348 52.9	S17 53.5
05	188 36.9	251 20.7	00.8	318 25.4	35.0	321 45.0	26.3	275 27.7	31.0			
06	203 39.4	266 19.8	S22 00.3	333 26.3	S17 35.4	336 47.1	S16 26.4	290 29.9	S22 31.0	Dubhe	193 47.6	N61 39.0
07	218 41.8	281 18.9	21 59.8	348 27.2	35.9	351 49.2	26.5	305 32.0	31.0	Elnath	278 08.4	N28 37.2
08	233 44.3	296 18.0	59.3	3 28.1	36.3	6 51.3	26.6	320 34.2	31.0	Eltanin	90 45.2	N51 29.2
S 09	248 46.8	311 17.1 ..	58.8	18 29.0 ..	36.7	21 53.4 ..	26.7	335 36.3 ..	31.0	Enif	33 44.4	N 9 57.5
U 10	263 49.2	326 16.2	58.3	33 29.9	37.1	36 55.5	26.8	350 38.5	31.0	Fomalhaut	15 20.8	S29 31.8
N 11	278 51.7	341 15.4	57.8	48 30.8	37.5	51 57.6	26.9	5 40.7	30.9			
D 12	293 54.2	356 14.5	S21 57.3	63 31.7	S17 37.9	66 59.7	S16 27.0	20 42.8	S22 30.9	Gacrux	171 57.2	S57 12.5
A 13	308 56.6	11 13.6	56.8	78 32.6	38.3	82 01.8	27.0	35 45.0	30.9	Gienah	175 49.0	S17 38.4
Y 14	323 59.1	26 12.7	56.3	93 33.5	38.7	97 03.9	27.1	50 47.1	30.9	Hadar	148 43.5	S60 27.2
15	339 01.6	41 11.8 ..	55.8	108 34.4 ..	39.2	112 06.0 ..	27.2	65 49.3 ..	30.9	Hamal	327 57.2	N23 32.8
16	354 04.0	56 10.9	55.3	123 35.3	39.6	127 08.1	27.3	80 51.4	30.9	Kaus Aust.	83 40.1	S34 22.3
17	9 06.5	71 10.1	54.8	138 36.1	40.0	142 10.2	27.4	95 53.6	30.9			
18	24 08.9	86 09.2	S21 54.3	153 37.0	S17 40.4	157 12.3	S16 27.5	110 55.8	S22 30.9	Kochab	137 20.7	N74 04.7
19	39 11.4	101 08.3	53.7	168 37.9	40.8	172 14.4	27.6	125 57.9	30.9	Markab	13 35.4	N15 18.1
20	54 13.9	116 07.4	53.2	183 38.8	41.2	187 16.5	27.7	141 00.1	30.9	Menkar	314 11.7	N 4 09.4
21	69 16.3	131 06.5 ..	52.7	198 39.7 ..	41.6	202 18.6 ..	27.8	156 02.2 ..	30.9	Menkent	148 43.0	S36 27.2
22	84 18.8	146 05.7	52.2	213 40.6	42.0	217 20.7	27.9	171 04.4	30.9	Miaplacidus	221 38.0	S69 47.4
23	99 21.3	161 04.8	51.7	228 41.5	42.4	232 22.8	28.0	186 06.6	30.9			
15 00	114 23.7	176 03.9	S21 51.2	243 42.4	S17 42.9	247 24.9	S16 28.1	201 08.7	S22 30.9	Mirfak	308 35.6	N49 55.5
01	129 26.2	191 03.0	50.6	258 43.3	43.3	262 27.0	28.2	216 10.9	30.9	Nunki	75 54.9	S26 16.3
02	144 28.7	206 02.2	50.1	273 44.2	43.7	277 29.1	28.3	231 13.0	30.9	Peacock	53 15.0	S56 40.6
03	159 31.1	221 01.3 ..	49.6	288 45.1 ..	44.1	292 31.2 ..	28.3	246 15.2 ..	30.9	Pollux	243 23.6	N27 58.7
04	174 33.6	236 00.4	49.1	303 46.0	44.5	307 33.3	28.4	261 17.4	30.9	Procyon	244 56.2	N 5 10.5
05	189 36.0	250 59.5	48.5	318 46.9	44.9	322 35.4	28.5	276 19.5	30.9			
06	204 38.5	265 58.7	S21 48.0	333 47.8	S17 45.3	337 37.5	S16 28.6	291 21.7	S22 30.9	Rasalhague	96 03.9	N12 32.9
07	219 41.0	280 57.8	47.5	348 48.7	45.7	352 39.6	28.7	306 23.8	30.9	Regulus	207 40.0	N11 52.6
08	234 43.4	295 56.9	47.0	3 49.6	46.1	7 41.7	28.8	321 26.0	30.8	Rigel	281 08.8	S 8 11.1
M 09	249 45.9	310 56.0 ..	46.4	18 50.5 ..	46.5	22 43.8 ..	28.9	336 28.2 ..	30.8	Rigil Kent.	139 47.6	S60 54.1
O 10	264 48.4	325 55.2	45.9	33 51.4	46.9	37 45.9	29.0	351 30.3	30.8	Sabik	102 09.3	S15 44.6
N 11	279 50.8	340 54.3	45.4	48 52.3	47.3	52 48.0	29.1	6 32.5	30.8			
D 12	294 53.3	355 53.4	S21 44.8	63 53.2	S17 47.8	67 50.1	S16 29.2	21 34.6	S22 30.8	Schedar	349 37.0	N56 38.3
A 13	309 55.8	10 52.5	44.3	78 54.0	48.2	82 52.2	29.3	36 36.8	30.8	Shaula	96 18.1	S37 06.7
Y 14	324 58.2	25 51.7	43.8	93 54.9	48.6	97 54.3	29.4	51 39.0	30.8	Sirius	258 30.6	S16 44.7
15	340 00.7	40 50.8 ..	43.2	108 55.8 ..	49.0	112 56.4 ..	29.5	66 41.1 ..	30.8	Spica	158 28.0	S11 15.2
16	355 03.2	55 49.9	42.7	123 56.7	49.4	127 58.5	29.5	81 43.3	30.8	Suhail	222 49.7	S43 30.3
17	10 05.6	70 49.1	42.2	138 57.6	49.8	143 00.7	29.6	96 45.4	30.8			
18	25 08.1	85 48.2	S21 41.6	153 58.5	S17 50.2	158 02.8	S16 29.7	111 47.6	S22 30.8	Vega	80 37.3	N38 48.1
19	40 10.5	100 47.3	41.1	168 59.4	50.6	173 04.9	29.8	126 49.8	30.8	Zuben'ubi	137 02.1	S16 06.8
20	55 13.0	115 46.4	40.5	184 00.3	51.0	188 07.0	29.9	141 51.9	30.8		SHA	Mer.Pass.
21	70 15.5	130 45.6 ..	40.0	199 01.2 ..	51.4	203 09.1 ..	30.0	156 54.1 ..	30.8		° ′	h m
22	85 17.9	145 44.7	39.5	214 02.1	51.8	218 11.2	30.1	171 56.2	30.8	Venus	63 00.5	12 15
23	100 20.4	160 43.8	38.9	229 03.0	52.2	233 13.3	30.2	186 58.4	30.8	Mars	129 56.3	7 46
	h m									Jupiter	133 09.9	7 33
Mer. Pass. 16 23.7		v −0.9	d 0.5	v 0.9	d 0.4	v 2.1	d 0.1	v 2.2	d 0.0	Saturn	86 52.3	10 37

UT	SUN GHA	SUN Dec	MOON GHA	v	MOON Dec	d	HP
d h	° ′	° ′	° ′	′	° ′	′	′
13 00	177 52.5	S21 31.1	224 56.9	12.9	S16 56.8	5.5	54.2
01	192 52.3	30.7	239 28.8	13.0	17 02.3	5.5	54.2
02	207 52.1	30.3	254 00.8	12.9	17 07.8	5.4	54.2
03	222 51.8 · ·	29.8	268 32.7	13.0	17 13.2	5.3	54.2
04	237 51.6	29.4	283 04.7	12.9	17 18.5	5.3	54.1
05	252 51.3	29.0	297 36.6	12.8	17 23.8	5.2	54.1
06	267 51.1	S21 28.6	312 08.4	12.9	S17 29.0	5.0	54.1
S 07	282 50.9	28.1	326 40.3	12.8	17 34.0	5.1	54.1
A 08	297 50.6	27.7	341 12.1	12.8	17 39.1	4.9	54.1
T 09	312 50.4 · ·	27.3	355 43.9	12.8	17 44.0	4.8	54.1
U 10	327 50.2	26.9	10 15.7	12.8	17 48.8	4.8	54.1
R 11	342 49.9	26.4	24 47.5	12.7	17 53.6	4.7	54.1
D 12	357 49.7	S21 26.0	39 19.2	12.7	S17 58.3	4.6	54.1
A 13	12 49.5	25.6	53 50.9	12.7	18 02.9	4.5	54.1
Y 14	27 49.2	25.1	68 22.6	12.7	18 07.4	4.5	54.1
15	42 49.0 · ·	24.7	82 54.3	12.7	18 11.9	4.3	54.1
16	57 48.8	24.3	97 26.0	12.6	18 16.2	4.3	54.1
17	72 48.5	23.9	111 57.6	12.6	18 20.5	4.2	54.0
18	87 48.3	S21 23.4	126 29.2	12.6	S18 24.7	4.1	54.0
19	102 48.1	23.0	141 00.8	12.6	18 28.8	4.0	54.0
20	117 47.9	22.5	155 32.4	12.5	18 32.8	4.0	54.0
21	132 47.6 · ·	22.1	170 03.9	12.6	18 36.8	3.8	54.0
22	147 47.4	21.7	184 35.5	12.5	18 40.6	3.8	54.0
23	162 47.2	21.2	199 07.0	12.5	18 44.4	3.7	54.0
14 00	177 46.9	S21 20.8	213 38.5	12.4	S18 48.1	3.6	54.0
01	192 46.7	20.4	228 09.9	12.5	18 51.7	3.5	54.0
02	207 46.5	19.9	242 41.4	12.4	18 55.2	3.4	54.0
03	222 46.2 · ·	19.5	257 12.8	12.5	18 58.6	3.4	54.0
04	237 46.0	19.0	271 44.3	12.4	19 02.0	3.2	54.0
05	252 45.8	18.6	286 15.7	12.3	19 05.2	3.2	54.0
06	267 45.6	S21 18.2	300 47.0	12.4	S19 08.4	3.1	54.0
07	282 45.3	17.7	315 18.4	12.3	19 11.5	3.0	54.0
08	297 45.1	17.3	329 49.7	12.4	19 14.5	2.9	54.0
S 09	312 44.9 · ·	16.8	344 21.1	12.3	19 17.4	2.8	54.0
U 10	327 44.6	16.4	358 52.4	12.3	19 20.2	2.7	54.0
N 11	342 44.4	15.9	13 23.7	12.2	19 22.9	2.7	54.0
D 12	357 44.2	S21 15.5	27 54.9	12.3	S19 25.6	2.5	54.0
A 13	12 44.0	15.0	42 26.2	12.3	19 28.1	2.5	54.0
Y 14	27 43.7	14.6	56 57.5	12.2	19 30.6	2.4	54.0
15	42 43.5 · ·	14.2	71 28.7	12.2	19 33.0	2.3	54.0
16	57 43.3	13.7	85 59.9	12.2	19 35.3	2.2	54.0
17	72 43.1	13.3	100 31.1	12.2	19 37.5	2.1	54.0
18	87 42.8	S21 12.8	115 02.3	12.2	S19 39.6	2.0	54.0
19	102 42.6	12.3	129 33.5	12.1	19 41.6	1.9	54.0
20	117 42.4	11.9	144 04.6	12.2	19 43.5	1.9	54.0
21	132 42.2 · ·	11.4	158 35.8	12.1	19 45.4	1.7	53.9
22	147 41.9	11.0	173 06.9	12.1	19 47.1	1.7	53.9
23	162 41.7	10.5	187 38.0	12.1	19 48.8	1.5	53.9
15 00	177 41.5	S21 10.1	202 09.1	12.1	S19 50.3	1.5	53.9
01	192 41.3	09.6	216 40.2	12.1	19 51.8	1.4	53.9
02	207 41.0	09.2	231 11.3	12.1	19 53.2	1.3	53.9
03	222 40.8 · ·	08.7	245 42.4	12.0	19 54.5	1.2	53.9
04	237 40.6	08.3	260 13.4	12.1	19 55.7	1.1	53.9
05	252 40.4	07.8	274 44.5	12.0	19 56.8	1.0	53.9
06	267 40.2	S21 07.4	289 15.5	12.0	S19 57.8	1.0	53.9
07	282 39.9	06.9	303 46.5	12.1	19 58.8	0.8	53.9
08	297 39.7	06.4	318 17.6	12.0	19 59.6	0.7	53.9
M 09	312 39.5 · ·	06.0	332 48.6	12.0	20 00.3	0.7	54.0
O 10	327 39.3	05.5	347 19.6	12.0	20 01.0	0.5	54.0
N 11	342 39.0	05.0	1 50.6	12.0	20 01.5	0.5	54.0
D 12	357 38.8	S21 04.6	16 21.6	12.0	S20 02.0	0.4	54.0
A 13	12 38.6	04.1	30 52.6	12.0	20 02.4	0.2	54.0
Y 14	27 38.4	03.6	45 23.6	11.9	20 02.6	0.2	54.0
15	42 38.2 · ·	03.2	59 54.5	12.0	20 02.8	0.1	54.0
16	57 38.0	02.7	74 25.5	12.0	20 02.9	0.0	54.0
17	72 37.7	02.2	88 56.5	11.9	20 02.9	0.1	54.0
18	87 37.5	S21 01.8	103 27.4	12.0	S20 02.8	0.1	54.0
19	102 37.3	01.3	117 58.4	12.0	20 02.7	0.3	54.0
20	117 37.1	00.8	132 29.4	11.9	20 02.4	0.4	54.0
21	132 36.9	21 00.4	147 00.3	12.0	20 02.0	0.5	54.0
22	147 36.6	20 59.9	161 31.3	11.9	20 01.5	0.5	54.0
23	162 36.4	S20 59.4	176 02.2	12.0	S20 01.0	0.7	54.0
	SD 16.3	d 0.4	SD 14.7		14.7		14.7

Lat.	Twilight Naut.	Twilight Civil	Sunrise	Moonrise 13	Moonrise 14	Moonrise 15	Moonrise 16
°	h m	h m	h m	h m	h m	h m	h m
N 72	08 03	09 56	■■	■■	08 41	■■	■■
N 70	07 48	09 21	■■	07 19	■■	09 03	■■
68	07 36	08 56	10 38	06 40	08 02	09 09	11 12
66	07 25	08 36	09 56	06 14	07 27	08 29	09 52
64	07 16	08 21	09 28	05 53	07 02	08 01	09 14
62	07 09	08 07	09 06	05 37	06 43	07 40	08 47
60	07 02	07 56	08 49	05 23	06 27	07 23	08 26
N 58	06 56	07 46	08 35	05 11	06 13	07 08	08 09
56	06 50	07 38	08 22	05 01	06 02	06 56	07 55
54	06 45	07 30	08 12	04 52	05 51	06 45	07 43
52	06 40	07 23	08 02	04 44	05 42	06 36	07 32
50	06 36	07 16	07 53	04 37	05 34	06 27	07 23
45	06 26	07 02	07 35	04 22	05 17	06 09	07 15
N 40	06 17	06 51	07 20	04 09	05 03	05 54	06 57
35	06 09	06 40	07 08	03 59	04 51	05 42	06 42
30	06 01	06 31	06 57	03 49	04 41	05 31	06 30
20	05 47	06 14	06 38	03 33	04 23	05 12	06 19
N 10	05 33	05 59	06 21	03 19	04 08	04 56	06 00
0	05 17	05 43	06 05	03 06	03 53	04 41	05 44
S 10	05 00	05 27	05 50	02 53	03 39	04 26	05 29
20	04 40	05 08	05 32	02 40	03 23	04 09	05 14
30	04 13	04 46	05 13	02 24	03 06	03 51	04 57
35	03 57	04 32	05 01	02 15	02 56	03 40	04 39
40	03 36	04 16	04 48	02 05	02 44	03 28	04 28
45	03 09	03 56	04 32	01 53	02 30	03 13	04 16
S 50	02 32	03 30	04 12	01 38	02 14	02 55	04 01
52	02 11	03 17	04 02	01 31	02 06	02 47	03 43
54	01 43	03 02	03 52	01 23	01 57	02 38	03 35
56	00 57	02 44	03 40	01 15	01 48	02 27	03 25
58	////	02 22	03 26	01 06	01 36	02 15	03 15
S 60	////	01 52	03 09	00 55	01 24	02 01	03 02

Lat.	Sunset	Twilight Civil	Twilight Naut.	Moonset 13	Moonset 14	Moonset 15	Moonset 16
°	h m	h m	h m	h m	h m	h m	h m
N 72	■■	14 23	16 16	09 45	■■	■■	■■
N 70	■■	14 58	16 31	11 08	11 01	■■	12 12
68	13 41	15 23	16 43	11 47	12 03	12 35	13 32
66	14 23	15 43	16 54	12 14	12 38	13 15	14 10
64	14 51	15 58	17 02	12 35	13 03	13 43	14 36
62	15 12	16 11	17 10	12 52	13 23	14 04	14 57
60	15 29	16 23	17 17	13 06	13 39	14 21	15 13
N 58	15 44	16 32	17 23	13 18	13 53	14 36	15 28
56	15 56	16 41	17 28	13 29	14 05	14 48	15 40
54	16 07	16 49	17 33	13 38	14 15	14 59	15 50
52	16 17	16 56	17 38	13 46	14 24	15 09	15 59
50	16 25	17 02	17 43	13 54	14 33	15 17	16 08
45	16 43	17 16	17 52	14 10	14 50	15 35	16 26
N 40	16 58	17 28	18 01	14 23	15 04	15 50	16 40
35	17 11	17 38	18 09	14 34	15 17	16 03	16 52
30	17 22	17 47	18 17	14 44	15 27	16 14	17 03
20	17 40	18 04	18 31	15 01	15 45	16 32	17 21
N 10	17 57	18 20	18 46	15 15	16 01	16 49	17 37
0	18 13	18 35	19 01	15 29	16 16	17 04	17 52
S 10	18 28	18 51	19 18	15 43	16 31	17 19	18 07
20	18 45	19 10	19 38	15 57	16 47	17 36	18 23
30	19 05	19 32	20 04	16 14	17 05	17 54	18 41
35	19 17	19 46	20 21	16 24	17 16	18 05	18 51
40	19 30	20 02	20 41	16 35	17 28	18 18	19 03
45	19 46	20 22	21 08	16 49	17 42	18 32	19 17
S 50	20 06	20 47	21 45	17 05	18 00	18 50	19 35
52	20 15	21 00	22 06	17 12	18 08	18 59	19 43
54	20 25	21 15	22 33	17 21	18 18	19 08	19 52
56	20 37	21 32	23 16	17 30	18 28	19 19	20 02
58	20 51	21 54	////	17 41	18 40	19 31	20 14
S 60	21 08	22 23	////	17 54	18 54	19 45	20 27

Day	SUN Eqn. of Time 00h	SUN Eqn. of Time 12h	SUN Mer. Pass.	MOON Mer. Pass. Upper	MOON Mer. Pass. Lower	Age	Phase
d	m s	m s	h m	h m	h m	d	%
13	08 29	08 41	12 09	09 18	21 41	26	11
14	08 52	09 03	12 09	10 05	22 28	27	6
15	09 14	09 24	12 09	10 52	23 16	28	2

UT	ARIES	VENUS −4·0		MARS +1·3		JUPITER −1·9		SATURN +0·5		STARS		
	GHA	GHA	Dec	GHA	Dec	GHA	Dec	GHA	Dec	Name	SHA	Dec
d h	° ′	° ′	° ′	° ′	° ′	° ′	° ′	° ′	° ′		° ′	° ′
16 00	115 22.9	175 43.0	S21 38.4	244 03.9	S17 52.6	248 15.4	S16 30.3	202 00.6	S22 30.8	Acamar	315 15.9	S40 14.4
01	130 25.3	190 42.1	37.8	259 04.8	53.0	263 17.5	30.4	217 02.7	30.8	Achernar	335 24.5	S57 09.2
02	145 27.8	205 41.2	37.3	274 05.7	53.4	278 19.6	30.5	232 04.9	30.8	Acrux	173 05.4	S63 11.6
03	160 30.3	220 40.4	.. 36.7	289 06.6	.. 53.8	293 21.7	.. 30.5	247 07.1	.. 30.8	Adhara	255 09.7	S29 00.0
04	175 32.7	235 39.5	36.2	304 07.5	54.2	308 23.8	30.6	262 09.2	30.7	Aldebaran	290 45.6	N16 32.5
05	190 35.2	250 38.6	35.6	319 08.3	54.6	323 25.9	30.7	277 11.4	30.7			
06	205 37.7	265 37.8	S21 35.1	334 09.2	S17 55.1	338 28.1	S16 30.8	292 13.5	S22 30.7	Alioth	166 17.9	N55 51.5
07	220 40.1	280 36.9	34.5	349 10.1	55.5	353 30.2	30.9	307 15.7	30.7	Alkaid	152 56.5	N49 13.2
T 08	235 42.6	295 36.0	34.0	4 11.0	55.9	8 32.3	31.0	322 17.9	30.7	Al Na'ir	27 40.3	S46 52.6
U 09	250 45.0	310 35.2	.. 33.4	19 11.9	.. 56.3	23 34.4	.. 31.1	337 20.0	.. 30.7	Alnilam	275 42.9	S 1 11.7
E 10	265 47.5	325 34.3	32.8	34 12.8	56.7	38 36.5	31.2	352 22.2	30.7	Alphard	217 52.7	S 8 44.3
S 11	280 50.0	340 33.5	32.3	49 13.7	57.1	53 38.6	31.3	7 24.3	30.7			
D 12	295 52.4	355 32.6	S21 31.7	64 14.6	S17 57.5	68 40.7	S16 31.4	22 26.5	S22 30.7	Alphecca	126 08.6	N26 39.2
A 13	310 54.9	10 31.7	31.2	79 15.5	57.9	83 42.8	31.5	37 28.7	30.7	Alpheratz	357 40.4	N29 11.4
Y 14	325 57.4	25 30.9	30.6	94 16.4	58.3	98 44.9	31.5	52 30.8	30.7	Altair	62 05.5	N 8 55.0
15	340 59.8	40 30.0	.. 30.0	109 17.3	.. 58.7	113 47.0	.. 31.6	67 33.0	.. 30.7	Ankaa	353 12.8	S42 12.8
16	356 02.3	55 29.2	29.5	124 18.2	59.1	128 49.2	31.7	82 35.1	30.7	Antares	112 22.7	S26 28.0
17	11 04.8	70 28.3	28.9	139 19.1	59.5	143 51.3	31.8	97 37.3	30.7			
18	26 07.2	85 27.4	S21 28.3	154 19.9	S17 59.9	158 53.4	S16 31.9	112 39.5	S22 30.7	Arcturus	145 53.0	N19 05.3
19	41 09.7	100 26.6	27.8	169 20.8	18 00.3	173 55.5	32.0	127 41.6	30.7	Atria	107 22.1	S69 03.2
20	56 12.2	115 25.7	27.2	184 21.7	00.7	188 57.6	32.1	142 43.8	30.7	Avior	234 16.0	S59 34.1
21	71 14.6	130 24.9	.. 26.6	199 22.6	.. 01.1	203 59.7	.. 32.2	157 46.0	.. 30.7	Bellatrix	278 28.4	N 6 21.7
22	86 17.1	145 24.0	26.1	214 23.5	01.5	219 01.8	32.3	172 48.1	30.7	Betelgeuse	270 57.6	N 7 24.4
23	101 19.5	160 23.1	25.5	229 24.4	01.9	234 03.9	32.3	187 50.3	30.6			
17 00	116 22.0	175 22.3	S21 24.9	244 25.3	S18 02.3	249 06.0	S16 32.4	202 52.4	S22 30.6	Canopus	263 54.2	S52 42.6
01	131 24.5	190 21.4	24.3	259 26.2	02.7	264 08.2	32.5	217 54.6	30.6	Capella	280 29.4	N46 00.8
02	146 26.9	205 20.6	23.8	274 27.1	03.1	279 10.3	32.6	232 56.8	30.6	Deneb	49 29.8	N45 20.8
03	161 29.4	220 19.7	.. 23.2	289 28.0	.. 03.5	294 12.4	.. 32.7	247 58.9	.. 30.6	Denebola	182 30.3	N14 28.2
04	176 31.9	235 18.9	22.6	304 28.9	03.9	309 14.5	32.8	263 01.1	30.6	Diphda	348 52.9	S17 53.5
05	191 34.3	250 18.0	22.0	319 29.8	04.3	324 16.6	32.9	278 03.3	30.6			
06	206 36.8	265 17.2	S21 21.5	334 30.6	S18 04.7	339 18.7	S16 33.0	293 05.4	S22 30.6	Dubhe	193 47.6	N61 39.0
W 07	221 39.3	280 16.3	20.9	349 31.5	05.1	354 20.8	33.1	308 07.6	30.6	Elnath	278 08.4	N28 37.2
E 08	236 41.7	295 15.4	20.3	4 32.4	05.5	9 23.0	33.1	323 09.7	30.6	Eltanin	90 45.2	N51 29.2
D 09	251 44.2	310 14.6	.. 19.7	19 33.3	.. 05.9	24 25.1	.. 33.2	338 11.9	.. 30.6	Enif	33 44.4	N 9 57.5
N 10	266 46.7	325 13.7	19.1	34 34.2	06.3	39 27.2	33.3	353 14.1	30.6	Fomalhaut	15 20.8	S29 31.8
E 11	281 49.1	340 12.9	18.5	49 35.1	06.7	54 29.3	33.4	8 16.2	30.6			
S 12	296 51.6	355 12.0	S21 18.0	64 36.0	S18 07.1	69 31.4	S16 33.5	23 18.4	S22 30.6	Gacrux	171 57.2	S57 12.5
D 13	311 54.0	10 11.2	17.4	79 36.9	07.4	84 33.5	33.6	38 20.6	30.6	Gienah	175 49.0	S17 38.4
A 14	326 56.5	25 10.3	16.8	94 37.8	07.8	99 35.6	33.7	53 22.7	30.6	Hadar	148 43.4	S60 27.2
Y 15	341 59.0	40 09.5	.. 16.2	109 38.7	.. 08.2	114 37.8	.. 33.8	68 24.9	.. 30.6	Hamal	327 57.2	N23 32.8
16	357 01.4	55 08.6	15.6	124 39.6	08.6	129 39.9	33.9	83 27.0	30.6	Kaus Aust.	83 40.1	S34 22.3
17	12 03.9	70 07.8	15.0	139 40.4	09.0	144 42.0	33.9	98 29.2	30.5			
18	27 06.4	85 06.9	S21 14.4	154 41.3	S18 09.4	159 44.1	S16 34.0	113 31.4	S22 30.5	Kochab	137 20.6	N74 04.7
19	42 08.8	100 06.1	13.8	169 42.2	09.8	174 46.2	34.1	128 33.5	30.5	Markab	13 35.4	N15 18.1
20	57 11.3	115 05.2	13.2	184 43.1	10.2	189 48.3	34.2	143 35.7	30.5	Menkar	314 11.7	N 4 09.4
21	72 13.8	130 04.4	.. 12.6	199 44.0	.. 10.6	204 50.5	.. 34.3	158 37.9	.. 30.5	Menkent	148 03.9	S36 27.2
22	87 16.2	145 03.6	12.0	214 44.9	11.0	219 52.6	34.4	173 40.0	30.5	Miaplacidus	221 38.0	S69 47.4
23	102 18.7	160 02.7	11.4	229 45.8	11.4	234 54.7	34.5	188 42.2	30.5			
18 00	117 21.1	175 01.9	S21 10.8	244 46.7	S18 11.8	249 56.8	S16 34.6	203 44.4	S22 30.5	Mirfak	308 35.6	N49 55.5
01	132 23.6	190 01.0	10.2	259 47.6	12.2	264 58.9	34.6	218 46.5	30.5	Nunki	75 54.8	S26 16.3
02	147 26.1	205 00.2	09.6	274 48.5	12.6	280 01.1	34.7	233 48.7	30.5	Peacock	53 15.0	S56 40.6
03	162 28.5	219 59.3	.. 09.0	289 49.3	.. 13.0	295 03.2	.. 34.8	248 50.8	.. 30.5	Pollux	243 23.6	N27 58.7
04	177 31.0	234 58.5	08.4	304 50.2	13.4	310 05.3	34.9	263 53.0	30.5	Procyon	244 56.2	N 5 10.5
05	192 33.5	249 57.6	07.8	319 51.1	13.8	325 07.4	35.0	278 55.2	30.5			
06	207 35.9	264 56.8	S21 07.2	334 52.0	S18 14.2	340 09.5	S16 35.1	293 57.3	S22 30.5	Rasalhague	96 03.9	N12 32.9
07	222 38.4	279 56.0	06.6	349 52.9	14.6	355 11.6	35.2	308 59.5	30.5	Regulus	207 40.0	N11 52.6
T 08	237 40.9	294 55.1	06.0	4 53.8	14.9	10 13.8	35.3	324 01.7	30.5	Rigel	281 08.8	S 8 11.1
H 09	252 43.3	309 54.3	.. 05.4	19 54.7	.. 15.3	25 15.9	.. 35.3	339 03.8	.. 30.5	Rigil Kent.	139 47.6	S60 54.1
U 10	267 45.8	324 53.4	04.8	34 55.6	15.7	40 18.0	35.4	354 06.0	30.5	Sabik	102 09.2	S15 44.6
R 11	282 48.3	339 52.6	04.2	49 56.5	16.1	55 20.1	35.5	9 08.2	30.4			
S 12	297 50.7	354 51.8	S21 03.5	64 57.3	S18 16.5	70 22.2	S16 35.6	24 10.3	S22 30.4	Schedar	349 37.0	N56 38.3
D 13	312 53.2	9 50.9	02.9	79 58.2	16.9	85 24.4	35.7	39 12.5	30.4	Shaula	96 18.0	S37 06.7
A 14	327 55.6	24 50.1	02.3	94 59.1	17.3	100 26.5	35.8	54 14.6	30.4	Sirius	258 30.6	S16 44.7
Y 15	342 58.1	39 49.2	.. 01.7	110 00.0	.. 17.7	115 28.6	.. 35.9	69 16.8	.. 30.4	Spica	158 27.9	S11 15.2
16	358 00.6	54 48.4	01.1	125 00.9	18.1	130 30.7	36.0	84 19.0	30.4	Suhail	222 49.7	S43 30.3
17	13 03.0	69 47.6	21 00.5	140 01.8	18.5	145 32.9	36.0	99 21.1	30.4			
18	28 05.5	84 46.7	S20 59.8	155 02.7	S18 18.9	160 35.0	S16 36.1	114 23.3	S22 30.4	Vega	80 37.3	N38 48.1
19	43 08.0	99 45.9	59.2	170 03.6	19.2	175 37.1	36.2	129 25.5	30.4	Zuben'ubi	137 02.1	S16 06.8
20	58 10.4	114 45.0	58.6	185 04.5	19.6	190 39.2	36.3	144 27.6	30.4		SHA	Mer. Pass.
21	73 12.9	129 44.2	.. 58.0	200 05.3	.. 20.0	205 41.3	.. 36.4	159 29.8	.. 30.4		° ′	h m
22	88 15.4	144 43.4	57.4	215 06.2	20.4	220 43.5	36.5	174 32.0	30.4	Venus	59 00.3	12 19
23	103 17.8	159 42.5	56.7	230 07.1	20.8	235 45.6	36.6	189 34.1	30.4	Mars	128 03.3	7 42
	h m									Jupiter	132 44.0	7 23
Mer. Pass. 16 11.9	v −0.9 d 0.6		v 0.9 d 0.4		v 2.1 d 0.1		v 2.2 d 0.0			Saturn	86 30.4	10 27

UT	SUN GHA	SUN Dec	MOON GHA	v	MOON Dec	d	HP
d h	° '	° '	° '	'	° '	'	'
16 00	177 36.2	S20 59.0	190 33.2	11.9	S20 00.3	0.7	54.0
01	192 36.0	58.5	205 04.1	12.0	19 59.6	0.8	54.0
02	207 35.8	58.0	219 35.1	11.9	19 58.8	1.0	54.0
03	222 35.6	.. 57.5	234 06.0	12.0	19 57.8	1.0	54.0
04	237 35.3	57.1	248 37.0	11.9	19 56.8	1.1	54.0
05	252 35.1	56.6	263 07.9	12.0	19 55.7	1.2	54.0
06	267 34.9	S20 56.1	277 38.9	11.9	S19 54.5	1.3	54.0
07	282 34.7	55.6	292 09.8	12.0	19 53.2	1.4	54.0
08	297 34.5	55.2	306 40.8	11.9	19 51.8	1.5	54.0
T 09	312 34.3	.. 54.7	321 11.7	12.0	19 50.3	1.6	54.0
U 10	327 34.1	54.2	335 42.7	12.0	19 48.7	1.6	54.0
E 11	342 33.8	53.7	350 13.7	11.9	19 47.1	1.8	54.0
S 12	357 33.6	S20 53.2	4 44.6	12.0	S19 45.3	1.8	54.0
D 13	12 33.4	52.8	19 15.6	12.0	19 43.5	2.0	54.0
A 14	27 33.2	52.3	33 46.6	12.0	19 41.5	2.0	54.0
Y 15	42 33.0	.. 51.8	48 17.6	12.0	19 39.5	2.1	54.0
16	57 32.8	51.3	62 48.6	12.0	19 37.4	2.3	54.1
17	72 32.6	50.8	77 19.6	12.0	19 35.1	2.3	54.1
18	87 32.4	S20 50.3	91 50.6	12.0	S19 32.8	2.4	54.1
19	102 32.2	49.9	106 21.6	12.0	19 30.4	2.5	54.1
20	117 31.9	49.4	120 52.6	12.1	19 27.9	2.5	54.1
21	132 31.7	.. 48.9	135 23.7	12.0	19 25.4	2.7	54.1
22	147 31.5	48.4	149 54.7	12.1	19 22.7	2.8	54.1
23	162 31.3	47.9	164 25.8	12.0	19 19.9	2.8	54.1
17 00	177 31.1	S20 47.4	178 56.8	12.1	S19 17.1	3.0	54.1
01	192 30.9	46.9	193 27.9	12.1	19 14.1	3.0	54.1
02	207 30.7	46.5	207 59.0	12.1	19 11.1	3.1	54.1
03	222 30.5	.. 46.0	222 30.1	12.1	19 08.0	3.2	54.1
04	237 30.3	45.5	237 01.2	12.1	19 04.8	3.3	54.1
05	252 30.1	45.0	251 32.3	12.1	19 01.5	3.4	54.1
06	267 29.9	S20 44.5	266 03.4	12.2	S18 58.1	3.5	54.2
W 07	282 29.6	44.0	280 34.6	12.1	18 54.6	3.6	54.2
E 08	297 29.4	43.5	295 05.7	12.2	18 51.0	3.6	54.2
D 09	312 29.2	.. 43.0	309 36.9	12.2	18 47.4	3.8	54.2
N 10	327 29.0	42.5	324 08.1	12.2	18 43.6	3.8	54.2
E 11	342 28.8	42.0	338 39.3	12.2	18 39.8	3.9	54.2
S 12	357 28.6	S20 41.5	353 10.5	12.2	S18 35.9	4.0	54.2
D 13	12 28.4	41.0	7 41.7	12.3	18 31.9	4.1	54.2
A 14	27 28.2	40.5	22 13.0	12.2	18 27.8	4.2	54.2
Y 15	42 28.0	.. 40.0	36 44.2	12.3	18 23.6	4.2	54.2
16	57 27.8	39.5	51 15.5	12.3	18 19.4	4.4	54.2
17	72 27.6	39.0	65 46.8	12.3	18 15.0	4.4	54.2
18	87 27.4	S20 38.5	80 18.1	12.3	S18 10.6	4.6	54.3
19	102 27.2	38.0	94 49.4	12.4	18 06.0	4.6	54.3
20	117 27.0	37.5	109 20.8	12.3	18 01.4	4.6	54.3
21	132 26.8	.. 37.0	123 52.1	12.4	17 56.8	4.8	54.3
22	147 26.6	36.5	138 23.5	12.4	17 52.0	4.9	54.3
23	162 26.4	36.0	152 54.9	12.4	17 47.1	4.9	54.3
18 00	177 26.2	S20 35.5	167 26.3	12.4	S17 42.2	5.0	54.3
01	192 26.0	35.0	181 57.7	12.5	17 37.2	5.1	54.3
02	207 25.8	34.5	196 29.2	12.4	17 32.1	5.2	54.3
03	222 25.6	.. 34.0	211 00.6	12.5	17 26.9	5.3	54.3
04	237 25.4	33.5	225 32.1	12.5	17 21.6	5.3	54.4
05	252 25.2	33.0	240 03.6	12.6	17 16.3	5.5	54.4
06	267 25.0	S20 32.5	254 35.2	12.5	S17 10.8	5.5	54.4
T 07	282 24.8	32.0	269 06.7	12.6	17 05.3	5.6	54.4
H 08	297 24.6	31.4	283 38.3	12.5	16 59.7	5.6	54.4
U 09	312 24.4	.. 30.9	298 09.8	12.6	16 54.1	5.8	54.4
R 10	327 24.2	30.4	312 41.4	12.7	16 48.3	5.8	54.4
S 11	342 24.0	29.9	327 13.1	12.6	16 42.5	5.9	54.4
D 12	357 23.8	S20 29.4	341 44.7	12.7	S16 36.6	6.0	54.4
A 13	12 23.6	28.9	356 16.4	12.6	16 30.6	6.0	54.5
Y 14	27 23.4	28.4	10 48.0	12.7	16 24.6	6.2	54.5
15	42 23.2	.. 27.9	25 19.7	12.7	16 18.4	6.2	54.5
16	57 23.0	27.3	39 51.4	12.8	16 12.2	6.3	54.5
17	72 22.8	26.8	54 23.2	12.7	16 05.9	6.3	54.5
18	87 22.6	S20 26.3	68 54.9	12.8	S15 59.6	6.5	54.5
19	102 22.4	25.8	83 26.7	12.8	15 53.1	6.5	54.5
20	117 22.2	25.3	97 58.5	12.9	15 46.6	6.6	54.5
21	132 22.0	.. 24.8	112 30.4	12.8	15 40.0	6.6	54.6
22	147 21.8	24.2	127 02.2	12.9	15 33.4	6.8	54.6
23	162 21.6	23.7	141 34.1	12.8	S15 26.6	6.8	54.6
	SD 16.3	d 0.5	SD 14.7		14.8		14.8

Twilight / Sunrise / Moonrise

Lat.	Twilight Naut.	Twilight Civil	Sunrise	Moonrise 16	Moonrise 17	Moonrise 18	Moonrise 19
°	h m	h m	h m	h m	h m	h m	h m
N 72	07 56	09 43	■■■	■■■	■■■	11 43	11 19
N 70	07 42	09 12	11 42	11 12	11 01	10 55	10 51
68	07 30	08 49	10 24	09 52	10 14	10 24	10 30
66	07 21	08 30	09 47	09 14	09 43	10 01	10 13
64	07 12	08 16	09 21	08 47	09 20	09 43	10 00
62	07 05	08 03	09 01	08 26	09 02	09 28	09 48
60	06 59	07 52	08 44	08 09	08 47	09 16	09 38
N 58	06 53	07 43	08 31	07 55	08 34	09 05	09 30
56	06 48	07 35	08 19	07 43	08 23	08 55	09 22
54	06 43	07 27	08 09	07 32	08 13	08 47	09 15
52	06 38	07 21	07 59	07 23	08 04	08 39	09 09
50	06 34	07 14	07 51	07 15	07 56	08 32	09 04
45	06 25	07 01	07 34	06 57	07 39	08 18	08 52
N 40	06 16	06 50	07 19	06 42	07 26	08 06	08 42
35	06 09	06 40	07 07	06 30	07 14	07 55	08 33
30	06 01	06 31	06 56	06 19	07 04	07 46	08 26
20	05 47	06 14	06 38	06 00	06 46	07 31	08 13
N 10	05 33	05 59	06 22	05 44	06 31	07 17	08 01
0	05 19	05 44	06 06	05 29	06 17	07 04	07 51
S 10	05 02	05 28	05 51	05 14	06 02	06 51	07 40
20	04 42	05 10	05 34	04 57	05 47	06 38	07 28
30	04 16	04 49	05 15	04 39	05 29	06 22	07 15
35	04 00	04 35	05 04	04 28	05 19	06 13	07 08
40	03 40	04 19	04 51	04 16	05 07	06 02	06 59
45	03 14	04 00	04 35	04 01	04 54	05 50	06 49
S 50	02 38	03 35	04 16	03 43	04 37	05 35	06 37
52	02 19	03 23	04 07	03 35	04 29	05 28	06 31
54	01 53	03 08	03 57	03 25	04 20	05 20	06 24
56	01 15	02 51	03 45	03 15	04 10	05 11	06 17
58	////	02 30	03 32	03 02	03 58	05 01	06 09
S 60	////	02 03	03 16	02 48	03 45	04 50	06 00

Sunset / Twilight / Moonset

Lat.	Sunset	Twilight Civil	Twilight Naut.	Moonset 16	Moonset 17	Moonset 18	Moonset 19
°	h m	h m	h m	h m	h m	h m	h m
N 72	■■■	14 38	16 25	■■■	■■■	14 59	17 00
N 70	12 39	15 09	16 39	12 12	14 02	15 46	17 27
68	13 57	15 32	16 51	13 32	14 49	16 16	17 46
66	14 34	15 51	17 00	14 10	15 19	16 38	18 02
64	15 00	16 05	17 08	14 36	15 42	16 56	18 15
62	15 20	16 18	17 16	14 57	16 00	17 10	18 26
60	15 36	16 28	17 22	15 13	16 15	17 23	18 35
N 58	15 50	16 38	17 28	15 28	16 27	17 33	18 43
56	16 02	16 46	17 33	15 40	16 38	17 42	18 50
54	16 12	16 53	17 38	15 50	16 48	17 50	18 56
52	16 21	17 00	17 42	15 59	16 56	17 57	19 02
50	16 30	17 06	17 46	16 08	17 04	18 04	19 07
45	16 47	17 20	17 56	16 26	17 20	18 18	19 18
N 40	17 01	17 31	18 04	16 40	17 33	18 29	19 27
35	17 13	17 41	18 12	16 52	17 45	18 39	19 35
30	17 24	17 50	18 19	17 03	17 54	18 47	19 41
20	17 42	18 06	18 33	17 21	18 11	19 02	19 53
N 10	17 59	18 21	18 47	17 37	18 26	19 15	20 03
0	18 14	18 36	19 02	17 52	18 40	19 27	20 13
S 10	18 29	18 52	19 18	18 07	18 53	19 38	20 22
20	18 46	19 09	19 38	18 23	19 08	19 51	20 32
30	19 05	19 31	20 03	18 41	19 24	20 05	20 44
35	19 16	19 44	20 19	18 51	19 34	20 14	20 50
40	19 29	20 00	20 39	19 03	19 45	20 23	20 58
45	19 44	20 19	21 05	19 17	19 58	20 34	21 06
S 50	20 03	20 44	21 40	19 35	20 14	20 47	21 17
52	20 12	20 56	22 00	19 43	20 21	20 53	21 21
54	20 22	21 10	22 24	19 52	20 29	21 00	21 27
56	20 34	21 27	23 01	20 02	20 38	21 08	21 32
58	20 47	21 48	////	20 14	20 48	21 16	21 39
S 60	21 02	22 14	////	20 27	21 00	21 26	21 46

SUN / MOON

Day	SUN Eqn. of Time 00h	SUN Eqn. of Time 12h	SUN Mer. Pass.	MOON Mer. Pass. Upper	MOON Mer. Pass. Lower	Age	Phase
d	m s	m s	h m	h m	h m	d	%
16	09 35	09 45	12 10	11 40	24 04	29	0
17	09 55	10 05	12 10	12 28	00 04	00	0
18	10 15	10 25	12 10	13 15	00 52	01	2

UT	ARIES GHA	VENUS −4·0 GHA	Dec	MARS +1·3 GHA	Dec	JUPITER −1·9 GHA	Dec	SATURN +0·5 GHA	Dec	STARS Name	SHA	Dec
19 00	118 20.3	174 41.7	S20 56.1	245 08.0	S18 21.2	250 47.7	S16 36.6	204 36.3	S22 30.4	Acamar	315 15.9	S40 14.4
01	133 22.8	189 40.9	55.5	260 08.9	21.6	265 49.8	36.7	219 38.5	30.4	Achernar	335 24.6	S57 09.2
02	148 25.2	204 40.0	54.9	275 09.8	22.0	280 52.0	36.8	234 40.6	30.4	Acrux	173 05.4	S63 11.6
03	163 27.7	219 39.2	.. 54.2	290 10.7	.. 22.4	295 54.1	.. 36.9	249 42.8	.. 30.4	Adhara	255 09.7	S29 00.0
04	178 30.1	234 38.4	53.6	305 11.6	22.7	310 56.2	37.0	264 45.0	30.4	Aldebaran	290 45.6	N16 32.5
05	193 32.6	249 37.5	53.0	320 12.4	23.1	325 58.3	37.1	279 47.1	30.3			
06	208 35.1	264 36.7	S20 52.3	335 13.3	S18 23.5	341 00.4	S16 37.2	294 49.3	S22 30.3	Alioth	166 17.9	N55 51.5
07	223 37.5	279 35.9	51.7	350 14.2	23.9	356 02.6	37.2	309 51.5	30.3	Alkaid	152 56.5	N49 13.2
F 08	238 40.0	294 35.1	51.1	5 15.1	24.3	11 04.7	37.3	324 53.6	30.3	Al Na'ir	27 40.3	S46 52.6
R 09	253 42.5	309 34.2	.. 50.4	20 16.0	.. 24.7	26 06.8	.. 37.4	339 55.8	.. 30.3	Alnilam	275 42.9	S 1 11.7
I 10	268 44.9	324 33.4	49.8	35 16.9	25.1	41 08.9	37.5	354 57.9	30.3	Alphard	217 52.7	S 8 44.3
D 11	283 47.4	339 32.6	49.2	50 17.8	25.5	56 11.1	37.6	10 00.1	30.3			
A 12	298 49.9	354 31.7	S20 48.5	65 18.7	S18 25.8	71 13.2	S16 37.7	25 02.3	S22 30.3	Alphecca	126 08.5	N26 39.2
Y 13	313 52.3	9 30.9	47.9	80 19.5	26.2	86 15.3	37.7	40 04.4	30.3	Alpheratz	357 40.4	N29 11.4
14	328 54.8	24 30.1	47.2	95 20.4	26.6	101 17.5	37.8	55 06.6	30.3	Altair	62 05.5	N 8 55.0
15	343 57.2	39 29.3	.. 46.6	110 21.3	.. 27.0	116 19.6	.. 37.9	70 08.8	.. 30.3	Ankaa	353 12.8	S42 12.8
16	358 59.7	54 28.4	46.0	125 22.2	27.4	131 21.7	38.0	85 10.9	30.3	Antares	112 22.7	S26 28.0
17	14 02.2	69 27.6	45.3	140 23.1	27.8	146 23.8	38.1	100 13.1	30.3			
18	29 04.6	84 26.8	S20 44.7	155 24.0	S18 28.2	161 26.0	S16 38.2	115 15.3	S22 30.3	Arcturus	145 52.9	N19 05.3
19	44 07.1	99 26.0	44.0	170 24.9	28.5	176 28.1	38.3	130 17.4	30.3	Atria	107 22.1	S69 03.2
20	59 09.6	114 25.1	43.4	185 25.7	28.9	191 30.2	38.3	145 19.6	30.3	Avior	234 16.0	S59 34.1
21	74 12.0	129 24.3	.. 42.7	200 26.6	.. 29.3	206 32.3	.. 38.4	160 21.8	.. 30.3	Bellatrix	278 28.4	N 6 21.7
22	89 14.5	144 23.5	42.1	215 27.5	29.7	221 34.5	38.5	175 23.9	30.2	Betelgeuse	270 57.6	N 7 24.4
23	104 17.0	159 22.7	41.4	230 28.4	30.1	236 36.6	38.6	190 26.1	30.2			
20 00	119 19.4	174 21.8	S20 40.8	245 29.3	S18 30.5	251 38.7	S16 38.7	205 28.3	S22 30.2	Canopus	263 54.2	S52 42.6
01	134 21.9	189 21.0	40.1	260 30.2	30.8	266 40.9	38.8	220 30.4	30.2	Capella	280 29.4	N46 00.8
02	149 24.4	204 20.2	39.5	275 31.1	31.2	281 43.0	38.8	235 32.6	30.2	Deneb	49 29.8	N45 20.8
03	164 26.8	219 19.4	.. 38.8	290 32.0	.. 31.6	296 45.1	.. 38.9	250 34.8	.. 30.2	Denebola	182 30.3	N14 28.2
04	179 29.3	234 18.5	38.2	305 32.8	32.0	311 47.2	39.0	265 36.9	30.2	Diphda	348 52.9	S17 53.5
05	194 31.7	249 17.7	37.5	320 33.7	32.4	326 49.4	39.1	280 39.1	30.2			
06	209 34.2	264 16.9	S20 36.8	335 34.6	S18 32.8	341 51.5	S16 39.2	295 41.3	S22 30.2	Dubhe	193 47.5	N61 39.0
07	224 36.7	279 16.1	36.2	350 35.5	33.1	356 53.6	39.3	310 43.4	30.2	Elnath	278 08.4	N28 37.2
S 08	239 39.1	294 15.3	35.5	5 36.4	33.5	11 55.8	39.3	325 45.6	30.2	Eltanin	90 45.2	N51 29.2
A 09	254 41.6	309 14.5	.. 34.9	20 37.3	.. 33.9	26 57.9	.. 39.4	340 47.8	.. 30.2	Enif	33 44.4	N 9 57.5
T 10	269 44.1	324 13.6	34.2	35 38.2	34.3	42 00.0	39.5	355 49.9	30.2	Fomalhaut	15 20.8	S29 31.8
U 11	284 46.5	339 12.8	33.5	50 39.0	34.7	57 02.2	39.6	10 52.1	30.2			
R 12	299 49.0	354 12.0	S20 32.9	65 39.9	S18 35.0	72 04.3	S16 39.7	25 54.3	S22 30.2	Gacrux	171 57.1	S57 12.5
D 13	314 51.5	9 11.2	32.2	80 40.8	35.4	87 06.4	39.8	40 56.4	30.2	Gienah	175 48.9	S17 38.4
A 14	329 53.9	24 10.4	31.5	95 41.7	35.8	102 08.5	39.8	55 58.6	30.1	Hadar	148 43.4	S60 27.2
Y 15	344 56.4	39 09.6	.. 30.9	110 42.6	.. 36.2	117 10.7	.. 39.9	71 00.8	.. 30.1	Hamal	327 57.2	N23 32.8
16	359 58.9	54 08.7	30.2	125 43.5	36.6	132 12.8	40.0	86 02.9	30.1	Kaus Aust.	83 40.1	S34 22.3
17	15 01.3	69 07.9	29.5	140 44.3	36.9	147 14.9	40.1	101 05.1	30.1			
18	30 03.8	84 07.1	S20 28.9	155 45.2	S18 37.3	162 17.1	S16 40.2	116 07.3	S22 30.1	Kochab	137 20.5	N74 04.7
19	45 06.2	99 06.3	28.2	170 46.1	37.7	177 19.2	40.3	131 09.5	30.1	Markab	13 35.4	N15 18.1
20	60 08.7	114 05.5	27.5	185 47.0	38.1	192 21.3	40.3	146 11.6	30.1	Menkar	314 11.7	N 4 09.4
21	75 11.2	129 04.7	.. 26.8	200 47.9	.. 38.5	207 23.5	.. 40.4	161 13.8	.. 30.1	Menkent	148 03.9	S36 27.2
22	90 13.6	144 03.9	26.2	215 48.8	38.8	222 25.6	40.5	176 16.0	30.1	Miaplacidus	221 38.0	S69 47.4
23	105 16.1	159 03.1	25.5	230 49.7	39.2	237 27.7	40.6	191 18.1	30.1			
21 00	120 18.6	174 02.2	S20 24.8	245 50.5	S18 39.6	252 29.9	S16 40.7	206 20.3	S22 30.1	Mirfak	308 35.6	N49 55.5
01	135 21.0	189 01.4	24.1	260 51.4	40.0	267 32.0	40.8	221 22.5	30.1	Nunki	75 54.8	S26 16.3
02	150 23.5	204 00.6	23.5	275 52.3	40.4	282 34.1	40.8	236 24.6	30.1	Peacock	53 15.0	S56 40.6
03	165 26.0	218 59.8	.. 22.8	290 53.2	.. 40.7	297 36.3	.. 40.9	251 26.8	.. 30.1	Pollux	243 23.6	N27 58.7
04	180 28.4	233 59.0	22.1	305 54.1	41.1	312 38.4	41.0	266 29.0	30.1	Procyon	244 56.1	N 5 10.5
05	195 30.9	248 58.2	21.4	320 55.0	41.5	327 40.5	41.1	281 31.1	30.1			
06	210 33.3	263 57.4	S20 20.7	335 55.8	S18 41.9	342 42.7	S16 41.2	296 33.3	S22 30.0	Rasalhague	96 03.8	N12 32.9
07	225 35.8	278 56.6	20.1	350 56.7	42.2	357 44.8	41.2	311 35.5	30.0	Regulus	207 39.9	N11 52.6
S 08	240 38.3	293 55.8	19.4	5 57.6	42.6	12 46.9	41.3	326 37.6	30.0	Rigel	281 08.8	S 8 11.1
U 09	255 40.7	308 55.0	.. 18.7	20 58.5	.. 43.0	27 49.1	.. 41.4	341 39.8	.. 30.0	Rigil Kent.	139 47.5	S60 54.1
N 10	270 43.2	323 54.2	18.0	35 59.4	43.4	42 51.2	41.5	356 42.0	30.0	Sabik	102 09.2	S15 44.6
D 11	285 45.7	338 53.4	17.3	51 00.3	43.7	57 53.4	41.6	11 44.1	30.0			
A 12	300 48.1	353 52.6	S20 16.6	66 01.2	S18 44.1	72 55.5	S16 41.7	26 46.3	S22 30.0	Schedar	349 37.1	N56 38.3
Y 13	315 50.6	8 51.8	15.9	81 02.0	44.5	87 57.6	41.7	41 48.5	30.0	Shaula	96 18.0	S37 06.7
14	330 53.1	23 51.0	15.2	96 02.9	44.9	102 59.8	41.8	56 50.7	30.0	Sirius	258 30.6	S16 44.7
15	345 55.5	38 50.1	.. 14.5	111 03.8	.. 45.2	118 01.9	.. 41.9	71 52.8	.. 30.0	Spica	158 27.9	S11 15.2
16	0 58.0	53 49.3	13.9	126 04.7	45.6	133 04.0	42.0	86 55.0	30.0	Suhail	222 49.7	S43 30.4
17	16 00.5	68 48.5	13.2	141 05.6	46.0	148 06.2	42.1	101 57.2	30.0			
18	31 02.9	83 47.7	S20 12.5	156 06.5	S18 46.4	163 08.3	S16 42.1	116 59.3	S22 30.0	Vega	80 37.2	N38 48.1
19	46 05.4	98 46.9	11.8	171 07.3	46.7	178 10.5	42.2	132 01.5	30.0	Zuben'ubi	137 02.0	S16 06.8
20	61 07.8	113 46.1	11.1	186 08.2	47.1	193 12.6	42.3	147 03.7	30.0			
21	76 10.3	128 45.3	.. 10.4	201 09.1	.. 47.5	208 14.7	.. 42.4	162 05.8	.. 30.0			
22	91 12.8	143 44.5	09.7	216 10.0	47.9	223 16.9	42.5	177 08.0	29.9			
23	106 15.2	158 43.7	09.0	231 10.9	48.2	238 19.0	42.5	192 10.2	29.9			

	SHA	Mer. Pass.
Venus	55 02.4	12 23
Mars	126 09.9	7 38
Jupiter	132 19.3	7 12
Saturn	86 08.8	10 17

Mer. Pass.	ARIES h m 16 00.1	VENUS v −0.8 d 0.7	MARS v 0.9 d 0.4	JUPITER v 2.1 d 0.1	SATURN v 2.2 d 0.0

UT	SUN GHA	SUN Dec	MOON GHA	v	MOON Dec	d	HP
d h	° ′	° ′	° ′	′	° ′	′	′
19 00	177 21.4	S20 23.2	156 05.9	12.9	S15 19.8	6.9	54.6
01	192 21.2	22.7	170 37.8	13.0	15 12.9	6.9	54.6
02	207 21.0	22.2	185 09.8	12.9	15 06.0	7.0	54.6
03	222 20.8	.. 21.6	199 41.7	13.0	14 59.0	7.1	54.6
04	237 20.6	21.1	214 13.7	13.0	14 51.9	7.2	54.7
05	252 20.5	20.6	228 45.7	13.0	14 44.7	7.2	54.7
06	267 20.3	S20 20.1	243 17.7	13.0	S14 37.5	7.3	54.7
07	282 20.1	19.5	257 49.7	13.0	14 30.2	7.4	54.7
08	297 19.9	19.0	272 21.7	13.1	14 22.8	7.4	54.7
F 09	312 19.7	.. 18.5	286 53.8	13.1	14 15.4	7.5	54.7
R 10	327 19.5	18.0	301 25.9	13.1	14 07.9	7.6	54.7
I 11	342 19.3	17.4	315 58.0	13.1	14 00.3	7.7	54.8
D 12	357 19.1	S20 16.9	330 30.1	13.1	S13 52.6	7.7	54.8
A 13	12 18.9	16.4	345 02.2	13.2	13 44.9	7.7	54.8
Y 14	27 18.7	15.8	359 34.4	13.2	13 37.2	7.9	54.8
15	42 18.5	.. 15.3	14 06.6	13.2	13 29.3	7.9	54.8
16	57 18.4	14.8	28 38.8	13.2	13 21.4	7.9	54.8
17	72 18.2	14.2	43 11.0	13.2	13 13.5	8.0	54.8
18	87 18.0	S20 13.7	57 43.2	13.3	S13 05.5	8.1	54.9
19	102 17.8	13.2	72 15.5	13.2	12 57.4	8.2	54.9
20	117 17.6	12.6	86 47.7	13.3	12 49.2	8.2	54.9
21	132 17.4	.. 12.1	101 20.0	13.3	12 41.0	8.3	54.9
22	147 17.2	11.6	115 52.3	13.3	12 32.7	8.3	54.9
23	162 17.0	11.0	130 24.6	13.4	12 24.4	8.4	54.9
20 00	177 16.9	S20 10.5	144 57.0	13.3	S12 16.0	8.4	55.0
01	192 16.7	10.0	159 29.3	13.4	12 07.6	8.5	55.0
02	207 16.5	09.4	174 01.7	13.4	11 59.1	8.6	55.0
03	222 16.3	.. 08.9	188 34.1	13.4	11 50.5	8.6	55.0
04	237 16.1	08.3	203 06.5	13.4	11 41.9	8.7	55.0
05	252 15.9	07.8	217 38.9	13.4	11 33.2	8.8	55.0
06	267 15.7	S20 07.3	232 11.3	13.5	S11 24.4	8.8	55.1
S 07	282 15.6	06.7	246 43.8	13.4	11 15.6	8.8	55.1
A 08	297 15.4	06.2	261 16.2	13.5	11 06.8	8.9	55.1
T 09	312 15.2	.. 05.6	275 48.7	13.5	10 57.9	9.0	55.1
U 10	327 15.0	05.1	290 21.2	13.5	10 48.9	9.0	55.1
R 11	342 14.8	04.6	304 53.7	13.5	10 39.9	9.0	55.1
D 12	357 14.6	S20 04.0	319 26.2	13.5	S10 30.9	9.1	55.2
A 13	12 14.5	03.5	333 58.7	13.6	10 21.8	9.2	55.2
Y 14	27 14.3	02.9	348 31.3	13.6	10 12.6	9.2	55.2
15	42 14.1	.. 02.4	3 03.8	13.6	10 03.4	9.3	55.2
16	57 13.9	01.8	17 36.4	13.5	9 54.1	9.3	55.2
17	72 13.7	01.3	32 08.9	13.6	9 44.8	9.4	55.3
18	87 13.6	S20 00.7	46 41.5	13.6	S 9 35.4	9.4	55.3
19	102 13.4	20 00.2	61 14.1	13.6	9 26.0	9.4	55.3
20	117 13.2	19 59.6	75 46.7	13.6	9 16.6	9.5	55.3
21	132 13.0	.. 59.1	90 19.3	13.6	9 07.1	9.6	55.3
22	147 12.8	58.5	104 51.9	13.6	8 57.5	9.6	55.4
23	162 12.7	58.0	119 24.5	13.7	8 47.9	9.6	55.4
21 00	177 12.5	S19 57.4	133 57.2	13.6	S 8 38.3	9.7	55.4
01	192 12.3	56.9	148 29.8	13.6	8 28.6	9.8	55.4
02	207 12.1	56.3	163 02.4	13.7	8 18.8	9.7	55.4
03	222 11.9	.. 55.8	177 35.1	13.6	8 09.1	9.9	55.5
04	237 11.8	55.2	192 07.7	13.7	7 59.2	9.8	55.5
05	252 11.6	54.7	206 40.4	13.7	7 49.4	9.9	55.5
06	267 11.4	S19 54.1	221 13.1	13.6	S 7 39.5	10.0	55.5
07	282 11.2	53.5	235 45.7	13.7	7 29.5	9.9	55.5
08	297 11.1	53.0	250 18.4	13.6	7 19.6	10.1	55.6
S 09	312 10.9	.. 52.4	264 51.0	13.7	7 09.5	10.0	55.6
U 10	327 10.7	51.9	279 23.7	13.7	6 59.5	10.1	55.6
N 11	342 10.5	51.3	293 56.4	13.7	6 49.4	10.2	55.6
D 12	357 10.4	S19 50.7	308 29.1	13.6	S 6 39.2	10.1	55.6
A 13	12 10.2	50.2	323 01.7	13.7	6 29.1	10.2	55.7
Y 14	27 10.0	49.6	337 34.4	13.7	6 18.9	10.3	55.7
15	42 09.8	.. 49.1	352 07.1	13.6	6 08.6	10.3	55.7
16	57 09.7	48.5	6 39.7	13.7	5 58.3	10.3	55.7
17	72 09.5	47.9	21 12.4	13.6	5 48.0	10.3	55.8
18	87 09.3	S19 47.4	35 45.0	13.7	S 5 37.7	10.4	55.8
19	102 09.1	46.8	50 17.7	13.6	5 27.3	10.4	55.8
20	117 09.0	46.2	64 50.3	13.7	5 16.9	10.4	55.8
21	132 08.8	.. 45.7	79 23.0	13.6	5 06.5	10.5	55.8
22	147 08.6	45.1	93 55.6	13.6	4 56.0	10.5	55.9
23	162 08.5	44.5	108 28.2	13.7	S 4 45.5	10.6	55.9
	SD 16.3	d 0.5	SD 14.9		15.0		15.2

Moonrise

Lat.	Twilight Naut.	Twilight Civil	Sunrise	19	20	21	22
°	h m	h m	h m	h m	h m	h m	h m
N 72	07 48	09 31	■■■	11 19	11 04	10 52	10 42
N 70	07 35	09 02	11 05	10 51	10 47	10 42	10 38
68	07 24	08 41	10 10	10 30	10 33	10 34	10 35
66	07 16	08 24	09 37	10 13	10 21	10 28	10 33
64	07 08	08 10	09 13	10 00	10 12	10 22	10 30
62	07 01	07 58	08 55	09 48	10 04	10 17	10 29
60	06 55	07 48	08 39	09 38	09 57	10 12	10 27
N 58	06 50	07 39	08 26	09 30	09 50	10 09	10 25
56	06 45	07 31	08 15	09 22	09 45	10 05	10 24
54	06 40	07 24	08 05	09 15	09 40	10 02	10 23
52	06 36	07 18	07 56	09 09	09 35	09 59	10 22
50	06 32	07 12	07 48	09 04	09 31	09 57	10 21
45	06 23	06 59	07 31	08 52	09 22	09 51	10 18
N 40	06 15	06 48	07 18	08 42	09 15	09 46	10 17
35	06 08	06 39	07 06	08 33	09 09	09 42	10 15
30	06 01	06 30	06 56	08 26	09 03	09 39	10 14
20	05 47	06 14	06 38	08 13	08 53	09 32	10 11
N 10	05 34	06 00	06 22	08 01	08 45	09 27	10 09
0	05 20	05 45	06 07	07 51	08 36	09 22	10 07
S 10	05 04	05 30	05 53	07 40	08 28	09 16	10 05
20	04 44	05 13	05 36	07 28	08 20	09 11	10 03
30	04 19	04 51	05 18	07 15	08 10	09 05	10 00
35	04 04	04 38	05 07	07 08	08 04	09 01	09 59
40	03 44	04 23	04 54	06 59	07 57	08 57	09 57
45	03 20	04 04	04 39	06 49	07 50	08 52	09 55
S 50	02 45	03 40	04 21	06 37	07 41	08 46	09 53
52	02 27	03 29	04 12	06 31	07 36	08 44	09 52
54	02 03	03 15	04 03	06 24	07 32	08 41	09 51
56	01 30	02 59	03 52	06 17	07 26	08 37	09 50
58	////	02 39	03 39	06 09	07 21	08 34	09 49
S 60	////	02 14	03 24	06 00	07 14	08 30	09 47

Moonset

Lat.	Sunset	Twilight Civil	Twilight Naut.	19	20	21	22
°	h m	h m	h m	h m	h m	h m	h m
N 72	■■■	14 52	16 35	17 00	18 50	20 35	22 21
N 70	13 18	15 21	16 48	17 27	19 05	20 43	22 21
68	14 13	15 42	16 59	17 46	19 18	20 49	22 22
66	14 46	15 59	17 07	18 02	19 28	20 55	22 23
64	15 09	16 13	17 15	18 15	19 36	20 59	22 23
62	15 28	16 24	17 22	18 26	19 44	21 03	22 24
60	15 43	16 35	17 28	18 35	19 50	21 06	22 24
N 58	15 56	16 43	17 33	18 43	19 55	21 09	22 25
56	16 08	16 51	17 38	18 50	20 00	21 12	22 25
54	16 18	16 58	17 42	18 56	20 04	21 14	22 25
52	16 26	17 05	17 47	19 02	20 08	21 16	22 26
50	16 34	17 11	17 50	19 07	20 12	21 18	22 26
45	16 51	17 23	17 59	19 18	20 19	21 22	22 26
N 40	17 05	17 34	18 07	19 27	20 26	21 26	22 27
35	17 16	17 44	18 15	19 35	20 31	21 29	22 27
30	17 27	17 52	18 21	19 41	20 36	21 31	22 27
20	17 44	18 08	18 35	19 53	20 44	21 36	22 28
N 10	18 00	18 22	18 48	20 03	20 52	21 40	22 28
0	18 15	18 37	19 02	20 13	20 58	21 43	22 29
S 10	18 29	18 52	19 18	20 22	21 05	21 47	22 29
20	18 45	19 09	19 37	20 32	21 12	21 51	22 30
30	19 04	19 30	20 02	20 44	21 20	21 55	22 30
35	19 15	19 43	20 18	20 50	21 25	21 58	22 30
40	19 27	19 58	20 37	20 58	21 30	22 00	22 30
45	19 42	20 17	21 01	21 06	21 36	22 04	22 31
S 50	20 00	20 40	21 35	21 17	21 43	22 07	22 31
52	20 09	20 52	21 53	21 21	21 46	22 09	22 31
54	20 18	21 06	22 16	21 27	21 50	22 11	22 31
56	20 29	21 21	22 48	21 32	21 54	22 13	22 32
58	20 42	21 41	23 59	21 39	21 58	22 15	22 32
S 60	20 57	22 05	////	21 46	22 03	22 18	22 32

	SUN Eqn. of Time 00h	SUN Eqn. of Time 12h	SUN Mer. Pass.	MOON Mer. Pass. Upper	MOON Mer. Pass. Lower	Age	Phase
Day							
d	m s	m s	h m	h m	h m	d	%
19	10 34	10 43	12 11	14 02	01 39	02	5
20	10 52	11 01	12 11	14 47	02 25	03	10
21	11 10	11 18	12 11	15 33	03 10	04	17

UT	ARIES	VENUS −3.9		MARS +1.3		JUPITER −1.9		SATURN +0.5		STARS		
	GHA	GHA	Dec	GHA	Dec	GHA	Dec	GHA	Dec	Name	SHA	Dec
d h	° ′	° ′	° ′	° ′	° ′	° ′	° ′	° ′	° ′		° ′	° ′
22 00	121 17.7	173 42.9	S20 08.3	246 11.8	S18 48.6	253 21.1	S16 42.6	207 12.3	S22 29.9	Acamar	315 15.9	S40 14.4
01	136 20.2	188 42.2	07.6	261 12.6	49.0	268 23.3	42.7	222 14.5	29.9	Achernar	335 24.6	S57 09.2
02	151 22.6	203 41.4	06.9	276 13.5	49.4	283 25.4	42.8	237 16.7	29.9	Acrux	173 05.4	S63 11.6
03	166 25.1	218 40.6	. . 06.2	291 14.4	. . 49.7	298 27.6	. . 42.9	252 18.9	. . 29.9	Adhara	255 09.7	S29 00.1
04	181 27.6	233 39.8	05.5	306 15.3	50.1	313 29.7	42.9	267 21.0	29.9	Aldebaran	290 45.6	N16 32.5
05	196 30.0	248 39.0	04.7	321 16.2	50.5	328 31.8	43.0	282 23.2	29.9			
06	211 32.5	263 38.2	S20 04.0	336 17.0	S18 50.8	343 34.0	S16 43.1	297 25.4	S22 29.9	Alioth	166 17.8	N55 51.5
07	226 35.0	278 37.4	03.3	351 17.9	51.2	358 36.1	43.2	312 27.5	29.9	Alkaid	152 56.5	N49 13.2
08	241 37.4	293 36.6	02.6	6 18.8	51.6	13 38.3	43.3	327 29.7	29.9	Al Na'ir	27 40.3	S46 52.6
M 09	256 39.9	308 35.8	. . 01.9	21 19.7	. . 52.0	28 40.4	. . 43.3	342 31.9	. . 29.9	Alnilam	275 42.9	S 1 11.7
O 10	271 42.3	323 35.0	01.2	36 20.6	52.3	43 42.5	43.4	357 34.0	29.9	Alphard	217 52.7	S 8 44.3
N 11	286 44.8	338 34.2	20 00.5	51 21.5	52.7	58 44.7	43.5	12 36.2	29.9			
D 12	301 47.3	353 33.4	S19 59.8	66 22.3	S18 53.1	73 46.8	S16 43.6	27 38.4	S22 29.9	Alphecca	126 08.5	N26 39.2
A 13	316 49.7	8 32.6	59.1	81 23.2	53.4	88 49.0	43.7	42 40.6	29.8	Alpheratz	357 40.4	N29 11.4
Y 14	331 52.2	23 31.8	58.3	96 24.1	53.8	103 51.1	43.7	57 42.7	29.8	Altair	62 05.5	N 8 55.0
15	346 54.7	38 31.0	. . 57.6	111 25.0	. . 54.2	118 53.3	. . 43.8	72 44.9	. . 29.8	Ankaa	353 12.8	S42 12.8
16	1 57.1	53 30.2	56.9	126 25.9	54.5	133 55.4	43.9	87 47.1	29.8	Antares	112 22.6	S26 28.1
17	16 59.6	68 29.5	56.2	141 26.8	54.9	148 57.5	44.0	102 49.2	29.8			
18	32 02.1	83 28.7	S19 55.5	156 27.6	S18 55.3	163 59.7	S16 44.1	117 51.4	S22 29.8	Arcturus	145 52.9	N19 05.3
19	47 04.5	98 27.9	54.7	171 28.5	55.6	179 01.8	44.1	132 53.6	29.8	Atria	107 22.0	S69 03.2
20	62 07.0	113 27.1	54.0	186 29.4	56.0	194 04.0	44.2	147 55.8	29.8	Avior	234 16.0	S59 34.1
21	77 09.4	128 26.3	. . 53.3	201 30.3	. . 56.4	209 06.1	. . 44.3	162 57.9	. . 29.8	Bellatrix	278 28.4	N 6 21.7
22	92 11.9	143 25.5	52.6	216 31.2	56.8	224 08.3	44.4	178 00.1	29.8	Betelgeuse	270 57.6	N 7 24.4
23	107 14.4	158 24.7	51.9	231 32.0	57.1	239 10.4	44.5	193 02.3	29.8			
23 00	122 16.8	173 23.9	S19 51.1	246 32.9	S18 57.5	254 12.6	S16 44.5	208 04.4	S22 29.8	Canopus	263 54.3	S52 42.6
01	137 19.3	188 23.2	50.4	261 33.8	57.9	269 14.7	44.6	223 06.6	29.8	Capella	280 29.5	N46 00.9
02	152 21.8	203 22.4	49.7	276 34.7	58.2	284 16.8	44.7	238 08.8	29.8	Deneb	49 29.8	N45 20.8
03	167 24.2	218 21.6	. . 48.9	291 35.6	. . 58.6	299 19.0	. . 44.8	253 11.0	. . 29.8	Denebola	182 30.3	N14 28.2
04	182 26.7	233 20.8	48.2	306 36.4	59.0	314 21.1	44.9	268 13.1	29.7	Diphda	348 52.9	S17 53.5
05	197 29.2	248 20.0	47.5	321 37.3	59.3	329 23.3	44.9	283 15.3	29.7			
06	212 31.6	263 19.2	S19 46.7	336 38.2	S18 59.7	344 25.4	S16 45.0	298 17.5	S22 29.7	Dubhe	193 47.5	N61 39.0
07	227 34.1	278 18.5	46.0	351 39.1	19 00.1	359 27.6	45.1	313 19.6	29.7	Elnath	278 08.4	N28 37.2
T 08	242 36.6	293 17.7	45.3	6 40.0	00.4	14 29.7	45.2	328 21.8	29.7	Eltanin	90 45.1	N51 29.2
U 09	257 39.0	308 16.9	. . 44.5	21 40.9	. . 00.8	29 31.9	. . 45.2	343 24.0	. . 29.7	Enif	33 44.4	N 9 57.5
E 10	272 41.5	323 16.1	43.8	36 41.7	01.1	44 34.0	45.3	358 26.2	29.7	Fomalhaut	15 20.9	S29 31.8
S 11	287 43.9	338 15.3	43.1	51 42.6	01.5	59 36.2	45.4	13 28.3	29.7			
D 12	302 46.4	353 14.6	S19 42.3	66 43.5	S19 01.9	74 38.3	S16 45.5	28 30.5	S22 29.7	Gacrux	171 57.1	S57 12.5
A 13	317 48.9	8 13.8	41.6	81 44.4	02.2	89 40.5	45.6	43 32.7	29.7	Gienah	175 48.9	S17 38.4
Y 14	332 51.3	23 13.0	40.9	96 45.3	02.6	104 42.6	45.6	58 34.8	29.7	Hadar	148 43.4	S60 27.2
15	347 53.8	38 12.2	. . 40.1	111 46.1	. . 03.0	119 44.7	. . 45.7	73 37.0	. . 29.7	Hamal	327 57.2	N23 32.8
16	2 56.3	53 11.5	39.4	126 47.0	03.3	134 46.9	45.8	88 39.2	29.7	Kaus Aust.	83 40.0	S34 22.3
17	17 58.7	68 10.7	38.6	141 47.9	03.7	149 49.0	45.9	103 41.4	29.7			
18	33 01.2	83 09.9	S19 37.9	156 48.8	S19 04.1	164 51.2	S16 45.9	118 43.5	S22 29.6	Kochab	137 20.5	N74 04.7
19	48 03.7	98 09.1	37.1	171 49.7	04.4	179 53.3	46.0	133 45.7	29.6	Markab	13 35.5	N15 18.1
20	63 06.1	113 08.3	36.4	186 50.5	04.8	194 55.5	46.1	148 47.9	29.6	Menkar	314 11.7	N 4 09.4
21	78 08.6	128 07.6	. . 35.6	201 51.4	. . 05.1	209 57.6	. . 46.2	163 50.1	. . 29.6	Menkent	148 03.9	S36 27.2
22	93 11.0	143 06.8	34.9	216 52.3	05.5	224 59.8	46.3	178 52.2	29.6	Miaplacidus	221 38.0	S69 47.5
23	108 13.5	158 06.0	34.2	231 53.2	05.9	240 01.9	46.3	193 54.4	29.6			
24 00	123 16.0	173 05.3	S19 33.4	246 54.1	S19 06.2	255 04.1	S16 46.4	208 56.6	S22 29.6	Mirfak	308 35.6	N49 55.5
01	138 18.4	188 04.5	32.7	261 54.9	06.6	270 06.2	46.5	223 58.7	29.6	Nunki	75 54.8	S26 16.3
02	153 20.9	203 03.7	31.9	276 55.8	07.0	285 08.4	46.6	239 00.9	29.6	Peacock	53 15.0	S56 40.6
03	168 23.4	218 02.9	. . 31.1	291 56.7	. . 07.3	300 10.5	. . 46.6	254 03.1	. . 29.6	Pollux	243 23.6	N27 58.7
04	183 25.8	233 02.2	30.4	306 57.6	07.7	315 12.7	46.7	269 05.3	29.6	Procyon	244 56.1	N 5 10.5
05	198 28.3	248 01.4	29.6	321 58.5	08.0	330 14.8	46.8	284 07.4	29.6			
06	213 30.8	263 00.6	S19 28.9	336 59.3	S19 08.4	345 17.0	S16 46.9	299 09.6	S22 29.6	Rasalhague	96 03.8	N12 32.9
W 07	228 33.2	277 59.9	28.1	352 00.2	08.8	0 19.2	46.9	314 11.8	29.6	Regulus	207 39.9	N11 52.6
E 08	243 35.7	292 59.1	27.4	7 01.1	09.1	15 21.3	47.0	329 14.0	29.6	Rigel	281 08.8	S 8 11.2
D 09	258 38.2	307 58.3	. . 26.6	22 02.0	. . 09.5	30 23.5	. . 47.1	344 16.1	. . 29.5	Rigil Kent.	139 47.5	S60 54.1
N 10	273 40.6	322 57.6	25.9	37 02.8	09.8	45 25.6	47.2	359 18.3	29.5	Sabik	102 09.2	S15 44.6
E 11	288 43.1	337 56.8	25.1	52 03.7	10.2	60 27.8	47.2	14 20.5	29.5			
S 12	303 45.5	352 56.0	S19 24.3	67 04.6	S19 10.6	75 29.9	S16 47.3	29 22.7	S22 29.5	Schedar	349 37.1	N56 38.3
D 13	318 48.0	7 55.3	23.6	82 05.5	10.9	90 32.1	47.4	44 24.8	29.5	Shaula	96 18.0	S37 06.7
A 14	333 50.5	22 54.5	22.8	97 06.4	11.3	105 34.2	47.5	59 27.0	29.5	Sirius	258 30.6	S16 44.7
Y 15	348 52.9	37 53.7	. . 22.0	112 07.2	. . 11.6	120 36.4	. . 47.6	74 29.2	. . 29.5	Spica	158 27.9	S11 15.2
16	3 55.4	52 53.0	21.3	127 08.1	12.0	135 38.5	47.6	89 31.4	29.5	Suhail	222 49.7	S43 30.4
17	18 57.9	67 52.2	20.5	142 09.0	12.3	150 40.7	47.7	104 33.5	29.5			
18	34 00.3	82 51.4	S19 19.7	157 09.9	S19 12.7	165 42.8	S16 47.8	119 35.7	S22 29.5	Vega	80 37.2	N38 48.0
19	49 02.8	97 50.7	19.0	172 10.8	13.1	180 45.0	47.9	134 37.9	29.5	Zuben'ubi	137 02.0	S16 06.8
20	64 05.3	112 49.9	18.2	187 11.6	13.4	195 47.1	47.9	149 40.1	29.5		SHA	Mer.Pass.
21	79 07.7	127 49.1	. . 17.4	202 12.5	. . 13.8	210 49.3	. . 48.0	164 42.2	. . 29.5		° ′	h m
22	94 10.2	142 48.4	16.7	217 13.4	14.1	225 51.5	48.1	179 44.4	29.5	Venus	51 07.1	12 27
23	109 12.7	157 47.6	15.9	232 14.3	14.5	240 53.6	48.2	194 46.6	29.4	Mars	124 16.1	7 33
	h m									Jupiter	131 55.7	7 02
Mer. Pass. 15 48.3		v −0.8	d 0.7	v 0.9	d 0.4	v 2.1	d 0.1	v 2.2	d 0.0	Saturn	85 47.6	10 06

UT	SUN GHA	SUN Dec	MOON GHA	v	MOON Dec	d	HP
d h	° ′	° ′	° ′	′	° ′	′	′
22 00	177 08.3	S19 44.0	123 00.9	13.6	S 4 34.9	10.5	55.9
01	192 08.1	43.4	137 33.5	13.6	4 24.4	10.6	55.9
02	207 08.0	42.8	152 06.1	13.6	4 13.8	10.6	56.0
03	222 07.8 ..	42.3	166 38.7	13.6	4 03.2	10.7	56.0
04	237 07.6	41.7	181 11.3	13.5	3 52.5	10.6	56.0
05	252 07.4	41.1	195 43.8	13.6	3 41.9	10.7	56.0
06	267 07.3	S19 40.6	210 16.4	13.6	S 3 31.2	10.8	56.1
07	282 07.1	40.0	224 49.0	13.5	3 20.4	10.7	56.1
M 08	297 06.9	39.4	239 21.5	13.5	3 09.7	10.8	56.1
O 09	312 06.8 ..	38.8	253 54.0	13.5	2 58.9	10.7	56.1
N 10	327 06.6	38.3	268 26.5	13.5	2 48.2	10.9	56.2
D 11	342 06.4	37.7	282 59.0	13.5	2 37.3	10.8	56.2
A 12	357 06.3	S19 37.1	297 31.5	13.4	S 2 26.5	10.8	56.2
Y 13	12 06.1	36.5	312 03.9	13.5	2 15.7	10.9	56.2
14	27 05.9	36.0	326 36.4	13.4	2 04.8	10.9	56.3
15	42 05.8 ..	35.4	341 08.8	13.4	1 53.9	10.9	56.3
16	57 05.6	34.8	355 41.2	13.4	1 43.0	10.9	56.3
17	72 05.4	34.2	10 13.6	13.4	1 32.1	11.0	56.3
18	87 05.3	S19 33.7	24 46.0	13.3	S 1 21.1	10.9	56.4
19	102 05.1	33.1	39 18.3	13.3	1 10.2	11.0	56.4
20	117 05.0	32.5	53 50.6	13.3	0 59.2	11.0	56.4
21	132 04.8 ..	31.9	68 22.9	13.3	0 48.2	11.0	56.5
22	147 04.6	31.3	82 55.2	13.2	0 37.2	11.0	56.5
23	162 04.5	30.7	97 27.4	13.2	0 26.2	11.0	56.5
23 00	177 04.3	S19 30.2	111 59.6	13.2	S 0 15.2	11.0	56.5
01	192 04.1	29.6	126 31.8	13.2	S 0 04.2	11.1	56.6
02	207 04.0	29.0	141 04.0	13.1	N 0 06.9	11.0	56.6
03	222 03.8 ..	28.4	155 36.1	13.1	0 17.9	11.1	56.6
04	237 03.7	27.8	170 08.2	13.1	0 29.0	11.1	56.6
05	252 03.5	27.2	184 40.3	13.1	0 40.1	11.1	56.7
06	267 03.3	S19 26.7	199 12.4	13.0	N 0 51.2	11.0	56.7
07	282 03.2	26.1	213 44.4	13.0	1 02.2	11.1	56.7
T 08	297 03.0	25.5	228 16.4	12.9	1 13.3	11.1	56.8
U 09	312 02.9 ..	24.9	242 48.3	12.9	1 24.4	11.0	56.8
E 10	327 02.7	24.3	257 20.2	12.9	1 35.5	11.1	56.8
S 11	342 02.5	23.7	271 52.1	12.8	1 46.6	11.1	56.8
D 12	357 02.4	S19 23.1	286 23.9	12.8	N 1 57.7	11.1	56.9
A 13	12 02.2	22.5	300 55.7	12.8	2 08.8	11.2	56.9
Y 14	27 02.1	21.9	315 27.5	12.7	2 20.0	11.1	56.9
15	42 01.9 ..	21.3	329 59.2	12.7	2 31.1	11.1	57.0
16	57 01.8	20.8	344 30.9	12.7	2 42.2	11.1	57.0
17	72 01.6	20.2	359 02.6	12.6	2 53.3	11.1	57.0
18	87 01.4	S19 19.6	13 34.2	12.6	N 3 04.4	11.1	57.1
19	102 01.3	19.0	28 05.8	12.5	3 15.5	11.1	57.1
20	117 01.1	18.4	42 37.3	12.5	3 26.6	11.0	57.1
21	132 01.0 ..	17.8	57 08.8	12.4	3 37.6	11.1	57.1
22	147 00.8	17.2	71 40.2	12.4	3 48.7	11.1	57.2
23	162 00.7	16.6	86 11.6	12.3	3 59.8	11.1	57.2
24 00	177 00.5	S19 16.0	100 42.9	12.3	N 4 10.9	11.0	57.2
01	192 00.4	15.4	115 14.2	12.3	4 21.9	11.1	57.3
02	207 00.2	14.8	129 45.5	12.2	4 33.0	11.0	57.3
03	222 00.1 ..	14.2	144 16.7	12.1	4 44.0	11.0	57.3
04	236 59.9	13.6	158 47.8	12.2	4 55.0	11.0	57.4
05	251 59.7	13.0	173 19.0	12.0	5 06.0	11.0	57.4
06	266 59.6	S19 12.4	187 50.0	12.0	N 5 17.0	11.0	57.4
W 07	281 59.4	11.8	202 21.0	11.9	5 28.0	10.7	57.5
E 08	296 59.3	11.2	216 51.9	11.9	5 39.0	10.9	57.5
D 09	311 59.1 ..	10.6	231 22.8	11.9	5 49.9	11.0	57.5
N 10	326 59.0	10.0	245 53.7	11.8	6 00.9	10.9	57.5
E 11	341 58.8	09.4	260 24.5	11.7	6 11.8	10.9	57.6
S 12	356 58.7	S19 08.8	274 55.2	11.6	N 6 22.7	10.9	57.6
D 13	11 58.5	08.2	289 25.8	11.7	6 33.6	10.8	57.6
A 14	26 58.4	07.6	303 56.5	11.5	6 44.4	10.8	57.7
Y 15	41 58.2 ..	07.0	318 27.0	11.5	6 55.2	10.7	57.7
16	56 58.1	06.3	332 57.5	11.4	7 06.1	10.7	57.7
17	71 57.9	05.7	347 27.9	11.4	7 16.8	10.8	57.8
18	86 57.8	S19 05.1	1 58.3	11.3	N 7 27.6	10.7	57.8
19	101 57.7	04.5	16 28.6	11.2	7 38.3	10.7	57.8
20	116 57.5	03.9	30 58.8	11.2	7 49.0	10.7	57.9
21	131 57.4 ..	03.3	45 29.0	11.1	7 59.7	10.6	57.9
22	146 57.2	02.7	59 59.1	11.1	8 10.3	10.7	57.9
23	161 57.1	02.1	74 29.2	11.0	N 8 21.0	10.5	58.0
	SD 16.3	d 0.6	SD 15.3		15.5		15.7

Lat.	Twilight Naut.	Twilight Civil	Sunrise	Moonrise 22	23	24	25
°	h m	h m	h m	h m	h m	h m	h m
N 72	07 39	09 18	■■■	10 42	10 32	10 22	10 11
N 70	07 28	08 52	10 41	10 38	10 34	10 31	10 27
68	07 18	08 33	09 57	10 35	10 36	10 37	10 40
66	07 10	08 17	09 27	10 33	10 38	10 43	10 50
64	07 03	08 04	09 06	10 30	10 39	10 48	10 59
62	06 57	07 53	08 48	10 29	10 40	10 52	11 07
60	06 51	07 43	08 34	10 27	10 41	10 56	11 13
N 58	06 46	07 35	08 21	10 25	10 42	10 59	11 19
56	06 41	07 28	08 11	10 24	10 43	11 02	11 25
54	06 37	07 21	08 01	10 23	10 43	11 05	11 29
52	06 33	07 15	07 53	10 22	10 44	11 07	11 33
50	06 30	07 09	07 45	10 21	10 45	11 10	11 37
45	06 21	06 57	07 29	10 18	10 46	11 14	11 46
N 40	06 14	06 47	07 16	10 17	10 47	11 19	11 53
35	06 07	06 37	07 05	10 15	10 48	11 22	11 59
30	06 00	06 29	06 55	10 14	10 49	11 25	12 04
20	05 47	06 14	06 38	10 11	10 50	11 31	12 14
N 10	05 35	06 00	06 22	10 09	10 52	11 36	12 22
0	05 21	05 46	06 08	10 07	10 53	11 40	12 30
S 10	05 05	05 31	05 54	10 05	10 54	11 45	12 38
20	04 47	05 15	05 38	10 03	10 55	11 50	12 46
30	04 23	04 54	05 21	10 00	10 57	11 56	12 56
35	04 07	04 42	05 10	09 59	10 58	11 59	13 02
40	03 49	04 27	04 58	09 57	10 59	12 03	13 08
45	03 25	04 09	04 44	09 55	11 00	12 07	13 16
S 50	02 52	03 46	04 26	09 53	11 02	12 12	13 25
52	02 35	03 35	04 18	09 52	11 03	12 15	13 29
54	02 14	03 22	04 08	09 51	11 03	12 18	13 34
56	01 45	03 07	03 58	09 50	11 04	12 20	13 39
58	00 54	02 48	03 46	09 49	11 05	12 24	13 45
S 60	////	02 26	03 32	09 47	11 06	12 28	13 51

Lat.	Sunset	Twilight Civil	Twilight Naut.	Moonset 22	23	24	25
°	h m	h m	h m	h m	h m	h m	h m
N 72	■■■	15 07	16 46	22 21	24 08	00 08	02 01
N 70	13 44	15 32	16 57	22 21	24 02	00 02	01 47
68	14 28	15 52	17 07	22 22	23 57	25 36	01 36
66	14 57	16 08	17 15	22 23	23 53	25 27	01 27
64	15 19	16 21	17 22	22 23	23 50	25 19	01 19
62	15 36	16 31	17 28	22 24	23 47	25 12	01 12
60	15 51	16 41	17 33	22 24	23 44	25 07	01 07
N 58	16 03	16 49	17 38	22 25	23 42	25 02	01 02
56	16 14	16 57	17 43	22 25	23 40	24 57	00 57
54	16 23	17 03	17 47	22 25	23 38	24 53	00 53
52	16 31	17 09	17 51	22 26	23 37	24 50	00 50
50	16 39	17 15	17 55	22 26	23 35	24 47	00 47
45	16 55	17 27	18 03	22 26	23 32	24 40	00 40
N 40	17 08	17 37	18 10	22 27	23 29	24 34	00 34
35	17 19	17 47	18 17	22 27	23 27	24 29	00 29
30	17 29	17 55	18 24	22 27	23 25	24 24	00 24
20	17 46	18 10	18 36	22 28	23 21	24 17	00 17
N 10	18 01	18 24	18 49	22 28	23 18	24 10	00 10
0	18 15	18 37	19 03	22 29	23 15	24 04	00 04
S 10	18 30	18 52	19 18	22 29	23 12	23 57	24 45
20	18 45	19 09	19 37	22 30	23 09	23 51	24 35
30	19 03	19 29	20 01	22 30	23 06	23 43	24 24
35	19 13	19 41	20 16	22 30	23 03	23 39	24 17
40	19 25	19 56	20 34	22 31	23 01	23 34	24 10
45	19 39	20 14	20 58	22 31	22 58	23 28	24 01
S 50	19 57	20 36	21 30	22 31	22 55	23 21	23 51
52	20 05	20 48	21 47	22 31	22 54	23 18	23 46
54	20 14	21 00	22 08	22 31	22 52	23 15	23 41
56	20 25	21 15	22 35	22 32	22 50	23 11	23 35
58	20 36	21 33	23 21	22 32	22 48	23 07	23 28
S 60	20 50	21 55	////	22 32	22 46	23 02	23 21

Day	SUN Eqn. of Time 00h	SUN Eqn. of Time 12h	Mer. Pass.	MOON Mer. Pass. Upper	MOON Mer. Pass. Lower	Age	Phase
d	m s	m s	h m	h m	h m	d	%
22	11 26	11 35	12 12	16 18	03 55	05	26
23	11 42	11 50	12 12	17 04	04 41	06	35
24	11 58	12 05	12 12	17 52	05 28	07	45

UT	ARIES GHA	VENUS −3·9 GHA	VENUS Dec	MARS +1·2 GHA	MARS Dec	JUPITER −1·9 GHA	JUPITER Dec	SATURN +0·5 GHA	SATURN Dec	STARS Name	SHA	Dec
d h	° ′	° ′	° ′	° ′	° ′	° ′	° ′	° ′	° ′		° ′	° ′
25 00	124 15.1	172 46.9	S19 15.1	247 15.1	S19 14.8	255 55.8	S16 48.2	209 48.7	S22 29.4	Acamar	315 15.9	S40 14.4
01	139 17.6	187 46.1	14.3	262 16.0	15.2	270 57.9	48.3	224 50.9	29.4	Achernar	335 24.6	S57 09.2
02	154 20.0	202 45.3	13.6	277 16.9	15.6	286 00.1	48.4	239 53.1	29.4	Acrux	173 05.3	S63 11.6
03	169 22.5	217 44.6	.. 12.8	292 17.8	.. 15.9	301 02.2	.. 48.5	254 55.3	.. 29.4	Adhara	255 09.7	S29 00.1
04	184 25.0	232 43.8	12.0	307 18.7	16.3	316 04.4	48.5	269 57.5	29.4	Aldebaran	290 45.6	N16 32.5
05	199 27.4	247 43.1	11.2	322 19.5	16.6	331 06.6	48.6	284 59.6	29.4			
T 06	214 29.9	262 42.3	S19 10.5	337 20.4	S19 17.0	346 08.7	S16 48.7	300 01.8	S22 29.4	Alioth	166 17.8	N55 51.5
H 07	229 32.4	277 41.6	09.7	352 21.3	17.3	1 10.9	48.8	315 04.0	29.4	Alkaid	152 56.4	N49 13.2
U 08	244 34.8	292 40.8	08.9	7 22.2	17.7	16 13.0	48.8	330 06.2	29.4	Al Na'ir	27 40.3	S46 52.6
R 09	259 37.3	307 40.0	.. 08.1	22 23.1	.. 18.0	31 15.2	.. 48.9	345 08.3	.. 29.4	Alnilam	275 42.9	S 1 11.7
S 10	274 39.8	322 39.3	07.3	37 23.9	18.4	46 17.3	49.0	0 10.5	29.4	Alphard	217 52.7	S 8 44.3
D 11	289 42.2	337 38.5	06.5	52 24.8	18.7	61 19.5	49.1	15 12.7	29.4			
A 12	304 44.7	352 37.8	S19 05.8	67 25.7	S19 19.1	76 21.7	S16 49.1	30 14.9	S22 29.4	Alphecca	126 08.5	N26 39.2
Y 13	319 47.1	7 37.0	05.0	82 26.6	19.5	91 23.8	49.2	45 17.0	29.3	Alpheratz	357 40.4	N29 11.4
14	334 49.6	22 36.3	04.2	97 27.4	19.8	106 26.0	49.3	60 19.2	29.3	Altair	62 05.5	N 8 55.0
15	349 52.1	37 35.5	.. 03.4	112 28.3	.. 20.2	121 28.1	.. 49.4	75 21.4	.. 29.3	Ankaa	353 12.9	S42 12.8
16	4 54.5	52 34.8	02.6	127 29.2	20.5	136 30.3	49.4	90 23.6	29.3	Antares	112 22.6	S26 28.1
17	19 57.0	67 34.0	01.8	142 30.1	20.9	151 32.5	49.5	105 25.7	29.3			
18	34 59.5	82 33.3	S19 01.0	157 30.9	S19 21.2	166 34.6	S16 49.6	120 27.9	S22 29.3	Arcturus	145 52.9	N19 05.3
19	50 01.9	97 32.5	19 00.2	172 31.8	21.6	181 36.8	49.6	135 30.1	29.3	Atria	107 22.0	S69 03.2
20	65 04.4	112 31.8	18 59.4	187 32.7	21.9	196 38.9	49.7	150 32.3	29.3	Avior	234 16.0	S59 34.2
21	80 06.9	127 31.0	.. 58.7	202 33.6	.. 22.3	211 41.1	.. 49.8	165 34.4	.. 29.3	Bellatrix	278 28.4	N 6 21.7
22	95 09.3	142 30.3	57.9	217 34.5	22.6	226 43.3	49.9	180 36.6	29.3	Betelgeuse	270 57.6	N 7 24.4
23	110 11.8	157 29.5	57.1	232 35.3	23.0	241 45.4	49.9	195 38.8	29.3			
26 00	125 14.3	172 28.8	S18 56.3	247 36.2	S19 23.3	256 47.6	S16 50.0	210 41.0	S22 29.3	Canopus	263 54.3	S52 42.6
01	140 16.7	187 28.0	55.5	262 37.1	23.7	271 49.7	50.1	225 43.1	29.2	Capella	280 29.5	N46 00.9
02	155 19.2	202 27.3	54.7	277 38.0	24.0	286 51.9	50.2	240 45.3	29.2	Deneb	49 29.8	N45 20.7
03	170 21.6	217 26.5	.. 53.9	292 38.8	.. 24.4	301 54.1	.. 50.2	255 47.5	.. 29.2	Denebola	182 30.3	N14 28.2
04	185 24.1	232 25.8	53.1	307 39.7	24.7	316 56.2	50.3	270 49.7	29.2	Diphda	348 52.9	S17 53.5
05	200 26.6	247 25.1	52.3	322 40.6	25.1	331 58.4	50.4	285 51.9	29.2			
F 06	215 29.0	262 24.3	S18 51.5	337 41.5	S19 25.4	347 00.6	S16 50.4	300 54.0	S22 29.2	Dubhe	193 47.5	N61 39.0
R 07	230 31.5	277 23.6	50.7	352 42.3	25.8	2 02.7	50.5	315 56.2	29.2	Elnath	278 08.4	N28 37.2
I 08	245 34.0	292 22.8	49.9	7 43.2	26.1	17 04.9	50.6	330 58.4	29.2	Eltanin	90 45.1	N51 29.2
D 09	260 36.4	307 22.1	.. 49.1	22 44.1	.. 26.5	32 07.0	.. 50.7	346 00.6	.. 29.2	Enif	33 44.4	N 9 57.5
A 10	275 38.9	322 21.3	48.3	37 45.0	26.8	47 09.2	50.7	1 02.7	29.2	Fomalhaut	15 20.9	S29 31.8
Y 11	290 41.4	337 20.6	47.4	52 45.8	27.2	62 11.4	50.8	16 04.9	29.2			
12	305 43.8	352 19.9	S18 46.6	67 46.7	S19 27.5	77 13.5	S16 50.9	31 07.1	S22 29.2	Gacrux	171 57.1	S57 12.6
13	320 46.3	7 19.1	45.8	82 47.6	27.9	92 15.7	51.0	46 09.3	29.2	Gienah	175 48.9	S17 38.4
14	335 48.8	22 18.4	45.0	97 48.5	28.2	107 17.9	51.0	61 11.5	29.2	Hadar	148 43.3	S60 27.2
15	350 51.2	37 17.6	.. 44.2	112 49.3	.. 28.6	122 20.0	.. 51.1	76 13.6	.. 29.2	Hamal	327 57.2	N23 32.8
16	5 53.7	52 16.9	43.4	127 50.2	28.9	137 22.2	51.2	91 15.8	29.1	Kaus Aust.	83 40.0	S34 22.3
17	20 56.1	67 16.2	42.6	142 51.1	29.2	152 24.4	51.3	106 18.0	29.1			
18	35 58.6	82 15.4	S18 41.8	157 52.0	S19 29.6	167 26.5	S16 51.3	121 20.2	S22 29.1	Kochab	137 20.4	N74 04.7
19	51 01.1	97 14.7	41.0	172 52.9	29.9	182 28.7	51.4	136 22.3	29.1	Markab	13 35.5	N15 18.1
20	66 03.5	112 14.0	40.1	187 53.7	30.3	197 30.9	51.5	151 24.5	29.1	Menkar	314 11.7	N 4 09.4
21	81 06.0	127 13.2	.. 39.3	202 54.6	.. 30.6	212 33.0	.. 51.5	166 26.7	.. 29.1	Menkent	148 03.8	S36 27.2
22	96 08.5	142 12.5	38.5	217 55.5	31.0	227 35.2	51.6	181 28.9	29.1	Miaplacidus	221 38.0	S69 47.5
23	111 10.9	157 11.8	37.7	232 56.4	31.3	242 37.4	51.7	196 31.1	29.1			
27 00	126 13.4	172 11.0	S18 36.9	247 57.2	S19 31.7	257 39.5	S16 51.8	211 33.2	S22 29.1	Mirfak	308 35.7	N49 55.5
01	141 15.9	187 10.3	36.1	262 58.1	32.0	272 41.7	51.8	226 35.4	29.1	Nunki	75 54.8	S26 16.3
02	156 18.3	202 09.6	35.2	277 59.0	32.4	287 43.9	51.9	241 37.6	29.1	Peacock	53 15.0	S56 40.5
03	171 20.8	217 08.8	.. 34.4	292 59.9	.. 32.7	302 46.0	.. 52.0	256 39.8	.. 29.1	Pollux	243 23.6	N27 58.7
04	186 23.3	232 08.1	33.6	308 00.7	33.0	317 48.2	52.0	271 41.9	29.1	Procyon	244 56.1	N 5 10.5
05	201 25.7	247 07.4	32.8	323 01.6	33.4	332 50.4	52.1	286 44.1	29.0			
S 06	216 28.2	262 06.6	S18 31.9	338 02.5	S19 33.7	347 52.5	S16 52.2	301 46.3	S22 29.0	Rasalhague	96 03.8	N12 32.9
A 07	231 30.6	277 05.9	31.1	353 03.4	34.1	2 54.7	52.3	316 48.5	29.0	Regulus	207 39.9	N11 52.6
T 08	246 33.1	292 05.2	30.3	8 04.2	34.4	17 56.9	52.3	331 50.7	29.0	Rigel	281 08.8	S 8 11.2
U 09	261 35.6	307 04.4	.. 29.5	23 05.1	.. 34.8	32 59.0	.. 52.4	346 52.8	.. 29.0	Rigil Kent.	139 47.5	S60 54.1
R 10	276 38.0	322 03.7	28.6	38 06.0	35.1	48 01.2	52.5	1 55.0	29.0	Sabik	102 09.2	S15 44.6
D 11	291 40.5	337 03.0	27.8	53 06.9	35.4	63 03.4	52.5	16 57.2	29.0			
A 12	306 43.0	352 02.3	S18 27.0	68 07.7	S19 35.8	78 05.6	S16 52.6	31 59.4	S22 29.0	Schedar	349 37.1	N56 38.3
Y 13	321 45.4	7 01.5	26.1	83 08.6	36.1	93 07.7	52.7	47 01.6	29.0	Shaula	96 18.0	S37 06.7
14	336 47.9	22 00.8	25.3	98 09.5	36.5	108 09.9	52.8	62 03.7	29.0	Sirius	258 30.6	S16 44.7
15	351 50.4	37 00.1	.. 24.5	113 10.3	.. 36.8	123 12.1	.. 52.8	77 05.9	.. 29.0	Spica	158 27.9	S11 15.2
16	6 52.8	51 59.4	23.6	128 11.2	37.2	138 14.2	52.9	92 08.1	29.0	Suhail	222 49.7	S43 30.4
17	21 55.3	66 58.6	22.8	143 12.1	37.5	153 16.4	53.0	107 10.3	29.0			
18	36 57.7	81 57.9	S18 22.0	158 13.0	S19 37.8	168 18.6	S16 53.0	122 12.5	S22 28.9	Vega	80 37.2	N38 48.0
19	52 00.2	96 57.2	21.1	173 13.8	38.2	183 20.8	53.1	137 14.6	28.9	Zuben'ubi	137 02.0	S16 06.8
20	67 02.7	111 56.5	20.3	188 14.7	38.5	198 22.9	53.2	152 16.8	28.9		SHA	Mer. Pass.
21	82 05.1	126 55.7	.. 19.5	203 15.6	.. 38.9	213 25.1	.. 53.2	167 19.0	.. 28.9		° ′	h m
22	97 07.6	141 55.0	18.6	218 16.5	39.2	228 27.3	53.3	182 21.2	28.9	Venus	47 14.5	12 31
23	112 10.1	156 54.3	17.8	233 17.3	39.5	243 29.4	53.4	197 23.4	28.9	Mars	122 22.0	7 29
	h m									Jupiter	131 33.3	6 52
Mer. Pass. 15 36.5	v −0.7 d 0.8			v 0.9 d 0.3		v 2.2 d 0.1		v 2.2 d 0.0		Saturn	85 26.7	9 56

UT	SUN GHA	SUN Dec	MOON GHA	v	MOON Dec	d	HP
d h	° ′	° ′	° ′	′	° ′	′	′
25 00	176 56.9	S19 01.5	88 59.2	10.9	N 8 31.5	10.6	58.0
01	191 56.8	00.8	103 29.1	10.8	8 42.1	10.5	58.0
02	206 56.6	19 00.2	117 58.9	10.8	8 52.6	10.5	58.1
03	221 56.5	18 59.6	132 28.7	10.7	9 03.1	10.4	58.1
04	236 56.3	59.0	146 58.4	10.7	9 13.5	10.4	58.1
05	251 56.2	58.4	161 28.1	10.5	9 23.9	10.4	58.2
06	266 56.1	S18 57.8	175 57.6	10.5	N 9 34.3	10.3	58.2
07	281 55.9	57.2	190 27.1	10.5	9 44.6	10.3	58.2
T 08	296 55.8	56.5	204 56.6	10.3	9 54.9	10.3	58.3
H 09	311 55.6 ..	55.9	219 25.9	10.3	10 05.2	10.2	58.3
U 10	326 55.5	55.3	233 55.2	10.2	10 15.4	10.1	58.3
R 11	341 55.3	54.7	248 24.4	10.1	10 25.5	10.1	58.4
S 12	356 55.2	S18 54.1	262 53.5	10.1	N10 35.6	10.1	58.4
D 13	11 55.1	53.4	277 22.6	10.0	10 45.7	10.0	58.4
A 14	26 54.9	52.8	291 51.6	9.9	10 55.7	10.0	58.5
Y 15	41 54.8 ..	52.2	306 20.5	9.8	11 05.7	9.9	58.5
16	56 54.6	51.6	320 49.3	9.7	11 15.6	9.9	58.5
17	71 54.5	51.0	335 18.0	9.7	11 25.5	9.8	58.6
18	86 54.4	S18 50.3	349 46.7	9.6	N11 35.3	9.7	58.6
19	101 54.2	49.7	4 15.3	9.5	11 45.0	9.7	58.6
20	116 54.1	49.1	18 43.8	9.4	11 54.7	9.7	58.7
21	131 53.9 ..	48.5	33 12.2	9.4	12 04.4	9.6	58.7
22	146 53.8	47.8	47 40.6	9.3	12 14.0	9.5	58.7
23	161 53.7	47.2	62 08.9	9.1	12 23.5	9.5	58.8
26 00	176 53.5	S18 46.6	76 37.0	9.1	N12 33.0	9.4	58.8
01	191 53.4	46.0	91 05.1	9.1	12 42.4	9.3	58.8
02	206 53.3	45.3	105 33.2	8.9	12 51.7	9.3	58.9
03	221 53.1 ..	44.7	120 01.1	8.9	13 01.0	9.2	58.9
04	236 53.0	44.1	134 29.0	8.7	13 10.2	9.1	58.9
05	251 52.9	43.4	148 56.7	8.7	13 19.3	9.1	59.0
06	266 52.7	S18 42.8	163 24.4	8.6	N13 28.4	9.0	59.0
07	281 52.6	42.2	177 52.0	8.5	13 37.4	9.0	59.0
F 08	296 52.5	41.6	192 19.5	8.5	13 46.4	8.8	59.1
R 09	311 52.3 ..	40.9	206 47.0	8.3	13 55.2	8.8	59.1
I 10	326 52.2	40.3	221 14.3	8.3	14 04.0	8.8	59.1
11	341 52.1	39.7	235 41.6	8.2	14 12.8	8.6	59.2
D 12	356 51.9	S18 39.0	250 08.8	8.1	N14 21.4	8.6	59.2
A 13	11 51.8	38.4	264 35.9	8.0	14 30.0	8.5	59.2
Y 14	26 51.7	37.7	279 02.9	7.9	14 38.5	8.4	59.3
15	41 51.5 ..	37.1	293 29.8	7.8	14 46.9	8.3	59.3
16	56 51.4	36.5	307 56.6	7.8	14 55.2	8.2	59.3
17	71 51.3	35.8	322 23.4	7.6	15 03.4	8.2	59.4
18	86 51.1	S18 35.2	336 50.0	7.6	N15 11.6	8.1	59.4
19	101 51.0	34.6	351 16.6	7.5	15 19.7	8.0	59.4
20	116 50.9	33.9	5 43.1	7.4	15 27.7	7.9	59.5
21	131 50.7 ..	33.3	20 09.5	7.3	15 35.6	7.8	59.5
22	146 50.6	32.6	34 35.8	7.2	15 43.4	7.7	59.5
23	161 50.5	32.0	49 02.0	7.2	15 51.1	7.6	59.5
27 00	176 50.4	S18 31.4	63 28.2	7.0	N15 58.7	7.6	59.6
01	191 50.2	30.7	77 54.2	7.0	16 06.3	7.4	59.6
02	206 50.1	30.1	92 20.2	6.9	16 13.7	7.3	59.6
03	221 50.0 ..	29.4	106 46.1	6.8	16 21.0	7.3	59.7
04	236 49.8	28.8	121 11.9	6.7	16 28.3	7.1	59.7
05	251 49.7	28.2	135 37.6	6.6	16 35.4	7.1	59.7
06	266 49.6	S18 27.5	150 03.2	6.5	N16 42.5	6.9	59.8
07	281 49.5	26.9	164 28.7	6.5	16 49.4	6.9	59.8
S 08	296 49.3	26.2	178 54.2	6.4	16 56.3	6.7	59.8
A 09	311 49.2 ..	25.6	193 19.6	6.3	17 03.0	6.6	59.9
T 10	326 49.1	24.9	207 44.9	6.2	17 09.6	6.6	59.9
U 11	341 49.0	24.3	222 10.1	6.1	17 16.2	6.4	59.9
R 12	356 48.8	S18 23.6	236 35.2	6.0	N17 22.6	6.3	59.9
D 13	11 48.7	23.0	251 00.2	6.0	17 28.9	6.2	60.0
A 14	26 48.6	22.3	265 25.2	5.9	17 35.1	6.1	60.0
Y 15	41 48.5 ..	21.7	279 50.1	5.8	17 41.2	6.0	60.0
16	56 48.3	21.0	294 14.9	5.7	17 47.2	5.8	60.1
17	71 48.2	20.4	308 39.6	5.7	17 53.0	5.8	60.1
18	86 48.1	S18 19.7	323 04.3	5.5	N17 58.8	5.6	60.1
19	101 48.0	19.1	337 28.8	5.5	18 04.4	5.5	60.1
20	116 47.9	18.4	351 53.3	5.4	18 09.9	5.4	60.2
21	131 47.7 ..	17.8	6 17.7	5.4	18 15.3	5.3	60.2
22	146 47.6	17.1	20 42.1	5.2	18 20.6	5.1	60.2
23	161 47.5	16.5	35 06.3	5.2	N18 25.7	5.0	60.2
SD	16.3	d 0.6	SD 15.9		16.1		16.3

Lat.	Twilight Naut.	Twilight Civil	Sunrise	Moonrise 25	26	27	28
°	h m	h m	h m	h m	h m	h m	h m
N 72	07 30	09 05	11 39	10 11	09 56	09 29	▭
N 70	07 19	08 42	10 21	10 27	10 23	10 20	10 19
68	07 11	08 24	09 43	10 40	10 44	10 53	11 12
66	07 03	08 09	09 17	10 50	11 00	11 17	11 45
64	06 57	07 57	08 57	10 59	11 14	11 36	12 09
62	06 51	07 47	08 41	11 07	11 25	11 51	12 28
60	06 46	07 38	08 27	11 13	11 35	12 04	12 44
N 58	06 42	07 30	08 16	11 19	11 44	12 15	12 58
56	06 38	07 23	08 06	11 25	11 51	12 25	13 09
54	06 34	07 17	07 57	11 29	11 58	12 34	13 19
52	06 30	07 11	07 49	11 33	12 04	12 42	13 28
50	06 27	07 06	07 42	11 37	12 10	12 49	13 37
45	06 19	06 55	07 26	11 46	12 22	13 04	13 54
N 40	06 12	06 45	07 14	11 53	12 32	13 16	14 08
35	06 05	06 36	07 03	11 59	12 40	13 27	14 20
30	05 59	06 28	06 53	12 04	12 48	13 36	14 31
20	05 47	06 14	06 37	12 14	13 01	13 52	14 49
N 10	05 35	06 00	06 23	12 22	13 12	14 06	15 05
0	05 22	05 47	06 09	12 30	13 23	14 20	15 20
S 10	05 07	05 33	05 55	12 38	13 34	14 33	15 35
20	04 49	05 17	05 40	12 46	13 46	14 48	15 51
30	04 26	04 57	05 23	12 56	13 59	15 04	16 09
35	04 11	04 45	05 13	13 02	14 07	15 14	16 20
40	03 53	04 31	05 02	13 08	14 16	15 25	16 33
45	03 30	04 14	04 48	13 16	14 27	15 38	16 47
S 50	02 59	03 52	04 31	13 25	14 39	15 54	17 05
52	02 43	03 41	04 23	13 29	14 45	16 01	17 14
54	02 24	03 29	04 14	13 34	14 52	16 10	17 23
56	01 58	03 15	04 04	13 39	14 59	16 19	17 34
58	01 19	02 58	03 53	13 45	15 08	16 30	17 46
S 60	////	02 37	03 40	13 51	15 17	16 42	18 00

Lat.	Sunset	Twilight Civil	Twilight Naut.	Moonset 25	26	27	28
°	h m	h m	h m	h m	h m	h m	h m
N 72	12 47	15 21	16 57	02 01	04 04	06 27	▭
N 70	14 05	15 44	17 07	01 47	03 38	05 37	07 42
68	14 43	16 02	17 15	01 36	03 19	05 05	06 49
66	15 09	16 17	17 23	01 27	03 04	04 42	06 17
64	15 29	16 29	17 29	01 19	02 51	04 24	05 53
62	15 45	16 39	17 35	01 12	02 40	04 09	05 34
60	15 58	16 48	17 39	01 07	02 31	03 57	05 19
N 58	16 10	16 55	17 44	01 02	02 24	03 46	05 06
56	16 20	17 02	17 48	00 57	02 17	03 37	04 54
54	16 29	17 09	17 52	00 53	02 11	03 28	04 44
52	16 37	17 14	17 56	00 50	02 05	03 21	04 36
50	16 44	17 20	17 59	00 47	02 00	03 14	04 28
45	16 59	17 31	18 07	00 40	01 49	03 00	04 11
N 40	17 12	17 41	18 14	00 34	01 40	02 49	03 57
35	17 22	17 49	18 20	00 29	01 33	02 39	03 45
30	17 32	17 57	18 26	00 24	01 26	02 30	03 35
20	17 48	18 11	18 38	00 17	01 14	02 15	03 18
N 10	18 03	18 25	18 50	00 10	01 04	02 02	03 02
0	18 16	18 38	19 03	00 04	00 55	01 50	02 48
S 10	18 30	18 52	19 18	24 45	00 45	01 37	02 34
20	18 44	19 08	19 36	24 35	00 35	01 24	02 18
30	19 01	19 28	19 59	24 24	00 24	01 10	02 01
35	19 11	19 39	20 13	24 17	00 17	01 01	01 51
40	19 23	19 53	20 31	24 10	00 10	00 51	01 39
45	19 36	20 10	20 54	24 01	00 01	00 40	01 26
S 50	19 53	20 32	21 24	23 51	24 26	00 26	01 09
52	20 01	20 43	21 40	23 46	24 19	00 19	01 01
54	20 10	20 55	21 59	23 41	24 12	00 12	00 52
56	20 19	21 09	22 24	23 35	24 04	00 04	00 43
58	20 31	21 25	23 00	23 28	23 56	24 32	00 32
S 60	20 44	21 46	////	23 21	23 45	24 19	00 19

	SUN			MOON			
Day	Eqn. of Time 00h	12h	Mer. Pass.	Mer. Pass. Upper	Lower	Age	Phase
d	m s	m s	h m	h m	h m	d	%
25	12 12	12 19	12 12	18 42	06 17	08	56
26	12 26	12 32	12 13	19 36	07 09	09	67
27	12 38	12 44	12 13	20 34	08 05	10	78

UT	ARIES	VENUS −3.9		MARS +1.2		JUPITER −2.0		SATURN +0.6		STARS		
d h	GHA	GHA	Dec	GHA	Dec	GHA	Dec	GHA	Dec	Name	SHA	Dec
28 00	127 12.5	171 53.6	S18 16.9	248 18.2	S19 39.9	258 31.6	S16 53.5	212 25.5	S22 28.9	Acamar	315 15.9	S40 14.4
01	142 15.0	186 52.8	16.1	263 19.1	40.2	273 33.8	53.5	227 27.7	28.9	Achernar	335 24.6	S57 09.2
02	157 17.5	201 52.1	15.3	278 20.0	40.6	288 36.0	53.6	242 29.9	28.9	Acrux	173 05.3	S63 11.6
03	172 19.9	216 51.4	.. 14.4	293 20.8	.. 40.9	303 38.1	.. 53.7	257 32.1	.. 28.9	Adhara	255 09.7	S29 00.1
04	187 22.4	231 50.7	13.6	308 21.7	41.2	318 40.3	53.7	272 34.3	28.9	Aldebaran	290 45.6	N16 32.5
05	202 24.9	246 50.0	12.7	323 22.6	41.6	333 42.5	53.8	287 36.4	28.9			
06	217 27.3	261 49.3	S18 11.9	338 23.5	S19 41.9	348 44.7	S16 53.9	302 38.6	S22 28.9	Alioth	166 17.8	N55 51.5
07	232 29.8	276 48.5	11.0	353 24.3	42.2	3 46.8	53.9	317 40.8	28.8	Alkaid	152 56.4	N49 13.2
S 08	247 32.2	291 47.8	10.2	8 25.2	42.6	18 49.0	54.0	332 43.0	28.8	Al Na'ir	27 40.3	S46 52.5
U 09	262 34.7	306 47.1	.. 09.3	23 26.1	.. 42.9	33 51.2	.. 54.1	347 45.2	.. 28.8	Alnilam	275 42.9	S 1 11.7
N 10	277 37.2	321 46.4	08.5	38 26.9	43.3	48 53.4	54.1	2 47.4	28.8	Alphard	217 52.7	S 8 44.3
11	292 39.6	336 45.7	07.6	53 27.8	43.6	63 55.5	54.2	17 49.5	28.8			
D 12	307 42.1	351 45.0	S18 06.8	68 28.7	S19 43.9	78 57.7	S16 54.3	32 51.7	S22 28.8	Alphecca	126 08.5	N26 39.2
A 13	322 44.6	6 44.2	05.9	83 29.6	44.3	93 59.9	54.4	47 53.9	28.8	Alpheratz	357 40.4	N29 11.4
Y 14	337 47.0	21 43.5	05.1	98 30.4	44.6	109 02.1	54.4	62 56.1	28.8	Altair	62 05.5	N 8 55.0
15	352 49.5	36 42.8	.. 04.2	113 31.3	.. 44.9	124 04.3	.. 54.5	77 58.3	.. 28.8	Ankaa	353 12.9	S42 12.8
16	7 52.0	51 42.1	03.4	128 32.2	45.3	139 06.4	54.6	93 00.4	28.8	Antares	112 22.6	S26 28.1
17	22 54.4	66 41.4	02.5	143 33.1	45.6	154 08.6	54.6	108 02.6	28.8			
18	37 56.9	81 40.7	S18 01.7	158 33.9	S19 45.9	169 10.8	S16 54.7	123 04.8	S22 28.8	Arcturus	145 52.9	N19 05.3
19	52 59.4	96 40.0	18 00.8	173 34.8	46.3	184 13.0	54.8	138 07.0	28.7	Atria	107 21.9	S69 03.1
20	68 01.8	111 39.3	17 59.9	188 35.7	46.6	199 15.1	54.8	153 09.2	28.7	Avior	234 16.0	S59 34.2
21	83 04.3	126 38.6	.. 59.1	203 36.5	.. 46.9	214 17.3	.. 54.9	168 11.4	.. 28.7	Bellatrix	278 28.4	N 6 21.7
22	98 06.7	141 37.8	58.2	218 37.4	47.3	229 19.5	55.0	183 13.5	28.7	Betelgeuse	270 57.6	N 7 24.4
23	113 09.2	156 37.1	57.4	233 38.3	47.6	244 21.7	55.0	198 15.7	28.7			
29 00	128 11.7	171 36.4	S17 56.5	248 39.2	S19 47.9	259 23.9	S16 55.1	213 17.9	S22 28.7	Canopus	263 54.3	S52 42.7
01	143 14.1	186 35.7	55.6	263 40.0	48.3	274 26.0	55.2	228 20.1	28.7	Capella	280 29.5	N46 00.9
02	158 16.6	201 35.0	54.8	278 40.9	48.6	289 28.2	55.2	243 22.3	28.7	Deneb	49 29.8	N45 20.7
03	173 19.1	216 34.3	.. 53.9	293 41.8	.. 48.9	304 30.4	.. 55.3	258 24.4	.. 28.7	Denebola	182 30.3	N14 28.2
04	188 21.5	231 33.6	53.0	308 42.7	49.3	319 32.6	55.4	273 26.6	28.7	Diphda	348 52.9	S17 53.5
05	203 24.0	246 32.9	52.2	323 43.5	49.6	334 34.8	55.4	288 28.8	28.7			
06	218 26.5	261 32.2	S17 51.3	338 44.4	S19 49.9	349 36.9	S16 55.5	303 31.0	S22 28.7	Dubhe	193 47.4	N61 39.0
07	233 28.9	276 31.5	50.4	353 45.3	50.3	4 39.1	55.6	318 33.2	28.7	Elnath	278 08.4	N28 37.2
08	248 31.4	291 30.8	49.6	8 46.1	50.6	19 41.3	55.7	333 35.4	28.6	Eltanin	90 45.1	N51 29.1
M 09	263 33.9	306 30.1	.. 48.7	23 47.0	.. 50.9	34 43.5	.. 55.7	348 37.5	.. 28.6	Enif	33 44.4	N 9 57.5
O 10	278 36.3	321 29.4	47.8	38 47.9	51.3	49 45.7	55.8	3 39.7	28.6	Fomalhaut	15 20.9	S29 31.8
N 11	293 38.8	336 28.7	47.0	53 48.8	51.6	64 47.8	55.9	18 41.9	28.6			
D 12	308 41.2	351 28.0	S17 46.1	68 49.6	S19 51.9	79 50.0	S16 55.9	33 44.1	S22 28.6	Gacrux	171 57.0	S57 12.6
A 13	323 43.7	6 27.3	45.2	83 50.5	52.3	94 52.2	56.0	48 46.3	28.6	Gienah	175 48.9	S17 38.4
Y 14	338 46.2	21 26.6	44.3	98 51.4	52.6	109 54.4	56.1	63 48.5	28.6	Hadar	148 43.3	S60 27.2
15	353 48.6	36 25.9	.. 43.5	113 52.2	.. 52.9	124 56.6	.. 56.1	78 50.6	.. 28.6	Hamal	327 57.2	N23 32.8
16	8 51.1	51 25.2	42.6	128 53.1	53.3	139 58.8	56.2	93 52.8	28.6	Kaus Aust.	83 40.0	S34 22.3
17	23 53.6	66 24.5	41.7	143 54.0	53.6	155 00.9	56.3	108 55.0	28.6			
18	38 56.0	81 23.8	S17 40.8	158 54.9	S19 53.9	170 03.1	S16 56.3	123 57.2	S22 28.6	Kochab	137 20.4	N74 04.7
19	53 58.5	96 23.1	40.0	173 55.7	54.2	185 05.3	56.4	138 59.4	28.6	Markab	13 35.5	N15 18.1
20	69 01.0	111 22.4	39.1	188 56.6	54.6	200 07.5	56.5	154 01.6	28.5	Menkar	314 11.7	N 4 09.4
21	84 03.4	126 21.7	.. 38.2	203 57.5	.. 54.9	215 09.7	.. 56.5	169 03.7	.. 28.5	Menkent	148 03.8	S36 27.2
22	99 05.9	141 21.0	37.3	218 58.3	55.2	230 11.9	56.6	184 05.9	28.5	Miaplacidus	221 38.0	S69 47.5
23	114 08.4	156 20.3	36.4	233 59.2	55.6	245 14.0	56.7	199 08.1	28.5			
30 00	129 10.8	171 19.6	S17 35.5	249 00.1	S19 55.9	260 16.2	S16 56.7	214 10.3	S22 28.5	Mirfak	308 35.7	N49 55.5
01	144 13.3	186 18.9	34.7	264 00.9	56.2	275 18.4	56.8	229 12.5	28.5	Nunki	75 54.8	S26 16.3
02	159 15.7	201 18.2	33.8	279 01.8	56.5	290 20.6	56.9	244 14.7	28.5	Peacock	53 15.0	S56 40.5
03	174 18.2	216 17.5	.. 32.9	294 02.7	.. 56.9	305 22.8	.. 56.9	259 16.9	.. 28.5	Pollux	243 23.6	N27 58.7
04	189 20.7	231 16.8	32.0	309 03.6	57.2	320 25.0	57.0	274 19.0	28.5	Procyon	244 56.1	N 5 10.5
05	204 23.1	246 16.2	31.1	324 04.4	57.5	335 27.2	57.1	289 21.2	28.5			
06	219 25.6	261 15.5	S17 30.2	339 05.3	S19 57.8	350 29.3	S16 57.1	304 23.4	S22 28.5	Rasalhague	96 03.8	N12 32.9
07	234 28.1	276 14.8	29.3	354 06.2	58.2	5 31.5	57.2	319 25.6	28.5	Regulus	207 39.9	N11 52.6
T 08	249 30.5	291 14.1	28.4	9 07.0	58.5	20 33.7	57.2	334 27.8	28.5	Rigel	281 08.8	S 8 11.2
U 09	264 33.0	306 13.4	.. 27.6	24 07.9	.. 58.8	35 35.9	.. 57.3	349 30.0	.. 28.4	Rigil Kent.	139 47.4	S60 54.1
E 10	279 35.5	321 12.7	26.7	39 08.8	59.2	50 38.1	57.4	4 32.2	28.4	Sabik	102 09.2	S15 44.6
S 11	294 37.9	336 12.0	25.8	54 09.7	59.5	65 40.3	57.4	19 34.3	28.4			
D 12	309 40.4	351 11.3	S17 24.9	69 10.5	S19 59.8	80 42.5	S16 57.5	34 36.5	S22 28.4	Schedar	349 37.1	N56 38.3
A 13	324 42.8	6 10.6	24.0	84 11.4	20 00.1	95 44.7	57.6	49 38.7	28.4	Shaula	96 18.0	S37 06.7
Y 14	339 45.3	21 10.0	23.1	99 12.3	00.5	110 46.8	57.6	64 40.9	28.4	Sirius	258 30.6	S16 44.8
15	354 47.8	36 09.3	.. 22.2	114 13.1	.. 00.8	125 49.0	.. 57.7	79 43.1	.. 28.4	Spica	158 27.8	S11 15.2
16	9 50.2	51 08.6	21.3	129 14.0	01.1	140 51.2	57.8	94 45.3	28.4	Suhail	222 49.7	S43 30.4
17	24 52.7	66 07.9	20.4	144 14.9	01.4	155 53.4	57.8	109 47.4	28.4			
18	39 55.2	81 07.2	S17 19.5	159 15.7	S20 01.7	170 55.6	S16 57.9	124 49.6	S22 28.4	Vega	80 37.2	N38 48.0
19	54 57.6	96 06.5	18.6	174 16.6	02.1	185 57.8	58.0	139 51.8	28.4	Zuben'ubi	137 02.0	S16 06.8
20	70 00.1	111 05.8	17.7	189 17.5	02.4	201 00.0	58.0	154 54.0	28.4		SHA	Mer.Pass.
21	85 02.6	126 05.2	.. 16.8	204 18.3	.. 02.7	216 02.2	.. 58.1	169 56.2	.. 28.3		° '	h m
22	100 05.0	141 04.5	15.9	219 19.2	03.0	231 04.4	58.2	184 58.4	28.3	Venus	43 24.8	12 34
23	115 07.5	156 03.8	15.0	234 20.1	03.4	246 06.6	58.2	200 00.6	28.3	Mars	120 27.5	7 25
	h m									Jupiter	131 12.2	6 41
Mer. Pass. 15 24.7		v −0.7	d 0.9	v 0.9	d 0.3	v 2.2	d 0.1	v 2.2	d 0.0	Saturn	85 06.2	9 45

UT	SUN GHA	SUN Dec	MOON GHA	v	MOON Dec	d	HP
d h	° ′	° ′	° ′	′	° ′	′	′
28 00	176 47.4	S18 15.8	49 30.5	5.1	N18 30.7	4.9	60.3
01	191 47.3	15.2	63 54.6	5.1	18 35.6	4.8	60.3
02	206 47.1	14.5	78 18.7	5.0	18 40.4	4.7	60.3
03	221 47.0	.. 13.8	92 42.7	4.9	18 45.1	4.5	60.3
04	236 46.9	13.2	107 06.6	4.8	18 49.6	4.4	60.4
05	251 46.8	12.5	121 30.4	4.8	18 54.0	4.3	60.4
06	266 46.7	S18 11.9	135 54.2	4.7	N18 58.3	4.1	60.4
07	281 46.6	11.2	150 17.9	4.6	19 02.4	4.0	60.4
08	296 46.4	10.6	164 41.5	4.6	19 06.4	3.9	60.5
S 09	311 46.3	.. 09.9	179 05.1	4.5	19 10.3	3.7	60.5
U 10	326 46.2	09.2	193 28.6	4.5	19 14.0	3.6	60.5
N 11	341 46.1	08.6	207 52.1	4.3	19 17.6	3.5	60.5
D 12	356 46.0	S18 07.9	222 15.4	4.4	N19 21.1	3.3	60.6
A 13	11 45.9	07.3	236 38.8	4.3	19 24.4	3.2	60.6
Y 14	26 45.7	06.6	251 02.1	4.2	19 27.6	3.1	60.6
15	41 45.6	.. 05.9	265 25.3	4.2	19 30.7	2.9	60.6
16	56 45.5	05.3	279 48.5	4.1	19 33.6	2.8	60.6
17	71 45.4	04.6	294 11.6	4.0	19 36.4	2.6	60.7
18	86 45.3	S18 03.9	308 34.6	4.1	N19 39.0	2.5	60.7
19	101 45.2	03.3	322 57.7	3.9	19 41.5	2.3	60.7
20	116 45.1	02.6	337 20.6	4.0	19 43.8	2.3	60.7
21	131 44.9	.. 01.9	351 43.6	3.8	19 46.1	2.0	60.7
22	146 44.8	01.3	6 06.4	3.9	19 48.1	1.9	60.7
23	161 44.7	18 00.6	20 29.3	3.8	19 50.0	1.8	60.8
29 00	176 44.6	S17 59.9	34 52.1	3.7	N19 51.8	1.7	60.8
01	191 44.5	59.3	49 14.8	3.8	19 53.5	1.4	60.8
02	206 44.4	58.6	63 37.6	3.7	19 54.9	1.4	60.8
03	221 44.3	.. 57.9	78 00.3	3.6	19 56.3	1.2	60.8
04	236 44.2	57.3	92 22.9	3.6	19 57.5	1.0	60.8
05	251 44.1	56.6	106 45.5	3.6	19 58.5	0.9	60.9
06	266 44.0	S17 55.9	121 08.1	3.6	N19 59.4	0.8	60.9
07	281 43.8	55.2	135 30.7	3.5	20 00.2	0.6	60.9
08	296 43.7	54.6	149 53.2	3.5	20 00.8	0.4	60.9
M 09	311 43.6	.. 53.9	164 15.7	3.5	20 01.2	0.3	60.9
O 10	326 43.5	53.2	178 38.2	3.5	20 01.5	0.2	60.9
N 11	341 43.4	52.5	193 00.7	3.4	20 01.7	0.0	60.9
D 12	356 43.3	S17 51.9	207 23.1	3.5	N20 01.7	0.1	61.0
A 13	11 43.2	51.2	221 45.6	3.4	20 01.6	0.3	61.0
Y 14	26 43.1	50.5	236 08.0	3.4	20 01.3	0.5	61.0
15	41 43.0	.. 49.8	250 30.4	3.4	20 00.8	0.6	61.0
16	56 42.9	49.2	264 52.8	3.4	20 00.2	0.7	61.0
17	71 42.8	48.5	279 15.2	3.4	19 59.5	0.9	61.0
18	86 42.7	S17 47.8	293 37.6	3.3	N19 58.6	1.1	61.0
19	101 42.6	47.1	307 59.9	3.4	19 57.5	1.2	61.0
20	116 42.5	46.5	322 22.3	3.4	19 56.3	1.3	61.0
21	131 42.4	.. 45.8	336 44.7	3.3	19 55.0	1.5	61.0
22	146 42.3	45.1	351 07.0	3.4	19 53.5	1.6	61.0
23	161 42.2	44.4	5 29.4	3.4	19 51.9	1.8	61.0
30 00	176 42.1	S17 43.7	19 51.8	3.4	N19 50.1	2.0	61.1
01	191 41.9	43.0	34 14.2	3.4	19 48.1	2.1	61.1
02	206 41.8	42.4	48 36.6	3.4	19 46.0	2.2	61.1
03	221 41.7	.. 41.7	62 59.0	3.4	19 43.8	2.4	61.1
04	236 41.6	41.0	77 21.4	3.4	19 41.4	2.6	61.1
05	251 41.5	40.3	91 43.8	3.5	19 38.8	2.7	61.1
06	266 41.4	S17 39.6	106 06.3	3.4	N19 36.1	2.8	61.1
07	281 41.3	38.9	120 28.7	3.5	19 33.3	3.0	61.1
T 08	296 41.2	38.3	134 51.2	3.5	19 30.3	3.1	61.1
U 09	311 41.1	.. 37.6	149 13.7	3.6	19 27.2	3.3	61.1
E 10	326 41.0	36.9	163 36.3	3.5	19 23.9	3.4	61.1
S 11	341 40.9	36.2	177 58.8	3.6	19 20.5	3.6	61.1
D 12	356 40.8	S17 35.5	192 21.4	3.6	N19 16.9	3.7	61.1
A 13	11 40.8	34.8	206 44.0	3.7	19 13.2	3.8	61.1
Y 14	26 40.7	34.1	221 06.7	3.7	19 09.4	4.0	61.1
15	41 40.6	.. 33.4	235 29.4	3.7	19 05.4	4.2	61.1
16	56 40.5	32.8	249 52.1	3.7	19 01.2	4.2	61.1
17	71 40.4	32.1	264 14.8	3.8	18 57.0	4.5	61.1
18	86 40.3	S17 31.4	278 37.6	3.8	N18 52.5	4.5	61.1
19	101 40.2	30.7	293 00.4	3.9	18 48.0	4.7	61.1
20	116 40.1	30.0	307 23.3	3.9	18 43.3	4.8	61.1
21	131 40.0	.. 29.3	321 46.2	4.0	18 38.5	5.0	61.0
22	146 39.9	28.6	336 09.2	4.0	18 33.5	5.1	61.0
23	161 39.8	27.9	350 32.2	4.0	N18 28.4	5.3	61.0
	SD 16.3	d 0.7	SD 16.5		16.6		16.6

Lat.	Twilight Naut.	Twilight Civil	Sunrise	Moonrise 28	29	30	31
°	h m	h m	h m	h m	h m	h m	h m
N 72	07 20	08 52	10 56	▭	▭	▭	13 40
N 70	07 11	08 31	10 03	10 19	10 36	12 24	14 34
68	07 03	08 15	09 30	11 12	11 57	13 20	15 06
66	06 57	08 02	09 07	11 45	12 35	13 53	15 30
64	06 51	07 50	08 49	12 09	13 02	14 17	15 49
62	06 46	07 41	08 33	12 28	13 23	14 36	16 04
60	06 41	07 33	08 21	12 44	13 40	14 52	16 17
N 58	06 37	07 25	08 10	12 58	13 54	15 05	16 28
56	06 33	07 19	08 01	13 09	14 06	15 17	16 37
54	06 30	07 13	07 52	13 19	14 17	15 27	16 45
52	06 27	07 08	07 45	13 28	14 27	15 36	16 53
50	06 24	07 03	07 38	13 37	14 35	15 44	17 00
45	06 16	06 52	07 23	13 54	14 53	16 01	17 14
N 40	06 10	06 42	07 11	14 08	15 08	16 15	17 26
35	06 04	06 34	07 01	14 20	15 21	16 27	17 36
30	05 58	06 27	06 52	14 31	15 32	16 37	17 45
20	05 47	06 13	06 36	14 49	15 50	16 55	18 00
N 10	05 35	06 01	06 23	15 05	16 07	17 10	18 13
0	05 23	05 48	06 10	15 20	16 22	17 25	18 26
S 10	05 08	05 34	05 56	15 35	16 37	17 39	18 38
20	04 51	05 19	05 42	15 51	16 54	17 55	18 51
30	04 29	05 00	05 26	16 09	17 13	18 12	19 06
35	04 15	04 48	05 16	16 20	17 24	18 23	19 15
40	03 58	04 35	05 05	16 33	17 37	18 34	19 25
45	03 36	04 18	04 52	16 47	17 52	18 48	19 37
S 50	03 07	03 58	04 36	17 05	18 10	19 05	19 51
52	02 52	03 47	04 29	17 14	18 18	19 13	19 57
54	02 33	03 36	04 20	17 23	18 28	19 22	20 04
56	02 10	03 23	04 11	17 34	18 39	19 32	20 13
58	01 38	03 07	04 00	17 46	18 52	19 43	20 22
S 60	00 17	02 47	03 48	18 00	19 06	19 56	20 32

Lat.	Sunset	Twilight Civil	Twilight Naut.	Moonset 28	29	30	31
°	h m	h m	h m	h m	h m	h m	h m
N 72	13 32	15 36	17 08	▭	▭	▭	10 53
N 70	14 25	15 56	17 17	07 42	09 35	09 59	09 58
68	14 57	16 13	17 24	06 49	08 14	09 03	09 25
66	15 20	16 26	17 31	06 17	07 36	08 29	08 59
64	15 39	16 37	17 36	05 53	07 09	08 05	08 41
62	15 54	16 46	17 41	05 34	06 48	07 45	08 25
60	16 06	16 54	17 46	05 19	06 31	07 29	08 12
N 58	16 17	17 02	17 50	05 06	06 17	07 16	08 00
56	16 26	17 08	17 54	04 54	06 05	07 04	07 50
54	16 35	17 14	17 57	04 44	05 54	06 53	07 42
52	16 42	17 19	18 00	04 36	05 44	06 44	07 34
50	16 49	17 24	18 03	04 28	05 36	06 36	07 27
45	17 03	17 35	18 10	04 11	05 18	06 19	07 11
N 40	17 15	17 44	18 17	03 57	05 03	06 04	06 59
35	17 26	17 52	18 23	03 45	04 51	05 52	06 48
30	17 35	18 00	18 28	03 35	04 40	05 41	06 38
20	17 50	18 13	18 40	03 18	04 21	05 23	06 22
N 10	18 04	18 26	18 51	03 02	04 05	05 07	06 08
0	18 17	18 38	19 04	02 48	03 49	04 52	05 54
S 10	18 30	18 52	19 18	02 34	03 34	04 37	05 40
20	18 44	19 07	19 35	02 18	03 18	04 21	05 26
30	19 00	19 26	19 57	02 01	02 59	04 02	05 09
35	19 09	19 37	20 11	01 51	02 48	03 51	04 59
40	19 20	19 51	20 28	01 39	02 35	03 39	04 48
45	19 33	20 07	20 49	01 26	02 20	03 24	04 35
S 50	19 49	20 27	21 18	01 09	02 02	03 06	04 19
52	19 56	20 37	21 33	01 01	01 53	02 57	04 11
54	20 05	20 49	21 50	00 52	01 44	02 48	04 03
56	20 14	21 02	22 13	00 43	01 33	02 37	03 53
58	20 24	21 17	22 43	00 32	01 21	02 25	03 42
S 60	20 37	21 36	00 10	00 19	01 06	02 10	03 30

Day	SUN Eqn. of Time 00h	SUN Eqn. of Time 12h	SUN Mer. Pass.	MOON Mer. Pass. Upper	MOON Mer. Pass. Lower	Age	Phase
d	m s	m s	h m	h m	h m	d	%
28	12 50	12 56	12 13	21 35	09 04	11	87
29	13 01	13 07	12 13	22 37	10 06	12	94
30	13 12	13 16	12 13	23 39	11 08	13	98

○

UT	ARIES GHA	VENUS −3.9 GHA	VENUS Dec	MARS +1.2 GHA	MARS Dec	JUPITER −2.0 GHA	JUPITER Dec	SATURN +0.6 GHA	SATURN Dec	STARS Name	SHA	Dec
31 00	130 10.0	171 03.1	S17 14.1	249 21.0	S20 03.7	261 08.8	S16 58.3	215 02.8	S22 28.3	Acamar	315 15.9	S40 14.4
01	145 12.4	186 02.4	13.2	264 21.8	04.0	276 10.9	58.4	230 04.9	28.3	Achernar	335 24.7	S57 09.2
02	160 14.9	201 01.8	12.3	279 22.7	04.3	291 13.1	58.4	245 07.1	28.3	Acrux	173 05.3	S63 11.7
03	175 17.3	216 01.1 ..	11.4	294 23.6 ..	04.6	306 15.3 ..	58.5	260 09.3 ..	28.3	Adhara	255 09.7	S29 00.1
04	190 19.8	231 00.4	10.5	309 24.4	05.0	321 17.5	58.5	275 11.5	28.3	Aldebaran	290 45.6	N16 32.5
05	205 22.3	245 59.7	09.6	324 25.3	05.3	336 19.7	58.6	290 13.7	28.3			
W 06	220 24.7	260 59.0	S17 08.7	339 26.2	S20 05.6	351 21.9	S16 58.7	305 15.9	S22 28.3	Alioth	166 17.7	N55 51.5
E 07	235 27.2	275 58.4	07.7	354 27.0	05.9	6 24.1	58.7	320 18.1	28.3	Alkaid	152 56.4	N49 13.2
D 08	250 29.7	290 57.7	06.8	9 27.9	06.3	21 26.3	58.8	335 20.2	28.3	Al Na'ir	27 40.3	S46 52.5
N 09	265 32.1	305 57.0 ..	05.9	24 28.8 ..	06.6	36 28.5 ..	58.9	350 22.4 ..	28.2	Alnilam	275 42.9	S 1 11.7
E 10	280 34.6	320 56.3	05.0	39 29.6	06.9	51 30.7	58.9	5 24.6	28.2	Alphard	217 52.7	S 8 44.4
S 11	295 37.1	335 55.7	04.1	54 30.5	07.2	66 32.9	59.0	20 26.8	28.2			
D 12	310 39.5	350 55.0	S17 03.2	69 31.4	S20 07.5	81 35.1	S16 59.1	35 29.0	S22 28.2	Alphecca	126 08.4	N26 39.2
A 13	325 42.0	5 54.3	02.3	84 32.3	07.9	96 37.3	59.1	50 31.2	28.2	Alpheratz	357 40.4	N29 11.4
Y 14	340 44.5	20 53.6	01.4	99 33.1	08.2	111 39.5	59.2	65 33.4	28.2	Altair	62 05.5	N 8 55.0
15	355 46.9	35 53.0	17 00.4	114 34.0 ..	08.5	126 41.7 ..	59.2	80 35.6 ..	28.2	Ankaa	353 12.9	S42 12.8
16	10 49.4	50 52.3	16 59.5	129 34.9	08.8	141 43.8	59.3	95 37.7	28.2	Antares	112 22.6	S26 28.1
17	25 51.8	65 51.6	58.6	144 35.7	09.1	156 46.0	59.4	110 39.9	28.2			
18	40 54.3	80 50.9	S16 57.7	159 36.6	S20 09.4	171 48.2	S16 59.4	125 42.1	S22 28.2	Arcturus	145 52.8	N19 05.3
19	55 56.8	95 50.3	56.8	174 37.5	09.8	186 50.4	59.5	140 44.3	28.1	Atria	107 21.8	S69 03.1
20	70 59.2	110 49.6	55.8	189 38.3	10.1	201 52.6	59.6	155 46.5	28.2	Avior	234 16.0	S59 34.2
21	86 01.7	125 48.9 ..	54.9	204 39.2 ..	10.4	216 54.8 ..	59.6	170 48.7 ..	28.1	Bellatrix	278 28.4	N 6 21.7
22	101 04.2	140 48.3	54.0	219 40.1	10.7	231 57.0	59.7	185 50.9	28.1	Betelgeuse	270 57.6	N 7 24.4
23	116 06.6	155 47.6	53.1	234 40.9	11.0	246 59.2	59.8	200 53.1	28.1			
1 00	131 09.1	170 46.9	S16 52.2	249 41.8	S20 11.3	262 01.4	S16 59.8	215 55.3	S22 28.1	Canopus	263 54.3	S52 42.7
01	146 11.6	185 46.3	51.2	264 42.7	11.7	277 03.6	59.9	230 57.4	28.1	Capella	280 29.5	N46 00.9
02	161 14.0	200 45.6	50.3	279 43.5	12.0	292 05.8	16 59.9	245 59.6	28.1	Deneb	49 29.8	N45 20.7
03	176 16.5	215 44.9 ..	49.4	294 44.4 ..	12.3	307 08.0	17 00.0	261 01.8 ..	28.1	Denebola	182 30.2	N14 28.2
04	191 19.0	230 44.3	48.5	309 45.3	12.6	322 10.2	00.1	276 04.0	28.1	Diphda	348 52.9	S17 53.5
05	206 21.4	245 43.6	47.5	324 46.1	12.9	337 12.4	00.1	291 06.2	28.1			
T 06	221 23.9	260 42.9	S16 46.6	339 47.0	S20 13.2	352 14.6	S17 00.2	306 08.4	S22 28.1	Dubhe	193 47.4	N61 39.0
H 07	236 26.3	275 42.3	45.7	354 47.9	13.6	7 16.8	00.3	321 10.6	28.1	Elnath	278 08.4	N28 37.2
U 08	251 28.8	290 41.6	44.7	9 48.7	13.9	22 19.0	00.3	336 12.8	28.0	Eltanin	90 45.1	N51 29.1
R 09	266 31.3	305 40.9 ..	43.8	24 49.6 ..	14.2	37 21.2 ..	00.4	351 15.0 ..	28.0	Enif	33 44.4	N 9 57.4
S 10	281 33.7	320 40.3	42.9	39 50.5	14.5	52 23.4	00.4	6 17.1	28.0	Fomalhaut	15 20.9	S29 31.8
D 11	296 36.2	335 39.6	41.9	54 51.3	14.8	67 25.6	00.5	21 19.3	28.0			
A 12	311 38.7	350 39.0	S16 41.0	69 52.2	S20 15.1	82 27.8	S17 00.6	36 21.5	S22 28.0	Gacrux	171 57.0	S57 12.6
Y 13	326 41.1	5 38.3	40.1	84 53.1	15.4	97 30.0	00.6	51 23.7	28.0	Gienah	175 48.8	S17 38.5
14	341 43.6	20 37.6	39.1	99 53.9	15.8	112 32.2	00.7	66 25.9	28.0	Hadar	148 43.2	S60 27.2
15	356 46.1	35 37.0 ..	38.2	114 54.8 ..	16.1	127 34.4 ..	00.7	81 28.1 ..	28.0	Hamal	327 57.2	N23 32.8
16	11 48.5	50 36.3	37.3	129 55.7	16.4	142 36.6	00.8	96 30.3	28.0	Kaus Aust.	83 40.0	S34 22.3
17	26 51.0	65 35.7	36.3	144 56.5	16.7	157 38.8	00.9	111 32.5	28.0			
18	41 53.4	80 35.0	S16 35.4	159 57.4	S20 17.0	172 41.0	S17 00.9	126 34.7	S22 28.0	Kochab	137 20.3	N74 04.7
19	56 55.9	95 34.3	34.5	174 58.3	17.3	187 43.2	01.0	141 36.9	28.0	Markab	13 35.5	N15 18.1
20	71 58.4	110 33.7	33.5	189 59.1	17.6	202 45.4	01.1	156 39.0	27.9	Menkar	314 11.7	N 4 09.4
21	87 00.8	125 33.0 ..	32.6	205 00.0 ..	17.9	217 47.6 ..	01.1	171 41.2 ..	27.9	Menkent	148 03.8	S36 27.2
22	102 03.3	140 32.4	31.6	220 00.9	18.2	232 49.8	01.2	186 43.4	27.9	Miaplacidus	221 38.0	S69 47.5
23	117 05.8	155 31.7	30.7	235 01.7	18.6	247 52.0	01.2	201 45.6	27.9			
2 00	132 08.2	170 31.1	S16 29.8	250 02.6	S20 18.9	262 54.2	S17 01.3	216 47.8	S22 27.9	Mirfak	308 35.7	N49 55.5
01	147 10.7	185 30.4	28.8	265 03.5	19.2	277 56.4	01.4	231 50.0	27.9	Nunki	75 54.8	S26 16.3
02	162 13.2	200 29.7	27.9	280 04.3	19.5	292 58.6	01.4	246 52.2	27.9	Peacock	53 14.9	S56 40.5
03	177 15.6	215 29.1 ..	26.9	295 05.2 ..	19.8	308 00.8 ..	01.5	261 54.4 ..	27.9	Pollux	243 23.6	N27 58.8
04	192 18.1	230 28.4	26.0	310 06.1	20.1	323 03.1	01.5	276 56.6	27.9	Procyon	244 56.1	N 5 10.5
05	207 20.6	245 27.8	25.0	325 06.9	20.4	338 05.3	01.6	291 58.8	27.9			
F 06	222 23.0	260 27.1	S16 24.1	340 07.8	S20 20.7	353 07.5	S17 01.7	307 01.0	S22 27.9	Rasalhague	96 03.8	N12 32.9
R 07	237 25.5	275 26.5	23.1	355 08.7	21.0	8 09.7	01.7	322 03.1	27.9	Regulus	207 39.9	N11 52.6
I 08	252 27.9	290 25.8	22.2	10 09.5	21.3	23 11.9	01.8	337 05.3	27.8	Rigel	281 08.8	S 8 11.2
D 09	267 30.4	305 25.2 ..	21.2	25 10.4 ..	21.7	38 14.1 ..	01.8	352 07.5 ..	27.8	Rigil Kent.	139 47.4	S60 54.1
A 10	282 32.9	320 24.5	20.3	40 11.3	22.0	53 16.3	01.9	7 09.7	27.8	Sabik	102 09.1	S15 44.6
Y 11	297 35.3	335 23.9	19.3	55 12.1	22.3	68 18.5	02.0	22 11.9	27.8			
12	312 37.8	350 23.2	S16 18.4	70 13.0	S20 22.6	83 20.7	S17 02.0	37 14.1	S22 27.8	Schedar	349 37.1	N56 38.3
13	327 40.3	5 22.6	17.4	85 13.9	22.9	98 22.9	02.1	52 16.3	27.8	Shaula	96 17.9	S37 06.7
14	342 42.7	20 21.9	16.5	100 14.7	23.2	113 25.1	02.1	67 18.5	27.8	Sirius	258 30.7	S16 44.8
15	357 45.2	35 21.3 ..	15.5	115 15.6 ..	23.5	128 27.3 ..	02.2	82 20.7 ..	27.8	Spica	158 27.8	S11 15.2
16	12 47.7	50 20.6	14.6	130 16.5	23.8	143 29.5	02.3	97 22.9	27.8	Suhail	222 49.7	S43 30.4
17	27 50.1	65 20.0	13.6	145 17.3	24.1	158 31.7	02.3	112 25.1	27.8			
18	42 52.6	80 19.4	S16 12.6	160 18.2	S20 24.4	173 33.9	S17 02.4	127 27.3	S22 27.8	Vega	80 37.2	N38 48.0
19	57 55.1	95 18.7	11.7	175 19.1	24.7	188 36.2	02.4	142 29.4	27.7	Zuben'ubi	137 01.9	S16 06.8
20	72 57.5	110 18.1	10.7	190 19.9	25.0	203 38.4	02.5	157 31.6	27.7		SHA	Mer.Pass.
21	88 00.0	125 17.4 ..	09.8	205 20.8 ..	25.3	218 40.6 ..	02.6	172 33.8 ..	27.7	Venus	39 37.8	12 37
22	103 02.4	140 16.8	08.8	220 21.7	25.6	233 42.8	02.6	187 36.0	27.7	Mars	118 32.7	7 21
23	118 04.9	155 16.1	07.8	235 22.5	25.9	248 45.0	02.7	202 38.2	27.7	Jupiter	130 52.3	6 31
Mer.Pass.	15 12.9	v −0.7	d 0.9	v 0.9	d 0.3	v 2.2	d 0.1	v 2.2	d 0.0	Saturn	84 46.2	9 35

UT	SUN GHA	SUN Dec	MOON GHA	MOON v	MOON Dec	MOON d	MOON HP
d h	° '	° '	° '	'	° '	'	'
31 00	176 39.7	S17 27.2	4 55.2	4.1	N18 23.1	5.3	61.0
01	191 39.6	26.5	19 18.3	4.2	18 17.8	5.6	61.0
02	206 39.5	25.8	33 41.5	4.2	18 12.2	5.6	61.0
03	221 39.4 ..	25.1	48 04.7	4.3	18 06.6	5.8	61.0
04	236 39.3	24.4	62 28.0	4.3	18 00.8	5.9	61.0
05	251 39.2	23.7	76 51.3	4.4	17 54.9	6.0	61.0
W 06	266 39.1	S17 23.0	91 14.7	4.4	N17 48.9	6.2	61.0
E 07	281 39.0	22.3	105 38.1	4.5	17 42.7	6.2	61.0
D 08	296 39.0	21.6	120 01.6	4.5	17 36.5	6.4	60.9
N 09	311 38.9 ..	20.9	134 25.1	4.6	17 30.1	6.6	60.9
E 10	326 38.8	20.2	148 48.7	4.7	17 23.5	6.6	60.9
S 11	341 38.7	19.5	163 12.4	4.7	17 16.9	6.8	60.9
D 12	356 38.6	S17 18.8	177 36.1	4.9	N17 10.1	6.9	60.9
A 13	11 38.5	18.1	192 00.0	4.8	17 03.2	7.0	60.9
Y 14	26 38.4	17.4	206 23.8	5.0	16 56.2	7.1	60.9
15	41 38.3 ..	16.7	220 47.8	5.0	16 49.1	7.3	60.9
16	56 38.2	16.0	235 11.8	5.0	16 41.8	7.3	60.8
17	71 38.2	15.3	249 35.8	5.2	16 34.5	7.5	60.8
18	86 38.1	S17 14.6	264 00.0	5.2	N16 27.0	7.6	60.8
19	101 38.0	13.9	278 24.2	5.3	16 19.4	7.7	60.8
20	116 37.9	13.2	292 48.5	5.4	16 11.7	7.8	60.8
21	131 37.8 ..	12.5	307 12.9	5.4	16 03.9	7.9	60.8
22	146 37.7	11.8	321 37.3	5.5	15 56.0	8.0	60.7
23	161 37.6	11.1	336 01.8	5.6	15 48.0	8.1	60.7
1 00	176 37.5	S17 10.4	350 26.4	5.6	N15 39.9	8.2	60.7
01	191 37.5	09.7	4 51.0	5.8	15 31.7	8.4	60.7
02	206 37.4	09.0	19 15.8	5.8	15 23.3	8.4	60.7
03	221 37.3 ..	08.3	33 40.6	5.9	15 14.9	8.5	60.6
04	236 37.2	07.5	48 05.5	6.0	15 06.4	8.6	60.6
05	251 37.1	06.8	62 30.5	6.0	14 57.8	8.7	60.6
T 06	266 37.0	S17 06.1	76 55.5	6.1	N14 49.1	8.8	60.6
H 07	281 37.0	05.4	91 20.6	6.3	14 40.3	8.9	60.5
U 08	296 36.9	04.7	105 45.9	6.2	14 31.4	9.0	60.5
R 09	311 36.8 ..	04.0	120 11.1	6.4	14 22.4	9.1	60.5
S 10	326 36.7	03.3	134 36.5	6.5	14 13.3	9.2	60.5
D 11	341 36.6	02.6	149 02.0	6.5	14 04.1	9.2	60.4
A 12	356 36.5	S17 01.9	163 27.5	6.6	N13 54.9	9.4	60.4
Y 13	11 36.5	01.1	177 53.1	6.7	13 45.5	9.4	60.4
14	26 36.4	17 00.4	192 18.8	6.8	13 36.1	9.5	60.4
15	41 36.3 ..	16 59.7	206 44.6	6.9	13 26.6	9.6	60.3
16	56 36.2	59.0	221 10.5	6.9	13 17.0	9.6	60.3
17	71 36.1	58.3	235 36.4	7.0	13 07.4	9.7	60.3
18	86 36.1	S16 57.6	250 02.4	7.1	N12 57.7	9.9	60.3
19	101 36.0	56.8	264 28.5	7.2	12 47.8	9.8	60.3
20	116 35.9	56.1	278 54.7	7.3	12 38.0	10.0	60.2
21	131 35.8 ..	55.4	293 21.0	7.4	12 28.0	10.0	60.2
22	146 35.8	54.7	307 47.4	7.4	12 18.0	10.1	60.1
23	161 35.7	54.0	322 13.8	7.5	12 07.9	10.2	60.1
2 00	176 35.6	S16 53.3	336 40.3	7.6	N11 57.7	10.2	60.1
01	191 35.5	52.5	351 06.9	7.7	11 47.5	10.3	60.1
02	206 35.4	51.8	5 33.6	7.8	11 37.2	10.3	60.0
03	221 35.4 ..	51.1	20 00.4	7.9	11 26.9	10.4	60.0
04	236 35.3	50.4	34 27.3	7.9	11 16.5	10.5	60.0
05	251 35.2	49.6	48 54.2	8.0	11 06.0	10.5	59.9
F 06	266 35.1	S16 48.9	63 21.2	8.1	N10 55.5	10.6	59.9
R 07	281 35.1	48.2	77 48.3	8.2	10 44.9	10.6	59.9
I 08	296 35.0	47.5	92 15.5	8.3	10 34.3	10.7	59.8
D 09	311 34.9 ..	46.8	106 42.8	8.3	10 23.6	10.8	59.8
A 10	326 34.8	46.0	121 10.1	8.5	10 12.8	10.7	59.8
Y 11	341 34.8	45.3	135 37.6	8.5	10 02.1	10.9	59.7
12	356 34.7	S16 44.6	150 05.1	8.6	N 9 51.2	10.9	59.7
13	11 34.6	43.8	164 32.7	8.6	9 40.3	10.9	59.7
14	26 34.6	43.1	179 00.3	8.8	9 29.4	11.0	59.6
15	41 34.5 ..	42.4	193 28.1	8.8	9 18.4	11.0	59.6
16	56 34.4	41.7	207 55.9	8.9	9 07.4	11.0	59.6
17	71 34.3	40.9	222 23.8	9.0	8 56.4	11.1	59.5
18	86 34.3	S16 40.2	236 51.8	9.0	N 8 45.3	11.2	59.5
19	101 34.2	39.5	251 19.8	9.2	8 34.1	11.1	59.5
20	116 34.1	38.8	265 48.0	9.2	8 23.0	11.2	59.4
21	131 34.1 ..	38.0	280 16.2	9.3	8 11.8	11.3	59.4
22	146 34.0	37.3	294 44.5	9.4	8 00.5	11.3	59.3
23	161 33.9	36.6	309 12.9	9.4	N 7 49.2	11.3	59.3
	SD 16.3	d 0.7	SD 16.6		16.5		16.3

Twilight / Moonrise

Lat.	Naut.	Civil	Sunrise	Moonrise 31	Moonrise 1	Moonrise 2	Moonrise 3
°	h m	h m	h m	h m	h m	h m	h m
N 72	07 10	08 39	10 27	13 40	16 13	18 24	20 23
N 70	07 02	08 20	09 46	14 34	16 39	18 37	20 28
68	06 55	08 05	09 17	15 06	16 59	18 48	20 32
66	06 49	07 53	08 56	15 30	17 14	18 57	20 36
64	06 44	07 43	08 40	15 49	17 27	19 04	20 39
62	06 40	07 34	08 26	16 04	17 37	19 11	20 41
60	06 36	07 27	08 14	16 17	17 47	19 16	20 44
N 58	06 32	07 20	08 04	16 28	17 54	19 21	20 46
56	06 29	07 14	07 55	16 37	18 01	19 26	20 47
54	06 26	07 08	07 47	16 45	18 08	19 29	20 49
52	06 23	07 03	07 40	16 53	18 13	19 33	20 50
50	06 20	06 59	07 34	17 00	18 18	19 36	20 52
45	06 14	06 49	07 20	17 14	18 29	19 43	20 54
N 40	06 08	06 40	07 09	17 26	18 38	19 49	20 57
35	06 02	06 32	06 59	17 36	18 46	19 54	20 59
30	05 57	06 25	06 50	17 45	18 52	19 58	21 01
20	05 46	06 13	06 36	18 00	19 04	20 05	21 04
N 10	05 35	06 01	06 22	18 13	19 14	20 12	21 07
0	05 23	05 48	06 10	18 26	19 24	20 18	21 09
S 10	05 10	05 35	05 58	18 38	19 33	20 24	21 12
20	04 53	05 21	05 44	18 51	19 43	20 31	21 15
30	04 32	05 03	05 28	19 06	19 55	20 38	21 18
35	04 18	04 52	05 19	19 15	20 01	20 42	21 20
40	04 02	04 39	05 09	19 25	20 09	20 47	21 22
45	03 41	04 23	04 57	19 37	20 18	20 53	21 24
S 50	03 14	04 03	04 42	19 51	20 28	20 59	21 27
52	03 00	03 54	04 34	19 57	20 33	21 02	21 28
54	02 43	03 43	04 27	20 04	20 38	21 06	21 30
56	02 22	03 31	04 18	20 13	20 44	21 10	21 31
58	01 54	03 16	04 08	20 22	20 51	21 14	21 33
S 60	01 10	02 58	03 56	20 32	20 58	21 18	21 35

Sunset / Twilight / Moonset

Lat.	Sunset	Civil	Naut.	Moonset 31	Moonset 1	Moonset 2	Moonset 3
°	h m	h m	h m	h m	h m	h m	h m
N 72	14 01	15 50	17 19	10 53	10 23	10 07	09 56
N 70	14 43	16 08	17 27	09 58	09 55	09 52	09 48
68	15 11	16 23	17 33	09 25	09 34	09 39	09 42
66	15 32	16 35	17 39	09 00	09 18	09 29	09 36
64	15 49	16 45	17 44	08 41	09 04	09 20	09 32
62	16 02	16 54	17 48	08 25	08 53	09 13	09 28
60	16 14	17 01	17 52	08 12	08 43	09 06	09 24
N 58	16 24	17 08	17 56	08 00	08 34	09 00	09 21
56	16 33	17 14	17 59	07 50	08 27	08 55	09 19
54	16 41	17 19	18 02	07 42	08 20	08 50	09 16
52	16 48	17 24	18 05	07 34	08 14	08 46	09 14
50	16 54	17 29	18 08	07 27	08 08	08 42	09 12
45	17 08	17 39	18 14	07 11	07 56	08 34	09 07
N 40	17 19	17 48	18 20	06 59	07 46	08 27	09 03
35	17 29	17 55	18 25	06 48	07 37	08 21	09 00
30	17 37	18 02	18 31	06 38	07 30	08 15	08 57
20	17 52	18 15	18 41	06 22	07 16	08 06	08 52
N 10	18 05	18 27	18 52	06 08	07 05	07 58	08 47
0	18 17	18 39	19 04	05 54	06 54	07 50	08 43
S 10	18 29	18 52	19 17	05 40	06 43	07 42	08 38
20	18 43	19 06	19 34	05 26	06 31	07 34	08 34
30	18 58	19 24	19 55	05 09	06 17	07 24	08 28
35	19 07	19 35	20 08	04 59	06 09	07 18	08 25
40	19 18	19 47	20 24	04 48	06 00	07 12	08 21
45	19 30	20 03	20 44	04 35	05 49	07 04	08 17
S 50	19 45	20 22	21 12	04 19	05 36	06 55	08 12
52	19 52	20 32	21 25	04 11	05 30	06 51	08 10
54	19 59	20 42	21 42	04 03	05 24	06 46	08 07
56	20 08	20 55	22 02	03 53	05 16	06 41	08 05
58	20 18	21 09	22 28	03 42	05 08	06 35	08 01
S 60	20 29	21 26	23 09	03 30	04 58	06 29	07 58

SUN / MOON

Day	Eqn. of Time 00h	Eqn. of Time 12h	Mer. Pass.	Mer. Pass. Upper	Mer. Pass. Lower	Age	Phase
d	m s	m s	h m	h m	h m	d	%
31	13 21	13 25	12 13	24 40	12 10	14	100
1	13 30	13 34	12 14	00 40	13 09	15	99
2	13 37	13 41	12 14	01 37	14 04	16	95

UT	ARIES GHA	VENUS −3.9 GHA	Dec	MARS +1.1 GHA	Dec	JUPITER −2.0 GHA	Dec	SATURN +0.6 GHA	Dec	STARS Name	SHA	Dec
3 00	133 07.4	170 15.5	S16 06.9	250 23.4	S20 26.3	263 47.2	S17 02.7	217 40.4	S22 27.7	Acamar	315 16.0	S40 14.4
01	148 09.8	185 14.8	05.9	265 24.3	26.6	278 49.4	02.8	232 42.6	27.7	Achernar	335 24.7	S57 09.1
02	163 12.3	200 14.2	05.0	280 25.1	26.9	293 51.6	02.9	247 44.8	27.7	Acrux	173 05.2	S63 11.7
03	178 14.8	215 13.6	.. 04.0	295 26.0	.. 27.2	308 53.8	.. 02.9	262 47.0	.. 27.7	Adhara	255 09.7	S29 00.1
04	193 17.2	230 12.9	03.0	310 26.9	27.5	323 56.0	03.0	277 49.2	27.7	Aldebaran	290 45.6	N16 32.5
05	208 19.7	245 12.3	02.1	325 27.7	27.8	338 58.3	03.0	292 51.4	27.7			
06	223 22.2	260 11.6	S16 01.1	340 28.6	S20 28.1	354 00.5	S17 03.1	307 53.6	S22 27.7	Alioth	166 17.7	N55 51.5
07	238 24.6	275 11.0	16 00.1	355 29.5	28.4	9 02.7	03.1	322 55.8	27.6	Alkaid	152 56.3	N49 13.2
S 08	253 27.1	290 10.4	15 59.2	10 30.3	28.7	24 04.9	03.2	337 58.0	27.6	Al Na'ir	27 40.3	S46 52.5
A 09	268 29.5	305 09.7	.. 58.2	25 31.2	.. 29.0	39 07.1	.. 03.3	353 00.2	.. 27.6	Alnilam	275 43.0	S 1 11.7
T 10	283 32.0	320 09.1	57.2	40 32.0	29.3	54 09.3	03.3	8 02.3	27.6	Alphard	217 52.7	S 8 44.4
U 11	298 34.5	335 08.5	56.3	55 32.9	29.6	69 11.5	03.4	23 04.5	27.6			
R 12	313 36.9	350 07.8	S15 55.3	70 33.8	S20 29.9	84 13.7	S17 03.4	38 06.7	S22 27.6	Alphecca	126 08.4	N26 39.2
D 13	328 39.4	5 07.2	54.3	85 34.6	30.2	99 16.0	03.5	53 08.9	27.6	Alpheratz	357 40.5	N29 11.4
A 14	343 41.9	20 06.6	53.3	100 35.5	30.5	114 18.2	03.6	68 11.1	27.6	Altair	62 05.5	N 8 55.0
Y 15	358 44.3	35 05.9	.. 52.4	115 36.4	.. 30.8	129 20.4	.. 03.6	83 13.3	.. 27.6	Ankaa	353 12.9	S42 12.8
16	13 46.8	50 05.3	51.4	130 37.2	31.1	144 22.6	03.7	98 15.5	27.6	Antares	112 22.5	S26 28.1
17	28 49.3	65 04.7	50.4	145 38.1	31.4	159 24.8	03.7	113 17.7	27.6			
18	43 51.7	80 04.0	S15 49.4	160 39.0	S20 31.7	174 27.0	S17 03.8	128 19.9	S22 27.5	Arcturus	145 52.8	N19 05.3
19	58 54.2	95 03.4	48.5	175 39.8	32.0	189 29.2	03.8	143 22.1	27.5	Atria	107 21.8	S69 03.1
20	73 56.7	110 02.8	47.5	190 40.7	32.3	204 31.5	03.9	158 24.3	27.5	Avior	234 16.1	S59 34.2
21	88 59.1	125 02.1	.. 46.5	205 41.6	.. 32.6	219 33.7	.. 04.0	173 26.5	.. 27.5	Bellatrix	278 28.4	N 6 21.7
22	104 01.6	140 01.5	45.5	220 42.4	32.9	234 35.9	04.0	188 28.7	27.5	Betelgeuse	270 57.7	N 7 24.4
23	119 04.0	155 00.9	44.6	235 43.3	33.2	249 38.1	04.1	203 30.9	27.5			
4 00	134 06.5	170 00.2	S15 43.6	250 44.2	S20 33.5	264 40.3	S17 04.1	218 33.1	S22 27.5	Canopus	263 54.3	S52 42.7
01	149 09.0	184 59.6	42.6	265 45.0	33.8	279 42.5	04.2	233 35.3	27.5	Capella	280 29.5	N46 00.9
02	164 11.4	199 59.0	41.6	280 45.9	34.1	294 44.8	04.2	248 37.5	27.5	Deneb	49 29.8	N45 20.7
03	179 13.9	214 58.4	.. 40.6	295 46.7	.. 34.4	309 47.0	.. 04.3	263 39.7	.. 27.5	Denebola	182 30.2	N14 28.2
04	194 16.4	229 57.7	39.6	310 47.6	34.7	324 49.2	04.4	278 41.9	27.5	Diphda	348 52.9	S17 53.5
05	209 18.8	244 57.1	38.7	325 48.5	35.0	339 51.4	04.4	293 44.0	27.4			
06	224 21.3	259 56.5	S15 37.7	340 49.3	S20 35.3	354 53.6	S17 04.4	308 46.2	S22 27.4	Dubhe	193 47.4	N61 39.0
07	239 23.8	274 55.8	36.7	355 50.2	35.6	9 55.8	04.5	323 48.4	27.4	Elnath	278 08.4	N28 37.2
S 08	254 26.2	289 55.2	35.7	10 51.1	35.9	24 58.1	04.6	338 50.6	27.4	Eltanin	90 45.1	N51 29.1
U 09	269 28.7	304 54.6	.. 34.7	25 51.9	.. 36.2	40 00.3	.. 04.6	353 52.8	.. 27.4	Enif	33 44.4	N 9 57.4
N 10	284 31.1	319 54.0	33.7	40 52.8	36.5	55 02.5	04.7	8 55.0	27.4	Fomalhaut	15 20.9	S29 31.8
D 11	299 33.6	334 53.3	32.7	55 53.7	36.8	70 04.7	04.8	23 57.2	27.4			
A 12	314 36.1	349 52.7	S15 31.8	70 54.5	S20 37.1	85 06.9	S17 04.8	38 59.4	S22 27.4	Gacrux	171 57.0	S57 12.6
Y 13	329 38.5	4 52.1	30.8	85 55.4	37.4	100 09.2	04.9	54 01.6	27.4	Gienah	175 48.8	S17 38.5
14	344 41.0	19 51.5	29.8	100 56.2	37.7	115 11.4	04.9	69 03.8	27.4	Hadar	148 43.2	S60 27.2
15	359 43.5	34 50.9	.. 28.8	115 57.1	.. 38.0	130 13.6	.. 05.0	84 06.0	.. 27.4	Hamal	327 57.2	N23 32.8
16	14 45.9	49 50.2	27.8	130 58.0	38.2	145 15.8	05.0	99 08.2	27.3	Kaus Aust.	83 40.0	S34 22.3
17	29 48.4	64 49.6	26.8	145 58.8	38.5	160 18.0	05.1	114 10.4	27.3			
18	44 50.9	79 49.0	S15 25.8	160 59.7	S20 38.8	175 20.3	S17 05.1	129 12.6	S22 27.3	Kochab	137 20.2	N74 04.7
19	59 53.3	94 48.4	24.8	176 00.6	39.1	190 22.5	05.2	144 14.8	27.3	Markab	13 35.5	N15 18.1
20	74 55.8	109 47.8	23.8	191 01.4	39.4	205 24.7	05.3	159 17.0	27.3	Menkar	314 11.7	N 4 09.4
21	89 58.3	124 47.1	.. 22.8	206 02.3	.. 39.7	220 26.9	.. 05.3	174 19.2	.. 27.3	Menkent	148 03.7	S36 27.3
22	105 00.7	139 46.5	21.8	221 03.1	40.0	235 29.1	05.4	189 21.4	27.3	Miaplacidus	221 38.0	S69 47.5
23	120 03.2	154 45.9	20.8	236 04.0	40.3	250 31.4	05.4	204 23.6	27.3			
5 00	135 05.6	169 45.3	S15 19.8	251 04.9	S20 40.6	265 33.6	S17 05.5	219 25.8	S22 27.3	Mirfak	308 35.7	N49 55.5
01	150 08.1	184 44.7	18.8	266 05.7	40.9	280 35.8	05.5	234 28.0	27.3	Nunki	75 54.7	S26 16.3
02	165 10.6	199 44.1	17.8	281 06.6	41.2	295 38.0	05.6	249 30.2	27.3	Peacock	53 14.9	S56 40.5
03	180 13.0	214 43.4	.. 16.8	296 07.5	.. 41.5	310 40.3	.. 05.6	264 32.4	.. 27.2	Pollux	243 23.6	N27 58.8
04	195 15.5	229 42.8	15.8	311 08.3	41.8	325 42.5	05.7	279 34.6	27.2	Procyon	244 56.1	N 5 10.5
05	210 18.0	244 42.2	14.8	326 09.2	42.1	340 44.7	05.8	294 36.8	27.2			
06	225 20.4	259 41.6	S15 13.8	341 10.1	S20 42.4	355 46.9	S17 05.9	309 39.0	S22 27.2	Rasalhague	96 03.8	N12 32.9
07	240 22.9	274 41.0	12.8	356 10.9	42.6	10 49.2	05.9	324 41.2	27.2	Regulus	207 39.9	N11 52.6
08	255 25.4	289 40.4	11.8	11 11.8	42.9	25 51.4	05.9	339 43.4	27.2	Rigel	281 08.8	S 8 11.2
M 09	270 27.8	304 39.8	.. 10.8	26 12.6	.. 43.2	40 53.6	.. 06.0	354 45.6	.. 27.2	Rigil Kent.	139 47.3	S60 54.1
O 10	285 30.3	319 39.1	09.8	41 13.5	43.5	55 55.8	06.0	9 47.8	27.2	Sabik	102 09.1	S15 44.7
N 11	300 32.8	334 38.5	08.8	56 14.4	43.8	70 58.1	06.1	24 50.0	27.2			
D 12	315 35.2	349 37.9	S15 07.8	71 15.2	S20 44.1	86 00.3	S17 06.1	39 52.2	S22 27.2	Schedar	349 37.2	N56 38.3
A 13	330 37.7	4 37.3	06.8	86 16.1	44.4	101 02.5	06.2	54 54.4	27.2	Shaula	96 17.9	S37 06.7
Y 14	345 40.1	19 36.7	05.8	101 17.0	44.7	116 04.7	06.2	69 56.6	27.1	Sirius	258 30.7	S16 44.8
15	0 42.6	34 36.1	.. 04.8	116 17.8	.. 45.0	131 07.0	.. 06.3	84 58.8	.. 27.1	Spica	158 27.8	S11 15.2
16	15 45.1	49 35.5	03.8	131 18.7	45.3	146 09.2	06.4	100 01.0	27.1	Suhail	222 49.6	S43 30.4
17	30 47.5	64 34.9	02.7	146 19.5	45.5	161 11.4	06.4	115 03.2	27.1			
18	45 50.0	79 34.3	S15 01.7	161 20.4	S20 45.8	176 13.7	S17 06.5	130 05.4	S22 27.1	Vega	80 37.2	N38 48.0
19	60 52.5	94 33.7	15 00.7	176 21.3	46.1	191 15.9	06.5	145 07.6	27.1	Zuben'ubi	137 01.9	S16 06.8
20	75 54.9	109 33.1	14 59.7	191 22.1	46.4	206 18.1	06.6	160 09.8	27.1		SHA	Mer. Pass.
21	90 57.4	124 32.5	.. 58.7	206 23.0	.. 46.7	221 20.3	.. 06.6	175 12.0	.. 27.1	Venus	35 53.7	12 41
22	105 59.9	139 31.8	57.7	221 23.9	47.0	236 22.6	06.7	190 14.1	27.1	Mars	116 37.6	7 17
23	121 02.3	154 31.2	56.7	236 24.7	47.3	251 24.8	06.7	205 16.3	27.1	Jupiter	130 33.8	6 20
Mer. Pass.	15 01.1	v −0.6	d 1.0	v 0.9	d 0.3	v 2.2	d 0.1	v 2.2	d 0.0	Saturn	84 26.6	9 24

UT	SUN GHA	SUN Dec	MOON GHA	v	Dec	d	HP
3 00	176 33.9	S16 35.8	323 41.3	9.5	N 7 37.9	11.3	59.3
01	191 33.8	35.1	338 09.8	9.6	7 26.6	11.3	59.2
02	206 33.7	34.4	352 38.4	9.7	7 15.3	11.4	59.2
03	221 33.6	.. 33.6	7 07.1	9.7	7 03.9	11.4	59.2
04	236 33.6	32.9	21 35.8	9.8	6 52.5	11.5	59.1
05	251 33.5	32.2	36 04.6	9.9	6 41.0	11.4	59.1
06	266 33.4	S16 31.4	50 33.5	10.0	N 6 29.6	11.5	59.0
S 07	281 33.4	30.7	65 02.5	10.0	6 18.1	11.5	59.0
A 08	296 33.3	30.0	79 31.5	10.1	6 06.6	11.5	59.0
T 09	311 33.3	.. 29.2	94 00.6	10.1	5 55.1	11.6	58.9
U 10	326 33.2	28.5	108 29.7	10.3	5 43.5	11.5	58.9
R 11	341 33.1	27.7	122 59.0	10.3	5 32.0	11.6	58.9
D 12	356 33.1	S16 27.0	137 28.3	10.3	N 5 20.4	11.6	58.8
A 13	11 33.0	26.3	151 57.6	10.5	5 08.8	11.5	58.8
Y 14	26 32.9	25.5	166 27.1	10.5	4 57.3	11.6	58.7
15	41 32.9	.. 24.8	180 56.6	10.5	4 45.7	11.7	58.7
16	56 32.8	24.0	195 26.1	10.7	4 34.0	11.6	58.7
17	71 32.7	23.3	209 55.8	10.7	4 22.4	11.6	58.6
18	86 32.7	S16 22.6	224 25.5	10.7	N 4 10.8	11.6	58.6
19	101 32.6	21.8	238 55.2	10.8	3 59.2	11.7	58.5
20	116 32.6	21.1	253 25.0	10.9	3 47.5	11.6	58.5
21	131 32.5	.. 20.3	267 54.9	10.9	3 35.9	11.7	58.5
22	146 32.4	19.6	282 24.8	11.0	3 24.2	11.6	58.4
23	161 32.4	18.9	296 54.8	11.1	3 12.6	11.6	58.4
4 00	176 32.3	S16 18.1	311 24.9	11.1	N 3 01.0	11.7	58.3
01	191 32.2	17.4	325 55.0	11.2	2 49.3	11.6	58.3
02	206 32.2	16.6	340 25.2	11.2	2 37.7	11.7	58.3
03	221 32.1	.. 15.9	354 55.4	11.3	2 26.0	11.6	58.2
04	236 32.0	15.1	9 25.7	11.3	2 14.4	11.6	58.2
05	251 32.0	14.4	23 56.0	11.4	2 02.8	11.7	58.1
06	266 32.0	S16 13.6	38 26.4	11.5	N 1 51.1	11.6	58.1
S 07	281 31.9	12.9	52 56.9	11.5	1 39.5	11.6	58.1
U 08	296 31.8	12.1	67 27.4	11.5	1 27.9	11.6	58.0
N 09	311 31.8	.. 11.4	81 57.9	11.6	1 16.3	11.6	58.0
D 10	326 31.7	10.6	96 28.5	11.7	1 04.7	11.6	57.9
A 11	341 31.7	09.9	110 59.2	11.7	0 53.1	11.5	57.9
Y 12	356 31.6	S16 09.1	125 29.9	11.8	N 0 41.6	11.6	57.9
13	11 31.6	08.4	140 00.7	11.8	0 30.0	11.5	57.8
14	26 31.5	07.6	154 31.5	11.8	0 18.5	11.5	57.8
15	41 31.4	06.9	169 02.3	11.9	N 0 07.0	11.5	57.7
16	56 31.4	06.1	183 33.2	11.9	S 0 04.5	11.5	57.7
17	71 31.3	05.4	198 04.1	12.0	0 16.0	11.5	57.7
18	86 31.3	S16 04.6	212 35.1	12.1	S 0 27.5	11.5	57.6
19	101 31.2	03.9	227 06.2	12.0	0 39.0	11.4	57.6
20	116 31.2	03.1	241 37.2	12.1	0 50.4	11.4	57.5
21	131 31.1	.. 02.4	256 08.3	12.2	1 01.8	11.4	57.5
22	146 31.1	01.6	270 39.5	12.2	1 13.2	11.4	57.5
23	161 31.0	00.9	285 10.7	12.2	1 24.6	11.3	57.4
5 00	176 31.0	S16 00.1	299 41.9	12.3	S 1 35.9	11.3	57.4
01	191 30.9	15 59.4	314 13.2	12.3	1 47.2	11.3	57.4
02	206 30.9	58.6	328 44.5	12.4	1 58.5	11.3	57.3
03	221 30.8	.. 57.8	343 15.9	12.4	2 09.8	11.2	57.3
04	236 30.8	57.1	357 47.3	12.4	2 21.0	11.3	57.2
05	251 30.7	56.3	12 18.7	12.4	2 32.3	11.1	57.2
06	266 30.7	S15 55.6	26 50.1	12.5	S 2 43.4	11.2	57.2
M 07	281 30.6	54.8	41 21.6	12.6	2 54.6	11.1	57.1
O 08	296 30.6	54.1	55 53.2	12.5	3 05.7	11.1	57.1
N 09	311 30.5	.. 53.3	70 24.7	12.6	3 16.8	11.1	57.0
10	326 30.5	52.5	84 56.3	12.6	3 27.9	11.0	57.0
11	341 30.4	51.8	99 27.9	12.7	3 38.9	11.0	57.0
D 12	356 30.4	S15 51.0	113 59.6	12.7	S 3 49.9	11.0	56.9
A 13	11 30.3	50.2	128 31.3	12.7	4 00.9	10.9	56.9
Y 14	26 30.3	49.5	143 03.0	12.7	4 11.8	10.9	56.9
15	41 30.2	.. 48.7	157 34.7	12.8	4 22.7	10.9	56.8
16	56 30.2	48.0	172 06.5	12.8	4 33.6	10.8	56.8
17	71 30.1	47.2	186 38.3	12.8	4 44.4	10.8	56.7
18	86 30.1	S15 46.4	201 10.1	12.9	S 4 55.2	10.8	56.7
19	101 30.0	45.7	215 42.0	12.8	5 06.0	10.7	56.7
20	116 30.0	44.9	230 13.8	12.9	5 16.7	10.6	56.6
21	131 29.9	.. 44.1	244 45.7	12.9	5 27.3	10.7	56.6
22	146 29.9	43.4	259 17.6	13.0	5 38.0	10.6	56.6
23	161 29.9	42.6	273 49.6	12.9	S 5 48.6	10.5	56.5
	SD 16.3	d 0.7	SD 16.0		15.8		15.5

Lat.	Twilight Naut.	Twilight Civil	Sunrise	Moonrise 3	4	5	6
°	h m	h m	h m	h m	h m	h m	h m
N 72	06 59	08 25	10 04	20 23	22 15	24 04	00 04
N 70	06 52	08 09	09 29	20 28	22 13	23 55	25 34
68	06 46	07 55	09 05	20 32	22 12	23 47	25 34
66	06 42	07 44	08 46	20 36	22 10	23 41	25 09
64	06 37	07 35	08 30	20 39	22 09	23 36	25 00
62	06 34	07 27	08 18	20 41	22 08	23 32	24 52
60	06 30	07 20	08 07	20 44	22 07	23 28	24 45
N 58	06 27	07 14	07 57	20 46	22 06	23 24	24 39
56	06 24	07 09	07 49	20 47	22 06	23 21	24 34
54	06 21	07 04	07 42	20 49	22 05	23 19	24 29
52	06 19	06 59	07 35	20 50	22 05	23 16	24 25
50	06 16	06 55	07 29	20 52	22 04	23 14	24 21
45	06 10	06 45	07 16	20 54	22 03	23 09	24 13
N 40	06 05	06 37	07 06	20 57	22 02	23 05	24 06
35	06 00	06 30	06 57	20 59	22 01	23 02	24 00
30	05 55	06 24	06 48	21 01	22 01	22 59	23 55
20	05 45	06 12	06 34	21 04	22 00	22 53	23 46
N 10	05 35	06 00	06 22	21 07	21 59	22 49	23 38
0	05 24	05 49	06 10	21 09	21 58	22 45	23 31
S 10	05 11	05 37	05 59	21 12	21 57	22 41	23 23
20	04 55	05 23	05 46	21 15	21 56	22 36	23 16
30	04 35	05 06	05 31	21 18	21 55	22 31	23 07
35	04 22	04 55	05 22	21 20	21 54	22 28	23 02
40	04 07	04 43	05 13	21 22	21 54	22 25	22 56
45	03 47	04 28	05 01	21 24	21 53	22 21	22 50
S 50	03 21	04 09	04 47	21 27	21 52	22 17	22 42
52	03 08	04 00	04 40	21 28	21 52	22 15	22 38
54	02 52	03 50	04 33	21 30	21 51	22 13	22 35
56	02 34	03 39	04 25	21 31	21 51	22 10	22 30
58	02 09	03 25	04 15	21 33	21 50	22 08	22 25
S 60	01 34	03 09	04 04	21 35	21 50	22 05	22 20

Lat.	Sunset	Twilight Civil	Twilight Naut.	Moonset 3	4	5	6
°	h m	h m	h m	h m	h m	h m	h m
N 72	14 25	16 04	17 31	09 56	09 46	09 36	09 25
N 70	15 00	16 21	17 37	09 48	09 44	09 41	09 37
68	15 24	16 34	17 43	09 42	09 43	09 44	09 46
66	15 43	16 44	17 47	09 36	09 42	09 48	09 53
64	15 58	16 54	17 52	09 32	09 42	09 51	10 00
62	16 11	17 01	17 55	09 28	09 41	09 53	10 05
60	16 22	17 08	17 59	09 24	09 40	09 55	10 10
N 58	16 31	17 15	18 02	09 21	09 40	09 57	10 14
56	16 39	17 20	18 05	09 19	09 39	09 59	10 18
54	16 47	17 25	18 07	09 16	09 39	10 00	10 22
52	16 53	17 30	18 10	09 14	09 38	10 02	10 25
50	16 59	17 34	18 12	09 12	09 38	10 03	10 28
45	17 12	17 43	18 18	09 07	09 37	10 06	10 34
N 40	17 23	17 51	18 23	09 03	09 36	10 08	10 39
35	17 32	17 58	18 28	09 00	09 36	10 10	10 44
30	17 40	18 05	18 33	08 57	09 35	10 12	10 48
20	17 54	18 16	18 43	08 52	09 34	10 15	10 55
N 10	18 06	18 28	18 53	08 47	09 33	10 18	11 01
0	18 17	18 39	19 04	08 43	09 33	10 20	11 07
S 10	18 29	18 51	19 17	08 38	09 32	10 23	11 13
20	18 42	19 05	19 32	08 34	09 31	10 26	11 19
30	18 56	19 22	19 52	08 28	09 30	10 29	11 26
35	19 05	19 32	20 05	08 25	09 29	10 31	11 30
40	19 15	19 44	20 20	08 21	09 28	10 33	11 34
45	19 26	19 59	20 40	08 17	09 28	10 35	11 40
S 50	19 40	20 17	21 05	08 12	09 26	10 38	11 46
52	19 46	20 26	21 18	08 10	09 26	10 39	11 49
54	19 54	20 36	21 33	08 07	09 25	10 40	11 53
56	20 02	20 47	21 51	08 05	09 25	10 42	11 58
58	20 11	21 01	22 15	08 01	09 24	10 44	12 00
S 60	20 22	21 17	22 48	07 58	09 24	10 46	12 05

Day	SUN Eqn. of Time 00h	12h	Mer. Pass.	MOON Mer. Pass. Upper	Lower	Age	Phase
d	m s	m s	h m	h m	h m	d	%
3	13 44	13 48	12 14	02 30	14 56	17	88
4	13 51	13 53	12 14	03 21	15 45	18	80
5	13 56	13 58	12 14	04 09	16 33	19	71

2018 FEBRUARY 6, 7, 8 (TUES., WED., THURS.)

UT	ARIES GHA	VENUS −3·9 GHA	Dec	MARS +1·1 GHA	Dec	JUPITER −2·0 GHA	Dec	SATURN +0·6 GHA	Dec	STARS Name	SHA	Dec
6 00	136 04.8	169 30.6	S14 55.7	251 25.6	S20 47.6	266 27.0	S17 06.8	220 18.5	S22 27.1	Acamar	315 16.0	S40 14.4
01	151 07.2	184 30.0	54.6	266 26.4	47.9	281 29.3	06.8	235 20.7	27.0	Achernar	335 24.7	S57 09.1
02	166 09.7	199 29.4	53.6	281 27.3	48.1	296 31.5	06.9	250 22.9	27.0	Acrux	173 05.2	S63 11.7
03	181 12.2	214 28.8 ..	52.6	296 28.2 ..	48.4	311 33.7 ..	06.9	265 25.1 ..	27.0	Adhara	255 09.7	S29 00.1
04	196 14.6	229 28.2	51.6	311 29.0	48.7	326 35.9	07.0	280 27.3	27.0	Aldebaran	290 45.6	N16 32.5
05	211 17.1	244 27.6	50.6	326 29.9	49.0	341 38.2	07.1	295 29.5	27.0			
06	226 19.6	259 27.0	S14 49.5	341 30.7	S20 49.3	356 40.4	S17 07.1	310 31.7	S22 27.0	Alioth	166 17.7	N55 51.5
07	241 22.0	274 26.4	48.5	356 31.6	49.4	11 42.6	07.2	325 34.0	27.0	Alkaid	152 56.3	N49 13.2
T 08	256 24.5	289 25.8	47.5	11 32.5	49.9	26 44.9	07.2	340 36.2	27.0	Al Na'ir	27 40.3	S46 52.5
U 09	271 27.0	304 25.2 ..	46.5	26 33.3 ..	50.1	41 47.1 ..	07.3	355 38.4 ..	27.0	Alnilam	275 43.0	S 1 11.7
E 10	286 29.4	319 24.6	45.5	41 34.2	50.4	56 49.3	07.3	10 40.6	27.0	Alphard	217 52.7	S 8 44.4
S 11	301 31.9	334 24.0	44.4	56 35.1	50.7	71 51.6	07.4	25 42.8	27.0			
D 12	316 34.4	349 23.4	S14 43.4	71 35.9	S20 51.0	86 53.8	S17 07.4	40 45.0	S22 26.9	Alphecca	126 08.4	N26 39.2
A 13	331 36.8	4 22.8	42.4	86 36.8	51.3	101 56.0	07.5	55 47.2	26.9	Alpheratz	357 40.5	N29 11.4
Y 14	346 39.3	19 22.2	41.4	101 37.6	51.6	116 58.3	07.5	70 49.4	26.9	Altair	62 05.5	N 8 55.0
15	1 41.7	34 21.6 ..	40.3	116 38.5 ..	51.8	132 00.5 ..	07.6	85 51.6 ..	26.9	Ankaa	353 12.9	S42 12.8
16	16 44.2	49 21.0	39.3	131 39.4	52.1	147 02.7	07.6	100 53.8	26.9	Antares	112 22.5	S26 28.1
17	31 46.7	64 20.4	38.3	146 40.2	52.4	162 05.0	07.7	115 56.0	26.9			
18	46 49.1	79 19.8	S14 37.3	161 41.1	S20 52.7	177 07.2	S17 07.7	130 58.2	S22 26.9	Arcturus	145 52.8	N19 05.2
19	61 51.6	94 19.2	36.2	176 41.9	53.0	192 09.4	07.8	146 00.4	26.9	Atria	107 21.7	S69 03.1
20	76 54.1	109 18.7	35.2	191 42.8	53.3	207 11.7	07.8	161 02.6	26.9	Avior	234 16.1	S59 34.2
21	91 56.5	124 18.1 ..	34.2	206 43.7 ..	53.5	222 13.9 ..	07.9	176 04.8 ..	26.9	Bellatrix	278 28.4	N 6 21.7
22	106 59.0	139 17.5	33.1	221 44.5	53.8	237 16.1	07.9	191 07.0	26.9	Betelgeuse	270 57.7	N 7 24.4
23	122 01.5	154 16.9	32.1	236 45.4	54.1	252 18.4	08.0	206 09.2	26.8			
7 00	137 03.9	169 16.3	S14 31.1	251 46.2	S20 54.4	267 20.6	S17 08.0	221 11.4	S22 26.8	Canopus	263 54.3	S52 42.7
01	152 06.4	184 15.7	30.0	266 47.1	54.7	282 22.8	08.1	236 13.6	26.8	Capella	280 29.5	N46 00.9
02	167 08.8	199 15.1	29.0	281 48.0	54.9	297 25.1	08.1	251 15.8	26.8	Deneb	49 29.8	N45 20.7
03	182 11.3	214 14.5 ..	28.0	296 48.8 ..	55.2	312 27.3 ..	08.2	266 18.0 ..	26.8	Denebola	182 30.2	N14 28.2
04	197 13.8	229 13.9	26.9	311 49.7	55.5	327 29.6	08.3	281 20.2	26.8	Diphda	348 52.9	S17 53.5
05	212 16.2	244 13.3	25.9	326 50.6	55.8	342 31.8	08.3	296 22.4	26.8			
06	227 18.7	259 12.7	S14 24.9	341 51.4	S20 56.1	357 34.0	S17 08.4	311 24.6	S22 26.8	Dubhe	193 47.3	N61 39.0
W 07	242 21.2	274 12.2	23.8	356 52.3	56.3	12 36.3	08.4	326 26.8	26.8	Elnath	278 08.4	N28 37.2
E 08	257 23.6	289 11.6	22.8	11 53.1	56.6	27 38.5	08.5	341 29.0	26.8	Eltanin	90 45.0	N51 29.1
D 09	272 26.1	304 11.0 ..	21.8	26 54.0 ..	56.9	42 40.7 ..	08.5	356 31.2 ..	26.7	Enif	33 44.4	N 9 57.4
N 10	287 28.6	319 10.4	20.7	41 54.9	57.2	57 43.0	08.6	11 33.4	26.7	Fomalhaut	15 20.9	S29 31.8
E 11	302 31.0	334 09.8	19.7	56 55.7	57.5	72 45.2	08.6	26 35.6	26.7			
S 12	317 33.5	349 09.2	S14 18.6	71 56.6	S20 57.7	87 47.5	S17 08.7	41 37.8	S22 26.7	Gacrux	171 56.9	S57 12.6
D 13	332 36.0	4 08.6	17.6	86 57.4	58.0	102 49.7	08.7	56 40.0	26.7	Gienah	175 48.8	S17 38.5
A 14	347 38.4	19 08.0	16.6	101 58.3	58.3	117 51.9	08.8	71 42.2	26.7	Hadar	148 43.2	S60 27.2
Y 15	2 40.9	34 07.5 ..	15.5	116 59.2 ..	58.6	132 54.2 ..	08.8	86 44.4 ..	26.7	Hamal	327 57.3	N23 32.7
16	17 43.3	49 06.9	14.5	132 00.0	58.9	147 56.4	08.9	101 46.6	26.7	Kaus Aust.	83 39.9	S34 22.3
17	32 45.8	64 06.3	13.4	147 00.9	59.1	162 58.7	08.9	116 48.8	26.7			
18	47 48.3	79 05.7	S14 12.4	162 01.7	S20 59.4	178 00.9	S17 09.0	131 51.0	S22 26.7	Kochab	137 20.1	N74 04.7
19	62 50.7	94 05.1	11.3	177 02.6	20 59.7	193 03.1	09.0	146 53.2	26.7	Markab	13 35.5	N15 18.1
20	77 53.2	109 04.5	10.3	192 03.5	21 00.0	208 05.4	09.1	161 55.4	26.6	Menkar	314 11.7	N 4 09.4
21	92 55.7	124 04.0 ..	09.2	207 04.3 ..	00.2	223 07.6 ..	09.1	176 57.6 ..	26.6	Menkent	148 03.7	S36 27.3
22	107 58.1	139 03.4	08.2	222 05.2	00.5	238 09.9	09.2	191 59.8	26.6	Miaplacidus	221 38.0	S69 47.6
23	123 00.6	154 02.8	07.1	237 06.0	00.8	253 12.1	09.2	207 02.0	26.6			
8 00	138 03.1	169 02.2	S14 06.1	252 06.9	S21 01.1	268 14.4	S17 09.3	222 04.3	S22 26.6	Mirfak	308 35.7	N49 55.5
01	153 05.5	184 01.6	05.0	267 07.8	01.3	283 16.6	09.3	237 06.5	26.6	Nunki	75 54.7	S26 16.3
02	168 08.0	199 01.1	04.0	282 08.6	01.6	298 18.8	09.4	252 08.7	26.6	Peacock	53 14.9	S56 40.5
03	183 10.5	214 00.5 ..	02.9	297 09.5 ..	01.9	313 21.1 ..	09.4	267 10.9 ..	26.6	Pollux	243 23.6	N27 58.8
04	198 12.9	228 59.9	01.9	312 10.3	02.2	328 23.3	09.5	282 13.1	26.6	Procyon	244 56.1	N 5 10.5
05	213 15.4	243 59.3	14 00.8	327 11.2	02.4	343 25.6	09.5	297 15.3	26.6			
06	228 17.8	258 58.8	S13 59.8	342 12.1	S21 02.7	358 27.8	S17 09.6	312 17.5	S22 26.5	Rasalhague	96 03.7	N12 32.8
07	243 20.3	273 58.2	58.7	357 12.9	03.0	13 30.1	09.6	327 19.7	26.5	Regulus	207 39.9	N11 52.6
T 08	258 22.8	288 57.6	57.7	12 13.8	03.3	28 32.3	09.7	342 21.9	26.5	Rigel	281 08.8	S 8 11.2
H 09	273 25.2	303 57.0 ..	56.6	27 14.6 ..	03.5	43 34.6 ..	09.7	357 24.1 ..	26.5	Rigil Kent.	139 47.3	S60 54.1
U 10	288 27.7	318 56.5	55.6	42 15.5	03.8	58 36.8	09.8	12 26.3	26.5	Sabik	102 09.1	S15 44.7
R 11	303 30.2	333 55.9	54.5	57 16.4	04.1	73 39.0	09.8	27 28.5	26.5			
S 12	318 32.6	348 55.3	S13 53.5	72 17.2	S21 04.3	88 41.3	S17 09.9	42 30.7	S22 26.5	Schedar	349 37.2	N56 38.3
D 13	333 35.1	3 54.7	52.4	87 18.1	04.6	103 43.5	09.9	57 32.9	26.5	Shaula	96 17.9	S37 06.7
A 14	348 37.6	18 54.2	51.4	102 18.9	04.9	118 45.8	10.0	72 35.1	26.5	Sirius	258 30.7	S16 44.8
Y 15	3 40.0	33 53.6 ..	50.3	117 19.8 ..	05.2	133 48.0 ..	10.0	87 37.3 ..	26.5	Spica	158 27.8	S11 15.3
16	18 42.5	48 53.0	49.2	132 20.7	05.4	148 50.3	10.0	102 39.5	26.5	Suhail	222 49.6	S43 30.5
17	33 45.0	63 52.4	48.2	147 21.5	05.7	163 52.5	10.1	117 41.7	26.4			
18	48 47.4	78 51.9	S13 47.1	162 22.4	S21 06.0	178 54.8	S17 10.1	132 44.0	S22 26.4	Vega	80 37.2	N38 48.0
19	63 49.9	93 51.3	46.1	177 23.2	06.2	193 57.0	10.2	147 46.2	26.4	Zuben'ubi	137 01.9	S16 06.8
20	78 52.3	108 50.7	45.0	192 24.1	06.5	208 59.3	10.2	162 48.4	26.4		SHA	Mer.Pass.
21	93 54.8	123 50.2 ..	43.9	207 25.0 ..	06.8	224 01.5 ..	10.3	177 50.6 ..	26.4	Venus	32 12.4	12 43
22	108 57.3	138 49.6	42.9	222 25.8	07.1	239 03.8	10.3	192 52.8	26.4	Mars	114 42.3	7 13
23	123 59.7	153 49.0	41.8	237 26.7	07.3	254 06.0	10.4	207 55.0	26.4	Jupiter	130 16.7	6 10
Mer. Pass. 14 49.3		v −0.6	d 1.0	v 0.9	d 0.3	v 2.2	d 0.1	v 2.2	d 0.0	Saturn	84 07.5	9 14

UT	SUN GHA	SUN Dec	MOON GHA	v	MOON Dec	d	HP
d h	° ′	° ′	° ′	′	° ′	′	′
6 00	176 29.8	S15 41.8	288 21.5	13.0	S 5 59.1	10.5	56.5
01	191 29.8	41.1	302 53.5	13.0	6 09.6	10.5	56.5
02	206 29.7	40.3	317 25.5	13.0	6 20.1	10.4	56.4
03	221 29.7	.. 39.5	331 57.5	13.1	6 30.5	10.4	56.4
04	236 29.6	38.8	346 29.6	13.0	6 40.9	10.3	56.3
05	251 29.6	38.0	1 01.6	13.1	6 51.2	10.3	56.3
T 06	266 29.6	S15 37.2	15 33.7	13.1	S 7 01.5	10.3	56.3
U 07	281 29.5	36.5	30 05.8	13.1	7 11.8	10.2	56.2
E 08	296 29.5	35.7	44 37.9	13.1	7 22.0	10.1	56.2
S 09	311 29.4	.. 34.9	59 10.0	13.1	7 32.1	10.1	56.2
D 10	326 29.4	34.1	73 42.1	13.2	7 42.2	10.1	56.1
A 11	341 29.4	33.4	88 14.3	13.1	7 52.3	10.0	56.1
Y 12	356 29.3	S15 32.6	102 46.4	13.2	S 8 02.3	9.9	56.1
13	11 29.3	31.8	117 18.6	13.2	8 12.2	10.0	56.0
14	26 29.2	31.1	131 50.8	13.2	8 22.2	9.8	56.0
15	41 29.2	.. 30.3	146 23.0	13.2	8 32.0	9.8	56.0
16	56 29.2	29.5	160 55.2	13.2	8 41.8	9.8	55.9
17	71 29.1	28.7	175 27.4	13.2	8 51.6	9.7	55.9
18	86 29.1	S15 28.0	189 59.6	13.2	S 9 01.3	9.6	55.9
19	101 29.0	27.2	204 31.8	13.3	9 10.9	9.6	55.8
20	116 29.0	26.4	219 04.1	13.2	9 20.5	9.6	55.8
21	131 29.0	.. 25.6	233 36.3	13.3	9 30.1	9.5	55.8
22	146 28.9	24.8	248 08.6	13.2	9 39.6	9.4	55.8
23	161 28.9	24.1	262 40.8	13.3	9 49.0	9.4	55.7
7 00	176 28.9	S15 23.3	277 13.1	13.3	S 9 58.4	9.3	55.7
01	191 28.8	22.5	291 45.4	13.2	10 07.7	9.3	55.7
02	206 28.8	21.7	306 17.6	13.3	10 17.0	9.2	55.6
03	221 28.8	.. 21.0	320 49.9	13.3	10 26.2	9.1	55.6
04	236 28.7	20.2	335 22.2	13.3	10 35.3	9.1	55.6
05	251 28.7	19.4	349 54.5	13.2	10 44.4	9.1	55.5
W 06	266 28.7	S15 18.6	4 26.7	13.3	S10 53.5	9.0	55.5
E 07	281 28.6	17.8	18 59.0	13.3	11 02.5	8.9	55.5
D 08	296 28.6	17.1	33 31.3	13.3	11 11.4	8.9	55.5
N 09	311 28.6	.. 16.3	48 03.6	13.3	11 20.3	8.8	55.4
E 10	326 28.5	15.5	62 35.9	13.3	11 29.1	8.7	55.4
S 11	341 28.5	14.7	77 08.2	13.2	11 37.8	8.7	55.4
D 12	356 28.5	S15 13.9	91 40.4	13.3	S11 46.5	8.6	55.3
A 13	11 28.4	13.1	106 12.7	13.3	11 55.1	8.6	55.3
Y 14	26 28.4	12.4	120 45.0	13.3	12 03.7	8.4	55.3
15	41 28.4	.. 11.6	135 17.3	13.2	12 12.1	8.5	55.3
16	56 28.3	10.8	149 49.5	13.3	12 20.6	8.3	55.2
17	71 28.3	10.0	164 21.8	13.3	12 28.9	8.4	55.2
18	86 28.3	S15 09.2	178 54.1	13.2	S12 37.3	8.2	55.2
19	101 28.2	08.4	193 26.3	13.3	12 45.5	8.2	55.2
20	116 28.2	07.6	207 58.6	13.2	12 53.7	8.1	55.1
21	131 28.2	.. 06.9	222 30.8	13.3	13 01.8	8.0	55.1
22	146 28.2	06.1	237 03.1	13.2	13 09.8	8.0	55.1
23	161 28.1	05.3	251 35.3	13.2	13 17.8	7.9	55.1
8 00	176 28.1	S15 04.5	266 07.5	13.3	S13 25.7	7.9	55.0
01	191 28.1	03.7	280 39.8	13.2	13 33.6	7.7	55.0
02	206 28.1	02.9	295 12.0	13.2	13 41.3	7.8	55.0
03	221 28.0	.. 02.1	309 44.2	13.2	13 49.1	7.6	55.0
04	236 28.0	01.3	324 16.4	13.2	13 56.7	7.6	55.0
05	251 28.0	15 00.5	338 48.6	13.1	14 04.3	7.5	54.9
T 06	266 27.9	S14 59.7	353 20.7	13.2	S14 11.8	7.4	54.9
H 07	281 27.9	59.0	7 52.9	13.2	14 19.2	7.4	54.9
U 08	296 27.9	58.2	22 25.1	13.1	14 26.6	7.3	54.9
R 09	311 27.9	.. 57.4	36 57.2	13.2	14 33.9	7.2	54.8
S 10	326 27.8	56.6	51 29.4	13.1	14 41.1	7.2	54.8
D 11	341 27.8	55.8	66 01.5	13.1	14 48.3	7.0	54.8
A 12	356 27.8	S14 55.0	80 33.6	13.1	S14 55.3	7.1	54.8
Y 13	11 27.8	54.2	95 05.7	13.1	15 02.4	6.9	54.8
14	26 27.8	53.4	109 37.8	13.1	15 09.3	6.9	54.7
15	41 27.7	.. 52.6	124 09.9	13.0	15 16.2	6.8	54.7
16	56 27.7	51.8	138 41.9	13.1	15 23.0	6.7	54.7
17	71 27.7	51.0	153 14.0	13.1	15 29.7	6.6	54.7
18	86 27.7	S14 50.2	167 46.0	13.1	S15 36.3	6.6	54.7
19	101 27.6	49.4	182 18.1	13.0	15 42.9	6.5	54.6
20	116 27.6	48.6	196 50.1	13.0	15 49.4	6.4	54.6
21	131 27.6	.. 47.8	211 22.1	13.0	15 55.8	6.4	54.6
22	146 27.6	47.0	225 54.1	13.1	16 02.2	6.2	54.6
23	161 27.6	46.2	240 26.1	12.9	S16 08.4	6.2	54.6
	SD 16.2	d 0.8	SD 15.3		15.1		14.9

Twilight / Moonrise

Lat.	Naut.	Civil	Sunrise	6	7	8	9
°	h m	h m	h m	h m	h m	h m	h m
N 72	06 47	08 12	09 43	00 04	01 52	03 43	05 48
N 70	06 42	07 57	09 14	25 34	01 34	03 14	04 54
68	06 37	07 45	08 52	25 20	01 20	02 52	04 21
66	06 34	07 35	08 35	25 09	01 09	02 35	03 58
64	06 30	07 27	08 21	25 00	01 00	02 21	03 39
62	06 27	07 20	08 09	24 52	00 52	02 10	03 24
60	06 24	07 14	07 59	24 45	00 45	02 00	03 11
N 58	06 21	07 08	07 51	24 39	00 39	01 51	03 00
56	06 19	07 03	07 43	24 34	00 34	01 44	02 51
54	06 16	06 58	07 36	24 29	00 29	01 37	02 42
52	06 14	06 54	07 30	24 25	00 25	01 31	02 35
50	06 12	06 50	07 24	24 21	00 21	01 26	02 28
45	06 07	06 42	07 13	24 13	00 13	01 14	02 14
N 40	06 02	06 34	07 03	24 06	00 06	01 05	02 02
35	05 58	06 28	06 54	24 00	00 00	00 57	01 52
30	05 53	06 22	06 46	23 55	24 49	00 49	01 43
20	05 44	06 10	06 33	23 46	24 37	00 37	01 28
N 10	05 35	06 00	06 22	23 38	24 26	00 26	01 15
0	05 24	05 49	06 11	23 31	24 16	00 16	01 02
S 10	05 12	05 38	06 00	23 23	24 06	00 06	00 50
20	04 57	05 24	05 48	23 16	23 56	24 37	00 37
30	04 38	05 08	05 34	23 07	23 44	24 22	00 22
35	04 26	04 58	05 26	23 02	23 37	24 14	00 14
40	04 11	04 47	05 16	22 56	23 29	24 04	00 04
45	03 53	04 33	05 05	22 50	23 20	23 53	24 29
S 50	03 28	04 15	04 52	22 42	23 09	23 39	24 13
52	03 16	04 07	04 46	22 38	23 04	23 33	24 06
54	03 02	03 57	04 39	22 35	22 58	23 26	23 57
56	02 44	03 46	04 31	22 30	22 52	23 18	23 48
58	02 23	03 34	04 23	22 25	22 45	23 09	23 38
S 60	01 54	03 19	04 13	22 20	22 38	22 59	23 25

Twilight / Moonset

Lat.	Sunset	Civil	Naut.	6	7	8	9
°	h m	h m	h m	h m	h m	h m	h m
N 72	14 46	16 18	17 43	09 25	09 13	08 58	08 28
N 70	15 16	16 33	17 48	09 37	09 32	09 28	09 24
68	15 37	16 44	17 52	09 46	09 47	09 51	09 57
66	15 54	16 54	17 56	09 53	10 00	10 09	10 21
64	16 08	17 02	17 59	10 00	10 10	10 23	10 41
62	16 20	17 09	18 03	10 05	10 19	10 35	10 56
60	16 30	17 16	18 05	10 10	10 27	10 46	11 09
N 58	16 38	17 21	18 08	10 14	10 33	10 55	11 21
56	16 46	17 26	18 10	10 18	10 39	11 03	11 31
54	16 53	17 31	18 13	10 22	10 45	11 10	11 39
52	16 59	17 35	18 15	10 25	10 49	11 16	11 46
50	17 04	17 39	18 17	10 28	10 54	11 22	11 54
45	17 16	17 47	18 22	10 34	11 03	11 35	12 09
N 40	17 26	17 54	18 27	10 39	11 11	11 45	12 22
35	17 35	18 01	18 31	10 44	11 18	11 54	12 32
30	17 42	18 07	18 35	10 48	11 24	12 02	12 42
20	17 55	18 18	18 44	10 55	11 35	12 15	12 58
N 10	18 07	18 28	18 53	11 01	11 44	12 27	13 12
0	18 18	18 39	19 04	11 07	11 53	12 39	13 25
S 10	18 29	18 50	19 16	11 13	12 01	12 50	13 38
20	18 40	19 03	19 31	11 19	12 11	13 02	13 52
30	18 54	19 19	19 50	11 26	12 21	13 15	14 08
35	19 02	19 29	20 02	11 30	12 27	13 23	14 18
40	19 11	19 41	20 16	11 34	12 34	13 32	14 29
45	19 19	19 54	20 34	11 40	12 43	13 43	14 41
S 50	19 35	20 12	20 58	11 46	12 52	13 56	14 57
52	19 41	20 20	21 10	11 49	12 57	14 02	15 04
54	19 48	20 29	21 24	11 53	13 02	14 09	15 12
56	19 55	20 40	21 41	11 56	13 08	14 16	15 21
58	20 04	20 52	22 02	12 00	13 14	14 24	15 31
S 60	20 14	21 07	22 30	12 05	13 21	14 34	15 43

SUN / MOON

Day	Eqn. of Time 00h	Eqn. of Time 12h	Mer. Pass.	Mer. Pass. Upper	Mer. Pass. Lower	Age	Phase
d	m s	m s	h m	h m	h m	d	%
6	14 01	14 03	12 14	04 56	17 19	20	62
7	14 04	14 06	12 14	05 42	18 05	21	52
8	14 08	14 09	12 14	06 27	18 51	22	42

UT	ARIES	VENUS −3·9		MARS +1·1		JUPITER −2·0		SATURN +0·6		STARS		
	GHA	GHA	Dec	GHA	Dec	GHA	Dec	GHA	Dec	Name	SHA	Dec
d h	° ′	° ′	° ′	° ′	° ′	° ′	° ′	° ′	° ′		° ′	° ′
9 00	139 02.2	168 48.5	S13 40.7	252 27.5	S21 07.6	269 08.3	S17 10.4	222 57.2	S22 26.4	Acamar	315 16.0	S40 14.4
01	154 04.7	183 47.9	39.7	267 28.4	07.9	284 10.5	10.5	237 59.4	26.4	Achernar	335 24.7	S57 09.1
02	169 07.1	198 47.3	38.6	282 29.3	08.1	299 12.8	10.5	253 01.6	26.4	Acrux	173 05.2	S63 11.7
03	184 09.6	213 46.8	. . 37.5	297 30.1	. . 08.4	314 15.0	. . 10.6	268 03.8	. . 26.3	Adhara	255 09.7	S29 00.1
04	199 12.1	228 46.2	36.5	312 31.0	08.7	329 17.3	10.6	283 06.0	26.3	Aldebaran	290 45.6	N16 32.5
05	214 14.5	243 45.6	35.4	327 31.8	08.9	344 19.5	10.7	298 08.2	26.3			
06	229 17.0	258 45.1	S13 34.3	342 32.7	S21 09.2	359 21.8	S17 10.7	313 10.4	S22 26.3	Alioth	166 17.6	N55 51.5
07	244 19.4	273 44.5	33.3	357 33.6	09.5	14 24.0	10.8	328 12.6	26.3	Alkaid	152 56.3	N49 13.2
08	259 21.9	288 43.9	32.2	12 34.4	09.7	29 26.3	10.8	343 14.9	26.3	Al Na'ir	27 40.3	S46 52.5
F 09	274 24.4	303 43.4	. . 31.1	27 35.3	. . 10.0	44 28.5	. . 10.9	358 17.1	. . 26.3	Alnilam	275 43.0	S 1 11.7
R 10	289 26.8	318 42.8	30.1	42 36.1	10.3	59 30.8	10.9	13 19.3	26.3	Alphard	217 52.7	S 8 44.4
I 11	304 29.3	333 42.2	29.0	57 37.0	10.5	74 33.0	11.0	28 21.5	26.3			
D 12	319 31.8	348 41.7	S13 27.9	72 37.8	S21 10.8	89 35.3	S17 11.0	43 23.7	S22 26.3	Alphecca	126 08.4	N26 39.2
A 13	334 34.2	3 41.1	26.8	87 38.7	11.1	104 37.5	11.0	58 25.9	26.3	Alpheratz	357 40.5	N29 11.4
Y 14	349 36.7	18 40.6	25.8	102 39.6	11.3	119 39.8	11.1	73 28.1	26.2	Altair	62 05.5	N 8 55.0
15	4 39.2	33 40.0	. . 24.7	117 40.4	. . 11.6	134 42.0	. . 11.1	88 30.3	. . 26.2	Ankaa	353 12.9	S42 12.8
16	19 41.6	48 39.4	23.6	132 41.3	11.9	149 44.3	11.2	103 32.5	26.2	Antares	112 22.5	S26 28.1
17	34 44.1	63 38.9	22.6	147 42.1	12.1	164 46.5	11.2	118 34.7	26.2			
18	49 46.6	78 38.3	S13 21.5	162 43.0	S21 12.4	179 48.8	S17 11.3	133 36.9	S22 26.2	Arcturus	145 52.8	N19 05.2
19	64 49.0	93 37.8	20.4	177 43.9	12.7	194 51.1	11.3	148 39.1	26.2	Atria	107 21.7	S69 03.1
20	79 51.5	108 37.2	19.3	192 44.7	12.9	209 53.3	11.4	163 41.4	26.2	Avior	234 16.1	S59 34.3
21	94 53.9	123 36.6	. . 18.2	207 45.6	. . 13.2	224 55.6	. . 11.4	178 43.6	. . 26.2	Bellatrix	278 28.4	N 6 21.7
22	109 56.4	138 36.1	17.2	222 46.4	13.5	239 57.8	11.5	193 45.8	26.2	Betelgeuse	270 57.7	N 7 24.4
23	124 58.9	153 35.5	16.1	237 47.3	13.7	255 00.1	11.5	208 48.0	26.2			
10 00	140 01.3	168 35.0	S13 15.0	252 48.2	S21 14.0	270 02.3	S17 11.6	223 50.2	S22 26.1	Canopus	263 54.3	S52 42.7
01	155 03.8	183 34.4	13.9	267 49.0	14.3	285 04.6	11.6	238 52.4	26.1	Capella	280 29.5	N46 00.9
02	170 06.3	198 33.9	12.8	282 49.9	14.5	300 06.8	11.7	253 54.6	26.1	Deneb	49 29.8	N45 20.7
03	185 08.7	213 33.3	. . 11.8	297 50.7	. . 14.8	315 09.1	. . 11.7	268 56.8	. . 26.1	Denebola	182 30.2	N14 28.2
04	200 11.2	228 32.7	10.7	312 51.6	15.0	330 11.4	11.7	283 59.0	26.1	Diphda	348 52.9	S17 53.5
05	215 13.7	243 32.2	09.6	327 52.4	15.3	345 13.6	11.8	299 01.2	26.1			
06	230 16.1	258 31.6	S13 08.5	342 53.3	S21 15.6	0 15.9	S17 11.8	314 03.5	S22 26.1	Dubhe	193 47.3	N61 39.0
07	245 18.6	273 31.1	07.4	357 54.2	15.8	15 18.1	11.9	329 05.7	26.1	Elnath	278 08.4	N28 37.2
S 08	260 21.1	288 30.5	06.4	12 55.0	16.1	30 20.4	11.9	344 07.9	26.1	Eltanin	90 45.0	N51 29.1
A 09	275 23.5	303 30.0	. . 05.3	27 55.9	. . 16.3	45 22.7	. . 12.0	359 10.1	. . 26.1	Enif	33 44.3	N 9 57.4
T 10	290 26.0	318 29.4	04.2	42 56.7	16.6	60 24.9	12.0	14 12.3	26.0	Fomalhaut	15 20.9	S29 31.8
U 11	305 28.4	333 28.9	03.1	57 57.6	16.9	75 27.2	12.1	29 14.5	26.0			
R 12	320 30.9	348 28.3	S13 02.0	72 58.5	S21 17.1	90 29.4	S17 12.1	44 16.7	S22 26.0	Gacrux	171 56.9	S57 12.6
D 13	335 33.4	3 27.8	13 00.9	87 59.3	17.4	105 31.7	12.2	59 18.9	26.0	Gienah	175 48.8	S17 38.5
A 14	350 35.8	18 27.2	12 59.8	103 00.2	17.6	120 34.0	12.2	74 21.1	26.0	Hadar	148 43.1	S60 27.2
Y 15	5 38.3	33 26.7	. . 58.7	118 01.0	. . 17.9	135 36.2	. . 12.2	89 23.4	. . 26.0	Hamal	327 57.3	N23 32.7
16	20 40.8	48 26.1	57.7	133 01.9	18.2	150 38.5	12.3	104 25.6	26.0	Kaus Aust.	83 39.9	S34 22.3
17	35 43.2	63 25.6	56.6	148 02.8	18.4	165 40.7	12.3	119 27.8	26.0			
18	50 45.7	78 25.0	S12 55.5	163 03.6	S21 18.7	180 43.0	S17 12.4	134 30.0	S22 26.0	Kochab	137 20.1	N74 04.7
19	65 48.2	93 24.5	54.4	178 04.5	18.9	195 45.3	12.4	149 32.2	26.0	Markab	13 35.5	N15 18.1
20	80 50.6	108 23.9	53.3	193 05.3	19.2	210 47.5	12.5	164 34.4	26.0	Menkar	314 11.8	N 4 09.4
21	95 53.1	123 23.4	. . 52.2	208 06.2	. . 19.5	225 49.8	. . 12.5	179 36.6	. . 25.9	Menkent	148 03.7	S36 27.3
22	110 55.5	138 22.8	51.1	223 07.0	19.7	240 52.0	12.6	194 38.8	25.9	Miaplacidus	221 38.0	S69 47.6
23	125 58.0	153 22.3	50.0	238 07.9	20.0	255 54.3	12.6	209 41.0	25.9			
11 00	141 00.5	168 21.8	S12 48.9	253 08.8	S21 20.2	270 56.6	S17 12.6	224 43.3	S22 25.9	Mirfak	308 35.8	N49 55.5
01	156 02.9	183 21.2	47.8	268 09.6	20.5	285 58.8	12.7	239 45.5	25.9	Nunki	75 54.7	S26 16.3
02	171 05.4	198 20.7	46.7	283 10.5	20.7	301 01.1	12.7	254 47.7	25.9	Peacock	53 14.9	S56 40.5
03	186 07.9	213 20.1	. . 45.6	298 11.3	. . 21.0	316 03.4	. . 12.8	269 49.9	. . 25.9	Pollux	243 23.6	N27 58.8
04	201 10.3	228 19.6	44.5	313 12.2	21.3	331 05.6	12.8	284 52.1	25.9	Procyon	244 56.1	N 5 10.5
05	216 12.8	243 19.0	43.4	328 13.1	21.5	346 07.9	12.9	299 54.3	25.9			
06	231 15.3	258 18.5	S12 42.3	343 13.9	S21 21.8	1 10.2	S17 12.9	314 56.5	S22 25.9	Rasalhague	96 03.7	N12 32.8
07	246 17.7	273 18.0	41.2	358 14.8	22.0	16 12.4	12.9	329 58.7	25.8	Regulus	207 39.9	N11 52.6
08	261 20.2	288 17.4	40.2	13 15.6	22.3	31 14.7	13.0	345 01.0	25.8	Rigel	281 08.9	S 8 11.2
S 09	276 22.7	303 16.9	. . 39.1	28 16.5	. . 22.5	46 17.0	. . 13.0	0 03.2	. . 25.8	Rigil Kent.	139 47.2	S60 54.2
U 10	291 25.1	318 16.3	38.0	43 17.3	22.8	61 19.2	13.1	15 05.4	25.8	Sabik	102 09.1	S15 44.7
N 11	306 27.6	333 15.8	36.9	58 18.2	23.0	76 21.5	13.1	30 07.6	25.8			
D 12	321 30.0	348 15.3	S12 35.7	73 19.1	S21 23.3	91 23.8	S17 13.2	45 09.8	S22 25.8	Schedar	349 37.2	N56 38.2
A 13	336 32.5	3 14.7	34.6	88 19.9	23.6	106 26.0	13.2	60 12.0	25.8	Shaula	96 17.9	S37 06.7
Y 14	351 35.0	18 14.2	33.5	103 20.8	23.8	121 28.3	13.3	75 14.2	25.8	Sirius	258 30.7	S16 44.8
15	6 37.4	33 13.6	. . 32.4	118 21.6	. . 24.1	136 30.6	. . 13.3	90 16.5	. . 25.8	Spica	158 27.8	S11 15.3
16	21 39.9	48 13.1	31.3	133 22.5	24.3	151 32.8	13.3	105 18.7	25.8	Suhail	222 49.6	S43 30.5
17	36 42.4	63 12.6	30.2	148 23.3	24.6	166 35.1	13.4	120 20.9	25.7			
18	51 44.8	78 12.0	S12 29.1	163 24.2	S21 24.8	181 37.4	S17 13.4	135 23.1	S22 25.7	Vega	80 37.1	N38 48.0
19	66 47.3	93 11.5	28.0	178 25.1	25.1	196 39.6	13.5	150 25.3	25.7	Zuben'ubi	137 01.9	S16 06.8
20	81 49.8	108 11.0	26.9	193 25.9	25.3	211 41.9	13.5	165 27.5	25.7		SHA	Mer. Pass.
21	96 52.2	123 10.4	. . 25.8	208 26.8	. . 25.6	226 44.2	. . 13.6	180 29.7	. . 25.7		° ′	h m
22	111 54.7	138 09.9	24.7	223 27.6	25.8	241 46.4	13.6	195 32.0	25.7	Venus	28 33.6	12 46
23	126 57.2	153 09.4	23.6	238 28.5	26.1	256 48.7	13.6	210 34.2	25.7	Mars	112 46.8	7 08
	h m									Jupiter	130 01.0	5 59
Mer. Pass. 14 37.5		v −0.6	d 1.1	v 0.9	d 0.3	v 2.3	d 0.0	v 2.2	d 0.0	Saturn	83 48.9	9 03

UT	SUN GHA	SUN Dec	MOON GHA	v	MOON Dec	d	HP
d h	° ′	° ′	° ′	′	° ′	′	′
9 00	176 27.5	S14 45.4	254 58.0	13.0	S16 14.6	6.2	54.6
01	191 27.5	44.6	269 30.0	12.9	16 20.8	6.0	54.5
02	206 27.5	43.8	284 01.9	12.9	16 26.8	6.0	54.5
03	221 27.5 ..	43.0	298 33.8	12.9	16 32.8	5.9	54.5
04	236 27.5	42.2	313 05.7	12.9	16 38.7	5.8	54.5
05	251 27.4	41.4	327 37.6	12.9	16 44.5	5.7	54.5
06	266 27.4 S14	40.6	342 09.5	12.8	S16 50.2	5.7	54.5
07	281 27.4	39.8	356 41.3	12.9	16 55.9	5.6	54.4
F 08	296 27.4	39.0	11 13.2	12.8	17 01.5	5.5	54.4
R 09	311 27.4 ..	38.2	25 45.0	12.8	17 07.0	5.4	54.4
I 10	326 27.4	37.4	40 16.8	12.8	17 12.4	5.3	54.4
11	341 27.3	36.6	54 48.6	12.8	17 17.7	5.3	54.4
D 12	356 27.3 S14	35.8	69 20.4	12.7	S17 23.0	5.2	54.4
A 13	11 27.3	35.0	83 52.1	12.8	17 28.2	5.0	54.4
Y 14	26 27.3	34.2	98 23.9	12.7	17 33.2	5.1	54.3
15	41 27.3 ..	33.4	112 55.6	12.7	17 38.3	4.9	54.3
16	56 27.3	32.6	127 27.3	12.7	17 43.2	4.9	54.3
17	71 27.3	31.8	141 59.0	12.7	17 48.1	4.7	54.3
18	86 27.2 S14	31.0	156 30.7	12.7	S17 52.8	4.7	54.3
19	101 27.2	30.2	171 02.4	12.6	17 57.5	4.6	54.3
20	116 27.2	29.3	185 34.0	12.7	18 02.1	4.6	54.3
21	131 27.2 ..	28.5	200 05.7	12.6	18 06.7	4.4	54.3
22	146 27.2	27.7	214 37.3	12.6	18 11.1	4.3	54.3
23	161 27.2	26.9	229 08.9	12.6	18 15.4	4.3	54.2
10 00	176 27.2 S14	26.1	243 40.5	12.5	S18 19.7	4.2	54.2
01	191 27.2	25.3	258 12.0	12.6	18 23.9	4.1	54.2
02	206 27.1	24.5	272 43.6	12.5	18 28.0	4.0	54.2
03	221 27.1 ..	23.7	287 15.1	12.6	18 32.0	4.0	54.2
04	236 27.1	22.9	301 46.7	12.5	18 36.0	3.8	54.2
05	251 27.1	22.1	316 18.2	12.4	18 39.8	3.8	54.2
06	266 27.1 S14	21.2	330 49.6	12.5	S18 43.6	3.7	54.2
S 07	281 27.1	20.4	345 21.1	12.5	18 47.3	3.6	54.2
A 08	296 27.1	19.6	359 52.6	12.4	18 50.9	3.5	54.2
T 09	311 27.1 ..	18.8	14 24.0	12.4	18 54.4	3.4	54.2
U 10	326 27.1	18.0	28 55.4	12.5	18 57.8	3.3	54.1
R 11	341 27.1	17.2	43 26.9	12.4	19 01.1	3.3	54.1
D 12	356 27.0 S14	16.4	57 58.3	12.3	S19 04.4	3.1	54.1
A 13	11 27.0	15.5	72 29.6	12.4	19 07.5	3.1	54.1
Y 14	26 27.0	14.7	87 01.0	12.4	19 10.6	3.0	54.1
15	41 27.0 ..	13.9	101 32.4	12.3	19 13.6	2.9	54.1
16	56 27.0	13.1	116 03.7	12.3	19 16.5	2.8	54.1
17	71 27.0	12.3	130 35.0	12.3	19 19.3	2.7	54.1
18	86 27.0 S14	11.5	145 06.3	12.3	S19 22.0	2.6	54.1
19	101 27.0	10.6	159 37.6	12.3	19 24.6	2.6	54.1
20	116 27.0	09.8	174 08.9	12.3	19 27.2	2.4	54.1
21	131 27.0 ..	09.0	188 40.2	12.2	19 29.6	2.4	54.1
22	146 27.0	08.2	203 11.4	12.3	19 32.0	2.3	54.1
23	161 27.0	07.4	217 42.7	12.2	19 34.3	2.2	54.1
11 00	176 27.0 S14	06.6	232 13.9	12.2	S19 36.5	2.0	54.1
01	191 27.0	05.7	246 45.1	12.2	19 38.5	2.1	54.1
02	206 27.0	04.9	261 16.3	12.2	19 40.6	1.9	54.1
03	221 27.0 ..	04.1	275 47.5	12.2	19 42.5	1.8	54.1
04	236 27.0	03.3	290 18.7	12.2	19 44.3	1.7	54.1
05	251 27.0	02.5	304 49.9	12.1	19 46.0	1.7	54.1
06	266 27.0 S14	01.6	319 21.0	12.2	S19 47.7	1.5	54.1
07	281 27.0	00.8	333 52.2	12.1	19 49.2	1.5	54.1
S 08	296 27.0 14	00.0	348 23.3	12.1	19 50.7	1.3	54.1
U 09	311 27.0 13	59.2	2 54.4	12.2	19 52.0	1.3	54.1
N 10	326 27.0	58.3	17 25.6	12.1	19 53.3	1.2	54.1
11	341 27.0	57.5	31 56.7	12.1	19 54.5	1.1	54.0
D 12	356 27.0 S13	56.7	46 27.8	12.0	S19 55.6	1.0	54.0
A 13	11 27.0	55.9	60 58.8	12.1	19 56.6	0.9	54.0
Y 14	26 27.0	55.0	75 29.9	12.1	19 57.5	0.8	54.0
15	41 27.0 ..	54.2	90 01.0	12.1	19 58.3	0.8	54.0
16	56 27.0	53.4	104 32.1	12.0	19 59.1	0.6	54.0
17	71 27.0	52.6	119 03.1	12.1	19 59.7	0.5	54.0
18	86 27.0 S13	51.7	133 34.2	12.0	S20 00.2	0.5	54.0
19	101 27.0	50.9	148 05.2	12.0	20 00.7	0.4	54.1
20	116 27.0	50.1	162 36.2	12.0	20 01.1	0.3	54.1
21	131 27.0 ..	49.3	177 07.2	12.1	20 01.3	0.2	54.1
22	146 27.0	48.4	191 38.3	12.0	20 01.5	0.1	54.1
23	161 27.0	47.6	206 09.3	12.0	S20 01.6	0.0	54.1
	SD 16.2 d 0.8		SD 14.8		14.7		14.7

Twilight and Moonrise

Lat.	Naut.	Civil	Sunrise	Moonrise 9	10	11	12
°	h m	h m	h m	h m	h m	h m	h m
N 72	06 35	07 58	09 24	05 48	■	■	■
N 70	06 31	07 45	08 59	04 54	06 37	08 30	■
68	06 28	07 35	08 39	04 21	05 46	06 59	07 51
66	06 25	07 26	08 24	03 58	05 14	06 21	07 12
64	06 22	07 19	08 11	03 39	04 51	05 54	06 45
62	06 20	07 12	08 01	03 24	04 32	05 33	06 23
60	06 17	07 07	07 52	03 11	04 17	05 16	06 06
N 58	06 15	07 02	07 44	03 00	04 04	05 02	05 52
56	06 13	06 57	07 37	02 51	03 53	04 50	05 40
54	06 11	06 53	07 30	02 42	03 43	04 39	05 29
52	06 09	06 49	07 25	02 35	03 35	04 30	05 19
50	06 08	06 46	07 20	02 28	03 27	04 21	05 11
45	06 03	06 38	07 08	02 14	03 10	04 04	04 53
N 40	05 59	06 31	06 59	02 02	02 57	03 49	04 38
35	05 55	06 25	06 51	01 52	02 45	03 37	04 25
30	05 51	06 19	06 44	01 43	02 35	03 26	04 15
20	05 43	06 09	06 32	01 28	02 18	03 07	03 56
N 10	05 34	05 59	06 21	01 15	02 03	02 51	03 40
0	05 25	05 49	06 11	01 02	01 49	02 36	03 24
S 10	05 13	05 39	06 00	00 50	01 35	02 22	03 09
20	04 59	05 26	05 49	00 37	01 20	02 06	02 53
30	04 41	05 11	05 36	00 22	01 03	01 47	02 34
35	04 29	05 02	05 29	00 14	00 54	01 37	02 23
40	04 15	04 51	05 20	00 04	00 42	01 25	02 11
45	03 58	04 38	05 10	24 29	00 29	01 10	01 56
S 50	03 35	04 21	04 57	24 13	00 13	00 53	01 38
52	03 24	04 13	04 52	24 06	00 06	00 45	01 30
54	03 11	04 04	04 45	23 57	24 35	00 35	01 20
56	02 55	03 54	04 38	23 48	24 25	00 25	01 10
58	02 35	03 43	04 30	23 38	24 13	00 13	00 57
S 60	02 10	03 29	04 21	23 25	24 00	00 00	00 43

Sunset, Twilight and Moonset

Lat.	Sunset	Civil	Naut.	Moonset 9	10	11	12
°	h m	h m	h m	h m	h m	h m	h m
N 72	15 06	16 32	17 55	08 28	■	■	■
N 70	15 31	16 45	17 59	09 24	09 18	09 04	■
68	15 50	16 55	18 02	09 57	10 09	10 35	11 22
66	16 06	17 04	18 05	10 21	10 41	11 13	12 01
64	16 18	17 11	18 08	10 41	11 05	11 40	12 29
62	16 29	17 17	18 10	10 56	11 24	12 01	12 50
60	16 38	17 23	18 12	11 09	11 40	12 18	13 07
N 58	16 46	17 28	18 14	11 21	11 53	12 32	13 21
56	16 53	17 32	18 16	11 31	12 04	12 45	13 33
54	16 59	17 36	18 18	11 39	12 14	12 55	13 44
52	17 04	17 40	18 20	11 47	12 23	13 05	13 53
50	17 10	17 43	18 22	11 54	12 31	13 13	14 02
45	17 21	17 51	18 26	12 09	12 48	13 31	14 20
N 40	17 30	17 58	18 30	12 22	13 02	13 46	14 34
35	17 38	18 04	18 34	12 32	13 14	13 59	14 47
30	17 45	18 09	18 38	12 42	13 24	14 09	14 58
20	17 57	18 19	18 46	12 58	13 42	14 28	15 16
N 10	18 07	18 29	18 54	13 12	13 57	14 44	15 32
0	18 18	18 39	19 04	13 25	14 12	15 00	15 47
S 10	18 28	18 50	19 15	13 38	14 26	15 15	16 03
20	18 39	19 02	19 29	13 52	14 42	15 31	16 19
30	18 52	19 19	19 47	14 08	15 00	15 50	16 37
35	18 59	19 26	19 58	14 18	15 10	16 00	16 48
40	19 08	19 37	20 12	14 29	15 22	16 13	17 00
45	19 18	19 50	20 29	14 41	15 36	16 27	17 14
S 50	19 30	20 06	20 52	14 57	15 53	16 45	17 32
52	19 36	20 14	21 03	15 04	16 01	16 54	17 40
54	19 42	20 22	21 16	15 12	16 10	17 03	17 50
56	19 49	20 32	21 31	15 21	16 21	17 14	18 00
58	19 57	20 44	21 50	15 31	16 32	17 26	18 12
S 60	20 06	20 57	22 14	15 43	16 46	17 40	18 26

SUN and MOON

Day	Eqn. of Time 00ʰ	12ʰ	Mer. Pass.	Mer. Pass. Upper	Lower	Age	Phase
d	m s	m s	h m	h m	h m	d	%
9	14 10	14 11	12 14	07 14	19 37	23	33
10	14 11	14 12	12 14	08 01	20 24	24	24
11	14 12	14 12	12 14	08 48	21 12	25	17

2018 FEBRUARY 12, 13, 14 (MON., TUES., WED.)

UT	ARIES	VENUS −3.9		MARS +1.0		JUPITER −2.1		SATURN +0.6		STARS		
	GHA	GHA	Dec	GHA	Dec	GHA	Dec	GHA	Dec	Name	SHA	Dec
d h	° ′	° ′	° ′	° ′	° ′	° ′	° ′	° ′	° ′		° ′	° ′
12 00	141 59.6	168 08.8	S12 22.5	253 29.4	S21 26.3	271 51.0	S17 13.7	225 36.4	S22 25.7	Acamar	315 16.0	S40 14.4
01	157 02.1	183 08.3	21.4	268 30.2	26.6	286 53.2	13.7	240 38.6	25.7	Achernar	335 24.7	S57 09.1
02	172 04.5	198 07.8	20.3	283 31.1	26.8	301 55.5	13.8	255 40.8	25.7	Acrux	173 05.1	S63 11.7
03	187 07.0	213 07.2	.. 19.2	298 31.9	.. 27.1	316 57.8	.. 13.8	270 43.0	.. 25.6	Adhara	255 09.7	S29 00.1
04	202 09.5	228 06.7	18.1	313 32.8	27.3	332 00.1	13.8	285 45.2	25.6	Aldebaran	290 45.6	N16 32.5
05	217 11.9	243 06.2	16.9	328 33.6	27.6	347 02.3	13.9	300 47.5	25.6			
06	232 14.4	258 05.6	S12 15.8	343 34.5	S21 27.8	2 04.6	S17 13.9	315 49.7	S22 25.6	Alioth	166 17.6	N55 51.5
07	247 16.9	273 05.1	14.7	358 35.4	28.1	17 06.9	14.0	330 51.9	25.6	Alkaid	152 56.2	N49 13.2
M 08	262 19.3	288 04.6	13.6	13 36.2	28.3	32 09.2	14.0	345 54.1	25.6	Al Na'ir	27 40.3	S46 52.5
O 09	277 21.8	303 04.0	.. 12.5	28 37.1	.. 28.6	47 11.4	.. 14.1	0 56.3	.. 25.6	Alnilam	275 43.0	S 1 11.7
N 10	292 24.3	318 03.5	11.4	43 37.9	28.8	62 13.7	14.1	15 58.5	25.6	Alphard	217 52.7	S 8 44.4
D 11	307 26.7	333 03.0	10.3	58 38.8	29.1	77 16.0	14.1	31 00.8	25.6			
A 12	322 29.2	348 02.4	S12 09.2	73 39.6	S21 29.3	92 18.2	S17 14.2	46 03.0	S22 25.6	Alphecca	126 08.3	N26 39.2
Y 13	337 31.7	3 01.9	08.0	88 40.5	29.6	107 20.5	14.2	61 05.2	25.5	Alpheratz	357 40.5	N29 11.4
14	352 34.1	18 01.4	06.9	103 41.4	29.8	122 22.8	14.3	76 07.4	25.5	Altair	62 05.4	N 8 55.0
15	7 36.6	33 00.9	.. 05.8	118 42.2	.. 30.1	137 25.1	.. 14.3	91 09.6	.. 25.5	Ankaa	353 12.9	S42 12.8
16	22 39.0	48 00.3	04.7	133 43.1	30.3	152 27.3	14.3	106 11.8	25.5	Antares	112 22.5	S26 28.1
17	37 41.5	62 59.8	03.6	148 43.9	30.6	167 29.6	14.4	121 14.1	25.5			
18	52 44.0	77 59.3	S12 02.5	163 44.8	S21 30.8	182 31.9	S17 14.4	136 16.3	S22 25.5	Arcturus	145 52.8	N19 05.2
19	67 46.4	92 58.8	01.3	178 45.6	31.1	197 34.2	14.5	151 18.5	25.5	Atria	107 21.6	S69 03.1
20	82 48.9	107 58.2	12 00.2	193 46.5	31.3	212 36.4	14.5	166 20.7	25.5	Avior	234 16.1	S59 34.3
21	97 51.4	122 57.7	11 59.1	208 47.4	.. 31.6	227 38.7	.. 14.5	181 22.9	.. 25.5	Bellatrix	278 28.5	N 6 21.7
22	112 53.8	137 57.2	58.0	223 48.2	31.8	242 41.0	14.6	196 25.1	25.5	Betelgeuse	270 57.7	N 7 24.4
23	127 56.3	152 56.7	56.9	238 49.1	32.0	257 43.3	14.6	211 27.4	25.5			
13 00	142 58.8	167 56.1	S11 55.7	253 49.9	S21 32.3	272 45.6	S17 14.7	226 29.6	S22 25.4	Canopus	263 54.4	S52 42.7
01	158 01.2	182 55.6	54.6	268 50.8	32.5	287 47.8	14.7	241 31.8	25.4	Capella	280 29.5	N46 00.9
02	173 03.7	197 55.1	53.5	283 51.7	32.8	302 50.1	14.8	256 34.0	25.4	Deneb	49 29.7	N45 20.7
03	188 06.1	212 54.6	.. 52.4	298 52.5	.. 33.0	317 52.4	.. 14.8	271 36.2	.. 25.4	Denebola	182 30.2	N14 28.2
04	203 08.6	227 54.1	51.2	313 53.4	33.3	332 54.7	14.8	286 38.4	25.4	Diphda	348 52.9	S17 53.5
05	218 11.1	242 53.5	50.1	328 54.2	33.5	347 56.9	14.9	301 40.7	25.4			
06	233 13.5	257 53.0	S11 49.0	343 55.1	S21 33.8	2 59.2	S17 14.9	316 42.9	S22 25.4	Dubhe	193 47.3	N61 39.1
07	248 16.0	272 52.5	47.9	358 55.9	34.0	18 01.5	15.0	331 45.1	25.4	Elnath	278 08.4	N28 37.2
T 08	263 18.5	287 52.0	46.7	13 56.8	34.2	33 03.8	15.0	346 47.3	25.4	Eltanin	90 45.0	N51 29.1
U 09	278 20.9	302 51.5	.. 45.6	28 57.7	.. 34.5	48 06.1	.. 15.0	1 49.5	.. 25.4	Enif	33 44.3	N 9 57.4
E 10	293 23.4	317 50.9	44.5	43 58.5	34.7	63 08.3	15.1	16 51.8	25.3	Fomalhaut	15 20.9	S29 31.8
S 11	308 25.9	332 50.4	43.4	58 59.4	35.0	78 10.6	15.1	31 54.0	25.3			
D 12	323 28.3	347 49.9	S11 42.2	74 00.2	S21 35.2	93 12.9	S17 15.2	46 56.2	S22 25.3	Gacrux	171 56.9	S57 12.6
A 13	338 30.8	2 49.4	41.1	89 01.1	35.5	108 15.2	15.2	61 58.4	25.3	Gienah	175 48.8	S17 38.5
Y 14	353 33.3	17 48.9	40.0	104 01.9	35.7	123 17.5	15.2	77 00.6	25.3	Hadar	148 43.1	S60 27.2
15	8 35.7	32 48.4	.. 38.8	119 02.8	.. 35.9	138 19.7	.. 15.3	92 02.8	.. 25.3	Hamal	327 57.3	N23 32.7
16	23 38.2	47 47.8	37.7	134 03.7	36.2	153 22.0	15.3	107 05.1	25.3	Kaus Aust.	83 39.9	S34 22.3
17	38 40.6	62 47.3	36.6	149 04.5	36.4	168 24.3	15.3	122 07.3	25.3			
18	53 43.1	77 46.8	S11 35.4	164 05.4	S21 36.7	183 26.6	S17 15.4	137 09.5	S22 25.3	Kochab	137 20.0	N74 04.7
19	68 45.6	92 46.3	34.3	179 06.2	36.9	198 28.9	15.4	152 11.7	25.3	Markab	13 35.5	N15 18.1
20	83 48.0	107 45.8	33.2	194 07.1	37.1	213 31.2	15.5	167 13.9	25.2	Menkar	314 11.8	N 4 09.4
21	98 50.5	122 45.3	.. 32.1	209 07.9	.. 37.4	228 33.4	.. 15.5	182 16.2	.. 25.2	Menkent	148 03.7	S36 27.3
22	113 53.0	137 44.8	30.9	224 08.8	37.6	243 35.7	15.5	197 18.4	25.2	Miaplacidus	221 38.0	S69 47.6
23	128 55.4	152 44.2	29.8	239 09.7	37.9	258 38.0	15.6	212 20.6	25.2			
14 00	143 57.9	167 43.7	S11 28.7	254 10.5	S21 38.1	273 40.3	S17 15.6	227 22.8	S22 25.2	Mirfak	308 35.8	N49 55.5
01	159 00.4	182 43.2	27.5	269 11.4	38.3	288 42.6	15.7	242 25.0	25.2	Nunki	75 54.7	S26 16.3
02	174 02.8	197 42.7	26.4	284 12.2	38.6	303 44.9	15.7	257 27.3	25.2	Peacock	53 14.9	S56 40.5
03	189 05.3	212 42.2	.. 25.2	299 13.1	.. 38.8	318 47.2	.. 15.7	272 29.5	.. 25.2	Pollux	243 23.6	N27 58.8
04	204 07.8	227 41.7	24.1	314 13.9	39.1	333 49.4	15.8	287 31.7	25.2	Procyon	244 56.1	N 5 10.5
05	219 10.2	242 41.2	23.0	329 14.8	39.3	348 51.7	15.8	302 33.9	25.2			
06	234 12.7	257 40.7	S11 21.8	344 15.7	S21 39.5	3 54.0	S17 15.8	317 36.1	S22 25.1	Rasalhague	96 03.7	N12 32.8
W 07	249 15.1	272 40.2	20.7	359 16.5	39.8	18 56.3	15.9	332 38.4	25.1	Regulus	207 39.8	N11 52.6
E 08	264 17.6	287 39.7	19.6	14 17.4	40.0	33 58.6	15.9	347 40.6	25.1	Rigel	281 08.9	S 8 11.2
D 09	279 20.1	302 39.1	.. 18.4	29 18.2	.. 40.2	49 00.9	.. 16.0	2 42.8	.. 25.1	Rigil Kent.	139 47.2	S60 54.2
N 10	294 22.5	317 38.6	17.3	44 19.1	40.5	64 03.2	16.0	17 45.0	25.1	Sabik	102 09.1	S15 44.7
E 11	309 25.0	332 38.1	16.1	59 19.9	40.7	79 05.4	16.0	32 47.3	25.1			
S 12	324 27.5	347 37.6	S11 15.0	74 20.8	S21 41.0	94 07.7	S17 16.1	47 49.5	S22 25.1	Schedar	349 37.2	N56 38.2
D 13	339 29.9	2 37.1	13.9	89 21.7	41.2	109 10.0	16.1	62 51.7	25.1	Shaula	96 17.8	S37 06.7
A 14	354 32.4	17 36.6	12.7	104 22.5	41.4	124 12.3	16.1	77 53.9	25.1	Sirius	258 30.7	S16 44.8
Y 15	9 34.9	32 36.1	.. 11.6	119 23.4	.. 41.7	139 14.6	.. 16.2	92 56.1	.. 25.1	Spica	158 27.7	S11 15.3
16	24 37.3	47 35.6	10.4	134 24.2	41.9	154 16.9	16.2	107 58.4	25.0	Suhail	222 49.6	S43 30.5
17	39 39.8	62 35.1	09.3	149 25.1	42.1	169 19.2	16.2	123 00.6	25.0			
18	54 42.2	77 34.6	S11 08.1	164 25.9	S21 42.4	184 21.5	S17 16.3	138 02.8	S22 25.0	Vega	80 37.1	N38 48.0
19	69 44.7	92 34.1	07.0	179 26.8	42.6	199 23.8	16.3	153 05.0	25.0	Zuben'ubi	137 01.8	S16 06.9
20	84 47.2	107 33.6	05.9	194 27.7	42.8	214 26.0	16.4	168 07.3	25.0		SHA	Mer.Pass.
21	99 49.6	122 33.1	.. 04.7	209 28.5	.. 43.1	229 28.3	.. 16.4	183 09.5	.. 25.0		° ′	h m
22	114 52.1	137 32.6	03.6	224 29.4	43.3	244 30.6	16.4	198 11.7	25.0	Venus	24 57.4	12 49
23	129 54.6	152 32.1	02.4	239 30.2	43.5	259 32.9	16.5	213 13.9	25.0	Mars	110 51.2	7 04
	h m									Jupiter	129 46.8	5 48
Mer.Pass. 14 25.7	v −0.5 d 1.1	v 0.9 d 0.2		v 2.3 d 0.0		v 2.2 d 0.0				Saturn	83 30.8	8 53

UT	SUN		MOON					Lat.	Twilight		Sunrise	Moonrise			
									Naut.	Civil		12	13	14	15
	GHA	Dec	GHA	v	Dec	d	HP	°	h m	h m	h m	h m	h m	h m	h m
d h	° ′	° ′	° ′	′	° ′	′	′	N 72	06 23	07 44	09 06	■■■	■■■	10 12	09 37
12 00	176 27.0	S13 46.8	220 40.3	12.0	S20 01.6	0.1	54.1	N 70	06 21	07 33	08 44	■■■	09 15	09 09	09 05
01	191 27.0	45.9	235 11.3	12.0	20 01.5	0.2	54.1	68	06 18	07 24	08 27	07 51	08 20	08 34	08 41
02	206 27.0	45.1	249 42.3	12.0	20 01.3	0.3	54.1	66	06 16	07 17	08 13	07 12	07 46	08 08	08 22
03	221 27.0	.. 44.3	264 13.3	12.0	20 01.0	0.4	54.1	64	06 14	07 10	08 02	06 45	07 22	07 48	08 07
04	236 27.0	43.4	278 44.3	12.0	20 00.6	0.5	54.1	62	06 12	07 04	07 52	06 23	07 03	07 32	07 54
05	251 27.0	42.6	293 15.3	11.9	20 00.1	0.6	54.1	60	06 11	06 59	07 44	06 06	06 47	07 19	07 43
06	266 27.0	S13 41.8	307 46.2	12.0	S19 59.5	0.6	54.1	N 58	06 09	06 55	07 36	05 52	06 33	07 07	07 34
07	281 27.0	41.0	322 17.2	12.0	19 58.9	0.8	54.1	56	06 07	06 51	07 30	05 40	06 22	06 57	07 26
08	296 27.0	40.1	336 48.2	12.0	19 58.1	0.8	54.1	54	06 06	06 47	07 24	05 29	06 12	06 48	07 18
M 09	311 27.0	.. 39.3	351 19.2	11.9	19 57.3	1.0	54.1	52	06 04	06 44	07 19	05 19	06 03	06 40	07 12
O 10	326 27.0	38.5	5 50.1	12.0	19 56.3	1.0	54.1	50	06 03	06 41	07 14	05 11	05 55	06 33	07 06
N 11	341 27.1	37.6	20 21.1	12.0	19 55.3	1.1	54.1	45	05 59	06 34	07 04	04 53	05 37	06 17	06 53
D 12	356 27.1	S13 36.8	34 52.1	12.0	S19 54.2	1.2	54.1	N 40	05 56	06 28	06 56	04 38	05 23	06 04	06 42
A 13	11 27.1	36.0	49 23.1	11.9	19 53.0	1.4	54.1	35	05 52	06 22	06 48	04 25	05 11	05 54	06 33
Y 14	26 27.1	35.1	63 54.0	12.0	19 51.6	1.4	54.1	30	05 49	06 17	06 42	04 15	05 01	05 44	06 25
15	41 27.1	.. 34.3	78 25.0	12.0	19 50.2	1.5	54.1	20	05 42	06 08	06 30	03 56	04 43	05 28	06 11
16	56 27.1	33.4	92 56.0	11.9	19 48.7	1.5	54.1	N 10	05 34	05 59	06 20	03 40	04 27	05 13	05 59
17	71 27.1	32.6	107 26.9	12.0	19 47.2	1.7	54.1	0	05 25	05 50	06 11	03 24	04 12	05 00	05 47
18	86 27.1	S13 31.8	121 57.9	12.0	S19 45.5	1.8	54.1	S 10	05 14	05 39	06 01	03 09	03 58	04 47	05 36
19	101 27.1	30.9	136 28.9	12.0	19 43.7	1.9	54.1	20	05 01	05 28	05 51	02 53	03 42	04 32	05 23
20	116 27.1	30.1	150 59.9	11.9	19 41.8	1.9	54.1	30	04 44	05 14	05 39	02 34	03 24	04 16	05 09
21	131 27.1	.. 29.3	165 30.8	12.0	19 39.9	2.1	54.2	35	04 33	05 05	05 32	02 23	03 13	04 06	05 01
22	146 27.2	28.4	180 01.8	12.0	19 37.8	2.1	54.2	40	04 20	04 55	05 24	02 11	03 01	03 55	04 52
23	161 27.2	27.6	194 32.8	12.0	19 35.7	2.2	54.2	45	04 03	04 42	05 14	01 56	02 47	03 42	04 41
13 00	176 27.2	S13 26.8	209 03.8	12.0	S19 33.5	2.4	54.2	S 50	03 42	04 27	05 03	01 38	02 30	03 26	04 28
01	191 27.2	25.9	223 34.8	12.0	19 31.1	2.4	54.2	52	03 31	04 20	04 57	01 30	02 21	03 19	04 21
02	206 27.2	25.1	238 05.8	12.0	19 28.7	2.5	54.2	54	03 19	04 11	04 52	01 20	02 12	03 11	04 14
03	221 27.2	.. 24.2	252 36.8	12.0	19 26.2	2.6	54.2	56	03 05	04 02	04 45	01 10	02 02	03 02	04 07
04	236 27.2	23.4	267 07.8	12.0	19 23.6	2.7	54.2	58	02 47	03 51	04 38	00 57	01 50	02 51	03 58
05	251 27.2	22.6	281 38.8	12.0	19 20.9	2.8	54.2	S 60	02 25	03 39	04 29	00 43	01 37	02 39	03 48
06	266 27.3	S13 21.7	296 09.8	12.0	S19 18.1	2.8	54.2	Lat.	Sunset	Twilight		Moonset			
07	281 27.3	20.9	310 40.8	12.1	19 15.3	3.0	54.2			Civil	Naut.	12	13	14	15
08	296 27.3	20.0	325 11.9	12.0	19 12.3	3.1	54.2								
T 09	311 27.3	.. 19.2	339 42.9	12.0	19 09.2	3.1	54.2	°	h m	h m	h m	h m	h m	h m	h m
U 10	326 27.3	18.3	354 13.9	12.1	19 06.1	3.2	54.3	N 72	15 24	16 46	18 07	■■■	■■■	12 20	14 33
E 11	341 27.3	17.5	8 45.0	12.1	19 02.9	3.4	54.3	N 70	15 46	16 57	18 10	■■■	11 38	13 23	15 05
S 12	356 27.3	S13 16.7	23 16.1	12.0	S18 59.5	3.4	54.3	68	16 03	17 06	18 12	11 22	12 33	13 58	15 28
D 13	11 27.4	15.8	37 47.1	12.1	18 56.1	3.5	54.3	66	16 17	17 13	18 14	12 01	13 06	14 23	15 46
A 14	26 27.4	15.0	52 18.2	12.1	18 52.6	3.6	54.3	64	16 28	17 20	18 16	12 29	13 30	14 42	16 00
Y 15	41 27.4	.. 14.1	66 49.3	12.1	18 49.0	3.7	54.3	62	16 37	17 25	18 17	12 50	13 49	14 58	16 12
16	56 27.4	13.3	81 20.4	12.1	18 45.3	3.7	54.3	60	16 46	17 30	18 19	13 07	14 05	15 11	16 23
17	71 27.4	12.4	95 51.5	12.1	18 41.6	3.9	54.3	N 58	16 53	17 34	18 21	13 21	14 18	15 22	16 31
18	86 27.4	S13 11.6	110 22.6	12.1	S18 37.7	3.9	54.3	56	16 59	17 38	18 22	13 33	14 29	15 32	16 39
19	101 27.5	10.7	124 53.7	12.2	18 33.8	4.1	54.3	54	17 05	17 42	18 24	13 44	14 39	15 41	16 46
20	116 27.5	09.9	139 24.9	12.1	18 29.7	4.1	54.4	52	17 10	17 45	18 25	13 53	14 48	15 48	16 52
21	131 27.5	.. 09.1	153 56.0	12.2	18 25.6	4.2	54.4	50	17 15	17 48	18 26	14 02	14 56	15 55	16 58
22	146 27.5	08.2	168 27.2	12.1	18 21.4	4.3	54.4	45	17 25	17 55	18 30	14 20	15 13	16 10	17 10
23	161 27.5	07.4	182 58.3	12.2	18 17.1	4.4	54.4	N 40	17 33	18 01	18 33	14 34	15 27	16 22	17 20
14 00	176 27.6	S13 06.5	197 29.5	12.2	S18 12.7	4.5	54.4	35	17 41	18 07	18 36	14 47	15 38	16 32	17 28
01	191 27.6	05.7	212 00.7	12.2	18 08.2	4.5	54.4	30	17 47	18 12	18 40	14 58	15 49	16 41	17 36
02	206 27.6	04.8	226 31.9	12.2	18 03.7	4.7	54.4	20	17 58	18 21	18 47	15 16	16 06	16 57	17 48
03	221 27.6	.. 04.0	241 03.1	12.2	17 59.0	4.7	54.4	N 10	18 08	18 30	18 55	15 32	16 21	17 10	17 59
04	236 27.6	03.1	255 34.3	12.3	17 54.3	4.8	54.4	0	18 18	18 39	19 03	15 47	16 35	17 23	18 10
05	251 27.7	02.3	270 05.6	12.2	17 49.5	4.9	54.5	S 10	18 27	18 49	19 14	16 03	16 50	17 35	18 20
06	266 27.7	S13 01.4	284 36.8	12.3	S17 44.6	5.0	54.5	20	18 37	19 00	19 27	16 19	17 05	17 49	18 31
W 07	281 27.7	13 00.6	299 08.1	12.3	17 39.6	5.1	54.5	30	18 49	19 14	19 44	16 37	17 22	18 04	18 43
E 08	296 27.7	12 59.7	313 39.4	12.3	17 34.5	5.1	54.5	35	18 56	19 23	19 55	16 48	17 32	18 13	18 51
D 09	311 27.7	.. 58.9	328 10.7	12.3	17 29.4	5.3	54.5	40	19 04	19 33	20 08	17 00	17 43	18 23	18 59
N 10	326 27.8	58.0	342 42.0	12.3	17 24.1	5.3	54.5	45	19 13	19 45	20 24	17 14	17 57	18 34	19 08
E 11	341 27.8	57.2	357 13.3	12.4	17 18.8	5.4	54.5	S 50	19 25	20 00	20 45	17 32	18 13	18 48	19 19
S 12	356 27.8	S12 56.3	11 44.7	12.3	S17 13.4	5.5	54.5	52	19 30	20 07	20 55	17 40	18 21	18 55	19 25
D 13	11 27.8	55.5	26 16.0	12.4	17 07.9	5.5	54.5	54	19 36	20 15	21 07	17 50	18 29	19 02	19 30
A 14	26 27.9	54.6	40 47.4	12.4	17 02.4	5.7	54.6	56	19 42	20 25	21 21	18 00	18 39	19 10	19 37
Y 15	41 27.9	.. 53.8	55 18.8	12.3	16 56.7	5.7	54.6	58	19 49	20 35	21 38	18 12	18 49	19 20	19 44
16	56 27.9	52.9	69 50.1	12.5	16 51.0	5.8	54.6	S 60	19 57	20 47	21 59	18 26	19 02	19 30	19 52
17	71 27.9	52.0	84 21.6	12.4	16 45.2	5.9	54.6								

									SUN			MOON			
18	86 28.0	S12 51.2	98 53.0	12.4	S16 39.3	6.0	54.6	Day	Eqn. of Time		Mer.	Mer. Pass.		Age	Phase
19	101 28.0	50.3	113 24.4	12.5	16 33.3	6.1	54.6		00ʰ	12ʰ	Pass.	Upper	Lower		
20	116 28.0	49.5	127 55.9	12.5	16 27.2	6.1	54.6	d	m s	m s	h m	h m	h m	d	%
21	131 28.0	.. 48.6	142 27.4	12.5	16 21.1	6.2	54.7	12	14 12	14 12	12 14	09 36	22 00	26	10
22	146 28.1	47.8	156 58.9	12.5	16 14.9	6.3	54.7	13	14 11	14 11	12 14	10 24	22 48	27	5
23	161 28.1	46.9	171 30.4	12.5	S16 08.6	6.4	54.7	14	14 10	14 09	12 14	11 11	23 35	28	2
	SD 16.2	d 0.8	SD 14.7		14.8		14.9									

UT	ARIES GHA	VENUS −3.9 GHA	VENUS Dec	MARS +1.0 GHA	MARS Dec	JUPITER −2.1 GHA	JUPITER Dec	SATURN +0.6 GHA	SATURN Dec	STARS Name	SHA	Dec
THURSDAY 15												
00	144 57.0	167 31.6	S11 01.3	254 31.1	S21 43.8	274 35.2	S17 16.5	228 16.1	S22 25.0	Acamar	315 16.0	S40 14.4
01	159 59.5	182 31.1	11 00.1	269 31.9	44.0	289 37.5	16.6	243 18.4	25.0	Achernar	335 24.8	S57 09.1
02	175 02.0	197 30.6	10 59.0	284 32.8	44.2	304 39.8	16.6	258 20.6	24.9	Acrux	173 05.1	S63 11.7
03	190 04.4	212 30.1	.. 57.8	299 33.7	.. 44.5	319 42.1	.. 16.6	273 22.8	.. 24.9	Adhara	255 09.7	S29 00.1
04	205 06.9	227 29.6	56.7	314 34.5	44.7	334 44.4	16.7	288 25.0	24.9	Aldebaran	290 45.7	N16 32.5
05	220 09.4	242 29.1	55.5	329 35.4	44.9	349 46.7	16.7	303 27.3	24.9			
06	235 11.8	257 28.6	S10 54.4	344 36.2	S21 45.2	4 49.0	S17 16.7	318 29.5	S22 24.9	Alioth	166 17.6	N55 51.5
07	250 14.3	272 28.1	53.2	359 37.1	45.4	19 51.3	16.8	333 31.7	24.9	Alkaid	152 56.2	N49 13.2
08	265 16.7	287 27.6	52.1	14 37.9	45.6	34 53.6	16.8	348 33.9	24.9	Al Na'ir	27 40.3	S46 52.5
09	280 19.2	302 27.1	.. 50.9	29 38.8	.. 45.9	49 55.9	.. 16.8	3 36.2	.. 24.9	Alnilam	275 43.0	S 1 11.7
10	295 21.7	317 26.6	49.8	44 39.7	46.1	64 58.1	16.9	18 38.4	24.9	Alphard	217 52.6	S 8 44.4
11	310 24.1	332 26.1	48.6	59 40.5	46.3	80 00.4	16.9	33 40.6	24.9			
12	325 26.6	347 25.6	S10 47.5	74 41.4	S21 46.6	95 02.7	S17 17.0	48 42.8	S22 24.8	Alphecca	126 08.3	N26 39.2
13	340 29.1	2 25.1	46.3	89 42.2	46.8	110 05.0	17.0	63 45.1	24.8	Alpheratz	357 40.5	N29 11.3
14	355 31.5	17 24.6	45.2	104 43.1	47.0	125 07.3	17.0	78 47.3	24.8	Altair	62 05.4	N 8 55.0
15	10 34.0	32 24.1	.. 44.0	119 43.9	.. 47.2	140 09.6	.. 17.1	93 49.5	.. 24.8	Ankaa	353 12.9	S42 12.8
16	25 36.5	47 23.6	42.8	134 44.8	47.5	155 11.9	17.1	108 51.7	24.8	Antares	112 22.4	S26 28.1
17	40 38.9	62 23.1	41.7	149 45.7	47.7	170 14.2	17.1	123 54.0	24.8			
18	55 41.4	77 22.6	S10 40.5	164 46.5	S21 47.9	185 16.5	S17 17.2	138 56.2	S22 24.8	Arcturus	145 52.7	N19 05.2
19	70 43.9	92 22.1	39.4	179 47.4	48.2	200 18.8	17.2	153 58.4	24.8	Atria	107 21.6	S69 03.1
20	85 46.3	107 21.6	38.2	194 48.2	48.4	215 21.1	17.2	169 00.6	24.8	Avior	234 16.1	S59 34.3
21	100 48.8	122 21.1	.. 37.1	209 49.1	.. 48.6	230 23.4	.. 17.3	184 02.9	.. 24.7	Bellatrix	278 28.5	N 6 21.7
22	115 51.2	137 20.6	35.9	224 49.9	48.8	245 25.7	17.3	199 05.1	24.7	Betelgeuse	270 57.7	N 7 24.4
23	130 53.7	152 20.2	34.7	239 50.8	49.1	260 28.0	17.3	214 07.3	24.7			
FRIDAY 16												
00	145 56.2	167 19.7	S10 33.6	254 51.7	S21 49.3	275 30.3	S17 17.4	229 09.5	S22 24.7	Canopus	263 54.4	S52 42.7
01	160 58.6	182 19.2	32.4	269 52.5	49.5	290 32.6	17.4	244 11.8	24.7	Capella	280 29.6	N46 00.9
02	176 01.1	197 18.7	31.3	284 53.4	49.7	305 34.9	17.4	259 14.0	24.7	Deneb	49 29.7	N45 20.6
03	191 03.6	212 18.2	.. 30.1	299 54.2	.. 50.0	320 37.2	.. 17.5	274 16.2	.. 24.7	Denebola	182 30.2	N14 28.2
04	206 06.0	227 17.7	28.9	314 55.1	50.2	335 39.5	17.5	289 18.4	24.7	Diphda	348 53.0	S17 53.5
05	221 08.5	242 17.2	27.8	329 55.9	50.4	350 41.8	17.5	304 20.7	24.7			
06	236 11.0	257 16.7	S10 26.6	344 56.8	S21 50.7	5 44.1	S17 17.6	319 22.9	S22 24.7	Dubhe	193 47.3	N61 39.1
07	251 13.4	272 16.2	25.5	359 57.7	50.9	20 46.4	17.6	334 25.1	24.6	Elnath	278 08.4	N28 37.2
08	266 15.9	287 15.7	24.3	14 58.5	51.1	35 48.7	17.6	349 27.3	24.6	Eltanin	90 45.0	N51 29.1
09	281 18.3	302 15.3	.. 23.1	29 59.4	.. 51.3	50 51.0	.. 17.7	4 29.6	.. 24.6	Enif	33 44.3	N 9 57.4
10	296 20.8	317 14.8	22.0	45 00.2	51.6	65 53.3	17.7	19 31.8	24.6	Fomalhaut	15 20.9	S29 31.7
11	311 23.3	332 14.3	20.8	60 01.1	51.8	80 55.6	17.7	34 34.0	24.6			
12	326 25.7	347 13.8	S10 19.6	75 01.9	S21 52.0	95 57.9	S17 17.8	49 36.3	S22 24.6	Gacrux	171 56.9	S57 12.7
13	341 28.2	2 13.3	18.5	90 02.8	52.2	111 00.2	17.8	64 38.5	24.6	Gienah	175 48.8	S17 38.5
14	356 30.7	17 12.8	17.3	105 03.7	52.4	126 02.5	17.9	79 40.7	24.6	Hadar	148 43.0	S60 27.3
15	11 33.1	32 12.3	.. 16.1	120 04.5	.. 52.7	141 04.8	.. 17.9	94 42.9	.. 24.6	Hamal	327 57.3	N23 32.7
16	26 35.6	47 11.9	15.0	135 05.4	52.9	156 07.1	17.9	109 45.2	24.6	Kaus Aust.	83 39.9	S34 22.3
17	41 38.1	62 11.4	13.8	150 06.2	53.1	171 09.4	18.0	124 47.4	24.5			
18	56 40.5	77 10.9	S10 12.6	165 07.1	S21 53.3	186 11.7	S17 18.0	139 49.6	S22 24.5	Kochab	137 20.0	N74 04.7
19	71 43.0	92 10.4	11.5	180 07.9	53.6	201 14.0	18.0	154 51.8	24.5	Markab	13 35.5	N15 18.1
20	86 45.5	107 09.9	10.3	195 08.8	53.8	216 16.3	18.1	169 54.1	24.5	Menkar	314 11.8	N 4 09.4
21	101 47.9	122 09.4	.. 09.1	210 09.7	.. 54.0	231 18.7	.. 18.1	184 56.3	.. 24.5	Menkent	148 03.6	S36 27.3
22	116 50.4	137 09.0	08.0	225 10.5	54.2	246 21.0	18.1	199 58.5	24.5	Miaplacidus	221 38.0	S69 47.6
23	131 52.8	152 08.5	06.8	240 11.4	54.4	261 23.3	18.1	215 00.8	24.5			
SATURDAY 17												
00	146 55.3	167 08.0	S10 05.6	255 12.2	S21 54.7	276 25.6	S17 18.2	230 03.0	S22 24.5	Mirfak	308 35.8	N49 55.5
01	161 57.8	182 07.5	04.5	270 13.1	54.9	291 27.9	18.2	245 05.2	24.5	Nunki	75 54.7	S26 16.3
02	177 00.2	197 07.0	03.3	285 13.9	55.1	306 30.2	18.2	260 07.5	24.5	Peacock	53 14.9	S56 40.5
03	192 02.7	212 06.5	.. 02.1	300 14.8	.. 55.3	321 32.5	.. 18.3	275 09.7	.. 24.4	Pollux	243 23.6	N27 58.8
04	207 05.2	227 06.1	10 00.9	315 15.7	55.5	336 34.8	18.3	290 11.9	24.4	Procyon	244 56.2	N 5 10.5
05	222 07.6	242 05.6	9 59.8	330 16.5	55.8	351 37.1	18.3	305 14.1	24.4			
06	237 10.1	257 05.1	S 9 58.6	345 17.4	S21 56.0	6 39.4	S17 18.4	320 16.4	S22 24.4	Rasalhague	96 03.7	N12 32.8
07	252 12.6	272 04.6	57.4	0 18.2	56.2	21 41.7	18.4	335 18.6	24.4	Regulus	207 39.8	N11 52.6
08	267 15.0	287 04.1	56.3	15 19.1	56.4	36 44.0	18.4	350 20.8	24.4	Rigel	281 08.9	S 8 11.2
09	282 17.5	302 03.7	.. 55.1	30 19.9	.. 56.6	51 46.3	.. 18.5	5 23.1	.. 24.4	Rigil Kent.	139 47.2	S60 54.2
10	297 20.0	317 03.2	53.9	45 20.8	56.9	66 48.6	18.5	20 25.3	24.4	Sabik	102 09.0	S15 44.7
11	312 22.4	332 02.7	52.7	60 21.7	57.1	81 51.0	18.5	35 27.5	24.4			
12	327 24.9	347 02.2	S 9 51.6	75 22.5	S21 57.3	96 53.3	S17 18.6	50 29.7	S22 24.4	Schedar	349 37.2	N56 38.2
13	342 27.3	2 01.8	50.4	90 23.4	57.5	111 55.6	18.6	65 32.0	24.3	Shaula	96 17.8	S37 06.7
14	357 29.8	17 01.3	49.2	105 24.2	57.7	126 57.9	18.6	80 34.2	24.3	Sirius	258 30.7	S16 44.8
15	12 32.3	32 00.8	.. 48.0	120 25.1	.. 58.0	142 00.2	.. 18.7	95 36.4	.. 24.3	Spica	158 27.7	S11 15.3
16	27 34.7	47 00.3	46.8	135 25.9	58.2	157 02.5	18.7	110 38.7	24.3	Suhail	222 49.6	S43 30.5
17	42 37.2	61 59.9	45.7	150 26.8	58.4	172 04.8	18.7	125 40.9	24.3			
18	57 39.7	76 59.4	S 9 44.5	165 27.7	S21 58.6	187 07.1	S17 18.8	140 43.1	S22 24.3	Vega	80 37.1	N38 47.9
19	72 42.1	91 58.9	43.3	180 28.5	58.8	202 09.4	18.8	155 45.4	24.3	Zuben'ubi	137 01.8	S16 06.9
20	87 44.6	106 58.4	42.1	195 29.4	59.0	217 11.8	18.8	170 47.6	24.3		SHA	Mer. Pass.
21	102 47.1	121 58.0	.. 41.0	210 30.2	.. 59.2	232 14.1	.. 18.9	185 49.8	.. 24.3		° ′	h m
22	117 49.5	136 57.5	39.8	225 31.1	59.5	247 16.4	18.9	200 52.1	24.3	Venus	21 23.5	12 51
23	132 52.0	151 57.0	38.6	240 31.9	59.7	262 18.7	18.9	215 54.3	24.2	Mars	108 55.5	7 00
	h m									Jupiter	129 34.1	5 37
Mer. Pass. 14 13.9	v −0.5 d 1.2			v 0.9 d 0.2		v 2.3 d 0.0		v 2.2 d 0.0		Saturn	83 13.4	8 42

UT	SUN GHA	SUN Dec	MOON GHA	v	Dec	d	HP
d h	° ′	° ′	° ′	′	° ′	′	′
15 00	176 28.1	S12 46.1	186 01.9	12.5	S16 02.2	6.4	54.7
01	191 28.1	45.2	200 33.4	12.6	15 55.8	6.5	54.7
02	206 28.2	44.3	215 05.0	12.6	15 49.3	6.6	54.7
03	221 28.2	.. 43.5	229 36.6	12.5	15 42.7	6.7	54.7
04	236 28.2	42.6	244 08.1	12.7	15 36.0	6.8	54.8
05	251 28.3	41.8	258 39.8	12.6	15 29.2	6.8	54.8
06	266 28.3	S12 40.9	273 11.4	12.6	S15 22.4	6.9	54.8
07	281 28.3	40.1	287 43.0	12.7	15 15.5	7.0	54.8
T 08	296 28.3	39.2	302 14.7	12.6	15 08.5	7.0	54.8
H 09	311 28.4	.. 38.3	316 46.3	12.7	15 01.5	7.1	54.8
U 10	326 28.4	37.5	331 18.0	12.7	14 54.4	7.2	54.8
R 11	341 28.4	36.6	345 49.7	12.8	14 47.2	7.3	54.9
S 12	356 28.5	S12 35.8	0 21.5	12.7	S14 39.9	7.3	54.9
D 13	11 28.5	34.9	14 53.2	12.7	14 32.6	7.4	54.9
A 14	26 28.5	34.0	29 24.9	12.8	14 25.2	7.5	54.9
Y 15	41 28.6	.. 33.2	43 56.7	12.8	14 17.7	7.6	54.9
16	56 28.6	32.3	58 28.5	12.8	14 10.1	7.6	54.9
17	71 28.6	31.5	73 00.3	12.8	S14 02.5	7.7	55.0
18	86 28.7	S12 30.6					
19	101 28.7	29.7					
20	116 28.7	28.9	A partial eclipse of				
21	131 28.8	.. 28.0	the Sun occurs on this				
22	146 28.8	27.1	date. See page 5.				
23	161 28.8	26.3					
16 00	176 28.9	S12 25.4	174 43.4	12.9	S13 07.3	8.2	55.1
01	191 28.9	24.5	189 15.3	13.0	12 59.1	8.2	55.1
02	206 28.9	23.7	203 47.3	12.9	12 50.9	8.3	55.1
03	221 29.0	.. 22.8	218 19.2	13.0	12 42.6	8.3	55.1
04	236 29.0	21.9	232 51.2	13.0	12 34.3	8.4	55.1
05	251 29.0	21.1	247 23.2	13.0	12 25.9	8.5	55.1
06	266 29.1	S12 20.2	261 55.2	13.0	S12 17.4	8.5	55.2
07	281 29.1	19.3	276 27.2	13.1	12 08.9	8.6	55.2
08	296 29.1	18.5	290 59.3	13.0	12 00.3	8.7	55.2
F 09	311 29.2	.. 17.6	305 31.3	13.1	11 51.6	8.7	55.2
R 10	326 29.2	16.7	320 03.4	13.1	11 42.9	8.7	55.2
I 11	341 29.3	15.9	334 35.5	13.0	11 34.2	8.9	55.3
D 12	356 29.3	S12 15.0	349 07.5	13.1	S11 25.3	8.9	55.3
A 13	11 29.3	14.1	3 39.6	13.2	11 16.4	8.9	55.3
Y 14	26 29.4	13.3	18 11.8	13.1	11 07.5	9.0	55.3
15	41 29.4	.. 12.4	32 43.9	13.1	10 58.5	9.0	55.3
16	56 29.5	11.5	47 16.0	13.2	10 49.5	9.2	55.3
17	71 29.5	10.7	61 48.2	13.2	10 40.3	9.1	55.4
18	86 29.5	S12 09.8	76 20.4	13.1	S10 31.2	9.2	55.4
19	101 29.6	08.9	90 52.5	13.2	10 22.0	9.3	55.4
20	116 29.6	08.0	105 24.7	13.2	10 12.7	9.3	55.4
21	131 29.7	.. 07.2	119 56.9	13.2	10 03.4	9.4	55.4
22	146 29.7	06.3	134 29.1	13.3	9 54.0	9.4	55.4
23	161 29.7	05.4	149 01.4	13.2	9 44.6	9.5	55.5
17 00	176 29.8	S12 04.5	163 33.6	13.2	S 9 35.1	9.5	55.5
01	191 29.8	03.7	178 05.8	13.3	9 25.6	9.6	55.5
02	206 29.9	02.8	192 38.1	13.2	9 16.0	9.6	55.5
03	221 29.9	.. 01.9	207 10.3	13.3	9 06.4	9.7	55.5
04	236 30.0	01.1	221 42.6	13.3	8 56.7	9.7	55.6
05	251 30.0	12 00.2	236 14.9	13.3	8 47.0	9.8	55.6
06	266 30.1	S11 59.3	250 47.2	13.3	S 8 37.2	9.8	55.6
07	281 30.1	58.4	265 19.5	13.3	8 27.4	9.8	55.6
S 08	296 30.1	57.6	279 51.8	13.3	8 17.6	9.9	55.6
A 09	311 30.2	.. 56.7	294 24.1	13.3	8 07.7	10.0	55.6
T 10	326 30.2	55.8	308 56.4	13.3	7 57.7	10.0	55.7
U 11	341 30.3	54.9	323 28.7	13.3	7 47.7	10.0	55.7
R 12	356 30.3	S11 54.0	338 01.0	13.3	S 7 37.7	10.0	55.7
D 13	11 30.4	53.2	352 33.3	13.4	7 27.7	10.1	55.7
A 14	26 30.4	52.3	7 05.7	13.3	7 17.6	10.2	55.7
Y 15	41 30.4	.. 51.4	21 38.0	13.3	7 07.4	10.2	55.8
16	56 30.5	50.5	36 10.3	13.4	6 57.2	10.2	55.8
17	71 30.5	49.7	50 42.7	13.3	6 47.0	10.3	55.8
18	86 30.6	S11 48.8	65 15.0	13.4	S 6 36.7	10.3	55.8
19	101 30.6	47.9	79 47.4	13.3	6 26.4	10.3	55.8
20	116 30.7	47.0	94 19.7	13.4	6 16.1	10.4	55.9
21	131 30.7	.. 46.1	108 52.1	13.3	6 05.7	10.4	55.9
22	146 30.8	45.3	123 24.4	13.4	5 55.3	10.4	55.9
23	161 30.8	44.4	137 56.8	13.3	S 5 44.9	10.5	55.9
	SD 16.2	d 0.9	SD 15.0		15.1		15.2

Lat.	Twilight Naut.	Twilight Civil	Sunrise	Moonrise 15	16	17	18
°	h m	h m	h m	h m	h m	h m	h m
N 72	06 10	07 30	08 48	09 37	09 21	09 08	08 58
N 70	06 09	07 21	08 29	09 05	09 00	08 56	08 52
68	06 08	07 13	08 14	08 41	08 44	08 46	08 48
66	06 07	07 07	08 02	08 22	08 32	08 38	08 44
64	06 06	07 01	07 52	08 07	08 21	08 31	08 40
62	06 04	06 56	07 43	07 54	08 11	08 25	08 38
60	06 03	06 52	07 36	07 43	08 03	08 20	08 35
N 58	06 02	06 48	07 29	07 34	07 56	08 16	08 33
56	06 01	06 45	07 23	07 26	07 50	08 11	08 31
54	06 00	06 41	07 18	07 18	07 45	08 08	08 29
52	05 59	06 38	07 13	07 12	07 40	08 04	08 27
50	05 58	06 36	07 09	07 06	07 35	08 01	08 26
45	05 55	06 29	07 00	06 53	07 25	07 55	08 23
N 40	05 52	06 24	06 52	06 42	07 17	07 49	08 20
35	05 50	06 19	06 45	06 33	07 10	07 44	08 17
30	05 47	06 15	06 39	06 25	07 03	07 40	08 15
20	05 40	06 06	06 29	06 11	06 52	07 32	08 12
N 10	05 33	05 58	06 19	05 59	06 43	07 26	08 08
0	05 25	05 49	06 11	05 47	06 34	07 20	08 05
S 10	05 15	05 40	06 02	05 36	06 25	07 14	08 02
20	05 03	05 29	05 52	05 23	06 15	07 07	07 59
30	04 47	05 16	05 41	05 09	06 04	06 59	07 56
35	04 36	05 08	05 35	05 01	05 58	06 55	07 53
40	04 24	04 59	05 27	04 52	05 50	06 50	07 51
45	04 09	04 47	05 19	04 41	05 42	06 44	07 48
S 50	03 49	04 33	05 08	04 28	05 32	06 38	07 45
52	03 39	04 26	05 03	04 21	05 27	06 34	07 43
54	03 28	04 18	04 58	04 14	05 22	06 31	07 42
56	03 14	04 10	04 52	04 07	05 16	06 27	07 40
58	02 59	04 00	04 45	03 58	05 09	06 23	07 38
S 60	02 39	03 48	04 37	03 48	05 02	06 18	07 36

Lat.	Sunset	Twilight Civil	Naut.	Moonset 15	16	17	18
°	h m	h m	h m	h m	h m	h m	h m
N 72	15 42	17 00	18 20	14 33	16 27	18 15	20 01
N 70	16 01	17 09	18 21	15 05	16 46	18 25	20 04
68	16 15	17 16	18 22	15 28	17 00	18 33	20 06
66	16 27	17 23	18 23	15 46	17 12	18 40	20 08
64	16 38	17 28	18 24	16 00	17 22	18 45	20 10
62	16 46	17 33	18 25	16 12	17 30	18 50	20 12
60	16 54	17 37	18 26	16 23	17 38	18 55	20 13
N 58	17 00	17 41	18 27	16 31	17 44	18 58	20 14
56	17 06	17 45	18 28	16 39	17 49	19 02	20 15
54	17 11	17 48	18 29	16 46	17 54	19 05	20 16
52	17 16	17 51	18 30	16 52	17 59	19 07	20 17
50	17 20	17 53	18 31	16 58	18 03	19 10	20 18
45	17 29	17 59	18 34	17 10	18 12	19 15	20 19
N 40	17 37	18 05	18 36	17 20	18 19	19 19	20 21
35	17 44	18 09	18 39	17 28	18 25	19 23	20 22
30	17 50	18 14	18 42	17 36	18 31	19 26	20 23
20	18 00	18 22	18 48	17 48	18 40	19 32	20 24
N 10	18 09	18 30	18 55	17 59	18 48	19 37	20 26
0	18 17	18 39	19 03	18 10	18 56	19 42	20 27
S 10	18 26	18 48	19 13	18 20	19 04	19 46	20 29
20	18 36	18 58	19 25	18 31	19 12	19 51	20 30
30	18 47	19 11	19 41	18 43	19 21	19 57	20 32
35	18 53	19 19	19 51	18 51	19 26	20 00	20 33
40	19 00	19 29	20 03	18 59	19 32	20 03	20 34
45	19 09	19 40	20 18	19 08	19 39	20 07	20 35
S 50	19 19	19 54	20 38	19 19	19 47	20 12	20 36
52	19 24	20 01	20 47	19 25	19 51	20 15	20 37
54	19 29	20 08	20 58	19 30	19 55	20 17	20 38
56	19 35	20 17	21 11	19 37	20 00	20 20	20 38
58	19 41	20 26	21 27	19 44	20 05	20 23	20 39
S 60	19 49	20 38	21 45	19 52	20 10	20 26	20 40

Day	SUN Eqn. of Time 00h	12h	Mer. Pass.	MOON Mer. Pass. Upper	Lower	Age	Phase
d	m s	m s	h m	h m	h m	d	%
15	14 08	14 06	12 14	11 59	24 22	29	0
16	14 05	14 03	12 14	12 45	00 22	01	0
17	14 01	13 59	12 14	13 31	01 08	02	3

UT	ARIES GHA	VENUS −3.9 GHA	VENUS Dec	MARS +0.9 GHA	MARS Dec	JUPITER −2.1 GHA	JUPITER Dec	SATURN +0.6 GHA	SATURN Dec	STARS Name	SHA	Dec
18 00	147 54.4	166 56.5	S 9 37.4	255 32.8	S21 59.9	277 21.0	S17 18.9	230 56.5	S22 24.2	Acamar	315 16.1	S40 14.4
01	162 56.9	181 56.1	36.2	270 33.7	22 00.1	292 23.3	19.0	245 58.8	24.2	Achernar	335 24.8	S57 09.1
02	177 59.4	196 55.6	35.0	285 34.5	00.3	307 25.6	19.0	261 01.0	24.2	Acrux	173 05.1	S63 11.8
03	193 01.8	211 55.1	.. 33.9	300 35.4	.. 00.5	322 28.0	.. 19.0	276 03.2	.. 24.2	Adhara	255 09.8	S29 00.2
04	208 04.3	226 54.7	32.7	315 36.2	00.8	337 30.3	19.1	291 05.4	24.2	Aldebaran	290 45.7	N16 32.5
05	223 06.8	241 54.2	31.5	330 37.1	01.0	352 32.6	19.1	306 07.7	24.2			
06	238 09.2	256 53.7	S 9 30.3	345 37.9	S22 01.2	7 34.9	S17 19.1	321 09.9	S22 24.2	Alioth	166 17.6	N55 51.5
07	253 11.7	271 53.3	29.1	0 38.8	01.4	22 37.2	19.2	336 12.1	24.2	Alkaid	152 56.2	N49 13.2
08	268 14.2	286 52.8	27.9	15 39.7	01.6	37 39.5	19.2	351 14.4	24.1	Al Na'ir	27 40.3	S46 52.5
S 09	283 16.6	301 52.3	.. 26.8	30 40.5	.. 01.8	52 41.8	.. 19.2	6 16.6	.. 24.1	Alnilam	275 43.0	S 1 11.7
U 10	298 19.1	316 51.8	25.6	45 41.4	02.0	67 44.2	19.2	21 18.8	24.1	Alphard	217 52.7	S 8 44.4
N 11	313 21.6	331 51.4	24.4	60 42.2	02.2	82 46.5	19.3	36 21.1	24.1			
D 12	328 24.0	346 50.9	S 9 23.2	75 43.1	S22 02.5	97 48.8	S17 19.3	51 23.3	S22 24.1	Alphecca	126 08.3	N26 39.1
A 13	343 26.5	1 50.4	22.0	90 44.0	02.7	112 51.1	19.3	66 25.5	24.1	Alpheratz	357 40.5	N29 11.3
Y 14	358 28.9	16 50.0	20.8	105 44.8	02.9	127 53.4	19.4	81 27.8	24.1	Altair	62 05.4	N 8 55.0
15	13 31.4	31 49.5	.. 19.6	120 45.7	.. 03.1	142 55.8	.. 19.4	96 30.0	.. 24.1	Ankaa	353 12.9	S42 12.8
16	28 33.9	46 49.0	18.5	135 46.5	03.3	157 58.1	19.4	111 32.2	24.1	Antares	112 22.4	S26 28.1
17	43 36.3	61 48.6	17.3	150 47.4	03.5	173 00.4	19.5	126 34.5	24.1			
18	58 38.8	76 48.1	S 9 16.1	165 48.2	S22 03.7	188 02.7	S17 19.5	141 36.7	S22 24.0	Arcturus	145 52.7	N19 05.2
19	73 41.3	91 47.6	14.9	180 49.1	03.9	203 05.0	19.5	156 38.9	24.0	Atria	107 21.5	S69 03.1
20	88 43.7	106 47.2	13.7	195 50.0	04.1	218 07.3	19.5	171 41.2	24.0	Avior	234 16.1	S59 34.3
21	103 46.2	121 46.7	.. 12.5	210 50.8	.. 04.3	233 09.7	.. 19.6	186 43.4	.. 24.0	Bellatrix	278 28.5	N 6 21.7
22	118 48.7	136 46.3	11.3	225 51.7	04.6	248 12.0	19.6	201 45.6	24.0	Betelgeuse	270 57.7	N 7 24.4
23	133 51.1	151 45.8	10.1	240 52.5	04.8	263 14.3	19.6	216 47.9	24.0			
19 00	148 53.6	166 45.3	S 9 08.9	255 53.4	S22 05.0	278 16.6	S17 19.7	231 50.1	S22 24.0	Canopus	263 54.4	S52 42.7
01	163 56.0	181 44.9	07.7	270 54.2	05.2	293 19.0	19.7	246 52.4	24.0	Capella	280 29.6	N46 00.9
02	178 58.5	196 44.4	06.6	285 55.1	05.4	308 21.3	19.7	261 54.6	24.0	Deneb	49 29.7	N45 20.6
03	194 01.0	211 43.9	.. 05.4	300 56.0	.. 05.6	323 23.6	.. 19.7	276 56.8	.. 24.0	Denebola	182 30.2	N14 28.2
04	209 03.4	226 43.5	04.2	315 56.8	05.8	338 25.9	19.8	291 59.1	23.9	Diphda	348 53.0	S17 53.5
05	224 05.9	241 43.0	03.0	330 57.7	06.0	353 28.2	19.8	307 01.3	23.9			
06	239 08.4	256 42.6	S 9 01.8	345 58.5	S22 06.2	8 30.6	S17 19.8	322 03.5	S22 23.9	Dubhe	193 47.3	N61 39.1
07	254 10.8	271 42.1	9 00.6	0 59.4	06.4	23 32.9	19.9	337 05.8	23.9	Elnath	278 08.5	N28 37.2
08	269 13.3	286 41.6	8 59.4	16 00.2	06.6	38 35.2	19.9	352 08.0	23.9	Eltanin	90 44.9	N51 29.1
M 09	284 15.8	301 41.2	.. 58.2	31 01.1	.. 06.8	53 37.5	.. 19.9	7 10.2	.. 23.9	Enif	33 44.3	N 9 57.4
O 10	299 18.2	316 40.7	57.0	46 02.0	07.0	68 39.9	19.9	22 12.5	23.9	Fomalhaut	15 20.9	S29 31.7
N 11	314 20.7	331 40.3	55.8	61 02.8	07.3	83 42.2	20.0	37 14.7	23.9			
D 12	329 23.2	346 39.8	S 8 54.6	76 03.7	S22 07.5	98 44.5	S17 20.0	52 16.9	S22 23.9	Gacrux	171 56.8	S57 12.7
A 13	344 25.6	1 39.3	53.4	91 04.5	07.7	113 46.8	20.0	67 19.2	23.9	Gienah	175 48.7	S17 38.5
Y 14	359 28.1	16 38.9	52.2	106 05.4	07.9	128 49.2	20.1	82 21.4	23.8	Hadar	148 43.0	S60 27.3
15	14 30.5	31 38.4	.. 51.0	121 06.3	.. 08.1	143 51.5	.. 20.1	97 23.7	.. 23.8	Hamal	327 57.3	N23 32.7
16	29 33.0	46 38.0	49.8	136 07.1	08.3	158 53.8	20.1	112 25.9	23.8	Kaus Aust.	83 39.9	S34 22.3
17	44 35.5	61 37.5	48.6	151 08.0	08.5	173 56.1	20.1	127 28.1	23.8			
18	59 37.9	76 37.1	S 8 47.4	166 08.8	S22 08.7	188 58.5	S17 20.2	142 30.4	S22 23.8	Kochab	137 19.9	N74 04.7
19	74 40.4	91 36.6	46.2	181 09.7	08.9	204 00.8	20.2	157 32.6	23.8	Markab	13 35.5	N15 18.1
20	89 42.9	106 36.1	45.0	196 10.5	09.1	219 03.1	20.2	172 34.8	23.8	Menkar	314 11.8	N 4 09.4
21	104 45.3	121 35.7	.. 43.8	211 11.4	.. 09.3	234 05.4	.. 20.2	187 37.1	.. 23.8	Menkent	148 03.6	S36 27.3
22	119 47.8	136 35.2	42.6	226 12.3	09.5	249 07.8	20.3	202 39.3	23.8	Miaplacidus	221 38.0	S69 47.6
23	134 50.3	151 34.8	41.4	241 13.1	09.7	264 10.1	20.3	217 41.6	23.7			
20 00	149 52.7	166 34.3	S 8 40.2	256 14.0	S22 09.9	279 12.4	S17 20.3	232 43.8	S22 23.7	Mirfak	308 35.8	N49 55.5
01	164 55.2	181 33.9	39.0	271 14.8	10.1	294 14.8	20.4	247 46.0	23.7	Nunki	75 54.7	S26 16.3
02	179 57.6	196 33.4	37.8	286 15.7	10.3	309 17.1	20.4	262 48.3	23.7	Peacock	53 14.8	S56 40.5
03	195 00.1	211 33.0	.. 36.6	301 16.5	.. 10.5	324 19.4	.. 20.4	277 50.5	.. 23.7	Pollux	243 23.6	N27 58.8
04	210 02.6	226 32.5	35.4	316 17.4	10.7	339 21.7	20.4	292 52.7	23.7	Procyon	244 56.2	N 5 10.5
05	225 05.0	241 32.1	34.2	331 18.3	10.9	354 24.1	20.5	307 55.0	23.7			
06	240 07.5	256 31.6	S 8 33.0	346 19.1	S22 11.1	9 26.4	S17 20.5	322 57.2	S22 23.7	Rasalhague	96 03.7	N12 32.8
07	255 10.0	271 31.2	31.8	1 20.0	11.3	24 28.7	20.5	337 59.5	23.7	Regulus	207 39.8	N11 52.6
08	270 12.4	286 30.7	30.6	16 20.8	11.5	39 31.1	20.5	353 01.7	23.7	Rigel	281 08.9	S 8 11.2
T 09	285 14.9	301 30.3	.. 29.4	31 21.7	.. 11.7	54 33.4	.. 20.6	8 03.9	.. 23.6	Rigil Kent.	139 47.1	S60 54.2
U 10	300 17.4	316 29.8	28.2	46 22.6	11.9	69 35.7	20.6	23 06.2	23.6	Sabik	102 09.0	S15 44.7
E 11	315 19.8	331 29.4	27.0	61 23.4	12.1	84 38.1	20.6	38 08.4	23.6			
S 12	330 22.3	346 28.9	S 8 25.8	76 24.3	S22 12.3	99 40.4	S17 20.7	53 10.7	S22 23.6	Schedar	349 37.3	N56 38.2
D 13	345 24.8	1 28.5	24.6	91 25.1	12.5	114 42.7	20.7	68 12.9	23.6	Shaula	96 17.8	S37 06.7
A 14	0 27.2	16 28.0	23.4	106 26.0	12.7	129 45.1	20.7	83 15.1	23.6	Sirius	258 30.7	S16 44.8
Y 15	15 29.7	31 27.6	.. 22.2	121 26.8	.. 12.9	144 47.4	.. 20.7	98 17.4	.. 23.6	Spica	158 27.7	S11 15.3
16	30 32.1	46 27.1	20.9	136 27.7	13.1	159 49.7	20.8	113 19.6	23.6	Suhail	222 49.7	S43 30.5
17	45 34.6	61 26.7	19.7	151 28.6	13.3	174 52.1	20.8	128 21.9	23.6			
18	60 37.1	76 26.2	S 8 18.5	166 29.4	S22 13.5	189 54.4	S17 20.8	143 24.1	S22 23.6	Vega	80 37.1	N38 47.9
19	75 39.5	91 25.8	17.3	181 30.3	13.7	204 56.7	20.8	158 26.3	23.5	Zuben'ubi	137 01.8	S16 06.9
20	90 42.0	106 25.3	16.1	196 31.1	13.9	219 59.1	20.9	173 28.6	23.5		SHA	Mer.Pass.
21	105 44.5	121 24.9	.. 14.9	211 32.0	.. 14.1	235 01.4	.. 20.9	188 30.8	.. 23.5	Venus	17 51.7	12 53
22	120 46.9	136 24.4	13.7	226 32.9	14.3	250 03.7	20.9	203 33.1	23.5	Mars	106 59.8	6 56
23	135 49.4	151 24.0	12.5	241 33.7	14.5	265 06.1	20.9	218 35.3	23.5	Jupiter	129 23.0	5 26
Mer.Pass. 14 02.1		v −0.5 d 1.2		v 0.9 d 0.2		v 2.3 d 0.0		v 2.2 d 0.0		Saturn	82 56.5	8 31

UT	SUN GHA	SUN Dec	MOON GHA	MOON v	MOON Dec	MOON d	MOON HP
d h	° ′	° ′	° ′	′	° ′	′	′
18 00	176 30.9	S11 43.5	152 29.1	13.4	S 5 34.4	10.5	55.9
01	191 30.9	42.6	167 01.5	13.3	5 23.9	10.5	56.0
02	206 31.0	41.7	181 33.8	13.3	5 13.4	10.6	56.0
03	221 31.0 ..	40.9	196 06.1	13.4	5 02.8	10.6	56.0
04	236 31.1	40.0	210 38.5	13.3	4 52.2	10.6	56.0
05	251 31.1	39.1	225 10.8	13.4	4 41.6	10.6	56.0
06	266 31.2	S11 38.2	239 43.2	13.3	S 4 31.0	10.7	56.1
07	281 31.2	37.3	254 15.5	13.3	4 20.3	10.7	56.1
08	296 31.3	36.4	268 47.8	13.3	4 09.6	10.8	56.1
S 09	311 31.3 ..	35.6	283 20.1	13.3	3 58.8	10.7	56.1
U 10	326 31.4	34.7	297 52.4	13.3	3 48.1	10.8	56.1
N 11	341 31.4	33.8	312 24.7	13.3	3 37.3	10.8	56.2
D 12	356 31.5	S11 32.9	326 57.0	13.3	S 3 26.5	10.8	56.2
A 13	11 31.5	32.0	341 29.3	13.3	3 15.7	10.9	56.2
Y 14	26 31.6	31.1	356 01.6	13.3	3 04.8	10.9	56.2
15	41 31.7 ..	30.2	10 33.9	13.3	2 53.9	10.8	56.2
16	56 31.7	29.4	25 06.2	13.2	2 43.1	11.0	56.3
17	71 31.8	28.5	39 38.4	13.3	2 32.1	10.9	56.3
18	86 31.8	S11 27.6	54 10.7	13.2	S 2 21.2	10.9	56.3
19	101 31.9	26.7	68 42.9	13.2	2 10.3	11.0	56.3
20	116 31.9	25.8	83 15.1	13.2	1 59.3	11.0	56.3
21	131 32.0 ..	24.9	97 47.3	13.2	1 48.3	11.0	56.4
22	146 32.0	24.0	112 19.5	13.2	1 37.3	11.0	56.4
23	161 32.1	23.2	126 51.7	13.1	1 26.3	11.0	56.4
19 00	176 32.1	S11 22.3	141 23.8	13.2	S 1 15.3	11.1	56.4
01	191 32.2	21.4	155 56.0	13.1	1 04.2	11.0	56.4
02	206 32.3	20.5	170 28.1	13.1	0 53.2	11.1	56.5
03	221 32.3 ..	19.6	185 00.2	13.1	0 42.1	11.1	56.5
04	236 32.4	18.7	199 32.3	13.1	0 31.0	11.0	56.5
05	251 32.4	17.8	214 04.4	13.1	0 20.0	11.1	56.5
06	266 32.5	S11 16.9	228 36.5	13.0	S 0 08.9	11.1	56.5
07	281 32.6	16.0	243 08.5	13.0	N 0 02.2	11.2	56.6
08	296 32.6	15.1	257 40.5	13.0	0 13.4	11.1	56.6
M 09	311 32.7 ..	14.3	272 12.5	13.0	0 24.5	11.1	56.6
O 10	326 32.7	13.4	286 44.5	13.0	0 35.6	11.1	56.6
N 11	341 32.8	12.5	301 16.5	12.9	0 46.7	11.1	56.6
D 12	356 32.8	S11 11.6	315 48.4	12.9	N 0 57.8	11.2	56.7
A 13	11 32.9	10.7	330 20.3	12.9	1 09.0	11.1	56.7
Y 14	26 33.0	09.8	344 52.2	12.8	1 20.1	11.1	56.7
15	41 33.0 ..	08.9	359 24.0	12.9	1 31.2	11.2	56.7
16	56 33.1	08.0	13 55.9	12.8	1 42.4	11.1	56.8
17	71 33.2	07.1	28 27.7	12.8	1 53.5	11.2	56.8
18	86 33.2	S11 06.2	42 59.5	12.7	N 2 04.7	11.1	56.8
19	101 33.3	05.3	57 31.2	12.7	2 15.8	11.1	56.8
20	116 33.3	04.4	72 02.9	12.7	2 26.9	11.1	56.8
21	131 33.4 ..	03.5	86 34.6	12.7	2 38.0	11.2	56.9
22	146 33.5	02.6	101 06.3	12.6	2 49.2	11.1	56.9
23	161 33.5	01.7	115 37.9	12.6	3 00.3	11.1	56.9
20 00	176 33.6	S11 00.9	130 09.5	12.6	N 3 11.4	11.1	56.9
01	191 33.7	11 00.0	144 41.1	12.5	3 22.5	11.1	56.9
02	206 33.7	10 59.1	159 12.6	12.5	3 33.6	11.0	57.0
03	221 33.8 ..	58.2	173 44.1	12.5	3 44.6	11.1	57.0
04	236 33.8	57.3	188 15.6	12.4	3 55.7	11.1	57.0
05	251 33.9	56.4	202 47.0	12.4	4 06.8	11.0	57.0
06	266 34.0	S10 55.5	217 18.4	12.4	N 4 17.8	11.1	57.1
07	281 34.0	54.6	231 49.8	12.3	4 28.9	11.0	57.1
08	296 34.1	53.7	246 21.1	12.3	4 39.9	11.0	57.1
T 09	311 34.2 ..	52.8	260 52.4	12.3	4 50.9	11.0	57.1
U 10	326 34.2	51.9	275 23.7	12.2	5 01.9	10.9	57.1
E 11	341 34.3	51.0	289 54.9	12.1	5 12.8	11.0	57.2
S 12	356 34.4	S10 50.1	304 26.0	12.2	N 5 23.8	10.9	57.2
D 13	11 34.4	49.2	318 57.2	12.1	5 34.7	10.9	57.2
A 14	26 34.5	48.3	333 28.3	12.0	5 45.6	10.9	57.2
Y 15	41 34.6 ..	47.4	347 59.3	12.0	5 56.5	10.9	57.3
16	56 34.6	46.5	2 30.3	12.0	6 07.4	10.8	57.3
17	71 34.7	45.6	17 01.3	11.9	6 18.2	10.9	57.3
18	86 34.8	S10 44.7	31 32.2	11.9	N 6 29.1	10.8	57.3
19	101 34.9	43.8	46 03.1	11.8	6 39.9	10.7	57.3
20	116 35.0	42.9	60 33.9	11.8	6 50.6	10.8	57.4
21	131 35.0 ..	42.0	75 04.7	11.7	7 01.4	10.7	57.4
22	146 35.1	41.1	89 35.4	11.7	7 12.1	10.7	57.4
23	161 35.1	40.2	104 06.1	11.6	N 7 22.8	10.7	57.4
	SD 16.2	d 0.9	SD 15.3		15.4		15.6

Lat.	Twilight Naut.	Twilight Civil	Sunrise	Moonrise 18	Moonrise 19	Moonrise 20	Moonrise 21
°	h m	h m	h m	h m	h m	h m	h m
N 72	05 57	07 16	08 31	08 58	08 48	08 38	08 27
N 70	05 57	07 08	08 15	08 52	08 48	08 44	08 40
68	05 57	07 02	08 02	08 48	08 48	08 49	08 51
66	05 57	06 57	07 51	08 44	08 49	08 54	09 00
64	05 57	06 52	07 42	08 40	08 49	08 58	09 08
62	05 56	06 48	07 34	08 38	08 49	09 01	09 14
60	05 56	06 44	07 27	08 35	08 49	09 04	09 20
N 58	05 55	06 41	07 21	08 33	08 49	09 06	09 25
56	05 55	06 38	07 16	08 31	08 49	09 09	09 30
54	05 54	06 35	07 11	08 29	08 50	09 11	09 34
52	05 53	06 33	07 07	08 27	08 50	09 13	09 37
50	05 53	06 30	07 03	08 26	08 50	09 14	09 41
45	05 51	06 25	06 55	08 23	08 50	09 18	09 48
N 40	05 49	06 20	06 48	08 20	08 50	09 21	09 54
35	05 46	06 16	06 42	08 17	08 50	09 24	10 00
30	05 44	06 12	06 36	08 15	08 51	09 27	10 04
20	05 39	06 04	06 27	08 12	08 51	09 31	10 13
N 10	05 32	05 57	06 18	08 08	08 51	09 35	10 20
0	05 25	05 49	06 10	08 05	08 51	09 38	10 27
S 10	05 16	05 41	06 02	08 02	08 52	09 42	10 34
20	05 04	05 31	05 54	07 59	08 52	09 46	10 41
30	04 49	05 19	05 43	07 56	08 52	09 50	10 50
35	04 40	05 11	05 38	07 53	08 53	09 53	10 55
40	04 28	05 02	05 31	07 51	08 53	09 56	11 00
45	04 14	04 52	05 23	07 48	08 53	09 59	11 07
S 50	03 55	04 39	05 13	07 45	08 54	10 03	11 15
52	03 46	04 32	05 09	07 43	08 54	10 05	11 18
54	03 36	04 25	05 04	07 42	08 54	10 07	11 23
56	03 24	04 17	04 59	07 40	08 54	10 10	11 29
58	03 09	04 08	04 52	07 38	08 54	10 12	11 32
S 60	02 52	03 58	04 46	07 36	08 55	10 15	11 38

Lat.	Sunset	Twilight Civil	Twilight Naut.	Moonset 18	Moonset 19	Moonset 20	Moonset 21
°	h m	h m	h m	h m	h m	h m	h m
N 72	15 58	17 14	18 33	20 01	21 48	23 39	25 36
N 70	16 15	17 21	18 32	20 04	21 44	23 27	25 15
68	16 28	17 27	18 32	20 06	21 41	23 18	24 58
66	16 38	17 33	18 32	20 08	21 38	23 11	24 45
64	16 47	17 37	18 32	20 10	21 36	23 04	24 34
62	16 55	17 41	18 33	20 12	21 34	22 59	24 25
60	17 01	17 45	18 33	20 13	21 33	22 54	24 17
N 58	17 07	17 48	18 34	20 14	21 31	22 50	24 10
56	17 12	17 51	18 34	20 15	21 30	22 46	24 04
54	17 17	17 53	18 35	20 16	21 29	22 43	23 58
52	17 21	17 56	18 35	20 17	21 28	22 40	23 53
50	17 25	17 58	18 36	20 18	21 27	22 37	23 49
45	17 33	18 03	18 38	20 19	21 25	22 31	23 39
N 40	17 40	18 08	18 40	20 21	21 23	22 26	23 31
35	17 46	18 12	18 42	20 22	21 21	22 22	23 25
30	17 52	18 16	18 44	20 23	21 20	22 19	23 19
20	18 01	18 23	18 49	20 24	21 18	22 12	23 08
N 10	18 09	18 31	18 55	20 26	21 16	22 06	22 59
0	18 17	18 38	19 03	20 27	21 14	22 01	22 51
S 10	18 25	18 47	19 12	20 29	21 12	21 56	22 42
20	18 34	18 56	19 23	20 30	21 10	21 50	22 33
30	18 44	19 08	19 38	20 32	21 07	21 44	22 23
35	18 50	19 16	19 47	20 33	21 06	21 40	22 17
40	18 56	19 24	19 58	20 34	21 04	21 36	22 10
45	19 04	19 35	20 13	20 35	21 03	21 31	22 03
S 50	19 13	19 48	20 31	20 36	21 00	21 26	21 53
52	19 18	19 54	20 40	20 37	20 59	21 23	21 49
54	19 22	20 01	20 50	20 38	20 58	21 20	21 44
56	19 28	20 09	21 02	20 38	20 57	21 17	21 39
58	19 34	20 18	21 16	20 39	20 56	21 13	21 33
S 60	19 40	20 28	21 32	20 40	20 54	21 09	21 27

	SUN Eqn. of Time 00h	SUN Eqn. of Time 12h	SUN Mer. Pass.	MOON Mer. Pass. Upper	MOON Mer. Pass. Lower	Age	Phase
Day							
d	m s	m s	h m	h m	h m	d	%
18	13 57	13 54	12 14	14 16	01 54	03	7
19	13 52	13 49	12 14	15 02	02 39	04	13
20	13 46	13 43	12 14	15 50	03 26	05	21

UT	ARIES GHA	VENUS −3.9 GHA	Dec	MARS +0.9 GHA	Dec	JUPITER −2.1 GHA	Dec	SATURN +0.6 GHA	Dec
21 00	150 51.9	166 23.5	S 8 11.3	256 34.6	S22 14.7	280 08.4	S17 21.0	233 37.5	S22 23.5
01	165 54.3	181 23.1	10.1	271 35.4	14.9	295 10.7	21.0	248 39.8	23.5
02	180 56.8	196 22.6	08.9	286 36.3	15.1	310 13.1	21.0	263 42.0	23.5
03	195 59.3	211 22.2 ..	07.6	301 37.1 ..	15.3	325 15.4 ..	21.0	278 44.3 ..	23.5
04	211 01.7	226 21.8	06.4	316 38.0	15.5	340 17.8	21.1	293 46.5	23.4
05	226 04.2	241 21.3	05.2	331 38.9	15.7	355 20.1	21.1	308 48.7	23.4
W 06	241 06.6	256 20.9	S 8 04.0	346 39.7	S22 15.9	10 22.4	S17 21.1	323 51.0	S22 23.4
E 07	256 09.1	271 20.4	02.8	1 40.6	16.1	25 24.8	21.1	338 53.2	23.4
D 08	271 11.6	286 20.0	01.6	16 41.4	16.3	40 27.1	21.2	353 55.5	23.4
N 09	286 14.0	301 19.5	8 00.4	31 42.3 ..	16.4	55 29.4 ..	21.2	8 57.7 ..	23.4
E 10	301 16.5	316 19.1	7 59.2	46 43.2	16.6	70 31.8	21.2	23 59.9	23.4
S 11	316 19.0	331 18.6	57.9	61 44.0	16.8	85 34.1	21.2	39 02.2	23.4
D 12	331 21.4	346 18.2	S 7 56.7	76 44.9	S22 17.0	100 36.5	S17 21.2	54 04.4	S22 23.4
A 13	346 23.9	1 17.8	55.5	91 45.7	17.2	115 38.8	21.3	69 06.7	23.4
Y 14	1 26.4	16 17.3	54.3	106 46.6	17.4	130 41.1	21.3	84 08.9	23.3
15	16 28.8	31 16.9 ..	53.1	121 47.5 ..	17.6	145 43.5 ..	21.3	99 11.2 ..	23.3
16	31 31.3	46 16.4	51.9	136 48.3	17.8	160 45.8	21.3	114 13.4	23.3
17	46 33.7	61 16.0	50.6	151 49.2	18.0	175 48.2	21.4	129 15.6	23.3
18	61 36.2	76 15.6	S 7 49.4	166 50.0	S22 18.2	190 50.5	S17 21.4	144 17.9	S22 23.3
19	76 38.7	91 15.1	48.2	181 50.9	18.4	205 52.9	21.4	159 20.1	23.3
20	91 41.1	106 14.7	47.0	196 51.7	18.6	220 55.2	21.4	174 22.4	23.3
21	106 43.6	121 14.2 ..	45.8	211 52.6 ..	18.8	235 57.5 ..	21.5	189 24.6 ..	23.3
22	121 46.1	136 13.8	44.6	226 53.5	18.9	250 59.9	21.5	204 26.9	23.3
23	136 48.5	151 13.4	43.3	241 54.3	19.1	266 02.2	21.5	219 29.1	23.3
22 00	151 51.0	166 12.9	S 7 42.1	256 55.2	S22 19.3	281 04.6	S17 21.5	234 31.4	S22 23.2
01	166 53.5	181 12.5	40.9	271 56.0	19.5	296 06.9	21.6	249 33.6	23.2
02	181 55.9	196 12.1	39.7	286 56.9	19.7	311 09.3	21.6	264 35.8	23.2
03	196 58.4	211 11.6 ..	38.5	301 57.8 ..	19.9	326 11.6 ..	21.6	279 38.1 ..	23.2
04	212 00.9	226 11.2	37.2	316 58.6	20.1	341 13.9	21.6	294 40.3	23.2
05	227 03.3	241 10.8	36.0	331 59.5	20.3	356 16.3	21.6	309 42.6	23.2
T 06	242 05.8	256 10.3	S 7 34.8	347 00.3	S22 20.5	11 18.6	S17 21.7	324 44.8	S22 23.2
H 07	257 08.2	271 09.9	33.6	2 01.2	20.7	26 21.0	21.7	339 47.1	23.2
U 08	272 10.7	286 09.4	32.4	17 02.1	20.8	41 23.3	21.7	354 49.3	23.2
R 09	287 13.2	301 09.0 ..	31.1	32 02.9 ..	21.0	56 25.7 ..	21.7	9 51.6 ..	23.1
S 10	302 15.6	316 08.6	29.9	47 03.8	21.2	71 28.0	21.8	24 53.8	23.1
11	317 18.1	331 08.1	28.7	62 04.6	21.4	86 30.4	21.8	39 56.0	23.1
D 12	332 20.6	346 07.7	S 7 27.5	77 05.5	S22 21.6	101 32.7	S17 21.8	54 58.3	S22 23.1
A 13	347 23.0	1 07.3	26.2	92 06.4	21.8	116 35.1	21.8	70 00.5	23.1
Y 14	2 25.5	16 06.8	25.0	107 07.2	22.0	131 37.4	21.8	85 02.8	23.1
15	17 28.0	31 06.4 ..	23.8	122 08.1 ..	22.2	146 39.8 ..	21.9	100 05.0 ..	23.1
16	32 30.4	46 06.0	22.6	137 08.9	22.3	161 42.1	21.9	115 07.3	23.1
17	47 32.9	61 05.5	21.3	152 09.8	22.5	176 44.5	21.9	130 09.5	23.1
18	62 35.3	76 05.1	S 7 20.1	167 10.7	S22 22.7	191 46.8	S17 21.9	145 11.8	S22 23.1
19	77 37.8	91 04.7	18.9	182 11.5	22.9	206 49.2	22.0	160 14.0	23.0
20	92 40.3	106 04.2	17.7	197 12.4	23.1	221 51.5	22.0	175 16.3	23.0
21	107 42.7	121 03.8 ..	16.4	212 13.2 ..	23.3	236 53.9 ..	22.0	190 18.5 ..	23.0
22	122 45.2	136 03.4	15.2	227 14.1	23.4	251 56.2	22.0	205 20.8	23.0
23	137 47.7	151 03.0	14.0	242 14.9	23.6	266 58.6	22.0	220 23.0	23.0
23 00	152 50.1	166 02.5	S 7 12.8	257 15.8	S22 23.8	282 00.9	S17 22.1	235 25.2	S22 23.0
01	167 52.6	181 02.1	11.5	272 16.7	24.0	297 03.3	22.1	250 27.5	23.0
02	182 55.1	196 01.7	10.3	287 17.5	24.2	312 05.6	22.1	265 29.7	23.0
03	197 57.5	211 01.2 ..	09.1	302 18.4 ..	24.4	327 08.0 ..	22.1	280 32.0 ..	23.0
04	213 00.0	226 00.8	07.8	317 19.2	24.6	342 10.3	22.1	295 34.2	23.0
05	228 02.5	241 00.4	06.6	332 20.1	24.7	357 12.7	22.2	310 36.5	22.9
06	243 04.9	256 00.0	S 7 05.4	347 21.0	S22 24.9	12 15.0	S17 22.2	325 38.7	S22 22.9
07	258 07.4	270 59.5	04.2	2 21.8	25.1	27 17.4	22.2	340 41.0	22.9
08	273 09.8	285 59.1	02.9	17 22.7	25.3	42 19.7	22.2	355 43.2	22.9
F 09	288 12.3	300 58.7 ..	01.7	32 23.5 ..	25.5	57 22.1 ..	22.2	10 45.5 ..	22.9
R 10	303 14.8	315 58.2	7 00.5	47 24.4	25.6	72 24.4	22.3	25 47.7	22.9
I 11	318 17.2	330 57.8	6 59.2	62 25.3	25.8	87 26.8	22.3	40 50.0	22.9
D 12	333 19.7	345 57.4	S 6 58.0	77 26.1	S22 26.0	102 29.2	S17 22.3	55 52.2	S22 22.9
A 13	348 22.2	0 57.0	56.8	92 27.0	26.2	117 31.5	22.3	70 54.5	22.9
Y 14	3 24.6	15 56.5	55.5	107 27.8	26.4	132 33.9	22.3	85 56.7	22.8
15	18 27.1	30 56.1 ..	54.3	122 28.7 ..	26.6	147 36.2 ..	22.4	100 59.0 ..	22.8
16	33 29.5	45 55.7	53.1	137 29.6	26.7	162 38.6	22.4	116 01.2	22.8
17	48 32.0	60 55.3	51.8	152 30.4	26.9	177 40.9	22.4	131 03.5	22.8
18	63 34.5	75 54.8	S 6 50.6	167 31.3	S22 27.1	192 43.3	S17 22.4	146 05.7	S22 22.8
19	78 37.0	90 54.4	49.4	182 32.1	27.3	207 45.6	22.4	161 08.0	22.8
20	93 39.4	105 54.0	48.1	197 33.0	27.4	222 48.0	22.5	176 10.2	22.8
21	108 41.9	120 53.6 ..	46.9	212 33.9 ..	27.6	237 50.4 ..	22.5	191 12.5 ..	22.8
22	123 44.3	135 53.1	45.7	227 34.7	27.8	252 52.7	22.5	206 14.7	22.8
23	138 46.8	150 52.7	44.4	242 35.6	28.0	267 55.1	22.5	221 17.0	22.8
Mer.Pass. 13 50.3		v −0.4	d 1.2	v 0.9	d 0.2	v 2.3	d 0.0	v 2.2	d 0.0

STARS

Name	SHA	Dec
Acamar	315 16.1	S40 14.4
Achernar	335 24.8	S57 09.1
Acrux	173 05.1	S63 11.8
Adhara	255 09.8	S29 00.2
Aldebaran	290 45.7	N16 32.5
Alioth	166 17.5	N55 51.5
Alkaid	152 56.2	N49 13.2
Al Na'ir	27 40.3	S46 52.5
Alnilam	275 43.0	S 1 11.7
Alphard	217 52.7	S 8 44.4
Alphecca	126 08.3	N26 39.1
Alpheratz	357 40.5	N29 11.3
Altair	62 05.4	N 8 54.9
Ankaa	353 12.9	S42 12.8
Antares	112 22.4	S26 28.1
Arcturus	145 52.7	N19 05.2
Atria	107 21.5	S69 03.1
Avior	234 16.1	S59 34.3
Bellatrix	278 28.5	N 6 21.7
Betelgeuse	270 57.7	N 7 24.4
Canopus	263 54.4	S52 42.7
Capella	280 29.6	N46 00.9
Deneb	49 29.7	N45 20.6
Denebola	182 30.1	N14 28.2
Diphda	348 53.0	S17 53.5
Dubhe	193 47.3	N61 39.1
Elnath	278 08.5	N28 37.2
Eltanin	90 44.9	N51 29.0
Enif	33 44.3	N 9 57.4
Fomalhaut	15 20.9	S29 31.7
Gacrux	171 56.8	S57 12.7
Gienah	175 48.7	S17 38.5
Hadar	148 43.0	S60 27.3
Hamal	327 57.3	N23 32.7
Kaus Aust.	83 39.8	S34 22.3
Kochab	137 19.8	N74 04.7
Markab	13 35.5	N15 18.0
Menkar	314 11.8	N 4 09.4
Menkent	148 03.6	S36 27.3
Miaplacidus	221 38.0	S69 47.6
Mirfak	308 35.8	N49 55.5
Nunki	75 54.6	S26 16.3
Peacock	53 14.8	S56 40.4
Pollux	243 23.6	N27 58.8
Procyon	244 56.2	N 5 10.5
Rasalhague	96 03.6	N12 32.8
Regulus	207 39.8	N11 52.6
Rigel	281 08.9	S 8 11.2
Rigil Kent.	139 47.1	S60 54.2
Sabik	102 09.0	S15 44.7
Schedar	349 37.3	N56 38.2
Shaula	96 17.8	S37 06.7
Sirius	258 30.7	S16 44.8
Spica	158 27.7	S11 15.3
Suhail	222 49.7	S43 30.5
Vega	80 37.1	N38 47.9
Zuben'ubi	137 01.8	S16 06.9

	SHA	Mer.Pass.
Venus	14 21.9	12 56
Mars	105 04.2	6 52
Jupiter	129 13.6	5 15
Saturn	82 40.4	8 21

UT	SUN GHA	SUN Dec	MOON GHA	v	MOON Dec	d	HP
d h	° ′	° ′	° ′	′	° ′	′	′
21 00	176 35.2	S10 39.3	118 36.7	11.6	N 7 33.5	10.6	57.5
01	191 35.3	38.4	133 07.3	11.5	7 44.1	10.6	57.5
02	206 35.3	37.5	147 37.8	11.5	7 54.7	10.6	57.5
03	221 35.4	.. 36.6	162 08.3	11.4	8 05.3	10.5	57.5
04	236 35.5	35.7	176 38.7	11.4	8 15.8	10.5	57.6
05	251 35.6	34.8	191 09.1	11.3	8 26.3	10.4	57.6
W 06	266 35.6	S10 33.8	205 39.4	11.3	N 8 36.7	10.4	57.6
E 07	281 35.7	32.9	220 09.7	11.2	8 47.2	10.4	57.6
D 08	296 35.8	32.0	234 39.9	11.2	8 57.6	10.3	57.6
N 09	311 35.8	.. 31.1	249 10.1	11.1	9 07.9	10.3	57.7
E 10	326 35.9	30.2	263 40.2	11.1	9 18.2	10.3	57.7
S 11	341 36.0	29.3	278 10.3	11.0	9 28.5	10.2	57.7
D 12	356 36.1	S10 28.4	292 40.3	10.9	N 9 38.7	10.2	57.7
A 13	11 36.1	27.5	307 10.2	10.9	9 48.9	10.1	57.8
Y 14	26 36.2	26.6	321 40.1	10.8	9 59.0	10.1	57.8
15	41 36.3	.. 25.7	336 09.9	10.8	10 09.1	10.1	57.8
16	56 36.4	24.8	350 39.7	10.7	10 19.2	10.0	57.8
17	71 36.4	23.9	5 09.4	10.7	10 29.2	9.9	57.9
18	86 36.5	S10 23.0	19 39.1	10.6	N10 39.1	9.9	57.9
19	101 36.6	22.1	34 08.7	10.5	10 49.0	9.9	57.9
20	116 36.7	21.2	48 38.2	10.5	10 58.9	9.8	57.9
21	131 36.7	.. 20.2	63 07.7	10.4	11 08.7	9.7	57.9
22	146 36.8	19.3	77 37.1	10.3	11 18.4	9.7	58.0
23	161 36.9	18.4	92 06.4	10.3	11 28.1	9.6	58.0
22 00	176 37.0	S10 17.5	106 35.7	10.2	N11 37.7	9.6	58.0
01	191 37.1	16.6	121 04.9	10.2	11 47.3	9.5	58.0
02	206 37.1	15.7	135 34.1	10.0	11 56.8	9.5	58.1
03	221 37.2	.. 14.8	150 03.1	10.1	12 06.3	9.4	58.1
04	236 37.3	13.9	164 32.2	9.9	12 15.7	9.4	58.1
05	251 37.4	13.0	179 01.1	9.9	12 25.1	9.2	58.1
T 06	266 37.4	S10 12.1	193 30.0	9.8	N12 34.3	9.3	58.2
H 07	281 37.5	11.1	207 58.8	9.8	12 43.6	9.1	58.2
U 08	296 37.6	10.2	222 27.6	9.7	12 52.7	9.1	58.2
R 09	311 37.7	.. 09.3	236 56.3	9.6	13 01.8	9.0	58.2
S 10	326 37.8	08.4	251 24.9	9.6	13 10.8	9.0	58.3
D 11	341 37.8	07.5	265 53.5	9.5	13 19.8	8.9	58.3
A 12	356 37.9	S10 06.6	280 22.0	9.4	N13 28.7	8.8	58.3
Y 13	11 38.0	05.7	294 50.4	9.3	13 37.5	8.8	58.3
14	26 38.1	04.8	309 18.7	9.3	13 46.3	8.6	58.3
15	41 38.2	.. 03.8	323 47.0	9.2	13 54.9	8.7	58.4
16	56 38.3	02.9	338 15.2	9.2	14 03.6	8.5	58.4
17	71 38.3	02.0	352 43.4	9.1	14 12.1	8.4	58.4
18	86 38.4	S10 01.1	7 11.5	9.0	N14 20.5	8.4	58.4
19	101 38.5	10 00.2	21 39.5	8.9	14 28.9	8.3	58.5
20	116 38.6	9 59.3	36 07.4	8.9	14 37.2	8.3	58.5
21	131 38.7	.. 58.4	50 35.3	8.8	14 45.5	8.1	58.5
22	146 38.7	57.4	65 03.1	8.7	14 53.6	8.1	58.5
23	161 38.8	56.5	79 30.8	8.7	15 01.7	8.0	58.6
23 00	176 38.9	S 9 55.6	93 58.5	8.5	N15 09.7	7.9	58.6
01	191 39.0	54.7	108 26.0	8.6	15 17.6	7.8	58.6
02	206 39.1	53.8	122 53.6	8.4	15 25.4	7.7	58.6
03	221 39.2	.. 52.9	137 21.0	8.4	15 33.1	7.7	58.6
04	236 39.3	52.0	151 48.4	8.3	15 40.8	7.5	58.7
05	251 39.3	51.0	166 15.7	8.2	15 48.3	7.5	58.7
F 06	266 39.4	S 9 50.1	180 42.9	8.2	N15 55.8	7.4	58.7
R 07	281 39.5	49.2	195 10.1	8.0	16 03.2	7.3	58.7
I 08	296 39.6	48.3	209 37.1	8.1	16 10.5	7.1	58.8
D 09	311 39.7	.. 47.4	224 04.2	7.9	16 17.6	7.2	58.8
A 10	326 39.8	46.4	238 31.1	7.9	16 24.8	7.0	58.8
Y 11	341 39.9	45.5	252 58.0	7.8	16 31.8	6.9	58.8
12	356 39.9	S 9 44.6	267 24.8	7.7	N16 38.7	6.8	58.9
13	11 40.0	43.7	281 51.5	7.7	16 45.5	6.7	58.9
14	26 40.1	42.8	296 18.2	7.6	16 52.2	6.6	58.9
15	41 40.2	.. 41.9	310 44.8	7.5	16 58.8	6.6	58.9
16	56 40.3	40.9	325 11.3	7.5	17 05.4	6.4	58.9
17	71 40.4	40.0	339 37.8	7.3	17 11.8	6.3	59.0
18	86 40.5	S 9 39.1	354 04.1	7.4	N17 18.1	6.2	59.0
19	101 40.6	38.2	8 30.5	7.2	17 24.3	6.1	59.0
20	116 40.7	37.2	22 56.7	7.2	17 30.4	6.0	59.0
21	131 40.7	.. 36.3	37 22.9	7.1	17 36.4	5.9	59.1
22	146 40.8	35.4	51 49.0	7.1	17 42.3	5.8	59.1
23	161 40.9	34.5	66 15.1	6.9	N17 48.1	5.7	59.1
	SD 16.2	d 0.9	SD 15.7		15.9		16.0

Twilight / Sunrise / Moonrise

Lat.	Naut.	Civil	Sunrise	Moonrise 21	22	23	24
°	h m	h m	h m	h m	h m	h m	h m
N 72	05 44	07 02	08 15	08 27	08 14	07 53	▭
N 70	05 45	06 56	08 00	08 40	08 37	08 33	08 30
68	05 46	06 51	07 49	08 51	08 54	09 01	09 14
66	05 47	06 46	07 40	09 00	09 09	09 22	09 44
64	05 48	06 43	07 32	09 08	09 21	09 39	10 06
62	05 48	06 39	07 25	09 14	09 31	09 53	10 24
60	05 48	06 36	07 19	09 20	09 40	10 05	10 39
N 58	05 48	06 34	07 14	09 25	09 47	10 15	10 52
56	05 48	06 31	07 09	09 30	09 54	10 24	11 03
54	05 48	06 29	07 05	09 34	10 00	10 32	11 12
52	05 48	06 27	07 01	09 37	10 06	10 39	11 21
50	05 47	06 25	06 58	09 41	10 11	10 46	11 29
45	05 46	06 20	06 50	09 48	10 22	11 00	11 45
N 40	05 45	06 16	06 44	09 54	10 31	11 12	11 59
35	05 43	06 13	06 38	10 00	10 38	11 22	12 11
30	05 41	06 09	06 33	10 04	10 45	11 30	12 21
20	05 37	06 03	06 25	10 13	10 57	11 46	12 38
N 10	05 31	05 56	06 17	10 20	11 08	11 59	12 54
0	05 25	05 49	06 10	10 27	11 18	12 11	13 08
S 10	05 16	05 41	06 03	10 34	11 28	12 24	13 23
20	05 06	05 32	05 55	10 41	11 38	12 37	13 38
30	04 52	05 21	05 46	10 50	11 51	12 53	13 56
35	04 43	05 14	05 40	10 55	11 58	13 02	14 06
40	04 32	05 06	05 34	11 00	12 06	13 12	14 18
45	04 19	04 56	05 27	11 07	12 16	13 25	14 33
S 50	04 02	04 44	05 19	11 15	12 27	13 40	14 50
52	03 53	04 38	05 15	11 18	12 33	13 47	14 58
54	03 44	04 32	05 10	11 23	12 39	13 54	15 07
56	03 33	04 25	05 05	11 27	12 45	14 03	15 17
58	03 20	04 16	05 00	11 32	12 53	14 13	15 29
S 60	03 04	04 07	04 54	11 38	13 01	14 24	15 43

Sunset / Twilight / Moonset

Lat.	Sunset	Civil	Naut.	Moonset 21	22	23	24
°	h m	h m	h m	h m	h m	h m	h m
N 72	16 14	17 27	18 46	25 36	01 36	03 47	▭
N 70	16 28	17 33	18 44	25 15	01 15	03 08	05 07
68	16 39	17 38	18 43	24 58	00 58	02 41	04 24
66	16 49	17 42	18 42	24 45	00 45	02 21	03 55
64	16 57	17 46	18 41	24 34	00 34	02 05	03 33
62	17 03	17 49	18 40	24 25	00 25	01 51	03 16
60	17 09	17 52	18 40	24 17	00 17	01 40	03 01
N 58	17 14	17 55	18 40	24 10	00 10	01 30	02 49
56	17 19	17 57	18 40	24 04	00 04	01 22	02 38
54	17 23	17 59	18 40	23 58	25 14	01 14	02 29
52	17 27	18 01	18 40	23 53	25 08	01 08	02 20
50	17 30	18 03	18 41	23 49	25 01	01 01	02 13
45	17 37	18 07	18 41	23 39	24 48	00 48	01 57
N 40	17 44	18 11	18 43	23 31	24 38	00 38	01 44
35	17 49	18 15	18 44	23 25	24 28	00 28	01 33
30	17 54	18 18	18 46	23 19	24 20	00 20	01 23
20	18 02	18 25	18 50	23 08	24 06	00 06	01 06
N 10	18 10	18 31	18 56	22 59	23 54	24 52	00 52
0	18 17	18 38	19 02	22 51	23 43	24 38	00 38
S 10	18 24	18 45	19 10	22 42	23 32	24 24	00 24
20	18 32	18 54	19 21	22 33	23 20	24 10	00 10
30	18 41	19 05	19 34	22 23	23 06	23 53	24 46
35	18 46	19 12	19 43	22 17	22 58	23 44	24 36
40	18 52	19 20	19 54	22 10	22 49	23 33	24 23
45	18 59	19 30	20 07	22 03	22 38	23 20	24 09
S 50	19 07	19 42	20 24	21 53	22 26	23 04	23 51
52	19 11	19 47	20 32	21 49	22 20	22 57	23 43
54	19 16	19 54	20 41	21 44	22 13	22 49	23 33
56	19 20	20 01	20 52	21 39	22 06	22 39	23 23
58	19 26	20 09	21 05	21 33	21 58	22 29	23 11
S 60	19 32	20 18	21 20	21 27	21 49	22 17	22 57

SUN / MOON

Day	Eqn. of Time 00h	Eqn. of Time 12h	Mer. Pass.	Mer. Pass. Upper	Mer. Pass. Lower	Age	Phase
d	m s	m s	h m	h m	h m	d	%
21	13 39	13 36	12 14	16 39	04 14	06	30
22	13 32	13 28	12 13	17 30	05 04	07	41
23	13 25	13 20	12 13	18 25	05 57	08	52

UT	ARIES	VENUS −3.9		MARS +0.9		JUPITER −2.1		SATURN +0.6		STARS		
	GHA	GHA	Dec	GHA	Dec	GHA	Dec	GHA	Dec	Name	SHA	Dec
d h	° ′	° ′	° ′	° ′	° ′	° ′	° ′	° ′	° ′		° ′	° ′
24 00	153 49.3	165 52.3	S 6 43.2	257 36.4	S22 28.2	282 57.4	S17 22.5	236 19.2	S22 22.7	Acamar	315 16.1	S40 14.4
01	168 51.7	180 51.9	42.0	272 37.3	28.3	297 59.8	22.6	251 21.5	22.7	Achernar	335 24.8	S57 09.1
02	183 54.2	195 51.5	40.7	287 38.2	28.5	313 02.2	22.6	266 23.7	22.7	Acrux	173 05.0	S63 11.8
03	198 56.7	210 51.0 . .	39.5	302 39.0 . .	28.7	328 04.5 . .	22.6	281 26.0 . .	22.7	Adhara	255 09.8	S29 00.2
04	213 59.1	225 50.6	38.3	317 39.9	28.9	343 06.9	22.6	296 28.2	22.7	Aldebaran	290 45.7	N16 32.5
05	229 01.6	240 50.2	37.0	332 40.7	29.0	358 09.2	22.6	311 30.5	22.7			
06	244 04.1	255 49.8	S 6 35.8	347 41.6	S22 29.2	13 11.6	S17 22.7	326 32.7	S22 22.7	Alioth	166 17.5	N55 51.6
07	259 06.5	270 49.4	34.6	2 42.5	29.4	28 14.0	22.7	341 35.0	22.7	Alkaid	152 56.1	N49 13.2
S 08	274 09.0	285 48.9	33.3	17 43.3	29.6	43 16.3	22.7	356 37.2	22.7	Al Na'ir	27 40.2	S46 52.4
A 09	289 11.5	300 48.5 . .	32.1	32 44.2 . .	29.8	58 18.7 . .	22.7	11 39.5 . .	22.7	Alnilam	275 43.0	S 1 11.7
T 10	304 13.9	315 48.1	30.8	47 45.0	29.9	73 21.0	22.7	26 41.7	22.6	Alphard	217 52.6	S 8 44.4
U 11	319 16.4	330 47.7	29.6	62 45.9	30.1	88 23.4	22.8	41 44.0	22.6			
R 12	334 18.8	345 47.3	S 6 28.4	77 46.8	S22 30.3	103 25.8	S17 22.8	56 46.2	S22 22.6	Alphecca	126 08.3	N26 39.1
D 13	349 21.3	0 46.8	27.1	92 47.6	30.5	118 28.1	22.8	71 48.5	22.6	Alpheratz	357 40.5	N29 11.3
A 14	4 23.8	15 46.4	25.9	107 48.5	30.6	133 30.5	22.8	86 50.7	22.6	Altair	62 05.4	N 8 54.9
Y 15	19 26.2	30 46.0 . .	24.7	122 49.4 . .	30.8	148 32.9 . .	22.8	101 53.0 . .	22.6	Ankaa	353 13.0	S42 12.7
16	34 28.7	45 45.6	23.4	137 50.2	31.0	163 35.2	22.8	116 55.2	22.6	Antares	112 22.4	S26 28.1
17	49 31.2	60 45.2	22.2	152 51.1	31.2	178 37.6	22.9	131 57.5	22.6			
18	64 33.6	75 44.7	S 6 20.9	167 51.9	S22 31.3	193 40.0	S17 22.9	146 59.7	S22 22.6	Arcturus	145 52.7	N19 05.2
19	79 36.1	90 44.3	19.7	182 52.8	31.5	208 42.3	22.9	162 02.0	22.5	Atria	107 21.4	S69 03.1
20	94 38.6	105 43.9	18.5	197 53.7	31.7	223 44.7	22.9	177 04.2	22.5	Avior	234 16.1	S59 34.3
21	109 41.0	120 43.5 . .	17.2	212 54.5 . .	31.8	238 47.0 . .	22.9	192 06.5 . .	22.5	Bellatrix	278 28.5	N 6 21.7
22	124 43.5	135 43.1	16.0	227 55.4	32.0	253 49.4	23.0	207 08.8	22.5	Betelgeuse	270 57.7	N 7 24.4
23	139 45.9	150 42.7	14.7	242 56.2	32.2	268 51.8	23.0	222 11.0	22.5			
25 00	154 48.4	165 42.3	S 6 13.5	257 57.1	S22 32.4	283 54.1	S17 23.0	237 13.3	S22 22.5	Canopus	263 54.5	S52 42.8
01	169 50.9	180 41.8	12.2	272 58.0	32.5	298 56.5	23.0	252 15.5	22.5	Capella	280 29.6	N46 00.9
02	184 53.3	195 41.4	11.0	287 58.8	32.7	313 58.9	23.0	267 17.8	22.5	Deneb	49 29.7	N45 20.6
03	199 55.8	210 41.0 . .	09.8	302 59.7 . .	32.9	329 01.2 . .	23.0	282 20.0 . .	22.5	Denebola	182 30.1	N14 28.2
04	214 58.3	225 40.6	08.5	318 00.5	33.0	344 03.6	23.1	297 22.3	22.5	Diphda	348 53.0	S17 53.5
05	230 00.7	240 40.2	07.3	333 01.4	33.2	359 06.0	23.1	312 24.5	22.4			
06	245 03.2	255 39.8	S 6 06.0	348 02.3	S22 33.4	14 08.4	S17 23.1	327 26.8	S22 22.4	Dubhe	193 47.2	N61 39.1
07	260 05.7	270 39.4	04.8	3 03.1	33.6	29 10.7	23.1	342 29.0	22.4	Elnath	278 08.5	N28 37.2
08	275 08.1	285 38.9	03.5	18 04.0	33.7	44 13.1	23.1	357 31.3	22.4	Eltanin	90 44.9	N51 29.0
S 09	290 10.6	300 38.5 . .	02.3	33 04.9 . .	33.9	59 15.5 . .	23.1	12 33.6 . .	22.4	Enif	33 44.3	N 9 57.4
U 10	305 13.1	315 38.1	6 01.1	48 05.7	34.1	74 17.8	23.2	27 35.8	22.4	Fomalhaut	15 20.9	S29 31.7
N 11	320 15.5	330 37.7	5 59.8	63 06.6	34.2	89 20.2	23.2	42 38.1	22.4			
D 12	335 18.0	345 37.3	S 5 58.6	78 07.4	S22 34.4	104 22.6	S17 23.2	57 40.3	S22 22.4	Gacrux	171 56.8	S57 12.7
A 13	350 20.4	0 36.9	57.3	93 08.3	34.6	119 24.9	23.2	72 42.6	22.4	Gienah	175 48.7	S17 38.5
Y 14	5 22.9	15 36.5	56.1	108 09.2	34.7	134 27.3	23.2	87 44.8	22.4	Hadar	148 42.9	S60 27.3
15	20 25.4	30 36.1 . .	54.8	123 10.0 . .	34.9	149 29.7 . .	23.2	102 47.1 . .	22.3	Hamal	327 57.3	N23 32.7
16	35 27.8	45 35.6	53.6	138 10.9	35.1	164 32.1	23.3	117 49.3	22.3	Kaus Aust.	83 39.8	S34 22.3
17	50 30.3	60 35.2	52.3	153 11.7	35.2	179 34.4	23.3	132 51.6	22.3			
18	65 32.8	75 34.8	S 5 51.1	168 12.6	S22 35.4	194 36.8	S17 23.3	147 53.8	S22 22.3	Kochab	137 19.8	N74 04.7
19	80 35.2	90 34.4	49.8	183 13.5	35.6	209 39.2	23.3	162 56.1	22.3	Markab	13 35.5	N15 18.0
20	95 37.7	105 34.0	48.6	198 14.3	35.7	224 41.5	23.3	177 58.4	22.3	Menkar	314 11.8	N 4 09.4
21	110 40.2	120 33.6 . .	47.3	213 15.2 . .	35.9	239 43.9 . .	23.3	193 00.6 . .	22.3	Menkent	148 03.6	S36 27.3
22	125 42.6	135 33.2	46.1	228 16.1	36.1	254 46.3	23.3	208 02.9	22.3	Miaplacidus	221 38.1	S69 47.7
23	140 45.1	150 32.8	44.8	243 16.9	36.2	269 48.7	23.4	223 05.1	22.3			
26 00	155 47.6	165 32.4	S 5 43.6	258 17.8	S22 36.4	284 51.0	S17 23.4	238 07.4	S22 22.2	Mirfak	308 35.9	N49 55.5
01	170 50.0	180 32.0	42.4	273 18.6	36.6	299 53.4	23.4	253 09.6	22.2	Nunki	75 54.6	S26 16.3
02	185 52.5	195 31.5	41.1	288 19.5	36.7	314 55.8	23.4	268 11.9	22.2	Peacock	53 14.8	S56 40.4
03	200 54.9	210 31.1 . .	39.9	303 20.4 . .	36.9	329 58.2 . .	23.4	283 14.2 . .	22.2	Pollux	243 23.6	N27 58.8
04	215 57.4	225 30.7	38.6	318 21.2	37.1	345 00.5	23.4	298 16.4	22.2	Procyon	244 56.2	N 5 10.5
05	230 59.9	240 30.3	37.4	333 22.1	37.2	0 02.9	23.5	313 18.7	22.2			
06	246 02.3	255 29.9	S 5 36.1	348 22.9	S22 37.4	15 05.3	S17 23.5	328 20.9	S22 22.2	Rasalhague	96 03.6	N12 32.8
07	261 04.8	270 29.5	34.9	3 23.8	37.6	30 07.7	23.5	343 23.2	22.2	Regulus	207 39.8	N11 52.6
08	276 07.3	285 29.1	33.6	18 24.7	37.7	45 10.0	23.5	358 25.4	22.2	Rigel	281 08.9	S 8 11.2
M 09	291 09.7	300 28.7 . .	32.4	33 25.5 . .	37.9	60 12.4 . .	23.5	13 27.7 . .	22.2	Rigil Kent.	139 47.1	S60 54.2
O 10	306 12.2	315 28.3	31.1	48 26.4	38.1	75 14.8	23.5	28 30.0	22.1	Sabik	102 09.0	S15 44.7
N 11	321 14.7	330 27.9	29.9	63 27.3	38.2	90 17.2	23.5	43 32.2	22.1			
D 12	336 17.1	345 27.5	S 5 28.6	78 28.1	S22 38.4	105 19.6	S17 23.6	58 34.5	S22 22.1	Schedar	349 37.3	N56 38.2
A 13	351 19.6	0 27.1	27.3	93 29.0	38.5	120 21.9	23.6	73 36.7	22.1	Shaula	96 17.7	S37 06.7
Y 14	6 22.1	15 26.7	26.1	108 29.8	38.7	135 24.3	23.6	88 39.0	22.1	Sirius	258 30.7	S16 44.8
15	21 24.5	30 26.3 . .	24.8	123 30.7 . .	38.9	150 26.7 . .	23.6	103 41.3 . .	22.1	Spica	158 27.7	S11 15.3
16	36 27.0	45 25.9	23.6	138 31.6	39.0	165 29.1	23.6	118 43.5	22.1	Suhail	222 49.7	S43 30.6
17	51 29.4	60 25.4	22.3	153 32.4	39.2	180 31.4	23.6	133 45.8	22.1			
18	66 31.9	75 25.0	S 5 21.1	168 33.3	S22 39.4	195 33.8	S17 23.6	148 48.0	S22 22.1	Vega	80 37.0	N38 47.9
19	81 34.4	90 24.6	19.8	183 34.2	39.5	210 36.2	23.7	163 50.3	22.1	Zuben'ubi	137 01.8	S16 06.9
20	96 36.8	105 24.2	18.6	198 35.0	39.7	225 38.6	23.7	178 52.6	22.0		SHA	Mer.Pass.
21	111 39.3	120 23.8 . .	17.3	213 35.9 . .	39.8	240 41.0 . .	23.7	193 54.8 . .	22.0		° ′	h m
22	126 41.8	135 23.4	16.1	228 36.7	40.0	255 43.4	23.7	208 57.1	22.0	Venus	10 53.8	12 58
23	141 44.2	150 23.0	14.8	243 37.6	40.2	270 45.7	23.7	223 59.3	22.0	Mars	103 08.7	6 48
	h m									Jupiter	129 05.7	5 04
Mer.Pass. 13 38.5		v −0.4	d 1.2	v 0.9	d 0.2	v 2.4	d 0.0	v 2.3	d 0.0	Saturn	82 24.8	8 10

SUN / MOON

UT	SUN GHA	SUN Dec	MOON GHA	v	MOON Dec	d	HP
d h	° ′	° ′	° ′	′	° ′	′	′
24 00	176 41.0	S 9 33.6	80 41.0	6.9	N17 53.8	5.6	59.1
01	191 41.1	32.6	95 06.9	6.9	17 59.4	5.5	59.1
02	206 41.2	31.7	109 32.8	6.8	18 04.9	5.3	59.1
03	221 41.3	. . 30.8	123 58.6	6.7	18 10.2	5.3	59.2
04	236 41.4	29.9	138 24.3	6.6	18 15.5	5.1	59.2
05	251 41.5	28.9	152 49.9	6.6	18 20.6	5.0	59.2
06	266 41.6	S 9 28.0	167 15.5	6.6	N18 25.6	4.9	59.2
07	281 41.7	27.1	181 41.1	6.4	18 30.5	4.8	59.3
08	296 41.7	26.2	196 06.5	6.4	18 35.3	4.7	59.3
09	311 41.8	. . 25.3	210 31.9	6.4	18 40.0	4.5	59.3
10	326 41.9	24.3	224 57.3	6.3	18 44.5	4.5	59.3
11	341 42.0	23.4	239 22.6	6.2	18 49.0	4.3	59.4
12	356 42.1	S 9 22.5	253 47.8	6.1	N18 53.3	4.2	59.4
13	11 42.2	21.6	268 12.9	6.2	18 57.5	4.0	59.4
14	26 42.3	20.6	282 38.1	6.0	19 01.5	4.0	59.4
15	41 42.4	. . 19.7	297 03.1	6.0	19 05.5	3.8	59.4
16	56 42.5	18.8	311 28.1	5.9	19 09.3	3.7	59.5
17	71 42.6	17.9	325 53.0	5.9	19 13.0	3.6	59.5
18	86 42.7	S 9 16.9	340 17.9	5.8	N19 16.6	3.4	59.5
19	101 42.8	16.0	354 42.7	5.8	19 20.0	3.3	59.5
20	116 42.9	15.1	9 07.5	5.8	19 23.3	3.2	59.5
21	131 43.0	. . 14.1	23 32.3	5.6	19 26.5	3.1	59.5
22	146 43.1	13.2	37 56.9	5.7	19 29.6	2.9	59.6
23	161 43.2	12.3	52 21.6	5.5	19 32.5	2.8	59.6
25 00	176 43.3	S 9 11.4	66 46.1	5.6	N19 35.3	2.7	59.6
01	191 43.4	10.4	81 10.7	5.5	19 38.0	2.6	59.6
02	206 43.5	09.5	95 35.2	5.4	19 40.6	2.4	59.6
03	221 43.6	. . 08.6	109 59.6	5.4	19 43.0	2.3	59.7
04	236 43.7	07.7	124 24.0	5.4	19 45.3	2.1	59.7
05	251 43.8	06.7	138 48.4	5.3	19 47.4	2.0	59.7
06	266 43.9	S 9 05.8	153 12.7	5.3	N19 49.4	1.9	59.7
07	281 44.0	04.9	167 37.0	5.2	19 51.3	1.8	59.7
08	296 44.1	03.9	182 01.2	5.2	19 53.1	1.6	59.7
09	311 44.1	. . 03.0	196 25.4	5.2	19 54.7	1.5	59.8
10	326 44.2	02.1	210 49.6	5.1	19 56.2	1.3	59.8
11	341 44.3	01.1	225 13.7	5.1	19 57.5	1.2	59.8
12	356 44.4	S 9 00.2	239 37.8	5.1	N19 58.7	1.1	59.8
13	11 44.5	8 59.3	254 01.9	5.0	19 59.8	0.9	59.8
14	26 44.6	58.4	268 25.9	5.0	20 00.7	0.8	59.8
15	41 44.8	. . 57.4	282 49.9	5.0	20 01.5	0.6	59.9
16	56 44.9	56.5	297 13.9	4.9	20 02.1	0.6	59.9
17	71 45.0	55.6	311 37.8	4.9	20 02.7	0.3	59.9
18	86 45.1	S 8 54.6	326 01.7	4.9	N20 03.0	0.3	59.9
19	101 45.2	53.7	340 25.6	4.9	20 03.3	0.1	59.9
20	116 45.3	52.8	354 49.5	4.9	20 03.4	0.1	59.9
21	131 45.4	. . 51.8	9 13.4	4.8	20 03.3	0.2	59.9
22	146 45.5	50.9	23 37.2	4.8	20 03.1	0.3	60.0
23	161 45.6	50.0	38 01.0	4.8	20 02.8	0.4	60.0
26 00	176 45.7	S 8 49.0	52 24.8	4.8	N20 02.4	0.6	60.0
01	191 45.8	48.1	66 48.6	4.8	20 01.8	0.8	60.0
02	206 45.9	47.2	81 12.4	4.7	20 01.0	0.9	60.0
03	221 46.0	. . 46.2	95 36.1	4.8	20 00.1	1.0	60.0
04	236 46.1	45.3	109 59.9	4.7	19 59.1	1.2	60.0
05	251 46.2	44.4	124 23.6	4.8	19 57.9	1.3	60.0
06	266 46.3	S 8 43.4	138 47.4	4.7	N19 56.6	1.4	60.1
07	281 46.4	42.5	153 11.1	4.7	19 55.2	1.6	60.1
08	296 46.5	41.6	167 34.8	4.7	19 53.6	1.7	60.1
09	311 46.6	. . 40.6	181 58.5	4.8	19 51.9	1.9	60.1
10	326 46.7	39.7	196 22.3	4.7	19 50.0	2.0	60.1
11	341 46.8	38.8	210 46.0	4.7	19 48.0	2.2	60.1
12	356 46.9	S 8 37.8	225 09.7	4.7	N19 45.8	2.2	60.1
13	11 47.0	36.9	239 33.4	4.7	19 43.6	2.5	60.1
14	26 47.1	35.9	253 57.1	4.8	19 41.1	2.5	60.1
15	41 47.2	. . 35.0	268 20.9	4.7	19 38.6	2.7	60.1
16	56 47.4	34.1	282 44.6	4.8	19 35.9	2.9	60.2
17	71 47.5	33.1	297 08.4	4.7	19 33.0	3.0	60.2
18	86 47.6	S 8 32.2	311 32.1	4.8	N19 30.0	3.1	60.2
19	101 47.7	31.3	325 55.9	4.8	19 26.9	3.3	60.2
20	116 47.8	30.3	340 19.7	4.8	19 23.6	3.4	60.2
21	131 47.9	. . 29.4	354 43.5	4.8	19 20.2	3.5	60.2
22	146 48.0	28.4	9 07.3	4.8	19 16.7	3.7	60.2
23	161 48.1	27.5	23 31.1	4.9	N19 13.0	3.8	60.2
	SD 16.2	d 0.9	SD 16.2		16.3		16.4

Day labels in left margin: 24 SATURDAY, 25 SUNDAY, 26 MONDAY

Twilight / Sunrise / Moonrise

Lat.	Naut.	Civil	Sunrise	Moonrise 24	25	26	27
°	h m	h m	h m	h m	h m	h m	h m
N 72	05 30	06 47	07 58	▢	▢	▢	▢
N 70	05 33	06 43	07 46	08 30	08 32	09 36	11 41
68	05 35	06 39	07 36	09 14	09 45	10 48	12 24
66	05 37	06 36	07 28	09 44	10 22	11 25	12 52
64	05 38	06 33	07 21	10 06	10 48	11 51	13 14
62	05 39	06 30	07 16	10 24	11 09	12 12	13 31
60	05 40	06 28	07 10	10 39	11 26	12 28	13 45
N 58	05 41	06 26	07 06	10 52	11 40	12 42	13 58
56	05 41	06 24	07 02	11 03	11 52	12 55	14 08
54	05 41	06 22	06 58	11 12	12 03	13 05	14 18
52	05 42	06 21	06 55	11 21	12 12	13 14	14 26
50	05 42	06 19	06 52	11 29	12 21	13 23	14 33
45	05 41	06 15	06 45	11 45	12 39	13 41	14 49
N 40	05 41	06 12	06 39	11 59	12 53	13 55	15 02
35	05 40	06 09	06 35	12 11	13 06	14 07	15 13
30	05 38	06 06	06 30	12 21	13 17	14 18	15 23
20	05 35	06 01	06 23	12 38	13 36	14 37	15 40
N 10	05 30	05 55	06 16	12 54	13 52	14 53	15 54
0	05 24	05 49	06 10	13 08	14 07	15 08	16 08
S 10	05 17	05 42	06 03	13 23	14 23	15 23	16 21
20	05 07	05 34	05 56	13 38	14 39	15 39	16 36
30	04 55	05 23	05 48	13 56	14 58	15 57	16 52
35	04 46	05 17	05 43	14 06	15 09	16 08	17 02
40	04 36	05 10	05 38	14 18	15 22	16 20	17 13
45	04 24	05 01	05 31	14 33	15 37	16 35	17 25
S 50	04 08	04 50	05 24	14 50	15 55	16 53	17 41
52	04 00	04 44	05 20	14 58	16 04	17 01	17 48
54	03 51	04 39	05 16	15 07	16 13	17 10	17 56
56	03 41	04 32	05 12	15 17	16 24	17 21	18 05
58	03 29	04 24	05 07	15 29	16 37	17 33	18 16
S 60	03 15	04 16	05 02	15 43	16 52	17 47	18 27

Sunset / Twilight / Moonset

Lat.	Sunset	Civil	Naut.	Moonset 24	25	26	27
°	h m	h m	h m	h m	h m	h m	h m
N 72	16 30	17 41	18 59	▢	▢	▢	▢
N 70	16 42	17 45	18 56	05 07	07 09	08 11	08 12
68	16 51	17 49	18 53	04 24	05 56	06 58	07 29
66	16 59	17 52	18 51	03 55	05 19	06 21	07 00
64	17 06	17 55	18 50	03 33	04 52	05 55	06 38
62	17 12	17 57	18 48	03 16	04 32	05 34	06 20
60	17 17	17 59	18 47	03 01	04 15	05 17	06 05
N 58	17 21	18 01	18 47	02 49	04 01	05 03	05 52
56	17 25	18 03	18 46	02 38	03 49	04 51	05 41
54	17 29	18 05	18 46	02 29	03 39	04 40	05 32
52	17 32	18 06	18 46	02 20	03 29	04 31	05 23
50	17 35	18 08	18 45	02 13	03 21	04 22	05 15
45	17 42	18 11	18 45	01 57	03 03	04 04	04 59
N 40	17 47	18 15	18 46	01 44	02 49	03 50	04 45
35	17 52	18 17	18 47	01 33	02 36	03 37	04 34
30	17 56	18 20	18 48	01 23	02 26	03 26	04 24
20	18 04	18 26	18 51	01 06	02 07	03 08	04 06
N 10	18 10	18 31	18 56	00 52	01 51	02 51	03 51
0	18 16	18 37	19 02	00 38	01 36	02 36	03 36
S 10	18 23	18 44	19 09	00 24	01 21	02 21	03 22
20	18 30	18 52	19 18	00 10	01 05	02 04	03 06
30	18 38	19 02	19 31	24 46	00 46	01 45	02 49
35	18 42	19 08	19 39	24 36	00 36	01 34	02 38
40	18 48	19 15	19 49	24 23	00 23	01 21	02 26
45	18 54	19 24	20 01	24 09	00 09	01 06	02 12
S 50	19 01	19 34	20 17	23 51	24 48	00 48	01 55
52	19 05	19 40	20 24	23 43	24 39	00 39	01 47
54	19 09	19 46	20 33	23 33	24 30	00 30	01 37
56	19 13	19 53	20 43	23 23	24 19	00 19	01 27
58	19 18	20 00	20 54	23 11	24 06	00 06	01 15
S 60	19 23	20 08	21 08	22 57	23 51	25 02	01 02

SUN / MOON

Day	Eqn. of Time 00h	Eqn. of Time 12h	Mer. Pass.	Mer. Pass. Upper	Mer. Pass. Lower	Age	Phase
d	m s	m s	h m	h m	h m	d	%
24	13 16	13 12	12 13	19 22	06 53	09	63
25	13 07	13 02	12 13	20 22	07 52	10	74
26	12 58	12 53	12 13	21 22	08 52	11	84

UT	ARIES GHA	VENUS −3.9 GHA	VENUS Dec	MARS +0.8 GHA	MARS Dec	JUPITER −2.2 GHA	JUPITER Dec	SATURN +0.6 GHA	SATURN Dec	STARS Name	SHA	Dec
27 00	156 46.7	165 22.6	S 5 13.6	258 38.5	S22 40.3	285 48.1	S17 23.7	239 01.6	S22 22.0	Acamar	315 16.1	S40 14.4
01	171 49.2	180 22.2	12.3	273 39.3	40.5	300 50.5	23.7	254 03.9	22.0	Achernar	335 24.8	S57 09.1
02	186 51.6	195 21.8	11.1	288 40.2	40.6	315 52.9	23.8	269 06.1	22.0	Acrux	173 05.0	S63 11.8
03	201 54.1	210 21.4	.. 09.8	303 41.1	.. 40.8	330 55.3	.. 23.8	284 08.4	.. 22.0	Adhara	255 09.8	S29 00.2
04	216 56.5	225 21.0	08.5	318 41.9	41.0	345 57.6	23.8	299 10.6	22.0	Aldebaran	290 45.7	N16 32.5
05	231 59.0	240 20.6	07.3	333 42.8	41.1	1 00.0	23.8	314 12.9	22.0			
06	247 01.5	255 20.2	S 5 06.0	348 43.6	S22 41.3	16 02.4	S17 23.8	329 15.2	S22 21.9	Alioth	166 17.5	N55 51.6
07	262 03.9	270 19.8	04.8	3 44.5	41.4	31 04.8	23.8	344 17.4	21.9	Alkaid	152 56.1	N49 13.2
T 08	277 06.4	285 19.4	03.5	18 45.4	41.6	46 07.2	23.8	359 19.7	21.9	Al Na'ir	27 40.2	S46 52.4
U 09	292 08.9	300 19.0	.. 02.3	33 46.2	.. 41.7	61 09.6	.. 23.8	14 21.9	.. 21.9	Alnilam	275 43.0	S 1 11.7
E 10	307 11.3	315 18.6	5 01.0	48 47.1	41.9	76 12.0	23.9	29 24.2	21.9	Alphard	217 52.6	S 8 44.4
S 11	322 13.8	330 18.2	4 59.7	63 48.0	42.1	91 14.3	23.9	44 26.5	21.9			
D 12	337 16.3	345 17.8	S 4 58.5	78 48.8	S22 42.2	106 16.7	S17 23.9	59 28.7	S22 21.9	Alphecca	126 08.2	N26 39.1
A 13	352 18.7	0 17.4	57.2	93 49.7	42.4	121 19.1	23.9	74 31.0	21.9	Alpheratz	357 40.5	N29 11.3
Y 14	7 21.2	15 17.0	56.0	108 50.5	42.5	136 21.5	23.9	89 33.2	21.9	Altair	62 05.4	N 8 54.9
15	22 23.7	30 16.6	.. 54.7	123 51.4	.. 42.7	151 23.9	.. 23.9	104 35.5	.. 21.8	Ankaa	353 13.0	S42 12.7
16	37 26.1	45 16.2	53.5	138 52.3	42.8	166 26.3	23.9	119 37.8	21.8	Antares	112 22.3	S26 28.1
17	52 28.6	60 15.8	52.2	153 53.1	43.0	181 28.7	23.9	134 40.0	21.8			
18	67 31.0	75 15.4	S 4 50.9	168 54.0	S22 43.2	196 31.0	S17 24.0	149 42.3	S22 21.8	Arcturus	145 52.6	N19 05.2
19	82 33.5	90 15.0	49.7	183 54.9	43.3	211 33.4	24.0	164 44.6	21.8	Atria	107 21.3	S69 03.1
20	97 36.0	105 14.6	48.4	198 55.7	43.5	226 35.8	24.0	179 46.8	21.8	Avior	234 16.2	S59 34.3
21	112 38.4	120 14.2	.. 47.2	213 56.6	.. 43.6	241 38.2	.. 24.0	194 49.1	.. 21.8	Bellatrix	278 28.5	N 6 21.7
22	127 40.9	135 13.8	45.9	228 57.5	43.8	256 40.6	24.0	209 51.3	21.8	Betelgeuse	270 57.7	N 7 24.4
23	142 43.4	150 13.4	44.6	243 58.3	43.9	271 43.0	24.0	224 53.6	21.8			
28 00	157 45.8	165 13.0	S 4 43.4	258 59.2	S22 44.1	286 45.4	S17 24.0	239 55.9	S22 21.8	Canopus	263 54.5	S52 42.8
01	172 48.3	180 12.6	42.1	274 00.0	44.2	301 47.8	24.0	254 58.1	21.7	Capella	280 29.6	N46 00.9
02	187 50.8	195 12.2	40.9	289 00.9	44.4	316 50.2	24.1	270 00.4	21.7	Deneb	49 29.7	N45 20.6
03	202 53.2	210 11.8	.. 39.6	304 01.8	.. 44.5	331 52.6	.. 24.1	285 02.7	.. 21.7	Denebola	182 30.1	N14 28.1
04	217 55.7	225 11.4	38.3	319 02.6	44.7	346 54.9	24.1	300 04.9	21.7	Diphda	348 53.0	S17 53.5
05	232 58.2	240 11.0	37.1	334 03.5	44.8	1 57.3	24.1	315 07.2	21.7			
06	248 00.6	255 10.6	S 4 35.8	349 04.4	S22 45.0	16 59.7	S17 24.1	330 09.5	S22 21.7	Dubhe	193 47.2	N61 39.1
W 07	263 03.1	270 10.3	34.6	4 05.2	45.2	32 02.1	24.1	345 11.7	21.7	Elnath	278 08.5	N28 37.2
E 08	278 05.5	285 09.9	33.3	19 06.1	45.3	47 04.5	24.1	0 14.0	21.7	Eltanin	90 44.8	N51 29.0
D 09	293 08.0	300 09.5	.. 32.0	34 07.0	.. 45.5	62 06.9	.. 24.1	15 16.3	.. 21.7	Enif	33 44.3	N 9 57.4
N 10	308 10.5	315 09.1	30.8	49 07.8	45.6	77 09.3	24.1	30 18.5	21.7	Fomalhaut	15 20.8	S29 31.7
E 11	323 12.9	330 08.7	29.5	64 08.7	45.8	92 11.7	24.2	45 20.8	21.6			
S 12	338 15.4	345 08.3	S 4 28.2	79 09.5	S22 45.9	107 14.1	S17 24.2	60 23.0	S22 21.6	Gacrux	171 56.8	S57 12.7
D 13	353 17.9	0 07.9	27.0	94 10.4	46.1	122 16.5	24.2	75 25.3	21.6	Gienah	175 48.7	S17 38.6
A 14	8 20.3	15 07.5	25.7	109 11.3	46.2	137 18.9	24.2	90 27.6	21.6	Hadar	148 42.9	S60 27.3
Y 15	23 22.8	30 07.1	.. 24.5	124 12.1	.. 46.4	152 21.3	.. 24.2	105 29.8	.. 21.6	Hamal	327 57.3	N23 32.7
16	38 25.3	45 06.7	23.2	139 13.0	46.5	167 23.7	24.2	120 32.1	21.6	Kaus Aust.	83 39.8	S34 22.3
17	53 27.7	60 06.3	21.9	154 13.9	46.7	182 26.1	24.2	135 34.4	21.6			
18	68 30.2	75 05.9	S 4 20.7	169 14.7	S22 46.8	197 28.4	S17 24.2	150 36.6	S22 21.6	Kochab	137 19.7	N74 04.7
19	83 32.7	90 05.5	19.4	184 15.6	47.0	212 30.8	24.2	165 38.9	21.6	Markab	13 35.5	N15 18.0
20	98 35.1	105 05.1	18.1	199 16.5	47.1	227 33.2	24.2	180 41.2	21.6	Menkar	314 11.8	N 4 09.4
21	113 37.6	120 04.7	.. 16.9	214 17.3	.. 47.3	242 35.6	.. 24.3	195 43.4	.. 21.5	Menkent	148 03.5	S36 27.3
22	128 40.0	135 04.3	15.6	229 18.2	47.4	257 38.0	24.3	210 45.7	21.5	Miaplacidus	221 38.1	S69 47.7
23	143 42.5	150 04.0	14.3	244 19.1	47.6	272 40.4	24.3	225 48.0	21.5			
1 00	158 45.0	165 03.6	S 4 13.1	259 19.9	S22 47.7	287 42.8	S17 24.3	240 50.2	S22 21.5	Mirfak	308 35.9	N49 55.5
01	173 47.4	180 03.2	11.8	274 20.8	47.8	302 45.2	24.3	255 52.5	21.5	Nunki	75 54.6	S26 16.3
02	188 49.9	195 02.8	10.6	289 21.6	48.0	317 47.6	24.3	270 54.8	21.5	Peacock	53 14.8	S56 40.4
03	203 52.4	210 02.4	.. 09.3	304 22.5	.. 48.1	332 50.0	.. 24.3	285 57.0	.. 21.5	Pollux	243 23.6	N27 58.8
04	218 54.8	225 02.0	08.0	319 23.4	48.3	347 52.4	24.3	300 59.3	21.5	Procyon	244 56.2	N 5 10.5
05	233 57.3	240 01.6	06.8	334 24.2	48.4	2 54.8	24.3	316 01.6	21.5			
06	248 59.8	255 01.2	S 4 05.5	349 25.1	S22 48.6	17 57.2	S17 24.3	331 03.8	S22 21.5	Rasalhague	96 03.6	N12 32.8
07	264 02.2	270 00.8	04.2	4 26.0	48.7	32 59.6	24.3	346 06.1	21.4	Regulus	207 39.8	N11 52.6
T 08	279 04.7	285 00.4	03.0	19 26.8	48.9	48 02.0	24.4	1 08.4	21.4	Rigel	281 08.9	S 8 11.2
H 09	294 07.1	300 00.0	.. 01.7	34 27.7	.. 49.0	63 04.4	.. 24.4	16 10.6	.. 21.4	Rigil Kent.	139 47.0	S60 54.2
U 10	309 09.6	314 59.7	4 00.4	49 28.6	49.2	78 06.8	24.4	31 12.9	21.4	Sabik	102 08.9	S15 44.7
R 11	324 12.1	329 59.3	3 59.2	64 29.4	49.3	93 09.2	24.4	46 15.2	21.4			
S 12	339 14.5	344 58.9	S 3 57.9	79 30.3	S22 49.5	108 11.6	S17 24.4	61 17.5	S22 21.4	Schedar	349 37.3	N56 38.2
D 13	354 17.0	359 58.5	56.6	94 31.2	49.6	123 14.0	24.4	76 19.7	21.4	Shaula	96 17.7	S37 06.7
A 14	9 19.5	14 58.1	55.4	109 32.0	49.7	138 16.4	24.4	91 22.0	21.4	Sirius	258 30.7	S16 44.8
Y 15	24 21.9	29 57.7	.. 54.1	124 32.9	.. 49.9	153 18.8	.. 24.4	106 24.3	.. 21.4	Spica	158 27.6	S11 15.3
16	39 24.4	44 57.3	52.8	139 33.8	50.0	168 21.2	24.4	121 26.5	21.4	Suhail	222 49.7	S43 30.6
17	54 26.9	59 56.9	51.6	154 34.6	50.2	183 23.6	24.4	136 28.8	21.3			
18	69 29.3	74 56.5	S 3 50.3	169 35.5	S22 50.3	198 26.0	S17 24.4	151 31.1	S22 21.3	Vega	80 37.0	N38 47.9
19	84 31.8	89 56.2	49.0	184 36.4	50.5	213 28.4	24.5	166 33.3	21.3	Zuben'ubi	137 01.7	S16 06.9
20	99 34.3	104 55.8	47.7	199 37.2	50.6	228 30.8	24.5	181 35.6	21.3		SHA	Mer.Pass.
21	114 36.7	119 55.4	.. 46.5	214 38.1	.. 50.7	243 33.3	.. 24.5	196 37.9	.. 21.3	Venus	7 27.2	12 59
22	129 39.2	134 55.0	45.2	229 39.0	50.9	258 35.7	24.5	211 40.1	21.3	Mars	101 13.3	6 44
23	144 41.6	149 54.6	43.9	244 39.8	51.0	273 38.1	24.5	226 42.4	21.3	Jupiter	128 59.5	4 52
Mer.Pass. 13 26.7		v −0.4 d 1.3		v 0.9 d 0.2		v 2.4 d 0.0		v 2.3 d 0.0		Saturn	82 10.0	7 59

SUN and MOON

UT (d h)	SUN GHA ° '	SUN Dec ° '	MOON GHA ° '	MOON v '	MOON Dec ° '	MOON d '	MOON HP '
27 00	176 48.2	S 8 26.6	37 55.0	4.9	N19 09.2	3.9	60.2
01	191 48.3	25.6	52 18.9	4.9	19 05.3	4.1	60.2
02	206 48.4	24.7	66 42.8	4.9	19 01.2	4.2	60.2
03	221 48.5	.. 23.7	81 06.7	4.9	18 57.0	4.3	60.2
04	236 48.7	22.8	95 30.6	5.0	18 52.7	4.5	60.2
05	251 48.8	21.9	109 54.6	5.0	18 48.2	4.6	60.2
06	266 48.9	S 8 20.9	124 18.6	5.0	N18 43.6	4.8	60.2
07	281 49.0	20.0	138 42.6	5.1	18 38.8	4.8	60.2
T 08	296 49.1	19.1	153 06.7	5.0	18 34.0	5.1	60.2
U 09	311 49.2	.. 18.1	167 30.7	5.2	18 28.9	5.1	60.2
E 10	326 49.3	17.2	181 54.9	5.1	18 23.8	5.3	60.2
S 11	341 49.4	16.2	196 19.0	5.2	18 18.5	5.3	60.2
D 12	356 49.5	S 8 15.3	210 43.2	5.2	N18 13.2	5.6	60.3
A 13	11 49.7	14.3	225 07.4	5.3	18 07.6	5.6	60.3
Y 14	26 49.8	13.4	239 31.7	5.3	18 02.0	5.8	60.3
15	41 49.9	.. 12.5	253 56.0	5.3	17 56.2	5.9	60.3
16	56 50.0	11.5	268 20.3	5.4	17 50.3	6.0	60.3
17	71 50.1	10.6	282 44.7	5.4	17 44.3	6.1	60.3
18	86 50.2	S 8 09.6	297 09.1	5.5	N17 38.2	6.3	60.2
19	101 50.3	08.7	311 33.6	5.5	17 31.9	6.4	60.2
20	116 50.4	07.8	325 58.1	5.5	17 25.5	6.5	60.2
21	131 50.6	.. 06.8	340 22.6	5.6	17 19.0	6.6	60.2
22	146 50.7	05.9	354 47.2	5.7	17 12.4	6.7	60.2
23	161 50.8	04.9	9 11.9	5.7	17 05.7	6.9	60.2
28 00	176 50.9	S 8 04.0	23 36.6	5.7	N16 58.8	7.0	60.2
01	191 51.0	03.0	38 01.3	5.8	16 51.8	7.1	60.2
02	206 51.1	02.1	52 26.1	5.8	16 44.7	7.1	60.2
03	221 51.2	.. 01.1	66 50.9	5.9	16 37.6	7.4	60.2
04	236 51.4	8 00.2	81 15.8	6.0	16 30.2	7.4	60.2
05	251 51.5	7 59.3	95 40.8	6.0	16 22.8	7.5	60.2
06	266 51.6	S 7 58.3	110 05.8	6.0	N16 15.3	7.7	60.2
W 07	281 51.7	57.4	124 30.8	6.1	16 07.6	7.7	60.2
E 08	296 51.8	56.4	138 55.9	6.2	15 59.9	7.9	60.2
D 09	311 51.9	.. 55.5	153 21.1	6.2	15 52.0	7.9	60.2
N 10	326 52.1	54.5	167 46.3	6.3	15 44.1	8.1	60.2
E 11	341 52.2	53.6	182 11.6	6.3	15 36.0	8.1	60.2
S 12	356 52.3	S 7 52.6	196 36.9	6.4	N15 27.9	8.3	60.2
D 13	11 52.4	51.7	211 02.3	6.4	15 19.6	8.4	60.2
A 14	26 52.5	50.8	225 27.7	6.5	15 11.2	8.4	60.1
Y 15	41 52.7	.. 49.8	239 53.2	6.6	15 02.8	8.6	60.1
16	56 52.8	48.9	254 18.8	6.6	14 54.2	8.7	60.1
17	71 52.9	47.9	268 44.4	6.7	14 45.5	8.7	60.1
18	86 53.0	S 7 47.0	283 10.1	6.8	N14 36.8	8.9	60.1
19	101 53.1	46.0	297 35.9	6.8	14 27.9	8.9	60.1
20	116 53.2	45.1	312 01.7	6.8	14 19.0	9.0	60.1
21	131 53.4	.. 44.1	326 27.5	7.0	14 10.0	9.2	60.1
22	146 53.5	43.2	340 53.5	7.0	14 00.8	9.2	60.1
23	161 53.6	42.2	355 19.5	7.0	13 51.6	9.2	60.0
1 00	176 53.7	S 7 41.3	9 45.5	7.1	N13 42.4	9.4	60.0
01	191 53.8	40.3	24 11.6	7.2	13 33.0	9.5	60.0
02	206 54.0	39.4	38 37.8	7.3	13 23.5	9.5	60.0
03	221 54.1	.. 38.4	53 04.1	7.3	13 14.0	9.7	60.0
04	236 54.2	37.5	67 30.4	7.4	13 04.3	9.7	60.0
05	251 54.3	36.5	81 56.8	7.4	12 54.6	9.7	60.0
06	266 54.5	S 7 35.6	96 23.2	7.5	N12 44.9	9.9	59.9
07	281 54.6	34.6	110 49.7	7.6	12 35.0	9.9	59.9
T 08	296 54.7	33.7	125 16.3	7.6	12 25.1	10.0	59.9
H 09	311 54.8	.. 32.7	139 42.9	7.7	12 15.1	10.1	59.9
U 10	326 54.9	31.8	154 09.6	7.8	12 05.0	10.2	59.9
R 11	341 55.1	30.8	168 36.4	7.8	11 54.8	10.2	59.9
S 12	356 55.2	S 7 29.9	183 03.2	7.9	N11 44.6	10.3	59.8
D 13	11 55.3	28.9	197 30.1	7.9	11 34.3	10.3	59.8
A 14	26 55.4	28.0	211 57.0	8.1	11 24.0	10.4	59.8
Y 15	41 55.6	.. 27.0	226 24.1	8.1	11 13.6	10.5	59.8
16	56 55.7	26.1	240 51.2	8.1	11 03.1	10.5	59.8
17	71 55.8	25.1	255 18.3	8.2	10 52.6	10.6	59.7
18	86 55.9	S 7 24.2	269 45.5	8.3	N10 42.0	10.7	59.7
19	101 56.1	23.2	284 12.8	8.4	10 31.3	10.7	59.7
20	116 56.2	22.3	298 40.2	8.4	10 20.6	10.8	59.7
21	131 56.3	.. 21.3	313 07.6	8.4	10 09.8	10.8	59.7
22	146 56.4	20.4	327 35.0	8.6	9 59.0	10.9	59.6
23	161 56.6	19.4	342 02.6	8.6	N 9 48.1	10.9	59.6
	SD 16.2	d 0.9	SD 16.4		16.4		16.3

Twilight, Sunrise, Moonrise

Lat.	Naut.	Civil	Sunrise	Moonrise 27	28	1	2
N 72	05 15	06 33	07 42	▭	13 11	15 29	17 34
N 70	05 20	06 30	07 32	11 41	13 47	15 48	17 43
68	05 23	06 27	07 24	12 24	14 13	16 03	17 51
66	05 26	06 25	07 17	12 52	14 32	16 15	17 57
64	05 28	06 23	07 11	13 14	14 48	16 25	18 02
62	05 30	06 21	07 06	13 31	15 01	16 34	18 07
60	05 32	06 20	07 02	13 45	15 12	16 41	18 10
N 58	05 33	06 18	06 58	13 58	15 21	16 48	18 14
56	05 34	06 17	06 54	14 08	15 29	16 53	18 17
54	05 35	06 16	06 51	14 18	15 37	16 58	18 20
52	05 35	06 14	06 48	14 26	15 43	17 03	18 22
50	05 36	06 13	06 46	14 33	15 49	17 07	18 24
45	05 36	06 10	06 40	14 49	16 02	17 16	18 29
N 40	05 37	06 08	06 35	15 02	16 13	17 24	18 33
35	05 36	06 06	06 31	15 13	16 22	17 30	18 37
30	05 35	06 03	06 27	15 23	16 29	17 36	18 40
20	05 33	05 58	06 21	15 40	16 43	17 45	18 45
N 10	05 29	05 54	06 15	15 54	16 55	17 54	18 50
0	05 24	05 48	06 09	16 08	17 06	18 02	18 55
S 10	05 18	05 42	06 03	16 21	17 17	18 10	18 59
20	05 09	05 35	05 57	16 36	17 29	18 18	19 04
30	04 57	05 26	05 50	16 52	17 42	18 28	19 09
35	04 50	05 20	05 46	17 02	17 50	18 33	19 12
40	04 40	05 13	05 41	17 13	17 59	18 39	19 16
45	04 29	05 05	05 36	17 25	18 09	18 47	19 20
S 50	04 14	04 55	05 29	17 41	18 21	18 55	19 25
52	04 07	04 50	05 26	17 48	18 27	18 59	19 27
54	03 59	04 45	05 22	17 56	18 33	19 04	19 29
56	03 50	04 39	05 18	18 05	18 40	19 08	19 32
58	03 39	04 32	05 14	18 16	18 48	19 14	19 35
S 60	03 26	04 24	05 09	18 27	18 57	19 20	19 38

Sunset, Twilight, Moonset

Lat.	Sunset	Civil	Naut.	Moonset 27	28	1	2
N 72	16 45	17 54	19 13	▭	08 46	08 26	08 13
N 70	16 55	17 57	19 08	08 12	08 09	08 05	08 02
68	17 03	17 59	19 04	07 29	07 42	07 49	07 52
66	17 09	18 02	19 01	07 00	07 22	07 35	07 44
64	17 15	18 03	18 58	06 38	07 06	07 24	07 38
62	17 20	18 05	18 56	06 20	06 52	07 15	07 32
60	17 25	18 07	18 55	06 05	06 40	07 06	07 27
N 58	17 28	18 08	18 53	05 52	06 30	06 59	07 22
56	17 32	18 09	18 52	05 41	06 21	06 53	07 18
54	17 35	18 11	18 51	05 32	06 13	06 47	07 15
52	17 38	18 12	18 51	05 23	06 06	06 42	07 11
50	17 40	18 13	18 50	05 15	06 00	06 37	07 08
45	17 46	18 15	18 49	04 59	05 46	06 26	07 02
N 40	17 51	18 18	18 49	04 45	05 35	06 18	06 56
35	17 55	18 20	18 49	04 34	05 25	06 10	06 51
30	17 58	18 22	18 50	04 24	05 16	06 04	06 47
20	18 05	18 27	18 52	04 06	05 01	05 52	06 40
N 10	18 10	18 32	18 56	03 51	04 48	05 42	06 33
0	18 16	18 37	19 01	03 36	04 36	05 33	06 27
S 10	18 21	18 43	19 07	03 22	04 23	05 23	06 21
20	18 27	18 50	19 16	03 06	04 10	05 13	06 14
30	18 34	18 59	19 27	02 49	03 55	05 01	06 07
35	18 39	19 04	19 35	02 38	03 46	04 54	06 02
40	18 43	19 11	19 44	02 26	03 35	04 46	05 57
45	18 49	19 19	19 55	02 12	03 23	04 37	05 51
S 50	18 55	19 29	20 09	01 55	03 09	04 26	05 44
52	18 58	19 33	20 16	01 47	03 02	04 21	05 41
54	19 02	19 39	20 24	01 37	02 54	04 15	05 37
56	19 05	19 44	20 33	01 27	02 45	04 09	05 33
58	19 09	19 51	20 44	01 15	02 36	04 01	05 28
S 60	19 14	19 59	20 56	01 02	02 24	03 53	05 28

SUN and MOON (daily data)

Day	Eqn. of Time 00h (m s)	Eqn. of Time 12h (m s)	Mer. Pass. (h m)	Mer. Pass. Upper (h m)	Mer. Pass. Lower (h m)	Age (d)	Phase (%)
27	12 47	12 42	12 13	22 22	09 52	12	91
28	12 37	12 31	12 13	23 19	10 51	13	97
1	12 25	12 20	12 12	24 15	11 47	14	100

UT (d h)	ARIES GHA	VENUS −3.9 GHA	Dec	MARS +0.8 GHA	Dec	JUPITER −2.2 GHA	Dec	SATURN +0.6 GHA	Dec	STARS Name	SHA	Dec
2 00	159 44.1	164 54.2	S 3 42.7	259 40.7	S22 51.2	288 40.5	S17 24.5	241 44.7	S22 21.3	Acamar	315 16.1	S40 14.4
01	174 46.6	179 53.8	41.4	274 41.5	51.3	303 42.9	24.5	256 47.0	21.3	Achernar	335 24.9	S57 09.1
02	189 49.0	194 53.4	40.1	289 42.4	51.5	318 45.3	24.5	271 49.2	21.2	Acrux	173 05.0	S63 11.8
03	204 51.5	209 53.1	.. 38.9	304 43.3	.. 51.5	333 47.7	.. 24.5	286 51.5	.. 21.2	Adhara	255 09.8	S29 00.2
04	219 54.0	224 52.7	37.6	319 44.1	51.7	348 50.1	24.5	301 53.8	21.2	Aldebaran	290 45.7	N16 32.5
05	234 56.4	239 52.3	36.3	334 45.0	51.9	3 52.5	24.5	316 56.0	21.2			
06	249 58.9	254 51.9	S 3 35.0	349 45.9	S22 52.0	18 54.9	S17 24.5	331 58.3	S22 21.2	Alioth	166 17.5	N55 51.6
07	265 01.4	269 51.5	33.8	4 46.7	52.2	33 57.3	24.5	347 00.6	21.2	Alkaid	152 56.1	N49 13.2
08	280 03.8	284 51.1	32.5	19 47.6	52.3	48 59.7	24.6	2 02.9	21.2	Al Na'ir	27 40.2	S46 52.4
F 09	295 06.3	299 50.7	.. 31.2	34 48.5	.. 52.4	64 02.1	.. 24.6	17 05.1	.. 21.2	Alnilam	275 43.1	S 1 11.7
R 10	310 08.7	314 50.4	30.0	49 49.3	52.6	79 04.5	24.6	32 07.4	21.2	Alphard	217 52.7	S 8 44.4
I 11	325 11.2	329 50.0	28.7	64 50.2	52.7	94 06.9	24.6	47 09.7	21.2			
D 12	340 13.7	344 49.6	S 3 27.4	79 51.1	S22 52.9	109 09.3	S17 24.6	62 11.9	S22 21.1	Alphecca	126 08.2	N26 39.1
A 13	355 16.1	359 49.2	26.2	94 51.9	53.0	124 11.8	24.6	77 14.2	21.1	Alpheratz	357 40.5	N29 11.3
Y 14	10 18.6	14 48.8	24.9	109 52.8	53.1	139 14.2	24.6	92 16.5	21.1	Altair	62 05.4	N 8 54.9
15	25 21.1	29 48.4	.. 23.6	124 53.7	.. 53.3	154 16.6	.. 24.6	107 18.8	.. 21.1	Ankaa	353 13.0	S42 12.7
16	40 23.5	44 48.1	22.3	139 54.5	53.4	169 19.0	24.6	122 21.0	21.1	Antares	112 22.3	S26 28.1
17	55 26.0	59 47.7	21.1	154 55.4	53.5	184 21.4	24.6	137 23.3	21.1			
18	70 28.5	74 47.3	S 3 19.8	169 56.3	S22 53.7	199 23.8	S17 24.6	152 25.6	S22 21.1	Arcturus	145 52.6	N19 05.2
19	85 30.9	89 46.9	18.5	184 57.1	53.8	214 26.2	24.6	167 27.8	21.1	Atria	107 21.3	S69 03.1
20	100 33.4	104 46.5	17.2	199 58.0	54.0	229 28.6	24.6	182 30.1	21.1	Avior	234 16.2	S59 34.4
21	115 35.9	119 46.1	.. 16.0	214 58.9	.. 54.1	244 31.1	.. 24.6	197 32.4	.. 21.1	Bellatrix	278 28.5	N 6 21.7
22	130 38.3	134 45.7	14.7	229 59.7	54.2	259 33.5	24.6	212 34.7	21.0	Betelgeuse	270 57.7	N 7 24.4
23	145 40.8	149 45.4	13.4	245 00.6	54.4	274 35.9	24.6	227 36.9	21.0			
3 00	160 43.2	164 45.0	S 3 12.2	260 01.5	S22 54.5	289 38.3	S17 24.7	242 39.2	S22 21.0	Canopus	263 54.5	S52 42.8
01	175 45.7	179 44.6	10.9	275 02.3	54.6	304 40.7	24.7	257 41.5	21.0	Capella	280 29.7	N46 00.9
02	190 48.2	194 44.2	09.6	290 03.2	54.8	319 43.1	24.7	272 43.8	21.0	Deneb	49 29.7	N45 20.6
03	205 50.6	209 43.8	.. 08.3	305 04.1	.. 54.9	334 45.5	.. 24.7	287 46.0	.. 21.0	Denebola	182 30.1	N14 28.2
04	220 53.1	224 43.5	07.1	320 04.9	55.0	349 47.9	24.7	302 48.3	21.0	Diphda	348 53.0	S17 53.5
05	235 55.6	239 43.1	05.8	335 05.8	55.2	4 50.4	24.7	317 50.6	21.0			
06	250 58.0	254 42.7	S 3 04.5	350 06.7	S22 55.3	19 52.8	S17 24.7	332 52.9	S22 21.0	Dubhe	193 47.2	N61 39.1
07	266 00.5	269 42.3	03.2	5 07.5	55.4	34 55.2	24.7	347 55.1	21.0	Elnath	278 08.5	N28 37.2
S 08	281 03.0	284 41.9	02.0	20 08.4	55.6	49 57.6	24.7	2 57.4	20.9	Eltanin	90 44.8	N51 29.0
A 09	296 05.4	299 41.5	3 00.7	35 09.3	.. 55.7	65 00.0	.. 24.7	17 59.7	.. 20.9	Enif	33 44.3	N 9 57.4
T 10	311 07.9	314 41.2	2 59.4	50 10.1	55.8	80 02.4	24.7	33 02.0	20.9	Fomalhaut	15 20.8	S29 31.7
U 11	326 10.3	329 40.8	58.1	65 11.0	56.0	95 04.9	24.7	48 04.2	20.9			
R 12	341 12.8	344 40.4	S 2 56.9	80 11.9	S22 56.1	110 07.3	S17 24.7	63 06.5	S22 20.9	Gacrux	171 56.8	S57 12.7
D 13	356 15.3	359 40.0	55.6	95 12.7	56.2	125 09.7	24.7	78 08.8	20.9	Gienah	175 48.7	S17 38.6
A 14	11 17.7	14 39.6	54.3	110 13.6	56.4	140 12.1	24.7	93 11.1	20.9	Hadar	148 42.9	S60 27.3
Y 15	26 20.2	29 39.3	.. 53.0	125 14.5	.. 56.5	155 14.5	.. 24.7	108 13.3	.. 20.9	Hamal	327 57.4	N23 32.7
16	41 22.7	44 38.9	51.8	140 15.4	56.6	170 16.9	24.7	123 15.6	20.9	Kaus Aust.	83 39.7	S34 22.3
17	56 25.1	59 38.5	50.5	155 16.2	56.8	185 19.4	24.7	138 17.9	20.9			
18	71 27.6	74 38.1	S 2 49.2	170 17.1	S22 56.9	200 21.8	S17 24.7	153 20.2	S22 20.8	Kochab	137 19.6	N74 04.7
19	86 30.1	89 37.7	47.9	185 18.0	57.0	215 24.2	24.7	168 22.4	20.8	Markab	13 35.5	N15 18.0
20	101 32.5	104 37.4	46.7	200 18.8	57.2	230 26.6	24.8	183 24.7	20.8	Menkar	314 11.8	N 4 09.4
21	116 35.0	119 37.0	.. 45.4	215 19.7	.. 57.3	245 29.0	.. 24.8	198 27.0	.. 20.8	Menkent	148 03.5	S36 27.4
22	131 37.5	134 36.6	44.1	230 20.6	57.4	260 31.5	24.8	213 29.3	20.8	Miaplacidus	221 38.1	S69 47.7
23	146 39.9	149 36.2	42.8	245 21.4	57.6	275 33.9	24.8	228 31.5	20.8			
4 00	161 42.4	164 35.8	S 2 41.5	260 22.3	S22 57.7	290 36.3	S17 24.8	243 33.8	S22 20.8	Mirfak	308 35.9	N49 55.5
01	176 44.8	179 35.5	40.3	275 23.2	57.8	305 38.7	24.8	258 36.1	20.8	Nunki	75 54.6	S26 16.3
02	191 47.3	194 35.1	39.0	290 24.0	57.9	320 41.1	24.8	273 38.4	20.8	Peacock	53 14.7	S56 40.4
03	206 49.8	209 34.7	.. 37.7	305 24.9	.. 58.1	335 43.6	.. 24.8	288 40.7	.. 20.8	Pollux	243 23.6	N27 58.8
04	221 52.2	224 34.3	36.4	320 25.8	58.2	350 46.0	24.8	303 42.9	20.7	Procyon	244 56.2	N 5 10.5
05	236 54.7	239 34.0	35.2	335 26.6	58.3	5 48.4	24.8	318 45.2	20.7			
06	251 57.2	254 33.6	S 2 33.9	350 27.5	S22 58.5	20 50.8	S17 24.8	333 47.5	S22 20.7	Rasalhague	96 03.6	N12 32.8
07	266 59.6	269 33.2	32.6	5 28.4	58.6	35 53.3	24.8	348 49.8	20.7	Regulus	207 39.8	N11 52.6
08	282 02.1	284 32.8	31.3	20 29.2	58.7	50 55.7	24.8	3 52.0	20.7	Rigel	281 08.9	S 8 11.2
S 09	297 04.6	299 32.4	.. 30.1	35 30.1	.. 58.8	65 58.1	.. 24.8	18 54.3	.. 20.7	Rigil Kent.	139 47.0	S60 54.2
U 10	312 07.0	314 32.1	28.8	50 31.0	59.0	81 00.5	24.8	33 56.6	20.7	Sabik	102 08.9	S15 44.7
N 11	327 09.5	329 31.7	27.5	65 31.8	59.1	96 03.0	24.8	48 58.9	20.7			
D 12	342 12.0	344 31.3	S 2 26.2	80 32.7	S22 59.2	111 05.4	S17 24.8	64 01.2	S22 20.7	Schedar	349 37.3	N56 38.2
A 13	357 14.4	359 30.9	24.9	95 33.6	59.4	126 07.8	24.8	79 03.4	20.6	Shaula	96 17.7	S37 06.7
Y 14	12 16.9	14 30.6	23.7	110 34.5	59.5	141 10.2	24.8	94 05.7	20.6	Sirius	258 30.7	S16 44.8
15	27 19.3	29 30.2	.. 22.4	125 35.3	.. 59.6	156 12.7	.. 24.8	109 08.0	.. 20.6	Spica	158 27.6	S11 15.3
16	42 21.8	44 29.8	21.1	140 36.2	59.7	171 15.1	24.8	124 10.3	20.6	Suhail	222 49.7	S43 30.6
17	57 24.3	59 29.4	19.8	155 37.1	22 59.9	186 17.5	24.8	139 12.6	20.6			
18	72 26.7	74 29.1	S 2 18.5	170 37.9	S23 00.0	201 19.9	S17 24.8	154 14.8	S22 20.6	Vega	80 37.0	N38 47.9
19	87 29.2	89 28.7	17.3	185 38.8	00.1	216 22.4	24.8	169 17.1	20.6	Zuben'ubi	137 01.7	S16 06.9
20	102 31.7	104 28.3	16.0	200 39.7	00.2	231 24.8	24.8	184 19.4	20.6		SHA	Mer. Pass.
21	117 34.1	119 27.9	.. 14.7	215 40.5	.. 00.4	246 27.2	.. 24.8	199 21.7	.. 20.6	Venus	4 01.7	13 01
22	132 36.6	134 27.6	13.4	230 41.4	00.5	261 29.6	24.8	214 24.0	20.6	Mars	99 18.2	6 40
23	147 39.1	149 27.2	12.1	245 42.3	00.6	276 32.1	24.8	229 26.2	20.6	Jupiter	128 55.0	4 41
Mer. Pass. 13 14.9		v −0.4	d 1.3	v 0.9	d 0.1	v 2.4	d 0.0	v 2.3	d 0.0	Saturn	81 56.0	7 48

UT	SUN GHA	Dec	MOON GHA	v	Dec	d	HP
d h	° ′	° ′	° ′	′	° ′	′	′
2 00	176 56.7	S 7 18.5	356 30.2	8.7	N 9 37.2	11.0	59.6
01	191 56.8	17.5	10 57.9	8.7	9 26.2	11.1	59.6
02	206 56.9	16.6	25 25.6	8.8	9 15.1	11.0	59.6
03	221 57.1	.. 15.6	39 53.4	8.8	9 04.1	11.2	59.5
04	236 57.2	14.7	54 21.2	9.0	8 52.9	11.1	59.5
05	251 57.3	13.7	68 49.2	8.9	8 41.8	11.2	59.5
06	266 57.4	S 7 12.7	83 17.1	9.1	N 8 30.6	11.3	59.5
07	281 57.6	11.8	97 45.2	9.1	8 19.3	11.3	59.4
F 08	296 57.7	10.8	112 13.3	9.2	8 08.0	11.3	59.4
R 09	311 57.8	.. 09.9	126 41.5	9.2	7 56.7	11.4	59.4
I 10	326 57.9	08.9	141 09.7	9.3	7 45.3	11.4	59.4
D 11	341 58.1	08.0	155 38.0	9.3	7 33.9	11.4	59.3
A 12	356 58.2	S 7 07.0	170 06.3	9.5	N 7 22.5	11.5	59.3
Y 13	11 58.3	06.1	184 34.8	9.4	7 11.0	11.5	59.3
14	26 58.5	05.1	199 03.2	9.6	6 59.5	11.5	59.3
15	41 58.6	.. 04.2	213 31.8	9.5	6 48.0	11.6	59.2
16	56 58.7	03.2	228 00.3	9.7	6 36.4	11.6	59.2
17	71 58.8	02.2	242 29.0	9.7	6 24.8	11.6	59.2
18	86 59.0	S 7 01.3	256 57.7	9.8	N 6 13.2	11.7	59.1
19	101 59.1	7 00.3	271 26.5	9.8	6 01.5	11.6	59.1
20	116 59.2	6 59.4	285 55.3	9.9	5 49.9	11.7	59.1
21	131 59.4	.. 58.4	300 24.2	9.9	5 38.2	11.7	59.1
22	146 59.5	57.5	314 53.1	10.0	5 26.5	11.7	59.0
23	161 59.6	56.5	329 22.1	10.0	5 14.8	11.8	59.0
3 00	176 59.8	S 6 55.5	343 51.1	10.1	N 5 03.0	11.7	59.0
01	191 59.9	54.6	358 20.2	10.2	4 51.3	11.8	58.9
02	207 00.0	53.6	12 49.4	10.2	4 39.5	11.8	58.9
03	222 00.1	.. 52.7	27 18.6	10.2	4 27.7	11.8	58.9
04	237 00.3	51.7	41 47.8	10.3	4 15.9	11.8	58.9
05	252 00.0	50.8	56 17.1	10.4	4 04.1	11.9	58.8
06	267 00.5	S 6 49.8	70 46.5	10.4	N 3 52.2	11.8	58.8
S 07	282 00.7	48.8	85 15.9	10.5	3 40.4	11.8	58.8
A 08	297 00.8	47.9	99 45.4	10.5	3 28.6	11.9	58.7
T 09	312 00.9	.. 46.9	114 14.9	10.6	3 16.7	11.8	58.7
U 10	327 01.1	46.0	128 44.5	10.6	3 04.9	11.9	58.7
R 11	342 01.2	45.0	143 14.1	10.6	2 53.0	11.8	58.6
D 12	357 01.3	S 6 44.1	157 43.7	10.7	N 2 41.2	11.9	58.6
A 13	12 01.5	43.1	172 13.4	10.8	2 29.3	11.9	58.6
Y 14	27 01.6	42.1	186 43.2	10.8	2 17.4	11.8	58.5
15	42 01.7	.. 41.2	201 13.0	10.9	2 05.6	11.9	58.5
16	57 01.9	40.2	215 42.9	10.9	1 53.7	11.8	58.5
17	72 02.0	39.3	230 12.8	10.9	1 41.9	11.9	58.4
18	87 02.1	S 6 38.3	244 42.7	11.0	N 1 30.0	11.8	58.4
19	102 02.3	37.3	259 12.7	11.0	1 18.2	11.8	58.4
20	117 02.4	36.4	273 42.7	11.1	1 06.4	11.9	58.3
21	132 02.5	.. 35.4	288 12.8	11.1	0 54.5	11.8	58.3
22	147 02.7	34.5	302 42.9	11.1	0 42.7	11.8	58.3
23	162 02.8	33.5	317 13.0	11.2	0 30.9	11.8	58.2
4 00	177 02.9	S 6 32.5	331 43.2	11.3	N 0 19.1	11.8	58.2
01	192 03.1	31.6	346 13.5	11.3	N 0 07.3	11.8	58.2
02	207 03.2	30.6	0 43.8	11.3	S 0 04.5	11.7	58.1
03	222 03.4	.. 29.6	15 14.1	11.3	0 16.2	11.8	58.1
04	237 03.5	28.7	29 44.4	11.4	0 28.0	11.7	58.1
05	252 03.6	27.7	44 14.8	11.5	0 39.7	11.7	58.0
06	267 03.8	S 6 26.8	58 45.3	11.4	S 0 51.4	11.7	58.0
07	282 03.9	25.8	73 15.7	11.5	1 03.1	11.6	58.0
S 08	297 04.0	24.8	87 46.2	11.6	1 14.7	11.7	57.9
U 09	312 04.2	.. 23.9	102 16.8	11.5	1 26.4	11.6	57.9
N 10	327 04.3	22.9	116 47.3	11.6	1 38.0	11.6	57.9
D 11	342 04.4	22.0	131 17.9	11.7	1 49.6	11.6	57.8
A 12	357 04.6	S 6 21.0	145 48.6	11.7	S 2 01.2	11.5	57.8
Y 13	12 04.7	20.0	160 19.3	11.7	2 12.7	11.6	57.8
14	27 04.9	19.1	174 50.0	11.7	2 24.3	11.5	57.7
15	42 05.0	.. 18.1	189 20.7	11.8	2 35.8	11.4	57.7
16	57 05.1	17.1	203 51.5	11.8	2 47.2	11.5	57.7
17	72 05.3	16.2	218 22.3	11.8	2 58.7	11.4	57.6
18	87 05.4	S 6 15.2	232 53.1	11.9	S 3 10.1	11.4	57.6
19	102 05.5	14.2	247 24.0	11.8	3 21.5	11.3	57.6
20	117 05.7	13.3	261 54.8	12.0	3 32.8	11.5	57.5
21	132 05.8	.. 12.3	276 25.8	11.9	3 44.2	11.2	57.5
22	147 06.0	11.4	290 56.7	12.0	3 55.4	11.3	57.5
23	162 06.1	10.4	305 27.7	12.0	S 4 06.7	11.2	57.4
	SD 16.2	d 1.0	SD 16.2		16.0		15.7

Twilight / Sunrise / Moonrise

Lat.	Naut.	Civil	Sunrise	Moonrise 2	3	4	5
°	h m	h m	h m	h m	h m	h m	h m
N 72	05 00	06 18	07 27	17 34	19 31	21 24	23 15
N 70	05 06	06 17	07 18	17 43	19 33	21 18	23 02
68	05 11	06 15	07 11	17 51	19 34	21 14	22 51
66	05 15	06 14	07 06	17 57	19 35	21 10	22 42
64	05 18	06 13	07 01	18 02	19 36	21 07	22 34
62	05 21	06 12	06 57	18 07	19 37	21 04	22 28
60	05 23	06 11	06 53	18 10	19 37	21 01	22 23
N 58	05 25	06 10	06 50	18 14	19 38	20 59	22 18
56	05 27	06 10	06 47	18 17	19 38	20 57	22 13
54	05 28	06 09	06 44	18 20	19 39	20 56	22 10
52	05 29	06 08	06 42	18 22	19 39	20 54	22 06
50	05 30	06 07	06 39	18 24	19 40	20 53	22 03
45	05 31	06 05	06 35	18 29	19 41	20 50	21 56
N 40	05 32	06 04	06 31	18 33	19 41	20 47	21 50
35	05 32	06 02	06 27	18 37	19 42	20 45	21 46
30	05 32	06 00	06 24	18 40	19 43	20 43	21 41
20	05 31	05 56	06 18	18 45	19 44	20 40	21 34
N 10	05 28	05 52	06 13	18 50	19 44	20 37	21 28
0	05 24	05 48	06 09	18 55	19 45	20 34	21 22
S 10	05 18	05 43	06 04	18 59	19 46	20 31	21 16
20	05 10	05 36	05 58	19 04	19 47	20 29	21 09
30	04 59	05 28	05 52	19 09	19 48	20 25	21 02
35	04 53	05 23	05 49	19 12	19 49	20 24	20 58
40	04 44	05 17	05 44	19 16	19 49	20 22	20 54
45	04 34	05 10	05 40	19 20	19 50	20 19	20 48
S 50	04 20	05 00	05 34	19 25	19 51	20 17	20 42
52	04 14	04 56	05 31	19 27	19 52	20 15	20 39
54	04 06	04 51	05 28	19 29	19 52	20 14	20 36
56	03 58	04 46	05 25	19 32	19 53	20 12	20 32
58	03 48	04 40	05 21	19 35	19 53	20 11	20 28
S 60	03 37	04 33	05 17	19 38	19 54	20 09	20 24

Sunset / Twilight / Moonset

Lat.	Sunset	Civil	Naut.	Moonset 2	3	4	5
°	h m	h m	h m	h m	h m	h m	h m
N 72	16 59	18 08	19 27	08 13	08 02	07 52	07 41
N 70	17 07	18 09	19 20	08 02	07 58	07 54	07 49
68	17 14	18 10	19 15	07 52	07 54	07 55	07 56
66	17 20	18 11	19 11	07 44	07 51	07 56	08 02
64	17 24	18 12	19 07	07 38	07 48	07 57	08 07
62	17 29	18 13	19 04	07 32	07 46	07 58	08 11
60	17 32	18 14	19 02	07 27	07 44	07 59	08 14
N 58	17 35	18 15	19 00	07 22	07 42	08 00	08 18
56	17 38	18 15	18 59	07 18	07 40	08 01	08 20
54	17 41	18 16	18 57	07 15	07 39	08 01	08 23
52	17 43	18 17	18 56	07 11	07 37	08 02	08 25
50	17 45	18 18	18 55	07 08	07 36	08 02	08 27
45	17 50	18 19	18 53	07 02	07 34	08 03	08 32
N 40	17 54	18 21	18 52	06 56	07 31	08 04	08 36
35	17 57	18 23	18 52	06 52	07 29	08 05	08 40
30	18 00	18 24	18 52	06 47	07 27	08 06	08 43
20	18 06	18 28	18 53	06 40	07 24	08 07	08 48
N 10	18 11	18 32	18 56	06 33	07 22	08 08	08 52
0	18 15	18 36	19 00	06 27	07 19	08 09	08 57
S 10	18 20	18 41	19 06	06 21	07 16	08 10	09 01
20	18 25	18 47	19 13	06 14	07 13	08 11	09 06
30	18 31	18 55	19 24	06 07	07 10	08 12	09 11
35	18 35	19 00	19 31	06 02	07 08	08 12	09 14
40	18 39	19 06	19 39	05 57	07 06	08 13	09 18
45	18 43	19 13	19 49	05 51	07 04	08 14	09 22
S 50	18 49	19 22	20 02	05 44	07 01	08 15	09 26
52	18 52	19 26	20 09	05 41	06 59	08 15	09 29
54	18 54	19 31	20 16	05 37	06 58	08 16	09 31
56	18 57	19 36	20 24	05 33	06 56	08 16	09 34
58	19 01	19 42	20 34	05 28	06 54	08 17	09 37
S 60	19 05	19 49	20 45	05 23	06 52	08 17	09 40

SUN / MOON

Day	Eqn. of Time 00h	12h	Mer. Pass.	Mer. Pass. Upper	Lower	Age	Phase
d	m s	m s	h m	h m	h m	d	%
2	12 14	12 07	12 12	00 15	12 41	15	100	◯
3	12 01	11 55	12 12	01 07	13 32	16	97	
4	11 48	11 42	12 12	01 57	14 21	17	92	

UT	ARIES	VENUS −3·9		MARS +0·7		JUPITER −2·2		SATURN +0·6		STARS		
	GHA	GHA	Dec	GHA	Dec	GHA	Dec	GHA	Dec	Name	SHA	Dec
d h	° ′	° ′	° ′	° ′	° ′	° ′	° ′	° ′	° ′		° ′	° ′
5 00	162 41.5	164 26.8	S 2 10.9	260 43.1	S23 00.7	291 34.5	S17 24.8	244 28.5	S22 20.5	Acamar	315 16.1	S40 14.4
01	177 44.0	179 26.4	09.6	275 44.0	00.9	306 36.9	24.8	259 30.8	20.5	Achernar	335 24.9	S57 09.1
02	192 46.4	194 26.0	08.3	290 44.9	01.0	321 39.4	24.8	274 33.1	20.5	Acrux	173 05.0	S63 11.8
03	207 48.9	209 25.7 ..	07.0	305 45.8 ..	01.1	336 41.8 ..	24.8	289 35.4 ..	20.5	Adhara	255 09.8	S29 00.2
04	222 51.4	224 25.3	05.7	320 46.6	01.2	351 44.2	24.8	304 37.6	20.5	Aldebaran	290 45.7	N16 32.5
05	237 53.8	239 24.9	04.5	335 47.5	01.3	6 46.7	24.8	319 39.9	20.5			
06	252 56.3	254 24.5	S 2 03.2	350 48.4	S23 01.5	21 49.1	S17 24.8	334 42.2	S22 20.5	Alioth	166 17.4	N55 51.6
07	267 58.8	269 24.2	01.9	5 49.2	01.6	36 51.5	24.9	349 44.5	20.5	Alkaid	152 56.1	N49 13.2
08	283 01.2	284 23.8	2 00.6	20 50.1	01.7	51 54.0	24.9	4 46.8	20.5	Al Na'ir	27 40.2	S46 52.4
M 09	298 03.7	299 23.4	1 59.3	35 51.0 ..	01.8	66 56.4 ..	24.9	19 49.1 ..	20.5	Alnilam	275 43.1	S 1 11.7
O 10	313 06.2	314 23.1	58.1	50 51.8	02.0	81 58.8	24.9	34 51.3	20.4	Alphard	217 52.7	S 8 44.4
N 11	328 08.6	329 22.7	56.8	65 52.7	02.1	97 01.2	24.9	49 53.6	20.4			
D 12	343 11.1	344 22.3	S 1 55.5	80 53.6	S23 02.2	112 03.7	S17 24.9	64 55.9	S22 20.4	Alphecca	126 08.2	N26 39.1
A 13	358 13.6	359 21.9	54.2	95 54.5	02.3	127 06.1	24.9	79 58.2	20.4	Alpheratz	357 40.5	N29 11.3
Y 14	13 16.0	14 21.6	52.9	110 55.3	02.4	142 08.5	24.9	95 00.5	20.4	Altair	62 05.3	N 8 54.9
15	28 18.5	29 21.2 ..	51.7	125 56.2 ..	02.6	157 11.0 ..	24.9	110 02.8 ..	20.4	Ankaa	353 13.0	S42 12.7
16	43 20.9	44 20.8	50.4	140 57.1	02.7	172 13.4	24.9	125 05.0	20.4	Antares	112 22.3	S26 28.1
17	58 23.4	59 20.4	49.1	155 57.9	02.8	187 15.8	24.9	140 07.3	20.4			
18	73 25.9	74 20.1	S 1 47.8	170 58.8	S23 02.9	202 18.3	S17 24.9	155 09.6	S22 20.4	Arcturus	145 52.6	N19 05.2
19	88 28.3	89 19.7	46.5	185 59.7	03.0	217 20.7	24.9	170 11.9	20.4	Atria	107 21.2	S69 03.1
20	103 30.8	104 19.3	45.2	201 00.6	03.2	232 23.2	24.9	185 14.2	20.3	Avior	234 16.2	S59 34.4
21	118 33.3	119 18.9 ..	44.0	216 01.4 ..	03.3	247 25.6 ..	24.9	200 16.5 ..	20.3	Bellatrix	278 28.5	N 6 21.7
22	133 35.7	134 18.6	42.7	231 02.3	03.4	262 28.0	24.9	215 18.7	20.3	Betelgeuse	270 57.8	N 7 24.4
23	148 38.2	149 18.2	41.4	246 03.2	03.5	277 30.5	24.9	230 21.0	20.3			
6 00	163 40.7	164 17.8	S 1 40.1	261 04.0	S23 03.6	292 32.9	S17 24.9	245 23.3	S22 20.3	Canopus	263 54.5	S52 42.8
01	178 43.1	179 17.5	38.8	276 04.9	03.7	307 35.3	24.9	260 25.6	20.3	Capella	280 29.7	N46 00.9
02	193 45.6	194 17.1	37.6	291 05.8	03.9	322 37.8	24.9	275 27.9	20.3	Deneb	49 29.7	N45 20.6
03	208 48.0	209 16.7 ..	36.3	306 06.7 ..	04.0	337 40.2 ..	24.9	290 30.2 ..	20.3	Denebola	182 30.1	N14 28.2
04	223 50.5	224 16.3	35.0	321 07.5	04.1	352 42.7	24.9	305 32.4	20.3	Diphda	348 53.0	S17 53.5
05	238 53.0	239 16.0	33.7	336 08.4	04.2	7 45.1	24.9	320 34.7	20.3			
06	253 55.4	254 15.6	S 1 32.4	351 09.3	S23 04.3	22 47.5	S17 24.9	335 37.0	S22 20.2	Dubhe	193 47.2	N61 39.1
07	268 57.9	269 15.2	31.1	6 10.1	04.4	37 50.0	24.9	350 39.3	20.2	Elnath	278 08.5	N28 37.2
T 08	284 00.4	284 14.9	29.9	21 11.0	04.6	52 52.4	24.9	5 41.6	20.2	Eltanin	90 44.8	N51 29.0
U 09	299 02.8	299 14.5 ..	28.6	36 11.9 ..	04.7	67 54.8 ..	24.9	20 43.9 ..	20.2	Enif	33 44.3	N 9 57.4
E 10	314 05.3	314 14.1	27.3	51 12.8	04.8	82 57.3	24.9	35 46.2	20.2	Fomalhaut	15 20.8	S29 31.7
S 11	329 07.8	329 13.7	26.0	66 13.6	04.9	97 59.7	24.9	50 48.4	20.2			
D 12	344 10.2	344 13.4	S 1 24.7	81 14.5	S23 05.0	113 02.2	S17 24.9	65 50.7	S22 20.2	Gacrux	171 56.7	S57 12.8
A 13	359 12.7	359 13.0	23.4	96 15.4	05.1	128 04.6	24.9	80 53.0	20.2	Gienah	175 48.7	S17 38.6
Y 14	14 15.2	14 12.6	22.2	111 16.2	05.3	143 07.0	24.9	95 55.3	20.2	Hadar	148 42.8	S60 27.3
15	29 17.6	29 12.3 ..	20.9	126 17.1 ..	05.4	158 09.5 ..	24.9	110 57.6 ..	20.2	Hamal	327 57.4	N23 32.7
16	44 20.1	44 11.9	19.6	141 18.0	05.5	173 11.9	24.9	125 59.9	20.2	Kaus Aust.	83 39.7	S34 22.3
17	59 22.5	59 11.5	18.3	156 18.9	05.6	188 14.4	24.9	141 02.2	20.1			
18	74 25.0	74 11.1	S 1 17.0	171 19.7	S23 05.7	203 16.8	S17 24.8	156 04.4	S22 20.1	Kochab	137 19.6	N74 04.7
19	89 27.5	89 10.8	15.7	186 20.6	05.8	218 19.3	24.8	171 06.7	20.1	Markab	13 35.5	N15 18.0
20	104 29.9	104 10.4	14.5	201 21.5	05.9	233 21.7	24.8	186 09.0	20.1	Menkar	314 11.9	N 4 09.4
21	119 32.4	119 10.0 ..	13.2	216 22.4 ..	06.0	248 24.1 ..	24.8	201 11.3 ..	20.1	Menkent	148 03.5	S36 27.4
22	134 34.9	134 09.7	11.9	231 23.2	06.2	263 26.6	24.8	216 13.6	20.1	Miaplacidus	221 38.1	S69 47.7
23	149 37.3	149 09.3	10.6	246 24.1	06.3	278 29.0	24.8	231 15.9	20.1			
7 00	164 39.8	164 08.9	S 1 09.3	261 25.0	S23 06.4	293 31.5	S17 24.8	246 18.2	S22 20.1	Mirfak	308 35.9	N49 55.5
01	179 42.3	179 08.6	08.0	276 25.8	06.5	308 33.9	24.8	261 20.5	20.1	Nunki	75 54.5	S26 16.3
02	194 44.7	194 08.2	06.8	291 26.7	06.6	323 36.4	24.8	276 22.7	20.1	Peacock	53 14.7	S56 40.4
03	209 47.2	209 07.8 ..	05.5	306 27.6 ..	06.7	338 38.8 ..	24.8	291 25.0 ..	20.0	Pollux	243 23.6	N27 58.8
04	224 49.7	224 07.4	04.2	321 28.5	06.8	353 41.3	24.8	306 27.3	20.0	Procyon	244 56.2	N 5 10.5
05	239 52.1	239 07.1	02.9	336 29.3	06.9	8 43.7	24.8	321 29.6	20.0			
06	254 54.6	254 06.7	S 1 01.6	351 30.2	S23 07.1	23 46.2	S17 24.8	336 31.9	S22 20.0	Rasalhague	96 03.5	N12 32.8
W 07	269 57.0	269 06.3	1 00.3	6 31.1	07.2	38 48.6	24.8	351 34.2	20.0	Regulus	207 39.8	N11 52.6
E 08	284 59.5	284 06.0	0 59.0	21 32.0	07.3	53 51.1	24.8	6 36.5	20.0	Rigel	281 09.0	S 8 11.2
D 09	300 02.0	299 05.6 ..	57.8	36 32.8 ..	07.4	68 53.5 ..	24.8	21 38.8 ..	20.0	Rigil Kent.	139 47.0	S60 54.2
N 10	315 04.4	314 05.2	56.5	51 33.7	07.5	83 55.9	24.8	36 41.1	20.0	Sabik	102 08.9	S15 44.7
E 11	330 06.9	329 04.9	55.2	66 34.6	07.6	98 58.4	24.8	51 43.3	20.0			
S 12	345 09.4	344 04.5	S 0 53.9	81 35.5	S23 07.7	114 00.8	S17 24.8	66 45.6	S22 20.0	Schedar	349 37.3	N56 38.2
D 13	0 11.8	359 04.1	52.6	96 36.3	07.8	129 03.3	24.8	81 47.9	19.9	Shaula	96 17.6	S37 06.7
A 14	15 14.3	14 03.8	51.3	111 37.2	07.9	144 05.7	24.8	96 50.2	19.9	Sirius	258 30.8	S16 44.8
Y 15	30 16.8	29 03.4 ..	50.0	126 38.1 ..	08.0	159 08.2 ..	24.8	111 52.5 ..	19.9	Spica	158 27.6	S11 15.3
16	45 19.2	44 03.0	48.8	141 38.9	08.1	174 10.6	24.8	126 54.8	19.9	Suhail	222 49.7	S43 30.6
17	60 21.7	59 02.6	47.5	156 39.8	08.3	189 13.1	24.8	141 57.1	19.9			
18	75 24.1	74 02.3	S 0 46.2	171 40.7	S23 08.4	204 15.5	S17 24.8	156 59.4	S22 19.9	Vega	80 37.0	N38 47.9
19	90 26.6	89 01.9	44.9	186 41.6	08.5	219 18.0	24.8	172 01.7	19.9	Zuben'ubi	137 01.7	S16 06.9
20	105 29.1	104 01.5	43.6	201 42.4	08.6	234 20.4	24.8	187 04.0	19.9		SHA	Mer. Pass.
21	120 31.5	119 01.2 ..	42.3	216 43.3 ..	08.7	249 22.9 ..	24.8	202 06.3 ..	19.9		° ′	h m
22	135 34.0	134 00.8	41.1	231 44.2	08.8	264 25.4	24.8	217 08.5	19.9	Venus	0 37.2	13 03
23	150 36.5	149 00.4	39.8	246 45.1	08.9	279 27.8	24.8	232 10.8	19.8	Mars	97 23.4	6 35
	h m									Jupiter	128 52.2	4 29
Mer. Pass. 13 03.1	v −0.4 d 1.3	v 0.9 d 0.1		v 2.4 d 0.0		v 2.3 d 0.0				Saturn	81 42.6	7 37

UT	SUN GHA	SUN Dec	MOON GHA	v	Dec	d	HP
d h	° ′	° ′	° ′	′	° ′	′	′
5 00	177 06.2	S 6 09.4	319 58.7	12.0	S 4 17.9	11.2	57.4
01	192 06.4	08.5	334 29.7	12.0	4 29.1	11.1	57.4
02	207 06.5	07.5	349 00.7	12.1	4 40.2	11.1	57.3
03	222 06.7 . .	06.5	3 31.8	12.1	4 51.3	11.1	57.3
04	237 06.8	05.6	18 02.9	12.1	5 02.4	11.0	57.2
05	252 06.9	04.6	32 34.0	12.1	5 13.4	11.0	57.2
06	267 07.1	S 6 03.6	47 05.1	12.2	S 5 24.4	11.0	57.2
07	282 07.2	02.7	61 36.3	12.2	5 35.4	10.9	57.1
08	297 07.4	01.7	76 07.5	12.2	5 46.3	10.9	57.1
M 09	312 07.5	6 00.7	90 38.7	12.2	5 57.2	10.8	57.1
O 10	327 07.7	5 59.8	105 09.9	12.2	6 08.0	10.8	57.0
N 11	342 07.8	58.8	119 41.1	12.3	6 18.8	10.7	57.0
D 12	357 07.9	S 5 57.8	134 12.4	12.3	S 6 29.5	10.7	57.0
A 13	12 08.1	56.9	148 43.7	12.3	6 40.2	10.6	56.9
Y 14	27 08.2	55.9	163 15.0	12.3	6 50.8	10.6	56.9
15	42 08.4 . .	54.9	177 46.3	12.3	7 01.4	10.6	56.9
16	57 08.5	54.0	192 17.6	12.4	7 12.0	10.5	56.8
17	72 08.7	53.0	206 49.0	12.3	7 22.5	10.4	56.8
18	87 08.8	S 5 52.0	221 20.3	12.4	S 7 32.9	10.4	56.8
19	102 08.9	51.1	235 51.7	12.4	7 43.3	10.4	56.7
20	117 09.1	50.1	250 23.1	12.4	7 53.7	10.3	56.7
21	132 09.2 . .	49.1	264 54.5	12.4	8 04.0	10.2	56.7
22	147 09.4	48.2	279 25.9	12.4	8 14.2	10.2	56.6
23	162 09.5	47.2	293 57.3	12.5	8 24.4	10.1	56.6
6 00	177 09.7	S 5 46.2	308 28.8	12.4	S 8 34.5	10.1	56.6
01	192 09.8	45.3	323 00.2	12.5	8 44.6	10.1	56.5
02	207 09.9	44.3	337 31.7	12.5	8 54.7	9.9	56.5
03	222 10.1 . .	43.3	352 03.1	12.5	9 04.6	10.0	56.5
04	237 10.2	42.4	6 34.6	12.5	9 14.6	9.8	56.4
05	252 10.4	41.4	21 06.1	12.5	9 24.4	9.8	56.4
06	267 10.5	S 5 40.4	35 37.6	12.5	S 9 34.2	9.8	56.4
07	282 10.7	39.5	50 09.1	12.5	9 44.0	9.7	56.3
T 08	297 10.8	38.5	64 40.6	12.6	9 53.7	9.6	56.3
U 09	312 11.0 . .	37.5	79 12.2	12.5	10 03.3	9.6	56.3
E 10	327 11.1	36.5	93 43.7	12.5	10 12.9	9.5	56.2
S 11	342 11.3	35.6	108 15.2	12.6	10 22.4	9.5	56.2
D 12	357 11.4	S 5 34.6	122 46.8	12.5	S10 31.9	9.3	56.2
A 13	12 11.5	33.6	137 18.3	12.6	10 41.2	9.4	56.1
Y 14	27 11.7	32.7	151 49.9	12.6	10 50.6	9.2	56.1
15	42 11.8 . .	31.7	166 21.5	12.6	10 59.8	9.3	56.1
16	57 12.0	30.7	180 53.0	12.6	11 09.1	9.1	56.0
17	72 12.1	29.8	195 24.6	12.6	11 18.2	9.1	56.0
18	87 12.3	S 5 28.8	209 56.2	12.5	S11 27.3	9.0	56.0
19	102 12.4	27.8	224 27.7	12.6	11 36.3	8.9	56.0
20	117 12.6	26.8	238 59.3	12.6	11 45.2	8.9	55.9
21	132 12.7 . .	25.9	253 30.9	12.6	11 54.1	8.8	55.9
22	147 12.9	24.9	268 02.5	12.6	12 02.9	8.8	55.9
23	162 13.0	23.9	282 34.1	12.6	12 11.7	8.7	55.8
7 00	177 13.2	S 5 23.0	297 05.7	12.5	S12 20.4	8.6	55.8
01	192 13.3	22.0	311 37.2	12.6	12 29.0	8.5	55.8
02	207 13.5	21.0	326 08.8	12.6	12 37.5	8.5	55.7
03	222 13.6 . .	20.0	340 40.4	12.6	12 46.0	8.4	55.7
04	237 13.8	19.1	355 12.0	12.6	12 54.4	8.4	55.7
05	252 13.9	18.1	9 43.6	12.6	13 02.8	8.2	55.7
06	267 14.1	S 5 17.1	24 15.2	12.6	S13 11.0	8.2	55.6
W 07	282 14.2	16.2	38 46.8	12.5	13 19.2	8.2	55.6
E 08	297 14.4	15.2	53 18.3	12.6	13 27.4	8.0	55.6
D 09	312 14.5 . .	14.2	67 49.9	12.6	13 35.4	8.0	55.6
N 10	327 14.7	13.2	82 21.5	12.6	13 43.4	7.9	55.5
E 11	342 14.8	12.3	96 53.1	12.6	13 51.3	7.9	55.5
S 12	357 15.0	S 5 11.3	111 24.7	12.5	S13 59.2	7.7	55.5
D 13	12 15.1	10.3	125 56.2	12.6	14 06.9	7.7	55.4
A 14	27 15.3	09.4	140 27.8	12.6	14 14.6	7.7	55.4
Y 15	42 15.4 . .	08.4	154 59.4	12.5	14 22.3	7.5	55.4
16	57 15.6	07.4	169 30.9	12.6	14 29.8	7.5	55.4
17	72 15.7	06.4	184 02.5	12.5	14 37.3	7.4	55.3
18	87 15.9	S 5 05.5	198 34.0	12.6	S14 44.7	7.3	55.3
19	102 16.0	04.5	213 05.6	12.5	14 52.0	7.3	55.3
20	117 16.2	03.5	227 37.1	12.5	14 59.3	7.1	55.2
21	132 16.3 . .	02.5	242 08.6	12.6	15 06.4	7.1	55.2
22	147 16.5	01.6	256 40.2	12.5	15 13.5	7.0	55.2
23	162 16.6	00.6	271 11.7	12.5	S15 20.5	7.0	55.2
	SD 16.1	d 1.0	SD 15.5		15.3		15.1

Lat.	Twilight Naut.	Twilight Civil	Sunrise	Moonrise 5	6	7	8
°	h m	h m	h m	h m	h m	h m	h m
N 72	04 45	06 03	07 11	23 15	25 08	01 08	03 09
N 70	04 53	06 03	07 04	23 02	24 44	00 44	02 27
68	04 59	06 03	06 59	22 51	24 26	00 26	01 59
66	05 04	06 03	06 54	22 42	24 11	00 11	01 37
64	05 08	06 03	06 50	22 34	23 59	25 21	01 21
62	05 12	06 03	06 47	22 28	23 49	25 07	01 07
60	05 14	06 03	06 44	22 23	23 41	24 55	00 55
N 58	05 17	06 02	06 41	22 18	23 33	24 45	00 45
56	05 19	06 02	06 39	22 13	23 27	24 36	00 36
54	05 21	06 02	06 37	22 10	23 21	24 29	00 29
52	05 22	06 01	06 35	22 06	23 15	24 22	00 22
50	05 24	06 01	06 33	22 03	23 11	24 15	00 15
45	05 26	06 00	06 29	21 56	23 00	24 02	00 02
N 40	05 28	05 59	06 26	21 50	22 52	23 51	24 48
35	05 29	05 58	06 23	21 46	22 45	23 42	24 37
30	05 29	05 57	06 21	21 41	22 38	23 33	24 27
20	05 28	05 54	06 16	21 34	22 27	23 19	24 11
N 10	05 26	05 51	06 12	21 28	22 18	23 07	23 56
0	05 23	05 47	06 08	21 22	22 09	22 56	23 43
S 10	05 18	05 43	06 04	21 16	22 00	22 44	23 29
20	05 11	05 37	05 59	21 09	21 50	22 32	23 15
30	05 02	05 30	05 54	21 02	21 40	22 18	22 59
35	04 55	05 26	05 51	20 58	21 33	22 10	22 49
40	04 48	05 20	05 48	20 54	21 26	22 01	22 39
45	04 38	05 14	05 44	20 48	21 18	21 51	22 26
S 50	04 26	05 06	05 39	20 42	21 09	21 38	22 11
52	04 20	05 02	05 37	20 39	21 04	21 32	22 04
54	04 13	04 58	05 34	20 36	20 59	21 25	21 56
56	04 06	04 53	05 31	20 32	20 54	21 18	21 47
58	03 57	04 47	05 28	20 28	20 48	21 10	21 37
S 60	03 46	04 41	05 25	20 24	20 41	21 01	21 25

Lat.	Sunset	Twilight Civil	Twilight Naut.	Moonset 5	6	7	8
°	h m	h m	h m	h m	h m	h m	h m
N 72	17 14	18 21	19 41	07 41	07 30	07 15	06 53
N 70	17 20	18 21	19 33	07 49	07 45	07 41	07 36
68	17 25	18 21	19 26	07 56	07 58	08 00	08 05
66	17 30	18 21	19 21	08 02	08 08	08 16	08 27
64	17 34	18 21	19 16	08 07	08 16	08 28	08 44
62	17 37	18 21	19 13	08 11	08 24	08 39	08 58
60	17 40	18 21	19 10	08 14	08 30	08 49	09 10
N 58	17 42	18 21	19 07	08 18	08 36	08 57	09 21
56	17 44	18 22	19 05	08 20	08 41	09 04	09 30
54	17 47	18 22	19 03	08 23	08 46	09 10	09 38
52	17 48	18 22	19 01	08 25	08 50	09 16	09 46
50	17 50	18 22	19 00	08 28	08 54	09 21	09 52
45	17 54	18 23	18 57	08 32	09 02	09 33	10 07
N 40	17 57	18 24	18 56	08 36	09 09	09 42	10 18
35	18 00	18 25	18 55	08 40	09 14	09 50	10 28
30	18 02	18 26	18 54	08 43	09 19	09 58	10 37
20	18 07	18 29	18 54	08 48	09 29	10 10	10 52
N 10	18 11	18 32	18 56	08 52	09 37	10 21	11 06
0	18 15	18 35	18 59	08 57	09 44	10 31	11 18
S 10	18 18	18 40	19 04	09 01	09 52	10 41	11 31
20	18 23	18 45	19 11	09 06	10 00	10 52	11 44
30	18 28	18 52	19 20	09 11	10 09	11 05	11 59
35	18 31	18 56	19 26	09 14	10 14	11 12	12 08
40	18 34	19 01	19 34	09 18	10 20	11 20	12 19
45	18 38	19 08	19 43	09 22	10 27	11 30	12 31
S 50	18 43	19 16	19 55	09 26	10 36	11 42	12 45
52	18 45	19 19	20 01	09 29	10 39	11 47	12 52
54	18 47	19 23	20 08	09 31	10 44	11 53	13 00
56	18 50	19 28	20 15	09 34	10 49	12 00	13 08
58	18 53	19 33	20 24	09 37	10 54	12 08	13 18
S 60	18 56	19 39	20 34	09 40	11 00	12 16	13 29

Day	SUN Eqn. of Time 00h	SUN Eqn. of Time 12h	SUN Mer. Pass.	MOON Mer. Pass. Upper	MOON Mer. Pass. Lower	Age	Phase
d	m s	m s	h m	h m	h m	d	%
5	11 35	11 29	12 11	02 45	15 09	18	86
6	11 22	11 15	12 11	03 33	15 56	19	78
7	11 08	11 00	12 11	04 20	16 43	20	69

UT	ARIES GHA	VENUS −3.9 GHA	Dec	MARS +0.7 GHA	Dec	JUPITER −2.2 GHA	Dec	SATURN +0.6 GHA	Dec	STARS Name	SHA	Dec
8 00	165 38.9	164 00.1	S 0 38.5	261 45.9	S23 09.0	294 30.3	S17 24.8	247 13.1	S22 19.8	Acamar	315 16.2	S40 14.4
01	180 41.4	178 59.7	37.2	276 46.8	09.1	309 32.7	24.8	262 15.4	19.8	Achernar	335 24.9	S57 09.0
02	195 43.9	193 59.3	35.9	291 47.7	09.2	324 35.2	24.8	277 17.7	19.8	Acrux	173 05.0	S63 11.9
03	210 46.3	208 59.0 ..	34.6	306 48.6 ..	09.3	339 37.6 ..	24.8	292 20.0 ..	19.8	Adhara	255 09.8	S29 00.2
04	225 48.8	223 58.6	33.3	321 49.4	09.4	354 40.1	24.8	307 22.3	19.8	Aldebaran	290 45.7	N16 32.5
05	240 51.3	238 58.2	32.1	336 50.3	09.5	9 42.5	24.8	322 24.6	19.8			
06	255 53.7	253 57.9	S 0 30.8	351 51.2	S23 09.6	24 45.0	S17 24.7	337 26.9	S22 19.8	Alioth	166 17.4	N55 51.6
07	270 56.2	268 57.5	29.5	6 52.1	09.7	39 47.4	24.7	352 29.2	19.8	Alkaid	152 56.0	N49 13.3
08	285 58.6	283 57.1	28.2	21 52.9	09.8	54 49.9	24.7	7 31.5	19.8	Al Na'ir	27 40.2	S46 52.4
09	301 01.1	298 56.8 ..	26.9	36 53.8 ..	09.9	69 52.3 ..	24.7	22 33.8 ..	19.8	Alnilam	275 43.1	S 1 11.7
10	316 03.6	313 56.4	25.6	51 54.7	10.0	84 54.8	24.7	37 36.0	19.7	Alphard	217 52.7	S 8 44.4
11	331 06.0	328 56.0	24.3	66 55.6	10.2	99 57.3	24.7	52 38.3	19.7			
12	346 08.5	343 55.7	S 0 23.0	81 56.4	S23 10.3	114 59.7	S17 24.7	67 40.6	S22 19.7	Alphecca	126 08.2	N26 39.1
13	1 11.0	358 55.3	21.8	96 57.3	10.4	130 02.2	24.7	82 42.9	19.7	Alpheratz	357 40.5	N29 11.3
14	16 13.4	13 54.9	20.5	111 58.2	10.5	145 04.6	24.7	97 45.2	19.7	Altair	62 05.3	N 8 54.9
15	31 15.9	28 54.6 ..	19.2	126 59.1 ..	10.6	160 07.1 ..	24.7	112 47.5 ..	19.7	Ankaa	353 13.0	S42 12.7
16	46 18.4	43 54.2	17.9	142 00.0	10.7	175 09.5	24.7	127 49.8	19.7	Antares	112 22.3	S26 28.1
17	61 20.8	58 53.8	16.6	157 00.8	10.8	190 12.0	24.7	142 52.1	19.7			
18	76 23.3	73 53.5	S 0 15.3	172 01.7	S23 10.9	205 14.5	S17 24.7	157 54.4	S22 19.7	Arcturus	145 52.6	N19 05.2
19	91 25.7	88 53.1	14.0	187 02.6	11.0	220 16.9	24.7	172 56.7	19.7	Atria	107 21.2	S69 03.1
20	106 28.2	103 52.7	12.8	202 03.5	11.1	235 19.4	24.7	187 59.0	19.6	Avior	234 16.2	S59 34.4
21	121 30.7	118 52.4 ..	11.5	217 04.3 ..	11.2	250 21.8 ..	24.7	203 01.3 ..	19.6	Bellatrix	278 28.6	N 6 21.7
22	136 33.1	133 52.0	10.2	232 05.2	11.3	265 24.3	24.7	218 03.6	19.6	Betelgeuse	270 57.8	N 7 24.4
23	151 35.6	148 51.6	08.9	247 06.1	11.4	280 26.8	24.7	233 05.9	19.6			
9 00	166 38.1	163 51.3	S 0 07.6	262 07.0	S23 11.5	295 29.2	S17 24.7	248 08.2	S22 19.6	Canopus	263 54.6	S52 42.8
01	181 40.5	178 50.9	06.3	277 07.8	11.6	310 31.7	24.7	263 10.5	19.6	Capella	280 29.7	N46 00.9
02	196 43.0	193 50.5	05.0	292 08.7	11.7	325 34.1	24.6	278 12.8	19.6	Deneb	49 29.6	N45 20.6
03	211 45.5	208 50.2 ..	03.8	307 09.6 ..	11.8	340 36.6 ..	24.6	293 15.1 ..	19.6	Denebola	182 30.1	N14 28.2
04	226 47.9	223 49.8	02.5	322 10.5	11.9	355 39.1	24.6	308 17.3	19.6	Diphda	348 53.0	S17 53.5
05	241 50.4	238 49.4	S 01.2	337 11.3	12.0	10 41.5	24.6	323 19.6	19.6			
06	256 52.9	253 49.1	N 0 00.1	352 12.2	S23 12.1	25 44.0	S17 24.6	338 21.9	S22 19.5	Dubhe	193 47.2	N61 39.2
07	271 55.3	268 48.7	01.4	7 13.1	12.2	40 46.5	24.6	353 24.2	19.5	Elnath	278 08.5	N28 37.2
08	286 57.8	283 48.3	02.7	22 14.0	12.3	55 48.9	24.6	8 26.5	19.5	Eltanin	90 44.8	N51 29.0
09	302 00.2	298 48.0 ..	04.0	37 14.9 ..	12.4	70 51.4 ..	24.6	23 28.8 ..	19.5	Enif	33 44.3	N 9 57.4
10	317 02.7	313 47.6	05.3	52 15.7	12.5	85 53.8	24.6	38 31.1	19.5	Fomalhaut	15 20.8	S29 31.7
11	332 05.2	328 47.2	06.5	67 16.6	12.6	100 56.3	24.6	53 33.4	19.5			
12	347 07.6	343 46.9	N 0 07.8	82 17.5	S23 12.7	115 58.8	S17 24.6	68 35.7	S22 19.5	Gacrux	171 56.7	S57 12.8
13	2 10.1	358 46.5	09.1	97 18.4	12.8	131 01.2	24.6	83 38.0	19.5	Gienah	175 48.7	S17 38.6
14	17 12.6	13 46.1	10.4	112 19.2	12.9	146 03.7	24.6	98 40.3	19.5	Hadar	148 42.8	S60 27.3
15	32 15.0	28 45.8 ..	11.7	127 20.1 ..	13.0	161 06.2 ..	24.6	113 42.6 ..	19.5	Hamal	327 57.4	N23 32.7
16	47 17.5	43 45.4	13.0	142 21.0	13.0	176 08.6	24.6	128 44.9	19.5	Kaus Aust.	83 39.7	S34 22.3
17	62 20.0	58 45.0	14.3	157 21.9	13.1	191 11.1	24.5	143 47.2	19.4			
18	77 22.4	73 44.7	N 0 15.6	172 22.8	S23 13.2	206 13.6	S17 24.5	158 49.5	S22 19.4	Kochab	137 19.5	N74 04.7
19	92 24.9	88 44.3	16.8	187 23.6	13.3	221 16.0	24.5	173 51.8	19.4	Markab	13 35.5	N15 18.0
20	107 27.4	103 43.9	18.1	202 24.5	13.4	236 18.5	24.5	188 54.1	19.4	Menkar	314 11.9	N 4 09.4
21	122 29.8	118 43.6 ..	19.4	217 25.4 ..	13.5	251 21.0 ..	24.5	203 56.4 ..	19.4	Menkent	148 03.5	S36 27.4
22	137 32.3	133 43.2	20.7	232 26.3	13.6	266 23.4	24.5	218 58.7	19.4	Miaplacidus	221 38.2	S69 47.7
23	152 34.7	148 42.8	22.0	247 27.2	13.7	281 25.9	24.5	234 01.0	19.4			
10 00	167 37.2	163 42.5	N 0 23.3	262 28.0	S23 13.8	296 28.4	S17 24.5	249 03.3	S22 19.4	Mirfak	308 35.9	N49 55.5
01	182 39.7	178 42.1	24.6	277 28.9	13.9	311 30.8	24.5	264 05.6	19.4	Nunki	75 54.5	S26 16.3
02	197 42.1	193 41.8	25.8	292 29.8	14.0	326 33.3	24.5	279 07.9	19.4	Peacock	53 14.7	S56 40.4
03	212 44.6	208 41.4 ..	27.1	307 30.7 ..	14.1	341 35.8 ..	24.5	294 10.2 ..	19.4	Pollux	243 23.6	N27 58.8
04	227 47.1	223 41.0	28.4	322 31.5	14.2	356 38.3	24.5	309 12.5	19.3	Procyon	244 56.2	N 5 10.5
05	242 49.5	238 40.7	29.7	337 32.4	14.3	11 40.7	24.5	324 14.8	19.3			
06	257 52.0	253 40.3	N 0 31.0	352 33.3	S23 14.4	26 43.2	S17 24.4	339 17.1	S22 19.3	Rasalhague	96 03.5	N12 32.8
07	272 54.5	268 39.9	32.3	7 34.2	14.5	41 45.7	24.4	354 19.4	19.3	Regulus	207 39.8	N11 52.6
08	287 56.9	283 39.6	33.6	22 35.1	14.6	56 48.1	24.4	9 21.7	19.3	Rigel	281 09.0	S 8 11.2
09	302 59.4	298 39.2 ..	34.9	37 35.9 ..	14.7	71 50.6 ..	24.4	24 24.0 ..	19.3	Rigil Kent.	139 46.9	S60 54.3
10	318 01.9	313 38.8	36.1	52 36.8	14.7	86 53.1	24.4	39 26.3	19.3	Sabik	102 08.9	S15 44.7
11	333 04.3	328 38.5	37.4	67 37.7	14.8	101 55.6	24.4	54 28.6	19.3			
12	348 06.8	343 38.1	N 0 38.7	82 38.6	S23 14.9	116 58.0	S17 24.4	69 30.9	S22 19.3	Schedar	349 37.3	N56 38.1
13	3 09.2	358 37.7	40.0	97 39.5	15.0	132 00.5	24.4	84 33.2	19.3	Shaula	96 17.6	S37 06.7
14	18 11.7	13 37.4	41.3	112 40.3	15.1	147 03.0	24.4	99 35.5	19.2	Sirius	258 30.8	S16 44.8
15	33 14.2	28 37.0 ..	42.6	127 41.2 ..	15.2	162 05.4 ..	24.4	114 37.8 ..	19.2	Spica	158 27.6	S11 15.3
16	48 16.6	43 36.6	43.9	142 42.1	15.3	177 07.9	24.4	129 40.1	19.2	Suhail	222 49.7	S43 30.6
17	63 19.1	58 36.3	45.2	157 43.0	15.4	192 10.4	24.4	144 42.4	19.2			
18	78 21.6	73 35.9	N 0 46.4	172 43.9	S23 15.5	207 12.9	S17 24.3	159 44.7	S22 19.2	Vega	80 36.9	N38 47.9
19	93 24.0	88 35.6	47.7	187 44.8	15.6	222 15.3	24.3	174 47.0	19.2	Zuben'ubi	137 01.7	S16 06.9
20	108 26.5	103 35.2	49.0	202 45.6	15.7	237 17.8	24.3	189 49.3	19.2		SHA	Mer. Pass.
21	123 29.0	118 34.8 ..	50.3	217 46.5 ..	15.7	252 20.3 ..	24.3	204 51.6 ..	19.2		° ′	h m
22	138 31.4	133 34.5	51.6	232 47.4	15.8	267 22.8	24.3	219 53.9	19.2	Venus	357 13.2	13 05
23	153 33.9	148 34.1	52.9	247 48.3	15.9	282 25.3	24.3	234 56.2	19.2	Mars	95 28.9	6 31
	h m									Jupiter	128 51.2	4 17
Mer. Pass.	12 51.4	v −0.4	d 1.3	v 0.9	d 0.1	v 2.5	d 0.0	v 2.3	d 0.0	Saturn	81 30.1	7 26

UT	SUN GHA	SUN Dec	MOON GHA	MOON v	MOON Dec	MOON d	MOON HP
d h	° ′	° ′	° ′	′	° ′	′	′
8 00	177 16.8	S 4 59.6	285 43.2	12.5	S15 27.5	6.8	55.2
01	192 16.9	58.6	300 14.7	12.5	15 34.3	6.8	55.1
02	207 17.1	57.7	314 46.2	12.5	15 41.1	6.7	55.1
03	222 17.2	.. 56.7	329 17.7	12.5	15 47.8	6.6	55.1
04	237 17.4	55.7	343 49.2	12.5	15 54.4	6.6	55.1
05	252 17.5	54.7	358 20.7	12.5	16 01.0	6.5	55.0
06	267 17.7	S 4 53.8	12 52.2	12.4	S16 07.5	6.4	55.0
07	282 17.8	52.8	27 23.6	12.5	16 13.9	6.3	55.0
08	297 18.0	51.8	41 55.1	12.4	16 20.2	6.2	55.0
T 09	312 18.1	.. 50.8	56 26.5	12.5	16 26.4	6.1	55.0
H 10	327 18.3	49.9	70 58.0	12.4	16 32.5	6.1	54.9
U 11	342 18.5	48.9	85 29.4	12.5	16 38.6	6.0	54.9
R 12	357 18.6	S 4 47.9	100 00.9	12.4	S16 44.6	5.9	54.9
S 13	12 18.8	46.9	114 32.3	12.4	16 50.5	5.8	54.9
D 14	27 18.9	46.0	129 03.7	12.4	16 56.3	5.7	54.9
A 15	42 19.1	.. 45.0	143 35.1	12.4	17 02.0	5.7	54.8
Y 16	57 19.2	44.0	158 06.5	12.4	17 07.7	5.6	54.8
17	72 19.4	43.0	172 37.9	12.4	17 13.3	5.4	54.8
18	87 19.5	S 4 42.1	187 09.3	12.4	S17 18.7	5.4	54.8
19	102 19.7	41.1	201 40.7	12.3	17 24.1	5.4	54.8
20	117 19.8	40.1	216 12.0	12.4	17 29.5	5.2	54.7
21	132 20.0	.. 39.1	230 43.4	12.3	17 34.7	5.2	54.7
22	147 20.2	38.2	245 14.7	12.3	17 39.9	5.0	54.7
23	162 20.3	37.2	259 46.1	12.3	17 44.9	5.0	54.7
9 00	177 20.5	S 4 36.2	274 17.4	12.3	S17 49.9	4.9	54.7
01	192 20.6	35.2	288 48.7	12.3	17 54.8	4.8	54.7
02	207 20.8	34.3	303 20.0	12.3	17 59.6	4.7	54.6
03	222 20.9	.. 33.3	317 51.3	12.3	18 04.3	4.7	54.6
04	237 21.1	32.3	332 22.6	12.3	18 09.0	4.5	54.6
05	252 21.3	31.3	346 53.9	12.3	18 13.5	4.5	54.6
06	267 21.4	S 4 30.3	1 25.2	12.3	S18 18.0	4.4	54.6
07	282 21.6	29.4	15 56.5	12.2	18 22.4	4.2	54.6
08	297 21.7	28.4	30 27.7	12.3	18 26.6	4.2	54.5
F 09	312 21.9	.. 27.4	44 59.0	12.2	18 30.8	4.2	54.5
R 10	327 22.0	26.4	59 30.2	12.2	18 35.0	4.0	54.5
I 11	342 22.2	25.5	74 01.4	12.3	18 39.0	3.9	54.5
D 12	357 22.4	S 4 24.5	88 32.7	12.2	S18 42.9	3.9	54.5
A 13	12 22.5	23.5	103 03.9	12.2	18 46.8	3.7	54.5
Y 14	27 22.7	22.5	117 35.1	12.2	18 50.5	3.7	54.5
15	42 22.8	.. 21.5	132 06.3	12.2	18 54.2	3.6	54.4
16	57 23.0	20.6	146 37.5	12.2	18 57.8	3.5	54.4
17	72 23.1	19.6	161 08.7	12.1	19 01.3	3.4	54.4
18	87 23.3	S 4 18.6	175 39.8	12.2	S19 04.7	3.3	54.4
19	102 23.5	17.6	190 11.0	12.2	19 08.0	3.3	54.4
20	117 23.6	16.6	204 42.2	12.1	19 11.3	3.1	54.4
21	132 23.8	.. 15.7	219 13.3	12.2	19 14.4	3.0	54.4
22	147 23.9	14.7	233 44.5	12.1	19 17.4	3.0	54.4
23	162 24.1	13.7	248 15.6	12.1	19 20.4	2.9	54.4
10 00	177 24.3	S 4 12.7	262 46.7	12.2	S19 23.3	2.7	54.3
01	192 24.4	11.8	277 17.9	12.1	19 26.0	2.7	54.3
02	207 24.6	10.8	291 49.0	12.1	19 28.7	2.6	54.3
03	222 24.7	.. 09.8	306 20.1	12.1	19 31.3	2.5	54.3
04	237 24.9	08.8	320 51.2	12.1	19 33.8	2.4	54.3
05	252 25.0	07.8	335 22.3	12.1	19 36.2	2.4	54.3
06	267 25.2	S 4 06.9	349 53.4	12.0	S19 38.6	2.2	54.3
07	282 25.4	05.9	4 24.4	12.1	19 40.8	2.1	54.3
S 08	297 25.5	04.9	18 55.5	12.1	19 42.9	2.1	54.3
A 09	312 25.7	.. 03.9	33 26.6	12.1	19 45.0	1.9	54.3
T 10	327 25.9	02.9	47 57.7	12.0	19 46.9	1.9	54.3
U 11	342 26.0	02.0	62 28.7	12.1	19 48.8	1.8	54.3
R 12	357 26.2	S 4 01.0	76 59.8	12.0	S19 50.6	1.7	54.3
D 13	12 26.3	4 00.0	91 30.8	12.1	19 52.3	1.6	54.2
A 14	27 26.5	3 59.0	106 01.9	12.0	19 53.9	1.4	54.2
Y 15	42 26.7	.. 58.0	120 32.9	12.0	19 55.3	1.5	54.2
16	57 26.8	57.1	135 03.9	12.1	19 56.8	1.3	54.2
17	72 27.0	56.1	149 35.0	12.0	19 58.1	1.2	54.2
18	87 27.1	S 3 55.1	164 06.0	12.0	S19 59.3	1.1	54.2
19	102 27.3	54.1	178 37.0	12.0	20 00.4	1.0	54.2
20	117 27.5	53.1	193 08.0	12.0	20 01.4	1.0	54.2
21	132 27.6	.. 52.1	207 39.0	12.0	20 02.4	0.8	54.2
22	147 27.8	51.2	222 10.0	12.1	20 03.2	0.8	54.2
23	162 28.0	50.2	236 41.1	12.0	S20 04.0	0.7	54.2
	SD 16.1	d 1.0	SD 15.0		14.8		14.8

Twilight / Sunrise / Moonrise

Lat.	Twilight Naut.	Twilight Civil	Sunrise	Moonrise 8	Moonrise 9	Moonrise 10	Moonrise 11
°	h m	h m	h m	h m	h m	h m	h m
N 72	04 28	05 48	06 55	03 09	■■■■	■■■■	■■■■
N 70	04 38	05 50	06 50	02 27	04 11	06 02	■■■■
68	04 46	05 51	06 46	01 59	03 27	04 47	05 49
66	04 52	05 52	06 43	01 37	02 58	04 10	05 08
64	04 57	05 53	06 40	01 21	02 37	03 44	04 40
62	05 02	05 53	06 37	01 07	02 19	03 24	04 19
60	05 06	05 54	06 35	00 55	02 05	03 07	04 01
N 58	05 09	05 54	06 33	00 45	01 53	02 54	03 47
56	05 11	05 54	06 31	00 36	01 42	02 42	03 34
54	05 14	05 55	06 30	00 29	01 33	02 31	03 24
52	05 16	05 55	06 28	00 22	01 24	02 22	03 14
50	05 17	05 55	06 27	00 15	01 17	02 14	03 05
45	05 21	05 55	06 24	00 02	01 01	01 56	02 47
N 40	05 23	05 54	06 21	24 48	00 48	01 42	02 32
35	05 25	05 54	06 19	24 37	00 37	01 30	02 20
30	05 26	05 53	06 17	24 27	00 27	01 19	02 09
20	05 26	05 52	06 14	24 11	00 11	01 01	01 50
N 10	05 25	05 49	06 10	23 56	24 45	00 45	01 33
0	05 22	05 47	06 07	23 43	24 30	00 30	01 18
S 10	05 18	05 43	06 04	23 29	24 16	00 16	01 03
20	05 13	05 38	06 00	23 15	24 00	00 00	00 47
30	05 04	05 32	05 56	22 59	23 42	24 28	00 28
35	04 58	05 28	05 54	22 49	23 31	24 17	00 17
40	04 51	05 24	05 51	22 39	23 20	24 04	00 04
45	04 43	05 18	05 48	22 26	23 06	23 50	24 39
S 50	04 32	05 11	05 44	22 11	22 48	23 32	24 21
52	04 26	05 08	05 42	22 04	22 40	23 23	24 12
54	04 20	05 04	05 40	21 56	22 31	23 14	24 03
56	04 13	05 00	05 38	21 47	22 21	23 03	23 52
58	04 05	04 55	05 35	21 37	22 10	22 51	23 40
S 60	03 56	04 49	05 32	21 25	21 57	22 37	23 26

Sunset / Twilight / Moonset

Lat.	Sunset	Twilight Civil	Twilight Naut.	Moonset 8	Moonset 9	Moonset 10	Moonset 11
°	h m	h m	h m	h m	h m	h m	h m
N 72	17 28	18 35	19 56	06 53	■■■■	■■■■	■■■■
N 70	17 33	18 33	19 46	07 36	07 30	07 18	■■■■
68	17 36	18 32	19 38	08 05	08 14	08 33	09 11
66	17 40	18 31	19 31	08 27	08 43	09 10	09 51
64	17 43	18 30	19 26	08 44	09 05	09 36	10 19
62	17 45	18 29	19 21	08 58	09 23	09 57	10 41
60	17 47	18 29	19 17	09 10	09 38	10 13	10 58
N 58	17 49	18 28	19 14	09 21	09 51	10 27	11 13
56	17 51	18 28	19 11	09 30	10 02	10 40	11 25
54	17 52	18 28	19 09	09 38	10 11	10 50	11 36
52	17 54	18 27	19 07	09 46	10 20	11 00	11 46
50	17 55	18 27	19 05	09 52	10 28	11 08	11 54
45	17 58	18 27	19 01	10 07	10 44	11 26	12 12
N 40	18 00	18 27	18 59	10 18	10 57	11 40	12 27
35	18 02	18 28	18 57	10 28	11 09	11 53	12 40
30	18 04	18 28	18 56	10 37	11 19	12 04	12 51
20	18 08	18 30	18 55	10 52	11 36	12 22	13 10
N 10	18 11	18 32	18 56	11 06	11 51	12 38	13 26
0	18 14	18 35	18 59	11 18	12 06	12 53	13 41
S 10	18 17	18 38	19 02	11 31	12 20	13 08	13 57
20	18 20	18 42	19 08	11 44	12 35	13 25	14 13
30	18 24	18 48	19 16	11 59	12 52	13 43	14 32
35	18 27	18 52	19 22	12 08	13 02	13 54	14 42
40	18 29	18 57	19 29	12 19	13 14	14 06	14 55
45	18 32	19 02	19 37	12 31	13 28	14 21	15 10
S 50	18 36	19 09	19 48	12 45	13 44	14 39	15 28
52	18 38	19 12	19 53	12 52	13 52	14 47	15 36
54	18 40	19 16	19 59	13 00	14 01	14 57	15 46
56	18 42	19 20	20 06	13 08	14 11	15 07	15 56
58	18 44	19 25	20 14	13 18	14 22	15 19	16 08
S 60	18 47	19 30	20 23	13 29	14 35	15 34	16 23

SUN / MOON

Day	SUN Eqn. of Time 00h	SUN Eqn. of Time 12h	SUN Mer. Pass.	MOON Mer. Pass. Upper	MOON Mer. Pass. Lower	Age	Phase
d	m s	m s	h m	h m	h m	d	%
8	10 53	10 46	12 11	05 07	17 30	21	59
9	10 38	10 31	12 11	05 54	18 18	22	50
10	10 23	10 16	12 10	06 42	19 06	23	40

2018 MARCH 11, 12, 13 (SUN., MON., TUES.)

UT	ARIES GHA	VENUS −3.9 GHA	Dec	MARS +0.6 GHA	Dec	JUPITER −2.2 GHA	Dec	SATURN +0.5 GHA	Dec
11 00	168 36.3	163 33.7	N 0 54.2	262 49.2	S23 16.0	297 27.7	S17 24.3	249 58.5	S22 19.2
01	183 38.8	178 33.4	55.5	277 50.0	16.1	312 30.2	24.3	265 00.8	19.1
02	198 41.3	193 33.0	56.7	292 50.9	16.2	327 32.7	24.3	280 03.1	19.1
03	213 43.7	208 32.6	.. 58.0	307 51.8	.. 16.3	342 35.2	.. 24.3	295 05.4	.. 19.1
04	228 46.2	223 32.3	0 59.3	322 52.7	16.4	357 37.6	24.3	310 07.7	19.1
05	243 48.7	238 31.9	1 00.6	337 53.6	16.5	12 40.1	24.2	325 10.0	19.1
06	258 51.1	253 31.5	N 1 01.9	352 54.4	S23 16.5	27 42.6	S17 24.2	340 12.3	S22 19.1
07	273 53.6	268 31.2	03.2	7 55.3	16.6	42 45.1	24.2	355 14.6	19.1
S 08	288 56.1	283 30.8	04.5	22 56.2	16.7	57 47.6	24.2	10 16.9	19.1
U 09	303 58.5	298 30.5	.. 05.7	37 57.1	.. 16.8	72 50.0	.. 24.2	25 19.3	.. 19.1
N 10	319 01.0	313 30.1	07.0	52 58.0	16.9	87 52.5	24.2	40 21.6	19.1
D 11	334 03.5	328 29.7	08.3	67 58.9	17.0	102 55.0	24.2	55 23.9	19.1
A 12	349 05.9	343 29.4	N 1 09.6	82 59.7	S23 17.1	117 57.5	S17 24.2	70 26.2	S22 19.0
Y 13	4 08.4	358 29.0	10.9	98 00.6	17.1	133 00.0	24.2	85 28.5	19.0
14	19 10.8	13 28.6	12.2	113 01.5	17.2	148 02.4	24.1	100 30.8	19.0
15	34 13.3	28 28.3	.. 13.5	128 02.4	.. 17.3	163 04.9	.. 24.1	115 33.1	.. 19.0
16	49 15.8	43 27.9	14.8	143 03.3	17.4	178 07.4	24.1	130 35.4	19.0
17	64 18.2	58 27.5	16.0	158 04.2	17.5	193 09.9	24.1	145 37.7	19.0
18	79 20.7	73 27.2	N 1 17.3	173 05.0	S23 17.6	208 12.4	S17 24.1	160 40.0	S22 19.0
19	94 23.2	88 26.8	18.6	188 05.9	17.7	223 14.8	24.1	175 42.3	19.0
20	109 25.6	103 26.4	19.9	203 06.8	17.7	238 17.3	24.1	190 44.6	19.0
21	124 28.1	118 26.1	.. 21.2	218 07.7	.. 17.8	253 19.8	.. 24.1	205 46.9	.. 19.0
22	139 30.6	133 25.7	22.5	233 08.6	17.9	268 22.3	24.1	220 49.2	18.9
23	154 33.0	148 25.4	23.8	248 09.5	18.0	283 24.8	24.1	235 51.5	18.9
12 00	169 35.5	163 25.0	N 1 25.0	263 10.3	S23 18.1	298 27.3	S17 24.0	250 53.8	S22 18.9
01	184 38.0	178 24.6	26.3	278 11.2	18.2	313 29.8	24.0	265 56.1	18.9
02	199 40.4	193 24.3	27.6	293 12.1	18.2	328 32.2	24.0	280 58.4	18.9
03	214 42.9	208 23.9	.. 28.9	308 13.0	.. 18.3	343 34.7	.. 24.0	296 00.8	.. 18.9
04	229 45.3	223 23.5	30.2	323 13.9	18.4	358 37.2	24.0	311 03.1	18.9
05	244 47.8	238 23.2	31.5	338 14.8	18.5	13 39.7	24.0	326 05.4	18.9
06	259 50.3	253 22.8	N 1 32.8	353 15.6	S23 18.6	28 42.2	S17 24.0	341 07.7	S22 18.9
07	274 52.7	268 22.4	34.0	8 16.5	18.6	43 44.7	24.0	356 10.0	18.9
08	289 55.2	283 22.1	35.3	23 17.4	18.7	58 47.2	23.9	11 12.3	18.9
M 09	304 57.7	298 21.7	.. 36.6	38 18.3	.. 18.8	73 49.6	.. 23.9	26 14.6	.. 18.8
O 10	320 00.1	313 21.3	37.9	53 19.2	18.9	88 52.1	23.9	41 16.9	18.8
N 11	335 02.6	328 21.0	39.2	68 20.1	19.0	103 54.6	23.9	56 19.2	18.8
D 12	350 05.1	343 20.6	N 1 40.5	83 21.0	S23 19.0	118 57.1	S17 23.9	71 21.5	S22 18.8
A 13	5 07.5	358 20.3	41.8	98 21.8	19.1	133 59.6	23.9	86 23.8	18.8
Y 14	20 10.0	13 19.9	43.0	113 22.7	19.2	149 02.1	23.9	101 26.1	18.8
15	35 12.4	28 19.5	.. 44.3	128 23.6	.. 19.3	164 04.6	.. 23.9	116 28.4	.. 18.8
16	50 14.9	43 19.2	45.6	143 24.5	19.4	179 07.1	23.8	131 30.8	18.8
17	65 17.4	58 18.8	46.9	158 25.4	19.4	194 09.6	23.8	146 33.1	18.8
18	80 19.8	73 18.4	N 1 48.2	173 26.3	S23 19.5	209 12.1	S17 23.8	161 35.4	S22 18.8
19	95 22.3	88 18.1	49.5	188 27.2	19.6	224 14.5	23.8	176 37.7	18.8
20	110 24.8	103 17.7	50.8	203 28.0	19.7	239 17.0	23.8	191 40.0	18.7
21	125 27.2	118 17.3	.. 52.0	218 28.9	.. 19.8	254 19.5	.. 23.8	206 42.3	.. 18.7
22	140 29.7	133 17.0	53.3	233 29.8	19.8	269 22.0	23.8	221 44.6	18.7
23	155 32.2	148 16.6	54.6	248 30.7	19.9	284 24.5	23.8	236 46.9	18.7
13 00	170 34.6	163 16.2	N 1 55.9	263 31.6	S23 20.0	299 27.0	S17 23.7	251 49.2	S22 18.7
01	185 37.1	178 15.9	57.2	278 32.5	20.1	314 29.5	23.7	266 51.5	18.7
02	200 39.6	193 15.5	58.5	293 33.4	20.1	329 32.0	23.7	281 53.9	18.7
03	215 42.0	208 15.2	1 59.8	308 34.2	.. 20.2	344 34.5	.. 23.7	296 56.2	.. 18.7
04	230 44.5	223 14.8	2 01.0	323 35.1	20.3	359 37.0	23.7	311 58.5	18.7
05	245 46.9	238 14.4	02.3	338 36.0	20.4	14 39.5	23.7	327 00.8	18.7
06	260 49.4	253 14.1	N 2 03.6	353 36.9	S23 20.5	29 42.0	S17 23.7	342 03.1	S22 18.7
07	275 51.9	268 13.7	04.9	8 37.8	20.5	44 44.5	23.6	357 05.4	18.6
08	290 54.3	283 13.3	06.2	23 38.7	20.6	59 47.0	23.6	12 07.7	18.6
T 09	305 56.8	298 13.0	.. 07.5	38 39.6	.. 20.7	74 49.5	.. 23.6	27 10.0	.. 18.6
U 10	320 59.3	313 12.6	08.8	53 40.5	20.8	89 51.9	23.6	42 12.3	18.6
E 11	336 01.7	328 12.2	10.0	68 41.3	20.8	104 54.4	23.6	57 14.7	18.6
S 12	351 04.2	343 11.9	N 2 11.3	83 42.2	S23 20.9	119 56.9	S17 23.6	72 17.0	S22 18.6
D 13	6 06.7	358 11.5	12.6	98 43.1	21.0	134 59.4	23.6	87 19.3	18.6
A 14	21 09.1	13 11.1	13.9	113 44.0	21.1	150 01.9	23.5	102 21.6	18.6
Y 15	36 11.6	28 10.8	.. 15.2	128 44.9	.. 21.1	165 04.4	.. 23.5	117 23.9	.. 18.6
16	51 14.1	43 10.4	16.5	143 45.8	21.2	180 06.9	23.5	132 26.2	18.6
17	66 16.5	58 10.1	17.7	158 46.7	21.3	195 09.4	23.5	147 28.5	18.6
18	81 19.0	73 09.7	N 2 19.0	173 47.6	S23 21.3	210 11.9	S17 23.5	162 30.8	S22 18.6
19	96 21.4	88 09.3	20.3	188 48.4	21.4	225 14.4	23.5	177 33.2	18.5
20	111 23.9	103 09.0	21.6	203 49.3	21.5	240 16.9	23.5	192 35.5	18.5
21	126 26.4	118 08.6	.. 22.9	218 50.2	.. 21.6	255 19.4	.. 23.4	207 37.8	.. 18.5
22	141 28.8	133 08.2	24.2	233 51.1	21.6	270 21.9	23.4	222 40.1	18.5
23	156 31.3	148 07.9	25.4	248 52.0	21.7	285 24.4	23.4	237 42.4	18.5
Mer.Pass.	h m 12 39.6	v −0.4 d 1.3		v 0.9 d 0.1		v 2.5 d 0.0		v 2.3 d 0.0	

STARS

Name	SHA	Dec
Acamar	315 16.2	S40 14.3
Achernar	335 24.9	S57 09.0
Acrux	173 04.9	S63 11.9
Adhara	255 09.9	S29 00.2
Aldebaran	290 45.8	N16 32.5
Alioth	166 17.4	N55 51.6
Alkaid	152 56.0	N49 13.3
Al Na'ir	27 40.2	S46 52.4
Alnilam	275 43.1	S 1 11.7
Alphard	217 52.7	S 8 44.4
Alphecca	126 08.1	N26 39.1
Alpheratz	357 40.5	N29 11.3
Altair	62 05.3	N 8 54.9
Ankaa	353 13.0	S42 12.7
Antares	112 22.2	S26 28.1
Arcturus	145 52.6	N19 05.2
Atria	107 21.1	S69 03.1
Avior	234 16.2	S59 34.4
Bellatrix	278 28.6	N 6 21.7
Betelgeuse	270 57.8	N 7 24.4
Canopus	263 54.6	S52 42.8
Capella	280 29.7	N46 00.9
Deneb	49 29.6	N45 20.5
Denebola	182 30.1	N14 28.2
Diphda	348 53.0	S17 53.5
Dubhe	193 47.2	N61 39.2
Elnath	278 08.6	N28 37.2
Eltanin	90 44.7	N51 29.0
Enif	33 44.3	N 9 57.4
Fomalhaut	15 20.8	S29 31.7
Gacrux	171 56.7	S57 12.8
Gienah	175 48.7	S17 38.6
Hadar	148 42.8	S60 27.4
Hamal	327 57.4	N23 32.7
Kaus Aust.	83 39.7	S34 22.3
Kochab	137 19.5	N74 04.7
Markab	13 35.5	N15 18.0
Menkar	314 11.9	N 4 09.4
Menkent	148 03.5	S36 27.4
Miaplacidus	221 38.2	S69 47.7
Mirfak	308 36.0	N49 55.5
Nunki	75 54.5	S26 16.3
Peacock	53 14.7	S56 40.4
Pollux	243 23.6	N27 58.8
Procyon	244 56.2	N 5 10.5
Rasalhague	96 03.5	N12 32.8
Regulus	207 39.8	N11 52.6
Rigel	281 09.0	S 8 11.2
Rigil Kent.	139 46.9	S60 54.3
Sabik	102 08.8	S15 44.7
Schedar	349 37.3	N56 38.1
Shaula	96 17.6	S37 06.7
Sirius	258 30.8	S16 44.8
Spica	158 27.6	S11 15.3
Suhail	222 49.7	S43 30.6
Vega	80 36.9	N38 47.9
Zuben'ubi	137 01.7	S16 06.9

	SHA	Mer.Pass.
Venus	353 49.5	h m 13 07
Mars	93 34.9	6 27
Jupiter	128 51.8	4 06
Saturn	81 18.3	7 15

UT	SUN GHA	SUN Dec	MOON GHA	v	MOON Dec	d	HP
d h	° ′	° ′	° ′	′	° ′	′	′
11 00	177 28.1	S 3 49.2	251 12.1	12.0	S20 04.7	0.5	54.2
01	192 28.3	48.2	265 43.1	12.0	20 05.2	0.5	54.2
02	207 28.4	47.2	280 14.1	12.0	20 05.7	0.4	54.2
03	222 28.6	.. 46.3	294 45.1	12.0	20 06.1	0.3	54.2
04	237 28.8	45.3	309 16.1	12.0	20 06.4	0.3	54.2
05	252 28.9	44.3	323 47.1	11.9	20 06.6	0.1	54.2
S 06	267 29.1	S 3 43.3	338 18.0	12.0	S20 06.7	0.0	54.2
U 07	282 29.3	42.3	352 49.0	12.0	20 06.7	0.1	54.2
N 08	297 29.4	41.4	7 20.0	12.0	20 06.6	0.2	54.2
D 09	312 29.6	.. 40.4	21 51.0	12.0	20 06.4	0.2	54.2
A 10	327 29.7	39.4	36 22.0	12.0	20 06.2	0.4	54.2
Y 11	342 29.9	38.4	50 53.0	12.0	20 05.8	0.5	54.2
12	357 30.1	S 3 37.4	65 24.0	12.0	S20 05.3	0.5	54.2
13	12 30.2	36.4	79 55.0	12.0	20 04.8	0.6	54.2
14	27 30.4	35.5	94 26.0	12.0	20 04.2	0.8	54.2
15	42 30.6	.. 34.5	108 57.0	12.0	20 03.4	0.8	54.2
16	57 30.7	33.5	123 28.0	12.0	20 02.6	0.9	54.2
17	72 30.9	32.5	137 59.0	11.9	20 01.7	1.0	54.2
18	87 31.1	S 3 31.5	152 29.9	12.0	S20 00.7	1.1	54.2
19	102 31.2	30.5	167 00.9	12.0	19 59.6	1.2	54.2
20	117 31.4	29.6	181 31.9	12.1	19 58.4	1.3	54.2
21	132 31.6	.. 28.6	196 03.0	12.0	19 57.1	1.4	54.2
22	147 31.7	27.6	210 34.0	12.0	19 55.7	1.5	54.2
23	162 31.9	26.6	225 05.0	12.0	19 54.2	1.6	54.2
12 00	177 32.1	S 3 25.6	239 36.0	12.0	S19 52.6	1.6	54.2
01	192 32.2	24.6	254 07.0	12.0	19 51.0	1.6	54.2
02	207 32.4	23.7	268 38.0	12.0	19 49.2	1.8	54.2
03	222 32.5	.. 22.7	283 09.0	12.1	19 47.4	2.0	54.2
04	237 32.7	21.7	297 40.1	12.0	19 45.4	2.0	54.2
05	252 32.9	20.7	312 11.1	12.0	19 43.4	2.1	54.2
M 06	267 33.0	S 3 19.7	326 42.1	12.1	S19 41.3	2.2	54.2
O 07	282 33.2	18.7	341 13.2	12.0	19 39.1	2.3	54.3
N 08	297 33.4	17.8	355 44.2	12.1	19 36.8	2.4	54.3
D 09	312 33.5	.. 16.8	10 15.3	12.0	19 34.4	2.5	54.3
A 10	327 33.7	15.8	24 46.3	12.0	19 31.9	2.6	54.3
Y 11	342 33.9	14.8	39 17.4	12.1	19 29.3	2.7	54.3
12	357 34.0	S 3 13.8	53 48.5	12.1	S19 26.6	2.7	54.3
13	12 34.2	12.8	68 19.6	12.0	19 23.9	2.9	54.3
14	27 34.4	11.9	82 50.6	12.1	19 21.0	2.9	54.3
15	42 34.6	.. 10.9	97 21.7	12.1	19 18.1	3.1	54.3
16	57 34.7	09.9	111 52.8	12.1	19 15.0	3.1	54.3
17	72 34.9	08.9	126 23.9	12.2	19 11.9	3.2	54.3
18	87 35.1	S 3 07.9	140 55.1	12.1	S19 08.7	3.3	54.3
19	102 35.2	06.9	155 26.2	12.1	19 05.4	3.4	54.3
20	117 35.4	06.0	169 57.3	12.1	19 02.0	3.5	54.4
21	132 35.6	.. 05.0	184 28.4	12.2	18 58.5	3.6	54.4
22	147 35.7	04.0	198 59.6	12.2	18 54.9	3.6	54.4
23	162 35.9	03.0	213 30.8	12.1	18 51.3	3.8	54.4
13 00	177 36.1	S 3 02.0	228 01.9	12.2	S18 47.5	3.8	54.4
01	192 36.2	01.0	242 33.1	12.2	18 43.7	4.0	54.4
02	207 36.4	3 00.0	257 04.3	12.2	18 39.7	4.0	54.4
03	222 36.6	2 59.1	271 35.5	12.2	18 35.7	4.1	54.4
04	237 36.7	58.1	286 06.7	12.2	18 31.6	4.2	54.4
05	252 36.9	57.1	300 37.9	12.2	18 27.4	4.3	54.4
T 06	267 37.1	S 2 56.1	315 09.1	12.2	S18 23.1	4.3	54.5
U 07	282 37.2	55.1	329 40.3	12.3	18 18.8	4.5	54.5
E 08	297 37.4	54.1	344 11.6	12.2	18 14.3	4.5	54.5
S 09	312 37.6	.. 53.1	358 42.8	12.3	18 09.8	4.7	54.5
D 10	327 37.8	52.2	13 14.1	12.3	18 05.1	4.7	54.5
A 11	342 37.9	51.2	27 45.4	12.2	18 00.4	4.8	54.5
Y 12	357 38.1	S 2 50.2	42 16.6	12.3	S17 55.6	4.9	54.5
13	12 38.3	49.2	56 47.9	12.3	17 50.7	4.9	54.5
14	27 38.4	48.2	71 19.2	12.4	17 45.8	5.1	54.6
15	42 38.6	.. 47.2	85 50.6	12.3	17 40.7	5.2	54.6
16	57 38.8	46.3	100 21.9	12.3	17 35.5	5.2	54.6
17	72 38.9	45.3	114 53.2	12.4	17 30.3	5.3	54.6
18	87 39.1	S 2 44.3	129 24.6	12.3	S17 25.0	5.4	54.6
19	102 39.3	43.3	143 55.9	12.4	17 19.6	5.5	54.6
20	117 39.5	42.3	158 27.3	12.4	17 14.1	5.5	54.6
21	132 39.6	.. 41.3	172 58.7	12.4	17 08.6	5.7	54.7
22	147 39.8	40.3	187 30.1	12.4	17 02.9	5.7	54.7
23	162 40.0	39.3	202 01.5	12.4	S16 57.2	5.8	54.7
	SD 16.1	d 1.0	SD 14.8		14.8		14.9

Lat.	Twilight Naut.	Twilight Civil	Sunrise	Moonrise 11	Moonrise 12	Moonrise 13	Moonrise 14
°	h m	h m	h m	h m	h m	h m	h m
N 72	04 12	05 33	06 40	■■	■■	■■	08 01
N 70	04 23	05 36	06 37	■■	07 36	07 26	07 20
68	04 33	05 39	06 34	05 49	06 25	06 43	06 52
66	04 40	05 41	06 31	05 08	05 48	06 14	06 30
64	04 47	05 42	06 29	04 40	05 22	05 52	06 13
62	04 52	05 44	06 28	04 19	05 02	05 35	05 59
60	04 56	05 45	06 26	04 01	04 45	05 20	05 47
N 58	05 00	05 46	06 25	03 47	04 31	05 08	05 37
56	05 03	05 47	06 24	03 34	04 19	04 57	05 28
54	05 06	05 47	06 22	03 24	04 09	04 47	05 20
52	05 09	05 48	06 21	03 14	04 00	04 39	05 13
50	05 11	05 48	06 20	03 05	03 51	04 31	05 06
45	05 15	05 49	06 18	02 47	03 33	04 15	04 52
N 40	05 18	05 50	06 17	02 32	03 19	04 01	04 40
35	05 21	05 50	06 15	02 20	03 06	03 50	04 30
30	05 24	05 50	06 14	02 09	02 56	03 40	04 22
20	05 24	05 49	06 11	01 50	02 37	03 23	04 07
N 10	05 23	05 48	06 09	01 33	02 21	03 08	03 54
0	05 22	05 46	06 06	01 18	02 06	02 54	03 41
S 10	05 19	05 43	06 04	01 03	01 51	02 40	03 29
20	05 14	05 39	06 01	00 47	01 35	02 25	03 16
30	05 06	05 34	05 58	00 28	01 16	02 07	03 00
35	05 01	05 31	05 56	00 17	01 06	01 57	02 52
40	04 55	05 27	05 54	00 04	00 53	01 46	02 42
45	04 47	05 22	05 52	24 39	00 39	01 32	02 30
S 50	04 37	05 16	05 49	24 21	00 21	01 16	02 15
52	04 32	05 13	05 47	24 12	00 12	01 08	02 09
54	04 27	05 10	05 46	24 03	00 03	00 59	02 02
56	04 20	05 06	05 44	23 52	24 49	00 49	01 53
58	04 13	05 02	05 42	23 40	24 38	00 38	01 43
S 60	04 05	04 57	05 40	23 26	24 25	00 25	01 32

Lat.	Sunset	Twilight Civil	Twilight Naut.	Moonset 11	Moonset 12	Moonset 13	Moonset 14
°	h m	h m	h m	h m	h m	h m	h m
N 72	17 42	18 49	20 12	■■	■■	■■	11 57
N 70	17 45	18 46	19 59	■■	09 03	10 53	12 37
68	17 47	18 43	19 49	09 11	10 14	11 43	13 04
66	17 50	18 41	19 41	09 51	10 50	12 03	13 25
64	17 52	18 39	19 35	10 19	11 16	12 25	13 41
62	17 53	18 37	19 30	10 41	11 36	12 42	13 55
60	17 55	18 36	19 25	10 58	11 53	12 56	14 06
N 58	17 56	18 35	19 21	11 13	12 07	13 08	14 16
56	17 57	18 34	19 18	11 25	12 18	13 19	14 25
54	17 58	18 33	19 15	11 36	12 29	13 28	14 32
52	17 59	18 33	19 12	11 46	12 38	13 36	14 39
50	18 00	18 32	19 10	11 54	12 46	13 44	14 45
45	18 02	18 31	19 05	12 12	13 04	13 59	14 58
N 40	18 04	18 31	19 02	12 27	13 18	14 12	15 09
35	18 05	18 30	19 00	12 40	13 30	14 23	15 18
30	18 06	18 30	18 58	12 51	13 41	14 33	15 27
20	18 09	18 31	18 56	13 10	13 59	14 49	15 40
N 10	18 11	18 32	18 56	13 26	14 15	15 03	15 53
0	18 13	18 34	18 58	13 41	14 29	15 17	16 04
S 10	18 15	18 36	19 01	13 57	14 44	15 30	16 15
20	18 18	18 40	19 06	14 13	14 59	15 44	16 27
30	18 21	18 45	19 13	14 32	15 17	16 00	16 41
35	18 23	18 48	19 18	14 42	15 28	16 10	16 49
40	18 25	18 52	19 24	14 55	15 40	16 20	16 57
45	18 27	18 56	19 31	15 10	15 53	16 33	17 08
S 50	18 30	19 02	19 41	15 28	16 10	16 48	17 20
52	18 31	19 05	19 46	15 36	16 18	16 55	17 26
54	18 33	19 08	19 51	15 46	16 27	17 03	17 33
56	18 34	19 12	19 57	15 56	16 37	17 11	17 40
58	18 36	19 16	20 04	16 08	16 49	17 21	17 48
S 60	18 38	19 20	20 12	16 23	17 02	17 33	17 57

Day	SUN Eqn. of Time 00ʰ	SUN Eqn. of Time 12ʰ	SUN Mer. Pass.	MOON Mer. Pass. Upper	MOON Mer. Pass. Lower	Age	Phase
d	m s	m s	h m	h m	h m	d	%
11	10 08	10 00	12 10	07 30	19 54	24	31
12	09 52	09 44	12 10	08 18	20 42	25	23
13	09 36	09 28	12 09	09 05	21 29	26	16

UT	ARIES GHA	VENUS −3.9 GHA	VENUS Dec	MARS +0.6 GHA	MARS Dec	JUPITER −2.3 GHA	JUPITER Dec	SATURN +0.5 GHA	SATURN Dec	STARS Name	SHA	Dec
14 00	171 33.8	163 07.5	N 2 26.7	263 52.9	S23 21.8	300 26.9	S17 23.4	252 44.7	S22 18.5	Acamar	315 16.2	S40 14.3
01	186 36.2	178 07.1	28.0	278 53.4	21.9	315 29.4	23.4	267 47.0	18.5	Achernar	335 24.9	S57 09.0
02	201 38.7	193 06.8	29.3	293 54.7	21.9	330 31.9	23.4	282 49.4	18.5	Acrux	173 04.9	S63 11.9
03	216 41.2	208 06.4 ..	30.6	308 55.6 ..	22.0	345 34.4 ..	23.4	297 51.7 ..	18.5	Adhara	255 09.9	S29 00.2
04	231 43.6	223 06.0	31.9	323 56.5	22.1	0 36.9	23.3	312 54.0	18.5	Aldebaran	290 45.8	N16 32.5
05	246 46.1	238 05.7	33.1	338 57.3	22.1	15 39.4	23.3	327 56.3	18.5			
06	261 48.5	253 05.3	N 2 34.4	353 58.2	S23 22.2	30 41.9	S17 23.3	342 58.6	S22 18.4	Alioth	166 17.4	N55 51.6
W 07	276 51.0	268 04.9	35.7	8 59.1	22.3	45 44.4	23.3	358 00.9	18.4	Alkaid	152 56.0	N49 13.3
E 08	291 53.5	283 04.6	37.0	24 00.0	22.3	60 46.9	23.3	13 03.3	18.4	Al Na'ir	27 40.2	S46 52.4
D 09	306 55.9	298 04.2 ..	38.3	39 00.9 ..	22.4	75 49.5 ..	23.3	28 05.6 ..	18.4	Alnilam	275 43.1	S 1 11.7
N 10	321 58.4	313 03.8	39.6	54 01.8	22.5	90 52.0	23.2	43 07.9	18.4	Alphard	217 52.7	S 8 44.5
E 11	337 00.9	328 03.5	40.8	69 02.7	22.6	105 54.5	23.2	58 10.2	18.4			
S 12	352 03.3	343 03.1	N 2 42.1	84 03.6	S23 22.6	120 57.0	S17 23.2	73 12.5	S22 18.4	Alphecca	126 08.1	N26 39.1
D 13	7 05.8	358 02.7	43.4	99 04.5	22.7	135 59.5	23.2	88 14.8	18.4	Alpheratz	357 40.5	N29 11.3
A 14	22 08.3	13 02.4	44.7	114 05.4	22.8	151 02.0	23.2	103 17.1	18.4	Altair	62 05.3	N 8 54.9
Y 15	37 10.7	28 02.0 ..	46.0	129 06.2 ..	22.8	166 04.5 ..	23.2	118 19.5 ..	18.4	Ankaa	353 13.0	S42 12.7
16	52 13.2	43 01.7	47.3	144 07.1	22.9	181 07.0	23.1	133 21.8	18.4	Antares	112 22.2	S26 28.1
17	67 15.7	58 01.3	48.5	159 08.0	23.0	196 09.5	23.1	148 24.1	18.3			
18	82 18.1	73 00.9	N 2 49.8	174 08.9	S23 23.0	211 12.0	S17 23.1	163 26.4	S22 18.3	Arcturus	145 52.6	N19 05.2
19	97 20.6	88 00.6	51.1	189 09.8	23.1	226 14.5	23.1	178 28.7	18.3	Atria	107 21.0	S69 03.2
20	112 23.0	103 00.2	52.4	204 10.7	23.2	241 17.0	23.1	193 31.1	18.3	Avior	234 16.3	S59 34.4
21	127 25.5	117 59.8 ..	53.7	219 11.6 ..	23.2	256 19.5 ..	23.1	208 33.4 ..	18.3	Bellatrix	278 28.6	N 6 21.7
22	142 28.0	132 59.5	54.9	234 12.5	23.3	271 22.0	23.0	223 35.7	18.3	Betelgeuse	270 57.8	N 7 24.4
23	157 30.4	147 59.1	56.2	249 13.4	23.4	286 24.5	23.0	238 38.0	18.3			
15 00	172 32.9	162 58.7	N 2 57.5	264 14.3	S23 23.4	301 27.0	S17 23.0	253 40.3	S22 18.3	Canopus	263 54.6	S52 42.8
01	187 35.4	177 58.4	2 58.8	279 15.2	23.5	316 29.6	23.0	268 42.6	18.3	Capella	280 29.7	N46 00.9
02	202 37.8	192 58.0	3 00.1	294 16.1	23.6	331 32.1	23.0	283 45.0	18.3	Deneb	49 29.6	N45 20.5
03	217 40.3	207 57.6 ..	01.4	309 16.9 ..	23.6	346 34.6 ..	23.0	298 47.3 ..	18.3	Denebola	182 30.1	N14 28.2
04	232 42.8	222 57.3	02.6	324 17.8	23.7	1 37.1	22.9	313 49.6	18.3	Diphda	348 53.0	S17 53.5
05	247 45.2	237 56.9	03.9	339 18.7	23.8	16 39.6	22.9	328 51.9	18.2			
06	262 47.7	252 56.5	N 3 05.2	354 19.6	S23 23.8	31 42.1	S17 22.9	343 54.2	S22 18.2	Dubhe	193 47.2	N61 39.2
T 07	277 50.2	267 56.2	06.5	9 20.5	23.9	46 44.6	22.9	358 56.6	18.2	Elnath	278 08.6	N28 37.2
H 08	292 52.6	282 55.8	07.8	24 21.4	24.0	61 47.1	22.9	13 58.9	18.2	Eltanin	90 44.7	N51 29.0
U 09	307 55.1	297 55.4 ..	09.0	39 22.3 ..	24.0	76 49.6 ..	22.8	29 01.2 ..	18.2	Enif	33 44.3	N 9 57.4
R 10	322 57.5	312 55.1	10.3	54 23.2	24.1	91 52.2	22.8	44 03.5	18.2	Fomalhaut	15 20.8	S29 31.7
11	338 00.0	327 54.7	11.6	69 24.1	24.1	106 54.7	22.8	59 05.8	18.2			
S 12	353 02.5	342 54.3	N 3 12.9	84 25.0	S23 24.2	121 57.2	S17 22.8	74 08.2	S22 18.2	Gacrux	171 56.7	S57 12.8
D 13	8 04.9	357 54.0	14.2	99 25.9	24.3	136 59.7	22.8	89 10.5	18.2	Gienah	175 48.7	S17 38.6
A 14	23 07.4	12 53.6	15.4	114 26.8	24.3	152 02.2	22.8	104 12.8	18.2	Hadar	148 42.8	S60 27.4
Y 15	38 09.9	27 53.2 ..	16.7	129 27.7 ..	24.4	167 04.7 ..	22.7	119 15.1 ..	18.2	Hamal	327 57.4	N23 32.7
16	53 12.3	42 52.9	18.0	144 28.6	24.5	182 07.2	22.7	134 17.4	18.1	Kaus Aust.	83 39.6	S34 22.3
17	68 14.8	57 52.5	19.3	159 29.5	24.5	197 09.7	22.7	149 19.8	18.1			
18	83 17.3	72 52.1	N 3 20.6	174 30.4	S23 24.6	212 12.3	S17 22.7	164 22.1	S22 18.1	Kochab	137 19.4	N74 04.7
19	98 19.7	87 51.8	21.8	189 31.2	24.6	227 14.8	22.7	179 24.4	18.1	Markab	13 35.4	N15 18.0
20	113 22.2	102 51.4	23.1	204 32.1	24.7	242 17.3	22.6	194 26.7	18.1	Menkar	314 11.9	N 4 09.4
21	128 24.6	117 51.0 ..	24.4	219 33.0 ..	24.8	257 19.8 ..	22.6	209 29.0 ..	18.1	Menkent	148 03.5	S36 27.4
22	143 27.1	132 50.7	25.7	234 33.9	24.8	272 22.3	22.6	224 31.4	18.1	Miaplacidus	221 38.2	S69 47.8
23	158 29.6	147 50.3	27.0	249 34.8	24.9	287 24.8	22.6	239 33.7	18.1			
16 00	173 32.0	162 49.9	N 3 28.2	264 35.7	S23 25.0	302 27.4	S17 22.6	254 36.0	S22 18.1	Mirfak	308 36.0	N49 55.5
01	188 34.5	177 49.6	29.5	279 36.6	25.0	317 29.9	22.6	269 38.3	18.1	Nunki	75 54.5	S26 16.3
02	203 37.0	192 49.2	30.8	294 37.5	25.1	332 32.4	22.5	284 40.7	18.1	Peacock	53 14.6	S56 40.4
03	218 39.4	207 48.8 ..	32.1	309 38.4 ..	25.1	347 34.9 ..	22.5	299 43.0 ..	18.1	Pollux	243 23.6	N27 58.8
04	233 41.9	222 48.5	33.4	324 39.3	25.2	2 37.4	22.5	314 45.3	18.0	Procyon	244 56.2	N 5 10.5
05	248 44.4	237 48.1	34.6	339 40.2	25.2	17 39.9	22.5	329 47.6	18.0			
06	263 46.8	252 47.7	N 3 35.9	354 41.1	S23 25.3	32 42.5	S17 22.5	344 49.9	S22 18.0	Rasalhague	96 03.5	N12 32.8
07	278 49.3	267 47.3	37.2	9 42.0	25.4	47 45.0	22.4	359 52.3	18.0	Regulus	207 39.8	N11 52.6
08	293 51.8	282 47.0	38.5	24 42.9	25.4	62 47.5	22.4	14 54.6	18.0	Rigel	281 09.0	S 8 11.2
F 09	308 54.2	297 46.6 ..	39.7	39 43.8 ..	25.5	77 50.0 ..	22.4	29 56.9 ..	18.0	Rigil Kent.	139 46.9	S60 54.3
R 10	323 56.7	312 46.2	41.0	54 44.7	25.5	92 52.5	22.4	44 59.2	18.0	Sabik	102 08.8	S15 44.7
I 11	338 59.1	327 45.9	42.3	69 45.6	25.6	107 55.1	22.4	60 01.6	18.0			
D 12	354 01.6	342 45.5	N 3 43.6	84 46.5	S23 25.7	122 57.6	S17 22.3	75 03.9	S22 18.0	Schedar	349 37.3	N56 38.1
A 13	9 04.1	357 45.1	44.9	99 47.4	25.7	138 00.1	22.3	90 06.2	18.0	Shaula	96 17.6	S37 06.7
Y 14	24 06.5	12 44.8	46.1	114 48.3	25.8	153 02.6	22.3	105 08.5	18.0	Sirius	258 30.8	S16 44.8
15	39 09.0	27 44.4 ..	47.4	129 49.2 ..	25.8	168 05.1 ..	22.3	120 10.9 ..	17.9	Spica	158 27.6	S11 15.3
16	54 11.5	42 44.0	48.7	144 50.1	25.9	183 07.7	22.3	135 13.2	17.9	Suhail	222 49.7	S43 30.6
17	69 13.9	57 43.7	50.0	159 51.0	25.9	198 10.2	22.2	150 15.5	17.9			
18	84 16.4	72 43.3	N 3 51.2	174 51.9	S23 26.0	213 12.7	S17 22.2	165 17.8	S22 17.9	Vega	80 36.9	N38 47.9
19	99 18.9	87 42.9	52.5	189 52.8	26.1	228 15.2	22.2	180 20.2	17.9	Zuben'ubi	137 01.6	S16 06.9
20	114 21.3	102 42.6	53.8	204 53.7	26.1	243 17.8	22.2	195 22.5	17.9		SHA	Mer.Pass.
21	129 23.8	117 42.2 ..	55.1	219 54.6 ..	26.2	258 20.3 ..	22.2	210 24.8 ..	17.9	Venus	350 25.8	13 08
22	144 26.2	132 41.8	56.3	234 55.5	26.2	273 22.8	22.1	225 27.1	17.9	Mars	91 41.4	6 23
23	159 28.7	147 41.5	57.6	249 56.4	26.3	288 25.3	22.1	240 29.5	17.9	Jupiter	128 54.1	3 54
Mer. Pass. 12 27.8		v −0.4 d 1.3		v 0.9 d 0.1		v 2.5 d 0.0		v 2.3 d 0.0		Saturn	81 07.4	7 04

UT	SUN GHA	SUN Dec	MOON GHA	v	Dec	d	HP
d h	° ′	° ′	° ′	′	° ′	′	′
14 00	177 40.1	S 2 38.4	216 32.9	12.5	S16 51.4	5.9	54.7
01	192 40.3	37.4	231 04.4	12.4	16 45.5	6.0	54.7
02	207 40.5	36.4	245 35.8	12.5	16 39.5	6.0	54.7
03	222 40.7	.. 35.4	260 07.3	12.4	16 33.5	6.2	54.7
04	237 40.8	34.4	274 38.7	12.5	16 27.3	6.2	54.8
05	252 41.0	33.4	289 10.2	12.5	16 21.1	6.3	54.8
W 06	267 41.2	S 2 32.4	303 41.7	12.5	S16 14.8	6.4	54.8
E 07	282 41.3	31.5	318 13.2	12.5	16 08.4	6.4	54.8
D 08	297 41.5	30.5	332 44.7	12.6	16 02.0	6.6	54.8
N 09	312 41.7	.. 29.5	347 16.3	12.5	15 55.4	6.6	54.8
E 10	327 41.9	28.5	1 47.8	12.6	15 48.8	6.7	54.9
S 11	342 42.0	27.5	16 19.4	12.5	15 42.1	6.7	54.9
D 12	357 42.2	S 2 26.5	30 50.9	12.6	S15 35.4	6.9	54.9
A 13	12 42.4	25.5	45 22.5	12.6	15 28.5	6.9	54.9
Y 14	27 42.5	24.6	59 54.1	12.6	15 21.6	7.0	54.9
15	42 42.7	.. 23.6	74 25.7	12.6	15 14.6	7.1	54.9
16	57 42.9	22.6	88 57.3	12.6	15 07.5	7.1	55.0
17	72 43.1	21.6	103 28.9	12.7	15 00.4	7.2	55.0
18	87 43.2	S 2 20.6	118 00.6	12.6	S14 53.2	7.3	55.0
19	102 43.4	19.6	132 32.2	12.7	14 45.9	7.4	55.0
20	117 43.6	18.6	147 03.9	12.7	14 38.5	7.4	55.0
21	132 43.8	.. 17.6	161 35.6	12.6	14 31.1	7.5	55.1
22	147 43.9	16.7	176 07.2	12.7	14 23.6	7.6	55.1
23	162 44.1	15.7	190 38.9	12.7	14 16.0	7.7	55.1
15 00	177 44.3	S 2 14.7	205 10.6	12.8	S14 08.3	7.7	55.1
01	192 44.4	13.7	219 42.4	12.7	14 00.6	7.8	55.1
02	207 44.6	12.7	234 14.1	12.7	13 52.8	7.9	55.2
03	222 44.8	.. 11.7	248 45.8	12.8	13 44.9	7.9	55.2
04	237 45.0	10.7	263 17.6	12.7	13 37.0	8.1	55.2
05	252 45.1	09.7	277 49.3	12.8	13 28.9	8.0	55.2
T 06	267 45.3	S 2 08.8	292 21.1	12.8	S13 20.9	8.2	55.2
H 07	282 45.5	07.8	306 52.9	12.8	13 12.7	8.2	55.3
U 08	297 45.7	06.8	321 24.7	12.8	13 04.5	8.3	55.3
R 09	312 45.8	.. 05.8	335 56.5	12.8	12 56.2	8.3	55.3
S 10	327 46.0	04.8	350 28.3	12.8	12 47.9	8.5	55.3
D 11	342 46.2	03.8	5 00.1	12.8	12 39.4	8.4	55.3
A 12	357 46.4	S 2 02.8	19 31.9	12.9	S12 31.0	8.6	55.4
Y 13	12 46.5	01.8	34 03.8	12.8	12 22.4	8.6	55.4
14	27 46.7	2 00.9	48 35.6	12.9	12 13.8	8.7	55.4
15	42 46.9	1 59.9	63 07.5	12.9	12 05.1	8.7	55.4
16	57 47.1	58.9	77 39.4	12.8	11 56.4	8.8	55.4
17	72 47.2	57.9	92 11.2	12.9	11 47.6	8.9	55.5
18	87 47.4	S 1 56.9	106 43.1	12.9	S11 38.7	8.9	55.5
19	102 47.6	55.9	121 15.0	12.9	11 29.8	9.0	55.5
20	117 47.8	54.9	135 46.9	12.9	11 20.8	9.0	55.5
21	132 47.9	.. 53.9	150 18.8	12.9	11 11.8	9.1	55.5
22	147 48.1	53.0	164 50.7	12.9	11 02.7	9.2	55.6
23	162 48.3	52.0	179 22.6	13.0	10 53.5	9.2	55.6
16 00	177 48.5	S 1 51.0	193 54.6	12.9	S10 44.3	9.3	55.6
01	192 48.6	50.0	208 26.5	12.9	10 35.0	9.3	55.6
02	207 48.8	49.0	222 58.4	13.0	10 25.7	9.4	55.6
03	222 49.0	.. 48.0	237 30.4	12.9	10 16.3	9.5	55.7
04	237 49.2	47.0	252 02.3	13.0	10 06.8	9.5	55.7
05	252 49.4	46.0	266 34.3	12.9	9 57.3	9.5	55.7
06	267 49.5	S 1 45.1	281 06.2	13.0	S 9 47.8	9.6	55.7
07	282 49.7	44.1	295 38.2	12.9	9 38.2	9.7	55.8
08	297 49.9	43.1	310 10.1	13.0	9 28.5	9.7	55.8
F 09	312 50.1	.. 42.1	324 42.1	13.0	9 18.8	9.8	55.8
R 10	327 50.2	41.1	339 14.1	13.0	9 09.0	9.8	55.8
I 11	342 50.4	40.1	353 46.1	12.9	8 59.2	9.9	55.8
D 12	357 50.6	S 1 39.1	8 18.0	13.0	S 8 49.3	9.9	55.9
A 13	12 50.8	38.1	22 50.0	13.0	8 39.4	9.9	55.9
Y 14	27 50.9	37.1	37 22.0	13.0	8 29.5	10.1	55.9
15	42 51.1	.. 36.2	51 54.0	12.9	8 19.4	10.0	55.9
16	57 51.3	35.2	66 25.9	13.0	8 09.4	10.1	56.0
17	72 51.5	34.2	80 57.9	13.0	7 59.3	10.2	56.0
18	87 51.7	S 1 33.2	95 29.9	13.0	S 7 49.1	10.2	56.0
19	102 51.8	32.2	110 01.9	13.0	7 38.9	10.2	56.0
20	117 52.0	31.2	124 33.9	13.0	7 28.7	10.3	56.0
21	132 52.2	.. 30.2	139 05.9	12.9	7 18.4	10.3	56.1
22	147 52.4	29.2	153 37.8	13.0	7 08.1	10.4	56.1
23	162 52.5	28.3	168 09.8	13.0	S 6 57.7	10.4	56.1
	SD 16.1	d 1.0	SD 15.0		15.1		15.2

Twilight / Sunrise / Moonrise

Lat.	Naut.	Civil	Sunrise	Moonrise 14	15	16	17
°	h m	h m	h m	h m	h m	h m	h m
N 72	03 54	05 18	06 25	08 01	07 39	07 25	07 13
N 70	04 08	05 22	06 23	07 20	07 15	07 10	07 06
68	04 19	05 26	06 21	06 52	06 56	06 58	06 59
66	04 28	05 29	06 20	06 30	06 41	06 48	06 54
64	04 35	05 32	06 19	06 13	06 28	06 40	06 49
62	04 42	05 34	06 18	05 59	06 18	06 33	06 45
60	04 47	05 36	06 17	05 47	06 09	06 26	06 42
N 58	04 51	05 37	06 16	05 37	06 01	06 21	06 39
56	04 55	05 39	06 16	05 28	05 54	06 16	06 36
54	04 59	05 40	06 15	05 20	05 47	06 12	06 33
52	05 02	05 41	06 15	05 13	05 42	06 08	06 31
50	05 04	05 42	06 14	05 06	05 37	06 04	06 29
45	05 10	05 44	06 13	04 52	05 25	05 56	06 25
N 40	05 13	05 45	06 12	04 40	05 16	05 49	06 21
35	05 16	05 46	06 11	04 30	05 08	05 44	06 18
30	05 19	05 46	06 10	04 22	05 01	05 38	06 15
20	05 21	05 47	06 09	04 07	04 49	05 30	06 10
N 10	05 22	05 46	06 07	03 54	04 38	05 22	06 05
0	05 21	05 45	06 06	03 41	04 28	05 15	06 01
S 10	05 19	05 43	06 04	03 29	04 18	05 07	05 57
20	05 15	05 40	06 02	03 16	04 07	05 00	05 52
30	05 08	05 36	06 00	03 00	03 55	04 51	05 47
35	05 04	05 34	05 59	02 52	03 48	04 45	05 44
40	04 58	05 30	05 57	02 42	03 40	04 40	05 41
45	04 51	05 26	05 56	02 30	03 30	04 33	05 37
S 50	04 42	05 21	05 54	02 15	03 19	04 25	05 32
52	04 38	05 19	05 53	02 09	03 13	04 21	05 30
54	04 33	05 16	05 51	02 01	03 07	04 17	05 28
56	04 28	05 13	05 49	01 53	03 01	04 12	05 25
58	04 21	05 09	05 49	01 43	02 53	04 07	05 22
S 60	04 14	05 05	05 47	01 32	02 45	04 01	05 19

Sunset / Twilight / Moonset

Lat.	Sunset	Civil	Naut.	Moonset 14	15	16	17
°	h m	h m	h m	h m	h m	h m	h m
N 72	17 56	19 03	20 28	11 57	13 56	15 47	17 35
N 70	17 57	18 58	20 13	12 37	14 19	16 00	17 41
68	17 58	18 54	20 02	13 04	14 37	16 11	17 45
66	18 00	18 51	19 52	13 25	14 51	16 19	17 49
64	18 00	18 48	19 45	13 41	15 02	16 26	17 52
62	18 01	18 45	19 38	13 55	15 12	16 32	17 55
60	18 02	18 43	19 33	14 06	15 21	16 38	17 57
N 58	18 03	18 42	19 28	14 16	15 28	16 42	17 59
56	18 03	18 40	19 24	14 25	15 34	16 47	18 01
54	18 04	18 39	19 20	14 32	15 40	16 50	18 03
52	18 04	18 38	19 17	14 39	15 45	16 54	18 04
50	18 05	18 37	19 15	14 45	15 50	16 57	18 05
45	18 06	18 35	19 09	14 58	16 00	17 03	18 08
N 40	18 07	18 34	19 05	15 09	16 08	17 09	18 11
35	18 07	18 33	19 02	15 18	16 15	17 14	18 13
30	18 08	18 32	19 00	15 27	16 22	17 18	18 15
20	18 10	18 32	18 57	15 40	16 32	17 25	18 18
N 10	18 11	18 32	18 56	15 53	16 42	17 31	18 21
0	18 12	18 33	18 57	16 04	16 51	17 37	18 23
S 10	18 14	18 35	18 59	16 15	16 59	17 43	18 26
20	18 15	18 37	19 03	16 27	17 08	17 49	18 28
30	18 17	18 41	19 09	16 41	17 19	17 56	18 31
35	18 18	18 44	19 13	16 49	17 25	18 00	18 33
40	18 20	18 47	19 19	16 57	17 32	18 04	18 35
45	18 21	18 51	19 25	17 08	17 40	18 09	18 37
S 50	18 23	18 56	19 34	17 20	17 49	18 15	18 40
52	18 24	18 58	19 43	17 26	17 53	18 18	18 41
54	18 25	19 01	19 43	17 33	17 58	18 21	18 42
56	18 26	19 04	19 49	17 40	18 04	18 25	18 44
58	18 28	19 07	19 55	17 48	18 09	18 28	18 45
S 60	18 29	19 11	20 02	17 57	18 16	18 32	18 47

SUN / MOON

Day	Eqn. of Time 00ʰ	12ʰ	Mer. Pass.	Mer. Pass. Upper	Lower	Age	Phase
d	m s	m s	h m	h m	h m	d	%
14	09 20	09 12	12 09	09 53	22 16	27	9
15	09 03	08 55	12 09	10 39	23 03	28	4
16	08 46	08 38	12 09	11 26	23 49	29	1

UT	ARIES GHA	VENUS −3.9 GHA	VENUS Dec	MARS +0.5 GHA	MARS Dec	JUPITER −2.3 GHA	JUPITER Dec	SATURN +0.5 GHA	SATURN Dec	STARS Name	SHA	Dec
17 00	174 31.2	162 41.1	N 3 58.9	264 57.3	S23 26.3	303 27.9	S17 22.1	255 31.8	S22 17.9	Acamar	315 16.2	S40 14.3
01	189 33.6	177 40.7	4 00.2	279 58.2	26.4	318 30.4	22.1	270 34.1	17.9	Achernar	335 24.9	S57 09.0
02	204 36.1	192 40.3	01.4	294 59.0	26.4	333 32.9	22.0	285 36.4	17.9	Acrux	173 04.9	S63 11.9
03	219 38.6	207 40.0 ..	02.7	309 59.9 ..	26.5	348 35.4 ..	22.0	300 38.8 ..	17.8	Adhara	255 09.9	S29 00.2
04	234 41.0	222 39.6	04.0	325 00.8	26.6	3 38.0	22.0	315 41.1	17.8	Aldebaran	290 45.8	N16 32.5
05	249 43.5	237 39.2	05.3	340 01.7	26.6	18 40.5	22.0	330 43.4	17.8			
S 06	264 46.0	252 38.9	N 4 06.5	355 02.6	S23 26.7	33 43.0	S17 22.0	345 45.7	S22 17.8	Alioth	166 17.4	N55 51.6
A 07	279 48.4	267 38.5	07.8	10 03.5	26.7	48 45.5	21.9	0 48.1	17.8	Alkaid	152 56.0	N49 13.3
T 08	294 50.9	282 38.1	09.1	25 04.4	26.8	63 48.1	21.9	15 50.4	17.8	Al Na'ir	27 40.2	S46 52.4
U 09	309 53.4	297 37.8 ..	10.4	40 05.3 ..	26.8	78 50.6 ..	21.9	30 52.7 ..	17.8	Alnilam	275 43.1	S 1 11.7
R 10	324 55.8	312 37.4	11.6	55 06.2	26.9	93 53.1	21.9	45 55.1	17.8	Alphard	217 52.7	S 8 44.5
D 11	339 58.3	327 37.0	12.9	70 07.1	26.9	108 55.6	21.9	60 57.4	17.8			
A 12	355 00.7	342 36.6	N 4 14.2	85 08.0	S23 27.0	123 58.2	S17 21.8	75 59.7	S22 17.8	Alphecca	126 08.1	N26 39.1
Y 13	10 03.2	357 36.3	15.5	100 08.9	27.0	139 00.7	21.8	91 02.0	17.8	Alpheratz	357 40.5	N29 11.3
14	25 05.7	12 35.9	16.7	115 09.8	27.1	154 03.2	21.8	106 04.4	17.8	Altair	62 05.3	N 8 54.9
15	40 08.1	27 35.5 ..	18.0	130 10.7 ..	27.1	169 05.8 ..	21.8	121 06.7 ..	17.7	Ankaa	353 13.0	S42 12.7
16	55 10.6	42 35.2	19.3	145 11.6	27.2	184 08.3	21.7	136 09.0	17.7	Antares	112 22.2	S26 28.1
17	70 13.1	57 34.8	20.6	160 12.6	27.2	199 10.8	21.7	151 11.4	17.7			
18	85 15.5	72 34.4	N 4 21.8	175 13.5	S23 27.3	214 13.4	S17 21.7	166 13.7	S22 17.7	Arcturus	145 52.6	N19 05.2
19	100 18.0	87 34.0	23.1	190 14.4	27.3	229 15.9	21.7	181 16.0	17.7	Atria	107 21.0	S69 03.2
20	115 20.5	102 33.7	24.4	205 15.3	27.4	244 18.4	21.7	196 18.3	17.7	Avior	234 16.3	S59 34.4
21	130 22.9	117 33.3 ..	25.6	220 16.2 ..	27.4	259 20.9 ..	21.6	211 20.7 ..	17.7	Bellatrix	278 28.6	N 6 21.7
22	145 25.4	132 32.9	26.9	235 17.1	27.5	274 23.5	21.6	226 23.0	17.7	Betelgeuse	270 57.8	N 7 24.4
23	160 27.8	147 32.6	28.2	250 18.0	27.5	289 26.0	21.6	241 25.3	17.7			
18 00	175 30.3	162 32.2	N 4 29.5	265 18.9	S23 27.6	304 28.5	S17 21.6	256 27.7	S22 17.7	Canopus	263 54.6	S52 42.8
01	190 32.8	177 31.8	30.7	280 19.8	27.6	319 31.1	21.5	271 30.0	17.7	Capella	280 29.8	N46 00.9
02	205 35.2	192 31.4	32.0	295 20.7	27.7	334 33.6	21.5	286 32.3	17.7	Deneb	49 29.6	N45 20.5
03	220 37.7	207 31.1 ..	33.3	310 21.6 ..	27.7	349 36.1 ..	21.5	301 34.7 ..	17.6	Denebola	182 30.1	N14 28.2
04	235 40.2	222 30.7	34.5	325 22.5	27.8	4 38.7	21.5	316 37.0	17.6	Diphda	348 53.0	S17 53.5
05	250 42.6	237 30.3	35.8	340 23.4	27.8	19 41.2	21.4	331 39.3	17.6			
S 06	265 45.1	252 30.0	N 4 37.1	355 24.3	S23 27.9	34 43.7	S17 21.4	346 41.6	S22 17.6	Dubhe	193 47.2	N61 39.2
U 07	280 47.6	267 29.6	38.4	10 25.2	27.9	49 46.3	21.4	1 44.0	17.6	Elnath	278 08.6	N28 37.2
N 08	295 50.0	282 29.2	39.6	25 26.1	28.0	64 48.8	21.4	16 46.3	17.6	Eltanin	90 44.7	N51 29.0
D 09	310 52.5	297 28.8 ..	40.9	40 27.0 ..	28.0	79 51.4 ..	21.4	31 48.6 ..	17.6	Enif	33 44.2	N 9 57.4
A 10	325 55.0	312 28.5	42.2	55 27.9	28.1	94 53.9	21.3	46 51.0	17.6	Fomalhaut	15 20.8	S29 31.7
Y 11	340 57.4	327 28.1	43.4	70 28.8	28.1	109 56.4	21.3	61 53.3	17.6			
12	355 59.9	342 27.7	N 4 44.7	85 29.7	S23 28.2	124 59.0	S17 21.3	76 55.6	S22 17.6	Gacrux	171 56.7	S57 12.8
13	11 02.3	357 27.3	46.0	100 30.6	28.2	140 01.5	21.3	91 58.0	17.6	Gienah	175 48.7	S17 38.6
14	26 04.8	12 27.0	47.3	115 31.5	28.3	155 04.0	21.2	107 00.3	17.6	Hadar	148 42.7	S60 27.4
15	41 07.3	27 26.6 ..	48.5	130 32.4 ..	28.3	170 06.6 ..	21.2	122 02.6 ..	17.5	Hamal	327 57.4	N23 32.7
16	56 09.7	42 26.2	49.8	145 33.3	28.3	185 09.1	21.2	137 05.0	17.5	Kaus Aust.	83 39.6	S34 22.3
17	71 12.2	57 25.9	51.1	160 34.2	28.4	200 11.6	21.2	152 07.3	17.5			
18	86 14.7	72 25.5	N 4 52.3	175 35.1	S23 28.4	215 14.2	S17 21.1	167 09.6	S22 17.5	Kochab	137 19.4	N74 04.7
19	101 17.1	87 25.1	53.6	190 36.0	28.5	230 16.7	21.1	182 12.0	17.5	Markab	13 35.4	N15 18.0
20	116 19.6	102 24.7	54.9	205 36.9	28.5	245 19.3	21.1	197 14.3	17.5	Menkar	314 11.9	N 4 09.4
21	131 22.1	117 24.4 ..	56.1	220 37.8 ..	28.6	260 21.8 ..	21.1	212 16.6 ..	17.5	Menkent	148 03.4	S36 27.4
22	146 24.5	132 24.0	57.4	235 38.7	28.6	275 24.3	21.0	227 19.0	17.5	Miaplacidus	221 38.2	S69 47.8
23	161 27.0	147 23.6	58.7	250 39.6	28.7	290 26.9	21.0	242 21.3	17.5			
19 00	176 29.4	162 23.2	N 4 59.9	265 40.6	S23 28.7	305 29.4	S17 21.0	257 23.6	S22 17.5	Mirfak	308 36.0	N49 55.5
01	191 31.9	177 22.9	5 01.2	280 41.5	28.8	320 32.0	21.0	272 26.0	17.5	Nunki	75 54.5	S26 16.3
02	206 34.4	192 22.5	02.5	295 42.4	28.8	335 34.5	20.9	287 28.3	17.5	Peacock	53 14.6	S56 40.4
03	221 36.8	207 22.1 ..	03.7	310 43.3 ..	28.8	350 37.0 ..	20.9	302 30.6 ..	17.5	Pollux	243 23.7	N27 58.8
04	236 39.3	222 21.7	05.0	325 44.2	28.9	5 39.6	20.9	317 33.0	17.4	Procyon	244 56.2	N 5 10.5
05	251 41.8	237 21.4	06.3	340 45.1	28.9	20 42.1	20.9	332 35.3	17.4			
M 06	266 44.2	252 21.0	N 5 07.5	355 46.0	S23 29.0	35 44.7	S17 20.8	347 37.6	S22 17.4	Rasalhague	96 03.5	N12 32.8
O 07	281 46.7	267 20.6	08.8	10 46.9	29.0	50 47.2	20.8	2 40.0	17.4	Regulus	207 39.8	N11 52.6
N 08	296 49.2	282 20.2	10.1	25 47.8	29.1	65 49.8	20.8	17 42.3	17.4	Rigel	281 09.0	S 8 11.2
D 09	311 51.6	297 19.9 ..	11.3	40 48.7 ..	29.1	80 52.3 ..	20.8	32 44.7 ..	17.4	Rigil Kent.	139 46.8	S60 54.3
A 10	326 54.1	312 19.5	12.6	55 49.6	29.1	95 54.8	20.7	47 47.0	17.4	Sabik	102 08.8	S15 44.7
Y 11	341 56.6	327 19.1	13.9	70 50.5	29.2	110 57.4	20.7	62 49.3	17.4			
12	356 59.0	342 18.7	N 5 15.1	85 51.4	S23 29.2	125 59.9	S17 20.7	77 51.7	S22 17.4	Schedar	349 37.4	N56 38.1
13	12 01.5	357 18.4	16.4	100 52.3	29.3	141 02.5	20.7	92 54.0	17.4	Shaula	96 17.5	S37 06.7
14	27 03.9	12 18.0	17.7	115 53.2	29.3	156 05.0	20.6	107 56.3	17.4	Sirius	258 30.8	S16 44.8
15	42 06.4	27 17.6 ..	18.9	130 54.2 ..	29.3	171 07.6 ..	20.6	122 58.7 ..	17.4	Spica	158 27.6	S11 15.3
16	57 08.9	42 17.2	20.2	145 55.1	29.4	186 10.1	20.6	138 01.0	17.3	Suhail	222 49.7	S43 30.6
17	72 11.3	57 16.9	21.5	160 56.0	29.4	201 12.7	20.6	153 03.3	17.3			
18	87 13.8	72 16.5	N 5 22.7	175 56.9	S23 29.5	216 15.2	S17 20.5	168 05.7	S22 17.3	Vega	80 36.9	N38 47.9
19	102 16.3	87 16.1	24.0	190 57.8	29.5	231 17.8	20.5	183 08.0	17.3	Zuben'ubi	137 01.6	S16 06.9
20	117 18.7	102 15.7	25.3	205 58.7	29.5	246 20.3	20.5	198 10.4	17.3		SHA	Mer. Pass.
21	132 21.2	117 15.3 ..	26.5	220 59.6 ..	29.6	261 22.8 ..	20.5	213 12.7 ..	17.3			
22	147 23.7	132 15.0	27.8	236 00.5	29.6	276 25.4	20.4	228 15.0	17.3	Venus	347 01.9	13 10
23	162 26.1	147 14.6	29.0	251 01.4	29.7	291 27.9	20.4	243 17.4	17.3	Mars	89 48.5	6 18
Mer. Pass. 12 16.0		v −0.4	d 1.3	v 0.9	d 0.0	v 2.5	d 0.0	v 2.3	d 0.0	Jupiter	128 58.2	3 41
										Saturn	80 57.3	6 53

UT	SUN GHA	SUN Dec	MOON GHA	v	MOON Dec	d	HP
d h	° ′	° ′	° ′	′	° ′	′	′
17 00	177 52.7	S 1 27.3	182 41.8	13.0	S 6 47.3	10.5	56.1
01	192 52.9	26.3	197 13.8	12.9	6 36.8	10.5	56.2
02	207 53.1	25.3	211 45.7	13.0	6 26.3	10.5	56.2
03	222 53.3	.. 24.3	226 17.7	12.9	6 15.8	10.6	56.2
04	237 53.4	23.3	240 49.6	13.0	6 05.2	10.6	56.2
05	252 53.6	22.3	255 21.6	12.9	5 54.6	10.6	56.2
06	267 53.8	S 1 21.3	269 53.5	13.0	S 5 44.0	10.7	56.3
S 07	282 54.0	20.3	284 25.5	12.9	5 33.3	10.7	56.3
A 08	297 54.1	19.4	298 57.4	13.0	5 22.6	10.8	56.3
T 09	312 54.3	.. 18.4	313 29.4	12.9	5 11.8	10.8	56.3
U 10	327 54.5	17.4	328 01.3	12.9	5 01.0	10.8	56.4
R 11	342 54.7	16.4	342 33.2	12.9	4 50.2	10.8	56.4
D 12	357 54.9	S 1 15.4	357 05.1	12.9	S 4 39.4	10.9	56.4
A 13	12 55.0	14.4	11 37.0	12.9	4 28.5	10.9	56.4
Y 14	27 55.2	13.4	26 08.9	12.9	4 17.6	11.0	56.5
15	42 55.4	.. 12.4	40 40.8	12.8	4 06.6	11.0	56.5
16	57 55.6	11.4	55 12.6	12.9	3 55.7	11.0	56.5
17	72 55.8	10.5	69 44.5	12.9	3 44.7	11.0	56.5
18	87 55.9	S 1 09.5	84 16.4	12.8	S 3 33.7	11.1	56.5
19	102 56.1	08.5	98 48.2	12.8	3 22.6	11.1	56.6
20	117 56.3	07.5	113 20.0	12.8	3 11.5	11.1	56.6
21	132 56.5	.. 06.5	127 51.8	12.8	3 00.4	11.1	56.6
22	147 56.7	05.5	142 23.6	12.8	2 49.3	11.1	56.6
23	162 56.8	04.5	156 55.4	12.8	2 38.2	11.2	56.7
18 00	177 57.0	S 1 03.5	171 27.2	12.7	S 2 27.0	11.2	56.7
01	192 57.2	02.5	185 58.9	12.8	2 15.8	11.2	56.7
02	207 57.4	01.6	200 30.7	12.7	2 04.6	11.2	56.7
03	222 57.6	1 00.6	215 02.4	12.7	1 53.4	11.2	56.7
04	237 57.7	0 59.6	229 34.1	12.7	1 42.2	11.3	56.8
05	252 57.9	58.6	244 05.8	12.7	1 30.9	11.3	56.8
06	267 58.1	S 0 57.6	258 37.5	12.6	S 1 19.6	11.3	56.8
S 07	282 58.3	56.6	273 09.1	12.6	1 08.3	11.3	56.8
U 08	297 58.5	55.6	287 40.7	12.7	0 57.0	11.3	56.9
N 09	312 58.6	.. 54.6	302 12.4	12.6	0 45.7	11.3	56.9
D 10	327 58.8	53.6	316 44.0	12.5	0 34.4	11.4	56.9
A 11	342 59.0	52.7	331 15.5	12.6	0 23.0	11.3	56.9
Y 12	357 59.2	S 0 51.7	345 47.1	12.5	S 0 11.7	11.4	56.9
13	12 59.4	50.7	0 18.6	12.5	S 0 00.3	11.3	57.0
14	27 59.5	49.7	14 50.1	12.5	N 0 11.0	11.4	57.0
15	42 59.7	.. 48.7	29 21.6	12.5	0 22.4	11.4	57.0
16	57 59.9	47.7	43 53.1	12.4	0 33.8	11.4	57.0
17	73 00.1	46.7	58 24.5	12.4	0 45.2	11.4	57.0
18	88 00.3	S 0 45.7	72 55.9	12.4	N 0 56.6	11.4	57.1
19	103 00.5	44.7	87 27.3	12.4	1 08.0	11.4	57.1
20	118 00.6	43.8	101 58.7	12.3	1 19.4	11.4	57.1
21	133 00.8	.. 42.8	116 30.0	12.3	1 30.8	11.4	57.1
22	148 01.0	41.8	131 01.3	12.3	1 42.2	11.4	57.2
23	163 01.2	40.8	145 32.6	12.2	1 53.6	11.4	57.2
19 00	178 01.4	S 0 39.8	160 03.8	12.3	N 2 05.0	11.4	57.2
01	193 01.5	38.8	174 35.1	12.2	2 16.4	11.4	57.2
02	208 01.7	37.8	189 06.3	12.1	2 27.8	11.4	57.2
03	223 01.9	.. 36.8	203 37.4	12.1	2 39.2	11.4	57.3
04	238 02.1	35.9	218 08.5	12.1	2 50.6	11.4	57.3
05	253 02.3	34.9	232 39.6	12.1	3 02.0	11.3	57.3
06	268 02.5	S 0 33.9	247 10.7	12.1	N 3 13.3	11.4	57.3
07	283 02.6	32.9	261 41.8	12.0	3 24.7	11.4	57.3
08	298 02.8	31.9	276 12.8	11.9	3 36.1	11.3	57.4
M 09	313 03.0	.. 30.9	290 43.7	12.0	3 47.4	11.4	57.4
O 10	328 03.2	29.9	305 14.7	11.9	3 58.8	11.3	57.4
N 11	343 03.4	28.9	319 45.6	11.8	4 10.1	11.3	57.4
D 12	358 03.5	S 0 27.9	334 16.4	11.9	N 4 21.4	11.3	57.4
A 13	13 03.7	27.0	348 47.3	11.7	4 32.7	11.3	57.5
Y 14	28 03.9	26.0	3 18.0	11.8	4 44.0	11.2	57.5
15	43 04.1	.. 25.0	17 48.8	11.7	4 55.2	11.3	57.5
16	58 04.3	24.0	32 19.5	11.7	5 06.5	11.2	57.5
17	73 04.5	23.0	46 50.2	11.6	5 17.7	11.2	57.5
18	88 04.6	S 0 22.0	61 20.8	11.6	N 5 28.9	11.2	57.6
19	103 04.8	21.0	75 51.4	11.6	5 40.1	11.2	57.6
20	118 05.0	20.0	90 22.0	11.5	5 51.3	11.1	57.6
21	133 05.2	.. 19.0	104 52.5	11.5	6 02.4	11.1	57.6
22	148 05.4	18.1	119 23.0	11.4	6 13.5	11.1	57.6
23	163 05.6	17.1	133 53.4	11.4	N 6 24.6	11.1	57.7
	SD 16.1	d 1.0	SD 15.4		15.5		15.7

Twilight / Moonrise

Lat.	Naut.	Civil	Sunrise	17	18	19	20
°	h m	h m	h m	h m	h m	h m	h m
N 72	03 35	05 02	06 09	07 13	07 03	06 53	06 42
N 70	03 52	05 08	06 09	07 06	07 01	06 57	06 53
68	04 05	05 13	06 09	06 59	07 00	07 01	07 02
66	04 15	05 18	06 09	06 54	06 59	07 04	07 09
64	04 24	05 21	06 08	06 49	06 58	07 06	07 16
62	04 31	05 24	06 08	06 45	06 57	07 09	07 21
60	04 37	05 27	06 08	06 42	06 56	07 11	07 26
N 58	04 43	05 29	06 08	06 39	06 56	07 12	07 31
56	04 47	05 31	06 08	06 36	06 55	07 14	07 34
54	04 51	05 33	06 08	06 33	06 54	07 15	07 38
52	04 54	05 34	06 08	06 31	06 54	07 17	07 41
50	04 58	05 35	06 08	06 29	06 53	07 18	07 44
45	05 04	05 38	06 07	06 25	06 52	07 21	07 50
N 40	05 09	05 40	06 07	06 21	06 51	07 23	07 56
35	05 12	05 42	06 07	06 18	06 51	07 25	08 00
30	05 15	05 43	06 06	06 15	06 50	07 27	08 04
20	05 18	05 44	06 06	06 10	06 49	07 30	08 11
N 10	05 20	05 44	06 05	06 05	06 48	07 32	08 18
0	05 20	05 44	06 05	06 01	06 47	07 35	08 24
S 10	05 19	05 43	06 04	05 57	06 47	07 37	08 30
20	05 16	05 41	06 03	05 52	06 46	07 40	08 36
30	05 10	05 38	06 02	05 47	06 45	07 43	08 43
35	05 06	05 36	06 01	05 44	06 44	07 45	08 48
40	05 02	05 33	06 01	05 41	06 44	07 47	08 53
45	04 56	05 30	06 00	05 37	06 43	07 50	08 58
S 50	04 48	05 26	05 58	05 32	06 42	07 53	09 05
52	04 44	05 24	05 58	05 30	06 41	07 54	09 08
54	04 39	05 22	05 57	05 28	06 41	07 56	09 12
56	04 35	05 19	05 56	05 25	06 41	07 57	09 16
58	04 29	05 16	05 56	05 22	06 40	07 59	09 20
S 60	04 22	05 13	05 55	05 19	06 39	08 01	09 25

Twilight / Moonset

Lat.	Sunset	Civil	Naut.	17	18	19	20
°	h m	h m	h m	h m	h m	h m	h m
N 72	18 09	19 17	20 45	17 35	19 24	21 16	23 13
N 70	18 09	19 11	20 28	17 41	19 23	21 07	22 55
68	18 09	19 05	20 14	17 45	19 21	21 00	22 41
66	18 09	19 01	20 03	17 49	19 20	20 54	22 29
64	18 09	18 57	19 54	17 52	19 19	20 49	22 20
62	18 09	18 54	19 47	17 55	19 19	20 44	22 12
60	18 09	18 51	19 41	17 57	19 18	20 41	22 05
N 58	18 09	18 49	19 35	17 59	19 17	20 37	21 58
56	18 09	18 47	19 31	18 01	19 17	20 34	21 53
54	18 09	18 45	19 27	18 03	19 16	20 32	21 48
52	18 10	18 43	19 23	18 04	19 16	20 29	21 44
50	18 10	18 42	19 20	18 05	19 16	20 27	21 40
45	18 10	18 39	19 13	18 08	19 15	20 22	21 31
N 40	18 10	18 37	19 08	18 11	19 14	20 18	21 24
35	18 10	18 35	19 04	18 13	19 13	20 15	21 18
30	18 10	18 34	19 02	18 15	19 13	20 12	21 13
20	18 10	18 32	18 58	18 18	19 12	20 07	21 03
N 10	18 11	18 32	18 56	18 21	19 11	20 02	20 55
0	18 11	18 32	18 56	18 23	19 10	19 58	20 48
S 10	18 12	18 33	18 57	18 26	19 09	19 54	20 40
20	18 13	18 35	19 00	18 28	19 08	19 49	20 32
30	18 14	18 37	19 05	18 31	19 07	19 44	20 23
35	18 14	18 39	19 09	18 33	19 07	19 41	20 17
40	18 15	18 42	19 14	18 35	19 06	19 38	20 11
45	18 16	18 45	19 19	18 37	19 05	19 34	20 05
S 50	18 17	18 49	19 27	18 40	19 04	19 29	19 56
52	18 17	18 51	19 31	18 41	19 04	19 27	19 52
54	18 18	18 53	19 35	18 42	19 03	19 25	19 48
56	18 18	18 56	19 40	18 44	19 03	19 22	19 44
58	18 19	18 58	19 46	18 45	19 02	19 19	19 38
S 60	18 20	19 02	19 52	18 47	19 01	19 16	19 33

SUN / MOON

Day	Eqn. of Time 00h	Eqn. of Time 12h	Mer. Pass.	Mer. Pass. Upper	Mer. Pass. Lower	Age	Phase
d	m s	m s	h m	h m	h m	d	%
17	08 29	08 21	12 08	12 12	24 35	30	0
18	08 12	08 04	12 08	12 59	00 35	01	1
19	07 55	07 46	12 08	13 46	01 22	02	4

UT	ARIES	VENUS −3.9		MARS +0.5		JUPITER −2.3		SATURN +0.5		STARS		
d h	GHA	GHA	Dec	GHA	Dec	GHA	Dec	GHA	Dec	Name	SHA	Dec
20 00	177 28.6	162 14.2 N 5 30.3		266 02.3 S23 29.7		306 30.5 S17 20.4		258 19.7 S22 17.3		Acamar	315 16.2	S40 14.3
01	192 31.1	177 13.8	31.6	281 03.2	29.7	321 33.0	20.3	273 22.0	17.3	Achernar	335 25.0	S57 09.0
02	207 33.5	192 13.5	32.8	296 04.2	29.8	336 35.6	20.3	288 24.4	17.3	Acrux	173 04.9	S63 11.9
03	222 36.0	207 13.1 ..	34.1	311 05.1 ..	29.8	351 38.1 ..	20.3	303 26.7 ..	17.3	Adhara	255 09.9	S29 00.2
04	237 38.4	222 12.7	35.4	326 06.0	29.9	6 40.7	20.3	318 29.1	17.3	Aldebaran	290 45.8	N16 32.5
05	252 40.9	237 12.3	36.6	341 06.9	29.9	21 43.2	20.2	333 31.4	17.2			
06	267 43.4	252 11.9 N 5 37.9		356 07.8 S23 29.9		36 45.8 S17 20.2		348 33.7 S22 17.2		Alioth	166 17.4	N55 51.6
T 07	282 45.8	267 11.6	39.1	11 08.7	30.0	51 48.3	20.2	3 36.1	17.2	Alkaid	152 56.0	N49 13.3
U 08	297 48.3	282 11.2	40.4	26 09.6	30.0	66 50.9	20.2	18 38.4	17.2	Al Na'ir	27 40.1	S46 52.3
E 09	312 50.8	297 10.8 ..	41.7	41 10.5 ..	30.0	81 53.4 ..	20.1	33 40.8 ..	17.2	Alnilam	275 43.1	S 1 11.7
S 10	327 53.2	312 10.4	42.9	56 11.4	30.1	96 56.0	20.1	48 43.1	17.2	Alphard	217 52.7	S 8 44.5
D 11	342 55.7	327 10.1	44.2	71 12.3	30.1	111 58.5	20.1	63 45.4	17.2			
A 12	357 58.2	342 09.7 N 5 45.5		86 13.3 S23 30.1		127 01.1 S17 20.0		78 47.8 S22 17.2		Alphecca	126 08.1	N26 39.1
Y 13	13 00.6	357 09.3	46.7	101 14.2	30.2	142 03.6	20.0	93 50.1	17.2	Alpheratz	357 40.5	N29 11.3
14	28 03.1	12 08.9	48.0	116 15.1	30.2	157 06.2	20.0	108 52.5	17.2	Altair	62 05.2	N 8 54.9
15	43 05.5	27 08.5 ..	49.2	131 16.0 ..	30.3	172 08.8 ..	20.0	123 54.8 ..	17.2	Ankaa	353 13.0	S42 12.6
16	58 08.0	42 08.2	50.5	146 16.9	30.3	187 11.3	19.9	138 57.1	17.2	Antares	112 22.2	S26 28.1
17	73 10.5	57 07.8	51.8	161 17.8	30.3	202 13.9	19.9	153 59.5	17.1			
18	88 12.9	72 07.4 N 5 53.0		176 18.7 S23 30.4		217 16.4 S17 19.9		169 01.8 S22 17.1		Arcturus	145 52.5	N19 05.2
19	103 15.4	87 07.0	54.3	191 19.6	30.4	232 19.0	19.9	184 04.2	17.1	Atria	107 20.9	S69 03.2
20	118 17.9	102 06.6	55.5	206 20.6	30.4	247 21.5	19.8	199 06.5	17.1	Avior	234 16.5	S59 34.4
21	133 20.3	117 06.3 ..	56.8	221 21.5 ..	30.5	262 24.1 ..	19.8	214 08.8 ..	17.1	Bellatrix	278 28.6	N 6 21.7
22	148 22.8	132 05.9	58.0	236 22.4	30.5	277 26.6	19.8	229 11.2	17.1	Betelgeuse	270 57.8	N 7 24.4
23	163 25.3	147 05.5 5 59.3		251 23.3	30.5	292 29.2	19.7	244 13.5	17.1			
21 00	178 27.7	162 05.1 N 6 00.6		266 24.2 S23 30.6		307 31.7 S17 19.7		259 15.9 S22 17.1		Canopus	263 54.7	S52 42.8
01	193 30.2	177 04.7	01.8	281 25.1	30.6	322 34.3	19.7	274 18.2	17.1	Capella	280 29.8	N46 00.9
02	208 32.7	192 04.3	03.1	296 26.0	30.6	337 36.9	19.7	289 20.6	17.1	Deneb	49 29.6	N45 20.5
03	223 35.1	207 04.0 ..	04.3	311 26.9 ..	30.7	352 39.4 ..	19.6	304 22.9 ..	17.1	Denebola	182 30.1	N14 28.2
04	238 37.6	222 03.6	05.6	326 27.9	30.7	7 42.0	19.6	319 25.2	17.1	Diphda	348 53.0	S17 53.5
05	253 40.0	237 03.2	06.8	341 28.8	30.7	22 44.5	19.6	334 27.6	17.1			
06	268 42.5	252 02.8 N 6 08.1		356 29.7 S23 30.8		37 47.1 S17 19.5		349 29.9 S22 17.0		Dubhe	193 47.2	N61 39.2
W 07	283 45.0	267 02.4	09.4	11 30.6	30.8	52 49.6	19.5	4 32.3	17.0	Elnath	278 08.6	N28 37.2
E 08	298 47.4	282 02.1	10.6	26 31.5	30.8	67 52.2	19.5	19 34.6	17.0	Eltanin	90 44.6	N51 29.0
D 09	313 49.9	297 01.7 ..	11.9	41 32.4 ..	30.9	82 54.8 ..	19.4	34 37.0 ..	17.0	Enif	33 44.2	N 9 57.4
N 10	328 52.4	312 01.3	13.1	56 33.3	30.9	97 57.3	19.4	49 39.3	17.0	Fomalhaut	15 20.8	S29 31.7
E 11	343 54.8	327 00.9	14.4	71 34.3	30.9	112 59.9	19.4	64 41.7	17.0			
S 12	358 57.3	342 00.5 N 6 15.6		86 35.2 S23 30.9		128 02.4 S17 19.4		79 44.0 S22 17.0		Gacrux	171 56.7	S57 12.8
D 13	13 59.8	357 00.1	16.9	101 36.1	31.0	143 05.0	19.3	94 46.3	17.0	Gienah	175 48.7	S17 38.6
A 14	29 02.2	11 59.8	18.1	116 37.0	31.0	158 07.6	19.3	109 48.7	17.0	Hadar	148 42.7	S60 27.4
Y 15	44 04.7	26 59.4 ..	19.4	131 37.9 ..	31.0	173 10.1 ..	19.3	124 51.0 ..	17.0	Hamal	327 57.4	N23 32.7
16	59 07.1	41 59.0	20.7	146 38.8	31.1	188 12.7	19.2	139 53.4	17.0	Kaus Aust.	83 39.6	S34 22.3
17	74 09.6	56 58.6	21.9	161 39.8	31.1	203 15.2	19.2	154 55.7	17.0			
18	89 12.1	71 58.2 N 6 23.2		176 40.7 S23 31.1		218 17.8 S17 19.2		169 58.1 S22 17.0		Kochab	137 19.3	N74 04.7
19	104 14.5	86 57.8	24.4	191 41.6	31.2	233 20.4	19.2	185 00.4	16.9	Markab	13 35.4	N15 18.0
20	119 17.0	101 57.5	25.7	206 42.5	31.2	248 22.9	19.1	200 02.8	16.9	Menkar	314 11.9	N 4 09.4
21	134 19.5	116 57.1 ..	26.9	221 43.4 ..	31.2	263 25.5 ..	19.1	215 05.1 ..	16.9	Menkent	148 03.4	S36 27.4
22	149 21.9	131 56.7	28.2	236 44.3	31.2	278 28.1	19.1	230 07.5	16.9	Miaplacidus	221 38.3	S69 47.8
23	164 24.4	146 56.3	29.4	251 45.3	31.3	293 30.6	19.0	245 09.8	16.9			
22 00	179 26.9	161 55.9 N 6 30.7		266 46.2 S23 31.3		308 33.2 S17 19.0		260 12.1 S22 16.9		Mirfak	308 36.0	N49 55.4
01	194 29.3	176 55.5	31.9	281 47.1	31.3	323 35.8	19.0	275 14.5	16.9	Nunki	75 54.4	S26 16.3
02	209 31.8	191 55.2	33.2	296 48.0	31.4	338 38.3	18.9	290 16.8	16.9	Peacock	53 14.6	S56 40.3
03	224 34.3	206 54.8 ..	34.4	311 48.9 ..	31.4	353 40.9 ..	18.9	305 19.2 ..	16.9	Pollux	243 23.7	N27 58.8
04	239 36.7	221 54.4	35.7	326 49.8	31.4	8 43.4	18.9	320 21.5	16.9	Procyon	244 56.3	N 5 10.5
05	254 39.2	236 54.0	36.9	341 50.8	31.4	23 46.0	18.8	335 23.9	16.9			
06	269 41.6	251 53.6 N 6 38.2		356 51.7 S23 31.5		38 48.6 S17 18.8		350 26.2 S22 16.9		Rasalhague	96 03.4	N12 32.8
T 07	284 44.1	266 53.2	39.4	11 52.6	31.5	53 51.1	18.8	5 28.6	16.9	Regulus	207 39.8	N11 52.6
H 08	299 46.6	281 52.8	40.7	26 53.5	31.5	68 53.7	18.8	20 30.9	16.9	Rigel	281 09.0	S 8 11.2
U 09	314 49.0	296 52.4 ..	41.9	41 54.4 ..	31.5	83 56.3 ..	18.7	35 33.3 ..	16.8	Rigil Kent.	139 46.8	S60 54.3
R 10	329 51.5	311 52.1	43.2	56 55.3	31.6	98 58.8	18.7	50 35.6	16.8	Sabik	102 08.8	S15 44.7
S 11	344 54.0	326 51.7	44.4	71 56.3	31.6	114 01.4	18.7	65 38.0	16.8			
S 12	359 56.4	341 51.3 N 6 45.7		86 57.2 S23 31.6		129 04.0 S17 18.6		80 40.3 S22 16.8		Schedar	349 37.4	N56 38.1
D 13	14 58.9	356 50.9	46.9	101 58.1	31.6	144 06.5	18.6	95 42.7	16.8	Shaula	96 17.5	S37 06.7
A 14	30 01.4	11 50.5	48.2	116 59.0	31.7	159 09.1	18.6	110 45.0	16.8	Sirius	258 30.8	S16 44.8
Y 15	45 03.8	26 50.1 ..	49.4	131 59.9 ..	31.7	174 11.7 ..	18.5	125 47.4 ..	16.8	Spica	158 27.6	S11 15.3
16	60 06.3	41 49.7	50.7	147 00.9	31.7	189 14.2	18.5	140 49.7	16.8	Suhail	222 49.8	S43 30.7
17	75 08.8	56 49.4	51.9	162 01.8	31.7	204 16.8	18.5	155 52.1	16.8			
18	90 11.2	71 49.0 N 6 53.2		177 02.7 S23 31.8		219 19.4 S17 18.4		170 54.4 S22 16.8		Vega	80 36.8	N38 47.9
19	105 13.7	86 48.6	54.4	192 03.6	31.8	234 22.0	18.4	185 56.8	16.8	Zuben'ubi	137 01.6	S16 06.9
20	120 16.1	101 48.2	55.7	207 04.5	31.8	249 24.5	18.4	200 59.1	16.8		SHA	Mer. Pass.
21	135 18.6	116 47.8 ..	56.9	222 05.5 ..	31.8	264 27.1 ..	18.3	216 01.5 ..	16.8		° ′	h m
22	150 21.1	131 47.4	58.2	237 06.4	31.9	279 29.7	18.3	231 03.8	16.7	Venus	343 37.4	13 12
23	165 23.5	146 47.0	59.4	252 07.3	31.9	294 32.2	18.3	246 06.2	16.7	Mars	87 56.5	6 14
	h m									Jupiter	129 04.0	3 29
Mer. Pass. 12 04.2		v −0.4	d 1.3	v 0.9	d 0.0	v 2.6	d 0.0	v 2.3	d 0.0	Saturn	80 48.2	6 42

UT	SUN GHA	SUN Dec	MOON GHA	v	MOON Dec	d	HP
d h	° ′	° ′	° ′	′	° ′	′	′
20 00	178 05.7	S 0 16.1	148 23.8	11.4	N 6 35.7	11.0	57.7
01	193 05.9	15.1	162 54.2	11.3	6 46.7	11.0	57.7
02	208 06.1	14.1	177 24.5	11.3	6 57.7	11.0	57.7
03	223 06.3	. . 13.1	191 54.8	11.2	7 08.7	10.9	57.7
04	238 06.5	12.1	206 25.0	11.2	7 19.6	11.0	57.8
05	253 06.7	11.1	220 55.2	11.1	7 30.6	10.9	57.8
06	268 06.8	S 0 10.1	235 25.3	11.1	N 7 41.5	10.8	57.8
07	283 07.0	09.2	249 55.4	11.0	7 52.3	10.8	57.8
08	298 07.2	08.2	264 25.4	11.0	8 03.1	10.8	57.8
09	313 07.4	. . 07.2	278 55.4	10.9	8 13.9	10.7	57.9
10	328 07.6	06.2	293 25.3	10.9	8 24.6	10.7	57.9
11	343 07.8	05.2	307 55.2	10.9	8 35.3	10.7	57.9
12	358 07.9	S 0 04.2	322 25.1	10.8	N 8 46.0	10.6	57.9
13	13 08.1	03.2	336 54.9	10.7	8 56.6	10.6	57.9
14	28 08.3	02.2	351 24.6	10.7	9 07.2	10.6	57.9
15	43 08.5	. . 01.3	5 54.3	10.7	9 17.8	10.5	58.0
16	58 08.7	S 00.3	20 24.0	10.6	9 28.3	10.4	58.0
17	73 08.9	N 00.7	34 53.6	10.5	9 38.7	10.4	58.0
18	88 09.1	N 0 01.7	49 23.1	10.5	N 9 49.1	10.4	58.0
19	103 09.2	02.7	63 52.6	10.5	9 59.5	10.3	58.0
20	118 09.4	03.7	78 22.1	10.4	10 09.8	10.2	58.0
21	133 09.6	. . 04.7	92 51.5	10.3	10 20.0	10.2	58.1
22	148 09.8	05.7	107 20.8	10.3	10 30.2	10.2	58.1
23	163 10.0	06.7	121 50.1	10.2	10 40.4	10.1	58.1
21 00	178 10.2	N 0 07.6	136 19.3	10.2	N10 50.5	10.1	58.1
01	193 10.3	08.6	150 48.5	10.1	11 00.6	10.0	58.1
02	208 10.5	09.6	165 17.6	10.1	11 10.6	9.9	58.1
03	223 10.7	. . 10.6	179 46.7	10.0	11 20.5	9.9	58.2
04	238 10.9	11.6	194 15.7	9.9	11 30.4	9.8	58.2
05	253 11.1	12.6	208 44.6	9.9	11 40.2	9.8	58.2
06	268 11.3	N 0 13.6	223 13.5	9.9	N11 50.0	9.7	58.2
07	283 11.5	14.6	237 42.4	9.8	11 59.7	9.6	58.2
08	298 11.6	15.5	252 11.2	9.7	12 09.3	9.6	58.2
09	313 11.8	. . 16.5	266 39.9	9.7	12 18.9	9.5	58.3
10	328 12.0	17.5	281 08.6	9.6	12 28.4	9.4	58.3
11	343 12.2	18.5	295 37.2	9.6	12 37.8	9.4	58.3
12	358 12.4	N 0 19.5	310 05.8	9.5	N12 47.2	9.3	58.3
13	13 12.6	20.5	324 34.3	9.4	12 56.5	9.3	58.3
14	28 12.8	21.5	339 02.7	9.4	13 05.8	9.1	58.3
15	43 12.9	. . 22.5	353 31.1	9.3	13 14.9	9.1	58.4
16	58 13.1	23.4	7 59.4	9.3	13 24.0	9.1	58.4
17	73 13.3	24.4	22 27.7	9.2	13 33.1	8.9	58.4
18	88 13.5	N 0 25.4	36 55.9	9.2	N13 42.0	8.9	58.4
19	103 13.7	26.4	51 24.1	9.1	13 50.9	8.8	58.4
20	118 13.9	27.4	65 52.2	9.0	13 59.7	8.7	58.4
21	133 14.1	. . 28.4	80 20.2	9.0	14 08.4	8.7	58.4
22	148 14.2	29.4	94 48.2	8.9	14 17.1	8.6	58.5
23	163 14.4	30.4	109 16.1	8.9	14 25.7	8.4	58.5
22 00	178 14.6	N 0 31.3	123 44.0	8.8	N14 34.1	8.5	58.5
01	193 14.8	32.3	138 11.8	8.7	14 42.6	8.3	58.5
02	208 15.0	33.3	152 39.5	8.7	14 50.9	8.2	58.5
03	223 15.2	34.3	167 07.2	8.7	14 59.1	8.2	58.5
04	238 15.4	35.3	181 34.9	8.5	15 07.3	8.1	58.5
05	253 15.5	36.3	196 02.4	8.5	15 15.4	7.9	58.6
06	268 15.7	N 0 37.3	210 29.9	8.5	N15 23.3	8.0	58.6
07	283 15.9	38.3	224 57.4	8.4	15 31.3	7.8	58.6
08	298 16.1	39.2	239 24.8	8.3	15 39.1	7.7	58.6
09	313 16.3	. . 40.2	253 52.1	8.3	15 46.8	7.6	58.6
10	328 16.5	41.2	268 19.4	8.2	15 54.4	7.6	58.6
11	343 16.7	42.2	282 46.6	8.2	16 02.0	7.4	58.6
12	358 16.9	N 0 43.2	297 13.8	8.1	N16 09.4	7.4	58.7
13	13 17.0	44.2	311 40.9	8.0	16 16.8	7.2	58.7
14	28 17.2	45.2	326 07.9	8.0	16 24.0	7.2	58.7
15	43 17.4	. . 46.1	340 34.9	7.9	16 31.2	7.0	58.7
16	58 17.6	47.1	355 01.8	7.9	16 38.2	7.0	58.7
17	73 17.8	48.1	9 28.7	7.8	16 45.2	6.9	58.7
18	88 18.0	N 0 49.1	23 55.5	7.8	N16 52.1	6.7	58.7
19	103 18.2	50.1	38 22.3	7.7	16 58.8	6.7	58.7
20	118 18.3	51.1	52 49.0	7.7	17 05.5	6.6	58.8
21	133 18.5	. . 52.1	67 15.7	7.6	17 12.1	6.4	58.8
22	148 18.7	53.0	81 42.3	7.5	17 18.5	6.4	58.8
23	163 18.9	54.0	96 08.8	7.5	N17 24.9	6.2	58.8
	SD 16.1	d 1.0	SD 15.8		15.9		16.0

Twilight / Sunrise / Moonrise

Lat.	Naut.	Civil	Sunrise	Moonrise 20	21	22	23
°	h m	h m	h m	h m	h m	h m	h m
N 72	03 15	04 45	05 54	06 42	06 29	06 10	05 15
N 70	03 35	04 54	05 55	06 53	06 48	06 44	06 39
68	03 50	05 00	05 56	07 02	07 04	07 09	07 19
66	04 02	05 06	05 57	07 09	07 17	07 28	07 46
64	04 12	05 10	05 58	07 16	07 28	07 44	08 07
62	04 20	05 14	05 58	07 21	07 37	07 57	08 24
60	04 27	05 17	05 59	07 26	07 45	08 08	08 38
N 58	04 33	05 20	06 00	07 31	07 52	08 17	08 51
56	04 39	05 23	06 00	07 34	07 58	08 26	09 01
54	04 43	05 25	06 00	07 38	08 03	08 33	09 11
52	04 47	05 27	06 01	07 41	08 08	08 40	09 19
50	04 51	05 29	06 01	07 44	08 13	08 46	09 26
45	04 58	05 32	06 02	07 50	08 23	09 00	09 43
N 40	05 04	05 35	06 02	07 56	08 31	09 11	09 56
35	05 08	05 37	06 03	08 00	08 38	09 20	10 07
30	05 11	05 39	06 03	08 04	08 45	09 29	10 17
20	05 16	05 41	06 03	08 11	08 56	09 43	10 34
N 10	05 18	05 43	06 04	08 18	09 05	09 56	10 49
0	05 19	05 43	06 04	08 24	09 14	10 08	11 03
S 10	05 19	05 43	06 04	08 30	09 24	10 20	11 17
20	05 16	05 42	06 04	08 36	09 33	10 32	11 32
30	05 12	05 40	06 04	08 43	09 45	10 47	11 50
35	05 09	05 39	06 04	08 48	09 51	10 56	12 00
40	05 05	05 37	06 04	08 53	09 59	11 06	12 12
45	05 00	05 34	06 03	08 58	10 08	11 17	12 26
S 50	04 53	05 31	06 03	09 05	10 18	11 32	12 42
52	04 49	05 29	06 03	09 08	10 23	11 38	12 50
54	04 46	05 28	06 03	09 12	10 29	11 45	12 59
56	04 41	05 25	06 03	09 16	10 35	11 54	13 09
58	04 36	05 23	06 02	09 20	10 42	12 03	13 21
S 60	04 31	05 21	06 02	09 25	10 50	12 14	13 34

Sunset / Twilight / Moonset

Lat.	Sunset	Civil	Naut.	Moonset 20	21	22	23
°	h m	h m	h m	h m	h m	h m	h m
N 72	18 23	19 32	21 04	23 13	25 21	01 21	04 11
N 70	18 22	19 23	20 43	22 55	24 49	00 49	02 48
68	18 20	19 17	20 27	22 41	24 25	00 25	02 09
66	18 19	19 11	20 15	22 29	24 07	00 07	01 42
64	18 18	19 06	20 05	22 20	23 52	25 22	01 22
62	18 17	19 02	19 56	22 12	23 40	25 05	01 05
60	18 17	18 58	19 49	22 05	23 29	24 51	00 51
N 58	18 16	18 55	19 43	21 58	23 20	24 40	00 40
56	18 16	18 53	19 37	21 53	23 12	24 29	00 29
54	18 15	18 51	19 33	21 48	23 05	24 20	00 20
52	18 15	18 48	19 28	21 44	22 59	24 12	00 12
50	18 14	18 47	19 25	21 40	22 53	24 05	00 05
45	18 14	18 43	19 17	21 31	22 41	23 50	24 56
N 40	18 13	18 40	19 12	21 24	22 31	23 37	24 42
35	18 12	18 38	19 07	21 18	22 22	23 27	24 30
30	18 12	18 36	19 04	21 13	22 15	23 17	24 20
20	18 11	18 33	18 59	21 03	22 01	23 01	24 01
N 10	18 11	18 32	18 56	20 55	21 50	22 47	23 45
0	18 10	18 31	18 55	20 48	21 39	22 34	23 30
S 10	18 10	18 31	18 56	20 40	21 29	22 21	23 00
20	18 10	18 32	18 58	20 32	21 18	22 07	23 00
30	18 10	18 34	19 02	20 23	21 05	21 51	22 42
35	18 10	18 35	19 05	20 17	20 57	21 41	22 31
40	18 10	18 37	19 09	20 11	20 49	21 31	22 19
45	18 10	18 39	19 14	20 05	20 39	21 18	22 05
S 50	18 10	18 42	19 20	19 56	20 27	21 03	21 47
52	18 10	18 44	19 24	19 52	20 22	20 56	21 39
54	18 10	18 46	19 27	19 48	20 16	20 49	21 30
56	18 11	18 48	19 32	19 44	20 09	20 40	21 20
58	18 11	18 50	19 36	19 38	20 01	20 30	21 08
S 60	18 11	18 52	19 42	19 33	19 53	20 19	20 54

	SUN Eqn. of Time 00h	12h	Mer. Pass.	MOON Mer. Pass. Upper	Lower	Age	Phase
Day	m s	m s	h m	h m	h m	d	%
20	07 37	07 29	12 07	14 36	02 11	03	10
21	07 20	07 11	12 07	15 27	03 01	04	17
22	07 02	06 53	12 07	16 21	03 53	05	27

UT	ARIES GHA	VENUS GHA	VENUS Dec	MARS GHA	MARS Dec	JUPITER GHA	JUPITER Dec	SATURN GHA	SATURN Dec	STARS Name	SHA	Dec
d h	° ′	° ′	° ′	° ′	° ′	° ′	° ′	° ′	° ′		° ′	° ′
23 00	180 26.0	161 46.6	N 7 00.7	267 08.2	S23 31.9	309 34.8	S17 18.3	261 08.5	S22 16.7	Acamar	315 16.2	S40 14.3
01	195 28.5	176 46.2	01.9	282 09.1	31.9	324 37.4	18.2	276 10.9	16.7	Achernar	335 25.0	S57 09.0
02	210 30.9	191 45.9	03.1	297 10.1	32.0	339 40.0	18.2	291 13.2	16.7	Acrux	173 04.9	S63 11.9
03	225 33.4	206 45.5	.. 04.4	312 11.0	.. 32.0	354 42.5	.. 18.2	306 15.6	.. 16.7	Adhara	255 09.9	S29 00.2
04	240 35.9	221 45.1	05.6	327 11.9	32.0	9 45.1	18.1	321 17.9	16.7	Aldebaran	290 45.8	N16 32.5
05	255 38.3	236 44.7	06.9	342 12.8	32.0	24 47.7	18.1	336 20.3	16.7			
F 06	270 40.8	251 44.3	N 7 08.1	357 13.8	S23 32.0	39 50.2	S17 18.1	351 22.6	S22 16.7	Alioth	166 17.4	N55 51.7
R 07	285 43.3	266 43.9	09.4	12 14.7	32.1	54 52.8	18.0	6 25.0	16.7	Alkaid	152 56.0	N49 13.3
I 08	300 45.7	281 43.5	10.6	27 15.6	32.1	69 55.4	18.0	21 27.3	16.7	Al Na'ir	27 40.1	S46 52.3
D 09	315 48.2	296 43.1	.. 11.9	42 16.5	.. 32.1	84 58.0	.. 18.0	36 29.7	.. 16.7	Alnilam	275 43.2	S 1 11.7
A 10	330 50.6	311 42.7	13.1	57 17.4	32.1	100 00.5	17.9	51 32.0	16.7	Alphard	217 52.7	S 8 44.5
Y 11	345 53.1	326 42.3	14.3	72 18.4	32.2	115 03.1	17.9	66 34.4	16.7			
12	0 55.6	341 41.9	N 7 15.6	87 19.3	S23 32.2	130 05.7	S17 17.9	81 36.7	S22 16.6	Alphecca	126 08.1	N26 39.2
13	15 58.0	356 41.6	16.8	102 20.2	32.2	145 08.3	17.8	96 39.1	16.6	Alpheratz	357 40.5	N29 11.2
14	31 00.5	11 41.2	18.1	117 21.1	32.2	160 10.8	17.8	111 41.4	16.6	Altair	62 05.2	N 8 54.9
15	46 03.0	26 40.8	.. 19.3	132 22.1	.. 32.2	175 13.4	.. 17.8	126 43.8	.. 16.6	Ankaa	353 13.0	S42 12.6
16	61 05.4	41 40.4	20.6	147 23.0	32.3	190 16.0	17.7	141 46.1	16.6	Antares	112 22.1	S26 28.1
17	76 07.9	56 40.0	21.8	162 23.9	32.3	205 18.6	17.7	156 48.5	16.6			
18	91 10.4	71 39.6	N 7 23.0	177 24.8	S23 32.3	220 21.1	S17 17.7	171 50.9	S22 16.6	Arcturus	145 52.5	N19 05.2
19	106 12.8	86 39.2	24.3	192 25.8	32.3	235 23.7	17.6	186 53.2	16.6	Atria	107 20.9	S69 03.2
20	121 15.3	101 38.8	25.5	207 26.7	32.3	250 26.3	17.6	201 55.6	16.6	Avior	234 16.4	S59 34.4
21	136 17.7	116 38.4	.. 26.8	222 27.6	.. 32.3	265 28.9	.. 17.6	216 57.9	.. 16.6	Bellatrix	278 28.6	N 6 21.7
22	151 20.2	131 38.0	28.0	237 28.5	32.4	280 31.5	17.5	232 00.3	16.6	Betelgeuse	270 57.8	N 7 24.4
23	166 22.7	146 37.6	29.2	252 29.5	32.4	295 34.0	17.5	247 02.6	16.6			
24 00	181 25.1	161 37.2	N 7 30.5	267 30.4	S23 32.4	310 36.6	S17 17.5	262 05.0	S22 16.6	Canopus	263 54.7	S52 42.8
01	196 27.6	176 36.8	31.7	282 31.3	32.4	325 39.2	17.4	277 07.3	16.6	Capella	280 29.8	N46 00.9
02	211 30.1	191 36.4	33.0	297 32.2	32.4	340 41.8	17.4	292 09.7	16.5	Deneb	49 29.5	N45 20.5
03	226 32.5	206 36.1	.. 34.2	312 33.2	.. 32.5	355 44.4	.. 17.4	307 12.0	.. 16.5	Denebola	182 30.1	N14 28.2
04	241 35.0	221 35.7	35.4	327 34.1	32.5	10 46.9	17.3	322 14.4	16.5	Diphda	348 53.0	S17 53.5
05	256 37.5	236 35.3	36.7	342 35.0	32.5	25 49.5	17.3	337 16.8	16.5			
S 06	271 39.9	251 34.9	N 7 37.9	357 35.9	S23 32.5	40 52.1	S17 17.3	352 19.1	S22 16.5	Dubhe	193 47.2	N61 39.2
A 07	286 42.4	266 34.5	39.1	12 36.9	32.5	55 54.7	17.2	7 21.5	16.5	Elnath	278 08.6	N28 37.2
T 08	301 44.9	281 34.1	40.4	27 37.8	32.5	70 57.3	17.2	22 23.8	16.5	Eltanin	90 44.6	N51 29.0
U 09	316 47.3	296 33.7	.. 41.6	42 38.7	.. 32.6	85 59.8	.. 17.1	37 26.2	.. 16.5	Enif	33 44.2	N 9 57.4
R 10	331 49.8	311 33.3	42.8	57 39.6	32.6	101 02.4	17.1	52 28.5	16.5	Fomalhaut	15 20.8	S29 31.6
D 11	346 52.2	326 32.9	44.1	72 40.6	32.6	116 05.0	17.1	67 30.9	16.5			
A 12	1 54.7	341 32.5	N 7 45.3	87 41.5	S23 32.6	131 07.6	S17 17.0	82 33.2	S22 16.5	Gacrux	171 56.7	S57 12.9
Y 13	16 57.2	356 32.1	46.6	102 42.4	32.6	146 10.2	17.0	97 35.6	16.5	Gienah	175 48.7	S17 38.6
14	31 59.6	11 31.7	47.8	117 43.4	32.6	161 12.8	17.0	112 38.0	16.5	Hadar	148 42.7	S60 27.4
15	47 02.1	26 31.3	.. 49.0	132 44.3	.. 32.6	176 15.3	.. 16.9	127 40.3	.. 16.5	Hamal	327 57.4	N23 32.7
16	62 04.6	41 30.9	50.3	147 45.2	32.7	191 17.9	16.9	142 42.7	16.4	Kaus Aust.	83 39.6	S34 22.3
17	77 07.0	56 30.5	51.5	162 46.1	32.7	206 20.5	16.9	157 45.0	16.4			
18	92 09.5	71 30.1	N 7 52.7	177 47.1	S23 32.7	221 23.1	S17 16.8	172 47.4	S22 16.4	Kochab	137 19.3	N74 04.8
19	107 12.0	86 29.7	54.0	192 48.0	32.7	236 25.7	16.8	187 49.8	16.4	Markab	13 35.4	N15 18.0
20	122 14.4	101 29.3	55.2	207 48.9	32.7	251 28.3	16.8	202 52.1	16.4	Menkar	314 11.9	N 4 09.4
21	137 16.9	116 28.9	.. 56.4	222 49.9	.. 32.7	266 30.8	.. 16.7	217 54.5	.. 16.4	Menkent	148 03.4	S36 27.4
22	152 19.4	131 28.5	57.7	237 50.8	32.7	281 33.4	16.7	232 56.8	16.4	Miaplacidus	221 38.3	S69 47.8
23	167 21.8	146 28.1	7 58.9	252 51.7	32.8	296 36.0	16.7	247 59.2	16.4			
25 00	182 24.3	161 27.7	N 8 00.1	267 52.6	S23 32.8	311 38.6	S17 16.6	263 01.5	S22 16.4	Mirfak	308 36.0	N49 55.4
01	197 26.7	176 27.3	01.4	282 53.6	32.8	326 41.2	16.6	278 03.9	16.4	Nunki	75 54.4	S26 16.3
02	212 29.2	191 26.9	02.6	297 54.5	32.8	341 43.8	16.5	293 06.3	16.4	Peacock	53 14.5	S56 40.3
03	227 31.7	206 26.5	.. 03.8	312 55.4	.. 32.8	356 46.4	.. 16.5	308 08.6	.. 16.4	Pollux	243 23.7	N27 58.8
04	242 34.1	221 26.1	05.0	327 56.4	32.8	11 49.0	16.5	323 11.0	16.4	Procyon	244 56.3	N 5 10.5
05	257 36.6	236 25.7	06.3	342 57.3	32.8	26 51.5	16.4	338 13.3	16.4			
S 06	272 39.1	251 25.3	N 8 07.5	357 58.2	S23 32.8	41 54.1	S17 16.4	353 15.7	S22 16.3	Rasalhague	96 03.4	N12 32.8
U 07	287 41.5	266 24.9	08.7	12 59.2	32.9	56 56.7	16.4	8 18.1	16.3	Regulus	207 39.8	N11 52.6
N 08	302 44.0	281 24.5	10.0	28 00.1	32.9	71 59.3	16.3	23 20.4	16.3	Rigel	281 09.0	S 8 11.2
D 09	317 46.5	296 24.1	.. 11.2	43 01.0	.. 32.9	87 01.9	.. 16.3	38 22.8	.. 16.3	Rigil Kent.	139 46.8	S60 54.3
A 10	332 48.9	311 23.7	12.4	58 01.9	32.9	102 04.5	16.3	53 25.1	16.3	Sabik	102 08.8	S15 44.7
Y 11	347 51.4	326 23.3	13.7	73 02.9	32.9	117 07.1	16.2	68 27.5	16.3			
12	2 53.9	341 22.9	N 8 14.9	88 03.8	S23 32.9	132 09.7	S17 16.2	83 29.9	S22 16.3	Schedar	349 37.4	N56 38.1
13	17 56.3	356 22.5	16.1	103 04.7	32.9	147 12.3	16.2	98 32.2	16.3	Shaula	96 17.5	S37 06.7
14	32 58.8	11 22.1	17.3	118 05.7	32.9	162 14.8	16.1	113 34.6	16.3	Sirius	258 30.9	S16 44.8
15	48 01.2	26 21.7	.. 18.6	133 06.6	.. 32.9	177 17.4	.. 16.1	128 36.9	.. 16.3	Spica	158 27.5	S11 15.4
16	63 03.7	41 21.3	19.8	148 07.5	32.9	192 20.0	16.0	143 39.3	16.3	Suhail	222 49.8	S43 30.7
17	78 06.2	56 20.9	21.0	163 08.5	33.0	207 22.6	16.0	158 41.7	16.3			
18	93 08.6	71 20.5	N 8 22.2	178 09.4	S23 33.0	222 25.2	S17 16.0	173 44.0	S22 16.3	Vega	80 36.8	N38 47.9
19	108 11.1	86 20.1	23.5	193 10.3	33.0	237 27.8	15.9	188 46.4	16.3	Zuben'ubi	137 01.6	S16 06.9
20	123 13.6	101 19.7	24.7	208 11.3	33.0	252 30.4	15.9	203 48.8	16.3		SHA	Mer. Pass.
21	138 16.0	116 19.3	.. 25.9	223 12.2	.. 33.0	267 33.0	.. 15.9	218 51.1	.. 16.2			h m
22	153 18.5	131 18.9	27.1	238 13.1	33.0	282 35.6	15.8	233 53.5	16.2	Venus	340 12.1	13 14
23	168 21.0	146 18.5	28.4	253 14.1	33.0	297 38.2	15.8	248 55.8	16.2	Mars	86 05.2	6 10
	h m									Jupiter	129 11.5	3 17
Mer. Pass.	11 52.4	v −0.4	d 1.2	v 0.9	d 0.0	v 2.6	d 0.0	v 2.4	d 0.0	Saturn	80 39.8	6 31

UT	SUN GHA	SUN Dec	MOON GHA	v	Dec	d	HP
d h	° ′	° ′	° ′	′	° ′	′	′
23 00	178 19.1	N 0 55.0	110 35.3	7.4	N17 31.1	6.2	58.8
01	193 19.3	56.0	125 01.7	7.4	17 37.3	6.0	58.8
02	208 19.5	57.0	139 28.1	7.3	17 43.3	6.0	58.8
03	223 19.7	.. 58.0	153 54.4	7.3	17 49.3	5.8	58.8
04	238 19.8	0 59.0	168 20.7	7.2	17 55.1	5.7	58.9
05	253 20.0	1 00.0	182 46.9	7.2	18 00.8	5.6	58.9
06	268 20.2	N 1 00.9	197 13.1	7.1	N18 06.4	5.5	58.9
07	283 20.4	01.9	211 39.2	7.1	18 11.9	5.4	58.9
08	298 20.6	02.9	226 05.3	7.0	18 17.3	5.2	58.9
F 09	313 20.8	.. 03.9	240 31.3	7.0	18 22.5	5.2	58.9
R 10	328 21.0	04.9	254 57.3	6.9	18 27.7	5.0	58.9
I 11	343 21.2	05.9	269 23.2	6.9	18 32.7	4.9	58.9
D 12	358 21.4	N 1 06.9	283 49.1	6.8	N18 37.6	4.8	58.9
A 13	13 21.5	07.8	298 14.9	6.8	18 42.4	4.7	59.0
Y 14	28 21.7	08.8	312 40.7	6.7	18 47.1	4.6	59.0
15	43 21.9	.. 09.8	327 06.4	6.7	18 51.7	4.5	59.0
16	58 22.1	10.8	341 32.1	6.6	18 56.2	4.3	59.0
17	73 22.3	11.8	355 57.7	6.6	19 00.5	4.2	59.0
18	88 22.5	N 1 12.8	10 23.3	6.6	N19 04.7	4.1	59.0
19	103 22.7	13.7	24 48.9	6.5	19 08.8	4.0	59.0
20	118 22.8	14.7	39 14.4	6.5	19 12.8	3.8	59.0
21	133 23.0	.. 15.7	53 39.9	6.4	19 16.6	3.7	59.0
22	148 23.2	16.7	68 05.3	6.4	19 20.3	3.6	59.0
23	163 23.4	17.7	82 30.7	6.4	19 23.9	3.5	59.1
24 00	178 23.6	N 1 18.7	96 56.1	6.3	N19 27.4	3.4	59.1
01	193 23.8	19.7	111 21.4	6.3	19 30.8	3.2	59.1
02	208 24.0	20.6	125 46.7	6.3	19 34.0	3.1	59.1
03	223 24.2	.. 21.6	140 12.0	6.2	19 37.1	3.0	59.1
04	238 24.4	22.6	154 37.2	6.2	19 40.1	2.8	59.1
05	253 24.5	23.6	169 02.4	6.1	19 42.9	2.7	59.1
06	268 24.7	N 1 24.6	183 27.5	6.2	N19 45.6	2.6	59.1
07	283 24.9	25.6	197 52.7	6.1	19 48.2	2.5	59.1
S 08	298 25.1	26.6	212 17.8	6.0	19 50.7	2.3	59.1
A 09	313 25.3	.. 27.5	226 42.8	6.0	19 53.0	2.2	59.1
T 10	328 25.5	28.5	241 07.8	6.1	19 55.2	2.1	59.2
U 11	343 25.7	29.5	255 32.9	5.9	19 57.3	1.9	59.2
R 12	358 25.9	N 1 30.5	269 57.8	6.0	N19 59.2	1.8	59.2
D 13	13 26.0	31.5	284 22.8	5.9	20 01.0	1.7	59.2
A 14	28 26.2	32.5	298 47.7	5.9	20 02.7	1.6	59.2
Y 15	43 26.4	.. 33.4	313 12.6	5.9	20 04.3	1.4	59.2
16	58 26.6	34.4	327 37.5	5.9	20 05.7	1.3	59.2
17	73 26.8	35.4	342 02.4	5.8	20 07.0	1.1	59.2
18	88 27.0	N 1 36.4	356 27.2	5.8	N20 08.1	1.1	59.2
19	103 27.2	37.4	10 52.1	5.8	20 09.2	0.8	59.2
20	118 27.4	38.4	25 16.9	5.8	20 10.0	0.8	59.2
21	133 27.6	.. 39.3	39 41.7	5.8	20 10.8	0.6	59.2
22	148 27.7	40.3	54 06.5	5.7	20 11.4	0.5	59.2
23	163 27.9	41.3	68 31.2	5.8	20 11.9	0.4	59.3
25 00	178 28.1	N 1 42.3	82 56.0	5.7	N20 12.3	0.2	59.3
01	193 28.3	43.3	97 20.7	5.7	20 12.5	0.1	59.3
02	208 28.5	44.3	111 45.5	5.7	20 12.6	0.1	59.3
03	223 28.7	.. 45.2	126 10.2	5.7	20 12.5	0.2	59.3
04	238 28.9	46.2	140 34.9	5.7	20 12.3	0.3	59.3
05	253 29.1	47.2	154 59.6	5.7	20 12.0	0.4	59.3
06	268 29.3	N 1 48.2	169 24.3	5.7	N20 11.6	0.6	59.3
07	283 29.4	49.2	183 49.0	5.7	20 11.0	0.8	59.3
08	298 29.6	50.2	198 13.7	5.7	20 10.2	0.8	59.3
S 09	313 29.8	.. 51.1	212 38.4	5.7	20 09.4	1.0	59.3
U 10	328 30.0	52.1	227 03.1	5.7	20 08.4	1.1	59.3
N 11	343 30.2	53.1	241 27.8	5.7	20 07.3	1.3	59.3
D 12	358 30.4	N 1 54.1	255 52.5	5.7	N20 06.0	1.4	59.3
A 13	13 30.6	55.1	270 17.2	5.7	20 04.6	1.5	59.3
Y 14	28 30.8	56.0	284 41.9	5.7	20 03.1	1.7	59.3
15	43 31.0	.. 57.0	299 06.6	5.8	20 01.4	1.8	59.3
16	58 31.1	58.0	313 31.4	5.7	19 59.6	1.9	59.4
17	73 31.3	1 59.0	327 56.1	5.7	19 57.7	2.1	59.4
18	88 31.5	N 2 00.0	342 20.8	5.8	N19 55.6	2.2	59.4
19	103 31.7	01.0	356 45.6	5.7	19 53.4	2.3	59.4
20	118 31.9	01.9	11 10.3	5.8	19 51.1	2.5	59.4
21	133 32.1	.. 02.9	25 35.1	5.8	19 48.6	2.5	59.4
22	148 32.3	03.9	39 59.9	5.8	19 46.1	2.8	59.4
23	163 32.5	04.9	54 24.7	5.8	N19 43.3	2.8	59.4
	SD 16.1	d 1.0	SD 16.1		16.1		16.2

Lat.	Twilight Naut.	Twilight Civil	Sunrise	Moonrise 23	24	25	26
°	h m	h m	h m	h m	h m	h m	h m
N 72	02 53	04 29	05 38	05 15	☐	☐	
N 70	03 17	04 39	05 41	06 39	06 33	☐	09 02
68	03 35	04 47	05 44	07 19	07 41	08 31	09 56
66	03 49	04 54	05 46	07 46	08 17	09 11	10 28
64	04 00	04 59	05 47	08 07	08 43	09 38	10 52
62	04 09	05 04	05 49	08 24	09 04	09 59	11 11
60	04 17	05 08	05 50	08 38	09 20	10 16	11 27
N 58	04 24	05 12	05 51	08 51	09 34	10 31	11 40
56	04 30	05 15	05 52	09 01	09 46	10 43	11 51
54	04 35	05 18	05 53	09 11	09 57	10 54	12 01
52	04 40	05 20	05 54	09 19	10 06	11 04	12 10
50	04 44	05 22	05 54	09 26	10 15	11 12	12 18
45	04 52	05 27	05 56	09 43	10 33	11 30	12 35
N 40	04 58	05 30	05 57	09 56	10 47	11 45	12 49
35	05 03	05 33	05 58	10 07	11 00	11 58	13 01
30	05 07	05 35	05 59	10 17	11 11	12 09	13 11
20	05 13	05 39	06 01	10 34	11 29	12 28	13 28
N 10	05 17	05 41	06 02	10 49	11 46	12 44	13 44
0	05 18	05 42	06 03	11 03	12 01	12 59	13 58
S 10	05 19	05 43	06 04	11 17	12 16	13 15	14 12
20	05 17	05 43	06 05	11 32	12 33	13 31	14 28
30	05 14	05 42	06 06	11 50	12 51	13 50	14 45
35	05 12	05 41	06 06	12 00	13 03	14 01	14 55
40	05 08	05 40	06 07	12 12	13 15	14 14	15 07
45	05 04	05 38	06 07	12 26	13 30	14 29	15 20
S 50	04 58	05 36	06 08	12 42	13 49	14 47	15 37
52	04 55	05 35	06 08	12 50	13 57	14 56	15 46
54	04 52	05 33	06 08	12 59	14 07	15 05	15 54
56	04 48	05 32	06 09	13 09	14 18	15 16	16 03
58	04 44	05 30	06 09	13 21	14 31	15 29	16 14
S 60	04 39	05 28	06 09	13 34	14 45	15 43	16 27

Lat.	Sunset	Twilight Civil	Twilight Naut.	Moonset 23	24	25	26
°	h m	h m	h m	h m	h m	h m	h m
N 72	18 37	19 47	21 25	04 11	☐	☐	☐
N 70	18 34	19 37	21 00	02 48	04 53	☐	06 30
68	18 31	19 28	20 41	02 09	03 46	04 58	05 36
66	18 29	19 21	20 27	01 42	03 10	04 19	05 03
64	18 27	19 15	20 15	01 22	02 44	03 51	04 39
62	18 25	19 10	20 05	01 05	02 24	03 30	04 19
60	18 24	19 06	19 57	00 51	02 08	03 13	04 03
N 58	18 23	19 02	19 50	00 40	01 54	02 58	03 50
56	18 22	18 59	19 44	00 29	01 42	02 46	03 38
54	18 21	18 56	19 39	00 20	01 32	02 35	03 28
52	18 20	18 54	19 34	00 12	01 22	02 25	03 19
50	18 19	18 52	19 30	00 05	01 14	02 17	03 11
45	18 17	18 47	19 21	24 56	00 56	01 58	02 54
N 40	18 16	18 43	19 15	24 42	00 42	01 43	02 39
35	18 15	18 40	19 10	24 30	00 30	01 31	02 27
30	18 14	18 38	19 06	24 19	00 19	01 20	02 17
20	18 12	18 34	19 00	24 01	00 01	01 01	01 58
N 10	18 11	18 32	18 56	23 45	24 44	00 44	01 42
0	18 10	18 30	18 54	23 30	24 29	00 29	01 27
S 10	18 08	18 29	18 54	23 16	24 13	00 13	01 12
20	18 07	18 29	18 55	23 00	23 57	24 56	00 56
30	18 06	18 30	18 58	22 42	23 38	24 38	00 38
35	18 06	18 31	19 00	22 31	23 26	24 27	00 27
40	18 05	18 32	19 04	22 19	23 14	24 15	00 15
45	18 04	18 34	19 08	22 05	22 59	24 00	00 00
S 50	18 04	18 36	19 14	21 47	22 40	23 42	24 51
52	18 03	18 37	19 16	21 39	22 31	23 33	24 44
54	18 03	18 38	19 20	21 30	22 21	23 24	24 35
56	18 03	18 40	19 23	21 20	22 10	23 13	24 26
58	18 02	18 41	19 27	21 08	21 58	23 01	24 15
S 60	18 02	18 43	19 32	20 54	21 43	22 47	24 03

Day	SUN Eqn. of Time 00h	SUN Eqn. of Time 12h	SUN Mer. Pass.	MOON Mer. Pass. Upper	MOON Mer. Pass. Lower	Age	Phase
d	m s	m s	h m	h m	h m	d	%
23	06 44	06 35	12 07	17 17	04 48	06	37
24	06 26	06 17	12 06	18 15	05 46	07	48
25	06 08	05 59	12 06	19 13	06 44	08	60

UT	ARIES	VENUS −3.9		MARS +0.4		JUPITER −2.3		SATURN +0.5		STARS		
	GHA	GHA	Dec	GHA	Dec	GHA	Dec	GHA	Dec	Name	SHA	Dec
d h	° ′	° ′	° ′	° ′	° ′	° ′	° ′	° ′	° ′		° ′	° ′
26 00	183 23.4	161 18.1	N 8 29.6	268 15.0	S23 33.0	312 40.8	S17 15.7	263 58.2	S22 16.2	Acamar	315 16.2	S40 14.3
01	198 25.9	176 17.7	30.8	283 15.9	33.0	327 43.4	15.7	279 00.6	16.2	Achernar	335 25.0	S57 08.9
02	213 28.3	191 17.3	32.0	298 16.9	33.0	342 46.0	15.7	294 02.9	16.2	Acrux	173 04.9	S63 12.0
03	228 30.8	206 16.9 . .	33.3	313 17.8 . .	33.0	357 48.6 . .	15.6	309 05.3 . .	16.2	Adhara	255 09.9	S29 00.2
04	243 33.3	221 16.5	34.5	328 18.7	33.0	12 51.1	15.6	324 07.7	16.2	Aldebaran	290 45.8	N16 32.5
05	258 35.7	236 16.1	35.7	343 19.7	33.1	27 53.7	15.6	339 10.0	16.2			
06	273 38.2	251 15.6	N 8 36.9	358 20.6	S23 33.1	42 56.3	S17 15.5	354 12.4	S22 16.2	Alioth	166 17.3	N55 51.7
07	288 40.7	266 15.2	38.1	13 21.5	33.1	57 58.9	15.5	9 14.8	16.2	Alkaid	152 55.9	N49 13.3
08	303 43.1	281 14.8	39.4	28 22.5	33.1	73 01.5	15.4	24 17.1	16.2	Al Na'ir	27 40.1	S46 52.3
M 09	318 45.6	296 14.4 . .	40.6	43 23.4 . .	33.1	88 04.1 . .	15.4	39 19.5 . .	16.2	Alnilam	275 43.2	S 1 11.7
O 10	333 48.1	311 14.0	41.8	58 24.3	33.1	103 06.7	15.4	54 21.9	16.2	Alphard	217 52.7	S 8 44.5
N 11	348 50.5	326 13.6	43.0	73 25.3	33.1	118 09.3	15.3	69 24.2	16.2			
D 12	3 53.0	341 13.2	N 8 44.3	88 26.2	S23 33.1	133 11.9	S17 15.3	84 26.6	S22 16.1	Alphecca	126 08.0	N26 39.2
A 13	18 55.5	356 12.8	45.5	103 27.2	33.1	148 14.5	15.2	99 28.9	16.1	Alpheratz	357 40.5	N29 11.2
Y 14	33 57.9	11 12.4	46.7	118 28.1	33.1	163 17.1	15.2	114 31.3	16.1	Altair	62 05.2	N 8 54.9
15	49 00.4	26 12.0 . .	47.9	133 29.0 . .	33.1	178 19.7 . .	15.2	129 33.7 . .	16.1	Ankaa	353 13.0	S42 12.6
16	64 02.8	41 11.6	49.1	148 30.0	33.1	193 22.3	15.1	144 36.0	16.1	Antares	112 22.1	S26 28.1
17	79 05.3	56 11.2	50.3	163 30.9	33.1	208 24.9	15.1	159 38.4	16.1			
18	94 07.8	71 10.8	N 8 51.6	178 31.8	S23 33.1	223 27.5	S17 15.1	174 40.8	S22 16.1	Arcturus	145 52.5	N19 05.2
19	109 10.2	86 10.4	52.8	193 32.8	33.1	238 30.1	15.0	189 43.1	16.1	Atria	107 20.8	S69 03.2
20	124 12.7	101 09.9	54.0	208 33.7	33.1	253 32.7	15.0	204 45.5	16.1	Avior	234 16.4	S59 34.4
21	139 15.2	116 09.5 . .	55.2	223 34.7 . .	33.1	268 35.3 . .	14.9	219 47.9 . .	16.1	Bellatrix	278 28.6	N 6 21.7
22	154 17.6	131 09.1	56.4	238 35.6	33.1	283 37.9	14.9	234 50.2	16.1	Betelgeuse	270 57.9	N 7 24.4
23	169 20.1	146 08.7	57.6	253 36.5	33.1	298 40.5	14.9	249 52.6	16.1			
27 00	184 22.6	161 08.3	N 8 58.9	268 37.5	S23 33.1	313 43.1	S17 14.8	264 55.0	S22 16.1	Canopus	263 54.7	S52 42.8
01	199 25.0	176 07.9	9 00.1	283 38.4	33.2	328 45.7	14.8	279 57.3	16.1	Capella	280 29.8	N46 00.9
02	214 27.5	191 07.5	01.3	298 39.3	33.2	343 48.3	14.7	294 59.7	16.1	Deneb	49 29.5	N45 20.5
03	229 30.0	206 07.1 . .	02.5	313 40.3 . .	33.2	358 50.9 . .	14.7	310 02.1 . .	16.0	Denebola	182 30.1	N14 28.2
04	244 32.4	221 06.7	03.7	328 41.2	33.2	13 53.5	14.7	325 04.5	16.0	Diphda	348 53.0	S17 53.4
05	259 34.9	236 06.3	04.9	343 42.2	33.2	28 56.1	14.6	340 06.8	16.0			
06	274 37.3	251 05.8	N 9 06.1	358 43.1	S23 33.2	43 58.7	S17 14.6	355 09.2	S22 16.0	Dubhe	193 47.2	N61 39.2
07	289 39.8	266 05.4	07.4	13 44.0	33.2	59 01.3	14.5	10 11.6	16.0	Elnath	278 08.6	N28 37.2
T 08	304 42.3	281 05.0	08.6	28 45.0	33.2	74 03.9	14.5	25 13.9	16.0	Eltanin	90 44.6	N51 29.0
U 09	319 44.7	296 04.6 . .	09.8	43 45.9 . .	33.2	89 06.5 . .	14.5	40 16.3 . .	16.0	Enif	33 44.2	N 9 57.4
E 10	334 47.2	311 04.2	11.0	58 46.9	33.2	104 09.1	14.4	55 18.7	16.0	Fomalhaut	15 20.8	S29 31.6
S 11	349 49.7	326 03.8	12.2	73 47.8	33.2	119 11.7	14.4	70 21.0	16.0			
D 12	4 52.1	341 03.4	N 9 13.4	88 48.7	S23 33.2	134 14.3	S17 14.3	85 23.4	S22 16.0	Gacrux	171 56.7	S57 12.9
A 13	19 54.6	356 03.0	14.6	103 49.7	33.2	149 17.0	14.3	100 25.8	16.0	Gienah	175 48.6	S17 38.6
Y 14	34 57.1	11 02.5	15.8	118 50.6	33.2	164 19.6	14.3	115 28.1	16.0	Hadar	148 42.7	S60 27.4
15	49 59.5	26 02.1 . .	17.1	133 51.6 . .	33.2	179 22.2 . .	14.2	130 30.5 . .	16.0	Hamal	327 57.4	N23 32.7
16	65 02.0	41 01.7	18.3	148 52.5	33.2	194 24.8	14.2	145 32.9	16.0	Kaus Aust.	83 39.5	S34 22.3
17	80 04.4	56 01.3	19.5	163 53.4	33.2	209 27.4	14.1	160 35.3	16.0			
18	95 06.9	71 00.9	N 9 20.7	178 54.4	S23 33.2	224 30.0	S17 14.1	175 37.6	S22 16.0	Kochab	137 19.3	N74 04.8
19	110 09.4	86 00.5	21.9	193 55.3	33.2	239 32.6	14.1	190 40.0	15.9	Markab	13 35.4	N15 18.0
20	125 11.8	101 00.0	23.1	208 56.3	33.2	254 35.2	14.0	205 42.4	15.9	Menkar	314 11.9	N 4 09.4
21	140 14.3	115 59.6 . .	24.3	223 57.2 . .	33.2	269 37.8 . .	14.0	220 44.7 . .	15.9	Menkent	148 03.4	S36 27.4
22	155 16.8	130 59.2	25.5	238 58.2	33.2	284 40.4	13.9	235 47.1	15.9	Miaplacidus	221 38.3	S69 47.8
23	170 19.2	145 58.8	26.7	253 59.1	33.2	299 43.0	13.9	250 49.5	15.9			
28 00	185 21.7	160 58.4	N 9 27.9	269 00.0	S23 33.2	314 45.6	S17 13.9	265 51.8	S22 15.9	Mirfak	308 36.0	N49 55.4
01	200 24.2	175 58.0	29.1	284 01.0	33.2	329 48.2	13.8	280 54.2	15.9	Nunki	75 54.4	S26 16.3
02	215 26.6	190 57.6	30.3	299 01.9	33.2	344 50.8	13.8	295 56.6	15.9	Peacock	53 14.5	S56 40.3
03	230 29.1	205 57.1 . .	31.5	314 02.9 . .	33.2	359 53.5 . .	13.7	310 59.0 . .	15.9	Pollux	243 23.7	N27 58.8
04	245 31.6	220 56.7	32.8	329 03.8	33.2	14 56.1	13.7	326 01.3	15.9	Procyon	244 56.3	N 5 10.5
05	260 34.0	235 56.3	34.0	344 04.8	33.2	29 58.7	13.7	341 03.7	15.9			
06	275 36.5	250 55.9	N 9 35.2	359 05.7	S23 33.1	45 01.3	S17 13.6	356 06.1	S22 15.9	Rasalhague	96 03.4	N12 32.8
W 07	290 38.9	265 55.5	36.4	14 06.6	33.1	60 03.9	13.6	11 08.5	15.9	Regulus	207 39.8	N11 52.6
E 08	305 41.4	280 55.0	37.6	29 07.6	33.1	75 06.5	13.5	26 10.8	15.9	Rigel	281 09.1	S 8 11.2
D 09	320 43.9	295 54.6 . .	38.8	44 08.5 . .	33.1	90 09.1 . .	13.5	41 13.2 . .	15.9	Rigil Kent.	139 46.8	S60 54.3
N 10	335 46.3	310 54.2	40.0	59 09.5	33.1	105 11.7	13.4	56 15.6	15.9	Sabik	102 08.7	S15 44.7
E 11	350 48.8	325 53.8	41.2	74 10.4	33.1	120 14.3	13.4	71 17.9	15.8			
S 12	5 51.3	340 53.4	N 9 42.4	89 11.4	S23 33.1	135 17.0	S17 13.3	86 20.3	S22 15.8	Schedar	349 37.3	N56 38.1
D 13	20 53.7	355 52.9	43.6	104 12.3	33.1	150 19.6	13.3	101 22.7	15.8	Shaula	96 17.4	S37 06.7
A 14	35 56.2	10 52.5	44.8	119 13.3	33.1	165 22.2	13.3	116 25.1	15.8	Sirius	258 30.9	S16 44.8
Y 15	50 58.7	25 52.1 . .	46.0	134 14.2 . .	33.1	180 24.8 . .	13.2	131 27.4 . .	15.8	Spica	158 27.5	S11 15.4
16	66 01.1	40 51.7	47.2	149 15.1	33.1	195 27.4	13.2	146 29.8	15.8	Suhail	222 49.8	S43 30.7
17	81 03.6	55 51.3	48.4	164 16.1	33.1	210 30.0	13.2	161 32.2	15.8			
18	96 06.1	70 50.8	N 9 49.6	179 17.0	S23 33.1	225 32.6	S17 13.1	176 34.6	S22 15.8	Vega	80 36.8	N38 47.9
19	111 08.5	85 50.4	50.8	194 18.0	33.1	240 35.2	13.1	191 36.9	15.8	Zuben'ubi	137 01.6	S16 06.9
20	126 11.0	100 50.0	52.0	209 18.9	33.1	255 37.9	13.0	206 39.3	15.8		SHA	Mer. Pass.
21	141 13.4	115 49.6 . .	53.2	224 19.9 . .	33.1	270 40.5 . .	13.0	221 41.7 . .	15.8		° ′	h m
22	156 15.9	130 49.2	54.4	239 20.8	33.1	285 43.1	12.9	236 44.1	15.8	Venus	336 45.7	13 16
23	171 18.4	145 48.7	55.6	254 21.8	33.1	300 45.7	12.9	251 46.4	15.8	Mars	84 14.9	6 05
	h m									Jupiter	129 20.6	3 05
Mer. Pass. 11 40.6		v −0.4	d 1.2	v 0.9	d 0.0	v 2.6	d 0.0	v 2.4	d 0.0	Saturn	80 32.4	6 19

UT	SUN GHA	SUN Dec	MOON GHA	v	Dec	d	HP
d h	° ′	° ′	° ′	′	° ′	′	′
26 00	178 32.7	N 2 05.9	68 49.5	5.9	N19 40.5	3.0	59.4
01	193 32.8	06.8	83 14.4	5.8	19 37.5	3.1	59.4
02	208 33.0	07.8	97 39.2	5.9	19 34.5	3.3	59.4
03	223 33.2	.. 08.8	112 04.1	5.9	19 31.1	3.4	59.4
04	238 33.4	09.8	126 29.0	5.9	19 27.7	3.5	59.4
05	253 33.6	10.8	140 53.9	5.9	19 24.2	3.6	59.4
06	268 33.8	N 2 11.8	155 18.8	6.0	N19 20.6	3.8	59.4
07	283 34.0	12.7	169 43.8	6.0	19 16.8	3.9	59.4
M 08	298 34.2	13.7	184 08.8	6.0	19 12.9	4.0	59.4
O 09	313 34.4	.. 14.7	198 33.8	6.1	19 08.9	4.1	59.4
N 10	328 34.5	15.7	212 58.9	6.0	19 04.8	4.3	59.4
D 11	343 34.7	16.7	227 23.9	6.1	19 00.5	4.4	59.4
A 12	358 34.9	N 2 17.6	241 49.0	6.1	N18 56.1	4.5	59.4
Y 13	13 35.1	18.6	256 14.1	6.2	18 51.6	4.7	59.4
14	28 35.3	19.6	270 39.3	6.2	18 46.9	4.8	59.4
15	43 35.5	.. 20.6	285 04.5	6.2	18 42.1	4.9	59.4
16	58 35.7	21.6	299 29.7	6.3	18 37.2	5.0	59.4
17	73 35.9	22.5	313 55.0	6.3	18 32.2	5.1	59.4
18	88 36.1	N 2 23.5	328 20.3	6.3	N18 27.1	5.3	59.4
19	103 36.3	24.5	342 45.6	6.4	18 21.8	5.4	59.4
20	118 36.4	25.5	357 11.0	6.4	18 16.4	5.5	59.4
21	133 36.6	.. 26.5	11 36.4	6.4	18 10.9	5.6	59.4
22	148 36.8	27.4	26 01.8	6.5	18 05.3	5.7	59.4
23	163 37.0	28.4	40 27.3	6.5	17 59.6	5.9	59.4
27 00	178 37.2	N 2 29.4	54 52.8	6.6	N17 53.7	6.0	59.4
01	193 37.4	30.4	69 18.4	6.6	17 47.7	6.0	59.4
02	208 37.6	31.4	83 44.0	6.6	17 41.7	6.2	59.4
03	223 37.8	.. 32.3	98 09.6	6.7	17 35.5	6.4	59.4
04	238 38.0	33.3	112 35.3	6.7	17 29.1	6.4	59.4
05	253 38.1	34.3	127 01.0	6.8	17 22.7	6.5	59.4
06	268 38.3	N 2 35.3	141 26.8	6.8	N17 16.2	6.7	59.4
07	283 38.5	36.2	155 52.6	6.8	17 09.5	6.7	59.4
T 08	298 38.7	37.2	170 18.4	6.9	17 02.8	6.9	59.4
U 09	313 38.9	.. 38.2	184 44.3	7.0	16 55.9	7.0	59.4
E 10	328 39.1	39.2	199 10.3	7.0	16 48.9	7.1	59.4
S 11	343 39.3	40.2	213 36.3	7.0	16 41.8	7.2	59.4
D 12	358 39.5	N 2 41.1	228 02.3	7.1	N16 34.6	7.3	59.4
A 13	13 39.7	42.1	242 28.4	7.2	16 27.3	7.4	59.4
Y 14	28 39.9	43.1	256 54.6	7.2	16 19.9	7.5	59.4
15	43 40.0	.. 44.1	271 20.8	7.2	16 12.4	7.6	59.4
16	58 40.2	45.1	285 47.0	7.3	16 04.8	7.7	59.4
17	73 40.4	46.0	300 13.3	7.3	15 57.1	7.8	59.4
18	88 40.6	N 2 47.0	314 39.6	7.4	N15 49.3	7.9	59.3
19	103 40.8	48.0	329 06.0	7.5	15 41.4	8.0	59.3
20	118 41.0	49.0	343 32.5	7.4	15 33.4	8.1	59.3
21	133 41.2	.. 49.9	357 58.9	7.6	15 25.3	8.2	59.3
22	148 41.4	50.9	12 25.5	7.6	15 17.1	8.3	59.3
23	163 41.6	51.9	26 52.1	7.6	15 08.8	8.4	59.3
28 00	178 41.7	N 2 52.9	41 18.7	7.7	N15 00.4	8.5	59.3
01	193 41.9	53.8	55 45.4	7.8	14 51.9	8.5	59.3
02	208 42.1	54.8	70 12.2	7.8	14 43.4	8.7	59.3
03	223 42.3	.. 55.8	84 39.0	7.8	14 34.7	8.7	59.3
04	238 42.5	56.8	99 05.8	7.9	14 26.0	8.9	59.3
05	253 42.7	57.8	113 32.7	8.0	14 17.1	8.9	59.3
06	268 42.9	N 2 58.7	127 59.7	8.0	N14 08.2	9.0	59.3
W 07	283 43.1	2 59.7	142 26.7	8.1	13 59.2	9.1	59.3
E 08	298 43.3	3 00.7	156 53.8	8.1	13 50.1	9.2	59.3
D 09	313 43.5	.. 01.7	171 20.9	8.2	13 40.9	9.2	59.2
N 10	328 43.6	02.6	185 48.1	8.2	13 31.7	9.4	59.2
E 11	343 43.8	03.6	200 15.3	8.3	13 22.3	9.4	59.2
S 12	358 44.0	N 3 04.6	214 42.6	8.4	N13 12.9	9.5	59.2
D 13	13 44.2	05.6	229 10.0	8.3	13 03.4	9.5	59.2
A 14	28 44.4	06.5	243 37.3	8.5	12 53.9	9.7	59.2
Y 15	43 44.6	.. 07.5	258 04.8	8.5	12 44.2	9.7	59.2
16	58 44.8	08.5	272 32.3	8.5	12 34.5	9.8	59.2
17	73 45.0	09.5	286 59.8	8.7	12 24.7	9.9	59.2
18	88 45.2	N 3 10.4	301 27.5	8.6	N12 14.8	9.9	59.2
19	103 45.3	11.4	315 55.1	8.7	12 04.9	10.0	59.1
20	118 45.5	12.4	330 22.8	8.8	11 54.9	10.1	59.1
21	133 45.7	.. 13.4	344 50.6	8.8	11 44.8	10.1	59.1
22	148 45.9	14.3	359 18.4	8.9	11 34.7	10.2	59.1
23	163 46.1	15.3	13 46.3	8.9	N11 24.5	10.3	59.1
	SD 16.1 d 1.0		SD 16.2		16.2		16.1

Lat.	Naut.	Civil	Sunrise	Moonrise 26	27	28	29
°	h m	h m	h m	h m	h m	h m	h m
N 72	02 29	04 12	05 23	▭	10 17	12 43	14 50
N 70	02 58	04 24	05 27	09 02	11 07	13 08	15 03
68	03 19	04 34	05 31	09 56	11 39	13 27	15 14
66	03 35	04 42	05 34	10 28	12 02	13 42	15 23
64	03 48	04 48	05 37	10 52	12 20	13 55	15 30
62	03 58	04 54	05 39	11 11	12 35	14 05	15 36
60	04 07	04 59	05 41	11 27	12 48	14 14	15 42
N 58	04 15	05 03	05 43	11 40	12 59	14 22	15 47
56	04 21	05 07	05 44	11 51	13 08	14 29	15 51
54	04 27	05 10	05 46	12 01	13 16	14 35	15 55
52	04 32	05 13	05 47	12 10	13 24	14 40	15 58
50	04 37	05 15	05 48	12 18	13 30	14 45	16 01
45	04 46	05 21	05 50	12 35	13 44	14 56	16 08
N 40	04 53	05 25	05 52	12 49	13 56	15 05	16 14
35	04 59	05 29	05 54	13 01	14 06	15 13	16 19
30	05 04	05 32	05 56	13 11	14 15	15 19	16 23
20	05 10	05 36	05 58	13 28	14 30	15 31	16 30
N 10	05 15	05 39	06 00	13 44	14 43	15 41	16 37
0	05 17	05 41	06 02	13 58	14 55	15 50	16 43
S 10	05 19	05 43	06 04	14 12	15 07	15 59	16 49
20	05 18	05 44	06 06	14 28	15 20	16 09	16 55
30	05 16	05 44	06 08	14 45	15 35	16 21	17 03
35	05 14	05 43	06 09	14 55	15 44	16 27	17 07
40	05 11	05 43	06 10	15 07	15 54	16 35	17 12
45	05 08	05 42	06 11	15 20	16 05	16 43	17 17
S 50	05 03	05 40	06 13	15 37	16 19	16 54	17 24
52	05 00	05 40	06 13	15 45	16 25	16 58	17 27
54	04 57	05 39	06 14	15 54	16 32	17 04	17 30
56	04 54	05 38	06 15	16 03	16 40	17 10	17 34
58	04 51	05 37	06 16	16 14	16 49	17 16	17 38
S 60	04 46	05 35	06 17	16 27	16 59	17 23	17 42

Lat.	Sunset	Civil	Naut.	Moonset 26	27	28	29
°	h m	h m	h m	h m	h m	h m	h m
N 72	18 51	20 03	21 48	▭	07 17	06 47	06 31
N 70	18 46	19 50	21 18	06 30	06 25	06 21	06 16
68	18 42	19 40	20 56	05 36	05 53	06 00	06 04
66	18 39	19 32	20 39	05 03	05 29	05 44	05 53
64	18 36	19 25	20 26	04 39	05 10	05 30	05 45
62	18 33	19 19	20 15	04 19	04 54	05 19	05 37
60	18 31	19 14	20 06	04 03	04 41	05 09	05 31
N 58	18 30	19 09	19 58	03 50	04 30	05 01	05 25
56	18 28	19 05	19 51	03 38	04 12	04 53	05 15
54	18 26	19 02	19 45	03 28	04 04	04 46	05 15
52	18 25	18 59	19 40	03 19	04 00	04 40	05 11
50	18 24	18 56	19 35	03 11	03 57	04 35	05 07
45	18 21	18 51	19 26	02 54	03 42	04 23	04 59
N 40	18 19	18 46	19 18	02 39	03 29	04 13	04 52
35	18 17	18 43	19 12	02 27	03 18	04 04	04 46
30	18 16	18 40	19 08	02 17	03 09	03 57	04 41
20	18 13	18 35	19 01	01 58	02 53	03 44	04 31
N 10	18 11	18 32	18 56	01 42	02 39	03 32	04 23
0	18 09	18 29	18 53	01 27	02 25	03 22	04 16
S 10	18 07	18 28	18 52	01 12	02 12	03 11	04 08
20	18 05	18 27	18 52	00 56	01 58	02 59	03 59
30	18 03	18 27	18 54	00 38	01 41	02 46	03 50
35	18 02	18 27	18 56	00 27	01 31	02 38	03 44
40	18 00	18 27	19 02	00 15	01 20	02 29	03 38
45	17 59	18 28	19 02	00 00	01 07	02 18	03 30
S 50	17 57	18 29	19 07	24 51	00 51	02 05	03 21
52	17 56	18 30	19 09	24 44	00 44	01 59	03 17
54	17 56	18 31	19 12	24 35	00 35	01 53	03 13
56	17 55	18 32	19 15	24 26	00 26	01 45	03 08
58	17 54	18 33	19 19	24 15	00 15	01 37	03 03
S 60	17 53	18 34	19 23	24 03	00 03	01 28	02 55

Day	Eqn. of Time 00h	Eqn. of Time 12h	Mer. Pass.	Mer. Pass. Upper	Mer. Pass. Lower	Age	Phase
d	m s	m s	h m	h m	h m	d	%
26	05 50	05 41	12 06	20 12	07 43	09	71
27	05 32	05 22	12 05	21 08	08 40	10	81
28	05 13	05 04	12 05	22 03	09 36	11	89

2018 MARCH 29, 30, 31 (THURS., FRI., SAT.)

UT	ARIES GHA	VENUS −3.9 GHA	VENUS Dec	MARS +0.3 GHA	MARS Dec	JUPITER −2.4 GHA	JUPITER Dec	SATURN +0.5 GHA	SATURN Dec	STARS Name	SHA	Dec
29 00	186 20.8	160 48.3	N 9 56.8	269 22.7	S23 33.1	315 48.3	S17 12.9	266 48.8	S22 15.8	Acamar	315 16.2	S40 14.3
01	201 23.3	175 47.9	58.0	284 23.7	33.1	330 50.9	12.8	281 51.2	15.8	Achernar	335 25.0	S57 08.9
02	216 25.8	190 47.5	9 59.2	299 24.6	33.0	345 53.6	12.8	296 53.6	15.8	Acrux	173 04.9	S63 12.0
03	231 28.2	205 47.0	10 00.4	314 25.6 ..	33.0	0 56.2 ..	12.7	311 55.9 ..	15.8	Adhara	255 10.0	S29 00.2
04	246 30.7	220 46.6	01.6	329 26.5	33.0	15 58.8	12.7	326 58.3	15.7	Aldebaran	290 45.8	N16 32.5
05	261 33.2	235 46.2	02.8	344 27.5	33.0	31 01.4	12.6	342 00.7	15.7			
06	276 35.6	250 45.8	N10 04.0	359 28.4	S23 33.0	46 04.0	S17 12.6	357 03.1	S22 15.7	Alioth	166 17.3	N55 51.7
07	291 38.1	265 45.3	05.1	14 29.4	33.0	61 06.6	12.6	12 05.5	15.7	Alkaid	152 55.9	N49 13.3
T 08	306 40.5	280 44.9	06.3	29 30.3	33.0	76 09.3	12.5	27 07.8	15.7	Al Na'ir	27 40.1	S46 52.3
H 09	321 43.0	295 44.5 ..	07.5	44 31.3 ..	33.0	91 11.9 ..	12.5	42 10.2 ..	15.7	Alnilam	275 43.2	S 1 11.7
U 10	336 45.5	310 44.1	08.7	59 32.2	33.0	106 14.5	12.4	57 12.6	15.7	Alphard	217 52.7	S 8 44.5
R 11	351 47.9	325 43.6	09.9	74 33.2	33.0	121 17.1	12.4	72 15.0	15.7			
S 12	6 50.4	340 43.2	N10 11.1	89 34.1	S23 33.0	136 19.7	S17 12.3	87 17.3	S22 15.7	Alphecca	126 08.0	N26 39.2
D 13	21 52.9	355 42.8	12.3	104 35.1	33.0	151 22.4	12.3	102 19.7	15.7	Alpheratz	357 40.5	N29 11.2
A 14	36 55.3	10 42.4	13.5	119 36.0	33.0	166 25.0	12.2	117 22.1	15.7	Altair	62 05.2	N 8 54.9
Y 15	51 57.8	25 41.9 ..	14.7	134 37.0 ..	32.9	181 27.6 ..	12.2	132 24.5 ..	15.7	Ankaa	353 13.0	S42 12.6
16	67 00.3	40 41.5	15.9	149 37.9	32.9	196 30.2	12.2	147 26.9	15.7	Antares	112 22.1	S26 28.1
17	82 02.7	55 41.1	17.1	164 38.9	32.9	211 32.8	12.1	162 29.2	15.7			
18	97 05.2	70 40.7	N10 18.3	179 39.8	S23 32.9	226 35.5	S17 12.1	177 31.6	S22 15.7	Arcturus	145 52.5	N19 05.2
19	112 07.7	85 40.2	19.4	194 40.8	32.9	241 38.1	12.0	192 34.0	15.7	Atria	107 20.8	S69 03.2
20	127 10.1	100 39.8	20.6	209 41.7	32.9	256 40.7	12.0	207 36.4	15.7	Avior	234 16.4	S59 34.5
21	142 12.6	115 39.4 ..	21.8	224 42.7 ..	32.9	271 43.3 ..	11.9	222 38.8 ..	15.6	Bellatrix	278 28.6	N 6 21.7
22	157 15.0	130 38.9	23.0	239 43.6	32.9	286 45.9	11.9	237 41.1	15.6	Betelgeuse	270 57.9	N 7 24.4
23	172 17.5	145 38.5	24.2	254 44.6	32.9	301 48.6	11.9	252 43.5	15.6			
30 00	187 20.0	160 38.1	N10 25.4	269 45.5	S23 32.9	316 51.2	S17 11.8	267 45.9	S22 15.6	Canopus	263 54.7	S52 42.8
01	202 22.4	175 37.6	26.6	284 46.5	32.8	331 53.8	11.8	282 48.3	15.6	Capella	280 29.8	N46 00.9
02	217 24.9	190 37.2	27.8	299 47.4	32.8	346 56.4	11.7	297 50.7	15.6	Deneb	49 29.5	N45 20.5
03	232 27.4	205 36.8 ..	28.9	314 48.4 ..	32.8	1 59.1 ..	11.7	312 53.0 ..	15.6	Denebola	182 30.1	N14 28.2
04	247 29.8	220 36.4	30.1	329 49.3	32.8	17 01.7	11.6	327 55.4	15.6	Diphda	348 53.0	S17 53.4
05	262 32.3	235 35.9	31.3	344 50.3	32.8	32 04.3	11.6	342 57.8	15.6			
06	277 34.8	250 35.5	N10 32.5	359 51.2	S23 32.8	47 06.9	S17 11.5	358 00.2	S22 15.6	Dubhe	193 47.2	N61 39.2
07	292 37.2	265 35.1	33.7	14 52.2	32.8	62 09.6	11.5	13 02.6	15.6	Elnath	278 08.7	N28 37.2
F 08	307 39.7	280 34.6	34.9	29 53.1	32.8	77 12.2	11.4	28 04.9	15.6	Eltanin	90 44.5	N51 29.0
R 09	322 42.1	295 34.2 ..	36.1	44 54.1 ..	32.7	92 14.8 ..	11.4	43 07.3 ..	15.6	Enif	33 44.2	N 9 57.4
I 10	337 44.6	310 33.8	37.2	59 55.1	32.7	107 17.4	11.4	58 09.7	15.6	Fomalhaut	15 20.8	S29 31.6
11	352 47.1	325 33.3	38.4	74 56.0	32.7	122 20.1	11.3	73 12.1	15.6			
D 12	7 49.5	340 32.9	N10 39.6	89 57.0	S23 32.7	137 22.7	S17 11.3	88 14.5	S22 15.6	Gacrux	171 56.7	S57 12.9
A 13	22 52.0	355 32.5	40.8	104 57.9	32.7	152 25.3	11.2	103 16.9	15.6	Gienah	175 48.6	S17 38.6
Y 14	37 54.5	10 32.0	42.0	119 58.9	32.7	167 27.9	11.2	118 19.2	15.6	Hadar	148 42.6	S60 27.4
15	52 56.9	25 31.6 ..	43.2	134 59.8 ..	32.7	182 30.6 ..	11.1	133 21.6 ..	15.5	Hamal	327 57.4	N23 32.7
16	67 59.4	40 31.2	44.3	150 00.8	32.6	197 33.2	11.1	148 24.0	15.5	Kaus Aust.	83 39.5	S34 22.3
17	83 01.9	55 30.7	45.5	165 01.7	32.6	212 35.8	11.0	163 26.4	15.5			
18	98 04.3	70 30.3	N10 46.7	180 02.7	S23 32.6	227 38.4	S17 11.0	178 28.8	S22 15.5	Kochab	137 19.2	N74 04.8
19	113 06.8	85 29.9	47.9	195 03.6	32.6	242 41.1	10.9	193 31.2	15.5	Markab	13 35.4	N15 18.0
20	128 09.3	100 29.4	49.0	210 04.6	32.6	257 43.7	10.9	208 33.5	15.5	Menkar	314 11.9	N 4 09.4
21	143 11.7	115 29.0 ..	50.2	225 05.6 ..	32.6	272 46.3 ..	10.9	223 35.9 ..	15.5	Menkent	148 03.4	S36 27.4
22	158 14.2	130 28.5	51.4	240 06.5	32.6	287 49.0	10.8	238 38.3	15.5	Miaplacidus	221 38.4	S69 47.8
23	173 16.6	145 28.1	52.6	255 07.5	32.5	302 51.6	10.8	253 40.7	15.5			
31 00	188 19.1	160 27.7	N10 53.8	270 08.4	S23 32.5	317 54.2	S17 10.7	268 43.1	S22 15.5	Mirfak	308 36.1	N49 55.4
01	203 21.6	175 27.2	54.9	285 09.4	32.5	332 56.8	10.7	283 45.5	15.5	Nunki	75 54.4	S26 16.3
02	218 24.0	190 26.8	56.1	300 10.3	32.5	347 59.5	10.6	298 47.8	15.5	Peacock	53 14.5	S56 40.3
03	233 26.5	205 26.4 ..	57.3	315 11.3 ..	32.5	3 02.1 ..	10.6	313 50.2 ..	15.5	Pollux	243 23.7	N27 58.8
04	248 29.0	220 25.9	58.5	330 12.3	32.5	18 04.7	10.5	328 52.6	15.5	Procyon	244 56.3	N 5 10.5
05	263 31.4	235 25.5	10 59.6	345 13.2	32.4	33 07.4	10.5	343 55.0	15.5			
06	278 33.9	250 25.0	N11 00.8	0 14.2	S23 32.4	48 10.0	S17 10.4	358 57.4	S22 15.5	Rasalhague	96 03.4	N12 32.8
07	293 36.4	265 24.6	02.0	15 15.1	32.4	63 12.6	10.4	13 59.8	15.5	Regulus	207 39.8	N11 52.6
S 08	308 38.8	280 24.2	03.2	30 16.1	32.4	78 15.3	10.3	29 02.2	15.5	Rigel	281 09.1	S 8 11.2
A 09	323 41.3	295 23.7 ..	04.3	45 17.1 ..	32.4	93 17.9 ..	10.3	44 04.5 ..	15.4	Rigil Kent.	139 46.7	S60 54.3
T 10	338 43.7	310 23.3	05.5	60 18.0	32.4	108 20.5	10.3	59 06.9	15.4	Sabik	102 08.7	S15 44.7
U 11	353 46.2	325 22.8	06.7	75 19.0	32.3	123 23.2	10.2	74 09.3	15.4			
R 12	8 48.7	340 22.4	N11 07.9	90 19.9	S23 32.3	138 25.8	S17 10.2	89 11.7	S22 15.4	Schedar	349 37.4	N56 38.1
D 13	23 51.1	355 22.0	09.0	105 20.9	32.3	153 28.4	10.1	104 14.1	15.4	Shaula	96 17.4	S37 06.7
A 14	38 53.6	10 21.5	10.2	120 21.9	32.3	168 31.1	10.1	119 16.5	15.4	Sirius	258 30.9	S16 44.8
Y 15	53 56.1	25 21.1 ..	11.4	135 22.8 ..	32.3	183 33.7 ..	10.0	134 18.9 ..	15.4	Spica	158 27.5	S11 15.4
16	68 58.5	40 20.6	12.5	150 23.8	32.3	198 36.3	10.0	149 21.2	15.4	Suhail	222 49.8	S43 30.7
17	84 01.0	55 20.2	13.7	165 24.7	32.2	213 39.0	09.9	164 23.6	15.4			
18	99 03.5	70 19.7	N11 14.9	180 25.7	S23 32.2	228 41.6	S17 09.9	179 26.0	S22 15.4	Vega	80 36.8	N38 47.9
19	114 05.9	85 19.3	16.0	195 26.7	32.2	243 44.2	09.8	194 28.4	15.4	Zuben'ubi	137 01.6	S16 06.9
20	129 08.4	100 18.9	17.2	210 27.6	32.2	258 46.9	09.8	209 30.8	15.4		SHA	Mer. Pass.
21	144 10.9	115 18.4 ..	18.4	225 28.6 ..	32.2	273 49.5 ..	09.7	224 33.2 ..	15.4	Venus	333 18.1	13 18
22	159 13.3	130 18.0	19.5	240 29.5	32.1	288 52.1	09.7	239 35.6	15.4	Mars	82 25.5	6 01
23	174 15.8	145 17.5	20.7	255 30.5	32.1	303 54.8	09.6	254 38.0	15.4	Jupiter	129 31.2	2 52
Mer. Pass. 11 28.8		v −0.4	d 1.2	v 1.0	d 0.0	v 2.6	d 0.0	v 2.4	d 0.0	Saturn	80 25.9	6 08

UT	SUN GHA	SUN Dec	MOON GHA	v	Dec	d	HP
d h	° '	° '	° '	'	° '	'	'
29 00	178 46.3	N 3 16.3	28 14.2	9.0	N11 14.2	10.3	59.1
01	193 46.5	17.3	42 42.2	9.1	11 03.9	10.4	59.1
02	208 46.7	18.2	57 10.3	9.0	10 53.5	10.4	59.1
03	223 46.9	.. 19.2	71 38.3	9.2	10 43.1	10.6	59.0
04	238 47.0	20.2	86 06.5	9.2	10 32.5	10.5	59.0
05	253 47.2	21.2	100 34.7	9.2	10 22.0	10.7	59.0
06	268 47.4	N 3 22.1	115 02.9	9.3	N10 11.3	10.6	59.0
T 07	283 47.6	23.1	129 31.2	9.4	10 00.7	10.8	59.0
H 08	298 47.8	24.1	143 59.6	9.4	9 49.9	10.8	59.0
U 09	313 48.0	.. 25.1	158 28.0	9.4	9 39.1	10.8	59.0
R 10	328 48.2	26.0	172 56.4	9.5	9 28.3	10.9	59.0
S 11	343 48.4	27.0	187 24.9	9.6	9 17.4	10.9	58.9
D 12	358 48.6	N 3 28.0	201 53.5	9.6	N 9 06.5	11.0	58.9
A 13	13 48.7	28.9	216 22.1	9.6	8 55.5	11.1	58.9
Y 14	28 48.9	29.9	230 50.7	9.7	8 44.4	11.0	58.9
15	43 49.1	.. 30.9	245 19.4	9.8	8 33.4	11.2	58.9
16	58 49.3	31.9	259 48.2	9.8	8 22.2	11.1	58.9
17	73 49.5	32.8	274 17.0	9.8	8 11.1	11.2	58.8
18	88 49.7	N 3 33.8	288 45.8	9.9	N 7 59.9	11.3	58.8
19	103 49.9	34.8	303 14.7	10.0	7 48.6	11.3	58.8
20	118 50.1	35.8	317 43.7	10.0	7 37.3	11.3	58.8
21	133 50.3	.. 36.7	332 12.7	10.0	7 26.0	11.3	58.8
22	148 50.4	37.7	346 41.7	10.1	7 14.7	11.4	58.7
23	163 50.6	38.7	1 10.8	10.1	7 03.3	11.5	58.7
30 00	178 50.8	N 3 39.6	15 39.9	10.2	N 6 51.8	11.4	58.7
01	193 51.0	40.6	30 09.1	10.3	6 40.4	11.5	58.7
02	208 51.2	41.6	44 38.3	10.3	6 28.9	11.5	58.7
03	223 51.4	.. 42.6	59 07.6	10.3	6 17.4	11.6	58.7
04	238 51.6	43.5	73 36.9	10.4	6 05.8	11.5	58.7
05	253 51.8	44.5	88 06.3	10.4	5 54.3	11.6	58.6
06	268 52.0	N 3 45.5	102 35.7	10.4	N 5 42.7	11.7	58.6
07	283 52.1	46.4	117 05.1	10.5	5 31.0	11.6	58.6
F 08	298 52.3	47.4	131 34.6	10.5	5 19.4	11.7	58.6
R 09	313 52.5	.. 48.4	146 04.1	10.6	5 07.7	11.7	58.6
I 10	328 52.7	49.3	160 33.7	10.6	4 56.0	11.7	58.5
D 11	343 52.9	50.3	175 03.3	10.6	4 44.3	11.7	58.5
A 12	358 53.1	N 3 51.3	189 32.9	10.7	N 4 32.6	11.8	58.5
Y 13	13 53.3	52.3	204 02.6	10.7	4 20.8	11.7	58.5
14	28 53.5	53.2	218 32.3	10.8	4 09.1	11.8	58.5
15	43 53.7	.. 54.2	233 02.1	10.8	3 57.3	11.8	58.4
16	58 53.8	55.2	247 31.9	10.8	3 45.5	11.8	58.4
17	73 54.0	56.1	262 01.7	10.9	3 33.7	11.8	58.4
18	88 54.2	N 3 57.1	276 31.6	10.9	N 3 21.9	11.8	58.4
19	103 54.4	58.1	291 01.5	11.0	3 10.1	11.9	58.3
20	118 54.6	3 59.0	305 31.5	11.0	2 58.2	11.8	58.3
21	133 54.8	4 00.0	320 01.5	11.0	2 46.4	11.9	58.3
22	148 55.0	01.0	334 31.5	11.0	2 34.5	11.8	58.3
23	163 55.2	02.0	349 01.5	11.1	2 22.7	11.9	58.3
31 00	178 55.3	N 4 02.9	3 31.6	11.1	N 2 10.8	11.8	58.2
01	193 55.5	03.9	18 01.7	11.2	1 59.0	11.9	58.2
02	208 55.7	04.9	32 31.9	11.2	1 47.1	11.8	58.2
03	223 55.9	.. 05.8	47 02.1	11.2	1 35.3	11.9	58.2
04	238 56.1	06.8	61 32.3	11.2	1 23.4	11.9	58.1
05	253 56.3	07.8	76 02.5	11.3	1 11.5	11.8	58.1
06	268 56.5	N 4 08.7	90 32.8	11.3	N 0 59.7	11.9	58.1
07	283 56.6	09.7	105 03.1	11.4	0 47.8	11.8	58.1
S 08	298 56.8	10.7	119 33.5	11.4	0 36.0	11.9	58.0
A 09	313 57.0	.. 11.6	134 03.9	11.3	0 24.1	11.8	58.0
T 10	328 57.2	12.6	148 34.2	11.5	0 12.3	11.8	58.0
U 11	343 57.4	13.6	163 04.7	11.4	N 0 00.5	11.8	58.0
R 12	358 57.6	N 4 14.5	177 35.1	11.5	S 0 11.3	11.8	57.9
D 13	13 57.8	15.5	192 05.6	11.5	0 23.1	11.8	57.9
A 14	28 58.0	16.5	206 36.1	11.5	0 34.9	11.8	57.9
Y 15	43 58.2	.. 17.4	221 06.6	11.6	0 46.7	11.8	57.9
16	58 58.3	18.4	235 37.2	11.6	0 58.5	11.7	57.8
17	73 58.5	19.4	250 07.8	11.6	1 10.2	11.8	57.8
18	88 58.7	N 4 20.3	264 38.4	11.6	S 1 22.0	11.7	57.8
19	103 58.9	21.3	279 09.0	11.7	1 33.7	11.7	57.8
20	118 59.1	22.3	293 39.7	11.6	1 45.4	11.7	57.7
21	133 59.3	.. 23.2	308 10.3	11.7	1 57.1	11.6	57.7
22	148 59.5	24.2	322 41.0	11.8	2 08.7	11.7	57.7
23	163 59.7	25.2	337 11.8	11.7	S 2 20.4	11.6	57.7
	SD 16.0	d 1.0	SD 16.1		15.9		15.8

Lat.	Twilight Naut.	Twilight Civil	Sunrise	Moonrise 29	30	31	1
°	h m	h m	h m	h m	h m	h m	h m
N 72	02 01	03 54	05 07	14 50	16 49	18 43	20 36
N 70	02 37	04 08	05 13	15 03	16 54	18 41	20 26
68	03 01	04 20	05 18	15 14	16 58	18 39	20 18
66	03 20	04 29	05 22	15 23	17 01	18 37	20 11
64	03 35	04 37	05 26	15 30	17 04	18 36	20 06
62	03 47	04 44	05 29	15 36	17 07	18 35	20 01
60	03 57	04 49	05 32	15 42	17 09	18 34	19 57
N 58	04 05	04 54	05 34	15 47	17 11	18 33	19 53
56	04 13	04 58	05 36	15 51	17 12	18 32	19 50
54	04 19	05 02	05 38	15 55	17 14	18 31	19 47
52	04 25	05 06	05 40	15 58	17 15	18 31	19 45
50	04 30	05 09	05 41	16 01	17 17	18 30	19 42
45	04 40	05 15	05 45	16 08	17 19	18 29	19 37
N 40	04 48	05 20	05 48	16 14	17 22	18 28	19 33
35	04 55	05 25	05 50	16 19	17 24	18 27	19 29
30	05 00	05 28	05 52	16 23	17 25	18 26	19 26
20	05 08	05 33	05 56	16 30	17 28	18 25	19 20
N 10	05 13	05 37	05 58	16 37	17 31	18 24	19 15
0	05 16	05 40	06 01	16 43	17 34	18 23	19 11
S 10	05 18	05 43	06 04	16 49	17 36	18 22	19 06
20	05 19	05 44	06 06	16 55	17 39	18 21	19 02
30	05 18	05 45	06 09	17 03	17 42	18 19	18 56
35	05 16	05 46	06 11	17 07	17 44	18 19	18 53
40	05 14	05 46	06 13	17 12	17 46	18 18	18 50
45	05 12	05 46	06 15	17 17	17 48	18 17	18 46
S 50	05 08	05 45	06 17	17 24	17 51	18 16	18 41
52	05 06	05 45	06 18	17 27	17 52	18 16	18 39
54	05 03	05 44	06 20	17 30	17 53	18 15	18 37
56	05 01	05 44	06 21	17 34	17 55	18 15	18 34
58	04 57	05 43	06 22	17 38	17 57	18 14	18 31
S 60	04 54	05 43	06 24	17 42	17 58	18 13	18 28

Lat.	Sunset	Twilight Civil	Twilight Naut.	Moonset 29	30	31	1
°	h m	h m	h m	h m	h m	h m	h m
N 72	19 05	20 19	22 16	06 31	06 19	06 08	05 57
N 70	18 58	20 04	21 38	06 16	06 12	06 07	06 02
68	18 53	19 52	21 12	06 04	06 05	06 06	06 07
66	18 49	19 42	20 52	05 53	06 00	06 05	06 10
64	18 45	19 34	20 37	05 45	05 56	06 05	06 13
62	18 42	19 27	20 25	05 37	05 52	06 04	06 16
60	18 39	19 21	20 14	05 31	05 48	06 04	06 18
N 58	18 36	19 16	20 06	05 25	05 45	06 03	06 20
56	18 34	19 12	19 58	05 20	05 42	06 03	06 22
54	18 32	19 08	19 51	05 15	05 40	06 02	06 24
52	18 30	19 04	19 46	05 11	05 38	06 02	06 25
50	18 29	19 01	19 40	05 07	05 36	06 02	06 27
45	18 25	18 55	19 30	04 59	05 31	06 01	06 30
N 40	18 22	18 49	19 22	04 52	05 27	06 00	06 32
35	18 20	18 45	19 15	04 46	05 24	06 00	06 35
30	18 17	18 41	19 10	04 41	05 21	05 59	06 37
20	18 14	18 36	19 02	04 31	05 16	05 59	06 40
N 10	18 11	18 32	18 56	04 23	05 12	05 58	06 43
0	18 08	18 28	18 52	04 16	05 07	05 57	06 46
S 10	18 05	18 26	18 50	04 08	05 03	05 56	06 49
20	18 02	18 24	18 50	03 59	04 58	05 56	06 52
30	17 59	18 23	18 51	03 50	04 53	05 55	06 55
35	17 57	18 23	18 52	03 44	04 50	05 54	06 57
40	17 55	18 22	18 54	03 38	04 46	05 53	06 59
45	17 53	18 23	18 56	03 30	04 42	05 53	07 02
S 50	17 51	18 23	19 00	03 21	04 37	05 52	07 05
52	17 50	18 23	19 02	03 17	04 35	05 51	07 06
54	17 48	18 23	19 04	03 13	04 32	05 51	07 08
56	17 47	18 24	19 07	03 08	04 30	05 50	07 09
58	17 45	18 24	19 10	03 02	04 27	05 50	07 11
S 60	17 44	18 25	19 13	02 55	04 23	05 49	07 13

	SUN			MOON			
Day	Eqn. of Time 00h	12h	Mer. Pass.	Mer. Pass. Upper	Lower	Age	Phase
d	m s	m s	h m	h m	h m	d	%
29	04 55	04 46	12 05	22 55	10 29	12	95
30	04 37	04 28	12 04	23 45	11 20	13	99
31	04 19	04 10	12 04	24 34	12 10	14	100 ○

UT	ARIES GHA	VENUS −3.9 GHA	Dec	MARS +0.3 GHA	Dec	JUPITER −2.4 GHA	Dec	SATURN +0.5 GHA	Dec	STARS Name	SHA	Dec
SUNDAY												
1 00	189 18.2	160 17.1	N11 21.9	270 31.5	S23 32.1	318 57.4	S17 09.6	269 40.4	S22 15.4	Acamar	315 16.3	S40 14.3
01	204 20.7	175 16.6	23.0	285 32.4	32.1	334 00.1	09.5	284 42.7	15.4	Achernar	335 25.0	S57 08.9
02	219 23.2	190 16.2	24.2	300 33.4	32.1	349 02.7	09.5	299 45.1	15.4	Acrux	173 04.9	S63 12.0
03	234 25.6	205 15.7 ..	25.4	315 34.3 ..	32.0	4 05.3 ..	09.4	314 47.5 ..	15.3	Adhara	255 10.0	S29 00.2
04	249 28.1	220 15.3	26.5	330 35.3	32.0	19 08.0	09.4	329 49.9	15.3	Aldebaran	290 45.9	N16 32.5
05	264 30.6	235 14.9	27.7	345 36.3	32.0	34 10.6	09.4	344 52.3	15.3			
06	279 33.0	250 14.4	N11 28.9	0 37.2	S23 32.0	49 13.2	S17 09.3	359 54.7	S22 15.3	Alioth	166 17.3	N55 51.7
07	294 35.5	265 14.0	30.0	15 38.2	31.9	64 15.9	09.3	14 57.1	15.3	Alkaid	152 55.9	N49 13.3
08	309 38.0	280 13.5	31.2	30 39.2	31.9	79 18.5	09.2	29 59.5	15.3	Al Na'ir	27 40.1	S46 52.3
S 09	324 40.4	295 13.1 ..	32.3	45 40.1 ..	31.9	94 21.2 ..	09.2	45 01.9 ..	15.3	Alnilam	275 43.2	S 1 11.7
U 10	339 42.9	310 12.6	33.5	60 41.1	31.9	109 23.8	09.1	60 04.2	15.3	Alphard	217 52.7	S 8 44.5
N 11	354 45.3	325 12.2	34.7	75 42.1	31.9	124 26.4	09.1	75 06.6	15.3			
D 12	9 47.8	340 11.7	N11 35.8	90 43.0	S23 31.8	139 29.1	S17 09.0	90 09.0	S22 15.3	Alphecca	126 08.0	N26 39.2
A 13	24 50.3	355 11.3	37.0	105 44.0	31.8	154 31.7	09.0	105 11.4	15.3	Alpheratz	357 40.5	N29 11.2
Y 14	39 52.7	10 10.8	38.2	120 45.0	31.8	169 34.4	08.9	120 13.8	15.3	Altair	62 05.2	N 8 54.9
15	54 55.2	25 10.4 ..	39.3	135 45.9 ..	31.8	184 37.0 ..	08.9	135 16.2 ..	15.3	Ankaa	353 13.0	S42 12.6
16	69 57.7	40 09.9	40.5	150 46.9	31.7	199 39.6	08.8	150 18.6	15.3	Antares	112 22.1	S26 28.1
17	85 00.1	55 09.5	41.6	165 47.9	31.7	214 42.3	08.8	165 21.0	15.3			
18	100 02.6	70 09.0	N11 42.8	180 48.8	S23 31.7	229 44.9	S17 08.7	180 23.4	S22 15.3	Arcturus	145 52.5	N19 05.2
19	115 05.1	85 08.6	43.9	195 49.8	31.7	244 47.6	08.7	195 25.8	15.3	Atria	107 20.7	S69 03.2
20	130 07.5	100 08.1	45.1	210 50.7	31.7	259 50.2	08.6	210 28.2	15.3	Avior	234 16.4	S59 34.5
21	145 10.0	115 07.7 ..	46.3	225 51.7 ..	31.6	274 52.8 ..	08.6	225 30.6 ..	15.3	Bellatrix	278 28.7	N 6 21.7
22	160 12.5	130 07.2	47.4	240 52.7	31.6	289 55.5	08.5	240 32.9	15.3	Betelgeuse	270 57.9	N 7 24.4
23	175 14.9	145 06.8	48.6	255 53.6	31.6	304 58.1	08.5	255 35.3	15.2			
MONDAY												
2 00	190 17.4	160 06.3	N11 49.7	270 54.6	S23 31.6	320 00.8	S17 08.4	270 37.7	S22 15.2	Canopus	263 54.8	S52 42.8
01	205 19.8	175 05.9	50.9	285 55.6	31.5	335 03.4	08.4	285 40.1	15.2	Capella	280 29.9	N46 00.9
02	220 22.3	190 05.4	52.0	300 56.6	31.5	350 06.1	08.3	300 42.5	15.2	Deneb	49 29.5	N45 20.5
03	235 24.8	205 04.9 ..	53.2	315 57.5 ..	31.5	5 08.7 ..	08.3	315 44.9 ..	15.2	Denebola	182 30.1	N14 28.2
04	250 27.2	220 04.5	54.3	330 58.5	31.5	20 11.4	08.2	330 47.3	15.2	Diphda	348 53.0	S17 53.4
05	265 29.7	235 04.0	55.5	345 59.5	31.4	35 14.0	08.2	345 49.7	15.2			
06	280 32.2	250 03.6	N11 56.6	1 00.4	S23 31.4	50 16.6	S17 08.1	0 52.1	S22 15.2	Dubhe	193 47.2	N61 39.3
07	295 34.6	265 03.1	57.8	16 01.4	31.4	65 19.3	08.1	15 54.5	15.2	Elnath	278 08.7	N28 37.2
08	310 37.1	280 02.7	11 58.9	31 02.4	31.4	80 21.9	08.0	30 56.9	15.2	Eltanin	90 44.5	N51 29.0
M 09	325 39.6	295 02.2	12 00.1	46 03.3 ..	31.3	95 24.6 ..	08.0	45 59.3 ..	15.2	Enif	33 44.2	N 9 57.4
O 10	340 42.0	310 01.8	01.2	61 04.3	31.3	110 27.2	07.9	61 01.7	15.2	Fomalhaut	15 20.8	S29 31.6
N 11	355 44.5	325 01.3	02.4	76 05.3	31.3	125 29.9	07.9	76 04.1	15.2			
D 12	10 47.0	340 00.8	N12 03.5	91 06.2	S23 31.2	140 32.5	S17 07.8	91 06.5	S22 15.2	Gacrux	171 56.7	S57 12.9
A 13	25 49.4	355 00.3	04.7	106 07.2	31.2	155 35.2	07.8	106 08.9	15.2	Gienah	175 48.6	S17 38.6
Y 14	40 51.9	9 59.9	05.8	121 08.2	31.2	170 37.8	07.7	121 11.3	15.2	Hadar	148 42.6	S60 27.5
15	55 54.3	24 59.5 ..	07.0	136 09.2 ..	31.2	185 40.5 ..	07.7	136 13.7 ..	15.2	Hamal	327 57.4	N23 32.7
16	70 56.8	39 59.0	08.1	151 10.1	31.1	200 43.1	07.6	151 16.0	15.2	Kaus Aust.	83 39.5	S34 22.3
17	85 59.3	54 58.6	09.3	166 11.1	31.1	215 45.8	07.6	166 18.4	15.2			
18	101 01.7	69 58.1	N12 10.4	181 12.1	S23 31.1	230 48.4	S17 07.5	181 20.8	S22 15.1	Kochab	137 19.2	N74 04.8
19	116 04.2	84 57.6	11.6	196 13.0	31.1	245 51.1	07.5	196 23.2	15.1	Markab	13 35.4	N15 18.0
20	131 06.7	99 57.2	12.7	211 14.0	31.0	260 53.7	07.4	211 25.6	15.1	Menkar	314 11.9	N 4 09.4
21	146 09.1	114 56.7 ..	13.9	226 15.0 ..	31.0	275 56.4 ..	07.4	226 28.0 ..	15.1	Menkent	148 03.4	S36 27.5
22	161 11.6	129 56.3	15.0	241 16.0	31.0	290 59.0	07.3	241 30.4	15.1	Miaplacidus	221 38.4	S69 47.8
23	176 14.1	144 55.8	16.1	256 16.9	30.9	306 01.7	07.3	256 32.8	15.1			
TUESDAY												
3 00	191 16.5	159 55.3	N12 17.3	271 17.9	S23 30.9	321 04.3	S17 07.2	271 35.2	S22 15.1	Mirfak	308 36.1	N49 55.4
01	206 19.0	174 54.9	18.4	286 18.9	30.9	336 07.0	07.2	286 37.6	15.1	Nunki	75 54.3	S26 16.3
02	221 21.4	189 54.4	19.6	301 19.8	30.9	351 09.6	07.1	301 40.0	15.1	Peacock	53 14.4	S56 40.3
03	236 23.9	204 54.0 ..	20.7	316 20.8 ..	30.8	6 12.3 ..	07.1	316 42.4 ..	15.1	Pollux	243 23.7	N27 58.8
04	251 26.4	219 53.5	21.9	331 21.8	30.8	21 14.9	07.0	331 44.8	15.1	Procyon	244 56.3	N 5 10.5
05	266 28.8	234 53.0	23.0	346 22.8	30.8	36 17.6	07.0	346 47.2	15.1			
06	281 31.3	249 52.6	N12 24.1	1 23.7	S23 30.7	51 20.2	S17 06.9	1 49.6	S22 15.1	Rasalhague	96 03.4	N12 32.8
07	296 33.8	264 52.1	25.3	16 24.7	30.7	66 22.9	06.9	16 52.0	15.1	Regulus	207 39.9	N11 52.6
T 08	311 36.2	279 51.6	26.4	31 25.7	30.7	81 25.5	06.8	31 54.4	15.1	Rigel	281 09.1	S 8 11.2
U 09	326 38.7	294 51.2 ..	27.5	46 26.7 ..	30.6	96 28.2 ..	06.8	46 56.8 ..	15.1	Rigil Kent.	139 46.7	S60 54.4
E 10	341 41.2	309 50.7	28.7	61 27.6	30.6	111 30.8	06.7	61 59.2	15.1	Sabik	102 08.7	S15 44.7
S 11	356 43.6	324 50.2	29.8	76 28.6	30.6	126 33.5	06.7	77 01.6	15.1			
D 12	11 46.1	339 49.8	N12 31.0	91 29.6	S23 30.6	141 36.1	S17 06.6	92 04.0	S22 15.1	Schedar	349 37.3	N56 38.0
A 13	26 48.6	354 49.3	32.1	106 30.6	30.5	156 38.8	06.5	107 06.4	15.1	Shaula	96 17.4	S37 06.7
Y 14	41 51.0	9 48.8	33.2	121 31.5	30.5	171 41.4	06.5	122 08.8	15.1	Sirius	258 30.9	S16 44.8
15	56 53.5	24 48.4 ..	34.4	136 32.5 ..	30.5	186 44.1 ..	06.4	137 11.2 ..	15.1	Spica	158 27.5	S11 15.4
16	71 55.9	39 47.9	35.5	151 33.5	30.4	201 46.7	06.4	152 13.6	15.0	Suhail	222 49.8	S43 30.7
17	86 58.4	54 47.4	36.6	166 34.5	30.4	216 49.4	06.3	167 16.0	15.0			
18	102 00.9	69 47.0	N12 37.8	181 35.4	S23 30.4	231 52.1	S17 06.3	182 18.4	S22 15.0	Vega	80 36.7	N38 47.9
19	117 03.3	84 46.5	38.9	196 36.4	30.3	246 54.7	06.2	197 20.8	15.0	Zuben'ubi	137 01.6	S16 07.0
20	132 05.8	99 46.0	40.0	211 37.4	30.3	261 57.4	06.2	212 23.2	15.0		SHA	Mer.Pass.
21	147 08.3	114 45.6 ..	41.2	226 38.4 ..	30.3	277 00.0 ..	06.1	227 25.6 ..	15.0			
22	162 10.7	129 45.1	42.3	241 39.4	30.2	292 02.7	06.1	242 28.0	15.0	Venus	329 48.9	13 20
23	177 13.2	144 44.6	43.4	256 40.3	30.2	307 05.3	06.0	257 30.4	15.0	Mars	80 37.2	5 56
Mer. Pass.	11 17.0	v −0.5	d 1.1	v 1.0	d 0.0	v 2.6	d 0.1	v 2.4	d 0.0	Jupiter	129 43.4	2 39
										Saturn	80 20.4	5 57

SUN / MOON

UT	SUN GHA	SUN Dec	MOON GHA	v	MOON Dec	d	HP
d h	° ′	° ′	° ′	′	° ′	′	′
1 00	178 59.8	N 4 26.1	351 42.5	11.7	S 2 32.0	11.6	57.6
01	194 00.0	27.1	6 13.2	11.8	2 43.6	11.5	57.6
02	209 00.2	28.1	20 44.0	11.8	2 55.1	11.6	57.6
03	224 00.4	.. 29.0	35 14.8	11.8	3 06.7	11.5	57.6
04	239 00.6	30.0	49 45.6	11.9	3 18.2	11.5	57.5
05	254 00.8	31.0	64 16.5	11.8	3 29.7	11.5	57.5
06	269 01.0	N 4 31.9	78 47.3	11.9	S 3 41.2	11.4	57.5
07	284 01.2	32.9	93 18.2	11.9	3 52.6	11.4	57.5
S 08	299 01.3	33.8	107 49.1	11.9	4 04.0	11.4	57.4
U 09	314 01.5	.. 34.8	122 20.0	11.9	4 15.4	11.3	57.4
N 10	329 01.7	35.8	136 50.9	11.9	4 26.7	11.3	57.4
D 11	344 01.9	36.7	151 21.8	12.0	4 38.0	11.3	57.3
A 12	359 02.1	N 4 37.7	165 52.8	11.9	S 4 49.3	11.2	57.3
Y 13	14 02.3	38.7	180 23.7	12.0	5 00.5	11.2	57.3
14	29 02.5	39.6	194 54.7	12.0	5 11.7	11.2	57.3
15	44 02.6	.. 40.6	209 25.7	12.0	5 22.9	11.1	57.2
16	59 02.8	41.6	223 56.7	12.0	5 34.0	11.1	57.2
17	74 03.0	42.5	238 27.7	12.0	5 45.1	11.0	57.2
18	89 03.2	N 4 43.5	252 58.7	12.0	S 5 56.1	11.0	57.2
19	104 03.4	44.4	267 29.7	12.0	6 07.1	11.0	57.1
20	119 03.6	45.4	282 00.8	12.0	6 18.1	10.9	57.1
21	134 03.8	.. 46.4	296 31.8	12.1	6 29.0	10.9	57.1
22	149 03.9	47.3	311 02.9	12.1	6 39.9	10.9	57.0
23	164 04.1	48.3	325 34.0	12.1	6 50.8	10.7	57.0
2 00	179 04.3	N 4 49.3	340 05.1	12.0	S 7 01.5	10.8	57.0
01	194 04.5	50.2	354 36.1	12.1	7 12.3	10.7	57.0
02	209 04.7	51.2	9 07.2	12.1	7 23.0	10.6	56.9
03	224 04.9	.. 52.1	23 38.3	12.2	7 33.6	10.7	56.9
04	239 05.1	53.1	38 09.5	12.1	7 44.3	10.5	56.9
05	254 05.2	54.1	52 40.6	12.1	7 54.8	10.5	56.8
06	269 05.4	N 4 55.0	67 11.7	12.1	S 8 05.3	10.5	56.8
07	284 05.6	56.0	81 42.8	12.2	8 15.8	10.4	56.8
M 08	299 05.8	56.9	96 14.0	12.1	8 26.2	10.3	56.8
O 09	314 06.0	.. 57.9	110 45.1	12.1	8 36.5	10.3	56.7
N 10	329 06.2	58.9	125 16.2	12.2	8 46.8	10.3	56.7
D 11	344 06.4	4 59.8	139 47.4	12.1	8 57.1	10.2	56.7
A 12	359 06.5	N 5 00.8	154 18.5	12.2	S 9 07.3	10.1	56.6
Y 13	14 06.7	01.7	168 49.7	12.1	9 17.4	10.1	56.6
14	29 06.9	02.7	183 20.8	12.2	9 27.5	10.0	56.6
15	44 07.1	.. 03.7	197 52.0	12.2	9 37.5	10.0	56.6
16	59 07.3	04.6	212 23.2	12.1	9 47.5	9.9	56.5
17	74 07.5	05.6	226 54.3	12.2	9 57.4	9.9	56.5
18	89 07.7	N 5 06.5	241 25.5	12.2	S10 07.3	9.7	56.5
19	104 07.8	07.5	255 56.7	12.1	10 17.0	9.8	56.5
20	119 08.0	08.5	270 27.8	12.2	10 26.8	9.7	56.4
21	134 08.2	.. 09.4	284 59.0	12.2	10 36.5	9.6	56.4
22	149 08.4	10.4	299 30.2	12.1	10 46.1	9.5	56.4
23	164 08.6	11.3	314 01.3	12.2	10 55.6	9.5	56.3
3 00	179 08.8	N 5 12.3	328 32.5	12.2	S11 05.1	9.4	56.3
01	194 08.9	13.3	343 03.7	12.1	11 14.5	9.4	56.3
02	209 09.1	14.2	357 34.8	12.2	11 23.9	9.3	56.3
03	224 09.3	.. 15.2	12 06.0	12.2	11 33.2	9.2	56.2
04	239 09.5	16.1	26 37.2	12.1	11 42.4	9.2	56.2
05	254 09.7	17.1	41 08.3	12.2	11 51.6	9.1	56.2
06	269 09.9	N 5 18.0	55 39.5	12.2	S12 00.7	9.0	56.1
07	284 10.0	19.0	70 10.7	12.1	12 09.7	9.0	56.1
T 08	299 10.2	20.0	84 41.8	12.2	12 18.7	8.8	56.1
U 09	314 10.4	.. 20.9	99 13.0	12.1	12 27.5	8.9	56.1
E 10	329 10.6	21.9	113 44.1	12.2	12 36.4	8.7	56.0
S 11	344 10.8	22.8	128 15.3	12.1	12 45.1	8.7	56.0
D 12	359 11.0	N 5 23.8	142 46.4	12.1	S12 53.8	8.6	56.0
A 13	14 11.1	24.7	157 17.5	12.2	13 02.4	8.6	56.0
Y 14	29 11.3	25.7	171 48.7	12.1	13 11.0	8.4	55.9
15	44 11.5	.. 26.7	186 19.8	12.1	13 19.4	8.4	55.9
16	59 11.7	27.6	200 50.9	12.2	13 27.8	8.4	55.9
17	74 11.9	28.6	215 22.1	12.1	13 36.2	8.2	55.9
18	89 12.1	N 5 29.5	229 53.2	12.1	S13 44.4	8.2	55.8
19	104 12.2	30.5	244 24.3	12.1	13 52.6	8.1	55.8
20	119 12.4	31.4	258 55.4	12.1	14 00.7	8.0	55.8
21	134 12.6	.. 32.4	273 26.5	12.1	14 08.7	8.0	55.8
22	149 12.8	33.3	287 57.6	12.1	14 16.7	7.8	55.7
23	164 13.0	34.3	302 28.7	12.1	S14 24.5	7.8	55.7
	SD 16.0	d 1.0	SD 15.6		15.4		15.3

Twilight / Moonrise

Lat.	Naut.	Civil	Sunrise	Moonrise 1	2	3	4
°	h m	h m	h m	h m	h m	h m	h m
N 72	01 26	03 36	04 51	20 36	22 29	24 29	00 29
N 70	02 14	03 53	04 59	20 26	22 10	23 55	25 42
68	02 43	04 06	05 05	20 18	21 55	23 32	25 05
66	03 05	04 17	05 11	20 11	21 43	23 13	24 39
64	03 21	04 26	05 15	20 06	21 33	22 58	24 19
62	03 35	04 33	05 19	20 01	21 25	22 46	24 03
60	03 46	04 40	05 23	19 57	21 18	22 36	23 49
N 58	03 56	04 45	05 26	19 53	21 11	22 27	23 38
56	04 04	04 50	05 28	19 50	21 06	22 19	23 28
54	04 11	04 55	05 31	19 47	21 01	22 12	23 19
52	04 17	04 59	05 33	19 45	20 56	22 05	23 11
50	04 23	05 02	05 35	19 42	20 52	21 59	23 04
45	04 34	05 09	05 39	19 37	20 43	21 47	22 49
N 40	04 43	05 15	05 43	19 33	20 36	21 37	22 36
35	04 50	05 20	05 46	19 29	20 30	21 29	22 26
30	04 56	05 24	05 48	19 26	20 24	21 21	22 16
20	05 05	05 31	05 53	19 20	20 15	21 08	22 01
N 10	05 11	05 36	05 57	19 15	20 06	20 57	21 47
0	05 15	05 40	06 00	19 11	19 59	20 46	21 34
S 10	05 18	05 43	06 04	19 06	19 51	20 36	21 21
20	05 20	05 45	06 07	19 02	19 43	20 25	21 08
30	05 20	05 47	06 11	18 56	19 34	20 12	20 52
35	05 19	05 48	06 13	18 53	19 28	20 05	20 43
40	05 17	05 49	06 16	18 50	19 22	19 56	20 33
45	05 15	05 49	06 19	18 46	19 15	19 47	20 21
S 50	05 12	05 50	06 22	18 41	19 07	19 35	20 07
52	05 11	05 50	06 23	18 39	19 03	19 30	20 00
54	05 09	05 50	06 25	18 37	18 59	19 24	19 53
56	05 07	05 50	06 27	18 34	18 55	19 18	19 44
58	05 04	05 50	06 29	18 31	18 50	19 10	19 35
S 60	05 01	05 50	06 31	18 28	18 44	19 02	19 24

Twilight / Moonset

Lat.	Sunset	Civil	Naut.	Moonset 1	2	3	4
°	h m	h m	h m	h m	h m	h m	h m
N 72	19 19	20 36	22 54	05 57	05 46	05 32	05 13
N 70	19 11	20 18	22 00	06 02	05 58	05 53	05 47
68	19 04	20 04	21 29	06 07	06 09	06 12	
66	18 58	19 53	21 06	06 10	06 16	06 22	06 31
64	18 54	19 44	20 49	06 13	06 22	06 33	06 46
62	18 50	19 36	20 35	06 16	06 28	06 42	06 59
60	18 46	19 29	20 23	06 18	06 34	06 50	07 11
N 58	18 43	19 23	20 14	06 20	06 38	06 58	07 20
56	18 40	19 18	20 05	06 22	06 42	07 04	07 29
54	18 38	19 14	19 58	06 24	06 46	07 10	07 36
52	18 35	19 10	19 52	06 25	06 49	07 15	07 43
50	18 33	19 06	19 46	06 27	06 52	07 19	07 49
45	18 29	18 59	19 34	06 30	06 59	07 29	08 02
N 40	18 25	18 52	19 25	06 32	07 05	07 38	08 13
35	18 22	18 48	19 18	06 35	07 09	07 45	08 23
30	18 19	18 43	19 12	06 37	07 14	07 51	08 31
20	18 15	18 37	19 03	06 40	07 21	08 03	08 45
N 10	18 11	18 32	18 56	06 43	07 28	08 12	08 58
0	18 07	18 28	18 52	06 46	07 34	08 21	09 09
S 10	18 03	18 24	18 49	06 49	07 40	08 31	09 21
20	18 00	18 22	18 47	06 52	07 46	08 40	09 34
30	17 56	18 19	18 47	06 55	07 54	08 52	09 48
35	17 53	18 19	18 48	06 57	07 58	08 58	09 56
40	17 51	18 18	18 49	06 59	08 03	09 05	10 06
45	17 48	18 17	18 51	07 02	08 09	09 14	10 17
S 50	17 44	18 16	18 54	07 05	08 16	09 25	10 31
52	17 43	18 16	18 55	07 06	08 19	09 29	10 37
54	17 41	18 16	18 57	07 08	08 22	09 35	10 44
56	17 39	18 16	18 59	07 09	08 26	09 41	10 52
58	17 37	18 16	19 01	07 11	08 31	09 47	11 01
S 60	17 35	18 16	19 04	07 13	08 35	09 55	11 11

SUN / MOON

	SUN Eqn. of Time 00h	12h	Mer. Pass.	MOON Mer. Pass. Upper	Lower	Age	Phase
Day	m s	m s	h m	h m	h m	d	%
1	04 01	03 52	12 04	00 34	12 58	15	99
2	03 43	03 34	12 04	01 22	13 46	16	95
3	03 25	03 17	12 03	02 10	14 34	17	90

2018 APRIL 4, 5, 6 (WED., THURS., FRI.)

UT	ARIES	VENUS −3·9		MARS +0·2		JUPITER −2·4		SATURN +0·5		STARS		
	GHA	GHA	Dec	GHA	Dec	GHA	Dec	GHA	Dec	Name	SHA	Dec
d h	° ′	° ′	° ′	° ′	° ′	° ′	° ′	° ′	° ′		° ′	° ′
4 00	192 15.7	159 44.2	N12 44.6	271 41.3	S23 30.2	322 08.0	S17 06.0	272 32.8	S22 15.0	Acamar	315 16.3	S40 14.3
01	207 18.1	174 43.7	45.7	286 42.3	30.1	337 10.6	05.9	287 35.2	15.0	Achernar	335 25.0	S57 08.9
02	222 20.6	189 43.2	46.8	301 43.3	30.1	352 13.3	05.9	302 37.6	15.0	Acrux	173 04.9	S63 12.0
03	237 23.1	204 42.7 ..	47.9	316 44.2 ..	30.1	7 16.0 ..	05.8	317 40.0 ..	15.0	Adhara	255 10.0	S29 00.2
04	252 25.5	219 42.3	49.1	331 45.2	30.0	22 18.6	05.8	332 42.4	15.0	Aldebaran	290 45.9	N16 32.5
05	267 28.0	234 41.8	50.2	346 46.2	30.0	37 21.3	05.7	347 44.8	15.0			
W 06	282 30.4	249 41.3	N12 51.3	1 47.2	S23 30.0	52 23.9	S17 05.7	2 47.2	S22 15.0	Alioth	166 17.3	N55 51.7
E 07	297 32.9	264 40.9	52.5	16 48.2	29.9	67 26.6	05.6	17 49.6	15.0	Alkaid	152 55.9	N49 13.3
D 08	312 35.4	279 40.4	53.6	31 49.1	29.9	82 29.3	05.5	32 52.0	15.0	Al Na'ir	27 40.0	S46 52.3
N 09	327 37.8	294 39.9 ..	54.7	46 50.1 ..	29.9	97 31.9 ..	05.5	47 54.4 ..	15.0	Alnilam	275 43.2	S 1 11.7
E 10	342 40.3	309 39.4	55.8	61 51.1	29.8	112 34.6	05.4	62 56.8	15.0	Alphard	217 52.7	S 8 44.5
S 11	357 42.8	324 39.0	57.0	76 52.1	29.8	127 37.2	05.4	77 59.2	15.0			
D 12	12 45.2	339 38.5	N12 58.1	91 53.1	S23 29.8	142 39.9	S17 05.3	93 01.6	S22 15.0	Alphecca	126 08.0	N26 39.2
A 13	27 47.7	354 38.0	12 59.2	106 54.0	29.7	157 42.6	05.3	108 04.1	15.0	Alpheratz	357 40.5	N29 11.2
Y 14	42 50.2	9 37.5	13 00.3	121 55.0	29.7	172 45.2	05.2	123 06.5	15.0	Altair	62 05.1	N 8 54.9
15	57 52.6	24 37.1 ..	01.5	136 56.0 ..	29.7	187 47.9 ..	05.2	138 08.9 ..	14.9	Ankaa	353 13.0	S42 12.6
16	72 55.1	39 36.6	02.6	151 57.0	29.6	202 50.5	05.1	153 11.3	14.9	Antares	112 22.1	S26 28.1
17	87 57.5	54 36.1	03.7	166 58.0	29.6	217 53.2	05.1	168 13.7	14.9			
18	103 00.0	69 35.6	N13 04.8	181 59.0	S23 29.5	232 55.9	S17 05.0	183 16.1	S22 14.9	Arcturus	145 52.5	N19 05.3
19	118 02.5	84 35.2	05.9	196 59.9	29.5	247 58.5	05.0	198 18.5	14.9	Atria	107 20.7	S69 03.2
20	133 04.9	99 34.7	07.1	212 00.9	29.5	263 01.2	04.9	213 20.9	14.9	Avior	234 16.5	S59 34.5
21	148 07.4	114 34.2 ..	08.2	227 01.9 ..	29.4	278 03.8 ..	04.9	228 23.3 ..	14.9	Bellatrix	278 28.7	N 6 21.7
22	163 09.9	129 33.7	09.3	242 02.9	29.4	293 06.5	04.8	243 25.7	14.9	Betelgeuse	270 57.9	N 7 24.4
23	178 12.3	144 33.2	10.4	257 03.9	29.4	308 09.2	04.7	258 28.1	14.9			
5 00	193 14.8	159 32.8	N13 11.5	272 04.9	S23 29.3	323 11.8	S17 04.7	273 30.5	S22 14.9	Canopus	263 54.8	S52 42.8
01	208 17.3	174 32.3	12.6	287 05.8	29.3	338 14.5	04.6	288 32.9	14.9	Capella	280 29.9	N46 00.9
02	223 19.7	189 31.8	13.8	302 06.8	29.2	353 17.2	04.6	303 35.3	14.9	Deneb	49 29.4	N45 20.5
03	238 22.2	204 31.3 ..	14.9	317 07.8 ..	29.2	8 19.8 ..	04.5	318 37.7 ..	14.9	Denebola	182 30.1	N14 28.2
04	253 24.7	219 30.8	16.0	332 08.8	29.2	23 22.5	04.5	333 40.1	14.9	Diphda	348 53.0	S17 53.4
05	268 27.1	234 30.4	17.1	347 09.8	29.1	38 25.2	04.4	348 42.5	14.9			
T 06	283 29.6	249 29.9	N13 18.2	2 10.8	S23 29.1	53 27.8	S17 04.4	3 44.9	S22 14.9	Dubhe	193 47.3	N61 39.3
H 07	298 32.0	264 29.4	19.3	17 11.8	29.1	68 30.5	04.3	18 47.4	14.9	Elnath	278 08.7	N28 37.2
U 08	313 34.5	279 28.9	20.4	32 12.7	29.0	83 33.2	04.3	33 49.8	14.9	Eltanin	90 44.5	N51 29.0
R 09	328 37.0	294 28.4 ..	21.6	47 13.7 ..	29.0	98 35.8 ..	04.2	48 52.2 ..	14.9	Enif	33 44.2	N 9 57.4
S 10	343 39.4	309 28.0	22.7	62 14.7	28.9	113 38.5	04.1	63 54.6	14.9	Fomalhaut	15 20.7	S29 31.6
D 11	358 41.9	324 27.5	23.8	77 15.7	28.9	128 41.1	04.1	78 57.0	14.9			
A 12	13 44.4	339 27.0	N13 24.9	92 16.7	S23 28.9	143 43.8	S17 04.0	93 59.4	S22 14.9	Gacrux	171 56.7	S57 12.9
Y 13	28 46.8	354 26.5	26.0	107 17.7	28.8	158 46.5	04.0	109 01.8	14.9	Gienah	175 48.6	S17 38.6
14	43 49.3	9 26.0	27.1	122 18.7	28.8	173 49.1	03.9	124 04.2	14.9	Hadar	148 42.6	S60 27.5
15	58 51.8	24 25.5 ..	28.2	137 19.6 ..	28.7	188 51.8 ..	03.9	139 06.6 ..	14.8	Hamal	327 57.4	N23 32.7
16	73 54.2	39 25.1	29.3	152 20.6	28.7	203 54.5	03.8	154 09.0	14.8	Kaus Aust.	83 39.5	S34 22.3
17	88 56.7	54 24.6	30.4	167 21.6	28.7	218 57.2	03.8	169 11.4	14.8			
18	103 59.2	69 24.1	N13 31.5	182 22.6	S23 28.6	233 59.8	S17 03.7	184 13.8	S22 14.8	Kochab	137 19.2	N74 04.8
19	119 01.6	84 23.6	32.7	197 23.6	28.6	249 02.5	03.6	199 16.3	14.8	Markab	13 35.4	N15 18.0
20	134 04.1	99 23.1	33.8	212 24.6	28.5	264 05.2	03.6	214 18.7	14.8	Menkar	314 11.9	N 4 09.4
21	149 06.5	114 22.6 ..	34.9	227 25.6 ..	28.5	279 07.8 ..	03.5	229 21.1 ..	14.8	Menkent	148 03.4	S36 27.5
22	164 09.0	129 22.1	36.0	242 26.6	28.5	294 10.5	03.5	244 23.5	14.8	Miaplacidus	221 38.5	S69 47.8
23	179 11.5	144 21.6	37.1	257 27.6	28.4	309 13.2	03.4	259 25.9	14.8			
6 00	194 13.9	159 21.2	N13 38.2	272 28.5	S23 28.4	324 15.8	S17 03.4	274 28.3	S22 14.8	Mirfak	308 36.1	N49 55.4
01	209 16.4	174 20.7	39.3	287 29.5	28.3	339 18.5	03.3	289 30.7	14.8	Nunki	75 54.3	S26 16.3
02	224 18.9	189 20.2	40.4	302 30.5	28.3	354 21.2	03.3	304 33.1	14.8	Peacock	53 14.4	S56 40.3
03	239 21.3	204 19.7 ..	41.5	317 31.5 ..	28.3	9 23.8 ..	03.2	319 35.5 ..	14.8	Pollux	243 23.7	N27 58.8
04	254 23.8	219 19.2	42.6	332 32.5	28.2	24 26.5	03.1	334 38.0	14.8	Procyon	244 56.3	N 5 10.5
05	269 26.3	234 18.7	43.7	347 33.5	28.2	39 29.2	03.1	349 40.4	14.8			
F 06	284 28.7	249 18.2	N13 44.8	2 34.5	S23 28.1	54 31.9	S17 03.0	4 42.8	S22 14.8	Rasalhague	96 03.3	N12 32.8
R 07	299 31.2	264 17.7	45.9	17 35.5	28.1	69 34.5	03.0	19 45.2	14.8	Regulus	207 39.9	N11 52.6
I 08	314 33.6	279 17.2	47.0	32 36.5	28.0	84 37.2	02.9	34 47.6	14.8	Rigel	281 09.1	S 8 11.2
D 09	329 36.1	294 16.7 ..	48.1	47 37.5 ..	28.0	99 39.9 ..	02.9	49 50.0 ..	14.8	Rigil Kent.	139 46.7	S60 54.4
A 10	344 38.6	309 16.3	49.2	62 38.5	28.0	114 42.5	02.8	64 52.4	14.8	Sabik	102 08.7	S15 44.7
Y 11	359 41.0	324 15.8	50.3	77 39.5	27.9	129 45.2	02.8	79 54.8	14.8			
12	14 43.5	339 15.3	N13 51.4	92 40.4	S23 27.9	144 47.9	S17 02.7	94 57.2	S22 14.8	Schedar	349 37.3	N56 38.0
13	29 46.0	354 14.8	52.5	107 41.4	27.8	159 50.6	02.6	109 59.7	14.8	Shaula	96 17.4	S37 06.7
14	44 48.4	9 14.3	53.6	122 42.4	27.8	174 53.2	02.6	125 02.1	14.8	Sirius	258 30.9	S16 44.8
15	59 50.9	24 13.8 ..	54.7	137 43.4 ..	27.7	189 55.9 ..	02.5	140 04.5 ..	14.8	Spica	158 27.5	S11 15.4
16	74 53.4	39 13.3	55.8	152 44.4	27.7	204 58.6	02.5	155 06.9	14.7	Suhail	222 49.8	S43 30.7
17	89 55.8	54 12.8	56.9	167 45.4	27.7	220 01.3	02.4	170 09.3	14.7			
18	104 58.3	69 12.3	N13 58.0	182 46.4	S23 27.6	235 03.9	S17 02.4	185 11.7	S22 14.7	Vega	80 36.7	N38 47.9
19	120 00.8	84 11.8	13 59.0	197 47.4	27.6	250 06.6	02.3	200 14.1	14.7	Zuben'ubi	137 01.5	S16 07.0
20	135 03.2	99 11.3	14 00.1	212 48.4	27.5	265 09.3	02.2	215 16.6	14.7		SHA	Mer.Pass.
21	150 05.7	114 10.8 ..	01.2	227 49.4 ..	27.5	280 12.0 ..	02.2	230 19.0 ..	14.7		° ′	h m
22	165 08.1	129 10.3	02.3	242 50.4	27.4	295 14.6	02.1	245 21.4	14.7	Venus	326 18.0	13 22
23	180 10.6	144 09.8	03.4	257 51.4	27.4	310 17.3	02.1	260 23.8	14.7	Mars	78 50.1	5 51
	h m									Jupiter	129 57.0	2 27
Mer. Pass. 11 05.2	v −0.5 d 1.1			v 1.0 d 0.0		v 2.7 d 0.1		v 2.4 d 0.0		Saturn	80 15.7	5 45

INDEX TO SELECTED STARS, 2018

Name	No	Mag	SHA	Dec		No	Name	Mag	SHA	Dec
Acamar	7	3·2	315	S 40		1	Alpheratz	2·1	358	N 29
Achernar	5	0·5	335	S 57		2	Ankaa	2·4	353	S 42
Acrux	30	1·3	173	S 63		3	Schedar	2·2	350	N 57
Adhara	19	1·5	255	S 29		4	Diphda	2·0	349	S 18
Aldebaran	10	0·9	291	N 17		5	Achernar	0·5	335	S 57
Alioth	32	1·8	166	N 56		6	Hamal	2·0	328	N 24
Alkaid	34	1·9	153	N 49		7	Acamar	3·2	315	S 40
Al Na'ir	55	1·7	28	S 47		8	Menkar	2·5	314	N 4
Alnilam	15	1·7	276	S 1		9	Mirfak	1·8	309	N 50
Alphard	25	2·0	218	S 9		10	Aldebaran	0·9	291	N 17
Alphecca	41	2·2	126	N 27		11	Rigel	0·1	281	S 8
Alpheratz	1	2·1	358	N 29		12	Capella	0·1	280	N 46
Altair	51	0·8	62	N 9		13	Bellatrix	1·6	278	N 6
Ankaa	2	2·4	353	S 42		14	Elnath	1·7	278	N 29
Antares	42	1·0	112	S 26		15	Alnilam	1·7	276	S 1
Arcturus	37	0·0	146	N 19		16	Betelgeuse	Var.*	271	N 7
Atria	43	1·9	107	S 69		17	Canopus	−0·7	264	S 53
Avior	22	1·9	234	S 60		18	Sirius	−1·5	259	S 17
Bellatrix	13	1·6	278	N 6		19	Adhara	1·5	255	S 29
Betelgeuse	16	Var.*	271	N 7		20	Procyon	0·4	245	N 5
Canopus	17	−0·7	264	S 53		21	Pollux	1·1	243	N 28
Capella	12	0·1	280	N 46		22	Avior	1·9	234	S 60
Deneb	53	1·3	49	N 45		23	Suhail	2·2	223	S 44
Denebola	28	2·1	183	N 14		24	Miaplacidus	1·7	222	S 70
Diphda	4	2·0	349	S 18		25	Alphard	2·0	218	S 9
Dubhe	27	1·8	194	N 62		26	Regulus	1·4	208	N 12
Elnath	14	1·7	278	N 29		27	Dubhe	1·8	194	N 62
Eltanin	47	2·2	91	N 51		28	Denebola	2·1	183	N 14
Enif	54	2·4	34	N 10		29	Gienah	2·6	176	S 18
Fomalhaut	56	1·2	15	S 30		30	Acrux	1·3	173	S 63
Gacrux	31	1·6	172	S 57		31	Gacrux	1·6	172	S 57
Gienah	29	2·6	176	S 18		32	Alioth	1·8	166	N 56
Hadar	35	0·6	149	S 60		33	Spica	1·0	158	S 11
Hamal	6	2·0	328	N 24		34	Alkaid	1·9	153	N 49
Kaus Australis	48	1·9	84	S 34		35	Hadar	0·6	149	S 60
Kochab	40	2·1	137	N 74		36	Menkent	2·1	148	S 36
Markab	57	2·5	14	N 15		37	Arcturus	0·0	146	N 19
Menkar	8	2·5	314	N 4		38	Rigil Kentaurus	−0·3	140	S 61
Menkent	36	2·1	148	S 36		39	Zubenelgenubi	2·8	137	S 16
Miaplacidus	24	1·7	222	S 70		40	Kochab	2·1	137	N 74
Mirfak	9	1·8	309	N 50		41	Alphecca	2·2	126	N 27
Nunki	50	2·0	76	S 26		42	Antares	1·0	112	S 26
Peacock	52	1·9	53	S 57		43	Atria	1·9	107	S 69
Pollux	21	1·1	243	N 28		44	Sabik	2·4	102	S 16
Procyon	20	0·4	245	N 5		45	Shaula	1·6	96	S 37
Rasalhague	46	2·1	96	N 13		46	Rasalhague	2·1	96	N 13
Regulus	26	1·4	208	N 12		47	Eltanin	2·2	91	N 51
Rigel	11	0·1	281	S 8		48	Kaus Australis	1·9	84	S 34
Rigil Kentaurus	38	−0·3	140	S 61		49	Vega	0·0	81	N 39
Sabik	44	2·4	102	S 16		50	Nunki	2·0	76	S 26
Schedar	3	2·2	350	N 57		51	Altair	0·8	62	N 9
Shaula	45	1·6	96	S 37		52	Peacock	1·9	53	S 57
Sirius	18	−1·5	259	S 17		53	Deneb	1·3	49	N 45
Spica	33	1·0	158	S 11		54	Enif	2·4	34	N 10
Suhail	23	2·2	223	S 44		55	Al Na'ir	1·7	28	S 47
Vega	49	0·0	81	N 39		56	Fomalhaut	1·2	15	S 30
Zubenelgenubi	39	2·8	137	S 16		57	Markab	2·5	14	N 15

*0·1 — 1·2

ALTITUDE CORRECTION TABLES 10°–90°—SUN, STARS, PLANETS

OCT.–MAR. **SUN** APR.–SEPT.						**STARS AND PLANETS**		**DIP**		
App. Alt.	Lower Limb	Upper Limb	App. Alt.	Lower Limb	Upper Limb	App Alt.	Corrⁿ	App. Alt.	Additional Corrⁿ	Ht. of Eye / Corrⁿ / Ht. of Eye / Corrⁿ / Ht. of Eye / Corrⁿ

SUN OCT.–MAR. (App. Alt. / Lower Limb / Upper Limb)

```
  °  ′        ′        ′
 9 33    +10·8   −21·5
 9 45    +10·9   −21·4
 9 56    +11·0   −21·3
10 08    +11·1   −21·2
10 20    +11·2   −21·1
10 33    +11·3   −21·0
10 46    +11·4   −20·9
11 00    +11·5   −20·8
11 15    +11·6   −20·7
11 30    +11·7   −20·6
11 45    +11·8   −20·5
12 01    +11·9   −20·4
12 18    +12·0   −20·3
12 36    +12·1   −20·2
12 54    +12·2   −20·1
13 14    +12·3   −20·0
13 34    +12·4   −19·9
13 55    +12·5   −19·8
14 17    +12·6   −19·7
14 41    +12·7   −19·6
15 05    +12·8   −19·5
15 31    +12·9   −19·4
15 59    +13·0   −19·3
16 27    +13·1   −19·2
16 58    +13·2   −19·1
17 30    +13·3   −19·0
18 05    +13·4   −18·9
18 41    +13·5   −18·8
19 20    +13·6   −18·7
20 02    +13·7   −18·6
20 46    +13·8   −18·5
21 34    +13·9   −18·4
22 25    +14·0   −18·3
23 20    +14·1   −18·2
24 20    +14·2   −18·1
25 24    +14·3   −18·0
26 34    +14·4   −17·9
27 50    +14·5   −17·8
29 13    +14·6   −17·7
30 44    +14·7   −17·6
32 24    +14·8   −17·5
34 15    +14·9   −17·4
36 17    +15·0   −17·3
38 34    +15·1   −17·2
41 06    +15·2   −17·1
43 56    +15·3   −17·0
47 07    +15·4   −16·9
50 43    +15·5   −16·8
54 46    +15·6   −16·7
59 21    +15·7   −16·6
64 28    +15·8   −16·5
70 10    +15·9   −16·4
76 24    +16·0   −16·3
83 05    +16·1   −16·2
90 00
```

SUN APR.–SEPT. (App. Alt. / Lower Limb / Upper Limb)

```
  °  ′        ′        ′
 9 39    +10·6   −21·2
 9 50    +10·7   −21·1
10 02    +10·8   −21·0
10 14    +10·9   −20·9
10 27    +11·0   −20·8
10 40    +11·1   −20·7
10 53    +11·2   −20·6
11 07    +11·3   −20·5
11 22    +11·4   −20·4
11 37    +11·5   −20·3
11 53    +11·6   −20·2
12 10    +11·7   −20·1
12 27    +11·8   −20·0
12 45    +11·9   −19·9
13 04    +12·0   −19·8
13 24    +12·1   −19·7
13 44    +12·2   −19·6
14 06    +12·3   −19·5
14 29    +12·4   −19·4
14 53    +12·5   −19·3
15 18    +12·6   −19·2
15 45    +12·7   −19·1
16 13    +12·8   −19·0
16 43    +12·9   −18·9
17 14    +13·0   −18·8
17 47    +13·1   −18·7
18 23    +13·2   −18·6
19 00    +13·3   −18·5
19 41    +13·4   −18·4
20 24    +13·5   −18·3
21 10    +13·6   −18·2
21 59    +13·7   −18·1
22 52    +13·8   −18·0
23 49    +13·9   −17·9
24 51    +14·0   −17·8
25 58    +14·1   −17·7
27 11    +14·2   −17·6
28 31    +14·3   −17·5
29 58    +14·4   −17·4
31 33    +14·5   −17·3
33 18    +14·6   −17·2
35 15    +14·7   −17·1
37 24    +14·8   −17·0
39 48    +14·9   −16·9
42 28    +15·0   −16·8
45 29    +15·1   −16·7
48 52    +15·2   −16·6
52 41    +15·3   −16·5
56 59    +15·4   −16·4
61 50    +15·5   −16·3
67 15    +15·6   −16·2
73 14    +15·7   −16·1
79 42    +15·8   −16·0
86 31    +15·9   −15·9
90 00
```

STARS AND PLANETS (App. Alt. / Corrⁿ)

```
  °  ′        ′
 9 55    −5·3
10 07    −5·2
10 20    −5·1
10 32    −5·0
10 46    −4·9
10 59    −4·8
11 14    −4·7
11 29    −4·6
11 44    −4·5
12 00    −4·4
12 17    −4·3
12 35    −4·2
12 53    −4·1
13 12    −4·0
13 32    −3·9
13 53    −3·8
14 16    −3·7
14 39    −3·6
15 03    −3·5
15 29    −3·4
15 56    −3·3
16 25    −3·2
16 55    −3·1
17 27    −3·0
18 01    −2·9
18 37    −2·8
19 16    −2·7
19 56    −2·6
20 40    −2·5
21 27    −2·4
22 17    −2·3
23 11    −2·2
24 09    −2·1
25 12    −2·0
26 20    −1·9
27 34    −1·8
28 54    −1·7
30 22    −1·6
31 58    −1·5
33 43    −1·4
35 38    −1·3
37 45    −1·2
40 06    −1·1
42 42    −1·0
45 34    −0·9
48 45    −0·8
52 16    −0·7
56 09    −0·6
60 26    −0·5
65 06    −0·4
70 09    −0·3
75 32    −0·2
81 12    −0·1
87 03     0·0
90 00
```

Additional Corrⁿ (App. Alt. / Additional Corrⁿ)

```
2018
VENUS
Jan. 1–July 11
   °  ′
   0   +0·1
  60

July 12–Aug. 30
Dec. 26–Dec. 31
   °  ′
   0   +0·2
  41   +0·1
  76

Aug. 31–Sept. 21
Dec. 3–Dec. 25
   °  ′
   0   +0·3
  34   +0·2
  60   +0·1
  80

Sept. 22–Oct. 7
Nov. 17–Dec. 2
   °  ′
   0   +0·4
  29   +0·3
  51   +0·2
  68   +0·1
  83

Oct. 8–Nov. 16
   °  ′
   0   +0·5
  26   +0·4
  46   +0·3
  60   +0·2
  73   +0·1
  84

MARS
Jan. 1–Apr. 15
Nov. 27–Dec. 31
   °  ′
   0   +0·1
  60

Apr. 16–June 4
Sept. 30–Nov. 26
   °  ′
   0   +0·2
  41   +0·1
  76

June 5–July 9
Aug. 23–Sept. 29
   °  ′
   0   +0·3
  34   +0·2
  60   +0·1
  80

July 10–Aug. 22
   °  ′
   0   +0·4
  29   +0·3
  51   +0·2
  68   +0·1
  83
```

DIP (Ht. of Eye / Corrⁿ)

```
   m      ′
 2·4   −2·8
 2·6
 2·8   −2·9
 3·0   −3·0
 3·2   −3·1
 3·4   −3·2
 3·6   −3·3
 3·8   −3·4
 4·0   −3·5
 4·3   −3·6
 4·5   −3·7
 4·7   −3·8
 5·0   −3·9
 5·2   −4·0
 5·5   −4·1
 5·8   −4·2
 6·1   −4·3
 6·3   −4·4
 6·6   −4·5
 6·9   −4·6
 7·2   −4·7
 7·5   −4·8
 7·9   −4·9
 8·2   −5·0
 8·5   −5·1
 8·8   −5·2
 9·2   −5·3
 9·5   −5·4
 9·9   −5·5
10·3   −5·6
10·6   −5·7
11·0   −5·8
11·4   −5·9
11·8   −6·0
12·2   −6·1
12·6   −6·2
13·0   −6·3
13·4   −6·4
13·8   −6·5
14·2   −6·6
14·7   −6·7
15·1   −6·8
15·5   −6·9
16·0   −7·0
16·5   −7·1
16·9   −7·2
17·4   −7·3
17·9   −7·4
18·4   −7·5
18·8   −7·6
19·3   −7·7
19·8   −7·8
20·4   −7·9
20·9   −8·0
21·4   −8·1
```

DIP (Ht. of Eye ft. / Corrⁿ)

```
  ft.
  8·0
  8·6
  9·2
  9·8
 10·5
 11·2
 11·9
 12·6
 13·3
 14·1
 14·9
 15·7
 16·5
 17·4
 18·3
 19·1
 20·1
 21·0
 22·0
 22·9
 23·9
 24·9
 26·0
 27·1
 28·1
 29·2
 30·4
 31·5
 32·7
 33·9
 35·1
 36·3
 37·6
 38·9
 40·1
 41·5
 42·8
 44·2
 45·5
 46·9
 48·4
 49·8
 51·3
 52·8
 54·3
 55·8
 57·4
 58·9
 60·5
 62·1
 63·8
 65·4
 67·1
 68·8
 70·5
```

DIP (Ht. of Eye / Corrⁿ)

```
   m      ′
 1·0   −1·8
 1·5   −2·2
 2·0   −2·5
 2·5   −2·8
 3·0   −3·0

See table
   ←

   m      ′
  20   −7·9
  22   −8·3
  24   −8·6
  26   −9·0
  28   −9·3

  30   −9·6
  32   −10·0
  34   −10·3
  36   −10·6
  38   −10·8

  40   −11·1
  42   −11·4
  44   −11·7
  46   −11·9
  48   −12·2

  ft.
   2   −1·4
   4   −1·9
   6   −2·4
   8   −2·7
  10   −3·1

See table
   ←

  ft.
  70   −8·1
  75   −8·4
  80   −8·7
  85   −8·9
  90   −9·2
  95   −9·5
 100   −9·7
 105   −9·9
 110   −10·2
 115   −10·4
 120   −10·6
 125   −10·8
 130   −11·1
 135   −11·3
 140   −11·5
 145   −11·7
 150   −11·9
 155   −12·1
```

App. Alt. = Apparent altitude = Sextant altitude corrected for index error and dip.

SUN and MOON

UT	SUN GHA	SUN Dec	MOON GHA	v	MOON Dec	d	HP
d h	° ′	° ′	° ′	′	° ′	′	′
4 00	179 13.2	N 5 35.2	316 59.8	12.1	S14 32.3	7.8	55.7
01	194 13.3	36.2	331 30.9	12.0	14 40.1	7.6	55.7
02	209 13.5	37.2	346 01.9	12.1	14 47.7	7.6	55.6
03	224 13.7	.. 38.1	0 33.0	12.1	14 55.3	7.5	55.6
04	239 13.9	39.1	15 04.1	12.0	15 02.8	7.4	55.6
05	254 14.1	40.0	29 35.1	12.1	15 10.2	7.3	55.6
06	269 14.3	N 5 41.0	44 06.2	12.0	S15 17.5	7.3	55.5
07	284 14.4	41.9	58 37.2	12.0	15 24.8	7.1	55.5
08	299 14.6	42.9	73 08.2	12.1	15 31.9	7.1	55.5
09	314 14.8	.. 43.8	87 39.3	12.0	15 39.0	7.0	55.5
10	329 15.0	44.8	102 10.3	12.0	15 46.0	7.0	55.4
11	344 15.2	45.7	116 41.3	12.0	15 53.0	6.8	55.4
12	359 15.3	N 5 46.7	131 12.3	12.0	S15 59.8	6.8	55.4
13	14 15.5	47.6	145 43.3	12.0	16 06.6	6.7	55.4
14	29 15.7	48.6	160 14.3	12.0	16 13.3	6.6	55.3
15	44 15.9	.. 49.5	174 45.3	12.0	16 19.9	6.5	55.3
16	59 16.1	50.5	189 16.3	12.0	16 26.4	6.4	55.3
17	74 16.3	51.4	203 47.3	12.0	16 32.8	6.4	55.3
18	89 16.4	N 5 52.4	218 18.3	11.9	S16 39.2	6.2	55.2
19	104 16.6	53.3	232 49.2	12.0	16 45.4	6.2	55.2
20	119 16.8	54.3	247 20.2	12.0	16 51.6	6.1	55.2
21	134 17.0	.. 55.2	261 51.2	11.9	16 57.7	6.0	55.2
22	149 17.2	56.2	276 22.1	11.9	17 03.7	5.9	55.2
23	164 17.3	57.2	290 53.0	12.0	17 09.6	5.8	55.1
5 00	179 17.5	N 5 58.1	305 24.0	11.9	S17 15.4	5.8	55.1
01	194 17.7	5 59.1	319 54.9	11.9	17 21.2	5.7	55.1
02	209 17.9	6 00.0	334 25.8	11.9	17 26.9	5.5	55.1
03	224 18.1	.. 01.0	348 56.7	12.0	17 32.4	5.5	55.1
04	239 18.2	01.9	3 27.7	11.9	17 37.9	5.4	55.0
05	254 18.4	02.8	17 58.6	11.9	17 43.3	5.3	55.0
06	269 18.6	N 6 03.8	32 29.5	11.8	S17 48.6	5.2	55.0
07	284 18.8	04.7	47 00.3	11.9	17 53.8	5.2	55.0
08	299 19.0	05.7	61 31.2	11.9	17 59.0	5.0	55.0
09	314 19.1	.. 06.6	76 02.1	11.9	18 04.0	5.0	54.9
10	329 19.3	07.6	90 33.0	11.9	18 09.0	4.8	54.9
11	344 19.5	08.5	105 03.9	11.8	18 13.8	4.8	54.9
12	359 19.7	N 6 09.5	119 34.7	11.9	S18 18.6	4.7	54.9
13	14 19.9	10.4	134 05.6	11.8	18 23.3	4.6	54.9
14	29 20.0	11.4	148 36.4	11.9	18 27.9	4.5	54.8
15	44 20.2	.. 12.3	163 07.3	11.8	18 32.4	4.4	54.8
16	59 20.4	13.3	177 38.1	11.9	18 36.8	4.3	54.8
17	74 20.6	14.2	192 09.0	11.8	18 41.1	4.3	54.8
18	89 20.8	N 6 15.2	206 39.8	11.8	S18 45.4	4.1	54.8
19	104 20.9	16.1	221 10.6	11.8	18 49.5	4.1	54.8
20	119 21.1	17.1	235 41.4	11.9	18 53.6	3.9	54.7
21	134 21.3	.. 18.0	250 12.3	11.8	18 57.5	3.9	54.7
22	149 21.5	19.0	264 43.1	11.8	19 01.4	3.8	54.7
23	164 21.7	19.9	279 13.9	11.8	19 05.2	3.7	54.7
6 00	179 21.8	N 6 20.9	293 44.7	11.8	S19 08.9	3.5	54.7
01	194 22.0	21.8	308 15.5	11.8	19 12.4	3.5	54.7
02	209 22.2	22.7	322 46.3	11.8	19 15.9	3.4	54.6
03	224 22.4	.. 23.7	337 17.1	11.8	19 19.3	3.4	54.6
04	239 22.5	24.6	351 47.9	11.8	19 22.7	3.2	54.6
05	254 22.7	25.6	6 18.7	11.8	19 25.9	3.1	54.6
06	269 22.9	N 6 26.5	20 49.5	11.8	S19 29.0	3.0	54.6
07	284 23.1	27.5	35 20.3	11.8	19 32.0	3.0	54.6
08	299 23.3	28.4	49 51.1	11.8	19 35.0	2.8	54.6
09	314 23.4	.. 29.4	64 21.9	11.8	19 37.8	2.8	54.6
10	329 23.6	30.3	78 52.7	11.8	19 40.6	2.6	54.5
11	344 23.8	31.2	93 23.5	11.7	19 43.2	2.6	54.5
12	359 24.0	N 6 32.2	107 54.2	11.8	S19 45.8	2.5	54.5
13	14 24.1	33.1	122 25.0	11.8	19 48.3	2.3	54.5
14	29 24.3	34.1	136 55.8	11.8	19 50.6	2.3	54.5
15	44 24.5	.. 35.0	151 26.6	11.8	19 52.9	2.2	54.5
16	59 24.7	36.0	165 57.4	11.8	19 55.1	2.1	54.5
17	74 24.9	36.9	180 28.2	11.7	19 57.2	2.0	54.5
18	89 25.0	N 6 37.8	194 58.9	11.8	S19 59.2	1.9	54.4
19	104 25.2	38.8	209 29.7	11.8	20 01.1	1.8	54.4
20	119 25.4	39.7	224 00.5	11.8	20 02.9	1.7	54.4
21	134 25.6	.. 40.7	238 31.3	11.8	20 04.6	1.6	54.4
22	149 25.7	41.6	253 02.1	11.8	20 06.2	1.6	54.4
23	164 25.9	42.6	267 32.9	11.8	S20 07.8	1.4	54.4
	SD 16.0	d 0.9	SD 15.1		15.0		14.9

Days: WEDNESDAY (4), THURSDAY (5), FRIDAY (6)

Twilight, Sunrise, Moonrise

Lat.	Naut.	Civil	Sunrise	Moonrise 4	5	6	7
°	h m	h m	h m	h m	h m	h m	h m
N 72	00 16	03 16	04 35	00 29	02 56	▮▮	▮▮
N 70	01 46	03 36	04 45	25 42	01 42	03 36	▮▮
68	02 23	03 52	04 53	25 05	01 05	02 32	03 45
66	02 48	04 04	04 59	24 39	00 39	01 57	03 03
64	03 07	04 14	05 05	24 19	00 19	01 32	02 34
62	03 23	04 23	05 09	24 03	00 03	01 12	02 12
60	03 35	04 30	05 14	23 49	24 56	00 56	01 55
N 58	03 46	04 36	05 17	23 38	24 43	00 43	01 40
56	03 55	04 42	05 21	23 28	24 31	00 31	01 28
54	04 02	04 47	05 23	23 19	24 21	00 21	01 17
52	04 09	04 51	05 26	23 11	24 12	00 12	01 07
50	04 15	04 55	05 28	23 04	24 04	00 04	00 58
45	04 28	05 04	05 34	22 49	23 46	24 40	00 40
N 40	04 38	05 10	05 38	22 36	23 32	24 25	00 25
35	04 46	05 16	05 42	22 26	23 20	24 12	00 12
30	04 52	05 21	05 45	22 16	23 10	24 01	00 01
20	05 02	05 28	05 50	22 01	22 52	23 42	24 31
N 10	05 09	05 34	05 55	21 47	22 37	23 26	24 14
0	05 15	05 39	05 59	21 34	22 22	23 11	23 59
S 10	05 18	05 43	06 04	21 21	22 08	22 55	23 43
20	05 21	05 46	06 08	21 08	21 53	22 39	23 27
30	05 21	05 49	06 13	20 52	21 35	22 20	23 08
35	05 21	05 50	06 16	20 43	21 25	22 09	22 57
40	05 20	05 52	06 19	20 33	21 13	21 57	22 44
45	05 19	05 53	06 22	20 21	20 59	21 42	22 29
S 50	05 17	05 54	06 27	20 07	20 43	21 24	22 11
52	05 16	05 55	06 29	20 00	20 35	21 16	22 02
54	05 14	05 55	06 31	19 53	20 26	21 06	21 53
56	05 13	05 56	06 33	19 44	20 17	20 55	21 42
58	05 11	05 56	06 36	19 35	20 05	20 43	21 29
S 60	05 09	05 57	06 38	19 24	19 53	20 29	21 15

Sunset, Twilight, Moonset

Lat.	Sunset	Civil	Naut.	Moonset 4	5	6	7
°	h m	h m	h m	h m	h m	h m	h m
N 72	19 33	20 54	////	05 13	04 25	▮▮	▮▮
N 70	19 23	20 33	22 28	05 47	05 40	05 26	▮▮
68	19 15	20 17	21 48	06 12	06 18	06 30	06 58
66	19 08	20 04	21 21	06 31	06 44	07 06	07 41
64	19 03	19 54	21 01	06 46	07 05	07 31	08 09
62	18 58	19 45	20 46	06 59	07 22	07 51	08 31
60	18 53	19 37	20 33	07 11	07 36	08 08	08 49
N 58	18 50	19 31	20 22	07 20	07 48	08 21	09 03
56	18 46	19 25	20 13	07 29	07 58	08 33	09 14
54	18 43	19 20	20 05	07 36	08 07	08 44	09 27
52	18 40	19 15	19 58	07 43	08 15	08 53	09 37
50	18 38	19 11	19 51	07 49	08 23	09 01	09 45
45	18 33	19 03	19 38	08 02	08 39	09 19	10 04
N 40	18 28	18 56	19 28	08 13	08 52	09 33	10 19
35	18 24	18 50	19 20	08 23	09 03	09 46	10 32
30	18 21	18 45	19 14	08 31	09 12	09 56	10 43
20	18 15	18 38	19 04	08 45	09 29	10 15	11 02
N 10	18 10	18 32	18 56	08 58	09 44	10 31	11 18
0	18 06	18 27	18 51	09 09	09 57	10 46	11 34
S 10	18 02	18 23	18 47	09 21	10 11	11 01	11 49
20	17 57	18 19	18 45	09 34	10 26	11 17	12 05
30	17 52	18 16	18 44	09 48	10 42	11 35	12 25
35	17 49	18 14	18 44	09 56	10 52	11 46	12 36
40	17 46	18 13	18 44	10 06	11 03	11 58	12 49
45	17 42	18 12	18 45	10 17	11 17	12 12	13 03
S 50	17 38	18 10	18 47	10 31	11 33	12 30	13 22
52	17 36	18 10	18 49	10 37	11 40	12 39	13 30
54	17 34	18 09	18 50	10 44	11 49	12 48	13 40
56	17 31	18 08	18 51	10 52	11 58	12 58	13 51
58	17 29	18 08	18 53	11 01	12 09	13 11	14 04
S 60	17 26	18 07	18 55	11 11	12 22	13 25	14 18

SUN and MOON

Day	Eqn. of Time 00h	Eqn. of Time 12h	Mer. Pass.	Mer. Pass. Upper	Mer. Pass. Lower	Age	Phase
d	m s	m s	h m	h m	h m	d	%
4	03 08	02 59	12 03	02 58	15 22	18	83
5	02 50	02 42	12 03	03 46	16 10	19	76
6	02 33	02 24	12 02	04 34	16 58	20	67

2018 APRIL 7, 8, 9 (SAT., SUN., MON.)

UT	ARIES GHA	VENUS −3.9 GHA	Dec	MARS +0.1 GHA	Dec	JUPITER −2.4 GHA	Dec	SATURN +0.5 GHA	Dec	STARS Name	SHA	Dec
7 00	195 13.1	159 09.3	N14 04.5	272 52.4	S23 27.3	325 20.0	S17 02.0	275 26.2	S22 14.7	Acamar	315 16.3	S40 14.3
01	210 15.5	174 08.8	05.6	287 53.4	27.3	340 22.7	02.0	290 28.6	14.7	Achernar	335 25.0	S57 08.9
02	225 18.0	189 08.3	06.7	302 54.4	27.3	355 25.3	01.9	305 31.0	14.7	Acrux	173 04.9	S63 12.0
03	240 20.5	204 07.8 ..	07.8	317 55.4 ..	27.2	10 28.0 ..	01.8	320 33.5 ..	14.7	Adhara	255 10.0	S29 00.2
04	255 22.9	219 07.3	08.9	332 56.4	27.2	25 30.7	01.8	335 35.9	14.7	Aldebaran	290 45.9	N16 32.5
05	270 25.4	234 06.8	09.9	347 57.4	27.1	40 33.4	01.7	350 38.3	14.7			
06	285 27.9	249 06.3	N14 11.0	2 58.4	S23 27.1	55 36.0	S17 01.7	5 40.7	S22 14.7	Alioth	166 17.3	N55 51.7
07	300 30.3	264 05.8	12.1	17 59.4	27.0	70 38.7	01.6	20 43.1	14.7	Alkaid	152 55.9	N49 13.4
S 08	315 32.8	279 05.3	13.2	33 00.4	27.0	85 41.4	01.5	35 45.5	14.7	Al Na'ir	27 40.0	S46 52.3
A 09	330 35.3	294 04.8 ..	14.3	48 01.4 ..	26.9	100 44.1 ..	01.5	50 48.0 ..	14.7	Alnilam	275 43.2	S 1 11.7
T 10	345 37.7	309 04.3	15.4	63 02.4	26.9	115 46.8	01.4	65 50.4	14.7	Alphard	217 52.7	S 8 44.5
U 11	0 40.2	324 03.8	16.4	78 03.4	26.8	130 49.4	01.4	80 52.8	14.7			
R 12	15 42.6	339 03.3	N14 17.5	93 04.4	S23 26.8	145 52.1	S17 01.3	95 55.2	S22 14.7	Alphecca	126 08.0	N26 39.2
D 13	30 45.1	354 02.8	18.6	108 05.4	26.7	160 54.8	01.3	110 57.6	14.7	Alpheratz	357 40.5	N29 11.2
A 14	45 47.6	9 02.3	19.7	123 06.4	26.7	175 57.5	01.2	126 00.0	14.7	Altair	62 05.1	N 8 54.9
Y 15	60 50.0	24 01.8 ..	20.8	138 07.4 ..	26.7	191 00.2 ..	01.1	141 02.5 ..	14.7	Ankaa	353 12.9	S42 12.6
16	75 52.5	39 01.3	21.9	153 08.4	26.6	206 02.9	01.1	156 04.9	14.7	Antares	112 22.0	S26 28.2
17	90 55.0	54 00.8	22.9	168 09.4	26.6	221 05.5	01.0	171 07.3	14.7			
18	105 57.4	69 00.3	N14 24.0	183 10.4	S23 26.5	236 08.2	S17 01.0	186 09.7	S22 14.7	Arcturus	145 52.5	N19 05.3
19	120 59.9	83 59.8	25.1	198 11.4	26.5	251 10.9	00.9	201 12.1	14.7	Atria	107 20.6	S69 03.2
20	136 02.4	98 59.3	26.2	213 12.4	26.4	266 13.6	00.9	216 14.6	14.6	Avior	234 16.5	S59 34.5
21	151 04.8	113 58.8 ..	27.3	228 13.4 ..	26.4	281 16.2 ..	00.8	231 17.0 ..	14.6	Bellatrix	278 28.7	N 6 21.7
22	166 07.3	128 58.3	28.3	243 14.4	26.3	296 18.9	00.7	246 19.4	14.6	Betelgeuse	270 57.9	N 7 24.4
23	181 09.7	143 57.8	29.4	258 15.4	26.3	311 21.6	00.7	261 21.8	14.6			
8 00	196 12.2	158 57.3	N14 30.5	273 16.4	S23 26.2	326 24.3	S17 00.6	276 24.2	S22 14.6	Canopus	263 54.8	S52 42.8
01	211 14.7	173 56.7	31.6	288 17.4	26.2	341 27.0	00.6	291 26.6	14.6	Capella	280 29.9	N46 00.9
02	226 17.1	188 56.2	32.6	303 18.4	26.1	356 29.7	00.5	306 29.1	14.6	Deneb	49 29.4	N45 20.5
03	241 19.6	203 55.7 ..	33.7	318 19.4 ..	26.1	11 32.3 ..	00.4	321 31.5 ..	14.6	Denebola	182 30.1	N14 28.2
04	256 22.1	218 55.2	34.8	333 20.4	26.0	26 35.0	00.4	336 33.9	14.6	Diphda	348 53.0	S17 53.4
05	271 24.5	233 54.7	35.8	348 21.4	26.0	41 37.7	00.3	351 36.3	14.6			
06	286 27.0	248 54.2	N14 36.9	3 22.4	S23 25.9	56 40.4	S17 00.3	6 38.7	S22 14.6	Dubhe	193 47.3	N61 39.3
07	301 29.5	263 53.7	38.0	18 23.4	25.9	71 43.1	00.2	21 41.2	14.6	Elnath	278 08.7	N28 37.2
S 08	316 31.9	278 53.2	39.1	33 24.4	25.8	86 45.8	00.1	36 43.6	14.6	Eltanin	90 44.5	N51 29.0
U 09	331 34.4	293 52.7 ..	40.1	48 25.4 ..	25.8	101 48.4 ..	00.1	51 46.0 ..	14.6	Enif	33 44.1	N 9 57.4
N 10	346 36.9	308 52.2	41.2	63 26.4	25.7	116 51.1	00.0	66 48.4	14.6	Fomalhaut	15 20.7	S29 31.6
D 11	1 39.3	323 51.6	42.3	78 27.4	25.7	131 53.8	17 00.0	81 50.8	14.6			
A 12	16 41.8	338 51.1	N14 43.3	93 28.4	S23 25.6	146 56.5	S16 59.9	96 53.3	S22 14.6	Gacrux	171 56.7	S57 12.9
Y 13	31 44.2	353 50.6	44.4	108 29.4	25.6	161 59.2	59.8	111 55.7	14.6	Gienah	175 48.6	S17 38.6
14	46 46.7	8 50.1	45.5	123 30.4	25.5	177 01.9	59.8	126 58.1	14.6	Hadar	148 42.6	S60 27.5
15	61 49.2	23 49.6 ..	46.5	138 31.4 ..	25.5	192 04.6 ..	59.7	142 00.5 ..	14.6	Hamal	327 57.4	N23 32.7
16	76 51.6	38 49.1	47.6	153 32.4	25.4	207 07.2	59.7	157 03.0	14.6	Kaus Aust.	83 39.4	S34 22.3
17	91 54.1	53 48.6	48.7	168 33.5	25.4	222 09.9	59.6	172 05.4	14.6			
18	106 56.6	68 48.1	N14 49.7	183 34.5	S23 25.3	237 12.6	S16 59.5	187 07.8	S22 14.6	Kochab	137 19.1	N74 04.8
19	121 59.0	83 47.5	50.8	198 35.5	25.3	252 15.3	59.5	202 10.2	14.6	Markab	13 35.4	N15 18.0
20	137 01.5	98 47.0	51.9	213 36.5	25.2	267 18.0	59.4	217 12.6	14.6	Menkar	314 11.9	N 4 09.4
21	152 04.0	113 46.5 ..	52.9	228 37.5 ..	25.2	282 20.7 ..	59.4	232 15.1 ..	14.6	Menkent	148 03.3	S36 27.5
22	167 06.4	128 46.0	54.0	243 38.5	25.1	297 23.4	59.3	247 17.5	14.6	Miaplacidus	221 38.5	S69 47.9
23	182 08.9	143 45.5	55.0	258 39.5	25.1	312 26.0	59.2	262 19.9	14.6			
9 00	197 11.4	158 45.0	N14 56.1	273 40.5	S23 25.0	327 28.7	S16 59.2	277 22.3	S22 14.6	Mirfak	308 36.1	N49 55.4
01	212 13.8	173 44.4	57.2	288 41.5	24.9	342 31.4	59.1	292 24.8	14.6	Nunki	75 54.3	S26 16.3
02	227 16.3	188 43.9	58.2	303 42.5	24.9	357 34.1	59.1	307 27.2	14.6	Peacock	53 14.4	S56 40.3
03	242 18.7	203 43.4	14 59.3	318 43.5 ..	24.8	12 36.8 ..	59.0	322 29.6 ..	14.5	Pollux	243 23.8	N27 58.8
04	257 21.2	218 42.9	15 00.3	333 44.5	24.8	27 39.5	58.9	337 32.0	14.5	Procyon	244 56.3	N 5 10.5
05	272 23.7	233 42.4	01.4	348 45.6	24.7	42 42.2	58.9	352 34.5	14.5			
06	287 26.1	248 41.8	N15 02.5	3 46.6	S23 24.7	57 44.9	S16 58.8	7 36.9	S22 14.5	Rasalhague	96 03.3	N12 32.8
07	302 28.6	263 41.3	03.5	18 47.6	24.6	72 47.6	58.8	22 39.3	14.5	Regulus	207 39.9	N11 52.6
M 08	317 31.1	278 40.8	04.6	33 48.6	24.6	87 50.3	58.7	37 41.7	14.5	Rigel	281 09.1	S 8 11.2
O 09	332 33.5	293 40.3 ..	05.6	48 49.6 ..	24.5	102 52.9 ..	58.6	52 44.2 ..	14.5	Rigil Kent.	139 46.7	S60 54.4
N 10	347 36.0	308 39.8	06.7	63 50.6	24.5	117 55.6	58.6	67 46.6	14.5	Sabik	102 08.6	S15 44.7
N 11	2 38.5	323 39.2	07.7	78 51.6	24.4	132 58.3	58.5	82 49.0	14.5			
D 12	17 40.9	338 38.7	N15 08.8	93 52.6	S23 24.4	148 01.0	S16 58.5	97 51.4	S22 14.5	Schedar	349 37.3	N56 38.0
A 13	32 43.4	353 38.2	09.8	108 53.6	24.3	163 03.7	58.4	112 53.9	14.5	Shaula	96 17.3	S37 06.7
Y 14	47 45.9	8 37.7	10.9	123 54.7	24.3	178 06.4	58.3	127 56.3	14.5	Sirius	258 30.9	S16 44.8
15	62 48.3	23 37.1 ..	11.9	138 55.7 ..	24.2	193 09.1 ..	58.3	142 58.7 ..	14.5	Spica	158 27.5	S11 15.4
16	77 50.8	38 36.6	13.0	153 56.7	24.1	208 11.8	58.2	158 01.1	14.5	Suhail	222 49.8	S43 30.7
17	92 53.2	53 36.1	14.0	168 57.7	24.1	223 14.5	58.2	173 03.6	14.5			
18	107 55.7	68 35.6	N15 15.1	183 58.7	S23 24.0	238 17.2	S16 58.1	188 06.0	S22 14.5	Vega	80 36.7	N38 47.9
19	122 58.2	83 35.0	16.1	198 59.7	24.0	253 19.9	58.0	203 08.4	14.5	Zuben'ubi	137 01.5	S16 07.0
20	138 00.6	98 34.5	17.2	214 00.7	23.9	268 22.6	58.0	218 10.9	14.5			
21	153 03.1	113 34.0 ..	18.2	229 01.8 ..	23.9	283 25.2 ..	57.9	233 13.3 ..	14.5		SHA	Mer.Pass.
22	168 05.6	128 33.5	19.3	244 02.8	23.8	298 27.9	57.8	248 15.7	14.5	Venus	322 45.0	13 25
23	183 08.0	143 32.9	20.3	259 03.8	23.8	313 30.6	57.8	263 18.1	14.5	Mars	77 04.2	5 47
Mer. Pass. 10 53.4		v −0.5	d 1.1	v 1.0	d 0.1	v 2.7	d 0.1	v 2.4	d 0.0	Jupiter	130 12.1	2 14
										Saturn	80 12.0	5 33

UT	SUN GHA	Dec	MOON GHA	v	Dec	d	HP
d h	° ′	° ′	° ′	′	° ′	′	′
7 00	179 26.1	N 6 43.5	282 03.7	11.8	S20 09.2	1.3	54.4
01	194 26.3	44.4	296 34.5	11.8	20 10.5	1.3	54.4
02	209 26.4	45.4	311 05.3	11.8	20 11.8	1.1	54.4
03	224 26.6	.. 46.3	325 36.1	11.8	20 12.9	1.1	54.4
04	239 26.8	47.3	340 06.9	11.8	20 14.0	0.9	54.4
05	254 27.0	48.2	354 37.7	11.8	20 14.9	0.9	54.3
06	269 27.1	N 6 49.1	9 08.5	11.8	S20 15.8	0.7	54.3
S 07	284 27.3	50.1	23 39.3	11.8	20 16.5	0.7	54.3
A 08	299 27.5	51.0	38 10.1	11.8	20 17.2	0.6	54.3
T 09	314 27.7	.. 52.0	52 40.9	11.9	20 17.8	0.5	54.3
U 10	329 27.8	52.9	67 11.8	11.8	20 18.3	0.4	54.3
R 11	344 28.0	53.8	81 42.6	11.8	20 18.7	0.2	54.3
D 12	359 28.2	N 6 54.8	96 13.4	11.9	S20 18.9	0.2	54.3
A 13	14 28.4	55.7	110 44.3	11.8	20 19.1	0.1	54.3
Y 14	29 28.5	56.7	125 15.1	11.9	20 19.2	0.1	54.3
15	44 28.7	.. 57.6	139 46.0	11.8	20 19.3	0.1	54.3
16	59 28.9	58.5	154 16.8	11.9	20 19.2	0.2	54.3
17	74 29.1	6 59.5	168 47.7	11.9	20 19.0	0.3	54.3
18	89 29.2	N 7 00.4	183 18.6	11.9	S20 18.7	0.4	54.3
19	104 29.4	01.3	197 49.5	11.8	20 18.3	0.4	54.3
20	119 29.6	02.3	212 20.3	11.9	20 17.9	0.6	54.3
21	134 29.8	.. 03.2	226 51.2	11.9	20 17.3	0.6	54.3
22	149 29.9	04.2	241 22.1	12.0	20 16.7	0.8	54.3
23	164 30.1	05.1	255 53.1	11.9	20 15.9	0.8	54.3
8 00	179 30.3	N 7 06.0	270 24.0	11.9	S20 15.1	1.0	54.3
01	194 30.5	07.0	284 54.9	11.9	20 14.1	1.1	54.3
02	209 30.6	07.9	299 25.8	12.0	20 13.1	1.1	54.3
03	224 30.8	.. 08.8	313 56.8	11.9	20 12.0	1.2	54.3
04	239 31.0	09.8	328 27.7	12.0	20 10.8	1.3	54.3
05	254 31.2	10.7	342 58.7	12.0	20 09.5	1.4	54.3
06	269 31.3	N 7 11.6	357 29.7	11.9	S20 08.1	1.5	54.3
07	284 31.5	12.6	12 00.6	12.0	20 06.6	1.6	54.3
S 08	299 31.7	13.5	26 31.6	12.0	20 05.0	1.7	54.3
U 09	314 31.9	.. 14.4	41 02.6	12.0	20 03.3	1.8	54.3
N 10	329 32.0	15.4	55 33.6	12.1	20 01.5	1.8	54.3
D 11	344 32.2	16.3	70 04.7	12.0	19 59.7	2.0	54.3
A 12	359 32.4	N 7 17.2	84 35.7	12.0	S19 57.7	2.0	54.3
Y 13	14 32.5	18.2	99 06.7	12.1	19 55.7	2.2	54.3
14	29 32.7	19.1	113 37.8	12.0	19 53.5	2.2	54.3
15	44 32.9	.. 20.0	128 08.8	12.1	19 51.3	2.4	54.3
16	59 33.1	21.0	142 39.9	12.1	19 48.9	2.4	54.3
17	74 33.2	21.9	157 11.0	12.1	19 46.5	2.5	54.3
18	89 33.4	N 7 22.8	171 42.1	12.1	S19 44.0	2.6	54.3
19	104 33.6	23.8	186 13.2	12.1	19 41.4	2.7	54.3
20	119 33.7	24.7	200 44.3	12.2	19 38.7	2.8	54.3
21	134 33.9	.. 25.6	215 15.5	12.1	19 35.9	2.8	54.3
22	149 34.1	26.6	229 46.6	12.2	19 33.1	3.0	54.3
23	164 34.3	27.5	244 17.8	12.2	19 30.1	3.1	54.3
9 00	179 34.4	N 7 28.4	258 49.0	12.1	S19 27.0	3.1	54.3
01	194 34.6	29.4	273 20.1	12.2	19 23.9	3.2	54.3
02	209 34.8	30.3	287 51.3	12.3	19 20.7	3.4	54.3
03	224 34.9	.. 31.2	302 22.6	12.2	19 17.3	3.4	54.3
04	239 35.1	32.2	316 53.8	12.2	19 13.9	3.5	54.3
05	254 35.3	33.1	331 25.0	12.3	19 10.4	3.6	54.3
06	269 35.5	N 7 34.0	345 56.3	12.2	S19 06.8	3.7	54.3
07	284 35.6	34.9	0 27.5	12.3	19 03.1	3.7	54.4
08	299 35.8	35.9	14 58.8	12.3	18 59.4	3.9	54.4
M 09	314 36.0	.. 36.8	29 30.1	12.3	18 55.5	4.0	54.4
O 10	329 36.1	37.7	44 01.4	12.3	18 51.5	4.0	54.4
N 11	344 36.3	38.7	58 32.7	12.4	18 47.5	4.1	54.4
D 12	359 36.5	N 7 39.6	73 04.1	12.3	S18 43.4	4.2	54.4
A 13	14 36.6	40.5	87 35.4	12.4	18 39.2	4.3	54.4
Y 14	29 36.8	41.5	102 06.8	12.3	18 34.9	4.4	54.4
15	44 37.0	.. 42.4	116 38.1	12.4	18 30.5	4.5	54.4
16	59 37.2	43.3	131 09.5	12.4	18 26.0	4.5	54.4
17	74 37.3	44.2	145 40.9	12.5	18 21.5	4.7	54.4
18	89 37.5	N 7 45.2	160 12.4	12.4	S18 16.8	4.7	54.5
19	104 37.7	46.1	174 43.8	12.4	18 12.1	4.8	54.5
20	119 37.8	47.0	189 15.2	12.5	18 07.3	4.9	54.5
21	134 38.0	.. 47.9	203 46.7	12.5	18 02.4	5.0	54.5
22	149 38.2	48.9	218 18.2	12.5	17 57.4	5.1	54.5
23	164 38.3	49.8	232 49.7	12.5	S17 52.3	5.1	54.5
	SD 16.0	d 0.9	SD 14.8		14.8		14.8

Lat.	Twilight Naut.	Civil	Sunrise	Moonrise 7	8	9	10
°	h m	h m	h m	h m	h m	h m	h m
N 72	////	02 55	04 19	■■■	■■■	■■■	06 36
N 70	01 10	03 19	04 30	■■■	■■■	05 49	05 38
68	02 01	03 37	04 40	03 45	04 31	04 54	05 04
66	02 31	03 51	04 48	03 03	03 50	04 21	04 39
64	02 53	04 02	04 54	02 34	03 22	03 56	04 20
62	03 10	04 12	05 00	02 12	03 01	03 37	04 04
60	03 24	04 20	05 05	01 55	02 43	03 21	03 51
N 58	03 36	04 28	05 09	01 40	02 28	03 08	03 39
56	03 45	04 34	05 13	01 28	02 16	02 56	03 29
54	03 54	04 39	05 16	01 17	02 05	02 46	03 20
52	04 02	04 44	05 19	01 07	01 55	02 37	03 13
50	04 08	04 49	05 22	00 58	01 47	02 29	03 05
45	04 22	04 58	05 28	00 40	01 28	02 12	02 50
N 40	04 33	05 06	05 33	00 25	01 13	01 58	02 38
35	04 41	05 12	05 38	00 12	01 01	01 46	02 27
30	04 49	05 17	05 41	00 01	00 50	01 35	02 18
20	05 00	05 26	05 48	24 31	00 31	01 17	02 01
N 10	05 08	05 32	05 53	24 14	00 14	01 01	01 47
0	05 14	05 38	05 59	23 59	24 47	00 47	01 34
S 10	05 18	05 42	06 04	23 43	24 32	00 32	01 21
20	05 21	05 47	06 09	23 27	24 16	00 16	01 06
30	05 23	05 51	06 15	23 08	23 58	24 50	00 50
35	05 23	05 53	06 18	22 57	23 48	24 41	00 41
40	05 23	05 55	06 22	22 44	23 35	24 30	00 30
45	05 23	05 57	06 26	22 29	23 21	24 17	00 17
S 50	05 21	05 59	06 31	22 11	23 04	24 01	00 01
52	05 21	06 00	06 34	22 02	22 56	23 54	24 57
54	05 20	06 01	06 36	21 53	22 46	23 46	24 50
56	05 19	06 03	06 39	21 42	22 36	23 37	24 43
58	05 17	06 03	06 42	21 29	22 24	23 26	24 34
S 60	05 16	06 04	06 46	21 15	22 10	23 14	24 25

Lat.	Sunset	Twilight Civil	Naut.	Moonset 7	8	9	10
°	h m	h m	h m	h m	h m	h m	h m
N 72	19 48	21 14	////	■■■	■■■	■■■	09 05
N 70	19 36	20 49	23 08	■■■	■■■	08 14	10 02
68	19 26	20 30	22 10	06 58	07 52	09 08	10 36
66	19 18	20 16	21 38	07 41	08 33	09 41	11 00
64	19 12	20 04	21 15	08 09	09 01	10 05	11 19
62	19 06	19 54	20 57	08 31	09 22	10 24	11 34
60	19 01	19 45	20 42	08 49	09 39	10 40	11 47
N 58	18 56	19 38	20 30	09 03	09 54	10 53	11 58
56	18 52	19 31	20 20	09 16	10 06	11 04	12 08
54	18 49	19 26	20 11	09 27	10 17	11 14	12 16
52	18 46	19 21	20 04	09 37	10 27	11 23	12 24
50	18 43	19 16	19 57	09 45	10 35	11 31	12 30
45	18 36	19 07	19 43	10 04	10 54	11 47	12 45
N 40	18 31	18 59	19 32	10 19	11 08	12 01	12 57
35	18 27	18 52	19 23	10 32	11 21	12 13	13 07
30	18 23	18 47	19 16	10 43	11 32	12 23	13 16
20	18 16	18 38	19 05	11 02	11 51	12 40	13 31
N 10	18 10	18 32	18 56	11 18	12 07	12 55	13 44
0	18 05	18 26	18 50	11 34	12 22	13 10	13 57
S 10	18 00	18 21	18 46	11 49	12 37	13 24	14 09
20	17 55	18 17	18 42	12 06	12 53	13 39	14 22
30	17 49	18 13	18 40	12 25	13 12	13 56	14 37
35	17 45	18 10	18 40	12 36	13 23	14 06	14 45
40	17 41	18 08	18 40	12 49	13 35	14 17	14 55
45	17 37	18 06	18 40	13 03	13 49	14 30	15 07
S 50	17 32	18 04	18 41	13 22	14 07	14 47	15 21
52	17 29	18 03	18 42	13 30	14 16	14 54	15 27
54	17 27	18 02	18 43	13 40	14 25	15 03	15 34
56	17 24	18 01	18 44	13 51	14 35	15 12	15 42
58	17 20	18 00	18 45	14 04	14 47	15 23	15 51
S 60	17 17	17 59	18 47	14 18	15 01	15 35	16 01

	SUN Eqn. of Time 00h	12h	Mer. Pass.	MOON Mer. Pass. Upper	Lower	Age	Phase
Day	m s	m s	h m	h m	h m	d	%
7	02 16	02 08	12 02	05 22	17 46	21	58
8	01 59	01 51	12 02	06 10	18 34	22	48
9	01 43	01 34	12 02	06 58	19 22	23	39

UT	ARIES	VENUS −3·9		MARS +0·1		JUPITER −2·4		SATURN +0·4		STARS		
	GHA	GHA	Dec	GHA	Dec	GHA	Dec	GHA	Dec	Name	SHA	Dec
d h	° ′	° ′	° ′	° ′	° ′	° ′	° ′	° ′	° ′		° ′	° ′
10 00	198 10.5	158 32.4	N15 21.4	274 04.8	S23 23.7	328 33.3	S16 57.7	278 20.6	S22 14.5	Acamar	315 16.3	S40 14.2
01	213 13.0	173 31.9	22.4	289 05.8	23.6	343 36.0	57.7	293 23.0	14.5	Achernar	335 25.0	S57 08.9
02	228 15.4	188 31.3	23.4	304 06.8	23.6	358 38.7	57.6	308 25.4	14.5	Acrux	173 04.9	S63 12.1
03	243 17.9	203 30.8 . .	24.5	319 07.9 . .	23.5	13 41.4 . .	57.5	323 27.9 . .	14.5	Adhara	255 10.0	S29 00.2
04	258 20.3	218 30.3	25.5	334 08.9	23.5	28 44.1	57.5	338 30.3	14.5	Aldebaran	290 45.9	N16 32.5
05	273 22.8	233 29.8	26.6	349 09.9	23.4	43 46.8	57.4	353 32.7	14.5			
06	288 25.3	248 29.2	N15 27.6	4 10.9	S23 23.4	58 49.5	S16 57.3	8 35.1	S22 14.5	Alioth	166 17.3	N55 51.7
07	303 27.7	263 28.7	28.7	19 11.9	23.3	73 52.2	57.3	23 37.6	14.5	Alkaid	152 55.9	N49 13.4
08	318 30.2	278 28.2	29.7	34 12.9	23.2	88 54.9	57.2	38 40.0	14.5	Al Na'ir	27 40.0	S46 52.3
09	333 32.7	293 27.6 . .	30.7	49 14.0 . .	23.2	103 57.6 . .	57.2	53 42.4 . .	14.5	Alnilam	275 43.2	S 1 11.7
10	348 35.1	308 27.1	31.8	64 15.0	23.1	119 00.3	57.1	68 44.9	14.5	Alphard	217 52.7	S 8 44.5
11	3 37.6	323 26.6	32.8	79 16.0	23.1	134 03.0	57.0	83 47.3	14.5			
12	18 40.1	338 26.0	N15 33.8	94 17.0	S23 23.0	149 05.7	S16 57.0	98 49.7	S22 14.5	Alphecca	126 08.0	N26 39.2
13	33 42.5	353 25.5	34.9	109 18.0	23.0	164 08.4	56.9	113 52.1	14.5	Alpheratz	357 40.5	N29 11.2
14	48 45.0	8 25.0	35.9	124 19.1	22.9	179 11.1	56.9	128 54.6	14.4	Altair	62 05.1	N 8 54.9
15	63 47.5	23 24.4 . .	37.0	139 20.1 . .	22.8	194 13.8 . .	56.8	143 57.0 . .	14.4	Ankaa	353 12.9	S42 12.5
16	78 49.9	38 23.9	38.0	154 21.1	22.8	209 16.5	56.7	158 59.4	14.4	Antares	112 22.0	S26 28.2
17	93 52.4	53 23.4	39.0	169 22.1	22.7	224 19.2	56.7	174 01.9	14.4			
18	108 54.8	68 22.8	N15 40.1	184 23.1	S23 22.7	239 21.9	S16 56.6	189 04.3	S22 14.4	Arcturus	145 52.5	N19 05.3
19	123 57.3	83 22.3	41.1	199 24.2	22.6	254 24.6	56.5	204 06.7	14.4	Atria	107 20.6	S69 03.2
20	138 59.8	98 21.8	42.1	214 25.2	22.5	269 27.3	56.5	219 09.2	14.4	Avior	234 16.5	S59 34.5
21	154 02.2	113 21.2 . .	43.2	229 26.2 . .	22.5	284 30.0 . .	56.4	234 11.6 . .	14.4	Bellatrix	278 28.7	N 6 21.7
22	169 04.7	128 20.7	44.2	244 27.2	22.4	299 32.7	56.3	249 14.0	14.4	Betelgeuse	270 57.9	N 7 24.4
23	184 07.2	143 20.1	45.2	259 28.2	22.4	314 35.4	56.3	264 16.5	14.4			
11 00	199 09.6	158 19.6	N15 46.2	274 29.3	S23 22.3	329 38.1	S16 56.2	279 18.9	S22 14.4	Canopus	263 54.9	S52 42.8
01	214 12.1	173 19.1	47.3	289 30.3	22.2	344 40.8	56.2	294 21.3	14.4	Capella	280 29.9	N46 00.9
02	229 14.6	188 18.5	48.3	304 31.3	22.2	359 43.5	56.1	309 23.8	14.4	Deneb	49 29.4	N45 20.5
03	244 17.0	203 18.0 . .	49.3	319 32.3 . .	22.1	14 46.2 . .	56.0	324 26.2 . .	14.4	Denebola	182 30.1	N14 28.2
04	259 19.5	218 17.4	50.3	334 33.4	22.1	29 48.9	56.0	339 28.6	14.4	Diphda	348 53.0	S17 53.4
05	274 21.9	233 16.9	51.4	349 34.4	22.0	44 51.6	55.9	354 31.1	14.4			
06	289 24.4	248 16.4	N15 52.4	4 35.4	S23 21.9	59 54.3	S16 55.8	9 33.5	S22 14.4	Dubhe	193 47.3	N61 39.3
07	304 26.9	263 15.8	53.4	19 36.4	21.9	74 57.0	55.7	24 35.9	14.4	Elnath	278 08.7	N28 37.2
08	319 29.3	278 15.3	54.4	34 37.5	21.8	89 59.7	55.7	39 38.4	14.4	Eltanin	90 44.4	N51 29.0
09	334 31.8	293 14.7 . .	55.5	49 38.5 . .	21.8	105 02.4 . .	55.7	54 40.8 . .	14.4	Enif	33 44.1	N 9 57.4
10	349 34.3	308 14.2	56.5	64 39.5	21.7	120 05.1	55.6	69 43.2	14.4	Fomalhaut	15 20.7	S29 31.6
11	4 36.7	323 13.7	57.5	79 40.5	21.6	135 07.8	55.5	84 45.7	14.4			
12	19 39.2	338 13.1	N15 58.5	94 41.6	S23 21.6	150 10.5	S16 55.5	99 48.1	S22 14.4	Gacrux	171 56.7	S57 13.0
13	34 41.7	353 12.6	15 59.6	109 42.6	21.5	165 13.2	55.4	114 50.5	14.4	Gienah	175 48.6	S17 38.7
14	49 44.1	8 12.0	16 00.6	124 43.6	21.5	180 15.9	55.3	129 53.0	14.4	Hadar	148 42.6	S60 27.5
15	64 46.6	23 11.5 . .	01.6	139 44.6 . .	21.4	195 18.6 . .	55.3	144 55.4 . .	14.4	Hamal	327 57.4	N23 32.7
16	79 49.1	38 10.9	02.6	154 45.7	21.3	210 21.3	55.2	159 57.8	14.4	Kaus Aust.	83 39.4	S34 22.3
17	94 51.5	53 10.4	03.6	169 46.7	21.3	225 24.0	55.1	175 00.3	14.4			
18	109 54.0	68 09.8	N16 04.6	184 47.7	S23 21.2	240 26.7	S16 55.1	190 02.7	S22 14.4	Kochab	137 19.1	N74 04.8
19	124 56.4	83 09.3	05.7	199 48.8	21.1	255 29.4	55.0	205 05.2	14.4	Markab	13 35.4	N15 18.0
20	139 58.9	98 08.7	06.7	214 49.8	21.1	270 32.1	54.9	220 07.6	14.4	Menkar	314 11.9	N 4 09.4
21	155 01.4	113 08.2 . .	07.7	229 50.8 . .	21.0	285 34.8 . .	54.9	235 10.0 . .	14.4	Menkent	148 03.3	S36 27.5
22	170 03.8	128 07.7	08.7	244 51.8	21.0	300 37.5	54.8	250 12.5	14.4	Miaplacidus	221 38.6	S69 47.9
23	185 06.3	143 07.1	09.7	259 52.9	20.9	315 40.2	54.8	265 14.9	14.4			
12 00	200 08.8	158 06.6	N16 10.7	274 53.9	S23 20.8	330 42.9	S16 54.7	280 17.3	S22 14.4	Mirfak	308 36.1	N49 55.4
01	215 11.2	173 06.0	11.7	289 54.9	20.8	345 45.6	54.6	295 19.8	14.4	Nunki	75 54.3	S26 16.3
02	230 13.7	188 05.5	12.7	304 56.0	20.7	0 48.3	54.6	310 22.2	14.4	Peacock	53 14.3	S56 40.3
03	245 16.2	203 04.9 . .	13.8	319 57.0 . .	20.6	15 51.0 . .	54.5	325 24.6 . .	14.4	Pollux	243 23.8	N27 58.8
04	260 18.6	218 04.4	14.8	334 58.0	20.6	30 53.7	54.4	340 27.1	14.4	Procyon	244 56.3	N 5 10.5
05	275 21.1	233 03.8	15.8	349 59.1	20.5	45 56.5	54.4	355 29.5	14.4			
06	290 23.6	248 03.3	N16 16.8	5 00.1	S23 20.5	60 59.2	S16 54.3	10 32.0	S22 14.4	Rasalhague	96 03.3	N12 32.8
07	305 26.0	263 02.7	17.8	20 01.1	20.4	76 01.9	54.2	25 34.4	14.4	Regulus	207 39.9	N11 52.6
08	320 28.5	278 02.1	18.8	35 02.2	20.3	91 04.6	54.2	40 36.8	14.3	Rigel	281 09.1	S 8 11.2
09	335 30.9	293 01.6 . .	19.8	50 03.2 . .	20.3	106 07.3 . .	54.1	55 39.3 . .	14.3	Rigil Kent.	139 46.7	S60 54.4
10	350 33.4	308 01.0	20.8	65 04.2	20.2	121 10.0	54.0	70 41.7	14.3	Sabik	102 08.6	S15 44.7
11	5 35.9	323 00.5	21.8	80 05.3	20.1	136 12.7	54.0	85 44.2	14.3			
12	20 38.3	337 59.9	N16 22.8	95 06.3	S23 20.1	151 15.4	S16 53.9	100 46.6	S22 14.3	Schedar	349 37.3	N56 38.0
13	35 40.8	352 59.4	23.8	110 07.3	20.0	166 18.1	53.8	115 49.0	14.3	Shaula	96 17.3	S37 06.8
14	50 43.3	7 58.8	24.8	125 08.4	19.9	181 20.8	53.8	130 51.5	14.3	Sirius	258 30.9	S16 44.8
15	65 45.7	22 58.3 . .	25.8	140 09.4 . .	19.9	196 23.5 . .	53.7	145 53.9 . .	14.3	Spica	158 27.5	S11 15.4
16	80 48.2	37 57.7	26.8	155 10.4	19.8	211 26.2	53.6	160 56.4	14.3	Suhail	222 49.9	S43 30.7
17	95 50.7	52 57.2	27.8	170 11.5	19.7	226 29.0	53.6	175 58.8	14.3			
18	110 53.1	67 56.6	N16 28.8	185 12.5	S23 19.7	241 31.7	S16 53.5	191 01.2	S22 14.3	Vega	80 36.7	N38 47.9
19	125 55.6	82 56.0	29.8	200 13.5	19.6	256 34.4	53.5	206 03.7	14.3	Zuben'ubi	137 01.5	S16 07.0
20	140 58.0	97 55.5	30.8	215 14.6	19.6	271 37.1	53.4	221 06.1	14.3		SHA	Mer.Pass.
21	156 00.5	112 54.9 . .	31.8	230 15.6 . .	19.5	286 39.8 . .	53.3	236 08.6 . .	14.3		° ′	h m
22	171 03.0	127 54.4	32.8	245 16.6	19.4	301 42.5	53.3	251 11.0	14.3	Venus	319 10.0	13 27
23	186 05.4	142 53.8	33.8	260 17.7	19.4	316 45.2	53.2	266 13.4	14.3	Mars	75 19.6	5 42
Mer.Pass.	h m 10 41.6	v −0.5	d 1.0	v 1.0	d 0.1	v 2.7	d 0.1	v 2.4	d 0.0	Jupiter	130 28.4	2 01
										Saturn	80 09.3	5 22

SUN / MOON

UT (d h)	SUN GHA	SUN Dec	MOON GHA	v	MOON Dec	d	HP
10 00	179 38.5	N 7 50.7	247 21.2	12.5	S17 47.2	5.3	54.5
01	194 38.7	51.6	261 52.7	12.5	17 41.9	5.3	54.5
02	209 38.8	52.6	276 24.2	12.6	17 36.6	5.4	54.6
03	224 39.0 . .	53.5	290 55.8	12.5	17 31.2	5.5	54.6
04	239 39.2	54.4	305 27.3	12.6	17 25.7	5.5	54.6
05	254 39.3	55.3	319 58.9	12.6	17 20.2	5.7	54.6
06	269 39.5	N 7 56.3	334 30.5	12.6	S17 14.5	5.7	54.6
07	284 39.7	57.2	349 02.1	12.6	17 08.8	5.8	54.6
T 08	299 39.8	58.1	3 33.7	12.6	17 03.0	5.9	54.6
U 09	314 40.0	7 59.0	18 05.3	12.7	16 57.1	6.0	54.7
E 10	329 40.2	8 00.0	32 37.0	12.6	16 51.1	6.1	54.7
S 11	344 40.3	00.9	47 08.6	12.7	16 45.0	6.1	54.7
D 12	359 40.5	N 8 01.8	61 40.3	12.7	S16 38.9	6.2	54.7
A 13	14 40.7	02.7	76 12.0	12.7	16 32.7	6.3	54.7
Y 14	29 40.8	03.7	90 43.7	12.7	16 26.4	6.4	54.7
15	44 41.0 . .	04.6	105 15.4	12.7	16 20.0	6.4	54.7
16	59 41.2	05.5	119 47.1	12.7	16 13.6	6.6	54.8
17	74 41.3	06.4	134 18.8	12.8	16 07.0	6.6	54.8
18	89 41.5	N 8 07.4	148 50.6	12.7	S16 00.4	6.7	54.8
19	104 41.7	08.3	163 22.3	12.8	15 53.7	6.7	54.8
20	119 41.8	09.2	177 54.1	12.8	15 47.0	6.9	54.8
21	134 42.0 . .	10.1	192 25.9	12.8	15 40.1	6.9	54.8
22	149 42.2	11.0	206 57.7	12.8	15 33.2	7.0	54.9
23	164 42.3	12.0	221 29.5	12.8	15 26.2	7.1	54.9
11 00	179 42.5	N 8 12.9	236 01.3	12.9	S15 19.1	7.1	54.9
01	194 42.7	13.8	250 33.2	12.8	15 12.0	7.2	54.9
02	209 42.8	14.7	265 05.0	12.9	15 04.8	7.3	54.9
03	224 43.0 . .	15.6	279 36.9	12.8	14 57.5	7.4	55.0
04	239 43.2	16.6	294 08.7	12.9	14 50.1	7.4	55.0
05	254 43.3	17.5	308 40.6	12.9	14 42.7	7.6	55.0
06	269 43.5	N 8 18.4	323 12.5	12.9	S14 35.1	7.5	55.0
W 07	284 43.7	19.3	337 44.4	12.9	14 27.6	7.7	55.0
E 08	299 43.8	20.2	352 16.3	12.9	14 19.9	7.7	55.1
D 09	314 44.0 . .	21.2	6 48.2	13.0	14 12.2	7.8	55.1
N 10	329 44.1	22.1	21 20.2	12.9	14 04.4	7.9	55.1
E 11	344 44.3	23.0	35 52.1	12.9	13 56.5	8.0	55.1
S 12	359 44.5	N 8 23.9	50 24.0	13.0	S13 48.5	8.0	55.1
D 13	14 44.6	24.8	64 56.0	13.0	13 40.5	8.0	55.2
A 14	29 44.8	25.7	79 28.0	12.9	13 32.5	8.2	55.2
Y 15	44 45.0 . .	26.7	93 59.9	13.0	13 24.3	8.2	55.2
16	59 45.1	27.6	108 31.9	13.0	13 16.1	8.3	55.3
17	74 45.3	28.5	123 03.9	13.0	13 07.8	8.4	55.3
18	89 45.5	N 8 29.4	137 35.9	13.0	S12 59.4	8.4	55.3
19	104 45.6	30.3	152 07.9	13.0	12 51.0	8.5	55.3
20	119 45.8	31.2	166 39.9	13.0	12 42.5	8.5	55.3
21	134 45.9 . .	32.2	181 11.9	13.0	12 34.0	8.7	55.3
22	149 46.1	33.1	195 43.9	13.0	12 25.3	8.6	55.4
23	164 46.3	34.0	210 15.9	13.1	12 16.7	8.8	55.4
12 00	179 46.4	N 8 34.9	224 48.0	13.0	S12 07.9	8.8	55.4
01	194 46.6	35.8	239 20.0	13.1	11 59.1	8.9	55.4
02	209 46.8	36.7	253 52.1	13.0	11 50.2	8.9	55.5
03	224 46.9 . .	37.6	268 24.1	13.0	11 41.3	9.0	55.5
04	239 47.1	38.6	282 56.1	13.1	11 32.3	9.1	55.5
05	254 47.2	39.5	297 28.2	13.0	11 23.2	9.1	55.5
06	269 47.4	N 8 40.4	312 00.2	13.1	S11 14.1	9.2	55.6
T 07	284 47.6	41.3	326 32.3	13.1	11 04.9	9.2	55.6
H 08	299 47.7	42.2	341 04.4	13.0	10 55.7	9.3	55.6
U 09	314 47.9 . .	43.1	355 36.4	13.1	10 46.4	9.4	55.6
R 10	329 48.0	44.0	10 08.5	13.0	10 37.0	9.4	55.7
S 11	344 48.2	44.9	24 40.5	13.1	10 27.6	9.5	55.7
D 12	359 48.4	N 8 45.9	39 12.6	13.1	S10 18.1	9.5	55.7
A 13	14 48.5	46.8	53 44.7	13.0	10 08.6	9.6	55.7
Y 14	29 48.7	47.7	68 16.7	13.1	9 59.0	9.7	55.8
15	44 48.8 . .	48.6	82 48.8	13.1	9 49.3	9.7	55.8
16	59 49.0	49.5	97 20.9	13.0	9 39.6	9.8	55.8
17	74 49.2	50.4	111 52.9	13.1	9 29.8	9.8	55.8
18	89 49.3	N 8 51.3	126 25.0	13.1	S 9 20.0	9.8	55.9
19	104 49.5	52.2	140 57.0	13.1	9 10.2	10.0	55.9
20	119 49.6	53.1	155 29.1	13.0	9 00.2	9.9	55.9
21	134 49.8 . .	54.0	170 01.1	13.1	8 50.3	10.1	56.0
22	149 50.0	55.0	184 33.2	13.0	8 40.2	10.0	56.0
23	164 50.1	55.9	199 05.2	13.0	S 8 30.2	10.2	56.0
	SD 16.0	d 0.9	SD 14.9		15.0		15.2

Twilight / Sunrise / Moonrise

Lat.	Twilight Naut.	Twilight Civil	Sunrise	Moonrise 10	11	12	13
N 72	////	02 33	04 02	06 36	06 02	05 45	05 32
N 70	////	03 01	04 16	05 38	05 32	05 26	05 21
68	01 34	03 22	04 27	05 04	05 09	05 11	05 12
66	02 12	03 38	04 36	04 39	04 51	04 59	05 05
64	02 37	03 51	04 44	04 20	04 36	04 49	04 58
62	02 57	04 02	04 50	04 04	04 24	04 40	04 53
60	03 12	04 11	04 56	03 51	04 14	04 32	04 48
N 58	03 25	04 19	05 01	03 39	04 05	04 26	04 44
56	03 36	04 26	05 05	03 29	03 57	04 20	04 40
54	03 46	04 32	05 09	03 20	03 49	04 15	04 37
52	03 54	04 37	05 13	03 13	03 43	04 10	04 34
50	04 01	04 42	05 16	03 05	03 37	04 05	04 31
45	04 16	04 52	05 23	02 50	03 25	03 56	04 25
N 40	04 28	05 01	05 29	02 38	03 14	03 48	04 20
35	04 37	05 08	05 34	02 27	03 05	03 41	04 15
30	04 45	05 14	05 38	02 18	02 57	03 35	04 12
20	04 57	05 23	05 45	02 01	02 44	03 25	04 05
N 10	05 06	05 31	05 52	01 47	02 32	03 16	03 59
0	05 13	05 37	05 58	01 34	02 21	03 07	03 53
S 10	05 18	05 42	06 04	01 21	02 10	02 58	03 48
20	05 22	05 48	06 10	01 06	01 58	02 49	03 42
30	05 25	05 52	06 17	00 50	01 44	02 39	03 35
35	05 26	05 55	06 20	00 41	01 36	02 33	03 31
40	05 26	05 58	06 25	00 30	01 27	02 26	03 26
45	05 26	06 00	06 30	00 17	01 16	02 17	03 21
S 50	05 26	06 03	06 36	00 01	01 03	02 08	03 15
52	05 26	06 05	06 39	24 57	00 57	02 03	03 12
54	05 25	06 06	06 42	24 50	00 50	01 58	03 09
56	05 24	06 07	06 45	24 43	00 43	01 53	03 05
58	05 24	06 09	06 49	24 34	00 34	01 46	03 01
S 60	05 23	06 11	06 53	24 25	00 25	01 39	02 57

Sunset / Twilight / Moonset

Lat.	Sunset	Twilight Civil	Twilight Naut.	Moonset 10	11	12	13
N 72	20 03	21 35	////	09 05	11 16	13 10	15 00
N 70	19 49	21 06	////	10 02	11 46	13 28	15 09
68	19 38	20 44	22 37	10 36	12 08	13 41	15 16
66	19 28	20 27	21 56	11 00	12 25	13 52	15 22
64	19 21	20 14	21 29	11 19	12 38	14 01	15 27
62	19 14	20 03	21 09	11 34	12 50	14 09	15 31
60	19 08	19 53	20 52	11 47	13 00	14 16	15 35
N 58	19 03	19 45	20 39	11 58	13 08	14 22	15 38
56	18 58	19 38	20 28	12 08	13 16	14 27	15 41
54	18 54	19 32	20 18	12 16	13 22	14 31	15 43
52	18 51	19 26	20 10	12 24	13 28	14 36	15 45
50	18 47	19 21	20 02	12 30	13 34	14 39	15 48
45	18 40	19 11	19 47	12 45	13 45	14 48	15 52
N 40	18 34	19 02	19 35	12 57	13 55	14 55	15 56
35	18 29	18 55	19 26	13 07	14 03	15 00	15 59
30	18 24	18 49	19 18	13 16	14 10	15 05	16 02
20	18 17	18 39	19 06	13 31	14 22	15 14	16 07
N 10	18 10	18 32	18 56	13 44	14 33	15 22	16 11
0	18 04	18 25	18 50	13 57	14 43	15 29	16 15
S 10	17 58	18 20	18 44	14 09	14 53	15 36	16 19
20	17 52	18 14	18 40	14 22	15 04	15 44	16 24
30	17 45	18 09	18 37	14 37	15 16	15 52	16 28
35	17 41	18 07	18 36	14 45	15 22	15 57	16 31
40	17 37	18 04	18 35	14 55	15 30	16 03	16 34
45	17 31	18 01	18 35	15 07	15 39	16 09	16 38
S 50	17 25	17 58	18 35	15 21	15 50	16 17	16 42
52	17 23	17 57	18 36	15 27	15 55	16 21	16 44
54	17 19	17 55	18 36	15 34	16 01	16 24	16 46
56	17 16	17 54	18 36	15 42	16 07	16 29	16 48
58	17 12	17 52	18 37	15 51	16 14	16 33	16 51
S 60	17 08	17 50	18 38	16 01	16 22	16 39	16 54

SUN / MOON

Day	SUN Eqn. of Time 00h	SUN Eqn. of Time 12h	SUN Mer. Pass.	MOON Mer. Pass. Upper	MOON Mer. Pass. Lower	Age	Phase
d	m s	m s	h m	h m	h m	d	%
10	01 26	01 18	12 01	07 45	20 09	24	30
11	01 10	01 02	12 01	08 32	20 55	25	21
12	00 55	00 47	12 01	09 18	21 41	26	14

UT (d h)	ARIES GHA	VENUS −3.9 GHA	Dec	MARS +0.0 GHA	Dec	JUPITER −2.4 GHA	Dec	SATURN +0.4 GHA	Dec	STARS Name	SHA	Dec
13 00	201 07.9	157 53.2	N16 34.8	275 18.7	S23 19.3	331 47.9	S16 53.1	281 15.9	S22 14.3	Acamar	315 16.3	S40 14.2
01	216 10.4	172 52.7	35.8	290 19.8	19.2	346 50.6	53.1	296 18.3	14.3	Achernar	335 25.0	S57 08.8
02	231 12.8	187 52.1	36.8	305 20.8	19.2	1 53.3	53.0	311 20.8	14.3	Acrux	173 04.9	S63 12.1
03	246 15.3	202 51.6 ..	37.8	320 21.8 ..	19.1	16 56.1 ..	52.9	326 23.2 ..	14.3	Adhara	255 10.0	S29 00.2
04	261 17.8	217 51.0	38.8	335 22.9	19.0	31 58.8	52.9	341 25.6	14.3	Aldebaran	290 45.9	N16 32.5
05	276 20.2	232 50.4	39.8	350 23.9	19.0	47 01.5	52.8	356 28.1	14.3			
06	291 22.7	247 49.9	N16 40.8	5 25.0	S23 18.9	62 04.2	S16 52.7	11 30.5	S22 14.3	Alioth	166 17.3	N55 51.7
07	306 25.2	262 49.3	41.8	20 26.0	18.8	77 06.9	52.7	26 33.0	14.3	Alkaid	152 55.9	N49 13.4
08	321 27.6	277 48.8	42.7	35 27.0	18.8	92 09.6	52.6	41 35.4	14.3	Al Na'ir	27 40.0	S46 52.2
F 09	336 30.1	292 48.2 ..	43.7	50 28.1 ..	18.7	107 12.3 ..	52.5	56 37.9 ..	14.3	Alnilam	275 43.2	S 1 11.7
R 10	351 32.5	307 47.6	44.7	65 29.1	18.6	122 15.0	52.5	71 40.3	14.3	Alphard	217 52.8	S 8 44.5
I 11	6 35.0	322 47.1	45.7	80 30.2	18.6	137 17.8	52.4	86 42.7	14.3			
D 12	21 37.5	337 46.5	N16 46.7	95 31.2	S23 18.5	152 20.5	S16 52.3	101 45.2	S22 14.3	Alphecca	126 08.0	N26 39.2
A 13	36 39.9	352 45.9	47.7	110 32.2	18.4	167 23.2	52.3	116 47.6	14.3	Alpheratz	357 40.4	N29 11.2
Y 14	51 42.4	7 45.4	48.7	125 33.3	18.3	182 25.9	52.2	131 50.1	14.3	Altair	62 05.1	N 8 54.9
15	66 44.9	22 44.8 ..	49.7	140 34.3 ..	18.3	197 28.6 ..	52.1	146 52.5 ..	14.3	Ankaa	353 12.9	S42 12.5
16	81 47.3	37 44.2	50.6	155 35.4	18.2	212 31.3	52.1	161 55.0	14.3	Antares	112 22.0	S26 28.2
17	96 49.8	52 43.7	51.6	170 36.4	18.1	227 34.0	52.0	176 57.4	14.3			
18	111 52.3	67 43.1	N16 52.6	185 37.4	S23 18.1	242 36.8	S16 51.9	191 59.9	S22 14.3	Arcturus	145 52.5	N19 05.3
19	126 54.7	82 42.5	53.6	200 38.5	18.0	257 39.5	51.9	207 02.3	14.3	Atria	107 20.5	S69 03.2
20	141 57.2	97 42.0	54.6	215 39.5	17.9	272 42.2	51.8	222 04.7	14.3	Avior	234 16.6	S59 34.5
21	156 59.6	112 41.4 ..	55.5	230 40.6 ..	17.9	287 44.9 ..	51.7	237 07.2 ..	14.3	Bellatrix	278 28.7	N 6 21.7
22	172 02.1	127 40.8	56.5	245 41.6	17.8	302 47.6	51.7	252 09.6	14.3	Betelgeuse	270 57.9	N 7 24.4
23	187 04.6	142 40.3	57.5	260 42.7	17.7	317 50.3	51.6	267 12.1	14.3			
14 00	202 07.0	157 39.7	N16 58.5	275 43.7	S23 17.7	332 53.1	S16 51.5	282 14.5	S22 14.3	Canopus	263 54.9	S52 42.8
01	217 09.5	172 39.1	16 59.5	290 44.8	17.6	347 55.8	51.5	297 17.0	14.3	Capella	280 29.9	N46 00.9
02	232 12.0	187 38.5	17 00.4	305 45.8	17.5	2 58.5	51.4	312 19.4	14.3	Deneb	49 29.4	N45 20.5
03	247 14.4	202 38.0 ..	01.4	320 46.9 ..	17.5	18 01.2 ..	51.3	327 21.9 ..	14.3	Denebola	182 30.1	N14 28.2
04	262 16.9	217 37.4	02.4	335 47.9	17.4	33 03.9	51.3	342 24.3	14.3	Diphda	348 53.0	S17 53.4
05	277 19.4	232 36.8	03.4	350 48.9	17.3	48 06.6	51.2	357 26.8	14.3			
06	292 21.8	247 36.3	N17 04.3	5 50.0	S23 17.2	63 09.4	S16 51.1	12 29.2	S22 14.3	Dubhe	193 47.3	N61 39.3
07	307 24.3	262 35.7	05.3	20 51.0	17.2	78 12.1	51.1	27 31.7	14.3	Elnath	278 08.7	N28 37.2
S 08	322 26.8	277 35.1	06.3	35 52.1	17.1	93 14.8	51.0	42 34.1	14.3	Eltanin	90 44.4	N51 29.0
A 09	337 29.2	292 34.5 ..	07.2	50 53.1 ..	17.0	108 17.5 ..	50.9	57 36.5 ..	14.3	Enif	33 44.1	N 9 57.4
T 10	352 31.7	307 34.0	08.2	65 54.2	17.0	123 20.2	50.8	72 39.0	14.3	Fomalhaut	15 20.7	S29 31.6
U 11	7 34.1	322 33.4	09.2	80 55.2	16.9	138 22.9	50.8	87 41.4	14.3			
R 12	22 36.6	337 32.8	N17 10.1	95 56.3	S23 16.8	153 25.7	S16 50.7	102 43.9	S22 14.3	Gacrux	171 56.7	S57 13.0
D 13	37 39.1	352 32.2	11.1	110 57.3	16.8	168 28.4	50.6	117 46.3	14.3	Gienah	175 48.6	S17 38.7
A 14	52 41.5	7 31.6	12.1	125 58.4	16.7	183 31.1	50.6	132 48.8	14.3	Hadar	148 42.6	S60 27.5
Y 15	67 44.0	22 31.1 ..	13.1	140 59.4 ..	16.6	198 33.8 ..	50.5	147 51.2 ..	14.3	Hamal	327 57.4	N23 32.7
16	82 46.5	37 30.5	14.0	156 00.5	16.5	213 36.5	50.4	162 53.7	14.2	Kaus Aust.	83 39.4	S34 22.3
17	97 48.9	52 29.9	15.0	171 01.5	16.5	228 39.3	50.4	177 56.1	14.2			
18	112 51.4	67 29.3	N17 15.9	186 02.6	S23 16.4	243 42.0	S16 50.3	192 58.6	S22 14.2	Kochab	137 19.1	N74 04.9
19	127 53.9	82 28.8	16.9	201 03.6	16.3	258 44.7	50.2	208 01.0	14.2	Markab	13 35.3	N15 18.0
20	142 56.3	97 28.2	17.9	216 04.7	16.3	273 47.4	50.2	223 03.5	14.2	Menkar	314 12.0	N 4 09.4
21	157 58.8	112 27.6 ..	18.8	231 05.7 ..	16.2	288 50.1 ..	50.1	238 05.9 ..	14.2	Menkent	148 03.3	S36 27.5
22	173 01.2	127 27.0	19.8	246 06.8	16.1	303 52.9	50.0	253 08.4	14.2	Miaplacidus	221 38.6	S69 47.9
23	188 03.7	142 26.4	20.8	261 07.8	16.0	318 55.6	50.0	268 10.8	14.2			
15 00	203 06.2	157 25.9	N17 21.7	276 08.9	S23 16.0	333 58.3	S16 49.9	283 13.3	S22 14.2	Mirfak	308 36.1	N49 55.4
01	218 08.6	172 25.3	22.7	291 09.9	15.9	349 01.0	49.8	298 15.7	14.2	Nunki	75 54.2	S26 16.3
02	233 11.1	187 24.7	23.6	306 11.0	15.8	4 03.7	49.8	313 18.2	14.2	Peacock	53 14.3	S56 40.3
03	248 13.6	202 24.1 ..	24.6	321 12.1 ..	15.7	19 06.5 ..	49.7	328 20.6 ..	14.2	Pollux	243 23.8	N27 58.8
04	263 16.0	217 23.5	25.5	336 13.1	15.7	34 09.2	49.6	343 23.1	14.2	Procyon	244 56.4	N 5 10.5
05	278 18.5	232 22.9	26.5	351 14.2	15.6	49 11.9	49.6	358 25.5	14.2			
06	293 21.0	247 22.4	N17 27.5	6 15.2	S23 15.5	64 14.6	S16 49.5	13 28.0	S22 14.2	Rasalhague	96 03.3	N12 32.8
07	308 23.4	262 21.8	28.4	21 16.3	15.5	79 17.4	49.4	28 30.4	14.2	Regulus	207 39.9	N11 52.6
08	323 25.9	277 21.2	29.4	36 17.3	15.4	94 20.1	49.3	43 32.9	14.2	Rigel	281 09.1	S 8 11.2
S 09	338 28.4	292 20.6 ..	30.3	51 18.4 ..	15.3	109 22.8 ..	49.3	58 35.3 ..	14.2	Rigil Kent.	139 46.6	S60 54.4
U 10	353 30.8	307 20.0	31.3	66 19.4	15.2	124 25.5	49.2	73 37.8	14.2	Sabik	102 08.6	S15 44.7
N 11	8 33.3	322 19.4	32.2	81 20.5	15.2	139 28.3	49.1	88 40.3	14.2			
D 12	23 35.7	337 18.8	N17 33.2	96 21.6	S23 15.1	154 31.0	S16 49.1	103 42.7	S22 14.2	Schedar	349 37.3	N56 38.0
A 13	38 38.2	352 18.3	34.1	111 22.6	15.0	169 33.7	49.0	118 45.2	14.2	Shaula	96 17.3	S37 06.8
Y 14	53 40.7	7 17.7	35.1	126 23.7	14.9	184 36.4	48.9	133 47.6	14.2	Sirius	258 31.0	S16 44.8
15	68 43.1	22 17.1 ..	36.0	141 24.7 ..	14.9	199 39.1 ..	48.9	148 50.1 ..	14.2	Spica	158 27.5	S11 15.4
16	83 45.6	37 16.5	37.0	156 25.8	14.8	214 41.9	48.8	163 52.5	14.2	Suhail	222 49.9	S43 30.7
17	98 48.1	52 15.9	37.9	171 26.8	14.7	229 44.6	48.7	178 55.0	14.2			
18	113 50.5	67 15.3	N17 38.9	186 27.9	S23 14.6	244 47.3	S16 48.7	193 57.4	S22 14.2	Vega	80 36.6	N38 47.9
19	128 53.0	82 14.7	39.8	201 29.0	14.6	259 50.0	48.6	208 59.9	14.2	Zuben'ubi	137 01.5	S16 07.0
20	143 55.5	97 14.1	40.7	216 30.0	14.5	274 52.8	48.5	224 02.3	14.2		SHA	Mer.Pass.
21	158 57.9	112 13.5 ..	41.7	231 31.1 ..	14.4	289 55.5 ..	48.4	239 04.8 ..	14.2	Venus	315 32.6	13 30
22	174 00.4	127 12.9	42.6	246 32.1	14.3	304 58.2	48.4	254 07.2	14.2	Mars	73 36.7	5 37
23	189 02.9	142 12.4	43.6	261 33.2	14.3	320 01.0	48.3	269 09.7	14.2	Jupiter	130 46.0	1 48
Mer.Pass. 10 29.8		v −0.6 d 1.0		v 1.0 d 0.1		v 2.7 d 0.1		v 2.4 d 0.0		Saturn	80 07.5	5 10

UT	SUN GHA	SUN Dec	MOON GHA	v	MOON Dec	d	HP
d h	° ′	° ′	° ′	′	° ′	′	′
13 00	179 50.3	N 8 56.8	213 37.2	13.1	S 8 20.0	10.1	56.0
01	194 50.4	57.7	228 09.3	13.0	8 09.9	10.3	56.1
02	209 50.6	58.6	242 41.3	13.0	7 59.6	10.2	56.1
03	224 50.7	8 59.5	257 13.3	13.0	7 49.4	10.3	56.1
04	239 50.9	9 00.4	271 45.3	13.0	7 39.1	10.4	56.1
05	254 51.1	01.3	286 17.3	13.0	7 28.7	10.4	56.2
06	269 51.2	N 9 02.2	300 49.3	13.0	S 7 18.3	10.5	56.2
07	284 51.4	03.1	315 21.3	13.0	7 07.8	10.5	56.2
08	299 51.5	04.0	329 53.3	12.9	6 57.3	10.5	56.3
F 09	314 51.7	.. 04.9	344 25.2	13.0	6 46.8	10.6	56.3
R 10	329 51.9	05.8	358 57.2	12.9	6 36.2	10.7	56.3
I 11	344 52.0	06.8	13 29.1	13.0	6 25.5	10.6	56.3
D 12	359 52.2	N 9 07.7	28 01.1	12.9	S 6 14.9	10.8	56.4
A 13	14 52.3	08.6	42 33.0	12.9	6 04.1	10.7	56.4
Y 14	29 52.5	09.5	57 04.9	12.9	5 53.4	10.8	56.4
15	44 52.6	.. 10.4	71 36.8	12.9	5 42.6	10.8	56.4
16	59 52.8	11.3	86 08.7	12.9	5 31.8	10.9	56.5
17	74 52.9	12.2	100 40.6	12.8	5 20.9	10.9	56.5
18	89 53.1	N 9 13.1	115 12.4	12.9	S 5 10.0	11.0	56.5
19	104 53.3	14.0	129 44.3	12.8	4 59.0	11.0	56.6
20	119 53.4	14.9	144 16.1	12.8	4 48.0	11.0	56.6
21	134 53.6	.. 15.8	158 47.9	12.8	4 37.0	11.0	56.6
22	149 53.7	16.7	173 19.7	12.8	4 26.0	11.1	56.6
23	164 53.9	17.6	187 51.5	12.7	4 14.9	11.1	56.7
14 00	179 54.0	N 9 18.5	202 23.2	12.7	S 4 03.8	11.2	56.7
01	194 54.2	19.4	216 54.9	12.8	3 52.6	11.2	56.7
02	209 54.3	20.3	231 26.7	12.7	3 41.4	11.2	56.8
03	224 54.5	.. 21.2	245 58.4	12.6	3 30.2	11.2	56.8
04	239 54.7	22.1	260 30.0	12.7	3 19.0	11.3	56.8
05	254 54.8	23.0	275 01.7	12.6	3 07.7	11.3	56.8
06	269 55.0	N 9 23.9	289 33.3	12.6	S 2 56.4	11.3	56.9
S 07	284 55.1	24.8	304 04.9	12.6	2 45.1	11.4	56.9
A 08	299 55.3	25.7	318 36.5	12.6	2 33.7	11.3	56.9
T 09	314 55.4	.. 26.6	333 08.1	12.5	2 22.4	11.4	57.0
U 10	329 55.6	27.5	347 39.6	12.6	2 11.0	11.4	57.0
R 11	344 55.7	28.4	2 11.2	12.4	1 59.6	11.5	57.0
D 12	359 55.9	N 9 29.3	16 42.6	12.5	S 1 48.1	11.4	57.0
A 13	14 56.0	30.2	31 14.1	12.4	1 36.7	11.5	57.1
Y 14	29 56.2	31.1	45 45.5	12.5	1 25.2	11.5	57.1
15	44 56.3	.. 32.0	60 17.0	12.3	1 13.7	11.6	57.1
16	59 56.5	32.9	74 48.3	12.4	1 02.1	11.5	57.2
17	74 56.7	33.8	89 19.7	12.3	0 50.6	11.5	57.2
18	89 56.8	N 9 34.7	103 51.0	12.3	S 0 39.1	11.6	57.2
19	104 57.0	35.6	118 22.3	12.3	0 27.5	11.6	57.2
20	119 57.1	36.5	132 53.6	12.2	0 15.9	11.6	57.3
21	134 57.3	.. 37.4	147 24.8	12.2	S 0 04.3	11.6	57.3
22	149 57.4	38.3	161 56.0	12.2	N 0 07.3	11.6	57.3
23	164 57.6	39.2	176 27.2	12.1	0 18.9	11.7	57.4
15 00	179 57.7	N 9 40.1	190 58.3	12.1	N 0 30.6	11.6	57.4
01	194 57.9	41.0	205 29.4	12.1	0 42.2	11.7	57.4
02	209 58.0	41.9	220 00.5	12.1	0 53.9	11.6	57.5
03	224 58.2	.. 42.8	234 31.6	12.0	1 05.5	11.7	57.5
04	239 58.3	43.7	249 02.6	11.9	1 17.2	11.7	57.5
05	254 58.5	44.6	263 33.5	12.0	1 28.9	11.6	57.5
06	269 58.6	N 9 45.4	278 04.5	11.8	N 1 40.5	11.7	57.6
07	284 58.8	46.3	292 35.3	11.9	1 52.2	11.7	57.6
08	299 58.9	47.2	307 06.2	11.8	2 03.9	11.7	57.6
S 09	314 59.1	.. 48.1	321 37.0	11.8	2 15.6	11.7	57.7
U 10	329 59.2	49.0	336 07.8	11.7	2 27.3	11.7	57.7
N 11	344 59.4	49.9	350 38.5	11.7	2 39.0	11.6	57.7
D 12	359 59.5	N 9 50.8	5 09.2	11.7	N 2 50.6	11.7	57.7
A 13	14 59.7	51.7	19 39.9	11.6	3 02.3	11.7	57.7
Y 14	29 59.8	52.6	34 10.5	11.6	3 14.0	11.7	57.8
15	45 00.0	.. 53.5	48 41.1	11.5	3 25.7	11.6	57.8
16	60 00.1	54.4	63 11.6	11.5	3 37.3	11.7	57.8
17	75 00.3	55.3	77 42.1	11.4	3 49.0	11.6	57.9
18	90 00.4	N 9 56.2	92 12.5	11.4	N 4 00.6	11.6	57.9
19	105 00.6	57.0	106 42.9	11.4	4 12.2	11.7	57.9
20	120 00.7	57.9	121 13.3	11.3	4 23.9	11.6	57.9
21	135 00.9	.. 58.8	135 43.6	11.3	4 35.5	11.6	58.0
22	150 01.0	9 59.7	150 13.9	11.2	4 47.1	11.6	58.0
23	165 01.2	N10 00.6	164 44.1	11.2	N 4 58.7	11.5	58.0
	SD 16.0	d 0.9	SD 15.4		15.5		15.7

Lat.	Twilight Naut.	Twilight Civil	Sunrise	Moonrise 13	14	15	16
°	h m	h m	h m	h m	h m	h m	h m
N 72	////	02 08	03 45	05 32	05 20	05 09	04 58
N 70	////	02 42	04 01	05 21	05 16	05 11	05 06
68	00 58	03 06	04 14	05 12	05 12	05 12	05 13
66	01 50	03 24	04 24	05 05	05 09	05 14	05 19
64	02 21	03 39	04 33	04 58	05 07	05 15	05 28
62	02 43	03 51	04 40	04 53	05 05	05 17	05 28
60	03 00	04 01	04 47	04 48	05 03	05 17	05 32
N 58	03 15	04 10	04 52	04 44	05 01	05 17	05 35
56	03 27	04 17	04 57	04 40	04 59	05 18	05 38
54	03 37	04 24	05 02	04 37	04 58	05 19	05 41
52	03 46	04 30	05 06	04 34	04 57	05 19	05 43
50	03 54	04 36	05 10	04 31	04 56	05 20	05 45
45	04 10	04 47	05 17	04 25	04 53	05 21	05 50
N 40	04 23	04 56	05 24	04 20	04 51	05 22	05 54
35	04 33	05 04	05 30	04 15	04 49	05 23	05 58
30	04 41	05 10	05 35	04 12	04 47	05 24	06 01
20	04 54	05 21	05 43	04 05	04 45	05 25	06 07
N 10	05 04	05 29	05 50	03 59	04 42	05 26	06 11
0	05 12	05 36	05 57	03 53	04 40	05 27	06 16
S 10	05 18	05 42	06 04	03 48	04 37	05 28	06 21
20	05 23	05 48	06 11	03 42	04 35	05 30	06 26
30	05 26	05 54	06 18	03 35	04 32	05 31	06 32
35	05 28	05 57	06 23	03 31	04 31	05 32	06 35
40	05 29	06 00	06 28	03 26	04 29	05 33	06 39
45	05 30	06 04	06 34	03 21	04 27	05 34	06 43
S 50	05 30	06 08	06 41	03 15	04 24	05 35	06 49
52	05 30	06 09	06 44	03 12	04 23	05 36	06 51
54	05 30	06 11	06 47	03 09	04 22	05 37	06 54
56	05 30	06 13	06 51	03 05	04 20	05 37	06 57
58	05 30	06 15	06 55	03 01	04 19	05 38	07 00
S 60	05 29	06 18	07 00	02 57	04 17	05 39	07 04

Lat.	Sunset	Twilight Civil	Twilight Naut.	Moonset 13	14	15	16
°	h m	h m	h m	h m	h m	h m	h m
N 72	20 19	22 00	////	15 00	16 50	18 42	20 40
N 70	20 02	21 24	////	15 09	16 51	18 36	20 26
68	19 49	20 59	23 19	15 16	16 52	18 32	20 14
66	19 39	20 40	22 17	15 22	16 53	18 28	20 05
64	19 30	20 25	21 44	15 27	16 54	18 24	19 57
62	19 22	20 12	21 21	15 31	16 55	18 22	19 51
60	19 15	20 02	21 03	15 35	16 56	18 19	19 45
N 58	19 10	19 53	20 48	15 38	16 56	18 17	19 40
56	19 05	19 45	20 36	15 41	16 57	18 15	19 35
54	19 00	19 38	20 25	15 43	16 57	18 13	19 31
52	18 56	19 32	20 16	15 45	16 57	18 11	19 27
50	18 52	19 26	20 08	15 48	16 58	18 10	19 24
45	18 44	19 15	19 52	15 52	16 59	18 07	19 18
N 40	18 37	19 05	19 39	15 56	16 59	18 04	19 11
35	18 32	18 58	19 29	15 59	17 00	18 02	19 06
30	18 27	18 51	19 20	16 02	17 00	18 00	19 01
20	18 18	18 40	19 07	16 07	17 01	17 56	18 53
N 10	18 10	18 32	18 57	16 11	17 02	17 53	18 47
0	18 04	18 25	18 49	16 15	17 02	17 50	18 40
S 10	17 57	18 18	18 43	16 19	17 03	17 47	18 34
20	17 50	18 12	18 38	16 24	17 03	17 44	18 27
30	17 42	18 06	18 34	16 28	17 04	17 41	18 20
35	17 37	18 03	18 32	16 31	17 05	17 39	18 15
40	17 32	17 59	18 31	16 34	17 05	17 36	18 10
45	17 26	17 56	18 30	16 38	17 05	17 34	18 04
S 50	17 19	17 52	18 29	16 42	17 06	17 31	17 57
52	17 16	17 50	18 29	16 44	17 06	17 29	17 54
54	17 12	17 48	18 29	16 46	17 07	17 28	17 50
56	17 09	17 46	18 29	16 48	17 07	17 26	17 47
58	17 04	17 44	18 30	16 51	17 07	17 24	17 42
S 60	16 59	17 42	18 30	16 54	17 08	17 22	17 37

Day	SUN Eqn. of Time 00h	SUN Eqn. of Time 12h	Mer. Pass.	MOON Mer. Pass. Upper	MOON Mer. Pass. Lower	Age	Phase
d	m s	m s	h m	h m	h m	d	%
13	00 39	00 32	12 01	10 04	22 28	27	8
14	00 24	00 17	12 00	10 51	23 15	28	3
15	00 09	00 02	12 00	11 39	24 03	29	1

2018 APRIL 16, 17, 18 (MON., TUES., WED.)

UT	ARIES GHA	VENUS −3·9 GHA	Dec	MARS −0·1 GHA	Dec	JUPITER −2·5 GHA	Dec	SATURN +0·4 GHA	Dec	STARS Name	SHA	Dec
16 00	204 05.3	157 11.8	N17 44.5	276 34.3	S23 14.2	335 03.7	S16 48.2	284 12.2	S22 14.2	Acamar	315 16.3	S40 14.2
01	219 07.8	172 11.2	45.5	291 35.3	14.1	350 06.4	48.2	299 14.6	14.2	Achernar	335 25.0	S57 08.8
02	234 10.2	187 10.6	46.4	306 36.4	14.0	5 09.1	48.1	314 17.1	14.2	Acrux	173 04.9	S63 12.1
03	249 12.7	202 10.0	.. 47.3	321 37.4	.. 14.0	20 11.9	48.0	329 19.5	.. 14.2	Adhara	255 10.1	S29 00.2
04	264 15.2	217 09.4	48.3	336 38.5	13.9	35 14.6	48.0	344 22.0	14.2	Aldebaran	290 45.9	N16 32.5
05	279 17.6	232 08.8	49.2	351 39.6	13.8	50 17.3	47.9	359 24.4	14.2			
06	294 20.1	247 08.2	N17 50.1	6 40.6	S23 13.7	65 20.0	S16 47.8	14 26.9	S22 14.2	Alioth	166 17.3	N55 51.8
07	309 22.6	262 07.6	51.1	21 41.7	13.7	80 22.8	47.7	29 29.3	14.2	Alkaid	152 55.9	N49 13.4
M 08	324 25.0	277 07.0	52.0	36 42.8	13.6	95 25.5	47.7	44 31.8	14.2	Al Na'ir	27 40.0	S46 52.2
O 09	339 27.5	292 06.4	.. 52.9	51 43.8	.. 13.5	110 28.2	.. 47.6	59 34.3	.. 14.2	Alnilam	275 43.3	S 1 11.7
N 10	354 30.0	307 05.8	53.9	66 44.9	13.4	125 31.0	47.5	74 36.7	14.2	Alphard	217 52.8	S 8 44.5
D 11	9 32.4	322 05.2	54.8	81 46.0	13.4	140 33.7	47.5	89 39.2	14.2			
A 12	24 34.9	337 04.6	N17 55.7	96 47.0	S23 13.3	155 36.4	S16 47.4	104 41.6	S22 14.2	Alphecca	126 07.9	N26 39.2
Y 13	39 37.3	352 04.0	56.7	111 48.1	13.2	170 39.1	47.3	119 44.1	14.2	Alpheratz	357 40.4	N29 11.2
14	54 39.8	7 03.4	57.6	126 49.1	13.1	185 41.9	47.3	134 46.5	14.2	Altair	62 05.1	N 8 54.9
15	69 42.3	22 02.8	.. 58.5	141 50.2	.. 13.1	200 44.6	.. 47.2	149 49.0	.. 14.2	Ankaa	353 12.9	S42 12.5
16	84 44.7	37 02.2	17 59.5	156 51.3	13.0	215 47.3	47.1	164 51.5	14.2	Antares	112 22.0	S26 28.2
17	99 47.2	52 01.6	18 00.4	171 52.3	12.9	230 50.1	47.0	179 53.9	14.2			
18	114 49.7	67 01.0	N18 01.3	186 53.4	S23 12.8	245 52.8	S16 47.0	194 56.4	S22 14.2	Arcturus	145 52.5	N19 05.3
19	129 52.1	82 00.4	02.2	201 54.5	12.7	260 55.5	46.9	209 58.8	14.2	Atria	107 20.5	S69 03.2
20	144 54.6	96 59.8	03.2	216 55.6	12.7	275 58.2	46.8	225 01.3	14.2	Avior	234 16.6	S59 34.5
21	159 57.1	111 59.2	.. 04.1	231 56.6	.. 12.6	291 01.0	.. 46.8	240 03.7	.. 14.2	Bellatrix	278 28.7	N 6 21.7
22	174 59.5	126 58.6	05.0	246 57.7	12.5	306 03.7	46.7	255 06.2	14.2	Betelgeuse	270 57.9	N 7 24.4
23	190 02.0	141 58.0	05.9	261 58.8	12.4	321 06.4	46.6	270 08.7	14.2			
17 00	205 04.5	156 57.4	N18 06.9	276 59.8	S23 12.4	336 09.2	S16 46.5	285 11.1	S22 14.2	Canopus	263 54.9	S52 42.8
01	220 06.9	171 56.8	07.8	292 00.9	12.3	351 11.9	46.5	300 13.6	14.2	Capella	280 29.9	N46 00.9
02	235 09.4	186 56.2	08.7	307 02.0	12.2	6 14.6	46.4	315 16.0	14.2	Deneb	49 29.3	N45 20.5
03	250 11.8	201 55.6	.. 09.6	322 03.0	.. 12.1	21 17.4	.. 46.3	330 18.5	.. 14.2	Denebola	182 30.1	N14 28.2
04	265 14.3	216 55.0	10.5	337 04.1	12.0	36 20.1	46.3	345 21.0	14.2	Diphda	348 53.0	S17 53.4
05	280 16.8	231 54.4	11.5	352 05.2	12.0	51 22.8	46.2	0 23.4	14.2			
06	295 19.2	246 53.8	N18 12.4	7 06.2	S23 11.9	66 25.6	S16 46.1	15 25.9	S22 14.2	Dubhe	193 47.3	N61 39.3
07	310 21.7	261 53.2	13.3	22 07.3	11.8	81 28.3	46.0	30 28.3	14.2	Elnath	278 08.7	N28 37.2
T 08	325 24.2	276 52.6	14.2	37 08.4	11.7	96 31.0	46.0	45 30.8	14.2	Eltanin	90 44.4	N51 29.0
U 09	340 26.6	291 52.0	.. 15.1	52 09.5	.. 11.7	111 33.8	.. 45.9	60 33.3	.. 14.2	Enif	33 44.1	N 9 57.4
E 10	355 29.1	306 51.3	16.0	67 10.5	11.6	126 36.5	45.8	75 35.7	14.2	Fomalhaut	15 20.7	S29 31.6
S 11	10 31.6	321 50.7	16.9	82 11.6	11.5	141 39.2	45.8	90 38.2	14.2			
D 12	25 34.0	336 50.1	N18 17.9	97 12.7	S23 11.4	156 42.0	S16 45.7	105 40.6	S22 14.2	Gacrux	171 56.7	S57 13.0
A 13	40 36.5	351 49.5	18.8	112 13.8	11.3	171 44.7	45.6	120 43.1	14.2	Gienah	175 48.6	S17 38.7
Y 14	55 38.9	6 48.9	19.7	127 14.8	11.3	186 47.4	45.5	135 45.6	14.2	Hadar	148 42.6	S60 27.5
15	70 41.4	21 48.3	.. 20.6	142 15.9	.. 11.2	201 50.2	.. 45.5	150 48.0	.. 14.2	Hamal	327 57.4	N23 32.7
16	85 43.9	36 47.7	21.5	157 17.0	11.1	216 52.9	45.4	165 50.5	14.2	Kaus Aust.	83 39.4	S34 22.3
17	100 46.3	51 47.1	22.4	172 18.1	11.0	231 55.6	45.3	180 53.0	14.2			
18	115 48.8	66 46.5	N18 23.3	187 19.1	S23 10.9	246 58.4	S16 45.3	195 55.4	S22 14.2	Kochab	137 19.1	N74 04.9
19	130 51.3	81 45.8	24.2	202 20.2	10.9	262 01.1	45.2	210 57.9	14.2	Markab	13 35.3	N15 18.0
20	145 53.7	96 45.2	25.1	217 21.3	10.8	277 03.8	45.1	226 00.3	14.2	Menkar	314 12.0	N 4 09.4
21	160 56.2	111 44.6	.. 26.0	232 22.4	.. 10.7	292 06.6	.. 45.0	241 02.8	.. 14.2	Menkent	148 03.3	S36 27.5
22	175 58.7	126 44.0	26.9	247 23.4	10.6	307 09.3	45.0	256 05.3	14.2	Miaplacidus	221 38.6	S69 47.9
23	191 01.1	141 43.4	27.8	262 24.5	10.5	322 12.0	44.9	271 07.7	14.2			
18 00	206 03.6	156 42.8	N18 28.7	277 25.6	S23 10.5	337 14.8	S16 44.8	286 10.2	S22 14.2	Mirfak	308 36.1	N49 55.4
01	221 06.1	171 42.2	29.6	292 26.7	10.4	352 17.5	44.8	301 12.7	14.2	Nunki	75 54.2	S26 16.2
02	236 08.5	186 41.5	30.5	307 27.7	10.3	7 20.2	44.7	316 15.1	14.2	Peacock	53 14.3	S56 40.3
03	251 11.0	201 40.9	.. 31.4	322 28.8	.. 10.2	22 23.0	.. 44.6	331 17.6	.. 14.2	Pollux	243 23.8	N27 58.8
04	266 13.4	216 40.3	32.3	337 29.9	10.1	37 25.7	44.5	346 20.1	14.2	Procyon	244 56.4	N 5 10.5
05	281 15.9	231 39.7	33.2	352 31.0	10.1	52 28.4	44.5	1 22.5	14.2			
06	296 18.4	246 39.1	N18 34.1	7 32.1	S23 10.0	67 31.2	S16 44.4	16 25.0	S22 14.2	Rasalhague	96 03.3	N12 32.8
07	311 20.8	261 38.5	35.0	22 33.1	09.9	82 33.9	44.3	31 27.5	14.2	Regulus	207 39.9	N11 52.6
W 08	326 23.3	276 37.8	35.9	37 34.2	09.8	97 36.7	44.2	46 29.9	14.2	Rigel	281 09.1	S 8 11.2
E 09	341 25.8	291 37.2	.. 36.8	52 35.3	.. 09.7	112 39.4	.. 44.2	61 32.4	.. 14.2	Rigil Kent.	139 46.6	S60 54.4
D 10	356 28.2	306 36.6	37.7	67 36.4	09.6	127 42.1	44.1	76 34.8	14.2	Sabik	102 08.6	S15 44.7
N 11	11 30.7	321 36.0	38.6	82 37.5	09.6	142 44.9	44.0	91 37.3	14.2			
E 12	26 33.2	336 35.4	N18 39.5	97 38.5	S23 09.5	157 47.6	S16 44.0	106 39.8	S22 14.2	Schedar	349 37.3	N56 38.0
S 13	41 35.6	351 34.7	40.4	112 39.6	09.4	172 50.3	43.9	121 42.2	14.2	Shaula	96 17.3	S37 06.8
D 14	56 38.1	6 34.1	41.3	127 40.7	09.3	187 53.1	43.8	136 44.7	14.2	Sirius	258 31.0	S16 44.8
A 15	71 40.6	21 33.5	.. 42.2	142 41.8	.. 09.2	202 55.8	.. 43.7	151 47.2	.. 14.2	Spica	158 27.5	S11 15.4
Y 16	86 43.0	36 32.9	43.1	157 42.9	09.2	217 58.6	43.7	166 49.6	14.2	Suhail	222 49.9	S43 30.7
17	101 45.5	51 32.3	43.9	172 44.0	09.1	233 01.3	43.6	181 52.1	14.2			
18	116 47.9	66 31.6	N18 44.8	187 45.0	S23 09.0	248 04.0	S16 43.5	196 54.6	S22 14.2	Vega	80 36.6	N38 47.9
19	131 50.4	81 31.0	45.7	202 46.1	08.9	263 06.8	43.4	211 57.0	14.2	Zuben'ubi	137 01.5	S16 07.0
20	146 52.9	96 30.4	46.6	217 47.2	08.8	278 09.5	43.4	226 59.5	14.2			
21	161 55.3	111 29.8	.. 47.5	232 48.3	.. 08.7	293 12.3	.. 43.3	242 02.0	.. 14.2		SHA	Mer. Pass.
22	176 57.8	126 29.1	48.4	247 49.4	08.7	308 15.0	43.2	257 04.4	14.2	Venus	311 53.0	13 33
23	192 00.3	141 28.5	49.3	262 50.5	08.6	323 17.7	43.2	272 06.9	14.2	Mars	71 55.4	5 32

	h m											
Mer. Pass.	10 18.0	v −0.6	d 0.9	v 1.1	d 0.1	v 2.7	d 0.1	v 2.5	d 0.0	Jupiter	131 04.7	1 35
										Saturn	80 06.7	4 58

SUN / MOON

UT	SUN GHA	SUN Dec	MOON GHA	v	MOON Dec	d	HP
d h	° '	° '	° '	'	° '	'	'
16 00	180 01.3	N10 01.5	179 14.3	11.1	N 5 10.2	11.6	58.0
01	195 01.5	02.4	193 44.4	11.1	5 21.8	11.5	58.1
02	210 01.6	03.3	208 14.5	11.0	5 33.3	11.5	58.1
03	225 01.8 ..	04.2	222 44.5	11.0	5 44.8	11.5	58.1
04	240 01.9	05.0	237 14.5	10.9	5 56.3	11.5	58.1
05	255 02.0	05.9	251 44.4	10.9	6 07.8	11.5	58.2
06	270 02.2	N10 06.8	266 14.3	10.8	N 6 19.3	11.4	58.2
07	285 02.3	07.7	280 44.1	10.8	6 30.7	11.4	58.2
08	300 02.5	08.6	295 13.9	10.7	6 42.1	11.4	58.2
M 09	315 02.6 ..	09.5	309 43.6	10.7	6 53.5	11.3	58.3
O 10	330 02.8	10.4	324 13.3	10.6	7 04.8	11.3	58.3
N 11	345 02.9	11.3	338 42.9	10.5	7 16.1	11.3	58.3
D 12	0 03.1	N10 12.1	353 12.4	10.6	N 7 27.4	11.3	58.3
A 13	15 03.2	13.0	7 42.0	10.4	7 38.7	11.2	58.3
Y 14	30 03.4	13.9	22 11.4	10.4	7 49.9	11.2	58.4
15	45 03.5 ..	14.8	36 40.8	10.4	8 01.1	11.1	58.4
16	60 03.7	15.7	51 10.2	10.3	8 12.2	11.2	58.4
17	75 03.8	16.5	65 39.5	10.2	8 23.4	11.0	58.4
18	90 03.9	N10 17.4	80 08.7	10.2	N 8 34.4	11.1	58.5
19	105 04.1	18.3	94 37.9	10.1	8 45.5	11.0	58.5
20	120 04.2	19.2	109 07.0	10.1	8 56.5	10.9	58.5
21	135 04.4 ..	20.1	123 36.1	10.0	9 07.4	11.0	58.5
22	150 04.5	21.0	138 05.1	9.9	9 18.4	10.8	58.5
23	165 04.7	21.9	152 34.0	9.9	9 29.2	10.9	58.6
17 00	180 04.8	N10 22.7	167 02.9	9.8	N 9 40.1	10.7	58.6
01	195 05.0	23.6	181 31.7	9.8	9 50.8	10.8	58.6
02	210 05.1	24.5	196 00.5	9.7	10 01.6	10.7	58.6
03	225 05.2 ..	25.4	210 29.2	9.7	10 12.3	10.6	58.6
04	240 05.4	26.3	224 57.9	9.6	10 22.9	10.6	58.7
05	255 05.7	27.1	239 26.5	9.5	10 33.5	10.5	58.7
06	270 05.7	N10 28.0	253 55.0	9.5	N10 44.0	10.5	58.7
07	285 05.8	28.9	268 23.5	9.4	10 54.5	10.4	58.7
T 08	300 06.0	29.8	282 51.9	9.4	11 04.9	10.4	58.7
U 09	315 06.1 ..	30.7	297 20.3	9.3	11 15.3	10.3	58.8
E 10	330 06.2	31.5	311 48.6	9.2	11 25.6	10.2	58.8
S 11	345 06.4	32.4	326 16.8	9.2	11 35.8	10.2	58.8
D 12	0 06.5	N10 33.3	340 45.0	9.1	N11 46.0	10.1	58.8
A 13	15 06.7	34.2	355 13.1	9.0	11 56.1	10.1	58.8
Y 14	30 06.8	35.1	9 41.1	9.0	12 06.2	10.0	58.9
15	45 07.0 ..	35.9	24 09.1	8.9	12 16.2	9.9	58.9
16	60 07.1	36.8	38 37.0	8.9	12 26.1	9.8	58.9
17	75 07.2	37.7	53 04.9	8.8	12 35.9	9.8	58.9
18	90 07.4	N10 38.6	67 32.7	8.7	N12 45.7	9.7	58.9
19	105 07.5	39.4	82 00.4	8.7	12 55.4	9.7	58.9
20	120 07.7	40.3	96 28.1	8.6	13 05.1	9.6	59.0
21	135 07.8 ..	41.2	110 55.7	8.6	13 14.7	9.5	59.0
22	150 07.9	42.1	125 23.3	8.4	13 24.2	9.4	59.0
23	165 08.1	42.9	139 50.7	8.5	13 33.6	9.3	59.0
18 00	180 08.2	N10 43.8	154 18.2	8.3	N13 42.9	9.3	59.0
01	195 08.4	44.7	168 45.5	8.3	13 52.2	9.2	59.0
02	210 08.5	45.6	183 12.8	8.3	14 01.4	9.1	59.0
03	225 08.6 ..	46.4	197 40.1	8.2	14 10.5	9.1	59.1
04	240 08.8	47.3	212 07.3	8.1	14 19.6	8.9	59.1
05	255 08.9	48.2	226 34.4	8.0	14 28.5	8.9	59.1
06	270 09.1	N10 49.1	241 01.4	8.0	N14 37.4	8.7	59.1
W 07	285 09.2	49.9	255 28.4	8.0	14 46.1	8.7	59.1
E 08	300 09.3	50.8	269 55.4	7.8	14 54.8	8.6	59.1
D 09	315 09.5 ..	51.7	284 22.2	7.8	15 03.4	8.6	59.1
N 10	330 09.6	52.6	298 49.0	7.8	15 12.0	8.4	59.2
E 11	345 09.7	53.4	313 15.8	7.7	15 20.4	8.3	59.2
S 12	0 09.9	N10 54.3	327 42.5	7.6	N15 28.7	8.2	59.2
D 13	15 10.0	55.2	342 09.1	7.6	15 36.9	8.2	59.2
A 14	30 10.2	56.0	356 35.7	7.5	15 45.1	8.0	59.2
Y 15	45 10.3 ..	56.9	11 02.2	7.4	15 53.1	8.0	59.2
16	60 10.4	57.8	25 28.6	7.4	16 01.1	7.9	59.2
17	75 10.6	58.6	39 55.0	7.4	16 09.0	7.7	59.2
18	90 10.7	N10 59.5	54 21.4	7.3	N16 16.7	7.7	59.2
19	105 10.8	11 00.4	68 47.7	7.2	16 24.4	7.5	59.3
20	120 11.0	01.3	83 13.9	7.1	16 31.9	7.5	59.3
21	135 11.1 ..	02.1	97 40.0	7.1	16 39.4	7.3	59.3
22	150 11.3	03.0	112 06.1	7.1	16 46.7	7.3	59.3
23	165 11.4	03.9	126 32.2	7.0	N16 54.0	7.1	59.3
	SD 16.0	d 0.9	SD 15.9		16.0		16.1

Twilight / Sunrise / Moonrise

Lat.	Naut.	Civil	Sunrise	Moonrise 16	17	18	19
°	h m	h m	h m	h m	h m	h m	h m
N 72	////	01 38	03 28	04 58	04 45	04 27	03 51
N 70	////	02 21	03 46	05 06	05 01	04 56	04 49
68	////	02 49	04 01	05 13	05 14	05 17	05 24
66	01 25	03 10	04 13	05 19	05 25	05 34	05 49
64	02 03	03 26	04 22	05 24	05 34	05 48	06 08
62	02 29	03 40	04 31	05 28	05 42	06 00	06 24
60	02 48	03 51	04 38	05 32	05 49	06 10	06 38
N 58	03 04	04 01	04 44	05 35	05 55	06 19	06 50
56	03 17	04 09	04 50	05 38	06 00	06 27	07 00
54	03 28	04 17	04 55	05 41	06 05	06 34	07 09
52	03 38	04 23	04 59	05 43	06 09	06 40	07 17
50	03 47	04 29	05 03	05 45	06 13	06 46	07 24
45	04 04	04 41	05 12	05 50	06 22	06 58	07 39
N 40	04 18	04 51	05 20	05 54	06 29	07 08	07 52
35	04 29	05 00	05 26	05 58	06 35	07 17	08 03
30	04 38	05 07	05 31	06 01	06 41	07 25	08 13
20	04 52	05 18	05 41	06 07	06 51	07 38	08 29
N 10	05 02	05 27	05 49	06 11	06 59	07 50	08 44
0	05 11	05 35	05 56	06 16	07 07	08 01	08 57
S 10	05 18	05 42	06 04	06 21	07 15	08 12	09 11
20	05 23	05 49	06 11	06 26	07 24	08 24	09 26
30	05 28	05 56	06 20	06 32	07 34	08 38	09 43
35	05 30	06 00	06 25	06 35	07 40	08 46	09 52
40	05 32	06 03	06 31	06 39	07 47	08 55	10 04
45	05 33	06 08	06 37	06 43	07 54	09 06	10 17
S 50	05 35	06 12	06 45	06 49	08 04	09 19	10 33
52	05 35	06 14	06 49	06 51	08 08	09 25	10 41
54	05 35	06 16	06 53	06 54	08 13	09 32	10 50
56	05 36	06 19	06 57	06 57	08 18	09 40	10 59
58	05 36	06 21	07 02	07 00	08 24	09 49	11 10
S 60	05 36	06 24	07 07	07 04	08 31	09 58	11 23

Sunset / Twilight / Moonset

Lat.	Sunset	Civil	Naut.	Moonset 16	17	18	19
°	h m	h m	h m	h m	h m	h m	h m
N 72	20 35	22 31	////	20 40	22 48	25 21	01 21
N 70	20 16	21 44	////	20 26	22 21	24 24	00 24
68	20 01	21 14	////	20 14	22 01	23 50	25 35
66	19 49	20 53	22 43	20 05	21 45	23 25	25 00
64	19 39	20 35	22 01	19 57	21 32	23 07	24 35
62	19 30	20 22	21 34	19 51	21 21	22 51	24 15
60	19 23	20 10	21 14	19 45	21 12	22 38	23 59
N 58	19 16	20 00	20 58	19 40	21 04	22 27	23 46
56	19 11	19 52	20 44	19 35	20 57	22 17	23 34
54	19 06	19 44	20 33	19 31	20 50	22 09	23 24
52	19 01	19 37	20 23	19 27	20 45	22 01	23 15
50	18 57	19 31	20 14	19 24	20 39	21 54	23 07
45	18 48	19 19	19 56	19 17	20 28	21 40	22 49
N 40	18 40	19 09	19 42	19 11	20 19	21 28	22 35
35	18 34	19 00	19 31	19 06	20 11	21 18	22 23
30	18 28	18 53	19 22	19 01	20 04	21 09	22 13
20	18 19	18 41	19 08	18 53	19 53	20 53	21 55
N 10	18 11	18 32	18 57	18 47	19 42	20 40	21 39
0	18 03	18 24	18 48	18 40	19 33	20 27	21 25
S 10	17 55	18 17	18 41	18 34	19 23	20 15	21 10
20	17 47	18 10	18 36	18 27	19 13	20 02	20 55
30	17 39	18 03	18 31	18 19	19 01	19 46	20 37
35	17 33	17 59	18 29	18 15	18 54	19 38	20 26
40	17 28	17 55	18 27	18 10	18 46	19 28	20 15
45	17 21	17 51	18 25	18 04	18 37	19 16	20 01
S 50	17 13	17 46	18 24	17 57	18 27	19 02	19 44
52	17 10	17 44	18 23	17 54	18 22	18 55	19 36
54	17 06	17 42	18 23	17 50	18 16	18 48	19 27
56	17 01	17 39	18 22	17 47	18 10	18 40	19 17
58	16 56	17 37	18 22	17 42	18 04	18 30	19 05
S 60	16 51	17 34	18 22	17 37	17 56	18 20	18 52

SUN / MOON

Day	SUN Eqn. of Time 00h	12h	Mer. Pass.	MOON Mer. Pass. Upper	Lower	Age	Phase
d	m s	m s	h m	h m	h m	d	%
16	00 05	00 12	12 00	12 28	00 03	00	0
17	00 19	00 26	12 00	13 20	00 54	01	3
18	00 33	00 39	11 59	14 14	01 47	02	8

UT (d h)	ARIES GHA	VENUS −3.9 GHA	VENUS Dec	MARS −0.1 GHA	MARS Dec	JUPITER −2.5 GHA	JUPITER Dec	SATURN +0.4 GHA	SATURN Dec	STARS Name	SHA	Dec
19 00	207 02.7	156 27.9	N18 50.1	277 51.6	S23 08.5	338 20.5	S16 43.1	287 09.4	S22 14.2	Acamar	315 16.3	S40 14.2
01	222 05.2	171 27.3	51.0	292 52.6	08.4	353 23.2	43.0	302 11.9	14.2	Achernar	335 25.0	S57 08.8
02	237 07.7	186 26.6	51.9	307 53.7	08.3	8 26.0	42.9	317 14.3	14.2	Acrux	173 04.9	S63 12.1
03	252 10.1	201 26.0 ..	52.8	322 54.8 ..	08.2	23 28.7 ..	42.9	332 16.8 ..	14.2	Adhara	255 10.1	S29 00.2
04	267 12.6	216 25.4	53.7	337 55.9	08.2	38 31.4	42.8	347 19.3	14.2	Aldebaran	290 45.9	N16 32.5
05	282 15.1	231 24.8	54.5	352 57.0	08.1	53 34.2	42.7	2 21.7	14.2			
06	297 17.5	246 24.1	N18 55.4	7 58.1	S23 08.0	68 36.9	S16 42.6	17 24.2	S22 14.2	Alioth	166 17.3	N55 51.8
T 07	312 20.0	261 23.5	56.3	22 59.2	07.9	83 39.7	42.6	32 26.7	14.2	Alkaid	152 55.9	N49 13.4
H 08	327 22.4	276 22.9	57.2	38 00.3	07.8	98 42.4	42.5	47 29.1	14.2	Al Na'ir	27 39.9	S46 52.2
U 09	342 24.9	291 22.2 ..	58.0	53 01.3 ..	07.7	113 45.1 ..	42.4	62 31.6 ..	14.2	Alnilam	275 43.3	S 1 11.7
R 10	357 27.4	306 21.6	58.9	68 02.4	07.7	128 47.9	42.3	77 34.1	14.2	Alphard	217 52.8	S 8 44.5
S 11	12 29.8	321 21.0	18 59.8	83 03.5	07.6	143 50.6	42.3	92 36.5	14.2			
D 12	27 32.3	336 20.3	N19 00.7	98 04.6	S23 07.5	158 53.4	S16 42.2	107 39.0	S22 14.2	Alphecca	126 07.9	N26 39.2
A 13	42 34.8	351 19.7	01.5	113 05.7	07.4	173 56.1	42.1	122 41.5	14.2	Alpheratz	357 40.4	N29 11.2
Y 14	57 37.2	6 19.1	02.4	128 06.8	07.3	188 58.9	42.1	137 44.0	14.2	Altair	62 05.0	N 8 54.9
15	72 39.7	21 18.4 ..	03.3	143 07.9 ..	07.2	204 01.6 ..	42.0	152 46.4 ..	14.2	Ankaa	353 12.9	S42 12.5
16	87 42.2	36 17.8	04.1	158 09.0	07.2	219 04.3	41.9	167 48.9	14.2	Antares	112 22.0	S26 28.2
17	102 44.6	51 17.2	05.0	173 10.1	07.1	234 07.1	41.8	182 51.4	14.2			
18	117 47.1	66 16.5	N19 05.9	188 11.2	S23 07.0	249 09.8	S16 41.8	197 53.8	S22 14.2	Arcturus	145 52.4	N19 05.3
19	132 49.5	81 15.9	06.7	203 12.3	06.9	264 12.6	41.7	212 56.3	14.2	Atria	107 20.4	S69 03.2
20	147 52.0	96 15.3	07.6	218 13.4	06.8	279 15.3	41.6	227 58.8	14.2	Avior	234 16.6	S59 34.5
21	162 54.5	111 14.6 ..	08.5	233 14.5 ..	06.7	294 18.1 ..	41.5	243 01.3 ..	14.2	Bellatrix	278 28.7	N 6 21.7
22	177 56.9	126 14.0	09.3	248 15.5	06.6	309 20.8	41.5	258 03.7	14.2	Betelgeuse	270 58.0	N 7 24.4
23	192 59.4	141 13.4	10.2	263 16.6	06.6	324 23.5	41.4	273 06.2	14.2			
20 00	208 01.9	156 12.7	N19 11.0	278 17.7	S23 06.5	339 26.3	S16 41.3	288 08.7	S22 14.2	Canopus	263 54.9	S52 42.8
01	223 04.3	171 12.1	11.9	293 18.8	06.4	354 29.0	41.2	303 11.1	14.2	Capella	280 29.9	N46 00.9
02	238 06.8	186 11.5	12.8	308 19.9	06.3	9 31.8	41.2	318 13.6	14.2	Deneb	49 29.3	N45 20.5
03	253 09.3	201 10.8 ..	13.6	323 21.0 ..	06.2	24 34.5 ..	41.1	333 16.1 ..	14.2	Denebola	182 30.1	N14 28.2
04	268 11.7	216 10.2	14.5	338 22.1	06.1	39 37.3	41.0	348 18.6	14.2	Diphda	348 52.9	S17 53.4
05	283 14.2	231 09.5	15.3	353 23.2	06.1	54 40.0	40.9	3 21.0	14.2			
06	298 16.7	246 08.9	N19 16.2	8 24.3	S23 06.0	69 42.8	S16 40.9	18 23.5	S22 14.2	Dubhe	193 47.3	N61 39.3
07	313 19.1	261 08.3	17.1	23 25.4	05.9	84 45.5	40.8	33 26.0	14.2	Elnath	278 08.7	N28 37.2
F 08	328 21.6	276 07.6	17.9	38 26.5	05.8	99 48.2	40.7	48 28.5	14.2	Eltanin	90 44.4	N51 29.1
R 09	343 24.0	291 07.0 ..	18.8	53 27.6 ..	05.7	114 51.0 ..	40.6	63 30.9 ..	14.2	Enif	33 44.1	N 9 57.4
I 10	358 26.5	306 06.3	19.6	68 28.7	05.6	129 53.7	40.6	78 33.4	14.2	Fomalhaut	15 20.7	S29 31.5
11	13 29.0	321 05.7	20.5	83 29.8	05.5	144 56.5	40.5	93 35.9	14.2			
D 12	28 31.4	336 05.1	N19 21.3	98 30.9	S23 05.4	159 59.2	S16 40.4	108 38.4	S22 14.2	Gacrux	171 56.7	S57 13.0
A 13	43 33.9	351 04.4	22.2	113 32.0	05.3	175 02.0	40.3	123 40.8	14.2	Gienah	175 48.6	S17 38.7
Y 14	58 36.4	6 03.8	23.0	128 33.1	05.3	190 04.7	40.3	138 43.3	14.2	Hadar	148 42.5	S60 27.6
15	73 38.8	21 03.1 ..	23.9	143 34.2 ..	05.2	205 07.5 ..	40.2	153 45.8 ..	14.2	Hamal	327 57.4	N23 32.7
16	88 41.3	36 02.5	24.7	158 35.3	05.1	220 10.2	40.1	168 48.3	14.2	Kaus Aust.	83 39.3	S34 22.3
17	103 43.8	51 01.8	25.6	173 36.4	05.0	235 13.0	40.0	183 50.7	14.2			
18	118 46.2	66 01.2	N19 26.4	188 37.5	S23 04.9	250 15.7	S16 40.0	198 53.2	S22 14.2	Kochab	137 19.1	N74 04.9
19	133 48.7	81 00.5	27.3	203 38.6	04.8	265 18.5	39.9	213 55.7	14.2	Markab	13 35.3	N15 18.0
20	148 51.2	95 59.9	28.1	218 39.7	04.8	280 21.2	39.8	228 58.2	14.2	Menkar	314 12.0	N 4 09.4
21	163 53.6	110 59.3 ..	28.9	233 40.8 ..	04.7	295 23.9 ..	39.7	244 00.6 ..	14.2	Menkent	148 03.3	S36 27.5
22	178 56.1	125 58.6	29.8	248 41.9	04.6	310 26.7	39.7	259 03.1	14.2	Miaplacidus	221 38.7	S69 47.9
23	193 58.5	140 58.0	30.6	263 43.0	04.5	325 29.4	39.6	274 05.6	14.2			
21 00	209 01.0	155 57.3	N19 31.5	278 44.1	S23 04.4	340 32.2	S16 39.5	289 08.1	S22 14.2	Mirfak	308 36.1	N49 55.4
01	224 03.5	170 56.7	32.3	293 45.2	04.3	355 34.9	39.4	304 10.6	14.2	Nunki	75 54.2	S26 16.2
02	239 05.9	185 56.0	33.1	308 46.3	04.2	10 37.7	39.4	319 13.0	14.2	Peacock	53 14.2	S56 40.3
03	254 08.4	200 55.4 ..	34.0	323 47.4 ..	04.1	25 40.4 ..	39.3	334 15.5 ..	14.2	Pollux	243 23.8	N27 58.8
04	269 10.9	215 54.7	34.8	338 48.5	04.1	40 43.2	39.2	349 18.0	14.2	Procyon	244 56.4	N 5 10.5
05	284 13.3	230 54.1	35.6	353 49.6	04.0	55 45.9	39.1	4 20.5	14.2			
06	299 15.8	245 53.4	N19 36.5	8 50.8	S23 03.9	70 48.7	S16 39.1	19 22.9	S22 14.2	Rasalhague	96 03.2	N12 32.8
07	314 18.3	260 52.8	37.3	23 51.9	03.8	85 51.4	39.0	34 25.4	14.2	Regulus	207 39.9	N11 52.6
S 08	329 20.7	275 52.1	38.2	38 53.0	03.7	100 54.2	38.9	49 27.9	14.2	Rigel	281 09.2	S 8 11.2
A 09	344 23.2	290 51.5 ..	39.0	53 54.1 ..	03.6	115 56.9 ..	38.8	64 30.4 ..	14.2	Rigil Kent.	139 46.6	S60 54.4
T 10	359 25.7	305 50.8	39.8	68 55.2	03.5	130 59.7	38.8	79 32.9	14.2	Sabik	102 08.6	S15 44.7
U 11	14 28.1	320 50.2	40.6	83 56.3	03.4	146 02.4	38.7	94 35.3	14.2			
R 12	29 30.6	335 49.5	N19 41.5	98 57.4	S23 03.3	161 05.2	S16 38.6	109 37.8	S22 14.2	Schedar	349 37.3	N56 38.0
D 13	44 33.0	350 48.9	42.3	113 58.5	03.3	176 07.9	38.5	124 40.3	14.2	Shaula	96 17.2	S37 06.8
A 14	59 35.5	5 48.2	43.1	128 59.6	03.2	191 10.7	38.5	139 42.8	14.2	Sirius	258 31.0	S16 44.8
Y 15	74 38.0	20 47.5 ..	44.0	144 00.7 ..	03.1	206 13.4 ..	38.4	154 45.3 ..	14.2	Spica	158 27.5	S11 15.4
16	89 40.4	35 46.9	44.8	159 01.8	03.0	221 16.2	38.3	169 47.7	14.2	Suhail	222 49.9	S43 30.7
17	104 42.9	50 46.2	45.6	174 02.9	02.9	236 18.9	38.2	184 50.2	14.2			
18	119 45.4	65 45.6	N19 46.4	189 04.1	S23 02.8	251 21.7	S16 38.2	199 52.7	S22 14.2	Vega	80 36.6	N38 47.9
19	134 47.8	80 44.9	47.3	204 05.2	02.7	266 24.4	38.1	214 55.2	14.2	Zuben'ubi	137 01.5	S16 07.0
20	149 50.3	95 44.3	48.1	219 06.3	02.6	281 27.2	38.0	229 57.7	14.2		SHA	Mer. Pass.
21	164 52.8	110 43.6 ..	48.9	234 07.4 ..	02.6	296 29.9 ..	37.9	245 00.1 ..	14.2		° ′	h m
22	179 55.2	125 42.9	49.7	249 08.5	02.5	311 32.7	37.8	260 02.6	14.2	Venus	308 10.9	13 36
23	194 57.7	140 42.3	50.5	264 09.6	02.4	326 35.4	37.8	275 05.1	14.2	Mars	70 15.9	5 26
										Jupiter	131 24.4	1 22
Mer. Pass.	h m 10 06.2	v −0.6	d 0.9	v 1.1	d 0.1	v 2.7	d 0.1	v 2.5	d 0.0	Saturn	80 06.8	4 47

UT	SUN GHA	SUN Dec	MOON GHA	v	Dec	d	HP
d h	° ′	° ′	° ′	′	° ′	′	′
19 00	180 11.5	N11 04.7	140 58.2	6.9	N17 01.1	7.1	59.3
01	195 11.7	05.6	155 24.1	6.9	17 08.2	6.9	59.3
02	210 11.8	06.5	169 50.0	6.9	17 15.1	6.8	59.3
03	225 11.9 ..	07.3	184 15.9	6.7	17 21.9	6.7	59.3
04	240 12.1	08.2	198 41.6	6.8	17 28.6	6.6	59.3
05	255 12.2	09.1	213 07.4	6.7	17 35.2	6.5	59.3
T 06	270 12.3 N11	09.9	227 33.1	6.6	N17 41.7	6.4	59.4
H 07	285 12.5	10.8	241 58.7	6.6	17 48.1	6.3	59.4
U 08	300 12.6	11.6	256 24.3	6.5	17 54.4	6.1	59.4
R 09	315 12.7 ..	12.5	270 49.8	6.5	18 00.5	6.0	59.4
S 10	330 12.9	13.4	285 15.3	6.4	18 06.5	6.0	59.4
D 11	345 13.0	14.2	299 40.7	6.4	18 12.5	5.8	59.4
A 12	0 13.1 N11	15.1	314 06.1	6.4	N18 18.3	5.6	59.4
Y 13	15 13.3	16.0	328 31.5	6.3	18 23.9	5.6	59.4
14	30 13.4	16.8	342 56.8	6.2	18 29.5	5.4	59.4
15	45 13.5 ..	17.7	357 22.0	6.2	18 34.9	5.4	59.4
16	60 13.7	18.6	11 47.2	6.2	18 40.3	5.2	59.4
17	75 13.8	19.4	26 12.4	6.1	18 45.5	5.0	59.4
18	90 13.9 N11	20.3	40 37.5	6.1	N18 50.5	5.0	59.4
19	105 14.1	21.1	55 02.6	6.1	18 55.5	4.8	59.4
20	120 14.2	22.0	69 27.7	6.0	19 00.3	4.7	59.4
21	135 14.3 ..	22.9	83 52.7	5.9	19 05.0	4.6	59.4
22	150 14.5	23.7	98 17.6	6.0	19 09.6	4.4	59.4
23	165 14.6	24.6	112 42.6	5.9	19 14.0	4.4	59.4
20 00	180 14.7 N11	25.4	127 07.5	5.8	N19 18.4	4.2	59.4
01	195 14.9	26.3	141 32.3	5.9	19 22.6	4.0	59.5
02	210 15.0	27.2	155 57.2	5.8	19 26.6	4.0	59.5
03	225 15.1 ..	28.0	170 22.0	5.8	19 30.6	3.8	59.5
04	240 15.3	28.9	184 46.8	5.7	19 34.4	3.7	59.5
05	255 15.4	29.7	199 11.5	5.7	19 38.1	3.5	59.5
06	270 15.5 N11	30.6	213 36.2	5.7	N19 41.6	3.4	59.5
F 07	285 15.7	31.4	228 00.9	5.7	19 45.0	3.3	59.5
R 08	300 15.8	32.3	242 25.6	5.6	19 48.3	3.2	59.5
I 09	315 15.9 ..	33.2	256 50.2	5.6	19 51.5	3.0	59.5
D 10	330 16.1	34.0	271 14.8	5.6	19 54.5	2.9	59.5
A 11	345 16.2	34.9	285 39.4	5.6	19 57.4	2.7	59.5
Y 12	0 16.3 N11	35.7	300 04.0	5.5	N20 00.1	2.6	59.5
13	15 16.4	36.6	314 28.5	5.6	20 02.7	2.5	59.5
14	30 16.6	37.4	328 53.1	5.5	20 05.2	2.4	59.5
15	45 16.7 ..	38.3	343 17.6	5.5	20 07.6	2.2	59.5
16	60 16.8	39.1	357 42.1	5.5	20 09.8	2.1	59.5
17	75 17.0	40.0	12 06.6	5.4	20 11.9	1.9	59.5
18	90 17.1 N11	40.9	26 31.0	5.5	N20 13.8	1.8	59.5
19	105 17.2	41.7	40 55.5	5.4	20 15.6	1.7	59.5
20	120 17.3	42.6	55 19.9	5.5	20 17.3	1.5	59.5
21	135 17.5 ..	43.4	69 44.4	5.4	20 18.8	1.4	59.5
22	150 17.6	44.3	84 08.8	5.4	20 20.2	1.3	59.5
23	165 17.7	45.1	98 33.2	5.4	20 21.5	1.1	59.5
21 00	180 17.9 N11	46.0	112 57.6	5.5	N20 22.6	1.0	59.5
01	195 18.0	46.8	127 22.1	5.4	20 23.6	0.8	59.5
02	210 18.1	47.7	141 46.5	5.4	20 24.4	0.7	59.5
03	225 18.2 ..	48.5	156 10.9	5.4	20 25.1	0.6	59.5
04	240 18.4	49.4	170 35.3	5.4	20 25.7	0.4	59.5
05	255 18.5	50.2	184 59.7	5.4	20 26.1	0.3	59.4
06	270 18.6 N11	51.1	199 24.1	5.4	N20 26.4	0.2	59.4
S 07	285 18.7	51.9	213 48.5	5.4	20 26.6	0.0	59.4
A 08	300 18.9	52.8	228 12.9	5.5	20 26.6	0.1	59.4
T 09	315 19.0 ..	53.6	242 37.4	5.4	20 26.5	0.3	59.4
U 10	330 19.1	54.5	257 01.8	5.5	20 26.2	0.3	59.4
R 11	345 19.2	55.3	271 26.3	5.4	20 25.9	0.6	59.4
D 12	0 19.4 N11	56.2	285 50.7	5.5	N20 25.3	0.6	59.4
A 13	15 19.5	57.0	300 15.2	5.5	20 24.7	0.8	59.4
Y 14	30 19.6	57.9	314 39.7	5.5	20 23.9	1.0	59.4
15	45 19.7 ..	58.7	329 04.2	5.5	20 22.9	1.1	59.4
16	60 19.9	11 59.5	343 28.7	5.5	20 21.8	1.2	59.4
17	75 20.0	12 00.4	357 53.2	5.5	20 20.6	1.3	59.4
18	90 20.1 N12	01.2	12 17.7	5.6	N20 19.3	1.5	59.4
19	105 20.2	02.1	26 42.3	5.6	20 17.8	1.6	59.4
20	120 20.4	02.9	41 06.9	5.6	20 16.2	1.8	59.4
21	135 20.5 ..	03.8	55 31.5	5.6	20 14.4	1.9	59.4
22	150 20.6	04.6	69 56.1	5.7	20 12.5	2.0	59.4
23	165 20.7	05.5	84 20.8	5.7	N20 10.5	2.2	59.4
	SD 15.9	d 0.9	SD 16.2		16.2		16.2

Lat.	Twilight Naut.	Twilight Civil	Sunrise	Moonrise 19	20	21	22
°	h m	h m	h m	h m	h m	h m	h m
N 72	////	00 57	03 10	03 51	☐	☐	☐
N 70	////	01 58	03 31	04 49	04 38	☐	06 21
68	////	02 32	03 48	05 24	05 40	06 18	07 35
66	00 49	02 56	04 01	05 49	06 15	07 00	08 12
64	01 43	03 14	04 12	06 08	06 40	07 29	08 38
62	02 13	03 29	04 21	06 24	07 00	07 51	08 58
60	02 36	03 41	04 29	06 38	07 16	08 08	09 15
N 58	02 53	03 52	04 36	06 50	07 30	08 23	09 29
56	03 08	04 01	04 42	07 00	07 42	08 36	09 41
54	03 20	04 09	04 48	07 09	07 52	08 47	09 51
52	03 30	04 16	04 53	07 17	08 02	08 57	10 01
50	03 39	04 23	04 57	07 24	08 10	09 05	10 09
45	03 58	04 36	05 07	07 39	08 28	09 24	10 27
N 40	04 13	04 47	05 15	07 52	08 42	09 39	10 41
35	04 24	04 56	05 22	08 03	08 55	09 52	10 54
30	04 34	05 03	05 28	08 13	09 05	10 03	11 04
20	04 49	05 16	05 38	08 29	09 24	10 22	11 23
N 10	05 01	05 26	05 47	08 44	09 40	10 39	11 39
0	05 10	05 34	05 56	08 57	09 55	10 55	11 53
S 10	05 18	05 42	06 04	09 11	10 11	11 10	12 08
20	05 24	05 50	06 12	09 26	10 27	11 27	12 24
30	05 30	05 58	06 22	09 43	10 46	11 47	12 43
35	05 32	06 02	06 28	09 52	10 57	11 58	12 53
40	05 35	06 06	06 34	10 04	11 10	12 11	13 05
45	05 37	06 11	06 41	10 17	11 25	12 26	13 20
S 50	05 39	06 17	06 50	10 33	11 43	12 45	13 37
52	05 40	06 19	06 54	10 41	11 52	12 54	13 46
54	05 40	06 22	06 58	10 50	12 01	13 04	13 55
56	05 41	06 25	07 03	10 59	12 12	13 15	14 05
58	05 42	06 28	07 08	11 10	12 25	13 28	14 17
S 60	05 43	06 31	07 14	11 23	12 40	13 43	14 31

Lat.	Sunset	Twilight Civil	Twilight Naut.	Moonset 19	20	21	22
°	h m	h m	h m	h m	h m	h m	h m
N 72	20 52	23 20	////	01 21	☐	☐	☐
N 70	20 30	22 07	////	00 24	02 36	☐	05 01
68	20 13	21 31	////	25 35	01 35	02 59	03 47
66	19 59	21 06	23 26	25 00	01 00	02 17	03 09
64	19 48	20 47	22 21	24 35	00 35	01 49	02 43
62	19 39	20 31	21 49	24 15	00 15	01 27	02 22
60	19 30	20 19	21 25	23 59	25 10	01 10	02 05
N 58	19 23	20 08	21 07	23 46	24 55	00 55	01 51
56	19 17	19 58	20 53	23 34	24 42	00 42	01 39
54	19 11	19 50	20 40	23 24	24 31	00 31	01 28
52	19 06	19 43	20 29	23 15	24 21	00 21	01 18
50	19 01	19 36	20 20	23 07	24 13	00 13	01 10
45	18 52	19 23	20 01	22 49	23 54	24 52	00 52
N 40	18 43	19 12	19 46	22 35	23 39	24 37	00 37
35	18 36	19 03	19 34	22 23	23 26	24 25	00 25
30	18 30	18 55	19 24	22 13	23 15	24 14	00 14
20	18 20	18 42	19 09	21 55	22 56	23 55	24 50
N 10	18 11	18 32	18 57	21 39	22 39	23 38	24 35
0	18 02	18 23	18 48	21 25	22 24	23 23	24 21
S 10	17 54	18 15	18 40	21 10	22 08	23 07	24 07
20	17 45	18 08	18 34	20 55	21 51	22 51	23 52
30	17 35	18 00	18 28	20 37	21 32	22 32	23 34
35	17 30	17 56	18 25	20 26	21 21	22 21	23 24
40	17 23	17 51	18 23	20 15	21 08	22 08	23 12
45	17 16	17 46	18 20	20 01	20 53	21 53	22 58
S 50	17 07	17 40	18 18	19 44	20 34	21 34	22 41
52	17 03	17 38	18 17	19 36	20 25	21 25	22 33
54	16 59	17 35	18 16	19 27	20 16	21 15	22 24
56	16 54	17 32	18 16	19 17	20 04	21 04	22 14
58	16 48	17 29	18 15	19 05	19 52	20 51	22 03
S 60	16 42	17 26	18 14	18 52	19 37	20 36	21 50

Day	SUN Eqn. of Time 00h	12h	SUN Mer. Pass.	MOON Mer. Pass. Upper	Lower	Age	Phase
d	m s	m s	h m	h m	h m	d	%
19	00 46	00 52	11 59	15 11	02 42	03	15
20	00 59	01 05	11 59	16 10	03 40	04	24
21	01 11	01 17	11 59	17 09	04 39	05	34

UT	ARIES GHA	VENUS −3.9 GHA	Dec	MARS −0.2 GHA	Dec	JUPITER −2.5 GHA	Dec	SATURN +0.4 GHA	Dec	STARS Name	SHA	Dec
22 00	210 00.1	155 41.6	N19 51.4	279 10.7	S23 02.3	341 38.2	S16 37.7	290 07.6	S22 14.2	Acamar	315 16.3	S40 14.2
01	225 02.6	170 41.0	52.2	294 11.8	02.2	356 40.9	37.6	305 10.1	14.2	Achernar	335 25.0	S57 08.8
02	240 05.1	185 40.3	53.0	309 13.0	02.1	11 43.7	37.5	320 12.5	14.2	Acrux	173 04.9	S63 12.1
03	255 07.5	200 39.7	.. 53.8	324 14.1	.. 02.0	26 46.4	.. 37.5	335 15.0	.. 14.2	Adhara	255 10.1	S29 00.2
04	270 10.0	215 39.0	54.6	339 15.2	01.9	41 49.2	37.4	350 17.5	14.2	Aldebaran	290 45.9	N16 32.5
05	285 12.5	230 38.3	55.4	354 16.3	01.8	56 51.9	37.3	5 20.0	14.2			
06	300 14.9	245 37.7	N19 56.3	9 17.4	S23 01.7	71 54.7	S16 37.2	20 22.5	S22 14.2	Alioth	166 17.3	N55 51.8
07	315 17.4	260 37.0	57.1	24 18.5	01.7	86 57.5	37.2	35 25.0	14.2	Alkaid	152 55.9	N49 13.4
S 08	330 19.9	275 36.3	57.9	39 19.6	01.6	102 00.2	37.1	50 27.4	14.2	Al Na'ir	27 39.9	S46 52.2
U 09	345 22.3	290 35.7	.. 58.7	54 20.8	.. 01.5	117 03.0	.. 37.0	65 29.9	.. 14.2	Alnilam	275 43.3	S 1 11.7
N 10	0 24.8	305 35.0	19 59.5	69 21.9	01.4	132 05.7	36.9	80 32.4	14.2	Alphard	217 52.8	S 8 44.5
D 11	15 27.3	320 34.4	20 00.3	84 23.0	01.3	147 08.5	36.9	95 34.9	14.2			
A 12	30 29.7	335 33.7	N20 01.1	99 24.1	S23 01.2	162 11.2	S16 36.8	110 37.4	S22 14.2	Alphecca	126 07.9	N26 39.2
Y 13	45 32.2	350 33.0	01.9	114 25.2	01.1	177 14.0	36.7	125 39.9	14.2	Alpheratz	357 40.4	N29 11.2
14	60 34.6	5 32.4	02.7	129 26.3	01.0	192 16.7	36.6	140 42.3	14.2	Altair	62 05.0	N 8 55.0
15	75 37.1	20 31.7	.. 03.5	144 27.5	.. 00.9	207 19.5	.. 36.5	155 44.8	.. 14.2	Ankaa	353 12.9	S42 12.5
16	90 39.6	35 31.0	04.3	159 28.6	00.8	222 22.2	36.5	170 47.3	14.2	Antares	112 21.9	S26 28.2
17	105 42.0	50 30.4	05.1	174 29.7	00.8	237 25.0	36.4	185 49.8	14.2			
18	120 44.5	65 29.7	N20 05.9	189 30.8	S23 00.7	252 27.7	S16 36.3	200 52.3	S22 14.2	Arcturus	145 52.4	N19 05.3
19	135 47.0	80 29.0	06.7	204 31.9	00.6	267 30.5	36.2	215 54.8	14.2	Atria	107 20.4	S69 03.3
20	150 49.4	95 28.4	07.5	219 33.1	00.5	282 33.3	36.2	230 57.2	14.2	Avior	234 16.7	S59 34.5
21	165 51.9	110 27.7	.. 08.3	234 34.2	.. 00.4	297 36.0	.. 36.1	245 59.7	.. 14.2	Bellatrix	278 28.7	N 6 21.7
22	180 54.4	125 27.0	09.1	249 35.3	00.3	312 38.8	36.0	261 02.2	14.2	Betelgeuse	270 58.0	N 7 24.4
23	195 56.8	140 26.4	09.9	264 36.4	00.2	327 41.5	35.9	276 04.7	14.2			
23 00	210 59.3	155 25.7	N20 10.7	279 37.5	S23 00.1	342 44.3	S16 35.9	291 07.2	S22 14.2	Canopus	263 55.0	S52 42.8
01	226 01.8	170 25.0	11.5	294 38.7	23 00.0	357 47.0	35.8	306 09.7	14.2	Capella	280 29.9	N46 00.9
02	241 04.2	185 24.4	12.3	309 39.8	22 59.9	12 49.8	35.7	321 12.2	14.2	Deneb	49 29.3	N45 20.5
03	256 06.7	200 23.7	.. 13.1	324 40.9	.. 59.8	27 52.5	.. 35.6	336 14.6	.. 14.2	Denebola	182 30.1	N14 28.2
04	271 09.1	215 23.0	13.9	339 42.0	59.7	42 55.3	35.5	351 17.1	14.2	Diphda	348 52.9	S17 53.4
05	286 11.6	230 22.3	14.7	354 43.2	59.7	57 58.1	35.5	6 19.6	14.2			
06	301 14.1	245 21.7	N20 15.5	9 44.3	S22 59.6	73 00.8	S16 35.4	21 22.1	S22 14.2	Dubhe	193 47.3	N61 39.3
07	316 16.5	260 21.0	16.3	24 45.4	59.5	88 03.6	35.3	36 24.6	14.2	Elnath	278 08.7	N28 37.2
08	331 19.0	275 20.3	17.1	39 46.5	59.4	103 06.3	35.2	51 27.1	14.2	Eltanin	90 44.3	N51 29.1
M 09	346 21.5	290 19.6	.. 17.9	54 47.7	.. 59.3	118 09.1	.. 35.2	66 29.6	.. 14.2	Enif	33 44.0	N 9 57.4
O 10	1 23.9	305 19.0	18.7	69 48.8	59.2	133 11.8	35.1	81 32.1	14.2	Fomalhaut	15 20.6	S29 31.5
N 11	16 26.4	320 18.3	19.4	84 49.9	59.1	148 14.6	35.0	96 34.5	14.2			
D 12	31 28.9	335 17.6	N20 20.2	99 51.0	S22 59.0	163 17.3	S16 34.9	111 37.0	S22 14.2	Gacrux	171 56.7	S57 13.0
A 13	46 31.3	350 16.9	21.0	114 52.2	58.9	178 20.1	34.9	126 39.5	14.2	Gienah	175 48.6	S17 38.7
Y 14	61 33.8	5 16.3	21.8	129 53.3	58.8	193 22.9	34.8	141 42.0	14.2	Hadar	148 42.5	S60 27.6
15	76 36.3	20 15.6	.. 22.6	144 54.4	.. 58.7	208 25.6	.. 34.7	156 44.5	.. 14.2	Hamal	327 57.4	N23 32.7
16	91 38.7	35 14.9	23.4	159 55.5	58.6	223 28.4	34.6	171 47.0	14.2	Kaus Aust.	83 39.3	S34 22.3
17	106 41.2	50 14.2	24.1	174 56.7	58.5	238 31.1	34.5	186 49.5	14.2			
18	121 43.6	65 13.6	N20 24.9	189 57.8	S22 58.5	253 33.9	S16 34.5	201 52.0	S22 14.2	Kochab	137 19.0	N74 04.9
19	136 46.1	80 12.9	25.7	204 58.9	58.4	268 36.6	34.4	216 54.4	14.2	Markab	13 35.3	N15 18.0
20	151 48.6	95 12.2	26.5	220 00.1	58.3	283 39.4	34.3	231 56.9	14.2	Menkar	314 11.9	N 4 09.4
21	166 51.0	110 11.5	.. 27.3	235 01.2	.. 58.2	298 42.2	.. 34.2	246 59.4	.. 14.2	Menkent	148 03.3	S36 27.5
22	181 53.5	125 10.9	28.0	250 02.3	58.1	313 44.9	34.2	262 01.9	14.2	Miaplacidus	221 38.7	S69 47.9
23	196 56.0	140 10.2	28.8	265 03.5	58.0	328 47.7	34.1	277 04.4	14.2			
24 00	211 58.4	155 09.5	N20 29.6	280 04.6	S22 57.9	343 50.4	S16 34.0	292 06.9	S22 14.2	Mirfak	308 36.1	N49 55.4
01	227 00.9	170 08.8	30.4	295 05.7	57.8	358 53.2	33.9	307 09.4	14.2	Nunki	75 54.2	S26 16.2
02	242 03.4	185 08.1	31.1	310 06.9	57.7	13 56.0	33.8	322 11.9	14.2	Peacock	53 14.2	S56 40.3
03	257 05.8	200 07.5	.. 31.9	325 08.0	.. 57.6	28 58.7	.. 33.8	337 14.4	.. 14.2	Pollux	243 23.8	N27 58.8
04	272 08.3	215 06.8	32.7	340 09.1	57.5	44 01.5	33.7	352 16.9	14.2	Procyon	244 56.4	N 5 10.5
05	287 10.7	230 06.1	33.4	355 10.3	57.4	59 04.2	33.6	7 19.3	14.2			
06	302 13.2	245 05.4	N20 34.2	10 11.4	S22 57.3	74 07.0	S16 33.5	22 21.8	S22 14.2	Rasalhague	96 03.2	N12 32.8
07	317 15.7	260 04.7	35.0	25 12.5	57.2	89 09.8	33.4	37 24.3	14.2	Regulus	207 39.9	N11 52.6
T 08	332 18.1	275 04.0	35.7	40 13.7	57.2	104 12.5	33.4	52 26.8	14.2	Rigel	281 09.2	S 8 11.2
U 09	347 20.6	290 03.4	.. 36.5	55 14.8	.. 57.1	119 15.3	.. 33.3	67 29.3	.. 14.2	Rigil Kent.	139 46.6	S60 54.5
E 10	2 23.1	305 02.7	37.3	70 15.9	57.0	134 18.0	33.2	82 31.8	14.2	Sabik	102 08.5	S15 44.7
S 11	17 25.5	320 02.0	38.0	85 17.1	56.9	149 20.8	33.1	97 34.3	14.2			
D 12	32 28.0	335 01.3	N20 38.8	100 18.2	S22 56.8	164 23.6	S16 33.1	112 36.8	S22 14.3	Schedar	349 37.3	N56 38.0
A 13	47 30.5	350 00.6	39.6	115 19.3	56.7	179 26.3	33.0	127 39.3	14.3	Shaula	96 17.2	S37 06.8
Y 14	62 32.9	4 59.9	40.3	130 20.5	56.6	194 29.1	32.9	142 41.8	14.3	Sirius	258 31.0	S16 44.8
15	77 35.4	19 59.2	.. 41.1	145 21.6	.. 56.5	209 31.8	.. 32.8	157 44.3	.. 14.3	Spica	158 27.5	S11 15.4
16	92 37.9	34 58.6	41.8	160 22.7	56.4	224 34.6	32.7	172 46.8	14.3	Suhail	222 49.9	S43 30.7
17	107 40.3	49 57.9	42.6	175 23.9	56.3	239 37.4	32.7	187 49.3	14.3			
18	122 42.8	64 57.2	N20 43.3	190 25.0	S22 56.2	254 40.1	S16 32.6	202 51.7	S22 14.3	Vega	80 36.6	N38 47.9
19	137 45.2	79 56.5	44.1	205 26.2	56.1	269 42.9	32.5	217 54.2	14.3	Zuben'ubi	137 01.5	S16 07.0
20	152 47.7	94 55.8	44.9	220 27.3	56.0	284 45.6	32.4	232 56.7	14.3			
21	167 50.2	109 55.1	.. 45.6	235 28.4	.. 55.9	299 48.4	.. 32.3	247 59.2	.. 14.3			
22	182 52.6	124 54.4	46.4	250 29.6	55.8	314 51.2	32.3	263 01.7	14.3			
23	197 55.1	139 53.7	47.1	265 30.7	55.7	329 53.9	32.2	278 04.2	14.3			

	SHA	Mer. Pass.
	° ′	h m
Venus	304 26.4	13 39
Mars	68 38.3	5 21
Jupiter	131 45.0	1 09
Saturn	80 07.9	4 35

	ARIES	VENUS	MARS	JUPITER	SATURN
Mer. Pass.	h m 9 54.4	v −0.7 d 0.8	v 1.1 d 0.1	v 2.8 d 0.1	v 2.5 d 0.0

UT	SUN GHA	SUN Dec	MOON GHA	v	Dec	d	HP
d h	° ′	° ′	° ′	′	° ′	′	′
22 00	180 20.9	N12 06.3	98 45.5	5.7	N20 08.3	2.2	59.4
01	195 21.0	07.1	113 10.2	5.7	20 06.1	2.5	59.4
02	210 21.1	08.0	127 34.9	5.8	20 03.6	2.5	59.4
03	225 21.2	.. 08.8	141 59.7	5.8	20 01.1	2.7	59.3
04	240 21.4	09.7	156 24.5	5.8	19 58.4	2.8	59.3
05	255 21.5	10.5	170 49.3	5.9	19 55.6	3.0	59.3
S 06	270 21.6	N12 11.4	185 14.2	5.8	N19 52.6	3.1	59.3
U 07	285 21.7	12.2	199 39.0	6.0	19 49.5	3.2	59.3
N 08	300 21.8	13.0	214 04.0	5.9	19 46.3	3.3	59.3
D 09	315 22.0	.. 13.9	228 28.9	6.0	19 43.0	3.5	59.3
A 10	330 22.1	14.7	242 53.9	6.1	19 39.5	3.6	59.3
Y 11	345 22.2	15.6	257 19.0	6.0	19 35.9	3.7	59.3
12	0 22.3	N12 16.4	271 44.0	6.2	N19 32.2	3.9	59.3
13	15 22.4	17.2	286 09.2	6.1	19 28.3	4.0	59.3
14	30 22.6	18.1	300 34.3	6.2	19 24.3	4.1	59.3
15	45 22.7	.. 18.9	314 59.5	6.2	19 20.2	4.2	59.3
16	60 22.8	19.7	329 24.7	6.3	19 16.0	4.4	59.3
17	75 22.9	20.6	343 50.0	6.3	19 11.6	4.4	59.2
18	90 23.0	N12 21.4	358 15.3	6.4	N19 07.2	4.6	59.2
19	105 23.2	22.3	12 40.7	6.4	19 02.6	4.8	59.2
20	120 23.3	23.1	27 06.1	6.5	18 57.8	4.8	59.2
21	135 23.4	.. 23.9	41 31.6	6.5	18 53.0	5.0	59.2
22	150 23.5	24.8	55 57.1	6.6	18 48.0	5.1	59.2
23	165 23.6	25.6	70 22.7	6.6	18 42.9	5.2	59.2
23 00	180 23.8	N12 26.4	84 48.3	6.6	N18 37.7	5.3	59.2
01	195 23.9	27.3	99 13.9	6.7	18 32.4	5.4	59.2
02	210 24.0	28.1	113 39.6	6.8	18 27.0	5.6	59.2
03	225 24.1	.. 28.9	128 05.4	6.8	18 21.4	5.6	59.2
04	240 24.2	29.8	142 31.2	6.8	18 15.8	5.8	59.1
05	255 24.4	30.6	156 57.0	7.0	18 10.0	5.9	59.1
M 06	270 24.5	N12 31.4	171 23.0	6.9	N18 04.1	6.0	59.1
O 07	285 24.6	32.3	185 48.9	7.0	17 58.1	6.1	59.1
N 08	300 24.7	33.1	200 14.9	7.1	17 52.0	6.3	59.1
D 09	315 24.8	.. 33.9	214 41.0	7.1	17 45.7	6.3	59.1
A 10	330 24.9	34.8	229 07.1	7.2	17 39.4	6.5	59.1
Y 11	345 25.1	35.6	243 33.3	7.3	17 32.9	6.5	59.1
12	0 25.2	N12 36.4	257 59.6	7.3	N17 26.4	6.7	59.1
13	15 25.3	37.3	272 25.9	7.3	17 19.7	6.8	59.1
14	30 25.4	38.1	286 52.2	7.4	17 12.9	6.8	59.0
15	45 25.5	.. 38.9	301 18.6	7.5	17 06.1	7.0	59.0
16	60 25.6	39.7	315 45.1	7.5	16 59.1	7.1	59.0
17	75 25.8	40.6	330 11.6	7.6	16 52.0	7.2	59.0
18	90 25.9	N12 41.4	344 38.2	7.6	N16 44.8	7.3	59.0
19	105 26.0	42.2	359 04.8	7.7	16 37.5	7.3	59.0
20	120 26.1	43.1	13 31.5	7.8	16 30.2	7.5	59.0
21	135 26.2	.. 43.9	27 58.3	7.8	16 22.7	7.6	59.0
22	150 26.3	44.7	42 25.1	7.9	16 15.1	7.7	58.9
23	165 26.4	45.5	56 52.0	7.9	16 07.4	7.7	58.9
24 00	180 26.6	N12 46.4	71 18.9	8.0	N15 59.7	7.9	58.9
01	195 26.7	47.2	85 45.9	8.0	15 51.8	8.0	58.9
02	210 26.8	48.0	100 12.9	8.2	15 43.8	8.0	58.9
03	225 26.9	.. 48.8	114 40.1	8.1	15 35.8	8.2	58.9
04	240 27.0	49.7	129 07.2	8.3	15 27.6	8.2	58.9
05	255 27.1	50.5	143 34.5	8.3	15 19.4	8.3	58.9
T 06	270 27.2	N12 51.3	158 01.8	8.3	N15 11.1	8.4	58.9
U 07	285 27.3	52.1	172 29.1	8.4	15 02.7	8.5	58.8
E 08	300 27.5	53.0	186 56.5	8.5	14 54.2	8.6	58.8
S 09	315 27.6	.. 53.8	201 24.0	8.5	14 45.6	8.7	58.8
D 10	330 27.7	54.6	215 51.5	8.6	14 36.9	8.7	58.8
A 11	345 27.8	55.4	230 19.1	8.7	14 28.2	8.8	58.8
Y 12	0 27.9	N12 56.3	244 46.8	8.7	N14 19.4	9.0	58.8
13	15 28.0	57.1	259 14.5	8.7	14 10.4	9.0	58.8
14	30 28.1	57.9	273 42.2	8.9	14 01.4	9.0	58.7
15	45 28.2	.. 58.7	288 10.1	8.9	13 52.4	9.2	58.7
16	60 28.4	12 59.5	302 38.0	8.9	13 43.2	9.2	58.7
17	75 28.5	13 00.4	317 05.9	9.0	13 34.0	9.3	58.7
18	90 28.6	N13 01.2	331 33.9	9.1	N13 24.7	9.4	58.7
19	105 28.7	02.0	346 02.0	9.1	13 15.3	9.4	58.7
20	120 28.8	02.8	0 30.1	9.2	13 05.9	9.5	58.7
21	135 28.9	.. 03.6	14 58.3	9.2	12 56.4	9.6	58.7
22	150 29.0	04.4	29 26.5	9.3	12 46.8	9.7	58.6
23	165 29.1	05.3	43 54.8	9.4	N12 37.1	9.7	58.6
	SD 15.9	d 0.8	SD 16.2		16.1		16.0

Twilight / Sunrise / Moonrise

Lat.	Naut.	Civil	Sunrise	22	23	24	25
°	h m	h m	h m	h m	h m	h m	h m
N 72	////	////	02 51	▭	07 13	10 07	12 17
N 70	////	01 31	03 16	06 21	08 37	10 39	12 34
68	////	02 13	03 34	07 35	09 15	11 02	12 48
66	////	02 40	03 49	08 12	09 42	11 20	12 59
64	01 19	03 01	04 01	08 38	10 03	11 35	13 08
62	01 57	03 18	04 12	08 58	10 19	11 47	13 16
60	02 22	03 32	04 21	09 15	10 33	11 57	13 23
N 58	02 42	03 43	04 28	09 29	10 45	12 06	13 29
56	02 58	03 53	04 35	09 41	10 55	12 14	13 34
54	03 11	04 02	04 41	09 51	11 04	12 21	13 39
52	03 22	04 09	04 47	10 01	11 12	12 27	13 43
50	03 32	04 16	04 52	10 09	11 19	12 33	13 47
45	03 52	04 31	05 02	10 27	11 35	12 45	13 55
N 40	04 08	04 42	05 11	10 41	11 47	12 55	14 02
35	04 20	04 52	05 18	10 54	11 58	13 03	14 08
30	04 31	05 00	05 25	11 04	12 07	13 11	14 13
20	04 47	05 13	05 36	11 23	12 23	13 24	14 22
N 10	04 59	05 24	05 46	11 39	12 37	13 35	14 30
0	05 09	05 34	05 55	11 53	12 51	13 45	14 37
S 10	05 18	05 42	06 04	12 08	13 04	13 56	14 45
20	05 25	05 51	06 13	12 24	13 18	14 07	14 53
30	05 31	05 59	06 24	12 43	13 34	14 20	15 01
35	05 34	06 04	06 30	12 53	13 43	14 27	15 07
40	05 37	06 09	06 37	13 05	13 53	14 35	15 12
45	05 40	06 15	06 45	13 20	14 06	14 45	15 19
S 50	05 43	06 21	06 54	13 37	14 21	14 57	15 27
52	05 44	06 24	06 59	13 46	14 28	15 02	15 31
54	05 45	06 27	07 04	13 55	14 36	15 08	15 35
56	05 47	06 30	07 09	14 05	14 44	15 15	15 39
58	05 48	06 34	07 15	14 17	14 54	15 22	15 44
S 60	05 49	06 38	07 22	14 31	15 05	15 30	15 50

Sunset / Twilight / Moonset

Lat.	Sunset	Civil	Naut.	22	23	24	25
°	h m	h m	h m	h m	h m	h m	h m
N 72	21 10	////	////	▭	06 10	05 12	04 52
N 70	20 45	22 35	////	05 01	04 45	04 38	04 33
68	20 25	21 49	////	03 47	04 06	04 14	04 18
66	20 10	21 20	////	03 09	03 39	03 55	04 05
64	19 57	20 58	22 46	02 43	03 17	03 40	03 55
62	19 47	20 41	22 05	02 22	03 00	03 27	03 46
60	19 38	20 27	21 38	02 05	02 46	03 16	03 38
N 58	19 30	20 15	21 18	01 51	02 34	03 06	03 31
56	19 23	20 05	21 01	01 39	02 23	02 58	03 25
54	19 17	19 56	20 48	01 28	02 14	02 50	03 20
52	19 11	19 49	20 36	01 18	02 05	02 44	03 15
50	19 06	19 42	20 26	01 10	01 58	02 37	03 11
45	18 55	19 27	20 06	00 52	01 42	02 24	03 01
N 40	18 46	19 15	19 50	00 37	01 29	02 13	02 53
35	18 39	19 05	19 37	00 25	01 17	02 04	02 46
30	18 32	18 57	19 27	00 14	01 07	01 56	02 40
20	18 21	18 43	19 10	24 50	00 50	01 41	02 29
N 10	18 11	18 32	18 58	24 35	00 35	01 29	02 19
0	18 02	18 23	18 47	24 21	00 21	01 17	02 10
S 10	17 53	18 14	18 39	24 07	00 07	01 05	02 01
20	17 43	18 06	18 32	23 52	24 52	00 52	01 52
30	17 32	17 57	18 25	23 34	24 38	00 38	01 41
35	17 26	17 52	18 22	23 24	24 29	00 29	01 34
40	17 19	17 47	18 19	23 12	24 19	00 19	01 27
45	17 11	17 41	18 16	22 58	24 08	00 08	01 18
S 50	17 02	17 35	18 13	22 41	23 54	25 08	01 08
52	16 57	17 32	18 12	22 33	23 47	25 03	01 03
54	16 52	17 29	18 10	22 24	23 40	24 58	00 58
56	16 47	17 26	18 09	22 14	23 31	24 52	00 52
58	16 41	17 22	18 08	22 03	23 22	24 45	00 45
S 60	16 34	17 18	18 07	21 50	23 12	24 37	00 37

SUN / MOON

Day	Eqn. of Time 00h	Eqn. of Time 12h	Mer. Pass.	Mer. Pass. Upper	Mer. Pass. Lower	Age	Phase
d	m s	m s	h m	h m	h m	d	%
22	01 23	01 29	11 59	18 07	05 38	06	45
23	01 35	01 40	11 58	19 04	06 36	07	57
24	01 46	01 51	11 58	19 58	07 31	08	68

UT	ARIES	VENUS −3.9		MARS −0.3		JUPITER −2.5		SATURN +0.4		STARS		
	GHA	GHA	Dec	GHA	Dec	GHA	Dec	GHA	Dec	Name	SHA	Dec
d h	° ′	° ′	° ′	° ′	° ′	° ′	° ′	° ′	° ′		° ′	° ′
25 00	212 57.6	154 53.0	N20 47.9	280 31.9	S22 55.6	344 56.7	S16 32.1	293 06.7	S22 14.3	Acamar	315 16.3	S40 14.2
01	228 00.0	169 52.4	48.6	295 33.0	55.6	359 59.4	32.0	308 09.2	14.3	Achernar	335 25.0	S57 08.8
02	243 02.5	184 51.7	49.4	310 34.1	55.5	15 02.2	32.0	323 11.7	14.3	Acrux	173 04.9	S63 12.1
03	258 05.0	199 51.0 ..	50.1	325 35.3 ..	55.4	30 05.0 ..	31.9	338 14.2 ..	14.3	Adhara	255 10.1	S29 00.2
04	273 07.4	214 50.3	50.9	340 36.4	55.3	45 07.7	31.8	353 16.7	14.3	Aldebaran	290 45.9	N16 32.5
05	288 09.9	229 49.6	51.6	355 37.6	55.2	60 10.5	31.7	8 19.2	14.3			
W 06	303 12.4	244 48.9	N20 52.4	10 38.7	S22 55.1	75 13.3	S16 31.6	23 21.7	S22 14.3	Alioth	166 17.3	N55 51.8
E 07	318 14.8	259 48.2	53.1	25 39.9	55.0	90 16.0	31.6	38 24.2	14.3	Alkaid	152 55.9	N49 13.4
D 08	333 17.3	274 47.5	53.8	40 41.0	54.9	105 18.8	31.5	53 26.7	14.3	Al Na'ir	27 39.9	S46 52.2
N 09	348 19.7	289 46.8 ..	54.6	55 42.1 ..	54.8	120 21.5 ..	31.4	68 29.2 ..	14.3	Alnilam	275 43.3	S 1 11.7
E 10	3 22.2	304 46.1	55.3	70 43.3	54.7	135 24.3	31.3	83 31.7	14.3	Alphard	217 52.8	S 8 44.5
S 11	18 24.7	319 45.4	56.1	85 44.4	54.6	150 27.1	31.2	98 34.2	14.3			
D 12	33 27.1	334 44.7	N20 56.8	100 45.6	S22 54.5	165 29.8	S16 31.2	113 36.7	S22 14.3	Alphecca	126 07.9	N26 39.2
A 13	48 29.6	349 44.0	57.5	115 46.7	54.4	180 32.6	31.1	128 39.2	14.3	Alpheratz	357 40.4	N29 11.2
Y 14	63 32.1	4 43.3	58.3	130 47.9	54.3	195 35.4	31.0	143 41.7	14.3	Altair	62 05.0	N 8 55.0
15	78 34.5	19 42.6 ..	59.0	145 49.0 ..	54.2	210 38.1 ..	30.9	158 44.1 ..	14.3	Ankaa	353 12.9	S42 12.5
16	93 37.0	34 41.9	20 59.8	160 50.2	54.1	225 40.9	30.8	173 46.6	14.3	Antares	112 21.9	S26 28.2
17	108 39.5	49 41.2	21 00.5	175 51.3	54.0	240 43.7	30.8	188 49.1	14.3			
18	123 41.9	64 40.5	N21 01.2	190 52.5	S22 53.9	255 46.4	S16 30.7	203 51.6	S22 14.3	Arcturus	145 52.4	N19 05.3
19	138 44.4	79 39.8	02.0	205 53.6	53.8	270 49.2	30.6	218 54.1	14.3	Atria	107 20.3	S69 03.3
20	153 46.8	94 39.1	02.7	220 54.8	53.7	285 51.9	30.5	233 56.6	14.3	Avior	234 16.7	S59 34.5
21	168 49.3	109 38.4 ..	03.4	235 55.9 ..	53.6	300 54.7 ..	30.4	248 59.1 ..	14.3	Bellatrix	278 28.7	N 6 21.7
22	183 51.8	124 37.7	04.2	250 57.1	53.5	315 57.5	30.4	264 01.6	14.3	Betelgeuse	270 58.0	N 7 24.4
23	198 54.2	139 37.0	04.9	265 58.2	53.5	331 00.2	30.3	279 04.1	14.3			
26 00	213 56.7	154 36.3	N21 05.6	280 59.4	S22 53.4	346 03.0	S16 30.2	294 06.6	S22 14.3	Canopus	263 55.0	S52 42.7
01	228 59.2	169 35.6	06.3	296 00.5	53.3	1 05.8	30.1	309 09.1	14.3	Capella	280 30.0	N46 00.8
02	244 01.6	184 34.9	07.1	311 01.7	53.2	16 08.5	30.1	324 11.6	14.3	Deneb	49 29.3	N45 20.5
03	259 04.1	199 34.2 ..	07.8	326 02.8 ..	53.1	31 11.3 ..	30.0	339 14.1 ..	14.3	Denebola	182 30.1	N14 28.2
04	274 06.6	214 33.5	08.5	341 04.0	53.0	46 14.1	29.9	354 16.6	14.3	Diphda	348 52.9	S17 53.4
05	289 09.0	229 32.8	09.2	356 05.1	52.9	61 16.8	29.8	9 19.1	14.3			
T 06	304 11.5	244 32.1	N21 10.0	11 06.3	S22 52.8	76 19.6	S16 29.7	24 21.6	S22 14.3	Dubhe	193 47.4	N61 39.4
H 07	319 14.0	259 31.4	10.7	26 07.4	52.7	91 22.4	29.7	39 24.1	14.3	Elnath	278 08.8	N28 37.2
U 08	334 16.4	274 30.7	11.4	41 08.6	52.6	106 25.1	29.6	54 26.6	14.3	Eltanin	90 44.3	N51 29.1
R 09	349 18.9	289 30.0 ..	12.1	56 09.7 ..	52.5	121 27.9 ..	29.5	69 29.1 ..	14.3	Enif	33 44.0	N 9 57.4
S 10	4 21.3	304 29.3	12.8	71 10.9	52.4	136 30.7	29.4	84 31.6	14.3	Fomalhaut	15 20.6	S29 31.5
D 11	19 23.8	319 28.6	13.5	86 12.0	52.3	151 33.4	29.3	99 34.1	14.3			
A 12	34 26.3	334 27.9	N21 14.3	101 13.2	S22 52.2	166 36.2	S16 29.3	114 36.6	S22 14.3	Gacrux	171 56.7	S57 13.0
Y 13	49 28.7	349 27.2	15.0	116 14.3	52.1	181 39.0	29.2	129 39.1	14.3	Gienah	175 48.6	S17 38.7
14	64 31.2	4 26.5	15.7	131 15.5	52.0	196 41.7	29.1	144 41.6	14.3	Hadar	148 42.5	S60 27.6
15	79 33.7	19 25.8 ..	16.4	146 16.7 ..	51.9	211 44.5 ..	29.0	159 44.1 ..	14.3	Hamal	327 57.4	N23 32.6
16	94 36.1	34 25.1	17.1	161 17.8	51.8	226 47.3	28.9	174 46.6	14.3	Kaus Aust.	83 39.3	S34 22.3
17	109 38.6	49 24.4	17.8	176 19.0	51.7	241 50.0	28.9	189 49.1	14.3			
18	124 41.1	64 23.7	N21 18.5	191 20.1	S22 51.6	256 52.8	S16 28.8	204 51.6	S22 14.4	Kochab	137 19.0	N74 04.9
19	139 43.5	79 22.9	19.2	206 21.3	51.5	271 55.6	28.7	219 54.1	14.4	Markab	13 35.3	N15 18.0
20	154 46.0	94 22.2	20.0	221 22.4	51.4	286 58.3	28.6	234 56.6	14.4	Menkar	314 11.9	N 4 09.4
21	169 48.4	109 21.5 ..	20.7	236 23.6 ..	51.3	302 01.1 ..	28.5	249 59.1 ..	14.4	Menkent	148 03.3	S36 27.5
22	184 50.9	124 20.8	21.4	251 24.8	51.2	317 03.9	28.5	265 01.6	14.4	Miaplacidus	221 38.8	S69 47.9
23	199 53.4	139 20.1	22.1	266 25.9	51.1	332 06.6	28.4	280 04.2	14.4			
27 00	214 55.8	154 19.4	N21 22.8	281 27.1	S22 51.0	347 09.4	S16 28.3	295 06.7	S22 14.4	Mirfak	308 36.1	N49 55.3
01	229 58.3	169 18.7	23.5	296 28.2	50.9	2 12.2	28.2	310 09.2	14.4	Nunki	75 54.1	S26 16.2
02	245 00.8	184 18.0	24.2	311 29.4	50.8	17 14.9	28.1	325 11.7	14.4	Peacock	53 14.1	S56 40.3
03	260 03.2	199 17.3 ..	24.9	326 30.6 ..	50.7	32 17.7 ..	28.1	340 14.2 ..	14.4	Pollux	243 23.8	N27 58.8
04	275 05.7	214 16.5	25.6	341 31.7	50.6	47 20.5	28.0	355 16.7	14.4	Procyon	244 56.4	N 5 10.5
05	290 08.2	229 15.8	26.3	356 32.9	50.5	62 23.2	27.9	10 19.2	14.4			
F 06	305 10.6	244 15.1	N21 27.0	11 34.1	S22 50.4	77 26.0	S16 27.8	25 21.7	S22 14.4	Rasalhague	96 03.2	N12 32.8
R 07	320 13.1	259 14.4	27.7	26 35.2	50.3	92 28.8	27.7	40 24.2	14.4	Regulus	207 39.9	N11 52.6
I 08	335 15.6	274 13.7	28.4	41 36.4	50.2	107 31.5	27.6	55 26.7	14.4	Rigel	281 09.2	S 8 11.2
D 09	350 18.0	289 13.0 ..	29.1	56 37.5 ..	50.2	122 34.3 ..	27.6	70 29.2 ..	14.4	Rigil Kent.	139 46.6	S60 54.5
A 10	5 20.5	304 12.3	29.8	71 38.7	50.1	137 37.1	27.5	85 31.7	14.4	Sabik	102 08.5	S15 44.7
Y 11	20 22.9	319 11.5	30.5	86 39.9	50.0	152 39.8	27.4	100 34.2	14.4			
12	35 25.4	334 10.8	N21 31.1	101 41.0	S22 49.9	167 42.6	S16 27.3	115 36.7	S22 14.4	Schedar	349 37.2	N56 38.0
13	50 27.9	349 10.1	31.8	116 42.2	49.8	182 45.4	27.2	130 39.2	14.4	Shaula	96 17.2	S37 06.8
14	65 30.3	4 09.4	32.5	131 43.4	49.7	197 48.1	27.2	145 41.7	14.4	Sirius	258 31.0	S16 44.8
15	80 32.8	19 08.7 ..	33.2	146 44.5 ..	49.6	212 50.9 ..	27.1	160 44.2 ..	14.4	Spica	158 27.5	S11 15.4
16	95 35.3	34 08.0	33.9	161 45.7	49.5	227 53.7	27.0	175 46.7	14.4	Suhail	222 50.0	S43 30.7
17	110 37.7	49 07.2	34.6	176 46.9	49.4	242 56.5	26.9	190 49.2	14.4			
18	125 40.2	64 06.5	N21 35.3	191 48.0	S22 49.3	257 59.2	S16 26.8	205 51.7	S22 14.4	Vega	80 36.5	N38 47.9
19	140 42.7	79 05.8	36.0	206 49.2	49.2	273 02.0	26.8	220 54.2	14.4	Zuben'ubi	137 01.5	S16 07.0
20	155 45.1	94 05.1	36.6	221 50.4	49.1	288 04.8	26.7	235 56.8	14.4		SHA	Mer. Pass.
21	170 47.6	109 04.4 ..	37.3	236 51.5 ..	49.0	303 07.5 ..	26.6	250 59.3 ..	14.4		° ′	h m
22	185 50.1	124 03.6	38.0	251 52.7	48.9	318 10.3	26.5	266 01.8	14.4	Venus	300 39.6	13 42
23	200 52.5	139 02.9	38.7	266 53.9	48.8	333 13.1	26.4	281 04.3	14.4	Mars	67 02.7	5 16
	h m									Jupiter	132 06.3	0 56
Mer. Pass. 9 42.6		v −0.7	d 0.7	v 1.2	d 0.1	v 2.8	d 0.1	v 2.5	d 0.0	Saturn	80 09.9	4 23

UT	SUN GHA	SUN Dec	MOON GHA	v	MOON Dec	d	HP
d h	° ′	° ′	° ′	′	° ′	′	′
25 00	180 29.2	N13 06.1	58 23.2	9.4	N12 27.4	9.8	58.6
01	195 29.3	06.9	72 51.6	9.5	12 17.6	9.9	58.6
02	210 29.5	07.7	87 20.1	9.5	12 07.7	9.9	58.6
03	225 29.6 ..	08.5	101 48.6	9.6	11 57.8	10.0	58.6
04	240 29.7	09.3	116 17.2	9.6	11 47.8	10.0	58.6
05	255 29.8	10.2	130 45.8	9.7	11 37.8	10.1	58.5
06	270 29.9	N13 11.0	145 14.5	9.8	N11 27.7	10.2	58.5
W 07	285 30.0	11.8	159 43.3	9.8	11 17.5	10.2	58.5
E 08	300 30.1	12.6	174 12.1	9.9	11 07.3	10.3	58.5
D 09	315 30.2 ..	13.4	188 41.0	9.9	10 57.0	10.4	58.5
N 10	330 30.3	14.2	203 09.9	9.9	10 46.6	10.4	58.5
E 11	345 30.4	15.0	217 38.8	10.1	10 36.2	10.4	58.4
S 12	0 30.5	N13 15.9	232 07.9	10.0	N10 25.8	10.5	58.4
D 13	15 30.6	16.7	246 36.9	10.2	10 15.3	10.6	58.4
A 14	30 30.7	17.5	261 06.1	10.2	10 04.7	10.6	58.4
Y 15	45 30.8 ..	18.3	275 35.3	10.2	9 54.1	10.7	58.4
16	60 31.0	19.1	290 04.5	10.3	9 43.4	10.7	58.4
17	75 31.1	19.9	304 33.8	10.3	9 32.7	10.7	58.4
18	90 31.2	N13 20.7	319 03.1	10.4	N 9 22.0	10.8	58.3
19	105 31.3	21.5	333 32.5	10.4	9 11.2	10.9	58.3
20	120 31.4	22.3	348 01.9	10.5	9 00.3	10.9	58.3
21	135 31.5 ..	23.2	2 31.4	10.5	8 49.4	10.9	58.3
22	150 31.6	24.0	17 00.9	10.6	8 38.5	11.0	58.3
23	165 31.7	24.8	31 30.5	10.6	8 27.5	11.0	58.3
26 00	180 31.8	N13 25.6	46 00.1	10.7	N 8 16.5	11.1	58.2
01	195 31.9	26.4	60 29.8	10.7	8 05.4	11.1	58.2
02	210 32.0	27.2	74 59.5	10.8	7 54.3	11.1	58.2
03	225 32.1 ..	28.0	89 29.3	10.8	7 43.2	11.2	58.2
04	240 32.2	28.8	103 59.1	10.9	7 32.0	11.2	58.2
05	255 32.3	29.6	118 29.0	10.9	7 20.8	11.2	58.2
06	270 32.4	N13 30.4	132 58.9	10.9	N 7 09.6	11.3	58.1
T 07	285 32.5	31.2	147 28.8	11.0	6 58.3	11.3	58.1
H 08	300 32.6	32.0	161 58.8	11.0	6 47.0	11.3	58.1
U 09	315 32.7 ..	32.8	176 28.8	11.1	6 35.7	11.4	58.1
R 10	330 32.8	33.6	190 58.9	11.1	6 24.3	11.4	58.1
S 11	345 32.9	34.4	205 29.0	11.1	6 12.9	11.4	58.1
D 12	0 33.0	N13 35.2	219 59.1	11.2	N 6 01.5	11.5	58.0
A 13	15 33.1	36.0	234 29.3	11.3	5 50.0	11.4	58.0
Y 14	30 33.2	36.8	248 59.6	11.2	5 38.6	11.5	58.0
15	45 33.3 ..	37.7	263 29.8	11.3	5 27.1	11.5	58.0
16	60 33.4	38.5	278 00.1	11.4	5 15.6	11.6	58.0
17	75 33.5	39.3	292 30.5	11.4	5 04.0	11.5	57.9
18	90 33.6	N13 40.1	307 00.9	11.4	N 4 52.5	11.6	57.9
19	105 33.7	40.9	321 31.3	11.4	4 40.9	11.6	57.9
20	120 33.8	41.7	336 01.7	11.5	4 29.3	11.6	57.9
21	135 33.9 ..	42.5	350 32.2	11.5	4 17.7	11.6	57.9
22	150 34.0	43.3	5 02.7	11.6	4 06.1	11.7	57.9
23	165 34.1	44.1	19 33.3	11.6	3 54.4	11.6	57.8
27 00	180 34.2	N13 44.9	34 03.9	11.6	N 3 42.8	11.7	57.8
01	195 34.3	45.7	48 34.5	11.6	3 31.1	11.7	57.8
02	210 34.4	46.4	63 05.1	11.7	3 19.4	11.7	57.8
03	225 34.5 ..	47.2	77 35.8	11.6	3 07.7	11.7	57.8
04	240 34.6	48.0	92 06.5	11.8	2 56.0	11.7	57.7
05	255 34.7	48.8	106 37.3	11.7	2 44.3	11.7	57.7
06	270 34.8	N13 49.6	121 08.0	11.8	N 2 32.6	11.7	57.7
F 07	285 34.9	50.4	135 38.8	11.9	2 20.9	11.8	57.7
R 08	300 35.0	51.2	150 09.7	11.8	2 09.1	11.7	57.7
I 09	315 35.1 ..	52.0	164 40.5	11.9	1 57.4	11.7	57.7
D 10	330 35.2	52.8	179 11.4	11.9	1 45.7	11.8	57.6
A 11	345 35.3	53.6	193 42.3	11.9	1 33.9	11.7	57.6
Y 12	0 35.4	N13 54.4	208 13.2	12.0	N 1 22.2	11.8	57.6
13	15 35.5	55.2	222 44.2	12.0	1 10.4	11.7	57.6
14	30 35.6	56.0	237 15.2	12.0	0 58.7	11.7	57.6
15	45 35.7 ..	56.8	251 46.2	12.0	0 47.0	11.8	57.5
16	60 35.8	57.6	266 17.2	12.0	0 35.2	11.7	57.5
17	75 35.9	58.4	280 48.2	12.1	0 23.5	11.7	57.5
18	90 36.0	N13 59.2	295 19.3	12.1	N 0 11.8	11.7	57.5
19	105 36.1	14 00.0	309 50.4	12.1	N 0 00.1	11.7	57.5
20	120 36.2	00.7	324 21.5	12.1	S 0 11.6	11.8	57.4
21	135 36.3 ..	01.5	338 52.6	12.2	0 23.4	11.6	57.4
22	150 36.4	02.3	353 23.8	12.1	0 35.0	11.7	57.4
23	165 36.5	03.1	7 54.9	12.2	S 0 46.7	11.7	57.4
	SD 15.9	d 0.8	SD 15.9		15.8		15.7

Lat.	Naut.	Civil	Sunrise	Moonrise 25	26	27	28
°	h m	h m	h m	h m	h m	h m	h m
N 72	////	////	02 31	12 17	14 16	16 10	18 02
N 70	////	00 53	03 00	12 34	14 24	16 11	17 55
68	////	01 52	03 21	12 48	14 31	16 11	17 50
66	////	02 25	03 37	12 59	14 36	16 12	17 45
64	00 47	02 48	03 51	13 08	14 41	16 12	17 41
62	01 39	03 07	04 02	13 16	14 45	16 12	17 38
60	02 08	03 22	04 12	13 23	14 48	16 13	17 35
N 58	02 30	03 34	04 21	13 29	14 51	16 13	17 33
56	02 48	03 45	04 28	13 34	14 54	16 13	17 30
54	03 02	03 54	04 35	13 39	14 57	16 13	17 28
52	03 15	04 03	04 40	13 43	14 59	16 13	17 27
50	03 25	04 10	04 46	13 47	15 01	16 14	17 25
45	03 47	04 26	04 57	13 55	15 05	16 14	17 21
N 40	04 03	04 38	05 07	14 02	15 09	16 14	17 18
35	04 16	04 48	05 15	14 08	15 12	16 14	17 16
30	04 27	04 57	05 22	14 13	15 15	16 15	17 14
20	04 44	05 11	05 34	14 22	15 19	16 15	17 10
N 10	04 58	05 23	05 45	14 30	15 24	16 16	17 07
0	05 08	05 33	05 54	14 37	15 27	16 16	17 03
S 10	05 18	05 43	06 04	14 45	15 31	16 16	17 00
20	05 26	05 52	06 14	14 53	15 36	16 17	16 57
30	05 33	06 01	06 26	15 01	15 40	16 17	16 53
35	05 37	06 06	06 32	15 07	15 43	16 18	16 51
40	05 40	06 12	06 40	15 12	15 46	16 18	16 49
45	05 44	06 18	06 48	15 19	15 50	16 18	16 46
S 50	05 47	06 25	06 59	15 27	15 54	16 19	16 43
52	05 49	06 28	07 04	15 31	15 56	16 19	16 42
54	05 50	06 32	07 09	15 35	15 58	16 19	16 40
56	05 52	06 36	07 15	15 39	16 00	16 20	16 38
58	05 53	06 40	07 21	15 44	16 03	16 20	16 36
S 60	05 55	06 44	07 29	15 50	16 06	16 20	16 34

Lat.	Sunset	Civil	Naut.	Moonset 25	26	27	28
°	h m	h m	h m	h m	h m	h m	h m
N 72	21 30	////	////	04 52	04 38	04 26	04 15
N 70	21 00	23 20	////	04 33	04 27	04 22	04 17
68	20 38	22 10	////	04 18	04 19	04 19	04 19
66	20 21	21 35	////	04 05	04 12	04 17	04 21
64	20 07	21 11	23 25	03 55	04 06	04 15	04 23
62	19 55	20 52	22 23	03 46	04 00	04 13	04 24
60	19 45	20 36	21 51	03 38	03 56	04 11	04 25
N 58	19 37	20 23	21 28	03 31	03 52	04 09	04 26
56	19 29	20 12	21 10	03 25	03 48	04 08	04 27
54	19 22	20 03	20 55	03 20	03 45	04 07	04 28
52	19 16	19 54	20 43	03 15	03 42	04 06	04 29
50	19 11	19 47	20 33	03 11	03 39	04 05	04 29
45	18 59	19 31	20 10	03 01	03 33	04 03	04 31
N 40	18 49	19 18	19 53	02 53	03 28	04 01	04 32
35	18 41	19 08	19 40	02 46	03 24	03 59	04 33
30	18 34	18 59	19 29	02 40	03 20	03 58	04 34
20	18 22	18 45	19 12	02 29	03 13	03 55	04 36
N 10	18 11	18 33	18 58	02 19	03 07	03 53	04 37
0	18 01	18 22	18 47	02 10	03 02	03 51	04 39
S 10	17 51	18 13	18 38	02 01	02 56	03 49	04 40
20	17 41	18 04	18 30	01 52	02 50	03 46	04 41
30	17 29	17 54	18 22	01 41	02 43	03 44	04 43
35	17 23	17 49	18 19	01 34	02 39	03 42	04 44
40	17 15	17 43	18 15	01 27	02 34	03 40	04 45
45	17 07	17 37	18 11	01 18	02 29	03 38	04 46
S 50	16 56	17 30	18 08	01 08	02 22	03 36	04 48
52	16 51	17 26	18 06	01 03	02 19	03 34	04 48
54	16 46	17 23	18 04	00 58	02 16	03 33	04 49
56	16 40	17 19	18 03	00 52	02 12	03 32	04 50
58	16 33	17 15	18 01	00 45	02 08	03 30	04 51
S 60	16 26	17 10	17 59	00 37	02 03	03 28	04 52

Day	Eqn. of Time 00h	Eqn. of Time 12h	Mer. Pass.	Mer. Pass. Upper	Mer. Pass. Lower	Age	Phase
d	m s	m s	h m	h m	h m	d	%
25	01 57	02 02	11 58	20 50	08 24	09	78
26	02 07	02 12	11 58	21 39	09 15	10	86
27	02 17	02 21	11 58	22 27	10 03	11	93

2018 APRIL 28, 29, 30 (SAT., SUN., MON.)

UT	ARIES	VENUS −3.9		MARS −0.3		JUPITER −2.5		SATURN +0.4		STARS		
	GHA	GHA	Dec	GHA	Dec	GHA	Dec	GHA	Dec	Name	SHA	Dec
d h	° ′	° ′	° ′	° ′	° ′	° ′	° ′	° ′	° ′		° ′	° ′
28 00	215 55.0	154 02.2	N21 39.4	281 55.1	S22 48.7	348 15.8	S16 26.4	296 06.8	S22 14.4	Acamar	315 16.3	S40 14.2
01	230 57.4	169 01.5	40.0	296 56.2	48.6	3 18.6	26.3	311 09.3	14.4	Achernar	335 25.0	S57 08.8
02	245 59.9	184 00.8	40.7	311 57.4	48.5	18 21.4	26.2	326 11.8	14.4	Acrux	173 04.9	S63 12.1
03	261 02.4	199 00.0 ..	41.4	326 58.6 ..	48.4	33 24.1 ..	26.1	341 14.3 ..	14.4	Adhara	255 10.1	S29 00.2
04	276 04.8	213 59.3	42.1	341 59.7	48.3	48 26.9	26.0	356 16.8	14.4	Aldebaran	290 45.9	N16 32.5
05	291 07.3	228 58.6	42.7	357 00.9	48.2	63 29.7	26.0	11 19.3	14.4			
06	306 09.8	243 57.9	N21 43.4	12 02.1	S22 48.1	78 32.5	S16 25.9	26 21.8	S22 14.4	Alioth	166 17.4	N55 51.8
07	321 12.2	258 57.1	44.1	27 03.3	48.0	93 35.2	25.8	41 24.3	14.4	Alkaid	152 55.9	N49 13.5
S 08	336 14.7	273 56.4	44.8	42 04.4	47.9	108 38.0	25.7	56 26.8	14.4	Al Na'ir	27 39.8	S46 52.2
A 09	351 17.2	288 55.7 ..	45.4	57 05.6 ..	47.8	123 40.8 ..	25.6	71 29.4 ..	14.4	Alnilam	275 43.3	S 1 11.7
T 10	6 19.6	303 55.0	46.1	72 06.8	47.7	138 43.5	25.5	86 31.9	14.4	Alphard	217 52.8	S 8 44.5
U 11	21 22.1	318 54.2	46.8	87 08.0	47.6	153 46.3	25.5	101 34.4	14.4			
R 12	36 24.5	333 53.5	N21 47.4	102 09.1	S22 47.5	168 49.1	S16 25.4	116 36.9	S22 14.5	Alphecca	126 07.9	N26 39.2
D 13	51 27.0	348 52.8	48.1	117 10.3	47.4	183 51.9	25.3	131 39.4	14.5	Alpheratz	357 40.4	N29 11.2
A 14	66 29.5	3 52.1	48.8	132 11.5	47.3	198 54.6	25.2	146 41.9	14.5	Altair	62 05.0	N 8 55.0
Y 15	81 31.9	18 51.3 ..	49.4	147 12.7 ..	47.2	213 57.4 ..	25.1	161 44.4 ..	14.5	Ankaa	353 12.9	S42 12.5
16	96 34.4	33 50.6	50.1	162 13.8	47.1	229 00.2	25.1	176 46.9	14.5	Antares	112 21.9	S26 28.2
17	111 36.9	48 49.9	50.8	177 15.0	47.0	244 02.9	25.0	191 49.4	14.5			
18	126 39.3	63 49.2	N21 51.4	192 16.2	S22 46.9	259 05.7	S16 24.9	206 51.9	S22 14.5	Arcturus	145 52.4	N19 05.3
19	141 41.8	78 48.4	52.1	207 17.4	46.8	274 08.5	24.8	221 54.5	14.5	Atria	107 20.3	S69 03.3
20	156 44.3	93 47.7	52.7	222 18.5	46.7	289 11.3	24.7	236 57.0	14.5	Avior	234 16.7	S59 34.5
21	171 46.7	108 47.0 ..	53.4	237 19.7 ..	46.6	304 14.0 ..	24.6	251 59.5 ..	14.5	Bellatrix	278 28.8	N 6 21.7
22	186 49.2	123 46.2	54.1	252 20.9	46.5	319 16.8	24.6	267 02.0	14.5	Betelgeuse	270 58.0	N 7 24.4
23	201 51.7	138 45.5	54.7	267 22.1	46.4	334 19.6	24.5	282 04.5	14.5			
29 00	216 54.1	153 44.8	N21 55.4	282 23.3	S22 46.3	349 22.3	S16 24.4	297 07.0	S22 14.5	Canopus	263 55.0	S52 42.7
01	231 56.6	168 44.0	56.0	297 24.4	46.2	4 25.1	24.3	312 09.5	14.5	Capella	280 30.0	N46 00.8
02	246 59.0	183 43.3	56.7	312 25.6	46.1	19 27.9	24.2	327 12.0	14.5	Deneb	49 29.2	N45 20.5
03	262 01.5	198 42.6 ..	57.3	327 26.8 ..	46.0	34 30.7 ..	24.2	342 14.5 ..	14.5	Denebola	182 30.1	N14 28.2
04	277 04.0	213 41.9	58.0	342 28.0	45.9	49 33.4	24.1	357 17.1	14.5	Diphda	348 52.9	S17 53.3
05	292 06.4	228 41.1	58.6	357 29.2	45.8	64 36.2	24.0	12 19.6	14.5			
06	307 08.9	243 40.4	N21 59.3	12 30.4	S22 45.7	79 39.0	S16 23.9	27 22.1	S22 14.5	Dubhe	193 47.4	N61 39.4
07	322 11.4	258 39.7	21 59.9	27 31.5	45.6	94 41.8	23.8	42 24.6	14.5	Elnath	278 08.8	N28 37.2
08	337 13.8	273 38.9	22 00.6	42 32.7	45.5	109 44.5	23.8	57 27.1	14.5	Eltanin	90 44.3	N51 29.1
S 09	352 16.3	288 38.2 ..	01.2	57 33.9 ..	45.4	124 47.3 ..	23.7	72 29.6 ..	14.5	Enif	33 44.0	N 9 57.4
U 10	7 18.8	303 37.5	01.9	72 35.1	45.3	139 50.1	23.6	87 32.1	14.5	Fomalhaut	15 20.6	S29 31.5
N 11	22 21.2	318 36.7	02.5	87 36.3	45.2	154 52.8	23.5	102 34.6	14.5			
D 12	37 23.7	333 36.0	N22 03.1	102 37.5	S22 45.1	169 55.6	S16 23.4	117 37.2	S22 14.5	Gacrux	171 56.7	S57 13.0
A 13	52 26.1	348 35.2	03.8	117 38.7	45.0	184 58.4	23.3	132 39.7	14.5	Gienah	175 48.7	S17 38.7
Y 14	67 28.6	3 34.5	04.4	132 39.8	44.9	200 01.2	23.3	147 42.2	14.5	Hadar	148 42.5	S60 27.6
15	82 31.1	18 33.8 ..	05.1	147 41.0 ..	44.8	215 03.9 ..	23.2	162 44.7 ..	14.5	Hamal	327 57.4	N23 32.6
16	97 33.5	33 33.0	05.7	162 42.2	44.7	230 06.7	23.1	177 47.2	14.5	Kaus Aust.	83 39.3	S34 22.3
17	112 36.0	48 32.3	06.3	177 43.4	44.6	245 09.5	23.0	192 49.7	14.5			
18	127 38.5	63 31.6	N22 07.0	192 44.6	S22 44.5	260 12.3	S16 22.9	207 52.2	S22 14.5	Kochab	137 19.0	N74 04.9
19	142 40.9	78 30.8	07.6	207 45.8	44.4	275 15.0	22.8	222 54.8	14.5	Markab	13 35.3	N15 18.0
20	157 43.4	93 30.1	08.2	222 47.0	44.3	290 17.8	22.8	237 57.3	14.5	Menkar	314 12.0	N 4 09.4
21	172 45.9	108 29.3 ..	08.9	237 48.2 ..	44.2	305 20.6 ..	22.7	252 59.8 ..	14.5	Menkent	148 03.3	S36 27.5
22	187 48.3	123 28.6	09.5	252 49.3	44.1	320 23.4	22.6	268 02.3	14.6	Miaplacidus	221 38.8	S69 47.9
23	202 50.8	138 27.9	10.1	267 50.5	44.0	335 26.1	22.5	283 04.8	14.6			
30 00	217 53.3	153 27.1	N22 10.8	282 51.7	S22 43.9	350 28.9	S16 22.4	298 07.3	S22 14.6	Mirfak	308 36.1	N49 55.5
01	232 55.7	168 26.4	11.4	297 52.9	43.8	5 31.7	22.4	313 09.9	14.6	Nunki	75 54.1	S26 16.2
02	247 58.2	183 25.6	12.0	312 54.1	43.7	20 34.5	22.3	328 12.4	14.6	Peacock	53 14.1	S56 40.3
03	263 00.6	198 24.9 ..	12.7	327 55.3 ..	43.6	35 37.2 ..	22.2	343 14.9 ..	14.6	Pollux	243 23.9	N27 58.8
04	278 03.1	213 24.2	13.3	342 56.5	43.5	50 40.0	22.1	358 17.4	14.6	Procyon	244 56.4	N 5 10.5
05	293 05.6	228 23.4	13.9	357 57.7	43.4	65 42.8	22.0	13 19.9	14.6			
06	308 08.0	243 22.7	N22 14.5	12 58.9	S22 43.3	80 45.6	S16 21.9	28 22.4	S22 14.6	Rasalhague	96 03.2	N12 32.8
07	323 10.5	258 21.9	15.1	28 00.1	43.2	95 48.3	21.9	43 25.0	14.6	Regulus	207 39.9	N11 52.6
08	338 13.0	273 21.2	15.8	43 01.3	43.1	110 51.1	21.8	58 27.5	14.6	Rigel	281 09.2	S 8 11.2
M 09	353 15.4	288 20.4 ..	16.4	58 02.5 ..	43.0	125 53.9 ..	21.7	73 30.0 ..	14.6	Rigil Kent.	139 46.6	S60 54.5
O 10	8 17.9	303 19.7	17.0	73 03.7	42.9	140 56.7	21.6	88 32.5	14.6	Sabik	102 08.5	S15 44.7
N 11	23 20.4	318 19.0	17.6	88 04.9	42.8	155 59.4	21.5	103 35.0	14.6			
D 12	38 22.8	333 18.2	N22 18.2	103 06.1	S22 42.7	171 02.2	S16 21.5	118 37.5	S22 14.6	Schedar	349 37.2	N56 37.9
A 13	53 25.3	348 17.5	18.9	118 07.2	42.6	186 05.0	21.4	133 40.1	14.6	Shaula	96 17.2	S37 06.8
Y 14	68 27.8	3 16.7	19.5	133 08.4	42.5	201 07.8	21.3	148 42.6	14.6	Sirius	258 31.0	S16 44.8
15	83 30.2	18 16.0 ..	20.1	148 09.6 ..	42.4	216 10.5 ..	21.2	163 45.1 ..	14.6	Spica	158 27.5	S11 15.4
16	98 32.7	33 15.2	20.7	163 10.8	42.3	231 13.3	21.1	178 47.6	14.6	Suhail	222 50.0	S43 30.7
17	113 35.1	48 14.5	21.3	178 12.0	42.2	246 16.1	21.0	193 50.1	14.6			
18	128 37.6	63 13.7	N22 21.9	193 13.2	S22 42.1	261 18.9	S16 21.0	208 52.6	S22 14.6	Vega	80 36.5	N38 47.9
19	143 40.1	78 13.0	22.5	208 14.4	42.0	276 21.6	20.9	223 55.2	14.6	Zuben'ubi	137 01.5	S16 07.0
20	158 42.5	93 12.2	23.1	223 15.6	41.9	291 24.4	20.8	238 57.7	14.6		SHA	Mer. Pass.
21	173 45.0	108 11.5 ..	23.8	238 16.8 ..	41.8	306 27.2 ..	20.7	254 00.2 ..	14.6		° ′	h m
22	188 47.5	123 10.7	24.4	253 18.0	41.7	321 30.0	20.6	269 02.7	14.6	Venus	296 50.7	13 46
23	203 49.9	138 10.0	25.0	268 19.2	41.6	336 32.7	20.5	284 05.2	14.6	Mars	65 29.2	5 10
	h m									Jupiter	132 28.2	0 42
Mer. Pass.	9 30.8	v −0.7	d 0.6	v 1.2	d 0.1	v 2.8	d 0.1	v 2.5	d 0.0	Saturn	80 12.9	4 11

SUN and MOON

UT	SUN GHA	SUN Dec	MOON GHA	v	MOON Dec	d	HP
28 00	180 36.6	N14 03.9	22 26.1	12.2	S 0 58.4	11.7	57.4
01	195 36.7	04.7	36 57.3	12.2	1 10.1	11.6	57.3
02	210 36.8	05.5	51 28.5	12.3	1 21.7	11.7	57.3
03	225 36.8	.. 06.3	65 59.8	12.2	1 33.4	11.6	57.3
04	240 36.9	07.1	80 31.0	12.3	1 45.0	11.6	57.3
05	255 37.0	07.8	95 02.3	12.2	1 56.6	11.6	57.3
06	270 37.1	N14 08.6	109 33.5	12.3	S 2 08.2	11.5	57.2
07	285 37.2	09.4	124 04.8	12.3	2 19.7	11.6	57.2
08	300 37.3	10.2	138 36.1	12.3	2 31.3	11.5	57.2
09	315 37.4	.. 11.0	153 07.4	12.4	2 42.8	11.5	57.2
10	330 37.5	11.8	167 38.8	12.3	2 54.3	11.5	57.1
11	345 37.6	12.6	182 10.1	12.3	3 05.8	11.5	57.1
12	0 37.7	N14 13.3	196 41.4	12.4	S 3 17.3	11.4	57.1
13	15 37.8	14.1	211 12.8	12.4	3 28.7	11.4	57.1
14	30 37.9	14.9	225 44.2	12.3	3 40.1	11.4	57.1
15	45 38.0	.. 15.7	240 15.5	12.4	3 51.5	11.4	57.0
16	60 38.0	16.5	254 46.9	12.4	4 02.9	11.3	57.0
17	75 38.1	17.3	269 18.3	12.4	4 14.2	11.3	57.0
18	90 38.2	N14 18.0	283 49.7	12.4	S 4 25.5	11.3	57.0
19	105 38.3	18.8	298 21.1	12.4	4 36.8	11.3	57.0
20	120 38.4	19.6	312 52.5	12.4	4 48.1	11.2	56.9
21	135 38.5	.. 20.4	327 23.9	12.4	4 59.3	11.2	56.9
22	150 38.6	21.2	341 55.3	12.4	5 10.5	11.1	56.9
23	165 38.7	21.9	356 26.7	12.5	5 21.6	11.2	56.9
29 00	180 38.8	N14 22.7	10 58.2	12.4	S 5 32.8	11.0	56.8
01	195 38.8	23.5	25 29.6	12.4	5 43.8	11.1	56.8
02	210 38.9	24.3	40 01.0	12.5	5 54.9	11.0	56.8
03	225 39.0	.. 25.0	54 32.5	12.4	6 05.9	11.0	56.8
04	240 39.1	25.8	69 03.9	12.4	6 16.9	10.9	56.8
05	255 39.2	26.6	83 35.3	12.5	6 27.8	10.9	56.7
06	270 39.3	N14 27.4	98 06.8	12.4	S 6 38.7	10.9	56.7
07	285 39.4	28.2	112 38.2	12.4	6 49.6	10.8	56.7
08	300 39.5	28.9	127 09.6	12.5	7 00.4	10.8	56.7
09	315 39.6	.. 29.7	141 41.1	12.4	7 11.2	10.7	56.7
10	330 39.6	30.5	156 12.5	12.4	7 21.9	10.7	56.6
11	345 39.7	31.3	170 43.9	12.5	7 32.6	10.7	56.6
12	0 39.8	N14 32.0	185 15.4	12.4	S 7 43.3	10.6	56.6
13	15 39.9	32.8	199 46.8	12.4	7 53.9	10.5	56.6
14	30 40.0	33.6	214 18.2	12.5	8 04.4	10.5	56.5
15	45 40.1	.. 34.4	228 49.7	12.4	8 14.9	10.5	56.5
16	60 40.2	35.1	243 21.1	12.4	8 25.4	10.4	56.5
17	75 40.2	35.9	257 52.5	12.4	8 35.8	10.4	56.5
18	90 40.3	N14 36.7	272 23.9	12.4	S 8 46.2	10.3	56.5
19	105 40.4	37.4	286 55.3	12.4	8 56.5	10.3	56.4
20	120 40.5	38.2	301 26.7	12.4	9 06.8	10.2	56.4
21	135 40.6	.. 39.0	315 58.1	12.4	9 17.0	10.1	56.4
22	150 40.7	39.8	330 29.5	12.4	9 27.1	10.1	56.4
23	165 40.7	40.5	345 00.9	12.4	9 37.2	10.1	56.3
30 00	180 40.8	N14 41.3	359 32.3	12.3	S 9 47.3	10.0	56.3
01	195 40.9	42.1	14 03.6	12.4	9 57.3	9.9	56.3
02	210 41.0	42.8	28 35.0	12.3	10 07.2	9.9	56.3
03	225 41.1	.. 43.6	43 06.3	12.4	10 17.1	9.9	56.3
04	240 41.2	44.4	57 37.7	12.3	10 27.0	9.7	56.2
05	255 41.2	45.1	72 09.0	12.4	10 36.7	9.8	56.2
06	270 41.3	N14 45.9	86 40.4	12.3	S10 46.5	9.6	56.2
07	285 41.4	46.7	101 11.7	12.3	10 56.1	9.6	56.2
08	300 41.5	47.4	115 43.0	12.3	11 05.7	9.6	56.1
09	315 41.6	.. 48.2	130 14.3	12.3	11 15.3	9.4	56.1
10	330 41.7	49.0	144 45.6	12.3	11 24.7	9.4	56.1
11	345 41.7	49.7	159 16.9	12.3	11 34.1	9.4	56.1
12	0 41.8	N14 50.5	173 48.2	12.2	S11 43.5	9.3	56.1
13	15 41.9	51.3	188 19.4	12.3	11 52.8	9.2	56.0
14	30 42.0	52.0	202 50.7	12.2	12 02.0	9.2	56.0
15	45 42.1	.. 52.8	217 21.9	12.3	12 11.2	9.1	56.0
16	60 42.1	53.5	231 53.2	12.2	12 20.3	9.0	56.0
17	75 42.2	54.3	246 24.4	12.2	12 29.3	9.0	55.9
18	90 42.3	N14 55.1	260 55.6	12.2	S12 38.3	8.8	55.9
19	105 42.4	55.8	275 26.8	12.2	12 47.1	8.9	55.9
20	120 42.5	56.6	289 58.0	12.2	12 56.0	8.7	55.9
21	135 42.5	.. 57.3	304 29.2	12.2	13 04.7	8.7	55.9
22	150 42.6	58.1	319 00.4	12.1	13 13.4	8.6	55.8
23	165 42.7	58.9	333 31.5	12.1	S13 22.0	8.6	55.8
	SD 15.9	d 0.8	SD 15.6		15.4		15.3

(28 = SATURDAY, 29 = SUNDAY, 30 = MONDAY)

Twilight, Sunrise, Moonrise

Lat.	Twilight Naut.	Twilight Civil	Sunrise	Moonrise 28	29	30	1
N 72	////	////	02 09	18 02	19 54	21 51	24 03
N 70	////	////	02 43	17 55	19 39	21 24	23 12
68	////	01 28	03 07	17 50	19 27	21 04	22 40
66	////	02 08	03 26	17 45	19 17	20 48	22 17
64	////	02 35	03 41	17 41	19 09	20 36	21 59
62	01 17	02 55	03 53	17 38	19 02	20 25	21 44
60	01 54	03 12	04 04	17 35	18 56	20 16	21 32
N 58	02 19	03 26	04 13	17 33	18 51	20 08	21 21
56	02 38	03 37	04 21	17 30	18 46	20 01	21 12
54	02 54	03 47	04 28	17 28	18 42	19 54	21 04
52	03 07	03 56	04 34	17 27	18 39	19 49	20 56
50	03 18	04 04	04 40	17 25	18 35	19 44	20 50
45	03 41	04 21	04 53	17 21	18 28	19 33	20 36
N 40	03 58	04 34	05 03	17 18	18 22	19 24	20 14
35	04 12	04 45	05 12	17 16	18 16	19 16	20 14
30	04 24	04 54	05 19	17 14	18 12	19 09	20 06
20	04 42	05 09	05 32	17 10	18 04	18 58	19 51
N 10	04 56	05 22	05 43	17 07	17 57	18 47	19 38
0	05 08	05 33	05 54	17 03	17 51	18 38	19 26
S 10	05 18	05 43	06 04	17 00	17 44	18 29	19 14
20	05 26	05 53	06 15	16 57	17 37	18 19	19 01
30	05 35	06 03	06 28	16 53	17 30	18 07	18 47
35	05 39	06 09	06 35	16 51	17 25	18 01	18 38
40	05 43	06 15	06 43	16 49	17 20	17 53	18 29
45	05 47	06 22	06 52	16 46	17 15	17 45	18 18
S 50	05 51	06 29	07 03	16 43	17 08	17 35	18 04
52	05 53	06 33	07 09	16 42	17 05	17 30	17 58
54	05 55	06 37	07 14	16 40	17 01	17 25	17 51
56	05 57	06 41	07 21	16 38	16 58	17 19	17 44
58	05 59	06 46	07 28	16 36	16 53	17 12	17 35
S 60	06 01	06 51	07 36	16 34	16 49	17 05	17 25

Sunset, Twilight, Moonset

Lat.	Sunset	Twilight Civil	Twilight Naut.	Moonset 28	29	30	1
N 72	21 52	////	////	04 15	04 03	03 49	03 32
N 70	21 16	////	////	04 17	04 12	04 06	04 00
68	20 51	22 35	////	04 19	04 19	04 19	04 21
66	20 32	21 52	////	04 21	04 25	04 30	04 37
64	20 16	21 23	////	04 23	04 31	04 40	04 51
62	20 03	21 02	22 45	04 24	04 35	04 48	05 03
60	19 53	20 45	22 05	04 25	04 39	04 55	05 13
N 58	19 43	20 31	21 39	04 26	04 43	05 01	05 21
56	19 35	20 19	21 19	04 27	04 46	05 06	05 29
54	19 28	20 09	21 03	04 28	04 49	05 11	05 36
52	19 21	20 00	20 50	04 29	04 51	05 15	05 42
50	19 15	19 52	20 38	04 29	04 54	05 19	05 48
45	19 03	19 35	20 15	04 31	04 59	05 28	05 59
N 40	18 53	19 22	19 57	04 32	05 03	05 35	06 09
35	18 44	19 11	19 43	04 33	05 07	05 42	06 18
30	18 36	19 01	19 31	04 34	05 10	05 47	06 27
20	18 23	18 46	19 13	04 36	05 16	05 57	06 39
N 10	18 11	18 33	18 59	04 37	05 21	06 05	06 50
0	18 01	18 22	18 47	04 39	05 26	06 13	07 01
S 10	17 50	18 12	18 37	04 40	05 31	06 21	07 12
20	17 39	18 02	18 28	04 41	05 36	06 30	07 23
30	17 27	17 51	18 20	04 43	05 42	06 40	07 36
35	17 20	17 46	18 16	04 44	05 45	06 45	07 44
40	17 11	17 39	18 11	04 45	05 49	06 52	07 54
45	17 02	17 33	18 07	04 46	05 53	06 59	08 03
S 50	16 51	17 25	18 03	04 48	05 59	07 08	08 16
52	16 45	17 21	18 01	04 48	06 01	07 12	08 21
54	16 40	17 17	17 59	04 49	06 04	07 17	08 28
56	16 33	17 13	17 57	04 50	06 07	07 22	08 35
58	16 26	17 08	17 55	04 51	06 10	07 28	08 43
S 60	16 18	17 03	17 52	04 52	06 14	07 34	08 52

SUN / MOON

Day	Eqn. of Time 00h	Eqn. of Time 12h	Mer. Pass.	Mer. Pass. Upper	Mer. Pass. Lower	Age	Phase
	m s	m s	h m	h m	h m	d	%
28	02 26	02 31	11 57	23 15	10 51	12	97
29	02 35	02 39	11 57	24 02	11 38	13	99
30	02 43	02 47	11 57	00 02	12 26	14	100

UT	ARIES GHA	VENUS −3.9 GHA	Dec	MARS −0.4 GHA	Dec	JUPITER −2.5 GHA	Dec	SATURN +0.3 GHA	Dec	STARS Name	SHA	Dec
d h	° ′	° ′	° ′	° ′	° ′	° ′	° ′	° ′	° ′		° ′	° ′
1 00	218 52.4	153 09.2	N22 25.6	283 20.4	S22 41.5	351 35.5	S16 20.5	299 07.8	S22 14.6	Acamar	315 16.3	S40 14.1
01	233 54.9	168 08.5	26.2	298 21.6	41.4	6 38.3	20.4	314 10.3	14.6	Achernar	335 24.9	S57 08.7
02	248 57.3	183 07.7	26.8	313 22.8	41.3	21 41.1	20.3	329 12.8	14.6	Acrux	173 05.0	S63 12.1
03	263 59.8	198 07.0	.. 27.4	328 24.0	.. 41.2	36 43.8	.. 20.2	344 15.3	.. 14.6	Adhara	255 10.1	S29 00.2
04	279 02.2	213 06.2	28.0	343 25.3	41.1	51 46.6	20.1	359 17.8	14.6	Aldebaran	290 45.9	N16 32.5
05	294 04.7	228 05.5	28.6	358 26.5	41.0	66 49.4	20.0	14 20.4	14.7			
06	309 07.2	243 04.7	N22 29.2	13 27.7	S22 40.9	81 52.2	S16 20.0	29 22.9	S22 14.7	Alioth	166 17.4	N55 51.8
07	324 09.6	258 04.0	29.8	28 28.9	40.8	96 55.0	19.9	44 25.4	14.7	Alkaid	152 55.9	N49 13.5
T 08	339 12.1	273 03.2	30.4	43 30.1	40.7	111 57.7	19.8	59 27.9	14.7	Al Na'ir	27 39.8	S46 52.2
U 09	354 14.6	288 02.5	.. 31.0	58 31.3	.. 40.6	127 00.5	.. 19.7	74 30.5	.. 14.7	Alnilam	275 43.3	S 1 11.7
E 10	9 17.0	303 01.7	31.6	73 32.5	40.5	142 03.3	19.6	89 33.0	14.7	Alphard	217 52.8	S 8 44.5
S 11	24 19.5	318 01.0	32.1	88 33.7	40.4	157 06.1	19.6	104 35.5	14.7			
D 12	39 22.0	333 00.2	N22 32.7	103 34.9	S22 40.3	172 08.8	S16 19.5	119 38.0	S22 14.7	Alphecca	126 07.9	N26 39.3
A 13	54 24.4	347 59.5	33.3	118 36.1	40.2	187 11.6	19.4	134 40.5	14.7	Alpheratz	357 40.4	N29 11.2
Y 14	69 26.9	2 58.7	33.9	133 37.3	40.1	202 14.4	19.3	149 43.1	14.7	Altair	62 04.9	N 8 55.0
15	84 29.4	17 58.0	.. 34.5	148 38.5	.. 40.0	217 17.2	.. 19.2	164 45.6	.. 14.7	Ankaa	353 12.8	S42 12.4
16	99 31.8	32 57.2	35.1	163 39.7	39.9	232 19.9	19.1	179 48.1	14.7	Antares	112 21.9	S26 28.2
17	114 34.3	47 56.5	35.7	178 40.9	39.8	247 22.7	19.1	194 50.6	14.7			
18	129 36.7	62 55.7	N22 36.3	193 42.1	S22 39.7	262 25.5	S16 19.0	209 53.2	S22 14.7	Arcturus	145 52.4	N19 05.3
19	144 39.2	77 54.9	36.8	208 43.4	39.5	277 28.3	18.9	224 55.7	14.7	Atria	107 20.3	S69 03.3
20	159 41.7	92 54.2	37.4	223 44.6	39.4	292 31.1	18.8	239 58.2	14.7	Avior	234 16.7	S59 34.5
21	174 44.1	107 53.4	.. 38.0	238 45.8	.. 39.3	307 33.8	.. 18.7	255 00.7	.. 14.7	Bellatrix	278 28.8	N 6 21.7
22	189 46.6	122 52.7	38.6	253 47.0	39.2	322 36.6	18.6	270 03.2	14.7	Betelgeuse	270 58.0	N 7 24.4
23	204 49.1	137 51.9	39.2	268 48.2	39.1	337 39.4	18.6	285 05.8	14.7			
2 00	219 51.5	152 51.2	N22 39.7	283 49.4	S22 39.0	352 42.2	S16 18.5	300 08.3	S22 14.7	Canopus	263 55.0	S52 42.7
01	234 54.0	167 50.4	40.3	298 50.6	38.9	7 44.9	18.4	315 10.8	14.7	Capella	280 30.0	N46 00.8
02	249 56.5	182 49.6	40.9	313 51.8	38.8	22 47.7	18.3	330 13.3	14.7	Deneb	49 29.2	N45 20.5
03	264 58.9	197 48.9	.. 41.5	328 53.1	.. 38.7	37 50.5	.. 18.2	345 15.9	.. 14.7	Denebola	182 30.1	N14 28.2
04	280 01.4	212 48.1	42.1	343 54.3	38.6	52 53.3	18.1	0 18.4	14.7	Diphda	348 52.9	S17 53.3
05	295 03.9	227 47.4	42.6	358 55.5	38.5	67 56.1	18.1	15 20.9	14.7			
06	310 06.3	242 46.6	N22 43.2	13 56.7	S22 38.4	82 58.8	S16 18.0	30 23.4	S22 14.7	Dubhe	193 47.4	N61 39.4
W 07	325 08.8	257 45.8	43.8	28 57.9	38.3	98 01.6	17.9	45 26.0	14.7	Elnath	278 08.8	N28 37.2
E 08	340 11.2	272 45.1	44.3	43 59.1	38.2	113 04.4	17.8	60 28.5	14.7	Eltanin	90 44.3	N51 29.1
D 09	355 13.7	287 44.3	.. 44.9	59 00.3	.. 38.1	128 07.2	.. 17.7	75 31.0	.. 14.8	Enif	33 44.0	N 9 57.4
N 10	10 16.2	302 43.6	45.5	74 01.6	38.0	143 09.9	17.6	90 33.5	14.8	Fomalhaut	15 20.6	S29 31.5
E 11	25 18.6	317 42.8	46.0	89 02.8	37.9	158 12.7	17.6	105 36.1	14.8			
S 12	40 21.1	332 42.0	N22 46.6	104 04.0	S22 37.8	173 15.5	S16 17.5	120 38.6	S22 14.8	Gacrux	171 56.7	S57 13.0
D 13	55 23.6	347 41.3	47.2	119 05.2	37.7	188 18.3	17.4	135 41.1	14.8	Gienah	175 48.7	S17 38.7
A 14	70 26.0	2 40.5	47.7	134 06.4	37.6	203 21.1	17.3	150 43.7	14.8	Hadar	148 42.5	S60 27.6
Y 15	85 28.5	17 39.7	.. 48.3	149 07.7	.. 37.5	218 23.8	.. 17.2	165 46.2	.. 14.8	Hamal	327 57.4	N23 32.6
16	100 31.0	32 39.0	48.9	164 08.9	37.4	233 26.6	17.1	180 48.7	14.8	Kaus Aust.	83 39.2	S34 22.3
17	115 33.4	47 38.2	49.4	179 10.1	37.3	248 29.4	17.1	195 51.2	14.8			
18	130 35.9	62 37.4	N22 50.0	194 11.3	S22 37.2	263 32.2	S16 17.0	210 53.8	S22 14.8	Kochab	137 19.0	N74 04.9
19	145 38.3	77 36.7	50.5	209 12.5	37.1	278 35.0	16.9	225 56.3	14.8	Markab	13 35.2	N15 18.0
20	160 40.8	92 35.9	51.1	224 13.8	37.0	293 37.7	16.8	240 58.8	14.8	Menkar	314 11.9	N 4 09.4
21	175 43.3	107 35.1	.. 51.6	239 15.0	.. 36.9	308 40.5	.. 16.7	256 01.3	.. 14.8	Menkent	148 03.3	S36 27.5
22	190 45.7	122 34.4	52.2	254 16.2	36.8	323 43.3	16.6	271 03.9	14.8	Miaplacidus	221 38.9	S69 47.9
23	205 48.2	137 33.6	52.8	269 17.4	36.7	338 46.1	16.6	286 06.4	14.8			
3 00	220 50.7	152 32.9	N22 53.3	284 18.7	S22 36.6	353 48.9	S16 16.5	301 08.9	S22 14.8	Mirfak	308 36.1	N49 55.3
01	235 53.1	167 32.1	53.9	299 19.9	36.5	8 51.6	16.4	316 11.5	14.8	Nunki	75 54.1	S26 16.2
02	250 55.6	182 31.3	54.4	314 21.1	36.4	23 54.4	16.3	331 14.0	14.8	Peacock	53 14.1	S56 40.2
03	265 58.1	197 30.5	.. 55.0	329 22.3	.. 36.3	38 57.2	.. 16.2	346 16.5	.. 14.8	Pollux	243 23.9	N27 58.8
04	281 00.5	212 29.8	55.5	344 23.6	36.2	54 00.0	16.1	1 19.0	14.8	Procyon	244 56.4	N 5 10.5
05	296 03.0	227 29.0	56.0	359 24.8	36.1	69 02.8	16.1	16 21.6	14.8			
06	311 05.5	242 28.2	N22 56.6	14 26.0	S22 36.0	84 05.5	S16 16.0	31 24.1	S22 14.8	Rasalhague	96 03.2	N12 32.8
07	326 07.9	257 27.5	57.1	29 27.2	35.9	99 08.3	15.9	46 26.6	14.8	Regulus	207 40.0	N11 52.6
T 08	341 10.4	272 26.7	57.7	44 28.5	35.8	114 11.1	15.8	61 29.2	14.8	Rigel	281 09.2	S 8 11.1
H 09	356 12.8	287 25.9	.. 58.2	59 29.7	.. 35.7	129 13.9	.. 15.7	76 31.7	.. 14.8	Rigil Kent.	139 46.6	S60 54.5
U 10	11 15.3	302 25.2	58.8	74 30.9	35.6	144 16.7	15.6	91 34.2	14.9	Sabik	102 08.5	S15 44.7
R 11	26 17.8	317 24.4	59.3	89 32.2	35.5	159 19.4	15.6	106 36.7	14.9			
S 12	41 20.2	332 23.6	N22 59.8	104 33.4	S22 35.4	174 22.2	S16 15.5	121 39.3	S22 14.9	Schedar	349 37.2	N56 37.9
D 13	56 22.7	347 22.9	23 00.4	119 34.6	35.3	189 25.0	15.4	136 41.8	14.9	Shaula	96 17.2	S37 06.8
A 14	71 25.2	2 22.1	00.9	134 35.8	35.2	204 27.8	15.3	151 44.3	14.9	Sirius	258 31.0	S16 44.8
Y 15	86 27.6	17 21.3	.. 01.4	149 37.1	.. 35.1	219 30.6	.. 15.2	166 46.9	.. 14.9	Spica	158 27.5	S11 15.4
16	101 30.1	32 20.5	02.0	164 38.3	35.0	234 33.3	15.1	181 49.4	14.9	Suhail	222 50.0	S43 30.7
17	116 32.6	47 19.8	02.5	179 39.5	34.9	249 36.1	15.1	196 51.9	14.9			
18	131 35.0	62 19.0	N23 03.1	194 40.8	S22 34.8	264 38.9	S16 15.0	211 54.5	S22 14.9	Vega	80 36.5	N38 47.9
19	146 37.5	77 18.2	03.6	209 42.0	34.7	279 41.7	14.9	226 57.0	14.9	Zuben'ubi	137 01.4	S16 07.0
20	161 40.0	92 17.4	04.1	224 43.2	34.6	294 44.5	14.8	241 59.5	14.9		SHA	Mer.Pass.
21	176 42.4	107 16.7	.. 04.6	239 44.5	.. 34.5	309 47.2	.. 14.7	257 02.1	.. 14.9			
22	191 44.9	122 15.9	05.2	254 45.7	34.4	324 50.0	14.6	272 04.6	14.9	Venus	292 59.6	13 49
23	206 47.3	137 15.1	05.7	269 46.9	34.3	339 52.8	14.5	287 07.1	14.9	Mars	63 57.9	5 04
	h m									Jupiter	132 50.6	0 29
Mer. Pass. 9 19.0		v −0.8 d 0.6		v 1.2 d 0.1		v 2.8 d 0.1		v 2.5 d 0.0		Saturn	80 16.8	3 59

SUN / MOON

UT	SUN GHA	SUN Dec	MOON GHA	v	MOON Dec	d	HP
d h	° ′	° ′	° ′	′	° ′	′	′
1 00	180 42.8	N14 59.6	348 02.6	12.2	S13 30.6	8.5	55.8
01	195 42.8	15 00.4	2 33.8	12.1	13 39.1	8.4	55.8
02	210 42.9	01.1	17 04.9	12.1	13 47.5	8.3	55.8
03	225 43.0	.. 01.9	31 36.0	12.1	13 55.8	8.3	55.7
04	240 43.1	02.7	46 07.1	12.1	14 04.1	8.1	55.7
05	255 43.2	03.4	60 38.2	12.1	14 12.2	8.2	55.7
06	270 43.2	N15 04.2	75 09.3	12.0	S14 20.4	8.0	55.7
07	285 43.3	04.9	89 40.3	12.1	14 28.4	7.9	55.6
08	300 43.4	05.7	104 11.4	12.0	14 36.3	7.9	55.6
09	315 43.5	.. 06.4	118 42.4	12.0	14 44.2	7.8	55.6
10	330 43.5	07.2	133 13.4	12.0	14 52.0	7.8	55.6
11	345 43.6	07.9	147 44.4	12.0	14 59.8	7.6	55.6
12	0 43.7	N15 08.7	162 15.4	12.0	S15 07.4	7.6	55.5
13	15 43.8	09.5	176 46.4	12.0	15 15.0	7.5	55.5
14	30 43.8	10.2	191 17.4	11.9	15 22.5	7.4	55.5
15	45 43.9	.. 11.0	205 48.3	12.0	15 29.9	7.4	55.5
16	60 44.0	11.7	220 19.3	11.9	15 37.3	7.2	55.5
17	75 44.1	12.5	234 50.2	11.9	15 44.5	7.2	55.4
18	90 44.1	N15 13.2	249 21.1	11.9	S15 51.7	7.1	55.4
19	105 44.2	14.0	263 52.0	11.9	15 58.8	7.0	55.4
20	120 44.3	14.7	278 22.9	11.9	16 05.8	6.9	55.4
21	135 44.3	.. 15.5	292 53.8	11.9	16 12.7	6.9	55.4
22	150 44.4	16.2	307 24.7	11.8	16 19.6	6.7	55.3
23	165 44.5	17.0	321 55.5	11.9	16 26.3	6.7	55.3
2 00	180 44.6	N15 17.7	336 26.4	11.8	S16 33.0	6.6	55.3
01	195 44.6	18.5	350 57.2	11.8	16 39.6	6.5	55.3
02	210 44.7	19.2	5 28.0	11.8	16 46.1	6.5	55.3
03	225 44.8	.. 20.0	19 58.8	11.8	16 52.6	6.3	55.2
04	240 44.9	20.7	34 29.6	11.8	16 58.9	6.3	55.2
05	255 44.9	21.4	49 00.4	11.8	17 05.2	6.1	55.2
06	270 45.0	N15 22.2	63 31.2	11.8	S17 11.3	6.1	55.2
07	285 45.1	22.9	78 02.0	11.7	17 17.4	6.0	55.2
08	300 45.1	23.7	92 32.7	11.8	17 23.4	5.9	55.1
09	315 45.2	.. 24.4	107 03.5	11.7	17 29.3	5.8	55.1
10	330 45.3	25.2	121 34.2	11.7	17 35.1	5.8	55.1
11	345 45.3	25.9	136 04.9	11.7	17 40.9	5.6	55.1
12	0 45.4	N15 26.7	150 35.6	11.7	S17 46.5	5.6	55.1
13	15 45.5	27.4	165 06.3	11.7	17 52.1	5.4	55.1
14	30 45.6	28.1	179 37.0	11.7	17 57.5	5.4	55.0
15	45 45.6	.. 28.9	194 07.7	11.7	18 02.9	5.3	55.0
16	60 45.7	29.6	208 38.4	11.6	18 08.2	5.2	55.0
17	75 45.8	30.4	223 09.0	11.7	18 13.4	5.1	55.0
18	90 45.8	N15 31.1	237 39.7	11.7	S18 18.5	5.0	55.0
19	105 45.9	31.8	252 10.4	11.6	18 23.5	4.9	55.0
20	120 46.0	32.6	266 41.0	11.6	18 28.4	4.9	54.9
21	135 46.0	.. 33.3	281 11.6	11.7	18 33.3	4.7	54.9
22	150 46.1	34.1	295 42.3	11.6	18 38.0	4.6	54.9
23	165 46.2	34.8	310 12.9	11.6	18 42.6	4.6	54.9
3 00	180 46.2	N15 35.5	324 43.5	11.6	S18 47.2	4.5	54.9
01	195 46.3	36.3	339 14.1	11.6	18 51.7	4.3	54.8
02	210 46.4	37.0	353 44.7	11.6	18 56.0	4.3	54.8
03	225 46.4	.. 37.8	8 15.3	11.6	19 00.3	4.2	54.8
04	240 46.5	38.5	22 45.9	11.5	19 04.5	4.1	54.8
05	255 46.6	39.2	37 16.4	11.6	19 08.6	4.0	54.8
06	270 46.6	N15 40.0	51 47.0	11.6	S19 12.6	3.9	54.8
07	285 46.7	40.7	66 17.6	11.6	19 16.5	3.8	54.8
08	300 46.8	41.4	80 48.2	11.5	19 20.3	3.7	54.7
09	315 46.8	.. 42.2	95 18.7	11.6	19 24.0	3.6	54.7
10	330 46.9	42.9	109 49.3	11.5	19 27.6	3.5	54.7
11	345 46.9	43.6	124 19.8	11.6	19 31.1	3.4	54.7
12	0 47.0	N15 44.4	138 50.4	11.5	S19 34.5	3.4	54.7
13	15 47.1	45.1	153 20.9	11.6	19 37.9	3.2	54.7
14	30 47.1	45.8	167 51.5	11.5	19 41.1	3.2	54.7
15	45 47.2	.. 46.6	182 22.0	11.6	19 44.3	3.0	54.6
16	60 47.3	47.3	196 52.6	11.5	19 47.3	3.0	54.6
17	75 47.3	48.0	211 23.1	11.5	19 50.3	2.8	54.6
18	90 47.4	N15 48.8	225 53.6	11.6	S19 53.1	2.8	54.6
19	105 47.4	49.5	240 24.2	11.5	19 55.9	2.6	54.6
20	120 47.5	50.2	254 54.7	11.6	19 58.5	2.6	54.6
21	135 47.6	.. 50.9	269 25.3	11.5	20 01.1	2.5	54.6
22	150 47.6	51.7	283 55.8	11.5	20 03.6	2.3	54.5
23	165 47.7	52.4	298 26.3	11.6	S20 05.9	2.3	54.5
	SD 15.9	d 0.7	SD 15.1		15.0		14.9

Column left label: TUESDAY (1), WEDNESDAY (2), THURSDAY (3)

Twilight / Sunrise / Moonrise

Lat.	Naut.	Civil	Sunrise	Moonrise 1	2	3	4
°	h m	h m	h m	h m	h m	h m	h m
N 72	////	////	01 45	24 03	00 03	■■■	■■■
N 70	////	////	02 26	23 12	25 06	01 06	■■■
68	////	00 56	02 53	22 40	24 13	00 13	01 36
66	////	01 50	03 14	22 17	23 41	24 54	00 54
64	////	02 21	03 30	21 59	23 17	24 26	00 26
62	00 50	02 44	03 44	21 44	22 58	24 04	00 04
60	01 37	03 02	03 56	21 32	22 43	23 46	24 40
N 58	02 06	03 17	04 05	21 21	22 30	23 32	24 25
56	02 28	03 29	04 14	21 12	22 19	23 19	24 12
54	02 45	03 40	04 22	21 04	22 09	23 08	24 00
52	02 59	03 50	04 29	20 56	22 00	22 59	23 50
50	03 11	03 58	04 35	20 50	21 52	22 50	23 42
45	03 35	04 16	04 48	20 36	21 36	22 32	23 23
N 40	03 54	04 30	04 59	20 24	21 22	22 17	23 07
35	04 09	04 41	05 08	20 14	21 11	22 04	22 55
30	04 21	04 51	05 16	20 06	21 00	21 53	22 43
20	04 40	05 07	05 30	19 51	20 43	21 34	22 24
N 10	04 55	05 21	05 42	19 38	20 28	21 18	22 07
0	05 07	05 32	05 54	19 26	20 14	21 03	21 51
S 10	05 18	05 43	06 05	19 14	20 00	20 48	21 36
20	05 27	05 53	06 16	19 01	19 45	20 31	21 19
30	05 36	06 05	06 30	18 47	19 28	20 13	21 00
35	05 41	06 11	06 37	18 38	19 19	20 02	20 49
40	05 45	06 17	06 46	18 29	19 07	19 50	20 36
45	05 50	06 25	06 56	18 18	18 54	19 35	20 21
S 50	05 55	06 34	07 08	18 04	18 38	19 17	20 02
52	05 57	06 38	07 14	17 58	18 31	19 09	19 53
54	06 00	06 42	07 20	17 51	18 22	18 59	19 43
56	06 02	06 46	07 27	17 44	18 13	18 49	19 32
58	06 05	06 52	07 34	17 35	18 02	18 37	19 20
S 60	06 07	06 57	07 43	17 25	17 50	18 23	19 05

Sunset / Twilight / Moonset

Lat.	Sunset	Civil	Naut.	Moonset 1	2	3	4
°	h m	h m	h m	h m	h m	h m	h m
N 72	22 17	////	////	03 32	03 00	■■■	■■■
N 70	21 33	////	////	04 00	03 52	03 38	■■■
68	21 04	23 11	////	04 21	04 24	04 32	04 50
66	20 43	22 10	////	04 37	04 48	05 04	05 32
64	20 26	21 37	////	04 51	05 07	05 29	06 01
62	20 12	21 13	23 16	05 03	05 22	05 48	06 23
60	20 00	20 54	22 21	05 13	05 35	06 03	06 40
N 58	19 50	20 39	21 51	05 21	05 46	06 17	06 55
56	19 41	20 26	21 29	05 29	05 56	06 28	07 08
54	19 33	20 15	21 11	05 36	06 04	06 38	07 19
52	19 26	20 06	20 57	05 42	06 12	06 47	07 29
50	19 20	19 57	20 44	05 47	06 19	06 55	07 37
45	19 07	19 39	20 20	05 59	06 34	07 13	07 56
N 40	18 56	19 25	20 01	06 09	06 46	07 27	08 11
35	18 46	19 13	19 46	06 18	06 57	07 39	08 24
30	18 38	19 03	19 34	06 26	07 06	07 49	08 35
20	18 24	18 47	19 14	06 39	07 22	08 07	08 54
N 10	18 12	18 34	18 59	06 51	07 36	08 23	09 11
0	18 01	18 22	18 47	07 01	07 49	08 38	09 26
S 10	17 49	18 11	18 36	07 12	08 02	08 52	09 42
20	17 37	18 00	18 26	07 23	08 16	09 08	09 59
30	17 24	17 49	18 17	07 36	08 32	09 26	10 18
35	17 16	17 43	18 13	07 44	08 42	09 37	10 29
40	17 08	17 36	18 08	07 53	08 52	09 49	10 42
45	16 58	17 28	18 03	08 03	09 05	10 03	10 57
S 50	16 45	17 20	17 58	08 16	09 20	10 20	11 15
52	16 40	17 16	17 56	08 21	09 27	10 29	11 24
54	16 34	17 11	17 53	08 28	09 35	10 38	11 34
56	16 27	17 07	17 51	08 35	09 44	10 48	11 45
58	16 19	17 02	17 48	08 43	09 54	11 00	11 57
S 60	16 10	16 56	17 46	08 52	10 06	11 14	12 12

SUN / MOON

Day	SUN Eqn. of Time 00h	12h	Mer. Pass.	MOON Mer. Pass. Upper	Lower	Age	Phase
d	m s	m s	h m	h m	h m	d %	
1	02 51	02 55	11 57	00 49	13 13	15 98	◯
2	02 58	03 02	11 57	01 37	14 02	16 94	
3	03 05	03 08	11 57	02 26	14 50	17 88	

2018 MAY 4, 5, 6 (FRI., SAT., SUN.)

UT	ARIES GHA	VENUS −3.9 GHA	Dec	MARS −0.5 GHA	Dec	JUPITER −2.5 GHA	Dec	SATURN +0.3 GHA	Dec	STARS Name	SHA	Dec
d h	° ′	° ′	° ′	° ′	° ′	° ′	° ′	° ′	° ′		° ′	° ′
4 00	221 49.8	152 14.3	N23 06.2	284 48.2	S22 34.2	354 55.6	S16 14.5	302 09.7	S22 14.9	Acamar	315 16.3	S40 14.1
01	236 52.3	167 13.6	06.7	299 49.4	34.0	9 58.4	14.4	317 12.2	14.9	Achernar	335 24.9	S57 08.7
02	251 54.7	182 12.8	07.3	314 50.6	33.9	25 01.1	14.3	332 14.7	14.9	Acrux	173 05.0	S63 12.2
03	266 57.2	197 12.0	. . 07.8	329 51.9	. . 33.8	40 03.9	. . 14.2	347 17.3	. . 14.9	Adhara	255 10.1	S29 00.2
04	281 59.7	212 11.2	08.3	344 53.1	33.7	55 06.7	14.1	2 19.8	14.9	Aldebaran	290 45.9	N16 32.5
05	297 02.1	227 10.5	08.8	359 54.4	33.6	70 09.5	14.0	17 22.3	14.9			
06	312 04.6	242 09.7	N23 09.4	14 55.6	S22 33.5	85 12.3	S16 14.0	32 24.9	S22 14.9	Alioth	166 17.4	N55 51.8
07	327 07.1	257 08.9	09.9	29 56.8	33.4	100 15.0	13.9	47 27.4	14.9	Alkaid	152 55.9	N49 13.5
08	342 09.5	272 08.1	10.4	44 58.1	33.3	115 17.8	13.8	62 29.9	14.9	Al Na'ir	27 39.8	S46 52.2
F 09	357 12.0	287 07.4	. . 10.9	59 59.3	. . 33.2	130 20.6	. . 13.7	77 32.5	. . 14.9	Alnilam	275 43.3	S 1 11.7
R 10	12 14.5	302 06.6	11.4	75 00.6	33.1	145 23.4	13.6	92 35.0	15.0	Alphard	217 52.8	S 8 44.5
I 11	27 16.9	317 05.8	11.9	90 01.8	33.0	160 26.2	13.5	107 37.5	15.0			
D 12	42 19.4	332 05.0	N23 12.4	105 03.0	S22 32.9	175 29.0	S16 13.5	122 40.1	S22 15.0	Alphecca	126 07.9	N26 39.3
A 13	57 21.8	347 04.2	13.0	120 04.3	32.8	190 31.7	13.4	137 42.6	15.0	Alpheratz	357 40.3	N29 11.2
Y 14	72 24.3	2 03.5	13.5	135 05.5	32.7	205 34.5	13.3	152 45.1	15.0	Altair	62 04.9	N 8 55.0
15	87 26.8	17 02.7	. . 14.0	150 06.8	. . 32.6	220 37.3	. . 13.2	167 47.7	. . 15.0	Ankaa	353 12.8	S42 12.4
16	102 29.2	32 01.9	14.5	165 08.0	32.5	235 40.1	13.1	182 50.2	15.0	Antares	112 21.9	S26 28.2
17	117 31.7	47 01.1	15.0	180 09.2	32.4	250 42.9	13.0	197 52.7	15.0			
18	132 34.2	62 00.3	N23 15.5	195 10.5	S22 32.3	265 45.6	S16 13.0	212 55.3	S22 15.0	Arcturus	145 52.4	N19 05.3
19	147 36.6	76 59.6	16.0	210 11.7	32.2	280 48.4	12.9	227 57.8	15.0	Atria	107 20.2	S69 03.4
20	162 39.1	91 58.8	16.5	225 13.0	32.1	295 51.2	12.8	243 00.3	15.0	Avior	234 16.8	S59 34.5
21	177 41.6	106 58.0	. . 17.0	240 14.2	. . 32.0	310 54.0	. . 12.7	258 02.9	. . 15.0	Bellatrix	278 28.8	N 6 21.7
22	192 44.0	121 57.2	17.5	255 15.5	31.9	325 56.8	12.6	273 05.4	15.0	Betelgeuse	270 58.0	N 7 24.4
23	207 46.5	136 56.4	18.0	270 16.7	31.8	340 59.5	12.5	288 07.9	15.0			
5 00	222 48.9	151 55.7	N23 18.5	285 18.0	S22 31.7	356 02.3	S16 12.5	303 10.5	S22 15.0	Canopus	263 55.0	S52 42.7
01	237 51.4	166 54.9	19.0	300 19.2	31.6	11 05.1	12.4	318 13.0	15.0	Capella	280 30.0	N46 00.8
02	252 53.9	181 54.1	19.5	315 20.5	31.5	26 07.9	12.3	333 15.6	15.0	Deneb	49 29.2	N45 20.5
03	267 56.3	196 53.3	. . 20.0	330 21.7	. . 31.4	41 10.7	. . 12.2	348 18.1	. . 15.0	Denebola	182 30.1	N14 28.2
04	282 58.8	211 52.5	20.5	345 23.0	31.3	56 13.5	12.1	3 20.6	15.0	Diphda	348 52.9	S17 53.3
05	298 01.3	226 51.7	21.0	0 24.2	31.2	71 16.2	12.0	18 23.2	15.0			
06	313 03.7	241 51.0	N23 21.5	15 25.5	S22 31.1	86 19.0	S16 11.9	33 25.7	S22 15.0	Dubhe	193 47.4	N61 39.4
07	328 06.2	256 50.2	22.0	30 26.7	31.0	101 21.8	11.9	48 28.2	15.0	Elnath	278 08.8	N28 37.2
S 08	343 08.7	271 49.4	22.5	45 28.0	30.9	116 24.6	11.8	63 30.8	15.1	Eltanin	90 44.2	N51 29.1
A 09	358 11.1	286 48.6	. . 22.9	60 29.2	. . 30.8	131 27.4	. . 11.7	78 33.3	. . 15.1	Enif	33 44.0	N 9 57.4
T 10	13 13.6	301 47.8	23.4	75 30.5	30.7	146 30.1	11.6	93 35.9	15.1	Fomalhaut	15 20.6	S29 31.5
U 11	28 16.1	316 47.0	23.9	90 31.7	30.6	161 32.9	11.5	108 38.4	15.1			
R 12	43 18.5	331 46.2	N23 24.4	105 33.0	S22 30.5	176 35.7	S16 11.4	123 40.9	S22 15.1	Gacrux	171 56.7	S57 13.1
D 13	58 21.0	346 45.5	24.9	120 34.2	30.4	191 38.5	11.4	138 43.5	15.1	Gienah	175 48.7	S17 38.7
A 14	73 23.4	1 44.7	25.4	135 35.5	30.3	206 41.3	11.3	153 46.0	15.1	Hadar	148 42.5	S60 27.6
Y 15	88 25.9	16 43.9	. . 25.9	150 36.7	. . 30.2	221 44.1	. . 11.2	168 48.5	. . 15.1	Hamal	327 57.4	N23 32.6
16	103 28.4	31 43.1	26.3	165 38.0	30.1	236 46.8	11.1	183 51.1	15.1	Kaus Aust.	83 39.2	S34 22.3
17	118 30.8	46 42.3	26.8	180 39.3	30.0	251 49.6	11.0	198 53.6	15.1			
18	133 33.3	61 41.5	N23 27.3	195 40.5	S22 29.9	266 52.4	S16 10.9	213 56.2	S22 15.1	Kochab	137 19.0	N74 05.0
19	148 35.8	76 40.7	27.8	210 41.8	29.8	281 55.2	10.9	228 58.7	15.1	Markab	13 35.2	N15 18.0
20	163 38.2	91 39.9	28.2	225 43.0	29.7	296 58.0	10.8	244 01.2	15.1	Menkar	314 11.9	N 4 09.4
21	178 40.7	106 39.1	. . 28.7	240 44.3	. . 29.6	312 00.8	. . 10.7	259 03.8	. . 15.1	Menkent	148 03.3	S36 27.6
22	193 43.2	121 38.4	29.2	255 45.5	29.5	327 03.5	10.6	274 06.3	15.1	Miaplacidus	221 38.9	S69 47.9
23	208 45.6	136 37.6	29.7	270 46.8	29.4	342 06.3	10.5	289 08.9	15.1			
6 00	223 48.1	151 36.8	N23 30.1	285 48.1	S22 29.3	357 09.1	S16 10.4	304 11.4	S22 15.1	Mirfak	308 36.1	N49 55.3
01	238 50.6	166 36.0	30.6	300 49.3	29.2	12 11.9	10.3	319 13.9	15.1	Nunki	75 54.1	S26 16.2
02	253 53.0	181 35.2	31.1	315 50.6	29.1	27 14.7	10.3	334 16.5	15.1	Peacock	53 14.0	S56 40.2
03	268 55.5	196 34.4	. . 31.5	330 51.8	. . 29.0	42 17.5	. . 10.2	349 19.0	. . 15.1	Pollux	243 23.9	N27 58.8
04	283 57.9	211 33.6	32.0	345 53.1	28.9	57 20.2	10.1	4 21.6	15.1	Procyon	244 56.4	N 5 10.5
05	299 00.4	226 32.8	32.5	0 54.4	28.8	72 23.0	10.0	19 24.1	15.2			
06	314 02.9	241 32.0	N23 32.9	15 55.6	S22 28.7	87 25.8	S16 09.9	34 26.7	S22 15.2	Rasalhague	96 03.1	N12 32.9
07	329 05.3	256 31.2	33.4	30 56.9	28.5	102 28.6	09.8	49 29.2	15.2	Regulus	207 40.0	N11 52.6
08	344 07.8	271 30.4	33.9	45 58.1	28.4	117 31.4	09.8	64 31.7	15.2	Rigel	281 09.2	S 8 11.1
S 09	359 10.3	286 29.7	. . 34.3	60 59.4	. . 28.3	132 34.1	. . 09.7	79 34.3	. . 15.2	Rigil Kent.	139 46.6	S60 54.5
U 10	14 12.7	301 28.9	34.8	76 00.7	28.2	147 36.9	09.6	94 36.8	15.2	Sabik	102 08.5	S15 44.7
N 11	29 15.2	316 28.1	35.2	91 01.9	28.1	162 39.7	09.5	109 39.4	15.2			
D 12	44 17.7	331 27.3	N23 35.7	106 03.2	S22 28.0	177 42.5	S16 09.4	124 41.9	S22 15.2	Schedar	349 37.2	N56 37.9
A 13	59 20.1	346 26.5	36.2	121 04.5	27.9	192 45.3	09.3	139 44.4	15.2	Shaula	96 17.1	S37 06.8
Y 14	74 22.6	1 25.7	36.6	136 05.7	27.8	207 48.1	09.2	154 47.0	15.2	Sirius	258 31.0	S16 44.8
15	89 25.1	16 24.9	. . 37.1	151 07.0	. . 27.7	222 50.8	. . 09.2	169 49.5	. . 15.2	Spica	158 27.5	S11 15.4
16	104 27.5	31 24.1	37.5	166 08.3	27.6	237 53.6	09.1	184 52.1	15.2	Suhail	222 50.0	S43 30.7
17	119 30.0	46 23.3	38.0	181 09.5	27.5	252 56.4	09.0	199 54.6	15.2			
18	134 32.4	61 22.5	N23 38.4	196 10.8	S22 27.4	267 59.2	S16 08.9	214 57.2	S22 15.2	Vega	80 36.5	N38 47.9
19	149 34.9	76 21.7	38.9	211 12.1	27.3	283 02.0	08.8	229 59.7	15.2	Zuben'ubi	137 01.4	S16 07.0
20	164 37.4	91 20.9	39.3	226 13.4	27.2	298 04.8	08.7	245 02.3	15.2		SHA	Mer. Pass.
21	179 39.8	106 20.1	. . 39.8	241 14.6	. . 27.1	313 07.5	. . 08.7	260 04.8	. . 15.2		° ′	h m
22	194 42.3	121 19.3	40.2	256 15.9	27.0	328 10.3	08.6	275 07.3	15.2	Venus	289 06.7	13 53
23	209 44.8	136 18.5	40.7	271 17.2	26.9	343 13.1	08.5	290 09.9	15.2	Mars	62 29.0	4 58
										Jupiter	133 13.4	0 16
Mer. Pass.	h m 9 07.2	v −0.8	d 0.5	v 1.3	d 0.1	v 2.8	d 0.1	v 2.5	d 0.0	Saturn	80 21.5	3 47

UT	SUN GHA	SUN Dec	MOON GHA	v	MOON Dec	d	HP
d h	° ′	° ′	° ′	′	° ′	′	′
4 00	180 47.8	N15 53.1	312 56.9	11.5	S20 08.2	2.2	54.5
01	195 47.8	53.8	327 27.4	11.6	20 10.4	2.1	54.5
02	210 47.9	54.6	341 58.0	11.5	20 12.5	1.9	54.5
03	225 47.9 ..	55.3	356 28.5	11.6	20 14.4	1.9	54.5
04	240 48.0	56.0	10 59.1	11.5	20 16.3	1.8	54.5
05	255 48.1	56.7	25 29.6	11.6	20 18.1	1.7	54.5
06	270 48.1	N15 57.5	40 00.2	11.5	S20 19.8	1.6	54.5
07	285 48.2	58.2	54 30.7	11.6	20 21.4	1.5	54.4
F 08	300 48.2	58.9	69 01.3	11.6	20 22.9	1.4	54.4
R 09	315 48.3	15 59.6	83 31.9	11.5	20 24.3	1.3	54.4
I 10	330 48.3	16 00.4	98 02.4	11.6	20 25.6	1.2	54.4
D 11	345 48.4	01.1	112 33.0	11.6	20 26.8	1.1	54.4
A 12	0 48.5	N16 01.8	127 03.6	11.6	S20 27.9	1.1	54.4
Y 13	15 48.5	02.5	141 34.2	11.6	20 29.0	0.9	54.4
14	30 48.6	03.3	156 04.8	11.6	20 29.9	0.8	54.4
15	45 48.6 ..	04.0	170 35.4	11.6	20 30.7	0.7	54.4
16	60 48.7	04.7	185 06.0	11.7	20 31.4	0.7	54.4
17	75 48.7	05.4	199 36.7	11.6	20 32.1	0.5	54.3
18	90 48.8	N16 06.1	214 07.3	11.6	S20 32.6	0.4	54.3
19	105 48.9	06.8	228 37.9	11.7	20 33.0	0.4	54.3
20	120 48.9	07.6	243 08.6	11.6	20 33.4	0.2	54.3
21	135 49.0 ..	08.3	257 39.2	11.7	20 33.6	0.1	54.3
22	150 49.0	09.0	272 09.9	11.7	20 33.7	0.1	54.3
23	165 49.1	09.7	286 40.6	11.7	20 33.8	0.1	54.3
5 00	180 49.1	N16 10.4	301 11.3	11.7	S20 33.7	0.1	54.3
01	195 49.2	11.1	315 42.0	11.7	20 33.6	0.2	54.3
02	210 49.2	11.9	330 12.7	11.7	20 33.4	0.4	54.3
03	225 49.3 ..	12.6	344 43.4	11.7	20 33.0	0.4	54.3
04	240 49.4	13.3	359 14.1	11.8	20 32.6	0.5	54.3
05	255 49.4	14.0	13 44.9	11.8	20 32.1	0.7	54.3
06	270 49.5	N16 14.7	28 15.7	11.7	S20 31.4	0.7	54.3
S 07	285 49.5	15.4	42 46.4	11.8	20 30.7	0.8	54.3
A 08	300 49.6	16.1	57 17.2	11.8	20 29.9	0.9	54.3
T 09	315 49.6 ..	16.9	71 48.0	11.8	20 29.0	1.0	54.2
U 10	330 49.7	17.6	86 18.8	11.8	20 28.0	1.1	54.2
R 11	345 49.7	18.3	100 49.6	11.9	20 26.9	1.2	54.2
D 12	0 49.8	N16 19.0	115 20.5	11.8	S20 25.7	1.3	54.2
A 13	15 49.8	19.7	129 51.3	11.9	20 24.4	1.4	54.2
Y 14	30 49.9	20.4	144 22.2	11.9	20 23.0	1.5	54.2
15	45 49.9 ..	21.1	158 53.1	11.9	20 21.5	1.5	54.2
16	60 50.0	21.8	173 24.0	11.9	20 20.0	1.7	54.2
17	75 50.0	22.5	187 54.9	12.0	20 18.3	1.8	54.2
18	90 50.1	N16 23.2	202 25.9	11.9	S20 16.5	1.8	54.2
19	105 50.1	24.0	216 56.8	12.0	20 14.7	2.0	54.2
20	120 50.2	24.7	231 27.8	12.0	20 12.7	2.0	54.2
21	135 50.2 ..	25.4	245 58.8	12.0	20 10.7	2.2	54.2
22	150 50.3	26.1	260 29.8	12.0	20 08.5	2.2	54.2
23	165 50.3	26.8	275 00.8	12.0	20 06.3	2.3	54.2
6 00	180 50.4	N16 27.5	289 31.8	12.1	S20 04.0	2.4	54.2
01	195 50.4	28.2	304 02.9	12.0	20 01.6	2.5	54.2
02	210 50.5	28.9	318 33.9	12.1	19 59.1	2.6	54.2
03	225 50.5 ..	29.6	333 05.0	12.1	19 56.5	2.7	54.2
04	240 50.6	30.3	347 36.1	12.2	19 53.8	2.8	54.2
05	255 50.6	31.0	2 07.3	12.1	19 51.0	2.8	54.2
06	270 50.7	N16 31.7	16 38.4	12.2	S19 48.2	3.0	54.2
07	285 50.7	32.4	31 09.6	12.2	19 45.2	3.0	54.2
S 08	300 50.8	33.1	45 40.8	12.2	19 42.2	3.2	54.2
U 09	315 50.8 ..	33.8	60 12.0	12.2	19 39.0	3.2	54.2
N 10	330 50.9	34.5	74 43.2	12.3	19 35.8	3.3	54.2
D 11	345 50.9	35.2	89 14.5	12.2	19 32.5	3.4	54.2
A 12	0 50.9	N16 35.9	103 45.7	12.3	S19 29.1	3.5	54.2
Y 13	15 51.0	36.6	118 17.0	12.3	19 25.6	3.6	54.2
14	30 51.0	37.3	132 48.3	12.3	19 22.0	3.7	54.2
15	45 51.1 ..	38.0	147 19.6	12.4	19 18.3	3.8	54.2
16	60 51.1	38.7	161 51.0	12.3	19 14.5	3.8	54.2
17	75 51.2	39.4	176 22.3	12.4	19 10.7	4.0	54.3
18	90 51.2	N16 40.1	190 53.7	12.4	S19 06.7	4.0	54.3
19	105 51.3	40.8	205 25.1	12.5	19 02.7	4.1	54.3
20	120 51.3	41.5	219 56.6	12.4	18 58.6	4.2	54.3
21	135 51.3 ..	42.2	234 28.0	12.5	18 54.4	4.3	54.3
22	150 51.4	42.9	248 59.5	12.5	18 50.1	4.4	54.3
23	165 51.4	43.6	263 31.0	12.5	S18 45.7	4.4	54.3
	SD 15.9	d 0.7	SD 14.8		14.8		14.8

Twilight / Sunrise / Moonrise

Lat.	Twilight Naut.	Twilight Civil	Sunrise	Moonrise 4	5	6	7
°	h m	h m	h m	h m	h m	h m	h m
N 72	////	////	01 15	■	■	■	■
N 70	////	////	02 07	■	■	04 36	04 02
68	////	////	02 39	01 36	02 36	03 06	03 18
66	////	01 29	03 02	00 54	01 50	02 27	02 49
64	////	02 06	03 20	00 20	01 20	02 00	02 27
62	////	02 32	03 35	00 04	00 58	01 39	02 09
60	01 19	02 52	03 48	24 40	00 40	01 22	01 54
N 58	01 53	03 08	03 58	24 25	00 25	01 08	01 42
56	02 17	03 22	04 08	24 12	00 12	00 55	01 31
54	02 36	03 33	04 16	24 00	00 00	00 45	01 21
52	02 51	03 43	04 23	23 50	24 35	00 35	01 13
50	03 04	03 52	04 30	23 42	24 27	00 27	01 05
45	03 30	04 11	04 44	23 23	24 08	00 08	00 49
N 40	03 50	04 26	04 55	23 07	23 54	24 35	00 35
35	04 05	04 38	05 05	22 55	23 41	24 24	00 24
30	04 18	04 48	05 14	22 43	23 30	24 14	00 14
20	04 38	05 05	05 29	22 24	23 11	23 56	24 39
N 10	04 54	05 19	05 41	22 07	22 55	23 41	24 26
0	05 07	05 32	05 53	21 51	22 40	23 27	24 14
S 10	05 18	05 43	06 05	21 36	22 24	23 13	24 01
20	05 28	05 54	06 17	21 19	22 08	22 58	23 48
30	05 38	06 06	06 31	21 00	21 49	22 40	23 33
35	05 43	06 13	06 39	20 49	21 38	22 30	23 24
40	05 48	06 20	06 49	20 36	21 26	22 19	23 14
45	05 53	06 28	06 59	20 21	21 11	22 05	23 02
S 50	05 59	06 38	07 12	20 02	20 53	21 48	22 48
52	06 02	06 42	07 18	19 53	20 44	21 40	22 41
54	06 04	06 47	07 25	19 43	20 34	21 32	22 34
56	06 07	06 52	07 32	19 32	20 24	21 22	22 26
58	06 10	06 57	07 41	19 20	20 11	21 10	22 16
S 60	06 13	07 03	07 50	19 05	19 57	20 57	22 05

Sunset / Twilight / Moonset

Lat.	Sunset	Twilight Civil	Twilight Naut.	Moonset 4	5	6	7
°	h m	h m	h m	h m	h m	h m	h m
N 72	22 50	////	////	■	■	■	■
N 70	21 52	////	////	■	■	05 12	07 24
68	21 18	////	////	04 50	05 31	06 41	08 07
66	20 54	22 31	////	05 32	06 17	07 20	08 35
64	20 35	21 51	////	06 01	06 47	07 46	08 57
62	20 20	21 24	////	06 23	07 09	08 07	09 14
60	20 08	21 04	22 40	06 40	07 27	08 24	09 29
N 58	19 57	20 47	22 04	06 55	07 42	08 38	09 41
56	19 47	20 33	21 39	07 08	07 55	08 50	09 51
54	19 39	20 22	21 20	07 19	08 06	09 01	10 01
52	19 31	20 11	21 04	07 29	08 16	09 10	10 09
50	19 25	20 02	20 51	07 37	08 25	09 18	10 16
45	19 10	19 43	20 24	07 56	08 44	09 36	10 32
N 40	18 59	19 28	20 05	08 11	08 59	09 51	10 45
35	18 49	19 16	19 49	08 24	09 12	10 03	10 56
30	18 40	19 05	19 36	08 35	09 23	10 14	11 06
20	18 25	18 48	19 16	08 54	09 43	10 32	11 22
N 10	18 12	18 34	19 00	09 11	09 59	10 48	11 36
0	18 00	18 22	18 47	09 26	10 15	11 03	11 50
S 10	17 48	18 10	18 35	09 42	10 30	11 18	12 03
20	17 36	17 59	18 25	09 59	10 47	11 33	12 17
30	17 22	17 47	18 15	10 18	11 06	11 51	12 33
35	17 13	17 40	18 10	10 29	11 17	12 02	12 43
40	17 04	17 33	18 05	10 42	11 30	12 14	12 53
45	16 53	17 25	18 00	10 57	11 45	12 28	13 06
S 50	16 40	17 15	17 54	11 15	12 03	12 45	13 21
52	16 34	17 11	17 51	11 24	12 12	12 53	13 28
54	16 28	17 06	17 48	11 33	12 22	13 02	13 35
56	16 20	17 01	17 46	11 45	12 33	13 12	13 45
58	16 12	16 55	17 43	11 57	12 45	13 24	13 55
S 60	16 02	16 49	17 39	12 12	13 00	13 37	14 06

SUN / MOON

Day	Eqn. of Time 00h	Eqn. of Time 12h	Mer. Pass.	Mer. Pass. Upper	Mer. Pass. Lower	Age	Phase
d	m s	m s	h m	h m	h m	d	%
4	03 11	03 14	11 57	03 15	15 39	18	82
5	03 16	03 19	11 57	04 03	16 27	19	74
6	03 21	03 24	11 57	04 51	17 15	20	65

UT	ARIES	VENUS −3·9		MARS −0·6		JUPITER −2·5		SATURN +0·3		STARS		
	GHA	GHA	Dec	GHA	Dec	GHA	Dec	GHA	Dec	Name	SHA	Dec
d h	° ′	° ′	° ′	° ′	° ′	° ′	° ′	° ′	° ′		° ′	° ′
7 00	224 47.2	151 17.7	N23 41.1	286 18.4	S22 26.8	358 15.9	S16 08.4	305 12.4	S22 15.2	Acamar	315 16.3	S40 14.1
01	239 49.7	166 16.9	41.6	301 19.7	26.7	13 18.7	08.3	320 15.0	15.3	Achernar	335 24.9	S57 08.7
02	254 52.2	181 16.1	42.0	316 21.0	26.6	28 21.5	08.2	335 17.5	15.3	Acrux	173 05.0	S63 12.2
03	269 54.6	196 15.3 . .	42.4	331 22.3 . .	26.5	43 24.2 . .	08.1	350 20.1 . .	15.3	Adhara	255 10.2	S29 00.2
04	284 57.1	211 14.5	42.9	346 23.5	26.4	58 27.0	08.1	5 22.6	15.3	Aldebaran	290 45.9	N16 32.5
05	299 59.5	226 13.7	43.3	1 24.8	26.3	73 29.8	08.0	20 25.2	15.3			
06	315 02.0	241 12.9	N23 43.8	16 26.1	S22 26.2	88 32.6	S16 07.9	35 27.7	S22 15.3	Alioth	166 17.4	N55 51.9
07	330 04.5	256 12.1	44.2	31 27.4	26.1	103 35.4	07.8	50 30.2	15.3	Alkaid	152 55.9	N49 13.5
08	345 06.9	271 11.3	44.6	46 28.6	26.0	118 38.2	07.7	65 32.8	15.3	Al Na'ir	27 39.8	S46 52.2
M 09	0 09.4	286 10.5 . .	45.1	61 29.9 . .	25.9	133 40.9 . .	07.6	80 35.3 . .	15.3	Alnilam	275 43.3	S 1 11.7
O 10	15 11.9	301 09.7	45.5	76 31.2	25.8	148 43.7	07.6	95 37.9	15.3	Alphard	217 52.8	S 8 44.5
N 11	30 14.3	316 08.9	45.9	91 32.5	25.7	163 46.5	07.5	110 40.4	15.3			
D 12	45 16.8	331 08.1	N23 46.4	106 33.7	S22 25.6	178 49.3	S16 07.4	125 43.0	S22 15.3	Alphecca	126 07.9	N26 39.3
A 13	60 19.3	346 07.3	46.8	121 35.0	25.5	193 52.1	07.3	140 45.5	15.3	Alpheratz	357 40.3	N29 11.2
Y 14	75 21.7	1 06.5	47.2	136 36.3	25.4	208 54.9	07.2	155 48.1	15.3	Altair	62 04.9	N 8 55.0
15	90 24.2	16 05.7 . .	47.6	151 37.6 . .	25.3	223 57.6 . .	07.1	170 50.6 . .	15.3	Ankaa	353 12.8	S42 12.4
16	105 26.7	31 04.9	48.1	166 38.9	25.2	239 00.4	07.1	185 53.2	15.3	Antares	112 21.9	S26 28.2
17	120 29.1	46 04.1	48.5	181 40.1	25.1	254 03.2	07.0	200 55.7	15.3			
18	135 31.6	61 03.3	N23 48.9	196 41.4	S22 25.0	269 06.0	S16 06.9	215 58.3	S22 15.3	Arcturus	145 52.4	N19 05.3
19	150 34.0	76 02.5	49.3	211 42.7	24.9	284 08.8	06.8	231 00.8	15.3	Atria	107 20.2	S69 03.3
20	165 36.5	91 01.7	49.8	226 44.0	24.8	299 11.6	06.7	246 03.4	15.4	Avior	234 16.8	S59 34.5
21	180 39.0	106 00.9 . .	50.2	241 45.3 . .	24.7	314 14.3 . .	06.6	261 05.9 . .	15.4	Bellatrix	278 28.8	N 6 21.7
22	195 41.4	121 00.1	50.6	256 46.6	24.6	329 17.1	06.5	276 08.5	15.4	Betelgeuse	270 58.0	N 7 24.4
23	210 43.9	135 59.3	51.0	271 47.8	24.5	344 19.9	06.5	291 11.0	15.4			
8 00	225 46.4	150 58.5	N23 51.4	286 49.1	S22 24.4	359 22.7	S16 06.4	306 13.5	S22 15.4	Canopus	263 55.1	S52 42.7
01	240 48.8	165 57.7	51.8	301 50.4	24.3	14 25.5	06.3	321 16.1	15.4	Capella	280 30.0	N46 00.8
02	255 51.3	180 56.9	52.3	316 51.7	24.2	29 28.3	06.2	336 18.6	15.4	Deneb	49 29.1	N45 20.5
03	270 53.8	195 56.1 . .	52.7	331 53.0 . .	24.1	44 31.1 . .	06.1	351 21.2 . .	15.4	Denebola	182 30.1	N14 28.2
04	285 56.2	210 55.3	53.1	346 54.3	24.0	59 33.8	06.0	6 23.7	15.4	Diphda	348 52.9	S17 53.3
05	300 58.7	225 54.5	53.5	1 55.6	23.9	74 36.6	06.0	21 26.3	15.4			
06	316 01.2	240 53.7	N23 53.9	16 56.8	S22 23.8	89 39.4	S16 05.9	36 28.8	S22 15.4	Dubhe	193 47.5	N61 39.4
07	331 03.6	255 52.9	54.3	31 58.1	23.7	104 42.2	05.8	51 31.4	15.4	Elnath	278 08.8	N28 37.2
T 08	346 06.1	270 52.1	54.7	46 59.4	23.6	119 45.0	05.7	66 33.9	15.4	Eltanin	90 44.2	N51 29.1
U 09	1 08.5	285 51.3 . .	55.1	62 00.7 . .	23.5	134 47.8 . .	05.6	81 36.5 . .	15.4	Enif	33 43.9	N 9 57.4
E 10	16 11.0	300 50.5	55.5	77 02.0	23.4	149 50.5	05.5	96 39.0	15.4	Fomalhaut	15 20.5	S29 31.5
S 11	31 13.5	315 49.7	55.9	92 03.3	23.3	164 53.3	05.4	111 41.6	15.4			
D 12	46 15.9	330 48.9	N23 56.3	107 04.6	S22 23.2	179 56.1	S16 05.4	126 44.1	S22 15.4	Gacrux	171 56.7	S57 13.1
A 13	61 18.4	345 48.1	56.7	122 05.9	23.1	194 58.9	05.3	141 46.7	15.5	Gienah	175 48.7	S17 38.7
Y 14	76 20.9	0 47.2	57.1	137 07.2	23.0	210 01.7	05.2	156 49.2	15.5	Hadar	148 42.5	S60 27.6
15	91 23.3	15 46.4 . .	57.5	152 08.5 . .	22.9	225 04.5 . .	05.1	171 51.8 . .	15.5	Hamal	327 57.4	N23 32.6
16	106 25.8	30 45.6	57.9	167 09.8	22.8	240 07.2	05.0	186 54.3	15.5	Kaus Aust.	83 39.2	S34 22.3
17	121 28.3	45 44.8	58.3	182 11.0	22.7	255 10.0	04.9	201 56.9	15.5			
18	136 30.7	60 44.0	N23 58.7	197 12.3	S22 22.6	270 12.8	S16 04.9	216 59.5	S22 15.5	Kochab	137 19.0	N74 05.0
19	151 33.2	75 43.2	59.1	212 13.6	22.5	285 15.6	04.8	232 02.0	15.5	Markab	13 35.2	N15 18.0
20	166 35.6	90 42.4	59.5	227 14.9	22.4	300 18.4	04.7	247 04.6	15.5	Menkar	314 11.9	N 4 09.4
21	181 38.1	105 41.6	23 59.9	242 16.2 . .	22.3	315 21.2 . .	04.6	262 07.1 . .	15.5	Menkent	148 03.3	S36 27.6
22	196 40.6	120 40.8	24 00.3	257 17.5	22.2	330 23.9	04.5	277 09.7	15.5	Miaplacidus	221 39.0	S69 47.9
23	211 43.0	135 40.0	00.7	272 18.8	22.1	345 26.7	04.4	292 12.2	15.5			
9 00	226 45.5	150 39.2	N24 01.1	287 20.1	S22 22.0	0 29.5	S16 04.3	307 14.8	S22 15.5	Mirfak	308 36.1	N49 55.3
01	241 48.0	165 38.4	01.5	302 21.4	21.9	15 32.3	04.3	322 17.3	15.5	Nunki	75 54.0	S26 16.2
02	256 50.4	180 37.5	01.8	317 22.7	21.8	30 35.1	04.2	337 19.9	15.5	Peacock	53 14.0	S56 40.2
03	271 52.9	195 36.7 . .	02.2	332 24.0 . .	21.7	45 37.9 . .	04.1	352 22.4 . .	15.5	Pollux	243 23.9	N27 58.8
04	286 55.4	210 35.9	02.6	347 25.3	21.6	60 40.6	04.0	7 25.0	15.5	Procyon	244 56.5	N 5 10.5
05	301 57.8	225 35.1	03.0	2 26.6	21.5	75 43.4	03.9	22 27.5	15.5			
06	317 00.3	240 34.3	N24 03.4	17 27.9	S22 21.4	90 46.2	S16 03.8	37 30.1	S22 15.5	Rasalhague	96 03.1	N12 32.9
W 07	332 02.8	255 33.5	03.8	32 29.2	21.3	105 49.0	03.7	52 32.6	15.5	Regulus	207 40.0	N11 52.6
E 08	347 05.2	270 32.7	04.1	47 30.5	21.2	120 51.8	03.7	67 35.2	15.6	Rigel	281 09.2	S 8 11.1
D 09	2 07.7	285 31.9 . .	04.5	62 31.8 . .	21.1	135 54.6 . .	03.6	82 37.7 . .	15.6	Rigil Kent.	139 46.6	S60 54.5
N 10	17 10.1	300 31.1	04.9	77 33.1	21.0	150 57.4	03.5	97 40.3	15.6	Sabik	102 08.5	S15 44.7
E 11	32 12.6	315 30.2	05.3	92 34.4	20.9	166 00.1	03.4	112 42.9	15.6			
S 12	47 15.1	330 29.4	N24 05.6	107 35.7	S22 20.8	181 02.9	S16 03.3	127 45.4	S22 15.6	Schedar	349 37.2	N56 37.9
D 13	62 17.5	345 28.6	06.0	122 37.0	20.7	196 05.7	03.2	142 48.0	15.6	Shaula	96 17.1	S37 06.8
A 14	77 20.0	0 27.8	06.4	137 38.3	20.6	211 08.5	03.2	157 50.5	15.6	Sirius	258 31.0	S16 44.8
Y 15	92 22.5	15 27.0 . .	06.7	152 39.7 . .	20.5	226 11.3 . .	03.1	172 53.1 . .	15.6	Spica	158 27.5	S11 15.4
16	107 24.9	30 26.2	07.1	167 41.0	20.4	241 14.1	03.0	187 55.6	15.6	Suhail	222 50.0	S43 30.7
17	122 27.4	45 25.4	07.5	182 42.3	20.3	256 16.8	02.9	202 58.2	15.6			
18	137 29.9	60 24.6	N24 07.9	197 43.6	S22 20.2	271 19.6	S16 02.8	218 00.7	S22 15.6	Vega	80 36.5	N38 48.0
19	152 32.3	75 23.7	08.2	212 44.9	20.1	286 22.4	02.7	233 03.3	15.6	Zuben'ubi	137 01.4	S16 07.0
20	167 34.8	90 22.9	08.6	227 46.2	20.0	301 25.2	02.6	248 05.8	15.6		SHA	Mer. Pass.
21	182 37.3	105 22.1 . .	08.9	242 47.5 . .	19.9	316 28.0 . .	02.6	263 08.4 . .	15.6		° ′	h m
22	197 39.7	120 21.3	09.3	257 48.8	19.8	331 30.8	02.5	278 11.0	15.6	Venus	285 12.2	13 57
23	212 42.2	135 20.5	09.7	272 50.1	19.7	346 33.5	02.4	293 13.5	15.6	Mars	61 02.8	4 52
	h m									Jupiter	133 36.3	0 02
Mer. Pass. 8 55.4		v −0.8	d 0.4	v 1.3	d 0.1	v 2.8	d 0.1	v 2.6	d 0.0	Saturn	80 27.2	3 34

UT	SUN GHA	SUN Dec	MOON GHA	v	MOON Dec	d	HP
d h	° ′	° ′	° ′	′	° ′	′	′
7 00	180 51.5	N16 44.3	278 02.5	12.5	S18 41.3	4.6	54.3
01	195 51.5	44.9	292 34.0	12.6	18 36.7	4.6	54.3
02	210 51.6	45.6	307 05.6	12.5	18 32.1	4.7	54.3
03	225 51.6 ..	46.3	321 37.1	12.6	18 27.4	4.8	54.3
04	240 51.6	47.0	336 08.7	12.6	18 22.6	4.9	54.3
05	255 51.7	47.7	350 40.3	12.7	18 17.7	4.9	54.3
06	270 51.7	N16 48.4	5 12.0	12.6	S18 12.8	5.1	54.3
07	285 51.8	49.1	19 43.6	12.7	18 07.7	5.1	54.3
08	300 51.8	49.8	34 15.3	12.7	18 02.6	5.2	54.4
M 09	315 51.8 ..	50.5	48 47.0	12.7	17 57.4	5.3	54.4
O 10	330 51.9	51.2	63 18.7	12.7	17 52.1	5.4	54.4
N 11	345 51.9	51.8	77 50.4	12.8	17 46.7	5.5	54.4
D 12	0 52.0	N16 52.5	92 22.2	12.8	S17 41.2	5.5	54.4
A 13	15 52.0	53.2	106 54.0	12.8	17 35.7	5.6	54.4
Y 14	30 52.0	53.9	121 25.8	12.8	17 30.1	5.7	54.4
15	45 52.1 ..	54.6	135 57.6	12.8	17 24.4	5.8	54.4
16	60 52.1	55.3	150 29.4	12.9	17 18.6	5.9	54.4
17	75 52.2	56.0	165 01.3	12.9	17 12.7	5.9	54.5
18	90 52.2	N16 56.7	179 33.2	12.9	S17 06.8	6.1	54.5
19	105 52.2	57.3	194 05.1	12.9	17 00.7	6.1	54.5
20	120 52.3	58.0	208 37.0	12.9	16 54.6	6.1	54.5
21	135 52.3 ..	58.7	223 08.9	13.0	16 48.5	6.3	54.5
22	150 52.3	16 59.4	237 40.9	13.0	16 42.2	6.3	54.5
23	165 52.4	17 00.1	252 12.9	12.9	16 35.9	6.4	54.5
8 00	180 52.4	N17 00.7	266 44.8	13.1	S16 29.5	6.5	54.5
01	195 52.5	01.4	281 16.9	13.0	16 23.0	6.6	54.6
02	210 52.5	02.1	295 48.9	13.0	16 16.4	6.6	54.6
03	225 52.5 ..	02.8	310 20.9	13.1	16 09.8	6.7	54.6
04	240 52.6	03.5	324 53.0	13.1	16 03.1	6.8	54.6
05	255 52.6	04.1	339 25.1	13.1	15 56.3	6.9	54.6
06	270 52.6	N17 04.8	353 57.2	13.1	S15 49.4	6.9	54.6
07	285 52.7	05.5	8 29.3	13.1	15 42.5	7.1	54.6
T 08	300 52.7	06.2	23 01.4	13.2	15 35.4	7.0	54.7
U 09	315 52.7 ..	06.9	37 33.6	13.1	15 28.4	7.2	54.7
E 10	330 52.8	07.5	52 05.7	13.2	15 21.2	7.2	54.7
S 11	345 52.8	08.2	66 37.9	13.2	15 14.0	7.3	54.7
D 12	0 52.8	N17 08.9	81 10.1	13.2	S15 06.7	7.4	54.7
A 13	15 52.9	09.6	95 42.3	13.3	14 59.3	7.5	54.7
Y 14	30 52.9	10.2	110 14.6	13.2	14 51.8	7.5	54.8
15	45 52.9 ..	10.9	124 46.8	13.3	14 44.3	7.6	54.8
16	60 53.0	11.6	139 19.1	13.2	14 36.7	7.6	54.8
17	75 53.0	12.3	153 51.3	13.3	14 29.1	7.8	54.8
18	90 53.0	N17 12.9	168 23.6	13.3	S14 21.3	7.8	54.8
19	105 53.1	13.6	182 55.9	13.3	14 13.5	7.8	54.9
20	120 53.1	14.3	197 28.2	13.4	14 05.7	8.0	54.9
21	135 53.1 ..	15.0	212 00.6	13.3	13 57.7	8.0	54.9
22	150 53.2	15.6	226 32.9	13.3	13 49.7	8.0	54.9
23	165 53.2	16.3	241 05.2	13.4	13 41.7	8.2	54.9
9 00	180 53.2	N17 17.0	255 37.6	13.4	S13 33.5	8.2	55.0
01	195 53.3	17.6	270 10.0	13.3	13 25.3	8.3	55.0
02	210 53.3	18.3	284 42.3	13.4	13 17.0	8.3	55.0
03	225 53.3 ..	19.0	299 14.7	13.4	13 08.7	8.4	55.0
04	240 53.3	19.6	313 47.1	13.4	13 00.3	8.5	55.0
05	255 53.4	20.3	328 19.5	13.5	12 51.8	8.5	55.1
06	270 53.4	N17 21.0	342 52.0	13.4	S12 43.3	8.6	55.1
W 07	285 53.4	21.6	357 24.4	13.4	12 34.7	8.6	55.1
E 08	300 53.5	22.3	11 56.8	13.4	12 26.1	8.8	55.1
D 09	315 53.5 ..	23.0	26 29.3	13.4	12 17.3	8.7	55.2
N 10	330 53.5	23.6	41 01.7	13.5	12 08.6	8.9	55.2
E 11	345 53.5	24.3	55 34.2	13.4	11 59.7	8.9	55.2
S 12	0 53.6	N17 25.0	70 06.6	13.5	S11 50.8	9.0	55.2
D 13	15 53.6	25.6	84 39.1	13.5	11 41.8	9.0	55.2
A 14	30 53.6	26.3	99 11.6	13.5	11 32.8	9.1	55.3
Y 15	45 53.7 ..	26.9	113 44.1	13.4	11 23.7	9.1	55.3
16	60 53.7	27.6	128 16.5	13.5	11 14.6	9.2	55.3
17	75 53.7	28.3	142 49.0	13.5	11 05.4	9.3	55.3
18	90 53.7	N17 28.9	157 21.5	13.5	S10 56.1	9.3	55.4
19	105 53.8	29.6	171 54.0	13.6	10 46.8	9.4	55.4
20	120 53.8	30.3	186 26.5	13.5	10 37.4	9.4	55.4
21	135 53.8 ..	30.9	200 59.0	13.5	10 28.0	9.5	55.4
22	150 53.8	31.6	215 31.5	13.5	10 18.5	9.6	55.5
23	165 53.9	32.2	230 04.0	13.5	S10 08.9	9.6	55.5
	SD 15.9	d 0.7	SD 14.8		14.9		15.0

Lat.	Twilight Naut.	Twilight Civil	Sunrise	Moonrise 7	Moonrise 8	Moonrise 9	Moonrise 10
°	h m	h m	h m	h m	h m	h m	h m
N 72	////	////	00 27	■■■	04 32	04 08	03 52
N 70	////	////	01 47	04 02	03 51	03 44	03 38
68	////	////	02 24	03 18	03 24	03 26	03 26
66	////	01 04	02 50	02 49	03 02	03 11	03 17
64	////	01 51	03 10	02 27	02 45	02 59	03 08
62	////	02 20	03 26	02 09	02 31	02 48	03 01
60	00 57	02 42	03 40	01 54	02 19	02 39	02 55
N 58	01 40	03 00	03 51	01 42	02 09	02 31	02 50
56	02 07	03 14	04 01	01 31	02 00	02 24	02 45
54	02 27	03 27	04 10	01 21	01 52	02 18	02 41
52	02 44	03 37	04 18	01 13	01 45	02 12	02 37
50	02 58	03 47	04 25	01 05	01 38	02 07	02 33
45	03 25	04 07	04 40	00 49	01 24	01 56	02 26
N 40	03 45	04 22	04 52	00 35	01 13	01 47	02 19
35	04 02	04 35	05 02	00 24	01 03	01 39	02 13
30	04 15	04 46	05 12	00 14	00 54	01 32	02 09
20	04 36	05 04	05 27	24 39	00 39	01 20	02 00
N 10	04 53	05 18	05 41	24 26	00 26	01 10	01 52
0	05 06	05 31	05 53	24 14	00 14	01 00	01 45
S 10	05 18	05 43	06 05	24 01	00 01	00 50	01 38
20	05 29	05 55	06 18	23 48	24 39	00 39	01 30
30	05 40	06 08	06 33	23 33	24 27	00 27	01 22
35	05 45	06 15	06 42	23 24	24 20	00 20	01 17
40	05 51	06 23	06 52	23 14	24 12	00 12	01 11
45	05 56	06 32	07 03	23 02	24 02	00 02	01 04
S 50	06 03	06 42	07 17	22 48	23 51	24 56	00 56
52	06 06	06 46	07 23	22 41	23 46	24 53	00 53
54	06 09	06 51	07 30	22 34	23 40	24 48	00 48
56	06 12	06 57	07 38	22 26	23 33	24 44	00 44
58	06 15	07 03	07 47	22 16	23 26	24 39	00 39
S 60	06 19	07 10	07 57	22 05	23 18	24 33	00 33

Lat.	Sunset	Twilight Civil	Twilight Naut.	Moonset 7	Moonset 8	Moonset 9	Moonset 10
°	h m	h m	h m	h m	h m	h m	h m
N 72	▭	▭	▭	■■■	08 31	10 30	12 21
N 70	22 12	////	////	07 24	09 11	10 53	12 33
68	21 33	////	////	08 07	09 38	11 10	12 44
66	21 06	22 58	////	08 35	09 58	11 24	12 52
64	20 45	22 06	////	08 57	10 14	11 35	12 59
62	20 29	21 36	////	09 14	10 28	11 45	13 05
60	20 15	21 13	23 04	09 29	10 39	11 53	13 10
N 58	20 03	20 55	22 17	09 41	10 49	12 00	13 14
56	19 53	20 40	21 49	09 51	10 57	12 07	13 18
54	19 44	20 28	21 28	10 01	11 05	12 12	13 22
52	19 36	20 17	21 11	10 09	11 12	12 17	13 25
50	19 29	20 07	20 57	10 16	11 18	12 22	13 28
45	19 14	19 47	20 29	10 32	11 31	12 32	13 35
N 40	19 02	19 32	20 08	10 45	11 42	12 40	13 40
35	18 51	19 19	19 52	10 56	11 51	12 47	13 45
30	18 42	19 08	19 38	11 06	11 59	12 53	13 49
20	18 26	18 49	19 17	11 22	12 13	13 04	13 55
N 10	18 13	18 35	19 00	11 36	12 25	13 13	14 01
0	18 00	18 22	18 47	11 50	12 36	13 22	14 07
S 10	17 47	18 09	18 35	12 03	12 47	13 30	14 13
20	17 34	17 57	18 24	12 17	12 59	13 39	14 18
30	17 19	17 44	18 13	12 33	13 13	13 50	14 25
35	17 11	17 37	18 08	12 43	13 20	13 56	14 29
40	17 01	17 30	18 02	12 53	13 29	14 02	14 33
45	16 49	17 21	17 56	13 06	13 40	14 10	14 38
S 50	16 36	17 11	17 49	13 21	13 52	14 19	14 44
52	16 29	17 06	17 47	13 28	13 58	14 24	14 47
54	16 22	17 01	17 44	13 36	14 04	14 28	14 50
56	16 14	16 55	17 40	13 45	14 11	14 33	14 53
58	16 05	16 49	17 37	13 55	14 19	14 39	14 57
S 60	15 55	16 42	17 33	14 06	14 28	14 46	15 01

Day	SUN Eqn. of Time 00h	SUN Eqn. of Time 12h	SUN Mer. Pass.	MOON Mer. Pass. Upper	MOON Mer. Pass. Lower	Age	Phase
d	m s	m s	h m	h m	h m	d	%
7	03 26	03 28	11 57	05 39	18 02	21	56
8	03 30	03 31	11 56	06 25	18 48	22	46
9	03 33	03 34	11 56	07 11	19 33	23	37

UT	ARIES GHA	VENUS −3·9 GHA	Dec	MARS −0·6 GHA	Dec	JUPITER −2·5 GHA	Dec	SATURN +0·3 GHA	Dec	STARS Name	SHA	Dec
d h 10 00	227 44.6	150 19.7	N24 10.0	287 51.4	S22 19.6	1 36.3	S16 02.3	308 16.1	S22 15.6	Acamar	315 16.3	S40 14.1
01	242 47.1	165 18.9	10.4	302 52.7	19.5	16 39.1	02.2	323 18.6	15.7	Achernar	335 24.9	S57 08.7
02	257 49.6	180 18.0	10.7	317 54.1	19.4	31 41.9	02.1	338 21.2	15.7	Acrux	173 05.0	S63 12.2
03	272 52.0	195 17.2 ..	11.1	332 55.4 ..	19.3	46 44.7 ..	02.1	353 23.7 ..	15.7	Adhara	255 10.2	S29 00.2
04	287 54.5	210 16.4	11.5	347 56.7	19.2	61 47.5	02.0	8 26.3	15.7	Aldebaran	290 45.9	N16 32.5
05	302 57.0	225 15.6	11.8	2 58.0	19.1	76 50.2	01.9	23 28.9	15.7			
06	317 59.4	240 14.8	N24 12.2	17 59.3	S22 19.0	91 53.0	S16 01.8	38 31.4	S22 15.7	Alioth	166 17.4	N55 51.9
07	333 01.9	255 14.0	12.5	33 00.6	18.9	106 55.8	01.7	53 34.0	15.7	Alkaid	152 55.9	N49 13.5
T 08	348 04.4	270 13.1	12.9	48 01.9	18.8	121 58.6	01.6	68 36.5	15.7	Al Na'ir	27 39.7	S46 52.1
H 09	3 06.8	285 12.3 ..	13.2	63 03.3 ..	18.7	137 01.4 ..	01.5	83 39.1 ..	15.7	Alnilam	275 43.3	S 1 11.7
U 10	18 09.3	300 11.5	13.6	78 04.6	18.6	152 04.2	01.5	98 41.6	15.7	Alphard	217 52.9	S 8 44.5
R 11	33 11.7	315 10.7	13.9	93 05.9	18.5	167 06.9	01.4	113 44.2	15.7			
S 12	48 14.2	330 09.9	N24 14.3	108 07.2	S22 18.4	182 09.7	S16 01.3	128 46.8	S22 15.7	Alphecca	126 07.9	N26 39.3
D 13	63 16.7	345 09.1	14.6	123 08.5	18.3	197 12.5	01.2	143 49.3	15.7	Alpheratz	357 40.3	N29 11.2
A 14	78 19.1	0 08.2	14.9	138 09.9	18.2	212 15.3	01.1	158 51.9	15.7	Altair	62 04.9	N 8 55.0
Y 15	93 21.6	15 07.4 ..	15.3	153 11.2 ..	18.1	227 18.1 ..	01.0	173 54.4 ..	15.7	Ankaa	353 12.8	S42 12.4
16	108 24.1	30 06.6	15.6	168 12.5	18.0	242 20.9	01.0	188 57.0	15.7	Antares	112 21.9	S26 28.2
17	123 26.5	45 05.8	16.0	183 13.8	18.0	257 23.6	00.9	203 59.6	15.7			
18	138 29.0	60 05.0	N24 16.3	198 15.1	S22 17.9	272 26.4	S16 00.8	219 02.1	S22 15.8	Arcturus	145 52.4	N19 05.3
19	153 31.5	75 04.2	16.6	213 16.5	17.8	287 29.2	00.7	234 04.7	15.8	Atria	107 20.2	S69 03.3
20	168 34.0	90 03.3	17.0	228 17.8	17.7	302 32.0	00.6	249 07.2	15.8	Avior	234 16.8	S59 34.5
21	183 36.4	105 02.5 ..	17.3	243 19.1 ..	17.6	317 34.8 ..	00.5	264 09.8 ..	15.8	Bellatrix	278 28.8	N 6 21.7
22	198 38.9	120 01.7	17.6	258 20.4	17.5	332 37.6	00.4	279 12.4	15.8	Betelgeuse	270 58.0	N 7 24.4
23	213 41.3	135 00.9	18.0	273 21.8	17.4	347 40.4	00.4	294 14.9	15.8			
11 00	228 43.8	150 00.1	N24 18.3	288 23.1	S22 17.3	2 43.1	S16 00.3	309 17.5	S22 15.8	Canopus	263 55.1	S52 42.7
01	243 46.2	164 59.2	18.6	303 24.4	17.2	17 45.9	00.2	324 20.0	15.8	Capella	280 30.0	N46 00.8
02	258 48.7	179 58.4	19.0	318 25.7	17.1	32 48.7	00.1	339 22.6	15.8	Deneb	49 29.1	N45 20.5
03	273 51.2	194 57.6 ..	19.3	333 27.1 ..	17.0	47 51.5	16 00.0	354 25.2 ..	15.8	Denebola	182 30.1	N14 28.2
04	288 53.6	209 56.8	19.6	348 28.4	16.9	62 54.3	15 59.9	9 27.7	15.8	Diphda	348 52.9	S17 53.3
05	303 56.1	224 56.0	20.0	3 29.7	16.8	77 57.1	59.9	24 30.3	15.8			
06	318 58.6	239 55.1	N24 20.3	18 31.0	S22 16.7	92 59.8	S15 59.8	39 32.8	S22 15.8	Dubhe	193 47.5	N61 39.4
07	334 01.0	254 54.3	20.6	33 32.4	16.6	108 02.6	59.7	54 35.4	15.8	Elnath	278 08.8	N28 37.2
08	349 03.5	269 53.5	20.9	48 33.7	16.5	123 05.4	59.6	69 38.0	15.8	Eltanin	90 44.2	N51 29.1
F 09	4 06.0	284 52.7 ..	21.2	63 35.0 ..	16.4	138 08.2 ..	59.5	84 40.5 ..	15.8	Enif	33 43.9	N 9 57.4
R 10	19 08.4	299 51.9	21.6	78 36.4	16.3	153 11.0	59.4	99 43.1	15.9	Fomalhaut	15 20.5	S29 31.5
I 11	34 10.9	314 51.0	21.9	93 37.7	16.2	168 13.8	59.3	114 45.7	15.9			
D 12	49 13.3	329 50.2	N24 22.2	108 39.0	S22 16.1	183 16.5	S15 59.3	129 48.2	S22 15.9	Gacrux	171 56.7	S57 13.1
A 13	64 15.8	344 49.4	22.5	123 40.4	16.0	198 19.3	59.2	144 50.8	15.9	Gienah	175 48.7	S17 38.7
Y 14	79 18.3	359 48.6	22.8	138 41.7	15.9	213 22.1	59.1	159 53.3	15.9	Hadar	148 42.5	S60 27.6
15	94 20.7	14 47.7 ..	23.1	153 43.0 ..	15.8	228 24.9 ..	59.0	174 55.9 ..	15.9	Hamal	327 57.4	N23 32.6
16	109 23.2	29 46.9	23.5	168 44.4	15.7	243 27.7	58.9	189 58.5	15.9	Kaus Aust.	83 39.2	S34 22.3
17	124 25.7	44 46.1	23.8	183 45.7	15.6	258 30.5	58.8	205 01.0	15.9			
18	139 28.1	59 45.3	N24 24.1	198 47.0	S22 15.5	273 33.2	S15 58.8	220 03.6	S22 15.9	Kochab	137 19.0	N74 05.0
19	154 30.6	74 44.4	24.4	213 48.4	15.4	288 36.0	58.7	235 06.2	15.9	Markab	13 35.2	N15 18.0
20	169 33.1	89 43.6	24.7	228 49.7	15.3	303 38.8	58.6	250 08.7	15.9	Menkar	314 11.9	N 4 09.4
21	184 35.5	104 42.8 ..	25.0	243 51.1 ..	15.2	318 41.6 ..	58.5	265 11.3 ..	15.9	Menkent	148 03.3	S36 27.6
22	199 38.0	119 42.0	25.3	258 52.4	15.1	333 44.4	58.4	280 13.8	15.9	Miaplacidus	221 39.0	S69 47.9
23	214 40.5	134 41.2	25.6	273 53.7	15.0	348 47.2	58.3	295 16.4	15.9			
12 00	229 42.9	149 40.3	N24 25.9	288 55.1	S22 14.9	3 49.9	S15 58.2	310 19.0	S22 15.9	Mirfak	308 36.1	N49 55.3
01	244 45.4	164 39.5	26.2	303 56.4	14.8	18 52.7	58.2	325 21.5	15.9	Nunki	75 54.0	S26 16.2
02	259 47.8	179 38.7	26.5	318 57.7	14.8	33 55.5	58.1	340 24.1	16.0	Peacock	53 13.9	S56 40.2
03	274 50.3	194 37.9 ..	26.8	333 59.1 ..	14.7	48 58.3 ..	58.0	355 26.7 ..	16.0	Pollux	243 23.9	N27 58.8
04	289 52.8	209 37.0	27.1	349 00.4	14.6	64 01.1	57.9	10 29.2	16.0	Procyon	244 56.5	N 5 10.5
05	304 55.2	224 36.2	27.4	4 01.8	14.5	79 03.9	57.8	25 31.8	16.0			
06	319 57.7	239 35.4	N24 27.7	19 03.1	S22 14.4	94 06.6	S15 57.7	40 34.4	S22 16.0	Rasalhague	96 03.1	N12 32.9
07	335 00.2	254 34.6	28.0	34 04.5	14.3	109 09.4	57.7	55 36.9	16.0	Regulus	207 40.0	N11 52.6
S 08	350 02.6	269 33.7	28.3	49 05.8	14.2	124 12.2	57.6	70 39.5	16.0	Rigel	281 09.2	S 8 11.1
A 09	5 05.1	284 32.9 ..	28.6	64 07.2 ..	14.1	139 15.0 ..	57.5	85 42.1 ..	16.0	Rigil Kent.	139 46.6	S60 54.5
T 10	20 07.6	299 32.1	28.9	79 08.5	14.0	154 17.8	57.4	100 44.6	16.0	Sabik	102 08.5	S15 44.7
U 11	35 10.0	314 31.3	29.2	94 09.8	13.9	169 20.5	57.3	115 47.2	16.0			
R 12	50 12.5	329 30.4	N24 29.4	109 11.2	S22 13.8	184 23.3	S15 57.2	130 49.8	S22 16.0	Schedar	349 37.1	N56 37.9
D 13	65 15.0	344 29.6	29.7	124 12.5	13.7	199 26.1	57.2	145 52.3	16.0	Shaula	96 17.1	S37 06.8
A 14	80 17.4	359 28.8	30.0	139 13.9	13.6	214 28.9	57.1	160 54.9	16.0	Sirius	258 31.1	S16 44.8
Y 15	95 19.9	14 28.0 ..	30.3	154 15.2 ..	13.5	229 31.7 ..	57.0	175 57.5 ..	16.0	Spica	158 27.5	S11 15.4
16	110 22.3	29 27.1	30.6	169 16.6	13.4	244 34.5	56.9	191 00.0	16.0	Suhail	222 50.0	S43 30.7
17	125 24.8	44 26.3	30.9	184 17.9	13.3	259 37.2	56.8	206 02.6	16.1			
18	140 27.3	59 25.5	N24 31.1	199 19.3	S22 13.2	274 40.0	S15 56.7	221 05.2	S22 16.1	Vega	80 36.4	N38 48.0
19	155 29.7	74 24.6	31.4	214 20.6	13.1	289 42.8	56.6	236 07.7	16.1	Zuben'ubi	137 01.4	S16 07.0
20	170 32.2	89 23.8	31.7	229 22.0	13.0	304 45.6	56.6	251 10.3	16.1			
21	185 34.7	104 23.0 ..	32.0	244 23.3 ..	12.9	319 48.4 ..	56.5	266 12.9 ..	16.1		SHA	Mer. Pass.
22	200 37.1	119 22.2	32.3	259 24.7	12.9	334 51.2	56.4	281 15.4	16.1	Venus	281 16.3	h m 14 01
23	215 39.6	134 21.3	32.5	274 26.0	12.8	349 53.9	56.3	296 18.0	16.1	Mars	59 39.3	4 46
Mer. Pass.	h m 8 43.6	v −0.8 d 0.3		v 1.3 d 0.1		v 2.8 d 0.1		v 2.6 d 0.0		Jupiter	133 59.4	23 45
										Saturn	80 33.7	3 22

UT	SUN GHA	SUN Dec	MOON GHA	v	MOON Dec	d	HP
d h	° '	° '	° '	'	° '	'	'
10 00	180 53.9	N17 32.9	244 36.5	13.5	S 9 59.3	9.6	55.5
01	195 53.9	33.5	259 09.0	13.4	9 49.7	9.7	55.6
02	210 53.9	34.2	273 41.4	13.5	9 40.0	9.8	55.6
03	225 54.0 ..	34.9	288 13.9	13.5	9 30.2	9.8	55.6
04	240 54.0	35.5	302 46.4	13.5	9 20.4	9.9	55.6
05	255 54.0	36.2	317 18.9	13.5	9 10.5	9.9	55.7
06	270 54.0	N17 36.8	331 51.4	13.5	S 9 00.6	10.0	55.7
T 07	285 54.0	37.5	346 23.9	13.4	8 50.6	10.0	55.7
H 08	300 54.1	38.1	0 56.3	13.5	8 40.6	10.1	55.7
U 09	315 54.1 ..	38.8	15 28.8	13.4	8 30.5	10.1	55.8
R 10	330 54.1	39.4	30 01.2	13.5	8 20.4	10.2	55.8
S 11	345 54.1	40.1	44 33.7	13.5	8 10.2	10.2	55.8
D 12	0 54.2	N17 40.7	59 06.1	13.5	S 8 00.0	10.3	55.9
A 13	15 54.2	41.4	73 38.6	13.4	7 49.7	10.3	55.9
Y 14	30 54.2	42.0	88 11.0	13.4	7 39.4	10.3	55.9
15	45 54.2 ..	42.7	102 43.4	13.4	7 29.1	10.4	56.0
16	60 54.2	43.3	117 15.8	13.4	7 18.7	10.5	56.0
17	75 54.3	44.0	131 48.2	13.5	7 08.2	10.5	56.0
18	90 54.3	N17 44.6	146 20.6	13.4	S 6 57.7	10.5	56.0
19	105 54.3	45.3	160 53.0	13.3	6 47.2	10.6	56.1
20	120 54.3	45.9	175 25.3	13.4	6 36.6	10.7	56.1
21	135 54.3 ..	46.6	189 57.7	13.3	6 25.9	10.6	56.1
22	150 54.4	47.2	204 30.0	13.3	6 15.3	10.7	56.2
23	165 54.4	47.9	219 02.3	13.3	6 04.6	10.8	56.2
11 00	180 54.4	N17 48.5	233 34.6	13.3	S 5 53.8	10.8	56.2
01	195 54.4	49.2	248 06.9	13.3	5 43.0	10.8	56.3
02	210 54.4	49.8	262 39.2	13.2	5 32.2	10.9	56.3
03	225 54.4 ..	50.5	277 11.4	13.2	5 21.3	10.9	56.3
04	240 54.5	51.1	291 43.6	13.3	5 10.4	10.9	56.4
05	255 54.5	51.7	306 15.9	13.1	4 59.5	11.0	56.4
06	270 54.5	N17 52.4	320 48.0	13.2	S 4 48.5	11.0	56.4
F 07	285 54.5	53.0	335 20.2	13.2	4 37.5	11.1	56.5
R 08	300 54.5	53.7	349 52.4	13.1	4 26.4	11.1	56.5
I 09	315 54.5 ..	54.3	4 24.5	13.1	4 15.3	11.1	56.5
D 10	330 54.6	54.9	18 56.6	13.1	4 04.2	11.2	56.6
A 11	345 54.6	55.6	33 28.7	13.0	3 53.0	11.1	56.6
Y 12	0 54.6	N17 56.2	48 00.7	13.1	S 3 41.9	11.3	56.6
13	15 54.6	56.9	62 32.8	13.0	3 30.6	11.2	56.7
14	30 54.6	57.5	77 04.8	12.9	3 19.4	11.3	56.7
15	45 54.6 ..	58.1	91 36.7	13.0	3 08.1	11.3	56.7
16	60 54.6	58.8	106 08.7	12.9	2 56.8	11.3	56.8
17	75 54.7	17 59.4	120 40.6	12.9	2 45.5	11.4	56.8
18	90 54.7	N18 00.0	135 12.5	12.9	S 2 34.1	11.4	56.8
19	105 54.7	00.7	149 44.4	12.8	2 22.7	11.4	56.9
20	120 54.7	01.3	164 16.2	12.8	2 11.3	11.5	56.9
21	135 54.7 ..	02.0	178 48.0	12.8	1 59.8	11.4	56.9
22	150 54.7	02.6	193 19.8	12.7	1 48.4	11.5	57.0
23	165 54.7	03.2	207 51.5	12.7	1 36.9	11.5	57.0
12 00	180 54.8	N18 03.9	222 23.2	12.7	S 1 25.4	11.6	57.0
01	195 54.8	04.5	236 54.9	12.6	1 13.8	11.5	57.1
02	210 54.8	05.1	251 26.5	12.6	1 02.3	11.6	57.1
03	225 54.8 ..	05.7	265 58.1	12.6	0 50.7	11.6	57.1
04	240 54.8	06.4	280 29.7	12.5	0 39.1	11.6	57.2
05	255 54.8	07.0	295 01.2	12.5	0 27.5	11.7	57.2
06	270 54.8	N18 07.6	309 32.7	12.5	S 0 15.8	11.6	57.2
S 07	285 54.8	08.3	324 04.2	12.4	S 0 04.2	11.7	57.3
A 08	300 54.9	08.9	338 35.6	12.3	N 0 07.5	11.7	57.3
T 09	315 54.9 ..	09.5	353 06.9	12.4	0 19.2	11.6	57.3
U 10	330 54.9	10.2	7 38.3	12.3	0 30.8	11.8	57.4
R 11	345 54.9	10.8	22 09.6	12.2	0 42.6	11.7	57.4
D 12	0 54.9	N18 11.4	36 40.8	12.2	N 0 54.3	11.7	57.4
A 13	15 54.9	12.0	51 12.0	12.2	1 06.0	11.7	57.5
Y 14	30 54.9	12.7	65 43.2	12.1	1 17.7	11.8	57.5
15	45 54.9 ..	13.3	80 14.3	12.1	1 29.5	11.7	57.5
16	60 54.9	13.9	94 45.4	12.0	1 41.2	11.8	57.6
17	75 54.9	14.5	109 16.4	12.0	1 53.0	11.8	57.6
18	90 54.9	N18 15.2	123 47.4	11.9	N 2 04.8	11.7	57.6
19	105 54.9	15.8	138 18.3	11.9	2 16.5	11.8	57.7
20	120 54.9	16.4	152 49.2	11.8	2 28.3	11.8	57.7
21	135 54.9 ..	17.0	167 20.0	11.8	2 40.1	11.8	57.7
22	150 55.0	17.6	181 50.8	11.7	2 51.9	11.8	57.8
23	165 55.0	18.3	196 21.5	11.7	N 3 03.7	11.7	57.8
	SD 15.9	d 0.6	SD 15.2		15.4		15.6

Lat.	Twilight Naut.	Twilight Civil	Sunrise	Moonrise 10	11	12	13
°	h m	h m	h m	h m	h m	h m	h m
N 72	▭	▭	▭	03 52	03 40	03 28	03 16
N 70	////	////	01 24	03 38	03 32	03 27	03 21
68	////	////	02 09	03 26	03 26	03 26	03 26
66	////	00 26	02 38	03 17	03 21	03 25	03 29
64	////	01 34	03 00	03 08	03 17	03 24	03 32
62	////	02 08	03 18	03 01	03 13	03 24	03 35
60	00 23	02 32	03 32	02 55	03 10	03 23	03 37
N 58	01 25	02 51	03 45	02 50	03 07	03 23	03 39
56	01 56	03 07	03 55	02 45	03 04	03 22	03 41
54	02 18	03 20	04 04	02 41	03 02	03 22	03 43
52	02 36	03 32	04 13	02 37	03 00	03 22	03 44
50	02 51	03 42	04 20	02 33	02 58	03 21	03 46
45	03 20	04 02	04 36	02 26	02 53	03 21	03 49
N 40	03 41	04 19	04 49	02 19	02 50	03 20	03 51
35	03 58	04 32	05 00	02 13	02 47	03 20	03 54
30	04 12	04 43	05 09	02 09	02 44	03 19	03 56
20	04 34	05 02	05 26	02 00	02 39	03 18	03 59
N 10	04 52	05 18	05 40	01 52	02 35	03 18	04 02
0	05 06	05 31	05 53	01 45	02 31	03 17	04 05
S 10	05 18	05 44	06 06	01 38	02 27	03 17	04 08
20	05 30	05 56	06 20	01 30	02 23	03 16	04 11
30	05 41	06 10	06 35	01 22	02 18	03 15	04 15
35	05 47	06 17	06 44	01 17	02 15	03 15	04 17
40	05 53	06 26	06 54	01 11	02 12	03 15	04 20
45	05 59	06 35	07 06	01 04	02 08	03 14	04 22
S 50	06 07	06 46	07 21	00 56	02 04	03 14	04 26
52	06 10	06 51	07 28	00 53	02 02	03 13	04 27
54	06 13	06 56	07 35	00 48	01 59	03 13	04 29
56	06 16	07 02	07 44	00 44	01 57	03 13	04 31
58	06 20	07 08	07 53	00 39	01 54	03 12	04 33
S 60	06 24	07 16	08 04	00 33	01 51	03 12	04 36

Lat.	Sunset	Twilight Civil	Twilight Naut.	Moonset 10	11	12	13
°	h m	h m	h m	h m	h m	h m	h m
N 72	▭	▭	▭	12 21	14 10	16 00	17 56
N 70	22 37	////	////	12 33	14 14	15 58	17 46
68	21 48	////	////	12 44	14 18	15 56	17 38
66	21 17	////	////	12 52	14 22	15 55	17 31
64	20 55	22 23	////	12 59	14 25	15 53	17 25
62	20 37	21 48	////	13 05	14 27	15 52	17 20
60	20 22	21 23	////	13 10	14 29	15 51	17 16
N 58	20 10	21 03	22 33	13 14	14 31	15 50	17 12
56	19 59	20 47	22 00	13 18	14 33	15 50	17 09
54	19 49	20 34	21 37	13 22	14 34	15 49	17 06
52	19 41	20 22	21 18	13 25	14 36	15 48	17 03
50	19 34	20 12	21 03	13 28	14 37	15 48	17 01
45	19 18	19 51	20 34	13 35	14 39	15 46	16 56
N 40	19 04	19 35	20 12	13 40	14 42	15 45	16 51
35	18 53	19 21	19 55	13 45	14 44	15 44	16 48
30	18 44	19 10	19 41	13 49	14 45	15 44	16 44
20	18 27	18 51	19 19	13 55	14 48	15 42	16 39
N 10	18 13	18 35	19 01	14 01	14 51	15 41	16 33
0	18 00	18 22	18 47	14 07	14 53	15 40	16 29
S 10	17 47	18 09	18 34	14 13	14 55	15 39	16 24
20	17 33	17 56	18 23	14 18	14 58	15 37	16 19
30	17 17	17 42	18 11	14 25	15 00	15 36	16 13
35	17 08	17 35	18 05	14 29	15 02	15 35	16 10
40	16 58	17 27	17 59	14 33	15 04	15 34	16 06
45	16 46	17 17	17 53	14 38	15 06	15 33	16 02
S 50	16 31	17 06	17 46	14 44	15 08	15 32	15 57
52	16 24	17 01	17 42	14 47	15 09	15 31	15 54
54	16 17	16 56	17 39	14 50	15 10	15 30	15 52
56	16 08	16 50	17 36	14 53	15 11	15 30	15 49
58	15 59	16 44	17 32	14 57	15 13	15 29	15 46
S 60	15 48	16 36	17 28	15 01	15 14	15 28	15 42

Day	SUN Eqn. of Time 00h	SUN Eqn. of Time 12h	SUN Mer. Pass.	MOON Mer. Pass. Upper	MOON Mer. Pass. Lower	Age	Phase
d	m s	m s	h m	h m	h m	d	%
10	03 35	03 37	11 56	07 56	20 19	24	27
11	03 38	03 38	11 56	08 42	21 05	25	19
12	03 39	03 39	11 56	09 28	21 52	26	11

UT	ARIES GHA	VENUS −3.9 GHA	Dec	MARS −0.7 GHA	Dec	JUPITER −2.5 GHA	Dec	SATURN +0.3 GHA	Dec	STARS Name	SHA	Dec
13 00	230 42.1	149 20.5	N24 32.8	289 27.4	S22 12.7	4 56.7	S15 56.2	311 20.6	S22 16.1	Acamar	315 16.3	S40 14.1
01	245 44.5	164 19.7	33.1	304 28.8	12.6	19 59.5	56.1	326 23.1	16.1	Achernar	335 24.9	S57 08.7
02	260 47.0	179 18.9	33.4	319 30.1	12.5	35 02.3	56.1	341 25.7	16.1	Acrux	173 05.0	S63 12.2
03	275 49.4	194 18.0	33.6	334 31.5	12.4	50 05.1	56.0	356 28.3	16.1	Adhara	255 10.2	S29 00.1
04	290 51.9	209 17.2	33.9	349 32.8	12.3	65 07.9	55.9	11 30.8	16.1	Aldebaran	290 45.9	N16 32.5
05	305 54.4	224 16.4	34.2	4 34.2	12.2	80 10.6	55.8	26 33.4	16.1			
06	320 56.8	239 15.5	N24 34.4	19 35.5	S22 12.1	95 13.4	S15 55.7	41 36.0	S22 16.1	Alioth	166 17.4	N55 51.9
07	335 59.3	254 14.7	34.7	34 36.9	12.0	110 16.2	55.6	56 38.5	16.1	Alkaid	152 55.9	N49 13.5
S 08	351 01.8	269 13.9	35.0	49 38.3	11.9	125 19.0	55.5	71 41.1	16.2	Al Na'ir	27 39.7	S46 52.1
U 09	6 04.2	284 13.1	35.2	64 39.6	11.8	140 21.8	55.5	86 43.7	16.2	Alnilam	275 43.3	S 1 11.7
N 10	21 06.7	299 12.2	35.5	79 41.0	11.7	155 24.5	55.4	101 46.2	16.2	Alphard	217 52.9	S 8 44.5
D 11	36 09.2	314 11.4	35.7	94 42.3	11.6	170 27.3	55.3	116 48.8	16.2			
A 12	51 11.6	329 10.6	N24 36.0	109 43.7	S22 11.5	185 30.1	S15 55.2	131 51.4	S22 16.2	Alphecca	126 07.9	N26 39.3
Y 13	66 14.1	344 09.7	36.3	124 45.1	11.4	200 32.9	55.1	146 54.0	16.2	Alpheratz	357 40.3	N29 11.2
14	81 16.6	359 08.9	36.5	139 46.4	11.3	215 35.7	55.0	161 56.5	16.2	Altair	62 04.9	N 8 55.0
15	96 19.0	14 08.1	36.8	154 47.8	11.3	230 38.5	55.0	176 59.1	16.2	Ankaa	353 12.8	S42 12.4
16	111 21.5	29 07.2	37.0	169 49.1	11.2	245 41.2	54.9	192 01.7	16.2	Antares	112 21.8	S26 28.2
17	126 23.9	44 06.4	37.3	184 50.5	11.1	260 44.0	54.8	207 04.2	16.2			
18	141 26.4	59 05.6	N24 37.5	199 51.9	S22 11.0	275 46.8	S15 54.7	222 06.8	S22 16.2	Arcturus	145 52.4	N19 05.3
19	156 28.9	74 04.8	37.8	214 53.2	10.9	290 49.6	54.6	237 09.4	16.2	Atria	107 20.1	S69 03.3
20	171 31.3	89 03.9	38.0	229 54.6	10.8	305 52.4	54.5	252 12.0	16.2	Avior	234 16.9	S59 34.5
21	186 33.8	104 03.1	38.3	244 56.0	10.7	320 55.1	54.5	267 14.5	16.2	Bellatrix	278 28.8	N 6 21.7
22	201 36.3	119 02.3	38.5	259 57.3	10.6	335 57.9	54.4	282 17.1	16.2	Betelgeuse	270 58.0	N 7 24.4
23	216 38.7	134 01.4	38.8	274 58.7	10.5	351 00.7	54.3	297 19.7	16.3			
14 00	231 41.2	149 00.6	N24 39.0	290 00.1	S22 10.4	6 03.5	S15 54.2	312 22.2	S22 16.3	Canopus	263 55.1	S52 42.7
01	246 43.7	163 59.8	39.3	305 01.4	10.3	21 06.3	54.1	327 24.8	16.3	Capella	280 30.0	N46 00.8
02	261 46.1	178 58.9	39.5	320 02.8	10.2	36 09.0	54.0	342 27.4	16.3	Deneb	49 29.1	N45 20.5
03	276 48.6	193 58.1	39.7	335 04.2	10.1	51 11.8	53.9	357 30.0	16.3	Denebola	182 30.1	N14 28.2
04	291 51.0	208 57.3	40.0	350 05.6	10.0	66 14.6	53.9	12 32.5	16.3	Diphda	348 52.8	S17 53.3
05	306 53.5	223 56.4	40.2	5 06.9	10.0	81 17.4	53.8	27 35.1	16.3			
06	321 56.0	238 55.6	N24 40.5	20 08.3	S22 09.9	96 20.2	S15 53.7	42 37.7	S22 16.3	Dubhe	193 47.5	N61 39.4
07	336 58.4	253 54.8	40.7	35 09.7	09.8	111 23.0	53.6	57 40.2	16.3	Elnath	278 08.8	N28 37.2
M 08	352 00.9	268 54.0	40.9	50 11.1	09.7	126 25.7	53.5	72 42.8	16.3	Eltanin	90 44.2	N51 29.1
O 09	7 03.4	283 53.1	41.2	65 12.4	09.6	141 28.5	53.4	87 45.4	16.3	Enif	33 43.9	N 9 57.4
N 10	22 05.8	298 52.3	41.4	80 13.8	09.5	156 31.3	53.4	102 48.0	16.3	Fomalhaut	15 20.5	S29 31.5
D 11	37 08.3	313 51.5	41.6	95 15.2	09.4	171 34.1	53.3	117 50.5	16.3			
A 12	52 10.8	328 50.6	N24 41.9	110 16.6	S22 09.3	186 36.9	S15 53.2	132 53.1	S22 16.3	Gacrux	171 56.7	S57 13.1
Y 13	67 13.2	343 49.8	42.1	125 17.9	09.2	201 39.6	53.1	147 55.7	16.4	Gienah	175 48.7	S17 38.7
14	82 15.7	358 49.0	42.3	140 19.3	09.1	216 42.4	53.0	162 58.3	16.4	Hadar	148 42.5	S60 27.7
15	97 18.2	13 48.1	42.5	155 20.7	09.0	231 45.2	52.9	178 00.8	16.4	Hamal	327 57.3	N23 32.6
16	112 20.6	28 47.3	42.8	170 22.1	08.9	246 48.0	52.9	193 03.4	16.4	Kaus Aust.	83 39.1	S34 22.3
17	127 23.1	43 46.5	43.0	185 23.4	08.9	261 50.8	52.8	208 06.0	16.4			
18	142 25.5	58 45.6	N24 43.2	200 24.8	S22 08.7	276 53.5	S15 52.7	223 08.6	S22 16.4	Kochab	137 19.0	N74 05.0
19	157 28.0	73 44.8	43.4	215 26.2	08.7	291 56.3	52.6	238 11.1	16.4	Markab	13 35.2	N15 18.0
20	172 30.5	88 44.0	43.7	230 27.6	08.6	306 59.1	52.5	253 13.7	16.4	Menkar	314 11.9	N 4 09.4
21	187 32.9	103 43.1	43.9	245 29.0	08.5	322 01.9	52.4	268 16.3	16.4	Menkent	148 03.3	S36 27.6
22	202 35.4	118 42.3	44.1	260 30.4	08.4	337 04.7	52.4	283 18.9	16.4	Miaplacidus	221 39.0	S69 47.9
23	217 37.9	133 41.5	44.3	275 31.7	08.3	352 07.4	52.3	298 21.4	16.4			
15 00	232 40.3	148 40.6	N24 44.5	290 33.1	S22 08.2	7 10.2	S15 52.2	313 24.0	S22 16.4	Mirfak	308 36.1	N49 55.3
01	247 42.8	163 39.8	44.7	305 34.5	08.1	22 13.0	52.1	328 26.6	16.4	Nunki	75 54.0	S26 16.2
02	262 45.3	178 39.0	44.9	320 35.9	08.0	37 15.8	52.0	343 29.2	16.4	Peacock	53 13.9	S56 40.2
03	277 47.7	193 38.1	45.2	335 37.3	08.0	52 18.6	51.9	358 31.7	16.5	Pollux	243 23.9	N27 58.8
04	292 50.2	208 37.3	45.4	350 38.7	07.9	67 21.3	51.9	13 34.3	16.5	Procyon	244 56.5	N 5 10.5
05	307 52.7	223 36.5	45.6	5 40.1	07.8	82 24.1	51.8	28 36.9	16.5			
06	322 55.1	238 35.6	N24 45.8	20 41.4	S22 07.7	97 26.9	S15 51.7	43 39.5	S22 16.5	Rasalhague	96 03.1	N12 32.9
07	337 57.6	253 34.8	46.0	35 42.8	07.6	112 29.7	51.6	58 42.0	16.5	Regulus	207 40.0	N11 52.6
T 08	353 00.0	268 34.0	46.2	50 44.2	07.5	127 32.5	51.5	73 44.6	16.5	Rigel	281 09.2	S 8 11.1
U 09	8 02.5	283 33.1	46.4	65 45.6	07.4	142 35.2	51.4	88 47.2	16.5	Rigil Kent.	139 46.6	S60 54.6
E 10	23 05.0	298 32.3	46.6	80 47.0	07.3	157 38.0	51.4	103 49.8	16.5	Sabik	102 08.4	S15 44.7
S 11	38 07.4	313 31.5	46.8	95 48.4	07.2	172 40.8	51.3	118 52.3	16.5			
D 12	53 09.9	328 30.6	N24 47.0	110 49.8	S22 07.1	187 43.6	S15 51.2	133 54.9	S22 16.5	Schedar	349 37.1	N56 37.9
A 13	68 12.4	343 29.8	47.2	125 51.2	07.1	202 46.4	51.1	148 57.5	16.5	Shaula	96 17.1	S37 06.8
Y 14	83 14.8	358 29.0	47.4	140 52.6	07.0	217 49.1	51.0	164 00.1	16.5	Sirius	258 31.1	S16 44.8
15	98 17.3	13 28.1	47.6	155 54.0	06.9	232 51.9	50.9	179 02.7	16.5	Spica	158 27.5	S11 15.4
16	113 19.8	28 27.3	47.8	170 55.4	06.8	247 54.7	50.9	194 05.2	16.5	Suhail	222 50.1	S43 30.7
17	128 22.2	43 26.5	48.0	185 56.8	06.7	262 57.5	50.8	209 07.8	16.6			
18	143 24.7	58 25.6	N24 48.2	200 58.1	S22 06.6	278 00.3	S15 50.7	224 10.4	S22 16.6	Vega	80 36.4	N38 48.0
19	158 27.2	73 24.8	48.4	215 59.5	06.5	293 03.0	50.6	239 13.0	16.6	Zuben'ubi	137 01.4	S16 07.0
20	173 29.6	88 23.9	48.6	231 00.9	06.4	308 05.8	50.5	254 15.5	16.6		SHA	Mer.Pass.
21	188 32.1	103 23.1	48.8	246 02.3	06.3	323 08.6	50.4	269 18.1	16.6	Venus	277 19.4	14 05
22	203 34.5	118 22.3	48.9	261 03.7	06.3	338 11.4	50.4	284 20.7	16.6	Mars	58 18.9	4 40
23	218 37.0	133 21.4	49.1	276 05.1	06.2	353 14.2	50.3	299 23.3	16.6	Jupiter	134 22.3	23 31
Mer. Pass.	8 31.9	v −0.8 d 0.2		v 1.4 d 0.1		v 2.8 d 0.1		v 2.6 d 0.0		Saturn	80 41.0	3 10

UT	SUN GHA	SUN Dec	MOON GHA	v	MOON Dec	d	HP
d h	° ′	° ′	° ′	′	° ′	′	′
13 00	180 55.0	N18 18.9	210 52.2	11.6	N 3 15.4	11.8	57.9
01	195 55.0	19.5	225 22.8	11.6	3 27.2	11.8	57.9
02	210 55.0	20.1	239 53.4	11.5	3 39.0	11.8	57.9
03	225 55.0 ..	20.7	254 23.9	11.5	3 50.8	11.7	58.0
04	240 55.0	21.4	268 54.4	11.4	4 02.5	11.8	58.0
05	255 55.0	22.0	283 24.8	11.3	4 14.3	11.8	58.0
06	270 55.0	N18 22.6	297 55.1	11.3	N 4 26.1	11.7	58.1
07	285 55.0	23.2	312 25.4	11.3	4 37.8	11.7	58.1
08	300 55.0	23.8	326 55.7	11.1	4 49.5	11.8	58.1
S 09	315 55.0 ..	24.4	341 25.8	11.2	5 01.3	11.7	58.2
U 10	330 55.0	25.1	355 56.0	11.0	5 13.0	11.7	58.2
N 11	345 55.0	25.7	10 26.0	11.0	5 24.7	11.7	58.2
D 12	0 55.0	N18 26.3	24 56.0	11.0	N 5 36.4	11.6	58.3
A 13	15 55.0	26.9	39 26.0	10.8	5 48.0	11.7	58.3
Y 14	30 55.0	27.5	53 55.8	10.9	5 59.7	11.6	58.3
15	45 55.0 ..	28.1	68 25.7	10.7	6 11.3	11.7	58.4
16	60 55.0	28.7	82 55.4	10.7	6 23.0	11.6	58.4
17	75 55.0	29.3	97 25.1	10.6	6 34.6	11.5	58.4
18	90 55.0	N18 30.0	111 54.7	10.6	N 6 46.1	11.6	58.5
19	105 55.0	30.6	126 24.3	10.5	6 57.7	11.5	58.5
20	120 55.0	31.2	140 53.8	10.4	7 09.2	11.5	58.5
21	135 55.0 ..	31.8	155 23.2	10.4	7 20.7	11.5	58.6
22	150 55.0	32.4	169 52.6	10.3	7 32.2	11.4	58.6
23	165 55.0	33.0	184 21.9	10.3	7 43.6	11.5	58.6
14 00	180 55.0	N18 33.6	198 51.2	10.1	N 7 55.1	11.4	58.6
01	195 55.0	34.2	213 20.3	10.1	8 06.5	11.3	58.7
02	210 55.0	34.8	227 49.4	10.0	8 17.8	11.3	58.7
03	225 55.0 ..	35.4	242 18.4	10.0	8 29.1	11.3	58.7
04	240 55.0	36.0	256 47.4	9.9	8 40.4	11.3	58.8
05	255 55.0	36.6	271 16.3	9.8	8 51.7	11.2	58.8
06	270 55.0	N18 37.2	285 45.1	9.8	N 9 02.9	11.2	58.8
07	285 55.0	37.8	300 13.9	9.6	9 14.1	11.1	58.9
08	300 55.0	38.4	314 42.5	9.6	9 25.2	11.1	58.9
M 09	315 55.0 ..	39.1	329 11.1	9.6	9 36.3	11.0	58.9
O 10	330 55.0	39.7	343 39.7	9.4	9 47.3	11.1	59.0
N 11	345 55.0	40.3	358 08.1	9.4	9 58.4	10.9	59.0
D 12	0 55.0	N18 40.9	12 36.5	9.3	N10 09.3	10.9	59.0
A 13	15 55.0	41.5	27 04.8	9.3	10 20.2	10.9	59.0
Y 14	30 55.0	42.1	41 33.1	9.1	10 31.1	10.8	59.1
15	45 55.0 ..	42.7	56 01.2	9.1	10 41.9	10.8	59.1
16	60 55.0	43.3	70 29.3	9.0	10 52.7	10.7	59.1
17	75 55.0	43.9	84 57.3	9.0	11 03.4	10.6	59.2
18	90 55.0	N18 44.4	99 25.3	8.8	N11 14.0	10.6	59.2
19	105 55.0	45.0	113 53.1	8.8	11 24.6	10.6	59.2
20	120 55.0	45.6	128 20.9	8.7	11 35.2	10.5	59.2
21	135 55.0 ..	46.2	142 48.6	8.7	11 45.7	10.4	59.3
22	150 55.0	46.8	157 16.3	8.5	11 56.1	10.4	59.3
23	165 55.0	47.4	171 43.8	8.5	12 06.5	10.3	59.3
15 00	180 55.0	N18 48.0	186 11.3	8.4	N12 16.8	10.2	59.3
01	195 55.0	48.6	200 38.7	8.4	12 27.0	10.2	59.4
02	210 54.9	49.2	215 06.1	8.2	12 37.2	10.1	59.4
03	225 54.9 ..	49.8	229 33.3	8.2	12 47.3	10.0	59.4
04	240 54.9	50.4	244 00.5	8.1	12 57.3	10.0	59.4
05	255 54.9	51.0	258 27.6	8.0	13 07.3	9.9	59.5
06	270 54.9	N18 51.6	272 54.6	8.0	N13 17.2	9.8	59.5
07	285 54.9	52.2	287 21.6	7.8	13 27.0	9.7	59.5
08	300 54.9	52.8	301 48.4	7.8	13 36.7	9.7	59.5
T 09	315 54.9 ..	53.3	316 15.2	7.7	13 46.4	9.6	59.6
U 10	330 54.9	53.9	330 41.9	7.7	13 56.0	9.5	59.6
E 11	345 54.9	54.5	345 08.6	7.6	14 05.5	9.4	59.6
S 12	0 54.9	N18 55.1	359 35.2	7.4	N14 14.9	9.4	59.6
D 13	15 54.9	55.7	14 01.6	7.4	14 24.3	9.2	59.7
A 14	30 54.9	56.3	28 28.0	7.4	14 33.5	9.2	59.7
Y 15	45 54.8 ..	56.9	42 54.4	7.2	14 42.7	9.1	59.7
16	60 54.8	57.5	57 20.6	7.2	14 51.8	9.0	59.7
17	75 54.8	58.0	71 46.8	7.1	15 00.8	8.9	59.7
18	90 54.8	N18 58.6	86 12.9	7.1	N15 09.7	8.8	59.8
19	105 54.8	59.2	100 39.0	6.9	15 18.5	8.7	59.8
20	120 54.8	18 59.8	115 04.9	6.9	15 27.2	8.7	59.8
21	135 54.8 ..	19 00.4	129 30.8	6.8	15 35.9	8.5	59.8
22	150 54.8	01.0	143 56.6	6.8	15 44.4	8.5	59.9
23	165 54.8	01.5	158 22.4	6.6	N15 52.9	8.3	59.9
	SD 15.9	d 0.6	SD 15.9		16.1		16.2

Lat.	Twilight Naut.	Twilight Civil	Sunrise	Moonrise 13	Moonrise 14	Moonrise 15	Moonrise 16
°	h m	h m	h m	h m	h m	h m	h m
N 72	▭	▭		03 16	03 04	02 48	02 21
N 70	////	////	00 55	03 21	03 16	03 10	03 03
68	////	////	01 53	03 26	03 26	03 27	03 31
66	////	////	02 26	03 29	03 34	03 41	03 52
64	////	01 16	02 51	03 32	03 41	03 53	04 10
62	////	01 56	03 10	03 35	03 47	04 03	04 24
60	////	02 23	03 25	03 37	03 53	04 12	04 36
N 58	01 08	02 43	03 38	03 39	03 57	04 19	04 47
56	01 45	03 00	03 49	03 41	04 02	04 26	04 56
54	02 09	03 14	03 59	03 43	04 05	04 32	05 04
52	02 29	03 26	04 08	03 44	04 09	04 37	05 12
50	02 45	03 37	04 16	03 46	04 12	04 42	05 18
45	03 15	03 58	04 32	03 49	04 19	04 53	05 32
N 40	03 38	04 15	04 46	03 51	04 25	05 02	05 44
35	03 55	04 29	04 57	03 54	04 30	05 10	05 54
30	04 10	04 41	05 07	03 56	04 34	05 16	06 03
20	04 33	05 01	05 24	03 59	04 42	05 28	06 19
N 10	04 51	05 17	05 39	04 02	04 49	05 39	06 32
0	05 06	05 31	05 53	04 05	04 55	05 49	06 45
S 10	05 19	05 44	06 06	04 08	05 02	05 58	06 58
20	05 31	05 58	06 21	04 11	05 09	06 09	07 12
30	05 43	06 12	06 37	04 15	05 17	06 21	07 27
35	05 49	06 20	06 47	04 17	05 22	06 29	07 37
40	05 55	06 28	06 57	04 20	05 27	06 37	07 47
45	06 02	06 38	07 10	04 22	05 33	06 46	08 00
S 50	06 10	06 50	07 25	04 26	05 41	06 58	08 15
52	06 14	06 55	07 32	04 27	05 44	07 03	08 22
54	06 17	07 01	07 40	04 29	05 48	07 09	08 30
56	06 21	07 07	07 49	04 31	05 52	07 16	08 39
58	06 25	07 14	07 59	04 33	05 57	07 23	08 49
S 60	06 30	07 22	08 11	04 36	06 02	07 32	09 01

Lat.	Sunset	Twilight Civil	Twilight Naut.	Moonset 13	Moonset 14	Moonset 15	Moonset 16
°	h m	h m	h m	h m	h m	h m	h m
N 72	▭	▭	▭	17 56	20 01	22 23	▭
N 70	23 10	////	////	17 46	19 40	21 43	23 57
68	22 04	////	////	17 38	19 24	21 15	23 08
66	21 29	////	////	17 31	19 11	20 55	22 37
64	21 05	22 43	////	17 25	19 01	20 38	22 14
62	20 45	22 00	////	17 20	18 52	20 25	21 55
60	20 29	21 33	////	17 16	18 44	20 13	21 40
N 58	20 16	21 11	22 50	17 12	18 37	20 04	21 28
56	20 05	20 54	22 11	17 09	18 31	19 55	21 16
54	19 55	20 40	21 46	17 06	18 26	19 47	21 07
52	19 46	20 28	21 26	17 03	18 21	19 40	20 58
50	19 38	20 17	21 10	17 01	18 17	19 34	20 50
45	19 21	19 55	20 39	16 56	18 08	19 21	20 34
N 40	19 07	19 38	20 16	16 51	18 00	19 10	20 20
35	18 56	19 24	19 58	16 48	17 53	19 01	20 09
30	18 46	19 12	19 43	16 44	17 47	18 53	19 59
20	18 28	18 52	19 20	16 39	17 37	18 39	19 42
N 10	18 14	18 36	19 02	16 33	17 29	18 26	19 27
0	18 00	18 22	18 47	16 29	17 20	18 15	19 13
S 10	17 46	18 08	18 34	16 24	17 12	18 04	18 59
20	17 32	17 55	18 22	16 19	17 03	17 52	18 44
30	17 15	17 41	18 10	16 13	16 53	17 38	18 27
35	17 06	17 33	18 03	16 10	16 48	17 30	18 17
40	16 55	17 24	17 57	16 06	16 41	17 21	18 06
45	16 42	17 14	17 50	16 02	16 34	17 10	17 53
S 50	16 27	17 03	17 42	15 57	16 25	16 57	17 37
52	16 20	16 57	17 39	15 54	16 20	16 51	17 29
54	16 12	16 52	17 35	15 52	16 16	16 45	17 21
56	16 03	16 45	17 31	15 49	16 11	16 37	17 11
58	15 53	16 38	17 27	15 46	16 05	16 29	17 01
S 60	15 41	16 30	17 22	15 42	15 59	16 20	16 48

Day	SUN Eqn. of Time 00h	SUN Eqn. of Time 12h	SUN Mer. Pass.	MOON Mer. Pass. Upper	MOON Mer. Pass. Lower	Age	Phase
d	m s	m s	h m	h m	h m	d	%
13	03 40	03 40	11 56	10 17	22 42	27	5
14	03 40	03 40	11 56	11 08	23 34	28	2
15	03 40	03 39	11 56	12 02	24 30	00	0

UT	ARIES GHA	VENUS −3.9 GHA	Dec	MARS −0.8 GHA	Dec	JUPITER −2.5 GHA	Dec	SATURN +0.3 GHA	Dec	STARS Name	SHA	Dec
16 00	233 39.5	148 20.6	N24 49.3	291 06.5	S22 06.1	8 16.9	S15 50.2	314 25.9	S22 16.6	Acamar	315 16.3	S40 14.1
01	248 41.9	163 19.8	49.5	306 07.9	06.0	23 19.7	50.1	329 28.4	16.6	Achernar	335 24.9	S57 08.7
02	263 44.4	178 18.9	49.7	321 09.3	05.9	38 22.5	50.0	344 31.0	16.6	Acrux	173 05.0	S63 12.2
03	278 46.9	193 18.1 ..	49.9	336 10.7 ..	05.8	53 25.3 ..	49.9	359 33.6 ..	16.6	Adhara	255 10.2	S29 00.1
04	293 49.3	208 17.3	50.1	351 12.1	05.7	68 28.1	49.9	14 36.2	16.6	Aldebaran	290 45.9	N16 32.5
05	308 51.8	223 16.4	50.2	6 13.5	05.6	83 30.8	49.8	29 38.8	16.6			
W 06	323 54.3	238 15.6	N24 50.4	21 14.9	S22 05.6	98 33.6	S15 49.7	44 41.3	S22 16.6	Alioth	166 17.4	N55 51.9
E 07	338 56.7	253 14.8	50.6	36 16.4	05.5	113 36.4	49.6	59 43.9	16.7	Alkaid	152 55.9	N49 13.5
D 08	353 59.2	268 13.9	50.8	51 17.8	05.4	128 39.2	49.5	74 46.5	16.7	Al Na'ir	27 39.7	S46 52.1
N 09	9 01.6	283 13.1 ..	50.9	66 19.2 ..	05.3	143 41.9 ..	49.4	89 49.1 ..	16.7	Alnilam	275 43.3	S 1 11.7
E 10	24 04.1	298 12.3	51.1	81 20.6	05.2	158 44.7	49.4	104 51.7	16.7	Alphard	217 52.9	S 8 44.5
S 11	39 06.6	313 11.4	51.3	96 22.0	05.1	173 47.5	49.3	119 54.2	16.7			
D 12	54 09.0	328 10.6	N24 51.5	111 23.4	S22 05.0	188 50.3	S15 49.2	134 56.8	S22 16.7	Alphecca	126 07.9	N26 39.3
A 13	69 11.5	343 09.7	51.6	126 24.8	04.9	203 53.1	49.1	149 59.4	16.7	Alpheratz	357 40.3	N29 11.2
Y 14	84 14.0	358 08.9	51.8	141 26.2	04.9	218 55.8	49.0	165 02.0	16.7	Altair	62 04.8	N 8 55.0
15	99 16.4	13 08.1 ..	52.0	156 27.6 ..	04.8	233 58.6 ..	48.9	180 04.6 ..	16.7	Ankaa	353 12.7	S42 12.4
16	114 18.9	28 07.2	52.1	171 29.0	04.7	249 01.4	48.9	195 07.1	16.7	Antares	112 21.8	S26 28.2
17	129 21.4	43 06.4	52.3	186 30.4	04.6	264 04.2	48.8	210 09.7	16.7			
18	144 23.8	58 05.6	N24 52.5	201 31.8	S22 04.5	279 06.9	S15 48.7	225 12.3	S22 16.7	Arcturus	145 52.4	N19 05.4
19	159 26.3	73 04.7	52.6	216 33.3	04.4	294 09.7	48.6	240 14.9	16.7	Atria	107 20.1	S69 03.3
20	174 28.8	88 03.9	52.8	231 34.7	04.3	309 12.5	48.5	255 17.5	16.8	Avior	234 16.9	S59 34.5
21	189 31.2	103 03.1 ..	52.9	246 36.1 ..	04.3	324 15.3 ..	48.4	270 20.1 ..	16.8	Bellatrix	278 28.8	N 6 21.7
22	204 33.7	118 02.2	53.1	261 37.5	04.2	339 18.1	48.4	285 22.6	16.8	Betelgeuse	270 58.0	N 7 24.4
23	219 36.1	133 01.4	53.3	276 38.9	04.1	354 20.8	48.3	300 25.2	16.8			
17 00	234 38.6	148 00.6	N24 53.4	291 40.3	S22 04.0	9 23.6	S15 48.2	315 27.8	S22 16.8	Canopus	263 55.1	S52 42.7
01	249 41.1	162 59.7	53.6	306 41.7	03.9	24 26.4	48.1	330 30.4	16.8	Capella	280 30.0	N46 00.8
02	264 43.5	177 58.9	53.7	321 43.2	03.8	39 29.2	48.0	345 33.0	16.8	Deneb	49 29.1	N45 20.5
03	279 46.0	192 58.0 ..	53.9	336 44.6 ..	03.7	54 31.9 ..	47.9	0 35.5 ..	16.8	Denebola	182 30.2	N14 28.3
04	294 48.5	207 57.2	54.0	351 46.0	03.7	69 34.7	47.9	15 38.1	16.8	Diphda	348 52.8	S17 53.3
05	309 50.9	222 56.4	54.2	6 47.4	03.6	84 37.5	47.8	30 40.7	16.8			
T 06	324 53.4	237 55.5	N24 54.3	21 48.8	S22 03.5	99 40.3	S15 47.7	45 43.3	S22 16.8	Dubhe	193 47.5	N61 39.4
H 07	339 55.9	252 54.7	54.5	36 50.3	03.4	114 43.0	47.6	60 45.9	16.8	Elnath	278 08.8	N28 37.2
U 08	354 58.3	267 53.9	54.6	51 51.7	03.3	129 45.8	47.5	75 48.5	16.8	Eltanin	90 44.1	N51 29.2
R 09	10 00.8	282 53.0 ..	54.8	66 53.1 ..	03.2	144 48.6 ..	47.4	90 51.1 ..	16.9	Enif	33 43.9	N 9 57.4
S 10	25 03.3	297 52.2	54.9	81 54.5	03.1	159 51.4	47.4	105 53.6	16.9	Fomalhaut	15 20.5	S29 31.4
D 11	40 05.7	312 51.4	55.1	96 55.9	03.1	174 54.2	47.3	120 56.2	16.9			
A 12	55 08.2	327 50.5	N24 55.2	111 57.4	S22 03.0	189 56.9	S15 47.2	135 58.8	S22 16.9	Gacrux	171 56.8	S57 13.1
Y 13	70 10.6	342 49.7	55.3	126 58.8	02.9	204 59.7	47.1	151 01.4	16.9	Gienah	175 48.7	S17 38.7
14	85 13.1	357 48.8	55.5	142 00.2	02.8	220 02.5	47.0	166 04.0	16.9	Hadar	148 42.5	S60 27.7
15	100 15.6	12 48.0 ..	55.6	157 01.6 ..	02.7	235 05.3 ..	46.9	181 06.6 ..	16.9	Hamal	327 57.3	N23 32.6
16	115 18.0	27 47.2	55.8	172 03.1	02.6	250 08.0	46.9	196 09.1	16.9	Kaus Aust.	83 39.1	S34 22.3
17	130 20.5	42 46.3	55.9	187 04.5	02.6	265 10.8	46.8	211 11.7	16.9			
18	145 23.0	57 45.5	N24 56.0	202 05.9	S22 02.5	280 13.6	S15 46.7	226 14.3	S22 16.9	Kochab	137 19.1	N74 05.0
19	160 25.4	72 44.7	56.2	217 07.4	02.4	295 16.4	46.6	241 16.9	16.9	Markab	13 35.1	N15 18.0
20	175 27.9	87 43.8	56.3	232 08.8	02.3	310 19.1	46.5	256 19.5	16.9	Menkar	314 11.9	N 4 09.4
21	190 30.4	102 43.0 ..	56.4	247 10.2 ..	02.2	325 21.9 ..	46.5	271 22.1 ..	16.9	Menkent	148 03.3	S36 27.6
22	205 32.8	117 42.1	56.5	262 11.6	02.1	340 24.7	46.4	286 24.7	17.0	Miaplacidus	221 39.1	S69 47.9
23	220 35.3	132 41.3	56.7	277 13.1	02.1	355 27.5	46.3	301 27.2	17.0			
18 00	235 37.8	147 40.5	N24 56.8	292 14.5	S22 02.0	10 30.2	S15 46.2	316 29.8	S22 17.0	Mirfak	308 36.1	N49 55.3
01	250 40.2	162 39.6	56.9	307 15.9	01.9	25 33.0	46.1	331 32.4	17.0	Nunki	75 54.0	S26 16.2
02	265 42.7	177 38.8	57.1	322 17.4	01.8	40 35.8	46.0	346 35.0	17.0	Peacock	53 13.9	S56 40.2
03	280 45.1	192 38.0 ..	57.2	337 18.8 ..	01.7	55 38.6 ..	46.0	1 37.6 ..	17.0	Pollux	243 23.9	N27 58.8
04	295 47.6	207 37.1	57.3	352 20.2	01.6	70 41.3	45.9	16 40.2	17.0	Procyon	244 56.5	N 5 10.5
05	310 50.1	222 36.3	57.4	7 21.7	01.6	85 44.1	45.8	31 42.8	17.0			
F 06	325 52.5	237 35.5	N24 57.5	22 23.1	S22 01.5	100 46.9	S15 45.7	46 45.3	S22 17.0	Rasalhague	96 03.1	N12 32.9
R 07	340 55.0	252 34.6	57.7	37 24.5	01.4	115 49.7	45.6	61 47.9	17.0	Regulus	207 40.0	N11 52.6
I 08	355 57.5	267 33.8	57.8	52 26.0	01.3	130 52.4	45.5	76 50.5	17.0	Rigel	281 09.2	S 8 11.1
D 09	10 59.9	282 32.9 ..	57.9	67 27.4 ..	01.2	145 55.2 ..	45.5	91 53.1 ..	17.0	Rigil Kent.	139 46.6	S60 54.6
A 10	26 02.4	297 32.1	58.0	82 28.9	01.1	160 58.0	45.4	106 55.7	17.0	Sabik	102 08.4	S15 44.7
Y 11	41 04.9	312 31.3	58.1	97 30.3	01.1	176 00.8	45.3	121 58.3	17.1			
12	56 07.3	327 30.4	N24 58.2	112 31.7	S22 01.0	191 03.5	S15 45.2	137 00.9	S22 17.1	Schedar	349 37.1	N56 37.9
13	71 09.8	342 29.6	58.3	127 33.2	00.9	206 06.3	45.1	152 03.5	17.1	Shaula	96 17.1	S37 06.8
14	86 12.3	357 28.8	58.4	142 34.6	00.8	221 09.1	45.1	167 06.0	17.1	Sirius	258 31.1	S16 44.8
15	101 14.7	12 27.9 ..	58.6	157 36.1 ..	00.7	236 11.9 ..	45.0	182 08.6 ..	17.1	Spica	158 27.5	S11 15.4
16	116 17.2	27 27.1	58.7	172 37.5	00.7	251 14.6	44.9	197 11.2	17.1	Suhail	222 50.1	S43 30.7
17	131 19.6	42 26.3	58.8	187 38.9	00.6	266 17.4	44.8	212 13.8	17.1			
18	146 22.1	57 25.4	N24 58.9	202 40.4	S22 00.5	281 20.2	S15 44.7	227 16.4	S22 17.1	Vega	80 36.4	N38 48.0
19	161 24.6	72 24.6	59.0	217 41.8	00.4	296 23.0	44.6	242 19.0	17.1	Zuben'ubi	137 01.4	S16 07.0
20	176 27.0	87 23.7	59.1	232 43.3	00.3	311 25.7	44.6	257 21.6	17.1			
21	191 29.5	102 22.9 ..	59.2	247 44.7 ..	00.3	326 28.5 ..	44.5	272 24.2 ..	17.1		SHA	Mer.Pass.
22	206 32.0	117 22.1	59.3	262 46.2	00.2	341 31.3	44.4	287 26.8	17.1	Venus	273 21.9	14 09
23	221 34.4	132 21.2	59.4	277 47.6	00.1	356 34.0	44.3	302 29.3	17.2	Mars	57 01.7	4 33
Mer.Pass.	h m 8 20.1	v −0.8	d 0.1	v 1.4	d 0.1	v 2.8	d 0.1	v 2.6	d 0.0	Jupiter	134 45.0	23 18
										Saturn	80 49.2	2 58

UT	SUN GHA	SUN Dec	MOON GHA	v	MOON Dec	d	HP
d h	° ′	° ′	° ′	′	° ′	′	′
16 00	180 54.7	N19 02.1	172 48.0	6.6	N16 01.2	8.3	59.9
01	195 54.7	02.7	187 13.6	6.5	16 09.5	8.1	59.9
02	210 54.7	03.3	201 39.1	6.5	16 17.6	8.0	59.9
03	225 54.7 ..	03.9	216 04.6	6.4	16 25.6	8.0	59.9
04	240 54.7	04.4	230 30.0	6.3	16 33.6	7.8	59.9
05	255 54.7	05.0	244 55.3	6.2	16 41.4	7.7	60.0
06	270 54.7	N19 05.6	259 20.5	6.2	N16 49.1	7.7	60.0
W 07	285 54.7	06.2	273 45.7	6.1	16 56.8	7.5	60.0
E 08	300 54.6	06.7	288 10.8	6.0	17 04.3	7.4	60.0
D 09	315 54.6 ..	07.3	302 35.8	6.0	17 11.7	7.3	60.0
N 10	330 54.6	07.9	317 00.8	5.9	17 19.0	7.1	60.0
E 11	345 54.6	08.5	331 25.7	5.8	17 26.1	7.1	60.0
S 12	0 54.6	N19 09.0	345 50.5	5.8	N17 33.2	7.0	60.1
D 13	15 54.6	09.6	0 15.3	5.7	17 40.2	6.8	60.1
A 14	30 54.6	10.2	14 40.0	5.7	17 47.0	6.7	60.1
Y 15	45 54.5 ..	10.8	29 04.7	5.6	17 53.7	6.6	60.1
16	60 54.5	11.3	43 29.3	5.5	18 00.3	6.5	60.1
17	75 54.5	11.9	57 53.8	5.5	18 06.8	6.3	60.1
18	90 54.5	N19 12.5	72 18.3	5.4	N18 13.1	6.2	60.1
19	105 54.5	13.0	86 42.7	5.3	18 19.3	6.2	60.1
20	120 54.5	13.6	101 07.0	5.3	18 25.5	5.9	60.2
21	135 54.4 ..	14.2	115 31.3	5.3	18 31.4	5.9	60.2
22	150 54.4	14.8	129 55.6	5.2	18 37.3	5.7	60.2
23	165 54.4	15.3	144 19.8	5.1	18 43.0	5.6	60.2
17 00	180 54.4	N19 15.9	158 43.9	5.1	N18 48.6	5.5	60.2
01	195 54.4	16.5	173 08.0	5.0	18 54.1	5.3	60.2
02	210 54.3	17.0	187 32.0	5.0	18 59.4	5.2	60.2
03	225 54.3 ..	17.6	201 56.0	5.0	19 04.6	5.1	60.2
04	240 54.3	18.2	216 20.0	4.9	19 09.7	5.0	60.2
05	255 54.3	18.7	230 43.9	4.8	19 14.7	4.8	60.2
06	270 54.3	N19 19.3	245 07.7	4.8	N19 19.5	4.7	60.2
T 07	285 54.3	19.8	259 31.5	4.8	19 24.2	4.5	60.2
H 08	300 54.2	20.4	273 55.3	4.7	19 28.7	4.4	60.2
U 09	315 54.2 ..	21.0	288 19.0	4.7	19 33.1	4.3	60.2
R 10	330 54.2	21.5	302 42.7	4.7	19 37.4	4.1	60.3
S 11	345 54.2	22.1	317 06.4	4.6	19 41.5	4.0	60.3
D 12	0 54.2	N19 22.7	331 30.0	4.6	N19 45.5	3.9	60.3
A 13	15 54.1	23.2	345 53.6	4.5	19 49.4	3.7	60.3
Y 14	30 54.1	23.8	0 17.1	4.5	19 53.1	3.6	60.3
15	45 54.1 ..	24.3	14 40.6	4.5	19 56.7	3.4	60.3
16	60 54.1	24.9	29 04.1	4.5	20 00.1	3.3	60.3
17	75 54.0	25.4	43 27.6	4.4	20 03.4	3.1	60.3
18	90 54.0	N19 26.0	57 51.0	4.4	N20 06.5	3.0	60.3
19	105 54.0	26.6	72 14.4	4.4	20 09.5	2.9	60.3
20	120 54.0	27.1	86 37.8	4.4	20 12.4	2.7	60.3
21	135 54.0 ..	27.7	101 01.2	4.3	20 15.1	2.6	60.3
22	150 53.9	28.2	115 24.5	4.4	20 17.7	2.4	60.3
23	165 53.9	28.8	129 47.9	4.3	20 20.1	2.3	60.3
18 00	180 53.9	N19 29.3	144 11.2	4.3	N20 22.4	2.2	60.3
01	195 53.9	29.9	158 34.5	4.2	20 24.6	2.0	60.3
02	210 53.8	30.4	172 57.7	4.3	20 26.6	1.8	60.3
03	225 53.8 ..	31.0	187 21.0	4.3	20 28.4	1.7	60.3
04	240 53.8	31.5	201 44.3	4.2	20 30.1	1.6	60.3
05	255 53.8	32.1	216 07.5	4.3	20 31.7	1.4	60.3
06	270 53.7	N19 32.6	230 30.8	4.2	N20 33.1	1.2	60.3
F 07	285 53.7	33.2	244 54.0	4.3	20 34.3	1.1	60.3
R 08	300 53.7	33.7	259 17.3	4.2	20 35.4	1.0	60.3
I 09	315 53.7 ..	34.3	273 40.5	4.3	20 36.4	0.8	60.3
D 10	330 53.6	34.8	288 03.8	4.2	20 37.2	0.7	60.2
A 11	345 53.6	35.4	302 27.0	4.2	20 37.9	0.5	60.2
Y 12	0 53.6	N19 35.9	316 50.2	4.3	N20 38.4	0.4	60.2
13	15 53.6	36.5	331 13.5	4.2	20 38.8	0.2	60.2
14	30 53.5	37.0	345 36.8	4.2	20 39.0	0.1	60.2
15	45 53.5 ..	37.6	0 00.0	4.3	20 39.1	0.0	60.2
16	60 53.5	38.1	14 23.3	4.3	20 39.1	0.3	60.2
17	75 53.5	38.7	28 46.6	4.3	20 38.8	0.3	60.2
18	90 53.4	N19 39.2	43 09.9	4.3	N20 38.5	0.5	60.2
19	105 53.4	39.7	57 33.2	4.4	20 38.0	0.7	60.2
20	120 53.4	40.3	71 56.6	4.3	20 37.3	0.8	60.2
21	135 53.3 ..	40.8	86 20.0	4.3	20 36.5	0.9	60.2
22	150 53.3	41.4	100 43.3	4.5	20 35.6	1.1	60.2
23	165 53.3	41.9	115 06.8	4.4	N20 34.5	1.2	60.2
	SD 15.8	d 0.6	SD 16.4		16.4		16.4

Twilight / Sunrise / Moonrise

Lat.	Naut.	Civil	Sunrise	16	17	18	19
°	h m	h m	h m	h m	h m	h m	h m
N 72	▢	▢	▢	02 21	▢	▢	▢
N 70	▢	▢	▢	03 03	02 51	▢	▢
68	////	////	01 36	03 31	03 41	04 07	05 11
66	////	////	02 15	03 52	04 12	04 49	05 53
64	////	00 53	02 41	04 10	04 36	05 18	06 22
62	////	01 43	03 01	04 24	04 55	05 40	06 43
60	////	02 13	03 18	04 36	05 10	05 58	07 01
N 58	00 48	02 35	03 32	04 47	05 23	06 13	07 16
56	01 33	02 53	03 44	04 56	05 35	06 25	07 28
54	02 01	03 08	03 54	05 04	05 45	06 36	07 39
52	02 22	03 21	04 03	05 12	05 54	06 46	07 49
50	02 39	03 32	04 12	05 18	06 02	06 55	07 58
45	03 11	03 55	04 29	05 32	06 19	07 14	08 16
N 40	03 34	04 12	04 43	05 44	06 33	07 29	08 31
35	03 53	04 27	04 55	05 54	06 45	07 42	08 44
30	04 08	04 39	05 06	06 03	06 56	07 53	08 55
20	04 31	05 00	05 23	06 19	07 14	08 13	09 14
N 10	04 50	05 16	05 39	06 32	07 30	08 30	09 31
0	05 05	05 31	05 53	06 45	07 44	08 45	09 46
S 10	05 19	05 45	06 07	06 58	07 59	09 01	10 02
20	05 32	05 59	06 22	07 12	08 15	09 18	10 19
30	05 44	06 13	06 39	07 27	08 34	09 38	10 38
35	05 51	06 22	06 49	07 37	08 45	09 49	10 49
40	05 58	06 31	07 00	07 47	08 57	10 02	11 01
45	06 05	06 41	07 13	08 00	09 12	10 18	11 17
S 50	06 14	06 53	07 29	08 15	09 29	10 37	11 35
52	06 17	06 59	07 37	08 22	09 38	10 46	11 44
54	06 21	07 05	07 45	08 30	09 47	10 56	11 53
56	06 25	07 12	07 54	08 39	09 58	11 08	12 04
58	06 30	07 19	08 05	08 49	10 10	11 21	12 17
S 60	06 35	07 27	08 17	09 01	10 25	11 36	12 31

Sunset / Twilight / Moonset

Lat.	Sunset	Civil	Naut.	16	17	18	19
°	h m	h m	h m	h m	h m	h m	h m
N 72	▢	▢	▢	23 57	▢	▢	▢
N 70	▢	▢	▢	23 57	▢	▢	▢
68	22 22	////	////	23 08	24 49	00 49	01 53
66	21 42	////	////	22 37	24 07	00 07	01 11
64	21 14	23 08	////	22 14	23 38	24 42	00 42
62	20 53	22 14	////	21 55	23 16	24 20	00 20
60	20 36	21 42	////	21 40	22 59	24 02	00 02
N 58	20 22	21 20	23 13	21 28	22 44	23 47	24 36
56	20 10	21 01	22 23	21 16	22 31	23 35	24 25
54	20 00	20 46	21 54	21 07	22 20	23 24	24 15
52	19 50	20 33	21 33	20 58	22 11	23 14	24 06
50	19 42	20 22	21 16	20 50	22 02	23 05	23 58
45	19 24	19 59	20 43	20 34	21 43	22 46	23 40
N 40	19 10	19 41	20 19	20 20	21 28	22 31	23 26
35	18 58	19 26	20 01	20 09	21 16	22 18	23 14
30	18 48	19 14	19 46	19 59	21 04	22 07	23 04
20	18 30	18 53	19 22	19 42	20 45	21 47	22 46
N 10	18 14	18 37	19 03	19 27	20 29	21 30	22 30
0	18 00	18 22	18 47	19 13	20 13	21 15	22 15
S 10	17 46	18 08	18 34	18 59	19 58	20 59	22 00
20	17 31	17 54	18 21	18 44	19 41	20 42	21 44
30	17 14	17 39	18 08	18 27	19 22	20 22	21 26
35	17 04	17 31	18 01	18 17	19 11	20 11	21 15
40	16 52	17 22	17 55	18 06	18 58	19 58	21 02
45	16 39	17 11	17 47	17 53	18 43	19 42	20 48
S 50	16 23	16 59	17 39	17 37	18 25	19 23	20 30
52	16 16	16 53	17 35	17 29	18 16	19 14	20 21
54	16 07	16 47	17 31	17 21	18 06	19 04	20 12
56	15 58	16 41	17 27	17 11	17 55	18 52	20 01
58	15 47	16 33	17 22	17 01	17 43	18 39	19 49
S 60	15 35	16 25	17 17	16 48	17 28	18 24	19 34

SUN / MOON

Day	Eqn. of Time 00h	Eqn. of Time 12h	Mer. Pass.	Mer. Pass. Upper	Mer. Pass. Lower	Age	Phase
d	m s	m s	h m	h m	h m	d	%
16	03 39	03 38	11 56	12 59	00 30	01	2
17	03 38	03 37	11 56	13 59	01 29	02	6
18	03 36	03 34	11 56	15 00	02 29	03	12

UT	ARIES GHA	VENUS −3.9 GHA	Dec	MARS −0.9 GHA	Dec	JUPITER −2.5 GHA	Dec	SATURN +0.2 GHA	Dec	STARS Name	SHA	Dec
19 00	236 36.9	147 20.4	N24 59.5	292 49.1	S22 00.0	11 36.8	S15 44.2	317 31.9	S22 17.2	Acamar	315 16.3	S40 14.0
01	251 39.4	162 19.6	59.6	307 50.5	21 59.9	26 39.6	44.2	332 34.5	17.2	Achernar	335 24.9	S57 08.6
02	266 41.8	177 18.7	59.7	322 52.0	59.9	41 42.4	44.1	347 37.1	17.2	Acrux	173 05.0	S63 12.2
03	281 44.3	192 17.9 ..	59.8	337 53.4 ..	59.8	56 45.1 ..	44.0	2 39.7 ..	17.2	Adhara	255 10.2	S29 00.1
04	296 46.8	207 17.1	59.9	352 54.9	59.7	71 47.9	43.9	17 42.3	17.2	Aldebaran	290 45.9	N16 32.5
05	311 49.2	222 16.2	24 59.9	7 56.3	59.6	86 50.7	43.8	32 44.9	17.2			
S 06	326 51.7	237 15.4	N25 00.0	22 57.8	S21 59.5	101 53.5	S15 43.7	47 47.5	S22 17.2	Alioth	166 17.4	N55 51.9
A 07	341 54.1	252 14.5	00.1	37 59.2	59.5	116 56.2	43.7	62 50.1	17.2	Alkaid	152 55.9	N49 13.5
T 08	356 56.6	267 13.7	00.2	53 00.7	59.4	131 59.0	43.6	77 52.7	17.2	Al Na'ir	27 39.6	S46 52.1
U 09	11 59.1	282 12.9 ..	00.3	68 02.1 ..	59.3	147 01.8 ..	43.5	92 55.2 ..	17.2	Alnilam	275 43.3	S 1 11.7
R 10	27 01.5	297 12.0	00.4	83 03.6	59.2	162 04.5	43.4	107 57.8	17.2	Alphard	217 52.9	S 8 44.5
D 11	42 04.0	312 11.2	00.5	98 05.0	59.1	177 07.3	43.3	123 00.4	17.2			
A 12	57 06.5	327 10.4	N25 00.5	113 06.5	S21 59.1	192 10.1	S15 43.3	138 03.0	S22 17.3	Alphecca	126 07.8	N26 39.3
Y 13	72 08.9	342 09.5	00.6	128 08.0	59.0	207 12.9	43.2	153 05.6	17.3	Alpheratz	357 40.2	N29 11.2
14	87 11.4	357 08.7	00.7	143 09.4	58.9	222 15.6	43.1	168 08.2	17.3	Altair	62 04.8	N 8 55.0
15	102 13.9	12 07.9 ..	00.8	158 10.9 ..	58.8	237 18.4 ..	43.0	183 10.8 ..	17.3	Ankaa	353 12.7	S42 12.3
16	117 16.3	27 07.0	00.9	173 12.3	58.7	252 21.2	42.9	198 13.4	17.3	Antares	112 21.8	S26 28.2
17	132 18.8	42 06.2	00.9	188 13.8	58.7	267 24.0	42.9	213 16.0	17.3			
18	147 21.2	57 05.3	N25 01.0	203 15.3	S21 58.6	282 26.7	S15 42.8	228 18.6	S22 17.3	Arcturus	145 52.4	N19 05.4
19	162 23.7	72 04.5	01.1	218 16.7	58.5	297 29.5	42.7	243 21.2	17.3	Atria	107 20.1	S69 03.4
20	177 26.2	87 03.7	01.2	233 18.2	58.4	312 32.3	42.6	258 23.8	17.3	Avior	234 16.9	S59 34.5
21	192 28.6	102 02.8 ..	01.2	248 19.6 ..	58.4	327 35.0 ..	42.5	273 26.4 ..	17.3	Bellatrix	278 28.8	N 6 21.7
22	207 31.1	117 02.0	01.3	263 21.1	58.3	342 37.8	42.4	288 28.9	17.3	Betelgeuse	270 58.0	N 7 24.4
23	222 33.6	132 01.2	01.4	278 22.6	58.2	357 40.6	42.4	303 31.5	17.3			
20 00	237 36.0	147 00.3	N25 01.4	293 24.0	S21 58.1	12 43.3	S15 42.3	318 34.1	S22 17.4	Canopus	263 55.1	S52 42.7
01	252 38.5	161 59.5	01.5	308 25.5	58.0	27 46.1	42.2	333 36.7	17.4	Capella	280 30.0	N46 00.8
02	267 41.0	176 58.7	01.6	323 27.0	58.0	42 48.9	42.1	348 39.3	17.4	Deneb	49 29.0	N45 20.6
03	282 43.4	191 57.8 ..	01.6	338 28.4 ..	57.9	57 51.7 ..	42.0	3 41.9 ..	17.4	Denebola	182 30.2	N14 28.3
04	297 45.9	206 57.0	01.7	353 29.9	57.8	72 54.4	42.0	18 44.5	17.4	Diphda	348 52.8	S17 53.3
05	312 48.4	221 56.2	01.8	8 31.4	57.7	87 57.2	41.9	33 47.1	17.4			
S 06	327 50.8	236 55.3	N25 01.8	23 32.8	S21 57.7	103 00.0	S15 41.8	48 49.7	S22 17.4	Dubhe	193 47.6	N61 39.4
U 07	342 53.3	251 54.5	01.9	38 34.3	57.6	118 02.7	41.7	63 52.3	17.4	Elnath	278 08.8	N28 37.2
N 08	357 55.7	266 53.7	01.9	53 35.8	57.5	133 05.5	41.6	78 54.9	17.4	Eltanin	90 44.1	N51 29.2
D 09	12 58.2	281 52.8 ..	02.0	68 37.2 ..	57.4	148 08.3 ..	41.6	93 57.5 ..	17.4	Enif	33 43.8	N 9 57.5
A 10	28 00.7	296 52.0	02.0	83 38.7	57.4	163 11.1	41.5	109 00.1	17.4	Fomalhaut	15 20.4	S29 31.4
Y 11	43 03.1	311 51.1	02.1	98 40.2	57.3	178 13.8	41.4	124 02.7	17.4			
12	58 05.6	326 50.3	N25 02.2	113 41.7	S21 57.2	193 16.6	S15 41.3	139 05.3	S22 17.5	Gacrux	171 56.8	S57 13.1
13	73 08.1	341 49.5	02.2	128 43.1	57.1	208 19.4	41.2	154 07.8	17.5	Gienah	175 48.7	S17 38.7
14	88 10.5	356 48.6	02.3	143 44.6	57.1	223 22.1	41.2	169 10.4	17.5	Hadar	148 42.5	S60 27.7
15	103 13.0	11 47.8 ..	02.3	158 46.1 ..	57.0	238 24.9 ..	41.1	184 13.0 ..	17.5	Hamal	327 57.3	N23 32.6
16	118 15.5	26 47.0	02.3	173 47.6	56.9	253 27.7	41.0	199 15.6	17.5	Kaus Aust.	83 39.1	S34 22.3
17	133 17.9	41 46.1	02.4	188 49.0	56.8	268 30.4	40.9	214 18.2	17.5			
18	148 20.4	56 45.3	N25 02.4	203 50.5	S21 56.8	283 33.2	S15 40.8	229 20.8	S22 17.5	Kochab	137 19.1	N74 05.0
19	163 22.9	71 44.5	02.5	218 52.0	56.7	298 36.0	40.8	244 23.4	17.5	Markab	13 35.1	N15 18.0
20	178 25.3	86 43.6	02.5	233 53.5	56.6	313 38.7	40.7	259 26.0	17.5	Menkar	314 11.9	N 4 09.4
21	193 27.8	101 42.8 ..	02.6	248 55.0 ..	56.5	328 41.5 ..	40.6	274 28.6 ..	17.5	Menkent	148 03.3	S36 27.6
22	208 30.2	116 42.0	02.6	263 56.4	56.5	343 44.3	40.5	289 31.2	17.5	Miaplacidus	221 39.1	S69 47.9
23	223 32.7	131 41.1	02.6	278 57.9	56.4	358 47.1	40.4	304 33.8	17.5			
21 00	238 35.2	146 40.3	N25 02.7	293 59.4	S21 56.3	13 49.8	S15 40.3	319 36.4	S22 17.6	Mirfak	308 36.1	N49 55.3
01	253 37.6	161 39.5	02.7	309 00.9	56.2	28 52.6	40.3	334 39.0	17.6	Nunki	75 53.9	S26 16.2
02	268 40.1	176 38.6	02.8	324 02.4	56.2	43 55.4	40.2	349 41.6	17.6	Peacock	53 13.8	S56 40.2
03	283 42.6	191 37.8 ..	02.8	339 03.8 ..	56.1	58 58.1 ..	40.1	4 44.2 ..	17.6	Pollux	243 23.9	N27 58.8
04	298 45.0	206 37.0	02.8	354 05.3	56.0	74 00.9	40.0	19 46.8	17.6	Procyon	244 56.5	N 5 10.5
05	313 47.5	221 36.1	02.9	9 06.8	56.0	89 03.7	39.9	34 49.4	17.6			
06	328 50.0	236 35.3	N25 02.9	24 08.3	S21 55.9	104 06.4	S15 39.9	49 52.0	S22 17.6	Rasalhague	96 03.1	N12 32.9
07	343 52.4	251 34.5	02.9	39 09.8	55.8	119 09.2	39.8	64 54.6	17.6	Regulus	207 40.0	N11 52.6
08	358 54.9	266 33.6	02.9	54 11.3	55.7	134 12.0	39.7	79 57.2	17.6	Rigel	281 09.2	S 8 11.1
M 09	13 57.4	281 32.8 ..	03.0	69 12.8 ..	55.7	149 14.7 ..	39.6	94 59.8 ..	17.6	Rigil Kent.	139 46.5	S60 54.6
O 10	28 59.8	296 32.0	03.0	84 14.3	55.6	164 17.5	39.5	110 02.4	17.6	Sabik	102 08.4	S15 44.7
N 11	44 02.3	311 31.1	03.0	99 15.7	55.5	179 20.3	39.5	125 05.0	17.6			
D 12	59 04.7	326 30.3	N25 03.0	114 17.2	S21 55.4	194 23.0	S15 39.4	140 07.6	S22 17.7	Schedar	349 37.0	N56 37.9
A 13	74 07.2	341 29.5	03.1	129 18.7	55.4	209 25.8	39.3	155 10.2	17.7	Shaula	96 17.0	S37 06.8
Y 14	89 09.7	356 28.6	03.1	144 20.2	55.3	224 28.6	39.2	170 12.8	17.7	Sirius	258 31.1	S16 44.8
15	104 12.1	11 27.8 ..	03.1	159 21.7 ..	55.2	239 31.3 ..	39.1	185 15.4 ..	17.7	Spica	158 27.5	S11 15.4
16	119 14.6	26 27.0	03.1	174 23.2	55.2	254 34.1	39.1	200 18.0	17.7	Suhail	222 50.1	S43 30.7
17	134 17.1	41 26.1	03.1	189 24.7	55.1	269 36.9	39.0	215 20.6	17.7			
18	149 19.5	56 25.3	N25 03.2	204 26.2	S21 55.0	284 39.6	S15 38.9	230 23.2	S22 17.7	Vega	80 36.4	N38 48.0
19	164 22.0	71 24.5	03.2	219 27.7	54.9	299 42.4	38.8	245 25.8	17.7	Zuben'ubi	137 01.4	S16 07.0
20	179 24.5	86 23.6	03.2	234 29.2	54.9	314 45.2	38.7	260 28.4	17.7		SHA	Mer.Pass.
21	194 26.9	101 22.8 ..	03.2	249 30.7 ..	54.8	329 47.9 ..	38.7	275 31.0 ..	17.7		° ′	h m
22	209 29.4	116 22.0	03.2	264 32.2	54.7	344 50.7	38.6	290 33.6	17.7	Venus	269 24.3	14 13
23	224 31.8	131 21.2	03.2	279 33.7	54.7	359 53.5	38.5	305 36.2	17.8	Mars	55 48.0	4 26
Mer.Pass.	h m 8 08.3	*v* −0.8	*d* 0.1	*v* 1.5	*d* 0.1	*v* 2.8	*d* 0.1	*v* 2.6	*d* 0.0	Jupiter	135 07.3	23 05
										Saturn	80 58.1	2 45

UT	SUN GHA	SUN Dec	MOON GHA	v	MOON Dec	d	HP
d h	° '	° '	° '	'	° '	'	'
19 00	180 53.3	N19 42.5	129 30.2	4.4	N20 33.3	1.4	60.1
01	195 53.2	43.0	143 53.6	4.5	20 31.9	1.5	60.1
02	210 53.2	43.5	158 17.1	4.5	20 30.4	1.7	60.1
03	225 53.2 . .	44.1	172 40.6	4.6	20 28.7	1.8	60.1
04	240 53.1	44.6	187 04.2	4.6	20 26.9	2.0	60.1
05	255 53.1	45.1	201 27.8	4.6	20 24.9	2.0	60.1
06	270 53.1	N19 45.7	215 51.4	4.6	N20 22.9	2.3	60.1
07	285 53.0	46.2	230 15.0	4.7	20 20.6	2.4	60.1
S 08	300 53.0	46.7	244 38.7	4.8	20 18.2	2.5	60.1
A 09	315 53.0 . .	47.3	259 02.5	4.7	20 15.7	2.6	60.0
T 10	330 53.0	47.8	273 26.2	4.8	20 13.1	2.8	60.0
U 11	345 52.9	48.3	287 50.0	4.9	20 10.3	3.0	60.0
R 12	0 52.9	N19 48.9	302 13.9	4.9	N20 07.3	3.1	60.0
D 13	15 52.9	49.4	316 37.8	4.9	20 04.2	3.2	60.0
A 14	30 52.8	49.9	331 01.7	5.0	20 01.0	3.3	60.0
Y 15	45 52.8 . .	50.5	345 25.7	5.0	19 57.7	3.5	60.0
16	60 52.8	51.0	359 49.7	5.1	19 54.2	3.6	60.0
17	75 52.7	51.5	14 13.8	5.2	19 50.6	3.8	59.9
18	90 52.7	N19 52.1	28 38.0	5.1	N19 46.8	3.9	59.9
19	105 52.7	52.6	43 02.1	5.3	19 42.9	4.0	59.9
20	120 52.6	53.1	57 26.4	5.3	19 38.9	4.1	59.9
21	135 52.6 . .	53.7	71 50.7	5.3	19 34.8	4.3	59.9
22	150 52.6	54.2	86 15.0	5.4	19 30.5	4.4	59.9
23	165 52.5	54.7	100 39.4	5.5	19 26.1	4.6	59.8
20 00	180 52.5	N19 55.2	115 03.9	5.5	N19 21.5	4.7	59.8
01	195 52.5	55.8	129 28.4	5.6	19 16.8	4.8	59.8
02	210 52.4	56.3	143 53.0	5.6	19 12.0	4.9	59.8
03	225 52.4 . .	56.8	158 17.6	5.7	19 07.1	5.0	59.8
04	240 52.4	57.3	172 42.3	5.8	19 02.1	5.2	59.8
05	255 52.3	57.8	187 07.1	5.8	18 56.9	5.3	59.7
06	270 52.3	N19 58.4	201 31.9	5.9	N18 51.6	5.4	59.7
07	285 52.2	58.9	215 56.8	6.0	18 46.2	5.6	59.7
S 08	300 52.2	59.4	230 21.8	6.0	18 40.6	5.6	59.7
U 09	315 52.2	19 59.9	244 46.8	6.1	18 35.0	5.8	59.7
N 10	330 52.1	20 00.5	259 11.9	6.2	18 29.2	5.9	59.7
D 11	345 52.1	01.0	273 37.1	6.2	18 23.3	6.0	59.6
A 12	0 52.1	N20 01.5	288 02.3	6.3	N18 17.3	6.2	59.6
Y 13	15 52.0	02.0	302 27.6	6.3	18 11.1	6.2	59.6
14	30 52.0	02.5	316 52.9	6.5	18 04.9	6.4	59.6
15	45 52.0 . .	03.0	331 18.4	6.5	17 58.5	6.4	59.6
16	60 51.9	03.6	345 43.9	6.6	17 52.1	6.6	59.5
17	75 51.9	04.1	0 09.5	6.6	17 45.5	6.7	59.5
18	90 51.8	N20 04.6	14 35.1	6.7	N17 38.8	6.8	59.5
19	105 51.8	05.1	29 00.8	6.8	17 32.0	6.9	59.5
20	120 51.8	05.6	43 26.6	6.9	17 25.1	7.0	59.5
21	135 51.7 . .	06.1	57 52.5	6.9	17 18.1	7.2	59.4
22	150 51.7	06.6	72 18.4	7.0	17 10.9	7.2	59.4
23	165 51.6	07.2	86 44.4	7.1	17 03.7	7.3	59.4
21 00	180 51.6	N20 07.7	101 10.5	7.2	N16 56.4	7.4	59.4
01	195 51.6	08.2	115 36.7	7.2	16 49.0	7.6	59.4
02	210 51.5	08.7	130 02.9	7.3	16 41.4	7.6	59.3
03	225 51.5 . .	09.2	144 29.2	7.4	16 33.8	7.7	59.3
04	240 51.4	09.7	158 55.6	7.4	16 26.1	7.9	59.3
05	255 51.4	10.2	173 22.0	7.6	16 18.2	7.9	59.3
06	270 51.4	N20 10.7	187 48.6	7.6	N16 10.3	8.0	59.3
07	285 51.3	11.2	202 15.2	7.7	16 02.3	8.1	59.2
08	300 51.3	11.7	216 41.9	7.7	15 54.2	8.2	59.2
M 09	315 51.2 . .	12.2	231 08.6	7.9	15 46.0	8.3	59.2
O 10	330 51.2	12.7	245 35.5	7.9	15 37.7	8.4	59.2
N 11	345 51.1	13.3	260 02.4	7.9	15 29.3	8.4	59.1
D 12	0 51.1	N20 13.8	274 29.3	8.1	N15 20.9	8.6	59.1
A 13	15 51.1	14.3	288 56.4	8.1	15 12.3	8.6	59.1
Y 14	30 51.0	14.8	303 23.5	8.2	15 03.7	8.7	59.1
15	45 51.0 . .	15.3	317 50.7	8.3	14 55.0	8.8	59.1
16	60 50.9	15.8	332 18.0	8.4	14 46.2	8.9	59.0
17	75 50.9	16.3	346 45.4	8.4	14 37.3	9.0	59.0
18	90 50.8	N20 16.8	1 12.8	8.5	N14 28.3	9.0	59.0
19	105 50.8	17.3	15 40.3	8.6	14 19.3	9.2	59.0
20	120 50.8	17.8	30 07.9	8.7	14 10.1	9.2	58.9
21	135 50.7 . .	18.3	44 35.6	8.7	14 00.9	9.2	58.9
22	150 50.7	18.8	59 03.3	8.8	13 51.7	9.4	58.9
23	165 50.6	19.3	73 31.1	8.9	N13 42.3	9.4	58.9
SD	15.8	d 0.5	SD 16.3		16.2		16.1

Twilight / Sunrise / Moonrise

Lat.	Twilight Naut.	Twilight Civil	Sunrise	Moonrise 19	Moonrise 20	Moonrise 21	Moonrise 22
°	h m	h m	h m	h m	h m	h m	h m
N 72	▭	▭	▭	▭	▭	07 29	09 49
N 70	▭	▭	▭	▭	06 00	08 11	10 10
68	////	////	01 17	05 11	06 50	08 39	10 27
66	////	////	02 02	05 53	07 21	09 00	10 40
64	////	00 15	02 32	06 22	07 44	09 17	10 51
62	////	01 29	02 54	06 43	08 03	09 31	11 01
60	////	02 03	03 11	07 01	08 18	09 42	11 09
N 58	00 13	02 28	03 26	07 16	08 31	09 52	11 16
56	01 21	02 47	03 39	07 28	08 42	10 01	11 22
54	01 52	03 02	03 50	07 39	08 51	10 09	11 27
52	02 15	03 16	03 59	07 49	09 00	10 16	11 32
50	02 33	03 27	04 08	07 58	09 08	10 22	11 37
45	03 06	03 51	04 26	08 16	09 24	10 35	11 46
N 40	03 31	04 10	04 41	08 31	09 38	10 46	11 54
35	03 50	04 25	04 53	08 44	09 49	10 56	12 01
30	04 06	04 37	05 04	08 55	09 59	11 04	12 07
20	04 30	04 58	05 22	09 14	10 17	11 18	12 18
N 10	04 49	05 16	05 38	09 31	10 32	11 30	12 27
0	05 05	05 31	05 53	09 46	10 46	11 42	12 35
S 10	05 20	05 45	06 08	10 02	11 00	11 54	12 44
20	05 33	06 00	06 23	10 19	11 15	12 06	12 53
30	05 46	06 15	06 41	10 38	11 32	12 20	13 03
35	05 53	06 24	06 51	10 49	11 42	12 28	13 09
40	06 00	06 33	07 03	11 01	11 53	12 37	13 16
45	06 08	06 44	07 16	11 17	12 06	12 48	13 23
S 50	06 17	06 57	07 33	11 35	12 22	13 01	13 33
52	06 21	07 03	07 41	11 44	12 30	13 07	13 37
54	06 25	07 09	07 50	11 53	12 38	13 14	13 42
56	06 29	07 16	08 00	12 04	12 48	13 21	13 47
58	06 34	07 24	08 11	12 17	12 58	13 29	13 53
S 60	06 40	07 33	08 24	12 31	13 11	13 39	13 59

Sunset / Twilight / Moonset

Lat.	Sunset	Twilight Civil	Twilight Naut.	Moonset 19	Moonset 20	Moonset 21	Moonset 22
°	h m	h m	h m	h m	h m	h m	h m
N 72	▭	▭	▭	▭	▭	03 41	03 14
N 70	▭	▭	▭	▭	03 09	02 58	02 51
68	22 42	////	////	01 53	02 19	02 29	02 33
66	21 54	////	////	01 11	01 47	02 07	02 18
64	21 24	////	////	00 42	01 24	01 50	02 06
62	21 01	22 28	////	00 20	01 05	01 35	01 56
60	20 43	21 52	////	00 02	00 49	01 23	01 47
N 58	20 28	21 28	////	24 36	00 36	01 12	01 39
56	20 16	21 08	22 36	24 25	00 25	01 03	01 32
54	20 05	20 52	22 03	24 15	00 15	00 55	01 26
52	19 55	20 38	21 40	24 06	00 06	00 47	01 21
50	19 46	20 27	21 22	23 58	24 40	00 40	01 15
45	19 28	20 03	20 48	23 40	24 26	00 26	01 05
N 40	19 13	19 44	20 23	23 26	24 14	00 14	00 55
35	19 00	19 29	20 04	23 14	24 04	00 04	00 47
30	18 49	19 16	19 48	23 04	23 55	24 41	00 41
20	18 31	18 55	19 23	22 46	23 39	24 28	00 28
N 10	18 15	18 37	19 04	22 30	23 26	24 18	00 18
0	18 00	18 22	18 48	22 15	23 13	24 08	00 08
S 10	17 45	18 08	18 33	22 00	23 00	23 58	24 53
20	17 30	17 53	18 20	21 44	22 46	23 47	24 45
30	17 12	17 38	18 07	21 26	22 30	23 34	24 37
35	17 02	17 29	18 00	21 15	22 21	23 27	24 32
40	16 51	17 19	17 52	21 02	22 10	23 19	24 26
45	16 36	17 09	17 45	20 48	21 58	23 09	24 20
S 50	16 19	16 56	17 36	20 30	21 42	22 57	24 12
52	16 12	16 50	17 32	20 21	21 35	22 52	24 08
54	16 03	16 43	17 28	20 12	21 27	22 46	24 04
56	15 53	16 36	17 23	20 01	21 18	22 39	24 00
58	15 42	16 29	17 18	19 49	21 08	22 31	23 55
S 60	15 29	16 20	17 13	19 34	20 56	22 22	23 49

SUN / MOON

Day	SUN Eqn. of Time 00h	SUN Eqn. of Time 12h	SUN Mer. Pass.	MOON Mer. Pass. Upper	MOON Mer. Pass. Lower	Age	Phase
d	m s	m s	h m	h m	h m	d	%
19	03 33	03 32	11 56	16 01	03 31	04	21
20	03 30	03 28	11 57	16 59	04 30	05	32
21	03 26	03 25	11 57	17 55	05 28	06	43

UT	ARIES GHA	VENUS −3.9 GHA	Dec	MARS −1.0 GHA	Dec	JUPITER −2.5 GHA	Dec	SATURN +0.2 GHA	Dec	STARS Name	SHA	Dec
22 00	239 34.3	146 20.3	N25 03.2	294 35.2	S21 54.6	14 56.2	S15 38.4	320 38.8	S22 17.8	Acamar	315 16.3	S40 14.0
01	254 36.8	161 19.5	03.2	309 36.7	54.5	29 59.0	38.3	335 41.4	17.8	Achernar	335 24.8	S57 08.6
02	269 39.2	176 18.7	03.2	324 38.2	54.5	45 01.8	38.3	350 44.0	17.8	Acrux	173 05.1	S63 12.2
03	284 41.7	191 17.8 ..	03.2	339 39.7 ..	54.4	60 04.5 ..	38.2	5 46.6 ..	17.8	Adhara	255 10.2	S29 00.1
04	299 44.2	206 17.0	03.2	354 41.2	54.3	75 07.3	38.1	20 49.2	17.8	Aldebaran	290 45.9	N16 32.5
05	314 46.6	221 16.2	03.2	9 42.7	54.2	90 10.1	38.0	35 51.8	17.8			
06	329 49.1	236 15.3	N25 03.2	24 44.2	S21 54.2	105 12.8	S15 38.0	50 54.4	S22 17.8	Alioth	166 17.5	N55 51.9
07	344 51.6	251 14.5	03.2	39 45.7	54.1	120 15.6	37.9	65 57.0	17.8	Alkaid	152 55.9	N49 13.6
08	359 54.0	266 13.7	03.2	54 47.2	54.0	135 18.4	37.8	80 59.6	17.8	Al Na'ir	27 39.6	S46 52.1
09	14 56.5	281 12.8 ..	03.2	69 48.7 ..	54.0	150 21.1 ..	37.7	96 02.2 ..	17.8	Alnilam	275 43.3	S 1 11.7
10	29 59.0	296 12.0	03.2	84 50.2	53.9	165 23.9	37.6	111 04.8	17.8	Alphard	217 52.9	S 8 44.4
11	45 01.4	311 11.2	03.2	99 51.7	53.8	180 26.6	37.6	126 07.4	17.9			
12	60 03.9	326 10.4	N25 03.2	114 53.2	S21 53.8	195 29.4	S15 37.5	141 10.0	S22 17.9	Alphecca	126 07.8	N26 39.3
13	75 06.3	341 09.5	03.2	129 54.7	53.7	210 32.2	37.4	156 12.6	17.9	Alpheratz	357 40.2	N29 11.2
14	90 08.8	356 08.7	03.2	144 56.2	53.6	225 34.9	37.3	171 15.2	17.9	Altair	62 04.8	N 8 55.0
15	105 11.3	11 07.9 ..	03.2	159 57.8 ..	53.6	240 37.7 ..	37.2	186 17.8 ..	17.9	Ankaa	353 12.7	S42 12.3
16	120 13.7	26 07.0	03.2	174 59.3	53.5	255 40.5	37.2	201 20.4	17.9	Antares	112 21.8	S26 28.2
17	135 16.2	41 06.2	03.2	190 00.8	53.4	270 43.2	37.1	216 23.0	17.9			
18	150 18.7	56 05.4	N25 03.2	205 02.3	S21 53.4	285 46.0	S15 37.0	231 25.6	S22 17.9	Arcturus	145 52.4	N19 05.4
19	165 21.1	71 04.6	03.1	220 03.8	53.3	300 48.8	36.9	246 28.2	17.9	Atria	107 20.0	S69 03.4
20	180 23.6	86 03.7	03.1	235 05.3	53.2	315 51.5	36.8	261 30.8	17.9	Avior	234 16.9	S59 34.5
21	195 26.1	101 02.9 ..	03.1	250 06.8 ..	53.2	330 54.3 ..	36.8	276 33.4 ..	17.9	Bellatrix	278 28.8	N 6 21.7
22	210 28.5	116 02.1	03.1	265 08.3	53.1	345 57.0	36.7	291 36.0	18.0	Betelgeuse	270 58.0	N 7 24.4
23	225 31.0	131 01.2	03.1	280 09.9	53.0	0 59.8	36.6	306 38.6	18.0			
23 00	240 33.5	146 00.4	N25 03.0	295 11.4	S21 53.0	16 02.6	S15 36.5	321 41.2	S22 18.0	Canopus	263 55.1	S52 42.6
01	255 35.9	160 59.6	03.0	310 12.9	52.9	31 05.3	36.4	336 43.8	18.0	Capella	280 30.0	N46 00.8
02	270 38.4	175 58.8	03.0	325 14.4	52.8	46 08.1	36.4	351 46.4	18.0	Deneb	49 29.0	N45 20.6
03	285 40.8	190 57.9 ..	03.0	340 15.9 ..	52.8	61 10.9 ..	36.3	6 49.0 ..	18.0	Denebola	182 30.2	N14 28.3
04	300 43.3	205 57.1	02.9	355 17.4	52.7	76 13.6	36.2	21 51.6	18.0	Diphda	348 52.8	S17 53.2
05	315 45.8	220 56.3	02.9	10 19.0	52.6	91 16.4	36.1	36 54.2	18.0			
06	330 48.2	235 55.4	N25 02.9	25 20.5	S21 52.6	106 19.1	S15 36.1	51 56.8	S22 18.0	Dubhe	193 47.6	N61 39.4
07	345 50.7	250 54.6	02.9	40 22.0	52.5	121 21.9	36.0	66 59.4	18.0	Elnath	278 08.8	N28 37.2
08	0 53.2	265 53.8	02.8	55 23.5	52.4	136 24.7	35.9	82 02.0	18.0	Eltanin	90 44.1	N51 29.2
09	15 55.6	280 53.0 ..	02.8	70 25.1 ..	52.4	151 27.4 ..	35.8	97 04.6 ..	18.1	Enif	33 43.8	N 9 57.5
10	30 58.1	295 52.1	02.8	85 26.6	52.3	166 30.2	35.7	112 07.2	18.1	Fomalhaut	15 20.4	S29 31.4
11	46 00.6	310 51.3	02.7	100 28.1	52.2	181 33.0	35.7	127 09.8	18.1			
12	61 03.0	325 50.5	N25 02.7	115 29.6	S21 52.2	196 35.7	S15 35.6	142 12.4	S22 18.1	Gacrux	171 56.8	S57 13.1
13	76 05.5	340 49.7	02.7	130 31.2	52.1	211 38.5	35.5	157 15.0	18.1	Gienah	175 48.7	S17 38.7
14	91 07.9	355 48.8	02.6	145 32.7	52.0	226 41.2	35.4	172 17.6	18.1	Hadar	148 42.5	S60 27.7
15	106 10.4	10 48.0 ..	02.6	160 34.2 ..	52.0	241 44.0 ..	35.4	187 20.2 ..	18.1	Hamal	327 57.3	N23 32.7
16	121 12.9	25 47.2	02.5	175 35.7	51.9	256 46.8	35.3	202 22.8	18.1	Kaus Aust.	83 39.1	S34 22.3
17	136 15.3	40 46.4	02.5	190 37.3	51.8	271 49.5	35.2	217 25.4	18.1			
18	151 17.8	55 45.5	N25 02.4	205 38.8	S21 51.8	286 52.3	S15 35.1	232 28.1	S22 18.1	Kochab	137 19.1	N74 05.1
19	166 20.3	70 44.7	02.4	220 40.3	51.7	301 55.0	35.0	247 30.7	18.1	Markab	13 35.1	N15 18.1
20	181 22.7	85 43.9	02.4	235 41.9	51.7	316 57.8	35.0	262 33.3	18.2	Menkar	314 11.9	N 4 09.4
21	196 25.2	100 43.1 ..	02.3	250 43.4 ..	51.6	332 00.6 ..	34.9	277 35.9 ..	18.2	Menkent	148 03.3	S36 27.6
22	211 27.7	115 42.2	02.3	265 44.9	51.5	347 03.3	34.8	292 38.5	18.2	Miaplacidus	221 39.2	S69 47.9
23	226 30.1	130 41.4	02.2	280 46.5	51.5	2 06.1	34.7	307 41.1	18.2			
24 00	241 32.6	145 40.6	N25 02.2	295 48.0	S21 51.4	17 08.8	S15 34.6	322 43.7	S22 18.2	Mirfak	308 36.1	N49 55.3
01	256 35.1	160 39.8	02.1	310 49.5	51.3	32 11.6	34.6	337 46.3	18.2	Nunki	75 53.9	S26 16.2
02	271 37.5	175 38.9	02.1	325 51.1	51.3	47 14.4	34.5	352 48.9	18.2	Peacock	53 13.8	S56 40.2
03	286 40.0	190 38.1 ..	02.0	340 52.6 ..	51.2	62 17.1 ..	34.4	7 51.5 ..	18.2	Pollux	243 23.9	N27 58.8
04	301 42.4	205 37.3	01.9	355 54.1	51.2	77 19.9	34.3	22 54.1	18.2	Procyon	244 56.5	N 5 10.5
05	316 44.9	220 36.5	01.9	10 55.7	51.1	92 22.6	34.3	37 56.7	18.2			
06	331 47.4	235 35.6	N25 01.8	25 57.2	S21 51.0	107 25.4	S15 34.2	52 59.3	S22 18.2	Rasalhague	96 03.1	N12 32.9
07	346 49.8	250 34.8	01.8	40 58.8	51.0	122 28.2	34.1	68 01.9	18.3	Regulus	207 40.0	N11 52.6
08	1 52.3	265 34.0	01.7	56 00.3	50.9	137 30.9	34.0	83 04.5	18.3	Rigel	281 09.2	S 8 11.1
09	16 54.8	280 33.2 ..	01.6	71 01.8 ..	50.8	152 33.7 ..	33.9	98 07.1 ..	18.3	Rigil Kent.	139 46.6	S60 54.6
10	31 57.2	295 32.3	01.6	86 03.4	50.8	167 36.4	33.9	113 09.7	18.3	Sabik	102 08.4	S15 44.7
11	46 59.7	310 31.5	01.5	101 04.9	50.7	182 39.2	33.8	128 12.4	18.3			
12	62 02.2	325 30.7	N25 01.4	116 06.5	S21 50.7	197 41.9	S15 33.7	143 15.0	S22 18.3	Schedar	349 37.0	N56 37.9
13	77 04.6	340 29.9	01.4	131 08.0	50.6	212 44.7	33.6	158 17.6	18.3	Shaula	96 17.0	S37 06.8
14	92 07.1	355 29.1	01.3	146 09.6	50.5	227 47.5	33.6	173 20.2	18.3	Sirius	258 31.1	S16 44.8
15	107 09.5	10 28.2 ..	01.2	161 11.1 ..	50.5	242 50.2 ..	33.5	188 22.8 ..	18.3	Spica	158 27.5	S11 15.4
16	122 12.0	25 27.4	01.2	176 12.6	50.4	257 53.0	33.4	203 25.4	18.3	Suhail	222 50.1	S43 30.7
17	137 14.5	40 26.6	01.1	191 14.2	50.4	272 55.7	33.3	218 28.0	18.3			
18	152 16.9	55 25.8	N25 01.0	206 15.7	S21 50.3	287 58.5	S15 33.3	233 30.6	S22 18.4	Vega	80 36.4	N38 48.0
19	167 19.4	70 25.0	00.9	221 17.3	50.2	303 01.2	33.2	248 33.2	18.4	Zuben'ubi	137 01.4	S16 07.0
20	182 21.9	85 24.1	00.9	236 18.8	50.2	318 04.0	33.1	263 35.8	18.4			
21	197 24.3	100 23.3 ..	00.8	251 20.4 ..	50.1	333 06.8 ..	33.0	278 38.4 ..	18.4		SHA	Mer.Pass.
22	212 26.8	115 22.5	00.7	266 21.9	50.1	348 09.5	32.9	293 41.0	18.4	Venus	265 27.0	14 17
23	227 29.3	130 21.7	00.6	281 23.5	50.0	3 12.3	32.9	308 43.7	18.4	Mars	54 37.9	4 19
										Jupiter	135 29.1	22 52
Mer. Pass. 7 56.5		v −0.8 d 0.0		v 1.5 d 0.1		v 2.8 d 0.1		v 2.6 d 0.0		Saturn	81 07.7	2 33

UT	SUN GHA	SUN Dec	MOON GHA	v	Dec	d	HP
d h	° ′	° ′	° ′	′	° ′	′	′
22 00	180 50.6	N20 19.8	87 59.0	8.9	N13 32.9	9.5	58.9
01	195 50.5	20.3	102 26.9	9.1	13 23.4	9.6	58.8
02	210 50.5	20.8	116 55.0	9.1	13 13.8	9.6	58.8
03	225 50.4 . .	21.2	131 23.1	9.1	13 04.2	9.7	58.8
04	240 50.4	21.7	145 51.2	9.3	12 54.5	9.8	58.8
05	255 50.3	22.2	160 19.5	9.3	12 44.7	9.8	58.7
06	270 50.3	N20 22.7	174 47.8	9.4	N12 34.9	9.9	58.7
07	285 50.3	23.2	189 16.2	9.4	12 25.0	9.9	58.7
T 08	300 50.2	23.7	203 44.6	9.6	12 15.1	10.1	58.7
U 09	315 50.2 . .	24.2	218 13.2	9.5	12 05.0	10.1	58.6
E 10	330 50.1	24.7	232 41.7	9.7	11 54.9	10.1	58.6
S 11	345 50.1	25.2	247 10.4	9.7	11 44.8	10.2	58.6
D 12	0 50.0	N20 25.7	261 39.1	9.8	N11 34.6	10.2	58.6
A 13	15 50.0	26.2	276 07.9	9.9	11 24.4	10.4	58.5
Y 14	30 49.9	26.7	290 36.8	9.9	11 14.0	10.3	58.5
15	45 49.9 . .	27.1	305 05.7	10.0	11 03.7	10.4	58.5
16	60 49.8	27.6	319 34.7	10.1	10 53.3	10.5	58.5
17	75 49.8	28.1	334 03.8	10.1	10 42.8	10.5	58.5
18	90 49.7	N20 28.6	348 32.9	10.2	N10 32.3	10.6	58.4
19	105 49.7	29.1	3 02.1	10.3	10 21.7	10.6	58.4
20	120 49.6	29.6	17 31.4	10.3	10 11.1	10.7	58.4
21	135 49.6 . .	30.1	32 00.7	10.4	10 00.4	10.7	58.4
22	150 49.5	30.5	46 30.1	10.4	9 49.7	10.8	58.3
23	165 49.5	31.0	60 59.5	10.5	9 38.9	10.8	58.3
23 00	180 49.4	N20 31.5	75 29.0	10.6	N 9 28.1	10.8	58.3
01	195 49.4	32.0	89 58.6	10.6	9 17.3	10.9	58.3
02	210 49.3	32.5	104 28.2	10.7	9 06.4	10.9	58.2
03	225 49.3 . .	32.9	118 57.9	10.8	8 55.5	11.0	58.2
04	240 49.2	33.4	133 27.7	10.8	8 44.5	11.0	58.2
05	255 49.2	33.9	147 57.5	10.8	8 33.5	11.0	58.2
06	270 49.1	N20 34.4	162 27.3	11.0	N 8 22.5	11.1	58.1
W 07	285 49.1	34.9	176 57.3	10.9	8 11.4	11.1	58.1
E 08	300 49.0	35.3	191 27.2	11.1	8 00.3	11.2	58.1
D 09	315 49.0 . .	35.8	205 57.3	11.1	7 49.1	11.2	58.1
N 10	330 48.9	36.3	220 27.4	11.1	7 37.9	11.2	58.0
E 11	345 48.9	36.8	234 57.5	11.2	7 26.7	11.2	58.0
S 12	0 48.8	N20 37.2	249 27.7	11.2	N 7 15.5	11.3	58.0
D 13	15 48.8	37.7	263 57.9	11.3	7 04.2	11.3	58.0
A 14	30 48.7	38.2	278 28.2	11.4	6 52.9	11.3	58.0
Y 15	45 48.6 . .	38.7	292 58.6	11.4	6 41.6	11.3	57.9
16	60 48.6	39.1	307 29.0	11.4	6 30.3	11.4	57.9
17	75 48.5	39.6	321 59.4	11.5	6 18.9	11.4	57.9
18	90 48.5	N20 40.1	336 29.9	11.5	N 6 07.5	11.4	57.9
19	105 48.4	40.5	351 00.4	11.6	5 56.1	11.5	57.8
20	120 48.4	41.0	5 31.0	11.7	5 44.6	11.4	57.8
21	135 48.3 . .	41.5	20 01.7	11.6	5 33.2	11.5	57.8
22	150 48.3	42.0	34 32.3	11.8	5 21.7	11.5	57.8
23	165 48.2	42.4	49 03.1	11.7	5 10.2	11.6	57.7
24 00	180 48.2	N20 42.9	63 33.8	11.8	N 4 58.6	11.5	57.7
01	195 48.1	43.4	78 04.6	11.9	4 47.1	11.5	57.7
02	210 48.0	43.8	92 35.5	11.9	4 35.6	11.6	57.7
03	225 48.0 . .	44.3	107 06.4	11.9	4 24.0	11.6	57.6
04	240 47.9	44.8	121 37.3	12.0	4 12.4	11.6	57.6
05	255 47.9	45.2	136 08.3	12.0	4 00.8	11.6	57.6
06	270 47.8	N20 45.7	150 39.3	12.1	N 3 49.2	11.6	57.6
T 07	285 47.8	46.1	165 10.4	12.0	3 37.6	11.6	57.5
H 08	300 47.7	46.6	179 41.4	12.2	3 26.0	11.7	57.5
U 09	315 47.6 . .	47.1	194 12.6	12.1	3 14.3	11.6	57.5
R 10	330 47.6	47.5	208 43.7	12.2	3 02.7	11.6	57.5
S 11	345 47.5	48.0	223 14.9	12.2	2 51.1	11.7	57.5
D 12	0 47.5	N20 48.4	237 46.1	12.3	N 2 39.4	11.6	57.4
A 13	15 47.4	48.9	252 17.4	12.3	2 27.8	11.7	57.4
Y 14	30 47.4	49.4	266 48.7	12.3	2 16.1	11.7	57.4
15	45 47.3 . .	49.8	281 20.0	12.4	2 04.4	11.6	57.4
16	60 47.2	50.3	295 51.4	12.4	1 52.8	11.7	57.3
17	75 47.2	50.7	310 22.8	12.4	1 41.1	11.7	57.3
18	90 47.1	N20 51.2	324 54.2	12.4	N 1 29.4	11.6	57.3
19	105 47.1	51.7	339 25.6	12.5	1 17.8	11.7	57.3
20	120 47.0	52.1	353 57.1	12.5	1 06.1	11.6	57.2
21	135 46.9 . .	52.6	8 28.6	12.5	0 54.5	11.7	57.2
22	150 46.9	53.0	23 00.1	12.6	0 42.8	11.7	57.2
23	165 46.8	53.5	37 31.7	12.5	N 0 31.1	11.6	57.2
	SD 15.8	d 0.5	SD 16.0		15.8		15.6

Lat.	Twilight Naut.	Twilight Civil	Sunrise	Moonrise 22	Moonrise 23	Moonrise 24	Moonrise 25
°	h m	h m	h m	h m	h m	h m	h m
N 72	▭	▭	▭	09 49	11 51	13 45	15 36
N 70	▭	▭	▭	10 10	12 02	13 49	15 32
68	////	////	00 54	10 27	12 11	13 51	15 29
66	////	////	01 50	10 40	12 18	13 53	15 26
64	////	////	02 23	10 51	12 24	13 55	15 22
62	////	01 15	02 46	11 01	12 30	13 57	15 22
60	////	01 54	03 05	11 09	12 34	13 58	15 20
N 58	////	02 20	03 21	11 16	12 38	13 59	15 18
56	01 08	02 41	03 34	11 22	12 42	14 00	15 17
54	01 43	02 57	03 45	11 27	12 45	14 01	15 16
52	02 08	03 11	03 55	11 32	12 48	14 02	15 15
50	02 27	03 23	04 04	11 37	12 51	14 03	15 14
45	03 03	03 48	04 23	11 46	12 56	14 05	15 12
N 40	03 28	04 07	04 38	11 54	13 01	14 06	15 10
35	03 48	04 23	04 51	12 01	13 05	14 07	15 08
30	04 04	04 36	05 02	12 07	13 09	14 08	15 07
20	04 29	04 58	05 21	12 18	13 15	14 10	15 04
N 10	04 49	05 15	05 38	12 27	13 20	14 12	15 02
0	05 05	05 31	05 53	12 35	13 26	14 14	15 01
S 10	05 20	05 46	06 08	12 44	13 31	14 15	14 59
20	05 34	06 01	06 24	12 53	13 36	14 17	14 57
30	05 48	06 17	06 43	13 03	13 42	14 19	14 55
35	05 55	06 26	06 53	13 09	13 46	14 20	14 53
40	06 02	06 36	07 05	13 16	13 50	14 22	14 52
45	06 11	06 47	07 20	13 23	13 55	14 23	14 50
S 50	06 20	07 00	07 37	13 33	14 00	14 25	14 48
52	06 24	07 06	07 45	13 37	14 03	14 26	14 48
54	06 29	07 13	07 54	13 42	14 05	14 27	14 47
56	06 33	07 20	08 05	13 47	14 08	14 28	14 46
58	06 39	07 29	08 16	13 53	14 12	14 29	14 44
S 60	06 44	07 38	08 30	13 59	14 16	14 30	14 43

Lat.	Sunset	Twilight Civil	Twilight Naut.	Moonset 22	Moonset 23	Moonset 24	Moonset 25
°	h m	h m	h m	h m	h m	h m	h m
N 72	▭	▭	▭	03 14	02 58	02 45	02 33
N 70	▭	▭	▭	02 51	02 45	02 39	02 33
68	23 08	////	////	02 33	02 34	02 34	02 34
66	22 07	////	////	02 18	02 25	02 30	02 34
64	21 33	////	////	02 06	02 18	02 26	02 34
62	21 09	22 43	////	01 56	02 11	02 23	02 34
60	20 50	22 02	////	01 47	02 05	02 21	02 34
N 58	20 34	21 35	////	01 39	02 00	02 18	02 35
56	20 21	21 15	22 50	01 32	01 56	02 16	02 35
54	20 09	20 58	22 12	01 26	01 52	02 14	02 35
52	19 59	20 43	21 47	01 21	01 48	02 13	02 35
50	19 50	20 31	21 28	01 15	01 45	02 11	02 35
45	19 31	20 06	20 52	01 05	01 38	02 07	02 35
N 40	19 16	19 47	20 26	00 55	01 32	02 04	02 35
35	19 03	19 31	20 06	00 47	01 26	02 02	02 36
30	18 51	19 18	19 50	00 41	01 22	02 00	02 36
20	18 32	18 56	19 25	00 28	01 14	01 56	02 36
N 10	18 16	18 38	19 05	00 18	01 06	01 52	02 36
0	18 00	18 22	18 48	00 08	01 00	01 49	02 36
S 10	17 45	18 08	18 33	24 53	00 53	01 45	02 36
20	17 29	17 53	18 20	24 45	00 45	01 42	02 36
30	17 11	17 36	18 06	24 37	00 37	01 37	02 37
35	17 00	17 27	17 58	24 32	00 32	01 35	02 37
40	16 48	17 17	17 51	24 26	00 26	01 32	02 37
45	16 34	17 06	17 42	24 20	00 20	01 29	02 37
S 50	16 16	16 53	17 33	24 12	00 12	01 25	02 37
52	16 08	16 47	17 29	24 08	00 08	01 23	02 37
54	15 59	16 40	17 24	24 04	00 04	01 21	02 37
56	15 48	16 33	17 20	24 00	00 00	01 19	02 37
58	15 37	16 24	17 14	23 55	25 17	01 17	02 37
S 60	15 23	16 15	17 09	23 49	25 14	01 14	02 37

Day	SUN Eqn. of Time 00h	SUN Eqn. of Time 12h	SUN Mer. Pass.	MOON Mer. Pass. Upper	MOON Mer. Pass. Lower	Age	Phase
d	m s	m s	h m	h m	h m	d	%
22	03 22	03 20	11 57	18 47	06 22	07	54
23	03 18	03 15	11 57	19 37	07 13	08	65
24	03 13	03 10	11 57	20 25	08 01	09	75

2018 MAY 25, 26, 27 (FRI., SAT., SUN.)

UT	ARIES GHA	VENUS −3.9 GHA	VENUS Dec	MARS −1·1 GHA	MARS Dec	JUPITER −2·5 GHA	JUPITER Dec	SATURN +0·2 GHA	SATURN Dec	STARS Name	SHA	Dec
25 00	242 31.7	145 20.9	N25 00.6	296 25.0	S21 50.0	18 15.0	S15 32.8	323 46.3	S22 18.4	Acamar	315 16.2	S40 14.0
01	257 34.2	160 20.0	00.5	311 26.6	49.9	33 17.8	32.7	338 48.9	18.4	Achernar	335 24.8	S57 08.6
02	272 36.7	175 19.2	00.4	326 28.2	49.8	48 20.5	32.6	353 51.5	18.4	Acrux	173 05.1	S63 12.2
03	287 39.1	190 18.4 ..	00.3	341 29.7 ..	49.8	63 23.3 ..	32.6	8 54.1 ..	18.4	Adhara	255 10.2	S29 00.1
04	302 41.6	205 17.6	00.2	356 31.3	49.7	78 26.1	32.5	23 56.7	18.4	Aldebaran	290 45.9	N16 32.5
05	317 44.0	220 16.8	00.1	11 32.8	49.7	93 28.8	32.4	38 59.3	18.5			
06	332 46.5	235 15.9	N25 00.0	26 34.4	S21 49.6	108 31.6	S15 32.3	54 01.9	S22 18.5	Alioth	166 17.5	N55 51.9
07	347 49.0	250 15.1	25 00.0	41 35.9	49.5	123 34.3	32.3	69 04.5	18.5	Alkaid	152 55.9	N49 13.6
08	2 51.4	265 14.3	24 59.9	56 37.5	49.5	138 37.1	32.2	84 07.1	18.5	Al Na'ir	27 39.6	S46 52.1
F 09	17 53.9	280 13.5 ..	59.8	71 39.1 ..	49.4	153 39.8 ..	32.1	99 09.7 ..	18.5	Alnilam	275 43.3	S 1 11.7
R 10	32 56.4	295 12.7	59.7	86 40.6	49.4	168 42.6	32.0	114 12.4	18.5	Alphard	217 52.9	S 8 44.4
I 11	47 58.8	310 11.8	59.6	101 42.2	49.3	183 45.3	31.9	129 15.0	18.5			
D 12	63 01.3	325 11.0	N24 59.5	116 43.7	S21 49.3	198 48.1	S15 31.9	144 17.6	S22 18.5	Alphecca	126 07.8	N26 39.3
A 13	78 03.8	340 10.2	59.4	131 45.3	49.2	213 50.9	31.8	159 20.2	18.5	Alpheratz	357 40.2	N29 11.2
Y 14	93 06.2	355 09.4	59.3	146 46.9	49.2	228 53.6	31.7	174 22.8	18.5	Altair	62 04.8	N 8 55.0
15	108 08.7	10 08.6 ..	59.2	161 48.4 ..	49.1	243 56.4 ..	31.6	189 25.4 ..	18.5	Ankaa	353 12.7	S42 12.3
16	123 11.2	25 07.8	59.1	176 50.0	49.0	258 59.1	31.6	204 28.0	18.6	Antares	112 21.8	S26 28.2
17	138 13.6	40 06.9	59.0	191 51.6	49.0	274 01.9	31.5	219 30.6	18.6			
18	153 16.1	55 06.1	N24 58.9	206 53.1	S21 48.9	289 04.6	S15 31.4	234 33.2	S22 18.6	Arcturus	145 52.4	N19 05.4
19	168 18.5	70 05.3	58.8	221 54.7	48.9	304 07.4	31.3	249 35.9	18.6	Atria	107 20.0	S69 03.4
20	183 21.0	85 04.5	58.7	236 56.3	48.8	319 10.1	31.3	264 38.5	18.6	Avior	234 17.0	S59 34.4
21	198 23.5	100 03.7 ..	58.6	251 57.8 ..	48.8	334 12.9 ..	31.2	279 41.1 ..	18.6	Bellatrix	278 28.8	N 6 21.7
22	213 25.9	115 02.9	58.5	266 59.4	48.7	349 15.6	31.1	294 43.7	18.6	Betelgeuse	270 58.0	N 7 24.4
23	228 28.4	130 02.1	58.4	282 01.0	48.7	4 18.4	31.0	309 46.3	18.6			
26 00	243 30.9	145 01.2	N24 58.2	297 02.5	S21 48.6	19 21.1	S15 31.0	324 48.9	S22 18.6	Canopus	263 55.1	S52 42.6
01	258 33.3	160 00.4	58.1	312 04.1	48.6	34 23.9	30.9	339 51.5	18.6	Capella	280 30.0	N46 00.8
02	273 35.8	174 59.6	58.0	327 05.7	48.5	49 26.6	30.8	354 54.1	18.7	Deneb	49 29.0	N45 20.6
03	288 38.3	189 58.8 ..	57.9	342 07.3 ..	48.4	64 29.4 ..	30.7	9 56.7 ..	18.7	Denebola	182 30.2	N14 28.3
04	303 40.7	204 58.0	57.8	357 08.8	48.4	79 32.2	30.7	24 59.4	18.7	Diphda	348 52.8	S17 53.2
05	318 43.2	219 57.2	57.7	12 10.4	48.3	94 34.9	30.6	40 02.0	18.7			
06	333 45.6	234 56.4	N24 57.6	27 12.0	S21 48.3	109 37.7	S15 30.5	55 04.6	S22 18.7	Dubhe	193 47.6	N61 39.4
07	348 48.1	249 55.5	57.4	42 13.6	48.2	124 40.4	30.4	70 07.2	18.7	Elnath	278 08.8	N28 37.2
S 08	3 50.6	264 54.7	57.3	57 15.1	48.2	139 43.2	30.3	85 09.8	18.7	Eltanin	90 44.1	N51 29.2
A 09	18 53.0	279 53.9 ..	57.2	72 16.7 ..	48.1	154 45.9 ..	30.3	100 12.4 ..	18.7	Enif	33 43.8	N 9 57.5
T 10	33 55.5	294 53.1	57.1	87 18.3	48.1	169 48.7	30.2	115 15.0	18.7	Fomalhaut	15 20.4	S29 31.4
U 11	48 58.0	309 52.3	57.0	102 19.9	48.0	184 51.4	30.1	130 17.6	18.7			
R 12	64 00.4	324 51.5	N24 56.8	117 21.5	S21 48.0	199 54.2	S15 30.0	145 20.3	S22 18.7	Gacrux	171 56.8	S57 13.1
D 13	79 02.9	339 50.7	56.7	132 23.0	47.9	214 56.9	30.0	160 22.9	18.8	Gienah	175 48.7	S17 38.7
A 14	94 05.4	354 49.9	56.6	147 24.6	47.9	229 59.7	29.9	175 25.5	18.8	Hadar	148 42.5	S60 27.7
Y 15	109 07.8	9 49.0 ..	56.4	162 26.2 ..	47.8	245 02.4 ..	29.8	190 28.1 ..	18.8	Hamal	327 57.3	N23 32.7
16	124 10.3	24 48.2	56.3	177 27.8	47.8	260 05.2	29.7	205 30.7	18.8	Kaus Aust.	83 39.1	S34 22.3
17	139 12.8	39 47.4	56.2	192 29.4	47.7	275 07.9	29.7	220 33.3	18.8			
18	154 15.2	54 46.6	N24 56.1	207 31.0	S21 47.7	290 10.7	S15 29.6	235 35.9	S22 18.8	Kochab	137 19.1	N74 05.1
19	169 17.7	69 45.8	55.9	222 32.5	47.6	305 13.4	29.5	250 38.6	18.8	Markab	13 35.1	N15 18.1
20	184 20.1	84 45.0	55.8	237 34.1	47.6	320 16.2	29.4	265 41.2	18.8	Menkar	314 11.9	N 4 09.4
21	199 22.6	99 44.2 ..	55.6	252 35.7 ..	47.5	335 18.9 ..	29.4	280 43.8 ..	18.8	Menkent	148 03.3	S36 27.6
22	214 25.1	114 43.4	55.5	267 37.3	47.5	350 21.7	29.3	295 46.4	18.8	Miaplacidus	221 39.2	S69 47.9
23	229 27.5	129 42.6	55.4	282 38.9	47.4	5 24.4	29.2	310 49.0	18.8			
27 00	244 30.0	144 41.8	N24 55.2	297 40.5	S21 47.4	20 27.2	S15 29.1	325 51.6	S22 18.9	Mirfak	308 36.0	N49 55.3
01	259 32.5	159 41.0	55.1	312 42.1	47.3	35 29.9	29.1	340 54.2	18.9	Nunki	75 53.9	S26 16.2
02	274 34.9	174 40.1	55.0	327 43.7	47.3	50 32.7	29.0	355 56.9	18.9	Peacock	53 13.8	S56 40.2
03	289 37.4	189 39.3 ..	54.8	342 45.3 ..	47.2	65 35.4 ..	28.9	10 59.5 ..	18.9	Pollux	243 23.9	N27 58.8
04	304 39.9	204 38.5	54.7	357 46.9	47.2	80 38.2	28.8	26 02.1	18.9	Procyon	244 56.5	N 5 10.5
05	319 42.3	219 37.7	54.5	12 48.5	47.1	95 40.9	28.8	41 04.7	18.9			
06	334 44.8	234 36.9	N24 54.4	27 50.1	S21 47.1	110 43.7	S15 28.7	56 07.3	S22 18.9	Rasalhague	96 03.0	N12 32.9
07	349 47.3	249 36.1	54.2	42 51.6	47.0	125 46.4	28.6	71 09.9	18.9	Regulus	207 40.0	N11 52.6
08	4 49.7	264 35.3	54.1	57 53.2	47.0	140 49.2	28.5	86 12.6	18.9	Rigel	281 09.2	S 8 11.1
S 09	19 52.2	279 34.5 ..	53.9	72 54.8 ..	46.9	155 51.9 ..	28.5	101 15.2 ..	18.9	Rigil Kent.	139 46.6	S60 54.6
U 10	34 54.6	294 33.7	53.8	87 56.4	46.9	170 54.7	28.4	116 17.8	19.0	Sabik	102 08.4	S15 44.7
N 11	49 57.1	309 32.9	53.6	102 58.0	46.8	185 57.4	28.3	131 20.4	19.0			
D 12	64 59.6	324 32.1	N24 53.5	117 59.6	S21 46.8	201 00.1	S15 28.3	146 23.0	S22 19.0	Schedar	349 37.0	N56 37.9
A 13	80 02.0	339 31.3	53.3	133 01.2	46.7	216 02.9	28.2	161 25.6	19.0	Shaula	96 17.0	S37 06.8
Y 14	95 04.5	354 30.5	53.1	148 02.8	46.7	231 05.6	28.1	176 28.2	19.0	Sirius	258 31.1	S16 44.7
15	110 07.0	9 29.7 ..	53.0	163 04.4 ..	46.6	246 08.4 ..	28.0	191 30.9 ..	19.0	Spica	158 27.5	S11 15.4
16	125 09.4	24 28.9	52.8	178 06.0	46.6	261 11.1	28.0	206 33.5	19.0	Suhail	222 50.1	S43 30.7
17	140 11.9	39 28.0	52.7	193 07.7	46.6	276 13.9	27.9	221 36.1	19.0			
18	155 14.4	54 27.2	N24 52.5	208 09.3	S21 46.5	291 16.6	S15 27.8	236 38.7	S22 19.0	Vega	80 36.3	N38 48.0
19	170 16.8	69 26.4	52.3	223 10.9	46.5	306 19.4	27.7	251 41.3	19.0	Zuben'ubi	137 01.4	S16 07.0
20	185 19.3	84 25.6	52.2	238 12.5	46.4	321 22.1	27.7	266 44.0	19.1		SHA	Mer.Pass.
21	200 21.7	99 24.8 ..	52.0	253 14.1 ..	46.4	336 24.9 ..	27.6	281 46.6 ..	19.1		° ′	h m
22	215 24.2	114 24.0	51.9	268 15.7	46.3	351 27.6	27.5	296 49.2	19.1	Venus	261 30.4	14 21
23	230 26.7	129 23.2	51.7	283 17.3	46.3	6 30.4	27.4	311 51.8	19.1	Mars	53 31.7	4 11
Mer.Pass.	h m 7 44.7	v −0.8	d 0.1	v 1.6	d 0.1	v 2.8	d 0.1	v 2.6	d 0.0	Jupiter	135 50.3	22 38
										Saturn	81 18.0	2 20

SUN and MOON

UT	SUN GHA	SUN Dec	MOON GHA	v	MOON Dec	d	HP
d h	° ′	° ′	° ′	′	° ′	′	′
25 00	180 46.8	N20 53.9	52 03.2	12.6	N 0 19.5	11.6	57.2
01	195 46.7	54.4	66 34.8	12.7	N 0 07.9	11.7	57.1
02	210 46.6	54.8	81 06.5	12.6	S 0 03.8	11.6	57.1
03	225 46.5 ..	55.3	95 38.1	12.7	0 15.4	11.6	57.1
04	240 46.5	55.7	110 09.8	12.7	0 27.0	11.6	57.1
05	255 46.5	56.2	124 41.5	12.7	0 38.6	11.6	57.0
06	270 46.4	N20 56.6	139 13.2	12.7	S 0 50.2	11.6	57.0
07	285 46.3	57.1	153 44.9	12.7	1 01.8	11.5	57.0
08	300 46.3	57.5	168 16.6	12.7	1 13.3	11.6	57.0
F 09	315 46.2 ..	58.0	182 48.4	12.8	1 24.9	11.5	56.9
R 10	330 46.1	58.4	197 20.2	12.8	1 36.4	11.5	56.9
I 11	345 46.1	58.9	211 52.0	12.8	1 47.9	11.6	56.9
D 12	0 46.0	N20 59.3	226 23.8	12.8	S 1 59.5	11.4	56.9
A 13	15 46.0	20 59.7	240 55.6	12.8	2 10.9	11.5	56.9
Y 14	30 45.9	21 00.2	255 27.4	12.9	2 22.4	11.5	56.8
15	45 45.8 ..	00.6	269 59.3	12.8	2 33.9	11.4	56.8
16	60 45.8	01.1	284 31.1	12.9	2 45.3	11.4	56.8
17	75 45.7	01.5	299 03.0	12.9	2 56.7	11.4	56.8
18	90 45.6	N21 02.0	313 34.9	12.9	S 3 08.1	11.4	56.7
19	105 45.6	02.4	328 06.8	12.9	3 19.5	11.3	56.7
20	120 45.5	02.8	342 38.7	12.9	3 30.8	11.3	56.7
21	135 45.4 ..	03.3	357 10.6	12.9	3 42.1	11.3	56.7
22	150 45.4	03.7	11 42.5	13.0	3 53.4	11.3	56.7
23	165 45.3	04.2	26 14.5	12.9	4 04.7	11.2	56.6
26 00	180 45.2	N21 04.6	40 46.4	13.0	S 4 15.9	11.2	56.6
01	195 45.2	05.0	55 18.4	12.9	4 27.1	11.2	56.6
02	210 45.1	05.5	69 50.3	13.0	4 38.3	11.2	56.6
03	225 45.0 ..	05.9	84 22.3	12.9	4 49.5	11.1	56.6
04	240 45.0	06.3	98 54.2	13.0	5 00.6	11.1	56.5
05	255 44.9	06.8	113 26.2	12.9	5 11.7	11.0	56.5
06	270 44.8	N21 07.2	127 58.1	13.0	S 5 22.7	11.1	56.5
07	285 44.8	07.6	142 30.1	13.0	5 33.8	11.0	56.5
S 08	300 44.7	08.1	157 02.1	13.0	5 44.8	10.9	56.4
A 09	315 44.6 ..	08.5	171 34.1	12.9	5 55.7	11.0	56.4
T 10	330 44.6	08.9	186 06.0	13.0	6 06.7	10.9	56.4
U 11	345 44.5	09.4	200 38.0	13.0	6 17.6	10.8	56.4
R 12	0 44.4	N21 09.8	215 10.0	12.9	S 6 28.4	10.8	56.4
D 13	15 44.4	10.2	229 41.9	13.0	6 39.2	10.8	56.3
A 14	30 44.3	10.6	244 13.9	13.0	6 50.0	10.7	56.3
Y 15	45 44.2 ..	11.1	258 45.9	12.9	7 00.7	10.7	56.3
16	60 44.2	11.5	273 17.8	13.0	7 11.4	10.7	56.3
17	75 44.1	11.9	287 49.8	12.9	7 22.1	10.6	56.3
18	90 44.0	N21 12.4	302 21.7	12.9	S 7 32.7	10.6	56.2
19	105 44.0	12.8	316 53.7	12.9	7 43.3	10.5	56.2
20	120 43.9	13.2	331 25.6	13.0	7 53.8	10.5	56.2
21	135 43.8 ..	13.6	345 57.6	12.9	8 04.3	10.5	56.2
22	150 43.8	14.0	0 29.5	12.9	8 14.8	10.4	56.2
23	165 43.7	14.5	15 01.4	13.0	8 25.2	10.3	56.1
27 00	180 43.6	N21 14.9	29 33.4	12.9	S 8 35.5	10.4	56.1
01	195 43.5	15.3	44 05.3	12.9	8 45.9	10.2	56.1
02	210 43.5	15.7	58 37.2	12.9	8 56.1	10.2	56.1
03	225 43.4 ..	16.2	73 09.1	12.8	9 06.3	10.2	56.1
04	240 43.3	16.6	87 40.9	12.9	9 16.5	10.1	56.0
05	255 43.3	17.0	102 12.8	12.9	9 26.6	10.1	56.0
06	270 43.2	N21 17.4	116 44.7	12.8	S 9 36.7	10.0	56.0
07	285 43.1	17.8	131 16.5	12.9	9 46.7	10.0	56.0
08	300 43.0	18.2	145 48.4	12.8	9 56.7	9.9	56.0
S 09	315 43.0 ..	18.7	160 20.2	12.9	10 06.6	9.8	55.9
U 10	330 42.9	19.1	174 52.1	12.8	10 16.4	9.8	55.9
N 11	345 42.8	19.5	189 23.9	12.8	10 26.2	9.8	55.9
D 12	0 42.7	N21 19.9	203 55.7	12.7	S10 36.0	9.7	55.9
A 13	15 42.7	20.3	218 27.4	12.8	10 45.7	9.6	55.9
Y 14	30 42.6	20.7	232 59.2	12.8	10 55.3	9.6	55.8
15	45 42.5 ..	21.1	247 31.0	12.7	11 04.9	9.5	55.8
16	60 42.5	21.6	262 02.7	12.8	11 14.4	9.5	55.8
17	75 42.4	22.0	276 34.5	12.7	11 23.9	9.4	55.8
18	90 42.3	N21 22.4	291 06.2	12.7	S11 33.3	9.3	55.8
19	105 42.2	22.8	305 37.9	12.7	11 42.6	9.3	55.7
20	120 42.2	23.2	320 09.6	12.6	11 51.9	9.2	55.7
21	135 42.1 ..	23.6	334 41.2	12.7	12 01.1	9.2	55.7
22	150 42.0	24.0	349 12.9	12.6	12 10.3	9.1	55.7
23	165 41.9	24.4	3 44.5	12.7	S12 19.4	9.0	55.7
	SD 15.8	d 0.4	SD 15.5		15.4		15.2

Twilight, Sunrise and Moonrise

Lat.	Twilight Naut.	Twilight Civil	Sunrise	Moonrise 25	26	27	28
°	h m	h m	h m	h m	h m	h m	h m
N 72	▭	▭	▭	15 36	17 26	19 19	21 23
N 70	▭	▭	▭	15 32	17 14	18 58	20 44
68	////	////	00 18	15 29	17 05	18 41	20 17
66	////	////	01 38	15 26	16 57	18 28	19 57
64	////	////	02 14	15 24	16 51	18 17	19 41
62	////	00 59	02 40	15 22	16 45	18 07	19 28
60	////	01 44	02 59	15 20	16 40	17 59	19 17
N 58	////	02 13	03 16	15 18	16 36	17 52	19 07
56	00 53	02 35	03 30	15 17	16 32	17 46	18 58
54	01 35	02 52	03 41	15 16	16 29	17 41	18 51
52	02 02	03 07	03 52	15 15	16 26	17 36	18 44
50	02 22	03 20	04 01	15 14	16 23	17 31	18 38
45	02 59	03 45	04 21	15 12	16 17	17 22	18 25
N 40	03 25	04 05	04 36	15 10	16 12	17 14	18 14
35	03 46	04 21	04 50	15 08	16 08	17 07	18 05
30	04 02	04 34	05 01	15 07	16 04	17 01	17 57
20	04 28	04 57	05 21	15 04	15 58	16 51	17 43
N 10	04 49	05 15	05 38	15 02	15 52	16 42	17 31
0	05 05	05 31	05 53	15 01	15 47	16 33	17 20
S 10	05 21	05 47	06 09	14 59	15 42	16 25	17 09
20	05 35	06 02	06 26	14 57	15 36	16 16	16 57
30	05 49	06 19	06 44	14 55	15 30	16 06	16 44
35	05 57	06 28	06 55	14 53	15 26	16 00	16 36
40	06 05	06 38	07 08	14 52	15 22	15 54	16 28
45	06 13	06 50	07 23	14 50	15 18	15 46	16 17
S 50	06 23	07 04	07 41	14 48	15 12	15 37	16 05
52	06 27	07 10	07 49	14 48	15 10	15 33	15 59
54	06 32	07 17	07 58	14 47	15 07	15 29	15 53
56	06 37	07 25	08 09	14 46	15 04	15 24	15 46
58	06 43	07 33	08 21	14 44	15 00	15 18	15 38
S 60	06 49	07 43	08 36	14 43	14 57	15 12	15 30

Sunset, Twilight and Moonset

Lat.	Sunset	Twilight Civil	Twilight Naut.	Moonset 25	26	27	28
°	h m	h m	h m	h m	h m	h m	h m
N 72	▭	▭	▭	02 33	02 21	02 08	01 52
N 70	▭	▭	▭	02 33	02 28	02 22	02 15
68	▭	▭	▭	02 34	02 33	02 33	02 33
66	22 20	////	////	02 34	02 38	02 42	02 47
64	21 42	////	////	02 34	02 41	02 49	02 59
62	21 16	23 01	////	02 34	02 45	02 56	03 09
60	20 56	22 12	////	02 34	02 48	03 02	03 18
N 58	20 40	21 43	////	02 35	02 50	03 07	03 26
56	20 26	21 21	23 06	02 35	02 53	03 12	03 33
54	20 14	21 03	22 22	02 35	02 55	03 16	03 39
52	20 03	20 48	21 54	02 35	02 57	03 20	03 44
50	19 54	20 35	21 33	02 35	02 59	03 23	03 49
45	19 34	20 10	20 56	02 35	03 03	03 30	04 00
N 40	19 18	19 50	20 29	02 35	03 06	03 37	04 09
35	19 05	19 34	20 09	02 36	03 09	03 42	04 17
30	18 53	19 20	19 52	02 36	03 11	03 47	04 24
20	18 33	18 57	19 26	02 36	03 15	03 55	04 36
N 10	18 16	18 39	19 06	02 36	03 19	04 02	04 46
0	18 01	18 23	18 49	02 36	03 23	04 09	04 56
S 10	17 45	18 07	18 33	02 36	03 26	04 16	05 06
20	17 28	17 52	18 19	02 36	03 30	04 23	05 16
30	17 10	17 35	18 05	02 37	03 34	04 32	05 28
35	16 59	17 26	17 57	02 37	03 37	04 36	05 35
40	16 46	17 16	17 49	02 37	03 40	04 42	05 45
45	16 31	17 04	17 40	02 37	03 43	04 48	05 52
S 50	16 13	16 50	17 31	02 37	03 47	04 56	06 03
52	16 05	16 44	17 26	02 37	03 49	05 00	06 09
54	15 55	16 37	17 22	02 37	03 51	05 03	06 14
56	15 44	16 29	17 16	02 37	03 53	05 08	06 21
58	15 32	16 20	17 11	02 37	03 56	05 13	06 28
S 60	15 18	16 11	17 05	02 37	03 58	05 18	06 36

SUN and MOON

Day	SUN Eqn. of Time 00h	SUN Eqn. of Time 12h	SUN Mer. Pass.	MOON Mer. Pass. Upper	MOON Mer. Pass. Lower	Age	Phase
d	m s	m s	h m	h m	h m	d	%
25	03 07	03 04	11 57	21 12	08 48	10	83
26	03 01	02 58	11 57	21 58	09 35	11	90
27	02 55	02 51	11 57	22 45	10 21	12	95

UT	ARIES	VENUS −3·9		MARS −1·1		JUPITER −2·5		SATURN +0·2		STARS		
	GHA	GHA	Dec	GHA	Dec	GHA	Dec	GHA	Dec	Name	SHA	Dec
d h	° ′	° ′	° ′	° ′	° ′	° ′	° ′	° ′	° ′		° ′	° ′
28 00	245 29.1	144 22.4	N24 51.5	298 18.9	S21 46.2	21 33.1	S15 27.4	326 54.4	S22 19.1	Acamar	315 16.2	S40 14.0
01	260 31.6	159 21.6	51.3	313 20.5	46.2	36 35.9	27.3	341 57.0	19.1	Achernar	335 24.8	S57 08.6
02	275 34.1	174 20.8	51.2	328 22.1	46.1	51 38.6	27.2	356 59.7	19.1	Acrux	173 05.1	S63 12.2
03	290 36.5	189 20.0 ..	51.0	343 23.7 ..	46.1	66 41.3 ..	27.1	12 02.3 ..	19.1	Adhara	255 10.2	S29 00.1
04	305 39.0	204 19.2	50.8	358 25.3	46.1	81 44.1	27.1	27 04.9	19.1	Aldebaran	290 45.9	N16 32.5
05	320 41.5	219 18.4	50.7	13 27.0	46.0	96 46.8	27.0	42 07.5	19.1			
06	335 43.9	234 17.6	N24 50.5	28 28.6	S21 46.0	111 49.6	S15 26.9	57 10.1	S22 19.1	Alioth	166 17.5	N55 51.9
07	350 46.4	249 16.8	50.3	43 30.2	45.9	126 52.3	26.8	72 12.7	19.2	Alkaid	152 55.9	N49 13.6
08	5 48.9	264 16.0	50.1	58 31.8	45.9	141 55.1	26.8	87 15.4	19.2	Al Na'ir	27 39.5	S46 52.1
M 09	20 51.3	279 15.2 ..	49.9	73 33.4 ..	45.8	156 57.8 ..	26.7	102 18.0 ..	19.2	Alnilam	275 43.3	S 1 11.7
O 10	35 53.8	294 14.4	49.8	88 35.0	45.8	172 00.6	26.6	117 20.6	19.2	Alphard	217 52.9	S 8 44.4
N 11	50 56.2	309 13.6	49.6	103 36.7	45.8	187 03.3	26.6	132 23.2	19.2			
D 12	65 58.7	324 12.8	N24 49.4	118 38.3	S21 45.7	202 06.0	S15 26.5	147 25.8	S22 19.2	Alphecca	126 07.8	N26 39.4
A 13	81 01.2	339 12.0	49.2	133 39.9	45.7	217 08.8	26.4	162 28.5	19.2	Alpheratz	357 40.2	N29 11.2
Y 14	96 03.6	354 11.2	49.0	148 41.5	45.6	232 11.5	26.3	177 31.1	19.2	Altair	62 04.8	N 8 55.0
15	111 06.1	9 10.4 ..	48.8	163 43.1 ..	45.6	247 14.3 ..	26.3	192 33.7 ..	19.2	Ankaa	353 12.7	S42 12.3
16	126 08.6	24 09.6	48.6	178 44.8	45.5	262 17.0	26.2	207 36.3	19.2	Antares	112 21.8	S26 28.2
17	141 11.0	39 08.8	48.5	193 46.4	45.5	277 19.8	26.1	222 38.9	19.3			
18	156 13.5	54 08.0	N24 48.3	208 48.0	S21 45.5	292 22.5	S15 26.0	237 41.6	S22 19.3	Arcturus	145 52.4	N19 05.4
19	171 16.0	69 07.2	48.1	223 49.6	45.4	307 25.2	26.0	252 44.2	19.3	Atria	107 20.0	S69 03.4
20	186 18.4	84 06.4	47.9	238 51.3	45.4	322 28.0	25.9	267 46.8	19.3	Avior	234 17.0	S59 34.4
21	201 20.9	99 05.6 ..	47.7	253 52.9 ..	45.3	337 30.7 ..	25.8	282 49.4 ..	19.3	Bellatrix	278 28.8	N 6 21.7
22	216 23.4	114 04.8	47.5	268 54.5	45.3	352 33.5	25.8	297 52.0	19.3	Betelgeuse	270 58.0	N 7 24.4
23	231 25.8	129 04.1	47.3	283 56.1	45.3	7 36.2	25.7	312 54.7	19.3			
29 00	246 28.3	144 03.3	N24 47.1	298 57.8	S21 45.2	22 38.9	S15 25.6	327 57.3	S22 19.3	Canopus	263 55.2	S52 42.6
01	261 30.7	159 02.5	46.9	313 59.4	45.2	37 41.7	25.5	342 59.9	19.3	Capella	280 30.0	N46 00.8
02	276 33.2	174 01.7	46.7	329 01.0	45.1	52 44.4	25.5	358 02.5	19.3	Deneb	49 29.0	N45 20.6
03	291 35.7	189 00.9 ..	46.5	344 02.7 ..	45.1	67 47.2 ..	25.4	13 05.1 ..	19.4	Denebola	182 30.2	N14 28.3
04	306 38.1	204 00.1	46.3	359 04.3	45.1	82 49.9	25.3	28 07.8	19.4	Diphda	348 52.7	S17 53.2
05	321 40.6	218 59.3	46.1	14 05.9	45.0	97 52.7	25.2	43 10.4	19.4			
06	336 43.1	233 58.5	N24 45.9	29 07.6	S21 45.0	112 55.4	S15 25.2	58 13.0	S22 19.4	Dubhe	193 47.6	N61 39.4
07	351 45.5	248 57.7	45.7	44 09.2	45.0	127 58.1	25.1	73 15.6	19.4	Elnath	278 08.8	N28 37.2
T 08	6 48.0	263 56.9	45.5	59 10.8	44.9	143 00.9	25.0	88 18.2	19.4	Eltanin	90 44.1	N51 29.2
U 09	21 50.5	278 56.1 ..	45.3	74 12.5 ..	44.9	158 03.6 ..	25.0	103 20.9 ..	19.4	Enif	33 43.8	N 9 57.5
E 10	36 52.9	293 55.3	45.0	89 14.1	44.8	173 06.4	24.9	118 23.5	19.4	Fomalhaut	15 20.4	S29 31.4
S 11	51 55.4	308 54.5	44.8	104 15.8	44.8	188 09.1	24.8	133 26.1	19.4			
D 12	66 57.8	323 53.7	N24 44.6	119 17.4	S21 44.8	203 11.8	S15 24.7	148 28.7	S22 19.4	Gacrux	171 56.8	S57 13.1
A 13	82 00.3	338 52.9	44.4	134 19.0	44.7	218 14.6	24.7	163 31.3	19.5	Gienah	175 48.7	S17 38.7
Y 14	97 02.8	353 52.2	44.2	149 20.7	44.7	233 17.3	24.6	178 34.0	19.5	Hadar	148 42.5	S60 27.7
15	112 05.2	8 51.4 ..	44.0	164 22.3 ..	44.7	248 20.0 ..	24.5	193 36.6 ..	19.5	Hamal	327 57.3	N23 32.7
16	127 07.7	23 50.6	43.8	179 24.0	44.6	263 22.8	24.4	208 39.2	19.5	Kaus Aust.	83 39.0	S34 22.3
17	142 10.2	38 49.8	43.5	194 25.6	44.6	278 25.5	24.4	223 41.8	19.5			
18	157 12.6	53 49.0	N24 43.3	209 27.3	S21 44.5	293 28.3	S15 24.3	238 44.5	S22 19.5	Kochab	137 19.1	N74 05.1
19	172 15.1	68 48.2	43.1	224 28.9	44.5	308 31.0	24.2	253 47.1	19.5	Markab	13 35.0	N15 18.1
20	187 17.6	83 47.4	42.9	239 30.5	44.4	323 33.7	24.2	268 49.7	19.5	Menkar	314 11.9	N 4 09.5
21	202 20.0	98 46.6 ..	42.7	254 32.2 ..	44.4	338 36.5 ..	24.1	283 52.3 ..	19.5	Menkent	148 03.3	S36 27.6
22	217 22.5	113 45.8	42.4	269 33.8	44.4	353 39.2	24.0	298 55.0	19.5	Miaplacidus	221 39.3	S69 47.9
23	232 25.0	128 45.0	42.2	284 35.5	44.4	8 42.0	23.9	313 57.6	19.6			
30 00	247 27.4	143 44.3	N24 42.0	299 37.1	S21 44.3	23 44.7	S15 23.9	329 00.2	S22 19.6	Mirfak	308 36.0	N49 55.3
01	262 29.9	158 43.5	41.8	314 38.8	44.3	38 47.4	23.8	344 02.8	19.6	Nunki	75 53.9	S26 16.2
02	277 32.3	173 42.7	41.5	329 40.4	44.3	53 50.2	23.7	359 05.4	19.6	Peacock	53 13.7	S56 40.2
03	292 34.8	188 41.9 ..	41.3	344 42.1 ..	44.2	68 52.9 ..	23.7	14 08.1 ..	19.6	Pollux	243 24.0	N27 58.8
04	307 37.3	203 41.1	41.1	359 43.7	44.2	83 55.6	23.6	29 10.7	19.6	Procyon	244 56.5	N 5 10.5
05	322 39.7	218 40.3	40.8	14 45.4	44.2	98 58.4	23.5	44 13.3	19.6			
06	337 42.2	233 39.5	N24 40.6	29 47.1	S21 44.1	114 01.1	S15 23.4	59 15.9	S22 19.6	Rasalhague	96 03.0	N12 32.9
W 07	352 44.7	248 38.8	40.4	44 48.7	44.1	129 03.8	23.4	74 18.6	19.6	Regulus	207 40.0	N11 52.6
E 08	7 47.1	263 38.0	40.1	59 50.4	44.1	144 06.6	23.3	89 21.2	19.6	Rigel	281 09.2	S 8 11.1
D 09	22 49.6	278 37.2 ..	39.9	74 52.0 ..	44.0	159 09.3 ..	23.2	104 23.8 ..	19.7	Rigil Kent.	139 46.6	S60 54.6
N 10	37 52.1	293 36.4	39.6	89 53.7	44.0	174 12.1	23.2	119 26.4	19.7	Sabik	102 08.4	S15 44.7
E 11	52 54.5	308 35.6	39.4	104 55.3	44.0	189 14.8	23.1	134 29.1	19.7			
S 12	67 57.0	323 34.8	N24 39.2	119 57.0	S21 43.9	204 17.5	S15 23.0	149 31.7	S22 19.7	Schedar	349 37.0	N56 37.9
D 13	82 59.5	338 34.1	38.9	134 58.7	43.9	219 20.3	23.0	164 34.3	19.7	Shaula	96 17.0	S37 06.8
A 14	98 01.9	353 33.3	38.7	150 00.3	43.9	234 23.0	22.9	179 36.9	19.7	Sirius	258 31.1	S16 44.7
Y 15	113 04.4	8 32.5 ..	38.4	165 02.0 ..	43.8	249 25.7 ..	22.8	194 39.6 ..	19.7	Spica	158 27.5	S11 15.4
16	128 06.8	23 31.7	38.2	180 03.7	43.8	264 28.5	22.7	209 42.2	19.7	Suhail	222 50.1	S43 30.7
17	143 09.3	38 30.9	37.9	195 05.3	43.8	279 31.2	22.7	224 44.8	19.7			
18	158 11.8	53 30.1	N24 37.7	210 07.0	S21 43.8	294 33.9	S15 22.6	239 47.4	S22 19.7	Vega	80 36.3	N38 48.0
19	173 14.2	68 29.4	37.4	225 08.6	43.7	309 36.7	22.5	254 50.1	19.8	Zuben'ubi	137 01.4	S16 07.0
20	188 16.7	83 28.6	37.2	240 10.3	43.7	324 39.4	22.5	269 52.7	19.8		SHA	Mer. Pass.
21	203 19.2	98 27.8 ..	36.9	255 12.0 ..	43.7	339 42.1 ..	22.4	284 55.3 ..	19.8		° ′	h m
22	218 21.6	113 27.0	36.7	270 13.7	43.6	354 44.9	22.3	299 57.9	19.8	Venus	257 35.0	14 25
23	233 24.1	128 26.2	36.4	285 15.3	43.6	9 47.6	22.2	315 00.6	19.8	Mars	52 29.5	4 04
Mer. Pass.	h m 7 32.9	v −0.8 d 0.2		v 1.6 d 0.0		v 2.7 d 0.1		v 2.6 d 0.0		Jupiter	136 10.7	22 25
										Saturn	81 29.0	2 08

SUN / MOON

UT	SUN GHA	SUN Dec	MOON GHA	v	MOON Dec	d	HP
28 00	180 41.9	N21 24.8	18 16.2	12.6	S12 28.4	9.0	55.6
01	195 41.8	25.2	32 47.8	12.6	12 37.4	8.9	55.6
02	210 41.7	25.6	47 19.4	12.5	12 46.3	8.9	55.6
03	225 41.6 ..	26.0	61 50.9	12.6	12 55.2	8.8	55.6
04	240 41.6	26.5	76 22.5	12.5	13 04.0	8.7	55.6
05	255 41.5	26.9	90 54.0	12.6	13 12.7	8.6	55.6
M 06	270 41.4	N21 27.3	105 25.6	12.5	S13 21.3	8.6	55.5
O 07	285 41.3	27.7	119 57.1	12.5	13 29.9	8.5	55.5
N 08	300 41.3	28.1	134 28.6	12.4	13 38.4	8.4	55.5
D 09	315 41.2 ..	28.5	149 00.0	12.5	13 46.8	8.4	55.5
A 10	330 41.1	28.9	163 31.5	12.4	13 55.2	8.3	55.5
Y 11	345 41.0	29.3	178 02.9	12.4	14 03.5	8.3	55.4
12	0 40.9	N21 29.7	192 34.3	12.4	S14 11.8	8.1	55.4
13	15 40.9	30.1	207 05.7	12.4	14 19.9	8.1	55.4
14	30 40.8	30.5	221 37.1	12.4	14 28.0	8.0	55.4
15	45 40.7 ..	30.9	236 08.5	12.3	14 36.0	8.0	55.4
16	60 40.6	31.3	250 39.8	12.4	14 44.0	7.8	55.4
17	75 40.6	31.6	265 11.2	12.3	14 51.8	7.8	55.3
18	90 40.5	N21 32.0	279 42.5	12.2	S14 59.6	7.7	55.3
19	105 40.4	32.4	294 13.7	12.3	15 07.3	7.7	55.3
20	120 40.3	32.8	308 45.0	12.3	15 15.0	7.5	55.3
21	135 40.2 ..	33.2	323 16.3	12.2	15 22.5	7.5	55.3
22	150 40.2	33.6	337 47.5	12.2	15 30.0	7.5	55.2
23	165 40.1	34.0	352 18.7	12.2	15 37.5	7.3	55.2
29 00	180 40.0	N21 34.4	6 49.9	12.2	S15 44.8	7.2	55.2
01	195 39.9	34.8	21 21.1	12.1	15 52.0	7.2	55.2
02	210 39.8	35.2	35 52.2	12.2	15 59.2	7.1	55.2
03	225 39.8 ..	35.6	50 23.4	12.1	16 06.3	7.0	55.2
04	240 39.7	36.0	64 54.5	12.1	16 13.3	7.0	55.1
05	255 39.6	36.3	79 25.6	12.1	16 20.3	6.8	55.1
T 06	270 39.5	N21 36.7	93 56.7	12.0	S16 27.1	6.8	55.1
U 07	285 39.4	37.1	108 27.7	12.1	16 33.9	6.7	55.1
E 08	300 39.4	37.5	122 58.8	12.0	16 40.6	6.6	55.1
S 09	315 39.3 ..	37.9	137 29.8	12.0	16 47.2	6.6	55.1
D 10	330 39.2	38.3	152 00.8	12.0	16 53.8	6.4	55.0
A 11	345 39.1	38.7	166 31.8	12.0	17 00.2	6.4	55.0
Y 12	0 39.0	N21 39.0	181 02.8	11.9	S17 06.6	6.2	55.0
13	15 38.9	39.4	195 33.7	12.0	17 12.8	6.2	55.0
14	30 38.9	39.8	210 04.7	11.9	17 19.0	6.1	55.0
15	45 38.8 ..	40.2	224 35.6	11.9	17 25.1	6.1	55.0
16	60 38.7	40.6	239 06.5	11.9	17 31.2	5.9	55.0
17	75 38.6	40.9	253 37.4	11.9	17 37.1	5.8	54.9
18	90 38.5	N21 41.3	268 08.3	11.8	S17 42.9	5.8	54.9
19	105 38.4	41.7	282 39.1	11.9	17 48.7	5.7	54.9
20	120 38.4	42.1	297 10.0	11.8	17 54.4	5.6	54.9
21	135 38.3 ..	42.5	311 40.8	11.8	18 00.0	5.5	54.9
22	150 38.2	42.8	326 11.6	11.8	18 05.5	5.4	54.9
23	165 38.1	43.2	340 42.4	11.8	18 10.9	5.3	54.8
30 00	180 38.0	N21 43.6	355 13.2	11.7	S18 16.2	5.2	54.8
01	195 37.9	44.0	9 43.9	11.8	18 21.4	5.2	54.8
02	210 37.9	44.3	24 14.7	11.7	18 26.6	5.0	54.8
03	225 37.8 ..	44.7	38 45.4	11.7	18 31.6	5.0	54.8
04	240 37.7	45.1	53 16.1	11.8	18 36.6	4.8	54.8
05	255 37.6	45.5	67 46.9	11.7	18 41.4	4.8	54.8
W 06	270 37.5	N21 45.8	82 17.6	11.6	S18 46.2	4.7	54.7
E 07	285 37.4	46.2	96 48.2	11.7	18 50.9	4.6	54.7
D 08	300 37.3	46.6	111 18.9	11.7	18 55.5	4.5	54.7
N 09	315 37.3 ..	46.9	125 49.6	11.6	19 00.0	4.4	54.7
E 10	330 37.2	47.3	140 20.2	11.6	19 04.4	4.3	54.7
S 11	345 37.1	47.7	154 50.8	11.7	19 08.7	4.2	54.7
D 12	0 37.0	N21 48.0	169 21.5	11.6	S19 12.9	4.2	54.7
A 13	15 36.9	48.4	183 52.1	11.6	19 17.1	4.0	54.6
Y 14	30 36.8	48.8	198 22.7	11.6	19 21.1	4.0	54.6
15	45 36.7 ..	49.1	212 53.3	11.6	19 25.1	3.8	54.6
16	60 36.6	49.5	227 23.9	11.5	19 28.9	3.8	54.6
17	75 36.6	49.9	241 54.4	11.6	19 32.7	3.6	54.6
18	90 36.5	N21 50.2	256 25.0	11.6	S19 36.3	3.6	54.6
19	105 36.4	50.6	270 55.6	11.5	19 39.9	3.4	54.6
20	120 36.3	51.0	285 26.1	11.6	19 43.3	3.4	54.6
21	135 36.2 ..	51.3	299 56.7	11.5	19 46.7	3.3	54.5
22	150 36.1	51.7	314 27.2	11.5	19 50.0	3.2	54.5
23	165 36.0	52.0	328 57.7	11.6	S19 53.2	3.1	54.5
	SD 15.8	d 0.4	SD 15.1		15.0		14.9

Twilight / Sunrise / Moonrise

Lat.	Naut.	Civil	Sunrise	Moonrise 28	29	30	31
N 72	▢	▢	▢	21 23	■	■	■
N 70	▢	▢	▢	20 44	22 36	■	■
68	▢	▢	▢	20 17	21 52	23 22	24 34
66	////	////	01 25	19 57	21 24	22 42	23 47
64	////	////	02 06	19 41	21 02	22 15	23 16
62	////	00 39	02 33	19 28	20 44	21 54	22 53
60	////	01 35	02 54	19 17	20 30	21 37	22 35
N 58	////	02 07	03 11	19 07	20 18	21 23	22 19
56	00 36	02 29	03 26	18 58	20 07	21 10	22 06
54	01 27	02 48	03 38	18 51	19 58	21 00	21 55
52	01 56	03 03	03 49	18 44	19 49	20 50	21 45
50	02 17	03 16	03 58	18 38	19 42	20 42	21 36
45	02 56	03 43	04 19	18 25	19 26	20 24	21 17
N 40	03 23	04 03	04 35	18 14	19 13	20 09	21 02
35	03 44	04 19	04 48	18 05	19 02	19 57	20 49
30	04 01	04 33	05 00	17 57	18 52	19 46	20 37
20	04 28	04 56	05 20	17 43	18 36	19 28	20 18
N 10	04 48	05 15	05 38	17 31	18 22	19 12	20 01
0	05 06	05 32	05 54	17 20	18 08	18 57	19 45
S 10	05 21	05 47	06 10	17 09	17 55	18 42	19 30
20	05 36	06 03	06 27	16 57	17 41	18 26	19 13
30	05 51	06 20	06 46	16 44	17 24	18 08	18 54
35	05 58	06 30	06 57	16 36	17 15	17 57	18 42
40	06 07	06 40	07 10	16 28	17 04	17 45	18 29
45	06 16	06 52	07 25	16 17	16 52	17 31	18 14
S 50	06 26	07 07	07 44	16 05	16 37	17 13	17 56
52	06 30	07 13	07 53	15 59	16 30	17 05	17 47
54	06 35	07 20	08 02	15 53	16 22	16 56	17 37
56	06 41	07 28	08 14	15 46	16 13	16 46	17 26
58	06 46	07 37	08 26	15 38	16 03	16 34	17 13
S 60	06 53	07 47	08 41	15 30	15 52	16 21	16 58

Sunset / Twilight / Moonset

Lat.	Sunset	Civil	Naut.	Moonset 28	29	30	31
N 72	▢	▢	▢	01 52	01 27	■	■
N 70	▢	▢	▢	02 15	02 07	01 54	■
68	▢	▢	▢	02 33	02 34	02 39	02 50
66	22 33	////	////	02 47	02 55	03 08	03 30
64	21 51	////	////	02 59	03 12	03 31	03 58
62	21 23	23 23	////	03 09	03 26	03 48	04 19
60	21 02	22 22	////	03 18	03 38	04 03	04 36
N 58	20 45	21 50	////	03 26	03 48	04 16	04 51
56	20 30	21 27	23 27	03 33	03 57	04 27	05 03
54	20 18	21 08	22 31	03 39	04 05	04 37	05 14
52	20 07	20 53	22 01	03 44	04 12	04 45	05 24
50	19 57	20 39	21 39	03 49	04 19	04 53	05 32
45	19 37	20 13	21 00	04 00	04 33	05 09	05 51
N 40	19 20	19 52	20 33	04 09	04 44	05 23	06 06
35	19 07	19 36	20 11	04 17	04 54	05 35	06 18
30	18 55	19 22	19 54	04 24	05 03	05 45	06 29
20	18 35	18 59	19 28	04 36	05 18	06 02	06 48
N 10	18 17	18 40	19 07	04 46	05 31	06 17	07 05
0	18 01	18 23	18 49	04 56	05 43	06 31	07 20
S 10	17 45	18 08	18 34	05 06	05 56	06 46	07 35
20	17 28	17 52	18 19	05 16	06 09	07 01	07 52
30	17 09	17 35	18 04	05 28	06 24	07 18	08 11
35	16 57	17 25	17 56	05 35	06 33	07 29	08 22
40	16 44	17 14	17 48	05 43	06 43	07 40	08 35
45	16 29	17 02	17 39	05 52	06 55	07 54	08 50
S 50	16 11	16 48	17 29	06 03	07 09	08 11	09 08
52	16 02	16 41	17 24	06 09	07 16	08 19	09 17
54	15 52	16 34	17 19	06 14	07 23	08 28	09 27
56	15 41	16 26	17 14	06 21	07 31	08 38	09 38
58	15 28	16 17	17 08	06 28	07 41	08 49	09 50
S 60	15 13	16 07	17 02	06 36	07 52	09 02	10 05

SUN / MOON

Day	Eqn. of Time 00h	12h	Mer. Pass.	Mer. Pass. Upper	Lower	Age	Phase
d	m s	m s	h m	h m	h m	d	%
28	02 48	02 44	11 57	23 32	11 08	13	99
29	02 40	02 36	11 57	24 20	11 56	14	100
30	02 32	02 28	11 58	00 20	12 44	15	99

UT	ARIES GHA	VENUS −3.9 GHA	Dec	MARS −1.2 GHA	Dec	JUPITER −2.5 GHA	Dec	SATURN +0.2 GHA	Dec	Name	SHA	Dec
31 00	248 26.6	143 25.5	N24 36.2	300 17.0	S21 43.6	24 50.3	S15 22.2	330 03.2	S22 19.8	Acamar	315 16.2	S40 14.0
01	263 29.0	158 24.7	35.9	315 18.7	43.5	39 53.1	22.1	345 05.8	19.8	Achernar	335 24.8	S57 08.6
02	278 31.5	173 23.9	35.7	330 20.3	43.5	54 55.8	22.0	0 08.4	19.8	Acrux	173 05.1	S63 12.2
03	293 34.0	188 23.1 ..	35.4	345 22.0 ..	43.5	69 58.5 ..	22.0	15 11.1 ..	19.8	Adhara	255 10.2	S29 00.1
04	308 36.4	203 22.3	35.1	0 23.7	43.5	85 01.3	21.9	30 13.7	19.8	Aldebaran	290 45.9	N16 32.5
05	323 38.9	218 21.6	34.9	15 25.4	43.4	100 04.0	21.8	45 16.3	19.9			
T 06	338 41.3	233 20.8	N24 34.6	30 27.0	S21 43.4	115 06.7	S15 21.8	60 18.9	S22 19.9	Alioth	166 17.5	N55 51.9
H 07	353 43.8	248 20.0	34.4	45 28.7	43.4	130 09.5	21.7	75 21.6	19.9	Alkaid	152 55.9	N49 13.6
U 08	8 46.3	263 19.2	34.1	60 30.4	43.4	145 12.2	21.6	90 24.2	19.9	Al Na'ir	27 39.5	S46 52.1
R 09	23 48.7	278 18.5 ..	33.8	75 32.1 ..	43.3	160 14.9 ..	21.6	105 26.8 ..	19.9	Alnilam	275 43.3	S 1 11.7
S 10	38 51.2	293 17.7	33.6	90 33.7	43.3	175 17.7	21.5	120 29.4	19.9	Alphard	217 52.9	S 8 44.4
D 11	53 53.7	308 16.9	33.3	105 35.4	43.3	190 20.4	21.4	135 32.1	19.9			
A 12	68 56.1	323 16.1	N24 33.0	120 37.1	S21 43.2	205 23.1	S15 21.3	150 34.7	S22 19.9	Alphecca	126 07.8	N26 39.4
Y 13	83 58.6	338 15.4	32.7	135 38.8	43.2	220 25.9	21.3	165 37.3	19.9	Alpheratz	357 40.1	N29 11.2
14	99 01.1	353 14.6	32.5	150 40.5	43.2	235 28.6	21.2	180 40.0	19.9	Altair	62 04.7	N 8 55.1
15	114 03.5	8 13.8 ..	32.2	165 42.2 ..	43.2	250 31.3 ..	21.1	195 42.6 ..	20.0	Ankaa	353 12.6	S42 12.3
16	129 06.0	23 13.0	31.9	180 43.8	43.1	265 34.0	21.1	210 45.2	20.0	Antares	112 21.8	S26 28.2
17	144 08.5	38 12.3	31.6	195 45.5	43.1	280 36.8	21.0	225 47.8	20.0			
18	159 10.9	53 11.5	N24 31.4	210 47.2	S21 43.1	295 39.5	S15 20.9	240 50.5	S22 20.0	Arcturus	145 52.4	N19 05.4
19	174 13.4	68 10.7	31.1	225 48.9	43.1	310 42.2	20.9	255 53.1	20.0	Atria	107 20.0	S69 03.4
20	189 15.8	83 10.0	30.8	240 50.6	43.0	325 45.0	20.8	270 55.7	20.0	Avior	234 17.0	S59 34.4
21	204 18.3	98 09.2 ..	30.5	255 52.3 ..	43.0	340 47.7 ..	20.7	285 58.3 ..	20.0	Bellatrix	278 28.8	N 6 21.7
22	219 20.8	113 08.4	30.3	270 54.0	43.0	355 50.4	20.7	301 01.0	20.0	Betelgeuse	270 58.0	N 7 24.4
23	234 23.2	128 07.6	30.0	285 55.7	43.0	10 53.1	20.6	316 03.6	20.0			
1 00	249 25.7	143 06.9	N24 29.7	300 57.3	S21 43.0	25 55.9	S15 20.5	331 06.2	S22 20.1	Canopus	263 55.2	S52 42.6
01	264 28.2	158 06.1	29.4	315 59.0	42.9	40 58.6	20.4	346 08.9	20.1	Capella	280 30.0	N46 00.8
02	279 30.6	173 05.3	29.1	331 00.7	42.9	56 01.3	20.4	1 11.5	20.1	Deneb	49 28.9	N45 20.6
03	294 33.1	188 04.6 ..	28.8	346 02.4 ..	42.9	71 04.1 ..	20.3	16 14.1 ..	20.1	Denebola	182 30.2	N14 28.3
04	309 35.6	203 03.8	28.5	1 04.1	42.9	86 06.8	20.2	31 16.7	20.1	Diphda	348 52.7	S17 53.2
05	324 38.0	218 03.0	28.2	16 05.8	42.8	101 09.5	20.2	46 19.4	20.1			
F 06	339 40.5	233 02.3	N24 28.0	31 07.5	S21 42.8	116 12.2	S15 20.1	61 22.0	S22 20.1	Dubhe	193 47.7	N61 39.4
R 07	354 42.9	248 01.5	27.7	46 09.2	42.8	131 15.0	20.0	76 24.6	20.1	Elnath	278 08.8	N28 37.2
I 08	9 45.4	263 00.7	27.4	61 10.9	42.8	146 17.7	20.0	91 27.3	20.1	Eltanin	90 44.1	N51 29.2
D 09	24 47.9	277 59.9 ..	27.1	76 12.6 ..	42.8	161 20.4 ..	19.9	106 29.9 ..	20.1	Enif	33 43.7	N 9 57.5
A 10	39 50.3	292 59.2	26.8	91 14.3	42.7	176 23.2	19.8	121 32.5	20.2	Fomalhaut	15 20.3	S29 31.4
Y 11	54 52.8	307 58.4	26.5	106 16.0	42.7	191 25.9	19.8	136 35.1	20.2			
12	69 55.3	322 57.7	N24 26.2	121 17.7	S21 42.7	206 28.6	S15 19.7	151 37.8	S22 20.2	Gacrux	171 56.8	S57 13.1
13	84 57.7	337 56.9	25.9	136 19.4	42.7	221 31.3	19.6	166 40.4	20.2	Gienah	175 48.7	S17 38.7
14	100 00.2	352 56.1	25.6	151 21.1	42.7	236 34.1	19.6	181 43.0	20.2	Hadar	148 42.5	S60 27.7
15	115 02.7	7 55.4 ..	25.3	166 22.8 ..	42.6	251 36.8 ..	19.5	196 45.7 ..	20.2	Hamal	327 57.2	N23 32.7
16	130 05.1	22 54.6	25.0	181 24.5	42.6	266 39.5	19.4	211 48.3	20.2	Kaus Aust.	83 39.0	S34 22.3
17	145 07.6	37 53.8	24.7	196 26.2	42.6	281 42.2	19.4	226 50.9	20.2			
18	160 10.1	52 53.1	N24 24.4	211 28.0	S21 42.6	296 45.0	S15 19.3	241 53.6	S22 20.2	Kochab	137 19.2	N74 05.1
19	175 12.5	67 52.3	24.1	226 29.7	42.6	311 47.7	19.2	256 56.2	20.2	Markab	13 35.0	N15 18.1
20	190 15.0	82 51.5	23.8	241 31.4	42.5	326 50.4	19.1	271 58.8	20.3	Menkar	314 11.9	N 4 09.5
21	205 17.4	97 50.8 ..	23.4	256 33.1 ..	42.5	341 53.1 ..	19.1	287 01.4 ..	20.3	Menkent	148 03.3	S36 27.6
22	220 19.9	112 50.0	23.1	271 34.8	42.5	356 55.9	19.0	302 04.1	20.3	Miaplacidus	221 39.3	S69 47.9
23	235 22.4	127 49.3	22.8	286 36.5	42.5	11 58.6	18.9	317 06.7	20.3			
2 00	250 24.8	142 48.5	N24 22.5	301 38.2	S21 42.5	27 01.3	S15 18.9	332 09.3	S22 20.3	Mirfak	308 36.0	N49 55.3
01	265 27.3	157 47.7	22.2	316 39.9	42.5	42 04.0	18.8	347 12.0	20.3	Nunki	75 53.9	S26 16.2
02	280 29.8	172 47.0	21.9	331 41.7	42.4	57 06.8	18.7	2 14.6	20.3	Peacock	53 13.7	S56 40.2
03	295 32.2	187 46.2 ..	21.6	346 43.4 ..	42.4	72 09.5 ..	18.7	17 17.2 ..	20.3	Pollux	243 24.0	N27 58.8
04	310 34.7	202 45.5	21.3	1 45.1	42.4	87 12.2	18.6	32 19.9	20.3	Procyon	244 56.5	N 5 10.5
05	325 37.2	217 44.7	20.9	16 46.8	42.4	102 14.9	18.5	47 22.5	20.4			
S 06	340 39.6	232 43.9	N24 20.6	31 48.5	S21 42.4	117 17.6	S15 18.5	62 25.1	S22 20.4	Rasalhague	96 03.0	N12 32.9
A 07	355 42.1	247 43.2	20.3	46 50.2	42.4	132 20.4	18.4	77 27.8	20.4	Regulus	207 40.0	N11 52.7
T 08	10 44.6	262 42.4	20.0	61 52.0	42.3	147 23.1	18.3	92 30.4	20.4	Rigel	281 09.2	S 8 11.1
U 09	25 47.0	277 41.7 ..	19.7	76 53.7 ..	42.3	162 25.8 ..	18.3	107 33.0 ..	20.4	Rigil Kent.	139 46.6	S60 54.6
R 10	40 49.5	292 40.9	19.3	91 55.4	42.3	177 28.5	18.2	122 35.6	20.4	Sabik	102 08.4	S15 44.7
D 11	55 51.9	307 40.1	19.0	106 57.1	42.3	192 31.3	18.1	137 38.3	20.4			
A 12	70 54.4	322 39.4	N24 18.7	121 58.9	S21 42.3	207 34.0	S15 18.1	152 40.9	S22 20.4	Schedar	349 36.9	N56 37.9
Y 13	85 56.9	337 38.6	18.3	137 00.6	42.3	222 36.7	18.0	167 43.5	20.4	Shaula	96 17.0	S37 06.8
14	100 59.3	352 37.9	18.0	152 02.3	42.3	237 39.4	17.9	182 46.2	20.4	Sirius	258 31.1	S16 44.7
15	116 01.8	7 37.1 ..	17.7	167 04.0 ..	42.2	252 42.1 ..	17.9	197 48.8 ..	20.5	Spica	158 27.5	S11 15.4
16	131 04.3	22 36.4	17.4	182 05.8	42.2	267 44.9	17.8	212 51.4	20.5	Suhail	222 50.2	S43 30.7
17	146 06.7	37 35.6	17.0	197 07.5	42.2	282 47.6	17.7	227 54.1	20.5			
18	161 09.2	52 34.9	N24 16.7	212 09.2	S21 42.2	297 50.3	S15 17.7	242 56.7	S22 20.5	Vega	80 36.3	N38 48.1
19	176 11.7	67 34.1	16.4	227 11.0	42.2	312 53.0	17.6	257 59.3	20.5	Zuben'ubi	137 01.4	S16 07.0
20	191 14.1	82 33.4	16.0	242 12.7	42.2	327 55.7	17.5	273 02.0	20.5		SHA	Mer.Pass.
21	206 16.6	97 32.6 ..	15.7	257 14.4 ..	42.2	342 58.5 ..	17.5	288 04.6 ..	20.5	Venus	253 41.2	14 28
22	221 19.1	112 31.9	15.3	272 16.2	42.2	358 01.2	17.4	303 07.2	20.5	Mars	51 31.6	3 56
23	236 21.5	127 31.1	15.0	287 17.9	42.1	13 03.9	17.3	318 09.9	20.5	Jupiter	136 30.2	22 12
Mer.Pass.	7 21.1 (h m)	v −0.8 d 0.3		v 1.7 d 0.0		v 2.7 d 0.1		v 2.6 d 0.0		Saturn	81 40.5	1 55

UT	SUN GHA	SUN Dec	MOON GHA	v	MOON Dec	d	HP
d h	° ′	° ′	° ′	′	° ′	′	′
31 00	180 35.9	N21 52.4	343 28.3	11.5	S19 56.3	2.9	54.5
01	195 35.9	52.8	357 58.8	11.5	19 59.2	2.9	54.5
02	210 35.8	53.1	12 29.3	11.5	20 02.1	2.8	54.5
03	225 35.7 ..	53.5	26 59.8	11.5	20 04.9	2.7	54.5
04	240 35.6	53.8	41 30.3	11.5	20 07.6	2.6	54.5
05	255 35.5	54.2	56 00.8	11.5	20 10.2	2.5	54.5
T 06	270 35.4	N21 54.5	70 31.3	11.5	S20 12.7	2.5	54.4
H 07	285 35.3	54.9	85 01.8	11.5	20 15.2	2.3	54.4
U 08	300 35.2	55.3	99 32.3	11.5	20 17.5	2.2	54.4
R 09	315 35.1 ..	55.6	114 02.8	11.5	20 19.7	2.1	54.4
S 10	330 35.0	56.0	128 33.3	11.5	20 21.8	2.0	54.4
D 11	345 34.9	56.3	143 03.8	11.5	20 23.8	1.9	54.4
A 12	0 34.9	N21 56.7	157 34.3	11.5	S20 25.7	1.9	54.4
Y 13	15 34.8	57.0	172 04.8	11.5	20 27.6	1.7	54.4
14	30 34.7	57.4	186 35.3	11.5	20 29.3	1.6	54.4
15	45 34.6 ..	57.7	201 05.8	11.5	20 30.9	1.5	54.4
16	60 34.5	58.1	215 36.3	11.5	20 32.4	1.5	54.3
17	75 34.4	58.4	230 06.8	11.5	20 33.9	1.3	54.3
18	90 34.3	N21 58.8	244 37.3	11.5	S20 35.2	1.2	54.3
19	105 34.2	59.1	259 07.8	11.6	20 36.4	1.2	54.3
20	120 34.1	59.5	273 38.4	11.5	20 37.6	1.0	54.3
21	135 34.0	21 59.8	288 08.9	11.5	20 38.6	1.0	54.3
22	150 33.9	22 00.2	302 39.4	11.5	20 39.6	0.8	54.3
23	165 33.8	00.5	317 09.9	11.6	20 40.4	0.8	54.3
1 00	180 33.8	N22 00.8	331 40.5	11.5	S20 41.2	0.6	54.3
01	195 33.7	01.2	346 11.0	11.6	20 41.8	0.6	54.3
02	210 33.6	01.5	0 41.6	11.6	20 42.4	0.4	54.3
03	225 33.5 ..	01.9	15 12.1	11.6	20 42.8	0.4	54.2
04	240 33.4	02.2	29 42.7	11.6	20 43.2	0.2	54.2
05	255 33.3	02.5	44 13.3	11.6	20 43.4	0.2	54.2
06	270 33.2	N22 02.9	58 43.9	11.6	S20 43.6	0.0	54.2
07	285 33.1	03.2	73 14.5	11.6	20 43.6	0.0	54.2
F 08	300 33.0	03.6	87 45.1	11.6	20 43.6	0.1	54.2
R 09	315 32.9 ..	03.9	102 15.7	11.6	20 43.5	0.3	54.2
I 10	330 32.8	04.2	116 46.3	11.7	20 43.2	0.3	54.2
D 11	345 32.7	04.6	131 17.0	11.6	20 42.9	0.4	54.2
A 12	0 32.6	N22 04.9	145 47.6	11.7	S20 42.5	0.5	54.2
Y 13	15 32.5	05.2	160 18.3	11.7	20 42.0	0.6	54.2
14	30 32.4	05.6	174 49.0	11.6	20 41.4	0.8	54.2
15	45 32.3 ..	05.9	189 19.6	11.8	20 40.6	0.8	54.2
16	60 32.2	06.2	203 50.4	11.7	20 39.8	0.9	54.2
17	75 32.1	06.6	218 21.1	11.7	20 38.9	1.0	54.2
18	90 32.0	N22 06.9	232 51.8	11.8	S20 37.9	1.1	54.2
19	105 31.9	07.2	247 22.6	11.7	20 36.8	1.2	54.2
20	120 31.9	07.6	261 53.3	11.8	20 35.6	1.3	54.1
21	135 31.8 ..	07.9	276 24.1	11.8	20 34.3	1.4	54.1
22	150 31.7	08.2	290 54.9	11.8	20 33.0	1.5	54.1
23	165 31.6	08.6	305 25.7	11.9	20 31.5	1.6	54.1
2 00	180 31.5	N22 08.9	319 56.6	11.8	S20 29.9	1.7	54.1
01	195 31.4	09.2	334 27.4	11.9	20 28.2	1.7	54.1
02	210 31.3	09.5	348 58.3	11.9	20 26.5	1.9	54.1
03	225 31.2 ..	09.9	3 29.2	11.9	20 24.6	1.9	54.1
04	240 31.1	10.2	18 00.1	11.9	20 22.7	2.1	54.1
05	255 31.0	10.5	32 31.0	12.0	20 20.6	2.1	54.1
06	270 30.9	N22 10.8	47 02.0	11.9	S20 18.5	2.3	54.1
S 07	285 30.8	11.2	61 32.9	12.0	20 16.2	2.3	54.1
A 08	300 30.7	11.5	76 03.9	12.0	20 13.9	2.4	54.1
T 09	315 30.6 ..	11.8	90 34.9	12.1	20 11.5	2.5	54.1
U 10	330 30.5	12.1	105 06.0	12.0	20 09.0	2.6	54.1
R 11	345 30.4	12.5	119 37.0	12.1	20 06.4	2.7	54.1
D 12	0 30.3	N22 12.8	134 08.1	12.1	S20 03.7	2.8	54.1
A 13	15 30.2	13.1	148 39.2	12.1	20 00.9	2.9	54.1
Y 14	30 30.1	13.4	163 10.3	12.1	19 58.0	3.0	54.1
15	45 30.0 ..	13.7	177 41.4	12.2	19 55.0	3.0	54.1
16	60 29.9	14.0	192 12.6	12.2	19 52.0	3.2	54.1
17	75 29.8	14.4	206 43.8	12.2	19 48.8	3.2	54.1
18	90 29.7	N22 14.7	221 15.0	12.2	S19 45.6	3.3	54.1
19	105 29.6	15.0	235 46.2	12.3	19 42.3	3.5	54.1
20	120 29.5	15.3	250 17.5	12.3	19 38.8	3.5	54.1
21	135 29.4 ..	15.6	264 48.8	12.3	19 35.3	3.6	54.1
22	150 29.3	15.9	279 20.1	12.3	19 31.7	3.7	54.1
23	165 29.2	16.2	293 51.4	12.4	S19 28.0	3.7	54.1
	SD 15.8	d 0.3	SD 14.8		14.8		14.7

Twilight / Sunrise / Moonrise

Lat.	Naut.	Civil	Sunrise	Moonrise 31	1	2	3
°	h m	h m	h m	h m	h m	h m	h m
N 72	□	□	□	■	■	■	■
N 70	□	□	□	■	■	■	02 29
68	□	□	□	24 34	00 34	01 15	01 32
66	////	////	01 13	23 47	24 31	00 31	00 58
64	////	////	01 58	23 16	24 02	00 02	00 33
62	////	////	02 27	22 53	23 40	24 14	00 14
60	////	01 26	02 49	22 35	23 22	23 58	24 25
N 58	////	02 00	03 07	22 19	23 07	23 44	24 14
56	////	02 25	03 22	22 06	22 54	23 33	24 04
54	01 19	02 44	03 35	21 55	22 43	23 22	23 55
52	01 50	03 00	03 46	21 45	22 33	23 13	23 47
50	02 13	03 13	03 56	21 36	22 24	23 05	23 40
45	02 53	03 40	04 17	21 17	22 05	22 48	23 25
N 40	03 21	04 01	04 33	21 02	21 50	22 33	23 12
35	03 42	04 18	04 47	20 49	21 37	22 21	23 02
30	04 00	04 32	04 59	20 37	21 26	22 11	22 52
20	04 27	04 56	05 20	20 18	21 06	21 53	22 36
N 10	04 48	05 15	05 38	20 01	20 50	21 37	22 22
0	05 06	05 32	05 54	19 45	20 34	21 22	22 09
S 10	05 22	05 48	06 11	19 30	20 18	21 07	21 55
20	05 37	06 04	06 28	19 13	20 01	20 51	21 41
30	05 52	06 22	06 48	18 54	19 42	20 33	21 25
35	06 00	06 31	06 59	18 42	19 31	20 22	21 15
40	06 09	06 42	07 12	18 29	19 18	20 10	21 05
45	06 18	06 55	07 28	18 14	19 03	19 56	20 52
S 50	06 29	07 09	07 47	17 56	18 44	19 38	20 36
52	06 33	07 16	07 56	17 47	18 35	19 30	20 29
54	06 38	07 24	08 06	17 37	18 25	19 20	20 21
56	06 44	07 32	08 18	17 26	18 14	19 10	20 12
58	06 50	07 41	08 31	17 13	18 01	18 58	20 01
S 60	06 56	07 52	08 46	16 58	17 46	18 44	19 49

Sunset / Twilight / Moonset

Lat.	Sunset	Civil	Naut.	Moonset 31	1	2	3
°	h m	h m	h m	h m	h m	h m	h m
N 72	□	□	□	■	■	■	
N 70	□	□	□	■	■	■	04 44
68	□	□	□	02 50	03 19	04 19	05 41
66	22 47	////	////	03 30	04 07	05 03	06 15
64	22 00	////	////	03 58	04 38	05 32	06 39
62	21 30	////	////	04 19	05 01	05 54	06 58
60	21 07	22 32	////	04 36	05 19	06 12	07 14
N 58	20 49	21 57	////	04 51	05 34	06 27	07 27
56	20 34	21 32	////	05 03	05 47	06 39	07 38
54	20 21	21 13	22 39	05 14	05 59	06 50	07 48
52	20 10	20 57	22 07	05 24	06 09	07 00	07 57
50	20 00	20 43	21 44	05 32	06 18	07 09	08 05
45	19 39	20 16	21 03	05 51	06 37	07 28	08 22
N 40	19 23	19 55	20 35	06 06	06 52	07 43	08 36
35	19 09	19 38	20 14	06 18	07 05	07 55	08 48
30	18 56	19 23	19 56	06 29	07 17	08 06	08 58
20	18 36	19 00	19 29	06 48	07 36	08 25	09 15
N 10	18 18	18 41	19 08	07 05	07 53	08 42	09 30
0	18 01	18 24	18 50	07 20	08 09	08 57	09 45
S 10	17 45	18 08	18 34	07 36	08 25	09 13	09 59
20	17 28	17 51	18 19	07 52	08 42	09 29	10 14
30	17 08	17 34	18 03	08 11	09 01	09 48	10 31
35	16 56	17 24	17 55	08 22	09 12	09 59	10 41
40	16 43	17 13	17 47	08 35	09 25	10 11	10 52
45	16 28	17 01	17 37	08 50	09 41	10 26	11 06
S 50	16 08	16 46	17 27	09 08	09 59	10 44	11 22
52	15 59	16 39	17 22	09 17	10 08	10 52	11 30
54	15 49	16 32	17 17	09 27	10 18	11 02	11 38
56	15 38	16 23	17 11	09 38	10 29	11 13	11 47
58	15 25	16 14	17 05	09 50	10 42	11 25	11 58
S 60	15 09	16 04	16 59	10 05	10 57	11 39	12 11

SUN / MOON

Day	Eqn. of Time 00ʰ	12ʰ	Mer. Pass.	Mer. Pass. Upper	Lower	Age	Phase
d	m s	m s	h m	h m	h m	d	%
31	02 24	02 20	11 58	01 08	13 33	16	97
1	02 15	02 11	11 58	01 57	14 21	17	92
2	02 06	02 01	11 58	02 46	15 10	18	87

UT	ARIES	VENUS −4.0		MARS −1.3		JUPITER −2.4		SATURN +0.1		STARS		
	GHA	GHA	Dec	GHA	Dec	GHA	Dec	GHA	Dec	Name	SHA	Dec
d h	° ′	° ′	° ′	° ′	° ′	° ′	° ′	° ′	° ′		° ′	° ′
3 00	251 24.0	142 30.4	N24 14.7	302 19.6	S21 42.1	28 06.6	S15 17.3	333 12.5	S22 20.6	Acamar	315 16.2	S40 14.0
01	266 26.4	157 29.6	14.3	317 21.4	42.1	43 09.3	17.2	348 15.1	20.6	Achernar	335 24.7	S57 08.6
02	281 28.9	172 28.8	14.0	332 23.1	42.1	58 12.1	17.1	3 17.8	20.6	Acrux	173 05.2	S63 12.3
03	296 31.4	187 28.1 . .	13.6	347 24.8 . .	42.1	73 14.8 . .	17.1	18 20.4 . .	20.6	Adhara	255 10.2	S29 00.1
04	311 33.8	202 27.4	13.3	2 26.6	42.1	88 17.5	17.0	33 23.0	20.6	Aldebaran	290 45.9	N16 32.5
05	326 36.3	217 26.6	12.9	17 28.3	42.1	103 20.2	16.9	48 25.7	20.6			
06	341 38.8	232 25.9	N24 12.6	32 30.1	S21 42.1	118 22.9	S15 16.9	63 28.3	S22 20.6	Alioth	166 17.5	N55 51.9
07	356 41.2	247 25.1	12.3	47 31.8	42.1	133 25.7	16.8	78 30.9	20.6	Alkaid	152 56.0	N49 13.6
08	11 43.7	262 24.4	11.9	62 33.5	42.1	148 28.4	16.8	93 33.6	20.6	Al Na'ir	27 39.5	S46 52.1
S 09	26 46.2	277 23.6 . .	11.6	77 35.3 . .	42.0	163 31.1 . .	16.7	108 36.2 . .	20.6	Alnilam	275 43.3	S 1 11.6
U 10	41 48.6	292 22.9	11.2	92 37.0	42.0	178 33.8	16.6	123 38.8	20.7	Alphard	217 52.9	S 8 44.4
N 11	56 51.1	307 22.1	10.8	107 38.8	42.0	193 36.5	16.6	138 41.5	20.7			
D 12	71 53.6	322 21.4	N24 10.5	122 40.5	S21 42.0	208 39.2	S15 16.5	153 44.1	S22 20.7	Alphecca	126 07.8	N26 39.4
A 13	86 56.0	337 20.6	10.1	137 42.3	42.0	223 42.0	16.4	168 46.7	20.7	Alpheratz	357 40.1	N29 11.2
Y 14	101 58.5	352 19.9	09.8	152 44.0	42.0	238 44.7	16.4	183 49.4	20.7	Altair	62 04.7	N 8 55.1
15	117 00.9	7 19.1 . .	09.4	167 45.8 . .	42.0	253 47.4 . .	16.3	198 52.0 . .	20.7	Ankaa	353 12.6	S42 12.3
16	132 03.4	22 18.4	09.1	182 47.5	42.0	268 50.1	16.2	213 54.6	20.7	Antares	112 21.8	S26 28.2
17	147 05.9	37 17.6	08.7	197 49.3	42.0	283 52.8	16.2	228 57.3	20.7			
18	162 08.3	52 16.9	N24 08.3	212 51.0	S21 42.0	298 55.5	S15 16.1	243 59.9	S22 20.7	Arcturus	145 52.4	N19 05.4
19	177 10.8	67 16.2	08.0	227 52.8	42.0	313 58.3	16.0	259 02.5	20.8	Atria	107 20.0	S69 03.4
20	192 13.3	82 15.4	07.6	242 54.5	42.0	329 01.0	16.0	274 05.2	20.8	Avior	234 17.0	S59 34.4
21	207 15.7	97 14.7 . .	07.3	257 56.3 . .	42.0	344 03.7 . .	15.9	289 07.8 . .	20.8	Bellatrix	278 28.8	N 6 21.7
22	222 18.2	112 13.9	06.9	272 58.1	42.0	359 06.4	15.8	304 10.4	20.8	Betelgeuse	270 58.0	N 7 24.4
23	237 20.7	127 13.2	06.5	287 59.8	42.0	14 09.1	15.8	319 13.1	20.8			
4 00	252 23.1	142 12.5	N24 06.2	303 01.6	S21 41.9	29 11.8	S15 15.7	334 15.7	S22 20.8	Canopus	263 55.2	S52 42.6
01	267 25.6	157 11.7	05.8	318 03.3	41.9	44 14.5	15.6	349 18.4	20.8	Capella	280 30.0	N46 00.8
02	282 28.0	172 11.0	05.4	333 05.1	41.9	59 17.3	15.6	4 21.0	20.8	Deneb	49 28.9	N45 20.6
03	297 30.5	187 10.2 . .	05.0	348 06.9 . .	41.9	74 20.0 . .	15.5	19 23.6 . .	20.8	Denebola	182 30.2	N14 28.3
04	312 33.0	202 09.5	04.7	3 08.6	41.9	89 22.7	15.5	34 26.3	20.9	Diphda	348 52.7	S17 53.2
05	327 35.4	217 08.8	04.3	18 10.4	41.9	104 25.4	15.4	49 28.9	20.9			
06	342 37.9	232 08.0	N24 03.9	33 12.1	S21 41.9	119 28.1	S15 15.3	64 31.5	S22 20.9	Dubhe	193 47.7	N61 39.4
07	357 40.4	247 07.3	03.5	48 13.9	41.9	134 30.8	15.3	79 34.2	20.9	Elnath	278 08.8	N28 37.2
08	12 42.8	262 06.5	03.2	63 15.7	41.9	149 33.5	15.2	94 36.8	20.9	Eltanin	90 44.1	N51 29.3
M 09	27 45.3	277 05.8 . .	02.8	78 17.4 . .	41.9	164 36.2 . .	15.1	109 39.4 . .	20.9	Enif	33 43.7	N 9 57.5
O 10	42 47.8	292 05.1	02.4	93 19.2	41.9	179 39.0	15.1	124 42.1	20.9	Fomalhaut	15 20.3	S29 31.4
N 11	57 50.2	307 04.3	02.0	108 21.0	41.9	194 41.7	15.0	139 44.7	20.9			
D 12	72 52.7	322 03.6	N24 01.6	123 22.7	S21 41.9	209 44.4	S15 14.9	154 47.4	S22 20.9	Gacrux	171 56.8	S57 13.1
A 13	87 55.2	337 02.9	01.3	138 24.5	41.9	224 47.1	14.9	169 50.0	20.9	Gienah	175 48.7	S17 38.7
Y 14	102 57.6	352 02.1	00.9	153 26.3	41.9	239 49.8	14.8	184 52.6	21.0	Hadar	148 42.6	S60 27.7
15	118 00.1	7 01.4 . .	00.5	168 28.1 . .	41.9	254 52.5 . .	14.7	199 55.3 . .	21.0	Hamal	327 57.2	N23 32.7
16	133 02.5	22 00.7	24 00.1	183 29.8	41.9	269 55.2	14.7	214 57.9	21.0	Kaus Aust.	83 39.0	S34 22.3
17	148 05.0	36 59.9	23 59.7	198 31.6	41.9	284 57.9	14.6	230 00.5	21.0			
18	163 07.5	51 59.2	N23 59.3	213 33.4	S21 41.9	300 00.6	S15 14.6	245 03.2	S22 21.0	Kochab	137 19.2	N74 05.1
19	178 09.9	66 58.5	58.9	228 35.2	41.9	315 03.4	14.5	260 05.8	21.0	Markab	13 35.0	N15 18.1
20	193 12.4	81 57.7	58.6	243 36.9	41.9	330 06.1	14.4	275 08.4	21.0	Menkar	314 11.8	N 4 09.5
21	208 14.9	96 57.0 . .	58.2	258 38.7 . .	41.9	345 08.8 . .	14.4	290 11.1 . .	21.0	Menkent	148 03.3	S36 27.6
22	223 17.3	111 56.3	57.8	273 40.5	41.9	0 11.5	14.3	305 13.7	21.0	Miaplacidus	221 39.3	S69 47.9
23	238 19.8	126 55.5	57.4	288 42.3	41.9	15 14.2	14.2	320 16.4	21.1			
5 00	253 22.3	141 54.8	N23 57.0	303 44.1	S21 41.9	30 16.9	S15 14.2	335 19.0	S22 21.1	Mirfak	308 36.0	N49 55.2
01	268 24.7	156 54.1	56.6	318 45.9	41.9	45 19.6	14.1	350 21.6	21.1	Nunki	75 53.8	S26 16.2
02	283 27.2	171 53.4	56.2	333 47.6	41.9	60 22.3	14.1	5 24.3	21.1	Peacock	53 13.6	S56 40.2
03	298 29.7	186 52.6 . .	55.8	348 49.4 . .	41.9	75 25.0 . .	14.0	20 26.9 . .	21.1	Pollux	243 24.0	N27 58.8
04	313 32.1	201 51.9	55.4	3 51.2	41.9	90 27.7	13.9	35 29.5	21.1	Procyon	244 56.5	N 5 10.5
05	328 34.6	216 51.2	55.0	18 53.0	41.9	105 30.4	13.9	50 32.2	21.1			
06	343 37.0	231 50.5	N23 54.6	33 54.8	S21 41.9	120 33.2	S15 13.8	65 34.8	S22 21.1	Rasalhague	96 03.0	N12 32.9
07	358 39.5	246 49.7	54.2	48 56.6	41.9	135 35.9	13.7	80 37.5	21.1	Regulus	207 40.0	N11 52.7
08	13 42.0	261 49.0	53.8	63 58.4	41.9	150 38.6	13.7	95 40.1	21.2	Rigel	281 09.2	S 8 11.1
T 09	28 44.4	276 48.3 . .	53.4	79 00.2 . .	41.9	165 41.3 . .	13.6	110 42.7 . .	21.2	Rigil Kent.	139 46.6	S60 54.6
U 10	43 46.9	291 47.6	53.0	94 01.9	42.0	180 44.0	13.6	125 45.4	21.2	Sabik	102 08.3	S15 44.7
E 11	58 49.4	306 46.8	52.6	109 03.7	42.0	195 46.7	13.5	140 48.0	21.2			
S 12	73 51.8	321 46.1	N23 52.1	124 05.5	S21 42.0	210 49.4	S15 13.4	155 50.7	S22 21.2	Schedar	349 36.9	N56 37.9
D 13	88 54.3	336 45.4	51.7	139 07.3	42.0	225 52.1	13.4	170 53.3	21.2	Shaula	96 16.9	S37 06.8
A 14	103 56.8	351 44.7	51.3	154 09.1	42.0	240 54.8	13.3	185 55.9	21.2	Sirius	258 31.1	S16 44.7
Y 15	118 59.2	6 43.9 . .	50.9	169 10.9 . .	42.0	255 57.5 . .	13.2	200 58.6 . .	21.2	Spica	158 27.5	S11 15.4
16	134 01.7	21 43.2	50.5	184 12.7	42.0	271 00.2	13.2	216 01.2	21.2	Suhail	222 50.2	S43 30.7
17	149 04.1	36 42.5	50.1	199 14.5	42.0	286 02.9	13.1	231 03.8	21.3			
18	164 06.6	51 41.8	N23 49.7	214 16.3	S21 42.0	301 05.6	S15 13.1	246 06.5	S22 21.3	Vega	80 36.3	N38 48.1
19	179 09.1	66 41.0	49.2	229 18.1	42.0	316 08.3	13.0	261 09.1	21.3	Zuben'ubi	137 01.4	S16 07.0
20	194 11.5	81 40.3	48.8	244 19.9	42.0	331 11.0	12.9	276 11.8	21.3		SHA	Mer. Pass.
21	209 14.0	96 39.6 . .	48.4	259 21.7 . .	42.0	346 13.8 . .	12.9	291 14.4 . .	21.3		° ′	h m
22	224 16.5	111 38.9	48.0	274 23.5	42.0	1 16.5	12.8	306 17.0	21.3	Venus	249 49.3	14 32
23	239 18.9	126 38.2	47.6	289 25.3	42.0	16 19.2	12.7	321 19.7	21.3	Mars	50 38.4	3 47
	h m									Jupiter	136 48.7	21 59
Mer. Pass. 7 09.3		v −0.7	d 0.4	v 1.8	d 0.0	v 2.7	d 0.1	v 2.6	d 0.0	Saturn	81 52.6	1 43

SUN and MOON

UT	SUN GHA	SUN Dec	MOON GHA	v	MOON Dec	d	HP
d h	° ′	° ′	° ′	′	° ′	′	′
3 00	180 29.1	N22 16.6	308 22.8	12.4	S19 24.3	3.9	54.1
01	195 29.0	16.9	322 54.2	12.4	19 20.4	4.0	54.1
02	210 28.9	17.2	337 25.6	12.4	19 16.4	4.0	54.1
03	225 28.8	.. 17.5	351 57.0	12.5	19 12.4	4.1	54.1
04	240 28.7	17.8	6 28.5	12.4	19 08.3	4.2	54.1
05	255 28.6	18.1	20 59.9	12.5	19 04.1	4.3	54.1
S 06	270 28.5	N22 18.4	35 31.4	12.6	S18 59.8	4.4	54.1
U 07	285 28.4	18.7	50 03.0	12.5	18 55.4	4.5	54.1
N 08	300 28.3	19.0	64 34.5	12.6	18 50.9	4.5	54.1
D 09	315 28.2	.. 19.3	79 06.1	12.6	18 46.4	4.7	54.1
A 10	330 28.0	19.6	93 37.7	12.7	18 41.7	4.7	54.1
Y 11	345 27.9	19.9	108 09.4	12.6	18 37.0	4.8	54.1
12	0 27.8	N22 20.2	122 41.0	12.7	S18 32.2	4.9	54.1
13	15 27.7	20.5	137 12.7	12.8	18 27.3	5.0	54.1
14	30 27.6	20.8	151 44.5	12.7	18 22.3	5.0	54.2
15	45 27.5	.. 21.1	166 16.2	12.8	18 17.3	5.2	54.2
16	60 27.4	21.4	180 48.0	12.8	18 12.1	5.2	54.2
17	75 27.3	21.7	195 19.8	12.8	18 06.9	5.3	54.2
18	90 27.2	N22 22.0	209 51.6	12.8	S18 01.6	5.4	54.2
19	105 27.1	22.3	224 23.4	12.9	17 56.2	5.4	54.2
20	120 27.0	22.6	238 55.3	12.9	17 50.8	5.6	54.2
21	135 26.9	.. 22.9	253 27.2	12.9	17 45.2	5.6	54.2
22	150 26.8	23.2	267 59.1	13.0	17 39.6	5.7	54.2
23	165 26.7	23.5	282 31.1	13.0	17 33.9	5.8	54.2
4 00	180 26.6	N22 23.8	297 03.1	13.0	S17 28.1	5.8	54.2
01	195 26.5	24.1	311 35.1	13.0	17 22.3	5.9	54.2
02	210 26.4	24.4	326 07.1	13.1	17 16.4	6.1	54.2
03	225 26.3	.. 24.7	340 39.2	13.1	17 10.3	6.0	54.2
04	240 26.2	25.0	355 11.3	13.1	17 04.3	6.2	54.3
05	255 26.1	25.3	9 43.4	13.1	16 58.1	6.3	54.3
M 06	270 26.0	N22 25.6	24 15.5	13.2	S16 51.8	6.3	54.3
O 07	285 25.8	25.9	38 47.7	13.1	16 45.5	6.4	54.3
N 08	300 25.7	26.2	53 19.8	13.3	16 39.1	6.4	54.3
D 09	315 25.6	.. 26.5	67 52.1	13.2	16 32.7	6.6	54.3
A 10	330 25.5	26.7	82 24.3	13.2	16 26.1	6.6	54.3
Y 11	345 25.4	27.0	96 56.5	13.3	16 19.5	6.7	54.3
12	0 25.3	N22 27.3	111 28.8	13.3	S16 12.8	6.8	54.3
13	15 25.2	27.6	126 01.1	13.4	16 06.0	6.8	54.3
14	30 25.1	27.9	140 33.5	13.3	15 59.2	6.9	54.4
15	45 25.0	.. 28.2	155 05.8	13.4	15 52.3	7.0	54.4
16	60 24.9	28.5	169 38.2	13.4	15 45.3	7.0	54.4
17	75 24.8	28.7	184 10.6	13.4	15 38.3	7.2	54.4
18	90 24.7	N22 29.0	198 43.0	13.5	S15 31.1	7.1	54.4
19	105 24.6	29.3	213 15.5	13.4	15 24.0	7.3	54.4
20	120 24.4	29.6	227 47.9	13.5	15 16.7	7.3	54.4
21	135 24.3	.. 29.9	242 20.4	13.5	15 09.4	7.4	54.4
22	150 24.2	30.2	256 52.9	13.6	15 02.0	7.5	54.5
23	165 24.1	30.4	271 25.5	13.5	14 54.5	7.5	54.5
5 00	180 24.0	N22 30.7	285 58.0	13.6	S14 47.0	7.7	54.5
01	195 23.9	31.0	300 30.6	13.6	14 39.3	7.6	54.5
02	210 23.8	31.3	315 03.2	13.6	14 31.7	7.8	54.5
03	225 23.7	.. 31.6	329 35.8	13.7	14 23.9	7.8	54.5
04	240 23.6	31.8	344 08.5	13.6	14 16.1	7.8	54.5
05	255 23.5	32.1	358 41.1	13.7	14 08.3	8.0	54.6
T 06	270 23.4	N22 32.4	13 13.8	13.7	S14 00.3	8.0	54.6
U 07	285 23.2	32.7	27 46.5	13.7	13 52.3	8.0	54.6
E 08	300 23.1	32.9	42 19.2	13.7	13 44.3	8.2	54.6
S 09	315 23.0	.. 33.2	56 51.9	13.8	13 36.1	8.2	54.6
D 10	330 22.9	33.5	71 24.7	13.7	13 27.9	8.2	54.6
A 11	345 22.8	33.7	85 57.4	13.8	13 19.7	8.3	54.7
Y 12	0 22.7	N22 34.0	100 30.2	13.8	S13 11.4	8.4	54.7
13	15 22.6	34.3	115 03.0	13.8	13 03.0	8.5	54.7
14	30 22.5	34.6	129 35.8	13.8	12 54.5	8.5	54.7
15	45 22.4	.. 34.8	144 08.6	13.9	12 46.0	8.5	54.7
16	60 22.2	35.1	158 41.5	13.8	12 37.5	8.6	54.7
17	75 22.1	35.4	173 14.3	13.9	12 28.9	8.7	54.8
18	90 22.0	N22 35.6	187 47.2	13.8	S12 20.2	8.8	54.8
19	105 21.9	35.9	202 20.0	13.9	12 11.4	8.8	54.8
20	120 21.8	36.2	216 52.9	13.9	12 02.6	8.8	54.8
21	135 21.7	.. 36.4	231 25.8	14.0	11 53.8	8.9	54.8
22	150 21.6	36.7	245 58.8	13.9	11 44.9	9.0	54.9
23	165 21.5	36.9	260 31.7	13.9	S11 35.9	9.0	54.9
	SD 15.8	d 0.3	SD 14.8		14.8		14.9

Twilight, Sunrise, Moonrise

Lat.	Twilight Naut.	Twilight Civil	Sunrise	Moonrise 3	4	5	6
°	h m	h m	h m	h m	h m	h m	h m
N 72	□	□	□	■	03 09	02 33	02 14
N 70	□	□	□	02 29	02 12	02 03	01 56
68	□	□	□	01 32	01 38	01 41	01 41
66	////	////	00 59	00 58	01 14	01 23	01 29
64	////	////	01 51	00 33	00 54	01 09	01 19
62	////	////	02 22	00 14	00 39	00 57	01 11
60	////	01 18	02 45	24 25	00 14	00 46	01 03
N 58	////	01 55	03 04	24 14	00 14	00 37	00 57
56	////	02 20	03 19	24 04	00 04	00 29	00 51
54	01 11	02 40	03 32	23 55	24 22	00 22	00 46
52	01 45	02 57	03 44	23 47	24 16	00 16	00 41
50	02 09	03 11	03 54	23 40	24 10	00 10	00 37
45	02 51	03 39	04 15	23 25	23 58	24 28	00 28
N 40	03 19	04 00	04 32	23 12	23 48	24 20	00 20
35	03 41	04 17	04 46	23 02	23 39	24 13	00 13
30	03 59	04 32	04 59	22 52	23 31	24 07	00 07
20	04 27	04 55	05 20	22 36	23 17	23 57	24 35
N 10	04 48	05 15	05 38	22 22	23 06	23 48	24 30
0	05 06	05 32	05 55	22 09	22 55	23 39	24 24
S 10	05 22	05 49	06 11	21 55	22 43	23 31	24 19
20	05 38	06 05	06 29	21 41	22 32	23 22	24 13
30	05 53	06 23	06 49	21 25	22 18	23 12	24 06
35	06 02	06 33	07 01	21 15	22 10	23 06	24 02
40	06 10	06 44	07 14	21 05	22 01	22 59	23 58
45	06 20	06 57	07 30	20 52	21 50	22 51	23 53
S 50	06 31	07 12	07 50	20 36	21 38	22 41	23 46
52	06 36	07 19	07 59	20 29	21 32	22 37	23 44
54	06 41	07 27	08 09	20 21	21 25	22 32	23 41
56	06 47	07 35	08 21	20 12	21 17	22 26	23 37
58	06 53	07 45	08 35	20 01	21 09	22 20	23 33
S 60	07 00	07 55	08 51	19 49	21 00	22 13	23 29

Sunset, Twilight, Moonset

Lat.	Sunset	Twilight Civil	Twilight Naut.	Moonset 3	4	5	6
°	h m	h m	h m	h m	h m	h m	h m
N 72	□	□	□	■	05 42	07 53	09 45
N 70	□	□	□	04 44	06 38	08 22	10 02
68	□	□	□	05 41	07 11	08 43	10 15
66	23 02	////	////	06 15	07 35	09 00	10 26
64	22 08	////	////	06 39	07 54	09 13	10 35
62	21 36	////	////	06 58	08 09	09 25	10 42
60	21 12	22 41	////	07 14	08 22	09 34	10 49
N 58	20 54	22 03	////	07 27	08 33	09 43	10 55
56	20 38	21 37	////	07 38	08 42	09 50	11 00
54	20 25	21 17	22 48	07 48	08 51	09 57	11 04
52	20 13	21 01	22 13	07 57	08 58	10 02	11 08
50	20 03	20 47	21 49	08 05	09 05	10 08	11 12
45	19 42	20 19	21 07	08 22	09 20	10 19	11 20
N 40	19 25	19 57	20 38	08 36	09 31	10 29	11 27
35	19 10	19 40	20 16	08 48	09 42	10 37	11 33
30	18 58	19 25	19 58	08 58	09 50	10 44	11 38
20	18 37	19 01	19 30	09 15	10 06	10 56	11 46
N 10	18 19	18 42	19 09	09 30	10 19	11 06	11 54
0	18 02	18 24	18 50	09 45	10 31	11 16	12 01
S 10	17 45	18 08	18 34	09 59	10 43	11 26	12 08
20	17 28	17 51	18 19	10 14	10 56	11 37	12 15
30	17 07	17 33	18 03	10 31	11 11	11 48	12 24
35	16 56	17 23	17 55	10 41	11 20	11 55	12 29
40	16 42	17 12	17 46	10 52	11 29	12 03	12 34
45	16 26	17 00	17 36	11 06	11 41	12 12	12 40
S 50	16 07	16 44	17 25	11 22	11 54	12 23	12 48
52	15 57	16 37	17 21	11 30	12 01	12 28	12 51
54	15 47	16 30	17 15	11 38	12 08	12 33	12 55
56	15 35	16 21	17 10	11 47	12 16	12 39	12 59
58	15 21	16 12	17 03	11 58	12 25	12 46	13 04
S 60	15 05	16 01	16 56	12 11	12 35	12 54	13 09

SUN and MOON data

Day	SUN Eqn. of Time 00h	SUN Eqn. of Time 12h	SUN Mer. Pass.	MOON Mer. Pass. Upper	MOON Mer. Pass. Lower	Age	Phase
d	m s	m s	h m	h m	h m	d	%
3	01 56	01 52	11 58	03 33	15 57	19	80
4	01 47	01 41	11 58	04 20	16 43	20	71
5	01 36	01 31	11 58	05 05	17 28	21	62

UT (d h)	ARIES GHA	VENUS −4.0 GHA	VENUS Dec	MARS −1.4 GHA	MARS Dec	JUPITER −2.4 GHA	JUPITER Dec	SATURN +0.1 GHA	SATURN Dec	STARS Name	SHA	Dec
6 00	254 21.4	141 37.5	N23 47.1	304 27.1	S21 42.1	31 21.9	S15 12.7	336 22.3	S22 21.3	Acamar	315 16.2	S40 13.9
01	269 23.9	156 36.7	46.7	319 28.9	42.1	46 24.6	12.6	351 25.0	21.3	Achernar	335 24.7	S57 08.5
02	284 26.3	171 36.0	46.3	334 30.8	42.1	61 27.3	12.6	6 27.6	21.3	Acrux	173 05.2	S63 12.3
03	299 28.8	186 35.3	.. 45.9	349 32.6	.. 42.1	76 30.0	.. 12.5	21 30.2	.. 21.4	Adhara	255 10.2	S29 00.1
04	314 31.3	201 34.6	45.4	4 34.4	42.1	91 32.7	12.4	36 32.9	21.4	Aldebaran	290 45.9	N16 32.5
05	329 33.7	216 33.9	45.0	19 36.2	42.1	106 35.4	12.4	51 35.5	21.4			
06	344 36.2	231 33.2	N23 44.6	34 38.0	S21 42.1	121 38.1	S15 12.3	66 38.2	S22 21.4	Alioth	166 17.5	N55 51.9
W 07	359 38.6	246 32.4	44.2	49 39.8	42.1	136 40.8	12.3	81 40.8	21.4	Alkaid	152 56.0	N49 13.6
E 08	14 41.1	261 31.7	43.7	64 41.6	42.1	151 43.5	12.2	96 43.4	21.4	Al Na'ir	27 39.4	S46 52.1
D 09	29 43.6	276 31.0	.. 43.3	79 43.4	.. 42.1	166 46.2	.. 12.1	111 46.1	.. 21.4	Alnilam	275 43.3	S 1 11.6
N 10	44 46.0	291 30.3	42.9	94 45.3	42.2	181 48.9	12.1	126 48.7	21.4	Alphard	217 52.9	S 8 44.4
E 11	59 48.5	306 29.6	42.4	109 47.1	42.2	196 51.6	12.0	141 51.4	21.4			
S 12	74 51.0	321 28.9	N23 42.0	124 48.9	S21 42.2	211 54.3	S15 12.0	156 54.0	S22 21.5	Alphecca	126 07.8	N26 39.4
D 13	89 53.4	336 28.2	41.6	139 50.7	42.2	226 57.0	11.9	171 56.6	21.5	Alpheratz	357 40.1	N29 11.2
A 14	104 55.9	351 27.5	41.1	154 52.5	42.2	241 59.7	11.8	186 59.3	21.5	Altair	62 04.7	N 8 55.1
Y 15	119 58.4	6 26.7	.. 40.7	169 54.3	.. 42.2	257 02.4	.. 11.8	202 01.9	.. 21.5	Ankaa	353 12.6	S42 12.3
16	135 00.8	21 26.0	40.2	184 56.2	42.2	272 05.1	11.7	217 04.6	21.5	Antares	112 21.8	S26 28.2
17	150 03.3	36 25.3	39.8	199 58.0	42.2	287 07.8	11.6	232 07.2	21.5			
18	165 05.8	51 24.6	N23 39.3	214 59.8	S21 42.3	302 10.5	S15 11.6	247 09.9	S22 21.5	Arcturus	145 52.4	N19 05.4
19	180 08.2	66 23.9	38.9	230 01.6	42.3	317 13.2	11.5	262 12.5	21.5	Atria	107 20.0	S69 03.4
20	195 10.7	81 23.2	38.5	245 03.5	42.3	332 15.9	11.5	277 15.1	21.5	Avior	234 17.1	S59 34.4
21	210 13.1	96 22.5	.. 38.0	260 05.3	.. 42.3	347 18.6	.. 11.4	292 17.8	.. 21.6	Bellatrix	278 28.8	N 6 21.8
22	225 15.6	111 21.8	37.6	275 07.1	42.3	2 21.3	11.3	307 20.4	21.6	Betelgeuse	270 58.0	N 7 24.4
23	240 18.1	126 21.1	37.1	290 09.0	42.3	17 24.0	11.3	322 23.1	21.6			
7 00	255 20.5	141 20.4	N23 36.7	305 10.8	S21 42.4	32 26.7	S15 11.2	337 25.7	S22 21.6	Canopus	263 55.2	S52 42.6
01	270 23.0	156 19.7	36.2	320 12.6	42.4	47 29.4	11.2	352 28.3	21.6	Capella	280 30.0	N46 00.8
02	285 25.5	171 19.0	35.8	335 14.4	42.4	62 32.1	11.1	7 31.0	21.6	Deneb	49 28.9	N45 20.6
03	300 27.9	186 18.3	.. 35.3	350 16.3	.. 42.4	77 34.8	.. 11.0	22 33.6	.. 21.6	Denebola	182 30.2	N14 28.3
04	315 30.4	201 17.6	34.9	5 18.1	42.4	92 37.5	11.0	37 36.3	21.6	Diphda	348 52.7	S17 53.2
05	330 32.9	216 16.8	34.4	20 20.0	42.4	107 40.2	10.9	52 38.9	21.6			
06	345 35.3	231 16.1	N23 33.9	35 21.8	S21 42.5	122 42.9	S15 10.9	67 41.6	S22 21.7	Dubhe	193 47.7	N61 39.4
T 07	0 37.8	246 15.4	33.5	50 23.6	42.5	137 45.6	10.8	82 44.2	21.7	Elnath	278 08.8	N28 37.2
H 08	15 40.2	261 14.7	33.0	65 25.5	42.5	152 48.3	10.8	97 46.8	21.7	Eltanin	90 44.1	N51 29.3
U 09	30 42.7	276 14.0	.. 32.6	80 27.3	.. 42.5	167 51.0	.. 10.7	112 49.5	.. 21.7	Enif	33 43.7	N 9 57.5
R 10	45 45.2	291 13.3	32.1	95 29.1	42.5	182 53.7	10.6	127 52.1	21.7	Fomalhaut	15 20.3	S29 31.4
11	60 47.6	306 12.6	31.7	110 31.0	42.5	197 56.4	10.6	142 54.8	21.7			
S 12	75 50.1	321 11.9	N23 31.2	125 32.8	S21 42.6	212 59.1	S15 10.5	157 57.4	S22 21.7	Gacrux	171 56.9	S57 13.1
D 13	90 52.6	336 11.2	30.7	140 34.7	42.6	228 01.8	10.5	173 00.1	21.7	Gienah	175 48.7	S17 38.7
A 14	105 55.0	351 10.5	30.3	155 36.5	42.6	243 04.5	10.4	188 02.7	21.7	Hadar	148 42.6	S60 27.8
Y 15	120 57.5	6 09.8	.. 29.8	170 38.4	.. 42.6	258 07.1	.. 10.3	203 05.3	.. 21.8	Hamal	327 57.2	N23 32.7
16	136 00.0	21 09.1	29.3	185 40.2	42.6	273 09.8	10.3	218 08.0	21.8	Kaus Aust.	83 39.0	S34 22.3
17	151 02.4	36 08.4	28.9	200 42.1	42.7	288 12.5	10.2	233 10.6	21.8			
18	166 04.9	51 07.8	N23 28.4	215 43.9	S21 42.7	303 15.2	S15 10.2	248 13.3	S22 21.8	Kochab	137 19.2	N74 05.1
19	181 07.4	66 07.1	27.9	230 45.8	42.7	318 17.9	10.1	263 15.9	21.8	Markab	13 35.0	N15 18.1
20	196 09.8	81 06.4	27.4	245 47.6	42.7	333 20.6	10.0	278 18.6	21.8	Menkar	314 11.8	N 4 09.5
21	211 12.3	96 05.7	.. 27.0	260 49.5	.. 42.8	348 23.3	.. 10.0	293 21.2	.. 21.8	Menkent	148 03.3	S36 27.6
22	226 14.7	111 05.0	26.5	275 51.3	42.8	3 26.0	09.9	308 23.8	21.8	Miaplacidus	221 39.4	S69 47.9
23	241 17.2	126 04.3	26.0	290 53.2	42.8	18 28.7	09.9	323 26.5	21.8			
8 00	256 19.7	141 03.6	N23 25.6	305 55.0	S21 42.8	33 31.4	S15 09.8	338 29.1	S22 21.9	Mirfak	308 36.0	N49 55.2
01	271 22.1	156 02.9	25.1	320 56.9	42.8	48 34.1	09.8	353 31.8	21.9	Nunki	75 53.8	S26 16.2
02	286 24.6	171 02.2	24.6	335 58.7	42.9	63 36.8	09.7	8 34.4	21.9	Peacock	53 13.6	S56 40.2
03	301 27.1	186 01.5	.. 24.1	351 00.6	.. 42.9	78 39.5	.. 09.6	23 37.1	.. 21.9	Pollux	243 24.0	N27 58.8
04	316 29.5	201 00.8	23.6	6 02.5	42.9	93 42.2	09.6	38 39.7	21.9	Procyon	244 56.5	N 5 10.5
05	331 32.0	216 00.1	23.2	21 04.3	42.9	108 44.9	09.5	53 42.4	21.9			
06	346 34.5	230 59.4	N23 22.7	36 06.2	S21 43.0	123 47.6	S15 09.5	68 45.0	S22 21.9	Rasalhague	96 03.0	N12 32.9
07	1 36.9	245 58.7	22.2	51 08.0	43.0	138 50.2	09.4	83 47.6	21.9	Regulus	207 40.1	N11 52.7
08	16 39.4	260 58.1	21.7	66 09.9	43.0	153 52.9	09.3	98 50.3	21.9	Rigel	281 09.2	S 8 11.0
F 09	31 41.9	275 57.4	.. 21.2	81 11.8	.. 43.0	168 55.6	.. 09.3	113 52.9	.. 22.0	Rigil Kent.	139 46.6	S60 54.6
R 10	46 44.3	290 56.7	20.7	96 13.6	43.1	183 58.3	09.2	128 55.6	22.0	Sabik	102 08.3	S15 44.7
I 11	61 46.8	305 56.0	20.2	111 15.5	43.1	199 01.0	09.2	143 58.2	22.0			
D 12	76 49.2	320 55.3	N23 19.8	126 17.4	S21 43.1	214 03.7	S15 09.1	159 00.9	S22 22.0	Schedar	349 36.9	N56 37.9
A 13	91 51.7	335 54.6	19.3	141 19.2	43.1	229 06.4	09.1	174 03.5	22.0	Shaula	96 16.9	S37 06.8
Y 14	106 54.2	350 53.9	18.8	156 21.1	43.2	244 09.1	09.0	189 06.2	22.0	Sirius	258 31.1	S16 44.7
15	121 56.6	5 53.2	.. 18.3	171 23.0	.. 43.2	259 11.8	.. 08.9	204 08.8	.. 22.0	Spica	158 27.5	S11 15.4
16	136 59.1	20 52.6	17.8	186 24.9	43.2	274 14.5	08.9	219 11.4	22.0	Suhail	222 50.2	S43 30.7
17	152 01.6	35 51.9	17.3	201 26.7	43.3	289 17.1	08.8	234 14.1	22.0			
18	167 04.0	50 51.2	N23 16.8	216 28.6	S21 43.3	304 19.8	S15 08.8	249 16.7	S22 22.1	Vega	80 36.3	N38 48.1
19	182 06.5	65 50.5	16.3	231 30.5	43.3	319 22.5	08.7	264 19.4	22.1	Zuben'ubi	137 01.4	S16 07.0
20	197 09.0	80 49.8	15.8	246 32.4	43.3	334 25.2	08.7	279 22.0	22.1		SHA	Mer.Pass.
21	212 11.4	95 49.1	.. 15.3	261 34.2	.. 43.4	349 27.9	.. 08.6	294 24.7	.. 22.1	Venus	245 59.8	14 35
22	227 13.9	110 48.5	14.8	276 36.1	43.4	4 30.6	08.5	309 27.3	22.1	Mars	49 50.2	3 39
23	242 16.3	125 47.8	14.3	291 38.0	43.4	19 33.3	08.5	324 30.0	22.1	Jupiter	137 06.2	21 46
Mer. Pass.	6 57.5	v −0.7	d 0.5	v 1.8	d 0.0	v 2.7	d 0.1	v 2.6	d 0.0	Saturn	82 05.2	1 30

UT	SUN		MOON					Lat.	Twilight		Sunrise	Moonrise			
									Naut.	Civil		6	7	8	9
	GHA	Dec	GHA	v	Dec	d	HP								
d h	° ′	° ′	° ′	′	° ′	′	′	N 72	h m	h m	h m	h m	h m	h m	h m
								°	▭	▭	▭	02 14	02 00	01 48	01 36
6 00	180 21.4	N22 37.2	275 04.6	14.0	S11 26.9	9.1	54.9	N 72	▭	▭	▭	02 14	02 00	01 48	01 36
01	195 21.2	37.5	289 37.6	13.9	11 17.8	9.2	54.9	N 70	▭	▭	▭	01 56	01 50	01 44	01 38
02	210 21.1	37.7	304 10.5	14.0	11 08.6	9.2	54.9	68	▭	▭	▭	01 41	01 41	01 40	01 40
03	225 21.0	.. 38.0	318 43.5	13.9	10 59.4	9.2	55.0	66	////	////	00 45	01 29	01 34	01 37	01 41
04	240 20.9	38.3	333 16.4	14.0	10 50.2	9.3	55.0	64	////	////	01 45	01 19	01 28	01 35	01 42
05	255 20.8	38.5	347 49.4	14.0	10 40.9	9.4	55.0	62	////	////	02 18	01 11	01 22	01 33	01 43
06	270 20.7	N22 38.8	2 22.4	14.0	S10 31.5	9.4	55.0	60	////	01 10	02 42	01 03	01 18	01 31	01 44
W 07	285 20.6	39.0	16 55.4	14.0	10 22.1	9.4	55.1	N 58	////	01 50	03 01	00 57	01 14	01 29	01 45
E 08	300 20.4	39.3	31 28.4	14.0	10 12.7	9.6	55.1	56	////	02 17	03 17	00 51	01 10	01 28	01 45
D 09	315 20.3	.. 39.5	46 01.4	14.0	10 03.1	9.5	55.1	54	01 04	02 38	03 30	00 46	01 07	01 26	01 46
N 10	330 20.2	39.8	60 34.4	14.0	9 53.6	9.6	55.1	52	01 41	02 54	03 42	00 41	01 04	01 25	01 47
E 11	345 20.1	40.1	75 07.4	14.0	9 44.0	9.7	55.2	50	02 06	03 09	03 52	00 37	01 01	01 24	01 47
S 12	0 20.0	N22 40.3	89 40.4	14.0	S 9 34.3	9.7	55.2	45	02 49	03 37	04 14	00 28	00 55	01 22	01 48
D 13	15 19.9	40.6	104 13.4	14.0	9 24.6	9.8	55.2	N 40	03 18	03 59	04 31	00 20	00 50	01 20	01 49
A 14	30 19.8	40.8	118 46.4	14.1	9 14.8	9.8	55.2	35	03 40	04 16	04 46	00 13	00 46	01 18	01 50
Y 15	45 19.6	.. 41.1	133 19.5	14.0	9 05.0	9.9	55.3	30	03 58	04 31	04 58	00 07	00 42	01 16	01 51
16	60 19.5	41.3	147 52.5	14.0	8 55.1	9.9	55.3	20	04 26	04 55	05 20	24 35	00 35	01 14	01 52
17	75 19.4	41.6	162 25.5	14.0	8 45.2	9.9	55.3	N 10	04 48	05 15	05 38	24 30	00 30	01 11	01 54
18	90 19.3	N22 41.8	176 58.5	14.0	S 8 35.3	10.0	55.3	0	05 07	05 33	05 55	24 24	00 24	01 09	01 55
19	105 19.2	42.1	191 31.5	14.0	8 25.3	10.1	55.4	S 10	05 23	05 49	06 12	24 19	00 19	01 07	01 56
20	120 19.1	42.3	206 04.5	14.0	8 15.2	10.1	55.4	20	05 39	06 06	06 30	24 13	00 13	01 04	01 57
21	135 19.0	.. 42.6	220 37.5	14.0	8 05.1	10.1	55.4	30	05 55	06 24	06 51	24 06	00 06	01 02	01 59
22	150 18.8	42.8	235 10.5	14.0	7 55.0	10.2	55.4	35	06 03	06 35	07 03	24 02	00 02	01 00	02 00
23	165 18.7	43.1	249 43.5	14.0	7 44.8	10.2	55.5	40	06 12	06 46	07 16	23 58	24 58	00 58	02 01
7 00	180 18.6	N22 43.3	264 16.5	14.0	S 7 34.6	10.3	55.5	45	06 22	06 59	07 32	23 53	24 56	00 56	02 02
01	195 18.5	43.6	278 49.5	14.0	7 24.3	10.3	55.5	S 50	06 33	07 14	07 52	23 46	24 54	00 54	02 03
02	210 18.4	43.8	293 22.5	14.0	7 14.0	10.4	55.5	52	06 38	07 21	08 02	23 44	24 53	00 53	02 04
03	225 18.3	.. 44.0	307 55.5	13.9	7 03.6	10.4	55.6	54	06 43	07 29	08 12	23 41	24 51	00 51	02 05
04	240 18.1	44.3	322 28.4	14.0	6 53.2	10.4	55.6	56	06 49	07 38	08 24	23 37	24 50	00 50	02 05
05	255 18.0	44.5	337 01.4	14.0	6 42.8	10.5	55.6	58	06 56	07 48	08 38	23 33	24 49	00 49	02 06
06	270 17.9	N22 44.8	351 34.4	13.9	S 6 32.3	10.5	55.7	S 60	07 03	07 59	08 55	23 29	24 47	00 47	02 07
T 07	285 17.8	45.0	6 07.3	13.9	6 21.8	10.6	55.7								
H 08	300 17.7	45.2	20 40.2	13.9	6 11.2	10.5	55.7	Lat.	Sunset	Twilight		Moonset			
U 09	315 17.6	.. 45.5	35 13.1	13.9	6 00.7	10.7	55.7			Civil	Naut.	6	7	8	9
R 10	330 17.4	45.7	49 46.0	13.9	5 50.0	10.7	55.8								
S 11	345 17.3	46.0	64 18.9	13.9	5 39.3	10.7	55.8	°	h m	h m	h m	h m	h m	h m	h m
D 12	0 17.2	N22 46.2	78 51.8	13.9	S 5 28.6	10.7	55.8	N 72	▭	▭	▭	09 45	11 32	13 20	15 10
A 13	15 17.1	46.4	93 24.7	13.8	5 17.9	10.8	55.9	N 70	▭	▭	▭	10 02	11 41	13 21	15 04
Y 14	30 17.0	46.7	107 57.5	13.8	5 07.1	10.8	55.9	68	▭	▭	▭	10 15	11 48	13 22	14 59
15	45 16.9	.. 46.9	122 30.3	13.8	4 56.3	10.9	55.9	66	23 17	////	////	10 26	11 53	13 23	14 55
16	60 16.7	47.1	137 03.1	13.8	4 45.4	10.8	56.0	64	22 15	////	////	10 35	11 58	13 24	14 52
17	75 16.6	47.4	151 35.9	13.8	4 34.6	11.0	56.0	62	21 41	////	////	10 42	12 02	13 24	14 49
18	90 16.5	N22 47.6	166 08.7	13.7	S 4 23.6	10.9	56.0	60	21 17	22 50	////	10 49	12 06	13 25	14 47
19	105 16.4	47.8	180 41.4	13.8	4 12.7	11.0	56.1	N 58	20 57	22 09	////	10 55	12 09	13 25	14 44
20	120 16.3	48.1	195 14.2	13.7	4 01.7	11.0	56.1	56	20 42	21 42	////	11 00	12 12	13 26	14 42
21	135 16.1	.. 48.3	209 46.9	13.7	3 50.7	11.0	56.1	54	20 28	21 21	22 56	11 04	12 14	13 26	14 41
22	150 16.0	48.5	224 19.6	13.6	3 39.7	11.1	56.1	52	20 16	21 04	22 18	11 08	12 16	13 26	14 39
23	165 15.9	48.8	238 52.2	13.7	3 28.6	11.1	56.2	50	20 06	20 50	21 53	11 12	12 18	13 27	14 37
8 00	180 15.8	N22 49.0	253 24.9	13.6	S 3 17.5	11.1	56.2	45	19 44	20 21	21 10	11 20	12 23	13 27	14 34
01	195 15.7	49.2	267 57.5	13.6	3 06.4	11.2	56.2	N 40	19 27	19 59	20 40	11 27	12 27	13 28	14 31
02	210 15.5	49.5	282 30.1	13.5	2 55.2	11.2	56.3	35	19 12	19 41	20 18	11 33	12 30	13 28	14 29
03	225 15.4	.. 49.7	297 02.6	13.6	2 44.0	11.2	56.3	30	18 59	19 27	20 00	11 38	12 33	13 29	14 27
04	240 15.3	49.9	311 35.2	13.5	2 32.8	11.2	56.3	20	18 38	19 02	19 31	11 46	12 37	13 30	14 24
05	255 15.2	50.1	326 07.7	13.4	2 21.6	11.3	56.4	N 10	18 20	18 43	19 09	11 54	12 42	13 30	14 20
06	270 15.1	N22 50.4	340 40.1	13.5	S 2 10.3	11.3	56.4	0	18 03	18 25	18 51	12 01	12 45	13 31	14 17
07	285 14.9	50.6	355 12.6	13.4	1 59.0	11.3	56.5	S 10	17 46	18 08	18 35	12 08	12 49	13 31	14 15
08	300 14.8	50.8	9 45.0	13.4	1 47.7	11.3	56.5	20	17 28	17 51	18 19	12 15	12 53	13 32	14 11
F 09	315 14.7	.. 51.0	24 17.4	13.3	1 36.4	11.4	56.5	30	17 07	17 33	18 03	12 24	12 58	13 32	14 08
R 10	330 14.6	51.3	38 49.7	13.3	1 25.0	11.3	56.6	35	16 55	17 23	17 55	12 29	13 01	13 33	14 06
I 11	345 14.5	51.5	53 22.0	13.3	1 13.7	11.4	56.6	40	16 41	17 12	17 46	12 34	13 04	13 33	14 03
D 12	0 14.3	N22 51.7	67 54.3	13.3	S 1 02.3	11.4	56.6	45	16 25	16 59	17 36	12 40	13 07	13 34	14 01
A 13	15 14.2	51.9	82 26.6	13.2	0 50.9	11.5	56.7	S 50	16 05	16 43	17 24	12 48	13 11	13 34	13 58
Y 14	30 14.1	52.1	96 58.8	13.1	0 39.4	11.4	56.7	52	15 56	16 36	17 19	12 51	13 13	13 34	13 56
15	45 14.0	.. 52.4	111 30.9	13.2	0 28.0	11.5	56.8	54	15 45	16 28	17 14	12 55	13 15	13 35	13 55
16	60 13.9	52.6	126 03.1	13.1	0 16.5	11.5	56.8	56	15 33	16 20	17 08	12 59	13 17	13 35	13 53
17	75 13.7	52.8	140 35.2	13.0	S 0 05.0	11.5	56.8	58	15 19	16 10	17 02	13 04	13 20	13 35	13 51
18	90 13.6	N22 53.0	155 07.2	13.0	N 0 06.5	11.5	56.8	S 60	15 02	15 59	16 55	13 09	13 23	13 35	13 49
19	105 13.5	53.2	169 39.2	13.0	0 18.0	11.5	56.9			SUN		MOON			
20	120 13.4	53.4	184 11.2	12.9	0 29.5	11.6	56.9	Day	Eqn. of Time		Mer.	Mer. Pass.		Age	Phase
21	135 13.3	.. 53.7	198 43.1	12.9	0 41.1	11.5	56.9		00ʰ	12ʰ	Pass.	Upper	Lower		
22	150 13.1	53.9	213 15.0	12.9	0 52.6	11.6	57.0	d	m s	m s	h m	h m	h m	d %	
23	165 13.0	54.1	227 46.9	12.8	N 1 04.2	11.6	57.0	6	01 26	01 20	11 59	05 50	18 12	22 53	
								7	01 15	01 09	11 59	06 35	18 57	23 43	
	SD 15.8	d 0.2	SD 15.0		15.2		15.4	8	01 03	00 58	11 59	07 20	19 43	24 33	

2018 JUNE 9, 10, 11 (SAT., SUN., MON.)

UT	ARIES GHA	VENUS −4.0 GHA	Dec	MARS −1.5 GHA	Dec	JUPITER −2.4 GHA	Dec	SATURN +0.1 GHA	Dec	STARS Name	SHA	Dec
d h	° ′	° ′	° ′	° ′	° ′	° ′	° ′	° ′	° ′		° ′	° ′
9 00	257 18.8	140 47.1	N23 13.8	306 39.9	S21 43.5	34 36.0	S15 08.4	339 32.6	S22 22.1	Acamar	315 16.2	S40 13.9
01	272 21.3	155 46.4	13.3	321 41.8	43.5	49 38.7	08.4	354 35.3	22.1	Achernar	335 24.7	S57 08.5
02	287 23.7	170 45.7	12.8	336 43.6	43.5	64 41.3	08.3	9 37.9	22.1	Acrux	173 05.2	S63 12.3
03	302 26.2	185 45.1	.. 12.3	351 45.5	.. 43.6	79 44.0	.. 08.3	24 40.5	.. 22.2	Adhara	255 10.2	S29 00.1
04	317 28.7	200 44.4	11.8	6 47.4	43.6	94 46.7	08.2	39 43.2	22.2	Aldebaran	290 45.9	N16 32.5
05	332 31.1	215 43.7	11.3	21 49.3	43.6	109 49.4	08.1	54 45.8	22.2			
06	347 33.6	230 43.0	N23 10.8	36 51.2	S21 43.7	124 52.1	S15 08.1	69 48.5	S22 22.2	Alioth	166 17.6	N55 52.0
07	2 36.1	245 42.3	10.3	51 53.1	43.7	139 54.8	08.0	84 51.1	22.2	Alkaid	152 56.0	N49 13.6
S 08	17 38.5	260 41.7	09.7	66 55.0	43.7	154 57.5	08.0	99 53.8	22.2	Al Na'ir	27 39.4	S46 52.1
A 09	32 41.0	275 41.0	.. 09.2	81 56.9	.. 43.8	170 00.1	.. 07.9	114 56.4	.. 22.2	Alnilam	275 43.3	S 1 11.6
T 10	47 43.5	290 40.3	08.7	96 58.8	43.8	185 02.8	07.9	129 59.1	22.2	Alphard	217 53.0	S 8 44.4
U 11	62 45.9	305 39.6	08.2	112 00.6	43.8	200 05.5	07.8	145 01.7	22.2			
R 12	77 48.4	320 39.0	N23 07.7	127 02.5	S21 43.9	215 08.2	S15 07.8	160 04.4	S22 22.3	Alphecca	126 07.8	N26 39.4
D 13	92 50.8	335 38.3	07.2	142 04.4	43.9	230 10.9	07.7	175 07.0	22.3	Alpheratz	357 40.1	N29 11.2
A 14	107 53.3	350 37.6	06.7	157 06.3	43.9	245 13.6	07.6	190 09.7	22.3	Altair	62 04.7	N 8 55.1
Y 15	122 55.8	5 36.9	.. 06.1	172 08.2	.. 44.0	260 16.2	.. 07.6	205 12.3	.. 22.3	Ankaa	353 12.5	S42 12.3
16	137 58.2	20 36.3	05.6	187 10.1	44.0	275 18.9	07.5	220 14.9	22.3	Antares	112 21.8	S26 28.2
17	153 00.7	35 35.6	05.1	202 12.0	44.0	290 21.6	07.5	235 17.6	22.3			
18	168 03.2	50 34.9	N23 04.6	217 13.9	S21 44.1	305 24.3	S15 07.4	250 20.2	S22 22.3	Arcturus	145 52.4	N19 05.4
19	183 05.6	65 34.3	04.1	232 15.8	44.1	320 27.0	07.4	265 22.9	22.3	Atria	107 20.0	S69 03.5
20	198 08.1	80 33.6	03.5	247 17.7	44.1	335 29.7	07.3	280 25.5	22.3	Avior	234 17.1	S59 34.4
21	213 10.6	95 32.9	.. 03.0	262 19.6	.. 44.2	350 32.3	.. 07.3	295 28.2	.. 22.4	Bellatrix	278 28.7	N 6 21.8
22	228 13.0	110 32.3	02.5	277 21.5	44.2	5 35.0	07.2	310 30.8	22.4	Betelgeuse	270 58.0	N 7 24.4
23	243 15.5	125 31.6	02.0	292 23.4	44.3	20 37.7	07.1	325 33.5	22.4			
10 00	258 17.9	140 30.9	N23 01.4	307 25.4	S21 44.3	35 40.4	S15 07.1	340 36.1	S22 22.4	Canopus	263 55.2	S52 42.6
01	273 20.4	155 30.3	00.9	322 27.3	44.3	50 43.1	07.0	355 38.8	22.4	Capella	280 30.0	N46 00.7
02	288 22.9	170 29.6	23 00.4	337 29.2	44.4	65 45.8	07.0	10 41.4	22.4	Deneb	49 28.9	N45 20.6
03	303 25.3	185 28.9	22 59.8	352 31.1	.. 44.4	80 48.4	.. 06.9	25 44.1	.. 22.4	Denebola	182 30.2	N14 28.3
04	318 27.8	200 28.3	59.3	7 33.0	44.5	95 51.1	06.9	40 46.7	22.4	Diphda	348 52.7	S17 53.2
05	333 30.3	215 27.6	58.8	22 34.9	44.5	110 53.8	06.8	55 49.4	22.4			
06	348 32.7	230 26.9	N22 58.2	37 36.8	S21 44.5	125 56.5	S15 06.8	70 52.0	S22 22.5	Dubhe	193 47.7	N61 39.4
07	3 35.2	245 26.3	57.7	52 38.7	44.6	140 59.2	06.7	85 54.7	22.5	Elnath	278 08.8	N28 37.1
S 08	18 37.7	260 25.6	57.2	67 40.7	44.6	156 01.8	06.7	100 57.3	22.5	Eltanin	90 44.0	N51 29.3
U 09	33 40.1	275 24.9	.. 56.6	82 42.6	.. 44.7	171 04.5	.. 06.6	116 00.0	.. 22.5	Enif	33 43.7	N 9 57.5
N 10	48 42.6	290 24.3	56.1	97 44.5	44.7	186 07.2	06.5	131 02.6	22.5	Fomalhaut	15 20.3	S29 31.4
D 11	63 45.1	305 23.6	55.6	112 46.4	44.7	201 09.9	06.5	146 05.3	22.5			
A 12	78 47.5	320 23.0	N22 55.0	127 48.3	S21 44.8	216 12.6	S15 06.4	161 07.9	S22 22.5	Gacrux	171 56.9	S57 13.1
Y 13	93 50.0	335 22.3	54.5	142 50.2	44.8	231 15.2	06.4	176 10.6	22.5	Gienah	175 48.7	S17 38.7
14	108 52.4	350 21.6	53.9	157 52.2	44.9	246 17.9	06.3	191 13.2	22.5	Hadar	148 42.6	S60 27.8
15	123 54.9	5 21.0	.. 53.4	172 54.1	.. 44.9	261 20.6	.. 06.3	206 15.8	.. 22.6	Hamal	327 57.2	N23 32.7
16	138 57.4	20 20.3	52.8	187 56.0	45.0	276 23.3	06.2	221 18.5	22.6	Kaus Aust.	83 39.0	S34 22.3
17	153 59.8	35 19.7	52.3	202 57.9	45.0	291 25.9	06.2	236 21.1	22.6			
18	169 02.3	50 19.0	N22 51.7	217 59.9	S21 45.0	306 28.6	S15 06.1	251 23.8	S22 22.6	Kochab	137 19.2	N74 05.1
19	184 04.8	65 18.3	51.2	233 01.8	45.1	321 31.3	06.1	266 26.4	22.6	Markab	13 35.0	N15 18.1
20	199 07.2	80 17.7	50.7	248 03.7	45.1	336 34.0	06.0	281 29.1	22.6	Menkar	314 11.8	N 4 09.5
21	214 09.7	95 17.0	.. 50.1	263 05.7	.. 45.2	351 36.7	.. 06.0	296 31.7	.. 22.6	Menkent	148 03.3	S36 27.6
22	229 12.2	110 16.4	49.5	278 07.6	45.2	6 39.3	05.9	311 34.4	22.6	Miaplacidus	221 39.4	S69 47.9
23	244 14.6	125 15.7	49.0	293 09.5	45.3	21 42.0	05.9	326 37.0	22.6			
11 00	259 17.1	140 15.1	N22 48.4	308 11.5	S21 45.3	36 44.7	S15 05.8	341 39.7	S22 22.7	Mirfak	308 36.0	N49 55.2
01	274 19.6	155 14.4	47.9	323 13.4	45.4	51 47.4	05.7	356 42.3	22.7	Nunki	75 53.8	S26 16.2
02	289 22.0	170 13.8	47.3	338 15.3	45.4	66 50.0	05.7	11 45.0	22.7	Peacock	53 13.6	S56 40.2
03	304 24.5	185 13.1	.. 46.8	353 17.3	.. 45.4	81 52.7	.. 05.6	26 47.6	.. 22.7	Pollux	243 24.0	N27 58.8
04	319 26.9	200 12.5	46.2	8 19.2	45.5	96 55.4	05.6	41 50.3	22.7	Procyon	244 56.5	N 5 10.5
05	334 29.4	215 11.8	45.7	23 21.1	45.5	111 58.1	05.5	56 52.9	22.7			
06	349 31.9	230 11.2	N22 45.1	38 23.1	S21 45.6	127 00.7	S15 05.5	71 55.6	S22 22.7	Rasalhague	96 03.0	N12 33.0
07	4 34.3	245 10.5	44.5	53 25.0	45.6	142 03.4	05.4	86 58.2	22.7	Regulus	207 40.1	N11 52.7
08	19 36.8	260 09.9	44.0	68 27.0	45.7	157 06.1	05.4	102 00.9	22.7	Rigel	281 09.2	S 8 11.0
M 09	34 39.3	275 09.2	.. 43.4	83 28.9	.. 45.7	172 08.8	.. 05.3	117 03.5	.. 22.8	Rigil Kent.	139 46.6	S60 54.7
O 10	49 41.7	290 08.6	42.9	98 30.9	45.8	187 11.4	05.3	132 06.2	22.8	Sabik	102 08.3	S15 44.7
N 11	64 44.2	305 07.9	42.3	113 32.8	45.8	202 14.1	05.2	147 08.8	22.8			
D 12	79 46.7	320 07.3	N22 41.7	128 34.8	S21 45.9	217 16.8	S15 05.1	162 11.5	S22 22.8	Schedar	349 36.8	N56 37.9
A 13	94 49.1	335 06.6	41.2	143 36.7	45.9	232 19.4	05.1	177 14.1	22.8	Shaula	96 16.9	S37 06.8
Y 14	109 51.6	350 06.0	40.6	158 38.7	46.0	247 22.1	05.1	192 16.8	22.8	Sirius	258 31.1	S16 44.7
15	124 54.1	5 05.3	.. 40.0	173 40.6	.. 46.0	262 24.8	.. 05.0	207 19.4	.. 22.8	Spica	158 27.5	S11 15.4
16	139 56.5	20 04.7	39.5	188 42.6	46.1	277 27.5	05.0	222 22.1	22.8	Suhail	222 50.2	S43 30.7
17	154 59.0	35 04.0	38.9	203 44.5	46.1	292 30.1	04.9	237 24.7	22.9			
18	170 01.4	50 03.4	N22 38.3	218 46.5	S21 46.2	307 32.8	S15 04.9	252 27.4	S22 22.9	Vega	80 36.3	N38 48.1
19	185 03.9	65 02.8	37.7	233 48.4	46.2	322 35.5	04.8	267 30.0	22.9	Zuben'ubi	137 01.4	S16 07.0
20	200 06.4	80 02.1	37.2	248 50.4	46.3	337 38.2	04.7	282 32.7	22.9			
21	215 08.8	95 01.5	.. 36.6	263 52.3	.. 46.3	352 40.8	.. 04.7	297 35.3	.. 22.9			
22	230 11.3	110 00.8	36.0	278 54.3	46.4	7 43.5	04.6	312 38.0	22.9			
23	245 13.8	125 00.2	35.4	293 56.3	46.5	22 46.2	04.6	327 40.6	22.9			

	SHA	Mer. Pass.
	° ′	h m
Venus	242 13.0	14 39
Mars	49 07.4	3 30
Jupiter	137 22.4	21 33
Saturn	82 18.2	1 17

	Aries	Venus	Mars	Jupiter	Saturn
Mer. Pass.	h m 6 45.7	v −0.7 d 0.5	v 1.9 d 0.0	v 2.7 d 0.1	v 2.6 d 0.0

UT	SUN GHA	SUN Dec	MOON GHA	v	MOON Dec	d	HP
d h	° ′	° ′	° ′	′	° ′	′	′
9 00	180 12.9	N22 54.3	242 18.7	12.7	N 1 15.8	11.6	57.1
01	195 12.8	54.5	256 50.4	12.7	1 27.4	11.6	57.1
02	210 12.6	54.7	271 22.1	12.7	1 39.0	11.6	57.1
03	225 12.5 ..	54.9	285 53.8	12.6	1 50.6	11.6	57.2
04	240 12.4	55.1	300 25.4	12.5	2 02.2	11.6	57.2
05	255 12.3	55.4	314 56.9	12.5	2 13.8	11.6	57.2
06	270 12.2	N22 55.6	329 28.4	12.5	N 2 25.4	11.6	57.3
07	285 12.0	55.8	343 59.9	12.4	2 37.0	11.7	57.3
S 08	300 11.9	56.0	358 31.3	12.4	2 48.7	11.6	57.4
A 09	315 11.8 ..	56.2	13 02.6	12.3	3 00.3	11.6	57.4
T 10	330 11.7	56.4	27 33.9	12.3	3 11.9	11.7	57.4
U 11	345 11.5	56.6	42 05.2	12.1	3 23.6	11.6	57.5
R 12	0 11.4	N22 56.8	56 36.3	12.2	N 3 35.2	11.7	57.5
D 13	15 11.3	57.0	71 07.5	12.0	3 46.9	11.6	57.6
A 14	30 11.2	57.2	85 38.5	12.0	3 58.5	11.6	57.6
Y 15	45 11.0 ..	57.4	100 09.5	12.0	4 10.1	11.6	57.6
16	60 10.9	57.6	114 40.5	11.9	4 21.7	11.7	57.7
17	75 10.8	57.7	129 11.4	11.8	4 33.4	11.6	57.7
18	90 10.7	N22 58.0	143 42.2	11.8	N 4 45.0	11.6	57.8
19	105 10.5	58.2	158 13.0	11.7	4 56.6	11.6	57.8
20	120 10.4	58.4	172 43.7	11.6	5 08.2	11.6	57.8
21	135 10.3 ..	58.6	187 14.3	11.6	5 19.8	11.5	57.9
22	150 10.2	58.8	201 44.9	11.5	5 31.3	11.6	57.9
23	165 10.1	59.0	216 15.4	11.4	5 42.9	11.5	57.9
10 00	180 09.9	N22 59.2	230 45.8	11.4	N 5 54.4	11.6	58.0
01	195 09.8	59.4	245 16.2	11.3	6 06.0	11.5	58.0
02	210 09.7	59.6	259 46.5	11.2	6 17.5	11.5	58.1
03	225 09.6	22 59.8	274 16.7	11.2	6 29.0	11.5	58.1
04	240 09.4	23 00.0	288 46.9	11.1	6 40.5	11.5	58.1
05	255 09.3	00.2	303 17.0	11.0	6 52.0	11.4	58.2
06	270 09.2	N23 00.4	317 47.0	11.0	N 7 03.4	11.4	58.2
07	285 09.1	00.5	332 17.0	10.8	7 14.8	11.4	58.2
S 08	300 08.9	00.7	346 46.8	10.9	7 26.2	11.4	58.3
U 09	315 08.8 ..	00.9	1 16.7	10.7	7 37.6	11.4	58.3
N 10	330 08.7	01.1	15 46.4	10.6	7 49.0	11.3	58.4
D 11	345 08.5	01.3	30 16.0	10.6	8 00.3	11.3	58.4
A 12	0 08.4	N23 01.5	44 45.6	10.5	N 8 11.6	11.3	58.4
Y 13	15 08.3	01.7	59 15.1	10.4	8 22.9	11.2	58.5
14	30 08.2	01.9	73 44.5	10.4	8 34.1	11.3	58.5
15	45 08.0 ..	02.0	88 13.9	10.3	8 45.4	11.1	58.6
16	60 07.9	02.2	102 43.2	10.1	8 56.5	11.2	58.6
17	75 07.8	02.4	117 12.3	10.2	9 07.7	11.1	58.6
18	90 07.7	N23 02.6	131 41.5	10.0	N 9 18.8	11.1	58.7
19	105 07.5	02.8	146 10.5	9.9	9 29.9	11.0	58.7
20	120 07.4	03.0	160 39.4	9.9	9 40.9	11.0	58.7
21	135 07.3 ..	03.1	175 08.3	9.8	9 51.9	11.0	58.8
22	150 07.2	03.3	189 37.1	9.7	10 02.9	10.9	58.8
23	165 07.0	03.5	204 05.8	9.6	10 13.8	10.9	58.9
11 00	180 06.9	N23 03.7	218 34.4	9.5	N10 24.7	10.8	58.9
01	195 06.8	03.9	233 02.9	9.5	10 35.5	10.8	58.9
02	210 06.6	04.0	247 31.4	9.3	10 46.3	10.7	59.0
03	225 06.5 ..	04.2	261 59.7	9.3	10 57.0	10.7	59.0
04	240 06.4	04.4	276 28.0	9.2	11 07.7	10.6	59.0
05	255 06.3	04.6	290 56.2	9.1	11 18.3	10.6	59.1
06	270 06.1	N23 04.7	305 24.3	9.0	N11 28.9	10.5	59.1
07	285 06.0	04.9	319 52.3	8.9	11 39.4	10.5	59.1
M 08	300 05.9	05.1	334 20.2	8.8	11 49.9	10.4	59.2
O 09	315 05.8 ..	05.3	348 48.0	8.8	12 00.3	10.4	59.2
N 10	330 05.6	05.4	3 15.8	8.6	12 10.7	10.3	59.3
11	345 05.5	05.6	17 43.4	8.6	12 21.0	10.2	59.3
D 12	0 05.4	N23 05.8	32 11.0	8.5	N12 31.2	10.2	59.3
A 13	15 05.2	05.9	46 38.5	8.4	12 41.4	10.1	59.4
Y 14	30 05.1	06.1	61 05.9	8.3	12 51.5	10.1	59.4
15	45 05.0 ..	06.3	75 33.2	8.2	13 01.6	10.0	59.4
16	60 04.9	06.5	90 00.4	8.1	13 11.6	9.9	59.5
17	75 04.7	06.6	104 27.5	8.0	13 21.5	9.8	59.5
18	90 04.6	N23 06.8	118 54.5	8.0	N13 31.3	9.8	59.5
19	105 04.5	07.0	133 21.5	7.8	13 41.1	9.7	59.6
20	120 04.3	07.1	147 48.3	7.8	13 50.8	9.6	59.6
21	135 04.2 ..	07.3	162 15.1	7.6	14 00.4	9.6	59.6
22	150 04.1	07.4	176 41.7	7.6	14 10.0	9.5	59.7
23	165 04.0	07.6	191 08.3	7.5	N14 19.5	9.4	59.7
	SD 15.8	d 0.2	SD 15.7		15.9		16.2

Lat.	Twilight Naut.	Twilight Civil	Sunrise	Moonrise 9	10	11	12
°	h m	h m	h m	h m	h m	h m	h m
N 72	☐	☐	☐	01 36	01 24	01 10	00 50
N 70	☐	☐	☐	01 38	01 32	01 26	01 19
68	☐	☐	☐	01 40	01 39	01 39	01 41
66	////	////	00 29	01 41	01 45	01 50	01 59
64	////	////	01 40	01 42	01 50	02 00	02 13
62	////	////	02 14	01 43	01 54	02 07	02 25
60	////	01 03	02 39	01 44	01 58	02 14	02 35
N 58	////	01 46	02 59	01 45	02 01	02 20	02 44
56	////	02 14	03 15	01 45	02 04	02 26	02 52
54	00 57	02 35	03 29	01 46	02 07	02 31	02 59
52	01 37	02 53	03 41	01 47	02 09	02 35	03 06
50	02 03	03 07	03 51	01 47	02 12	02 39	03 12
45	02 47	03 36	04 13	01 48	02 17	02 48	03 24
N 40	03 17	03 58	04 31	01 49	02 21	02 55	03 35
35	03 40	04 16	04 46	01 50	02 24	03 02	03 43
30	03 58	04 31	04 58	01 51	02 28	03 07	03 51
20	04 26	04 55	05 20	01 52	02 33	03 17	04 05
N 10	04 49	05 16	05 39	01 54	02 38	03 26	04 17
0	05 07	05 33	05 56	01 55	02 43	03 34	04 28
S 10	05 24	05 50	06 13	01 56	02 48	03 42	04 40
20	05 40	06 07	06 31	01 57	02 53	03 51	04 52
30	05 56	06 26	06 52	01 59	02 59	04 01	05 06
35	06 04	06 36	07 04	02 00	03 02	04 07	05 14
40	06 13	06 47	07 18	02 01	03 06	04 14	05 24
45	06 24	07 01	07 34	02 02	03 10	04 21	05 35
S 50	06 35	07 16	07 55	02 03	03 16	04 31	05 48
52	06 40	07 24	08 04	02 04	03 18	04 35	05 55
54	06 46	07 32	08 15	02 05	03 21	04 40	06 02
56	06 52	07 40	08 27	02 05	03 24	04 46	06 09
58	06 58	07 50	08 42	02 06	03 27	04 52	06 18
S 60	07 05	08 02	08 58	02 07	03 31	04 59	06 28

Lat.	Sunset	Twilight Civil	Twilight Naut.	Moonset 9	10	11	12
°	h m	h m	h m	h m	h m	h m	h m
N 72	☐	☐	☐	15 10	17 08	19 19	22 07
N 70	☐	☐	☐	15 04	16 54	18 51	21 00
68	☐	☐	☐	14 59	16 42	18 31	20 24
66	23 37	////	////	14 55	16 32	18 14	19 59
64	22 21	////	////	14 52	16 25	18 01	19 39
62	21 46	////	////	14 49	16 18	17 50	19 23
60	21 20	22 58	////	14 47	16 12	17 40	19 10
N 58	21 01	22 14	////	14 44	16 07	17 32	18 58
56	20 44	21 46	////	14 42	16 02	17 25	18 48
54	20 31	21 24	23 04	14 41	15 58	17 18	18 40
52	20 19	21 07	22 23	14 39	15 54	17 12	18 32
50	20 08	20 52	21 56	14 37	15 51	17 07	18 25
45	19 46	20 23	21 12	14 34	15 44	16 56	18 10
N 40	19 28	20 01	20 42	14 31	15 38	16 47	17 58
35	19 13	19 43	20 20	14 29	15 33	16 39	17 47
30	19 01	19 28	20 01	14 27	15 28	16 32	17 38
20	18 39	19 04	19 33	14 24	15 20	16 20	17 22
N 10	18 20	18 43	19 10	14 20	15 13	16 09	17 09
0	18 03	18 26	18 52	14 17	15 07	15 59	16 56
S 10	17 46	18 09	18 35	14 15	15 00	15 49	16 43
20	17 28	17 52	18 19	14 11	14 53	15 39	16 29
30	17 07	17 33	18 03	14 08	14 46	15 27	16 15
35	16 55	17 23	17 54	14 06	14 41	15 20	16 05
40	16 41	17 11	17 45	14 03	14 36	15 13	15 55
45	16 24	16 56	17 35	14 01	14 30	15 03	15 43
S 50	16 04	16 42	17 24	13 58	14 23	14 53	15 29
52	15 55	16 35	17 19	13 56	14 20	14 48	15 21
54	15 44	16 27	17 13	13 55	14 16	14 42	15 14
56	15 31	16 18	17 07	13 53	14 13	14 36	15 05
58	15 17	16 08	17 01	13 51	14 08	14 29	14 56
S 60	15 00	15 57	16 53	13 49	14 03	14 21	14 45

Day	SUN Eqn. of Time 00h	SUN Eqn. of Time 12h	SUN Mer. Pass.	MOON Mer. Pass. Upper	MOON Mer. Pass. Lower	Age	Phase
d	m s	m s	h m	h m	h m	d	%
9	00 52	00 46	11 59	08 06	20 30	25	23
10	00 40	00 34	11 59	08 55	21 20	26	15
11	00 28	00 22	12 00	09 46	22 14	27	8

UT	ARIES GHA	VENUS −4·0 GHA	Dec	MARS −1·6 GHA	Dec	JUPITER −2·4 GHA	Dec	SATURN +0·1 GHA	Dec	STARS Name	SHA	Dec
12 00	260 16.2	139 59.6	N22 34.9	308 58.2	S21 46.5	37 48.8	S15 04.5	342 43.3	S22 22.9	Acamar	315 16.2	S40 13.9
01	275 18.7	154 58.9	34.3	324 00.2	46.6	52 51.5	04.5	357 45.9	22.9	Achernar	335 24.7	S57 08.5
02	290 21.2	169 58.3	33.7	339 02.1	46.6	67 54.2	04.4	12 48.6	23.0	Acrux	173 05.2	S63 12.3
03	305 23.6	184 57.6 ..	33.1	354 04.1 ..	46.7	82 56.8 ..	04.4	27 51.2 ..	23.0	Adhara	255 10.2	S29 00.0
04	320 26.1	199 57.0	32.5	9 06.1	46.7	97 59.5	04.3	42 53.9	23.0	Aldebaran	290 45.9	N16 32.5
05	335 28.5	214 56.4	31.9	24 08.0	46.8	113 02.2	04.3	57 56.5	23.0			
06	350 31.0	229 55.7	N22 31.4	39 10.0	S21 46.8	128 04.8	S15 04.2	72 59.2	S22 23.0	Alioth	166 17.6	N55 52.0
07	5 33.5	244 55.1	30.8	54 12.0	46.9	143 07.5	04.2	88 01.8	23.0	Alkaid	152 56.0	N49 13.6
T 08	20 35.9	259 54.5	30.2	69 13.9	47.0	158 10.2	04.1	103 04.5	23.0	Al Na'ir	27 39.4	S46 52.1
U 09	35 38.4	274 53.8 ..	29.6	84 15.9 ..	47.0	173 12.8 ..	04.1	118 07.1 ..	23.0	Alnilam	275 43.3	S 1 11.6
E 10	50 40.9	289 53.2	29.0	99 17.9	47.1	188 15.5	04.0	133 09.8	23.0	Alphard	217 53.0	S 8 44.4
S 11	65 43.3	304 52.6	28.4	114 19.9	47.1	203 18.2	04.0	148 12.5	23.1			
D 12	80 45.8	319 51.9	N22 27.8	129 21.8	S21 47.2	218 20.9	S15 03.9	163 15.1	S22 23.1	Alphecca	126 07.8	N26 39.4
A 13	95 48.3	334 51.3	27.2	144 23.8	47.2	233 23.5	03.9	178 17.8	23.1	Alpheratz	357 40.0	N29 11.3
Y 14	110 50.7	349 50.7	26.7	159 25.8	47.3	248 26.2	03.8	193 20.4	23.1	Altair	62 04.7	N 8 55.1
15	125 53.2	4 50.0 ..	26.1	174 27.8 ..	47.4	263 28.9 ..	03.8	208 23.1 ..	23.1	Ankaa	353 12.5	S42 12.2
16	140 55.7	19 49.4	25.5	189 29.8	47.4	278 31.5	03.7	223 25.7	23.1	Antares	112 21.8	S26 28.2
17	155 58.1	34 48.8	24.9	204 31.7	47.5	293 34.2	03.7	238 28.4	23.1			
18	171 00.6	49 48.1	N22 24.3	219 33.7	S21 47.5	308 36.8	S15 03.6	253 31.0	S22 23.1	Arcturus	145 52.4	N19 05.4
19	186 03.0	64 47.5	23.7	234 35.7	47.6	323 39.5	03.6	268 33.7	23.1	Atria	107 19.9	S69 03.5
20	201 05.5	79 46.9	23.1	249 37.7	47.7	338 42.2	03.5	283 36.3	23.2	Avior	234 17.1	S59 34.4
21	216 08.0	94 46.3 ..	22.5	264 39.7 ..	47.7	353 44.8 ..	03.5	298 39.0 ..	23.2	Bellatrix	278 28.7	N 6 21.8
22	231 10.4	109 45.6	21.9	279 41.7	47.8	8 47.5	03.4	313 41.6	23.2	Betelgeuse	270 58.0	N 7 24.4
23	246 12.9	124 45.0	21.3	294 43.6	47.8	23 50.2	03.4	328 44.3	23.2			
13 00	261 15.4	139 44.4	N22 20.7	309 45.6	S21 47.9	38 52.8	S15 03.3	343 46.9	S22 23.2	Canopus	263 55.2	S52 42.5
01	276 17.8	154 43.8	20.1	324 47.6	48.0	53 55.5	03.3	358 49.6	23.2	Capella	280 29.9	N46 00.7
02	291 20.3	169 43.1	19.5	339 49.6	48.0	68 58.2	03.2	13 52.2	23.2	Deneb	49 28.8	N45 20.6
03	306 22.8	184 42.5 ..	18.9	354 51.6 ..	48.1	84 00.8 ..	03.2	28 54.9 ..	23.2	Denebola	182 30.2	N14 28.3
04	321 25.2	199 41.9	18.2	9 53.6	48.2	99 03.5	03.1	43 57.5	23.2	Diphda	348 52.6	S17 53.2
05	336 27.7	214 41.3	17.6	24 55.6	48.2	114 06.1	03.1	59 00.2	23.3			
06	351 30.2	229 40.6	N22 17.0	39 57.6	S21 48.3	129 08.8	S15 03.0	74 02.8	S22 23.3	Dubhe	193 47.8	N61 39.4
W 07	6 32.6	244 40.0	16.4	54 59.6	48.3	144 11.5	03.0	89 05.5	23.3	Elnath	278 08.7	N28 37.1
E 08	21 35.1	259 39.4	15.8	70 01.6	48.4	159 14.1	02.9	104 08.1	23.3	Eltanin	90 44.0	N51 29.3
D 09	36 37.5	274 38.8 ..	15.2	85 03.6 ..	48.5	174 16.8 ..	02.9	119 10.8 ..	23.3	Enif	33 43.7	N 9 57.5
N 10	51 40.0	289 38.2	14.6	100 05.6	48.5	189 19.5	02.8	134 13.5	23.3	Fomalhaut	15 20.2	S29 31.4
E 11	66 42.5	304 37.5	14.0	115 07.6	48.6	204 22.1	02.8	149 16.1	23.3			
S 12	81 44.9	319 36.9	N22 13.4	130 09.6	S21 48.7	219 24.8	S15 02.7	164 18.8	S22 23.3	Gacrux	171 56.9	S57 13.2
D 13	96 47.4	334 36.3	12.7	145 11.6	48.8	234 27.4	02.7	179 21.4	23.4	Gienah	175 48.8	S17 38.7
A 14	111 49.9	349 35.7	12.1	160 13.6	48.8	249 30.1	02.7	194 24.1	23.4	Hadar	148 42.6	S60 27.8
Y 15	126 52.3	4 35.1 ..	11.5	175 15.6 ..	48.9	264 32.8 ..	02.6	209 26.7 ..	23.4	Hamal	327 57.2	N23 32.7
16	141 54.8	19 34.5	10.9	190 17.6	48.9	279 35.4	02.6	224 29.4	23.4	Kaus Aust.	83 39.0	S34 22.3
17	156 57.3	34 33.8	10.3	205 19.6	49.0	294 38.1	02.5	239 32.0	23.4			
18	171 59.7	49 33.2	N22 09.6	220 21.6	S21 49.1	309 40.7	S15 02.5	254 34.7	S22 23.4	Kochab	137 19.3	N74 05.1
19	187 02.2	64 32.6	09.0	235 23.6	49.1	324 43.4	02.4	269 37.3	23.4	Markab	13 34.9	N15 18.1
20	202 04.7	79 32.0	08.4	250 25.7	49.2	339 46.1	02.4	284 40.0	23.4	Menkar	314 11.8	N 4 09.5
21	217 07.1	94 31.4 ..	07.8	265 27.7 ..	49.3	354 48.7 ..	02.3	299 42.6 ..	23.4	Menkent	148 03.3	S36 27.6
22	232 09.6	109 30.8	07.1	280 29.7	49.4	9 51.4	02.3	314 45.3	23.5	Miaplacidus	221 39.5	S69 47.9
23	247 12.0	124 30.2	06.5	295 31.7	49.4	24 54.0	02.2	329 47.9	23.5			
14 00	262 14.5	139 29.6	N22 05.9	310 33.7	S21 49.5	39 56.7	S15 02.2	344 50.6	S22 23.5	Mirfak	308 35.9	N49 55.2
01	277 17.0	154 28.9	05.3	325 35.7	49.6	54 59.3	02.1	359 53.3	23.5	Nunki	75 53.8	S26 16.2
02	292 19.4	169 28.3	04.6	340 37.7	49.6	70 02.0	02.1	14 55.9	23.5	Peacock	53 13.6	S56 40.2
03	307 21.9	184 27.7 ..	04.0	355 39.8 ..	49.7	85 04.7 ..	02.0	29 58.6 ..	23.5	Pollux	243 24.0	N27 58.8
04	322 24.4	199 27.1	03.4	10 41.8	49.8	100 07.3	02.0	45 01.2	23.5	Procyon	244 56.5	N 5 10.5
05	337 26.8	214 26.5	02.7	25 43.8	49.9	115 10.0	01.9	60 03.9	23.5			
06	352 29.3	229 25.9	N22 02.1	40 45.8	S21 49.9	130 12.6	S15 01.9	75 06.5	S22 23.5	Rasalhague	96 03.0	N12 33.0
T 07	7 31.8	244 25.3	01.5	55 47.9	50.0	145 15.3	01.8	90 09.2	23.6	Regulus	207 40.1	N11 52.7
H 08	22 34.2	259 24.7	00.8	70 49.9	50.1	160 17.9	01.8	105 11.8	23.6	Rigel	281 09.2	S 8 11.0
U 09	37 36.7	274 24.1	22 00.2	85 51.9 ..	50.1	175 20.6 ..	01.7	120 14.5 ..	23.6	Rigil Kent.	139 46.6	S60 54.7
R 10	52 39.2	289 23.5	21 59.6	100 53.9	50.2	190 23.2	01.7	135 17.1	23.6	Sabik	102 08.3	S15 44.7
S 11	67 41.6	304 22.9	58.9	115 56.0	50.3	205 25.9	01.7	150 19.8	23.6			
D 12	82 44.1	319 22.3	N21 58.3	130 58.0	S21 50.4	220 28.6	S15 01.6	165 22.4	S22 23.6	Schedar	349 36.8	N56 37.9
A 13	97 46.5	334 21.7	57.7	146 00.0	50.4	235 31.2	01.6	180 25.1	23.6	Shaula	96 16.9	S37 06.8
Y 14	112 49.0	349 21.1	57.0	161 02.1	50.5	250 33.9	01.5	195 27.8	23.6	Sirius	258 31.1	S16 44.7
15	127 51.5	4 20.5 ..	56.4	176 04.1 ..	50.6	265 36.5 ..	01.5	210 30.4 ..	23.6	Spica	158 27.5	S11 15.4
16	142 53.9	19 19.9	55.7	191 06.1	50.7	280 39.2	01.4	225 33.1	23.7	Suhail	222 50.2	S43 30.7
17	157 56.4	34 19.3	55.1	206 08.2	50.7	295 41.8	01.4	240 35.7	23.7			
18	172 58.9	49 18.7	N21 54.4	221 10.2	S21 50.8	310 44.5	S15 01.3	255 38.4	S22 23.7	Vega	80 36.3	N38 48.1
19	188 01.3	64 18.1	53.8	236 12.3	50.9	325 47.1	01.3	270 41.0	23.7	Zuben'ubi	137 01.4	S16 07.0
20	203 03.8	79 17.5	53.1	251 14.3	51.0	340 49.8	01.2	285 43.7	23.7		SHA	Mer.Pass.
21	218 06.3	94 16.9 ..	52.5	266 16.3 ..	51.1	355 52.4 ..	01.2	300 46.3 ..	23.7			
22	233 08.7	109 16.3	51.9	281 18.4	51.1	10 55.1	01.1	315 49.0	23.7	Venus	238 29.0	14 42
23	248 11.2	124 15.7	51.2	296 20.4	51.2	25 57.7	01.1	330 51.7	23.7	Mars	48 30.3	3 21
Mer.Pass. 6ʰ 33.9ᵐ		v −0.6	d 0.6	v 2.0	d 0.1	v 2.7	d 0.0	v 2.7	d 0.0	Jupiter	137 37.5	21 21
										Saturn	82 31.6	1 05

UT	SUN GHA	SUN Dec	MOON GHA	v	MOON Dec	d	HP
	° ′	° ′	° ′	′	° ′	′	′
d h							
12 00	180 03.8	N23 07.8	205 34.8	7.4	N14 28.9	9.3	59.7
01	195 03.7	07.9	220 01.2	7.2	14 38.2	9.2	59.8
02	210 03.6	08.1	234 27.4	7.3	14 47.4	9.2	59.8
03	225 03.4	08.3	248 53.7	7.1	14 56.6	9.0	59.8
04	240 03.3	08.4	263 19.8	7.0	15 05.6	9.0	59.9
05	255 03.2	08.6	277 45.8	6.9	15 14.6	8.9	59.9
06	270 03.0	N23 08.7	292 11.7	6.9	N15 23.5	8.8	59.9
07	285 02.9	08.9	306 37.6	6.7	15 32.3	8.7	60.0
08	300 02.8	09.0	321 03.3	6.7	15 41.0	8.6	60.0
09	315 02.7	09.2	335 29.0	6.5	15 49.6	8.5	60.0
10	330 02.5	09.4	349 54.5	6.5	15 58.1	8.5	60.0
11	345 02.4	09.5	4 20.0	6.4	16 06.6	8.3	60.1
12	0 02.3	N23 09.7	18 45.4	6.3	N16 14.9	8.2	60.1
13	15 02.1	09.8	33 10.7	6.2	16 23.1	8.2	60.1
14	30 02.0	10.0	47 35.9	6.2	16 31.3	8.0	60.2
15	45 01.9	10.1	62 01.1	6.0	16 39.3	7.9	60.2
16	60 01.7	10.3	76 26.1	6.0	16 47.2	7.8	60.2
17	75 01.6	10.4	90 51.1	5.8	16 55.0	7.7	60.2
18	90 01.5	N23 10.6	105 15.9	5.8	N17 02.7	7.6	60.3
19	105 01.3	10.7	119 40.7	5.7	17 10.3	7.5	60.3
20	120 01.2	10.9	134 05.4	5.6	17 17.8	7.4	60.3
21	135 01.1	11.0	148 30.0	5.6	17 25.2	7.3	60.3
22	150 01.0	11.2	162 54.6	5.4	17 32.5	7.1	60.4
23	165 00.8	11.3	177 19.0	5.4	17 39.6	7.1	60.4
13 00	180 00.7	N23 11.4	191 43.4	5.3	N17 46.7	6.9	60.4
01	195 00.6	11.6	206 07.7	5.2	17 53.6	6.8	60.4
02	210 00.4	11.7	220 31.9	5.1	18 00.4	6.7	60.5
03	225 00.3	11.9	234 56.0	5.1	18 07.1	6.5	60.5
04	240 00.2	12.0	249 20.1	4.9	18 13.6	6.5	60.5
05	255 00.0	12.2	263 44.0	4.9	18 20.1	6.3	60.5
06	269 59.9	N23 12.3	278 07.9	4.9	N18 26.4	6.2	60.5
07	284 59.8	12.4	292 31.8	4.7	18 32.6	6.0	60.6
08	299 59.6	12.6	306 55.5	4.7	18 38.6	5.9	60.6
09	314 59.5	12.7	321 19.2	4.6	18 44.5	5.9	60.6
10	329 59.4	12.9	335 42.8	4.6	18 50.4	5.6	60.6
11	344 59.2	13.0	350 06.4	4.4	18 56.0	5.6	60.6
12	359 59.1	N23 13.1	4 29.8	4.4	N19 01.6	5.4	60.7
13	14 59.0	13.3	18 53.2	4.4	19 07.0	5.3	60.7
14	29 58.8	13.4	33 16.6	4.3	19 12.3	5.1	60.7
15	44 58.7	13.5	47 39.9	4.2	19 17.4	5.0	60.7
16	59 58.6	13.7	62 03.1	4.1	19 22.4	4.9	60.7
17	74 58.5	13.8	76 26.2	4.1	19 27.3	4.7	60.7
18	89 58.3	N23 13.9	90 49.3	4.1	N19 32.0	4.6	60.8
19	104 58.2	14.1	105 12.4	4.0	19 36.6	4.4	60.8
20	119 58.1	14.2	119 35.4	3.9	19 41.0	4.3	60.8
21	134 57.9	14.3	133 58.3	3.8	19 45.3	4.2	60.8
22	149 57.8	14.5	148 21.1	3.9	19 49.5	4.0	60.8
23	164 57.7	14.6	162 44.0	3.7	19 53.5	3.9	60.8
14 00	179 57.5	N23 14.7	177 06.7	3.8	N19 57.4	3.7	60.8
01	194 57.4	14.8	191 29.5	3.6	20 01.1	3.6	60.9
02	209 57.3	15.0	205 52.1	3.7	20 04.7	3.5	60.9
03	224 57.1	15.1	220 14.8	3.6	20 08.2	3.2	60.9
04	239 57.0	15.2	234 37.4	3.5	20 11.4	3.2	60.9
05	254 56.9	15.3	248 59.9	3.5	20 14.6	3.0	60.9
06	269 56.7	N23 15.5	263 22.4	3.5	N20 17.6	2.8	60.9
07	284 56.6	15.6	277 44.9	3.5	20 20.4	2.7	60.9
08	299 56.5	15.7	292 07.4	3.4	20 23.1	2.5	60.9
09	314 56.3	15.8	306 29.8	3.3	20 25.6	2.4	60.9
10	329 56.2	16.0	320 52.1	3.4	20 28.0	2.3	60.9
11	344 56.1	16.1	335 14.5	3.3	20 30.3	2.1	61.0
12	359 55.9	N23 16.2	349 36.8	3.3	N20 32.4	1.9	61.0
13	14 55.8	16.3	3 59.1	3.3	20 34.3	1.8	61.0
14	29 55.7	16.4	18 21.4	3.2	20 36.1	1.6	61.0
15	44 55.5	16.6	32 43.6	3.3	20 37.7	1.4	61.0
16	59 55.4	16.7	47 05.9	3.2	20 39.1	1.4	61.0
17	74 55.3	16.8	61 28.1	3.2	20 40.5	1.1	61.0
18	89 55.1	N23 16.9	75 50.3	3.2	N20 41.6	1.0	61.0
19	104 55.0	17.0	90 12.5	3.2	20 42.6	0.9	61.0
20	119 54.9	17.1	104 34.7	3.1	20 43.5	0.6	61.0
21	134 54.7	17.2	118 56.8	3.2	20 44.1	0.6	61.0
22	149 54.6	17.4	133 19.0	3.2	20 44.7	0.4	61.0
23	164 54.4	17.5	147 41.2	3.1	N20 45.1	0.2	61.0
	SD 15.8	d 0.1	SD 16.4		16.5		16.6

Twilight / Sunrise / Moonrise

Lat.	Naut.	Civil	Sunrise	Moonrise 12	13	14	15
°	h m	h m	h m	h m	h m	h m	h m
N 72	□	□	□	00 50	00 02	□	□
N 70	□	□	□	01 19	01 10	00 44	□
68	□	□	□	01 41	01 47	02 02	02 46
66	□	□	□	01 59	02 13	02 40	03 31
64	////	////	01 35	02 13	02 33	03 07	04 01
62	////	////	02 12	02 25	02 50	03 28	04 23
60	////	00 57	02 37	02 35	03 04	03 45	04 42
N 58	////	01 43	02 57	02 44	03 16	03 59	04 57
56	////	02 12	03 14	02 52	03 26	04 11	05 10
54	00 56	02 34	03 28	02 59	03 36	04 22	05 21
52	01 35	02 51	03 40	03 06	03 44	04 32	05 31
50	02 02	03 06	03 50	03 12	03 51	04 40	05 40
45	02 46	03 36	04 13	03 24	04 07	04 59	05 59
N 40	03 16	03 58	04 31	03 35	04 20	05 13	06 15
35	03 39	04 16	04 45	03 43	04 31	05 26	06 28
30	03 58	04 31	04 58	03 51	04 41	05 37	06 39
20	04 26	04 56	05 20	04 05	04 58	05 56	06 59
N 10	04 49	05 16	05 39	04 17	05 13	06 13	07 16
0	05 08	05 34	05 56	04 28	05 27	06 28	07 32
S 10	05 25	05 51	06 14	04 40	05 41	06 44	07 47
20	05 41	06 08	06 32	04 52	05 56	07 01	08 05
30	05 57	06 27	06 53	05 06	06 13	07 20	08 24
35	06 06	06 37	07 05	05 14	06 23	07 32	08 36
40	06 15	06 49	07 19	05 24	06 35	07 45	08 49
45	06 25	07 02	07 36	05 35	06 49	08 00	09 04
S 50	06 37	07 18	07 56	05 48	07 06	08 19	09 24
52	06 42	07 25	08 06	05 55	07 14	08 28	09 33
54	06 47	07 33	08 17	06 02	07 22	08 38	09 43
56	06 53	07 42	08 30	06 09	07 32	08 49	09 54
58	07 00	07 53	08 44	06 18	07 44	09 02	10 07
S 60	07 07	08 04	09 01	06 28	07 57	09 18	10 23

Sunset / Twilight / Moonset

Lat.	Sunset	Civil	Naut.	Moonset 12	13	14	15
°	h m	h m	h m	h m	h m	h m	h m
N 72	□	□	□	22 07	□	□	□
N 70	□	□	□	21 00	23 33	□	□
68	□	□	□	20 24	22 16	23 44	24 27
66	□	□	□	19 59	21 39	22 59	23 49
64	22 26	////	////	19 39	21 12	22 29	23 22
62	21 49	////	////	19 23	20 51	22 06	23 02
60	21 24	23 05	////	19 10	20 35	21 48	22 45
N 58	21 03	22 18	////	18 58	20 21	21 33	22 30
56	20 47	21 49	////	18 48	20 09	21 20	22 18
54	20 33	21 27	23 10	18 40	19 58	21 09	22 07
52	20 21	21 09	22 26	18 32	19 49	20 59	21 58
50	20 10	20 54	21 59	18 25	19 40	20 50	21 49
45	19 48	20 25	21 14	18 10	19 23	20 31	21 31
N 40	19 30	20 02	20 44	17 58	19 08	20 15	21 16
35	19 15	19 44	20 21	17 47	18 56	20 02	21 04
30	19 02	19 29	20 03	17 38	18 45	19 51	20 53
20	18 40	19 05	19 34	17 22	18 27	19 31	20 34
N 10	18 21	18 44	19 11	17 09	18 11	19 14	20 17
0	18 04	18 26	18 52	16 56	17 56	18 58	20 01
S 10	17 46	18 09	18 36	16 43	17 41	18 42	19 46
20	17 28	17 52	18 20	16 29	17 25	18 25	19 29
30	17 07	17 33	18 03	16 14	17 07	18 06	19 10
35	16 55	17 23	17 55	16 05	16 56	17 54	18 58
40	16 41	17 11	17 45	15 55	16 44	17 41	18 45
45	16 24	16 56	17 35	15 43	16 29	17 25	18 30
S 50	16 04	16 42	17 23	15 28	16 12	17 06	18 11
52	15 54	16 35	17 18	15 21	16 04	16 57	18 02
54	15 43	16 26	17 13	15 14	15 54	16 47	17 52
56	15 30	16 17	17 06	15 05	15 44	16 35	17 41
58	15 16	16 07	17 00	14 56	15 32	16 22	17 28
S 60	14 59	15 56	16 52	14 45	15 19	16 07	17 13

Day	SUN Eqn. of Time 00ʰ	12ʰ	Mer. Pass.	MOON Mer. Pass. Upper	Lower	Age	Phase
d	m s	m s	h m	h m	h m	d	%
12	00 16	00 09	12 00	10 42	23 11	28	3
13	00 03	00 03	12 00	11 41	24 12	29	0
14	00 10	00 16	12 00	12 43	00 12	01	1

(Phase: new moon ●)

UT	ARIES GHA	VENUS −4.0 GHA	Dec	MARS −1.7 GHA	Dec	JUPITER −2.4 GHA	Dec	SATURN +0.1 GHA	Dec	Name	SHA	Dec
15 00	263 13.7	139 15.1	N21 50.6	311 22.5	S21 51.3	41 00.4	S15 01.1	345 54.3	S22 23.8	Acamar	315 16.1	S40 13.9
01	278 16.1	154 14.5	49.9	326 24.5	51.4	56 03.0	01.0	0 57.0	23.8	Achernar	335 24.6	S57 08.5
02	293 18.6	169 13.9	49.2	341 26.6	51.5	71 05.7	01.0	15 59.6	23.8	Acrux	173 05.3	S63 12.3
03	308 21.0	184 13.3 ..	48.6	356 28.6 ..	51.5	86 08.3 ..	00.9	31 02.3 ..	23.8	Adhara	255 10.2	S29 00.0
04	323 23.5	199 12.7	47.9	11 30.7	51.6	101 11.0	00.9	46 04.9	23.8	Aldebaran	290 45.8	N16 32.5
05	338 26.0	214 12.1	47.3	26 32.7	51.7	116 13.6	00.8	61 07.6	23.8			
06	353 28.4	229 11.5	N21 46.6	41 34.8	S21 51.8	131 16.3	S15 00.8	76 10.2	S22 23.8	Alioth	166 17.6	N55 52.0
07	8 30.9	244 10.9	46.0	56 36.8	51.8	146 18.9	00.7	91 12.9	23.8	Alkaid	152 56.0	N49 13.6
08	23 33.4	259 10.3	45.3	71 38.9	51.9	161 21.6	00.7	106 15.5	23.8	Al Na'ir	27 39.3	S46 52.1
F 09	38 35.8	274 09.8 ..	44.6	86 40.9 ..	52.0	176 24.2 ..	00.6	121 18.2 ..	23.9	Alnilam	275 43.3	S 1 11.6
R 10	53 38.3	289 09.2	44.0	101 43.0	52.1	191 26.9	00.6	136 20.9	23.9	Alphard	217 53.0	S 8 44.4
I 11	68 40.8	304 08.6	43.3	116 45.1	52.2	206 29.5	00.6	151 23.5	23.9			
D 12	83 43.2	319 08.0	N21 42.7	131 47.1	S21 52.3	221 32.2	S15 00.5	166 26.2	S22 23.9	Alphecca	126 07.8	N26 39.4
A 13	98 45.7	334 07.4	42.0	146 49.2	52.3	236 34.8	00.5	181 28.8	23.9	Alpheratz	357 40.0	N29 11.3
Y 14	113 48.1	349 06.8	41.3	161 51.2	52.4	251 37.5	00.4	196 31.5	23.9	Altair	62 04.6	N 8 55.1
15	128 50.6	4 06.2 ..	40.7	176 53.3 ..	52.5	266 40.1 ..	00.4	211 34.1 ..	23.9	Ankaa	353 12.5	S42 12.2
16	143 53.1	19 05.6	40.0	191 55.4	52.6	281 42.8	00.3	226 36.8	23.9	Antares	112 21.7	S26 28.2
17	158 55.5	34 05.1	39.3	206 57.4	52.7	296 45.4	00.3	241 39.5	23.9			
18	173 58.0	49 04.5	N21 38.7	221 59.5	S21 52.8	311 48.1	S15 00.2	256 42.1	S22 24.0	Arcturus	145 52.4	N19 05.4
19	189 00.5	64 03.9	38.0	237 01.6	52.8	326 50.7	00.2	271 44.8	24.0	Atria	107 19.9	S69 03.5
20	204 02.9	79 03.3	37.3	252 03.6	52.9	341 53.4	00.2	286 47.4	24.0	Avior	234 17.1	S59 34.4
21	219 05.4	94 02.7 ..	36.7	267 05.7 ..	53.0	356 56.0 ..	00.1	301 50.1 ..	24.0	Bellatrix	278 28.7	N 6 21.8
22	234 07.9	109 02.1	36.0	282 07.8	53.1	11 58.6	00.1	316 52.7	24.0	Betelgeuse	270 58.0	N 7 24.4
23	249 10.3	124 01.6	35.3	297 09.9	53.2	27 01.3	00.0	331 55.4	24.0			
16 00	264 12.8	139 01.0	N21 34.6	312 11.9	S21 53.3	42 03.9	S15 00.0	346 58.0	S22 24.0	Canopus	263 55.2	S52 42.5
01	279 15.3	154 00.4	34.0	327 14.0	53.4	57 06.6	14 59.9	2 00.7	24.0	Capella	280 29.9	N46 00.7
02	294 17.7	168 59.8	33.3	342 16.1	53.5	72 09.2	59.9	17 03.4	24.1	Deneb	49 28.8	N45 20.7
03	309 20.2	183 59.2 ..	32.6	357 18.2 ..	53.5	87 11.9 ..	59.9	32 06.0 ..	24.1	Denebola	182 30.2	N14 28.3
04	324 22.6	198 58.7	31.9	12 20.2	53.6	102 14.5	59.8	47 08.7	24.1	Diphda	348 52.6	S17 53.2
05	339 25.1	213 58.1	31.3	27 22.3	53.7	117 17.2	59.8	62 11.3	24.1			
06	354 27.6	228 57.5	N21 30.6	42 24.4	S21 53.8	132 19.8	S14 59.7	77 14.0	S22 24.1	Dubhe	193 47.8	N61 39.4
07	9 30.0	243 56.9	29.9	57 26.5	53.9	147 22.4	59.7	92 16.6	24.1	Elnath	278 08.7	N28 37.1
S 08	24 32.5	258 56.4	29.2	72 28.6	54.0	162 25.1	59.6	107 19.3	24.1	Eltanin	90 44.0	N51 29.3
A 09	39 35.0	273 55.8 ..	28.5	87 30.6 ..	54.1	177 27.7 ..	59.6	122 22.0 ..	24.1	Enif	33 43.6	N 9 57.5
T 10	54 37.4	288 55.2	27.8	102 32.7	54.2	192 30.4	59.6	137 24.6	24.1	Fomalhaut	15 20.2	S29 31.4
U 11	69 39.9	303 54.6	27.2	117 34.8	54.3	207 33.0	59.5	152 27.3	24.2			
R 12	84 42.4	318 54.1	N21 26.5	132 36.9	S21 54.3	222 35.6	S14 59.5	167 29.9	S22 24.2	Gacrux	171 56.9	S57 13.2
D 13	99 44.8	333 53.5	25.8	147 39.0	54.4	237 38.3	59.4	182 32.6	24.2	Gienah	175 48.8	S17 38.7
A 14	114 47.3	348 52.9	25.1	162 41.1	54.5	252 40.9	59.4	197 35.2	24.2	Hadar	148 42.6	S60 27.8
Y 15	129 49.8	3 52.4 ..	24.4	177 43.2 ..	54.6	267 43.6 ..	59.3	212 37.9 ..	24.2	Hamal	327 57.1	N23 32.7
16	144 52.2	18 51.8	23.7	192 45.3	54.7	282 46.2	59.3	227 40.5	24.2	Kaus Aust.	83 38.9	S34 22.3
17	159 54.7	33 51.2	23.0	207 47.4	54.8	297 48.8	59.3	242 43.2	24.2			
18	174 57.1	48 50.6	N21 22.3	222 49.5	S21 54.9	312 51.5	S14 59.2	257 45.9	S22 24.2	Kochab	137 19.3	N74 05.2
19	189 59.6	63 50.1	21.7	237 51.6	55.0	327 54.1	59.2	272 48.5	24.2	Markab	13 34.9	N15 18.1
20	205 02.1	78 49.5	21.0	252 53.7	55.1	342 56.8	59.1	287 51.2	24.3	Menkar	314 11.8	N 4 09.5
21	220 04.5	93 48.9 ..	20.3	267 55.8 ..	55.2	357 59.4 ..	59.1	302 53.8 ..	24.3	Menkent	148 03.3	S36 27.6
22	235 07.0	108 48.4	19.6	282 57.9	55.3	13 02.0	59.0	317 56.5	24.3	Miaplacidus	221 39.5	S69 47.9
23	250 09.5	123 47.8	18.9	298 00.0	55.4	28 04.7	59.0	332 59.2	24.3			
17 00	265 11.9	138 47.3	N21 18.2	313 02.1	S21 55.5	43 07.3	S14 59.0	348 01.8	S22 24.3	Mirfak	308 35.9	N49 55.2
01	280 14.4	153 46.7	17.5	328 04.2	55.6	58 10.0	58.9	3 04.5	24.3	Nunki	75 53.8	S26 16.2
02	295 16.9	168 46.1	16.8	343 06.3	55.7	73 12.6	58.9	18 07.1	24.3	Peacock	53 13.5	S56 40.2
03	310 19.3	183 45.6 ..	16.1	358 08.4 ..	55.8	88 15.2 ..	58.8	33 09.8 ..	24.3	Pollux	243 24.0	N27 58.8
04	325 21.8	198 45.0	15.4	13 10.5	55.9	103 17.9	58.8	48 12.4	24.4	Procyon	244 56.5	N 5 10.5
05	340 24.3	213 44.4	14.7	28 12.6	56.0	118 20.5	58.8	63 15.1	24.4			
06	355 26.7	228 43.9	N21 14.0	43 14.7	S21 56.1	133 23.1	S14 58.7	78 17.8	S22 24.4	Rasalhague	96 03.0	N12 33.0
07	10 29.2	243 43.3	13.3	58 16.8	56.1	148 25.8	58.7	93 20.4	24.4	Regulus	207 40.1	N11 52.7
08	25 31.6	258 42.8	12.6	73 18.9	56.2	163 28.4	58.6	108 23.1	24.4	Rigel	281 09.2	S 8 11.0
S 09	40 34.1	273 42.2 ..	11.9	88 21.1 ..	56.3	178 31.1 ..	58.6	123 25.7 ..	24.4	Rigil Kent.	139 46.6	S60 54.7
U 10	55 36.6	288 41.6	11.2	103 23.2	56.4	193 33.7	58.6	138 28.4	24.4	Sabik	102 08.3	S15 44.7
N 11	70 39.0	303 41.1	10.4	118 25.3	56.5	208 36.3	58.5	153 31.0	24.4			
D 12	85 41.5	318 40.5	N21 09.7	133 27.4	S21 56.6	223 39.0	S14 58.5	168 33.7	S22 24.4	Schedar	349 36.7	N56 37.9
A 13	100 44.0	333 40.0	09.0	148 29.5	56.7	238 41.6	58.4	183 36.4	24.5	Shaula	96 16.9	S37 06.8
Y 14	115 46.4	348 39.4	08.3	163 31.7	56.8	253 44.2	58.4	198 39.0	24.5	Sirius	258 31.1	S16 44.7
15	130 48.9	3 38.9 ..	07.6	178 33.8 ..	56.9	268 46.9 ..	58.3	213 41.7 ..	24.5	Spica	158 27.5	S11 15.4
16	145 51.4	18 38.3	06.9	193 35.9	57.0	283 49.5	58.3	228 44.3	24.5	Suhail	222 50.2	S43 30.7
17	160 53.8	33 37.8	06.2	208 38.0	57.1	298 52.1	58.3	243 47.0	24.5			
18	175 56.3	48 37.2	N21 05.5	223 40.1	S21 57.3	313 54.8	S14 58.2	258 49.6	S22 24.5	Vega	80 36.2	N38 48.1
19	190 58.8	63 36.7	04.8	238 42.3	57.4	328 57.4	58.2	273 52.3	24.5	Zuben'ubi	137 01.4	S16 07.0
20	206 01.2	78 36.1	04.0	253 44.4	57.5	344 00.0	58.1	288 55.0	24.5		SHA	Mer.Pass.
21	221 03.7	93 35.5 ..	03.3	268 46.5 ..	57.6	359 02.7 ..	58.1	303 57.6 ..	24.5		° ′	h m
22	236 06.1	108 35.0	02.6	283 48.7	57.7	14 05.3	58.1	319 00.3	24.6	Venus	234 48.2	14 45
23	251 08.6	123 34.5	01.9	298 50.8	57.8	29 07.9	58.0	334 02.9	24.6	Mars	47 59.1	3 11
	h m									Jupiter	137 51.1	21 08
Mer. Pass.	6 22.1	v −0.6	d 0.7	v 2.1	d 0.1	v 2.6	d 0.0	v 2.7	d 0.0	Saturn	82 45.3	0 52

UT	SUN GHA	SUN Dec	MOON GHA	v	MOON Dec	d	HP
d h	° ′	° ′	° ′	′	° ′	′	′
15 00	179 54.3	N23 17.6	162 03.3	3.2	N20 45.3	0.0	61.0
01	194 54.2	17.7	176 25.5	3.2	20 45.3	0.1	61.0
02	209 54.0	17.8	190 47.7	3.1	20 45.2	0.2	61.0
03	224 53.9 ..	17.9	205 09.8	3.2	20 45.0	0.4	61.0
04	239 53.8	18.0	219 32.0	3.2	20 44.6	0.6	61.0
05	254 53.6	18.1	233 54.2	3.2	20 44.0	0.7	61.0
06	269 53.5	N23 18.2	248 16.4	3.2	N20 43.3	0.9	61.0
07	284 53.4	18.3	262 38.6	3.2	20 42.4	1.0	61.0
08	299 53.2	18.4	277 00.8	3.2	20 41.4	1.2	61.0
F 09	314 53.1 ..	18.5	291 23.0	3.3	20 40.2	1.3	61.0
R 10	329 53.0	18.6	305 45.3	3.3	20 38.9	1.5	61.0
I 11	344 52.8	18.8	320 07.6	3.3	20 37.4	1.6	61.0
D 12	359 52.7	N23 18.9	334 29.9	3.3	N20 35.8	1.8	61.0
A 13	14 52.6	19.0	348 52.2	3.4	20 34.0	2.0	60.9
Y 14	29 52.4	19.1	3 14.6	3.4	20 32.0	2.1	60.9
15	44 52.3 ..	19.2	17 37.0	3.4	20 29.9	2.3	60.9
16	59 52.2	19.3	31 59.4	3.4	20 27.6	2.4	60.9
17	74 52.0	19.4	46 21.8	3.5	20 25.2	2.5	60.9
18	89 51.9	N23 19.5	60 44.3	3.5	N20 22.7	2.7	60.9
19	104 51.8	19.6	75 06.8	3.6	20 20.0	2.9	60.9
20	119 51.6	19.6	89 29.4	3.6	20 17.1	3.0	60.9
21	134 51.5 ..	19.7	103 52.0	3.6	20 14.1	3.2	60.9
22	149 51.4	19.8	118 14.6	3.7	20 10.9	3.3	60.9
23	164 51.2	19.9	132 37.3	3.7	20 07.6	3.4	60.9
16 00	179 51.1	N23 20.0	147 00.0	3.8	N20 04.2	3.6	60.8
01	194 50.9	20.1	161 22.8	3.8	20 00.6	3.8	60.8
02	209 50.8	20.2	175 45.6	3.9	19 56.8	3.9	60.8
03	224 50.7 ..	20.3	190 08.5	4.0	19 52.9	4.0	60.8
04	239 50.5	20.4	204 31.5	3.9	19 48.9	4.2	60.8
05	254 50.4	20.5	218 54.4	4.1	19 44.7	4.3	60.8
06	269 50.3	N23 20.6	233 17.5	4.1	N19 40.4	4.4	60.8
07	284 50.1	20.7	247 40.6	4.2	19 36.0	4.6	60.8
S 08	299 50.0	20.8	262 03.8	4.2	19 31.4	4.8	60.7
A 09	314 49.9 ..	20.8	276 27.0	4.3	19 26.6	4.8	60.7
T 10	329 49.7	20.9	290 50.3	4.3	19 21.8	5.0	60.7
U 11	344 49.6	21.0	305 13.6	4.4	19 16.8	5.2	60.7
R 12	359 49.5	N23 21.1	319 37.0	4.5	N19 11.6	5.3	60.7
D 13	14 49.3	21.2	334 00.5	4.5	19 06.3	5.4	60.7
A 14	29 49.2	21.3	348 24.0	4.6	19 00.9	5.5	60.6
Y 15	44 49.0 ..	21.3	2 47.6	4.7	18 55.4	5.7	60.6
16	59 48.9	21.4	17 11.3	4.8	18 49.7	5.8	60.6
17	74 48.8	21.5	31 35.1	4.8	18 43.9	5.9	60.6
18	89 48.6	N23 21.6	45 58.9	4.9	N18 38.0	6.1	60.6
19	104 48.5	21.7	60 22.8	4.9	18 31.9	6.2	60.5
20	119 48.4	21.8	74 46.7	5.1	18 25.7	6.3	60.5
21	134 48.2 ..	21.8	89 10.8	5.1	18 19.4	6.4	60.5
22	149 48.1	21.9	103 34.9	5.2	18 13.0	6.5	60.5
23	164 48.0	22.0	117 59.1	5.3	18 06.5	6.7	60.5
17 00	179 47.8	N23 22.1	132 23.4	5.3	N17 59.8	6.8	60.4
01	194 47.7	22.1	146 47.7	5.4	17 53.0	6.9	60.4
02	209 47.6	22.2	161 12.1	5.6	17 46.1	7.0	60.4
03	224 47.4 ..	22.3	175 36.7	5.6	17 39.1	7.2	60.4
04	239 47.3	22.4	190 01.3	5.6	17 31.9	7.2	60.3
05	254 47.1	22.4	204 25.9	5.8	17 24.7	7.4	60.3
06	269 47.0	N23 22.5	218 50.7	5.8	N17 17.3	7.5	60.3
07	284 46.9	22.6	233 15.5	5.9	17 09.8	7.5	60.3
08	299 46.7	22.7	247 40.4	6.0	17 02.3	7.7	60.2
S 09	314 46.6 ..	22.7	262 05.4	6.1	16 54.6	7.8	60.2
U 10	329 46.5	22.8	276 30.5	6.2	16 46.8	7.9	60.2
N 11	344 46.3	22.9	290 55.7	6.3	16 38.9	8.0	60.2
D 12	359 46.2	N23 22.9	305 21.0	6.3	N16 30.9	8.1	60.2
A 13	14 46.1	23.0	319 46.3	6.4	16 22.8	8.2	60.1
Y 14	29 45.9	23.1	334 11.7	6.6	16 14.6	8.4	60.1
15	44 45.8 ..	23.1	348 37.3	6.6	16 06.2	8.4	60.1
16	59 45.6	23.2	3 02.9	6.6	15 57.8	8.5	60.1
17	74 45.5	23.3	17 28.5	6.8	15 49.3	8.5	60.0
18	89 45.4	N23 23.3	31 54.3	6.9	N15 40.8	8.7	60.0
19	104 45.2	23.4	46 20.2	6.9	15 32.1	8.8	60.0
20	119 45.1	23.4	60 46.1	7.1	15 23.3	8.9	59.9
21	134 45.0 ..	23.5	75 12.2	7.1	15 14.4	8.9	59.9
22	149 44.8	23.6	89 38.3	7.2	15 05.5	9.1	59.9
23	164 44.7	23.6	104 04.5	7.3	N14 56.4	9.1	59.9
	SD 15.8	d 0.1	SD 16.6		16.5		16.4

Lat.	Twilight Naut.	Twilight Civil	Sunrise	Moonrise 15	Moonrise 16	Moonrise 17	Moonrise 18
°	h m	h m	h m	h m	h m	h m	h m
N 72	▭	▭	▭	▭	▭	04 27	07 12
N 70	▭	▭	▭	▭	03 00	05 31	07 39
68	▭	▭	▭	02 46	04 15	06 06	08 00
66	▭	▭	▭	03 31	04 52	06 32	08 16
64	////	////	01 33	04 01	05 18	06 51	08 29
62	////	////	02 10	04 23	05 39	07 07	08 40
60	////	00 52	02 36	04 42	05 55	07 20	08 50
N 58	////	01 41	02 56	04 57	06 09	07 32	08 58
56	////	02 11	03 13	05 10	06 21	07 42	09 05
54	00 48	02 33	03 27	05 21	06 32	07 50	09 11
52	01 33	02 51	03 39	05 31	06 41	07 58	09 17
50	02 00	03 06	03 50	05 40	06 50	08 05	09 22
45	02 46	03 35	04 13	05 59	07 07	08 20	09 34
N 40	03 16	03 58	04 31	06 15	07 22	08 32	09 43
35	03 39	04 16	04 46	06 28	07 34	08 43	09 51
30	03 58	04 31	04 59	06 39	07 45	08 52	09 58
20	04 27	04 56	05 21	06 59	08 03	09 07	10 10
N 10	04 49	05 16	05 39	07 16	08 19	09 21	10 20
0	05 08	05 34	05 57	07 32	08 34	09 34	10 30
S 10	05 25	05 52	06 14	07 47	08 49	09 46	10 40
20	05 41	06 09	06 33	08 05	09 05	10 00	10 50
30	05 58	06 28	06 54	08 24	09 23	10 15	11 02
35	06 07	06 38	07 06	08 36	09 34	10 24	11 09
40	06 16	06 50	07 21	08 49	09 46	10 35	11 16
45	06 26	07 03	07 37	09 04	10 00	10 47	11 25
S 50	06 38	07 19	07 58	09 24	10 17	11 01	11 36
52	06 43	07 27	08 08	09 33	10 26	11 08	11 41
54	06 49	07 35	08 19	09 43	10 35	11 15	11 47
56	06 55	07 44	08 31	09 54	10 45	11 23	11 53
58	07 02	07 54	08 46	10 07	10 57	11 33	11 59
S 60	07 09	08 06	09 04	10 23	11 10	11 43	12 07

Lat.	Sunset	Twilight Civil	Twilight Naut.	Moonset 15	Moonset 16	Moonset 17	Moonset 18
°	h m	h m	h m	h m	h m	h m	h m
N 72	▭	▭	▭	▭	▭	02 23	01 38
N 70	▭	▭	▭	▭	01 42	01 18	01 09
68	▭	▭	▭	24 27	00 42	00 47	00 47
66	▭	▭	▭	23 49	24 16	00 16	00 30
64	22 30	////	////	23 22	23 55	24 15	00 15
62	21 52	////	////	23 02	23 39	24 03	00 03
60	21 26	23 11	////	22 45	23 25	23 53	24 14
N 58	21 05	22 21	////	22 30	23 13	23 44	24 08
56	20 49	21 51	////	22 18	23 03	23 36	24 03
54	20 34	21 29	23 15	22 07	22 54	23 29	23 58
52	20 22	21 11	22 29	21 58	22 45	23 23	23 53
50	20 11	20 56	22 01	21 49	22 38	23 17	23 49
45	19 49	20 26	21 16	21 31	22 22	23 05	23 41
N 40	19 31	20 04	20 45	21 16	22 09	22 54	23 33
35	19 16	19 46	20 22	21 04	21 58	22 46	23 27
30	19 03	19 30	20 04	20 53	21 48	22 38	23 22
20	18 41	19 05	19 35	20 34	21 31	22 24	23 12
N 10	18 22	18 45	19 12	20 17	21 17	22 12	23 03
0	18 04	18 27	18 53	20 01	21 03	22 01	22 55
S 10	17 47	18 10	18 36	19 46	20 49	21 49	22 47
20	17 28	17 52	18 20	19 29	20 34	21 37	22 38
30	17 07	17 34	18 04	19 10	20 16	21 23	22 28
35	16 55	17 23	17 55	18 58	20 06	21 15	22 22
40	16 41	17 11	17 45	18 45	19 55	21 06	22 16
45	16 24	16 58	17 35	18 30	19 41	20 55	22 08
S 50	16 03	16 42	17 23	18 11	19 24	20 41	21 59
52	15 54	16 34	17 18	18 02	19 16	20 35	21 54
54	15 42	16 25	17 12	17 52	19 08	20 28	21 49
56	15 30	16 17	17 06	17 41	18 58	20 20	21 44
58	15 15	16 07	17 00	17 28	18 46	20 12	21 38
S 60	14 58	15 55	16 52	17 13	18 33	20 02	21 31

	SUN Eqn. of Time 00ʰ	SUN Eqn. of Time 12ʰ	SUN Mer. Pass.	MOON Mer. Pass. Upper	MOON Mer. Pass. Lower	Age	Phase
Day							
d	m s	m s	h m	h m	h m	d	%
15	00 22	00 29	12 00	13 46	01 15	02	4
16	00 35	00 42	12 01	14 48	02 18	03	10
17	00 48	00 55	12 01	15 47	03 18	04	19

UT	ARIES	VENUS −4.0		MARS −1.8		JUPITER −2.4		SATURN +0.1		STARS		
	GHA	GHA	Dec	GHA	Dec	GHA	Dec	GHA	Dec	Name	SHA	Dec
d h	° ′	° ′	° ′	° ′	° ′	° ′	° ′	° ′	° ′		° ′	° ′
18 00	266 11.1	138 33.9	N21 01.2	313 52.9	S21 57.9	44 10.6	S14 58.0	349 05.6	S22 24.6	Acamar	315 16.1	S40 13.9
01	281 13.5	153 33.4	21 00.4	328 55.1	58.0	59 13.2	57.9	4 08.3	24.6	Achernar	335 24.6	S57 08.5
02	296 16.0	168 32.8	20 59.7	343 57.2	58.1	74 15.8	57.9	19 10.9	24.6	Acrux	173 05.3	S63 12.3
03	311 18.5	183 32.3	.. 59.0	358 59.3	.. 58.2	89 18.4	.. 57.9	34 13.6	.. 24.6	Adhara	255 10.2	S29 00.0
04	326 20.9	198 31.7	58.3	14 01.5	58.3	104 21.1	57.8	49 16.2	24.6	Aldebaran	290 45.8	N16 32.5
05	341 23.4	213 31.2	57.6	29 03.6	58.4	119 23.7	57.8	64 18.9	24.6			
06	356 25.9	228 30.6	N20 56.8	44 05.8	S21 58.5	134 26.3	S14 57.8	79 21.5	S22 24.7	Alioth	166 17.6	N55 52.0
07	11 28.3	243 30.1	56.1	59 07.9	58.6	149 29.0	57.7	94 24.2	24.7	Alkaid	152 56.0	N49 13.6
08	26 30.8	258 29.5	55.4	74 10.0	58.7	164 31.6	57.7	109 26.9	24.7	Al Na'ir	27 39.3	S46 52.1
M 09	41 33.2	273 29.0	.. 54.7	89 12.2	.. 58.8	179 34.2	.. 57.6	124 29.5	.. 24.7	Alnilam	275 43.3	S 1 11.6
O 10	56 35.7	288 28.5	53.9	104 14.3	58.9	194 36.9	57.6	139 32.2	24.7	Alphard	217 53.0	S 8 44.4
N 11	71 38.2	303 27.9	53.2	119 16.5	59.0	209 39.5	57.6	154 34.8	24.7			
D 12	86 40.6	318 27.4	N20 52.5	134 18.6	S21 59.1	224 42.1	S14 57.5	169 37.5	S22 24.7	Alphecca	126 07.8	N26 39.4
A 13	101 43.1	333 26.8	51.7	149 20.8	59.3	239 44.7	57.5	184 40.2	24.7	Alpheratz	357 40.0	N29 11.3
Y 14	116 45.6	348 26.3	51.0	164 22.9	59.4	254 47.4	57.4	199 42.8	24.7	Altair	62 04.6	N 8 55.1
15	131 48.0	3 25.8	.. 50.3	179 25.1	.. 59.5	269 50.0	.. 57.4	214 45.5	.. 24.8	Ankaa	353 12.5	S42 12.2
16	146 50.5	18 25.2	49.5	194 27.2	59.6	284 52.6	57.4	229 48.1	24.8	Antares	112 21.7	S26 28.2
17	161 53.0	33 24.7	48.8	209 29.4	59.7	299 55.2	57.3	244 50.8	24.8			
18	176 55.4	48 24.1	N20 48.1	224 31.5	S21 59.8	314 57.9	S14 57.3	259 53.5	S22 24.8	Arcturus	145 52.5	N19 05.4
19	191 57.9	63 23.6	47.3	239 33.7	21 59.9	330 00.5	57.3	274 56.1	24.8	Atria	107 19.9	S69 03.5
20	207 00.4	78 23.1	46.6	254 35.8	22 00.0	345 03.1	57.2	289 58.8	24.8	Avior	234 17.1	S59 34.4
21	222 02.8	93 22.5	.. 45.9	269 38.0	.. 00.1	0 05.7	.. 57.2	305 01.4	.. 24.8	Bellatrix	278 28.7	N 6 21.8
22	237 05.3	108 22.0	45.1	284 40.2	00.3	15 08.4	57.1	320 04.1	24.8	Betelgeuse	270 58.0	N 7 24.4
23	252 07.7	123 21.5	44.4	299 42.3	00.4	30 11.0	57.1	335 06.8	24.9			
19 00	267 10.2	138 20.9	N20 43.6	314 44.5	S22 00.5	45 13.6	S14 57.1	350 09.4	S22 24.9	Canopus	263 55.2	S52 42.5
01	282 12.7	153 20.4	42.9	329 46.7	00.6	60 16.2	57.0	5 12.1	24.9	Capella	280 29.9	N46 00.7
02	297 15.1	168 19.9	42.1	344 48.8	00.7	75 18.9	57.0	20 14.7	24.9	Deneb	49 28.8	N45 20.7
03	312 17.6	183 19.3	.. 41.4	359 51.0	.. 00.8	90 21.5	.. 57.0	35 17.4	.. 24.9	Denebola	182 30.2	N14 28.3
04	327 20.1	198 18.8	40.7	14 53.2	00.9	105 24.1	56.9	50 20.0	24.9	Diphda	348 52.6	S17 53.1
05	342 22.5	213 18.3	39.9	29 55.3	01.0	120 26.7	56.9	65 22.7	24.9			
06	357 25.0	228 17.8	N20 39.2	44 57.5	S22 01.2	135 29.4	S14 56.8	80 25.4	S22 24.9	Dubhe	193 47.8	N61 39.4
07	12 27.5	243 17.2	38.4	59 59.7	01.3	150 32.0	56.8	95 28.0	24.9	Elnath	278 08.7	N28 37.1
T 08	27 29.9	258 16.7	37.7	75 01.8	01.4	165 34.6	56.8	110 30.7	25.0	Eltanin	90 44.0	N51 29.3
U 09	42 32.4	273 16.2	.. 36.9	90 04.0	.. 01.5	180 37.2	.. 56.7	125 33.3	.. 25.0	Enif	33 43.6	N 9 57.6
E 10	57 34.9	288 15.7	36.2	105 06.2	01.6	195 39.9	56.7	140 36.0	25.0	Fomalhaut	15 20.2	S29 31.3
S 11	72 37.3	303 15.1	35.4	120 08.4	01.7	210 42.5	56.7	155 38.7	25.0			
D 12	87 39.8	318 14.6	N20 34.7	135 10.5	S22 01.9	225 45.1	S14 56.6	170 41.3	S22 25.0	Gacrux	171 56.9	S57 13.2
A 13	102 42.3	333 14.1	33.9	150 12.7	02.0	240 47.7	56.6	185 44.0	25.0	Gienah	175 48.8	S17 38.7
Y 14	117 44.7	348 13.6	33.2	165 14.9	02.1	255 50.3	56.5	200 46.6	25.0	Hadar	148 42.6	S60 27.8
15	132 47.2	3 13.0	.. 32.4	180 17.1	.. 02.2	270 53.0	.. 56.5	215 49.3	.. 25.0	Hamal	327 57.1	N23 32.7
16	147 49.6	18 12.5	31.6	195 19.3	02.3	285 55.6	56.5	230 52.0	25.0	Kaus Aust.	83 38.9	S34 22.3
17	162 52.1	33 12.0	30.9	210 21.5	02.4	300 58.2	56.4	245 54.6	25.1			
18	177 54.6	48 11.5	N20 30.1	225 23.6	S22 02.6	316 00.8	S14 56.4	260 57.3	S22 25.1	Kochab	137 19.4	N74 05.2
19	192 57.0	63 11.0	29.4	240 25.8	02.7	331 03.4	56.4	275 59.9	25.1	Markab	13 34.9	N15 18.1
20	207 59.5	78 10.4	28.6	255 28.0	02.8	346 06.1	56.3	291 02.6	25.1	Menkar	314 11.8	N 4 09.5
21	223 02.0	93 09.9	.. 27.9	270 30.2	.. 02.9	1 08.7	.. 56.3	306 05.3	.. 25.1	Menkent	148 03.3	S36 27.6
22	238 04.4	108 09.4	27.1	285 32.4	03.0	16 11.3	56.3	321 07.9	25.1	Miaplacidus	221 39.5	S69 47.8
23	253 06.9	123 08.9	26.3	300 34.6	03.2	31 13.9	56.2	336 10.6	25.1			
20 00	268 09.3	138 08.4	N20 25.6	315 36.8	S22 03.3	46 16.5	S14 56.2	351 13.2	S22 25.1	Mirfak	308 35.9	N49 55.2
01	283 11.8	153 07.9	24.8	330 39.0	03.4	61 19.1	56.2	6 15.9	25.2	Nunki	75 53.8	S26 16.2
02	298 14.3	168 07.3	24.0	345 41.2	03.5	76 21.8	56.1	21 18.6	25.2	Peacock	53 13.5	S56 40.3
03	313 16.7	183 06.8	.. 23.3	0 43.4	.. 03.7	91 24.4	.. 56.1	36 21.2	.. 25.2	Pollux	243 24.0	N27 58.8
04	328 19.2	198 06.3	22.5	15 45.6	03.8	106 27.0	56.0	51 23.9	25.2	Procyon	244 56.5	N 5 10.5
05	343 21.7	213 05.8	21.7	30 47.8	03.9	121 29.6	56.0	66 26.5	25.2			
06	358 24.1	228 05.3	N20 21.0	45 50.0	S22 04.0	136 32.2	S14 56.0	81 29.2	S22 25.2	Rasalhague	96 03.0	N12 33.0
W 07	13 26.6	243 04.8	20.2	60 52.2	04.1	151 34.8	55.9	96 31.9	25.2	Regulus	207 40.1	N11 52.7
E 08	28 29.1	258 04.3	19.4	75 54.4	04.3	166 37.5	55.9	111 34.5	25.2	Rigel	281 09.1	S 8 11.0
D 09	43 31.5	273 03.8	.. 18.7	90 56.6	.. 04.4	181 40.1	.. 55.9	126 37.2	.. 25.2	Rigil Kent.	139 46.6	S60 54.7
N 10	58 34.0	288 03.3	17.9	105 58.8	04.5	196 42.7	55.8	141 39.8	25.3	Sabik	102 08.3	S15 44.7
E 11	73 36.5	303 02.7	17.1	121 01.0	04.6	211 45.3	55.8	156 42.5	25.3			
S 12	88 38.9	318 02.2	N20 16.3	136 03.2	S22 04.8	226 47.9	S14 55.8	171 45.2	S22 25.3	Schedar	349 36.7	N56 37.9
D 13	103 41.4	333 01.7	15.6	151 05.4	04.9	241 50.5	55.7	186 47.8	25.3	Shaula	96 16.9	S37 06.8
A 14	118 43.8	348 01.2	14.8	166 07.6	05.0	256 53.1	55.7	201 50.5	25.3	Sirius	258 31.1	S16 44.7
Y 15	133 46.3	3 00.7	.. 14.0	181 09.8	.. 05.1	271 55.8	.. 55.7	216 53.1	.. 25.3	Spica	158 27.5	S11 15.4
16	148 48.8	18 00.2	13.2	196 12.0	05.3	286 58.4	55.6	231 55.8	25.3	Suhail	222 50.2	S43 30.6
17	163 51.2	32 59.7	12.5	211 14.2	05.4	302 01.0	55.6	246 58.5	25.3			
18	178 53.7	47 59.2	N20 11.7	226 16.5	S22 05.5	317 03.6	S14 55.6	262 01.1	S22 25.4	Vega	80 36.2	N38 48.2
19	193 56.2	62 58.7	10.9	241 18.7	05.7	332 06.2	55.5	277 03.8	25.4	Zuben'ubi	137 01.4	S16 07.0
20	208 58.6	77 58.2	10.1	256 20.9	05.8	347 08.8	55.5	292 06.5	25.4		SHA	Mer.Pass.
21	224 01.1	92 57.7	.. 09.3	271 23.1	.. 05.9	2 11.4	.. 55.5	307 09.1	.. 25.4		° ′	h m
22	239 03.6	107 57.2	08.6	286 25.3	06.0	17 14.0	55.4	322 11.8	25.4	Venus	231 10.7	14 47
23	254 06.0	122 56.7	07.8	301 27.6	06.2	32 16.7	55.4	337 14.4	25.4	Mars	47 34.3	3 01
	h m									Jupiter	138 03.4	20 55
Mer. Pass. 6 10.3		v −0.5	d 0.8	v 2.2	d 0.1	v 2.6	d 0.0	v 2.7	d 0.0	Saturn	82 59.2	0 39

UT	SUN GHA	SUN Dec	MOON GHA	v	MOON Dec	d	HP
d h	° ′	° ′	° ′	′	° ′	′	′
18 00	179 44.6	N23 23.7	118 30.8	7.4	N14 47.3	9.2	59.8
01	194 44.4	23.7	132 57.2	7.5	14 38.1	9.3	59.8
02	209 44.3	23.8	147 23.7	7.5	14 28.8	9.4	59.8
03	224 44.1 ..	23.9	161 50.2	7.7	14 19.4	9.5	59.7
04	239 44.0	23.9	176 16.9	7.7	14 09.9	9.5	59.7
05	254 43.9	24.0	190 43.6	7.8	14 00.4	9.6	59.7
06	269 43.7	N23 24.0	205 10.4	7.9	N13 50.8	9.7	59.7
07	284 43.6	24.1	219 37.3	8.0	13 41.1	9.8	59.6
08	299 43.5	24.1	234 04.3	8.1	13 31.3	9.8	59.6
M 09	314 43.3 ..	24.2	248 31.4	8.2	13 21.5	9.9	59.6
O 10	329 43.2	24.2	262 58.6	8.2	13 11.6	10.0	59.5
N 11	344 43.1	24.3	277 25.8	8.4	13 01.6	10.0	59.5
D 12	359 42.9	N23 24.3	291 53.2	8.4	N12 51.6	10.2	59.5
A 13	14 42.8	24.4	306 20.6	8.5	12 41.4	10.1	59.4
Y 14	29 42.6	24.4	320 48.1	8.6	12 31.3	10.3	59.4
15	44 42.5 ..	24.5	335 15.7	8.7	12 21.0	10.3	59.4
16	59 42.4	24.5	349 43.4	8.7	12 10.7	10.3	59.4
17	74 42.2	24.6	4 11.1	8.9	12 00.4	10.5	59.3
18	89 42.1	N23 24.6	18 39.0	8.9	N11 49.9	10.4	59.3
19	104 42.0	24.7	33 06.9	9.0	11 39.5	10.6	59.3
20	119 41.8	24.7	47 34.9	9.1	11 28.9	10.6	59.2
21	134 41.7 ..	24.8	62 03.0	9.2	11 18.3	10.6	59.2
22	149 41.6	24.8	76 31.2	9.2	11 07.7	10.7	59.2
23	164 41.4	24.9	90 59.4	9.4	10 57.0	10.8	59.1
19 00	179 41.3	N23 24.9	105 27.8	9.4	N10 46.2	10.8	59.1
01	194 41.1	24.9	119 56.2	9.4	10 35.4	10.8	59.1
02	209 41.0	25.0	134 24.6	9.6	10 24.6	10.9	59.0
03	224 40.9 ..	25.0	148 53.2	9.6	10 13.7	11.0	59.0
04	239 40.7	25.1	163 21.8	9.8	10 02.7	11.0	59.0
05	254 40.6	25.1	177 50.6	9.8	9 51.7	11.0	58.9
06	269 40.5	N23 25.1	192 19.4	9.8	N 9 40.7	11.1	58.9
07	284 40.3	25.2	206 48.2	10.0	9 29.6	11.1	58.9
T 08	299 40.2	25.2	221 17.2	10.0	9 18.5	11.1	58.8
U 09	314 40.1 ..	25.2	235 46.2	10.1	9 07.4	11.2	58.8
E 10	329 39.9	25.3	250 15.3	10.1	8 56.2	11.2	58.8
S 11	344 39.8	25.3	264 44.4	10.3	8 45.0	11.3	58.7
D 12	359 39.6	N23 25.4	279 13.7	10.3	N 8 33.7	11.3	58.7
A 13	14 39.5	25.4	293 43.0	10.3	8 22.4	11.3	58.7
Y 14	29 39.4	25.4	308 12.3	10.5	8 11.1	11.4	58.6
15	44 39.2 ..	25.4	322 41.8	10.5	7 59.7	11.4	58.6
16	59 39.1	25.5	337 11.3	10.6	7 48.3	11.4	58.6
17	74 39.0	25.5	351 40.9	10.6	7 36.9	11.5	58.5
18	89 38.8	N23 25.6	6 10.5	10.7	N 7 25.4	11.5	58.5
19	104 38.7	25.6	20 40.2	10.8	7 14.0	11.6	58.5
20	119 38.6	25.6	35 10.0	10.8	7 02.5	11.5	58.5
21	134 38.4 ..	25.6	49 39.8	10.9	6 50.9	11.6	58.4
22	149 38.3	25.6	64 09.7	11.0	6 39.4	11.6	58.4
23	164 38.1	25.7	78 39.7	11.0	6 27.8	11.6	58.4
20 00	179 38.0	N23 25.7	93 09.7	11.1	N 6 16.2	11.6	58.3
01	194 37.9	25.7	107 39.8	11.2	6 04.6	11.6	58.3
02	209 37.7	25.7	122 10.0	11.2	5 53.0	11.7	58.3
03	224 37.6 ..	25.8	136 40.2	11.2	5 41.3	11.7	58.2
04	239 37.5	25.8	151 10.4	11.3	5 29.6	11.7	58.2
05	254 37.3	25.8	165 40.7	11.4	5 18.0	11.7	58.2
06	269 37.2	N23 25.8	180 11.1	11.5	N 5 06.3	11.7	58.1
W 07	284 37.1	25.9	194 41.6	11.4	4 54.6	11.8	58.1
E 08	299 36.9	25.9	209 12.0	11.6	4 42.8	11.7	58.1
D 09	314 36.8 ..	25.9	223 42.6	11.6	4 31.1	11.7	58.0
N 10	329 36.6	25.9	238 13.2	11.6	4 19.4	11.8	58.0
E 11	344 36.5	25.9	252 43.8	11.7	4 07.6	11.8	58.0
S 12	359 36.4	N23 25.9	267 14.5	11.8	N 3 55.8	11.7	57.9
D 13	14 36.2	26.0	281 45.3	11.8	3 44.1	11.8	57.9
A 14	29 36.1	26.0	296 16.1	11.8	3 32.3	11.8	57.9
Y 15	44 36.0 ..	26.0	310 46.9	11.9	3 20.5	11.8	57.8
16	59 35.8	26.0	325 17.8	12.0	3 08.7	11.7	57.8
17	74 35.7	26.0	339 48.8	11.9	2 57.0	11.8	57.8
18	89 35.6	N23 26.0	354 19.7	12.1	N 2 45.2	11.8	57.7
19	104 35.4	26.0	8 50.8	12.1	2 33.4	11.8	57.7
20	119 35.3	26.0	23 21.9	12.1	2 21.6	11.8	57.7
21	134 35.1 ..	26.1	37 53.0	12.1	2 09.8	11.7	57.6
22	149 35.0	26.1	52 24.1	12.2	1 58.0	11.8	57.6
23	164 34.9	26.1	66 55.3	12.3	N 1 46.2	11.7	57.6
	SD 15.8	d 0.0	SD 16.2	16.0	15.8		

Twilight / Sunrise / Moonrise

Lat.	Naut.	Civil	Sunrise	18	19	20	21
°	h m	h m	h m	h m	h m	h m	h m
N 72	☐	☐	☐	07 12	09 22	11 21	13 13
N 70	☐	☐	☐	07 39	09 37	11 27	13 12
68	☐	☐	☐	08 00	09 48	11 31	13 11
66	☐	☐	☐	08 16	09 58	11 35	13 09
64	////	////	01 31	08 29	10 06	11 39	13 08
62	////	////	02 09	08 40	10 12	11 41	13 08
60	////	00 50	02 36	08 50	10 18	11 44	13 07
N 58	////	01 40	02 56	08 58	10 23	11 46	13 06
56	////	02 10	03 13	09 05	10 28	11 48	13 06
54	00 45	02 33	03 27	09 11	10 32	11 50	13 05
52	01 32	02 51	03 39	09 17	10 35	11 51	13 05
50	02 00	03 06	03 50	09 22	10 39	11 53	13 05
45	02 46	03 35	04 13	09 34	10 46	11 56	13 04
N 40	03 16	03 58	04 31	09 43	10 52	11 58	13 03
35	03 40	04 16	04 46	09 51	10 57	12 01	13 02
30	03 58	04 32	04 59	09 58	11 01	12 03	13 02
20	04 27	04 57	05 21	10 10	11 09	12 06	13 01
N 10	04 50	05 17	05 40	10 20	11 16	12 09	13 00
0	05 09	05 35	05 58	10 30	11 22	12 12	12 59
S 10	05 26	05 52	06 15	10 40	11 29	12 15	12 59
20	05 42	06 10	06 34	10 50	11 36	12 18	12 58
30	05 59	06 29	06 55	11 02	11 43	12 21	12 57
35	06 07	06 39	07 07	11 09	11 48	12 23	12 57
40	06 17	06 51	07 21	11 16	11 53	12 26	12 56
45	06 27	07 04	07 38	11 25	11 59	12 28	12 56
S 50	06 39	07 21	07 59	11 36	12 05	12 31	12 55
52	06 44	07 28	08 09	11 41	12 09	12 33	12 55
54	06 50	07 36	08 20	11 47	12 12	12 34	12 54
56	06 56	07 45	08 33	11 53	12 16	12 36	12 54
58	07 03	07 56	08 48	11 59	12 20	12 38	12 54
S 60	07 10	08 07	09 05	12 07	12 25	12 40	12 53

Sunset / Twilight / Moonset

Lat.	Sunset	Civil	Naut.	18	19	20	21
°	h m	h m	h m	h m	h m	h m	h m
N 72	☐	☐	☐	01 38	01 18	01 04	00 51
N 70	☐	☐	☐	01 09	01 02	00 56	00 50
68	☐	☐	☐	00 47	00 49	00 49	00 48
66	☐	☐	☐	00 30	00 38	00 43	00 47
64	22 32	////	////	00 15	00 29	00 38	00 46
62	21 54	////	////	00 03	00 21	00 34	00 45
60	21 27	23 14	////	24 14	00 14	00 30	00 44
N 58	21 07	22 23	////	24 08	00 08	00 27	00 44
56	20 50	21 53	////	24 03	00 03	00 24	00 43
54	20 36	21 30	23 18	23 58	24 21	00 21	00 43
52	20 23	21 12	22 31	23 53	24 19	00 19	00 42
50	20 12	20 57	22 03	23 49	24 17	00 17	00 42
45	19 50	20 27	21 17	23 41	24 12	00 12	00 41
N 40	19 32	20 05	20 46	23 33	24 08	00 08	00 40
35	19 17	19 46	20 23	23 27	24 04	00 04	00 39
30	19 04	19 31	20 05	23 22	24 01	00 01	00 38
20	18 42	19 06	19 35	23 12	23 56	24 37	00 37
N 10	18 23	18 46	19 13	23 03	23 51	24 36	00 36
0	18 05	18 28	18 54	22 55	23 46	24 35	00 35
S 10	17 48	18 10	18 37	22 47	23 42	24 34	00 34
20	17 29	17 53	18 21	22 38	23 37	24 33	00 33
30	17 08	17 34	18 04	22 28	23 31	24 31	00 31
35	16 55	17 24	17 55	22 22	23 28	24 30	00 30
40	16 41	17 12	17 46	22 16	23 24	24 30	00 30
45	16 24	16 58	17 35	22 08	23 19	24 28	00 28
S 50	16 04	16 42	17 24	21 59	23 14	24 27	00 27
52	15 54	16 35	17 18	21 54	23 12	24 27	00 27
54	15 43	16 26	17 13	21 49	23 09	24 26	00 26
56	15 30	16 17	17 07	21 44	23 06	24 25	00 25
58	15 15	16 07	17 00	21 38	23 03	24 24	00 24
S 60	14 58	15 55	16 52	21 31	22 59	24 24	00 24

SUN / MOON

Day	Eqn. of Time 00ʰ	Eqn. of Time 12ʰ	Mer. Pass.	Mer. Pass. Upper	Mer. Pass. Lower	Age	Phase
d	m s	m s	h m	h m	h m	d	%
18	01 01	01 08	12 01	16 43	04 15	05	29
19	01 15	01 21	12 01	17 34	05 09	06	40
20	01 28	01 34	12 02	18 23	05 59	07	51

UT	ARIES GHA	VENUS −4.0 GHA	Dec	MARS −1.9 GHA	Dec	JUPITER −2.4 GHA	Dec	SATURN +0.0 GHA	Dec	STARS Name	SHA	Dec
d h	° ′	° ′	° ′	° ′	° ′	° ′	° ′	° ′	° ′		° ′	° ′
21 00	269 08.5	137 56.2	N20 07.0	316 29.8	S22 06.3	47 19.3	S14 55.4	352 17.1	S22 25.4	Acamar	315 16.1	S40 13.9
01	284 11.0	152 55.7	06.2	331 32.0	06.4	62 21.9	55.3	7 19.8	25.4	Achernar	335 24.6	S57 08.5
02	299 13.4	167 55.2	05.4	346 34.2	06.6	77 24.5	55.3	22 22.4	25.4	Acrux	173 05.3	S63 12.3
03	314 15.9	182 54.7 ..	04.6	1 36.5 ..	06.7	92 27.1 ..	55.3	37 25.1 ..	25.5	Adhara	255 10.2	S29 00.0
04	329 18.3	197 54.2	03.9	16 38.7	06.8	107 29.7	55.2	52 27.7	25.5	Aldebaran	290 45.8	N16 32.5
05	344 20.8	212 53.7	03.1	31 40.9	07.0	122 32.3	55.2	67 30.4	25.5			
T 06	359 23.3	227 53.2	N20 02.3	46 43.2	S22 07.1	137 34.9	S14 55.2	82 33.1	S22 25.5	Alioth	166 17.6	N55 52.0
H 07	14 25.7	242 52.7	01.5	61 45.4	07.2	152 37.5	55.1	97 35.7	25.5	Alkaid	152 56.0	N49 13.6
U 08	29 28.2	257 52.2	20 00.7	76 47.6	07.4	167 40.1	55.1	112 38.4	25.5	Al Na'ir	27 39.3	S46 52.1
R 09	44 30.7	272 51.7	19 59.9	91 49.9 ..	07.5	182 42.8 ..	55.1	127 41.0 ..	25.5	Alnilam	275 43.3	S 1 11.6
S 10	59 33.1	287 51.2	59.1	106 52.1	07.6	197 45.4	55.0	142 43.7	25.5	Alphard	217 53.0	S 8 44.4
D 11	74 35.6	302 50.8	58.3	121 54.3	07.8	212 48.0	55.0	157 46.4	25.5			
A 12	89 38.1	317 50.3	N19 57.5	136 56.6	S22 07.9	227 50.6	S14 55.0	172 49.0	S22 25.6	Alphecca	126 07.8	N26 39.4
Y 13	104 40.5	332 49.8	56.7	151 58.8	08.0	242 53.2	54.9	187 51.7	25.6	Alpheratz	357 40.0	N29 11.3
14	119 43.0	347 49.3	55.9	167 01.0	08.2	257 55.8	54.9	202 54.3	25.6	Altair	62 04.6	N 8 55.1
15	134 45.4	2 48.8 ..	55.1	182 03.3 ..	08.3	272 58.4 ..	54.9	217 57.0 ..	25.6	Ankaa	353 12.4	S42 12.2
16	149 47.9	17 48.3	54.3	197 05.5	08.4	288 01.0	54.8	232 59.7	25.6	Antares	112 21.7	S26 28.2
17	164 50.4	32 47.8	53.5	212 07.8	08.6	303 03.6	54.8	248 02.3	25.6			
18	179 52.8	47 47.3	N19 52.7	227 10.0	S22 08.7	318 06.2	S14 54.8	263 05.0	S22 25.6	Arcturus	145 52.5	N19 05.4
19	194 55.3	62 46.8	51.9	242 12.3	08.8	333 08.8	54.7	278 07.7	25.6	Atria	107 19.9	S69 03.5
20	209 57.8	77 46.4	51.1	257 14.5	09.0	348 11.4	54.7	293 10.3	25.7	Avior	234 17.2	S59 34.4
21	225 00.2	92 45.9 ..	50.3	272 16.8 ..	09.1	3 14.0 ..	54.7	308 13.0 ..	25.7	Bellatrix	278 28.7	N 6 21.8
22	240 02.7	107 45.4	49.5	287 19.0	09.3	18 16.6	54.6	323 15.6	25.7	Betelgeuse	270 58.0	N 7 24.4
23	255 05.2	122 44.9	48.7	302 21.3	09.4	33 19.2	54.6	338 18.3	25.7			
22 00	270 07.6	137 44.4	N19 47.9	317 23.5	S22 09.5	48 21.8	S14 54.6	353 21.0	S22 25.7	Canopus	263 55.2	S52 42.5
01	285 10.1	152 43.9	47.1	332 25.8	09.7	63 24.5	54.6	8 23.6	25.7	Capella	280 29.9	N46 00.7
02	300 12.6	167 43.5	46.3	347 28.0	09.8	78 27.1	54.5	23 26.3	25.7	Deneb	49 28.8	N45 20.7
03	315 15.0	182 43.0 ..	45.5	2 30.3 ..	09.9	93 29.7 ..	54.5	38 28.9 ..	25.7	Denebola	182 30.3	N14 28.3
04	330 17.5	197 42.5	44.7	17 32.6	10.1	108 32.3	54.5	53 31.6	25.7	Diphda	348 52.6	S17 53.1
05	345 19.9	212 42.0	43.9	32 34.8	10.2	123 34.9	54.4	68 34.3	25.8			
F 06	0 22.4	227 41.5	N19 43.1	47 37.1	S22 10.4	138 37.5	S14 54.4	83 36.9	S22 25.8	Dubhe	193 47.8	N61 39.4
R 07	15 24.9	242 41.1	42.3	62 39.3	10.5	153 40.1	54.4	98 39.6	25.8	Elnath	278 08.7	N28 37.1
I 08	30 27.3	257 40.6	41.5	77 41.6	10.7	168 42.7	54.3	113 42.3	25.8	Eltanin	90 44.0	N51 29.4
D 09	45 29.8	272 40.1 ..	40.7	92 43.9 ..	10.8	183 45.3 ..	54.3	128 44.9 ..	25.8	Enif	33 43.6	N 9 57.6
A 10	60 32.3	287 39.6	39.8	107 46.1	10.9	198 47.9	54.3	143 47.6	25.8	Fomalhaut	15 20.2	S29 31.3
Y 11	75 34.7	302 39.2	39.0	122 48.4	11.1	213 50.5	54.2	158 50.2	25.8			
12	90 37.2	317 38.7	N19 38.2	137 50.7	S22 11.2	228 53.1	S14 54.2	173 52.9	S22 25.8	Gacrux	171 57.0	S57 13.2
13	105 39.7	332 38.2	37.4	152 52.9	11.4	243 55.7	54.2	188 55.6	25.9	Gienah	175 48.8	S17 38.7
14	120 42.1	347 37.7	36.6	167 55.2	11.5	258 58.3	54.2	203 58.2	25.9	Hadar	148 42.6	S60 27.8
15	135 44.6	2 37.3 ..	35.8	182 57.5 ..	11.7	274 00.9 ..	54.1	219 00.9 ..	25.9	Hamal	327 57.1	N23 32.7
16	150 47.0	17 36.8	34.9	197 59.8	11.8	289 03.5	54.1	234 03.5	25.9	Kaus Aust.	83 38.9	S34 22.3
17	165 49.5	32 36.3	34.1	213 02.0	11.9	304 06.1	54.1	249 06.2	25.9			
18	180 52.0	47 35.9	N19 33.3	228 04.3	S22 12.1	319 08.7	S14 54.0	264 08.9	S22 25.9	Kochab	137 19.4	N74 05.2
19	195 54.4	62 35.4	32.5	243 06.6	12.2	334 11.3	54.0	279 11.5	25.9	Markab	13 34.9	N15 18.1
20	210 56.9	77 34.9	31.7	258 08.9	12.4	349 13.9	54.0	294 14.2	25.9	Menkar	314 11.7	N 4 09.5
21	225 59.4	92 34.5 ..	30.8	273 11.2 ..	12.5	4 16.5 ..	53.9	309 16.9 ..	25.9	Menkent	148 03.3	S36 27.6
22	241 01.8	107 34.0	30.0	288 13.4	12.7	19 19.1	53.9	324 19.5	26.0	Miaplacidus	221 39.6	S69 47.8
23	256 04.3	122 33.5	29.2	303 15.7	12.8	34 21.7	53.9	339 22.2	26.0			
23 00	271 06.8	137 33.1	N19 28.4	318 18.0	S22 13.0	49 24.3	S14 53.9	354 24.8	S22 26.0	Mirfak	308 35.9	N49 55.2
01	286 09.2	152 32.6	27.5	333 20.3	13.1	64 26.9	53.8	9 27.5	26.0	Nunki	75 53.8	S26 16.2
02	301 11.7	167 32.1	26.7	348 22.6	13.3	79 29.5	53.8	24 30.2	26.0	Peacock	53 13.5	S56 40.3
03	316 14.2	182 31.7 ..	25.9	3 24.9 ..	13.4	94 32.0 ..	53.8	39 32.8 ..	26.0	Pollux	243 24.0	N27 58.8
04	331 16.6	197 31.2	25.1	18 27.2	13.6	109 34.6	53.7	54 35.5	26.0	Procyon	244 56.5	N 5 10.5
05	346 19.1	212 30.7	24.2	33 29.5	13.7	124 37.2	53.7	69 38.1	26.0			
S 06	1 21.5	227 30.3	N19 23.4	48 31.8	S22 13.9	139 39.8	S14 53.7	84 40.8	S22 26.0	Rasalhague	96 03.0	N12 33.0
A 07	16 24.0	242 29.8	22.6	63 34.0	14.0	154 42.4	53.7	99 43.5	26.1	Regulus	207 40.1	N11 52.7
T 08	31 26.5	257 29.4	21.7	78 36.3	14.2	169 45.0	53.6	114 46.1	26.1	Rigel	281 09.1	S 8 11.0
U 09	46 28.9	272 28.9 ..	20.9	93 38.6 ..	14.3	184 47.6 ..	53.6	129 48.8 ..	26.1	Rigil Kent.	139 46.6	S60 54.7
R 10	61 31.4	287 28.4	20.1	108 40.9	14.5	199 50.2	53.6	144 51.5	26.1	Sabik	102 08.3	S15 44.7
D 11	76 33.9	302 28.0	19.3	123 43.2	14.6	214 52.8	53.5	159 54.1	26.1			
A 12	91 36.3	317 27.5	N19 18.4	138 45.5	S22 14.8	229 55.4	S14 53.5	174 56.8	S22 26.1	Schedar	349 36.7	N56 37.9
Y 13	106 38.8	332 27.1	17.6	153 47.8	14.9	244 58.0	53.5	189 59.4	26.1	Shaula	96 16.9	S37 06.8
14	121 41.3	347 26.6	16.7	168 50.1	15.1	260 00.6	53.5	205 02.1	26.1	Sirius	258 31.1	S16 44.7
15	136 43.7	2 26.2 ..	15.9	183 52.4 ..	15.2	275 03.2 ..	53.4	220 04.8 ..	26.2	Spica	158 27.5	S11 15.4
16	151 46.2	17 25.7	15.1	198 54.8	15.4	290 05.8	53.4	235 07.4	26.2	Suhail	222 50.3	S43 30.6
17	166 48.7	32 25.3	14.2	213 57.1	15.5	305 08.4	53.4	250 10.1	26.2			
18	181 51.1	47 24.8	N19 13.4	228 59.4	S22 15.7	320 11.0	S14 53.3	265 12.8	S22 26.2	Vega	80 36.2	N38 48.2
19	196 53.6	62 24.4	12.6	244 01.7	15.8	335 13.5	53.3	280 15.4	26.2	Zuben'ubi	137 01.4	S16 07.0
20	211 56.0	77 23.9	11.7	259 04.0	16.0	350 16.1	53.3	295 18.1	26.2		SHA	Mer. Pass.
21	226 58.5	92 23.4 ..	10.9	274 06.3 ..	16.1	5 18.7 ..	53.3	310 20.7 ..	26.2		° ′	h m
22	242 01.0	107 23.0	10.0	289 08.6	16.3	20 21.3	53.2	325 23.4	26.2	Venus	227 36.8	14 50
23	257 03.4	122 22.6	09.2	304 10.9	16.4	35 23.9	53.2	340 26.1	26.2	Mars	47 15.9	2 50
	h m									Jupiter	138 14.2	20 43
Mer. Pass.	5 58.5	v −0.5	d 0.8	v 2.3	d 0.1	v 2.6	d 0.0	v 2.7	d 0.0	Saturn	83 13.3	0 27

UT	SUN GHA	SUN Dec	MOON GHA	v	MOON Dec	d	HP
d h	° ′	° ′	° ′	′	° ′	′	′
21 00	179 34.7	N23 26.1	81 26.6	12.3	N 1 34.5	11.8	57.5
01	194 34.6	26.1	95 57.9	12.3	1 22.7	11.8	57.5
02	209 34.5	26.1	110 29.2	12.3	1 10.9	11.7	57.5
03	224 34.3	.. 26.1	125 00.5	12.4	0 59.2	11.8	57.5
04	239 34.2	26.1	139 31.9	12.5	0 47.4	11.7	57.4
05	254 34.1	26.1	154 03.4	12.4	0 35.7	11.8	57.4
06	269 33.9	N23 26.1	168 34.8	12.5	N 0 23.9	11.7	57.4
T 07	284 33.8	26.1	183 06.3	12.5	0 12.2	11.7	57.3
H 08	299 33.6	26.1	197 37.8	12.6	N 0 00.5	11.7	57.3
U 09	314 33.5	.. 26.1	212 09.4	12.6	S 0 11.2	11.7	57.3
R 10	329 33.4	26.1	226 41.0	12.6	0 22.9	11.7	57.2
S 11	344 33.2	26.1	241 12.6	12.7	0 34.6	11.7	57.2
D 12	359 33.1	N23 26.1	255 44.3	12.7	S 0 46.3	11.8	57.2
A 13	14 33.0	26.1	270 16.0	12.7	0 57.9	11.6	57.1
Y 14	29 32.8	26.1	284 47.7	12.7	1 09.5	11.6	57.1
15	44 32.7	.. 26.1	299 19.4	12.8	1 21.1	11.6	57.1
16	59 32.6	26.1	313 51.2	12.8	1 32.7	11.6	57.1
17	74 32.4	26.1	328 23.0	12.8	1 44.3	11.6	57.0
18	89 32.3	N23 26.1	342 54.8	12.8	S 1 55.9	11.5	57.0
19	104 32.2	26.1	357 26.6	12.9	2 07.4	11.5	57.0
20	119 32.0	26.1	11 58.5	12.9	2 18.9	11.5	56.9
21	134 31.9	.. 26.1	26 30.4	12.9	2 30.4	11.5	56.9
22	149 31.7	26.1	41 02.3	12.9	2 41.9	11.4	56.9
23	164 31.6	26.1	55 34.2	12.9	2 53.3	11.4	56.9
22 00	179 31.5	N23 26.0	70 06.1	13.0	S 3 04.7	11.4	56.8
01	194 31.4	26.0	84 38.1	13.0	3 16.1	11.4	56.8
02	209 31.2	26.0	99 10.1	13.0	3 27.5	11.3	56.8
03	224 31.1	.. 26.0	113 42.1	13.0	3 38.8	11.3	56.7
04	239 30.9	26.0	128 14.1	13.0	3 50.1	11.3	56.7
05	254 30.8	26.0	142 46.1	13.0	4 01.4	11.3	56.7
06	269 30.7	N23 26.0	157 18.1	13.1	S 4 12.7	11.2	56.7
07	284 30.5	26.0	171 50.2	13.1	4 23.9	11.2	56.6
F 08	299 30.4	25.9	186 22.3	13.0	4 35.1	11.2	56.6
R 09	314 30.3	.. 25.9	200 54.3	13.1	4 46.3	11.1	56.6
I 10	329 30.1	25.9	215 26.4	13.1	4 57.4	11.1	56.5
11	344 30.0	25.9	229 58.5	13.1	5 08.5	11.1	56.5
D 12	359 29.9	N23 25.9	244 30.6	13.2	S 5 19.6	11.0	56.5
A 13	14 29.7	25.9	259 02.8	13.1	5 30.6	11.0	56.5
Y 14	29 29.6	25.8	273 34.9	13.1	5 41.6	10.9	56.4
15	44 29.4	.. 25.8	288 07.0	13.2	5 52.5	11.0	56.4
16	59 29.3	25.8	302 39.2	13.1	6 03.5	10.8	56.4
17	74 29.2	25.8	317 11.3	13.2	6 14.3	10.9	56.4
18	89 29.0	N23 25.8	331 43.5	13.1	S 6 25.2	10.8	56.3
19	104 28.9	25.7	346 15.6	13.2	6 36.0	10.8	56.3
20	119 28.8	25.7	0 47.8	13.2	6 46.8	10.7	56.3
21	134 28.6	.. 25.7	15 20.0	13.1	6 57.5	10.7	56.3
22	149 28.5	25.7	29 52.1	13.2	7 08.2	10.6	56.2
23	164 28.4	25.6	44 24.3	13.2	7 18.8	10.6	56.2
23 00	179 28.2	N23 25.6	58 56.5	13.1	S 7 29.4	10.6	56.2
01	194 28.1	25.6	73 28.6	13.2	7 40.0	10.5	56.2
02	209 28.0	25.5	88 00.8	13.2	7 50.5	10.4	56.1
03	224 27.8	.. 25.5	102 33.0	13.2	8 00.9	10.5	56.1
04	239 27.7	25.5	117 05.2	13.2	8 11.4	10.4	56.1
05	254 27.6	25.5	131 37.3	13.2	8 21.8	10.3	56.1
06	269 27.4	N23 25.4	146 09.5	13.2	S 8 32.1	10.3	56.0
07	284 27.3	25.4	160 41.7	13.1	8 42.4	10.2	56.0
S 08	299 27.2	25.4	175 13.8	13.2	8 52.6	10.2	56.0
A 09	314 27.0	.. 25.3	189 46.0	13.1	9 02.8	10.1	56.0
T 10	329 26.9	25.3	204 18.1	13.2	9 12.9	10.1	55.9
U 11	344 26.8	25.3	218 50.3	13.1	9 23.0	10.1	55.9
R 12	359 26.6	N23 25.2	233 22.4	13.2	S 9 33.1	9.9	55.9
D 13	14 26.5	25.2	247 54.6	13.1	9 43.0	10.0	55.9
A 14	29 26.4	25.2	262 26.7	13.1	9 53.0	9.9	55.8
Y 15	44 26.2	.. 25.1	276 58.8	13.1	10 02.9	9.8	55.8
16	59 26.1	25.1	291 30.9	13.1	10 12.7	9.8	55.8
17	74 25.9	25.0	306 03.0	13.1	10 22.5	9.7	55.8
18	89 25.8	N23 25.0	320 35.1	13.1	S10 32.2	9.6	55.7
19	104 25.7	25.0	335 07.2	13.1	10 41.8	9.7	55.7
20	119 25.5	24.9	349 39.3	13.0	10 51.5	9.5	55.7
21	134 25.4	.. 24.9	4 11.3	13.1	11 01.0	9.5	55.7
22	149 25.3	24.8	18 43.4	13.0	11 10.5	9.4	55.7
23	164 25.1	24.8	33 15.4	13.1	S11 19.9	9.4	55.6
	SD 15.8	d 0.0	SD 15.6		15.4		15.2

Twilight / Sunrise / Moonrise

Lat.	Twilight Naut.	Twilight Civil	Sunrise	Moonrise 21	22	23	24
°	h m	h m	h m	h m	h m	h m	h m
N 72	□	□	□	13 13	15 03	16 54	18 52
N 70	□	□	□	13 12	14 54	16 37	18 21
68	□	□	□	13 11	14 47	16 23	17 58
66	□	□	□	13 09	14 41	16 11	17 40
64	////	////	01 31	13 08	14 36	16 02	17 26
62	////	////	02 10	13 08	14 32	15 54	17 14
60	////	00 49	02 36	13 07	14 28	15 47	17 04
N 58	////	01 41	02 57	13 06	14 25	15 41	16 55
56	////	02 11	03 13	13 06	14 22	15 36	16 48
54	00 45	02 33	03 28	13 05	14 19	15 31	16 41
52	01 33	02 51	03 40	13 05	14 17	15 26	16 35
50	02 01	03 06	03 51	13 05	14 14	15 23	16 29
45	02 46	03 36	04 13	13 04	14 10	15 14	16 17
N 40	03 17	03 59	04 32	13 03	14 06	15 07	16 07
35	03 40	04 17	04 47	13 02	14 02	15 01	15 59
30	03 59	04 32	05 00	13 02	13 59	14 56	15 52
20	04 28	04 57	05 22	13 01	13 54	14 47	15 39
N 10	04 51	05 18	05 41	13 00	13 50	14 39	15 28
0	05 10	05 36	05 58	12 59	13 46	14 32	15 18
S 10	05 27	05 53	06 16	12 59	13 42	14 24	15 08
20	05 43	06 10	06 34	12 58	13 37	14 17	14 57
30	05 59	06 29	06 56	12 57	13 32	14 08	14 45
35	06 08	06 40	07 08	12 57	13 30	14 03	14 38
40	06 18	06 52	07 22	12 56	13 26	13 57	14 30
45	06 28	07 05	07 39	12 56	13 23	13 51	14 20
S 50	06 40	07 21	08 00	12 55	13 18	13 43	14 09
52	06 45	07 29	08 10	12 55	13 16	13 39	14 04
54	06 51	07 37	08 21	12 54	13 14	13 35	13 58
56	06 57	07 46	08 34	12 54	13 12	13 31	13 52
58	07 04	07 56	08 48	12 54	13 09	13 26	13 45
S 60	07 11	08 08	09 06	12 53	13 06	13 21	13 37

Sunset / Twilight / Moonset

Lat.	Sunset	Twilight Civil	Twilight Naut.	Moonset 21	22	23	24
°	h m	h m	h m	h m	h m	h m	h m
N 72	□	□	□	00 51	00 40	00 27	00 12 / 23 51
N 70	□	□	□	00 50	00 44	00 38	00 31
68	□	□	□	00 48	00 48	00 47	00 47
66	□	□	□	00 47	00 51	00 54	00 59
64	22 33	////	////	00 46	00 53	01 01	01 10
62	21 54	////	////	00 45	00 56	01 06	01 19
60	21 28	23 14	////	00 44	00 58	01 11	01 26
N 58	21 07	22 23	////	00 44	01 00	01 16	01 33
56	20 51	21 53	////	00 43	01 01	01 19	01 39
54	20 36	21 31	23 18	00 43	01 03	01 23	01 45
52	20 24	21 13	22 31	00 42	01 04	01 26	01 50
50	20 13	20 58	22 03	00 42	01 05	01 29	01 54
45	19 51	20 28	21 18	00 41	01 08	01 35	02 04
N 40	19 32	20 05	20 47	00 40	01 10	01 40	02 12
35	19 17	19 47	20 24	00 39	01 12	01 45	02 19
30	19 04	19 32	20 05	00 38	01 14	01 49	02 25
20	18 42	19 07	19 36	00 37	01 17	01 56	02 36
N 10	18 23	18 46	19 13	00 36	01 19	02 02	02 45
0	18 06	18 28	18 54	00 35	01 22	02 08	02 54
S 10	17 48	18 11	18 37	00 34	01 24	02 13	03 03
20	17 30	17 54	18 21	00 33	01 27	02 20	03 12
30	17 08	17 35	18 05	00 31	01 30	02 27	03 23
35	16 56	17 24	17 56	00 30	01 31	02 31	03 29
40	16 42	17 12	17 47	00 30	01 33	02 35	03 36
45	16 25	16 59	17 36	00 28	01 35	02 41	03 45
S 50	16 04	16 43	17 24	00 27	01 38	02 47	03 55
52	15 54	16 35	17 19	00 27	01 39	02 50	03 59
54	15 43	16 27	17 13	00 26	01 41	02 53	04 04
56	15 30	16 18	17 07	00 25	01 42	02 57	04 10
58	15 16	16 08	17 00	00 24	01 44	03 01	04 17
S 60	14 58	15 56	16 53	00 24	01 46	03 06	04 24

SUN and MOON

Day	SUN Eqn. of Time 00h	SUN Eqn. of Time 12h	SUN Mer. Pass.	MOON Mer. Pass. Upper	MOON Mer. Pass. Lower	Age	Phase
d	m s	m s	h m	h m	h m	d	%
21	01 41	01 47	12 02	19 11	06 47	08	61
22	01 54	02 00	12 02	19 57	07 34	09	71
23	02 07	02 13	12 02	20 43	08 20	10	80

UT	ARIES GHA	VENUS −4.0 GHA	Dec	MARS −2.0 GHA	Dec	JUPITER −2.3 GHA	Dec	SATURN +0.0 GHA	Dec	STARS Name	SHA	Dec
24 00	272 05.9	137 22.1	N19 08.3	319 13.2	S22 16.6	50 26.5	S14 53.2	355 28.7	S22 26.3	Acamar	315 16.1	S40 13.8
01	287 08.4	152 21.7	07.5	334 15.6	16.8	65 29.1	53.2	10 31.4	26.3	Achernar	335 24.5	S57 08.5
02	302 10.8	167 21.2	06.7	349 17.9	16.9	80 31.7	53.1	25 34.1	26.3	Acrux	173 05.3	S63 12.3
03	317 13.3	182 20.8 ..	05.8	4 20.2 ..	17.1	95 34.3 ..	53.1	40 36.7 ..	26.3	Adhara	255 10.2	S29 00.0
04	332 15.8	197 20.3	05.0	19 22.5	17.2	110 36.9	53.1	55 39.4	26.3	Aldebaran	290 45.8	N16 32.5
05	347 18.2	212 19.9	04.1	34 24.9	17.4	125 39.4	53.1	70 42.0	26.3			
06	2 20.7	227 19.4	N19 03.3	49 27.2	S22 17.5	140 42.0	S14 53.0	85 44.7	S22 26.3	Alioth	166 17.7	N55 52.0
07	17 23.2	242 19.0	02.4	64 29.5	17.7	155 44.6	53.0	100 47.4	26.3	Alkaid	152 56.1	N49 13.7
08	32 25.6	257 18.5	01.6	79 31.8	17.9	170 47.2	53.0	115 50.0	26.3	Al Na'ir	27 39.3	S46 52.1
S 09	47 28.1	272 18.1	19 00.7	94 34.2 ..	18.0	185 49.8 ..	52.9	130 52.7 ..	26.4	Alnilam	275 43.3	S 1 11.6
U 10	62 30.5	287 17.7	18 59.9	109 36.5	18.2	200 52.4	52.9	145 55.4	26.4	Alphard	217 53.0	S 8 44.4
N 11	77 33.0	302 17.2	59.0	124 38.8	18.3	215 55.0	52.9	160 58.0	26.4			
D 12	92 35.5	317 16.8	N18 58.2	139 41.2	S22 18.5	230 57.6	S14 52.9	176 00.7	S22 26.4	Alphecca	126 07.9	N26 39.4
A 13	107 37.9	332 16.3	57.3	154 43.5	18.7	246 00.1	52.8	191 03.3	26.4	Alpheratz	357 39.9	N29 11.3
Y 14	122 40.4	347 15.9	56.4	169 45.8	18.8	261 02.7	52.8	206 06.0	26.4	Altair	62 04.6	N 8 55.1
15	137 42.9	2 15.5 ..	55.6	184 48.2 ..	19.0	276 05.3 ..	52.8	221 08.7 ..	26.4	Ankaa	353 12.4	S42 12.2
16	152 45.3	17 15.0	54.7	199 50.5	19.1	291 07.9	52.8	236 11.3	26.4	Antares	112 21.7	S26 28.2
17	167 47.8	32 14.6	53.9	214 52.8	19.3	306 10.5	52.7	251 14.0	26.5			
18	182 50.3	47 14.2	N18 53.0	229 55.2	S22 19.5	321 13.1	S14 52.7	266 16.7	S22 26.5	Arcturus	145 52.5	N19 05.4
19	197 52.7	62 13.7	52.2	244 57.5	19.6	336 15.7	52.7	281 19.3	26.5	Atria	107 19.9	S69 03.5
20	212 55.2	77 13.3	51.3	259 59.9	19.8	351 18.2	52.7	296 22.0	26.5	Avior	234 17.2	S59 34.3
21	227 57.6	92 12.8 ..	50.4	275 02.2 ..	20.0	6 20.8 ..	52.6	311 24.6 ..	26.5	Bellatrix	278 28.7	N 6 21.8
22	243 00.1	107 12.4	49.6	290 04.5	20.1	21 23.4	52.6	326 27.3	26.5	Betelgeuse	270 58.0	N 7 24.4
23	258 02.6	122 12.0	48.7	305 06.9	20.3	36 26.0	52.6	341 30.0	26.5			
25 00	273 05.0	137 11.6	N18 47.8	320 09.2	S22 20.4	51 28.6	S14 52.6	356 32.6	S22 26.5	Canopus	263 55.2	S52 42.5
01	288 07.5	152 11.1	47.0	335 11.6	20.6	66 31.2	52.5	11 35.3	26.5	Capella	280 29.9	N46 00.7
02	303 10.0	167 10.7	46.1	350 13.9	20.8	81 33.7	52.5	26 38.0	26.6	Deneb	49 28.6	N45 20.7
03	318 12.4	182 10.3 ..	45.3	5 16.3 ..	20.9	96 36.3 ..	52.5	41 40.6 ..	26.6	Denebola	182 30.3	N14 28.3
04	333 14.9	197 09.8	44.4	20 18.6	21.1	111 38.9	52.5	56 43.3	26.6	Diphda	348 52.5	S17 53.1
05	348 17.4	212 09.4	43.5	35 21.0	21.3	126 41.5	52.4	71 45.9	26.6			
06	3 19.8	227 09.0	N18 42.7	50 23.4	S22 21.4	141 44.1	S14 52.4	86 48.6	S22 26.6	Dubhe	193 47.9	N61 39.4
07	18 22.3	242 08.6	41.8	65 25.7	21.6	156 46.6	52.4	101 51.3	26.6	Elnath	278 08.7	N28 37.1
08	33 24.8	257 08.1	40.9	80 28.1	21.8	171 49.2	52.4	116 53.9	26.6	Eltanin	90 44.0	N51 29.4
M 09	48 27.2	272 07.7 ..	40.0	95 30.4 ..	21.9	186 51.8 ..	52.3	131 56.6 ..	26.6	Enif	33 43.6	N 9 57.6
O 10	63 29.7	287 07.3	39.2	110 32.8	22.1	201 54.4	52.3	146 59.3	26.6	Fomalhaut	15 20.1	S29 31.3
N 11	78 32.1	302 06.9	38.3	125 35.2	22.3	216 57.0	52.3	162 01.9	26.7			
D 12	93 34.6	317 06.4	N18 37.4	140 37.5	S22 22.4	231 59.5	S14 52.3	177 04.6	S22 26.7	Gacrux	171 57.0	S57 13.2
A 13	108 37.1	332 06.0	36.6	155 39.9	22.6	247 02.1	52.2	192 07.2	26.7	Gienah	175 48.8	S17 38.7
Y 14	123 39.5	347 05.6	35.7	170 42.3	22.8	262 04.7	52.2	207 09.9	26.7	Hadar	148 42.7	S60 27.8
15	138 42.0	2 05.2 ..	34.8	185 44.6 ..	23.0	277 07.3 ..	52.2	222 12.6 ..	26.7	Hamal	327 57.1	N23 32.7
16	153 44.5	17 04.7	33.9	200 47.0	23.1	292 09.9	52.2	237 15.2	26.7	Kaus Aust.	83 38.9	S34 22.3
17	168 46.9	32 04.3	33.1	215 49.4	23.3	307 12.4	52.2	252 17.9	26.7			
18	183 49.4	47 03.9	N18 32.2	230 51.7	S22 23.5	322 15.0	S14 52.1	267 20.6	S22 26.7	Kochab	137 19.4	N74 05.2
19	198 51.9	62 03.5	31.3	245 54.1	23.6	337 17.6	52.1	282 23.2	26.8	Markab	13 34.8	N15 18.2
20	213 54.3	77 03.1	30.4	260 56.5	23.8	352 20.2	52.1	297 25.9	26.8	Menkar	314 11.7	N 4 09.5
21	228 56.8	92 02.7 ..	29.5	275 58.9 ..	24.0	7 22.7 ..	52.1	312 28.5 ..	26.8	Menkent	148 03.3	S36 27.6
22	243 59.3	107 02.2	28.7	291 01.2	24.2	22 25.3	52.0	327 31.2	26.8	Miaplacidus	221 39.6	S69 47.8
23	259 01.7	122 01.8	27.8	306 03.6	24.3	37 27.9	52.0	342 33.9	26.8			
26 00	274 04.2	137 01.4	N18 26.9	321 06.0	S22 24.5	52 30.5	S14 52.0	357 36.5	S22 26.8	Mirfak	308 35.8	N49 55.2
01	289 06.6	152 01.0	26.0	336 08.4	24.7	67 33.0	52.0	12 39.2	26.8	Nunki	75 53.7	S26 16.2
02	304 09.1	167 00.6	25.1	351 10.8	24.8	82 35.6	52.0	27 41.9	26.8	Peacock	53 13.4	S56 40.3
03	319 11.6	182 00.2 ..	24.3	6 13.1 ..	25.0	97 38.2 ..	51.9	42 44.5 ..	26.8	Pollux	243 24.0	N27 58.8
04	334 14.0	196 59.8	23.4	21 15.5	25.2	112 40.8	51.9	57 47.2	26.9	Procyon	244 56.5	N 5 10.5
05	349 16.5	211 59.3	22.5	36 17.9	25.4	127 43.3	51.9	72 49.8	26.9			
06	4 19.0	226 58.9	N18 21.6	51 20.3	S22 25.5	142 45.9	S14 51.9	87 52.5	S22 26.9	Rasalhague	96 03.0	N12 33.0
07	19 21.4	241 58.5	20.7	66 22.7	25.7	157 48.5	51.8	102 55.2	26.9	Regulus	207 40.1	N11 52.7
08	34 23.9	256 58.1	19.8	81 25.1	25.9	172 51.1	51.8	117 57.8	26.9	Rigel	281 09.1	S 8 11.0
T 09	49 26.4	271 57.7 ..	18.9	96 27.5 ..	26.1	187 53.6 ..	51.8	133 00.5 ..	26.9	Rigil Kent.	139 46.7	S60 54.7
U 10	64 28.8	286 57.3	18.0	111 29.9	26.2	202 56.2	51.8	148 03.2	26.9	Sabik	102 08.3	S15 44.7
E 11	79 31.3	301 56.9	17.2	126 32.3	26.4	217 58.8	51.8	163 05.8	26.9			
S 12	94 33.8	316 56.5	N18 16.3	141 34.7	S22 26.6	233 01.4	S14 51.7	178 08.5	S22 26.9	Schedar	349 36.6	N56 37.9
D 13	109 36.2	331 56.1	15.4	156 37.1	26.8	248 03.9	51.7	193 11.2	27.0	Shaula	96 16.9	S37 06.8
A 14	124 38.7	346 55.7	14.5	171 39.5	26.9	263 06.5	51.7	208 13.8	27.0	Sirius	258 31.1	S16 44.6
Y 15	139 41.1	1 55.3 ..	13.6	186 41.9 ..	27.1	278 09.1 ..	51.7	223 16.5 ..	27.0	Spica	158 27.6	S11 15.4
16	154 43.6	16 54.9	12.7	201 44.3	27.3	293 11.6	51.6	238 19.1	27.0	Suhail	222 50.3	S43 30.6
17	169 46.1	31 54.5	11.8	216 46.7	27.5	308 14.2	51.6	253 21.8	27.0			
18	184 48.5	46 54.1	N18 10.9	231 49.1	S22 27.7	323 16.8	S14 51.6	268 24.5	S22 27.0	Vega	80 36.2	N38 48.2
19	199 51.0	61 53.7	10.0	246 51.5	27.8	338 19.4	51.6	283 27.1	27.0	Zuben'ubi	137 01.4	S16 07.0
20	214 53.5	76 53.3	09.1	261 53.9	28.0	353 21.9	51.6	298 29.8	27.0		SHA	Mer. Pass.
21	229 55.9	91 52.9 ..	08.2	276 56.3 ..	28.2	8 24.5 ..	51.5	313 32.5 ..	27.1			h m
22	244 58.4	106 52.5	07.3	291 58.7	28.4	23 27.1	51.5	328 35.1	27.1	Venus	224 06.5	14 52
23	260 00.9	121 52.1	06.4	307 01.1	28.6	38 29.6	51.5	343 37.8	27.1	Mars	47 04.2	2 39
	h m									Jupiter	138 23.5	20 31
Mer. Pass.	5 46.7	v −0.4	d 0.9	v 2.4	d 0.2	v 2.6	d 0.0	v 2.7	d 0.0	Saturn	83 27.6	0 14

UT	SUN GHA	SUN Dec	MOON GHA	v	MOON Dec	d	HP
d h	° ′	° ′	° ′	′	° ′	′	′
24 00	179 25.0	N23 24.7	47 47.5	13.0	S11 29.3	9.3	55.6
01	194 24.9	24.7	62 19.5	13.0	11 38.6	9.3	55.6
02	209 24.7	24.7	76 51.5	13.0	11 47.9	9.2	55.6
03	224 24.6	. . 24.6	91 23.5	12.9	11 57.1	9.1	55.5
04	239 24.5	24.6	105 55.4	13.0	12 06.2	9.1	55.5
05	254 24.3	24.5	120 27.4	13.0	12 15.3	9.0	55.5
06	269 24.2	N23 24.5	134 59.4	12.9	S12 24.3	9.0	55.5
07	284 24.1	24.4	149 31.3	12.9	12 33.3	8.9	55.5
08	299 23.9	24.4	164 03.2	12.9	12 42.2	8.8	55.4
S 09	314 23.8	. . 24.3	178 35.1	12.9	12 51.0	8.8	55.4
U 10	329 23.7	24.3	193 07.0	12.9	12 59.8	8.7	55.4
N 11	344 23.5	24.2	207 38.9	12.8	13 08.5	8.6	55.4
D 12	359 23.4	N23 24.2	222 10.7	12.9	S13 17.1	8.6	55.4
A 13	14 23.3	24.1	236 42.6	12.8	13 25.7	8.5	55.3
Y 14	29 23.1	24.1	251 14.4	12.8	13 34.2	8.4	55.3
15	44 23.0	. . 24.0	265 46.2	12.8	13 42.6	8.4	55.3
16	59 22.9	23.9	280 18.0	12.8	13 51.0	8.2	55.3
17	74 22.7	23.9	294 49.8	12.7	13 59.2	8.3	55.3
18	89 22.6	N23 23.8	309 21.5	12.7	S14 07.5	8.1	55.2
19	104 22.5	23.8	323 53.2	12.8	14 15.6	8.1	55.2
20	119 22.3	23.7	338 25.0	12.7	14 23.7	8.0	55.2
21	134 22.2	. . 23.7	352 56.7	12.6	14 31.7	8.0	55.2
22	149 22.1	23.6	7 28.3	12.7	14 39.7	7.8	55.2
23	164 21.9	23.5	22 00.0	12.6	14 47.5	7.8	55.2
25 00	179 21.8	N23 23.5	36 31.6	12.6	S14 55.3	7.8	55.1
01	194 21.7	23.4	51 03.2	12.7	15 03.1	7.6	55.1
02	209 21.6	23.3	65 34.9	12.5	15 10.7	7.6	55.1
03	224 21.4	. . 23.3	80 06.4	12.6	15 18.3	7.5	55.1
04	239 21.3	23.2	94 38.0	12.5	15 25.8	7.4	55.1
05	254 21.2	23.2	109 09.5	12.6	15 33.2	7.4	55.0
06	269 21.0	N23 23.1	123 41.1	12.5	S15 40.6	7.2	55.0
07	284 20.9	23.0	138 12.6	12.4	15 47.8	7.2	55.0
08	299 20.8	23.0	152 44.0	12.5	15 55.0	7.2	55.0
M 09	314 20.6	. . 22.9	167 15.5	12.5	16 02.2	7.0	55.0
O 10	329 20.5	22.8	181 47.0	12.4	16 09.2	7.0	55.0
N 11	344 20.4	22.8	196 18.4	12.4	16 16.2	6.9	54.9
D 12	359 20.2	N23 22.7	210 49.8	12.4	S16 23.1	6.8	54.9
A 13	14 20.1	22.6	225 21.2	12.3	16 29.9	6.7	54.9
Y 14	29 20.0	22.5	239 52.5	12.4	16 36.6	6.6	54.9
15	44 19.8	. . 22.5	254 23.9	12.3	16 43.2	6.6	54.9
16	59 19.7	22.4	268 55.2	12.3	16 49.8	6.5	54.9
17	74 19.6	22.3	283 26.5	12.3	16 56.3	6.4	54.9
18	89 19.4	N23 22.2	297 57.8	12.2	S17 02.7	6.3	54.8
19	104 19.3	22.2	312 29.0	12.3	17 09.0	6.2	54.8
20	119 19.2	22.1	327 00.3	12.2	17 15.2	6.2	54.8
21	134 19.0	. . 22.0	341 31.5	12.2	17 21.4	6.1	54.8
22	149 18.9	21.9	356 02.7	12.2	17 27.5	6.0	54.8
23	164 18.8	21.9	10 33.9	12.2	17 33.5	5.9	54.8
26 00	179 18.7	N23 21.8	25 05.1	12.1	S17 39.4	5.8	54.7
01	194 18.5	21.7	39 36.2	12.1	17 45.2	5.7	54.7
02	209 18.4	21.6	54 07.3	12.1	17 50.9	5.6	54.7
03	224 18.3	. . 21.6	68 38.4	12.1	17 56.5	5.6	54.7
04	239 18.1	21.5	83 09.5	12.1	18 02.1	5.5	54.7
05	254 18.0	21.4	97 40.6	12.0	18 07.6	5.4	54.7
06	269 17.9	N23 21.3	112 11.6	12.1	S18 13.0	5.3	54.7
07	284 17.7	21.2	126 42.7	12.0	18 18.3	5.2	54.6
08	299 17.6	21.1	141 13.7	12.0	18 23.5	5.1	54.6
T 09	314 17.5	. . 21.1	155 44.7	12.0	18 28.6	5.0	54.6
U 10	329 17.3	21.0	170 15.7	11.9	18 33.6	5.0	54.6
E 11	344 17.2	20.9	184 46.6	12.0	18 38.6	4.8	54.6
S 12	359 17.1	N23 20.8	199 17.6	11.9	S18 43.4	4.8	54.6
D 13	14 17.0	20.7	213 48.5	11.9	18 48.2	4.7	54.6
A 14	29 16.8	20.6	228 19.4	11.9	18 52.9	4.6	54.6
Y 15	44 16.7	. . 20.5	242 50.3	11.9	18 57.5	4.5	54.5
16	59 16.6	20.4	257 21.2	11.9	19 02.0	4.4	54.5
17	74 16.4	20.3	271 52.1	11.8	19 06.4	4.3	54.5
18	89 16.3	N23 20.3	286 22.9	11.9	S19 10.7	4.2	54.5
19	104 16.2	20.2	300 53.8	11.8	19 14.9	4.1	54.5
20	119 16.0	20.1	315 24.6	11.8	19 19.0	4.1	54.5
21	134 15.9	. . 20.0	329 55.4	11.8	19 23.1	3.9	54.5
22	149 15.8	19.9	344 26.2	11.8	19 27.0	3.8	54.5
23	164 15.7	19.8	358 57.0	11.7	S19 30.8	3.8	54.4
	SD 15.8	d 0.1	SD 15.1		15.0		14.9

Twilight / Sunrise / Moonrise

Lat.	Twilight Naut.	Twilight Civil	Sunrise	Moonrise 24	25	26	27
°	h m	h m	h m	h m	h m	h m	h m
N 72	▮	▮	▮	18 52	21 18	▬	▬
N 70	▮	▮	▮	18 21	20 09	22 12	▬
68	▮	▮	▮	17 58	19 33	21 05	22 26
66	▮	▮	▮	17 40	19 07	20 29	21 40
64	////	////	01 33	17 26	18 48	20 04	21 10
62	////	////	02 11	17 14	18 32	19 44	20 47
60	////	00 52	02 37	17 04	18 18	19 27	20 29
N 58	////	01 42	02 58	16 55	18 07	19 14	20 14
56	////	02 12	03 14	16 48	17 57	19 02	20 01
54	00 48	02 34	03 29	16 41	17 48	18 52	19 50
52	01 34	02 52	03 41	16 35	17 40	18 43	19 40
50	02 02	03 07	03 52	16 29	17 33	18 34	19 31
45	02 47	03 37	04 14	16 17	17 19	18 17	19 12
N 40	03 18	04 00	04 32	16 07	17 06	18 03	18 57
35	03 41	04 18	04 47	15 59	16 56	17 51	18 44
30	04 00	04 33	05 00	15 52	16 47	17 41	18 33
20	04 29	04 58	05 22	15 39	16 31	17 23	18 13
N 10	04 51	05 18	05 41	15 28	16 18	17 07	17 57
0	05 10	05 36	05 59	15 18	16 05	16 53	17 41
S 10	05 27	05 54	06 16	15 08	15 52	16 38	17 26
20	05 43	06 11	06 35	14 57	15 39	16 23	17 09
30	06 00	06 30	06 56	14 45	15 24	16 05	16 50
35	06 09	06 40	07 08	14 38	15 15	15 55	16 39
40	06 18	06 52	07 23	14 30	15 05	15 43	16 26
45	06 28	07 06	07 39	14 20	14 53	15 30	16 11
S 50	06 40	07 22	08 00	14 09	14 39	15 13	15 53
52	06 45	07 29	08 10	14 04	14 32	15 05	15 44
54	06 51	07 37	08 21	13 58	14 25	14 56	15 35
56	06 57	07 46	08 34	13 52	14 17	14 47	15 24
58	07 04	07 57	08 48	13 45	14 07	14 36	15 11
S 60	07 11	08 08	09 06	13 37	13 57	14 23	14 57

Sunset / Twilight / Moonset

Lat.	Sunset	Twilight Civil	Twilight Naut.	Moonset 24	25	26	27
°	h m	h m	h m	h m	h m	h m	h m
N 72	▮	▮	▮	(00 12 / 23 51)	23 04	▬	▬
N 70	▮	▮	▮	00 31	00 24	(00 13 / 23 50)	▬
68	▮	▮	▮	00 47	00 47	00 50	00 58
66	▮	▮	▮	00 59	01 06	01 16	01 34
64	22 32	////	////	01 10	01 21	01 37	02 00
62	21 54	////	////	01 19	01 34	01 53	02 20
60	21 28	23 12	////	01 26	01 44	02 07	02 37
N 58	21 07	22 23	////	01 33	01 54	02 19	02 51
56	20 51	21 53	////	01 39	02 02	02 29	03 03
54	20 36	21 31	23 17	01 45	02 09	02 38	03 13
52	20 24	21 13	22 31	01 50	02 16	02 46	03 21
50	20 13	20 58	22 03	01 54	02 22	02 54	03 31
45	19 51	20 28	21 18	02 04	02 35	03 09	03 49
N 40	19 33	20 06	20 47	02 12	02 46	03 22	04 03
35	19 18	19 48	20 24	02 19	02 55	03 33	04 15
30	19 05	19 32	20 06	02 25	03 03	03 43	04 26
20	18 43	19 07	19 37	02 36	03 17	04 00	04 45
N 10	18 24	18 47	19 14	02 45	03 29	04 14	05 01
0	18 06	18 29	18 55	02 54	03 40	04 28	05 16
S 10	17 49	18 12	18 38	03 03	03 52	04 42	05 31
20	17 30	17 54	18 22	03 12	04 04	04 56	05 47
30	17 09	17 36	18 05	03 23	04 18	05 13	06 06
35	16 57	17 25	17 57	03 29	04 27	05 23	06 17
40	16 43	17 13	17 47	03 36	04 36	05 34	06 29
45	16 26	17 00	17 37	03 45	04 47	05 47	06 44
S 50	16 05	16 44	17 25	03 55	05 00	06 03	07 02
52	15 55	16 36	17 20	03 59	05 06	06 11	07 10
54	15 44	16 28	17 14	04 04	05 13	06 19	07 20
56	15 32	16 19	17 08	04 10	05 21	06 28	07 31
58	15 17	16 09	17 01	04 17	05 30	06 39	07 43
S 60	14 59	15 57	16 54	04 24	05 40	06 52	07 57

SUN / MOON

Day	SUN Eqn. of Time 00h	SUN Eqn. of Time 12h	SUN Mer. Pass.	MOON Mer. Pass. Upper	MOON Mer. Pass. Lower	Age	Phase
d	m s	m s	h m	h m	h m	d	%
24	02 20	02 26	12 02	21 29	09 06	11	87
25	02 32	02 39	12 03	22 16	09 53	12	93
26	02 45	02 51	12 03	23 04	10 40	13	97

UT	ARIES GHA	VENUS −4.1 GHA	Dec	MARS −2.1 GHA	Dec	JUPITER −2.3 GHA	Dec	SATURN +0.0 GHA	Dec	STARS Name	SHA	Dec
27 00	275 03.3	136 51.7	N18 05.5	322 03.5	S22 28.7	53 32.2	S14 51.5	358 40.4	S22 27.1	Acamar	315 16.1	S40 13.8
01	290 05.8	151 51.3	04.6	337 05.9	28.9	68 34.8	51.5	13 43.1	27.1	Achernar	335 24.5	S57 08.4
02	305 08.2	166 50.9	03.7	352 08.3	29.1	83 37.3	51.4	28 45.8	27.1	Acrux	173 05.4	S63 12.3
03	320 10.7	181 50.5	02.8	7 10.8	29.3	98 39.9	51.4	43 48.4	27.1	Adhara	255 10.2	S29 00.0
04	335 13.2	196 50.1	01.9	22 13.2	29.5	113 42.5	51.4	58 51.1	27.1	Aldebaran	290 45.8	N16 32.5
05	350 15.6	211 49.7	01.0	37 15.6	29.7	128 45.0	51.4	73 53.8	27.1			
W 06	5 18.1	226 49.3	N18 00.1	52 18.0	S22 29.8	143 47.6	S14 51.4	88 56.4	S22 27.2	Alioth	166 17.7	N55 52.0
E 07	20 20.6	241 48.9	17 59.2	67 20.4	30.0	158 50.2	51.3	103 59.1	27.2	Alkaid	152 56.1	N49 13.7
D 08	35 23.0	256 48.5	58.3	82 22.9	30.2	173 52.7	51.3	119 01.7	27.2	Al Na'ir	27 39.2	S46 52.1
N 09	50 25.5	271 48.1	57.4	97 25.3	30.4	188 55.3	51.3	134 04.4	27.2	Alnilam	275 43.2	S 1 11.6
E 10	65 28.0	286 47.7	56.5	112 27.7	30.6	203 57.9	51.3	149 07.1	27.2	Alphard	217 53.0	S 8 44.4
S 11	80 30.4	301 47.4	55.6	127 30.1	30.8	219 00.4	51.3	164 09.7	27.2			
D 12	95 32.9	316 47.0	N17 54.7	142 32.6	S22 30.9	234 03.0	S14 51.2	179 12.4	S22 27.2	Alphecca	126 07.9	N26 39.5
A 13	110 35.4	331 46.6	53.7	157 35.0	31.1	249 05.6	51.2	194 15.1	27.2	Alpheratz	357 39.9	N29 11.3
Y 14	125 37.8	346 46.2	52.8	172 37.4	31.3	264 08.1	51.2	209 17.7	27.2	Altair	62 04.6	N 8 55.1
15	140 40.3	1 45.8	51.9	187 39.9	31.5	279 10.7	51.2	224 20.4	27.3	Ankaa	353 12.4	S42 12.2
16	155 42.7	16 45.4	51.0	202 42.3	31.7	294 13.3	51.2	239 23.0	27.3	Antares	112 21.7	S26 28.2
17	170 45.2	31 45.0	50.1	217 44.7	31.9	309 15.8	51.1	254 25.7	27.3			
18	185 47.7	46 44.7	N17 49.2	232 47.2	S22 32.1	324 18.4	S14 51.1	269 28.4	S22 27.3	Arcturus	145 52.5	N19 05.5
19	200 50.1	61 44.3	48.3	247 49.6	32.2	339 21.0	51.1	284 31.0	27.3	Atria	107 19.9	S69 03.5
20	215 52.6	76 43.9	47.4	262 52.0	32.4	354 23.5	51.1	299 33.7	27.3	Avior	234 17.2	S59 34.3
21	230 55.1	91 43.5	46.4	277 54.5	32.6	9 26.1	51.1	314 36.4	27.3	Bellatrix	278 28.7	N 6 21.8
22	245 57.5	106 43.1	45.5	292 56.9	32.8	24 28.6	51.1	329 39.0	27.3	Betelgeuse	270 58.0	N 7 24.4
23	261 00.0	121 42.7	44.6	307 59.4	33.0	39 31.2	51.0	344 41.7	27.4			
28 00	276 02.5	136 42.4	N17 43.7	323 01.8	S22 33.2	54 33.8	S14 51.0	359 44.4	S22 27.4	Canopus	263 55.2	S52 42.5
01	291 04.9	151 42.0	42.8	338 04.3	33.4	69 36.3	51.0	14 47.0	27.4	Capella	280 29.9	N46 00.7
02	306 07.4	166 41.6	41.9	353 06.7	33.6	84 38.9	51.0	29 49.7	27.4	Deneb	49 28.7	N45 20.7
03	321 09.9	181 41.2	40.9	8 09.2	33.8	99 41.4	51.0	44 52.3	27.4	Denebola	182 30.3	N14 28.3
04	336 12.3	196 40.8	40.0	23 11.6	34.0	114 44.0	50.9	59 55.0	27.4	Diphda	348 52.5	S17 53.1
05	351 14.8	211 40.5	39.1	38 14.1	34.1	129 46.6	50.9	74 57.7	27.4			
T 06	6 17.2	226 40.1	N17 38.2	53 16.5	S22 34.3	144 49.1	S14 50.9	90 00.3	S22 27.4	Dubhe	193 47.9	N61 39.4
H 07	21 19.7	241 39.7	37.3	68 19.0	34.5	159 51.7	50.9	105 03.0	27.4	Elnath	278 08.7	N28 37.1
U 08	36 22.2	256 39.3	36.3	83 21.4	34.7	174 54.2	50.9	120 05.7	27.5	Eltanin	90 44.0	N51 29.4
R 09	51 24.6	271 39.0	35.4	98 23.9	34.9	189 56.8	50.9	135 08.3	27.5	Enif	33 43.6	N 9 57.6
S 10	66 27.1	286 38.6	34.5	113 26.3	35.1	204 59.4	50.8	150 11.0	27.5	Fomalhaut	15 20.1	S29 31.3
D 11	81 29.6	301 38.2	33.6	128 28.8	35.3	220 01.9	50.8	165 13.6	27.5			
A 12	96 32.0	316 37.9	N17 32.6	143 31.3	S22 35.5	235 04.5	S14 50.8	180 16.3	S22 27.5	Gacrux	171 57.0	S57 13.2
Y 13	111 34.5	331 37.5	31.7	158 33.7	35.7	250 07.0	50.8	195 19.0	27.5	Gienah	175 48.8	S17 38.7
14	126 37.0	346 37.1	30.8	173 36.2	35.9	265 09.6	50.8	210 21.6	27.5	Hadar	148 42.7	S60 27.8
15	141 39.4	1 36.7	29.9	188 38.7	36.1	280 12.1	50.8	225 24.3	27.5	Hamal	327 57.0	N23 32.7
16	156 41.9	16 36.4	28.9	203 41.1	36.3	295 14.7	50.7	240 27.0	27.5	Kaus Aust.	83 38.9	S34 22.3
17	171 44.4	31 36.0	28.0	218 43.6	36.5	310 17.3	50.7	255 29.6	27.6			
18	186 46.8	46 35.6	N17 27.1	233 46.1	S22 36.7	325 19.8	S14 50.7	270 32.3	S22 27.6	Kochab	137 19.5	N74 05.2
19	201 49.3	61 35.3	26.1	248 48.5	36.9	340 22.4	50.7	285 34.9	27.6	Markab	13 34.8	N15 18.2
20	216 51.7	76 34.9	25.2	263 51.0	37.0	355 24.9	50.7	300 37.6	27.6	Menkar	314 11.7	N 4 09.5
21	231 54.2	91 34.5	24.3	278 53.5	37.2	10 27.5	50.7	315 40.3	27.6	Menkent	148 03.3	S36 27.6
22	246 56.7	106 34.2	23.3	293 55.9	37.4	25 30.0	50.6	330 42.9	27.6	Miaplacidus	221 39.6	S69 47.8
23	261 59.1	121 33.8	22.4	308 58.4	37.6	40 32.6	50.6	345 45.6	27.6			
29 00	277 01.6	136 33.5	N17 21.5	324 00.9	S22 37.8	55 35.1	S14 50.6	0 48.3	S22 27.6	Mirfak	308 35.8	N49 55.2
01	292 04.1	151 33.1	20.5	339 03.4	38.0	70 37.7	50.6	15 50.9	27.7	Nunki	75 53.7	S26 16.2
02	307 06.5	166 32.7	19.6	354 05.9	38.2	85 40.3	50.6	30 53.6	27.7	Peacock	53 13.4	S56 40.3
03	322 09.0	181 32.4	18.7	9 08.3	38.4	100 42.8	50.6	45 56.3	27.7	Pollux	243 24.0	N27 58.8
04	337 11.5	196 32.0	17.7	24 10.8	38.6	115 45.4	50.5	60 58.9	27.7	Procyon	244 56.5	N 5 10.5
05	352 13.9	211 31.6	16.8	39 13.3	38.8	130 47.9	50.5	76 01.6	27.7			
F 06	7 16.4	226 31.3	N17 15.8	54 15.8	S22 39.0	145 50.5	S14 50.5	91 04.2	S22 27.7	Rasalhague	96 03.0	N12 33.0
R 07	22 18.9	241 30.9	14.9	69 18.3	39.2	160 53.0	50.5	106 06.9	27.7	Regulus	207 40.1	N11 52.7
I 08	37 21.3	256 30.6	14.0	84 20.8	39.4	175 55.6	50.5	121 09.6	27.7	Rigel	281 09.1	S 8 11.0
D 09	52 23.8	271 30.2	13.0	99 23.3	39.6	190 58.1	50.5	136 12.2	27.7	Rigil Kent.	139 46.7	S60 54.7
A 10	67 26.2	286 29.9	12.1	114 25.8	39.8	206 00.7	50.5	151 14.9	27.8	Sabik	102 08.3	S15 44.7
Y 11	82 28.7	301 29.5	11.1	129 28.2	40.0	221 03.2	50.4	166 17.6	27.8			
12	97 31.2	316 29.2	N17 10.2	144 30.7	S22 40.2	236 05.8	S14 50.4	181 20.2	S22 27.8	Schedar	349 36.6	N56 37.9
13	112 33.6	331 28.8	09.3	159 33.2	40.4	251 08.3	50.4	196 22.9	27.8	Shaula	96 16.9	S37 06.8
14	127 36.1	346 28.4	08.3	174 35.7	40.6	266 10.9	50.4	211 25.5	27.8	Sirius	258 31.1	S16 44.6
15	142 38.6	1 28.1	07.4	189 38.2	40.8	281 13.4	50.4	226 28.2	27.8	Spica	158 27.6	S11 15.4
16	157 41.0	16 27.7	06.4	204 40.7	41.0	296 16.0	50.3	241 30.9	27.8	Suhail	222 50.3	S43 30.6
17	172 43.5	31 27.4	05.5	219 43.2	41.2	311 18.5	50.3	256 33.5	27.8			
18	187 46.0	46 27.0	N17 04.5	234 45.7	S22 41.4	326 21.1	S14 50.3	271 36.2	S22 27.8	Vega	80 36.2	N38 48.2
19	202 48.4	61 26.7	03.6	249 48.2	41.6	341 23.6	50.3	286 38.9	27.9	Zuben'ubi	137 01.4	S16 07.0
20	217 50.9	76 26.3	02.6	264 50.7	41.8	356 26.2	50.3	301 41.5	27.9		SHA	Mer. Pass.
21	232 53.3	91 26.0	01.7	279 53.2	42.1	11 28.7	50.3	316 44.2	27.9	Venus	220 39.9	14 54
22	247 55.8	106 25.6	17 00.7	294 55.8	42.3	26 31.3	50.3	331 46.8	27.9	Mars	46 59.4	2 27
23	262 58.3	121 25.3	N16 59.8	309 58.3	42.5	41 33.8	50.3	346 49.5	27.9	Jupiter	138 31.3	20 18
Mer. Pass. 5 34.9		v −0.4 d 0.9		v 2.5 d 0.2		v 2.6 d 0.0		v 2.7 d 0.0		Saturn	83 41.9	0 01

UT	SUN GHA	SUN Dec	MOON GHA	v	MOON Dec	d	HP
d h	° '	° '	° '	'	° '	'	'
27 00	179 15.5	N23 19.7	13 27.7	11.8	S19 34.6	3.7	54.4
01	194 15.4	19.6	27 58.5	11.8	19 38.3	3.5	54.4
02	209 15.3	19.5	42 29.3	11.7	19 41.8	3.5	54.4
03	224 15.1 ..	19.4	57 00.0	11.7	19 45.3	3.4	54.4
04	239 15.0	19.3	71 30.7	11.7	19 48.7	3.3	54.4
05	254 14.9	19.2	86 01.4	11.7	19 52.0	3.2	54.4
W 06	269 14.8	N23 19.1	100 32.1	11.7	S19 55.2	3.1	54.4
E 07	284 14.6	19.0	115 02.8	11.7	19 58.3	3.0	54.4
D 08	299 14.5	18.9	129 33.5	11.7	20 01.3	2.9	54.4
N 09	314 14.4 ..	18.8	144 04.2	11.6	20 04.2	2.8	54.3
E 10	329 14.2	18.7	158 34.8	11.7	20 07.0	2.7	54.3
S 11	344 14.1	18.6	173 05.5	11.6	20 09.7	2.6	54.3
D 12	359 14.0	N23 18.5	187 36.1	11.7	S20 12.3	2.6	54.3
A 13	14 13.9	18.4	202 06.8	11.6	20 14.9	2.4	54.3
Y 14	29 13.7	18.3	216 37.4	11.6	20 17.3	2.3	54.3
15	44 13.6 ..	18.2	231 08.0	11.7	20 19.6	2.2	54.3
16	59 13.5	18.1	245 38.7	11.6	20 21.8	2.2	54.3
17	74 13.3	18.0	260 09.3	11.6	20 24.0	2.0	54.3
18	89 13.2	N23 17.9	274 39.9	11.6	S20 26.0	2.0	54.3
19	104 13.1	17.7	289 10.5	11.6	20 28.0	1.8	54.2
20	119 13.0	17.6	303 41.1	11.6	20 29.8	1.8	54.2
21	134 12.8 ..	17.5	318 11.7	11.6	20 31.6	1.6	54.2
22	149 12.7	17.4	332 42.3	11.6	20 33.2	1.6	54.2
23	164 12.6	17.3	347 12.9	11.6	20 34.8	1.4	54.2
28 00	179 12.4	N23 17.2	1 43.5	11.6	S20 36.2	1.4	54.2
01	194 12.3	17.1	16 14.1	11.6	20 37.6	1.3	54.2
02	209 12.2	17.0	30 44.7	11.6	20 38.9	1.1	54.2
03	224 12.1 ..	16.9	45 15.3	11.6	20 40.0	1.1	54.2
04	239 11.9	16.7	59 45.9	11.6	20 41.1	1.0	54.2
05	254 11.8	16.6	74 16.5	11.6	20 42.1	0.8	54.2
06	269 11.7	N23 16.5	88 47.1	11.6	S20 42.9	0.8	54.2
T 07	284 11.6	16.4	103 17.7	11.6	20 43.7	0.7	54.2
H 08	299 11.4	16.3	117 48.3	11.6	20 44.4	0.6	54.1
U 09	314 11.3 ..	16.1	132 18.9	11.7	20 45.0	0.5	54.1
R 10	329 11.2	16.0	146 49.6	11.6	20 45.5	0.3	54.1
S 11	344 11.0	15.9	161 20.2	11.6	20 45.8	0.3	54.1
D 12	359 10.9	N23 15.8	175 50.8	11.6	S20 46.1	0.2	54.1
A 13	14 10.8	15.7	190 21.4	11.7	20 46.3	0.1	54.1
Y 14	29 10.7	15.5	204 52.1	11.6	20 46.4	0.0	54.1
15	44 10.5 ..	15.4	219 22.7	11.7	20 46.4	0.2	54.1
16	59 10.4	15.3	233 53.4	11.6	20 46.3	0.2	54.1
17	74 10.3	15.2	248 24.0	11.7	20 46.1	0.3	54.1
18	89 10.2	N23 15.0	262 54.7	11.7	S20 45.8	0.4	54.1
19	104 10.0	14.9	277 25.4	11.7	20 45.4	0.5	54.1
20	119 09.9	14.8	291 56.1	11.7	20 44.9	0.6	54.1
21	134 09.8 ..	14.7	306 26.8	11.7	20 44.3	0.7	54.1
22	149 09.7	14.5	320 57.5	11.7	20 43.6	0.7	54.1
23	164 09.5	14.4	335 28.2	11.7	20 42.9	0.9	54.1
29 00	179 09.4	N23 14.3	349 58.9	11.8	S20 42.0	1.0	54.1
01	194 09.3	14.2	4 29.7	11.7	20 41.0	1.1	54.1
02	209 09.2	14.0	19 00.4	11.8	20 39.9	1.1	54.0
03	224 09.0 ..	13.9	33 31.2	11.8	20 38.8	1.3	54.0
04	239 08.9	13.8	48 02.0	11.8	20 37.5	1.4	54.0
05	254 08.8	13.6	62 32.8	11.8	20 36.1	1.4	54.0
06	269 08.7	N23 13.5	77 03.6	11.8	S20 34.7	1.6	54.0
F 07	284 08.5	13.4	91 34.4	11.9	20 33.1	1.6	54.0
R 08	299 08.4	13.2	106 05.3	11.8	20 31.5	1.8	54.0
I 09	314 08.3 ..	13.1	120 36.1	11.9	20 29.7	1.8	54.0
D 10	329 08.2	12.9	135 07.0	11.9	20 27.9	1.9	54.0
A 11	344 08.0	12.8	149 37.9	11.9	20 26.0	2.1	54.0
Y 12	359 07.9	N23 12.7	164 08.8	11.9	S20 23.9	2.1	54.0
13	14 07.8	12.5	178 39.7	12.0	20 21.8	2.2	54.0
14	29 07.7	12.4	193 10.7	12.0	20 19.6	2.3	54.0
15	44 07.5 ..	12.3	207 41.7	11.9	20 17.3	2.4	54.0
16	59 07.4	12.1	222 12.6	12.0	20 14.9	2.5	54.0
17	74 07.3	12.0	236 43.6	12.1	20 12.4	2.6	54.0
18	89 07.2	N23 11.8	251 14.7	12.0	S20 09.8	2.6	54.0
19	104 07.0	11.7	265 45.7	12.1	20 07.2	2.8	54.0
20	119 06.9	11.5	280 16.8	12.1	20 04.4	2.9	54.0
21	134 06.8 ..	11.4	294 47.9	12.1	20 01.5	2.9	54.0
22	149 06.7	11.3	309 19.0	12.1	19 58.6	3.1	54.0
23	164 06.5	11.1	323 50.1	12.2	S19 55.5	3.1	54.0
	SD 15.8	d 0.1	SD 14.8		14.7		14.7

Lat.	Twilight Naut.	Twilight Civil	Sunrise	Moonrise 27	28	29	30
°	h m	h m	h m	h m	h m	h m	h m
N 72	▭	▭	▭	▬▬	▬▬	▬▬	
N 70	▭	▭	▭	▬▬	▬▬	▬▬	01 05
68	▭	▭	▭	22 26	23 19	23 43	23 51
66	▭	▭	▭	21 40	22 32	23 04	23 23
64	////	////	01 36	21 10	22 01	22 38	23 02
62	////	////	02 13	20 47	21 38	22 17	22 45
60	////	00 57	02 39	20 29	21 20	22 00	22 30
N 58	////	01 45	02 59	20 14	21 04	21 46	22 18
56	////	02 14	03 16	20 01	20 51	21 33	22 07
54	00 52	02 36	03 30	19 50	20 40	21 23	21 58
52	01 36	02 54	03 42	19 40	20 30	21 13	21 49
50	02 04	03 09	03 53	19 31	20 21	21 05	21 42
45	02 49	03 38	04 16	19 12	20 02	20 46	21 25
N 40	03 19	04 01	04 33	18 57	19 46	20 32	21 12
35	03 42	04 19	04 48	18 44	19 33	20 19	21 01
30	04 01	04 34	05 01	18 33	19 22	20 08	20 51
20	04 30	04 59	05 23	18 13	19 03	19 50	20 34
N 10	04 52	05 19	05 42	17 57	18 46	19 33	20 19
0	05 11	05 37	06 00	17 41	18 30	19 18	20 05
S 10	05 28	05 54	06 17	17 26	18 14	19 03	19 51
20	05 44	06 11	06 35	17 09	17 57	18 46	19 36
30	06 00	06 30	06 56	16 50	17 37	18 27	19 19
35	06 09	06 41	07 09	16 39	17 26	18 16	19 09
40	06 18	06 52	07 23	16 26	17 13	18 04	18 58
45	06 28	07 06	07 39	16 11	16 58	17 49	18 44
S 50	06 40	07 22	08 00	15 53	16 39	17 31	18 28
52	06 45	07 29	08 10	15 44	16 30	17 22	18 20
54	06 51	07 37	08 21	15 35	16 20	17 13	18 11
56	06 57	07 46	08 33	15 24	16 09	17 02	18 01
58	07 04	07 56	08 48	15 11	15 56	16 49	17 50
S 60	07 11	08 08	09 05	14 57	15 41	16 35	17 37

Lat.	Sunset	Twilight Civil	Twilight Naut.	Moonset 27	28	29	30
°	h m	h m	h m	h m	h m	h m	h m
N 72	▭	▭	▭	▬▬	▬▬	▬▬	
N 70	▭	▭	▭	▬▬	▬▬	▬▬	01 59
68	▭	▭	▭	00 58	01 18	02 05	03 22
66	▭	▭	▭	01 34	02 04	02 53	03 59
64	22 29	////	////	02 00	02 34	03 23	04 26
62	21 53	////	////	02 20	02 57	03 46	04 46
60	21 27	23 08	////	02 37	03 15	04 04	05 03
N 58	21 07	22 21	////	02 51	03 30	04 20	05 17
56	20 50	21 52	////	03 03	03 43	04 33	05 29
54	20 36	21 30	23 13	03 13	03 55	04 44	05 40
52	20 24	21 12	22 29	03 22	04 05	04 54	05 49
50	20 13	20 58	22 02	03 31	04 14	05 03	05 57
45	19 51	20 28	21 18	03 49	04 33	05 22	06 15
N 40	19 33	20 06	20 47	04 03	04 48	05 37	06 29
35	19 18	19 48	20 24	04 15	05 01	05 50	06 42
30	19 05	19 33	20 06	04 26	05 12	06 01	06 52
20	18 43	19 08	19 37	04 45	05 32	06 21	07 10
N 10	18 24	18 47	19 14	05 01	05 49	06 37	07 26
0	18 07	18 29	18 56	05 16	06 05	06 53	07 41
S 10	17 50	18 12	18 39	05 31	06 20	07 09	07 56
20	17 31	17 55	18 23	05 47	06 37	07 25	08 11
30	17 10	17 37	18 06	06 06	06 57	07 45	08 29
35	16 58	17 26	17 58	06 17	07 08	07 56	08 40
40	16 44	17 14	17 48	06 29	07 21	08 09	08 52
45	16 27	17 01	17 38	06 44	07 36	08 24	09 06
S 50	16 07	16 45	17 26	07 02	07 55	08 42	09 23
52	15 57	16 38	17 21	07 10	08 04	08 51	09 31
54	15 46	16 30	17 16	07 20	08 14	09 01	09 40
56	15 33	16 21	17 10	07 31	08 25	09 12	09 50
58	15 19	16 10	17 03	07 43	08 38	09 24	10 01
S 60	15 01	15 59	16 55	07 57	08 54	09 39	10 14

Day	SUN Eqn. of Time 00h	SUN Eqn. of Time 12h	SUN Mer. Pass.	MOON Mer. Pass. Upper	MOON Mer. Pass. Lower	Age	Phase
d	m s	m s	h m	h m	h m	d	%
27	02 58	03 04	12 03	23 53	11 29	14	99
28	03 10	03 16	12 03	24 41	12 17	15	100
29	03 22	03 28	12 03	00 41	13 06	16	98

2018 JUNE 30, JULY 1, 2 (SAT., SUN., MON.)

UT	ARIES GHA	VENUS −4·1 GHA	Dec	MARS −2·2 GHA	Dec	JUPITER −2·3 GHA	Dec	SATURN +0·0 GHA	Dec	STARS Name	SHA	Dec
d h	° ′	° ′	° ′	° ′	° ′	° ′	° ′	° ′	° ′		° ′	° ′
30 00	278 00.7	136 25.0	N16 58.8	325 00.8	S22 42.7	56 36.4	S14 50.2	1 52.2	S22 27.9	Acamar	315 16.0	S40 13.8
01	293 03.2	151 24.6	57.9	340 03.3	42.9	71 38.9	50.2	16 54.8	27.9	Achernar	335 24.5	S57 08.4
02	308 05.7	166 24.3	56.9	355 05.8	43.1	86 41.4	50.2	31 57.5	27.9	Acrux	173 05.4	S63 12.3
03	323 08.1	181 23.9 ..	56.0	10 08.3 ..	43.3	101 44.0 ..	50.2	47 00.2 ..	27.9	Adhara	255 10.2	S29 00.0
04	338 10.6	196 23.6	55.0	25 10.8	43.5	116 46.5	50.2	62 02.8	28.0	Aldebaran	290 45.8	N16 32.6
05	353 13.1	211 23.2	54.1	40 13.3	43.7	131 49.1	50.2	77 05.5	28.0			
06	8 15.5	226 22.9	N16 53.1	55 15.9	S22 43.9	146 51.6	S14 50.2	92 08.1	S22 28.0	Alioth	166 17.7	N55 52.0
07	23 18.0	241 22.6	52.2	70 18.4	44.1	161 54.2	50.2	107 10.8	28.0	Alkaid	152 56.1	N49 13.7
S 08	38 20.5	256 22.2	51.2	85 20.9	44.3	176 56.7	50.1	122 13.5	28.0	Al Na'ir	27 39.2	S46 52.1
A 09	53 22.9	271 21.9 ..	50.2	100 23.4 ..	44.5	191 59.3 ..	50.1	137 16.1 ..	28.0	Alnilam	275 43.2	S 1 11.6
T 10	68 25.4	286 21.5	49.3	115 26.0	44.7	207 01.8	50.1	152 18.8	28.0	Alphard	217 53.0	S 8 44.4
U 11	83 27.8	301 21.2	48.3	130 28.5	44.9	222 04.4	50.1	167 21.5	28.0			
R 12	98 30.3	316 20.9	N16 47.4	145 31.0	S22 45.2	237 06.9	S14 50.1	182 24.1	S22 28.1	Alphecca	126 07.9	N26 39.5
D 13	113 32.8	331 20.5	46.4	160 33.5	45.4	252 09.4	50.1	197 26.8	28.1	Alpheratz	357 39.9	N29 11.3
A 14	128 35.2	346 20.2	45.4	175 36.1	45.6	267 12.0	50.1	212 29.4	28.1	Altair	62 04.6	N 8 55.2
Y 15	143 37.7	1 19.8 ..	44.5	190 38.6 ..	45.8	282 14.5 ..	50.0	227 32.1 ..	28.1	Ankaa	353 12.3	S42 12.2
16	158 40.2	16 19.5	43.5	205 41.1	46.0	297 17.1	50.0	242 34.8	28.1	Antares	112 21.7	S26 28.2
17	173 42.6	31 19.2	42.6	220 43.7	46.2	312 19.6	50.0	257 37.4	28.1			
18	188 45.1	46 18.8	N16 41.6	235 46.2	S22 46.4	327 22.1	S14 50.0	272 40.1	S22 28.1	Arcturus	145 52.5	N19 05.5
19	203 47.6	61 18.5	40.6	250 48.7	46.6	342 24.7	50.0	287 42.8	28.1	Atria	107 19.9	S69 03.5
20	218 50.0	76 18.2	39.7	265 51.3	46.8	357 27.2	50.0	302 45.4	28.1	Avior	234 17.2	S59 34.3
21	233 52.5	91 17.9 ..	38.7	280 53.8 ..	47.1	12 29.8 ..	50.0	317 48.1 ..	28.2	Bellatrix	278 28.7	N 6 21.8
22	248 55.0	106 17.5	37.7	295 56.3	47.3	27 32.3	50.0	332 50.7	28.2	Betelgeuse	270 57.9	N 7 24.5
23	263 57.4	121 17.2	36.8	310 58.9	47.5	42 34.9	50.0	347 53.4	28.2			
1 00	278 59.9	136 16.9	N16 35.8	326 01.4	S22 47.7	57 37.4	S14 49.9	2 56.1	S22 28.2	Canopus	263 55.2	S52 42.4
01	294 02.3	151 16.5	34.8	341 04.0	47.9	72 39.9	49.9	17 58.7	28.2	Capella	280 29.8	N46 00.7
02	309 04.8	166 16.2	33.9	356 06.5	48.1	87 42.5	49.9	33 01.4	28.2	Deneb	49 28.7	N45 20.7
03	324 07.3	181 15.9 ..	32.9	11 09.1 ..	48.3	102 45.0 ..	49.9	48 04.1 ..	28.2	Denebola	182 30.3	N14 28.3
04	339 09.7	196 15.6	31.9	26 11.6	48.5	117 47.5	49.9	63 06.7	28.2	Diphda	348 52.5	S17 53.1
05	354 12.2	211 15.2	31.0	41 14.2	48.8	132 50.1	49.9	78 09.4	28.2			
06	9 14.7	226 14.9	N16 30.0	56 16.7	S22 49.0	147 52.6	S14 49.9	93 12.0	S22 28.3	Dubhe	193 47.9	N61 39.4
07	24 17.1	241 14.6	29.0	71 19.3	49.2	162 55.2	49.9	108 14.7	28.3	Elnath	278 08.7	N28 37.1
08	39 19.6	256 14.3	28.0	86 21.8	49.4	177 57.7	49.9	123 17.4	28.3	Eltanin	90 44.0	N51 29.4
S 09	54 22.1	271 13.9 ..	27.1	101 24.4 ..	49.6	193 00.2 ..	49.8	138 20.0 ..	28.3	Enif	33 43.5	N 9 57.6
U 10	69 24.5	286 13.6	26.1	116 26.9	49.8	208 02.8	49.8	153 22.7	28.3	Fomalhaut	15 20.1	S29 31.3
N 11	84 27.0	301 13.3	25.1	131 29.5	50.1	223 05.3	49.8	168 25.4	28.3			
D 12	99 29.5	316 13.0	N16 24.1	146 32.1	S22 50.3	238 07.8	S14 49.8	183 28.0	S22 28.3	Gacrux	171 57.0	S57 13.2
A 13	114 31.9	331 12.6	23.2	161 34.6	50.5	253 10.4	49.8	198 30.7	28.3	Gienah	175 48.8	S17 38.7
Y 14	129 34.4	346 12.3	22.2	176 37.2	50.7	268 12.9	49.8	213 33.3	28.4	Hadar	148 42.7	S60 27.8
15	144 36.8	1 12.0 ..	21.2	191 39.7 ..	50.9	283 15.5 ..	49.8	228 36.0 ..	28.4	Hamal	327 57.0	N23 32.7
16	159 39.3	16 11.7	20.2	206 42.3	51.1	298 18.0	49.8	243 38.7	28.4	Kaus Aust.	83 38.9	S34 22.3
17	174 41.8	31 11.4	19.3	221 44.9	51.4	313 20.5	49.8	258 41.3	28.4			
18	189 44.2	46 11.1	N16 18.3	236 47.4	S22 51.6	328 23.1	S14 49.7	273 44.0	S22 28.4	Kochab	137 19.5	N74 05.2
19	204 46.7	61 10.7	17.3	251 50.0	51.8	343 25.6	49.7	288 46.7	28.4	Markab	13 34.8	N15 18.2
20	219 49.2	76 10.4	16.3	266 52.6	52.0	358 28.1	49.7	303 49.3	28.4	Menkar	314 11.7	N 4 09.5
21	234 51.6	91 10.1 ..	15.3	281 55.2 ..	52.2	13 30.7 ..	49.7	318 52.0 ..	28.4	Menkent	148 03.4	S36 27.6
22	249 54.1	106 09.8	14.4	296 57.7	52.5	28 33.2	49.7	333 54.6	28.4	Miaplacidus	221 39.7	S69 47.8
23	264 56.6	121 09.5	13.4	312 00.3	52.7	43 35.7	49.7	348 57.3	28.5			
2 00	279 59.0	136 09.2	N16 12.4	327 02.9	S22 52.9	58 38.3	S14 49.7	4 00.0	S22 28.5	Mirfak	308 35.8	N49 55.2
01	295 01.5	151 08.9	11.4	342 05.5	53.1	73 40.8	49.7	19 02.6	28.5	Nunki	75 53.7	S26 16.2
02	310 03.9	166 08.6	10.4	357 08.0	53.3	88 43.3	49.7	34 05.3	28.5	Peacock	53 13.4	S56 40.3
03	325 06.4	181 08.2 ..	09.4	12 10.6 ..	53.6	103 45.8 ..	49.7	49 07.9 ..	28.5	Pollux	243 24.0	N27 58.8
04	340 08.9	196 07.9	08.5	27 13.2	53.8	118 48.4	49.7	64 10.6	28.5	Procyon	244 56.5	N 5 10.6
05	355 11.3	211 07.6	07.5	42 15.8	54.0	133 50.9	49.7	79 13.3	28.5			
06	10 13.8	226 07.3	N16 06.5	57 18.4	S22 54.2	148 53.4	S14 49.6	94 15.9	S22 28.5	Rasalhague	96 03.0	N12 33.0
07	25 16.3	241 07.0	05.5	72 21.0	54.4	163 56.0	49.6	109 18.6	28.5	Regulus	207 40.1	N11 52.7
08	40 18.7	256 06.7	04.5	87 23.5	54.7	178 58.5	49.6	124 21.3	28.6	Rigel	281 09.1	S 8 11.0
M 09	55 21.2	271 06.4 ..	03.5	102 26.1 ..	54.9	194 01.0 ..	49.6	139 23.9 ..	28.6	Rigil Kent.	139 46.7	S60 54.7
O 10	70 23.7	286 06.1	02.5	117 28.7	55.1	209 03.6	49.6	154 26.6	28.6	Sabik	102 08.3	S15 44.7
N 11	85 26.1	301 05.8	01.5	132 31.3	55.3	224 06.1	49.6	169 29.2	28.6			
D 12	100 28.6	316 05.5	N16 00.5	147 33.9	S22 55.6	239 08.6	S14 49.6	184 31.9	S22 28.6	Schedar	349 36.6	N56 37.9
A 13	115 31.1	331 05.2	15 59.6	162 36.5	55.8	254 11.1	49.6	199 34.6	28.6	Shaula	96 16.9	S37 06.9
Y 14	130 33.5	346 04.9	58.6	177 39.1	56.0	269 13.7	49.6	214 37.2	28.6	Sirius	258 31.1	S16 44.6
15	145 36.0	1 04.6 ..	57.6	192 41.7 ..	56.2	284 16.2 ..	49.6	229 39.9 ..	28.6	Spica	158 27.6	S11 15.4
16	160 38.4	16 04.3	56.6	207 44.3	56.5	299 18.7	49.6	244 42.6	28.6	Suhail	222 50.3	S43 30.6
17	175 40.9	31 04.0	55.6	222 46.9	56.7	314 21.3	49.6	259 45.2	28.7			
18	190 43.4	46 03.7	N15 54.6	237 49.5	S22 56.9	329 23.8	S14 49.5	274 47.9	S22 28.7	Vega	80 36.2	N38 48.2
19	205 45.8	61 03.4	53.6	252 52.1	57.1	344 26.3	49.5	289 50.5	28.7	Zuben'ubi	137 01.4	S16 07.0
20	220 48.3	76 03.1	52.6	267 54.7	57.4	359 28.8	49.5	304 53.2	28.7		SHA	Mer. Pass.
21	235 50.8	91 02.8 ..	51.6	282 57.3 ..	57.6	14 31.4 ..	49.5	319 55.9 ..	28.7		° ′	h m
22	250 53.2	106 02.5	50.6	297 59.9	57.8	29 33.9	49.5	334 58.5	28.7	Venus	217 17.0	14 55
23	265 55.7	121 02.2	49.6	313 02.5	58.0	44 36.4	49.5	350 01.2	28.7	Mars	47 01.6	2 16
Mer. Pass.	h m 5 23.1	v −0.3 d 1.0		v 2.6 d 0.2		v 2.5 d 0.0		v 2.7 d 0.0		Jupiter Saturn	138 37.5 83 56.2	20 06 23 44

UT	SUN GHA	SUN Dec	MOON GHA	v	MOON Dec	d	HP
d h	° '	° '	° '	'	° '	'	'
30 00	179 06.4	N23 11.0	338 21.3	12.2	S19 52.4	3.2	54.0
01	194 06.3	10.8	352 52.5	12.2	19 49.2	3.3	54.0
02	209 06.2	10.7	7 23.7	12.2	19 45.9	3.5	54.0
03	224 06.1	.. 10.5	21 54.9	12.3	19 42.4	3.4	54.0
04	239 05.9	10.4	36 26.2	12.3	19 39.0	3.6	54.0
05	254 05.8	10.2	50 57.5	12.3	19 35.4	3.7	54.0
06	269 05.7	N23 10.1	65 28.8	12.3	S19 31.7	3.8	54.0
07	284 05.6	09.9	80 00.1	12.3	19 27.9	3.8	54.0
S 08	299 05.4	09.8	94 31.4	12.4	19 24.1	4.0	54.0
A 09	314 05.3	.. 09.6	109 02.8	12.4	19 20.1	4.0	54.0
T 10	329 05.2	09.5	123 34.2	12.5	19 16.1	4.1	54.0
U 11	344 05.1	09.3	138 05.7	12.4	19 12.0	4.2	54.0
R 12	359 05.0	N23 09.2	152 37.1	12.5	S19 07.8	4.3	54.0
D 13	14 04.8	09.0	167 08.6	12.5	19 03.5	4.4	54.0
A 14	29 04.7	08.8	181 40.1	12.5	18 59.1	4.4	54.0
Y 15	44 04.6	.. 08.7	196 11.6	12.6	18 54.7	4.6	54.0
16	59 04.5	08.5	210 43.2	12.6	18 50.1	4.6	54.0
17	74 04.3	08.4	225 14.8	12.6	18 45.5	4.7	54.0
18	89 04.2	N23 08.2	239 46.4	12.7	S18 40.8	4.8	54.0
19	104 04.1	08.0	254 18.1	12.6	18 36.0	4.9	54.0
20	119 04.0	07.9	268 49.7	12.8	18 31.1	4.9	54.0
21	134 03.9	.. 07.7	283 21.5	12.7	18 26.2	5.1	54.0
22	149 03.7	07.6	297 53.2	12.7	18 21.1	5.1	54.0
23	164 03.6	07.4	312 24.9	12.8	18 16.0	5.2	54.0
1 00	179 03.5	N23 07.2	326 56.7	12.9	S18 10.8	5.3	54.0
01	194 03.4	07.1	341 28.6	12.8	18 05.5	5.4	54.0
02	209 03.3	06.9	356 00.4	12.9	18 00.1	5.4	54.0
03	224 03.1	.. 06.7	10 32.3	12.9	17 54.7	5.6	54.1
04	239 03.0	06.6	25 04.2	12.9	17 49.1	5.6	54.1
05	254 02.9	06.4	39 36.1	13.0	17 43.5	5.7	54.1
06	269 02.8	N23 06.2	54 08.1	13.0	S17 37.8	5.7	54.1
07	284 02.7	06.1	68 40.1	13.0	17 32.1	5.9	54.1
S 08	299 02.5	05.9	83 12.1	13.0	17 26.2	5.9	54.1
U 09	314 02.4	.. 05.7	97 44.1	13.1	17 20.3	6.0	54.1
N 10	329 02.3	05.6	112 16.2	13.1	17 14.3	6.1	54.1
D 11	344 02.2	05.4	126 48.3	13.2	17 08.2	6.1	54.1
A 12	359 02.1	N23 05.2	141 20.5	13.1	S17 02.1	6.3	54.1
Y 13	14 01.9	05.1	155 52.6	13.2	16 55.8	6.3	54.1
14	29 01.8	04.9	170 24.8	13.2	16 49.5	6.3	54.1
15	44 01.7	.. 04.7	184 57.0	13.3	16 43.2	6.5	54.1
16	59 01.6	04.5	199 29.3	13.3	16 36.7	6.5	54.1
17	74 01.5	04.4	214 01.6	13.3	16 30.2	6.6	54.1
18	89 01.3	N23 04.2	228 33.9	13.3	S16 23.6	6.7	54.1
19	104 01.2	04.0	243 06.2	13.4	16 16.9	6.7	54.2
20	119 01.1	03.8	257 38.6	13.4	16 10.2	6.9	54.2
21	134 01.0	.. 03.6	272 11.0	13.4	16 03.3	6.8	54.2
22	149 00.9	03.5	286 43.4	13.4	15 56.5	7.0	54.2
23	164 00.7	03.3	301 15.8	13.5	15 49.5	7.0	54.2
2 00	179 00.6	N23 03.1	315 48.3	13.5	S15 42.5	7.1	54.2
01	194 00.5	02.9	330 20.8	13.5	15 35.4	7.2	54.2
02	209 00.4	02.7	344 53.3	13.6	15 28.2	7.2	54.2
03	224 00.3	.. 02.6	359 25.9	13.6	15 21.0	7.3	54.2
04	239 00.2	02.4	13 58.5	13.6	15 13.7	7.4	54.2
05	254 00.0	02.2	28 31.1	13.6	15 06.3	7.4	54.2
06	268 59.9	N23 02.0	43 03.7	13.7	S14 58.9	7.5	54.2
07	283 59.8	01.8	57 36.4	13.7	14 51.4	7.6	54.3
M 08	298 59.7	01.6	72 09.1	13.7	14 43.8	7.7	54.3
O 09	313 59.6	.. 01.5	86 41.8	13.7	14 36.1	7.7	54.3
N 10	328 59.4	01.3	101 14.5	13.8	14 28.4	7.7	54.3
D 11	343 59.3	01.1	115 47.3	13.8	14 20.7	7.9	54.3
A 12	358 59.2	N23 00.9	130 20.1	13.8	S14 12.8	7.8	54.3
Y 13	13 59.1	00.7	144 52.9	13.8	14 05.0	8.0	54.3
14	28 59.0	00.5	159 25.7	13.9	13 57.0	8.0	54.3
15	43 58.9	.. 00.3	173 58.6	13.9	13 49.0	8.1	54.3
16	58 58.7	23 00.1	188 31.5	13.9	13 40.9	8.1	54.4
17	73 58.6	22 59.9	203 04.4	13.9	13 32.8	8.2	54.4
18	88 58.5	N22 59.7	217 37.3	14.0	S13 24.6	8.3	54.4
19	103 58.4	59.6	232 10.3	13.9	13 16.3	8.3	54.4
20	118 58.3	59.4	246 43.2	14.0	13 08.0	8.4	54.4
21	133 58.2	.. 59.2	261 16.2	14.1	12 59.6	8.5	54.4
22	148 58.1	59.0	275 49.3	14.0	12 51.1	8.5	54.4
23	163 57.9	58.8	290 22.3	14.1	S12 42.6	8.5	54.5
SD	15.8	d 0.2	SD 14.7		14.7		14.8

Twilight / Moonrise

Lat.	Naut.	Civil	Sunrise	Moonrise 30	1	2	3
°	h m	h m	h m	h m	h m	h m	h m
N 72	□	□	□	■	■	00 58	00 35
N 70	□	□	□	01 05	00 32	00 21	00 13
68	□	□	□	23 51	23 55	23 56	23 55
66	////	////	00 19	23 23	23 35	23 42	23 46
64	////	////	01 41	23 02	23 18	23 30	23 39
62	////	////	02 17	22 45	23 05	23 20	23 32
60	////	01 03	02 42	22 30	22 53	23 11	23 26
N 58	////	01 48	03 02	22 18	22 43	23 04	23 21
56	////	02 17	03 18	22 07	22 35	22 57	23 17
54	00 58	02 38	03 32	21 58	22 27	22 51	23 13
52	01 40	02 56	03 44	21 49	22 20	22 46	23 09
50	02 06	03 11	03 55	21 42	22 14	22 41	23 06
45	02 51	03 40	04 17	21 26	22 00	22 31	22 59
N 40	03 21	04 02	04 35	21 12	21 49	22 22	22 52
35	03 43	04 20	04 50	21 01	21 39	22 14	22 47
30	04 02	04 35	05 02	20 51	21 31	22 08	22 42
20	04 31	05 00	05 24	20 34	21 16	21 56	22 34
N 10	04 53	05 20	05 43	20 19	21 03	21 46	22 27
0	05 12	05 38	06 00	20 05	20 51	21 36	22 21
S 10	05 28	05 55	06 17	19 51	20 39	21 27	22 14
20	05 44	06 12	06 36	19 36	20 26	21 17	22 07
30	06 00	06 30	06 57	19 19	20 12	21 05	21 58
35	06 09	06 41	07 09	19 09	20 03	20 58	21 54
40	06 18	06 52	07 23	18 58	19 53	20 50	21 48
45	06 28	07 05	07 39	18 44	19 42	20 41	21 42
S 50	06 40	07 21	08 00	18 28	19 28	20 30	21 35
52	06 45	07 29	08 09	18 20	19 21	20 25	21 31
54	06 51	07 37	08 20	18 11	19 14	20 20	21 27
56	06 57	07 45	08 32	18 01	19 06	20 14	21 23
58	07 03	07 55	08 47	17 50	18 57	20 07	21 18
S 60	07 10	08 07	09 04	17 37	18 46	19 59	21 13

Sunset / Twilight / Moonset

Lat.	Sunset	Civil	Naut.	Moonset 30	1	2	3
°	h m	h m	h m	h m	h m	h m	h m
N 72	□	□	□	■	■	05 21	07 17
N 70	□	□	□	01 59	04 10	05 57	07 37
68	□	□	□	03 22	04 50	06 22	07 53
66	23 40	////	////	03 59	05 18	06 41	08 06
64	22 25	////	////	04 26	05 39	06 57	08 17
62	21 50	////	////	04 46	05 55	07 09	08 26
60	21 25	23 03	////	05 03	06 09	07 20	08 34
N 58	21 05	22 18	////	05 17	06 21	07 30	08 41
56	20 49	21 50	////	05 29	06 32	07 38	08 47
54	20 35	21 29	23 08	05 40	06 41	07 45	08 52
52	20 23	21 11	22 27	05 49	06 49	07 52	08 57
50	20 12	20 57	22 01	05 57	06 56	07 58	09 01
45	19 50	20 28	21 17	06 15	07 12	08 10	09 10
N 40	19 33	20 05	20 47	06 29	07 24	08 21	09 18
35	19 18	19 48	20 24	06 42	07 35	08 30	09 25
30	19 05	19 33	20 06	06 52	07 44	08 37	09 31
20	18 43	19 08	19 37	07 10	08 01	08 51	09 41
N 10	18 25	18 48	19 15	07 26	08 15	09 02	09 50
0	18 08	18 30	18 56	07 41	08 28	09 13	09 58
S 10	17 50	18 13	18 39	07 56	08 41	09 24	10 06
20	17 32	17 56	18 24	08 11	08 55	09 36	10 15
30	17 11	17 38	18 07	08 29	09 10	09 49	10 24
35	16 59	17 27	17 59	08 40	09 20	09 56	10 30
40	16 45	17 16	17 50	08 52	09 30	10 05	10 36
45	16 29	17 02	17 39	09 06	09 42	10 15	10 44
S 50	16 08	16 47	17 28	09 23	09 57	10 27	10 52
52	15 59	16 39	17 23	09 31	10 04	10 32	10 57
54	15 48	16 31	17 17	09 40	10 12	10 38	11 01
56	15 35	16 22	17 11	09 50	10 20	10 45	11 06
58	15 21	16 12	17 05	10 01	10 30	10 53	11 11
S 60	15 04	16 01	16 57	10 14	10 41	11 01	11 18

SUN / MOON

Day	SUN Eqn. of Time 00ʰ	SUN Eqn. of Time 12ʰ	SUN Mer. Pass.	MOON Mer. Pass. Upper	MOON Mer. Pass. Lower	Age	Phase
d	m s	m s	h m	h m	h m	d	%
30	03 34	03 40	12 04	01 29	13 53	17	95
1	03 46	03 52	12 04	02 16	14 40	18	91
2	03 57	04 03	12 04	03 02	15 25	19	84

UT	ARIES GHA	VENUS −4.1 GHA	Dec	MARS −2.3 GHA	Dec	JUPITER −2.3 GHA	Dec	SATURN +0.0 GHA	Dec	STARS Name	SHA	Dec
d h 3 00	280 58.2	136 01.9	N15 48.6	328 05.1	S22 58.3	59 38.9	S14 49.5	5 03.8	S22 28.7	Acamar	315 16.0	S40 13.8
01	296 00.6	151 01.6	47.6	343 07.7	58.5	74 41.5	49.5	20 06.5	28.7	Achernar	335 24.4	S57 08.4
02	311 03.1	166 01.3	46.6	358 10.4	58.7	89 44.0	49.5	35 09.2	28.8	Acrux	173 05.4	S63 12.3
03	326 05.6	181 01.0 ..	45.6	13 13.0 ..	59.0	104 46.5 ..	49.5	50 11.8 ..	28.8	Adhara	255 10.2	S29 00.0
04	341 08.0	196 00.7	44.6	28 15.6	59.2	119 49.0	49.5	65 14.5	28.8	Aldebaran	290 45.7	N16 32.6
05	356 10.5	211 00.4	43.6	43 18.2	59.4	134 51.6	49.5	80 17.2	28.8			
06	11 12.9	226 00.1	N15 42.6	58 20.8	S22 59.6	149 54.1	S14 49.5	95 19.8	S22 28.8	Alioth	166 17.7	N55 52.0
07	26 15.4	240 59.8	41.6	73 23.4	22 59.9	164 56.6	49.5	110 22.5	28.8	Alkaid	152 56.1	N49 13.7
T 08	41 17.9	255 59.6	40.6	88 26.1	23 00.1	179 59.1	49.4	125 25.1	28.8	Al Na'ir	27 39.2	S46 52.1
U 09	56 20.3	270 59.3 ..	39.6	103 28.7 ..	00.3	195 01.6 ..	49.4	140 27.8 ..	28.8	Alnilam	275 43.2	S 1 11.6
E 10	71 22.8	285 59.0	38.6	118 31.3	00.6	210 04.2	49.4	155 30.5	28.8	Alphard	217 53.0	S 8 44.4
S 11	86 25.3	300 58.7	37.6	133 33.9	00.8	225 06.7	49.4	170 33.1	28.9			
D 12	101 27.7	315 58.4	N15 36.6	148 36.6	S23 01.0	240 09.2	S14 49.4	185 35.8	S22 28.9	Alphecca	126 07.9	N26 39.5
A 13	116 30.2	330 58.1	35.6	163 39.2	01.2	255 11.7	49.4	200 38.4	28.9	Alpheratz	357 39.9	N29 11.3
Y 14	131 32.7	345 57.8	34.6	178 41.8	01.5	270 14.3	49.4	215 41.1	28.9	Altair	62 04.6	N 8 55.2
15	146 35.1	0 57.6 ..	33.6	193 44.4 ..	01.7	285 16.8 ..	49.4	230 43.8 ..	28.9	Ankaa	353 12.3	S42 12.2
16	161 37.6	15 57.3	32.6	208 47.1	01.9	300 19.3	49.4	245 46.4	28.9	Antares	112 21.7	S26 28.2
17	176 40.0	30 57.0	31.6	223 49.7	02.2	315 21.8	49.4	260 49.1	28.9			
18	191 42.5	45 56.7	N15 30.5	238 52.3	S23 02.4	330 24.3	S14 49.4	275 51.8	S22 28.9	Arcturus	145 52.5	N19 05.5
19	206 45.0	60 56.4	29.5	253 55.0	02.6	345 26.9	49.4	290 54.4	29.0	Atria	107 19.9	S69 03.6
20	221 47.4	75 56.1	28.5	268 57.6	02.9	0 29.4	49.4	305 57.1	29.0	Avior	234 17.2	S59 34.3
21	236 49.9	90 55.9 ..	27.5	284 00.3 ..	03.1	15 31.9 ..	49.4	320 59.7 ..	29.0	Bellatrix	278 28.7	N 6 21.8
22	251 52.4	105 55.6	26.5	299 02.9	03.3	30 34.4	49.4	336 02.4	29.0	Betelgeuse	270 57.9	N 7 24.5
23	266 54.8	120 55.3	25.5	314 05.5	03.6	45 36.9	49.4	351 05.1	29.0			
4 00	281 57.3	135 55.0	N15 24.5	329 08.2	S23 03.8	60 39.4	S14 49.4	6 07.7	S22 29.0	Canopus	263 55.2	S52 42.4
01	296 59.8	150 54.7	23.5	344 10.8	04.0	75 42.0	49.4	21 10.4	29.0	Capella	280 29.8	N46 00.7
02	312 02.2	165 54.5	22.5	359 13.5	04.3	90 44.5	49.3	36 13.0	29.0	Deneb	49 28.7	N45 20.8
03	327 04.7	180 54.2 ..	21.4	14 16.1 ..	04.5	105 47.0 ..	49.3	51 15.7 ..	29.0	Denebola	182 30.3	N14 28.3
04	342 07.2	195 53.9	20.4	29 18.8	04.7	120 49.5	49.3	66 18.4	29.1	Diphda	348 52.5	S17 53.1
05	357 09.6	210 53.6	19.4	44 21.4	05.0	135 52.0	49.3	81 21.0	29.1			
06	12 12.1	225 53.4	N15 18.4	59 24.1	S23 05.2	150 54.5	S14 49.3	96 23.7	S22 29.1	Dubhe	193 47.9	N61 39.4
W 07	27 14.5	240 53.1	17.4	74 26.7	05.5	165 57.1	49.3	111 26.3	29.1	Elnath	278 08.7	N28 37.1
E 08	42 17.0	255 52.8	16.4	89 29.4	05.7	180 59.6	49.3	126 29.0	29.1	Eltanin	90 44.0	N51 29.4
D 09	57 19.5	270 52.5 ..	15.3	104 32.0 ..	05.9	196 02.1 ..	49.3	141 31.7 ..	29.1	Enif	33 43.5	N 9 57.6
N 10	72 21.9	285 52.3	14.3	119 34.7	06.2	211 04.6	49.3	156 34.3	29.1	Fomalhaut	15 20.1	S29 31.3
E 11	87 24.4	300 52.0	13.3	134 37.3	06.4	226 07.1	49.3	171 37.0	29.1			
S 12	102 26.9	315 51.7	N15 12.3	149 40.0	S23 06.6	241 09.6	S14 49.3	186 39.6	S22 29.1	Gacrux	171 57.1	S57 13.2
D 13	117 29.3	330 51.5	11.3	164 42.7	06.9	256 12.1	49.3	201 42.3	29.2	Gienah	175 48.8	S17 38.7
A 14	132 31.8	345 51.2	10.2	179 45.3	07.1	271 14.7	49.3	216 45.0	29.2	Hadar	148 42.7	S60 27.8
Y 15	147 34.3	0 50.9 ..	09.2	194 48.0 ..	07.4	286 17.2 ..	49.3	231 47.6 ..	29.2	Hamal	327 57.0	N23 32.7
16	162 36.7	15 50.7	08.2	209 50.7	07.6	301 19.7	49.3	246 50.3	29.2	Kaus Aust.	83 38.9	S34 22.4
17	177 39.2	30 50.4	07.2	224 53.3	07.8	316 22.2	49.3	261 53.0	29.2			
18	192 41.7	45 50.1	N15 06.2	239 56.0	S23 08.1	331 24.7	S14 49.3	276 55.6	S22 29.2	Kochab	137 19.6	N74 05.2
19	207 44.1	60 49.9	05.1	254 58.7	08.3	346 27.2	49.3	291 58.3	29.2	Markab	13 34.8	N15 18.2
20	222 46.6	75 49.6	04.1	270 01.3	08.5	1 29.7	49.3	307 00.9	29.2	Menkar	314 11.7	N 4 09.6
21	237 49.0	90 49.3 ..	03.1	285 04.0 ..	08.8	16 32.2 ..	49.3	322 03.6 ..	29.2	Menkent	148 03.4	S36 27.6
22	252 51.5	105 49.1	02.1	300 06.7	09.0	31 34.8	49.3	337 06.3	29.3	Miaplacidus	221 39.7	S69 47.8
23	267 54.0	120 48.8	01.0	315 09.3	09.3	46 37.3	49.3	352 08.9	29.3			
5 00	282 56.4	135 48.5	N15 00.0	330 12.0	S23 09.5	61 39.8	S14 49.3	7 11.6	S22 29.3	Mirfak	308 35.7	N49 55.2
01	297 58.9	150 48.3	14 59.0	345 14.7	09.8	76 42.3	49.3	22 14.2	29.3	Nunki	75 53.7	S26 16.2
02	313 01.4	165 48.0	57.9	0 17.4	10.0	91 44.8	49.3	37 16.9	29.3	Peacock	53 13.4	S56 40.3
03	328 03.8	180 47.8 ..	56.9	15 20.1 ..	10.2	106 47.3 ..	49.3	52 19.6 ..	29.3	Pollux	243 23.9	N27 58.8
04	343 06.3	195 47.5	55.9	30 22.7	10.5	121 49.8	49.3	67 22.2	29.3	Procyon	244 56.5	N 5 10.6
05	358 08.8	210 47.2	54.9	45 25.4	10.7	136 52.3	49.3	82 24.9	29.3			
06	13 11.2	225 47.0	N14 53.8	60 28.1	S23 11.0	151 54.8	S14 49.3	97 27.5	S22 29.3	Rasalhague	96 03.0	N12 33.0
T 07	28 13.7	240 46.7	52.8	75 30.8	11.2	166 57.3	49.3	112 30.2	29.4	Regulus	207 40.1	N11 52.7
H 08	43 16.1	255 46.5	51.8	90 33.5	11.4	181 59.8	49.3	127 32.9	29.4	Rigel	281 09.1	S 8 11.0
U 09	58 18.6	270 46.2 ..	50.7	105 36.2 ..	11.7	197 02.4 ..	49.3	142 35.5 ..	29.4	Rigil Kent.	139 46.7	S60 54.7
R 10	73 21.1	285 46.0	49.7	120 38.9	11.9	212 04.9	49.2	157 38.2	29.4	Sabik	102 08.3	S15 44.7
S 11	88 23.5	300 45.7	48.7	135 41.5	12.2	227 07.4	49.2	172 40.8	29.4			
D 12	103 26.0	315 45.4	N14 47.6	150 44.2	S23 12.4	242 09.9	S14 49.2	187 43.5	S22 29.4	Schedar	349 36.5	N56 37.9
A 13	118 28.5	330 45.2	46.6	165 46.9	12.7	257 12.4	49.2	202 46.2	29.4	Shaula	96 16.9	S37 06.9
Y 14	133 30.9	345 45.0	45.6	180 49.6	12.9	272 14.9	49.2	217 48.8	29.4	Sirius	258 31.1	S16 44.6
15	148 33.4	0 44.7 ..	44.5	195 52.3 ..	13.2	287 17.4 ..	49.2	232 51.5 ..	29.4	Spica	158 27.6	S11 15.4
16	163 35.9	15 44.4	43.5	210 55.0	13.4	302 19.9	49.2	247 54.1	29.5	Suhail	222 50.3	S43 30.6
17	178 38.3	30 44.2	42.5	225 57.7	13.6	317 22.4	49.2	262 56.8	29.5			
18	193 40.8	45 43.9	N14 41.4	241 00.4	S23 13.9	332 24.9	S14 49.2	277 59.5	S22 29.5	Vega	80 36.2	N38 48.2
19	208 43.3	60 43.7	40.4	256 03.1	14.1	347 27.4	49.2	293 02.1	29.5	Zuben'ubi	137 01.4	S16 07.0
20	223 45.7	75 43.4	39.3	271 05.8	14.4	2 29.9	49.2	308 04.8	29.5		SHA	Mer.Pass.
21	238 48.2	90 43.2 ..	38.3	286 08.5 ..	14.6	17 32.4 ..	49.2	323 07.4 ..	29.5	Venus	213 57.7	14 57
22	253 50.6	105 42.9	37.3	301 11.2	14.9	32 34.9	49.2	338 10.1	29.5	Mars	47 10.9	2 03
23	268 53.1	120 42.7	36.2	316 13.9	15.1	47 37.4	49.2	353 12.8	29.5	Jupiter	138 42.1	19 54
Mer.Pass.	h m 5 11.3	v −0.3	d 1.0	v 2.7	d 0.2	v 2.5	d 0.0	v 2.7	d 0.0	Saturn	84 10.4	23 31

UT	SUN GHA	SUN Dec	MOON GHA	v	MOON Dec	d	HP
d h	° ′	° ′	° ′	′	° ′	′	′
3 00	178 57.8	N22 58.6	304 55.4	14.0	S12 34.1	8.6	54.5
01	193 57.7	58.4	319 28.4	14.1	12 25.5	8.7	54.5
02	208 57.6	58.2	334 01.5	14.1	12 16.8	8.7	54.5
03	223 57.5	.. 58.0	348 34.6	14.2	12 08.1	8.8	54.5
04	238 57.4	57.8	3 07.8	14.1	11 59.3	8.8	54.5
05	253 57.2	57.6	17 40.9	14.2	11 50.5	8.9	54.5
06	268 57.1	N22 57.4	32 14.1	14.2	S11 41.6	9.0	54.6
07	283 57.0	57.2	46 47.3	14.2	11 32.6	9.0	54.6
08	298 56.9	57.0	61 20.5	14.2	11 23.6	9.0	54.6
09	313 56.8	.. 56.8	75 53.7	14.2	11 14.6	9.1	54.6
10	328 56.7	56.6	90 26.9	14.3	11 05.5	9.2	54.6
11	343 56.6	56.4	105 00.2	14.3	10 56.3	9.2	54.6
12	358 56.4	N22 56.2	119 33.5	14.3	S10 47.1	9.2	54.7
13	13 56.3	56.0	134 06.7	14.3	10 37.9	9.3	54.7
14	28 56.2	55.7	148 40.0	14.3	10 28.6	9.4	54.7
15	43 56.1	.. 55.5	163 13.3	14.3	10 19.2	9.4	54.7
16	58 56.0	55.3	177 46.6	14.4	10 09.8	9.5	54.7
17	73 55.9	55.1	192 20.0	14.3	10 00.3	9.5	54.7
18	88 55.8	N22 54.9	206 53.3	14.4	S 9 50.8	9.5	54.8
19	103 55.7	54.7	221 26.7	14.3	9 41.3	9.6	54.8
20	118 55.5	54.5	236 00.0	14.4	9 31.7	9.6	54.8
21	133 55.4	.. 54.3	250 33.4	14.4	9 22.1	9.7	54.8
22	148 55.3	54.1	265 06.8	14.3	9 12.4	9.8	54.8
23	163 55.2	53.9	279 40.1	14.4	9 02.6	9.7	54.9
4 00	178 55.1	N22 53.6	294 13.5	14.4	S 8 52.9	9.9	54.9
01	193 55.0	53.4	308 46.9	14.4	8 43.0	9.8	54.9
02	208 54.9	53.2	323 20.3	14.4	8 33.2	9.9	54.9
03	223 54.8	.. 53.0	337 53.7	14.4	8 23.3	10.0	54.9
04	238 54.6	52.8	352 27.1	14.5	8 13.3	10.0	55.0
05	253 54.5	52.6	7 00.6	14.4	8 03.3	10.0	55.0
06	268 54.4	N22 52.3	21 34.0	14.4	S 7 53.3	10.1	55.0
07	283 54.3	52.1	36 07.4	14.4	7 43.2	10.1	55.0
08	298 54.2	51.9	50 40.8	14.5	7 33.1	10.1	55.0
09	313 54.1	.. 51.7	65 14.3	14.4	7 23.0	10.2	55.1
10	328 54.0	51.5	79 47.7	14.4	7 12.8	10.2	55.1
11	343 53.9	51.3	94 21.1	14.4	7 02.6	10.3	55.1
12	358 53.8	N22 51.0	108 54.5	14.5	S 6 52.3	10.3	55.1
13	13 53.6	50.8	123 28.0	14.4	6 42.0	10.3	55.2
14	28 53.5	50.6	138 01.4	14.4	6 31.7	10.4	55.2
15	43 53.4	.. 50.4	152 34.8	14.4	6 21.3	10.4	55.2
16	58 53.3	50.1	167 08.2	14.4	6 10.9	10.5	55.2
17	73 53.2	49.9	181 41.6	14.4	6 00.4	10.5	55.3
18	88 53.1	N22 49.7	196 15.0	14.4	S 5 49.9	10.5	55.3
19	103 53.0	49.5	210 48.4	14.4	5 39.4	10.5	55.3
20	118 52.9	49.2	225 21.8	14.4	5 28.9	10.6	55.3
21	133 52.8	.. 49.0	239 55.2	14.4	5 18.3	10.6	55.4
22	148 52.6	48.8	254 28.6	14.3	5 07.7	10.6	55.4
23	163 52.5	48.5	269 01.9	14.4	4 57.1	10.7	55.4
5 00	178 52.4	N22 48.3	283 35.3	14.3	S 4 46.4	10.7	55.4
01	193 52.3	48.1	298 08.6	14.3	4 35.7	10.7	55.5
02	208 52.2	47.9	312 42.0	14.3	4 25.0	10.8	55.5
03	223 52.1	.. 47.6	327 15.3	14.3	4 14.2	10.8	55.5
04	238 52.0	47.4	341 48.6	14.3	4 03.4	10.8	55.5
05	253 51.9	47.2	356 21.9	14.3	3 52.6	10.8	55.6
06	268 51.8	N22 46.9	10 55.2	14.2	S 3 41.8	10.9	55.6
07	283 51.7	46.7	25 28.4	14.3	3 30.9	10.9	55.6
08	298 51.6	46.4	40 01.7	14.2	3 20.0	10.9	55.6
09	313 51.5	.. 46.2	54 34.9	14.2	3 09.1	11.0	55.7
10	328 51.3	46.0	69 08.1	14.2	2 58.1	10.9	55.7
11	343 51.2	45.7	83 41.3	14.2	2 47.2	11.0	55.7
12	358 51.1	N22 45.5	98 14.5	14.1	S 2 36.2	11.0	55.8
13	13 51.0	45.3	112 47.6	14.1	2 25.2	11.1	55.8
14	28 50.9	45.0	127 20.7	14.1	2 14.1	11.0	55.8
15	43 50.8	.. 44.8	141 53.8	14.1	2 03.1	11.1	55.8
16	58 50.7	44.5	156 26.9	14.1	1 52.0	11.1	55.9
17	73 50.6	44.3	171 00.0	14.0	1 40.9	11.1	55.9
18	88 50.5	N22 44.1	185 33.0	14.0	S 1 29.8	11.1	55.9
19	103 50.4	43.8	200 06.0	14.0	1 18.7	11.2	56.0
20	118 50.3	43.6	214 39.0	13.9	1 07.5	11.2	56.0
21	133 50.2	.. 43.3	229 11.9	14.0	0 56.3	11.1	56.0
22	148 50.1	43.1	243 44.9	13.8	0 45.2	11.2	56.1
23	163 50.0	42.8	258 17.7	13.9	S 0 34.0	11.3	56.1
	SD 15.8	d 0.2	SD 14.9		15.0		15.2

Left column day labels: **3 / TUESDAY**, **4 / WEDNESDAY**, **5 / THURSDAY**

Lat.	Twilight Naut.	Twilight Civil	Sunrise	Moonrise 3	4	5	6
°	h m	h m	h m	h m	h m	h m	h m
N 72	▭	▭	▭	00 35	00 19	(00 07 / 23 55)	23 43
N 70	▭	▭	▭	00 13	00 06	(00 00 / 23 54)	23 48
68	▭	▭	▭	23 55	23 55	23 54	23 53
66	////	////	00 41	23 46	23 50	23 53	23 57
64	////	////	01 47	23 39	23 46	23 53	24 00
62	////	////	02 21	23 32	23 43	23 52	24 03
60	////	01 11	02 46	23 26	23 40	23 52	24 05
N 58	////	01 53	03 05	23 21	23 37	23 52	24 07
56	////	02 20	03 21	23 17	23 35	23 52	24 09
54	01 05	02 41	03 35	23 13	23 32	23 51	24 11
52	01 44	02 59	03 47	23 09	23 30	23 51	24 13
50	02 10	03 13	03 57	23 06	23 29	23 51	24 14
45	02 53	03 42	04 19	22 59	23 25	23 51	24 17
N 40	03 23	04 04	04 36	22 52	23 22	23 50	24 20
35	03 45	04 21	04 51	22 47	23 19	23 50	24 22
30	04 03	04 36	05 04	22 42	23 16	23 50	24 24
20	04 32	05 01	05 25	22 34	23 12	23 49	24 28
N 10	04 54	05 21	05 44	22 27	23 08	23 49	24 31
0	05 12	05 38	06 01	22 21	23 04	23 49	24 34
S 10	05 29	05 55	06 18	22 14	23 01	23 48	24 38
20	05 44	06 12	06 36	22 07	22 57	23 48	24 41
30	06 00	06 30	06 56	21 58	22 53	23 48	24 45
35	06 09	06 40	07 08	21 54	22 50	23 48	24 47
40	06 18	06 52	07 22	21 48	22 47	23 47	24 50
45	06 28	07 05	07 39	21 42	22 44	23 47	24 52
S 50	06 39	07 21	07 59	21 35	22 40	23 47	24 54
52	06 44	07 28	08 08	21 31	22 38	23 47	24 58
54	06 50	07 36	08 19	21 27	22 36	23 47	25 00
56	06 56	07 44	08 31	21 23	22 34	23 47	25 02
58	07 02	07 54	08 45	21 18	22 31	23 46	25 04
S 60	07 09	08 05	09 02	21 13	22 29	23 46	25 06

Lat.	Sunset	Twilight Civil	Twilight Naut.	Moonset 3	4	5	6
°	h m	h m	h m	h m	h m	h m	h m
N 72	▭	▭	▭	07 17	09 04	10 49	12 35
N 70	▭	▭	▭	07 37	09 15	10 53	12 32
68	▭	▭	▭	07 53	09 25	10 56	12 30
66	23 23	////	////	08 06	09 32	10 59	12 28
64	22 20	////	////	08 17	09 39	11 01	12 26
62	21 47	////	////	08 26	09 44	11 03	12 25
60	21 22	22 56	////	08 34	09 49	11 05	12 24
N 58	21 03	22 15	////	08 41	09 53	11 07	12 23
56	20 47	21 47	////	08 47	09 57	11 08	12 22
54	20 34	21 27	23 02	08 52	10 00	11 10	12 21
52	20 22	21 10	22 24	08 57	10 03	11 11	12 20
50	20 11	20 55	21 58	09 01	10 06	11 12	12 20
45	19 50	20 27	21 15	09 10	10 12	11 14	12 18
N 40	19 32	20 05	20 46	09 18	10 17	11 16	12 17
35	19 18	19 47	20 23	09 25	10 21	11 18	12 16
30	19 05	19 32	20 05	09 31	10 24	11 19	12 15
20	18 44	19 08	19 37	09 41	10 31	11 21	12 13
N 10	18 25	18 48	19 15	09 50	10 36	11 24	12 12
0	18 08	18 31	18 57	09 58	10 42	11 26	12 10
S 10	17 51	18 14	18 40	10 06	10 47	11 28	12 09
20	17 33	17 57	18 24	10 15	10 52	11 30	12 07
30	17 12	17 39	18 08	10 24	10 58	11 32	12 06
35	17 00	17 28	18 00	10 30	11 02	11 33	12 05
40	16 47	17 17	17 51	10 36	11 06	11 35	12 04
45	16 30	17 04	17 41	10 44	11 11	11 36	12 02
S 50	16 10	16 49	17 30	10 52	11 16	11 38	12 01
52	16 01	16 41	17 25	10 57	11 19	11 39	12 00
54	15 50	16 33	17 19	11 01	11 21	11 40	11 59
56	15 38	16 25	17 13	11 06	11 24	11 41	11 59
58	15 24	16 15	17 07	11 11	11 28	11 43	11 58
S 60	15 07	16 04	17 00	11 18	11 31	11 44	11 57

Day	SUN Eqn. of Time 00h	SUN Eqn. of Time 12h	SUN Mer. Pass.	MOON Mer. Pass. Upper	MOON Mer. Pass. Lower	Age	Phase
d	m s	m s	h m	h m	h m	d	%
3	04 08	04 14	12 04	03 47	16 09	20	77
4	04 19	04 25	12 04	04 31	16 53	21	68
5	04 30	04 35	12 05	05 15	17 37	22	59

UT	ARIES GHA	VENUS −4.1 GHA	Dec	MARS −2.4 GHA	Dec	JUPITER −2.3 GHA	Dec	SATURN +0.1 GHA	Dec	STARS Name	SHA	Dec
6 00	283 55.6	135 42.5	N14 35.2	331 16.7	S23 15.4	62 39.9	S14 49.2	8 15.4	S22 29.5	Acamar	315 16.0	S40 13.8
01	298 58.0	150 42.2	34.1	346 19.4	15.6	77 42.4	49.2	23 18.1	29.6	Achernar	335 24.4	S57 08.4
02	314 00.5	165 42.0	33.1	1 22.1	15.9	92 44.9	49.2	38 20.7	29.6	Acrux	173 05.5	S63 12.3
03	329 03.0	180 41.7	.. 32.1	16 24.8	.. 16.1	107 47.4	.. 49.2	53 23.4	.. 29.6	Adhara	255 10.2	S28 59.9
04	344 05.4	195 41.5	31.0	31 27.5	16.4	122 49.9	49.2	68 26.1	29.6	Aldebaran	290 45.7	N16 32.6
05	359 07.9	210 41.2	30.0	46 30.2	16.6	137 52.4	49.2	83 28.7	29.6			
06	14 10.4	225 41.0	N14 28.9	61 32.9	S23 16.8	152 54.9	S14 49.2	98 31.4	S22 29.6	Alioth	166 17.7	N55 52.0
07	29 12.8	240 40.8	27.9	76 35.7	17.1	167 57.4	49.2	113 34.0	29.6	Alkaid	152 56.1	N49 13.7
08	44 15.3	255 40.5	26.8	91 38.4	17.3	182 59.9	49.2	128 36.7	29.6	Al Na'ir	27 39.1	S46 52.1
F 09	59 17.7	270 40.3	.. 25.8	106 41.1	.. 17.6	198 02.4	.. 49.2	143 39.4	.. 29.6	Alnilam	275 43.2	S 1 11.6
R 10	74 20.2	285 40.0	24.7	121 43.8	17.8	213 04.9	49.2	158 42.0	29.7	Alphard	217 53.0	S 8 44.4
I 11	89 22.7	300 39.8	23.7	136 46.5	18.1	228 07.4	49.2	173 44.7	29.7			
D 12	104 25.1	315 39.6	N14 22.7	151 49.3	S23 18.3	243 09.9	S14 49.2	188 47.3	S22 29.7	Alphecca	126 07.9	N26 39.5
A 13	119 27.6	330 39.3	21.6	166 52.0	18.6	258 12.4	49.2	203 50.0	29.7	Alpheratz	357 39.8	N29 11.3
Y 14	134 30.1	345 39.1	20.6	181 54.7	18.8	273 14.9	49.2	218 52.6	29.7	Altair	62 04.6	N 8 55.2
15	149 32.5	0 38.9	.. 19.5	196 57.4	.. 19.1	288 17.4	.. 49.2	233 55.3	.. 29.7	Ankaa	353 12.3	S42 12.2
16	164 35.0	15 38.6	18.5	212 00.2	19.3	303 19.9	49.2	248 58.0	29.7	Antares	112 21.7	S26 28.2
17	179 37.5	30 38.4	17.4	227 02.9	19.6	318 22.4	49.2	264 00.6	29.7			
18	194 39.9	45 38.2	N14 16.4	242 05.6	S23 19.8	333 24.9	S14 49.2	279 03.3	S22 29.7	Arcturus	145 52.5	N19 05.5
19	209 42.4	60 37.9	15.3	257 08.4	20.1	348 27.4	49.2	294 05.9	29.8	Atria	107 19.9	S69 03.6
20	224 44.9	75 37.7	14.3	272 11.1	20.3	3 29.9	49.2	309 08.6	29.8	Avior	234 17.2	S59 34.3
21	239 47.3	90 37.5	.. 13.2	287 13.8	.. 20.6	18 32.4	.. 49.3	324 11.3	.. 29.8	Bellatrix	278 28.6	N 6 21.8
22	254 49.8	105 37.2	12.2	302 16.6	20.8	33 34.9	49.3	339 13.9	29.8	Betelgeuse	270 57.9	N 7 24.5
23	269 52.2	120 37.0	11.1	317 19.3	21.1	48 37.4	49.3	354 16.6	29.8			
7 00	284 54.7	135 36.8	N14 10.0	332 22.1	S23 21.4	63 39.9	S14 49.3	9 19.2	S22 29.8	Canopus	263 55.2	S52 42.4
01	299 57.2	150 36.5	. 09.0	347 24.8	21.6	78 42.4	49.3	24 21.9	29.8	Capella	280 29.8	N46 00.7
02	314 59.6	165 36.3	07.9	2 27.6	21.9	93 44.9	49.3	39 24.6	29.8	Deneb	49 28.7	N45 20.8
03	330 02.1	180 36.1	.. 06.9	17 30.3	.. 22.1	108 47.4	.. 49.3	54 27.2	.. 29.8	Denebola	182 30.3	N14 28.3
04	345 04.6	195 35.9	05.8	32 33.0	22.4	123 49.9	49.3	69 29.9	29.8	Diphda	348 52.4	S17 53.1
05	0 07.0	210 35.6	04.8	47 35.8	22.6	138 52.4	49.3	84 32.5	29.9			
06	15 09.5	225 35.4	N14 03.7	62 38.5	S23 22.9	153 54.9	S14 49.3	99 35.2	S22 29.9	Dubhe	193 47.9	N61 39.4
07	30 12.0	240 35.2	02.7	77 41.3	23.1	168 57.4	49.3	114 37.8	29.9	Elnath	278 08.6	N28 37.1
S 08	45 14.4	255 35.0	01.6	92 44.0	23.4	183 59.9	49.3	129 40.5	29.9	Eltanin	90 44.0	N51 29.4
A 09	60 16.9	270 34.7	14 00.5	107 46.8	.. 23.6	199 02.4	.. 49.3	144 43.2	.. 29.9	Enif	33 43.5	N 9 57.6
T 10	75 19.4	285 34.5	13 59.5	122 49.6	23.9	214 04.8	49.3	159 45.8	29.9	Fomalhaut	15 20.0	S29 31.3
U 11	90 21.8	300 34.3	58.4	137 52.3	24.1	229 07.3	49.3	174 48.5	29.9			
R 12	105 24.3	315 34.1	N13 57.4	152 55.1	S23 24.4	244 09.8	S14 49.3	189 51.1	S22 29.9	Gacrux	171 57.1	S57 13.2
D 13	120 26.7	330 33.8	56.3	167 57.8	24.7	259 12.3	49.3	204 53.8	30.0	Gienah	175 48.8	S17 38.6
A 14	135 29.2	345 33.6	55.2	183 00.6	24.9	274 14.8	49.3	219 56.5	30.0	Hadar	148 42.7	S60 27.8
Y 15	150 31.7	0 33.4	.. 54.2	198 03.4	.. 25.2	289 17.3	.. 49.3	234 59.1	.. 30.0	Hamal	327 57.0	N23 32.7
16	165 34.1	15 33.2	53.1	213 06.1	25.4	304 19.8	49.3	250 01.8	30.0	Kaus Aust.	83 38.9	S34 22.4
17	180 36.6	30 33.0	52.1	228 08.9	25.7	319 22.3	49.3	265 04.4	30.0			
18	195 39.1	45 32.8	N13 51.0	243 11.6	S23 25.9	334 24.8	S14 49.3	280 07.1	S22 30.0	Kochab	137 19.6	N74 05.2
19	210 41.5	60 32.5	49.9	258 14.4	26.2	349 27.3	49.3	295 09.7	30.0	Markab	13 34.7	N15 18.2
20	225 44.0	75 32.3	48.9	273 17.2	26.4	4 29.8	49.3	310 12.4	30.0	Menkar	314 11.6	N 4 09.6
21	240 46.5	90 32.1	.. 47.8	288 19.9	.. 26.7	19 32.2	.. 49.3	325 15.1	.. 30.0	Menkent	148 03.4	S36 27.6
22	255 48.9	105 31.9	46.7	303 22.7	27.0	34 34.7	49.3	340 17.7	30.1	Miaplacidus	221 39.7	S69 47.8
23	270 51.4	120 31.7	45.7	318 25.5	27.2	49 37.2	49.3	355 20.4	30.1			
8 00	285 53.8	135 31.5	N13 44.6	333 28.3	S23 27.5	64 39.7	S14 49.3	10 23.0	S22 30.1	Mirfak	308 35.7	N49 55.2
01	300 56.3	150 31.3	43.5	348 31.0	27.7	79 42.2	49.3	25 25.7	30.1	Nunki	75 53.7	S26 16.2
02	315 58.8	165 31.0	42.5	3 33.8	28.0	94 44.7	49.3	40 28.4	30.1	Peacock	53 13.3	S56 40.3
03	331 01.2	180 30.8	.. 41.4	18 36.6	.. 28.2	109 47.2	.. 49.3	55 31.0	.. 30.1	Pollux	243 23.9	N27 58.8
04	346 03.7	195 30.6	40.3	33 39.4	28.5	124 49.7	49.3	70 33.7	30.1	Procyon	244 56.5	N 5 10.6
05	1 06.2	210 30.4	39.3	48 42.2	28.8	139 52.1	49.4	85 36.3	30.1			
06	16 08.6	225 30.2	N13 38.2	63 44.9	S23 29.0	154 54.6	S14 49.4	100 39.0	S22 30.1	Rasalhague	96 03.0	N12 33.0
07	31 11.1	240 30.0	37.1	78 47.7	29.3	169 57.1	49.4	115 41.6	30.2	Regulus	207 40.1	N11 52.7
S 08	46 13.6	255 29.8	36.1	93 50.5	29.5	184 59.6	49.4	130 44.3	30.2	Rigel	281 09.1	S 8 11.0
U 09	61 16.0	270 29.6	.. 35.0	108 53.3	.. 29.8	200 02.1	.. 49.4	145 47.0	.. 30.2	Rigil Kent.	139 46.7	S60 54.7
N 10	76 18.5	285 29.4	33.9	123 56.1	30.1	215 04.6	49.4	160 49.6	30.2	Sabik	102 08.3	S15 44.7
D 11	91 21.0	300 29.2	32.8	138 58.9	30.3	230 07.1	49.4	175 52.3	30.2			
A 12	106 23.4	315 29.0	N13 31.8	154 01.7	S23 30.6	245 09.5	S14 49.4	190 54.9	S22 30.2	Schedar	349 36.5	N56 37.9
Y 13	121 25.9	330 28.8	30.7	169 04.4	30.8	260 12.0	49.4	205 57.6	30.2	Shaula	96 16.9	S37 06.9
14	136 28.3	345 28.6	29.6	184 07.2	31.1	275 14.5	49.4	221 00.2	30.2	Sirius	258 31.1	S16 44.6
15	151 30.8	0 28.4	.. 28.5	199 10.0	.. 31.4	290 17.0	.. 49.4	236 02.9	.. 30.2	Spica	158 27.6	S11 15.4
16	166 33.3	15 28.1	27.5	214 12.8	31.6	305 19.5	49.4	251 05.6	30.3	Suhail	222 50.3	S43 30.6
17	181 35.7	30 27.9	26.4	229 15.6	31.9	320 22.0	49.4	266 08.2	30.3			
18	196 38.2	45 27.7	N13 25.3	244 18.4	S23 32.1	335 24.4	S14 49.4	281 10.9	S22 30.3	Vega	80 36.2	N38 48.2
19	211 40.7	60 27.5	24.2	259 21.2	32.4	350 26.9	49.4	296 13.5	30.3	Zuben'ubi	137 01.4	S16 07.0
20	226 43.1	75 27.3	23.2	274 24.0	32.7	5 29.4	49.4	311 16.2	30.3		SHA	Mer.Pass.
21	241 45.6	90 27.1	.. 22.1	289 26.8	.. 32.9	20 31.9	.. 49.4	326 18.8	.. 30.3	Venus	210 42.1	14 58
22	256 48.1	105 26.9	21.0	304 29.6	33.2	35 34.4	49.4	341 21.5	30.3	Mars	47 27.4	1 50
23	271 50.5	120 26.8	19.9	319 32.4	33.5	50 36.8	49.5	356 24.2	30.3	Jupiter	138 45.2	19 42
Mer. Pass.	4 59.5	v −0.2	d 1.1	v 2.8	d 0.3	v 2.5	d 0.0	v 2.7	d 0.0	Saturn	84 24.5	23 19

SUN and MOON

UT	SUN GHA	SUN Dec	MOON GHA	v	Dec	d	HP
d h	° ′	° ′	° ′	′	° ′	′	′
6 00	178 49.9	N22 42.6	272 50.6	13.8	S 0 22.7	11.2	56.1
01	193 49.7	42.3	287 23.4	13.8	0 11.5	11.2	56.1
02	208 49.6	42.1	301 56.2	13.8	S 0 00.3	11.3	56.2
03	223 49.5	41.8	316 29.0	13.7	N 0 11.0	11.2	56.2
04	238 49.4	41.6	331 01.7	13.7	0 22.2	11.3	56.2
05	253 49.3	41.3	345 34.4	13.7	0 33.5	11.3	56.3
06	268 49.2	N22 41.1	0 07.1	13.6	N 0 44.8	11.3	56.3
07	283 49.1	40.8	14 39.7	13.6	0 56.1	11.3	56.3
F 08	298 49.0	40.6	29 12.3	13.5	1 07.4	11.3	56.4
R 09	313 48.9	40.3	43 44.8	13.5	1 18.7	11.3	56.4
I 10	328 48.8	40.1	58 17.3	13.5	1 30.0	11.4	56.4
D 11	343 48.7	39.8	72 49.8	13.4	1 41.4	11.3	56.5
A 12	358 48.6	N22 39.6	87 22.2	13.4	N 1 52.7	11.4	56.5
Y 13	13 48.5	39.3	101 54.6	13.3	2 04.1	11.3	56.5
14	28 48.4	39.1	116 26.9	13.3	2 15.4	11.3	56.6
15	43 48.3	38.8	130 59.2	13.2	2 26.7	11.4	56.6
16	58 48.2	38.5	145 31.4	13.2	2 38.1	11.3	56.6
17	73 48.1	38.3	160 03.6	13.2	2 49.4	11.4	56.7
18	88 48.0	N22 38.0	174 35.8	13.1	N 3 00.8	11.4	56.7
19	103 47.9	37.8	189 07.9	13.0	3 12.2	11.3	56.8
20	118 47.8	37.5	203 39.9	13.0	3 23.5	11.4	56.8
21	133 47.7	37.3	218 11.9	13.0	3 34.9	11.3	56.8
22	148 47.6	37.0	232 43.9	12.9	3 46.2	11.3	56.9
23	163 47.5	36.7	247 15.8	12.8	3 57.5	11.4	56.9
7 00	178 47.4	N22 36.5	261 47.6	12.8	N 4 08.9	11.3	56.9
01	193 47.3	36.2	276 19.4	12.7	4 20.2	11.4	57.0
02	208 47.2	35.9	290 51.1	12.7	4 31.6	11.3	57.0
03	223 47.1	35.7	305 22.8	12.6	4 42.9	11.3	57.0
04	238 46.9	35.4	319 54.4	12.6	4 54.2	11.3	57.1
05	253 46.8	35.1	334 26.0	12.5	5 05.5	11.3	57.1
06	268 46.7	N22 34.9	348 57.5	12.4	N 5 16.8	11.3	57.2
S 07	283 46.6	34.6	3 28.9	12.4	5 28.1	11.3	57.2
A 08	298 46.5	34.3	18 00.3	12.3	5 39.4	11.2	57.2
T 09	313 46.4	34.1	32 31.6	12.3	5 50.6	11.3	57.3
U 10	328 46.3	33.8	47 02.9	12.2	6 01.9	11.2	57.3
R 11	343 46.2	33.5	61 34.1	12.1	6 13.1	11.2	57.3
D 12	358 46.1	N22 33.3	76 05.2	12.1	N 6 24.3	11.2	57.4
A 13	13 46.0	33.0	90 36.3	12.0	6 35.5	11.2	57.4
Y 14	28 45.9	32.7	105 07.3	11.9	6 46.7	11.2	57.5
15	43 45.8	32.4	119 38.2	11.9	6 57.9	11.1	57.5
16	58 45.7	32.2	134 09.1	11.7	7 09.0	11.1	57.5
17	73 45.6	31.9	148 39.8	11.8	7 20.1	11.2	57.6
18	88 45.5	N22 31.6	163 10.6	11.6	N 7 31.3	11.0	57.6
19	103 45.4	31.3	177 41.2	11.6	7 42.3	11.1	57.6
20	118 45.3	31.1	192 11.8	11.5	7 53.4	11.0	57.7
21	133 45.2	30.8	206 42.3	11.4	8 04.4	11.0	57.7
22	148 45.1	30.5	221 12.7	11.4	8 15.4	11.0	57.8
23	163 45.0	30.2	235 43.1	11.3	8 26.4	11.0	57.8
8 00	178 44.9	N22 29.9	250 13.4	11.2	N 8 37.4	10.9	57.8
01	193 44.9	29.7	264 43.6	11.1	8 48.3	10.9	57.9
02	208 44.8	29.4	279 13.7	11.1	8 59.2	10.8	57.9
03	223 44.7	29.1	293 43.8	11.0	9 10.0	10.8	58.0
04	238 44.6	28.8	308 13.8	10.8	9 20.9	10.8	58.0
05	253 44.5	28.5	322 43.6	10.9	9 31.7	10.7	58.0
06	268 44.4	N22 28.3	337 13.5	10.7	N 9 42.4	10.7	58.1
07	283 44.3	28.0	351 43.2	10.6	9 53.1	10.7	58.1
S 08	298 44.2	27.7	6 12.8	10.6	10 03.8	10.7	58.2
U 09	313 44.1	27.4	20 42.4	10.5	10 14.5	10.6	58.2
N 10	328 44.0	27.1	35 11.9	10.4	10 25.1	10.5	58.2
D 11	343 43.9	26.8	49 41.3	10.3	10 35.6	10.5	58.3
A 12	358 43.8	N22 26.5	64 10.6	10.3	N10 46.1	10.5	58.3
Y 13	13 43.7	26.3	78 39.9	10.1	10 56.6	10.5	58.3
14	28 43.6	26.0	93 09.0	10.1	11 07.1	10.3	58.4
15	43 43.5	25.7	107 38.1	9.9	11 17.4	10.4	58.4
16	58 43.4	25.4	122 07.0	9.9	11 27.8	10.3	58.5
17	73 43.3	25.1	136 35.9	9.8	11 38.1	10.2	58.5
18	88 43.2	N22 24.8	151 04.7	9.7	N11 48.3	10.2	58.5
19	103 43.1	24.5	165 33.4	9.6	11 58.5	10.1	58.6
20	118 43.0	24.2	180 02.0	9.6	12 08.6	10.1	58.6
21	133 42.9	23.9	194 30.6	9.4	12 18.7	10.0	58.7
22	148 42.8	23.6	208 59.0	9.3	12 28.7	10.0	58.7
23	163 42.7	23.3	223 27.3	9.3	N12 38.7	9.9	58.7
	SD 15.8	d 0.3	SD 15.4		15.6		15.9

Twilight and Moonrise

Lat.	Twilight Naut.	Twilight Civil	Sunrise	Moonrise 6	7	8	9
°	h m	h m	h m	h m	h m	h m	h m
N 72	□	□	□	23 43	23 30	23 14	22 48
N 70	□	□	□	23 48	23 42	23 36	23 28
68	□	□	□	23 53	23 52	23 53	23 56
66	////	////	00 57	23 57	24 01	00 01	00 07
64	////	////	01 54	24 00	00 00	00 08	00 19
62	////	////	02 26	24 03	00 03	00 14	00 29
60	////	01 19	02 50	24 05	00 05	00 20	00 37
N 58	////	01 58	03 09	24 07	00 07	00 24	00 45
56	////	02 25	03 24	24 09	00 09	00 29	00 52
54	01 13	02 45	03 38	24 11	00 11	00 32	00 57
52	01 49	03 02	03 49	24 13	00 13	00 36	01 03
50	02 14	03 16	03 59	24 14	00 14	00 39	01 08
45	02 56	03 44	04 21	24 17	00 17	00 46	01 18
N 40	03 25	04 06	04 38	24 20	00 20	00 52	01 27
35	03 47	04 23	04 53	24 22	00 22	00 57	01 35
30	04 05	04 38	05 05	24 24	00 24	01 01	01 42
20	04 33	05 02	05 26	24 28	00 28	01 09	01 53
N 10	04 55	05 21	05 44	24 31	00 31	01 16	02 04
0	05 13	05 39	06 01	24 34	00 34	01 22	02 14
S 10	05 29	05 55	06 18	24 38	00 38	01 29	02 23
20	05 45	06 12	06 36	24 41	00 41	01 36	02 34
30	06 00	06 30	06 56	24 45	00 45	01 44	02 46
35	06 09	06 40	07 08	24 47	00 47	01 49	02 53
40	06 17	06 51	07 22	24 50	00 50	01 54	03 01
45	06 27	07 04	07 38	24 52	00 52	02 00	03 11
S 50	06 38	07 19	07 57	24 54	00 54	02 08	03 22
52	06 43	07 26	08 07	24 55	00 55	02 11	03 28
54	06 49	07 34	08 17	25 00	01 00	02 15	03 33
56	06 54	07 43	08 29	25 02	01 02	02 19	03 40
58	07 01	07 52	08 43	25 04	01 04	02 24	03 47
S 60	07 07	08 03	08 59	25 06	01 06	02 29	03 56

Sunset, Twilight and Moonset

Lat.	Sunset	Twilight Civil	Twilight Naut.	Moonset 6	7	8	9
°	h m	h m	h m	h m	h m	h m	h m
N 72	□	□	□	12 35	14 25	16 26	18 44
N 70	□	□	□	12 32	14 15	16 05	18 05
68	□	□	□	12 30	14 07	15 50	17 38
66	23 08	////	////	12 28	14 00	15 37	17 18
64	22 14	////	////	12 26	13 54	15 26	17 02
62	21 43	////	////	12 25	13 49	15 17	16 48
60	21 19	22 48	////	12 24	13 45	15 10	16 37
N 58	21 00	22 10	////	12 23	13 41	15 03	16 27
56	20 45	21 44	////	12 22	13 38	14 57	16 18
54	20 32	21 24	22 55	12 21	13 35	14 52	16 11
52	20 20	21 07	22 19	12 20	13 32	14 47	16 04
50	20 10	20 53	21 55	12 20	13 30	14 43	15 58
45	19 49	20 25	21 13	12 18	13 24	14 33	15 45
N 40	19 31	20 04	20 45	12 17	13 20	14 26	15 34
35	19 17	19 46	20 23	12 16	13 16	14 19	15 25
30	19 05	19 32	20 05	12 15	13 13	14 13	15 17
20	18 44	19 08	19 37	12 13	13 07	14 03	15 03
N 10	18 25	18 48	19 15	12 12	13 02	13 55	14 51
0	18 09	18 31	18 57	12 10	12 57	13 46	14 39
S 10	17 52	18 15	18 41	12 09	12 52	13 38	14 28
20	17 34	17 58	18 25	12 07	12 47	13 29	14 16
30	17 14	17 40	18 10	12 06	12 41	13 20	14 02
35	17 02	17 30	18 01	12 05	12 38	13 14	13 54
40	16 48	17 19	17 53	12 04	12 34	13 07	13 45
45	16 32	17 06	17 43	12 02	12 30	13 00	13 35
S 50	16 13	16 51	17 32	12 01	12 24	12 51	13 22
52	16 03	16 44	17 27	12 00	12 22	12 47	13 16
54	15 53	16 36	17 22	11 59	12 19	12 42	13 10
56	15 41	16 27	17 16	11 59	12 17	12 37	13 03
58	15 27	16 18	17 10	11 58	12 13	12 32	12 54
S 60	15 11	16 07	17 03	11 57	12 10	12 25	12 45

SUN and MOON

Day	SUN Eqn. of Time 00h	12h	Mer. Pass.	MOON Mer. Pass. Upper	Lower	Age	Phase
d	m s	m s	h m	h m	h m	d	%
6	04 40	04 45	12 05	06 00	18 22	23	48
7	04 50	04 55	12 05	06 46	19 10	24	38
8	05 00	05 05	12 05	07 34	20 00	25	28

UT	ARIES	VENUS −4.1		MARS −2.4		JUPITER −2.2		SATURN +0.1		STARS		
	GHA	GHA	Dec	GHA	Dec	GHA	Dec	GHA	Dec	Name	SHA	Dec
d h	° ′	° ′	° ′	° ′	° ′	° ′	° ′	° ′	° ′		° ′	° ′
9 00	286 53.0	135 26.6	N13 18.9	334 35.2	S23 33.7	65 39.3	S14 49.5	11 26.8	S22 30.3	Acamar	315 16.0	S40 13.8
01	301 55.5	150 26.4	17.8	349 38.0	34.0	80 41.8	49.5	26 29.5	30.4	Achernar	335 24.4	S57 08.4
02	316 57.9	165 26.2	16.7	4 40.8	34.2	95 44.3	49.5	41 32.1	30.4	Acrux	173 05.5	S63 12.3
03	332 00.4	180 26.0 ..	15.6	19 43.7 ..	34.5	110 46.8 ..	49.5	56 34.8 ..	30.4	Adhara	255 10.2	S28 59.7
04	347 02.8	195 25.8	14.5	34 46.5	34.8	125 49.2	49.5	71 37.4	30.4	Aldebaran	290 45.7	N16 32.6
05	2 05.3	210 25.6	13.5	49 49.3	35.0	140 51.7	49.5	86 40.1	30.4			
06	17 07.8	225 25.4	N13 12.4	64 52.1	S23 35.3	155 54.2	S14 49.5	101 42.8	S22 30.4	Alioth	166 17.8	N55 52.0
M 07	32 10.2	240 25.2	11.3	79 54.9	35.6	170 56.7	49.5	116 45.4	30.4	Alkaid	152 56.1	N49 13.7
O 08	47 12.7	255 25.0	10.2	94 57.7	35.8	185 59.2	49.5	131 48.1	30.4	Al Na'ir	27 39.1	S46 52.1
N 09	62 15.2	270 24.8 ..	09.1	110 00.5 ..	36.1	201 01.6 ..	49.5	146 50.7 ..	30.4	Alnilam	275 43.2	S 1 11.6
D 10	77 17.6	285 24.6	08.0	125 03.4	36.3	216 04.1	49.5	161 53.4	30.4	Alphard	217 53.0	S 8 44.4
A 11	92 20.1	300 24.4	07.0	140 06.2	36.6	231 06.6	49.5	176 56.0	30.5			
Y 12	107 22.6	315 24.2	N13 05.9	155 09.0	S23 36.9	246 09.1	S14 49.5	191 58.7	S22 30.5	Alphecca	126 07.9	N26 39.5
13	122 25.0	330 24.1	04.8	170 11.8	37.1	261 11.5	49.6	207 01.3	30.5	Alpheratz	357 39.8	N29 11.3
14	137 27.5	345 23.9	03.7	185 14.6	37.4	276 14.0	49.6	222 04.0	30.5	Altair	62 04.6	N 8 55.2
15	152 30.0	0 23.7 ..	02.6	200 17.5 ..	37.7	291 16.5 ..	49.6	237 06.7 ..	30.5	Ankaa	353 12.3	S42 12.2
16	167 32.4	15 23.5	01.5	215 20.3	37.9	306 19.0	49.6	252 09.3	30.5	Antares	112 21.7	S26 28.2
17	182 34.9	30 23.3	13 00.4	230 23.1	38.2	321 21.4	49.6	267 12.0	30.5			
18	197 37.3	45 23.1	N12 59.4	245 25.9	S23 38.5	336 23.9	S14 49.6	282 14.6	S22 30.5	Arcturus	145 52.5	N19 05.5
19	212 39.8	60 22.9	58.3	260 28.8	38.7	351 26.4	49.6	297 17.3	30.5	Atria	107 20.0	S69 03.6
20	227 42.3	75 22.8	57.2	275 31.6	39.0	6 28.9	49.6	312 19.9	30.6	Avior	234 17.2	S59 34.3
21	242 44.7	90 22.6	56.1	290 34.4 ..	39.3	21 31.3 ..	49.6	327 22.6 ..	30.6	Bellatrix	278 28.6	N 6 21.8
22	257 47.2	105 22.4	55.0	305 37.3	39.5	36 33.8	49.6	342 25.2	30.6	Betelgeuse	270 57.9	N 7 24.5
23	272 49.7	120 22.2	53.9	320 40.1	39.8	51 36.3	49.6	357 27.9	30.6			
10 00	287 52.1	135 22.0	N12 52.8	335 42.9	S23 40.1	66 38.8	S14 49.7	12 30.6	S22 30.6	Canopus	263 55.2	S52 42.4
01	302 54.6	150 21.8	51.7	350 45.8	40.3	81 41.2	49.7	27 33.2	30.6	Capella	280 29.8	N46 00.7
02	317 57.1	165 21.7	50.6	5 48.6	40.6	96 43.7	49.7	42 35.9	30.6	Deneb	49 28.7	N45 20.8
03	332 59.5	180 21.5 ..	49.5	20 51.5 ..	40.9	111 46.2 ..	49.7	57 38.5 ..	30.6	Denebola	182 30.3	N14 28.3
04	348 02.0	195 21.3	48.5	35 54.3	41.1	126 48.7	49.7	72 41.2	30.6	Diphda	348 52.4	S17 53.1
05	3 04.4	210 21.1	47.4	50 57.2	41.4	141 51.1	49.7	87 43.8	30.7			
06	18 06.9	225 20.9	N12 46.3	66 00.0	S23 41.7	156 53.6	S14 49.7	102 46.5	S22 30.7	Dubhe	193 48.0	N61 39.4
T 07	33 09.4	240 20.8	45.2	81 02.8	41.9	171 56.1	49.7	117 49.1	30.7	Elnath	278 08.6	N28 37.1
U 08	48 11.8	255 20.6	44.1	96 05.7	42.2	186 58.5	49.7	132 51.8	30.7	Eltanin	90 44.0	N51 29.4
E 09	63 14.3	270 20.4 ..	43.0	111 08.5 ..	42.5	202 01.0 ..	49.7	147 54.5 ..	30.7	Enif	33 43.5	N 9 57.6
S 10	78 16.8	285 20.2	41.9	126 11.4	42.7	217 03.5	49.7	162 57.1	30.7	Fomalhaut	15 20.0	S29 31.3
D 11	93 19.2	300 20.1	40.8	141 14.2	43.0	232 05.9	49.7	177 59.8	30.7			
A 12	108 21.7	315 19.9	N12 39.7	156 17.1	S23 43.3	247 08.4	S14 49.8	193 02.4	S22 30.7	Gacrux	171 57.1	S57 13.2
Y 13	123 24.2	330 19.7	38.6	171 19.9	43.5	262 10.9	49.8	208 05.1	30.7	Gienah	175 48.8	S17 38.6
14	138 26.6	345 19.6	37.5	186 22.8	43.8	277 13.4	49.8	223 07.7	30.8	Hadar	148 42.8	S60 27.8
15	153 29.1	0 19.4 ..	36.4	201 25.7 ..	44.1	292 15.8 ..	49.8	238 10.4 ..	30.8	Hamal	327 57.0	N23 32.7
16	168 31.6	15 19.2	35.3	216 28.5	44.3	307 18.3	49.8	253 13.0	30.8	Kaus Aust.	83 38.9	S34 22.4
17	183 34.0	30 19.0	34.2	231 31.4	44.6	322 20.8	49.8	268 15.7	30.8			
18	198 36.5	45 18.9	N12 33.1	246 34.2	S23 44.9	337 23.2	S14 49.8	283 18.4	S22 30.8	Kochab	137 19.7	N74 05.2
19	213 38.9	60 18.7	32.0	261 37.1	45.1	352 25.7	49.8	298 21.0	30.8	Markab	13 34.7	N15 18.2
20	228 41.4	75 18.5	30.9	276 39.9	45.4	7 28.2	49.8	313 23.7	30.8	Menkar	314 11.6	N 4 09.6
21	243 43.9	90 18.4 ..	29.8	291 42.8 ..	45.7	22 30.6 ..	49.8	328 26.3 ..	30.8	Menkent	148 03.4	S36 27.6
22	258 46.3	105 18.2	28.7	306 45.7	46.0	37 33.1	49.9	343 29.0	30.8	Miaplacidus	221 39.7	S69 47.8
23	273 48.8	120 18.0	27.6	321 48.5	46.2	52 35.6	49.9	358 31.6	30.8			
11 00	288 51.3	135 17.9	N12 26.5	336 51.4	S23 46.5	67 38.0	S14 49.9	13 34.3	S22 30.9	Mirfak	308 35.7	N49 55.5
01	303 53.7	150 17.7	25.4	351 54.3	46.8	82 40.5	49.9	28 36.9	30.9	Nunki	75 53.7	S26 16.2
02	318 56.2	165 17.5	24.3	6 57.1	47.0	97 43.0	49.9	43 39.6	30.9	Peacock	53 13.3	S56 40.3
03	333 58.7	180 17.4 ..	23.2	22 00.0 ..	47.3	112 45.4 ..	49.9	58 42.2 ..	30.9	Pollux	243 23.9	N27 58.8
04	349 01.1	195 17.2	22.1	37 02.9	47.6	127 47.9	49.9	73 44.9	30.9	Procyon	244 56.5	N 5 10.6
05	4 03.6	210 17.0	21.0	52 05.8	47.8	142 50.3	49.9	88 47.6	30.9			
06	19 06.1	225 16.9	N12 19.9	67 08.6	S23 48.1	157 52.8	S14 49.9	103 50.2	S22 30.9	Rasalhague	96 03.0	N12 33.0
W 07	34 08.5	240 16.7	18.8	82 11.5	48.4	172 55.3	50.0	118 52.9	30.9	Regulus	207 40.1	N11 52.7
E 08	49 11.0	255 16.6	17.7	97 14.4	48.7	187 57.7	50.0	133 55.5	30.9	Rigel	281 09.1	S 8 10.9
D 09	64 13.4	270 16.4 ..	16.6	112 17.3 ..	48.9	203 00.2 ..	50.0	148 58.2 ..	31.0	Rigil Kent.	139 46.8	S60 54.7
N 10	79 15.9	285 16.2	15.5	127 20.1	49.2	218 02.7	50.0	164 00.8	31.0	Sabik	102 08.3	S15 44.7
E 11	94 18.4	300 16.1	14.4	142 23.0	49.5	233 05.1	50.0	179 03.5	31.0			
S 12	109 20.8	315 15.9	N12 13.3	157 25.9	S23 49.7	248 07.6	S14 50.0	194 06.1	S22 31.0	Schedar	349 36.5	N56 38.0
D 13	124 23.3	330 15.8	12.1	172 28.8	50.0	263 10.0	50.0	209 08.8	31.0	Shaula	96 16.9	S37 06.9
A 14	139 25.8	345 15.6	11.0	187 31.7	50.3	278 12.5	50.0	224 11.4	31.0	Sirius	258 31.1	S16 44.6
Y 15	154 28.2	0 15.5 ..	09.9	202 34.6 ..	50.6	293 15.0 ..	50.1	239 14.1 ..	31.0	Spica	158 27.6	S11 15.4
16	169 30.7	15 15.3	08.8	217 37.5	50.8	308 17.4	50.1	254 16.7	31.0	Suhail	222 50.3	S43 30.6
17	184 33.2	30 15.2	07.7	232 40.3	51.1	323 19.9	50.1	269 19.4	31.0			
18	199 35.6	45 15.0	N12 06.6	247 43.2	S23 51.4	338 22.3	S14 50.1	284 22.1	S22 31.1	Vega	80 36.2	N38 48.3
19	214 38.1	60 14.8	05.5	262 46.1	51.6	353 24.8	50.1	299 24.7	31.1	Zuben'ubi	137 01.5	S16 07.0
20	229 40.6	75 14.7	04.4	277 49.0	51.9	8 27.3	50.1	314 27.4	31.1		SHA	Mer. Pass.
21	244 43.0	90 14.5 ..	03.3	292 51.9 ..	52.2	23 29.7 ..	50.1	329 30.0 ..	31.1		° ′	h m
22	259 45.5	105 14.4	02.2	307 54.8	52.5	38 32.2	50.1	344 32.7	31.1	Venus	207 29.9	14 59
23	274 47.9	120 14.2	01.0	322 57.7	52.7	53 34.6	50.2	359 35.3	31.1	Mars	47 50.8	1 37
	h m									Jupiter	138 46.6	19 30
Mer. Pass.	4 47.7	v −0.2	d 1.1	v 2.9	d 0.3	v 2.5	d 0.0	v 2.7	d 0.0	Saturn	84 38.4	23 06

UT	SUN GHA	Dec	MOON GHA	v	Dec	d	HP
d h	° ′	° ′	° ′	′	° ′	′	′
9 00	178 42.6	N22 23.0	237 55.6	9.1	N12 48.6	9.8	58.8
01	193 42.5	22.8	252 23.7	9.1	12 58.4	9.8	58.8
02	208 42.4	22.5	266 51.8	9.0	13 08.2	9.7	58.9
03	223 42.4 ..	22.2	281 19.8	8.9	13 17.9	9.7	58.9
04	238 42.3	21.9	295 47.7	8.7	13 27.6	9.6	58.9
05	253 42.2	21.6	310 15.4	8.7	13 37.2	9.5	59.0
06	268 42.1	N22 21.3	324 43.1	8.6	N13 46.7	9.5	59.0
07	283 42.0	21.0	339 10.7	8.5	13 56.2	9.4	59.1
M 08	298 41.9	20.7	353 38.2	8.4	14 05.6	9.3	59.1
O 09	313 41.8 ..	20.4	8 05.6	8.3	14 14.9	9.2	59.1
N 10	328 41.7	20.1	22 32.9	8.2	14 24.1	9.2	59.2
D 11	343 41.6	19.8	37 00.1	8.1	14 33.3	9.1	59.2
A 12	358 41.5	N22 19.4	51 27.2	8.0	N14 42.4	9.0	59.2
Y 13	13 41.4	19.1	65 54.2	8.0	14 51.4	8.9	59.3
14	28 41.3	18.8	80 21.2	7.8	15 00.3	8.9	59.3
15	43 41.2 ..	18.5	94 48.0	7.7	15 09.2	8.8	59.4
16	58 41.1	18.2	109 14.7	7.6	15 18.0	8.7	59.4
17	73 41.1	17.9	123 41.3	7.6	15 26.7	8.6	59.4
18	88 41.0	N22 17.6	138 07.9	7.4	N15 35.3	8.5	59.5
19	103 40.9	17.3	152 34.3	7.3	15 43.8	8.4	59.5
20	118 40.8	17.0	167 00.6	7.3	15 52.2	8.4	59.5
21	133 40.7 ..	16.7	181 26.9	7.1	16 00.6	8.2	59.6
22	148 40.6	16.4	195 53.0	7.0	16 08.8	8.2	59.6
23	163 40.5	16.1	210 19.0	7.0	16 17.0	8.1	59.7
10 00	178 40.4	N22 15.8	224 45.0	6.8	N16 25.1	7.9	59.7
01	193 40.3	15.4	239 10.8	6.8	16 33.0	7.9	59.7
02	208 40.2	15.1	253 36.6	6.6	16 40.9	7.8	59.8
03	223 40.1 ..	14.8	268 02.2	6.6	16 48.7	7.7	59.8
04	238 40.0	14.5	282 27.8	6.4	16 56.4	7.6	59.8
05	253 40.0	14.2	296 53.2	6.4	17 04.0	7.4	59.9
06	268 39.9	N22 13.9	311 18.6	6.3	N17 11.4	7.4	59.9
07	283 39.8	13.6	325 43.9	6.2	17 18.8	7.3	59.9
T 08	298 39.7	13.2	340 09.1	6.0	17 26.1	7.1	60.0
U 09	313 39.6 ..	12.9	354 34.1	6.0	17 33.2	7.1	60.0
E 10	328 39.5	12.6	8 59.1	5.9	17 40.3	6.9	60.0
S 11	343 39.4	12.3	23 24.0	5.8	17 47.2	6.9	60.1
D 12	358 39.3	N22 12.0	37 48.8	5.7	N17 54.1	6.7	60.1
A 13	13 39.3	11.6	52 13.5	5.7	18 00.8	6.6	60.1
Y 14	28 39.2	11.3	66 38.2	5.5	18 07.4	6.5	60.2
15	43 39.1 ..	11.0	81 02.7	5.4	18 13.9	6.3	60.2
16	58 39.0	10.7	95 27.1	5.4	18 20.2	6.3	60.2
17	73 38.9	10.4	109 51.5	5.2	18 26.5	6.1	60.3
18	88 38.8	N22 10.0	124 15.7	5.2	N18 32.6	6.0	60.3
19	103 38.7	09.7	138 39.9	5.1	18 38.6	5.9	60.3
20	118 38.6	09.4	153 04.0	5.0	18 44.5	5.8	60.4
21	133 38.6 ..	09.1	167 28.0	4.9	18 50.3	5.6	60.4
22	148 38.5	08.7	181 51.9	4.9	18 55.9	5.5	60.4
23	163 38.4	08.4	196 15.8	4.7	19 01.4	5.4	60.5
11 00	178 38.3	N22 08.1	210 39.5	4.7	N19 06.8	5.2	60.5
01	193 38.2	07.8	225 03.2	4.6	19 12.0	5.2	60.5
02	208 38.1	07.4	239 26.8	4.5	19 17.2	4.9	60.5
03	223 38.0 ..	07.1	253 50.3	4.5	19 22.1	4.9	60.6
04	238 38.0	06.8	268 13.8	4.3	19 27.0	4.7	60.6
05	253 37.9	06.4	282 37.1	4.3	19 31.7	4.6	60.6
06	268 37.8	N22 06.1	297 00.4	4.2	N19 36.3	4.4	60.6
W 07	283 37.7	05.8	311 23.6	4.2	19 40.7	4.3	60.7
E 08	298 37.6	05.4	325 46.8	4.1	19 45.0	4.2	60.7
D 09	313 37.5 ..	05.1	340 09.9	4.0	19 49.2	4.0	60.7
N 10	328 37.5	04.8	354 32.9	3.9	19 53.2	3.9	60.7
E 11	343 37.4	04.4	8 55.8	3.9	19 57.1	3.8	60.8
S 12	358 37.3	N22 04.1	23 18.7	3.8	N20 00.9	3.6	60.8
D 13	13 37.2	03.8	37 41.5	3.7	20 04.5	3.4	60.8
A 14	28 37.1	03.4	52 04.2	3.7	20 07.9	3.3	60.8
Y 15	43 37.0 ..	03.1	66 26.9	3.7	20 11.2	3.2	60.9
16	58 37.0	02.8	80 49.6	3.5	20 14.4	3.0	60.9
17	73 36.9	02.4	95 12.1	3.6	20 17.4	2.9	60.9
18	88 36.8	N22 02.1	109 34.7	3.4	N20 20.3	2.7	60.9
19	103 36.7	01.7	123 57.1	3.4	20 23.0	2.6	61.0
20	118 36.6	01.4	138 19.5	3.4	20 25.6	2.4	61.0
21	133 36.5 ..	01.1	152 41.9	3.3	20 28.0	2.3	61.0
22	148 36.5	00.7	167 04.2	3.3	20 30.3	2.1	61.0
23	163 36.4	00.4	181 26.5	3.2	N20 32.4	1.9	61.1
	SD 15.8	d 0.3	SD 16.1		16.4		16.6

Moonrise

Lat.	Twilight Naut.	Civil	Sunrise	9	10	11	12
°	h m	h m	h m	h m	h m	h m	h m
N 72	□	□	□	22 48	□	□	□
N 70	□	□	□	23 28	23 16	□	□
68	□	□	□	23 56	24 05	00 05	00 30
66	////	////	01 12	00 07	00 18	00 36	01 13
64	////	////	02 01	00 19	00 35	01 00	01 42
62	////	////	02 32	00 29	00 49	01 19	02 04
60	////	01 29	02 54	00 37	01 01	01 34	02 22
N 58	////	02 04	03 13	00 45	01 11	01 47	02 37
56	////	02 30	03 28	00 52	01 20	01 59	02 50
54	01 21	02 49	03 41	00 57	01 29	02 09	03 01
52	01 55	03 05	03 52	01 03	01 36	02 18	03 11
50	02 19	03 19	04 02	01 08	01 42	02 26	03 20
45	02 59	03 47	04 23	01 18	01 57	02 43	03 38
N 40	03 27	04 08	04 40	01 27	02 08	02 57	03 54
35	03 49	04 25	04 54	01 35	02 19	03 09	04 07
30	04 07	04 39	05 06	01 42	02 27	03 19	04 18
20	04 34	05 03	05 27	01 53	02 43	03 37	04 38
N 10	04 55	05 22	05 45	02 04	02 56	03 53	04 55
0	05 13	05 39	06 02	02 14	03 09	04 08	05 11
S 10	05 29	05 56	06 18	02 23	03 22	04 23	05 27
20	05 45	06 12	06 36	02 34	03 35	04 39	05 44
30	06 00	06 30	06 56	02 46	03 51	04 58	06 03
35	06 08	06 39	07 07	02 53	04 00	05 08	06 15
40	06 17	06 50	07 21	03 01	04 11	05 21	06 28
45	06 26	07 03	07 36	03 11	04 23	05 35	06 44
S 50	06 37	07 18	07 56	03 22	04 38	05 53	07 03
52	06 42	07 25	08 05	03 28	04 45	06 02	07 12
54	06 47	07 32	08 15	03 33	04 53	06 11	07 23
56	06 52	07 41	08 26	03 40	05 02	06 22	07 37
58	06 59	07 50	08 40	03 47	05 12	06 34	07 47
S 60	07 05	08 01	08 55	03 56	05 24	06 49	08 03

Moonset

Lat.	Sunset	Twilight Civil	Naut.	9	10	11	12
°	h m	h m	h m	h m	h m	h m	h m
N 72	□	□	□	18 44	□	□	□
N 70	□	□	□	18 05	20 19	□	□
68	□	□	□	17 38	19 31	21 15	22 23
66	22 55	////	////	17 18	19 00	20 32	21 39
64	22 07	////	////	17 02	18 37	20 03	21 10
62	21 38	////	////	16 48	18 19	19 41	20 48
60	21 15	22 39	////	16 37	18 03	19 24	20 30
N 58	20 57	22 05	////	16 27	17 51	19 09	20 15
56	20 42	21 40	////	16 18	17 40	18 56	20 02
54	20 29	21 21	22 47	16 11	17 30	18 45	19 51
52	20 18	21 05	22 15	16 04	17 21	18 35	19 41
50	20 08	20 51	21 52	15 58	17 14	18 26	19 32
45	19 47	20 24	21 11	15 45	16 57	18 08	19 13
N 40	19 30	20 03	20 43	15 34	16 44	17 53	18 58
35	19 16	19 45	20 21	15 25	16 32	17 40	18 45
30	19 04	19 31	20 04	15 17	16 22	17 29	18 33
20	18 43	19 08	19 37	15 03	16 05	17 10	18 14
N 10	18 26	18 48	19 15	14 51	15 50	16 53	17 57
0	18 09	18 31	18 57	14 39	15 37	16 38	17 41
S 10	17 53	18 15	18 41	14 28	15 23	16 22	17 25
20	17 35	17 59	18 26	14 16	15 08	16 05	17 08
30	17 15	17 41	18 11	14 02	14 51	15 46	16 48
35	17 04	17 31	18 03	13 54	14 41	15 35	16 36
40	16 50	17 21	17 54	13 45	14 30	15 22	16 23
45	16 35	17 08	17 45	13 35	14 17	15 07	16 07
S 50	16 16	16 53	17 34	13 22	14 00	14 49	15 48
52	16 06	16 46	17 29	13 16	13 53	14 40	15 39
54	15 56	16 39	17 24	13 10	13 45	14 30	15 29
56	15 45	16 30	17 19	13 03	13 35	14 19	15 17
58	15 31	16 21	17 13	12 54	13 25	14 07	15 04
S 60	15 16	16 11	17 06	12 45	13 13	13 52	14 48

Day	SUN Eqn. of Time 00h	12h	Mer. Pass.	MOON Mer. Pass. Upper	Lower	Age	Phase
d	m s	m s	h m	h m	h m	d	%
9	05 09	05 14	12 05	08 26	20 54	26	18
10	05 18	05 22	12 05	09 23	21 52	27	10
11	05 27	05 31	12 06	10 23	22 54	28	4

UT	ARIES	VENUS −4·2		MARS −2·5		JUPITER −2·2		SATURN +0·1		STARS		
	GHA	GHA	Dec	GHA	Dec	GHA	Dec	GHA	Dec	Name	SHA	Dec
d h	° ′	° ′	° ′	° ′	° ′	° ′	° ′	° ′	° ′		° ′	° ′
12 00	289 50.4	135 14.1 N11 59.9		338 00.6 S23 53.0		68 37.1 S14 50.2		14 38.0 S22 31.1		Acamar	315 15.9	S40 13.8
01	304 52.9	150 13.9	58.8	353 03.5	53.3	83 39.6	50.2	29 40.6	31.1	Achernar	335 24.3	S57 08.4
02	319 55.3	165 13.8	57.7	8 06.4	53.5	98 42.0	50.2	44 43.3	31.1	Acrux	173 05.5	S63 12.3
03	334 57.8	180 13.6 .. 56.6		23 09.3 .. 53.8		113 44.5 .. 50.2		59 45.9 .. 31.1		Adhara	255 10.2	S28 59.9
04	350 00.3	195 13.5	55.5	38 12.2	54.1	128 46.9	50.2	74 48.6	31.2	Aldebaran	290 45.7	N16 32.6
05	5 02.7	210 13.3	54.4	53 15.1	54.4	143 49.4	50.2	89 51.2	31.2			
06	20 05.2	225 13.2 N11 53.2		68 18.0 S23 54.6		158 51.8 S14 50.3		104 53.9 S22 31.2		Alioth	166 17.8	N55 52.0
07	35 07.7	240 13.1	52.1	83 20.9	54.9	173 54.3	50.3	119 56.5	31.2	Alkaid	152 56.2	N49 13.7
T 08	50 10.1	255 12.9	51.0	98 23.8	55.2	188 56.8	50.3	134 59.2	31.2	Al Na'ir	27 39.1	S46 52.1
H 09	65 12.6	270 12.8 .. 49.9		113 26.7 .. 55.5		203 59.2 .. 50.3		150 01.8 .. 31.2		Alnilam	275 43.2	S 1 11.5
U 10	80 15.1	285 12.6	48.8	128 29.6	55.7	219 01.7	50.3	165 04.5	31.2	Alphard	217 53.0	S 8 44.4
R 11	95 17.5	300 12.5	47.7	143 32.5	56.0	234 04.1	50.3	180 07.1	31.2			
S 12	110 20.0	315 12.3 N11 46.5		158 35.4 S23 56.3		249 06.6 S14 50.3		195 09.8 S22 31.2		Alphecca	126 07.9	N26 39.5
D 13	125 22.4	330 12.2	45.4	173 38.4	56.6	264 09.0	50.4	210 12.5	31.3	Alpheratz	357 39.8	N29 11.4
A 14	140 24.9	345 12.1	44.3	188 41.3	56.8	279 11.5	50.4	225 15.1	31.3	Altair	62 04.5	N 8 55.2
Y 15	155 27.4	0 11.9 .. 43.2		203 44.2 .. 57.1		294 13.9 .. 50.4		240 17.8 .. 31.3		Ankaa	353 12.2	S42 12.2
16	170 29.8	15 11.8	42.1	218 47.1	57.4	309 16.4	50.4	255 20.4	31.3	Antares	112 21.7	S26 28.2
17	185 32.3	30 11.6	41.0	233 50.0	57.7	324 18.8	50.4	270 23.1	31.3			
18	200 34.8	45 11.5 N11 39.8		248 52.9 S23 57.9		339 21.3 S14 50.4		285 25.7 S22 31.3		Arcturus	145 52.5	N19 05.5
19	215 37.2	60 11.4	38.7	263 55.9	58.2	354 23.7	50.4	300 28.4	31.3	Atria	107 20.0	S69 03.6
20	230 39.7	75 11.2	37.6	278 58.8	58.5	9 26.2	50.5	315 31.0	31.3	Avior	234 17.2	S59 34.3
21	245 42.2	90 11.1 .. 36.5		294 01.7 .. 58.7		24 28.6 .. 50.5		330 33.7 .. 31.3		Bellatrix	278 28.6	N 6 21.8
22	260 44.6	105 11.0	35.3	309 04.6	59.0	39 31.1	50.5	345 36.3	31.4	Betelgeuse	270 57.9	N 7 24.5
23	275 47.1	120 10.8	34.2	324 07.5	59.3	54 33.6	50.5	0 39.0	31.4			
13 00	290 49.6	135 10.7 N11 33.1		339 10.5 S23 59.6		69 36.0 S14 50.5		15 41.6 S22 31.4		Canopus	263 55.2	S52 42.4
01	305 52.0	150 10.5	32.0	354 13.4 23 59.8		84 38.5	50.5	30 44.3	31.4	Capella	280 29.8	N46 00.7
02	320 54.5	165 10.4	30.9	9 16.3 24 00.1		99 40.9	50.6	45 46.9	31.4	Deneb	49 28.7	N45 20.8
03	335 56.9	180 10.3 .. 29.7		24 19.3 .. 00.4		114 43.4 .. 50.6		60 49.6 .. 31.4		Denebola	182 30.3	N14 28.3
04	350 59.4	195 10.1	28.6	39 22.2	00.7	129 45.8	50.6	75 52.2	31.4	Diphda	348 52.4	S17 53.1
05	6 01.9	210 10.0	27.5	54 25.1	00.9	144 48.2	50.6	90 54.9	31.4			
06	21 04.3	225 09.9 N11 26.4		69 28.0 S24 01.2		159 50.7 S14 50.6		105 57.5 S22 31.4		Dubhe	193 48.0	N61 39.4
07	36 06.8	240 09.8	25.2	84 31.0	01.5	174 53.1	50.6	121 00.2	31.4	Elnath	278 08.6	N28 37.1
08	51 09.3	255 09.6	24.1	99 33.9	01.8	189 55.6	50.6	136 02.8	31.5	Eltanin	90 44.0	N51 29.5
F 09	66 11.7	270 09.5 .. 23.0		114 36.9 .. 02.1		204 58.0 .. 50.7		151 05.5 .. 31.5		Enif	33 43.5	N 9 57.6
R 10	81 14.2	285 09.4	21.9	129 39.8	02.3	220 00.5	50.7	166 08.1	31.5	Fomalhaut	15 20.0	S29 31.3
I 11	96 16.7	300 09.2	20.7	144 42.7	02.6	235 02.9	50.7	181 10.8	31.5			
D 12	111 19.1	315 09.1 N11 19.6		159 45.7 S24 02.9		250 05.4 S14 50.7		196 13.4 S22 31.5		Gacrux	171 57.1	S57 13.2
A 13	126 21.6	330 09.0	18.5	174 48.6	03.2	265 07.8	50.7	211 16.1	31.5	Gienah	175 48.8	S17 38.6
Y 14	141 24.0	345 08.9	17.3	189 51.5	03.4	280 10.3	50.7	226 18.7	31.5	Hadar	148 42.8	S60 27.8
15	156 26.5	0 08.7 .. 16.2		204 54.5 .. 03.7		295 12.7 .. 50.8		241 21.4 .. 31.5		Hamal	327 56.9	N23 32.7
16	171 29.0	15 08.6	15.1	219 57.4	04.0	310 15.2	50.8	256 24.0	31.5	Kaus Aust.	83 38.9	S34 22.4
17	186 31.4	30 08.5	14.0	235 00.4	04.3	325 17.6	50.8	271 26.7	31.6			
18	201 33.9	45 08.4 N11 12.8		250 03.3 S24 04.5		340 20.1 S14 50.8		286 29.3 S22 31.6		Kochab	137 19.7	N74 05.2
19	216 36.4	60 08.2	11.7	265 06.3	04.8	355 22.5	50.8	301 32.0	31.6	Markab	13 34.7	N15 18.2
20	231 38.8	75 08.1	10.6	280 09.2	05.1	10 24.9	50.9	316 34.6	31.6	Menkar	314 11.6	N 4 09.6
21	246 41.3	90 08.0 .. 09.4		295 12.2 .. 05.4		25 27.4 .. 50.9		331 37.3 .. 31.6		Menkent	148 03.4	S36 27.6
22	261 43.8	105 07.9	08.3	310 15.1	05.6	40 29.8	50.9	346 39.9	31.6	Miaplacidus	221 39.7	S69 47.8
23	276 46.2	120 07.8	07.2	325 18.1	05.9	55 32.3	50.9	1 42.6	31.6			
14 00	291 48.7	135 07.6 N11 06.0		340 21.0 S24 06.2		70 34.7 S14 50.9		16 45.2 S22 31.6		Mirfak	308 35.6	N49 55.2
01	306 51.2	150 07.5	04.9	355 24.0	06.5	85 37.2	50.9	31 47.9	31.6	Nunki	75 53.7	S26 16.2
02	321 53.6	165 07.4	03.8	10 26.9	06.7	100 39.6	51.0	46 50.5	31.7	Peacock	53 13.3	S56 40.3
03	336 56.1	180 07.3 .. 02.6		25 29.9 .. 07.0		115 42.0 .. 51.0		61 53.2 .. 31.7		Pollux	243 23.9	N27 58.8
04	351 58.5	195 07.2	01.5	40 32.8	07.3	130 44.5	51.0	76 55.8	31.7	Procyon	244 56.5	N 5 10.6
05	7 01.0	210 07.1 11 00.4		55 35.8	07.6	145 46.9	51.0	91 58.5	31.7			
06	22 03.5	225 06.9 N10 59.2		70 38.8 S24 07.9		160 49.4 S14 51.0		107 01.1 S22 31.7		Rasalhague	96 02.9	N12 33.1
07	37 05.9	240 06.8	58.1	85 41.7	08.1	175 51.8	51.0	122 03.8	31.7	Regulus	207 40.1	N11 52.7
S 08	52 08.4	255 06.7	57.0	100 44.7	08.4	190 54.3	51.1	137 06.4	31.7	Rigel	281 09.0	S 8 10.9
A 09	67 10.9	270 06.6 .. 55.8		115 47.7 .. 08.7		205 56.7 .. 51.1		152 09.1 .. 31.7		Rigil Kent.	139 46.8	S60 54.7
T 10	82 13.3	285 06.5	54.7	130 50.6	09.0	220 59.1	51.1	167 11.7	31.7	Sabik	102 08.3	S15 44.7
U 11	97 15.8	300 06.4	53.5	145 53.6	09.2	236 01.6	51.1	182 14.4	31.7			
R 12	112 18.3	315 06.3 N10 52.4		160 56.5 S24 09.5		251 04.0 S14 51.1		197 17.0 S22 31.8		Schedar	349 36.4	N56 38.0
D 13	127 20.7	330 06.2	51.3	175 59.5	09.8	266 06.5	51.2	212 19.7	31.8	Shaula	96 16.9	S37 06.9
A 14	142 23.2	345 06.0	50.1	191 02.5	10.1	281 08.9	51.2	227 22.3	31.8	Sirius	258 31.0	S16 44.6
Y 15	157 25.7	0 05.9 .. 49.0		206 05.5 .. 10.3		296 11.3 .. 51.2		242 25.0 .. 31.8		Spica	158 27.6	S11 15.4
16	172 28.1	15 05.8	47.9	221 08.4	10.6	311 13.8	51.2	257 27.6	31.8	Suhail	222 50.3	S43 30.6
17	187 30.6	30 05.7	46.7	236 11.4	10.9	326 16.2	51.2	272 30.3	31.8			
18	202 33.0	45 05.6 N10 45.6		251 14.4 S24 11.2		341 18.6 S14 51.3		287 32.9 S22 31.8		Vega	80 36.2	N38 48.3
19	217 35.5	60 05.5	44.4	266 17.3	11.5	356 21.1	51.3	302 35.6	31.8	Zuben'ubi	137 01.5	S16 07.0
20	232 38.0	75 05.4	43.3	281 20.3	11.7	11 23.5	51.3	317 38.2	31.8		SHA	Mer.Pass.
21	247 40.4	90 05.3 .. 42.2		296 23.3 .. 12.0		26 26.0 .. 51.3		332 40.9 .. 31.9			° ′	h m
22	262 42.9	105 05.2	41.0	311 26.3	12.3	41 28.4	51.3	347 43.5	31.9	Venus	204 21.1	14 59
23	277 45.4	120 05.1	39.9	326 29.2	12.6	56 30.8	51.4	2 46.2	31.9	Mars	48 20.9	1 23
	h m									Jupiter	138 46.5	19 18
Mer.Pass. 4 35.9		v −0.1 d 1.1		v 2.9 d 0.3		v 2.4 d 0.0		v 2.7 d 0.0		Saturn	84 52.1	22 53

SUN and MOON

UT	SUN GHA	SUN Dec	MOON GHA	v	MOON Dec	d	HP
d h	° ′	° ′	° ′	′	° ′	′	′
12 00	178 36.3	N22 00.0	195 48.7	3.2	N20 34.3	1.8	61.0
01	193 36.2	21 59.7	210 10.9	3.1	20 36.1	1.7	61.1
02	208 36.1	59.3	224 33.0	3.1	20 37.8	1.5	61.1
03	223 36.1 ..	59.0	238 55.1	3.1	20 39.3	1.3	61.1
04	238 36.0	58.6	253 17.2	3.1	20 40.6	1.2	61.1
05	253 35.9	58.3	267 39.3	3.0	20 41.8	1.0	61.1
06	268 35.8	N21 58.0	282 01.3	2.9	N20 42.8	0.9	61.1
07	283 35.7	57.6	296 23.2	3.0	20 43.7	0.7	61.2
T 08	298 35.7	57.3	310 45.2	2.9	20 44.4	0.6	61.2
H 09	313 35.6 ..	56.9	325 07.1	2.9	20 45.0	0.4	61.2
U 10	328 35.5	56.6	339 29.0	2.9	20 45.4	0.2	61.2
R 11	343 35.4	56.2	353 50.9	2.9	20 45.6	0.1	61.2
S 12	358 35.3	N21 55.9	8 12.8	2.8	N20 45.7	0.1	61.2
D 13	13 35.3	55.5	22 34.6	2.8	20 45.6	0.2	61.2
A 14	28 35.2	55.2	36 56.4	2.9	20 45.4	0.4	61.2
Y 15	43 35.1 ..	54.8	51 18.3	2.8	20 45.0	0.6	61.3
16	58 35.0	54.4	65 40.1	2.8	20 44.4	0.7	61.3
17	73 34.9	54.1	80 01.9	2.8	20 43.7	0.9	61.3
18	88 34.9	N21 53.7	94 23.7	2.8	N20 42.8	1.0	61.3
19	103 34.8	53.4	108 45.5	2.8	20 41.8	1.2	61.3
20	118 34.7	53.0	123 07.3	2.7	20 40.6	1.3	61.3
21	133 34.6 ..	52.7	137 29.0	2.8	20 39.3	1.6	61.3
22	148 34.6	52.3	151 50.8	2.8	20 37.7	1.6	61.3
23	163 34.5	52.0	166 12.6	2.9	N20 36.1	1.9	61.3
13 00	178 34.4	N21 51.6					
01	193 34.3	51.2					
02	208 34.3	50.9					
03	223 34.2 ..	50.5	A partial eclipse of				
04	238 34.1	50.2	the Sun occurs on this				
05	253 34.0	49.8	date. See page 5.				
06	268 33.9	N21 49.4	266 45.6	3.0	N20 20.0	3.0	61.3
07	283 33.9	49.1	281 07.6	2.9	20 17.0	3.0	61.3
F 08	298 33.8	48.7	295 29.5	3.0	20 14.0	3.3	61.3
R 09	313 33.7 ..	48.3	309 51.5	3.0	20 10.7	3.4	61.3
I 10	328 33.6	48.0	324 13.5	3.1	20 07.3	3.5	61.3
D 11	343 33.6	47.6	338 35.6	3.0	20 03.8	3.7	61.3
A 12	358 33.5	N21 47.2	352 57.6	3.1	N20 00.1	3.9	61.3
Y 13	13 33.4	46.9	7 19.7	3.2	19 56.2	4.0	61.3
14	28 33.4	46.5	21 41.9	3.2	19 52.2	4.1	61.3
15	43 33.3 ..	46.1	36 04.1	3.2	19 48.1	4.3	61.3
16	58 33.2	45.8	50 26.3	3.3	19 43.8	4.5	61.3
17	73 33.1	45.4	64 48.6	3.3	19 39.3	4.6	61.3
18	88 33.1	N21 45.0	79 10.9	3.4	N19 34.7	4.7	61.3
19	103 33.0	44.7	93 33.3	3.4	19 30.0	4.9	61.3
20	118 32.9	44.3	107 55.7	3.5	19 25.1	5.0	61.3
21	133 32.8 ..	43.9	122 18.2	3.5	19 20.1	5.2	61.3
22	148 32.8	43.5	136 40.7	3.5	19 14.9	5.3	61.3
23	163 32.7	43.2	151 03.2	3.7	19 09.6	5.5	61.3
14 00	178 32.6	N21 42.8	165 25.9	3.6	N19 04.1	5.6	61.3
01	193 32.6	42.4	179 48.5	3.8	18 58.5	5.8	61.3
02	208 32.5	42.0	194 11.3	3.8	18 52.7	5.8	61.3
03	223 32.4 ..	41.7	208 34.1	3.9	18 46.9	6.1	61.2
04	238 32.3	41.3	222 57.0	3.9	18 40.8	6.1	61.2
05	253 32.3	40.9	237 19.9	4.0	18 34.7	6.3	61.2
06	268 32.2	N21 40.5	251 42.9	4.0	N18 28.4	6.4	61.2
07	283 32.1	40.2	266 05.9	4.2	18 22.0	6.6	61.2
S 08	298 32.1	39.8	280 29.1	4.1	18 15.4	6.7	61.2
A 09	313 32.0 ..	39.4	294 52.2	4.3	18 08.7	6.8	61.2
T 10	328 31.9	39.0	309 15.5	4.3	18 01.9	6.9	61.1
U 11	343 31.9	38.6	323 38.8	4.4	17 55.0	7.1	61.1
R 12	358 31.8	N21 38.3	338 02.2	4.5	N17 47.9	7.2	61.1
D 13	13 31.7	37.9	352 25.7	4.6	17 40.7	7.3	61.1
A 14	28 31.6	37.5	6 49.3	4.6	17 33.4	7.4	61.1
Y 15	43 31.6 ..	37.1	21 12.9	4.7	17 26.0	7.6	61.1
16	58 31.5	36.7	35 36.6	4.8	17 18.4	7.7	61.1
17	73 31.4	36.3	50 00.4	4.9	17 10.7	7.8	61.0
18	88 31.4	N21 35.9	64 24.3	4.9	N17 02.9	7.9	61.0
19	103 31.3	35.6	78 48.2	5.0	16 55.0	8.0	61.0
20	118 31.2	35.2	93 12.2	5.1	16 47.0	8.1	61.0
21	133 31.2 ..	34.8	107 36.3	5.2	16 38.9	8.3	61.0
22	148 31.1	34.4	122 00.5	5.3	16 30.6	8.3	61.0
23	163 31.0	34.0	136 24.8	5.3	N16 22.3	8.5	60.9
	SD 15.8	d 0.4	SD 16.7		16.7		16.7

Twilight, Sunrise and Moonrise

Lat.	Twilight Naut.	Civil	Sunrise	Moonrise 12	13	14	15
°	h m	h m	h m	h m	h m	h m	h m
N 72	□	□	□	□	□		04 14
N 70	□	□	□	□	□	02 33	04 53
68	□	□	□	00 30	01 36	03 22	05 19
66	////	////	01 26	01 13	02 19	03 53	05 39
64	////	////	02 09	01 42	02 48	04 16	05 56
62	////	00 30	02 38	02 04	03 10	04 34	06 09
60	////	01 38	03 00	02 22	03 28	04 50	06 20
N 58	////	02 11	03 17	02 37	03 43	05 02	06 30
56	00 28	02 35	03 32	02 50	03 55	05 13	06 38
54	01 30	02 54	03 44	03 01	04 06	05 23	06 46
52	02 01	03 09	03 55	03 11	04 16	05 32	06 53
50	02 23	03 23	04 05	03 20	04 25	05 40	06 59
45	03 02	03 50	04 26	03 38	04 44	05 56	07 12
N 40	03 30	04 10	04 42	03 54	04 59	06 10	07 23
35	03 51	04 27	04 56	04 07	05 12	06 21	07 32
30	04 08	04 41	05 08	04 18	05 23	06 31	07 40
20	04 35	05 04	05 28	04 38	05 42	06 48	07 54
N 10	04 56	05 23	05 46	04 55	05 59	07 03	08 06
0	05 14	05 40	06 02	05 11	06 14	07 17	08 17
S 10	05 30	05 56	06 18	05 27	06 30	07 31	08 28
20	05 44	06 12	06 35	05 44	06 47	07 46	08 40
30	05 59	06 29	06 55	06 03	07 06	08 03	08 54
35	06 07	06 39	07 06	06 15	07 17	08 13	09 02
40	06 16	06 49	07 19	06 28	07 30	08 24	09 11
45	06 25	07 02	07 35	06 44	07 45	08 37	09 21
S 50	06 35	07 16	07 53	07 03	08 04	08 54	09 34
52	06 40	07 23	08 02	07 12	08 12	09 01	09 40
54	06 45	07 30	08 12	07 23	08 22	09 09	09 46
56	06 50	07 38	08 23	07 34	08 33	09 19	09 53
58	06 56	07 47	08 36	07 47	08 46	09 29	10 01
S 60	07 03	07 57	08 51	08 03	09 01	09 42	10 10

Sunset, Twilight and Moonset

Lat.	Sunset	Twilight Civil	Naut.	Moonset 12	13	14	15
°	h m	h m	h m	h m	h m	h m	h m
N 72	□	□	□	□	□		(00 06 / 23 39)
N 70	□	□	□	□	23 39	23 26	23 18
68	□	□	□	22 23	22 49	22 58	23 01
66	22 42	////	////	21 39	22 17	22 37	22 48
64	22 00	////	////	21 10	21 54	22 20	22 36
62	21 32	23 31	////	20 48	21 35	22 06	22 27
60	21 11	22 31	////	20 30	21 19	21 54	22 18
N 58	20 53	21 59	////	20 15	21 06	21 43	22 11
56	20 39	21 35	23 34	20 02	20 54	21 34	22 05
54	20 26	21 17	22 39	19 51	20 44	21 26	21 59
52	20 15	21 01	22 09	19 41	20 35	21 19	21 53
50	20 04	20 48	21 47	19 32	20 27	21 12	21 49
45	19 45	20 21	21 08	19 13	20 10	20 58	21 38
N 40	19 29	20 01	20 41	18 58	19 56	20 46	21 30
35	19 15	19 44	20 20	18 45	19 44	20 36	21 22
30	19 03	19 30	20 03	18 33	19 33	20 27	21 15
20	18 43	19 07	19 36	18 14	19 15	20 12	21 04
N 10	18 26	18 48	19 15	17 57	18 59	19 59	20 54
0	18 09	18 32	18 58	17 41	18 44	19 46	20 44
S 10	17 53	18 16	18 42	17 25	18 29	19 33	20 34
20	17 36	18 00	18 27	17 08	18 13	19 19	20 24
30	17 17	17 43	18 12	16 48	17 55	19 04	20 12
35	17 05	17 33	18 04	16 36	17 44	18 54	20 05
40	16 52	17 22	17 56	16 23	17 31	18 44	19 57
45	16 37	17 10	17 47	16 07	17 17	18 31	19 48
S 50	16 18	16 56	17 37	15 48	16 59	18 16	19 36
52	16 10	16 49	17 32	15 39	16 50	18 09	19 31
54	16 00	16 42	17 27	15 29	16 40	18 01	19 25
56	15 48	16 34	17 22	15 15	16 30	17 52	19 19
58	15 36	16 25	17 16	15 04	16 17	17 42	19 12
S 60	15 20	16 15	17 09	14 48	16 03	17 31	19 03

SUN and MOON

Day	SUN Eqn. of Time 00ʰ	12ʰ	Mer. Pass.	MOON Mer. Pass. Upper	Lower	Age	Phase
d	m s	m s	h m	h m	h m	d	%
12	05 35	05 38	12 06	11 26	23 58	29	1
13	05 42	05 46	12 06	12 29	25 01	00	0
14	05 49	05 53	12 06	13 32	01 01	01	3

2018 JULY 15, 16, 17 (SUN., MON., TUES.)

UT	ARIES	VENUS −4·2		MARS −2·6		JUPITER −2·2		SATURN +0·1		STARS		
	GHA	GHA	Dec	GHA	Dec	GHA	Dec	GHA	Dec	Name	SHA	Dec
d h	° ′	° ′	° ′	° ′	° ′	° ′	° ′	° ′	° ′		° ′	° ′
15 00	292 47.8	135 05.0	N10 38.7	341 32.2	S24 12.8	71 33.3	S14 51.4	17 48.8	S22 31.9	Acamar	315 15.9	S40 13.8
01	307 50.3	150 04.9	37.6	356 35.2	13.1	86 35.7	51.4	32 51.5	31.9	Achernar	335 24.3	S57 08.4
02	322 52.8	165 04.8	36.4	11 38.2	13.4	101 38.1	51.4	47 54.1	31.9	Acrux	173 05.5	S63 12.3
03	337 55.2	180 04.7 . .	35.3	26 41.2 . .	13.7	116 40.6 . .	51.4	62 56.8 . .	31.9	Adhara	255 10.2	S28 59.9
04	352 57.7	195 04.6	34.2	41 44.2	13.9	131 43.0	51.5	77 59.4	31.9	Aldebaran	290 45.7	N16 32.6
05	8 00.2	210 04.5	33.0	56 47.1	14.2	146 45.4	51.5	93 02.1	31.9			
06	23 02.6	225 04.4	N10 31.9	71 50.1	S24 14.5	161 47.9	S14 51.5	108 04.7	S22 31.9	Alioth	166 17.8	N55 52.0
07	38 05.1	240 04.3	30.7	86 53.1	14.8	176 50.3	51.5	123 07.4	32.0	Alkaid	152 56.2	N49 13.7
08	53 07.5	255 04.2	29.6	101 56.1	15.1	191 52.7	51.5	138 10.0	32.0	Al Na'ir	27 39.1	S46 52.1
S 09	68 10.0	270 04.1 . .	28.4	116 59.1 . .	15.3	206 55.2 . .	51.6	153 12.7 . .	32.0	Alnilam	275 43.2	S 1 11.5
U 10	83 12.5	285 04.0	27.3	132 02.1	15.6	221 57.6	51.6	168 15.3	32.0	Alphard	217 53.0	S 8 44.3
N 11	98 14.9	300 03.9	26.1	147 05.1	15.9	237 00.0	51.6	183 17.9	32.0			
D 12	113 17.4	315 03.8	N10 25.0	162 08.1	S24 16.2	252 02.5	S14 51.6	198 20.6	S22 32.0	Alphecca	126 07.9	N26 39.5
A 13	128 19.9	330 03.7	23.9	177 11.0	16.4	267 04.9	51.6	213 23.2	32.0	Alpheratz	357 39.8	N29 11.4
Y 14	143 22.3	345 03.6	22.7	192 14.0	16.7	282 07.3	51.7	228 25.9	32.0	Altair	62 04.5	N 8 55.2
15	158 24.8	0 03.5 . .	21.6	207 17.0 . .	17.0	297 09.8 . .	51.7	243 28.5 . .	32.0	Ankaa	353 12.2	S42 12.2
16	173 27.3	15 03.4	20.4	222 20.0	17.3	312 12.2	51.7	258 31.2	32.0	Antares	112 21.7	S26 28.2
17	188 29.7	30 03.3	19.3	237 23.0	17.6	327 14.6	51.7	273 33.8	32.1			
18	203 32.2	45 03.2	N10 18.1	252 26.0	S24 17.8	342 17.1	S14 51.8	288 36.5	S22 32.1	Arcturus	145 52.5	N19 05.5
19	218 34.6	60 03.1	17.0	267 29.0	18.1	357 19.5	51.8	303 39.1	32.1	Atria	107 20.0	S69 03.6
20	233 37.1	75 03.0	15.8	282 32.0	18.4	12 21.9	51.8	318 41.8	32.1	Avior	234 17.2	S59 34.2
21	248 39.6	90 02.9 . .	14.7	297 35.0 . .	18.7	27 24.3 . .	51.8	333 44.4 . .	32.1	Bellatrix	278 28.6	N 6 21.8
22	263 42.0	105 02.8	13.5	312 38.0	18.9	42 26.8	51.8	348 47.1	32.1	Betelgeuse	270 57.9	N 7 24.5
23	278 44.5	120 02.8	12.4	327 41.0	19.2	57 29.2	51.9	3 49.7	32.1			
16 00	293 47.0	135 02.7	N10 11.2	342 44.0	S24 19.5	72 31.6	S14 51.9	18 52.4	S22 32.1	Canopus	263 55.1	S52 42.4
01	308 49.4	150 02.6	10.1	357 47.0	19.8	87 34.1	51.9	33 55.0	32.1	Capella	280 29.7	N46 00.7
02	323 51.9	165 02.5	08.9	12 50.0	20.1	102 36.5	51.9	48 57.7	32.2	Deneb	49 28.7	N45 20.8
03	338 54.4	180 02.4 . .	07.8	27 53.1 . .	20.3	117 38.9 . .	52.0	64 00.3 . .	32.2	Denebola	182 30.3	N14 28.3
04	353 56.8	195 02.3	06.6	42 56.1	20.6	132 41.3	52.0	79 02.9	32.2	Diphda	348 52.4	S17 53.1
05	8 59.3	210 02.2	05.5	57 59.1	20.9	147 43.8	52.0	94 05.6	32.2			
06	24 01.8	225 02.1	N10 04.3	73 02.1	S24 21.2	162 46.2	S14 52.0	109 08.2	S22 32.2	Dubhe	193 48.0	N61 39.4
07	39 04.2	240 02.1	03.2	88 05.1	21.4	177 48.6	52.0	124 10.9	32.2	Elnath	278 08.6	N28 37.1
08	54 06.7	255 02.0	02.0	103 08.1	21.7	192 51.0	52.1	139 13.5	32.2	Eltanin	90 44.0	N51 29.5
M 09	69 09.1	270 01.9	10 00.8	118 11.1 . .	22.0	207 53.5 . .	52.1	154 16.2 . .	32.2	Enif	33 43.4	N 9 57.6
O 10	84 11.6	285 01.8	9 59.7	133 14.1	22.3	222 55.9	52.1	169 18.8	32.2	Fomalhaut	15 20.0	S29 31.3
N 11	99 14.1	300 01.7	58.5	148 17.1	22.6	237 58.3	52.1	184 21.5	32.2			
D 12	114 16.5	315 01.6	N 9 57.4	163 20.2	S24 22.8	253 00.7	S14 52.2	199 24.1	S22 32.3	Gacrux	171 57.1	S57 13.1
A 13	129 19.0	330 01.6	56.2	178 23.2	23.1	268 03.2	52.2	214 26.8	32.3	Gienah	175 48.8	S17 38.6
Y 14	144 21.5	345 01.5	55.1	193 26.2	23.4	283 05.6	52.2	229 29.4	32.3	Hadar	148 42.8	S60 27.8
15	159 23.9	0 01.4 . .	53.9	208 29.2 . .	23.7	298 08.0 . .	52.2	244 32.1 . .	32.3	Hamal	327 56.9	N23 32.8
16	174 26.4	15 01.3	52.8	223 32.2	23.9	313 10.4	52.3	259 34.7	32.3	Kaus Aust.	83 38.8	S34 22.4
17	189 28.9	30 01.2	51.6	238 35.3	24.2	328 12.9	52.3	274 37.3	32.3			
18	204 31.3	45 01.2	N 9 50.4	253 38.3	S24 24.5	343 15.3	S14 52.3	289 40.0	S22 32.3	Kochab	137 19.8	N74 05.2
19	219 33.8	60 01.1	49.3	268 41.3	24.8	358 17.7	52.3	304 42.6	32.3	Markab	13 34.7	N15 18.2
20	234 36.3	75 01.0	48.1	283 44.3	25.0	13 20.1	52.4	319 45.3	32.3	Menkar	314 11.6	N 4 09.6
21	249 38.7	90 00.9 . .	47.0	298 47.3 . .	25.3	28 22.5 . .	52.4	334 47.9 . .	32.4	Menkent	148 03.4	S36 27.6
22	264 41.2	105 00.8	45.8	313 50.4	25.6	43 25.0	52.4	349 50.6	32.4	Miaplacidus	221 39.8	S69 47.7
23	279 43.6	120 00.8	44.7	328 53.4	25.9	58 27.4	52.4	4 53.2	32.4			
17 00	294 46.1	135 00.7	N 9 43.5	343 56.4	S24 26.2	73 29.8	S14 52.5	19 55.9	S22 32.4	Mirfak	308 35.6	N49 55.2
01	309 48.6	150 00.6	42.3	358 59.5	26.4	88 32.2	52.5	34 58.5	32.4	Nunki	75 53.7	S26 16.2
02	324 51.0	165 00.6	41.2	14 02.5	26.7	103 34.6	52.5	50 01.1	32.4	Peacock	53 13.3	S56 40.3
03	339 53.5	180 00.5 . .	40.0	29 05.5 . .	27.0	118 37.1 . .	52.5	65 03.8 . .	32.4	Pollux	243 23.9	N27 58.8
04	354 56.0	195 00.4	38.9	44 08.5	27.3	133 39.5	52.6	80 06.4	32.4	Procyon	244 56.5	N 5 10.6
05	9 58.4	210 00.4	37.7	59 11.6	27.5	148 41.9	52.6	95 09.1	32.4			
06	25 00.9	225 00.3	N 9 36.5	74 14.6	S24 27.8	163 44.3	S14 52.6	110 11.7	S22 32.4	Rasalhague	96 02.9	N12 33.1
07	40 03.4	240 00.2	35.4	89 17.6	28.1	178 46.7	52.6	125 14.4	32.5	Regulus	207 40.1	N11 52.7
08	55 05.8	255 00.1	34.2	104 20.7	28.4	193 49.2	52.7	140 17.0	32.5	Rigel	281 09.0	S 8 10.9
T 09	70 08.3	270 00.1 . .	33.1	119 23.7 . .	28.6	208 51.6 . .	52.7	155 19.7 . .	32.5	Rigil Kent.	139 46.8	S60 54.7
U 10	85 10.7	285 00.0	31.9	134 26.8	28.9	223 54.0	52.7	170 22.3	32.5	Sabik	102 08.3	S15 44.7
E 11	100 13.2	299 59.9	30.7	149 29.8	29.2	238 56.4	52.7	185 24.9	32.5			
S 12	115 15.7	314 59.9	N 9 29.6	164 32.8	S24 29.5	253 58.8	S14 52.8	200 27.6	S22 32.5	Schedar	349 36.4	N56 38.0
D 13	130 18.1	329 59.8	28.4	179 35.9	29.8	269 01.2	52.8	215 30.2	32.5	Shaula	96 16.9	S37 06.9
A 14	145 20.6	344 59.7	27.2	194 38.9	30.0	284 03.7	52.8	230 32.9	32.5	Sirius	258 31.0	S16 44.6
Y 15	160 23.1	359 59.7 . .	26.1	209 41.9 . .	30.3	299 06.1 . .	52.8	245 35.5 . .	32.5	Spica	158 27.6	S11 15.3
16	175 25.5	14 59.6	24.9	224 45.0	30.6	314 08.5	52.9	260 38.2	32.5	Suhail	222 50.3	S43 30.5
17	190 28.0	29 59.6	23.7	239 48.0	30.9	329 10.9	52.9	275 40.8	32.6			
18	205 30.5	44 59.5	N 9 22.6	254 51.1	S24 31.1	344 13.3	S14 52.9	290 43.4	S22 32.6	Vega	80 36.2	N38 48.3
19	220 32.9	59 59.4	21.4	269 54.1	31.4	359 15.7	52.9	305 46.1	32.6	Zuben'ubi	137 01.5	S16 07.0
20	235 35.4	74 59.4	20.2	284 57.2	31.7	14 18.2	53.0	320 48.7	32.6		SHA	Mer.Pass.
21	250 37.9	89 59.3 . .	19.1	300 00.2 . .	32.0	29 20.6 . .	53.0	335 51.4 . .	32.6		° ′	h m
22	265 40.3	104 59.2	17.9	315 03.3	32.2	44 23.0	53.0	350 54.0	32.6	Venus	201 15.7	15 00
23	280 42.8	119 59.2	16.7	330 06.3	32.5	59 25.4	53.0	5 56.7	32.6	Mars	48 57.1	1 09
	h m									Jupiter	138 44.7	19 07
Mer.Pass. 4 24.1		v −0.1	d 1.2	v 3.0	d 0.3	v 2.4	d 0.0	v 2.6	d 0.0	Saturn	85 05.4	22 41

UT	SUN GHA	SUN Dec	MOON GHA	v	Dec	d	HP
d h	° ′	° ′	° ′	′	° ′	′	′
15 00	178 31.0	N21 33.6	150 49.1	5.4	N16 13.8	8.6	60.9
01	193 30.9	33.2	165 13.5	5.6	16 05.2	8.7	60.9
02	208 30.8	32.8	179 38.1	5.6	15 56.5	8.7	60.9
03	223 30.8 . .	32.4	194 02.7	5.6	15 47.8	8.9	60.8
04	238 30.7	32.1	208 27.3	5.8	15 38.9	9.0	60.8
05	253 30.6	31.7	222 52.1	5.9	15 29.9	9.1	60.8
06	268 30.6	N21 31.3	237 17.0	5.9	N15 20.8	9.2	60.8
07	283 30.5	30.9	251 41.9	6.0	15 11.6	9.2	60.7
08	298 30.5	30.5	266 06.9	6.2	15 02.4	9.4	60.7
S 09	313 30.4 . .	30.1	280 32.1	6.2	14 53.0	9.5	60.7
U 10	328 30.3	29.7	294 57.3	6.3	14 43.5	9.5	60.7
N 11	343 30.3	29.3	309 22.6	6.3	14 34.0	9.7	60.6
D 12	358 30.2	N21 28.9	323 47.9	6.5	N14 24.3	9.7	60.6
A 13	13 30.1	28.5	338 13.4	6.6	14 14.6	9.8	60.6
Y 14	28 30.1	28.1	352 39.0	6.6	14 04.8	9.9	60.6
15	43 30.0 . .	27.7	7 04.6	6.7	13 54.9	10.0	60.5
16	58 29.9	27.3	21 30.3	6.9	13 44.9	10.0	60.5
17	73 29.9	26.9	35 56.2	6.9	13 34.9	10.2	60.5
18	88 29.8	N21 26.5	50 22.1	7.0	N13 24.7	10.2	60.5
19	103 29.8	26.1	64 48.1	7.1	13 14.5	10.3	60.4
20	118 29.7	25.7	79 14.2	7.2	13 04.2	10.3	60.4
21	133 29.6 . .	25.3	93 40.4	7.2	12 53.9	10.5	60.4
22	148 29.6	24.9	108 06.6	7.4	12 43.4	10.5	60.3
23	163 29.5	24.5	122 33.0	7.4	12 32.9	10.6	60.3
16 00	178 29.5	N21 24.1	136 59.4	7.5	N12 22.3	10.6	60.3
01	193 29.4	23.7	151 25.9	7.7	12 11.7	10.7	60.2
02	208 29.3	23.3	165 52.6	7.7	12 01.0	10.8	60.2
03	223 29.3 . .	22.9	180 19.3	7.8	11 50.2	10.8	60.2
04	238 29.2	22.4	194 46.1	7.8	11 39.4	10.9	60.2
05	253 29.2	22.0	209 12.9	8.0	11 28.5	11.0	60.1
06	268 29.1	N21 21.6	223 39.9	8.1	N11 17.5	11.0	60.1
07	283 29.0	21.2	238 07.0	8.1	11 06.5	11.0	60.1
08	298 29.0	20.8	252 34.1	8.2	10 55.5	11.2	60.0
M 09	313 28.9 . .	20.4	267 01.3	8.3	10 44.3	11.1	60.0
O 10	328 28.9	20.0	281 28.6	8.4	10 33.2	11.3	60.0
N 11	343 28.8	19.6	295 56.0	8.5	10 21.9	11.2	59.9
D 12	358 28.7	N21 19.2	310 23.5	8.5	N10 10.7	11.4	59.9
A 13	13 28.7	18.8	324 51.0	8.7	9 59.3	11.3	59.9
Y 14	28 28.6	18.3	339 18.7	8.7	9 48.0	11.4	59.8
15	43 28.6 . .	17.9	353 46.4	8.8	9 36.6	11.5	59.8
16	58 28.5	17.5	8 14.2	8.9	9 25.1	11.5	59.8
17	73 28.5	17.1	22 42.1	9.0	9 13.6	11.5	59.7
18	88 28.4	N21 16.7	37 10.1	9.0	N 9 02.1	11.6	59.7
19	103 28.3	16.3	51 38.1	9.1	8 50.5	11.6	59.6
20	118 28.3	15.8	66 06.2	9.2	8 38.9	11.7	59.6
21	133 28.2 . .	15.4	80 34.4	9.3	8 27.2	11.7	59.6
22	148 28.2	15.0	95 02.7	9.4	8 15.5	11.7	59.5
23	163 28.1	14.6	109 31.1	9.4	8 03.8	11.8	59.5
17 00	178 28.1	N21 14.2	123 59.5	9.5	N 7 52.0	11.7	59.5
01	193 28.0	13.7	138 28.0	9.6	7 40.3	11.8	59.4
02	208 28.0	13.3	152 56.6	9.7	7 28.5	11.9	59.4
03	223 27.9 . .	12.9	167 25.3	9.7	7 16.6	11.9	59.4
04	238 27.8	12.5	181 54.0	9.8	7 04.7	11.8	59.3
05	253 27.8	12.1	196 22.8	9.9	6 52.9	12.0	59.3
06	268 27.7	N21 11.6	210 51.7	10.0	N 6 40.9	11.9	59.2
07	283 27.7	11.2	225 20.7	10.0	6 29.0	12.0	59.2
08	298 27.6	10.8	239 49.7	10.1	6 17.0	11.9	59.2
T 09	313 27.6 . .	10.4	254 18.8	10.1	6 05.1	12.0	59.1
U 10	328 27.5	09.9	268 47.9	10.3	5 53.1	12.0	59.1
E 11	343 27.5	09.5	283 17.2	10.3	5 41.1	12.1	59.1
S 12	358 27.4	N21 09.1	297 46.5	10.3	N 5 29.0	12.0	59.0
D 13	13 27.4	08.7	312 15.8	10.5	5 17.0	12.1	59.0
A 14	28 27.3	08.2	326 45.3	10.5	5 04.9	12.0	58.9
Y 15	43 27.3 . .	07.8	341 14.8	10.5	4 52.9	12.1	58.9
16	58 27.2	07.4	355 44.3	10.6	4 40.8	12.1	58.9
17	73 27.2	06.9	10 13.9	10.7	4 28.7	12.1	58.8
18	88 27.1	N21 06.5	24 43.6	10.8	N 4 16.6	12.1	58.8
19	103 27.1	06.1	39 13.4	10.8	4 04.5	12.1	58.8
20	118 27.0	05.6	53 43.2	10.8	3 52.4	12.1	58.7
21	133 27.0 . .	05.2	68 13.0	11.0	3 40.3	12.1	58.7
22	148 26.9	04.8	82 43.0	11.0	3 28.2	12.1	58.6
23	163 26.9	04.3	97 13.0	11.0	N 3 16.1	12.1	58.6
	SD 15.8	d 0.4	SD 16.5		16.3		16.1

Lat.	Twilight Naut.	Twilight Civil	Sunrise	Moonrise 15	Moonrise 16	Moonrise 17	Moonrise 18
°	h m	h m	h m	h m	h m	h m	h m
N 72	▭	▭	▭	04 14	06 40	08 47	10 45
N 70	▭	▭	▭	04 53	06 59	08 56	10 46
68	▭	▭	▭	05 19	07 14	09 03	10 47
66	////	////	01 39	05 39	07 26	09 09	10 48
64	////	////	02 18	05 56	07 37	09 15	10 48
62	////	00 56	02 45	06 09	07 45	09 19	10 49
60	////	01 48	03 05	06 20	07 53	09 23	10 50
N 58	////	02 18	03 22	06 30	07 59	09 26	10 50
56	00 52	02 41	03 36	06 38	08 05	09 29	10 50
54	01 39	02 59	03 48	06 46	08 10	09 32	10 51
52	02 07	03 14	03 59	06 53	08 14	09 34	10 51
50	02 28	03 27	04 09	06 59	08 19	09 36	10 51
45	03 06	03 53	04 28	07 12	08 28	09 41	10 52
N 40	03 33	04 13	04 44	07 23	08 35	09 45	10 52
35	03 54	04 29	04 58	07 32	08 41	09 48	10 53
30	04 10	04 43	05 10	07 40	08 47	09 51	10 53
20	04 37	05 05	05 29	07 54	08 57	09 57	10 54
N 10	04 57	05 24	05 47	08 06	09 05	10 01	10 55
0	05 14	05 40	06 02	08 17	09 13	10 06	10 55
S 10	05 30	05 56	06 18	08 28	09 21	10 10	10 56
20	05 44	06 11	06 35	08 40	09 29	10 14	10 57
30	05 59	06 28	06 54	08 54	09 39	10 20	10 57
35	06 06	06 38	07 05	09 02	09 44	10 23	10 58
40	06 14	06 48	07 18	09 11	09 51	10 26	10 58
45	06 23	07 00	07 33	09 21	09 58	10 30	10 59
S 50	06 33	07 14	07 51	09 34	10 07	10 35	11 00
52	06 38	07 20	07 59	09 40	10 11	10 37	11 00
54	06 43	07 27	08 09	09 46	10 15	10 39	11 00
56	06 48	07 35	08 20	09 53	10 20	10 42	11 01
58	06 53	07 44	08 32	10 01	10 25	10 44	11 01
S 60	06 59	07 54	08 47	10 10	10 31	10 48	11 02

Lat.	Sunset	Twilight Civil	Twilight Naut.	Moonset 15	Moonset 16	Moonset 17	Moonset 18
°	h m	h m	h m	h m	h m	h m	h m
N 72	▭	▭	▭	{ 00 06 / 23 39 }	23 23	23 10	22 57
N 70	▭	▭	▭	23 18	23 12	23 06	23 00
68	▭	▭	▭	23 01	23 02	23 02	23 01
66	22 29	////	////	22 48	22 55	22 59	23 03
64	21 52	////	////	22 36	22 48	22 57	23 04
62	21 26	23 10	////	22 27	22 42	22 55	23 05
60	21 05	22 22	////	22 18	22 37	22 53	23 06
N 58	20 49	21 52	////	22 11	22 33	22 51	23 07
56	20 35	21 30	23 15	22 05	22 29	22 49	23 08
54	20 23	21 12	22 31	21 59	22 25	22 48	23 09
52	20 12	20 58	22 03	21 53	22 22	22 47	23 10
50	20 03	20 45	21 43	21 49	22 19	22 46	23 10
45	19 43	20 19	21 05	21 38	22 13	22 43	23 11
N 40	19 27	19 59	20 39	21 30	22 07	22 41	23 13
35	19 14	19 43	20 18	21 22	22 02	22 39	23 13
30	19 02	19 29	20 01	21 15	21 58	22 37	23 14
20	18 43	19 07	19 35	21 04	21 51	22 35	23 16
N 10	18 25	18 48	19 15	20 54	21 45	22 32	23 17
0	18 10	18 32	18 58	20 44	21 38	22 30	23 18
S 10	17 54	18 16	18 42	20 34	21 32	22 27	23 19
20	17 37	18 01	18 28	20 24	21 26	22 24	23 21
30	17 18	17 44	18 14	20 12	21 18	22 21	23 22
35	17 07	17 35	18 06	20 05	21 14	22 20	23 23
40	16 55	17 25	17 58	19 57	21 09	22 17	23 24
45	16 40	17 13	17 49	19 48	21 03	22 15	23 25
S 50	16 22	16 59	17 39	19 36	20 56	22 12	23 26
52	16 13	16 52	17 35	19 31	20 52	22 11	23 26
54	16 03	16 45	17 30	19 25	20 49	22 09	23 27
56	15 53	16 37	17 25	19 19	20 45	22 08	23 28
58	15 40	16 29	17 19	19 12	20 40	22 06	23 29
S 60	15 26	16 19	17 13	19 03	20 35	22 04	23 29

Day	SUN Eqn. of Time 00ʰ	SUN Eqn. of Time 12ʰ	SUN Mer. Pass.	MOON Mer. Pass. Upper	MOON Mer. Pass. Lower	Age	Phase
d	m s	m s	h m	h m	h m	d	%
15	05 56	05 59	12 06	14 31	02 02	02	8
16	06 02	06 05	12 06	15 26	02 59	03	16
17	06 08	06 10	12 06	16 18	03 52	04	26

2018 JULY 18, 19, 20 (WED., THURS., FRI.)

UT	ARIES	VENUS −4·2		MARS −2·7		JUPITER −2·2		SATURN +0·1		STARS		
	GHA	GHA	Dec	GHA	Dec	GHA	Dec	GHA	Dec	Name	SHA	Dec
d h	° ′	° ′	° ′	° ′	° ′	° ′	° ′	° ′	° ′		° ′	° ′
18 00	295 45.2	134 59.1	N 9 15.6	345 09.4	S24 32.8	74 27.8	S14 53.1	20 59.3	S22 32.6	Acamar	315 15.9	S40 13.7
01	310 47.7	149 59.1	14.4	0 12.4	33.1	89 30.2	53.1	36 01.9	32.6	Achernar	335 24.2	S57 08.4
02	325 50.2	164 59.0	13.2	15 15.5	33.3	104 32.6	53.1	51 04.6	32.7	Acrux	173 05.6	S63 12.3
03	340 52.6	179 59.0	. . 12.1	30 18.5	. . 33.6	119 35.1	. . 53.1	66 07.2	. . 32.7	Adhara	255 10.2	S28 59.9
04	355 55.1	194 58.9	10.9	45 21.6	33.9	134 37.5	53.2	81 09.9	32.7	Aldebaran	290 45.6	N16 32.6
05	10 57.6	209 58.8	09.7	60 24.6	34.2	149 39.9	53.2	96 12.5	32.7			
06	26 00.0	224 58.8	N 9 08.6	75 27.7	S24 34.4	164 42.3	S14 53.2	111 15.2	S22 32.7	Alioth	166 17.8	N55 52.0
W 07	41 02.5	239 58.7	07.4	90 30.7	34.7	179 44.7	53.3	126 17.8	32.7	Alkaid	152 56.2	N49 13.7
E 08	56 05.0	254 58.7	06.2	105 33.8	35.0	194 47.1	53.3	141 20.4	32.7	Al Na'ir	27 39.0	S46 52.1
D 09	71 07.4	269 58.6	. . 05.1	120 36.8	. . 35.3	209 49.5	. . 53.3	156 23.1	. . 32.7	Alnilam	275 43.1	S 1 11.5
N 10	86 09.9	284 58.6	03.9	135 39.9	35.5	224 51.9	53.3	171 25.7	32.7	Alphard	217 53.0	S 8 44.3
N 11	101 12.4	299 58.5	02.7	150 43.0	35.8	239 54.3	53.4	186 28.4	32.7			
S 12	116 14.8	314 58.5	N 9 01.6	165 46.0	S24 36.1	254 56.7	S14 53.4	201 31.0	S22 32.8	Alphecca	126 07.9	N26 39.5
S 13	131 17.3	329 58.4	9 00.4	180 49.1	36.4	269 59.2	53.4	216 33.7	32.8	Alpheratz	357 39.7	N29 11.4
D 14	146 19.7	344 58.4	8 59.2	195 52.1	36.6	285 01.6	53.5	231 36.3	32.8	Altair	62 04.5	N 8 55.2
A 15	161 22.2	359 58.3	. . 58.0	210 55.2	. . 36.9	300 04.0	. . 53.5	246 38.9	. . 32.8	Ankaa	353 12.2	S42 12.2
Y 16	176 24.7	14 58.3	56.9	225 58.3	37.2	315 06.4	53.5	261 41.6	32.8	Antares	112 21.8	S26 28.2
17	191 27.1	29 58.2	55.7	241 01.3	37.5	330 08.8	53.5	276 44.2	32.8			
18	206 29.6	44 58.2	N 8 54.5	256 04.4	S24 37.7	345 11.2	S14 53.6	291 46.9	S22 32.8	Arcturus	145 52.5	N19 05.5
19	221 32.1	59 58.1	53.4	271 07.5	38.0	0 13.6	53.6	306 49.5	32.8	Atria	107 20.0	S69 03.6
20	236 34.5	74 58.1	52.2	286 10.5	38.3	15 16.0	53.6	321 52.1	32.8	Avior	234 17.2	S59 34.2
21	251 37.0	89 58.0	. . 51.0	301 13.6	. . 38.6	30 18.4	. . 53.7	336 54.8	. . 32.8	Bellatrix	278 28.6	N 6 21.8
22	266 39.5	104 58.0	49.8	316 16.7	38.8	45 20.8	53.7	351 57.4	32.9	Betelgeuse	270 57.9	N 7 24.5
23	281 41.9	119 57.9	48.7	331 19.7	39.1	60 23.2	53.7	7 00.1	32.9			
19 00	296 44.4	134 57.9	N 8 47.5	346 22.8	S24 39.4	75 25.6	S14 53.7	22 02.7	S22 32.9	Canopus	263 55.1	S52 42.3
01	311 46.8	149 57.9	46.3	1 25.9	39.7	90 28.0	53.8	37 05.3	32.9	Capella	280 29.7	N46 00.7
02	326 49.3	164 57.8	45.1	16 28.9	39.9	105 30.5	53.8	52 08.0	32.9	Deneb	49 28.6	N45 20.8
03	341 51.8	179 57.8	. . 44.0	31 32.0	. . 40.2	120 32.9	. . 53.8	67 10.6	. . 32.9	Denebola	182 30.3	N14 28.3
04	356 54.2	194 57.7	42.8	46 35.1	40.5	135 35.3	53.9	82 13.3	32.9	Diphda	348 52.3	S17 53.1
05	11 56.7	209 57.7	41.6	61 38.2	40.7	150 37.7	53.9	97 15.9	32.9			
06	26 59.2	224 57.6	N 8 40.4	76 41.2	S24 41.0	165 40.1	S14 53.9	112 18.6	S22 32.9	Dubhe	193 48.0	N61 39.4
T 07	42 01.6	239 57.6	39.3	91 44.3	41.3	180 42.5	53.9	127 21.2	32.9	Elnath	278 08.6	N28 37.1
H 08	57 04.1	254 57.6	38.1	106 47.4	41.6	195 44.9	54.0	142 23.8	33.0	Eltanin	90 44.1	N51 29.5
U 09	72 06.6	269 57.5	. . 36.9	121 50.5	. . 41.8	210 47.3	. . 54.0	157 26.5	. . 33.0	Enif	33 43.4	N 9 57.7
R 10	87 09.0	284 57.5	35.7	136 53.5	42.1	225 49.7	54.0	172 29.1	33.0	Fomalhaut	15 19.9	S29 31.3
S 11	102 11.5	299 57.5	34.5	151 56.6	42.4	240 52.1	54.1	187 31.8	33.0			
D 12	117 14.0	314 57.4	N 8 33.4	166 59.7	S24 42.7	255 54.5	S14 54.1	202 34.4	S22 33.0	Gacrux	171 57.2	S57 13.1
A 13	132 16.4	329 57.4	32.2	182 02.8	42.9	270 56.9	54.1	217 37.0	33.0	Gienah	175 48.9	S17 38.6
A 14	147 18.9	344 57.3	31.0	197 05.9	43.2	285 59.3	54.2	232 39.7	33.0	Hadar	148 42.8	S60 27.8
Y 15	162 21.3	359 57.3	. . 29.8	212 08.9	. . 43.5	301 01.7	. . 54.2	247 42.3	. . 33.0	Hamal	327 56.9	N23 32.8
16	177 23.8	14 57.3	28.7	227 12.0	43.7	316 04.1	54.2	262 44.9	33.0	Kaus Aust.	83 38.9	S34 22.4
17	192 26.3	29 57.2	27.5	242 15.1	44.0	331 06.5	54.2	277 47.6	33.0			
18	207 28.7	44 57.2	N 8 26.3	257 18.2	S24 44.3	346 08.9	S14 54.3	292 50.2	S22 33.1	Kochab	137 19.8	N74 05.2
19	222 31.2	59 57.2	25.1	272 21.3	44.6	1 11.3	54.3	307 52.9	33.1	Markab	13 34.7	N15 18.2
20	237 33.7	74 57.1	23.9	287 24.4	44.8	16 13.7	54.3	322 55.5	33.1	Menkar	314 11.6	N 4 09.6
21	252 36.1	89 57.1	. . 22.8	302 27.5	. . 45.1	31 16.1	. . 54.4	337 58.1	. . 33.1	Menkent	148 03.4	S36 27.6
22	267 38.6	104 57.1	21.6	317 30.5	45.4	46 18.5	54.4	353 00.8	33.1	Miaplacidus	221 39.8	S69 47.7
23	282 41.1	119 57.1	20.4	332 33.6	45.6	61 20.9	54.4	8 03.4	33.1			
20 00	297 43.5	134 57.0	N 8 19.2	347 36.7	S24 45.9	76 23.3	S14 54.5	23 06.1	S22 33.1	Mirfak	308 35.6	N49 55.2
01	312 46.0	149 57.0	18.0	2 39.8	46.2	91 25.7	54.5	38 08.7	33.1	Nunki	75 53.7	S26 16.2
02	327 48.5	164 57.0	16.9	17 42.9	46.5	106 28.1	54.5	53 11.3	33.1	Peacock	53 13.3	S56 40.3
03	342 50.9	179 56.9	. . 15.7	32 46.0	. . 46.7	121 30.5	. . 54.6	68 14.0	. . 33.1	Pollux	243 23.9	N27 58.8
04	357 53.4	194 56.9	14.5	47 49.1	47.0	136 32.9	54.6	83 16.6	33.2	Procyon	244 56.5	N 5 10.6
05	12 55.8	209 56.9	13.3	62 52.2	47.3	151 35.3	54.6	98 19.3	33.2			
06	27 58.3	224 56.9	N 8 12.1	77 55.3	S24 47.5	166 37.7	S14 54.6	113 21.9	S22 33.2	Rasalhague	96 03.0	N12 33.1
07	43 00.8	239 56.8	10.9	92 58.4	47.8	181 40.1	54.7	128 24.5	33.2	Regulus	207 40.1	N11 52.7
08	58 03.2	254 56.8	09.8	108 01.5	48.1	196 42.5	54.7	143 27.2	33.2	Rigel	281 09.0	S 8 10.9
F 09	73 05.7	269 56.8	. . 08.6	123 04.6	. .* 48.3	211 44.9	. . 54.7	158 29.8	. . 33.2	Rigil Kent.	139 46.8	S60 54.7
R 10	88 08.2	284 56.7	07.4	138 07.6	48.6	226 47.3	54.8	173 32.4	33.2	Sabik	102 08.3	S15 44.7
I 11	103 10.6	299 56.7	06.2	153 10.7	48.9	241 49.7	54.8	188 35.1	33.2			
D 12	118 13.1	314 56.7	N 8 05.0	168 13.8	S24 49.2	256 52.1	S14 54.8	203 37.7	S22 33.2	Schedar	349 36.4	N56 38.0
A 13	133 15.6	329 56.7	03.8	183 16.9	49.4	271 54.4	54.9	218 40.4	33.2	Shaula	96 16.9	S37 06.9
Y 14	148 18.0	344 56.7	02.6	198 20.0	49.7	286 56.8	54.9	233 43.0	33.3	Sirius	258 31.0	S16 44.6
15	163 20.5	359 56.6	. . 01.5	213 23.1	. . 50.0	301 59.2	. . 54.9	248 45.6	. . 33.3	Spica	158 27.6	S11 15.3
16	178 22.9	14 56.6	8 00.3	228 26.2	50.2	317 01.6	55.0	263 48.3	33.3	Suhail	222 50.3	S43 30.5
17	193 25.4	29 56.6	7 59.1	243 29.3	50.5	332 04.0	55.0	278 50.9	33.3			
18	208 27.9	44 56.6	N 7 57.9	258 32.4	S24 50.8	347 06.4	S14 55.0	293 53.5	S22 33.3	Vega	80 36.2	N38 48.3
19	223 30.3	59 56.6	56.7	273 35.5	51.0	2 08.8	55.1	308 56.2	33.3	Zuben'ubi	137 01.5	S16 07.0
20	238 32.8	74 56.6	55.5	288 38.6	51.3	17 11.2	55.1	323 58.8	33.3		SHA	Mer. Pass.
21	253 35.3	89 56.5	. . 54.3	303 41.8	. . 51.6	32 13.6	. . 55.1	339 01.5	. . 33.3		° ′	h m
22	268 37.7	104 56.5	53.2	318 44.9	51.8	47 16.0	55.2	354 04.1	33.3	Venus	198 13.5	15 00
23	283 40.2	119 56.5	52.0	333 48.0	52.1	62 18.4	55.2	9 06.7	33.3	Mars	49 38.4	0 54
	h m									Jupiter	138 41.3	18 55
Mer. Pass. 4 12.4		v 0.0	d 1.2	v 3.1	d 0.3	v 2.4	d 0.0	v 2.6	d 0.0	Saturn	85 18.3	22 28

UT	SUN GHA	SUN Dec	MOON GHA	v	MOON Dec	d	HP
d h	° ′	° ′	° ′	′	° ′	′	′
18 00	178 26.8	N21 03.9	111 43.0	11.1	N 3 04.0	12.2	58.6
01	193 26.8	03.5	126 13.1	11.2	2 51.8	12.1	58.5
02	208 26.7	03.0	140 43.3	11.2	2 39.7	12.1	58.5
03	223 26.7	.. 02.6	155 13.5	11.2	2 27.6	12.1	58.4
04	238 26.6	02.2	169 43.7	11.3	2 15.5	12.1	58.4
05	253 26.6	01.7	184 14.0	11.4	2 03.4	12.1	58.4
W 06	268 26.5	N21 01.3	198 44.4	11.4	N 1 51.3	12.1	58.3
E 07	283 26.5	00.8	213 14.8	11.5	1 39.2	12.1	58.3
D 08	298 26.4	00.4	227 45.3	11.5	1 27.1	12.0	58.3
N 09	313 26.4	21 00.0	242 15.8	11.6	1 15.1	12.1	58.2
E 10	328 26.3	20 59.5	256 46.4	11.6	1 03.0	12.1	58.2
S 11	343 26.3	59.1	271 17.0	11.6	0 50.9	12.0	58.1
D 12	358 26.2	N20 58.6	285 47.6	11.7	N 0 38.9	12.0	58.1
A 13	13 26.2	58.2	300 18.3	11.8	0 26.9	12.1	58.1
Y 14	28 26.1	57.7	314 49.1	11.8	0 14.8	12.0	58.0
15	43 26.1	.. 57.3	329 19.9	11.8	N 0 02.8	11.9	58.0
16	58 26.0	56.9	343 50.7	11.9	S 0 09.1	12.0	58.0
17	73 26.0	56.4	358 21.6	11.9	0 21.1	12.0	57.9
18	88 26.0	N20 56.0	12 52.5	12.0	S 0 33.1	11.9	57.9
19	103 25.9	55.5	27 23.5	11.9	0 45.0	11.9	57.8
20	118 25.9	55.1	41 54.4	12.1	0 56.9	11.9	57.8
21	133 25.8	.. 54.6	56 25.5	12.1	1 08.8	11.9	57.8
22	148 25.8	54.2	70 56.6	12.1	1 20.7	11.8	57.7
23	163 25.7	53.7	85 27.7	12.1	1 32.5	11.8	57.7
19 00	178 25.7	N20 53.3	99 58.8	12.2	S 1 44.3	11.8	57.7
01	193 25.6	52.8	114 30.0	12.2	1 56.1	11.8	57.6
02	208 25.6	52.4	129 01.2	12.2	2 07.9	11.8	57.6
03	223 25.6	.. 51.9	143 32.4	12.3	2 19.7	11.7	57.5
04	238 25.5	51.5	158 03.7	12.3	2 31.4	11.7	57.5
05	253 25.5	51.0	172 35.0	12.4	2 43.1	11.6	57.5
T 06	268 25.4	N20 50.6	187 06.4	12.3	S 2 54.7	11.7	57.4
H 07	283 25.4	50.1	201 37.7	12.4	3 06.4	11.6	57.4
U 08	298 25.3	49.7	216 09.1	12.4	3 18.0	11.6	57.4
R 09	313 25.3	.. 49.2	230 40.5	12.5	3 29.6	11.5	57.3
S 10	328 25.3	48.7	245 12.0	12.5	3 41.1	11.5	57.3
D 11	343 25.2	48.3	259 43.5	12.5	3 52.6	11.5	57.3
A 12	358 25.2	N20 47.8	274 15.0	12.5	S 4 04.1	11.4	57.2
Y 13	13 25.1	47.4	288 46.5	12.5	4 15.5	11.4	57.2
14	28 25.1	46.9	303 18.0	12.6	4 26.9	11.4	57.1
15	43 25.1	.. 46.5	317 49.6	12.6	4 38.3	11.3	57.1
16	58 25.0	46.0	332 21.2	12.6	4 49.6	11.3	57.1
17	73 25.0	45.5	346 52.8	12.7	5 00.9	11.3	57.0
18	88 24.9	N20 45.1	1 24.5	12.6	S 5 12.2	11.2	57.0
19	103 24.9	44.6	15 56.1	12.7	5 23.4	11.2	57.0
20	118 24.9	44.2	30 27.8	12.7	5 34.6	11.2	56.9
21	133 24.8	.. 43.7	44 59.5	12.7	5 45.8	11.1	56.9
22	148 24.8	43.2	59 31.2	12.7	5 56.9	11.0	56.9
23	163 24.8	42.8	74 02.9	12.8	6 07.9	11.0	56.8
20 00	178 24.7	N20 42.3	88 34.7	12.7	S 6 18.9	11.0	56.8
01	193 24.7	41.8	103 06.4	12.8	6 29.9	10.9	56.8
02	208 24.6	41.4	117 38.2	12.8	6 40.8	10.9	56.7
03	223 24.6	.. 40.9	132 10.0	12.8	6 51.7	10.9	56.7
04	238 24.6	40.4	146 41.8	12.8	7 02.6	10.8	56.7
05	253 24.5	40.0	161 13.6	12.8	7 13.4	10.7	56.6
F 06	268 24.5	N20 39.5	175 45.4	12.8	S 7 24.1	10.7	56.6
R 07	283 24.5	39.0	190 17.2	12.8	7 34.8	10.7	56.6
I 08	298 24.4	38.6	204 49.0	12.9	7 45.5	10.6	56.5
D 09	313 24.4	.. 38.1	219 20.9	12.8	7 56.1	10.5	56.5
A 10	328 24.3	37.6	233 52.7	12.9	8 06.6	10.5	56.5
Y 11	343 24.3	37.2	248 24.6	12.9	8 17.1	10.5	56.4
12	358 24.3	N20 36.7	262 56.5	12.8	S 8 27.6	10.4	56.4
13	13 24.2	36.2	277 28.3	12.9	8 38.0	10.3	56.4
14	28 24.2	35.7	292 00.2	12.9	8 48.3	10.3	56.3
15	43 24.2	.. 35.3	306 32.1	12.9	8 58.6	10.3	56.3
16	58 24.1	34.8	321 04.0	12.9	9 08.9	10.2	56.3
17	73 24.1	34.3	335 35.9	12.9	9 19.1	10.1	56.2
18	88 24.1	N20 33.8	350 07.8	12.9	S 9 29.2	10.1	56.2
19	103 24.0	33.4	4 39.7	12.9	9 39.3	10.0	56.2
20	118 24.0	32.9	19 11.6	12.9	9 49.3	10.0	56.2
21	133 24.0	.. 32.4	33 43.5	12.9	9 59.3	9.9	56.1
22	148 23.9	31.9	48 15.4	12.9	10 09.2	9.9	56.1
23	163 23.9	31.5	62 47.3	12.9	S10 19.1	9.8	56.1
	SD 15.8	d 0.5	SD 15.8		15.6		15.4

Lat.	Twilight Naut.	Twilight Civil	Sunrise	Moonrise 18	Moonrise 19	Moonrise 20	Moonrise 21
°	h m	h m	h m	h m	h m	h m	h m
N 72	▭	▭	▭	10 45	12 38	14 30	16 25
N 70	▭	▭	▭	10 46	12 32	14 15	15 59
68	////	////	00 45	10 47	12 27	14 04	15 40
66	////	////	01 52	10 48	12 22	13 54	15 24
64	////	////	02 27	10 48	12 19	13 46	15 12
62	////	01 15	02 52	10 49	12 16	13 40	15 01
60	////	01 58	03 11	10 50	12 13	13 34	14 52
N 58	////	02 25	03 27	10 50	12 11	13 29	14 44
56	01 08	02 47	03 41	10 50	12 09	13 24	14 37
54	01 48	03 04	03 53	10 51	12 07	13 20	14 31
52	02 14	03 18	04 03	10 51	12 05	13 16	14 26
50	02 34	03 31	04 12	10 51	12 03	13 13	14 21
45	03 10	03 56	04 31	10 52	12 00	13 06	14 11
N 40	03 36	04 15	04 47	10 52	11 57	13 00	14 01
35	03 56	04 31	05 00	10 53	11 55	12 55	13 53
30	04 12	04 45	05 11	10 53	11 53	12 50	13 47
20	04 38	05 07	05 31	10 54	11 49	12 43	13 35
N 10	04 58	05 25	05 47	10 55	11 46	12 36	13 25
0	05 15	05 41	06 03	10 55	11 43	12 30	13 16
S 10	05 30	05 56	06 18	10 56	11 40	12 23	13 07
20	05 44	06 11	06 34	10 57	11 37	12 17	12 57
30	05 58	06 27	06 53	10 57	11 34	12 09	12 46
35	06 05	06 36	07 04	10 58	11 32	12 05	12 39
40	06 13	06 46	07 16	10 58	11 29	12 00	12 32
45	06 21	06 58	07 30	10 59	11 27	11 55	12 24
S 50	06 31	07 11	07 48	11 00	11 24	11 48	12 15
52	06 35	07 17	07 56	11 00	11 22	11 45	12 09
54	06 40	07 24	08 06	11 00	11 21	11 42	12 04
56	06 45	07 32	08 16	11 01	11 19	11 38	11 58
58	06 50	07 40	08 28	11 01	11 17	11 34	11 52
S 60	06 56	07 50	08 42	11 02	11 15	11 29	11 45

Lat.	Sunset	Twilight Civil	Twilight Naut.	Moonset 18	Moonset 19	Moonset 20	Moonset 21
°	h m	h m	h m	h m	h m	h m	h m
N 72	▭	▭	▭	22 57	22 45	22 31	22 13
N 70	▭	▭	▭	23 00	22 54	22 47	22 40
68	23 17	////	////	23 01	23 01	23 00	23 01
66	22 17	////	////	23 03	23 07	23 11	23 16
64	21 43	////	////	23 04	23 12	23 20	23 31
62	21 19	22 53	////	23 05	23 16	23 28	23 42
60	21 00	22 12	////	23 06	23 20	23 35	23 52
N 58	20 44	21 45	////	23 07	23 24	23 41	24 00
56	20 31	21 24	23 00	23 08	23 27	23 46	24 08
54	20 19	21 08	22 22	23 09	23 29	23 51	24 14
52	20 09	20 53	21 57	23 10	23 32	23 55	24 20
50	20 00	20 41	21 38	23 10	23 34	23 59	24 26
45	19 41	20 16	21 02	23 11	23 39	24 08	00 08
N 40	19 25	19 57	20 36	23 13	23 43	24 15	00 15
35	19 12	19 41	20 16	23 13	23 47	24 21	00 21
30	19 01	19 28	20 00	23 14	23 50	24 26	00 26
20	18 42	19 06	19 34	23 16	23 56	24 36	00 36
N 10	18 25	18 48	19 14	23 17	24 01	00 01	00 44
0	18 10	18 32	18 58	23 18	24 05	00 05	00 52
S 10	17 55	18 17	18 43	23 19	24 10	00 10	01 00
20	17 38	18 02	18 29	23 21	24 15	00 15	01 08
30	17 20	17 46	18 15	23 22	24 21	00 21	01 18
35	17 09	17 37	18 08	23 23	24 24	00 24	01 23
40	16 57	17 27	18 00	23 24	24 28	00 28	01 30
45	16 43	17 15	17 52	23 25	24 32	00 32	01 37
S 50	16 25	17 02	17 42	23 26	24 37	00 37	01 46
52	16 17	16 56	17 38	23 26	24 39	00 39	01 50
54	16 08	16 49	17 33	23 27	24 42	00 42	01 54
56	15 57	16 41	17 29	23 28	24 45	00 45	01 59
58	15 45	16 33	17 23	23 29	24 48	00 48	02 05
S 60	15 31	16 24	17 17	23 29	24 52	00 52	02 11

	SUN			MOON			
Day	Eqn. of Time 00ʰ	Eqn. of Time 12ʰ	Mer. Pass.	Mer. Pass. Upper	Mer. Pass. Lower	Age	Phase
d	m s	m s	h m	h m	h m	d	%
18	06 13	06 15	12 06	17 07	04 42	05	36
19	06 17	06 19	12 06	17 54	05 31	06	47
20	06 21	06 23	12 06	18 41	06 18	07	57

2018 JULY 21, 22, 23 (SAT., SUN., MON.)

UT (d h)	ARIES GHA	VENUS −4·2 GHA	Dec	MARS −2·7 GHA	Dec	JUPITER −2·2 GHA	Dec	SATURN +0·1 GHA	Dec	STARS Name	SHA	Dec
21 00	298 42.7	134 56.5	N 7 50.8	348 51.1	S24 52.4	77 20.8	S14 55.2	24 09.4	S22 33.4	Acamar	315 15.9	S40 13.7
01	313 45.1	149 56.5	49.6	3 54.2	52.6	92 23.2	55.3	39 12.0	33.4	Achernar	335 24.2	S57 08.4
02	328 47.6	164 56.5	48.4	18 57.3	52.9	107 25.5	55.3	54 14.6	33.4	Acrux	173 05.6	S63 12.3
03	343 50.1	179 56.5 ..	47.2	34 00.4 ..	53.2	122 27.9 ..	55.3	69 17.3 ..	33.4	Adhara	255 10.2	S28 59.9
04	358 52.5	194 56.4	46.0	49 03.5	53.4	137 30.3	55.4	84 19.9	33.4	Aldebaran	290 45.6	N16 32.6
05	13 55.0	209 56.4	44.8	64 06.6	53.7	152 32.7	55.4	99 22.5	33.4			
06	28 57.4	224 56.4	N 7 43.7	79 09.7	S24 54.0	167 35.1	S14 55.4	114 25.2	S22 33.4	Alioth	166 17.8	N55 52.0
07	43 59.9	239 56.4	42.5	94 12.8	54.2	182 37.5	55.5	129 27.8	33.4	Alkaid	152 56.2	N49 13.7
S 08	59 02.4	254 56.4	41.3	109 15.9	54.5	197 39.9	55.5	144 30.4	33.4	Al Na'ir	27 39.0	S46 52.1
A 09	74 04.8	269 56.4 ..	40.1	124 19.0 ..	54.8	212 42.3 ..	55.5	159 33.1 ..	33.4	Alnilam	275 43.1	S 1 11.5
T 10	89 07.3	284 56.4	38.9	139 22.2	55.0	227 44.7	55.6	174 35.7	33.5	Alphard	217 53.0	S 8 44.3
U 11	104 09.8	299 56.4	37.7	154 25.3	55.3	242 47.1	55.6	189 38.4	33.5			
R 12	119 12.2	314 56.4	N 7 36.5	169 28.4	S24 55.6	257 49.4	S14 55.6	204 41.0	S22 33.5	Alphecca	126 07.9	N26 39.5
D 13	134 14.7	329 56.4	35.3	184 31.5	55.8	272 51.8	55.7	219 43.6	33.5	Alpheratz	357 39.7	N29 11.4
A 14	149 17.2	344 56.3	34.1	199 34.6	56.1	287 54.2	55.7	234 46.3	33.5	Altair	62 04.5	N 8 55.2
Y 15	164 19.6	359 56.3 ..	32.9	214 37.7 ..	56.4	302 56.6 ..	55.7	249 48.9 ..	33.5	Ankaa	353 12.1	S42 12.2
16	179 22.1	14 56.3	31.7	229 40.9	56.6	317 59.0	55.7	264 51.5	33.5	Antares	112 21.8	S26 28.2
17	194 24.6	29 56.3	30.6	244 44.0	56.9	333 01.4	55.8	279 54.2	33.5			
18	209 27.0	44 56.3	N 7 29.4	259 47.1	S24 57.2	348 03.8	S14 55.8	294 56.8	S22 33.5	Arcturus	145 52.6	N19 05.5
19	224 29.5	59 56.3	28.2	274 50.2	57.4	3 06.1	55.9	309 59.4	33.5	Atria	107 20.0	S69 03.6
20	239 31.9	74 56.3	27.0	289 53.3	57.7	18 08.5	55.9	325 02.1	33.6	Avior	234 17.2	S59 34.2
21	254 34.4	89 56.3 ..	25.8	304 56.4 ..	58.0	33 10.9 ..	56.0	340 04.7 ..	33.6	Bellatrix	278 28.6	N 6 21.8
22	269 36.9	104 56.3	24.6	319 59.6	58.2	48 13.3	56.0	355 07.3	33.6	Betelgeuse	270 57.8	N 7 24.5
23	284 39.3	119 56.3	23.4	335 02.7	58.5	63 15.7	56.0	10 10.0	33.6			
22 00	299 41.8	134 56.3	N 7 22.2	350 05.8	S24 58.7	78 18.1	S14 56.1	25 12.6	S22 33.6	Canopus	263 55.1	S52 42.3
01	314 44.3	149 56.3	21.0	5 08.9	59.0	93 20.5	56.1	40 15.2	33.6	Capella	280 29.7	N46 00.7
02	329 46.7	164 56.3	19.8	20 12.1	59.3	108 22.8	56.1	55 17.9	33.6	Deneb	49 28.6	N45 20.9
03	344 49.2	179 56.3 ..	18.6	35 15.2 ..	59.5	123 25.2 ..	56.2	70 20.5 ..	33.6	Denebola	182 30.3	N14 28.3
04	359 51.7	194 56.3	17.4	50 18.3	24 59.8	138 27.6	56.2	85 23.1	33.6	Diphda	348 52.3	S17 53.0
05	14 54.1	209 56.3	16.2	65 21.4	25 00.1	153 30.0	56.2	100 25.8	33.6			
06	29 56.6	224 56.3	N 7 15.0	80 24.5	S25 00.3	168 32.4	S14 56.3	115 28.4	S22 33.7	Dubhe	193 48.0	N61 39.3
07	44 59.0	239 56.3	13.8	95 27.7	00.6	183 34.7	56.3	130 31.0	33.7	Elnath	278 08.5	N28 37.1
S 08	60 01.5	254 56.3	12.7	110 30.8	00.8	198 37.1	56.3	145 33.7	33.7	Eltanin	90 44.1	N51 29.5
U 09	75 04.0	269 56.3 ..	11.5	125 33.9 ..	01.1	213 39.5 ..	56.4	160 36.3 ..	33.7	Enif	33 43.4	N 9 57.7
N 10	90 06.4	284 56.3	10.3	140 37.1	01.4	228 41.9	56.4	175 38.9	33.7	Fomalhaut	15 19.9	S29 31.3
D 11	105 08.9	299 56.3	09.1	155 40.2	01.6	243 44.3	56.5	190 41.6	33.7			
A 12	120 11.4	314 56.3	N 7 07.9	170 43.3	S25 01.9	258 46.7	S14 56.5	205 44.2	S22 33.7	Gacrux	171 57.2	S57 13.1
Y 13	135 13.8	329 56.4	06.7	185 46.4	02.2	273 49.0	56.6	220 46.8	33.7	Gienah	175 48.9	S17 38.6
14	150 16.3	344 56.4	05.5	200 49.6	02.4	288 51.4	56.6	235 49.5	33.7	Hadar	148 42.9	S60 27.8
15	165 18.8	359 56.4 ..	04.3	215 52.7 ..	02.7	303 53.8 ..	56.6	250 52.1 ..	33.7	Hamal	327 56.9	N23 32.8
16	180 21.2	14 56.4	03.1	230 55.8	02.9	318 56.2	56.6	265 54.7	33.8	Kaus Aust.	83 38.9	S34 22.4
17	195 23.7	29 56.4	01.9	245 59.0	03.2	333 58.5	56.7	280 57.4	33.8			
18	210 26.2	44 56.4	N 7 00.7	261 02.1	S25 03.5	349 00.9	S14 56.7	296 00.0	S22 33.8	Kochab	137 19.9	N74 05.2
19	225 28.6	59 56.4	6 59.5	276 05.2	03.7	4 03.3	56.8	311 02.6	33.8	Markab	13 34.6	N15 18.3
20	240 31.1	74 56.4	58.3	291 08.4	04.0	19 05.7	56.8	326 05.3	33.8	Menkar	314 11.5	N 4 09.6
21	255 33.5	89 56.4 ..	57.1	306 11.5 ..	04.2	34 08.1 ..	56.8	341 07.9 ..	33.8	Menkent	148 03.4	S36 27.6
22	270 36.0	104 56.4	55.9	321 14.6	04.5	49 10.4	56.9	356 10.5	33.8	Miaplacidus	221 39.8	S69 47.7
23	285 38.5	119 56.5	54.7	336 17.8	04.7	64 12.8	56.9	11 13.2	33.8			
23 00	300 40.9	134 56.5	N 6 53.5	351 20.9	S25 05.0	79 15.2	S14 56.9	26 15.8	S22 33.8	Mirfak	308 35.6	N49 55.2
01	315 43.4	149 56.5	52.3	6 24.0	05.3	94 17.6	57.0	41 18.4	33.8	Nunki	75 53.7	S26 16.2
02	330 45.9	164 56.5	51.1	21 27.2	05.5	109 19.9	57.0	56 21.1	33.8	Peacock	53 13.2	S56 40.3
03	345 48.3	179 56.5 ..	49.9	36 30.3 ..	05.8	124 22.3 ..	57.1	71 23.7 ..	33.9	Pollux	243 23.9	N27 58.8
04	0 50.8	194 56.5	48.7	51 33.4	06.0	139 24.7	57.1	86 26.3	33.9	Procyon	244 56.5	N 5 10.6
05	15 53.3	209 56.6	47.5	66 36.6	06.3	154 27.1	57.1	101 29.0	33.9			
06	30 55.7	224 56.6	N 6 46.3	81 39.7	S25 06.6	169 29.4	S14 57.2	116 31.6	S22 33.9	Rasalhague	96 03.0	N12 33.1
07	45 58.2	239 56.6	45.1	96 42.9	06.8	184 31.8	57.2	131 34.2	33.9	Regulus	207 40.1	N11 52.7
08	61 00.7	254 56.6	43.9	111 46.0	07.1	199 34.2	57.2	146 36.8	33.9	Rigel	281 09.0	S 8 10.9
M 09	76 03.1	269 56.6 ..	42.7	126 49.1 ..	07.3	214 36.6 ..	57.3	161 39.5 ..	33.9	Rigil Kent.	139 46.9	S60 54.7
O 10	91 05.6	284 56.6	41.5	141 52.3	07.6	229 38.9	57.3	176 42.1	33.9	Sabik	102 08.3	S15 44.7
N 11	106 08.0	299 56.7	40.3	156 55.4	07.8	244 41.3	57.4	191 44.7	33.9			
D 12	121 10.5	314 56.7	N 6 39.1	171 58.6	S25 08.1	259 43.7	S14 57.4	206 47.4	S22 33.9	Schedar	349 36.3	N56 38.0
A 13	136 13.0	329 56.7	37.9	187 01.7	08.3	274 46.1	57.4	221 50.0	34.0	Shaula	96 16.9	S37 06.9
Y 14	151 15.4	344 56.7	36.7	202 04.9	08.6	289 48.4	57.5	236 52.6	34.0	Sirius	258 31.0	S16 44.6
15	166 17.9	359 56.7 ..	35.5	217 08.0 ..	08.9	304 50.8 ..	57.5	251 55.3 ..	34.0	Spica	158 27.6	S11 15.3
16	181 20.4	14 56.8	34.3	232 11.1	09.1	319 53.2	57.6	266 57.9	34.0	Suhail	222 50.3	S43 30.5
17	196 22.8	29 56.8	33.1	247 14.3	09.4	334 55.6	57.6	282 00.5	34.0			
18	211 25.3	44 56.8	N 6 31.9	262 17.4	S25 09.6	349 57.9	S14 57.6	297 03.2	S22 34.0	Vega	80 36.2	N38 48.3
19	226 27.8	59 56.8	30.7	277 20.6	09.9	5 00.3	57.7	312 05.8	34.0	Zuben'ubi	137 01.5	S16 07.0
20	241 30.2	74 56.9	29.5	292 23.7	10.1	20 02.7	57.7	327 08.4	34.0			
21	256 32.7	89 56.9 ..	28.3	307 26.9 ..	10.4	35 05.0 ..	57.7	342 11.0 ..	34.0			
22	271 35.1	104 56.9	27.1	322 30.0	10.6	50 07.4	57.8	357 13.7	34.0			
23	286 37.6	119 56.9	25.9	337 33.2	10.9	65 09.8	57.8	12 16.3	34.1			
Mer.Pass.	h m 4 00.6	v 0.0	d 1.2	v 3.1	d 0.3	v 2.4	d 0.0	v 2.6	d 0.0			

	SHA	Mer.Pass.
	° '	h m
Venus	195 14.5	15 00
Mars	50 24.0	0 39
Jupiter	138 36.3	18 44
Saturn	85 30.8	22 15

UT	SUN GHA	Dec	MOON GHA	v	Dec	d	HP
d h	° ′	° ′	° ′	′	° ′	′	′
21 00	178 23.9	N20 31.0	77 19.2	12.9	S10 28.9	9.7	56.0
01	193 23.9	30.5	91 51.1	12.9	10 38.6	9.7	56.0
02	208 23.8	30.0	106 23.0	12.9	10 48.3	9.6	56.0
03	223 23.8 ..	29.5	120 54.9	12.9	10 57.9	9.6	55.9
04	238 23.8	29.1	135 26.8	12.9	11 07.5	9.5	55.9
05	253 23.7	28.6	149 58.7	12.8	11 17.0	9.4	55.9
S 06	268 23.7	N20 28.1	164 30.5	12.9	S11 26.4	9.4	55.9
A 07	283 23.7	27.6	179 02.4	12.9	11 35.8	9.3	55.8
T 08	298 23.6	27.1	193 34.3	12.9	11 45.1	9.3	55.8
U 09	313 23.6 ..	26.6	208 06.2	12.8	11 54.4	9.2	55.8
R 10	328 23.6	26.2	222 38.0	12.9	12 03.6	9.1	55.8
D 11	343 23.6	25.7	237 09.9	12.8	12 12.7	9.1	55.7
A 12	358 23.5	N20 25.2	251 41.7	12.9	S12 21.8	9.0	55.7
Y 13	13 23.5	24.7	266 13.6	12.8	12 30.8	8.9	55.7
14	28 23.5	24.2	280 45.4	12.8	12 39.7	8.9	55.6
15	43 23.4 ..	23.7	295 17.2	12.9	12 48.6	8.8	55.6
16	58 23.4	23.2	309 49.1	12.8	12 57.4	8.7	55.6
17	73 23.4	22.8	324 20.9	12.8	13 06.1	8.7	55.6
18	88 23.4	N20 22.3	338 52.7	12.8	S13 14.8	8.5	55.5
19	103 23.3	21.8	353 24.5	12.7	13 23.3	8.6	55.5
20	118 23.3	21.3	7 56.2	12.8	13 31.9	8.4	55.5
21	133 23.3 ..	20.8	22 28.0	12.8	13 40.3	8.4	55.5
22	148 23.3	20.3	36 59.8	12.7	13 48.7	8.3	55.4
23	163 23.2	19.8	51 31.5	12.7	13 57.0	8.3	55.4
22 00	178 23.2	N20 19.3	66 03.2	12.8	S14 05.3	8.1	55.4
01	193 23.2	18.8	80 35.0	12.7	14 13.4	8.1	55.4
02	208 23.1	18.3	95 06.7	12.7	14 21.5	8.1	55.3
03	223 23.1 ..	17.8	109 38.4	12.7	14 29.6	7.9	55.3
04	238 23.1	17.3	124 10.1	12.6	14 37.5	7.9	55.3
05	253 23.1	16.8	138 41.7	12.7	14 45.4	7.8	55.3
S 06	268 23.0	N20 16.3	153 13.4	12.6	S14 53.2	7.8	55.3
U 07	283 23.0	15.8	167 45.0	12.7	15 01.0	7.6	55.2
N 08	298 23.0	15.4	182 16.7	12.6	15 08.6	7.6	55.2
D 09	313 23.0 ..	14.9	196 48.3	12.6	15 16.2	7.5	55.2
A 10	328 23.0	14.4	211 19.9	12.6	15 23.7	7.4	55.2
Y 11	343 22.9	13.9	225 51.5	12.5	15 31.1	7.4	55.1
12	358 22.9	N20 13.4	240 23.0	12.6	S15 38.5	7.3	55.1
13	13 22.9	12.9	254 54.6	12.5	15 45.8	7.2	55.1
14	28 22.8	12.4	269 26.1	12.6	15 53.0	7.1	55.1
15	43 22.8 ..	11.9	283 57.7	12.5	16 00.1	7.0	55.1
16	58 22.8	11.3	298 29.2	12.5	16 07.1	7.0	55.0
17	73 22.8	10.8	313 00.7	12.5	16 14.1	6.9	55.0
18	88 22.8	N20 10.3	327 32.2	12.4	S16 21.0	6.8	55.0
19	103 22.8	09.8	342 03.6	12.5	16 27.8	6.7	55.0
20	118 22.7	09.3	356 35.1	12.4	16 34.5	6.6	55.0
21	133 22.7 ..	08.8	11 06.5	12.4	16 41.1	6.6	54.9
22	148 22.7	08.3	25 37.9	12.4	16 47.7	6.5	54.9
23	163 22.7	07.8	40 09.3	12.4	16 54.2	6.4	54.9
23 00	178 22.7	N20 07.3	54 40.7	12.4	S17 00.6	6.3	54.9
01	193 22.6	06.8	69 12.1	12.3	17 06.9	6.2	54.9
02	208 22.6	06.3	83 43.4	12.4	17 13.1	6.2	54.8
03	223 22.6 ..	05.8	98 14.8	12.3	17 19.3	6.0	54.8
04	238 22.6	05.3	112 46.1	12.3	17 25.3	6.0	54.8
05	253 22.6	04.8	127 17.4	12.3	17 31.3	5.9	54.8
M 06	268 22.5	N20 04.3	141 48.7	12.2	S17 37.2	5.8	54.8
O 07	283 22.5	03.7	156 19.9	12.3	17 43.0	5.8	54.8
N 08	298 22.5	03.2	170 51.2	12.2	17 48.8	5.6	54.7
D 09	313 22.5 ..	02.7	185 23.4	12.2	17 54.4	5.6	54.7
A 10	328 22.5	02.2	199 53.6	12.2	18 00.0	5.4	54.7
Y 11	343 22.5	01.7	214 24.8	12.2	18 05.4	5.4	54.7
12	358 22.4	N20 01.2	228 56.0	12.2	S18 10.8	5.3	54.7
13	13 22.4	00.7	243 27.2	12.2	18 16.1	5.2	54.7
14	28 22.4	20 00.2	257 58.4	12.1	18 21.3	5.1	54.6
15	43 22.4	19 59.6	272 29.5	12.1	18 26.4	5.1	54.6
16	58 22.4	59.1	287 00.6	12.1	18 31.5	4.9	54.6
17	73 22.4	58.6	301 31.7	12.1	18 36.4	4.9	54.6
18	88 22.4	N19 58.1	316 02.8	12.1	S18 41.3	4.7	54.6
19	103 22.3	57.6	330 33.9	12.1	18 46.0	4.7	54.5
20	118 22.3	57.0	345 05.0	12.0	18 50.7	4.6	54.5
21	133 22.3 ..	56.5	359 36.0	12.1	18 55.3	4.5	54.5
22	148 22.3	56.0	14 07.1	12.0	18 59.8	4.4	54.5
23	163 22.3	55.5	28 38.1	12.0	S19 04.2	4.3	54.5
	SD 15.8	d 0.5	SD 15.2		15.0		14.9

Twilight / Sunrise / Moonrise

Lat.	Twilight Naut.	Civil	Sunrise	Moonrise 21	22	23	24
°	h m	h m	h m	h m	h m	h m	h m
N 72	□	□	□	16 25	18 34	■■	■■
N 70	□	□	□	15 59	17 46	19 40	■■
68	////	////	01 13	15 40	17 15	18 48	20 13
66	////	////	02 05	15 24	16 52	18 16	19 31
64	////	////	02 36	15 12	16 34	17 52	19 02
62	////	01 31	02 59	15 01	16 20	17 34	18 40
60	////	02 07	03 18	14 52	16 08	17 18	18 23
N 58	////	02 33	03 33	14 44	15 57	17 05	18 08
56	01 23	02 53	03 46	14 37	15 48	16 54	17 55
54	01 57	03 09	03 57	14 31	15 40	16 44	17 44
52	02 21	03 23	04 07	14 26	15 32	16 36	17 34
50	02 39	03 35	04 16	14 21	15 26	16 28	17 26
45	03 14	03 59	04 34	14 10	15 12	16 11	17 07
N 40	03 39	04 18	04 49	14 01	15 00	15 58	16 52
35	03 59	04 33	05 02	13 53	14 51	15 46	16 40
30	04 14	04 46	05 13	13 47	14 42	15 36	16 29
20	04 39	05 08	05 32	13 35	14 27	15 19	16 10
N 10	04 59	05 25	05 48	13 25	14 15	15 04	15 53
0	05 15	05 41	06 03	13 16	14 03	14 50	15 38
S 10	05 30	05 55	06 18	13 07	13 51	14 36	15 23
20	05 43	06 10	06 34	12 57	13 38	14 21	15 07
30	05 57	06 26	06 52	12 46	13 24	14 05	14 48
35	06 04	06 35	07 02	12 39	13 16	13 55	14 37
40	06 11	06 44	07 14	12 32	13 06	13 44	14 25
45	06 19	06 55	07 28	12 24	12 55	13 30	14 10
S 50	06 28	07 08	07 45	12 14	12 42	13 15	13 52
52	06 32	07 14	07 53	12 09	12 36	13 07	13 44
54	06 37	07 21	08 02	12 04	12 29	12 59	13 34
56	06 41	07 28	08 12	11 58	12 22	12 50	13 24
58	06 46	07 36	08 23	11 52	12 13	12 39	13 12
S 60	06 52	07 45	08 36	11 45	12 03	12 27	12 58

Sunset / Twilight / Moonset

Lat.	Sunset	Twilight Civil	Naut.	Moonset 21	22	23	24
°	h m	h m	h m	h m	h m	h m	h m
N 72	□	□	□	22 13	21 41	■■	■■
N 70	□	□	□	22 40	22 31	22 15	■■
68	22 53	////	////	23 01	23 03	23 08	23 23
66	22 05	////	////	23 17	23 26	23 41	24 06
64	21 34	////	////	23 31	23 45	24 05	00 05
62	21 12	22 38	////	23 42	24 00	00 00	00 24
60	20 54	22 03	////	23 52	24 13	00 13	00 39
N 58	20 39	21 38	////	24 00	00 00	00 24	00 53
56	20 26	21 18	22 46	24 08	00 08	00 33	01 04
54	20 15	21 02	22 14	24 14	00 14	00 42	01 14
52	20 05	20 49	21 51	24 20	00 20	00 49	01 23
50	19 56	20 37	21 32	24 26	00 26	00 56	01 31
45	19 38	20 13	20 58	00 08	00 38	01 11	01 48
N 40	19 23	19 54	20 33	00 15	00 48	01 23	02 03
35	19 11	19 39	20 14	00 21	00 56	01 34	02 14
30	19 00	19 26	19 58	00 26	01 04	01 43	02 25
20	18 41	19 05	19 33	00 36	01 16	01 59	02 43
N 10	18 25	18 47	19 14	00 44	01 28	02 13	03 00
0	18 10	18 32	18 58	00 52	01 38	02 26	03 13
S 10	17 55	18 18	18 43	01 00	01 49	02 38	03 28
20	17 40	18 03	18 30	01 08	02 00	02 52	03 44
30	17 22	17 47	18 16	01 18	02 14	03 08	04 02
35	17 11	17 39	18 09	01 23	02 21	03 18	04 12
40	16 59	17 29	18 02	01 29	02 30	03 28	04 24
45	16 46	17 18	17 54	01 37	02 40	03 41	04 39
S 50	16 29	17 05	17 45	01 46	02 52	03 56	04 56
52	16 21	16 59	17 41	01 50	02 58	04 03	05 04
54	16 12	16 53	17 37	01 54	03 04	04 11	05 13
56	16 02	16 46	17 32	01 59	03 11	04 20	05 24
58	15 50	16 38	17 27	02 05	03 19	04 30	05 36
S 60	15 37	16 29	17 22	02 11	03 28	04 42	05 45

SUN / MOON

Day	SUN Eqn. of Time 00ʰ	12ʰ	Mer. Pass.	MOON Mer. Pass. Upper	Lower	Age	Phase
d	m s	m s	h m	h m	h m	d	%
21	06 24	06 26	12 06	19 27	07 04	08	67
22	06 27	06 28	12 06	20 14	07 51	09	76
23	06 29	06 30	12 07	21 02	08 38	10	84

UT	ARIES	VENUS −4.2		MARS −2.8		JUPITER −2.1		SATURN +0.2		STARS		
	GHA	GHA	Dec	GHA	Dec	GHA	Dec	GHA	Dec	Name	SHA	Dec
d h	° ′	° ′	° ′	° ′	° ′	° ′	° ′	° ′	° ′		° ′	° ′
24 00	301 40.1	134 57.0	N 6 24.7	352 36.3	S25 11.1	80 12.1	S14 57.9	27 18.9	S22 34.1	Acamar	315 15.8	S40 13.7
01	316 42.5	149 57.0	23.4	7 39.5	11.4	95 14.5	57.9	42 21.6	34.1	Achernar	335 24.2	S57 08.4
02	331 45.0	164 57.0	22.2	22 42.6	11.7	110 16.9	57.9	57 24.2	34.1	Acrux	173 05.6	S63 12.3
03	346 47.5	179 57.1	. . 21.0	37 45.7	. . 11.9	125 19.3	. . 58.0	72 26.8	. . 34.1	Adhara	255 10.2	S28 59.9
04	1 49.9	194 57.1	19.8	52 48.9	12.2	140 21.6	58.0	87 29.4	34.1	Aldebaran	290 45.6	N16 32.6
05	16 52.4	209 57.1	18.6	67 52.0	12.4	155 24.0	58.1	102 32.1	34.1			
06	31 54.9	224 57.2	N 6 17.4	82 55.2	S25 12.7	170 26.4	S14 58.1	117 34.7	S22 34.1	Alioth	166 17.9	N55 52.0
07	46 57.3	239 57.2	16.2	97 58.3	12.9	185 28.7	58.1	132 37.3	34.1	Alkaid	152 56.2	N49 13.7
T 08	61 59.8	254 57.2	15.0	113 01.5	13.2	200 31.1	58.2	147 40.0	34.1	Al Na'ir	27 39.0	S46 52.1
U 09	77 02.3	269 57.3	. . 13.8	128 04.7	. . 13.4	215 33.5	. . 58.2	162 42.6	. . 34.2	Alnilam	275 43.1	S 1 11.5
E 10	92 04.7	284 57.3	12.6	143 07.8	13.7	230 35.8	58.3	177 45.2	34.2	Alphard	217 53.0	S 8 44.3
S 11	107 07.2	299 57.3	11.4	158 11.0	13.9	245 38.2	58.3	192 47.8	34.2			
D 12	122 09.6	314 57.4	N 6 10.2	173 14.1	S25 14.2	260 40.6	S14 58.4	207 50.5	S22 34.2	Alphecca	126 07.9	N26 39.5
A 13	137 12.1	329 57.4	09.0	188 17.3	14.4	275 42.9	58.4	222 53.1	34.2	Alpheratz	357 39.7	N29 11.4
Y 14	152 14.6	344 57.4	07.8	203 20.4	14.7	290 45.3	58.4	237 55.7	34.2	Altair	62 04.5	N 8 55.2
15	167 17.0	359 57.5	. . 06.6	218 23.6	. . 14.9	305 47.7	. . 58.5	252 58.4	. . 34.2	Ankaa	353 12.1	S42 12.2
16	182 19.5	14 57.5	05.4	233 26.7	15.2	320 50.0	58.5	268 01.0	34.2	Antares	112 21.8	S26 28.2
17	197 22.0	29 57.5	04.2	248 29.9	15.4	335 52.4	58.6	283 03.6	34.2			
18	212 24.4	44 57.6	N 6 02.9	263 33.0	S25 15.7	350 54.7	S14 58.6	298 06.2	S22 34.2	Arcturus	145 52.6	N19 05.5
19	227 26.9	59 57.6	01.7	278 36.2	15.9	5 57.1	58.6	313 08.9	34.2	Atria	107 20.0	S69 03.6
20	242 29.4	74 57.7	6 00.5	293 39.3	16.2	20 59.5	58.7	328 11.5	34.3	Avior	234 17.2	S59 34.2
21	257 31.8	89 57.7	5 59.3	308 42.5	. . 16.4	36 01.8	. . 58.7	343 14.1	. . 34.3	Bellatrix	278 28.5	N 6 21.8
22	272 34.3	104 57.7	58.1	323 45.7	16.7	51 04.2	58.8	358 16.8	34.3	Betelgeuse	270 57.8	N 7 24.5
23	287 36.8	119 57.8	56.9	338 48.8	16.9	66 06.6	58.8	13 19.4	34.3			
25 00	302 39.2	134 57.8	N 5 55.7	353 52.0	S25 17.1	81 08.9	S14 58.8	28 22.0	S22 34.3	Canopus	263 55.1	S52 42.3
01	317 41.7	149 57.9	54.5	8 55.1	17.4	96 11.3	58.9	43 24.6	34.3	Capella	280 29.7	N46 00.7
02	332 44.1	164 57.9	53.3	23 58.3	17.6	111 13.7	58.9	58 27.3	34.3	Deneb	49 28.6	N45 20.9
03	347 46.6	179 57.9	. . 52.1	39 01.5	. . 17.9	126 16.0	. . 59.0	73 29.9	. . 34.3	Denebola	182 30.3	N14 28.3
04	2 49.1	194 58.0	50.9	54 04.6	18.1	141 18.4	59.0	88 32.5	34.3	Diphda	348 52.3	S17 53.0
05	17 51.5	209 58.0	49.7	69 07.8	18.4	156 20.7	59.1	103 35.1	34.3			
06	32 54.0	224 58.1	N 5 48.4	84 10.9	S25 18.6	171 23.1	S14 59.1	118 37.8	S22 34.4	Dubhe	193 48.0	N61 39.3
W 07	47 56.5	239 58.1	47.2	99 14.1	18.9	186 25.5	59.1	133 40.4	34.4	Elnath	278 08.5	N28 37.1
E 08	62 58.9	254 58.2	46.0	114 17.3	19.1	201 27.8	59.2	148 43.0	34.4	Eltanin	90 44.1	N51 29.5
D 09	78 01.4	269 58.2	. . 44.8	129 20.4	. . 19.4	216 30.2	. . 59.2	163 45.6	. . 34.4	Enif	33 43.4	N 9 57.7
N 10	93 03.9	284 58.3	43.6	144 23.6	19.6	231 32.5	59.3	178 48.3	34.4	Fomalhaut	15 19.9	S29 31.3
E 11	108 06.3	299 58.3	42.4	159 26.7	19.8	246 34.9	59.3	193 50.9	34.4			
S 12	123 08.8	314 58.4	N 5 41.2	174 29.9	S25 20.1	261 37.3	S14 59.4	208 53.5	S22 34.4	Gacrux	171 57.2	S57 13.1
D 13	138 11.3	329 58.4	40.0	189 33.1	20.3	276 39.6	59.4	223 56.1	34.4	Gienah	175 48.9	S17 38.6
A 14	153 13.7	344 58.5	38.8	204 36.2	20.6	291 42.0	59.4	238 58.8	34.4	Hadar	148 42.9	S60 27.8
Y 15	168 16.2	359 58.5	. . 37.5	219 39.4	. . 20.8	306 44.3	. . 59.5	254 01.4	. . 34.4	Hamal	327 56.8	N23 32.8
16	183 18.6	14 58.6	36.3	234 42.6	21.1	321 46.7	59.5	269 04.0	34.4	Kaus Aust.	83 38.8	S34 22.4
17	198 21.1	29 58.6	35.1	249 45.7	21.3	336 49.0	59.6	284 06.6	34.5			
18	213 23.6	44 58.7	N 5 33.9	264 48.9	S25 21.5	351 51.4	S14 59.6	299 09.3	S22 34.5	Kochab	137 19.9	N74 05.2
19	228 26.0	59 58.7	32.7	279 52.0	21.8	6 53.8	59.7	314 11.9	34.5	Markab	13 34.6	N15 18.3
20	243 28.5	74 58.7	31.5	294 55.2	22.0	21 56.1	59.7	329 14.5	34.5	Menkar	314 11.5	N 4 09.6
21	258 31.0	89 58.8	. . 30.3	309 58.4	. . 22.3	36 58.5	. . 59.7	344 17.1	. . 34.5	Menkent	148 03.4	S36 27.6
22	273 33.4	104 58.9	29.1	325 01.5	22.5	52 00.8	59.8	359 19.8	34.5	Miaplacidus	221 39.8	S69 47.7
23	288 35.9	119 58.9	27.8	340 04.7	22.7	67 03.2	59.8	14 22.4	34.5			
26 00	303 38.4	134 59.0	N 5 26.6	355 07.9	S25 23.0	82 05.5	S14 59.9	29 25.0	S22 34.5	Mirfak	308 35.5	N49 55.2
01	318 40.8	149 59.0	25.4	10 11.0	23.2	97 07.9	14 59.9	44 27.6	34.5	Nunki	75 53.7	S26 16.2
02	333 43.3	164 59.1	24.2	25 14.2	23.5	112 10.2	15 00.0	59 30.3	34.5	Peacock	53 13.2	S56 40.3
03	348 45.8	179 59.2	. . 23.0	40 17.4	. . 23.7	127 12.6	. . 00.0	74 32.9	. . 34.6	Pollux	243 23.9	N27 58.8
04	3 48.2	194 59.2	21.8	55 20.5	23.9	142 15.0	00.1	89 35.5	34.6	Procyon	244 56.4	N 5 10.6
05	18 50.7	209 59.3	20.6	70 23.7	24.2	157 17.3	00.1	104 38.1	34.6			
06	33 53.1	224 59.3	N 5 19.4	85 26.9	S25 24.4	172 19.7	S15 00.1	119 40.8	S22 34.6	Rasalhague	96 03.0	N12 33.1
07	48 55.6	239 59.4	18.1	100 30.0	24.7	187 22.0	00.2	134 43.4	34.6	Regulus	207 40.1	N11 52.7
T 08	63 58.1	254 59.5	16.9	115 33.2	24.9	202 24.4	00.2	149 46.0	34.6	Rigel	281 09.0	S 8 10.9
H 09	79 00.5	269 59.5	. . 15.7	130 36.4	. . 25.1	217 26.7	. . 00.3	164 48.6	. . 34.6	Rigil Kent.	139 46.9	S60 54.7
U 10	94 03.0	284 59.6	14.5	145 39.6	25.4	232 29.1	00.3	179 51.3	34.6	Sabik	102 08.3	S15 44.7
R 11	109 05.5	299 59.6	13.3	160 42.7	25.6	247 31.4	00.4	194 53.9	34.6			
S 12	124 07.9	314 59.7	N 5 12.1	175 45.9	S25 25.8	262 33.8	S15 00.4	209 56.5	S22 34.6	Schedar	349 36.3	N56 38.0
D 13	139 10.4	329 59.8	10.9	190 49.1	26.1	277 36.1	00.5	224 59.1	34.6	Shaula	96 16.9	S37 06.9
A 14	154 12.9	344 59.8	09.6	205 52.2	26.3	292 38.5	00.5	240 01.7	34.7	Sirius	258 31.0	S16 44.5
Y 15	169 15.3	359 59.9	. . 08.4	220 55.4	. . 26.6	307 40.8	. . 00.5	255 04.4	. . 34.7	Spica	158 27.6	S11 15.3
16	184 17.8	15 00.0	07.2	235 58.6	26.8	322 43.2	00.6	270 07.0	34.7	Suhail	222 50.3	S43 30.5
17	199 20.2	30 00.0	06.0	251 01.7	27.0	337 45.5	00.6	285 09.6	34.7			
18	214 22.7	45 00.1	N 5 04.8	266 04.9	S25 27.3	352 47.9	S15 00.7	300 12.2	S22 34.7	Vega	80 36.2	N38 48.3
19	229 25.2	60 00.2	03.6	281 08.1	27.5	7 50.2	00.7	315 14.9	34.7	Zuben'ubi	137 01.5	S16 07.0
20	244 27.6	75 00.2	02.3	296 11.3	27.7	22 52.6	00.8	330 17.5	34.7		SHA	Mer. Pass.
21	259 30.1	90 00.3	5 01.1	311 14.4	. . 28.0	37 54.9	. . 00.8	345 20.1	. . 34.7		° ′	h m
22	274 32.6	105 00.4	4 59.9	326 17.6	28.2	52 57.3	00.9	0 22.7	34.7	Venus	192 18.6	15 00
23	289 35.0	120 00.4	N 4 58.7	341 20.8	28.4	67 59.6	00.9	15 25.3	34.7	Mars	51 12.8	0 24
	h m									Jupiter	138 29.7	18 32
Mer. Pass. 3 48.8		v 0.0	d 1.2	v 3.2	d 0.2	v 2.4	d 0.0	v 2.6	d 0.0	Saturn	85 42.8	22 03

UT	SUN GHA	SUN Dec	MOON GHA	MOON v	MOON Dec	MOON d	MOON HP
d h	° ′	° ′	° ′	′	° ′	′	′
24 00	178 22.3	N19 55.0	43 09.1	12.0	S19 08.5	4.2	54.5
01	193 22.3	54.4	57 40.1	12.0	19 12.7	4.2	54.5
02	208 22.2	53.9	72 11.1	11.9	19 16.9	4.0	54.5
03	223 22.2 ..	53.4	86 42.0	12.0	19 20.9	4.0	54.4
04	238 22.2	52.9	101 13.0	11.9	19 24.9	3.8	54.4
05	253 22.2	52.4	115 43.9	11.9	19 28.7	3.8	54.4
06	268 22.2	N19 51.8	130 14.8	12.0	S19 32.5	3.7	54.4
07	283 22.2	51.3	144 45.8	11.9	19 36.2	3.5	54.4
T 08	298 22.2	50.8	159 16.7	11.9	19 39.7	3.5	54.4
U 09	313 22.2 ..	50.3	173 47.6	11.8	19 43.2	3.4	54.4
E 10	328 22.2	49.7	188 18.4	11.9	19 46.6	3.3	54.4
S 11	343 22.1	49.2	202 49.3	11.9	19 49.9	3.2	54.3
D 12	358 22.1	N19 48.7	217 20.2	11.8	S19 53.1	3.1	54.3
A 13	13 22.1	48.1	231 51.0	11.9	19 56.2	3.0	54.3
Y 14	28 22.1	47.6	246 21.9	11.8	19 59.2	3.0	54.3
15	43 22.1 ..	47.1	260 52.7	11.8	20 02.2	2.8	54.3
16	58 22.1	46.6	275 23.5	11.8	20 05.0	2.7	54.3
17	73 22.1	46.0	289 54.3	11.8	20 07.7	2.7	54.3
18	88 22.1	N19 45.5	304 25.1	11.8	S20 10.4	2.5	54.3
19	103 22.1	45.0	318 55.9	11.8	20 12.9	2.5	54.3
20	118 22.1	44.4	333 26.7	11.8	20 15.4	2.3	54.3
21	133 22.1 ..	43.9	347 57.5	11.7	20 17.7	2.3	54.2
22	148 22.0	43.4	2 28.2	11.8	20 20.0	2.1	54.2
23	163 22.0	42.8	16 59.0	11.8	20 22.1	2.1	54.2
25 00	178 22.0	N19 42.3	31 29.8	11.7	S20 24.2	2.0	54.2
01	193 22.0	41.8	46 00.5	11.8	20 26.2	1.8	54.2
02	208 22.0	41.2	60 31.3	11.7	20 28.0	1.8	54.2
03	223 22.0 ..	40.7	75 02.0	11.8	20 29.8	1.7	54.2
04	238 22.0	40.2	89 32.8	11.7	20 31.5	1.6	54.2
05	253 22.0	39.6	104 03.5	11.7	20 33.1	1.5	54.2
06	268 22.0	N19 39.1	118 34.2	11.8	S20 34.6	1.4	54.2
W 07	283 22.0	38.5	133 05.0	11.7	20 36.0	1.2	54.2
E 08	298 22.0	38.0	147 35.7	11.7	20 37.2	1.2	54.1
D 09	313 22.0 ..	37.5	162 06.4	11.7	20 38.4	1.1	54.1
N 10	328 22.0	36.9	176 37.1	11.8	20 39.5	1.0	54.1
E 11	343 22.0	36.4	191 07.9	11.7	20 40.5	1.0	54.1
S 12	358 22.0	N19 35.8	205 38.6	11.7	S20 41.5	0.8	54.1
D 13	13 22.0	35.3	220 09.3	11.7	20 42.3	0.7	54.1
A 14	28 22.0	34.8	234 40.0	11.8	20 43.0	0.6	54.1
Y 15	43 22.0 ..	34.2	249 10.8	11.7	20 43.6	0.5	54.1
16	58 22.0	33.7	263 41.5	11.7	20 44.1	0.4	54.1
17	73 22.0	33.1	278 12.2	11.7	20 44.5	0.4	54.1
18	88 22.0	N19 32.6	292 42.9	11.8	S20 44.9	0.2	54.1
19	103 22.0	32.0	307 13.7	11.7	20 45.1	0.1	54.1
20	118 21.9	31.5	321 44.4	11.7	20 45.2	0.0	54.1
21	133 21.9 ..	30.9	336 15.1	11.8	20 45.2	0.0	54.1
22	148 21.9	30.4	350 45.9	11.7	20 45.2	0.2	54.1
23	163 21.9	29.8	5 16.6	11.8	20 45.0	0.2	54.1
26 00	178 21.9	N19 29.3	19 47.4	11.8	S20 44.8	0.4	54.0
01	193 21.9	28.7	34 18.2	11.7	20 44.4	0.4	54.0
02	208 21.9	28.2	48 48.9	11.8	20 44.0	0.6	54.0
03	223 21.9 ..	27.6	63 19.7	11.8	20 43.4	0.6	54.0
04	238 21.9	27.1	77 50.5	11.8	20 42.8	0.8	54.0
05	253 21.9	26.5	92 21.3	11.8	20 42.0	0.8	54.0
06	268 21.9	N19 26.0	106 52.1	11.8	S20 41.2	1.0	54.0
T 07	283 21.9	25.4	121 22.9	11.8	20 40.2	1.0	54.0
H 08	298 21.9	24.9	135 53.7	11.8	20 39.2	1.1	54.0
U 09	313 21.9 ..	24.3	150 24.5	11.9	20 38.1	1.2	54.0
R 10	328 22.0	23.8	164 55.4	11.8	20 36.9	1.3	54.0
S 11	343 22.0	23.2	179 26.2	11.9	20 35.6	1.5	54.0
D 12	358 22.0	N19 22.7	193 57.1	11.9	S20 34.1	1.5	54.0
A 13	13 22.0	22.1	208 28.0	11.8	20 32.6	1.6	54.0
Y 14	28 22.0	21.6	222 58.8	11.9	20 31.0	1.7	54.0
15	43 22.0 ..	21.0	237 29.7	12.0	20 29.3	1.8	54.0
16	58 22.0	20.4	252 00.7	11.9	20 27.5	1.9	54.0
17	73 22.0	19.9	266 31.6	11.9	20 25.6	1.9	54.0
18	88 22.0	N19 19.3	281 02.5	12.0	S20 23.7	2.1	54.0
19	103 22.0	18.8	295 33.5	11.9	20 21.6	2.2	54.0
20	118 22.0	18.2	310 04.4	12.0	20 19.4	2.2	54.0
21	133 22.0 ..	17.7	324 35.4	12.0	20 17.2	2.4	54.0
22	148 22.0	17.1	339 06.4	12.1	20 14.8	2.5	54.0
23	163 22.0	16.5	353 37.5	12.0	S20 12.3	2.5	54.0
	SD 15.8	d 0.5	SD 14.8		14.7		14.7

Twilight / Sunrise / Moonrise

Lat.	Twilight Naut.	Twilight Civil	Sunrise	Moonrise 24	Moonrise 25	Moonrise 26	Moonrise 27
°	h m	h m	h m	h m	h m	h m	h m
N 72	▭	▭	▭	■	■	■	■
N 70	▭	▭	▭	■	■	■	22 51
68	////	////	01 35	20 13	21 17	21 50	22 02
66	////	////	02 17	19 31	20 29	21 08	21 31
64	////	00 43	02 46	19 02	19 58	20 40	21 08
62	////	01 45	03 07	18 40	19 35	20 18	20 49
60	////	02 17	03 24	18 22	19 17	20 00	20 34
N 58	00 39	02 41	03 39	18 08	19 01	19 46	20 21
56	01 36	02 59	03 51	17 55	18 48	19 33	20 10
54	02 06	03 15	04 02	17 44	18 37	19 22	20 00
52	02 28	03 28	04 11	17 34	18 27	19 12	19 51
50	02 45	03 39	04 20	17 26	18 18	19 04	19 43
45	03 18	04 03	04 37	17 07	17 59	18 45	19 26
N 40	03 42	04 21	04 52	16 52	17 43	18 30	19 12
35	04 01	04 36	05 04	16 40	17 30	18 17	19 00
30	04 17	04 48	05 15	16 29	17 19	18 06	18 50
20	04 41	05 09	05 33	16 10	16 59	17 47	18 32
N 10	05 00	05 26	05 48	15 53	16 42	17 30	18 17
0	05 16	05 41	06 03	15 38	16 26	17 15	18 02
S 10	05 29	05 55	06 17	15 23	16 11	16 59	17 48
20	05 42	06 09	06 33	15 07	15 54	16 43	17 32
30	05 55	06 24	06 50	14 48	15 34	16 23	17 15
35	06 02	06 33	07 00	14 37	15 23	16 12	17 04
40	06 09	06 42	07 11	14 25	15 10	15 59	16 52
45	06 17	06 53	07 25	14 10	14 55	15 44	16 38
S 50	06 25	07 05	07 41	13 52	14 36	15 26	16 21
52	06 29	07 11	07 49	13 44	14 27	15 17	16 13
54	06 33	07 17	07 57	13 34	14 17	15 07	16 04
56	06 37	07 24	08 07	13 24	14 06	14 56	15 54
58	06 42	07 31	08 18	13 12	13 53	14 43	15 42
S 60	06 47	07 40	08 30	12 58	13 38	14 29	15 29

Sunset / Twilight / Moonset

Lat.	Sunset	Twilight Civil	Twilight Naut.	Moonset 24	Moonset 25	Moonset 26	Moonset 27
°	h m	h m	h m	h m	h m	h m	h m
N 72	▭	▭	▭	■	■	■	■
N 70	▭	▭	▭	■	■	■	■
68	22 33	////	////	23 23	23 59	25 07	01 07
66	21 52	////	////	24 06	00 06	00 48	01 49
64	21 25	23 19	////	00 05	00 35	01 18	02 17
62	21 04	22 24	////	00 24	00 57	01 41	02 38
60	20 47	21 53	////	00 39	01 15	02 00	02 55
N 58	20 33	21 30	23 24	00 53	01 29	02 15	03 10
56	20 21	21 12	22 34	01 04	01 42	02 28	03 22
54	20 10	20 57	22 05	01 14	01 53	02 40	03 33
52	20 01	20 44	21 44	01 23	02 03	02 50	03 43
50	19 53	20 33	21 26	01 31	02 12	02 59	03 51
45	19 35	20 10	20 54	01 48	02 31	03 18	04 10
N 40	19 21	19 52	20 30	02 03	02 46	03 33	04 24
35	19 09	19 37	20 11	02 14	02 59	03 46	04 37
30	18 58	19 24	19 56	02 25	03 10	03 58	04 48
20	18 40	19 04	19 32	02 43	03 29	04 17	05 07
N 10	18 24	18 47	19 13	02 59	03 46	04 34	05 23
0	18 10	18 32	18 58	03 13	04 01	04 50	05 38
S 10	17 56	18 18	18 44	03 28	04 17	05 06	05 53
20	17 41	18 04	18 31	03 44	04 34	05 23	06 09
30	17 23	17 49	18 18	04 02	04 53	05 42	06 28
35	17 13	17 41	18 11	04 12	05 04	05 53	06 38
40	17 02	17 31	18 04	04 24	05 17	06 06	06 51
45	16 49	17 21	17 57	04 39	05 32	06 21	07 05
S 50	16 32	17 08	17 48	04 56	05 51	06 40	07 23
52	16 25	17 03	17 44	05 04	06 00	06 49	07 31
54	16 16	16 57	17 41	05 13	06 10	06 59	07 40
56	16 07	16 50	17 36	05 24	06 21	07 10	07 51
58	15 56	16 42	17 32	05 36	06 34	07 23	08 02
S 60	15 43	16 34	17 27	05 49	06 49	07 38	08 16

SUN / MOON

Day	SUN Eqn. of Time 00ʰ	SUN Eqn. of Time 12ʰ	SUN Mer. Pass.	MOON Mer. Pass. Upper	MOON Mer. Pass. Lower	Age	Phase
d	m s	m s	h m	h m	h m	d	%
24	06 31	06 31	12 07	21 50	09 26	11	90
25	06 32	06 32	12 07	22 38	10 14	12	95
26	06 32	06 32	12 07	23 26	11 02	13	98

UT	ARIES GHA	VENUS −4.3 GHA	Dec	MARS −2.8 GHA	Dec	JUPITER −2.1 GHA	Dec	SATURN +0.2 GHA	Dec	STARS Name	SHA	Dec
27 00	304 37.5	135 00.5	N 4 57.5	356 23.9	S25 28.7	83 02.0	S15 01.0	30 28.0	S22 34.8	Acamar	315 15.8	S40 13.7
01	319 40.0	150 00.6	56.3	11 27.1	28.9	98 04.3	01.0	45 30.6	34.8	Achernar	335 24.1	S57 08.4
02	334 42.4	165 00.6	55.0	26 30.3	29.1	113 06.7	01.1	60 33.2	34.8	Acrux	173 05.6	S63 12.2
03	349 44.9	180 00.7 ..	53.8	41 33.5 ..	29.4	128 09.0 ..	01.1	75 35.8 ..	34.8	Adhara	255 10.1	S28 59.9
04	4 47.4	195 00.8	52.6	56 36.6	29.6	143 11.4	01.1	90 38.5	34.8	Aldebaran	290 45.6	N16 32.6
05	19 49.8	210 00.8	51.4	71 39.8	29.8	158 13.7	01.2	105 41.1	34.8			
06	34 52.3	225 00.9	N 4 50.2	86 43.0	S25 30.1	173 16.1	S15 01.2	120 43.7	S22 34.8	Alioth	166 17.9	N55 52.0
07	49 54.7	240 01.0	49.0	101 46.2	30.3	188 18.4	01.3	135 46.3	34.8	Alkaid	152 56.2	N49 13.7
08	64 57.2	255 01.1	47.7	116 49.3	30.5	203 20.8	01.3	150 48.9	34.8	Al Na'ir	27 39.0	S46 52.1
F 09	79 59.7	270 01.1 ..	46.5	131 52.5 ..	30.7	218 23.1 ..	01.4	165 51.6 ..	34.8	Alnilam	275 43.1	S 1 11.5
R 10	95 02.1	285 01.2	45.3	146 55.7	31.0	233 25.4	01.4	180 54.2	34.8	Alphard	217 53.0	S 8 44.3
I 11	110 04.6	300 01.3	44.1	161 58.9	31.2	248 27.8	01.5	195 56.8	34.9			
D 12	125 07.1	315 01.4	N 4 42.9	177 02.0	S25 31.4	263 30.1	S15 01.5	210 59.4	S22 34.9	Alphecca	126 07.9	N26 39.5
A 13	140 09.5	330 01.4	41.7	192 05.2	31.7	278 32.5	01.6	226 02.0	34.9	Alpheratz	357 39.7	N29 11.4
Y 14	155 12.0	345 01.5	40.4	207 08.4	31.9	293 34.8	01.6	241 04.7	34.9	Altair	62 04.5	N 8 55.2
15	170 14.5	0 01.6 ..	39.2	222 11.6 ..	32.1	308 37.2 ..	01.7	256 07.3 ..	34.9	Ankaa	353 12.1	S42 12.1
16	185 16.9	15 01.7	38.0	237 14.7	32.3	323 39.5	01.7	271 09.9	34.9	Antares	112 21.8	S26 28.2
17	200 19.4	30 01.8	36.8	252 17.9	32.6	338 41.9	01.8	286 12.5	34.9			
18	215 21.9	45 01.8	N 4 35.6	267 21.1	S25 32.8	353 44.2	S15 01.8	301 15.1	S22 34.9	Arcturus	145 52.6	N19 05.5
19	230 24.3	60 01.9	34.3	282 24.3	33.0	8 46.5	01.9	316 17.8	34.9	Atria	107 20.1	S69 03.6
20	245 26.8	75 02.0	33.1	297 27.4	33.3	23 48.9	01.9	331 20.4	34.9	Avior	234 17.2	S59 34.2
21	260 29.2	90 02.1 ..	31.9	312 30.6 ..	33.5	38 51.2 ..	01.9	346 23.0 ..	35.0	Bellatrix	278 28.5	N 6 21.9
22	275 31.7	105 02.2	30.7	327 33.8	33.7	53 53.6	02.0	1 25.6	35.0	Betelgeuse	270 57.8	N 7 24.5
23	290 34.2	120 02.2	29.5	342 37.0	33.9	68 55.9	02.0	16 28.2	35.0			
28 00	305 36.6	135 02.3	N 4 28.2	357 40.2	S25 34.2	83 58.3	S15 02.1	31 30.9	S22 35.0	Canopus	263 55.1	S52 42.3
01	320 39.1	150 02.4	27.0	12 43.3	34.4	99 00.6	02.1	46 33.5	35.0	Capella	280 29.6	N46 00.7
02	335 41.6	165 02.5	25.8	27 46.5	34.6	114 02.9	02.2	61 36.1	35.0	Deneb	49 28.6	N45 20.9
03	350 44.0	180 02.6 ..	24.6	42 49.7 ..	34.8	129 05.3 ..	02.2	76 38.7 ..	35.0	Denebola	182 30.3	N14 28.3
04	5 46.5	195 02.7	23.4	57 52.9	35.1	144 07.6	02.3	91 41.3	35.0	Diphda	348 52.3	S17 53.0
05	20 49.0	210 02.7	22.1	72 56.0	35.3	159 10.0	02.3	106 43.9	35.0			
06	35 51.4	225 02.8	N 4 20.9	87 59.2	S25 35.5	174 12.3	S15 02.4	121 46.6	S22 35.0	Dubhe	193 48.0	N61 39.3
07	50 53.9	240 02.9	19.7	103 02.4	35.7	189 14.6	02.4	136 49.2	35.0	Elnath	278 08.5	N28 37.1
08	65 56.4	255 03.0	18.5	118 05.6	35.9	204 17.0	02.5	151 51.8	35.1	Eltanin	90 44.1	N51 29.5
S 09	80 58.8	270 03.1 ..	17.3	133 08.8 ..	36.2	219 19.3 ..	02.5	166 54.4 ..	35.1	Enif	33 43.4	N 9 57.7
A 10	96 01.3	285 03.2	16.0	148 11.9	36.4	234 21.6	02.6	181 57.0	35.1	Fomalhaut	15 19.9	S29 31.3
T 11	111 03.7	300 03.3	14.8	163 15.1	36.6	249 24.0	02.6	196 59.7	35.1			
U R 12	126 06.2	315 03.4	N 4 13.6	178 18.3	S25 36.8	264 26.3	S15 02.7	212 02.3	S22 35.1	Gacrux	171 57.2	S57 13.1
D 13	141 08.7	330 03.5	12.4	193 21.5	37.0	279 28.7	02.7	227 04.9	35.1	Gienah	175 48.9	S17 38.6
A 14	156 11.1	345 03.5	11.2	208 24.7	37.3	294 31.0	02.8	242 07.5	35.1	Hadar	148 42.9	S60 27.8
Y 15	171 13.6	0 03.6 ..	09.9	223 27.8 ..	37.5	309 33.3 ..	02.8	257 10.1 ..	35.1	Hamal	327 56.8	N23 32.8
16	186 16.1	15 03.7	08.7	238 31.0	37.7	324 35.7	02.9	272 12.7	35.1	Kaus Aust.	83 38.8	S34 22.4
17	201 18.5	30 03.8	07.5	253 34.2	37.9	339 38.0	02.9	287 15.4	35.1			
18	216 21.0	45 03.9	N 4 06.3	268 37.4	S25 38.1	354 40.3	S15 03.0	302 18.0	S22 35.1	Kochab	137 20.0	N74 05.2
19	231 23.5	60 04.0	05.1	283 40.6	38.4	9 42.7	03.0	317 20.6	35.2	Markab	13 34.6	N15 18.3
20	246 25.9	75 04.1	03.8	298 43.7	38.6	24 45.0	03.1	332 23.2	35.2	Menkar	314 11.5	N 4 09.6
21	261 28.4	90 04.2 ..	02.6	313 46.9 ..	38.8	39 47.4 ..	03.1	347 25.8 ..	35.2	Menkent	148 03.5	S36 27.6
22	276 30.8	105 04.3	01.4	328 50.1	39.0	54 49.7	03.2	2 28.4	35.2	Miaplacidus	221 39.8	S69 47.7
23	291 33.3	120 04.4	4 00.2	343 53.3	39.2	69 52.0	03.2	17 31.1	35.2			
29 00	306 35.8	135 04.5	N 3 58.9	358 56.5	S25 39.5	84 54.4	S15 03.3	32 33.7	S22 35.2	Mirfak	308 35.5	N49 55.2
01	321 38.2	150 04.6	57.7	13 59.6	39.7	99 56.7	03.3	47 36.3	35.2	Nunki	75 53.7	S26 16.2
02	336 40.7	165 04.7	56.5	29 02.8	39.9	114 59.0	03.4	62 38.9	35.2	Peacock	53 13.2	S56 40.4
03	351 43.2	180 04.8 ..	55.3	44 06.0 ..	40.1	130 01.4 ..	03.4	77 41.5 ..	35.2	Pollux	243 23.9	N27 58.8
04	6 45.6	195 04.9	54.0	59 09.2	40.3	145 03.7	03.5	92 44.1	35.2	Procyon	244 56.4	N 5 10.6
05	21 48.1	210 05.0	52.8	74 12.4	40.5	160 06.0	03.5	107 46.8	35.3			
06	36 50.6	225 05.1	N 3 51.6	89 15.5	S25 40.7	175 08.4	S15 03.6	122 49.4	S22 35.3	Rasalhague	96 03.0	N12 33.1
07	51 53.0	240 05.2	50.4	104 18.7	41.0	190 10.7	03.6	137 52.0	35.3	Regulus	207 40.1	N11 52.7
08	66 55.5	255 05.3	49.2	119 21.9	41.2	205 13.0	03.7	152 54.6	35.3	Rigel	281 09.0	S 8 10.9
S 09	81 58.0	270 05.4 ..	47.9	134 25.1 ..	41.4	220 15.4 ..	03.7	167 57.2 ..	35.3	Rigil Kent.	139 46.9	S60 54.7
U 10	97 00.4	285 05.5	46.7	149 28.3	41.6	235 17.7	03.8	182 59.8	35.3	Sabik	102 08.3	S15 44.7
N 11	112 02.9	300 05.6	45.5	164 31.4	41.8	250 20.0	03.8	198 02.4	35.3			
D 12	127 05.3	315 05.7	N 3 44.3	179 34.6	S25 42.0	265 22.3	S15 03.9	213 05.1	S22 35.3	Schedar	349 36.3	N56 38.0
A 13	142 07.8	330 05.8	43.0	194 37.8	42.2	280 24.7	03.9	228 07.7	35.3	Shaula	96 16.9	S37 06.9
Y 14	157 10.3	345 05.9	41.8	209 41.0	42.4	295 27.0	04.0	243 10.3	35.3	Sirius	258 31.0	S16 44.5
15	172 12.7	0 06.0 ..	40.6	224 44.2 ..	42.7	310 29.3 ..	04.0	258 12.9 ..	35.3	Spica	158 27.6	S11 15.3
16	187 15.2	15 06.1	39.4	239 47.3	42.9	325 31.7	04.1	273 15.5	35.4	Suhail	222 50.3	S43 30.5
17	202 17.7	30 06.2	38.1	254 50.5	43.1	340 34.0	04.1	288 18.1	35.4			
18	217 20.1	45 06.3	N 3 36.9	269 53.7	S25 43.3	355 36.3	S15 04.2	303 20.7	S22 35.4	Vega	80 36.2	N38 48.3
19	232 22.6	60 06.4	35.7	284 56.9	43.5	10 38.7	04.2	318 23.4	35.4	Zuben'ubi	137 01.5	S16 07.0
20	247 25.1	75 06.5	34.5	300 00.1	43.7	25 41.0	04.3	333 26.0	35.4		SHA	Mer. Pass.
21	262 27.5	90 06.6 ..	33.2	315 03.3 ..	43.9	40 43.3 ..	04.3	348 28.6 ..	35.4	Venus	189 25.7	15 00
22	277 30.0	105 06.7	32.0	330 06.4	44.1	55 45.6	04.4	3 31.2	35.4	Mars	52 05.3	0 09
23	292 32.5	120 06.8	30.8	345 09.6	44.3	70 48.0	04.4	18 33.8	35.4	Jupiter	138 21.6	18 21
Mer. Pass. 3 37.0		v 0.1	d 1.2	v 3.2	d 0.2	v 2.3	d 0.0	v 2.6	d 0.0	Saturn	85 54.2	21 50

UT	SUN GHA	SUN Dec	MOON GHA	v	MOON Dec	d	HP
d h	° ′	° ′	° ′	′	° ′	′	′
27 00	178 22.0	N19 16.0	8 08.5	12.0	S20 09.8	2.6	54.0
01	193 22.0	15.4	22 39.5	12.1	20 07.2	2.8	54.0
02	208 22.0	14.8	37 10.6	12.1	20 04.4	2.8	54.0
03	223 22.0 ..	14.3	51 41.7	12.1	20 01.6	2.9	54.0
04	238 22.0	13.7	66 12.8	12.1	19 58.7	3.0	54.0
05	253 22.0	13.2	80 43.9	12.2	19 55.7	3.1	54.0
06	268 22.0	N19 12.6	95 15.1	12.2	S19 52.6	3.2	54.0
07	283 22.1	12.0	109 46.3	12.2	19 49.4	3.3	54.0
F 08	298 22.1	11.5	124 17.5	12.2	19 46.1	3.4	54.0
R 09	313 22.1 ..	10.9	138 48.7	12.2	19 42.7	3.4	54.0
I 10	328 22.1	10.3	153 19.9	12.3	19 39.3	3.6	54.0
D 11	343 22.1	09.8	167 51.2	12.2	19 35.7	3.6	54.0
A 12	358 22.1	N19 09.2	182 22.4	12.3	S19 32.1	3.7	54.0
Y 13	13 22.1	08.6	196 53.7	12.3	19 28.4	3.9	54.0
14	28 22.1	08.1	211 25.0	12.4	19 24.5	3.9	54.0
15	43 22.1 ..	07.5	225 56.4	12.4	19 20.6	4.0	54.0
16	58 22.1	06.9	240 27.8	12.3	19 16.6	4.1	54.0
17	73 22.1	06.3	254 59.1	12.5	19 12.5	4.1	54.0
18	88 22.2	N19 05.8	269 30.6	12.4	S19 08.4	4.3	54.0
19	103 22.2	05.2	284 02.0	12.5	19 04.1	4.3	54.0
20	118 22.2	04.6	298 33.5	12.4	18 59.8	4.5	54.0
21	133 22.2 ..	04.1	313 04.9	12.6	18 55.3	4.5	54.0
22	148 22.2	03.5	327 36.5	12.5	18 50.8	4.6	54.0
23	163 22.2	02.9	342 08.0	12.6	18 46.2	4.7	54.0
28 00	178 22.2	N19 02.3	356 39.6	12.5	S18 41.5	4.7	54.0
01	193 22.2	01.8	11 11.1	12.7	18 36.8	4.9	54.0
02	208 22.2	01.2	25 42.8	12.6	18 31.9	4.9	54.0
03	223 22.3 ..	00.6	40 14.4	12.7	18 27.0	5.1	54.0
04	238 22.3	19 00.0	54 46.1	12.7	18 21.9	5.1	54.0
05	253 22.3	18 59.5	69 17.8	12.7	18 16.8	5.2	54.0
06	268 22.3	N18 58.9	83 49.5	12.7	S18 11.6	5.2	54.0
S 07	283 22.3	58.3	98 21.2	12.8	18 06.4	5.4	54.0
A 08	298 22.3	57.7	112 53.0	12.8	18 01.0	5.4	54.0
T 09	313 22.3 ..	57.1	127 24.8	12.8	17 55.6	5.5	54.0
U 10	328 22.4	56.6	141 56.6	12.9	17 50.1	5.6	54.0
R 11	343 22.4	56.0	156 28.5	12.9	17 44.5	5.7	54.0
D 12	358 22.4	N18 55.4	171 00.4	12.9	S17 38.8	5.8	54.0
A 13	13 22.4	54.8	185 32.3	12.9	17 33.0	5.8	54.1
Y 14	28 22.4	54.2	200 04.2	13.0	17 27.2	5.9	54.1
15	43 22.4 ..	53.6	214 36.2	13.0	17 21.3	6.0	54.1
16	58 22.4	53.1	229 08.2	13.0	17 15.3	6.1	54.1
17	73 22.5	52.5	243 40.2	13.0	17 09.2	6.1	54.1
18	88 22.5	N18 51.9	258 12.2	13.1	S17 03.1	6.2	54.1
19	103 22.5	51.3	272 44.3	13.1	16 56.9	6.3	54.1
20	118 22.5	50.7	287 16.4	13.2	16 50.6	6.4	54.1
21	133 22.5 ..	50.1	301 48.6	13.1	16 44.2	6.5	54.1
22	148 22.5	49.6	316 20.7	13.2	16 37.7	6.5	54.1
23	163 22.6	49.0	330 52.9	13.2	16 31.2	6.6	54.1
29 00	178 22.6	N18 48.4	345 25.1	13.3	S16 24.6	6.6	54.1
01	193 22.6	47.8	359 57.4	13.3	16 18.0	6.8	54.1
02	208 22.6	47.2	14 29.7	13.3	16 11.2	6.8	54.1
03	223 22.6 ..	46.6	29 02.0	13.3	16 04.4	6.9	54.1
04	238 22.7	46.0	43 34.3	13.4	15 57.5	6.9	54.1
05	253 22.7	45.4	58 06.7	13.4	15 50.6	7.1	54.1
06	268 22.7	N18 44.8	72 39.1	13.4	S15 43.5	7.1	54.2
07	283 22.7	44.3	87 11.5	13.4	15 36.4	7.1	54.2
S 08	298 22.7	43.7	101 43.9	13.5	15 29.3	7.3	54.2
U 09	313 22.8 ..	43.1	116 16.4	13.5	15 22.0	7.3	54.2
N 10	328 22.8	42.5	130 48.9	13.5	15 14.7	7.4	54.2
D 11	343 22.8	41.9	145 21.4	13.6	15 07.3	7.4	54.2
A 12	358 22.8	N18 41.3	159 54.0	13.6	S14 59.9	7.5	54.2
Y 13	13 22.8	40.7	174 26.6	13.6	14 52.4	7.6	54.2
14	28 22.9	40.1	188 59.2	13.6	14 44.8	7.6	54.2
15	43 22.9 ..	39.5	203 31.8	13.7	14 37.2	7.7	54.2
16	58 22.9	38.9	218 04.5	13.6	14 29.5	7.8	54.2
17	73 22.9	38.3	232 37.1	13.8	14 21.7	7.8	54.2
18	88 23.0	N18 37.7	247 09.9	13.7	S14 13.9	7.9	54.3
19	103 23.0	37.1	261 42.6	13.8	14 06.0	8.0	54.3
20	118 23.0	36.5	276 15.4	13.8	13 58.0	8.0	54.3
21	133 23.0 ..	35.9	290 48.2	13.8	13 50.0	8.1	54.3
22	148 23.0	35.3	305 21.0	13.8	13 41.9	8.1	54.3
23	163 23.1	34.7	319 53.8	13.9	S13 33.8	8.3	54.3
	SD 15.8	d 0.6	SD 14.7		14.7		14.8

Lat.	Twilight Naut.	Twilight Civil	Sunrise	Moonrise 27	Moonrise 28	Moonrise 29	Moonrise 30
°	h m	h m	h m	h m	h m	h m	h m
N 72	▭	▭	▭	▬	23 22	22 54	22 37
N 70	////	////	00 34	22 51	22 37	22 28	22 21
68	////	////	01 53	22 02	22 07	22 08	22 08
66	////	////	02 29	21 31	21 44	21 52	21 58
64	////	01 12	02 55	21 08	21 26	21 39	21 49
62	////	01 58	03 15	20 49	21 12	21 28	21 41
60	////	02 27	03 31	20 34	20 59	21 19	21 35
N 58	01 06	02 49	03 45	20 21	20 48	21 11	21 29
56	01 48	03 06	03 56	20 10	20 39	21 03	21 24
54	02 14	03 21	04 06	20 00	20 31	20 57	21 19
52	02 35	03 33	04 16	19 51	20 23	20 51	21 15
50	02 51	03 44	04 24	19 43	20 16	20 45	21 11
45	03 23	04 06	04 41	19 26	20 02	20 34	21 03
N 40	03 46	04 24	04 55	19 12	19 50	20 24	20 56
35	04 04	04 38	05 06	19 00	19 40	20 16	20 49
30	04 19	04 50	05 17	18 50	19 31	20 09	20 44
20	04 42	05 10	05 34	18 32	19 15	19 56	20 35
N 10	05 01	05 27	05 49	18 17	19 02	19 45	20 27
0	05 16	05 41	06 03	18 02	18 49	19 35	20 19
S 10	05 29	05 55	06 17	17 48	18 36	19 24	20 11
20	05 42	06 08	06 31	17 32	18 23	19 13	20 03
30	05 54	06 23	06 48	17 15	18 07	19 00	19 54
35	06 00	06 31	06 58	17 04	17 58	18 53	19 48
40	06 07	06 40	07 09	16 52	17 48	18 44	19 42
45	06 14	06 50	07 22	16 38	17 35	18 35	19 35
S 50	06 22	07 02	07 37	16 21	17 20	18 23	19 26
52	06 26	07 07	07 45	16 13	17 13	18 17	19 22
54	06 29	07 13	07 53	16 04	17 06	18 11	19 18
56	06 33	07 19	08 02	15 54	16 57	18 04	19 13
58	06 38	07 26	08 12	15 42	16 47	17 56	19 07
S 60	06 42	07 34	08 24	15 29	16 36	17 47	19 01

Lat.	Sunset	Twilight Civil	Twilight Naut.	Moonset 27	Moonset 28	Moonset 29	Moonset 30
°	h m	h m	h m	h m	h m	h m	h m
N 72	▭	▭	▭	▬	▬	02 51	04 53
N 70	23 22	////	////	▬	01 45	03 35	05 18
68	22 15	////	////	01 07	02 33	04 04	05 36
66	21 40	////	////	01 49	03 04	04 26	05 51
64	21 16	22 54	////	02 17	03 27	04 43	06 03
62	20 56	22 11	////	02 38	03 45	04 57	06 14
60	20 40	21 43	////	02 55	04 00	05 09	06 22
N 58	20 27	21 22	23 01	03 10	04 12	05 20	06 30
56	20 15	21 05	22 22	03 22	04 23	05 29	06 37
54	20 05	20 51	21 56	03 33	04 33	05 36	06 43
52	19 57	20 39	21 36	03 43	04 41	05 44	06 48
50	19 49	20 28	21 20	03 51	04 49	05 50	06 53
45	19 32	20 06	20 49	04 10	05 05	06 04	07 03
N 40	19 18	19 49	20 26	04 24	05 19	06 15	07 12
35	19 06	19 34	20 08	04 37	05 30	06 24	07 20
30	18 56	19 22	19 54	04 48	05 40	06 33	07 26
20	18 39	19 02	19 30	05 07	05 57	06 47	07 37
N 10	18 24	18 46	19 12	05 23	06 11	07 00	07 47
0	18 10	18 32	18 57	05 38	06 25	07 11	07 56
S 10	17 56	18 18	18 44	05 53	06 39	07 23	08 05
20	17 42	18 05	18 32	06 09	06 53	07 35	08 15
30	17 25	17 51	18 19	06 28	07 10	07 49	08 26
35	17 16	17 43	18 13	06 38	07 20	07 57	08 32
40	17 05	17 34	18 07	06 51	07 31	08 06	08 39
45	16 52	17 24	17 59	07 05	07 43	08 17	08 47
S 50	16 36	17 12	17 51	07 23	07 59	08 30	08 57
52	16 29	17 07	17 48	07 31	08 06	08 36	09 02
54	16 21	17 01	17 44	07 40	08 14	08 43	09 07
56	16 12	16 54	17 40	07 51	08 23	08 50	09 12
58	16 02	16 47	17 36	08 02	08 34	08 58	09 19
S 60	15 50	16 39	17 31	08 16	08 46	09 08	09 25

Day	SUN Eqn. of Time 00h	SUN Eqn. of Time 12h	SUN Mer. Pass.	MOON Mer. Pass. Upper	MOON Mer. Pass. Lower	Age	Phase
d	m s	m s	h m	h m	h m	d	%
27	06 32	06 32	12 07	24 14	11 50	14	100
28	06 31	06 31	12 07	00 14	12 37	15	100
29	06 30	06 29	12 06	01 00	13 23	16	98

UT	ARIES	VENUS −4.3		MARS −2.8		JUPITER −2.1		SATURN +0.2		STARS		
	GHA	GHA	Dec	GHA	Dec	GHA	Dec	GHA	Dec	Name	SHA	Dec
d h	° ′	° ′	° ′	° ′	° ′	° ′	° ′	° ′	° ′		° ′	° ′
30 00	307 34.9	135 07.0 N 3 29.6		0 12.8 S25 44.5		85 50.3 S15 04.5		33 36.4 S22 35.4		Acamar	315 15.8	S40 13.7
01	322 37.4	150 07.1	28.3	15 16.0	44.7	100 52.6	04.5	48 39.0	35.4	Achernar	335 24.1	S57 08.4
02	337 39.8	165 07.2	27.1	30 19.2	44.9	115 54.9	04.6	63 41.6	35.4	Acrux	173 05.7	S63 12.2
03	352 42.3	180 07.3 . .	25.9	45 22.3 . .	45.2	130 57.3 . .	04.7	78 44.3 . .	35.5	Adhara	255 10.1	S28 59.8
04	7 44.8	195 07.4	24.7	60 25.5	45.4	145 59.6	04.7	93 46.9	35.5	Aldebaran	290 45.6	N16 32.6
05	22 47.2	210 07.5	23.4	75 28.7	45.6	161 01.9	04.8	108 49.5	35.5			
06	37 49.7	225 07.6 N 3 22.2		90 31.9 S25 45.8		176 04.2 S15 04.8		123 52.1 S22 35.5		Alioth	166 17.9	N55 52.0
07	52 52.2	240 07.7	21.0	105 35.1	46.0	191 06.6	04.9	138 54.7	35.5	Alkaid	152 56.3	N49 13.7
08	67 54.6	255 07.9	19.8	120 38.2	46.2	206 08.9	04.9	153 57.3	35.5	Al Na'ir	27 39.0	S46 52.1
M 09	82 57.1	270 08.0 . .	18.5	135 41.4 . .	46.4	221 11.2 . .	05.0	168 59.9 . .	35.5	Alnilam	275 43.1	S 1 11.5
O 10	97 59.6	285 08.1	17.3	150 44.6	46.6	236 13.5	05.0	184 02.5	35.5	Alphard	217 53.0	S 8 44.3
N 11	113 02.0	300 08.2	16.1	165 47.8	46.8	251 15.9	05.1	199 05.2	35.5			
D 12	128 04.5	315 08.3 N 3 14.9		180 51.0 S25 47.0		266 18.2 S15 05.1		214 07.8 S22 35.5		Alphecca	126 08.0	N26 39.5
A 13	143 06.9	330 08.4	13.6	195 54.1	47.2	281 20.5	05.2	229 10.4	35.5	Alpheratz	357 39.7	N29 11.4
Y 14	158 09.4	345 08.5	12.4	210 57.3	47.4	296 22.8	05.2	244 13.0	35.6	Altair	62 04.5	N 8 55.2
15	173 11.9	0 08.7 . .	11.2	226 00.5 . .	47.6	311 25.2 . .	05.3	259 15.6 . .	35.6	Ankaa	353 12.1	S42 12.1
16	188 14.3	15 08.8	10.0	241 03.7	47.8	326 27.5	05.3	274 18.2	35.6	Antares	112 21.8	S26 28.2
17	203 16.8	30 08.9	08.7	256 06.9	48.0	341 29.8	05.4	289 20.8	35.6			
18	218 19.3	45 09.0 N 3 07.5		271 10.0 S25 48.2		356 32.1 S15 05.4		304 23.4 S22 35.6		Arcturus	145 52.6	N19 05.5
19	233 21.7	60 09.1	06.3	286 13.2	48.4	11 34.5	05.5	319 26.1	35.6	Atria	107 20.1	S69 03.7
20	248 24.2	75 09.3	05.1	301 16.4	48.6	26 36.8	05.6	334 28.7	35.6	Avior	234 17.2	S59 34.2
21	263 26.7	90 09.4 . .	03.8	316 19.6 . .	48.8	41 39.1 . .	05.6	349 31.3 . .	35.6	Bellatrix	278 28.5	N 6 21.9
22	278 29.1	105 09.5	02.6	331 22.8	49.0	56 41.4	05.7	4 33.9	35.6	Betelgeuse	270 57.8	N 7 24.5
23	293 31.6	120 09.6	01.4	346 25.9	49.2	71 43.7	05.7	19 36.5	35.6			
31 00	308 34.1	135 09.7 N 3 00.2		1 29.1 S25 49.4		86 46.1 S15 05.8		34 39.1 S22 35.6		Canopus	263 55.1	S52 42.3
01	323 36.5	150 09.9	2 58.9	16 32.3	49.6	101 48.4	05.8	49 41.7	35.7	Capella	280 29.6	N46 00.7
02	338 39.0	165 10.0	57.7	31 35.5	49.8	116 50.7	05.9	64 44.3	35.7	Deneb	49 28.6	N45 20.9
03	353 41.4	180 10.1 . .	56.5	46 38.7 . .	50.0	131 53.0 . .	05.9	79 46.9 . .	35.7	Denebola	182 30.3	N14 28.3
04	8 43.9	195 10.2	55.2	61 41.8	50.2	146 55.3	06.0	94 49.5	35.7	Diphda	348 52.3	S17 53.0
05	23 46.4	210 10.4	54.0	76 45.0	50.4	161 57.7	06.0	109 52.2	35.7			
06	38 48.8	225 10.5 N 2 52.8		91 48.2 S25 50.6		177 00.0 S15 06.1		124 54.8 S22 35.7		Dubhe	193 48.0	N61 39.3
07	53 51.3	240 10.6	51.6	106 51.4	50.8	192 02.3	06.1	139 57.4	35.7	Elnath	278 08.5	N28 37.1
08	68 53.8	255 10.8	50.3	121 54.6	51.0	207 04.6	06.2	155 00.0	35.7	Eltanin	90 44.1	N51 29.5
T 09	83 56.2	270 10.9 . .	49.1	136 57.7 . .	51.2	222 06.9 . .	06.3	170 02.6 . .	35.7	Enif	33 43.4	N 9 57.7
U 10	98 58.7	285 11.0	47.9	152 00.9	51.3	237 09.2	06.3	185 05.2	35.7	Fomalhaut	15 19.9	S29 31.3
E 11	114 01.2	300 11.1	46.7	167 04.1	51.5	252 11.6	06.4	200 07.8	35.7			
S 12	129 03.6	315 11.3 N 2 45.4		182 07.3 S25 51.7		267 13.9 S15 06.4		215 10.4 S22 35.8		Gacrux	171 57.2	S57 13.1
D 13	144 06.1	330 11.4	44.2	197 10.5	51.9	282 16.2	06.5	230 13.0	35.8	Gienah	175 48.9	S17 38.6
A 14	159 08.5	345 11.5	43.0	212 13.6	52.1	297 18.5	06.5	245 15.6	35.8	Hadar	148 42.9	S60 27.8
Y 15	174 11.0	0 11.7 . .	41.7	227 16.8 . .	52.3	312 20.8 . .	06.6	260 18.2 . .	35.8	Hamal	327 56.8	N23 32.8
16	189 13.5	15 11.8	40.5	242 20.0	52.5	327 23.1	06.6	275 20.9	35.8	Kaus Aust.	83 38.9	S34 22.4
17	204 15.9	30 11.9	39.3	257 23.2	52.7	342 25.5	06.7	290 23.5	35.8			
18	219 18.4	45 12.1 N 2 38.1		272 26.3 S25 52.9		357 27.8 S15 06.8		305 26.1 S22 35.8		Kochab	137 20.1	N74 05.2
19	234 20.9	60 12.2	36.8	287 29.5	53.1	12 30.1	06.8	320 28.7	35.8	Markab	13 34.6	N15 18.3
20	249 23.3	75 12.3	35.6	302 32.7	53.3	27 32.4	06.9	335 31.3	35.8	Menkar	314 11.5	N 4 09.6
21	264 25.8	90 12.5 . .	34.4	317 35.9 . .	53.5	42 34.7 . .	06.9	350 33.9 . .	35.8	Menkent	148 03.5	S36 27.6
22	279 28.3	105 12.6	33.2	332 39.1	53.6	57 37.0	07.0	5 36.5	35.8	Miaplacidus	221 39.8	S69 47.7
23	294 30.7	120 12.7	31.9	347 42.2	53.8	72 39.4	07.0	20 39.1	35.9			
1 00	309 33.2	135 12.9 N 2 30.7		2 45.4 S25 54.0		87 41.7 S15 07.1		35 41.7 S22 35.9		Mirfak	308 35.5	N49 55.2
01	324 35.7	150 13.0	29.5	17 48.6	54.2	102 44.0	07.1	50 44.3	35.9	Nunki	75 53.7	S26 16.2
02	339 38.1	165 13.1	28.2	32 51.8	54.4	117 46.3	07.2	65 46.9	35.9	Peacock	53 13.2	S56 40.4
03	354 40.6	180 13.3 . .	27.0	47 54.9 . .	54.6	132 48.6 . .	07.3	80 49.5 . .	35.9	Pollux	243 23.9	N27 58.8
04	9 43.0	195 13.4	25.8	62 58.1	54.8	147 50.9	07.3	95 52.1	35.9	Procyon	244 56.4	N 5 10.6
05	24 45.5	210 13.5	24.6	78 01.3	54.9	162 53.2	07.4	110 54.7	35.9			
06	39 48.0	225 13.7 N 2 23.3		93 04.5 S25 55.1		177 55.5 S15 07.4		125 57.4 S22 35.9		Rasalhague	96 03.0	N12 33.1
W 07	54 50.4	240 13.8	22.1	108 07.6	55.3	192 57.9	07.5	141 00.0	35.9	Regulus	207 40.1	N11 52.7
E 08	69 52.9	255 14.0	20.9	123 10.8	55.5	208 00.2	07.5	156 02.6	35.9	Rigel	281 08.9	S 8 10.9
D 09	84 55.4	270 14.1 . .	19.6	138 14.0 . .	55.7	223 02.5 . .	07.6	171 05.2 . .	35.9	Rigil Kent.	139 46.9	S60 54.7
N 10	99 57.8	285 14.2	18.4	153 17.2	55.9	238 04.8	07.7	186 07.8	36.0	Sabik	102 08.3	S15 44.7
E 11	115 00.3	300 14.4	17.2	168 20.3	56.1	253 07.1	07.7	201 10.4	36.0			
S 12	130 02.8	315 14.5 N 2 16.0		183 23.5 S25 56.2		268 09.4 S15 07.8		216 13.0 S22 36.0		Schedar	349 36.2	N56 38.0
D 13	145 05.2	330 14.7	14.7	198 26.7	56.4	283 11.7	07.8	231 15.6	36.0	Shaula	96 16.9	S37 06.9
A 14	160 07.7	345 14.8	13.5	213 29.9	56.6	298 14.0	07.9	246 18.2	36.0	Sirius	258 31.0	S16 44.5
Y 15	175 10.2	0 15.0 . .	12.3	228 33.0 . .	56.8	313 16.3 . .	07.9	261 20.8 . .	36.0	Spica	158 27.7	S11 15.3
16	190 12.6	15 15.1	11.0	243 36.2	57.0	328 18.6	08.0	276 23.4	36.0	Suhail	222 50.3	S43 30.5
17	205 15.1	30 15.3	09.8	258 39.4	57.1	343 21.0	08.1	291 26.0	36.0			
18	220 17.5	45 15.4 N 2 08.6		273 42.5 S25 57.3		358 23.3 S15 08.1		306 28.6 S22 36.0		Vega	80 36.2	N38 48.3
19	235 20.0	60 15.5	07.4	288 45.7	57.5	13 25.6	08.2	321 31.2	36.0	Zuben'ubi	137 01.5	S16 07.0
20	250 22.5	75 15.7	06.1	303 48.9	57.7	28 27.9	08.2	336 33.8	36.0		SHA	Mer.Pass.
21	265 24.9	90 15.8 . .	04.9	318 52.1 . .	57.9	43 30.2 . .	08.3	351 36.4 . .	36.1		° ′	h m
22	280 27.4	105 16.0	03.7	333 55.2	58.0	58 32.5	08.3	6 39.0	36.1	Venus	186 35.7	14 59
23	295 29.9	120 16.1	02.4	348 58.4	58.2	73 34.8	08.4	21 41.6	36.1	Mars	52 55.1	23 49
	h m									Jupiter	138 12.0	18 10
Mer.Pass. 3 25.2		v 0.1	d 1.2	v 3.2	d 0.2	v 2.3	d 0.1	v 2.6	d 0.0	Saturn	86 05.1	21 38

UT	SUN GHA	SUN Dec	MOON GHA	v	Dec	d	HP
d h	° ′	° ′	° ′	′	° ′	′	′
30 00	178 23.1	N18 34.1	334 26.7	13.9	S13 25.5	8.2	54.3
01	193 23.1	33.5	348 59.6	13.9	13 17.3	8.3	54.3
02	208 23.1	32.9	3 32.5	13.9	13 09.0	8.4	54.3
03	223 23.2 ..	32.3	18 05.4	14.0	13 00.6	8.5	54.3
04	238 23.2	31.7	32 38.4	14.0	12 52.1	8.5	54.4
05	253 23.2	31.1	47 11.4	14.0	12 43.6	8.5	54.4
06	268 23.2	N18 30.5	61 44.4	14.0	S12 35.1	8.7	54.4
07	283 23.3	29.9	76 17.4	14.1	12 26.4	8.6	54.4
M 08	298 23.3	29.3	90 50.5	14.1	12 17.8	8.8	54.4
O 09	313 23.3 ..	28.7	105 23.6	14.1	12 09.0	8.7	54.4
N 10	328 23.4	28.1	119 56.7	14.1	12 00.3	8.9	54.4
D 11	343 23.4	27.5	134 29.8	14.1	11 51.4	8.9	54.4
A 12	358 23.4	N18 26.9	149 02.9	14.2	S11 42.5	8.9	54.5
Y 13	13 23.4	26.3	163 36.1	14.2	11 33.6	9.0	54.5
14	28 23.5	25.7	178 09.3	14.2	11 24.6	9.0	54.5
15	43 23.5 ..	25.0	192 42.5	14.2	11 15.6	9.1	54.5
16	58 23.5	24.4	207 15.7	14.3	11 06.5	9.2	54.5
17	73 23.5	23.8	221 48.9	14.3	10 57.3	9.2	54.5
18	88 23.6	N18 23.2	236 22.2	14.3	S10 48.1	9.2	54.5
19	103 23.6	22.6	250 55.4	14.3	10 38.9	9.3	54.5
20	118 23.6	22.0	265 28.7	14.3	10 29.6	9.4	54.6
21	133 23.7 ..	21.4	280 02.0	14.4	10 20.2	9.4	54.6
22	148 23.7	20.8	294 35.4	14.4	10 10.8	9.4	54.6
23	163 23.7	20.2	309 08.7	14.4	10 01.4	9.5	54.6
31 00	178 23.8	N18 19.6	323 42.1	14.3	S 9 51.9	9.5	54.6
01	193 23.8	18.9	338 15.4	14.4	9 42.4	9.6	54.6
02	208 23.8	18.3	352 48.8	14.4	9 32.8	9.6	54.6
03	223 23.9 ..	17.7	7 22.2	14.4	9 23.2	9.7	54.7
04	238 23.9	17.1	21 55.6	14.5	9 13.5	9.7	54.7
05	253 23.9	16.5	36 29.1	14.4	9 03.8	9.8	54.7
06	268 23.9	N18 15.9	51 02.5	14.5	S 8 54.0	9.8	54.7
07	283 24.0	15.2	65 36.0	14.4	8 44.2	9.8	54.7
T 08	298 24.0	14.6	80 09.4	14.5	8 34.4	9.9	54.7
U 09	313 24.0 ..	14.0	94 42.9	14.5	8 24.5	9.9	54.7
E 10	328 24.1	13.4	109 16.4	14.5	8 14.6	10.0	54.8
S 11	343 24.1	12.8	123 49.9	14.5	8 04.6	10.0	54.8
D 12	358 24.1	N18 12.2	138 23.4	14.5	S 7 54.6	10.0	54.8
A 13	13 24.2	11.5	152 56.9	14.5	7 44.6	10.1	54.8
Y 14	28 24.2	10.9	167 30.4	14.5	7 34.5	10.1	54.8
15	43 24.2 ..	10.3	182 03.9	14.5	7 24.4	10.1	54.8
16	58 24.3	09.7	196 37.4	14.6	7 14.3	10.2	54.9
17	73 24.3	09.1	211 11.0	14.5	7 04.1	10.2	54.9
18	88 24.4	N18 08.4	225 44.5	14.6	S 6 53.9	10.3	54.9
19	103 24.4	07.8	240 18.1	14.5	6 43.6	10.3	54.9
20	118 24.4	07.2	254 51.6	14.6	6 33.3	10.3	54.9
21	133 24.5 ..	06.6	269 25.2	14.5	6 23.0	10.3	55.0
22	148 24.5	05.9	283 58.7	14.6	6 12.7	10.4	55.0
23	163 24.5	05.3	298 32.3	14.6	6 02.3	10.4	55.0
1 00	178 24.6	N18 04.7	313 05.9	14.5	S 5 51.9	10.5	55.0
01	193 24.6	04.1	327 39.4	14.6	5 41.4	10.5	55.0
02	208 24.6	03.4	342 13.0	14.6	5 30.9	10.5	55.0
03	223 24.7 ..	02.8	356 46.6	14.5	5 20.4	10.5	55.1
04	238 24.7	02.2	11 20.1	14.6	5 09.9	10.6	55.1
05	253 24.8	01.5	25 53.7	14.5	4 59.3	10.6	55.1
06	268 24.8	N18 00.9	40 27.2	14.6	S 4 48.7	10.6	55.1
W 07	283 24.8	18 00.3	55 00.8	14.5	4 38.1	10.6	55.1
E 08	298 24.9	17 59.7	69 34.3	14.6	4 27.5	10.7	55.2
D 09	313 24.9 ..	59.0	84 07.9	14.5	4 16.8	10.7	55.2
N 10	328 25.0	58.4	98 41.4	14.5	4 06.1	10.7	55.2
E 11	343 25.0	57.8	113 14.9	14.6	3 55.4	10.8	55.2
S 12	358 25.0	N17 57.1	127 48.5	14.5	S 3 44.6	10.7	55.2
D 13	13 25.1	56.5	142 22.0	14.5	3 33.9	10.8	55.3
A 14	28 25.1	55.9	156 55.5	14.5	3 23.1	10.9	55.3
Y 15	43 25.2 ..	55.2	171 29.0	14.5	3 12.2	10.8	55.3
16	58 25.2	54.6	186 02.5	14.5	3 01.4	10.8	55.3
17	73 25.2	54.0	200 36.0	14.4	2 50.6	10.9	55.4
18	88 25.3	N17 53.3	215 09.4	14.5	S 2 39.7	10.9	55.4
19	103 25.3	52.7	229 42.9	14.4	2 28.8	10.9	55.4
20	118 25.4	52.1	244 16.3	14.5	2 17.9	11.0	55.4
21	133 25.4 ..	51.4	258 49.8	14.4	2 06.9	10.9	55.4
22	148 25.4	50.8	273 23.2	14.4	1 56.0	11.0	55.5
23	163 25.5	50.2	287 56.6	14.3	S 1 45.0	10.9	55.5
	SD 15.8	d 0.6	SD 14.8		14.9		15.1

Lat.	Twilight Naut.	Twilight Civil	Sunrise	Moonrise 30	31	1	2
°	h m	h m	h m	h m	h m	h m	h m
N 72	□	□	□	22 37	22 24	22 12	22 00
N 70	////	////	01 16	22 21	22 15	22 09	22 03
68	////	////	02 09	22 08	22 08	22 07	22 06
66	////	////	02 41	21 58	22 02	22 05	22 08
64	////	01 33	03 05	21 49	21 57	22 03	22 10
62	////	02 11	03 23	21 41	21 52	22 02	22 12
60	////	02 37	03 38	21 35	21 48	22 01	22 13
N 58	01 24	02 57	03 51	21 29	21 45	22 00	22 14
56	01 59	03 13	04 02	21 24	21 42	21 59	22 16
54	02 23	03 27	04 11	21 19	21 39	21 58	22 17
52	02 42	03 38	04 20	21 15	21 36	21 57	22 18
50	02 57	03 49	04 28	21 11	21 34	21 56	22 18
45	03 27	04 10	04 44	21 03	21 29	21 55	22 20
N 40	03 49	04 27	04 57	20 56	21 25	21 53	22 22
35	04 07	04 41	05 09	20 49	21 21	21 52	22 23
30	04 21	04 52	05 18	20 44	21 18	21 51	22 25
20	04 44	05 11	05 35	20 35	21 12	21 49	22 27
N 10	05 01	05 27	05 49	20 27	21 07	21 48	22 29
0	05 16	05 41	06 03	20 19	21 03	21 46	22 31
S 10	05 29	05 54	06 16	20 11	20 58	21 45	22 33
20	05 40	06 07	06 30	20 03	20 53	21 44	22 35
30	05 52	06 21	06 46	19 54	20 48	21 42	22 37
35	05 58	06 29	06 55	19 48	20 44	21 41	22 38
40	06 04	06 37	07 06	19 42	20 41	21 40	22 40
45	06 11	06 47	07 18	19 35	20 36	21 38	22 42
S 50	06 18	06 58	07 33	19 26	20 31	21 37	22 44
52	06 22	07 03	07 40	19 22	20 29	21 36	22 45
54	06 25	07 08	07 48	19 18	20 26	21 35	22 46
56	06 29	07 14	07 56	19 13	20 23	21 35	22 47
58	06 33	07 21	08 06	19 07	20 20	21 34	22 49
S 60	06 37	07 29	08 17	19 01	20 16	21 33	22 50

Lat.	Sunset	Twilight Civil	Twilight Naut.	Moonset 30	31	1	2
°	h m	h m	h m	h m	h m	h m	h m
N 72	□	□	□	04 53	06 42	08 27	10 10
N 70	22 48	////	////	05 18	06 56	08 33	10 10
68	21 59	////	////	05 36	07 07	08 38	10 10
66	21 28	////	////	05 51	07 17	08 43	10 10
64	21 06	22 34	////	06 03	07 25	08 46	10 10
62	20 48	21 59	////	06 14	07 31	08 50	10 09
60	20 33	21 34	////	06 22	07 37	08 52	10 09
N 58	20 21	21 14	22 44	06 30	07 42	08 55	10 09
56	20 10	20 58	22 11	06 37	07 46	08 57	10 09
54	20 00	20 45	21 48	06 43	07 50	08 59	10 09
52	19 52	20 33	21 29	06 48	07 54	09 01	10 09
50	19 44	20 23	21 14	06 53	07 57	09 02	10 09
45	19 28	20 02	20 44	07 03	08 04	09 06	10 09
N 40	19 15	19 45	20 23	07 12	08 10	09 09	10 09
35	19 04	19 32	20 05	07 19	08 15	09 11	10 08
30	18 54	19 20	19 51	07 26	08 20	09 14	10 08
20	18 38	19 01	19 29	07 37	08 27	09 17	10 08
N 10	18 23	18 45	19 11	07 47	08 34	09 21	10 08
0	18 10	18 32	18 57	07 56	08 40	09 24	10 08
S 10	17 57	18 19	18 44	08 05	08 46	09 27	10 07
20	17 43	18 06	18 32	08 15	08 53	09 30	10 07
30	17 27	17 52	18 21	08 26	09 00	09 34	10 07
35	17 18	17 45	18 15	08 32	09 05	09 36	10 07
40	17 07	17 36	18 09	08 39	09 09	09 38	10 06
45	16 55	17 27	18 02	08 47	09 15	09 41	10 06
S 50	16 40	17 16	17 55	08 57	09 21	09 44	10 06
52	16 33	17 11	17 52	09 02	09 24	09 45	10 06
54	16 26	17 05	17 48	09 07	09 28	09 47	10 06
56	16 17	16 59	17 45	09 12	09 31	09 49	10 05
58	16 07	16 52	17 41	09 19	09 35	09 51	10 05
S 60	15 56	16 45	17 36	09 25	09 40	09 53	10 05

Day	SUN Eqn. of Time 00h	SUN Eqn. of Time 12h	SUN Mer. Pass.	MOON Mer. Pass. Upper	MOON Mer. Pass. Lower	Age	Phase
d	m s	m s	h m	h m	h m	d	%
30	06 28	06 26	12 06	01 45	14 08	17	94
31	06 25	06 23	12 06	02 30	14 51	18	88
1	06 22	06 20	12 06	03 13	15 35	19	81

UT	ARIES GHA	VENUS −4.3 GHA	Dec	MARS −2.7 GHA	Dec	JUPITER −2.1 GHA	Dec	SATURN +0.2 GHA	Dec	Name	SHA	Dec
THURSDAY												
2 00	310 32.3	135 16.3	N 2 01.2	4 01.6	S25 58.4	88 37.1	S15 08.5	36 44.2	S22 36.1	Acamar	315 15.8	S40 13.7
01	325 34.8	150 16.4	2 00.0	19 04.8	58.6	103 39.4	08.5	51 46.9	36.1	Achernar	335 24.1	S57 08.4
02	340 37.3	165 16.6	1 58.7	34 07.9	58.7	118 41.7	08.6	66 49.5	36.1	Acrux	173 05.7	S63 12.2
03	355 39.7	180 16.7	.. 57.5	49 11.1	.. 58.9	133 44.0	.. 08.6	81 52.1	.. 36.1	Adhara	255 10.1	S28 59.8
04	10 42.2	195 16.9	56.3	64 14.3	59.1	148 46.3	08.7	96 54.7	36.1	Aldebaran	290 45.5	N16 32.6
05	25 44.6	210 17.0	55.1	79 17.4	59.3	163 48.6	08.7	111 57.3	36.1			
06	40 47.1	225 17.2	N 1 53.8	94 20.6	S25 59.4	178 50.9	S15 08.8	126 59.9	S22 36.1	Alioth	166 17.9	N55 52.0
07	55 49.6	240 17.3	52.6	109 23.8	59.6	193 53.2	08.9	142 02.5	36.1	Alkaid	152 56.3	N49 13.7
08	70 52.0	255 17.5	51.4	124 26.9	25 59.8	208 55.5	08.9	157 05.1	36.2	Al Na'ir	27 39.0	S46 52.1
09	85 54.5	270 17.6	.. 50.1	139 30.1	26 00.0	223 57.9	.. 09.0	172 07.7	.. 36.2	Alnilam	275 43.1	S 1 11.5
10	100 57.0	285 17.8	48.9	154 33.3	00.1	239 00.2	09.0	187 10.3	36.2	Alphard	217 53.0	S 8 44.3
11	115 59.4	300 18.0	47.7	169 36.4	00.3	254 02.5	09.1	202 12.9	36.2			
12	131 01.9	315 18.1	N 1 46.5	184 39.6	S26 00.5	269 04.8	S15 09.2	217 15.5	S22 36.2	Alphecca	126 08.0	N26 39.5
13	146 04.4	330 18.3	45.2	199 42.8	00.7	284 07.1	09.2	232 18.1	36.2	Alpheratz	357 39.6	N29 11.4
14	161 06.8	345 18.4	44.0	214 46.0	00.8	299 09.4	09.3	247 20.7	36.2	Altair	62 04.5	N 8 55.3
15	176 09.3	0 18.6	.. 42.8	229 49.1	.. 01.0	314 11.7	.. 09.3	262 23.3	.. 36.2	Ankaa	353 12.0	S42 12.1
16	191 11.8	15 18.7	41.5	244 52.3	01.2	329 14.0	09.4	277 25.9	36.2	Antares	112 21.8	S26 28.2
17	206 14.2	30 18.9	40.3	259 55.5	01.3	344 16.3	09.5	292 28.5	36.2			
18	221 16.7	45 19.1	N 1 39.1	274 58.6	S26 01.5	359 18.6	S15 09.5	307 31.1	S22 36.2	Arcturus	145 52.6	N19 05.5
19	236 19.1	60 19.2	37.8	290 01.8	01.7	14 20.9	09.6	322 33.7	36.2	Atria	107 20.1	S69 03.7
20	251 21.6	75 19.4	36.6	305 04.9	01.8	29 23.2	09.6	337 36.3	36.3	Avior	234 17.2	S59 34.1
21	266 24.1	90 19.5	.. 35.4	320 08.1	.. 02.0	44 25.5	.. 09.7	352 38.9	.. 36.3	Bellatrix	278 28.5	N 6 21.9
22	281 26.5	105 19.7	34.2	335 11.3	02.2	59 27.8	09.8	7 41.5	36.3	Betelgeuse	270 57.8	N 7 24.5
23	296 29.0	120 19.9	32.9	350 14.4	02.3	74 30.1	09.8	22 44.1	36.3			
FRIDAY												
3 00	311 31.5	135 20.0	N 1 31.7	5 17.6	S26 02.5	89 32.4	S15 09.9	37 46.7	S22 36.3	Canopus	263 55.1	S52 42.3
01	326 33.9	150 20.2	30.5	20 20.8	02.7	104 34.7	09.9	52 49.3	36.3	Capella	280 29.6	N46 00.7
02	341 36.4	165 20.3	29.2	35 23.9	02.8	119 37.0	10.0	67 51.9	36.3	Deneb	49 28.6	N45 20.9
03	356 38.9	180 20.5	.. 28.0	50 27.1	.. 03.0	134 39.3	.. 10.1	82 54.5	.. 36.3	Denebola	182 30.4	N14 28.3
04	11 41.3	195 20.7	26.8	65 30.3	03.2	149 41.6	10.1	97 57.1	36.3	Diphda	348 52.2	S17 53.0
05	26 43.8	210 20.8	25.5	80 33.4	03.3	164 43.9	10.2	112 59.7	36.3			
06	41 46.2	225 21.0	N 1 24.3	95 36.6	S26 03.5	179 46.2	S15 10.3	128 02.3	S22 36.3	Dubhe	193 48.1	N61 39.3
07	56 48.7	240 21.2	23.1	110 39.7	03.7	194 48.5	10.3	143 04.9	36.4	Elnath	278 08.5	N28 37.2
08	71 51.2	255 21.3	21.9	125 42.9	03.8	209 50.8	10.4	158 07.5	36.4	Eltanin	90 44.1	N51 29.5
09	86 53.6	270 21.5	.. 20.6	140 46.1	.. 04.0	224 53.1	.. 10.4	173 10.1	.. 36.4	Enif	33 43.4	N 9 57.7
10	101 56.1	285 21.7	19.4	155 49.2	04.2	239 55.4	10.5	188 12.7	36.4	Fomalhaut	15 19.9	S29 31.3
11	116 58.6	300 21.8	18.2	170 52.4	04.3	254 57.7	10.5	203 15.3	36.4			
12	132 01.0	315 22.0	N 1 16.9	185 55.6	S26 04.5	270 00.0	S15 10.6	218 17.9	S22 36.4	Gacrux	171 57.3	S57 13.1
13	147 03.5	330 22.2	15.7	200 58.7	04.6	285 02.3	10.7	233 20.5	36.4	Gienah	175 48.9	S17 38.6
14	162 06.0	345 22.3	14.5	216 01.9	04.8	300 04.6	10.7	248 23.1	36.4	Hadar	148 43.0	S60 27.8
15	177 08.4	0 22.5	.. 13.2	231 05.0	.. 05.0	315 06.8	.. 10.8	263 25.7	.. 36.4	Hamal	327 56.8	N23 32.8
16	192 10.9	15 22.7	12.0	246 08.2	05.1	330 09.1	10.8	278 28.3	36.4	Kaus Aust.	83 38.9	S34 22.4
17	207 13.4	30 22.8	10.8	261 11.3	05.3	345 11.4	10.9	293 30.9	36.4			
18	222 15.8	45 23.0	N 1 09.6	276 14.5	S26 05.4	0 13.7	S15 11.0	308 33.5	S22 36.5	Kochab	137 20.1	N74 05.2
19	237 18.3	60 23.2	08.3	291 17.7	05.6	15 16.0	11.0	323 36.1	36.5	Markab	13 34.6	N15 18.3
20	252 20.7	75 23.4	07.1	306 20.8	05.7	30 18.3	11.1	338 38.7	36.5	Menkar	314 11.4	N 4 09.6
21	267 23.2	90 23.5	.. 05.9	321 24.0	.. 05.9	45 20.6	.. 11.1	353 41.3	.. 36.5	Menkent	148 03.5	S36 27.6
22	282 25.7	105 23.7	04.6	336 27.1	06.1	60 22.9	11.2	8 43.9	36.5	Miaplacidus	221 39.8	S69 47.6
23	297 28.1	120 23.9	03.4	351 30.3	06.2	75 25.2	11.3	23 46.5	36.5			
SATURDAY												
4 00	312 30.6	135 24.1	N 1 02.2	6 33.4	S26 06.4	90 27.5	S15 11.3	38 49.1	S22 36.5	Mirfak	308 35.4	N49 55.2
01	327 33.1	150 24.2	1 00.9	21 36.6	06.5	105 29.8	11.4	53 51.7	36.5	Nunki	75 53.7	S26 16.2
02	342 35.5	165 24.4	0 59.7	36 39.7	06.7	120 32.1	11.5	68 54.3	36.5	Peacock	53 13.2	S56 40.4
03	357 38.0	180 24.6	.. 58.5	51 42.9	.. 06.8	135 34.4	.. 11.5	83 56.9	.. 36.5	Pollux	243 23.9	N27 58.8
04	12 40.5	195 24.8	57.3	66 46.1	07.0	150 36.7	11.6	98 59.5	36.5	Procyon	244 56.4	N 5 10.6
05	27 42.9	210 24.9	56.0	81 49.2	07.1	165 39.0	11.6	114 02.1	36.5			
06	42 45.4	225 25.1	N 0 54.8	96 52.4	S26 07.3	180 41.2	S15 11.7	129 04.7	S22 36.6	Rasalhague	96 03.0	N12 33.1
07	57 47.9	240 25.3	53.6	111 55.5	07.4	195 43.5	11.8	144 07.3	36.6	Regulus	207 40.1	N11 52.7
08	72 50.3	255 25.5	52.3	126 58.7	07.6	210 45.8	11.8	159 09.9	36.6	Rigel	281 08.9	S 8 10.9
09	87 52.8	270 25.6	.. 51.1	142 01.8	.. 07.7	225 48.1	.. 11.9	174 12.5	.. 36.6	Rigil Kent.	139 47.0	S60 54.7
10	102 55.2	285 25.8	49.9	157 05.0	07.9	240 50.4	12.0	189 15.1	36.6	Sabik	102 08.3	S15 44.7
11	117 57.7	300 26.0	48.6	172 08.1	08.0	255 52.7	12.0	204 17.7	36.6			
12	133 00.2	315 26.2	N 0 47.4	187 11.3	S26 08.2	270 55.0	S15 12.1	219 20.3	S22 36.6	Schedar	349 36.2	N56 38.0
13	148 02.6	330 26.4	46.2	202 14.4	08.3	285 57.3	12.1	234 22.9	36.6	Shaula	96 16.9	S37 06.9
14	163 05.1	345 26.6	45.0	217 17.6	08.5	300 59.6	12.2	249 25.5	36.6	Sirius	258 31.0	S16 44.5
15	178 07.6	0 26.7	.. 43.7	232 20.7	.. 08.6	316 01.9	.. 12.3	264 28.0	.. 36.6	Spica	158 27.7	S11 15.3
16	193 10.0	15 26.9	42.5	247 23.9	08.8	331 04.1	12.3	279 30.6	36.6	Suhail	222 50.3	S43 30.5
17	208 12.5	30 27.1	41.3	262 27.0	08.9	346 06.4	12.4	294 33.2	36.7			
18	223 15.0	45 27.3	N 0 40.0	277 30.1	S26 09.1	1 08.7	S15 12.5	309 35.8	S22 36.7	Vega	80 36.2	N38 48.4
19	238 17.4	60 27.5	38.8	292 33.3	09.2	16 11.0	12.5	324 38.4	36.7	Zuben'ubi	137 01.5	S16 07.0
20	253 19.9	75 27.7	37.6	307 36.4	09.4	31 13.3	12.6	339 41.0	36.7		SHA	Mer. Pass.
21	268 22.3	90 27.8	.. 36.3	322 39.6	.. 09.5	46 15.6	.. 12.6	354 43.6	.. 36.7		° ′	h m
22	283 24.8	105 28.0	35.1	337 42.7	09.7	61 17.9	12.7	9 46.2	36.7	Venus	183 48.5	14 59
23	298 27.3	120 28.2	33.9	352 45.9	09.8	76 20.2	12.8	24 48.8	36.7	Mars	53 46.1	23 34
	h m									Jupiter	138 00.9	17 59
Mer. Pass.	3 13.4	v 0.2	d 1.2	v 3.2	d 0.2	v 2.3	d 0.1	v 2.6	d 0.0	Saturn	86 15.2	21 25

SUN and MOON

UT	SUN GHA	SUN Dec	MOON GHA	v	MOON Dec	d	HP
d h	° ′	° ′	° ′	′	° ′	′	′
2 00	178 25.5	N17 49.5	302 29.9	14.4	S 1 34.1	11.0	55.5
01	193 25.6	48.9	317 03.3	14.4	1 23.1	11.1	55.5
02	208 25.6	48.2	331 36.7	14.3	1 12.0	11.0	55.6
03	223 25.7	.. 47.6	346 10.0	14.3	1 01.0	11.0	55.6
04	238 25.7	47.0	0 43.3	14.3	0 50.0	11.1	55.6
05	253 25.8	46.3	15 16.6	14.2	0 38.9	11.0	55.6
T 06	268 25.8	N17 45.7	29 49.8	14.3	S 0 27.9	11.1	55.7
H 07	283 25.8	45.0	44 23.1	14.2	0 16.8	11.1	55.7
U 08	298 25.9	44.4	58 56.3	14.2	S 0 05.7	11.1	55.7
R 09	313 25.9	.. 43.8	73 29.5	14.2	N 0 05.4	11.1	55.7
S 10	328 26.0	43.1	88 02.7	14.1	0 16.5	11.1	55.8
D 11	343 26.0	42.5	102 35.8	14.1	0 27.6	11.1	55.8
A 12	358 26.1	N17 41.8	117 08.9	14.1	N 0 38.7	11.1	55.8
Y 13	13 26.1	41.2	131 42.0	14.1	0 49.8	11.1	55.8
14	28 26.2	40.5	146 15.1	14.0	1 00.9	11.2	55.9
15	43 26.2	.. 39.9	160 48.1	14.1	1 12.1	11.1	55.9
16	58 26.3	39.3	175 21.2	13.9	1 23.2	11.2	55.9
17	73 26.3	38.6	189 54.1	14.0	1 34.4	11.1	55.9
18	88 26.4	N17 38.0	204 27.1	13.9	N 1 45.5	11.1	56.0
19	103 26.4	37.3	219 00.0	13.9	1 56.6	11.2	56.0
20	118 26.4	36.7	233 32.9	13.8	2 07.8	11.1	56.0
21	133 26.5	.. 36.0	248 05.7	13.8	2 18.9	11.2	56.0
22	148 26.5	35.4	262 38.5	13.8	2 30.1	11.1	56.1
23	163 26.6	34.7	277 11.3	13.7	2 41.2	11.2	56.1
3 00	178 26.6	N17 34.1	291 44.0	13.7	N 2 52.4	11.1	56.1
01	193 26.7	33.4	306 16.7	13.7	3 03.5	11.2	56.1
02	208 26.7	32.8	320 49.4	13.6	3 14.7	11.1	56.2
03	223 26.8	.. 32.1	335 22.0	13.6	3 25.8	11.1	56.2
04	238 26.8	31.5	349 54.6	13.6	3 36.9	11.2	56.2
05	253 26.9	30.8	4 27.2	13.5	3 48.1	11.1	56.3
F 06	268 26.9	N17 30.2	18 59.7	13.4	N 3 59.2	11.1	56.3
R 07	283 27.0	29.5	33 32.1	13.4	4 10.3	11.1	56.3
I 08	298 27.0	28.9	48 04.5	13.4	4 21.4	11.1	56.3
D 09	313 27.1	.. 28.2	62 36.9	13.3	4 32.5	11.1	56.4
A 10	328 27.1	27.5	77 09.2	13.3	4 43.6	11.1	56.4
Y 11	343 27.2	26.9	91 41.5	13.2	4 54.7	11.0	56.4
12	358 27.3	N17 26.2	106 13.7	13.2	N 5 05.7	11.1	56.5
13	13 27.3	25.6	120 45.9	13.1	5 16.8	11.0	56.5
14	28 27.4	24.9	135 18.0	13.1	5 27.8	11.0	56.5
15	43 27.4	.. 24.3	149 50.1	13.1	5 38.8	11.0	56.6
16	58 27.5	23.6	164 22.2	12.9	5 49.8	11.0	56.6
17	73 27.5	23.0	178 54.1	13.0	6 00.8	11.0	56.6
18	88 27.6	N17 22.3	193 26.1	12.8	N 6 11.8	11.0	56.7
19	103 27.6	21.6	207 57.9	12.9	6 22.8	10.9	56.7
20	118 27.7	21.0	222 29.8	12.7	6 33.7	10.9	56.7
21	133 27.7	.. 20.3	237 01.5	12.7	6 44.6	10.9	56.7
22	148 27.8	19.7	251 33.2	12.7	6 55.5	10.9	56.8
23	163 27.8	19.0	266 04.9	12.6	7 06.4	10.9	56.8
4 00	178 27.9	N17 18.3	280 36.5	12.5	N 7 17.3	10.8	56.8
01	193 28.0	17.7	295 08.0	12.5	7 28.1	10.8	56.9
02	208 28.0	17.0	309 39.5	12.4	7 38.9	10.8	56.9
03	223 28.1	.. 16.3	324 10.9	12.4	7 49.7	10.8	56.9
04	238 28.1	15.7	338 42.3	12.2	8 00.5	10.7	57.0
05	253 28.2	15.0	353 13.5	12.3	8 11.2	10.7	57.0
S 06	268 28.2	N17 14.4	7 44.8	12.1	N 8 21.9	10.7	57.0
A 07	283 28.3	13.7	22 15.9	12.1	8 32.6	10.6	57.1
T 08	298 28.3	13.0	36 47.0	12.1	8 43.2	10.7	57.1
U 09	313 28.4	.. 12.4	51 18.1	11.9	8 53.9	10.5	57.1
R 10	328 28.5	11.7	65 49.0	11.9	9 04.4	10.6	57.2
D 11	343 28.5	11.0	80 19.9	11.9	9 15.0	10.5	57.2
A 12	358 28.6	N17 10.4	94 50.8	11.7	N 9 25.5	10.5	57.2
Y 13	13 28.6	09.7	109 21.5	11.7	9 36.0	10.4	57.3
14	28 28.7	09.0	123 52.2	11.6	9 46.4	10.5	57.3
15	43 28.8	.. 08.4	138 22.8	11.6	9 56.9	10.3	57.3
16	58 28.8	07.7	152 53.4	11.5	10 07.2	10.4	57.4
17	73 28.9	07.0	167 23.9	11.4	10 17.6	10.2	57.4
18	88 28.9	N17 06.3	181 54.3	11.3	N10 27.8	10.3	57.4
19	103 29.0	05.7	196 24.6	11.2	10 38.1	10.2	57.5
20	118 29.1	05.0	210 54.8	11.2	10 48.3	10.2	57.5
21	133 29.1	.. 04.3	225 25.0	11.1	10 58.5	10.1	57.5
22	148 29.2	03.7	239 55.1	11.1	11 08.6	10.1	57.6
23	163 29.2	03.0	254 25.2	10.9	N11 18.7	10.0	57.6
	SD 15.8	d 0.7	SD 15.2		15.4		15.6

Twilight, Sunrise and Moonrise

Lat.	Twilight Naut.	Twilight Civil	Sunrise	Moonrise 2	3	4	5
°	h m	h m	h m	h m	h m	h m	h m
N 72	▭	▭	▭	22 00	21 48	21 34	21 14
N 70	////	////	01 42	22 03	21 57	21 51	21 44
68	////	////	02 25	22 06	22 05	22 05	22 07
66	////	00 52	02 53	22 08	22 12	22 17	22 25
64	////	01 50	03 14	22 10	22 17	22 27	22 39
62	////	02 23	03 31	22 12	22 22	22 35	22 52
60	00 47	02 46	03 45	22 13	22 26	22 42	23 02
N 58	01 40	03 04	03 57	22 14	22 30	22 49	23 11
56	02 10	03 20	04 07	22 16	22 34	22 54	23 19
54	02 31	03 33	04 17	22 17	22 37	22 59	23 27
52	02 49	03 44	04 25	22 18	22 39	23 04	23 33
50	03 03	03 54	04 32	22 18	22 42	23 08	23 39
45	03 32	04 14	04 47	22 20	22 47	23 17	23 52
N 40	03 53	04 30	05 00	22 22	22 52	23 25	24 02
35	04 10	04 43	05 11	22 23	22 56	23 32	24 11
30	04 23	04 54	05 20	22 25	23 00	23 37	24 19
20	04 45	05 13	05 36	22 27	23 06	23 48	24 33
N 10	05 02	05 28	05 50	22 29	23 11	23 57	24 45
0	05 16	05 41	06 03	22 31	23 17	24 05	00 05
S 10	05 28	05 53	06 15	22 33	23 22	24 14	00 14
20	05 39	06 06	06 29	22 35	23 28	24 23	00 23
30	05 50	06 19	06 44	22 37	23 34	24 33	00 33
35	05 56	06 26	06 53	22 38	23 38	24 39	00 39
40	06 02	06 34	07 03	22 40	23 42	24 46	00 46
45	06 08	06 43	07 14	22 42	23 47	24 54	00 54
S 50	06 15	06 54	07 29	22 44	23 53	25 04	01 04
52	06 18	06 58	07 35	22 45	23 56	25 09	01 09
54	06 21	07 03	07 42	22 46	23 59	25 14	01 14
56	06 24	07 09	07 51	22 47	24 02	00 02	01 20
58	06 28	07 15	08 00	22 49	24 06	00 06	01 26
S 60	06 31	07 22	08 10	22 50	24 10	00 10	01 33

Sunset, Twilight and Moonset

Lat.	Sunset	Twilight Civil	Twilight Naut.	Moonset 2	3	4	5
°	h m	h m	h m	h m	h m	h m	h m
N 72	▭	▭	▭	10 10	11 57	13 50	15 55
N 70	22 24	////	////	10 10	11 50	13 34	15 26
68	21 44	////	////	10 10	11 44	13 21	15 04
66	21 17	23 09	////	10 10	11 39	13 11	14 47
64	20 56	22 17	////	10 10	11 35	13 03	14 34
62	20 39	21 47	////	10 09	11 31	12 55	14 22
60	20 26	21 24	23 15	10 09	11 28	12 49	14 12
N 58	20 14	21 06	22 28	10 09	11 25	12 44	14 04
56	20 04	20 51	22 00	10 09	11 23	12 39	13 57
54	19 55	20 38	21 39	10 09	11 21	12 34	13 50
52	19 47	20 27	21 22	10 09	11 19	12 30	13 44
50	19 39	20 18	21 07	10 09	11 17	12 27	13 39
45	19 24	19 58	20 40	10 09	11 13	12 19	13 29
N 40	19 12	19 42	20 19	10 09	11 10	12 12	13 18
35	19 01	19 29	20 02	10 08	11 07	12 07	13 09
30	18 52	19 18	19 49	10 08	11 04	12 02	13 02
20	18 36	18 59	19 27	10 08	11 00	11 54	12 50
N 10	18 22	18 44	19 10	10 08	10 56	11 46	12 39
0	18 10	18 31	18 56	10 08	10 53	11 39	12 29
S 10	17 57	18 19	18 44	10 07	10 49	11 33	12 19
20	17 44	18 07	18 33	10 07	10 45	11 25	12 09
30	17 29	17 54	18 22	10 07	10 41	11 17	11 56
35	17 20	17 47	18 17	10 07	10 38	11 12	11 49
40	17 10	17 39	18 11	10 06	10 36	11 07	11 41
45	16 58	17 30	18 05	10 06	10 32	11 00	11 32
S 50	16 44	17 19	17 58	10 06	10 28	10 53	11 21
52	16 38	17 15	17 55	10 06	10 27	10 50	11 16
54	16 31	17 10	17 52	10 06	10 25	10 46	11 10
56	16 23	17 04	17 49	10 05	10 23	10 42	11 04
58	16 13	16 58	17 46	10 05	10 20	10 37	10 57
S 60	16 03	16 51	17 42	10 05	10 18	10 32	10 49

SUN and MOON

Day	SUN Eqn. of Time 00h	SUN Eqn. of Time 12h	SUN Mer. Pass.	MOON Mer. Pass. Upper	MOON Mer. Pass. Lower	Age	Phase
d	m s	m s	h m	h m	h m	d	%
2	06 18	06 16	12 06	03 57	16 19	20	73
3	06 14	06 11	12 06	04 42	17 05	21	63
4	06 09	06 06	12 06	05 28	17 52	22	53

UT	ARIES	VENUS −4.4		MARS −2.7		JUPITER −2.1		SATURN +0.2		STARS		
	GHA	GHA	Dec	GHA	Dec	GHA	Dec	GHA	Dec	Name	SHA	Dec
d h	° ′	° ′	° ′	° ′	° ′	° ′	° ′	° ′	° ′		° ′	° ′
5 00	313 29.7	135 28.4	N 0 32.7	7 49.0	S26 09.9	91 22.4	S15 12.8	39 51.4	S22 36.7	Acamar	315 15.7	S40 13.7
01	328 32.2	150 28.6	31.4	22 52.2	10.1	106 24.7	12.9	54 54.0	36.7	Achernar	335 24.0	S57 08.4
02	343 34.7	165 28.8	30.2	37 55.3	10.2	121 27.0	13.0	69 56.6	36.7	Acrux	173 05.7	S63 12.2
03	358 37.1	180 29.0	.. 29.0	52 58.4	.. 10.4	136 29.3	.. 13.0	84 59.2	.. 36.7	Adhara	255 10.1	S28 59.8
04	13 39.6	195 29.2	27.7	68 01.6	10.5	151 31.6	13.1	100 01.8	36.7	Aldebaran	290 45.5	N16 32.6
05	28 42.1	210 29.3	26.5	83 04.7	10.7	166 33.9	13.2	115 04.4	36.8			
06	43 44.5	225 29.5	N 0 25.3	98 07.9	S26 10.8	181 36.2	S15 13.2	130 07.0	S22 36.8	Alioth	166 17.9	N55 51.9
07	58 47.0	240 29.7	24.0	113 11.0	10.9	196 38.4	13.3	145 09.6	36.8	Alkaid	152 56.3	N49 13.7
08	73 49.5	255 29.9	22.8	128 14.2	11.1	211 40.7	13.3	160 12.2	36.8	Al Na'ir	27 38.9	S46 52.1
S 09	88 51.9	270 30.1	.. 21.6	143 17.3	.. 11.2	226 43.0	.. 13.4	175 14.8	.. 36.8	Alnilam	275 43.0	S 1 11.5
U 10	103 54.4	285 30.3	20.4	158 20.4	11.4	241 45.3	13.5	190 17.3	36.8	Alphard	217 53.0	S 8 44.3
N 11	118 56.8	300 30.5	19.1	173 23.6	11.5	256 47.6	13.5	205 19.9	36.8			
D 12	133 59.3	315 30.7	N 0 17.9	188 26.7	S26 11.6	271 49.9	S15 13.6	220 22.5	S22 36.8	Alphecca	126 08.0	N26 39.5
A 13	149 01.8	330 30.9	16.7	203 29.8	11.8	286 52.1	13.7	235 25.1	36.8	Alpheratz	357 39.6	N29 11.5
Y 14	164 04.2	345 31.1	15.4	218 33.0	11.9	301 54.4	13.7	250 27.7	36.8	Altair	62 04.5	N 8 55.3
15	179 06.7	0 31.3	.. 14.2	233 36.1	.. 12.0	316 56.7	.. 13.8	265 30.3	.. 36.8	Ankaa	353 12.0	S42 12.2
16	194 09.2	15 31.5	13.0	248 39.2	12.2	331 59.0	13.9	280 32.9	36.8	Antares	112 21.8	S26 28.2
17	209 11.6	30 31.7	11.8	263 42.4	12.3	347 01.3	13.9	295 35.5	36.9			
18	224 14.1	45 31.9	N 0 10.5	278 45.5	S26 12.5	2 03.6	S15 14.0	310 38.1	S22 36.9	Arcturus	145 52.6	N19 05.5
19	239 16.6	60 32.1	09.3	293 48.6	12.6	17 05.8	14.1	325 40.7	36.9	Atria	107 20.1	S69 03.7
20	254 19.0	75 32.3	08.1	308 51.8	12.7	32 08.1	14.1	340 43.3	36.9	Avior	234 17.2	S59 34.1
21	269 21.5	90 32.5	.. 06.8	323 54.9	.. 12.9	47 10.4	.. 14.2	355 45.9	.. 36.9	Bellatrix	278 28.5	N 6 21.9
22	284 24.0	105 32.7	05.6	338 58.0	13.0	62 12.7	14.3	10 48.5	36.9	Betelgeuse	270 57.8	N 7 24.5
23	299 26.4	120 32.8	04.4	354 01.2	13.1	77 15.0	14.3	25 51.0	36.9			
6 00	314 28.9	135 33.0	N 0 03.1	9 04.3	S26 13.2	92 17.2	S15 14.4	40 53.6	S22 36.9	Canopus	263 55.0	S52 42.3
01	329 31.3	150 33.3	01.9	24 07.4	13.4	107 19.5	14.5	55 56.2	36.9	Capella	280 29.6	N46 00.7
02	344 33.8	165 33.5	N 00.7	39 10.6	13.5	122 21.8	14.5	70 58.8	36.9	Deneb	49 28.6	N45 20.9
03	359 36.3	180 33.7	S 00.5	54 13.7	.. 13.6	137 24.1	.. 14.6	86 01.4	.. 36.9	Denebola	182 30.4	N14 28.3
04	14 38.7	195 33.9	01.8	69 16.8	13.8	152 26.4	14.6	101 04.0	37.0	Diphda	348 52.2	S17 53.0
05	29 41.2	210 34.1	03.0	84 20.0	13.9	167 28.6	14.7	116 06.6	37.0			
06	44 43.7	225 34.3	S 0 04.2	99 23.1	S26 14.0	182 30.9	S15 14.8	131 09.2	S22 37.0	Dubhe	193 48.1	N61 39.3
07	59 46.1	240 34.5	05.5	114 26.2	14.2	197 33.2	14.8	146 11.8	37.0	Elnath	278 08.4	N28 37.1
08	74 48.6	255 34.7	06.7	129 29.3	14.3	212 35.5	14.9	161 14.4	37.0	Eltanin	90 44.1	N51 29.6
M 09	89 51.1	270 34.9	.. 07.9	144 32.5	.. 14.4	227 37.7	.. 15.0	176 16.9	.. 37.0	Enif	33 43.4	N 9 57.7
O 10	104 53.5	285 35.1	09.1	159 35.6	14.5	242 40.0	15.0	191 19.5	37.0	Fomalhaut	15 19.8	S29 31.3
N 11	119 56.0	300 35.3	10.4	174 38.7	14.7	257 42.3	15.1	206 22.1	37.0			
D 12	134 58.4	315 35.5	S 0 11.6	189 41.8	S26 14.8	272 44.6	S15 15.2	221 24.7	S22 37.0	Gacrux	171 57.3	S57 13.1
A 13	150 00.9	330 35.7	12.8	204 44.9	14.9	287 46.9	15.2	236 27.3	37.0	Gienah	175 48.9	S17 38.6
Y 14	165 03.4	345 35.9	14.1	219 48.1	15.0	302 49.1	15.3	251 29.9	37.0	Hadar	148 43.0	S60 27.8
15	180 05.8	0 36.1	.. 15.3	234 51.2	.. 15.2	317 51.4	.. 15.4	266 32.5	.. 37.0	Hamal	327 56.7	N23 32.8
16	195 08.3	15 36.3	16.5	249 54.3	15.3	332 53.7	15.4	281 35.1	37.1	Kaus Aust.	83 38.9	S34 22.4
17	210 10.8	30 36.5	17.7	264 57.4	15.4	347 56.0	15.5	296 37.7	37.1			
18	225 13.2	45 36.7	S 0 19.0	280 00.6	S26 15.5	2 58.2	S15 15.6	311 40.3	S22 37.1	Kochab	137 20.2	N74 05.2
19	240 15.7	60 36.9	20.2	295 03.7	15.7	18 00.5	15.6	326 42.8	37.1	Markab	13 34.6	N15 18.3
20	255 18.2	75 37.2	21.4	310 06.8	15.8	33 02.8	15.7	341 45.4	37.1	Menkar	314 11.4	N 4 09.6
21	270 20.6	90 37.4	.. 22.7	325 09.9	.. 15.9	48 05.1	.. 15.8	356 48.0	.. 37.1	Menkent	148 03.5	S36 27.6
22	285 23.1	105 37.6	23.9	340 13.0	16.0	63 07.3	15.8	11 50.6	37.1	Miaplacidus	221 39.8	S69 47.6
23	300 25.6	120 37.8	25.1	355 16.1	16.1	78 09.6	15.9	26 53.2	37.1			
7 00	315 28.0	135 38.0	S 0 26.3	10 19.3	S26 16.3	93 11.9	S15 16.0	41 55.8	S22 37.1	Mirfak	308 35.4	N49 55.2
01	330 30.5	150 38.2	27.6	25 22.4	16.4	108 14.1	16.0	56 58.4	37.1	Nunki	75 53.7	S26 16.2
02	345 32.9	165 38.4	28.8	40 25.5	16.5	123 16.4	16.1	72 01.0	37.1	Peacock	53 13.2	S56 40.4
03	0 35.4	180 38.6	.. 30.0	55 28.6	.. 16.6	138 18.7	.. 16.2	87 03.5	.. 37.1	Pollux	243 23.8	N27 58.8
04	15 37.9	195 38.9	31.3	70 31.7	16.7	153 21.0	16.3	102 06.1	37.2	Procyon	244 56.4	N 5 10.6
05	30 40.3	210 39.1	32.5	85 34.8	16.9	168 23.2	16.3	117 08.7	37.2			
06	45 42.8	225 39.3	S 0 33.7	100 37.9	S26 17.0	183 25.5	S15 16.4	132 11.3	S22 37.2	Rasalhague	96 03.0	N12 33.1
07	60 45.3	240 39.5	34.9	115 41.0	17.1	198 27.8	16.5	147 13.9	37.2	Regulus	207 40.1	N11 52.7
T 08	75 47.7	255 39.7	36.2	130 44.2	17.2	213 30.0	16.5	162 16.5	37.2	Rigel	281 08.9	S 8 10.9
U 09	90 50.2	270 39.9	.. 37.4	145 47.3	.. 17.3	228 32.3	.. 16.6	177 19.1	.. 37.2	Rigil Kent.	139 47.0	S60 54.7
E 10	105 52.7	285 40.2	38.6	160 50.4	17.4	243 34.6	16.7	192 21.7	37.2	Sabik	102 08.3	S15 44.7
S 11	120 55.1	300 40.4	39.9	175 53.5	17.5	258 36.9	16.7	207 24.2	37.2			
D 12	135 57.6	315 40.6	S 0 41.1	190 56.6	S26 17.7	273 39.1	S15 16.8	222 26.8	S22 37.2	Schedar	349 36.2	N56 38.1
A 13	151 00.1	330 40.8	42.3	205 59.7	17.8	288 41.4	16.9	237 29.4	37.2	Shaula	96 16.9	S37 06.9
Y 14	166 02.5	345 41.0	43.5	221 02.8	17.9	303 43.7	16.9	252 32.0	37.2	Sirius	258 30.9	S16 44.5
15	181 05.0	0 41.3	.. 44.8	236 05.9	.. 18.0	318 45.9	.. 17.0	267 34.6	.. 37.2	Spica	158 27.7	S11 15.3
16	196 07.4	15 41.5	46.0	251 09.0	18.1	333 48.2	17.1	282 37.2	37.3	Suhail	222 50.3	S43 30.4
17	211 09.9	30 41.7	47.2	266 12.1	18.2	348 50.5	17.1	297 39.8	37.3			
18	226 12.4	45 41.9	S 0 48.4	281 15.2	S26 18.3	3 52.7	S15 17.2	312 42.3	S22 37.3	Vega	80 36.2	N38 48.4
19	241 14.8	60 42.1	49.7	296 18.3	18.4	18 55.0	17.3	327 44.9	37.3	Zuben'ubi	137 01.5	S16 07.0
20	256 17.3	75 42.4	50.9	311 21.4	18.5	33 57.3	17.3	342 47.5	37.3		SHA	Mer. Pass.
21	271 19.8	90 42.6	.. 52.1	326 24.5	.. 18.7	48 59.5	.. 17.4	357 50.1	.. 37.3		° ′	h m
22	286 22.2	105 42.8	53.4	341 27.6	18.8	64 01.8	17.5	12 52.7	37.3	Venus	181 04.2	14 58
23	301 24.7	120 43.0	54.6	356 30.7	18.9	79 04.1	17.6	27 55.3	37.3	Mars	54 35.4	23 19
	h m									Jupiter	137 48.4	17 48
Mer. Pass.	3 01.6	v 0.2	d 1.2	v 3.1	d 0.1	v 2.3	d 0.1	v 2.6	d 0.0	Saturn	86 24.8	21 13

UT	SUN GHA	SUN Dec	MOON GHA	v	MOON Dec	d	HP
d h	° ′	° ′	° ′	′	° ′	′	′
5 00	178 29.3	N17 02.3	268 55.1	10.9	N11 28.7	10.0	57.6
01	193 29.4	01.6	283 25.0	10.8	11 38.7	9.9	57.7
02	208 29.4	01.0	297 54.8	10.7	11 48.6	9.9	57.7
03	223 29.5	17 00.3	312 24.5	10.6	11 58.5	9.8	57.7
04	238 29.5	16 59.6	326 54.1	10.6	12 08.3	9.8	57.8
05	253 29.6	58.9	341 23.7	10.4	12 18.1	9.7	57.8
06	268 29.7	N16 58.3	355 53.1	10.4	N12 27.8	9.7	57.9
07	283 29.7	57.6	10 22.5	10.3	12 37.5	9.6	57.9
08	298 29.8	56.9	24 51.8	10.2	12 47.1	9.6	57.9
S 09	313 29.9 ..	56.2	39 21.0	10.2	12 56.7	9.5	58.0
U 10	328 29.9	55.6	53 50.2	10.0	13 06.2	9.4	58.0
N 11	343 30.0	54.9	68 19.2	10.0	13 15.6	9.4	58.0
D 12	358 30.1	N16 54.2	82 48.2	9.9	N13 25.0	9.3	58.1
A 13	13 30.1	53.5	97 17.1	9.8	13 34.3	9.2	58.1
Y 14	28 30.2	52.8	111 45.9	9.7	13 43.5	9.2	58.1
15	43 30.3 ..	52.2	126 14.6	9.6	13 52.7	9.2	58.2
16	58 30.3	51.5	140 43.2	9.6	14 01.9	9.0	58.2
17	73 30.4	50.8	155 11.8	9.4	14 10.9	9.0	58.2
18	88 30.4	N16 50.1	169 40.2	9.4	N14 19.9	8.9	58.3
19	103 30.5	49.4	184 08.6	9.2	14 28.8	8.9	58.3
20	118 30.6	48.7	198 36.8	9.2	14 37.7	8.7	58.4
21	133 30.6 ..	48.1	213 05.0	9.1	14 46.4	8.7	58.4
22	148 30.7	47.4	227 33.1	9.0	14 55.1	8.7	58.4
23	163 30.8	46.7	242 01.1	8.9	15 03.8	8.5	58.5
6 00	178 30.8	N16 46.0	256 29.0	8.8	N15 12.3	8.5	58.5
01	193 30.9	45.3	270 56.8	8.8	15 20.8	8.4	58.5
02	208 31.0	44.6	285 24.6	8.6	15 29.2	8.3	58.6
03	223 31.1 ..	44.0	299 52.2	8.5	15 37.5	8.2	58.6
04	238 31.1	43.3	314 19.7	8.5	15 45.7	8.2	58.6
05	253 31.2	42.6	328 47.2	8.3	15 53.9	8.0	58.7
06	268 31.3	N16 41.9	343 14.5	8.3	N16 01.9	8.0	58.7
07	283 31.3	41.2	357 41.8	8.2	16 09.9	7.9	58.8
08	298 31.4	40.5	12 09.0	8.1	16 17.8	7.8	58.8
M 09	313 31.5 ..	39.8	26 36.1	8.0	16 25.6	7.7	58.8
O 10	328 31.5	39.1	41 03.1	7.9	16 33.3	7.7	58.9
N 11	343 31.6	38.5	55 30.0	7.8	16 41.0	7.5	58.9
D 12	358 31.7	N16 37.8	69 56.8	7.7	N16 48.5	7.4	58.9
A 13	13 31.7	37.1	84 23.5	7.6	16 55.9	7.4	59.0
Y 14	28 31.8	36.4	98 50.1	7.6	17 03.3	7.2	59.0
15	43 31.9 ..	35.7	113 16.7	7.4	17 10.5	7.2	59.0
16	58 32.0	35.0	127 43.1	7.3	17 17.7	7.0	59.1
17	73 32.0	34.3	142 09.4	7.3	17 24.7	7.0	59.1
18	88 32.1	N16 33.6	156 35.7	7.2	N17 31.7	6.8	59.1
19	103 32.2	32.9	171 01.9	7.0	17 38.5	6.8	59.2
20	118 32.2	32.2	185 27.9	7.0	17 45.3	6.6	59.2
21	133 32.3 ..	31.5	199 53.9	6.9	17 51.9	6.6	59.3
22	148 32.4	30.8	214 19.8	6.8	17 58.5	6.4	59.3
23	163 32.5	30.1	228 45.6	6.7	18 04.9	6.3	59.3
7 00	178 32.5	N16 29.4	243 11.3	6.7	N18 11.2	6.3	59.4
01	193 32.6	28.7	257 37.0	6.5	18 17.5	6.1	59.4
02	208 32.7	28.1	272 02.5	6.5	18 23.6	6.0	59.4
03	223 32.8 ..	27.4	286 28.0	6.3	18 29.6	5.9	59.5
04	238 32.8	26.7	300 53.3	6.3	18 35.5	5.7	59.5
05	253 32.9	26.0	315 18.6	6.2	18 41.2	5.7	59.5
06	268 33.0	N16 25.3	329 43.8	6.1	N18 46.9	5.5	59.6
07	283 33.1	24.6	344 08.9	6.0	18 52.4	5.4	59.6
08	298 33.1	23.9	358 33.9	5.9	18 57.8	5.3	59.6
T 09	313 33.2 ..	23.2	12 58.8	5.9	19 03.1	5.2	59.7
U 10	328 33.3	22.5	27 23.7	5.7	19 08.3	5.1	59.7
E 11	343 33.4	21.8	41 48.4	5.7	19 13.4	4.9	59.7
S 12	358 33.4	N16 21.1	56 13.1	5.6	N19 18.3	4.8	59.8
D 13	13 33.5	20.4	70 37.7	5.5	19 23.1	4.7	59.8
A 14	28 33.6	19.7	85 02.2	5.4	19 27.8	4.6	59.8
Y 15	43 33.7 ..	19.0	99 26.6	5.4	19 32.4	4.4	59.9
16	58 33.7	18.2	113 51.0	5.3	19 36.8	4.3	59.9
17	73 33.8	17.5	128 15.3	5.2	19 41.1	4.2	59.9
18	88 33.9	N16 16.8	142 39.5	5.1	N19 45.3	4.0	60.0
19	103 34.0	16.1	157 03.6	5.1	19 49.3	3.9	60.0
20	118 34.1	15.4	171 27.7	5.0	19 53.2	3.8	60.0
21	133 34.1 ..	14.7	185 51.7	4.9	19 57.0	3.6	60.1
22	148 34.2	14.0	200 15.6	4.8	20 00.6	3.5	60.1
23	163 34.3	13.3	214 39.4	4.8	N20 04.1	3.4	60.1
	SD 15.8	d 0.7	SD 15.8		16.1		16.3

Lat.	Twilight Naut.	Twilight Civil	Sunrise	Moonrise 5	6	7	8
°	h m	h m	h m	h m	h m	h m	h m
N 72	////	////	00 56	21 14	20 26	□	□
N 70	////	////	02 04	21 44	21 35	21 11	□
68	////	////	02 39	22 07	22 12	22 26	23 07
66	////	01 23	03 04	22 25	22 38	23 04	23 53
64	////	02 06	03 24	22 39	22 59	23 31	24 23
62	////	02 34	03 39	22 52	23 15	23 51	24 45
60	01 14	02 55	03 52	23 02	23 29	24 08	00 08
N 58	01 54	03 12	04 03	23 11	23 41	24 23	00 23
56	02 20	03 27	04 13	23 19	23 52	24 35	00 35
54	02 40	03 39	04 22	23 27	24 01	00 01	00 46
52	02 56	03 49	04 29	23 33	24 09	00 09	00 55
50	03 10	03 58	04 36	23 39	24 17	00 17	01 04
45	03 36	04 18	04 51	23 52	24 32	00 32	01 22
N 40	03 56	04 33	05 03	24 02	00 02	00 46	01 37
35	04 12	04 46	05 13	24 11	00 11	00 57	01 49
30	04 26	04 56	05 22	24 19	00 19	01 07	02 00
20	04 46	05 14	05 37	24 33	00 33	01 23	02 19
N 10	05 02	05 28	05 50	24 45	00 45	01 38	02 36
0	05 16	05 41	06 02	00 05	00 57	01 52	02 51
S 10	05 27	05 53	06 15	00 14	01 08	02 06	03 07
20	05 38	06 04	06 27	00 23	01 21	02 21	03 24
30	05 48	06 17	06 42	00 33	01 35	02 39	03 43
35	05 53	06 24	06 50	00 39	01 43	02 49	03 54
40	05 59	06 31	07 00	00 46	01 53	03 00	04 07
45	06 04	06 39	07 11	00 54	02 04	03 14	04 23
S 50	06 10	06 49	07 24	01 04	02 17	03 31	04 41
52	06 13	06 54	07 30	01 09	02 24	03 39	04 50
54	06 16	06 58	07 37	01 14	02 31	03 47	05 00
56	06 19	07 04	07 44	01 20	02 39	03 57	05 12
58	06 22	07 09	07 53	01 26	02 47	04 09	05 25
S 60	06 25	07 16	08 03	01 33	02 58	04 22	05 40

Lat.	Sunset	Twilight Civil	Twilight Naut.	Moonset 5	6	7	8
°	h m	h m	h m	h m	h m	h m	h m
N 72	23 02	////	////	15 55	18 36	□	□
N 70	22 03	////	////	15 26	17 28	19 54	□
68	21 29	////	////	15 04	16 52	18 39	20 06
66	21 05	22 42	////	14 47	16 26	18 02	19 21
64	20 46	22 02	////	14 34	16 06	17 35	18 51
62	20 31	21 35	////	14 22	15 50	17 15	18 29
60	20 18	21 14	22 51	14 12	15 37	16 58	18 10
N 58	20 07	20 57	22 14	14 04	15 25	16 44	17 55
56	19 57	20 44	21 49	13 57	15 16	16 32	17 42
54	19 49	20 32	21 30	13 50	15 07	16 22	17 31
52	19 41	20 21	21 14	13 44	14 59	16 12	17 21
50	19 35	20 12	21 01	13 39	14 52	16 04	17 12
45	19 20	19 53	20 34	13 27	14 37	15 46	16 53
N 40	19 08	19 38	20 14	13 18	14 25	15 32	16 38
35	18 58	19 26	19 59	13 09	14 14	15 20	16 24
30	18 49	19 15	19 46	13 02	14 05	15 09	16 13
20	18 34	18 58	19 25	12 50	13 49	14 51	15 54
N 10	18 21	18 43	19 09	12 39	13 35	14 35	15 37
0	18 09	18 31	18 56	12 29	13 23	14 20	15 21
S 10	17 57	18 19	18 45	12 19	13 10	14 05	15 05
20	17 45	18 08	18 34	12 09	12 56	13 49	14 48
30	17 30	17 55	18 24	11 56	12 41	13 31	14 28
35	17 22	17 49	18 19	11 49	12 32	13 20	14 17
40	17 13	17 41	18 14	11 41	12 21	13 08	14 03
45	17 02	17 33	18 08	11 32	12 09	12 54	13 48
S 50	16 49	17 23	18 02	11 21	11 55	12 36	13 29
52	16 42	17 19	17 59	11 16	11 48	12 28	13 20
54	16 36	17 14	17 57	11 10	11 40	12 19	13 10
56	16 28	17 09	17 54	11 04	11 32	12 09	12 58
58	16 19	17 03	17 51	10 57	11 22	11 57	12 45
S 60	16 10	16 57	17 47	10 49	11 12	11 44	12 30

	SUN			MOON			
Day	Eqn. of Time 00h	Eqn. of Time 12h	Mer. Pass.	Mer. Pass. Upper	Mer. Pass. Lower	Age	Phase
d	m s	m s	h m	h m	h m	d	%
5	06 03	06 00	12 06	06 17	18 43	23	42
6	05 57	05 53	12 06	07 10	19 37	24	31
7	05 50	05 46	12 06	08 06	20 36	25	21

2018 AUGUST 8, 9, 10 (WED., THURS., FRI.)

UT	ARIES GHA	VENUS −4.4 GHA	Dec	MARS −2.6 GHA	Dec	JUPITER −2.1 GHA	Dec	SATURN +0.2 GHA	Dec	STARS Name	SHA	Dec
8 00	316 27.2	135 43.3	S 0 55.8	11 33.8	S26 19.0	94 06.3	S15 17.6	42 57.8	S22 37.3	Acamar	315 15.7	S40 13.7
01	331 29.6	150 43.5	57.0	26 36.9	19.1	109 08.6	17.7	58 00.4	37.3	Achernar	335 24.0	S57 08.4
02	346 32.1	165 43.7	58.3	41 40.0	19.2	124 10.9	17.8	73 03.0	37.3	Acrux	173 05.7	S63 12.2
03	1 34.6	180 43.9	0 59.5	56 43.1 ..	19.3	139 13.1 ..	17.8	88 05.6 ..	37.3	Adhara	255 10.1	S28 59.8
04	16 37.0	195 44.2	1 00.7	71 46.2	19.4	154 15.4	17.9	103 08.2	37.4	Aldebaran	290 45.5	N16 32.6
05	31 39.5	210 44.4	01.9	86 49.3	19.5	169 17.7	18.0	118 10.8	37.4			
W 06	46 41.9	225 44.6	S 1 03.2	101 52.4	S26 19.6	184 19.9	S15 18.0	133 13.4	S22 37.4	Alioth	166 18.0	N55 51.9
E 07	61 44.4	240 44.9	04.4	116 55.5	19.7	199 22.2	18.1	148 15.9	37.4	Alkaid	152 56.3	N49 13.7
D 08	76 46.9	255 45.1	05.6	131 58.6	19.8	214 24.5	18.2	163 18.5	37.4	Al Na'ir	27 38.9	S46 52.1
N 09	91 49.3	270 45.3 ..	06.8	147 01.7 ..	19.9	229 26.7 ..	18.2	178 21.1 ..	37.4	Alnilam	275 43.0	S 1 11.5
E 10	106 51.8	285 45.5	08.1	162 04.7	20.0	244 29.0	18.3	193 23.7	37.4	Alphard	217 53.0	S 8 44.3
S 11	121 54.3	300 45.8	09.3	177 07.8	20.1	259 31.3	18.4	208 26.3	37.4			
D 12	136 56.7	315 46.0	S 1 10.5	192 10.9	S26 20.2	274 33.5	S15 18.5	223 28.8	S22 37.4	Alphecca	126 08.0	N26 39.5
A 13	151 59.2	330 46.2	11.7	207 14.0	20.3	289 35.8	18.5	238 31.4	37.4	Alpheratz	357 39.6	N29 11.5
Y 14	167 01.7	345 46.5	13.0	222 17.1	20.4	304 38.0	18.6	253 34.0	37.4	Altair	62 04.5	N 8 55.3
15	182 04.1	0 46.7 ..	14.2	237 20.2 ..	20.5	319 40.3 ..	18.7	268 36.6 ..	37.4	Ankaa	353 12.0	S42 12.1
16	197 06.6	15 46.9	15.4	252 23.3	20.6	334 42.6	18.7	283 39.2	37.5	Antares	112 21.8	S26 28.2
17	212 09.1	30 47.2	16.6	267 26.4	20.7	349 44.8	18.8	298 41.8	37.5			
18	227 11.5	45 47.4	S 1 17.9	282 29.4	S26 20.8	4 47.1	S15 18.9	313 44.3	S22 37.5	Arcturus	145 52.6	N19 05.5
19	242 14.0	60 47.6	19.1	297 32.5	20.9	19 49.4	18.9	328 46.9	37.5	Atria	107 20.2	S69 03.7
20	257 16.4	75 47.9	20.3	312 35.6	21.0	34 51.6	19.0	343 49.5	37.5	Avior	234 17.2	S59 34.1
21	272 18.9	90 48.1 ..	21.6	327 38.7 ..	21.1	49 53.9 ..	19.1	358 52.1 ..	37.5	Bellatrix	278 28.4	N 6 21.9
22	287 21.4	105 48.4	22.8	342 41.8	21.2	64 56.1	19.2	13 54.7	37.5	Betelgeuse	270 57.7	N 7 24.5
23	302 23.8	120 48.6	24.0	357 44.8	21.3	79 58.4	19.2	28 57.2	37.5			
9 00	317 26.3	135 48.8	S 1 25.2	12 47.9	S26 21.4	95 00.7	S15 19.3	43 59.8	S22 37.5	Canopus	263 55.0	S52 42.2
01	332 28.8	150 49.1	26.4	27 51.0	21.5	110 02.9	19.4	59 02.4	37.5	Capella	280 29.5	N46 00.7
02	347 31.2	165 49.3	27.7	42 54.1	21.6	125 05.2	19.4	74 05.0	37.5	Deneb	49 28.6	N45 20.9
03	2 33.7	180 49.5 ..	28.9	57 57.2 ..	21.7	140 07.4 ..	19.5	89 07.6 ..	37.5	Denebola	182 30.4	N14 28.3
04	17 36.2	195 49.8	30.1	73 00.2	21.8	155 09.7	19.6	104 10.2	37.6	Diphda	348 52.2	S17 53.0
05	32 38.6	210 50.0	31.3	88 03.3	21.9	170 12.0	19.7	119 12.7	37.6			
T 06	47 41.1	225 50.3	S 1 32.6	103 06.4	S26 22.0	185 14.2	S15 19.7	134 15.3	S22 37.6	Dubhe	193 48.1	N61 39.3
H 07	62 43.5	240 50.5	33.8	118 09.5	22.0	200 16.5	19.8	149 17.9	37.6	Elnath	278 08.4	N28 37.2
U 08	77 46.0	255 50.8	35.0	133 12.5	22.1	215 18.7	19.9	164 20.5	37.6	Eltanin	90 44.1	N51 29.6
R 09	92 48.5	270 51.0 ..	36.2	148 15.6 ..	22.2	230 21.0 ..	19.9	179 23.0 ..	37.6	Enif	33 43.4	N 9 57.7
S 10	107 50.9	285 51.2	37.5	163 18.7	22.3	245 23.2	20.0	194 25.6	37.6	Fomalhaut	15 19.8	S29 31.3
D 11	122 53.4	300 51.5	38.7	178 21.7	22.4	260 25.5	20.1	209 28.2	37.6			
A 12	137 55.9	315 51.7	S 1 39.9	193 24.8	S26 22.5	275 27.8	S15 20.2	224 30.8	S22 37.6	Gacrux	171 57.3	S57 13.1
Y 13	152 58.3	330 52.0	41.1	208 27.9	22.6	290 30.0	20.2	239 33.4	37.6	Gienah	175 48.9	S17 38.6
14	168 00.8	345 52.2	42.4	223 30.9	22.7	305 32.3	20.3	254 35.9	37.6	Hadar	148 43.0	S60 27.8
15	183 03.3	0 52.5 ..	43.6	238 34.0 ..	22.8	320 34.5 ..	20.4	269 38.5 ..	37.6	Hamal	327 56.7	N23 32.8
16	198 05.7	15 52.7	44.8	253 37.1	22.8	335 36.8	20.4	284 41.1	37.7	Kaus Aust.	83 38.9	S34 22.4
17	213 08.2	30 53.0	46.0	268 40.1	22.9	350 39.0	20.5	299 43.7	37.7			
18	228 10.7	45 53.2	S 1 47.3	283 43.2	S26 23.0	5 41.3	S15 20.6	314 46.3	S22 37.7	Kochab	137 20.2	N74 05.2
19	243 13.1	60 53.5	48.5	298 46.3	23.1	20 43.5	20.7	329 48.8	37.7	Markab	13 34.6	N15 18.3
20	258 15.6	75 53.7	49.7	313 49.3	23.2	35 45.8	20.7	344 51.4	37.7	Menkar	314 11.4	N 4 09.7
21	273 18.0	90 53.9 ..	50.9	328 52.4 ..	23.3	50 48.1 ..	20.8	359 54.0 ..	37.7	Menkent	148 03.5	S36 27.6
22	288 20.5	105 54.2	52.1	343 55.4	23.4	65 50.3	20.9	14 56.6	37.7	Miaplacidus	221 39.8	S69 47.6
23	303 23.0	120 54.4	53.4	358 58.5	23.4	80 52.6	21.0	29 59.1	37.7			
10 00	318 25.4	135 54.7	S 1 54.6	14 01.6	S26 23.5	95 54.8	S15 21.0	45 01.7	S22 37.7	Mirfak	308 35.4	N49 55.2
01	333 27.9	150 55.0	55.8	29 04.6	23.6	110 57.1	21.1	60 04.3	37.7	Nunki	75 53.7	S26 16.2
02	348 30.4	165 55.2	57.0	44 07.7	23.7	125 59.3	21.2	75 06.9	37.7	Peacock	53 13.2	S56 40.4
03	3 32.8	180 55.5 ..	58.3	59 10.7 ..	23.8	141 01.6 ..	21.2	90 09.5 ..	37.7	Pollux	243 23.8	N27 58.8
04	18 35.3	195 55.7	1 59.5	74 13.8	23.8	156 03.8	21.3	105 12.0	37.8	Procyon	244 56.4	N 5 10.6
05	33 37.8	210 56.0	2 00.7	89 16.8	23.9	171 06.1	21.4	120 14.6	37.8			
F 06	48 40.2	225 56.2	S 2 01.9	104 19.9	S26 24.0	186 08.3	S15 21.5	135 17.2	S22 37.8	Rasalhague	96 03.0	N12 33.1
R 07	63 42.7	240 56.5	03.2	119 22.9	24.1	201 10.6	21.5	150 19.8	37.8	Regulus	207 40.1	N11 52.7
I 08	78 45.2	255 56.7	04.4	134 26.0	24.2	216 12.8	21.6	165 22.3	37.8	Rigel	281 08.9	S 8 10.9
D 09	93 47.6	270 57.0 ..	05.6	149 29.0 ..	24.2	231 15.1 ..	21.7	180 24.9 ..	37.8	Rigil Kent.	139 47.0	S60 54.7
A 10	108 50.1	285 57.2	06.8	164 32.1	24.3	246 17.3	21.8	195 27.5	37.8	Sabik	102 08.3	S15 44.7
Y 11	123 52.5	300 57.5	08.0	179 35.1	24.4	261 19.6	21.8	210 30.1	37.8			
12	138 55.0	315 57.7	S 2 09.3	194 38.2	S26 24.5	276 21.8	S15 21.9	225 32.6	S22 37.8	Schedar	349 36.1	N56 38.1
13	153 57.5	330 58.0	10.5	209 41.2	24.5	291 24.1	22.0	240 35.2	37.8	Shaula	96 16.9	S37 06.9
14	168 59.9	345 58.3	11.7	224 44.3	24.6	306 26.3	22.1	255 37.8	37.8	Sirius	258 30.9	S16 44.5
15	184 02.4	0 58.5 ..	12.9	239 47.3 ..	24.7	321 28.6 ..	22.1	270 40.4 ..	37.8	Spica	158 27.7	S11 15.3
16	199 04.9	15 58.8	14.1	254 50.4	24.8	336 30.8	22.2	285 42.9	37.9	Suhail	222 50.3	S43 30.4
17	214 07.3	30 59.0	15.4	269 53.4	24.8	351 33.1	22.3	300 45.5	37.9			
18	229 09.8	45 59.3	S 2 16.6	284 56.4	S26 24.9	6 35.3	S15 22.3	315 48.1	S22 37.9	Vega	80 36.2	N38 48.4
19	244 12.3	60 59.6	17.8	299 59.5	25.0	21 37.6	22.4	330 50.7	37.9	Zuben'ubi	137 01.5	S16 07.0
20	259 14.7	75 59.8	19.0	315 02.5	25.1	36 39.8	22.5	345 53.2	37.9		SHA	Mer.Pass.
21	274 17.2	91 00.1 ..	20.2	330 05.6 ..	25.1	51 42.1 ..	22.6	0 55.8 ..	37.9		° ′	h m
22	289 19.7	106 00.4	21.5	345 08.6	25.2	66 44.3	22.6	15 58.4	37.9	Venus	178 22.5	14 57
23	304 22.1	121 00.6	22.7	0 11.6	25.3	81 46.6	22.7	31 01.0	37.9	Mars	55 21.6	23 04
	h m									Jupiter	137 34.4	17 37
Mer. Pass.	2 49.8	v 0.2	d 1.2	v 3.1	d 0.1	v 2.3	d 0.1	v 2.6	d 0.0	Saturn	86 33.5	21 00

UT	SUN GHA	SUN Dec	MOON GHA	v	MOON Dec	d	HP
d h	° ′	° ′	° ′	′	° ′	′	′
8 00	178 34.4	N16 12.6	229 03.2	4.7	N20 07.5	3.2	60.1
01	193 34.5	11.9	243 26.9	4.6	20 10.7	3.1	60.2
02	208 34.5	11.2	257 50.5	4.6	20 13.8	3.0	60.2
03	223 34.6 ..	10.5	272 14.1	4.5	20 16.8	2.8	60.2
04	238 34.7	09.8	286 37.6	4.4	20 19.6	2.7	60.3
05	253 34.8	09.1	301 01.0	4.4	20 22.3	2.5	60.3
06	268 34.9	N16 08.4	315 24.4	4.3	N20 24.8	2.4	60.3
W 07	283 34.9	07.6	329 47.7	4.3	20 27.2	2.2	60.3
E 08	298 35.0	06.9	344 11.0	4.2	20 29.4	2.1	60.4
D 09	313 35.1 ..	06.2	358 34.2	4.1	20 31.5	2.0	60.4
N 10	328 35.2	05.5	12 57.3	4.1	20 33.5	1.8	60.4
E 11	343 35.3	04.8	27 20.4	4.0	20 35.3	1.6	60.5
S 12	358 35.3	N16 04.1	41 43.4	4.0	N20 36.9	1.5	60.5
D 13	13 35.4	03.4	56 06.4	4.0	20 38.4	1.4	60.5
A 14	28 35.5	02.7	70 29.4	3.9	20 39.8	1.2	60.5
Y 15	43 35.6 ..	02.0	84 52.3	3.8	20 41.0	1.1	60.6
16	58 35.7	01.2	99 15.1	3.8	20 42.1	0.9	60.6
17	73 35.8	16 00.5	113 37.9	3.8	20 42.9	0.8	60.6
18	88 35.8	N15 59.8	128 00.7	3.7	N20 43.8	0.6	60.6
19	103 35.9	59.1	142 23.4	3.7	20 44.4	0.4	60.7
20	118 36.0	58.4	156 46.1	3.7	20 44.8	0.3	60.7
21	133 36.1 ..	57.7	171 08.8	3.6	20 45.1	0.2	60.7
22	148 36.2	56.9	185 31.4	3.6	20 45.3	0.0	60.7
23	163 36.3	56.2	199 54.0	3.5	20 45.3	0.2	60.7
9 00	178 36.4	N15 55.5	214 16.5	3.5	N20 45.1	0.3	60.8
01	193 36.4	54.8	228 39.0	3.5	20 44.8	0.4	60.8
02	208 36.5	54.1	243 01.5	3.5	20 44.4	0.6	60.8
03	223 36.6 ..	53.4	257 24.0	3.5	20 43.8	0.8	60.8
04	238 36.7	52.6	271 46.5	3.4	20 43.0	0.9	60.8
05	253 36.8	51.9	286 08.9	3.4	20 42.1	1.1	60.9
06	268 36.9	N15 51.2	300 31.3	3.4	N20 41.0	1.3	60.9
T 07	283 37.0	50.5	314 53.7	3.4	20 39.7	1.3	60.9
H 08	298 37.0	49.8	329 16.1	3.3	20 38.4	1.6	60.9
U 09	313 37.1 ..	49.0	343 38.4	3.4	20 36.8	1.7	60.9
R 10	328 37.2	48.3	358 00.8	3.3	20 35.1	1.8	61.0
S 11	343 37.3	47.6	12 23.1	3.4	20 33.3	2.1	61.0
D 12	358 37.4	N15 46.9	26 45.5	3.3	N20 31.2	2.1	61.0
A 13	13 37.5	46.1	41 07.8	3.3	20 29.1	2.3	61.0
Y 14	28 37.6	45.4	55 30.1	3.4	20 26.8	2.5	61.0
15	43 37.7 ..	44.7	69 52.5	3.3	20 24.3	2.7	61.0
16	58 37.7	44.0	84 14.8	3.3	20 21.6	2.7	61.1
17	73 37.8	43.2	98 37.1	3.4	20 18.9	3.0	61.1
18	88 37.9	N15 42.5	112 59.5	3.3	N20 15.9	3.1	61.1
19	103 38.0	41.8	127 21.8	3.4	20 12.8	3.2	61.1
20	118 38.1	41.1	141 44.2	3.3	20 09.6	3.4	61.1
21	133 38.2 ..	40.3	156 06.5	3.4	20 06.2	3.6	61.1
22	148 38.3	39.6	170 28.9	3.4	20 02.6	3.7	61.1
23	163 38.4	38.9	184 51.3	3.4	19 58.9	3.8	61.1
10 00	178 38.5	N15 38.2	199 13.7	3.4	N19 55.1	4.0	61.1
01	193 38.6	37.4	213 36.1	3.5	19 51.1	4.2	61.2
02	208 38.7	36.7	227 58.6	3.5	19 46.9	4.3	61.2
03	223 38.7 ..	36.0	242 21.1	3.4	19 42.6	4.4	61.2
04	238 38.8	35.2	256 43.5	3.6	19 38.2	4.7	61.2
05	253 38.9	34.5	271 06.1	3.5	19 33.5	4.7	61.2
06	268 39.0	N15 33.8	285 28.6	3.6	N19 28.8	4.9	61.2
F 07	283 39.1	33.1	299 51.2	3.6	19 23.9	5.0	61.2
R 08	298 39.2	32.3	314 13.8	3.6	19 18.9	5.2	61.2
I 09	313 39.3 ..	31.6	328 36.4	3.7	19 13.7	5.4	61.2
D 10	328 39.4	30.9	342 59.1	3.7	19 08.3	5.4	61.2
A 11	343 39.5	30.1	357 21.8	3.8	19 02.9	5.7	61.2
Y 12	358 39.6	N15 29.4	11 44.6	3.8	N18 57.2	5.7	61.2
13	13 39.7	28.7	26 07.4	3.8	18 51.5	5.9	61.2
14	28 39.8	27.9	40 30.2	3.9	18 45.6	6.1	61.2
15	43 39.9 ..	27.2	54 53.1	3.9	18 39.5	6.2	61.2
16	58 40.0	26.5	69 16.0	3.9	18 33.3	6.3	61.2
17	73 40.1	25.7	83 38.9	4.0	18 27.0	6.4	61.2
18	88 40.2	N15 25.0	98 01.9	4.1	N18 20.6	6.6	61.2
19	103 40.2	24.2	112 25.0	4.1	18 14.0	6.7	61.2
20	118 40.3	23.5	126 48.1	4.2	18 07.3	6.9	61.2
21	133 40.4 ..	22.8	141 11.3	4.2	18 00.4	7.0	61.2
22	148 40.5	22.0	155 34.5	4.3	17 53.4	7.1	61.2
23	163 40.6	21.3	169 57.8	4.3	N17 46.3	7.3	61.2
	SD 15.8	d 0.7	SD 16.5		16.6		16.7

Lat.	Twilight Naut.	Twilight Civil	Sunrise	Moonrise 8	Moonrise 9	Moonrise 10	Moonrise 11
°	h m	h m	h m	h m	h m	h m	h m
N 72	////	////	01 34	▭	▭	▭	00 47
N 70	////	////	02 23	▭	23 16	25 53	01 53
68	////	00 26	02 53	23 07	24 35	00 35	02 29
66	////	01 45	03 15	23 53	25 13	01 13	02 55
64	////	02 20	03 33	24 23	00 23	01 39	03 15
62	00 23	02 45	03 47	00 23	00 45	02 00	03 31
60	01 34	03 05	03 59	00 08	01 03	02 17	03 44
N 58	02 07	03 20	04 10	00 23	01 19	02 31	03 55
56	02 30	03 33	04 19	00 35	01 32	02 43	04 05
54	02 48	03 45	04 27	00 46	01 43	02 54	04 14
52	03 03	03 55	04 34	00 55	01 53	03 03	04 22
50	03 16	04 03	04 41	01 04	02 02	03 11	04 29
45	03 41	04 22	04 54	01 22	02 21	03 29	04 44
N 40	04 00	04 36	05 06	01 37	02 36	03 44	04 56
35	04 15	04 48	05 15	01 49	02 49	03 56	05 07
30	04 28	04 58	05 24	02 00	03 01	04 07	05 16
20	04 48	05 15	05 38	02 19	03 20	04 25	05 31
N 10	05 03	05 29	05 51	02 36	03 37	04 41	05 45
0	05 16	05 41	06 02	02 51	03 53	04 56	05 58
S 10	05 27	05 52	06 14	03 07	04 09	05 11	06 11
20	05 36	06 03	06 26	03 24	04 26	05 27	06 24
30	05 46	06 14	06 39	03 43	04 46	05 46	06 40
35	05 51	06 21	06 47	03 54	04 58	05 56	06 49
40	05 55	06 28	06 56	04 07	05 11	06 08	06 59
45	06 01	06 35	07 06	04 23	05 26	06 23	07 11
S 50	06 06	06 45	07 19	04 41	05 46	06 40	07 26
52	06 08	06 49	07 25	04 50	05 55	06 49	07 32
54	06 11	06 53	07 31	05 00	06 05	06 58	07 40
56	06 13	06 58	07 38	05 12	06 16	07 08	07 48
58	06 16	07 03	07 46	05 25	06 29	07 20	07 58
S 60	06 19	07 09	07 55	05 40	06 45	07 34	08 08

Lat.	Sunset	Twilight Civil	Twilight Naut.	Moonset 8	Moonset 9	Moonset 10	Moonset 11
°	h m	h m	h m	h m	h m	h m	h m
N 72	22 28	////	////	▭	▭	22 51	22 02
N 70	21 44	////	////	▭	22 10	21 43	21 34
68	21 15	23 23	////	20 06	20 51	21 06	21 12
66	20 53	22 20	////	19 21	20 12	20 40	20 55
64	20 36	21 47	////	18 51	19 45	20 19	20 41
62	20 22	21 23	23 28	18 29	19 24	20 03	20 29
60	20 10	21 04	22 32	18 10	19 07	19 49	20 18
N 58	20 00	20 49	22 01	17 55	18 53	19 37	20 10
56	19 51	20 36	21 39	17 42	18 41	19 26	20 02
54	19 43	20 25	21 21	17 31	18 30	19 17	19 55
52	19 36	20 15	21 06	17 21	18 20	19 09	19 48
50	19 29	20 06	20 54	17 12	18 12	19 02	19 43
45	19 16	19 48	20 30	16 53	17 53	18 46	19 30
N 40	19 05	19 34	20 10	16 38	17 38	18 33	19 20
35	18 55	19 22	19 55	16 24	17 26	18 21	19 11
30	18 47	19 12	19 43	16 13	17 15	18 12	19 03
20	18 33	18 56	19 23	15 54	16 56	17 55	18 49
N 10	18 20	18 42	19 08	15 37	16 39	17 40	18 37
0	18 09	18 30	18 55	15 21	16 23	17 26	18 26
S 10	17 58	18 19	18 45	15 05	16 08	17 12	18 15
20	17 46	18 08	18 35	14 48	15 51	16 57	18 03
30	17 32	17 57	18 25	14 28	15 31	16 39	17 49
35	17 24	17 51	18 21	14 17	15 20	16 29	17 40
40	17 15	17 44	18 16	14 03	15 07	16 17	17 31
45	17 05	17 36	18 11	13 48	14 52	16 04	17 20
S 50	16 53	17 27	18 06	13 29	14 33	15 47	17 07
52	16 47	17 23	18 03	13 20	14 24	15 39	17 00
54	16 41	17 19	18 01	13 10	14 14	15 30	16 53
56	16 34	17 14	17 58	12 58	14 02	15 20	16 46
58	16 26	17 09	17 56	12 45	13 49	15 08	16 37
S 60	16 17	17 03	17 53	12 30	13 34	14 55	16 27

	SUN			MOON			
Day	Eqn. of Time 00ʰ	Eqn. of Time 12ʰ	Mer. Pass.	Mer. Pass. Upper	Mer. Pass. Lower	Age	Phase
d	m s	m s	h m	h m	h m	d	%
8	05 43	05 39	12 06	09 06	21 37	26	12	●
9	05 35	05 31	12 06	10 08	22 40	27	6	
10	05 26	05 22	12 05	11 11	23 42	28	1	

UT (d h)	ARIES GHA	VENUS GHA	VENUS Dec	MARS GHA	MARS Dec	JUPITER GHA	JUPITER Dec	SATURN GHA	SATURN Dec	Name	SHA	Dec
11 00	319 24.6	136 00.9	S 2 23.9	15 14.7	S26 25.3	96 48.8	S15 22.8	46 03.5	S22 37.9	Acamar	315 15.7	S40 13.7
01	334 27.0	151 01.1	25.1	30 17.7	25.4	111 51.1	22.9	61 06.1	37.9	Achernar	335 24.0	S57 08.4
02	349 29.5	166 01.4	26.3	45 20.7	25.5	126 53.3	22.9	76 08.7	37.9	Acrux	173 05.8	S63 12.2
03	4 32.0	181 01.7	.. 27.6	60 23.8	.. 25.5	141 55.6	.. 23.0	91 11.3	.. 37.9	Adhara	255 10.1	S28 59.8
04	19 34.4	196 01.9	28.8	75 26.8	25.6	156 57.8	23.1	106 13.8	38.0	Aldebaran	290 45.5	N16 32.6
05	34 36.9	211 02.2	30.0	90 29.8	25.7	172 00.0	23.2	121 16.4	38.0			
S 06	49 39.4	226 02.5	S 2 31.2	105 32.9	S26 25.7	187 02.3	S15 23.2	136 19.0	S22 38.0	Alioth	166 18.0	N55 51.9
A 07	64 41.8	241 02.7	32.4	120 35.9	25.8	202 04.5	23.3	151 21.5	38.0	Alkaid	152 56.3	N49 13.7
T 08	79 44.3	256 03.0	33.7	135 38.9	25.9	217 06.8	23.4	166 24.1	38.0	Al Na'ir	27 38.9	S46 52.1
U 09	94 46.8	271 03.3	.. 34.9	150 41.9	.. 25.9	232 09.0	.. 23.4	181 26.7	.. 38.0	Alnilam	275 43.0	S 1 11.5
R 10	109 49.2	286 03.5	36.1	165 45.0	26.0	247 11.3	23.5	196 29.3	38.0	Alphard	217 53.0	S 8 44.3
D 11	124 51.7	301 03.8	37.3	180 48.0	26.1	262 13.5	23.6	211 31.8	38.0			
A 12	139 54.2	316 04.1	S 2 38.5	195 51.0	S26 26.1	277 15.8	S15 23.7	226 34.4	S22 38.0	Alphecca	126 08.0	N26 39.5
Y 13	154 56.6	331 04.4	39.8	210 54.0	26.2	292 18.0	23.8	241 37.0	38.0	Alpheratz	357 39.6	N29 11.5
14	169 59.1	346 04.6	41.0	225 57.0	26.3	307 20.2	23.8	256 39.5	38.0	Altair	62 04.5	N 8 55.3
15	185 01.5	1 04.9	.. 42.2	241 00.1	.. 26.3	322 22.5	.. 23.9	271 42.1	.. 38.0	Ankaa	353 12.0	S42 12.2
16	200 04.0	16 05.2	43.4	256 03.1	26.4	337 24.7	24.0	286 44.7	38.1	Antares	112 21.8	S26 28.2
17	215 06.5	31 05.4	44.6	271 06.1	26.4	352 27.0	24.1	301 47.3	38.1			
18	230 08.9	46 05.7	S 2 45.8	286 09.1	S26 26.5	7 29.2	S15 24.1	316 49.8	S22 38.1	Arcturus	145 52.6	N19 05.5
19	245 11.4	61 06.0	47.1	301 12.1	26.6	22 31.5	24.2	331 52.4	38.1	Atria	107 20.2	S69 03.7
20	260 13.9	76 06.3	48.3	316 15.2	26.6	37 33.7	24.3	346 55.0	38.1	Avior	234 17.2	S59 34.1
21	275 16.3	91 06.5	.. 49.5	331 18.2	.. 26.7	52 35.9	.. 24.4	1 57.5	.. 38.1	Bellatrix	278 28.4	N 6 21.9
22	290 18.8	106 06.8	50.7	346 21.2	26.7	67 38.2	24.5	17 00.1	38.1	Betelgeuse	270 57.7	N 7 24.5
23	305 21.3	121 07.1	51.9	1 24.2	26.8	82 40.4	24.5	32 02.7	38.1			
12 00	320 23.7	136 07.4	S 2 53.1	16 27.2	S26 26.8	97 42.7	S15 24.6	47 05.3	S22 38.1	Canopus	263 55.0	S52 42.2
01	335 26.2	151 07.6	54.4	31 30.2	26.9	112 44.9	24.7	62 07.8	38.1	Capella	280 29.5	N46 00.7
02	350 28.6	166 07.9	55.6	46 33.2	27.0	127 47.1	24.8	77 10.4	38.1	Deneb	49 28.6	N45 21.0
03	5 31.1	181 08.2	.. 56.8	61 36.2	.. 27.0	142 49.4	.. 24.8	92 13.0	.. 38.1	Denebola	182 30.4	N14 28.3
04	20 33.6	196 08.5	58.0	76 39.2	27.1	157 51.6	24.9	107 15.5	38.1	Diphda	348 52.2	S17 53.0
05	35 36.0	211 08.8	2 59.2	91 42.2	27.1	172 53.9	25.0	122 18.1	38.2			
S 06	50 38.5	226 09.0	S 3 00.4	106 45.2	S26 27.2	187 56.1	S15 25.1	137 20.7	S22 38.2	Dubhe	193 48.1	N61 39.3
U 07	65 41.0	241 09.3	01.7	121 48.2	27.2	202 58.3	25.1	152 23.2	38.2	Elnath	278 08.4	N28 37.2
N 08	80 43.4	256 09.6	02.9	136 51.2	27.3	218 00.6	25.2	167 25.8	38.2	Eltanin	90 44.2	N51 29.6
D 09	95 45.9	271 09.9	.. 04.1	151 54.2	.. 27.3	233 02.8	.. 25.3	182 28.4	.. 38.2	Enif	33 43.4	N 9 57.7
A 10	110 48.4	286 10.2	05.3	166 57.2	27.4	248 05.1	25.4	197 30.9	38.2	Fomalhaut	15 19.8	S29 31.3
Y 11	125 50.8	301 10.4	06.5	182 00.2	27.4	263 07.3	25.4	212 33.5	38.2			
12	140 53.3	316 10.7	S 3 07.7	197 03.2	S26 27.5	278 09.5	S15 25.5	227 36.1	S22 38.2	Gacrux	171 57.3	S57 13.1
13	155 55.8	331 11.0	08.9	212 06.2	27.5	293 11.8	25.6	242 38.6	38.2	Gienah	175 48.9	S17 38.6
14	170 58.2	346 11.3	10.2	227 09.2	27.6	308 14.0	25.7	257 41.2	38.2	Hadar	148 43.0	S60 27.8
15	186 00.7	1 11.6	.. 11.4	242 12.2	.. 27.6	323 16.2	.. 25.8	272 43.8	.. 38.2	Hamal	327 56.7	N23 32.8
16	201 03.1	16 11.9	12.6	257 15.2	27.7	338 18.5	25.8	287 46.3	38.2	Kaus Aust.	83 38.9	S34 22.4
17	216 05.6	31 12.2	13.8	272 18.2	27.7	353 20.7	25.9	302 48.9	38.3			
18	231 08.1	46 12.4	S 3 15.0	287 21.2	S26 27.8	8 22.9	S15 26.0	317 51.5	S22 38.3	Kochab	137 20.3	N74 05.2
19	246 10.5	61 12.7	16.2	302 24.2	27.8	23 25.2	26.1	332 54.1	38.3	Markab	13 34.5	N15 18.3
20	261 13.0	76 13.0	17.4	317 27.2	27.9	38 27.4	26.1	347 56.6	38.3	Menkar	314 11.4	N 4 09.7
21	276 15.5	91 13.3	.. 18.7	332 30.2	.. 27.9	53 29.7	.. 26.2	2 59.2	.. 38.3	Menkent	148 03.5	S36 27.6
22	291 17.9	106 13.6	19.9	347 33.2	28.0	68 31.9	26.3	18 01.8	38.3	Miaplacidus	221 39.8	S69 47.6
23	306 20.4	121 13.9	21.1	2 36.1	28.0	83 34.1	26.4	33 04.3	38.3			
13 00	321 22.9	136 14.2	S 3 22.3	17 39.1	S26 28.1	98 36.4	S15 26.5	48 06.9	S22 38.3	Mirfak	308 35.3	N49 55.3
01	336 25.3	151 14.5	23.5	32 42.1	28.1	113 38.6	26.5	63 09.4	38.3	Nunki	75 53.7	S26 16.2
02	351 27.8	166 14.8	24.7	47 45.1	28.1	128 40.8	26.6	78 12.0	38.3	Peacock	53 13.2	S56 40.4
03	6 30.2	181 15.0	.. 25.9	62 48.1	.. 28.2	143 43.1	.. 26.7	93 14.6	.. 38.3	Pollux	243 23.8	N27 58.8
04	21 32.7	196 15.3	27.2	77 51.0	28.2	158 45.3	26.8	108 17.1	38.3	Procyon	244 56.4	N 5 10.6
05	36 35.2	211 15.6	28.4	92 54.0	28.3	173 47.5	26.8	123 19.7	38.3			
M 06	51 37.6	226 15.9	S 3 29.6	107 57.0	S26 28.3	188 49.8	S15 26.9	138 22.3	S22 38.4	Rasalhague	96 03.0	N12 33.1
O 07	66 40.1	241 16.2	30.8	123 00.0	28.3	203 52.0	27.0	153 24.8	38.4	Regulus	207 40.1	N11 52.7
N 08	81 42.6	256 16.5	32.0	138 02.9	28.4	218 54.2	27.1	168 27.4	38.4	Rigel	281 08.9	S 8 10.8
D 09	96 45.0	271 16.8	.. 33.2	153 05.9	.. 28.4	233 56.5	.. 27.2	183 30.0	.. 38.4	Rigil Kent.	139 47.0	S60 54.7
A 10	111 47.5	286 17.1	34.4	168 08.9	28.5	248 58.7	27.2	198 32.5	38.4	Sabik	102 08.3	S15 44.7
Y 11	126 50.0	301 17.4	35.6	183 11.9	28.5	264 00.9	27.3	213 35.1	38.4			
12	141 52.4	316 17.7	S 3 36.8	198 14.8	S26 28.5	279 03.1	S15 27.4	228 37.7	S22 38.4	Schedar	349 36.1	N56 38.1
13	156 54.9	331 18.0	38.1	213 17.8	28.6	294 05.4	27.5	243 40.2	38.4	Shaula	96 16.9	S37 06.9
14	171 57.4	346 18.3	39.3	228 20.8	28.6	309 07.6	27.5	258 42.8	38.4	Sirius	258 30.9	S16 44.5
15	186 59.8	1 18.6	.. 40.5	243 23.7	.. 28.6	324 09.8	.. 27.6	273 45.4	.. 38.4	Spica	158 27.7	S11 15.3
16	202 02.3	16 18.9	41.7	258 26.7	28.7	339 12.1	27.7	288 47.9	38.4	Suhail	222 50.3	S43 30.4
17	217 04.7	31 19.2	42.9	273 29.7	28.7	354 14.3	27.8	303 50.5	38.4			
18	232 07.2	46 19.5	S 3 44.1	288 32.6	S26 28.8	9 16.5	S15 27.9	318 53.0	S22 38.5	Vega	80 36.3	N38 48.4
19	247 09.7	61 19.8	45.3	303 35.6	28.8	24 18.8	27.9	333 55.6	38.5	Zuben'ubi	137 01.6	S16 07.0
20	262 12.1	76 20.1	46.5	318 38.6	28.8	39 21.0	28.0	348 58.2	38.5			
21	277 14.6	91 20.4	.. 47.7	333 41.5	.. 28.9	54 23.2	.. 28.1	4 00.7	.. 38.5		SHA	Mer.Pass.
22	292 17.1	106 20.7	48.9	348 44.5	28.9	69 25.4	28.2	19 03.3	38.5	Venus	175 43.6	14 55
23	307 19.5	121 21.0	50.2	3 47.4	28.9	84 27.7	28.3	34 05.9	38.5	Mars	56 03.5	22 50
Mer.Pass.	h m 2 38.0	v 0.3 d 1.2		v 3.0 d 0.1		v 2.2 d 0.1		v 2.6 d 0.0		Jupiter	137 18.9	17 27
										Saturn	86 41.5	20 48

UT	SUN		MOON					Lat.	Twilight		Sunrise	Moonrise			
									Naut.	Civil		11	12	13	14
	GHA	Dec	GHA	v	Dec	d	HP								
d h	° ′	° ′	° ′	′	° ′	′	′	N 72	////	////	02 01	00 47	03 41	05 59	08 04
11 00	178 40.7	N15 20.6	184 21.1	4.4	N17 39.0	7.3	61.2	N 70	////	////	02 40	01 53	04 08	06 12	08 09
01	193 40.8	19.8	198 44.5	4.4	17 31.7	7.5	61.2	68	////	01 15	03 06	02 29	04 28	06 23	08 13
02	208 40.9	19.1	213 07.9	4.5	17 24.2	7.7	61.2	66	////	02 04	03 26	02 55	04 44	06 32	08 16
03	223 41.0 ..	18.3	227 31.4	4.5	17 16.5	7.7	61.2	64	////	02 34	03 42	03 15	04 57	06 39	08 18
04	238 41.1	17.6	241 54.9	4.7	17 08.8	7.9	61.2	62	01 07	02 56	03 55	03 31	05 08	06 46	08 21
05	253 41.2	16.9	256 18.6	4.6	N17 00.9	8.0	61.2	60	01 51	03 14	04 07	03 44	05 17	06 51	08 23
06	268 41.3	N15 16.1						N 58	02 18	03 28	04 16	03 55	05 26	06 56	08 24
S 07	283 41.4	15.4						56	02 39	03 40	04 25	04 05	05 33	07 00	08 26
A 08	298 41.5	14.6	A partial eclipse of					54	02 56	03 51	04 32	04 14	05 39	07 04	08 27
T 09	313 41.6 ..	13.9	the Sun occurs on this					52	03 10	04 00	04 39	04 22	05 45	07 08	08 28
U 10	328 41.7	13.1	date. See page 5.					50	03 22	04 08	04 45	04 29	05 50	07 11	08 30
R 11	343 41.8	12.4						45	03 45	04 26	04 58	04 44	06 01	07 18	08 32
D 12	358 41.9	N15 11.7	357 05.7	5.1	N16 02.5	8.8	61.1	N 40	04 04	04 39	05 09	04 56	06 10	07 23	08 34
A 13	13 42.0	10.9	11 29.8	5.2	15 53.7	9.0	61.1	35	04 18	04 51	05 18	05 07	06 18	07 28	08 36
Y 14	28 42.1	10.2	25 54.0	5.3	15 44.7	9.0	61.1	30	04 30	05 00	05 26	05 16	06 25	07 32	08 38
15	43 42.2 ..	09.4	40 18.3	5.4	15 35.7	9.1	61.1	20	04 49	05 16	05 39	05 31	06 37	07 40	08 40
16	58 42.3	08.7	54 42.7	5.4	15 26.6	9.2	61.1	N 10	05 03	05 29	05 51	05 45	06 47	07 46	08 43
17	73 42.4	07.9	69 07.1	5.5	15 17.4	9.4	61.1	0	05 15	05 40	06 02	05 58	06 57	07 52	08 45
18	88 42.5	N15 07.2	83 31.6	5.6	N15 08.0	9.4	61.1	S 10	05 26	05 51	06 12	06 11	07 06	07 59	08 47
19	103 42.6	06.4	97 56.2	5.6	14 58.6	9.6	61.1	20	05 35	06 01	06 24	06 24	07 17	08 05	08 50
20	118 42.7	05.7	112 20.8	5.7	14 49.0	9.6	61.0	30	05 43	06 12	06 37	06 40	07 28	08 12	08 53
21	133 42.8 ..	05.0	126 45.5	5.8	14 39.4	9.7	61.0	35	05 48	06 18	06 44	06 49	07 35	08 17	08 54
22	148 42.9	04.2	141 10.3	5.9	14 29.7	9.8	61.0	40	05 52	06 24	06 52	06 59	07 43	08 21	08 56
23	163 43.0	03.5	155 35.2	5.9	14 19.9	10.0	61.0	45	05 57	06 31	07 02	07 11	07 52	08 27	08 58
12 00	178 43.1	N15 02.7	170 00.1	6.1	N14 09.9	10.0	61.0	S 50	06 01	06 40	07 14	07 26	08 02	08 33	09 01
01	193 43.2	02.0	184 25.2	6.1	13 59.9	10.1	61.0	52	06 03	06 43	07 19	07 32	08 07	08 36	09 02
02	208 43.3	01.2	198 50.3	6.1	13 49.8	10.2	61.0	54	06 06	06 47	07 25	07 40	08 13	08 40	09 03
03	223 43.4	15 00.5	213 15.4	6.3	13 39.6	10.2	60.9	56	06 08	06 52	07 32	07 48	08 19	08 43	09 04
04	238 43.6	14 59.7	227 40.7	6.3	13 29.4	10.4	60.9	58	06 10	06 57	07 39	07 58	08 26	08 47	09 06
05	253 43.7	59.0	242 06.0	6.4	13 19.0	10.4	60.9	S 60	06 13	07 02	07 48	08 08	08 33	08 52	09 08
06	268 43.8	N14 58.2	256 31.4	6.5	N13 08.6	10.6	60.9	Lat.	Sunset	Twilight		Moonset			
S 07	283 43.9	57.5	270 56.9	6.6	12 58.0	10.6	60.9			Civil	Naut.	11	12	13	14
U 08	298 44.0	56.7	285 22.5	6.6	12 47.4	10.6	60.8	°	h m	h m	h m	h m	h m	h m	h m
N 09	313 44.1 ..	56.0	299 48.1	6.7	12 36.8	10.8	60.8	N 72	22 02	////	////	22 02	21 42	21 27	21 15
D 10	328 44.2	55.2	314 13.8	6.8	12 26.0	10.8	60.8	N 70	21 26	////	////	21 34	21 26	21 20	21 14
A 11	343 44.3	54.4	328 39.6	6.9	12 15.2	10.9	60.8	68	21 01	22 46	////	21 12	21 14	21 14	21 14
Y 12	358 44.4	N14 53.7	343 05.5	6.9	N12 04.3	11.0	60.8	66	20 41	22 01	////	20 55	21 03	21 09	21 13
13	13 44.5	52.9	357 31.4	7.0	11 53.3	11.1	60.7	64	20 26	21 33	////	20 41	20 54	21 05	21 13
14	28 44.6	52.2	11 57.4	7.1	11 42.2	11.1	60.7	62	20 13	21 11	22 55	20 29	20 47	21 01	21 13
15	43 44.7 ..	51.4	26 23.5	7.2	11 31.1	11.2	60.7	60	20 02	20 54	22 15	20 18	20 40	20 58	21 12
16	58 44.8	50.7	40 49.7	7.3	11 19.9	11.2	60.7	N 58	19 52	20 40	21 48	20 10	20 34	20 55	21 12
17	73 44.9	49.9	55 16.0	7.3	11 08.7	11.3	60.6	56	19 44	20 28	21 28	20 02	20 29	20 52	21 12
18	88 45.0	N14 49.2	69 42.3	7.4	N10 57.4	11.4	60.6	54	19 37	20 18	21 12	19 55	20 24	20 50	21 12
19	103 45.1	48.4	84 08.7	7.5	10 46.0	11.4	60.6	52	19 30	20 09	20 59	19 48	20 20	20 47	21 12
20	118 45.2	47.7	98 35.2	7.6	10 34.6	11.5	60.6	50	19 24	20 00	20 47	19 43	20 16	20 45	21 11
21	133 45.4 ..	46.9	113 01.8	7.6	10 23.1	11.5	60.5	45	19 11	19 44	20 23	19 30	20 08	20 41	21 11
22	148 45.5	46.1	127 28.4	7.8	10 11.6	11.6	60.5	N 40	19 01	19 30	20 06	19 20	20 01	20 37	21 11
23	163 45.6	45.4	141 55.2	7.8	10 00.0	11.7	60.5	35	18 52	19 19	19 51	19 11	19 55	20 34	21 11
13 00	178 45.7	N14 44.6	156 22.0	7.8	N 9 48.3	11.7	60.5	30	18 44	19 09	19 40	19 03	19 49	20 31	21 10
01	193 45.8	43.9	170 48.8	8.0	9 36.6	11.7	60.4	20	18 31	18 54	19 21	18 49	19 40	20 26	21 10
02	208 45.9	43.1	185 15.8	8.0	9 24.9	11.8	60.4	N 10	18 19	18 41	19 06	18 37	19 32	20 22	21 10
03	223 46.0 ..	42.3	199 42.8	8.1	9 13.1	11.9	60.4	0	18 08	18 30	18 55	18 26	19 24	20 18	21 09
04	238 46.1	41.6	214 09.9	8.2	9 01.2	11.8	60.3	S 10	17 58	18 19	18 45	18 15	19 16	20 14	21 09
05	253 46.2	40.8	228 37.1	8.2	8 49.4	12.0	60.3	20	17 47	18 09	18 35	18 03	19 07	20 09	21 08
06	268 46.3	N14 40.1	243 04.3	8.4	N 8 37.4	11.9	60.3	30	17 34	17 59	18 27	17 49	18 57	20 04	21 08
07	283 46.4	39.3	257 31.7	8.4	8 25.5	12.1	60.3	35	17 27	17 53	18 23	17 40	18 52	20 01	21 07
08	298 46.6	38.5	271 59.1	8.4	8 13.4	12.0	60.2	40	17 18	17 46	18 18	17 31	18 45	19 57	21 07
M 09	313 46.7 ..	37.8	286 26.5	8.6	8 01.4	12.1	60.2	45	17 09	17 39	18 14	17 20	18 37	19 53	21 07
O 10	328 46.8	37.0	300 54.1	8.6	7 49.3	12.1	60.2	S 50	16 57	17 31	18 09	17 07	18 28	19 48	21 06
N 11	343 46.9	36.2	315 21.7	8.7	7 37.2	12.2	60.1	52	16 52	17 27	18 07	17 00	18 24	19 46	21 06
D 12	358 47.0	N14 35.5	329 49.4	8.7	N 7 25.0	12.1	60.1	54	16 46	17 23	18 05	16 53	18 19	19 44	21 05
A 13	13 47.1	34.7	344 17.1	8.8	7 12.9	12.2	60.1	56	16 39	17 19	18 03	16 46	18 14	19 41	21 05
Y 14	28 47.2	34.0	358 44.9	8.9	7 00.7	12.3	60.0	58	16 32	17 14	18 01	16 37	18 08	19 38	21 05
15	43 47.3 ..	33.2	13 12.8	9.0	6 48.4	12.2	60.0	S 60	16 23	17 09	17 59	16 27	18 01	19 35	21 04
16	58 47.5	32.4	27 40.8	9.0	6 36.2	12.3	60.0								
17	73 47.6	31.7	42 08.8	9.1	6 23.9	12.4	59.9			SUN			MOON		
18	88 47.7	N14 30.9	56 36.9	9.2	N 6 11.5	12.3	59.9	Day	Eqn. of Time		Mer.	Mer. Pass.		Age	Phase
19	103 47.8	30.1	71 05.1	9.3	5 59.2	12.4	59.9		00ʰ	12ʰ	Pass.	Upper	Lower		
20	118 47.9	29.4	85 33.4	9.3	5 46.8	12.3	59.8	d	m s	m s	h m	h m	h m	d	%
21	133 48.0 ..	28.6	100 01.7	9.3	5 34.5	12.4	59.8	11	05 17	05 13	12 05	12 12	24 42	00	0
22	148 48.1	27.8	114 30.0	9.5	5 22.1	12.4	59.8	12	05 08	05 03	12 05	13 10	00 42	01	2
23	163 48.3	27.1	128 58.5	9.5	N 5 09.7	12.5	59.7	13	04 57	04 52	12 05	14 05	01 38	02	6
	SD 15.8	d 0.8	SD 16.7		16.6		16.4									

UT d h	ARIES GHA	VENUS −4.4 GHA	VENUS Dec	MARS −2.5 GHA	MARS Dec	JUPITER −2.0 GHA	JUPITER Dec	SATURN +0.3 GHA	SATURN Dec	Name	SHA	Dec
14 00	322 22.0	136 21.3	S 3 51.4	18 50.4	S26 28.9	99 29.9	S15 28.3	49 08.4	S22 38.5	Acamar	315 15.6	S40 13.7
01	337 24.5	151 21.6	52.6	33 53.3	29.0	114 32.1	28.4	64 11.0	38.5	Achernar	335 23.9	S57 08.4
02	352 26.9	166 21.9	53.8	48 56.3	29.0	129 34.4	28.5	79 13.5	38.5	Acrux	173 05.8	S63 12.2
03	7 29.4	181 22.2	.. 55.0	63 59.2	.. 29.0	144 36.6	.. 28.6	94 16.1	.. 38.5	Adhara	255 10.1	S28 59.8
04	22 31.9	196 22.5	56.2	79 02.2	29.1	159 38.8	28.7	109 18.7	38.5	Aldebaran	290 45.5	N16 32.6
05	37 34.3	211 22.8	57.4	94 05.1	29.1	174 41.0	28.7	124 21.2	38.5			
06	52 36.8	226 23.1	S 3 58.6	109 08.1	S26 29.1	189 43.3	S15 28.8	139 23.8	S22 38.5	Alioth	166 18.0	N55 51.9
07	67 39.2	241 23.4	3 59.8	124 11.0	29.2	204 45.5	28.9	154 26.4	38.6	Alkaid	152 56.3	N49 13.7
08	82 41.7	256 23.7	4 01.0	139 14.0	29.2	219 47.7	29.0	169 28.9	38.6	Al Na'ir	27 38.9	S46 52.1
09	97 44.2	271 24.1	.. 02.2	154 16.9	.. 29.2	234 49.9	.. 29.1	184 31.5	.. 38.6	Alnilam	275 43.0	S 1 11.5
10	112 46.6	286 24.4	03.4	169 19.9	29.2	249 52.2	29.1	199 34.0	38.6	Alphard	217 53.0	S 8 44.3
11	127 49.1	301 24.7	04.7	184 22.8	29.3	264 54.4	29.2	214 36.6	38.6			
12	142 51.6	316 25.0	S 4 05.9	199 25.8	S26 29.3	279 56.6	S15 29.3	229 39.2	S22 38.6	Alphecca	126 08.0	N26 39.5
13	157 54.0	331 25.3	07.1	214 28.7	29.3	294 58.8	29.4	244 41.7	38.6	Alpheratz	357 39.6	N29 11.5
14	172 56.5	346 25.6	08.3	229 31.6	29.3	310 01.1	29.5	259 44.3	38.6	Altair	62 04.5	N 8 55.3
15	187 59.0	1 25.9	.. 09.5	244 34.6	.. 29.4	325 03.3	.. 29.5	274 46.8	.. 38.6	Ankaa	353 11.9	S42 12.2
16	203 01.4	16 26.2	10.7	259 37.5	29.4	340 05.5	29.6	289 49.4	38.6	Antares	112 21.8	S26 28.2
17	218 03.9	31 26.5	11.9	274 40.4	29.4	355 07.7	29.7	304 52.0	38.6			
18	233 06.3	46 26.9	S 4 13.1	289 43.4	S26 29.4	10 10.0	S15 29.8	319 54.5	S22 38.6	Arcturus	145 52.6	N19 05.5
19	248 08.8	61 27.2	14.3	304 46.3	29.4	25 12.2	29.9	334 57.1	38.7	Atria	107 20.2	S69 03.7
20	263 11.3	76 27.5	15.5	319 49.2	29.5	40 14.4	29.9	349 59.6	38.7	Avior	234 17.2	S59 34.1
21	278 13.7	91 27.8	.. 16.7	334 52.2	.. 29.5	55 16.6	.. 30.0	5 02.2	.. 38.7	Bellatrix	278 28.4	N 6 21.9
22	293 16.2	106 28.1	17.9	349 55.1	29.5	70 18.8	30.1	20 04.8	38.7	Betelgeuse	270 57.7	N 7 24.5
23	308 18.7	121 28.4	19.1	4 58.0	29.5	85 21.1	30.2	35 07.3	38.7			
15 00	323 21.1	136 28.8	S 4 20.3	20 01.0	S26 29.5	100 23.3	S15 30.3	50 09.9	S22 38.7	Canopus	263 55.0	S52 42.2
01	338 23.6	151 29.1	21.5	35 03.9	29.6	115 25.5	30.4	65 12.4	38.7	Capella	280 29.5	N46 00.7
02	353 26.1	166 29.4	22.7	50 06.8	29.6	130 27.7	30.4	80 15.0	38.7	Deneb	49 28.6	N45 21.0
03	8 28.5	181 29.7	.. 23.9	65 09.7	.. 29.6	145 30.0	.. 30.5	95 17.5	.. 38.7	Denebola	182 30.4	N14 28.3
04	23 31.0	196 30.0	25.1	80 12.7	29.6	160 32.2	30.6	110 20.1	38.7	Diphda	348 52.2	S17 53.0
05	38 33.5	211 30.3	26.3	95 15.6	29.6	175 34.4	30.7	125 22.7	38.7			
06	53 35.9	226 30.7	S 4 27.5	110 18.5	S26 29.6	190 36.6	S15 30.8	140 25.2	S22 38.7	Dubhe	193 48.1	N61 39.3
07	68 38.4	241 31.0	28.8	125 21.4	29.7	205 38.8	30.8	155 27.8	38.7	Elnath	278 08.4	N28 37.2
08	83 40.8	256 31.3	30.0	140 24.3	29.7	220 41.1	30.9	170 30.3	38.8	Eltanin	90 44.2	N51 29.6
09	98 43.3	271 31.6	.. 31.2	155 27.2	.. 29.7	235 43.3	.. 31.0	185 32.9	.. 38.8	Enif	33 43.3	N 9 57.7
10	113 45.8	286 32.0	32.4	170 30.2	29.7	250 45.5	31.1	200 35.4	38.8	Fomalhaut	15 19.8	S29 31.3
11	128 48.2	301 32.3	33.6	185 33.1	29.7	265 47.7	31.2	215 38.0	38.8			
12	143 50.7	316 32.6	S 4 34.8	200 36.0	S26 29.7	280 49.9	S15 31.2	230 40.6	S22 38.8	Gacrux	171 57.3	S57 13.1
13	158 53.2	331 32.9	36.0	215 38.9	29.7	295 52.1	31.3	245 43.1	38.8	Gienah	175 48.9	S17 38.6
14	173 55.6	346 33.3	37.2	230 41.8	29.8	310 54.4	31.4	260 45.7	38.8	Hadar	148 43.1	S60 27.8
15	188 58.1	1 33.6	.. 38.4	245 44.7	.. 29.8	325 56.6	.. 31.5	275 48.2	.. 38.8	Hamal	327 56.7	N23 32.8
16	204 00.6	16 33.9	39.6	260 47.6	29.8	340 58.8	31.6	290 50.8	38.8	Kaus Aust.	83 38.9	S34 22.4
17	219 03.0	31 34.2	40.8	275 50.5	29.8	356 01.0	31.7	305 53.3	38.8			
18	234 05.5	46 34.6	S 4 42.0	290 53.4	S26 29.8	11 03.2	S15 31.7	320 55.9	S22 38.8	Kochab	137 20.3	N74 05.2
19	249 07.9	61 34.9	43.2	305 56.3	29.8	26 05.5	31.8	335 58.4	38.8	Markab	13 34.5	N15 18.3
20	264 10.4	76 35.2	44.4	320 59.2	29.8	41 07.7	31.9	351 01.0	38.8	Menkar	314 11.3	N 4 09.7
21	279 12.9	91 35.5	.. 45.6	336 02.1	.. 29.8	56 09.9	.. 32.0	6 03.6	.. 38.9	Menkent	148 03.5	S36 27.6
22	294 15.3	106 35.9	46.8	351 05.0	29.8	71 12.1	32.1	21 06.1	38.9	Miaplacidus	221 39.8	S69 47.6
23	309 17.8	121 36.2	48.0	6 07.9	29.8	86 14.3	32.2	36 08.7	38.9			
16 00	324 20.3	136 36.5	S 4 49.2	21 10.8	S26 29.8	101 16.5	S15 32.2	51 11.2	S22 38.9	Mirfak	308 35.3	N49 55.3
01	339 22.7	151 36.9	50.4	36 13.7	29.8	116 18.7	32.3	66 13.8	38.9	Nunki	75 53.7	S26 16.2
02	354 25.2	166 37.2	51.6	51 16.6	29.8	131 21.0	32.4	81 16.3	38.9	Peacock	53 13.2	S56 40.4
03	9 27.7	181 37.5	.. 52.8	66 19.5	.. 29.9	146 23.2	.. 32.5	96 18.9	.. 38.9	Pollux	243 23.8	N27 58.8
04	24 30.1	196 37.9	54.0	81 22.4	29.9	161 25.4	32.6	111 21.4	38.9	Procyon	244 56.4	N 5 10.6
05	39 32.6	211 38.2	55.2	96 25.3	29.9	176 27.6	32.7	126 24.0	38.9			
06	54 35.1	226 38.5	S 4 56.4	111 28.2	S26 29.9	191 29.8	S15 32.7	141 26.5	S22 38.9	Rasalhague	96 03.0	N12 33.1
07	69 37.5	241 38.9	57.6	126 31.1	29.9	206 32.0	32.8	156 29.1	38.9	Regulus	207 40.1	N11 52.7
08	84 40.0	256 39.2	4 58.8	141 33.9	29.9	221 34.2	32.9	171 31.7	38.9	Rigel	281 08.8	S 8 10.8
09	99 42.4	271 39.5	5 00.0	156 36.8	.. 29.9	236 36.5	.. 33.0	186 34.2	.. 38.9	Rigil Kent.	139 47.1	S60 54.7
10	114 44.9	286 39.9	01.2	171 39.7	29.9	251 38.7	33.1	201 36.8	39.0	Sabik	102 08.4	S15 44.7
11	129 47.4	301 40.2	02.4	186 42.6	29.9	266 40.9	33.2	216 39.3	39.0			
12	144 49.8	316 40.6	S 5 03.5	201 45.5	S26 29.9	281 43.1	S15 33.2	231 41.9	S22 39.0	Schedar	349 36.1	N56 38.1
13	159 52.3	331 40.9	04.7	216 48.4	29.9	296 45.3	33.3	246 44.4	39.0	Shaula	96 16.9	S37 06.9
14	174 54.8	346 41.2	05.9	231 51.2	29.9	311 47.5	33.4	261 47.0	39.0	Sirius	258 30.9	S16 44.5
15	189 57.2	1 41.6	.. 07.1	246 54.1	.. 29.9	326 49.7	.. 33.5	276 49.5	.. 39.0	Spica	158 27.7	S11 15.3
16	204 59.7	16 41.9	08.3	261 57.0	29.9	341 51.9	33.6	291 52.1	39.0	Suhail	222 50.3	S43 30.4
17	220 02.2	31 42.3	09.5	276 59.9	29.9	356 54.2	33.7	306 54.6	39.0			
18	235 04.6	46 42.6	S 5 10.7	292 02.7	S26 29.9	11 56.4	S15 33.7	321 57.2	S22 39.0	Vega	80 36.3	N38 48.4
19	250 07.1	61 42.9	11.9	307 05.6	29.9	26 58.6	33.8	336 59.7	39.0	Zuben'ubi	137 01.6	S16 07.0
20	265 09.6	76 43.3	13.1	322 08.5	29.9	42 00.8	33.9	352 02.3	39.0			
21	280 12.0	91 43.6	.. 14.3	337 11.3	.. 29.8	57 03.0	.. 34.0	7 04.8	.. 39.0		SHA	Mer. Pass.
22	295 14.5	106 44.0	15.5	352 14.2	29.8	72 05.2	34.1	22 07.4	39.0	Venus	173 07.6	14 54
23	310 16.9	121 44.3	16.7	7 17.1	29.8	87 07.4	34.2	37 09.7	39.1	Mars	56 39.8	22 36

Mer. Pass.	h m 2 26.2	v 0.3	d 1.2	v 2.9	d 0.0	v 2.2	d 0.1	v 2.6	d 0.0	Jupiter	137 02.2	17 16
										Saturn	86 48.7	20 36

SUN / MOON

UT	SUN GHA	SUN Dec	MOON GHA	v	MOON Dec	d	HP
d h	° ′	° ′	° ′	′	° ′	′	′
14 00	178 48.4	N14 26.3	143 27.0	9.5	N 4 57.2	12.4	59.7
01	193 48.5	25.5	157 55.5	9.6	4 44.8	12.5	59.7
02	208 48.6	24.8	172 24.1	9.7	4 32.3	12.4	59.6
03	223 48.7	.. 24.0	186 52.8	9.8	4 19.9	12.5	59.6
04	238 48.8	23.2	201 21.6	9.8	4 07.4	12.5	59.6
05	253 48.9	22.4	215 50.4	9.9	3 54.9	12.5	59.5
06	268 49.1	N14 21.7	230 19.3	9.9	N 3 42.4	12.4	59.5
07	283 49.2	20.9	244 48.2	10.0	3 30.0	12.5	59.4
08	298 49.3	20.1	259 17.2	10.0	3 17.5	12.5	59.4
09	313 49.4	.. 19.4	273 46.2	10.1	3 05.0	12.5	59.4
10	328 49.5	18.6	288 15.3	10.2	2 52.5	12.5	59.3
11	343 49.6	17.8	302 44.5	10.2	2 40.0	12.5	59.3
12	358 49.8	N14 17.0	317 13.7	10.3	N 2 27.5	12.5	59.3
13	13 49.9	16.3	331 43.0	10.3	2 15.0	12.5	59.2
14	28 50.0	15.5	346 12.3	10.4	2 02.5	12.5	59.2
15	43 50.1	.. 14.7	0 41.7	10.4	1 50.0	12.5	59.1
16	58 50.2	14.0	15 11.1	10.5	1 37.5	12.4	59.1
17	73 50.4	13.2	29 40.6	10.5	1 25.1	12.5	59.1
18	88 50.5	N14 12.4	44 10.1	10.6	N 1 12.6	12.4	59.0
19	103 50.6	11.6	58 39.7	10.6	1 00.2	12.5	59.0
20	118 50.7	10.9	73 09.3	10.7	0 47.7	12.4	58.9
21	133 50.8	.. 10.1	87 39.0	10.8	0 35.3	12.4	58.9
22	148 50.9	09.3	102 08.8	10.7	0 22.9	12.4	58.9
23	163 51.1	08.5	116 38.5	10.9	N 0 10.5	12.4	58.8
15 00	178 51.2	N14 07.7	131 08.4	10.8	S 0 01.9	12.3	58.8
01	193 51.3	07.0	145 38.2	10.9	0 14.2	12.4	58.8
02	208 51.4	06.2	160 08.1	11.0	0 26.6	12.3	58.7
03	223 51.6	.. 05.4	174 38.1	11.0	0 38.9	12.3	58.7
04	238 51.7	04.6	189 08.1	11.1	0 51.2	12.3	58.6
05	253 51.8	03.9	203 38.2	11.0	1 03.5	12.3	58.6
06	268 51.9	N14 03.1	218 08.2	11.2	S 1 15.8	12.2	58.6
07	283 52.0	02.3	232 38.4	11.1	1 28.0	12.2	58.5
08	298 52.2	01.5	247 08.5	11.2	1 40.2	12.2	58.5
09	313 52.3	14 00.7	261 38.7	11.3	1 52.4	12.1	58.4
10	328 52.4	13 59.9	276 09.0	11.3	2 04.5	12.2	58.4
11	343 52.5	59.2	290 39.3	11.3	2 16.7	12.1	58.4
12	358 52.7	N13 58.4	305 09.6	11.4	S 2 28.8	12.0	58.3
13	13 52.8	57.6	319 40.0	11.3	2 40.8	12.1	58.3
14	28 52.9	56.8	334 10.3	11.5	2 52.9	12.0	58.2
15	43 53.0	.. 56.0	348 40.8	11.4	3 04.9	11.9	58.2
16	58 53.2	55.3	3 11.2	11.5	3 16.8	12.0	58.2
17	73 53.3	54.5	17 41.7	11.6	3 28.8	11.9	58.1
18	88 53.4	N13 53.7	32 12.3	11.5	S 3 40.7	11.8	58.1
19	103 53.5	52.9	46 42.8	11.6	3 52.5	11.9	58.0
20	118 53.6	52.1	61 13.4	11.6	4 04.4	11.8	58.0
21	133 53.8	.. 51.3	75 44.0	11.7	4 16.2	11.7	58.0
22	148 53.9	50.5	90 14.7	11.6	4 27.9	11.7	57.9
23	163 54.0	49.8	104 45.3	11.7	4 39.6	11.7	57.9
16 00	178 54.2	N13 49.0	119 16.0	11.8	S 4 51.3	11.6	57.8
01	193 54.3	48.2	133 46.8	11.7	5 02.9	11.6	57.8
02	208 54.4	47.4	148 17.5	11.8	5 14.5	11.6	57.8
03	223 54.5	.. 46.6	162 48.3	11.8	5 26.1	11.5	57.7
04	238 54.7	45.8	177 19.1	11.9	5 37.6	11.4	57.7
05	253 54.8	45.0	191 50.0	11.8	5 49.0	11.4	57.6
06	268 54.9	N13 44.2	206 20.8	11.9	S 6 00.4	11.4	57.6
07	283 55.0	43.5	220 51.7	11.9	6 11.8	11.3	57.6
08	298 55.2	42.7	235 22.6	11.9	6 23.1	11.3	57.5
09	313 55.3	.. 41.9	249 53.5	11.9	6 34.4	11.2	57.5
10	328 55.4	41.1	264 24.4	12.0	6 45.6	11.2	57.5
11	343 55.6	40.3	278 55.4	12.0	6 56.8	11.1	57.4
12	358 55.7	N13 39.5	293 26.4	12.0	S 7 07.9	11.1	57.4
13	13 55.8	38.7	307 57.4	12.0	7 19.0	11.0	57.3
14	28 55.9	37.9	322 28.4	12.0	7 30.0	11.0	57.3
15	43 56.1	.. 37.1	336 59.4	12.1	7 41.0	10.9	57.3
16	58 56.2	36.3	351 30.5	12.0	7 51.9	10.9	57.2
17	73 56.3	35.5	6 01.5	12.1	8 02.8	10.8	57.2
18	88 56.5	N13 34.7	20 32.6	12.1	S 8 13.6	10.7	57.1
19	103 56.6	33.9	35 03.7	12.1	8 24.3	10.7	57.1
20	118 56.7	33.2	49 34.8	12.2	8 35.0	10.6	57.1
21	133 56.9	.. 32.4	64 06.0	12.1	8 45.6	10.6	57.0
22	148 57.0	31.6	78 37.1	12.1	8 56.2	10.6	57.0
23	163 57.1	30.8	93 08.2	12.2	S 9 06.8	10.4	57.0
	SD 15.8	d 0.8	SD 16.1		15.9		15.6

Day labels (left margin): 14 = TUESDAY; 15 = WEDNESDAY; 16 = THURSDAY

Sunrise / Moonrise

Lat.	Twilight Naut.	Twilight Civil	Sunrise	Moonrise 14	15	16	17
°	h m	h m	h m	h m	h m	h m	h m
N 72	////	////	02 24	08 04	10 03	11 59	13 55
N 70	////	////	02 56	08 09	10 00	11 47	13 34
68	////	01 43	03 19	08 13	09 57	11 38	13 17
66	////	02 21	03 37	08 16	09 55	11 31	13 04
64	////	02 47	03 52	08 18	09 53	11 25	12 53
62	01 31	03 06	04 04	08 21	09 52	11 20	12 44
60	02 06	03 22	04 14	08 23	09 50	11 15	12 36
N 58	02 30	03 36	04 23	08 24	09 49	11 11	12 29
56	02 48	03 47	04 31	08 26	09 48	11 07	12 23
54	03 04	03 57	04 38	08 27	09 47	11 04	12 18
52	03 16	04 06	04 44	08 28	09 46	11 01	12 13
50	03 28	04 13	04 49	08 30	09 45	10 58	12 09
45	03 50	04 29	05 01	08 32	09 44	10 53	11 59
N 40	04 07	04 42	05 11	08 34	09 42	10 48	11 51
35	04 21	04 53	05 20	08 36	09 41	10 44	11 45
30	04 32	05 02	05 27	08 38	09 40	10 40	11 39
20	04 50	05 17	05 40	08 40	09 38	10 34	11 28
N 10	05 04	05 29	05 51	08 43	09 37	10 29	11 20
0	05 15	05 40	06 01	08 45	09 35	10 24	11 11
S 10	05 25	05 50	06 11	08 47	09 34	10 19	11 03
20	05 33	05 59	06 22	08 50	09 32	10 13	10 54
30	05 41	06 09	06 34	08 53	09 31	10 07	10 45
35	05 45	06 15	06 41	08 54	09 30	10 04	10 39
40	05 49	06 20	06 48	08 56	09 28	10 00	10 32
45	05 52	06 27	06 57	08 58	09 27	09 56	10 25
S 50	05 56	06 35	07 08	09 01	09 26	09 51	10 16
52	05 58	06 38	07 13	09 02	09 25	09 48	10 12
54	06 00	06 42	07 19	09 03	09 24	09 45	10 08
56	06 02	06 46	07 25	09 04	09 24	09 43	10 03
58	06 04	06 50	07 32	09 06	09 23	09 39	09 57
S 60	06 06	06 55	07 40	09 08	09 22	09 36	09 51

Sunset / Moonset

Lat.	Sunset	Twilight Civil	Twilight Naut.	Moonset 14	15	16	17
°	h m	h m	h m	h m	h m	h m	h m
N 72	21 40	////	////	21 15	21 02	20 49	20 32
N 70	21 09	23 33	////	21 14	21 08	21 02	20 55
68	20 47	22 20	////	21 14	21 13	21 12	21 12
66	20 29	21 44	////	21 13	21 17	21 21	21 27
64	20 15	21 19	23 37	21 13	21 21	21 29	21 39
62	20 03	21 00	22 32	21 13	21 24	21 35	21 49
60	19 53	20 44	21 59	21 12	21 27	21 41	21 57
N 58	19 45	20 31	21 36	21 12	21 29	21 46	22 05
56	19 37	20 20	21 18	21 12	21 31	21 51	22 12
54	19 30	20 11	21 03	21 12	21 33	21 55	22 18
52	19 24	20 02	20 51	21 12	21 35	21 58	22 23
50	19 19	19 54	20 40	21 11	21 36	22 02	22 28
45	19 07	19 39	20 18	21 11	21 40	22 09	22 39
N 40	18 57	19 26	20 01	21 11	21 43	22 15	22 48
35	18 49	19 15	19 47	21 11	21 45	22 20	22 56
30	18 41	19 06	19 36	21 10	21 48	22 25	23 02
20	18 29	18 52	19 19	21 10	21 52	22 33	23 14
N 10	18 18	18 40	19 05	21 09	21 55	22 40	23 24
0	18 08	18 29	18 54	21 09	21 58	22 47	23 34
S 10	17 58	18 20	18 44	21 09	22 02	22 53	23 44
20	17 47	18 10	18 36	21 08	22 05	23 00	23 54
30	17 36	18 00	18 28	21 08	22 09	23 08	24 06
35	17 29	17 55	18 25	21 07	22 11	23 13	24 13
40	17 21	17 49	18 21	21 07	22 14	23 19	24 21
45	17 12	17 43	18 17	21 07	22 17	23 25	24 30
S 50	17 01	17 35	18 13	21 06	22 21	23 32	24 41
52	16 56	17 32	18 12	21 06	22 22	23 36	24 46
54	16 51	17 28	18 10	21 05	22 24	23 40	24 52
56	16 45	17 24	18 08	21 05	22 26	23 44	24 58
58	16 38	17 20	18 06	21 05	22 28	23 48	25 06
S 60	16 30	17 15	18 04	21 04	22 31	23 54	25 14

SUN and MOON

Day	SUN Eqn. of Time 00h	SUN Eqn. of Time 12h	SUN Mer. Pass.	MOON Mer. Pass. Upper	MOON Mer. Pass. Lower	Age	Phase
d	m s	m s	h m	h m	h m	d %	
14	04 47	04 41	12 05	14 57	02 31	03 13	
15	04 35	04 30	12 04	15 47	03 22	04 22	
16	04 24	04 18	12 04	16 35	04 11	05 32	◐

UT	ARIES	VENUS −4·5		MARS −2·4		JUPITER −2·0		SATURN +0·3		STARS		
	GHA	GHA	Dec	GHA	Dec	GHA	Dec	GHA	Dec	Name	SHA	Dec
d h	° ′	° ′	° ′	° ′	° ′	° ′	° ′	° ′	° ′		° ′	° ′
17 00	325 19.4	136 44.7	S 5 17.9	22 19.9	S26 29.8	102 09.6	S15 34.2	52 12.5	S22 39.1	Acamar	315 15.6	S40 13.7
01	340 21.9	151 45.0	19.1	37 22.8	29.8	117 11.8	34.3	67 15.0	39.1	Achernar	335 23.9	S57 08.4
02	355 24.3	166 45.4	20.3	52 25.7	29.8	132 14.0	34.4	82 17.6	39.1	Acrux	173 05.8	S63 12.2
03	10 26.8	181 45.7	. . 21.5	67 28.5	. . 29.8	147 16.3	. . 34.5	97 20.1	. . 39.1	Adhara	255 10.1	S28 59.8
04	25 29.3	196 46.1	22.7	82 31.4	29.8	162 18.5	34.6	112 22.7	39.1	Aldebaran	290 45.4	N16 32.6
05	40 31.7	211 46.4	23.9	97 34.2	29.8	177 20.7	34.7	127 25.2	39.1			
06	55 34.2	226 46.8	S 5 25.1	112 37.1	S26 29.8	192 22.9	S15 34.8	142 27.8	S22 39.1	Alioth	166 18.0	N55 51.9
07	70 36.7	241 47.1	26.2	127 40.0	29.8	207 25.1	34.8	157 30.3	39.1	Alkaid	152 56.4	N49 13.7
08	85 39.1	256 47.5	27.4	142 42.8	29.8	222 27.3	34.9	172 32.9	39.1	Al Na'ir	27 38.9	S46 52.1
F 09	100 41.6	271 47.8	. . 28.6	157 45.7	. . 29.7	237 29.5	. . 35.0	187 35.4	. . 39.1	Alnilam	275 43.0	S 1 11.5
R 10	115 44.0	286 48.2	29.8	172 48.5	29.7	252 31.7	35.1	202 38.0	39.1	Alphard	217 53.0	S 8 44.3
I 11	130 46.5	301 48.5	31.0	187 51.4	29.7	267 33.9	35.2	217 40.5	39.1			
D 12	145 49.0	316 48.9	S 5 32.2	202 54.2	S26 29.7	282 36.1	S15 35.3	232 43.1	S22 39.2	Alphecca	126 08.0	N26 39.5
A 13	160 51.4	331 49.2	33.4	217 57.1	29.7	297 38.3	35.3	247 45.6	39.2	Alpheratz	357 39.6	N29 11.5
Y 14	175 53.9	346 49.6	34.6	232 59.9	29.7	312 40.5	35.4	262 48.2	39.2	Altair	62 04.5	N 8 55.3
15	190 56.4	1 49.9	. . 35.8	248 02.8	. . 29.7	327 42.7	. . 35.5	277 50.7	. . 39.2	Ankaa	353 11.9	S42 12.2
16	205 58.8	16 50.3	37.0	263 05.6	29.7	342 44.9	35.6	292 53.3	39.2	Antares	112 21.9	S26 28.2
17	221 01.3	31 50.6	38.2	278 08.4	29.6	357 47.1	35.7	307 55.8	39.2			
18	236 03.8	46 51.0	S 5 39.3	293 11.3	S26 29.6	12 49.4	S15 35.8	322 58.4	S22 39.2	Arcturus	145 52.7	N19 05.5
19	251 06.2	61 51.4	40.5	308 14.1	29.6	27 51.6	35.9	338 00.9	39.2	Atria	107 20.3	S69 03.7
20	266 08.7	76 51.7	41.7	323 17.0	29.6	42 53.8	35.9	353 03.5	39.2	Avior	234 17.2	S59 34.1
21	281 11.2	91 52.1	. . 42.9	338 19.8	. . 29.6	57 56.0	. . 36.0	8 06.0	. . 39.2	Bellatrix	278 28.4	N 6 21.9
22	296 13.6	106 52.4	44.1	353 22.6	29.6	72 58.2	36.1	23 08.6	39.2	Betelgeuse	270 57.7	N 7 24.5
23	311 16.1	121 52.8	45.3	8 25.5	29.5	88 00.4	36.2	38 11.1	39.2			
18 00	326 18.5	136 53.1	S 5 46.5	23 28.3	S26 29.5	103 02.6	S15 36.3	53 13.6	S22 39.2	Canopus	263 54.9	S52 42.2
01	341 21.0	151 53.5	47.7	38 31.1	29.5	118 04.8	36.4	68 16.2	39.3	Capella	280 29.4	N46 00.7
02	356 23.5	166 53.9	48.9	53 34.0	29.5	133 07.0	36.5	83 18.7	39.3	Deneb	49 28.6	N45 21.0
03	11 25.9	181 54.2	. . 50.0	68 36.8	. . 29.5	148 09.2	. . 36.5	98 21.3	. . 39.3	Denebola	182 30.4	N14 28.3
04	26 28.4	196 54.6	51.2	83 39.6	29.4	163 11.4	36.6	113 23.8	39.3	Diphda	348 52.1	S17 53.0
05	41 30.9	211 55.0	52.4	98 42.4	29.4	178 13.6	36.7	128 26.4	39.3			
06	56 33.3	226 55.3	S 5 53.6	113 45.3	S26 29.4	193 15.8	S15 36.8	143 28.9	S22 39.3	Dubhe	193 48.1	N61 39.2
07	71 35.8	241 55.7	54.8	128 48.1	29.4	208 18.0	36.9	158 31.5	39.3	Elnath	278 08.3	N28 37.2
S 08	86 38.3	256 56.1	56.0	143 50.9	29.4	223 20.2	37.0	173 34.0	39.3	Eltanin	90 44.2	N51 29.6
A 09	101 40.7	271 56.4	. . 57.2	158 53.7	. . 29.3	238 22.4	. . 37.1	188 36.6	. . 39.3	Enif	33 43.3	N 9 57.7
T 10	116 43.2	286 56.8	58.3	173 56.5	29.3	253 24.6	37.1	203 39.1	39.3	Fomalhaut	15 19.8	S29 31.3
U 11	131 45.6	301 57.2	5 59.5	188 59.4	29.3	268 26.8	37.2	218 41.7	39.3			
R 12	146 48.1	316 57.5	S 6 00.7	204 02.2	S26 29.3	283 29.0	S15 37.3	233 44.2	S22 39.3	Gacrux	171 57.4	S57 13.1
D 13	161 50.6	331 57.9	01.9	219 05.0	29.2	298 31.2	37.4	248 46.7	39.3	Gienah	175 48.9	S17 38.6
A 14	176 53.0	346 58.3	03.1	234 07.8	29.2	313 33.4	37.5	263 49.3	39.4	Hadar	148 43.1	S60 27.8
Y 15	191 55.5	1 58.6	. . 04.3	249 10.6	. . 29.2	328 35.6	. . 37.6	278 51.8	. . 39.4	Hamal	327 56.6	N23 32.8
16	206 58.0	16 59.0	05.5	264 13.4	29.2	343 37.8	37.7	293 54.4	39.4	Kaus Aust.	83 38.9	S34 22.4
17	222 00.4	31 59.4	06.6	279 16.2	29.1	358 40.0	37.8	308 56.9	39.4			
18	237 02.9	46 59.7	S 6 07.8	294 19.0	S26 29.1	13 42.2	S15 37.8	323 59.5	S22 39.4	Kochab	137 20.4	N74 05.2
19	252 05.4	62 00.1	09.0	309 21.8	29.1	28 44.4	37.9	339 02.0	39.4	Markab	13 34.5	N15 18.4
20	267 07.8	77 00.5	10.2	324 24.6	29.1	43 46.6	38.0	354 04.5	39.4	Menkar	314 11.3	N 4 09.7
21	282 10.3	92 00.9	. . 11.4	339 27.5	. . 29.0	58 48.8	. . 38.1	9 07.1	. . 39.4	Menkent	148 03.6	S36 27.6
22	297 12.8	107 01.2	12.6	354 30.3	29.0	73 51.0	38.2	24 09.6	39.4	Miaplacidus	221 39.8	S69 47.6
23	312 15.2	122 01.6	13.7	9 33.1	29.0	88 53.2	38.3	39 12.2	39.4			
19 00	327 17.7	137 02.0	S 6 14.9	24 35.9	S26 28.9	103 55.4	S15 38.4	54 14.7	S22 39.4	Mirfak	308 35.3	N49 55.3
01	342 20.1	152 02.4	16.1	39 38.7	28.9	118 57.6	38.5	69 17.3	39.4	Nunki	75 53.7	S26 16.2
02	357 22.6	167 02.7	17.3	54 41.4	28.9	133 59.8	38.5	84 19.8	39.4	Peacock	53 13.2	S56 40.4
03	12 25.1	182 03.1	. . 18.5	69 44.2	. . 28.8	149 02.0	. . 38.6	99 22.3	. . 39.4	Pollux	243 23.8	N27 58.8
04	27 27.5	197 03.5	19.6	84 47.0	28.8	164 04.2	38.7	114 24.9	39.5	Procyon	244 56.4	N 5 10.6
05	42 30.0	212 03.9	20.8	99 49.8	28.8	179 06.4	38.8	129 27.4	39.5			
06	57 32.5	227 04.2	S 6 22.0	114 52.6	S26 28.7	194 08.6	S15 38.9	144 30.0	S22 39.5	Rasalhague	96 03.0	N12 33.1
07	72 34.9	242 04.6	23.2	129 55.4	28.7	209 10.8	39.0	159 32.5	39.5	Regulus	207 40.1	N11 52.7
08	87 37.4	257 05.0	24.4	144 58.2	28.7	224 12.9	39.1	174 35.1	39.5	Rigel	281 08.8	S 8 10.8
S 09	102 39.9	272 05.4	. . 25.5	160 01.0	. . 28.6	239 15.1	. . 39.2	189 37.6	. . 39.5	Rigil Kent.	139 47.1	S60 54.7
U 10	117 42.3	287 05.8	26.7	175 03.8	28.6	254 17.3	39.2	204 40.1	39.5	Sabik	102 08.4	S15 44.7
N 11	132 44.8	302 06.2	27.9	190 06.5	28.6	269 19.5	39.3	219 42.7	39.5			
D 12	147 47.3	317 06.5	S 6 29.1	205 09.3	S26 28.5	284 21.7	S15 39.4	234 45.2	S22 39.5	Schedar	349 36.1	N56 38.1
A 13	162 49.7	332 06.9	30.3	220 12.1	28.5	299 23.9	39.5	249 47.8	39.5	Shaula	96 16.9	S37 06.9
Y 14	177 52.2	347 07.3	31.4	235 14.9	28.5	314 26.1	39.6	264 50.3	39.5	Sirius	258 30.9	S16 44.5
15	192 54.6	2 07.7	. . 32.6	250 17.7	. . 28.4	329 28.3	. . 39.7	279 52.8	. . 39.5	Spica	158 27.7	S11 15.3
16	207 57.1	17 08.1	33.8	265 20.4	28.4	344 30.5	39.8	294 55.4	39.5	Suhail	222 50.3	S43 30.4
17	222 59.6	32 08.5	35.0	280 23.2	28.3	359 32.7	39.9	309 57.9	39.6			
18	238 02.0	47 08.9	S 6 36.1	295 26.0	S26 28.3	14 34.9	S15 40.0	325 00.5	S22 39.6	Vega	80 36.3	N38 48.4
19	253 04.5	62 09.2	37.3	310 28.8	28.3	29 37.1	40.0	340 03.0	39.6	Zuben'ubi	137 01.6	S16 06.9
20	268 07.0	77 09.6	38.5	325 31.5	28.2	44 39.3	40.1	355 05.5	39.6		SHA	Mer.Pass.
21	283 09.4	92 10.0	. . 39.7	340 34.3	. . 28.2	59 41.5	. . 40.2	10 08.1	. . 39.6		° ′	h m
22	298 11.9	107 10.4	40.9	355 37.1	28.1	74 43.7	40.3	25 10.6	39.6	Venus	170 34.6	14 52
23	313 14.4	122 10.8	42.0	10 39.8	28.1	89 45.8	40.4	40 13.2	39.6	Mars	57 09.7	22 22
	h m									Jupiter	136 44.0	17 05
Mer.Pass.	2 14.4	v 0.4	d 1.2	v 2.8	d 0.0	v 2.2	d 0.1	v 2.5	d 0.0	Saturn	86 55.1	20 24

UT	SUN GHA	SUN Dec	MOON GHA	v	MOON Dec	d	HP
d h	° ′	° ′	° ′	′	° ′	′	′
17 00	178 57.3	N13 30.0	107 39.4	12.2	S 9 17.2	10.4	56.9
01	193 57.4	29.2	122 10.6	12.1	9 27.6	10.4	56.9
02	208 57.5	28.4	136 41.7	12.2	9 38.0	10.3	56.9
03	223 57.6	.. 27.6	151 12.9	12.2	9 48.3	10.2	56.8
04	238 57.8	26.8	165 44.1	12.2	9 58.5	10.1	56.8
05	253 57.9	26.0	180 15.3	12.2	10 08.6	10.1	56.7
F 06	268 58.0	N13 25.2	194 46.5	12.3	S10 18.7	10.1	56.7
R 07	283 58.2	24.4	209 17.8	12.2	10 28.8	10.0	56.7
I 08	298 58.3	23.6	223 49.0	12.2	10 38.8	9.9	56.6
D 09	313 58.4	.. 22.8	238 20.2	12.2	10 48.7	9.8	56.6
A 10	328 58.6	22.0	252 51.4	12.3	10 58.5	9.8	56.6
Y 11	343 58.7	21.2	267 22.7	12.2	11 08.3	9.7	56.5
12	358 58.8	N13 20.4	281 53.9	12.3	S11 18.0	9.6	56.5
13	13 59.0	19.6	296 25.2	12.2	11 27.6	9.6	56.5
14	28 59.1	18.8	310 56.4	12.3	11 37.2	9.5	56.4
15	43 59.3	.. 18.0	325 27.7	12.3	11 46.7	9.5	56.4
16	58 59.4	17.2	339 59.0	12.2	11 56.2	9.4	56.4
17	73 59.5	16.4	354 30.2	12.3	12 05.6	9.3	56.3
18	88 59.7	N13 15.6	9 01.5	12.3	S12 14.9	9.2	56.3
19	103 59.8	14.8	23 32.8	12.2	12 24.1	9.2	56.3
20	118 59.9	14.0	38 04.0	12.3	12 33.3	9.1	56.2
21	134 00.1	.. 13.2	52 35.3	12.3	12 42.4	9.0	56.2
22	149 00.2	12.4	67 06.6	12.2	12 51.4	8.9	56.2
23	164 00.3	11.6	81 37.8	12.3	13 00.3	8.9	56.1
18 00	179 00.5	N13 10.8	96 09.1	12.2	S13 09.2	8.8	56.1
01	194 00.6	10.0	110 40.3	12.3	13 18.0	8.7	56.1
02	209 00.8	09.2	125 11.6	12.3	13 26.7	8.7	56.0
03	224 00.9	.. 08.3	139 42.9	12.2	13 35.4	8.6	56.0
04	239 01.0	07.5	154 14.1	12.3	13 44.0	8.5	56.0
05	254 01.2	06.7	168 45.4	12.3	13 52.5	8.4	55.9
S 06	269 01.3	N13 05.9	183 16.6	12.3	S14 00.9	8.4	55.9
A 07	284 01.4	05.1	197 47.9	12.2	14 09.3	8.3	55.9
T 08	299 01.6	04.3	212 19.1	12.3	14 17.6	8.2	55.8
U 09	314 01.7	.. 03.5	226 50.4	12.2	14 25.8	8.1	55.8
R 10	329 01.9	02.7	241 21.6	12.2	14 33.9	8.0	55.8
D 11	344 02.0	01.9	255 52.8	12.2	14 41.9	8.0	55.8
A 12	359 02.1	N13 01.1	270 24.0	12.3	S14 49.9	7.9	55.7
Y 13	14 02.3	13 00.3	284 55.3	12.2	14 57.8	7.8	55.7
14	29 02.4	12 59.5	299 26.5	12.2	15 05.6	7.8	55.7
15	44 02.6	.. 58.7	313 57.7	12.2	15 13.4	7.6	55.6
16	59 02.7	57.8	328 28.9	12.2	15 21.0	7.6	55.6
17	74 02.8	57.0	343 00.1	12.2	15 28.6	7.5	55.6
18	89 03.0	N12 56.2	357 31.3	12.1	S15 36.1	7.4	55.6
19	104 03.1	55.4	12 02.4	12.2	15 43.5	7.3	55.5
20	119 03.3	54.6	26 33.6	12.2	15 50.8	7.3	55.5
21	134 03.4	.. 53.8	41 04.8	12.1	15 58.1	7.1	55.5
22	149 03.6	53.0	55 35.9	12.2	16 05.2	7.1	55.4
23	164 03.7	52.2	70 07.1	12.1	16 12.3	7.0	55.4
19 00	179 03.8	N12 51.3	84 38.2	12.2	S16 19.3	6.9	55.4
01	194 04.0	50.5	99 09.4	12.1	16 26.2	6.9	55.4
02	209 04.1	49.7	113 40.5	12.1	16 33.1	6.7	55.3
03	224 04.3	.. 48.9	128 11.6	12.1	16 39.8	6.7	55.3
04	239 04.4	48.1	142 42.7	12.1	16 46.5	6.6	55.3
05	254 04.6	47.3	157 13.8	12.1	16 53.1	6.5	55.3
S 06	269 04.7	N12 46.5	171 44.9	12.1	S16 59.6	6.4	55.2
U 07	284 04.8	45.6	186 16.0	12.1	17 06.0	6.3	55.2
N 08	299 05.0	44.8	200 47.1	12.0	17 12.3	6.2	55.2
D 09	314 05.1	.. 44.0	215 18.1	12.1	17 18.5	6.2	55.2
A 10	329 05.3	43.2	229 49.2	12.0	17 24.7	6.0	55.1
Y 11	344 05.4	42.4	244 20.2	12.1	17 30.7	6.0	55.1
12	359 05.6	N12 41.6	258 51.3	12.0	S17 36.7	5.9	55.1
13	14 05.7	40.7	273 22.3	12.0	17 42.6	5.8	55.1
14	29 05.9	39.9	287 53.3	12.0	17 48.4	5.7	55.0
15	44 06.0	.. 39.1	302 24.3	12.1	17 54.1	5.6	55.0
16	59 06.2	38.3	316 55.4	11.9	17 59.7	5.6	55.0
17	74 06.3	37.5	331 26.3	12.0	18 05.3	5.4	55.0
18	89 06.4	N12 36.7	345 57.3	12.0	S18 10.7	5.4	55.0
19	104 06.6	35.8	0 28.3	12.0	18 16.1	5.2	54.9
20	119 06.7	35.0	14 59.3	11.9	18 21.3	5.2	54.9
21	134 06.9	.. 34.2	29 30.2	12.0	18 26.5	5.1	54.9
22	149 07.0	33.4	44 01.2	11.9	18 31.6	5.0	54.9
23	164 07.2	32.6	58 32.1	11.9	S18 36.6	4.9	54.9
	SD 15.8	d 0.8	SD 15.4		15.2		15.0

Twilight / Sunrise / Moonrise

Lat.	Twilight Naut.	Twilight Civil	Sunrise	Moonrise 17	18	19	20
°	h m	h m	h m	h m	h m	h m	h m
N 72	////	////	02 44	13 55	15 59	■	■
N 70	////	01 12	03 11	13 34	15 21	17 13	■
68	////	02 04	03 31	13 17	14 55	16 30	18 00
66	////	02 36	03 48	13 04	14 35	16 01	17 20
64	01 03	02 59	04 01	12 53	14 19	15 40	16 53
62	01 50	03 16	04 12	12 44	14 06	15 22	16 32
60	02 19	03 31	04 21	12 36	13 54	15 08	16 15
N 58	02 40	03 43	04 29	12 29	13 45	14 56	16 00
56	02 57	03 54	04 37	12 23	13 36	14 45	15 48
54	03 11	04 03	04 43	12 18	13 29	14 36	15 38
52	03 23	04 11	04 49	12 13	13 22	14 27	15 28
50	03 34	04 18	04 54	12 09	13 16	14 20	15 20
45	03 55	04 33	05 05	11 59	13 03	14 04	15 02
N 40	04 11	04 45	05 14	11 51	12 52	13 51	14 47
35	04 24	04 56	05 22	11 45	12 43	13 40	14 35
30	04 34	05 04	05 29	11 39	12 35	13 31	14 24
20	04 51	05 18	05 41	11 28	12 22	13 14	14 06
N 10	05 04	05 29	05 51	11 20	12 10	13 00	13 50
0	05 15	05 39	06 00	11 11	11 59	12 47	13 35
S 10	05 23	05 48	06 10	11 03	11 48	12 33	13 20
20	05 31	05 57	06 20	10 54	11 36	12 19	13 04
30	05 38	06 06	06 31	10 45	11 23	12 03	12 46
35	05 42	06 11	06 37	10 39	11 15	11 54	12 35
40	05 45	06 17	06 44	10 32	11 06	11 43	12 23
45	05 48	06 22	06 53	10 25	10 56	11 30	12 09
S 50	05 51	06 29	07 03	10 16	10 44	11 15	11 51
52	05 53	06 32	07 07	10 12	10 38	11 08	11 43
54	05 55	06 36	07 12	10 08	10 32	11 01	11 34
56	05 55	06 39	07 18	10 03	10 25	10 52	11 24
58	05 57	06 43	07 24	09 57	10 17	10 42	11 12
S 60	05 58	06 47	07 31	09 51	10 09	10 31	10 59

Sunset / Twilight / Moonset

Lat.	Sunset	Twilight Civil	Twilight Naut.	Moonset 17	18	19	20
°	h m	h m	h m	h m	h m	h m	h m
N 72	21 19	////	////	20 32	20 07	■	■
N 70	20 53	22 45	////	20 55	20 46	20 34	■
68	20 33	21 58	////	21 12	21 14	21 18	21 28
66	20 18	21 28	////	21 27	21 35	21 47	22 08
64	20 05	21 06	22 55	21 39	21 51	22 09	22 36
62	19 54	20 49	22 12	21 49	22 05	22 27	22 57
60	19 45	20 34	21 45	21 57	22 17	22 42	23 14
N 58	19 37	20 23	21 25	22 05	22 27	22 54	23 29
56	19 30	20 12	21 08	22 12	22 36	23 05	23 41
54	19 24	20 03	20 55	22 18	22 44	23 15	23 52
52	19 18	19 55	20 43	22 23	22 51	23 24	24 01
50	19 13	19 48	20 33	22 28	22 58	23 31	24 10
45	19 02	19 33	20 12	22 39	23 12	23 48	24 28
N 40	18 53	19 21	19 56	22 48	23 23	24 01	00 01
35	18 45	19 12	19 43	22 56	23 33	24 13	00 13
30	18 38	19 03	19 33	23 02	23 42	24 23	00 23
20	18 27	18 49	19 16	23 14	23 56	24 40	00 40
N 10	18 17	18 38	19 03	23 24	24 09	00 09	00 55
0	18 07	18 28	18 53	23 34	24 22	00 22	01 10
S 10	17 58	18 19	18 44	23 44	24 34	00 34	01 24
20	17 48	18 11	18 37	23 54	24 47	00 47	01 39
30	17 37	18 02	18 30	24 06	00 06	01 02	01 57
35	17 31	17 57	18 27	24 13	00 13	01 11	02 07
40	17 24	17 52	18 23	24 21	00 21	01 21	02 18
45	17 16	17 46	18 20	24 30	00 30	01 33	02 32
S 50	17 06	17 39	18 17	24 41	00 41	01 47	02 49
52	17 01	17 36	18 16	24 46	00 46	01 54	02 57
54	16 56	17 33	18 15	24 52	00 52	02 01	03 06
56	16 51	17 30	18 13	24 58	00 58	02 09	03 16
58	16 44	17 26	18 12	25 06	01 06	02 19	03 27
S 60	16 37	17 21	18 10	25 14	01 14	02 30	03 40

SUN and MOON

Day	SUN Eqn. of Time 00h	12h	Mer. Pass.	MOON Mer. Pass. Upper	Lower	Age	Phase
d	m s	m s	h m	h m	h m	d	%
17	04 11	04 05	12 04	17 23	04 59	06	42
18	03 58	03 52	12 04	18 10	05 46	07	52
19	03 45	03 38	12 04	18 58	06 34	08	62

UT	ARIES	VENUS −4.5		MARS −2.4		JUPITER −2.0		SATURN +0.3		STARS		
	GHA	GHA	Dec	GHA	Dec	GHA	Dec	GHA	Dec	Name	SHA	Dec
d h	° ′	° ′	° ′	° ′	° ′	° ′	° ′	° ′	° ′		° ′	° ′
20 00	328 16.8	137 11.2	S 6 43.2	25 42.6	S26 28.1	104 48.0	S15 40.5	55 15.7	S22 39.6	Acamar	315 15.6	S40 13.7
01	343 19.3	152 11.6	44.4	40 45.4	28.0	119 50.2	40.6	70 18.2	39.6	Achernar	335 23.9	S57 08.4
02	358 21.8	167 12.0	45.6	55 48.1	28.0	134 52.4	40.7	85 20.8	39.6	Acrux	173 05.8	S63 12.2
03	13 24.2	182 12.4 ..	46.7	70 50.9 ..	27.9	149 54.6 ..	40.8	100 23.3 ..	39.6	Adhara	255 10.0	S28 59.8
04	28 26.7	197 12.8	47.9	85 53.7	27.9	164 56.8	40.8	115 25.8	39.6	Aldebaran	290 45.4	N16 32.6
05	43 29.1	212 13.1	49.1	100 56.4	27.8	179 59.0	40.9	130 28.4	39.6			
06	58 31.6	227 13.5	S 6 50.2	115 59.2	S26 27.8	195 01.2	S15 41.0	145 30.9	S22 39.6	Alioth	166 18.0	N55 51.9
07	73 34.1	242 13.9	51.4	131 01.9	27.7	210 03.4	41.1	160 33.5	39.7	Alkaid	152 56.4	N49 13.6
08	88 36.5	257 14.3	52.6	146 04.7	27.7	225 05.6	41.2	175 36.0	39.7	Al Na'ir	27 38.9	S46 52.1
M 09	103 39.0	272 14.7 ..	53.8	161 07.4 ..	27.6	240 07.8 ..	41.3	190 38.5 ..	39.7	Alnilam	275 42.9	S 1 11.5
O 10	118 41.5	287 15.1	54.9	176 10.2	27.6	255 09.9	41.4	205 41.1	39.7	Alphard	217 53.0	S 8 44.3
N 11	133 43.9	302 15.5	56.1	191 12.9	27.6	270 12.1	41.5	220 43.6	39.7			
D 12	148 46.4	317 15.9	S 6 57.3	206 15.7	S26 27.5	285 14.3	S15 41.6	235 46.1	S22 39.7	Alphecca	126 08.0	N26 39.5
A 13	163 48.9	332 16.3	58.5	221 18.4	27.5	300 16.5	41.6	250 48.7	39.7	Alpheratz	357 39.5	N29 11.5
Y 14	178 51.3	347 16.7	6 59.6	236 21.2	27.4	315 18.7	41.7	265 51.2	39.7	Altair	62 04.5	N 8 55.3
15	193 53.8	2 17.1	7 00.8	251 23.9 ..	27.4	330 20.9 ..	41.8	280 53.7 ..	39.7	Ankaa	353 11.9	S42 12.2
16	208 56.2	17 17.5	02.0	266 26.7	27.3	345 23.1	41.9	295 56.3	39.7	Antares	112 21.9	S26 28.2
17	223 58.7	32 17.9	03.1	281 29.4	27.3	0 25.3	42.0	310 58.8	39.7			
18	239 01.2	47 18.3	S 7 04.3	296 32.1	S26 27.2	15 27.4	S15 42.1	326 01.4	S22 39.7	Arcturus	145 52.7	N19 05.5
19	254 03.6	62 18.7	05.5	311 34.9	27.2	30 29.6	42.2	341 03.9	39.7	Atria	107 20.3	S69 03.7
20	269 06.1	77 19.1	06.6	326 37.6	27.1	45 31.8	42.3	356 06.4	39.8	Avior	234 17.2	S59 34.1
21	284 08.6	92 19.5 ..	07.8	341 40.3 ..	27.1	60 34.0 ..	42.4	11 09.0 ..	39.8	Bellatrix	278 28.4	N 6 21.9
22	299 11.0	107 20.0	09.0	356 43.1	27.0	75 36.2	42.5	26 11.5	39.8	Betelgeuse	270 57.7	N 7 24.5
23	314 13.5	122 20.4	10.1	11 45.8	26.9	90 38.4	42.5	41 14.0	39.8			
21 00	329 16.0	137 20.8	S 7 11.3	26 48.5	S26 26.9	105 40.6	S15 42.6	56 16.6	S22 39.8	Canopus	263 54.9	S52 42.2
01	344 18.4	152 21.2	12.5	41 51.3	26.8	120 42.7	42.7	71 19.1	39.8	Capella	280 29.4	N46 00.7
02	359 20.9	167 21.6	13.7	56 54.0	26.8	135 44.9	42.8	86 21.6	39.8	Deneb	49 28.6	N45 21.0
03	14 23.4	182 22.0 ..	14.8	71 56.7 ..	26.7	150 47.1 ..	42.9	101 24.2 ..	39.8	Denebola	182 30.4	N14 28.3
04	29 25.8	197 22.4	16.0	86 59.4	26.7	165 49.3	43.0	116 26.7	39.8	Diphda	348 52.1	S17 53.0
05	44 28.3	212 22.8	17.2	102 02.2	26.6	180 51.5	43.1	131 29.2	39.8			
06	59 30.7	227 23.2	S 7 18.3	117 04.9	S26 26.6	195 53.7	S15 43.2	146 31.8	S22 39.8	Dubhe	193 48.1	N61 39.2
07	74 33.2	242 23.6	19.5	132 07.6	26.5	210 55.9	43.3	161 34.3	39.8	Elnath	278 08.3	N28 37.2
T 08	89 35.7	257 24.0	20.6	147 10.3	26.4	225 58.0	43.4	176 36.8	39.8	Eltanin	90 44.2	N51 29.6
U 09	104 38.1	272 24.5 ..	21.8	162 13.0 ..	26.4	241 00.2 ..	43.5	191 39.4 ..	39.8	Enif	33 43.3	N 9 57.8
E 10	119 40.6	287 24.9	23.0	177 15.8	26.3	256 02.4	43.5	206 41.9	39.9	Fomalhaut	15 19.8	S29 31.3
S 11	134 43.1	302 25.3	24.1	192 18.5	26.3	271 04.6	43.6	221 44.4	39.9			
D 12	149 45.5	317 25.7	S 7 25.3	207 21.2	S26 26.2	286 06.8	S15 43.7	236 47.0	S22 39.9	Gacrux	171 57.4	S57 13.1
A 13	164 48.0	332 26.1	26.5	222 23.9	26.1	301 09.0	43.8	251 49.5	39.9	Gienah	175 48.9	S17 38.6
Y 14	179 50.5	347 26.5	27.6	237 26.6	26.1	316 11.1	43.9	266 52.0	39.9	Hadar	148 43.1	S60 27.8
15	194 52.9	2 26.9 ..	28.8	252 29.3 ..	26.0	331 13.3 ..	44.0	281 54.6 ..	39.9	Hamal	327 56.6	N23 32.9
16	209 55.4	17 27.4	30.0	267 32.0	26.0	346 15.5	44.1	296 57.1	39.9	Kaus Aust.	83 38.9	S34 22.4
17	224 57.9	32 27.8	31.1	282 34.7	25.9	1 17.7	44.2	311 59.6	39.9			
18	240 00.3	47 28.2	S 7 32.3	297 37.4	S26 25.8	16 19.9	S15 44.3	327 02.2	S22 39.9	Kochab	137 20.5	N74 05.2
19	255 02.8	62 28.6	33.4	312 40.1	25.8	31 22.0	44.4	342 04.7	39.9	Markab	13 34.5	N15 18.4
20	270 05.2	77 29.0	34.6	327 42.8	25.7	46 24.2	44.5	357 07.2	39.9	Menkar	314 11.3	N 4 09.7
21	285 07.7	92 29.5 ..	35.8	342 45.5 ..	25.6	61 26.4 ..	44.5	12 09.7 ..	39.9	Menkent	148 03.6	S36 27.6
22	300 10.2	107 29.9	36.9	357 48.2	25.6	76 28.6	44.6	27 12.3	39.9	Miaplacidus	221 39.8	S69 47.6
23	315 12.6	122 30.3	38.1	12 50.9	25.5	91 30.8	44.7	42 14.8	40.0			
22 00	330 15.1	137 30.7	S 7 39.3	27 53.6	S26 25.5	106 32.9	S15 44.8	57 17.3	S22 40.0	Mirfak	308 35.2	N49 55.3
01	345 17.6	152 31.2	40.4	42 56.3	25.4	121 35.1	44.9	72 19.9	40.0	Nunki	75 53.7	S26 16.3
02	0 20.0	167 31.6	41.6	57 59.0	25.3	136 37.3	45.0	87 22.4	40.0	Peacock	53 13.2	S56 40.4
03	15 22.5	182 32.0 ..	42.7	73 01.7 ..	25.3	151 39.5 ..	45.1	102 24.9 ..	40.0	Pollux	243 23.8	N27 58.8
04	30 25.0	197 32.4	43.9	88 04.4	25.2	166 41.7	45.2	117 27.5	40.0	Procyon	244 56.3	N 5 10.6
05	45 27.4	212 32.9	45.0	103 07.1	25.1	181 43.8	45.3	132 30.0	40.0			
06	60 29.9	227 33.3	S 7 46.2	118 09.8	S26 25.1	196 46.0	S15 45.4	147 32.5	S22 40.0	Rasalhague	96 03.0	N12 33.1
W 07	75 32.4	242 33.7	47.4	133 12.5	25.0	211 48.2	45.5	162 35.0	40.0	Regulus	207 40.1	N11 52.7
E 08	90 34.8	257 34.1	48.5	148 15.1	24.9	226 50.4	45.6	177 37.6	40.0	Rigel	281 08.8	S 8 10.8
D 09	105 37.3	272 34.6 ..	49.7	163 17.8 ..	24.8	241 52.5 ..	45.7	192 40.1 ..	40.0	Rigil Kent.	139 47.1	S60 54.7
N 10	120 39.7	287 35.0	50.8	178 20.5	24.8	256 54.7	45.7	207 42.6	40.0	Sabik	102 08.4	S15 44.7
E 11	135 42.2	302 35.4	52.0	193 23.2	24.7	271 56.9	45.8	222 45.2	40.0			
S 12	150 44.7	317 35.9	S 7 53.1	208 25.9	S26 24.6	286 59.1	S15 45.9	237 47.7	S22 40.0	Schedar	349 36.0	N56 38.1
D 13	165 47.1	332 36.3	54.3	223 28.5	24.6	302 01.3	46.0	252 50.2	40.1	Shaula	96 16.9	S37 06.9
A 14	180 49.6	347 36.7	55.5	238 31.2	24.5	317 03.4	46.1	267 52.7	40.1	Sirius	258 30.9	S16 44.5
Y 15	195 52.1	2 37.2 ..	56.6	253 33.9 ..	24.4	332 05.6 ..	46.2	282 55.3 ..	40.1	Spica	158 27.7	S11 15.3
16	210 54.5	17 37.6	57.8	268 36.6	24.3	347 07.8	46.3	297 57.8	40.1	Suhail	222 50.3	S43 30.4
17	225 57.0	32 38.0	7 58.9	283 39.2	24.3	2 10.0	46.4	313 00.3	40.1			
18	240 59.5	47 38.5	S 8 00.1	298 41.9	S26 24.2	17 12.1	S15 46.5	328 02.9	S22 40.1	Vega	80 36.3	N38 48.4
19	256 01.9	62 38.9	01.2	313 44.6	24.1	32 14.3	46.6	343 05.4	40.1	Zuben'ubi	137 01.6	S16 06.9
20	271 04.4	77 39.3	02.4	328 47.2	24.0	47 16.5	46.7	358 07.9	40.1		SHA	Mer. Pass.
21	286 06.8	92 39.8 ..	03.5	343 49.9 ..	24.0	62 18.7 ..	46.8	13 10.4 ..	40.1		° ′	h m
22	301 09.3	107 40.2	04.7	358 52.6	23.9	77 20.8	46.9	28 13.0	40.1	Venus	168 04.8	14 50
23	316 11.8	122 40.7	05.8	13 55.2	23.8	92 23.0	47.0	43 15.5	40.1	Mars	57 32.6	22 09
	h m									Jupiter	136 24.6	16 55
Mer. Pass. 2 02.6		v 0.4	d 1.2	v 2.7	d 0.1	v 2.2	d 0.1	v 2.5	d 0.0	Saturn	87 00.6	20 11

UT	SUN		MOON					Lat.	Twilight		Sunrise	Moonrise			
									Naut.	Civil		20	21	22	23
	GHA	Dec	GHA	v	Dec	d	HP	°	h m	h m	h m	h m	h m	h m	h m
d h	° ′	° ′	° ′	′	° ′	′	′	N 72	////	////	03 02	■■■■	■■■■	■■■■	■■■■
20 00	179 07.3	N12 31.7	73 03.0	12.0	S18 41.5	4.8	54.8	N 70	////	01 44	03 26	■■■■	■■■■	■■■■	21 12
01	194 07.5	30.9	87 34.0	11.9	18 46.3	4.7	54.8	68	////	02 23	03 44	18 00	19 13	19 55	20 12
02	209 07.6	30.1	102 04.9	11.9	18 51.0	4.6	54.8	66	////	02 50	03 58	17 20	18 25	19 10	19 37
03	224 07.8 ..	29.3	116 35.8	11.9	18 55.6	4.6	54.8	64	01 31	03 10	04 10	16 53	17 54	18 40	19 12
04	239 07.9	28.4	131 06.7	11.9	19 00.2	4.4	54.8	62	02 07	03 26	04 20	16 32	17 31	18 18	18 52
05	254 08.1	27.6	145 37.6	11.8	19 04.6	4.4	54.7	60	02 31	03 40	04 28	16 15	17 13	18 00	18 36
06	269 08.2	N12 26.8	160 08.4	11.9	S19 09.0	4.2	54.7	N 58	02 50	03 51	04 36	16 00	16 57	17 45	18 23
07	284 08.4	26.0	174 39.3	11.9	19 13.2	4.2	54.7	56	03 06	04 01	04 42	15 48	16 44	17 32	18 11
08	299 08.5	25.1	189 10.2	11.8	19 17.4	4.1	54.7	54	03 19	04 09	04 48	15 38	16 33	17 20	18 00
M 09	314 08.7 ..	24.3	203 41.0	11.9	19 21.5	4.0	54.7	52	03 30	04 17	04 54	15 28	16 23	17 10	17 51
O 10	329 08.8	23.5	218 11.9	11.8	19 25.5	3.8	54.6	50	03 39	04 23	04 58	15 20	16 14	17 02	17 43
N 11	344 09.0	22.7	232 42.7	11.8	19 29.3	3.8	54.6	45	03 59	04 37	05 09	15 02	15 55	16 43	17 25
D 12	359 09.1	N12 21.8	247 13.5	11.9	S19 33.1	3.7	54.6	N 40	04 14	04 49	05 17	14 47	15 39	16 27	17 11
A 13	14 09.3	21.0	261 44.4	11.8	19 36.8	3.6	54.6	35	04 26	04 58	05 24	14 35	15 26	16 14	16 59
Y 14	29 09.4	20.2	276 15.2	11.8	19 40.4	3.5	54.6	30	04 36	05 06	05 31	14 24	15 15	16 03	16 48
15	44 09.6 ..	19.4	290 46.0	11.8	19 43.9	3.5	54.6	20	04 52	05 19	05 42	14 06	14 56	15 44	16 30
16	59 09.7	18.5	305 16.8	11.8	19 47.4	3.3	54.5	N 10	05 04	05 30	05 51	13 50	14 39	15 27	16 14
17	74 09.9	17.7	319 47.6	11.8	19 50.7	3.2	54.5	0	05 14	05 39	06 00	13 35	14 23	15 11	15 59
18	89 10.0	N12 16.9	334 18.4	11.8	S19 53.9	3.1	54.5	S 10	05 22	05 47	06 08	13 20	14 07	14 55	15 44
19	104 10.2	16.1	348 49.2	11.8	19 57.0	3.1	54.5	20	05 29	05 55	06 17	13 04	13 50	14 39	15 28
20	119 10.3	15.2	3 20.0	11.7	20 00.1	2.9	54.5	30	05 35	06 03	06 28	12 46	13 31	14 19	15 10
21	134 10.5 ..	14.4	17 50.7	11.8	20 03.0	2.9	54.5	35	05 38	06 08	06 34	12 35	13 20	14 08	14 59
22	149 10.6	13.6	32 21.5	11.8	20 05.9	2.7	54.5	40	05 41	06 13	06 40	12 23	13 07	13 55	14 47
23	164 10.8	12.7	46 52.3	11.7	20 08.6	2.7	54.4	45	05 43	06 18	06 48	12 09	12 52	13 40	14 32
21 00	179 10.9	N12 11.9	61 23.0	11.8	S20 11.3	2.5	54.4	S 50	05 46	06 24	06 57	11 51	12 33	13 21	14 15
01	194 11.1	11.1	75 53.8	11.8	20 13.8	2.5	54.4	52	05 47	06 26	07 01	11 43	12 24	13 12	14 06
02	209 11.3	10.3	90 24.6	11.7	20 16.3	2.4	54.4	54	05 48	06 29	07 06	11 34	12 15	13 02	13 57
03	224 11.4 ..	09.4	104 55.3	11.8	20 18.7	2.2	54.4	56	05 49	06 32	07 11	11 24	12 03	12 51	13 46
04	239 11.6	08.6	119 26.1	11.7	20 20.9	2.2	54.4	58	05 50	06 36	07 17	11 12	11 51	12 38	13 34
05	254 11.7	07.8	133 56.8	11.7	20 23.1	2.1	54.4	S 60	05 51	06 40	07 23	10 59	11 36	12 23	13 20

UT	SUN		MOON					Lat.	Sunset	Twilight		Moonset			
										Civil	Naut.	20	21	22	23
	GHA	Dec	GHA	v	Dec	d	HP	°	h m	h m	h m	h m	h m	h m	h m
06	269 11.9	N12 06.9	148 27.5	11.8	S20 25.2	2.0	54.4	N 72	21 00	23 35	////	■■■■	■■■■	■■■■	■■■■
07	284 12.0	06.1	162 58.3	11.7	20 27.2	1.8	54.3	N 70	20 37	22 15	////	■■■■	■■■■	■■■■	23 16
08	299 12.2	05.3	177 29.0	11.8	20 29.0	1.8	54.3	68	20 20	21 38	////	21 28	21 55	22 54	24 16
T 09	314 12.3 ..	04.4	191 59.8	11.7	20 30.8	1.7	54.3	66	20 06	21 13	23 39	22 08	22 44	23 38	24 50
U 10	329 12.5	03.6	206 30.5	11.7	20 32.5	1.6	54.3	64	19 54	20 53	22 29	22 36	23 14	24 08	00 08
E 11	344 12.6	02.8	221 01.2	11.8	20 34.1	1.5	54.3	62	19 45	20 38	21 55	22 57	23 37	24 30	00 30
S 12	359 12.8	N12 01.9	235 32.0	11.7	S20 35.6	1.4	54.3	60	19 36	20 25	21 32	23 14	23 56	24 48	00 48
D 13	14 13.0	01.1	250 02.7	11.7	20 37.0	1.3	54.3	N 58	19 29	20 14	21 13	23 29	24 11	00 11	01 03
A 14	29 13.1	12 00.3	264 33.4	11.8	20 38.3	1.2	54.3	56	19 23	20 04	20 58	23 41	24 24	00 24	01 16
Y 15	44 13.3	11 59.4	279 04.2	11.7	20 39.5	1.1	54.3	54	19 17	19 56	20 46	23 52	24 36	00 36	01 27
16	59 13.4	58.6	293 34.9	11.8	20 40.6	1.0	54.2	52	19 12	19 48	20 35	24 01	00 01	00 46	01 37
17	74 13.6	57.8	308 05.7	11.7	20 41.6	0.9	54.2	50	19 07	19 42	20 25	24 10	00 10	00 55	01 46
18	89 13.7	N11 56.9	322 36.4	11.7	S20 42.5	0.9	54.2	45	18 57	19 28	20 06	24 28	00 28	01 14	02 04
19	104 13.9	56.1	337 07.1	11.8	20 43.4	0.7	54.2	N 40	18 48	19 17	19 51	00 01	00 43	01 29	02 19
20	119 14.0	55.3	351 37.9	11.7	20 44.1	0.6	54.2	35	18 41	19 08	19 39	00 13	00 56	01 43	02 32
21	134 14.2 ..	54.4	6 08.6	11.8	20 44.7	0.5	54.2	30	18 35	19 00	19 29	00 23	01 07	01 54	02 43
22	149 14.4	53.6	20 39.4	11.7	20 45.2	0.5	54.2	20	18 24	18 47	19 14	00 40	01 26	02 13	03 02
23	164 14.5	52.7	35 10.1	11.8	20 45.7	0.3	54.2	N 10	18 15	18 37	19 02	00 55	01 42	02 30	03 19
22 00	179 14.7	N11 51.9	49 40.9	11.7	S20 46.0	0.2	54.2	0	18 06	18 28	18 52	01 10	01 58	02 46	03 34
01	194 14.8	51.1	64 11.6	11.8	20 46.2	0.0	54.2	S 10	17 58	18 19	18 44	01 24	02 13	03 02	03 50
02	209 15.0	50.2	78 42.4	11.8	20 46.4	0.0	54.2	20	17 49	18 11	18 37	01 39	02 30	03 19	04 06
03	224 15.2 ..	49.4	93 13.2	11.8	20 46.4	0.1	54.2	30	17 39	18 03	18 31	01 57	02 49	03 39	04 25
04	239 15.3	48.6	107 44.0	11.7	20 46.3	0.1	54.1	35	17 33	17 59	18 29	02 07	03 00	03 50	04 36
05	254 15.5	47.7	122 14.7	11.8	20 46.2	0.3	54.1	40	17 27	17 54	18 26	02 18	03 13	04 03	04 49
06	269 15.6	N11 46.9	136 45.5	11.8	S20 45.9	0.3	54.1	45	17 19	17 49	18 24	02 32	03 28	04 18	05 04
W 07	284 15.8	46.0	151 16.3	11.8	20 45.6	0.5	54.1	S 50	17 10	17 43	18 21	02 49	03 46	04 37	05 22
E 08	299 15.9	45.2	165 47.1	11.8	20 45.1	0.5	54.1	52	17 06	17 41	18 20	02 57	03 55	04 46	05 30
D 09	314 16.1 ..	44.4	180 17.9	11.9	20 44.6	0.6	54.1	54	17 01	17 38	18 19	03 06	04 04	04 56	05 40
N 10	329 16.3	43.5	194 48.8	11.8	20 44.0	0.8	54.1	56	16 56	17 35	18 18	03 16	04 15	05 07	05 51
E 11	344 16.4	42.7	209 19.6	11.8	20 43.2	0.8	54.1	58	16 51	17 32	18 17	03 27	04 28	05 20	06 03
S 12	359 16.6	N11 41.8	223 50.4	11.9	S20 42.4	0.9	54.1	S 60	16 44	17 28	18 17	03 40	04 43	05 35	06 17
D 13	14 16.7	41.0	238 21.3	11.8	20 41.5	1.1	54.1								
A 14	29 16.9	40.2	252 52.1	11.9	20 40.4	1.1	54.1								
Y 15	44 17.1 ..	39.3	267 23.0	11.9	20 39.3	1.2	54.1								
16	59 17.2	38.5	281 53.9	11.8	20 38.1	1.3	54.1								
17	74 17.4	37.6	296 24.7	11.9	20 36.8	1.4	54.1								

UT	SUN		MOON						SUN			MOON			
18	89 17.6	N11 36.8	310 55.6	11.9	S20 35.4	1.5	54.1	Day	Eqn. of Time		Mer.	Mer. Pass.		Age	Phase
19	104 17.7	35.9	325 26.5	12.0	20 33.9	1.6	54.1		00ʰ	12ʰ	Pass.	Upper	Lower		
20	119 17.9	35.1	339 57.5	11.9	20 32.3	1.7	54.1	d	m s	m s	h m	h m	h m	d %	
21	134 18.0 ..	34.3	354 28.4	11.9	20 30.6	1.8	54.1	20	03 31	03 24	12 03	19 46	07 22	09 71	
22	149 18.2	33.4	8 59.3	12.0	20 28.8	1.9	54.1	21	03 17	03 09	12 03	20 35	08 10	10 79	
23	164 18.4	32.6	23 30.3	12.0	S20 26.9	2.0	54.1	22	03 02	02 54	12 03	21 23	08 59	11 86	
	SD 15.8	d 0.8	SD 14.9		14.8		14.7									

UT	ARIES GHA	VENUS −4.5 GHA	Dec	MARS −2.3 GHA	Dec	JUPITER −2.0 GHA	Dec	SATURN +0.3 GHA	Dec	STARS Name	SHA	Dec
23 00	331 14.2	137 41.1	S 8 07.0	28 57.9	S26 23.7	107 25.2	S15 47.0	58 18.0	S22 40.1	Acamar	315 15.6	S40 13.7
01	346 16.7	152 41.5	08.1	44 00.5	23.7	122 27.4	47.1	73 20.5	40.1	Achernar	335 23.8	S57 08.4
02	1 19.2	167 42.0	09.3	59 03.2	23.6	137 29.5	47.2	88 23.1	40.1	Acrux	173 05.8	S63 12.2
03	16 21.6	182 42.4	.. 10.4	74 05.8	.. 23.5	152 31.7	.. 47.3	103 25.6	.. 40.2	Adhara	255 10.0	S28 59.8
04	31 24.1	197 42.9	11.6	89 08.5	23.4	167 33.9	47.4	118 28.1	40.2	Aldebaran	290 45.4	N16 32.6
05	46 26.6	212 43.3	12.7	104 11.2	23.4	182 36.0	47.5	133 30.6	40.2			
T 06	61 29.0	227 43.7	S 8 13.9	119 13.8	S26 23.3	197 38.2	S15 47.6	148 33.2	S22 40.2	Alioth	166 18.0	N55 51.9
H 07	76 31.5	242 44.2	15.0	134 16.5	23.2	212 40.4	47.7	163 35.7	40.2	Alkaid	152 56.4	N49 13.6
U 08	91 34.0	257 44.6	16.2	149 19.1	23.1	227 42.6	47.8	178 38.2	40.2	Al Na'ir	27 38.9	S46 52.1
R 09	106 36.4	272 45.1	.. 17.3	164 21.8	.. 23.0	242 44.7	.. 47.9	193 40.7	.. 40.2	Alnilam	275 42.9	S 1 11.4
S 10	121 38.9	287 45.5	18.5	179 24.4	23.0	257 46.9	48.0	208 43.3	40.2	Alphard	217 52.9	S 8 44.3
D 11	136 41.3	302 46.0	19.6	194 27.0	22.9	272 49.1	48.1	223 45.8	40.2			
A 12	151 43.8	317 46.4	S 8 20.8	209 29.7	S26 22.8	287 51.3	S15 48.2	238 48.3	S22 40.2	Alphecca	126 08.1	N26 39.5
Y 13	166 46.3	332 46.9	21.9	224 32.3	22.7	302 53.4	48.3	253 50.8	40.2	Alpheratz	357 39.5	N29 11.5
14	181 48.7	347 47.3	23.1	239 35.0	22.6	317 55.6	48.4	268 53.4	40.2	Altair	62 04.5	N 8 55.3
15	196 51.2	2 47.8	.. 24.2	254 37.6	.. 22.5	332 57.8	.. 48.4	283 55.9	.. 40.2	Ankaa	353 11.9	S42 12.2
16	211 53.7	17 48.2	25.4	269 40.2	22.5	347 59.9	48.5	298 58.4	40.2	Antares	112 21.9	S26 28.2
17	226 56.1	32 48.7	26.5	284 42.9	22.4	3 02.1	48.6	314 00.9	40.3			
18	241 58.6	47 49.1	S 8 27.7	299 45.5	S26 22.3	18 04.3	S15 48.7	329 03.5	S22 40.3	Arcturus	145 52.7	N19 05.5
19	257 01.1	62 49.6	28.8	314 48.1	22.2	33 06.4	48.8	344 06.0	40.3	Atria	107 20.3	S69 03.7
20	272 03.5	77 50.0	30.0	329 50.8	22.1	48 08.6	48.9	359 08.5	40.3	Avior	234 17.1	S59 34.0
21	287 06.0	92 50.5	.. 31.1	344 53.4	.. 22.0	63 10.8	.. 49.0	14 11.0	.. 40.3	Bellatrix	278 28.3	N 6 21.9
22	302 08.5	107 51.0	32.2	359 56.0	21.9	78 13.0	49.1	29 13.6	40.3	Betelgeuse	270 57.6	N 7 24.5
23	317 10.9	122 51.4	33.4	14 58.6	21.9	93 15.1	49.2	44 16.1	40.3			
24 00	332 13.4	137 51.9	S 8 34.5	30 01.3	S26 21.8	108 17.3	S15 49.3	59 18.6	S22 40.3	Canopus	263 54.9	S52 42.2
01	347 15.8	152 52.3	35.7	45 03.9	21.7	123 19.5	49.4	74 21.1	40.3	Capella	280 29.4	N46 00.7
02	2 18.3	167 52.8	36.8	60 06.5	21.6	138 21.6	49.5	89 23.6	40.3	Deneb	49 28.6	N45 21.0
03	17 20.8	182 53.2	.. 38.0	75 09.1	.. 21.5	153 23.8	.. 49.6	104 26.2	.. 40.3	Denebola	182 30.4	N14 28.3
04	32 23.2	197 53.7	39.1	90 11.8	21.4	168 26.0	49.7	119 28.7	40.3	Diphda	348 52.1	S17 53.0
05	47 25.7	212 54.2	40.2	105 14.4	21.3	183 28.1	49.8	134 31.2	40.3			
F 06	62 28.2	227 54.6	S 8 41.4	120 17.0	S26 21.2	198 30.3	S15 49.9	149 33.7	S22 40.4	Dubhe	193 48.1	N61 39.2
R 07	77 30.6	242 55.1	42.5	135 19.6	21.1	213 32.5	50.0	164 36.2	40.4	Elnath	278 08.3	N28 37.2
I 08	92 33.1	257 55.5	43.7	150 22.2	21.1	228 34.6	50.1	179 38.8	40.4	Eltanin	90 44.2	N51 29.6
D 09	107 35.6	272 56.0	.. 44.8	165 24.8	.. 21.0	243 36.8	.. 50.2	194 41.3	.. 40.4	Enif	33 43.3	N 9 57.8
A 10	122 38.0	287 56.5	45.9	180 27.4	20.9	258 39.0	50.2	209 43.8	40.4	Fomalhaut	15 19.8	S29 31.3
Y 11	137 40.5	302 56.9	47.1	195 30.0	20.8	273 41.1	50.3	224 46.3	40.4			
12	152 42.9	317 57.4	S 8 48.2	210 32.6	S26 20.7	288 43.3	S15 50.4	239 48.8	S22 40.4	Gacrux	171 57.4	S57 13.0
13	167 45.4	332 57.9	49.4	225 35.3	20.6	303 45.5	50.5	254 51.4	40.4	Gienah	175 48.9	S17 38.6
14	182 47.9	347 58.3	50.5	240 37.9	20.5	318 47.6	50.6	269 53.9	40.4	Hadar	148 43.1	S60 27.8
15	197 50.3	2 58.8	.. 51.6	255 40.5	.. 20.4	333 49.8	.. 50.7	284 56.4	.. 40.4	Hamal	327 56.6	N23 32.9
16	212 52.8	17 59.3	52.8	270 43.1	20.3	348 51.9	50.8	299 58.9	40.4	Kaus Aust.	83 38.9	S34 22.4
17	227 55.3	32 59.8	53.9	285 45.7	20.2	3 54.1	50.9	315 01.4	40.4			
18	242 57.7	48 00.2	S 8 55.1	300 48.3	S26 20.1	18 56.3	S15 51.0	330 04.0	S22 40.4	Kochab	137 20.5	N74 05.2
19	258 00.2	63 00.7	56.2	315 50.8	20.0	33 58.4	51.1	345 06.5	40.4	Markab	13 34.5	N15 18.4
20	273 02.7	78 01.2	57.3	330 53.4	19.9	49 00.6	51.2	0 09.0	40.4	Menkar	314 11.3	N 4 09.7
21	288 05.1	93 01.6	.. 58.5	345 56.0	.. 19.8	64 02.8	.. 51.3	15 11.5	.. 40.5	Menkent	148 03.6	S36 27.6
22	303 07.6	108 02.1	8 59.6	0 58.6	19.7	79 04.9	51.4	30 14.0	40.5	Miaplacidus	221 39.8	S69 47.5
23	318 10.1	123 02.6	9 00.7	16 01.2	19.6	94 07.1	51.5	45 16.6	40.5			
25 00	333 12.5	138 03.1	S 9 01.9	31 03.8	S26 19.5	109 09.3	S15 51.6	60 19.1	S22 40.5	Mirfak	308 35.2	N49 55.3
01	348 15.0	153 03.5	03.0	46 06.4	19.4	124 11.4	51.7	75 21.6	40.5	Nunki	75 53.7	S26 16.3
02	3 17.4	168 04.0	04.1	61 09.0	19.3	139 13.6	51.8	90 24.1	40.5	Peacock	53 13.2	S56 40.4
03	18 19.9	183 04.5	.. 05.3	76 11.6	.. 19.2	154 15.7	.. 51.9	105 26.6	.. 40.5	Pollux	243 23.7	N27 58.8
04	33 22.4	198 05.0	06.4	91 14.1	19.1	169 17.9	52.0	120 29.1	40.5	Procyon	244 56.3	N 5 10.6
05	48 24.8	213 05.4	07.5	106 16.7	19.0	184 20.1	52.1	135 31.7	40.5			
S 06	63 27.3	228 05.9	S 9 08.7	121 19.3	S26 18.9	199 22.2	S15 52.2	150 34.2	S22 40.5	Rasalhague	96 03.0	N12 33.1
A 07	78 29.8	243 06.4	09.8	136 21.9	18.8	214 24.4	52.3	165 36.7	40.5	Regulus	207 40.1	N11 52.7
T 08	93 32.2	258 06.9	10.9	151 24.5	18.7	229 26.5	52.4	180 39.2	40.5	Rigel	281 08.8	S 8 10.8
U 09	108 34.7	273 07.4	.. 12.1	166 27.0	.. 18.6	244 28.7	.. 52.4	195 41.7	.. 40.5	Rigil Kent.	139 47.1	S60 54.7
R 10	123 37.2	288 07.9	13.2	181 29.6	18.5	259 30.9	52.5	210 44.2	40.5	Sabik	102 08.4	S15 44.7
D 11	138 39.6	303 08.3	14.3	196 32.2	18.4	274 33.0	52.6	225 46.8	40.6			
A 12	153 42.1	318 08.8	S 9 15.4	211 34.8	S26 18.3	289 35.2	S15 52.7	240 49.3	S22 40.6	Schedar	349 36.0	N56 38.2
Y 13	168 44.6	333 09.3	16.6	226 37.3	18.2	304 37.4	52.8	255 51.8	40.6	Shaula	96 17.0	S37 06.9
14	183 47.0	348 09.8	17.7	241 39.9	18.1	319 39.5	52.9	270 54.3	40.6	Sirius	258 30.8	S16 44.5
15	198 49.5	3 10.3	.. 18.8	256 42.5	.. 18.0	334 41.7	.. 53.0	285 56.8	.. 40.6	Spica	158 27.7	S11 15.3
16	213 51.9	18 10.8	20.0	271 45.0	17.9	349 43.8	53.1	300 59.3	40.6	Suhail	222 50.3	S43 30.4
17	228 54.4	33 11.3	21.1	286 47.6	17.8	4 46.0	53.2	316 01.9	40.6			
18	243 56.9	48 11.7	S 9 22.2	301 50.1	S26 17.7	19 48.1	S15 53.3	331 04.4	S22 40.6	Vega	80 36.3	N38 48.4
19	258 59.3	63 12.2	23.3	316 52.7	17.6	34 50.3	53.4	346 06.9	40.6	Zuben'ubi	137 01.6	S16 06.9
20	274 01.8	78 12.7	24.5	331 55.3	17.5	49 52.5	53.5	1 09.4	40.6		SHA	Mer. Pass.
21	289 04.3	93 13.2	.. 25.6	346 57.8	.. 17.4	64 54.6	.. 53.6	16 11.9	.. 40.6	Venus	165 38.5	14 48
22	304 06.7	108 13.7	26.7	2 00.4	17.3	79 56.8	53.7	31 14.4	40.6	Mars	57 47.9	21 56
23	319 09.2	123 14.2	27.8	17 02.9	17.2	94 58.9	53.8	46 16.9	40.6	Jupiter	136 03.9	16 44
Mer. Pass. 1 50.8		v 0.5	d 1.1	v 2.6	d 0.1	v 2.2	d 0.1	v 2.5	d 0.0	Saturn	87 05.2	19 59

UT	SUN GHA	SUN Dec	MOON GHA	v	MOON Dec	d	HP
d h	° ′	° ′	° ′	′	° ′	′	′
23 00	179 18.5	N11 31.7	38 01.3	12.0	S20 24.9	2.0	54.1
01	194 18.7	30.9	52 32.3	12.0	20 22.9	2.2	54.1
02	209 18.9	30.0	67 03.3	12.0	20 20.7	2.3	54.1
03	224 19.0	. . 29.2	81 34.3	12.0	20 18.4	2.3	54.0
04	239 19.2	28.3	96 05.3	12.1	20 16.1	2.5	54.0
05	254 19.3	27.5	110 36.4	12.0	20 13.6	2.5	54.0
06	269 19.5	N11 26.6	125 07.4	12.1	S20 11.1	2.6	54.0
07	284 19.7	25.8	139 38.5	12.1	20 08.5	2.8	54.0
08	299 19.8	24.9	154 09.6	12.1	20 05.7	2.8	54.0
T 09	314 20.0	. . 24.1	168 40.7	12.1	20 02.9	2.9	54.0
H 10	329 20.2	23.2	183 11.8	12.2	20 00.0	3.0	54.0
U 11	344 20.3	22.4	197 43.0	12.1	19 57.0	3.1	54.0
R 12	359 20.5	N11 21.6	212 14.1	12.2	S19 53.9	3.2	54.0
S 13	14 20.7	20.7	226 45.3	12.2	19 50.7	3.2	54.0
D 14	29 20.8	19.9	241 16.5	12.2	19 47.5	3.4	54.0
A 15	44 21.0	. . 19.0	255 47.7	12.3	19 44.1	3.5	54.0
Y 16	59 21.2	18.2	270 19.0	12.2	19 40.6	3.5	54.0
17	74 21.3	17.3	284 50.2	12.3	19 37.1	3.7	54.0
18	89 21.5	N11 16.5	299 21.5	12.3	S19 33.4	3.7	54.0
19	104 21.7	15.6	313 52.8	12.3	19 29.7	3.8	54.0
20	119 21.8	14.8	328 24.1	12.3	19 25.9	3.9	54.0
21	134 22.0	. . 13.9	342 55.4	12.4	19 22.0	4.0	54.1
22	149 22.2	13.0	357 26.8	12.4	19 18.0	4.1	54.1
23	164 22.3	12.2	11 58.2	12.4	19 13.9	4.2	54.1
24 00	179 22.5	N11 11.3	26 29.6	12.4	S19 09.7	4.2	54.1
01	194 22.7	10.5	41 01.0	12.4	19 05.5	4.4	54.1
02	209 22.8	09.6	55 32.4	12.5	19 01.1	4.4	54.1
03	224 23.0	. . 08.8	70 03.9	12.5	18 56.7	4.6	54.1
04	239 23.2	07.9	84 35.4	12.5	18 52.1	4.6	54.1
05	254 23.3	07.1	99 06.9	12.5	18 47.5	4.7	54.1
06	269 23.5	N11 06.2	113 38.4	12.6	S18 42.8	4.7	54.1
07	284 23.7	05.4	128 10.0	12.6	18 38.1	4.9	54.1
08	299 23.8	04.5	142 41.6	12.6	18 33.2	5.0	54.1
F 09	314 24.0	. . 03.7	157 13.2	12.6	18 28.2	5.0	54.1
R 10	329 24.2	02.8	171 44.8	12.7	18 23.2	5.1	54.1
I 11	344 24.3	01.9	186 16.5	12.6	18 18.1	5.2	54.1
D 12	359 24.5	N11 01.1	200 48.1	12.7	S18 12.9	5.3	54.1
A 13	14 24.7	11 00.2	215 19.8	12.7	18 07.6	5.4	54.1
Y 14	29 24.9	10 59.4	229 51.5	12.8	18 02.2	5.4	54.1
15	44 25.0	. . 58.5	244 23.3	12.8	17 56.8	5.6	54.1
16	59 25.2	57.7	258 55.1	12.8	17 51.2	5.6	54.1
17	74 25.4	56.8	273 26.9	12.8	17 45.6	5.7	54.1
18	89 25.5	N10 55.9	287 58.7	12.8	S17 39.9	5.8	54.1
19	104 25.7	55.1	302 30.5	12.9	17 34.1	5.8	54.1
20	119 25.9	54.2	317 02.4	12.9	17 28.3	5.9	54.2
21	134 26.0	. . 53.4	331 34.3	12.9	17 22.4	6.1	54.2
22	149 26.2	52.5	346 06.2	12.9	17 16.3	6.1	54.2
23	164 26.4	51.7	0 38.1	13.0	17 10.2	6.1	54.2
25 00	179 26.6	N10 50.8	15 10.1	13.0	S17 04.1	6.3	54.2
01	194 26.7	49.9	29 42.1	13.0	16 57.8	6.3	54.2
02	209 26.9	49.1	44 14.1	13.1	16 51.5	6.4	54.2
03	224 27.1	. . 48.2	58 46.2	13.0	16 45.1	6.5	54.2
04	239 27.3	47.4	73 18.2	13.1	16 38.6	6.6	54.2
05	254 27.4	46.5	87 50.3	13.2	16 32.0	6.6	54.2
06	269 27.6	N10 45.6	102 22.5	13.1	S16 25.4	6.7	54.2
07	284 27.8	44.8	116 54.6	13.2	16 18.7	6.8	54.2
S 08	299 27.9	43.9	131 26.8	13.2	16 11.9	6.8	54.2
A 09	314 28.1	. . 43.1	145 59.0	13.3	16 05.1	7.0	54.2
T 10	329 28.3	42.2	160 31.2	13.3	15 58.1	7.0	54.2
U 11	344 28.5	41.3	175 03.5	13.3	15 51.1	7.0	54.2
R 12	359 28.6	N10 40.5	189 35.7	13.3	S15 44.1	7.2	54.3
D 13	14 28.8	39.6	204 08.0	13.3	15 36.9	7.2	54.3
A 14	29 29.0	38.7	218 40.3	13.4	15 29.7	7.3	54.3
Y 15	44 29.2	. . 37.9	233 12.7	13.4	15 22.4	7.3	54.3
16	59 29.3	37.0	247 45.1	13.4	15 15.1	7.5	54.3
17	74 29.5	36.1	262 17.5	13.4	15 07.6	7.5	54.3
18	89 29.7	N10 35.3	276 49.9	13.5	S15 00.1	7.5	54.3
19	104 29.9	34.4	291 22.3	13.5	14 52.6	7.7	54.3
20	119 30.0	33.5	305 54.8	13.5	14 44.9	7.7	54.3
21	134 30.2	. . 32.7	320 27.3	13.5	14 37.2	7.7	54.3
22	149 30.4	31.8	334 59.8	13.6	14 29.5	7.9	54.3
23	164 30.6	30.9	349 32.4	13.5	S14 21.6	7.9	54.4
	SD 15.8	d 0.9	SD 14.7		14.7		14.8

Twilight / Moonrise

Lat.	Naut.	Civil	Sunrise	Moonrise 23	24	25	26
°	h m	h m	h m	h m	h m	h m	h m
N 72	////	01 13	03 19	■■■	21 53	21 14	20 54
N 70	////	02 08	03 39	21 12	20 53	20 43	20 35
68	////	02 40	03 55	20 12	20 18	20 20	20 21
66	01 04	03 03	04 08	19 37	19 53	20 03	20 09
64	01 52	03 21	04 19	19 12	19 33	19 48	19 59
62	02 21	03 36	04 28	18 52	19 17	19 36	19 50
60	02 43	03 48	04 36	18 36	19 04	19 25	19 42
N 58	03 00	03 58	04 42	18 23	18 52	19 16	19 36
56	03 14	04 07	04 48	18 11	18 42	19 08	19 30
54	03 26	04 15	04 54	18 00	18 33	19 01	19 24
52	03 36	04 22	04 58	17 51	18 26	18 55	19 20
50	03 45	04 28	05 03	17 43	18 18	18 49	19 15
45	04 03	04 41	05 12	17 25	18 03	18 36	19 06
N 40	04 18	04 52	05 20	17 11	17 50	18 26	18 58
35	04 29	05 00	05 27	16 59	17 40	18 17	18 51
30	04 38	05 08	05 32	16 48	17 30	18 09	18 45
20	04 53	05 20	05 42	16 30	17 14	17 55	18 35
N 10	05 05	05 30	05 51	16 14	17 00	17 43	18 26
0	05 14	05 38	05 59	15 59	16 46	17 32	18 17
S 10	05 21	05 46	06 07	15 44	16 33	17 21	18 09
20	05 27	05 53	06 15	15 28	16 18	17 09	17 59
30	05 32	06 00	06 25	15 10	16 02	16 55	17 49
35	05 35	06 04	06 30	14 59	15 52	16 47	17 43
40	05 37	06 08	06 36	14 47	15 41	16 38	17 36
45	05 39	06 13	06 43	14 32	15 29	16 27	17 28
S 50	05 40	06 18	06 51	14 15	15 13	16 14	17 18
52	05 41	06 20	06 55	14 06	15 05	16 08	17 14
54	05 42	06 23	06 59	13 57	14 57	16 02	17 09
56	05 42	06 25	07 04	13 46	14 48	15 54	17 03
58	05 43	06 28	07 09	13 34	14 37	15 46	16 57
S 60	05 43	06 32	07 15	13 20	14 25	15 36	16 50

Twilight / Moonset

Lat.	Sunset	Civil	Naut.	Moonset 23	24	25	26
°	h m	h m	h m	h m	h m	h m	h m
N 72	20 42	22 39	////	■■■	■■■	00 13	02 28
N 70	20 22	21 50	////	23 16	25 12	01 12	02 57
68	20 07	21 20	////	24 16	00 16	01 46	03 19
66	19 54	20 58	22 51	24 50	00 50	02 11	03 36
64	19 44	20 41	22 07	00 08	01 15	02 30	03 50
62	19 35	20 27	21 40	00 30	01 34	02 45	04 01
60	19 28	20 15	21 19	00 48	01 50	02 58	04 11
N 58	19 21	20 05	21 02	01 03	02 03	03 09	04 19
56	19 15	19 56	20 49	01 16	02 15	03 19	04 27
54	19 10	19 48	20 37	01 27	02 25	03 28	04 33
52	19 05	19 42	20 27	01 37	02 34	03 35	04 39
50	19 01	19 35	20 18	01 46	02 42	03 42	04 45
45	18 52	19 23	20 00	02 04	02 59	03 57	04 56
N 40	18 44	19 12	19 46	02 19	03 13	04 08	05 06
35	18 38	19 04	19 35	02 32	03 25	04 19	05 14
30	18 32	18 56	19 26	02 43	03 35	04 28	05 21
20	18 22	18 45	19 11	03 02	03 52	04 43	05 33
N 10	18 14	18 35	19 00	03 19	04 08	04 56	05 44
0	18 06	18 27	18 51	03 34	04 22	05 09	05 54
S 10	17 58	18 19	18 44	03 50	04 36	05 21	06 04
20	17 50	18 12	18 38	04 06	04 51	05 34	06 15
30	17 41	18 05	18 33	04 25	05 09	05 49	06 26
35	17 35	18 01	18 31	04 36	05 19	05 58	06 33
40	17 29	17 57	18 29	04 49	05 30	06 07	06 41
45	17 23	17 53	18 27	05 04	05 44	06 19	06 50
S 50	17 14	17 47	18 25	05 22	06 00	06 33	07 01
52	17 11	17 45	18 25	05 30	06 08	06 39	07 06
54	17 07	17 43	18 24	05 40	06 16	06 46	07 12
56	17 02	17 40	18 24	05 51	06 26	06 54	07 18
58	16 57	17 37	18 23	06 03	06 37	07 03	07 25
S 60	16 51	17 34	18 23	06 17	06 49	07 13	07 32

SUN / MOON

Day	SUN Eqn. of Time 00h	SUN Eqn. of Time 12h	SUN Mer. Pass.	MOON Mer. Pass. Upper	MOON Mer. Pass. Lower	Age	Phase
d	m s	m s	h m	h m	h m	d %	
23	02 46	02 38	12 03	22 11	09 47	12 92	
24	02 30	02 22	12 02	22 57	10 34	13 96	
25	02 14	02 06	12 02	23 43	11 20	14 99	◯

2018 AUGUST 26, 27, 28 (SUN., MON., TUES.)

UT	ARIES	VENUS −4·6		MARS −2·2		JUPITER −2·0		SATURN +0·3		STARS		
	GHA	GHA	Dec	GHA	Dec	GHA	Dec	GHA	Dec	Name	SHA	Dec
d h	° ′	° ′	° ′	° ′	° ′	° ′	° ′	° ′	° ′		° ′	° ′
26 00	334 11.7	138 14.7	S 9 29.0	32 05.5	S26 17.1	110 01.1	S15 53.9	61 19.4	S22 40.6	Acamar	315 15.5	S40 13.7
01	349 14.1	153 15.2	30.1	47 08.0	16.9	125 03.2	54.0	76 22.0	40.7	Achernar	335 23.8	S57 08.4
02	4 16.6	168 15.7	31.2	62 10.6	16.8	140 05.4	54.1	91 24.5	40.7	Acrux	173 05.9	S63 12.1
03	19 19.0	183 16.2	.. 32.3	77 13.1	.. 16.7	155 07.6	.. 54.2	106 27.0	.. 40.7	Adhara	255 10.0	S28 59.7
04	34 21.5	198 16.7	33.5	92 15.7	16.6	170 09.7	54.3	121 29.5	40.7	Aldebaran	290 45.4	N16 32.6
05	49 24.0	213 17.2	34.6	107 18.2	16.5	185 11.9	54.4	136 32.0	40.7			
06	64 26.4	228 17.7	S 9 35.7	122 20.8	S26 16.4	200 14.0	S15 54.5	151 34.5	S22 40.7	Alioth	166 18.0	N55 51.9
07	79 28.9	243 18.2	36.8	137 23.3	16.3	215 16.2	54.6	166 37.0	40.7	Alkaid	152 56.4	N49 13.6
08	94 31.4	258 18.7	38.0	152 25.8	16.2	230 18.3	54.7	181 39.6	40.7	Al Na'ir	27 38.9	S46 52.2
S 09	109 33.8	273 19.2	.. 39.1	167 28.4	.. 16.1	245 20.5	.. 54.8	196 42.1	.. 40.7	Alnilam	275 42.9	S 1 11.4
U 10	124 36.3	288 19.7	40.2	182 30.9	15.9	260 22.7	54.9	211 44.6	40.7	Alphard	217 52.9	S 8 44.3
N 11	139 38.8	303 20.2	41.3	197 33.5	15.8	275 24.8	55.0	226 47.1	40.7			
D 12	154 41.2	318 20.7	S 9 42.4	212 36.0	S26 15.7	290 27.0	S15 55.1	241 49.6	S22 40.7	Alphecca	126 08.1	N26 39.5
A 13	169 43.7	333 21.2	43.6	227 38.5	15.6	305 29.1	55.2	256 52.1	40.7	Alpheratz	357 39.5	N29 11.5
Y 14	184 46.2	348 21.7	44.7	242 41.1	15.5	320 31.3	55.3	271 54.6	40.7	Altair	62 04.5	N 8 55.3
15	199 48.6	3 22.2	.. 45.8	257 43.6	.. 15.4	335 33.4	.. 55.4	286 57.1	.. 40.8	Ankaa	353 11.9	S42 12.2
16	214 51.1	18 22.7	46.9	272 46.1	15.3	350 35.6	55.5	301 59.6	40.8	Antares	112 21.9	S26 28.2
17	229 53.5	33 23.2	48.0	287 48.6	15.1	5 37.7	55.6	317 02.2	40.8			
18	244 56.0	48 23.7	S 9 49.1	302 51.2	S26 15.0	20 39.9	S15 55.7	332 04.7	S22 40.8	Arcturus	145 52.7	N19 05.5
19	259 58.5	63 24.2	50.3	317 53.7	14.9	35 42.0	55.8	347 07.2	40.8	Atria	107 20.4	S69 03.7
20	275 00.9	78 24.7	51.4	332 56.2	14.8	50 44.2	55.9	2 09.7	40.8	Avior	234 17.1	S59 34.0
21	290 03.4	93 25.2	.. 52.5	347 58.7	.. 14.7	65 46.3	.. 56.0	17 12.2	.. 40.8	Bellatrix	278 28.3	N 6 21.9
22	305 05.9	108 25.8	53.6	3 01.2	14.6	80 48.5	56.1	32 14.7	40.8	Betelgeuse	270 57.6	N 7 24.5
23	320 08.3	123 26.3	54.7	18 03.8	14.4	95 50.6	56.2	47 17.2	40.8			
27 00	335 10.8	138 26.8	S 9 55.8	33 06.3	S26 14.3	110 52.8	S15 56.3	62 19.7	S22 40.8	Canopus	263 54.9	S52 42.2
01	350 13.3	153 27.3	57.0	48 08.8	14.2	125 54.9	56.3	77 22.2	40.8	Capella	280 29.4	N46 00.7
02	5 15.7	168 27.8	58.1	63 11.3	14.1	140 57.1	56.4	92 24.7	40.8	Deneb	49 28.6	N45 21.0
03	20 18.2	183 28.3	9 59.2	78 13.8	.. 14.0	155 59.2	.. 56.5	107 27.3	.. 40.8	Denebola	182 30.4	N14 28.3
04	35 20.6	198 28.8	10 00.3	93 16.3	13.8	171 01.4	56.6	122 29.8	40.8	Diphda	348 52.1	S17 53.0
05	50 23.1	213 29.4	01.4	108 18.8	13.7	186 03.5	56.7	137 32.3	40.9			
06	65 25.6	228 29.9	S10 02.5	123 21.3	S26 13.6	201 05.7	S15 56.8	152 34.8	S22 40.9	Dubhe	193 48.1	N61 39.2
07	80 28.0	243 30.4	03.6	138 23.9	13.5	216 07.8	56.9	167 37.3	40.9	Elnath	278 08.3	N28 37.2
08	95 30.5	258 30.9	04.7	153 26.4	13.3	231 10.0	57.0	182 39.8	40.9	Eltanin	90 44.3	N51 29.6
M 09	110 33.0	273 31.4	.. 05.9	168 28.9	.. 13.2	246 12.1	.. 57.1	197 42.3	.. 40.9	Enif	33 43.3	N 9 57.8
O 10	125 35.4	288 31.9	07.0	183 31.4	13.1	261 14.3	57.2	212 44.8	40.9	Fomalhaut	15 19.7	S29 31.3
N 11	140 37.9	303 32.5	08.1	198 33.9	13.0	276 16.4	57.3	227 47.3	40.9			
D 12	155 40.4	318 33.0	S10 09.2	213 36.4	S26 12.9	291 18.6	S15 57.4	242 49.8	S22 40.9	Gacrux	171 57.4	S57 13.0
A 13	170 42.8	333 33.5	10.3	228 38.9	12.7	306 20.7	57.5	257 52.3	40.9	Gienah	175 48.9	S17 38.6
Y 14	185 45.3	348 34.0	11.4	243 41.4	12.6	321 22.9	57.6	272 54.8	40.9	Hadar	148 43.2	S60 27.8
15	200 47.8	3 34.6	.. 12.5	258 43.8	.. 12.5	336 25.0	.. 57.7	287 57.3	.. 40.9	Hamal	327 56.6	N23 32.9
16	215 50.2	18 35.1	13.6	273 46.3	12.4	351 27.2	57.8	302 59.9	40.9	Kaus Aust.	83 38.9	S34 22.4
17	230 52.7	33 35.6	14.7	288 48.8	12.2	6 29.3	57.9	318 02.4	40.9			
18	245 55.1	48 36.1	S10 15.8	303 51.3	S26 12.1	21 31.5	S15 58.0	333 04.9	S22 40.9	Kochab	137 20.6	N74 05.2
19	260 57.6	63 36.7	16.9	318 53.8	12.0	36 33.6	58.1	348 07.4	40.9	Markab	13 34.5	N15 18.4
20	276 00.1	78 37.2	18.0	333 56.3	11.8	51 35.8	58.2	3 09.9	41.0	Menkar	314 11.3	N 4 09.7
21	291 02.5	93 37.7	.. 19.2	348 58.8	.. 11.7	66 37.9	.. 58.3	18 12.4	.. 41.0	Menkent	148 03.6	S36 27.6
22	306 05.0	108 38.3	20.3	4 01.3	11.6	81 40.1	58.4	33 14.9	41.0	Miaplacidus	221 39.8	S69 47.5
23	321 07.5	123 38.8	21.4	19 03.7	11.5	96 42.2	58.5	48 17.4	41.0			
28 00	336 09.9	138 39.3	S10 22.5	34 06.2	S26 11.3	111 44.4	S15 58.6	63 19.9	S22 41.0	Mirfak	308 35.2	N49 55.3
01	351 12.4	153 39.9	23.6	49 08.7	11.2	126 46.5	58.7	78 22.4	41.0	Nunki	75 53.7	S26 16.3
02	6 14.9	168 40.4	24.7	64 11.2	11.1	141 48.7	58.8	93 24.9	41.0	Peacock	53 13.2	S56 40.5
03	21 17.3	183 40.9	.. 25.8	79 13.7	.. 10.9	156 50.8	.. 58.9	108 27.4	.. 41.0	Pollux	243 23.7	N27 58.8
04	36 19.8	198 41.5	26.9	94 16.1	10.8	171 52.9	59.0	123 29.9	41.0	Procyon	244 56.3	N 5 10.6
05	51 22.3	213 42.0	28.0	109 18.6	10.7	186 55.1	59.1	138 32.4	41.0			
06	66 24.7	228 42.5	S10 29.1	124 21.1	S26 10.6	201 57.2	S15 59.2	153 34.9	S22 41.0	Rasalhague	96 03.1	N12 33.1
07	81 27.2	243 43.1	30.2	139 23.5	10.4	216 59.4	59.3	168 37.4	41.0	Regulus	207 40.1	N11 52.7
08	96 29.6	258 43.6	31.3	154 26.0	10.3	232 01.5	59.4	183 39.9	41.0	Rigel	281 08.8	S 8 10.8
T 09	111 32.1	273 44.2	.. 32.4	169 28.5	.. 10.2	247 03.7	.. 59.5	198 42.4	.. 41.0	Rigil Kent.	139 47.2	S60 54.7
U 10	126 34.6	288 44.7	33.5	184 30.9	10.0	262 05.8	59.6	213 44.9	41.1	Sabik	102 08.4	S15 44.7
E 11	141 37.0	303 45.2	34.6	199 33.4	09.9	277 08.0	59.7	228 47.4	41.1			
S 12	156 39.5	318 45.8	S10 35.7	214 35.9	S26 09.8	292 10.1	S15 59.8	243 49.9	S22 41.1	Schedar	349 36.0	N56 38.2
D 13	171 42.0	333 46.3	36.8	229 38.3	09.6	307 12.2	15 59.9	258 52.5	41.1	Shaula	96 17.0	S37 06.9
A 14	186 44.4	348 46.8	37.9	244 40.8	09.5	322 14.4	16 00.0	273 55.0	41.1	Sirius	258 30.8	S16 44.4
Y 15	201 46.9	3 47.4	.. 39.0	259 43.2	.. 09.4	337 16.5	.. 00.1	288 57.5	.. 41.1	Spica	158 27.7	S11 15.3
16	216 49.4	18 48.0	40.1	274 45.7	09.2	352 18.7	00.2	304 00.0	41.1	Suhail	222 50.3	S43 30.4
17	231 51.8	33 48.5	41.2	289 48.2	09.1	7 20.8	00.3	319 02.5	41.1			
18	246 54.3	48 49.1	S10 42.3	304 50.6	S26 08.9	22 23.0	S16 00.4	334 05.0	S22 41.1	Vega	80 36.3	N38 48.4
19	261 56.7	63 49.6	43.4	319 53.1	08.8	37 25.1	00.5	349 07.5	41.1	Zuben'ubi	137 01.6	S16 06.9
20	276 59.2	78 50.2	44.5	334 55.5	08.7	52 27.2	00.6	4 10.0	41.1		SHA	Mer. Pass.
21	292 01.7	93 50.7	.. 45.6	349 58.0	.. 08.5	67 29.4	.. 00.7	19 12.5	.. 41.1		° ′	h m
22	307 04.1	108 51.3	46.6	5 00.4	08.4	82 31.5	00.8	34 15.0	41.1	Venus	163 16.0	14 46
23	322 06.6	123 51.8	47.7	20 02.9	08.3	97 33.7	00.9	49 17.5	41.1	Mars	57 55.5	21 44
	h m									Jupiter	135 42.0	16 34
Mer. Pass.	1 39.0	v 0.5	d 1.1	v 2.5	d 0.1	v 2.1	d 0.1	v 2.5	d 0.0	Saturn	87 08.9	19 47

UT	SUN GHA	SUN Dec	MOON GHA	v	Dec	d	HP
d h	° ′	° ′	° ′	′	° ′	′	′
26 00	179 30.7	N10 30.1	4 04.9	13.6	S14 13.7	7.9	54.4
01	194 30.9	29.2	18 37.5	13.6	14 05.8	8.0	54.4
02	209 31.1	28.3	33 10.1	13.7	13 57.8	8.1	54.4
03	224 31.3	.. 27.5	47 42.8	13.6	13 49.7	8.2	54.4
04	239 31.4	26.6	62 15.4	13.7	13 41.5	8.2	54.4
05	254 31.6	25.7	76 48.1	13.7	13 33.3	8.3	54.4
06	269 31.8	N10 24.9	91 20.8	13.8	S13 25.0	8.3	54.4
07	284 32.0	24.0	105 53.6	13.7	13 16.7	8.4	54.4
S 08	299 32.2	23.1	120 26.3	13.8	13 08.3	8.5	54.4
U 09	314 32.3	22.3	134 59.1	13.8	12 59.8	8.5	54.5
N 10	329 32.5	21.4	149 31.9	13.8	12 51.3	8.6	54.5
D 11	344 32.7	20.5	164 04.7	13.8	12 42.7	8.7	54.5
A 12	359 32.9	N10 19.6	178 37.5	13.9	S12 34.0	8.6	54.5
Y 13	14 33.0	18.8	193 10.4	13.9	12 25.4	8.8	54.5
14	29 33.2	17.9	207 43.3	13.9	12 16.6	8.8	54.5
15	44 33.4	.. 17.0	222 16.2	13.9	12 07.8	8.9	54.5
16	59 33.6	16.2	236 49.1	13.9	11 58.9	8.9	54.5
17	74 33.8	15.3	251 22.0	14.0	11 50.0	9.0	54.5
18	89 33.9	N10 14.4	265 55.0	14.0	S11 41.0	9.0	54.6
19	104 34.1	13.6	280 28.0	14.0	11 32.0	9.1	54.6
20	119 34.3	12.7	295 01.0	14.0	11 22.9	9.2	54.6
21	134 34.5	.. 11.8	309 34.0	14.0	11 13.7	9.2	54.6
22	149 34.7	10.9	324 07.0	14.1	11 04.5	9.2	54.6
23	164 34.8	10.1	338 40.1	14.0	10 55.3	9.3	54.6
27 00	179 35.0	N10 09.2	353 13.1	14.1	S10 46.0	9.3	54.6
01	194 35.2	08.3	7 46.2	14.1	10 36.7	9.4	54.6
02	209 35.4	07.4	22 19.3	14.2	10 27.3	9.5	54.7
03	224 35.6	.. 06.6	36 52.5	14.1	10 17.8	9.5	54.7
04	239 35.7	05.7	51 25.6	14.1	10 08.3	9.5	54.7
05	254 35.9	04.8	65 58.7	14.2	9 58.8	9.6	54.7
06	269 36.1	N10 03.9	80 31.9	14.2	S 9 49.2	9.6	54.7
07	284 36.3	03.1	95 05.1	14.2	9 39.6	9.7	54.7
08	299 36.5	02.2	109 38.3	14.2	9 29.9	9.8	54.7
M 09	314 36.6	.. 01.3	124 11.5	14.2	9 20.1	9.7	54.8
O 10	329 36.8	10 00.4	138 44.7	14.2	9 10.4	9.9	54.8
N 11	344 37.0	9 59.6	153 17.9	14.3	9 00.5	9.8	54.8
D 12	359 37.2	N 9 58.7	167 51.2	14.2	S 8 50.7	9.9	54.8
A 13	14 37.4	57.8	182 24.4	14.3	8 40.8	10.0	54.8
Y 14	29 37.5	56.9	196 57.7	14.3	8 30.8	9.9	54.8
15	44 37.7	.. 56.0	211 31.0	14.3	8 20.9	10.1	54.8
16	59 37.9	55.2	226 04.3	14.3	8 10.8	10.0	54.9
17	74 38.1	54.3	240 37.6	14.3	8 00.8	10.1	54.9
18	89 38.3	N 9 53.4	255 10.9	14.3	S 7 50.7	10.2	54.9
19	104 38.5	52.5	269 44.2	14.4	7 40.5	10.2	54.9
20	119 38.6	51.7	284 17.6	14.3	7 30.3	10.2	54.9
21	134 38.8	.. 50.8	298 50.9	14.3	7 20.1	10.3	54.9
22	149 39.0	49.9	313 24.2	14.4	7 09.8	10.3	54.9
23	164 39.2	49.0	327 57.6	14.3	6 59.5	10.3	55.0
28 00	179 39.4	N 9 48.1	342 30.9	14.4	S 6 49.2	10.3	55.0
01	194 39.6	47.3	357 04.3	14.4	6 38.9	10.4	55.0
02	209 39.8	46.4	11 37.7	14.3	6 28.5	10.5	55.0
03	224 39.9	.. 45.5	26 11.0	14.4	6 18.0	10.4	55.0
04	239 40.1	44.6	40 44.4	14.4	6 07.6	10.5	55.0
05	254 40.3	43.7	55 17.8	14.4	5 57.1	10.6	55.1
06	269 40.5	N 9 42.9	69 51.2	14.4	S 5 46.5	10.5	55.1
07	284 40.7	42.0	84 24.6	14.4	5 36.0	10.6	55.1
T 08	299 40.9	41.1	98 58.0	14.4	5 25.4	10.6	55.1
U 09	314 41.0	.. 40.2	113 31.4	14.3	5 14.8	10.7	55.1
E 10	329 41.2	39.3	128 04.7	14.4	5 04.1	10.6	55.1
S 11	344 41.4	38.4	142 38.1	14.4	4 53.5	10.7	55.2
D 12	359 41.6	N 9 37.6	157 11.5	14.4	S 4 42.8	10.8	55.2
A 13	14 41.8	36.7	171 44.9	14.4	4 32.0	10.7	55.2
Y 14	29 42.0	35.8	186 18.3	14.4	4 21.3	10.8	55.2
15	44 42.2	.. 34.9	200 51.7	14.4	4 10.5	10.8	55.2
16	59 42.3	34.0	215 25.1	14.4	3 59.7	10.8	55.2
17	74 42.5	33.1	229 58.5	14.3	3 48.9	10.9	55.3
18	89 42.7	N 9 32.3	244 31.8	14.4	S 3 38.0	10.8	55.3
19	104 42.9	31.4	259 05.2	14.4	3 27.2	10.9	55.3
20	119 43.1	30.5	273 38.6	14.3	3 16.3	10.9	55.3
21	134 43.3	.. 29.6	288 11.9	14.4	3 05.4	11.0	55.3
22	149 43.5	28.7	302 45.3	14.3	2 54.4	10.9	55.3
23	164 43.7	27.8	317 18.6	14.3	S 2 43.5	11.0	55.4
	SD 15.9	d 0.9	SD 14.8		14.9		15.0

Lat.	Twilight Naut.	Twilight Civil	Sunrise	Moonrise 26	27	28	29
°	h m	h m	h m	h m	h m	h m	h m
N 72	////	01 48	03 35	20 54	20 40	20 27	20 15
N 70	////	02 29	03 53	20 35	20 29	20 23	20 17
68	////	02 56	04 07	20 21	20 23	20 19	20 19
66	01 34	03 16	04 18	20 09	20 13	20 16	20 19
64	02 10	03 32	04 28	19 58	20 07	20 13	20 20
62	02 35	03 45	04 36	19 50	20 01	20 11	20 21
60	02 54	03 56	04 43	19 42	19 56	20 09	20 21
N 58	03 09	04 06	04 49	19 36	19 52	20 07	20 22
56	03 22	04 14	04 54	19 30	19 48	20 06	20 22
54	03 33	04 21	04 59	19 24	19 45	20 04	20 23
52	03 42	04 27	05 03	19 20	19 42	20 03	20 23
50	03 51	04 33	05 07	19 15	19 39	20 02	20 24
45	04 08	04 45	05 16	19 06	19 33	19 59	20 25
N 40	04 21	04 55	05 23	18 58	19 28	19 57	20 25
35	04 32	05 03	05 29	18 51	19 24	19 55	20 26
30	04 41	05 10	05 34	18 45	19 20	19 53	20 27
20	04 54	05 21	05 43	18 35	19 13	19 50	20 28
N 10	05 05	05 30	05 51	18 26	19 07	19 48	20 29
0	05 13	05 37	05 58	18 17	19 01	19 45	20 30
S 10	05 19	05 44	06 05	18 09	18 56	19 43	20 31
20	05 25	05 51	06 13	17 59	18 50	19 40	20 32
30	05 29	05 57	06 21	17 49	18 43	19 38	20 33
35	05 31	06 00	06 26	17 43	18 39	19 36	20 33
40	05 33	06 04	06 31	17 36	18 35	19 34	20 34
45	05 34	06 08	06 38	17 28	18 29	19 32	20 35
S 50	05 35	06 12	06 45	17 18	18 23	19 29	20 36
52	05 35	06 14	06 48	17 14	18 20	19 28	20 37
54	05 35	06 16	06 52	17 09	18 17	19 27	20 37
56	05 35	06 18	06 56	17 03	18 13	19 25	20 38
58	05 35	06 21	07 01	16 57	18 10	19 23	20 38
S 60	05 35	06 23	07 06	16 50	18 05	19 22	20 39

Lat.	Sunset	Twilight Civil	Twilight Naut.	Moonset 26	27	28	29
°	h m	h m	h m	h m	h m	h m	h m
N 72	20 24	22 06	////	02 28	04 21	06 07	07 52
N 70	20 07	21 29	////	02 57	04 38	06 16	07 53
68	19 53	21 03	23 31	03 19	04 51	06 23	07 55
66	19 43	20 44	22 22	03 36	05 02	06 29	07 56
64	19 33	20 28	21 49	03 50	05 11	06 34	07 57
62	19 26	20 16	21 25	04 01	05 19	06 38	07 58
60	19 19	20 05	21 06	04 11	05 26	06 41	07 58
N 58	19 13	19 56	20 52	04 19	05 31	06 45	07 59
56	19 08	19 48	20 39	04 27	05 37	06 48	07 59
54	19 03	19 41	20 28	04 33	05 41	06 50	08 00
52	18 59	19 34	20 19	04 39	05 45	06 53	08 01
50	18 55	19 29	20 11	04 45	05 49	06 55	08 01
45	18 46	19 17	19 54	04 56	05 57	06 59	08 02
N 40	18 40	19 08	19 41	05 06	06 04	07 03	08 03
35	18 34	19 00	19 31	05 14	06 10	07 06	08 03
30	18 28	18 53	19 22	05 21	06 15	07 09	08 04
20	18 20	18 42	19 08	05 33	06 24	07 14	08 05
N 10	18 12	18 33	18 58	05 44	06 31	07 19	08 06
0	18 05	18 26	18 50	05 54	06 39	07 23	08 07
S 10	17 58	18 19	18 44	06 04	06 46	07 27	08 07
20	17 51	18 13	18 39	06 15	06 53	07 31	08 08
30	17 42	18 06	18 34	06 26	07 02	07 36	08 09
35	17 38	18 03	18 33	06 33	07 07	07 38	08 09
40	17 32	18 00	18 31	06 41	07 12	07 42	08 10
45	17 26	17 56	18 30	06 50	07 19	07 45	08 11
S 50	17 19	17 52	18 29	07 01	07 26	07 49	08 11
52	17 15	17 50	18 29	07 06	07 30	07 51	08 12
54	17 12	17 48	18 29	07 12	07 34	07 53	08 12
56	17 08	17 46	18 29	07 18	07 38	07 56	08 12
58	17 03	17 43	18 29	07 25	07 43	07 58	08 13
S 60	16 58	17 41	18 29	07 32	07 48	08 01	08 13

	SUN			MOON			
Day	Eqn. of Time 00h	12h	Mer. Pass.	Mer. Pass. Upper	Lower	Age	Phase
d	m s	m s	h m	h m	h m	d	%
26	01 57	01 49	12 02	24 28	12 06	15	100
27	01 40	01 32	12 02	00 28	12 50	16	99
28	01 23	01 14	12 01	01 12	13 34	17	96

2018 AUGUST 29, 30, 31 (WED., THURS., FRI.)

UT	ARIES	VENUS −4.6		MARS −2.1		JUPITER −1.9		SATURN +0.4		STARS		
	GHA	GHA	Dec	GHA	Dec	GHA	Dec	GHA	Dec	Name	SHA	Dec
d h	° ′	° ′	° ′	° ′	° ′	° ′	° ′	° ′	° ′		° ′	° ′
29 00	337 09.1	138 52.4	S10 48.8	35 05.3	S26 08.1	112 35.8	S16 01.0	64 20.0	S22 41.1	Acamar	315 15.5	S40 13.7
01	352 11.5	153 52.9	49.9	50 07.7	08.0	127 37.9	01.1	79 22.5	41.2	Achernar	335 23.8	S57 08.4
02	7 14.0	168 53.5	51.0	65 10.2	07.8	142 40.1	01.2	94 25.0	41.2	Acrux	173 05.9	S63 12.1
03	22 16.5	183 54.0 ..	52.1	80 12.6 ..	07.7	157 42.2 ..	01.3	109 27.5 ..	41.2	Adhara	255 10.0	S28 59.7
04	37 18.9	198 54.6	53.2	95 15.1	07.6	172 44.4	01.4	124 30.0	41.2	Aldebaran	290 45.3	N16 32.6
05	52 21.4	213 55.1	54.3	110 17.5	07.4	187 46.5	01.5	139 32.5	41.2			
W 06	67 23.9	228 55.7	S10 55.4	125 19.9	S26 07.3	202 48.6	S16 01.6	154 35.0	S22 41.2	Alioth	166 18.1	N55 51.9
E 07	82 26.3	243 56.3	56.5	140 22.4	07.1	217 50.8	01.7	169 37.5	41.2	Alkaid	152 56.4	N49 13.6
D 08	97 28.8	258 56.8	57.6	155 24.8	07.0	232 52.9	01.8	184 40.0	41.2	Al Na'ir	27 38.9	S46 52.2
N 09	112 31.2	273 57.4 ..	58.7	170 27.2 ..	06.8	247 55.1 ..	01.9	199 42.5 ..	41.2	Alnilam	275 42.9	S 1 11.4
E 10	127 33.7	288 57.9	10 59.7	185 29.7	06.7	262 57.2	02.1	214 45.0	41.2	Alphard	217 52.9	S 8 44.3
S 11	142 36.2	303 58.5	11 00.8	200 32.1	06.6	277 59.3	02.2	229 47.5	41.2			
D 12	157 38.6	318 59.1	S11 01.9	215 34.5	S26 06.4	293 01.5	S16 02.3	244 50.0	S22 41.2	Alphecca	126 08.1	N26 39.5
A 13	172 41.1	333 59.6	03.0	230 36.9	06.3	308 03.6	02.4	259 52.5	41.2	Alpheratz	357 39.5	N29 11.5
Y 14	187 43.6	349 00.2	04.1	245 39.4	06.1	323 05.8	02.5	274 55.0	41.2	Altair	62 04.5	N 8 55.3
15	202 46.0	4 00.8 ..	05.2	260 41.8 ..	06.0	338 07.9 ..	02.6	289 57.5 ..	41.2	Ankaa	353 11.9	S42 12.2
16	217 48.5	19 01.3	06.3	275 44.2	05.8	353 10.0	02.7	305 00.0	41.3	Antares	112 21.9	S26 28.2
17	232 51.0	34 01.9	07.3	290 46.6	05.7	8 12.2	02.8	320 02.5	41.3			
18	247 53.4	49 02.5	S11 08.4	305 49.0	S26 05.5	23 14.3	S16 02.9	335 05.0	S22 41.3	Arcturus	145 52.7	N19 05.5
19	262 55.9	64 03.0	09.5	320 51.4	05.4	38 16.4	03.0	350 07.5	41.3	Atria	107 20.4	S69 03.7
20	277 58.3	79 03.6	10.6	335 53.9	05.3	53 18.6	03.1	5 10.0	41.3	Avior	234 17.1	S59 34.0
21	293 00.8	94 04.2 ..	11.7	350 56.3 ..	05.1	68 20.7 ..	03.2	20 12.5 ..	41.3	Bellatrix	278 28.3	N 6 21.9
22	308 03.3	109 04.7	12.8	5 58.7	05.0	83 22.8	03.3	35 14.9	41.3	Betelgeuse	270 57.6	N 7 24.6
23	323 05.7	124 05.3	13.9	21 01.1	04.8	98 25.0	03.4	50 17.4	41.3			
30 00	338 08.2	139 05.9	S11 14.9	36 03.5	S26 04.7	113 27.1	S16 03.5	65 19.9	S22 41.3	Canopus	263 54.8	S52 42.2
01	353 10.7	154 06.5	16.0	51 05.9	04.5	128 29.3	03.6	80 22.4	41.3	Capella	280 29.3	N46 00.7
02	8 13.1	169 07.0	17.1	66 08.3	04.4	143 31.4	03.7	95 24.9	41.3	Deneb	49 28.7	N45 21.0
03	23 15.6	184 07.6 ..	18.2	81 10.7 ..	04.2	158 33.5 ..	03.8	110 27.4 ..	41.3	Denebola	182 30.4	N14 28.3
04	38 18.1	199 08.2	19.3	96 13.1	04.1	173 35.7	03.9	125 29.9	41.3	Diphda	348 52.1	S17 53.0
05	53 20.5	214 08.8	20.3	111 15.5	03.9	188 37.8	04.0	140 32.4	41.3			
T 06	68 23.0	229 09.4	S11 21.4	126 17.9	S26 03.8	203 39.9	S16 04.1	155 34.9	S22 41.3	Dubhe	193 48.1	N61 39.2
H 07	83 25.5	244 09.9	22.5	141 20.3	03.6	218 42.1	04.2	170 37.4	41.4	Elnath	278 08.3	N28 37.2
U 08	98 27.9	259 10.5	23.6	156 22.7	03.5	233 44.2	04.3	185 39.9	41.4	Eltanin	90 44.3	N51 29.6
R 09	113 30.4	274 11.1 ..	24.6	171 25.1 ..	03.3	248 46.3 ..	04.4	200 42.4 ..	41.4	Enif	33 43.3	N 9 57.8
S 10	128 32.8	289 11.7	25.7	186 27.5	03.2	263 48.5	04.5	215 44.9	41.4	Fomalhaut	15 19.7	S29 31.3
D 11	143 35.3	304 12.3	26.8	201 29.9	03.0	278 50.6	04.6	230 47.4	41.4			
A 12	158 37.8	319 12.8	S11 27.9	216 32.3	S26 02.8	293 52.7	S16 04.7	245 49.9	S22 41.4	Gacrux	171 57.4	S57 13.0
Y 13	173 40.2	334 13.4	29.0	231 34.7	02.7	308 54.9	04.8	260 52.4	41.4	Gienah	175 49.0	S17 38.6
14	188 42.7	349 14.0	30.0	246 37.1	02.5	323 57.0	04.9	275 54.9	41.4	Hadar	148 43.2	S60 27.8
15	203 45.2	4 14.6 ..	31.1	261 39.4 ..	02.4	338 59.1 ..	05.0	290 57.4 ..	41.4	Hamal	327 56.6	N23 32.9
16	218 47.6	19 15.2	32.2	276 41.8	02.2	354 01.3	05.1	305 59.9	41.4	Kaus Aust.	83 38.9	S34 22.4
17	233 50.1	34 15.8	33.3	291 44.2	02.1	9 03.4	05.2	321 02.4	41.4			
18	248 52.6	49 16.4	S11 34.3	306 46.6	S26 01.9	24 05.5	S16 05.3	336 04.9	S22 41.4	Kochab	137 20.6	N74 05.2
19	263 55.0	64 17.0	35.4	321 49.0	01.8	39 07.6	05.4	351 07.3	41.4	Markab	13 34.5	N15 18.4
20	278 57.5	79 17.6	36.5	336 51.4	01.6	54 09.8	05.5	6 09.8	41.4	Menkar	314 11.2	N 4 09.7
21	293 59.9	94 18.2 ..	37.5	351 53.7 ..	01.5	69 11.9 ..	05.6	21 12.3 ..	41.4	Menkent	148 03.6	S36 27.6
22	309 02.4	109 18.7	38.6	6 56.1	01.3	84 14.0	05.7	36 14.8	41.5	Miaplacidus	221 39.8	S69 47.5
23	324 04.9	124 19.3	39.7	21 58.5	01.1	99 16.2	05.8	51 17.3	41.5			
31 00	339 07.3	139 19.9	S11 40.8	37 00.9	S26 01.0	114 18.3	S16 05.9	66 19.8	S22 41.5	Mirfak	308 35.1	N49 55.3
01	354 09.8	154 20.5	41.8	52 03.2	00.8	129 20.4	06.0	81 22.3	41.5	Nunki	75 53.7	S26 16.3
02	9 12.3	169 21.1	42.9	67 05.6	00.7	144 22.6	06.1	96 24.8	41.5	Peacock	53 13.2	S56 40.5
03	24 14.7	184 21.7 ..	44.0	82 08.0 ..	00.5	159 24.7 ..	06.3	111 27.3 ..	41.5	Pollux	243 23.7	N27 58.8
04	39 17.2	199 22.3	45.0	97 10.3	00.3	174 26.8	06.4	126 29.8	41.5	Procyon	244 56.3	N 5 10.6
05	54 19.7	214 22.9	46.1	112 12.7	00.2	189 28.9	06.5	141 32.3	41.5			
F 06	69 22.1	229 23.5	S11 47.2	127 15.1	S26 00.0	204 31.1	S16 06.6	156 34.8	S22 41.5	Rasalhague	96 03.1	N12 33.1
R 07	84 24.6	244 24.1	48.2	142 17.4	25 59.9	219 33.2	06.7	171 37.3	41.5	Regulus	207 40.1	N11 52.7
I 08	99 27.1	259 24.7	49.3	157 19.8	59.7	234 35.3	06.8	186 39.7	41.5	Rigel	281 08.7	S 8 10.8
D 09	114 29.5	274 25.3 ..	50.4	172 22.1 ..	59.5	249 37.5 ..	06.9	201 42.2 ..	41.5	Rigil Kent.	139 47.2	S60 54.7
A 10	129 32.0	289 26.0	51.4	187 24.5	59.4	264 39.6	07.0	216 44.7	41.5	Sabik	102 08.4	S15 44.7
Y 11	144 34.4	304 26.6	52.5	202 26.9	59.2	279 41.7	07.1	231 47.2	41.5			
12	159 36.9	319 27.2	S11 53.6	217 29.2	S25 59.1	294 43.8	S16 07.2	246 49.7	S22 41.5	Schedar	349 36.0	N56 38.2
13	174 39.4	334 27.8	54.6	232 31.6	58.9	309 46.0	07.3	261 52.2	41.6	Shaula	96 17.0	S37 06.9
14	189 41.8	349 28.4	55.7	247 33.9	58.7	324 48.1	07.4	276 54.7	41.6	Sirius	258 30.8	S16 44.4
15	204 44.3	4 29.0 ..	56.7	262 36.3 ..	58.6	339 50.2 ..	07.5	291 57.2 ..	41.6	Spica	158 27.8	S11 15.3
16	219 46.8	19 29.6	57.8	277 38.6	58.4	354 52.4	07.6	306 59.7	41.6	Suhail	222 50.3	S43 30.3
17	234 49.2	34 30.2	58.9	292 41.0	58.2	9 54.5	07.7	322 02.2	41.6			
18	249 51.7	49 30.8	S11 59.9	307 43.3	S25 58.1	24 56.6	S16 07.8	337 04.6	S22 41.6	Vega	80 36.3	N38 48.4
19	264 54.2	64 31.4	12 01.0	322 45.6	57.9	39 58.7	07.9	352 07.1	41.6	Zuben'ubi	137 01.6	S16 06.9
20	279 56.6	79 32.1	02.0	337 48.0	57.7	55 00.9	08.0	7 09.6	41.6		SHA	Mer. Pass.
21	294 59.1	94 32.7 ..	03.1	352 50.3 ..	57.6	70 03.0 ..	08.1	22 12.1 ..	41.6		° ′	h m
22	310 01.6	109 33.3	04.2	7 52.7	57.4	85 05.1	08.2	37 14.6	41.6	Venus	160 57.7	14 43
23	325 04.0	124 33.9	05.2	22 55.0	57.2	100 07.2	08.3	52 17.1	41.6	Mars	57 55.3	21 32
	h m									Jupiter	135 18.9	16 24
Mer. Pass. 1 27.2	*v* 0.6 *d* 1.1			*v* 2.4 *d* 0.2		*v* 2.1 *d* 0.1		*v* 2.5 *d* 0.0		Saturn	87 11.7	19 35

SUN and MOON

UT (d h)	SUN GHA	SUN Dec	MOON GHA	v	MOON Dec	d	HP
29 00	179 43.8	N 9 26.9	331 51.9	14.4	S 2 32.5	11.0	55.4
01	194 44.0	26.0	346 25.3	14.3	2 21.5	11.0	55.4
02	209 44.2	25.2	0 58.6	14.3	2 10.5	11.0	55.4
03	224 44.4 ..	24.3	15 31.9	14.3	1 59.5	11.0	55.4
04	239 44.6	23.4	30 05.2	14.3	1 48.5	11.1	55.5
05	254 44.8	22.5	44 38.5	14.3	1 37.4	11.0	55.5
06	269 45.0 N 9 21.6		59 11.8	14.2	S 1 26.4	11.1	55.5
W 07	284 45.2	20.7	73 45.0	14.3	1 15.3	11.1	55.5
E 08	299 45.3	19.8	88 18.3	14.2	1 04.2	11.1	55.5
D 09	314 45.5 ..	18.9	102 51.5	14.2	0 53.1	11.1	55.6
N 10	329 45.7	18.1	117 24.7	14.2	0 42.0	11.1	55.6
E 11	344 45.9	17.2	131 57.9	14.2	0 30.9	11.1	55.6
S 12	359 46.1 N 9 16.3		146 31.1	14.2	S 0 19.8	11.2	55.6
D 13	14 46.3	15.4	161 04.3	14.1	S 0 08.6	11.1	55.6
A 14	29 46.5	14.5	175 37.4	14.1	N 0 02.5	11.2	55.6
Y 15	44 46.7 ..	13.6	190 10.5	14.1	0 13.7	11.1	55.7
16	59 46.9	12.7	204 43.6	14.1	0 24.8	11.2	55.7
17	74 47.1	11.8	219 16.7	14.1	0 36.0	11.2	55.7
18	89 47.2 N 9 10.9		233 49.8	14.1	N 0 47.2	11.1	55.7
19	104 47.4	10.0	248 22.9	14.0	0 58.3	11.2	55.7
20	119 47.6	09.2	262 55.9	14.0	1 09.5	11.2	55.8
21	134 47.8 ..	08.3	277 28.9	14.0	1 20.7	11.2	55.8
22	149 48.0	07.4	292 01.9	13.9	1 31.9	11.1	55.8
23	164 48.2	06.5	306 34.8	14.0	1 43.0	11.2	55.8
30 00	179 48.4 N 9 05.6		321 07.8	13.9	N 1 54.2	11.2	55.9
01	194 48.6	04.7	335 40.7	13.8	2 05.4	11.2	55.9
02	209 48.8	03.8	350 13.5	13.9	2 16.6	11.2	55.9
03	224 49.0 ..	02.9	4 46.4	13.8	2 27.8	11.1	55.9
04	239 49.2	02.0	19 19.2	13.8	2 38.9	11.2	55.9
05	254 49.3	01.1	33 52.0	13.8	2 50.1	11.2	56.0
06	269 49.5 N 9 00.2		48 24.8	13.7	N 3 01.3	11.1	56.0
T 07	284 49.7 8 59.3		62 57.5	13.7	3 12.4	11.2	56.0
H 08	299 49.9	58.4	77 30.2	13.7	3 23.6	11.1	56.0
U 09	314 50.1 ..	57.5	92 02.9	13.6	3 34.7	11.2	56.0
R 10	329 50.3	56.6	106 35.5	13.6	3 45.9	11.1	56.1
S 11	344 50.5	55.7	121 08.1	13.6	3 57.0	11.1	56.1
D 12	359 50.7 N 8 54.9		135 40.7	13.5	N 4 08.1	11.1	56.1
A 13	14 50.9	54.0	150 13.2	13.5	4 19.2	11.1	56.1
Y 14	29 51.1	53.1	164 45.7	13.5	4 30.3	11.1	56.2
15	44 51.3 ..	52.2	179 18.2	13.4	4 41.4	11.0	56.2
16	59 51.5	51.3	193 50.6	13.4	4 52.4	11.1	56.2
17	74 51.7	50.4	208 23.0	13.3	5 03.5	11.0	56.2
18	89 51.9 N 8 49.5		222 55.3	13.3	N 5 14.5	11.1	56.2
19	104 52.0	48.6	237 27.6	13.3	5 25.6	11.0	56.3
20	119 52.2	47.7	251 59.9	13.2	5 36.6	11.0	56.3
21	134 52.4 ..	46.8	266 32.1	13.2	5 47.6	10.9	56.3
22	149 52.6	45.9	281 04.3	13.1	5 58.5	11.0	56.3
23	164 52.8	45.0	295 36.4	13.1	6 09.5	10.9	56.4
31 00	179 53.0 N 8 44.1		310 08.5	13.1	N 6 20.4	10.9	56.4
01	194 53.2	43.2	324 40.6	13.0	6 31.3	10.9	56.4
02	209 53.4	42.3	339 12.6	13.0	6 42.2	10.9	56.4
03	224 53.6 ..	41.4	353 44.6	12.9	6 53.1	10.8	56.5
04	239 53.8	40.5	8 16.5	12.8	7 03.9	10.8	56.5
05	254 54.0	39.6	22 48.3	12.9	7 14.7	10.8	56.5
06	269 54.2 N 8 38.7		37 20.2	12.7	N 7 25.5	10.8	56.5
F 07	284 54.4	37.8	51 51.9	12.8	7 36.3	10.7	56.5
R 08	299 54.6	36.9	66 23.7	12.6	7 47.0	10.7	56.6
I 09	314 54.8 ..	36.0	80 55.3	12.6	7 57.7	10.7	56.6
D 10	329 55.0	35.1	95 26.9	12.6	8 08.4	10.7	56.6
A 11	344 55.2	34.2	109 58.5	12.5	8 19.1	10.6	56.6
Y 12	359 55.4 N 8 33.3		124 30.0	12.5	N 8 29.7	10.6	56.7
13	14 55.6	32.4	139 01.5	12.4	8 40.3	10.5	56.7
14	29 55.8	31.5	153 32.9	12.3	8 50.8	10.6	56.7
15	44 55.9 ..	30.6	168 04.2	12.3	9 01.4	10.4	56.7
16	59 56.1	29.7	182 35.5	12.3	9 11.8	10.5	56.8
17	74 56.3	28.8	197 06.8	12.2	9 22.3	10.4	56.8
18	89 56.5 N 8 27.9		211 38.0	12.1	N 9 32.7	10.4	56.8
19	104 56.7	27.0	226 09.1	12.1	9 43.1	10.3	56.8
20	119 56.9	26.1	240 40.2	12.0	9 53.4	10.3	56.9
21	134 57.1 ..	25.2	255 11.2	11.9	10 03.7	10.2	56.9
22	149 57.3	24.3	269 42.1	11.9	10 13.9	10.3	56.9
23	164 57.5	23.3	284 13.0	11.9	N10 24.2	10.1	56.9
	SD 15.9 d 0.9		SD 15.2		15.3		15.4

Twilight / Sunrise / Moonrise

Lat.	Twilight Naut.	Twilight Civil	Sunrise	Moonrise 29	30	31	1
°	h m	h m	h m	h m	h m	h m	h m
N 72	////	02 15	03 51	20 15	20 03	19 50	19 32
N 70	////	02 47	04 06	20 17	20 11	20 05	19 58
68	01 08	03 10	04 18	20 18	20 17	20 17	20 17
66	01 56	03 28	04 28	20 19	20 22	20 27	20 33
64	02 25	03 42	04 37	20 20	20 27	20 35	20 46
62	02 47	03 54	04 44	20 21	20 31	20 42	20 57
60	03 04	04 04	04 50	20 21	20 34	20 49	21 06
N 58	03 18	04 13	04 55	20 22	20 37	20 54	21 15
56	03 30	04 20	05 00	20 22	20 40	20 59	21 22
54	03 40	04 27	05 04	20 23	20 42	21 04	21 29
52	03 48	04 33	05 08	20 23	20 45	21 08	21 34
50	03 56	04 38	05 12	20 24	20 47	21 11	21 40
45	04 12	04 49	05 19	20 25	20 51	21 19	21 51
N 40	04 24	04 58	05 26	20 25	20 55	21 26	22 01
35	04 34	05 05	05 31	20 26	20 58	21 32	22 09
30	04 42	05 11	05 36	20 27	21 01	21 37	22 17
20	04 55	05 21	05 44	20 28	21 06	21 46	22 29
N 10	05 05	05 30	05 51	20 29	21 11	21 54	22 41
0	05 12	05 36	05 57	20 30	21 15	22 02	22 51
S 10	05 18	05 42	06 04	20 31	21 19	22 09	23 02
20	05 22	05 48	06 10	20 32	21 24	22 17	23 13
30	05 26	05 54	06 18	20 33	21 29	22 27	23 26
35	05 27	05 57	06 22	20 33	21 32	22 32	23 34
40	05 28	06 00	06 27	20 34	21 35	22 38	23 43
45	05 29	06 03	06 32	20 35	21 40	22 46	23 53
S 50	05 29	06 06	06 39	20 36	21 44	22 54	24 05
52	05 29	06 08	06 42	20 37	21 47	22 58	24 11
54	05 29	06 09	06 45	20 37	21 49	23 03	24 18
56	05 28	06 11	06 49	20 38	21 52	23 08	24 25
58	05 28	06 13	06 53	20 38	21 55	23 13	24 33
S 60	05 27	06 15	06 57	20 39	21 58	23 19	24 42

Sunset / Twilight / Moonset

Lat.	Sunset	Twilight Civil	Twilight Naut.	Moonset 29	30	31	1
°	h m	h m	h m	h m	h m	h m	h m
N 72	20 07	21 40	////	07 52	09 37	11 27	13 26
N 70	19 52	21 09	////	07 53	09 32	11 14	13 02
68	19 40	20 47	22 43	07 55	09 28	11 04	12 44
66	19 31	20 30	21 59	07 56	09 24	10 55	12 29
64	19 23	20 16	21 32	07 57	09 21	10 48	12 17
62	19 16	20 05	21 11	07 58	09 19	10 42	12 07
60	19 10	19 55	20 54	07 58	09 17	10 37	11 58
N 58	19 05	19 47	20 41	07 59	09 15	10 32	11 51
56	19 00	19 40	20 30	08 00	09 13	10 28	11 44
54	18 56	19 33	20 20	08 00	09 11	10 24	11 38
52	18 52	19 27	20 11	08 01	09 10	10 21	11 33
50	18 48	19 22	20 04	08 01	09 09	10 18	11 28
45	18 41	19 11	19 48	08 02	09 06	10 11	11 18
N 40	18 35	19 03	19 36	08 03	09 03	10 05	11 09
35	18 30	18 56	19 26	08 03	09 01	10 01	11 02
30	18 25	18 49	19 18	08 04	09 00	09 56	10 55
20	18 17	18 39	19 06	08 05	08 56	09 49	10 43
N 10	18 10	18 32	18 56	08 06	08 54	09 43	10 34
0	18 04	18 25	18 49	08 07	08 51	09 37	10 25
S 10	17 58	18 19	18 43	08 07	08 48	09 31	10 16
20	17 51	18 13	18 39	08 08	08 46	09 25	10 06
30	17 44	18 08	18 36	08 09	08 43	09 18	09 55
35	17 40	18 05	18 35	08 09	08 41	09 14	09 49
40	17 35	18 02	18 34	08 10	08 39	09 09	09 42
45	17 30	17 59	18 33	08 11	08 36	09 04	09 33
S 50	17 23	17 56	18 33	08 11	08 34	08 57	09 23
52	17 20	17 54	18 33	08 12	08 33	08 54	09 19
54	17 17	17 53	18 34	08 12	08 31	08 51	09 14
56	17 13	17 51	18 34	08 12	08 29	08 47	09 08
58	17 09	17 49	18 35	08 13	08 28	08 43	09 02
S 60	17 05	17 47	18 36	08 13	08 26	08 39	08 55

SUN / MOON

Day	SUN Eqn. of Time 00h	12h	Mer. Pass.	MOON Mer. Pass. Upper	Lower	Age	Phase
d	m s	m s	h m	h m	h m	d	%
29	01 05	00 56	12 01	01 56	14 18	18	91
30	00 47	00 38	12 01	02 40	15 03	19	85
31	00 28	00 19	12 00	03 26	15 49	20	77

UT	ARIES GHA	VENUS −4·6 GHA	Dec	MARS −2·1 GHA	Dec	JUPITER −1·9 GHA	Dec	SATURN +0·4 GHA	Dec	STARS Name	SHA	Dec
d h	° ′	° ′	° ′	° ′	° ′	° ′	° ′	° ′	° ′		° ′	° ′
1 00	340 06.5	139 34.5	S12 06.3	37 57.3	S25 57.1	115 09.4	S16 08.4	67 19.6	S22 41.6	Acamar	315 15.5	S40 13.7
01	355 08.9	154 35.2	07.3	52 59.7	56.9	130 11.5	08.5	82 22.1	41.6	Achernar	335 23.8	S57 08.4
02	10 11.4	169 35.8	08.4	68 02.0	56.7	145 13.6	08.6	97 24.5	41.6	Acrux	173 05.9	S63 12.1
03	25 13.9	184 36.4 ..	09.5	83 04.3 ..	56.6	160 15.7 ..	08.7	112 27.0 ..	41.6	Adhara	255 10.0	S28 59.7
04	40 16.3	199 37.0	10.5	98 06.7	56.4	175 17.9	08.9	127 29.5	41.7	Aldebaran	290 45.3	N16 32.6
05	55 18.8	214 37.6	11.6	113 09.0	56.2	190 20.0	09.0	142 32.0	41.7			
06	70 21.3	229 38.3	S12 12.6	128 11.3	S25 56.1	205 22.1	S16 09.1	157 34.5	S22 41.7	Alioth	166 18.1	N55 51.9
S 07	85 23.7	244 38.9	13.7	143 13.7	55.9	220 24.2	09.2	172 37.0	41.7	Alkaid	152 56.5	N49 13.6
A 08	100 26.2	259 39.5	14.7	158 16.0	55.7	235 26.3	09.3	187 39.5	41.7	Al Na'ir	27 38.9	S46 52.2
T 09	115 28.7	274 40.1 ..	15.8	173 18.3 ..	55.6	250 28.5 ..	09.4	202 42.0 ..	41.7	Alnilam	275 42.9	S 1 11.4
U 10	130 31.1	289 40.8	16.8	188 20.6	55.4	265 30.6	09.5	217 44.4	41.7	Alphard	217 52.9	S 8 44.3
R 11	145 33.6	304 41.4	17.9	203 22.9	55.2	280 32.7	09.6	232 46.9	41.7			
D 12	160 36.0	319 42.0	S12 18.9	218 25.3	S25 55.0	295 34.8	S16 09.7	247 49.4	S22 41.7	Alphecca	126 08.1	N26 39.5
A 13	175 38.5	334 42.7	20.0	233 27.6	54.9	310 37.0	09.8	262 51.9	41.7	Alpheratz	357 39.5	N29 11.6
Y 14	190 41.0	349 43.3	21.0	248 29.9	54.7	325 39.1	09.9	277 54.4	41.7	Altair	62 04.6	N 8 55.3
15	205 43.4	4 43.9 ..	22.1	263 32.2 ..	54.5	340 41.2 ..	10.0	292 56.9 ..	41.7	Ankaa	353 11.8	S42 12.2
16	220 45.9	19 44.6	23.1	278 34.5	54.3	355 43.3	10.1	307 59.4	41.7	Antares	112 21.9	S26 28.2
17	235 48.4	34 45.2	24.2	293 36.8	54.2	10 45.4	10.2	323 01.8	41.7			
18	250 50.8	49 45.8	S12 25.2	308 39.2	S25 54.0	25 47.6	S16 10.3	338 04.3	S22 41.7	Arcturus	145 52.7	N19 05.5
19	265 53.3	64 46.5	26.3	323 41.5	53.8	40 49.7	10.4	353 06.8	41.7	Atria	107 20.5	S69 03.7
20	280 55.8	79 47.1	27.3	338 43.8	53.7	55 51.8	10.5	8 09.3	41.8	Avior	234 17.1	S59 34.0
21	295 58.2	94 47.8 ..	28.4	353 46.1 ..	53.5	70 53.9 ..	10.6	23 11.8 ..	41.8	Bellatrix	278 28.3	N 6 21.9
22	311 00.7	109 48.4	29.4	8 48.4	53.3	85 56.0	10.7	38 14.3	41.8	Betelgeuse	270 57.6	N 7 24.6
23	326 03.2	124 49.0	30.5	23 50.7	53.1	100 58.2	10.9	53 16.7	41.8			
2 00	341 05.6	139 49.7	S12 31.5	38 53.0	S25 52.9	116 00.3	S16 11.0	68 19.2	S22 41.8	Canopus	263 54.8	S52 42.2
01	356 08.1	154 50.3	32.6	53 55.3	52.8	131 02.4	11.1	83 21.7	41.8	Capella	280 29.3	N46 00.7
02	11 10.5	169 51.0	33.6	68 57.6	52.6	146 04.5	11.2	98 24.2	41.8	Deneb	49 28.7	N45 21.1
03	26 13.0	184 51.6 ..	34.6	83 59.9 ..	52.4	161 06.6 ..	11.3	113 26.7 ..	41.8	Denebola	182 30.4	N14 28.3
04	41 15.5	199 52.3	35.7	99 02.2	52.2	176 08.8	11.4	128 29.2	41.8	Diphda	348 52.1	S17 53.0
05	56 17.9	214 52.9	36.7	114 04.5	52.1	191 10.9	11.5	143 31.6	41.8			
06	71 20.4	229 53.6	S12 37.8	129 06.8	S25 51.9	206 13.0	S16 11.6	158 34.1	S22 41.8	Dubhe	193 48.1	N61 39.2
07	86 22.9	244 54.2	38.8	144 09.0	51.7	221 15.1	11.7	173 36.6	41.8	Elnath	278 08.2	N28 37.2
08	101 25.3	259 54.9	39.9	159 11.3	51.5	236 17.2	11.8	188 39.1	41.8	Eltanin	90 44.3	N51 29.6
S 09	116 27.8	274 55.5 ..	40.9	174 13.6 ..	51.3	251 19.4 ..	11.9	203 41.6 ..	41.8	Enif	33 43.3	N 9 57.8
U 10	131 30.3	289 56.2	41.9	189 15.9	51.2	266 21.5	12.0	218 44.1	41.8	Fomalhaut	15 19.7	S29 31.3
N 11	146 32.7	304 56.8	43.0	204 18.2	51.0	281 23.6	12.1	233 46.5	41.9			
D 12	161 35.2	319 57.5	S12 44.0	219 20.5	S25 50.8	296 25.7	S16 12.2	248 49.0	S22 41.9	Gacrux	171 57.4	S57 13.0
A 13	176 37.7	334 58.1	45.0	234 22.8	50.6	311 27.8	12.3	263 51.5	41.9	Gienah	175 49.0	S17 38.5
Y 14	191 40.1	349 58.8	46.1	249 25.0	50.4	326 29.9	12.4	278 54.0	41.9	Hadar	148 43.2	S60 27.8
15	206 42.6	4 59.4 ..	47.1	264 27.3 ..	50.3	341 32.1 ..	12.5	293 56.5 ..	41.9	Hamal	327 56.5	N23 32.9
16	221 45.0	20 00.1	48.2	279 29.6	50.1	356 34.2	12.7	308 58.9	41.9	Kaus Aust.	83 39.0	S34 22.4
17	236 47.5	35 00.8	49.2	294 31.9	49.9	11 36.3	12.8	324 01.4	41.9			
18	251 50.0	50 01.4	S12 50.2	309 34.1	S25 49.7	26 38.4	S16 12.9	339 03.9	S22 41.9	Kochab	137 20.7	N74 05.2
19	266 52.4	65 02.1	51.3	324 36.4	49.5	41 40.5	13.0	354 06.4	41.9	Markab	13 34.5	N15 18.4
20	281 54.9	80 02.8	52.3	339 38.7	49.3	56 42.6	13.1	9 08.9	41.9	Menkar	314 11.2	N 4 09.7
21	296 57.4	95 03.4 ..	53.4	354 41.0 ..	49.2	71 44.8 ..	13.2	24 11.3 ..	41.9	Menkent	148 03.6	S36 27.6
22	311 59.8	110 04.1	54.4	9 43.2	49.0	86 46.9	13.3	39 13.8	41.9	Miaplacidus	221 39.8	S69 47.5
23	327 02.3	125 04.7	55.4	24 45.5	48.8	101 49.0	13.4	54 16.3	41.9			
3 00	342 04.8	140 05.4	S12 56.4	39 47.8	S25 48.6	116 51.1	S16 13.5	69 18.8	S22 41.9	Mirfak	308 35.1	N49 55.3
01	357 07.2	155 06.1	57.5	54 50.0	48.4	131 53.2	13.6	84 21.3	41.9	Nunki	75 53.7	S26 16.3
02	12 09.7	170 06.8	58.5	69 52.3	48.2	146 55.3	13.7	99 23.7	41.9	Peacock	53 13.2	S56 40.5
03	27 12.1	185 07.4	12 59.5	84 54.6 ..	48.1	161 57.4 ..	13.8	114 26.2 ..	42.0	Pollux	243 23.7	N27 58.8
04	42 14.6	200 08.1	13 00.5	99 56.8	47.9	176 59.6	13.9	129 28.7	42.0	Procyon	244 56.3	N 5 10.6
05	57 17.1	215 08.8	01.6	114 59.1	47.7	192 01.7	14.0	144 31.2	42.0			
06	72 19.5	230 09.4	S13 02.6	130 01.3	S25 47.5	207 03.8	S16 14.1	159 33.7	S22 42.0	Rasalhague	96 03.1	N12 33.1
07	87 22.0	245 10.1	03.6	145 03.6	47.3	222 05.9	14.3	174 36.1	42.0	Regulus	207 40.1	N11 52.7
08	102 24.5	260 10.8	04.7	160 05.8	47.1	237 08.0	14.4	189 38.6	42.0	Rigel	281 08.7	S 8 10.8
M 09	117 26.9	275 11.5 ..	05.7	175 08.1 ..	46.9	252 10.1 ..	14.5	204 41.1 ..	42.0	Rigil Kent.	139 47.2	S60 54.7
O 10	132 29.4	290 12.1	06.7	190 10.3	46.7	267 12.2	14.6	219 43.6	42.0	Sabik	102 08.4	S15 44.7
N 11	147 31.9	305 12.8	07.7	205 12.6	46.5	282 14.3	14.7	234 46.0	42.0			
D 12	162 34.3	320 13.5	S13 08.8	220 14.8	S25 46.4	297 16.5	S16 14.8	249 48.5	S22 42.0	Schedar	349 36.0	N56 38.2
A 13	177 36.8	335 14.2	09.8	235 17.1	46.2	312 18.6	14.9	264 51.0	42.0	Shaula	96 17.0	S37 06.9
Y 14	192 39.3	350 14.9	10.8	250 19.3	46.0	327 20.7	15.0	279 53.5	42.0	Sirius	258 30.8	S16 44.4
15	207 41.7	5 15.6 ..	11.8	265 21.6 ..	45.8	342 22.8 ..	15.1	294 56.0 ..	42.0	Spica	158 27.8	S11 15.3
16	222 44.2	20 16.2	12.9	280 23.8	45.6	357 24.9	15.2	309 58.4	42.0	Suhail	222 50.2	S43 30.3
17	237 46.6	35 16.9	13.9	295 26.1	45.4	12 27.0	15.3	325 00.9	42.0			
18	252 49.1	50 17.6	S13 14.9	310 28.3	S25 45.2	27 29.1	S16 15.4	340 03.4	S22 42.0	Vega	80 36.4	N38 48.5
19	267 51.6	65 18.3	15.9	325 30.5	45.0	42 31.2	15.5	355 05.9	42.1	Zuben'ubi	137 01.6	S16 06.9
20	282 54.0	80 19.0	16.9	340 32.8	44.8	57 33.3	15.6	10 08.3	42.1		SHA	Mer.Pass.
21	297 56.5	95 19.7 ..	18.0	355 35.0 ..	44.6	72 35.4 ..	15.8	25 10.8 ..	42.1		° ′	h m
22	312 59.0	110 20.4	19.0	10 37.2	44.4	87 37.6	15.9	40 13.3	42.1	Venus	158 44.1	14 40
23	328 01.4	125 21.1	20.0	25 39.5	44.2	102 39.7	16.0	55 15.8	42.1	Mars	57 47.4	21 21
	h m									Jupiter	134 54.7	16 14
Mer. Pass.	1 15.4	*v* 0.7	*d* 1.0	*v* 2.3 *d* 0.2		*v* 2.1 *d* 0.1		*v* 2.5 *d* 0.0		Saturn	87 13.6	19 24

UT	SUN GHA	SUN Dec	MOON GHA	v	MOON Dec	d	HP
d h	° ′	° ′	° ′	′	° ′	′	′
1 00	179 57.7	N 8 22.4	298 43.9	11.7	N10 34.3	10.2	57.0
01	194 57.9	21.5	313 14.6	11.7	10 44.5	10.0	57.0
02	209 58.1	20.6	327 45.3	11.7	10 54.5	10.1	57.0
03	224 58.3 ..	19.7	342 16.0	11.5	11 04.6	10.0	57.1
04	239 58.5	18.8	356 46.5	11.6	11 14.6	9.9	57.1
05	254 58.7	17.9	11 17.1	11.4	11 24.5	9.9	57.1
06	269 58.9	N 8 17.0	25 47.5	11.4	N11 34.4	9.8	57.1
07	284 59.1	16.1	40 17.9	11.3	11 44.2	9.8	57.2
S 08	299 59.3	15.2	54 48.2	11.3	11 54.0	9.7	57.2
A 09	314 59.5 ..	14.3	69 18.5	11.2	12 03.7	9.7	57.2
T 10	329 59.7	13.4	83 48.7	11.1	12 13.4	9.7	57.2
U 11	344 59.9	12.5	98 18.8	11.0	12 23.1	9.5	57.3
R 12	0 00.0	N 8 11.6	112 48.8	11.0	N12 32.6	9.5	57.3
D 13	15 00.3	10.7	127 18.8	10.9	12 42.1	9.5	57.3
A 14	30 00.5	09.8	141 48.7	10.9	12 51.6	9.4	57.3
Y 15	45 00.7 ..	08.8	156 18.6	10.7	13 01.0	9.3	57.4
16	60 00.9	07.9	170 48.3	10.7	13 10.3	9.3	57.4
17	75 01.1	07.0	185 18.0	10.6	13 19.6	9.2	57.4
18	90 01.3	N 8 06.1	199 47.6	10.6	N13 28.8	9.2	57.5
19	105 01.5	05.2	214 17.2	10.5	13 38.0	9.1	57.5
20	120 01.7	04.3	228 46.7	10.4	13 47.1	9.0	57.5
21	135 01.9 ..	03.4	243 16.1	10.3	13 56.1	9.0	57.5
22	150 02.1	02.5	257 45.4	10.3	14 05.1	8.9	57.6
23	165 02.3	01.6	272 14.7	10.2	14 14.0	8.8	57.6
2 00	180 02.5	N 8 00.7	286 43.9	10.1	N14 22.8	8.8	57.6
01	195 02.7	7 59.8	301 13.0	10.0	14 31.6	8.6	57.6
02	210 02.9	58.8	315 42.0	10.0	14 40.2	8.7	57.7
03	225 03.1 ..	57.9	330 11.0	9.9	14 48.9	8.5	57.7
04	240 03.3	57.0	344 39.9	9.8	14 57.4	8.5	57.7
05	255 03.5	56.1	359 08.7	9.7	15 05.9	8.4	57.8
06	270 03.7	N 7 55.2	13 37.4	9.7	N15 14.3	8.3	57.8
07	285 03.9	54.3	28 06.1	9.6	15 22.6	8.2	57.8
S 08	300 04.1	53.4	42 34.7	9.5	15 30.8	8.2	57.8
U 09	315 04.3 ..	52.5	57 03.2	9.4	15 39.0	8.1	57.9
N 10	330 04.5	51.6	71 31.6	9.4	15 47.1	8.0	57.9
D 11	345 04.7	50.6	86 00.0	9.2	15 55.1	7.9	57.9
A 12	0 04.9	N 7 49.7	100 28.2	9.2	N16 03.0	7.8	58.0
Y 13	15 05.1	48.8	114 56.4	9.1	16 10.8	7.8	58.0
14	30 05.3	47.9	129 24.5	9.1	16 18.6	7.6	58.0
15	45 05.5 ..	47.0	143 52.6	8.9	16 26.2	7.6	58.0
16	60 05.7	46.1	158 20.5	8.9	16 33.8	7.5	58.1
17	75 05.9	45.2	172 48.4	8.8	16 41.3	7.4	58.1
18	90 06.1	N 7 44.2	187 16.2	8.7	N16 48.7	7.3	58.1
19	105 06.3	43.3	201 43.9	8.7	16 56.0	7.2	58.2
20	120 06.5	42.4	216 11.6	8.6	17 03.2	7.2	58.2
21	135 06.7 ..	41.5	230 39.2	8.4	17 10.4	7.0	58.2
22	150 06.9	40.6	245 06.6	8.5	17 17.4	7.0	58.2
23	165 07.1	39.7	259 34.1	8.3	17 24.4	6.8	58.3
3 00	180 07.3	N 7 38.8	274 01.4	8.2	N17 31.2	6.8	58.3
01	195 07.5	37.8	288 28.6	8.2	17 38.0	6.6	58.3
02	210 07.7	36.9	302 55.8	8.1	17 44.6	6.6	58.4
03	225 07.9 ..	36.0	317 22.9	8.0	17 51.2	6.4	58.4
04	240 08.1	35.1	331 49.9	8.0	17 57.6	6.4	58.4
05	255 08.4	34.2	346 16.9	7.8	18 04.0	6.2	58.4
06	270 08.6	N 7 33.3	0 43.7	7.8	N18 10.2	6.2	58.5
07	285 08.8	32.3	15 10.5	7.7	18 16.4	6.0	58.5
M 08	300 09.0	31.4	29 37.2	7.6	18 22.4	6.0	58.5
O 09	315 09.2 ..	30.5	44 03.8	7.6	18 28.4	5.8	58.6
N 10	330 09.4	29.6	58 30.4	7.5	18 34.2	5.7	58.6
D 11	345 09.6	28.7	72 56.9	7.4	18 39.9	5.6	58.6
A 12	0 09.8	N 7 27.8	87 23.3	7.3	N18 45.5	5.5	58.6
Y 13	15 10.0	26.8	101 49.6	7.3	18 51.0	5.4	58.7
14	30 10.2	25.9	116 15.9	7.1	18 56.4	5.3	58.7
15	45 10.4 ..	25.0	130 42.0	7.1	19 01.7	5.2	58.7
16	60 10.6	24.1	145 08.1	7.1	19 06.9	5.0	58.8
17	75 10.8	23.2	159 34.2	6.9	19 11.9	5.0	58.8
18	90 11.0	N 7 22.2	174 00.1	6.9	N19 16.9	4.8	58.8
19	105 11.2	21.3	188 26.0	6.8	19 21.7	4.7	58.8
20	120 11.4	20.4	202 51.8	6.8	19 26.4	4.6	58.9
21	135 11.6 ..	19.5	217 17.6	6.6	19 31.0	4.4	58.9
22	150 11.8	18.6	231 43.2	6.6	19 35.4	4.4	58.9
23	165 12.0	17.6	246 08.8	6.6	N19 39.8	4.2	59.0
	SD 15.9	d 0.9	SD 15.6		15.8		16.0

Twilight / Sunrise / Moonrise

Lat.	Naut.	Civil	Sunrise	Moonrise 1	2	3	4
°	h m	h m	h m	h m	h m	h m	h m
N 72	////	02 37	04 06	19 32	19 00	▭	▭
N 70	////	03 04	04 19	19 58	19 49	19 33	
68	01 39	03 24	04 29	20 17	20 20	20 29	20 54
66	02 15	03 40	04 38	20 33	20 43	21 02	21 39
64	02 40	03 53	04 45	20 46	21 02	21 27	22 08
62	02 59	04 03	04 52	20 57	21 17	21 47	22 33
60	03 14	04 12	04 57	21 06	21 30	22 03	22 49
N 58	03 27	04 20	05 02	21 15	21 41	22 16	23 04
56	03 37	04 27	05 06	21 22	21 51	22 28	23 17
54	03 46	04 33	05 10	21 29	21 59	22 38	23 28
52	03 55	04 38	05 13	21 34	22 07	22 47	23 38
50	04 02	04 43	05 16	21 40	22 14	22 56	23 47
45	04 16	04 53	05 23	21 51	22 29	23 13	24 06
N 40	04 28	05 01	05 28	22 01	22 41	23 27	24 22
35	04 37	05 07	05 33	22 09	22 51	23 40	24 35
30	04 44	05 13	05 37	22 17	23 01	23 50	24 46
20	04 56	05 22	05 45	22 29	23 17	24 09	00 09
N 10	05 05	05 29	05 51	22 41	23 31	24 25	00 25
0	05 11	05 36	05 56	22 51	23 44	24 40	00 40
S 10	05 16	05 41	06 02	23 02	23 57	24 55	00 55
20	05 20	05 46	06 08	23 13	24 11	00 11	01 11
30	05 22	05 50	06 14	23 26	24 28	00 28	01 30
35	05 23	05 53	06 18	23 34	24 37	00 37	01 41
40	05 24	05 55	06 22	23 43	24 48	00 48	01 54
45	05 24	05 57	06 27	23 53	25 01	01 01	02 08
S 50	05 23	06 00	06 33	24 05	00 05	01 17	02 27
52	05 22	06 01	06 35	24 11	00 11	01 24	02 35
54	05 22	06 02	06 38	24 18	00 18	01 33	02 45
56	05 21	06 04	06 41	24 25	00 25	01 42	02 56
58	05 20	06 05	06 45	24 33	00 33	01 52	03 08
S 60	05 19	06 07	06 49	24 42	00 42	02 05	03 23

Sunset / Twilight / Moonset

Lat.	Sunset	Civil	Naut.	Moonset 1	2	3	4
°	h m	h m	h m	h m	h m	h m	h m
N 72	19 50	21 16	////	13 26	15 46	▭	▭
N 70	19 38	20 51	23 17	13 02	14 58	17 09	▭
68	19 28	20 32	22 13	12 44	14 28	16 13	17 50
66	19 19	20 17	21 39	12 29	14 05	15 40	17 05
64	19 12	20 04	21 16	12 17	13 47	15 16	16 36
62	19 06	19 54	20 58	12 07	13 33	14 57	16 13
60	19 01	19 45	20 43	11 58	13 21	14 41	15 55
N 58	18 56	19 38	20 31	11 51	13 10	14 28	15 27...
56	18 52	19 31	20 20	11 44	13 01	14 17	15 27
54	18 48	19 25	20 11	11 38	12 53	14 07	15 16
52	18 45	19 20	20 03	11 33	12 46	13 58	15 06
50	18 42	19 16	19 56	11 28	12 39	13 50	14 57
45	18 36	19 06	19 42	11 18	12 25	13 33	14 39
N 40	18 30	18 58	19 31	11 09	12 14	13 19	14 24
35	18 26	18 51	19 22	11 02	12 04	13 08	14 11
30	18 21	18 46	19 14	10 55	11 56	12 57	13 59
20	18 15	18 37	19 03	10 44	11 41	12 40	13 40
N 10	18 09	18 30	18 54	10 34	11 28	12 25	13 23
0	18 03	18 24	18 48	10 25	11 16	12 10	13 08
S 10	17 58	18 19	18 43	10 16	11 04	11 56	12 52
20	17 52	18 14	18 40	10 06	10 51	11 41	12 35
30	17 45	18 10	18 37	09 55	10 37	11 23	12 16
35	17 42	18 07	18 37	09 49	10 28	11 13	12 05
40	17 38	18 05	18 36	09 42	10 19	11 02	11 52
45	17 33	18 03	18 37	09 33	10 08	10 48	11 36
S 50	17 28	18 00	18 38	09 23	09 54	10 31	11 18
52	17 25	17 59	18 38	09 19	09 48	10 24	11 09
54	17 22	17 58	18 39	09 14	09 41	10 15	10 59
56	17 19	17 57	18 40	09 08	09 33	10 05	10 48
58	17 16	17 55	18 41	09 02	09 24	09 54	10 35
S 60	17 12	17 54	18 42	08 55	09 15	09 42	10 20

SUN / MOON

Day	Eqn. of Time 00h	12h	Mer. Pass.	Mer. Pass. Upper	Lower	Age	Phase
d	m s	m s	h m	h m	h m	d	%
1	00 10	00 00	12 00	04 13	16 38	21	67
2	00 10	00 19	12 00	05 04	17 30	22	57
3	00 29	00 39	11 59	05 57	18 25	23	46

UT	ARIES GHA	VENUS −4.7 GHA	Dec	MARS −2.0 GHA	Dec	JUPITER −1.9 GHA	Dec	SATURN +0.4 GHA	Dec	STARS Name	SHA	Dec
TUESDAY												
4 00	343 03.9	140 21.8	S13 21.0	40 41.7	S25 44.1	117 41.8	S16 16.1	70 18.2	S22 42.1	Acamar	315 15.5	S40 13.7
01	358 06.4	155 22.5	22.0	55 43.9	43.9	132 43.9	16.2	85 20.7	42.1	Achernar	335 23.7	S57 08.4
02	13 08.8	170 23.1	23.1	70 46.2	43.7	147 46.0	16.3	100 23.2	42.1	Acrux	173 05.9	S63 12.1
03	28 11.3	185 23.8 ..	24.1	85 48.4 ..	43.5	162 48.1 ..	16.4	115 25.7 ..	42.1	Adhara	255 09.9	S28 59.7
04	43 13.8	200 24.5	25.1	100 50.6	43.3	177 50.2	16.5	130 28.1	42.1	Aldebaran	290 45.3	N16 32.7
05	58 16.2	215 25.2	26.1	115 52.8	43.1	192 52.3	16.6	145 30.6	42.1			
06	73 18.7	230 25.9	S13 27.1	130 55.1	S25 42.9	207 54.4	S16 16.7	160 33.1	S22 42.1	Alioth	166 18.1	N55 51.8
07	88 21.1	245 26.6	28.1	145 57.3	42.7	222 56.5	16.8	175 35.6	42.1	Alkaid	152 56.5	N49 13.6
08	103 23.6	260 27.3	29.1	160 59.5	42.5	237 58.6	16.9	190 38.0	42.1	Al Na'ir	27 38.9	S46 52.2
09	118 26.1	275 28.0 ..	30.2	176 01.7 ..	42.3	253 00.8 ..	17.0	205 40.5 ..	42.1	Alnilam	275 42.8	S 1 11.4
10	133 28.5	290 28.8	31.2	191 03.9	42.1	268 02.9	17.2	220 43.0	42.1	Alphard	217 52.9	S 8 44.3
11	148 31.0	305 29.5	32.2	206 06.2	41.9	283 05.0	17.3	235 45.4	42.2			
12	163 33.5	320 30.2	S13 33.2	221 08.4	S25 41.7	298 07.1	S16 17.4	250 47.9	S22 42.2	Alphecca	126 08.1	N26 39.5
13	178 35.9	335 30.9	34.2	236 10.6	41.5	313 09.2	17.5	265 50.4	42.2	Alpheratz	357 39.5	N29 11.6
14	193 38.4	350 31.6	35.2	251 12.8	41.3	328 11.3	17.6	280 52.9	42.2	Altair	62 04.6	N 8 55.3
15	208 40.9	5 32.3 ..	36.2	266 15.0 ..	41.1	343 13.4 ..	17.7	295 55.3 ..	42.2	Ankaa	353 11.8	S42 12.2
16	223 43.3	20 33.0	37.2	281 17.2	40.9	358 15.5	17.8	310 57.8	42.2	Antares	112 21.9	S26 28.2
17	238 45.8	35 33.7	38.2	296 19.4	40.7	13 17.6	17.9	326 00.3	42.2			
18	253 48.3	50 34.4	S13 39.2	311 21.6	S25 40.5	28 19.7	S16 18.0	341 02.8	S22 42.2	Arcturus	145 52.7	N19 05.5
19	268 50.7	65 35.1	40.2	326 23.8	40.3	43 21.8	18.1	356 05.2	42.2	Atria	107 20.5	S69 03.7
20	283 53.2	80 35.9	41.3	341 26.0	40.1	58 23.9	18.2	11 07.7	42.2	Avior	234 17.1	S59 34.0
21	298 55.6	95 36.6 ..	42.3	356 28.2 ..	39.9	73 26.0 ..	18.3	26 10.2 ..	42.2	Bellatrix	278 28.3	N 6 21.9
22	313 58.1	110 37.3	43.3	11 30.4	39.7	88 28.1	18.5	41 12.6	42.2	Betelgeuse	270 57.6	N 7 24.6
23	329 00.6	125 38.0	44.3	26 32.6	39.5	103 30.2	18.6	56 15.1	42.2			
WEDNESDAY												
5 00	344 03.0	140 38.7	S13 45.3	41 34.8	S25 39.3	118 32.3	S16 18.7	71 17.6	S22 42.2	Canopus	263 54.8	S52 42.2
01	359 05.5	155 39.5	46.3	56 37.0	39.1	133 34.4	18.8	86 20.1	42.2	Capella	280 29.3	N46 00.7
02	14 08.0	170 40.2	47.3	71 39.2	38.9	148 36.5	18.9	101 22.5	42.2	Deneb	49 28.7	N45 21.1
03	29 10.4	185 40.9 ..	48.3	86 41.4 ..	38.7	163 38.7 ..	19.0	116 25.0 ..	42.3	Denebola	182 30.4	N14 28.3
04	44 12.9	200 41.6	49.3	101 43.6	38.5	178 40.8	19.1	131 27.5	42.3	Diphda	348 52.1	S17 53.0
05	59 15.4	215 42.3	50.3	116 45.8	38.3	193 42.9	19.2	146 29.9	42.3			
06	74 17.8	230 43.1	S13 51.3	131 48.0	S25 38.1	208 45.0	S16 19.3	161 32.4	S22 42.3	Dubhe	193 48.1	N61 39.1
07	89 20.3	245 43.8	52.3	146 50.2	37.9	223 47.1	19.4	176 34.9	42.3	Elnath	278 08.2	N28 37.2
08	104 22.7	260 44.5	53.3	161 52.4	37.7	238 49.2	19.5	191 37.3	42.3	Eltanin	90 44.3	N51 29.6
09	119 25.2	275 45.3 ..	54.3	176 54.5 ..	37.5	253 51.3 ..	19.7	206 39.8 ..	42.3	Enif	33 43.3	N 9 57.8
10	134 27.7	290 46.0	55.3	191 56.7	37.3	268 53.4	19.8	221 42.3	42.3	Fomalhaut	15 19.7	S29 31.3
11	149 30.1	305 46.7	56.3	206 58.9	37.0	283 55.5	19.9	236 44.7	42.3			
12	164 32.6	320 47.5	S13 57.3	222 01.1	S25 36.8	298 57.6	S16 20.0	251 47.2	S22 42.3	Gacrux	171 57.4	S57 13.0
13	179 35.1	335 48.2	58.3	237 03.2	36.6	313 59.7	20.1	266 49.7	42.3	Gienah	175 49.0	S17 38.5
14	194 37.5	350 48.9	13 59.3	252 05.4	36.4	329 01.8	20.2	281 52.1	42.3	Hadar	148 43.2	S60 27.8
15	209 40.0	5 49.7	14 00.3	267 07.6 ..	36.2	344 03.9 ..	20.3	296 54.6 ..	42.3	Hamal	327 56.5	N23 32.9
16	224 42.5	20 50.4	01.3	282 09.8	36.0	359 06.0	20.4	311 57.1	42.3	Kaus Aust.	83 39.0	S34 22.4
17	239 44.9	35 51.2	02.2	297 11.9	35.8	14 08.1	20.5	326 59.6	42.3			
18	254 47.4	50 51.9	S14 03.2	312 14.1	S25 35.6	29 10.2	S16 20.6	342 02.0	S22 42.3	Kochab	137 20.7	N74 05.2
19	269 49.9	65 52.6	04.2	327 16.3	35.4	44 12.3	20.8	357 04.5	42.4	Markab	13 34.5	N15 18.4
20	284 52.3	80 53.4	05.2	342 18.4	35.2	59 14.4	20.9	12 07.0	42.4	Menkar	314 11.2	N 4 09.7
21	299 54.8	95 54.1 ..	06.2	357 20.6 ..	35.0	74 16.5 ..	21.0	27 09.4 ..	42.4	Menkent	148 03.6	S36 27.6
22	314 57.2	110 54.9	07.2	12 22.8	34.8	89 18.6	21.1	42 11.9	42.4	Miaplacidus	221 39.8	S69 47.5
23	329 59.7	125 55.6	08.2	27 24.9	34.5	104 20.7	21.2	57 14.4	42.4			
THURSDAY												
6 00	345 02.2	140 56.4	S14 09.2	42 27.1	S25 34.3	119 22.8	S16 21.3	72 16.8	S22 42.4	Mirfak	308 35.1	N49 55.3
01	0 04.6	155 57.1	10.2	57 29.3	34.1	134 24.9	21.4	87 19.3	42.4	Nunki	75 53.7	S26 16.3
02	15 07.1	170 57.9	11.2	72 31.4	33.9	149 27.0	21.5	102 21.8	42.4	Peacock	53 13.2	S56 40.5
03	30 09.6	185 58.6 ..	12.1	87 33.6 ..	33.7	164 29.1 ..	21.6	117 24.2 ..	42.4	Pollux	243 23.7	N27 58.8
04	45 12.0	200 59.4	13.1	102 35.7	33.5	179 31.2	21.7	132 26.7	42.4	Procyon	244 56.3	N 5 10.6
05	60 14.5	216 00.1	14.1	117 37.9	33.3	194 33.3	21.8	147 29.1	42.4			
06	75 17.0	231 00.9	S14 15.1	132 40.0	S25 33.1	209 35.4	S16 22.0	162 31.6	S22 42.4	Rasalhague	96 03.1	N12 33.1
07	90 19.4	246 01.6	16.1	147 42.2	32.9	224 37.5	22.1	177 34.1	42.4	Regulus	207 40.1	N11 52.7
08	105 21.9	261 02.4	17.1	162 44.3	32.6	239 39.6	22.2	192 36.5	42.4	Rigel	281 08.7	S 8 10.8
09	120 24.4	276 03.2 ..	18.1	177 46.5 ..	32.4	254 41.7 ..	22.3	207 39.0 ..	42.4	Rigil Kent.	139 47.3	S60 54.7
10	135 26.8	291 03.9	19.0	192 48.6	32.2	269 43.8	22.4	222 41.5	42.4	Sabik	102 08.4	S15 44.7
11	150 29.3	306 04.7	20.0	207 50.8	32.0	284 45.9	22.5	237 43.9	42.5			
12	165 31.7	321 05.4	S14 21.0	222 52.9	S25 31.8	299 48.0	S16 22.6	252 46.4	S22 42.5	Schedar	349 35.9	N56 38.2
13	180 34.2	336 06.2	22.0	237 55.1	31.6	314 50.1	22.7	267 48.9	42.5	Shaula	96 17.0	S37 06.9
14	195 36.7	351 07.0	23.0	252 57.2	31.3	329 52.1	22.8	282 51.3	42.5	Sirius	258 30.8	S16 44.4
15	210 39.1	6 07.7 ..	23.9	267 59.4 ..	31.1	344 54.2 ..	23.0	297 53.8 ..	42.5	Spica	158 27.8	S11 15.3
16	225 41.6	21 08.5	24.9	283 01.5	30.9	359 56.3	23.1	312 56.3	42.5	Suhail	222 50.2	S43 30.3
17	240 44.1	36 09.3	25.9	298 03.6	30.7	14 58.4	23.2	327 58.7	42.5			
18	255 46.5	51 10.0	S14 26.9	313 05.8	S25 30.5	30 00.5	S16 23.3	343 01.2	S22 42.5	Vega	80 36.4	N38 48.5
19	270 49.0	66 10.8	27.9	328 07.9	30.3	45 02.6	23.4	358 03.6	42.5	Zuben'ubi	137 01.6	S16 06.9
20	285 51.5	81 11.6	28.8	343 10.0	30.0	60 04.7	23.5	13 06.1	42.5		SHA	Mer. Pass.
21	300 53.9	96 12.4 ..	29.8	358 12.2 ..	29.8	75 06.8 ..	23.6	28 08.6 ..	42.5	Venus	156 35.7	14 37
22	315 56.4	111 13.1	30.8	13 14.3	29.6	90 08.9	23.7	43 11.0	42.5	Mars	57 31.8	21 11
23	330 58.9	126 13.9	31.8	28 16.4	29.4	105 11.0	23.8	58 13.5	42.5	Jupiter	134 29.3	16 04
Mer. Pass.	h m 1 03.6	v 0.7	d 1.0	v 2.2	d 0.2	v 2.1	d 0.1	v 2.5	d 0.0	Saturn	87 14.5	19 12

UT	SUN GHA	Dec	MOON GHA	v	Dec	d	HP
d h	° ′	° ′	° ′	′	° ′	′	′
4 00	180 12.2	N 7 16.7	260 34.4	6.4	N19 44.0	4.1	59.0
01	195 12.4	15.8	274 59.8	6.4	19 48.1	4.0	59.0
02	210 12.6	14.9	289 25.2	6.4	19 52.1	3.9	59.0
03	225 12.9	.. 14.0	303 50.6	6.2	19 56.0	3.7	59.1
04	240 13.1	13.0	318 15.8	6.2	19 59.7	3.6	59.1
05	255 13.3	12.1	332 41.0	6.2	20 03.3	3.5	59.1
06	270 13.5	N 7 11.2	347 06.2	6.0	N20 06.8	3.3	59.2
07	285 13.7	10.3	1 31.2	6.0	20 10.1	3.2	59.2
T 08	300 13.9	09.4	15 56.2	6.0	20 13.3	3.1	59.2
U 09	315 14.1	.. 08.4	30 21.2	5.9	20 16.4	3.0	59.2
E 10	330 14.3	07.5	44 46.1	5.8	20 19.4	2.8	59.3
S 11	345 14.5	06.6	59 10.9	5.8	20 22.2	2.7	59.3
D 12	0 14.7	N 7 05.7	73 35.7	5.7	N20 24.9	2.6	59.3
A 13	15 14.9	04.7	88 00.4	5.6	20 27.5	2.4	59.3
Y 14	30 15.1	03.8	102 25.0	5.6	20 29.9	2.3	59.4
15	45 15.3	.. 02.9	116 49.6	5.6	20 32.2	2.2	59.4
16	60 15.5	02.0	131 14.2	5.5	20 34.4	2.0	59.4
17	75 15.7	01.1	145 38.7	5.4	20 36.4	1.9	59.4
18	90 16.0	N 7 00.1	160 03.1	5.4	N20 38.3	1.7	59.5
19	105 16.2	6 59.2	174 27.5	5.4	20 40.0	1.6	59.5
20	120 16.4	58.3	188 51.9	5.3	20 41.6	1.5	59.5
21	135 16.6	.. 57.4	203 16.2	5.2	20 43.1	1.4	59.6
22	150 16.8	56.4	217 40.4	5.2	20 44.5	1.1	59.6
23	165 17.0	55.5	232 04.6	5.2	20 45.6	1.1	59.6
5 00	180 17.2	N 6 54.6	246 28.8	5.1	N20 46.7	0.9	59.6
01	195 17.4	53.7	260 52.9	5.1	20 47.6	0.8	59.7
02	210 17.6	52.7	275 17.0	5.0	20 48.4	0.6	59.7
03	225 17.8	.. 51.8	289 41.0	5.0	20 49.0	0.5	59.7
04	240 18.0	50.9	304 05.0	4.9	20 49.5	0.4	59.7
05	255 18.2	49.9	318 28.9	5.0	20 49.9	0.2	59.8
06	270 18.4	N 6 49.0	332 52.9	4.9	N20 50.1	0.0	59.8
W 07	285 18.7	48.1	347 16.8	4.8	20 50.1	0.1	59.8
E 08	300 18.9	47.2	1 40.6	4.8	20 50.0	0.2	59.8
D 09	315 19.1	.. 46.2	16 04.4	4.8	20 49.8	0.4	59.8
N 10	330 19.3	45.3	30 28.2	4.8	20 49.4	0.5	59.9
E 11	345 19.5	44.4	44 52.0	4.7	20 48.9	0.7	59.9
S 12	0 19.7	N 6 43.5	59 15.7	4.8	N20 48.2	0.8	59.9
D 13	15 19.9	42.5	73 39.5	4.7	20 47.4	0.9	59.9
A 14	30 20.1	41.6	88 03.2	4.6	20 46.5	1.1	60.0
Y 15	45 20.3	.. 40.7	102 26.8	4.7	20 45.4	1.3	60.0
16	60 20.5	39.7	116 50.5	4.6	20 44.1	1.4	60.0
17	75 20.7	38.8	131 14.1	4.6	20 42.7	1.5	60.0
18	90 21.0	N 6 37.9	145 37.7	4.6	N20 41.2	1.7	60.0
19	105 21.2	37.0	160 01.3	4.6	20 39.5	1.8	60.1
20	120 21.4	36.0	174 24.9	4.6	20 37.7	2.0	60.1
21	135 21.6	.. 35.1	188 48.5	4.5	20 35.7	2.2	60.1
22	150 21.8	34.2	203 12.0	4.6	20 33.5	2.2	60.1
23	165 22.0	33.2	217 35.6	4.5	20 31.3	2.5	60.1
6 00	180 22.2	N 6 32.3	231 59.1	4.5	N20 28.8	2.5	60.2
01	195 22.4	31.4	246 22.6	4.6	20 26.3	2.7	60.2
02	210 22.6	30.5	260 46.2	4.5	20 23.6	2.9	60.2
03	225 22.8	.. 29.5	275 09.7	4.5	20 20.7	3.0	60.2
04	240 23.1	28.6	289 33.2	4.5	20 17.7	3.2	60.2
05	255 23.3	27.7	303 56.7	4.5	20 14.5	3.3	60.3
06	270 23.5	N 6 26.7	318 20.2	4.6	N20 11.2	3.4	60.3
07	285 23.7	25.8	332 43.8	4.5	20 07.8	3.6	60.3
T 08	300 23.9	24.9	347 07.3	4.5	20 04.2	3.7	60.3
H 09	315 24.1	.. 23.9	1 30.8	4.6	20 00.5	3.9	60.3
U 10	330 24.3	23.0	15 54.4	4.5	19 56.6	4.0	60.3
R 11	345 24.5	22.1	30 17.9	4.6	19 52.6	4.2	60.4
S 12	0 24.7	N 6 21.1	44 41.5	4.6	N19 48.4	4.3	60.4
D 13	15 25.0	20.2	59 05.1	4.5	19 44.1	4.4	60.4
A 14	30 25.2	19.3	73 28.6	4.6	19 39.7	4.6	60.4
Y 15	45 25.4	.. 18.3	87 52.2	4.7	19 35.1	4.8	60.4
16	60 25.6	17.4	102 15.9	4.6	19 30.3	4.9	60.4
17	75 25.8	16.5	116 39.5	4.6	19 25.4	5.0	60.5
18	90 26.0	N 6 15.5	131 03.1	4.7	N19 20.4	5.1	60.5
19	105 26.2	14.6	145 26.8	4.7	19 15.3	5.3	60.5
20	120 26.4	13.7	159 50.5	4.7	19 10.0	5.4	60.5
21	135 26.6	.. 12.7	174 14.2	4.8	19 04.6	5.6	60.5
22	150 26.9	11.8	188 38.0	4.7	18 59.0	5.7	60.5
23	165 27.1	10.9	203 01.7	4.8	N18 53.3	5.9	60.5
	SD 15.9	d 0.9	SD 16.2		16.3		16.5

Lat.	Twilight Naut.	Civil	Sunrise	Moonrise 4	5	6	7
°	h m	h m	h m	h m	h m	h m	h m
N 72	////	02 57	04 20	☐	☐		
N 70	01 16	03 20	04 31	☐	☐	22 53	25 13
68	02 03	03 37	04 40	20 54	21 59	23 43	25 40
66	02 32	03 51	04 48	21 39	22 43	24 15	00 15
64	02 53	04 02	04 54	22 08	23 12	24 38	00 38
62	03 10	04 12	04 59	22 31	23 34	24 56	00 56
60	03 23	04 20	05 04	22 49	23 52	25 12	01 12
N 58	03 35	04 27	05 08	23 04	24 07	00 07	01 25
56	03 45	04 33	05 12	23 17	24 20	00 20	01 36
54	03 53	04 38	05 15	23 28	24 31	00 31	01 45
52	04 00	04 43	05 18	23 38	24 41	00 41	01 54
50	04 07	04 47	05 21	23 47	24 50	00 50	02 02
45	04 20	04 56	05 26	24 06	00 06	01 08	02 18
N 40	04 31	05 04	05 31	24 22	00 22	01 24	02 32
35	04 39	05 10	05 35	24 35	00 35	01 36	02 44
30	04 46	05 15	05 39	24 46	00 46	01 48	02 54
20	04 57	05 23	05 45	00 09	01 06	02 07	03 11
N 10	05 05	05 29	05 51	00 25	01 23	02 24	03 26
0	05 10	05 35	05 55	00 40	01 39	02 39	03 40
S 10	05 15	05 39	06 00	00 55	01 55	02 55	03 54
20	05 17	05 43	06 05	01 11	02 12	03 12	04 09
30	05 19	05 47	06 11	01 30	02 32	03 31	04 26
35	05 19	05 49	06 14	01 41	02 43	03 42	04 36
40	05 19	05 50	06 17	01 54	02 56	03 55	04 47
45	05 18	05 52	06 21	02 08	03 12	04 10	05 01
S 50	05 17	05 54	06 26	02 27	03 32	04 29	05 17
52	05 16	05 55	06 28	02 35	03 41	04 37	05 24
54	05 15	05 55	06 31	02 45	03 51	04 47	05 33
56	05 13	05 56	06 33	02 56	04 03	04 58	05 42
58	05 12	05 57	06 36	03 08	04 16	05 11	05 53
S 60	05 10	05 58	06 40	03 23	04 32	05 26	06 05

Lat.	Sunset	Twilight Civil	Naut.	Moonset 4	5	6	7
°	h m	h m	h m	h m	h m	h m	h m
N 72	19 34	20 55	////	☐	☐	☐	20 31
N 70	19 23	20 33	22 31	☐	☐	20 05	19 50
68	19 15	20 17	21 49	17 50	18 50	19 14	19 22
66	19 08	20 04	21 21	17 05	18 07	18 42	19 01
64	19 02	19 53	21 01	16 36	17 37	18 18	18 43
62	18 56	19 43	20 45	16 13	17 15	17 59	18 29
60	18 52	19 36	20 31	15 55	16 57	17 43	18 17
N 58	18 48	19 29	20 20	15 40	16 42	17 30	18 06
56	18 44	19 23	20 11	15 27	16 29	17 19	17 57
54	18 41	19 18	20 03	15 16	16 18	17 08	17 49
52	18 38	19 13	19 55	15 06	16 08	16 59	17 42
50	18 36	19 09	19 49	14 57	15 59	16 51	17 35
45	18 30	19 00	19 36	14 39	15 40	16 34	17 21
N 40	18 25	18 53	19 26	14 24	15 24	16 20	17 09
35	18 21	18 47	19 17	14 11	15 11	16 08	16 59
30	18 18	18 42	19 10	13 59	15 00	15 57	16 50
20	18 12	18 34	19 00	13 40	14 40	15 39	16 35
N 10	18 07	18 28	18 52	13 23	14 23	15 23	16 21
0	18 02	18 23	18 47	13 08	14 07	15 08	16 08
S 10	17 57	18 18	18 43	12 52	13 51	14 53	15 55
20	17 52	18 15	18 40	12 35	13 34	14 37	15 42
30	17 47	18 11	18 39	12 16	13 15	14 18	15 26
35	17 44	18 09	18 39	12 05	13 03	14 08	15 16
40	17 41	18 08	18 39	11 52	12 50	13 55	15 06
45	17 37	18 06	18 40	11 36	12 34	13 40	14 53
S 50	17 32	18 04	18 42	11 18	12 15	13 22	14 38
52	17 30	18 04	18 43	11 09	12 06	13 14	14 31
54	17 28	18 03	18 44	10 59	11 55	13 04	14 23
56	17 25	18 02	18 45	10 48	11 44	12 53	14 14
58	17 22	18 01	18 47	10 35	11 30	12 41	14 04
S 60	17 19	18 01	18 49	10 20	11 15	12 26	13 52

Day	SUN Eqn. of Time 00ʰ	12ʰ	Mer. Pass.	MOON Mer. Pass. Upper	Lower	Age	Phase
d	m s	m s	h m	h m	h m	d %	
4	00 49	00 58	11 59	06 54	19 23	24 35	
5	01 08	01 18	11 59	07 53	20 23	25 24	
6	01 28	01 39	11 58	08 54	21 24	26 15	

UT	ARIES GHA	VENUS −4.7 GHA	Dec	MARS −1.9 GHA	Dec	JUPITER −1.9 GHA	Dec	SATURN +0.4 GHA	Dec	STARS Name	SHA	Dec
FRIDAY 7 00	346 01.3	141 14.7	S14 32.7	43 18.6	S25 29.2	120 13.1	S16 23.9	73 16.0	S22 42.5	Acamar	315 15.4	S40 13.7
01	1 03.8	156 15.5	33.7	58 20.7	29.0	135 15.2	24.1	88 18.4	42.5	Achernar	335 23.7	S57 08.4
02	16 06.2	171 16.2	34.7	73 22.8	28.7	150 17.3	24.2	103 20.9	42.5	Acrux	173 05.9	S63 12.1
03	31 08.7	186 17.0	.. 35.6	88 24.9	.. 28.5	165 19.4	.. 24.3	118 23.3	.. 42.6	Adhara	255 09.9	S28 59.7
04	46 11.2	201 17.8	36.6	103 27.0	28.3	180 21.5	24.4	133 25.8	42.6	Aldebaran	290 45.3	N16 32.7
05	61 13.6	216 18.6	37.6	118 29.2	28.1	195 23.6	24.5	148 28.3	42.6			
06	76 16.1	231 19.4	S14 38.6	133 31.3	S25 27.9	210 25.7	S16 24.6	163 30.7	S22 42.6	Alioth	166 18.1	N55 51.8
07	91 18.6	246 20.2	39.5	148 33.4	27.6	225 27.8	24.7	178 33.2	42.6	Alkaid	152 56.5	N49 13.6
08	106 21.0	261 21.0	40.5	163 35.5	27.4	240 29.8	24.8	193 35.6	42.6	Al Na'ir	27 38.9	S46 52.2
09	121 23.5	276 21.7	.. 41.5	178 37.6	.. 27.2	255 31.9	.. 24.9	208 38.1	.. 42.6	Alnilam	275 42.8	S 1 11.4
10	136 26.0	291 22.5	42.4	193 39.7	27.0	270 34.0	25.1	223 40.6	42.6	Alphard	217 52.9	S 8 44.3
11	151 28.4	306 23.3	43.4	208 41.9	26.7	285 36.1	25.2	238 43.0	42.6			
12	166 30.9	321 24.1	S14 44.4	223 44.0	S25 26.5	300 38.2	S16 25.3	253 45.5	S22 42.6	Alphecca	126 08.1	N26 39.5
13	181 33.3	336 24.9	45.3	238 46.1	26.3	315 40.3	25.4	268 47.9	42.6	Alpheratz	357 39.5	N29 11.6
14	196 35.8	351 25.7	46.3	253 48.2	26.1	330 42.4	25.5	283 50.4	42.6	Altair	62 04.6	N 8 55.3
15	211 38.3	6 26.5	.. 47.3	268 50.3	.. 25.9	345 44.5	.. 25.6	298 52.9	.. 42.6	Ankaa	353 11.8	S42 12.2
16	226 40.7	21 27.3	48.2	283 52.4	25.6	0 46.6	25.7	313 55.3	42.6	Antares	112 21.9	S26 28.2
17	241 43.2	36 28.1	49.2	298 54.5	25.4	15 48.7	25.8	328 57.8	42.6			
18	256 45.7	51 28.9	S14 50.1	313 56.6	S25 25.2	30 50.8	S16 25.9	344 00.2	S22 42.6	Arcturus	145 52.7	N19 05.5
19	271 48.1	66 29.7	51.1	328 58.7	25.0	45 52.9	26.1	359 02.7	42.6	Atria	107 20.5	S69 03.7
20	286 50.6	81 30.5	52.1	344 00.8	24.7	60 54.9	26.2	14 05.1	42.7	Avior	234 17.0	S59 34.0
21	301 53.1	96 31.3	.. 53.0	359 02.9	.. 24.5	75 57.0	.. 26.3	29 07.6	.. 42.7	Bellatrix	278 28.2	N 6 21.9
22	316 55.5	111 32.1	54.0	14 05.0	24.3	90 59.1	26.4	44 10.1	42.7	Betelgeuse	270 57.5	N 7 24.6
23	331 58.0	126 32.9	54.9	29 07.1	24.0	106 01.2	26.5	59 12.5	42.7			
SATURDAY 8 00	347 00.5	141 33.7	S14 55.9	44 09.2	S25 23.8	121 03.3	S16 26.6	74 15.0	S22 42.7	Canopus	263 54.8	S52 42.1
01	2 02.9	156 34.5	56.9	59 11.3	23.6	136 05.4	26.7	89 17.4	42.7	Capella	280 29.2	N46 00.7
02	17 05.4	171 35.4	57.8	74 13.4	23.4	151 07.5	26.8	104 19.9	42.7	Deneb	49 28.7	N45 21.1
03	32 07.8	186 36.2	.. 58.8	89 15.5	.. 23.1	166 09.6	.. 27.0	119 22.3	.. 42.7	Denebola	182 30.4	N14 28.3
04	47 10.3	201 37.0	14 59.7	104 17.5	22.9	181 11.7	27.1	134 24.8	42.7	Diphda	348 52.0	S17 53.0
05	62 12.8	216 37.8	15 00.7	119 19.6	22.7	196 13.7	27.2	149 27.3	42.7			
06	77 15.2	231 38.6	S15 01.6	134 21.7	S25 22.4	211 15.8	S16 27.3	164 29.7	S22 42.7	Dubhe	193 48.1	N61 39.1
07	92 17.7	246 39.4	02.6	149 23.8	22.2	226 17.9	27.4	179 32.2	42.7	Elnath	278 08.2	N28 37.2
08	107 20.2	261 40.3	03.5	164 25.9	22.0	241 20.0	27.5	194 34.6	42.7	Eltanin	90 44.4	N51 29.6
09	122 22.6	276 41.1	.. 04.5	179 28.0	.. 21.8	256 22.1	.. 27.6	209 37.1	.. 42.7	Enif	33 43.3	N 9 57.8
10	137 25.1	291 41.9	05.4	194 30.0	21.5	271 24.2	27.7	224 39.5	42.7	Fomalhaut	15 19.7	S29 31.3
11	152 27.6	306 42.7	06.4	209 32.1	21.3	286 26.3	27.9	239 42.0	42.7			
12	167 30.0	321 43.5	S15 07.3	224 34.2	S25 21.1	301 28.4	S16 28.0	254 44.5	S22 42.7	Gacrux	171 57.4	S57 13.0
13	182 32.5	336 44.4	08.3	239 36.3	20.8	316 30.4	28.1	269 46.9	42.8	Gienah	175 49.0	S17 38.5
14	197 35.0	351 45.2	09.2	254 38.4	20.6	331 32.5	28.2	284 49.4	42.8	Hadar	148 43.2	S60 27.7
15	212 37.4	6 46.0	.. 10.2	269 40.4	.. 20.4	346 34.6	.. 28.3	299 51.8	.. 42.8	Hamal	327 56.5	N23 32.9
16	227 39.9	21 46.9	11.1	284 42.5	20.1	1 36.7	28.4	314 54.3	42.8	Kaus Aust.	83 39.0	S34 22.4
17	242 42.3	36 47.7	12.1	299 44.6	19.9	16 38.8	28.5	329 56.7	42.8			
18	257 44.8	51 48.5	S15 13.0	314 46.6	S25 19.7	31 40.9	S16 28.6	344 59.2	S22 42.8	Kochab	137 20.8	N74 05.2
19	272 47.3	66 49.4	14.0	329 48.7	19.4	46 43.0	28.8	0 01.6	42.8	Markab	13 34.5	N15 18.4
20	287 49.7	81 50.2	14.9	344 50.8	19.2	61 45.0	28.9	15 04.1	42.8	Menkar	314 11.2	N 4 09.7
21	302 52.2	96 51.0	.. 15.9	359 52.8	.. 19.0	76 47.1	.. 29.0	30 06.5	.. 42.8	Menkent	148 03.6	S36 27.6
22	317 54.7	111 51.9	16.8	14 54.9	18.7	91 49.2	29.1	45 09.0	42.8	Miaplacidus	221 39.7	S69 47.5
23	332 57.1	126 52.7	17.7	29 57.0	18.5	106 51.3	29.2	60 11.4	42.8			
SUNDAY 9 00	347 59.6	141 53.5	S15 18.7	44 59.0	S25 18.3	121 53.4	S16 29.3	75 13.9	S22 42.8	Mirfak	308 35.0	N49 55.3
01	3 02.1	156 54.4	19.6	60 01.1	18.0	136 55.5	29.4	90 16.4	42.8	Nunki	75 53.8	S26 16.3
02	18 04.5	171 55.2	20.6	75 03.1	17.8	151 57.6	29.5	105 18.8	42.8	Peacock	53 13.2	S56 40.5
03	33 07.0	186 56.1	.. 21.5	90 05.2	.. 17.6	166 59.6	.. 29.7	120 21.3	.. 42.8	Pollux	243 23.7	N27 58.8
04	48 09.4	201 56.9	22.4	105 07.2	17.3	182 01.7	29.8	135 23.7	42.8	Procyon	244 56.2	N 5 10.6
05	63 11.9	216 57.8	23.4	120 09.3	17.1	197 03.8	29.9	150 26.2	42.9			
06	78 14.4	231 58.6	S15 24.3	135 11.3	S25 16.9	212 05.9	S16 30.0	165 28.6	S22 42.9	Rasalhague	96 03.1	N12 33.1
07	93 16.8	246 59.5	25.2	150 13.4	16.6	227 08.0	30.1	180 31.1	42.9	Regulus	207 40.1	N11 52.7
08	108 19.3	262 00.3	26.2	165 15.4	16.4	242 10.1	30.2	195 33.5	42.9	Rigel	281 08.7	S 8 10.8
09	123 21.8	277 01.2	.. 27.1	180 17.5	.. 16.1	257 12.1	.. 30.3	210 36.0	.. 42.9	Rigil Kent.	139 47.3	S60 54.7
10	138 24.2	292 02.0	28.1	195 19.5	15.9	272 14.2	30.4	225 38.4	42.9	Sabik	102 08.5	S15 44.7
11	153 26.7	307 02.9	29.0	210 21.6	15.7	287 16.3	30.6	240 40.9	42.9			
12	168 29.2	322 03.7	S15 29.9	225 23.6	S25 15.4	302 18.4	S16 30.7	255 43.3	S22 42.9	Schedar	349 35.9	N56 38.2
13	183 31.6	337 04.6	30.8	240 25.7	15.2	317 20.5	30.8	270 45.8	42.9	Shaula	96 17.0	S37 06.9
14	198 34.1	352 05.5	31.8	255 27.7	14.9	332 22.6	30.9	285 48.2	42.9	Sirius	258 30.7	S16 44.4
15	213 36.6	7 06.3	.. 32.7	270 29.8	.. 14.7	347 24.6	.. 31.0	300 50.7	.. 42.9	Spica	158 27.8	S11 15.3
16	228 39.0	22 07.2	33.6	285 31.8	14.5	2 26.7	31.1	315 53.1	42.9	Suhail	222 50.2	S43 30.3
17	243 41.5	37 08.1	34.6	300 33.8	14.2	17 28.8	31.2	330 55.6	42.9			
18	258 43.9	52 08.9	S15 35.5	315 35.9	S25 14.0	32 30.9	S16 31.3	345 58.0	S22 42.9	Vega	80 36.4	N38 48.5
19	273 46.4	67 09.8	36.4	330 37.9	13.7	47 33.0	31.5	1 00.5	42.9	Zuben'ubi	137 01.7	S16 06.9
20	288 48.9	82 10.7	37.4	345 39.9	13.5	62 35.0	31.6	16 02.9	42.9			
21	303 51.3	97 11.5	.. 38.3	0 42.0	.. 13.3	77 37.1	.. 31.7	31 05.4	.. 42.9		SHA	Mer. Pass.
22	318 53.8	112 12.4	39.2	15 44.0	13.0	92 39.2	31.8	46 07.8	43.0	Venus	154 33.3	14 33
23	333 56.3	127 13.3	40.1	30 46.0	12.8	107 41.3	31.9	61 10.3	43.0	Mars	57 08.7	21 00
Mer. Pass.	h m 0 51.8	v 0.8	d 0.9	v 2.1	d 0.2	v 2.1	d 0.1	v 2.5	d 0.0	Jupiter	134 02.9	15 54
										Saturn	87 14.5	19 00

UT	SUN GHA	SUN Dec	MOON GHA	v	MOON Dec	d	HP
d h	° ′	° ′	° ′	′	° ′	′	′
7 00	180 27.3	N 6 09.9	217 25.5	4.9	N18 47.4	5.9	60.5
01	195 27.5	09.0	231 49.4	4.8	18 41.5	6.2	60.5
02	210 27.7	08.1	246 13.2	4.9	18 35.3	6.2	60.6
03	225 27.9	.. 07.1	260 37.1	4.9	18 29.1	6.4	60.6
04	240 28.1	06.2	275 01.0	5.0	18 22.7	6.5	60.6
05	255 28.3	05.3	289 25.0	5.0	18 16.2	6.6	60.6
06	270 28.6 N 6 04.3		303 49.0	5.0	N18 09.6	6.8	60.6
07	285 28.8	03.4	318 13.0	5.0	18 02.8	6.9	60.6
08	300 29.0	02.5	332 37.0	5.1	17 55.9	7.0	60.6
F 09	315 29.2	.. 01.5	347 01.1	5.2	17 48.9	7.2	60.6
R 10	330 29.4	6 00.6	1 25.3	5.2	17 41.7	7.3	60.6
I 11	345 29.6	5 59.6	15 49.5	5.2	17 34.4	7.4	60.6
D 12	0 29.8 N 5 58.7		30 13.7	5.2	N17 27.0	7.5	60.6
A 13	15 30.0	57.8	44 37.9	5.3	17 19.5	7.7	60.6
Y 14	30 30.3	56.8	59 02.2	5.4	17 11.8	7.7	60.7
15	45 30.5	.. 55.9	73 26.6	5.4	17 04.1	7.9	60.7
16	60 30.7	55.0	87 51.0	5.4	16 56.2	8.0	60.7
17	75 30.9	54.0	102 15.4	5.5	16 48.2	8.2	60.7
18	90 31.1 N 5 53.1		116 39.9	5.5	N16 40.0	8.2	60.7
19	105 31.3	52.2	131 04.4	5.6	16 31.8	8.4	60.7
20	120 31.5	51.2	145 29.0	5.7	16 23.4	8.5	60.7
21	135 31.7	.. 50.3	159 53.7	5.6	16 14.9	8.6	60.7
22	150 32.0	49.3	174 18.3	5.8	16 06.3	8.7	60.7
23	165 32.2	48.4	188 43.1	5.8	15 57.6	8.8	60.7
8 00	180 32.4 N 5 47.5		203 07.9	5.8	N15 48.8	8.9	60.7
01	195 32.6	46.5	217 32.7	5.9	15 39.9	9.0	60.7
02	210 32.8	45.6	231 57.6	5.9	15 30.9	9.2	60.7
03	225 33.0	.. 44.6	246 22.5	6.0	15 21.7	9.2	60.7
04	240 33.2	43.7	260 47.5	6.1	15 12.5	9.4	60.7
05	255 33.5	42.8	275 12.6	6.1	15 03.1	9.4	60.7
06	270 33.7 N 5 41.8		289 37.7	6.1	N14 53.7	9.6	60.7
S 07	285 33.9	40.9	304 02.8	6.3	14 44.1	9.6	60.7
A 08	300 34.1	39.9	318 28.1	6.2	14 34.5	9.7	60.7
T 09	315 34.3	.. 39.0	332 53.3	6.4	14 24.8	9.9	60.7
U 10	330 34.5	38.1	347 18.7	6.4	14 14.9	9.9	60.7
R 11	345 34.7	37.1	1 44.1	6.4	14 05.0	10.1	60.7
D 12	0 35.0 N 5 36.2		16 09.5	6.5	N13 54.9	10.1	60.7
A 13	15 35.2	35.2	30 35.0	6.6	13 44.8	10.2	60.7
Y 14	30 35.4	34.3	45 00.6	6.6	13 34.6	10.3	60.6
15	45 35.6	.. 33.4	59 26.2	6.7	13 24.3	10.4	60.6
16	60 35.8	32.4	73 51.9	6.8	13 13.9	10.5	60.6
17	75 36.0	31.5	88 17.7	6.8	13 03.4	10.5	60.6
18	90 36.2 N 5 30.5		102 43.5	6.8	N12 52.9	10.7	60.6
19	105 36.5	29.6	117 09.3	7.0	12 42.2	10.7	60.6
20	120 36.7	28.7	131 35.3	6.9	12 31.5	10.8	60.6
21	135 36.9	.. 27.7	146 01.2	7.1	12 20.7	10.9	60.6
22	150 37.1	26.8	160 27.3	7.1	12 09.8	10.9	60.6
23	165 37.3	25.8	174 53.4	7.2	11 58.9	11.0	60.6
9 00	180 37.5 N 5 24.9		189 19.6	7.2	N11 47.9	11.1	60.6
01	195 37.8	23.9	203 45.8	7.3	11 36.8	11.2	60.6
02	210 38.0	23.0	218 12.1	7.3	11 25.6	11.3	60.5
03	225 38.2	.. 22.1	232 38.4	7.5	11 14.3	11.3	60.5
04	240 38.4	21.1	247 04.9	7.4	11 03.0	11.4	60.5
05	255 38.6	20.2	261 31.3	7.6	10 51.6	11.4	60.5
06	270 38.8 N 5 19.2		275 57.9	7.6	N10 40.2	11.5	60.5
07	285 39.1	18.3	290 24.5	7.6	10 28.7	11.6	60.5
08	300 39.3	17.3	304 51.1	7.7	10 17.1	11.6	60.5
S 09	315 39.5	.. 16.4	319 17.8	7.8	10 05.5	11.7	60.4
U 10	330 39.7	15.5	333 44.6	7.8	9 53.8	11.8	60.4
N 11	345 39.9	14.5	348 11.4	7.9	9 42.0	11.8	60.4
D 12	0 40.1 N 5 13.6		2 38.3	8.0	N 9 30.2	11.8	60.4
A 13	15 40.3	12.6	17 05.3	8.0	9 18.4	11.9	60.4
Y 14	30 40.6	11.7	31 32.3	8.1	9 06.5	12.0	60.4
15	45 40.8	.. 10.7	45 59.4	8.1	8 54.5	12.0	60.3
16	60 41.0	09.8	60 26.5	8.2	8 42.5	12.1	60.3
17	75 41.2	08.8	74 53.7	8.3	8 30.4	12.1	60.3
18	90 41.4 N 5 07.9		89 21.0	8.3	N 8 18.3	12.1	60.3
19	105 41.6	07.0	103 48.3	8.3	8 06.2	12.2	60.3
20	120 41.9	06.0	118 15.6	8.5	7 54.0	12.2	60.3
21	135 42.1	.. 05.1	132 43.1	8.4	7 41.8	12.3	60.2
22	150 42.3	04.1	147 10.5	8.6	7 29.5	12.3	60.2
23	165 42.5	03.2	161 38.1	8.6	N 7 17.2	12.4	60.2
	SD 15.9	d 0.9	SD 16.5		16.5		16.5

Twilight / Sunrise / Moonrise

Lat.	Naut.	Civil	Sunrise	7	8	9	10
°	h m	h m	h m	h m	h m	h m	h m
N 72	00 34	03 16	04 34	▭	00 33	03 02	05 14
N 70	01 47	03 35	04 44	25 13	01 13	03 21	05 22
68	02 23	03 50	04 51	25 40	01 40	03 36	05 30
66	02 47	04 02	04 57	00 15	02 00	03 49	05 35
64	03 06	04 12	05 03	00 38	02 16	03 59	05 40
62	03 20	04 20	05 07	00 56	02 30	04 08	05 45
60	03 33	04 28	05 11	01 12	02 41	04 15	05 48
N 58	03 43	04 34	05 15	01 25	02 51	04 21	05 52
56	03 52	04 39	05 18	01 36	03 00	04 27	05 55
54	03 59	04 44	05 20	01 45	03 07	04 32	05 57
52	04 06	04 48	05 23	01 54	03 14	04 37	05 59
50	04 12	04 52	05 25	02 02	03 20	04 41	06 02
45	04 25	05 00	05 30	02 18	03 33	04 50	06 06
N 40	04 34	05 07	05 34	02 32	03 44	04 58	06 10
35	04 42	05 12	05 38	02 44	03 54	05 04	06 14
30	04 48	05 17	05 41	02 54	04 02	05 10	06 16
20	04 58	05 24	05 46	03 11	04 16	05 19	06 22
N 10	05 05	05 29	05 50	03 26	04 28	05 28	06 26
0	05 10	05 34	05 54	03 40	04 39	05 36	06 30
S 10	05 13	05 37	05 58	03 54	04 50	05 44	06 34
20	05 15	05 40	06 03	04 09	05 02	05 52	06 39
30	05 15	05 43	06 07	04 26	05 16	06 02	06 44
35	05 15	05 44	06 10	04 36	05 24	06 07	06 47
40	05 14	05 46	06 13	04 47	05 33	06 14	06 50
45	05 13	05 47	06 16	05 01	05 44	06 21	06 54
S 50	05 10	05 48	06 20	05 17	05 56	06 30	06 59
52	05 09	05 48	06 22	05 24	06 02	06 34	07 01
54	05 07	05 48	06 24	05 33	06 09	06 38	07 03
56	05 06	05 49	06 26	05 42	06 16	06 43	07 05
58	05 04	05 49	06 28	05 53	06 24	06 48	07 08
S 60	05 01	05 49	06 31	06 05	06 33	06 54	07 11

Sunset / Twilight / Moonset

Lat.	Sunset	Civil	Naut.	7	8	9	10
°	h m	h m	h m	h m	h m	h m	h m
N 72	19 18	20 35	23 00	20 31	20 03	19 46	19 32
N 70	19 09	20 17	22 01	19 50	19 42	19 35	19 28
68	19 02	20 02	21 28	19 22	19 25	19 25	19 25
66	18 56	19 51	21 04	19 01	19 11	19 18	19 22
64	18 51	19 41	20 47	18 43	19 00	19 11	19 20
62	18 47	19 33	20 32	18 29	18 50	19 06	19 18
60	18 43	19 26	20 20	18 17	18 42	19 01	19 16
N 58	18 39	19 20	20 10	18 06	18 34	18 56	19 15
56	18 36	19 15	20 02	17 57	18 28	18 52	19 13
54	18 34	19 10	19 54	17 49	18 22	18 49	19 12
52	18 31	19 06	19 48	17 42	18 16	18 45	19 11
50	18 29	19 02	19 42	17 35	18 12	18 42	19 10
45	18 24	18 54	19 30	17 21	18 01	18 36	19 08
N 40	18 21	18 48	19 20	17 09	17 52	18 31	19 06
35	18 17	18 43	19 13	16 59	17 45	18 26	19 04
30	18 14	18 38	19 07	16 50	17 38	18 22	19 02
20	18 09	18 31	18 57	16 35	17 26	18 15	19 00
N 10	18 05	18 26	18 51	16 21	17 16	18 08	18 57
0	18 01	18 22	18 46	16 08	17 06	18 02	18 55
S 10	17 57	18 18	18 43	15 55	16 57	17 56	18 53
20	17 53	18 15	18 41	15 42	16 46	17 49	18 50
30	17 49	18 13	18 40	15 26	16 34	17 42	18 48
35	17 46	18 12	18 41	15 16	16 27	17 37	18 46
40	17 43	18 10	18 42	15 06	16 19	17 32	18 44
45	17 40	18 10	18 44	14 53	16 10	17 26	18 42
S 50	17 36	18 09	18 46	14 38	15 58	17 19	18 39
52	17 35	18 08	18 47	14 31	15 53	17 16	18 38
54	17 33	18 08	18 49	14 23	15 47	17 12	18 37
56	17 31	18 08	18 51	14 14	15 40	17 08	18 35
58	17 28	18 08	18 53	14 04	15 33	17 04	18 33
S 60	17 26	18 07	18 56	13 52	15 25	16 59	18 32

SUN / MOON

Day	Eqn. of Time 00h	12h	Mer. Pass.	Mer. Pass. Upper	Lower	Age	Phase
d	m s	m s	h m	h m	h m	d	%
7	01 49	01 59	11 58	09 54	22 24	27	7
8	02 09	02 19	11 58	10 53	23 21	28	2
9	02 30	02 40	11 57	11 49	24 16	29	0

UT	ARIES GHA	VENUS −4.7 GHA	Dec	MARS −1.8 GHA	Dec	JUPITER −1.9 GHA	Dec	SATURN +0.4 GHA	Dec	STARS Name	SHA	Dec
10 00	348 58.7	142 14.1	S15 41.1	45 48.0	S25 12.5	122 43.4	S16 32.0	76 12.7	S22 43.0	Acamar	315 15.4	S40 13.7
01	4 01.2	157 15.0	42.0	60 50.1	12.3	137 45.4	32.1	91 15.2	43.0	Achernar	335 23.7	S57 08.4
02	19 03.7	172 15.9	42.9	75 52.1	12.0	152 47.5	32.3	106 17.6	43.0	Acrux	173 05.9	S63 12.1
03	34 06.1	187 16.8 ..	43.8	90 54.1 ..	11.8	167 49.6 ..	32.4	121 20.1 ..	43.0	Adhara	255 09.9	S28 59.7
04	49 08.6	202 17.7	44.7	105 56.1	11.6	182 51.7	32.5	136 22.5	43.0	Aldebaran	290 45.2	N16 32.7
05	64 11.0	217 18.5	45.7	120 58.2	11.3	197 53.8	32.6	151 25.0	43.0			
06	79 13.5	232 19.4	S15 46.6	136 00.2	S25 11.1	212 55.8	S16 32.7	166 27.4	S22 43.0	Alioth	166 18.1	N55 51.8
07	94 16.0	247 20.3	47.5	151 02.2	10.8	227 57.9	32.8	181 29.8	43.0	Alkaid	152 56.5	N49 13.6
08	109 18.4	262 21.2	48.4	166 04.2	10.6	243 00.0	32.9	196 32.3	43.0	Al Na'ir	27 38.9	S46 52.2
M 09	124 20.9	277 22.1 ..	49.3	181 06.2 ..	10.3	258 02.1 ..	33.1	211 34.7 ..	43.0	Alnilam	275 42.8	S 1 11.4
O 10	139 23.4	292 23.0	50.3	196 08.2	10.1	273 04.1	33.2	226 37.2	43.0	Alphard	217 52.9	S 8 44.2
N 11	154 25.8	307 23.9	51.2	211 10.3	09.8	288 06.2	33.3	241 39.6	43.0			
D 12	169 28.3	322 24.8	S15 52.1	226 12.3	S25 09.6	303 08.3	S16 33.4	256 42.1	S22 43.0	Alphecca	126 08.1	N26 39.5
A 13	184 30.8	337 25.7	53.0	241 14.3	09.3	318 10.4	33.5	271 44.5	43.0	Alpheratz	357 39.5	N29 11.6
Y 14	199 33.2	352 26.5	53.9	256 16.3	09.1	333 12.5	33.6	286 47.0	43.0	Altair	62 04.6	N 8 55.3
15	214 35.7	7 27.4 ..	54.8	271 18.3 ..	08.8	348 14.5 ..	33.7	301 49.4 ..	43.0	Ankaa	353 11.8	S42 12.2
16	229 38.2	22 28.3	55.7	286 20.3	08.6	3 16.6	33.9	316 51.9	43.1	Antares	112 22.0	S26 28.2
17	244 40.6	37 29.2	56.7	301 22.3	08.4	18 18.7	34.0	331 54.3	43.1			
18	259 43.1	52 30.1	S15 57.6	316 24.3	S25 08.1	33 20.8	S16 34.1	346 56.8	S22 43.1	Arcturus	145 52.7	N19 05.5
19	274 45.5	67 31.0	58.5	331 26.3	07.9	48 22.8	34.2	1 59.2	43.1	Atria	107 20.6	S69 03.7
20	289 48.0	82 32.0	15 59.4	346 28.3	07.6	63 24.9	34.3	17 01.6	43.1	Avior	234 17.0	S59 34.0
21	304 50.5	97 32.9	16 00.3	1 30.3 ..	07.4	78 27.0 ..	34.4	32 04.1 ..	43.1	Bellatrix	278 28.2	N 6 21.9
22	319 52.9	112 33.8	01.2	16 32.3	07.1	93 29.1	34.5	47 06.5	43.1	Betelgeuse	270 57.5	N 7 24.6
23	334 55.4	127 34.7	02.1	31 34.3	06.9	108 31.1	34.7	62 09.0	43.1			
11 00	349 57.9	142 35.6	S16 03.0	46 36.3	S25 06.6	123 33.2	S16 34.8	77 11.4	S22 43.1	Canopus	263 54.7	S52 42.1
01	5 00.3	157 36.5	03.9	61 38.3	06.4	138 35.3	34.9	92 13.9	43.1	Capella	280 29.2	N46 00.7
02	20 02.8	172 37.4	04.8	76 40.3	06.1	153 37.4	35.0	107 16.3	43.1	Deneb	49 28.7	N45 21.1
03	35 05.3	187 38.3 ..	05.7	91 42.3 ..	05.9	168 39.4 ..	35.1	122 18.7 ..	43.1	Denebola	182 30.4	N14 28.3
04	50 07.7	202 39.2	06.6	106 44.2	05.6	183 41.5	35.2	137 21.2	43.1	Diphda	348 52.0	S17 53.0
05	65 10.2	217 40.2	07.5	121 46.2	05.3	198 43.6	35.3	152 23.6	43.1			
06	80 12.6	232 41.1	S16 08.4	136 48.2	S25 05.1	213 45.7	S16 35.4	167 26.1	S22 43.1	Dubhe	193 48.1	N61 39.1
07	95 15.1	247 42.0	09.3	151 50.2	04.8	228 47.7	35.6	182 28.5	43.1	Elnath	278 08.2	N28 37.2
T 08	110 17.6	262 42.9	10.2	166 52.2	04.6	243 49.8	35.7	197 31.0	43.1	Eltanin	90 44.4	N51 29.6
U 09	125 20.0	277 43.8 ..	11.1	181 54.2 ..	04.3	258 51.9 ..	35.8	212 33.4 ..	43.2	Enif	33 43.3	N 9 57.8
E 10	140 22.5	292 44.8	12.0	196 56.2	04.1	273 54.0	35.9	227 35.8	43.2	Fomalhaut	15 19.7	S29 31.3
S 11	155 25.0	307 45.7	12.9	211 58.1	03.8	288 56.0	36.0	242 38.3	43.2			
D 12	170 27.4	322 46.6	S16 13.8	227 00.1	S25 03.6	303 58.1	S16 36.1	257 40.7	S22 43.2	Gacrux	171 57.5	S57 13.0
A 13	185 29.9	337 47.6	14.7	242 02.1	03.3	319 00.2	36.3	272 43.2	43.2	Gienah	175 49.0	S17 38.5
Y 14	200 32.4	352 48.5	15.6	257 04.1	03.1	334 02.2	36.4	287 45.6	43.2	Hadar	148 43.3	S60 27.7
15	215 34.8	7 49.4 ..	16.5	272 06.0 ..	02.8	349 04.3 ..	36.5	302 48.1 ..	43.2	Hamal	327 56.5	N23 32.9
16	230 37.3	22 50.4	17.4	287 08.0	02.6	4 06.4	36.6	317 50.5	43.2	Kaus Aust.	83 39.0	S34 22.4
17	245 39.8	37 51.3	18.3	302 10.0	02.3	19 08.5	36.7	332 52.9	43.2			
18	260 42.2	52 52.2	S16 19.2	317 12.0	S25 02.0	34 10.5	S16 36.8	347 55.4	S22 43.2	Kochab	137 20.8	N74 05.1
19	275 44.7	67 53.2	20.1	332 13.9	01.8	49 12.6	36.9	2 57.8	43.2	Markab	13 34.5	N15 18.4
20	290 47.1	82 54.1	21.0	347 15.9	01.5	64 14.7	37.1	18 00.3	43.2	Menkar	314 11.2	N 4 09.7
21	305 49.6	97 55.1 ..	21.9	2 17.9 ..	01.3	79 16.7 ..	37.2	33 02.7 ..	43.2	Menkent	148 03.7	S36 27.6
22	320 52.1	112 56.0	22.8	17 19.8	01.0	94 18.8	37.3	48 05.1	43.2	Miaplacidus	221 39.7	S69 47.4
23	335 54.5	127 57.0	23.7	32 21.8	00.8	109 20.9	37.4	63 07.6	43.2			
12 00	350 57.0	142 57.9	S16 24.5	47 23.7	S25 00.5	124 23.0	S16 37.5	78 10.0	S22 43.2	Mirfak	308 35.0	N49 55.3
01	5 59.5	157 58.9	25.4	62 25.7	00.2	139 25.0	37.6	93 12.5	43.2	Nunki	75 53.8	S26 16.3
02	21 01.9	172 59.8	26.3	77 27.7	25 00.0	154 27.1	37.8	108 14.9	43.2	Peacock	53 13.3	S56 40.5
03	36 04.4	188 00.8 ..	27.2	92 29.6	24 59.7	169 29.2 ..	37.9	123 17.3 ..	43.3	Pollux	243 23.6	N27 58.8
04	51 06.9	203 01.7	28.1	107 31.6	59.5	184 31.2	38.0	138 19.8	43.3	Procyon	244 56.2	N 5 10.6
05	66 09.3	218 02.7	29.0	122 33.5	59.2	199 33.3	38.1	153 22.2	43.3			
06	81 11.8	233 03.6	S16 29.9	137 35.5	S24 58.9	214 35.4	S16 38.2	168 24.7	S22 43.3	Rasalhague	96 03.1	N12 33.1
W 07	96 14.2	248 04.6	30.7	152 37.4	58.7	229 37.4	38.3	183 27.1	43.3	Regulus	207 40.1	N11 52.7
E 08	111 16.7	263 05.5	31.6	167 39.4	58.4	244 39.5	38.4	198 29.5	43.3	Rigel	281 08.6	S 8 10.8
D 09	126 19.2	278 06.5 ..	32.5	182 41.3 ..	58.2	259 41.6 ..	38.6	213 32.0 ..	43.3	Rigil Kent.	139 47.3	S60 54.7
N 10	141 21.6	293 07.5	33.4	197 43.3	57.9	274 43.7	38.7	228 34.4	43.3	Sabik	102 08.5	S15 44.7
E 11	156 24.1	308 08.4	34.3	212 45.2	57.6	289 45.7	38.8	243 36.8	43.3			
S 12	171 26.6	323 09.4	S16 35.1	227 47.2	S24 57.4	304 47.8	S16 38.9	258 39.3	S22 43.3	Schedar	349 35.9	N56 38.2
D 13	186 29.0	338 10.4	36.0	242 49.1	57.1	319 49.9	39.0	273 41.7	43.3	Shaula	96 17.1	S37 06.9
A 14	201 31.5	353 11.3	36.9	257 51.1	56.8	334 51.9	39.1	288 44.2	43.3	Sirius	258 30.7	S16 44.4
Y 15	216 34.0	8 12.3 ..	37.8	272 53.0 ..	56.6	349 54.0 ..	39.3	303 46.6 ..	43.3	Spica	158 27.8	S11 15.3
16	231 36.4	23 13.3	38.6	287 55.0	56.3	4 56.1	39.4	318 49.0	43.3	Suhail	222 50.2	S43 30.3
17	246 38.9	38 14.3	39.5	302 56.9	56.1	19 58.1	39.5	333 51.5	43.3			
18	261 41.4	53 15.2	S16 40.4	317 58.8	S24 55.8	35 00.2	S16 39.6	348 53.9	S22 43.3	Vega	80 36.4	N38 48.5
19	276 43.8	68 16.2	41.3	333 00.8	55.5	50 02.3	39.7	3 56.3	43.3	Zuben'ubi	137 01.7	S16 06.9
20	291 46.3	83 17.2	42.1	348 02.7	55.3	65 04.3	39.8	18 58.8	43.4		SHA	Mer.Pass.
21	306 48.7	98 18.2 ..	43.0	3 04.7 ..	55.0	80 06.4 ..	39.9	34 01.2 ..	43.4	Venus	152 37.7	14 29
22	321 51.2	113 19.2	43.9	18 06.6	54.7	95 08.5	40.1	49 03.6	43.4	Mars	56 38.4	20 51
23	336 53.7	128 20.2	44.8	33 08.5	54.5	110 10.5	40.2	64 06.1	43.4	Jupiter	133 35.4	15 44
Mer.Pass.	h m 0 40.0	v 0.9	d 0.9	v 2.0	d 0.3	v 2.1	d 0.1	v 2.4	d 0.0	Saturn	87 13.6	18 48

UT	SUN GHA	Dec	MOON GHA	v	Dec	d	HP
d h	° ′	° ′	° ′	′	° ′	′	′
10 00	180 42.7	N 5 02.2	176 05.7	8.6	N 7 04.8	12.3	60.2
01	195 43.0	01.3	190 33.3	8.7	6 52.5	12.4	60.2
02	210 43.2	5 00.3	205 01.0	8.8	6 40.1	12.5	60.1
03	225 43.4	4 59.4	219 28.8	8.8	6 27.6	12.5	60.1
04	240 43.6	58.4	233 56.6	8.9	6 15.1	12.5	60.1
05	255 43.8	57.5	248 24.5	8.9	6 02.6	12.5	60.1
06	270 44.0	N 4 56.5	262 52.4	9.0	N 5 50.1	12.5	60.0
07	285 44.3	55.6	277 20.4	9.0	5 37.6	12.6	60.0
M 08	300 44.5	54.6	291 48.4	9.1	5 25.0	12.6	60.0
O 09	315 44.7	.. 53.7	306 16.5	9.1	5 12.4	12.6	60.0
N 10	330 44.9	52.8	320 44.6	9.2	4 59.8	12.7	59.9
D 11	345 45.1	51.8	335 12.8	9.3	4 47.1	12.6	59.9
A 12	0 45.3	N 4 50.9	349 41.1	9.3	N 4 34.5	12.7	59.9
Y 13	15 45.6	49.9	4 09.4	9.3	4 21.8	12.7	59.9
14	30 45.8	49.0	18 37.7	9.4	4 09.1	12.7	59.8
15	45 46.0	.. 48.0	33 06.1	9.4	3 56.4	12.7	59.8
16	60 46.2	47.1	47 34.5	9.5	3 43.7	12.7	59.8
17	75 46.4	46.1	62 03.0	9.6	3 31.0	12.8	59.8
18	90 46.7	N 4 45.2	76 31.6	9.6	N 3 18.2	12.7	59.7
19	105 46.9	44.2	91 00.2	9.6	3 05.5	12.7	59.7
20	120 47.1	43.3	105 28.8	9.7	2 52.8	12.8	59.7
21	135 47.3	.. 42.3	119 57.5	9.7	2 40.0	12.7	59.6
22	150 47.5	41.4	134 26.2	9.8	2 27.3	12.8	59.6
23	165 47.7	40.4	148 55.0	9.8	2 14.5	12.7	59.6
11 00	180 48.0	N 4 39.5	163 23.8	9.8	N 2 01.8	12.8	59.6
01	195 48.2	38.5	177 52.6	9.9	1 49.0	12.7	59.5
02	210 48.4	37.6	192 21.5	10.0	1 36.3	12.8	59.5
03	225 48.6	.. 36.6	206 50.5	10.0	1 23.5	12.7	59.5
04	240 48.8	35.7	221 19.5	10.0	1 10.8	12.7	59.4
05	255 49.1	34.7	235 48.5	10.1	0 58.1	12.8	59.4
06	270 49.3	N 4 33.8	250 17.6	10.1	N 0 45.3	12.7	59.4
07	285 49.5	32.8	264 46.7	10.1	0 32.6	12.7	59.3
T 08	300 49.7	31.9	279 15.8	10.2	0 19.9	12.7	59.3
U 09	315 49.9	.. 30.9	293 45.0	10.2	N 0 07.2	12.7	59.3
E 10	330 50.1	30.0	308 14.2	10.3	S 0 05.5	12.6	59.2
S 11	345 50.4	29.0	322 43.5	10.3	0 18.1	12.7	59.2
D 12	0 50.6	N 4 28.1	337 12.8	10.3	S 0 30.8	12.6	59.2
A 13	15 50.8	27.1	351 42.1	10.4	0 43.4	12.6	59.1
Y 14	30 51.0	26.2	6 11.5	10.4	0 56.0	12.6	59.1
15	45 51.2	.. 25.2	20 40.9	10.4	1 08.6	12.6	59.1
16	60 51.5	24.3	35 10.3	10.5	1 21.2	12.5	59.0
17	75 51.7	23.3	49 39.8	10.5	1 33.7	12.5	59.0
18	90 51.9	N 4 22.4	64 09.3	10.6	S 1 46.2	12.5	59.0
19	105 52.1	21.4	78 38.9	10.5	1 58.7	12.5	58.9
20	120 52.3	20.4	93 08.4	10.7	2 11.2	12.5	58.9
21	135 52.6	.. 19.5	107 38.1	10.6	2 23.7	12.4	58.9
22	150 52.8	18.5	122 07.7	10.7	2 36.1	12.4	58.8
23	165 53.0	17.6	136 37.4	10.7	2 48.5	12.3	58.8
12 00	180 53.2	N 4 16.6	151 07.1	10.7	S 3 00.8	12.4	58.8
01	195 53.4	15.7	165 36.8	10.7	3 13.2	12.2	58.7
02	210 53.7	14.7	180 06.5	10.8	3 25.4	12.3	58.7
03	225 53.9	.. 13.8	194 36.3	10.8	3 37.7	12.2	58.7
04	240 54.1	12.8	209 06.1	10.9	3 49.9	12.2	58.6
05	255 54.3	11.9	223 36.0	10.8	4 02.1	12.2	58.6
06	270 54.5	N 4 10.9	238 05.8	10.9	S 4 14.3	12.1	58.6
W 07	285 54.8	10.0	252 35.7	10.9	4 26.4	12.1	58.5
E 08	300 55.0	09.0	267 05.6	11.0	4 38.5	12.0	58.5
D 09	315 55.2	.. 08.1	281 35.6	10.9	4 50.5	12.0	58.4
N 10	330 55.4	07.1	296 05.5	11.0	5 02.5	11.9	58.4
E 11	345 55.6	06.1	310 35.5	11.0	5 14.4	11.9	58.4
S 12	0 55.9	N 4 05.2	325 05.5	11.0	S 5 26.3	11.9	58.3
D 13	15 56.1	04.2	339 35.5	11.1	5 38.2	11.8	58.3
A 14	30 56.3	03.3	354 05.6	11.1	5 50.0	11.8	58.3
Y 15	45 56.5	.. 02.3	8 35.7	11.0	6 01.8	11.7	58.2
16	60 56.7	01.4	23 05.7	11.2	6 13.5	11.7	58.2
17	75 57.0	4 00.4	37 35.9	11.1	6 25.2	11.6	58.2
18	90 57.2	N 3 59.5	52 06.0	11.1	S 6 36.8	11.6	58.1
19	105 57.4	58.5	66 36.1	11.2	6 48.4	11.5	58.1
20	120 57.6	57.6	81 06.3	11.2	6 59.9	11.5	58.0
21	135 57.8	.. 56.6	95 36.5	11.2	7 11.4	11.4	58.0
22	150 58.1	55.6	110 06.7	11.2	7 22.8	11.4	58.0
23	165 58.3	54.7	124 36.9	11.2	S 7 34.2	11.3	57.9
	SD 15.9	d 1.0	SD 16.3		16.1		15.9

Lat.	Twilight Naut.	Civil	Sunrise	Moonrise 10	11	12	13
°	h m	h m	h m	h m	h m	h m	h m
N 72	01 26	03 33	04 48	05 14	07 18	09 17	11 17
N 70	02 12	03 49	04 56	05 22	07 18	09 10	11 00
68	02 40	04 02	05 04	05 30	07 18	09 04	10 47
66	03 01	04 13	05 07	05 35	07 19	08 59	10 36
64	03 17	04 21	05 11	05 40	07 19	08 55	10 27
62	03 31	04 29	05 15	05 45	07 19	08 51	10 20
60	03 41	04 35	05 18	05 48	07 19	08 48	10 13
N 58	03 51	04 41	05 21	05 52	07 20	08 45	10 08
56	03 59	04 45	05 23	05 55	07 20	08 43	10 02
54	04 06	04 50	05 26	05 57	07 20	08 40	09 58
52	04 12	04 53	05 28	05 59	07 20	08 38	09 54
50	04 17	04 57	05 30	06 02	07 20	08 37	09 50
45	04 29	05 04	05 34	06 06	07 21	08 33	09 42
N 40	04 37	05 10	05 37	06 10	07 21	08 29	09 36
35	04 44	05 14	05 40	06 14	07 21	08 26	09 30
30	04 50	05 18	05 42	06 16	07 21	08 24	09 25
20	04 59	05 24	05 47	06 22	07 22	08 20	09 16
N 10	05 05	05 29	05 50	06 26	07 22	08 16	09 09
0	05 09	05 33	05 53	06 30	07 22	08 13	09 02
S 10	05 11	05 36	05 57	06 34	07 23	08 09	08 55
20	05 12	05 38	06 00	06 39	07 23	08 06	08 48
30	05 12	05 40	06 03	06 44	07 23	08 02	08 39
35	05 11	05 40	06 05	06 47	07 24	07 59	08 35
40	05 09	05 41	06 08	06 50	07 24	07 57	08 29
45	05 07	05 41	06 10	06 54	07 24	07 54	08 23
S 50	05 04	05 41	06 13	06 59	07 25	07 50	08 16
52	05 02	05 41	06 15	07 01	07 25	07 49	08 12
54	05 00	05 41	06 16	07 03	07 25	07 47	08 09
56	04 58	05 41	06 18	07 05	07 26	07 45	08 05
58	04 55	05 41	06 20	07 08	07 26	07 43	08 00
S 60	04 52	05 40	06 22	07 11	07 26	07 40	07 55

Lat.	Sunset	Twilight Civil	Naut.	Moonset 10	11	12	13
°	h m	h m	h m	h m	h m	h m	h m
N 72	19 02	20 16	22 17	19 32	19 19	19 05	18 50
N 70	18 55	20 01	21 36	19 28	19 22	19 15	19 08
68	18 49	19 48	21 09	19 25	19 24	19 23	19 23
66	18 44	19 38	20 49	19 22	19 26	19 30	19 35
64	18 40	19 30	20 33	19 20	19 28	19 36	19 45
62	18 37	19 22	20 20	19 18	19 29	19 41	19 53
60	18 34	19 16	20 10	19 16	19 31	19 45	20 01
N 58	18 31	19 11	20 00	19 15	19 32	19 49	20 07
56	18 29	19 06	19 53	19 13	19 33	19 53	20 13
54	18 26	19 02	19 46	19 12	19 34	19 56	20 19
52	18 24	18 59	19 40	19 11	19 35	19 58	20 23
50	18 23	18 55	19 35	19 10	19 36	20 01	20 28
45	18 19	18 48	19 24	19 08	19 37	20 07	20 37
N 40	18 16	18 43	19 15	19 06	19 39	20 11	20 45
35	18 13	18 38	19 08	19 04	19 40	20 16	20 51
30	18 11	18 35	19 03	19 02	19 41	20 19	20 57
20	18 06	18 29	18 54	19 00	19 43	20 25	21 08
N 10	18 03	18 24	18 49	18 57	19 45	20 31	21 17
0	18 00	18 21	18 45	18 55	19 46	20 36	21 25
S 10	17 57	18 18	18 42	18 53	19 48	20 41	21 34
20	17 54	18 16	18 41	18 50	19 50	20 47	21 43
30	17 50	18 14	18 42	18 48	19 51	20 53	21 53
35	17 48	18 14	18 43	18 46	19 53	20 57	22 00
40	17 46	18 13	18 45	18 44	19 54	21 01	22 06
45	17 44	18 13	18 47	18 42	19 55	21 06	22 14
S 50	17 41	18 13	18 51	18 39	19 57	21 12	22 24
52	17 40	18 13	18 52	18 38	19 58	21 15	22 29
54	17 38	18 13	18 54	18 37	19 58	21 18	22 34
56	17 36	18 14	18 57	18 35	19 59	21 21	22 39
58	17 35	18 14	19 00	18 33	20 00	21 24	22 45
S 60	17 33	18 14	19 03	18 32	20 01	21 29	22 52

Day	SUN Eqn. of Time 00h	12h	Mer. Pass.	MOON Mer. Pass. Upper	Lower	Age	Phase
d	m s	m s	h m	h m	h m	d	%
10	02 50	03 01	11 57	12 43	00 16	01	1
11	03 11	03 22	11 57	13 34	01 09	02	4
12	03 32	03 43	11 56	14 24	02 00	03	10

UT	ARIES GHA	VENUS −4·7 GHA	Dec	MARS −1·7 GHA	Dec	JUPITER −1·9 GHA	Dec	SATURN +0·4 GHA	Dec	STARS Name	SHA	Dec
d h	° ′	° ′	° ′	° ′	° ′	° ′	° ′	° ′	° ′		° ′	° ′
13 00	351 56.1	143 21.1	S16 45.6	48 10.4	S24 54.2	125 12.6	S16 40.3	79 08.5	S22 43.4	Acamar	315 15.4	S40 13.7
01	6 58.6	158 22.1	46.5	63 12.4	53.9	140 14.7	40.4	94 10.9	43.4	Achernar	335 23.7	S57 08.4
02	22 01.1	173 23.1	47.4	78 14.3	53.7	155 16.7	40.5	109 13.4	43.4	Acrux	173 05.9	S63 12.1
03	37 03.5	188 24.1	.. 48.2	93 16.2	.. 53.4	170 18.8	.. 40.6	124 15.8	.. 43.4	Adhara	255 09.9	S28 59.7
04	52 06.0	203 25.1	49.1	108 18.2	53.1	185 20.9	40.8	139 18.3	43.4	Aldebaran	290 45.2	N16 32.7
05	67 08.5	218 26.1	50.0	123 20.1	52.9	200 22.9	40.9	154 20.7	43.4			
06	82 10.9	233 27.1	S16 50.8	138 22.0	S24 52.6	215 25.0	S16 41.0	169 23.1	S22 43.4	Alioth	166 18.1	N55 51.8
07	97 13.4	248 28.1	51.7	153 23.9	52.3	230 27.0	41.1	184 25.6	43.4	Alkaid	152 56.5	N49 13.6
T 08	112 15.9	263 29.1	52.5	168 25.8	52.1	245 29.1	41.2	199 28.0	43.4	Al Na'ir	27 38.9	S46 52.2
H 09	127 18.3	278 30.1	.. 53.4	183 27.8	.. 51.8	260 31.2	.. 41.3	214 30.4	.. 43.4	Alnilam	275 42.8	S 1 11.4
U 10	142 20.8	293 31.1	54.3	198 29.7	51.5	275 33.2	41.5	229 32.9	43.4	Alphard	217 52.9	S 8 44.2
R 11	157 23.2	308 32.1	55.1	213 31.6	51.3	290 35.3	41.6	244 35.3	43.4			
S 12	172 25.7	323 33.1	S16 56.0	228 33.5	S24 51.0	305 37.4	S16 41.7	259 37.7	S22 43.4	Alphecca	126 08.2	N26 39.5
D 13	187 28.2	338 34.1	56.8	243 35.4	50.7	320 39.4	41.8	274 40.2	43.4	Alpheratz	357 39.5	N29 11.6
A 14	202 30.6	353 35.1	57.7	258 37.3	50.5	335 41.5	41.9	289 42.6	43.4	Altair	62 04.6	N 8 55.3
Y 15	217 33.1	8 36.2	.. 58.6	273 39.3	.. 50.2	350 43.6	.. 42.0	304 45.0	.. 43.5	Ankaa	353 11.8	S42 12.2
16	232 35.6	23 37.2	16 59.4	288 41.2	49.9	5 45.6	42.2	319 47.4	43.5	Antares	112 22.0	S26 28.2
17	247 38.0	38 38.2	17 00.3	303 43.1	49.6	20 47.7	42.3	334 49.9	43.5			
18	262 40.5	53 39.2	S17 01.1	318 45.0	S24 49.4	35 49.7	S16 42.4	349 52.3	S22 43.5	Arcturus	145 52.7	N19 05.5
19	277 43.0	68 40.2	02.0	333 46.9	49.1	50 51.8	42.5	4 54.7	43.5	Atria	107 20.6	S69 03.7
20	292 45.4	83 41.2	02.8	348 48.8	48.8	65 53.9	42.6	19 57.2	43.5	Avior	234 17.0	S59 33.9
21	307 47.9	98 42.3	.. 03.7	3 50.7	.. 48.6	80 55.9	.. 42.7	34 59.6	.. 43.5	Bellatrix	278 28.2	N 6 21.9
22	322 50.3	113 43.3	04.5	18 52.6	48.3	95 58.0	42.9	50 02.1	43.5	Betelgeuse	270 57.5	N 7 24.6
23	337 52.8	128 44.3	05.4	33 54.5	48.0	111 00.1	43.0	65 04.5	43.5			
14 00	352 55.3	143 45.4	S17 06.2	48 56.4	S24 47.7	126 02.1	S16 43.1	80 06.9	S22 43.5	Canopus	263 54.7	S52 42.1
01	7 57.7	158 46.4	07.1	63 58.3	47.5	141 04.2	43.2	95 09.3	43.5	Capella	280 29.2	N46 00.7
02	23 00.2	173 47.4	07.9	79 00.2	47.2	156 06.2	43.3	110 11.8	43.5	Deneb	49 28.7	N45 21.1
03	38 02.7	188 48.5	.. 08.8	94 02.1	.. 46.9	171 08.3	.. 43.4	125 14.2	.. 43.5	Denebola	182 30.4	N14 28.3
04	53 05.1	203 49.5	09.6	109 04.0	46.6	186 10.4	43.6	140 16.6	43.5	Diphda	348 52.0	S17 53.0
05	68 07.6	218 50.5	10.5	124 05.9	46.4	201 12.4	43.7	155 19.0	43.5			
06	83 10.1	233 51.6	S17 11.3	139 07.8	S24 46.1	216 14.5	S16 43.8	170 21.5	S22 43.5	Dubhe	193 48.1	N61 39.1
07	98 12.5	248 52.6	12.2	154 09.7	45.8	231 16.5	43.9	185 23.9	43.5	Elnath	278 08.1	N28 37.2
08	113 15.0	263 53.6	13.0	169 11.6	45.5	246 18.6	44.0	200 26.3	43.5	Eltanin	90 44.4	N51 29.6
F 09	128 17.5	278 54.7	.. 13.8	184 13.4	.. 45.3	261 20.7	.. 44.1	215 28.8	.. 43.6	Enif	33 43.3	N 9 57.8
R 10	143 19.9	293 55.7	14.7	199 15.3	45.0	276 22.7	44.3	230 31.2	43.6	Fomalhaut	15 19.7	S29 31.3
I 11	158 22.4	308 56.8	15.5	214 17.2	44.7	291 24.8	44.4	245 33.6	43.6			
D 12	173 24.8	323 57.8	S17 16.4	229 19.1	S24 44.4	306 26.8	S16 44.5	260 36.1	S22 43.6	Gacrux	171 57.5	S57 13.0
A 13	188 27.3	338 58.9	17.2	244 21.0	44.2	321 28.9	44.6	275 38.5	43.6	Gienah	175 49.0	S17 38.5
Y 14	203 29.8	353 59.9	18.0	259 22.9	43.9	336 31.0	44.7	290 40.9	43.6	Hadar	148 43.3	S60 27.7
15	218 32.2	9 01.0	.. 18.9	274 24.7	.. 43.6	351 33.0	.. 44.8	305 43.3	.. 43.6	Hamal	327 56.5	N23 32.9
16	233 34.7	24 02.1	19.7	289 26.6	43.3	6 35.1	45.0	320 45.8	43.6	Kaus Aust.	83 39.0	S34 22.4
17	248 37.2	39 03.1	20.5	304 28.5	43.1	21 37.1	45.1	335 48.2	43.6			
18	263 39.6	54 04.2	S17 21.4	319 30.4	S24 42.8	36 39.2	S16 45.2	350 50.6	S22 43.6	Kochab	137 20.9	N74 05.1
19	278 42.1	69 05.2	22.2	334 32.3	42.5	51 41.2	45.3	5 53.0	43.6	Markab	13 34.5	N15 18.4
20	293 44.6	84 06.3	23.0	349 34.1	42.2	66 43.3	45.4	20 55.5	43.6	Menkar	314 11.1	N 4 09.7
21	308 47.0	99 07.4	.. 23.9	4 36.0	.. 41.9	81 45.4	.. 45.6	35 57.9	.. 43.6	Menkent	148 03.7	S36 27.6
22	323 49.5	114 08.4	24.7	19 37.9	41.7	96 47.4	45.7	51 00.3	43.6	Miaplacidus	221 39.7	S69 47.4
23	338 52.0	129 09.5	25.5	34 39.7	41.4	111 49.5	45.8	66 02.8	43.6			
15 00	353 54.4	144 10.6	S17 26.4	49 41.6	S24 41.1	126 51.5	S16 45.9	81 05.2	S22 43.6	Mirfak	308 35.0	N49 55.3
01	8 56.9	159 11.7	27.2	64 43.5	40.8	141 53.6	46.0	96 07.6	43.6	Nunki	75 53.8	S26 16.3
02	23 59.3	174 12.7	28.0	79 45.4	40.5	156 55.6	46.1	111 10.0	43.6	Peacock	53 13.3	S56 40.5
03	39 01.8	189 13.8	.. 28.8	94 47.2	.. 40.3	171 57.7	.. 46.3	126 12.5	.. 43.6	Pollux	243 23.6	N27 58.7
04	54 04.3	204 14.9	29.7	109 49.1	40.0	186 59.8	46.4	141 14.9	43.7	Procyon	244 56.2	N 5 10.6
05	69 06.7	219 16.0	30.5	124 50.9	39.7	202 01.8	46.5	156 17.3	43.7			
06	84 09.2	234 17.1	S17 31.3	139 52.8	S24 39.4	217 03.9	S16 46.6	171 19.7	S22 43.7	Rasalhague	96 03.1	N12 33.1
07	99 11.7	249 18.1	32.1	154 54.7	39.1	232 05.9	46.7	186 22.2	43.7	Regulus	207 40.1	N11 52.7
S 08	114 14.1	264 19.2	33.0	169 56.5	38.8	247 08.0	46.8	201 24.6	43.7	Rigel	281 08.6	S 8 10.8
A 09	129 16.6	279 20.3	.. 33.8	184 58.4	.. 38.6	262 10.0	.. 47.0	216 27.0	.. 43.7	Rigil Kent.	139 47.3	S60 54.7
T 10	144 19.1	294 21.4	34.6	200 00.2	38.3	277 12.1	47.1	231 29.4	43.7	Sabik	102 08.5	S15 44.7
U 11	159 21.5	309 22.5	35.4	215 02.1	38.0	292 14.1	47.2	246 31.9	43.7			
R 12	174 24.0	324 23.6	S17 36.2	230 04.0	S24 37.7	307 16.2	S16 47.3	261 34.3	S22 43.7	Schedar	349 35.9	N56 38.3
D 13	189 26.4	339 24.7	37.0	245 05.8	37.4	322 18.3	47.4	276 36.7	43.7	Shaula	96 17.1	S37 06.9
A 14	204 28.9	354 25.8	37.9	260 07.7	37.1	337 20.3	47.6	291 39.1	43.7	Sirius	258 30.7	S16 44.4
Y 15	219 31.4	9 26.9	.. 38.7	275 09.5	.. 36.9	352 22.4	.. 47.7	306 41.5	.. 43.7	Spica	158 27.8	S11 15.3
16	234 33.8	24 28.0	39.5	290 11.4	36.6	7 24.4	47.8	321 44.0	43.7	Suhail	222 50.2	S43 30.3
17	249 36.3	39 29.1	40.3	305 13.2	36.3	22 26.5	47.9	336 46.4	43.7			
18	264 38.8	54 30.2	S17 41.1	320 15.1	S24 36.0	37 28.5	S16 48.0	351 48.8	S22 43.7	Vega	80 36.4	N38 48.5
19	279 41.2	69 31.3	41.9	335 16.9	35.7	52 30.6	48.1	6 51.2	43.7	Zuben'ubi	137 01.7	S16 06.9
20	294 43.7	84 32.4	42.7	350 18.8	35.4	67 32.6	48.3	21 53.7	43.7		SHA	Mer. Pass.
21	309 46.2	99 33.5	.. 43.6	5 20.6	.. 35.1	82 34.7	.. 48.4	36 56.1	.. 43.7		° ′	h m
22	324 48.6	114 34.7	44.4	20 22.4	34.9	97 36.7	48.5	51 58.5	43.8	Venus	150 50.1	14 24
23	339 51.1	129 35.8	45.2	35 24.3	34.6	112 38.8	48.6	67 00.9	43.8	Mars	56 01.1	20 42
	h m									Jupiter	133 06.8	15 34
Mer. Pass. 0 28.2	v 1.1 d 0.8			v 1.9 d 0.3		v 2.1 d 0.1		v 2.4 d 0.0		Saturn	87 11.6	18 37

UT	SUN GHA	SUN Dec	MOON GHA	v	Dec	d	HP
d h	° ′	° ′	° ′	′	° ′	′	′
13 00	180 58.5	N 3 53.7	139 07.1	11.3	S 7 45.5	11.2	57.9
01	195 58.7	52.8	153 37.4	11.2	7 56.7	11.2	57.9
02	210 58.9	51.8	168 07.6	11.3	8 07.9	11.2	57.8
03	225 59.2	.. 50.9	182 37.9	11.3	8 19.1	11.1	57.8
04	240 59.4	49.9	197 08.2	11.3	8 30.2	11.0	57.7
05	255 59.6	49.0	211 38.5	11.3	8 41.2	10.9	57.7
06	270 59.8	N 3 48.0	226 08.8	11.3	S 8 52.1	10.9	57.7
07	286 00.1	47.0	240 39.1	11.4	9 03.0	10.9	57.6
T 08	301 00.3	46.1	255 09.5	11.3	9 13.9	10.8	57.6
H 09	316 00.5	.. 45.1	269 39.8	11.4	9 24.7	10.7	57.6
U 10	331 00.7	44.2	284 10.2	11.3	9 35.4	10.6	57.5
R 11	346 00.9	43.2	298 40.5	11.4	9 46.0	10.6	57.5
S 12	1 01.2	N 3 42.3	313 10.9	11.4	S 9 56.6	10.6	57.5
D 13	16 01.4	41.3	327 41.3	11.4	10 07.2	10.4	57.4
A 14	31 01.6	40.3	342 11.7	11.4	10 17.6	10.4	57.4
Y 15	46 01.8	.. 39.4	356 42.1	11.4	10 28.0	10.3	57.3
16	61 02.0	38.4	11 12.5	11.4	10 38.3	10.3	57.3
17	76 02.3	37.5	25 42.9	11.4	10 48.6	10.2	57.3
18	91 02.5	N 3 36.5	40 13.3	11.5	S10 58.8	10.1	57.2
19	106 02.7	35.6	54 43.8	11.4	11 08.9	10.1	57.2
20	121 02.9	34.6	69 14.2	11.5	11 19.0	9.9	57.2
21	136 03.2	.. 33.6	83 44.7	11.4	11 28.9	9.9	57.1
22	151 03.4	32.7	98 15.1	11.5	11 38.8	9.9	57.1
23	166 03.6	31.7	112 45.6	11.4	11 48.7	9.7	57.0
14 00	181 03.8	N 3 30.8	127 16.0	11.5	S11 58.4	9.7	57.0
01	196 04.0	29.8	141 46.5	11.5	12 08.1	9.6	57.0
02	211 04.3	28.8	156 17.0	11.4	12 17.7	9.6	56.9
03	226 04.5	.. 27.9	170 47.4	11.5	12 27.3	9.4	56.9
04	241 04.7	26.9	185 17.9	11.5	12 36.7	9.4	56.9
05	256 04.9	26.0	199 48.4	11.5	12 46.1	9.3	56.8
06	271 05.1	N 3 25.0	214 18.9	11.5	S12 55.4	9.3	56.8
07	286 05.4	24.0	228 49.4	11.5	13 04.7	9.1	56.8
F 08	301 05.6	23.1	243 19.9	11.5	13 13.8	9.1	56.7
R 09	316 05.8	.. 22.1	257 50.4	11.4	13 22.9	9.0	56.7
I 10	331 06.0	21.2	272 20.8	11.5	13 31.9	8.9	56.7
11	346 06.3	20.2	286 51.3	11.5	13 40.8	8.9	56.6
D 12	1 06.5	N 3 19.2	301 21.8	11.5	S13 49.7	8.8	56.6
A 13	16 06.7	18.3	315 52.3	11.5	13 58.5	8.6	56.6
Y 14	31 06.9	17.3	330 22.8	11.5	14 07.1	8.6	56.5
15	46 07.1	.. 16.4	344 53.3	11.5	14 15.7	8.6	56.5
16	61 07.4	15.4	359 23.8	11.5	14 24.3	8.4	56.5
17	76 07.6	14.4	13 54.3	11.5	14 32.7	8.4	56.4
18	91 07.8	N 3 13.5	28 24.8	11.5	S14 41.1	8.2	56.4
19	106 08.0	12.5	42 55.3	11.5	14 49.3	8.2	56.3
20	121 08.3	11.6	57 25.8	11.5	14 57.5	8.1	56.3
21	136 08.5	.. 10.6	71 56.3	11.5	15 05.6	8.0	56.3
22	151 08.7	09.6	86 26.8	11.5	15 13.6	8.0	56.3
23	166 08.9	08.7	100 57.3	11.5	15 21.6	7.8	56.2
15 00	181 09.1	N 3 07.7	115 27.8	11.5	S15 29.4	7.8	56.2
01	196 09.4	06.8	129 58.3	11.5	15 37.2	7.7	56.2
02	211 09.6	05.8	144 28.8	11.4	15 44.9	7.6	56.1
03	226 09.8	.. 04.8	158 59.2	11.5	15 52.5	7.5	56.1
04	241 10.0	03.9	173 29.7	11.5	16 00.0	7.4	56.1
05	256 10.3	02.9	188 00.2	11.5	16 07.4	7.3	56.0
06	271 10.5	N 3 02.0	202 30.7	11.5	S16 14.7	7.2	56.0
07	286 10.7	01.0	217 01.2	11.4	16 21.9	7.2	56.0
S 08	301 10.9	3 00.0	231 31.6	11.5	16 29.1	7.1	55.9
A 09	316 11.2	2 59.1	246 02.1	11.5	16 36.2	6.9	55.9
T 10	331 11.4	58.1	260 32.6	11.5	16 43.1	6.9	55.9
U 11	346 11.6	57.1	275 03.1	11.4	16 50.0	6.8	55.8
R 12	1 11.8	N 2 56.2	289 33.5	11.5	S16 56.8	6.7	55.8
D 13	16 12.0	55.2	304 04.0	11.5	17 03.5	6.6	55.8
A 14	31 12.3	54.3	318 34.5	11.4	17 10.1	6.5	55.8
Y 15	46 12.5	.. 53.3	333 04.9	11.5	17 16.6	6.5	55.7
16	61 12.7	52.3	347 35.4	11.4	17 23.1	6.3	55.7
17	76 12.9	51.4	2 05.8	11.5	17 29.4	6.2	55.7
18	91 13.2	N 2 50.4	16 36.3	11.4	S17 35.6	6.2	55.6
19	106 13.4	49.4	31 06.7	11.5	17 41.8	6.1	55.6
20	121 13.6	48.5	45 37.2	11.4	17 47.9	5.9	55.6
21	136 13.8	.. 47.5	60 07.6	11.5	17 53.8	5.9	55.6
22	151 14.0	46.6	74 38.1	11.4	17 59.7	5.8	55.5
23	166 14.3	45.6	89 08.5	11.4	S18 05.5	5.7	55.5
	SD 15.9	d 1.0	SD 15.7		15.4		15.2

Twilight / Moonrise

Lat.	Naut.	Civil	Sunrise	Moonrise 13	14	15	16
°	h m	h m	h m	h m	h m	h m	h m
N 72	01 58	03 49	05 02	11 17	13 21	15 52	▬
N 70	02 32	04 03	05 08	11 00	12 50	14 44	16 54
68	02 56	04 14	05 13	10 47	12 28	14 08	15 43
66	03 14	04 23	05 16	10 36	12 11	13 42	15 06
64	03 29	04 31	05 20	10 27	11 57	13 22	14 41
62	03 40	04 37	05 23	10 20	11 45	13 06	14 20
60	03 50	04 43	05 25	10 13	11 35	12 53	14 04
N 58	03 58	04 47	05 27	10 08	11 27	12 41	13 50
56	04 06	04 52	05 29	10 02	11 19	12 32	13 38
54	04 12	04 55	05 31	09 58	11 12	12 23	13 28
52	04 18	04 59	05 33	09 54	11 06	12 15	13 19
50	04 22	05 01	05 34	09 50	11 01	12 08	13 11
45	04 33	05 08	05 37	09 42	10 49	11 53	12 53
N 40	04 40	05 13	05 40	09 36	10 40	11 41	12 39
35	04 47	05 17	05 42	09 30	10 31	11 30	12 27
30	04 52	05 20	05 44	09 25	10 24	11 21	12 17
20	04 59	05 25	05 47	09 16	10 12	11 06	11 59
N 10	05 04	05 29	05 50	09 09	10 01	10 52	11 43
0	05 08	05 32	05 52	09 02	09 51	10 40	11 28
S 10	05 09	05 34	05 55	08 55	09 41	10 27	11 14
20	05 10	05 35	05 57	08 48	09 30	10 14	10 59
30	05 08	05 36	06 00	08 39	09 18	09 58	10 41
35	05 07	05 36	06 01	08 35	09 11	09 50	10 31
40	05 04	05 36	06 03	08 29	09 03	09 40	10 19
45	05 01	05 35	06 05	08 23	08 54	09 28	10 05
S 50	04 57	05 35	06 07	08 16	08 43	09 14	09 48
52	04 55	05 34	06 08	08 12	08 38	09 07	09 41
54	04 53	05 34	06 09	08 09	08 33	09 00	09 32
56	04 50	05 33	06 10	08 05	08 26	08 52	09 22
58	04 47	05 32	06 11	08 00	08 20	08 43	09 11
S 60	04 43	05 31	06 13	07 55	08 12	08 32	08 58

Sunset / Twilight / Moonset

Lat.	Sunset	Civil	Naut.	Moonset 13	14	15	16
°	h m	h m	h m	h m	h m	h m	h m
N 72	18 46	19 58	21 46	18 50	18 28	17 39	▬
N 70	18 41	19 45	21 14	19 08	19 00	18 48	18 20
68	18 36	19 34	20 51	19 23	19 23	19 25	19 31
66	18 33	19 26	20 34	19 35	19 41	19 51	20 08
64	18 30	19 18	20 20	19 45	19 56	20 12	20 34
62	18 27	19 12	20 08	19 53	20 09	20 28	20 55
60	18 25	19 07	19 59	20 01	20 19	20 42	21 12
N 58	18 22	19 02	19 51	20 07	20 28	20 54	21 26
56	18 21	18 58	19 44	20 13	20 37	21 04	21 38
54	18 19	18 55	19 38	20 19	20 44	21 13	21 48
52	18 17	18 51	19 32	20 23	20 50	21 22	21 58
50	18 16	18 49	19 27	20 28	20 56	21 29	22 06
45	18 13	18 43	19 18	20 37	21 09	21 45	22 24
N 40	18 11	18 38	19 10	20 45	21 20	21 58	22 39
35	18 09	18 34	19 04	20 51	21 29	22 09	22 51
30	18 07	18 31	18 59	20 57	21 37	22 18	23 02
20	18 04	18 26	18 51	21 08	21 51	22 35	23 21
N 10	18 01	18 22	18 47	21 17	22 03	22 49	23 37
0	17 59	18 20	18 44	21 25	22 14	23 03	23 52
S 10	17 57	18 18	18 42	21 34	22 26	23 17	24 07
20	17 54	18 16	18 42	21 43	22 38	23 31	24 24
30	17 52	18 16	18 44	21 53	22 52	23 48	24 42
35	17 51	18 16	18 45	22 00	23 00	23 58	24 53
40	17 49	18 16	18 47	22 06	23 09	24 09	00 09
45	17 47	18 17	18 51	22 14	23 20	24 22	00 22
S 50	17 45	18 17	18 55	22 24	23 33	24 38	00 38
52	17 44	18 18	18 57	22 29	23 39	24 46	00 46
54	17 43	18 19	19 00	22 34	23 46	24 54	00 54
56	17 42	18 19	19 03	22 39	23 54	25 04	01 04
58	17 41	18 20	19 06	22 45	24 03	00 03	01 15
S 60	17 40	18 21	19 10	22 52	24 12	00 12	01 27

SUN and MOON

Day	SUN Eqn. of Time 00h	12h	Mer. Pass.	MOON Mer. Pass. Upper	Lower	Age	Phase
d	m s	m s	h m	h m	h m	d	%
13	03 54	04 04	11 56	15 14	02 49	04	18
14	04 15	04 25	11 56	16 02	03 38	05	26
15	04 36	04 47	11 55	16 51	04 27	06	36

UT	ARIES GHA	VENUS −4.8 GHA	Dec	MARS −1.7 GHA	Dec	JUPITER −1.9 GHA	Dec	SATURN +0.4 GHA	Dec	STARS Name	SHA	Dec
16 00	354 53.6	144 36.9	S17 46.0	50 26.1	S24 34.3	127 40.8	S16 48.7	82 03.4	S22 43.8	Acamar	315 15.4	S40 13.7
01	9 56.0	159 38.0	46.8	65 28.0	34.0	142 42.9	48.9	97 05.8	43.8	Achernar	335 23.6	S57 08.4
02	24 58.5	174 39.1	47.6	80 29.8	33.7	157 44.9	49.0	112 08.2	43.8	Acrux	173 05.9	S63 12.1
03	40 00.9	189 40.2 ..	48.4	95 31.6 ..	33.4	172 47.0 ..	49.1	127 10.6 ..	43.8	Adhara	255 09.9	S28 59.7
04	55 03.4	204 41.4	49.2	110 33.5	33.1	187 49.0	49.2	142 13.0	43.8	Aldebaran	290 45.2	N16 32.7
05	70 05.9	219 42.5	50.0	125 35.3	32.8	202 51.1	49.3	157 15.5	43.8			
06	85 08.3	234 43.6	S17 50.8	140 37.1	S24 32.6	217 53.1	S16 49.4	172 17.9	S22 43.8	Alioth	166 18.1	N55 51.8
07	100 10.8	249 44.8	51.6	155 39.0	32.3	232 55.2	49.6	187 20.3	43.8	Alkaid	152 56.5	N49 13.6
08	115 13.3	264 45.9	52.4	170 40.8	32.0	247 57.2	49.7	202 22.7	43.8	Al Na'ir	27 38.9	S46 52.2
S 09	130 15.7	279 47.0 ..	53.2	185 42.6 ..	31.7	262 59.3 ..	49.8	217 25.1 ..	43.8	Alnilam	275 42.8	S 1 11.4
U 10	145 18.2	294 48.2	54.0	200 44.5	31.4	278 01.4	49.9	232 27.6	43.8	Alphard	217 52.9	S 8 44.2
N 11	160 20.7	309 49.3	54.8	215 46.3	31.1	293 03.4	50.0	247 30.0	43.8			
D 12	175 23.1	324 50.5	S17 55.6	230 48.1	S24 30.8	308 05.5	S16 50.2	262 32.4	S22 43.8	Alphecca	126 08.2	N26 39.5
A 13	190 25.6	339 51.6	56.4	245 49.9	30.5	323 07.5	50.3	277 34.8	43.8	Alpheratz	357 39.4	N29 11.6
Y 14	205 28.1	354 52.7	57.2	260 51.8	30.2	338 09.6	50.4	292 37.2	43.8	Altair	62 04.6	N 8 55.3
15	220 30.5	9 53.9 ..	58.0	275 53.6 ..	29.9	353 11.6 ..	50.5	307 39.7 ..	43.8	Ankaa	353 11.8	S42 12.2
16	235 33.0	24 55.0	58.8	290 55.4	29.6	8 13.7	50.6	322 42.1	43.8	Antares	112 22.0	S26 28.2
17	250 35.4	39 56.2	17 59.6	305 57.2	29.4	23 15.7	50.8	337 44.5	43.9			
18	265 37.9	54 57.3	S18 00.4	320 59.0	S24 29.1	38 17.7	S16 50.9	352 46.9	S22 43.9	Arcturus	145 52.8	N19 05.5
19	280 40.4	69 58.5	01.1	336 00.9	28.8	53 19.8	51.0	7 49.3	43.9	Atria	107 20.7	S69 03.7
20	295 42.8	84 59.7	01.9	351 02.7	28.5	68 21.8	51.1	22 51.7	43.9	Avior	234 17.0	S59 33.9
21	310 45.3	100 00.8 ..	02.7	6 04.5 ..	28.2	83 23.9 ..	51.2	37 54.2 ..	43.9	Bellatrix	278 28.2	N 6 21.9
22	325 47.8	115 02.0	03.5	21 06.3	27.9	98 25.9	51.3	52 56.6	43.9	Betelgeuse	270 57.5	N 7 24.6
23	340 50.2	130 03.1	04.3	36 08.1	27.6	113 28.0	51.5	67 59.0	43.9			
17 00	355 52.7	145 04.3	S18 05.1	51 09.9	S24 27.3	128 30.0	S16 51.6	83 01.4	S22 43.9	Canopus	263 54.7	S52 42.1
01	10 55.2	160 05.5	05.9	66 11.7	27.0	143 32.1	51.7	98 03.8	43.9	Capella	280 29.1	N46 00.7
02	25 57.6	175 06.6	06.6	81 13.5	26.7	158 34.1	51.8	113 06.3	43.9	Deneb	49 28.7	N45 21.1
03	41 00.1	190 07.8 ..	07.4	96 15.4 ..	26.4	173 36.2 ..	51.9	128 08.7 ..	43.9	Denebola	182 30.4	N14 28.3
04	56 02.5	205 09.0	08.2	111 17.2	26.1	188 38.2	52.1	143 11.1	43.9	Diphda	348 52.0	S17 53.0
05	71 05.0	220 10.2	09.0	126 19.0	25.8	203 40.3	52.2	158 13.5	43.9			
06	86 07.5	235 11.3	S18 09.8	141 20.8	S24 25.5	218 42.3	S16 52.3	173 15.9	S22 43.9	Dubhe	193 48.0	N61 39.1
07	101 09.9	250 12.5	10.5	156 22.6	25.2	233 44.4	52.4	188 18.3	43.9	Elnath	278 08.1	N28 37.2
08	116 12.4	265 13.7	11.3	171 24.4	24.9	248 46.4	52.5	203 20.8	43.9	Eltanin	90 44.4	N51 29.6
M 09	131 14.9	280 14.9 ..	12.1	186 26.2 ..	24.6	263 48.5 ..	52.7	218 23.2 ..	43.9	Enif	33 43.3	N 9 57.8
O 10	146 17.3	295 16.1	12.9	201 28.0	24.3	278 50.5	52.8	233 25.6	43.9	Fomalhaut	15 19.7	S29 31.3
N 11	161 19.8	310 17.3	13.7	216 29.8	24.0	293 52.6	52.9	248 28.0	43.9			
D 12	176 22.3	325 18.5	S18 14.4	231 31.6	S24 23.7	308 54.6	S16 53.0	263 30.4	S22 43.9	Gacrux	171 57.5	S57 12.9
A 13	191 24.7	340 19.6	15.2	246 33.4	23.4	323 56.6	53.1	278 32.8	44.0	Gienah	175 49.0	S17 38.5
Y 14	206 27.2	355 20.8	16.0	261 35.2	23.1	338 58.7	53.3	293 35.2	44.0	Hadar	148 43.3	S60 27.7
15	221 29.7	10 22.0 ..	16.7	276 37.0 ..	22.9	354 00.7 ..	53.4	308 37.7 ..	44.0	Hamal	327 56.5	N23 32.9
16	236 32.1	25 23.2	17.5	291 38.7	22.6	9 02.8	53.5	323 40.1	44.0	Kaus Aust.	83 39.0	S34 22.4
17	251 34.6	40 24.4	18.3	306 40.5	22.3	24 04.8	53.6	338 42.5	44.0			
18	266 37.0	55 25.6	S18 19.0	321 42.3	S24 22.0	39 06.9	S16 53.7	353 44.9	S22 44.0	Kochab	137 20.9	N74 05.1
19	281 39.5	70 26.8	19.8	336 44.1	21.7	54 08.9	53.9	8 47.3	44.0	Markab	13 34.5	N15 18.4
20	296 42.0	85 28.1	20.6	351 45.9	21.4	69 11.0	54.0	23 49.7	44.0	Menkar	314 11.1	N 4 09.7
21	311 44.4	100 29.3 ..	21.3	6 47.7 ..	21.1	84 13.0 ..	54.1	38 52.1 ..	44.0	Menkent	148 03.7	S36 27.6
22	326 46.9	115 30.5	22.1	21 49.5	20.8	99 15.1	54.2	53 54.6	44.0	Miaplacidus	221 39.6	S69 47.4
23	341 49.4	130 31.7	22.9	36 51.3	20.5	114 17.1	54.3	68 57.0	44.0			
18 00	356 51.8	145 32.9	S18 23.6	51 53.0	S24 20.2	129 19.1	S16 54.5	83 59.4	S22 44.0	Mirfak	308 35.0	N49 55.5
01	11 54.3	160 34.1	24.4	66 54.8	19.8	144 21.2	54.6	99 01.8	44.0	Nunki	75 53.8	S26 16.3
02	26 56.8	175 35.3	25.2	81 56.6	19.5	159 23.2	54.7	114 04.2	44.0	Peacock	53 13.3	S56 40.5
03	41 59.2	190 36.6 ..	25.9	96 58.4 ..	19.2	174 25.3 ..	54.8	129 06.6 ..	44.0	Pollux	243 23.6	N27 58.7
04	57 01.7	205 37.8	26.7	112 00.2	18.9	189 27.3	54.9	144 09.0	44.0	Procyon	244 56.2	N 5 10.6
05	72 04.2	220 39.0	27.4	127 01.9	18.6	204 29.4	55.1	159 11.4	44.0			
06	87 06.6	235 40.2	S18 28.2	142 03.7	S24 18.3	219 31.4	S16 55.2	174 13.9	S22 44.0	Rasalhague	96 03.2	N12 33.1
07	102 09.1	250 41.5	28.9	157 05.5	18.0	234 33.4	55.3	189 16.3	44.0	Regulus	207 40.0	N11 52.7
08	117 11.5	265 42.7	29.7	172 07.3	17.7	249 35.5	55.4	204 18.7	44.1	Rigel	281 08.6	S 8 10.8
T 09	132 14.0	280 43.9 ..	30.4	187 09.0 ..	17.4	264 37.5 ..	55.5	219 21.1 ..	44.1	Rigil Kent.	139 47.3	S60 54.7
U 10	147 16.5	295 45.2	31.2	202 10.8	17.1	279 39.6	55.7	234 23.5	44.1	Sabik	102 08.5	S15 44.7
E 11	162 18.9	310 46.4	31.9	217 12.6	16.8	294 41.6	55.8	249 25.9	44.1			
S 12	177 21.4	325 47.7	S18 32.7	232 14.4	S24 16.5	309 43.7	S16 55.9	264 28.3	S22 44.1	Schedar	349 35.9	N56 38.3
D 13	192 23.9	340 48.9	33.4	247 16.1	16.2	324 45.7	56.0	279 30.7	44.1	Shaula	96 17.1	S37 06.9
A 14	207 26.3	355 50.2	34.2	262 17.9	15.9	339 47.7	56.1	294 33.1	44.1	Sirius	258 30.7	S16 44.4
Y 15	222 28.8	10 51.4 ..	34.9	277 19.7 ..	15.6	354 49.8 ..	56.3	309 35.6 ..	44.1	Spica	158 27.8	S11 15.3
16	237 31.3	25 52.7	35.7	292 21.4	15.3	9 51.8	56.4	324 38.0	44.1	Suhail	222 50.2	S43 30.3
17	252 33.7	40 53.9	36.4	307 23.2	15.0	24 53.9	56.5	339 40.4	44.1			
18	267 36.2	55 55.2	S18 37.2	322 24.9	S24 14.7	39 55.9	S16 56.6	354 42.8	S22 44.1	Vega	80 36.4	N38 48.5
19	282 38.6	70 56.4	37.9	337 26.7	14.4	54 57.9	56.7	9 45.2	44.1	Zuben'ubi	137 01.7	S16 06.9
20	297 41.1	85 57.7	38.7	352 28.5	14.1	70 00.0	56.9	24 47.6	44.1		SHA	Mer. Pass.
21	312 43.6	100 58.9 ..	39.4	7 30.2 ..	13.8	85 02.0 ..	57.0	39 50.0 ..	44.1		° ′	h m
22	327 46.0	116 00.2	40.1	22 32.0	13.5	100 04.1	57.1	54 52.4	44.1	Venus	149 11.6	14 19
23	342 48.5	131 01.5	40.9	37 33.7	13.1	115 06.1	57.2	69 54.8	44.1	Mars	55 17.2	20 33
	h m									Jupiter	132 37.3	15 24
Mer. Pass. 0 16.4	v 1.2 d 0.8			v 1.8 d 0.3		v 2.0 d 0.1		v 2.4 d 0.0		Saturn	87 08.7	18 25

UT	SUN GHA	SUN Dec	MOON GHA	v	MOON Dec	d	HP
d h	° ′	° ′	° ′	′	° ′	′	′
16 00	181 14.5	N 2 44.6	103 38.9	11.5	S18 11.2	5.5	55.5
01	196 14.7	43.7	118 09.4	11.4	18 16.7	5.5	55.4
02	211 14.9	42.7	132 39.8	11.4	18 22.2	5.4	55.4
03	226 15.2	.. 41.7	147 10.2	11.5	18 27.6	5.4	55.4
04	241 15.4	40.8	161 40.7	11.4	18 33.0	5.2	55.4
05	256 15.6	39.8	176 11.1	11.4	18 38.2	5.1	55.3
S 06	271 15.8	N 2 38.8	190 41.5	11.4	S18 43.3	5.0	55.3
U 07	286 16.1	37.9	205 11.9	11.4	18 48.3	4.9	55.3
N 08	301 16.3	36.9	219 42.3	11.5	18 53.2	4.9	55.3
D 09	316 16.5	.. 36.0	234 12.8	11.4	18 58.1	4.7	55.2
A 10	331 16.7	35.0	248 43.2	11.4	19 02.8	4.6	55.2
Y 11	346 16.9	34.0	263 13.6	11.4	19 07.4	4.6	55.2
12	1 17.2	N 2 33.1	277 44.0	11.4	S19 12.0	4.4	55.2
13	16 17.4	32.1	292 14.4	11.4	19 16.4	4.4	55.1
14	31 17.6	31.1	306 44.8	11.5	19 20.8	4.2	55.1
15	46 17.8	.. 30.2	321 15.3	11.4	19 25.0	4.2	55.1
16	61 18.1	29.2	335 45.7	11.4	19 29.2	4.0	55.1
17	76 18.3	28.2	350 16.1	11.4	19 33.2	4.0	55.0
18	91 18.5	N 2 27.3	4 46.5	11.4	S19 37.2	3.8	55.0
19	106 18.7	26.3	19 16.9	11.4	19 41.0	3.8	55.0
20	121 19.0	25.3	33 47.3	11.4	19 44.8	3.7	55.0
21	136 19.2	.. 24.4	48 17.7	11.5	19 48.5	3.5	55.0
22	151 19.4	23.4	62 48.2	11.4	19 52.0	3.5	54.9
23	166 19.6	22.4	77 18.6	11.4	19 55.5	3.4	54.9
17 00	181 19.9	N 2 21.5	91 49.0	11.4	S19 58.9	3.3	54.9
01	196 20.1	20.5	106 19.4	11.4	20 02.2	3.1	54.9
02	211 20.3	19.6	120 49.8	11.5	20 05.3	3.1	54.9
03	226 20.5	.. 18.6	135 20.3	11.4	20 08.4	3.0	54.8
04	241 20.7	17.6	149 50.7	11.4	20 11.4	2.9	54.8
05	256 21.0	16.7	164 21.1	11.4	20 14.3	2.7	54.8
M 06	271 21.2	N 2 15.7	178 51.5	11.5	S20 17.0	2.7	54.8
O 07	286 21.4	14.7	193 22.0	11.4	20 19.7	2.6	54.8
N 08	301 21.6	13.8	207 52.4	11.4	20 22.3	2.5	54.7
D 09	316 21.9	.. 12.8	222 22.8	11.5	20 24.8	2.4	54.7
A 10	331 22.1	11.8	236 53.3	11.4	20 27.2	2.2	54.7
Y 11	346 22.3	10.9	251 23.7	11.5	20 29.4	2.2	54.7
12	1 22.5	N 2 09.9	265 54.2	11.4	S20 31.6	2.1	54.7
13	16 22.8	08.9	280 24.6	11.5	20 33.7	2.0	54.7
14	31 23.0	08.0	294 55.1	11.5	20 35.7	1.9	54.6
15	46 23.2	.. 07.0	309 25.6	11.4	20 37.6	1.8	54.6
16	61 23.4	06.0	323 56.0	11.5	20 39.4	1.7	54.6
17	76 23.6	05.1	338 26.5	11.5	20 41.1	1.5	54.6
18	91 23.9	N 2 04.1	352 57.0	11.5	S20 42.6	1.5	54.6
19	106 24.1	03.1	7 27.5	11.5	20 44.1	1.4	54.5
20	121 24.3	02.2	21 58.0	11.5	20 45.5	1.3	54.5
21	136 24.5	.. 01.2	36 28.5	11.5	20 46.8	1.2	54.5
22	151 24.8	2 00.2	50 59.0	11.5	20 48.0	1.1	54.5
23	166 25.0	1 59.3	65 29.5	11.5	20 49.1	1.0	54.5
18 00	181 25.2	N 1 58.3	80 00.0	11.6	S20 50.1	0.9	54.5
01	196 25.4	57.3	94 30.6	11.5	20 51.0	0.8	54.5
02	211 25.7	56.4	109 01.1	11.6	20 51.8	0.7	54.5
03	226 25.9	.. 55.4	123 31.7	11.5	20 52.5	0.6	54.4
04	241 26.1	54.4	138 02.2	11.6	20 53.1	0.5	54.4
05	256 26.3	53.5	152 32.8	11.6	20 53.6	0.4	54.4
T 06	271 26.6	N 1 52.5	167 03.4	11.6	S20 54.0	0.3	54.4
U 07	286 26.8	51.5	181 34.0	11.6	20 54.3	0.2	54.4
E 08	301 27.0	50.6	196 04.6	11.6	20 54.5	0.1	54.4
S 09	316 27.2	.. 49.6	210 35.2	11.6	20 54.6	0.0	54.4
D 10	331 27.4	48.6	225 05.8	11.6	20 54.6	0.1	54.4
A 11	346 27.7	47.6	239 36.4	11.7	20 54.5	0.2	54.4
Y 12	1 27.9	N 1 46.7	254 07.1	11.6	S20 54.3	0.3	54.3
13	16 28.1	45.7	268 37.7	11.7	20 54.0	0.4	54.3
14	31 28.3	44.7	283 08.4	11.7	20 53.6	0.5	54.3
15	46 28.6	.. 43.8	297 39.1	11.7	20 53.1	0.6	54.3
16	61 28.8	42.8	312 09.8	11.7	20 52.5	0.6	54.3
17	76 29.0	41.8	326 40.5	11.7	20 51.9	0.8	54.3
18	91 29.2	N 1 40.9	341 11.2	11.8	S20 51.1	0.9	54.3
19	106 29.5	39.9	355 42.0	11.7	20 50.2	1.0	54.3
20	121 29.7	38.9	10 12.7	11.8	20 49.2	1.0	54.3
21	136 29.9	.. 38.0	24 43.5	11.8	20 48.2	1.2	54.3
22	151 30.1	37.0	39 14.3	11.8	20 47.0	1.3	54.3
23	166 30.3	36.0	53 45.1	11.8	S20 45.7	1.3	54.2
	SD 15.9	d 1.0	SD 15.0		14.9		14.8

Moonrise

Lat.	Twilight Naut.	Twilight Civil	Sunrise	16	17	18	19
°	h m	h m	h m	h m	h m	h m	h m
N 72	02 23	04 05	05 16	■■	■■	■■	■■
N 70	02 51	04 16	05 20	16 54	■■	■■	■■
68	03 11	04 26	05 23	15 43	17 06	18 01	18 23
66	03 27	04 33	05 26	15 06	16 18	17 11	17 44
64	03 39	04 40	05 28	14 41	15 48	16 40	17 16
62	03 50	04 45	05 30	14 20	15 25	16 16	16 55
60	03 58	04 50	05 32	14 04	15 06	15 58	16 38
N 58	04 06	04 54	05 34	13 50	14 51	15 42	16 23
56	04 12	04 58	05 35	13 38	14 38	15 29	16 11
54	04 18	05 01	05 36	13 28	14 27	15 17	16 00
52	04 23	05 04	05 38	13 19	14 17	15 07	15 50
50	04 27	05 06	05 39	13 11	14 08	14 58	15 42
45	04 37	05 11	05 41	12 53	13 49	14 39	15 24
N 40	04 44	05 15	05 43	12 39	13 33	14 23	15 09
35	04 49	05 19	05 44	12 27	13 20	14 10	14 56
30	04 54	05 22	05 46	12 17	13 09	13 59	14 45
20	05 00	05 26	05 48	11 59	12 50	13 39	14 26
N 10	05 04	05 29	05 50	11 43	12 33	13 22	14 10
0	05 07	05 31	05 51	11 28	12 17	13 06	13 54
S 10	05 07	05 32	05 53	11 14	12 02	12 50	13 39
20	05 07	05 32	05 54	10 59	11 45	12 33	13 22
30	05 04	05 32	05 56	10 41	11 26	12 13	13 03
35	05 02	05 32	05 57	10 31	11 15	12 02	12 52
40	04 59	05 31	05 58	10 19	11 02	11 49	12 40
45	04 56	05 30	05 59	10 05	10 47	11 33	12 25
S 50	04 50	05 28	06 00	09 48	10 28	11 14	12 06
52	04 48	05 27	06 01	09 41	10 20	11 05	11 58
54	04 45	05 26	06 01	09 32	10 10	10 55	11 48
56	04 42	05 25	06 02	09 22	09 59	10 44	11 37
58	04 38	05 24	06 03	09 11	09 46	10 31	11 24
S 60	04 33	05 22	06 04	08 58	09 32	10 15	11 09

Moonset

Lat.	Sunset	Twilight Civil	Twilight Naut.	16	17	18	19
°	h m	h m	h m	h m	h m	h m	h m
N 72	18 31	19 41	21 20	■■	■■	■■	■■
N 70	18 27	19 30	20 54	18 20	■■	■■	■■
68	18 24	19 21	20 34	19 31	19 50	20 37	21 54
66	18 21	19 13	20 19	20 08	20 38	21 26	22 33
64	18 19	19 07	20 07	20 34	21 09	21 57	23 00
62	18 17	19 02	19 57	20 55	21 32	22 20	23 21
60	18 15	18 57	19 49	21 12	21 50	22 39	23 38
N 58	18 14	18 53	19 41	21 26	22 06	22 54	23 52
56	18 13	18 50	19 35	21 38	22 19	23 08	24 15
54	18 11	18 47	19 29	21 48	22 30	23 19	24 15
52	18 10	18 44	19 25	21 58	22 40	23 29	24 24
50	18 09	18 42	19 20	22 06	22 49	23 38	24 31
45	18 07	18 37	19 11	22 24	23 08	23 57	24 51
N 40	18 06	18 33	19 05	22 39	23 24	24 13	00 13
35	18 04	18 30	18 59	22 51	23 37	24 26	00 26
30	18 03	18 27	18 55	23 02	23 48	24 37	00 37
20	18 01	18 23	18 49	23 21	24 08	00 08	00 57
N 10	17 59	18 20	18 45	23 37	24 25	00 25	01 14
0	17 58	18 18	18 42	23 52	24 41	00 41	01 29
S 10	17 56	18 17	18 42	24 07	00 07	00 57	01 45
20	17 55	18 17	18 43	24 24	00 24	01 14	02 02
30	17 53	18 17	18 45	24 42	00 42	01 33	02 21
35	17 53	18 18	18 47	24 53	00 53	01 45	02 33
40	17 52	18 19	18 50	00 09	01 06	01 58	02 46
45	17 51	18 20	18 54	00 22	01 20	02 13	03 01
S 50	17 50	18 22	19 00	00 38	01 38	02 32	03 19
52	17 49	18 23	19 02	00 46	01 47	02 41	03 28
54	17 49	18 24	19 05	00 54	01 57	02 51	03 38
56	17 48	18 25	19 09	01 04	02 07	03 03	03 49
58	17 47	18 27	19 13	01 15	02 20	03 16	04 02
S 60	17 47	18 28	19 17	01 27	02 34	03 31	04 17

Day	SUN Eqn. of Time 00ʰ	SUN Eqn. of Time 12ʰ	SUN Mer. Pass.	MOON Mer. Pass. Upper	MOON Mer. Pass. Lower	Age	Phase
d	m s	m s	h m	h m	h m	d	%
16	04 58	05 08	11 55	17 40	05 16	07	46
17	05 19	05 30	11 55	18 29	06 05	08	55
18	05 40	05 51	11 54	19 18	06 54	09	65

UT	ARIES	VENUS −4.8		MARS −1.6		JUPITER −1.8		SATURN +0.5		STARS		
d h	GHA	GHA	Dec	GHA	Dec	GHA	Dec	GHA	Dec	Name	SHA	Dec
19 00	357 51.0	146 02.7	S18 41.6	52 35.5	S24 12.8	130 08.1	S16 57.3	84 57.2	S22 44.1	Acamar	315 15.4	S40 13.7
01	12 53.4	161 04.0	42.4	67 37.3	12.5	145 10.2	57.5	99 59.6	44.1	Achernar	335 23.6	S57 08.5
02	27 55.9	176 05.3	43.1	82 39.0	12.2	160 12.2	57.6	115 02.1	44.1	Acrux	173 05.9	S63 12.0
03	42 58.4	191 06.6 ..	43.8	97 40.8 ..	11.9	175 14.3 ..	57.7	130 04.5 ..	44.1	Adhara	255 09.8	S28 59.7
04	58 00.8	206 07.8	44.6	112 42.5	11.6	190 16.3	57.8	145 06.9	44.2	Aldebaran	290 45.2	N16 32.7
05	73 03.3	221 09.1	45.3	127 44.3	11.3	205 18.3	57.9	160 09.3	44.2			
W 06	88 05.8	236 10.4	S18 46.0	142 46.0	S24 11.0	220 20.4	S16 58.1	175 11.7	S22 44.2	Alioth	166 18.1	N55 51.8
E 07	103 08.2	251 11.7	46.8	157 47.8	10.7	235 22.4	58.2	190 14.1	44.2	Alkaid	152 56.5	N49 13.5
D 08	118 10.7	266 13.0	47.5	172 49.5	10.4	250 24.5	58.3	205 16.5	44.2	Al Na'ir	27 38.9	S46 52.2
N 09	133 13.1	281 14.3 ..	48.2	187 51.3 ..	10.0	265 26.5 ..	58.4	220 18.9 ..	44.2	Alnilam	275 42.7	S 1 11.4
E 10	148 15.6	296 15.5	48.9	202 53.0	09.7	280 28.5	58.5	235 21.3	44.2	Alphard	217 52.9	S 8 44.2
S 11	163 18.1	311 16.8	49.7	217 54.7	09.4	295 30.6	58.7	250 23.7	44.2			
D 12	178 20.5	326 18.1	S18 50.4	232 56.5	S24 09.1	310 32.6	S16 58.8	265 26.1	S22 44.2	Alphecca	126 08.2	N26 39.5
A 13	193 23.0	341 19.4	51.1	247 58.2	08.8	325 34.6	58.9	280 28.5	44.2	Alpheratz	357 39.4	N29 11.6
Y 14	208 25.5	356 20.7	51.8	263 00.0	08.5	340 36.7	59.0	295 30.9	44.2	Altair	62 04.6	N 8 55.3
15	223 27.9	11 22.0 ..	52.6	278 01.7 ..	08.2	355 38.7 ..	59.1	310 33.3 ..	44.2	Ankaa	353 11.8	S42 12.2
16	238 30.4	26 23.3	53.3	293 03.4	07.9	10 40.7	59.3	325 35.7	44.2	Antares	112 22.0	S26 28.2
17	253 32.9	41 24.7	54.0	308 05.2	07.6	25 42.8	59.4	340 38.2	44.2			
18	268 35.3	56 26.0	S18 54.7	323 06.9	S24 07.2	40 44.8	S16 59.5	355 40.6	S22 44.2	Arcturus	145 52.8	N19 05.4
19	283 37.8	71 27.3	55.4	338 08.6	06.9	55 46.9	59.6	10 43.0	44.2	Atria	107 20.7	S69 03.7
20	298 40.3	86 28.6	56.2	353 10.4	06.6	70 48.9	59.7	25 45.4	44.2	Avior	234 16.9	S59 33.9
21	313 42.7	101 29.9 ..	56.9	8 12.1 ..	06.3	85 50.9	16 59.9	40 47.8 ..	44.2	Bellatrix	278 28.2	N 6 21.9
22	328 45.2	116 31.2	57.6	23 13.8	06.0	100 53.0	17 00.0	55 50.2	44.2	Betelgeuse	270 57.5	N 7 24.6
23	343 47.6	131 32.5	58.3	38 15.6	05.7	115 55.0	00.1	70 52.6	44.2			
20 00	358 50.1	146 33.9	S18 59.0	53 17.3	S24 05.4	130 57.0	S17 00.2	85 55.0	S22 44.3	Canopus	263 54.6	S52 42.1
01	13 52.6	161 35.2	18 59.7	68 19.0	05.0	145 59.1	00.3	100 57.4	44.3	Capella	280 29.1	N46 00.7
02	28 55.0	176 36.5	19 00.4	83 20.8	04.7	161 01.1	00.5	115 59.8	44.3	Deneb	49 28.7	N45 21.1
03	43 57.5	191 37.8 ..	01.2	98 22.5 ..	04.4	176 03.1 ..	00.6	131 02.2 ..	44.3	Denebola	182 30.4	N14 28.3
04	59 00.0	206 39.2	01.9	113 24.2	04.1	191 05.2	00.7	146 04.6	44.3	Diphda	348 52.0	S17 53.0
05	74 02.4	221 40.5	02.6	128 25.9	03.8	206 07.2	00.8	161 07.0	44.3			
T 06	89 04.9	236 41.9	S19 03.3	143 27.7	S24 03.5	221 09.2	S17 01.0	176 09.4	S22 44.3	Dubhe	193 48.0	N61 39.1
H 07	104 07.4	251 43.2	04.0	158 29.4	03.1	236 11.3	01.1	191 11.8	44.3	Elnath	278 08.1	N28 37.2
U 08	119 09.8	266 44.5	04.7	173 31.1	02.8	251 13.3	01.2	206 14.2	44.3	Eltanin	90 44.5	N51 29.6
R 09	134 12.3	281 45.9 ..	05.4	188 32.8 ..	02.5	266 15.3 ..	01.3	221 16.6 ..	44.3	Enif	33 43.4	N 9 57.8
S 10	149 14.8	296 47.2	06.1	203 34.5	02.2	281 17.4	01.4	236 19.0	44.3	Fomalhaut	15 19.7	S29 31.4
D 11	164 17.2	311 48.6	06.8	218 36.3	01.9	296 19.4	01.6	251 21.4	44.3			
A 12	179 19.7	326 49.9	S19 07.5	233 38.0	S24 01.6	311 21.4	S17 01.7	266 23.8	S22 44.3	Gacrux	171 57.5	S57 12.9
Y 13	194 22.1	341 51.3	08.2	248 39.7	01.2	326 23.5	01.8	281 26.2	44.3	Gienah	175 49.0	S17 38.5
14	209 24.6	356 52.6	08.9	263 41.4	00.9	341 25.5	01.9	296 28.6	44.3	Hadar	148 43.3	S60 27.7
15	224 27.1	11 54.0 ..	09.6	278 43.1 ..	00.6	356 27.5 ..	02.0	311 31.0 ..	44.3	Hamal	327 56.4	N23 32.9
16	239 29.5	26 55.4	10.3	293 44.8	00.3	11 29.6	02.2	326 33.4	44.3	Kaus Aust.	83 39.0	S34 22.4
17	254 32.0	41 56.7	11.0	308 46.5	24 00.0	26 31.6	02.3	341 35.8	44.3			
18	269 34.5	56 58.1	S19 11.7	323 48.2	S23 59.6	41 33.6	S17 02.4	356 38.2	S22 44.3	Kochab	137 21.0	N74 05.1
19	284 36.9	71 59.5	12.4	338 50.0	59.3	56 35.7	02.5	11 40.6	44.3	Markab	13 34.5	N15 18.4
20	299 39.4	87 00.8	13.1	353 51.7	59.0	71 37.7	02.7	26 43.0	44.3	Menkar	314 11.1	N 4 09.7
21	314 41.9	102 02.2 ..	13.8	8 53.4 ..	58.7	86 39.7 ..	02.8	41 45.4 ..	44.4	Menkent	148 03.7	S36 27.5
22	329 44.3	117 03.6	14.4	23 55.1	58.4	101 41.8	02.9	56 47.8	44.4	Miaplacidus	221 39.6	S69 47.4
23	344 46.8	132 05.0	15.1	38 56.8	58.0	116 43.8	03.0	71 50.2	44.4			
21 00	359 49.2	147 06.3	S19 15.8	53 58.5	S23 57.7	131 45.8	S17 03.1	86 52.6	S22 44.4	Mirfak	308 34.9	N49 55.4
01	14 51.7	162 07.7	16.5	69 00.2	57.4	146 47.9	03.3	101 55.0	44.4	Nunki	75 53.8	S26 16.3
02	29 54.2	177 09.1	17.2	84 01.9	57.1	161 49.9	03.4	116 57.4	44.4	Peacock	53 13.3	S56 40.5
03	44 56.6	192 10.5 ..	17.9	99 03.6 ..	56.7	176 51.9 ..	03.5	131 59.8 ..	44.4	Pollux	243 23.6	N27 58.7
04	59 59.1	207 11.9	18.6	114 05.3	56.4	191 54.0	03.6	147 02.2	44.4	Procyon	244 56.2	N 5 10.6
05	75 01.6	222 13.3	19.2	129 07.0	56.1	206 56.0	03.7	162 04.6	44.4			
F 06	90 04.0	237 14.7	S19 19.9	144 08.7	S23 55.8	221 58.0	S17 03.9	177 07.0	S22 44.4	Rasalhague	96 03.2	N12 33.1
R 07	105 06.5	252 16.1	20.6	159 10.4	55.5	237 00.1	04.0	192 09.4	44.4	Regulus	207 40.0	N11 52.7
I 08	120 09.0	267 17.5	21.3	174 12.1	55.1	252 02.1	04.1	207 11.8	44.4	Rigel	281 08.6	S 8 10.8
D 09	135 11.4	282 18.9 ..	22.0	189 13.8 ..	54.8	267 04.1 ..	04.2	222 14.2 ..	44.4	Rigil Kent.	139 47.4	S60 54.6
A 10	150 13.9	297 20.3	22.6	204 15.5	54.5	282 06.1	04.4	237 16.6	44.4	Sabik	102 08.5	S15 44.7
Y 11	165 16.4	312 21.7	23.3	219 17.2	54.2	297 08.2	04.5	252 19.0	44.4			
12	180 18.8	327 23.1	S19 24.0	234 18.8	S23 53.8	312 10.2	S17 04.6	267 21.4	S22 44.4	Schedar	349 35.9	N56 38.3
13	195 21.3	342 24.5	24.6	249 20.5	53.5	327 12.2	04.7	282 23.8	44.4	Shaula	96 17.1	S37 06.9
14	210 23.7	357 25.9	25.3	264 22.2	53.2	342 14.3	04.8	297 26.2	44.4	Sirius	258 30.7	S16 44.4
15	225 26.2	12 27.3 ..	26.0	279 23.9 ..	52.9	357 16.3 ..	05.0	312 28.6 ..	44.4	Spica	158 27.8	S11 15.3
16	240 28.7	27 28.8	26.7	294 25.6	52.5	12 18.3	05.1	327 31.0	44.4	Suhail	222 50.1	S43 30.3
17	255 31.1	42 30.2	27.3	309 27.3	52.2	27 20.3	05.2	342 33.4	44.4			
18	270 33.6	57 31.6	S19 28.0	324 29.0	S23 51.9	42 22.4	S17 05.3	357 35.8	S22 44.5	Vega	80 36.5	N38 48.5
19	285 36.1	72 33.0	28.7	339 30.6	51.6	57 24.4	05.4	12 38.2	44.5	Zuben'ubi	137 01.7	S16 06.9
20	300 38.5	87 34.5	29.3	354 32.3	51.2	72 26.4	05.6	27 40.6	44.5		SHA	Mer. Pass.
21	315 41.0	102 35.9 ..	30.0	9 34.0 ..	50.9	87 28.5 ..	05.7	42 43.0 ..	44.5	Venus	147 43.8	14 12
22	330 43.5	117 37.3	30.7	24 35.7	50.6	102 30.5	05.8	57 45.4	44.5	Mars	54 27.2	20 25
23	345 45.9	132 38.8	31.3	39 37.4	50.2	117 32.5	05.9	72 47.8	44.5	Jupiter	132 06.9	15 14
Mer. Pass.	h m 0 04.6	v 1.4	d 0.7	v 1.7	d 0.3	v 2.0	d 0.1	v 2.4	d 0.0	Saturn	87 04.9	18 13

UT	SUN GHA	SUN Dec	MOON GHA	v	MOON Dec	d	HP
d h	° '	° '	° '	'	° '	'	'
19 00	181 30.6	N 1 35.1	68 15.9	11.8	S20 44.4	1.5	54.2
01	196 30.8	34.1	82 46.7	11.8	20 42.9	1.5	54.2
02	211 31.0	33.1	97 17.5	11.9	20 41.4	1.7	54.2
03	226 31.2	.. 32.2	111 48.4	11.9	20 39.7	1.7	54.2
04	241 31.5	31.2	126 19.3	11.9	20 38.0	1.9	54.2
05	256 31.7	30.2	140 50.2	11.9	20 36.1	1.9	54.2
W 06	271 31.9	N 1 29.2	155 21.1	11.9	S20 34.2	2.0	54.2
E 07	286 32.1	28.3	169 52.0	11.9	20 32.2	2.2	54.2
D 08	301 32.4	27.3	184 22.9	12.0	20 30.0	2.2	54.2
N 09	316 32.6	.. 26.3	198 53.9	12.0	20 27.8	2.3	54.2
E 10	331 32.8	25.4	213 24.9	12.0	20 25.5	2.4	54.2
S 11	346 33.0	24.4	227 55.9	12.0	20 23.1	2.5	54.2
D 12	1 33.2	N 1 23.4	242 26.9	12.0	S20 20.6	2.6	54.2
A 13	16 33.5	22.5	256 57.9	12.1	20 18.0	2.7	54.2
Y 14	31 33.7	21.5	271 29.0	12.1	20 15.3	2.8	54.2
15	46 33.9	.. 20.5	286 00.1	12.1	20 12.5	2.9	54.2
16	61 34.1	19.6	300 31.2	12.1	20 09.6	2.9	54.2
17	76 34.4	18.6	315 02.3	12.1	20 06.7	3.1	54.2
18	91 34.6	N 1 17.6	329 33.4	12.2	S20 03.6	3.1	54.2
19	106 34.8	16.6	344 04.6	12.2	20 00.5	3.3	54.2
20	121 35.0	15.7	358 35.8	12.2	19 57.2	3.3	54.2
21	136 35.3	.. 14.7	13 07.0	12.2	19 53.9	3.5	54.2
22	151 35.5	13.7	27 38.2	12.2	19 50.4	3.5	54.2
23	166 35.7	12.8	42 09.4	12.3	19 46.9	3.6	54.2
20 00	181 35.9	N 1 11.8	56 40.7	12.3	S19 43.3	3.7	54.2
01	196 36.1	10.8	71 12.0	12.3	19 39.6	3.8	54.2
02	211 36.4	09.9	85 43.3	12.3	19 35.8	3.9	54.2
03	226 36.6	.. 08.9	100 14.6	12.3	19 31.9	3.9	54.2
04	241 36.8	07.9	114 45.9	12.4	19 28.0	4.1	54.2
05	256 37.0	06.9	129 17.3	12.4	19 23.9	4.1	54.2
T 06	271 37.3	N 1 06.0	143 48.7	12.4	S19 19.8	4.3	54.2
H 07	286 37.5	05.0	158 20.1	12.4	19 15.5	4.3	54.2
U 08	301 37.7	04.0	172 51.5	12.5	19 11.2	4.4	54.2
R 09	316 37.9	.. 03.1	187 23.0	12.5	19 06.8	4.5	54.2
S 10	331 38.2	02.1	201 54.5	12.5	19 02.3	4.6	54.2
D 11	346 38.4	01.1	216 26.0	12.5	18 57.7	4.7	54.2
A 12	1 38.6	N 1 00.1	230 57.5	12.6	S18 53.0	4.7	54.2
Y 13	16 38.8	0 59.2	245 29.1	12.6	18 48.3	4.9	54.2
14	31 39.0	58.2	260 00.7	12.6	18 43.4	4.9	54.2
15	46 39.3	.. 57.2	274 32.3	12.6	18 38.5	5.0	54.2
16	61 39.5	56.3	289 03.9	12.6	18 33.5	5.1	54.2
17	76 39.7	55.3	303 35.5	12.7	18 28.4	5.2	54.2
18	91 39.9	N 0 54.3	318 07.2	12.7	S18 23.2	5.3	54.2
19	106 40.2	53.4	332 38.9	12.7	18 17.9	5.3	54.2
20	121 40.4	52.4	347 10.6	12.8	18 12.6	5.5	54.2
21	136 40.6	.. 51.4	1 42.4	12.7	18 07.1	5.5	54.2
22	151 40.8	50.4	16 14.1	12.8	18 01.6	5.6	54.2
23	166 41.0	49.5	30 45.9	12.8	17 56.0	5.7	54.2
21 00	181 41.3	N 0 48.5	45 17.7	12.9	S17 50.3	5.7	54.2
01	196 41.5	47.5	59 49.6	12.8	17 44.6	5.9	54.2
02	211 41.7	46.6	74 21.4	12.9	17 38.7	5.9	54.2
03	226 41.9	.. 45.6	88 53.3	12.9	17 32.8	6.0	54.2
04	241 42.2	44.6	103 25.2	12.9	17 26.8	6.1	54.2
05	256 42.4	43.6	117 57.1	13.0	17 20.7	6.2	54.3
F 06	271 42.6	N 0 42.7	132 29.1	13.0	S17 14.5	6.2	54.3
R 07	286 42.8	41.7	147 01.1	13.0	17 08.3	6.3	54.3
I 08	301 43.0	40.7	161 33.1	13.0	17 02.0	6.4	54.3
D 09	316 43.3	.. 39.8	176 05.1	13.1	16 55.6	6.5	54.3
A 10	331 43.5	38.8	190 37.2	13.0	16 49.1	6.6	54.3
Y 11	346 43.7	37.8	205 09.2	13.1	16 42.5	6.6	54.3
12	1 43.9	N 0 36.8	219 41.3	13.2	S16 35.9	6.7	54.3
13	16 44.2	35.9	234 13.5	13.1	16 29.2	6.8	54.3
14	31 44.4	34.9	248 45.6	13.2	16 22.4	6.9	54.3
15	46 44.6	.. 33.9	263 17.8	13.2	16 15.5	6.9	54.3
16	61 44.8	33.0	277 50.0	13.2	16 08.6	7.0	54.3
17	76 45.0	32.0	292 22.2	13.2	16 01.6	7.1	54.3
18	91 45.3	N 0 31.0	306 54.4	13.3	S15 54.5	7.1	54.4
19	106 45.5	30.0	321 26.7	13.3	15 47.4	7.3	54.4
20	121 45.7	29.1	335 59.0	13.3	15 40.1	7.3	54.4
21	136 45.9	.. 28.1	350 31.3	13.3	15 32.8	7.3	54.4
22	151 46.2	27.1	5 03.6	13.4	15 25.5	7.5	54.4
23	166 46.4	26.2	19 36.0	13.3	S15 18.0	7.5	54.4
	SD 16.0 d 1.0		SD 14.8		14.8		14.8

Lat.	Twilight Naut.	Twilight Civil	Sunrise	Moonrise 19	Moonrise 20	Moonrise 21	Moonrise 22
°	h m	h m	h m	h m	h m	h m	h m
N 72	02 44	04 20	05 29	■■■■	■■■■	19 38	19 13
N 70	03 07	04 29	05 32	■■■■	19 13	19 00	18 51
68	03 25	04 37	05 34	18 23	18 31	18 33	18 34
66	03 38	04 43	05 35	17 44	18 02	18 13	18 20
64	03 50	04 49	05 37	17 16	17 40	17 56	18 08
62	03 59	04 53	05 38	16 55	17 23	17 43	17 58
60	04 07	04 57	05 39	16 38	17 08	17 31	17 49
N 58	04 13	05 01	05 40	16 23	16 56	17 21	17 42
56	04 19	05 04	05 41	16 11	16 45	17 12	17 35
54	04 24	05 06	05 42	16 00	16 35	17 04	17 29
52	04 28	05 09	05 42	15 50	16 27	16 57	17 24
50	04 32	05 11	05 43	15 42	16 19	16 51	17 19
45	04 40	05 15	05 44	15 24	16 03	16 37	17 08
N 40	04 47	05 18	05 45	15 09	15 49	16 26	16 59
35	04 51	05 21	05 46	14 56	15 38	16 16	16 52
30	04 55	05 23	05 47	14 45	15 28	16 08	16 45
20	05 01	05 26	05 48	14 26	15 11	15 53	16 33
N 10	05 04	05 28	05 49	14 10	14 56	15 40	16 23
0	05 06	05 30	05 50	13 54	14 42	15 28	16 14
S 10	05 06	05 30	05 51	13 39	14 28	15 16	16 04
20	05 04	05 30	05 52	13 22	14 12	15 03	15 54
30	05 01	05 28	05 52	13 03	13 55	14 48	15 42
35	04 58	05 27	05 53	12 52	13 45	14 39	15 35
40	04 54	05 26	05 53	12 40	13 33	14 30	15 27
45	04 50	05 24	05 53	12 25	13 20	14 18	15 18
S 50	04 44	05 21	05 54	12 06	13 03	14 04	15 07
52	04 41	05 20	05 54	11 58	12 55	13 57	15 02
54	04 37	05 19	05 54	11 48	12 46	13 50	14 56
56	04 33	05 17	05 54	11 37	12 37	13 42	14 50
58	04 29	05 15	05 54	11 25	12 25	13 32	14 43
S 60	04 24	05 13	05 54	11 09	12 12	13 22	14 35

Lat.	Sunset	Twilight Civil	Twilight Naut.	Moonset 19	Moonset 20	Moonset 21	Moonset 22
°	h m	h m	h m	h m	h m	h m	h m
N 72	18 15	19 24	20 57	■■■■	■■■■	23 54	25 53
N 70	18 13	19 15	20 35	■■■■	22 42	24 31	00 31
68	18 11	19 07	20 19	21 54	23 24	24 57	00 57
66	18 10	19 01	20 06	22 33	23 52	25 16	01 16
64	18 08	18 56	19 55	23 00	24 13	00 13	01 32
62	18 07	18 52	19 46	23 21	24 30	00 30	01 45
60	18 05	18 48	19 38	23 38	24 44	00 44	01 56
N 58	18 05	18 45	19 32	23 52	24 56	00 56	02 06
56	18 05	18 42	19 26	24 04	00 04	01 07	02 14
54	18 04	18 39	19 21	24 15	00 15	01 16	02 21
52	18 03	18 37	19 17	24 24	00 24	01 24	02 28
50	18 03	18 35	19 13	24 33	00 33	01 32	02 34
45	18 02	18 31	19 05	24 51	00 51	01 47	02 47
N 40	18 01	18 28	18 59	00 13	01 05	02 00	02 57
35	18 00	18 25	18 55	00 26	01 17	02 11	03 06
30	17 59	18 23	18 51	00 37	01 28	02 21	03 14
20	17 58	18 20	18 46	00 57	01 46	02 37	03 27
N 10	17 57	18 18	18 43	01 14	02 02	02 51	03 39
0	17 57	18 17	18 41	01 29	02 17	03 04	03 50
S 10	17 56	18 17	18 41	01 45	02 32	03 17	04 01
20	17 56	18 18	18 43	02 02	02 48	03 31	04 13
30	17 55	18 19	18 47	02 21	03 06	03 47	04 26
35	17 55	18 20	18 50	02 33	03 17	03 57	04 36
40	17 55	18 22	18 53	02 46	03 29	04 07	04 42
45	17 54	18 24	18 58	03 01	03 43	04 19	04 52
S 50	17 54	18 26	19 04	03 19	04 00	04 34	05 04
52	17 54	18 28	19 07	03 28	04 08	04 41	05 10
54	17 54	18 29	19 11	03 38	04 17	04 49	05 16
56	17 54	18 31	19 15	03 49	04 27	04 58	05 23
58	17 54	18 33	19 20	04 02	04 39	05 07	05 30
S 60	17 54	18 35	19 25	04 17	04 52	05 19	05 39

	SUN			MOON			
Day	Eqn. of Time 00h	12h	Mer. Pass.	Mer. Pass. Upper	Mer. Pass. Lower	Age	Phase
d	m s	m s	h m	h m	h m	d	%
19	06 02	06 13	11 54	20 06	07 42	10	73
20	06 23	06 34	11 53	20 53	08 29	11	81
21	06 45	06 55	11 53	21 39	09 16	12	88

2018 SEPTEMBER 22, 23, 24 (SAT., SUN., MON.)

UT	ARIES GHA	VENUS −4.8 GHA	Dec	MARS −1.5 GHA	Dec	JUPITER −1.8 GHA	Dec	SATURN +0.5 GHA	Dec	STARS Name	SHA	Dec
22 00	0 48.4	147 40.2	S19 32.0	54 39.0	S23 49.9	132 34.5	S17 06.1	87 50.2	S22 44.5	Acamar	315 15.3	S40 13.7
01	15 50.8	162 41.7	32.6	69 40.7	49.6	147 36.6	06.2	102 52.6	44.5	Achernar	335 23.6	S57 08.5
02	30 53.3	177 43.1	33.3	84 42.4	49.3	162 38.6	06.3	117 55.0	44.5	Acrux	173 05.9	S63 12.0
03	45 55.8	192 44.6 ..	33.9	99 44.1 ..	48.9	177 40.6 ..	06.4	132 57.4 ..	44.5	Adhara	255 09.8	S28 59.7
04	60 58.2	207 46.0	34.6	114 45.7	48.6	192 42.6	06.5	147 59.8	44.5	Aldebaran	290 45.2	N16 32.7
05	76 00.7	222 47.5	35.3	129 47.4	48.3	207 44.7	06.7	163 02.2	44.5			
S 06	91 03.2	237 48.9	S19 35.9	144 49.1	S23 47.9	222 46.7	S17 06.8	178 04.5	S22 44.5	Alioth	166 18.1	N55 51.7
A 07	106 05.6	252 50.4	36.6	159 50.8	47.6	237 48.7	06.9	193 06.9	44.5	Alkaid	152 56.5	N49 13.5
T 08	121 08.1	267 51.8	37.2	174 52.4	47.3	252 50.8	07.0	208 09.3	44.5	Al Na'ir	27 38.9	S46 52.2
U 09	136 10.6	282 53.3 ..	37.9	189 54.1 ..	47.0	267 52.8 ..	07.2	223 11.7 ..	44.5	Alnilam	275 42.7	S 1 11.4
R 10	151 13.0	297 54.8	38.5	204 55.8	46.6	282 54.8	07.3	238 14.1	44.5	Alphard	217 52.8	S 8 44.2
D 11	166 15.5	312 56.2	39.2	219 57.4	46.3	297 56.8	07.4	253 16.5	44.5			
A 12	181 18.0	327 57.7	S19 39.8	234 59.1	S23 46.0	312 58.9	S17 07.5	268 18.9	S22 44.5	Alphecca	126 08.2	N26 39.5
Y 13	196 20.4	342 59.2	40.5	250 00.8	45.6	328 00.9	07.6	283 21.3	44.5	Alpheratz	357 39.4	N29 11.6
14	211 22.9	358 00.7	41.1	265 02.4	45.3	343 02.9	07.8	298 23.7	44.5	Altair	62 04.6	N 8 55.3
15	226 25.3	13 02.1 ..	41.7	280 04.1 ..	45.0	358 04.9 ..	07.9	313 26.1 ..	44.6	Ankaa	353 11.8	S42 12.2
16	241 27.8	28 03.6	42.4	295 05.8	44.6	13 07.0	08.0	328 28.5	44.6	Antares	112 22.0	S26 28.2
17	256 30.3	43 05.1	43.0	310 07.4	44.3	28 09.0	08.1	343 30.9	44.6			
18	271 32.7	58 06.6	S19 43.7	325 09.1	S23 44.0	43 11.0	S17 08.3	358 33.3	S22 44.6	Arcturus	145 52.8	N19 05.4
19	286 35.2	73 08.1	44.3	340 10.7	43.6	58 13.0	08.4	13 35.7	44.6	Atria	107 20.7	S69 03.7
20	301 37.7	88 09.6	44.9	355 12.4	43.3	73 15.1	08.5	28 38.1	44.6	Avior	234 16.9	S59 33.9
21	316 40.1	103 11.1 ..	45.6	10 14.1 ..	43.0	88 17.1 ..	08.6	43 40.4 ..	44.6	Bellatrix	278 28.1	N 6 21.9
22	331 42.6	118 12.6	46.2	25 15.7	42.6	103 19.1	08.7	58 42.8	44.6	Betelgeuse	270 57.4	N 7 24.6
23	346 45.1	133 14.1	46.8	40 17.4	42.3	118 21.1	08.9	73 45.2	44.6			
23 00	1 47.5	148 15.6	S19 47.5	55 19.0	S23 42.0	133 23.1	S17 09.0	88 47.6	S22 44.6	Canopus	263 54.6	S52 42.1
01	16 50.0	163 17.1	48.1	70 20.7	41.6	148 25.2	09.1	103 50.0	44.6	Capella	280 29.1	N46 00.7
02	31 52.5	178 18.6	48.7	85 22.3	41.3	163 27.2	09.2	118 52.4	44.6	Deneb	49 28.8	N45 21.1
03	46 54.9	193 20.1 ..	49.4	100 24.0 ..	41.0	178 29.2 ..	09.4	133 54.8 ..	44.6	Denebola	182 30.4	N14 28.3
04	61 57.4	208 21.6	50.0	115 25.6	40.6	193 31.2	09.5	148 57.2	44.6	Diphda	348 52.0	S17 53.0
05	76 59.8	223 23.1	50.6	130 27.3	40.3	208 33.3	09.6	163 59.6	44.6			
S 06	92 02.3	238 24.7	S19 51.2	145 28.9	S23 39.9	223 35.3	S17 09.7	179 02.0	S22 44.6	Dubhe	193 48.0	N61 39.0
U 07	107 04.8	253 26.2	51.9	160 30.6	39.6	238 37.3	09.9	194 04.4	44.6	Elnath	278 08.1	N28 37.2
N 08	122 07.2	268 27.7	52.5	175 32.2	39.3	253 39.3	10.0	209 06.7	44.6	Eltanin	90 44.5	N51 29.6
D 09	137 09.7	283 29.2 ..	53.1	190 33.9 ..	38.9	268 41.3 ..	10.1	224 09.1 ..	44.6	Enif	33 43.4	N 9 57.8
A 10	152 12.2	298 30.8	53.7	205 35.5	38.6	283 43.4	10.2	239 11.5	44.6	Fomalhaut	15 19.7	S29 31.4
Y 11	167 14.6	313 32.3	54.3	220 37.1	38.3	298 45.4	10.3	254 13.9	44.6			
12	182 17.1	328 33.8	S19 55.0	235 38.8	S23 37.9	313 47.4	S17 10.5	269 16.3	S22 44.6	Gacrux	171 57.5	S57 12.9
13	197 19.6	343 35.4	55.6	250 40.4	37.6	328 49.4	10.6	284 18.7	44.7	Gienah	175 49.0	S17 38.5
14	212 22.0	358 36.9	56.2	265 42.1	37.2	343 51.5	10.7	299 21.1	44.7	Hadar	148 43.3	S60 27.7
15	227 24.5	13 38.5 ..	56.8	280 43.7 ..	36.9	358 53.5 ..	10.8	314 23.5 ..	44.7	Hamal	327 56.4	N23 32.9
16	242 26.9	28 40.0	57.4	295 45.3	36.6	13 55.5	11.0	329 25.9	44.7	Kaus Aust.	83 39.1	S34 22.4
17	257 29.4	43 41.5	58.0	310 47.0	36.2	28 57.5	11.1	344 28.2	44.7			
18	272 31.9	58 43.1	S19 58.6	325 48.6	S23 35.9	43 59.5	S17 11.2	359 30.6	S22 44.7	Kochab	137 21.0	N74 05.1
19	287 34.3	73 44.7	59.2	340 50.2	35.5	59 01.6	11.3	14 33.0	44.7	Markab	13 34.5	N15 18.5
20	302 36.8	88 46.2	19 59.9	355 51.9	35.2	74 03.6	11.4	29 35.4	44.7	Menkar	314 11.1	N 4 09.7
21	317 39.3	103 47.8	20 00.5	10 53.5 ..	34.9	89 05.6 ..	11.6	44 37.8 ..	44.7	Menkent	148 03.7	S36 27.5
22	332 41.7	118 49.3	01.1	25 55.1	34.5	104 07.6	11.7	59 40.2	44.7	Miaplacidus	221 39.6	S69 47.4
23	347 44.2	133 50.9	01.7	40 56.8	34.2	119 09.6	11.8	74 42.6	44.7			
24 00	2 46.7	148 52.5	S20 02.3	55 58.4	S23 33.8	134 11.7	S17 11.9	89 45.0	S22 44.7	Mirfak	308 34.9	N49 55.4
01	17 49.1	163 54.0	02.9	71 00.0	33.5	149 13.7	12.1	104 47.3	44.7	Nunki	75 53.8	S26 16.3
02	32 51.6	178 55.6	03.5	86 01.7	33.2	164 15.7	12.2	119 49.7	44.7	Peacock	53 13.3	S56 40.5
03	47 54.1	193 57.2 ..	04.1	101 03.3 ..	32.8	179 17.7 ..	12.3	134 52.1 ..	44.7	Pollux	243 23.5	N27 58.7
04	62 56.5	208 58.8	04.7	116 04.9	32.5	194 19.7	12.4	149 54.5	44.7	Procyon	244 56.1	N 5 10.6
05	77 59.0	224 00.4	05.3	131 06.5	32.1	209 21.8	12.6	164 56.9	44.7			
M 06	93 01.4	239 01.9	S20 05.9	146 08.2	S23 31.8	224 23.8	S17 12.7	179 59.3	S22 44.7	Rasalhague	96 03.2	N12 33.1
O 07	108 03.9	254 03.5	06.5	161 09.8	31.4	239 25.8	12.8	195 01.7	44.7	Regulus	207 40.0	N11 52.7
N 08	123 06.4	269 05.1	07.1	176 11.4	31.1	254 27.8	12.9	210 04.0	44.7	Rigel	281 08.6	S 8 10.8
D 09	138 08.8	284 06.7 ..	07.6	191 13.0 ..	30.8	269 29.8 ..	13.0	225 06.4 ..	44.7	Rigil Kent.	139 47.4	S60 54.6
A 10	153 11.3	299 08.3	08.2	206 14.6	30.4	284 31.8	13.2	240 08.8	44.7	Sabik	102 08.5	S15 44.7
Y 11	168 13.8	314 09.9	08.8	221 16.3	30.1	299 33.9	13.3	255 11.2	44.7			
12	183 16.2	329 11.5	S20 09.4	236 17.9	S23 29.7	314 35.9	S17 13.4	270 13.6	S22 44.8	Schedar	349 35.9	N56 38.3
13	198 18.7	344 13.1	10.0	251 19.5	29.4	329 37.9	13.5	285 16.0	44.8	Shaula	96 17.1	S37 06.9
14	213 21.2	359 14.7	10.6	266 21.1	29.0	344 39.9	13.7	300 18.4	44.8	Sirius	258 30.6	S16 44.4
15	228 23.6	14 16.3 ..	11.2	281 22.7 ..	28.7	359 41.9 ..	13.8	315 20.7 ..	44.8	Spica	158 27.8	S11 15.3
16	243 26.1	29 17.9	11.8	296 24.3	28.3	14 43.9	13.9	330 23.1	44.8	Suhail	222 50.1	S43 30.3
17	258 28.5	44 19.6	12.3	311 26.0	28.0	29 46.0	14.0	345 25.5	44.8			
18	273 31.0	59 21.2	S20 12.9	326 27.6	S23 27.7	44 48.0	S17 14.2	0 27.9	S22 44.8	Vega	80 36.5	N38 48.5
19	288 33.5	74 22.8	13.5	341 29.2	27.3	59 50.0	14.3	15 30.3	44.8	Zuben'ubi	137 01.7	S16 06.9
20	303 35.9	89 24.4	14.1	356 30.8	27.0	74 52.0	14.4	30 32.7	44.8		SHA	Mer.Pass.
21	318 38.4	104 26.1 ..	14.6	11 32.4 ..	26.6	89 54.0 ..	14.5	45 35.0 ..	44.8		° '	h m
22	333 40.9	119 27.7	15.2	26 34.0	26.3	104 56.0	14.7	60 37.4	44.8	Venus	146 28.1	14 06
23	348 43.3	134 29.3	15.8	41 35.6	25.9	119 58.1	14.8	75 39.8	44.8	Mars	53 31.5	20 17
Mer. Pass.	23 48.9	v 1.5	d 0.6	v 1.6 d 0.3		v 2.0 d 0.1		v 2.4 d 0.0		Jupiter	131 35.6	15 04
										Saturn	87 00.1	18 02

UT	SUN GHA	SUN Dec	MOON GHA	v	MOON Dec	d	HP
d h	° '	° '	° '	'	° '	'	'
22 00	181 46.6	N 0 25.2	34 08.3	13.4	S15 10.5	7.6	54.4
01	196 46.8	24.2	48 40.7	13.5	15 02.9	7.6	54.4
02	211 47.0	23.2	63 13.2	13.4	14 55.3	7.8	54.4
03	226 47.3 ..	22.3	77 45.6	13.5	14 47.5	7.8	54.5
04	241 47.5	21.3	92 18.1	13.4	14 39.7	7.8	54.5
05	256 47.7	20.3	106 50.5	13.5	14 31.9	8.0	54.5
06	271 47.9	N 0 19.3	121 23.0	13.6	S14 23.9	8.0	54.5
07	286 48.1	18.4	135 55.6	13.5	14 15.9	8.0	54.5
08	301 48.4	17.4	150 28.1	13.6	14 07.9	8.1	54.5
09	316 48.6 ..	16.4	165 00.7	13.5	13 59.8	8.2	54.5
10	331 48.8	15.5	179 33.2	13.7	13 51.6	8.3	54.5
11	346 49.0	14.5	194 06.9	13.6	13 43.3	8.3	54.5
12	1 49.3	N 0 13.5	208 38.5	13.6	S13 35.0	8.4	54.6
13	16 49.5	12.5	223 11.1	13.7	13 26.6	8.5	54.6
14	31 49.7	11.6	237 43.8	13.7	13 18.1	8.5	54.6
15	46 49.9 ..	10.6	252 16.5	13.7	13 09.6	8.6	54.6
16	61 50.1	09.6	266 49.2	13.7	13 01.0	8.6	54.6
17	76 50.4	08.7	281 21.9	13.7	12 52.4	8.7	54.6
18	91 50.6	N 0 07.7	295 54.6	13.8	S12 43.7	8.8	54.6
19	106 50.8	06.7	310 27.4	13.7	12 34.9	8.8	54.6
20	121 51.0	05.7	325 00.1	13.8	12 26.1	8.8	54.7
21	136 51.2 ..	04.8	339 32.9	13.8	12 17.3	9.0	54.7
22	151 51.5	03.8	354 05.7	13.8	12 08.3	9.0	54.7
23	166 51.7	02.8	8 38.5	13.9	11 59.3	9.0	54.7
23 00	181 51.9	N 0 01.8	23 11.4	13.8	S11 50.3	9.1	54.7
01	196 52.1	N 0 00.9	37 44.2	13.9	11 41.2	9.2	54.7
02	211 52.3	S 0 00.1	52 17.1	13.9	11 32.0	9.2	54.7
03	226 52.6 ..	01.1	66 50.0	13.9	11 22.8	9.3	54.8
04	241 52.8	02.0	81 22.9	13.9	11 13.5	9.3	54.8
05	256 53.0	03.0	95 55.8	13.9	11 04.2	9.4	54.8
06	271 53.2	S 0 04.0	110 28.7	13.9	S10 54.8	9.5	54.8
07	286 53.4	05.0	125 01.6	14.0	10 45.3	9.5	54.8
08	301 53.7	05.9	139 34.6	13.9	10 35.8	9.5	54.8
09	316 53.9 ..	06.9	154 07.5	14.0	10 26.3	9.6	54.9
10	331 54.1	07.9	168 40.5	14.0	10 16.7	9.6	54.9
11	346 54.3	08.9	183 13.5	14.0	10 07.1	9.7	54.9
12	1 54.5	S 0 09.8	197 46.5	14.0	S 9 57.4	9.8	54.9
13	16 54.8	10.8	212 19.5	14.0	9 47.6	9.8	54.9
14	31 55.0	11.8	226 52.5	14.0	9 37.8	9.8	54.9
15	46 55.2 ..	12.7	241 25.5	14.1	9 28.0	9.9	54.9
16	61 55.4	13.7	255 58.6	14.0	9 18.1	9.9	55.0
17	76 55.6	14.7	270 31.6	14.1	9 08.2	10.0	55.0
18	91 55.9	S 0 15.7	285 04.7	14.0	S 8 58.2	10.1	55.0
19	106 56.1	16.6	299 37.7	14.1	8 48.1	10.0	55.0
20	121 56.3	17.6	314 10.8	14.1	8 38.1	10.1	55.0
21	136 56.5 ..	18.6	328 43.9	14.1	8 28.0	10.2	55.0
22	151 56.7	19.6	343 17.0	14.1	8 17.8	10.2	55.1
23	166 57.0	20.5	357 50.1	14.0	8 07.6	10.3	55.1
24 00	181 57.2	S 0 21.5	12 23.1	14.2	S 7 57.3	10.2	55.1
01	196 57.4	22.5	26 56.3	14.1	7 47.1	10.4	55.1
02	211 57.6	23.4	41 29.4	14.1	7 36.7	10.3	55.1
03	226 57.8 ..	24.4	56 02.5	14.1	7 26.4	10.4	55.1
04	241 58.1	25.4	70 35.6	14.1	7 16.0	10.5	55.2
05	256 58.3	26.4	85 08.7	14.1	7 05.5	10.5	55.2
06	271 58.5	S 0 27.3	99 41.8	14.1	S 6 55.0	10.5	55.2
07	286 58.7	28.3	114 14.9	14.2	6 44.5	10.6	55.2
08	301 58.9	29.3	128 48.1	14.1	6 33.9	10.5	55.2
09	316 59.1 ..	30.3	143 21.2	14.1	6 23.4	10.7	55.3
10	331 59.4	31.2	157 54.3	14.1	6 12.7	10.6	55.3
11	346 59.6	32.2	172 27.4	14.2	6 02.1	10.7	55.3
12	1 59.8	S 0 33.2	187 00.6	14.1	S 5 51.4	10.8	55.3
13	17 00.0	34.2	201 33.7	14.1	5 40.6	10.7	55.3
14	32 00.2	35.1	216 06.8	14.1	5 29.9	10.8	55.3
15	47 00.5 ..	36.1	230 39.9	14.2	5 19.1	10.8	55.4
16	62 00.7	37.1	245 13.1	14.1	5 08.3	10.9	55.4
17	77 00.9	38.0	259 46.2	14.1	4 57.4	10.9	55.4
18	92 01.1	S 0 39.0	274 19.3	14.1	S 4 46.5	10.9	55.4
19	107 01.3	40.0	288 52.4	14.1	4 35.6	10.9	55.5
20	122 01.5	41.0	303 25.5	14.1	4 24.7	11.0	55.5
21	137 01.8 ..	41.9	317 58.6	14.1	4 13.7	11.0	55.5
22	152 02.0	42.9	332 31.7	14.1	4 02.7	11.0	55.5
23	167 02.2	43.9	347 04.8	14.0	S 3 51.7	11.1	55.5
	SD 16.0 d 1.0		SD 14.9		15.0		15.1

Left-margin day labels: **S A T U R D A Y** (22), **S U N D A Y** (23), **M O N D A Y** (24).

Lat.	Twilight Naut.	Twilight Civil	Sunrise	Moonrise 22	23	24	25
°	h m	h m	h m	h m	h m	h m	h m
N 72	03 04	04 34	05 42	19 13	18 57	18 43	18 31
N 70	03 23	04 42	05 43	18 51	18 44	18 37	18 30
68	03 38	04 48	05 44	18 34	18 33	18 32	18 30
66	03 50	04 53	05 45	18 20	18 24	18 27	18 30
64	04 00	04 58	05 45	18 08	18 16	18 23	18 29
62	04 08	05 01	05 46	17 58	18 10	18 20	18 29
60	04 14	05 05	05 46	17 49	18 04	18 17	18 29
N 58	04 20	05 07	05 47	17 42	17 59	18 14	18 29
56	04 25	05 10	05 47	17 35	17 55	18 12	18 29
54	04 30	05 12	05 47	17 29	17 50	18 09	18 29
52	04 34	05 14	05 47	17 24	17 47	18 08	18 29
50	04 37	05 15	05 48	17 19	17 43	18 06	18 29
45	04 44	05 19	05 48	17 08	17 36	18 03	18 28
N 40	04 50	05 21	05 48	16 59	17 30	17 59	18 28
35	04 54	05 23	05 49	16 52	17 25	17 57	18 28
30	04 57	05 25	05 49	16 45	17 20	17 54	18 28
20	05 01	05 27	05 49	16 33	17 12	17 50	18 28
N 10	05 04	05 28	05 49	16 23	17 05	17 46	18 27
0	05 04	05 28	05 49	16 14	16 58	17 43	18 27
S 10	05 04	05 28	05 49	16 04	16 52	17 39	18 27
20	05 01	05 27	05 49	15 54	16 44	17 35	18 27
30	04 57	05 25	05 48	15 42	16 36	17 31	18 27
35	04 54	05 23	05 48	15 35	16 31	17 29	18 27
40	04 49	05 21	05 48	15 27	16 26	17 26	18 27
45	04 44	05 18	05 47	15 18	16 20	17 23	18 26
S 50	04 37	05 15	05 47	15 07	16 12	17 19	18 26
52	04 33	05 13	05 47	15 02	16 09	17 17	18 26
54	04 29	05 11	05 46	14 56	16 05	17 15	18 26
56	04 25	05 09	05 46	14 50	16 01	17 13	18 26
58	04 20	05 07	05 46	14 43	15 56	17 10	18 26
S 60	04 14	05 04	05 45	14 35	15 51	17 08	18 26

Lat.	Sunset	Twilight Civil	Twilight Naut.	Moonset 22	23	24	25
°	h m	h m	h m	h m	h m	h m	h m
N 72	18 00	19 08	20 36	25 53	01 53	03 43	05 29
N 70	17 59	19 00	20 18	00 31	02 14	03 54	05 33
68	17 59	18 54	20 04	00 57	02 30	04 03	05 36
66	17 58	18 49	19 52	01 16	02 43	04 11	05 39
64	17 58	18 45	19 43	01 32	02 54	04 17	05 41
62	17 57	18 42	19 35	01 45	03 03	04 22	05 43
60	17 57	18 39	19 28	01 56	03 11	04 27	05 45
N 58	17 57	18 36	19 23	02 06	03 18	04 31	05 46
56	17 57	18 34	19 18	02 14	03 24	04 35	05 48
54	17 57	18 32	19 13	02 21	03 29	04 38	05 49
52	17 56	18 30	19 10	02 28	03 34	04 41	05 50
50	17 56	18 28	19 06	02 34	03 38	04 44	05 51
45	17 56	18 25	19 00	02 47	03 48	04 50	05 53
N 40	17 56	18 23	18 54	02 57	03 55	04 55	05 55
35	17 56	18 21	18 50	03 06	04 02	04 59	05 57
30	17 56	18 19	18 47	03 14	04 08	05 03	05 58
20	17 55	18 17	18 43	03 27	04 18	05 09	06 00
N 10	17 55	18 16	18 41	03 39	04 27	05 14	06 02
0	17 56	18 16	18 40	03 50	04 35	05 20	06 04
S 10	17 56	18 17	18 41	04 01	04 43	05 25	06 06
20	17 56	18 18	18 44	04 13	04 52	05 30	06 08
30	17 57	18 21	18 48	04 26	05 02	05 36	06 10
35	17 57	18 22	18 52	04 33	05 07	05 40	06 11
40	17 58	18 25	18 56	04 42	05 14	05 44	06 13
45	17 58	18 27	19 02	04 52	05 21	05 48	06 14
S 50	17 59	18 31	19 09	05 04	05 30	05 54	06 16
52	17 59	18 33	19 13	05 10	05 34	05 56	06 17
54	17 59	18 35	19 17	05 16	05 39	05 59	06 18
56	18 00	18 37	19 21	05 23	05 44	06 02	06 19
58	18 00	18 40	19 27	05 30	05 49	06 05	06 20
S 60	18 01	18 42	19 33	05 39	05 55	06 09	06 21

	SUN Eqn. of Time 00h	12h	Mer. Pass.	MOON Mer. Pass. Upper	Lower	Age	Phase
Day	m s	m s	h m	h m	h m	d	%
d							
22	07 06	07 17	11 53	22 24	10 02	13	93
23	07 27	07 38	11 52	23 09	10 47	14	97
24	07 48	07 59	11 52	23 53	11 31	15	99

UT	ARIES GHA	VENUS −4.8 GHA	Dec	MARS −1.4 GHA	Dec	JUPITER −1.8 GHA	Dec	SATURN +0.5 GHA	Dec	STARS Name	SHA	Dec
25 00	3 45.8	149 31.0	S20 16.4	56 37.2	S23 25.6	135 00.1	S17 14.9	90 42.2	S22 44.8	Acamar	315 15.3	S40 13.7
01	18 48.3	164 32.6	16.9	71 38.8	25.2	150 02.1	15.0	105 44.6	44.8	Achernar	335 23.6	S57 08.5
02	33 50.7	179 34.2	17.5	86 40.4	24.9	165 04.1	15.1	120 47.0	44.8	Acrux	173 05.9	S63 12.0
03	48 53.2	194 35.9	.. 18.1	101 42.0	.. 24.5	180 06.1	.. 15.3	135 49.3	.. 44.8	Adhara	255 09.8	S28 59.7
04	63 55.7	209 37.5	18.6	116 43.6	24.2	195 08.1	15.4	150 51.7	44.8	Aldebaran	290 45.1	N16 32.7
05	78 58.1	224 39.2	19.2	131 45.3	23.8	210 10.1	15.5	165 54.1	44.8			
06	94 00.6	239 40.8	S20 19.8	146 46.9	S23 23.5	225 12.2	S17 15.6	180 56.5	S22 44.8	Alioth	166 18.1	N55 51.7
T 07	109 03.0	254 42.5	20.3	161 48.5	23.1	240 14.2	15.8	195 58.9	44.8	Alkaid	152 56.5	N49 13.5
U 08	124 05.5	269 44.2	20.9	176 50.1	22.8	255 16.2	15.9	211 01.2	44.8	Al Na'ir	27 38.9	S46 52.3
E 09	139 08.0	284 45.8	.. 21.5	191 51.6	.. 22.4	270 18.2	.. 16.0	226 03.6	.. 44.8	Alnilam	275 42.7	S 1 11.4
S 10	154 10.4	299 47.5	22.0	206 53.2	22.1	285 20.2	16.1	241 06.0	44.8	Alphard	217 52.8	S 8 44.2
D 11	169 12.9	314 49.1	22.6	221 54.8	21.7	300 22.2	16.3	256 08.4	44.9			
A 12	184 15.4	329 50.8	S20 23.1	236 56.4	S23 21.4	315 24.2	S17 16.4	271 10.8	S22 44.9	Alphecca	126 08.2	N26 39.5
Y 13	199 17.8	344 52.5	23.7	251 58.0	21.0	330 26.3	16.5	286 13.1	44.9	Alpheratz	357 39.4	N29 11.6
14	214 20.3	359 54.2	24.2	266 59.6	20.7	345 28.3	16.6	301 15.5	44.9	Altair	62 04.6	N 8 55.3
15	229 22.8	14 55.9	.. 24.8	282 01.2	.. 20.3	0 30.3	.. 16.8	316 17.9	.. 44.9	Ankaa	353 11.8	S42 12.3
16	244 25.2	29 57.5	25.4	297 02.8	20.0	15 32.3	16.9	331 20.3	44.9	Antares	112 22.0	S26 28.2
17	259 27.7	44 59.2	25.9	312 04.4	19.6	30 34.3	17.0	346 22.7	44.9			
18	274 30.1	60 00.9	S20 26.4	327 06.0	S23 19.3	45 36.3	S17 17.1	1 25.0	S22 44.9	Arcturus	145 52.8	N19 05.4
19	289 32.6	75 02.6	27.0	342 07.6	18.9	60 38.3	17.2	16 27.4	44.9	Atria	107 20.8	S69 03.7
20	304 35.1	90 04.3	27.5	357 09.2	18.6	75 40.3	17.4	31 29.8	44.9	Avior	234 16.9	S59 33.9
21	319 37.5	105 06.0	.. 28.1	12 10.8	.. 18.2	90 42.4	.. 17.5	46 32.2	.. 44.9	Bellatrix	278 28.1	N 6 21.9
22	334 40.0	120 07.7	28.6	27 12.3	17.9	105 44.4	17.6	61 34.6	44.9	Betelgeuse	270 57.4	N 7 24.6
23	349 42.5	135 09.4	29.2	42 13.9	17.5	120 46.4	17.7	76 36.9	44.9			
26 00	4 44.9	150 11.1	S20 29.7	57 15.5	S23 17.1	135 48.4	S17 17.9	91 39.3	S22 44.9	Canopus	263 54.6	S52 42.1
01	19 47.4	165 12.8	30.3	72 17.1	16.8	150 50.4	18.0	106 41.7	44.9	Capella	280 29.1	N46 00.7
02	34 49.9	180 14.5	30.8	87 18.7	16.4	165 52.4	18.1	121 44.1	44.9	Deneb	49 28.8	N45 21.1
03	49 52.3	195 16.2	.. 31.3	102 20.3	.. 16.1	180 54.4	.. 18.2	136 46.5	.. 44.9	Denebola	182 30.4	N14 28.3
04	64 54.8	210 18.0	31.9	117 21.8	15.7	195 56.4	18.4	151 48.8	44.9	Diphda	348 52.0	S17 53.0
05	79 57.3	225 19.7	32.4	132 23.4	15.4	210 58.5	18.5	166 51.2	44.9			
06	94 59.7	240 21.4	S20 32.9	147 25.0	S23 15.0	226 00.5	S17 18.6	181 53.6	S22 44.9	Dubhe	193 48.0	N61 39.0
W 07	110 02.2	255 23.1	33.5	162 26.6	14.7	241 02.5	18.7	196 56.0	44.9	Elnath	278 08.0	N28 37.2
E 08	125 04.6	270 24.9	34.0	177 28.2	14.3	256 04.5	18.9	211 58.3	44.9	Eltanin	90 44.5	N51 29.6
D 09	140 07.1	285 26.6	.. 34.5	192 29.7	.. 14.0	271 06.5	.. 19.0	227 00.7	.. 44.9	Enif	33 43.4	N 9 57.8
N 10	155 09.6	300 28.3	35.0	207 31.3	13.6	286 08.5	19.1	242 03.1	44.9	Fomalhaut	15 19.7	S29 31.4
E 11	170 12.0	315 30.1	35.6	222 32.9	13.2	301 10.5	19.2	257 05.5	45.0			
S 12	185 14.5	330 31.8	S20 36.1	237 34.5	S23 12.9	316 12.5	S17 19.4	272 07.8	S22 45.0	Gacrux	171 57.5	S57 12.9
D 13	200 17.0	345 33.6	36.6	252 36.0	12.5	331 14.5	19.5	287 10.2	45.0	Gienah	175 49.0	S17 38.5
A 14	215 19.4	0 35.3	37.1	267 37.6	12.2	346 16.5	19.6	302 12.6	45.0	Hadar	148 43.4	S60 27.7
Y 15	230 21.9	15 37.1	.. 37.7	282 39.2	.. 11.8	1 18.6	.. 19.7	317 15.0	.. 45.0	Hamal	327 56.4	N23 33.0
16	245 24.4	30 38.8	38.2	297 40.7	11.4	16 20.6	19.9	332 17.3	45.0	Kaus Aust.	83 39.1	S34 22.4
17	260 26.8	45 40.6	38.7	312 42.3	11.1	31 22.6	20.0	347 19.7	45.0			
18	275 29.3	60 42.3	S20 39.2	327 43.9	S23 10.7	46 24.6	S17 20.1	2 22.1	S22 45.0	Kochab	137 21.0	N74 05.1
19	290 31.7	75 44.1	39.7	342 45.4	10.4	61 26.6	20.2	17 24.5	45.0	Markab	13 34.5	N15 18.5
20	305 34.2	90 45.9	40.2	357 47.0	10.0	76 28.6	20.3	32 26.8	45.0	Menkar	314 11.1	N 4 09.7
21	320 36.7	105 47.6	.. 40.8	12 48.6	.. 09.7	91 30.6	.. 20.5	47 29.2	.. 45.0	Menkent	148 03.7	S36 27.5
22	335 39.1	120 49.4	41.3	27 50.1	09.3	106 32.6	20.6	62 31.6	45.0	Miaplacidus	221 39.6	S69 47.4
23	350 41.6	135 51.2	41.8	42 51.7	08.9	121 34.6	20.7	77 34.0	45.0			
27 00	5 44.1	150 53.0	S20 42.3	57 53.3	S23 08.6	136 36.6	S17 20.8	92 36.3	S22 45.0	Mirfak	308 34.9	N49 55.4
01	20 46.5	165 54.8	42.8	72 54.8	08.2	151 38.6	21.0	107 38.7	45.0	Nunki	75 53.8	S26 16.3
02	35 49.0	180 56.5	43.3	87 56.4	07.8	166 40.6	21.1	122 41.1	45.0	Peacock	53 13.3	S56 40.6
03	50 51.5	195 58.3	.. 43.8	102 57.9	.. 07.5	181 42.7	.. 21.2	137 43.5	.. 45.0	Pollux	243 23.5	N27 58.7
04	65 53.9	211 00.1	44.3	117 59.5	07.1	196 44.7	21.3	152 45.8	45.0	Procyon	244 56.1	N 5 10.6
05	80 56.4	226 01.9	44.8	133 01.1	06.8	211 46.7	21.5	167 48.2	45.0			
06	95 58.9	241 03.7	S20 45.3	148 02.6	S23 06.4	226 48.7	S17 21.6	182 50.6	S22 45.0	Rasalhague	96 03.2	N12 33.1
T 07	111 01.3	256 05.5	45.8	163 04.2	06.0	241 50.7	21.7	197 53.0	45.0	Regulus	207 40.0	N11 52.7
H 08	126 03.8	271 07.3	46.3	178 05.7	05.7	256 52.7	21.8	212 55.3	45.0	Rigel	281 08.5	S 8 10.8
U 09	141 06.2	286 09.1	.. 46.8	193 07.3	.. 05.3	271 54.7	.. 22.0	227 57.7	.. 45.0	Rigil Kent.	139 47.4	S60 54.6
R 10	156 08.7	301 10.9	47.3	208 08.8	05.0	286 56.7	22.1	243 00.1	45.0	Sabik	102 08.5	S15 44.7
S 11	171 11.2	316 12.8	47.8	223 10.4	04.6	301 58.7	22.2	258 02.4	45.1			
D 12	186 13.6	331 14.6	S20 48.3	238 11.9	S23 04.2	317 00.7	S17 22.3	273 04.8	S22 45.1	Schedar	349 35.9	N56 38.3
A 13	201 16.1	346 16.4	48.8	253 13.5	03.9	332 02.7	22.5	288 07.2	45.1	Shaula	96 17.1	S37 06.9
Y 14	216 18.6	1 18.2	49.2	268 15.0	03.5	347 04.7	22.6	303 09.6	45.1	Sirius	258 30.6	S16 44.4
15	231 21.0	16 20.0	.. 49.7	283 16.6	.. 03.1	2 06.7	.. 22.7	318 11.9	.. 45.1	Spica	158 27.8	S11 15.3
16	246 23.5	31 21.9	50.2	298 18.1	02.8	17 08.7	22.8	333 14.3	45.1	Suhail	222 50.1	S43 30.3
17	261 26.0	46 23.7	50.7	313 19.7	02.4	32 10.7	23.0	348 16.7	45.1			
18	276 28.4	61 25.5	S20 51.2	328 21.2	S23 02.0	47 12.7	S17 23.1	3 19.1	S22 45.1	Vega	80 36.5	N38 48.5
19	291 30.9	76 27.4	51.7	343 22.8	01.7	62 14.8	23.2	18 21.4	45.1	Zuben'ubi	137 01.7	S16 06.9
20	306 33.4	91 29.2	52.1	358 24.3	01.3	77 16.8	23.3	33 23.8	45.1		SHA	Mer.Pass.
21	321 35.8	106 31.1	.. 52.6	13 25.9	.. 00.9	92 18.8	.. 23.5	48 26.2	.. 45.1		° ′	h m
22	336 38.3	121 32.9	53.1	28 27.4	00.6	107 20.8	23.6	63 28.5	45.1	Venus	145 26.2	13 58
23	351 40.7	136 34.8	53.6	43 29.0	00.2	122 22.8	23.7	78 30.9	45.1	Mars	52 30.6	20 09
Mer. Pass. 23 37.1		v 1.7	d 0.5	v 1.6	d 0.4	v 2.0	d 0.1	v 2.4	d 0.0	Jupiter	131 03.5	14 55
										Saturn	86 54.4	17 51

UT	SUN GHA	SUN Dec	MOON GHA	v	MOON Dec	d	HP
25 00	182 02.4	S 0 44.9	1 37.8	14.1	S 3 40.6	11.0	55.5
01	197 02.6	45.8	16 10.9	14.1	3 29.6	11.1	55.6
02	212 02.9	46.8	30 44.0	14.0	3 18.5	11.1	55.6
03	227 03.1	.. 47.8	45 17.0	14.1	3 07.4	11.2	55.6
04	242 03.3	48.7	59 50.1	14.0	2 56.2	11.1	55.6
05	257 03.5	49.7	74 23.1	14.0	2 45.1	11.2	55.6
06	272 03.7	S 0 50.7	88 56.1	14.0	S 2 33.9	11.2	55.6
07	287 03.9	51.7	103 29.1	14.0	2 22.7	11.2	55.7
T 08	302 04.2	52.6	118 02.1	14.0	2 11.5	11.3	55.7
U 09	317 04.4	.. 53.6	132 35.1	14.0	2 00.2	11.2	55.7
E 10	332 04.6	54.6	147 08.1	13.9	1 49.0	11.3	55.7
S 11	347 04.8	55.6	161 41.0	14.0	1 37.7	11.3	55.7
D 12	2 05.0	S 0 56.5	176 14.0	13.9	S 1 26.4	11.3	55.8
A 13	17 05.2	57.5	190 46.9	13.9	1 15.1	11.3	55.8
Y 14	32 05.5	58.5	205 19.8	13.9	1 03.8	11.3	55.8
15	47 05.7	0 59.5	219 52.7	13.9	0 52.5	11.3	55.8
16	62 05.9	1 00.4	234 25.6	13.9	0 41.2	11.4	55.8
17	77 06.1	01.4	248 58.5	13.8	0 29.8	11.3	55.9
18	92 06.3	S 1 02.4	263 31.3	13.8	S 0 18.5	11.4	55.9
19	107 06.5	03.3	278 04.1	13.8	S 0 07.1	11.4	55.9
20	122 06.8	04.3	292 36.9	13.8	N 0 04.3	11.3	55.9
21	137 07.0	.. 05.3	307 09.7	13.8	0 15.6	11.4	55.9
22	152 07.2	06.3	321 42.5	13.7	0 27.0	11.4	56.0
23	167 07.4	07.2	336 15.2	13.7	0 38.4	11.4	56.0
26 00	182 07.6	S 1 08.2	350 47.9	13.7	N 0 49.8	11.4	56.0
01	197 07.8	09.2	5 20.6	13.7	1 01.2	11.4	56.0
02	212 08.1	10.2	19 53.3	13.6	1 12.6	11.5	56.0
03	227 08.3	.. 11.1	34 25.9	13.6	1 24.1	11.4	56.1
04	242 08.5	12.1	48 58.5	13.6	1 35.5	11.4	56.1
05	257 08.7	13.1	63 31.1	13.6	1 46.9	11.4	56.1
06	272 08.9	S 1 14.1	78 03.7	13.5	N 1 58.3	11.4	56.1
W 07	287 09.1	15.0	92 36.2	13.6	2 09.7	11.4	56.1
E 08	302 09.3	16.0	107 08.8	13.4	2 21.1	11.4	56.2
D 09	317 09.6	.. 17.0	121 41.2	13.5	2 32.5	11.4	56.2
N 10	332 09.8	17.9	136 13.7	13.4	2 43.9	11.4	56.2
E 11	347 10.0	18.9	150 46.1	13.4	2 55.3	11.4	56.2
S 12	2 10.2	S 1 19.9	165 18.5	13.4	N 3 06.7	11.4	56.2
D 13	17 10.4	20.9	179 50.9	13.3	3 18.1	11.4	56.3
A 14	32 10.6	21.8	194 23.2	13.3	3 29.5	11.4	56.3
Y 15	47 10.9	.. 22.8	208 55.5	13.3	3 40.9	11.3	56.3
16	62 11.1	23.8	223 27.8	13.2	3 52.2	11.4	56.3
17	77 11.3	24.8	238 00.0	13.2	4 03.6	11.3	56.3
18	92 11.5	S 1 25.7	252 32.2	13.2	N 4 14.9	11.4	56.4
19	107 11.7	26.7	267 04.4	13.1	4 26.3	11.3	56.4
20	122 11.9	27.7	281 36.5	13.1	4 37.6	11.3	56.4
21	137 12.1	.. 28.6	296 08.6	13.1	4 48.9	11.3	56.4
22	152 12.4	29.6	310 40.7	13.0	5 00.2	11.3	56.4
23	167 12.6	30.6	325 12.7	12.9	5 11.5	11.2	56.5
27 00	182 12.8	S 1 31.6	339 44.6	13.0	N 5 22.7	11.3	56.5
01	197 13.0	32.5	354 16.6	12.9	5 34.0	11.2	56.5
02	212 13.2	33.5	8 48.5	12.9	5 45.2	11.2	56.5
03	227 13.4	.. 34.5	23 20.4	12.8	5 56.4	11.2	56.5
04	242 13.6	35.5	37 52.2	12.7	6 07.6	11.2	56.6
05	257 13.8	36.4	52 23.9	12.8	6 18.8	11.1	56.6
06	272 14.1	S 1 37.4	66 55.7	12.7	N 6 29.9	11.1	56.6
07	287 14.3	38.4	81 27.4	12.6	6 41.0	11.1	56.6
T 08	302 14.5	39.3	95 59.0	12.6	6 52.1	11.1	56.6
H 09	317 14.7	.. 40.3	110 30.6	12.6	7 03.2	11.0	56.7
U 10	332 14.9	41.3	125 02.2	12.5	7 14.2	11.0	56.7
R 11	347 15.1	42.3	139 33.7	12.5	7 25.2	11.0	56.7
S 12	2 15.3	S 1 43.2	154 05.2	12.4	N 7 36.2	11.0	56.7
D 13	17 15.6	44.2	168 36.6	12.4	7 47.2	10.9	56.8
A 14	32 15.8	45.2	183 08.0	12.3	7 58.1	10.9	56.8
Y 15	47 16.0	.. 46.2	197 39.3	12.3	8 09.0	10.9	56.8
16	62 16.2	47.1	212 10.6	12.2	8 19.9	10.8	56.8
17	77 16.4	48.1	226 41.8	12.2	8 30.7	10.8	56.8
18	92 16.6	S 1 49.1	241 13.0	12.1	N 8 41.5	10.7	56.9
19	107 16.8	50.0	255 44.1	12.1	8 52.2	10.8	56.9
20	122 17.0	51.0	270 15.2	12.0	9 03.0	10.7	56.9
21	137 17.2	.. 52.0	284 46.2	12.0	9 13.7	10.6	56.9
22	152 17.5	53.0	299 17.2	12.0	9 24.3	10.6	56.9
23	167 17.7	53.9	313 48.2	11.8	N 9 34.9	10.6	57.0
	SD 16.0	d 1.0	SD 15.2		15.3		15.5

Twilight / Sunrise / Moonrise

Lat.	Twilight Naut.	Twilight Civil	Sunrise	Moonrise 25	Moonrise 26	Moonrise 27	Moonrise 28
°	h m	h m	h m	h m	h m	h m	h m
N 72	03 21	04 48	05 56	18 31	18 18	18 05	17 48
N 70	03 38	04 54	05 55	18 30	18 24	18 17	18 10
68	03 51	04 59	05 55	18 30	18 29	18 28	18 27
66	04 01	05 03	05 54	18 30	18 33	18 36	18 41
64	04 09	05 06	05 54	18 30	18 36	18 44	18 53
62	04 16	05 09	05 54	18 29	18 39	18 50	19 03
60	04 22	05 12	05 53	18 29	18 42	18 55	19 12
N 58	04 27	05 14	05 53	18 29	18 44	19 00	19 19
56	04 32	05 16	05 53	18 29	18 46	19 05	19 26
54	04 36	05 17	05 53	18 29	18 48	19 08	19 32
52	04 39	05 19	05 52	18 29	18 50	19 12	19 37
50	04 42	05 20	05 52	18 29	18 51	19 15	19 42
45	04 48	05 22	05 52	18 28	18 54	19 22	19 53
N 40	04 53	05 24	05 51	18 28	18 57	19 28	20 02
35	04 56	05 26	05 51	18 28	19 00	19 33	20 10
30	04 59	05 27	05 50	18 28	19 02	19 38	20 17
20	05 02	05 28	05 50	18 28	19 06	19 46	20 28
N 10	05 03	05 28	05 49	18 27	19 09	19 53	20 39
0	05 03	05 27	05 48	18 27	19 13	19 59	20 49
S 10	05 02	05 26	05 47	18 27	19 16	20 06	20 58
20	04 58	05 24	05 46	18 27	19 19	20 13	21 09
30	04 53	05 21	05 45	18 27	19 23	20 22	21 21
35	04 49	05 19	05 44	18 27	19 26	20 26	21 28
40	04 44	05 16	05 43	18 27	19 28	20 32	21 36
45	04 38	05 12	05 42	18 26	19 32	20 38	21 46
S 50	04 30	05 08	05 40	18 26	19 35	20 46	21 57
52	04 26	05 06	05 40	18 26	19 37	20 49	22 03
54	04 21	05 04	05 39	18 26	19 39	20 53	22 09
56	04 16	05 01	05 38	18 26	19 41	20 57	22 15
58	04 11	04 58	05 37	18 26	19 43	21 02	22 23
S 60	04 04	04 54	05 36	18 26	19 46	21 08	22 31

Sunset / Twilight / Moonset

Lat.	Sunset	Twilight Civil	Twilight Naut.	Moonset 25	Moonset 26	Moonset 27	Moonset 28
°	h m	h m	h m	h m	h m	h m	h m
N 72	17 44	18 52	20 17	05 29	07 16	09 06	11 04
N 70	17 45	18 46	20 01	05 33	07 13	08 56	10 43
68	17 46	18 41	19 49	05 36	07 10	08 47	10 27
66	17 47	18 38	19 39	05 39	07 08	08 40	10 14
64	17 47	18 34	19 31	05 41	07 07	08 34	10 04
62	17 48	18 32	19 24	05 43	07 05	08 29	09 55
60	17 48	18 29	19 19	05 45	07 04	08 25	09 47
N 58	17 48	18 27	19 14	05 46	07 03	08 21	09 40
56	17 49	18 26	19 09	05 48	07 02	08 17	09 34
54	17 49	18 24	19 06	05 49	07 01	08 14	09 29
52	17 49	18 23	19 02	05 50	07 00	08 11	09 24
50	17 50	18 22	18 59	05 51	06 59	08 09	09 20
45	17 50	18 19	18 54	05 53	06 57	08 03	09 10
N 40	17 51	18 18	18 49	05 55	06 56	07 59	09 02
35	17 51	18 17	18 46	05 56	06 55	07 55	08 56
30	17 52	18 16	18 43	05 58	06 54	07 51	08 50
20	17 53	18 15	18 40	06 00	06 52	07 45	08 40
N 10	17 54	18 15	18 39	06 02	06 50	07 40	08 31
0	17 55	18 15	18 39	06 04	06 49	07 35	08 23
S 10	17 56	18 17	18 41	06 06	06 47	07 30	08 14
20	17 57	18 19	18 45	06 08	06 46	07 25	08 06
30	17 58	18 22	18 50	06 10	06 44	07 19	07 56
35	17 59	18 25	18 54	06 11	06 43	07 15	07 50
40	18 00	18 27	18 59	06 12	06 41	07 11	07 43
45	18 02	18 31	19 06	06 14	06 40	07 07	07 36
S 50	18 03	18 36	19 14	06 16	06 38	07 01	07 27
52	18 04	18 38	19 18	06 17	06 37	06 59	07 22
54	18 05	18 40	19 23	06 18	06 37	06 56	07 17
56	18 06	18 43	19 28	06 19	06 36	06 53	07 13
58	18 07	18 46	19 34	06 20	06 35	06 50	07 07
S 60	18 08	18 50	19 41	06 21	06 33	06 46	07 01

SUN / MOON

Day	Eqn. of Time 00h	Eqn. of Time 12h	Mer. Pass.	Mer. Pass. Upper	Mer. Pass. Lower	Age	Phase
d	m s	m s	h m	h m	h m	d	%
25	08 09	08 20	11 52	24 38	12 16	16	100
26	08 30	08 40	11 51	00 38	13 01	17	98
27	08 51	09 01	11 51	01 24	13 47	18	94

UT	ARIES GHA	VENUS −4·8 GHA	Dec	MARS −1·4 GHA	Dec	JUPITER −1·8 GHA	Dec	SATURN +0·5 GHA	Dec	STARS Name	SHA	Dec
d h	° ′	° ′	° ′	° ′	° ′	° ′	° ′	° ′	° ′		° ′	° ′
28 00	6 43.2	151 36.6	S20 54.0	58 30.5	S22 59.8	137 24.8	S17 23.8	93 33.3	S22 45.1	Acamar	315 15.3	S40 13.7
01	21 45.7	166 38.5	54.5	73 32.0	59.5	152 26.8	24.0	108 35.6	45.1	Achernar	335 23.6	S57 08.5
02	36 48.1	181 40.3	55.0	88 33.6	59.1	167 28.8	24.1	123 38.0	45.1	Acrux	173 05.9	S63 12.0
03	51 50.6	196 42.2 ..	55.5	103 35.1 ..	58.7	182 30.8 ..	24.2	138 40.4 ..	45.1	Adhara	255 09.8	S28 59.7
04	66 53.1	211 44.1	55.9	118 36.7	58.4	197 32.8	24.3	153 42.8	45.1	Aldebaran	290 45.1	N16 32.7
05	81 55.5	226 45.9	56.4	133 38.2	58.0	212 34.8	24.5	168 45.1	45.1			
06	96 58.0	241 47.8	S20 56.9	148 39.7	S22 57.6	227 36.8	S17 24.6	183 47.5	S22 45.1	Alioth	166 18.1	N55 51.7
07	112 00.5	256 49.7	57.3	163 41.3	57.3	242 38.8	24.7	198 49.9	45.1	Alkaid	152 56.5	N49 13.5
08	127 02.9	271 51.6	57.8	178 42.8	56.9	257 40.8	24.8	213 52.2	45.1	Al Na'ir	27 38.9	S46 52.3
F 09	142 05.4	286 53.5 ..	58.2	193 44.3 ..	56.5	272 42.8 ..	25.0	228 54.6 ..	45.1	Alnilam	275 42.7	S 1 11.4
R 10	157 07.8	301 55.3	58.7	208 45.9	56.2	287 44.8	25.1	243 57.0	45.1	Alphard	217 52.8	S 8 44.2
I 11	172 10.3	316 57.2	59.2	223 47.4	55.8	302 46.8	25.2	258 59.3	45.1			
D 12	187 12.8	331 59.1	S20 59.6	238 48.9	S22 55.4	317 48.8	S17 25.3	274 01.7	S22 45.1	Alphecca	126 08.2	N26 39.5
A 13	202 15.2	347 01.0	21 00.1	253 50.5	55.0	332 50.8	25.5	289 04.1	45.2	Alpheratz	357 39.4	N29 11.7
Y 14	217 17.7	2 02.9	00.5	268 52.0	54.7	347 52.8	25.6	304 06.4	45.2	Altair	62 04.6	N 8 55.3
15	232 20.2	17 04.8 ..	01.0	283 53.5 ..	54.3	2 54.8 ..	25.7	319 08.8 ..	45.2	Ankaa	353 11.8	S42 12.3
16	247 22.6	32 06.7	01.4	298 55.0	53.9	17 56.8	25.8	334 11.2	45.2	Antares	112 22.0	S26 28.2
17	262 25.1	47 08.6	01.9	313 56.6	53.6	32 58.8	26.0	349 13.5	45.2			
18	277 27.6	62 10.6	S21 02.3	328 58.1	S22 53.2	48 00.8	S17 26.1	4 15.9	S22 45.2	Arcturus	145 52.8	N19 05.4
19	292 30.0	77 12.5	02.8	343 59.6	52.8	63 02.8	26.2	19 18.3	45.2	Atria	107 20.8	S69 03.7
20	307 32.5	92 14.4	03.2	359 01.1	52.4	78 04.8	26.3	34 20.6	45.2	Avior	234 16.9	S59 33.9
21	322 35.0	107 16.3 ..	03.7	14 02.7 ..	52.1	93 06.8 ..	26.5	49 23.0 ..	45.2	Bellatrix	278 28.1	N 6 21.9
22	337 37.4	122 18.2	04.1	29 04.2	51.7	108 08.8	26.6	64 25.4	45.2	Betelgeuse	270 57.4	N 7 24.6
23	352 39.9	137 20.2	04.5	44 05.7	51.3	123 10.8	26.7	79 27.7	45.2			
29 00	7 42.3	152 22.1	S21 05.0	59 07.2	S22 51.0	138 12.8	S17 26.8	94 30.1	S22 45.2	Canopus	263 54.6	S52 42.1
01	22 44.8	167 24.0	05.4	74 08.7	50.6	153 14.8	27.0	109 32.5	45.2	Capella	280 29.0	N46 00.7
02	37 47.3	182 26.0	05.8	89 10.3	50.2	168 16.8	27.1	124 34.8	45.2	Deneb	49 28.8	N45 21.2
03	52 49.7	197 27.9 ..	06.3	104 11.8 ..	49.8	183 18.8 ..	27.2	139 37.2 ..	45.2	Denebola	182 30.4	N14 28.2
04	67 52.2	212 29.9	06.7	119 13.3	49.5	198 20.8	27.3	154 39.6	45.2	Diphda	348 52.0	S17 53.0
05	82 54.7	227 31.8	07.1	134 14.8	49.1	213 22.8	27.5	169 41.9	45.2			
06	97 57.1	242 33.8	S21 07.6	149 16.3	S22 48.7	228 24.8	S17 27.6	184 44.3	S22 45.2	Dubhe	193 48.0	N61 39.0
07	112 59.6	257 35.7	08.0	164 17.9	48.3	243 26.8	27.7	199 46.7	45.2	Elnath	278 08.0	N28 37.2
S 08	128 02.1	272 37.7	08.4	179 19.4	48.0	258 28.8	27.8	214 49.0	45.2	Eltanin	90 44.6	N51 29.6
A 09	143 04.5	287 39.7 ..	08.8	194 20.9 ..	47.6	273 30.8 ..	28.0	229 51.4 ..	45.2	Enif	33 43.4	N 9 57.8
T 10	158 07.0	302 41.6	09.3	209 22.4	47.2	288 32.8	28.1	244 53.7	45.2	Fomalhaut	15 19.7	S29 31.4
U 11	173 09.4	317 43.6	09.7	224 23.9	46.8	303 34.8	28.2	259 56.1	45.2			
R 12	188 11.9	332 45.6	S21 10.1	239 25.4	S22 46.5	318 36.8	S17 28.3	274 58.5	S22 45.2	Gacrux	171 57.5	S57 12.9
D 13	203 14.4	347 47.5	10.5	254 26.9	46.1	333 38.8	28.5	290 00.8	45.2	Gienah	175 49.0	S17 38.5
A 14	218 16.8	2 49.5	10.9	269 28.4	45.7	348 40.8	28.6	305 03.2	45.2	Hadar	148 43.4	S60 27.7
Y 15	233 19.3	17 51.5 ..	11.4	284 29.9 ..	45.3	3 42.8 ..	28.7	320 05.6 ..	45.3	Hamal	327 56.4	N23 33.0
16	248 21.8	32 53.5	11.8	299 31.4	45.0	18 44.8	28.8	335 07.9	45.3	Kaus Aust.	83 39.1	S34 22.4
17	263 24.2	47 55.5	12.2	314 33.0	44.6	33 46.8	29.0	350 10.3	45.3			
18	278 26.7	62 57.5	S21 12.6	329 34.5	S22 44.2	48 48.8	S17 29.1	5 12.7	S22 45.3	Kochab	137 21.1	N74 05.1
19	293 29.2	77 59.5	13.0	344 36.0	43.8	63 50.8	29.2	20 15.0	45.3	Markab	13 34.5	N15 18.5
20	308 31.6	93 01.5	13.4	359 37.5	43.4	78 52.8	29.3	35 17.4	45.3	Menkar	314 11.1	N 4 09.7
21	323 34.1	108 03.5 ..	13.8	14 39.0 ..	43.1	93 54.8 ..	29.5	50 19.7 ..	45.3	Menkent	148 03.7	S36 27.5
22	338 36.6	123 05.5	14.2	29 40.5	42.7	108 56.8	29.6	65 22.1	45.3	Miaplacidus	221 39.5	S69 47.4
23	353 39.0	138 07.5	14.6	44 42.0	42.3	123 58.8	29.7	80 24.5	45.3			
30 00	8 41.5	153 09.5	S21 15.0	59 43.5	S22 41.9	139 00.8	S17 29.8	95 26.8	S22 45.3	Mirfak	308 34.9	N49 55.4
01	23 43.9	168 11.5	15.4	74 45.0	41.5	154 02.8	30.0	110 29.2	45.3	Nunki	75 53.9	S26 16.3
02	38 46.4	183 13.5	15.8	89 46.5	41.2	169 04.8	30.1	125 31.5	45.3	Peacock	53 13.4	S56 40.6
03	53 48.9	198 15.6 ..	16.2	104 48.0 ..	40.8	184 06.8 ..	30.2	140 33.9 ..	45.3	Pollux	243 23.5	N27 58.7
04	68 51.3	213 17.6	16.6	119 49.5	40.4	199 08.8	30.3	155 36.3	45.3	Procyon	244 56.1	N 5 10.6
05	83 53.8	228 19.6	17.0	134 51.0	40.0	214 10.8	30.5	170 38.6	45.3			
06	98 56.3	243 21.7	S21 17.4	149 52.5	S22 39.6	229 12.8	S17 30.6	185 41.0	S22 45.3	Rasalhague	96 03.2	N12 33.1
07	113 58.7	258 23.7	17.8	164 54.0	39.3	244 14.8	30.7	200 43.3	45.3	Regulus	207 40.0	N11 52.6
08	129 01.2	273 25.7	18.2	179 55.5	38.9	259 16.8	30.8	215 45.7	45.3	Rigel	281 08.5	S 8 10.8
S 09	144 03.7	288 27.8 ..	18.5	194 56.9 ..	38.5	274 18.8 ..	31.0	230 48.1 ..	45.3	Rigil Kent.	139 47.4	S60 54.6
U 10	159 06.1	303 29.8	18.9	209 58.4	38.1	289 20.8	31.1	245 50.4	45.3	Sabik	102 08.6	S15 44.7
N 11	174 08.6	318 31.9	19.3	224 59.9	37.7	304 22.7	31.2	260 52.8	45.3			
D 12	189 11.1	333 33.9	S21 19.7	240 01.4	S22 37.3	319 24.7	S17 31.3	275 55.1	S22 45.3	Schedar	349 35.8	N56 38.3
A 13	204 13.5	348 36.0	20.1	255 02.9	37.0	334 26.7	31.5	290 57.5	45.3	Shaula	96 17.2	S37 06.9
Y 14	219 16.0	3 38.0	20.5	270 04.4	36.6	349 28.7	31.6	305 59.9	45.3	Sirius	258 30.6	S16 44.4
15	234 18.4	18 40.1 ..	20.8	285 05.9 ..	36.2	4 30.7 ..	31.7	321 02.2 ..	45.3	Spica	158 27.8	S11 15.3
16	249 20.9	33 42.2	21.2	300 07.4	35.8	19 32.7	31.8	336 04.6	45.3	Suhail	222 50.1	S43 30.2
17	264 23.4	48 44.3	21.6	315 08.9	35.4	34 34.7	32.0	351 06.9	45.3			
18	279 25.8	63 46.3	S21 22.0	330 10.3	S22 35.0	49 36.7	S17 32.1	6 09.3	S22 45.3	Vega	80 36.5	N38 48.5
19	294 28.3	78 48.4	22.3	345 11.8	34.7	64 38.7	32.2	21 11.7	45.4	Zuben'ubi	137 01.7	S16 06.9
20	309 30.8	93 50.5	22.7	0 13.3	34.3	79 40.7	32.3	36 14.0	45.4		SHA	Mer. Pass.
21	324 33.2	108 52.6 ..	23.1	15 14.8 ..	33.9	94 42.7 ..	32.5	51 16.4 ..	45.4		° ′	h m
22	339 35.7	123 54.7	23.4	30 16.3	33.5	109 44.7	32.6	66 18.7	45.4	Venus	144 39.8	13 49
23	354 38.3	138 56.8	23.8	45 17.8	33.1	124 46.7	32.7	81 21.1	45.4	Mars	51 24.9	20 01
	h m									Jupiter	130 30.5	14 45
Mer. Pass. 23 25.3	v 2.0 d 0.4			v 1.5 d 0.4		v 2.0 d 0.1		v 2.4 d 0.0		Saturn	86 47.8	17 39

UT	SUN GHA	SUN Dec	MOON GHA	MOON v	MOON Dec	MOON d	MOON HP
d h	° ′	° ′	° ′	′	° ′	′	′
28 00	182 17.9	S 1 54.9	328 19.0	11.8	N 9 45.5	10.5	57.0
01	197 18.1	55.9	342 49.8	11.8	9 56.0	10.5	57.0
02	212 18.3	56.9	357 20.6	11.7	10 06.5	10.4	57.0
03	227 18.5	.. 57.8	11 51.3	11.7	10 16.9	10.4	57.0
04	242 18.7	58.8	26 22.0	11.6	10 27.3	10.4	57.1
05	257 18.9	1 59.8	40 52.6	11.5	10 37.7	10.3	57.1
06	272 19.2	S 2 00.7	55 23.1	11.5	N10 48.0	10.2	57.1
07	287 19.4	01.7	69 53.6	11.4	10 58.2	10.2	57.1
08	302 19.6	02.7	84 24.0	11.4	11 08.4	10.2	57.1
F 09	317 19.8	.. 03.7	98 54.4	11.3	11 18.6	10.1	57.2
R 10	332 20.0	04.6	113 24.7	11.3	11 28.7	10.1	57.2
I 11	347 20.2	05.6	127 55.0	11.2	11 38.8	10.0	57.2
D 12	2 20.4	S 2 06.6	142 25.2	11.1	N11 48.8	9.9	57.2
A 13	17 20.6	07.5	156 55.3	11.1	11 58.7	9.9	57.2
Y 14	32 20.8	08.5	171 25.4	11.0	12 08.6	9.8	57.3
15	47 21.0	.. 09.5	185 55.4	11.0	12 18.4	9.8	57.3
16	62 21.3	10.5	200 25.4	10.9	12 28.2	9.7	57.3
17	77 21.5	11.4	214 55.3	10.8	12 37.9	9.7	57.3
18	92 21.7	S 2 12.4	229 25.1	10.8	N12 47.6	9.6	57.3
19	107 21.9	13.4	243 54.9	10.7	12 57.2	9.5	57.4
20	122 22.1	14.4	258 24.6	10.6	13 06.7	9.5	57.4
21	137 22.3	.. 15.3	272 54.2	10.6	13 16.2	9.4	57.4
22	152 22.5	16.3	287 23.8	10.5	13 25.6	9.4	57.4
23	167 22.7	17.3	301 53.3	10.5	13 35.0	9.2	57.4
29 00	182 22.9	S 2 18.2	316 22.8	10.4	N13 44.2	9.2	57.5
01	197 23.1	19.2	330 52.2	10.3	13 53.4	9.2	57.5
02	212 23.3	20.2	345 21.5	10.3	14 02.6	9.1	57.5
03	227 23.6	.. 21.2	359 50.8	10.2	14 11.7	9.0	57.5
04	242 23.8	22.1	14 20.0	10.1	14 20.7	8.9	57.5
05	257 24.0	23.1	28 49.1	10.1	14 29.6	8.9	57.6
06	272 24.2	S 2 24.1	43 18.2	10.0	N14 38.5	8.7	57.6
S 07	287 24.4	25.0	57 47.2	9.9	14 47.2	8.8	57.6
A 08	302 24.6	26.0	72 16.1	9.9	14 56.0	8.6	57.6
T 09	317 24.8	.. 27.0	86 45.0	9.8	15 04.6	8.5	57.6
U 10	332 25.0	28.0	101 13.8	9.7	15 13.1	8.5	57.7
R 11	347 25.2	28.9	115 42.5	9.7	15 21.6	8.4	57.7
D 12	2 25.4	S 2 29.9	130 11.2	9.6	N15 30.0	8.3	57.7
A 13	17 25.6	30.9	144 39.8	9.6	15 38.3	8.3	57.7
Y 14	32 25.8	31.8	159 08.4	9.5	15 46.6	8.1	57.7
15	47 26.1	.. 32.8	173 36.9	9.4	15 54.7	8.1	57.8
16	62 26.3	33.8	188 05.3	9.3	16 02.8	8.0	57.8
17	77 26.5	34.8	202 33.6	9.3	16 10.8	7.9	57.8
18	92 26.7	S 2 35.7	217 01.9	9.2	N16 18.7	7.8	57.8
19	107 26.9	36.7	231 30.1	9.1	16 26.5	7.7	57.8
20	122 27.1	37.7	245 58.2	9.1	16 34.2	7.7	57.9
21	137 27.3	.. 38.6	260 26.3	9.0	16 41.9	7.5	57.9
22	152 27.5	39.6	274 54.3	9.0	16 49.4	7.5	57.9
23	167 27.7	40.6	289 22.3	8.8	16 56.9	7.4	57.9
30 00	182 27.9	S 2 41.5	303 50.1	8.8	N17 04.3	7.2	57.9
01	197 28.1	42.5	318 17.9	8.8	17 11.5	7.2	58.0
02	212 28.3	43.5	332 45.7	8.7	17 18.7	7.1	58.0
03	227 28.5	.. 44.5	347 13.4	8.6	17 25.8	7.0	58.0
04	242 28.7	45.4	1 41.0	8.5	17 32.8	6.9	58.0
05	257 28.9	46.4	16 08.5	8.5	17 39.7	6.7	58.0
06	272 29.1	S 2 47.4	30 36.0	8.4	N17 46.4	6.7	58.1
07	287 29.4	48.3	45 03.4	8.4	17 53.1	6.6	58.1
08	302 29.6	49.3	59 30.8	8.3	17 59.7	6.5	58.1
S 09	317 29.8	.. 50.3	73 58.1	8.2	18 06.2	6.4	58.1
U 10	332 30.0	51.3	88 25.3	8.1	18 12.6	6.3	58.1
N 11	347 30.2	52.2	102 52.4	8.1	18 18.9	6.2	58.2
D 12	2 30.4	S 2 53.2	117 19.5	8.1	N18 25.1	6.0	58.2
A 13	17 30.6	54.2	131 46.6	7.9	18 31.1	6.0	58.2
Y 14	32 30.8	55.1	146 13.5	7.9	18 37.1	5.9	58.2
15	47 31.0	.. 56.1	160 40.4	7.9	18 43.0	5.7	58.2
16	62 31.2	57.1	175 07.3	7.7	18 48.7	5.7	58.2
17	77 31.4	58.0	189 34.0	7.8	18 54.4	5.5	58.3
18	92 31.6	S 2 59.0	204 00.8	7.6	N18 59.9	5.4	58.3
19	107 31.8	3 00.0	218 27.4	7.6	19 05.3	5.3	58.3
20	122 32.0	01.0	232 54.0	7.6	19 10.6	5.2	58.3
21	137 32.2	.. 01.9	247 20.6	7.4	19 15.8	5.1	58.3
22	152 32.4	02.9	261 47.0	7.5	19 20.9	5.0	58.4
23	167 32.6	03.9	276 13.5	7.3	N19 25.9	4.8	58.4
	SD 16.0	d 1.0	SD 15.6		15.7		15.8

Lat.	Twilight Naut.	Twilight Civil	Sunrise	Moonrise 28	Moonrise 29	Moonrise 30	Moonrise 1
°	h m	h m	h m	h m	h m	h m	h m
N 72	03 38	05 02	06 09	17 48	17 20	▭	▭
N 70	03 52	05 06	06 07	18 10	18 01	17 45	▭
68	04 03	05 10	06 05	18 27	18 28	18 33	18 49
66	04 11	05 13	06 04	18 41	18 50	19 05	19 33
64	04 19	05 15	06 02	18 53	19 07	19 28	20 02
62	04 25	05 17	06 01	19 03	19 21	19 46	20 24
60	04 30	05 19	06 00	19 12	19 33	20 02	20 42
N 58	04 34	05 20	05 59	19 19	19 43	20 15	20 57
56	04 38	05 22	05 59	19 26	19 52	20 26	21 10
54	04 41	05 23	05 58	19 32	20 00	20 36	21 22
52	04 44	05 24	05 57	19 37	20 08	20 45	21 32
50	04 47	05 24	05 57	19 42	20 14	20 53	21 40
45	04 52	05 26	05 55	19 53	20 28	21 10	21 59
N 40	04 56	05 27	05 54	20 02	20 40	21 24	22 15
35	04 58	05 28	05 53	20 10	20 50	21 36	22 28
30	05 00	05 28	05 52	20 17	20 59	21 46	22 39
20	05 03	05 28	05 50	20 28	21 14	22 04	22 59
N 10	05 03	05 28	05 49	20 39	21 28	22 20	23 16
0	05 02	05 26	05 47	20 49	21 40	22 35	23 32
S 10	05 00	05 24	05 45	20 58	21 53	22 50	23 48
20	04 56	05 21	05 43	21 09	22 07	23 05	24 05
30	04 49	05 17	05 41	21 21	22 22	23 24	24 25
35	04 45	05 14	05 40	21 28	22 31	23 35	24 36
40	04 39	05 11	05 38	21 36	22 42	23 47	24 50
45	04 32	05 07	05 36	21 46	22 54	24 01	00 01
S 50	04 23	05 01	05 34	21 57	23 09	24 19	00 19
52	04 18	04 59	05 33	22 03	23 16	24 28	00 28
54	04 13	04 56	05 32	22 09	23 24	24 37	00 37
56	04 08	04 53	05 30	22 15	23 33	24 48	00 48
58	04 01	04 49	05 29	22 23	23 43	25 00	01 00
S 60	03 54	04 45	05 27	22 31	23 54	25 14	01 14

Lat.	Sunset	Twilight Civil	Twilight Naut.	Moonset 28	Moonset 29	Moonset 30	Moonset 1
°	h m	h m	h m	h m	h m	h m	h m
N 72	17 29	18 36	19 59	11 04	13 17	▭	▭
N 70	17 32	18 32	19 46	10 43	12 38	14 46	▭
68	17 33	18 29	19 35	10 27	12 11	13 58	15 40
66	17 35	18 26	19 27	10 14	11 51	13 28	14 57
64	17 37	18 24	19 20	10 04	11 35	13 05	14 28
62	17 38	18 22	19 14	09 55	11 21	12 47	14 05
60	17 39	18 20	19 09	09 47	11 10	12 32	13 48
N 58	17 40	18 19	19 05	09 40	11 00	12 19	13 33
56	17 41	18 18	19 01	09 34	10 52	12 08	13 20
54	17 42	18 17	18 58	09 29	10 44	11 59	13 09
52	17 42	18 16	18 55	09 24	10 37	11 50	12 59
50	17 43	18 15	18 53	09 20	10 31	11 42	12 50
45	17 45	18 14	18 48	09 10	10 18	11 26	12 32
N 40	17 46	18 13	18 44	09 02	10 07	11 13	12 17
35	17 47	18 12	18 42	08 56	09 58	11 01	12 04
30	17 48	18 12	18 40	08 50	09 50	10 52	11 53
20	17 50	18 12	18 38	08 40	09 36	10 35	11 34
N 10	17 52	18 13	18 37	08 31	09 24	10 20	11 17
0	17 54	18 14	18 38	08 23	09 13	10 06	11 02
S 10	17 55	18 16	18 41	08 14	09 02	09 52	10 46
20	17 58	18 20	18 45	08 06	08 50	09 37	10 30
30	18 00	18 24	18 52	07 56	08 36	09 21	10 11
35	18 02	18 27	18 57	07 50	08 28	09 11	09 59
40	18 03	18 30	19 02	07 43	08 19	09 00	09 44
45	18 05	18 35	19 10	07 36	08 08	08 47	09 32
S 50	18 08	18 40	19 19	07 27	07 56	08 31	09 13
52	18 09	18 43	19 24	07 22	07 50	08 23	09 05
54	18 10	18 46	19 29	07 18	07 43	08 15	08 55
56	18 12	18 49	19 35	07 13	07 36	08 06	08 44
58	18 13	18 53	19 41	07 07	07 28	07 55	08 32
S 60	18 15	18 57	19 49	07 01	07 19	07 43	08 17

Day	SUN Eqn. of Time 00h	SUN Eqn. of Time 12h	SUN Mer. Pass.	MOON Mer. Pass. Upper	MOON Mer. Pass. Lower	Age	Phase
d	m s	m s	h m	h m	h m	d	%
28	09 11	09 21	11 51	02 11	14 35	19	88
29	09 31	09 41	11 50	03 01	15 26	20	80
30	09 51	10 01	11 50	03 53	16 20	21	71

UT (d h)	ARIES GHA	VENUS −4.7 GHA	Dec	MARS −1.3 GHA	Dec	JUPITER −1.8 GHA	Dec	SATURN +0.5 GHA	Dec	STARS Name	SHA	Dec
1 00	9 40.6	153 58.9	S21 24.1	60 19.2	S22 32.7	139 48.7	S17 32.8	96 23.4	S22 45.4	Acamar	315 15.3	S40 13.7
01	24 43.1	169 01.0	24.5	75 20.7	32.4	154 50.7	33.0	111 25.8	45.4	Achernar	335 23.6	S57 08.5
02	39 45.6	184 03.1	24.9	90 22.2	32.0	169 52.7	33.1	126 28.2	45.4	Acrux	173 05.9	S63 12.0
03	54 48.0	199 05.2 ..	25.2	105 23.7 ..	31.6	184 54.7 ..	33.2	141 30.5 ..	45.4	Adhara	255 09.7	S28 59.7
04	69 50.5	214 07.3	25.6	120 25.2	31.2	199 56.6	33.4	156 32.9	45.4	Aldebaran	290 45.1	N16 32.7
05	84 52.9	229 09.4	25.9	135 26.6	30.8	214 58.6	33.5	171 35.2	45.4			
M 06	99 55.4	244 11.5	S21 26.3	150 28.1	S22 30.4	230 00.6	S17 33.6	186 37.6	S22 45.4	Alioth	166 18.1	N55 51.7
O 07	114 57.9	259 13.6	26.6	165 29.6	30.0	245 02.6	33.7	201 39.9	45.4	Alkaid	152 56.6	N49 13.5
N 08	130 00.3	274 15.7	27.0	180 31.1	29.6	260 04.6	33.9	216 42.3	45.4	Al Na'ir	27 38.9	S46 52.3
D 09	145 02.8	289 17.9 ..	27.3	195 32.5 ..	29.3	275 06.6 ..	34.0	231 44.7 ..	45.4	Alnilam	275 42.7	S 1 11.4
A 10	160 05.3	304 20.0	27.7	210 34.0	28.9	290 08.6	34.1	246 47.0	45.4	Alphard	217 52.8	S 8 44.2
Y 11	175 07.7	319 22.1	28.0	225 35.5	28.5	305 10.6	34.2	261 49.4	45.4			
12	190 10.2	334 24.3	S21 28.4	240 37.0	S22 28.1	320 12.6	S17 34.3	276 51.7	S22 45.4	Alphecca	126 08.2	N26 39.5
13	205 12.7	349 26.4	28.7	255 38.4	27.7	335 14.6	34.5	291 54.1	45.4	Alpheratz	357 39.4	N29 11.7
14	220 15.1	4 28.6	29.0	270 39.9	27.3	350 16.6	34.6	306 56.4	45.4	Altair	62 04.7	N 8 55.3
15	235 17.6	19 30.7 ..	29.4	285 41.4 ..	26.9	5 18.6 ..	34.7	321 58.8 ..	45.4	Ankaa	353 11.8	S42 12.3
16	250 20.0	34 32.9	29.7	300 42.8	26.5	20 20.5	34.9	337 01.1	45.4	Antares	112 22.1	S26 28.2
17	265 22.5	49 35.0	30.0	315 44.3	26.1	35 22.5	35.0	352 03.5	45.4			
18	280 25.0	64 37.2	S21 30.4	330 45.8	S22 25.8	50 24.5	S17 35.1	7 05.8	S22 45.4	Arcturus	145 52.8	N19 05.4
19	295 27.4	79 39.3	30.7	345 47.2	25.4	65 26.5	35.2	22 08.2	45.4	Atria	107 20.9	S69 03.7
20	310 29.9	94 41.5	31.0	0 48.7	25.0	80 28.5	35.4	37 10.6	45.4	Avior	234 16.8	S59 33.9
21	325 32.4	109 43.7 ..	31.4	15 50.2 ..	24.6	95 30.5 ..	35.5	52 12.9 ..	45.4	Bellatrix	278 28.1	N 6 21.9
22	340 34.8	124 45.9	31.7	30 51.6	24.2	110 32.5	35.6	67 15.3	45.4	Betelgeuse	270 57.4	N 7 24.6
23	355 37.3	139 48.0	32.0	45 53.1	23.8	125 34.5	35.7	82 17.6	45.4			
2 00	10 39.8	154 50.2	S21 32.3	60 54.6	S22 23.4	140 36.5	S17 35.9	97 20.0	S22 45.5	Canopus	263 54.5	S52 42.1
01	25 42.2	169 52.4	32.7	75 56.0	23.0	155 38.5	36.0	112 22.3	45.5	Capella	280 29.0	N46 00.7
02	40 44.7	184 54.6	33.0	90 57.5	22.6	170 40.4	36.1	127 24.7	45.5	Deneb	49 28.8	N45 21.2
03	55 47.2	199 56.8 ..	33.3	105 58.9 ..	22.2	185 42.4 ..	36.2	142 27.0 ..	45.5	Denebola	182 30.3	N14 28.2
04	70 49.6	214 59.0	33.6	121 00.4	21.8	200 44.4	36.4	157 29.4	45.5	Diphda	348 52.0	S17 53.0
05	85 52.1	230 01.2	33.9	136 01.9	21.4	215 46.4	36.5	172 31.7	45.5			
T 06	100 54.5	245 03.4	S21 34.2	151 03.3	S22 21.0	230 48.4	S17 36.6	187 34.1	S22 45.5	Dubhe	193 48.0	N61 39.0
U 07	115 57.0	260 05.6	34.5	166 04.8	20.7	245 50.4	36.8	202 36.4	45.5	Elnath	278 08.0	N28 37.2
E 08	130 59.5	275 07.8	34.8	181 06.2	20.3	260 52.4	36.9	217 38.8	45.5	Eltanin	90 44.6	N51 29.6
S 09	146 01.9	290 10.0 ..	35.1	196 07.7 ..	19.9	275 54.4 ..	37.0	232 41.1 ..	45.5	Enif	33 43.4	N 9 57.8
D 10	161 04.4	305 12.2	35.5	211 09.1	19.5	290 56.4	37.1	247 43.5	45.5	Fomalhaut	15 19.7	S29 31.4
A 11	176 06.9	320 14.4	35.8	226 10.6	19.1	305 58.3	37.3	262 45.8	45.5			
Y 12	191 09.3	335 16.7	S21 36.1	241 12.0	S22 18.7	321 00.3	S17 37.4	277 48.2	S22 45.5	Gacrux	171 57.5	S57 12.9
13	206 11.8	350 18.9	36.4	256 13.5	18.3	336 02.3	37.5	292 50.5	45.5	Gienah	175 48.9	S17 38.5
14	221 14.3	5 21.1	36.7	271 14.9	17.9	351 04.3	37.6	307 52.9	45.5	Hadar	148 43.4	S60 27.7
15	236 16.7	20 23.4 ..	36.9	286 16.4 ..	17.5	6 06.3 ..	37.8	322 55.2 ..	45.5	Hamal	327 56.4	N23 33.0
16	251 19.2	35 25.6	37.2	301 17.8	17.1	21 08.3	37.9	337 57.6	45.5	Kaus Aust.	83 39.1	S34 22.4
17	266 21.7	50 27.8	37.5	316 19.3	16.7	36 10.3	38.0	352 59.9	45.5			
18	281 24.1	65 30.1	S21 37.8	331 20.7	S22 16.3	51 12.3	S17 38.1	8 02.3	S22 45.5	Kochab	137 21.1	N74 05.0
19	296 26.6	80 32.3	38.1	346 22.2	15.9	66 14.2	38.3	23 04.6	45.5	Markab	13 34.5	N15 18.5
20	311 29.0	95 34.6	38.4	1 23.6	15.5	81 16.2	38.4	38 07.0	45.5	Menkar	314 11.0	N 4 09.7
21	326 31.5	110 36.8 ..	38.7	16 25.1 ..	15.1	96 18.2 ..	38.5	53 09.3 ..	45.5	Menkent	148 03.7	S36 27.5
22	341 34.0	125 39.1	39.0	31 26.5	14.7	111 20.2	38.6	68 11.7	45.5	Miaplacidus	221 39.5	S69 47.4
23	356 36.4	140 41.4	39.2	46 28.0	14.3	126 22.2	38.8	83 14.0	45.5			
3 00	11 38.9	155 43.6	S21 39.5	61 29.4	S22 13.9	141 24.2	S17 38.9	98 16.4	S22 45.5	Mirfak	308 34.8	N49 55.4
01	26 41.4	170 45.9	39.7	76 30.9	13.5	156 26.2	39.0	113 18.7	45.5	Nunki	75 53.9	S26 16.3
02	41 43.8	185 48.2	40.1	91 32.3	13.1	171 28.1	39.1	128 21.1	45.5	Peacock	53 13.4	S56 40.6
03	56 46.3	200 50.5 ..	40.4	106 33.7 ..	12.7	186 30.1 ..	39.3	143 23.4 ..	45.5	Pollux	243 23.5	N27 58.7
04	71 48.8	215 52.7	40.6	121 35.2	12.3	201 32.1	39.4	158 25.8	45.5	Procyon	244 56.1	N 5 10.6
05	86 51.2	230 55.0	40.9	136 36.6	11.9	216 34.1	39.5	173 28.1	45.5			
W 06	101 53.7	245 57.3	S21 41.2	151 38.1	S22 11.5	231 36.1	S17 39.7	188 30.5	S22 45.6	Rasalhague	96 03.2	N12 33.1
E 07	116 56.2	260 59.6	41.4	166 39.5	11.1	246 38.1	39.8	203 32.8	45.6	Regulus	207 40.0	N11 52.6
D 08	131 58.6	276 01.9	41.7	181 40.9	10.7	261 40.1	39.9	218 35.2	45.6	Rigel	281 08.5	S 8 10.8
N 09	147 01.1	291 04.2 ..	42.0	196 42.4 ..	10.3	276 42.0 ..	40.0	233 37.5 ..	45.6	Rigil Kent.	139 47.4	S60 54.6
E 10	162 03.5	306 06.5	42.2	211 43.8	09.9	291 44.0	40.2	248 39.9	45.6	Sabik	102 08.6	S15 44.7
S 11	177 06.0	321 08.8	42.5	226 45.3	09.5	306 46.0	40.3	263 42.2	45.6			
D 12	192 08.5	336 11.1	S21 42.7	241 46.7	S22 09.1	321 48.0	S17 40.4	278 44.6	S22 45.6	Schedar	349 35.8	N56 38.4
A 13	207 10.9	351 13.4	43.0	256 48.1	08.7	336 50.0	40.5	293 46.9	45.6	Shaula	96 17.2	S37 06.9
Y 14	222 13.4	6 15.8	43.3	271 49.6	08.3	351 52.0	40.7	308 49.3	45.6	Sirius	258 30.6	S16 44.4
15	237 15.9	21 18.1 ..	43.5	286 51.0 ..	07.9	6 53.9 ..	40.8	323 51.6 ..	45.6	Spica	158 27.8	S11 15.3
16	252 18.3	36 20.4	43.8	301 52.4	07.5	21 55.9	40.9	338 54.0	45.6	Suhail	222 50.1	S43 30.2
17	267 20.8	51 22.7	44.0	316 53.8	07.1	36 57.9	41.0	353 56.3	45.6			
18	282 23.3	66 25.1	S21 44.3	331 55.3	S22 06.7	51 59.9	S17 41.2	8 58.6	S22 45.6	Vega	80 36.5	N38 48.5
19	297 25.7	81 27.4	44.5	346 56.7	06.3	67 01.9	41.3	24 01.0	45.6	Zuben'ubi	137 01.7	S16 06.9
20	312 28.2	96 29.8	44.7	1 58.1	05.9	82 03.9	41.4	39 03.3	45.6		SHA	Mer.Pass.
21	327 30.6	111 32.1 ..	45.0	16 59.6 ..	05.5	97 05.9 ..	41.5	54 05.7 ..	45.6		° ′	h m
22	342 33.1	126 34.4	45.2	32 01.0	05.1	112 07.8	41.7	69 08.0	45.6	Venus	144 10.5	13 39
23	357 35.6	141 36.8	45.5	47 02.4	04.7	127 09.8	41.8	84 10.4	45.6	Mars	50 14.8	19 54
Mer.Pass.	h m 23 13.5	v 2.2	d 0.3	v 1.5	d 0.4	v 2.0	d 0.1	v 2.4	d 0.0	Jupiter	129 56.7	14 36
										Saturn	86 40.2	17 28

SUN / MOON

UT	SUN GHA	SUN Dec	MOON GHA	v	Dec	d	HP
d h	° ′	° ′	° ′	′	° ′	′	′
1 00	182 32.8	S 3 04.8	290 39.8	7.3	N19 30.7	4.8	58.4
01	197 33.0	05.8	305 06.1	7.3	19 35.5	4.6	58.4
02	212 33.2	06.8	319 32.4	7.2	19 40.1	4.5	58.4
03	227 33.4 . .	07.7	333 58.6	7.1	19 44.6	4.4	58.5
04	242 33.6	08.7	348 24.7	7.1	19 49.0	4.2	58.5
05	257 33.8	09.7	2 50.8	7.0	19 53.2	4.2	58.5
06	272 34.0	S 3 10.6	17 16.8	7.0	N19 57.4	4.0	58.5
07	287 34.2	11.6	31 42.8	6.9	20 01.4	3.9	58.5
M 08	302 34.4	12.6	46 08.7	6.9	20 05.3	3.7	58.6
O 09	317 34.6 . .	13.6	60 34.6	6.8	20 09.0	3.7	58.6
N 10	332 34.8	14.5	75 00.4	6.8	20 12.7	3.5	58.6
D 11	347 35.1	15.5	89 26.2	6.7	20 16.2	3.4	58.6
A 12	2 35.3	S 3 16.5	103 51.9	6.7	N20 19.6	3.3	58.6
Y 13	17 35.5	17.4	118 17.6	6.6	20 22.9	3.1	58.6
14	32 35.7	18.4	132 43.2	6.6	20 26.0	3.1	58.7
15	47 35.9 . .	19.4	147 08.8	6.5	20 29.1	2.8	58.7
16	62 36.1	20.3	161 34.3	6.5	20 31.9	2.8	58.7
17	77 36.3	21.3	175 59.8	6.4	20 34.7	2.6	58.7
18	92 36.5	S 3 22.3	190 25.2	6.4	N20 37.3	2.5	58.7
19	107 36.7	23.2	204 50.6	6.4	20 39.8	2.4	58.8
20	122 36.9	24.2	219 16.0	6.3	20 42.2	2.3	58.8
21	137 37.1 . .	25.2	233 41.3	6.3	20 44.5	2.1	58.8
22	152 37.3	26.2	248 06.6	6.2	20 46.6	1.9	58.8
23	167 37.5	27.1	262 31.8	6.2	20 48.5	1.9	58.8
2 00	182 37.7	S 3 28.1	276 57.0	6.2	N20 50.4	1.7	58.8
01	197 37.9	29.1	291 22.2	6.1	20 52.1	1.6	58.9
02	212 38.1	30.0	305 47.3	6.1	20 53.7	1.4	58.9
03	227 38.3 . .	31.0	320 12.4	6.1	20 55.1	1.3	58.9
04	242 38.5	32.0	334 37.5	6.0	20 56.4	1.2	58.9
05	257 38.7	32.9	349 02.5	6.0	20 57.6	1.0	58.9
06	272 38.9	S 3 33.9	3 27.5	6.0	N20 58.6	0.9	58.9
07	287 39.1	34.9	17 52.5	5.9	20 59.5	0.8	59.0
T 08	302 39.3	35.8	32 17.4	6.0	21 00.3	0.6	59.0
U 09	317 39.5 . .	36.8	46 42.4	5.9	21 00.9	0.5	59.0
E 10	332 39.7	37.8	61 07.3	5.8	21 01.4	0.4	59.0
S 11	347 39.9	38.7	75 32.1	5.9	21 01.8	0.2	59.0
D 12	2 40.1	S 3 39.7	89 57.0	5.8	N21 02.0	0.1	59.0
A 13	17 40.2	40.7	104 21.8	5.8	21 02.1	0.1	59.1
Y 14	32 40.4	41.6	118 46.6	5.8	21 02.0	0.2	59.1
15	47 40.6 . .	42.6	133 11.4	5.7	21 01.8	0.3	59.1
16	62 40.8	43.6	147 36.1	5.8	21 01.5	0.5	59.1
17	77 41.0	44.5	162 00.9	5.7	21 01.0	0.6	59.1
18	92 41.2	S 3 45.5	176 25.6	5.7	N21 00.4	0.8	59.1
19	107 41.4	46.5	190 50.3	5.7	20 59.6	0.9	59.2
20	122 41.6	47.4	205 15.0	5.7	20 58.7	1.0	59.2
21	137 41.8 . .	48.4	219 39.7	5.7	20 57.7	1.2	59.2
22	152 42.0	49.4	234 04.4	5.6	20 56.5	1.3	59.2
23	167 42.2	50.3	248 29.0	5.7	20 55.2	1.4	59.2
3 00	182 42.4	S 3 51.3	262 53.7	5.6	N20 53.8	1.6	59.2
01	197 42.6	52.3	277 18.3	5.7	20 52.2	1.8	59.2
02	212 42.8	53.2	291 43.0	5.6	20 50.4	1.8	59.3
03	227 43.0 . .	54.2	306 07.6	5.7	20 48.6	2.0	59.3
04	242 43.2	55.2	320 32.3	5.6	20 46.6	2.2	59.3
05	257 43.4	56.1	334 56.9	5.6	20 44.4	2.3	59.3
06	272 43.6	S 3 57.1	349 21.5	5.6	N20 42.1	2.4	59.3
W 07	287 43.8	58.1	3 46.1	5.7	20 39.7	2.6	59.3
E 08	302 44.0	3 59.0	18 10.8	5.6	20 37.1	2.7	59.4
D 09	317 44.2 . .	4 00.0	32 35.4	5.7	20 34.4	2.8	59.4
N 10	332 44.4	01.0	47 00.1	5.6	20 31.6	3.0	59.4
E 11	347 44.6	01.9	61 24.7	5.6	20 28.6	3.1	59.4
S 12	2 44.8	S 4 02.9	75 49.3	5.7	N20 25.5	3.3	59.4
D 13	17 45.0	03.9	90 14.0	5.6	20 22.2	3.3	59.4
A 14	32 45.2	04.8	104 38.7	5.7	20 18.9	3.6	59.4
Y 15	47 45.3 . .	05.8	119 03.4	5.6	20 15.3	3.6	59.4
16	62 45.5	06.8	133 28.0	5.7	20 11.7	3.8	59.5
17	77 45.7	07.7	147 52.7	5.8	20 07.9	4.0	59.5
18	92 45.9	S 4 08.7	162 17.5	5.7	N20 03.9	4.1	59.5
19	107 46.1	09.7	176 42.2	5.7	19 59.8	4.2	59.5
20	122 46.3	10.6	191 06.9	5.8	19 55.6	4.3	59.5
21	137 46.5 . .	11.6	205 31.7	5.8	19 51.3	4.5	59.5
22	152 46.7	12.5	219 56.5	5.8	19 46.8	4.6	59.5
23	167 46.9	13.5	234 21.3	5.8	N19 42.2	4.7	59.5
	SD 16.0	d 1.0	SD 16.0		16.1		16.2

Twilight / Sunrise / Moonrise

Lat.	Twilight Naut.	Twilight Civil	Sunrise	Moonrise 1	Moonrise 2	Moonrise 3	Moonrise 4
°	h m	h m	h m	h m	h m	h m	h m
N 72	03 54	05 15	06 23	▭	▭	▭	21 22
N 70	04 05	05 18	06 19	▭	▭	19 50	22 26
68	04 14	05 21	06 16	18 49	19 37	21 09	23 01
66	04 22	05 22	06 13	19 33	20 25	21 47	23 26
64	04 28	05 24	06 11	20 02	20 57	22 13	23 45
62	04 33	05 25	06 09	20 24	21 20	22 34	24 01
60	04 37	05 26	06 07	20 42	21 38	22 50	24 14
N 58	04 41	05 27	06 06	20 57	21 54	23 04	24 26
56	04 44	05 28	06 05	21 10	22 07	23 17	24 35
54	04 47	05 28	06 03	21 22	22 19	23 27	24 44
52	04 49	05 29	06 02	21 32	22 29	23 36	24 52
50	04 51	05 29	06 01	21 40	22 38	23 45	24 59
45	04 56	05 30	05 59	21 59	22 57	24 02	00 02
N 40	04 59	05 30	05 57	22 15	23 13	24 17	00 17
35	05 01	05 30	05 55	22 28	23 26	24 29	00 29
30	05 02	05 30	05 54	22 39	23 37	24 40	00 40
20	05 03	05 29	05 51	22 59	23 57	24 58	00 58
N 10	05 03	05 28	05 49	23 16	24 14	00 14	01 14
0	05 01	05 25	05 46	23 32	24 30	00 30	01 29
S 10	04 58	05 22	05 44	23 48	24 46	00 46	01 44
20	04 53	05 19	05 41	24 05	00 05	01 04	02 00
30	04 45	05 13	05 37	24 25	00 25	01 23	02 18
35	04 40	05 10	05 35	24 36	00 36	01 35	02 29
40	04 34	05 06	05 33	24 50	00 50	01 48	02 41
45	04 26	05 01	05 30	00 01	01 05	02 04	02 55
S 50	04 16	04 55	05 27	00 19	01 25	02 23	03 13
52	04 11	04 52	05 26	00 28	01 34	02 32	03 21
54	04 05	04 48	05 24	00 37	01 44	02 42	03 30
56	03 59	04 45	05 22	00 48	01 56	02 54	03 40
58	03 52	04 40	05 20	01 00	02 09	03 07	03 52
S 60	03 43	04 36	05 18	01 14	02 25	03 23	04 05

Sunset / Twilight / Moonset

Lat.	Sunset	Twilight Civil	Twilight Naut.	Moonset 1	Moonset 2	Moonset 3	Moonset 4
°	h m	h m	h m	h m	h m	h m	h m
N 72	17 14	18 21	19 42	▭	▭	▭	19 15
N 70	17 18	18 18	19 30	▭	▭	18 44	18 11
68	17 21	18 16	19 22	15 40	16 54	17 25	17 35
66	17 24	18 14	19 15	14 57	16 05	16 47	17 09
64	17 26	18 13	19 09	14 28	15 34	16 20	16 49
62	17 28	18 12	19 04	14 05	15 11	15 59	16 32
60	17 30	18 11	19 00	13 48	14 52	15 42	16 19
N 58	17 32	18 10	18 56	13 33	14 37	15 28	16 07
56	17 33	18 10	18 53	13 20	14 23	15 16	15 56
54	17 34	18 09	18 50	13 09	14 12	15 05	15 47
52	17 35	18 09	18 48	12 59	14 02	14 55	15 39
50	17 37	18 08	18 46	12 50	13 53	14 47	15 32
45	17 39	18 08	18 42	12 32	13 33	14 28	15 16
N 40	17 41	18 08	18 39	12 17	13 18	14 13	15 03
35	17 43	18 08	18 37	12 04	13 04	14 01	14 52
30	17 44	18 08	18 36	11 53	12 53	13 50	14 42
20	17 47	18 09	18 35	11 34	12 33	13 31	14 25
N 10	17 50	18 11	18 35	11 17	12 16	13 14	14 11
0	17 53	18 13	18 37	11 02	12 00	12 58	13 57
S 10	17 55	18 16	18 41	10 46	11 43	12 43	13 43
20	17 58	18 20	18 46	10 30	11 26	12 26	13 28
30	18 02	18 26	18 54	10 11	11 06	12 07	13 11
35	18 04	18 29	18 59	09 59	10 54	11 55	13 01
40	18 06	18 34	19 06	09 47	10 41	11 42	12 49
45	18 09	18 39	19 14	09 32	10 25	11 27	12 35
S 50	18 12	18 45	19 24	09 13	10 06	11 08	12 19
52	18 14	18 48	19 29	09 05	09 56	10 59	12 11
54	18 16	18 52	19 35	08 55	09 46	10 49	12 02
56	18 18	18 56	19 42	08 44	09 34	10 37	11 52
58	18 20	19 00	19 49	08 32	09 21	10 24	11 41
S 60	18 22	19 05	19 58	08 17	09 05	10 09	11 28

SUN / MOON

Day	Eqn. of Time 00h	Eqn. of Time 12h	Mer. Pass.	Mer. Pass. Upper	Mer. Pass. Lower	Age	Phase
d	m s	m s	h m	h m	h m	d	%
1	10 11	10 21	11 50	04 48	17 17	22	60
2	10 30	10 40	11 49	05 46	18 15	23	49
3	10 49	10 59	11 49	06 44	19 14	24	38

2018 OCTOBER 4, 5, 6 (THURS., FRI., SAT.)

UT	ARIES GHA	VENUS −4.7 GHA	Dec	MARS −1.2 GHA	Dec	JUPITER −1.8 GHA	Dec	SATURN +0.5 GHA	Dec	STARS Name	SHA	Dec
4 00	12 38.0	156 39.2	S21 45.7	62 03.8	S22 04.3	142 11.8	S17 41.9	99 12.7	S22 45.6	Acamar	315 15.3	S40 13.7
01	27 40.5	171 41.5	45.9	77 05.3	03.9	157 13.8	42.1	114 15.1	45.6	Achernar	335 23.5	S57 08.5
02	42 43.0	186 43.9	46.2	92 06.7	03.5	172 15.8	42.2	129 17.4	45.6	Acrux	173 05.9	S63 12.0
03	57 45.4	201 46.2 ..	46.4	107 08.1 ..	03.1	187 17.7 ..	42.3	144 19.8 ..	45.6	Adhara	255 09.7	S28 59.7
04	72 47.9	216 48.6	46.6	122 09.5	02.7	202 19.7	42.4	159 22.1	45.6	Aldebaran	290 45.1	N16 32.7
05	87 50.4	231 51.0	46.9	137 11.0	02.3	217 21.7	42.6	174 24.4	45.6			
06	102 52.8	246 53.4	S21 47.1	152 12.4	S22 01.9	232 23.7	S17 42.7	189 26.8	S22 45.6	Alioth	166 18.1	N55 51.7
T 07	117 55.3	261 55.8	47.3	167 13.8	01.5	247 25.7	42.8	204 29.1	45.6	Alkaid	152 56.6	N49 13.5
H 08	132 57.8	276 58.1	47.5	182 15.2	01.0	262 27.7	42.9	219 31.5	45.6	Al Na'ir	27 38.9	S46 52.3
U 09	148 00.2	292 00.5 ..	47.7	197 16.6 ..	00.6	277 29.6 ..	43.1	234 33.8 ..	45.6	Alnilam	275 42.6	S 1 11.4
R 10	163 02.7	307 02.9	48.0	212 18.1	22 00.2	292 31.6	43.2	249 36.2	45.6	Alphard	217 52.8	S 8 44.2
S 11	178 05.1	322 05.3	48.2	227 19.5	21 59.8	307 33.6	43.3	264 38.5	45.6			
D 12	193 07.6	337 07.7	S21 48.4	242 20.9	S21 59.4	322 35.6	S17 43.4	279 40.8	S22 45.6	Alphecca	126 08.2	N26 39.5
A 13	208 10.1	352 10.1	48.6	257 22.3	59.0	337 37.6	43.6	294 43.2	45.6	Alpheratz	357 39.4	N29 11.7
Y 14	223 12.5	7 12.5	48.8	272 23.7	58.6	352 39.5	43.7	309 45.5	45.7	Altair	62 04.7	N 8 55.3
15	238 15.0	22 14.9 ..	49.0	287 25.1 ..	58.2	7 41.5 ..	43.8	324 47.9 ..	45.7	Ankaa	353 11.7	S42 12.3
16	253 17.5	37 17.4	49.2	302 26.6	57.8	22 43.5	44.0	339 50.2	45.7	Antares	112 22.1	S26 28.2
17	268 19.9	52 19.8	49.4	317 28.0	57.4	37 45.5	44.1	354 52.6	45.7			
18	283 22.4	67 22.2	S21 49.6	332 29.4	S21 57.0	52 47.5	S17 44.2	9 54.9	S22 45.7	Arcturus	145 52.8	N19 05.4
19	298 24.9	82 24.6	49.8	347 30.8	56.6	67 49.4	44.3	24 57.2	45.7	Atria	107 20.9	S69 03.7
20	313 27.3	97 27.1	50.0	2 32.2	56.1	82 51.4	44.5	39 59.6	45.7	Avior	234 16.8	S59 33.9
21	328 29.8	112 29.5 ..	50.2	17 33.6 ..	55.7	97 53.4 ..	44.6	55 01.9 ..	45.7	Bellatrix	278 28.0	N 6 21.9
22	343 32.3	127 31.9	50.4	32 35.0	55.3	112 55.4	44.7	70 04.3	45.7	Betelgeuse	270 57.3	N 7 24.6
23	358 34.7	142 34.4	50.6	47 36.4	54.9	127 57.4	44.8	85 06.6	45.7			
5 00	13 37.2	157 36.8	S21 50.8	62 37.8	S21 54.5	142 59.3	S17 45.0	100 08.9	S22 45.7	Canopus	263 54.5	S52 42.1
01	28 39.6	172 39.3	51.0	77 39.2	54.1	158 01.3	45.1	115 11.3	45.7	Capella	280 29.0	N46 00.7
02	43 42.1	187 41.7	51.2	92 40.7	53.7	173 03.3	45.2	130 13.6	45.7	Deneb	49 28.8	N45 21.2
03	58 44.6	202 44.2 ..	51.4	107 42.1 ..	53.3	188 05.3 ..	45.3	145 16.0 ..	45.7	Denebola	182 30.3	N14 28.2
04	73 47.0	217 46.6	51.5	122 43.5	52.9	203 07.3	45.5	160 18.3	45.7	Diphda	348 52.0	S17 53.0
05	88 49.5	232 49.1	51.7	137 44.9	52.5	218 09.2	45.6	175 20.6	45.7			
06	103 52.0	247 51.6	S21 51.9	152 46.3	S21 52.0	233 11.2	S17 45.7	190 23.0	S22 45.7	Dubhe	193 47.9	N61 39.0
07	118 54.4	262 54.1	52.1	167 47.7	51.6	248 13.2	45.9	205 25.3	45.7	Elnath	278 08.0	N28 37.2
F 08	133 56.9	277 56.5	52.3	182 49.1	51.2	263 15.2	46.0	220 27.7	45.7	Eltanin	90 44.6	N51 29.6
R 09	148 59.4	292 59.0 ..	52.4	197 50.5 ..	50.8	278 17.2 ..	46.1	235 30.0 ..	45.7	Enif	33 43.4	N 9 57.8
I 10	164 01.8	308 01.5	52.6	212 51.9	50.4	293 19.1	46.2	250 32.3	45.7	Fomalhaut	15 19.7	S29 31.4
D 11	179 04.3	323 04.0	52.8	227 53.3	50.0	308 21.1	46.4	265 34.7	45.7			
A 12	194 06.7	338 06.5	S21 52.9	242 54.7	S21 49.6	323 23.1	S17 46.5	280 37.0	S22 45.7	Gacrux	171 57.5	S57 12.9
Y 13	209 09.2	353 09.0	53.1	257 56.1	49.2	338 25.1	46.6	295 39.4	45.7	Gienah	175 48.9	S17 38.5
14	224 11.7	8 11.5	53.3	272 57.5	48.7	353 27.0	46.7	310 41.7	45.7	Hadar	148 43.4	S60 27.6
15	239 14.1	23 14.0 ..	53.4	287 58.9 ..	48.3	8 29.0 ..	46.9	325 44.0 ..	45.7	Hamal	327 56.4	N23 33.0
16	254 16.6	38 16.5	53.6	303 00.3	47.9	23 31.0	47.0	340 46.4	45.7	Kaus Aust.	83 39.1	S34 22.4
17	269 19.1	53 19.0	53.7	318 01.7	47.5	38 33.0	47.1	355 48.7	45.7			
18	284 21.5	68 21.5	S21 53.9	333 03.1	S21 47.1	53 34.9	S17 47.3	10 51.1	S22 45.7	Kochab	137 21.2	N74 05.0
19	299 24.0	83 24.0	54.1	348 04.5	46.7	68 36.9	47.4	25 53.4	45.7	Markab	13 34.5	N15 18.5
20	314 26.5	98 26.5	54.2	3 05.9	46.2	83 38.9	47.5	40 55.7	45.7	Menkar	314 11.0	N 4 09.7
21	329 28.9	113 29.1 ..	54.4	18 07.2 ..	45.8	98 40.9 ..	47.6	55 58.1 ..	45.7	Menkent	148 03.7	S36 27.5
22	344 31.4	128 31.6	54.5	33 08.6	45.4	113 42.9	47.8	71 00.4	45.7	Miaplacidus	221 39.4	S69 47.4
23	359 33.9	143 34.1	54.6	48 10.0	45.0	128 44.8	47.9	86 02.7	45.7			
6 00	14 36.3	158 36.7	S21 54.8	63 11.4	S21 44.6	143 46.8	S17 48.0	101 05.1	S22 45.8	Mirfak	308 34.8	N49 55.4
01	29 38.8	173 39.2	54.7	78 12.8	44.2	158 48.8	48.1	116 07.4	45.8	Nunki	75 53.9	S26 16.3
02	44 41.2	188 41.8	55.1	93 14.2	43.7	173 50.8	48.3	131 09.7	45.8	Peacock	53 13.4	S56 40.6
03	59 43.7	203 44.3 ..	55.2	108 15.6 ..	43.3	188 52.7 ..	48.4	146 12.1 ..	45.8	Pollux	243 23.5	N27 58.7
04	74 46.2	218 46.9	55.3	123 17.0	42.9	203 54.7	48.5	161 14.4	45.8	Procyon	244 56.1	N 5 10.6
05	89 48.6	233 49.4	55.5	138 18.4	42.5	218 56.7	48.6	176 16.8	45.8			
06	104 51.1	248 52.0	S21 55.6	153 19.8	S21 42.1	233 58.7	S17 48.8	191 19.1	S22 45.8	Rasalhague	96 03.2	N12 33.1
S 07	119 53.6	263 54.5	55.7	168 21.1	41.7	249 00.6	48.9	206 21.4	45.8	Regulus	207 40.0	N11 52.6
A 08	134 56.0	278 57.1	55.9	183 22.5	41.2	264 02.6	49.0	221 23.8	45.8	Rigel	281 08.5	S 8 10.8
T 09	149 58.5	293 59.7 ..	56.0	198 23.9 ..	40.8	279 04.6 ..	49.2	236 26.1 ..	45.8	Rigil Kent.	139 47.4	S60 54.6
U 10	165 01.0	309 02.3	56.1	213 25.3	40.4	294 06.6	49.3	251 28.4	45.8	Sabik	102 08.6	S15 44.7
R 11	180 03.4	324 04.8	56.2	228 26.7	40.0	309 08.5	49.4	266 30.8	45.8			
D 12	195 05.9	339 07.4	S21 56.4	243 28.1	S21 39.6	324 10.5	S17 49.5	281 33.1	S22 45.8	Schedar	349 35.8	N56 38.4
A 13	210 08.4	354 10.0	56.5	258 29.4	39.1	339 12.5	49.7	296 35.4	45.8	Shaula	96 17.2	S37 06.9
Y 14	225 10.8	9 12.6	56.6	273 30.8	38.7	354 14.5	49.8	311 37.8	45.8	Sirius	258 30.6	S16 44.4
15	240 13.3	24 15.2 ..	56.7	288 32.2 ..	38.3	9 16.4 ..	49.9	326 40.1 ..	45.8	Spica	158 27.8	S11 15.3
16	255 15.7	39 17.8	56.8	303 33.6	37.9	24 18.4	50.0	341 42.4	45.8	Suhail	222 50.0	S43 30.2
17	270 18.2	54 20.4	56.9	318 35.0	37.5	39 20.4	50.2	356 44.8	45.8			
18	285 20.7	69 23.0	S21 57.0	333 36.3	S21 37.0	54 22.3	S17 50.3	11 47.1	S22 45.8	Vega	80 36.6	N38 48.5
19	300 23.1	84 25.6	57.1	348 37.7	36.6	69 24.3	50.4	26 49.4	45.8	Zuben'ubi	137 01.7	S16 06.9
20	315 25.6	99 28.2	57.2	3 39.1	36.2	84 26.3	50.6	41 51.8	45.8		SHA	Mer. Pass.
21	330 28.1	114 30.9 ..	57.3	18 40.5 ..	35.8	99 28.3 ..	50.7	56 54.1 ..	45.8		° ′	h m
22	345 30.5	129 33.5	57.4	33 41.8	35.4	114 30.2	50.8	71 56.4	45.8	Venus	143 59.6	13 27
23	0 33.0	144 36.1	57.5	48 43.2	34.9	129 32.2	50.9	86 58.8	45.8	Mars	49 00.7	19 48
	h m									Jupiter	129 22.2	14 26
Mer. Pass. 23 01.7	*v* 2.5 *d* 0.2			*v* 1.4 *d* 0.4		*v* 2.0 *d* 0.1		*v* 2.3 *d* 0.0		Saturn	86 31.8	17 17

UT	SUN GHA	SUN Dec	MOON GHA	v	Dec	d	HP
4 00	182 47.1	S 4 14.5	248 46.1	5.8	N19 37.5	4.9	59.6
01	197 47.3	15.4	263 10.9	5.9	19 32.6	5.0	59.6
02	212 47.5	16.4	277 35.8	5.9	19 27.6	5.2	59.6
03	227 47.7	.. 17.4	292 00.7	5.9	19 22.4	5.2	59.6
04	242 47.9	18.3	306 25.6	5.9	19 17.2	5.5	59.6
05	257 48.1	19.3	320 50.5	6.0	19 11.7	5.5	59.6
T 06	272 48.2	S 4 20.3	335 15.5	6.0	N19 06.2	5.6	59.6
H 07	287 48.4	21.2	349 40.5	6.0	19 00.6	5.8	59.6
U 08	302 48.6	22.2	4 05.6	6.0	18 54.8	5.9	59.6
R 09	317 48.8	.. 23.2	18 30.5	6.1	18 48.9	6.1	59.7
S 10	332 49.0	24.1	32 55.6	6.1	18 42.8	6.2	59.7
D 11	347 49.2	25.1	47 20.7	6.1	18 36.6	6.3	59.7
A 12	2 49.4	S 4 26.0	61 45.8	6.2	N18 30.3	6.4	59.7
Y 13	17 49.6	27.0	76 11.0	6.2	18 23.9	6.5	59.7
14	32 49.8	28.0	90 36.2	6.2	18 17.4	6.7	59.7
15	47 50.0	.. 28.9	105 01.4	6.3	18 10.7	6.8	59.7
16	62 50.2	29.9	119 26.7	6.3	18 03.9	6.9	59.7
17	77 50.3	30.9	133 52.0	6.4	17 57.0	7.0	59.7
18	92 50.5	S 4 31.8	148 17.4	6.4	N17 50.0	7.1	59.7
19	107 50.7	32.8	162 42.8	6.4	17 42.9	7.3	59.7
20	122 50.9	33.8	177 08.2	6.4	17 35.6	7.4	59.7
21	137 51.1	.. 34.7	191 33.6	6.5	17 28.2	7.5	59.8
22	152 51.3	35.7	205 59.1	6.6	17 20.7	7.6	59.8
23	167 51.5	36.6	220 24.7	6.5	17 13.1	7.7	59.8
5 00	182 51.7	S 4 37.6	234 50.2	6.7	N17 05.4	7.9	59.8
01	197 51.9	38.6	249 15.9	6.6	16 57.5	7.9	59.8
02	212 52.0	39.5	263 41.5	6.7	16 49.6	8.1	59.8
03	227 52.2	.. 40.5	278 07.2	6.8	16 41.5	8.2	59.8
04	242 52.4	41.5	292 33.0	6.8	16 33.3	8.3	59.8
05	257 52.6	42.4	306 58.8	6.8	16 25.0	8.4	59.8
F 06	272 52.8	S 4 43.4	321 24.6	6.9	N16 16.6	8.5	59.8
R 07	287 53.0	44.3	335 50.5	6.9	16 08.1	8.6	59.8
I 08	302 53.2	45.3	350 16.4	7.0	15 59.5	8.7	59.8
D 09	317 53.4	.. 46.3	4 42.4	7.0	15 50.8	8.8	59.8
A 10	332 53.6	47.2	19 08.4	7.0	15 42.0	8.9	59.8
Y 11	347 53.7	48.2	33 34.4	7.2	15 33.1	9.0	59.8
12	2 53.9	S 4 49.1	48 00.6	7.1	N15 24.1	9.1	59.8
13	17 54.1	50.1	62 26.7	7.2	15 15.0	9.3	59.8
14	32 54.3	51.1	76 52.9	7.3	15 05.7	9.3	59.8
15	47 54.5	.. 52.0	91 19.2	7.2	14 56.4	9.4	59.8
16	62 54.7	53.0	105 45.4	7.4	14 47.0	9.5	59.8
17	77 54.9	54.0	120 11.8	7.4	14 37.5	9.6	59.8
18	92 55.0	S 4 54.9	134 38.2	7.4	N14 27.9	9.7	59.8
19	107 55.2	55.9	149 04.6	7.5	14 18.2	9.8	59.8
20	122 55.4	56.8	163 31.1	7.5	14 08.4	9.9	59.8
21	137 55.6	.. 57.8	177 57.6	7.6	13 58.5	9.9	59.8
22	152 55.8	58.8	192 24.2	7.6	13 48.6	10.1	59.8
23	167 56.0	4 59.7	206 50.8	7.7	13 38.5	10.1	59.8
6 00	182 56.2	S 5 00.7	221 17.5	7.8	N13 28.4	10.3	59.8
01	197 56.3	01.6	235 44.3	7.7	13 18.1	10.3	59.8
02	212 56.5	02.6	250 11.0	7.9	13 07.8	10.4	59.8
03	227 56.7	.. 03.6	264 37.9	7.8	12 57.4	10.4	59.8
04	242 56.9	04.5	279 04.7	8.0	12 47.0	10.6	59.8
05	257 57.1	05.5	293 31.7	7.9	12 36.4	10.6	59.8
S 06	272 57.3	S 5 06.4	307 58.6	8.0	N12 25.8	10.7	59.8
A 07	287 57.4	07.4	322 25.6	8.1	12 15.1	10.8	59.8
T 08	302 57.6	08.4	336 52.7	8.1	12 04.3	10.9	59.8
U 09	317 57.8	.. 09.3	351 19.8	8.2	11 53.4	10.9	59.8
R 10	332 58.0	10.3	5 47.0	8.2	11 42.5	11.0	59.8
D 11	347 58.2	11.2	20 14.2	8.3	11 31.5	11.1	59.8
A 12	2 58.4	S 5 12.2	34 41.5	8.3	N11 20.4	11.1	59.8
Y 13	17 58.5	13.1	49 08.8	8.4	11 09.3	11.2	59.8
14	32 58.7	14.1	63 36.2	8.4	10 58.1	11.3	59.8
15	47 58.9	.. 15.1	78 03.6	8.4	10 46.8	11.3	59.8
16	62 59.1	16.0	92 31.0	8.5	10 35.5	11.4	59.8
17	77 59.3	17.0	106 58.5	8.6	10 24.1	11.5	59.8
18	92 59.5	S 5 17.9	121 26.1	8.6	N10 12.6	11.5	59.8
19	107 59.6	18.9	135 53.7	8.6	10 01.1	11.6	59.8
20	122 59.8	19.9	150 21.3	8.7	9 49.5	11.7	59.8
21	138 00.0	.. 20.8	164 49.0	8.8	9 37.8	11.7	59.8
22	153 00.2	21.8	179 16.8	8.8	9 26.1	11.8	59.8
23	168 00.4	22.7	193 44.6	8.8	N 9 14.4	11.8	59.8
	SD 16.0	d 1.0	SD 16.3		16.3		16.3

Lat.	Twilight Naut.	Twilight Civil	Sunrise	Moonrise 4	5	6	7
°	h m	h m	h m	h m	h m	h m	h m
N 72	04 09	05 29	06 36	21 22	24 09	00 09	02 24
N 70	04 18	05 30	06 31	22 26	24 36	00 36	02 38
68	04 26	05 31	06 27	23 01	24 56	00 56	02 48
66	04 32	05 32	06 23	23 26	25 11	01 11	02 57
64	04 37	05 32	06 20	23 46	25 24	01 24	03 05
62	04 41	05 33	06 17	24 01	00 01	01 35	03 11
60	04 45	05 33	06 15	24 14	00 14	01 44	03 16
N 58	04 48	05 33	06 13	24 26	00 26	01 52	03 21
56	04 50	05 34	06 11	24 35	00 35	02 00	03 25
54	04 53	05 34	06 09	24 44	00 44	02 06	03 29
52	04 54	05 34	06 07	24 52	00 52	02 12	03 33
50	04 56	05 34	06 06	24 59	00 59	02 17	03 36
45	04 59	05 33	06 03	00 02	01 14	02 28	03 42
N 40	05 02	05 33	06 00	00 17	01 26	02 37	03 48
35	05 03	05 32	05 58	00 29	01 36	02 44	03 53
30	05 04	05 32	05 56	00 40	01 45	02 51	03 57
20	05 04	05 30	05 52	00 58	02 01	03 03	04 04
N 10	05 03	05 27	05 48	01 14	02 14	03 13	04 11
0	05 00	05 24	05 45	01 29	02 27	03 23	04 17
S 10	04 56	05 21	05 42	01 44	02 40	03 33	04 23
20	04 50	05 16	05 38	02 00	02 53	03 43	04 29
30	04 41	05 10	05 34	02 18	03 08	03 54	04 37
35	04 36	05 06	05 31	02 29	03 17	04 01	04 41
40	04 29	05 01	05 28	02 41	03 28	04 09	04 46
45	04 20	04 55	05 25	02 55	03 39	04 17	04 51
S 50	04 09	04 48	05 21	03 13	03 54	04 28	04 58
52	04 03	04 44	05 19	03 21	04 00	04 33	05 01
54	03 57	04 41	05 17	03 30	04 08	04 38	05 04
56	03 50	04 36	05 14	03 40	04 16	04 44	05 07
58	03 42	04 32	05 12	03 52	04 25	04 51	05 12
S 60	03 33	04 26	05 09	04 05	04 36	04 58	05 16

Lat.	Sunset	Twilight Civil	Twilight Naut.	Moonset 4	5	6	7
°	h m	h m	h m	h m	h m	h m	h m
N 72	16 58	18 05	19 25	19 15	18 28	18 06	17 51
N 70	17 04	18 04	19 16	18 11	17 59	17 51	17 43
68	17 08	18 04	19 09	17 35	17 38	17 38	17 37
66	17 12	18 03	19 03	17 09	17 21	17 28	17 32
64	17 16	18 03	18 58	16 49	17 07	17 19	17 28
62	17 18	18 02	18 54	16 32	16 55	17 12	17 24
60	17 21	18 02	18 51	16 19	16 45	17 05	17 21
N 58	17 23	18 02	18 48	16 07	16 36	16 59	17 18
56	17 25	18 02	18 45	15 56	16 28	16 54	17 16
54	17 27	18 02	18 43	15 47	16 21	16 49	17 13
52	17 29	18 02	18 41	15 39	16 15	16 45	17 11
50	17 30	18 02	18 40	15 32	16 09	16 41	17 09
45	17 33	18 03	18 37	15 16	15 57	16 33	17 05
N 40	17 36	18 03	18 35	15 03	15 47	16 26	17 01
35	17 39	18 04	18 33	14 52	15 38	16 20	16 58
30	17 41	18 05	18 32	14 42	15 30	16 14	16 55
20	17 45	18 07	18 32	14 25	15 17	16 05	16 50
N 10	17 48	18 09	18 34	14 11	15 05	15 57	16 46
0	17 52	18 12	18 37	13 57	14 54	15 49	16 42
S 10	17 55	18 16	18 41	13 43	14 43	15 41	16 38
20	17 59	18 21	18 47	13 28	14 30	15 33	16 33
30	18 04	18 28	18 56	13 11	14 17	15 23	16 28
35	18 06	18 32	19 02	13 01	14 08	15 17	16 25
40	18 09	18 37	19 09	12 49	13 59	15 11	16 21
45	18 13	18 43	19 18	12 35	13 48	15 03	16 18
S 50	18 17	18 50	19 30	12 19	13 35	14 54	16 13
52	18 19	18 54	19 35	12 11	13 29	14 50	16 11
54	18 21	18 58	19 42	12 02	13 22	14 45	16 08
56	18 24	19 02	19 49	11 52	13 14	14 40	16 05
58	18 26	19 07	19 57	11 41	13 06	14 34	16 03
S 60	18 29	19 13	20 07	11 28	12 56	14 27	15 59

	SUN			MOON			
Day	Eqn. of Time 00h	12h	Mer. Pass.	Mer. Pass. Upper	Lower	Age	Phase
d	m s	m s	h m	h m	h m	d	%
4	11 08	11 17	11 49	07 43	20 12	25	27
5	11 26	11 35	11 48	08 40	21 08	26	17
6	11 44	11 53	11 48	09 36	22 03	27	9

2018 OCTOBER 7, 8, 9 (SUN., MON., TUES.)

UT	ARIES GHA	VENUS −4·6 GHA	Dec	MARS −1·1 GHA	Dec	JUPITER −1·8 GHA	Dec	SATURN +0·5 GHA	Dec	STARS Name	SHA	Dec
d h	° ′	° ′	° ′	° ′	° ′	° ′	° ′	° ′	° ′		° ′	° ′
7 00	15 35.5	159 38.7	S21 57.6	63 44.6	S21 34.5	144 34.2	S17 51.1	102 01.1	S22 45.8	Acamar	315 15.3	S40 13.7
01	30 37.9	174 41.4	57.7	78 46.0	34.1	159 36.2	51.2	117 03.4	45.8	Achernar	335 23.5	S57 08.5
02	45 40.4	189 44.0	57.8	93 47.3	33.7	174 38.1	51.3	132 05.8	45.8	Acrux	173 05.9	S63 12.0
03	60 42.8	204 46.6 ..	57.9	108 48.7 ..	33.2	189 40.1 ..	51.4	147 08.1 ..	45.8	Adhara	255 09.7	S28 59.7
04	75 45.3	219 49.3	58.0	123 50.1	32.8	204 42.1	51.6	162 10.4	45.8	Aldebaran	290 45.1	N16 32.7
05	90 47.8	234 51.9	58.1	138 51.5	32.4	219 44.0	51.7	177 12.8	45.8			
S 06	105 50.2	249 54.6	S21 58.2	153 52.8	S21 32.0	234 46.0	S17 51.8	192 15.1	S22 45.8	Alioth	166 18.1	N55 51.7
U 07	120 52.7	264 57.3	58.2	168 54.2	31.5	249 48.0	51.9	207 17.4	45.8	Alkaid	152 56.6	N49 13.5
N 08	135 55.2	279 59.9	58.3	183 55.6	31.1	264 50.0	52.1	222 19.8	45.8	Al Na'ir	27 38.9	S46 52.3
D 09	150 57.6	295 02.6 ..	58.4	198 56.9 ..	30.7	279 51.9 ..	52.2	237 22.1 ..	45.8	Alnilam	275 42.6	S 1 11.4
A 10	166 00.1	310 05.2	58.5	213 58.3	30.3	294 53.9	52.3	252 24.4	45.8	Alphard	217 52.8	S 8 44.2
Y 11	181 02.6	325 07.9	58.5	228 59.7	29.8	309 55.9	52.5	267 26.8	45.8			
12	196 05.0	340 10.6	S21 58.6	244 01.0	S21 29.4	324 57.8	S17 52.6	282 29.1	S22 45.8	Alphecca	126 08.3	N26 39.5
13	211 07.5	355 13.3	58.7	259 02.4	29.0	339 59.8	52.7	297 31.4	45.9	Alpheratz	357 39.4	N29 11.7
14	226 10.0	10 16.0	58.7	274 03.8	28.6	355 01.8	52.8	312 33.7	45.9	Altair	62 04.7	N 8 55.3
15	241 12.4	25 18.7 ..	58.8	289 05.1 ..	28.1	10 03.8 ..	53.0	327 36.1 ..	45.9	Ankaa	353 11.7	S42 12.3
16	256 14.9	40 21.3	58.9	304 06.5	27.7	25 05.7	53.1	342 38.4	45.9	Antares	112 22.1	S26 28.2
17	271 17.3	55 24.0	58.9	319 07.9	27.3	40 07.7	53.2	357 40.7	45.9			
18	286 19.8	70 26.7	S21 59.0	334 09.2	S21 26.9	55 09.7	S17 53.3	12 43.1	S22 45.9	Arcturus	145 52.8	N19 05.4
19	301 22.3	85 29.4	59.0	349 10.6	26.4	70 11.6	53.5	27 45.4	45.9	Atria	107 20.9	S69 03.7
20	316 24.7	100 32.2	59.1	4 11.9	26.0	85 13.6	53.6	42 47.7	45.9	Avior	234 16.8	S59 33.9
21	331 27.2	115 34.9 ..	59.1	19 13.3 ..	25.6	100 15.6 ..	53.7	57 50.1 ..	45.9	Bellatrix	278 28.0	N 6 21.9
22	346 29.7	130 37.6	59.2	34 14.7	25.1	115 17.6	53.9	72 52.4	45.9	Betelgeuse	270 57.3	N 7 24.6
23	1 32.1	145 40.3	59.2	49 16.0	24.7	130 19.5	54.0	87 54.7	45.9			
8 00	16 34.6	160 43.0	S21 59.3	64 17.4	S21 24.3	145 21.5	S17 54.1	102 57.0	S22 45.9	Canopus	263 54.5	S52 42.1
01	31 37.1	175 45.7	59.3	79 18.7	23.9	160 23.5	54.2	117 59.4	45.9	Capella	280 28.9	N46 00.7
02	46 39.5	190 48.5	59.4	94 20.1	23.4	175 25.4	54.4	133 01.7	45.9	Deneb	49 28.9	N45 21.2
03	61 42.0	205 51.2 ..	59.4	109 21.4 ..	23.0	190 27.4 ..	54.5	148 04.0 ..	45.9	Denebola	182 30.3	N14 28.2
04	76 44.4	220 54.0	59.4	124 22.8	22.6	205 29.4	54.6	163 06.4	45.9	Diphda	348 52.0	S17 53.0
05	91 46.9	235 56.7	59.5	139 24.2	22.1	220 31.3	54.7	178 08.7	45.9			
M 06	106 49.4	250 59.4	S21 59.5	154 25.5	S21 21.7	235 33.3	S17 54.9	193 11.0	S22 45.9	Dubhe	193 47.9	N61 39.0
O 07	121 51.8	266 02.2	59.5	169 26.9	21.3	250 35.3	55.0	208 13.3	45.9	Elnath	278 07.9	N28 37.2
N 08	136 54.3	281 04.9	59.5	184 28.2	20.8	265 37.2	55.1	223 15.7	45.9	Eltanin	90 44.6	N51 29.6
D 09	151 56.8	296 07.7 ..	59.6	199 29.6 ..	20.4	280 39.2 ..	55.3	238 18.0 ..	45.9	Enif	33 43.4	N 9 57.8
A 10	166 59.2	311 10.5	59.6	214 30.9	20.0	295 41.2	55.4	253 20.3	45.9	Fomalhaut	15 19.7	S29 31.4
Y 11	182 01.7	326 13.2	59.6	229 32.3	19.6	310 43.1	55.5	268 22.6	45.9			
12	197 04.2	341 16.0	S21 59.6	244 33.6	S21 19.1	325 45.1	S17 55.6	283 25.0	S22 45.9	Gacrux	171 57.5	S57 12.9
13	212 06.6	356 18.8	59.7	259 35.0	18.7	340 47.1	55.8	298 27.3	45.9	Gienah	175 48.9	S17 38.5
14	227 09.1	11 21.6	59.7	274 36.3	18.3	355 49.1	55.9	313 29.6	45.9	Hadar	148 43.4	S60 27.6
15	242 11.6	26 24.3 ..	59.7	289 37.7 ..	17.8	10 51.0 ..	56.0	328 32.0 ..	45.9	Hamal	327 56.4	N23 33.0
16	257 14.0	41 27.1	59.7	304 39.0	17.4	25 53.0	56.1	343 34.3	45.9	Kaus Aust.	83 39.1	S34 22.4
17	272 16.5	56 29.9	59.7	319 40.4	17.0	40 55.0	56.3	358 36.6	45.9			
18	287 18.9	71 32.7	S21 59.7	334 41.7	S21 16.5	55 56.9	S17 56.4	13 38.9	S22 45.9	Kochab	137 21.2	N74 05.0
19	302 21.4	86 35.5	59.7	349 43.1	16.1	70 58.9	56.5	28 41.3	45.9	Markab	13 34.5	N15 18.5
20	317 23.9	101 38.3	59.7	4 44.4	15.7	86 00.9	56.7	43 43.6	45.9	Menkar	314 11.0	N 4 09.7
21	332 26.3	116 41.1 ..	59.7	19 45.7 ..	15.2	101 02.8 ..	56.8	58 45.9 ..	45.9	Menkent	148 03.7	S36 27.5
22	347 28.8	131 43.9	59.7	34 47.1	14.8	116 04.8	56.9	73 48.2	45.9	Miaplacidus	221 39.4	S69 47.4
23	2 31.3	146 46.7	59.7	49 48.4	14.4	131 06.8	57.0	88 50.6	45.9			
9 00	17 33.7	161 49.5	S21 59.7	64 49.8	S21 13.9	146 08.7	S17 57.2	103 52.9	S22 45.9	Mirfak	308 34.8	N49 55.4
01	32 36.2	176 52.4	59.7	79 51.1	13.5	161 10.7	57.3	118 55.2	45.9	Nunki	75 53.9	S26 16.3
02	47 38.7	191 55.2	59.7	94 52.5	13.0	176 12.7	57.4	133 57.5	45.9	Peacock	53 13.4	S56 40.6
03	62 41.1	206 58.0 ..	59.6	109 53.8 ..	12.6	191 14.6 ..	57.5	148 59.9 ..	45.9	Pollux	243 23.4	N27 58.7
04	77 43.6	222 00.9	59.6	124 55.1	12.2	206 16.6	57.7	164 02.2	45.9	Procyon	244 56.0	N 5 10.6
05	92 46.0	237 03.7	59.6	139 56.5	11.7	221 18.5	57.8	179 04.5	45.9			
T 06	107 48.5	252 06.5	S21 59.6	154 57.8	S21 11.3	236 20.5	S17 57.9	194 06.8	S22 45.9	Rasalhague	96 03.3	N12 33.1
U 07	122 51.0	267 09.4	59.6	169 59.2	10.9	251 22.5	58.1	209 09.1	45.9	Regulus	207 39.9	N11 52.6
E 08	137 53.4	282 12.2	59.5	185 00.5	10.4	266 24.4	58.2	224 11.5	46.0	Rigel	281 08.5	S 8 10.8
S 09	152 55.9	297 15.1 ..	59.5	200 01.8 ..	10.0	281 26.4 ..	58.3	239 13.8 ..	46.0	Rigil Kent.	139 47.5	S60 54.6
D 10	167 58.4	312 17.9	59.5	215 03.2	09.6	296 28.4	58.4	254 16.1	46.0	Sabik	102 08.6	S15 44.7
A 11	183 00.8	327 20.8	59.4	230 04.5	09.1	311 30.3	58.6	269 18.4	46.0			
Y 12	198 03.3	342 23.6	S21 59.4	245 05.8	S21 08.7	326 32.3	S17 58.7	284 20.8	S22 46.0	Schedar	349 35.8	N56 38.4
13	213 05.8	357 26.5	59.4	260 07.2	08.2	341 34.3	58.8	299 23.1	46.0	Shaula	96 17.2	S37 06.9
14	228 08.2	12 29.4	59.3	275 08.5	07.8	356 36.2	58.9	314 25.4	46.0	Sirius	258 30.5	S16 44.4
15	243 10.7	27 32.3 ..	59.3	290 09.8 ..	07.4	11 38.2 ..	59.1	329 27.7 ..	46.0	Spica	158 27.8	S11 15.3
16	258 13.2	42 35.1	59.2	305 11.2	06.9	26 40.2	59.2	344 30.1	46.0	Suhail	222 50.0	S43 30.2
17	273 15.6	57 38.0	59.2	320 12.5	06.5	41 42.1	59.3	359 32.4	46.0			
18	288 18.1	72 40.9	S21 59.2	335 13.8	S21 06.0	56 44.1	S17 59.5	14 34.7	S22 46.0	Vega	80 36.6	N38 48.5
19	303 20.5	87 43.8	59.1	350 15.2	05.6	71 46.1	59.6	29 37.0	46.0	Zuben'ubi	137 01.7	S16 06.9
20	318 23.0	102 46.7	59.0	5 16.5	05.2	86 48.0	59.7	44 39.3	46.0		SHA	Mer. Pass.
21	333 25.5	117 49.6 ..	59.0	20 17.8 ..	04.7	101 50.0	17 59.8	59 41.7 ..	46.0	Venus	144 08.4	13 15
22	348 27.9	132 52.5	58.9	35 19.1	04.3	116 51.9	18 00.0	74 44.0	46.0	Mars	47 42.8	19 41
23	3 30.4	147 55.4	58.9	50 20.5	03.8	131 53.9	S18 00.1	89 46.3	46.0	Jupiter	128 46.9	14 17
Mer. Pass.	22 49.9	v 2.8	d 0.0	v 1.3	d 0.4	v 2.0	d 0.1	v 2.3	d 0.0	Saturn	86 22.4	17 06

UT	SUN GHA	SUN Dec	MOON GHA	v	MOON Dec	d	HP
	° ′	° ′	° ′	′	° ′	′	′
7 00	183 00.5	S 5 23.7	208 12.4	8.9	N 9 02.6	11.9	59.7
01	198 00.7	24.6	222 40.3	8.9	8 50.7	11.9	59.7
02	213 00.9	25.6	237 08.2	8.9	8 38.8	12.0	59.7
03	228 01.1	.. 26.6	251 36.1	9.1	8 26.8	12.0	59.7
04	243 01.3	27.5	266 04.2	9.0	8 14.8	12.0	59.7
05	258 01.4	28.5	280 32.2	9.1	8 02.8	12.1	59.7
S 06	273 01.6	S 5 29.4	295 00.3	9.2	N 7 50.7	12.2	59.7
07	288 01.8	30.4	309 28.5	9.1	7 38.5	12.1	59.7
U 08	303 02.0	31.3	323 56.6	9.3	7 26.4	12.3	59.7
N 09	318 02.2	.. 32.3	338 24.9	9.2	7 14.1	12.2	59.7
D 10	333 02.3	33.3	352 53.1	9.3	7 01.9	12.3	59.6
A 11	348 02.5	34.2	7 21.4	9.4	6 49.6	12.4	59.6
Y 12	3 02.7	S 5 35.2	21 49.8	9.4	N 6 37.2	12.3	59.6
13	18 02.9	36.1	36 18.2	9.4	6 24.9	12.4	59.6
14	33 03.1	37.1	50 46.6	9.5	6 12.5	12.5	59.6
15	48 03.2	.. 38.0	65 15.1	9.5	6 00.0	12.5	59.6
16	63 03.4	39.0	79 43.6	9.6	5 47.5	12.4	59.6
17	78 03.6	39.9	94 12.2	9.6	5 35.1	12.6	59.6
18	93 03.8	S 5 40.9	108 40.8	9.6	N 5 22.5	12.5	59.5
19	108 03.9	41.9	123 09.4	9.6	5 10.0	12.6	59.5
20	123 04.1	42.8	137 38.0	9.7	4 57.4	12.6	59.5
21	138 04.3	.. 43.8	152 06.7	9.8	4 44.8	12.6	59.5
22	153 04.5	44.7	166 35.5	9.8	4 32.2	12.6	59.5
23	168 04.7	45.7	181 04.3	9.8	4 19.6	12.7	59.5
8 00	183 04.8	S 5 46.6	195 33.1	9.8	N 4 06.9	12.7	59.5
01	198 05.0	47.6	210 01.9	9.9	3 54.2	12.7	59.4
02	213 05.2	48.5	224 30.8	9.9	3 41.5	12.7	59.4
03	228 05.4	.. 49.5	238 59.7	10.0	3 28.8	12.7	59.4
04	243 05.5	50.4	253 28.7	9.9	3 16.1	12.7	59.4
05	258 05.7	51.4	267 57.6	10.1	3 03.4	12.8	59.4
M 06	273 05.9	S 5 52.4	282 26.7	10.0	N 2 50.6	12.7	59.3
07	288 06.1	53.3	296 55.7	10.1	2 37.9	12.8	59.3
O 08	303 06.2	54.3	311 24.8	10.1	2 25.1	12.7	59.3
N 09	318 06.4	.. 55.2	325 53.9	10.1	2 12.4	12.8	59.3
D 10	333 06.6	56.2	340 23.0	10.2	1 59.6	12.8	59.3
A 11	348 06.8	57.1	354 52.2	10.2	1 46.8	12.8	59.3
Y 12	3 06.9	S 5 58.1	9 21.4	10.2	N 1 34.0	12.7	59.2
13	18 07.1	5 59.0	23 50.6	10.2	1 21.3	12.8	59.2
14	33 07.3	6 00.0	38 19.8	10.3	1 08.5	12.8	59.2
15	48 07.5	.. 00.9	52 49.1	10.3	0 55.7	12.8	59.2
16	63 07.6	01.9	67 18.4	10.4	0 42.9	12.7	59.2
17	78 07.8	02.8	81 47.8	10.3	0 30.2	12.8	59.1
18	93 08.0	S 6 03.8	96 17.1	10.4	N 0 17.4	12.8	59.1
19	108 08.1	04.7	110 46.5	10.4	N 0 04.6	12.7	59.1
20	123 08.3	05.7	125 15.9	10.4	S 0 08.1	12.7	59.1
21	138 08.5	.. 06.6	139 45.3	10.5	0 20.8	12.8	59.0
22	153 08.7	07.6	154 14.8	10.5	0 33.6	12.7	59.0
23	168 08.8	08.5	168 44.3	10.5	0 46.3	12.7	59.0
9 00	183 09.0	S 6 09.5	183 13.8	10.5	S 0 59.0	12.7	59.0
01	198 09.2	10.4	197 43.3	10.5	1 11.7	12.6	59.0
02	213 09.3	11.4	212 12.8	10.6	1 24.3	12.7	58.9
03	228 09.5	.. 12.3	226 42.4	10.6	1 37.0	12.6	58.9
04	243 09.7	13.3	241 12.0	10.6	1 49.6	12.6	58.9
05	258 09.9	14.2	255 41.6	10.6	2 02.2	12.6	58.9
T 06	273 10.0	S 6 15.2	270 11.2	10.6	S 2 14.8	12.6	58.8
07	288 10.2	16.1	284 40.8	10.7	2 27.4	12.5	58.8
U 08	303 10.4	17.1	299 10.5	10.7	2 39.9	12.6	58.8
E 09	318 10.5	.. 18.0	313 40.2	10.7	2 52.5	12.5	58.8
S 10	333 10.7	19.0	328 09.9	10.7	3 05.0	12.4	58.7
D 11	348 10.9	19.9	342 39.6	10.7	3 17.4	12.5	58.7
A 12	3 11.1	S 6 20.9	357 09.3	10.7	S 3 29.9	12.4	58.7
Y 13	18 11.2	21.8	11 39.0	10.8	3 42.3	12.3	58.7
14	33 11.4	22.8	26 08.8	10.7	3 54.6	12.4	58.6
15	48 11.6	.. 23.7	40 38.5	10.8	4 07.0	12.3	58.6
16	63 11.7	24.7	55 08.3	10.8	4 19.3	12.3	58.6
17	78 11.9	25.6	69 38.1	10.8	4 31.6	12.2	58.5
18	93 12.1	S 6 26.6	84 07.9	10.8	S 4 43.8	12.2	58.5
19	108 12.2	27.5	98 37.7	10.9	4 56.0	12.2	58.5
20	123 12.4	28.5	113 07.6	10.8	5 08.2	12.1	58.5
21	138 12.6	.. 29.4	127 37.4	10.9	5 20.3	12.1	58.4
22	153 12.7	30.4	142 07.3	10.8	5 32.4	12.1	58.4
23	168 12.9	31.3	156 37.1	10.9	S 5 44.5	12.0	58.4
	SD 16.0	d 1.0	SD 16.2		16.1		16.0

Twilight / Sunrise / Moonrise

Lat.	Naut.	Civil	Sunrise	Moonrise 7	8	9	10
°	h m	h m	h m	h m	h m	h m	h m
N 72	04 23	05 42	06 50	02 24	04 30	06 31	08 32
N 70	04 31	05 42	06 43	02 38	04 34	06 28	08 20
68	04 37	05 42	06 37	02 48	04 38	06 25	08 10
66	04 42	05 41	06 33	02 57	04 41	06 22	08 02
64	04 46	05 41	06 29	03 05	04 43	06 20	07 55
62	04 49	05 41	06 25	03 11	04 46	06 19	07 50
60	04 52	05 40	06 22	03 16	04 47	06 17	07 45
N 58	04 54	05 40	06 19	03 21	04 49	06 16	07 40
56	04 56	05 39	06 17	03 25	04 51	06 14	07 36
54	04 58	05 39	06 14	03 29	04 52	06 13	07 33
52	05 00	05 39	06 12	03 33	04 53	06 12	07 30
50	05 01	05 38	06 11	03 36	04 54	06 11	07 27
45	05 03	05 37	06 06	03 42	04 57	06 10	07 21
N 40	05 05	05 36	06 03	03 48	04 59	06 08	07 16
35	05 05	05 35	06 00	03 53	05 00	06 07	07 11
30	05 06	05 33	05 57	03 57	05 02	06 05	07 08
20	05 05	05 31	05 53	04 04	05 05	06 03	07 01
N 10	05 03	05 27	05 48	04 11	05 07	06 01	06 55
0	04 59	05 23	05 44	04 17	05 09	06 00	06 50
S 10	04 54	05 19	05 40	04 23	05 11	05 58	06 44
20	04 47	05 13	05 35	04 29	05 14	05 56	06 39
30	04 38	05 06	05 30	04 37	05 16	05 55	06 32
35	04 31	05 01	05 27	04 41	05 18	05 54	06 29
40	04 24	04 56	05 23	04 46	05 20	05 52	06 25
45	04 14	04 49	05 19	04 51	05 22	05 51	06 20
S 50	04 01	04 41	05 14	04 58	05 24	05 49	06 14
52	03 55	04 37	05 12	05 01	05 25	05 48	06 12
54	03 49	04 33	05 09	05 04	05 26	05 48	06 09
56	03 41	04 28	05 07	05 07	05 28	05 47	06 06
58	03 32	04 23	05 03	05 12	05 29	05 46	06 03
S 60	03 22	04 16	05 00	05 16	05 31	05 45	05 59

Sunset / Twilight / Moonset

Lat.	Sunset	Civil	Naut.	Moonset 7	8	9	10
°	h m	h m	h m	h m	h m	h m	h m
N 72	16 43	17 51	19 09	17 51	17 37	17 23	17 08
N 70	16 50	17 51	19 02	17 43	17 36	17 29	17 22
68	16 56	17 52	18 56	17 37	17 36	17 35	17 33
66	17 01	17 52	18 51	17 32	17 36	17 39	17 43
64	17 05	17 53	18 47	17 28	17 36	17 43	17 51
62	17 09	17 53	18 44	17 24	17 36	17 46	17 58
60	17 12	17 54	18 42	17 21	17 35	17 49	18 04
N 58	17 15	17 54	18 39	17 18	17 35	17 52	18 09
56	17 17	17 54	18 37	17 16	17 35	17 54	18 14
54	17 20	17 55	18 36	17 13	17 35	17 56	18 18
52	17 22	17 55	18 34	17 11	17 35	17 58	18 22
50	17 24	17 56	18 33	17 09	17 35	18 00	18 26
45	17 28	17 57	18 31	17 05	17 35	18 04	18 33
N 40	17 31	17 59	18 30	17 01	17 34	18 07	18 40
35	17 35	18 00	18 29	16 58	17 34	18 10	18 45
30	17 37	18 01	18 29	16 55	17 34	18 12	18 50
20	17 42	18 04	18 30	16 50	17 34	18 16	18 59
N 10	17 47	18 08	18 32	16 46	17 34	18 20	19 06
0	17 51	18 12	18 36	16 42	17 33	18 24	19 14
S 10	17 55	18 16	18 41	16 38	17 33	18 27	19 21
20	18 00	18 22	18 48	16 33	17 33	18 31	19 28
30	18 05	18 30	18 58	16 28	17 32	18 35	19 37
35	18 09	18 34	19 04	16 25	17 32	18 38	19 42
40	18 13	18 40	19 12	16 22	17 32	18 40	19 48
45	18 17	18 47	19 22	16 18	17 31	18 44	19 54
S 50	18 22	18 55	19 35	16 13	17 31	18 48	20 02
52	18 24	18 59	19 41	16 11	17 31	18 49	20 06
54	18 27	19 03	19 48	16 08	17 31	18 51	20 10
56	18 30	19 08	19 56	16 06	17 30	18 54	20 15
58	18 33	19 14	20 05	16 03	17 30	18 56	20 20
S 60	18 37	19 20	20 16	15 59	17 30	18 59	20 25

SUN / MOON

Day	Eqn. of Time 00ʰ	12ʰ	Mer. Pass.	MOON Mer. Pass. Upper	Lower	Age	Phase
d	m s	m s	h m	h m	h m	d	%
7	12 02	12 10	11 48	10 29	22 56	28	4
8	12 19	12 27	11 48	11 21	23 47	29	1
9	12 36	12 44	11 47	12 12	24 37	00	0 ●

UT	ARIES GHA	VENUS −4·6 GHA	Dec	MARS −1·1 GHA	Dec	JUPITER −1·8 GHA	Dec	SATURN +0·5 GHA	Dec	STARS Name	SHA	Dec
10 00	18 32.9	162 58.3	S21 58.8	65 21.8	S21 03.4	146 55.9	S18 00.2	104 48.6	S22 46.0	Acamar	315 15.2	S40 13.8
01	33 35.3	178 01.2	58.7	80 23.1	03.0	161 57.8	00.3	119 50.9	46.0	Achernar	335 23.5	S57 08.6
02	48 37.8	193 04.1	58.7	95 24.4	02.5	176 59.8	00.5	134 53.3	46.0	Acrux	173 05.9	S63 11.9
03	63 40.3	208 07.1 ..	58.6	110 25.8 ..	02.1	192 01.8 ..	00.6	149 55.6 ..	46.0	Adhara	255 09.7	S28 59.7
04	78 42.7	223 10.0	58.5	125 27.1	01.6	207 03.7	00.7	164 57.9	46.0	Aldebaran	290 45.0	N16 32.7
05	93 45.2	238 12.9	58.5	140 28.4	01.2	222 05.7	00.9	180 00.2	46.0			
06	108 47.7	253 15.9	S21 58.4	155 29.7	S21 00.8	237 07.6	S18 01.0	195 02.5	S22 46.0	Alioth	166 18.1	N55 51.7
W 07	123 50.1	268 18.8	58.3	170 31.1	21 00.3	252 09.6	01.1	210 04.9	46.0	Alkaid	152 56.6	N49 13.4
E 08	138 52.6	283 21.7	58.2	185 32.4	20 59.9	267 11.6	01.2	225 07.2	46.0	Al Na'ir	27 38.9	S46 52.3
D 09	153 55.0	298 24.7 ..	58.1	200 33.7 ..	59.4	282 13.5 ..	01.4	240 09.5 ..	46.0	Alnilam	275 42.6	S 1 11.4
N 10	168 57.5	313 27.6	58.1	215 35.0	59.0	297 15.5	01.5	255 11.8	46.0	Alphard	217 52.7	S 8 44.2
E 11	184 00.0	328 30.6	58.0	230 36.4	58.5	312 17.5	01.6	270 14.1	46.0			
S 12	199 02.4	343 33.5	S21 57.9	245 37.7	S20 58.1	327 19.4	S18 01.7	285 16.5	S22 46.0	Alphecca	126 08.3	N26 39.5
D 13	214 04.9	358 36.5	57.8	260 39.0	57.6	342 21.4	01.9	300 18.8	46.0	Alpheratz	357 39.4	N29 11.7
A 14	229 07.4	13 39.5	57.7	275 40.3	57.2	357 23.3	02.0	315 21.1	46.0	Altair	62 04.7	N 8 55.3
Y 15	244 09.8	28 42.4 ..	57.6	290 41.6 ..	56.8	12 25.3 ..	02.1	330 23.4 ..	46.0	Ankaa	353 11.7	S42 12.3
16	259 12.3	43 45.4	57.5	305 42.9	56.3	27 27.3	02.3	345 25.7	46.0	Antares	112 22.1	S26 28.2
17	274 14.8	58 48.4	57.4	320 44.3	55.9	42 29.2	02.4	0 28.1	46.0			
18	289 17.2	73 51.3	S21 57.3	335 45.6	S20 55.4	57 31.2	S18 02.5	15 30.4	S22 46.0	Arcturus	145 52.8	N19 05.4
19	304 19.7	88 54.3	57.2	350 46.9	55.0	72 33.1	02.6	30 32.7	46.0	Atria	107 21.0	S69 03.7
20	319 22.1	103 57.3	57.1	5 48.2	54.5	87 35.1	02.8	45 35.0	46.0	Avior	234 16.7	S59 33.9
21	334 24.6	119 00.3 ..	57.0	20 49.5 ..	54.1	102 37.1 ..	02.9	60 37.3 ..	46.0	Bellatrix	278 28.0	N 6 21.9
22	349 27.1	134 03.3	56.9	35 50.8	53.6	117 39.0	03.0	75 39.6	46.0	Betelgeuse	270 57.3	N 7 24.6
23	4 29.5	149 06.3	56.7	50 52.1	53.2	132 41.0	03.2	90 42.0	46.0			
11 00	19 32.0	164 09.3	S21 56.6	65 53.5	S20 52.7	147 42.9	S18 03.3	105 44.3	S22 46.0	Canopus	263 54.4	S52 42.1
01	34 34.5	179 12.3	56.5	80 54.8	52.3	162 44.9	03.4	120 46.6	46.0	Capella	280 28.9	N46 00.7
02	49 36.9	194 15.3	56.4	95 56.1	51.8	177 46.9	03.5	135 48.9	46.0	Deneb	49 28.9	N45 21.2
03	64 39.4	209 18.3 ..	56.3	110 57.4 ..	51.4	192 48.8 ..	03.7	150 51.2 ..	46.0	Denebola	182 30.3	N14 28.2
04	79 41.9	224 21.3	56.1	125 58.7	51.0	207 50.8	03.8	165 53.5	46.0	Diphda	348 52.0	S17 53.0
05	94 44.3	239 24.4	56.0	141 00.0	50.5	222 52.7	03.9	180 55.9	46.0			
06	109 46.8	254 27.4	S21 55.9	156 01.3	S20 50.1	237 54.7	S18 04.0	195 58.2	S22 46.0	Dubhe	193 47.9	N61 39.0
07	124 49.3	269 30.4	55.7	171 02.6	49.6	252 56.7	04.2	211 00.5	46.1	Elnath	278 07.9	N28 37.2
T 08	139 51.7	284 33.5	55.6	186 03.9	49.2	267 58.6	04.3	226 02.8	46.1	Eltanin	90 44.7	N51 29.6
H 09	154 54.2	299 36.5 ..	55.5	201 05.2 ..	48.7	283 00.6 ..	04.4	241 05.1 ..	46.1	Enif	33 43.4	N 9 57.8
U 10	169 56.6	314 39.5	55.3	216 06.5	48.3	298 02.5	04.6	256 07.4	46.1	Fomalhaut	15 19.7	S29 31.4
R 11	184 59.1	329 42.6	55.2	231 07.8	47.8	313 04.5	04.7	271 09.7	46.1			
S 12	200 01.6	344 45.6	S21 55.0	246 09.2	S20 47.4	328 06.5	S18 04.8	286 12.1	S22 46.1	Gacrux	171 57.4	S57 12.8
D 13	215 04.0	359 48.7	54.9	261 10.5	46.9	343 08.4	04.9	301 14.4	46.1	Gienah	175 48.9	S17 38.5
A 14	230 06.5	14 51.7	54.7	276 11.8	46.5	358 10.4	05.1	316 16.7	46.1	Hadar	148 43.4	S60 27.6
Y 15	245 09.0	29 54.8 ..	54.6	291 13.1 ..	46.0	13 12.3 ..	05.2	331 19.0 ..	46.1	Hamal	327 56.4	N23 33.0
16	260 11.4	44 57.9	54.4	306 14.4	45.6	28 14.3	05.3	346 21.3	46.1	Kaus Aust.	83 39.2	S34 22.4
17	275 13.9	60 00.9	54.3	321 15.7	45.1	43 16.3	05.4	1 23.6	46.1			
18	290 16.4	75 04.0	S21 54.1	336 17.0	S20 44.7	58 18.2	S18 05.6	16 25.9	S22 46.1	Kochab	137 21.2	N74 05.0
19	305 18.8	90 07.1	53.9	351 18.3	44.2	73 20.2	05.7	31 28.3	46.1	Markab	13 34.5	N15 18.5
20	320 21.3	105 10.1	53.8	6 19.6	43.7	88 22.1	05.8	46 30.6	46.1	Menkar	314 11.0	N 4 09.7
21	335 23.7	120 13.2 ..	53.6	21 20.9 ..	43.3	103 24.1 ..	06.0	61 32.9 ..	46.1	Menkent	148 03.7	S36 27.5
22	350 26.2	135 16.3	53.4	36 22.2	42.8	118 26.0	06.1	76 35.2	46.1	Miaplacidus	221 39.4	S69 47.3
23	5 28.7	150 19.4	53.3	51 23.5	42.4	133 28.0	06.2	91 37.5	46.1			
12 00	20 31.1	165 22.5	S21 53.1	66 24.8	S20 41.9	148 30.0	S18 06.3	106 39.8	S22 46.1	Mirfak	308 34.8	N49 55.4
01	35 33.6	180 25.6	52.9	81 26.1	41.5	163 31.9	06.5	121 42.1	46.1	Nunki	75 53.9	S26 16.3
02	50 36.1	195 28.7	52.7	96 27.4	41.0	178 33.9	06.6	136 44.5	46.1	Peacock	53 13.5	S56 40.6
03	65 38.5	210 31.8 ..	52.6	111 28.7 ..	40.6	193 35.8 ..	06.7	151 46.8 ..	46.1	Pollux	243 23.4	N27 58.7
04	80 41.0	225 34.9	52.4	126 30.0	40.1	208 37.8	06.8	166 49.1	46.1	Procyon	244 56.0	N 5 10.6
05	95 43.5	240 38.0	52.2	141 31.2	39.7	223 39.7	07.0	181 51.4	46.1			
06	110 45.9	255 41.1	S21 52.0	156 32.5	S20 39.2	238 41.7	S18 07.1	196 53.7	S22 46.1	Rasalhague	96 03.3	N12 33.1
07	125 48.4	270 44.2	51.8	171 33.8	38.8	253 43.7	07.2	211 56.0	46.1	Regulus	207 39.9	N11 52.6
08	140 50.9	285 47.4	51.6	186 35.1	38.3	268 45.6	07.4	226 58.3	46.1	Rigel	281 08.4	S 8 10.8
F 09	155 53.3	300 50.5 ..	51.4	201 36.4 ..	37.8	283 47.6 ..	07.5	242 00.6 ..	46.1	Rigil Kent.	139 47.5	S60 54.6
R 10	170 55.8	315 53.6	51.2	216 37.7	37.4	298 49.5	07.6	257 02.9	46.1	Sabik	102 08.6	S15 44.7
I 11	185 58.2	330 56.8	51.0	231 39.0	36.9	313 51.5	07.7	272 05.3	46.1			
D 12	201 00.7	345 59.9	S21 50.8	246 40.3	S20 36.5	328 53.4	S18 07.9	287 07.6	S22 46.1	Schedar	349 35.8	N56 38.4
A 13	216 03.2	1 03.0	50.6	261 41.6	36.0	343 55.4	08.0	302 09.9	46.1	Shaula	96 17.2	S37 06.9
Y 14	231 05.6	16 06.2	50.4	276 42.9	35.6	358 57.3	08.1	317 12.2	46.1	Sirius	258 30.5	S16 44.4
15	246 08.1	31 09.3 ..	50.2	291 44.2 ..	35.1	13 59.3 ..	08.2	332 14.5 ..	46.1	Spica	158 27.8	S11 15.3
16	261 10.6	46 12.5	50.0	306 45.5	34.7	29 01.3	08.4	347 16.8	46.1	Suhail	222 50.0	S43 30.2
17	276 13.0	61 15.6	49.7	321 46.7	34.2	44 03.2	08.5	2 19.1	46.1			
18	291 15.5	76 18.8	S21 49.5	336 48.0	S20 33.7	59 05.2	S18 08.6	17 21.4	S22 46.1	Vega	80 36.6	N38 48.5
19	306 18.0	91 22.0	49.3	351 49.3	33.3	74 07.1	08.8	32 23.7	46.1	Zuben'ubi	137 01.7	S16 06.9
20	321 20.4	106 25.1	49.1	6 50.6	32.8	89 09.1	08.9	47 26.0	46.1			
21	336 22.9	121 28.3 ..	48.9	21 51.9 ..	32.4	104 11.0 ..	09.0	62 28.4 ..	46.1		SHA	Mer. Pass.
22	351 25.4	136 31.5	48.6	36 53.2	31.9	119 13.0	09.1	77 30.7	46.1	Venus	° ′ 144 37.3	h m 13 01
23	6 27.8	151 34.7	48.4	51 54.5	31.4	134 14.9	09.3	92 33.0	46.1	Mars	46 21.5	19 35
h m Mer. Pass. 22 38.1		v 3.0	d 0.1	v 1.3	d 0.5	v 2.0	d 0.1	v 2.3	d 0.0	Jupiter	128 10.9	14 07
										Saturn	86 12.3	16 54

UT	SUN GHA	SUN Dec	MOON GHA	v	MOON Dec	d	HP
d h	° ′	° ′	° ′	′	° ′	′	′
10 00	183 13.1	S 6 32.3	171 07.0	10.9	S 5 56.5	11.9	58.4
01	198 13.2	33.2	185 36.9	10.9	6 08.4	11.9	58.3
02	213 13.4	34.2	200 06.8	10.9	6 20.3	11.9	58.3
03	228 13.6	.. 35.1	214 36.7	10.9	6 32.2	11.8	58.3
04	243 13.7	36.1	229 06.6	10.9	6 44.0	11.8	58.2
05	258 13.9	37.0	243 36.5	10.9	6 55.8	11.7	58.2
W 06	273 14.1	S 6 38.0	258 06.4	10.9	S 7 07.5	11.7	58.2
E 07	288 14.2	38.9	272 36.3	11.0	7 19.2	11.6	58.2
D 08	303 14.4	39.9	287 06.3	11.0	7 30.8	11.6	58.1
N 09	318 14.6	.. 40.8	301 36.2	11.0	7 42.4	11.5	58.1
E 10	333 14.7	41.8	316 06.2	10.9	7 53.9	11.5	58.1
S 11	348 14.8	42.7	330 36.1	11.0	8 05.4	11.4	58.0
D 12	3 15.1	S 6 43.6	345 06.1	10.9	S 8 16.8	11.4	58.0
A 13	18 15.2	44.6	359 36.0	11.0	8 28.2	11.3	58.0
Y 14	33 15.4	45.5	14 06.0	10.9	8 39.5	11.2	57.9
15	48 15.6	.. 46.5	28 35.9	11.0	8 50.7	11.2	57.9
16	63 15.7	47.4	43 05.9	11.0	9 01.9	11.1	57.9
17	78 15.9	48.4	57 35.9	11.0	9 13.0	11.1	57.8
18	93 16.0	S 6 49.3	72 05.9	10.9	S 9 24.1	11.0	57.8
19	108 16.2	50.3	86 35.8	11.0	9 35.1	11.0	57.8
20	123 16.4	51.2	101 05.8	11.0	9 46.1	10.8	57.8
21	138 16.5	.. 52.2	115 35.8	11.0	9 56.9	10.8	57.7
22	153 16.7	53.1	130 05.8	10.9	10 07.7	10.8	57.7
23	168 16.9	54.0	144 35.7	11.0	10 18.5	10.7	57.7
11 00	183 17.0	S 6 55.0	159 05.7	11.0	S10 29.2	10.6	57.6
01	198 17.2	55.9	173 35.7	11.0	10 39.8	10.5	57.6
02	213 17.3	56.9	188 05.7	11.0	10 50.3	10.5	57.6
03	228 17.5	.. 57.8	202 35.7	10.9	11 00.8	10.4	57.5
04	243 17.7	58.7	217 05.6	11.0	11 11.2	10.4	57.5
05	258 17.8	6 59.7	231 35.6	11.0	11 21.6	10.2	57.5
T 06	273 18.0	S 7 00.6	246 05.6	11.0	S11 31.8	10.2	57.4
H 07	288 18.2	01.6	260 35.6	11.0	11 42.0	10.2	57.4
U 08	303 18.3	02.5	275 05.6	10.9	11 52.2	10.0	57.4
R 09	318 18.5	.. 03.5	289 35.5	11.0	12 02.2	10.0	57.3
S 10	333 18.6	04.4	304 05.5	11.0	12 12.2	9.9	57.3
D 11	348 18.8	05.4	318 35.5	10.9	12 22.1	9.8	57.3
A 12	3 19.0	S 7 06.3	333 05.4	11.0	S12 31.9	9.8	57.2
Y 13	18 19.1	07.2	347 35.4	11.0	12 41.7	9.7	57.2
14	33 19.3	08.2	2 05.4	10.9	12 51.4	9.6	57.2
15	48 19.4	.. 09.1	16 35.3	11.0	13 01.0	9.5	57.2
16	63 19.6	10.1	31 05.3	10.9	13 10.5	9.4	57.1
17	78 19.8	11.0	45 35.2	11.0	13 19.9	9.4	57.1
18	93 19.9	S 7 11.9	60 05.2	10.9	S13 29.3	9.3	57.1
19	108 20.1	12.9	74 35.1	10.9	13 38.6	9.2	57.0
20	123 20.2	13.8	89 05.0	11.0	13 47.8	9.1	57.0
21	138 20.4	.. 14.8	103 35.0	10.9	13 56.9	9.0	57.0
22	153 20.5	15.7	118 04.9	10.9	14 05.9	9.0	56.9
23	168 20.7	16.7	132 34.8	11.0	14 14.9	8.8	56.9
12 00	183 20.9	S 7 17.6	147 04.8	10.9	S14 23.7	8.8	56.9
01	198 21.0	18.5	161 34.7	10.9	14 32.5	8.7	56.8
02	213 21.2	19.5	176 04.6	10.9	14 41.2	8.6	56.8
03	228 21.3	.. 20.4	190 34.5	10.9	14 49.8	8.5	56.8
04	243 21.5	21.4	205 04.4	10.9	14 58.3	8.5	56.7
05	258 21.6	22.3	219 34.3	10.9	15 06.8	8.3	56.7
F 06	273 21.8	S 7 23.2	234 04.2	10.9	S15 15.1	8.3	56.7
R 07	288 22.0	24.2	248 34.1	10.9	15 23.4	8.2	56.6
I 08	303 22.1	25.1	263 04.0	10.9	15 31.6	8.1	56.6
D 09	318 22.3	.. 26.0	277 33.9	10.9	15 39.7	8.0	56.6
A 10	333 22.4	27.0	292 03.8	10.9	15 47.7	7.9	56.6
Y 11	348 22.6	27.9	306 33.7	10.9	15 55.6	7.8	56.5
12	3 22.7	S 7 28.9	321 03.6	10.8	S16 03.4	7.7	56.5
13	18 22.9	29.8	335 33.4	10.9	16 11.1	7.6	56.5
14	33 23.0	30.7	350 03.3	10.9	16 18.7	7.6	56.4
15	48 23.2	.. 31.7	4 33.2	10.8	16 26.3	7.4	56.4
16	63 23.3	32.6	19 03.0	10.9	16 33.7	7.4	56.4
17	78 23.5	33.5	33 32.9	10.9	16 41.1	7.3	56.3
18	93 23.7	S 7 34.5	48 02.7	10.9	S16 48.4	7.1	56.3
19	108 23.8	35.4	62 32.6	10.8	16 55.5	7.1	56.3
20	123 24.0	36.4	77 02.4	10.9	17 02.6	7.0	56.2
21	138 24.1	.. 37.3	91 32.3	10.8	17 09.6	6.9	56.2
22	153 24.3	38.2	106 02.1	10.9	17 16.5	6.8	56.2
23	168 24.4	39.2	120 31.9	10.9	S17 23.3	6.7	56.2
	SD 16.0	d 0.9	SD 15.8		15.6		15.4

Lat.	Twilight Naut.	Twilight Civil	Sunrise	Moonrise 10	11	12	13
°	h m	h m	h m	h m	h m	h m	h m
N 72	04 37	05 55	07 04	08 32	10 36	12 54	■■■
N 70	04 43	05 54	06 56	08 20	10 12	12 08	14 14
68	04 48	05 52	06 48	08 10	09 54	11 38	13 19
66	04 51	05 51	06 42	08 02	09 40	11 16	12 47
64	04 54	05 50	06 37	07 55	09 28	10 58	12 23
62	04 57	05 48	06 33	07 50	09 18	10 44	12 04
60	04 59	05 47	06 29	07 45	09 10	10 32	11 48
N 58	05 01	05 46	06 26	07 40	09 03	10 22	11 35
56	05 02	05 45	06 23	07 36	08 56	10 13	11 24
54	05 04	05 45	06 20	07 33	08 50	10 05	11 14
52	05 05	05 44	06 18	07 30	08 45	09 57	11 05
50	05 05	05 43	06 15	07 27	08 40	09 51	10 57
45	05 07	05 41	06 10	07 21	08 30	09 37	10 41
N 40	05 08	05 39	06 06	07 16	08 22	09 26	10 27
35	05 08	05 37	06 02	07 11	08 15	09 16	10 15
30	05 07	05 35	05 59	07 08	08 08	09 08	10 05
20	05 06	05 31	05 53	07 01	07 58	08 53	09 48
N 10	05 03	05 27	05 48	06 55	07 48	08 41	09 33
0	04 58	05 23	05 43	06 50	07 39	08 29	09 19
S 10	04 53	05 17	05 38	06 44	07 31	08 18	09 05
20	04 45	05 11	05 33	06 39	07 22	08 05	08 50
30	04 34	05 02	05 27	06 32	07 11	07 51	08 33
35	04 27	04 57	05 23	06 29	07 05	07 43	08 24
40	04 18	04 51	05 19	06 25	06 58	07 34	08 12
45	04 08	04 44	05 14	06 20	06 50	07 23	07 59
S 50	03 54	04 35	05 08	06 14	06 41	07 10	07 43
52	03 48	04 30	05 05	06 12	06 37	07 04	07 36
54	03 40	04 25	05 02	06 09	06 32	06 58	07 28
56	03 32	04 20	04 59	06 06	06 27	06 50	07 18
58	03 22	04 14	04 55	06 03	06 21	06 42	07 08
S 60	03 10	04 07	04 51	05 59	06 14	06 33	06 56

Lat.	Sunset	Twilight Civil	Twilight Naut.	Moonset 10	11	12	13
°	h m	h m	h m	h m	h m	h m	h m
N 72	16 27	17 36	18 54	17 08	16 48	16 14	■■■
N 70	16 36	17 38	18 48	17 22	17 13	17 02	16 40
68	16 43	17 40	18 44	17 33	17 32	17 32	17 35
66	16 50	17 41	18 40	17 43	17 48	17 55	18 08
64	16 55	17 42	18 37	17 51	18 00	18 14	18 32
62	16 59	17 44	18 35	17 58	18 11	18 28	18 52
60	17 03	17 45	18 33	18 04	18 21	18 41	19 08
N 58	17 07	17 46	18 31	18 09	18 29	18 52	19 21
56	17 10	17 47	18 30	18 14	18 36	19 02	19 33
54	17 12	17 48	18 29	18 18	18 42	19 10	19 43
52	17 15	17 49	18 28	18 22	18 48	19 19	19 52
50	17 17	17 50	18 27	18 26	18 53	19 25	20 00
45	17 22	17 52	18 26	18 33	19 05	19 39	20 17
N 40	17 27	17 54	18 25	18 40	19 14	19 51	20 32
35	17 31	17 56	18 25	18 45	19 22	20 02	20 44
30	17 34	17 58	18 26	18 50	19 30	20 11	20 54
20	17 40	18 02	18 27	18 59	19 42	20 27	21 12
N 10	17 45	18 06	18 31	19 06	19 53	20 40	21 28
0	17 50	18 11	18 35	19 14	20 03	20 53	21 43
S 10	17 55	18 16	18 41	19 21	20 14	21 06	21 58
20	18 01	18 23	18 49	19 28	20 25	21 20	22 14
30	18 07	18 32	19 00	19 37	20 37	21 36	22 32
35	18 11	18 37	19 07	19 42	20 44	21 45	22 43
40	18 15	18 43	19 16	19 48	20 53	21 56	22 55
45	18 21	18 51	19 27	19 54	21 03	22 08	23 09
S 50	18 27	19 00	19 41	20 02	21 14	22 23	23 27
52	18 29	19 05	19 47	20 06	21 20	22 30	23 35
54	18 33	19 09	19 55	20 10	21 26	22 38	23 45
56	18 36	19 15	20 04	20 15	21 33	22 47	23 55
58	18 40	19 21	20 14	20 20	21 40	22 57	24 07
S 60	18 44	19 29	20 26	20 25	21 49	23 09	24 21

	SUN Eqn. of Time 00ʰ	12ʰ	Mer. Pass.	MOON Mer. Pass. Upper	Lower	Age	Phase
Day							
d	m s	m s	h m	h m	h m	d	%
10	12 52	13 00	11 47	13 02	00 37	01	2
11	13 08	13 15	11 47	13 51	01 27	02	7
12	13 23	13 31	11 46	14 41	02 16	03	13

UT	ARIES GHA	VENUS −4.5 GHA	Dec	MARS −1.0 GHA	Dec	JUPITER −1.8 GHA	Dec	SATURN +0.5 GHA	Dec	STARS Name	SHA	Dec
13 00	21 30.3	166 37.8	S21 48.2	66 55.7	S20 31.0	149 16.9	S18 09.4	107 35.3	S22 46.1	Acamar	315 15.2	S40 13.8
01	36 32.7	181 41.0	47.9	81 57.0	30.5	164 18.8	09.5	122 37.6	46.1	Achernar	335 23.5	S57 08.6
02	51 35.2	196 44.2	47.7	96 58.3	30.1	179 20.8	09.7	137 39.9	46.1	Acrux	173 05.9	S63 11.9
03	66 37.7	211 47.4 ..	47.5	111 59.6 ..	29.6	194 22.8 ..	09.8	152 42.2 ..	46.1	Adhara	255 09.7	S28 59.7
04	81 40.1	226 50.6	47.2	127 00.9	29.1	209 24.7	09.9	167 44.5	46.1	Aldebaran	290 45.0	N16 32.7
05	96 42.6	241 53.8	47.0	142 02.2	28.7	224 26.7	10.0	182 46.8	46.1			
06	111 45.1	256 57.0	S21 46.7	157 03.4	S20 28.2	239 28.6	S18 10.2	197 49.1	S22 46.1	Alioth	166 18.1	N55 51.6
S 07	126 47.5	272 00.2	46.5	172 04.7	27.8	254 30.6	10.3	212 51.4	46.1	Alkaid	152 56.6	N49 13.4
A 08	141 50.0	287 03.4	46.2	187 06.0	27.3	269 32.5	10.4	227 53.8	46.1	Al Na'ir	27 39.0	S46 52.3
T 09	156 52.5	302 06.6 ..	46.0	202 07.3 ..	26.8	284 34.5 ..	10.5	242 56.1 ..	46.1	Alnilam	275 42.6	S 1 11.4
U 10	171 54.9	317 09.9	45.7	217 08.5	26.4	299 36.4	10.7	257 58.4	46.1	Alphard	217 52.7	S 8 44.2
R 11	186 57.4	332 13.1	45.4	232 09.8	25.9	314 38.4	10.8	273 00.7	46.1			
D 12	201 59.8	347 16.3	S21 45.2	247 11.1	S20 25.5	329 40.3	S18 10.9	288 03.0	S22 46.1	Alphecca	126 08.3	N26 39.5
A 13	217 02.3	2 19.5	44.9	262 12.4	25.0	344 42.3	11.1	303 05.3	46.1	Alpheratz	357 39.4	N29 11.7
Y 14	232 04.8	17 22.8	44.6	277 13.7	24.5	359 44.2	11.2	318 07.6	46.1	Altair	62 04.7	N 8 55.3
15	247 07.2	32 26.0 ..	44.4	292 14.9 ..	24.1	14 46.2 ..	11.3	333 09.9 ..	46.1	Ankaa	353 11.8	S42 12.3
16	262 09.7	47 29.2	44.1	307 16.2	23.6	29 48.1	11.4	348 12.2	46.1	Antares	112 22.1	S26 28.2
17	277 12.2	62 32.5	43.8	322 17.5	23.1	44 50.1	11.6	3 14.5	46.1			
18	292 14.6	77 35.7	S21 43.6	337 18.8	S20 22.7	59 52.0	S18 11.7	18 16.8	S22 46.1	Arcturus	145 52.8	N19 05.4
19	307 17.1	92 39.0	43.3	352 20.0	22.2	74 54.0	11.8	33 19.1	46.2	Atria	107 21.0	S69 03.6
20	322 19.6	107 42.2	43.0	7 21.3	21.8	89 55.9	11.9	48 21.4	46.2	Avior	234 16.7	S59 33.9
21	337 22.0	122 45.5 ..	42.7	22 22.6 ..	21.3	104 57.9 ..	12.1	63 23.7 ..	46.2	Bellatrix	278 28.0	N 6 21.9
22	352 24.5	137 48.7	42.4	37 23.8	20.8	119 59.9	12.2	78 26.0	46.2	Betelgeuse	270 57.3	N 7 24.6
23	7 27.0	152 52.0	42.1	52 25.1	20.4	135 01.8	12.3	93 28.3	46.2			
14 00	22 29.4	167 55.3	S21 41.8	67 26.4	S20 19.9	150 03.8	S18 12.5	108 30.7	S22 46.2	Canopus	263 54.4	S52 42.1
01	37 31.9	182 58.5	41.5	82 27.7	19.4	165 05.7	12.6	123 33.0	46.2	Capella	280 28.9	N46 00.7
02	52 34.3	198 01.8	41.2	97 28.9	19.0	180 07.7	12.7	138 35.3	46.2	Deneb	49 28.9	N45 21.2
03	67 36.8	213 05.1 ..	40.9	112 30.2 ..	18.5	195 09.6 ..	12.8	153 37.6 ..	46.2	Denebola	182 30.3	N14 28.2
04	82 39.3	228 08.4	40.6	127 31.5	18.0	210 11.6	13.0	168 39.9	46.2	Diphda	348 52.0	S17 53.0
05	97 41.7	243 11.7	40.3	142 32.7	17.6	225 13.5	13.1	183 42.2	46.2			
06	112 44.2	258 15.0	S21 40.0	157 34.0	S20 17.1	240 15.5	S18 13.2	198 44.5	S22 46.2	Dubhe	193 47.9	N61 38.9
07	127 46.7	273 18.2	39.7	172 35.3	16.6	255 17.4	13.3	213 46.8	46.2	Elnath	278 07.9	N28 37.2
S 08	142 49.1	288 21.5	39.4	187 36.5	16.2	270 19.4	13.5	228 49.1	46.2	Eltanin	90 44.7	N51 29.6
U 09	157 51.6	303 24.8 ..	39.1	202 37.8 ..	15.7	285 21.3 ..	13.6	243 51.4 ..	46.2	Enif	33 43.4	N 9 57.8
N 10	172 54.1	318 28.1	38.8	217 39.1	15.2	300 23.3	13.7	258 53.7	46.2	Fomalhaut	15 19.7	S29 31.4
D 11	187 56.5	333 31.4	38.5	232 40.3	14.8	315 25.2	13.9	273 56.0	46.2			
A 12	202 59.0	348 34.8	S21 38.1	247 41.6	S20 14.3	330 27.2	S18 14.0	288 58.3	S22 46.2	Gacrux	171 57.4	S57 12.8
Y 13	218 01.5	3 38.1	37.8	262 42.9	13.8	345 29.1	14.1	304 00.6	46.2	Gienah	175 48.9	S17 38.5
14	233 03.9	18 41.4	37.5	277 44.1	13.4	0 31.1	14.2	319 02.9	46.2	Hadar	148 43.4	S60 27.6
15	248 06.4	33 44.7 ..	37.2	292 45.4 ..	12.9	15 33.0 ..	14.4	334 05.2 ..	46.2	Hamal	327 56.3	N23 33.0
16	263 08.8	48 48.0	36.8	307 46.6	12.4	30 35.0	14.5	349 07.5	46.2	Kaus Aust.	83 39.2	S34 22.4
17	278 11.3	63 51.4	36.5	322 47.9	12.0	45 36.9	14.6	4 09.8	46.2			
18	293 13.8	78 54.7	S21 36.1	337 49.2	S20 11.5	60 38.9	S18 14.7	19 12.1	S22 46.2	Kochab	137 21.2	N74 05.0
19	308 16.2	93 58.0	35.8	352 50.4	11.0	75 40.8	14.9	34 14.4	46.2	Markab	13 34.5	N15 18.5
20	323 18.7	109 01.4	35.5	7 51.7	10.5	90 42.8	15.0	49 16.7	46.2	Menkar	314 11.0	N 4 09.7
21	338 21.2	124 04.7 ..	35.1	22 52.9 ..	10.1	105 44.7 ..	15.1	64 19.0 ..	46.2	Menkent	148 03.7	S36 27.5
22	353 23.6	139 08.0	34.8	37 54.2	09.6	120 46.7	15.3	79 21.3	46.2	Miaplacidus	221 39.3	S69 47.3
23	8 26.1	154 11.4	34.4	52 55.5	09.1	135 48.6	15.4	94 23.6	46.2			
15 00	23 28.6	169 14.7	S21 34.1	67 56.7	S20 08.7	150 50.6	S18 15.5	109 25.9	S22 46.2	Mirfak	308 34.7	N49 55.4
01	38 31.0	184 18.1	33.7	82 58.0	08.2	165 52.5	15.6	124 28.2	46.2	Nunki	75 53.9	S26 16.3
02	53 33.5	199 21.4	33.4	97 59.2	07.7	180 54.4	15.8	139 30.5	46.2	Peacock	53 13.5	S56 40.6
03	68 36.0	214 24.8 ..	33.0	113 00.5 ..	07.3	195 56.4 ..	15.9	154 32.8 ..	46.2	Pollux	243 23.4	N27 58.7
04	83 38.4	229 28.2	32.6	128 01.7	06.8	210 58.3	16.0	169 35.1	46.2	Procyon	244 56.0	N 5 10.6
05	98 40.9	244 31.5	32.3	143 03.0	06.3	226 00.3	16.2	184 37.4	46.2			
06	113 43.3	259 34.9	S21 31.9	158 04.3	S20 05.8	241 02.2	S18 16.3	199 39.7	S22 46.2	Rasalhague	96 03.3	N12 33.1
07	128 45.8	274 38.3	31.5	173 05.5	05.4	256 04.2	16.4	214 42.0	46.2	Regulus	207 39.9	N11 52.6
08	143 48.3	289 41.7	31.2	188 06.8	04.9	271 06.1	16.5	229 44.3	46.2	Rigel	281 08.4	S 8 10.8
M 09	158 50.7	304 45.0 ..	30.8	203 08.0 ..	04.4	286 08.1 ..	16.7	244 46.6 ..	46.2	Rigil Kent.	139 47.5	S60 54.6
O 10	173 53.2	319 48.4	30.4	218 09.3	03.9	301 10.0	16.8	259 48.9	46.2	Sabik	102 08.6	S15 44.7
N 11	188 55.7	334 51.8	30.0	233 10.5	03.5	316 12.0	16.9	274 51.2	46.2			
D 12	203 58.1	349 55.2	S21 29.6	248 11.8	S20 03.0	331 13.9	S18 17.0	289 53.5	S22 46.2	Schedar	349 35.8	N56 38.4
A 13	219 00.6	4 58.6	29.3	263 13.0	02.5	346 15.9	17.2	304 55.8	46.2	Shaula	96 17.2	S37 06.9
Y 14	234 03.1	20 02.0	28.9	278 14.3	02.0	1 17.8	17.3	319 58.1	46.2	Sirius	258 30.5	S16 44.4
15	249 05.5	35 05.4 ..	28.5	293 15.5 ..	01.6	16 19.8 ..	17.4	335 00.4 ..	46.2	Spica	158 27.8	S11 15.3
16	264 08.0	50 08.8	28.1	308 16.8	01.1	31 21.7	17.6	350 02.7	46.2	Suhail	222 50.0	S43 30.2
17	279 10.4	65 12.2	27.7	323 18.0	00.6	46 23.7	17.7	5 05.0	46.2			
18	294 12.9	80 15.6	S21 27.3	338 19.3	S20 00.1	61 25.6	S18 17.8	20 07.3	S22 46.2	Vega	80 36.6	N38 48.5
19	309 15.4	95 19.0	26.9	353 20.5	19 59.7	76 27.6	17.9	35 09.6	46.2	Zuben'ubi	137 01.7	S16 06.9
20	324 17.8	110 22.4	26.5	8 21.8	59.2	91 29.5	18.1	50 11.9	46.2		SHA	Mer. Pass.
21	339 20.3	125 25.8 ..	26.1	23 23.0 ..	58.7	106 31.4 ..	18.2	65 14.2 ..	46.2		° ′	h m
22	354 22.8	140 29.3	25.7	38 24.3	58.2	121 33.4	18.3	80 16.5	46.2	Venus	145 25.9	12 46
23	9 25.2	155 32.7	25.3	53 25.5	57.8	136 35.3	18.4	95 18.8	46.2	Mars	44 57.0	19 29
	h m									Jupiter	127 34.3	13 58
Mer. Pass. 22 26.4		v 3.3	d 0.3	v 1.3	d 0.5	v 1.9	d 0.1	v 2.3	d 0.0	Saturn	86 01.2	16 43

UT	SUN GHA	SUN Dec	MOON GHA	v	MOON Dec	d	HP
d h	° ′	° ′	° ′	′	° ′	′	′
13 00	183 24.6	S 7 40.1	135 01.8	10.8	S17 30.0	6.6	56.1
01	198 24.7	41.0	149 31.6	10.8	17 36.6	6.5	56.1
02	213 24.9	42.0	164 01.4	10.9	17 43.1	6.4	56.1
03	228 25.0	.. 42.9	178 31.3	10.8	17 49.5	6.3	56.0
04	243 25.2	43.8	193 01.1	10.8	17 55.8	6.2	56.0
05	258 25.3	44.8	207 30.9	10.8	18 02.0	6.1	56.0
06	273 25.5	S 7 45.7	222 00.7	10.9	S18 08.1	6.0	56.0
07	288 25.6	46.6	236 30.6	10.8	18 14.1	6.0	55.9
08	303 25.8	47.6	251 00.4	10.8	18 20.1	5.8	55.9
09	318 25.9	.. 48.5	265 30.2	10.8	18 25.9	5.7	55.9
10	333 26.1	49.4	280 00.0	10.8	18 31.6	5.6	55.8
11	348 26.2	50.4	294 29.8	10.8	18 37.2	5.5	55.8
12	3 26.4	S 7 51.3	308 59.6	10.9	S18 42.7	5.5	55.8
13	18 26.5	52.2	323 29.5	10.8	18 48.2	5.3	55.8
14	33 26.7	53.2	337 59.3	10.8	18 53.5	5.2	55.7
15	48 26.8	.. 54.1	352 29.1	10.8	18 58.7	5.1	55.7
16	63 27.0	55.0	6 58.9	10.8	19 03.8	5.0	55.7
17	78 27.1	56.0	21 28.7	10.8	19 08.8	5.0	55.6
18	93 27.3	S 7 56.9	35 58.5	10.9	S19 13.8	4.8	55.6
19	108 27.4	57.8	50 28.4	10.8	19 18.6	4.7	55.6
20	123 27.6	58.8	64 58.2	10.8	19 23.3	4.6	55.6
21	138 27.7	7 59.7	79 28.0	10.8	19 27.9	4.5	55.5
22	153 27.9	8 00.6	93 57.8	10.9	19 32.4	4.4	55.5
23	168 28.0	01.6	108 27.7	10.8	19 36.8	4.3	55.5
14 00	183 28.2	S 8 02.5	122 57.5	10.8	S19 41.1	4.2	55.5
01	198 28.3	03.4	137 27.3	10.9	19 45.3	4.2	55.4
02	213 28.4	04.4	151 57.2	10.8	19 49.5	4.0	55.4
03	228 28.6	.. 05.3	166 27.0	10.9	19 53.5	3.9	55.4
04	243 28.7	06.2	180 56.9	10.8	19 57.4	3.8	55.4
05	258 28.9	07.2	195 26.7	10.9	20 01.2	3.6	55.3
06	273 29.0	S 8 08.1	209 56.6	10.8	S20 04.8	3.6	55.3
07	288 29.2	09.0	224 26.4	10.9	20 08.4	3.5	55.3
08	303 29.3	09.9	238 56.3	10.9	20 11.9	3.4	55.3
09	318 29.5	.. 10.9	253 26.2	10.9	20 15.3	3.3	55.2
10	333 29.6	11.8	267 56.1	10.9	20 18.6	3.2	55.2
11	348 29.8	12.7	282 26.0	10.9	20 21.8	3.0	55.2
12	3 29.9	S 8 13.7	296 55.9	10.9	S20 24.8	3.0	55.2
13	18 30.1	14.6	311 25.8	10.9	20 27.8	2.9	55.2
14	33 30.2	15.5	325 55.7	10.9	20 30.7	2.7	55.1
15	48 30.3	.. 16.4	340 25.6	10.9	20 33.4	2.7	55.1
16	63 30.5	17.4	354 55.5	11.0	20 36.1	2.6	55.1
17	78 30.6	18.3	9 25.5	10.9	20 38.7	2.4	55.1
18	93 30.8	S 8 19.2	23 55.4	11.0	S20 41.1	2.4	55.0
19	108 30.9	20.2	38 25.4	10.9	20 43.5	2.2	55.0
20	123 31.0	21.1	52 55.3	11.0	20 45.7	2.2	55.0
21	138 31.2	.. 22.0	67 25.3	11.0	20 47.9	2.0	55.0
22	153 31.3	22.9	81 55.3	11.0	20 49.9	1.9	55.0
23	168 31.5	23.9	96 25.3	11.0	20 51.8	1.9	54.9
15 00	183 31.6	S 8 24.8	110 55.3	11.1	S20 53.7	1.7	54.9
01	198 31.8	25.7	125 25.4	11.0	20 55.4	1.6	54.9
02	213 31.9	26.6	139 55.4	11.0	20 57.0	1.6	54.9
03	228 32.0	.. 27.6	154 25.4	11.1	20 58.6	1.4	54.9
04	243 32.2	28.5	168 55.5	11.1	21 00.0	1.3	54.8
05	258 32.3	29.4	183 25.6	11.1	21 01.3	1.2	54.8
06	273 32.5	S 8 30.3	197 55.7	11.1	S21 02.5	1.1	54.8
07	288 32.6	31.3	212 25.8	11.1	21 03.6	1.0	54.8
08	303 32.7	32.2	226 55.9	11.1	21 04.6	1.0	54.8
09	318 32.9	.. 33.1	241 26.0	11.2	21 05.6	0.8	54.8
10	333 33.0	34.0	255 56.2	11.2	21 06.4	0.7	54.7
11	348 33.1	35.0	270 26.4	11.2	21 07.1	0.6	54.7
12	3 33.3	S 8 35.9	284 56.6	11.2	S21 07.7	0.5	54.7
13	18 33.4	36.8	299 26.8	11.2	21 08.2	0.4	54.7
14	33 33.6	37.7	313 57.0	11.2	21 08.6	0.3	54.7
15	48 33.7	.. 38.7	328 27.2	11.3	21 08.9	0.1	54.7
16	63 33.8	39.6	342 57.5	11.2	21 09.0	0.1	54.6
17	78 34.0	40.5	357 27.7	11.3	21 09.1	0.0	54.6
18	93 34.1	S 8 41.4	11 58.0	11.3	S21 09.1	0.1	54.6
19	108 34.3	42.4	26 28.3	11.4	21 09.0	0.2	54.6
20	123 34.4	43.3	40 58.7	11.3	21 08.8	0.3	54.6
21	138 34.5	.. 44.2	55 29.0	11.4	21 08.5	0.4	54.6
22	153 34.7	45.1	69 59.4	11.4	21 08.1	0.5	54.6
23	168 34.8	46.0	84 29.8	11.4	S21 07.6	0.6	54.5
	SD 16.1	d 0.9	SD 15.2		15.0		14.9

Moonrise

Lat.	Twilight Naut.	Twilight Civil	Sunrise	13	14	15	16
°	h m	h m	h m	h m	h m	h m	h m
N 72	04 50	06 09	07 19	▬▬▬	▬▬▬	▬▬▬	▬▬▬
N 70	04 55	06 05	07 08	14 14	▬▬▬	▬▬▬	▬▬▬
68	04 58	06 03	07 00	13 19	14 54	16 05	16 37
66	05 01	06 00	06 52	12 47	14 07	15 10	15 50
64	05 03	05 58	06 46	12 23	13 37	14 37	15 19
62	05 05	05 56	06 41	12 04	13 15	14 13	14 56
60	05 06	05 54	06 37	11 48	12 56	13 53	14 38
N 58	05 07	05 53	06 33	11 35	12 41	13 37	14 23
56	05 08	05 51	06 29	11 24	12 28	13 24	14 10
54	05 09	05 50	06 26	11 14	12 17	13 12	13 58
52	05 10	05 49	06 23	11 05	12 07	13 02	13 48
50	05 10	05 47	06 20	10 57	11 58	12 52	13 39
45	05 11	05 45	06 14	10 41	11 40	12 33	13 20
N 40	05 11	05 42	06 09	10 27	11 24	12 17	13 05
35	05 10	05 39	06 05	10 15	11 11	12 04	12 52
30	05 09	05 37	06 01	10 05	11 00	11 52	12 40
20	05 07	05 32	05 54	09 48	10 41	11 32	12 21
N 10	05 03	05 27	05 48	09 33	10 25	11 15	12 03
0	04 58	05 22	05 43	09 19	10 09	10 59	11 48
S 10	04 51	05 16	05 37	09 05	09 54	10 42	11 32
20	04 42	05 08	05 31	08 50	09 37	10 25	11 15
30	04 30	04 59	05 23	08 33	09 18	10 05	10 55
35	04 23	04 53	05 19	08 24	09 07	09 54	10 44
40	04 13	04 46	05 14	08 12	08 55	09 41	10 30
45	04 02	04 38	05 08	07 59	08 40	09 25	10 15
S 50	03 47	04 28	05 02	07 43	08 22	09 06	09 56
52	03 40	04 23	04 58	07 36	08 13	08 57	09 47
54	03 32	04 18	04 55	07 28	08 04	08 46	09 37
56	03 22	04 12	04 51	07 18	07 53	08 35	09 25
58	03 12	04 05	04 47	07 08	07 41	08 22	09 12
S 60	02 59	03 57	04 42	06 56	07 26	08 06	08 56

Moonset

Lat.	Sunset	Twilight Civil	Twilight Naut.	13	14	15	16
°	h m	h m	h m	h m	h m	h m	h m
N 72	16 11	17 21	18 39	▬▬▬	▬▬▬	▬▬▬	▬▬▬
N 70	16 22	17 25	18 35	16 40	▬▬▬	▬▬▬	▬▬▬
68	16 31	17 28	18 32	17 35	17 44	18 16	19 25
66	16 38	17 30	18 29	18 08	18 31	19 11	20 12
64	16 44	17 33	18 27	18 32	19 01	19 44	20 42
62	16 50	17 35	18 26	18 52	19 24	20 08	21 05
60	16 56	17 36	18 24	19 08	19 43	20 28	21 23
N 58	16 58	17 38	18 23	19 21	19 58	20 44	21 38
56	17 02	17 40	18 22	19 33	20 11	20 57	21 51
54	17 05	17 41	18 22	19 43	20 22	21 09	22 03
52	17 08	17 42	18 21	19 52	20 32	21 19	22 13
50	17 11	17 44	18 21	20 00	20 41	21 29	22 21
45	17 17	17 47	18 21	20 17	21 00	21 48	22 40
N 40	17 22	17 49	18 21	20 32	21 16	22 04	22 55
35	17 27	17 52	18 22	20 44	21 29	22 17	23 08
30	17 31	17 55	18 22	20 54	21 40	22 29	23 19
20	17 37	18 00	18 25	21 12	22 00	22 49	23 39
N 10	17 43	18 05	18 29	21 28	22 17	23 06	23 55
0	17 49	18 10	18 34	21 43	22 33	23 22	24 11
S 10	17 55	18 17	18 41	21 58	22 49	23 38	24 26
20	18 02	18 24	18 50	22 14	23 06	23 56	24 43
30	18 09	18 34	19 02	22 32	23 26	24 16	00 16
35	18 14	18 39	19 10	22 43	23 37	24 27	00 27
40	18 19	18 46	19 20	22 55	23 50	24 40	00 40
45	18 24	18 55	19 31	23 09	24 06	00 06	00 56
S 50	18 31	19 05	19 46	23 27	24 25	00 25	01 15
52	18 35	19 10	19 54	23 35	24 34	00 34	01 24
54	18 38	19 16	20 02	23 44	24 44	00 44	01 35
56	18 42	19 22	20 12	23 55	24 55	00 55	01 46
58	18 47	19 29	20 23	24 07	00 07	01 09	01 59
S 60	18 52	19 37	20 36	24 21	00 21	01 24	02 15

Day	SUN Eqn. of Time 00h	SUN Eqn. of Time 12h	SUN Mer. Pass.	MOON Mer. Pass. Upper	MOON Mer. Pass. Lower	Age	Phase
d	m s	m s	h m	h m	h m	d	%
13	13 38	13 45	11 46	15 31	03 06	04	21
14	13 52	13 59	11 46	16 21	03 56	05	29
15	14 06	14 13	11 46	17 10	04 46	06	38

2018 OCTOBER 16, 17, 18 (TUES., WED., THURS.)

UT	ARIES	VENUS −4·3		MARS −0·9		JUPITER −1·8		SATURN +0·5		STARS		
	GHA	GHA	Dec	GHA	Dec	GHA	Dec	GHA	Dec	Name	SHA	Dec
d h	° ′	° ′	° ′	° ′	° ′	° ′	° ′	° ′	° ′		° ′	° ′
16 00	24 27.7	170 36.1	S21 24.9	68 26.8	S19 57.3	151 37.3	S18 18.6	110 21.1	S22 46.2	Acamar	315 15.2	S40 13.8
01	39 30.2	185 39.5	24.4	83 28.0	56.8	166 39.2	18.7	125 23.4	46.2	Achernar	335 23.5	S57 08.6
02	54 32.6	200 43.0	24.0	98 29.2	56.3	181 41.2	18.8	140 25.7	46.2	Acrux	173 05.9	S63 11.9
03	69 35.1	215 46.4	.. 23.6	113 30.5	.. 55.9	196 43.1	.. 19.0	155 28.0	.. 46.2	Adhara	255 09.6	S28 59.7
04	84 37.6	230 49.9	23.2	128 31.7	55.4	211 45.1	19.1	170 30.3	46.2	Aldebaran	290 45.0	N16 32.7
05	99 40.0	245 53.3	22.8	143 33.0	54.9	226 47.0	19.2	185 32.6	46.2			
T 06	114 42.5	260 56.7	S21 22.3	158 34.2	S19 54.4	241 49.0	S18 19.3	200 34.9	S22 46.2	Alioth	166 18.1	N55 51.6
U 07	129 44.9	276 00.2	21.9	173 35.5	53.9	256 50.9	19.5	215 37.2	46.2	Alkaid	152 56.6	N49 13.4
E 08	144 47.4	291 03.6	21.5	188 36.7	53.5	271 52.8	19.6	230 39.5	46.2	Al Na'ir	27 39.0	S46 52.3
S 09	159 49.9	306 07.1	.. 21.0	203 37.9	.. 53.0	286 54.8	.. 19.7	245 41.8	.. 46.2	Alnilam	275 42.5	S 1 11.4
D 10	174 52.3	321 10.6	20.6	218 39.2	52.5	301 56.7	19.8	260 44.1	46.2	Alphard	217 52.7	S 8 44.2
A 11	189 54.8	336 14.0	20.2	233 40.4	52.0	316 58.7	20.0	275 46.4	46.2			
Y 12	204 57.3	351 17.5	S21 19.7	248 41.7	S19 51.6	332 00.6	S18 20.1	290 48.7	S22 46.2	Alphecca	126 08.3	N26 39.4
13	219 59.7	6 21.0	19.3	263 42.9	51.1	347 02.6	20.2	305 51.0	46.2	Alpheratz	357 39.4	N29 11.7
14	235 02.2	21 24.4	18.8	278 44.1	50.6	2 04.5	20.4	320 53.3	46.2	Altair	62 04.7	N 8 55.3
15	250 04.7	36 27.9	.. 18.4	293 45.4	.. 50.1	17 06.5	.. 20.5	335 55.6	.. 46.2	Ankaa	353 11.7	S42 12.3
16	265 07.1	51 31.4	17.9	308 46.6	49.6	32 08.4	20.6	350 57.9	46.2	Antares	112 22.1	S26 28.2
17	280 09.6	66 34.9	17.5	323 47.9	49.2	47 10.3	20.7	6 00.2	46.2			
18	295 12.1	81 38.3	S21 17.0	338 49.1	S19 48.7	62 12.3	S18 20.9	21 02.5	S22 46.2	Arcturus	145 52.8	N19 05.4
19	310 14.5	96 41.8	16.5	353 50.3	48.2	77 14.2	21.0	36 04.7	46.2	Atria	107 21.0	S69 03.6
20	325 17.0	111 45.3	16.1	8 51.6	47.7	92 16.2	21.1	51 07.0	46.2	Avior	234 16.6	S59 33.9
21	340 19.4	126 48.8	.. 15.6	23 52.8	.. 47.2	107 18.1	.. 21.2	66 09.3	.. 46.2	Bellatrix	278 28.0	N 6 21.9
22	355 21.9	141 52.3	15.1	38 54.0	46.7	122 20.1	21.4	81 11.6	46.2	Betelgeuse	270 57.3	N 7 24.6
23	10 24.4	156 55.8	14.7	53 55.3	46.3	137 22.0	21.5	96 13.9	46.2			
17 00	25 26.8	171 59.3	S21 14.2	68 56.5	S19 45.8	152 23.9	S18 21.6	111 16.2	S22 46.2	Canopus	263 54.4	S52 42.1
01	40 29.3	187 02.8	13.7	83 57.7	45.3	167 25.9	21.8	126 18.5	46.2	Capella	280 28.8	N46 00.7
02	55 31.8	202 06.3	13.2	98 59.0	44.8	182 27.8	21.9	141 20.8	46.2	Deneb	49 28.9	N45 21.2
03	70 34.2	217 09.8	.. 12.8	114 00.2	.. 44.3	197 29.8	.. 22.0	156 23.1	.. 46.2	Denebola	182 30.3	N14 28.2
04	85 36.7	232 13.3	12.3	129 01.4	43.8	212 31.7	22.1	171 25.4	46.2	Diphda	348 52.0	S17 53.1
05	100 39.2	247 16.8	11.8	144 02.7	43.4	227 33.7	22.3	186 27.7	46.2			
W 06	115 41.6	262 20.4	S21 11.3	159 03.9	S19 42.9	242 35.6	S18 22.4	201 30.0	S22 46.2	Dubhe	193 47.9	N61 38.9
E 07	130 44.1	277 23.9	10.8	174 05.1	42.4	257 37.5	22.5	216 32.3	46.2	Elnath	278 07.9	N28 37.2
D 08	145 46.6	292 27.4	10.3	189 06.3	41.9	272 39.5	22.6	231 34.6	46.2	Eltanin	90 44.7	N51 29.6
N 09	160 49.0	307 30.9	.. 09.8	204 07.6	.. 41.4	287 41.4	.. 22.8	246 36.9	.. 46.2	Enif	33 43.4	N 9 57.8
E 10	175 51.5	322 34.5	09.3	219 08.8	40.9	302 43.4	22.9	261 39.1	46.2	Fomalhaut	15 19.8	S29 31.4
S 11	190 53.9	337 38.0	08.8	234 10.0	40.5	317 45.3	23.0	276 41.4	46.2			
D 12	205 56.4	352 41.5	S21 08.3	249 11.3	S19 40.0	332 47.3	S18 23.2	291 43.7	S22 46.2	Gacrux	171 57.4	S57 12.8
A 13	220 58.9	7 45.1	07.8	264 12.5	39.5	347 49.2	23.3	306 46.0	46.2	Gienah	175 48.9	S17 38.5
Y 14	236 01.3	22 48.6	07.3	279 13.7	39.0	2 51.1	23.4	321 48.3	46.2	Hadar	148 43.4	S60 27.6
15	251 03.8	37 52.1	.. 06.8	294 14.9	.. 38.5	17 53.1	.. 23.5	336 50.6	.. 46.3	Hamal	327 56.3	N23 33.0
16	266 06.3	52 55.7	06.3	309 16.2	38.0	32 55.0	23.7	351 52.9	46.3	Kaus Aust.	83 39.2	S34 22.4
17	281 08.7	67 59.2	05.8	324 17.4	37.5	47 57.0	23.8	6 55.2	46.3			
18	296 11.2	83 02.8	S21 05.3	339 18.6	S19 37.1	62 58.9	S18 23.9	21 57.5	S22 46.2	Kochab	137 21.3	N74 05.0
19	311 13.7	98 06.3	04.7	354 19.8	36.6	78 00.8	24.0	36 59.8	46.3	Markab	13 34.5	N15 18.5
20	326 16.1	113 09.9	04.2	9 21.1	36.1	93 02.8	24.2	52 02.1	46.3	Menkar	314 11.0	N 4 09.7
21	341 18.6	128 13.5	.. 03.7	24 22.3	.. 35.6	108 04.7	.. 24.3	67 04.4	.. 46.3	Menkent	148 03.7	S36 27.5
22	356 21.0	143 17.0	03.2	39 23.5	35.1	123 06.7	24.4	82 06.6	46.3	Miaplacidus	221 39.3	S69 47.3
23	11 23.5	158 20.6	02.6	54 24.7	34.6	138 08.6	24.6	97 08.9	46.3			
18 00	26 26.0	173 24.1	S21 02.1	69 26.0	S19 34.1	153 10.6	S18 24.7	112 11.2	S22 46.3	Mirfak	308 34.7	N49 55.4
01	41 28.4	188 27.7	01.6	84 27.2	33.6	168 12.5	24.8	127 13.5	46.3	Nunki	75 53.9	S26 16.3
02	56 30.9	203 31.3	01.0	99 28.4	33.2	183 14.4	24.9	142 15.8	46.3	Peacock	53 13.5	S56 40.6
03	71 33.4	218 34.9	21 00.5	114 29.6	.. 32.7	198 16.4	.. 25.1	157 18.1	.. 46.3	Pollux	243 23.4	N27 58.7
04	86 35.8	233 38.4	20 59.9	129 30.8	32.2	213 18.3	25.2	172 20.4	46.3	Procyon	244 56.0	N 5 10.6
05	101 38.3	248 42.0	59.4	144 32.1	31.7	228 20.3	25.3	187 22.7	46.3			
T 06	116 40.8	263 45.6	S20 58.8	159 33.3	S19 31.2	243 22.2	S18 25.4	202 25.0	S22 46.3	Rasalhague	96 03.3	N12 33.1
H 07	131 43.2	278 49.2	58.3	174 34.5	30.7	258 24.1	25.6	217 27.3	46.3	Regulus	207 39.9	N11 52.6
U 08	146 45.7	293 52.8	57.7	189 35.7	30.2	273 26.1	25.7	232 29.5	46.3	Rigel	281 08.4	S 8 10.8
R 09	161 48.2	308 56.4	.. 57.2	204 36.9	.. 29.7	288 28.0	.. 25.8	247 31.8	.. 46.3	Rigil Kent.	139 47.5	S60 54.5
S 10	176 50.6	324 00.0	56.6	219 38.2	29.2	303 30.0	26.0	262 34.1	46.3	Sabik	102 08.6	S15 44.7
D 11	191 53.1	339 03.6	56.1	234 39.4	28.7	318 31.9	26.1	277 36.4	46.3			
A 12	206 55.5	354 07.2	S20 55.5	249 40.6	S19 28.3	333 33.8	S18 26.2	292 38.7	S22 46.3	Schedar	349 35.8	N56 38.4
Y 13	221 58.0	9 10.8	54.9	264 41.8	27.8	348 35.8	26.3	307 41.0	46.3	Shaula	96 17.2	S37 06.9
14	237 00.5	24 14.4	54.4	279 43.0	27.3	3 37.7	26.5	322 43.3	46.3	Sirius	258 30.5	S16 44.4
15	252 02.9	39 18.0	.. 53.8	294 44.2	.. 26.8	18 39.6	.. 26.6	337 45.6	.. 46.3	Spica	158 27.8	S11 15.3
16	267 05.4	54 21.6	53.2	309 45.5	26.3	33 41.6	26.7	352 47.9	46.3	Suhail	222 49.9	S43 30.2
17	282 07.9	69 25.2	52.7	324 46.7	25.8	48 43.5	26.8	7 50.1	46.3			
18	297 10.3	84 28.8	S20 52.1	339 47.9	S19 25.3	63 45.5	S18 27.0	22 52.4	S22 46.3	Vega	80 36.6	N38 48.5
19	312 12.8	99 32.4	51.5	354 49.0	24.8	78 47.4	27.1	37 54.7	46.3	Zuben'ubi	137 01.7	S16 06.9
20	327 15.3	114 36.0	50.9	9 50.3	24.3	93 49.3	27.2	52 57.0	46.3		SHA	Mer.Pass.
21	342 17.7	129 39.6	.. 50.3	24 51.5	.. 23.8	108 51.3	.. 27.4	67 59.3	.. 46.3		° ′	h m
22	357 20.2	144 43.3	49.7	39 52.7	23.3	123 53.2	27.5	83 01.6	46.3	Venus	146 32.5	12 29
23	12 22.7	159 46.9	49.2	54 53.9	22.8	138 55.2	27.6	98 03.9	46.3	Mars	43 29.7	19 23
	h m									Jupiter	126 57.1	13 49
Mer. Pass. 22 14.6		v 3.5	d 0.5	v 1.2	d 0.5	v 1.9	d 0.1	v 2.3	d 0.0	Saturn	85 49.4	16 32

UT	SUN		MOON					Lat.	Twilight		Sunrise	Moonrise			
									Naut.	Civil		16	17	18	19
	GHA	Dec	GHA	v	Dec	d	HP								
d h	° ′	° ′	° ′	′	° ′	′	′	N °	h m	h m	h m	h m	h m	h m	h m
16 00	183 34.9	S 8 47.0	99 00.2	11.4	S21 07.0	0.8	54.5	N 72	05 04	06 22	07 34	■■■	■■■	18 14	17 37
01	198 35.1	47.9	113 30.6	11.5	21 06.2	0.8	54.5	N 70	05 06	06 17	07 21		17 44	17 21	17 09
02	213 35.2	48.8	128 01.1	11.4	21 05.4	0.9	54.5	68	05 09	06 13	07 11	16 37	16 46	16 49	16 48
03	228 35.3	.. 49.7	142 31.5	11.5	21 04.5	1.0	54.5	66	05 10	06 10	07 02	15 50	16 12	16 24	16 32
04	243 35.5	50.6	157 02.0	11.5	21 03.5	1.1	54.5	64	05 12	06 07	06 55	15 19	15 47	16 06	16 18
05	258 35.6	51.6	171 32.5	11.6	21 02.4	1.2	54.5	62	05 13	06 04	06 49	14 56	15 28	15 50	16 06
06	273 35.7	S 8 52.5	186 03.1	11.5	S21 01.2	1.3	54.5	60	05 13	06 01	06 44	14 38	15 12	15 37	15 56
07	288 35.9	53.4	200 33.6	11.6	20 59.9	1.4	54.4	N 58	05 14	05 59	06 39	14 23	14 58	15 26	15 48
08	303 36.0	54.3	215 04.2	11.6	20 58.5	1.5	54.4	56	05 14	05 57	06 35	14 10	14 47	15 16	15 40
T 09	318 36.1	.. 55.2	229 34.8	11.7	20 57.0	1.6	54.4	54	05 14	05 55	06 31	13 58	14 36	15 07	15 33
U 10	333 36.3	56.2	244 05.5	11.6	20 55.4	1.7	54.4	52	05 15	05 54	06 28	13 48	14 27	15 00	15 27
E 11	348 36.4	57.1	258 36.1	11.7	20 53.7	1.8	54.4	50	05 15	05 52	06 25	13 39	14 19	14 53	15 21
S 12	3 36.5	S 8 58.0	273 06.8	11.7	S20 51.9	1.9	54.4	45	05 14	05 48	06 18	13 20	14 02	14 38	15 09
D 13	18 36.7	58.9	287 37.5	11.7	20 50.0	2.0	54.4	N 40	05 14	05 45	06 12	13 05	13 47	14 25	14 59
A 14	33 36.8	8 59.8	302 08.2	11.8	20 48.0	2.1	54.4	35	05 12	05 42	06 07	12 52	13 35	14 15	14 51
Y 15	48 36.9	9 00.8	316 39.0	11.8	20 45.9	2.2	54.4	30	05 11	05 39	06 03	12 40	13 24	14 05	14 43
16	63 37.1	01.7	331 09.8	11.8	20 43.7	2.3	54.4	20	05 07	05 33	05 55	12 21	13 06	13 49	14 30
17	78 37.2	02.6	345 40.6	11.8	20 41.4	2.4	54.3	N 10	05 03	05 27	05 49	12 03	12 50	13 35	14 19
18	93 37.3	S 9 03.5	0 11.4	11.8	S20 39.0	2.4	54.3	0	04 57	05 21	05 42	11 48	12 35	13 22	14 08
19	108 37.5	04.4	14 42.2	11.9	20 36.6	2.6	54.3	S 10	04 49	05 14	05 35	11 32	12 21	13 09	13 57
20	123 37.6	05.3	29 13.1	11.9	20 34.0	2.7	54.3	20	04 40	05 06	05 28	11 15	12 05	12 55	13 45
21	138 37.7	.. 06.3	43 44.0	12.0	20 31.3	2.7	54.3	30	04 27	04 56	05 20	10 55	11 46	12 39	13 32
22	153 37.9	07.2	58 15.0	11.9	20 28.6	2.9	54.3	35	04 18	04 49	05 15	10 44	11 36	12 29	13 25
23	168 38.0	08.1	72 45.9	12.0	20 25.7	2.9	54.3	40	04 08	04 42	05 10	10 30	11 23	12 19	13 16
17 00	183 38.1	S 9 09.0	87 16.9	12.0	S20 22.8	3.0	54.3	45	03 56	04 33	05 03	10 15	11 09	12 06	13 05
01	198 38.2	09.9	101 47.9	12.1	20 19.8	3.2	54.3	S 50	03 40	04 21	04 55	09 56	10 51	11 51	12 53
02	213 38.4	10.8	116 19.0	12.0	20 16.6	3.2	54.3	52	03 32	04 16	04 52	09 47	10 43	11 43	12 47
03	228 38.5	.. 11.8	130 50.0	12.1	20 13.4	3.3	54.3	54	03 23	04 10	04 48	09 37	10 33	11 35	12 41
04	243 38.6	12.7	145 21.1	12.1	20 10.1	3.4	54.3	56	03 13	04 04	04 43	09 25	10 23	11 26	12 34
05	258 38.8	13.6	159 52.2	12.2	20 06.7	3.5	54.3	58	03 01	03 56	04 39	09 12	10 11	11 16	12 25
06	273 38.9	S 9 14.5	174 23.4	12.2	S20 03.2	3.6	54.3	S 60	02 47	03 47	04 33	08 56	09 57	11 04	12 16

UT	SUN		MOON					Lat.	Sunset	Twilight		Moonset			
	GHA	Dec	GHA	v	Dec	d	HP			Civil	Naut.	16	17	18	19
d h	° ′	° ′	° ′	′	° ′	′	′	N °	h m	h m	h m	h m	h m	h m	h m
W 07	288 39.0	15.4	188 54.6	12.2	19 59.6	3.7	54.3	N 72	15 55	17 07	18 25	■■■	■■■	21 05	23 16
E 08	303 39.1	16.3	203 25.8	12.2	19 55.9	3.8	54.3	N 70	16 08	17 12	18 22	■■■	19 58	21 57	23 43
D 09	318 39.3	.. 17.2	217 57.0	12.3	19 52.1	3.8	54.3	68	16 18	17 16	18 20	19 25	20 55	22 29	24 03
N 10	333 39.4	18.2	232 28.3	12.2	19 48.3	4.0	54.3	66	16 27	17 20	18 19	20 12	21 28	22 52	24 19
E 11	348 39.5	19.1	246 59.5	12.4	19 44.3	4.0	54.3	64	16 34	17 23	18 18	20 42	21 53	23 10	24 32
S 12	3 39.7	S 9 20.0	261 30.9	12.3	S19 40.3	4.1	54.3	62	16 40	17 26	18 17	21 05	22 12	23 25	24 42
D 13	18 39.8	20.9	276 02.2	12.4	19 36.2	4.3	54.3	60	16 46	17 28	18 16	21 23	22 28	23 38	24 52
A 14	33 39.9	21.8	290 33.6	12.4	19 31.9	4.3	54.2	N 58	16 50	17 30	18 16	21 38	22 41	23 49	25 00
Y 15	48 40.0	.. 22.7	305 05.0	12.4	19 27.6	4.4	54.2	56	16 55	17 32	18 15	21 51	22 52	23 58	25 07
16	63 40.2	23.6	319 36.4	12.5	19 23.2	4.4	54.2	54	16 58	17 34	18 15	22 03	23 02	24 06	00 06
17	78 40.3	24.5	334 07.9	12.4	19 18.8	4.6	54.2	52	17 02	17 36	18 15	22 13	23 11	24 13	00 13
18	93 40.4	S 9 25.5	348 39.3	12.6	S19 14.2	4.7	54.2	50	17 05	17 38	18 15	22 21	23 19	24 20	00 20
19	108 40.5	26.4	3 10.9	12.5	19 09.5	4.7	54.2	45	17 12	17 42	18 16	22 40	23 36	24 34	00 34
20	123 40.7	27.3	17 42.4	12.6	19 04.8	4.9	54.2	N 40	17 18	17 45	18 17	22 55	23 50	24 46	00 46
21	138 40.8	.. 28.2	32 14.0	12.6	18 59.9	4.9	54.2	35	17 23	17 48	18 18	23 08	24 01	00 01	00 56
22	153 40.9	29.1	46 45.6	12.6	18 55.0	5.0	54.2	30	17 27	17 51	18 19	23 19	24 11	00 11	01 04
23	168 41.0	30.0	61 17.2	12.7	18 50.0	5.1	54.2	20	17 35	17 57	18 23	23 39	24 29	00 29	01 19
18 00	183 41.2	S 9 30.9	75 48.9	12.6	S18 44.9	5.1	54.2	N 10	17 42	18 03	18 28	23 55	24 44	00 44	01 32
01	198 41.3	31.8	90 20.5	12.8	18 39.8	5.3	54.2	0	17 49	18 10	18 34	24 11	00 11	00 58	01 44
02	213 41.4	32.7	104 52.3	12.7	18 34.5	5.3	54.3	S 10	17 55	18 17	18 42	24 26	00 26	01 12	01 56
03	228 41.5	.. 33.6	119 24.0	12.8	18 29.2	5.4	54.3	20	18 03	18 25	18 51	24 43	00 43	01 27	02 09
04	243 41.6	34.6	133 55.8	12.8	18 23.8	5.6	54.3	30	18 11	18 36	19 05	00 16	01 02	01 44	02 24
05	258 41.8	35.5	148 27.6	12.8	18 18.2	5.5	54.3	35	18 16	18 42	19 13	00 27	01 13	01 54	02 32
06	273 41.9	S 9 36.4	162 59.4	12.8	S18 12.7	5.7	54.3	40	18 22	18 50	19 23	00 40	01 25	02 06	02 42
07	288 42.0	37.3	177 31.2	12.9	18 07.0	5.8	54.3	45	18 28	18 59	19 36	00 56	01 40	02 19	02 53
T 08	303 42.1	38.2	192 03.1	12.9	18 01.2	5.8	54.3	S 50	18 36	19 10	19 52	01 15	01 59	02 35	03 06
H 09	318 42.3	.. 39.1	206 35.0	13.0	17 55.4	5.9	54.3	52	18 40	19 16	20 00	01 24	02 07	02 43	03 12
U 10	333 42.4	40.0	221 07.0	12.9	17 49.5	6.0	54.3	54	18 44	19 22	20 09	01 35	02 17	02 51	03 19
R 11	348 42.5	40.9	235 38.9	13.0	17 43.5	6.1	54.3	56	18 49	19 29	20 20	01 46	02 27	03 00	03 27
S 12	3 42.6	S 9 41.8	250 10.9	13.0	S17 37.4	6.1	54.3	58	18 54	19 36	20 32	01 59	02 40	03 11	03 36
D 13	18 42.7	42.7	264 42.9	13.1	17 31.3	6.3	54.3	S 60	18 59	19 45	20 46	02 15	02 54	03 23	03 45
A 14	33 42.9	43.6	279 15.0	13.1	17 25.0	6.3	54.3								
Y 15	48 43.0	.. 44.5	293 47.1	13.1	17 18.7	6.4	54.3								
16	63 43.1	45.4	308 19.2	13.1	17 12.3	6.4	54.3								
17	78 43.2	46.4	322 51.3	13.1	17 05.9	6.6	54.3								

									SUN			MOON			
18	93 43.3	S 9 47.3	337 23.4	13.2	S16 59.3	6.6	54.3								
19	108 43.5	48.2	351 55.6	13.2	16 52.7	6.7	54.3	Day	Eqn. of Time		Mer.	Mer. Pass.		Age	Phase
20	123 43.6	49.1	6 27.8	13.3	16 46.0	6.8	54.3		00ʰ	12ʰ	Pass.	Upper	Lower		
21	138 43.7	.. 50.0	21 00.1	13.2	16 39.2	6.8	54.3	d	m s	m s	h m	h m	h m	d	%
22	153 43.8	50.9	35 32.3	13.3	16 32.4	6.9	54.3	16	14 19	14 26	11 46	17 59	05 35	07	48
23	168 43.9	S 9 51.8	50 04.6	13.3	S16 25.5	7.0	54.4	17	14 32	14 38	11 45	18 47	06 23	08	57
	SD 16.1	d 0.9	SD 14.8		14.8		14.8	18	14 44	14 50	11 45	19 33	07 10	09	66

UT	ARIES GHA	VENUS −4.2 GHA	VENUS Dec	MARS −0.9 GHA	MARS Dec	JUPITER −1.8 GHA	JUPITER Dec	SATURN +0.5 GHA	SATURN Dec	STARS Name	SHA	Dec
d h	° ′	° ′	° ′	° ′	° ′	° ′	° ′	° ′	° ′		° ′	° ′
19 00	27 25.1	174 50.5	S20 48.6	69 55.2	S19 22.3	153 57.1	S18 27.7	113 06.2	S22 46.3	Acamar	315 15.2	S40 13.8
01	42 27.6	189 54.1	48.0	84 56.4	21.9	168 59.0	27.9	128 08.4	46.3	Achernar	335 23.5	S57 08.6
02	57 30.0	204 57.8	47.4	99 57.6	21.4	184 01.0	28.0	143 10.7	46.3	Acrux	173 05.9	S63 11.9
03	72 32.5	220 01.4 ..	46.8	114 58.8 ..	20.9	199 02.9 ..	28.1	158 13.0 ..	46.3	Adhara	255 09.6	S28 59.7
04	87 35.0	235 05.0	46.2	130 00.0	20.4	214 04.8	28.2	173 15.3	46.3	Aldebaran	290 45.0	N16 32.7
05	102 37.4	250 08.7	45.6	145 01.2	19.9	229 06.8	28.4	188 17.6	46.3			
06	117 39.9	265 12.3	S20 45.0	160 02.4	S19 19.4	244 08.7	S18 28.5	203 19.9	S22 46.3	Alioth	166 18.1	N55 51.6
07	132 42.4	280 16.0	44.4	175 03.6	18.9	259 10.7	28.6	218 22.2	46.3	Alkaid	152 56.6	N49 13.4
F 08	147 44.8	295 19.6	43.7	190 04.8	18.4	274 12.6	28.7	233 24.4	46.3	Al Na'ir	27 39.0	S46 52.3
R 09	162 47.3	310 23.3 ..	43.1	205 06.0 ..	17.9	289 14.5 ..	28.9	248 26.7 ..	46.3	Alnilam	275 42.5	S 1 11.4
I 10	177 49.8	325 26.9	42.5	220 07.2	17.4	304 16.5	29.0	263 29.0	46.3	Alphard	217 52.7	S 8 44.3
D 11	192 52.2	340 30.6	41.9	235 08.5	16.9	319 18.4	29.1	278 31.3	46.3			
A 12	207 54.7	355 34.2	S20 41.3	250 09.7	S19 16.4	334 20.3	S18 29.3	293 33.6	S22 46.3	Alphecca	126 08.3	N26 39.4
Y 13	222 57.1	10 37.9	40.6	265 10.9	15.9	349 22.3	29.4	308 35.9	46.3	Alpheratz	357 39.4	N29 11.7
14	237 59.6	25 41.5	40.0	280 12.1	15.4	4 24.2	29.5	323 38.1	46.3	Altair	62 04.7	N 8 55.3
15	253 02.1	40 45.2 ..	39.4	295 13.3 ..	14.9	19 26.1 ..	29.6	338 40.4 ..	46.3	Ankaa	353 11.8	S42 12.3
16	268 04.5	55 48.9	38.8	310 14.5	14.4	34 28.1	29.8	353 42.7	46.3	Antares	112 22.1	S26 28.2
17	283 07.0	70 52.5	38.1	325 15.7	13.9	49 30.0	29.9	8 45.0	46.3			
18	298 09.5	85 56.2	S20 37.5	340 16.9	S19 13.4	64 32.0	S18 30.0	23 47.3	S22 46.3	Arcturus	145 52.8	N19 05.4
19	313 11.9	100 59.9	36.9	355 18.1	12.9	79 33.9	30.1	38 49.6	46.3	Atria	107 21.0	S69 03.6
20	328 14.4	116 03.5	36.2	10 19.3	12.4	94 35.8	30.3	53 51.9	46.3	Avior	234 16.6	S59 33.9
21	343 16.9	131 07.2 ..	35.6	25 20.5 ..	11.9	109 37.8 ..	30.4	68 54.1 ..	46.3	Bellatrix	278 27.9	N 6 21.9
22	358 19.3	146 10.9	34.9	40 21.7	11.4	124 39.7	30.5	83 56.4	46.3	Betelgeuse	270 57.2	N 7 24.6
23	13 21.8	161 14.5	34.3	55 22.9	10.9	139 41.6	30.7	98 58.7	46.3			
20 00	28 24.3	176 18.2	S20 33.6	70 24.1	S19 10.4	154 43.6	S18 30.8	114 01.0	S22 46.3	Canopus	263 54.3	S52 42.1
01	43 26.7	191 21.9	33.0	85 25.3	09.9	169 45.5	30.9	129 03.3	46.3	Capella	280 28.8	N46 00.7
02	58 29.2	206 25.6	32.3	100 26.5	09.4	184 47.4	31.0	144 05.6	46.3	Deneb	49 28.9	N45 21.2
03	73 31.6	221 29.3 ..	31.7	115 27.7 ..	08.9	199 49.4 ..	31.2	159 07.8 ..	46.3	Denebola	182 30.3	N14 28.2
04	88 34.1	236 33.0	31.0	130 28.9	08.4	214 51.3	31.3	174 10.1	46.3	Diphda	348 52.0	S17 53.1
05	103 36.6	251 36.6	30.3	145 30.1	07.9	229 53.2	31.4	189 12.4	46.3			
06	118 39.0	266 40.3	S20 29.7	160 31.3	S19 07.4	244 55.2	S18 31.5	204 14.7	S22 46.3	Dubhe	193 47.8	N61 38.9
07	133 41.5	281 44.0	29.0	175 32.5	06.9	259 57.1	31.7	219 17.0	46.3	Elnath	278 07.8	N28 37.2
S 08	148 44.0	296 47.7	28.4	190 33.7	06.4	274 59.1	31.8	234 19.2	46.3	Eltanin	90 44.7	N51 29.6
A 09	163 46.4	311 51.4 ..	27.7	205 34.9 ..	05.9	290 01.0 ..	31.9	249 21.5 ..	46.3	Enif	33 43.4	N 9 57.8
T 10	178 48.9	326 55.1	27.0	220 36.1	05.4	305 02.9	32.0	264 23.8	46.3	Fomalhaut	15 19.8	S29 31.4
U 11	193 51.4	341 58.8	26.3	235 37.3	04.9	320 04.9	32.2	279 26.1	46.3			
R 12	208 53.8	357 02.5	S20 25.7	250 38.5	S19 04.4	335 06.8	S18 32.3	294 28.4	S22 46.3	Gacrux	171 57.4	S57 12.8
D 13	223 56.3	12 06.2	25.0	265 39.7	03.9	350 08.7	32.4	309 30.7	46.3	Gienah	175 48.9	S17 38.5
A 14	238 58.7	27 09.9	24.3	280 40.9	03.4	5 10.7	32.6	324 32.9	46.3	Hadar	148 43.4	S60 27.6
Y 15	254 01.2	42 13.6 ..	23.6	295 42.1 ..	02.9	20 12.6 ..	32.7	339 35.2 ..	46.3	Hamal	327 56.3	N23 33.0
16	269 03.7	57 17.4	22.9	310 43.3	02.4	35 14.5	32.8	354 37.5	46.3	Kaus Aust.	83 39.2	S34 22.4
17	284 06.1	72 21.1	22.2	325 44.4	01.9	50 16.5	32.9	9 39.8	46.3			
18	299 08.6	87 24.8	S20 21.5	340 45.6	S19 01.4	65 18.4	S18 33.1	24 42.1	S22 46.3	Kochab	137 21.3	N74 04.9
19	314 11.1	102 28.5	20.8	355 46.8	00.9	80 20.3	33.2	39 44.3	46.3	Markab	13 34.5	N15 18.5
20	329 13.5	117 32.2	20.2	10 48.0	19 00.4	95 22.3	33.3	54 46.6	46.3	Menkar	314 11.0	N 4 09.7
21	344 16.0	132 35.9 ..	19.5	25 49.2	18 59.9	110 24.2 ..	33.4	69 48.9 ..	46.3	Menkent	148 03.7	S36 27.5
22	359 18.5	147 39.6	18.8	40 50.4	59.4	125 26.1	33.6	84 51.2	46.3	Miaplacidus	221 39.2	S69 47.3
23	14 20.9	162 43.4	18.0	55 51.6	58.9	140 28.1	33.7	99 53.5	46.3			
21 00	29 23.4	177 47.1	S20 17.3	70 52.8	S18 58.4	155 30.0	S18 33.8	114 55.7	S22 46.3	Mirfak	308 34.7	N49 55.5
01	44 25.9	192 50.8	16.6	85 54.0	57.9	170 31.9	33.9	129 58.0	46.3	Nunki	75 54.0	S26 16.3
02	59 28.3	207 54.5	15.9	100 55.2	57.4	185 33.9	34.1	145 00.3	46.3	Peacock	53 13.5	S56 40.6
03	74 30.8	222 58.3 ..	15.2	115 56.4 ..	56.8	200 35.8 ..	34.2	160 02.6 ..	46.3	Pollux	243 23.3	N27 58.7
04	89 33.2	238 02.0	14.5	130 57.5	56.3	215 37.7	34.3	175 04.9	46.3	Procyon	244 55.9	N 5 10.6
05	104 35.7	253 05.7	13.8	145 58.7	55.8	230 39.7	34.5	190 07.1	46.3			
06	119 38.2	268 09.5	S20 13.1	160 59.9	S18 55.3	245 41.6	S18 34.6	205 09.4	S22 46.3	Rasalhague	96 03.3	N12 33.1
07	134 40.6	283 13.2	12.3	176 01.1	54.8	260 43.5	34.7	220 11.7	46.3	Regulus	207 39.9	N11 52.6
S 08	149 43.1	298 16.9	11.6	191 02.3	54.3	275 45.5	34.8	235 14.0	46.3	Rigel	281 08.4	S 8 10.8
U 09	164 45.6	313 20.7 ..	10.9	206 03.5 ..	53.8	290 47.4 ..	35.0	250 16.2 ..	46.3	Rigil Kent.	139 47.5	S60 54.5
N 10	179 48.0	328 24.4	10.2	221 04.7	53.3	305 49.3	35.1	265 18.5	46.3	Sabik	102 08.6	S15 44.7
D 11	194 50.5	343 28.1	09.4	236 05.9	52.8	320 51.2	35.2	280 20.8	46.3			
A 12	209 53.0	358 31.9	S20 08.7	251 07.0	S18 52.3	335 53.2	S18 35.3	295 23.1	S22 46.3	Schedar	349 35.8	N56 38.4
Y 13	224 55.4	13 35.6	08.0	266 08.2	51.8	350 55.1	35.5	310 25.4	46.3	Shaula	96 17.3	S37 06.9
14	239 57.9	28 39.4	07.2	281 09.4	51.3	5 57.0	35.6	325 27.6	46.3	Sirius	258 30.4	S16 44.4
15	255 00.4	43 43.1 ..	06.5	296 10.6 ..	50.8	20 59.0 ..	35.7	340 29.9 ..	46.3	Spica	158 27.8	S11 15.3
16	270 02.8	58 46.9	05.8	311 11.8	50.3	36 00.9	35.8	355 32.2	46.3	Suhail	222 49.9	S43 30.2
17	285 05.3	73 50.6	05.0	326 13.0	49.7	51 02.8	36.0	10 34.5	46.3			
18	300 07.7	88 54.4	S20 04.3	341 14.2	S18 49.2	66 04.8	S18 36.1	25 36.7	S22 46.3	Vega	80 36.7	N38 48.5
19	315 10.2	103 58.1	03.5	356 15.3	48.7	81 06.7	36.2	40 39.0	46.3	Zuben'ubi	137 01.7	S16 06.9
20	330 12.7	119 01.9	02.8	11 16.5	48.2	96 08.6	36.4	55 41.3	46.3		SHA	Mer.Pass.
21	345 15.1	134 05.6 ..	02.0	26 17.7 ..	47.7	111 10.6 ..	36.5	70 43.6 ..	46.3		° ′	h m
22	0 17.6	149 09.4	01.3	41 18.9	47.2	126 12.5	36.6	85 45.9	46.3	Venus	147 54.0	12 12
23	15 20.1	164 13.1	00.5	56 20.1	46.7	141 14.4	36.7	100 48.1	46.3	Mars	41 59.8	19 17
	h m									Jupiter	126 19.3	13 39
Mer.Pass. 22 02.8	v 3.7 d 0.7			v 1.2 d 0.5		v 1.9 d 0.1		v 2.3 d 0.0		Saturn	85 36.7	16 21

UT	SUN GHA	SUN Dec	MOON GHA	v	Dec	d	HP
d h	° ′	° ′	° ′	′	° ′	′	′
19 00	183 44.0	S 9 52.7	64 36.9	13.3	S16 18.5	7.1	54.4
01	198 44.2	53.6	79 09.2	13.4	16 11.4	7.2	54.4
02	213 44.3	54.5	93 41.6	13.4	16 04.2	7.2	54.4
03	228 44.4	.. 55.4	108 14.0	13.4	15 57.0	7.3	54.4
04	243 44.5	56.3	122 46.4	13.4	15 49.7	7.3	54.4
05	258 44.6	57.2	137 18.8	13.5	15 42.4	7.5	54.4
06	273 44.7	S 9 58.1	151 51.3	13.4	S15 34.9	7.5	54.4
07	288 44.9	59.0	166 23.7	13.5	15 27.4	7.5	54.4
F 08	303 45.0	9 59.9	180 56.2	13.6	15 19.9	7.7	54.4
R 09	318 45.1	10 00.8	195 28.8	13.5	15 12.2	7.7	54.5
I 10	333 45.2	01.7	210 01.3	13.6	15 04.5	7.8	54.5
11	348 45.3	02.6	224 33.9	13.6	14 56.7	7.9	54.5
D 12	3 45.4	S10 03.5	239 06.5	13.6	S14 48.8	7.9	54.5
A 13	18 45.5	04.4	253 39.1	13.6	14 40.9	8.0	54.5
Y 14	33 45.7	05.3	268 11.7	13.7	14 32.9	8.0	54.5
15	48 45.8	.. 06.2	282 44.4	13.6	14 24.9	8.1	54.5
16	63 45.9	07.1	297 17.0	13.7	14 16.8	8.2	54.5
17	78 46.0	08.0	311 49.7	13.7	14 08.6	8.3	54.5
18	93 46.1	S10 08.9	326 22.4	13.8	S14 00.3	8.3	54.6
19	108 46.2	09.8	340 55.2	13.7	13 52.0	8.4	54.6
20	123 46.3	10.7	355 27.9	13.8	13 43.6	8.5	54.6
21	138 46.5	.. 11.6	10 00.7	13.8	13 35.1	8.5	54.6
22	153 46.6	12.5	24 33.5	13.8	13 26.6	8.5	54.6
23	168 46.7	13.4	39 06.3	13.8	13 18.1	8.7	54.6
20 00	183 46.8	S10 14.3	53 39.1	13.9	S13 09.4	8.7	54.6
01	198 46.9	15.2	68 12.0	13.8	13 00.7	8.8	54.7
02	213 47.0	16.1	82 44.8	13.9	12 51.9	8.8	54.7
03	228 47.1	.. 17.0	97 17.7	13.9	12 43.1	8.9	54.7
04	243 47.2	17.9	111 50.6	13.9	12 34.2	8.9	54.7
05	258 47.4	18.8	126 23.5	13.9	12 25.3	9.0	54.7
06	273 47.4	S10 19.7	140 56.4	13.9	S12 16.3	9.1	54.7
S 07	288 47.6	20.6	155 29.3	14.0	12 07.2	9.1	54.7
A 08	303 47.7	21.5	170 02.3	14.0	11 58.1	9.2	54.8
T 09	318 47.8	.. 22.4	184 35.3	13.9	11 48.9	9.2	54.8
U 10	333 47.9	23.3	199 08.2	14.0	11 39.7	9.3	54.8
R 11	348 48.0	24.2	213 41.2	14.0	11 30.4	9.4	54.8
D 12	3 48.1	S10 25.1	228 14.2	14.0	S11 21.0	9.4	54.8
A 13	18 48.2	26.0	242 47.2	14.0	11 11.6	9.4	54.8
Y 14	33 48.3	26.9	257 20.2	14.1	11 02.2	9.6	54.9
15	48 48.4	.. 27.8	271 53.3	14.0	10 52.6	9.5	54.9
16	63 48.5	28.6	286 26.3	14.1	10 43.1	9.6	54.9
17	78 48.6	29.5	300 59.4	14.0	10 33.5	9.7	54.9
18	93 48.7	S10 30.4	315 32.4	14.1	S10 23.8	9.7	54.9
19	108 48.8	31.3	330 05.5	14.1	10 14.1	9.8	54.9
20	123 48.9	32.2	344 38.6	14.1	10 04.3	9.9	55.0
21	138 49.1	.. 33.1	359 11.7	14.1	9 54.4	9.8	55.0
22	153 49.2	34.0	13 44.8	14.1	9 44.6	10.0	55.0
23	168 49.3	34.9	28 17.9	14.1	9 34.6	9.9	55.0
21 00	183 49.4	S10 35.8	42 51.0	14.1	S 9 24.7	10.1	55.0
01	198 49.5	36.7	57 24.1	14.1	9 14.6	10.1	55.1
02	213 49.6	37.6	71 57.2	14.1	9 04.5	10.1	55.1
03	228 49.7	.. 38.5	86 30.3	14.1	8 54.4	10.1	55.1
04	243 49.8	39.4	101 03.4	14.2	8 44.3	10.3	55.1
05	258 49.9	40.2	115 36.6	14.1	8 34.0	10.2	55.1
06	273 50.0	S10 41.1	130 09.7	14.1	S 8 23.8	10.3	55.2
07	288 50.1	42.0	144 42.8	14.2	8 13.5	10.4	55.2
08	303 50.2	42.9	159 16.0	14.1	8 03.1	10.4	55.2
S 09	318 50.3	.. 43.8	173 49.1	14.1	7 52.7	10.4	55.2
U 10	333 50.4	44.7	188 22.2	14.2	7 42.3	10.5	55.2
N 11	348 50.5	45.6	202 55.4	14.1	7 31.8	10.5	55.3
D 12	3 50.6	S10 46.5	217 28.5	14.1	S 7 21.3	10.6	55.3
A 13	18 50.7	47.4	232 01.6	14.2	7 10.7	10.6	55.3
Y 14	33 50.8	48.2	246 34.8	14.1	7 00.1	10.6	55.3
15	48 50.9	.. 49.1	261 07.9	14.1	6 49.5	10.7	55.3
16	63 51.0	50.0	275 41.0	14.1	6 38.8	10.7	55.4
17	78 51.1	50.9	290 14.1	14.1	6 28.1	10.8	55.4
18	93 51.2	S10 51.8	304 47.2	14.2	S 6 17.3	10.8	55.4
19	108 51.3	52.7	319 20.4	14.1	6 06.5	10.8	55.4
20	123 51.4	53.6	333 53.5	14.1	5 55.7	10.9	55.5
21	138 51.5	.. 54.4	348 26.6	14.0	5 44.8	10.9	55.5
22	153 51.6	55.3	2 59.6	14.1	5 33.9	10.9	55.5
23	168 51.7	56.2	17 32.7	14.1	S 5 23.0	11.0	55.5
	SD 16.1	d 0.9	SD 14.8		14.9		15.1

Lat.	Twilight Naut.	Twilight Civil	Sunrise	Moonrise 19	20	21	22
°	h m	h m	h m	h m	h m	h m	h m
N 72	05 16	06 35	07 49	17 37	17 17	17 02	16 49
N 70	05 18	06 29	07 34	17 09	17 01	16 53	16 46
68	05 19	06 23	07 22	16 48	16 47	16 45	16 44
66	05 19	06 19	07 13	16 32	16 36	16 39	16 42
64	05 20	06 15	07 04	16 18	16 27	16 34	16 40
62	05 20	06 12	06 57	16 06	16 19	16 29	16 38
60	05 20	06 09	06 51	15 56	16 12	16 25	16 37
N 58	05 20	06 06	06 46	15 48	16 06	16 21	16 36
56	05 20	06 03	06 41	15 40	16 00	16 18	16 35
54	05 20	06 01	06 37	15 33	15 55	16 15	16 34
52	05 20	05 59	06 33	15 27	15 51	16 12	16 33
50	05 19	05 57	06 30	15 21	15 47	16 10	16 32
45	05 18	05 52	06 22	15 09	15 38	16 05	16 30
N 40	05 17	05 48	06 16	14 59	15 31	16 00	16 29
35	05 15	05 44	06 10	14 51	15 24	15 56	16 28
30	05 13	05 41	06 05	14 43	15 19	15 53	16 27
20	05 08	05 34	05 56	14 30	15 09	15 47	16 25
N 10	05 03	05 27	05 47	14 19	15 01	15 42	16 23
0	04 56	05 20	05 41	14 08	14 53	15 37	16 22
S 10	04 48	05 13	05 34	13 57	14 45	15 32	16 20
20	04 37	05 04	05 26	13 45	14 36	15 27	16 18
30	04 23	04 52	05 17	13 32	14 26	15 21	16 16
35	04 14	04 45	05 11	13 25	14 21	15 17	16 15
40	04 03	04 37	05 05	13 16	14 14	15 14	16 14
45	03 50	04 27	04 58	13 05	14 07	15 09	16 13
S 50	03 33	04 15	04 49	12 53	13 57	15 03	16 11
52	03 24	04 09	04 45	12 47	13 53	15 01	16 10
54	03 15	04 03	04 41	12 41	13 49	14 58	16 09
56	03 04	03 55	04 36	12 34	13 43	14 55	16 09
58	02 51	03 47	04 30	12 25	13 38	14 52	16 08
S 60	02 35	03 38	04 24	12 16	13 31	14 48	16 06

Lat.	Sunset	Twilight Civil	Twilight Naut.	Moonset 19	20	21	22
°	h m	h m	h m	h m	h m	h m	h m
N 72	15 39	16 53	18 11	23 16	25 09	01 09	02 57
N 70	15 54	16 59	18 10	23 43	25 24	01 24	03 04
68	16 06	17 05	18 09	24 03	00 03	01 36	03 10
66	16 16	17 09	18 08	24 19	00 19	01 46	03 15
64	16 24	17 13	18 08	24 32	00 32	01 54	03 19
62	16 31	17 17	18 08	24 42	00 42	02 01	03 22
60	16 37	17 20	18 08	24 52	00 52	02 07	03 25
N 58	16 43	17 23	18 08	25 00	01 00	02 13	03 28
56	16 47	17 25	18 08	25 07	01 07	02 17	03 30
54	16 52	17 28	18 09	00 06	01 13	02 22	03 32
52	16 56	17 30	18 09	00 13	01 19	02 25	03 34
50	17 00	17 32	18 10	00 20	01 24	02 29	03 36
45	17 07	17 37	18 11	00 34	01 35	02 36	03 39
N 40	17 13	17 41	18 12	00 46	01 44	02 43	03 43
35	17 19	17 45	18 14	00 56	01 51	02 48	03 45
30	17 24	17 48	18 16	01 04	01 58	02 52	03 48
20	17 33	17 55	18 21	01 19	02 10	03 00	03 52
N 10	17 41	18 02	18 27	01 32	02 20	03 07	03 55
0	17 48	18 09	18 34	01 44	02 30	03 14	03 58
S 10	17 56	18 17	18 42	01 56	02 39	03 20	04 02
20	18 04	18 26	18 53	02 09	02 49	03 27	04 05
30	18 13	18 38	19 07	02 24	03 00	03 35	04 09
35	18 19	18 45	19 16	02 32	03 07	03 40	04 11
40	18 25	18 53	19 27	02 42	03 14	03 45	04 14
45	18 32	19 03	19 41	02 53	03 23	03 50	04 16
S 50	18 41	19 16	19 58	03 06	03 33	03 57	04 20
52	18 45	19 22	20 07	03 12	03 38	04 00	04 21
54	18 50	19 28	20 17	03 19	03 43	04 04	04 23
56	18 55	19 36	20 28	03 27	03 49	04 08	04 25
58	19 01	19 44	20 42	03 36	03 55	04 12	04 27
S 60	19 07	19 54	20 58	03 45	04 03	04 17	04 29

Day	SUN Eqn. of Time 00h	12h	Mer. Pass.	MOON Mer. Pass. Upper	Lower	Age	Phase
d	m s	m s	h m	h m	h m	d	%
19	14 56	15 02	11 45	20 19	07 56	10	75
20	15 07	15 12	11 45	21 03	08 41	11	83
21	15 17	15 22	11 45	21 48	09 25	12	89

2018 OCTOBER 22, 23, 24 (MON., TUES., WED.)

UT	ARIES GHA	VENUS −4.2 GHA	Dec	MARS −0.8 GHA	Dec	JUPITER −1.8 GHA	Dec	SATURN +0.5 GHA	Dec	STARS Name	SHA	Dec
d h 22 00	30 22.5	179 16.9	S19 59.8	71 21.2	S18 46.2	156 16.4	S18 36.9	115 50.4	S22 46.3	Acamar	315 15.2	S40 13.8
01	45 25.0	194 20.7	59.0	86 22.4	45.7	171 18.3	37.0	130 52.7	46.3	Achernar	335 23.5	S57 08.6
02	60 27.5	209 24.4	58.2	101 23.6	45.2	186 20.2	37.1	145 55.0	46.3	Acrux	173 05.8	S63 11.9
03	75 29.9	224 28.2 ..	57.5	116 24.8 ..	44.6	201 22.1 ..	37.2	160 57.2 ..	46.3	Adhara	255 09.6	S28 59.7
04	90 32.4	239 31.9	56.7	131 26.0	44.1	216 24.1	37.4	175 59.5	46.3	Aldebaran	290 45.0	N16 32.7
05	105 34.8	254 35.7	55.9	146 27.1	43.6	231 26.0	37.5	191 01.8	46.3			
06	120 37.3	269 39.5	S19 55.2	161 28.3	S18 43.1	246 27.9	S18 37.6	206 04.1	S22 46.3	Alioth	166 18.1	N55 51.6
07	135 39.8	284 43.2	54.4	176 29.5	42.6	261 29.9	37.7	221 06.3	46.3	Alkaid	152 56.6	N49 13.4
08	150 42.2	299 47.0	53.6	191 30.7	42.1	276 31.8	37.9	236 08.6	46.3	Al Na'ir	27 39.0	S46 52.3
M 09	165 44.7	314 50.8 ..	52.8	206 31.9 ..	41.6	291 33.7 ..	38.0	251 10.9 ..	46.3	Alnilam	275 42.5	S 1 11.4
O 10	180 47.2	329 54.6	52.1	221 33.0	41.1	306 35.7	38.1	266 13.2	46.3	Alphard	217 52.7	S 8 44.3
N 11	195 49.6	344 58.3	51.3	236 34.2	40.5	321 37.6	38.2	281 15.4	46.3			
D 12	210 52.1	0 02.1	S19 50.5	251 35.4	S18 40.0	336 39.5	S18 38.4	296 17.7	S22 46.3	Alphecca	126 08.3	N26 39.4
A 13	225 54.6	15 05.9	49.7	266 36.6	39.5	351 41.4	38.5	311 20.0	46.3	Alpheratz	357 39.4	N29 11.7
Y 14	240 57.0	30 09.6	48.9	281 37.7	39.0	6 43.4	38.6	326 22.3	46.3	Altair	62 04.8	N 8 55.3
15	255 59.5	45 13.4 ..	48.1	296 38.9 ..	38.5	21 45.3 ..	38.8	341 24.5 ..	46.3	Ankaa	353 11.8	S42 12.4
16	271 02.0	60 17.2	47.3	311 40.1	38.0	36 47.2	38.9	356 26.8	46.3	Antares	112 22.1	S26 28.2
17	286 04.4	75 21.0	46.5	326 41.3	37.5	51 49.2	39.0	11 29.1	46.3			
18	301 06.9	90 24.8	S19 45.8	341 42.4	S18 36.9	66 51.1	S18 39.1	26 31.3	S22 46.3	Arcturus	145 52.8	N19 05.4
19	316 09.3	105 28.5	45.0	356 43.6	36.4	81 53.0	39.3	41 33.6	46.3	Atria	107 21.1	S69 03.6
20	331 11.8	120 32.3	44.2	11 44.8	35.9	96 54.9	39.4	56 35.9	46.3	Avior	234 16.6	S59 33.9
21	346 14.3	135 36.1 ..	43.4	26 46.0 ..	35.4	111 56.9 ..	39.5	71 38.2 ..	46.3	Bellatrix	278 27.9	N 6 21.9
22	1 16.7	150 39.9	42.6	41 47.1	34.9	126 58.8	39.6	86 40.4	46.3	Betelgeuse	270 57.2	N 7 24.6
23	16 19.2	165 43.7	41.7	56 48.3	34.4	142 00.7	39.8	101 42.7	46.3			
23 00	31 21.7	180 47.4	S19 40.9	71 49.5	S18 33.9	157 02.7	S18 39.9	116 45.0	S22 46.3	Canopus	263 54.3	S52 42.2
01	46 24.1	195 51.2	40.1	86 50.6	33.3	172 04.6	40.0	131 47.3	46.3	Capella	280 28.8	N46 00.7
02	61 26.6	210 55.0	39.3	101 51.8	32.8	187 06.5	40.1	146 49.5	46.3	Deneb	49 29.0	N45 21.2
03	76 29.1	225 58.8 ..	38.5	116 53.0 ..	32.3	202 08.4 ..	40.3	161 51.8 ..	46.3	Denebola	182 30.3	N14 28.2
04	91 31.5	241 02.6	37.7	131 54.2	31.8	217 10.4	40.4	176 54.1	46.3	Diphda	348 52.0	S17 53.1
05	106 34.0	256 06.4	36.9	146 55.3	31.3	232 12.3	40.5	191 56.3	46.3			
06	121 36.4	271 10.2	S19 36.1	161 56.5	S18 30.8	247 14.2	S18 40.6	206 58.6	S22 46.3	Dubhe	193 47.8	N61 38.9
07	136 38.9	286 14.0	35.2	176 57.7	30.2	262 16.2	40.8	222 00.9	46.3	Elnath	278 07.8	N28 37.2
T 08	151 41.4	301 17.7	34.4	191 58.8	29.7	277 18.1	40.9	237 03.2	46.3	Eltanin	90 44.8	N51 29.6
U 09	166 43.8	316 21.5 ..	33.6	207 00.0 ..	29.2	292 20.0 ..	41.0	252 05.4 ..	46.3	Enif	33 43.5	N 9 57.8
E 10	181 46.3	331 25.3	32.8	222 01.2	28.7	307 21.9	41.1	267 07.7	46.3	Fomalhaut	15 19.8	S29 31.4
S 11	196 48.8	346 29.1	31.9	237 02.3	28.2	322 23.9	41.3	282 10.0	46.3			
D 12	211 51.2	1 32.9	S19 31.1	252 03.5	S18 27.6	337 25.8	S18 41.4	297 12.2	S22 46.3	Gacrux	171 57.4	S57 12.8
A 13	226 53.7	16 36.7	30.3	267 04.7	27.1	352 27.7	41.5	312 14.5	46.3	Gienah	175 48.9	S17 38.5
Y 14	241 56.2	31 40.5	29.4	282 05.8	26.6	7 29.6	41.7	327 16.8	46.3	Hadar	148 43.4	S60 27.6
15	256 58.6	46 44.3 ..	28.6	297 07.0 ..	26.1	22 31.6 ..	41.8	342 19.1 ..	46.3	Hamal	327 56.3	N23 33.0
16	272 01.1	61 48.1	27.8	312 08.2	25.6	37 33.5	41.9	357 21.3	46.3	Kaus Aust.	83 39.2	S34 22.4
17	287 03.6	76 51.9	26.9	327 09.3	25.0	52 35.4	42.0	12 23.6	46.3			
18	302 06.0	91 55.7	S19 26.1	342 10.5	S18 24.5	67 37.3	S18 42.2	27 25.9	S22 46.3	Kochab	137 21.3	N74 04.9
19	317 08.5	106 59.5	25.2	357 11.7	24.0	82 39.3	42.3	42 28.1	46.3	Markab	13 34.5	N15 18.5
20	332 10.9	122 03.3	24.4	12 12.8	23.5	97 41.2	42.4	57 30.4	46.3	Menkar	314 11.0	N 4 09.7
21	347 13.4	137 07.1 ..	23.5	27 14.0 ..	23.0	112 43.1 ..	42.5	72 32.7 ..	46.3	Menkent	148 03.7	S36 27.5
22	2 15.9	152 10.9	22.7	42 15.2	22.4	127 45.1	42.7	87 34.9	46.3	Miaplacidus	221 39.2	S69 47.3
23	17 18.3	167 14.7	21.8	57 16.3	21.9	142 47.0	42.8	102 37.2	46.3			
24 00	32 20.8	182 18.5	S19 21.0	72 17.5	S18 21.4	157 48.9	S18 42.9	117 39.5	S22 46.3	Mirfak	308 34.7	N49 55.5
01	47 23.3	197 22.3	20.1	87 18.7	20.9	172 50.8	43.0	132 41.8	46.3	Nunki	75 54.0	S26 16.3
02	62 25.7	212 26.1	19.3	102 19.8	20.4	187 52.8	43.2	147 44.0	46.3	Peacock	53 13.6	S56 40.6
03	77 28.2	227 29.9 ..	18.4	117 21.0 ..	19.8	202 54.7 ..	43.3	162 46.3 ..	46.3	Pollux	243 23.3	N27 58.7
04	92 30.7	242 33.7	17.5	132 22.1	19.3	217 56.6	43.4	177 48.6	46.3	Procyon	244 55.9	N 5 10.6
05	107 33.1	257 37.5	16.7	147 23.3	18.8	232 58.5	43.5	192 50.8	46.3			
06	122 35.6	272 41.3	S19 15.8	162 24.5	S18 18.3	248 00.5	S18 43.7	207 53.1	S22 46.3	Rasalhague	96 03.3	N12 33.1
W 07	137 38.0	287 45.1	15.0	177 25.6	17.7	263 02.4	43.8	222 55.4	46.2	Regulus	207 39.9	N11 52.6
E 08	152 40.5	302 48.9	14.1	192 26.8	17.2	278 04.3	43.9	237 57.6	46.2	Rigel	281 08.4	S 8 10.8
D 09	167 43.0	317 52.7 ..	13.2	207 27.9 ..	16.7	293 06.2 ..	44.0	252 59.9 ..	46.2	Rigil Kent.	139 47.5	S60 54.5
N 10	182 45.4	332 56.5	12.3	222 29.1	16.2	308 08.2	44.2	268 02.2	46.2	Sabik	102 08.6	S15 44.7
E 11	197 47.9	348 00.3	11.5	237 30.3	15.7	323 10.1	44.3	283 04.4	46.2			
S 12	212 50.4	3 04.1	S19 10.6	252 31.4	S18 15.1	338 12.0	S18 44.4	298 06.7	S22 46.2	Schedar	349 35.8	N56 38.5
D 13	227 52.8	18 07.9	09.7	267 32.6	14.6	353 13.9	44.5	313 09.0	46.2	Shaula	96 17.3	S37 06.9
A 14	242 55.3	33 11.7	08.8	282 33.7	14.1	8 15.9	44.7	328 11.2	46.2	Sirius	258 30.4	S16 44.4
Y 15	257 57.8	48 15.5 ..	08.0	297 34.9 ..	13.6	23 17.8 ..	44.8	343 13.5 ..	46.2	Spica	158 27.8	S11 15.3
16	273 00.2	63 19.3	07.1	312 36.0	13.0	38 19.7	44.9	358 15.8	46.2	Suhail	222 49.9	S43 30.2
17	288 02.7	78 23.1	06.2	327 37.2	12.5	53 21.6	45.1	13 18.0	46.2			
18	303 05.2	93 26.9	S19 05.3	342 38.4	S18 12.0	68 23.6	S18 45.2	28 20.3	S22 46.2	Vega	80 36.7	N38 48.5
19	318 07.6	108 30.8	04.4	357 39.5	11.5	83 25.5	45.3	43 22.6	46.2	Zuben'ubi	137 01.8	S16 06.9
20	333 10.1	123 34.6	03.5	12 40.7	10.9	98 27.4	45.4	58 24.8	46.2		SHA	Mer. Pass.
21	348 12.5	138 38.4 ..	02.7	27 41.8 ..	10.4	113 29.3 ..	45.5	73 27.1 ..	46.2		° ′	h m
22	3 15.0	153 42.2	01.8	42 43.0	09.9	128 31.2	45.7	88 29.4	46.2	Venus	149 25.8	11 54
23	18 17.5	168 46.0	00.9	57 44.1	09.3	143 33.2	45.8	103 31.6	46.2	Mars	40 27.8	19 11
Mer. Pass.	h m 21 51.0	v 3.8	d 0.8	v 1.2	d 0.5	v 1.9	d 0.1	v 2.3	d 0.0	Jupiter	125 41.0	13 30
										Saturn	85 23.3	16 11

UT	SUN GHA	SUN Dec	MOON GHA	v	MOON Dec	d	HP
d h	° ′	° ′	° ′	′	° ′	′	′
22 00	183 51.8	S10 57.1	32 05.8	14.1	S 5 12.0	11.0	55.5
01	198 51.9	58.0	46 38.9	14.0	5 01.0	11.0	55.6
02	213 52.0	58.9	61 11.9	14.1	4 50.0	11.1	55.6
03	228 52.1	10 59.8	75 45.0	14.0	4 38.9	11.1	55.6
04	243 52.2	11 00.6	90 18.0	14.0	4 27.8	11.1	55.6
05	258 52.3	01.5	104 51.0	14.0	4 16.7	11.2	55.7
06	273 52.4	S11 02.4	119 24.0	14.0	S 4 05.5	11.2	55.7
07	288 52.5	03.3	133 57.0	14.0	3 54.3	11.2	55.7
08	303 52.6	04.2	148 30.0	14.0	3 43.1	11.2	55.7
M 09	318 52.7	05.1	163 03.0	13.9	3 31.9	11.3	55.8
O 10	333 52.8	05.9	177 35.9	14.0	3 20.6	11.3	55.8
N 11	348 52.8	06.8	192 08.9	13.9	3 09.3	11.3	55.8
D 12	3 52.9	S11 07.7	206 41.8	13.9	S 2 58.0	11.4	55.8
A 13	18 53.0	08.6	221 14.7	13.9	2 46.6	11.3	55.9
Y 14	33 53.1	09.5	235 47.6	13.8	2 35.3	11.4	55.9
15	48 53.2	10.3	250 20.4	13.9	2 23.9	11.4	55.9
16	63 53.3	11.2	264 53.3	13.8	2 12.5	11.4	55.9
17	78 53.4	12.1	279 26.1	13.8	2 01.1	11.5	55.9
18	93 53.5	S11 13.0	293 58.9	13.8	S 1 49.6	11.5	56.0
19	108 53.6	13.9	308 31.7	13.8	1 38.1	11.4	56.0
20	123 53.7	14.7	323 04.5	13.7	1 26.7	11.5	56.0
21	138 53.8	15.6	337 37.2	13.7	1 15.2	11.6	56.0
22	153 53.9	16.5	352 09.9	13.7	1 03.6	11.5	56.1
23	168 54.0	17.4	6 42.6	13.7	0 52.1	11.6	56.1
23 00	183 54.1	S11 18.3	21 15.3	13.7	S 0 40.5	11.5	56.1
01	198 54.1	19.1	35 48.0	13.6	0 29.0	11.6	56.1
02	213 54.2	20.0	50 20.6	13.6	0 17.4	11.6	56.2
03	228 54.3	20.9	64 53.2	13.5	S 0 05.8	11.6	56.2
04	243 54.4	21.8	79 25.7	13.6	N 0 05.8	11.6	56.2
05	258 54.5	22.6	93 58.3	13.5	0 17.4	11.6	56.2
06	273 54.6	S11 23.5	108 30.8	13.5	N 0 29.0	11.7	56.3
07	288 54.7	24.4	123 03.3	13.4	0 40.7	11.6	56.3
T 08	303 54.8	25.3	137 35.7	13.4	0 52.3	11.7	56.3
U 09	318 54.9	26.1	152 08.1	13.4	1 04.0	11.6	56.3
E 10	333 54.9	27.0	166 40.5	13.4	1 15.6	11.7	56.4
S 11	348 55.0	27.9	181 12.9	13.3	1 27.3	11.6	56.4
D 12	3 55.1	S11 28.8	195 45.2	13.3	N 1 38.9	11.7	56.4
A 13	18 55.2	29.6	210 17.5	13.3	1 50.6	11.7	56.4
Y 14	33 55.3	30.5	224 49.8	13.2	2 02.3	11.7	56.5
15	48 55.4	31.4	239 22.0	13.2	2 14.0	11.6	56.5
16	63 55.5	32.3	253 54.2	13.1	2 25.6	11.7	56.5
17	78 55.5	33.1	268 26.3	13.1	2 37.3	11.7	56.5
18	93 55.6	S11 34.0	282 58.4	13.1	N 2 49.0	11.6	56.6
19	108 55.7	34.9	297 30.5	13.0	3 00.6	11.7	56.6
20	123 55.8	35.8	312 02.5	13.0	3 12.3	11.7	56.6
21	138 55.9	36.6	326 34.5	13.0	3 24.0	11.6	56.6
22	153 56.0	37.5	341 06.5	12.9	3 35.6	11.7	56.7
23	168 56.1	38.4	355 38.4	12.9	3 47.3	11.6	56.7
24 00	183 56.1	S11 39.2	10 10.3	12.8	N 3 58.9	11.7	56.7
01	198 56.2	40.1	24 42.1	12.8	4 10.6	11.6	56.7
02	213 56.3	41.0	39 13.9	12.8	4 22.2	11.6	56.8
03	228 56.4	41.8	53 45.7	12.7	4 33.8	11.6	56.8
04	243 56.5	42.7	68 17.4	12.6	4 45.4	11.6	56.8
05	258 56.6	43.6	82 49.0	12.6	4 57.0	11.6	56.8
06	273 56.6	S11 44.5	97 20.6	12.6	N 5 08.6	11.6	56.9
W 07	288 56.7	45.3	111 52.2	12.5	5 20.2	11.5	56.9
E 08	303 56.8	46.2	126 23.7	12.5	5 31.7	11.6	56.9
D 09	318 56.9	47.1	140 55.2	12.4	5 43.3	11.5	56.9
N 10	333 57.0	47.9	155 26.6	12.4	5 54.8	11.5	57.0
E 11	348 57.0	48.8	169 58.0	12.3	6 06.3	11.5	57.0
S 12	3 57.1	S11 49.7	184 29.3	12.3	N 6 17.8	11.4	57.0
D 13	18 57.2	50.5	199 00.6	12.3	6 29.2	11.5	57.0
A 14	33 57.3	51.4	213 31.9	12.1	6 40.7	11.4	57.1
Y 15	48 57.4	52.3	228 03.0	12.2	6 52.1	11.4	57.1
16	63 57.4	53.1	242 34.2	12.1	7 03.5	11.4	57.1
17	78 57.5	54.0	257 05.3	12.0	7 14.8	11.4	57.1
18	93 57.6	S11 54.9	271 36.3	12.0	N 7 26.2	11.3	57.2
19	108 57.7	55.7	286 07.3	11.9	7 37.5	11.3	57.2
20	123 57.7	56.6	300 38.2	11.8	7 48.8	11.2	57.2
21	138 57.8	57.5	315 09.0	11.8	8 00.0	11.3	57.2
22	153 57.9	58.3	329 39.8	11.8	8 11.3	11.2	57.2
23	168 58.0	59.2	344 10.6	11.7	N 8 22.5	11.1	57.3
	SD 16.1 d 0.9		SD 15.2		15.4		15.5

Lat.	Twilight Naut.	Twilight Civil	Sunrise	Moonrise 22	23	24	25
°	h m	h m	h m	h m	h m	h m	h m
N 72	05 29	06 48	08 04	16 49	16 36	16 22	16 05
N 70	05 29	06 40	07 47	16 46	16 39	16 32	16 24
68	05 29	06 34	07 34	16 44	16 42	16 40	16 38
66	05 28	06 28	07 23	16 42	16 44	16 47	16 51
64	05 28	06 24	07 14	16 40	16 46	16 52	17 00
62	05 28	06 19	07 06	16 38	16 47	16 57	17 09
60	05 27	06 16	06 59	16 37	16 49	17 02	17 17
N 58	05 26	06 12	06 53	16 36	16 50	17 06	17 24
56	05 26	06 09	06 48	16 35	16 51	17 09	17 30
54	05 25	06 06	06 43	16 34	16 53	17 12	17 35
52	05 24	06 04	06 38	16 33	16 54	17 15	17 40
50	05 24	06 01	06 35	16 32	16 54	17 18	17 44
45	05 22	05 56	06 26	16 30	16 56	17 24	17 54
N 40	05 20	05 51	06 19	16 29	16 58	17 28	18 01
35	05 17	05 47	06 13	16 28	16 59	17 33	18 08
30	05 15	05 43	06 07	16 27	17 01	17 36	18 14
20	05 09	05 35	05 58	16 25	17 03	17 43	18 25
N 10	05 03	05 28	05 49	16 23	17 05	17 48	18 34
0	04 55	05 20	05 41	16 22	17 07	17 54	18 43
S 10	04 46	05 11	05 33	16 20	17 09	17 59	18 52
20	04 35	05 01	05 24	16 18	17 11	18 05	19 01
30	04 20	04 49	05 14	16 16	17 13	18 12	19 12
35	04 10	04 41	05 08	16 15	17 15	18 16	19 19
40	03 59	04 33	05 01	16 14	17 16	18 20	19 26
45	03 44	04 22	04 53	16 13	17 18	18 25	19 34
S 50	03 26	04 09	04 43	16 11	17 20	18 32	19 45
52	03 16	04 02	04 39	16 10	17 21	18 35	19 49
54	03 06	03 55	04 34	16 09	17 23	18 38	19 55
56	02 54	03 47	04 29	16 09	17 24	18 41	20 01
58	02 40	03 38	04 22	16 08	17 25	18 45	20 07
S 60	02 22	03 28	04 16	16 06	17 27	18 50	20 15

Lat.	Sunset	Twilight Civil	Twilight Naut.	Moonset 22	23	24	25
°	h m	h m	h m	h m	h m	h m	h m
N 72	15 23	16 38	17 57	02 57	04 45	06 36	08 33
N 70	15 40	16 47	17 58	03 04	04 45	06 28	08 17
68	15 53	16 53	17 58	03 10	04 45	06 22	08 04
66	16 04	16 59	17 59	03 15	04 45	06 17	07 53
64	16 14	17 04	17 59	03 19	04 45	06 13	07 44
62	16 22	17 08	18 00	03 22	04 44	06 09	07 36
60	16 29	17 12	18 00	03 25	04 44	06 06	07 30
N 58	16 35	17 15	18 01	03 28	04 44	06 03	07 24
56	16 40	17 18	18 02	03 30	04 44	06 00	07 19
54	16 45	17 21	18 02	03 32	04 44	05 58	07 14
52	16 49	17 24	18 03	03 34	04 44	05 56	07 10
50	16 53	17 26	18 04	03 36	04 44	05 54	07 06
45	17 02	17 32	18 06	03 39	04 44	05 50	06 58
N 40	17 09	17 37	18 08	03 43	04 44	05 47	06 51
35	17 16	17 41	18 11	03 45	04 44	05 44	06 46
30	17 21	17 45	18 13	03 48	04 44	05 41	06 41
20	17 31	17 53	18 19	03 52	04 43	05 37	06 32
N 10	17 39	18 01	18 26	03 55	04 43	05 33	06 24
0	17 48	18 09	18 33	03 58	04 43	05 29	06 17
S 10	17 56	18 18	18 43	04 02	04 43	05 25	06 10
20	18 05	18 28	18 54	04 05	04 43	05 22	06 02
30	18 15	18 40	19 10	04 09	04 42	05 17	05 54
35	18 21	18 48	19 19	04 11	04 42	05 15	05 49
40	18 28	18 57	19 31	04 14	04 42	05 12	05 43
45	18 36	19 08	19 46	04 16	04 42	05 08	05 37
S 50	18 46	19 21	20 05	04 20	04 42	05 04	05 29
52	18 51	19 28	20 14	04 21	04 42	05 02	05 25
54	18 56	19 35	20 25	04 23	04 41	05 00	05 21
56	19 01	19 43	20 37	04 25	04 41	04 58	05 17
58	19 08	19 52	20 52	04 27	04 41	04 56	05 12
S 60	19 15	20 03	21 09	04 29	04 41	04 53	05 07

Day	SUN Eqn. of Time 00h	SUN Eqn. of Time 12h	SUN Mer. Pass.	MOON Mer. Pass. Upper	MOON Mer. Pass. Lower	Age	Phase
d	m s	m s	h m	h m	h m	d	%
22	15 27	15 32	11 44	22 32	10 10	13	95
23	15 36	15 40	11 44	23 18	10 55	14	98
24	15 44	15 48	11 44	24 05	11 41	15	100

UT	ARIES	VENUS −4.3		MARS −0.7		JUPITER −1.7		SATURN +0.5		STARS		
	GHA	GHA	Dec	GHA	Dec	GHA	Dec	GHA	Dec	Name	SHA	Dec
25 00	33 19.9	183 49.8	S19 00.0	72 45.3	S18 08.8	158 35.1	S18 45.9	118 33.9	S22 46.2	Acamar	315 15.2	S40 13.8
01	48 22.4	198 53.6	18 59.1	87 46.4	08.3	173 37.0	46.1	133 36.2	46.2	Achernar	335 23.5	S57 08.6
02	63 24.9	213 57.4	58.2	102 47.6	07.8	188 38.9	46.2	148 38.4	46.2	Acrux	173 05.8	S63 11.9
03	78 27.3	229 01.2 ..	57.3	117 48.8 ..	07.2	203 40.9 ..	46.3	163 40.7 ..	46.2	Adhara	255 09.6	S28 59.7
04	93 29.8	244 05.0	56.4	132 49.9	06.7	218 42.8	46.4	178 43.0	46.2	Aldebaran	290 45.0	N16 32.7
05	108 32.3	259 08.8	55.5	147 51.1	06.2	233 44.7	46.6	193 45.2	46.2			
06	123 34.7	274 12.6	S18 54.6	162 52.2	S18 05.7	248 46.6	S18 46.7	208 47.5	S22 46.2	Alioth	166 18.1	N55 51.6
07	138 37.2	289 16.4	53.7	177 53.4	05.1	263 48.6	46.8	223 49.8	46.2	Alkaid	152 56.6	N49 13.4
T 08	153 39.7	304 20.2	52.8	192 54.5	04.6	278 50.5	46.9	238 52.0	46.2	Al Na'ir	27 39.0	S46 52.3
H 09	168 42.1	319 24.0 ..	51.9	207 55.7 ..	04.1	293 52.4 ..	47.1	253 54.3 ..	46.2	Alnilam	275 42.5	S 1 11.4
U 10	183 44.6	334 27.9	50.9	222 56.8	03.5	308 54.3	47.2	268 56.6	46.2	Alphard	217 52.6	S 8 44.3
R 11	198 47.0	349 31.7	50.0	237 58.0	03.0	323 56.3	47.3	283 58.8	46.2			
S 12	213 49.5	4 35.5	S18 49.1	252 59.1	S18 02.5	338 58.2	S18 47.4	299 01.1	S22 46.2	Alphecca	126 08.3	N26 39.4
D 13	228 52.0	19 39.3	48.2	268 00.3	02.0	354 00.1	47.6	314 03.3	46.2	Alpheratz	357 39.4	N29 11.7
A 14	243 54.4	34 43.1	47.3	283 01.4	01.4	9 02.0	47.7	329 05.6	46.2	Altair	62 04.8	N 8 55.3
Y 15	258 56.9	49 46.9 ..	46.4	298 02.6 ..	00.9	24 03.9 ..	47.8	344 07.9 ..	46.2	Ankaa	353 11.8	S42 12.4
16	273 59.4	64 50.7	45.5	313 03.7	18 00.4	39 05.9	47.9	359 10.1	46.2	Antares	112 22.1	S26 28.2
17	289 01.8	79 54.5	44.5	328 04.9	17 59.8	54 07.8	48.1	14 12.4	46.2			
18	304 04.3	94 58.3	S18 43.6	343 06.0	S17 59.3	69 09.7	S18 48.2	29 14.7	S22 46.2	Arcturus	145 52.8	N19 05.3
19	319 06.8	110 02.1	42.7	358 07.2	58.8	84 11.6	48.3	44 16.9	46.2	Atria	107 21.1	S69 03.6
20	334 09.2	125 05.9	41.8	13 08.3	58.2	99 13.5	48.4	59 19.2	46.2	Avior	234 16.5	S59 33.9
21	349 11.7	140 09.7 ..	40.8	28 09.5 ..	57.7	114 15.5 ..	48.6	74 21.5 ..	46.2	Bellatrix	278 27.9	N 6 21.9
22	4 14.1	155 13.5	39.9	43 10.6	57.2	129 17.4	48.7	89 23.7	46.2	Betelgeuse	270 57.2	N 7 24.5
23	19 16.6	170 17.3	39.0	58 11.8	56.6	144 19.3	48.8	104 26.0	46.2			
26 00	34 19.1	185 21.1	S18 38.1	73 12.9	S17 56.1	159 21.3	S18 48.9	119 28.2	S22 46.2	Canopus	263 54.3	S52 42.2
01	49 21.5	200 24.9	37.1	88 14.0	55.6	174 23.2	49.1	134 30.5	46.2	Capella	280 28.8	N46 00.7
02	64 24.0	215 28.7	36.2	103 15.2	55.0	189 25.1	49.2	149 32.8	46.2	Deneb	49 29.0	N45 21.2
03	79 26.5	230 32.5 ..	35.3	118 16.3 ..	54.5	204 27.0 ..	49.3	164 35.0 ..	46.2	Denebola	182 30.3	N14 28.2
04	94 28.9	245 36.3	34.3	133 17.5	54.0	219 28.9	49.4	179 37.3	46.2	Diphda	348 52.0	S17 53.1
05	109 31.4	260 40.1	33.4	148 18.6	53.4	234 30.8	49.6	194 39.6	46.2			
06	124 33.9	275 43.9	S18 32.4	163 19.8	S17 52.9	249 32.8	S18 49.7	209 41.8	S22 46.2	Dubhe	193 47.8	N61 38.9
07	139 36.3	290 47.7	31.5	178 20.9	52.4	264 34.7	49.8	224 44.1	46.2	Elnath	278 07.8	N28 37.2
08	154 38.8	305 51.5	30.6	193 22.1	51.8	279 36.6	49.9	239 46.3	46.2	Eltanin	90 44.8	N51 29.6
F 09	169 41.3	320 55.3 ..	29.6	208 23.2 ..	51.3	294 38.5 ..	50.1	254 48.6 ..	46.2	Enif	33 43.5	N 9 57.8
R 10	184 43.7	335 59.1	28.7	223 24.3	50.8	309 40.4	50.2	269 50.9	46.2	Fomalhaut	15 19.8	S29 31.4
I 11	199 46.2	351 02.9	27.7	238 25.5	50.2	324 42.4	50.3	284 53.1	46.2			
D 12	214 48.6	6 06.7	S18 26.8	253 26.6	S17 49.7	339 44.3	S18 50.4	299 55.4	S22 46.2	Gacrux	171 57.4	S57 12.8
A 13	229 51.1	21 10.5	25.8	268 27.8	49.2	354 46.2	50.6	314 57.6	46.2	Gienah	175 48.9	S17 38.5
Y 14	244 53.6	36 14.3	24.9	283 28.9	48.6	9 48.1	50.7	329 59.9	46.2	Hadar	148 43.4	S60 27.6
15	259 56.0	51 18.1 ..	23.9	298 30.1 ..	48.1	24 50.0 ..	50.8	345 02.2 ..	46.2	Hamal	327 56.3	N23 33.0
16	274 58.5	66 21.9	23.0	313 31.2	47.6	39 52.0	50.9	0 04.4	46.2	Kaus Aust.	83 39.2	S34 22.4
17	290 01.0	81 25.7	22.0	328 32.3	47.0	54 53.9	51.1	15 06.7	46.2			
18	305 03.4	96 29.5	S18 21.1	343 33.5	S17 46.5	69 55.8	S18 51.2	30 08.9	S22 46.2	Kochab	137 21.3	N74 04.9
19	320 05.9	111 33.3	20.1	358 34.6	46.0	84 57.7	51.3	45 11.2	46.2	Markab	13 34.5	N15 18.5
20	335 08.4	126 37.1	19.2	13 35.8	45.4	99 59.6	51.4	60 13.5	46.2	Menkar	314 11.0	N 4 09.7
21	350 10.8	141 40.9 ..	18.2	28 36.9 ..	44.9	115 01.6 ..	51.6	75 15.7 ..	46.2	Menkent	148 03.7	S36 27.5
22	5 13.3	156 44.7	17.3	43 38.0	44.3	130 03.5	51.7	90 18.0	46.2	Miaplacidus	221 39.1	S69 47.3
23	20 15.8	171 48.5	16.3	58 39.2	43.8	145 05.4	51.8	105 20.2	46.2			
27 00	35 18.2	186 52.2	S18 15.3	73 40.3	S17 43.3	160 07.3	S18 51.9	120 22.5	S22 46.2	Mirfak	308 34.7	N49 55.5
01	50 20.7	201 56.0	14.4	88 41.5	42.7	175 09.2	52.1	135 24.8	46.2	Nunki	75 54.0	S26 16.3
02	65 23.1	216 59.8	13.4	103 42.6	42.2	190 11.2	52.2	150 27.0	46.2	Peacock	53 13.6	S56 40.6
03	80 25.6	232 03.6 ..	12.4	118 43.7 ..	41.7	205 13.1 ..	52.3	165 29.3 ..	46.2	Pollux	243 23.3	N27 58.7
04	95 28.1	247 07.4	11.5	133 44.9	41.1	220 15.0	52.4	180 31.5	46.2	Procyon	244 55.9	N 5 10.6
05	110 30.5	262 11.2	10.5	148 46.0	40.6	235 16.9	52.6	195 33.8	46.2			
06	125 33.0	277 15.0	S18 09.5	163 47.1	S17 40.0	250 18.8	S18 52.7	210 36.1	S22 46.2	Rasalhague	96 03.3	N12 33.1
07	140 35.5	292 18.8	08.6	178 48.3	39.5	265 20.8	52.8	225 38.3	46.2	Regulus	207 39.8	N11 52.6
S 08	155 37.9	307 22.5	07.6	193 49.4	39.0	280 22.7	52.9	240 40.6	46.2	Rigel	281 08.4	S 8 10.8
A 09	170 40.4	322 26.3 ..	06.6	208 50.5 ..	38.4	295 24.6 ..	53.1	255 42.8 ..	46.2	Rigil Kent.	139 47.5	S60 54.5
T 10	185 42.9	337 30.1	05.7	223 51.7	37.9	310 26.5	53.2	270 45.1	46.2	Sabik	102 08.6	S15 44.7
U 11	200 45.3	352 33.9	04.7	238 52.8	37.3	325 28.4	53.3	285 47.3	46.2			
R 12	215 47.8	7 37.7	S18 03.7	253 54.0	S17 36.8	340 30.3	S18 53.4	300 49.6	S22 46.2	Schedar	349 35.8	N56 38.5
D 13	230 50.2	22 41.5	02.7	268 55.1	36.3	355 32.3	53.6	315 51.9	46.2	Shaula	96 17.3	S37 06.9
A 14	245 52.7	37 45.2	01.8	283 56.2	35.7	10 34.2	53.7	330 54.1	46.2	Sirius	258 30.4	S16 44.5
Y 15	260 55.2	52 49.0	18 00.8	298 57.4 ..	35.2	25 36.1 ..	53.8	345 56.4 ..	46.2	Spica	158 27.8	S11 15.3
16	275 57.6	67 52.8	17 59.8	313 58.5	34.6	40 38.0	53.9	0 58.6	46.2	Suhail	222 49.9	S43 30.2
17	291 00.1	82 56.6	58.8	328 59.6	34.1	55 39.9	54.1	16 00.9	46.2			
18	306 02.6	98 00.3	S17 57.8	344 00.8	S17 33.6	70 41.9	S18 54.2	31 03.1	S22 46.2	Vega	80 36.7	N38 48.5
19	321 05.0	113 04.1	56.9	359 01.9	33.0	85 43.8	54.3	46 05.4	46.1	Zuben'ubi	137 01.8	S16 06.9
20	336 07.5	128 07.9	55.9	14 03.0	32.5	100 45.7	54.4	61 07.7	46.1			
21	351 10.0	143 11.7 ..	54.9	29 04.2 ..	31.9	115 47.6 ..	54.6	76 09.9 ..	46.1		SHA	Mer.Pass.
22	6 12.4	158 15.4	53.9	44 05.3	31.4	130 49.5	54.7	91 12.2	46.1	Venus	151 02.0	11 36
23	21 14.9	173 19.2	52.9	59 06.4	30.8	145 51.4	54.8	106 14.4	46.1	Mars	38 53.8	19 06
	h m									Jupiter	125 02.2	13 21
Mer.Pass. 21 39.2	v 3.8 d 0.9			v 1.1 d 0.5		v 1.9 d 0.1		v 2.3 d 0.0		Saturn	85 09.2	16 00

UT	SUN GHA	SUN Dec	MOON GHA	v	Dec	d	HP
d h	° ′	° ′	° ′	′	° ′	′	′
25 00	183 58.1	S12 00.0	358 41.3	11.6	N 8 33.6	11.1	57.3
01	198 58.1	00.9	13 11.9	11.6	8 44.7	11.1	57.3
02	213 58.2	01.8	27 42.5	11.6	8 55.8	11.1	57.3
03	228 58.3	.. 02.6	42 13.1	11.4	9 06.9	11.0	57.4
04	243 58.4	03.5	56 43.5	11.4	9 17.9	11.0	57.4
05	258 58.4	04.4	71 13.9	11.4	9 28.9	10.9	57.4
06	273 58.5	S12 05.2	85 44.3	11.3	N 9 39.8	10.9	57.4
07	288 58.6	06.1	100 14.6	11.2	9 50.7	10.9	57.5
08	303 58.6	06.9	114 44.8	11.2	10 01.6	10.8	57.5
T 09	318 58.7	.. 07.8	129 15.0	11.1	10 12.4	10.8	57.5
H 10	333 58.8	08.7	143 45.1	11.0	10 23.2	10.7	57.5
U 11	348 58.9	09.5	158 15.1	11.0	10 33.9	10.7	57.5
R 12	3 58.9	S12 10.4	172 45.1	11.0	N10 44.6	10.6	57.6
S 13	18 59.0	11.2	187 15.1	10.8	10 55.2	10.6	57.6
D 14	33 59.1	12.1	201 44.9	10.8	11 05.8	10.5	57.6
A 15	48 59.2	.. 13.0	216 14.7	10.8	11 16.3	10.5	57.6
Y 16	63 59.2	13.8	230 44.5	10.6	11 26.8	10.4	57.7
17	78 59.3	14.7	245 14.1	10.6	11 37.2	10.4	57.7
18	93 59.4	S12 15.5	259 43.7	10.6	N11 47.6	10.3	57.7
19	108 59.4	16.4	274 13.3	10.5	11 57.9	10.3	57.7
20	123 59.5	17.2	288 42.8	10.4	12 08.2	10.2	57.7
21	138 59.6	.. 18.1	303 12.2	10.3	12 18.4	10.1	57.8
22	153 59.6	19.0	317 41.5	10.3	12 28.5	10.1	57.8
23	168 59.7	19.8	332 10.8	10.2	12 38.6	10.1	57.8
26 00	183 59.8	S12 20.7	346 40.0	10.2	N12 48.7	9.9	57.8
01	198 59.9	21.5	1 09.2	10.1	12 58.6	9.9	57.8
02	213 59.9	22.4	15 38.3	10.0	13 08.5	9.8	57.9
03	229 00.0	.. 23.2	30 07.3	9.9	13 18.3	9.8	57.9
04	244 00.1	24.1	44 36.2	9.9	13 28.1	9.7	57.9
05	259 00.1	24.9	59 05.1	9.8	13 37.8	9.6	57.9
06	274 00.2	S12 25.8	73 33.9	9.8	N13 47.4	9.6	57.9
07	289 00.3	26.6	88 02.7	9.7	13 57.0	9.5	58.0
08	304 00.3	27.5	102 31.4	9.6	14 06.5	9.4	58.0
F 09	319 00.4	.. 28.3	117 00.0	9.5	14 15.9	9.4	58.0
R 10	334 00.5	29.2	131 28.5	9.5	14 25.3	9.2	58.0
I 11	349 00.5	30.1	145 57.0	9.4	14 34.5	9.2	58.0
D 12	4 00.6	S12 30.9	160 25.4	9.3	N14 43.7	9.1	58.1
A 13	19 00.6	31.8	174 53.7	9.3	14 52.8	9.1	58.1
Y 14	34 00.7	32.6	189 22.0	9.2	15 01.9	8.9	58.1
15	49 00.8	.. 33.5	203 50.2	9.2	15 10.8	8.9	58.1
16	64 00.8	34.3	218 18.4	9.0	15 19.7	8.8	58.1
17	79 00.9	35.2	232 46.4	9.0	15 28.5	8.7	58.2
18	94 01.0	S12 36.0	247 14.4	9.0	N15 37.2	8.6	58.2
19	109 01.0	36.9	261 42.4	8.8	15 45.8	8.6	58.2
20	124 01.1	37.7	276 10.2	8.8	15 54.4	8.4	58.2
21	139 01.2	.. 38.6	290 38.0	8.8	16 02.8	8.4	58.2
22	154 01.2	39.4	305 05.8	8.6	16 11.2	8.3	58.2
23	169 01.3	40.2	319 33.4	8.6	16 19.5	8.2	58.3
27 00	184 01.3	S12 41.1	334 01.0	8.5	N16 27.7	8.1	58.3
01	199 01.4	41.9	348 28.5	8.5	16 35.8	8.0	58.3
02	214 01.5	42.8	2 56.0	8.4	16 43.8	7.9	58.3
03	229 01.5	.. 43.6	17 23.4	8.3	16 51.7	7.8	58.3
04	244 01.6	44.5	31 50.7	8.3	16 59.5	7.7	58.3
05	259 01.6	45.3	46 18.0	8.2	17 07.2	7.6	58.4
06	274 01.7	S12 46.2	60 45.2	8.1	N17 14.8	7.5	58.4
07	289 01.8	47.0	75 12.3	8.1	17 22.3	7.5	58.4
S 08	304 01.8	47.9	89 39.4	8.0	17 29.8	7.3	58.4
A 09	319 01.9	.. 48.7	104 06.4	7.9	17 37.1	7.2	58.4
T 10	334 01.9	49.6	118 33.3	7.9	17 44.3	7.1	58.4
U 11	349 02.0	50.4	133 00.2	7.8	17 51.4	7.0	58.5
R 12	4 02.0	S12 51.2	147 27.0	7.8	N17 58.4	6.9	58.5
D 13	19 02.1	52.1	161 53.8	7.7	18 05.3	6.8	58.5
A 14	34 02.2	52.9	176 20.5	7.6	18 12.1	6.7	58.5
Y 15	49 02.2	.. 53.8	190 47.1	7.6	18 18.8	6.6	58.5
16	64 02.3	54.6	205 13.7	7.5	18 25.4	6.5	58.5
17	79 02.3	55.4	219 40.2	7.4	18 31.9	6.3	58.6
18	94 02.4	S12 56.3	234 06.6	7.4	N18 38.2	6.3	58.6
19	109 02.4	57.1	248 33.0	7.3	18 44.5	6.1	58.6
20	124 02.5	58.0	262 59.3	7.3	18 50.6	6.1	58.6
21	139 02.5	.. 58.8	277 25.6	7.2	18 56.7	5.9	58.6
22	154 02.6	12 59.7	291 51.8	7.2	19 02.6	5.8	58.6
23	169 02.6	S13 00.5	306 18.0	7.0	N19 08.4	5.6	58.6
	SD 16.1	d 0.9	SD 15.7		15.8		15.9

Twilight / Sunrise / Moonrise

Lat.	Naut.	Civil	Sunrise	25	26	27	28
°	h m	h m	h m	h m	h m	h m	h m
N 72	05 42	07 02	08 21	16 05	15 41	▭	▭
N 70	05 40	06 52	08 01	16 24	16 14	15 58	▭
68	05 39	06 44	07 46	16 38	16 38	16 40	16 48
66	05 37	06 38	07 33	16 51	16 57	17 08	17 30
64	05 36	06 32	07 23	17 01	17 12	17 30	17 59
62	05 35	06 27	07 14	17 09	17 25	17 48	18 21
60	05 34	06 23	07 07	17 17	17 36	18 02	18 39
N 58	05 33	06 19	07 00	17 24	17 46	18 15	18 54
56	05 32	06 15	06 54	17 30	17 54	18 25	19 06
54	05 30	06 12	06 49	17 35	18 02	18 35	19 18
52	05 29	06 09	06 44	17 40	18 08	18 44	19 27
50	05 28	06 06	06 39	17 44	18 14	18 51	19 36
45	05 25	06 00	06 30	17 54	18 28	19 08	19 55
N 40	05 23	05 54	06 22	18 01	18 39	19 21	20 10
35	05 20	05 49	06 15	18 08	18 48	19 33	20 23
30	05 17	05 45	06 09	18 14	18 56	19 43	20 35
20	05 10	05 36	05 59	18 25	19 11	20 00	20 54
N 10	05 03	05 28	05 49	18 34	19 23	20 15	21 11
0	04 55	05 19	05 41	18 43	19 35	20 30	21 27
S 10	04 45	05 10	05 32	18 52	19 47	20 44	21 43
20	04 33	04 59	05 22	19 01	20 00	21 00	22 00
30	04 16	04 46	05 11	19 12	20 14	21 17	22 20
35	04 06	04 38	05 04	19 19	20 23	21 28	22 31
40	03 54	04 28	04 57	19 26	20 33	21 40	22 45
45	03 38	04 17	04 48	19 34	20 44	21 54	23 00
S 50	03 19	04 02	04 38	19 45	20 59	22 11	23 20
52	03 09	03 56	04 33	19 49	21 05	22 19	23 29
54	02 57	03 48	04 27	19 55	21 12	22 29	23 39
56	02 44	03 39	04 21	20 01	21 21	22 39	23 51
58	02 29	03 30	04 15	20 07	21 30	22 51	24 05
S 60	02 09	03 18	04 07	20 15	21 41	23 04	24 20

Sunset / Twilight / Moonset

Lat.	Sunset	Civil	Naut.	25	26	27	28
°	h m	h m	h m	h m	h m	h m	h m
N 72	15 06	16 24	17 44	08 33	10 44	▭	▭
N 70	15 25	16 34	17 46	08 17	10 13	12 20	▭
68	15 41	16 42	17 48	08 04	09 50	11 40	13 29
66	15 53	16 49	17 49	07 53	09 32	11 12	12 48
64	16 04	16 55	17 50	07 44	09 17	10 51	12 19
62	16 13	17 00	17 52	07 36	09 05	10 34	11 58
60	16 20	17 04	17 53	07 30	08 55	10 20	11 40
N 58	16 27	17 08	17 54	07 24	08 46	10 08	11 26
56	16 33	17 12	17 55	07 19	08 38	09 58	11 13
54	16 38	17 15	17 57	07 14	08 31	09 49	11 02
52	16 43	17 18	17 58	07 10	08 25	09 40	10 53
50	16 48	17 21	17 59	07 06	08 20	09 33	10 44
45	16 57	17 27	18 02	06 58	08 08	09 18	10 24
N 40	17 05	17 33	18 05	06 51	07 58	09 05	10 11
35	17 12	17 38	18 08	06 46	07 49	08 54	09 58
30	17 18	17 43	18 11	06 41	07 42	08 44	09 47
20	17 29	17 51	18 17	06 32	07 29	08 28	09 28
N 10	17 38	18 00	18 25	06 24	07 18	08 14	09 12
0	17 47	18 09	18 33	06 17	07 08	08 01	08 57
S 10	17 56	18 18	18 43	06 10	06 57	07 48	08 42
20	18 06	18 29	18 56	06 02	06 46	07 34	08 25
30	18 18	18 43	19 12	05 54	06 33	07 17	08 06
35	18 24	18 51	19 22	05 49	06 26	07 08	07 56
40	18 32	19 00	19 35	05 43	06 18	06 57	07 43
45	18 41	19 12	19 51	05 37	06 08	06 45	07 28
S 50	18 51	19 27	20 11	05 29	05 57	06 30	07 10
52	18 56	19 34	20 21	05 25	05 51	06 23	07 01
54	19 02	19 41	20 33	05 21	05 45	06 15	06 52
56	19 08	19 50	20 46	05 17	05 39	06 06	06 42
58	19 15	20 00	21 02	05 12	05 32	05 56	06 30
S 60	19 23	20 12	21 22	05 07	05 23	05 45	06 16

SUN / MOON

Day	Eqn. of Time 00h	Eqn. of Time 12h	Mer. Pass.	Mer. Pass. Upper	Mer. Pass. Lower	Age	Phase
d	m s	m s	h m	h m	h m	d	%
25	15 52	15 56	11 44	00 05	12 30	16	99
26	15 59	16 02	11 44	00 55	13 21	17	96
27	16 05	16 08	11 44	01 48	14 15	18	91

UT	ARIES GHA	VENUS −4.3 GHA	Dec	MARS −0.7 GHA	Dec	JUPITER −1.7 GHA	Dec	SATURN +0.6 GHA	Dec	STARS Name	SHA	Dec
28 00	36 17.4	188 23.0	S17 51.9	74 07.5	S17 30.3	160 53.4	S18 54.9	121 16.7	S22 46.1	Acamar	315 15.2	S40 13.8
01	51 19.8	203 26.7	51.0	89 08.7	29.8	175 55.3	55.1	136 18.9	46.1	Achernar	335 23.5	S57 08.6
02	66 22.3	218 30.5	50.0	104 09.8	29.2	190 57.2	55.2	151 21.2	46.1	Acrux	173 05.8	S63 11.9
03	81 24.7	233 34.3	.. 49.0	119 10.9	.. 28.7	205 59.1	.. 55.3	166 23.4	.. 46.1	Adhara	255 09.5	S28 59.7
04	96 27.2	248 38.0	48.0	134 12.1	28.1	221 01.0	55.4	181 25.7	46.1	Aldebaran	290 44.9	N16 32.7
05	111 29.7	263 41.8	47.0	149 13.2	27.6	236 02.9	55.6	196 28.0	46.1			
06	126 32.1	278 45.6	S17 46.0	164 14.3	S17 27.0	251 04.9	S18 55.7	211 30.2	S22 46.1	Alioth	166 18.1	N55 51.5
07	141 34.6	293 49.3	45.0	179 15.5	26.5	266 06.8	55.8	226 32.5	46.1	Alkaid	152 56.5	N49 13.3
08	156 37.1	308 53.1	44.0	194 16.6	26.0	281 08.7	55.9	241 34.7	46.1	Al Na'ir	27 39.0	S46 52.3
S 09	171 39.5	323 56.8	.. 43.0	209 17.7	.. 25.4	296 10.6	.. 56.1	256 37.0	.. 46.1	Alnilam	275 42.5	S 1 11.5
U 10	186 42.0	339 00.6	42.0	224 18.8	24.9	311 12.5	56.2	271 39.2	46.1	Alphard	217 52.6	S 8 44.3
N 11	201 44.5	354 04.3	41.0	239 20.0	24.3	326 14.4	56.3	286 41.5	46.1			
D 12	216 46.9	9 08.1	S17 40.0	254 21.1	S17 23.8	341 16.4	S18 56.4	301 43.7	S22 46.1	Alphecca	126 08.3	N26 39.4
A 13	231 49.4	24 11.9	39.0	269 22.2	23.2	356 18.3	56.6	316 46.0	46.1	Alpheratz	357 39.4	N29 11.7
Y 14	246 51.9	39 15.6	38.0	284 23.3	22.7	11 20.2	56.7	331 48.2	46.1	Altair	62 04.8	N 8 55.3
15	261 54.3	54 19.4	.. 37.0	299 24.5	.. 22.1	26 22.1	.. 56.8	346 50.5	.. 46.1	Ankaa	353 11.8	S42 12.4
16	276 56.8	69 23.1	36.0	314 25.6	21.6	41 24.0	56.9	1 52.8	46.1	Antares	112 22.1	S26 28.2
17	291 59.2	84 26.9	35.0	329 26.7	21.0	56 25.9	57.1	16 55.0	46.1			
18	307 01.7	99 30.6	S17 34.0	344 27.9	S17 20.5	71 27.9	S18 57.2	31 57.3	S22 46.1	Arcturus	145 52.8	N19 05.3
19	322 04.2	114 34.3	33.0	359 29.0	20.0	86 29.8	57.3	46 59.5	46.1	Atria	107 21.1	S69 03.6
20	337 06.6	129 38.1	32.0	14 30.1	19.4	101 31.7	57.4	62 01.8	46.1	Avior	234 16.5	S59 33.9
21	352 09.1	144 41.8	.. 31.0	29 31.2	.. 18.9	116 33.6	.. 57.6	77 04.0	.. 46.1	Bellatrix	278 27.9	N 6 21.9
22	7 11.6	159 45.6	30.0	44 32.4	18.3	131 35.5	57.7	92 06.3	46.1	Betelgeuse	270 57.2	N 7 24.5
23	22 14.0	174 49.3	29.0	59 33.5	17.8	146 37.4	57.8	107 08.5	46.1			
29 00	37 16.5	189 53.1	S17 28.0	74 34.6	S17 17.2	161 39.3	S18 57.9	122 10.8	S22 46.1	Canopus	263 54.3	S52 42.2
01	52 19.0	204 56.8	27.0	89 35.7	16.7	176 41.3	58.1	137 13.0	46.1	Capella	280 28.7	N46 00.7
02	67 21.4	220 00.5	26.0	104 36.8	16.1	191 43.2	58.2	152 15.3	46.1	Deneb	49 29.0	N45 21.2
03	82 23.9	235 04.3	.. 25.0	119 38.0	.. 15.6	206 45.1	.. 58.3	167 17.5	.. 46.1	Denebola	182 30.2	N14 28.2
04	97 26.4	250 08.0	24.0	134 39.1	15.0	221 47.0	58.4	182 19.8	46.1	Diphda	348 52.0	S17 53.1
05	112 28.8	265 11.7	23.0	149 40.2	14.5	236 48.9	58.6	197 22.0	46.1			
06	127 31.3	280 15.5	S17 22.0	164 41.3	S17 13.9	251 50.8	S18 58.7	212 24.3	S22 46.1	Dubhe	193 47.7	N61 38.9
07	142 33.7	295 19.2	21.0	179 42.5	13.4	266 52.7	58.8	227 26.5	46.1	Elnath	278 07.8	N28 37.2
08	157 36.2	310 22.9	19.9	194 43.6	12.8	281 54.7	58.9	242 28.8	46.1	Eltanin	90 44.8	N51 29.6
M 09	172 38.7	325 26.6	.. 18.9	209 44.7	.. 12.3	296 56.6	.. 59.1	257 31.0	.. 46.1	Enif	33 43.5	N 9 57.8
O 10	187 41.1	340 30.4	17.9	224 45.8	11.7	311 58.5	59.2	272 33.3	46.1	Fomalhaut	15 19.8	S29 31.4
N 11	202 43.6	355 34.1	16.9	239 46.9	11.2	327 00.4	59.3	287 35.6	46.1			
D 12	217 46.1	10 37.8	S17 15.9	254 48.1	S17 10.6	342 02.3	S18 59.4	302 37.8	S22 46.1	Gacrux	171 57.3	S57 12.8
A 13	232 48.5	25 41.5	14.9	269 49.2	10.1	357 04.2	59.6	317 40.1	46.1	Gienah	175 48.9	S17 38.5
Y 14	247 51.0	40 45.2	13.9	284 50.3	09.5	12 06.1	59.7	332 42.3	46.1	Hadar	148 43.4	S60 27.5
15	262 53.5	55 48.9	.. 12.8	299 51.4	.. 09.0	27 08.1	.. 59.8	347 44.6	.. 46.1	Hamal	327 56.3	N23 33.0
16	277 55.9	70 52.7	11.8	314 52.5	08.4	42 10.0	18 59.9	2 46.8	46.1	Kaus Aust.	83 39.2	S34 22.4
17	292 58.4	85 56.4	10.8	329 53.7	07.9	57 11.9	19 00.0	17 49.1	46.1			
18	308 00.8	101 00.1	S17 09.8	344 54.8	S17 07.3	72 13.8	S19 00.2	32 51.3	S22 46.1	Kochab	137 21.3	N74 04.9
19	323 03.3	116 03.8	08.8	359 55.9	06.8	87 15.7	00.3	47 53.6	46.1	Markab	13 34.5	N15 18.5
20	338 05.8	131 07.5	07.8	14 57.0	06.2	102 17.6	00.4	62 55.8	46.1	Menkar	314 10.9	N 4 09.7
21	353 08.2	146 11.2	.. 06.7	29 58.1	.. 05.7	117 19.5	.. 00.5	77 58.1	.. 46.1	Menkent	148 03.7	S36 27.5
22	8 10.7	161 14.9	05.7	44 59.2	05.1	132 21.5	00.7	93 00.3	46.1	Miaplacidus	221 39.1	S69 47.3
23	23 13.2	176 18.6	04.7	60 00.4	04.6	147 23.4	00.8	108 02.6	46.1			
30 00	38 15.6	191 22.3	S17 03.7	75 01.5	S17 04.0	162 25.3	S19 00.9	123 04.8	S22 46.0	Mirfak	308 34.7	N49 55.5
01	53 18.1	206 26.0	02.7	90 02.6	03.5	177 27.2	01.0	138 07.1	46.0	Nunki	75 54.0	S26 16.3
02	68 20.6	221 29.7	01.6	105 03.7	02.9	192 29.1	01.2	153 09.3	46.0	Peacock	53 13.6	S56 40.6
03	83 23.0	236 33.4	17 00.6	120 04.8	.. 02.3	207 31.0	.. 01.3	168 11.6	.. 46.0	Pollux	243 23.3	N27 58.7
04	98 25.5	251 37.1	16 59.6	135 05.9	01.8	222 32.9	01.4	183 13.8	46.0	Procyon	244 55.9	N 5 10.6
05	113 28.0	266 40.8	58.6	150 07.1	01.2	237 34.8	01.5	198 16.1	46.0			
06	128 30.4	281 44.4	S16 57.5	165 08.2	S17 00.7	252 36.8	S19 01.7	213 18.3	S22 46.0	Rasalhague	96 03.3	N12 33.1
07	143 32.9	296 48.1	56.5	180 09.3	17 00.1	267 38.7	01.8	228 20.5	46.0	Regulus	207 39.8	N11 52.6
T 08	158 35.3	311 51.8	55.5	195 10.4	16 59.6	282 40.6	01.9	243 22.8	46.0	Rigel	281 08.3	S 8 10.8
U 09	173 37.8	326 55.5	.. 54.5	210 11.5	.. 59.0	297 42.5	.. 02.0	258 25.0	.. 46.0	Rigil Kent.	139 47.5	S60 54.5
E 10	188 40.3	341 59.2	53.4	225 12.6	58.5	312 44.4	02.2	273 27.3	46.0	Sabik	102 08.7	S15 44.7
S 11	203 42.7	357 02.9	52.4	240 13.7	57.9	327 46.3	02.3	288 29.5	46.0			
D 12	218 45.2	12 06.5	S16 51.4	255 14.9	S16 57.4	342 48.2	S19 02.4	303 31.8	S22 46.0	Schedar	349 35.8	N56 38.5
A 13	233 47.7	27 10.2	50.4	270 16.0	56.8	357 50.1	02.5	318 34.0	46.0	Shaula	96 17.3	S37 06.9
Y 14	248 50.1	42 13.9	49.3	285 17.1	56.2	12 52.1	02.7	333 36.3	46.0	Sirius	258 30.4	S16 44.5
15	263 52.6	57 17.5	.. 48.3	300 18.2	.. 55.7	27 54.0	.. 02.8	348 38.5	.. 46.0	Spica	158 27.8	S11 15.3
16	278 55.1	72 21.2	47.3	315 19.3	55.1	42 55.9	02.9	3 40.8	46.0	Suhail	222 49.8	S43 30.2
17	293 57.5	87 24.9	46.3	330 20.4	54.6	57 57.8	03.0	18 43.0	46.0			
18	309 00.0	102 28.5	S16 45.2	345 21.5	S16 54.0	72 59.7	S19 03.1	33 45.3	S22 46.0	Vega	80 36.7	N38 48.4
19	324 02.5	117 32.2	44.2	0 22.6	53.5	88 01.6	03.3	48 47.5	46.0	Zuben'ubi	137 01.7	S16 06.9
20	339 04.9	132 35.9	43.2	15 23.8	52.9	103 03.5	03.4	63 49.8	46.0		SHA	Mer. Pass.
21	354 07.4	147 39.5	.. 42.1	30 24.9	.. 52.3	118 05.4	.. 03.5	78 52.0	.. 46.0	Venus	152 36.6	11 18
22	9 09.8	162 43.2	41.1	45 26.0	51.8	133 07.3	03.6	93 54.3	46.0	Mars	37 18.1	19 00
23	24 12.3	177 46.8	40.1	60 27.1	51.2	148 09.3	03.8	108 56.5	46.0	Jupiter	124 22.8	13 12
Mer. Pass. 21 27.4		v 3.7	d 1.0	v 1.1	d 0.6	v 1.9	d 0.1	v 2.3	d 0.0	Saturn	84 54.3	15 49

UT	SUN GHA	SUN Dec	MOON GHA	v	MOON Dec	d	HP	Lat.	Twilight Naut.	Twilight Civil	Sunrise	Moonrise 28	Moonrise 29	Moonrise 30	Moonrise 31
	° '	° '	° '	'	° '	'	'	°	h m	h m	h m	h m	h m	h m	h m
d h								N 72	05 54	07 15	08 38	▭	▭	▭	19 47
28 00	184 02.7	S13 01.3	320 44.0	7.1	N19 14.0	5.6	58.6	N 70	05 51	07 04	08 15	▭	▭	▭	20 33
01	199 02.8	02.2	335 10.1	7.0	19 19.6	5.4	58.7	68	05 48	06 55	07 58	16 48	17 21	18 43	21 03
02	214 02.8	03.0	349 36.1	6.9	19 25.0	5.4	58.7	66	05 46	06 47	07 44	17 30	18 14	19 28	21 25
03	229 02.9 ..	03.8	4 02.0	6.9	19 30.4	5.2	58.7	64	05 44	06 40	07 32	17 59	18 47	19 57	21 43
04	244 02.9	04.7	18 27.9	6.8	19 35.6	5.1	58.7	62	05 42	06 35	07 23	18 21	19 11	20 19	21 57
05	259 03.0	05.5	32 53.7	6.8	19 40.7	4.9	58.7	60	05 41	06 30	07 14	18 39	19 30	20 37	22 10
06	274 03.0	S13 06.4	47 19.5	6.7	N19 45.6	4.9	58.7	N 58	05 39	06 25	07 07	18 54	19 46	20 52	22 10
07	289 03.1	07.2	61 45.2	6.7	19 50.5	4.7	58.7	56	05 37	06 21	07 00	19 06	19 59	21 05	22 21
08	304 03.1	08.0	76 10.9	6.6	19 55.2	4.6	58.7	54	05 36	06 17	06 54	19 18	20 11	21 16	22 30
S 09	319 03.2 ..	08.9	90 36.5	6.6	19 59.8	4.4	58.7	52	05 34	06 14	06 49	19 27	20 22	21 26	22 39
U 10	334 03.2	09.7	105 02.1	6.6	20 04.2	4.4	58.8	50	05 33	06 11	06 44	19 36	20 31	21 35	22 46
N 11	349 03.3	10.5	119 27.7	6.5	20 08.6	4.2	58.8	45	05 29	06 04	06 34	19 55	20 50	21 54	23 02
D 12	4 03.3	S13 11.4	133 53.2	6.4	N20 12.8	4.1	58.8	N 40	05 26	05 58	06 25	20 10	21 06	22 09	23 16
A 13	19 03.4	12.2	148 18.6	6.4	20 16.9	3.9	58.8	35	05 22	05 52	06 18	20 23	21 20	22 22	23 27
Y 14	34 03.4	13.0	162 44.0	6.4	20 20.8	3.9	58.8	30	05 19	05 47	06 11	20 35	21 32	22 33	23 37
15	49 03.5 ..	13.9	177 09.4	6.3	20 24.7	3.7	58.8	20	05 11	05 37	06 00	20 54	21 52	22 52	23 53
16	64 03.5	14.7	191 34.7	6.3	20 28.4	3.5	58.8	N 10	05 03	05 28	05 50	21 11	22 09	23 09	24 08
17	79 03.6	15.5	206 00.0	6.2	20 31.9	3.5	58.8	0	04 54	05 19	05 40	21 27	22 26	23 24	24 22
18	94 03.6	S13 16.4	220 25.2	6.2	N20 35.4	3.3	58.9	S 10	04 44	05 09	05 31	21 43	22 42	23 40	24 35
19	109 03.6	17.2	234 50.4	6.2	20 38.7	3.1	58.9	20	04 30	04 57	05 20	22 00	23 00	23 56	24 50
20	124 03.7	18.0	249 15.6	6.1	20 41.8	3.1	58.9	30	04 13	04 43	05 08	22 20	23 20	24 16	00 16
21	139 03.7 ..	18.9	263 40.7	6.1	20 44.9	2.9	58.9	35	04 02	04 34	05 01	22 31	23 32	24 27	00 27
22	154 03.8	19.7	278 05.8	6.1	20 47.8	2.8	58.9	40	03 49	04 24	04 53	22 45	23 45	24 39	00 39
23	169 03.8	20.5	292 30.9	6.0	20 50.6	2.6	58.9	45	03 33	04 12	04 44	23 00	24 01	00 01	00 55
29 00	184 03.9	S13 21.4	306 55.9	6.0	N20 53.2	2.5	58.9	S 50	03 12	03 56	04 32	23 20	24 21	00 21	01 13
01	199 03.9	22.2	321 20.9	6.0	20 55.7	2.4	58.9	52	03 01	03 49	04 27	23 29	24 30	00 30	01 22
02	214 04.0	23.0	335 45.9	6.0	20 58.1	2.2	58.9	54	02 49	03 41	04 21	23 39	24 41	00 41	01 31
03	229 04.0 ..	23.9	350 10.9	5.9	21 00.3	2.1	58.9	56	02 34	03 31	04 14	23 51	24 53	00 53	01 42
04	244 04.1	24.7	4 35.8	5.9	21 02.4	2.0	59.0	58	02 17	03 21	04 07	24 05	00 05	01 07	01 55
05	259 04.1	25.5	19 00.7	5.8	21 04.4	1.8	59.0	S 60	01 55	03 08	03 59	24 20	00 20	01 23	02 09
06	274 04.1	S13 26.3	33 25.5	5.9	N21 06.2	1.7	59.0	Lat.	Sunset	Twilight Civil	Twilight Naut.	Moonset 28	Moonset 29	Moonset 30	Moonset 31
07	289 04.2	27.2	47 50.4	5.8	21 07.9	1.5	59.0								
08	304 04.2	28.0	62 15.2	5.8	21 09.4	1.4	59.0	°	h m	h m	h m	h m	h m	h m	h m
M 09	319 04.3 ..	28.8	76 40.0	5.8	21 10.8	1.3	59.0	N 72	14 48	16 11	17 32	▭	▭	▭	▭
O 10	334 04.3	29.7	91 04.8	5.8	21 12.1	1.1	59.0	N 70	15 11	16 22	17 35	▭	▭	▭	16 37
N 11	349 04.3	30.5	105 29.6	5.7	21 13.2	1.0	59.0	68	15 28	16 31	17 37	13 29	14 59	15 40	15 51
D 12	4 04.4	S13 31.3	119 54.3	5.8	N21 14.2	0.9	59.0	66	15 42	16 39	17 40	12 48	14 06	14 55	15 20
A 13	19 04.4	32.1	134 19.1	5.7	21 15.1	0.7	59.0	64	15 54	16 46	17 42	12 19	13 33	14 25	14 58
Y 14	34 04.5	33.0	148 43.8	5.7	21 15.8	0.6	59.0	62	16 04	16 52	17 44	11 58	13 09	14 03	14 39
15	49 04.5 ..	33.8	163 08.5	5.7	21 16.4	0.4	59.0	60	16 12	16 57	17 46	11 40	12 50	13 44	14 24
16	64 04.5	34.6	177 33.2	5.7	21 16.8	0.3	59.1	N 58	16 20	17 01	17 47	11 26	12 34	13 29	14 11
17	79 04.6	35.4	191 57.9	5.6	21 17.1	0.2	59.1	56	16 26	17 05	17 49	11 13	12 21	13 16	14 00
18	94 04.6	S13 36.3	206 22.5	5.7	N21 17.3	0.0	59.1	54	16 32	17 09	17 51	11 02	12 09	13 05	13 50
19	109 04.7	37.1	220 47.2	5.7	21 17.3	0.2	59.1	52	16 37	17 13	17 52	10 53	11 58	12 55	13 41
20	124 04.7	37.9	235 11.9	5.6	21 17.1	0.2	59.1	50	16 42	17 16	17 54	10 44	11 49	12 46	13 33
21	139 04.7 ..	38.7	249 36.5	5.7	21 16.9	0.4	59.1	45	16 53	17 23	17 58	10 26	11 30	12 27	13 16
22	154 04.8	39.5	264 01.2	5.7	21 16.5	0.6	59.1	N 40	17 01	17 29	18 01	10 11	11 14	12 11	13 02
23	169 04.8	40.4	278 25.9	5.6	21 15.9	0.7	59.1	35	17 09	17 35	18 05	09 58	11 00	11 58	12 50
30 00	184 04.9	S13 41.2	292 50.5	5.7	N21 15.2	0.8	59.1	30	17 16	17 40	18 08	09 47	10 49	11 47	12 40
01	199 04.9	42.0	307 15.2	5.6	21 14.4	1.0	59.1	20	17 27	17 50	18 16	09 28	10 29	11 27	12 22
02	214 04.9	42.8	321 39.8	5.7	21 13.4	1.1	59.1	N 10	17 37	17 59	18 24	09 12	10 11	11 10	12 07
03	229 05.0 ..	43.7	336 04.5	5.7	21 12.3	1.2	59.1	0	17 47	18 08	18 33	08 57	09 55	10 54	11 52
04	244 05.0	44.5	350 29.2	5.6	21 11.1	1.4	59.1	S 10	17 57	18 19	18 44	08 42	09 39	10 37	11 37
05	259 05.0	45.3	4 53.8	5.7	21 09.7	1.5	59.1	20	18 08	18 30	18 57	08 25	09 21	10 20	11 21
06	274 05.1	S13 46.1	19 18.5	5.7	N21 08.2	1.7	59.1	30	18 20	18 45	19 15	08 06	09 01	10 00	11 03
07	289 05.1	46.9	33 43.2	5.7	21 06.5	1.8	59.1	35	18 27	18 54	19 26	07 56	08 49	09 48	10 52
T 08	304 05.1	47.8	48 07.9	5.7	21 04.7	2.0	59.1	40	18 35	19 04	19 39	07 43	08 36	09 35	10 40
U 09	319 05.2 ..	48.6	62 32.6	5.8	21 02.7	2.1	59.1	45	18 45	19 17	19 56	07 28	08 20	09 19	10 25
E 10	334 05.2	49.4	76 57.4	5.7	21 00.6	2.2	59.2	S 50	18 56	19 32	20 18	07 10	08 00	09 00	10 08
S 11	349 05.2	50.2	91 22.1	5.8	20 58.4	2.3	59.2	52	19 02	19 40	20 28	07 02	07 51	08 50	09 59
D 12	4 05.3	S13 51.0	105 46.9	5.7	N20 56.1	2.6	59.2	54	19 08	19 48	20 41	06 52	07 40	08 40	09 50
A 13	19 05.3	51.8	120 11.6	5.8	20 53.5	2.6	59.2	56	19 15	19 58	20 55	06 42	07 28	08 28	09 39
Y 14	34 05.3	52.7	134 36.4	5.8	20 50.9	2.8	59.2	58	19 22	20 09	21 13	06 30	07 15	08 14	09 27
15	49 05.4 ..	53.5	149 01.2	5.9	20 48.1	2.9	59.2	S 60	19 31	20 21	21 36	06 16	06 59	07 58	09 13
16	64 05.4	54.3	163 26.1	5.9	20 45.2	3.0	59.2								
17	79 05.4	55.1	177 50.9	5.9	20 42.2	3.2	59.2			SUN			MOON		
18	94 05.5	S13 55.9	192 15.8	5.9	N20 39.0	3.3	59.2	Day	Eqn. of Time 00h	Eqn. of Time 12h	Mer. Pass.	Mer. Pass. Upper	Mer. Pass. Lower	Age	Phase
19	109 05.5	56.7	206 40.7	5.9	20 35.7	3.5	59.2								
20	124 05.5	57.5	221 05.6	5.9	20 32.2	3.6	59.2	d	m s	m s	h m	h m	h m	d	%
21	139 05.5 ..	58.4	235 30.5	6.0	20 28.6	3.7	59.2	28	16 11	16 13	11 44	02 43	15 12	19	83
22	154 05.6	13 59.2	249 55.5	6.0	20 24.9	3.9	59.2	29	16 15	16 17	11 44	03 41	16 10	20	74
23	169 05.6	S14 00.0	264 20.5	6.1	N20 21.0	4.0	59.2	30	16 19	16 21	11 44	04 40	17 09	21	64
	SD 16.1	d 0.8	SD 16.0		16.1		16.1									

UT	ARIES	VENUS −4·2		MARS −0·6		JUPITER −1·7		SATURN +0·6		STARS		
	GHA	GHA	Dec	GHA	Dec	GHA	Dec	GHA	Dec	Name	SHA	Dec
d h	° ′	° ′	° ′	° ′	° ′	° ′	° ′	° ′	° ′		° ′	° ′
31 00	39 14.8	192 50.5	S16 39.0	75 28.2	S16 50.7	163 11.2	S19 03.9	123 58.8	S22 46.0	Acamar	315 15.2	S40 13.8
01	54 17.2	207 54.1	38.0	90 29.3	50.1	178 13.1	04.0	139 01.0	46.0	Achernar	335 23.5	S57 08.7
02	69 19.7	222 57.8	37.0	105 30.4	49.6	193 15.0	04.1	154 03.2	46.0	Acrux	173 05.8	S63 11.9
03	84 22.2	238 01.4 . .	36.0	120 31.5 . .	49.0	208 16.9 . .	04.3	169 05.5 . .	46.0	Adhara	255 05.5	S28 59.7
04	99 24.6	253 05.0	34.9	135 32.6	48.4	223 18.8	04.4	184 07.7	46.0	Aldebaran	290 44.9	N16 32.7
05	114 27.1	268 08.7	33.9	150 33.7	47.9	238 20.7	04.5	199 10.0	46.0			
06	129 29.6	283 12.3	S16 32.9	165 34.8	S16 47.3	253 22.6	S19 04.6	214 12.2	S22 46.0	Alioth	166 18.0	N55 51.5
W 07	144 32.0	298 16.0	31.8	180 36.0	46.8	268 24.5	04.8	229 14.5	46.0	Alkaid	152 56.5	N49 13.3
E 08	159 34.5	313 19.6	30.8	195 37.1	46.2	283 26.4	04.9	244 16.7	46.0	Al Na'ir	27 39.0	S46 52.4
D 09	174 37.0	328 23.2 . .	29.8	210 38.2 . .	45.6	298 28.4 . .	05.0	259 19.0 . .	46.0	Alnilam	275 42.5	S 1 11.5
N 10	189 39.4	343 26.8	28.7	225 39.3	45.1	313 30.3	05.1	274 21.2	46.0	Alphard	217 52.6	S 8 44.3
E 11	204 41.9	358 30.5	27.7	240 40.4	44.5	328 32.2	05.2	289 23.5	46.0			
S 12	219 44.3	13 34.1	S16 26.7	255 41.5	S16 44.0	343 34.1	S19 05.4	304 25.7	S22 46.0	Alphecca	126 08.3	N26 39.4
D 13	234 46.8	28 37.7	25.6	270 42.6	43.4	358 36.0	05.5	319 27.9	46.0	Alpheratz	357 39.4	N29 11.7
A 14	249 49.3	43 41.3	24.6	285 43.7	42.8	13 37.9	05.6	334 30.2	46.0	Altair	62 04.8	N 8 55.3
Y 15	264 51.7	58 44.9 . .	23.6	300 44.8 . .	42.3	28 39.8 . .	05.7	349 32.4 . .	46.0	Ankaa	353 11.8	S42 12.4
16	279 54.2	73 48.6	22.5	315 45.9	41.7	43 41.7	05.9	4 34.7	46.0	Antares	112 22.1	S26 28.2
17	294 56.7	88 52.2	21.5	330 47.0	41.2	58 43.6	06.0	19 36.9	46.0			
18	309 59.1	103 55.8	S16 20.5	345 48.1	S16 40.6	73 45.5	S19 06.1	34 39.2	S22 45.9	Arcturus	145 52.8	N19 05.3
19	325 01.6	118 59.4	19.4	0 49.2	40.0	88 47.5	06.2	49 41.4	45.9	Atria	107 21.1	S69 03.6
20	340 04.1	134 03.0	18.4	15 50.3	39.5	103 49.4	06.4	64 43.7	45.9	Avior	234 16.5	S59 33.9
21	355 06.5	149 06.6 . .	17.4	30 51.4 . .	38.9	118 51.3 . .	06.5	79 45.9 . .	45.9	Bellatrix	278 27.9	N 6 21.9
22	10 09.0	164 10.2	16.3	45 52.5	38.3	133 53.2	06.6	94 48.1	45.9	Betelgeuse	270 57.2	N 7 24.5
23	25 11.5	179 13.8	15.3	60 53.6	37.8	148 55.1	06.7	109 50.4	45.9			
1 00	40 13.9	194 17.4	S16 14.3	75 54.7	S16 37.2	163 57.0	S19 06.9	124 52.6	S22 45.9	Canopus	263 54.2	S52 42.2
01	55 16.4	209 21.0	13.3	90 55.8	36.7	178 58.9	07.0	139 54.9	45.9	Capella	280 28.7	N46 00.7
02	70 18.8	224 24.6	12.2	105 57.0	36.1	194 00.8	07.1	154 57.1	45.9	Deneb	49 29.0	N45 21.2
03	85 21.3	239 28.1 . .	11.2	120 58.1 . .	35.5	209 02.7 . .	07.2	169 59.4 . .	45.9	Denebola	182 30.2	N14 28.2
04	100 23.8	254 31.7	10.2	135 59.2	35.0	224 04.6	07.3	185 01.6	45.9	Diphda	348 52.0	S17 53.1
05	115 26.2	269 35.3	09.1	151 00.3	34.4	239 06.5	07.5	200 03.8	45.9			
06	130 28.7	284 38.9	S16 08.1	166 01.4	S16 33.8	254 08.5	S19 07.6	215 06.1	S22 45.9	Dubhe	193 47.7	N61 38.8
07	145 31.2	299 42.5	07.1	181 02.5	33.3	269 10.4	07.7	230 08.3	45.9	Elnath	278 07.8	N28 37.2
T 08	160 33.6	314 46.0	06.0	196 03.6	32.7	284 12.3	07.8	245 10.6	45.9	Eltanin	90 44.8	N51 29.6
H 09	175 36.1	329 49.6 . .	05.0	211 04.7 . .	32.1	299 14.2 . .	08.0	260 12.8 . .	45.9	Enif	33 43.5	N 9 57.8
U 10	190 38.6	344 53.2	04.0	226 05.8	31.6	314 16.1	08.1	275 15.0	45.9	Fomalhaut	15 19.8	S29 31.5
R 11	205 41.0	359 56.7	02.9	241 06.9	31.0	329 18.0	08.2	290 17.3	45.9			
S 12	220 43.5	15 00.3	S16 01.9	256 08.0	S16 30.4	344 19.9	S19 08.3	305 19.5	S22 45.9	Gacrux	171 57.3	S57 12.8
D 13	235 45.9	30 03.9	16 00.9	271 09.1	29.9	359 21.8	08.5	320 21.8	45.9	Gienah	175 48.8	S17 38.5
A 14	250 48.4	45 07.4	15 59.8	286 10.2	29.3	14 23.7	08.6	335 24.0	45.9	Hadar	148 43.3	S60 27.5
Y 15	265 50.9	60 11.0 . .	58.8	301 11.3 . .	28.7	29 25.6 . .	08.7	350 26.3 . .	45.9	Hamal	327 56.3	N23 33.0
16	280 53.3	75 14.5	57.8	316 12.4	28.2	44 27.5	08.8	5 28.5	45.9	Kaus Aust.	83 39.2	S34 22.4
17	295 55.8	90 18.1	56.7	331 13.5	27.6	59 29.4	08.9	20 30.7	45.9			
18	310 58.3	105 21.6	S15 55.7	346 14.6	S16 27.1	74 31.4	S19 09.1	35 33.0	S22 45.9	Kochab	137 21.3	N74 04.9
19	326 00.7	120 25.2	54.7	1 15.7	26.5	89 33.3	09.2	50 35.2	45.9	Markab	13 34.5	N15 18.5
20	341 03.2	135 28.7	53.6	16 16.8	25.9	104 35.2	09.3	65 37.5	45.9	Menkar	314 10.9	N 4 09.7
21	356 05.7	150 32.2 . .	52.6	31 17.9 . .	25.3	119 37.1 . .	09.4	80 39.7 . .	45.9	Menkent	148 03.7	S36 27.5
22	11 08.1	165 35.8	51.6	46 18.9	24.8	134 39.0	09.6	95 41.9	45.9	Miaplacidus	221 39.0	S69 47.3
23	26 10.6	180 39.3	50.6	61 20.0	24.2	149 40.9	09.7	110 44.2	45.9			
2 00	41 13.1	195 42.8	S15 49.5	76 21.1	S16 23.6	164 42.8	S19 09.8	125 46.4	S22 45.9	Mirfak	308 34.6	N49 55.5
01	56 15.5	210 46.4	48.5	91 22.2	23.1	179 44.7	09.9	140 48.7	45.9	Nunki	75 54.0	S26 16.3
02	71 18.0	225 49.9	47.5	106 23.3	22.5	194 46.6	10.0	155 50.9	45.9	Peacock	53 13.6	S56 40.6
03	86 20.4	240 53.4 . .	46.4	121 24.4 . .	21.9	209 48.5 . .	10.2	170 53.1 . .	45.9	Pollux	243 23.2	N27 58.7
04	101 22.9	255 56.9	45.4	136 25.5	21.4	224 50.4	10.3	185 55.4	45.9	Procyon	244 55.9	N 5 10.6
05	116 25.4	271 00.4	44.4	151 26.6	20.8	239 52.3	10.4	200 57.6	45.9			
06	131 27.8	286 04.0	S15 43.4	166 27.7	S16 20.2	254 54.2	S19 10.5	215 59.9	S22 45.8	Rasalhague	96 03.3	N12 33.1
07	146 30.3	301 07.5	42.3	181 28.8	19.7	269 56.1	10.7	231 02.1	45.8	Regulus	207 39.8	N11 52.6
08	161 32.8	316 11.0	41.3	196 29.9	19.1	284 58.1	10.8	246 04.3	45.8	Rigel	281 08.3	S 8 10.8
F 09	176 35.2	331 14.5 . .	40.3	211 31.0 . .	18.5	300 00.0 . .	10.9	261 06.6 . .	45.8	Rigil Kent.	139 47.5	S60 54.5
R 10	191 37.7	346 18.0	39.2	226 32.1	18.0	315 01.9	11.0	276 08.8	45.8	Sabik	102 08.7	S15 44.7
I 11	206 40.2	1 21.5	38.2	241 33.2	17.4	330 03.8	11.2	291 11.1	45.8			
D 12	221 42.6	16 25.0	S15 37.2	256 34.3	S16 16.8	345 05.7	S19 11.3	306 13.3	S22 45.8	Schedar	349 35.8	N56 38.5
A 13	236 45.1	31 28.5	36.2	271 35.4	16.2	0 07.6	11.4	321 15.5	45.8	Shaula	96 17.3	S37 06.9
Y 14	251 47.6	46 32.0	35.1	286 36.5	15.7	15 09.5	11.5	336 17.8	45.8	Sirius	258 30.4	S16 44.5
15	266 50.0	61 35.4 . .	34.1	301 37.6 . .	15.1	30 11.4 . .	11.6	351 20.0 . .	45.8	Spica	158 27.7	S11 15.3
16	281 52.5	76 38.9	33.1	316 38.7	14.5	45 13.3	11.8	6 22.2	45.8	Suhail	222 49.8	S43 30.2
17	296 54.9	91 42.4	32.1	331 39.7	14.0	60 15.2	11.9	21 24.5	45.8			
18	311 57.4	106 45.9	S15 31.0	346 40.8	S16 13.4	75 17.1	S19 12.0	36 26.7	S22 45.8	Vega	80 36.7	N38 48.4
19	326 59.9	121 49.4	30.0	1 41.9	12.8	90 19.0	12.1	51 29.0	45.8	Zuben'ubi	137 01.7	S16 06.9
20	342 02.3	136 52.8	29.0	16 43.0	12.2	105 20.9	12.3	66 31.2	45.8		SHA	Mer.Pass.
21	357 04.8	151 56.3 . .	28.0	31 44.1 . .	11.7	120 22.8 . .	12.4	81 33.4 . .	45.8		° ′	h m
22	12 07.3	166 59.8	27.0	46 45.2	11.1	135 24.7	12.5	96 35.7	45.8	Venus	154 03.5	11 00
23	27 09.7	182 03.2	25.9	61 46.3	10.5	150 26.6	12.6	111 37.9	45.8	Mars	35 40.8	18 55
	h m									Jupiter	123 43.1	13 03
Mer. Pass. 21 15.6		v 3.6	d 1.0	v 1.1	d 0.6	v 1.9	d 0.1	v 2.2	d 0.0	Saturn	84 38.7	15 38

UT	SUN GHA	SUN Dec	MOON GHA	v	MOON Dec	d	HP
d h	° ′	° ′	° ′	′	° ′	′	′
31 00	184 05.6	S14 00.8	278 45.6	6.0	N20 17.0	4.1	59.2
01	199 05.7	01.6	293 10.6	6.1	20 12.9	4.3	59.2
02	214 05.7	02.4	307 35.7	6.1	20 08.6	4.4	59.2
03	229 05.7	.. 03.2	322 00.8	6.2	20 04.2	4.5	59.2
04	244 05.7	04.0	336 26.0	6.2	19 59.7	4.6	59.2
05	259 05.8	04.9	350 51.2	6.2	19 55.1	4.8	59.2
W 06	274 05.8	S14 05.7	5 16.4	6.3	N19 50.3	4.9	59.2
E 07	289 05.8	06.5	19 41.7	6.3	19 45.4	5.1	59.2
D 08	304 05.8	07.3	34 07.0	6.3	19 40.3	5.1	59.2
N 09	319 05.9	.. 08.1	48 32.3	6.4	19 35.2	5.3	59.2
E 10	334 05.9	08.9	62 57.7	6.4	19 29.9	5.4	59.2
S 11	349 05.9	09.7	77 23.1	6.5	19 24.5	5.6	59.2
D 12	4 05.9	S14 10.5	91 48.6	6.5	N19 18.9	5.6	59.2
A 13	19 06.0	11.3	106 14.1	6.5	19 13.3	5.8	59.2
Y 14	34 06.0	12.1	120 39.6	6.6	19 07.5	5.9	59.2
15	49 06.0	.. 12.9	135 05.2	6.6	19 01.6	6.1	59.2
16	64 06.0	13.8	149 30.8	6.7	18 55.5	6.1	59.2
17	79 06.1	14.6	163 56.5	6.7	18 49.4	6.3	59.2
18	94 06.1	S14 15.4	178 22.2	6.8	N18 43.1	6.4	59.2
19	109 06.1	16.2	192 48.0	6.8	18 36.7	6.5	59.2
20	124 06.1	17.0	207 13.8	6.8	18 30.2	6.6	59.2
21	139 06.1	.. 17.8	221 39.6	6.9	18 23.6	6.8	59.2
22	154 06.2	18.6	236 05.5	7.0	18 16.8	6.9	59.2
23	169 06.2	19.4	250 31.5	7.0	18 09.9	6.9	59.2
1 00	184 06.2	S14 20.2	264 57.5	7.0	N18 03.0	7.1	59.2
01	199 06.2	21.0	279 23.5	7.1	17 55.9	7.2	59.2
02	214 06.2	21.8	293 49.6	7.1	17 48.7	7.4	59.2
03	229 06.3	.. 22.6	308 15.7	7.2	17 41.3	7.4	59.2
04	244 06.3	23.4	322 41.9	7.3	17 33.9	7.5	59.2
05	259 06.3	24.2	337 08.2	7.3	17 26.4	7.7	59.2
T 06	274 06.3	S14 25.0	351 34.5	7.3	N17 18.7	7.7	59.2
H 07	289 06.3	25.8	6 00.8	7.4	17 11.0	7.9	59.2
U 08	304 06.4	26.6	20 27.2	7.5	17 03.1	7.9	59.2
R 09	319 06.4	.. 27.4	34 53.7	7.5	16 55.2	8.1	59.2
S 10	334 06.4	28.2	49 20.2	7.5	16 47.1	8.2	59.2
D 11	349 06.4	29.0	63 46.7	7.7	16 38.9	8.3	59.2
A 12	4 06.4	S14 29.8	78 13.4	7.6	N16 30.6	8.4	59.2
Y 13	19 06.4	30.6	92 40.0	7.7	16 22.2	8.4	59.2
14	34 06.4	31.4	107 06.7	7.8	16 13.8	8.6	59.2
15	49 06.5	.. 32.2	121 33.5	7.8	16 05.2	8.7	59.2
16	64 06.5	33.0	136 00.3	7.9	15 56.5	8.8	59.2
17	79 06.5	33.8	150 27.2	7.9	15 47.7	8.8	59.2
18	94 06.5	S14 34.6	164 54.1	8.0	N15 38.9	9.0	59.2
19	109 06.5	35.4	179 21.1	8.0	15 29.9	9.1	59.2
20	124 06.5	36.2	193 48.1	8.1	15 20.8	9.1	59.2
21	139 06.5	.. 37.0	208 15.2	8.2	15 11.7	9.3	59.2
22	154 06.6	37.8	222 42.4	8.2	15 02.4	9.3	59.2
23	169 06.6	38.6	237 09.6	8.2	14 53.1	9.4	59.2
2 00	184 06.6	S14 39.4	251 36.8	8.3	N14 43.7	9.5	59.2
01	199 06.6	40.1	266 04.1	8.4	14 34.2	9.6	59.2
02	214 06.6	40.9	280 31.5	8.4	14 24.6	9.7	59.2
03	229 06.6	.. 41.7	294 58.9	8.5	14 14.9	9.8	59.2
04	244 06.6	42.5	309 26.4	8.5	14 05.1	9.8	59.2
05	259 06.6	43.3	323 53.9	8.6	13 55.3	9.9	59.2
F 06	274 06.6	S14 44.1	338 21.5	8.6	N13 45.4	10.1	59.2
R 07	289 06.6	44.9	352 49.1	8.7	13 35.3	10.1	59.2
I 08	304 06.7	45.7	7 16.8	8.7	13 25.2	10.1	59.1
D 09	319 06.7	.. 46.5	21 44.5	8.8	13 15.1	10.3	59.1
A 10	334 06.7	47.3	36 12.3	8.8	13 04.8	10.3	59.1
Y 11	349 06.7	48.1	50 40.1	8.9	12 54.5	10.4	59.1
12	4 06.7	S14 48.8	65 08.0	9.0	N12 44.1	10.5	59.1
13	19 06.7	49.6	79 36.0	9.0	12 33.6	10.5	59.1
14	34 06.7	50.4	94 04.0	9.0	12 23.1	10.6	59.1
15	49 06.7	.. 51.2	108 32.0	9.1	12 12.5	10.7	59.1
16	64 06.7	52.0	123 00.1	9.2	12 01.8	10.8	59.1
17	79 06.7	52.8	137 28.3	9.1	11 51.0	10.8	59.1
18	94 06.7	S14 53.6	151 56.4	9.3	N11 40.2	10.9	59.1
19	109 06.7	54.4	166 24.7	9.3	11 29.3	10.9	59.1
20	124 06.7	55.1	180 53.0	9.3	11 18.4	11.0	59.1
21	139 06.7	.. 55.9	195 21.3	9.4	11 07.4	11.1	59.1
22	154 06.7	56.7	209 49.7	9.5	10 56.3	11.2	59.1
23	169 06.7	57.5	224 18.2	9.5	N10 45.1	11.2	59.1
	SD 16.1	d 0.8	SD 16.1		16.1		16.1

Lat.	Twilight Naut.	Civil	Sunrise	Moonrise 31	1	2	3
°	h m	h m	h m	h m	h m	h m	h m
N 72	06 06	07 29	08 56	▭	21 26	23 46	25 52
N 70	06 02	07 16	08 30	19 47	22 02	24 04	00 04
68	05 58	07 05	08 10	20 33	22 27	24 18	00 18
66	05 55	06 56	07 55	21 03	22 46	24 29	00 29
64	05 52	06 49	07 42	21 25	23 01	24 39	00 39
62	05 50	06 42	07 31	21 43	23 14	24 47	00 47
60	05 47	06 37	07 22	21 57	23 25	24 54	00 54
N 58	05 45	06 32	07 14	22 10	23 34	25 00	01 00
56	05 43	06 27	07 07	22 21	23 42	25 05	01 05
54	05 41	06 23	07 00	22 30	23 49	25 10	01 10
52	05 39	06 19	06 55	22 39	23 56	25 15	01 15
50	05 37	06 15	06 49	22 46	24 02	00 02	01 18
45	05 33	06 08	06 38	23 02	24 14	00 14	01 27
N 40	05 29	06 01	06 29	23 16	24 25	00 25	01 34
35	05 25	05 55	06 21	23 27	24 33	00 33	01 40
30	05 21	05 49	06 14	23 37	24 41	00 41	01 45
20	05 13	05 39	06 01	23 53	24 54	00 54	01 55
N 10	05 04	05 29	05 50	24 08	00 08	01 06	02 03
0	04 54	05 19	05 40	24 22	00 22	01 17	02 10
S 10	04 43	05 08	05 30	24 35	00 35	01 28	02 18
20	04 28	04 55	05 18	24 50	00 50	01 39	02 25
30	04 10	04 40	05 05	00 16	01 06	01 53	02 35
35	03 59	04 31	04 58	00 27	01 16	02 00	02 40
40	03 45	04 20	04 49	00 39	01 27	02 09	02 46
45	03 27	04 07	04 39	00 55	01 40	02 19	02 52
S 50	03 05	03 51	04 27	01 13	01 56	02 31	03 01
52	02 53	03 43	04 21	01 22	02 03	02 37	03 04
54	02 40	03 34	04 15	01 32	02 11	02 43	03 09
56	02 24	03 24	04 07	01 42	02 20	02 50	03 13
58	02 05	03 12	03 59	01 55	02 30	02 57	03 18
S 60	01 41	02 58	03 50	02 09	02 42	03 06	03 24

Lat.	Sunset	Twilight Civil	Naut.	Moonset 31	1	2	3
°	h m	h m	h m	h m	h m	h m	h m
N 72	14 30	15 57	17 20	▭	16 56	16 29	16 11
N 70	14 56	16 10	17 24	16 37	16 20	16 09	16 01
68	15 16	16 21	17 28	15 51	15 54	15 53	15 52
66	15 31	16 29	17 31	15 20	15 33	15 41	15 45
64	15 44	16 37	17 34	14 58	15 17	15 30	15 39
62	15 55	16 44	17 36	14 39	15 04	15 21	15 34
60	16 04	16 49	17 39	14 24	14 52	15 13	15 29
N 58	16 12	16 55	17 41	14 11	14 42	15 06	15 25
56	16 20	16 59	17 43	14 00	14 33	15 00	15 21
54	16 26	17 04	17 45	13 50	14 25	14 54	15 18
52	16 32	17 07	17 47	13 41	14 18	14 49	15 15
50	16 37	17 11	17 49	13 33	14 12	14 44	15 12
45	16 48	17 19	17 54	13 16	13 58	14 34	15 06
N 40	16 58	17 26	17 58	13 02	13 47	14 26	15 01
35	17 06	17 32	18 02	12 50	13 37	14 19	14 57
30	17 13	17 38	18 06	12 40	13 29	14 13	14 53
20	17 26	17 48	18 14	12 22	13 14	14 01	14 46
N 10	17 37	17 58	18 23	12 07	13 01	13 52	14 40
0	17 47	18 08	18 33	11 52	12 48	13 42	14 35
S 10	17 58	18 19	18 45	11 37	12 36	13 33	14 29
20	18 09	18 32	18 59	11 21	12 23	13 23	14 23
30	18 22	18 47	19 17	11 03	12 07	13 12	14 16
35	18 30	18 57	19 29	10 52	11 58	13 05	14 12
40	18 39	19 08	19 43	10 40	11 48	12 58	14 07
45	18 49	19 21	20 01	10 25	11 36	12 49	14 01
S 50	19 02	19 38	20 24	10 08	11 21	12 38	13 55
52	19 07	19 46	20 36	09 59	11 14	12 33	13 52
54	19 14	19 55	20 49	09 50	11 07	12 27	13 49
56	19 21	20 05	21 05	09 39	10 58	12 21	13 45
58	19 29	20 17	21 25	09 27	10 49	12 14	13 41
S 60	19 39	20 31	21 51	09 13	10 37	12 06	13 36

Day	SUN Eqn. of Time 00h	12h	Mer. Pass.	MOON Mer. Pass. Upper	Lower	Age	Phase
d	m s	m s	h m	h m	h m	d	%
31	16 22	16 24	11 44	05 38	18 07	22	52
1	16 25	16 26	11 44	06 35	19 03	23	41
2	16 26	16 27	11 44	07 30	19 56	24	30

UT	ARIES	VENUS −4.3		MARS −0.5		JUPITER −1.7		SATURN +0.6		STARS		
	GHA	GHA	Dec	GHA	Dec	GHA	Dec	GHA	Dec	Name	SHA	Dec
d h	° '	° '	° '	° '	° '	° '	° '	° '	° '		° '	° '
3 00	42 12.2	197 06.7	S15 24.9	76 47.4	S16 10.0	165 28.5	S19 12.7	126 40.1	S22 45.8	Acamar	315 15.2	S40 13.9
01	57 14.7	212 10.1	23.9	91 48.5	09.4	180 30.5	12.9	141 42.4	45.8	Achernar	335 23.5	S57 08.7
02	72 17.1	227 13.6	22.9	106 49.6	08.8	195 32.4	13.0	156 44.6	45.8	Acrux	173 05.8	S63 11.9
03	87 19.6	242 17.1 . .	21.9	121 50.7 . .	08.2	210 34.3 . .	13.1	171 46.9 . .	45.8	Adhara	255 09.5	S28 59.7
04	102 22.0	257 20.5	20.8	136 51.7	07.7	225 36.2	13.2	186 49.1	45.8	Aldebaran	290 44.9	N16 32.7
05	117 24.5	272 23.9	19.8	151 52.8	07.1	240 38.1	13.4	201 51.3	45.8			
06	132 27.0	287 27.4	S15 18.8	166 53.9	S16 06.5	255 40.0	S19 13.5	216 53.6	S22 45.8	Alioth	166 18.0	N55 51.5
07	147 29.4	302 30.8	17.8	181 55.0	05.9	270 41.9	13.6	231 55.8	45.8	Alkaid	152 56.5	N49 13.3
S 08	162 31.9	317 34.3	16.8	196 56.1	05.4	285 43.8	13.7	246 58.0	45.8	Al Na'ir	27 39.1	S46 52.4
A 09	177 34.4	332 37.7 . .	15.7	211 57.2 . .	04.8	300 45.7 . .	13.8	262 00.3 . .	45.8	Alnilam	275 42.4	S 1 11.5
T 10	192 36.8	347 41.1	14.7	226 58.3	04.2	315 47.6	14.0	277 02.5	45.8	Alphard	217 52.6	S 8 44.3
U 11	207 39.3	2 44.5	13.7	241 59.4	03.6	330 49.5	14.1	292 04.7	45.8			
R 12	222 41.8	17 48.0	S15 12.7	257 00.5	S16 03.1	345 51.4	S19 14.2	307 07.0	S22 45.8	Alphecca	126 08.3	N26 39.4
D 13	237 44.2	32 51.4	11.7	272 01.5	02.5	0 53.3	14.3	322 09.2	45.8	Alpheratz	357 39.5	N29 11.7
A 14	252 46.7	47 54.8	10.7	287 02.6	01.9	15 55.2	14.5	337 11.5	45.7	Altair	62 04.8	N 8 55.3
Y 15	267 49.2	62 58.2 . .	09.7	302 03.7 . .	01.3	30 57.1 . .	14.6	352 13.7 . .	45.7	Ankaa	353 11.8	S42 12.4
16	282 51.6	78 01.6	08.7	317 04.8	00.8	45 59.0	14.7	7 15.9	45.7	Antares	112 22.1	S26 28.2
17	297 54.1	93 05.0	07.6	332 05.9	16 00.2	61 00.9	14.8	22 18.2	45.7			
18	312 56.5	108 08.4	S15 06.6	347 07.0	S15 59.6	76 02.8	S19 14.9	37 20.4	S22 45.7	Arcturus	145 52.8	N19 05.3
19	327 59.0	123 11.8	05.6	2 08.1	59.0	91 04.7	15.1	52 22.6	45.7	Atria	107 21.1	S69 03.6
20	343 01.5	138 15.2	04.6	17 09.1	58.5	106 06.6	15.2	67 24.9	45.7	Avior	234 16.4	S59 33.9
21	358 03.9	153 18.6 . .	03.6	32 10.2 . .	57.9	121 08.5 . .	15.3	82 27.1 . .	45.7	Bellatrix	278 27.9	N 6 21.9
22	13 06.4	168 22.0	02.6	47 11.3	57.3	136 10.4	15.4	97 29.3	45.7	Betelgeuse	270 57.1	N 7 24.5
23	28 08.9	183 25.4	01.6	62 12.4	56.7	151 12.4	15.6	112 31.6	45.7			
4 00	43 11.3	198 28.8	S15 00.6	77 13.5	S15 56.1	166 14.3	S19 15.7	127 33.8	S22 45.7	Canopus	263 54.2	S52 42.2
01	58 13.8	213 32.2	14 59.6	92 14.6	55.6	181 16.2	15.8	142 36.0	45.7	Capella	280 28.7	N46 00.8
02	73 16.3	228 35.6	58.6	107 15.7	55.0	196 18.1	15.9	157 38.3	45.7	Deneb	49 29.0	N45 21.2
03	88 18.7	243 38.9 . .	57.6	122 16.7 . .	54.4	211 20.0 . .	16.0	172 40.5 . .	45.7	Denebola	182 30.2	N14 28.1
04	103 21.2	258 42.3	56.6	137 17.8	53.8	226 21.9	16.2	187 42.7	45.7	Diphda	348 52.0	S17 53.1
05	118 23.6	273 45.7	55.6	152 18.9	53.3	241 23.8	16.3	202 45.0	45.7			
06	133 26.1	288 49.0	S14 54.6	167 20.0	S15 52.7	256 25.7	S19 16.4	217 47.2	S22 45.7	Dubhe	193 47.7	N61 38.8
07	148 28.6	303 52.4	53.6	182 21.1	52.1	271 27.6	16.5	232 49.4	45.7	Elnath	278 07.7	N28 37.2
08	163 31.0	318 55.7	52.6	197 22.1	51.5	286 29.5	16.7	247 51.7	45.7	Eltanin	90 44.8	N51 29.6
S 09	178 33.5	333 59.1 . .	51.6	212 23.2 . .	50.9	301 31.4 . .	16.8	262 53.9 . .	45.7	Enif	33 43.5	N 9 57.8
U 10	193 36.0	349 02.5	50.6	227 24.3	50.4	316 33.3	16.9	277 56.1	45.7	Fomalhaut	15 19.8	S29 31.5
N 11	208 38.4	4 05.8	49.6	242 25.4	49.8	331 35.2	17.0	292 58.4	45.7			
D 12	223 40.9	19 09.1	S14 48.6	257 26.5	S15 49.2	346 37.1	S19 17.1	308 00.6	S22 45.7	Gacrux	171 57.3	S57 12.8
A 13	238 43.4	34 12.5	47.6	272 27.6	48.6	1 39.0	17.3	323 02.8	45.7	Gienah	175 48.8	S17 38.5
Y 14	253 45.8	49 15.8	46.6	287 28.6	48.0	16 40.9	17.4	338 05.1	45.7	Hadar	148 43.3	S60 27.5
15	268 48.3	64 19.2 . .	45.6	302 29.7 . .	47.5	31 42.8 . .	17.5	353 07.3 . .	45.7	Hamal	327 56.3	N23 33.0
16	283 50.8	79 22.5	44.6	317 30.8	46.9	46 44.7	17.6	8 09.5	45.7	Kaus Aust.	83 39.3	S34 22.4
17	298 53.2	94 25.8	43.6	332 31.9	46.3	61 46.6	17.7	23 11.8	45.7			
18	313 55.7	109 29.1	S14 42.6	347 33.0	S15 45.7	76 48.5	S19 17.9	38 14.0	S22 45.6	Kochab	137 21.3	N74 04.9
19	328 58.1	124 32.5	41.6	2 34.0	45.1	91 50.4	18.0	53 16.2	45.6	Markab	13 34.5	N15 18.5
20	344 00.6	139 35.8	40.6	17 35.1	44.5	106 52.3	18.1	68 18.5	45.6	Menkar	314 10.9	N 4 09.7
21	359 03.1	154 39.1 . .	39.6	32 36.2 . .	44.0	121 54.2 . .	18.2	83 20.7 . .	45.6	Menkent	148 03.7	S36 27.4
22	14 05.5	169 42.4	38.6	47 37.3	43.4	136 56.1	18.4	98 22.9	45.6	Miaplacidus	221 39.0	S69 47.3
23	29 08.0	184 45.7	37.6	62 38.4	42.8	151 58.0	18.5	113 25.1	45.6			
5 00	44 10.5	199 49.0	S14 36.7	77 39.4	S15 42.2	166 59.9	S19 18.6	128 27.4	S22 45.6	Mirfak	308 34.6	N49 55.5
01	59 12.9	214 52.3	35.7	92 40.5	41.6	182 01.8	18.7	143 29.6	45.6	Nunki	75 54.0	S26 16.3
02	74 15.4	229 55.6	34.7	107 41.6	41.0	197 03.7	18.8	158 31.8	45.6	Peacock	53 13.6	S56 40.6
03	89 17.9	244 58.9 . .	33.7	122 42.7 . .	40.5	212 05.6 . .	19.0	173 34.1 . .	45.6	Pollux	243 23.2	N27 58.7
04	104 20.3	260 02.2	32.7	137 43.7	39.9	227 07.5	19.1	188 36.3	45.6	Procyon	244 55.8	N 5 10.6
05	119 22.8	275 05.5	31.7	152 44.8	39.3	242 09.4	19.2	203 38.5	45.6			
06	134 25.2	290 08.8	S14 30.8	167 45.9	S15 38.7	257 11.3	S19 19.3	218 40.8	S22 45.6	Rasalhague	96 03.3	N12 33.1
07	149 27.7	305 12.0	29.8	182 47.0	38.1	272 13.2	19.4	233 43.0	45.6	Regulus	207 39.8	N11 52.6
08	164 30.2	320 15.3	28.8	197 48.1	37.5	287 15.1	19.6	248 45.2	45.6	Rigel	281 08.3	S 8 10.8
M 09	179 32.6	335 18.6 . .	27.8	212 49.1 . .	37.0	302 17.0 . .	19.7	263 47.5 . .	45.6	Rigil Kent.	139 47.5	S60 54.5
O 10	194 35.1	350 21.9	26.8	227 50.2	36.4	317 18.9	19.8	278 49.7	45.6	Sabik	102 08.7	S15 44.7
N 11	209 37.6	5 25.1	25.9	242 51.3	35.8	332 20.8	19.9	293 51.9	45.6			
D 12	224 40.0	20 28.4	S14 24.9	257 52.4	S15 35.2	347 22.7	S19 20.1	308 54.1	S22 45.6	Schedar	349 35.9	N56 38.5
A 13	239 42.5	35 31.7	23.9	272 53.4	34.6	2 24.6	20.2	323 56.4	45.6	Shaula	96 17.3	S37 06.9
Y 14	254 45.0	50 34.9	22.9	287 54.5	34.0	17 26.5	20.3	338 58.6	45.6	Sirius	258 30.3	S16 44.5
15	269 47.4	65 38.2 . .	22.0	302 55.6 . .	33.5	32 28.4 . .	20.4	354 00.8 . .	45.6	Spica	158 27.7	S11 15.3
16	284 49.9	80 41.4	21.0	317 56.7	32.9	47 30.3	20.5	9 03.1	45.6	Suhail	222 49.8	S43 30.2
17	299 52.4	95 44.7	20.0	332 57.7	32.3	62 32.2	20.7	24 05.3	45.6			
18	314 54.8	110 47.9	S14 19.1	347 58.8	S15 31.7	77 34.1	S19 20.8	39 07.5	S22 45.6	Vega	80 36.7	N38 48.4
19	329 57.3	125 51.1	18.1	2 59.9	31.1	92 36.0	20.9	54 09.7	45.6	Zuben'ubi	137 01.7	S16 06.9
20	344 59.7	140 54.4	17.1	18 01.0	30.5	107 37.9	21.0	69 12.0	45.5		SHA	Mer.Pass.
21	0 02.2	155 57.6 . .	16.2	33 02.0 . .	29.9	122 39.8 . .	21.1	84 14.2 . .	45.5		° '	h m
22	15 04.7	171 00.8	15.2	48 03.1	29.3	137 41.7	21.3	99 16.4	45.5	Venus	155 17.5	10 44
23	30 07.1	186 04.0	14.2	63 04.2	28.8	152 43.6	21.4	114 18.7	45.5	Mars	34 02.2	18 50
	h m									Jupiter	123 02.9	12 53
Mer. Pass. 21 03.8		v 3.3	d 1.0	v 1.1	d 0.6	v 1.9	d 0.1	v 2.2	d 0.0	Saturn	84 22.5	15 27

SUN / MOON

UT	SUN GHA	SUN Dec	MOON GHA	v	MOON Dec	d	HP
d h	° ′	° ′	° ′	′	° ′	′	′
3 00	184 06.7	S14 58.3	238 46.7	9.5	N10 33.9	11.2	59.1
01	199 06.7	59.1	253 15.2	9.6	10 22.7	11.3	59.0
02	214 06.8	14 59.8	267 43.8	9.6	10 11.4	11.4	59.0
03	229 06.8	15 00.6	282 12.4	9.7	10 00.0	11.4	59.0
04	244 06.8	01.4	296 41.1	9.7	9 48.6	11.5	59.0
05	259 06.8	02.2	311 09.8	9.8	9 37.1	11.5	59.0
06	274 06.8	S15 03.0	325 38.6	9.8	N 9 25.6	11.6	59.0
07	289 06.8	03.8	340 07.4	9.9	9 14.0	11.7	59.0
S 08	304 06.8	04.5	354 36.3	9.9	9 02.3	11.6	59.0
A 09	319 06.8	.. 05.3	9 05.2	9.9	8 50.7	11.8	59.0
T 10	334 06.8	06.1	23 34.1	10.0	8 38.9	11.7	59.0
U 11	349 06.8	06.9	38 03.1	10.0	8 27.2	11.9	59.0
R 12	4 06.8	S15 07.6	52 32.1	10.1	N 8 15.3	11.8	59.0
D 13	19 06.7	08.4	67 01.2	10.1	8 03.5	11.9	58.9
A 14	34 06.7	09.2	81 30.3	10.1	7 51.6	12.0	58.9
Y 15	49 06.7	.. 10.0	95 59.4	10.2	7 39.6	12.0	58.9
16	64 06.7	10.8	110 28.6	10.3	7 27.6	12.0	58.9
17	79 06.7	11.5	124 57.9	10.2	7 15.6	12.1	58.9
18	94 06.7	S15 12.3	139 27.1	10.3	N 7 03.5	12.1	58.9
19	109 06.7	13.1	153 56.4	10.4	6 51.4	12.1	58.9
20	124 06.7	13.9	168 25.8	10.4	6 39.3	12.2	58.9
21	139 06.7	.. 14.6	182 55.2	10.4	6 27.1	12.2	58.9
22	154 06.7	15.4	197 24.6	10.4	6 14.9	12.2	58.9
23	169 06.7	16.2	211 54.0	10.5	6 02.7	12.3	58.8
4 00	184 06.7	S15 17.0	226 23.5	10.5	N 5 50.4	12.2	58.8
01	199 06.7	17.7	240 53.0	10.6	5 38.2	12.4	58.8
02	214 06.7	18.5	255 22.6	10.6	5 25.8	12.3	58.8
03	229 06.7	.. 19.3	269 52.2	10.6	5 13.5	12.4	58.8
04	244 06.7	20.1	284 21.8	10.6	5 01.1	12.4	58.8
05	259 06.7	20.8	298 51.4	10.7	4 48.7	12.4	58.8
06	274 06.7	S15 21.6	313 21.1	10.7	N 4 36.3	12.4	58.8
07	289 06.7	22.4	327 50.8	10.8	4 23.9	12.5	58.7
S 08	304 06.6	23.1	342 20.6	10.7	4 11.4	12.5	58.7
U 09	319 06.6	.. 23.9	356 50.3	10.8	3 59.0	12.5	58.7
N 10	334 06.6	24.7	11 20.1	10.9	3 46.5	12.5	58.7
D 11	349 06.6	25.4	25 50.0	10.8	3 34.0	12.6	58.7
A 12	4 06.6	S15 26.2	40 19.8	10.9	N 3 21.4	12.5	58.7
Y 13	19 06.6	27.0	54 49.7	10.9	3 08.9	12.6	58.7
14	34 06.6	27.7	69 19.6	10.9	2 56.3	12.5	58.7
15	49 06.6	.. 28.5	83 49.5	11.0	2 43.8	12.6	58.6
16	64 06.6	29.3	98 19.5	10.9	2 31.2	12.6	58.6
17	79 06.6	30.0	112 49.4	11.0	2 18.6	12.6	58.6
18	94 06.5	S15 30.8	127 19.4	11.1	N 2 06.0	12.5	58.6
19	109 06.5	31.6	141 49.5	11.0	1 53.5	12.6	58.6
20	124 06.5	32.3	156 19.5	11.1	1 40.9	12.6	58.6
21	139 06.5	.. 33.1	170 49.6	11.1	1 28.3	12.6	58.6
22	154 06.5	33.9	185 19.7	11.1	1 15.7	12.7	58.5
23	169 06.5	34.6	199 49.8	11.1	1 03.0	12.6	58.5
5 00	184 06.5	S15 35.4	214 19.9	11.1	N 0 50.4	12.6	58.5
01	199 06.4	36.2	228 50.0	11.2	0 37.8	12.6	58.5
02	214 06.4	36.9	243 20.2	11.1	0 25.2	12.6	58.5
03	229 06.4	.. 37.7	257 50.3	11.2	N 0 12.6	12.6	58.5
04	244 06.4	38.4	272 20.5	11.2	0 00.0	12.6	58.5
05	259 06.4	39.2	286 50.7	11.3	S 0 12.6	12.5	58.4
06	274 06.4	S15 40.0	301 21.0	11.2	S 0 25.1	12.6	58.4
07	289 06.3	40.7	315 51.2	11.2	0 37.7	12.6	58.4
08	304 06.3	41.5	330 21.4	11.3	0 50.3	12.5	58.4
M 09	319 06.3	.. 42.2	344 51.7	11.3	1 02.8	12.6	58.4
O 10	334 06.3	43.0	359 22.0	11.3	1 15.4	12.5	58.4
N 11	349 06.3	43.8	13 52.3	11.3	1 27.9	12.5	58.3
D 12	4 06.3	S15 44.5	28 22.6	11.3	S 1 40.4	12.5	58.3
A 13	19 06.2	45.3	42 52.9	11.3	1 52.9	12.5	58.3
Y 14	34 06.2	46.0	57 23.2	11.3	2 05.4	12.5	58.3
15	49 06.2	.. 46.8	71 53.5	11.3	2 17.9	12.5	58.3
16	64 06.2	47.5	86 23.8	11.4	2 30.4	12.4	58.2
17	79 06.2	48.3	100 54.2	11.3	2 42.8	12.4	58.2
18	94 06.1	S15 49.1	115 24.5	11.4	S 2 55.2	12.4	58.2
19	109 06.1	49.8	129 54.9	11.3	3 07.6	12.4	58.2
20	124 06.1	50.6	144 25.2	11.4	3 20.0	12.3	58.2
21	139 06.1	.. 51.3	158 55.6	11.4	3 32.3	12.3	58.2
22	154 06.0	52.1	173 26.0	11.4	3 44.6	12.3	58.1
23	169 06.0	52.8	187 56.4	11.3	S 3 56.9	12.3	58.1
	SD 16.2	d 0.8	SD 16.1		16.0		15.9

Twilight / Moonrise

Lat.	Naut.	Civil	Sunrise	Moonrise 3	4	5	6
°	h m	h m	h m	h m	h m	h m	h m
N 72	06 18	07 42	09 16	25 52	01 52	03 52	05 50
N 70	06 12	07 28	08 45	00 04	02 00	03 52	05 42
68	06 08	07 16	08 23	00 18	02 06	03 52	05 36
66	06 03	07 06	08 06	00 29	02 11	03 51	05 30
64	06 00	06 57	07 52	00 39	02 16	03 51	05 26
62	05 57	06 50	07 40	00 47	02 20	03 51	05 22
60	05 54	06 44	07 30	00 54	02 23	03 51	05 18
N 58	05 51	06 38	07 21	01 00	02 26	03 51	05 15
56	05 49	06 33	07 13	01 05	02 29	03 51	05 13
54	05 46	06 28	07 06	01 10	02 31	03 51	05 10
52	05 44	06 24	07 00	01 15	02 33	03 51	05 08
50	05 42	06 20	06 54	01 18	02 35	03 51	05 05
45	05 37	06 11	06 42	01 27	02 39	03 51	05 02
N 40	05 32	06 04	06 32	01 34	02 43	03 51	04 58
35	05 27	05 57	06 24	01 40	02 46	03 51	04 55
30	05 23	05 51	06 16	01 45	02 49	03 51	04 52
20	05 14	05 40	06 03	01 55	02 53	03 51	04 48
N 10	05 04	05 29	05 51	02 03	02 57	03 51	04 44
0	04 54	05 19	05 40	02 10	03 01	03 51	04 40
S 10	04 42	05 07	05 29	02 18	03 05	03 51	04 36
20	04 27	04 54	05 17	02 25	03 09	03 51	04 32
30	04 07	04 38	05 03	02 35	03 14	03 51	04 28
35	03 55	04 28	04 55	02 40	03 16	03 51	04 25
40	03 41	04 16	04 46	02 46	03 19	03 51	04 22
45	03 22	04 02	04 35	02 52	03 23	03 51	04 19
S 50	02 58	03 45	04 22	03 01	03 27	03 51	04 15
52	02 46	03 36	04 15	03 04	03 29	03 51	04 14
54	02 31	03 27	04 08	03 09	03 31	03 51	04 12
56	02 14	03 16	04 01	03 13	03 33	03 52	04 10
58	01 53	03 03	03 52	03 18	03 36	03 52	04 07
S 60	01 24	02 49	03 42	03 24	03 39	03 52	04 05

Twilight / Moonset

Lat.	Sunset	Civil	Naut.	Moonset 3	4	5	6
°	h m	h m	h m	h m	h m	h m	h m
N 72	14 10	15 43	17 08	16 11	15 56	15 42	15 27
N 70	14 41	15 58	17 13	16 01	15 53	15 45	15 37
68	15 03	16 10	17 18	15 52	15 50	15 48	15 46
66	15 20	16 20	17 22	15 45	15 48	15 50	15 53
64	15 35	16 29	17 26	15 39	15 46	15 53	15 59
62	15 46	16 36	17 29	15 34	15 44	15 54	16 05
60	15 57	16 42	17 32	15 29	15 43	15 56	16 09
N 58	16 05	16 48	17 35	15 25	15 42	15 57	16 13
56	16 13	16 53	17 38	15 21	15 40	15 59	16 17
54	16 20	16 58	17 40	15 18	15 39	16 00	16 23
52	16 26	17 02	17 42	15 15	15 38	16 01	16 23
50	16 32	17 06	17 45	15 12	15 37	16 02	16 26
45	16 44	17 15	17 50	15 06	15 36	16 04	16 32
N 40	16 54	17 23	17 55	15 01	15 34	16 05	16 37
35	17 03	17 29	17 59	14 57	15 32	16 07	16 41
30	17 11	17 36	18 04	14 53	15 31	16 08	16 45
20	17 24	17 47	18 13	14 46	15 29	16 10	16 52
N 10	17 36	17 58	18 23	14 40	15 27	16 12	16 57
0	17 47	18 08	18 33	14 35	15 25	16 14	17 03
S 10	17 58	18 20	18 46	14 29	15 23	16 16	17 09
20	18 10	18 34	19 01	14 23	15 21	16 18	17 15
30	18 25	18 50	19 20	14 16	15 18	16 20	17 22
35	18 33	19 00	19 33	14 12	15 17	16 22	17 25
40	18 42	19 12	19 48	14 07	15 15	16 23	17 30
45	18 53	19 26	20 06	14 01	15 14	16 25	17 35
S 50	19 07	19 44	20 31	13 55	15 11	16 27	17 44
52	19 13	19 52	20 43	13 52	15 10	16 28	17 44
54	19 20	20 02	20 58	13 49	15 09	16 29	17 47
56	19 28	20 13	21 16	13 45	15 08	16 30	17 51
58	19 37	20 26	21 38	13 41	15 06	16 31	17 55
S 60	19 47	20 41	22 08	13 36	15 05	16 33	17 59

SUN / MOON

Day	Eqn. of Time 00h	12h	Mer. Pass.	Mer. Pass. Upper	Lower	Age	Phase
d	m s	m s	h m	h m	h m	d	%
3	16 27	16 27	11 44	08 22	20 48	25	20
4	16 27	16 26	11 44	09 13	21 38	26	12
5	16 26	16 25	11 44	10 03	22 27	27	6

UT	ARIES GHA	VENUS −4.4 GHA	Dec	MARS −0.5 GHA	Dec	JUPITER −1.7 GHA	Dec	SATURN +0.6 GHA	Dec	STARS Name	SHA	Dec
d h	° ′	° ′	° ′	° ′	° ′	° ′	° ′	° ′	° ′		° ′	° ′
6 00	45 09.6	201 07.3	S14 13.3	78 05.2	S15 28.2	167 45.5	S19 21.5	129 20.9	S22 45.5	Acamar	315 15.2	S40 13.9
01	60 12.1	216 10.5	12.3	93 06.3	27.6	182 47.4	21.6	144 23.1	45.5	Achernar	335 23.5	S57 08.7
02	75 14.5	231 13.7	11.3	108 07.4	27.0	197 49.3	21.7	159 25.3	45.5	Acrux	173 05.7	S63 11.9
03	90 17.0	246 16.9	.. 10.4	123 08.5	.. 26.4	212 51.2	.. 21.9	174 27.6	.. 45.5	Adhara	255 09.5	S28 59.8
04	105 19.5	261 20.1	09.4	138 09.5	25.8	227 53.1	22.0	189 29.8	45.5	Aldebaran	290 44.9	N16 32.7
05	120 21.9	276 23.3	08.5	153 10.6	25.2	242 55.0	22.1	204 32.0	45.5			
06	135 24.4	291 26.5	S14 07.5	168 11.7	S15 24.6	257 56.9	S19 22.2	219 34.3	S22 45.5	Alioth	166 18.0	N55 51.5
07	150 26.9	306 29.7	06.6	183 12.8	24.1	272 58.8	22.3	234 36.5	45.5	Alkaid	152 56.5	N49 13.3
T 08	165 29.3	321 32.9	05.6	198 13.8	23.5	288 00.7	22.5	249 38.7	45.5	Al Na'ir	27 39.1	S46 52.4
U 09	180 31.8	336 36.1	.. 04.7	213 14.9	.. 22.9	303 02.6	.. 22.6	264 40.9	.. 45.5	Alnilam	275 42.4	S 1 11.5
E 10	195 34.2	351 39.3	03.7	228 16.0	22.3	318 04.5	22.7	279 43.2	45.5	Alphard	217 52.6	S 8 44.3
S 11	210 36.7	6 42.4	02.8	243 17.0	21.7	333 06.4	22.8	294 45.4	45.5			
D 12	225 39.2	21 45.6	S14 01.8	258 18.1	S15 21.1	348 08.3	S19 23.0	309 47.6	S22 45.5	Alphecca	126 08.3	N26 39.4
A 13	240 41.6	36 48.8	14 00.9	273 19.2	20.5	3 10.2	23.1	324 49.8	45.5	Alpheratz	357 39.5	N29 11.8
Y 14	255 44.1	51 52.0	13 59.9	288 20.2	19.9	18 12.1	23.2	339 52.1	45.5	Altair	62 04.8	N 8 55.3
15	270 46.6	66 55.1	.. 59.0	303 21.3	.. 19.3	33 14.0	.. 23.3	354 54.3	.. 45.5	Ankaa	353 11.8	S42 12.4
16	285 49.0	81 58.3	58.0	318 22.4	18.7	48 15.9	23.4	9 56.5	45.5	Antares	112 22.1	S26 28.2
17	300 51.5	97 01.4	57.1	333 23.5	18.2	63 17.8	23.6	24 58.7	45.5			
18	315 54.0	112 04.6	S13 56.1	348 24.5	S15 17.6	78 19.7	S19 23.7	40 01.0	S22 45.5	Arcturus	145 52.8	N19 05.3
19	330 56.4	127 07.7	55.2	3 25.6	17.0	93 21.6	23.8	55 03.2	45.5	Atria	107 21.2	S69 03.6
20	345 58.9	142 10.9	54.3	18 26.7	16.4	108 23.5	23.9	70 05.4	45.4	Avior	234 16.4	S59 33.9
21	1 01.3	157 14.0	.. 53.3	33 27.7	.. 15.8	123 25.4	.. 24.0	85 07.7	.. 45.4	Bellatrix	278 27.8	N 6 21.9
22	16 03.8	172 17.2	52.4	48 28.8	15.2	138 27.3	24.2	100 09.9	45.4	Betelgeuse	270 57.1	N 7 24.5
23	31 06.3	187 20.3	51.4	63 29.9	14.6	153 29.2	24.3	115 12.1	45.4			
7 00	46 08.7	202 23.4	S13 50.5	78 30.9	S15 14.0	168 31.1	S19 24.4	130 14.3	S22 45.4	Canopus	263 54.2	S52 42.2
01	61 11.2	217 26.6	49.6	93 32.0	13.4	183 33.0	24.5	145 16.6	45.4	Capella	280 28.7	N46 00.8
02	76 13.7	232 29.7	48.6	108 33.1	12.8	198 34.9	24.6	160 18.8	45.4	Deneb	49 29.1	N45 21.2
03	91 16.1	247 32.8	.. 47.7	123 34.1	.. 12.2	213 36.8	.. 24.8	175 21.0	.. 45.4	Denebola	182 30.2	N14 28.1
04	106 18.6	262 35.9	46.8	138 35.2	11.6	228 38.7	24.9	190 23.2	45.4	Diphda	348 52.0	S17 53.1
05	121 21.1	277 39.0	45.9	153 36.3	11.1	243 40.6	25.0	205 25.5	45.4			
06	136 23.5	292 42.2	S13 44.9	168 37.3	S15 10.5	258 42.5	S19 25.1	220 27.7	S22 45.4	Dubhe	193 47.6	N61 38.8
W 07	151 26.0	307 45.3	44.0	183 38.4	09.9	273 44.4	25.2	235 29.9	45.4	Elnath	278 07.7	N28 37.2
E 08	166 28.5	322 48.4	43.1	198 39.5	09.3	288 46.3	25.4	250 32.1	45.4	Eltanin	90 44.9	N51 29.5
D 09	181 30.9	337 51.5	.. 42.2	213 40.5	.. 08.7	303 48.2	.. 25.5	265 34.4	.. 45.4	Enif	33 43.5	N 9 57.8
N 10	196 33.4	352 54.6	41.2	228 41.6	08.1	318 50.1	25.6	280 36.6	45.4	Fomalhaut	15 19.8	S29 31.5
E 11	211 35.8	7 57.6	40.3	243 42.7	07.5	333 52.0	25.7	295 38.8	45.4			
S 12	226 38.3	23 00.7	S13 39.4	258 43.7	S15 06.9	348 53.9	S19 25.8	310 41.0	S22 45.4	Gacrux	171 57.3	S57 12.8
D 13	241 40.8	38 03.8	38.5	273 44.8	06.3	3 55.8	26.0	325 43.2	45.4	Gienah	175 48.8	S17 38.5
A 14	256 43.2	53 06.9	37.6	288 45.8	05.7	18 57.7	26.1	340 45.5	45.4	Hadar	148 43.3	S60 27.5
Y 15	271 45.7	68 10.0	.. 36.7	303 46.9	.. 05.1	33 59.6	.. 26.2	355 47.7	.. 45.4	Hamal	327 56.3	N23 33.0
16	286 48.2	83 13.0	35.7	318 48.0	04.5	49 01.5	26.3	10 49.9	45.4	Kaus Aust.	83 39.3	S34 22.4
17	301 50.6	98 16.1	34.8	333 49.0	03.9	64 03.4	26.4	25 52.1	45.4			
18	316 53.1	113 19.2	S13 33.9	348 50.1	S15 03.3	79 05.3	S19 26.6	40 54.4	S22 45.4	Kochab	137 21.4	N74 04.8
19	331 55.6	128 22.2	33.0	3 51.2	02.7	94 07.2	26.7	55 56.6	45.3	Markab	13 34.5	N15 18.5
20	346 58.0	143 25.3	32.1	18 52.2	02.1	109 09.1	26.8	70 58.8	45.3	Menkar	314 10.9	N 4 09.7
21	2 00.5	158 28.3	.. 31.2	33 53.3	.. 01.5	124 11.0	.. 26.9	86 01.0	.. 45.3	Menkent	148 03.7	S36 27.4
22	17 03.0	173 31.4	30.3	48 54.4	00.9	139 12.9	27.0	101 03.3	45.3	Miaplacidus	221 38.9	S69 47.3
23	32 05.4	188 34.4	29.4	63 55.4	15 00.3	154 14.8	27.2	116 05.5	45.3			
8 00	47 07.9	203 37.5	S13 28.5	78 56.5	S14 59.7	169 16.7	S19 27.3	131 07.7	S22 45.3	Mirfak	308 34.6	N49 55.5
01	62 10.3	218 40.5	27.6	93 57.5	59.1	184 18.6	27.4	146 09.9	45.3	Nunki	75 54.0	S26 16.3
02	77 12.8	233 43.6	26.7	108 58.6	58.5	199 20.5	27.5	161 12.1	45.3	Peacock	53 13.7	S56 40.6
03	92 15.3	248 46.6	.. 25.8	123 59.7	.. 58.0	214 22.4	.. 27.6	176 14.4	.. 45.3	Pollux	243 23.2	N27 58.7
04	107 17.7	263 49.6	24.9	139 00.7	57.4	229 24.3	27.8	191 16.6	45.3	Procyon	244 55.8	N 5 10.6
05	122 20.2	278 52.6	24.0	154 01.8	56.8	244 26.2	27.9	206 18.8	45.3			
06	137 22.7	293 55.7	S13 23.1	169 02.8	S14 56.2	259 28.1	S19 28.0	221 21.0	S22 45.3	Rasalhague	96 03.4	N12 33.1
07	152 25.1	308 58.7	22.2	184 03.9	55.6	274 30.0	28.1	236 23.3	45.3	Regulus	207 39.8	N11 52.6
T 08	167 27.6	324 01.7	21.3	199 05.0	55.0	289 31.9	28.2	251 25.5	45.3	Rigel	281 08.3	S 8 10.8
H 09	182 30.1	339 04.7	.. 20.4	214 06.0	.. 54.4	304 33.8	.. 28.4	266 27.7	.. 45.3	Rigil Kent.	139 47.5	S60 54.5
U 10	197 32.5	354 07.7	19.5	229 07.1	53.8	319 35.6	28.5	281 29.9	45.3	Sabik	102 08.7	S15 44.7
R 11	212 35.0	9 10.7	18.7	244 08.1	53.2	334 37.5	28.6	296 32.1	45.3			
S 12	227 37.4	24 13.7	S13 17.8	259 09.2	S14 52.6	349 39.4	S19 28.7	311 34.4	S22 45.3	Schedar	349 35.9	N56 38.5
D 13	242 39.9	39 16.7	16.9	274 10.3	52.0	4 41.3	28.8	326 36.6	45.3	Shaula	96 17.3	S37 06.9
A 14	257 42.4	54 19.7	16.0	289 11.3	51.4	19 43.2	29.0	341 38.8	45.3	Sirius	258 30.3	S16 44.5
Y 15	272 44.8	69 22.6	.. 15.1	304 12.4	.. 50.8	34 45.1	.. 29.1	356 41.0	.. 45.3	Spica	158 27.7	S11 15.3
16	287 47.3	84 25.6	14.3	319 13.4	50.2	49 47.0	29.2	11 43.2	45.2	Suhail	222 49.8	S43 30.2
17	302 49.8	99 28.6	13.4	334 14.5	49.6	64 48.9	29.3	26 45.5	45.2			
18	317 52.2	114 31.6	S13 12.5	349 15.6	S14 49.0	79 50.8	S19 29.4	41 47.7	S22 45.2	Vega	80 36.8	N38 48.4
19	332 54.7	129 34.5	11.6	4 16.6	48.4	94 52.7	29.6	56 49.9	45.2	Zuben'ubi	137 01.7	S16 06.9
20	347 57.2	144 37.5	10.8	19 17.7	47.8	109 54.6	29.7	71 52.1	45.2		SHA	Mer.Pass.
21	2 59.6	159 40.5	.. 09.9	34 18.7	.. 47.2	124 56.5	.. 29.8	86 54.3	.. 45.2		° ′	h m
22	18 02.1	174 43.4	09.0	49 19.8	46.6	139 58.4	29.9	101 56.6	45.2	Venus	156 14.7	10 28
23	33 04.6	189 46.4	08.1	64 20.8	46.0	155 00.3	30.0	116 58.8	45.2	Mars	32 22.2	18 45
	h m									Jupiter	122 22.4	12 44
Mer.Pass. 20 52.0	v 3.1	d 0.9	v 1.1	d 0.6	v 1.9	d 0.1	v 2.2	d 0.0	Saturn	84 05.6	15 17

UT	SUN GHA	SUN Dec	MOON GHA	v	MOON Dec	d	HP
d h	° ′	° ′	° ′	′	° ′	′	′
6 00	184 06.0	S15 53.6	202 26.7	11.4	S 4 09.2	12.2	58.1
01	199 06.0	54.3	216 57.1	11.4	4 21.4	12.2	58.1
02	214 05.9	55.1	231 27.5	11.4	4 33.6	12.2	58.1
03	229 05.9	.. 55.8	245 57.9	11.4	4 45.8	12.1	58.0
04	244 05.9	56.6	260 28.3	11.4	4 57.9	12.1	58.0
05	259 05.9	57.3	274 58.7	11.4	5 10.0	12.1	58.0
06	274 05.8	S15 58.1	289 29.1	11.3	S 5 22.1	12.0	58.0
07	289 05.8	58.8	303 59.4	11.4	5 34.1	12.0	58.0
08	304 05.8	15 59.6	318 29.8	11.4	5 46.1	12.0	57.9
09	319 05.8	16 00.3	333 00.2	11.4	5 58.1	11.9	57.9
10	334 05.7	01.1	347 30.6	11.4	6 10.0	11.9	57.9
11	349 05.7	01.8	2 01.0	11.4	6 21.9	11.9	57.9
12	4 05.7	S16 02.6	16 31.4	11.3	S 6 33.8	11.8	57.9
13	19 05.7	03.3	31 01.7	11.4	6 45.6	11.7	57.8
14	34 05.6	04.1	45 32.1	11.4	6 57.3	11.7	57.8
15	49 05.6	.. 04.8	60 02.5	11.3	7 09.0	11.7	57.8
16	64 05.6	05.5	74 32.8	11.4	7 20.7	11.6	57.8
17	79 05.5	06.3	89 03.2	11.4	7 32.3	11.6	57.8
18	94 05.5	S16 07.0	103 33.6	11.3	S 7 43.9	11.6	57.7
19	109 05.5	07.8	118 03.9	11.3	7 55.5	11.4	57.7
20	124 05.5	08.5	132 34.2	11.4	8 06.9	11.5	57.7
21	139 05.4	.. 09.3	147 04.6	11.3	8 18.4	11.4	57.7
22	154 05.4	10.0	161 34.9	11.3	8 29.8	11.3	57.6
23	169 05.4	10.7	176 05.2	11.3	8 41.1	11.3	57.6
7 00	184 05.3	S16 11.5	190 35.5	11.3	S 8 52.4	11.2	57.6
01	199 05.3	12.2	205 05.8	11.3	9 03.6	11.2	57.6
02	214 05.3	13.0	219 36.1	11.3	9 14.8	11.1	57.6
03	229 05.2	.. 13.7	234 06.4	11.3	9 25.9	11.0	57.5
04	244 05.2	14.4	248 36.7	11.3	9 36.9	11.0	57.5
05	259 05.2	15.2	263 07.0	11.2	9 47.9	11.0	57.5
06	274 05.1	S16 15.9	277 37.2	11.3	S 9 58.9	10.8	57.5
07	289 05.1	16.7	292 07.5	11.2	10 09.7	10.9	57.4
08	304 05.1	17.4	306 37.7	11.2	10 20.6	10.7	57.4
09	319 05.0	.. 18.1	321 07.9	11.2	10 31.3	10.7	57.4
10	334 05.0	18.9	335 38.1	11.3	10 42.0	10.7	57.4
11	349 04.9	19.6	350 08.4	11.1	10 52.7	10.5	57.3
12	4 04.9	S16 20.3	4 38.5	11.2	S11 03.2	10.5	57.3
13	19 04.9	21.1	19 08.7	11.2	11 13.7	10.5	57.3
14	34 04.8	21.8	33 38.9	11.1	11 24.2	10.3	57.3
15	49 04.8	.. 22.5	48 09.0	11.2	11 34.5	10.3	57.2
16	64 04.8	23.3	62 39.2	11.1	11 44.8	10.3	57.2
17	79 04.7	24.0	77 09.3	11.1	11 55.1	10.1	57.2
18	94 04.7	S16 24.7	91 39.4	11.1	S12 05.2	10.1	57.2
19	109 04.6	25.5	106 09.5	11.1	12 15.3	10.0	57.2
20	124 04.6	26.2	120 39.6	11.1	12 25.3	10.0	57.1
21	139 04.6	.. 26.9	135 09.7	11.1	12 35.3	9.9	57.1
22	154 04.5	27.7	149 39.8	11.0	12 45.2	9.8	57.1
23	169 04.5	28.4	164 09.8	11.1	12 55.0	9.7	57.1
8 00	184 04.4	S16 29.1	178 39.9	11.0	S13 04.7	9.6	57.0
01	199 04.4	29.9	193 09.9	11.0	13 14.3	9.6	57.0
02	214 04.4	30.6	207 39.9	11.0	13 23.9	9.5	57.0
03	229 04.3	.. 31.3	222 09.9	11.0	13 33.4	9.4	57.0
04	244 04.3	32.0	236 39.9	10.9	13 42.8	9.4	56.9
05	259 04.2	32.8	251 09.8	11.0	13 52.2	9.2	56.9
06	274 04.2	S16 33.5	265 39.8	10.9	S14 01.4	9.2	56.9
07	289 04.2	34.2	280 09.7	11.0	14 10.6	9.1	56.9
08	304 04.1	35.0	294 39.6	11.0	14 19.7	9.0	56.8
09	319 04.1	.. 35.7	309 09.6	10.8	14 28.7	9.0	56.8
10	334 04.0	36.4	323 39.4	10.9	14 37.7	8.8	56.8
11	349 04.0	37.1	338 09.3	10.9	14 46.5	8.8	56.8
12	4 03.9	S16 37.9	352 39.2	10.8	S14 55.3	8.7	56.7
13	19 03.9	38.6	7 09.0	10.9	15 04.0	8.6	56.7
14	34 03.8	39.3	21 38.9	10.8	15 12.6	8.5	56.7
15	49 03.8	.. 40.0	36 08.7	10.8	15 21.1	8.4	56.7
16	64 03.7	40.7	50 38.5	10.8	15 29.5	8.3	56.6
17	79 03.7	41.5	65 08.3	10.8	15 37.8	8.3	56.6
18	94 03.6	S16 42.2	79 38.1	10.8	S15 46.1	8.2	56.6
19	109 03.6	42.9	94 07.9	10.7	15 54.3	8.0	56.6
20	124 03.6	43.6	108 37.6	10.8	16 02.3	8.0	56.5
21	139 03.5	.. 44.3	123 07.4	10.7	16 10.3	7.9	56.5
22	154 03.5	45.1	137 37.1	10.7	16 18.2	7.8	56.5
23	169 03.4	45.8	152 06.8	10.7	S16 26.0	7.7	56.4
	SD 16.2	d 0.7	SD 15.8		15.6		15.5

Rows by day: 6 = TUESDAY, 7 = WEDNESDAY, 8 = THURSDAY.

Lat.	Twilight Naut.	Twilight Civil	Sunrise	Moonrise 6	7	8	9
°	h m	h m	h m	h m	h m	h m	h m
N 72	06 29	07 56	09 37	05 50	07 52	10 02	▬▬
N 70	06 22	07 40	09 01	05 42	07 34	09 28	11 31
68	06 17	07 26	08 36	05 36	07 20	09 04	10 49
66	06 12	07 15	08 17	05 30	07 08	08 46	10 21
64	06 08	07 06	08 01	05 26	06 59	08 31	09 59
62	06 04	06 58	07 48	05 22	06 51	08 18	09 42
60	06 00	06 51	07 37	05 18	06 44	08 08	09 28
N 58	05 57	06 44	07 28	05 15	06 38	07 59	09 16
56	05 54	06 39	07 19	05 13	06 33	07 51	09 06
54	05 51	06 34	07 12	05 10	06 28	07 44	08 56
52	05 49	06 29	07 05	05 08	06 24	07 37	08 48
50	05 46	06 25	06 59	05 06	06 20	07 32	08 41
45	05 40	06 15	06 46	05 02	06 11	07 19	08 25
N 40	05 35	06 07	06 36	04 58	06 04	07 09	08 12
35	05 30	06 00	06 27	04 55	05 58	07 01	08 02
30	05 25	05 53	06 18	04 52	05 53	06 53	07 52
20	05 15	05 41	06 04	04 48	05 44	06 40	07 36
N 10	05 05	05 30	05 52	04 44	05 36	06 29	07 22
0	04 54	05 19	05 40	04 40	05 29	06 18	07 08
S 10	04 41	05 06	05 28	04 36	05 22	06 08	06 55
20	04 25	04 52	05 16	04 32	05 14	05 57	06 41
30	04 05	04 35	05 01	04 28	05 05	05 44	06 26
35	03 52	04 25	04 52	04 25	05 00	05 37	06 16
40	03 36	04 13	04 42	04 23	04 55	05 29	06 06
45	03 17	03 58	04 31	04 19	04 48	05 19	05 54
S 50	02 51	03 39	04 17	04 15	04 41	05 08	05 39
52	02 38	03 30	04 10	04 14	04 37	05 03	05 32
54	02 23	03 20	04 03	04 12	04 33	04 57	05 24
56	02 04	03 09	03 54	04 10	04 29	04 50	05 16
58	01 40	02 55	03 45	04 07	04 24	04 43	05 06
S 60	01 06	02 39	03 34	04 05	04 19	04 35	04 55

Lat.	Sunset	Twilight Civil	Twilight Naut.	Moonset 6	7	8	9
°	h m	h m	h m	h m	h m	h m	h m
N 72	13 49	15 30	16 56	15 27	15 09	14 42	▬▬
N 70	14 25	15 47	17 03	15 37	15 28	15 17	14 59
68	14 50	16 00	17 09	15 46	15 44	15 42	15 42
66	15 10	16 11	17 14	15 53	15 57	16 02	16 11
64	15 25	16 21	17 19	15 59	16 07	16 18	16 33
62	15 38	16 29	17 23	16 05	16 16	16 31	16 51
60	15 49	16 36	17 26	16 09	16 24	16 42	17 05
N 58	15 59	16 42	17 29	16 13	16 31	16 52	17 18
56	16 07	16 48	17 32	16 17	16 37	17 00	17 29
54	16 15	16 53	17 35	16 20	16 43	17 08	17 38
52	16 21	16 58	17 38	16 23	16 48	17 15	17 47
50	16 27	17 02	17 41	16 26	16 52	17 21	17 54
45	16 40	17 11	17 46	16 32	17 02	17 35	18 11
N 40	16 51	17 20	17 52	16 37	17 10	17 46	18 24
35	17 00	17 27	17 57	16 41	17 17	17 55	18 36
30	17 09	17 34	18 02	16 45	17 23	18 03	18 46
20	17 23	17 46	18 12	16 52	17 34	18 18	19 03
N 10	17 35	17 57	18 22	16 58	17 44	18 31	19 19
0	17 47	18 09	18 34	17 03	17 53	18 42	19 33
S 10	17 59	18 21	18 47	17 09	18 02	18 54	19 47
20	18 12	18 35	19 03	17 15	18 11	19 07	20 02
30	18 27	18 53	19 23	17 22	18 22	19 22	20 20
35	18 36	19 03	19 36	17 25	18 28	19 30	20 30
40	18 46	19 15	19 52	17 30	18 36	19 40	20 42
45	18 57	19 30	20 12	17 35	18 44	19 51	20 55
S 50	19 12	19 49	20 38	17 41	18 54	20 05	21 12
52	19 19	19 58	20 51	17 44	18 59	20 12	21 20
54	19 26	20 09	21 07	17 47	19 04	20 19	21 29
56	19 34	20 21	21 26	17 51	19 10	20 27	21 39
58	19 44	20 34	21 51	17 55	19 17	20 36	21 50
S 60	19 55	20 51	22 28	17 59	19 24	20 46	22 03

Day	SUN Eqn. of Time 00h	SUN Eqn. of Time 12h	SUN Mer. Pass.	MOON Mer. Pass. Upper	MOON Mer. Pass. Lower	Age	Phase
d	m s	m s	h m	h m	h m	d	%
6	16 24	16 23	11 44	10 52	23 16	28	2
7	16 21	16 20	11 44	11 41	24 06	29	0
8	16 18	16 16	11 44	12 30	00 06	01	1

UT	ARIES GHA	VENUS −4.6 GHA	Dec	MARS −0.4 GHA	Dec	JUPITER −1.7 GHA	Dec	SATURN +0.6 GHA	Dec	STARS Name	SHA	Dec
9 00	48 07.0	204 49.3	S13 07.3	79 21.9	S14 45.4	170 02.2	S19 30.2	132 01.0	S22 45.2	Acamar	315 15.2	S40 13.9
01	63 09.5	219 52.3	06.4	94 23.0	44.8	185 04.1	30.3	147 03.2	45.2	Achernar	335 23.5	S57 08.7
02	78 11.9	234 55.2	05.6	109 24.0	44.2	200 06.0	30.4	162 05.4	45.2	Acrux	173 05.7	S63 11.8
03	93 14.4	249 58.2 ..	04.7	124 25.1 ..	43.6	215 07.9 ..	30.5	177 07.7 ..	45.2	Adhara	255 09.4	S28 59.8
04	108 16.9	265 01.1	03.8	139 26.1	43.0	230 09.8	30.6	192 09.9	45.2	Aldebaran	290 44.9	N16 32.7
05	123 19.3	280 04.0	03.0	154 27.2	42.4	245 11.7	30.7	207 12.1	45.2			
06	138 21.8	295 06.9	S13 02.1	169 28.2	S14 41.8	260 13.6	S19 30.9	222 14.3	S22 45.2	Alioth	166 18.0	N55 51.5
F 07	153 24.3	310 09.9	01.3	184 29.3	41.1	275 15.5	31.0	237 16.5	45.2	Alkaid	152 56.5	N49 13.3
R 08	168 26.7	325 12.8	13 00.4	199 30.4	40.5	290 17.4	31.1	252 18.8	45.2	Al Na'ir	27 39.1	S46 52.4
I 09	183 29.2	340 15.7	12 59.6	214 31.4 ..	39.9	305 19.3 ..	31.2	267 21.0 ..	45.2	Alnilam	275 42.4	S 1 11.5
D 10	198 31.7	355 18.6	58.7	229 32.5	39.3	320 21.1	31.3	282 23.2	45.2	Alphard	217 52.5	S 8 44.3
A 11	213 34.1	10 21.5	57.9	244 33.5	38.7	335 23.0	31.5	297 25.4	45.2			
Y 12	228 36.6	25 24.4	S12 57.0	259 34.6	S14 38.1	350 24.9	S19 31.6	312 27.6	S22 45.2	Alphecca	126 08.3	N26 39.3
13	243 39.1	40 27.3	56.2	274 35.6	37.5	5 26.8	31.7	327 29.9	45.1	Alpheratz	357 39.5	N29 11.8
14	258 41.5	55 30.2	55.3	289 36.7	36.9	20 28.7	31.8	342 32.1	45.1	Altair	62 04.8	N 8 55.3
15	273 44.0	70 33.1 ..	54.5	304 37.7 ..	36.3	35 30.6 ..	31.9	357 34.3 ..	45.1	Ankaa	353 11.8	S42 12.4
16	288 46.4	85 36.0	53.6	319 38.8	35.7	50 32.5	32.1	12 36.5	45.1	Antares	112 22.1	S26 28.2
17	303 48.9	100 38.9	52.8	334 39.8	35.1	65 34.4	32.2	27 38.7	45.1			
18	318 51.4	115 41.8	S12 52.0	349 40.9	S14 34.5	80 36.3	S19 32.3	42 40.9	S22 45.1	Arcturus	145 52.8	N19 05.3
19	333 53.8	130 44.6	51.1	4 41.9	33.9	95 38.2	32.4	57 43.2	45.1	Atria	107 21.2	S69 03.5
20	348 56.3	145 47.5	50.3	19 43.0	33.3	110 40.1	32.5	72 45.4	45.1	Avior	234 16.4	S59 33.9
21	3 58.8	160 50.4 ..	49.5	34 44.1 ..	32.7	125 42.0 ..	32.6	87 47.6 ..	45.1	Bellatrix	278 27.8	N 6 21.9
22	19 01.2	175 53.2	48.6	49 45.1	32.1	140 43.9	32.8	102 49.8	45.1	Betelgeuse	270 57.1	N 7 24.5
23	34 03.7	190 56.1	47.8	64 46.2	31.5	155 45.8	32.9	117 52.0	45.1			
10 00	49 06.2	205 59.0	S12 47.0	79 47.2	S14 30.9	170 47.7	S19 33.0	132 54.2	S22 45.1	Canopus	263 54.1	S52 42.2
01	64 08.6	221 01.8	46.1	94 48.3	30.3	185 49.6	33.1	147 56.5	45.1	Capella	280 28.6	N46 00.8
02	79 11.1	236 04.7	45.3	109 49.3	29.7	200 51.5	33.2	162 58.7	45.1	Deneb	49 29.1	N45 21.2
03	94 13.6	251 07.5 ..	44.5	124 50.4 ..	29.1	215 53.4 ..	33.4	178 00.9 ..	45.1	Denebola	182 30.2	N14 28.1
04	109 16.0	266 10.3	43.7	139 51.4	28.4	230 55.2	33.5	193 03.1	45.1	Diphda	348 52.0	S17 53.1
05	124 18.5	281 13.2	42.9	154 52.5	27.8	245 57.1	33.6	208 05.3	45.1			
06	139 20.9	296 16.0	S12 42.0	169 53.5	S14 27.2	260 59.0	S19 33.7	223 07.5	S22 45.1	Dubhe	193 47.6	N61 38.8
S 07	154 23.4	311 18.8	41.2	184 54.6	26.6	276 00.9	33.8	238 09.8	45.1	Elnath	278 07.7	N28 37.2
A 08	169 25.9	326 21.7	40.4	199 55.6	26.0	291 02.8	34.0	253 12.0	45.0	Eltanin	90 44.9	N51 29.5
T 09	184 28.3	341 24.5 ..	39.6	214 56.7 ..	25.4	306 04.7 ..	34.1	268 14.2 ..	45.0	Enif	33 43.5	N 9 57.8
U 10	199 30.8	356 27.3	38.8	229 57.7	24.8	321 06.6	34.2	283 16.4	45.0	Fomalhaut	15 19.8	S29 31.5
R 11	214 33.3	11 30.1	38.0	244 58.8	24.2	336 08.5	34.3	298 18.6	45.0			
D 12	229 35.7	26 32.9	S12 37.2	259 59.8	S14 23.6	351 10.4	S19 34.4	313 20.8	S22 45.0	Gacrux	171 57.3	S57 12.8
A 13	244 38.2	41 35.7	36.4	275 00.9	23.0	6 12.3	34.5	328 23.1	45.0	Gienah	175 48.8	S17 38.5
Y 14	259 40.7	56 38.5	35.6	290 01.9	22.4	21 14.2	34.7	343 25.3	45.0	Hadar	148 43.3	S60 27.5
15	274 43.1	71 41.3 ..	34.8	305 03.0 ..	21.8	36 16.1 ..	34.8	358 27.5 ..	45.0	Hamal	327 56.3	N23 33.0
16	289 45.6	86 44.1	34.0	320 04.0	21.2	51 18.0	34.9	13 29.7	45.0	Kaus Aust.	83 39.3	S34 22.4
17	304 48.0	101 46.9	33.2	335 05.1	20.5	66 19.9	35.0	28 31.9	45.0			
18	319 50.5	116 49.7	S12 32.4	350 06.1	S14 19.9	81 21.8	S19 35.1	43 34.1	S22 45.0	Kochab	137 21.4	N74 04.8
19	334 53.0	131 52.5	31.6	5 07.2	19.3	96 23.7	35.3	58 36.3	45.0	Markab	13 34.6	N15 18.5
20	349 55.4	146 55.3	30.8	20 08.2	18.7	111 25.5	35.4	73 38.6	45.0	Menkar	314 10.9	N 4 09.7
21	4 57.9	161 58.0 ..	30.0	35 09.3 ..	18.1	126 27.4 ..	35.5	88 40.8 ..	45.0	Menkent	148 03.7	S36 27.4
22	20 00.4	177 00.8	29.2	50 10.3	17.5	141 29.3	35.6	103 43.0	45.0	Miaplacidus	221 38.9	S69 47.3
23	35 02.8	192 03.6	28.4	65 11.4	16.9	156 31.2	35.7	118 45.2	45.0			
11 00	50 05.3	207 06.3	S12 27.6	80 12.4	S14 16.3	171 33.1	S19 35.8	133 47.4	S22 45.0	Mirfak	308 34.6	N49 55.5
01	65 07.8	222 09.1	26.8	95 13.5	15.7	186 35.0	36.0	148 49.6	45.0	Nunki	75 54.0	S26 16.3
02	80 10.2	237 11.8	26.1	110 14.5	15.1	201 36.9	36.1	163 51.8	44.9	Peacock	53 13.7	S56 40.6
03	95 12.7	252 14.6 ..	25.3	125 15.5 ..	14.4	216 38.8 ..	36.2	178 54.1 ..	44.9	Pollux	243 23.2	N27 58.7
04	110 15.2	267 17.3	24.5	140 16.6	13.8	231 40.7	36.3	193 56.3	44.9	Procyon	244 55.8	N 5 10.6
05	125 17.6	282 20.1	23.7	155 17.6	13.2	246 42.6	36.4	208 58.5	44.9			
06	140 20.1	297 22.8	S12 23.0	170 18.7	S14 12.6	261 44.5	S19 36.6	224 00.7	S22 44.9	Rasalhague	96 03.4	N12 33.1
07	155 22.5	312 25.5	22.2	185 19.7	12.0	276 46.4	36.7	239 02.9	44.9	Regulus	207 39.7	N11 52.5
S 08	170 25.0	327 28.3	21.4	200 20.8	11.4	291 48.3	36.8	254 05.1	44.9	Rigel	281 08.3	S 8 10.9
U 09	185 27.5	342 31.0 ..	20.6	215 21.8 ..	10.8	306 50.2 ..	36.9	269 07.3 ..	44.9	Rigil Kent.	139 47.4	S60 54.4
N 10	200 29.9	357 33.7	19.9	230 22.9	10.2	321 52.0	37.0	284 09.6	44.9	Sabik	102 08.7	S15 44.7
D 11	215 32.4	12 36.4	19.1	245 23.9	09.5	336 53.9	37.1	299 11.8	44.9			
A 12	230 34.9	27 39.2	S12 18.3	260 25.0	S14 08.9	351 55.8	S19 37.3	314 14.0	S22 44.9	Schedar	349 35.9	N56 38.5
Y 13	245 37.3	42 41.9	17.6	275 26.0	08.3	6 57.7	37.4	329 16.2	44.9	Shaula	96 17.3	S37 06.9
14	260 39.8	57 44.6	16.8	290 27.1	07.7	21 59.6	37.5	344 18.4	44.9	Sirius	258 30.3	S16 44.5
15	275 42.3	72 47.3 ..	16.1	305 28.1 ..	07.1	37 01.5 ..	37.6	359 20.6 ..	44.9	Spica	158 27.7	S11 15.3
16	290 44.7	87 50.0	15.3	320 29.1	06.5	52 03.4	37.7	14 22.8	44.9	Suhail	222 49.7	S43 30.2
17	305 47.2	102 52.7	14.5	335 30.2	05.9	67 05.3	37.9	29 25.0	44.9			
18	320 49.7	117 55.4	S12 13.8	350 31.2	S14 05.3	82 07.2	S19 38.0	44 27.3	S22 44.9	Vega	80 36.8	N38 48.4
19	335 52.1	132 58.1	13.0	5 32.3	04.6	97 09.1	38.1	59 29.5	44.9	Zuben'ubi	137 01.7	S16 06.9
20	350 54.6	148 00.7	12.3	20 33.3	04.0	112 11.0	38.2	74 31.7	44.8		SHA	Mer. Pass.
21	5 57.0	163 03.4 ..	11.5	35 34.4 ..	03.4	127 12.9 ..	38.3	89 33.9 ..	44.8		° '	h m
22	20 59.5	178 06.1	10.8	50 35.4	02.8	142 14.8	38.4	104 36.1	44.8	Venus	156 52.8	10 14
23	36 02.0	193 08.8	10.1	65 36.4	02.2	157 16.6	38.6	119 38.3	44.8	Mars	30 41.1	18 40
	h m									Jupiter	121 41.5	12 35
Mer. Pass.	20 40.2	v 2.8	d 0.8	v 1.0	d 0.6	v 1.9	d 0.1	v 2.2	d 0.0	Saturn	83 48.1	15 06

UT	SUN GHA	SUN Dec	MOON GHA	v	MOON Dec	d	HP
9 00	184 03.4	S16 46.5	166 36.5	10.7	S16 33.7	7.6	56.4
01	199 03.3	47.2	181 06.2	10.7	16 41.3	7.6	56.4
02	214 03.3	47.9	195 35.9	10.7	16 48.9	7.4	56.4
03	229 03.2	.. 48.7	210 05.6	10.6	16 56.3	7.3	56.3
04	244 03.2	49.4	224 35.2	10.7	17 03.6	7.3	56.3
05	259 03.1	50.1	239 04.9	10.6	17 10.9	7.1	56.3
06	274 03.1	S16 50.8	253 34.5	10.6	S17 18.0	7.1	56.3
07	289 03.0	51.5	268 04.1	10.7	17 25.1	7.0	56.2
08	304 02.9	52.2	282 33.8	10.6	17 32.1	6.8	56.2
F 09	319 02.9	.. 52.9	297 03.4	10.6	17 38.9	6.8	56.2
R 10	334 02.8	53.7	311 33.0	10.5	17 45.7	6.6	56.2
I 11	349 02.8	54.4	326 02.5	10.6	17 52.3	6.6	56.1
D 12	4 02.7	S16 55.1	340 32.1	10.5	S17 58.9	6.5	56.1
A 13	19 02.7	55.8	355 01.7	10.5	18 05.4	6.4	56.1
Y 14	34 02.6	56.5	9 31.2	10.6	18 11.8	6.2	56.1
15	49 02.6	.. 57.2	24 00.8	10.5	18 18.0	6.2	56.0
16	64 02.5	57.9	38 30.3	10.6	18 24.2	6.1	56.0
17	79 02.5	58.6	52 59.9	10.5	18 30.3	6.0	56.0
18	94 02.4	S16 59.3	67 29.4	10.5	S18 36.3	5.8	56.0
19	109 02.3	17 00.1	81 58.9	10.5	18 42.1	5.8	55.9
20	124 02.3	00.8	96 28.4	10.5	18 47.9	5.7	55.9
21	139 02.2	.. 01.5	110 57.9	10.5	18 53.6	5.6	55.9
22	154 02.2	02.2	125 27.4	10.5	18 59.2	5.4	55.9
23	169 02.1	02.9	139 56.9	10.5	19 04.6	5.4	55.8
10 00	184 02.1	S17 03.6	154 26.4	10.5	S19 10.0	5.3	55.8
01	199 02.0	04.3	168 55.9	10.5	19 15.3	5.1	55.8
02	214 01.9	05.0	183 25.4	10.4	19 20.4	5.1	55.8
03	229 01.9	.. 05.7	197 54.8	10.5	19 25.5	4.9	55.8
04	244 01.8	06.4	212 24.3	10.5	19 30.4	4.9	55.7
05	259 01.8	07.1	226 53.8	10.5	19 35.3	4.7	55.7
06	274 01.7	S17 07.8	241 23.3	10.4	S19 40.0	4.7	55.7
07	289 01.6	08.5	255 52.7	10.5	19 44.7	4.5	55.7
S 08	304 01.6	09.2	270 22.2	10.5	19 49.2	4.4	55.6
A 09	319 01.5	.. 09.9	284 51.7	10.4	19 53.6	4.4	55.6
T 10	334 01.5	10.6	299 21.1	10.5	19 58.0	4.2	55.6
U 11	349 01.4	11.3	313 50.6	10.5	20 02.2	4.1	55.6
R 12	4 01.3	S17 12.0	328 20.1	10.4	S20 06.3	4.0	55.5
D 13	19 01.3	12.7	342 49.5	10.5	20 10.3	3.9	55.5
A 14	34 01.2	13.4	357 19.0	10.5	20 14.2	3.8	55.5
Y 15	49 01.1	.. 14.1	11 48.5	10.5	20 18.0	3.7	55.5
16	64 01.1	14.8	26 18.0	10.4	20 21.7	3.6	55.4
17	79 01.0	15.5	40 47.4	10.5	20 25.3	3.5	55.4
18	94 00.9	S17 16.2	55 16.9	10.5	S20 28.8	3.3	55.4
19	109 00.9	16.9	69 46.4	10.5	20 32.1	3.3	55.4
20	124 00.8	17.6	84 15.9	10.5	20 35.4	3.2	55.4
21	139 00.7	.. 18.3	98 45.4	10.5	20 38.6	3.0	55.3
22	154 00.7	19.0	113 14.9	10.6	20 41.6	3.0	55.3
23	169 00.6	19.7	127 44.5	10.5	20 44.6	2.8	55.3
11 00	184 00.5	S17 20.4	142 14.0	10.5	S20 47.4	2.8	55.3
01	199 00.5	21.1	156 43.5	10.5	20 50.2	2.6	55.3
02	214 00.4	21.8	171 13.0	10.6	20 52.8	2.5	55.2
03	229 00.3	.. 22.5	185 42.6	10.6	20 55.3	2.4	55.2
04	244 00.3	23.2	200 12.2	10.5	20 57.7	2.3	55.2
05	259 00.2	23.8	214 41.7	10.6	21 00.0	2.2	55.2
06	274 00.1	S17 24.5	229 11.3	10.6	S21 02.2	2.1	55.1
07	289 00.1	25.2	243 40.9	10.6	21 04.3	2.0	55.1
08	304 00.0	25.9	258 10.5	10.6	21 06.3	1.9	55.1
S 09	318 59.9	.. 26.6	272 40.1	10.7	21 08.2	1.8	55.1
U 10	333 59.9	27.3	287 09.8	10.6	21 10.0	1.6	55.1
N 11	348 59.8	28.0	301 39.4	10.7	21 11.6	1.6	55.0
D 12	3 59.7	S17 28.7	316 09.1	10.6	S21 13.2	1.4	55.0
A 13	18 59.6	29.4	330 38.7	10.7	21 14.6	1.4	55.0
Y 14	33 59.6	30.0	345 08.4	10.7	21 16.0	1.2	55.0
15	48 59.5	.. 30.7	359 38.1	10.8	21 17.2	1.2	55.0
16	63 59.4	31.4	14 07.9	10.7	21 18.4	1.0	54.9
17	78 59.4	32.1	28 37.6	10.7	21 19.4	0.9	54.9
18	93 59.3	S17 32.8	43 07.3	10.8	S21 20.3	0.8	54.9
19	108 59.2	33.5	57 37.1	10.8	21 21.1	0.7	54.9
20	123 59.1	34.1	72 06.9	10.8	21 21.8	0.7	54.9
21	138 59.1	.. 34.8	86 36.7	10.9	21 22.5	0.5	54.9
22	153 59.0	35.5	101 06.6	10.8	21 23.0	0.4	54.8
23	168 58.9	36.2	115 36.4	10.9	S21 23.4	0.2	54.8
	SD 16.2	d 0.7	SD 15.3		15.1		15.0

Lat.	Twilight Naut.	Civil	Sunrise	Moonrise 9	10	11	12
N 72	06 41	08 10	10 02	▮▮▮	▮▮▮	▮▮▮	▮▮▮
N 70	06 33	07 51	09 18	11 31	▮▮▮	▮▮▮	▮▮▮
68	06 26	07 36	08 49	10 49	12 31	14 02	14 51
66	06 20	07 24	08 28	10 21	11 49	13 03	13 54
64	06 15	07 14	08 11	09 59	11 21	12 29	13 20
62	06 11	07 05	07 57	09 42	10 59	12 05	12 55
60	06 07	06 57	07 45	09 28	10 42	11 45	12 36
N 58	06 03	06 51	07 35	09 16	10 27	11 29	12 20
56	05 59	06 45	07 26	09 06	10 15	11 15	12 06
54	05 56	06 39	07 18	08 56	10 04	11 03	11 54
52	05 53	06 34	07 11	08 48	09 54	10 53	11 44
50	05 50	06 29	07 04	08 41	09 45	10 44	11 34
45	05 44	06 19	06 51	08 25	09 27	10 24	11 15
N 40	05 38	06 11	06 39	08 12	09 12	10 08	10 59
35	05 32	06 03	06 29	08 02	09 00	09 55	10 45
30	05 27	05 56	06 21	07 52	08 49	09 43	10 33
20	05 16	05 43	06 06	07 36	08 30	09 23	10 13
N 10	05 06	05 31	05 53	07 22	08 14	09 06	09 56
0	04 54	05 19	05 40	07 08	07 59	08 49	09 39
S 10	04 40	05 06	05 28	06 55	07 44	08 33	09 23
20	04 24	04 51	05 14	06 41	07 28	08 16	09 05
30	04 02	04 33	04 59	06 26	07 09	07 56	08 45
35	03 49	04 22	04 50	06 16	06 59	07 45	08 34
40	03 33	04 09	04 39	06 06	06 47	07 31	08 20
45	03 12	03 54	04 27	05 54	06 32	07 16	08 04
S 50	02 45	03 34	04 12	05 39	06 15	06 57	07 45
52	02 31	03 24	04 05	05 32	06 07	06 48	07 35
54	02 14	03 14	03 57	05 24	05 57	06 37	07 25
56	01 53	03 01	03 48	05 16	05 47	06 26	07 13
58	01 26	02 47	03 38	05 06	05 35	06 13	06 59
S 60	00 43	02 29	03 27	04 55	05 22	05 57	06 43

Lat.	Sunset	Twilight Civil	Naut.	Moonset 9	10	11	12
N 72	13 25	15 16	16 46	▮▮▮	▮▮▮	▮▮▮	▮▮▮
N 70	14 09	15 35	16 54	14 59	▮▮▮	▮▮▮	▮▮▮
68	14 37	15 50	17 01	15 42	15 45	15 59	16 54
66	14 59	16 03	17 07	16 11	16 27	16 58	17 51
64	15 16	16 13	17 12	16 33	16 56	17 32	18 24
62	15 30	16 22	17 16	16 51	17 18	17 57	18 49
60	15 42	16 30	17 20	17 05	17 36	18 17	19 08
N 58	15 52	16 36	17 24	17 18	17 51	18 33	19 24
56	16 01	16 43	17 28	17 29	18 04	18 46	19 38
54	16 09	16 48	17 31	17 38	18 15	18 58	19 50
52	16 16	16 53	17 34	17 47	18 24	19 09	20 00
50	16 23	16 58	17 37	17 54	18 33	19 18	20 09
45	16 37	17 08	17 43	18 11	18 52	19 38	20 29
N 40	16 48	17 17	17 49	18 24	19 07	19 54	20 45
35	16 58	17 25	17 55	18 36	19 20	20 08	20 58
30	17 07	17 32	18 00	18 48	19 31	20 19	21 10
20	17 22	17 45	18 11	19 03	19 51	20 40	21 30
N 10	17 35	17 57	18 22	19 19	20 08	20 57	21 47
0	17 47	18 09	18 34	19 33	20 23	21 14	22 03
S 10	18 00	18 22	18 48	19 47	20 39	21 30	22 19
20	18 14	18 37	19 05	20 02	20 56	21 47	22 36
30	18 29	18 55	19 26	20 20	21 15	22 08	22 56
35	18 39	19 06	19 40	20 30	21 27	22 19	23 08
40	18 51	19 19	19 56	20 42	21 40	22 33	23 21
45	19 02	19 35	20 17	20 55	21 55	22 49	23 36
S 50	19 17	19 55	20 45	21 12	22 14	23 08	23 55
52	19 24	20 05	20 59	21 20	22 23	23 18	24 04
54	19 32	20 16	21 16	21 29	22 33	23 28	24 14
56	19 41	20 28	21 37	21 39	22 44	23 40	24 26
58	19 51	20 43	22 06	21 50	22 57	23 54	24 39
S 60	20 03	21 01	22 54	22 03	23 12	24 10	00 10

Day	SUN Eqn. of Time 00h	12h	Mer. Pass.	MOON Mer. Pass. Upper	Lower	Age	Phase
d	m s	m s	h m	h m	h m	d	%
9	16 14	16 11	11 44	13 21	00 55	02	4
10	16 08	16 05	11 44	14 11	01 46	03	9
11	16 02	15 59	11 44	15 02	02 36	04	15

2018 NOVEMBER 12, 13, 14 (MON., TUES., WED.)

UT	ARIES	VENUS −4·7		MARS −0·4		JUPITER −1·7		SATURN +0·6		STARS		
	GHA	GHA	Dec	GHA	Dec	GHA	Dec	GHA	Dec	Name	SHA	Dec
d h	° ′	° ′	° ′	° ′	° ′	° ′	° ′	° ′	° ′		° ′	° ′
12 00	51 04.4	208 11.4	S12 09.3	80 37.5	S14 01.6	172 18.5	S19 38.7	134 40.5	S22 44.8	Acamar	315 15.2	S40 13.9
01	66 06.9	223 14.1	08.6	95 38.5	01.0	187 20.4	38.8	149 42.7	44.8	Achernar	335 23.5	S57 08.7
02	81 09.4	238 16.8	07.8	110 39.6	14 00.3	202 22.3	38.9	164 45.0	44.8	Acrux	173 05.7	S63 11.8
03	96 11.8	253 19.4	. . 07.1	125 40.6	13 59.7	217 24.2	. . 39.0	179 47.2	. . 44.8	Adhara	255 09.4	S28 59.8
04	111 14.3	268 22.1	06.4	140 41.7	59.1	232 26.1	39.1	194 49.4	44.8	Aldebaran	290 44.9	N16 32.7
05	126 16.8	283 24.7	05.6	155 42.7	58.5	247 28.0	39.3	209 51.6	44.8			
06	141 19.2	298 27.3	S12 04.9	170 43.7	S13 57.9	262 29.9	S19 39.4	224 53.8	S22 44.8	Alioth	166 18.0	N55 51.5
07	156 21.7	313 30.0	04.2	185 44.8	57.3	277 31.8	39.5	239 56.0	44.8	Alkaid	152 56.5	N49 13.2
08	171 24.2	328 32.6	03.4	200 45.8	56.6	292 33.7	39.6	254 58.2	44.8	Al Na'ir	27 39.1	S46 52.4
M 09	186 26.6	343 35.3	. . 02.7	215 46.9	. . 56.0	307 35.6	. . 39.7	270 00.4	. . 44.8	Alnilam	275 42.4	S 1 11.5
O 10	201 29.1	358 37.9	02.0	230 47.9	55.4	322 37.4	39.8	285 02.6	44.8	Alphard	217 52.5	S 8 44.3
N 11	216 31.5	13 40.5	01.3	245 49.0	54.8	337 39.3	40.0	300 04.9	44.8			
D 12	231 34.0	28 43.1	S12 00.6	260 50.0	S13 54.2	352 41.2	S19 40.1	315 07.1	S22 44.8	Alphecca	126 08.3	N26 39.3
A 13	246 36.5	43 45.7	11 59.8	275 51.0	53.6	7 43.1	40.2	330 09.3	44.7	Alpheratz	357 39.5	N29 11.8
Y 14	261 38.9	58 48.4	59.1	290 52.1	52.9	22 45.0	40.3	345 11.5	44.7	Altair	62 04.8	N 8 55.3
15	276 41.4	73 51.0	. . 58.4	305 53.1	. . 52.3	37 46.9	. . 40.4	0 13.7	. . 44.7	Ankaa	353 11.8	S42 12.4
16	291 43.9	88 53.6	57.7	320 54.2	51.7	52 48.8	40.6	15 15.9	44.7	Antares	112 22.1	S26 28.2
17	306 46.3	103 56.2	57.0	335 55.2	51.1	67 50.7	40.7	30 18.1	44.7			
18	321 48.8	118 58.8	S11 56.3	350 56.2	S13 50.5	82 52.6	S19 40.8	45 20.3	S22 44.7	Arcturus	145 52.7	N19 05.3
19	336 51.3	134 01.4	55.6	5 57.3	49.9	97 54.5	40.9	60 22.5	44.7	Atria	107 21.2	S69 03.5
20	351 53.7	149 03.9	54.9	20 58.3	49.2	112 56.4	41.0	75 24.7	44.7	Avior	234 16.3	S59 33.9
21	6 56.2	164 06.5	. . 54.2	35 59.4	. . 48.6	127 58.2	. . 41.1	90 27.0	. . 44.7	Bellatrix	278 27.8	N 6 21.9
22	21 58.6	179 09.1	53.5	51 00.4	48.0	143 00.1	41.3	105 29.2	44.7	Betelgeuse	270 57.1	N 7 24.5
23	37 01.1	194 11.7	52.8	66 01.4	47.4	158 02.0	41.4	120 31.4	44.7			
13 00	52 03.6	209 14.3	S11 52.1	81 02.5	S13 46.8	173 03.9	S19 41.5	135 33.6	S22 44.7	Canopus	263 54.1	S52 42.2
01	67 06.0	224 16.8	51.4	96 03.5	46.1	188 05.8	41.6	150 35.8	44.7	Capella	280 28.6	N46 00.8
02	82 08.5	239 19.4	50.7	111 04.5	45.5	203 07.7	41.7	165 38.0	44.7	Deneb	49 29.1	N45 21.2
03	97 11.0	254 22.0	. . 50.0	126 05.6	. . 44.9	218 09.6	. . 41.8	180 40.2	. . 44.7	Denebola	182 30.1	N14 28.1
04	112 13.4	269 24.5	49.3	141 06.6	44.3	233 11.5	42.0	195 42.4	44.7	Diphda	348 52.0	S17 53.1
05	127 15.9	284 27.1	48.6	156 07.7	43.7	248 13.4	42.1	210 44.6	44.7			
06	142 18.4	299 29.6	S11 47.9	171 08.7	S13 43.0	263 15.3	S19 42.2	225 46.8	S22 44.6	Dubhe	193 47.6	N61 38.8
07	157 20.8	314 32.2	47.2	186 09.7	42.4	278 17.2	42.3	240 49.0	44.6	Elnath	278 07.7	N28 37.2
T 08	172 23.3	329 34.7	46.6	201 10.8	41.8	293 19.0	42.4	255 51.2	44.6	Eltanin	90 44.9	N51 29.5
U 09	187 25.8	344 37.2	. . 45.9	216 11.8	. . 41.2	308 20.9	. . 42.5	270 53.5	. . 44.6	Enif	33 43.5	N 9 57.8
E 10	202 28.2	359 39.8	45.2	231 12.8	40.6	323 22.8	42.7	285 55.7	44.6	Fomalhaut	15 19.8	S29 31.5
S 11	217 30.7	14 42.3	44.5	246 13.9	39.9	338 24.7	42.8	300 57.9	44.6			
D 12	232 33.1	29 44.8	S11 43.8	261 14.9	S13 39.3	353 26.6	S19 42.9	316 00.1	S22 44.6	Gacrux	171 57.2	S57 12.7
A 13	247 35.6	44 47.4	43.2	276 16.0	38.7	8 28.5	43.0	331 02.3	44.6	Gienah	175 48.8	S17 38.5
Y 14	262 38.1	59 49.9	42.5	291 17.0	38.1	23 30.4	43.1	346 04.5	44.6	Hadar	148 43.3	S60 27.5
15	277 40.5	74 52.4	. . 41.8	306 18.0	. . 37.5	38 32.3	. . 43.2	1 06.7	. . 44.6	Hamal	327 56.3	N23 33.0
16	292 43.0	89 54.9	41.2	321 19.1	36.8	53 34.2	43.4	16 08.9	44.6	Kaus Aust.	83 39.3	S34 22.4
17	307 45.5	104 57.4	40.5	336 20.1	36.2	68 36.1	43.5	31 11.1	44.6			
18	322 47.9	119 59.9	S11 39.8	351 21.1	S13 35.6	83 37.9	S19 43.6	46 13.3	S22 44.6	Kochab	137 21.4	N74 04.8
19	337 50.4	135 02.4	39.2	6 22.2	35.0	98 39.8	43.7	61 15.5	44.6	Markab	13 34.6	N15 18.5
20	352 52.9	150 04.9	38.5	21 23.2	34.3	113 41.7	43.8	76 17.7	44.6	Menkar	314 10.9	N 4 09.7
21	7 55.3	165 07.4	. . 37.9	36 24.2	. . 33.7	128 43.6	. . 43.9	91 19.9	. . 44.6	Menkent	148 03.6	S36 27.4
22	22 57.8	180 09.9	37.2	51 25.3	33.1	143 45.5	44.1	106 22.2	44.5	Miaplacidus	221 38.8	S69 47.3
23	38 00.3	195 12.4	36.6	66 26.3	32.5	158 47.4	44.2	121 24.4	44.5			
14 00	53 02.7	210 14.8	S11 35.9	81 27.4	S13 31.9	173 49.3	S19 44.3	136 26.6	S22 44.5	Mirfak	308 34.6	N49 55.5
01	68 05.2	225 17.3	35.3	96 28.4	31.2	188 51.2	44.4	151 28.8	44.5	Nunki	75 54.0	S26 16.3
02	83 07.6	240 19.8	34.6	111 29.4	30.6	203 53.1	44.5	166 31.0	44.5	Peacock	53 13.7	S56 40.6
03	98 10.1	255 22.2	. . 34.0	126 30.5	. . 30.0	218 54.9	. . 44.6	181 33.2	. . 44.5	Pollux	243 23.1	N27 58.7
04	113 12.6	270 24.7	33.3	141 31.5	29.4	233 56.8	44.7	196 35.4	44.5	Procyon	244 55.8	N 5 10.5
05	128 15.0	285 27.2	32.7	156 32.5	28.7	248 58.7	44.9	211 37.6	44.5			
06	143 17.5	300 29.6	S11 32.0	171 33.6	S13 28.1	264 00.6	S19 45.0	226 39.8	S22 44.5	Rasalhague	96 03.4	N12 33.1
W 07	158 20.0	315 32.1	31.4	186 34.6	27.5	279 02.5	45.1	241 42.0	44.5	Regulus	207 39.7	N11 52.5
E 08	173 22.4	330 34.5	30.8	201 35.6	26.9	294 04.4	45.2	256 44.2	44.5	Rigel	281 08.2	S 8 10.9
D 09	188 24.9	345 37.0	. . 30.1	216 36.7	. . 26.2	309 06.3	. . 45.3	271 46.4	. . 44.5	Rigil Kent.	139 47.4	S60 54.4
N 10	203 27.4	0 39.4	29.5	231 37.7	25.6	324 08.2	45.4	286 48.6	44.5	Sabik	102 08.7	S15 44.7
E 11	218 29.8	15 41.8	28.9	246 38.7	25.0	339 10.1	45.6	301 50.8	44.5			
S 12	233 32.3	30 44.3	S11 28.3	261 39.8	S13 24.4	354 11.9	S19 45.7	316 53.0	S22 44.4	Schedar	349 35.9	N56 38.5
D 13	248 34.8	45 46.7	27.6	276 40.8	23.7	9 13.8	45.8	331 55.2	44.4	Shaula	96 17.3	S37 06.9
A 14	263 37.2	60 49.1	27.0	291 41.8	23.1	24 15.7	45.9	346 57.4	44.4	Sirius	258 30.3	S16 44.5
Y 15	278 39.7	75 51.6	. . 26.4	306 42.9	. . 22.5	39 17.6	. . 46.0	1 59.7	. . 44.4	Spica	158 27.7	S11 15.3
16	293 42.1	90 54.0	25.8	321 43.9	21.9	54 19.5	46.1	17 01.9	44.4	Suhail	222 49.7	S43 30.3
17	308 44.6	105 56.4	25.2	336 44.9	21.2	69 21.4	46.3	32 04.1	44.4			
18	323 47.1	120 58.8	S11 24.5	351 46.0	S13 20.6	84 23.3	S19 46.4	47 06.3	S22 44.4	Vega	80 36.8	N38 48.4
19	338 49.5	136 01.2	23.9	6 47.0	20.0	99 25.2	46.5	62 08.5	44.4	Zuben'ubi	137 01.7	S16 06.9
20	353 52.0	151 03.6	23.3	21 48.0	19.4	114 27.1	46.6	77 10.7	44.4		SHA	Mer.Pass.
21	8 54.5	166 06.0	. . 22.7	36 49.0	. . 18.7	129 28.9	. . 46.7	92 12.9	. . 44.4		° ′	h m
22	23 56.9	181 08.4	22.1	51 50.1	18.1	144 30.8	46.8	107 15.1	44.4	Venus	157 10.7	10 01
23	38 59.4	196 10.8	21.5	66 51.1	17.5	159 32.7	46.9	122 17.3	44.4	Mars	28 58.9	18 35
	h m									Jupiter	121 00.3	12 26
Mer.Pass. 20 28.4		v 2.5	d 0.7	v 1.0	d 0.6	v 1.9	d 0.1	v 2.2	d 0.0	Saturn	83 30.0	14 56

UT	SUN GHA	SUN Dec	MOON GHA	v	Dec	d	HP
	° '	° '	° '	'	° '	'	'
d h							
12 00	183 58.8	S17 36.9	130 06.3	10.9	S21 23.6	0.2	54.8
01	198 58.8	37.6	144 36.2	10.9	21 23.8	0.1	54.8
02	213 58.7	38.2	159 06.1	10.9	21 23.9	0.0	54.8
03	228 58.6	.. 38.9	173 36.0	11.0	21 23.9	0.1	54.8
04	243 58.5	39.6	188 06.0	11.0	21 23.8	0.3	54.7
05	258 58.4	40.3	202 36.0	11.0	21 23.5	0.3	54.7
06	273 58.4	S17 41.0	217 06.0	11.0	S21 23.2	0.4	54.7
07	288 58.3	41.6	231 36.0	11.1	21 22.8	0.6	54.7
08	303 58.2	42.3	246 06.1	11.1	21 22.2	0.6	54.7
M 09	318 58.1	.. 43.0	260 36.2	11.1	21 21.6	0.8	54.7
O 10	333 58.0	43.7	275 06.3	11.1	21 20.8	0.8	54.6
N 11	348 58.0	44.3	289 36.4	11.2	21 20.0	1.0	54.6
D 12	3 57.9	S17 45.0	304 06.6	11.2	S21 19.0	1.0	54.6
A 13	18 57.8	45.7	318 36.8	11.2	21 18.0	1.2	54.6
Y 14	33 57.7	46.4	333 07.0	11.2	21 16.8	1.2	54.6
15	48 57.6	.. 47.0	347 37.2	11.3	21 15.6	1.4	54.6
16	63 57.6	47.7	2 07.5	11.3	21 14.2	1.4	54.6
17	78 57.5	48.4	16 37.8	11.4	21 12.8	1.6	54.5
18	93 57.4	S17 49.0	31 08.2	11.3	S21 11.2	1.7	54.5
19	108 57.3	49.7	45 38.5	11.4	21 09.5	1.7	54.5
20	123 57.2	50.4	60 08.9	11.4	21 07.8	1.9	54.5
21	138 57.2	.. 51.1	74 39.3	11.5	21 05.9	1.9	54.5
22	153 57.1	51.7	89 09.8	11.5	21 04.0	2.1	54.5
23	168 57.0	52.4	103 40.3	11.5	21 01.9	2.1	54.5
13 00	183 56.9	S17 53.1	118 10.8	11.5	S20 59.8	2.3	54.5
01	198 56.8	53.7	132 41.3	11.6	20 57.5	2.3	54.5
02	213 56.7	54.4	147 11.9	11.6	20 55.2	2.5	54.4
03	228 56.6	.. 55.1	161 42.5	11.6	20 52.7	2.5	54.4
04	243 56.6	55.7	176 13.1	11.7	20 50.2	2.7	54.4
05	258 56.5	56.4	190 43.8	11.7	20 47.5	2.7	54.4
06	273 56.4	S17 57.1	205 14.5	11.8	S20 44.8	2.8	54.4
07	288 56.3	57.7	219 45.3	11.7	20 42.0	2.9	54.4
T 08	303 56.2	58.4	234 16.0	11.8	20 39.1	3.1	54.4
U 09	318 56.1	.. 59.1	248 46.8	11.9	20 36.0	3.1	54.4
E 10	333 56.0	17 59.7	263 17.7	11.8	20 32.9	3.2	54.4
S 11	348 55.9	18 00.4	277 48.5	12.0	20 29.7	3.3	54.4
D 12	3 55.9	S18 01.0	292 19.5	11.9	S20 26.4	3.4	54.3
A 13	18 55.8	01.7	306 50.4	12.0	20 23.0	3.5	54.3
Y 14	33 55.7	02.4	321 21.4	12.0	20 19.5	3.6	54.3
15	48 55.6	.. 03.0	335 52.4	12.0	20 15.9	3.6	54.3
16	63 55.5	03.7	350 23.4	12.1	20 12.3	3.8	54.3
17	78 55.4	04.3	4 54.5	12.1	20 08.5	3.9	54.3
18	93 55.3	S18 05.0	19 25.6	12.2	S20 04.6	3.9	54.3
19	108 55.2	05.7	33 56.8	12.2	20 00.7	4.0	54.3
20	123 55.1	06.3	48 28.0	12.2	19 56.7	4.2	54.3
21	138 55.0	.. 07.0	62 59.2	12.3	19 52.5	4.2	54.3
22	153 54.9	07.6	77 30.5	12.2	19 48.3	4.3	54.3
23	168 54.9	08.3	92 01.7	12.4	19 44.0	4.4	54.3
14 00	183 54.8	S18 08.9	106 33.1	12.3	S19 39.6	4.5	54.3
01	198 54.7	09.6	121 04.4	12.4	19 35.1	4.5	54.3
02	213 54.6	10.3	135 35.8	12.5	19 30.6	4.7	54.3
03	228 54.5	.. 10.9	150 07.3	12.5	19 25.9	4.7	54.3
04	243 54.4	11.6	164 38.8	12.5	19 21.2	4.9	54.3
05	258 54.3	12.2	179 10.3	12.5	19 16.3	4.9	54.2
06	273 54.2	S18 12.9	193 41.8	12.6	S19 11.4	5.0	54.2
07	288 54.1	13.5	208 13.4	12.6	19 06.4	5.1	54.2
W 08	303 54.0	14.2	222 45.0	12.7	19 01.3	5.1	54.2
E 09	318 53.9	.. 14.8	237 16.7	12.6	18 56.2	5.3	54.2
D 10	333 53.8	15.5	251 48.3	12.8	18 50.9	5.3	54.2
N 11	348 53.7	16.1	266 20.1	12.7	18 45.6	5.5	54.2
E 12	3 53.6	S18 16.8	280 51.8	12.8	S18 40.1	5.5	54.2
S 13	18 53.5	17.4	295 23.6	12.9	18 34.6	5.5	54.2
D 14	33 53.4	18.1	309 55.5	12.8	18 29.1	5.7	54.2
A 15	48 53.3	.. 18.7	324 27.3	12.9	18 23.4	5.8	54.2
Y 16	63 53.2	19.4	338 59.2	13.0	18 17.6	5.8	54.2
17	78 53.1	20.0	353 31.2	12.9	18 11.8	5.9	54.2
18	93 53.0	S18 20.6	8 03.1	13.0	S18 05.9	6.0	54.2
19	108 52.9	21.3	22 35.1	13.1	17 59.9	6.1	54.2
20	123 52.8	21.9	37 07.2	13.0	17 53.8	6.1	54.2
21	138 52.7	.. 22.6	51 39.2	13.1	17 47.7	6.2	54.2
22	153 52.6	23.2	66 11.3	13.2	17 41.5	6.3	54.2
23	168 52.5	23.9	80 43.5	13.2	S17 35.2	6.4	54.2
	SD 16.2	d 0.7	SD 14.9		14.8		14.8

Lat.	Twilight Naut.	Twilight Civil	Sunrise	Moonrise 12	13	14	15
°	h m	h m	h m	h m	h m	h m	h m
N 72	06 52	08 24	10 32	■■■	■■■	■■■	16 08
N 70	06 43	08 03	09 36	■■■	■■■	15 48	15 31
68	06 35	07 47	09 03	14 51	15 03	15 05	15 05
66	06 28	07 33	08 39	13 54	14 22	14 37	14 45
64	06 22	07 22	08 21	13 20	13 54	14 15	14 29
62	06 17	07 13	08 05	12 55	13 32	13 57	14 15
60	06 13	07 04	07 53	12 36	13 14	13 42	14 04
N 58	06 09	06 57	07 42	12 20	13 00	13 30	13 54
56	06 05	06 50	07 32	12 06	12 47	13 19	13 45
54	06 01	06 44	07 24	11 54	12 36	13 10	13 37
52	05 58	06 39	07 16	11 44	12 26	13 01	13 30
50	05 55	06 34	07 09	11 34	12 17	12 53	13 24
45	05 48	06 23	06 55	11 15	11 59	12 37	13 10
N 40	05 41	06 14	06 43	10 59	11 44	12 24	12 59
35	05 35	06 06	06 32	10 45	11 31	12 12	12 49
30	05 29	05 58	06 23	10 33	11 20	12 02	12 41
20	05 18	05 44	06 08	10 13	11 00	11 45	12 26
N 10	05 06	05 32	05 54	09 56	10 44	11 30	12 14
0	04 54	05 19	05 41	09 39	10 28	11 16	12 01
S 10	04 39	05 05	05 28	09 23	10 12	11 01	11 49
20	04 22	04 50	05 13	09 05	09 56	10 46	11 37
30	04 00	04 31	04 57	08 45	09 36	10 29	11 22
35	03 46	04 20	04 47	08 34	09 25	10 19	11 13
40	03 29	04 06	04 36	08 20	09 12	10 07	11 03
45	03 07	03 50	04 23	08 04	08 57	09 53	10 52
S 50	02 38	03 29	04 08	07 45	08 38	09 36	10 38
52	02 23	03 19	04 00	07 35	08 29	09 29	10 31
54	02 05	03 07	03 52	07 25	08 19	09 20	10 24
56	01 43	02 54	03 42	07 13	08 08	09 10	10 16
58	01 11	02 38	03 32	06 59	07 55	08 58	10 07
S 60	00 05	02 19	03 19	06 43	07 40	08 45	09 56

Lat.	Sunset	Twilight Civil	Twilight Naut.	Moonset 12	13	14	15
°	h m	h m	h m	h m	h m	h m	h m
N 72	12 55	15 03	16 35	■■■	■■■	■■■	20 31
N 70	13 51	15 24	16 45	■■■	■■■	19 15	21 07
68	14 24	15 41	16 53	16 54	18 22	19 57	21 32
66	14 48	15 54	16 59	17 51	19 03	20 26	21 52
64	15 07	16 06	17 05	18 24	19 31	20 47	22 07
62	15 22	16 15	17 10	18 49	19 52	21 04	22 20
60	15 35	16 24	17 15	19 08	20 10	21 18	22 31
N 58	15 46	16 31	17 19	19 24	20 24	21 30	22 40
56	15 56	16 38	17 23	19 38	20 37	21 41	22 48
54	16 04	16 44	17 27	19 50	20 47	21 50	22 55
52	16 12	16 49	17 30	20 00	20 57	21 58	23 02
50	16 19	16 54	17 33	20 09	21 06	22 05	23 08
45	16 33	17 05	17 40	20 29	21 24	22 21	23 20
N 40	16 45	17 14	17 47	20 45	21 38	22 34	23 31
35	16 56	17 23	17 53	20 58	21 51	22 45	23 40
30	17 05	17 30	17 59	21 10	22 02	22 54	23 47
20	17 21	17 44	18 10	21 30	22 20	23 11	24 01
N 10	17 35	17 57	18 22	21 47	22 36	23 25	24 12
0	17 48	18 10	18 35	22 03	22 51	23 38	24 23
S 10	18 01	18 23	18 49	22 19	23 06	23 51	24 34
20	18 15	18 39	19 07	22 36	23 22	24 05	00 05
30	18 32	18 58	19 29	22 56	23 40	24 21	00 21
35	18 42	19 09	19 43	23 08	23 51	24 30	00 30
40	18 53	19 23	20 01	23 21	24 03	00 03	00 40
45	19 06	19 40	20 22	23 36	24 17	00 17	00 53
S 50	19 22	20 01	20 52	23 55	24 35	00 35	01 08
52	19 30	20 11	21 07	24 04	00 04	00 43	01 15
54	19 39	20 23	21 26	24 14	00 14	00 52	01 23
56	19 48	20 36	21 49	24 26	00 26	01 02	01 31
58	19 58	20 52	22 22	24 39	00 39	01 14	01 41
S 60	20 11	21 12	////	00 10	00 54	01 27	01 52

Day	SUN Eqn. of Time 00h	SUN Eqn. of Time 12h	Mer. Pass.	MOON Mer. Pass. Upper	MOON Mer. Pass. Lower	Age	Phase
d	m s	m s	h m	h m	h m	d	%
12	15 55	15 44	11 44	15 51	03 26	05	22
13	15 48	15 44	11 44	16 40	04 16	06	31
14	15 39	15 35	11 44	17 27	05 03	07	40

UT	ARIES GHA	VENUS −4·8 GHA	Dec	MARS −0·3 GHA	Dec	JUPITER −1·7 GHA	Dec	SATURN +0·6 GHA	Dec	STARS Name	SHA	Dec
15 00	54 01.9	211 13.2	S11 20.9	81 52.1	S13 16.8	174 34.6	S19 47.1	137 19.5	S22 44.4	Acamar	315 15.1	S40 13.9
01	69 04.3	226 15.5	20.3	96 53.2	16.2	189 36.5	47.2	152 21.7	44.4	Achernar	335 23.6	S57 08.7
02	84 06.8	241 17.9	19.7	111 54.2	15.6	204 38.4	47.3	167 23.9	44.4	Acrux	173 05.6	S63 11.8
03	99 09.2	256 20.3 ..	19.1	126 55.2 ..	15.0	219 40.3 ..	47.4	182 26.1 ..	44.3	Adhara	255 09.4	S28 59.8
04	114 11.7	271 22.7	18.5	141 56.3	14.3	234 42.2	47.5	197 28.3	44.3	Aldebaran	290 44.8	N16 32.7
05	129 14.2	286 25.0	17.9	156 57.3	13.7	249 44.0	47.6	212 30.5	44.3			
06	144 16.6	301 27.4	S11 17.3	171 58.3	S13 13.1	264 45.9	S19 47.8	227 32.7	S22 44.3	Alioth	166 17.9	N55 51.4
07	159 19.1	316 29.8	16.7	186 59.4	12.5	279 47.8	47.9	242 34.9	44.3	Alkaid	152 56.5	N49 13.2
T 08	174 21.6	331 32.1	16.1	202 00.4	11.8	294 49.7	48.0	257 37.1	44.3	Al Na'ir	27 39.1	S46 52.4
H 09	189 24.0	346 34.5 ..	15.6	217 01.4 ..	11.2	309 51.6 ..	48.1	272 39.3 ..	44.3	Alnilam	275 42.4	S 1 11.5
U 10	204 26.5	1 36.8	15.0	232 02.4	10.6	324 53.5	48.2	287 41.5	44.3	Alphard	217 52.5	S 8 44.3
R 11	219 29.0	16 39.2	14.4	247 03.5	09.9	339 55.4	48.3	302 43.7	44.3			
S 12	234 31.4	31 41.5	S11 13.8	262 04.5	S13 09.3	354 57.3	S19 48.4	317 45.9	S22 44.3	Alphecca	126 08.3	N26 39.3
D 13	249 33.9	46 43.8	13.2	277 05.5	08.7	9 59.2	48.6	332 48.1	44.3	Alpheratz	357 39.5	N29 11.8
A 14	264 36.4	61 46.2	12.7	292 06.6	08.0	25 01.0	48.7	347 50.3	44.3	Altair	62 04.8	N 8 55.3
Y 15	279 38.8	76 48.5 ..	12.1	307 07.6 ..	07.4	40 02.9 ..	48.8	2 52.5 ..	44.3	Ankaa	353 11.8	S42 12.4
16	294 41.3	91 50.8	11.5	322 08.6	06.8	55 04.8	48.9	17 54.7	44.3	Antares	112 22.1	S26 28.2
17	309 43.7	106 53.1	11.0	337 09.6	06.2	70 06.7	49.0	32 57.0	44.3			
18	324 46.2	121 55.5	S11 10.4	352 10.7	S13 05.5	85 08.6	S19 49.1	47 59.2	S22 44.3	Arcturus	145 52.7	N19 05.3
19	339 48.7	136 57.8	09.8	7 11.7	04.9	100 10.5	49.3	63 01.4	44.2	Atria	107 21.2	S69 03.5
20	354 51.1	152 00.1	09.3	22 12.7	04.3	115 12.4	49.4	78 03.6	44.2	Avior	234 16.3	S59 33.9
21	9 53.6	167 02.4 ..	08.7	37 13.8 ..	03.6	130 14.3 ..	49.5	93 05.8 ..	44.2	Bellatrix	278 27.8	N 6 21.9
22	24 56.1	182 04.7	08.1	52 14.8	03.0	145 16.1	49.6	108 08.0	44.2	Betelgeuse	270 57.1	N 7 24.5
23	39 58.5	197 07.0	07.6	67 15.8	02.4	160 18.0	49.7	123 10.2	44.2			
16 00	55 01.0	212 09.3	S11 07.0	82 16.8	S13 01.7	175 19.9	S19 49.8	138 12.4	S22 44.2	Canopus	263 54.1	S52 42.2
01	70 03.5	227 11.6	06.5	97 17.9	01.1	190 21.8	49.9	153 14.6	44.2	Capella	280 28.6	N46 00.8
02	85 05.9	242 13.9	05.9	112 18.9	13 00.5	205 23.7	50.1	168 16.8	44.2	Deneb	49 29.1	N45 21.2
03	100 08.4	257 16.1 ..	05.4	127 19.9	12 59.8	220 25.6 ..	50.2	183 19.0 ..	44.2	Denebola	182 30.1	N14 28.1
04	115 10.9	272 18.4	04.8	142 20.9	59.2	235 27.5	50.3	198 21.2	44.2	Diphda	348 52.0	S17 53.1
05	130 13.3	287 20.7	04.3	157 22.0	58.6	250 29.4	50.4	213 23.4	44.2			
06	145 15.8	302 23.0	S11 03.7	172 23.0	S12 58.0	265 31.2	S19 50.5	228 25.6	S22 44.2	Dubhe	193 47.5	N61 38.8
07	160 18.2	317 25.2	03.2	187 24.0	57.3	280 33.1	50.6	243 27.8	44.2	Elnath	278 07.7	N28 37.2
08	175 20.7	332 27.5	02.7	202 25.1	56.7	295 35.0	50.7	258 30.0	44.2	Eltanin	90 44.9	N51 29.5
F 09	190 23.2	347 29.8 ..	02.1	217 26.1 ..	56.1	310 36.9 ..	50.9	273 32.2 ..	44.1	Enif	33 43.5	N 9 57.8
R 10	205 25.6	2 32.0	01.6	232 27.1	55.4	325 38.8	51.0	288 34.4	44.1	Fomalhaut	15 19.9	S29 31.5
I 11	220 28.1	17 34.3	01.1	247 28.1	54.8	340 40.7	51.1	303 36.6	44.1			
D 12	235 30.6	32 36.5	S11 00.5	262 29.2	S12 54.2	355 42.6	S19 51.2	318 38.8	S22 44.1	Gacrux	171 57.2	S57 12.7
A 13	250 33.0	47 38.8	11 00.0	277 30.2	53.5	10 44.4	51.3	333 41.0	44.1	Gienah	175 48.7	S17 38.5
Y 14	265 35.5	62 41.0	10 59.5	292 31.2	52.9	25 46.3	51.4	348 43.2	44.1	Hadar	148 43.3	S60 27.5
15	280 38.0	77 43.2 ..	59.0	307 32.2 ..	52.3	40 48.2 ..	51.5	3 45.4 ..	44.1	Hamal	327 56.3	N23 33.0
16	295 40.4	92 45.5	58.4	322 33.3	51.6	55 50.1	51.7	18 47.6	44.1	Kaus Aust.	83 39.3	S34 22.4
17	310 42.9	107 47.7	57.9	337 34.3	51.0	70 52.0	51.8	33 49.8	44.1			
18	325 45.3	122 49.9	S10 57.4	352 35.3	S12 50.4	85 53.9	S19 51.9	48 52.0	S22 44.1	Kochab	137 21.3	N74 04.8
19	340 47.8	137 52.1	56.9	7 36.3	49.7	100 55.8	52.0	63 54.2	44.1	Markab	13 34.6	N15 18.5
20	355 50.3	152 54.4	56.4	22 37.4	49.1	115 57.7	52.1	78 56.4	44.1	Menkar	314 10.9	N 4 09.7
21	10 52.7	167 56.6 ..	55.8	37 38.4 ..	48.4	130 59.5 ..	52.2	93 58.6 ..	44.1	Menkent	148 03.6	S36 27.4
22	25 55.2	182 58.8	55.3	52 39.4	47.8	146 01.4	52.3	109 00.8	44.1	Miaplacidus	221 38.8	S69 47.3
23	40 57.7	198 01.0	54.8	67 40.4	47.2	161 03.3	52.5	124 03.0	44.0			
17 00	56 00.1	213 03.2	S10 54.3	82 41.5	S12 46.5	176 05.2	S19 52.6	139 05.2	S22 44.0	Mirfak	308 34.6	N49 55.6
01	71 02.6	228 05.4	53.8	97 42.5	45.9	191 07.1	52.7	154 07.4	44.0	Nunki	75 54.0	S26 16.3
02	86 05.1	243 07.6	53.3	112 43.5	45.3	206 09.0	52.8	169 09.6	44.0	Peacock	53 13.7	S56 40.6
03	101 07.5	258 09.8 ..	52.8	127 44.5 ..	44.6	221 10.9 ..	52.9	184 11.8 ..	44.0	Pollux	243 23.1	N27 58.7
04	116 10.0	273 12.0	52.3	142 45.6	44.0	236 12.7	53.0	199 14.0	44.0	Procyon	244 55.7	N 5 10.5
05	131 12.5	288 14.2	51.8	157 46.6	43.4	251 14.6	53.1	214 16.2	44.0			
06	146 14.9	303 16.3	S10 51.3	172 47.6	S12 42.7	266 16.5	S19 53.3	229 18.4	S22 44.0	Rasalhague	96 03.4	N12 33.1
07	161 17.4	318 18.5	50.8	187 48.6	42.1	281 18.4	53.4	244 20.6	44.0	Regulus	207 39.7	N11 52.5
S 08	176 19.8	333 20.7	50.4	202 49.6	41.5	296 20.3	53.5	259 22.8	44.0	Rigel	281 08.2	S 8 10.9
A 09	191 22.3	348 22.9 ..	49.9	217 50.7 ..	40.8	311 22.2 ..	53.6	274 25.0 ..	44.0	Rigil Kent.	139 47.4	S60 54.4
T 10	206 24.8	3 25.0	49.4	232 51.7	40.2	326 24.1	53.7	289 27.2	44.0	Sabik	102 08.7	S15 44.7
U 11	221 27.2	18 27.2	48.9	247 52.7	39.5	341 25.9	53.8	304 29.4	44.0			
R 12	236 29.7	33 29.4	S10 48.4	262 53.7	S12 38.9	356 27.8	S19 53.9	319 31.6	S22 44.0	Schedar	349 35.9	N56 38.6
D 13	251 32.2	48 31.5	47.9	277 54.8	38.3	11 29.7	54.1	334 33.8	43.9	Shaula	96 17.3	S37 06.9
A 14	266 34.6	63 33.7	47.5	292 55.8	37.6	26 31.6	54.2	349 36.0	43.9	Sirius	258 30.3	S16 44.5
Y 15	281 37.1	78 35.8 ..	47.0	307 56.8 ..	37.0	41 33.5 ..	54.3	4 38.2 ..	43.9	Spica	158 27.7	S11 15.3
16	296 39.6	93 38.0	46.5	322 57.8	36.4	56 35.4	54.4	19 40.4	43.9	Suhail	222 49.7	S43 30.3
17	311 42.0	108 40.1	46.0	337 58.8	35.7	71 37.3	54.5	34 42.6	43.9			
18	326 44.5	123 42.2	S10 45.6	352 59.9	S12 35.1	86 39.1	S19 54.6	49 44.8	S22 43.9	Vega	80 36.8	N38 48.4
19	341 47.0	138 44.4	45.1	8 00.9	34.4	101 41.0	54.7	64 47.0	43.9	Zuben'ubi	137 01.7	S16 06.9
20	356 49.4	153 46.5	44.6	23 01.9	33.8	116 42.9	54.9	79 49.1	43.9			
21	11 51.9	168 48.6 ..	44.2	38 02.9 ..	33.2	131 44.8 ..	55.0	94 51.3 ..	43.9		SHA	Mer. Pass.
22	26 54.3	183 50.7	43.7	53 04.0	32.5	146 46.7	55.1	109 53.5	43.9	Venus	157 08.3	9 50
23	41 56.8	198 52.9	43.2	68 05.0	31.9	161 48.6	55.2	124 55.7	43.9	Mars	27 15.8	18 30
	h m									Jupiter	120 18.9	12 17
Mer. Pass. 20 16.6	v 2.2 d 0.5			v 1.0 d 0.6		v 1.9 d 0.1		v 2.2 d 0.0		Saturn	83 11.4	14 45

UT	SUN GHA	SUN Dec	MOON GHA	MOON v	MOON Dec	MOON d	MOON HP
d h	° ′	° ′	° ′	′	° ′	′	′
15 00	183 52.4	S18 24.5	95 15.7	13.2	S17 28.8	6.5	54.2
01	198 52.3	25.1	109 47.9	13.2	17 22.3	6.5	54.2
02	213 52.2	25.8	124 20.1	13.3	17 15.8	6.6	54.2
03	228 52.1 ..	26.4	138 52.4	13.3	17 09.2	6.7	54.2
04	243 52.0	27.1	153 24.7	13.3	17 02.5	6.7	54.3
05	258 51.9	27.7	167 57.0	13.4	16 55.8	6.9	54.3
06	273 51.8	S18 28.3	182 29.4	13.4	S16 48.9	6.9	54.3
07	288 51.7	29.0	197 01.8	13.4	16 42.0	7.0	54.3
T 08	303 51.6	29.6	211 34.2	13.5	16 35.0	7.0	54.3
H 09	318 51.5 ..	30.3	226 06.7	13.5	16 28.0	7.1	54.3
U 10	333 51.4	30.9	240 39.2	13.5	16 20.9	7.2	54.3
R 11	348 51.3	31.5	255 11.7	13.6	16 13.7	7.3	54.3
S 12	3 51.2	S18 32.2	269 44.3	13.6	S16 06.4	7.3	54.3
D 13	18 51.1	32.8	284 16.9	13.6	15 59.1	7.5	54.3
A 14	33 51.0	33.4	298 49.5	13.7	15 51.6	7.4	54.3
Y 15	48 50.8 ..	34.1	313 22.2	13.6	15 44.2	7.6	54.3
16	63 50.7	34.7	327 54.8	13.7	15 36.6	7.6	54.3
17	78 50.6	35.3	342 27.5	13.8	15 29.0	7.7	54.3
18	93 50.5	S18 36.0	357 00.3	13.7	S15 21.3	7.7	54.3
19	108 50.4	36.6	11 33.0	13.8	15 13.6	7.9	54.3
20	123 50.3	37.2	26 05.8	13.8	15 05.7	7.9	54.4
21	138 50.2 ..	37.9	40 38.6	13.9	14 57.8	7.9	54.4
22	153 50.1	38.5	55 11.5	13.8	14 49.9	8.0	54.4
23	168 50.0	39.1	69 44.3	13.9	14 41.9	8.1	54.4
16 00	183 49.9	S18 39.7	84 17.2	14.0	S14 33.8	8.2	54.4
01	198 49.8	40.4	98 50.2	13.9	14 25.6	8.2	54.4
02	213 49.6	41.0	113 23.1	14.0	14 17.4	8.3	54.4
03	228 49.5 ..	41.6	127 56.1	14.0	14 09.1	8.3	54.4
04	243 49.4	42.3	142 29.1	14.0	14 00.8	8.4	54.4
05	258 49.3	42.9	157 02.1	14.0	13 52.4	8.5	54.4
06	273 49.2	S18 43.5	171 35.1	14.1	S13 43.9	8.5	54.5
07	288 49.1	44.1	186 08.2	14.1	13 35.4	8.6	54.5
08	303 49.0	44.7	200 41.3	14.1	13 26.8	8.7	54.5
F 09	318 48.9 ..	45.4	215 14.4	14.1	13 18.1	8.7	54.5
R 10	333 48.7	46.0	229 47.5	14.1	13 09.4	8.7	54.5
I 11	348 48.6	46.6	244 20.6	14.2	13 00.7	8.9	54.5
D 12	3 48.5	S18 47.2	258 53.8	14.2	S12 51.8	8.9	54.5
A 13	18 48.4	47.9	273 27.0	14.2	12 42.9	8.9	54.5
Y 14	33 48.3	48.5	288 00.2	14.2	12 34.0	9.0	54.6
15	48 48.2 ..	49.1	302 33.4	14.3	12 25.0	9.1	54.6
16	63 48.1	49.7	317 06.7	14.3	12 15.9	9.1	54.6
17	78 47.9	50.3	331 39.9	14.3	12 06.8	9.2	54.6
18	93 47.8	S18 51.0	346 13.2	14.3	S11 57.6	9.2	54.6
19	108 47.7	51.6	0 46.5	14.3	11 48.4	9.3	54.6
20	123 47.6	52.2	15 19.8	14.3	11 39.1	9.4	54.6
21	138 47.5 ..	52.8	29 53.1	14.3	11 29.7	9.3	54.7
22	153 47.3	53.4	44 26.4	14.4	11 20.4	9.5	54.7
23	168 47.2	54.0	58 59.8	14.3	11 10.9	9.5	54.7
17 00	183 47.1	S18 54.6	73 33.1	14.4	S11 01.4	9.6	54.7
01	198 47.0	55.3	88 06.5	14.4	10 51.8	9.6	54.7
02	213 46.9	55.9	102 39.9	14.4	10 42.2	9.6	54.7
03	228 46.8 ..	56.5	117 13.3	14.4	10 32.6	9.7	54.8
04	243 46.6	57.1	131 46.7	14.4	10 22.9	9.8	54.8
05	258 46.5	57.7	146 20.1	14.4	10 13.1	9.8	54.8
06	273 46.4	S18 58.3	160 53.5	14.5	S10 03.3	9.9	54.8
07	288 46.3	58.9	175 27.0	14.4	9 53.4	9.9	54.8
S 08	303 46.1	18 59.5	190 00.4	14.5	9 43.5	9.9	54.9
A 09	318 46.0	19 00.2	204 33.9	14.4	9 33.6	10.1	54.9
T 10	333 45.9	00.8	219 07.3	14.5	9 23.5	10.0	54.9
U 11	348 45.8	01.4	233 40.8	14.4	9 13.5	10.1	54.9
R 12	3 45.7	S19 02.0	248 14.2	14.5	S 9 03.4	10.2	54.9
D 13	18 45.5	02.6	262 47.7	14.5	8 53.2	10.1	54.9
A 14	33 45.4	03.2	277 21.2	14.4	8 43.1	10.3	55.0
Y 15	48 45.3 ..	03.8	291 54.6	14.5	8 32.8	10.3	55.0
16	63 45.2	04.4	306 28.1	14.5	8 22.5	10.3	55.0
17	78 45.0	05.0	321 01.6	14.5	8 12.2	10.4	55.0
18	93 44.9	S19 05.6	335 35.1	14.5	S 8 01.8	10.4	55.1
19	108 44.8	06.2	350 08.6	14.4	7 51.4	10.4	55.1
20	123 44.7	06.8	4 42.0	14.5	7 41.0	10.5	55.1
21	138 44.5 ..	07.4	19 15.5	14.5	7 30.5	10.5	55.1
22	153 44.4	08.0	33 49.0	14.5	7 19.9	10.5	55.1
23	168 44.3	08.6	48 22.5	14.4	S 7 09.4	10.6	55.2
	SD 16.2	d 0.6	SD 14.8		14.9		15.0

Lat.	Twilight Naut.	Twilight Civil	Sunrise	Moonrise 15	Moonrise 16	Moonrise 17	Moonrise 18
°	h m	h m	h m	h m	h m	h m	h m
N 72	07 03	08 39	11 27	16 08	15 42	15 24	15 09
N 70	06 52	08 15	09 56	15 31	15 20	15 11	15 03
68	06 43	07 57	09 17	15 05	15 03	15 01	14 58
66	06 36	07 42	08 51	14 45	14 49	14 52	14 54
64	06 30	07 30	08 30	14 29	14 38	14 45	14 51
62	06 24	07 20	08 14	14 15	14 28	14 39	14 48
60	06 19	07 11	08 00	14 04	14 20	14 33	14 45
N 58	06 14	07 03	07 48	13 54	14 13	14 28	14 43
56	06 10	06 56	07 38	13 45	14 06	14 24	14 41
54	06 06	06 50	07 29	13 37	14 00	14 20	14 39
52	06 02	06 44	07 21	13 30	13 55	14 17	14 37
50	05 59	06 38	07 14	13 24	13 50	14 14	14 36
45	05 51	06 27	06 59	13 10	13 40	14 07	14 32
N 40	05 44	06 17	06 46	12 59	13 31	14 01	14 29
35	05 38	06 08	06 35	12 49	13 24	13 56	14 27
30	05 31	06 00	06 26	12 41	13 17	13 51	14 24
20	05 19	05 46	06 09	12 26	13 06	13 43	14 21
N 10	05 07	05 33	05 55	12 14	12 56	13 37	14 17
0	04 54	05 19	05 41	12 01	12 46	13 30	14 14
S 10	04 39	05 05	05 27	11 49	12 37	13 24	14 11
20	04 21	04 49	05 13	11 37	12 27	13 17	14 07
30	03 58	04 29	04 55	11 22	12 15	13 09	14 03
35	03 43	04 17	04 45	11 13	12 08	13 04	14 01
40	03 26	04 03	04 34	11 03	12 01	12 59	13 59
45	03 03	03 46	04 20	10 52	11 52	12 53	13 56
S 50	02 32	03 24	04 03	10 38	11 41	12 46	13 52
52	02 16	03 14	03 56	10 31	11 36	12 43	13 51
54	01 57	03 01	03 47	10 24	11 31	12 39	13 49
56	01 31	02 47	03 37	10 16	11 24	12 35	13 47
58	00 54	02 30	03 26	10 07	11 17	12 30	13 45
S 60	////	02 10	03 12	09 56	11 10	12 25	13 42

Lat.	Sunset	Twilight Civil	Twilight Naut.	Moonset 15	Moonset 16	Moonset 17	Moonset 18
°	h m	h m	h m	h m	h m	h m	h m
N 72	12 02	14 50	16 26	20 31	22 30	24 20	00 20
N 70	13 33	15 13	16 36	21 07	22 50	24 30	00 30
68	14 11	15 32	16 45	21 32	23 06	24 39	00 39
66	14 38	15 46	16 53	21 52	23 19	24 46	00 46
64	14 58	15 59	16 59	22 07	23 29	24 52	00 52
62	15 15	16 09	17 05	22 20	23 38	24 57	00 57
60	15 29	16 18	17 10	22 31	23 45	25 02	01 02
N 58	15 40	16 26	17 15	22 40	23 52	25 05	01 05
56	15 51	16 33	17 19	22 48	23 58	25 09	01 09
54	16 00	16 39	17 23	22 55	24 03	00 03	01 12
52	16 08	16 45	17 26	23 02	24 08	00 08	01 15
50	16 15	16 50	17 30	23 08	24 12	00 12	01 17
45	16 30	17 02	17 38	23 20	24 21	00 21	01 23
N 40	16 43	17 12	17 45	23 31	24 29	00 29	01 28
35	16 54	17 21	17 51	23 40	24 35	00 35	01 32
30	17 03	17 29	17 58	23 47	24 41	00 41	01 35
20	17 20	17 43	18 10	24 01	00 01	00 50	01 41
N 10	17 35	17 57	18 22	24 12	00 12	00 59	01 46
0	17 48	18 10	18 36	24 23	00 23	01 07	01 51
S 10	18 02	18 25	18 51	24 34	00 34	01 15	01 56
20	18 17	18 41	19 09	00 05	00 45	01 24	02 01
30	18 34	19 01	19 32	00 21	00 58	01 33	02 07
35	18 45	19 13	19 47	00 30	01 06	01 39	02 10
40	18 56	19 27	20 05	00 41	01 14	01 45	02 14
45	19 10	19 44	20 28	00 53	01 24	01 52	02 18
S 50	19 27	20 06	20 59	01 08	01 36	02 01	02 23
52	19 35	20 17	21 15	01 15	01 42	02 05	02 26
54	19 44	20 30	21 35	01 23	01 48	02 09	02 28
56	19 54	20 44	22 02	01 31	01 54	02 14	02 31
58	20 06	21 01	22 42	01 41	02 02	02 19	02 34
S 60	20 19	21 23	////	01 52	02 10	02 25	02 38

	SUN Eqn. of Time 00h	SUN Eqn. of Time 12h	SUN Mer. Pass.	MOON Mer. Pass. Upper	MOON Mer. Pass. Lower	Age	Phase
Day							
d	m s	m s	h m	h m	h m	d %	
15	15 30	15 25	11 45	18 12	05 50	08 49	
16	15 20	15 14	11 45	18 57	06 35	09 58	
17	15 09	15 03	11 45	19 41	07 19	10 68	

UT	ARIES	VENUS −4·8		MARS −0·2		JUPITER −1·7		SATURN +0·6		STARS		
	GHA	GHA	Dec	GHA	Dec	GHA	Dec	GHA	Dec	Name	SHA	Dec
d h	° ′	° ′	° ′	° ′	° ′	° ′	° ′	° ′	° ′		° ′	° ′
18 00	56 59.3	213 55.0	S10 42.8	83 06.0	S12 31.3	176 50.5	S19 55.3	139 57.9	S22 43.9	Acamar	315 15.1	S40 13.9
01	72 01.7	228 57.1	42.3	98 07.0	30.6	191 52.3	55.4	155 00.1	43.9	Achernar	335 23.6	S57 08.7
02	87 04.2	243 59.2	41.9	113 08.0	30.0	206 54.2	55.5	170 02.3	43.8	Acrux	173 05.6	S63 11.8
03	102 06.7	259 01.3 ..	41.4	128 09.1 ..	29.3	221 56.1 ..	55.6	185 04.5 ..	43.8	Adhara	255 09.4	S28 59.8
04	117 09.1	274 03.4	41.0	143 10.1	28.7	236 58.0	55.8	200 06.7	43.8	Aldebaran	290 44.8	N16 32.7
05	132 11.6	289 05.5	40.5	158 11.1	28.1	251 59.9	55.9	215 08.9	43.8			
06	147 14.1	304 07.6	S10 40.1	173 12.1	S12 27.4	267 01.8	S19 56.0	230 11.1	S22 43.8	Alioth	166 17.9	N55 51.4
07	162 16.5	319 09.7	39.6	188 13.1	26.8	282 03.7	56.1	245 13.3	43.8	Alkaid	152 56.5	N49 13.2
08	177 19.0	334 11.8	39.2	203 14.2	26.1	297 05.5	56.2	260 15.5	43.8	Al Na'ir	27 39.1	S46 52.4
S 09	192 21.4	349 13.8 ..	38.8	218 15.2 ..	25.5	312 07.4 ..	56.3	275 17.7 ..	43.8	Alnilam	275 42.4	S 1 11.5
U 10	207 23.9	4 15.9	38.3	233 16.2	24.9	327 09.3	56.4	290 19.9	43.8	Alphard	217 52.5	S 8 44.3
N 11	222 26.4	19 18.0	37.9	248 17.2	24.2	342 11.2	56.6	305 22.1	43.8			
D 12	237 28.8	34 20.1	S10 37.5	263 18.2	S12 23.6	357 13.1	S19 56.7	320 24.3	S22 43.8	Alphecca	126 08.3	N26 39.3
A 13	252 31.3	49 22.1	37.0	278 19.3	22.9	12 15.0	56.8	335 26.5	43.8	Alpheratz	357 39.5	N29 11.8
Y 14	267 33.8	64 24.2	36.6	293 20.3	22.3	27 16.8	56.9	350 28.7	43.8	Altair	62 04.9	N 8 55.3
15	282 36.2	79 26.3 ..	36.2	308 21.3 ..	21.6	42 18.7 ..	57.0	5 30.9 ..	43.7	Ankaa	353 11.8	S42 12.5
16	297 38.7	94 28.3	35.8	323 22.3	21.0	57 20.6	57.1	20 33.1	43.7	Antares	112 22.1	S26 28.2
17	312 41.2	109 30.4	35.3	338 23.3	20.4	72 22.5	57.2	35 35.3	43.7			
18	327 43.6	124 32.4	S10 34.9	353 24.3	S12 19.7	87 24.4	S19 57.3	50 37.5	S22 43.7	Arcturus	145 52.7	N19 05.2
19	342 46.1	139 34.5	34.5	8 25.4	19.1	102 26.3	57.5	65 39.7	43.7	Atria	107 21.2	S69 03.5
20	357 48.6	154 36.5	34.1	23 26.4	18.4	117 28.2	57.6	80 41.9	43.7	Avior	234 16.3	S59 33.9
21	12 51.0	169 38.5 ..	33.7	38 27.4 ..	17.8	132 30.0 ..	57.7	95 44.1 ..	43.7	Bellatrix	278 27.8	N 6 21.9
22	27 53.5	184 40.6	33.2	53 28.4	17.2	147 31.9	57.8	110 46.3	43.7	Betelgeuse	270 57.0	N 7 24.5
23	42 55.9	199 42.6	32.8	68 29.4	16.5	162 33.8	57.9	125 48.4	43.7			
19 00	57 58.4	214 44.6	S10 32.4	83 30.5	S12 15.9	177 35.7	S19 58.0	140 50.6	S22 43.7	Canopus	263 54.1	S52 42.3
01	73 00.9	229 46.7	32.0	98 31.5	15.2	192 37.6	58.1	155 52.8	43.7	Capella	280 28.6	N46 00.8
02	88 03.3	244 48.7	31.6	113 32.5	14.6	207 39.5	58.2	170 55.0	43.7	Deneb	49 29.1	N45 21.2
03	103 05.8	259 50.7 ..	31.2	128 33.5 ..	13.9	222 41.3 ..	58.4	185 57.2 ..	43.6	Denebola	182 30.1	N14 28.1
04	118 08.3	274 52.7	30.8	143 34.5	13.3	237 43.2	58.5	200 59.4	43.6	Diphda	348 52.0	S17 53.1
05	133 10.7	289 54.7	30.4	158 35.5	12.7	252 45.1	58.6	216 01.6	43.6			
06	148 13.2	304 56.7	S10 30.0	173 36.6	S12 12.0	267 47.0	S19 58.7	231 03.8	S22 43.6	Dubhe	193 47.5	N61 38.8
07	163 15.7	319 58.7	29.6	188 37.6	11.4	282 48.9	58.8	246 06.0	43.6	Elnath	278 07.6	N28 37.2
08	178 18.1	335 00.7	29.2	203 38.6	10.7	297 50.8	58.9	261 08.2	43.6	Eltanin	90 44.9	N51 29.5
M 09	193 20.6	350 02.7 ..	28.8	218 39.6 ..	10.1	312 52.7 ..	59.0	276 10.4 ..	43.6	Enif	33 43.6	N 9 57.8
O 10	208 23.0	5 04.7	28.4	233 40.6	09.4	327 54.5	59.1	291 12.6	43.6	Fomalhaut	15 19.9	S29 31.5
N 11	223 25.5	20 06.7	28.1	248 41.6	08.8	342 56.4	59.3	306 14.8	43.6			
D 12	238 28.0	35 08.7	S10 27.7	263 42.7	S12 08.1	357 58.3	S19 59.4	321 17.0	S22 43.6	Gacrux	171 57.2	S57 12.7
A 13	253 30.4	50 10.7	27.3	278 43.7	07.5	13 00.2	59.5	336 19.2	43.6	Gienah	175 48.7	S17 38.5
Y 14	268 32.9	65 12.7	26.9	293 44.7	06.9	28 02.1	59.6	351 21.4	43.6	Hadar	148 43.2	S60 27.5
15	283 35.4	80 14.6 ..	26.5	308 45.7 ..	06.2	43 04.0 ..	59.7	6 23.6 ..	43.6	Hamal	327 56.3	N23 33.0
16	298 37.8	95 16.6	26.2	323 46.7	05.6	58 05.8	59.8	21 25.7	43.5	Kaus Aust.	83 39.3	S34 22.4
17	313 40.3	110 18.6	25.8	338 47.7	04.9	73 07.7	19 59.9	36 27.9	43.5			
18	328 42.8	125 20.5	S10 25.4	353 48.8	S12 04.3	88 09.6	S20 00.0	51 30.1	S22 43.5	Kochab	137 21.3	N74 04.8
19	343 45.2	140 22.5	25.0	8 49.8	03.6	103 11.5	00.2	66 32.3	43.5	Markab	13 34.6	N15 18.5
20	358 47.7	155 24.5	24.7	23 50.8	03.0	118 13.4	00.3	81 34.5	43.5	Menkar	314 10.9	N 4 09.7
21	13 50.2	170 26.4 ..	24.3	38 51.8 ..	02.3	133 15.3 ..	00.4	96 36.7 ..	43.5	Menkent	148 03.6	S36 27.4
22	28 52.6	185 28.4	23.9	53 52.8	01.7	148 17.1	00.5	111 38.9	43.5	Miaplacidus	221 38.7	S69 47.3
23	43 55.1	200 30.3	23.6	68 53.8	01.0	163 19.0	00.6	126 41.1	43.5			
20 00	58 57.5	215 32.2	S10 23.2	83 54.8	S12 00.4	178 20.9	S20 00.7	141 43.3	S22 43.5	Mirfak	308 34.6	N49 55.6
01	74 00.0	230 34.2	22.9	98 55.9	11 59.7	193 22.8	00.8	156 45.5	43.5	Nunki	75 54.1	S26 16.3
02	89 02.5	245 36.1	22.5	113 56.9	59.1	208 24.7	00.9	171 47.7	43.5	Peacock	53 13.8	S56 40.6
03	104 04.9	260 38.1 ..	22.2	128 57.9 ..	58.5	223 26.6 ..	01.1	186 49.9 ..	43.5	Pollux	243 23.1	N27 58.7
04	119 07.4	275 40.0	21.8	143 58.9	57.8	238 28.4	01.2	201 52.1	43.4	Procyon	244 55.7	N 5 10.5
05	134 09.9	290 41.9	21.4	158 59.9	57.2	253 30.3	01.3	216 54.3	43.4			
06	149 12.3	305 43.8	S10 21.1	174 00.9	S11 56.5	268 32.2	S20 01.4	231 56.4	S22 43.4	Rasalhague	96 03.4	N12 33.0
07	164 14.8	320 45.8	20.8	189 01.9	55.9	283 34.1	01.5	246 58.6	43.4	Regulus	207 39.7	N11 52.5
08	179 17.3	335 47.7	20.4	204 03.0	55.2	298 36.0	01.6	262 00.8	43.4	Rigel	281 08.2	S 8 10.9
T 09	194 19.7	350 49.6 ..	20.1	219 04.0 ..	54.6	313 37.9 ..	01.7	277 03.0 ..	43.4	Rigil Kent.	139 47.4	S60 54.4
U 10	209 22.2	5 51.5	19.7	234 05.0	53.9	328 39.7	01.8	292 05.2	43.4	Sabik	102 08.7	S15 44.7
E 11	224 24.7	20 53.4	19.4	249 06.0	53.3	343 41.6	01.9	307 07.4	43.4			
S 12	239 27.1	35 55.3	S10 19.1	264 07.0	S11 52.6	358 43.5	S20 02.1	322 09.6	S22 43.4	Schedar	349 35.9	N56 38.6
D 13	254 29.6	50 57.2	18.7	279 08.0	52.0	13 45.4	02.2	337 11.8	43.4	Shaula	96 17.3	S37 06.9
A 14	269 32.0	65 59.1	18.4	294 09.0	51.3	28 47.3	02.3	352 14.0	43.4	Sirius	258 30.2	S16 44.5
Y 15	284 34.5	81 01.0 ..	18.1	309 10.1 ..	50.7	43 49.2 ..	02.4	7 16.2 ..	43.4	Spica	158 27.7	S11 15.3
16	299 37.0	96 02.9	17.7	324 11.1	50.0	58 51.0	02.5	22 18.4	43.3	Suhail	222 49.6	S43 30.3
17	314 39.4	111 04.8	17.4	339 12.1	49.4	73 52.9	02.6	37 20.6	43.3			
18	329 41.9	126 06.6	S10 17.1	354 13.1	S11 48.7	88 54.8	S20 02.7	52 22.7	S22 43.3	Vega	80 36.8	N38 48.4
19	344 44.4	141 08.5	16.8	9 14.1	48.1	103 56.7	02.8	67 24.9	43.3	Zuben'ubi	137 01.7	S16 06.9
20	359 46.8	156 10.4	16.4	24 15.1	47.4	118 58.6	02.9	82 27.1	43.3		SHA	Mer. Pass.
21	14 49.3	171 12.3 ..	16.1	39 16.1 ..	46.8	134 00.5 ..	03.1	97 29.3 ..	43.3		° ′	h m
22	29 51.8	186 14.1	15.8	54 17.1	46.1	149 02.3	03.2	112 31.5	43.3	Venus	156 46.2	9 40
23	44 54.2	201 16.0	15.5	69 18.2	45.5	164 04.2	03.3	127 33.7	43.3	Mars	25 32.0	18 25
	h m									Jupiter	119 37.3	12 08
Mer. Pass. 20 04.8		v 2.0	d 0.4	v 1.0	d 0.6	v 1.9	d 0.1	v 2.2	d 0.0	Saturn	82 52.2	14 34

UT	SUN GHA	SUN Dec	MOON GHA	v	MOON Dec	d	HP
d h	° ′	° ′	° ′	′	° ′	′	′
18 00	183 44.1	S19 09.2	62 55.9	14.5	S 6 58.8	10.7	55.2
01	198 44.0	09.8	77 29.4	14.5	6 48.1	10.7	55.2
02	213 43.9	10.4	92 02.9	14.4	6 37.4	10.7	55.2
03	228 43.8	.. 11.0	106 36.3	14.5	6 26.7	10.8	55.3
04	243 43.6	11.6	121 09.8	14.4	6 15.9	10.8	55.3
05	258 43.5	12.2	135 43.2	14.4	6 05.1	10.9	55.3
06	273 43.4	S19 12.8	150 16.6	14.5	S 5 54.2	10.8	55.3
07	288 43.2	13.4	164 50.1	14.4	5 43.4	10.9	55.4
S 08	303 43.1	14.0	179 23.5	14.4	5 32.5	11.0	55.4
U 09	318 43.0	.. 14.6	193 56.9	14.4	5 21.5	11.0	55.4
N 10	333 42.9	15.2	208 30.3	14.3	5 10.5	11.0	55.4
D 11	348 42.8	15.8	223 03.7	14.3	4 59.5	11.0	55.5
A 12	3 42.6	S19 16.4	237 37.0	14.4	S 4 48.5	11.1	55.5
Y 13	18 42.5	17.0	252 10.4	14.3	4 37.4	11.1	55.5
14	33 42.3	17.6	266 43.7	14.4	4 26.3	11.2	55.5
15	48 42.2	.. 18.1	281 17.1	14.3	4 15.1	11.2	55.6
16	63 42.1	18.7	295 50.4	14.3	4 03.9	11.2	55.6
17	78 41.9	19.3	310 23.7	14.2	3 52.7	11.2	55.6
18	93 41.8	S19 19.9	324 56.9	14.3	S 3 41.5	11.2	55.6
19	108 41.7	20.5	339 30.2	14.2	3 30.3	11.3	55.7
20	123 41.5	21.1	354 03.4	14.3	3 19.0	11.3	55.7
21	138 41.4	.. 21.7	8 36.7	14.2	3 07.7	11.4	55.7
22	153 41.3	22.3	23 09.9	14.1	2 56.3	11.3	55.7
23	168 41.1	22.9	37 43.0	14.2	2 45.0	11.4	55.8
19 00	183 41.0	S19 23.4	52 16.2	14.1	S 2 33.6	11.4	55.8
01	198 40.8	24.0	66 49.3	14.1	2 22.2	11.5	55.8
02	213 40.7	24.6	81 22.4	14.1	2 10.7	11.4	55.9
03	228 40.6	.. 25.2	95 55.5	14.1	1 59.3	11.5	55.9
04	243 40.4	25.8	110 28.6	14.0	1 47.8	11.5	55.9
05	258 40.3	26.4	125 01.6	14.0	1 36.3	11.5	55.9
06	273 40.2	S19 26.9	139 34.6	14.0	S 1 24.8	11.6	56.0
07	288 40.0	27.5	154 07.6	13.9	1 13.2	11.5	56.0
08	303 39.9	28.1	168 40.5	14.0	1 01.7	11.6	56.0
M 09	318 39.7	.. 28.7	183 13.5	13.9	0 50.1	11.6	56.1
O 10	333 39.6	29.3	197 46.4	13.8	0 38.5	11.6	56.1
N 11	348 39.5	29.8	212 19.2	13.8	0 26.9	11.6	56.1
D 12	3 39.3	S19 30.4	226 52.0	13.8	S 0 15.3	11.7	56.1
A 13	18 39.2	31.0	241 24.8	13.8	S 0 03.6	11.6	56.2
Y 14	33 39.0	31.6	255 57.6	13.7	N 0 08.0	11.7	56.2
15	48 38.9	.. 32.1	270 30.3	13.7	0 19.7	11.7	56.2
16	63 38.8	32.7	285 03.0	13.6	0 31.4	11.6	56.3
17	78 38.6	33.3	299 35.6	13.7	0 43.0	11.7	56.3
18	93 38.5	S19 33.9	314 08.3	13.5	N 0 54.7	11.8	56.3
19	108 38.3	34.4	328 40.8	13.6	1 06.5	11.7	56.4
20	123 38.2	35.0	343 13.4	13.5	1 18.2	11.7	56.4
21	138 38.0	.. 35.6	357 45.9	13.4	1 29.9	11.7	56.4
22	153 37.9	36.2	12 18.3	13.5	1 41.6	11.8	56.5
23	168 37.8	36.7	26 50.8	13.3	1 53.4	11.7	56.5
20 00	183 37.6	S19 37.3	41 23.1	13.4	N 2 05.1	11.8	56.5
01	198 37.5	37.9	55 55.5	13.2	2 16.9	11.7	56.5
02	213 37.3	38.5	70 27.7	13.3	2 28.6	11.8	56.6
03	228 37.2	.. 39.0	85 00.0	13.2	2 40.4	11.7	56.6
04	243 37.0	39.6	99 32.2	13.1	2 52.1	11.8	56.6
05	258 36.9	40.2	114 04.3	13.1	3 03.9	11.8	56.7
06	273 36.7	S19 40.7	128 36.4	13.1	N 3 15.7	11.7	56.7
07	288 36.6	41.3	143 08.5	13.0	3 27.4	11.8	56.7
T 08	303 36.4	41.9	157 40.5	13.0	3 39.2	11.7	56.8
U 09	318 36.3	.. 42.4	172 12.5	12.9	3 50.9	11.8	56.8
E 10	333 36.2	43.0	186 44.4	12.8	4 02.7	11.7	56.8
S 11	348 36.0	43.5	201 16.2	12.8	4 14.4	11.8	56.9
D 12	3 35.9	S19 44.1	215 48.0	12.8	N 4 26.2	11.7	56.9
A 13	18 35.7	44.7	230 19.8	12.7	4 37.9	11.7	56.9
Y 14	33 35.6	45.2	244 51.5	12.6	4 49.6	11.7	57.0
15	48 35.4	.. 45.8	259 23.1	12.6	5 01.3	11.7	57.0
16	63 35.3	46.4	273 54.7	12.6	5 13.0	11.7	57.0
17	78 35.1	46.9	288 26.3	12.4	5 24.7	11.7	57.0
18	93 35.0	S19 47.5	302 57.7	12.5	N 5 36.4	11.7	57.1
19	108 34.8	48.0	317 29.2	12.3	5 48.1	11.7	57.1
20	123 34.7	48.6	332 00.5	12.3	5 59.8	11.6	57.1
21	138 34.5	.. 49.2	346 31.8	12.3	6 11.4	11.6	57.2
22	153 34.4	49.7	1 03.1	12.2	6 23.0	11.6	57.2
23	168 34.2	50.3	15 34.3	12.1	N 6 34.6	11.6	57.2
	SD 16.2	d 0.6	SD 15.1		15.3		15.5

Lat.	Twilight Naut.	Twilight Civil	Sunrise	Moonrise 18	19	20	21
°	h m	h m	h m	h m	h m	h m	h m
N 72	07 13	08 53	■■■	15 09	14 55	14 42	14 26
N 70	07 01	08 27	10 17	15 03	14 56	14 48	14 40
68	06 52	08 07	09 32	14 58	14 56	14 54	14 51
66	06 44	07 51	09 02	14 54	14 56	14 58	15 01
64	06 36	07 38	08 40	14 51	14 56	15 02	15 09
62	06 30	07 27	08 22	14 48	14 56	15 06	15 16
60	06 25	07 17	08 08	14 45	14 57	15 09	15 22
N 58	06 20	07 09	07 55	14 43	14 57	15 11	15 28
56	06 15	07 01	07 44	14 41	14 57	15 14	15 32
54	06 11	06 55	07 35	14 39	14 57	15 16	15 37
52	06 07	06 48	07 27	14 37	14 57	15 18	15 41
50	06 03	06 43	07 19	14 36	14 57	15 20	15 44
45	05 55	06 31	07 03	14 32	14 57	15 23	15 52
N 40	05 47	06 20	06 49	14 29	14 57	15 27	15 58
35	05 40	06 11	06 38	14 27	14 58	15 30	16 04
30	05 34	06 03	06 28	14 24	14 58	15 32	16 09
20	05 21	05 48	06 11	14 21	14 58	15 37	16 18
N 10	05 08	05 34	05 56	14 17	14 58	15 41	16 25
0	04 54	05 20	05 42	14 14	14 58	15 44	16 33
S 10	04 39	05 05	05 27	14 11	14 59	15 48	16 40
20	04 20	04 48	05 12	14 07	14 59	15 52	16 48
30	03 56	04 28	04 54	14 03	14 59	15 57	16 57
35	03 41	04 15	04 44	14 01	14 59	16 00	17 02
40	03 22	04 01	04 32	13 59	15 00	16 03	17 08
45	02 59	03 43	04 17	13 56	15 00	16 06	17 15
S 50	02 26	03 20	04 00	13 52	15 00	16 11	17 24
52	02 09	03 09	03 51	13 51	15 00	16 13	17 27
54	01 48	02 56	03 42	13 49	15 01	16 15	17 32
56	01 20	02 41	03 32	13 47	15 01	16 17	17 37
58	00 32	02 23	03 20	13 45	15 01	16 20	17 42
S 60	////	02 00	03 06	13 42	15 01	16 23	17 48

Lat.	Sunset	Twilight Civil	Twilight Naut.	Moonset 18	19	20	21
°	h m	h m	h m	h m	h m	h m	h m
N 72	■■■	14 37	16 16	00 20	02 07	03 55	05 50
N 70	13 12	15 03	16 28	00 30	02 10	03 52	05 38
68	13 58	15 23	16 38	00 39	02 12	03 48	05 28
66	14 28	15 39	16 46	00 46	02 15	03 46	05 20
64	14 50	15 52	16 53	00 52	02 17	03 43	05 14
62	15 08	16 03	17 00	00 57	02 18	03 41	05 08
60	15 23	16 13	17 05	01 02	02 20	03 40	05 03
N 58	15 35	16 21	17 10	01 05	02 21	03 38	04 58
56	15 46	16 29	17 15	01 09	02 22	03 37	04 55
54	15 55	16 36	17 19	01 12	02 24	03 36	04 51
52	16 04	16 42	17 23	01 15	02 24	03 35	04 48
50	16 11	16 47	17 27	01 17	02 25	03 34	04 45
45	16 28	17 00	17 36	01 23	02 26	03 31	04 39
N 40	16 41	17 10	17 43	01 28	02 28	03 30	04 34
35	16 52	17 19	17 50	01 32	02 29	03 28	04 29
30	17 02	17 28	17 57	01 35	02 30	03 27	04 25
20	17 19	17 43	18 10	01 41	02 32	03 24	04 19
N 10	17 35	17 57	18 23	01 46	02 34	03 22	04 13
0	17 49	18 11	18 36	01 51	02 35	03 20	04 07
S 10	18 03	18 26	18 52	01 56	02 37	03 18	04 02
20	18 19	18 43	19 11	02 01	02 38	03 16	03 56
30	18 37	19 03	19 35	02 07	02 40	03 14	03 49
35	18 48	19 16	19 50	02 10	02 41	03 12	03 45
40	19 00	19 31	20 09	02 14	02 42	03 11	03 41
45	19 14	19 49	20 33	02 18	02 43	03 09	03 36
S 50	19 32	20 12	21 06	02 23	02 45	03 07	03 30
52	19 40	20 23	21 23	02 26	02 45	03 06	03 27
54	19 50	20 36	21 45	02 28	02 46	03 04	03 24
56	20 00	20 52	22 15	02 31	02 47	03 03	03 21
58	20 13	21 10	23 08	02 34	02 48	03 02	03 17
S 60	20 27	21 33	////	02 38	02 49	03 00	03 13

Day	SUN Eqn. of Time 00ʰ	12ʰ	Mer. Pass.	MOON Mer. Pass. Upper	Lower	Age	Phase
d	m s	m s	h m	h m	h m	d	%
18	14 57	14 51	11 45	20 25	08 03	11	76
19	14 44	14 38	11 45	21 09	08 47	12	84
20	14 31	14 24	11 46	21 56	09 32	13	91

UT	ARIES GHA	VENUS −4.8 GHA	Dec	MARS −0.2 GHA	Dec	JUPITER −1.7 GHA	Dec	SATURN +0.6 GHA	Dec
21 00	59 56.7	216 17.8	S10 15.2	84 19.2	S11 44.8	179 06.1	S20 03.4	142 35.9	S22 43.3
01	74 59.1	231 19.7	14.9	99 20.2	44.2	194 08.0	03.5	157 38.1	43.3
02	90 01.6	246 21.6	14.5	114 21.2	43.5	209 09.9	03.6	172 40.3	43.3
03	105 04.1	261 23.4 ..	14.2	129 22.2 ..	42.9	224 11.8 ..	03.7	187 42.5 ..	43.2
04	120 06.5	276 25.3	13.9	144 23.2	42.2	239 13.6	03.8	202 44.6	43.2
05	135 09.0	291 27.1	13.6	159 24.2	41.6	254 15.5	03.9	217 46.8	43.2
W 06	150 11.5	306 28.9	S10 13.3	174 25.2	S11 40.9	269 17.4	S20 04.1	232 49.0	S22 43.2
E 07	165 13.9	321 30.8	13.0	189 26.2	40.3	284 19.3	04.2	247 51.2	43.2
D 08	180 16.4	336 32.6	12.7	204 27.3	39.6	299 21.2	04.3	262 53.4	43.2
N 09	195 18.9	351 34.4 ..	12.4	219 28.3 ..	39.0	314 23.1 ..	04.4	277 55.6 ..	43.2
E 10	210 21.3	6 36.3	12.1	234 29.3	38.3	329 24.9	04.5	292 57.8	43.2
S 11	225 23.8	21 38.1	11.9	249 30.3	37.7	344 26.8	04.6	308 00.0	43.2
D 12	240 26.3	36 39.9	S10 11.6	264 31.3	S11 37.0	359 28.7	S20 04.7	323 02.2	S22 43.2
A 13	255 28.7	51 41.7	11.3	279 32.3	36.4	14 30.6	04.8	338 04.4	43.2
Y 14	270 31.2	66 43.5	11.0	294 33.3	35.7	29 32.5	04.9	353 06.5	43.2
15	285 33.6	81 45.3 ..	10.7	309 34.3 ..	35.1	44 34.4 ..	05.1	8 08.7 ..	43.1
16	300 36.1	96 47.1	10.4	324 35.3	34.4	59 36.2	05.2	23 10.9	43.1
17	315 38.6	111 48.9	10.2	339 36.4	33.8	74 38.1	05.3	38 13.1	43.1
18	330 41.0	126 50.7	S10 09.9	354 37.4	S11 33.1	89 40.0	S20 05.4	53 15.3	S22 43.1
19	345 43.5	141 52.5	09.6	9 38.4	32.5	104 41.9	05.5	68 17.5	43.1
20	0 46.0	156 54.3	09.3	24 39.4	31.8	119 43.8	05.6	83 19.7	43.1
21	15 48.4	171 56.1 ..	09.1	39 40.4 ..	31.2	134 45.6 ..	05.7	98 21.9 ..	43.1
22	30 50.9	186 57.9	08.8	54 41.4	30.5	149 47.5	05.8	113 24.1	43.1
23	45 53.4	201 59.7	08.5	69 42.4	29.8	164 49.4	05.9	128 26.2	43.1
22 00	60 55.8	217 01.5	S10 08.2	84 43.4	S11 29.2	179 51.3	S20 06.0	143 28.4	S22 43.1
01	75 58.3	232 03.3	08.0	99 44.4	28.5	194 53.2	06.2	158 30.6	43.1
02	91 00.8	247 05.0	07.7	114 45.4	27.9	209 55.1	06.3	173 32.8	43.0
03	106 03.2	262 06.8 ..	07.5	129 46.5 ..	27.2	224 56.9 ..	06.4	188 35.0 ..	43.0
04	121 05.7	277 08.6	07.2	144 47.5	26.6	239 58.8	06.5	203 37.2	43.0
05	136 08.1	292 10.3	06.9	159 48.5	25.9	255 00.7	06.6	218 39.4	43.0
T 06	151 10.6	307 12.1	S10 06.7	174 49.5	S11 25.3	270 02.6	S20 06.7	233 41.6	S22 43.0
H 07	166 13.1	322 13.8	06.4	189 50.5	24.6	285 04.5	06.8	248 43.8	43.0
U 08	181 15.5	337 15.6	06.2	204 51.5	24.0	300 06.4	06.9	263 45.9	43.0
R 09	196 18.0	352 17.3 ..	05.9	219 52.5 ..	23.3	315 08.2 ..	07.0	278 48.1 ..	43.0
R 10	211 20.5	7 19.1	05.7	234 53.5	22.6	330 10.1	07.1	293 50.3	43.0
11	226 22.9	22 20.8	05.5	249 54.5	22.0	345 12.0	07.3	308 52.5	43.0
S 12	241 25.4	37 22.6	S10 05.2	264 55.5	S11 21.3	0 13.9	S20 07.4	323 54.7	S22 43.0
D 13	256 27.9	52 24.3	05.0	279 56.5	20.7	15 15.8	07.5	338 56.9	42.9
A 14	271 30.3	67 26.0	04.7	294 57.5	20.0	30 17.6	07.6	353 59.1	42.9
Y 15	286 32.8	82 27.8 ..	04.5	309 58.6 ..	19.4	45 19.5 ..	07.7	9 01.2 ..	42.9
16	301 35.2	97 29.5	04.3	324 59.6	18.7	60 21.4	07.8	24 03.4	42.9
17	316 37.7	112 31.2	04.0	340 00.6	18.1	75 23.3	07.9	39 05.6	42.9
18	331 40.2	127 32.9	S10 03.8	355 01.6	S11 17.4	90 25.2	S20 08.0	54 07.8	S22 42.9
19	346 42.6	142 34.7	03.6	10 02.6	16.7	105 27.1	08.1	69 10.0	42.9
20	1 45.1	157 36.4	03.3	25 03.6	16.1	120 28.9	08.2	84 12.2	42.9
21	16 47.6	172 38.1 ..	03.1	40 04.6 ..	15.4	135 30.8 ..	08.3	99 14.4 ..	42.9
22	31 50.0	187 39.8	02.9	55 05.6	14.8	150 32.7	08.5	114 16.6	42.9
23	46 52.5	202 41.5	02.7	70 06.6	14.1	165 34.6	08.6	129 18.7	42.9
23 00	61 55.0	217 43.2	S10 02.4	85 07.6	S11 13.5	180 36.5	S20 08.7	144 20.9	S22 42.8
01	76 57.4	232 44.9	02.2	100 08.6	12.8	195 38.3	08.8	159 23.1	42.8
02	91 59.9	247 46.6	02.0	115 09.6	12.2	210 40.2	08.9	174 25.3	42.8
03	107 02.4	262 48.3 ..	01.8	130 10.6 ..	11.5	225 42.1 ..	09.0	189 27.5 ..	42.8
04	122 04.8	277 50.0	01.6	145 11.6	10.8	240 44.0	09.1	204 29.7	42.8
05	137 07.3	292 51.7	01.4	160 12.7	10.2	255 45.9	09.2	219 31.9	42.8
F 06	152 09.7	307 53.3	S10 01.2	175 13.7	S11 09.5	270 47.8	S20 09.3	234 34.0	S22 42.8
R 07	167 12.2	322 55.0	01.0	190 14.7	08.9	285 49.6	09.5	249 36.2	42.8
I 08	182 14.7	337 56.7	00.8	205 15.7	08.2	300 51.5	09.6	264 38.4	42.8
D 09	197 17.1	352 58.4 ..	00.6	220 16.7 ..	07.5	315 53.4 ..	09.7	279 40.6 ..	42.8
A 10	212 19.6	8 00.0	00.4	235 17.7	06.9	330 55.3	09.8	294 42.8	42.8
Y 11	227 22.1	23 01.7	00.2	250 18.7	06.2	345 57.2	09.9	309 45.0	42.7
12	242 24.5	38 03.4	S10 00.0	265 19.7	S11 05.6	0 59.0	S20 10.0	324 47.2	S22 42.7
13	257 27.0	53 05.0	9 59.8	280 20.7	04.9	16 00.9	10.1	339 49.3	42.7
14	272 29.5	68 06.7	59.6	295 21.7	04.3	31 02.8	10.2	354 51.5	42.7
15	287 31.9	83 08.3 ..	59.4	310 22.7 ..	03.6	46 04.7 ..	10.3	9 53.7 ..	42.7
16	302 34.4	98 10.0	59.2	325 23.7	02.9	61 06.6	10.4	24 55.9	42.7
17	317 36.9	113 11.6	59.0	340 24.7	02.3	76 08.4	10.5	39 58.1	42.7
18	332 39.3	128 13.3	S 9 58.8	355 25.7	S11 01.6	91 10.3	S20 10.7	55 00.3	S22 42.7
19	347 41.8	143 14.9	58.6	10 26.7	01.0	106 12.2	10.8	70 02.5	42.7
20	2 44.2	158 16.5	58.5	25 27.7	11 00.3	121 14.1	10.9	85 04.6	42.7
21	17 46.7	173 18.2 ..	58.3	40 28.7	10 59.6	136 16.0 ..	11.0	100 06.8 ..	42.6
22	32 49.2	188 19.8	58.1	55 29.8	59.0	151 17.9	11.1	115 09.0	42.6
23	47 51.6	203 21.4	57.9	70 30.8	58.3	166 19.7	11.2	130 11.2	42.6
Mer. Pass.	h m 19 53.0	v 1.7	d 0.2	v 1.0	d 0.7	v 1.9	d 0.1	v 2.2	d 0.0

STARS

Name	SHA	Dec
Acamar	315 15.2	S40 13.9
Achernar	335 23.6	S57 08.8
Acrux	173 05.6	S63 11.8
Adhara	255 09.4	S28 59.8
Aldebaran	290 44.8	N16 32.7
Alioth	166 17.9	N55 51.4
Alkaid	152 56.5	N49 13.2
Al Na'ir	27 39.2	S46 52.4
Alnilam	275 42.3	S 1 11.5
Alphard	217 52.4	S 8 44.3
Alphecca	126 08.3	N26 39.3
Alpheratz	357 39.5	N29 11.8
Altair	62 04.9	N 8 55.3
Ankaa	353 11.8	S42 12.5
Antares	112 22.1	S26 28.2
Arcturus	145 52.7	N19 05.2
Atria	107 21.2	S69 03.5
Avior	234 16.2	S59 33.9
Bellatrix	278 27.8	N 6 21.9
Betelgeuse	270 57.0	N 7 24.5
Canopus	263 54.1	S52 42.3
Capella	280 28.6	N46 00.8
Deneb	49 29.2	N45 21.2
Denebola	182 30.1	N14 28.1
Diphda	348 52.0	S17 53.1
Dubhe	193 47.4	N61 38.8
Elnath	278 07.6	N28 37.2
Eltanin	90 44.9	N51 29.5
Enif	33 43.6	N 9 57.8
Fomalhaut	15 19.9	S29 31.5
Gacrux	171 57.1	S57 12.7
Gienah	175 48.7	S17 38.5
Hadar	148 43.2	S60 27.5
Hamal	327 56.3	N23 33.0
Kaus Aust.	83 39.3	S34 22.4
Kochab	137 21.3	N74 04.7
Markab	13 34.6	N15 18.5
Menkar	314 10.9	N 4 09.7
Menkent	148 03.6	S36 27.4
Miaplacidus	221 38.6	S69 47.4
Mirfak	308 34.6	N49 55.6
Nunki	75 54.1	S26 16.3
Peacock	53 13.8	S56 40.6
Pollux	243 23.1	N27 58.7
Procyon	244 55.7	N 5 10.5
Rasalhague	96 03.4	N12 33.0
Regulus	207 39.6	N11 52.5
Rigel	281 08.2	S 8 10.9
Rigil Kent.	139 47.4	S60 54.4
Sabik	102 08.7	S15 44.7
Schedar	349 35.9	N56 38.6
Shaula	96 17.3	S37 06.9
Sirius	258 30.2	S16 44.5
Spica	158 27.6	S11 15.3
Suhail	222 49.6	S43 30.3
Vega	80 36.8	N38 48.4
Zuben'ubi	137 01.7	S16 06.9

	SHA	Mer. Pass.
	° '	h m
Venus	156 05.7	9 31
Mars	23 47.6	18 20
Jupiter	118 55.5	11 59
Saturn	82 32.6	14 24

UT	SUN GHA	Dec	MOON GHA	v	Dec	d	HP
d h	° ′	° ′	° ′	′	° ′	′	′
21 00	183 34.0	S19 50.8	30 05.4	12.0	N 6 46.2	11.6	57.3
01	198 33.9	51.4	44 36.4	12.0	6 57.8	11.5	57.3
02	213 33.7	51.9	59 07.4	12.0	7 09.3	11.6	57.3
03	228 33.6	.. 52.5	73 38.4	11.8	7 20.9	11.5	57.4
04	243 33.4	53.0	88 09.2	11.8	7 32.4	11.4	57.4
05	258 33.3	53.6	102 40.0	11.8	7 43.8	11.5	57.4
06	273 33.1	S19 54.1	117 10.8	11.7	N 7 55.3	11.4	57.5
W 07	288 33.0	54.7	131 41.5	11.6	8 06.7	11.4	57.5
E 08	303 32.8	55.3	146 12.1	11.5	8 18.1	11.4	57.5
D 09	318 32.7	.. 55.8	160 42.6	11.5	8 29.5	11.3	57.6
N 10	333 32.5	56.4	175 13.1	11.4	8 40.8	11.4	57.6
E 11	348 32.3	56.9	189 43.5	11.3	8 52.2	11.2	57.6
S 12	3 32.2	S19 57.4	204 13.8	11.3	N 9 03.4	11.3	57.7
D 13	18 32.0	58.0	218 44.1	11.2	9 14.7	11.2	57.7
A 14	33 31.9	58.5	233 14.3	11.1	9 25.9	11.2	57.7
Y 15	48 31.7	.. 59.1	247 44.4	11.0	9 37.1	11.1	57.7
16	63 31.6	19 59.6	262 14.4	11.0	9 48.2	11.1	57.8
17	78 31.4	20 00.2	276 44.4	10.9	9 59.3	11.1	57.8
18	93 31.2	S20 00.7	291 14.3	10.8	N10 10.4	11.0	57.8
19	108 31.1	01.3	305 44.1	10.8	10 21.4	11.0	57.9
20	123 30.9	01.8	320 13.9	10.7	10 32.4	10.9	57.9
21	138 30.8	.. 02.4	334 43.6	10.6	10 43.3	10.9	57.9
22	153 30.6	02.9	349 13.2	10.5	10 54.2	10.8	58.0
23	168 30.4	03.4	3 42.7	10.5	11 05.0	10.8	58.0
22 00	183 30.3	S20 04.0	18 12.2	10.3	N11 15.8	10.7	58.0
01	198 30.1	04.5	32 41.5	10.3	11 26.5	10.7	58.0
02	213 30.0	05.1	47 10.8	10.3	11 37.2	10.7	58.1
03	228 29.8	.. 05.6	61 40.1	10.1	11 47.9	10.6	58.1
04	243 29.6	06.1	76 09.2	10.1	11 58.5	10.5	58.1
05	258 29.5	06.7	90 38.3	10.0	12 09.0	10.5	58.2
06	273 29.3	S20 07.2	105 07.3	9.9	N12 19.5	10.4	58.2
T 07	288 29.1	07.7	119 36.2	9.8	12 29.9	10.4	58.2
H 08	303 29.0	08.3	134 05.0	9.7	12 40.3	10.3	58.3
U 09	318 28.8	.. 08.8	148 33.7	9.7	12 50.6	10.2	58.3
R 10	333 28.7	09.4	163 02.4	9.6	13 00.8	10.2	58.3
S 11	348 28.5	09.9	177 31.0	9.5	13 11.0	10.1	58.3
D 12	3 28.3	S20 10.4	191 59.5	9.4	N13 21.1	10.1	58.4
A 13	18 28.2	11.0	206 27.9	9.4	13 31.2	10.0	58.4
Y 14	33 28.0	11.5	220 56.3	9.3	13 41.2	9.9	58.4
15	48 27.8	.. 12.0	235 24.6	9.1	13 51.1	9.8	58.5
16	63 27.7	12.5	249 52.7	9.1	14 00.9	9.8	58.5
17	78 27.5	13.1	264 20.8	9.1	14 10.7	9.7	58.5
18	93 27.3	S20 13.6	278 48.9	8.9	N14 20.4	9.6	58.5
19	108 27.2	14.1	293 16.8	8.9	14 30.0	9.6	58.6
20	123 27.0	14.7	307 44.7	8.7	14 39.6	9.5	58.6
21	138 26.8	.. 15.2	322 12.4	8.7	14 49.1	9.4	58.6
22	153 26.7	15.7	336 40.1	8.6	14 58.5	9.3	58.6
23	168 26.5	16.2	351 07.7	8.6	15 07.8	9.2	58.7
23 00	183 26.3	S20 16.8	5 35.3	8.4	N15 17.0	9.2	58.7
01	198 26.1	17.3	20 02.7	8.4	15 26.2	9.1	58.7
02	213 26.0	17.8	34 30.1	8.3	15 35.3	9.0	58.7
03	228 25.8	.. 18.3	48 57.4	8.2	15 44.3	8.9	58.8
04	243 25.6	18.9	63 24.6	8.1	15 53.2	8.8	58.8
05	258 25.5	19.4	77 51.7	8.0	16 02.0	8.7	58.8
06	273 25.3	S20 19.9	92 18.7	8.0	N16 10.7	8.7	58.8
F 07	288 25.1	20.4	106 45.7	7.9	16 19.4	8.5	58.9
R 08	303 24.9	20.9	121 12.6	7.8	16 27.9	8.5	58.9
I 09	318 24.8	.. 21.5	135 39.4	7.7	16 36.4	8.3	58.9
D 10	333 24.6	22.0	150 06.1	7.6	16 44.7	8.3	58.9
A 11	348 24.4	22.5	164 32.7	7.6	16 53.0	8.1	59.0
Y 12	3 24.3	S20 23.0	178 59.3	7.4	N17 01.1	8.1	59.0
13	18 24.1	23.5	193 25.7	7.4	17 09.2	8.0	59.0
14	33 23.9	24.1	207 52.1	7.4	17 17.2	7.9	59.0
15	48 23.7	.. 24.6	222 18.5	7.2	17 25.1	7.7	59.0
16	63 23.6	25.1	236 44.7	7.2	17 32.8	7.7	59.1
17	78 23.4	25.6	251 10.9	7.1	17 40.5	7.5	59.1
18	93 23.2	S20 26.1	265 37.0	7.0	N17 48.0	7.5	59.1
19	108 23.1	26.6	280 05.0	6.9	17 55.5	7.3	59.1
20	123 22.9	27.1	294 28.9	6.9	18 02.8	7.2	59.2
21	138 22.7	.. 27.6	308 54.8	6.8	18 10.0	7.2	59.2
22	153 22.5	28.2	323 20.6	6.7	18 17.2	7.0	59.2
23	168 22.3	28.7	337 46.3	6.6	N18 24.2	6.9	59.2
	SD 16.2	d 0.5	SD 15.7		15.9		16.1

Lat.	Twilight Naut.	Civil	Sunrise	Moonrise 21	22	23	24
°	h m	h m	h m	h m	h m	h m	h m
N 72	07 23	09 07	■	14 26	14 05	13 24	☐
N 70	07 10	08 38	10 44	14 40	14 30	14 17	13 42
68	07 00	08 17	09 47	14 51	14 50	14 50	14 53
66	06 51	08 00	09 13	15 01	15 06	15 14	15 30
64	06 43	07 45	08 49	15 09	15 19	15 33	15 56
62	06 36	07 34	08 30	15 16	15 30	15 49	16 17
60	06 30	07 23	08 15	15 22	15 39	16 02	16 34
N 58	06 25	07 15	08 02	15 28	15 47	16 13	16 48
56	06 20	07 07	07 50	15 32	15 55	16 23	17 00
54	06 15	07 00	07 40	15 37	16 01	16 32	17 11
52	06 11	06 53	07 32	15 41	16 07	16 40	17 21
50	06 07	06 47	07 24	15 44	16 12	16 47	17 29
45	05 58	06 34	07 07	15 52	16 24	17 02	17 47
N 40	05 50	06 23	06 53	15 58	16 34	17 15	18 02
35	05 43	06 14	06 41	16 04	16 42	17 25	18 15
30	05 36	06 05	06 31	16 09	16 49	17 35	18 26
20	05 23	05 49	06 13	16 18	17 02	17 51	18 45
N 10	05 09	05 35	05 57	16 25	17 13	18 05	19 01
0	04 55	05 20	05 42	16 33	17 24	18 19	19 17
S 10	04 39	05 05	05 28	16 40	17 35	18 32	19 33
20	04 19	04 48	05 12	16 48	17 46	18 47	19 49
30	03 55	04 27	04 53	16 57	17 59	19 04	20 09
35	03 39	04 14	04 42	17 02	18 07	19 14	20 21
40	03 20	03 58	04 30	17 08	18 16	19 25	20 33
45	02 55	03 40	04 15	17 15	18 26	19 38	20 48
S 50	02 21	03 16	03 56	17 24	18 39	19 54	21 07
52	02 03	03 04	03 48	17 27	18 44	20 02	21 16
54	01 40	02 51	03 38	17 32	18 51	20 10	21 26
56	01 07	02 35	03 27	17 37	18 58	20 20	21 38
58	////	02 15	03 14	17 42	19 06	20 31	21 51
S 60	////	01 51	02 59	17 48	19 16	20 43	22 07

Lat.	Sunset	Twilight Civil	Naut.	Moonset 21	22	23	24
°	h m	h m	h m	h m	h m	h m	h m
N 72	■	14 24	16 08	05 50	07 56	10 29	☐
N 70	12 47	14 53	16 21	05 38	07 32	09 38	12 12
68	13 45	15 15	16 32	05 28	07 14	09 06	11 02
66	14 18	15 32	16 41	05 20	06 59	08 42	10 25
64	14 42	15 46	16 48	05 14	06 47	08 24	09 59
62	15 01	15 58	16 55	05 08	06 37	08 09	09 39
60	15 17	16 08	17 01	05 03	06 29	07 57	09 23
N 58	15 30	16 17	17 07	04 58	06 21	07 46	09 09
56	15 41	16 25	17 12	04 55	06 15	07 37	08 57
54	15 51	16 32	17 16	04 51	06 09	07 28	08 47
52	16 00	16 39	17 21	04 48	06 04	07 21	08 37
50	16 08	16 45	17 25	04 45	05 59	07 14	08 29
45	16 25	16 57	17 34	04 39	05 49	07 00	08 12
N 40	16 39	17 08	17 42	04 34	05 40	06 49	07 57
35	16 51	17 18	17 56	04 29	05 33	06 39	07 45
30	17 01	17 27	17 56	04 25	05 26	06 30	07 35
20	17 19	17 43	18 10	04 19	05 15	06 15	07 17
N 10	17 35	17 57	18 23	04 13	05 06	06 02	07 01
0	17 50	18 12	18 37	04 07	04 57	05 50	06 46
S 10	18 05	18 27	18 54	04 02	04 48	05 38	06 32
20	18 21	18 45	19 13	03 56	04 38	05 25	06 16
30	18 40	19 06	19 38	03 49	04 27	05 10	05 58
35	18 51	19 19	19 54	03 45	04 21	05 01	05 47
40	19 04	19 34	20 13	03 41	04 14	04 52	05 35
45	19 18	19 53	20 38	03 36	04 06	04 40	05 22
S 50	19 37	20 17	21 13	03 30	03 56	04 27	05 04
52	19 45	20 29	21 32	03 27	03 51	04 20	04 56
54	19 55	20 43	21 55	03 24	03 46	04 13	04 48
56	20 06	20 59	22 29	03 21	03 41	04 05	04 38
58	20 19	21 19	////	03 17	03 35	03 57	04 26
S 60	20 34	21 44	////	03 13	03 28	03 47	04 13

Day	SUN Eqn. of Time 00h	12h	Mer. Pass.	MOON Mer. Pass. Upper	Lower	Age	Phase
d	m s	m s	h m	h m	h m	d	%
21	14 16	14 09	11 46	22 45	10 20	14	96
22	14 01	13 54	11 46	23 37	11 10	15	99
23	13 46	13 37	11 46	24 32	12 04	16	100

2018 NOVEMBER 24, 25, 26 (SAT., SUN., MON.)

UT	ARIES	VENUS −4·9		MARS −0·1		JUPITER −1·7		SATURN +0·5		STARS		
	GHA	GHA	Dec	GHA	Dec	GHA	Dec	GHA	Dec	Name	SHA	Dec
d h	° ′	° ′	° ′	° ′	° ′	° ′	° ′	° ′	° ′		° ′	° ′
24 00	62 54.1	218 23.1	S 9 57.7	85 31.8	S10 57.7	181 21.6	S20 11.3	145 13.4	S22 42.6	Acamar	315 15.2	S40 13.9
01	77 56.6	233 24.7	57.6	100 32.8	57.0	196 23.5	11.4	160 15.6	42.6	Achernar	335 23.6	S57 08.8
02	92 59.0	248 26.3	57.4	115 33.8	56.3	211 25.4	11.5	175 17.7	42.6	Acrux	173 05.5	S63 11.8
03	108 01.5	263 27.9	.. 57.2	130 34.8	.. 55.7	226 27.3	.. 11.6	190 19.9	.. 42.6	Adhara	255 09.3	S28 59.8
04	123 04.0	278 29.5	57.1	145 35.8	55.0	241 29.1	11.7	205 22.1	42.6	Aldebaran	290 44.8	N16 32.7
05	138 06.4	293 31.1	56.9	160 36.8	54.4	256 31.0	11.8	220 24.3	42.6			
06	153 08.9	308 32.7	S 9 56.7	175 37.8	S10 53.7	271 32.9	S20 12.0	235 26.5	S22 42.6	Alioth	166 17.9	N55 51.4
S 07	168 11.4	323 34.3	56.6	190 38.8	53.0	286 34.8	12.1	250 28.7	42.5	Alkaid	152 56.4	N49 13.2
A 08	183 13.8	338 35.9	56.4	205 39.8	52.4	301 36.7	12.2	265 30.8	42.5	Al Na'ir	27 39.2	S46 52.4
T 09	198 16.3	353 37.5	.. 56.3	220 40.8	.. 51.7	316 38.5	.. 12.3	280 33.0	.. 42.5	Alnilam	275 42.3	S 1 11.5
U 10	213 18.7	8 39.1	56.1	235 41.8	51.1	331 40.4	12.4	295 35.2	42.5	Alphard	217 52.4	S 8 44.3
R 11	228 21.2	23 40.7	55.9	250 42.8	50.4	346 42.3	12.5	310 37.4	42.5			
D 12	243 23.7	38 42.3	S 9 55.8	265 43.8	S10 49.7	1 44.2	S20 12.6	325 39.6	S22 42.5	Alphecca	126 08.3	N26 39.3
A 13	258 26.1	53 43.9	55.6	280 44.8	49.1	16 46.1	12.7	340 41.8	42.5	Alpheratz	357 39.5	N29 11.8
Y 14	273 28.6	68 45.5	55.5	295 45.8	48.4	31 47.9	12.8	355 43.9	42.5	Altair	62 04.9	N 8 55.3
15	288 31.1	83 47.1	.. 55.3	310 46.8	.. 47.7	46 49.8	.. 12.9	10 46.1	.. 42.5	Ankaa	353 11.9	S42 12.5
16	303 33.5	98 48.6	55.2	325 47.8	47.1	61 51.7	13.0	25 48.3	42.5	Antares	112 22.1	S26 28.2
17	318 36.0	113 50.2	55.1	340 48.8	46.4	76 53.6	13.1	40 50.5	42.5			
18	333 38.5	128 51.8	S 9 54.9	355 49.8	S10 45.8	91 55.5	S20 13.3	55 52.7	S22 42.4	Arcturus	145 52.7	N19 05.2
19	348 40.9	143 53.3	54.8	10 50.8	45.1	106 57.3	13.4	70 54.9	42.4	Atria	107 21.2	S69 03.5
20	3 43.4	158 54.9	54.6	25 51.8	44.4	121 59.2	13.5	85 57.0	42.4	Avior	234 16.2	S59 34.0
21	18 45.9	173 56.5	.. 54.5	40 52.8	.. 43.8	137 01.1	.. 13.6	100 59.2	.. 42.4	Bellatrix	278 27.7	N 6 21.9
22	33 48.3	188 58.0	54.4	55 53.8	43.1	152 03.0	13.7	116 01.4	42.4	Betelgeuse	270 57.0	N 7 24.5
23	48 50.8	203 59.6	54.2	70 54.8	42.4	167 04.9	13.8	131 03.6	42.4			
25 00	63 53.2	219 01.1	S 9 54.1	85 55.8	S10 41.8	182 06.7	S20 13.9	146 05.8	S22 42.4	Canopus	263 54.0	S52 42.3
01	78 55.7	234 02.7	54.0	100 56.9	41.1	197 08.6	14.0	161 08.0	42.4	Capella	280 28.5	N46 00.8
02	93 58.2	249 04.2	53.8	115 57.9	40.5	212 10.5	14.1	176 10.1	42.4	Deneb	49 29.2	N45 21.2
03	109 00.6	264 05.8	.. 53.7	130 58.9	.. 39.8	227 12.4	.. 14.2	191 12.3	.. 42.4	Denebola	182 30.1	N14 28.1
04	124 03.1	279 07.3	53.6	145 59.9	39.1	242 14.3	14.3	206 14.5	42.3	Diphda	348 52.0	S17 53.1
05	139 05.6	294 08.8	53.5	161 00.9	38.5	257 16.2	14.4	221 16.7	42.3			
06	154 08.0	309 10.4	S 9 53.4	176 01.9	S10 37.8	272 18.0	S20 14.6	236 18.9	S22 42.3	Dubhe	193 47.4	N61 38.7
07	169 10.5	324 11.9	53.2	191 02.9	37.1	287 19.9	14.7	251 21.0	42.3	Elnath	278 07.6	N28 37.2
S 08	184 13.0	339 13.4	53.1	206 03.9	36.5	302 21.8	14.8	266 23.2	42.3	Eltanin	90 44.9	N51 29.5
U 09	199 15.4	354 14.9	.. 52.9	221 04.9	.. 35.8	317 23.7	.. 14.9	281 25.4	.. 42.3	Enif	33 43.6	N 9 57.8
N 10	214 17.9	9 16.5	52.9	236 05.9	35.1	332 25.6	15.0	296 27.6	42.3	Fomalhaut	15 19.9	S29 31.5
D 11	229 20.3	24 18.0	52.8	251 06.9	34.5	347 27.4	15.1	311 29.8	42.3			
A 12	244 22.8	39 19.5	S 9 52.7	266 07.9	S10 33.8	2 29.3	S20 15.2	326 32.0	S22 42.3	Gacrux	171 57.1	S57 12.7
Y 13	259 25.3	54 21.0	52.6	281 08.9	33.1	17 31.2	15.3	341 34.1	42.2	Gienah	175 48.7	S17 38.5
14	274 27.7	69 22.5	52.5	296 09.9	32.5	32 33.1	15.4	356 36.3	42.2	Hadar	148 43.2	S60 27.5
15	289 30.2	84 24.0	.. 52.4	311 10.9	.. 31.8	47 35.0	.. 15.5	11 38.5	.. 42.2	Hamal	327 56.3	N23 33.1
16	304 32.7	99 25.5	52.3	326 11.9	31.1	62 36.8	15.6	26 40.7	42.2	Kaus Aust.	83 39.3	S34 22.4
17	319 35.1	114 27.0	52.2	341 12.9	30.5	77 38.7	15.7	41 42.9	42.2			
18	334 37.6	129 28.5	S 9 52.1	356 13.9	S10 29.8	92 40.6	S20 15.8	56 45.0	S22 42.2	Kochab	137 21.3	N74 04.7
19	349 40.1	144 30.0	52.0	11 14.9	29.1	107 42.5	15.9	71 47.2	42.2	Markab	13 34.6	N15 18.5
20	4 42.5	159 31.5	51.9	26 15.9	28.5	122 44.4	16.1	86 49.4	42.2	Menkar	314 10.9	N 4 09.7
21	19 45.0	174 33.0	.. 51.8	41 16.9	.. 27.8	137 46.2	.. 16.2	101 51.6	.. 42.2	Menkent	148 03.6	S36 27.4
22	34 47.5	189 34.5	51.7	56 17.9	27.2	152 48.1	16.3	116 53.8	42.2	Miaplacidus	221 38.6	S69 47.4
23	49 49.9	204 36.0	51.6	71 18.9	26.5	167 50.0	16.4	131 55.9	42.1			
26 00	64 52.4	219 37.4	S 9 51.5	86 19.9	S10 25.8	182 51.9	S20 16.5	146 58.1	S22 42.1	Mirfak	308 34.5	N49 55.6
01	79 54.8	234 38.9	51.4	101 20.9	25.2	197 53.8	16.6	162 00.3	42.1	Nunki	75 54.1	S26 16.3
02	94 57.3	249 40.4	51.3	116 21.9	24.5	212 55.6	16.7	177 02.5	42.1	Peacock	53 13.8	S56 40.6
03	109 59.8	264 41.9	.. 51.3	131 22.9	.. 23.8	227 57.5	.. 16.8	192 04.7	.. 42.1	Pollux	243 23.0	N27 58.6
04	125 02.2	279 43.3	51.2	146 23.9	23.2	242 59.4	16.9	207 06.8	42.1	Procyon	244 55.7	N 5 10.5
05	140 04.7	294 44.8	51.1	161 24.9	22.5	258 01.3	17.0	222 09.0	42.1			
06	155 07.2	309 46.3	S 9 51.0	176 25.9	S10 21.8	273 03.2	S20 17.1	237 11.2	S22 42.1	Rasalhague	96 03.4	N12 33.0
07	170 09.6	324 47.7	50.9	191 26.9	21.1	288 05.0	17.2	252 13.4	42.1	Regulus	207 39.6	N11 52.5
08	185 12.1	339 49.2	50.9	206 27.9	20.5	303 06.9	17.3	267 15.6	42.1	Rigel	281 08.2	S 8 10.9
M 09	200 14.6	354 50.6	.. 50.8	221 28.9	.. 19.8	318 08.8	.. 17.4	282 17.7	.. 42.0	Rigil Kent.	139 47.3	S60 54.4
O 10	215 17.0	9 52.1	50.7	236 29.9	19.1	333 10.7	17.5	297 19.9	42.0	Sabik	102 08.7	S15 44.7
N 11	230 19.5	24 53.5	50.7	251 30.9	18.5	348 12.6	17.7	312 22.1	42.0			
D 12	245 22.0	39 55.0	S 9 50.6	266 31.9	S10 17.8	3 14.4	S20 17.8	327 24.3	S22 42.0	Schedar	349 35.9	N56 38.6
A 13	260 24.4	54 56.4	50.5	281 32.9	17.1	18 16.3	17.9	342 26.5	42.0	Shaula	96 17.3	S37 06.9
Y 14	275 26.9	69 57.8	50.5	296 33.9	16.5	33 18.2	18.0	357 28.6	42.0	Sirius	258 30.2	S16 44.5
15	290 29.3	84 59.3	.. 50.4	311 34.9	.. 15.8	48 20.1	.. 18.1	12 30.8	.. 42.0	Spica	158 27.6	S11 15.3
16	305 31.8	100 00.7	50.3	326 35.9	15.1	63 22.0	18.2	27 33.0	42.0	Suhail	222 49.6	S43 30.3
17	320 34.3	115 02.1	50.3	341 36.9	14.5	78 23.8	18.3	42 35.2	42.0			
18	335 36.7	130 03.6	S 9 50.2	356 37.9	S10 13.8	93 25.7	S20 18.4	57 37.4	S22 42.0	Vega	80 36.8	N38 48.4
19	350 39.2	145 05.0	50.2	11 38.9	13.1	108 27.6	18.5	72 39.5	41.9	Zuben'ubi	137 01.7	S16 06.9
20	5 41.7	160 06.4	50.1	26 39.9	12.5	123 29.5	18.6	87 41.7	41.9		SHA	Mer. Pass.
21	20 44.1	175 07.8	.. 50.1	41 40.9	.. 11.8	138 31.4	.. 18.7	102 43.9	.. 41.9		° ′	h m
22	35 46.6	190 09.3	50.0	56 41.9	11.1	153 33.2	18.8	117 46.1	41.9	Venus	155 07.9	9 23
23	50 49.1	205 10.7	50.0	71 42.9	10.5	168 35.1	18.9	132 48.3	41.9	Mars	22 02.6	18 15
	h m									Jupiter	118 13.5	11 50
Mer. Pass. 19 41.2		v 1.5	d 0.1	v 1.0	d 0.7	v 1.9	d 0.1	v 2.2	d 0.0	Saturn	82 12.5	14 14

UT	SUN GHA	SUN Dec	MOON GHA	v	MOON Dec	d	HP
d h	° ′	° ′	° ′	′	° ′	′	′
24 00	183 22.2	S20 29.2	352 11.9	6.6	N18 31.1	6.8	59.2
01	198 22.0	29.7	6 37.5	6.5	18 37.9	6.6	59.3
02	213 21.8	30.2	21 03.0	6.4	18 44.5	6.6	59.3
03	228 21.6	.. 30.7	35 28.4	6.4	18 51.1	6.4	59.3
04	243 21.4	31.2	49 53.8	6.3	18 57.5	6.3	59.3
05	258 21.3	31.7	64 19.1	6.2	19 03.8	6.2	59.3
06	273 21.1	S20 32.2	78 44.3	6.1	N19 10.0	6.1	59.3
S 07	288 20.9	32.7	93 09.4	6.1	19 16.1	5.9	59.4
A 08	303 20.7	33.2	107 34.5	6.1	19 22.0	5.8	59.4
T 09	318 20.5	.. 33.7	121 59.6	5.9	19 27.8	5.7	59.4
U 10	333 20.4	34.2	136 24.5	5.9	19 33.5	5.6	59.4
R 11	348 20.2	34.7	150 49.4	5.9	19 39.1	5.4	59.4
D 12	3 20.0	S20 35.2	165 14.3	5.7	N19 44.5	5.4	59.4
A 13	18 19.8	35.7	179 39.0	5.8	19 49.9	5.2	59.5
Y 14	33 19.6	36.2	194 03.8	5.6	19 55.1	5.0	59.5
15	48 19.5	.. 36.7	208 28.4	5.6	20 00.1	4.9	59.5
16	63 19.3	37.2	222 53.0	5.5	20 05.0	4.8	59.5
17	78 19.1	37.7	237 17.6	5.5	20 09.8	4.7	59.5
18	93 18.9	S20 38.2	251 42.1	5.4	N20 14.5	4.5	59.5
19	108 18.7	38.7	266 06.5	5.4	20 19.0	4.4	59.5
20	123 18.5	39.2	280 30.9	5.3	20 23.4	4.3	59.6
21	138 18.4	.. 39.7	294 55.2	5.3	20 27.7	4.1	59.6
22	153 18.2	40.2	309 19.5	5.3	20 31.8	4.0	59.6
23	168 18.0	40.7	323 43.8	5.2	20 35.8	3.8	59.6
25 00	183 17.8	S20 41.2	338 08.0	5.1	N20 39.6	3.7	59.6
01	198 17.6	41.7	352 32.1	5.1	20 43.3	3.6	59.6
02	213 17.4	42.2	6 56.2	5.1	20 46.9	3.4	59.6
03	228 17.2	.. 42.7	21 20.3	5.0	20 50.3	3.3	59.6
04	243 17.1	43.2	35 44.3	5.0	20 53.6	3.1	59.6
05	258 16.9	43.7	50 08.3	5.0	20 56.7	3.0	59.7
06	273 16.7	S20 44.2	64 32.3	4.9	N20 59.7	2.9	59.7
S 07	288 16.5	44.7	78 56.2	4.9	21 02.6	2.7	59.7
U 08	303 16.3	45.1	93 20.1	4.8	21 05.3	2.5	59.7
N 09	318 16.1	.. 45.6	107 43.9	4.8	21 07.8	2.5	59.7
D 10	333 15.9	46.1	122 07.7	4.8	21 10.3	2.2	59.7
A 11	348 15.7	46.6	136 31.5	4.8	21 12.5	2.2	59.7
Y 12	3 15.5	S20 47.1	150 55.3	4.7	N21 14.7	1.9	59.7
13	18 15.4	47.6	165 19.0	4.8	21 16.6	1.9	59.7
14	33 15.2	48.1	179 42.8	4.6	21 18.5	1.7	59.7
15	48 15.0	.. 48.5	194 06.4	4.7	21 20.2	1.5	59.7
16	63 14.8	49.0	208 30.1	4.7	21 21.7	1.4	59.7
17	78 14.6	49.5	222 53.8	4.6	21 23.1	1.2	59.8
18	93 14.4	S20 50.0	237 17.4	4.6	N21 24.3	1.1	59.8
19	108 14.2	50.5	251 41.0	4.7	21 25.4	1.0	59.8
20	123 14.0	51.0	266 04.7	4.6	21 26.4	0.8	59.8
21	138 13.8	.. 51.4	280 28.3	4.5	21 27.2	0.6	59.8
22	153 13.6	51.9	294 51.8	4.6	21 27.8	0.5	59.8
23	168 13.4	52.4	309 15.4	4.6	21 28.3	0.4	59.8
26 00	183 13.2	S20 52.9	323 39.0	4.6	N21 28.7	0.2	59.8
01	198 13.1	53.3	338 02.6	4.5	21 28.9	0.0	59.8
02	213 12.9	53.8	352 26.1	4.6	21 28.9	0.1	59.8
03	228 12.7	.. 54.3	6 49.7	4.6	21 28.8	0.2	59.8
04	243 12.5	54.8	21 13.3	4.5	21 28.6	0.4	59.8
05	258 12.3	55.2	35 36.8	4.6	21 28.2	0.6	59.8
06	273 12.1	S20 55.7	50 00.4	4.6	N21 27.6	0.7	59.8
07	288 11.9	56.2	64 24.0	4.6	21 26.9	0.8	59.8
08	303 11.7	56.7	78 47.6	4.6	21 26.1	1.0	59.8
M 09	318 11.5	.. 57.1	93 11.2	4.6	21 25.1	1.2	59.8
O 10	333 11.3	57.6	107 34.8	4.6	21 23.9	1.2	59.8
N 11	348 11.1	58.1	121 58.4	4.6	21 22.7	1.5	59.8
D 12	3 10.9	S20 58.5	136 22.0	4.7	N21 21.2	1.6	59.8
A 13	18 10.7	59.0	150 45.7	4.7	21 19.6	1.7	59.8
Y 14	33 10.5	20 59.5	165 09.4	4.7	21 17.9	1.9	59.8
15	48 10.3	21 00.0	179 33.1	4.7	21 16.0	2.0	59.8
16	63 10.1	00.4	193 56.8	4.7	21 14.0	2.2	59.8
17	78 09.9	00.9	208 20.5	4.8	21 11.8	2.3	59.8
18	93 09.7	S21 01.4	222 44.3	4.7	N21 09.5	2.5	59.8
19	108 09.5	01.8	237 08.0	4.9	21 07.0	2.6	59.8
20	123 09.3	02.3	251 31.9	4.8	21 04.4	2.8	59.8
21	138 09.1	.. 02.7	265 55.7	4.9	21 01.6	2.9	59.8
22	153 08.9	03.2	280 19.6	4.9	20 58.7	3.1	59.8
23	168 08.7	03.7	294 43.5	4.9	N20 55.6	3.2	59.8
	SD 16.2	d 0.5	SD 16.2		16.3		16.3

Lat.	Twilight Naut.	Twilight Civil	Sunrise	Moonrise 24	25	26	27
°	h m	h m	h m	h m	h m	h m	h m
N 72	07 33	09 21	■■■	□	□	□	□
N 70	07 19	08 49	11 30	13 42	□	□	17 00
68	07 07	08 26	10 02	14 53	15 10	16 15	18 05
66	06 58	08 08	09 25	15 30	16 04	17 08	18 40
64	06 49	07 53	08 58	15 56	16 37	17 41	19 06
62	06 42	07 40	08 38	16 17	17 01	18 05	19 26
60	06 36	07 29	08 22	16 34	17 20	18 24	19 42
N 58	06 30	07 20	08 08	16 48	17 36	18 39	19 56
56	06 25	07 12	07 56	17 00	17 50	18 53	20 07
54	06 20	07 04	07 46	17 11	18 02	19 05	20 18
52	06 15	06 57	07 36	17 21	18 12	19 15	20 27
50	06 11	06 51	07 28	17 29	18 21	19 24	20 35
45	06 02	06 38	07 11	17 47	18 41	19 44	20 52
N 40	05 53	06 26	06 56	18 02	18 57	19 59	21 06
35	05 45	06 16	06 44	18 15	19 11	20 13	21 18
30	05 38	06 07	06 33	18 26	19 23	20 24	21 29
20	05 24	05 51	06 15	18 45	19 43	20 44	21 47
N 10	05 10	05 36	05 59	19 01	20 01	21 01	22 02
0	04 55	05 21	05 43	19 17	20 17	21 18	22 17
S 10	04 39	05 05	05 28	19 33	20 34	21 34	22 32
20	04 19	04 47	05 11	19 49	20 51	21 51	22 47
30	03 53	04 26	04 52	20 09	21 12	22 11	23 05
35	03 37	04 12	04 41	20 20	21 24	22 23	23 15
40	03 17	03 56	04 28	20 33	21 38	22 36	23 27
45	02 52	03 37	04 12	20 48	21 54	22 52	23 41
S 50	02 16	03 12	03 53	21 07	22 14	23 11	23 58
52	01 56	03 00	03 44	21 16	22 24	23 20	24 06
54	01 31	02 46	03 34	21 26	22 34	23 31	24 15
56	00 54	02 29	03 23	21 38	22 47	23 42	24 24
58	////	02 08	03 09	21 51	23 01	23 55	24 36
S 60	////	01 41	02 54	22 07	23 17	24 11	00 11

Lat.	Sunset	Twilight Civil	Twilight Naut.	Moonset 24	25	26	27
°	h m	h m	h m	h m	h m	h m	h m
N 72	■■■	14 12	16 00	□	□	□	□
N 70	12 04	14 44	16 14	12 12	□	□	15 13
68	13 31	15 07	16 26	11 02	12 50	13 52	14 07
66	14 09	15 26	16 35	10 25	11 56	12 59	13 31
64	14 35	15 41	16 44	09 59	11 23	12 26	13 05
62	14 55	15 53	16 51	09 39	10 59	12 02	12 45
60	15 12	16 04	16 58	09 23	10 40	11 43	12 28
N 58	15 25	16 13	17 03	09 09	10 24	11 27	12 14
56	15 37	16 22	17 09	08 57	10 11	11 13	12 02
54	15 48	16 29	17 14	08 47	09 59	11 01	11 51
52	15 57	16 36	17 18	08 37	09 49	10 51	11 42
50	16 05	16 42	17 22	08 29	09 39	10 41	11 33
45	16 23	16 56	17 32	08 12	09 20	10 22	11 15
N 40	16 37	17 07	17 40	07 57	09 04	10 06	11 01
35	16 50	17 17	17 48	07 45	08 51	09 52	10 48
30	17 00	17 26	17 56	07 35	08 39	09 40	10 37
20	17 19	17 43	18 10	07 17	08 19	09 20	10 18
N 10	17 35	17 58	18 24	07 01	08 02	09 03	10 02
0	17 51	18 13	18 38	06 46	07 45	08 46	09 46
S 10	18 06	18 29	18 55	06 32	07 29	08 29	09 31
20	18 23	18 47	19 15	06 16	07 12	08 12	09 14
30	18 42	19 09	19 41	05 58	06 52	07 51	08 55
35	18 53	19 22	19 57	05 47	06 40	07 39	08 43
40	19 06	19 38	20 17	05 36	06 27	07 26	08 31
45	19 22	19 58	20 43	05 22	06 11	07 09	08 15
S 50	19 41	20 23	21 20	05 04	05 52	06 49	07 56
52	19 50	20 35	21 40	04 56	05 42	06 40	07 47
54	20 01	20 50	22 05	04 48	05 32	06 29	07 37
56	20 12	21 07	22 45	04 38	05 20	06 17	07 26
58	20 26	21 28	////	04 26	05 07	06 02	07 13
S 60	20 42	21 56	////	04 13	04 51	05 46	06 58

Day	SUN Eqn. of Time 00ʰ	12ʰ	Mer. Pass.	MOON Mer. Pass. Upper	Lower	Age	Phase
d	m s	m s	h m	h m	h m	d	%
24	13 29	13 20	11 47	00 32	13 01	17	98
25	13 12	13 03	11 47	01 31	14 01	18	93
26	12 53	12 44	11 47	02 32	15 02	19	86

UT	ARIES GHA	VENUS −4.9 GHA	Dec	MARS −0.1 GHA	Dec	JUPITER −1.7 GHA	Dec	SATURN +0.5 GHA	Dec	STARS Name	SHA	Dec
27 00	65 51.5	220 12.1	S 9 49.9	86 43.9	S10 09.8	183 37.0	S20 19.0	147 50.4	S22 41.9	Acamar	315 15.1	S40 14.0
01	80 54.0	235 13.5	49.9	101 44.9	09.1	198 38.9	19.2	162 52.6	41.9	Achernar	335 23.6	S57 08.8
02	95 56.5	250 14.9	49.8	116 45.9	08.4	213 40.8	19.3	177 54.8	41.9	Acrux	173 05.5	S63 11.8
03	110 58.9	265 16.3 ..	49.8	131 46.9 ..	07.8	228 42.6 ..	19.4	192 57.0 ..	41.9	Adhara	255 09.3	S28 59.8
04	126 01.4	280 17.7	49.8	146 47.9	07.1	243 44.5	19.5	207 59.1	41.8	Aldebaran	290 44.8	N16 32.7
05	141 03.8	295 19.1	49.7	161 48.9	06.4	258 46.4	19.6	223 01.3	41.8			
06	156 06.3	310 20.5	S 9 49.7	176 49.9	S10 05.8	273 48.3	S20 19.7	238 03.5	S22 41.8	Alioth	166 17.8	N55 51.4
T 07	171 08.8	325 21.9	49.6	191 50.8	05.1	288 50.2	19.8	253 05.7	41.8	Alkaid	152 56.4	N49 13.2
U 08	186 11.2	340 23.3	49.6	206 51.8	04.4	303 52.0	19.9	268 07.9	41.8	Al Na'ir	27 39.2	S46 52.4
E 09	201 13.7	355 24.6 ..	49.6	221 52.8 ..	03.8	318 53.9 ..	20.0	283 10.0 ..	41.8	Alnilam	275 42.3	S 1 11.5
S 10	216 16.2	10 26.0	49.6	236 53.8	03.1	333 55.8	20.1	298 12.2	41.8	Alphard	217 52.4	S 8 44.3
D 11	231 18.6	25 27.4	49.5	251 54.8	02.4	348 57.7	20.2	313 14.4	41.8			
A 12	246 21.1	40 28.8	S 9 49.5	266 55.8	S10 01.7	3 59.6	S20 20.3	328 16.6	S22 41.8	Alphecca	126 08.3	N26 39.3
Y 13	261 23.6	55 30.1	49.5	281 56.8	01.1	19 01.4	20.4	343 18.7	41.7	Alpheratz	357 39.5	N29 11.8
14	276 26.0	70 31.5	49.5	296 57.8	10 00.4	34 03.3	20.5	358 20.9	41.7	Altair	62 04.9	N 8 55.3
15	291 28.5	85 32.9 ..	49.4	311 58.8	9 59.7	49 05.2 ..	20.6	13 23.1 ..	41.7	Ankaa	353 11.9	S42 12.5
16	306 31.0	100 34.3	49.4	326 59.8	59.1	64 07.1	20.7	28 25.3	41.7	Antares	112 22.1	S26 28.2
17	321 33.4	115 35.6	49.4	342 00.8	58.4	79 08.9	20.9	43 27.5	41.7			
18	336 35.9	130 37.0	S 9 49.4	357 01.8	S 9 57.7	94 10.8	S20 21.0	58 29.6	S22 41.7	Arcturus	145 52.7	N19 05.2
19	351 38.3	145 38.3	49.4	12 02.8	57.0	109 12.7	21.1	73 31.8	41.7	Atria	107 21.2	S69 03.5
20	6 40.8	160 39.7	49.4	27 03.8	56.4	124 14.6	21.2	88 34.0	41.7	Avior	234 16.1	S59 34.0
21	21 43.3	175 41.0 ..	49.3	42 04.8 ..	55.7	139 16.5 ..	21.3	103 36.2 ..	41.7	Bellatrix	278 27.7	N 6 21.9
22	36 45.7	190 42.4	49.3	57 05.8	55.0	154 18.3	21.4	118 38.3	41.7	Betelgeuse	270 57.0	N 7 24.5
23	51 48.2	205 43.7	49.3	72 06.8	54.4	169 20.2	21.5	133 40.5	41.6			
28 00	66 50.7	220 45.1	S 9 49.3	87 07.8	S 9 53.7	184 22.1	S20 21.6	148 42.7	S22 41.6	Canopus	263 54.0	S52 42.3
01	81 53.1	235 46.4	49.3	102 08.8	53.0	199 24.0	21.7	163 44.9	41.6	Capella	280 28.5	N46 00.8
02	96 55.6	250 47.8	49.3	117 09.8	52.3	214 25.9	21.8	178 47.0	41.6	Deneb	49 29.2	N45 21.2
03	111 58.1	265 49.1 ..	49.3	132 10.8 ..	51.7	229 27.7 ..	21.9	193 49.2 ..	41.6	Denebola	182 30.0	N14 28.1
04	127 00.5	280 50.4	49.3	147 11.8	51.0	244 29.6	22.0	208 51.4	41.6	Diphda	348 52.0	S17 53.1
05	142 03.0	295 51.7	49.3	162 12.8	50.3	259 31.5	22.1	223 53.6	41.6			
06	157 05.5	310 53.1	S 9 49.3	177 13.8	S 9 49.6	274 33.4	S20 22.2	238 55.8	S22 41.6	Dubhe	193 47.4	N61 38.7
W 07	172 07.9	325 54.4	49.3	192 14.8	49.0	289 35.3	22.3	253 57.9	41.6	Elnath	278 07.6	N28 37.2
E 08	187 10.4	340 55.7	49.3	207 15.8	48.3	304 37.1	22.4	269 00.1	41.5	Eltanin	90 44.9	N51 29.5
D 09	202 12.8	355 57.0 ..	49.3	222 16.8 ..	47.6	319 39.0 ..	22.5	284 02.3 ..	41.5	Enif	33 43.6	N 9 57.8
N 10	217 15.3	10 58.4	49.4	237 17.8	47.0	334 40.9	22.6	299 04.5	41.5	Fomalhaut	15 19.9	S29 31.5
E 11	232 17.8	25 59.7	49.4	252 18.7	46.3	349 42.8	22.8	314 06.6	41.5			
S 12	247 20.2	41 01.0	S 9 49.4	267 19.7	S 9 45.6	4 44.7	S20 22.9	329 08.8	S22 41.5	Gacrux	171 57.1	S57 12.7
D 13	262 22.7	56 02.3	49.4	282 20.7	44.9	19 46.5	23.0	344 11.0	41.5	Gienah	175 48.7	S17 38.6
A 14	277 25.2	71 03.6	49.4	297 21.7	44.3	34 48.4	23.1	359 13.2	41.5	Hadar	148 43.2	S60 27.5
Y 15	292 27.6	86 04.9 ..	49.4	312 22.7 ..	43.6	49 50.3 ..	23.2	14 15.3 ..	41.5	Hamal	327 56.3	N23 33.1
16	307 30.1	101 06.2	49.5	327 23.7	42.9	64 52.2	23.3	29 17.5	41.5	Kaus Aust.	83 39.3	S34 22.4
17	322 32.6	116 07.5	49.5	342 24.7	42.2	79 54.0	23.4	44 19.7	41.4			
18	337 35.0	131 08.8	S 9 49.5	357 25.7	S 9 41.6	94 55.9	S20 23.5	59 21.9	S22 41.4	Kochab	137 21.3	N74 04.7
19	352 37.5	146 10.1	49.5	12 26.7	40.9	109 57.8	23.6	74 24.0	41.4	Markab	13 34.6	N15 18.5
20	7 39.9	161 11.4	49.5	27 27.7	40.2	124 59.7	23.7	89 26.2	41.4	Menkar	314 10.9	N 4 09.7
21	22 42.4	176 12.6 ..	49.6	42 28.7 ..	39.5	140 01.6 ..	23.8	104 28.4 ..	41.4	Menkent	148 03.6	S36 27.4
22	37 44.9	191 13.9	49.6	57 29.7	38.9	155 03.4	23.9	119 30.6	41.4	Miaplacidus	221 38.5	S69 47.4
23	52 47.3	206 15.2	49.6	72 30.7	38.2	170 05.3	24.0	134 32.7	41.4			
29 00	67 49.8	221 16.5	S 9 49.7	87 31.7	S 9 37.5	185 07.2	S20 24.1	149 34.9	S22 41.4	Mirfak	308 34.5	N49 55.6
01	82 52.3	236 17.8	49.7	102 32.7	36.8	200 09.1	24.2	164 37.1	41.4	Nunki	75 54.1	S26 16.3
02	97 54.7	251 19.0	49.8	117 33.7	36.2	215 11.0	24.3	179 39.3	41.3	Peacock	53 13.8	S56 40.6
03	112 57.2	266 20.3 ..	49.8	132 34.7 ..	35.5	230 12.8 ..	24.4	194 41.4 ..	41.3	Pollux	243 23.0	N27 58.6
04	127 59.7	281 21.6	49.8	147 35.7	34.8	245 14.7	24.5	209 43.6	41.3	Procyon	244 55.7	N 5 10.5
05	143 02.1	296 22.8	49.9	162 36.6	34.1	260 16.6	24.6	224 45.8	41.3			
06	158 04.6	311 24.1	S 9 49.9	177 37.6	S 9 33.5	275 18.5	S20 24.7	239 48.0	S22 41.3	Rasalhague	96 03.4	N12 33.0
T 07	173 07.1	326 25.4	49.9	192 38.6	32.8	290 20.4	24.8	254 50.1	41.3	Regulus	207 39.6	N11 52.5
H 08	188 09.5	341 26.6	50.0	207 39.6	32.1	305 22.2	25.0	269 52.3	41.3	Rigel	281 08.2	S 8 10.9
U 09	203 12.0	356 27.9 ..	50.0	222 40.6 ..	31.4	320 24.1 ..	25.1	284 54.5 ..	41.3	Rigil Kent.	139 47.3	S60 54.4
R 10	218 14.4	11 29.1	50.1	237 41.6	30.7	335 26.0	25.2	299 56.7	41.3	Sabik	102 08.7	S15 44.7
S 11	233 16.9	26 30.4	50.1	252 42.6	30.1	350 27.9	25.3	314 58.8	41.2			
12	248 19.4	41 31.6	S 9 50.2	267 43.6	S 9 29.4	5 29.7	S20 25.4	330 01.0	S22 41.2	Schedar	349 35.9	N56 38.6
D 13	263 21.8	56 32.9	50.2	282 44.6	28.7	20 31.6	25.5	345 03.2	41.2	Shaula	96 17.3	S37 06.9
A 14	278 24.3	71 34.1	50.3	297 45.6	28.0	35 33.5	25.6	0 05.4	41.2	Sirius	258 30.2	S16 44.6
Y 15	293 26.8	86 35.4 ..	50.4	312 46.6 ..	27.4	50 35.4 ..	25.7	15 07.5 ..	41.2	Spica	158 27.6	S11 15.3
16	308 29.2	101 36.6	50.4	327 47.6	26.7	65 37.3	25.8	30 09.7	41.2	Suhail	222 49.6	S43 30.3
17	323 31.7	116 37.8	50.5	342 48.6	26.0	80 39.1	25.9	45 11.9	41.2			
18	338 34.2	131 39.1	S 9 50.5	357 49.6	S 9 25.3	95 41.0	S20 26.0	60 14.1	S22 41.2	Vega	80 36.8	N38 48.3
19	353 36.6	146 40.3	50.6	12 50.5	24.7	110 42.9	26.1	75 16.2	41.1	Zuben'ubi	137 01.7	S16 06.9
20	8 39.1	161 41.5	50.7	27 51.5	24.0	125 44.8	26.2	90 18.4	41.1		SHA	Mer. Pass.
21	23 41.6	176 42.7 ..	50.7	42 52.5 ..	23.3	140 46.7 ..	26.3	105 20.6 ..	41.1	Venus	153 54.4	9 16
22	38 44.0	191 44.0	50.8	57 53.5	22.6	155 48.5	26.4	120 22.7	41.1	Mars	20 17.1	18 10
23	53 46.5	206 45.2	50.9	72 54.5	21.9	170 50.4	26.5	135 24.9	41.1	Jupiter	117 31.4	11 41
Mer. Pass. 19 29.4		v 1.3	d 0.0	v 1.0	d 0.7	v 1.9	d 0.1	v 2.2	d 0.0	Saturn	81 52.0	14 03

UT	SUN GHA	Dec	MOON GHA	v	Dec	d	HP
d h	° ′	° ′	° ′	′	° ′	′	′
27 00	183 08.5	S21 04.1	309 07.4	5.0	N20 52.4	3.3	59.8
01	198 08.3	04.6	323 31.4	5.0	20 49.1	3.5	59.8
02	213 08.1	05.0	337 55.4	5.0	20 45.6	3.6	59.8
03	228 07.9	.. 05.5	352 19.4	5.1	20 42.0	3.8	59.8
04	243 07.7	06.0	6 43.5	5.1	20 38.2	3.9	59.8
05	258 07.5	06.4	21 07.6	5.2	20 34.3	4.0	59.8
06	273 07.3	S21 06.9	35 31.8	5.2	N20 30.3	4.2	59.8
07	288 07.1	07.3	49 56.0	5.3	20 26.1	4.3	59.8
08	303 06.9	07.8	64 20.3	5.3	20 21.8	4.5	59.8
09	318 06.7	.. 08.3	78 44.6	5.3	20 17.3	4.5	59.7
10	333 06.5	08.7	93 08.9	5.4	20 12.8	4.8	59.7
11	348 06.3	09.2	107 33.3	5.5	20 08.0	4.8	59.7
12	3 06.1	S21 09.6	121 57.8	5.5	N20 03.2	5.0	59.7
13	18 05.9	10.1	136 22.3	5.5	19 58.2	5.2	59.7
14	33 05.7	10.5	150 46.8	5.6	19 53.0	5.2	59.7
15	48 05.5	.. 11.0	165 11.4	5.7	19 47.8	5.4	59.7
16	63 05.3	11.4	179 36.1	5.7	19 42.4	5.5	59.7
17	78 05.0	11.9	194 00.8	5.8	19 36.9	5.7	59.7
18	93 04.8	S21 12.3	208 25.6	5.8	N19 31.2	5.8	59.7
19	108 04.6	12.8	222 50.4	5.9	19 25.4	5.9	59.7
20	123 04.4	13.2	237 15.3	5.9	19 19.5	6.0	59.7
21	138 04.2	.. 13.7	251 40.2	6.0	19 13.5	6.1	59.7
22	153 04.0	14.1	266 05.2	6.1	19 07.4	6.3	59.7
23	168 03.8	14.6	280 30.3	6.1	19 01.1	6.4	59.6
28 00	183 03.6	S21 15.0	294 55.4	6.2	N18 54.7	6.5	59.6
01	198 03.4	15.4	309 20.6	6.2	18 48.2	6.7	59.6
02	213 03.2	15.9	323 45.8	6.3	18 41.5	6.8	59.6
03	228 03.0	.. 16.3	338 11.1	6.4	18 34.7	6.8	59.6
04	243 02.8	16.8	352 36.5	6.4	18 27.9	7.0	59.6
05	258 02.5	17.2	7 01.9	6.5	18 20.9	7.1	59.6
06	273 02.3	S21 17.7	21 27.4	6.6	N18 13.8	7.3	59.6
07	288 02.1	18.1	35 53.0	6.6	18 06.5	7.3	59.6
08	303 01.9	18.5	50 18.6	6.7	17 59.2	7.5	59.6
09	318 01.7	.. 19.0	64 44.3	6.8	17 51.7	7.5	59.5
10	333 01.5	19.4	79 10.1	6.8	17 44.2	7.7	59.5
11	348 01.3	19.8	93 35.9	6.9	17 36.5	7.8	59.5
12	3 01.1	S21 20.3	108 01.8	7.0	N17 28.7	7.9	59.5
13	18 00.8	20.7	122 27.8	7.1	17 20.8	8.0	59.5
14	33 00.6	21.2	136 53.9	7.1	17 12.8	8.1	59.5
15	48 00.4	.. 21.6	151 20.0	7.1	17 04.7	8.2	59.5
16	63 00.2	22.0	165 46.1	7.3	16 56.5	8.3	59.5
17	78 00.0	22.5	180 12.4	7.3	16 48.2	8.4	59.5
18	92 59.8	S21 22.9	194 38.7	7.4	N16 39.8	8.5	59.4
19	107 59.6	23.3	209 05.1	7.4	16 31.3	8.7	59.4
20	122 59.3	23.7	223 31.5	7.6	16 22.6	8.7	59.4
21	137 59.1	.. 24.2	237 58.1	7.6	16 13.9	8.8	59.4
22	152 58.9	24.6	252 24.7	7.6	16 05.1	8.9	59.4
23	167 58.7	25.0	266 51.3	7.8	15 56.2	9.0	59.4
29 00	182 58.5	S21 25.5	281 18.1	7.8	N15 47.2	9.1	59.4
01	197 58.3	25.9	295 44.9	7.9	15 38.1	9.1	59.3
02	212 58.1	26.3	310 11.8	7.9	15 29.0	9.3	59.3
03	227 57.8	.. 26.7	324 38.7	8.0	15 19.7	9.4	59.3
04	242 57.6	27.2	339 05.7	8.1	15 10.3	9.4	59.3
05	257 57.4	27.6	353 32.8	8.2	15 00.9	9.5	59.3
06	272 57.2	S21 28.0	8 00.0	8.2	N14 51.4	9.6	59.3
07	287 57.0	28.4	22 27.2	8.3	14 41.8	9.7	59.3
08	302 56.7	28.9	36 54.5	8.4	14 32.1	9.8	59.3
09	317 56.5	.. 29.3	51 21.9	8.4	14 22.3	9.9	59.2
10	332 56.3	29.7	65 49.3	8.5	14 12.4	9.9	59.2
11	347 56.1	30.1	80 16.8	8.6	14 02.5	10.0	59.2
12	2 55.9	S21 30.5	94 44.4	8.6	N13 52.5	10.1	59.2
13	17 55.6	31.0	109 12.0	8.8	13 42.4	10.2	59.2
14	32 55.4	31.4	123 39.8	8.7	13 32.2	10.3	59.2
15	47 55.2	.. 31.8	138 07.5	8.9	13 21.9	10.3	59.1
16	62 55.0	32.2	152 35.4	8.9	13 11.6	10.4	59.1
17	77 54.8	32.6	167 03.3	9.0	13 01.2	10.4	59.1
18	92 54.5	S21 33.1	181 31.3	9.0	N12 50.8	10.6	59.1
19	107 54.3	33.5	195 59.3	9.2	12 40.2	10.6	59.1
20	122 54.1	33.9	210 27.5	9.1	12 29.6	10.6	59.1
21	137 53.9	.. 34.3	224 55.6	9.3	12 19.0	10.8	59.1
22	152 53.6	34.7	239 23.9	9.3	12 08.2	10.8	59.0
23	167 53.4	35.1	253 52.2	9.4	N11 57.4	10.8	59.0
	SD 16.2	d 0.4	SD 16.3		16.2		16.1

T U E S D A Y (27) • W E D N E S D A Y (28) • T H U R S D A Y (29)

Lat.	Twilight Naut.	Civil	Sunrise	Moonrise 27	28	29	30
°	h m	h m	h m	h m	h m	h m	h m
N 72	07 42	09 36	■	▢	18 43	21 15	23 24
N 70	07 27	09 00	■	17 00	19 31	21 38	23 35
68	07 15	08 35	10 18	18 05	20 02	21 55	23 44
66	07 04	08 15	09 36	18 40	20 24	22 09	23 51
64	06 55	08 00	09 07	19 06	20 42	22 21	23 57
62	06 48	07 46	08 46	19 26	20 57	22 30	24 03
60	06 41	07 35	08 28	19 42	21 09	22 38	24 07
N 58	06 35	07 25	08 14	19 56	21 19	22 46	24 11
56	06 29	07 17	08 01	20 07	21 29	22 52	24 15
54	06 24	07 09	07 51	20 18	21 37	22 58	24 18
52	06 19	07 02	07 41	20 27	21 44	23 03	24 21
50	06 15	06 55	07 32	20 35	21 51	23 07	24 24
45	06 05	06 41	07 14	20 52	22 04	23 17	24 29
N 40	05 56	06 29	06 59	21 06	22 16	23 26	24 34
35	05 48	06 19	06 47	21 18	22 26	23 33	24 38
30	05 40	06 10	06 36	21 29	22 34	23 39	24 42
20	05 26	05 53	06 17	21 47	22 49	23 49	24 48
N 10	05 11	05 37	06 00	22 02	23 02	23 59	24 53
0	04 56	05 22	05 44	22 17	23 14	24 08	00 08
S 10	04 39	05 06	05 28	22 32	23 26	24 16	00 16
20	04 19	04 47	05 11	22 47	23 38	24 25	00 25
30	03 52	04 25	04 52	23 05	23 53	24 36	00 36
35	03 36	04 11	04 40	23 15	24 01	00 01	00 42
40	03 15	03 55	04 27	23 27	24 11	00 11	00 49
45	02 49	03 35	04 11	23 41	24 22	00 22	00 57
S 50	02 11	03 09	03 51	23 58	24 35	00 35	01 06
52	01 50	02 56	03 41	24 06	00 06	00 42	01 11
54	01 23	02 41	03 31	24 15	00 15	00 49	01 16
56	00 38	02 24	03 19	24 24	00 24	00 56	01 21
58	////	02 02	03 05	24 36	00 36	01 05	01 27
S 60	////	01 32	02 48	00 11	00 49	01 15	01 34

Lat.	Sunset	Twilight Civil	Naut.	Moonset 27	28	29	30
°	h m	h m	h m	h m	h m	h m	h m
N 72	■	13 59	15 53	▢	15 31	14 53	14 32
N 70		14 35	16 08	15 13	14 42	14 28	14 19
68	13 17	15 00	16 21	14 07	14 10	14 10	14 08
66	14 00	15 20	16 31	13 31	13 46	13 54	13 59
64	14 28	15 36	16 40	13 05	13 28	13 42	13 51
62	14 50	15 49	16 48	12 43	13 13	13 31	13 45
60	15 07	16 00	16 54	12 28	13 00	13 22	13 39
N 58	15 21	16 10	17 01	12 14	12 48	13 14	13 34
56	15 34	16 19	17 06	12 02	12 39	13 07	13 29
54	15 45	16 27	17 11	11 52	12 30	13 01	13 25
52	15 54	16 34	17 16	11 42	12 22	12 55	13 22
50	16 03	16 40	17 21	11 33	12 15	12 50	13 18
45	16 21	16 54	17 31	11 15	12 00	12 38	13 11
N 40	16 36	17 06	17 40	11 01	11 48	12 29	13 05
35	16 49	17 16	17 48	10 48	11 37	12 21	12 59
30	17 00	17 26	17 55	10 37	11 28	12 14	12 55
20	17 19	17 43	18 10	10 18	11 12	12 01	12 46
N 10	17 36	17 58	18 24	10 02	10 58	11 50	12 39
0	17 52	18 14	18 40	09 46	10 44	11 40	12 32
S 10	18 07	18 30	18 57	09 31	10 31	11 29	12 25
20	18 25	18 49	19 17	09 14	10 17	11 18	12 18
30	18 45	19 11	19 44	08 55	10 00	11 05	12 09
35	18 56	19 25	20 01	08 43	09 50	10 58	12 04
40	19 10	19 42	20 21	08 31	09 39	10 49	11 58
45	19 26	20 02	20 48	08 15	09 26	10 39	11 52
S 50	19 46	20 28	21 26	07 56	09 10	10 27	11 44
52	19 55	20 41	21 47	07 47	09 03	10 21	11 40
54	20 06	20 56	22 16	07 37	08 54	10 15	11 36
56	20 18	21 14	23 03	07 26	08 45	10 08	11 31
58	20 32	21 36	////	07 13	08 34	10 00	11 26
S 60	20 49	22 07	////	06 58	08 22	09 51	11 20

Day	SUN Eqn. of Time 00h	12h	Mer. Pass.	MOON Mer. Pass. Upper	Lower	Age	Phase
d	m s	m s	h m	h m	h m	d %	
27	12 34	12 25	11 48	03 32	16 02	20 77	
28	12 15	12 05	11 48	04 31	16 59	21 67	
29	11 54	11 44	11 48	05 27	17 54	22 56	

UT	ARIES GHA	VENUS GHA	VENUS Dec	MARS GHA	MARS Dec	JUPITER GHA	JUPITER Dec	SATURN GHA	SATURN Dec	STARS Name	SHA	Dec
30 00	68 48.9	221 46.4	S 9 50.9	87 55.5	S 9 21.3	185 52.3	S20 26.6	150 27.1	S22 41.1	Acamar	315 15.2	S40 14.0
01	83 51.4	236 47.6	51.0	102 56.5	20.6	200 54.2	26.7	165 29.3	41.1	Achernar	335 23.6	S57 08.8
02	98 53.9	251 48.8	51.1	117 57.5	19.9	215 56.0	26.8	180 31.4	41.1	Acrux	173 05.4	S63 11.8
03	113 56.3	266 50.0	.. 51.2	132 58.5	.. 19.2	230 57.9	.. 26.9	195 33.6	.. 41.1	Adhara	255 09.3	S28 59.8
04	128 58.8	281 51.2	51.2	147 59.5	18.6	245 59.8	27.0	210 35.8	41.0	Aldebaran	290 44.8	N16 32.7
05	144 01.3	296 52.4	51.3	163 00.5	17.9	261 01.7	27.1	225 38.0	41.0			
06	159 03.7	311 53.6	S 9 51.4	178 01.5	S 9 17.2	276 03.6	S20 27.2	240 40.1	S22 41.0	Alioth	166 17.8	N55 51.4
07	174 06.2	326 54.8	51.5	193 02.4	16.5	291 05.4	27.3	255 42.3	41.0	Alkaid	152 56.4	N49 13.1
08	189 08.7	341 56.0	51.5	208 03.4	15.8	306 07.3	27.4	270 44.5	41.0	Al Na'ir	27 39.2	S46 52.4
F 09	204 11.1	356 57.2	.. 51.6	223 04.4	.. 15.2	321 09.2	.. 27.5	285 46.6	.. 41.0	Alnilam	275 42.3	S 1 11.5
R 10	219 13.6	11 58.4	51.7	238 05.4	14.5	336 11.1	27.7	300 48.8	41.0	Alphard	217 52.4	S 8 44.4
I 11	234 16.0	26 59.6	51.8	253 06.4	13.8	351 13.0	27.8	315 51.0	41.0			
D 12	249 18.5	42 00.8	S 9 51.9	268 07.4	S 9 13.1	6 14.8	S20 27.9	330 53.2	S22 41.0	Alphecca	126 08.3	N26 39.2
A 13	264 21.0	57 02.0	52.0	283 08.4	12.4	21 16.7	28.0	345 55.3	40.9	Alpheratz	357 39.5	N29 11.8
Y 14	279 23.4	72 03.1	52.1	298 09.4	11.8	36 18.6	28.1	0 57.5	40.9	Altair	62 04.9	N 8 55.3
15	294 25.9	87 04.3	.. 52.2	313 10.4	.. 11.1	51 20.5	.. 28.2	15 59.7	.. 40.9	Ankaa	353 11.9	S42 12.5
16	309 28.4	102 05.5	52.3	328 11.4	10.4	66 22.3	28.3	31 01.9	40.9	Antares	112 22.1	S26 28.2
17	324 30.8	117 06.7	52.4	343 12.4	09.7	81 24.2	28.4	46 04.0	40.9			
18	339 33.3	132 07.8	S 9 52.5	358 13.4	S 9 09.0	96 26.1	S20 28.5	61 06.2	S22 40.9	Arcturus	145 52.7	N19 05.2
19	354 35.8	147 09.0	52.6	13 14.3	08.4	111 28.0	28.6	76 08.4	40.9	Atria	107 21.2	S69 03.5
20	9 38.2	162 10.2	52.7	28 15.3	07.7	126 29.9	28.7	91 10.5	40.9	Avior	234 16.1	S59 34.0
21	24 40.7	177 11.3	.. 52.8	43 16.3	.. 07.0	141 31.7	.. 28.8	106 12.7	.. 40.8	Bellatrix	278 27.7	N 6 21.9
22	39 43.2	192 12.5	52.9	58 17.3	06.3	156 33.6	28.9	121 14.9	40.8	Betelgeuse	270 57.0	N 7 24.5
23	54 45.6	207 13.7	53.0	73 18.3	05.6	171 35.5	29.0	136 17.1	40.8			
1 00	69 48.1	222 14.8	S 9 53.1	88 19.3	S 9 05.0	186 37.4	S20 29.1	151 19.2	S22 40.8	Canopus	263 54.0	S52 42.3
01	84 50.5	237 16.0	53.2	103 20.3	04.3	201 39.2	29.2	166 21.4	40.8	Capella	280 28.5	N46 00.8
02	99 53.0	252 17.1	53.3	118 21.3	03.6	216 41.1	29.3	181 23.6	40.8	Deneb	49 29.2	N45 21.2
03	114 55.5	267 18.3	.. 53.4	133 22.3	.. 02.9	231 43.0	.. 29.4	196 25.7	.. 40.8	Denebola	182 30.0	N14 28.0
04	129 57.9	282 19.4	53.5	148 23.3	02.2	246 44.9	29.5	211 27.9	40.8	Diphda	348 52.0	S17 53.2
05	145 00.4	297 20.6	53.6	163 24.2	01.6	261 46.8	29.6	226 30.1	40.7			
06	160 02.9	312 21.7	S 9 53.7	178 25.2	S 9 00.9	276 48.6	S20 29.7	241 32.3	S22 40.7	Dubhe	193 47.3	N61 38.7
07	175 05.3	327 22.8	53.9	193 26.2	9 00.2	291 50.5	29.8	256 34.4	40.7	Elnath	278 07.6	N28 37.2
08	190 07.8	342 24.0	54.0	208 27.2	8 59.5	306 52.4	29.9	271 36.6	40.7	Eltanin	90 44.9	N51 29.4
S 09	205 10.3	357 25.1	.. 54.1	223 28.2	.. 58.8	321 54.3	.. 30.0	286 38.8	.. 40.7	Enif	33 43.6	N 9 57.8
A 10	220 12.7	12 26.2	54.2	238 29.2	58.1	336 56.2	30.1	301 40.9	40.7	Fomalhaut	15 19.9	S29 31.5
T 11	235 15.2	27 27.4	54.3	253 30.2	57.5	351 58.0	30.2	316 43.1	40.7			
U 12	250 17.7	42 28.5	S 9 54.5	268 31.2	S 8 56.8	6 59.9	S20 30.3	331 45.3	S22 40.7	Gacrux	171 57.0	S57 12.7
R 13	265 20.1	57 29.6	54.6	283 32.2	56.1	22 01.8	30.4	346 47.4	40.7	Gienah	175 48.6	S17 38.6
D 14	280 22.6	72 30.7	54.7	298 33.1	55.4	37 03.7	30.5	1 49.6	40.6	Hadar	148 43.1	S60 27.5
A 15	295 25.0	87 31.9	.. 54.8	313 34.1	.. 54.7	52 05.5	.. 30.6	16 51.8	... 40.6	Hamal	327 56.3	N23 33.1
Y 16	310 27.5	102 33.0	55.0	328 35.1	54.0	67 07.4	30.7	31 54.0	40.6	Kaus Aust.	83 39.3	S34 22.4
17	325 30.0	117 34.1	55.1	343 36.1	53.4	82 09.3	30.8	46 56.1	40.6			
18	340 32.4	132 35.2	S 9 55.2	358 37.1	S 8 52.7	97 11.2	S20 30.9	61 58.3	S22 40.6	Kochab	137 21.3	N74 04.7
19	355 34.9	147 36.3	55.4	13 38.1	52.0	112 13.1	31.0	77 00.5	40.6	Markab	13 34.6	N15 18.5
20	10 37.4	162 37.4	55.5	28 39.1	51.3	127 14.9	31.1	92 02.6	40.6	Menkar	314 10.9	N 4 09.7
21	25 39.8	177 38.5	.. 55.6	43 40.1	.. 50.6	142 16.8	.. 31.2	107 04.8	.. 40.6	Menkent	148 03.5	S36 27.4
22	40 42.3	192 39.6	55.8	58 41.1	50.0	157 18.7	31.3	122 07.0	40.5	Miaplacidus	221 38.5	S69 47.4
23	55 44.8	207 40.7	55.9	73 42.0	49.3	172 20.6	31.5	137 09.2	40.5			
2 00	70 47.2	222 41.8	S 9 56.1	88 43.0	S 8 48.6	187 22.4	S20 31.6	152 11.3	S22 40.5	Mirfak	308 34.5	N49 55.6
01	85 49.7	237 42.9	56.2	103 44.0	47.9	202 24.3	31.7	167 13.5	40.5	Nunki	75 54.1	S26 16.3
02	100 52.1	252 44.0	56.3	118 45.0	47.2	217 26.2	31.8	182 15.7	40.5	Peacock	53 13.8	S56 40.6
03	115 54.6	267 45.1	.. 56.5	133 46.0	.. 46.5	232 28.1	.. 31.9	197 17.8	.. 40.5	Pollux	243 23.0	N27 58.6
04	130 57.1	282 46.2	56.6	148 47.0	45.8	247 30.0	32.0	212 20.0	40.5	Procyon	244 55.6	N 5 10.5
05	145 59.5	297 47.3	56.8	163 48.0	45.2	262 31.8	32.1	227 22.2	40.5			
06	161 02.0	312 48.4	S 9 56.9	178 49.0	S 8 44.5	277 33.7	S20 32.2	242 24.3	S22 40.4	Rasalhague	96 03.4	N12 33.0
07	176 04.5	327 49.4	57.1	193 49.9	43.8	292 35.6	32.3	257 26.5	40.4	Regulus	207 39.6	N11 52.5
08	191 06.9	342 50.5	57.2	208 50.9	43.1	307 37.5	32.4	272 28.7	40.4	Rigel	281 08.2	S 8 10.9
S 09	206 09.4	357 51.6	.. 57.4	223 51.9	.. 42.4	322 39.4	.. 32.5	287 30.8	.. 40.4	Rigil Kent.	139 47.3	S60 54.4
U 10	221 11.9	12 52.7	57.5	238 52.9	41.7	337 41.2	32.6	302 33.0	40.4	Sabik	102 08.7	S15 44.7
N 11	236 14.3	27 53.8	57.7	253 53.9	41.1	352 43.1	32.7	317 35.2	40.4			
D 12	251 16.8	42 54.8	S 9 57.9	268 54.9	S 8 40.4	7 45.0	S20 32.8	332 37.4	S22 40.4	Schedar	349 36.0	N56 38.6
A 13	266 19.3	57 55.9	58.0	283 55.9	39.7	22 46.9	32.9	347 39.5	40.4	Shaula	96 17.3	S37 06.9
Y 14	281 21.7	72 57.0	58.2	298 56.9	39.0	37 48.7	33.0	2 41.7	40.3	Sirius	258 30.2	S16 44.6
15	296 24.2	87 58.0	58.3	313 57.8	38.3	52 50.6	33.1	17 43.9	.. 40.3	Spica	158 27.6	S11 15.3
16	311 26.6	102 59.1	58.5	328 58.8	37.6	67 52.5	33.2	32 46.0	40.3	Suhail	222 49.5	S43 30.3
17	326 29.1	118 00.1	58.7	343 59.8	36.9	82 54.4	33.3	47 48.2	40.3			
18	341 31.6	133 01.2	S 9 58.8	359 00.8	S 8 36.3	97 56.3	S20 33.4	62 50.4	S22 40.3	Vega	80 36.8	N38 48.3
19	356 34.1	148 02.2	59.0	14 01.8	35.6	112 58.1	33.5	77 52.5	40.3	Zuben'ubi	137 01.6	S16 06.9
20	11 36.5	163 03.3	59.2	29 02.8	34.9	128 00.0	33.6	92 54.7	40.3			
21	26 39.0	178 04.3	.. 59.3	44 03.8	.. 34.2	143 01.9	.. 33.7	107 56.9	.. 40.3		SHA	Mer. Pass.
22	41 41.4	193 05.4	59.5	59 04.7	33.5	158 03.8	33.8	122 59.0	40.2	Venus	152 26.7	9 10
23	56 43.9	208 06.4	59.7	74 05.7	32.8	173 05.6	33.9	138 01.2	40.2	Mars	18 31.2	18 06
	h m									Jupiter	116 49.3	11 32
Mer. Pass. 19 17.6		v 1.1	d 0.1	v 1.0	d 0.7	v 1.9	d 0.1	v 2.2	d 0.0	Saturn	81 31.1	13 53

UT	SUN GHA	SUN Dec	MOON GHA	v	MOON Dec	d	HP
d h	° ′	° ′	° ′	′	° ′	′	′
30 00	182 53.2	S21 35.5	268 20.6	9.4	N11 46.6	10.9	59.0
01	197 53.0	35.9	282 49.0	9.5	11 35.7	11.0	59.0
02	212 52.8	36.3	297 17.5	9.6	11 24.7	11.1	59.0
03	227 52.5	36.8	311 46.1	9.6	11 13.6	11.0	59.0
04	242 52.3	37.2	326 14.7	9.7	11 02.6	11.2	58.9
05	257 52.1	37.6	340 43.4	9.7	10 51.4	11.2	58.9
06	272 51.9	S21 38.0	355 12.1	9.8	N10 40.2	11.3	58.9
07	287 51.6	38.4	9 40.9	9.9	10 28.9	11.3	58.9
08	302 51.4	38.8	24 09.8	9.9	10 17.6	11.3	58.9
F 09	317 51.2	39.2	38 38.7	10.0	10 06.3	11.5	58.9
R 10	332 50.9	39.6	53 07.7	10.1	9 54.8	11.4	58.8
I 11	347 50.7	40.0	67 36.8	10.1	9 43.4	11.5	58.8
D 12	2 50.5	S21 40.4	82 05.9	10.1	N 9 31.9	11.6	58.8
A 13	17 50.3	40.8	96 35.0	10.2	9 20.3	11.6	58.8
Y 14	32 50.0	41.2	111 04.2	10.3	9 08.7	11.6	58.8
15	47 49.8	41.6	125 33.5	10.3	8 57.1	11.7	58.8
16	62 49.6	42.0	140 02.8	10.4	8 45.4	11.8	58.7
17	77 49.4	42.4	154 32.2	10.4	8 33.6	11.7	58.7
18	92 49.1	S21 42.8	169 01.6	10.5	N 8 21.9	11.8	58.7
19	107 48.9	43.2	183 31.1	10.5	8 10.1	11.9	58.7
20	122 48.7	43.6	198 00.6	10.6	7 58.2	11.9	58.7
21	137 48.4	44.0	212 30.2	10.7	7 46.3	11.9	58.6
22	152 48.2	44.4	226 59.9	10.6	7 34.4	11.9	58.6
23	167 48.0	44.8	241 29.5	10.8	7 22.5	12.0	58.6
1 00	182 47.7	S21 45.2	255 59.3	10.7	N 7 10.5	12.0	58.6
01	197 47.5	45.6	270 29.0	10.9	6 58.5	12.1	58.6
02	212 47.3	46.0	284 58.9	10.8	6 46.4	12.1	58.6
03	227 47.1	46.4	299 28.7	10.9	6 34.3	12.1	58.5
04	242 46.8	46.8	313 58.6	11.0	6 22.2	12.1	58.5
05	257 46.6	47.1	328 28.6	11.0	6 10.1	12.2	58.5
06	272 46.4	S21 47.5	342 58.6	11.1	N 5 57.9	12.2	58.5
07	287 46.1	47.9	357 28.7	11.0	5 45.7	12.2	58.5
S 08	302 45.9	48.3	11 58.7	11.2	5 33.5	12.2	58.5
A 09	317 45.7	48.7	26 28.9	11.1	5 21.3	12.2	58.4
T 10	332 45.4	49.1	40 59.0	11.2	5 09.1	12.3	58.4
U 11	347 45.2	49.5	55 29.2	11.3	4 56.8	12.3	58.4
R 12	2 45.0	S21 49.9	69 59.5	11.3	N 4 44.5	12.3	58.4
D 13	17 44.7	50.2	84 29.8	11.3	4 32.2	12.3	58.4
A 14	32 44.5	50.6	99 00.1	11.4	4 19.9	12.4	58.3
Y 15	47 44.2	51.0	113 30.5	11.4	4 07.5	12.3	58.3
16	62 44.0	51.4	128 00.9	11.4	3 55.2	12.4	58.3
17	77 43.8	51.8	142 31.3	11.4	3 42.8	12.4	58.3
18	92 43.5	S21 52.2	157 01.7	11.5	N 3 30.4	12.4	58.3
19	107 43.3	52.5	171 32.2	11.6	3 18.0	12.4	58.3
20	122 43.1	52.9	186 02.8	11.5	3 05.6	12.4	58.2
21	137 42.8	53.3	200 33.3	11.6	2 53.2	12.4	58.2
22	152 42.6	53.7	215 03.9	11.6	2 40.8	12.4	58.2
23	167 42.4	54.0	229 34.5	11.7	2 28.4	12.5	58.2
2 00	182 42.1	S21 54.4	244 05.2	11.6	N 2 15.9	12.4	58.2
01	197 41.9	54.8	258 35.8	11.7	2 03.5	12.4	58.1
02	212 41.6	55.2	273 06.5	11.8	1 51.1	12.5	58.1
03	227 41.4	55.5	287 37.3	11.7	1 38.6	12.4	58.1
04	242 41.2	55.9	302 08.0	11.8	1 26.2	12.5	58.1
05	257 40.9	56.3	316 38.8	11.8	1 13.7	12.4	58.1
06	272 40.7	S21 56.7	331 09.6	11.8	N 1 01.3	12.4	58.0
07	287 40.4	57.0	345 40.4	11.9	0 48.9	12.5	58.0
S 08	302 40.2	57.4	0 11.3	11.8	0 36.4	12.4	58.0
U 09	317 40.0	57.8	14 42.1	11.9	0 24.0	12.4	58.0
N 10	332 39.7	58.1	29 13.0	11.9	N 0 11.6	12.5	58.0
D 11	347 39.5	58.5	43 43.9	11.9	S 0 00.9	12.4	57.9
A 12	2 39.2	S21 58.9	58 14.8	12.0	S 0 13.3	12.4	57.9
Y 13	17 39.0	59.3	72 45.8	11.9	0 25.7	12.4	57.9
14	32 38.8	21 59.6	87 16.7	12.0	0 38.1	12.4	57.9
15	47 38.5	22 00.0	101 47.7	12.0	0 50.5	12.3	57.9
16	62 38.3	00.3	116 18.7	12.0	1 02.8	12.4	57.9
17	77 38.0	00.7	130 49.7	12.0	1 15.2	12.4	57.8
18	92 37.8	S22 01.1	145 20.7	12.0	S 1 27.6	12.3	57.8
19	107 37.6	01.4	159 51.7	12.1	1 39.9	12.3	57.8
20	122 37.3	01.8	174 22.8	12.0	1 52.2	12.3	57.8
21	137 37.1	02.2	188 53.8	12.1	2 04.5	12.3	57.8
22	152 36.8	02.5	203 24.9	12.1	2 16.8	12.3	57.7
23	167 36.6	02.9	217 56.0	12.0	S 2 29.1	12.2	57.7
SD	16.2	d 0.4	SD 16.0		15.9		15.8

Lat.	Twilight Naut.	Twilight Civil	Sunrise	Moonrise 30	1	2	3
°	h m	h m	h m	h m	h m	h m	h m
N 72	07 51	09 50	▪▪	23 24	25 24	01 24	03 20
N 70	07 34	09 11	▪▪	23 35	25 26	01 26	03 15
68	07 21	08 43	10 36	23 44	25 29	01 29	03 11
66	07 10	08 23	09 46	23 51	25 30	01 30	03 08
64	07 01	08 06	09 16	23 57	25 32	01 32	03 05
62	06 53	07 52	08 53	24 03	00 03	01 33	03 02
60	06 46	07 40	08 35	24 07	00 07	01 34	03 00
N 58	06 39	07 30	08 20	24 11	00 11	01 35	02 58
56	06 33	07 21	08 07	24 15	00 15	01 36	02 56
54	06 28	07 13	07 55	24 18	00 18	01 37	02 55
52	06 23	07 06	07 45	24 21	00 21	01 38	02 53
50	06 18	06 59	07 37	24 24	00 24	01 39	02 52
45	06 08	06 45	07 18	24 29	00 29	01 40	02 49
N 40	05 59	06 32	07 02	24 34	00 34	01 41	02 47
35	05 50	06 22	06 49	24 38	00 38	01 42	02 45
30	05 43	06 12	06 38	24 42	00 42	01 43	02 44
20	05 28	05 55	06 19	24 48	00 48	01 45	02 41
N 10	05 13	05 39	06 01	24 53	00 53	01 46	02 38
0	04 57	05 23	05 45	00 08	00 59	01 48	02 36
S 10	04 40	05 06	05 29	00 16	01 04	01 49	02 33
20	04 19	04 47	05 12	00 25	01 09	01 51	02 31
30	03 52	04 24	04 51	00 36	01 15	01 52	02 28
35	03 35	04 10	04 39	00 42	01 19	01 53	02 27
40	03 13	03 54	04 26	00 49	01 23	01 54	02 25
45	02 46	03 33	04 09	00 57	01 28	01 56	02 23
S 50	02 07	03 06	03 49	01 06	01 33	01 57	02 20
52	01 45	02 53	03 39	01 11	01 36	01 58	02 19
54	01 15	02 38	03 28	01 16	01 38	01 59	02 18
56	00 18	02 19	03 16	01 21	01 41	02 00	02 17
58	////	01 55	03 01	01 27	01 45	02 00	02 15
S 60	////	01 23	02 44	01 34	01 49	02 02	02 14

Lat.	Sunset	Twilight Civil	Twilight Naut.	Moonset 30	1	2	3
°	h m	h m	h m	h m	h m	h m	h m
N 72	▪▪	13 48	15 47	14 32	14 16	14 01	13 47
N 70	▪▪	14 27	16 03	14 19	14 10	14 02	13 54
68	13 02	14 54	16 16	14 08	14 06	14 03	14 01
66	13 51	15 15	16 27	13 59	14 02	14 04	14 04
64	14 22	15 31	16 36	13 51	13 58	14 04	14 10
62	14 45	15 45	16 45	13 45	13 56	14 05	14 14
60	15 03	15 57	16 52	13 39	13 53	14 05	14 18
N 58	15 18	16 07	16 58	13 34	13 51	14 06	14 21
56	15 31	16 16	17 04	13 29	13 49	14 06	14 24
54	15 42	16 25	17 10	13 25	13 47	14 07	14 26
52	15 52	16 32	17 15	13 22	13 45	14 07	14 28
50	16 01	16 39	17 19	13 18	13 44	14 07	14 30
45	16 20	16 53	17 30	13 11	13 40	14 08	14 35
N 40	16 35	17 05	17 39	13 05	13 37	14 08	14 39
35	16 48	17 16	17 47	12 59	13 35	14 09	14 42
30	17 00	17 26	17 55	12 55	13 33	14 09	14 45
20	17 19	17 43	18 10	12 46	13 29	14 10	14 50
N 10	17 37	17 59	18 25	12 39	13 25	14 10	14 54
0	17 53	18 15	18 41	12 32	13 22	14 11	14 59
S 10	18 09	18 32	18 59	12 25	13 19	14 11	15 03
20	18 27	18 51	19 20	12 18	13 15	14 12	15 07
30	18 47	19 14	19 47	12 09	13 11	14 12	15 12
35	18 59	19 28	20 04	12 04	13 09	14 13	15 15
40	19 14	19 45	20 25	11 58	13 06	14 13	15 18
45	19 29	20 06	20 53	11 52	13 03	14 13	15 22
S 50	19 50	20 32	21 33	11 44	12 59	14 14	15 27
52	20 00	20 46	21 55	11 40	12 58	14 14	15 29
54	20 11	21 02	22 26	11 36	12 56	14 14	15 31
56	20 23	21 21	23 31	11 31	12 54	14 14	15 34
58	20 38	21 44	////	11 26	12 51	14 15	15 37
S 60	20 56	22 18	////	11 20	12 49	14 15	15 40

Day	SUN Eqn. of Time 00ʰ	SUN Eqn. of Time 12ʰ	Mer. Pass.	MOON Mer. Pass. Upper	MOON Mer. Pass. Lower	Age	Phase
d	m s	m s	h m	h m	h m	d	%
30	11 33	11 22	11 49	06 20	18 45	23	45
1	11 11	11 00	11 49	07 10	19 35	24	34
2	10 49	10 37	11 49	07 59	20 23	25	24

UT	ARIES	VENUS −4·9		MARS +0·0		JUPITER −1·7		SATURN +0·5		STARS		
	GHA	GHA	Dec	GHA	Dec	GHA	Dec	GHA	Dec	Name	SHA	Dec
d h	° ′	° ′	° ′	° ′	° ′	° ′	° ′	° ′	° ′		° ′	° ′
3 00	71 46.4	223 07.5	S 9 59.8	89 06.7	S 8 32.1	188 07.5	S20 34.0	153 03.4	S22 40.2	Acamar	315 15.2	S40 14.0
01	86 48.8	238 08.5	10 00.0	104 07.7	31.5	203 09.4	34.1	168 05.5	40.2	Achernar	335 23.6	S57 08.8
02	101 51.3	253 09.6	00.2	119 08.7	30.8	218 11.3	34.2	183 07.7	40.2	Acrux	173 05.4	S63 11.8
03	116 53.7	268 10.6 ..	00.4	134 09.7 ..	30.1	233 13.2 ..	34.3	198 09.9 ..	40.2	Adhara	255 09.3	S28 59.9
04	131 56.2	283 11.6	00.6	149 10.7	29.4	248 15.0	34.4	213 12.0	40.2	Aldebaran	290 44.8	N16 32.7
05	146 58.7	298 12.7	00.7	164 11.6	28.7	263 16.9	34.5	228 14.2	40.2			
06	162 01.1	313 13.7	S10 00.9	179 12.6	S 8 28.0	278 18.8	S20 34.6	243 16.4	S22 40.1	Alioth	166 17.8	N55 51.3
07	177 03.6	328 14.7	01.1	194 13.6	27.3	293 20.7	34.7	258 18.6	40.1	Alkaid	152 56.4	N49 13.1
08	192 06.1	343 15.7	01.3	209 14.6	26.7	308 22.5	34.8	273 20.7	40.1	Al Na'ir	27 39.2	S46 52.4
M 09	207 08.5	358 16.8 ..	01.5	224 15.6 ..	26.0	323 24.4 ..	34.9	288 22.9 ..	40.1	Alnilam	275 42.3	S 1 11.5
O 10	222 11.0	13 17.8	01.7	239 16.6	25.3	338 26.3	35.0	303 25.1	40.1	Alphard	217 52.3	S 8 44.4
N 11	237 13.5	28 18.8	01.8	254 17.6	24.6	353 28.2	35.1	318 27.2	40.1			
D 12	252 15.9	43 19.8	S10 02.0	269 18.5	S 8 23.9	8 30.1	S20 35.2	333 29.4	S22 40.1	Alphecca	126 08.2	N26 39.2
A 13	267 18.4	58 20.8	02.2	284 19.5	23.2	23 31.9	35.3	348 31.6	40.1	Alpheratz	357 39.5	N29 11.8
Y 14	282 20.9	73 21.8	02.4	299 20.5	22.5	38 33.8	35.4	3 33.7	40.0	Altair	62 04.9	N 8 55.3
15	297 23.3	88 22.8 ..	02.6	314 21.5 ..	21.8	53 35.7 ..	35.5	18 35.9 ..	40.0	Ankaa	353 11.9	S42 12.5
16	312 25.8	103 23.9	02.8	329 22.5	21.2	68 37.6	35.6	33 38.1	40.0	Antares	112 22.1	S26 28.2
17	327 28.2	118 24.9	03.0	344 23.5	20.5	83 39.5	35.7	48 40.2	40.0			
18	342 30.7	133 25.9	S10 03.2	359 24.5	S 8 19.8	98 41.3	S20 35.8	63 42.4	S22 40.0	Arcturus	145 52.7	N19 05.2
19	357 33.2	148 26.9	03.4	14 25.4	19.1	113 43.2	35.9	78 44.6	40.0	Atria	107 21.1	S69 03.5
20	12 35.6	163 27.9	03.6	29 26.4	18.4	128 45.1	36.0	93 46.7	40.0	Avior	234 16.1	S59 34.0
21	27 38.1	178 28.8 ..	03.8	44 27.4 ..	17.7	143 47.0 ..	36.1	108 48.9 ..	39.9	Bellatrix	278 27.7	N 6 21.9
22	42 40.6	193 29.8	04.0	59 28.4	17.0	158 48.8	36.2	123 51.1	39.9	Betelgeuse	270 57.0	N 7 24.5
23	57 43.0	208 30.8	04.2	74 29.4	16.3	173 50.7	36.3	138 53.2	39.9			
4 00	72 45.5	223 31.8	S10 04.4	89 30.4	S 8 15.6	188 52.6	S20 36.4	153 55.4	S22 39.9	Canopus	263 54.0	S52 42.3
01	87 48.0	238 32.8	04.6	104 31.3	15.0	203 54.5	36.5	168 57.6	39.9	Capella	280 28.5	N46 00.8
02	102 50.4	253 33.8	04.8	119 32.3	14.3	218 56.4	36.6	183 59.7	39.9	Deneb	49 29.2	N45 21.1
03	117 52.9	268 34.8 ..	05.0	134 33.3 ..	13.6	233 58.2 ..	36.7	199 01.9 ..	39.9	Denebola	182 30.0	N14 28.0
04	132 55.4	283 35.8	05.2	149 34.3	12.9	249 00.1	36.8	214 04.1	39.9	Diphda	348 52.0	S17 53.2
05	147 57.8	298 36.7	05.5	164 35.3	12.2	264 02.0	36.9	229 06.2	39.8			
06	163 00.3	313 37.7	S10 05.7	179 36.3	S 8 11.5	279 03.9	S20 37.0	244 08.4	S22 39.8	Dubhe	193 47.3	N61 38.7
07	178 02.7	328 38.7	05.9	194 37.2	10.8	294 05.7	37.1	259 10.6	39.8	Elnath	278 07.6	N28 37.2
T 08	193 05.2	343 39.7	06.1	209 38.2	10.1	309 07.6	37.2	274 12.7	39.8	Eltanin	90 45.0	N51 29.4
U 09	208 07.7	358 40.6 ..	06.3	224 39.2 ..	09.4	324 09.5 ..	37.3	289 14.9 ..	39.8	Enif	33 43.6	N 9 57.8
E 10	223 10.1	13 41.6	06.5	239 40.2	08.8	339 11.4	37.4	304 17.1	39.8	Fomalhaut	15 19.9	S29 31.5
S 11	238 12.6	28 42.6	06.8	254 41.2	08.1	354 13.3	37.5	319 19.2	39.8			
D 12	253 15.1	43 43.5	S10 07.0	269 42.2	S 8 07.4	9 15.1	S20 37.6	334 21.4	S22 39.8	Gacrux	171 57.0	S57 12.7
A 13	268 17.5	58 44.5	07.2	284 43.1	06.7	24 17.0	37.7	349 23.6	39.7	Gienah	175 48.6	S17 38.6
Y 14	283 20.0	73 45.4	07.4	299 44.1	06.0	39 18.9	37.8	4 25.7	39.7	Hadar	148 43.1	S60 27.4
15	298 22.5	88 46.4 ..	07.6	314 45.1 ..	05.3	54 20.8 ..	37.9	19 27.9 ..	39.7	Hamal	327 56.3	N23 33.1
16	313 24.9	103 47.3	07.9	329 46.1	04.6	69 22.6	38.0	34 30.1	39.7	Kaus Aust.	83 39.3	S34 22.4
17	328 27.4	118 48.3	08.1	344 47.1	03.9	84 24.5	38.1	49 32.2	39.7			
18	343 29.8	133 49.2	S10 08.3	359 48.1	S 8 03.2	99 26.4	S20 38.2	64 34.4	S22 39.7	Kochab	137 21.2	N74 04.7
19	358 32.3	148 50.2	08.6	14 49.0	02.5	114 28.3	38.3	79 36.5	39.7	Markab	13 34.6	N15 18.5
20	13 34.8	163 51.1	08.8	29 50.0	01.9	129 30.2	38.4	94 38.7	39.6	Menkar	314 10.9	N 4 09.7
21	28 37.2	178 52.1 ..	09.0	44 51.0 ..	01.2	144 32.0 ..	38.5	109 40.9 ..	39.6	Menkent	148 03.5	S36 27.4
22	43 39.7	193 53.0	09.2	59 52.0	8 00.5	159 33.9	38.6	124 43.0	39.6	Miaplacidus	221 38.5	S69 47.4
23	58 42.2	208 54.0	09.5	74 53.0	7 59.8	174 35.8	38.7	139 45.2	39.6			
5 00	73 44.6	223 54.9	S10 09.7	89 54.0	S 7 59.1	189 37.7	S20 38.8	154 47.4	S22 39.6	Mirfak	308 34.5	N49 55.6
01	88 47.1	238 55.8	10.0	104 54.9	58.4	204 39.6	38.9	169 49.5	39.6	Nunki	75 54.1	S26 16.3
02	103 49.6	253 56.8	10.2	119 55.9	57.7	219 41.4	39.0	184 51.7	39.6	Peacock	53 13.8	S56 40.6
03	118 52.0	268 57.7 ..	10.4	134 56.9 ..	57.0	234 43.3 ..	39.1	199 53.9 ..	39.5	Pollux	243 23.0	N27 58.6
04	133 54.5	283 58.6	10.7	149 57.9	56.3	249 45.2	39.2	214 56.0	39.5	Procyon	244 55.6	N 5 10.5
05	148 57.0	298 59.5	10.9	164 58.9	55.6	264 47.1	39.3	229 58.2	39.5			
06	163 59.4	314 00.5	S10 11.2	179 59.9	S 7 54.9	279 48.9	S20 39.4	245 00.4	S22 39.5	Rasalhague	96 03.4	N12 33.0
W 07	179 01.9	329 01.4	11.4	195 00.8	54.3	294 50.8	39.5	260 02.5	39.5	Regulus	207 39.5	N11 52.5
E 08	194 04.3	344 02.3	11.6	210 01.8	53.6	309 52.7	39.6	275 04.7	39.5	Rigel	281 08.2	S 8 10.9
D 09	209 06.8	359 03.2 ..	11.9	225 02.8 ..	52.9	324 54.6 ..	39.7	290 06.9 ..	39.5	Rigil Kent.	139 47.3	S60 54.4
N 10	224 09.3	14 04.1	12.1	240 03.8	52.2	339 56.5	39.8	305 09.0	39.5	Sabik	102 08.7	S15 44.7
E 11	239 11.7	29 05.1	12.4	255 04.8	51.5	354 58.3	39.9	320 11.2	39.4			
S 12	254 14.2	44 06.0	S10 12.6	270 05.7	S 7 50.8	10 00.2	S20 40.0	335 13.4	S22 39.4	Schedar	349 36.0	N56 38.6
S 13	269 16.7	59 06.9	12.9	285 06.7	50.1	25 02.1	40.1	350 15.5	39.4	Shaula	96 17.3	S37 06.9
D 14	284 19.1	74 07.8	13.1	300 07.7	49.4	40 04.0	40.2	5 17.7	39.4	Sirius	258 30.2	S16 44.6
A 15	299 21.6	89 08.7 ..	13.4	315 08.7 ..	48.7	55 05.8 ..	40.3	20 19.8 ..	39.4	Spica	158 27.6	S11 15.4
Y 16	314 24.1	104 09.6	13.6	330 09.7	48.0	70 07.7	40.4	35 22.0	39.4	Suhail	222 49.5	S43 30.3
17	329 26.5	119 10.5	13.9	345 10.6	47.3	85 09.6	40.5	50 24.2	39.4			
18	344 29.0	134 11.4	S10 14.2	0 11.6	S 7 46.6	100 11.5	S20 40.6	65 26.3	S22 39.3	Vega	80 36.9	N38 48.3
19	359 31.5	149 12.3	14.4	15 12.6	45.9	115 13.4	40.7	80 28.5	39.3	Zuben'ubi	137 01.6	S16 06.9
20	14 33.9	164 13.2	14.7	30 13.6	45.3	130 15.2	40.8	95 30.7	39.3		SHA	Mer.Pass.
21	29 36.4	179 14.1 ..	14.9	45 14.6 ..	44.6	145 17.1 ..	40.9	110 32.8 ..	39.3		° ′	h m
22	44 38.8	194 15.0	15.2	60 15.5	43.9	160 19.0	41.0	125 35.0	39.3	Venus	150 46.3	9 05
23	59 41.3	209 15.9	15.5	75 16.5	43.2	175 20.9	41.1	140 37.2	39.3	Mars	16 44.9	18 01
	h m									Jupiter	116 07.1	11 23
Mer. Pass. 19 05.8		v 1.0 d 0.2		v 1.0 d 0.7		v 1.9 d 0.1		v 2.2 d 0.0		Saturn	81 09.9	13 42

UT	SUN GHA	SUN Dec	MOON GHA	v	Dec	d	HP
d h	° ′	° ′	° ′	′	° ′	′	′
3 00	182 36.3	S22 03.2	232 27.0	12.1	S 2 41.3	12.2	57.7
01	197 36.1	03.6	246 58.1	12.1	2 53.5	12.2	57.7
02	212 35.8	04.0	261 29.2	12.1	3 05.7	12.2	57.7
03	227 35.6	.. 04.3	276 00.3	12.1	3 17.9	12.2	57.6
04	242 35.4	04.7	290 31.4	12.1	3 30.1	12.1	57.6
05	257 35.1	05.0	305 02.5	12.2	3 42.2	12.1	57.6
06	272 34.9	S22 05.4	319 33.7	12.1	S 3 54.3	12.1	57.6
07	287 34.6	05.7	334 04.8	12.1	4 06.4	12.1	57.6
M 08	302 34.4	06.1	348 35.9	12.1	4 18.5	12.0	57.5
O 09	317 34.1	.. 06.4	3 07.0	12.2	4 30.5	12.0	57.5
N 10	332 33.9	06.8	17 38.2	12.1	4 42.5	12.0	57.5
D 11	347 33.6	07.1	32 09.3	12.1	4 54.5	11.9	57.5
A 12	2 33.4	S22 07.5	46 40.4	12.2	S 5 06.4	11.9	57.5
Y 13	17 33.1	07.8	61 11.6	12.1	5 18.3	11.9	57.4
14	32 32.9	08.2	75 42.7	12.1	5 30.2	11.8	57.4
15	47 32.6	.. 08.5	90 13.8	12.1	5 42.0	11.8	57.4
16	62 32.4	08.9	104 44.9	12.2	5 53.8	11.8	57.4
17	77 32.1	09.2	119 16.1	12.1	6 05.6	11.7	57.4
18	92 31.9	S22 09.6	133 47.2	12.1	S 6 17.3	11.7	57.3
19	107 31.6	09.9	148 18.3	12.1	6 29.0	11.7	57.3
20	122 31.4	10.3	162 49.4	12.1	6 40.7	11.6	57.3
21	137 31.1	.. 10.6	177 20.5	12.1	6 52.3	11.5	57.3
22	152 30.9	11.0	191 51.6	12.1	7 03.8	11.6	57.3
23	167 30.6	11.3	206 22.7	12.1	7 15.4	11.5	57.2
4 00	182 30.4	S22 11.6	220 53.8	12.0	S 7 26.9	11.4	57.2
01	197 30.1	12.0	235 24.8	12.1	7 38.3	11.4	57.2
02	212 29.9	12.3	249 55.9	12.1	7 49.7	11.4	57.2
03	227 29.6	.. 12.7	264 27.0	12.0	8 01.1	11.3	57.2
04	242 29.4	13.0	278 58.0	12.0	8 12.4	11.2	57.1
05	257 29.1	13.3	293 29.0	12.1	8 23.6	11.2	57.1
06	272 28.9	S22 13.7	308 00.1	12.0	S 8 34.8	11.2	57.1
07	287 28.6	14.0	322 31.1	12.0	8 46.0	11.1	57.1
T 08	302 28.4	14.3	337 02.1	12.0	8 57.1	11.1	57.1
U 09	317 28.1	.. 14.7	351 33.1	11.9	9 08.2	11.0	57.0
E 10	332 27.9	15.0	6 04.0	12.0	9 19.2	10.9	57.0
S 11	347 27.6	15.3	20 35.0	11.9	9 30.1	11.0	57.0
D 12	2 27.4	S22 15.7	35 05.9	12.0	S 9 41.1	10.8	57.0
A 13	17 27.1	16.0	49 36.9	11.9	9 51.9	10.8	57.0
Y 14	32 26.9	16.3	64 07.8	11.9	10 02.7	10.7	56.9
15	47 26.6	.. 16.7	78 38.7	11.9	10 13.4	10.7	56.9
16	62 26.3	17.0	93 09.6	11.9	10 24.1	10.6	56.9
17	77 26.1	17.3	107 40.5	11.8	10 34.7	10.6	56.9
18	92 25.8	S22 17.7	122 11.3	11.9	S10 45.3	10.5	56.9
19	107 25.6	18.0	136 42.2	11.8	10 55.8	10.5	56.8
20	122 25.3	18.3	151 13.0	11.8	11 06.3	10.3	56.8
21	137 25.1	.. 18.6	165 43.8	11.8	11 16.6	10.4	56.8
22	152 24.8	19.0	180 14.6	11.8	11 27.0	10.2	56.8
23	167 24.6	19.3	194 45.4	11.7	11 37.2	10.2	56.8
5 00	182 24.3	S22 19.6	209 16.1	11.7	S11 47.4	10.1	56.7
01	197 24.0	19.9	223 46.8	11.7	11 57.5	10.1	56.7
02	212 23.8	20.2	238 17.5	11.7	12 07.6	10.0	56.7
03	227 23.5	.. 20.6	252 48.2	11.7	12 17.6	9.9	56.7
04	242 23.3	20.9	267 18.9	11.7	12 27.5	9.8	56.7
05	257 23.0	21.2	281 49.6	11.6	12 37.4	9.8	56.6
06	272 22.7	S22 21.5	296 20.2	11.6	S12 47.2	9.7	56.6
07	287 22.5	21.8	310 50.8	11.6	12 56.9	9.7	56.6
W 08	302 22.2	22.2	325 21.4	11.6	13 06.6	9.5	56.6
E 09	317 22.0	.. 22.5	339 52.0	11.5	13 16.1	9.5	56.6
D 10	332 21.7	22.8	354 22.5	11.6	13 25.6	9.5	56.5
N 11	347 21.5	23.1	8 53.1	11.5	13 35.1	9.3	56.5
E 12	2 21.2	S22 23.4	23 23.6	11.5	S13 44.4	9.3	56.5
S 13	17 20.9	23.7	37 54.1	11.4	13 53.7	9.2	56.5
D 14	32 20.7	24.1	52 24.5	11.5	14 02.9	9.2	56.5
A 15	47 20.4	.. 24.4	66 55.0	11.4	14 12.1	9.0	56.4
Y 16	62 20.2	24.7	81 25.4	11.4	14 21.1	9.0	56.4
17	77 19.9	25.0	95 55.8	11.4	14 30.1	8.9	56.4
18	92 19.6	S22 25.3	110 26.2	11.4	S14 39.0	8.9	56.4
19	107 19.4	25.6	124 56.6	11.3	14 47.9	8.7	56.4
20	122 19.1	25.9	139 26.9	11.3	14 56.6	8.7	56.3
21	137 18.8	.. 26.2	153 57.2	11.3	15 05.3	8.5	56.3
22	152 18.6	26.5	168 27.5	11.3	15 13.8	8.6	56.3
23	167 18.3	26.8	182 57.8	11.2	S15 22.4	8.4	56.3
	SD 16.3	d 0.3	SD 15.7		15.5		15.4

Twilight / Moonrise

Lat.	Naut.	Civil	Sunrise	Moonrise 3	4	5	6
°	h m	h m	h m	h m	h m	h m	h m
N 72	07 59	10 03	▬	03 20	05 17	07 21	09 48
N 70	07 41	09 20	▬	03 15	05 04	06 55	08 52
68	07 27	08 51	10 55	03 11	04 53	06 35	08 19
66	07 16	08 30	09 57	03 08	04 44	06 20	07 55
64	07 06	08 12	09 24	03 05	04 36	06 07	07 37
62	06 58	07 58	09 00	03 02	04 30	05 57	07 21
60	06 50	07 45	08 41	03 00	04 24	05 48	07 09
N 58	06 43	07 35	08 25	02 58	04 20	05 40	06 58
56	06 37	07 25	08 11	02 56	04 15	05 33	06 48
54	06 32	07 17	08 00	02 55	04 11	05 27	06 40
52	06 27	07 10	07 50	02 53	04 08	05 21	06 32
50	06 22	07 03	07 40	02 52	04 05	05 16	06 26
45	06 11	06 48	07 21	02 49	03 58	05 05	06 11
N 40	06 01	06 35	07 05	02 47	03 52	04 57	06 00
35	05 53	06 24	06 52	02 45	03 47	04 49	05 50
30	05 45	06 14	06 40	02 44	03 43	04 42	05 41
20	05 29	05 57	06 20	02 41	03 36	04 31	05 26
N 10	05 14	05 40	06 03	02 38	03 29	04 21	05 13
0	04 58	05 24	05 46	02 36	03 23	04 12	05 01
S 10	04 40	05 07	05 30	02 33	03 18	04 02	04 48
20	04 19	04 48	05 12	02 31	03 11	03 53	04 36
30	03 51	04 24	04 51	02 28	03 04	03 42	04 21
35	03 34	04 10	04 39	02 27	03 00	03 35	04 12
40	03 12	03 53	04 25	02 25	02 56	03 28	04 03
45	02 44	03 32	04 08	02 23	02 50	03 20	03 52
S 50	02 03	03 04	03 47	02 20	02 44	03 10	03 38
52	01 40	02 50	03 37	02 19	02 41	03 05	03 32
54	01 07	02 34	03 26	02 18	02 38	03 00	03 25
56	////	02 15	03 13	02 17	02 35	02 54	03 17
58	////	01 50	02 58	02 15	02 31	02 48	03 09
S 60	////	01 15	02 40	02 14	02 26	02 41	02 59

Sunset / Twilight / Moonset

Lat.	Sunset	Civil	Naut.	Moonset 3	4	5	6
°	h m	h m	h m	h m	h m	h m	h m
N 72	▬	13 36	15 41	13 47	13 30	13 07	12 24
N 70	▬	14 20	15 58	13 54	13 45	13 35	13 20
68	12 45	14 48	16 12	14 01	13 58	13 56	13 20
66	13 43	15 10	16 24	14 06	14 08	14 12	14 19
64	14 16	15 28	16 34	14 10	14 17	14 26	14 38
62	14 40	15 42	16 42	14 14	14 25	14 37	14 54
60	14 59	15 54	16 50	14 18	14 31	14 47	15 07
N 58	15 15	16 05	16 57	14 21	14 37	14 56	15 19
56	15 29	16 15	17 03	14 24	14 42	15 03	15 29
54	15 40	16 23	17 08	14 26	14 47	15 10	15 37
52	15 51	16 30	17 13	14 28	14 51	15 16	15 45
50	16 00	16 37	17 18	14 30	14 55	15 22	15 52
45	16 19	16 52	17 29	14 35	15 03	15 34	16 08
N 40	16 35	17 05	17 39	14 39	15 10	15 44	16 20
35	16 48	17 16	17 47	14 42	15 16	15 52	16 31
30	17 00	17 26	17 55	14 45	15 21	16 00	16 43
20	17 20	17 44	18 11	14 50	15 31	16 13	16 57
N 10	17 37	18 00	18 26	14 54	15 39	16 24	17 11
0	17 54	18 16	18 42	14 59	15 46	16 35	17 24
S 10	18 11	18 33	19 00	15 03	15 54	16 46	17 38
20	18 28	18 53	19 22	15 07	16 02	16 57	17 52
30	18 49	19 16	19 49	15 12	16 12	17 10	18 09
35	19 02	19 31	20 07	15 15	16 17	17 18	18 18
40	19 17	19 48	20 29	15 18	16 23	17 27	18 29
45	19 33	20 09	20 57	15 22	16 30	17 37	18 42
S 50	19 54	20 37	21 38	15 27	16 39	17 50	18 58
52	20 04	20 51	22 02	15 29	16 43	17 55	19 05
54	20 16	21 07	22 36	15 31	16 47	18 02	19 13
56	20 28	21 27	////	15 34	16 52	18 09	19 23
58	20 44	21 52	////	15 37	16 58	18 17	19 33
S 60	21 02	22 29	////	15 40	17 04	18 26	19 45

SUN / MOON

Day	Eqn. of Time 00h	12h	Mer. Pass.	Mer. Pass. Upper	Lower	Age	Phase
d	m s	m s	h m	h m	h m	d	%
3	10 26	10 14	11 50	08 47	21 11	26	15
4	10 02	09 50	11 50	09 35	21 59	27	8
5	09 38	09 25	11 51	10 23	22 48	28	4

UT	ARIES GHA	VENUS −4·8 GHA	Dec	MARS +0·1 GHA	Dec	JUPITER −1·7 GHA	Dec	SATURN +0·5 GHA	Dec	STARS Name	SHA	Dec
d h	° ′	° ′	° ′	° ′	° ′	° ′	° ′	° ′	° ′		° ′	° ′
6 00	74 43.8	224 16.8	S10 15.7	90 17.5	S 7 42.5	190 22.8	S20 41.2	155 39.3	S22 39.3	Acamar	315 15.2	S40 14.0
01	89 46.2	239 17.6	16.0	105 18.5	41.8	205 24.6	41.3	170 41.5	39.3	Achernar	335 23.7	S57 08.8
02	104 48.7	254 18.5	16.3	120 19.5	41.1	220 26.5	41.4	185 43.7	39.2	Acrux	173 05.3	S63 11.8
03	119 51.2	269 19.4 ..	16.5	135 20.5 ..	40.4	235 28.4 ..	41.5	200 45.8 ..	39.2	Adhara	255 09.3	S28 59.9
04	134 53.6	284 20.3	16.8	150 21.4	39.7	250 30.3	41.6	215 48.0	39.2	Aldebaran	290 44.8	N16 32.7
05	149 56.1	299 21.2	17.1	165 22.4	39.0	265 32.1	41.7	230 50.1	39.2			
06	164 58.6	314 22.0	S10 17.3	180 23.4	S 7 38.3	280 34.0	S20 41.8	245 52.3	S22 39.2	Alioth	166 17.7	N55 51.3
07	180 01.0	329 22.9	17.6	195 24.4	37.6	295 35.9	41.9	260 54.5	39.2	Alkaid	152 56.3	N49 13.1
T 08	195 03.5	344 23.8	17.9	210 25.4	36.9	310 37.8	42.0	275 56.6	39.2	Al Na'ir	27 39.2	S46 52.4
H 09	210 06.0	359 24.6 ..	18.2	225 26.3 ..	36.2	325 39.7 ..	42.0	290 58.8 ..	39.1	Alnilam	275 42.3	S 1 11.5
U 10	225 08.4	14 25.5	18.4	240 27.3	35.5	340 41.5	42.1	306 01.0	39.1	Alphard	217 52.3	S 8 44.4
R 11	240 10.9	29 26.4	18.7	255 28.3	34.8	355 43.4	42.2	321 03.1	39.1			
S 12	255 13.3	44 27.2	S10 19.0	270 29.3	S 7 34.1	10 45.3	S20 42.3	336 05.3	S22 39.1	Alphecca	126 08.2	N26 39.2
D 13	270 15.8	59 28.1	19.3	285 30.2	33.5	25 47.2	42.4	351 07.4	39.1	Alpheratz	357 39.5	N29 11.8
A 14	285 18.3	74 29.0	19.5	300 31.2	32.8	40 49.0	42.5	6 09.6	39.1	Altair	62 04.9	N 8 55.3
Y 15	300 20.7	89 29.8 ..	19.8	315 32.2 ..	32.1	55 50.9 ..	42.6	21 11.8 ..	39.1	Ankaa	353 11.9	S42 12.5
16	315 23.2	104 30.7	20.1	330 33.2	31.4	70 52.8	42.7	36 13.9	39.0	Antares	112 22.1	S26 28.2
17	330 25.7	119 31.5	20.4	345 34.2	30.7	85 54.7	42.8	51 16.1	39.0			
18	345 28.1	134 32.4	S10 20.7	0 35.1	S 7 30.0	100 56.6	S20 42.9	66 18.3	S22 39.0	Arcturus	145 52.6	N19 05.2
19	0 30.6	149 33.2	21.0	15 36.1	29.3	115 58.4	43.0	81 20.4	39.0	Atria	107 21.1	S69 03.4
20	15 33.1	164 34.1	21.2	30 37.1	28.6	131 00.3	43.1	96 22.6	39.0	Avior	234 16.1	S59 34.0
21	30 35.5	179 34.9 ..	21.5	45 38.1 ..	27.9	146 02.2 ..	43.2	111 24.7 ..	39.0	Bellatrix	278 27.7	N 6 21.9
22	45 38.0	194 35.8	21.8	60 39.1	27.2	161 04.1	43.3	126 26.9	39.0	Betelgeuse	270 57.0	N 7 24.5
23	60 40.4	209 36.6	22.1	75 40.0	26.5	176 06.0	43.4	141 29.1	38.9			
7 00	75 42.9	224 37.4	S10 22.4	90 41.0	S 7 25.8	191 07.8	S20 43.5	156 31.2	S22 38.9	Canopus	263 54.0	S52 42.4
01	90 45.4	239 38.3	22.7	105 42.0	25.1	206 09.7	43.6	171 33.4	38.9	Capella	280 28.5	N46 00.8
02	105 47.8	254 39.1	23.0	120 43.0	24.4	221 11.6	43.7	186 35.6	38.9	Deneb	49 29.2	N45 21.1
03	120 50.3	269 39.9 ..	23.3	135 44.0 ..	23.7	236 13.5 ..	43.8	201 37.7 ..	38.9	Denebola	182 30.0	N14 28.0
04	135 52.8	284 40.8	23.6	150 44.9	23.0	251 15.3	43.9	216 39.9	38.9	Diphda	348 52.0	S17 53.2
05	150 55.2	299 41.6	23.9	165 45.9	22.3	266 17.2	44.0	231 42.0	38.9			
06	165 57.7	314 42.4	S10 24.2	180 46.9	S 7 21.6	281 19.1	S20 44.1	246 44.2	S22 38.9	Dubhe	193 47.2	N61 38.7
07	181 00.2	329 43.3	24.5	195 47.9	20.9	296 21.0	44.2	261 46.4	38.8	Elnath	278 07.5	N28 37.2
08	196 02.6	344 44.1	24.8	210 48.8	20.2	311 22.9	44.3	276 48.5	38.8	Eltanin	90 45.0	N51 29.4
F 09	211 05.1	359 44.9 ..	25.1	225 49.8 ..	19.5	326 24.7 ..	44.4	291 50.7 ..	38.8	Enif	33 43.6	N 9 57.8
R 10	226 07.6	14 45.7	25.4	240 50.8	18.8	341 26.6	44.5	306 52.9	38.8	Fomalhaut	15 19.9	S29 31.5
I 11	241 10.0	29 46.5	25.7	255 51.8	18.1	356 28.5	44.6	321 55.0	38.8			
D 12	256 12.5	44 47.4	S10 26.0	270 52.8	S 7 17.5	11 30.4	S20 44.7	336 57.2	S22 38.8	Gacrux	171 57.0	S57 12.7
A 13	271 14.9	59 48.2	26.3	285 53.7	16.8	26 32.3	44.8	351 59.3	38.8	Gienah	175 48.6	S17 38.6
Y 14	286 17.4	74 49.0	26.6	300 54.7	16.1	41 34.1	44.9	7 01.5	38.7	Hadar	148 43.1	S60 27.4
15	301 19.9	89 49.8 ..	26.9	315 55.7 ..	15.4	56 36.0 ..	45.0	22 03.7 ..	38.7	Hamal	327 56.3	N23 33.1
16	316 22.3	104 50.6	27.2	330 56.7	14.7	71 37.9	45.1	37 05.8	38.7	Kaus Aust.	83 39.3	S34 22.4
17	331 24.8	119 51.4	27.5	345 57.6	14.0	86 39.8	45.2	52 08.0	38.7			
18	346 27.3	134 52.2	S10 27.8	0 58.6	S 7 13.3	101 41.6	S20 45.3	67 10.1	S22 38.7	Kochab	137 21.2	N74 04.6
19	1 29.7	149 53.0	28.1	15 59.6	12.6	116 43.5	45.4	82 12.3	38.7	Markab	13 34.6	N15 18.5
20	16 32.2	164 53.8	28.5	31 00.6	11.9	131 45.4	45.5	97 14.5	38.7	Menkar	314 10.9	N 4 09.7
21	31 34.7	179 54.6 ..	28.8	46 01.6 ..	11.2	146 47.3 ..	45.5	112 16.6 ..	38.6	Menkent	148 03.5	S36 27.4
22	46 37.1	194 55.4	29.1	61 02.5	10.5	161 49.2	45.6	127 18.8	38.6	Miaplacidus	221 38.4	S69 47.4
23	61 39.6	209 56.2	29.4	76 03.5	09.8	176 51.0	45.7	142 21.0	38.6			
8 00	76 42.1	224 57.0	S10 29.7	91 04.5	S 7 09.1	191 52.9	S20 45.8	157 23.1	S22 38.6	Mirfak	308 34.5	N49 55.6
01	91 44.5	239 57.8	30.0	106 05.5	08.4	206 54.8	45.9	172 25.3	38.6	Nunki	75 54.1	S26 16.3
02	106 47.0	254 58.6	30.3	121 06.4	07.7	221 56.7	46.0	187 27.4	38.6	Peacock	53 13.9	S56 40.6
03	121 49.4	269 59.4 ..	30.7	136 07.4 ..	07.0	236 58.6 ..	46.1	202 29.6 ..	38.6	Pollux	243 22.9	N27 58.6
04	136 51.9	285 00.1	31.0	151 08.4	06.3	252 00.4	46.2	217 31.8	38.5	Procyon	244 55.6	N 5 10.5
05	151 54.4	300 00.9	31.3	166 09.4	05.6	267 02.3	46.3	232 33.9	38.5			
06	166 56.8	315 01.7	S10 31.6	181 10.3	S 7 04.9	282 04.2	S20 46.4	247 36.1	S22 38.5	Rasalhague	96 03.4	N12 33.0
07	181 59.3	330 02.5	32.0	196 11.3	04.2	297 06.1	46.5	262 38.2	38.5	Regulus	207 39.5	N11 52.5
S 08	197 01.8	345 03.3	32.3	211 12.3	03.5	312 08.0	46.6	277 40.4	38.5	Rigel	281 08.2	S 8 10.9
A 09	212 04.2	0 04.0 ..	32.6	226 13.3 ..	02.8	327 09.8 ..	46.7	292 42.6 ..	38.5	Rigil Kent.	139 47.2	S60 54.4
T 10	227 06.7	15 04.8	32.9	241 14.3	02.1	342 11.7	46.8	307 44.7	38.4	Sabik	102 08.6	S15 44.7
U 11	242 09.2	30 05.6	33.3	256 15.2	01.4	357 13.6	46.9	322 46.9	38.4			
R 12	257 11.6	45 06.3	S10 33.6	271 16.2	S 7 00.7	12 15.5	S20 47.0	337 49.0	S22 38.4	Schedar	349 36.0	N56 38.6
D 13	272 14.1	60 07.1	33.9	286 17.2	7 00.0	27 17.3	47.1	352 51.2	38.4	Shaula	96 17.3	S37 06.9
A 14	287 16.6	75 07.9	34.3	301 18.2	6 59.3	42 19.2	47.2	7 53.4	38.4	Sirius	258 30.1	S16 44.6
Y 15	302 19.0	90 08.6 ..	34.6	316 19.1 ..	58.6	57 21.1 ..	47.3	22 55.5 ..	38.4	Spica	158 27.5	S11 15.4
16	317 21.5	105 09.4	34.9	331 20.1	57.9	72 23.0	47.4	37 57.7	38.4	Suhail	222 49.5	S43 30.3
17	332 23.9	120 10.2	35.3	346 21.1	57.2	87 24.9	47.5	52 59.8	38.3			
18	347 26.4	135 10.9	S10 35.6	1 22.1	S 6 56.5	102 26.7	S20 47.6	68 02.0	S22 38.3	Vega	80 36.9	N38 48.3
19	2 28.9	150 11.7	35.9	16 23.0	55.8	117 28.6	47.7	83 04.2	38.3	Zuben'ubi	137 01.6	S16 06.9
20	17 31.3	165 12.4	36.3	31 24.0	55.1	132 30.5	47.8	98 06.3	38.3		SHA	Mer. Pass.
21	32 33.8	180 13.2 ..	36.6	46 25.0 ..	54.4	147 32.4 ..	47.9	113 08.5 ..	38.3		° ′	h m
22	47 36.3	195 13.9	36.9	61 26.0	53.7	162 34.3	48.0	128 10.6	38.3	Venus	148 54.5	9 01
23	62 38.7	210 14.7	37.3	76 26.9	53.0	177 36.1	48.0	143 12.8	38.3	Mars	14 58.1	17 56
	h m									Jupiter	115 24.9	11 14
Mer. Pass. 18 54.0		v 0.8	d 0.3	v 1.0	d 0.7	v 1.9	d 0.1	v 2.2	d 0.0	Saturn	80 48.3	13 32

SUN / MOON

UT (d h)	SUN GHA	SUN Dec	MOON GHA	v	MOON Dec	d	HP
6 00	182 18.1	S22 27.1	197 28.0	11.3	S15 30.8	8.3	56.3
01	197 17.8	27.4	211 58.3	11.2	15 39.1	8.3	56.2
02	212 17.5	27.7	226 28.5	11.1	15 47.4	8.1	56.2
03	227 17.3	.. 28.0	240 58.6	11.2	15 55.5	8.1	56.2
04	242 17.0	28.3	255 28.8	11.2	16 03.6	8.0	56.2
05	257 16.7	28.7	269 59.0	11.1	16 11.6	7.9	56.2
06	272 16.5	S22 29.0	284 29.1	11.1	S16 19.5	7.9	56.1
07	287 16.2	29.3	298 59.2	11.1	16 27.4	7.7	56.1
08	302 15.9	29.6	313 29.3	11.0	16 35.1	7.6	56.1
09	317 15.7	.. 29.8	327 59.3	11.0	16 42.7	7.6	56.1
10	332 15.4	30.1	342 29.3	11.1	16 50.3	7.5	56.1
11	347 15.2	30.4	356 59.4	11.0	16 57.8	7.3	56.0
12	2 14.9	S22 30.7	11 29.4	10.9	S17 05.1	7.3	56.0
13	17 14.6	31.0	25 59.3	11.0	17 12.4	7.2	56.0
14	32 14.4	31.3	40 29.3	10.9	17 19.6	7.1	56.0
15	47 14.1	.. 31.6	54 59.2	10.9	17 26.7	7.0	56.0
16	62 13.8	31.9	69 29.1	10.9	17 33.7	7.0	55.9
17	77 13.6	32.2	83 59.0	10.9	17 40.7	6.8	55.9
18	92 13.3	S22 32.5	98 28.9	10.9	S17 47.5	6.7	55.9
19	107 13.0	32.8	112 58.8	10.8	17 54.2	6.7	55.9
20	122 12.8	33.1	127 28.6	10.8	18 00.9	6.5	55.9
21	137 12.5	.. 33.4	141 58.4	10.8	18 07.4	6.4	55.8
22	152 12.2	33.7	156 28.2	10.8	18 13.8	6.4	55.8
23	167 12.0	33.9	170 58.0	10.8	18 20.2	6.2	55.8
7 00	182 11.7	S22 34.2	185 27.8	10.8	S18 26.4	6.2	55.8
01	197 11.4	34.5	199 57.6	10.7	18 32.6	6.0	55.8
02	212 11.1	34.8	214 27.3	10.7	18 38.6	6.0	55.7
03	227 10.9	.. 35.1	228 57.0	10.7	18 44.6	5.9	55.7
04	242 10.6	35.4	243 26.7	10.7	18 50.5	5.7	55.7
05	257 10.3	35.7	257 56.4	10.7	18 56.2	5.7	55.7
06	272 10.1	S22 35.9	272 26.1	10.7	S19 01.9	5.5	55.7
07	287 09.8	36.2	286 55.8	10.6	19 07.4	5.5	55.6
08	302 09.5	36.5	301 25.4	10.7	19 12.9	5.4	55.6
09	317 09.3	.. 36.8	315 55.1	10.6	19 18.3	5.2	55.6
10	332 09.0	37.1	330 24.7	10.6	19 23.5	5.2	55.6
11	347 08.7	37.3	344 54.3	10.6	19 28.7	5.0	55.6
12	2 08.5	S22 37.6	359 23.9	10.6	S19 33.7	5.0	55.5
13	17 08.2	37.9	13 53.5	10.6	19 38.7	4.8	55.5
14	32 07.9	38.2	28 23.1	10.5	19 43.5	4.8	55.5
15	47 07.6	.. 38.4	42 52.6	10.5	19 48.3	4.6	55.5
16	62 07.4	38.7	57 22.2	10.6	19 52.9	4.6	55.5
17	77 07.1	39.0	71 51.8	10.5	19 57.5	4.4	55.5
18	92 06.8	S22 39.3	86 21.3	10.5	S20 01.9	4.3	55.4
19	107 06.5	39.5	100 50.8	10.6	20 06.2	4.3	55.4
20	122 06.3	39.8	115 20.4	10.5	20 10.5	4.1	55.4
21	137 06.0	.. 40.1	129 49.9	10.5	20 14.6	4.0	55.4
22	152 05.7	40.4	144 19.4	10.5	20 18.6	3.9	55.4
23	167 05.5	40.6	158 48.9	10.5	20 22.5	3.8	55.3
8 00	182 05.2	S22 40.9	173 18.4	10.5	S20 26.3	3.7	55.3
01	197 04.9	41.2	187 47.9	10.5	20 30.0	3.6	55.3
02	212 04.6	41.4	202 17.4	10.5	20 33.6	3.5	55.3
03	227 04.4	.. 41.7	216 46.9	10.5	20 37.1	3.4	55.3
04	242 04.1	42.0	231 16.4	10.5	20 40.5	3.3	55.2
05	257 03.8	42.2	245 45.9	10.5	20 43.8	3.1	55.2
06	272 03.5	S22 42.5	260 15.4	10.5	S20 46.9	3.1	55.2
07	287 03.3	42.7	274 44.9	10.5	20 50.0	3.0	55.2
08	302 03.0	43.0	289 14.4	10.5	20 53.0	2.8	55.2
09	317 02.7	.. 43.3	303 43.9	10.5	20 55.8	2.7	55.2
10	332 02.4	43.5	318 13.4	10.5	20 58.5	2.7	55.1
11	347 02.2	43.8	332 42.9	10.5	21 01.2	2.5	55.1
12	2 01.9	S22 44.1	347 12.4	10.5	S21 03.7	2.4	55.1
13	17 01.6	44.3	1 41.9	10.5	21 06.1	2.3	55.1
14	32 01.3	44.6	16 11.4	10.6	21 08.4	2.2	55.1
15	47 01.1	.. 44.8	30 41.0	10.5	21 10.6	2.1	55.1
16	62 00.8	45.1	45 10.5	10.5	21 12.7	2.0	55.0
17	77 00.5	45.3	59 40.0	10.6	21 14.7	1.9	55.0
18	92 00.2	S22 45.6	74 09.6	10.5	S21 16.6	1.8	55.0
19	107 00.0	45.8	88 39.1	10.6	21 18.4	1.7	55.0
20	121 59.7	46.1	103 08.7	10.5	21 20.1	1.5	55.0
21	136 59.4	.. 46.3	117 38.2	10.6	21 21.6	1.5	54.9
22	151 59.1	46.6	132 07.8	10.6	21 23.1	1.3	54.9
23	166 58.8	46.9	146 37.4	10.6	S21 24.4	1.3	54.9
	SD 16.3 d 0.3		SD 15.3		15.1		15.0

Day labels (left margin): **THURSDAY** (6), **FRIDAY** (7), **SATURDAY** (8)

Twilight / Sunrise / Moonrise

Lat.	Naut.	Civil	Sunrise	Moonrise 6	7	8	9
N 72	08 06	10 17	■■	09 48	■■	■■	■■
N 70	07 48	09 29	■■	08 52	11 13	■■	■■
68	07 33	08 58	11 18	08 19	10 04	11 44	12 58
66	07 21	08 36	10 06	07 55	09 27	10 49	11 51
64	07 11	08 18	09 31	07 37	09 02	10 17	11 16
62	07 02	08 03	09 06	07 21	08 42	09 53	10 50
60	06 54	07 50	08 46	07 09	08 25	09 34	10 30
N 58	06 47	07 39	08 30	06 58	08 11	09 18	10 14
56	06 41	07 29	08 16	06 48	08 00	09 04	10 00
54	06 35	07 21	08 04	06 40	07 49	08 53	09 48
52	06 30	07 13	07 53	06 32	07 40	08 42	09 37
50	06 25	07 06	07 44	06 26	07 32	08 33	09 28
45	06 14	06 51	07 24	06 11	07 15	08 14	09 08
N 40	06 04	06 38	07 08	06 00	07 01	07 58	08 51
35	05 55	06 27	06 55	05 50	06 49	07 45	08 38
30	05 47	06 16	06 43	05 41	06 38	07 34	08 26
20	05 31	05 58	06 22	05 26	06 20	07 14	08 05
N 10	05 16	05 42	06 04	05 13	06 05	06 57	07 48
0	04 59	05 25	05 48	05 01	05 50	06 41	07 31
S 10	04 41	05 08	05 31	04 48	05 36	06 25	07 15
20	04 19	04 48	05 13	04 36	05 21	06 08	06 57
30	03 51	04 24	04 51	04 21	05 03	05 49	06 37
35	03 33	04 10	04 39	04 12	04 53	05 37	06 25
40	03 11	03 52	04 25	04 03	04 41	05 24	06 11
45	02 42	03 31	04 07	03 52	04 28	05 09	05 55
S 50	02 00	03 02	03 46	03 38	04 11	04 50	05 36
52	01 36	02 48	03 36	03 32	04 04	04 41	05 26
54	01 00	02 32	03 24	03 25	03 55	04 31	05 16
56	////	02 11	03 11	03 17	03 45	04 20	05 04
58	////	01 45	02 55	03 09	03 34	04 08	04 50
S 60	////	01 07	02 36	02 59	03 22	03 53	04 34

Sunset / Twilight / Moonset

Lat.	Sunset	Civil	Naut.	Moonset 6	7	8	9
N 72	■■	13 26	15 37	12 24	■■	■■	■■
N 70	■■	14 13	15 55	13 20	12 43	■■	■■
68	12 24	14 44	16 09	13 54	13 54	13 58	14 29
66	13 36	15 07	16 32	14 19	14 30	14 53	15 35
64	14 12	15 25	16 32	14 38	14 57	15 26	16 11
62	14 37	15 40	16 41	14 53	15 17	15 50	16 36
60	14 57	15 53	16 48	15 07	15 34	16 09	16 56
N 58	15 13	16 04	16 55	15 19	15 48	16 25	17 13
56	15 27	16 13	17 02	15 29	16 00	16 39	17 27
54	15 39	16 22	17 07	15 37	16 10	16 51	17 39
52	15 49	16 30	17 13	15 45	16 20	17 01	17 50
50	15 59	16 37	17 18	15 52	16 28	17 10	17 59
45	16 18	16 52	17 29	16 08	16 46	17 30	18 19
N 40	16 35	17 05	17 39	16 20	17 01	17 46	18 35
35	16 48	17 16	17 48	16 31	17 13	18 00	18 49
30	17 00	17 26	17 56	16 41	17 24	18 11	19 01
20	17 20	17 44	18 12	16 57	17 43	18 31	19 21
N 10	17 38	18 01	18 27	17 11	17 59	18 49	19 39
0	17 55	18 18	18 44	17 24	18 15	19 05	19 55
S 10	18 12	18 35	19 02	17 38	18 30	19 21	20 12
20	18 30	18 55	19 24	17 52	18 46	19 39	20 29
30	18 52	19 19	19 52	18 09	19 05	19 59	20 49
35	19 04	19 34	20 10	18 18	19 16	20 11	21 01
40	19 19	19 51	20 32	18 29	19 29	20 24	21 15
45	19 36	20 13	21 01	18 42	19 44	20 40	21 31
S 50	19 57	20 41	21 44	18 58	20 02	21 00	21 50
52	20 08	20 55	22 09	19 05	20 10	21 09	22 00
54	20 20	21 12	22 45	19 13	20 20	21 20	22 10
56	20 33	21 33	////	19 23	20 31	21 31	22 22
58	20 49	21 59	////	19 33	20 44	21 45	22 36
S 60	21 08	22 39	////	19 45	20 58	22 01	22 52

SUN / MOON

Day	Eqn. of Time 00h	12h	Mer. Pass.	Mer. Pass. Upper	Lower	Age	Phase
d	m s	m s	h m	h m	h m	d	%
6	09 13	09 00	11 51	11 12	23 37	29	1
7	08 47	08 34	11 51	12 02	24 28	00	0
8	08 21	08 08	11 52	12 53	00 28	01	1

Phase: ● (New Moon)

UT	ARIES	VENUS −4·8		MARS +0·1		JUPITER −1·7		SATURN +0·5		STARS		
	GHA	GHA	Dec	GHA	Dec	GHA	Dec	GHA	Dec	Name	SHA	Dec
d h	° ′	° ′	° ′	° ′	° ′	° ′	° ′	° ′	° ′		° ′	° ′
9 00	77 41.2	225 15.4	S10 37.6	91 27.9	S 6 52.3	192 38.0	S20 48.1	158 15.0	S22 38.2	Acamar	315 15.2	S40 14.0
01	92 43.7	240 16.2	38.0	106 28.9	51.6	207 39.9	48.2	173 17.1	38.2	Achernar	335 23.7	S57 08.8
02	107 46.1	255 16.9	38.3	121 29.9	50.9	222 41.8	48.3	188 19.3	38.2	Acrux	173 05.3	S63 11.8
03	122 48.6	270 17.7	.. 38.7	136 30.8	.. 50.2	237 43.7	.. 48.4	203 21.4	.. 38.2	Adhara	255 09.3	S28 59.9
04	137 51.1	285 18.4	39.0	151 31.8	49.5	252 45.5	48.5	218 23.6	38.2	Aldebaran	290 44.8	N16 32.7
05	152 53.5	300 19.2	39.3	166 32.8	48.8	267 47.4	48.6	233 25.8	38.2			
06	167 56.0	315 19.9	S10 39.7	181 33.8	S 6 48.1	282 49.3	S20 48.7	248 27.9	S22 38.2	Alioth	166 17.7	N55 51.3
07	182 58.4	330 20.6	40.0	196 34.7	47.4	297 51.2	48.8	263 30.1	38.1	Alkaid	152 56.3	N49 13.1
08	198 00.9	345 21.4	40.4	211 35.7	46.7	312 53.0	48.9	278 32.2	38.1	Al Na'ir	27 39.3	S46 52.4
S 09	213 03.4	0 22.1	.. 40.7	226 36.7	.. 46.0	327 54.9	.. 49.0	293 34.4	.. 38.1	Alnilam	275 42.3	S 1 11.5
U 10	228 05.8	15 22.8	41.1	241 37.7	45.3	342 56.8	49.1	308 36.6	38.1	Alphard	217 52.3	S 8 44.4
N 11	243 08.3	30 23.5	41.4	256 38.6	44.6	357 58.7	49.2	323 38.7	38.1			
D 12	258 10.8	45 24.3	S10 41.8	271 39.6	S 6 43.9	13 00.6	S20 49.3	338 40.9	S22 38.1	Alphecca	126 08.2	N26 39.2
A 13	273 13.2	60 25.0	42.2	286 40.6	43.2	28 02.4	49.4	353 43.0	38.1	Alpheratz	357 39.5	N29 11.8
Y 14	288 15.7	75 25.7	42.5	301 41.6	42.5	43 04.3	49.5	8 45.2	38.0	Altair	62 04.9	N 8 55.3
15	303 18.2	90 26.4	.. 42.9	316 42.5	.. 41.8	58 06.2	.. 49.6	23 47.4	.. 38.0	Ankaa	353 11.9	S42 12.5
16	318 20.6	105 27.2	43.2	331 43.5	41.1	73 08.1	49.7	38 49.5	38.0	Antares	112 22.1	S26 28.2
17	333 23.1	120 27.9	43.6	346 44.5	40.4	88 10.0	49.8	53 51.7	38.0			
18	348 25.6	135 28.6	S10 43.9	1 45.5	S 6 39.7	103 11.8	S20 49.9	68 53.8	S22 38.0	Arcturus	145 52.6	N19 05.1
19	3 28.0	150 29.3	44.3	16 46.4	39.0	118 13.7	49.9	83 56.0	38.0	Atria	107 21.1	S69 03.4
20	18 30.5	165 30.0	44.7	31 47.4	38.3	133 15.6	50.0	98 58.1	37.9	Avior	234 16.0	S59 34.0
21	33 32.9	180 30.7	.. 45.0	46 48.4	.. 37.6	148 17.5	.. 50.1	114 00.3	.. 37.9	Bellatrix	278 27.7	N 6 21.9
22	48 35.4	195 31.4	45.4	61 49.3	36.9	163 19.4	50.2	129 02.5	37.9	Betelgeuse	270 56.9	N 7 24.5
23	63 37.9	210 32.1	45.7	76 50.3	36.2	178 21.2	50.3	144 04.6	37.9			
10 00	78 40.3	225 32.8	S10 46.1	91 51.3	S 6 35.5	193 23.1	S20 50.4	159 06.8	S22 37.9	Canopus	263 54.0	S52 42.4
01	93 42.8	240 33.5	46.5	106 52.3	34.8	208 25.0	50.5	174 08.9	37.9	Capella	280 28.5	N46 00.8
02	108 45.3	255 34.2	46.8	121 53.2	34.1	223 26.9	50.6	189 11.1	37.9	Deneb	49 29.2	N45 21.1
03	123 47.7	270 34.9	.. 47.2	136 54.2	.. 33.4	238 28.8	.. 50.7	204 13.3	.. 37.8	Denebola	182 29.9	N14 28.0
04	138 50.2	285 35.6	47.6	151 55.2	32.7	253 30.6	50.8	219 15.4	37.8	Diphda	348 52.0	S17 53.2
05	153 52.7	300 36.3	47.9	166 56.2	32.0	268 32.5	50.9	234 17.6	37.8			
06	168 55.1	315 37.0	S10 48.3	181 57.1	S 6 31.3	283 34.4	S20 51.0	249 19.7	S22 37.8	Dubhe	193 47.2	N61 38.7
07	183 57.6	330 37.7	48.7	196 58.1	30.6	298 36.3	51.1	264 21.9	37.8	Elnath	278 07.5	N28 37.2
08	199 00.0	345 38.4	49.1	211 59.1	29.9	313 38.2	51.2	279 24.1	37.8	Eltanin	90 45.0	N51 29.4
M 09	214 02.5	0 39.1	.. 49.4	227 00.1	.. 29.2	328 40.0	.. 51.3	294 26.2	.. 37.8	Enif	33 43.6	N 9 57.8
O 10	229 05.0	15 39.8	49.8	242 01.0	28.5	343 41.9	51.4	309 28.4	37.7	Fomalhaut	15 19.9	S29 31.5
N 11	244 07.4	30 40.5	50.2	257 02.0	27.8	358 43.8	51.5	324 30.5	37.7			
D 12	259 09.9	45 41.2	S10 50.6	272 03.0	S 6 27.1	13 45.7	S20 51.6	339 32.7	S22 37.7	Gacrux	171 56.9	S57 12.7
A 13	274 12.4	60 41.8	50.9	287 03.9	26.4	28 47.6	51.6	354 34.8	37.7	Gienah	175 48.6	S17 38.6
Y 14	289 14.8	75 42.5	51.3	302 04.9	25.7	43 49.4	51.7	9 37.0	37.7	Hadar	148 43.0	S60 27.4
15	304 17.3	90 43.2	.. 51.7	317 05.9	.. 24.9	58 51.3	.. 51.8	24 39.2	.. 37.7	Hamal	327 56.3	N23 33.1
16	319 19.8	105 43.9	52.1	332 06.9	24.2	73 53.2	51.9	39 41.3	37.6	Kaus Aust.	83 39.3	S34 22.4
17	334 22.2	120 44.5	52.4	347 07.8	23.5	88 55.1	52.0	54 43.5	37.6			
18	349 24.7	135 45.2	S10 52.8	2 08.8	S 6 22.8	103 57.0	S20 52.1	69 45.6	S22 37.6	Kochab	137 21.2	N74 04.6
19	4 27.2	150 45.9	53.2	17 09.8	22.1	118 58.8	52.2	84 47.8	37.6	Markab	13 34.6	N15 18.5
20	19 29.6	165 46.6	53.6	32 10.8	21.4	134 00.7	52.3	99 49.9	37.6	Menkar	314 10.9	N 4 09.7
21	34 32.1	180 47.2	.. 54.0	47 11.7	.. 20.7	149 02.6	.. 52.4	114 52.1	.. 37.6	Menkent	148 03.5	S36 27.4
22	49 34.5	195 47.9	54.4	62 12.7	20.0	164 04.5	52.5	129 54.3	37.6	Miaplacidus	221 38.4	S69 47.4
23	64 37.0	210 48.6	54.7	77 13.7	19.3	179 06.4	52.6	144 56.4	37.5			
11 00	79 39.5	225 49.2	S10 55.1	92 14.6	S 6 18.6	194 08.2	S20 52.7	159 58.6	S22 37.5	Mirfak	308 34.5	N49 55.6
01	94 41.9	240 49.9	55.5	107 15.6	17.9	209 10.1	52.8	175 00.7	37.5	Nunki	75 54.1	S26 16.3
02	109 44.4	255 50.5	55.9	122 16.6	17.2	224 12.0	52.9	190 02.9	37.5	Peacock	53 13.9	S56 40.6
03	124 46.9	270 51.2	.. 56.3	137 17.6	.. 16.5	239 13.9	.. 53.0	205 05.0	.. 37.5	Pollux	243 22.9	N27 58.6
04	139 49.3	285 51.9	56.7	152 18.5	15.8	254 15.8	53.0	220 07.2	37.5	Procyon	244 55.6	N 5 10.5
05	154 51.8	300 52.5	57.1	167 19.5	15.1	269 17.6	53.1	235 09.4	37.4			
06	169 54.3	315 53.2	S10 57.5	182 20.5	S 6 14.4	284 19.5	S20 53.2	250 11.5	S22 37.4	Rasalhague	96 03.4	N12 33.0
07	184 56.7	330 53.8	57.9	197 21.4	13.7	299 21.4	53.3	265 13.7	37.4	Regulus	207 39.5	N11 52.4
T 08	199 59.2	345 54.5	58.2	212 22.4	13.0	314 23.3	53.4	280 15.8	37.4	Rigel	281 08.1	S 8 10.9
U 09	215 01.7	0 55.1	.. 58.6	227 23.4	.. 12.3	329 25.2	.. 53.5	295 18.0	.. 37.4	Rigil Kent.	139 47.2	S60 54.4
E 10	230 04.1	15 55.7	59.0	242 24.4	11.6	344 27.0	53.6	310 20.1	37.4	Sabik	102 08.6	S15 44.7
S 11	245 06.6	30 56.4	59.4	257 25.3	10.9	359 28.9	53.7	325 22.3	37.4			
D 12	260 09.0	45 57.0	S10 59.8	272 26.3	S 6 10.2	14 30.8	S20 53.8	340 24.5	S22 37.3	Schedar	349 36.0	N56 38.6
A 13	275 11.5	60 57.7	11 00.2	287 27.3	09.5	29 32.7	53.9	355 26.6	37.3	Shaula	96 17.3	S37 06.8
Y 14	290 14.0	75 58.3	00.6	302 28.2	08.8	44 34.6	54.0	10 28.8	37.3	Sirius	258 30.1	S16 44.6
15	305 16.4	90 59.0	01.0	317 29.2	08.1	59 36.4	54.1	25 30.9	37.3	Spica	158 27.5	S11 15.4
16	320 18.9	105 59.6	01.4	332 30.2	07.3	74 38.3	54.2	40 33.1	37.3	Suhail	222 49.5	S43 30.3
17	335 21.4	121 00.2	01.8	347 31.2	06.6	89 40.2	54.3	55 35.2	37.3			
18	350 23.8	136 00.9	S11 02.2	2 32.1	S 6 05.9	104 42.1	S20 54.4	70 37.4	S22 37.2	Vega	80 36.9	N38 48.3
19	5 26.3	151 01.5	02.6	17 33.1	05.2	119 44.0	54.4	85 39.6	37.2	Zuben'ubi	137 01.6	S16 07.0
20	20 28.8	166 02.1	03.0	32 34.1	04.5	134 45.8	54.5	100 41.7	37.2		SHA	Mer. Pass.
21	35 31.2	181 02.7	.. 03.4	47 35.0	.. 03.8	149 47.7	.. 54.6	115 43.9	.. 37.2		° ′	h m
22	50 33.7	196 03.4	03.8	62 36.0	03.1	164 49.6	54.7	130 46.0	37.2	Venus	146 52.5	8 57
23	65 36.2	211 04.0	04.2	77 37.0	02.4	179 51.5	54.8	145 48.2	37.2	Mars	13 11.0	17 51
	h m									Jupiter	114 42.8	11 05
Mer. Pass. 18 42.2	*v* 0.7 *d* 0.4			*v* 1.0 *d* 0.7		*v* 1.9 *d* 0.1		*v* 2.2 *d* 0.0		Saturn	80 26.4	13 22

SUN and MOON

UT	SUN GHA	SUN Dec	MOON GHA	v	Dec	d	HP
d h	° ′	° ′	° ′	′	° ′	′	′
9 00	181 58.6	S22 47.1	161 07.0	10.6	S21 25.7	1.1	54.9
01	196 58.3	47.4	175 36.6	10.6	21 26.8	1.0	54.9
02	211 58.0	47.6	190 06.2	10.7	21 27.8	0.9	54.9
03	226 57.7	.. 47.8	204 35.9	10.6	21 28.7	0.8	54.9
04	241 57.5	48.1	219 05.5	10.7	21 29.5	0.7	54.8
05	256 57.2	48.3	233 35.2	10.7	21 30.2	0.6	54.8
06	271 56.9	S22 48.6	248 04.9	10.7	S21 30.8	0.5	54.8
07	286 56.6	48.8	262 34.6	10.7	21 31.3	0.4	54.8
08	301 56.3	49.1	277 04.3	10.8	21 31.7	0.3	54.8
S 09	316 56.1	.. 49.3	291 34.1	10.7	21 32.0	0.2	54.8
U 10	331 55.8	49.6	306 03.8	10.8	21 32.2	0.2	54.7
N 11	346 55.5	49.8	320 33.6	10.8	21 32.2	0.0	54.7
D 12	1 55.2	S22 50.0	335 03.4	10.8	S21 32.2	0.2	54.7
A 13	16 54.9	50.3	349 33.2	10.9	21 32.0	0.2	54.7
Y 14	31 54.7	50.5	4 03.1	10.8	21 31.8	0.4	54.7
15	46 54.4	.. 50.8	18 32.9	10.9	21 31.4	0.4	54.7
16	61 54.1	51.0	33 02.8	10.9	21 31.0	0.6	54.7
17	76 53.8	51.2	47 32.7	10.9	21 30.4	0.7	54.6
18	91 53.5	S22 51.5	62 02.6	11.0	S21 29.7	0.7	54.6
19	106 53.2	51.7	76 32.6	11.0	21 29.0	0.9	54.6
20	121 53.0	51.9	91 02.6	11.0	21 28.1	1.0	54.6
21	136 52.7	.. 52.2	105 32.6	11.0	21 27.1	1.1	54.6
22	151 52.4	52.4	120 02.6	11.1	21 26.0	1.2	54.6
23	166 52.1	52.6	134 32.7	11.0	21 24.8	1.3	54.6
10 00	181 51.8	S22 52.9	149 02.7	11.2	S21 23.5	1.4	54.5
01	196 51.6	53.1	163 32.9	11.1	21 22.1	1.5	54.5
02	211 51.3	53.3	178 03.0	11.2	21 20.6	1.6	54.5
03	226 51.0	.. 53.6	192 33.2	11.2	21 19.0	1.7	54.5
04	241 50.7	53.8	207 03.4	11.2	21 17.3	1.8	54.5
05	256 50.4	54.0	221 33.6	11.3	21 15.5	1.9	54.5
06	271 50.1	S22 54.2	236 03.9	11.3	S21 13.6	2.0	54.5
07	286 49.9	54.5	250 34.2	11.3	21 11.6	2.1	54.5
08	301 49.6	54.7	265 04.5	11.3	21 09.5	2.2	54.4
M 09	316 49.3	.. 54.9	279 34.8	11.4	21 07.3	2.3	54.4
O 10	331 49.0	55.1	294 05.2	11.5	21 05.0	2.4	54.4
N 11	346 48.7	55.4	308 35.7	11.4	21 02.6	2.5	54.4
D 12	1 48.4	S22 55.6	323 06.1	11.5	S21 00.1	2.6	54.4
A 13	16 48.1	55.8	337 36.6	11.5	20 57.5	2.7	54.4
Y 14	31 47.9	56.0	352 07.1	11.6	20 54.8	2.7	54.4
15	46 47.6	.. 56.2	6 37.7	11.6	20 52.1	2.9	54.4
16	61 47.3	56.5	21 08.3	11.6	20 49.2	3.0	54.4
17	76 47.0	56.7	35 38.9	11.7	20 46.2	3.1	54.3
18	91 46.7	S22 56.9	50 09.6	11.7	S20 43.1	3.2	54.3
19	106 46.4	57.1	64 40.3	11.7	20 39.9	3.3	54.3
20	121 46.1	57.3	79 11.0	11.8	20 36.6	3.3	54.3
21	136 45.9	.. 57.5	93 41.8	11.8	20 33.3	3.5	54.3
22	151 45.6	57.8	108 12.6	11.9	20 29.8	3.5	54.3
23	166 45.3	58.0	122 43.5	11.8	20 26.3	3.7	54.3
11 00	181 45.0	S22 58.2	137 14.3	12.0	S20 22.6	3.7	54.3
01	196 44.7	58.4	151 45.3	11.9	20 18.9	3.9	54.3
02	211 44.4	58.6	166 16.2	12.0	20 15.0	3.9	54.3
03	226 44.1	.. 58.8	180 47.2	12.1	20 11.1	4.0	54.3
04	241 43.9	59.0	195 18.3	12.1	20 07.1	4.1	54.2
05	256 43.6	59.2	209 49.4	12.1	20 03.0	4.2	54.2
06	271 43.3	S22 59.4	224 20.5	12.1	S19 58.8	4.3	54.2
07	286 43.0	59.6	238 51.6	12.2	19 54.5	4.4	54.2
08	301 42.7	22 59.8	253 22.8	12.3	19 50.1	4.4	54.2
T 09	316 42.4	23 00.1	267 54.1	12.3	19 45.7	4.6	54.2
U 10	331 42.1	00.3	282 25.4	12.3	19 41.1	4.6	54.2
E 11	346 41.8	00.5	296 56.7	12.3	19 36.5	4.7	54.2
S 12	1 41.5	S23 00.7	311 28.0	12.4	S19 31.8	4.9	54.2
D 13	16 41.3	00.9	325 59.4	12.5	19 26.9	4.9	54.2
A 14	31 41.0	01.1	340 30.9	12.5	19 22.0	5.0	54.2
Y 15	46 40.7	.. 01.3	355 02.4	12.5	19 17.0	5.0	54.2
16	61 40.4	01.5	9 33.9	12.5	19 12.0	5.2	54.2
17	76 40.1	01.7	24 05.4	12.6	19 06.8	5.2	54.2
18	91 39.8	S23 01.9	38 37.0	12.7	S19 01.6	5.3	54.2
19	106 39.5	02.1	53 08.7	12.7	18 56.3	5.5	54.2
20	121 39.2	02.3	67 40.4	12.7	18 50.8	5.4	54.2
21	136 38.9	.. 02.5	82 12.1	12.8	18 45.4	5.6	54.1
22	151 38.7	02.6	96 43.9	12.8	18 39.8	5.7	54.1
23	166 38.4	02.8	111 15.7	12.8	S18 34.1	5.7	54.1
SD	16.3	d 0.2	SD 14.9		14.8		14.8

Twilight, Sunrise and Moonrise

Lat.	Twilight Naut.	Twilight Civil	Sunrise	Moonrise 9	10	11	12
°	h m	h m	h m	h m	h m	h m	h m
N 72	08 12	10 29	■	■	■	■	14 45
N 70	07 53	09 37	■	■	■	14 22	13 53
68	07 38	09 05	■	12 58	13 19	13 22	13 21
66	07 26	08 41	10 15	11 51	12 28	12 47	12 57
64	07 15	08 22	09 37	11 16	11 57	12 22	12 38
62	07 06	08 07	09 11	10 50	11 33	12 03	12 38
60	06 58	07 54	08 51	10 30	11 14	11 46	12 10
N 58	06 51	07 43	08 34	10 14	10 59	11 33	11 59
56	06 44	07 33	08 20	10 00	10 45	11 21	11 49
54	06 38	07 24	08 07	09 48	10 34	11 11	11 41
52	06 33	07 16	07 57	09 37	10 23	11 01	11 33
50	06 28	07 09	07 47	09 28	10 14	10 53	11 26
45	06 16	06 53	07 27	09 08	09 55	10 36	11 11
N 40	06 06	06 40	07 11	08 51	09 39	10 21	10 59
35	05 57	06 29	06 57	08 38	09 26	10 09	10 48
30	05 49	06 19	06 45	08 26	09 14	09 58	10 39
20	05 33	06 00	06 24	08 05	08 54	09 40	10 23
N 10	05 17	05 43	06 06	07 48	08 37	09 24	10 09
0	05 00	05 27	05 49	07 31	08 21	09 09	09 56
S 10	04 42	05 09	05 32	07 15	08 05	08 54	09 43
20	04 20	04 49	05 13	06 57	07 47	08 38	09 29
30	03 51	04 25	04 52	06 37	07 27	08 20	09 12
35	03 33	04 10	04 39	06 25	07 16	08 09	09 03
40	03 11	03 52	04 25	06 11	07 02	07 56	08 52
45	02 41	03 30	04 07	05 55	06 47	07 42	08 40
S 50	01 58	03 01	03 45	05 36	06 27	07 24	08 24
52	01 32	02 47	03 35	05 26	06 18	07 15	08 17
54	00 53	02 30	03 23	05 16	06 08	07 06	08 09
56	////	02 09	03 09	05 04	05 56	06 55	08 00
58	////	01 41	02 53	04 50	05 42	06 43	07 50
S 60	////	00 59	02 34	04 34	05 26	06 29	07 38

Sunset, Twilight and Moonset

Lat.	Sunset	Twilight Civil	Twilight Naut.	Moonset 9	10	11	12
°	h m	h m	h m	h m	h m	h m	h m
N 72	■	13 16	15 33	■	■	■	17 41
N 70	■	14 08	15 52	■	■	16 28	18 32
68	■	14 40	16 07	14 29	15 51	17 27	19 03
66	13 30	15 04	16 20	15 35	16 41	18 01	19 27
64	14 08	15 23	16 30	16 11	17 12	18 26	19 45
62	14 34	15 38	16 39	16 36	17 36	18 45	19 59
60	14 55	15 51	16 47	16 56	17 54	19 01	20 12
N 58	15 11	16 02	16 55	17 13	18 10	19 14	20 23
56	15 26	16 12	17 01	17 27	18 23	19 25	20 32
54	15 38	16 21	17 07	17 39	18 34	19 35	20 40
52	15 49	16 29	17 13	17 50	18 45	19 44	20 47
50	15 59	16 36	17 18	17 59	18 54	19 52	20 54
45	16 18	16 52	17 29	18 19	19 13	20 09	21 08
N 40	16 35	17 05	17 39	18 35	19 28	20 23	21 20
35	16 48	17 17	17 48	18 49	19 41	20 35	21 29
30	17 01	17 27	17 57	19 01	19 52	20 45	21 38
20	17 21	17 45	18 13	19 21	20 12	21 02	21 53
N 10	17 39	18 02	18 28	19 39	20 29	21 18	22 06
0	17 56	18 19	18 45	19 55	20 44	21 32	22 18
S 10	18 14	18 37	19 04	20 12	21 00	21 46	22 30
20	18 32	18 57	19 26	20 29	21 17	22 01	22 42
30	18 54	19 21	19 54	20 49	21 36	22 18	22 57
35	19 07	19 36	20 13	21 01	21 47	22 28	23 05
40	19 21	19 54	20 35	21 15	22 00	22 39	23 14
45	19 39	20 16	21 05	21 31	22 15	22 53	23 26
S 50	20 01	20 45	21 49	21 50	22 33	23 09	23 39
52	20 11	20 59	22 14	22 00	22 42	23 16	23 45
54	20 23	21 17	22 54	22 10	22 52	23 25	23 52
56	20 37	21 38	////	22 22	23 02	23 34	24 00
58	20 53	22 06	////	22 36	23 15	23 45	24 08
S 60	21 13	22 49	////	22 52	23 30	23 57	24 18

SUN and MOON data

Day	SUN Eqn. of Time 00h	SUN Eqn. of Time 12h	SUN Mer. Pass.	MOON Mer. Pass. Upper	MOON Mer. Pass. Lower	Age	Phase
d	m s	m s	h m	h m	h m	d	%
9	07 55	07 41	11 52	13 43	01 18	02	5
10	07 28	07 14	11 53	14 33	02 08	03	10
11	07 01	06 47	11 53	15 20	02 57	04	16

UT	ARIES	VENUS −4·8		MARS +0·2		JUPITER −1·7		SATURN +0·5		STARS		
d h	GHA	GHA	Dec	GHA	Dec	GHA	Dec	GHA	Dec	Name	SHA	Dec
	° ′	° ′	° ′	° ′	° ′	° ′	° ′	° ′	° ′		° ′	° ′
12 00	80 38.6	226 04.6	S11 04.7	92 38.0	S 6 01.7	194 53.4	S20 54.9	160 50.3	S22 37.2	Acamar	315 15.2	S40 14.0
01	95 41.1	241 05.2	05.1	107 38.9	01.0	209 55.2	55.0	175 52.5	37.1	Achernar	335 23.7	S57 08.8
02	110 43.5	256 05.8	05.5	122 39.9	6 00.3	224 57.1	55.1	190 54.7	37.1	Acrux	173 05.3	S63 11.8
03	125 46.0	271 06.5 ..	05.9	137 40.9	5 59.6	239 59.0 ..	55.2	205 56.8 ..	37.1	Adhara	255 09.2	S28 59.9
04	140 48.5	286 07.1	06.3	152 41.8	58.9	255 00.9	55.3	220 59.0	37.1	Aldebaran	290 44.8	N16 32.7
05	155 50.9	301 07.7	06.7	167 42.8	58.2	270 02.8	55.4	236 01.1	37.1			
W 06	170 53.4	316 08.3	S11 07.1	182 43.8	S 5 57.5	285 04.6	S20 55.5	251 03.3	S22 37.1	Alioth	166 17.7	N55 51.3
E 07	185 55.9	331 08.9	07.5	197 44.7	56.8	300 06.5	55.6	266 05.4	37.0	Alkaid	152 56.3	N49 13.1
D 08	200 58.3	346 09.5	07.9	212 45.7	56.1	315 08.4	55.6	281 07.6	37.0	Al Na'ir	27 39.3	S46 52.4
N 09	216 00.8	1 10.1 ..	08.4	227 46.7 ..	55.4	330 10.3 ..	55.7	296 09.7 ..	37.0	Alnilam	275 42.3	S 1 11.5
E 10	231 03.3	16 10.7	08.8	242 47.7	54.6	345 12.2	55.8	311 11.9	37.0	Alphard	217 52.3	S 8 44.4
S 11	246 05.7	31 11.3	09.2	257 48.6	53.9	0 14.0	55.9	326 14.1	37.0			
D 12	261 08.2	46 11.9	S11 09.6	272 49.6	S 5 53.2	15 15.9	S20 56.0	341 16.2	S22 37.0	Alphecca	126 08.2	N26 39.2
A 13	276 10.6	61 12.5	10.0	287 50.6	52.5	30 17.8	56.1	356 18.4	36.9	Alpheratz	357 39.6	N29 11.8
Y 14	291 13.1	76 13.1	10.4	302 51.5	51.8	45 19.7	56.2	11 20.5	36.9	Altair	62 04.9	N 8 55.2
15	306 15.6	91 13.7 ..	10.9	317 52.5 ..	51.1	60 21.6 ..	56.3	26 22.7 ..	36.9	Ankaa	353 11.9	S42 12.5
16	321 18.0	106 14.3	11.3	332 53.5	50.4	75 23.5	56.4	41 24.8	36.9	Antares	112 22.1	S26 28.2
17	336 20.5	121 14.9	11.7	347 54.4	49.7	90 25.3	56.5	56 27.0	36.9			
18	351 23.0	136 15.5	S11 12.1	2 55.4	S 5 49.0	105 27.2	S20 56.6	71 29.1	S22 36.9	Arcturus	145 52.6	N19 05.1
19	6 25.4	151 16.1	12.5	17 56.4	48.3	120 29.1	56.7	86 31.3	36.8	Atria	107 21.1	S69 03.4
20	21 27.9	166 16.7	13.0	32 57.4	47.6	135 31.0	56.7	101 33.5	36.8	Avior	234 16.0	S59 34.0
21	36 30.4	181 17.3 ..	13.4	47 58.3 ..	46.9	150 32.9 ..	56.8	116 35.6 ..	36.8	Bellatrix	278 27.7	N 6 21.8
22	51 32.8	196 17.9	13.8	62 59.3	46.2	165 34.7	56.9	131 37.8	36.8	Betelgeuse	270 56.9	N 7 24.5
23	66 35.3	211 18.5	14.2	78 00.3	45.5	180 36.6	57.0	146 39.9	36.8			
13 00	81 37.8	226 19.0	S11 14.7	93 01.2	S 5 44.8	195 38.5	S20 57.1	161 42.1	S22 36.8	Canopus	263 53.9	S52 42.4
01	96 40.2	241 19.6	15.1	108 02.2	44.0	210 40.4	57.2	176 44.2	36.8	Capella	280 28.4	N46 00.8
02	111 42.7	256 20.2	15.5	123 03.2	43.3	225 42.3	57.3	191 46.4	36.7	Deneb	49 29.3	N45 21.1
03	126 45.1	271 20.8 ..	15.9	138 04.1 ..	42.6	240 44.1 ..	57.4	206 48.5 ..	36.7	Denebola	182 29.9	N14 28.0
04	141 47.6	286 21.4	16.4	153 05.1	41.9	255 46.0	57.5	221 50.7	36.7	Diphda	348 52.0	S17 53.2
05	156 50.1	301 21.9	16.8	168 06.1	41.2	270 47.9	57.6	236 52.9	36.7			
T 06	171 52.5	316 22.5	S11 17.2	183 07.0	S 5 40.5	285 49.8	S20 57.7	251 55.0	S22 36.7	Dubhe	193 47.1	N61 38.7
H 07	186 55.0	331 23.1	17.7	198 08.0	39.8	300 51.7	57.8	266 57.2	36.7	Elnath	278 07.5	N28 37.2
U 08	201 57.5	346 23.6	18.1	213 09.0	39.1	315 53.5	57.8	281 59.3	36.6	Eltanin	90 45.0	N51 29.4
R 09	216 59.9	1 24.2 ..	18.5	228 09.9 ..	38.4	330 55.4 ..	57.9	297 01.5 ..	36.6	Enif	33 43.6	N 9 57.8
S 10	232 02.4	16 24.8	19.0	243 10.9	37.7	345 57.3	58.0	312 03.6	36.6	Fomalhaut	15 19.9	S29 31.5
D 11	247 04.9	31 25.3	19.4	258 11.9	37.0	0 59.2	58.1	327 05.8	36.6			
A 12	262 07.3	46 25.9	S11 19.8	273 12.9	S 5 36.3	16 01.1	S20 58.2	342 07.9	S22 36.6	Gacrux	171 56.9	S57 12.7
Y 13	277 09.8	61 26.5	20.3	288 13.8	35.6	31 03.0	58.3	357 10.1	36.6	Gienah	175 48.5	S17 38.6
14	292 12.3	76 27.0	20.7	303 14.8	34.8	46 04.8	58.4	12 12.2	36.5	Hadar	148 43.0	S60 27.4
15	307 14.7	91 27.6 ..	21.1	318 15.8 ..	34.1	61 06.7 ..	58.5	27 14.4 ..	36.5	Hamal	327 56.3	N23 33.1
16	322 17.2	106 28.1	21.6	333 16.7	33.4	76 08.6	58.6	42 16.6	36.5	Kaus Aust.	83 39.3	S34 22.4
17	337 19.6	121 28.7	22.0	348 17.7	32.7	91 10.5	58.7	57 18.7	36.5			
18	352 22.1	136 29.2	S11 22.4	3 18.7	S 5 32.0	106 12.4	S20 58.8	72 20.9	S22 36.5	Kochab	137 21.1	N74 04.6
19	7 24.6	151 29.8	22.9	18 19.6	31.3	121 14.2	58.8	87 23.0	36.5	Markab	13 34.7	N15 18.5
20	22 27.0	166 30.4	23.3	33 20.6	30.6	136 16.1	58.9	102 25.2	36.4	Menkar	314 10.9	N 4 09.7
21	37 29.5	181 30.9 ..	23.8	48 21.6 ..	29.9	151 18.0 ..	59.0	117 27.3 ..	36.4	Menkent	148 03.4	S36 27.4
22	52 32.0	196 31.4	24.2	63 22.5	29.2	166 19.9	59.1	132 29.5	36.4	Miaplacidus	221 38.3	S69 47.4
23	67 34.4	211 32.0	24.7	78 23.5	28.5	181 21.8	59.2	147 31.6	36.4			
14 00	82 36.9	226 32.5	S11 25.1	93 24.5	S 5 27.8	196 23.7	S20 59.3	162 33.8	S22 36.4	Mirfak	308 34.5	N49 55.6
01	97 39.4	241 33.1	25.5	108 25.4	27.1	211 25.5	59.4	177 35.9	36.4	Nunki	75 54.1	S26 16.3
02	112 41.8	256 33.6	26.0	123 26.4	26.3	226 27.4	59.5	192 38.1	36.3	Peacock	53 13.9	S56 40.5
03	127 44.3	271 34.2 ..	26.4	138 27.4 ..	25.6	241 29.3 ..	59.6	207 40.3 ..	36.3	Pollux	243 22.9	N27 58.6
04	142 46.8	286 34.7	26.9	153 28.3	24.9	256 31.2	59.7	222 42.4	36.3	Procyon	244 55.6	N 5 10.5
05	157 49.2	301 35.2	27.3	168 29.3	24.2	271 33.1	59.8	237 44.6	36.3			
F 06	172 51.7	316 35.8	S11 27.8	183 30.3	S 5 23.5	286 34.9	S20 59.9	252 46.7	S22 36.3	Rasalhague	96 03.4	N12 33.0
R 07	187 54.1	331 36.3	28.2	198 31.2	22.8	301 36.8	20 59.9	267 48.9	36.3	Regulus	207 39.5	N11 52.4
I 08	202 56.6	346 36.8	28.7	213 32.2	22.1	316 38.7	21 00.0	282 51.0	36.2	Rigel	281 08.1	S 8 10.9
D 09	217 59.1	1 37.4 ..	29.1	228 33.2 ..	21.4	331 40.6 ..	00.1	297 53.2 ..	36.2	Rigil Kent.	139 47.2	S60 54.4
A 10	233 01.5	16 37.9	29.6	243 34.1	20.7	346 42.5	00.2	312 55.3	36.2	Sabik	102 08.6	S15 44.7
Y 11	248 04.0	31 38.4	30.0	258 35.1	20.0	1 44.4	00.3	327 57.5	36.2			
12	263 06.5	46 38.9	S11 30.5	273 36.1	S 5 19.2	16 46.2	S21 00.4	342 59.6	S22 36.2	Schedar	349 36.0	N56 38.6
13	278 08.9	61 39.5	30.9	288 37.0	18.5	31 48.1	00.5	358 01.8	36.2	Shaula	96 17.3	S37 06.8
14	293 11.4	76 40.0	31.4	303 38.0	17.8	46 50.0	00.6	13 03.9	36.1	Sirius	258 30.1	S16 44.6
15	308 13.9	91 40.5 ..	31.8	318 39.0 ..	17.1	61 51.9 ..	00.7	28 06.1 ..	36.1	Spica	158 27.5	S11 15.4
16	323 16.3	106 41.0	32.3	333 39.9	16.4	76 53.8	00.7	43 08.3	36.1	Suhail	222 49.4	S43 30.4
17	338 18.8	121 41.6	32.8	348 40.9	15.7	91 55.7	00.8	58 10.4	36.1			
18	353 21.2	136 42.1	S11 33.2	3 41.9	S 5 15.0	106 57.5	S21 00.9	73 12.6	S22 36.1	Vega	80 36.9	N38 48.3
19	8 23.7	151 42.6	33.7	18 42.8	14.3	121 59.4	01.0	88 14.7	36.1	Zuben'ubi	137 01.6	S16 07.0
20	23 26.2	166 43.1	34.1	33 43.8	13.6	137 01.3	01.1	103 16.9	36.0		SHA	Mer.Pass.
21	38 28.6	181 43.6 ..	34.6	48 44.8 ..	12.9	152 03.2 ..	01.2	118 19.0 ..	36.0	Venus	144 41.3	8 54
22	53 31.1	196 44.1	35.0	63 45.7	12.2	167 05.1	01.3	133 21.2	36.0	Mars	11 23.5	17 47
23	68 33.3	211 44.6	35.5	78 46.7	11.4	182 06.9	01.4	148 23.3	36.0	Jupiter	114 00.7	10 56
Mer.Pass. 18 30.4		v 0.6	d 0.4	v 1.0	d 0.7	v 1.9	d 0.1	v 2.2	d 0.0	Saturn	80 04.3	13 11

UT	SUN GHA	SUN Dec	MOON GHA	v	MOON Dec	d	HP
d h	° ′	° ′	° ′	′	° ′	′	′
12 00	181 38.1	S23 03.0	125 47.5	12.9	S18 28.4	5.8	54.1
01	196 37.8	03.2	140 19.4	12.9	18 22.6	5.9	54.1
02	211 37.5	03.4	154 51.3	13.0	18 16.7	6.0	54.1
03	226 37.2	.. 03.6	169 23.3	13.0	18 10.7	6.1	54.1
04	241 36.9	03.8	183 55.3	13.1	18 04.6	6.1	54.1
05	256 36.6	04.0	198 27.4	13.1	17 58.5	6.2	54.1
06	271 36.3	S23 04.2	212 59.5	13.1	S17 52.3	6.3	54.1
W 07	286 36.0	04.4	227 31.6	13.2	17 46.0	6.4	54.1
E 08	301 35.7	04.6	242 03.8	13.2	17 39.6	6.4	54.1
D 09	316 35.5	.. 04.7	256 36.0	13.2	17 33.2	6.5	54.1
N 10	331 35.2	04.9	271 08.2	13.3	17 26.7	6.6	54.1
E 11	346 34.9	05.1	285 40.5	13.3	17 20.1	6.7	54.1
S 12	1 34.6	S23 05.3	300 12.8	13.4	S17 13.4	6.7	54.1
D 13	16 34.3	05.5	314 45.2	13.4	17 06.7	6.8	54.1
A 14	31 34.0	05.7	329 17.6	13.5	16 59.9	6.9	54.1
Y 15	46 33.7	.. 05.8	343 50.1	13.4	16 53.0	7.0	54.1
16	61 33.4	06.0	358 22.5	13.6	16 46.0	7.0	54.1
17	76 33.1	06.2	12 55.1	13.5	16 39.0	7.1	54.1
18	91 32.8	S23 06.4	27 27.6	13.6	S16 31.9	7.2	54.1
19	106 32.5	06.6	42 00.2	13.7	16 24.7	7.2	54.1
20	121 32.2	06.7	56 32.9	13.6	16 17.5	7.3	54.1
21	136 31.9	.. 06.9	71 05.5	13.7	16 10.2	7.4	54.1
22	151 31.6	07.1	85 38.2	13.8	16 02.8	7.4	54.1
23	166 31.4	07.3	100 11.0	13.8	15 55.4	7.5	54.1
13 00	181 31.1	S23 07.4	114 43.8	13.8	S15 47.9	7.6	54.1
01	196 30.8	07.6	129 16.6	13.8	15 40.3	7.7	54.1
02	211 30.5	07.8	143 49.4	13.9	15 32.6	7.7	54.1
03	226 30.2	.. 08.0	158 22.3	13.9	15 24.9	7.8	54.1
04	241 29.9	08.1	172 55.2	14.0	15 17.1	7.8	54.2
05	256 29.6	08.3	187 28.2	14.0	15 09.3	7.9	54.2
06	271 29.3	S23 08.5	202 01.2	14.0	S15 01.4	8.0	54.2
T 07	286 29.0	08.6	216 34.2	14.1	14 53.4	8.0	54.2
H 08	301 28.7	08.8	231 07.3	14.0	14 45.4	8.1	54.2
U 09	316 28.4	.. 09.0	245 40.3	14.2	14 37.3	8.2	54.2
R 10	331 28.1	09.1	260 13.5	14.1	14 29.1	8.2	54.2
S 11	346 27.8	09.3	274 46.6	14.2	14 20.9	8.3	54.2
D 12	1 27.5	S23 09.5	289 19.8	14.2	S14 12.6	8.4	54.2
A 13	16 27.2	09.6	303 53.0	14.3	14 04.2	8.4	54.2
Y 14	31 26.9	09.8	318 26.3	14.2	13 55.8	8.4	54.2
15	46 26.6	.. 10.0	332 59.5	14.3	13 47.4	8.6	54.2
16	61 26.3	10.1	347 32.8	14.4	13 38.8	8.5	54.2
17	76 26.0	10.3	2 06.2	14.3	13 30.3	8.7	54.2
18	91 25.7	S23 10.4	16 39.5	14.4	S13 21.6	8.7	54.2
19	106 25.4	10.6	31 12.9	14.4	13 12.9	8.7	54.2
20	121 25.2	10.8	45 46.3	14.5	13 04.2	8.8	54.3
21	136 24.9	.. 10.9	60 19.8	14.4	12 55.4	8.9	54.3
22	151 24.6	11.1	74 53.2	14.5	12 46.5	8.9	54.3
23	166 24.3	11.2	89 26.7	14.5	12 37.6	9.0	54.3
14 00	181 24.0	S23 11.4	104 00.2	14.6	S12 28.6	9.1	54.3
01	196 23.7	11.5	118 33.8	14.5	12 19.5	9.0	54.3
02	211 23.4	11.7	133 07.3	14.6	12 10.5	9.2	54.3
03	226 23.1	.. 11.8	147 40.9	14.6	12 01.3	9.2	54.3
04	241 22.8	12.0	162 14.5	14.7	11 52.1	9.2	54.3
05	256 22.5	12.1	176 48.2	14.6	11 42.9	9.3	54.3
06	271 22.2	S23 12.3	191 21.8	14.7	S11 33.6	9.4	54.4
07	286 21.9	12.4	205 55.4	14.7	11 24.2	9.3	54.4
08	301 21.6	12.6	220 29.2	14.7	11 14.9	9.5	54.4
F 09	316 21.3	.. 12.7	235 02.9	14.7	11 05.4	9.5	54.4
R 10	331 21.0	12.9	249 36.6	14.8	10 55.9	9.5	54.4
I 11	346 20.7	13.0	264 10.4	14.7	10 46.4	9.6	54.4
D 12	1 20.4	S23 13.2	278 44.1	14.8	S10 36.8	9.7	54.4
A 13	16 20.1	13.3	293 17.9	14.8	10 27.1	9.7	54.4
Y 14	31 19.8	13.5	307 51.7	14.8	10 17.4	9.7	54.5
15	46 19.5	.. 13.6	322 25.5	14.9	10 07.7	9.8	54.5
16	61 19.2	13.7	336 59.4	14.8	9 57.9	9.8	54.5
17	76 18.9	13.9	351 33.2	14.9	9 48.1	9.9	54.5
18	91 18.6	S23 14.0	6 07.1	14.8	S 9 38.2	9.9	54.5
19	106 18.3	14.2	20 40.9	14.9	9 28.3	9.9	54.5
20	121 18.0	14.3	35 14.8	14.9	9 18.4	10.0	54.6
21	136 17.7	.. 14.4	49 48.7	14.9	9 08.4	10.1	54.6
22	151 17.4	14.6	64 22.6	14.9	8 58.3	10.1	54.6
23	166 17.1	14.7	78 56.5	14.9	S 8 48.2	10.1	54.6
	SD 16.3	d 0.2	SD 14.7		14.8		14.8

Lat.	Naut.	Civil	Sunrise	Moonrise 12	13	14	15
°	h m	h m	h m	h m	h m	h m	h m
N 72	08 17	10 40	■■	14 45	14 07	13 46	13 30
N 70	07 58	09 44	■■	13 53	13 40	13 30	13 21
68	07 42	09 10	■■	13 21	13 19	13 17	13 14
66	07 29	08 46	10 23	12 57	13 03	13 06	13 08
64	07 19	08 27	09 43	12 38	12 49	12 57	13 03
62	07 09	08 11	09 16	12 23	12 38	12 49	12 58
60	07 01	07 58	08 55	12 10	12 28	12 42	12 54
N 58	06 54	07 46	08 38	11 59	12 19	12 36	12 50
56	06 47	07 36	08 23	11 49	12 12	12 31	12 47
54	06 41	07 27	08 11	11 41	12 05	12 26	12 44
52	06 35	07 19	08 00	11 33	11 59	12 22	12 42
50	06 30	07 12	07 50	11 26	11 53	12 18	12 40
45	06 19	06 56	07 30	11 11	11 42	12 09	12 34
N 40	06 09	06 43	07 13	10 59	11 32	12 02	12 30
35	05 59	06 31	06 59	10 48	11 23	11 56	12 26
30	05 51	06 21	06 47	10 39	11 16	11 50	12 23
20	05 35	06 02	06 26	10 23	11 03	11 41	12 17
N 10	05 19	05 45	06 08	10 09	10 51	11 32	12 12
0	05 02	05 28	05 50	09 56	10 41	11 24	12 07
S 10	04 43	05 10	05 33	09 43	10 30	11 17	12 03
20	04 21	04 50	05 14	09 29	10 19	11 08	11 58
30	03 52	04 25	04 53	09 12	10 05	10 58	11 52
35	03 34	04 10	04 40	09 03	09 58	10 53	11 48
40	03 11	03 52	04 25	08 52	09 49	10 47	11 45
45	02 41	03 30	04 07	08 40	09 39	10 39	11 40
S 50	01 56	03 01	03 45	08 24	09 27	10 30	11 35
52	01 30	02 46	03 34	08 17	09 21	10 26	11 32
54	00 48	02 28	03 22	08 09	09 14	10 22	11 30
56	////	02 07	03 08	08 00	09 07	10 16	11 27
58	////	01 38	02 52	07 50	08 59	10 11	11 23
S 60	////	00 53	02 32	07 38	08 50	10 04	11 20

Lat.	Sunset	Civil	Naut.	Moonset 12	13	14	15
°	h m	h m	h m	h m	h m	h m	h m
N 72	■■	13 08	15 31	17 41	19 52	21 44	23 29
N 70	■■	14 04	15 50	18 32	20 18	21 58	23 36
68	■■	14 38	16 06	19 03	20 38	22 10	23 42
66	13 25	15 02	16 19	19 27	20 53	22 20	23 46
64	14 05	15 22	16 29	19 45	21 06	22 27	23 50
62	14 32	15 37	16 39	19 59	21 16	22 34	23 53
60	14 53	15 51	16 47	20 12	21 25	22 40	23 56
N 58	15 11	16 02	16 54	20 23	21 33	22 45	23 59
56	15 25	16 12	17 01	20 32	21 40	22 50	24 01
54	15 37	16 21	17 07	20 40	21 46	22 54	24 03
52	15 48	16 29	17 13	20 47	21 52	22 58	24 05
50	15 58	16 36	17 18	20 54	21 57	23 01	24 06
45	16 19	16 52	17 29	21 08	22 08	23 08	24 10
N 40	16 35	17 06	17 40	21 20	22 17	23 14	24 13
35	16 49	17 17	17 49	21 29	22 24	23 20	24 15
30	17 01	17 28	17 57	21 38	22 31	23 24	24 18
20	17 22	17 46	18 14	21 53	22 43	23 32	24 22
N 10	17 41	18 03	18 30	22 06	22 53	23 39	24 25
0	17 58	18 20	18 47	22 18	23 02	23 45	24 28
S 10	18 15	18 38	19 05	22 30	23 11	23 51	24 31
20	18 34	18 59	19 28	22 42	23 21	23 58	24 34
30	18 56	19 23	19 57	22 57	23 32	24 06	00 06
35	19 09	19 38	20 15	23 05	23 39	24 10	00 10
40	19 24	19 56	20 38	23 14	23 46	24 15	00 15
45	19 41	20 19	21 08	23 26	23 54	24 21	00 21
S 50	20 04	20 48	21 53	23 39	24 05	00 05	00 27
52	20 14	21 03	22 20	23 45	24 09	00 09	00 31
54	20 27	21 20	23 02	23 52	24 14	00 14	00 34
56	20 40	21 42	////	24 00	00 00	00 20	00 38
58	20 57	22 11	////	24 08	00 08	00 26	00 42
S 60	21 17	22 57	////	24 18	00 18	00 34	00 47

Day	SUN Eqn. of Time 00ʰ	12ʰ	Mer. Pass.	MOON Mer. Pass. Upper	Lower	Age	Phase
d	m s	m s	h m	h m	h m	d	%
12	06 33	06 19	11 54	16 07	03 44	05	23
13	06 05	05 51	11 54	16 51	04 29	06	32
14	05 36	05 22	11 55	17 35	05 13	07	41

UT	ARIES GHA	VENUS −4.8 GHA	Dec	MARS +0.2 GHA	Dec	JUPITER −1.7 GHA	Dec	SATURN +0.5 GHA	Dec	STARS Name	SHA	Dec
15 00	83 36.0	226 45.1	S11 36.0	93 47.7	S 5 10.7	197 08.8	S21 01.5	163 25.5	S22 36.0	Acamar	315 15.2	S40 14.0
01	98 38.5	241 45.6	36.4	108 48.6	10.0	212 10.7	01.5	178 27.6	36.0	Achernar	335 23.7	S57 08.8
02	113 41.0	256 46.1	36.9	123 49.6	09.3	227 12.6	01.6	193 29.8	35.9	Acrux	173 05.2	S63 11.8
03	128 43.4	271 46.7 ..	37.3	138 50.6 ..	08.6	242 14.5 ..	01.7	208 31.9 ..	35.9	Adhara	255 09.2	S28 59.9
04	143 45.9	286 47.2	37.8	153 51.5	07.9	257 16.4	01.8	223 34.1	35.9	Aldebaran	290 44.8	N16 32.7
05	158 48.4	301 47.7	38.3	168 52.5	07.2	272 18.2	01.9	238 36.3	35.9			
S 06	173 50.8	316 48.1	S11 38.7	183 53.5	S 5 06.5	287 20.1	S21 02.0	253 38.4	S22 35.9	Alioth	166 17.6	N55 51.3
A 07	188 53.3	331 48.6	39.2	198 54.4	05.8	302 22.0	02.1	268 40.6	35.9	Alkaid	152 56.3	N49 13.1
T 08	203 55.7	346 49.1	39.7	213 55.4	05.0	317 23.9	02.2	283 42.7	35.8	Al Na'ir	27 39.3	S46 52.4
U 09	218 58.2	1 49.6 ..	40.1	228 56.4 ..	04.3	332 25.8 ..	02.3	298 44.9 ..	35.8	Alnilam	275 42.2	S 1 11.6
R 10	234 00.7	16 50.1	40.6	243 57.3	03.6	347 27.7	02.4	313 47.0	35.8	Alphard	217 52.2	S 8 44.4
D 11	249 03.1	31 50.6	41.1	258 58.3	02.9	2 29.5	02.4	328 49.2	35.8			
A 12	264 05.6	46 51.1	S11 41.5	273 59.3	S 5 02.2	17 31.4	S21 02.5	343 51.3	S22 35.8	Alphecca	126 08.2	N26 39.2
Y 13	279 08.1	61 51.6	42.0	289 00.2	01.5	32 33.3	02.6	358 53.5	35.8	Alpheratz	357 39.6	N29 11.8
14	294 10.5	76 52.1	42.5	304 01.2	00.8	47 35.2	02.7	13 55.6	35.7	Altair	62 04.9	N 8 55.2
15	309 13.0	91 52.6 ..	42.9	319 02.2	5 00.1	62 37.1 ..	02.8	28 57.8 ..	35.7	Ankaa	353 11.9	S42 12.5
16	324 15.5	106 53.0	43.4	334 03.1	4 59.4	77 39.0	02.9	43 59.9	35.7	Antares	112 22.0	S26 28.2
17	339 17.9	121 53.5	43.9	349 04.1	58.6	92 40.8	03.0	59 02.1	35.7			
18	354 20.4	136 54.0	S11 44.4	4 05.1	S 4 57.9	107 42.7	S21 03.1	74 04.2	S22 35.7	Arcturus	145 52.6	N19 05.1
19	9 22.8	151 54.5	44.8	19 06.0	57.2	122 44.6	03.1	89 06.4	35.7	Atria	107 21.1	S69 03.4
20	24 25.3	166 55.0	45.3	34 07.0	56.5	137 46.5	03.2	104 08.5	35.6	Avior	234 16.0	S59 34.1
21	39 27.8	181 55.4 ..	45.8	49 08.0 ..	55.8	152 48.4 ..	03.3	119 10.7 ..	35.6	Bellatrix	278 27.7	N 6 21.8
22	54 30.2	196 55.9	46.3	64 08.9	55.1	167 50.3	03.4	134 12.8	35.6	Betelgeuse	270 56.9	N 7 24.5
23	69 32.7	211 56.4	46.7	79 09.9	54.4	182 52.1	03.5	149 15.0	35.6			
16 00	84 35.2	226 56.9	S11 47.2	94 10.9	S 4 53.7	197 54.0	S21 03.6	164 17.2	S22 35.6	Canopus	263 53.9	S52 42.4
01	99 37.6	241 57.3	47.7	109 11.8	53.0	212 55.9	03.7	179 19.3	35.6	Capella	280 28.4	N46 00.9
02	114 40.1	256 57.8	48.2	124 12.8	52.2	227 57.8	03.8	194 21.5	35.5	Deneb	49 29.3	N45 21.1
03	129 42.6	271 58.3 ..	48.6	139 13.7 ..	51.5	242 59.7 ..	03.9	209 23.6 ..	35.5	Denebola	182 29.9	N14 28.0
04	144 45.0	286 58.7	49.1	154 14.7	50.8	258 01.6	03.9	224 25.8	35.5	Diphda	348 52.1	S17 53.2
05	159 47.5	301 59.2	49.6	169 15.7	50.1	273 03.4	04.0	239 27.9	35.5			
S 06	174 50.0	316 59.7	S11 50.1	184 16.6	S 4 49.4	288 05.3	S21 04.1	254 30.1	S22 35.5	Dubhe	193 47.1	N61 38.7
U 07	189 52.4	332 00.1	50.6	199 17.6	48.7	303 07.2	04.2	269 32.2	35.5	Elnath	278 07.5	N28 37.2
N 08	204 54.9	347 00.6	51.0	214 18.6	48.0	318 09.1	04.3	284 34.4	35.4	Eltanin	90 45.0	N51 29.3
D 09	219 57.3	2 01.0 ..	51.5	229 19.5 ..	47.3	333 11.0 ..	04.4	299 36.5 ..	35.4	Enif	33 43.6	N 9 57.8
A 10	234 59.8	17 01.5	52.0	244 20.5	46.5	348 12.9	04.5	314 38.7	35.4	Fomalhaut	15 20.0	S29 31.5
Y 11	250 02.3	32 01.9	52.5	259 21.5	45.8	3 14.7	04.6	329 40.8	35.4			
12	265 04.7	47 02.4	S11 53.0	274 22.4	S 4 45.1	18 16.6	S21 04.7	344 43.0	S22 35.4	Gacrux	171 56.8	S57 12.7
13	280 07.2	62 02.9	53.5	289 23.4	44.4	33 18.5	04.7	359 45.1	35.4	Gienah	175 48.5	S17 38.6
14	295 09.7	77 03.3	53.9	304 24.4	43.7	48 20.4	04.8	14 47.3	35.3	Hadar	148 43.0	S60 27.4
15	310 12.1	92 03.8 ..	54.4	319 25.3 ..	43.0	63 22.3 ..	04.9	29 49.4 ..	35.3	Hamal	327 56.3	N23 33.1
16	325 14.6	107 04.2	54.9	334 26.3	42.3	78 24.2	05.0	44 51.6	35.3	Kaus Aust.	83 39.3	S34 22.4
17	340 17.1	122 04.6	55.4	349 27.3	41.6	93 26.0	05.1	59 53.7	35.3			
18	355 19.5	137 05.1	S11 55.9	4 28.2	S 4 40.8	108 27.9	S21 05.2	74 55.9	S22 35.3	Kochab	137 21.1	N74 04.6
19	10 22.0	152 05.5	56.4	19 29.2	40.1	123 29.8	05.3	89 58.0	35.3	Markab	13 34.7	N15 18.5
20	25 24.5	167 06.0	56.9	34 30.1	39.4	138 31.7	05.4	105 00.2	35.2	Menkar	314 10.9	N 4 09.7
21	40 26.9	182 06.4 ..	57.4	49 31.1 ..	38.7	153 33.6 ..	05.4	120 02.3 ..	35.2	Menkent	148 03.4	S36 27.4
22	55 29.4	197 06.9	57.8	64 32.1	38.0	168 35.5	05.5	135 04.5	35.2	Miaplacidus	221 38.3	S69 47.4
23	70 31.8	212 07.3	58.3	79 33.0	37.3	183 37.3	05.6	150 06.7	35.2			
17 00	85 34.3	227 07.7	S11 58.8	94 34.0	S 4 36.6	198 39.2	S21 05.7	165 08.8	S22 35.2	Mirfak	308 34.5	N49 55.7
01	100 36.8	242 08.2	59.3	109 35.0	35.9	213 41.1	05.8	180 11.0	35.1	Nunki	75 54.1	S26 16.3
02	115 39.2	257 08.6	11 59.8	124 35.9	35.1	228 43.0	05.9	195 13.1	35.1	Peacock	53 13.9	S56 40.5
03	130 41.7	272 09.0	12 00.3	139 36.9 ..	34.4	243 44.9 ..	06.0	210 15.3 ..	35.1	Pollux	243 22.9	N27 58.6
04	145 44.2	287 09.5	00.8	154 37.9	33.7	258 46.8	06.1	225 17.4	35.1	Procyon	244 55.5	N 5 10.5
05	160 46.6	302 09.9	01.3	169 38.8	33.0	273 48.7	06.1	240 19.6	35.1			
M 06	175 49.1	317 10.3	S12 01.8	184 39.8	S 4 32.3	288 50.5	S21 06.2	255 21.7	S22 35.1	Rasalhague	96 03.3	N12 33.0
O 07	190 51.6	332 10.7	02.3	199 40.7	31.6	303 52.4	06.3	270 23.9	35.0	Regulus	207 39.4	N11 52.4
N 08	205 54.0	347 11.2	02.8	214 41.7	30.9	318 54.3	06.4	285 26.0	35.0	Rigel	281 08.1	S 8 11.0
D 09	220 56.5	2 11.6 ..	03.3	229 42.7 ..	30.2	333 56.2 ..	06.5	300 28.2 ..	35.0	Rigil Kent.	139 47.1	S60 54.4
A 10	235 58.9	17 12.0	03.8	244 43.6	29.4	348 58.1	06.6	315 30.3	35.0	Sabik	102 08.6	S15 44.7
Y 11	251 01.4	32 12.4	04.3	259 44.6	28.7	4 00.0	06.7	330 32.5	35.0			
12	266 03.9	47 12.9	S12 04.8	274 45.6	S 4 28.0	19 01.8	S21 06.7	345 34.6	S22 35.0	Schedar	349 36.1	N56 38.6
13	281 06.3	62 13.3	05.2	289 46.5	27.3	34 03.7	06.8	0 36.8	34.9	Shaula	96 17.3	S37 06.8
14	296 08.8	77 13.7	05.7	304 47.5	26.6	49 05.6	06.9	15 38.9	34.9	Sirius	258 30.1	S16 44.6
15	311 11.3	92 14.1 ..	06.2	319 48.4 ..	25.9	64 07.5 ..	07.0	30 41.1 ..	34.9	Spica	158 27.5	S11 15.4
16	326 13.7	107 14.5	06.7	334 49.4	25.2	79 09.4	07.1	45 43.2	34.9	Suhail	222 49.4	S43 30.4
17	341 16.2	122 14.9	07.2	349 50.4	24.4	94 11.3	07.2	60 45.4	34.9			
18	356 18.7	137 15.3	S12 07.7	4 51.3	S 4 23.7	109 13.2	S21 07.3	75 47.5	S22 34.8	Vega	80 36.9	N38 48.3
19	11 21.1	152 15.7	08.2	19 52.3	23.0	124 15.0	07.4	90 49.7	34.8	Zuben'ubi	137 01.6	S16 07.0
20	26 23.6	167 16.2	08.7	34 53.3	22.3	139 16.9	07.4	105 51.8	34.8		SHA	Mer.Pass.
21	41 26.1	182 16.6 ..	09.3	49 54.2 ..	21.6	154 18.8 ..	07.5	120 54.0 ..	34.8			
22	56 28.5	197 17.0	09.8	64 55.2	20.9	169 20.7	07.6	135 56.1	34.8	Venus	142 21.7	8 52
23	71 31.0	212 17.4	10.3	79 56.2	20.2	184 22.6	07.7	150 58.3	34.8	Mars	9 35.7	17 42
Mer.Pass. 18 18.6		v 0.5	d 0.5	v 1.0	d 0.7	v 1.9	d 0.1	v 2.2	d 0.0	Jupiter	113 18.8	10 47
										Saturn	79 42.0	13 01

UT	SUN GHA	SUN Dec	MOON GHA	v	MOON Dec	d	HP
d h	° ′	° ′	° ′	′	° ′	′	′
15 00	181 16.8	S23 14.9	93 30.4	15.0	S 8 38.1	10.2	54.6
01	196 16.5	15.0	108 04.4	14.9	8 27.9	10.2	54.6
02	211 16.2	15.1	122 38.3	14.9	8 17.7	10.3	54.7
03	226 15.9	. . 15.3	137 12.2	15.0	8 07.4	10.2	54.7
04	241 15.6	15.4	151 46.2	14.9	7 57.2	10.4	54.7
05	256 15.3	15.5	166 20.1	15.0	7 46.8	10.4	54.7
06	271 15.0	S23 15.7	180 54.1	14.9	S 7 36.4	10.4	54.7
S 07	286 14.7	15.8	195 28.0	15.0	7 26.0	10.4	54.7
A 08	301 14.4	15.9	210 02.0	15.0	7 15.6	10.5	54.8
T 09	316 14.1	. . 16.0	224 36.0	14.9	7 05.1	10.5	54.8
U 10	331 13.8	16.2	239 09.9	15.0	6 54.6	10.6	54.8
R 11	346 13.5	16.3	253 43.9	15.0	6 44.0	10.6	54.8
D 12	1 13.2	S23 16.4	268 17.9	14.9	S 6 33.4	10.6	54.9
A 13	16 12.9	16.5	282 51.8	15.0	6 22.8	10.6	54.9
Y 14	31 12.6	16.7	297 25.8	14.9	6 12.2	10.7	54.9
15	46 12.3	. . 16.8	311 59.7	15.0	6 01.5	10.8	54.9
16	61 12.0	16.9	326 33.7	14.9	5 50.7	10.7	54.9
17	76 11.7	17.0	341 07.6	15.0	5 40.0	10.8	55.0
18	91 11.4	S23 17.2	355 41.6	14.9	S 5 29.2	10.8	55.0
19	106 11.1	17.3	10 15.5	15.0	5 18.4	10.9	55.0
20	121 10.8	17.4	24 49.5	14.9	5 07.5	10.9	55.0
21	136 10.5	. . 17.5	39 23.4	14.9	4 56.6	10.9	55.0
22	151 10.2	17.6	53 57.3	14.9	4 45.7	10.9	55.1
23	166 09.9	17.8	68 31.2	14.9	4 34.8	11.0	55.1
16 00	181 09.6	S23 17.9	83 05.1	14.9	S 4 23.8	11.0	55.1
01	196 09.3	18.0	97 39.0	14.8	4 12.8	11.1	55.1
02	211 09.0	18.1	112 12.8	14.9	4 01.7	11.0	55.2
03	226 08.7	. . 18.2	126 46.7	14.8	3 50.7	11.1	55.2
04	241 08.4	18.3	141 20.5	14.9	3 39.6	11.1	55.2
05	256 08.1	18.4	155 54.4	14.8	3 28.5	11.1	55.2
06	271 07.8	S23 18.5	170 28.2	14.8	S 3 17.4	11.2	55.3
07	286 07.5	18.7	185 02.0	14.7	3 06.2	11.2	55.3
08	301 07.1	18.8	199 35.7	14.8	2 55.0	11.2	55.3
S 09	316 06.8	. . 18.9	214 09.5	14.7	2 43.8	11.2	55.3
U 10	331 06.5	19.0	228 43.2	14.7	2 32.6	11.2	55.4
N 11	346 06.2	19.1	243 16.9	14.7	2 21.4	11.3	55.4
D 12	1 05.9	S23 19.2	257 50.6	14.7	S 2 10.1	11.3	55.4
A 13	16 05.6	19.3	272 24.3	14.7	1 58.8	11.3	55.5
Y 14	31 05.3	19.4	286 58.0	14.6	1 47.5	11.3	55.5
15	46 05.0	. . 19.5	301 31.6	14.6	1 36.2	11.4	55.5
16	61 04.7	19.6	316 05.2	14.6	1 24.8	11.4	55.5
17	76 04.4	19.7	330 38.8	14.5	1 13.4	11.3	55.6
18	91 04.1	S23 19.8	345 12.3	14.5	S 1 02.1	11.5	55.6
19	106 03.8	19.9	359 45.8	14.5	0 50.6	11.4	55.6
20	121 03.5	20.0	14 19.3	14.5	0 39.2	11.4	55.7
21	136 03.2	. . 20.1	28 52.8	14.4	0 27.8	11.4	55.7
22	151 02.9	20.2	43 26.2	14.4	0 16.4	11.5	55.7
23	166 02.6	20.3	57 59.6	14.4	S 0 04.9	11.5	55.7
17 00	181 02.3	S23 20.4	72 33.0	14.3	N 0 06.6	11.5	55.8
01	196 02.0	20.5	87 06.3	14.3	0 18.1	11.5	55.8
02	211 01.7	20.6	101 39.6	14.3	0 29.6	11.5	55.8
03	226 01.4	. . 20.7	116 12.9	14.2	0 41.1	11.5	55.9
04	241 01.1	20.8	130 46.1	14.2	0 52.6	11.5	55.9
05	256 00.8	20.9	145 19.3	14.1	1 04.1	11.6	55.9
06	271 00.5	S23 21.0	159 52.4	14.1	N 1 15.7	11.5	56.0
07	286 00.2	21.1	174 25.5	14.1	1 27.2	11.6	56.0
08	300 59.9	21.2	188 58.6	14.0	1 38.8	11.6	56.0
M 09	315 59.5	. . 21.3	203 31.6	14.0	1 50.4	11.5	56.1
O 10	330 59.2	21.3	218 04.6	14.0	2 01.9	11.6	56.1
N 11	345 58.9	21.4	232 37.6	13.9	2 13.5	11.6	56.1
D 12	0 58.6	S23 21.5	247 10.5	13.8	N 2 25.1	11.6	56.2
A 13	15 58.3	21.6	261 43.3	13.8	2 36.7	11.5	56.2
Y 14	30 58.0	21.7	276 16.1	13.8	2 48.2	11.6	56.2
15	45 57.7	. . 21.8	290 48.9	13.7	2 59.8	11.6	56.3
16	60 57.4	21.9	305 21.6	13.7	3 11.4	11.6	56.3
17	75 57.1	21.9	319 54.3	13.6	3 23.0	11.6	56.3
18	90 56.8	S23 22.0	334 26.9	13.5	N 3 34.6	11.6	56.4
19	105 56.5	22.1	348 59.4	13.5	3 46.2	11.6	56.4
20	120 56.2	22.2	3 31.9	13.5	3 57.8	11.6	56.4
21	135 55.9	. . 22.3	18 04.4	13.4	4 09.4	11.5	56.5
22	150 55.6	22.3	32 36.8	13.4	4 20.9	11.6	56.5
23	165 55.3	22.4	47 09.2	13.3	N 4 32.5	11.6	56.5
	SD 16.3	*d* 0.1	SD 14.9		15.1		15.3

Lat.	Twilight Naut.	Twilight Civil	Sunrise	Moonrise 15	Moonrise 16	Moonrise 17	Moonrise 18
°	h m	h m	h m	h m	h m	h m	h m
N 72	08 21	10 49	■	13 30	13 16	13 02	12 48
N 70	08 01	09 49	■	13 21	13 13	13 06	12 58
68	07 46	09 14	■	13 14	13 11	13 08	13 06
66	07 33	08 49	10 29	13 08	13 09	13 11	13 13
64	07 22	08 30	09 47	13 03	13 08	13 13	13 19
62	07 12	08 14	09 19	12 58	13 06	13 15	13 24
60	07 04	08 01	08 58	12 54	13 05	13 16	13 28
N 58	06 56	07 49	08 41	12 50	13 04	13 17	13 32
56	06 50	07 39	08 26	12 47	13 03	13 19	13 36
54	06 43	07 30	08 13	12 44	13 02	13 20	13 39
52	06 38	07 22	08 02	12 42	13 01	13 21	13 42
50	06 33	07 14	07 53	12 40	13 00	13 22	13 44
45	06 21	06 58	07 32	12 34	12 59	13 24	13 50
N 40	06 11	06 45	07 15	12 30	12 58	13 25	13 55
35	06 01	06 33	07 01	12 26	12 56	13 27	13 59
30	05 53	06 22	06 49	12 23	12 55	13 28	14 03
20	05 36	06 04	06 28	12 17	12 54	13 31	14 09
N 10	05 20	05 46	06 09	12 12	12 52	13 33	14 15
0	05 03	05 29	05 52	12 07	12 51	13 35	14 21
S 10	04 44	05 11	05 34	12 03	12 49	13 37	14 26
20	04 22	04 51	05 15	11 58	12 48	13 39	14 32
30	03 53	04 26	04 54	11 52	12 46	13 41	14 39
35	03 34	04 11	04 41	11 48	12 45	13 43	14 43
40	03 11	03 53	04 26	11 45	12 44	13 44	14 47
45	02 41	03 30	04 08	11 40	12 42	13 46	14 53
S 50	01 56	03 01	03 45	11 35	12 41	13 49	14 59
52	01 28	02 46	03 34	11 32	12 40	13 50	15 02
54	00 44	02 28	03 22	11 30	12 39	13 51	15 05
56	////	02 06	03 08	11 27	12 38	13 52	15 08
58	////	01 37	02 51	11 23	12 37	13 53	15 12
S 60	////	00 48	02 31	11 20	12 36	13 55	15 17

Lat.	Sunset	Twilight Civil	Twilight Naut.	Moonset 15	Moonset 16	Moonset 17	Moonset 18
°	h m	h m	h m	h m	h m	h m	h m
N 72	■	13 02	15 30	23 29	25 15	01 15	03 04
N 70	■	14 02	15 50	23 36	25 15	01 15	02 56
68	■	14 37	16 05	23 42	25 14	01 14	02 50
66	13 22	15 02	16 18	23 46	25 14	01 14	02 45
64	14 04	15 21	16 29	23 50	25 14	01 14	02 41
62	14 32	15 37	16 39	23 53	25 14	01 14	02 37
60	14 53	15 51	16 47	23 56	25 13	01 13	02 33
N 58	15 10	16 02	16 55	23 59	25 13	01 13	02 31
56	15 25	16 12	17 01	24 01	00 01	01 13	02 28
54	15 38	16 21	17 08	24 03	00 03	01 13	02 26
52	15 49	16 30	17 13	24 05	00 05	01 13	02 24
50	15 59	16 37	17 18	24 06	00 06	01 13	02 22
45	16 19	16 53	17 30	24 10	00 10	01 13	02 18
N 40	16 36	17 06	17 40	24 13	00 13	01 13	02 14
35	16 50	17 18	17 50	24 15	00 15	01 12	02 11
30	17 02	17 29	17 59	24 18	00 18	01 12	02 09
20	17 23	17 47	18 15	24 22	00 22	01 12	02 04
N 10	17 42	18 05	18 31	24 25	00 25	01 12	02 00
0	17 59	18 22	18 48	24 28	00 28	01 11	01 56
S 10	18 17	18 40	19 07	24 31	00 31	01 11	01 53
20	18 36	19 00	19 30	24 34	00 34	01 11	01 49
30	18 58	19 25	19 59	00 06	00 38	01 11	01 44
35	19 11	19 40	20 17	00 10	00 40	01 10	01 42
40	19 26	19 59	20 40	00 15	00 43	01 10	01 39
45	19 44	20 21	21 11	00 21	00 45	01 10	01 35
S 50	20 06	20 51	21 56	00 27	00 49	01 10	01 31
52	20 17	21 06	22 24	00 31	00 50	01 09	01 29
54	20 29	21 24	23 09	00 34	00 52	01 09	01 27
56	20 43	21 46	////	00 38	00 54	01 09	01 25
58	21 00	22 15	////	00 42	00 56	01 09	01 23
S 60	21 20	23 04	////	00 47	00 58	01 09	01 20

Day	SUN Eqn. of Time 00^h	SUN Eqn. of Time 12^h	SUN Mer. Pass.	MOON Mer. Pass. Upper	MOON Mer. Pass. Lower	MOON Age	MOON Phase
d	m s	m s	h m	h m	h m	d %	
15	05 08	04 53	11 55	18 18	05 56	08 50	
16	04 39	04 24	11 56	19 01	06 39	09 60	
17	04 10	03 55	11 56	19 45	07 23	10 69	

UT	ARIES	VENUS −4·7		MARS +0·3		JUPITER −1·8		SATURN +0·5		STARS		
	GHA	GHA	Dec	GHA	Dec	GHA	Dec	GHA	Dec	Name	SHA	Dec
d h	° ′	° ′	° ′	° ′	° ′	° ′	° ′	° ′	° ′		° ′	° ′
18 00	86 33.4	227 17.8	S12 10.8	94 57.1	S 4 19.4	199 24.5	S21 07.8	166 00.4	S22 34.7	Acamar	315 15.2	S40 14.0
01	101 35.9	242 18.2	11.3	109 58.1	18.7	214 26.3	07.9	181 02.6	34.7	Achernar	335 23.7	S57 08.8
02	116 38.4	257 18.6	11.8	124 59.0	18.0	229 28.2	08.0	196 04.7	34.7	Acrux	173 05.2	S63 11.8
03	131 40.8	272 19.0	. . 12.3	140 00.0	. . 17.3	244 30.1	. . 08.0	211 06.9	. . 34.7	Adhara	255 09.2	S28 59.9
04	146 43.3	287 19.4	12.8	155 01.0	16.6	259 32.0	08.1	226 09.0	34.7	Aldebaran	290 44.8	N16 32.7
05	161 45.8	302 19.8	13.3	170 01.9	15.9	274 33.9	08.2	241 11.2	34.7			
06	176 48.2	317 20.2	S12 13.8	185 02.9	S 4 15.2	289 35.8	S21 08.3	256 13.3	S22 34.6	Alioth	166 17.6	N55 51.3
07	191 50.7	332 20.6	14.3	200 03.9	14.4	304 37.7	08.4	271 15.5	34.6	Alkaid	152 56.2	N49 13.0
T 08	206 53.2	347 20.9	14.8	215 04.8	13.7	319 39.5	08.5	286 17.6	34.6	Al Na'ir	27 39.3	S46 52.4
U 09	221 55.6	2 21.3	. . 15.3	230 05.8	. . 13.0	334 41.4	. . 08.6	301 19.8	. . 34.6	Alnilam	275 42.2	S 1 11.6
E 10	236 58.1	17 21.7	15.8	245 06.7	12.3	349 43.3	08.6	316 21.9	34.6	Alphard	217 52.2	S 8 44.4
S 11	252 00.6	32 22.1	16.3	260 07.7	11.6	4 45.2	08.7	331 24.1	34.5			
D 12	267 03.0	47 22.5	S12 16.8	275 08.7	S 4 10.9	19 47.1	S21 08.8	346 26.2	S22 34.5	Alphecca	126 08.2	N26 39.2
A 13	282 05.5	62 22.9	17.4	290 09.6	10.2	34 49.0	08.9	1 28.4	34.5	Alpheratz	357 39.6	N29 11.8
Y 14	297 07.9	77 23.3	17.9	305 10.6	09.4	49 50.9	09.0	16 30.5	34.5	Altair	62 04.9	N 8 55.2
15	312 10.4	92 23.6	. . 18.4	320 11.5	. . 08.7	64 52.7	. . 09.1	31 32.7	. . 34.5	Ankaa	353 12.0	S42 12.5
16	327 12.9	107 24.0	18.9	335 12.5	08.0	79 54.6	09.2	46 34.8	34.5	Antares	112 22.0	S26 28.2
17	342 15.3	122 24.4	19.4	350 13.5	07.3	94 56.5	09.2	61 37.0	34.4			
18	357 17.8	137 24.8	S12 19.9	5 14.4	S 4 06.6	109 58.4	S21 09.3	76 39.1	S22 34.4	Arcturus	145 52.6	N19 05.1
19	12 20.3	152 25.2	20.4	20 15.4	05.9	125 00.3	09.4	91 41.3	34.4	Atria	107 21.0	S69 03.4
20	27 22.7	167 25.5	20.9	35 16.4	05.2	140 02.2	09.5	106 43.4	34.4	Avior	234 16.0	S59 34.1
21	42 25.2	182 25.9	. . 21.5	50 17.3	. . 04.4	155 04.1	. . 09.6	121 45.6	. . 34.4	Bellatrix	278 27.7	N 6 21.8
22	57 27.7	197 26.3	22.0	65 18.3	03.7	170 05.9	09.7	136 47.7	34.3	Betelgeuse	270 56.9	N 7 24.5
23	72 30.1	212 26.6	22.5	80 19.2	03.0	185 07.8	09.8	151 49.9	34.3			
19 00	87 32.6	227 27.0	S12 23.0	95 20.2	S 4 02.3	200 09.7	S21 09.8	166 52.0	S22 34.3	Canopus	263 53.9	S52 42.4
01	102 35.0	242 27.4	23.5	110 21.2	01.6	215 11.6	09.9	181 54.2	34.3	Capella	280 28.4	N46 00.9
02	117 37.5	257 27.7	24.0	125 22.1	00.9	230 13.5	10.0	196 56.3	34.3	Deneb	49 29.3	N45 21.1
03	132 40.0	272 28.1	. . 24.6	140 23.1	4 00.2	245 15.4	. . 10.1	211 58.5	. . 34.2	Denebola	182 29.9	N14 28.0
04	147 42.4	287 28.5	25.1	155 24.0	3 59.4	260 17.3	10.2	227 00.6	34.2	Diphda	348 52.1	S17 53.2
05	162 44.9	302 28.8	25.6	170 25.0	58.7	275 19.2	10.3	242 02.8	34.2			
06	177 47.4	317 29.2	S12 26.1	185 26.0	S 3 58.0	290 21.0	S21 10.4	257 04.9	S22 34.2	Dubhe	193 47.0	N61 38.7
W 07	192 49.8	332 29.6	26.6	200 26.9	57.3	305 22.9	10.4	272 07.1	34.2	Elnath	278 07.5	N28 37.2
E 08	207 52.3	347 29.9	27.2	215 27.9	56.6	320 24.8	10.5	287 09.2	34.2	Eltanin	90 45.0	N51 29.3
D 09	222 54.8	2 30.3	. . 27.7	230 28.9	. . 55.9	335 26.7	. . 10.6	302 11.4	. . 34.1	Enif	33 43.6	N 9 57.8
N 10	237 57.2	17 30.6	28.2	245 29.8	55.1	350 28.6	10.7	317 13.5	34.1	Fomalhaut	15 20.0	S29 31.5
E 11	252 59.7	32 31.0	28.7	260 30.8	54.4	5 30.5	10.8	332 15.7	34.1			
S 12	268 02.2	47 31.3	S12 29.2	275 31.7	S 3 53.7	20 32.4	S21 10.9	347 17.8	S22 34.1	Gacrux	171 56.8	S57 12.7
D 13	283 04.6	62 31.7	29.8	290 32.7	53.0	35 34.2	10.9	2 20.0	34.1	Gienah	175 48.5	S17 38.6
A 14	298 07.1	77 32.0	30.3	305 33.7	52.3	50 36.1	11.0	17 22.1	34.1	Hadar	148 42.9	S60 27.4
Y 15	313 09.5	92 32.4	. . 30.8	320 34.6	. . 51.6	65 38.0	. . 11.1	32 24.3	. . 34.0	Hamal	327 56.3	N23 33.1
16	328 12.0	107 32.7	31.3	335 35.6	50.8	80 39.9	11.2	47 26.4	34.0	Kaus Aust.	83 39.3	S34 22.4
17	343 14.5	122 33.1	31.9	350 36.5	50.1	95 41.8	11.3	62 28.6	34.0			
18	358 16.9	137 33.4	S12 32.4	5 37.5	S 3 49.4	110 43.7	S21 11.4	77 30.7	S22 34.0	Kochab	137 21.1	N74 04.6
19	13 19.4	152 33.8	32.9	20 38.5	48.7	125 45.6	11.5	92 32.9	34.0	Markab	13 34.7	N15 18.5
20	28 21.9	167 34.1	33.4	35 39.4	48.0	140 47.5	11.5	107 35.0	33.9	Menkar	314 10.9	N 4 09.7
21	43 24.3	182 34.4	. . 34.0	50 40.4	. . 47.3	155 49.3	. . 11.6	122 37.2	. . 33.9	Menkent	148 03.4	S36 27.4
22	58 26.8	197 34.8	34.5	65 41.3	46.6	170 51.2	11.7	137 39.3	33.9	Miaplacidus	221 38.2	S69 47.5
23	73 29.3	212 35.1	35.0	80 42.3	45.8	185 53.1	11.8	152 41.5	33.9			
20 00	88 31.7	227 35.5	S12 35.5	95 43.3	S 3 45.1	200 55.0	S21 11.9	167 43.6	S22 33.9	Mirfak	308 34.5	N49 55.7
01	103 34.2	242 35.8	36.1	110 44.2	44.4	215 56.9	12.0	182 45.8	33.9	Nunki	75 54.1	S26 16.3
02	118 36.7	257 36.1	36.6	125 45.2	43.7	230 58.8	12.0	197 47.9	33.8	Peacock	53 13.9	S56 40.5
03	133 39.1	272 36.5	. . 37.1	140 46.1	. . 43.0	246 00.7	. . 12.1	212 50.1	. . 33.8	Pollux	243 22.9	N27 58.6
04	148 41.6	287 36.8	37.6	155 47.1	42.3	261 02.6	12.2	227 52.2	33.8	Procyon	244 55.5	N 5 10.5
05	163 44.0	302 37.1	38.2	170 48.1	41.5	276 04.4	12.3	242 54.4	33.8			
06	178 46.5	317 37.4	S12 38.7	185 49.0	S 3 40.8	291 06.3	S21 12.4	257 56.5	S22 33.8	Rasalhague	96 03.3	N12 32.9
07	193 49.0	332 37.8	39.2	200 50.0	40.1	306 08.2	12.5	272 58.7	33.7	Regulus	207 39.4	N11 52.4
T 08	208 51.4	347 38.1	39.8	215 50.9	39.4	321 10.1	12.6	288 00.8	33.7	Rigel	281 08.1	S 8 11.0
H 09	223 53.9	2 38.4	. . 40.3	230 51.9	. . 38.7	336 12.0	. . 12.6	303 03.0	. . 33.7	Rigil Kent.	139 47.1	S60 54.4
U 10	238 56.4	17 38.7	40.8	245 52.9	38.0	351 13.9	12.7	318 05.1	33.7	Sabik	102 08.6	S15 44.7
R 11	253 58.8	32 39.1	41.4	260 53.8	37.2	6 15.8	12.8	333 07.3	33.7			
S 12	269 01.3	47 39.4	S12 41.9	275 54.8	S 3 36.5	21 17.7	S21 12.9	348 09.4	S22 33.6	Schedar	349 36.1	N56 38.6
D 13	284 03.8	62 39.7	42.4	290 55.7	35.8	36 19.5	13.0	3 11.6	33.6	Shaula	96 17.3	S37 06.8
A 14	299 06.2	77 40.0	43.0	305 56.7	35.1	51 21.4	13.1	18 13.7	33.6	Sirius	258 30.1	S16 44.6
Y 15	314 08.7	92 40.3	. . 43.5	320 57.7	. . 34.4	66 23.3	. . 13.1	33 15.9	. . 33.6	Spica	158 27.5	S11 15.4
16	329 11.2	107 40.7	44.0	335 58.6	33.7	81 25.2	13.2	48 18.0	33.6	Suhail	222 49.4	S43 30.4
17	344 13.6	122 41.0	44.6	350 59.6	32.9	96 27.1	13.3	63 20.2	33.6			
18	359 16.1	137 41.3	S12 45.1	6 00.5	S 3 32.2	111 29.0	S21 13.4	78 22.3	S22 33.5	Vega	80 36.9	N38 48.2
19	14 18.5	152 41.6	45.6	21 01.5	31.5	126 30.9	13.5	93 24.5	33.5	Zuben'ubi	137 01.5	S16 07.0
20	29 21.0	167 41.9	46.2	36 02.5	30.8	141 32.8	13.6	108 26.6	33.5		SHA	Mer. Pass.
21	44 23.5	182 42.2	. . 46.7	51 03.4	. . 30.1	156 34.6	. . 13.6	123 28.8	. . 33.5		° ′	h m
22	59 25.9	197 42.5	47.2	66 04.4	29.4	171 36.5	13.7	138 30.9	33.5	Venus	139 54.4	8 50
23	74 28.4	212 42.8	47.8	81 05.3	28.6	186 38.4	13.8	153 33.1	33.4	Mars	7 47.6	17 38
	h m									Jupiter	112 37.1	10 38
Mer. Pass. 18 06.9		v 0.4	d 0.5	v 1.0	d 0.7	v 1.9	d 0.1	v 2.1	d 0.0	Saturn	79 19.5	12 51

UT	SUN GHA	Dec	MOON GHA	v	Dec	d	HP
18 00	180 55.0	S23 22.5	61 41.5	13.2	N 4 44.1	11.5	56.6
01	195 54.7	22.6	76 13.7	13.2	4 55.6	11.6	56.6
02	210 54.3	22.6	90 45.9	13.1	5 07.2	11.6	56.6
03	225 54.0 ..	22.7	105 18.0	13.1	5 18.8	11.5	56.7
04	240 53.7	22.8	119 50.1	13.0	5 30.3	11.5	56.7
05	255 53.4	22.9	134 22.1	12.9	5 41.8	11.5	56.7
T 06	270 53.1	S23 22.9	148 54.0	12.9	N 5 53.3	11.5	56.8
U 07	285 52.8	23.0	163 25.9	12.8	6 04.8	11.5	56.8
E 08	300 52.5	23.1	177 57.7	12.8	6 16.3	11.5	56.9
S 09	315 52.2 ..	23.2	192 29.5	12.6	6 27.8	11.5	56.9
D 10	330 51.9	23.2	207 01.1	12.7	6 39.3	11.4	56.9
A 11	345 51.6	23.3	221 32.8	12.5	6 50.7	11.4	57.0
Y 12	0 51.3	S23 23.4	236 04.3	12.5	N 7 02.1	11.5	57.0
13	15 51.0	23.4	250 35.8	12.4	7 13.6	11.4	57.0
14	30 50.7	23.5	265 07.2	12.4	7 25.0	11.3	57.1
15	45 50.4 ..	23.6	279 38.6	12.3	7 36.3	11.4	57.1
16	60 50.1	23.6	294 09.9	12.2	7 47.7	11.3	57.2
17	75 49.7	23.7	308 41.1	12.1	7 59.0	11.3	57.2
18	90 49.4	S23 23.7	323 12.2	12.1	N 8 10.3	11.3	57.2
19	105 49.1	23.8	337 43.3	11.9	8 21.6	11.2	57.3
20	120 48.8	23.9	352 14.2	12.0	8 32.8	11.3	57.3
21	135 48.5 ..	23.9	6 45.2	11.8	8 44.1	11.2	57.3
22	150 48.2	24.0	21 16.0	11.8	8 55.3	11.1	57.4
23	165 47.9	24.1	35 46.8	11.6	9 06.4	11.2	57.4
19 00	180 47.6	S23 24.1	50 17.4	11.6	N 9 17.6	11.1	57.5
01	195 47.3	24.2	64 48.0	11.6	9 28.7	11.1	57.5
02	210 47.0	24.2	79 18.6	11.4	9 39.8	11.0	57.5
03	225 46.7 ..	24.3	93 49.0	11.4	9 50.8	11.0	57.6
04	240 46.4	24.3	108 19.4	11.3	10 01.8	11.0	57.6
05	255 46.1	24.4	122 49.7	11.2	10 12.8	10.9	57.6
W 06	270 45.8	S23 24.4	137 19.9	11.1	N10 23.7	10.9	57.7
E 07	285 45.4	24.5	151 50.0	11.0	10 34.6	10.9	57.7
D 08	300 45.1	24.5	166 20.0	11.0	10 45.5	10.8	57.8
N 09	315 44.8 ..	24.6	180 50.0	10.9	10 56.3	10.8	57.8
E 10	330 44.5	24.6	195 19.9	10.7	11 07.1	10.7	57.8
S 11	345 44.2	24.7	209 49.6	10.7	11 17.8	10.7	57.9
D 12	0 43.9	S23 24.7	224 19.3	10.6	N11 28.5	10.6	57.9
A 13	15 43.6	24.8	238 48.9	10.6	11 39.1	10.6	57.9
Y 14	30 43.3	24.8	253 18.5	10.4	11 49.7	10.6	58.0
15	45 43.0 ..	24.9	267 47.9	10.3	12 00.3	10.5	58.0
16	60 42.7	24.9	282 17.2	10.3	12 10.8	10.4	58.1
17	75 42.4	25.0	296 46.5	10.2	12 21.2	10.4	58.1
18	90 42.1	S23 25.0	311 15.7	10.0	N12 31.6	10.4	58.1
19	105 41.7	25.1	325 44.7	10.0	12 42.0	10.2	58.2
20	120 41.4	25.1	340 13.7	9.9	12 52.2	10.3	58.2
21	135 41.1 ..	25.1	354 42.6	9.8	13 02.5	10.1	58.2
22	150 40.8	25.2	9 11.4	9.7	13 12.6	10.1	58.3
23	165 40.5	25.2	23 40.1	9.6	13 22.7	10.1	58.3
20 00	180 40.2	S23 25.3	38 08.7	9.6	N13 32.8	10.0	58.4
01	195 39.9	25.3	52 37.3	9.4	13 42.8	9.9	58.4
02	210 39.6	25.3	67 05.7	9.3	13 52.7	9.8	58.4
03	225 39.3 ..	25.4	81 34.0	9.2	14 02.5	9.8	58.5
04	240 39.0	25.4	96 02.2	9.2	14 12.3	9.7	58.5
05	255 38.7	25.4	110 30.4	9.0	14 22.0	9.7	58.5
T 06	270 38.3	S23 25.5	124 58.4	9.0	N14 31.7	9.6	58.6
H 07	285 38.0	25.5	139 26.4	8.8	14 41.3	9.5	58.6
U 08	300 37.7	25.5	153 54.2	8.8	14 50.8	9.4	58.7
R 09	315 37.4 ..	25.6	168 22.0	8.7	15 00.2	9.4	58.7
S 10	330 37.1	25.6	182 49.7	8.5	15 09.6	9.3	58.7
D 11	345 36.8	25.6	197 17.2	8.5	15 18.9	9.2	58.8
A 12	0 36.5	S23 25.6	211 44.7	8.4	N15 28.1	9.1	58.8
Y 13	15 36.2	25.7	226 12.1	8.3	15 37.2	9.0	58.8
14	30 35.9	25.7	240 39.4	8.1	15 46.2	9.0	58.9
15	45 35.6 ..	25.7	255 06.5	8.1	15 55.2	8.9	58.9
16	60 35.3	25.8	269 33.6	8.0	16 04.1	8.8	58.9
17	75 34.9	25.8	284 00.6	7.9	16 12.9	8.7	59.0
18	90 34.6	S23 25.8	298 27.5	7.8	N16 21.6	8.6	59.0
19	105 34.3	25.8	312 54.3	7.7	16 30.2	8.5	59.0
20	120 34.0	25.8	327 21.0	7.6	16 38.7	8.4	59.1
21	135 33.7 ..	25.9	341 47.6	7.5	16 47.1	8.4	59.1
22	150 33.4	25.9	356 14.1	7.4	16 55.5	8.2	59.1
23	165 33.1	25.9	10 40.5	7.3	N17 03.7	8.1	59.2
	SD 16.3	d 0.0	SD 15.5		15.8		16.0

Lat.	Twilight Naut.	Civil	Sunrise	Moonrise 18	19	20	21
°	h m	h m	h m	h m	h m	h m	h m
N 72	08 24	10 55	■■■	12 48	12 30	12 03	▭
N 70	08 04	09 53	■■■	12 58	12 49	12 37	12 18
68	07 48	09 18	■■■	13 06	13 04	13 02	13 03
66	07 35	08 52	10 33	13 13	13 16	13 22	13 33
64	07 24	08 33	09 51	13 19	13 26	13 37	13 55
62	07 14	08 16	09 22	13 24	13 35	13 50	14 13
60	07 06	08 03	09 01	13 28	13 43	14 02	14 28
N 58	06 58	07 51	08 43	13 32	13 49	14 11	14 41
56	06 52	07 41	08 28	13 36	13 55	14 20	14 52
54	06 46	07 32	08 16	13 39	14 01	14 28	15 02
52	06 40	07 24	08 05	13 42	14 06	14 34	15 11
50	06 35	07 16	07 55	13 44	14 10	14 41	15 19
45	06 23	07 00	07 34	13 50	14 20	14 54	15 35
N 40	06 12	06 47	07 17	13 55	14 28	15 05	15 49
35	06 03	06 35	07 03	13 59	14 35	15 15	16 01
30	05 54	06 24	06 51	14 03	14 41	15 23	16 11
20	05 38	06 05	06 29	14 09	14 51	15 38	16 29
N 10	05 22	05 48	06 11	14 15	15 01	15 50	16 45
0	05 05	05 31	05 53	14 21	15 10	16 02	16 59
S 10	04 46	05 13	05 36	14 26	15 19	16 15	17 14
20	04 23	04 52	05 17	14 32	15 28	16 28	17 30
30	03 54	04 27	04 55	14 39	15 39	16 43	17 48
35	03 35	04 12	04 42	14 43	15 46	16 51	17 59
40	03 12	03 54	04 27	14 47	15 53	17 01	18 11
45	02 41	03 31	04 09	14 53	16 02	17 13	18 25
S 50	01 56	03 01	03 46	14 59	16 12	17 27	18 43
52	01 28	02 46	03 35	15 02	16 17	17 34	18 52
54	00 41	02 28	03 23	15 05	16 22	17 42	19 01
56	////	02 06	03 09	15 08	16 28	17 50	19 12
58	////	01 36	02 52	15 12	16 35	18 00	19 24
S 60	////	00 46	02 31	15 17	16 42	18 10	19 38

Lat.	Sunset	Twilight Civil	Naut.	Moonset 18	19	20	21
°	h m	h m	h m	h m	h m	h m	h m
N 72	■■■	12 59	15 30	03 04	05 01	07 16	▭
N 70	■■■	14 01	15 50	02 56	04 44	06 43	08 58
68	■■■	14 37	16 06	02 50	04 31	06 19	08 14
66	13 21	15 02	16 19	02 45	04 20	06 01	07 45
64	14 04	15 22	16 30	02 41	04 11	05 46	07 23
62	14 32	15 38	16 40	02 37	04 03	05 34	07 06
60	14 53	15 51	16 48	02 33	03 57	05 23	06 51
N 58	15 11	16 03	16 56	02 31	03 51	05 14	06 39
56	15 26	16 13	17 02	02 28	03 46	05 06	06 28
54	15 38	16 22	17 09	02 26	03 41	04 59	06 19
52	15 50	16 30	17 14	02 24	03 37	04 53	06 11
50	15 59	16 38	17 19	02 22	03 33	04 47	06 03
45	16 20	16 54	17 31	02 18	03 25	04 35	05 47
N 40	16 37	17 08	17 42	02 14	03 18	04 25	05 34
35	16 51	17 19	17 51	02 11	03 13	04 17	05 23
30	17 04	17 30	18 00	02 09	03 07	04 09	05 14
20	17 25	17 49	18 16	02 04	02 59	03 56	04 57
N 10	17 43	18 06	18 33	02 00	02 51	03 45	04 43
0	18 01	18 23	18 50	01 56	02 44	03 34	04 29
S 10	18 18	18 41	19 09	01 53	02 36	03 24	04 16
20	18 37	19 02	19 31	01 49	02 29	03 13	04 01
30	18 59	19 27	20 00	01 44	02 20	03 00	03 45
35	19 12	19 42	20 19	01 42	02 15	02 52	03 35
40	19 28	20 00	20 42	01 39	02 09	02 44	03 24
45	19 46	20 23	21 13	01 35	02 03	02 34	03 12
S 50	20 08	20 53	21 58	01 31	01 55	02 23	02 56
52	20 19	21 08	22 26	01 29	01 51	02 17	02 49
54	20 31	21 26	23 13	01 27	01 47	02 11	02 41
56	20 46	21 48	////	01 25	01 43	02 05	02 32
58	21 02	22 18	////	01 23	01 38	01 57	02 22
S 60	21 23	23 09	////	01 20	01 33	01 49	02 11

Day	SUN Eqn. of Time 00ʰ	12ʰ	Mer. Pass.	MOON Mer. Pass. Upper	Lower	Age	Phase
d	m s	m s	h m	h m	h m	d	%
18	03 40	03 26	11 57	20 32	08 08	11	79
19	03 11	02 56	11 57	21 22	08 57	12	87
20	02 41	02 27	11 58	22 16	09 48	13	93

2018 DECEMBER 21, 22, 23 (FRI., SAT., SUN.)

UT	ARIES	VENUS −4·7		MARS +0·3		JUPITER −1·8		SATURN +0·5		STARS		
	GHA	GHA	Dec	GHA	Dec	GHA	Dec	GHA	Dec	Name	SHA	Dec
d h	° ′	° ′	° ′	° ′	° ′	° ′	° ′	° ′	° ′		° ′	° ′
21 00	89 30.9	227 43.1	S12 48.3	96 06.3	S 3 27.9	201 40.3	S21 13.9	168 35.2	S22 33.4	Acamar	315 15.2	S40 14.1
01	104 33.3	242 43.4	48.8	111 07.3	27.2	216 42.2	14.0	183 37.4	33.4	Achernar	335 23.8	S57 08.8
02	119 35.8	257 43.7	49.4	126 08.2	26.5	231 44.1	14.1	198 39.5	33.4	Acrux	173 05.1	S63 11.8
03	134 38.3	272 44.0 ..	49.9	141 09.2 ..	25.8	246 46.0 ..	14.1	213 41.7 ..	33.4	Adhara	255 09.2	S29 00.0
04	149 40.7	287 44.3	50.5	156 10.1	25.1	261 47.9	14.2	228 43.8	33.4	Aldebaran	290 44.7	N16 32.7
05	164 43.2	302 44.6	51.0	171 11.1	24.3	276 49.8	14.3	243 46.0	33.3			
06	179 45.6	317 44.9	S12 51.5	186 12.1	S 3 23.6	291 51.6	S21 14.4	258 48.1	S22 33.3	Alioth	166 17.6	N55 51.3
07	194 48.1	332 45.2	52.1	201 13.0	22.9	306 53.5	14.5	273 50.3	33.3	Alkaid	152 56.2	N49 13.0
08	209 50.6	347 45.5	52.6	216 14.0	22.2	321 55.4	14.6	288 52.4	33.3	Al Na'ir	27 39.3	S46 52.4
F 09	224 53.0	2 45.8 ..	53.2	231 14.9 ..	21.5	336 57.3 ..	14.6	303 54.6 ..	33.3	Alnilam	275 42.2	S 1 11.6
R 10	239 55.5	17 46.1	53.7	246 15.9	20.8	351 59.2	14.7	318 56.7	33.2	Alphard	217 52.2	S 8 44.4
I 11	254 58.0	32 46.4	54.2	261 16.8	20.0	7 01.1	14.8	333 58.9	33.2			
D 12	270 00.4	47 46.7	S12 54.8	276 17.8	S 3 19.3	22 03.0	S21 14.9	349 01.0	S22 33.2	Alphecca	126 08.2	N26 39.1
A 13	285 02.9	62 47.0	55.3	291 18.8	18.6	37 04.9	15.0	4 03.2	33.2	Alpheratz	357 39.6	N29 11.8
Y 14	300 05.4	77 47.3	55.9	306 19.7	17.9	52 06.7	15.0	19 05.3	33.2	Altair	62 04.9	N 8 55.2
15	315 07.8	92 47.5 ..	56.4	321 20.7 ..	17.2	67 08.6 ..	15.1	34 07.5 ..	33.1	Ankaa	353 12.0	S42 12.5
16	330 10.3	107 47.8	57.0	336 21.6	16.4	82 10.5	15.2	49 09.6	33.1	Antares	112 22.0	S26 28.2
17	345 12.8	122 48.1	57.5	351 22.6	15.7	97 12.4	15.3	64 11.8	33.1			
18	0 15.2	137 48.4	S12 58.0	6 23.6	S 3 15.0	112 14.3	S21 15.4	79 13.9	S22 33.1	Arcturus	145 52.5	N19 05.1
19	15 17.7	152 48.7	58.6	21 24.5	14.3	127 16.2	15.5	94 16.0	33.1	Atria	107 21.0	S69 03.4
20	30 20.1	167 49.0	59.1	36 25.5	13.6	142 18.1	15.5	109 18.2	33.0	Avior	234 15.9	S59 34.1
21	45 22.6	182 49.2	12 59.7	51 26.4 ..	12.9	157 20.0 ..	15.6	124 20.3 ..	33.0	Bellatrix	278 27.7	N 6 21.8
22	60 25.1	197 49.5	13 00.2	66 27.4	12.1	172 21.9	15.7	139 22.5	33.0	Betelgeuse	270 56.9	N 7 24.5
23	75 27.5	212 49.8	00.8	81 28.3	11.4	187 23.8	15.8	154 24.6	33.0			
22 00	90 30.0	227 50.1	S13 01.3	96 29.3	S 3 10.7	202 25.6	S21 15.9	169 26.8	S22 33.0	Canopus	263 53.9	S52 42.4
01	105 32.5	242 50.3	01.9	111 30.3	10.0	217 27.5	16.0	184 28.9	33.0	Capella	280 28.4	N46 00.9
02	120 34.9	257 50.6	02.4	126 31.2	09.3	232 29.4	16.0	199 31.1	32.9	Deneb	49 29.3	N45 21.1
03	135 37.4	272 50.9 ..	03.0	141 32.2 ..	08.6	247 31.3 ..	16.1	214 33.2 ..	32.9	Denebola	182 29.8	N14 28.0
04	150 39.9	287 51.1	03.5	156 33.1	07.8	262 33.2	16.2	229 35.4	32.9	Diphda	348 52.1	S17 53.2
05	165 42.3	302 51.4	04.1	171 34.1	07.1	277 35.1	16.3	244 37.5	32.9			
06	180 44.8	317 51.7	S13 04.6	186 35.1	S 3 06.4	292 37.0	S21 16.4	259 39.7	S22 32.9	Dubhe	193 47.0	N61 38.7
07	195 47.3	332 51.9	05.2	201 36.0	05.7	307 38.9	16.4	274 41.8	32.8	Elnath	278 07.5	N28 37.2
S 08	210 49.7	347 52.2	05.7	216 37.0	05.0	322 40.8	16.5	289 44.0	32.8	Eltanin	90 45.0	N51 29.3
A 09	225 52.2	2 52.5 ..	06.2	231 37.9 ..	04.2	337 42.6 ..	16.6	304 46.1 ..	32.8	Enif	33 43.6	N 9 57.8
T 10	240 54.6	17 52.7	06.8	246 38.9	03.5	352 44.5	16.7	319 48.3	32.8	Fomalhaut	15 20.0	S29 31.5
U 11	255 57.1	32 53.0	07.3	261 39.8	02.8	7 46.4	16.8	334 50.4	32.8			
R 12	270 59.6	47 53.2	S13 07.9	276 40.8	S 3 02.1	22 48.3	S21 16.9	349 52.6	S22 32.7	Gacrux	171 56.8	S57 12.8
D 13	286 02.0	62 53.5	08.5	291 41.8	01.4	37 50.2	16.9	4 54.7	32.7	Gienah	175 48.5	S17 38.6
A 14	301 04.5	77 53.8	09.0	306 42.7	3 00.7	52 52.1	17.0	19 56.9	32.7	Hadar	148 42.9	S60 27.4
Y 15	316 07.0	92 54.0 ..	09.6	321 43.7	2 59.9	67 54.0 ..	17.1	34 59.0 ..	32.7	Hamal	327 56.3	N23 33.1
16	331 09.4	107 54.3	10.1	336 44.6	59.2	82 55.9	17.2	50 01.2	32.7	Kaus Aust.	83 39.3	S34 22.4
17	346 11.9	122 54.5	10.7	351 45.6	58.5	97 57.8	17.3	65 03.3	32.6			
18	1 14.4	137 54.8	S13 11.2	6 46.5	S 2 57.8	112 59.7	S21 17.3	80 05.5	S22 32.6	Kochab	137 21.0	N74 04.6
19	16 16.8	152 55.0	11.8	21 47.5	57.1	128 01.6	17.4	95 07.6	32.6	Markab	13 34.7	N15 18.5
20	31 19.3	167 55.3	12.3	36 48.5	56.3	143 03.4	17.5	110 09.8	32.6	Menkar	314 10.9	N 4 09.7
21	46 21.8	182 55.5 ..	12.9	51 49.4 ..	55.6	158 05.3 ..	17.6	125 11.9 ..	32.6	Menkent	148 03.4	S36 27.4
22	61 24.2	197 55.8	13.4	66 50.4	54.9	173 07.2	17.7	140 14.0	32.5	Miaplacidus	221 38.2	S69 47.5
23	76 26.7	212 56.0	14.0	81 51.3	54.2	188 09.1	17.7	155 16.2	32.5			
23 00	91 29.1	227 56.2	S13 14.5	96 52.3	S 2 53.5	203 11.0	S21 17.8	170 18.3	S22 32.5	Mirfak	308 34.5	N49 55.7
01	106 31.6	242 56.5	15.1	111 53.2	52.8	218 12.9	17.9	185 20.5	32.5	Nunki	75 54.1	S26 16.3
02	121 34.1	257 56.7	15.6	126 54.2	52.0	233 14.8	18.0	200 22.6	32.5	Peacock	53 13.9	S56 40.5
03	136 36.5	272 57.0 ..	16.2	141 55.2 ..	51.3	248 16.7 ..	18.1	215 24.8 ..	32.5	Pollux	243 22.8	N27 58.6
04	151 39.0	287 57.2	16.7	156 56.1	50.6	263 18.6	18.2	230 26.9	32.4	Procyon	244 55.5	N 5 10.5
05	166 41.5	302 57.4	17.3	171 57.1	49.9	278 20.5	18.2	245 29.1	32.4			
06	181 43.9	317 57.7	S13 17.9	186 58.0	S 2 49.2	293 22.4	S21 18.3	260 31.2	S22 32.4	Rasalhague	96 03.3	N12 32.9
07	196 46.4	332 57.9	18.4	201 59.0	48.4	308 24.2	18.4	275 33.4	32.4	Regulus	207 39.4	N11 52.4
08	211 48.9	347 58.1	19.0	216 59.9	47.7	323 26.1	18.5	290 35.5	32.4	Rigel	281 08.1	S 8 11.0
S 09	226 51.3	2 58.4 ..	19.5	232 00.9 ..	47.0	338 28.0 ..	18.6	305 37.7 ..	32.3	Rigil Kent.	139 47.1	S60 54.4
U 10	241 53.8	17 58.6	20.1	247 01.9	46.3	353 29.9	18.6	320 39.8	32.3	Sabik	102 08.6	S15 44.7
N 11	256 56.3	32 58.8	20.6	262 02.8	45.6	8 31.8	18.7	335 42.0	32.3			
D 12	271 58.7	47 59.1	S13 21.2	277 03.8	S 2 44.8	23 33.7	S21 18.8	350 44.1	S22 32.3	Schedar	349 36.1	N56 38.6
A 13	287 01.2	62 59.3	21.8	292 04.7	44.1	38 35.6	18.9	5 46.3	32.3	Shaula	96 17.3	S37 06.8
Y 14	302 03.6	77 59.5	22.3	307 05.7	43.4	53 37.5	19.0	20 48.4	32.2	Sirius	258 30.1	S16 44.7
15	317 06.1	92 59.7 ..	22.9	322 06.6 ..	42.7	68 39.4 ..	19.0	35 50.6 ..	32.2	Spica	158 27.4	S11 15.4
16	332 08.6	108 00.0	23.4	337 07.6	42.0	83 41.3	19.1	50 52.7	32.2	Suhail	222 49.4	S43 30.4
17	347 11.0	123 00.2	24.0	352 08.6	41.3	98 43.2	19.2	65 54.9	32.2			
18	2 13.5	138 00.4	S13 24.6	7 09.5	S 2 40.5	113 45.0	S21 19.3	80 57.0	S22 32.2	Vega	80 36.9	N38 48.2
19	17 16.0	153 00.6	25.1	22 10.5	39.8	128 46.9	19.4	95 59.1	32.1	Zuben'ubi	137 01.5	S16 07.0
20	32 18.4	168 00.8	25.7	37 11.4	39.1	143 48.8	19.4	111 01.3	32.1		SHA	Mer.Pass.
21	47 20.9	183 01.1 ..	26.2	52 12.4 ..	38.4	158 50.7 ..	19.5	126 03.4 ..	32.1		° ′	h m
22	62 23.4	198 01.3	26.8	67 13.3	37.7	173 52.6	19.6	141 05.6	32.1	Venus	137 20.0	8 48
23	77 25.8	213 01.5	27.4	82 14.3	36.9	188 54.5	19.7	156 07.7	32.1	Mars	5 59.3	17 33
	h m									Jupiter	111 55.6	10 29
Mer.Pass. 17 55.1		v 0.3	d 0.6	v 1.0	d 0.7	v 1.9	d 0.1	v 2.1	d 0.0	Saturn	78 56.8	12 40

SUN / MOON

UT	SUN GHA	SUN Dec	MOON GHA	MOON v	MOON Dec	MOON d	MOON HP
d h	° ′	° ′	° ′	′	° ′	′	′
21 00	180 32.8	S23 25.9	25 06.8	7.2	N17 11.8	8.1	59.2
01	195 32.5	25.9	39 33.0	7.1	17 19.9	7.9	59.2
02	210 32.2	26.0	53 59.1	7.0	17 27.8	7.9	59.3
03	225 31.9	.. 26.0	68 25.1	7.0	17 35.7	7.7	59.3
04	240 31.5	26.0	82 51.1	6.8	17 43.4	7.7	59.3
05	255 31.2	26.0	97 16.9	6.7	17 51.1	7.5	59.4
06	270 30.9	S23 26.0	111 42.6	6.7	N17 58.6	7.5	59.4
07	285 30.6	26.0	126 08.3	6.5	18 06.1	7.3	59.4
08	300 30.3	26.0	140 33.8	6.5	18 13.4	7.2	59.5
F 09	315 30.0	.. 26.1	154 59.3	6.4	18 20.6	7.1	59.5
R 10	330 29.7	26.1	169 24.7	6.3	18 27.7	7.0	59.5
I 11	345 29.4	26.1	183 50.0	6.1	18 34.7	6.8	59.6
D 12	0 29.1	S23 26.1	198 15.1	6.1	N18 41.5	6.8	59.6
A 13	15 28.8	26.1	212 40.2	6.1	18 48.3	6.6	59.6
Y 14	30 28.5	26.1	227 05.3	5.9	18 54.9	6.6	59.7
15	45 28.1	.. 26.1	241 30.2	5.8	19 01.5	6.4	59.7
16	60 27.8	26.1	255 55.0	5.8	19 07.9	6.3	59.7
17	75 27.5	26.1	270 19.8	5.6	19 14.2	6.1	59.7
18	90 27.2	S23 26.1	284 44.4	5.6	N19 20.3	6.1	59.8
19	105 26.9	26.1	299 09.0	5.5	19 26.4	5.9	59.8
20	120 26.6	26.1	313 33.5	5.4	19 32.3	5.7	59.8
21	135 26.3	.. 26.1	327 57.9	5.3	19 38.0	5.7	59.9
22	150 26.0	26.1	342 22.2	5.3	19 43.7	5.5	59.9
23	165 25.7	26.1	356 46.5	5.2	19 49.2	5.4	59.9
22 00	180 25.4	S23 26.1	11 10.7	5.1	N19 54.6	5.3	59.9
01	195 25.0	26.1	25 34.8	5.0	19 59.9	5.1	60.0
02	210 24.7	26.1	39 58.8	4.9	20 05.0	5.0	60.0
03	225 24.4	.. 26.1	54 22.7	4.9	20 10.0	4.9	60.0
04	240 24.1	26.1	68 46.6	4.8	20 14.9	4.7	60.0
05	255 23.8	26.1	83 10.4	4.7	20 19.6	4.6	60.1
06	270 23.5	S23 26.1	97 34.1	4.7	N20 24.2	4.4	60.1
07	285 23.2	26.1	111 57.8	4.6	20 28.6	4.3	60.1
S 08	300 22.9	26.1	126 21.4	4.5	20 32.9	4.2	60.1
A 09	315 22.6	.. 26.1	140 44.9	4.4	20 37.1	4.0	60.2
T 10	330 22.3	26.1	155 08.3	4.4	20 41.1	3.9	60.2
U 11	345 21.9	26.1	169 31.7	4.4	20 45.0	3.8	60.2
R 12	0 21.6	S23 26.0	183 55.1	4.2	N20 48.8	3.5	60.2
D 13	15 21.3	26.0	198 18.3	4.3	20 52.3	3.5	60.2
A 14	30 21.0	26.0	212 41.6	4.1	20 55.8	3.3	60.3
Y 15	45 20.7	.. 26.0	227 04.7	4.1	20 59.1	3.1	60.3
16	60 20.4	26.0	241 27.8	4.1	21 02.2	3.0	60.3
17	75 20.1	26.0	255 50.9	4.0	21 05.2	2.9	60.3
18	90 19.8	S23 26.0	270 13.9	3.9	N21 08.1	2.7	60.3
19	105 19.5	25.9	284 36.8	3.9	21 10.8	2.5	60.4
20	120 19.2	25.9	298 59.7	3.9	21 13.3	2.4	60.4
21	135 18.8	.. 25.9	313 22.6	3.8	21 15.7	2.3	60.4
22	150 18.5	25.9	327 45.4	3.8	21 18.0	2.1	60.4
23	165 18.2	25.9	342 08.2	3.7	21 20.1	1.9	60.4
23 00	180 17.9	S23 25.9	356 30.9	3.7	N21 22.0	1.8	60.5
01	195 17.6	25.8	10 53.6	3.6	21 23.8	1.6	60.5
02	210 17.3	25.8	25 16.2	3.7	21 25.4	1.5	60.5
03	225 17.0	.. 25.8	39 38.9	3.6	21 26.9	1.3	60.5
04	240 16.7	25.8	54 01.5	3.5	21 28.2	1.2	60.5
05	255 16.4	25.7	68 24.0	3.6	21 29.4	1.0	60.5
06	270 16.1	S23 25.7	82 46.6	3.5	N21 30.4	0.8	60.5
07	285 15.7	25.7	97 09.1	3.4	21 31.2	0.7	60.6
08	300 15.4	25.7	111 31.5	3.5	21 31.9	0.5	60.6
S 09	315 15.1	.. 25.6	125 54.0	3.5	21 32.4	0.4	60.6
U 10	330 14.8	25.6	140 16.5	3.4	21 32.8	0.2	60.6
N 11	345 14.5	25.6	154 38.9	3.4	21 33.0	0.0	60.6
D 12	0 14.2	S23 25.5	169 01.3	3.4	N21 33.0	0.1	60.6
A 13	15 13.9	25.5	183 23.7	3.4	21 32.9	0.2	60.6
Y 14	30 13.6	25.5	197 46.1	3.4	21 32.7	0.5	60.6
15	45 13.3	.. 25.4	212 08.5	3.3	21 32.2	0.6	60.6
16	60 13.0	25.4	226 30.8	3.4	21 31.6	0.7	60.7
17	75 12.6	25.4	240 53.2	3.4	21 30.9	0.9	60.7
18	90 12.3	S23 25.3	255 15.6	3.4	N21 30.0	1.1	60.7
19	105 12.0	25.3	269 38.0	3.3	21 28.9	1.2	60.7
20	120 11.7	25.3	284 00.3	3.4	21 27.7	1.4	60.7
21	135 11.4	.. 25.2	298 22.7	3.4	21 26.3	1.5	60.7
22	150 11.1	25.2	312 45.1	3.4	21 24.8	1.7	60.7
23	165 10.8	25.2	327 07.5	3.4	N21 23.1	1.9	60.7
	SD 16.3	d 0.0	SD 16.2		16.4		16.5

Twilight / Sunrise / Moonrise

Lat.	Twilight Naut.	Twilight Civil	Sunrise	Moonrise 21	Moonrise 22	Moonrise 23	Moonrise 24
°	h m	h m	h m	h m	h m	h m	h m
N 72	08 26	10 58	■■■	☐	☐	☐	☐
N 70	08 06	09 55	■■■	12 18	☐	☐	☐
68	07 50	09 19	■■■	13 03	13 10	13 46	15 25
66	07 37	08 54	10 35	13 33	13 56	14 45	16 09
64	07 26	08 34	09 52	13 55	14 26	15 19	16 38
62	07 16	08 18	09 24	14 13	14 49	15 44	17 01
60	07 08	08 05	09 02	14 28	15 07	16 04	17 19
N 58	07 00	07 53	08 45	14 41	15 23	16 20	17 33
56	06 53	07 43	08 30	14 52	15 36	16 34	17 46
54	06 47	07 33	08 17	15 02	15 47	16 46	17 57
52	06 41	07 25	08 06	15 11	15 57	16 56	18 07
50	06 36	07 18	07 56	15 19	16 06	17 06	18 16
45	06 24	07 02	07 36	15 35	16 26	17 26	18 34
N 40	06 14	06 48	07 19	15 49	16 41	17 42	18 50
35	06 05	06 36	07 04	16 01	16 55	17 56	19 02
30	05 56	06 26	06 52	16 11	17 06	18 08	19 13
20	05 39	06 07	06 31	16 29	17 26	18 28	19 33
N 10	05 23	05 49	06 12	16 45	17 43	18 46	19 49
0	05 06	05 32	05 55	16 59	18 00	19 02	20 05
S 10	04 47	05 14	05 37	17 14	18 16	19 19	20 20
20	04 24	04 54	05 18	17 30	18 34	19 37	20 37
30	03 55	04 29	04 56	17 48	18 54	19 57	20 56
35	03 37	04 13	04 43	17 59	19 06	20 09	21 07
40	03 13	03 55	04 28	18 11	19 19	20 23	21 19
45	02 43	03 32	04 10	18 25	19 35	20 39	21 34
S 50	01 57	03 03	03 47	18 43	19 55	20 59	21 53
52	01 29	02 47	03 36	18 52	20 05	21 09	22 01
54	00 42	02 29	03 24	19 01	20 15	21 20	22 11
56	////	02 07	03 10	19 12	20 27	21 32	22 22
58	////	01 37	02 53	19 24	20 41	21 46	22 34
S 60	////	00 46	02 32	19 38	20 58	22 02	22 48

Sunset / Twilight / Moonset

Lat.	Sunset	Twilight Civil	Twilight Naut.	Moonset 21	Moonset 22	Moonset 23	Moonset 24
°	h m	h m	h m	h m	h m	h m	h m
N 72	■■■	12 59	15 31	☐	☐	☐	☐
N 70	■■■	14 02	15 51	08 58	☐	☐	☐
68	■■■	14 38	16 07	08 14	10 12	11 46	12 18
66	13 22	15 03	16 20	07 45	09 26	10 47	11 34
64	14 05	15 23	16 31	07 23	08 56	10 13	11 04
62	14 33	15 39	16 41	07 06	08 34	09 48	10 42
60	14 55	15 53	16 49	06 51	08 16	09 28	10 23
N 58	15 12	16 04	16 57	06 39	08 00	09 12	10 08
56	15 27	16 15	17 04	06 28	07 48	08 58	09 55
54	15 40	16 24	17 10	06 19	07 36	08 46	09 44
52	15 51	16 32	17 16	06 11	07 26	08 35	09 34
50	16 01	16 39	17 21	06 03	07 18	08 26	09 25
45	16 22	16 55	17 33	05 47	06 59	08 06	09 05
N 40	16 38	17 09	17 43	05 34	06 44	07 50	08 50
35	16 53	17 21	17 53	05 23	06 31	07 36	08 37
30	17 05	17 31	18 01	05 14	06 19	07 24	08 25
20	17 26	17 50	18 18	04 57	06 00	07 04	08 06
N 10	17 45	18 08	18 34	04 43	05 43	06 46	07 48
0	18 02	18 25	18 51	04 29	05 28	06 29	07 32
S 10	18 20	18 43	19 10	04 16	05 12	06 13	07 16
20	18 39	19 03	19 33	04 01	04 55	05 55	06 58
30	19 01	19 28	20 02	03 45	04 36	05 34	06 39
35	19 14	19 44	20 21	03 35	04 25	05 22	06 27
40	19 29	20 02	20 44	03 24	04 12	05 09	06 13
45	19 47	20 25	21 14	03 12	03 57	04 52	05 57
S 50	20 10	20 54	22 00	02 56	03 39	04 32	05 37
52	20 21	21 10	22 28	02 49	03 30	04 23	05 28
54	20 33	21 28	23 15	02 41	03 20	04 12	05 17
56	20 47	21 50	////	02 32	03 09	04 00	05 05
58	21 04	22 20	////	02 22	02 57	03 46	04 51
S 60	21 25	23 11	////	02 11	02 42	03 29	04 35

SUN / MOON

Day	SUN Eqn. of Time 00h	SUN Eqn. of Time 12h	SUN Mer. Pass.	MOON Mer. Pass. Upper	MOON Mer. Pass. Lower	Age	Phase
d	m s	m s	h m	h m	h m	d	%
21	02 12	01 57	11 58	23 13	10 44	14	98
22	01 42	01 27	11 59	24 15	11 44	15	100
23	01 12	00 57	11 59	00 15	12 46	16	99

UT	ARIES	VENUS -4.7		MARS $+0.4$		JUPITER -1.8		SATURN $+0.5$		STARS		
	GHA	GHA	Dec	GHA	Dec	GHA	Dec	GHA	Dec	Name	SHA	Dec
d h	° ′	° ′	° ′	° ′	° ′	° ′	° ′	° ′	° ′		° ′	° ′
24 00	92 28.3	228 01.7	S13 27.9	97 15.2	S 2 36.2	203 56.4	S21 19.8	171 09.9	S22 32.0	Acamar	315 15.2	S40 14.1
01	107 30.8	243 01.9	28.5	112 16.2	35.5	218 58.3	19.8	186 12.0	32.0	Achernar	335 23.8	S57 08.9
02	122 33.2	258 02.1	29.0	127 17.2	34.8	234 00.2	19.9	201 14.2	32.0	Acrux	173 05.1	S63 11.8
03	137 35.7	273 02.3 . .	29.6	142 18.1 . .	34.1	249 02.1 . .	20.0	216 16.3 . .	32.0	Adhara	255 09.2	S29 00.0
04	152 38.1	288 02.6	30.2	157 19.1	33.3	264 04.0	20.1	231 18.5	32.0	Aldebaran	290 44.7	N16 32.7
05	167 40.6	303 02.8	30.7	172 20.0	32.6	279 05.9	20.2	246 20.6	31.9			
06	182 43.1	318 03.0	S13 31.3	187 21.0	S 2 31.9	294 07.8	S21 20.2	261 22.8	S22 31.9	Alioth	166 17.5	N55 51.3
07	197 45.5	333 03.2	31.9	202 21.9	31.2	309 09.6	20.3	276 24.9	31.9	Alkaid	152 56.2	N49 13.0
08	212 48.0	348 03.4	32.4	217 22.9	30.5	324 11.5	20.4	291 27.1	31.9	Al Na'ir	27 39.3	S46 52.4
M 09	227 50.5	3 03.6 . .	33.0	232 23.8 . .	29.8	339 13.4 . .	20.5	306 29.2 . .	31.9	Alnilam	275 42.2	S 1 11.6
O 10	242 52.9	18 03.8	33.5	247 24.8	29.0	354 15.3	20.6	321 31.4	31.8	Alphard	217 52.2	S 8 44.4
N 11	257 55.4	33 04.0	34.1	262 25.8	28.3	9 17.2	20.6	336 33.5	31.8			
D 12	272 57.9	48 04.2	S13 34.7	277 26.7	S 2 27.6	24 19.1	S21 20.7	351 35.6	S22 31.8	Alphecca	126 08.1	N26 39.1
A 13	288 00.3	63 04.4	35.2	292 27.7	26.9	39 21.0	20.8	6 37.8	31.8	Alpheratz	357 39.6	N29 11.8
Y 14	303 02.8	78 04.6	35.8	307 28.6	26.2	54 22.9	20.9	21 39.9	31.8	Altair	62 04.9	N 8 55.2
15	318 05.3	93 04.8 . .	36.4	322 29.6 . .	25.4	69 24.8 . .	21.0	36 42.1 . .	31.7	Ankaa	353 12.0	S42 12.5
16	333 07.7	108 05.0	36.9	337 30.5	24.7	84 26.7	21.0	51 44.2	31.7	Antares	112 22.0	S26 28.2
17	348 10.2	123 05.2	37.5	352 31.5	24.0	99 28.6	21.1	66 46.4	31.7			
18	3 12.6	138 05.4	S13 38.1	7 32.4	S 2 23.3	114 30.5	S21 21.2	81 48.5	S22 31.7	Arcturus	145 52.5	N19 05.1
19	18 15.1	153 05.5	38.6	22 33.4	22.6	129 32.4	21.3	96 50.7	31.7	Atria	107 21.0	S69 03.4
20	33 17.6	168 05.7	39.2	37 34.4	21.8	144 34.2	21.4	111 52.8	31.6	Avior	234 15.9	S59 34.1
21	48 20.0	183 05.9 . .	39.8	52 35.3 . .	21.1	159 36.1 . .	21.4	126 55.0 . .	31.6	Bellatrix	278 27.6	N 6 21.8
22	63 22.5	198 06.1	40.3	67 36.3	20.4	174 38.0	21.5	141 57.1	31.6	Betelgeuse	270 56.9	N 7 24.5
23	78 25.0	213 06.3	40.9	82 37.2	19.7	189 39.9	21.6	156 59.3	31.6			
25 00	93 27.4	228 06.5	S13 41.5	97 38.2	S 2 19.0	204 41.8	S21 21.7	172 01.4	S22 31.6	Canopus	263 53.9	S52 42.5
01	108 29.9	243 06.7	42.0	112 39.1	18.2	219 43.7	21.8	187 03.6	31.5	Capella	280 28.4	N46 00.9
02	123 32.4	258 06.8	42.6	127 40.1	17.5	234 45.6	21.8	202 05.7	31.5	Deneb	49 29.3	N45 21.1
03	138 34.8	273 07.0 . .	43.2	142 41.0 . .	16.8	249 47.5 . .	21.9	217 07.9 . .	31.5	Denebola	182 29.8	N14 28.0
04	153 37.3	288 07.2	43.7	157 42.0	16.1	264 49.4	22.0	232 10.0	31.5	Diphda	348 52.1	S17 53.2
05	168 39.8	303 07.4	44.3	172 43.0	15.4	279 51.3	22.1	247 12.1	31.5			
06	183 42.2	318 07.6	S13 44.9	187 43.9	S 2 14.6	294 53.2	S21 22.1	262 14.3	S22 31.4	Dubhe	193 47.0	N61 38.7
07	198 44.7	333 07.7	45.4	202 44.9	13.9	309 55.1	22.2	277 16.4	31.4	Elnath	278 07.5	N28 37.2
T 08	213 47.1	348 07.9	46.0	217 45.8	13.2	324 57.0	22.3	292 18.6	31.4	Eltanin	90 44.9	N51 29.3
U 09	228 49.6	3 08.1 . .	46.6	232 46.8 . .	12.5	339 58.9 . .	22.4	307 20.7 . .	31.4	Enif	33 43.6	N 9 57.8
E 10	243 52.1	18 08.3	47.2	247 47.7	11.8	355 00.8	22.5	322 22.9	31.4	Fomalhaut	15 20.0	S29 31.5
S 11	258 54.5	33 08.4	47.7	262 48.7	11.0	10 02.7	22.5	337 25.0	31.3			
D 12	273 57.0	48 08.6	S13 48.3	277 49.6	S 2 10.3	25 04.5	S21 22.6	352 27.2	S22 31.3	Gacrux	171 56.7	S57 12.8
A 13	288 59.5	63 08.8	48.9	292 50.6	09.6	40 06.4	22.7	7 29.3	31.3	Gienah	175 48.4	S17 38.6
Y 14	304 01.9	78 08.9	49.4	307 51.5	08.9	55 08.3	22.8	22 31.5	31.3	Hadar	148 42.8	S60 27.4
15	319 04.4	93 09.1 . .	50.0	322 52.5 . .	08.2	70 10.2 . .	22.9	37 33.6 . .	31.3	Hamal	327 56.3	N23 33.1
16	334 06.9	108 09.3	50.6	337 53.5	07.5	85 12.1	22.9	52 35.8	31.2	Kaus Aust.	83 39.3	S34 22.4
17	349 09.3	123 09.4	51.1	352 54.4	06.7	100 14.0	23.0	67 37.9	31.2			
18	4 11.8	138 09.6	S13 51.7	7 55.4	S 2 06.0	115 15.9	S21 23.1	82 40.1	S22 31.2	Kochab	137 21.0	N74 04.5
19	19 14.2	153 09.8	52.3	22 56.3	05.3	130 17.8	23.2	97 42.2	31.2	Markab	13 34.7	N15 18.5
20	34 16.7	168 09.9	52.9	37 57.3	04.6	145 19.7	23.2	112 44.3	31.2	Menkar	314 10.9	N 4 09.7
21	49 19.2	183 10.1 . .	53.4	52 58.2 . .	03.9	160 21.6 . .	23.3	127 46.5 . .	31.1	Menkent	148 03.3	S36 27.4
22	64 21.6	198 10.2	54.0	67 59.2	03.1	175 23.5	23.4	142 48.6	31.1	Miaplacidus	221 38.2	S69 47.5
23	79 24.1	213 10.4	54.6	83 00.1	02.4	190 25.4	23.5	157 50.8	31.1			
26 00	94 26.6	228 10.6	S13 55.1	98 01.1	S 2 01.7	205 27.3	S21 23.6	172 52.9	S22 31.1	Mirfak	308 34.5	N49 55.7
01	109 29.0	243 10.7	55.7	113 02.0	01.0	220 29.2	23.6	187 55.1	31.1	Nunki	75 54.0	S26 16.3
02	124 31.5	258 10.9	56.3	128 03.0	2 00.3	235 31.1	23.7	202 57.2	31.0	Peacock	53 13.9	S56 40.5
03	139 34.0	273 11.0 . .	56.9	143 03.9 . .	1 59.5	250 33.0 . .	23.8	217 59.4 . .	31.0	Pollux	243 22.8	N27 58.6
04	154 36.4	288 11.2	57.4	158 04.9	58.8	265 34.9	23.9	233 01.5	31.0	Procyon	244 55.5	N 5 10.4
05	169 38.9	303 11.3	58.0	173 05.9	58.1	280 36.8	23.9	248 03.7	31.0			
06	184 41.4	318 11.5	S13 58.6	188 06.8	S 1 57.4	295 38.7	S21 24.0	263 05.8	S22 31.0	Rasalhague	96 03.3	N12 32.9
W 07	199 43.8	333 11.6	59.2	203 07.8	56.7	310 40.5	24.1	278 08.0	30.9	Regulus	207 39.4	N11 52.4
E 08	214 46.3	348 11.8	13 59.7	218 08.7	55.9	325 42.4	24.2	293 10.1	30.9	Rigel	281 08.1	S 8 11.0
D 09	229 48.7	3 11.9	14 00.3	233 09.7 . .	55.2	340 44.3 . .	24.3	308 12.2 . .	30.9	Rigil Kent.	139 47.0	S60 54.4
N 10	244 51.2	18 12.1	00.9	248 10.6	54.5	355 46.2	24.3	323 14.4	30.9	Sabik	102 08.6	S15 44.7
E 11	259 53.7	33 12.2	01.5	263 11.6	53.8	10 48.1	24.4	338 16.5	30.9			
S 12	274 56.1	48 12.3	S14 02.0	278 12.5	S 1 53.1	25 50.0	S21 24.5	353 18.7	S22 30.8	Schedar	349 36.1	N56 38.6
S 13	289 58.6	63 12.5	02.6	293 13.5	52.3	40 51.9	24.6	8 20.8	30.8	Shaula	96 17.2	S37 06.8
D 14	305 01.1	78 12.6	03.2	308 14.4	51.6	55 53.8	24.6	23 23.0	30.8	Sirius	258 30.1	S16 44.7
A 15	320 03.5	93 12.8 . .	03.8	323 15.4 . .	50.9	70 55.7 . .	24.7	38 25.1 . .	30.8	Spica	158 27.4	S11 15.4
Y 16	335 06.0	108 12.9	04.3	338 16.3	50.2	85 57.6	24.8	53 27.3	30.8	Suhail	222 49.3	S43 30.4
17	350 08.5	123 13.0	04.9	353 17.3	49.5	100 59.5	24.9	68 29.4	30.7			
18	5 10.9	138 13.2	S14 05.5	8 18.2	S 1 48.7	116 01.4	S21 25.0	83 31.6	S22 30.7	Vega	80 36.9	N38 48.2
19	20 13.4	153 13.3	06.1	23 19.2	48.0	131 03.3	25.0	98 33.7	30.7	Zuben'ubi	137 01.5	S16 07.0
20	35 15.9	168 13.4	06.6	38 20.1	47.3	146 05.2	25.1	113 35.9	30.7		SHA	Mer. Pass.
21	50 18.3	183 13.6 . .	07.2	53 21.1 . .	46.6	161 07.1 . .	25.2	128 38.0 . .	30.7		° ′	h m
22	65 20.8	198 13.7	07.8	68 22.1	45.9	176 09.0	25.3	143 40.2	30.6	Venus	134 39.0	8 47
23	80 23.2	213 13.8	08.4	83 23.0	45.1	191 10.9	25.3	158 42.3	30.6	Mars	4 10.7	17 28
	h m									Jupiter	111 14.4	10 20
Mer. Pass. 17 43.3		v 0.2	d 0.6	v 1.0	d 0.7	v 1.9	d 0.1	v 2.1	d 0.0	Saturn	78 34.0	12 30

SUN and MOON

UT	SUN GHA	SUN Dec	MOON GHA	v	MOON Dec	d	HP
24 00	180 10.5	S23 25.1	341 29.9	3.4	N21 21.2	2.0	60.7
01	195 10.2	25.1	355 52.3	3.4	21 19.2	2.2	60.7
02	210 09.9	25.0	10 14.7	3.5	21 17.0	2.3	60.7
03	225 09.5 ..	25.0	24 37.2	3.5	21 14.7	2.5	60.7
04	240 09.2	24.9	38 59.7	3.4	21 12.2	2.7	60.7
05	255 08.9	24.9	53 22.1	3.6	21 09.5	2.8	60.7
06	270 08.6	S23 24.9	67 44.7	3.5	N21 06.7	2.9	60.7
07	285 08.3	24.8	82 07.2	3.6	21 03.8	3.2	60.7
M 08	300 08.0	24.8	96 29.8	3.6	21 00.6	3.2	60.7
O 09	315 07.7 ..	24.7	110 52.4	3.6	20 57.4	3.5	60.7
N 10	330 07.4	24.7	125 15.0	3.7	20 53.9	3.5	60.7
D 11	345 07.1	24.6	139 37.7	3.6	20 50.4	3.8	60.7
A 12	0 06.8	S23 24.6	154 00.3	3.8	N20 46.6	3.8	60.7
Y 13	15 06.5	24.5	168 23.1	3.7	20 42.8	4.1	60.7
14	30 06.1	24.5	182 45.8	3.9	20 38.7	4.2	60.7
15	45 05.8 ..	24.4	197 08.7	3.8	20 34.5	4.3	60.7
16	60 05.5	24.4	211 31.5	3.9	20 30.2	4.5	60.7
17	75 05.2	24.3	225 54.4	4.0	20 25.7	4.6	60.7
18	90 04.9	S23 24.3	240 17.4	3.9	N20 21.1	4.8	60.7
19	105 04.6	24.2	254 40.3	4.1	20 16.3	4.9	60.7
20	120 04.3	24.1	269 03.4	4.1	20 11.4	5.1	60.7
21	135 04.0 ..	24.1	283 26.5	4.1	20 06.3	5.2	60.7
22	150 03.7	24.0	297 49.6	4.2	20 01.1	5.4	60.7
23	165 03.4	24.0	312 12.8	4.3	19 55.7	5.4	60.7
25 00	180 03.0	S23 23.9	326 36.1	4.3	N19 50.3	5.7	60.7
01	195 02.7	23.8	340 59.4	4.4	19 44.6	5.8	60.7
02	210 02.4	23.8	355 22.8	4.4	19 38.8	5.9	60.7
03	225 02.1 ..	23.7	9 46.2	4.5	19 32.9	6.0	60.7
04	240 01.8	23.7	24 09.7	4.5	19 26.9	6.2	60.7
05	255 01.5	23.6	38 33.2	4.6	19 20.7	6.4	60.6
06	270 01.2	S23 23.5	52 56.8	4.7	N19 14.3	6.4	60.6
07	285 00.9	23.5	67 20.5	4.8	19 07.9	6.6	60.6
T 08	300 00.6	23.4	81 44.3	4.8	19 01.3	6.7	60.6
U 09	315 00.3 ..	23.3	96 08.1	4.8	18 54.6	6.9	60.6
E 10	330 00.0	23.3	110 31.9	5.0	18 47.7	7.0	60.6
S 11	344 59.6	23.2	124 55.9	5.0	18 40.7	7.1	60.6
D 12	359 59.3	S23 23.1	139 19.9	5.1	N18 33.6	7.2	60.6
A 13	14 59.0	23.1	153 44.0	5.2	18 26.4	7.4	60.6
Y 14	29 58.7	23.0	168 08.2	5.2	18 19.0	7.4	60.5
15	44 58.4 ..	22.9	182 32.4	5.3	18 11.6	7.6	60.5
16	59 58.1	22.8	196 56.7	5.4	18 04.0	7.8	60.5
17	74 57.8	22.8	211 21.1	5.5	17 56.2	7.8	60.5
18	89 57.5	S23 22.7	225 45.6	5.5	N17 48.4	8.0	60.5
19	104 57.2	22.6	240 10.1	5.6	17 40.4	8.1	60.5
20	119 56.9	22.5	254 34.7	5.7	17 32.3	8.2	60.5
21	134 56.6 ..	22.5	268 59.4	5.8	17 24.1	8.3	60.5
22	149 56.2	22.4	283 24.2	5.8	17 15.8	8.4	60.4
23	164 55.9	22.3	297 49.0	6.0	17 07.4	8.5	60.4
26 00	179 55.6	S23 22.2	312 14.0	6.0	N16 58.9	8.6	60.4
01	194 55.3	22.1	326 39.0	6.1	16 50.3	8.8	60.4
02	209 55.0	22.1	341 04.1	6.2	16 41.5	8.8	60.4
03	224 54.7 ..	22.0	355 29.3	6.2	16 32.7	9.0	60.4
04	239 54.4	21.9	9 54.5	6.3	16 23.7	9.1	60.3
05	254 54.1	21.8	24 19.8	6.5	16 14.6	9.1	60.3
06	269 53.8	S23 21.7	38 45.3	6.5	N16 05.5	9.3	60.3
07	284 53.5	21.6	53 10.8	6.5	15 56.2	9.3	60.3
W 08	299 53.2	21.6	67 36.3	6.7	15 46.9	9.5	60.3
E 09	314 52.9 ..	21.5	82 02.0	6.8	15 37.4	9.5	60.2
D 10	329 52.5	21.4	96 27.8	6.8	15 27.9	9.7	60.2
N 11	344 52.2	21.3	110 53.6	6.9	15 18.2	9.7	60.2
E 12	359 51.9	S23 21.2	125 19.5	7.0	N15 08.5	9.8	60.2
S 13	14 51.6	21.1	139 45.5	7.1	14 58.7	9.9	60.2
D 14	29 51.3	21.0	154 11.6	7.2	14 48.8	10.0	60.1
A 15	44 51.0 ..	20.9	168 37.8	7.2	14 38.8	10.1	60.1
Y 16	59 50.7	20.8	183 04.0	7.3	14 28.7	10.1	60.1
17	74 50.4	20.8	197 30.3	7.4	14 18.5	10.2	60.1
18	89 50.1	S23 20.7	211 56.7	7.5	N14 08.3	10.4	60.1
19	104 49.8	20.6	226 23.2	7.6	13 57.9	10.4	60.0
20	119 49.5	20.5	240 49.8	7.7	13 47.5	10.5	60.0
21	134 49.2 ..	20.4	255 16.5	7.7	13 37.0	10.5	60.0
22	149 48.8	20.3	269 43.2	7.9	13 26.5	10.7	60.0
23	164 48.5	20.2	284 10.1	7.9	N13 15.8	10.7	59.9
	SD 16.3	d 0.1	SD 16.5		16.5		16.4

Twilight, Sunrise and Moonrise

Lat.	Naut.	Civil	Sunrise	Moonrise 24	25	26	27
N 72	08 27	10 57	████	▭	▭	18 36	20 54
N 70	08 07	09 55	████	▭	16 46	19 05	21 09
68	07 51	09 20	████	15 25	17 27	19 27	21 21
66	07 38	08 55	10 35	16 09	17 54	19 44	21 30
64	07 27	08 35	09 53	16 38	18 15	19 57	21 38
62	07 17	08 19	09 25	17 01	18 32	20 09	21 45
60	07 09	08 06	09 03	17 19	18 46	20 19	21 51
N 58	07 01	07 54	08 46	17 33	18 58	20 27	21 56
56	06 55	07 44	08 31	17 46	19 08	20 35	22 00
54	06 48	07 35	08 19	17 57	19 18	20 41	22 04
52	06 43	07 26	08 07	18 07	19 26	20 47	22 08
50	06 37	07 19	07 58	18 16	19 33	20 52	22 11
45	06 26	07 03	07 37	18 34	19 48	21 04	22 18
N 40	06 15	06 49	07 20	18 50	20 01	21 14	22 24
35	06 06	06 38	07 06	19 02	20 12	21 22	22 30
30	05 57	06 27	06 53	19 13	20 21	21 29	22 34
20	05 41	06 08	06 32	19 33	20 38	21 41	22 42
N 10	05 25	05 51	06 14	19 49	20 52	21 52	22 49
0	05 08	05 34	05 56	20 05	21 05	22 02	22 55
S 10	04 49	05 16	05 39	20 20	21 18	22 12	23 02
20	04 26	04 55	05 20	20 37	21 32	22 23	23 09
30	03 57	04 30	04 58	20 56	21 48	22 35	23 16
35	03 38	04 15	04 45	21 07	21 57	22 42	23 21
40	03 15	03 57	04 30	21 19	22 08	22 50	23 26
45	02 44	03 34	04 12	21 34	22 20	22 59	23 32
S 50	01 59	03 04	03 49	21 53	22 35	23 10	23 39
52	01 31	02 49	03 38	22 01	22 42	23 15	23 42
54	00 45	02 31	03 26	22 11	22 50	23 21	23 45
56	////	02 09	03 12	22 22	22 59	23 27	23 49
58	////	01 39	02 55	22 34	23 09	23 34	23 53
S 60	////	00 49	02 34	22 48	23 20	23 42	23 58

Sunset, Twilight and Moonset

Lat.	Sunset	Civil	Naut.	Moonset 24	25	26	27
N 72	████	13 03	15 33	▭	▭	13 18	12 53
N 70	████	14 05	15 53	▭	13 05	12 47	12 36
68	████	14 40	16 09	12 18	12 24	12 24	12 23
66	13 25	15 05	16 22	11 34	11 56	12 06	12 12
64	14 07	15 25	16 33	11 04	11 34	11 52	12 03
62	14 35	15 41	16 43	10 42	11 17	11 39	11 55
60	14 57	15 54	16 51	10 23	11 02	11 28	11 48
N 58	15 14	16 06	16 59	10 07	10 49	11 19	11 42
56	15 29	16 16	17 06	09 55	10 39	11 11	11 36
54	15 42	16 25	17 12	09 44	10 29	11 04	11 31
52	15 53	16 34	17 17	09 34	10 20	10 57	11 27
50	16 03	16 41	17 23	09 25	10 13	10 51	11 23
45	16 23	16 57	17 34	09 06	09 56	10 38	11 14
N 40	16 40	17 11	17 45	08 50	09 43	10 28	11 06
35	16 54	17 22	17 54	08 37	09 31	10 19	11 00
30	17 07	17 33	18 03	08 25	09 21	10 10	10 54
20	17 28	17 52	18 19	08 06	09 03	09 56	10 45
N 10	17 46	18 09	18 36	07 48	08 48	09 44	10 36
0	18 04	18 26	18 53	07 32	08 34	09 32	10 28
S 10	18 21	18 44	19 12	07 16	08 19	09 21	10 19
20	18 40	19 05	19 34	06 58	08 04	09 08	10 10
30	19 02	19 30	20 03	06 38	07 46	08 54	10 00
35	19 15	19 45	20 22	06 27	07 35	08 45	09 54
40	19 30	20 03	20 45	06 14	07 23	08 35	09 47
45	19 48	20 26	21 15	05 57	07 09	08 24	09 40
S 50	20 11	20 55	22 01	05 37	06 51	08 10	09 30
52	20 22	21 11	22 29	05 28	06 43	08 04	09 25
54	20 34	21 28	23 15	05 18	06 34	07 57	09 20
56	20 48	21 51	////	05 05	06 23	07 49	09 15
58	21 05	22 20	////	04 51	06 11	07 39	09 09
S 60	21 25	23 10	////	04 35	05 58	07 29	09 02

SUN and MOON

Day	SUN Eqn. of Time 00h	12h	Mer. Pass.	MOON Mer. Pass. Upper	Lower	Age	Phase
24	00 43	00 28	12 00		13 48	17	96
25	00 13	00 02	12 00	02 19	14 49	18	89
26	00 17	00 32	12 01	03 19	15 47	19	81

UT	ARIES	VENUS −4.7		MARS +0.4		JUPITER −1.8		SATURN +0.5	
d h	GHA	GHA	Dec	GHA	Dec	GHA	Dec	GHA	Dec
27 00	95 25.7	228 14.0	S14 08.9	98 24.0	S 1 44.4	206 12.8	S21 25.4	173 44.4	S22 30.6
01	110 28.2	243 14.1	09.5	113 24.9	43.7	221 14.7	25.5	188 46.6	30.6
02	125 30.6	258 14.2	10.1	128 25.9	43.0	236 16.6	25.6	203 48.7	30.5
03	140 33.1	273 14.3 ..	10.7	143 26.8 ..	42.3	251 18.5 ..	25.6	218 50.9 ..	30.5
04	155 35.6	288 14.5	11.2	158 27.8	41.5	266 20.4	25.7	233 53.0	30.5
05	170 38.0	303 14.6	11.8	173 28.7	40.8	281 22.3	25.8	248 55.2	30.5
06	185 40.5	318 14.7	S14 12.4	188 29.7	S 1 40.1	296 24.2	S21 25.9	263 57.3	S22 30.5
T 07	200 43.0	333 14.8	13.0	203 30.6	39.4	311 26.0	26.0	278 59.5	30.4
H 08	215 45.4	348 14.9	13.6	218 31.6	38.7	326 27.9	26.0	294 01.6	30.4
U 09	230 47.9	3 15.1 ..	14.1	233 32.5 ..	37.9	341 29.8 ..	26.1	309 03.8 ..	30.4
R 10	245 50.4	18 15.2	14.7	248 33.5	37.2	356 31.7	26.2	324 05.9	30.4
S 11	260 52.8	33 15.3	15.3	263 34.4	36.5	11 33.6	26.3	339 08.1	30.4
D 12	275 55.3	48 15.4	S14 15.9	278 35.4	S 1 35.8	26 35.5	S21 26.3	354 10.2	S22 30.3
A 13	290 57.7	63 15.5	16.4	293 36.3	35.1	41 37.4	26.4	9 12.3	30.3
Y 14	306 00.2	78 15.6	17.0	308 37.3	34.3	56 39.3	26.5	24 14.5	30.3
15	321 02.7	93 15.7 ..	17.6	323 38.2 ..	33.6	71 41.2 ..	26.6	39 16.6 ..	30.3
16	336 05.1	108 15.9	18.2	338 39.2	32.9	86 43.1	26.6	54 18.8	30.3
17	351 07.6	123 16.0	18.8	353 40.1	32.2	101 45.0	26.7	69 20.9	30.2
18	6 10.1	138 16.1	S14 19.3	8 41.1	S 1 31.5	116 46.9	S21 26.8	84 23.1	S22 30.2
19	21 12.5	153 16.2	19.9	23 42.0	30.7	131 48.8	26.9	99 25.2	30.2
20	36 15.0	168 16.3	20.5	38 43.0	30.0	146 50.7	26.9	114 27.4	30.2
21	51 17.5	183 16.4 ..	21.1	53 44.0 ..	29.3	161 52.6 ..	27.0	129 29.5 ..	30.2
22	66 19.9	198 16.5	21.6	68 44.9	28.6	176 54.5	27.1	144 31.7	30.1
23	81 22.4	213 16.6	22.2	83 45.9	27.9	191 56.4	27.2	159 33.8	30.1
28 00	96 24.8	228 16.7	S14 22.8	98 46.8	S 1 27.1	206 58.3	S21 27.2	174 35.9	S22 30.1
01	111 27.3	243 16.8	23.4	113 47.8	26.4	222 00.2	27.3	189 38.1	30.1
02	126 29.8	258 16.9	24.0	128 48.7	25.7	237 02.1	27.4	204 40.2	30.0
03	141 32.2	273 17.0 ..	24.5	143 49.7 ..	25.0	252 04.0 ..	27.5	219 42.4 ..	30.0
04	156 34.7	288 17.1	25.1	158 50.6	24.2	267 05.9	27.5	234 44.5	30.0
05	171 37.2	303 17.2	25.7	173 51.6	23.5	282 07.8	27.6	249 46.7	30.0
06	186 39.6	318 17.3	S14 26.3	188 52.5	S 1 22.8	297 09.7	S21 27.7	264 48.8	S22 30.0
F 07	201 42.1	333 17.4	26.9	203 53.5	22.1	312 11.6	27.8	279 51.0	29.9
R 08	216 44.6	348 17.5	27.4	218 54.4	21.4	327 13.5	27.9	294 53.1	29.9
I 09	231 47.0	3 17.6 ..	28.0	233 55.4 ..	20.6	342 15.4 ..	27.9	309 55.3 ..	29.9
D 10	246 49.5	18 17.7	28.6	248 56.3	19.9	357 17.3	28.0	324 57.4	29.9
A 11	261 52.0	33 17.7	29.2	263 57.3	19.2	12 19.2	28.1	339 59.6	29.9
Y 12	276 54.4	48 17.8	S14 29.8	278 58.2	S 1 18.5	27 21.1	S21 28.2	355 01.7	S22 29.8
13	291 56.9	63 17.9	30.3	293 59.2	17.8	42 23.0	28.2	10 03.8	29.8
14	306 59.3	78 18.0	30.9	309 00.1	17.0	57 24.9	28.3	25 06.0	29.8
15	322 01.8	93 18.1 ..	31.5	324 01.1 ..	16.3	72 26.8 ..	28.4	40 08.1 ..	29.8
16	337 04.3	108 18.2	32.1	339 02.0	15.6	87 28.7	28.5	55 10.3	29.8
17	352 06.7	123 18.3	32.7	354 03.0	14.9	102 30.6	28.5	70 12.4	29.7
18	7 09.2	138 18.3	S14 33.3	9 03.9	S 1 14.2	117 32.5	S21 28.6	85 14.6	S22 29.7
19	22 11.7	153 18.4	33.8	24 04.9	13.4	132 34.4	28.7	100 16.7	29.7
20	37 14.1	168 18.5	34.4	39 05.8	12.7	147 36.3	28.8	115 18.9	29.7
21	52 16.6	183 18.6 ..	35.0	54 06.8 ..	12.0	162 38.2 ..	28.8	130 21.0 ..	29.6
22	67 19.1	198 18.6	35.6	69 07.7	11.3	177 40.1	28.9	145 23.2	29.6
23	82 21.5	213 18.7	36.2	84 08.7	10.6	192 42.0	29.0	160 25.3	29.6
29 00	97 24.0	228 18.8	S14 36.7	99 09.6	S 1 09.8	207 43.9	S21 29.1	175 27.4	S22 29.6
01	112 26.4	243 18.9	37.3	114 10.6	09.1	222 45.8	29.1	190 29.6	29.6
02	127 28.9	258 18.9	37.9	129 11.5	08.4	237 47.7	29.2	205 31.7	29.5
03	142 31.4	273 19.0 ..	38.5	144 12.5 ..	07.7	252 49.6 ..	29.3	220 33.9 ..	29.5
04	157 33.8	288 19.1	39.1	159 13.4	07.0	267 51.5	29.4	235 36.0	29.5
05	172 36.3	303 19.2	39.6	174 14.4	06.2	282 53.4	29.4	250 38.2	29.5
06	187 38.8	318 19.2	S14 40.2	189 15.3	S 1 05.5	297 55.3	S21 29.5	265 40.3	S22 29.5
S 07	202 41.2	333 19.3	40.8	204 16.3	04.8	312 57.2	29.6	280 42.5	29.4
A 08	217 43.7	348 19.4	41.4	219 17.2	04.1	327 59.1	29.6	295 44.6	29.4
T 09	232 46.2	3 19.4 ..	42.0	234 18.2 ..	03.4	343 01.0 ..	29.7	310 46.8 ..	29.4
U 10	247 48.6	18 19.5	42.6	249 19.1	02.6	358 02.9	29.8	325 48.9	29.4
R 11	262 51.1	33 19.5	43.1	264 20.1	01.9	13 04.8	29.9	340 51.0	29.3
D 12	277 53.6	48 19.6	S14 43.7	279 21.0	S 1 01.2	28 06.7	S21 29.9	355 53.2	S22 29.3
A 13	292 56.0	63 19.7	44.3	294 22.0	1 00.5	43 08.6	30.0	10 55.3	29.3
Y 14	307 58.5	78 19.7	44.9	309 22.9	0 59.8	58 10.5	30.1	25 57.5	29.3
15	323 00.9	93 19.8 ..	45.5	324 23.9 ..	59.0	73 12.4 ..	30.2	40 59.6 ..	29.3
16	338 03.4	108 19.8	46.1	339 24.8	58.3	88 14.3	30.2	56 01.8	29.2
17	353 05.9	123 19.9	46.6	354 25.8	57.6	103 16.2	30.3	71 03.9	29.2
18	8 08.3	138 20.0	S14 47.2	9 26.7	S 0 56.9	118 18.1	S21 30.4	86 06.1	S22 29.2
19	23 10.8	153 20.0	47.8	24 27.7	56.2	133 20.0	30.5	101 08.2	29.2
20	38 13.3	168 20.1	48.4	39 28.6	55.4	148 21.9	30.5	116 10.4	29.2
21	53 15.7	183 20.1 ..	49.0	54 29.6 ..	54.7	163 23.8 ..	30.6	131 12.5 ..	29.1
22	68 18.2	198 20.2	49.5	69 30.5	54.0	178 25.7	30.7	146 14.6	29.1
23	83 20.7	213 20.2	50.1	84 31.5	53.3	193 27.6	30.8	161 16.8	29.1
Mer. Pass.	h m 17 31.5	v 0.1	d 0.6	v 1.0	d 0.7	v 1.9	d 0.1	v 2.1	d 0.0

STARS

Name	SHA	Dec
Acamar	315 15.2	S40 14.1
Achernar	335 23.8	S57 08.9
Acrux	173 05.0	S63 11.8
Adhara	255 09.2	S29 00.0
Aldebaran	290 44.7	N16 32.7
Alioth	166 17.5	N55 51.2
Alkaid	152 56.1	N49 13.0
Al Na'ir	27 39.3	S46 52.4
Alnilam	275 42.2	S 1 11.6
Alphard	217 52.2	S 8 44.5
Alphecca	126 08.1	N26 39.1
Alpheratz	357 39.6	N29 11.8
Altair	62 04.9	N 8 55.2
Ankaa	353 12.0	S42 12.5
Antares	112 22.0	S26 28.2
Arcturus	145 52.5	N19 05.1
Atria	107 20.9	S69 03.4
Avior	234 15.9	S59 34.1
Bellatrix	278 27.6	N 6 21.8
Betelgeuse	270 56.9	N 7 24.5
Canopus	263 53.9	S52 42.5
Capella	280 28.4	N46 00.9
Deneb	49 29.3	N45 21.1
Denebola	182 29.8	N14 27.9
Diphda	348 52.1	S17 53.2
Dubhe	193 46.9	N61 38.7
Elnath	278 07.5	N28 37.2
Eltanin	90 44.9	N51 29.3
Enif	33 43.7	N 9 57.8
Fomalhaut	15 20.0	S29 31.5
Gacrux	171 56.7	S57 12.8
Gienah	175 48.4	S17 38.6
Hadar	148 42.8	S60 27.4
Hamal	327 56.3	N23 33.1
Kaus Aust.	83 39.2	S34 22.4
Kochab	137 20.9	N74 04.5
Markab	13 34.7	N15 18.5
Menkar	314 10.9	N 4 09.7
Menkent	148 03.3	S36 27.5
Miaplacidus	221 38.1	S69 47.5
Mirfak	308 34.6	N49 55.7
Nunki	75 54.0	S26 16.3
Peacock	53 13.9	S56 40.5
Pollux	243 22.8	N27 58.6
Procyon	244 55.5	N 5 10.4
Rasalhague	96 03.3	N12 32.9
Regulus	207 39.3	N11 52.4
Rigel	281 08.1	S 8 11.0
Rigil Kent.	139 47.0	S60 54.4
Sabik	102 08.6	S15 44.7
Schedar	349 36.1	N56 38.6
Shaula	96 17.2	S37 06.8
Sirius	258 30.1	S16 44.7
Spica	158 27.4	S11 15.4
Suhail	222 49.3	S43 30.4
Vega	80 36.9	N38 48.2
Zuben'ubi	137 01.5	S16 07.0

	SHA	Mer. Pass.
	° ′	h m
Venus	131 51.9	8 47
Mars	2 22.0	17 24
Jupiter	110 33.5	10 11
Saturn	78 11.1	12 20

UT	SUN GHA	SUN Dec	MOON GHA	v	MOON Dec	d	HP
d h	° ′	° ′	° ′	′	° ′	′	′
27 00	179 48.2	S23 20.1	298 37.0	8.0	N13 05.1	10.8	59.9
01	194 47.9	20.0	313 04.0	8.0	12 54.3	10.9	59.9
02	209 47.6	19.9	327 31.0	8.2	12 43.4	10.9	59.9
03	224 47.3	.. 19.8	341 58.2	8.2	12 32.5	11.0	59.9
04	239 47.0	19.7	356 25.4	8.3	12 21.5	11.0	59.9
05	254 46.7	19.6	10 52.7	8.4	12 10.5	11.1	59.8
06	269 46.4	S23 19.5	25 20.1	8.5	N11 59.4	11.2	59.8
07	284 46.1	19.4	39 47.6	8.6	11 48.2	11.3	59.8
08	299 45.8	19.3	54 15.2	8.6	11 36.9	11.3	59.7
09	314 45.5	.. 19.2	68 42.8	8.7	11 25.6	11.3	59.7
10	329 45.2	19.0	83 10.5	8.8	11 14.3	11.5	59.7
11	344 44.9	18.9	97 38.3	8.9	11 02.8	11.4	59.7
12	359 44.5	S23 18.8	112 06.2	8.9	N10 51.4	11.6	59.6
13	14 44.2	18.7	126 34.1	9.0	10 39.8	11.6	59.6
14	29 43.9	18.6	141 02.1	9.1	10 28.2	11.6	59.6
15	44 43.6	.. 18.5	155 30.2	9.2	10 16.6	11.7	59.6
16	59 43.3	18.4	169 58.4	9.2	10 04.9	11.7	59.5
17	74 43.0	18.3	184 26.6	9.3	9 53.2	11.8	59.5
18	89 42.7	S23 18.2	198 54.9	9.4	N 9 41.4	11.8	59.5
19	104 42.4	18.0	213 23.3	9.4	9 29.6	11.9	59.4
20	119 42.1	17.9	227 51.7	9.6	9 17.7	11.9	59.4
21	134 41.8	.. 17.8	242 20.3	9.6	9 05.8	11.9	59.4
22	149 41.5	17.7	256 48.9	9.6	8 53.9	12.0	59.4
23	164 41.2	17.6	271 17.5	9.8	8 41.9	12.0	59.3
28 00	179 40.9	S23 17.5	285 46.3	9.8	N 8 29.9	12.1	59.3
01	194 40.6	17.3	300 15.1	9.8	8 17.8	12.1	59.3
02	209 40.3	17.2	314 43.9	10.0	8 05.7	12.1	59.3
03	224 40.0	.. 17.1	329 12.9	10.0	7 53.6	12.2	59.2
04	239 39.6	17.0	343 41.9	10.0	7 41.4	12.2	59.2
05	254 39.3	16.9	358 10.9	10.2	7 29.2	12.2	59.2
06	269 39.0	S23 16.7	12 40.1	10.2	N 7 17.0	12.2	59.1
07	284 38.7	16.6	27 09.3	10.2	7 04.8	12.3	59.1
08	299 38.4	16.5	41 38.5	10.3	6 52.5	12.3	59.1
09	314 38.1	.. 16.4	56 07.8	10.4	6 40.2	12.3	59.1
10	329 37.8	16.2	70 37.2	10.5	6 27.9	12.4	59.0
11	344 37.5	16.1	85 06.7	10.5	6 15.5	12.4	59.0
12	359 37.2	S23 16.0	99 36.2	10.5	N 6 03.1	12.3	59.0
13	14 36.9	15.8	114 05.7	10.6	5 50.8	12.5	58.9
14	29 36.6	15.7	128 35.3	10.7	5 38.3	12.4	58.9
15	44 36.3	.. 15.6	143 05.0	10.7	5 25.9	12.4	58.9
16	59 36.0	15.5	157 34.7	10.8	5 13.5	12.5	58.9
17	74 35.7	15.3	172 04.5	10.8	5 01.0	12.5	58.8
18	89 35.4	S23 15.2	186 34.3	10.9	N 4 48.5	12.5	58.8
19	104 35.1	15.1	201 04.2	11.0	4 36.0	12.5	58.8
20	119 34.8	14.9	215 34.2	10.9	4 23.5	12.5	58.7
21	134 34.5	.. 14.8	230 04.1	11.1	4 11.0	12.5	58.7
22	149 34.1	14.7	244 34.2	11.1	3 58.5	12.6	58.7
23	164 33.8	14.5	259 04.3	11.1	3 45.9	12.5	58.7
29 00	179 33.5	S23 14.4	273 34.4	11.2	N 3 33.4	12.5	58.6
01	194 33.2	14.2	288 04.6	11.2	3 20.9	12.6	58.6
02	209 32.9	14.1	302 34.8	11.3	3 08.3	12.5	58.6
03	224 32.6	.. 14.0	317 05.1	11.3	2 55.8	12.6	58.5
04	239 32.3	13.8	331 35.4	11.4	2 43.2	12.6	58.5
05	254 32.0	13.7	346 05.8	11.4	2 30.6	12.5	58.5
06	269 31.7	S23 13.5	0 36.2	11.4	N 2 18.1	12.6	58.5
07	284 31.4	13.4	15 06.6	11.5	2 05.5	12.5	58.4
08	299 31.1	13.2	29 37.1	11.5	1 53.0	12.6	58.4
09	314 30.8	.. 13.1	44 07.6	11.6	1 40.4	12.6	58.4
10	329 30.5	13.0	58 38.2	11.6	1 27.9	12.6	58.3
11	344 30.2	12.8	73 08.8	11.6	1 15.3	12.5	58.3
12	359 29.9	S23 12.7	87 39.4	11.7	N 1 02.8	12.6	58.3
13	14 29.6	12.5	102 10.1	11.7	0 50.2	12.5	58.2
14	29 29.3	12.4	116 40.8	11.7	0 37.7	12.5	58.2
15	44 29.0	.. 12.2	131 11.5	11.8	0 25.2	12.5	58.2
16	59 28.7	12.1	145 42.3	11.8	0 12.7	12.5	58.2
17	74 28.4	11.9	160 13.1	11.9	N 0 00.2	12.5	58.1
18	89 28.1	S23 11.8	174 44.0	11.8	S 0 12.3	12.5	58.1
19	104 27.8	11.6	189 14.8	11.9	0 24.8	12.4	58.1
20	119 27.5	11.5	203 45.7	11.9	0 37.2	12.5	58.0
21	134 27.2	.. 11.3	218 16.6	12.0	0 49.7	12.4	58.0
22	149 26.9	11.1	232 47.6	12.0	1 02.1	12.4	58.0
23	164 26.6	11.0	247 18.6	12.0	S 1 14.5	12.4	58.0
	SD 16.3	d 0.1	SD 16.2		16.1		15.9

Lat.	Twilight Naut.	Twilight Civil	Sunrise	Moonrise 27	28	29	30
°	h m	h m	h m	h m	h m	h m	h m
N 72	08 26	10 53	■■	20 54	22 59	24 57	00 57
N 70	08 07	09 54	■■	21 09	23 04	24 54	00 54
68	07 51	09 20	■■	21 21	23 08	24 54	00 52
66	07 38	08 55	10 33	21 30	23 12	24 50	00 50
64	07 27	08 35	09 52	21 38	23 15	24 49	00 49
62	07 18	08 19	09 25	21 45	23 18	24 48	00 48
60	07 09	08 06	09 03	21 51	23 20	24 46	00 46
N 58	07 02	07 55	08 46	21 56	23 22	24 45	00 45
56	06 55	07 44	08 32	22 00	23 24	24 45	00 45
54	06 49	07 35	08 19	22 04	23 25	24 44	00 44
52	06 44	07 27	08 08	22 08	23 27	24 43	00 43
50	06 38	07 20	07 58	22 11	23 28	24 43	00 43
45	06 27	07 04	07 38	22 18	23 31	24 41	00 41
N 40	06 16	06 50	07 21	22 24	23 33	24 40	00 40
35	06 07	06 39	07 07	22 30	23 35	24 39	00 39
30	05 58	06 28	06 55	22 34	23 37	24 38	00 38
20	05 42	06 10	06 34	22 42	23 40	24 37	00 37
N 10	05 26	05 52	06 15	22 49	23 43	24 35	00 35
0	05 09	05 35	05 58	22 55	23 46	24 34	00 34
S 10	04 50	05 17	05 40	23 02	23 48	24 33	00 33
20	04 28	04 57	05 21	23 09	23 51	24 32	00 32
30	03 59	04 32	04 59	23 16	23 54	24 31	00 31
35	03 40	04 17	04 47	23 21	23 56	24 30	00 30
40	03 17	03 59	04 32	23 26	23 58	24 29	00 29
45	02 47	03 36	04 14	23 32	24 01	00 01	00 28
S 50	02 02	03 07	03 51	23 39	24 04	00 04	00 27
52	01 34	02 52	03 41	23 42	24 05	00 05	00 27
54	00 50	02 34	03 28	23 45	24 06	00 06	00 26
56	////	02 12	03 14	23 49	24 08	00 08	00 25
58	////	01 43	02 58	23 53	24 10	00 10	00 25
S 60	////	00 55	02 37	23 58	24 12	00 12	00 24

Lat.	Sunset	Twilight Civil	Twilight Naut.	Moonset 27	28	29	30
°	h m	h m	h m	h m	h m	h m	h m
N 72	■■	13 11	15 37	12 53	12 35	12 20	12 06
N 70	■■	14 09	15 56	12 36	12 27	12 19	12 11
68	■■	14 44	16 12	12 23	12 21	12 18	12 16
66	13 30	15 08	16 25	12 12	12 15	12 17	12 19
64	14 11	15 28	16 36	12 03	12 10	12 17	12 23
62	14 38	15 44	16 45	11 55	12 06	12 16	12 25
60	15 00	15 57	16 54	11 48	12 03	12 16	12 28
N 58	15 17	16 09	17 01	11 42	12 00	12 15	12 30
56	15 32	16 19	17 08	11 36	11 57	12 15	12 32
54	15 44	16 28	17 14	11 31	11 54	12 14	12 34
52	15 55	16 36	17 20	11 27	11 52	12 14	12 35
50	16 05	16 43	17 25	11 23	11 50	12 14	12 37
45	16 25	16 59	17 36	11 14	11 45	12 13	12 40
N 40	16 42	17 13	17 47	11 06	11 41	12 12	12 43
35	16 56	17 24	17 56	11 00	11 37	12 12	12 45
30	17 08	17 35	18 05	10 54	11 34	12 11	12 47
20	17 29	17 54	18 21	10 45	11 29	12 11	12 51
N 10	17 48	18 11	18 37	10 36	11 24	12 10	12 54
0	18 05	18 28	18 54	10 28	11 20	12 09	12 57
S 10	18 23	18 46	19 13	10 19	11 15	12 08	13 00
20	18 42	19 06	19 35	10 10	11 10	12 08	13 03
30	19 03	19 31	20 04	10 00	11 05	12 07	13 07
35	19 16	19 46	20 23	09 54	11 01	12 06	13 09
40	19 31	20 04	20 46	09 47	10 58	12 05	13 11
45	19 49	20 26	21 16	09 40	10 53	12 05	13 14
S 50	20 11	20 56	22 01	09 30	10 48	12 04	13 17
52	20 22	21 11	22 28	09 25	10 46	12 03	13 19
54	20 34	21 28	23 11	09 21	10 43	12 03	13 20
56	20 48	21 50	////	09 15	10 40	12 02	13 22
58	21 05	22 19	////	09 09	10 37	12 02	13 24
S 60	21 25	23 07	////	09 02	10 33	12 01	13 27

Day	SUN Eqn. of Time 00h	SUN Eqn. of Time 12h	SUN Mer. Pass.	MOON Mer. Pass. Upper	MOON Mer. Pass. Lower	Age	Phase
d	m s	m s	h m	h m	h m	d	%
27	00 46	01 01	12 01	04 15	16 42	20	71
28	01 16	01 31	12 02	05 08	17 33	21	60
29	01 45	02 00	12 02	05 58	18 22	22	49

2018 DEC. 30, 31, JAN. 1 (SUN., MON., TUES.)

UT	ARIES GHA	VENUS −4.6 GHA	Dec	MARS +0.5 GHA	Dec	JUPITER −1.8 GHA	Dec	SATURN +0.5 GHA	Dec	STARS Name	SHA	Dec
30 00	98 23.1	228 20.3	S14 50.7	99 32.4	S 0 52.6	208 29.5	S21 30.8	176 18.9	S22 29.1	Acamar	315 15.2	S40 14.1
01	113 25.6	243 20.3	51.3	114 33.4	51.8	223 31.4	30.9	191 21.1	29.0	Achernar	335 23.8	S57 08.9
02	128 28.1	258 20.4	51.9	129 34.3	51.1	238 33.3	31.0	206 23.2	29.0	Acrux	173 05.0	S63 11.9
03	143 30.5	273 20.4 ..	52.5	144 35.3 ..	50.4	253 35.2 ..	31.1	221 25.4 ..	29.0	Adhara	255 09.2	S29 00.0
04	158 33.0	288 20.5	53.0	159 36.2	49.7	268 37.1	31.1	236 27.5	29.0	Aldebaran	290 44.7	N16 32.7
05	173 35.4	303 20.5	53.6	174 37.2	48.9	283 39.0	31.2	251 29.7	29.0			
06	188 37.9	318 20.5	S14 54.2	189 38.1	S 0 48.2	298 40.9	S21 31.3	266 31.8	S22 28.9	Alioth	166 17.5	N55 51.2
07	203 40.4	333 20.6	54.8	204 39.0	47.5	313 42.8	31.3	281 34.0	28.9	Alkaid	152 56.1	N49 13.0
S 08	218 42.8	348 20.6	55.4	219 40.0	46.8	328 44.7	31.4	296 36.1	28.9	Al Na'ir	27 39.3	S46 52.4
U 09	233 45.3	3 20.7 ..	56.0	234 40.9 ..	46.1	343 46.6 ..	31.5	311 38.2 ..	28.9	Alnilam	275 42.2	S 1 11.6
N 10	248 47.8	18 20.7	56.5	249 41.9	45.3	358 48.5	31.6	326 40.4	28.9	Alphard	217 52.1	S 8 44.5
D 11	263 50.2	33 20.7	57.1	264 42.8	44.6	13 50.4	31.6	341 42.5	28.8			
A 12	278 52.7	48 20.8	S14 57.7	279 43.8	S 0 43.9	28 52.3	S21 31.7	356 44.7	S22 28.8	Alphecca	126 08.1	N26 39.1
Y 13	293 55.2	63 20.8	58.3	294 44.7	43.2	43 54.2	31.8	11 46.8	28.8	Alpheratz	357 39.6	N29 11.8
14	308 57.6	78 20.8	58.9	309 45.7	42.5	58 56.1	31.9	26 49.0	28.8	Altair	62 04.9	N 8 55.2
15	324 00.1	93 20.9	14 59.5	324 46.6 ..	41.7	73 58.0 ..	31.9	41 51.1 ..	28.7	Ankaa	353 12.0	S42 12.5
16	339 02.5	108 20.9	15 00.0	339 47.6	41.0	88 59.9	32.0	56 53.3	28.7	Antares	112 22.0	S26 28.2
17	354 05.0	123 20.9	00.6	354 48.5	40.3	104 01.8	32.1	71 55.4	28.7			
18	9 07.5	138 21.0	S15 01.2	9 49.5	S 0 39.6	119 03.7	S21 32.2	86 57.6	S22 28.7	Arcturus	145 52.5	N19 05.1
19	24 09.9	153 21.0	01.8	24 50.4	38.9	134 05.6	32.2	101 59.7	28.7	Atria	107 20.9	S69 03.3
20	39 12.4	168 21.0	02.4	39 51.4	38.1	149 07.5	32.3	117 01.8	28.6	Avior	234 15.9	S59 34.1
21	54 14.9	183 21.0 ..	03.0	54 52.3 ..	37.4	164 09.4 ..	32.4	132 04.0 ..	28.6	Bellatrix	278 27.6	N 6 21.8
22	69 17.3	198 21.1	03.5	69 53.3	36.7	179 11.3	32.4	147 06.1	28.6	Betelgeuse	270 56.9	N 7 24.5
23	84 19.8	213 21.1	04.1	84 54.2	36.0	194 13.2	32.5	162 08.3	28.6			
31 00	99 22.3	228 21.1	S15 04.7	99 55.2	S 0 35.3	209 15.1	S21 32.6	177 10.4	S22 28.5	Canopus	263 53.9	S52 42.5
01	114 24.7	243 21.1	05.3	114 56.1	34.5	224 17.0	32.7	192 12.6	28.5	Capella	280 28.4	N46 00.9
02	129 27.2	258 21.2	05.9	129 57.1	33.8	239 18.9	32.7	207 14.7	28.5	Deneb	49 29.3	N45 21.0
03	144 29.7	273 21.2 ..	06.4	144 58.0 ..	33.1	254 20.8 ..	32.8	222 16.9 ..	28.5	Denebola	182 29.8	N14 27.9
04	159 32.1	288 21.2	07.0	159 58.9	32.4	269 22.7	32.9	237 19.0	28.5	Diphda	348 52.1	S17 53.2
05	174 34.6	303 21.2	07.6	174 59.9	31.7	284 24.6	33.0	252 21.2	28.4			
06	189 37.0	318 21.2	S15 08.2	190 00.8	S 0 30.9	299 26.5	S21 33.0	267 23.3	S22 28.4	Dubhe	193 46.9	N61 38.7
07	204 39.5	333 21.3	08.8	205 01.8	30.2	314 28.4	33.1	282 25.4	28.4	Elnath	278 07.5	N28 37.2
08	219 42.0	348 21.3	09.4	220 02.7	29.5	329 30.3	33.2	297 27.6	28.4	Eltanin	90 44.9	N51 29.3
M 09	234 44.4	3 21.3 ..	09.9	235 03.7 ..	28.8	344 32.3 ..	33.2	312 29.7 ..	28.4	Enif	33 43.7	N 9 57.8
O 10	249 46.9	18 21.3	10.5	250 04.6	28.1	359 34.2	33.3	327 31.9	28.3	Fomalhaut	15 20.0	S29 31.5
N 11	264 49.4	33 21.3	11.1	265 05.6	27.3	14 36.1	33.4	342 34.0	28.3			
D 12	279 51.8	48 21.3	S15 11.7	280 06.5	S 0 26.6	29 38.0	S21 33.5	357 36.2	S22 28.3	Gacrux	171 56.7	S57 12.8
A 13	294 54.3	63 21.3	12.3	295 07.5	25.9	44 39.9	33.5	12 38.3	28.3	Gienah	175 48.4	S17 38.7
Y 14	309 56.8	78 21.3	12.9	310 08.4	25.2	59 41.8	33.6	27 40.5	28.2	Hadar	148 42.8	S60 27.4
15	324 59.2	93 21.4 ..	13.4	325 09.4 ..	24.5	74 43.7 ..	33.7	42 42.6 ..	28.2	Hamal	327 56.3	N23 33.1
16	340 01.7	108 21.4	14.0	340 10.3	23.7	89 45.6	33.7	57 44.8	28.2	Kaus Aust.	83 39.2	S34 22.4
17	355 04.2	123 21.4	14.6	355 11.3	23.0	104 47.5	33.8	72 46.9	28.2			
18	10 06.6	138 21.4	S15 15.2	10 12.2	S 0 22.3	119 49.4	S21 33.9	87 49.0	S22 28.2	Kochab	137 20.9	N74 04.5
19	25 09.1	153 21.4	15.8	25 13.1	21.6	134 51.3	34.0	102 51.2	28.1	Markab	13 34.7	N15 18.5
20	40 11.5	168 21.4	16.4	40 14.1	20.9	149 53.2	34.0	117 53.3	28.1	Menkar	314 10.9	N 4 09.7
21	55 14.0	183 21.4 ..	16.9	55 15.0 ..	20.1	164 55.1 ..	34.1	132 55.5 ..	28.1	Menkent	148 03.3	S36 27.5
22	70 16.5	198 21.4	17.5	70 16.0	19.4	179 57.0	34.2	147 57.6	28.1	Miaplacidus	221 38.1	S69 47.5
23	85 18.9	213 21.4	18.1	85 16.9	18.7	194 58.9	34.2	162 59.8	28.0			
1 00	100 21.4	228 21.4	S15 18.7	100 17.9	S 0 18.0	210 00.8	S21 34.3	178 01.9	S22 28.0	Mirfak	308 34.6	N49 55.7
01	115 23.9	243 21.4	19.3	115 18.8	17.2	225 02.7	34.4	193 04.1	28.0	Nunki	75 54.0	S26 16.3
02	130 26.3	258 21.4	19.8	130 19.8	16.5	240 04.6	34.5	208 06.2	28.0	Peacock	53 13.9	S56 40.5
03	145 28.8	273 21.4 ..	20.4	145 20.7 ..	15.8	255 06.5 ..	34.5	223 08.3 ..	28.0	Pollux	243 22.8	N27 58.6
04	160 31.3	288 21.4	21.0	160 21.7	15.1	270 08.4	34.6	238 10.5	27.9	Procyon	244 55.5	N 5 10.4
05	175 33.7	303 21.4	21.6	175 22.6	14.4	285 10.3	34.7	253 12.6	27.9			
06	190 36.2	318 21.3	S15 22.2	190 23.6	S 0 13.6	300 12.2	S21 34.7	268 14.8	S22 27.9	Rasalhague	96 03.3	N12 32.9
07	205 38.6	333 21.3	22.8	205 24.5	12.9	315 14.1	34.8	283 16.9	27.9	Regulus	207 39.3	N11 52.4
T 08	220 41.1	348 21.3	23.3	220 25.4	12.2	330 16.1	34.9	298 19.1	27.8	Rigel	281 08.1	S 8 11.0
U 09	235 43.6	3 21.3 ..	23.9	235 26.4 ..	11.5	345 18.0 ..	35.0	313 21.2 ..	27.8	Rigil Kent.	139 46.9	S60 54.4
E 10	250 46.0	18 21.3	24.5	250 27.3	10.8	0 19.9	35.0	328 23.4	27.8	Sabik	102 08.6	S15 44.7
S 11	265 48.5	33 21.3	25.1	265 28.3	10.0	15 21.8	35.1	343 25.5	27.8			
D 12	280 51.0	48 21.3	S15 25.7	280 29.2	S 0 09.3	30 23.7	S21 35.2	358 27.7	S22 27.7	Schedar	349 36.2	N56 38.6
A 13	295 53.4	63 21.3	26.2	295 30.2	08.6	45 25.6	35.2	13 29.8	27.7	Shaula	96 17.2	S37 06.8
Y 14	310 55.9	78 21.3	26.8	310 31.1	07.9	60 27.5	35.3	28 31.9	27.7	Sirius	258 30.1	S16 44.7
15	325 58.4	93 21.2 ..	27.4	325 32.1 ..	07.2	75 29.4 ..	35.4	43 34.1 ..	27.7	Spica	158 27.4	S11 15.4
16	341 00.8	108 21.2	28.0	340 33.0	06.4	90 31.3	35.5	58 36.2	27.7	Suhail	222 49.3	S43 30.4
17	356 03.3	123 21.2	28.6	355 34.0	05.7	105 33.2	35.5	73 38.4	27.6			
18	11 05.8	138 21.2	S15 29.2	10 34.9	S 0 05.0	120 35.1	S21 35.6	88 40.5	S22 27.6	Vega	80 36.8	N38 48.2
19	26 08.2	153 21.2	29.7	25 35.8	04.3	135 37.0	35.7	103 42.7	27.6	Zuben'ubi	137 01.4	S16 07.0
20	41 10.7	168 21.1	30.3	40 36.8	03.6	150 38.9	35.7	118 44.8	27.6		SHA	Mer. Pass.
21	56 13.1	183 21.1 ..	30.8	55 37.7 ..	02.8	165 40.8 ..	35.8	133 47.0 ..	27.5		° ′	h m
22	71 15.6	198 21.1	31.5	70 38.7	02.1	180 42.7	35.9	148 49.1	27.5	Venus	128 58.9	8 47
23	86 18.1	213 21.1	32.1	85 39.6	01.4	195 44.6	35.9	163 51.3	27.5	Mars	0 32.9	17 19
	h m									Jupiter	109 52.9	10 02
Mer. Pass. 17 19.7	v 0.0 d 0.6			v 0.9 d 0.7		v 1.9 d 0.1		v 2.1 d 0.0		Saturn	77 48.2	12 10

UT	SUN GHA	Dec	MOON GHA	v	Dec	d	HP
d h	° ′	° ′	° ′	′	° ′	′	′
30 00	179 26.3	S23 10.8	261 49.6	12.0	S 1 26.9	12.3	57.9
01	194 26.0	10.7	276 20.6	12.1	1 39.2	12.4	57.9
02	209 25.7	10.5	290 51.7	12.0	1 51.6	12.3	57.9
03	224 25.4 ..	10.3	305 22.7	12.1	2 03.9	12.3	57.8
04	239 25.0	10.2	319 53.8	12.2	2 16.2	12.3	57.8
05	254 24.7	10.0	334 25.0	12.2	2 28.5	12.3	57.8
06	269 24.4	S23 09.9	348 56.1	12.2	S 2 40.8	12.2	57.8
07	284 24.1	09.7	3 27.3	12.1	2 53.0	12.2	57.7
08	299 23.8	09.5	17 58.4	12.2	3 05.2	12.2	57.7
S 09	314 23.5 ..	09.4	32 29.6	12.2	3 17.4	12.1	57.7
U 10	329 23.2	09.2	47 00.8	12.3	3 29.5	12.2	57.6
N 11	344 22.9	09.0	61 32.1	12.2	3 41.7	12.1	57.6
D 12	359 22.6	S23 08.9	76 03.3	12.3	S 3 53.8	12.0	57.6
A 13	14 22.3	08.7	90 34.6	12.2	4 05.8	12.1	57.6
Y 14	29 22.0	08.5	105 05.8	12.3	4 17.9	12.0	57.5
15	44 21.7 ..	08.4	119 37.1	12.3	4 29.9	11.9	57.5
16	59 21.4	08.2	134 08.4	12.3	4 41.8	12.0	57.5
17	74 21.1	08.0	148 39.7	12.3	4 53.8	11.9	57.5
18	89 20.8	S23 07.9	163 11.0	12.4	S 5 05.7	11.8	57.4
19	104 20.5	07.7	177 42.4	12.3	5 17.5	11.8	57.4
20	119 20.2	07.5	192 13.7	12.3	5 29.3	11.8	57.4
21	134 19.9 ..	07.3	206 45.0	12.4	5 41.1	11.8	57.3
22	149 19.6	07.2	221 16.4	12.3	5 52.9	11.7	57.3
23	164 19.3	07.0	235 47.7	12.4	6 04.6	11.7	57.3
31 00	179 19.0	S23 06.8	250 19.1	12.3	S 6 16.3	11.6	57.3
01	194 18.7	06.6	264 50.4	12.4	6 27.9	11.6	57.2
02	209 18.4	06.5	279 21.8	12.4	6 39.5	11.5	57.2
03	224 18.1 ..	06.3	293 53.2	12.3	6 51.0	11.5	57.2
04	239 17.8	06.1	308 24.5	12.4	7 02.5	11.5	57.2
05	254 17.5	05.9	322 55.9	12.4	7 14.0	11.4	57.1
06	269 17.2	S23 05.7	337 27.3	12.4	S 7 25.4	11.4	57.1
07	284 16.9	05.6	351 58.7	12.3	7 36.8	11.3	57.1
08	299 16.6	05.4	6 30.0	12.4	7 48.1	11.3	57.1
M 09	314 16.3 ..	05.2	21 01.4	12.4	7 59.4	11.2	57.0
O 10	329 16.0	05.0	35 32.8	12.3	8 10.6	11.2	57.0
N 11	344 15.7	04.8	50 04.1	12.4	8 21.8	11.1	57.0
D 12	359 15.4	S23 04.6	64 35.5	12.3	S 8 32.9	11.1	56.9
A 13	14 15.1	04.4	79 06.8	12.4	8 44.0	11.0	56.9
Y 14	29 14.8	04.3	93 38.2	12.3	8 55.0	11.0	56.9
15	44 14.5 ..	04.1	108 09.5	12.4	9 06.0	10.9	56.9
16	59 14.2	03.9	122 40.9	12.3	9 16.9	10.9	56.8
17	74 13.9	03.7	137 12.2	12.3	9 27.8	10.8	56.8
18	89 13.6	S23 03.5	151 43.5	12.4	S 9 38.6	10.8	56.8
19	104 13.3	03.3	166 14.9	12.3	9 49.4	10.7	56.8
20	119 13.1	03.1	180 46.2	12.3	10 00.1	10.6	56.7
21	134 12.8 ..	02.9	195 17.5	12.3	10 10.7	10.6	56.7
22	149 12.5	02.7	209 48.8	12.2	10 21.3	10.5	56.7
23	164 12.2	02.5	224 20.0	12.3	10 31.8	10.5	56.7
1 00	179 11.9	S23 02.3	238 51.3	12.3	S10 42.3	10.4	56.6
01	194 11.6	02.1	253 22.6	12.2	10 52.7	10.3	56.6
02	209 11.3	01.9	267 53.8	12.3	11 03.0	10.3	56.6
03	224 11.0 ..	01.7	282 25.1	12.2	11 13.3	10.3	56.6
04	239 10.7	01.5	296 56.3	12.2	11 23.6	10.1	56.6
05	254 10.4	01.3	311 27.5	12.2	11 33.7	10.1	56.5
06	269 10.1	S23 01.1	325 58.7	12.2	S11 43.8	10.1	56.5
07	284 09.8	00.9	340 29.9	12.1	11 53.9	9.9	56.5
T 08	299 09.5	00.7	355 01.0	12.2	12 03.8	9.9	56.5
U 09	314 09.2 ..	00.5	9 32.2	12.1	12 13.7	9.9	56.4
E 10	329 08.9	00.3	24 03.3	12.1	12 23.6	9.7	56.4
S 11	344 08.6	23 00.1	38 34.4	12.1	12 33.3	9.7	56.4
D 12	359 08.3	S22 59.9	53 05.5	12.1	S12 43.0	9.7	56.4
A 13	14 08.0	59.7	67 36.6	12.1	12 52.7	9.5	56.3
Y 14	29 07.7	59.5	82 07.7	12.0	13 02.2	9.5	56.3
15	44 07.4 ..	59.3	96 38.7	12.1	13 11.7	9.5	56.3
16	59 07.1	59.1	111 09.8	12.0	13 21.2	9.3	56.3
17	74 06.8	58.9	125 40.8	12.0	13 30.5	9.3	56.2
18	89 06.5	S22 58.7	140 11.8	12.0	S13 39.8	9.2	56.2
19	104 06.2	58.5	154 42.8	11.9	13 49.0	9.1	56.2
20	119 05.9	58.3	169 13.7	12.0	13 58.1	9.1	56.2
21	134 05.6 ..	58.0	183 44.7	11.9	14 07.2	9.0	56.2
22	149 05.4	57.8	198 15.6	11.9	14 16.2	8.9	56.1
23	164 05.1	57.6	212 46.5	11.9	S14 25.1	8.8	56.1
	SD 16.3	d 0.2	SD 15.7		15.5		15.4

Lat.	Twilight Naut.	Civil	Sunrise	Moonrise 30	31	1	2
°	h m	h m	h m	h m	h m	h m	h m
N 72	08 25	10 46	■	00 57	02 52	04 52	07 04
N 70	08 06	09 51	■	00 54	02 42	04 31	06 24
68	07 50	09 18	■	00 52	02 33	04 14	05 56
66	07 38	08 54	10 30	00 50	02 26	04 01	05 36
64	07 27	08 35	09 51	00 49	02 20	03 51	05 19
62	07 18	08 19	09 24	00 48	02 15	03 41	05 06
60	07 09	08 06	09 03	00 46	02 11	03 34	04 54
N 58	07 02	07 54	08 46	00 45	02 07	03 27	04 44
56	06 56	07 44	08 31	00 44	02 04	03 21	04 36
54	06 50	07 36	08 19	00 44	02 00	03 15	04 28
52	06 44	07 28	08 08	00 43	01 58	03 10	04 21
50	06 39	07 20	07 59	00 43	01 55	03 06	04 15
45	06 27	07 04	07 38	00 41	01 50	02 57	04 02
N 40	06 17	06 51	07 22	00 40	01 45	02 49	03 51
35	06 08	06 40	07 08	00 39	01 41	02 42	03 42
30	05 59	06 29	06 56	00 38	01 38	02 36	03 34
20	05 43	06 11	06 35	00 37	01 32	02 26	03 20
N 10	05 27	05 54	06 16	00 35	01 27	02 17	03 08
0	05 11	05 37	05 59	00 34	01 22	02 09	02 57
S 10	04 52	05 19	05 42	00 33	01 17	02 01	02 46
20	04 30	04 59	05 23	00 32	01 12	01 52	02 34
30	04 01	04 34	05 01	00 31	01 06	01 43	02 21
35	03 42	04 19	04 49	00 30	01 03	01 37	02 13
40	03 20	04 01	04 34	00 29	00 59	01 31	02 04
45	02 50	03 39	04 16	00 28	00 55	01 23	01 54
S 50	02 05	03 10	03 54	00 27	00 50	01 15	01 41
52	01 39	02 55	03 43	00 27	00 48	01 11	01 36
54	00 57	02 38	03 31	00 26	00 45	01 06	01 29
56	////	02 16	03 17	00 25	00 43	01 01	01 22
58	////	01 48	03 01	00 25	00 40	00 56	01 15
S 60	////	01 02	02 41	00 24	00 36	00 50	01 06

Lat.	Sunset	Twilight Civil	Naut.	Moonset 30	31	1	2
°	h m	h m	h m	h m	h m	h m	h m
N 72	■	13 20	15 41	12 06	11 50	11 30	10 58
N 70	■	14 15	16 01	12 11	12 02	11 53	11 40
68	■	14 48	16 16	12 16	12 13	12 10	12 08
66	13 37	15 13	16 29	12 19	12 21	12 25	12 30
64	14 16	15 32	16 39	12 23	12 29	12 36	12 47
62	14 43	15 47	16 49	12 25	12 35	12 46	13 01
60	15 03	16 00	16 57	12 28	12 41	12 55	13 13
N 58	15 20	16 12	17 04	12 30	12 45	13 03	13 24
56	15 35	16 22	17 11	12 32	12 50	13 10	13 33
54	15 47	16 31	17 17	12 34	12 54	13 16	13 41
52	15 58	16 39	17 22	12 35	12 57	13 21	13 48
50	16 08	16 46	17 27	12 37	13 01	13 26	13 55
45	16 28	17 02	17 39	12 40	13 08	13 37	14 09
N 40	16 44	17 15	17 49	12 43	13 14	13 46	14 21
35	16 58	17 26	17 58	12 45	13 19	13 53	14 31
30	17 10	17 37	18 07	12 47	13 23	14 00	14 39
20	17 31	17 55	18 23	12 51	13 31	14 12	14 55
N 10	17 50	18 12	18 39	12 54	13 38	14 22	15 08
0	18 07	18 29	18 55	12 57	13 44	14 32	15 20
S 10	18 24	18 47	19 14	13 00	13 51	14 42	15 33
20	18 43	19 07	19 36	13 03	13 58	14 52	15 46
30	19 04	19 32	20 05	13 07	14 06	15 04	16 02
35	19 17	19 47	20 23	13 09	14 10	15 11	16 11
40	19 32	20 05	20 46	13 11	14 16	15 19	16 21
45	19 50	20 27	21 16	13 14	14 22	15 28	16 33
S 50	20 12	20 56	22 00	13 17	14 29	15 39	16 47
52	20 22	21 10	22 26	13 19	14 33	15 45	16 54
54	20 34	21 28	23 07	13 20	14 36	15 50	17 02
56	20 48	21 49	////	13 22	14 40	15 57	17 10
58	21 04	22 17	////	13 24	14 45	16 04	17 20
S 60	21 24	23 01	////	13 27	14 50	16 12	17 31

	SUN Eqn. of Time 00h	12h	Mer. Pass.	MOON Mer. Pass. Upper	Lower	Age	Phase
Day	m s	m s	h m	h m	h m	d	%
30	02 14	02 29	12 02	06 46	19 09	23	38
31	02 43	02 58	12 03	07 33	19 57	24	28
1	03 12	03 26	12 03	08 21	20 45	25	19

EXPLANATION

PRINCIPLE AND ARRANGEMENT

1. *Object.* The object of this Almanac is to provide, in a convenient form, the data required for the practice of astronomical navigation at sea.

2. *Principle.* The main contents of the Almanac consist of data from which the *Greenwich Hour Angle* (GHA) and the *Declination* (Dec) of all the bodies used for navigation can be obtained for any instant of *Universal Time* (UT, specifically UT1, or previously Greenwich Mean Time (GMT)).

The *Local Hour Angle* (LHA) can then be obtained by means of the formula:

$$\text{LHA} = \text{GHA} \begin{array}{c} - \text{ west} \\ + \text{ east} \end{array} \text{longitude}$$

The remaining data consist of: times of rising and setting of the Sun and Moon, and times of twilight; miscellaneous calendarial and planning data and auxiliary tables, including a list of Standard Times; corrections to be applied to observed altitude.

For the Sun, Moon, and planets, the GHA and Dec are tabulated directly for each hour of UT throughout the year. For the stars, the *Sidereal Hour Angle* (SHA) is given, and the GHA is obtained from:

$$\text{GHA Star} = \text{GHA Aries} + \text{SHA Star}$$

The SHA and Dec of the stars change slowly and may be regarded as constant over periods of several days. GHA Aries, or the Greenwich Hour Angle of the first point of Aries (the Vernal Equinox), is tabulated for each hour. Permanent tables give the appropriate increments and corrections to the tabulated hourly values of GHA and Dec for the minutes and seconds of UT.

The six-volume series of *Sight Reduction Tables for Marine Navigation* (published in U.S.A. as Pub. No. 229) has been designed for the solution of the navigational triangle and is intended for use with *The Nautical Almanac*.

Two alternative procedures for sight reduction are described on pages 277–318. The first requires the use of programmable calculators or computers, while the second uses a set of concise tables that is given on pages 286–317.

The tabular accuracy is $0\rlap{.}'1$ throughout. The time argument on the daily pages of this Almanac is UT1 denoted throughout by UT. This scale may differ from the broadcast time signals (UTC) by an amount which, if ignored, will introduce an error of up to $0\rlap{.}'2$ in longitude determined from astronomical observations. The difference arises because the time argument depends on the variable rate of rotation of the Earth while the broadcast time signals are based on an atomic time-scale. Step adjustments of exactly one second are made to the time signals as required (normally at 24^{h} on December 31 and June 30) so that the difference between the time signals and UT, as used in this Almanac, may not exceed $0\rlap{.}^{\text{s}}9$. Those who require to reduce observations to a precision of better than 1^{s} must therefore obtain the correction (DUT1) to the time signals from coding in the signal, or from other sources; the required time is given by UT1=UTC+DUT1 to a precision of $0\rlap{.}^{\text{s}}1$. Alternatively, the longitude, when determined from astronomical observations, may be corrected by the corresponding amount shown in the following table:

Correction to time signals	Correction to longitude
$-0\rlap{.}^{\text{s}}9$ to $-0\rlap{.}^{\text{s}}7$	$0\rlap{.}'2$ to east
$-0\rlap{.}^{\text{s}}6$ to $-0\rlap{.}^{\text{s}}3$	$0\rlap{.}'1$ to east
$-0\rlap{.}^{\text{s}}2$ to $+0\rlap{.}^{\text{s}}2$	no correction
$+0\rlap{.}^{\text{s}}3$ to $+0\rlap{.}^{\text{s}}6$	$0\rlap{.}'1$ to west
$+0\rlap{.}^{\text{s}}7$ to $+0\rlap{.}^{\text{s}}9$	$0\rlap{.}'2$ to west

3. *Lay-out.* The ephemeral data for three days are presented on an opening of two pages: the left-hand page contains the data for the planets and stars; the right-hand page contains the data for the Sun and Moon, together with times of twilight, sunrise, sunset, moonrise and moonset.

The remaining contents are arranged as follows: for ease of reference the altitude-correction tables are given on pages A2, A3, A4, xxxiv and xxxv; calendar, Moon's phases, eclipses, and planet notes (i.e. data of general interest) precede the main tabulations. The Explanation is followed by information on standard times, star charts and list of star positions, sight reduction procedures and concise sight reduction tables, polar phenomena information and graphs, tables of increments and corrections and other auxiliary tables that are frequently used.

MAIN DATA

4. *Daily pages.* The daily pages give the GHA of Aries, the GHA and Dec of the Sun, Moon, and the four navigational planets, for each hour of UT. For the Moon, values of v and d are also tabulated for each hour to facilitate the correction of GHA and Dec to intermediate times; v and d for the Sun and planets change so slowly that they are given, at the foot of the appropriate columns, once only on the page; v is zero for Aries and negligible for the Sun, and is omitted. The SHA and Dec of the 57 selected stars, arranged in alphabetical order of proper name, are also given.

5. *Stars.* The SHA and Dec of 173 stars, including the 57 selected stars, are tabulated for each month on pages 268–273; no interpolation is required and the data can be used in precisely the same way as those for the selected stars on the daily pages. The stars are arranged in order of SHA.

The list of 173 includes all stars down to magnitude 3·0, together with a few fainter ones to fill the larger gaps. The 57 selected stars have been chosen from amongst these on account of brightness and distribution in the sky; they will suffice for the majority of observations.

The 57 selected stars are known by their proper names, but they are also numbered in descending order of SHA. In the list of 173 stars, the constellation names are always given on the left-hand page; on the facing page proper names are given where well-known names exist. Numbers for the selected stars are given in both columns.

An index to the selected stars, containing lists in both alphabetical and numerical order, is given on page xxxiii and is also reprinted on the bookmark.

6. *Increments and corrections.* The tables printed on tinted paper (pages ii–xxxi) at the back of the Almanac provide the increments and corrections for minutes and seconds to be applied to the hourly values of GHA and Dec. They consist of sixty tables, one for each minute, separated into two parts: increments to GHA for Sun and planets, Aries, and Moon for every minute and second; and, for each minute, corrections to be applied to GHA and Dec corresponding to the values of v and d given on the daily pages.

The increments are based on the following adopted hourly rates of increase of the GHA: Sun and planets, $15°$ precisely; Aries, $15° \ 02\!\!\cdot\!\!46$; Moon, $14° \ 19\!\!\cdot\!\!0$. The values of v on the daily pages are the excesses of the actual hourly motions over the adopted values; they are generally positive, except for Venus. The tabulated hourly values of the Sun's GHA have been adjusted to reduce to a minimum the error caused by treating v as negligible. The values of d on the daily pages are the hourly differences of the Dec. For the Moon, the true values of v and d are given for each hour; otherwise mean values are given for the three days on the page.

7. *Method of entry.* The UT of an observation is expressed as a day and hour, followed by a number of minutes and seconds. The tabular values of GHA and Dec, and, where necessary, the corresponding values of v and d, are taken directly from the daily pages for the day and hour of UT; this hour is always *before* the time of observation. SHA and Dec of the selected stars are also taken from the daily pages.

The table of Increments and Corrections for the minute of UT is then selected. For the GHA, the increment for minutes and seconds is taken from the appropriate column opposite the seconds of UT; the v-correction is taken from the second part of the same table opposite the value of v as given on the daily pages. Both increment and v-correction are to be added to the GHA, except for Venus when v is prefixed by a minus sign and the v-correction is to be subtracted. For the Dec there is no increment, but a d-correction is applied in the same way as the v-correction; d is given without sign on the daily pages and the sign of the correction is to be supplied by inspection of the Dec column. In many cases the correction may be applied mentally.

8. *Examples.* (a) Sun and Moon. Required the GHA and Dec of the Sun and Moon on 2018 May 23 at 15^h 47^m 13^s UT.

	SUN			MOON			
	GHA	Dec	d	GHA	v	Dec	d
	° ′	° ′	′	° ′	′	° ′	′
Daily page, May 23^d 15^h	45 48·6	N 20 38·7	0·5	292 58·6	11·4	N 6 41·6	11·3
Increments for 47^m 13^s	11 48·3			11 16·0			
v or d corrections for 47^m		+0·4		+9·0		−8·9	
Sum for May 23^d 15^h 47^m 13^s	57 36·9	N 20 39·1		304 23·6		N 6 32·7	

(b) Planets. Required the LHA and Dec of (i) Venus on 2018 May 23 at 13^h 15^m 58^s UT in longitude E 90° 54′; (ii) Mars on 2018 May 23 at 8^h 12^m 57^s UT in longitude W 70° 00′.

		VENUS					MARS			
		GHA	v	Dec	d		GHA	v	Dec	d
		° ′	′	° ′	′		° ′	′	° ′	′
Daily page, May 23^d	(13^h)	340 49·7	−0·8	N 25 02·7	0·0	(8^h)	55 23·5	1·5	S 21 52·4	0·1
Increments (planets)	(15^m 58^s)	3 59·5				(12^m 57^s)	3 14·3			
v or d corrections	(15^m)	−0·2		+0·0		(12^m)	+0·3		+0·0	
Sum = GHA and Dec.		344 49·0		N 25 02·7			58 38·1		S 21 52·4	
Longitude	(east)	+ 90 54·0				(west)	− 70 00·0			
Multiples of 360°		−360					+360			
LHA planet		75 43·0					348 38·1			

(c) Stars. Required the GHA and Dec of (i) *Arcturus* on 2018 May 23 at 22^h 39^m 35^s UT; (ii) *Vega* on 2018 May 23 at 7^h 54^m 09^s UT.

		Arcturus			*Vega*	
		GHA	Dec		GHA	Dec
		° ′	° ′		° ′	° ′
Daily page (SHA and Dec)		145 52·4	N 19 05·4		80 36·4	N 38 48·0
Daily page (GHA Aries)	(22^h)	211 27·7		(7^h)	345 50·7	
Increments (Aries)	(39^m 35^s)	9 55·4		(54^m 09^s)	13 34·5	
Sum = GHA star		367 15·5			440 01·6	
Multiples of 360°		−360			−360	
GHA star		7 15·5			80 01·6	

9. *Polaris (Pole Star) tables.* The tables on pages 274–276 provide means by which the latitude can be deduced from an observed altitude of *Polaris*, and they also give its azimuth; their use is explained and illustrated on those pages. They are based on the following formula:

$$\text{Latitude} - H_O = -p\cos h + \tfrac{1}{2}p\sin p \sin^2 h \tan(\text{latitude})$$

where

H_O = Apparent altitude (corrected for refraction)

p = polar distance of *Polaris* = 90° − Dec

h = local hour angle of *Polaris* = LHA Aries + SHA

a_0, which is a function of LHA Aries only, is the value of both terms of the above formula calculated for mean values of the SHA (316° 13′) and Dec (N 89° 20′·4) of *Polaris*, for a mean latitude of 50°, and adjusted by the addition of a constant (58′·8).

a_1, which is a function of LHA Aries and latitude, is the excess of the value of the second term over its mean value for latitude 50°, increased by a constant (0ʹ6) to make it always positive. a_2, which is a function of LHA Aries and date, is the correction to the first term for the variation of *Polaris* from its adopted mean position; it is increased by a constant (0ʹ6) to make it positive. The sum of the added constants is 1°, so that:

$$\text{Latitude} = \text{Apparent altitude (corrected for refraction)} - 1° + a_0 + a_1 + a_2$$

RISING AND SETTING PHENOMENA

10. *General.* On the right-hand daily pages are given the times of sunrise and sunset, of the beginning and end of civil and nautical twilights, and of moonrise and moonset for a range of latitudes from N 72° to S 60°. These times, which are given to the nearest minute, are strictly the UT of the phenomena on the Greenwich meridian; they are given for every day for moonrise and moonset, but only for the middle day of the three on each page for the solar phenomena.

They are approximately the Local Mean Times (LMT) of the corresponding phenomena on other meridians; they can be formally interpolated if desired. The UT of a phenomenon is obtained from the LMT by:

$$\text{UT} = \text{LMT} \genfrac{}{}{0pt}{}{+ \text{ west}}{- \text{ east}} \text{ longitude}$$

in which the longitude must first be converted to time by the table on page i or otherwise. Interpolation for latitude can be done mentally or with the aid of Table I on page xxxii.

The following symbols are used to indicate the conditions under which, in high latitudes, some of the phenomena do not occur:

☐ Sun or Moon remains continuously above the horizon;

■ Sun or Moon remains continuously below the horizon;

//// twilight lasts all night.

Basis of the tabulations. At sunrise and sunset 16ʹ is allowed for semi-diameter and 34ʹ for horizontal refraction, so that at the times given the Sun's upper limb is on the visible horizon; all times refer to phenomena as seen from sea level with a clear horizon.

At the times given for the beginning and end of twilight, the Sun's zenith distance is 96° for civil, and 102° for nautical twilight. The degree of illumination at the times given for civil twilight (in good conditions and in the absence of other illumination) is such that the brightest stars are visible and the horizon is clearly defined. At the times given for nautical twilight, the horizon is in general not visible, and it is too dark for observation with a marine sextant.

Times corresponding to other depressions of the Sun may be obtained by interpolation or, for depressions of more than 12°, less reliably, by extrapolation; times so obtained will be subject to considerable uncertainty near extreme conditions.

At moonrise and moonset, allowance is made for semi-diameter, parallax, and refraction (34ʹ), so that at the times given the Moon's upper limb is on the visible horizon as seen from sea level.

Polar phenomena. Information and graphs concerning the rising and setting of the Sun and Moon and the duration of civil twilight for high latitudes are given on pages 320–325.

11. *Sunrise, sunset, twilight.* The tabulated times may be regarded, without serious error, as the LMT of the phenomena on any of the three days on the page and in any longitude. Precise times may normally be obtained by interpolating the tabular values for latitude and to the correct day and longitude, the latter being expressed as a fraction of a day by dividing it by 360°, positive for west and negative for east longitudes. In the extreme conditions near ☐, ■ or //// interpolation may not be possible in one direction, but accurate times are of little value in these circumstances.

Examples. Required the UT of (a) the beginning of morning twilights and sunrise on 2018 January 13 for latitude S 48° 55ʹ, longitude E 75° 18ʹ; (b) sunset and the end of evening twilights on 2018 January 15 for latitude N 67° 10ʹ, longitude W 168° 05ʹ.

		Twilight		Sunrise		Sunset	Twilight	
	(a)	Nautical	Civil		(b)		Civil	Nautical
From p. 19		d h m	d h m	d h m		d h m	d h m	d h m
LMT for Lat	S 45°	13 03 09	13 03 56	13 04 32	N 66°	15 14 23	15 15 43	15 16 54
Corr. to	S 48° 55′	−27	−20	−16	N 67° 10′	−22	−12	−6
(p. xxxii, Table I)								
Long (p. i)	E 75° 18′	−5 01	−5 01	−5 01	W 168° 05′	+11 12	+11 12	+11 12
UT		12 21 41	12 22 35	12 23 15		16 01 13	16 02 43	16 04 00

The LMT are strictly for January 14 (middle date on page) and 0° longitude; for more precise times it is necessary to interpolate, but rounding errors may accumulate to about 2^m.

(a) to January $13^d - 75°/360°$ = Jan. $12^d{\cdot}8$, i.e. $\frac{1}{3}(1{\cdot}2) = 0{\cdot}4$ backwards towards the data for the same latitude interpolated similarly from page 17; the corrections are -3^m to nautical twilight, -2^m to civil twilight and -2^m to sunrise.

(b) to January $15^d + 168°/360°$ = Jan. $15^d{\cdot}5$, i.e. $\frac{1}{3}(1{\cdot}5) = 0{\cdot}5$ forwards towards the data for the same latitude interpolated similarly from page 21; the corrections are $+7^m$ to sunset, $+4^m$ to civil twilight, and $+3^m$ to nautical twilight.

12. *Moonrise, moonset.* Precise times of moonrise and moonset are rarely needed; a glance at the tables will generally give sufficient indication of whether the Moon is available for observation and of the hours of rising and setting. If needed, precise times may be obtained as follows. Interpolate for latitude, using Table I on page xxxii, on the day wanted and also on the preceding day in east longitudes or the following day in west longitudes; take the difference between these times and interpolate for longitude by applying to the time for the day wanted the correction from Table II on page xxxii, so that the resulting time is between the two times used. In extreme conditions near ☐ or ◼ interpolation for latitude or longitude may be possible only in one direction; accurate times are of little value in these circumstances.

To facilitate this interpolation, the times of moonrise and moonset are given for four days on each page; where no phenomenon occurs during a particular day (as happens once a month) the time of the phenomenon on the following day, increased by 24^h, is given; extra care must be taken when interpolating between two values, when one of those values exceeds 24^h. In practice it suffices to use the daily difference between the times for the nearest tabular latitude, and generally, to enter Table II with the nearest tabular arguments as in the examples below.

Examples. Required the UT of moonrise and moonset in latitude S 47° 10′, longitudes E 124° 00′ and W 78° 31′ on 2018 January 5.

	Longitude E 124° 00′		Longitude W 78° 31′	
	Moonrise	Moonset	Moonrise	Moonset
	d h m	d h m	d h m	d h m
LMT for Lat. S 45°	5 22 24	5 08 18	5 22 24	5 08 18
Lat correction (p. xxxii, Table I)	+04	−04	+04	−04
Long correction (p. xxxii, Table II)	−13	−27	+07	+16
Correct LMT	5 22 15	5 07 47	5 22 35	5 08 30
Longitude (p. i)	−8 16	−8 16	+5 14	+5 14
UT	5 13 59	4 23 31	6 03 49	5 13 44

ALTITUDE CORRECTION TABLES

13. *General.* In general, two corrections are given for application to altitudes observed with a marine sextant; additional corrections are required for Venus and Mars and also for very low altitudes.

Tables of the correction for dip of the horizon, due to height of eye above sea level, are given on pages A2 and xxxiv. Strictly this correction should be applied first and subtracted from the sextant altitude to give apparent altitude, which is the correct argument for the other tables.

Separate tables are given of the second correction for the Sun, for stars and planets (on pages A2 and A3), and for the Moon (on pages xxxiv and xxxv). For the Sun, values are given for both lower and upper limbs, for two periods of the year. The star tables are used for the planets, but additional corrections for parallax (page A2) are required for Venus and Mars. The Moon tables are in two parts: the main correction is a function of apparent altitude only and is tabulated for the lower limb (30′ must be subtracted to obtain the correction for the upper limb); the other, which is given for both lower and upper limbs, depends also on the horizontal parallax, which has to be taken from the daily pages.

An additional correction, given on page A4, is required for the change in the refraction, due to variations of pressure and temperature from the adopted standard conditions; it may generally be ignored for altitudes greater than 10°, except possibly in extreme conditions. The correction tables for the Sun, stars, and planets are in two parts; only those for altitudes greater than 10° are reprinted on the bookmark.

14. *Critical tables.* Some of the altitude correction tables are arranged as critical tables. In these, an interval of apparent altitude (or height of eye) corresponds to a single value of the correction; no interpolation is required. At a "critical" entry the upper of the two possible values of the correction is to be taken. For example, in the table of dip, a correction of −4′1 corresponds to all values of the height of eye from 5·3 to 5·5 metres (17·5 to 18·3 feet) inclusive.

15. *Examples.* The following examples illustrate the use of the altitude correction tables; the sextant altitudes given are assumed to be taken on 2018 March 9 with a marine sextant at height 5·4 metres (18 feet), temperature −3°C and pressure 982 mb, the Moon sights being taken at about 10^h UT.

	SUN lower limb	SUN upper limb	MOON lower limb	MOON upper limb	VENUS	*Polaris*
	° ′	° ′	° ′	° ′	° ′	° ′
Sextant altitude	21 19·7	3 20·2	33 27·6	26 06·7	4 32·6	49 36·5
Dip, height 5·4 metres (18 feet)	−4·1	−4·1	−4·1	−4·1	−4·1	−4·1
Main correction	+13·8	−29·6	+57·4	+60·5	−10·8	−0·8
−30′ for upper limb (Moon)	—	—	—	−30·0	—	—
L, U correction for Moon	—	—	+1·4	+1·6	—	—
Additional correction for Venus	—	—	—	—	+0·1	—
Additional refraction correction	−0·1	−0·6	−0·1	−0·1	−0·5	0·0
Corrected sextant altitude	21 29·3	2 45·9	34 22·2	26 34·6	4 17·3	49 31·6

The main corrections have been taken out with apparent altitude (sextant altitude corrected for index error and dip) as argument, interpolating where possible. These refinements are rarely necessary.

16. *Composition of the Corrections.* The table for the dip of the sea horizon is based on the formula:

Correction for dip $= -1\!\cdot\!76\sqrt{\text{(height of eye in metres)}} = -0\!\cdot\!97\sqrt{\text{(height of eye in feet)}}$

The correction table for the Sun includes the effects of semi-diameter, parallax and mean refraction.

The correction tables for the stars and planets allow for the effect of mean refraction.

The phase correction for Venus has been incorporated in the tabulations for GHA and Dec, and no correction for phase is required. The additional corrections for Venus and Mars allow for parallax. Alternatively, the correction for parallax may be calculated from $p \cos H$, where p is the parallax and H is the altitude. In 2018 the values for p are:

	Jan. 1	July 11	Aug. 30	Sept. 21	Oct. 7	Nov. 16	Dec. 2	Dec. 25	Dec. 31
Venus	0′1	0′2	0′3	0′4	0′5	0′4	0′3	0′2	

	Jan. 1	Apr. 15	June 4	July 9	Aug. 22	Sept. 29	Nov. 26	Dec. 31
Mars	0′1	0′2	0′3	0′4	0′3	0′2	0′1	

The correction table for the Moon includes the effect of semi-diameter, parallax, augmentation and mean refraction.

Mean refraction is calculated for a temperature of $10°C$ ($50°F$), a pressure of $1010\,\text{mb}$ ($29·83$ inches), humidity of 80% and wavelength $0·50169\,\mu\text{m}$.

17. *Bubble sextant observations.* When observing with a bubble sextant, no correction is necessary for dip, semi-diameter, or augmentation. The altitude corrections for the stars and planets on page A2 and on the bookmark should be used for the Sun as well as for the stars and planets; for the Moon, it is easiest to take the mean of the corrections for lower and upper limbs and subtract $15'$ from the altitude; the correction for dip must not be applied.

AUXILIARY AND PLANNING DATA

18. *Sun and Moon.* On the daily pages are given: hourly values of the horizontal parallax of the Moon; the semi-diameters and the times of meridian passage of both Sun and Moon over the Greenwich meridian; the equation of time; the age of the Moon, the percent (%) illuminated and a symbol indicating the phase. The times of the phases of the Moon are given in UT on page 4. For the Moon, the semi-diameters for each of the three days are given at the foot of the column; for the Sun a single value is sufficient. Table II on page xxxii may be used for interpolating the time of the Moon's meridian passage for longitude. The equation of time is given daily at 00^h and 12^h UT. The sign is *positive* for unshaded values and *negative* for shaded values. To obtain apparent time add the equation of time to mean time when the sign is *positive*. Subtract the equation of time from mean time when the sign is *negative*. At 12^h UT, when the sign is *positive*, meridian passage of the Sun occurs *before* 12^h UT, otherwise it occurs *after* 12^h UT.

19. *Planets.* The magnitudes of the planets are given immediately following their names in the headings on the daily pages; also given, for the middle day of the three on the page, are their SHA at 00^h UT and their times of meridian passage.

The planet notes and diagram on pages 8 and 9 provide descriptive information as to the suitability of the planets for observation during the year, and of their positions and movements.

20. *Stars.* The time of meridian passage of the first point of Aries over the Greenwich meridian is given on the daily pages, for the middle day of the three on the page, to 0^m1. The interval between successive meridian passages is $23^h\,56^m1$ (24^h less 3^m9), so that times for intermediate days and other meridians can readily be derived. If a precise time is required, it may be obtained by finding the UT at which LHA Aries is zero.

The meridian passage of a star occurs when its LHA is zero, that is when LHA Aries + SHA = $360°$. An approximate time can be obtained from the planet diagram on page 9.

The star charts on pages 266 and 267 are intended to assist identification. They show the relative positions of the stars in the sky as seen from the Earth and include all 173 stars used in the Almanac, together with a few others to complete the main constellation configurations. The local meridian at any time may be located on the chart by means of its SHA which is $360°$ − LHA Aries, or west longitude − GHA Aries.

21. *Star globe.* To set a star globe on which is printed a scale of LHA Aries, first set the globe for latitude and then rotate about the polar axis until the scale under the edge of the meridian circle reads LHA Aries.

To mark the positions of the Sun, Moon, and planets on the star globe, take the difference GHA Aries − GHA body and use this along the LHA Aries scale, in conjunction with the declination, to plot the position. GHA Aries − GHA body is most conveniently found by taking the difference when the GHA of the body is small (less than $15°$), which happens once a day.

22. *Calendar.* On page 4 are given lists of ecclesiastical festivals, and of the principal anniversaries and holidays in the United Kingdom and the United States of America. The calendar on page 5 includes the day of the year as well as the day of the week.

Brief particulars are given, at the foot of page 5, of the solar and lunar eclipses occurring during the year; the times given are in UT. The principal features of the more important solar eclipses are shown on the maps on pages 6 and 7.

23. *Standard times.* The lists on pages 262–265 give the standard times used in most countries. In general no attempt is made to give details of the beginning and end of summer time, since they are liable to frequent changes at short notice. For the latest information consult Admiralty List of Radio Signals Volume 2 (NP 282) corrected by Section VI of the weekly edition of Admiralty Notices to Mariners.

The Date or Calendar Line is an arbitrary line, on either side of which the date differs by one day; when crossing this line on a westerly course, the date must be advanced one day; when crossing it on an easterly course, the date must be put back one day. The line is a modification of the line of the 180th meridian, and is drawn so as to include, as far as possible, islands of any one group, etc., on the same side of the line. It may be traced by starting at the South Pole and joining up to the following positions:

Lat	S 51·0	S 45·0	S 15·0	S 5·0	N 48·0	N 53·0	N 65·5
Long	180·0	W 172·5	W 172·5	180·0	180·0	E 170·0	W 169·0

thence through the middle of the Diomede Islands to Lat N 68°·0, Long W 169°·0, passing east of Ostrov Vrangelya (Wrangel Island) to Lat N 75°·0, Long 180°·0, and thence to the North Pole.

ACCURACY

24. *Main data.* The quantities tabulated in this Almanac are generally correct to the nearest 0·1; the exception is the Sun's GHA which is deliberately adjusted by up to 0·15 to reduce the error due to ignoring the v-correction. The GHA and Dec at intermediate times cannot be obtained to this precision, since at least two quantities must be added; moreover, the v- and d-corrections are based on mean values of v and d and are taken from tables for the whole minute only. The largest error that can occur in the GHA or Dec of any body other than the Sun or Moon is less than 0·2; it may reach 0·25 for the GHA of the Sun and 0·3 for that of the Moon.

In practice, it may be expected that only one third of the values of GHA and Dec taken out will have errors larger than 0·05 and less than one tenth will have errors larger than 0·1.

25. *Altitude corrections.* The errors in the altitude corrections are nominally of the same order as those in GHA and Dec, as they result from the addition of several quantities each correctly rounded off to 0·1. But the actual values of the dip and of the refraction at low altitudes may, in extreme atmospheric conditions, differ considerably from the mean values used in the tables.

USE OF THIS ALMANAC IN 2019

This Almanac may be used for the Sun and stars in 2019 in the following manner.

For the Sun, take out the GHA and Dec for the same date but for a time $5^h 48^m 00^s$ *earlier* than the UT of observation; add 87° 00' to the GHA so obtained. The error, mainly due to planetary perturbations of the Earth, is unlikely to exceed 0·4.

For the stars, calculate the GHA and Dec for the same date and the same time, but *subtract* 15·1 from the GHA so found. The error due to incomplete correction for precession and nutation is unlikely to exceed 0·4. If preferred, the same result can be obtained by using a time $5^h 48^m 00^s$ earlier than the UT of observation (as for the Sun) and adding 86° 59·2 to the GHA (or adding 87° as for the Sun and subtracting 0·8, for precession, from the SHA of the star).

The Almanac cannot be so used for the Moon or planets.

LIST I — PLACES FAST ON UTC (mainly those EAST OF GREENWICH)

The times given } *added* to UTC to give Standard Time
below should be } *subtracted* from Standard Time to give UTC.

Place	h	m
Admiralty Islands	10	
Afghanistan	04	30
Albania*	01	
Algeria	01	
Amirante Islands	04	
Andaman Islands	05	30
Angola	01	
Armenia	04	
Australia		
Australian Capital Territory*	10	
New South Wales*[1]	10	
Northern Territory	09	30
Queensland	10	
South Australia*	09	30
Tasmania*	10	
Victoria*	10	
Western Australia	08	
Whitsunday Islands	10	
Austria*†	01	
Azerbaijan	04	
Bahrain	03	
Balearic Islands*†	01	
Bangladesh	06	
Belarus	03	
Belgium*†	01	
Benin	01	
Bosnia and Herzegovina*	01	
Botswana, Republic of	02	
Brunei	08	
Bulgaria*†	02	
Burma (Myanmar)	06	30
Burundi	02	
Cambodia	07	
Cameroon Republic	01	
Caroline Islands[2]	10	
Central African Republic	01	
Chad	01	
Chagos Archipelago & Diego Garcia	06	
Chatham Islands*	12	45
China, People's Republic of	08	
Christmas Island, Indian Ocean	07	
Cocos (Keeling) Islands	06	30
Comoro Islands (Comoros)	03	
Congo, Democratic Republic		
West: Kinshasa, Equateur	01	
East: Orientale, Kasai, Kivu, Shaba	02	
Congo Republic	01	
Corsica*†	01	
Crete*†	02	
Croatia*†	01	
Cyprus†: Ercan*, Larnaca*	02	
Czech Republic*†	01	

Place	h	m
Denmark*†	01	
Djibouti	03	
Egypt, Arab Republic of	02	
Equatorial Guinea, Republic of	01	
Bioko	01	
Eritrea	03	
Estonia*†	02	
Ethiopia	03	
Fiji*	12	
Finland*†	02	
France*†	01	
Gabon	01	
Georgia	04	
Germany*†	01	
Gibraltar*	01	
Greece*†	02	
Guam	10	
Hong Kong	08	
Hungary*†	01	
India	05	30
Indonesia, Republic of		
Bangka, Billiton, Java, West and		
Central Kalimantan, Madura, Sumatra	07	
Bali, Flores, South, North and East		
Kalimantan, Lombok, Sulawesi,		
Sumba, Sumbawa, West Timor	08	
Aru, Irian Jaya, Kai, Moluccas		
Tanimbar	09	
Iran*	03	30
Iraq	03	
Israel*	02	
Italy*†	01	
Jan Mayen Island*	01	
Japan	09	
Jordan	02	
Kazakhstan		
Western: Aktau, Uralsk, Atyrau	05	
Eastern & Central: Kzyl-Orda, Astana	06	
Kenya	03	
Kerguelen Islands	05	
Kiribati Republic		
Gilbert Islands	12	
Phoenix Islands[3]	13	
Line Islands[3]	14	
Korea, North	08	30
Korea, South	09	
Kuwait	03	
Kyrgyzstan	06	
Laccadive Islands	05	30
Laos	07	

---

* Daylight-saving time may be kept in these places.   † For Summer time dates see List II footnotes.

[1] Except Broken Hill Area* which keeps $09^h 30^m$.

[2] Except Pohnpei, Pingelap and Kosrae which keep 11^h and Palau which keeps 09^h.

[3] The Line and Phoenix Is. not part of the Kiribati Republic may keep other time zones.

LIST I — (*continued*)

	h	m		h	m
Latvia*†	02		Norilsk, Krasnoyarsk, Dikson,		
Lebanon*	02		Novosibirsk, Tomsk	07	
Lesotho	02		Irkutsk, Bratsk, Ulan-Ude	08	
Libya	02		Tiksi, Yakutsk, Chita	09	
Liechtenstein*	01		Vladivostok, Khabarovsk, Okhotsk	10	
Lithuania*†	02		Severo-Kurilsk, Magadan,		
Lord Howe Island*	10	30	Sakhalin Island	11	
Luxembourg*†	01		Petropavlovsk-K., Anadyr	12	
Macau	08		Rwanda	02	
Macedonia*, former Yugoslav Republic	01		Ryukyu Islands	09	
Madagascar, Democratic Republic of	03				
Malawi	02		Samoa*	13	
Malaysia, Malaya, Sabah, Sarawak	08		Santa Cruz Islands	11	
Maldives, Republic of The	05		Sardinia*†	01	
Malta*†	01		Saudi Arabia	03	
Mariana Islands	10		Schouten Islands	09	
Marshall Islands	12		Serbia*	01	
Mauritius	04		Seychelles	04	
Moldova*	02		Sicily*†	01	
Monaco*	01		Singapore	08	
Mongolia*	08		Slovakia*†	01	
Montenegro*	01		Slovenia*†	01	
Mozambique	02		Socotra	03	
			Solomon Islands	11	
Namibia*	01		Somalia Republic	03	
Nauru	12		South Africa, Republic of	02	
Nepal	05	45	Spain*†	01	
Netherlands, The*†	01		Spanish Possessions in North Africa*	01	
New Caledonia	11		Spitsbergen (Svalbard)*	01	
New Zealand*	12		Sri Lanka	05	30
Nicobar Islands	05	30	Sudan, Republic of	03	
Niger	01		Swaziland	02	
Nigeria, Republic of	01		Sweden*†	01	
Norfolk Island	11		Switzerland*	01	
Norway*	01		Syria (Syrian Arab Republic)*	02	
Novaya Zemlya	03				
			Taiwan	08	
Okinawa	09		Tajikistan	05	
Oman	04		Tanzania	03	
			Thailand	07	
Pagalu (Annobon Islands)	01		Timor-Leste	09	
Pakistan	05		Tonga	13	
Palau Islands	09		Tunisia	01	
Papua New Guinea [1]	10		Turkey	03	
Pescadores Islands	08		Turkmenistan	05	
Philippine Republic	08		Tuvalu	12	
Poland*†	01				
			Uganda	03	
Qatar	03		Ukraine*	02	
			United Arab Emirates	04	
Reunion	04		Uzbekistan	05	
Romania*†	02				
Russia [2]			Vanuatu, Republic of	11	
Kaliningrad	02		Vietnam, Socialist Republic of	07	
Moscow, St. Petersburg, Volgograd,					
Arkhangelsk	03		Yemen	03	
Samara, Astrakhan	04				
Ekaterinburg, Ufa, Perm, Novyy Port	05		Zambia, Republic of	02	
Omsk	06		Zimbabwe	02	

* Daylight-saving time may be kept in these places.   † For Summer time dates see List II footnotes.
[1] Excluding the Autonomous Region of Bougainville which keeps 11^{h}.
[2] The boundaries between the zones are irregular; listed are chief towns in each zone.

LIST II — PLACES NORMALLY KEEPING UTC

Ascension Island	Ghana	Irish Republic*†	Morocco*	Sierra Leone
Burkina-Faso	Great Britain†	Ivory Coast	Portugal*†	Togo Republic
Canary Islands*†	Guinea-Bissau	Liberia	Principe	Tristan da Cunha
Channel Islands†	Guinea Republic	Madeira*†	St. Helena	
Faeroes*, The	Iceland	Mali	São Tomé	
Gambia, The	Ireland, Northern†	Mauritania	Senegal	

* Daylight-saving time may be kept in these places.

† Summer time (daylight-saving time), one hour in advance of UTC, will be kept from 2018 March 25^d 01^h to October 28^d 01^h UTC (Ninth Summer Time Directive of the European Union). Ratification by member countries has not been verified.

LIST III — PLACES SLOW ON UTC (WEST OF GREENWICH)

The times given ⎫ *subtracted* from UTC to give Standard Time
below should be ⎰ *added* to Standard Time to give UTC.

	h	m		h	m
American Samoa	11		Canada (*continued*)		
Argentina ... ... ,..	03		Prince Edward Island*	04	
Austral (Tubuai) Islands[1]	10		Quebec, east of long. W. 63°	04	
Azores*†	01		west of long. W. 63°* ...	05	
			Saskatchewan	06	
Bahamas*	05		Yukon*	08	
Barbados	04		Cape Verde Islands	01	
Belize	06		Cayman Islands	05	
Bermuda*	04		Chile*	04	
Bolivia	04		Colombia	05	
Brazil			Cook Islands	10	
Fernando de Noronha I., Trindade I.,			Costa Rica	06	
Oceanic Is.	02		Cuba*	05	
N and NE coastal states, Tocantins,			Curaçao Island	04	
Minas Gerais*, Goiás*, Brasilia*,					
S and E coastal states*	03		Dominican Republic	04	
Amazonas[2], Mato Grosso do Sul*,					
Mato Grosso*, Rondônia, Roraima	04		Easter Island (I. de Pascua)*	06	
Acre	05		Ecuador	05	
British Antarctic Territory[3,4]	03		El Salvador	06	
Canada[4]‡			Falkland Islands	03	
Alberta*	07		Fernando de Noronha Island	02	
British Columbia*	08		French Guiana	03	
Labrador*	04				
Manitoba*	06		Galápagos Islands	06	
New Brunswick*	04		Greenland		
Newfoundland*	03	30	Danmarkshavn, Mesters Vig	00	
Nunavut*			General*	03	
east of long. W. 85°	05		Scoresby Sound*	01	
long. W. 85° to W. 102°	06		Thule*, Pituffik*	04	
west of long. W. 102°	07		Grenada	04	
Northwest Territories*	07		Guadeloupe	04	
Nova Scotia*	04		Guatemala	06	
Ontario, east of long. W. 90°*	05		Guyana, Republic of	04	
Ontario, west of long. W. 90°* ...	06				

* Daylight-saving time may be kept in these places.   ‡ Dates for DST are given at the end of List III.

[1] This is the legal standard time, but local mean time is generally used.

[2] Except the cities of Eirunepe, Benjamin Constant and Tabatinga which keep 05^h.

[3] Stations may use UTC.

[4] Some areas may keep another time zone.

LIST III — (continued)

	h	m		h	m
Haiti	05		United States of America‡(continued)		
Honduras	06		Idaho, southern part	07	
			northern part	08	
Jamaica	05		Illinois	06	
Johnston Island	10		Indiana 2	05	
Juan Fernandez Islands*	04		Iowa	06	
			Kansas 2	06	
Leeward Islands	04		Kentucky, eastern part	05	
			western part	06	
Marquesas Islands	09	30	Louisiana	06	
Martinique	04		Maine	05	
Mexico			Maryland	05	
General*	06		Massachusetts	05	
Quintana Roo	05		Michigan 2	05	
Baja California Sur*, Chihuahua*			Minnesota	06	
Nayarit*, Sinaloa* and Sonara ...	07		Mississippi	06	
Baja California Norte*	08		Missouri	06	
Midway Islands	11		Montana	07	
			Nebraska, eastern part	06	
Nicaragua	06		western part	07	
Niue	11		Nevada	08	
			New Hampshire	05	
Panama, Republic of	05		New Jersey	05	
Paraguay*	04		New Mexico	07	
Peru	05		New York	05	
Pitcairn Island	08		North Carolina	05	
Puerto Rico	04		North Dakota, eastern part	06	
			western part	07	
St. Pierre and Miquelon*	03		Ohio	05	
Society Islands	10		Oklahoma	06	
South Georgia	02		Oregon 2	08	
Suriname	03		Pennsylvania	05	
			Rhode Island	05	
Trindade Island, South Atlantic ...	02		South Carolina	05	
Trinidad and Tobago	04		South Dakota, eastern part	06	
Tuamotu Archipelago	10		western part	07	
Tubuai (Austral) Islands	10		Tennessee, eastern part	05	
Turks and Caicos Islands	04		western part	06	
			Texas 2	06	
United States of America‡			Utah	07	
Alabama	06		Vermont	05	
Alaska	09		Virginia	05	
Aleutian Islands, east of W. 169° 30′	09		Washington D.C.	05	
Aleutian Islands, west of W. 169° 30′	10		Washington	08	
Arizona 1	07		West Virginia	05	
Arkansas	06		Wisconsin	06	
California	08		Wyoming	07	
Colorado	07		Uruguay	03	
Connecticut	05				
Delaware	05		Venezuela	04	
District of Columbia	05		Virgin Islands	04	
Florida 2	05				
Georgia	05		Windward Islands	04	
Hawaii 1	10				

* Daylight-saving time may be kept in these places.

‡ Daylight-saving (Summer) time, one hour fast on the time given, is kept during 2018 from March 11 (second Sunday) to November 4 (first Sunday), changing at $02^h\ 00^m$ local clock time.

1 Exempt from keeping daylight-saving time, except for a portion of Arizona.

2 A small portion of the state is in another time zone.

NORTHERN STARS

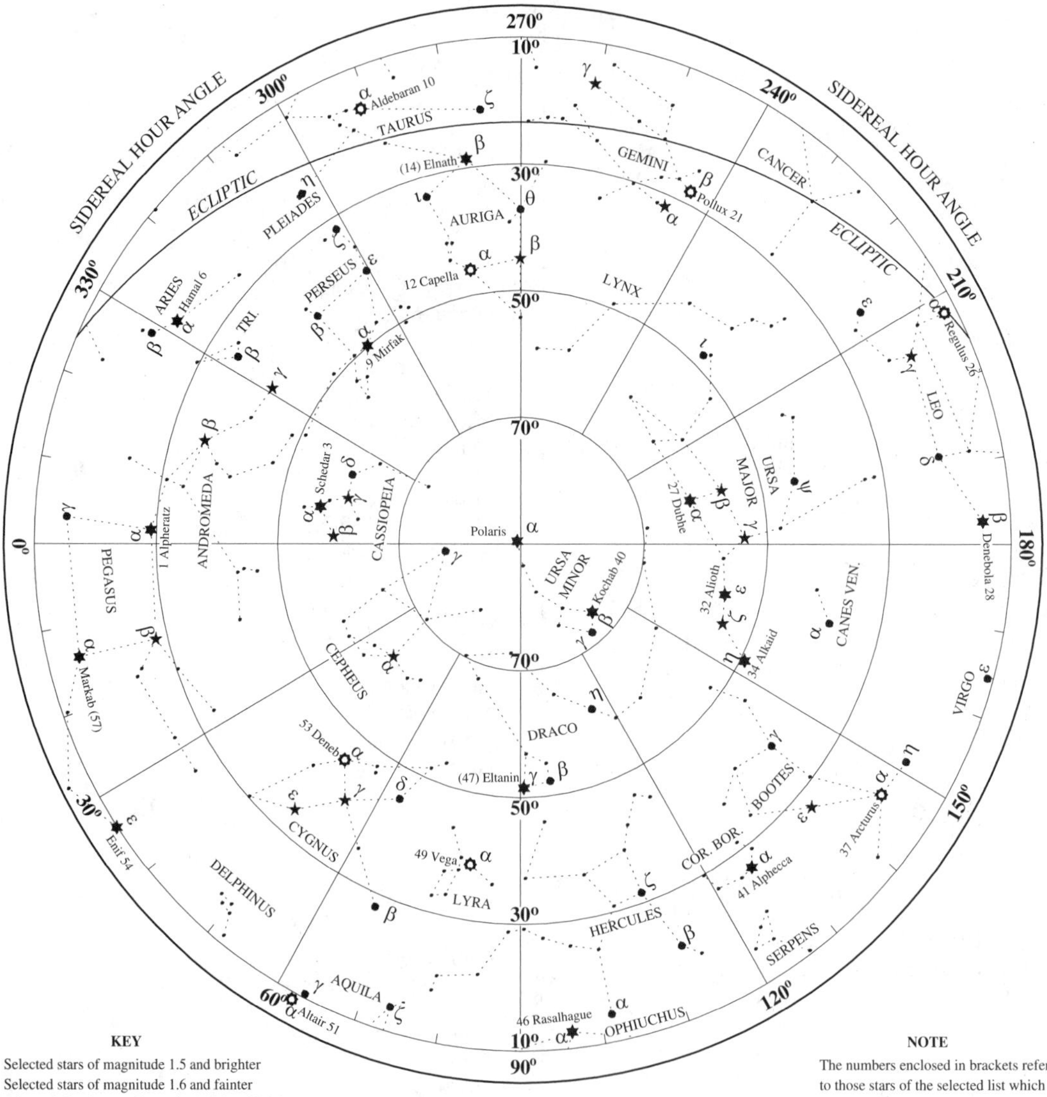

SIDEREAL HOUR ANGLE

270°
10°

300°

SIDEREAL HOUR ANGLE

240°

α Aldebaran 10 ζ
TAURUS
(14) Elnath β
30°
ECLIPTIC
GEMINI
β Pollux 21
CANCER
210°
330°
η
PLEIADES
ι
θ
AURIGA
β
CANCER
ECLIPTIC
ζ
α
ε
12 Capella
β
LYNX
 γ
Regulus 26
PERSEUS
β
α
LYNX
γ
ε
LEO
TRI
β
9 Mirfak
ι
δ
ARIES α Hamal 6
γ
β
ψ
180°
β
δ Schedar 3
CANES VEN.
β Denebola 28
ANDROMEDA
α
ζ
δ
URSA MAJOR
γ
32 Alioth
β α 27 Dubhe
γ
ζ
ι Alpheratz
CASSIOPEIA
β
Polaris α
URSA MINOR
ε
PEGASUS
γ
Kochab 40
α
34 Alkaid
CANES VEN.
α
ε
150°
β Markab (57)
CEPHEUS
γ
η
BOOTES
ε
VIRGO
γ
53 Deneb α
δ
DRACO
η
γ
37 Arcturus α
30°
ε
(47) Eltanin γ β
CYGNUS
γ
COR. BOR.
α Alphecca
ε Enif 54
49 Vega α
HERCULES
ζ
SERPENS
DELPHINUS
LYRA
β
β
120°
γ
AQUILA
60°
Altair 51
ζ
46 Rasalhague
α
10°
OPHIUCHUS
90°

KEY

✧ Selected stars of magnitude 1.5 and brighter
★ Selected stars of magnitude 1.6 and fainter
★ Other tabulated stars of magnitude 2.5 and brighter
● Other tabulated stars of magnitude 2.6 and fainter
· Untabulated stars

NOTE

The numbers enclosed in brackets refer to those stars of the selected list which are not used in Sight Reduction Tables A.P. 3270, N.P. 303.

EQUATORIAL STARS (SHA 0° to 180°)

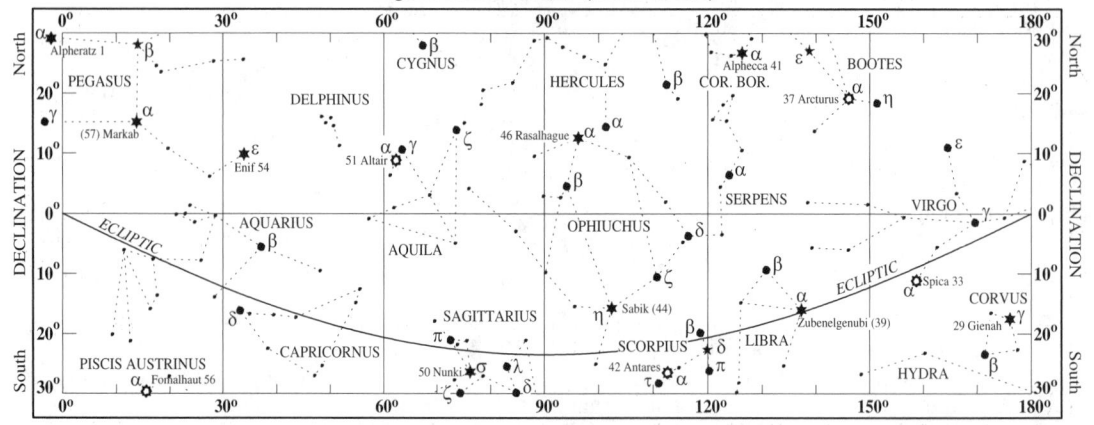

SOUTHERN STARS

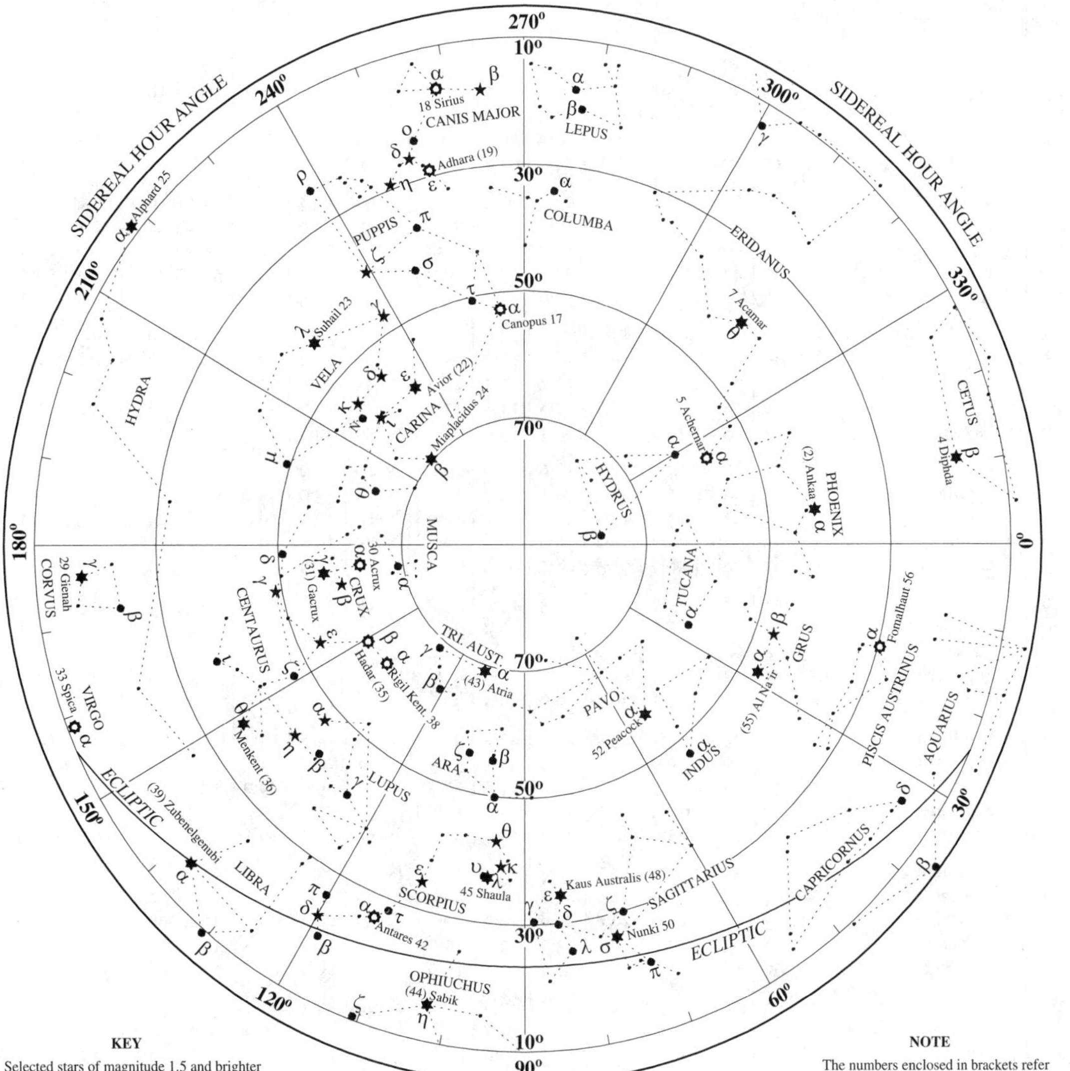

(circular star chart showing southern constellations with SIDEREAL HOUR ANGLE markings 0° to 330° around the perimeter and declination circles at 10°, 30°, 50°, 70°; constellations labelled include CANIS MAJOR, LEPUS, COLUMBA, ERIDANUS, PUPPIS, CETUS, HYDRA, VELA, CARINA, PHOENIX, HYDRUS, MUSCA, CRUX, CENTAURUS, TUCANA, GRUS, PISCIS AUSTRINUS, AQUARIUS, CORVUS, VIRGO, TRI. AUST., PAVO, INDUS, LUPUS, ARA, LIBRA, SCORPIUS, SAGITTARIUS, CAPRICORNUS, OPHIUCHUS. Labelled stars include 18 Sirius, Adhara (19), Alphard 25, Subail 23, Canopus 17, Avior (22), Miaplacidus 24, 7 Acamar, 5 Achernar, (2) Ankaa, 4 Diphda, 30 Acrux, (31) Gacrux, 29 Gienah, 33 Spica, Menkent (36), Hadar (35), Rigil Kent. 38, (43) Atria, 52 Peacock, Fomalhaut 56, (55) Al Na'ir, (39) Zubenelgenubi, 45 Shaula, Kaus Australis (48), Nunki 50, Antares 42, (44) Sabik)

KEY

- ✿ Selected stars of magnitude 1.5 and brighter
- ★ Selected stars of magnitude 1.6 and fainter
- ★ Other tabulated stars of magnitude 2.5 and brighter
- ● Other tabulated stars of magnitude 2.6 and fainter
- · Untabulated stars

NOTE

The numbers enclosed in brackets refer to those stars of the selected list which are not used in Sight Reduction Tables A.P. 3270, N.P. 303.

EQUATORIAL STARS (SHA 180° to 360°)

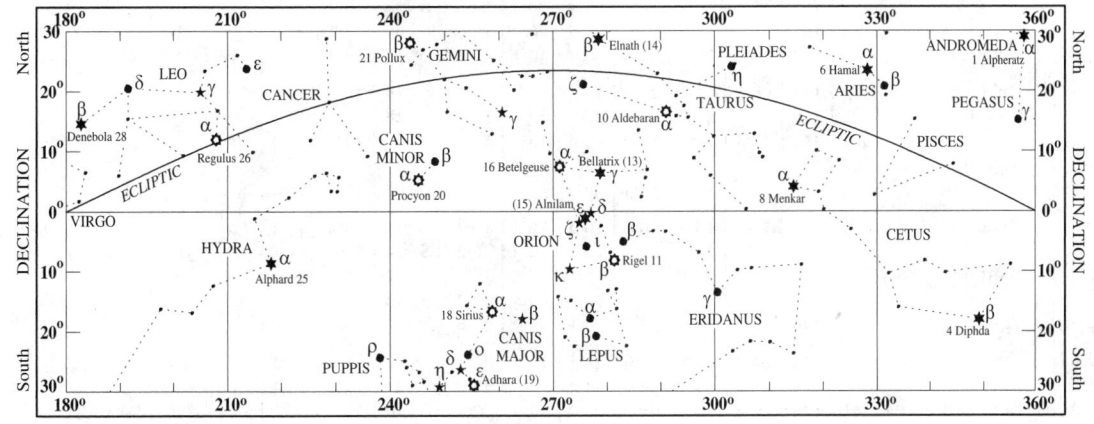

(rectangular star chart with DECLINATION axis from North 30° to South 30° and SIDEREAL HOUR ANGLE axis from 180° to 360°; constellations labelled include LEO, CANCER, GEMINI, ANDROMEDA, PLEIADES, TAURUS, ARIES, PEGASUS, PISCES, CANIS MINOR, ORION, CETUS, VIRGO, HYDRA, CANIS MAJOR, LEPUS, ERIDANUS, PUPPIS. Labelled stars include Denebola 28, Regulus 26, 21 Pollux, Elnath (14), 6 Hamal, 1 Alpheratz, 10 Aldebaran, 16 Betelgeuse, Bellatrix (13), 8 Menkar, Procyon 20, (15) Alnilam, Rigel 11, Alphard 25, 18 Sirius, Adhara (19), 4 Diphda)

SIDEREAL HOUR ANGLE

Mag.	Name and Number			SHA JAN.	FEB.	MAR.	APR.	MAY	JUNE		Declination JAN.	FEB.	MAR.	APR.	MAY	JUNE
			°	′	′	′	′	′	′	°	′	′	′	′	′	′
3·2	γ Cephei		4	58·8	59·3	59·5	59·3	58·7	57·9	N 77	44·2	44·1	43·9	43·8	43·7	43·7
2·5	α Pegasi	57	13	35·4	35·5	35·5	35·3	35·2	34·9	N 15	18·1	18·1	18·0	18·0	18·0	18·1
2·4	β Pegasi		13	50·6	50·6	50·6	50·5	50·3	50·0	N 28	10·9	10·8	10·7	10·7	10·7	10·8
1·2	α Piscis Aust.	56	15	20·8	20·9	20·8	20·7	20·5	20·2	S 29	31·8	31·8	31·7	31·6	31·5	31·4
2·1	β Gruis		19	04·6	04·6	04·6	04·4	04·1	03·8	S 46	47·6	47·5	47·4	47·3	47·2	47·1
2·9	α Tucanæ		25	05·1	05·1	05·0	04·8	04·4	04·0	S 60	10·4	10·3	10·1	10·0	09·8	09·8
1·7	α Gruis	55	27	40·3	40·3	40·2	40·0	39·7	39·4	S 46	52·6	52·5	52·4	52·2	52·1	52·1
2·9	δ Capricorni		32	60·0	60·0	59·9	59·7	59·5	59·2	S 16	02·8	02·8	02·7	02·7	02·6	02·5
2·4	ε Pegasi	54	33	44·4	44·3	44·3	44·1	43·9	43·6	N 9	57·5	57·4	57·4	57·4	57·4	57·5
2·9	β Aquarii		36	52·9	52·8	52·7	52·6	52·4	52·1	S 5	29·5	29·5	29·5	29·5	29·4	29·3
2·4	α Cephei		40	15·4	15·5	15·3	15·0	14·6	14·2	N 62	39·9	39·7	39·6	39·5	39·5	39·6
2·5	ε Cygni		48	16·3	16·3	16·2	16·0	15·7	15·5	N 34	02·4	02·2	02·1	02·1	02·2	02·3
1·3	α Cygni	53	49	29·8	29·7	29·6	29·4	29·1	28·8	N 45	20·8	20·7	20·5	20·5	20·5	20·7
3·1	α Indi		50	18·4	18·3	18·1	17·8	17·5	17·2	S 47	13·7	13·6	13·5	13·4	13·4	13·4
1·9	α Pavonis	52	53	15·0	14·9	14·6	14·3	13·9	13·5	S 56	40·6	40·5	40·4	40·3	40·2	40·2
2·2	γ Cygni		54	17·4	17·3	17·1	16·9	16·6	16·4	N 40	19·0	18·8	18·7	18·7	18·7	18·9
0·8	α Aquilæ	51	62	05·5	05·4	05·3	05·1	04·9	04·7	N 8	55·0	55·0	54·9	54·9	55·0	55·1
2·7	γ Aquilæ		63	13·7	13·6	13·5	13·3	13·1	12·9	N 10	39·5	39·4	39·4	39·4	39·5	39·6
2·9	δ Cygni		63	37·5	37·4	37·2	36·9	36·6	36·4	N 45	10·6	10·4	10·3	10·3	10·4	10·5
3·1	β Cygni		67	08·8	08·7	08·5	08·2	08·0	07·8	N 27	59·9	59·8	59·7	59·7	59·8	59·9
2·9	π Sagittarii		72	18·0	17·9	17·7	17·5	17·2	17·0	S 20	59·6	59·6	59·6	59·5	59·5	59·5
3·0	ζ Aquilæ		73	26·9	26·8	26·6	26·4	26·2	26·0	N 13	53·5	53·4	53·4	53·4	53·4	53·6
2·6	ζ Sagittarii		74	04·3	04·1	03·9	03·6	03·4	03·2	S 29	51·1	51·1	51·1	51·0	51·0	51·0
2·0	σ Sagittarii	50	75	54·9	54·7	54·5	54·2	54·0	53·8	S 26	16·3	16·3	16·3	16·3	16·2	16·2
0·0	α Lyræ	49	80	37·3	37·1	36·9	36·6	36·4	36·2	N 38	48·1	48·0	47·9	47·9	48·0	48·1
2·8	λ Sagittarii		82	44·3	44·1	43·9	43·7	43·4	43·3	S 25	24·5	24·5	24·5	24·5	24·5	24·5
1·9	ε Sagittarii	48	83	40·1	39·9	39·6	39·4	39·1	38·9	S 34	22·3	22·3	22·3	22·3	22·3	22·3
2·7	δ Sagittarii		84	28·4	28·2	27·9	27·7	27·5	27·3	S 29	49·0	49·0	49·0	49·0	49·0	49·0
3·0	γ Sagittarii		88	16·1	15·9	15·6	15·4	15·2	15·0	S 30	25·2	25·2	25·2	25·2	25·2	25·2
2·2	γ Draconis	47	90	45·2	45·0	44·7	44·4	44·2	44·0	N 51	29·2	29·1	29·0	29·0	29·2	29·3
2·8	β Ophiuchi		93	55·0	54·8	54·6	54·4	54·2	54·1	N 4	33·7	33·6	33·6	33·6	33·7	33·8
2·4	κ Scorpii		94	04·6	04·3	04·0	03·8	03·5	03·4	S 39	02·1	02·1	02·1	02·1	02·1	02·2
1·9	θ Scorpii		95	21·4	21·1	20·8	20·6	20·3	20·1	S 43	00·3	00·2	00·2	00·3	00·3	00·4
2·1	α Ophiuchi	46	96	03·9	03·7	03·5	03·3	03·1	03·0	N 12	32·9	32·8	32·8	32·8	32·9	33·0
1·6	λ Scorpii	45	96	18·1	17·8	17·6	17·3	17·1	16·9	S 37	06·7	06·7	06·7	06·8	06·8	06·8
3·0	α Aræ		96	42·1	41·8	41·5	41·2	40·9	40·7	S 49	53·1	53·1	53·1	53·1	53·1	53·2
2·7	υ Scorpii		96	60·7	60·5	60·2	59·9	59·7	59·5	S 37	18·3	18·3	18·3	18·4	18·4	18·4
2·8	β Draconis		97	18·0	17·7	17·4	17·1	16·9	16·8	N 52	17·3	17·1	17·1	17·1	17·2	17·4
2·8	β Aræ		98	18·7	18·4	18·0	17·7	17·4	17·2	S 55	32·4	32·4	32·4	32·4	32·5	32·6
Var.‡	α Herculis		101	08·4	08·2	08·0	07·8	07·6	07·5	N 14	22·3	22·2	22·1	22·2	22·2	22·3
2·4	η Ophiuchi	44	102	09·3	09·0	08·8	08·6	08·4	08·3	S 15	44·6	44·7	44·7	44·7	44·7	44·7
3·1	ζ Aræ		104	58·9	58·6	58·2	57·9	57·6	57·4	S 56	00·7	00·7	00·7	00·8	00·9	01·0
2·3	ε Scorpii		107	10·5	10·2	10·0	09·7	09·5	09·4	S 34	19·3	19·3	19·3	19·3	19·4	19·4
1·9	α Triang. Aust.	43	107	22·1	21·6	21·0	20·5	20·1	19·9	S 69	03·2	03·1	03·2	03·2	03·3	03·5
2·8	ζ Herculis		109	30·9	30·7	30·5	30·3	30·1	30·1	N 31	34·2	34·1	34·1	34·1	34·2	34·4
2·6	ζ Ophiuchi		110	28·1	27·9	27·7	27·5	27·3	27·2	S 10	36·0	36·1	36·1	36·1	36·1	36·1
2·8	τ Scorpii		110	45·3	45·1	44·8	44·6	44·5	44·4	S 28	14·9	15·0	15·0	15·0	15·1	15·1
2·8	β Herculis		112	15·5	15·3	15·0	14·8	14·7	14·6	N 21	27·1	27·0	26·9	27·0	27·1	27·2
1·0	α Scorpii	42	112	22·7	22·5	22·2	22·0	21·8	21·7	S 26	28·0	28·1	28·1	28·2	28·2	28·2
2·7	η Draconis		113	57·0	56·7	56·3	56·0	55·8	55·8	N 61	28·3	28·2	28·2	28·3	28·4	28·6
2·7	δ Ophiuchi		116	11·0	10·8	10·6	10·4	10·3	10·2	S 3	44·3	44·3	44·4	44·4	44·4	44·3
2·6	β Scorpii		118	23·1	22·8	22·6	22·4	22·3	22·2	S 19	51·0	51·1	51·1	51·2	51·2	51·2
2·3	δ Scorpii		119	39·4	39·1	38·9	38·7	38·5	38·5	S 22	40·1	40·2	40·2	40·3	40·3	40·3
2·9	π Scorpii		120	01·2	00·9	00·7	00·5	00·4	00·3	S 26	09·7	09·7	09·8	09·8	09·9	09·9
2·8	β Trianguli Aust.		120	49·4	48·9	48·5	48·1	47·9	47·8	S 63	28·7	28·7	28·8	28·9	29·0	29·1
2·6	α Serpentis		123	43·0	42·8	42·6	42·4	42·3	42·2	N 6	22·2	22·2	22·1	22·1	22·2	22·3
2·8	γ Lupi		125	55·2	54·9	54·6	54·4	54·3	54·2	S 41	13·3	13·3	13·4	13·5	13·5	13·6
2·2	α Coronæ Bor.	41	126	08·6	08·3	08·1	08·0	07·9	07·8	N 26	39·2	39·2	39·1	39·2	39·3	39·4

‡ 2·9 — 3·6

Mag.	Name and Number		SHA							Declination						
			°	JULY	AUG.	SEPT.	OCT.	NOV.	DEC.	°	JULY	AUG.	SEPT.	OCT.	NOV.	DEC.
			°	′	′	′	′	′	′	°	′	′	′	′	′	′
3·2	γ Cephei		4	57·1	56·6	56·4	56·5	57·0	57·6	N 77	43·8	43·9	44·1	44·3	44·5	44·5
2·5	Markab	57	13	34·7	34·5	34·5	34·5	34·6	34·7	N 15	18·2	18·3	18·4	18·5	18·5	18·5
2·4	Scheat		13	49·8	49·6	49·6	49·6	49·7	49·8	N 28	10·9	11·0	11·1	11·2	11·3	11·2
1·2	Fomalhaut	56	15	20·0	19·8	19·7	19·7	19·8	20·0	S 29	31·3	31·3	31·3	31·4	31·5	31·5
2·1	β Gruis		19	03·5	03·3	03·2	03·3	03·4	03·6	S 46	47·1	47·1	47·2	47·3	47·4	47·4
2·9	α Tucanæ		25	03·6	03·4	03·3	03·4	03·7	03·9	S 60	09·8	09·9	10·0	10·1	10·2	10·2
1·7	Al Na'ir	55	27	39·1	38·9	38·9	39·0	39·1	39·3	S 46	52·1	52·1	52·2	52·3	52·4	52·4
2·9	δ Capricorni		32	59·0	58·9	58·9	59·0	59·1	59·2	S 16	02·5	02·4	02·4	02·5	02·5	02·5
2·4	Enif	54	33	43·5	43·4	43·3	43·4	43·5	43·6	N 9	57·6	57·7	57·8	57·8	57·8	57·8
2·9	β Aquarii		36	51·9	51·8	51·8	51·9	52·0	52·1	S 5	29·3	29·2	29·2	29·2	29·2	29·3
2·4	Alderamin		40	14·0	13·9	14·1	14·3	14·6	15·0	N 62	39·8	39·9	40·1	40·2	40·3	40·2
2·5	ε Cygni		48	15·3	15·3	15·3	15·5	15·6	15·7	N 34	02·4	02·6	02·7	02·7	02·7	02·7
1·3	Deneb	53	49	28·7	28·6	28·7	28·9	29·1	29·3	N 45	20·8	21·0	21·1	21·2	21·2	21·1
3·1	α Indi		50	16·9	16·8	16·9	17·1	17·2	17·4	S 47	13·4	13·5	13·6	13·6	13·6	13·6
1·9	Peacock	52	53	13·3	13·2	13·3	13·5	13·7	13·9	S 56	40·3	40·4	40·5	40·6	40·6	40·5
2·2	γ Cygni		54	16·3	16·2	16·3	16·5	16·7	16·8	N 40	19·0	19·2	19·3	19·4	19·3	19·3
0·8	Altair	51	62	04·5	04·5	04·6	04·7	04·8	04·9	N 8	55·2	55·3	55·3	55·3	55·3	55·2
2·7	γ Aquilæ		63	12·7	12·7	12·8	12·9	13·0	13·1	N 10	39·7	39·8	39·8	39·8	39·8	39·7
2·9	δ Cygni		63	36·3	36·3	36·5	36·7	36·9	37·0	N 45	10·7	10·8	10·9	11·0	10·9	10·8
3·1	Albireo		67	07·7	07·7	07·8	08·0	08·1	08·2	N 28	00·1	00·2	00·3	00·3	00·3	00·2
2·9	π Sagittarii		72	16·9	16·9	17·0	17·1	17·2	17·3	S 20	59·5	59·5	59·5	59·5	59·5	59·5
3·0	ζ Aquilæ		73	25·9	25·9	26·0	26·2	26·3	26·3	N 13	53·7	53·7	53·8	53·8	53·8	53·7
2·6	ζ Sagittarii		74	03·0	03·0	03·1	03·3	03·4	03·4	S 29	51·0	51·1	51·1	51·1	51·1	51·1
2·0	Nunki	50	75	53·7	53·7	53·8	53·9	54·0	54·1	S 26	16·2	16·2	16·3	16·3	16·3	16·3
0·0	Vega	49	80	36·2	36·3	36·4	36·6	36·8	36·9	N 38	48·3	48·4	48·5	48·5	48·4	48·3
2·8	λ Sagittarii		82	43·2	43·2	43·3	43·5	43·6	43·6	S 25	24·5	24·5	24·5	24·5	24·5	24·5
1·9	Kaus Australis	48	83	38·8	38·9	39·0	39·2	39·3	39·3	S 34	22·4	22·4	22·4	22·4	22·4	22·4
2·7	δ Sagittarii		84	27·2	27·2	27·3	27·5	27·6	27·6	S 29	49·0	49·1	49·1	49·1	49·1	49·0
3·0	γ Sagittarii		88	14·9	14·9	15·1	15·2	15·3	15·3	S 30	25·2	25·3	25·3	25·3	25·3	25·3
2·2	Eltanin	47	90	44·0	44·2	44·4	44·7	44·9	45·0	N 51	29·5	29·6	29·6	29·6	29·5	29·4
2·8	β Ophiuchi		93	54·1	54·1	54·2	54·4	54·5	54·4	N 4	33·8	33·9	33·9	33·9	33·8	33·7
2·4	κ Scorpii		94	03·3	03·4	03·5	03·7	03·8	03·8	S 39	02·2	02·3	02·3	02·3	02·2	02·2
1·9	θ Scorpii		95	20·1	20·2	20·3	20·5	20·6	20·6	S 43	00·4	00·5	00·5	00·5	00·4	00·4
2·1	Rasalhague	46	96	02·9	03·0	03·1	03·3	03·4	03·4	N 12	33·1	33·1	33·1	33·1	33·1	33·0
1·6	Shaula	45	96	16·9	16·9	17·1	17·2	17·3	17·3	S 37	06·9	06·9	06·9	06·9	06·9	06·8
3·0	α Aræ		96	40·7	40·8	41·0	41·2	41·3	41·3	S 49	53·3	53·4	53·4	53·4	53·3	53·2
2·7	υ Scorpii		96	59·5	59·6	59·7	59·9	60·0	59·9	S 37	18·5	18·5	18·5	18·5	18·5	18·4
2·8	β Draconis		97	16·8	17·0	17·3	17·5	17·7	17·8	N 52	17·6	17·7	17·7	17·7	17·5	17·4
2·8	β Aræ		98	17·1	17·2	17·5	17·7	17·8	17·8	S 55	32·7	32·8	32·8	32·8	32·7	32·6
Var.‡	α Herculis		101	07·5	07·6	07·7	07·8	07·9	07·9	N 14	22·4	22·5	22·5	22·5	22·4	22·3
2·4	Sabik	44	102	08·3	08·4	08·5	08·6	08·7	08·6	S 15	44·7	44·7	44·7	44·7	44·7	44·7
3·1	ζ Aræ		104	57·4	57·5	57·8	58·0	58·1	58·0	S 56	01·1	01·1	01·1	01·1	01·0	00·9
2·3	ε Scorpii		107	09·4	09·5	09·7	09·8	09·9	09·8	S 34	19·5	19·5	19·5	19·5	19·4	19·4
1·9	Atria	43	107	20·0	20·2	20·6	21·0	21·2	21·1	S 69	03·6	03·7	03·7	03·6	03·5	03·4
2·8	ζ Herculis		109	30·1	30·2	30·4	30·5	30·6	30·6	N 31	34·5	34·5	34·6	34·5	34·4	34·2
2·6	ζ Ophiuchi		110	27·2	27·3	27·4	27·6	27·6	27·5	S 10	36·1	36·0	36·0	36·0	36·1	36·1
2·8	τ Scorpii		110	44·4	44·4	44·6	44·7	44·8	44·7	S 28	15·1	15·1	15·1	15·1	15·1	15·1
2·8	β Herculis		112	14·7	14·8	14·9	15·0	15·1	15·0	N 21	27·3	27·3	27·3	27·3	27·2	27·1
1·0	Antares	42	112	21·7	21·8	22·0	22·1	22·1	22·1	S 26	28·2	28·2	28·2	28·2	28·2	28·2
2·7	η Draconis		113	55·9	56·2	56·6	56·9	57·1	57·0	N 61	28·7	28·8	28·8	28·7	28·5	28·3
2·7	δ Ophiuchi		116	10·2	10·3	10·4	10·5	10·5	10·5	S 3	44·3	44·3	44·2	44·3	44·3	44·4
2·6	β Scorpii		118	22·2	22·3	22·4	22·5	22·6	22·5	S 19	51·2	51·2	51·2	51·2	51·2	51·2
2·3	Dschubba		119	38·5	38·6	38·7	38·8	38·8	38·7	S 22	40·3	40·3	40·3	40·3	40·3	40·3
2·9	π Scorpii		120	00·3	00·4	00·6	00·7	00·7	00·6	S 26	09·9	09·9	09·9	09·9	09·8	09·8
2·8	β Trianguli Aust.		120	47·9	48·2	48·5	48·7	48·8	48·6	S 63	29·2	29·3	29·3	29·2	29·1	29·0
2·6	α Serpentis		123	42·3	42·4	42·5	42·6	42·6	42·5	N 6	22·3	22·3	22·4	22·3	22·3	22·2
2·8	γ Lupi		125	54·2	54·4	54·6	54·7	54·7	54·5	S 41	13·7	13·7	13·7	13·6	13·5	13·5
2·2	Alphecca	41	126	07·9	08·0	08·2	08·3	08·3	08·2	N 26	39·5	39·5	39·5	39·5	39·3	39·2

‡ 2·9 — 3·6

Mag.	Name and Number	No.	SHA °	JAN.	FEB.	MAR.	APR.	MAY	JUNE	Dec.	JAN.	FEB.	MAR.	APR.	MAY	JUNE
3·1	γ Ursæ Minoris		129	50·0	49·5	48·9	48·6	48·5	48·6	N 71	46·0	46·0	46·0	46·1	46·3	46·4
2·9	γ Trianguli Aust.		129	51·3	50·7	50·2	49·8	49·6	49·6	S 68	44·3	44·3	44·4	44·5	44·6	44·8
2·6	β Libræ		130	30·6	30·4	30·2	30·0	29·9	29·9	S 9	26·8	26·9	26·9	26·9	26·9	26·9
2·7	β Lupi		135	04·5	04·2	03·9	03·7	03·6	03·6	S 43	12·0	12·1	12·2	12·3	12·4	12·4
2·8	α Libræ	39	137	02·1	01·8	01·6	01·5	01·4	01·4	S 16	06·8	06·9	06·9	07·0	07·0	07·0
2·1	β Ursæ Minoris	40	137	20·7	20·0	19·4	19·1	19·0	19·3	N 74	04·7	04·7	04·7	04·9	05·0	05·2
2·4	ε Bootis		138	33·7	33·5	33·3	33·1	33·1	33·1	N 26	59·9	59·8	59·8	59·9	60·0	60·1
2·3	α Lupi		139	13·2	12·9	12·6	12·4	12·3	12·3	S 47	27·5	27·6	27·7	27·8	27·9	28·0
−0·3	α Centauri	38	139	47·6	47·2	46·9	46·6	46·6	46·6	S 60	54·1	54·2	54·3	54·4	54·6	54·7
2·3	η Centauri		140	50·4	50·1	49·8	49·7	49·6	49·6	S 42	13·9	13·9	14·0	14·1	14·2	14·3
3·0	γ Bootis		141	48·3	48·0	47·8	47·6	47·6	47·6	N 38	13·7	13·6	13·6	13·7	13·9	14·0
0·0	α Bootis	37	145	53·0	52·8	52·6	52·5	52·4	52·4	N 19	05·3	05·2	05·2	05·3	05·4	05·4
2·1	θ Centauri	36	148	03·9	03·7	03·5	03·3	03·3	03·3	S 36	27·2	27·3	27·4	27·5	27·6	27·6
0·6	β Centauri	35	148	43·5	43·1	42·8	42·6	42·5	42·6	S 60	27·2	27·2	27·4	27·7	27·7	27·8
2·6	ζ Centauri		150	50·0	49·7	49·5	49·4	49·3	49·4	S 47	22·3	22·3	22·5	22·6	22·7	22·8
2·7	η Bootis		151	07·1	06·8	06·7	06·6	06·5	06·6	N 18	18·4	18·4	18·4	18·4	18·5	18·6
1·9	η Ursæ Majoris	34	152	56·5	56·2	56·0	55·9	55·9	56·0	N 49	13·2	13·2	13·3	13·4	13·5	13·6
2·3	ε Centauri		154	44·5	44·1	43·9	43·8	43·7	43·8	S 53	33·1	33·2	33·3	33·5	33·6	33·7
1·0	α Virginis	33	158	28·0	27·7	27·6	27·5	27·5	27·5	S 11	15·2	15·3	15·3	15·4	15·4	15·4
2·3	ζ Ursæ Majoris		158	50·5	50·2	50·0	49·9	49·9	50·1	N 54	49·7	49·7	49·8	49·9	50·0	50·1
2·8	ι Centauri		159	35·8	35·6	35·4	35·3	35·3	35·4	S 36	48·1	48·3	48·4	48·5	48·6	48·6
2·8	ε Virginis		164	14·0	13·8	13·7	13·6	13·6	13·7	N 10	51·7	51·7	51·6	51·7	51·7	51·8
2·9	α Canum Venat.		165	47·1	46·9	46·7	46·7	46·7	46·8	N 38	13·1	13·1	13·1	13·3	13·4	13·4
1·8	ε Ursæ Majoris	32	166	17·9	17·6	17·4	17·3	17·4	17·6	N 55	51·5	51·5	51·6	51·8	51·9	52·0
1·3	β Crucis		167	48·1	47·7	47·5	47·4	47·5	47·7	S 59	46·9	47·0	47·2	47·3	47·4	47·5
2·9	γ Virginis		169	21·5	21·3	21·1	21·1	21·1	21·2	S 1	32·9	32·9	33·0	33·0	33·0	33·0
2·2	γ Centauri		169	22·1	21·9	21·7	21·7	21·7	21·8	S 49	03·2	03·3	03·5	03·6	03·7	03·8
2·7	α Muscæ		170	25·5	25·0	24·8	24·7	24·9	25·2	S 69	13·7	13·8	14·0	14·2	14·3	14·4
2·7	β Corvi		171	10·0	09·7	09·6	09·6	09·6	09·7	S 23	29·6	29·7	29·8	29·9	29·9	30·0
1·6	γ Crucis	31	171	57·2	56·9	56·7	56·7	56·8	56·9	S 57	12·5	12·6	12·8	13·0	13·1	13·2
1·3	α Crucis	30	173	05·5	05·1	04·9	04·9	05·0	05·2	S 63	11·6	11·7	11·9	12·1	12·2	12·3
2·6	γ Corvi	29	175	49·0	48·8	48·7	48·6	48·7	48·8	S 17	38·4	38·5	38·6	38·7	38·7	38·7
2·6	δ Centauri		177	40·3	40·1	40·0	39·9	40·0	40·2	S 50	49·1	49·2	49·4	49·5	49·6	49·7
2·4	γ Ursæ Majoris		181	18·5	18·2	18·1	18·1	18·2	18·4	N 53	35·5	35·5	35·6	35·7	35·8	35·9
2·1	β Leonis	28	182	30·4	30·2	30·1	30·1	30·1	30·2	N 14	28·2	28·2	28·2	28·2	28·2	28·3
2·6	δ Leonis		191	14·0	13·9	13·8	13·8	13·9	14·0	N 20	25·4	25·3	25·4	25·4	25·5	25·5
3·0	ψ Ursæ Majoris		192	20·0	19·7	19·7	19·7	19·8	20·0	N 44	23·8	23·9	23·9	24·1	24·1	24·2
1·8	α Ursæ Majoris	27	193	47·6	47·3	47·2	47·3	47·5	47·8	N 61	39·0	39·1	39·2	39·3	39·4	39·4
2·4	β Ursæ Majoris		194	16·2	16·0	15·9	15·9	16·1	16·3	N 56	16·9	17·0	17·1	17·2	17·3	17·3
2·7	μ Velorum		198	06·4	06·3	06·2	06·3	06·5	06·7	S 49	30·8	30·9	31·1	31·2	31·3	31·3
2·8	θ Carinæ		199	05·3	05·1	05·1	05·2	05·5	05·8	S 64	29·1	29·3	29·5	29·6	29·7	29·7
2·3	γ Leonis		204	45·5	45·3	45·3	45·4	45·5	45·6	N 19	44·9	44·9	44·9	45·0	45·0	45·0
1·4	α Leonis	26	207	40·0	39·8	39·8	39·9	40·0	40·1	N 11	52·6	52·6	52·6	52·6	52·6	52·7
3·0	ε Leonis		213	16·8	16·7	16·7	16·8	16·9	17·0	N 23	41·3	41·3	41·3	41·4	41·4	41·4
3·1	N Velorum		217	02·8	02·8	02·9	03·1	03·3	03·6	S 57	06·8	06·9	07·1	07·2	07·3	07·2
2·0	α Hydræ	25	217	52·7	52·7	52·7	52·8	52·9	53·0	S 8	44·3	44·4	44·4	44·5	44·5	44·4
2·5	κ Velorum		219	19·3	19·3	19·4	19·6	19·8	20·0	S 55	05·2	05·4	05·5	05·7	05·7	05·6
2·2	ι Carinæ		220	35·7	35·7	35·8	36·1	36·3	36·6	S 59	21·0	21·2	21·3	21·4	21·5	21·4
1·7	β Carinæ	24	221	38·0	38·0	38·2	38·6	39·1	39·5	S 69	47·4	47·6	47·8	47·9	47·9	47·9
2·2	λ Velorum	23	222	49·7	49·6	49·7	49·9	50·1	50·2	S 43	30·3	30·5	30·6	30·7	30·7	30·7
3·1	ι Ursæ Majoris		224	53·3	53·2	53·3	53·4	53·6	53·7	N 47	58·0	58·1	58·2	58·3	58·3	58·3
2·0	δ Velorum		228	41·4	41·4	41·5	41·8	42·0	42·2	S 54	46·5	46·7	46·8	46·9	46·9	46·9
1·9	ε Carinæ	22	234	16·1	16·1	16·3	16·6	16·9	17·1	S 59	34·1	34·3	34·4	34·5	34·5	34·4
1·8	γ Velorum		237	28·2	28·2	28·4	28·6	28·8	28·9	S 47	23·5	23·6	23·8	23·8	23·8	23·7
2·8	ρ Puppis		237	55·1	55·0	55·1	55·3	55·4	55·5	S 24	21·5	21·7	21·7	21·8	21·7	21·6
2·3	ζ Puppis		238	56·3	56·3	56·5	56·7	56·8	57·0	S 40	03·4	03·5	03·6	03·7	03·6	03·5
1·1	β Geminorum	21	243	23·6	23·6	23·6	23·8	23·9	24·0	N 27	58·7	58·8	58·8	58·8	58·8	58·8
0·4	α Canis Minoris	20	244	56·2	56·1	56·2	56·4	56·5	56·5	N 5	10·5	10·5	10·5	10·5	10·5	10·5

Mag.	Name and Number		SHA							Declination						
				JULY	AUG.	SEPT.	OCT.	NOV.	DEC.		JULY	AUG.	SEPT.	OCT.	NOV.	DEC.
			°	′	′	′	′	′	′	°	′	′	′	′	′	′
3·1	γ Ursæ Minoris		129	49·0	49·5	50·0	50·4	50·5	50·4	N 71	46·5	46·5	46·5	46·3	46·1	45·9
2·9	γ Trianguli Aust.		129	49·8	50·1	50·5	50·8	50·8	50·5	S 68	44·9	44·9	44·9	44·8	44·6	44·5
2·6	β Libræ		130	29·9	30·0	30·2	30·2	30·2	30·1	S 9	26·9	26·9	26·8	26·8	26·9	26·9
2·7	β Lupi		135	03·7	03·9	04·0	04·1	04·1	03·9	S 43	12·5	12·5	12·4	12·4	12·3	12·3
2·8	Zubenelgenubi	39	137	01·5	01·6	01·7	01·7	01·7	01·6	S 16	07·0	07·0	06·9	06·9	06·9	07·0
2·1	Kochab	40	137	19·8	20·3	20·9	21·2	21·4	21·1	N 74	05·2	05·2	05·1	05·0	04·8	04·6
2·4	ε Bootis		138	33·1	33·3	33·4	33·5	33·5	33·3	N 26	60·2	60·2	60·2	60·1	59·9	59·8
2·3	α Lupi		139	12·4	12·6	12·8	12·9	12·8	12·6	S 47	28·1	28·1	28·0	27·9	27·8	27·8
−0·3	Rigil Kent.	38	139	46·8	47·1	47·3	47·5	47·4	47·1	S 60	54·7	54·7	54·7	54·6	54·4	54·4
2·3	η Centauri		140	49·7	49·8	50·0	50·1	50·0	49·8	S 42	14·3	14·3	14·3	14·2	14·1	14·1
3·0	γ Bootis		141	47·7	47·9	48·0	48·1	48·1	47·9	N 38	14·0	14·0	14·0	13·9	13·7	13·6
0·0	Arcturus	37	145	52·5	52·6	52·7	52·8	52·7	52·6	N 19	05·5	05·5	05·5	05·4	05·3	05·1
2·1	Menkent	36	148	03·4	03·5	03·7	03·7	03·6	03·4	S 36	27·6	27·6	27·6	27·5	27·4	27·4
0·6	Hadar	35	148	42·8	43·1	43·3	43·4	43·3	43·0	S 60	27·8	27·8	27·7	27·6	27·5	27·4
2·6	ζ Centauri		150	49·5	49·7	49·8	49·9	49·8	49·5	S 47	22·8	22·8	22·7	22·6	22·5	22·5
2·7	η Bootis		151	06·7	06·8	06·9	06·9	06·8	06·6	N 18	18·6	18·6	18·6	18·5	18·4	18·3
1·9	Alkaid	34	152	56·2	56·3	56·5	56·6	56·5	56·3	N 49	13·7	13·7	13·6	13·4	13·2	13·1
2·3	ε Centauri		154	44·0	44·2	44·4	44·4	44·3	44·0	S 53	33·7	33·7	33·6	33·5	33·4	33·3
1·0	Spica	33	158	27·6	27·7	27·8	27·8	27·7	27·5	S 11	15·4	15·3	15·3	15·3	15·3	15·4
2·3	Mizar		158	50·2	50·5	50·6	50·7	50·5	50·3	N 54	50·2	50·1	50·0	49·8	49·7	49·5
2·8	ι Centauri		159	35·5	35·6	35·7	35·7	35·6	35·4	S 36	48·6	48·6	48·5	48·4	48·4	48·4
2·8	ε Virginis		164	13·8	13·8	13·9	13·9	13·8	13·6	N 10	51·8	51·8	51·8	51·8	51·7	51·5
2·9	Cor Caroli		165	46·9	47·0	47·1	47·1	47·0	46·8	N 38	13·5	13·4	13·3	13·2	13·1	12·9
1·8	Alioth	32	166	17·8	18·0	18·1	18·1	18·0	17·7	N 55	52·0	51·9	51·8	51·6	51·4	51·3
1·3	Mimosa		167	47·9	48·2	48·3	48·3	48·1	47·7	S 59	47·5	47·5	47·4	47·2	47·1	47·1
2·9	γ Virginis		169	21·3	21·3	21·4	21·4	21·2	21·0	S 1	32·9	32·9	32·9	32·9	33·0	33·1
2·2	Muhlifain		169	22·0	22·1	22·2	22·2	22·0	21·8	S 49	03·8	03·7	03·6	03·5	03·4	03·4
2·7	α Muscæ		170	25·5	25·9	26·1	26·1	25·8	25·3	S 69	14·4	14·4	14·2	14·1	14·0	13·9
2·7	β Corvi		171	09·8	09·9	09·9	09·9	09·7	09·5	S 23	29·9	29·9	29·8	29·8	29·8	29·8
1·6	Gacrux	31	171	57·1	57·3	57·5	57·4	57·2	56·9	S 57	13·2	13·1	13·0	12·8	12·7	12·7
1·3	Acrux	30	173	05·5	05·8	05·9	05·9	05·6	05·2	S 63	12·3	12·2	12·1	11·9	11·8	11·8
2·6	Gienah	29	175	48·8	48·9	49·0	48·9	48·8	48·5	S 17	38·6	38·6	38·5	38·5	38·5	38·6
2·6	δ Centauri		177	40·4	40·5	40·6	40·5	40·3	40·0	S 50	49·7	49·6	49·4	49·3	49·3	49·3
2·4	Phecda		181	18·6	18·7	18·7	18·7	18·4	18·1	N 53	35·9	35·8	35·6	35·5	35·3	35·2
2·1	Denebola	28	182	30·3	30·4	30·4	30·3	30·1	29·9	N 14	28·3	28·3	28·3	28·2	28·1	28·0
2·6	δ Leonis		191	14·1	14·1	14·1	14·0	13·8	13·5	N 20	25·5	25·5	25·5	25·4	25·3	25·2
3·0	ψ Ursæ Majoris		192	20·1	20·1	20·0	19·8	19·5	19·2	N 44	24·1	24·1	24·0	23·8	23·7	23·6
1·8	Dubhe	27	193	48·0	48·1	48·1	47·9	47·5	47·1	N 61	39·4	39·3	39·1	38·9	38·8	38·7
2·4	Merak		194	16·5	16·6	16·5	16·4	16·1	15·7	N 56	17·3	17·2	17·0	16·9	16·7	16·6
2·7	μ Velorum		198	06·8	06·9	06·9	06·8	06·5	06·2	S 49	31·2	31·1	31·0	30·9	30·8	30·9
2·8	θ Carinæ		199	06·1	06·3	06·3	06·1	05·7	05·3	S 64	29·7	29·5	29·4	29·3	29·2	29·3
2·3	Algieba		204	45·6	45·6	45·6	45·4	45·2	44·9	N 19	45·0	45·0	44·9	44·9	44·8	44·7
1·4	Regulus	26	207	40·1	40·1	40·1	39·9	39·7	39·4	N 11	52·7	52·7	52·7	52·6	52·5	52·4
3·0	ε Leonis		213	17·0	17·0	16·9	16·8	16·5	16·3	N 23	41·4	41·4	41·3	41·3	41·2	41·1
3·1	N Velorum		217	03·7	03·8	03·7	03·4	03·1	02·7	S 57	07·1	07·0	06·8	06·7	06·7	06·8
2·0	Alphard	25	217	53·0	53·0	52·9	52·7	52·5	52·3	S 8	44·4	44·3	44·2	44·2	44·3	44·4
2·5	κ Velorum		219	20·2	20·2	20·1	19·9	19·5	19·2	S 55	05·5	05·4	05·2	05·1	05·2	05·3
2·2	ι Carinæ		220	36·8	36·8	36·7	36·4	36·0	35·7	S 59	21·3	21·2	21·0	20·9	20·9	21·0
1·7	Miaplacidus	24	221	39·8	39·8	39·7	39·3	38·8	38·3	S 69	47·7	47·6	47·4	47·3	47·3	47·4
2·2	Suhail	23	222	50·3	50·3	50·2	50·0	49·7	49·4	S 43	30·6	30·4	30·3	30·2	30·3	30·4
3·1	ι Ursæ Majoris		224	53·8	53·7	53·5	53·3	52·9	52·6	N 47	58·2	58·1	58·0	57·9	57·8	57·8
2·0	δ Velorum		228	42·3	42·3	42·2	41·9	41·5	41·2	S 54	46·7	46·6	46·4	46·4	46·4	46·5
1·9	Avior	22	234	17·2	17·2	17·0	16·7	16·3	16·0	S 59	34·2	34·1	33·9	33·9	33·9	34·1
1·8	γ Velorum		237	29·0	28·9	28·7	28·5	28·2	27·9	S 47	23·6	23·4	23·3	23·2	23·3	23·4
2·8	ρ Puppis		237	55·5	55·4	55·3	55·1	54·8	54·6	S 24	21·5	21·4	21·3	21·3	21·4	21·5
2·3	ζ Puppis		238	57·0	56·9	56·7	56·5	56·2	56·0	S 40	03·4	03·3	03·2	03·1	03·2	03·3
1·1	Pollux	21	243	23·9	23·8	23·6	23·4	23·1	22·9	N 27	58·8	58·8	58·7	58·7	58·7	58·6
0·4	Procyon	20	244	56·5	56·4	56·2	56·0	55·8	55·6	N 5	10·6	10·6	10·6	10·6	10·5	10·5

Mag.	Name and Number		SHA							Declination						
			JAN.	FEB.	MAR.	APR.	MAY	JUNE		JAN.	FEB.	MAR.	APR.	MAY	JUNE
		°	′	′	′	′	′	′	°	′	′	′	′	′	′
1·6	α Geminorum	246	03·7	03·6	03·7	03·9	04·0	04·1	N 31	50·7	50·7	50·8	50·8	50·8	50·8
3·3	σ Puppis	247	32·5	32·6	32·7	33·0	33·1	33·3	S 43	20·4	20·6	20·7	20·7	20·7	20·6
2·9	β Canis Minoris	247	57·9	57·9	58·0	58·1	58·2	58·3	N 8	15·0	14·9	14·9	14·9	15·0	15·0
2·4	η Canis Majoris	248	47·6	47·6	47·7	47·9	48·0	48·1	S 29	20·5	20·6	20·7	20·7	20·7	20·6
2·7	π Puppis	250	33·0	33·0	33·1	33·3	33·5	33·6	S 37	08·0	08·1	08·2	08·2	08·2	08·1
1·8	δ Canis Majoris	252	42·9	42·9	43·0	43·2	43·3	43·4	S 26	25·5	25·6	25·7	25·7	25·7	25·6
3·0	o Canis Majoris	254	03·1	03·1	03·2	03·4	03·5	03·6	S 23	51·8	51·9	52·0	52·0	51·9	51·8
1·5	ε Canis Majoris 19	255	09·7	09·7	09·9	10·0	10·2	10·2	S 29	00·0	00·1	00·2	00·2	00·1	00·0
2·9	τ Puppis	257	23·8	23·9	24·1	24·3	24·6	24·7	S 50	38·4	38·5	38·6	38·6	38·5	38·4
−1·5	α Canis Majoris 18	258	30·6	30·7	30·8	31·0	31·1	31·1	S 16	44·7	44·8	44·8	44·8	44·8	44·7
1·9	γ Geminorum	260	18·6	18·6	18·7	18·8	18·9	18·9	N 16	22·8	22·8	22·8	22·8	22·8	22·8
−0·7	α Carinæ 17	263	54·2	54·4	54·6	54·9	55·1	55·2	S 52	42·6	42·7	42·8	42·8	42·7	42·5
2·0	β Canis Majoris	264	07·4	07·4	07·6	07·7	07·8	07·8	S 17	58·2	58·2	58·3	58·3	58·2	58·1
2·6	θ Aurigæ	269	45·6	45·6	45·8	45·9	46·0	46·0	N 37	12·6	12·7	12·7	12·7	12·7	12·6
1·9	β Aurigæ	269	47·0	47·1	47·2	47·4	47·6	47·5	N 44	56·8	56·8	56·9	56·9	56·8	56·7
Var.‡	α Orionis 16	270	57·6	57·7	57·8	57·9	58·0	58·0	N 7	24·4	24·4	24·4	24·4	24·4	24·4
2·1	κ Orionis	272	50·7	50·7	50·8	51·0	51·1	51·1	S 9	40·1	40·1	40·1	40·1	40·1	40·0
1·9	ζ Orionis	274	34·8	34·9	35·0	35·1	35·2	35·2	S 1	56·2	56·3	56·3	56·3	56·2	56·2
2·6	α Columbæ	274	55·2	55·3	55·5	55·7	55·8	55·8	S 34	04·2	04·3	04·3	04·3	04·2	04·0
3·0	ζ Tauri	275	19·0	19·1	19·2	19·3	19·4	19·4	N 21	09·0	09·0	09·0	09·0	09·0	09·0
1·7	ε Orionis 15	275	42·9	43·0	43·1	43·2	43·3	43·3	S 1	11·7	11·7	11·7	11·7	11·7	11·6
2·8	ι Orionis	275	55·1	55·2	55·3	55·5	55·5	55·5	S 5	54·2	54·2	54·2	54·2	54·2	54·1
2·6	α Leporis	276	36·9	37·0	37·2	37·3	37·4	37·4	S 17	48·9	48·9	49·0	48·9	48·9	48·7
2·2	δ Orionis	276	45·9	46·0	46·1	46·3	46·3	46·3	S 0	17·4	17·4	17·5	17·4	17·4	17·3
2·8	β Leporis	277	44·5	44·6	44·8	44·9	45·0	45·0	S 20	45·0	45·1	45·1	45·1	45·0	44·9
1·7	β Tauri 14	278	08·4	08·4	08·6	08·7	08·8	08·7	N 28	37·2	37·2	37·2	37·2	37·2	37·1
1·6	γ Orionis 13	278	28·4	28·5	28·6	28·7	28·8	28·7	N 6	21·7	21·7	21·7	21·7	21·7	21·8
0·1	α Aurigæ 12	280	29·4	29·5	29·7	29·9	30·0	29·9	N 46	00·8	00·9	00·9	00·9	00·8	00·7
0·1	β Orionis 11	281	08·8	08·9	09·0	09·1	09·2	09·2	S 8	11·1	11·2	11·2	11·2	11·1	11·0
2·8	β Eridani	282	48·8	48·9	49·0	49·2	49·2	49·2	S 5	04·1	04·1	04·1	04·1	04·0	04·0
2·7	ι Aurigæ	285	27·3	27·4	27·6	27·7	27·8	27·7	N 33	11·5	11·5	11·5	11·5	11·5	11·4
0·9	α Tauri 10	290	45·6	45·6	45·8	45·9	45·9	45·8	N 16	32·5	32·5	32·5	32·5	32·5	32·5
2·9	ε Persei	300	13·9	14·0	14·2	14·3	14·3	14·2	N 40	03·6	03·7	03·6	03·6	03·5	03·5
3·0	γ Eridani	300	16·9	17·0	17·1	17·2	17·2	17·2	S 13	27·8	27·8	27·8	27·7	27·7	27·5
2·9	ζ Persei	301	10·9	11·0	11·1	11·3	11·3	11·1	N 31	56·1	56·1	56·1	56·0	56·0	56·0
2·9	η Tauri	302	51·5	51·7	51·8	51·9	51·9	51·8	N 24	09·5	09·5	09·5	09·4	09·4	09·4
1·8	α Persei 9	308	35·6	35·8	36·0	36·1	36·1	35·9	N 49	55·5	55·5	55·5	55·4	55·3	55·2
Var.§	β Persei	312	39·7	39·9	40·0	40·1	40·1	39·9	N 41	01·5	01·5	01·4	01·3	01·3	01·2
2·5	α Ceti 8	314	11·7	11·8	11·9	12·0	11·9	11·8	N 4	09·4	09·4	09·4	09·4	09·4	09·5
3·2	θ Eridani 7	315	15·9	16·0	16·2	16·3	16·3	16·1	S 40	14·4	14·4	14·3	14·2	14·1	13·9
2·0	α Ursæ Minoris	316	12·3	25·5	37·6	44·8	44·0	36·3	N 89	20·6	20·6	20·6	20·4	20·3	20·2
3·0	β Trianguli	327	20·7	20·8	21·0	21·0	20·9	20·7	N 35	04·3	04·3	04·2	04·2	04·1	04·1
2·0	α Arietis 6	327	57·2	57·3	57·4	57·4	57·3	57·2	N 23	32·8	32·7	32·7	32·7	32·6	32·7
2·3	γ Andromedæ	328	44·8	45·0	45·1	45·2	45·1	44·9	N 42	25·0	25·0	24·9	24·8	24·7	24·7
2·9	α Hydri	330	10·1	10·4	10·7	10·8	10·7	10·4	S 61	29·4	29·4	29·3	29·1	28·9	28·7
2·6	β Arietis	331	05·5	05·6	05·7	05·7	05·6	05·4	N 20	53·7	53·6	53·6	53·6	53·6	53·6
0·5	α Eridani 5	335	24·5	24·8	24·9	25·0	24·9	24·6	S 57	09·2	09·1	09·0	08·8	08·7	08·5
2·7	δ Cassiopeiæ	338	14·9	15·1	15·3	15·3	15·2	14·8	N 60	19·9	19·8	19·7	19·6	19·5	19·4
2·1	β Andromedæ	342	18·9	19·1	19·1	19·1	19·0	18·8	N 35	43·0	42·9	42·9	42·8	42·7	42·8
Var.‖	γ Cassiopeiæ	345	32·9	33·2	33·3	33·3	33·1	32·8	N 60	49·0	48·9	48·8	48·7	48·6	48·6
2·0	β Ceti 4	348	52·9	52·9	53·0	53·0	52·8	52·6	S 17	53·5	53·5	53·5	53·4	53·3	53·2
2·2	α Cassiopeiæ 3	349	37·0	37·2	37·3	37·3	37·1	36·8	N 56	38·3	38·2	38·1	38·0	37·9	37·9
2·4	α Phœnicis 2	353	12·8	12·9	13·0	12·9	12·8	12·5	S 42	12·8	12·8	12·7	12·5	12·4	12·2
2·8	β Hydri	353	21·0	21·5	21·7	21·6	21·2	20·5	S 77	09·6	09·5	09·3	09·1	08·9	08·8
2·8	γ Pegasi	356	27·8	27·8	27·9	27·8	27·7	27·4	N 15	17·0	16·9	16·9	16·9	16·9	17·0
2·3	β Cassiopeiæ	357	27·9	28·1	28·2	28·2	27·9	27·5	N 59	15·1	15·0	14·9	14·8	14·7	14·7
2·1	α Andromedæ 1	357	40·4	40·5	40·5	40·4	40·3	40·0	N 29	11·4	11·4	11·3	11·2	11·2	11·3

‡ 0·1 — 1·2   § 2·1 — 3·4   ‖ Irregular variable; 2016 mag. 2·2

Mag.	Name and Number	SHA °	JULY	AUG.	SEPT.	OCT.	NOV.	DEC.	Declination	JULY	AUG.	SEPT.	OCT.	NOV.	DEC.
1·6	Castor	246	04·0	03·9	03·7	03·4	03·1	02·9	N 31	50·8	50·7	50·7	50·6	50·6	50·6
3·3	σ Puppis	247	33·3	33·2	33·0	32·7	32·4	32·2	S 43	20·4	20·3	20·2	20·1	20·2	20·3
2·9	β Canis Minoris	247	58·2	58·1	57·9	57·7	57·5	57·3	N 8	15·0	15·1	15·1	15·1	15·0	14·9
2·4	η Canis Majoris	248	48·1	48·0	47·8	47·6	47·3	47·1	S 29	20·4	20·3	20·2	20·2	20·3	20·4
2·7	π Puppis	250	33·6	33·5	33·3	33·0	32·8	32·6	S 37	07·9	07·8	07·7	07·7	07·7	07·9
1·8	Wezen	252	43·3	43·2	43·0	42·8	42·6	42·4	S 26	25·4	25·3	25·2	25·2	25·3	25·4
3·0	o Canis Majoris	254	03·5	03·4	03·2	03·0	02·8	02·6	S 23	51·7	51·6	51·5	51·5	51·6	51·7
1·5	Adhara 19	255	10·2	10·1	09·9	09·6	09·4	09·2	S 28	59·9	59·8	59·7	59·7	59·8	59·9
2·9	τ Puppis	257	24·6	24·5	24·3	24·0	23·7	23·5	S 50	38·2	38·1	38·0	38·0	38·1	38·2
−1·5	Sirius 18	258	31·0	30·9	30·7	30·5	30·3	30·1	S 16	44·6	44·5	44·4	44·4	44·5	44·6
1·9	Alhena	260	18·8	18·7	18·5	18·3	18·0	17·8	N 16	22·9	22·9	22·9	22·9	22·8	22·8
−0·7	Canopus 17	263	55·1	55·0	54·7	54·4	54·1	53·9	S 52	42·4	42·2	42·1	42·1	42·2	42·4
2·0	Mirzam	264	07·8	07·6	07·4	07·2	07·0	06·8	S 17	58·0	57·9	57·8	57·8	57·9	58·0
2·6	θ Aurigæ	269	45·9	45·7	45·4	45·1	44·9	44·7	N 37	12·6	12·6	12·6	12·6	12·6	12·6
1·9	Menkalinan	269	47·4	47·1	46·9	46·6	46·3	46·1	N 44	56·7	56·7	56·7	56·6	56·6	56·7
Var.‡	Betelgeuse 16	270	57·9	57·7	57·5	57·3	57·1	56·9	N 7	24·5	24·5	24·6	24·6	24·5	24·5
2·1	κ Orionis	272	50·9	50·8	50·6	50·4	50·2	50·0	S 9	39·9	39·8	39·8	39·8	39·8	39·9
1·9	Alnitak	274	35·1	34·9	34·7	34·5	34·3	34·1	S 1	56·1	56·0	56·0	56·0	56·0	56·1
2·6	Phact	274	55·7	55·5	55·3	55·0	54·8	54·7	S 34	03·9	03·8	03·7	03·7	03·8	04·0
3·0	ζ Tauri	275	19·2	19·0	18·8	18·6	18·4	18·2	N 21	09·0	09·1	09·1	09·1	09·1	09·1
1·7	Alnilam 15	275	43·2	43·0	42·8	42·6	42·4	42·2	S 1	11·5	11·5	11·4	11·4	11·5	11·5
2·8	ι Orionis	275	55·4	55·2	55·0	54·8	54·6	54·5	S 5	54·0	53·9	53·9	53·9	53·9	54·0
2·6	α Leporis	276	37·3	37·1	36·9	36·6	36·5	36·3	S 17	48·6	48·5	48·5	48·5	48·6	48·7
2·2	δ Orionis	276	46·2	46·0	45·8	45·6	45·4	45·3	S 0	17·3	17·2	17·1	17·2	17·2	17·3
2·8	β Leporis	277	44·9	44·7	44·5	44·3	44·1	44·0	S 20	44·8	44·6	44·6	44·6	44·7	44·8
1·7	Elnath 14	278	08·6	08·4	08·1	07·9	07·7	07·5	N 28	37·1	37·2	37·2	37·2	37·2	37·2
1·6	Bellatrix 13	278	28·6	28·4	28·2	28·0	27·8	27·7	N 6	21·8	21·9	21·9	21·9	21·9	21·8
0·1	Capella 12	280	29·7	29·5	29·2	28·9	28·6	28·4	N 46	00·7	00·7	00·7	00·7	00·8	00·8
0·1	Rigel 11	281	09·0	08·8	08·6	08·4	08·2	08·1	S 8	10·9	10·8	10·8	10·8	10·9	11·0
2·8	β Eridani	282	49·0	48·8	48·6	48·4	48·2	48·1	S 5	03·9	03·8	03·7	03·8	03·8	03·9
2·7	ι Aurigæ	285	27·5	27·3	27·0	26·8	26·5	26·4	N 33	11·4	11·5	11·5	11·5	11·6	11·6
0·9	Aldebaran 10	290	45·7	45·5	45·2	45·0	44·8	44·8	N 16	32·6	32·6	32·7	32·7	32·7	32·7
2·9	ε Persei	300	13·9	13·7	13·4	13·1	13·0	12·9	N 40	03·5	03·5	03·6	03·6	03·7	03·8
3·0	γ Eridani	300	17·0	16·8	16·5	16·4	16·2	16·2	S 13	27·4	27·3	27·3	27·3	27·4	27·5
2·9	ζ Persei	301	10·9	10·7	10·4	10·2	10·0	10·0	N 31	56·0	56·1	56·1	56·2	56·2	56·3
2·9	Alcyone	302	51·6	51·3	51·1	50·9	50·8	50·7	N 24	09·5	09·5	09·6	09·6	09·7	09·7
1·8	Mirfak 9	308	35·6	35·3	35·0	34·7	34·6	34·5	N 49	55·2	55·3	55·3	55·4	55·6	55·6
Var.§	Algol	312	39·7	39·4	39·1	38·9	38·8	38·7	N 41	01·3	01·3	01·4	01·5	01·6	01·7
2·5	Menkar 8	314	11·6	11·4	11·1	11·0	10·9	10·9	N 4	09·6	09·7	09·7	09·7	09·7	09·7
3·2	Acamar 7	315	15·9	15·6	15·4	15·2	15·1	15·2	S 40	13·8	13·7	13·7	13·8	13·9	14·0
2·0	Polaris	315	83·7	69·0	55·3	45·3	41·0	44·9	N 89	20·1	20·1	20·2	20·4	20·6	20·7
3·0	β Trianguli	327	20·5	20·2	20·0	19·8	19·8	19·8	N 35	04·2	04·3	04·4	04·5	04·5	04·6
2·0	Hamal 6	327	56·9	56·7	56·5	56·3	56·3	56·3	N 23	32·7	32·8	32·9	33·0	33·0	33·1
2·3	Almak	328	44·6	44·3	44·0	43·9	43·8	43·9	N 42	24·8	24·8	25·0	25·1	25·2	25·3
2·9	α Hydri	330	10·1	09·7	09·4	09·2	09·2	09·3	S 61	28·6	28·6	28·7	28·8	28·9	29·1
2·6	Sheratan	331	05·2	05·0	04·8	04·7	04·6	04·7	N 20	53·7	53·8	53·9	53·9	54·0	54·0
0·5	Achernar 5	335	24·3	23·9	23·7	23·5	23·5	23·7	S 57	08·4	08·4	08·4	08·6	08·7	08·8
2·7	Ruchbah	338	14·4	14·1	13·8	13·6	13·6	13·8	N 60	19·5	19·6	19·7	19·9	20·0	20·1
2·1	Mirach	342	18·5	18·2	18·1	18·0	18·0	18·0	N 35	42·8	42·9	43·1	43·2	43·3	43·3
Var.‖	γ Cassiopeiæ	345	32·4	32·0	31·8	31·7	31·7	31·9	N 60	48·6	48·7	48·9	49·1	49·2	49·3
2·0	Diphda 4	348	52·4	52·2	52·0	52·0	52·0	52·1	S 17	53·1	53·0	53·0	53·0	53·1	53·2
2·2	Schedar 3	349	36·4	36·1	35·9	35·8	35·9	36·0	N 56	38·0	38·1	38·3	38·4	38·6	38·6
2·4	Ankaa 2	353	12·2	12·0	11·8	11·7	11·8	11·9	S 42	12·2	12·2	12·2	12·3	12·4	12·5
2·8	β Hydri	353	19·7	19·0	18·5	18·5	18·8	19·4	S 77	08·8	08·8	08·9	09·1	09·2	09·3
2·8	Algenib	356	27·2	27·0	26·9	26·8	26·9	26·9	N 15	17·1	17·2	17·3	17·3	17·3	17·3
2·3	Caph	357	27·2	26·9	26·7	26·7	26·8	27·0	N 59	14·8	14·9	15·1	15·3	15·4	15·5
2·1	Alpheratz 1	357	39·8	39·6	39·5	39·4	39·5	39·6	N 29	11·4	11·5	11·6	11·7	11·8	11·8

‡ 0·1 — 1·2   § 2·1 — 3·4   ‖ Irregular variable; 2016 mag. 2·2

POLARIS (POLE STAR) TABLES, 2018
FOR DETERMINING LATITUDE FROM SEXTANT ALTITUDE AND FOR AZIMUTH

LHA ARIES	0° – 9°	10° – 19°	20° – 29°	30° – 39°	40° – 49°	50° – 59°	60° – 69°	70° – 79°	80° – 89°	90° – 99°	100° – 109°	110° – 119°
	a_0	a_0	a_0	a_0	a_0	a_0	a_0	a_0	a_0	a_0	a_0	a_0
°	° ′	° ′	° ′	° ′	° ′	° ′	° ′	° ′	° ′	° ′	° ′	° ′
0	0 30·3	0 26·0	0 22·6	0 20·4	0 19·3	0 19·4	0 20·8	0 23·3	0 26·9	0 31·5	0 37·0	0 43·1
1	29·9	25·6	22·3	20·2	19·2	19·5	21·0	23·6	27·4	32·0	37·6	43·7
2	29·4	25·2	22·1	20·0	19·2	19·6	21·2	24·0	27·8	32·6	38·1	44·3
3	28·9	24·9	21·8	19·9	19·2	19·7	21·4	24·3	28·2	33·1	38·7	45·0
4	28·5	24·5	21·6	19·8	19·2	19·8	21·7	24·6	28·7	33·6	39·3	45·6
5	0 28·0	0 24·2	0 21·3	0 19·7	0 19·2	0 20·0	0 21·9	0 25·0	0 29·1	0 34·2	0 39·9	0 46·3
6	27·6	23·8	21·1	19·6	19·2	20·1	22·2	25·4	29·6	34·7	40·6	47·0
7	27·2	23·5	20·9	19·5	19·3	20·3	22·4	25·8	30·1	35·3	41·2	47·6
8	26·8	23·2	20·7	19·4	19·3	20·4	22·7	26·1	30·6	35·8	41·8	48·3
9	26·4	22·9	20·5	19·3	19·4	20·6	23·0	26·5	31·0	36·4	42·4	48·9
10	0 26·0	0 22·6	0 20·4	0 19·3	0 19·4	0 20·8	0 23·3	0 26·9	0 31·5	0 37·0	0 43·1	0 49·6

Lat.	a_1	a_1	a_1	a_1	a_1	a_1	a_1	a_1	a_1	a_1	a_1	a_1
°	′	′	′	′	′	′	′	′	′	′	′	′
0	0·5	0·5	0·6	0·6	0·6	0·6	0·6	0·5	0·5	0·4	0·4	0·4
10	·5	·5	·6	·6	·6	·6	·6	·5	·5	·5	·4	·4
20	·5	·6	·6	·6	·6	·6	·6	·5	·5	·5	·5	·4
30	·5	·6	·6	·6	·6	·6	·6	·6	·5	·5	·5	·5
40	0·6	0·6	0·6	0·6	0·6	0·6	0·6	0·6	0·6	0·6	0·5	0·5
45	·6	·6	·6	·6	·6	·6	·6	·6	·6	·6	·6	·6
50	·6	·6	·6	·6	·6	·6	·6	·6	·6	·6	·6	·6
55	·6	·6	·6	·6	·6	·6	·6	·6	·6	·6	·6	·6
60	·6	·6	·6	·6	·6	·6	·6	·6	·7	·7	·7	·7
62	0·7	0·6	0·6	0·6	0·6	0·6	0·6	0·6	0·7	0·7	0·7	0·7
64	·7	·6	·6	·6	·6	·6	·6	·7	·7	·7	·8	·8
66	·7	·7	·6	·6	·6	·6	·6	·7	·7	·7	·8	·8
68	0·7	0·7	0·6	0·6	0·6	0·6	0·6	0·7	0·7	0·8	0·8	0·9

Month	a_2	a_2	a_2	a_2	a_2	a_2	a_2	a_2	a_2	a_2	a_2	a_2
	′	′	′	′	′	′	′	′	′	′	′	′
Jan.	0·8	0·8	0·8	0·8	0·8	0·8	0·8	0·8	0·7	0·7	0·7	0·7
Feb.	·7	·7	·8	·8	·8	·8	·9	·9	·9	·8	·8	·8
Mar.	·5	·6	·7	·7	·8	·8	·8	·9	·9	·9	·9	0·9
Apr.	0·4	0·4	0·5	0·6	0·6	0·7	0·8	0·8	0·9	0·9	0·9	1·0
May	·3	·3	·4	·4	·5	·5	·6	·7	·7	·8	·9	0·9
June	·2	·3	·3	·3	·4	·4	·5	·5	·6	·7	·7	·8
July	0·3	0·3	0·3	0·3	0·3	0·3	0·4	0·4	0·5	0·5	0·6	0·6
Aug.	·4	·4	·4	·3	·3	·3	·3	·3	·4	·4	·4	·5
Sept.	·6	·5	·5	·5	·4	·4	·4	·3	·3	·3	·3	·3
Oct.	0·8	0·7	0·7	0·6	0·6	0·5	0·5	0·4	0·4	0·3	0·3	0·3
Nov.	0·9	0·9	0·9	0·8	·7	·7	·6	·5	·5	·4	·4	·3
Dec.	1·1	1·0	1·0	1·0	0·9	0·9	0·8	0·7	0·6	0·5	0·5	0·4

Lat.	AZIMUTH											
°	°	°	°	°	°	°	°	°	°	°	°	°
0	0·4	0·3	0·2	0·1	0·0	359·9	359·8	359·7	359·6	359·5	359·4	359·4
20	0·4	0·3	0·2	0·1	0·0	359·9	359·7	359·6	359·5	359·5	359·4	359·3
40	0·5	0·4	0·3	0·1	0·0	359·8	359·7	359·5	359·4	359·3	359·2	359·2
50	0·7	0·5	0·3	0·2	0·0	359·8	359·6	359·5	359·3	359·2	359·1	359·0
55	0·7	0·6	0·4	0·2	0·0	359·8	359·6	359·4	359·2	359·1	359·0	358·9
60	0·8	0·6	0·4	0·2	0·0	359·7	359·5	359·3	359·1	359·0	358·8	358·7
65	1·0	0·8	0·5	0·2	0·0	359·7	359·4	359·2	359·0	358·8	358·6	358·5

Latitude = Apparent altitude (corrected for refraction) $-1° + a_0 + a_1 + a_2$

The table is entered with LHA Aries to determine the column to be used; each column refers to a range of 10°. a_0 is taken, with mental interpolation, from the upper table with the units of LHA Aries in degrees as argument; a_1, a_2 are taken, without interpolation, from the second and third tables with arguments latitude and month respectively. a_0, a_1, a_2, are always positive. The final table gives the azimuth of *Polaris*.

LHA ARIES	120° – 129°	130° – 139°	140° – 149°	150° – 159°	160° – 169°	170° – 179°	180° – 189°	190° – 199°	200° – 209°	210° – 219°	220° – 229°	230° – 239°
°	a_0	a_0	a_0	a_0	a_0	a_0	a_0	a_0	a_0	a_0	a_0	a_0
0	0 49·6	0 56·5	1 03·4	1 10·1	1 16·5	1 22·4	1 27·5	1 31·8	1 35·1	1 37·3	1 38·3	1 38·2
1	50·3	57·1	04·0	10·8	17·1	22·9	28·0	32·2	35·4	37·4	38·4	38·1
2	51·0	57·8	04·7	11·4	17·7	23·5	28·4	32·5	35·6	37·6	38·4	38·0
3	51·7	58·5	05·4	12·1	18·3	24·0	28·9	32·9	35·9	37·7	38·4	37·9
4	52·3	59·2	06·1	12·7	18·9	24·5	29·3	33·2	36·1	37·8	38·4	37·8
5	0 53·0	0 59·9	1 06·8	1 13·4	1 19·5	1 25·0	1 29·8	1 33·6	1 36·3	1 37·9	1 38·4	1 37·7
6	53·7	1 00·6	07·4	14·0	20·1	25·6	30·2	33·9	36·5	38·0	38·4	37·5
7	54·4	01·3	08·1	14·6	20·7	26·1	30·6	34·2	36·7	38·1	38·3	37·4
8	55·1	02·0	08·8	15·3	21·3	26·6	31·0	34·5	36·9	38·2	38·3	37·2
9	55·8	02·7	09·4	15·9	21·8	27·0	31·4	34·8	37·1	38·3	38·2	37·0
10	0 56·5	1 03·4	1 10·1	1 16·5	1 22·4	1 27·5	1 31·8	1 35·1	1 37·3	1 38·3	1 38·2	1 36·8

Lat.	a_1	a_1	a_1	a_1	a_1	a_1	a_1	a_1	a_1	a_1	a_1	a_1
°	′	′	′	′	′	′	′	′	′	′	′	′
0	0·3	0·3	0·3	0·4	0·4	0·4	0·5	0·5	0·6	0·6	0·6	0·6
10	·4	·4	·4	·4	·4	·5	·5	·5	·6	·6	·6	·6
20	·4	·4	·4	·4	·5	·5	·5	·6	·6	·6	·6	·6
30	·5	·5	·5	·5	·5	·5	·5	·6	·6	·6	·6	·6
40	0·5	0·5	0·5	0·5	0·5	0·6	0·6	0·6	0·6	0·6	0·6	0·6
45	·6	·6	·6	·6	·6	·6	·6	·6	·6	·6	·6	·6
50	·6	·6	·6	·6	·6	·6	·6	·6	·6	·6	·6	·6
55	·7	·7	·7	·6	·6	·6	·6	·6	·6	·6	·6	·6
60	·7	·7	·7	·7	·7	·7	·6	·6	·6	·6	·6	·6
62	0·8	0·8	0·8	0·7	0·7	0·7	0·7	0·6	0·6	0·6	0·6	0·6
64	·8	·8	·8	·8	·7	·7	·7	·6	·6	·6	·6	·6
66	·8	·8	·8	·8	·8	·7	·7	·7	·6	·6	·6	·6
68	0·9	0·9	0·9	0·9	0·8	0·8	0·7	0·7	0·6	0·6	0·6	0·6

Month	a_2	a_2	a_2	a_2	a_2	a_2	a_2	a_2	a_2	a_2	a_2	a_2
	′	′	′	′	′	′	′	′	′	′	′	′
Jan.	0·6	0·6	0·6	0·5	0·5	0·5	0·4	0·4	0·4	0·4	0·4	0·4
Feb.	·8	·7	·7	·7	·6	·6	·5	·5	·4	·4	·4	·4
Mar.	0·9	0·9	0·8	·8	·8	·7	·7	·6	·5	·5	·4	·4
Apr.	1·0	1·0	1·0	0·9	0·9	0·9	0·8	0·8	0·7	0·6	0·6	0·5
May	0·9	1·0	1·0	1·0	1·0	1·0	0·9	·9	·8	·8	·7	·7
June	·8	0·9	0·9	0·9	1·0	1·0	1·0	·9	·9	·9	·8	·8
July	0·7	0·7	0·8	0·8	0·9	0·9	0·9	0·9	0·9	0·9	0·9	0·9
Aug.	·5	·6	·6	·7	·7	·7	·8	·8	·8	·9	·9	·9
Sept.	·4	·4	·4	·5	·5	·6	·6	·7	·7	·7	·8	·8
Oct.	0·3	0·3	0·3	0·3	0·3	0·4	0·4	0·5	0·5	0·6	0·6	0·7
Nov.	·3	·2	·2	·2	·2	·2	·3	·3	·3	·4	·5	·5
Dec.	0·3	0·3	0·2	0·2	0·2	0·1	0·1	0·2	0·2	0·2	0·3	0·3

Lat.	AZIMUTH											
°	°	°	°	°	°	°	°	°	°	°	°	°
0	359·3	359·3	359·4	359·4	359·4	359·5	359·6	359·7	359·8	359·9	0·0	0·1
20	359·3	359·3	359·3	359·3	359·4	359·5	359·6	359·7	359·8	359·9	0·0	0·1
40	359·1	359·1	359·2	359·2	359·3	359·4	359·5	359·6	359·7	359·9	0·0	0·2
50	359·0	359·0	359·0	359·0	359·1	359·2	359·4	359·5	359·7	359·8	0·0	0·2
55	358·9	358·8	358·9	358·9	359·0	359·1	359·3	359·5	359·6	359·8	0·0	0·2
60	358·7	358·7	358·7	358·8	358·9	359·0	359·2	359·4	359·6	359·8	0·0	0·3
65	358·5	358·4	358·5	358·6	358·7	358·8	359·0	359·3	359·5	359·8	0·0	0·3

ILLUSTRATION

On 2018 April 21 at 23ʰ 18ᵐ 56ˢ UT in longitude W 37° 14′ the apparent altitude (corrected for refraction), H_O, of Polaris was 49° 31′·6

From the daily pages:	°	′
GHA Aries (23ʰ)	194	57·7
Increment (18ᵐ 56ˢ)	4	44·8
Longitude (west)	−37	14
LHA Aries	162	29

	°	′
H_O	49	31·6
a_0 (argument 162° 29′)	1	18·0
a_1 (Lat 50° approx.)		0·6
a_2 (April)		0·9
Sum − 1° = Lat =	49	51·1

POLARIS (POLE STAR) TABLES, 2018
FOR DETERMINING LATITUDE FROM SEXTANT ALTITUDE AND FOR AZIMUTH

LHA ARIES	240° – 249°	250° – 259°	260° – 269°	270° – 279°	280° – 289°	290° – 299°	300° – 309°	310° – 319°	320° – 329°	330° – 339°	340° – 349°	350° – 359°
°	a_0	a_0	a_0	a_0	a_0	a_0	a_0	a_0	a_0	a_0	a_0	a_0
	° ′	° ′	° ′	° ′	° ′	° ′	° ′	° ′	° ′	° ′	° ′	° ′
0	I 36·8	I 34·4	I 30·8	I 26·3	I 21·0	I 15·0	I 08·5	I 01·7	0 54·8	0 48·0	0 41·5	0 35·6
I	36·6	34·1	30·4	25·8	20·4	14·4	07·8	01·0	54·1	47·3	40·9	35·0
2	36·4	33·8	30·0	25·3	19·9	13·7	07·1	I 00·3	53·4	46·7	40·3	34·5
3	36·2	33·4	29·6	24·8	19·3	13·1	06·5	0 59·6	52·7	46·0	39·7	33·9
4	36·0	33·1	29·2	24·3	18·7	12·4	05·8	58·9	52·0	45·4	39·1	33·4
5	I 35·8	I 32·7	I 28·7	I 23·8	I 18·1	I 11·8	I 05·1	0 58·2	0 51·4	0 44·7	0 38·5	0 32·9
6	35·5	32·4	28·3	23·2	17·5	11·1	04·4	57·5	50·7	44·1	37·9	32·3
7	35·2	32·0	27·8	22·7	16·9	10·5	03·7	56·8	50·0	43·4	37·3	31·8
8	35·0	31·6	27·3	22·1	16·2	09·8	03·1	56·2	49·3	42·8	36·7	31·3
9	34·7	31·2	26·8	21·6	15·6	09·2	02·4	55·5	48·7	42·2	36·1	30·8
10	I 34·4	I 30·8	I 26·3	I 21·0	I 15·0	I 08·5	I 01·7	0 54·8	0 48·0	0 41·5	0 35·6	0 30·3

Lat.	a_1	a_1	a_1	a_1	a_1	a_1	a_1	a_1	a_1	a_1	a_1	a_1
°	′	′	′	′	′	′	′	′	′	′	′	′
0	0·6	0·5	0·5	0·4	0·4	0·4	0·3	0·3	0·3	0·4	0·4	0·4
10	·6	·5	·5	·5	·4	·4	·4	·4	·4	·4	·4	·5
20	·6	·5	·5	·5	·5	·4	·4	·4	·4	·4	·5	·5
30	·6	·6	·5	·5	·5	·5	·5	·5	·5	·5	·5	·5
40	0·6	0·6	0·6	0·6	0·5	0·5	0·5	0·5	0·5	0·5	0·5	0·6
45	·6	·6	·6	·6	·6	·6	·6	·6	·6	·6	·6	·6
50	·6	·6	·6	·6	·6	·6	·6	·6	·6	·6	·6	·6
55	·6	·6	·6	·6	·6	·6	·7	·7	·7	·6	·6	·6
60	·6	·6	·7	·7	·7	·7	·7	·7	·7	·7	·7	·7
62	0·6	0·6	0·7	0·7	0·7	0·7	0·8	0·8	0·8	0·7	0·7	0·7
64	·6	·7	·7	·7	·8	·8	·8	·8	·8	·8	·7	·7
66	·6	·7	·7	·7	·8	·8	·8	·8	·8	·8	·8	·7
68	0·6	0·7	0·7	0·8	0·8	0·9	0·9	0·9	0·9	0·9	0·8	0·8

Month	a_2	a_2	a_2	a_2	a_2	a_2	a_2	a_2	a_2	a_2	a_2	a_2
	′	′	′	′	′	′	′	′	′	′	′	′
Jan.	0·4	0·4	0·5	0·5	0·5	0·5	0·6	0·6	0·6	0·7	0·7	0·7
Feb.	·3	·3	·3	·4	·4	·4	·4	·5	·5	·5	·6	·6
Mar.	·4	·3	·3	·3	·3	·3	·3	·3	·4	·4	·4	·5
Apr.	0·4	0·4	0·3	0·3	0·3	0·2	0·2	0·2	0·2	0·3	0·3	0·3
May	·6	·5	·5	·4	·3	·3	·3	·2	·2	·2	·2	·2
June	·7	·7	·6	·5	·5	·4	·4	·3	·3	·3	·2	·2
July	0·8	0·8	0·7	0·7	0·6	0·6	0·5	0·5	0·4	0·4	0·3	0·3
Aug.	·9	·9	·8	·8	·8	·7	·7	·6	·6	·5	·5	·5
Sept.	·8	·9	·9	·9	·9	·9	·8	·8	·8	·7	·7	·6
Oct.	0·7	0·8	0·8	0·9	0·9	0·9	0·9	0·9	0·9	0·9	0·9	0·8
Nov.	·6	·7	·7	·8	·8	·9	·9	I·0	I·0	I·0	I·0	I·0
Dec.	0·4	0·5	0·6	0·7	0·7	0·8	0·9	0·9	I·0	I·0	I·0	I·1

Lat.	AZIMUTH											
°	°	°	°	°	°	°	°	°	°	°	°	°
0	0·2	0·3	0·4	0·5	0·6	0·6	0·7	0·7	0·6	0·6	0·6	0·5
20	0·3	0·4	0·5	0·5	0·6	0·7	0·7	0·7	0·7	0·7	0·6	0·5
40	0·3	0·4	0·6	0·7	0·8	0·8	0·9	0·9	0·8	0·8	0·7	0·7
50	0·4	0·5	0·7	0·8	0·9	I·0	I·0	I·0	I·0	I·0	0·9	0·8
55	0·4	0·6	0·7	0·9	I·0	I·1	I·1	I·2	I·1	I·1	I·0	0·9
60	0·5	0·7	0·9	I·0	I·1	I·2	I·3	I·3	I·3	I·2	I·1	I·0
65	0·6	0·8	I·0	I·2	I·4	I·5	I·5	I·6	I·5	I·5	I·4	I·2

Latitude = Apparent altitude (corrected for refraction) $-1° + a_0 + a_1 + a_2$

The table is entered with LHA Aries to determine the column to be used; each column refers to a range of 10°. a_0 is taken, with mental interpolation, from the upper table with the units of LHA Aries in degrees as argument; a_1, a_2 are taken, without interpolation, from the second and third tables with arguments latitude and month respectively. a_0, a_1, a_2, are always positive. The final table gives the azimuth of *Polaris*.

SIGHT REDUCTION PROCEDURES
METHODS AND FORMULAE FOR DIRECT COMPUTATION

1. *Introduction.* In this section formulae and methods are provided for *calculating* position at sea from observed altitudes taken with a marine sextant using a computer or programmable calculator.

The method uses analogous concepts and similar terminology as that used in *manual* methods of astro-navigation, where position is found by plotting position lines from their intercept and azimuth on a marine chart.

The algorithms are presented in standard algebra suitable for translating into the programming language of the user's computer. The basic ephemeris data may be taken directly from the main tabular pages of a current version of *The Nautical Almanac*. Formulae are given for calculating altitude and azimuth from the *GHA* and *Dec* of a body, and the estimated position of the observer. Formulae are also given for reducing sextant observations to observed altitudes by applying the corrections for dip, refraction, parallax and semi-diameter.

The intercept and azimuth obtained from each observation determine a position line, and the observer should lie on or close to each position line. The method of least squares is used to calculate the fix by finding the position where the sum of the squares of the distances from the position lines is a minimum. The use of least squares has other advantages. For example, it is possible to improve the estimated position at the time of fix by repeating the calculation. It is also possible to include more observations in the solution and to reject doubtful ones.

2. *Notation.*

GHA = Greenwich hour angle. The range of GHA is from $0°$ to $360°$ starting at $0°$ on the Greenwich meridian increasing to the west, back to $360°$ on the Greenwich meridian.

SHA = sidereal hour angle. The range is $0°$ to $360°$.

Dec = declination. The sign convention for declination is north is positive, south is negative. The range is from $-90°$ at the south celestial pole to $+90°$ at the north celestial pole.

$Long$ = longitude. The sign convention is east is positive, west is negative. The range is $-180°$ to $+180°$.

Lat = latitude. The sign convention is north is positive, south is negative. The range is from $-90°$ to $+90°$.

LHA = $GHA + Long$ = local hour angle. The LHA increases to the west from $0°$ on the local meridian to $360°$.

H_C = calculated altitude. Above the horizon is positive, below the horizon is negative. The range is from $-90°$ in the nadir to $+90°$ in the zenith.

H_S = sextant altitude.

H = apparent altitude = sextant altitude corrected for instrumental error and dip.

H_O = observed altitude = apparent altitude corrected for refraction and, in appropriate cases, corrected for parallax and semi-diameter.

Z = Z_n = true azimuth. Z is measured from true north through east, south, west and back to north. The range is from $0°$ to $360°$.

I = sextant index error.

D = dip of horizon.

R = atmospheric refraction.

HP = horizontal parallax of the Sun, Moon, Venus or Mars.
PA = parallax in altitude of the Sun, Moon, Venus or Mars.
SD = semi-diameter of the Sun or Moon.
p = intercept = $H_O - H_C$. Towards is positive, away is negative.
T = course or track, measured as for azimuth from the north.
V = speed in knots.

3. *Entering Basic Data.*   When quantities such as *GHA* are entered, which in *The Nautical Almanac* are given in degrees and minutes, convert them to degrees and decimals of a degree by dividing the minutes by 60 and adding to the degrees; for example, if $GHA = 123°\ 45\!.\!6$, enter the two numbers 123 and 45·6 into the memory and set $GHA = 123 + 45\cdot6/60 = 123\!°\!7600$. Although four decimal places of a degree are shown in the examples, it is assumed that full precision is maintained in the calculations.

When using a computer or programmable calculator, write a subroutine to convert degrees and minutes to degrees and decimals. Scientific calculators usually have a special key for this purpose. For quantities like *Dec* which require a minus sign for southern declination, change the sign from plus to minus after the value has been converted to degrees and decimals, *e.g.* $Dec = S\,0°\ 12\!.\!3 = S\,0\!°\!2050 = -0\!°\!2050$. Other quantities which require conversion are semi-diameter, horizontal parallax, longitude and latitude.

4. *Interpolation of GHA and Dec*   The *GHA* and *Dec* of the Sun, Moon and planets are interpolated to the time of observation by direct calculation as follows: If the universal time is $a^h\ b^m\ c^s$, form the interpolation factor $x = b/60 + c/3600$. Enter the tabular value GHA_0 for the preceding hour (a) and the tabular value GHA_1 for the following hour ($a + 1$) then the interpolated value *GHA* is given by

$$GHA = GHA_0 + x(GHA_1 - GHA_0)$$

If the *GHA* passes through 360° between tabular values, add 360° to GHA_1 before interpolation. If the interpolated value exceeds 360°, subtract 360° from *GHA*.

Similarly for declination, enter the tabular value Dec_0 for the preceding hour (a) and the tabular value Dec_1 for the following hour ($a + 1$), then the interpolated value *Dec* is given by
$$Dec = Dec_0 + x(Dec_1 - Dec_0)$$

5. *Example.* (a) Find the *GHA* and *Dec* of the Sun on 2018 February 13 at $14^h\ 47^m\ 13^s$ UT.

The interpolation factor $x = 47/60 + 13/3600 = 0\!^h\!7869$

page 39 $14^h\ GHA_0 = 26°\ 27\!.\!4 = 26\!°\!4567$

$15^h\ GHA_1 = 41°\ 27\!.\!4 = 41\!°\!4567$

$14\!^h\!7869\ GHA = 26\cdot4567 + 0\cdot7869(41\cdot4567 - 26\cdot4567) = 38\!°\!2608$

$14^h\ Dec_0 = S\,13°\ 15\!.\!0 = -13\!°\!2500$

$15^h\ Dec_1 = S\,13°\ 14\!.\!1 = -13\!°\!2350$

$14\!^h\!7869\ Dec = -13\cdot2500 + 0\cdot7869(-13\cdot2350 + 13\cdot2500) = -13\!°\!2382$

GHA Aries is interpolated in the same way as *GHA* of a body. For a star the *SHA* and *Dec* are taken from the tabular page and do not require interpolation, then

$$GHA = GHA\ \text{Aries} + SHA$$

where *GHA* Aries is interpolated to the time of observation.

(b) Find the *GHA* and *Dec* of *Vega* on 2018 February 13 at 14^h 47^m 13^s UT.

The interpolation factor $x = 0^h7869$ as in the previous example

page 38 14^h *GHA* Aries$_0$ = 353° 33′3 = 353°5550

15^h *GHA* Aries$_1$ = 8° 35′7 = 368°5950   (360° added)

14^h7869 *GHA* Aries = 353·5550 + 0·7869(368·5950 − 353·5550) = 365°3906

SHA = 80° 37′1 = 80°6183

GHA = *GHA* Aries + *SHA* = 86°0090   (multiple of 360° removed)

Dec = N 38° 48′0 = +38°8000

6. *The calculated altitude and azimuth.* The calculated altitude H_C and true azimuth Z are determined from the *GHA* and *Dec* interpolated to the time of observation and from the *Long* and *Lat* estimated at the time of observation as follows:

Step 1.   Calculate the local hour angle

$$LHA = GHA + Long$$

Add or subtract multiples of 360° to set *LHA* in the range 0° to 360°.

Step 2.   Calculate S, C and the altitude H_C from

$$S = \sin Dec$$
$$C = \cos Dec \cos LHA$$
$$H_C = \sin^{-1}(S \sin Lat + C \cos Lat)$$

where $\sin^{-1}$ is the inverse function of sine.

Step 3.   Calculate X and A from

$$X = (S \cos Lat - C \sin Lat)/ \cos H_C$$
If $X > +1$ set $X = +1$
If $X < -1$ set $X = -1$
$$A = \cos^{-1} X$$

where $\cos^{-1}$ is the inverse function of cosine.

Step 4.   Determine the azimuth Z

If $LHA > 180°$ then $Z = A$
Otherwise $Z = 360° - A$

7. *Example.* Find the calculated altitude H_C and azimuth Z when

$$GHA = 53°\quad Dec = S\,15°\quad Lat = N\,32°\quad Long = W\,16°$$

For the calculation

$$GHA = 53°0000\quad Dec = -15°0000\quad Lat = +32°0000\quad Long = -16°0000$$

Step 1. $LHA = 53·0000 - 16·0000 = 37·0000$

Step 2. $S = -0·2588$

$C = +0·9659 \times 0·7986 = 0·7714$

$\sin H_C = -0·2588 \times 0·5299 + 0·7714 \times 0·8480 = 0·5171$

$H_C = 31°1346$

Step 3. $$X = (-0 \cdot 2588 \times 0 \cdot 8480 - 0 \cdot 7714 \times 0 \cdot 5299)/0 \cdot 8560 = -0 \cdot 7340$$
$$A = 137°2239$$

Step 4.   Since $LHA \leq 180°$ then $Z = 360° - A = 222°7761$

8. *Reduction from sextant altitude to observed altitude.*   The sextant altitude H_S is corrected for both dip and index error to produce the apparent altitude. The observed altitude H_O is calculated by applying a correction for refraction. For the Sun, Moon, Venus and Mars a correction for parallax is also applied to H, and for the Sun and Moon a further correction for semi-diameter is required. The corrections are calculated as follows:

Step 1.   Calculate dip

$$D = 0°0293 \sqrt{h}$$

where h is the height of eye above the horizon in metres.

Step 2.   Calculate apparent altitude

$$H = H_S + I - D$$

where I is the sextant index error.

Step 3.   Calculate refraction (R) at a standard temperature of $10°$ Celsius (C) and pressure of 1010 millibars (mb)

$$R_0 = 0°0167/\tan(H + 7 \cdot 32/(H + 4 \cdot 32))$$

If the temperature $T°$ C and pressure P mb are known calculate the refraction from

$$R = fR_0 \qquad \text{where} \qquad f = 0 \cdot 28P/(T + 273)$$
$$\text{otherwise set} \qquad R = R_0$$

Step 4.   Calculate the parallax in altitude (PA) from the horizontal parallax (HP) and the apparent altitude (H) for the Sun, Moon, Venus and Mars as follows:

$$PA = HP \cos H$$

For the Sun $HP = 0°0024$. This correction is very small and could be ignored.

For the Moon HP is taken for the nearest hour from the main tabular page and converted to degrees.

For Venus and Mars the HP is taken from the critical table at the bottom of page 259 and converted to degrees.

For the navigational stars and the remaining planets, Jupiter and Saturn set $PA = 0$.

If an error of $0'2$ is significant the expression for the parallax in altitude for the Moon should include a small correction OB for the oblateness of the Earth as follows:

$$PA = HP \cos H + OB$$
$$\text{where} \quad OB = -0°0032 \sin^2 Lat \cos H + 0°0032 \sin(2Lat) \cos Z \sin H$$

At mid-latitudes and for altitudes of the Moon below $60°$ a simple approximation to OB is

$$OB = -0°0017 \cos H$$

Step 5.   Calculate the semi-diameter for the Sun and Moon as follows:

Sun: *SD* is taken from the main tabular page and converted to degrees.

Moon: $SD = 0°2724HP$ where *HP* is taken for the nearest hour from the main tabular page and converted to degrees.

Step 6.   Calculate the observed altitude

$$H_O = H - R + PA \pm SD$$

where the plus sign is used if the lower limb of the Sun or Moon was observed and the minus sign if the upper limb was observed.

9. *Example.*   The following example illustrates how to use a calculator to reduce the sextant altitude (H_S) to observed altitude (H_O); the sextant altitudes given are assumed to be taken on 2018 March 9 with a marine sextant, zero index error, at height 5·4 m, temperature $-3°$ C and pressure 982 mb, the Moon sights are assumed to be taken at 10^h UT.

Body limb	Sun lower	Sun upper	Moon lower	Moon upper	Venus —	*Polaris* —
Sextant altitude: H_S	21·3283	3·3367	33·4600	26·1117	4·5433	49·6083
Step 1. Dip: $D = 0·0293\sqrt{h}$	0·0681	0·0681	0·0681	0·0681	0·0681	0·0681
Step 2. Apparent altitude: $H = H_S + I - D$	21·2602	3·2686	33·3919	26·0436	4·4752	49·5402
Step 3. Refraction: R_0	0·0423	0·2256	0·0251	0·0338	0·1798	0·0142
f	1·0184	1·0184	1·0184	1·0184	1·0184	1·0184
$R = fR_0$	0·0431	0·2298	0·0256	0·0344	0·1831	0·0144
Step 4. Parallax:			(54′5)	(54′5)	(0′1)	
HP	0·0024	0·0024	0·9083	0·9083	0·0017	—
Parallax in altitude: $PA = HP \cos H$	0·0022	0·0024	0·7584	0·8161	0·0017	—
Step 5. Semi-diameter: Sun : $SD = 16·1/60$	0·2683	0·2683	—	—	—	—
Moon : $SD = 0·2724HP$	—	—	0·2474	0·2474	—	—
Step 6. Observed altitude: $H_O = H - R + PA \pm SD$	21·4877	2·7729	34·3721	26·5779	4·2938	49·5258

Note that for the Moon the correction for the oblateness of the Earth of about $-0°0017 \cos H$, which equals $-0°0014$ for the lower limb and $-0°0015$ for the upper limb, has been ignored in the above calculation.

10. *Position from intercept and azimuth using a chart.*   An estimate is made of the position at the adopted time of fix. The position at the time of observation is then calculated by dead reckoning from the time of fix. For example, if the course (track) *T* and the speed *V* (in knots) of the observer are constant, then *Long* and *Lat* at the time of observation are calculated from

$$Long = L_F + t\,(V/60)\sin T / \cos B_F$$
$$Lat = B_F + t\,(V/60)\cos T$$

where L_F and B_F are the estimated longitude and latitude at the time of fix and t is the time interval in hours from the time of fix to the time of observation, t is positive if the time of observation is after the time of fix and negative if it was before.

The position line of an observation is plotted on a chart using the intercept

$$p = H_O - H_C$$

and azimuth Z with origin at the calculated position (*Long, Lat*) at the time of observation, where H_C and Z are calculated using the method in section 6, page 279. Starting from this calculated position a line is drawn on the chart along the direction of the azimuth to the body. Convert p to nautical miles by multiplying by 60. The position line is drawn at right angles to the azimuth line, distance p from (*Long, Lat*) towards the body if p is positive and distance p away from the body if p is negative. Provided there are no gross errors the navigator should be somewhere on or near the position line at the time of observation. Two or more position lines are required to determine a fix.

11. *Position from intercept and azimuth by calculation.* The position of the fix may be calculated from two or more sextant observations as follows.

If p_1, Z_1, are the intercept and azimuth of the first observation, p_2, Z_2, of the second observation and so on, form the summations

$$A = \cos^2 Z_1 + \cos^2 Z_2 + \cdots$$
$$B = \cos Z_1 \sin Z_1 + \cos Z_2 \sin Z_2 + \cdots$$
$$C = \sin^2 Z_1 + \sin^2 Z_2 + \cdots$$
$$D = p_1 \cos Z_1 + p_2 \cos Z_2 + \cdots$$
$$E = p_1 \sin Z_1 + p_2 \sin Z_2 + \cdots$$

where the number of terms in each summation is equal to the number of observations.

With $G = A\,C - B^2$, an improved estimate of the position at the time of fix (L_I, B_I) is given by

$$L_I = L_F + (A\,E - B\,D)/(G\cos B_F), \qquad B_I = B_F + (C\,D - B\,E)/G$$

Calculate the distance d between the initial estimated position (L_F, B_F) at the time of fix and the improved estimated position (L_I, B_I) in nautical miles from

$$d = 60\sqrt{((L_I - L_F)^2 \cos^2 B_F + (B_I - B_F)^2)}$$

If d exceeds about 20 nautical miles set $L_F = L_I$, $B_F = B_I$ and repeat the calculation until d, the distance between the position at the previous estimate and the improved estimate, is less than about 20 nautical miles.

12. *Example of direct computation.* Using the method described above, calculate the position of a ship on 2018 July 4 at $21^h\,00^m\,00^s$ UT from the marine sextant observations of the three stars *Regulus* (No. 26) at $20^h\,39^m\,23^s$ UT, *Antares* (No. 42) at $20^h\,45^m\,47^s$ UT and *Kochab* (No. 40) at $21^h\,10^m\,34^s$ UT, where the observed altitudes of the three stars corrected for the effects of refraction, dip and instrumental error, are $27°\!.0675$, $25°\!.9580$ and $47°\!.5384$ respectively. The ship was travelling at a constant speed of 20 knots on a course of $325°$ during the period of observation, and the position of the ship at the time of fix $21^h\,00^m\,00^s$ UT is only known to the nearest whole degree W $15°$, N $32°$.

Intermediate values for the first iteration are shown in the table. *GHA* Aries was interpolated from the nearest tabular values on page 132. For the first iteration set $L_F = -15°0000$, $B_F = +32°0000$ at the time of fix at $21^h\ 00^m\ 00^s$ UT.

First Iteration

Body	Regulus	Antares	Kochab
No.	26	42	40
time of observation	$20^h\ 39^m\ 23^s$	$20^h\ 45^m\ 47^s$	$21^h\ 10^m\ 34^s$
H_O	27·0675	25·9580	47·5384
interpolation factor	0·6564	0·7631	0·1761
GHA Aries	232·6488	234·2530	240·4657
SHA (page 132)	207·6683	112·3617	137·3267
GHA	80·3171	346·6147	17·7923
Dec (page 132)	+11·8783	−26·4700	+74·0867
t	−0·3436	−0·2369	+0·1761
Long	−14·9225	−14·9466	−15·0397
Lat	+31·9062	+31·9353	+32·0481
Z	267·3864	151·8828	358·8738
H_C	27·0444	25·6522	47·9385
p	+0·0231	+0·3058	−0·4001

$$A = 1·7796 \quad B = -0·3898 \quad C = 1·2204 \quad D = -0·6708 \quad E = 0·1289 \quad G = 2·0199$$
$$(AE - BD)/(G\cos B_F) = -0·0187, \qquad (CD - BE)/G = -0·3804$$

An improved estimate of the position at the time of fix is

$$L_I = L_F - 0·0187 = -15·0187 \quad \text{and} \quad B_I = B_F - 0·3804 = +31·6196$$

Since the distance between the previous estimated position and the improved estimate $d = 22·8$ nautical miles set $L_F = -15·0187$, and $B_F = +31·6196$ and repeat the calculation. The table shows the intermediate values of the calculation for the second iteration. In each iteration the quantities H_O, *GHA*, *Dec* and t do not change.

Second Iteration

Body	Regulus	Antares	Kochab
No.	26	42	40
Long	−14·9416	−14·9655	−15·0582
Lat	+31·5258	+31·5549	+31·6677
Z	267·5701	151·7791	358·8895
H_C	27·0773	25·9800	47·5585
p	−0·0098	−0·0220	−0·0201

$$A = 1·7778 \quad B = -0·3937 \quad C = 1·2222 \quad D = -0·0003 \quad E = -0·0002 \quad G = 2·0178$$
$$(AE - BD)/(G\cos B_F) = -0·0003, \qquad (CD - BE)/G = -0·0002$$

An improved estimate of the position at the time of fix is

$$L_I = L_F - 0·0003 = -15·0190 \quad \text{and} \quad B_I = B_F - 0·0002 = +31·6194$$

The distance between the previous estimated position and the improved estimated position, $d = 0·02$ nautical miles, is so small that a third iteration would produce a negligible improvement to the estimate of the position.

USE OF CONCISE SIGHT REDUCTION TABLES

1. *Introduction.* The concise sight reduction tables given on pages 286 to 317 are intended for use when neither more extensive tables nor electronic computing aids are available. These "NAO sight reduction tables" provide for the reduction of the local hour angle and declination of a celestial object to azimuth and altitude, referred to an assumed position on the Earth, for use in the intercept method of celestial navigation which is now standard practice.

2. *Form of tables.* Entries in the reduction table are at a fixed interval of one degree for all latitudes and hour angles. A compact arrangement results from division of the navigational triangle into two right spherical triangles, so that the table has to be entered twice. Assumed latitude and local hour angle are the arguments for the first entry. The reduction table responds with the intermediate arguments A, B, and Z_1, where A is used as one of the arguments for the second entry to the table, B has to be incremented by the declination to produce the quantity F, and Z_1 is a component of the azimuth angle. The reduction table is then reentered with A and F and yields H, P, and Z_2 where H is the altitude, P is the complement of the parallactic angle, and Z_2 is the second component of the azimuth angle. It is usually necessary to adjust the tabular altitude for the fractional parts of the intermediate entering arguments to derive computed altitude, and an auxiliary table is provided for the purpose. Rules governing signs of the quantities which must be added or subtracted are given in the instructions and summarized on each tabular page. Azimuth angle is the sum of two components and is converted to true azimuth by familiar rules, repeated at the bottom of the tabular pages.

Tabular altitude and intermediate quantities are given to the nearest minute of arc, although errors of $2'$ in computed altitude may accrue during adjustment for the minutes parts of entering arguments. Components of azimuth angle are stated to $0°1$; for derived true azimuth, only whole degrees are warranted. Since objects near the zenith are difficult to observe with a marine sextant, they should be avoided; altitudes greater than about $80°$ are not suited to reduction by this method.

In many circumstances, the accuracy provided by these tables is sufficient. However, to maintain the full accuracy ($0'1$) of the ephemeral data in the almanac throughout their reduction to altitude and azimuth, more extensive tables or a calculator should be used.

3. *Use of Tables.*

Step 1. Determine the Greenwich hour angle (GHA) and Declination (Dec) of the body from the almanac. Select an assumed latitude (Lat) of integral degrees nearest to the estimated latitude. Choose an assumed longitude nearest to the estimated longitude such that the local hour angle

$$LHA = GHA \; {- \text{ west} \atop + \text{ east}} \; \text{longitude}$$

has integral degrees.

Step 2. Enter the reduction table with Lat and LHA as arguments. Record the quantities A, B and Z_1. Apply the rules for the sign of B and Z_1: B is minus if $90° < LHA < 270°$: Z_1 has the same sign as B. Set $A° =$ nearest whole degree of A and $A' =$ minutes part of A. This step may be repeated for all reductions before leaving the latitude opening of the table.

Step 3. Record the declination Dec. Apply the rules for the sign of Dec: Dec is minus if the name of Dec (*i.e.* N or S) is contrary to latitude. Add B and Dec algebraically to produce F. If F is negative, the object is below the horizon (in sight reduction, this can occur when the objects are close to the horizon). Regard F as positive until step 7. Set $F° =$ nearest whole degree of F and $F' =$ minutes part of F.

Step 4.   Enter the reduction table a second time with $A°$ and $F°$ as arguments and record H, P, and Z_2. Set $P° =$ nearest whole degree of P and $Z_2° =$ nearest whole degree of Z_2.

Step 5.   Enter the auxiliary table with F' and $P°$ as arguments to obtain $corr_1$ to H for F'. Apply the rule for the sign of $corr_1$: $corr_1$ is minus if $F < 90°$ and $F' > 29'$ or if $F > 90°$ and $F' < 30'$, otherwise $corr_1$ is plus.

Step 6.   Enter the auxiliary table with A' and $Z_2°$ as arguments to obtain $corr_2$ to H for A'. Apply the rule for the sign of $corr_2$: $corr_2$ is minus if $A' < 30'$, otherwise $corr_2$ is plus.

Step 7.   Calculate the computed altitude H_C as the sum of H, $corr_1$ and $corr_2$. Apply the rule for the sign of H_C: H_C is minus if F is negative.

Step 8.   Apply the rule for the sign of Z_2: Z_2 is minus if $F > 90°$. If F is negative, replace Z_2 by $180° - Z_2$. Set the azimuth angle Z equal to the algebraic sum of Z_1 and Z_2 and ignore the resulting sign. Obtain the true azimuth Z_n from the rules

$$\text{For N latitude, if} \quad LHA > 180° \quad\quad Z_n = Z$$
$$\text{if} \quad LHA < 180° \quad\quad Z_n = 360° - Z$$

$$\text{For S latitude, if} \quad LHA > 180° \quad\quad Z_n = 180° - Z$$
$$\text{if} \quad LHA < 180° \quad\quad Z_n = 180° + Z$$

Observed altitude H_O is compared with H_C to obtain the altitude difference, which, with Z_n, is used to plot the position line.

4. *Example.*   (a) Required the altitude and azimuth of *Schedar* on 2018 February 4 at UT 06^h 32^m from the estimated position 5° east, 53° north.

1. Assumed latitude $Lat =$ 53° N
    From the almanac $GHA =$ 222° 00′
    Assumed longitude   5° 00′ E
    Local hour angle $LHA =$ 227

2. Reduction table, 1st entry
    $(Lat, LHA) = (53, 227)$ $A =$ 26   07 $A° = 26, A' = 7$
                                     $B = -27$ 12 $Z_1 = -49·4,$ $90° < LHA < 270°$
3. From the almanac $Dec = +56$ 38 Lat and Dec same
    $Sum = B + Dec$ $F = +29$ 26 $F° = 29, F' = 26$

4. Reduction table, 2nd entry
    $(A°, F°) = (26, 29)$ $H =$ 25   50 $P° = 61$
                                                        $Z_2 = 76·3, Z_2° = 76$
5. Auxiliary table, 1st entry
    $(F', P°) = (26, 61)$ $corr_1 =$ $+23$ $F < 90°, F' < 29'$
    Sum   26   13
6. Auxiliary table, 2nd entry
    $(A', Z_2°) = (7, 76)$ $corr_2 =$ -2 $A' < 30'$
7. Sum = computed altitude $H_C = +26°$ 11′ $F > 0°$

8. Azimuth, first component $Z_1 = -49·4$ same sign as B
               second component $Z_2 = +76·3$ $F < 90°, F > 0°$
    Sum = azimuth angle $Z =$ 26·9

    True azimuth $Z_n =$ 027°   N Lat, $LHA > 180°$

continued on page 318

SIGHT REDUCTION TABLE

B: (−) for 90° < LHA < 270°
Dec:(−) for Lat. contrary name

Z1: same sign as B
Z2: (−) for F > 90°

Lat./A	0°			1°			2°			3°			4°			5°			Lat./A	
LHA/F	A/H	B/P	Z1/Z2	A/H	B/P	Z1/Z2	A/H	B/P	Z1/Z2	A/H	B/P	Z1/Z2	A/H	B/P	Z1/Z2	A/H	B/P	Z1/Z2	LHA	LHA
0	0 00	90 00	90.0	0 00	89 00	90.0	0 00	88 00	90.0	0 00	87 00	90.0	0 00	86 00	90.0	0 00	85 00	90.0	180	360
1	1 00	90 00	90.0	1 00	89 00	90.0	1 00	88 00	90.0	1 00	87 00	89.9	1 00	86 00	89.9	1 00	85 00	89.9	181	359
2	2 00	90 00	90.0	2 00	89 00	90.0	2 00	88 00	89.9	2 00	87 00	89.9	2 00	86 00	89.9	2 59	85 00	89.8	182	358
3	3 00	90 00	90.0	3 00	89 00	89.9	3 00	88 00	89.9	3 00	87 00	89.8	3 00	86 00	89.8	3 59	85 00	89.7	183	357
4	4 00	90 00	90.0	4 00	89 00	89.9	4 00	88 00	89.9	4 00	87 00	89.8	4 59	85 59	89.7	4 59	84 59	89.7	184	356
5	5 00	90 00	90.0	5 00	89 00	89.9	5 00	88 00	89.8	5 00	86 59	89.7	5 59	85 59	89.7	5 59	84 59	89.6	185	355
6	6 00	90 00	90.0	6 00	89 00	89.9	6 00	87 59	89.8	6 59	86 59	89.7	6 59	85 59	89.6	6 58	84 58	89.5	186	354
7	7 00	90 00	90.0	7 00	89 00	89.9	7 00	87 59	89.8	7 59	86 59	89.6	7 59	85 58	89.5	7 58	84 58	89.4	187	353
8	8 00	90 00	90.0	8 00	88 59	89.8	8 00	87 59	89.7	8 59	86 58	89.6	8 59	85 58	89.4	8 58	84 57	89.3	188	352
9	9 00	90 00	90.0	9 00	88 59	89.8	9 00	87 59	89.7	9 59	86 58	89.6	9 59	85 57	89.4	9 58	84 56	89.2	189	351
10	10 00	90 00	90.0	10 00	88 59	89.8	10 00	87 59	89.7	10 59	86 57	89.5	10 58	85 56	89.3	10 57	84 55	89.1	190	350
11	11 00	90 00	90.0	11 00	88 59	89.8	11 00	87 58	89.6	11 59	86 57	89.5	11 58	85 55	89.2	11 57	84 54	89.0	191	349
12	12 00	90 00	90.0	12 00	88 59	89.8	12 00	87 58	89.6	12 59	86 56	89.4	12 58	85 54	89.1	12 57	84 53	88.9	192	348
13	13 00	90 00	90.0	13 00	88 58	89.8	13 00	87 57	89.5	13 59	86 55	89.4	13 58	85 53	89.1	13 57	84 51	88.8	193	347
14	14 00	90 00	90.0	14 00	88 58	89.7	14 59	87 57	89.5	14 59	86 54	89.3	14 58	85 52	89.0	14 56	84 49	88.7	194	346
15	15 00	90 00	90.0	15 00	88 58	89.7	15 59	87 56	89.5	15 59	86 53	89.3	15 58	85 49	88.9	15 56	84 48	88.6	195	345
16	16 00	90 00	90.0	16 00	88 58	89.7	16 59	87 56	89.4	16 59	86 52	89.2	16 57	85 48	88.8	16 56	84 46	88.6	196	344
17	17 00	90 00	90.0	17 00	88 57	89.7	17 59	87 55	89.4	17 58	86 51	89.1	17 57	85 46	88.7	17 56	84 45	88.5	197	343
18	18 00	90 00	90.0	18 00	88 57	89.7	18 59	87 54	89.4	18 58	86 50	89.1	18 57	85 45	88.7	18 55	84 43	88.4	198	342
19	19 00	90 00	90.0	19 00	88 57	89.6	19 59	87 53	89.3	19 58	86 48	89.0	19 57	85 43	88.6	19 55	84 41	88.3	199	341
20	20 00	90 00	90.0	20 00	88 56	89.6	20 59	87 52	89.3	20 58	86 47	89.0	20 57	85 41	88.5	20 55	84 39	88.2	200	340
21	21 00	90 00	90.0	21 00	88 56	89.6	21 59	87 51	89.2	21 58	86 46	88.9	21 57	85 39	88.5	21 55	84 34	88.1	201	339
22	22 00	90 00	90.0	22 00	88 55	89.6	22 59	87 51	89.2	22 58	86 44	88.8	22 56	85 37	88.4	22 54	84 32	88.0	202	338
23	23 00	90 00	90.0	23 00	88 55	89.6	23 59	87 50	89.2	23 58	86 43	88.8	23 56	85 35	88.3	23 54	84 29	87.9	203	337
24	24 00	90 00	90.0	24 00	88 54	89.5	23 59	87 49	89.1	24 58	86 41	88.7	24 56	85 33	88.2	24 54	84 26	87.8	204	336
25	25 00	90 00	90.0	25 00	88 54	89.5	24 59	87 48	89.1	25 58	86 40	88.6	25 56	85 31	88.1	25 54	84 24	87.7	205	335
26	26 00	90 00	90.0	26 00	88 53	89.5	25 59	87 47	89.0	26 58	86 38	88.5	26 56	85 28	88.1	26 53	84 20	87.6	206	334
27	27 00	90 00	90.0	27 00	88 53	89.5	26 59	87 45	89.0	27 57	86 36	88.5	27 56	85 26	88.0	27 53	84 17	87.5	207	333
28	28 00	90 00	90.0	28 00	88 52	89.4	27 59	87 44	89.0	28 57	86 34	88.4	28 55	85 23	87.9	28 53	84 14	87.3	208	332
29	29 00	90 00	90.0	29 00	88 51	89.4	28 59	87 43	88.9	29 57	86 32	88.3	29 55	85 20	87.8	29 52	84 10	87.2	209	331
30	30 00	90 00	90.0	30 00	88 51	89.4	29 59	87 41	88.8	30 57	86 30	88.3	30 55	85 17	87.7	30 52	84 07	87.1	210	330
31	31 00	90 00	90.0	31 00	88 50	89.4	30 59	87 39	88.8	31 57	86 28	88.2	31 55	85 14	87.6	31 52	84 03	87.0	211	329
32	32 00	90 00	90.0	32 00	88 49	89.4	31 59	87 37	88.8	32 57	86 25	88.1	32 55	85 11	87.5	32 52	83 59	86.9	212	328
33	33 00	90 00	90.0	33 00	88 48	89.3	32 59	87 35	88.7	33 57	86 23	88.1	33 54	85 07	87.3	33 51	83 54	86.8	213	327
34	34 00	90 00	90.0	34 00	88 48	89.3	33 59	87 34	88.7	34 57	86 20	88.0	34 54	85 04	87.2	34 51	83 50	86.6	214	326
35	35 00	90 00	90.0	35 00	88 47	89.3	34 59	87 34	88.6	35 57	86 18	87.9	35 54	85 00	87.1	35 51	83 45	86.5	215	325
36	36 00	90 00	90.0	36 00	88 46	89.2	35 58	87 32	88.5	36 56	86 15	87.8	36 54	84 56	87.0	36 50	83 40	86.4	216	324
37	37 00	90 00	90.0	37 00	88 45	89.2	36 58	87 30	88.5	37 56	86 12	87.7	37 53	84 52	86.9	37 50	83 35	86.2	217	323
38	38 00	90 00	90.0	38 00	88 44	89.2	37 58	87 28	88.4	38 56	86 09	87.6	38 53	84 49	86.8	38 49	83 29	86.1	218	322
39	39 00	90 00	90.0	39 00	88 43	89.2	38 58	87 26	88.4	39 56	86 05	87.5	39 53	84 47	86.7	39 49	83 23	86.0	219	321
40	40 00	90 00	90.0	40 00	88 42	89.1	39 58	87 23	88.3	40 56	86 02	87.4	40 53	84 42	86.5	40 49	83 17	85.8	220	320
41	41 00	90 00	90.0	41 00	88 41	89.1	40 58	87 21	88.3	41 56	85 58	87.3	41 52	84 37	86.4	41 48	83 11	85.7	221	319
42	42 00	90 00	90.0	42 00	88 39	89.1	41 58	87 19	88.2	42 56	85 58	87.3	42 52	84 37	86.4	42 48	83 17	85.5	222	318
43	43 00	90 00	90.0	43 00	88 38	89.1	42 58	87 16	88.1	43 55	85 54	87.2	43 52	84 32	86.3	43 48	83 11	85.4	223	317
44	44 00	90 00	90.0	43 59	88 37	89.0	43 58	87 13	88.1	44 55	85 50	87.1	44 52	84 27	86.1	43 48	83 04	85.2	224	316
45	45 00	90 00	90.0	44 59	88 35	89.0	44 58	87 10	88.0	44 55	85 46	87.0	44 52	84 21	86.0	44 47	82 57	85.0	225	315

Lat./A	LHA/F	0° A/H	0° B/P	0° Z_1/Z_2	1° A/H	1° B/P	1° Z_1/Z_2	2° A/H	2° B/P	2° Z_1/Z_2	3° A/H	3° B/P	3° Z_1/Z_2	4° A/H	4° B/P	4° Z_1/Z_2	5° A/H	5° B/P	5° Z_1/Z_2	LHA	A
45	135	45 00	90 00	90·0	44 59	88 35	89·0	44 58	87 10	88·0	44 55	85 46	87·0	44 52	84 21	86·0	44 47	82 57	85·0	225	315
46	134	46 00	90 00	90·0	45 59	88 34	89·0	45 58	87 07	87·9	45 55	85 41	86·9	45 51	84 15	85·9	45 46	82 49	84·8	226	314
47	133	47 00	90 00	90·0	46 59	88 32	88·9	46 58	87 04	87·9	46 55	85 36	86·8	46 51	84 09	85·7	46 46	82 41	84·7	227	313
48	132	48 00	90 00	90·0	47 59	88 30	88·9	47 58	87 01	87·8	47 55	85 31	86·7	47 51	84 02	85·6	47 46	82 33	84·5	228	312
49	131	49 00	90 00	90·0	48 59	88 29	88·8	48 58	86 57	87·7	48 55	85 26	86·6	48 50	83 55	85·4	48 45	82 24	84·3	229	311
50	130	50 00	90 00	90·0	49 59	88 27	88·8	49 58	86 53	87·6	49 54	85 20	86·4	49 50	83 47	85·2	49 44	82 15	84·1	230	310
51	129	51 00	90 00	90·0	50 59	88 25	88·8	50 57	86 49	87·5	50 54	85 14	86·3	50 50	83 40	85·1	50 44	82 05	83·9	231	309
52	128	52 00	90 00	90·0	51 59	88 23	88·7	51 57	86 45	87·4	51 54	85 08	86·2	51 49	83 31	84·9	51 43	81 55	83·6	232	308
53	127	53 00	90 00	90·0	52 59	88 20	88·7	52 57	86 41	87·3	52 54	85 01	86·0	52 49	83 22	84·7	52 43	81 44	83·4	233	307
54	126	54 00	90 00	90·0	53 59	88 18	88·6	53 57	86 36	87·2	53 54	84 54	85·9	53 49	83 13	84·5	53 42	81 32	83·2	234	306
55	125	55 00	90 00	90·0	54 59	88 15	88·6	54 57	86 31	87·1	54 54	84 47	85·7	54 48	83 03	84·3	54 41	81 20	82·9	235	305
56	124	56 00	90 00	90·0	55 59	88 13	88·5	55 57	86 26	87·0	55 53	84 39	85·6	55 48	82 52	84·1	55 41	81 06	82·6	236	304
57	123	57 00	90 00	90·0	56 59	88 10	88·5	56 57	86 20	86·9	56 53	84 30	85·4	56 47	82 41	83·9	56 40	80 52	82·4	237	303
58	122	58 00	90 00	90·0	57 59	88 07	88·4	57 57	86 14	86·8	57 52	84 21	85·2	57 47	82 29	83·6	57 39	80 38	82·1	238	302
59	121	59 00	90 00	90·0	58 59	88 04	88·3	58 56	86 07	86·7	58 52	84 11	85·0	58 46	82 16	83·4	58 38	80 22	81·7	239	301
60	120	60 00	90 00	90·0	59 59	88 00	88·3	59 56	86 00	86·6	59 52	84 01	84·8	59 46	82 02	83·1	59 37	80 05	81·4	240	300
61	119	61 00	90 00	90·0	60 59	87 56	88·2	60 56	85 53	86·4	60 52	83 50	84·6	60 45	81 48	82·8	60 37	79 46	81·1	241	299
62	118	62 00	90 00	90·0	61 59	87 52	88·1	61 56	85 45	86·2	61 51	83 38	84·4	61 44	81 32	82·5	61 36	79 27	80·7	242	298
63	117	63 00	90 00	90·0	62 59	87 48	88·0	62 56	85 36	86·1	62 51	83 25	84·1	62 44	81 15	82·2	62 35	79 06	80·3	243	297
64	116	64 00	90 00	90·0	63 59	87 43	88·0	63 56	85 27	85·9	63 50	83 11	83·9	63 43	80 56	81·9	63 33	78 43	79·9	244	296
65	115	65 00	90 00	90·0	64 59	87 38	87·9	64 56	85 17	85·7	64 50	82 56	83·6	64 42	80 36	81·6	64 32	78 18	79·4	245	295
66	114	66 00	90 00	90·0	65 59	87 33	87·8	65 55	85 06	85·5	65 49	82 39	83·3	65 41	80 15	81·1	65 31	77 52	78·9	246	294
67	113	67 00	90 00	90·0	66 59	87 27	87·6	66 55	84 54	85·3	66 49	82 22	83·0	66 40	79 51	80·7	66 29	77 23	78·4	247	293
68	112	68 00	90 00	90·0	67 59	87 20	87·5	67 55	84 40	85·1	67 48	82 02	82·6	67 39	79 26	80·2	67 28	76 51	77·8	248	292
69	111	69 00	90 00	90·0	68 59	87 13	87·4	68 55	84 26	84·8	68 48	81 41	82·2	68 38	78 58	79·7	68 26	76 17	77·2	249	291
70	110	70 00	90 00	90·0	69 59	87 05	87·3	69 54	84 10	84·5	69 47	81 17	81·8	69 37	78 27	79·1	69 25	75 39	76·5	250	290
71	109	71 00	90 00	90·0	70 58	86 56	87·1	70 54	83 53	84·2	70 46	80 51	81·4	70 36	77 53	78·5	70 23	74 58	75·8	251	289
72	108	72 00	90 00	90·0	71 58	86 46	86·9	71 54	83 33	83·9	71 46	80 22	80·8	71 35	77 15	77·9	71 20	74 12	75·0	252	288
73	107	73 00	90 00	90·0	72 58	86 35	86·7	72 53	83 11	83·5	72 45	79 50	80·3	72 33	76 33	77·1	72 18	73 23	74·1	253	287
74	106	74 00	90 00	90·0	73 58	86 23	86·5	73 53	82 47	83·1	73 44	79 14	79·7	73 31	75 46	76·3	73 15	72 23	73·1	254	286
75	105	75 00	90 00	90·0	74 58	86 09	86·3	74 52	82 19	82·6	74 43	78 33	78·9	74 29	74 53	75·4	74 12	71 19	72·0	255	285
76	104	76 00	90 00	90·0	75 58	85 52	86·0	75 52	81 47	82·0	75 41	77 47	78·1	75 27	73 53	74·4	75 09	70 07	70·7	256	284
77	103	77 00	90 00	90·0	76 58	85 34	85·7	76 51	81 11	81·4	76 40	76 53	77·2	76 25	72 44	73·2	76 05	68 45	69·3	257	283
78	102	78 00	90 00	90·0	77 58	85 12	85·3	77 50	80 28	80·7	77 38	75 51	76·2	77 22	71 25	71·8	77 01	67 01	67·7	258	282
79	101	79 00	90 00	90·0	78 57	84 46	84·9	78 49	79 38	79·8	78 36	74 39	74·9	78 18	69 52	70·3	77 56	65 22	65·8	259	281
80	100	80 00	90 00	90·0	79 57	84 16	84·3	79 48	78 38	78·8	79 34	73 12	73·5	79 14	68 04	68·4	78 50	63 16	63·7	260	280
81	99	81 00	90 00	90·0	80 57	83 38	83·7	80 47	77 25	77·6	80 31	71 29	71·7	80 09	65 55	66·2	79 43	60 47	61·2	261	279
82	98	82 00	90 00	90·0	81 56	82 51	82·9	81 45	75 55	76·1	81 28	69 22	69·6	81 04	63 19	63·6	80 34	57 51	58·2	262	278
83	97	83 00	90 00	90·0	82 56	81 51	81·9	82 43	74 01	74·1	82 23	66 44	66·9	81 57	60 04	60·4	81 24	54 20	54·6	263	277
84	96	84 00	90 00	90·0	83 55	80 31	80·6	83 41	71 32	71·6	83 18	63 22	63·5	82 48	56 13	56·4	82 12	50 04	50·3	264	276
85	95	85 00	90 00	90·0	84 54	78 40	78·7	84 37	68 10	68·3	84 10	58 59	59·1	83 36	51 16	51·4	82 56	44 53	45·1	265	275
86	94	86 00	90 00	90·0	85 53	75 57	76·0	85 32	63 24	63·5	85 00	53 05	53·2	84 21	45 01	45·1	83 36	38 34	38·7	266	274
87	93	87 00	90 00	90·0	86 50	71 33	71·6	86 24	56 17	56·3	85 45	44 58	45·0	85 00	36 49	36·9	84 10	30 53	31·0	267	273
88	92	88 00	90 00	90·0	87 46	63 26	63·4	87 10	44 59	45·0	86 24	33 40	33·7	85 32	26 31	26·6	84 37	21 45	21·8	268	272
89	91	89 00	90 00	90·0	88 35	45 00	45·0	87 46	26 33	26·6	86 50	18 25	18·4	85 53	14 01	14·0	84 54	11 17	11·3	269	271
90	90	90 00	0 00	0·0	89 00	0 00	0·0	88 00	0 00	0·0	87 00	0 00	0·0	86 00	0 00	0·0	85 00	0 00	0·0	270	270

N. Lat.: for LHA > 180° ... $Z_n = Z$
for LHA < 180° ... $Z_n = 360° - Z$

S. Lat.: for LHA > 180° ... $Z_n = 180° - Z$
for LHA < 180° ... $Z_n = 180° + Z$

SIGHT REDUCTION TABLE

B: (−) for 90° < LHA < 270°
Dec:(−) for Lat. contrary name

Z₁: same sign as B
Z₂: (−) for F > 90°

LHA	F	6° A/H	6° B/P	6° Z₁/Z₂	7° A/H	7° B/P	7° Z₁/Z₂	8° A/H	8° B/P	8° Z₁/Z₂	9° A/H	9° B/P	9° Z₁/Z₂	10° A/H	10° B/P	10° Z₁/Z₂	11° A/H	11° B/P	11° Z₁/Z₂	LHA	A
0	180	0 00	84 00	90·0	0 00	83 00	90·0	0 00	82 00	90·0	0 00	81 00	90·0	0 00	80 00	90·0	0 00	79 00	90·0	180	360
1	179	1 00	84 00	89·9	1 00	83 00	89·9	0 59	82 00	89·9	0 59	81 00	89·8	0 59	80 00	89·8	0 59	79 00	89·8	181	359
2	178	1 59	84 00	89·8	1 59	83 00	89·8	1 59	82 00	89·7	1 59	81 00	89·7	1 58	80 00	89·7	1 58	79 00	89·6	182	358
3	177	2 59	84 00	89·7	2 59	82 59	89·7	2 58	81 59	89·6	2 58	80 59	89·5	2 57	79 59	89·5	2 57	78 59	89·4	183	357
4	176	3 59	83 59	89·6	3 58	82 59	89·6	3 58	81 59	89·4	3 57	80 59	89·4	3 56	79 59	89·3	3 56	78 58	89·2	184	356
5	175	4 58	83 59	89·5	4 58	82 58	89·5	4 57	81 58	89·3	4 56	80 58	89·2	4 55	79 58	89·1	4 54	78 58	89·0	185	355
6	174	5 58	83 58	89·4	5 57	82 58	89·3	5 56	81 57	89·2	5 56	80 57	89·1	5 55	79 57	89·0	5 53	78 56	88·9	186	354
7	173	6 58	83 57	89·3	6 57	82 57	89·1	6 56	81 56	89·0	6 55	80 56	88·9	6 54	79 56	88·8	6 52	78 55	88·7	187	353
8	172	7 57	83 56	89·2	7 56	82 56	89·0	7 55	81 55	88·9	7 54	80 55	88·7	7 53	79 54	88·6	7 51	78 54	88·5	188	352
9	171	8 57	83 56	89·1	8 56	82 55	88·9	8 55	81 54	88·7	8 53	80 53	88·6	8 52	79 53	88·4	8 50	78 52	88·3	189	351
10	170	9 57	83 54	88·9	9 55	82 54	88·8	9 54	81 53	88·6	9 53	80 52	88·4	9 51	79 51	88·2	9 49	78 50	88·1	190	350
11	169	10 56	83 53	88·8	10 55	82 52	88·6	10 53	81 51	88·5	10 52	80 50	88·3	10 50	79 49	88·1	10 48	78 48	87·9	191	349
12	168	11 56	83 52	88·7	11 55	82 51	88·5	11 53	81 49	88·3	11 51	80 48	88·1	11 49	79 47	87·9	11 47	78 46	87·7	192	348
13	167	12 56	83 51	88·6	12 54	82 49	88·4	12 52	81 48	88·2	12 50	80 46	87·9	12 48	79 45	87·7	12 45	78 43	87·5	193	347
14	166	13 55	83 49	88·5	13 54	82 47	88·3	13 52	81 46	88·0	13 49	80 44	87·8	13 47	79 42	87·5	13 44	78 40	87·3	194	346
15	165	14 55	83 47	88·4	14 53	82 45	88·1	14 51	81 43	87·9	14 49	80 41	87·6	14 46	79 39	87·3	14 43	78 37	87·1	195	345
16	164	15 55	83 46	88·3	15 53	82 43	88·0	15 50	81 41	87·7	15 48	80 39	87·4	15 45	79 36	87·1	15 42	78 34	86·9	196	344
17	163	16 54	83 44	88·2	16 52	82 41	87·9	16 50	81 38	87·6	16 47	80 36	87·3	16 44	79 33	87·0	16 41	78 31	86·7	197	343
18	162	17 54	83 42	88·1	17 52	82 39	87·7	17 49	81 36	87·4	17 46	80 33	87·1	17 43	79 30	86·8	17 39	78 27	86·5	198	342
19	161	18 54	83 39	87·9	18 51	82 36	87·6	18 48	81 33	87·3	18 45	80 29	86·9	18 42	79 26	86·6	18 38	78 23	86·2	199	341
20	160	19 53	83 37	87·8	19 51	82 33	87·5	19 48	81 30	87·1	19 45	80 26	86·7	19 41	79 22	86·4	19 37	78 19	86·0	200	340
21	159	20 53	83 35	87·7	20 50	82 30	87·3	20 47	81 26	86·9	20 44	80 22	86·6	20 40	79 18	86·2	20 36	78 14	85·8	201	339
22	158	21 52	83 32	87·6	21 50	82 27	87·2	21 46	81 23	86·8	21 43	80 18	86·4	21 39	79 14	86·0	21 35	78 10	85·6	202	338
23	157	22 52	83 29	87·5	22 49	82 24	87·0	22 46	81 19	86·6	22 42	80 14	86·2	22 38	79 09	85·8	22 33	78 05	85·4	203	337
24	156	23 52	83 26	87·3	23 49	82 21	86·9	23 45	81 15	86·5	23 41	80 10	86·0	23 37	79 05	85·6	23 32	77 59	85·1	204	336
25	155	24 51	83 23	87·2	24 48	82 17	86·7	24 44	81 11	86·3	24 40	80 05	85·8	24 36	79 00	85·4	24 31	77 54	84·9	205	335
26	154	25 51	83 20	87·1	25 48	82 13	86·6	25 44	81 07	86·1	25 39	80 00	85·6	25 35	78 54	85·2	25 29	77 48	84·7	206	334
27	153	26 50	83 16	87·0	26 47	82 09	86·4	26 43	81 02	85·9	26 38	79 55	85·4	26 33	78 48	84·9	26 28	77 42	84·4	207	333
28	152	27 50	83 13	86·8	27 46	82 05	86·3	27 42	80 57	85·8	27 37	79 50	85·2	27 32	78 42	84·7	27 27	77 35	84·2	208	332
29	151	28 50	83 09	86·7	28 46	82 01	86·1	28 41	80 52	85·6	28 37	79 44	85·0	28 31	78 36	84·5	28 25	77 28	84·0	209	331
30	150	29 49	83 05	86·5	29 45	81 56	86·0	29 41	80 47	85·4	29 36	79 38	84·8	29 30	78 29	84·3	29 24	77 21	83·7	210	330
31	149	30 49	83 01	86·4	30 45	81 51	85·8	30 40	80 41	85·2	30 35	79 32	84·6	30 29	78 23	84·0	30 22	77 13	83·5	211	329
32	148	31 48	82 56	86·3	31 44	81 46	85·6	31 39	80 35	85·0	31 34	79 25	84·4	31 27	78 15	83·8	31 21	77 05	83·2	212	328
33	147	32 48	82 51	86·1	32 43	81 40	85·5	32 38	80 29	84·8	32 33	79 18	84·2	32 26	78 08	83·6	32 19	76 57	82·9	213	327
34	146	33 47	82 46	86·0	33 43	81 35	85·3	33 38	80 23	84·6	33 32	79 11	84·0	33 25	78 00	83·3	33 18	76 48	82·7	214	326
35	145	34 47	82 41	85·8	34 42	81 29	85·1	34 37	80 16	84·4	34 30	79 03	83·7	34 24	77 51	83·1	34 16	76 39	82·4	215	325
36	144	35 46	82 36	85·7	35 41	81 22	84·9	35 36	80 09	84·2	35 29	78 55	83·5	35 22	77 42	82·8	35 14	76 29	82·1	216	324
37	143	36 46	82 30	85·5	36 41	81 16	84·8	36 35	80 01	84·0	36 28	78 47	83·3	36 21	77 33	82·5	36 13	76 19	81·8	217	323
38	142	37 45	82 24	85·3	37 40	81 09	84·6	37 34	79 53	83·8	37 27	78 38	83·0	37 19	77 23	82·2	37 11	76 09	81·5	218	322
39	141	38 45	82 18	85·2	38 39	81 01	84·4	38 33	79 45	83·6	38 26	78 29	82·8	38 18	77 13	82·0	38 09	75 57	81·2	219	321
40	140	39 44	82 11	85·0	39 39	80 54	84·2	39 32	79 36	83·3	39 25	78 19	82·5	39 16	77 02	81·7	39 07	75 46	80·9	220	320
41	139	40 44	82 04	84·8	40 38	80 46	84·0	40 31	79 27	83·1	40 23	78 09	82·3	40 15	76 51	81·4	40 05	75 33	80·6	221	319
42	138	41 43	81 57	84·6	41 37	80 37	83·7	41 30	79 17	82·9	41 22	77 58	82·0	41 13	76 39	81·1	41 04	75 21	80·3	222	318
43	137	42 43	81 49	84·4	42 36	80 28	83·5	42 29	79 07	82·6	42 21	77 47	81·7	42 12	76 27	80·8	42 02	75 07	79·9	223	317
44	136	43 42	81 41	84·2	43 35	80 19	83·3	43 28	78 57	82·3	43 19	77 35	81·4	43 10	76 14	80·5	43 00	74 53	79·6	224	316
45	135	44 41	81 33	84·0	44 34	80 09	83·1	44 27	78 46	82·1	44 18	77 22	81·1	44 08	76 00	80·1	43 57	74 38	79·2	225	315

Lat./A LHA/F	6° A/H	6° B/P	6° Z_1/Z_2	7° A/H	7° B/P	7° Z_1/Z_2	8° A/H	8° B/P	8° Z_1/Z_2	9° A/H	9° B/P	9° Z_1/Z_2	10° A/H	10° B/P	10° Z_1/Z_2	11° A/H	11° B/P	11° Z_1/Z_2	Lat./A LHA
45 135	44 41	81 33	84·0	44 34	80 09	83·1	44 27	78 46	82·1	44 18	77 22	81·1	44 08	76 00	80·1	43 57	74 38	79·2	225 315
46 134	45 41	81 24	83·8	45 34	79 59	82·8	45 26	78 34	81·8	45 16	77 09	80·8	45 06	75 45	79·8	44 55	74 22	78·8	226 314
47 133	46 40	81 14	83·6	46 33	79 48	82·6	46 24	78 21	81·5	46 15	76 56	80·5	46 04	75 30	79·5	45 53	74 05	78·4	227 313
48 132	47 39	81 04	83·4	47 32	79 36	82·3	47 23	78 08	81·2	47 13	76 41	80·1	47 03	75 14	79·1	46 51	73 48	78·0	228 312
49 131	48 38	80 54	83·1	48 31	79 24	82·0	48 22	77 55	80·9	48 12	76 26	79·8	48 01	74 57	78·7	47 48	73 30	77·6	229 311
50 130	49 38	80 43	82·9	49 30	79 11	81·7	49 20	77 40	80·6	49 10	76 09	79·4	48 58	74 40	78·3	48 46	73 10	77·2	230 310
51 129	50 37	80 31	82·6	50 29	78 58	81·4	50 19	77 25	80·2	50 08	75 52	79·1	49 56	74 21	77·9	49 43	72 50	76·7	231 309
52 128	51 36	80 19	82·4	51 28	78 43	81·1	51 18	77 08	79·9	51 06	75 34	78·7	50 54	74 01	77·5	50 40	72 29	76·3	232 308
53 127	52 35	80 06	82·1	52 26	78 28	80·8	52 16	76 51	79·5	52 04	75 15	78·3	51 52	73 40	77·0	51 37	72 06	75·8	233 307
54 126	53 34	79 52	81·8	53 25	78 12	80·5	53 14	76 33	79·2	53 02	74 55	77·8	52 49	73 18	76·6	52 35	71 42	75·3	234 306
55 125	54 33	79 37	81·5	54 24	77 55	80·1	54 13	76 14	78·9	54 00	74 34	77·4	53 47	72 55	76·1	53 31	71 17	74·8	235 305
56 124	55 32	79 21	81·2	55 22	77 37	79·8	55 11	75 54	78·3	54 58	74 11	76·9	54 44	72 30	75·6	54 28	70 50	74·2	236 304
57 123	56 31	79 05	80·9	56 21	77 18	79·4	56 09	75 32	77·9	55 56	73 47	76·5	55 41	72 04	75·0	55 25	70 22	73·6	237 303
58 122	57 30	78 47	80·5	57 19	76 57	79·0	57 07	75 09	77·4	56 53	73 22	75·9	56 38	71 36	74·5	56 21	69 51	73·0	238 302
59 121	58 29	78 28	80·1	58 18	76 35	78·5	58 05	74 44	77·0	57 51	72 54	75·4	57 35	71 06	73·9	57 17	69 19	72·4	239 301
60 120	59 28	78 08	79·7	59 16	76 12	78·1	59 03	74 18	76·4	58 48	72 25	74·8	58 32	70 34	73·3	58 13	68 45	71·7	240 300
61 119	60 26	77 46	79·3	60 14	75 47	77·6	60 01	73 50	75·9	59 45	71 54	74·2	59 28	70 01	72·6	59 09	68 09	71·0	241 299
62 118	61 25	77 23	78·9	61 12	75 21	77·1	60 58	73 20	75·3	60 42	71 21	73·6	60 24	69 25	71·9	60 05	67 31	70·3	242 298
63 117	62 23	76 58	78·4	62 10	74 52	76·5	61 56	72 48	74·7	61 39	70 46	72·9	61 20	68 46	71·2	61 00	66 49	69·5	243 297
64 116	63 22	76 31	77·9	63 08	74 21	76·0	62 53	72 13	74·1	62 35	70 08	72·2	62 16	68 05	70·4	61 55	66 05	68·6	244 296
65 115	64 20	76 02	77·4	64 06	73 48	75·4	63 50	71 36	73·4	63 32	69 27	71·5	63 12	67 21	69·6	62 50	65 18	67·7	245 295
66 114	65 18	75 31	76·8	65 03	73 12	74·7	64 47	70 56	72·6	64 28	68 43	70·6	64 07	66 34	68·7	63 44	64 27	66·8	246 294
67 113	66 16	74 57	76·2	66 01	72 33	74·0	65 43	70 13	71·8	65 23	67 56	69·8	65 02	65 43	67·8	64 38	63 33	65·8	247 293
68 112	67 14	74 20	75·5	66 58	71 51	73·2	66 40	69 26	71·0	66 19	67 05	68·8	65 56	64 48	66·7	65 32	62 35	64·7	248 292
69 111	68 12	73 39	74·8	67 55	71 05	72·4	67 36	68 35	70·1	67 14	66 09	67·8	66 50	63 48	65·7	66 25	61 31	63·6	249 291
70 110	69 09	72 55	74·0	68 51	70 15	71·5	68 31	67 40	69·1	68 09	65 09	66·7	67 44	62 44	64·5	67 17	60 23	62·3	250 290
71 109	70 07	72 06	73·1	69 48	69 20	70·5	69 27	66 39	68·0	69 03	64 03	65·6	68 37	61 34	63·2	68 09	59 10	61·0	251 289
72 108	71 03	71 13	72·2	70 44	68 20	69·4	70 21	65 33	66·8	69 57	62 52	64·3	69 29	60 17	61·9	69 00	57 50	59·6	252 288
73 107	72 00	70 14	71·1	71 39	67 13	68·3	71 16	64 20	65·5	70 50	61 33	62·9	70 21	58 54	60·4	69 50	56 23	58·0	253 287
74 106	72 56	69 08	70·0	72 34	65 59	67·0	72 09	62 59	64·1	71 42	60 07	61·4	71 12	57 24	58·8	70 40	54 49	56·4	254 286
75 105	73 52	67 54	68·7	73 29	64 37	65·5	73 03	61 30	62·6	72 34	58 32	59·7	72 02	55 44	57·1	71 28	53 06	54·5	255 285
76 104	74 48	66 31	67·3	74 23	63 05	64·0	73 55	59 51	60·8	73 24	56 47	57·9	72 51	53 55	55·1	72 16	51 13	52·6	256 284
77 103	75 42	64 57	65·6	75 16	61 22	62·2	74 46	58 00	58·9	74 14	54 51	55·9	73 39	51 55	53·1	73 02	49 10	50·4	257 283
78 102	76 36	63 11	63·8	76 08	59 22	60·2	75 37	55 57	56·8	75 04	52 42	53·6	74 26	49 42	50·8	73 47	46 56	48·1	258 282
79 101	77 29	61 09	61·7	76 59	57 14	57·9	76 26	53 38	54·4	75 49	50 18	51·2	75 11	47 16	48·2	74 30	44 28	45·5	259 281
80 100	78 21	58 49	59·3	77 49	54 44	55·3	77 13	51 01	51·7	76 35	47 38	48·4	75 54	44 34	45·4	75 11	41 47	42·7	260 280
81 99	79 12	56 06	56·6	78 37	51 52	52·4	77 59	48 04	48·7	77 18	44 39	45·4	76 35	41 35	42·4	75 49	38 50	39·7	261 279
82 98	80 01	52 56	53·4	79 23	48 35	49·1	78 42	44 43	45·3	77 59	41 18	41·9	77 13	38 17	39·0	76 26	35 36	36·4	262 278
83 97	80 47	49 13	49·6	80 07	44 47	45·2	79 23	40 56	41·4	78 37	37 35	38·1	77 49	34 39	35·2	76 59	32 05	32·8	263 277
84 96	81 31	44 51	45·2	80 47	40 24	40·8	80 01	36 38	37·1	79 12	33 25	33·9	78 21	30 40	31·2	77 29	28 16	28·8	264 276
85 95	82 12	39 40	39·9	81 24	35 22	35·7	80 34	31 48	32·2	79 43	28 49	29·2	78 50	26 18	26·7	77 56	24 09	24·6	265 275
86 94	82 48	33 34	33·8	81 57	29 36	29·8	81 04	26 24	26·7	80 09	23 46	24·1	79 14	21 35	21·9	78 18	19 44	20·1	266 274
87 93	83 18	26 28	26·6	82 23	23 05	23·3	81 28	20 25	20·6	80 31	18 17	18·5	79 34	16 32	16·8	78 36	15 04	15·4	267 273
88 92	83 41	18 22	18·5	82 43	15 52	16·0	81 45	13 57	14·1	80 47	12 26	12·6	79 48	11 12	11·4	78 49	10 11	10·4	268 272
89 91	83 55	9 26	9·5	82 56	8 05	8·2	81 56	7 05	7·1	80 57	6 17	6·4	79 57	5 39	5·7	78 57	5 08	5·2	269 271
90 90	84 00	0 00	0·0	83 00	0 00	0·0	82 00	0 00	0·0	81 00	0 00	0·0	80 00	0 00	0·0	79 00	0 00	0·0	270 270

N. Lat: for LHA > 180° ... $Z_n = Z$
for LHA < 180° ... $Z_n = 360° - Z$

S. Lat: for LHA > 180° ... $Z_n = 180° - Z$
for LHA < 180° ... $Z_n = 180° + Z$

SIGHT REDUCTION TABLE

B: (−) for 90° < LHA < 270°
Dec:(−) for Lat. contrary name

Z1: same sign as B
Z2: (−) for F > 90°

Lat. / A	12°			13°			14°			15°			16°			17°			Lat. / A
LHA/F	A/H	B/P	Z1/Z2	A/H	B/P	Z1/Z2	A/H	B/P	Z1/Z2	A/H	B/P	Z1/Z2	A/H	B/P	Z1/Z2	A/H	B/P	Z1/Z2	LHA
0 / 180	0 00	78 00	90·0	0 00	77 00	90·0	0 00	76 00	90·0	0 00	75 00	90·0	0 00	74 00	90·0	0 00	73 00	90·0	180 / 360
1 / 179	0 59	78 00	89·8	0 58	77 00	89·8	0 58	76 00	89·8	0 58	75 00	89·7	0 58	74 00	89·7	0 57	73 00	89·7	181 / 359
2 / 178	1 57	78 00	89·6	1 57	77 00	89·5	1 56	76 00	89·5	1 56	75 00	89·5	1 55	74 00	89·4	1 55	73 00	89·4	182 / 358
3 / 177	2 56	77 59	89·4	2 55	76 59	89·3	2 54	75 59	89·3	2 54	74 59	89·2	2 53	73 59	89·2	2 52	72 59	89·1	183 / 357
4 / 176	3 55	77 58	89·2	3 54	76 58	89·1	3 53	75 58	89·0	3 52	74 58	89·0	3 51	73 58	88·9	3 49	72 58	88·8	184 / 356
5 / 175	4 53	77 57	89·0	4 52	76 57	88·9	4 51	75 57	88·8	4 50	74 57	88·7	4 48	73 57	88·6	4 47	72 56	88·5	185 / 355
6 / 174	5 52	77 56	88·7	5 51	76 56	88·6	5 49	75 56	88·5	5 48	74 55	88·4	5 46	73 55	88·3	5 44	72 55	88·2	186 / 354
7 / 173	6 51	77 55	88·5	6 49	76 54	88·4	6 47	75 54	88·3	6 46	74 54	88·2	6 44	73 53	88·1	6 42	72 53	87·9	187 / 353
8 / 172	7 49	77 53	88·3	7 48	76 53	88·2	7 46	75 52	88·1	7 44	74 52	87·9	7 41	73 51	87·8	7 39	72 51	87·6	188 / 352
9 / 171	8 48	77 51	88·1	8 46	76 51	88·0	8 44	75 50	87·8	8 41	74 49	87·7	8 39	73 49	87·5	8 36	72 48	87·3	189 / 351
10 / 170	9 47	77 49	87·9	9 44	76 48	87·7	9 42	75 48	87·6	9 39	74 47	87·4	9 37	73 46	87·2	9 34	72 45	87·0	190 / 350
11 / 169	10 45	77 47	87·7	10 43	76 46	87·5	10 40	75 45	87·3	10 37	74 44	87·1	10 34	73 43	86·9	10 31	72 42	86·7	191 / 349
12 / 168	11 44	77 44	87·5	11 41	76 43	87·3	11 38	75 42	87·1	11 35	74 41	86·9	11 32	73 40	86·6	11 28	72 39	86·4	192 / 348
13 / 167	12 43	77 42	87·3	12 40	76 40	87·0	12 36	75 39	86·8	12 33	74 37	86·6	12 29	73 36	86·4	12 25	72 35	86·1	193 / 347
14 / 166	13 41	77 39	87·0	13 38	76 37	86·8	13 35	75 35	86·5	13 31	74 34	86·3	13 27	73 32	86·1	13 23	72 31	85·8	194 / 346
15 / 165	14 40	77 35	86·8	14 36	76 33	86·6	14 33	75 32	86·3	14 29	74 30	86·0	14 24	73 28	85·8	14 20	72 26	85·5	195 / 345
16 / 164	15 38	77 32	86·6	15 35	76 30	86·3	15 31	75 28	86·0	15 26	74 25	85·8	15 22	73 23	85·5	15 17	72 21	85·2	196 / 344
17 / 163	16 37	77 28	86·4	16 33	76 26	86·1	16 29	75 23	85·8	16 24	74 21	85·5	16 19	73 19	85·2	16 14	72 16	84·9	197 / 343
18 / 162	17 36	77 24	86·1	17 31	76 21	85·8	17 27	75 19	85·5	17 22	74 16	85·2	17 17	73 13	84·9	17 11	72 11	84·6	198 / 342
19 / 161	18 34	77 20	85·9	18 30	76 17	85·6	18 25	75 14	85·2	18 20	74 11	84·9	18 14	73 08	84·6	18 08	72 05	84·3	199 / 341
20 / 160	19 33	77 15	85·7	19 28	76 12	85·3	19 23	75 09	85·0	19 17	74 05	84·6	19 12	73 02	84·3	19 05	71 59	83·9	200 / 340
21 / 159	20 31	77 10	85·4	20 26	76 07	85·1	20 21	75 03	84·7	20 15	73 59	84·3	20 09	72 56	84·0	20 03	71 52	83·6	201 / 339
22 / 158	21 30	77 05	85·2	21 24	76 01	84·8	21 19	74 57	84·4	21 13	73 53	84·0	21 06	72 49	83·6	21 00	71 45	83·3	202 / 338
23 / 157	22 28	77 00	85·0	22 23	75 55	84·5	22 17	74 51	84·1	22 10	73 46	83·7	22 04	72 42	83·3	21 56	71 38	82·9	203 / 337
24 / 156	23 27	76 54	84·7	23 21	75 49	84·3	23 15	74 44	83·9	23 08	73 39	83·4	23 01	72 34	83·0	22 53	71 30	82·6	204 / 336
25 / 155	24 25	76 48	84·5	24 19	75 43	84·0	24 13	74 37	83·6	24 06	73 32	83·1	23 58	72 27	82·7	23 50	71 22	82·2	205 / 335
26 / 154	25 23	76 42	84·2	25 17	75 36	83·7	25 10	74 30	83·3	25 03	73 24	82·8	24 55	72 18	82·3	24 47	71 13	81·9	206 / 334
27 / 153	26 22	76 35	84·0	26 15	75 28	83·5	26 08	74 22	83·0	26 01	73 16	82·5	25 52	72 10	82·0	25 44	71 04	81·5	207 / 333
28 / 152	27 20	76 28	83·7	27 13	75 21	83·2	27 06	74 14	82·7	26 58	73 07	82·2	26 50	72 00	81·7	26 41	70 54	81·2	208 / 332
29 / 151	28 18	76 20	83·4	28 11	75 13	82·9	28 04	74 05	82·4	27 55	72 58	81·8	27 47	71 51	81·3	27 37	70 44	80·8	209 / 331
30 / 150	29 17	76 13	83·2	29 09	75 04	82·6	29 01	73 56	82·0	28 53	72 48	81·5	28 44	71 41	81·0	28 34	70 33	80·4	210 / 330
31 / 149	30 15	76 04	82·9	30 07	74 56	82·3	29 59	73 47	81·7	29 50	72 38	81·2	29 41	71 30	80·6	29 30	70 22	80·0	211 / 329
32 / 148	31 13	75 56	82·6	31 05	74 46	82·0	30 57	73 37	81·4	30 47	72 28	80·8	30 37	71 19	80·2	30 27	70 11	79·6	212 / 328
33 / 147	32 11	75 47	82·3	32 03	74 37	81·7	31 54	73 26	81·1	31 44	72 17	80·5	31 34	71 07	79·9	31 23	69 58	79·2	213 / 327
34 / 146	33 09	75 37	82·0	33 01	74 26	81·4	32 52	73 16	80·7	32 41	72 05	80·1	32 31	70 55	79·5	32 20	69 45	78·8	214 / 326
35 / 145	34 08	75 27	81·7	33 59	74 16	81·0	33 49	73 04	80·4	33 39	71 53	79·7	33 28	70 42	79·1	33 16	69 32	78·4	215 / 325
36 / 144	35 06	75 17	81·4	34 56	74 04	80·7	34 46	72 52	80·0	34 36	71 40	79·4	34 24	70 29	78·7	34 12	69 18	78·0	216 / 324
37 / 143	36 04	75 06	81·1	35 54	73 53	80·4	35 44	72 40	79·7	35 33	71 27	79·0	35 21	70 15	78·3	35 08	69 03	77·6	217 / 323
38 / 142	37 02	74 54	80·8	36 52	73 40	80·0	36 41	72 27	79·3	36 30	71 13	78·6	36 17	70 00	77·8	36 04	68 48	77·1	218 / 322
39 / 141	38 00	74 42	80·4	37 49	73 27	79·7	37 38	72 13	78·9	37 26	70 59	78·2	37 13	69 45	77·4	37 00	68 32	76·7	219 / 321
40 / 140	38 57	74 30	80·1	38 47	73 14	79·3	38 35	71 58	78·5	38 23	70 43	77·7	38 10	69 29	77·0	37 56	68 15	76·2	220 / 320
41 / 139	39 55	74 16	79·8	39 44	72 59	78·9	39 32	71 43	78·1	39 19	70 27	77·3	39 06	69 12	76·5	38 51	67 57	75·7	221 / 319
42 / 138	40 53	74 02	79·4	40 41	72 45	78·5	40 29	71 27	77·7	40 16	70 10	76·9	40 02	68 54	76·1	39 47	67 38	75·3	222 / 318
43 / 137	41 51	73 48	79·0	41 39	72 29	78·2	41 26	71 11	77·3	41 12	69 53	76·4	40 58	68 35	75·6	40 42	67 19	74·7	223 / 317
44 / 136	42 48	73 32	78·6	42 36	72 12	77·7	42 23	70 53	76·9	42 09	69 34	76·0	41 54	68 16	75·1	41 38	66 58	74·2	224 / 316
45 / 135	43 46	73 16	78·3	43 33	71 55	77·3	43 19	70 35	76·4	43 05	69 15	75·5	42 49	67 56	74·6	42 33	66 37	73·7	225 / 315

Lat. / A		12°			13°			14°			15°			16°			17°			Lat. / A	
LHA/F		A/H	B/P	Z_1/Z_2	A/H	B/P	Z_1/Z_2	A/H	B/P	Z_1/Z_2	A/H	B/P	Z_1/Z_2	A/H	B/P	Z_1/Z_2	A/H	B/P	Z_1/Z_2	LHA	
45	135	43 46	73 16	78·3	43 33	71 55	77·3	43 19	70 35	76·4	43 05	69 15	75·5	42 49	67 56	74·6	42 33	66 37	73·7	225	315
46	134	44 43	72 59	77·8	44 30	71 37	76·9	44 16	70 15	75·9	44 01	68 54	75·0	43 45	67 34	74·1	43 28	66 15	73·2	226	314
47	133	45 40	72 41	77·4	45 27	71 18	76·4	45 12	69 55	75·5	44 57	68 33	74·5	44 40	67 12	73·5	44 23	65 51	72·6	227	313
48	132	46 38	72 23	77·0	46 24	70 58	76·0	46 09	69 34	75·0	45 53	68 11	74·0	45 35	66 48	73·0	45 17	65 27	72·0	228	312
49	131	47 35	72 03	76·5	47 20	70 37	75·5	47 05	69 11	74·4	46 48	67 47	73·4	46 30	66 23	72·4	46 12	65 01	71·4	229	311
50	130	48 32	71 42	76·1	48 17	70 15	75·0	48 01	68 48	73·9	47 44	67 22	72·9	47 25	65 58	71·8	47 06	64 34	70·8	230	310
51	129	49 29	71 20	75·6	49 13	69 51	74·5	48 57	68 23	73·4	48 39	66 56	72·3	48 20	65 30	71·2	48 00	64 05	70·1	231	309
52	128	50 25	70 57	75·1	50 09	69 27	73·9	49 52	67 57	72·8	49 34	66 29	71·7	49 15	65 02	70·6	48 54	63 35	69·5	232	308
53	127	51 22	70 33	74·6	51 06	69 01	73·4	50 48	67 30	72·2	50 29	66 00	71·0	50 09	64 31	69·9	49 48	63 04	68·8	233	307
54	126	52 19	70 07	74·0	52 02	68 33	72·8	51 43	67 01	71·6	51 24	65 30	70·4	51 03	64 00	69·2	50 41	62 31	68·1	234	306
55	125	53 15	69 40	73·5	52 57	68 04	72·2	52 38	66 30	70·9	52 18	64 58	69·7	51 57	63 26	68·5	51 34	61 56	67·3	235	305
56	124	54 11	69 11	72·9	53 53	67 34	71·6	53 33	65 58	70·3	53 12	64 24	69·0	52 50	62 51	67·8	52 27	61 20	66·6	236	304
57	123	55 07	68 41	72·2	54 48	67 02	70·9	54 28	65 24	69·6	54 06	63 48	68·3	53 43	62 14	67·0	53 19	60 42	65·8	237	303
58	122	56 03	68 09	71·6	55 43	66 28	70·2	55 22	64 48	68·8	55 00	63 11	67·5	54 36	61 35	66·2	54 12	60 03	64·9	238	302
59	121	56 59	67 34	70·9	56 38	65 51	69·5	56 16	64 10	68·1	55 53	62 31	66·7	55 29	60 54	65·4	55 03	59 18	64·1	239	301
60	120	57 54	66 58	70·2	57 33	65 13	68·7	57 10	63 30	67·3	56 46	61 49	65·9	56 21	60 10	64·5	55 55	58 33	63·1	240	300
61	119	58 49	66 20	69·4	58 27	64 32	67·9	58 04	62 47	66·4	57 39	61 04	65·0	57 13	59 24	63·6	56 46	57 46	62·2	241	299
62	118	59 44	65 38	68·6	59 21	63 49	67·1	58 57	62 02	65·5	58 31	60 17	64·0	58 05	58 35	62·6	57 36	56 56	61·2	242	298
63	117	60 38	64 55	67·8	60 15	63 03	66·2	59 50	61 13	64·6	59 23	59 27	63·1	58 55	57 43	61·6	58 26	56 03	60·2	243	297
64	116	61 32	64 08	66·9	61 08	62 14	65·2	60 42	60 22	63·6	60 15	58 34	62·0	59 46	56 49	60·5	59 16	55 06	59·1	244	296
65	115	62 26	63 18	66·0	62 01	61 21	64·2	61 34	59 28	62·6	61 06	57 37	61·0	60 36	55 51	59·4	60 05	54 04	57·9	245	295
66	114	63 20	62 25	65·0	62 53	60 25	63·2	62 26	58 30	61·5	61 56	56 37	59·8	61 25	54 49	58·2	60 53	53 04	56·7	246	294
67	113	64 13	61 27	63·9	63 45	59 25	62·1	63 16	57 27	60·3	62 46	55 34	58·6	62 14	53 44	57·0	61 41	51 57	55·4	247	293
68	112	65 05	60 26	62·8	64 37	58 21	60·9	64 07	56 21	59·1	63 35	54 25	57·4	63 02	52 34	55·7	62 27	50 47	54·1	248	292
69	111	65 57	59 20	61·6	65 27	57 13	59·6	64 56	55 10	57·8	64 23	53 13	56·0	63 49	51 20	54·3	63 14	49 32	52·7	249	291
70	110	66 48	58 08	60·3	66 18	55 55	58·3	65 45	53 55	56·4	65 11	51 55	54·6	64 36	50 01	52·9	63 59	48 12	51·2	250	290
71	109	67 39	56 52	58·9	67 07	54 40	56·8	66 33	52 33	54·9	65 58	50 33	53·1	65 21	48 38	51·3	64 43	46 48	49·7	251	289
72	108	68 28	55 29	57·4	67 55	53 14	55·3	67 20	51 06	53·3	66 44	49 04	51·5	66 06	47 08	49·7	65 26	45 18	48·0	252	288
73	107	69 18	53 59	55·8	68 43	51 42	53·7	68 07	49 33	51·6	67 29	47 29	49·8	66 49	45 33	48·0	66 08	43 43	46·3	253	287
74	106	70 06	52 22	54·1	69 30	50 03	51·9	68 52	47 52	49·8	68 12	45 49	47·9	67 31	43 52	46·1	66 49	42 02	44·4	254	286
75	105	70 53	50 36	52·2	70 15	48 16	50·0	69 36	46 04	47·9	68 55	44 00	46·0	68 12	42 04	44·2	67 29	40 15	42·5	255	285
76	104	71 38	48 42	50·2	70 59	46 20	47·9	70 18	44 08	45·9	69 36	42 05	43·9	68 52	40 09	42·1	68 07	38 21	40·5	256	284
77	103	72 23	46 37	48·0	71 42	44 15	45·7	70 59	42 03	43·7	70 15	40 01	41·7	69 30	38 07	39·9	68 43	36 13	38·3	257	283
78	102	73 06	44 22	45·6	72 23	42 00	43·4	71 38	39 49	41·3	70 53	37 49	39·4	70 06	35 57	37·6	69 18	34 13	36·0	258	282
79	101	73 47	41 55	43·1	73 02	39 34	40·8	72 16	37 26	38·8	71 28	35 27	36·9	70 40	33 38	35·2	69 50	31 58	33·6	259	281
80	100	74 26	39 15	40·3	73 39	36 57	38·1	72 51	34 51	36·1	72 02	32 57	34·3	71 12	31 12	32·6	70 21	29 36	31·1	260	280
81	99	75 02	36 21	37·3	74 14	34 07	35·1	73 24	32 06	33·2	72 34	30 17	31·5	71 42	28 37	29·9	70 50	27 06	28·4	261	279
82	98	75 37	33 13	34·1	74 46	31 05	32·0	73 55	29 11	30·2	73 03	27 27	28·5	72 09	25 53	27·0	71 16	24 29	25·7	262	278
83	97	76 08	29 50	30·6	75 16	27 50	28·6	74 23	26 03	26·9	73 29	24 27	25·4	72 34	23 02	24·0	71 39	21 44	22·8	263	277
84	96	76 36	26 11	26·8	75 42	24 22	25·0	74 48	22 45	23·5	73 52	21 19	22·1	72 56	20 02	20·9	72 00	18 53	19·8	264	276
85	95	77 01	22 18	22·8	76 05	20 41	21·3	75 09	19 16	19·9	74 12	18 01	18·7	73 15	16 54	17·6	72 18	15 55	16·7	265	275
86	94	77 22	18 10	18·6	76 25	16 49	17·3	75 27	15 38	16·1	74 29	14 36	15·1	73 31	13 40	14·2	72 33	12 51	13·5	266	274
87	93	77 38	13 50	14·1	76 40	12 46	13·1	75 41	11 51	12·2	74 43	11 03	11·4	73 44	10 21	10·8	72 45	9 43	10·2	267	273
88	92	77 50	9 19	9·5	76 51	8 36	8·8	75 52	7 58	8·2	74 52	7 25	7·7	73 53	6 56	7·2	72 53	6 31	6·8	268	272
89	91	77 58	4 42	4·8	76 58	4 19	4·4	75 58	4 00	4·1	74 58	3 44	3·9	73 58	3 29	3·6	72 58	3 16	3·4	269	271
90	90	78 00	0 00	0·0	77 00	0 00	0·0	76 00	0 00	0·0	75 00	0 00	0·0	74 00	0 00	0·0	73 00	0 00	0·0	270	270

N. Lat.: for LHA > 180° … $Z_n = Z$
for LHA < 180° … $Z_n = 360° - Z$

S. Lat.: for LHA > 180° … $Z_n = 180° - Z$
for LHA < 180° … $Z_n = 180° + Z$

SIGHT REDUCTION TABLE

B: (−) for 90° < LHA < 270°
Dec:(−) for Lat. contrary name

Z₁: same sign as B
Z₂: (−) for F > 90°

Lat./A LHA/F	18° A/H	18° B/P	18° Z₁/Z₂	19° A/H	19° B/P	19° Z₁/Z₂	20° A/H	20° B/P	20° Z₁/Z₂	21° A/H	21° B/P	21° Z₁/Z₂	22° A/H	22° B/P	22° Z₁/Z₂	23° A/H	23° B/P	23° Z₁/Z₂	Lat./A LHA
0 / 180	0 00	72 00	90·0	0 00	71 00	90·0	0 00	70 00	90·0	0 00	69 00	90·0	0 00	68 00	90·0	0 00	67 00	90·0	180 / 360
1 / 179	0 57	72 00	89·7	0 57	71 00	89·7	0 56	70 00	89·7	0 56	69 00	89·6	0 56	68 00	89·6	0 55	67 00	89·6	181 / 359
2 / 178	1 54	71 59	89·4	1 53	70 59	89·3	1 53	69 59	89·3	1 52	68 59	89·3	1 51	67 59	89·2	1 50	66 59	89·2	182 / 358
3 / 177	2 51	71 59	89·1	2 50	70 59	89·0	2 49	69 58	89·0	2 48	68 58	88·9	2 47	67 58	88·9	2 46	66 58	88·8	183 / 357
4 / 176	3 48	71 58	88·8	3 47	70 57	88·7	3 46	69 57	88·6	3 44	68 57	88·6	3 42	67 57	88·5	3 41	66 57	88·4	184 / 356
5 / 175	4 45	71 56	88·5	4 44	70 56	88·4	4 42	69 56	88·3	4 40	68 56	88·2	4 38	67 55	88·1	4 36	66 55	88·0	185 / 355
6 / 174	5 42	71 54	88·1	5 40	70 54	88·0	5 38	69 54	87·9	5 36	68 54	87·8	5 34	67 53	87·7	5 31	66 53	87·6	186 / 354
7 / 173	6 39	71 52	87·8	6 37	70 52	87·7	6 35	69 52	87·6	6 32	68 51	87·5	6 29	67 51	87·3	6 26	66 51	87·3	187 / 353
8 / 172	7 36	71 50	87·5	7 34	70 50	87·3	7 31	69 49	87·2	7 28	68 49	87·1	7 25	67 48	87·0	7 22	66 48	86·9	188 / 352
9 / 171	8 33	71 47	87·2	8 30	70 47	87·0	8 27	69 46	86·9	8 24	68 46	86·8	8 20	67 45	86·6	8 17	66 45	86·5	189 / 351
10 / 170	9 30	71 44	86·9	9 27	70 44	86·7	9 23	69 43	86·5	9 20	68 42	86·4	9 16	67 42	86·2	9 12	66 41	86·1	190 / 350
11 / 169	10 27	71 41	86·6	10 24	70 40	86·4	10 20	69 39	86·2	10 16	68 39	86·0	10 11	67 38	85·8	10 07	66 37	85·7	191 / 349
12 / 168	11 24	71 37	86·2	11 20	70 36	86·0	11 16	69 35	85·8	11 12	68 34	85·6	11 07	67 33	85·4	11 02	66 32	85·3	192 / 348
13 / 167	12 21	71 33	85·9	12 17	70 32	85·7	12 12	69 31	85·5	12 07	68 30	85·3	12 02	67 29	85·1	11 57	66 28	84·8	193 / 347
14 / 166	13 18	71 29	85·6	13 13	70 28	85·3	13 08	69 26	85·1	13 03	68 25	84·9	12 58	67 24	84·7	12 52	66 22	84·4	194 / 346
15 / 165	14 15	71 24	85·3	14 10	70 23	85·0	14 05	69 21	84·8	13 59	68 20	84·5	13 53	67 18	84·3	13 47	66 17	84·0	195 / 345
16 / 164	15 12	71 19	84·9	15 06	70 18	84·7	15 01	69 16	84·4	14 55	68 14	84·1	14 48	67 12	83·9	14 42	66 10	83·6	196 / 344
17 / 163	16 09	71 14	84·6	16 03	70 12	84·3	15 57	69 10	84·0	15 50	68 08	83·7	15 44	67 06	83·5	15 37	66 04	83·2	197 / 343
18 / 162	17 05	71 08	84·3	16 59	70 06	84·0	16 53	69 03	83·7	16 46	68 01	83·4	16 39	66 59	83·1	16 32	65 57	82·8	198 / 342
19 / 161	18 02	71 02	83·9	17 56	69 59	83·6	17 49	68 57	83·3	17 42	67 54	83·0	17 34	66 52	82·7	17 26	65 49	82·3	199 / 341
20 / 160	18 59	70 56	83·6	18 52	69 53	83·3	18 45	68 50	82·9	18 37	67 47	82·6	18 29	66 44	82·2	18 21	65 41	81·9	200 / 340
21 / 159	19 56	70 49	83·2	19 48	69 45	82·9	19 41	68 42	82·5	19 33	67 39	82·2	19 24	66 36	81·8	19 16	65 33	81·5	201 / 339
22 / 158	20 52	70 41	82·9	20 45	69 38	82·5	20 37	68 34	82·1	20 28	67 31	81·8	20 19	66 27	81·4	20 10	65 24	81·0	202 / 338
23 / 157	21 49	70 33	82·5	21 41	69 29	82·1	21 32	68 26	81·7	21 24	67 22	81·4	21 14	66 18	81·0	21 05	65 15	80·6	203 / 337
24 / 156	22 45	70 25	82·2	22 37	69 21	81·8	22 28	68 17	81·3	22 19	67 12	80·9	22 09	66 09	80·5	21 59	65 05	80·1	204 / 336
25 / 155	23 42	70 17	81·8	23 33	69 12	81·4	23 24	68 07	80·9	23 14	67 03	80·5	23 04	65 58	80·1	22 54	64 54	79·7	205 / 335
26 / 154	24 38	70 07	81·4	24 29	69 02	81·0	24 20	67 57	80·5	24 09	66 52	80·1	23 59	65 48	79·6	23 48	64 43	79·2	206 / 334
27 / 153	25 35	69 58	81·1	25 25	68 52	80·6	25 15	67 47	80·1	25 05	66 42	79·7	24 54	65 36	79·2	24 42	64 31	78·7	207 / 333
28 / 152	26 31	69 48	80·7	26 21	68 42	80·2	26 11	67 36	79·7	26 00	66 30	79·2	25 48	65 25	78·7	25 36	64 19	78·3	208 / 332
29 / 151	27 27	69 37	80·3	27 17	68 31	79·8	27 06	67 24	79·3	26 55	66 18	78·8	26 43	65 12	78·3	26 30	64 07	77·8	209 / 331
30 / 150	28 24	69 26	79·9	28 13	68 19	79·4	28 01	67 12	78·8	27 50	66 06	78·3	27 37	64 59	77·8	27 24	63 53	77·3	210 / 330
31 / 149	29 20	69 14	79·5	29 09	68 07	78·9	28 57	67 00	78·4	28 44	65 53	77·8	28 31	64 46	77·3	28 18	63 39	76·8	211 / 329
32 / 148	30 16	69 02	79·1	30 04	67 54	78·5	29 52	66 46	77·9	29 39	65 40	77·4	29 26	64 32	76·8	29 12	63 25	76·3	212 / 328
33 / 147	31 12	68 49	78·7	31 00	67 41	78·1	30 47	66 32	77·5	30 34	65 24	76·9	30 20	64 17	76·3	30 05	63 09	75·8	213 / 327
34 / 146	32 08	68 36	78·2	31 55	67 27	77·6	31 42	66 18	77·0	31 28	65 09	76·4	31 14	64 01	75·8	30 59	62 53	75·2	214 / 326
35 / 145	33 04	68 22	77·8	32 51	67 12	77·2	32 37	66 03	76·5	32 23	64 54	75·9	32 08	63 45	75·3	31 52	62 36	74·7	215 / 325
36 / 144	33 59	68 07	77·3	33 46	66 57	76·7	33 32	65 47	76·0	33 17	64 37	75·4	33 01	63 28	74·8	32 45	62 19	74·2	216 / 324
37 / 143	34 55	67 52	76·9	34 41	66 41	76·2	34 26	65 30	75·5	34 11	64 20	74·9	33 55	63 10	74·2	33 38	62 01	73·6	217 / 323
38 / 142	35 50	67 36	76·4	35 36	66 24	75·7	35 21	65 13	75·0	35 05	64 02	74·4	34 48	62 51	73·7	34 31	61 41	73·0	218 / 322
39 / 141	36 46	67 19	76·0	36 31	66 06	75·2	36 15	64 54	74·5	35 59	63 43	73·8	35 42	62 32	73·1	35 24	61 21	72·4	219 / 321
40 / 140	37 41	67 01	75·5	37 26	65 48	74·7	37 10	64 35	74·0	36 52	63 23	73·3	36 35	62 12	72·6	36 17	61 01	71·8	220 / 320
41 / 139	38 36	66 42	75·0	38 20	65 29	74·2	38 04	64 15	73·4	37 46	63 02	72·7	37 28	61 50	72·0	37 09	60 39	71·2	221 / 319
42 / 138	39 31	66 23	74·5	39 15	65 08	73·7	38 58	63 54	72·9	38 40	62 41	72·1	38 21	61 28	71·4	38 01	60 16	70·6	222 / 318
43 / 137	40 26	66 03	73·9	40 09	64 47	73·1	39 51	63 33	72·3	39 33	62 18	71·5	39 13	61 05	70·7	38 53	59 52	70·0	223 / 317
44 / 136	41 21	65 42	73·4	41 03	64 25	72·5	40 45	63 10	71·7	40 26	61 55	70·9	40 06	60 41	70·1	39 45	59 27	69·3	224 / 316
45 / 135	42 16	65 19	72·8	41 57	64 02	72·0	41 38	62 46	71·1	41 19	61 30	70·3	40 58	60 15	69·5	40 37	59 01	68·7	225 / 315

Lat./A		18°			19°			20°			21°			22°			23°			Lat./A	
LHA/F		A/H	B/P	Z_1/Z_2	A/H	B/P	Z_1/Z_2	A/H	B/P	Z_1/Z_2	A/H	B/P	Z_1/Z_2	A/H	B/P	Z_1/Z_2	A/H	B/P	Z_1/Z_2	LHA	
45	135	42 16	65 19	72.8	41 57	64 02	72.0	41 38	62 46	71.1	41 19	61 30	70.3	40 58	60 15	69.5	40 37	59 01	68.7	225	315
46	134	43 10	64 56	72.3	42 51	63 38	71.4	42 32	62 21	70.5	42 11	61 05	69.6	41 50	59 49	68.8	41 28	58 34	68.0	226	314
47	133	44 04	64 32	71.7	43 45	63 15	70.8	43 25	61 55	69.9	43 04	60 38	69.0	42 42	59 21	68.1	42 19	58 06	67.3	227	313
48	132	44 58	64 06	71.1	44 38	62 46	70.1	44 18	61 27	69.2	43 56	60 11	68.3	43 33	58 53	67.4	43 10	57 37	66.5	228	312
49	131	45 52	63 39	70.4	45 32	62 18	69.5	45 10	60 59	68.5	44 48	59 40	67.6	44 24	58 22	66.7	44 00	57 06	65.8	229	311
50	130	46 46	63 11	69.8	46 25	61 49	68.8	46 03	60 29	67.8	45 39	59 09	66.9	45 15	57 51	65.9	44 50	56 34	65.0	230	310
51	129	47 39	62 42	69.1	47 17	61 19	68.1	46 55	59 57	67.1	46 31	58 37	66.1	46 06	57 18	65.2	45 40	56 00	64.2	231	309
52	128	48 33	62 11	68.4	48 10	60 47	67.4	47 46	59 25	66.4	47 22	58 05	65.4	46 56	56 44	64.4	46 30	55 25	63.4	232	308
53	127	49 25	61 38	67.7	49 02	60 13	66.6	48 38	58 50	65.6	48 13	57 28	64.6	47 46	56 07	63.6	47 19	54 48	62.6	233	307
54	126	50 18	61 04	67.0	49 54	59 38	65.9	49 29	58 14	64.8	49 03	56 51	63.7	48 36	55 30	62.7	48 08	54 10	61.7	234	306
55	125	51 10	60 28	66.2	50 46	59 01	65.1	50 20	57 36	64.0	49 53	56 12	62.9	49 25	54 50	61.9	48 56	53 30	60.8	235	305
56	124	52 03	59 50	65.4	51 37	58 23	64.2	51 10	56 56	63.1	50 43	55 32	62.0	50 14	54 09	61.0	49 44	52 48	59.9	236	304
57	123	52 54	59 11	64.6	52 28	57 42	63.4	52 00	56 15	62.2	51 32	54 49	61.1	51 02	53 26	60.0	50 32	52 04	59.0	237	303
58	122	53 46	58 29	63.7	53 18	56 59	62.5	52 50	55 31	61.3	52 21	54 05	60.2	51 50	52 41	59.1	51 19	51 18	58.0	238	302
59	121	54 37	57 45	62.8	54 08	56 14	61.5	53 39	54 45	60.4	53 09	53 18	59.2	52 38	51 53	58.1	52 06	50 30	57.0	239	301
60	120	55 27	56 59	61.8	54 58	55 27	60.6	54 28	53 57	59.4	53 57	52 30	58.2	53 25	51 04	57.0	52 52	49 40	55.9	240	300
61	119	56 17	56 10	60.9	55 47	54 37	59.6	55 16	53 06	58.3	54 44	51 38	57.1	54 11	50 12	55.9	53 37	48 48	54.8	241	299
62	118	57 07	55 19	59.8	56 36	53 45	58.5	56 04	52 13	57.2	55 31	50 44	56.0	54 57	49 17	54.8	54 22	47 53	53.7	242	298
63	117	57 56	54 25	58.8	57 24	52 49	57.4	56 51	51 17	56.1	56 17	49 47	54.9	55 42	48 20	53.7	55 06	46 55	52.5	243	297
64	116	58 44	53 27	57.6	58 12	51 51	56.3	57 38	50 18	55.0	57 03	48 48	53.7	56 27	47 20	52.5	55 50	45 55	51.3	244	296
65	115	59 32	52 27	56.5	58 58	50 50	55.1	58 24	49 16	53.7	57 47	47 45	52.5	57 10	46 17	51.2	56 32	44 52	50.0	245	295
66	114	60 19	51 23	55.2	59 45	49 45	53.8	59 09	48 11	52.5	58 32	46 39	51.2	57 53	45 11	49.9	57 14	43 47	48.7	246	294
67	113	61 06	50 15	53.9	60 30	48 37	52.5	59 53	47 02	51.1	59 15	45 30	49.8	58 36	44 02	48.6	57 55	42 38	47.4	247	293
68	112	61 52	49 04	52.6	61 15	47 25	51.1	60 36	45 50	49.8	59 57	44 18	48.4	59 17	42 50	47.2	58 36	41 26	46.0	248	292
69	111	62 37	47 48	51.2	61 58	46 09	49.7	61 19	44 33	48.3	60 39	43 02	47.0	59 57	41 34	45.7	59 15	40 10	44.5	249	291
70	110	63 21	46 28	49.7	62 41	44 48	48.2	62 01	43 13	46.8	61 19	41 42	45.4	60 36	40 15	44.1	59 53	38 52	43.0	250	290
71	109	64 04	45 03	48.1	63 23	43 24	46.6	62 41	41 49	45.2	61 58	40 18	43.9	61 15	38 52	42.6	60 30	37 29	41.4	251	289
72	108	64 45	43 34	46.4	64 04	41 54	44.9	63 21	40 20	43.5	62 37	38 50	42.2	61 52	37 25	40.9	61 06	36 03	39.7	252	288
73	107	65 26	41 59	44.7	64 44	40 20	43.2	63 59	38 46	41.8	63 14	37 18	40.5	62 27	35 53	39.2	61 41	34 34	38.0	253	287
74	106	66 06	40 19	42.9	65 21	38 41	41.4	64 36	37 08	40.0	63 49	35 41	38.7	63 02	34 18	37.4	62 14	33 00	36.3	254	286
75	105	66 44	38 32	40.9	65 58	36 56	39.5	65 11	35 25	38.1	64 23	33 59	36.8	63 35	32 39	35.6	62 47	31 23	34.4	255	285
76	104	67 20	36 40	38.9	66 33	35 05	37.4	65 45	33 37	36.1	64 56	32 13	34.8	64 07	30 55	33.6	63 16	29 41	32.5	256	284
77	103	67 55	34 42	36.8	67 07	33 09	35.3	66 18	31 43	34.0	65 27	30 22	32.8	64 37	29 06	31.6	63 45	27 55	30.6	257	283
78	102	68 29	32 37	34.5	67 39	31 07	33.1	66 48	29 44	31.9	65 57	28 26	30.7	65 05	27 14	29.4	64 13	26 06	28.5	258	282
79	101	69 00	30 25	32.2	68 09	29 00	30.8	67 17	27 40	29.6	66 25	26 26	28.5	65 32	25 17	27.4	64 38	24 12	26.4	259	281
80	100	69 29	28 07	29.7	68 37	26 46	28.4	67 44	25 30	27.3	66 50	24 20	26.2	65 56	23 15	25.2	65 02	22 15	24.3	260	280
81	99	69 57	25 43	27.1	69 03	24 26	25.9	68 09	23 15	24.8	67 14	22 10	23.8	66 19	21 10	22.9	65 23	20 14	22.1	261	279
82	98	70 21	23 11	24.5	69 27	22 00	23.3	68 31	20 56	22.3	67 36	19 56	21.4	66 40	19 00	20.6	65 43	18 09	19.8	262	278
83	97	70 44	20 34	21.7	69 48	19 29	20.7	68 51	18 31	19.7	67 55	17 37	18.9	66 58	16 47	18.1	66 01	16 01	17.4	263	277
84	96	71 03	17 50	18.8	70 07	16 53	17.9	69 09	16 01	17.1	68 12	15 14	16.3	67 14	14 30	15.7	66 16	13 51	15.1	264	276
85	95	71 20	15 01	15.8	70 23	14 12	15.0	69 25	13 28	14.3	68 26	12 48	13.7	67 28	12 10	13.1	66 29	11 36	12.6	265	275
86	94	71 35	12 07	12.8	70 36	11 27	12.1	69 37	10 51	11.6	68 38	10 18	11.0	67 39	9 48	10.6	66 40	9 20	10.1	266	274
87	93	71 46	9 09	9.6	70 46	8 39	9.1	69 47	8 11	8.7	68 48	7 46	8.3	67 48	7 23	8.0	66 49	7 02	7.6	267	273
88	92	71 54	6 08	6.4	70 54	5 47	6.1	69 54	5 29	5.8	68 55	5 12	5.6	67 55	4 56	5.3	66 55	4 42	5.1	268	272
89	91	71 58	3 04	3.2	70 58	2 54	3.1	69 59	2 45	2.9	68 59	2 36	2.8	67 59	2 28	2.7	66 59	2 21	2.6	269	271
90	90	72 00	0 00	0.0	71 00	0 00	0.0	70 00	0 00	0.0	69 00	0 00	0.0	68 00	0 00	0.0	67 00	0 00	0.0	270	270

N. Lat.: for LHA > 180° ... Z_n = Z / for LHA < 180° ... Z_n = 360° − Z

S. Lat.: for LHA > 180° ... Z_n = 180° − Z / for LHA < 180° ... Z_n = 180° + Z

SIGHT REDUCTION TABLE

B: (−) for 90° < LHA < 270°
Dec:(−) for Lat. contrary name

Z₁: same sign as B
Z₂:(−) for F > 90°

Lat./A LHA/F	24° A/H	B/P	Z₁/Z₂	25° A/H	B/P	Z₁/Z₂	26° A/H	B/P	Z₁/Z₂	27° A/H	B/P	Z₁/Z₂	28° A/H	B/P	Z₁/Z₂	29° A/H	B/P	Z₁/Z₂	Lat./A LHA
0 / 180	0 00	66 00	90·0	0 00	65 00	90·0	0 00	64 00	90·0	0 00	63 00	90·0	0 00	62 00	90·0	0 00	61 00	90·0	180 / 360
1 / 179	0 55	66 00	89·6	0 54	65 00	89·6	0 54	64 00	89·6	0 53	63 00	89·5	0 53	62 00	89·5	0 52	61 00	89·5	181 / 359
2 / 178	1 50	65 59	89·2	1 49	64 59	89·2	1 48	63 59	89·1	1 47	62 59	89·1	1 46	61 59	89·1	1 45	60 59	89·0	182 / 358
3 / 177	2 44	65 58	88·8	2 43	64 58	88·7	2 42	63 58	88·7	2 40	62 58	88·6	2 39	61 58	88·6	2 37	60 58	88·5	183 / 357
4 / 176	3 39	65 57	88·4	3 37	64 57	88·3	3 36	63 57	88·3	3 34	62 57	88·2	3 32	61 57	88·1	3 30	60 58	88·1	184 / 356
5 / 175	4 34	65 55	88·0	4 32	64 55	87·9	4 30	63 55	87·8	4 27	62 55	87·7	4 25	61 55	87·6	4 22	60 54	87·6	185 / 355
6 / 174	5 29	65 53	87·6	5 26	64 53	87·5	5 23	63 53	87·4	5 21	62 52	87·3	5 18	61 52	87·2	5 15	60 52	87·1	186 / 354
7 / 173	6 24	65 50	87·1	6 20	64 50	87·0	6 17	63 50	86·9	6 14	62 50	86·8	6 11	61 49	86·7	6 07	60 49	86·6	187 / 353
8 / 172	7 18	65 47	86·7	7 15	64 47	86·6	7 11	63 47	86·5	7 07	62 46	86·3	7 04	61 46	86·2	6 59	60 46	86·1	188 / 352
9 / 171	8 13	65 44	86·3	8 09	64 44	86·2	8 05	63 43	86·0	8 01	62 43	85·9	7 56	61 42	85·7	7 52	60 42	85·6	189 / 351
10 / 170	9 08	65 40	85·9	9 03	64 40	85·7	8 59	63 39	85·6	8 54	62 39	85·4	8 49	61 38	85·3	8 44	60 38	85·1	190 / 350
11 / 169	10 02	65 36	85·5	9 57	64 35	85·3	9 52	63 35	85·1	9 47	62 34	85·0	9 42	61 33	84·8	9 36	60 33	84·6	191 / 349
12 / 168	10 57	65 32	85·1	10 52	64 31	84·9	10 46	63 30	84·7	10 41	62 29	84·5	10 35	61 28	84·3	10 29	60 28	84·1	192 / 348
13 / 167	11 52	65 27	84·6	11 46	64 26	84·4	11 40	63 25	84·2	11 34	62 23	84·0	11 27	61 23	83·8	11 21	60 22	83·6	193 / 347
14 / 166	12 46	65 21	84·2	12 40	64 20	84·0	12 34	63 19	83·8	12 27	62 18	83·5	12 20	61 17	83·3	12 13	60 16	83·1	194 / 346
15 / 165	13 41	65 15	83·8	13 34	64 14	83·5	13 27	63 13	83·3	13 20	62 11	83·1	13 13	61 10	82·8	13 05	60 09	82·6	195 / 345
16 / 164	14 35	65 09	83·3	14 28	64 07	83·1	14 21	63 06	82·8	14 13	62 04	82·6	14 05	61 03	82·3	13 57	60 02	82·1	196 / 344
17 / 163	15 29	65 02	82·9	15 22	64 00	82·6	15 14	62 59	82·4	15 06	61 57	82·1	14 58	60 56	81·8	14 49	59 54	81·6	197 / 343
18 / 162	16 24	64 55	82·5	16 16	63 53	82·2	16 08	62 51	81·9	15 59	61 49	81·6	15 50	60 47	81·3	15 41	59 46	81·0	198 / 342
19 / 161	17 18	64 47	82·0	17 10	63 45	81·7	17 01	62 43	81·4	16 52	61 41	81·1	16 42	60 39	80·8	16 33	59 37	80·5	199 / 341
20 / 160	18 12	64 39	81·6	18 03	63 36	81·3	17 54	62 34	80·9	17 45	61 32	80·6	17 35	60 30	80·3	17 24	59 28	80·0	200 / 340
21 / 159	19 07	64 30	81·1	18 57	63 28	80·8	18 47	62 25	80·4	18 37	61 23	80·1	18 27	60 20	79·8	18 16	59 18	79·5	201 / 339
22 / 158	20 01	64 21	80·7	19 51	63 18	80·3	19 41	62 15	80·0	19 30	61 13	79·6	19 19	60 10	79·3	19 08	59 08	78·9	202 / 338
23 / 157	20 55	64 11	80·2	20 44	63 08	79·8	20 34	62 05	79·5	20 22	61 02	79·1	20 11	59 59	78·7	19 59	58 57	78·4	203 / 337
24 / 156	21 49	64 01	79·7	21 38	62 58	79·3	21 27	61 54	79·0	21 15	60 51	78·6	21 03	59 48	78·2	20 50	58 45	77·8	204 / 336
25 / 155	22 43	63 50	79·3	22 31	62 46	78·9	22 19	61 43	78·4	22 07	60 39	78·0	21 55	59 36	77·7	21 42	58 33	77·3	205 / 335
26 / 154	23 36	63 39	78·8	23 25	62 35	78·4	23 12	61 31	77·9	22 59	60 27	77·5	22 46	59 24	77·1	22 33	58 20	76·7	206 / 334
27 / 153	24 30	63 27	78·3	24 18	62 22	77·8	24 05	61 18	77·4	23 52	60 14	77·0	23 38	59 10	76·5	23 24	58 07	76·1	207 / 333
28 / 152	25 24	63 14	77·8	25 11	62 10	77·3	24 57	61 05	76·9	24 44	60 01	76·4	24 29	58 57	76·0	24 15	57 53	75·5	208 / 332
29 / 151	26 17	63 01	77·3	26 04	61 56	76·8	25 50	60 51	76·3	25 36	59 47	75·9	25 21	58 42	75·4	25 05	57 38	75·0	209 / 331
30 / 150	27 11	62 48	76·8	26 57	61 42	76·3	26 42	60 37	75·8	26 27	59 32	75·3	26 12	58 27	74·8	25 56	57 23	74·4	210 / 330
31 / 149	28 04	62 33	76·3	27 50	61 27	75·8	27 35	60 22	75·2	27 19	59 16	74·7	27 03	58 11	74·2	26 46	57 07	73·8	211 / 329
32 / 148	28 57	62 18	75·7	28 42	61 12	75·2	28 27	60 06	74·7	28 10	59 00	74·2	27 54	57 55	73·7	27 37	56 50	73·1	212 / 328
33 / 147	29 50	62 02	75·2	29 35	60 56	74·7	29 19	59 49	74·1	29 02	58 43	73·6	28 45	57 38	73·1	28 27	56 32	72·5	213 / 327
34 / 146	30 43	61 46	74·7	30 27	60 39	74·1	30 10	59 32	73·5	29 53	58 25	73·0	29 35	57 20	72·4	29 17	56 14	71·9	214 / 326
35 / 145	31 36	61 28	74·1	31 19	60 21	73·5	31 02	59 14	72·9	30 44	58 07	72·4	30 26	57 01	71·8	30 07	55 55	71·2	215 / 325
36 / 144	32 29	61 10	73·5	32 11	60 02	72·9	31 53	58 55	72·3	31 35	57 48	71·7	31 16	56 41	71·2	30 56	55 35	70·6	216 / 324
37 / 143	33 21	60 52	73·0	33 03	59 43	72·3	32 45	58 35	71·7	32 26	57 28	71·1	32 06	56 21	70·5	31 46	55 14	69·9	217 / 323
38 / 142	34 13	60 32	72·4	33 55	59 23	71·7	33 36	58 15	71·1	33 16	57 07	70·5	32 56	55 59	69·9	32 35	54 53	69·3	218 / 322
39 / 141	35 05	60 11	71·8	34 47	59 02	71·1	34 27	57 53	70·5	34 06	56 45	69·8	33 45	55 37	69·2	33 24	54 30	68·6	219 / 321
40 / 140	35 58	59 50	71·2	35 38	58 40	70·5	35 17	57 31	69·8	34 56	56 22	69·1	34 35	55 14	68·5	34 12	54 07	67·9	220 / 320
41 / 139	36 49	59 28	70·5	36 29	58 17	69·8	36 08	57 08	69·1	35 46	55 59	68·5	35 24	54 50	67·8	35 01	53 42	67·1	221 / 319
42 / 138	37 41	59 04	69·9	37 20	57 54	69·2	36 58	56 43	68·5	36 36	55 34	67·8	36 13	54 25	67·1	35 49	53 17	66·4	222 / 318
43 / 137	38 32	58 40	69·2	38 11	57 29	68·5	37 48	56 18	67·8	37 25	55 08	67·1	37 02	53 59	66·4	36 37	52 50	65·7	223 / 317
44 / 136	39 23	58 15	68·6	39 01	57 03	67·8	38 38	55 52	67·1	38 14	54 41	66·3	37 50	53 32	65·7	37 25	52 23	64·9	224 / 316
45 / 135	40 14	57 48	67·9	39 51	56 36	67·1	39 28	55 24	66·3	39 03	54 13	65·6	38 38	53 04	64·9	38 12	51 54	64·1	225 / 315

| | | 24° | | | 25° | | | 26° | | | 27° | | | 28° | | | 29° | | | | |
Lat./A	LHA/F	A/H	B/P	Z_1/Z_2	A/H	B/P	Z_1/Z_2	A/H	B/P	Z_1/Z_2	A/H	B/P	Z_1/Z_2	A/H	B/P	Z_1/Z_2	A/H	B/P	Z_1/Z_2	LHA	Lat./A
135	45	40 14	57 48	67·9	39 51	56 36	67·1	39 28	55 24	66·3	39 03	54 13	65·6	38 38	53 04	64·9	38 12	51 54	64·1	225	315
134	46	41 05	57 21	67·2	40 41	56 08	66·4	40 17	54 56	65·6	39 52	53 44	64·8	39 26	52 34	64·1	38 59	51 25	63·3	226	314
133	47	41 55	56 52	66·4	41 31	55 38	65·6	41 06	54 26	64·8	40 40	53 14	64·0	40 13	52 04	63·3	39 46	50 54	62·5	227	313
132	48	42 45	56 22	65·7	42 22	55 08	64·9	41 54	53 55	64·0	41 28	52 43	63·3	41 00	51 33	62·5	40 32	50 22	61·7	228	312
131	49	43 35	55 50	64·9	43 09	54 36	64·1	42 43	53 22	63·2	42 15	52 10	62·4	41 47	50 59	61·6	41 18	49 48	60·9	229	311
130	50	44 25	55 17	64·1	43 58	54 02	63·3	43 31	52 49	62·4	43 03	51 36	61·6	42 34	50 24	60·8	42 04	49 14	60·0	230	310
129	51	45 14	54 43	63·3	44 47	53 28	62·4	44 18	52 13	61·6	43 49	51 00	60·7	43 20	49 48	59·9	42 49	48 38	59·1	231	309
128	52	46 03	54 08	62·5	45 35	52 52	61·6	45 06	51 37	60·7	44 36	50 23	59·8	44 06	49 11	59·0	43 34	48 00	58·2	232	308
127	53	46 51	53 30	61·6	46 22	52 14	60·7	45 52	50 59	59·8	45 22	49 45	58·9	44 51	48 32	58·1	44 18	47 21	57·2	233	307
126	54	47 39	52 51	60·8	47 09	51 34	59·8	46 39	50 19	58·9	46 07	49 05	58·0	45 35	47 52	57·1	45 02	46 41	56·3	234	306
125	55	48 27	52 11	59·8	47 56	50 53	58·9	47 25	49 37	58·0	46 53	48 23	57·0	46 19	47 10	56·2	45 46	45 59	55·3	235	305
124	56	49 14	51 28	58·9	48 43	50 11	57·9	48 10	48 54	57·0	47 37	47 40	56·1	47 03	46 27	55·2	46 29	45 15	54·3	236	304
123	57	50 01	50 44	57·9	49 28	49 26	56·9	48 55	48 09	56·0	48 21	46 54	55·0	47 46	45 41	54·1	47 11	44 30	53·3	237	303
122	58	50 47	49 58	56·9	50 14	48 39	55·9	49 40	47 22	54·9	49 05	46 07	54·0	48 29	44 54	53·1	47 53	43 43	52·2	238	302
121	59	51 33	49 09	55·9	50 58	47 51	54·9	50 23	46 34	53·9	49 48	45 18	52·9	49 11	44 05	52·0	48 34	42 54	51·1	239	301
120	60	52 18	48 19	54·8	51 43	47 01	53·8	51 07	45 43	52·8	50 31	44 28	51·8	49 53	43 14	50·9	49 14	42 03	50·0	240	300
119	61	53 02	47 26	53·7	52 26	46 07	52·7	51 49	44 50	51·7	51 12	43 35	50·7	50 33	42 22	49·7	49 54	41 10	48·8	241	299
118	62	53 46	46 31	52·6	53 09	45 12	51·5	52 31	43 54	50·5	51 53	42 39	49·5	51 13	41 27	48·6	50 33	40 16	47·6	242	298
117	63	54 29	45 33	51·4	53 51	44 14	50·3	53 13	42 57	49·3	52 33	41 42	48·3	51 53	40 30	47·3	51 12	39 19	46·4	243	297
116	64	55 12	44 33	50·2	54 33	43 11	49·1	53 53	41 57	48·1	53 13	40 40	47·1	52 31	39 30	46·1	51 49	38 20	45·2	244	296
115	65	55 53	43 30	48·9	55 15	42 11	47·8	54 33	40 55	46·8	53 51	39 40	45·8	53 09	38 29	44·8	52 26	37 19	43·9	245	295
114	66	56 34	42 25	47·6	55 53	41 06	46·5	55 12	39 50	45·4	54 29	38 36	44·4	53 46	37 25	43·5	53 02	36 16	42·6	246	294
113	67	57 14	41 16	46·2	56 32	39 58	45·1	55 50	38 42	44·1	55 06	37 29	43·1	54 22	36 19	42·1	53 37	35 11	41·2	247	293
112	68	57 53	40 05	44·8	57 10	38 47	43·7	56 27	37 32	42·7	55 42	36 19	41·7	54 57	35 10	40·7	54 11	34 03	39·8	248	292
111	69	58 32	38 50	43·3	57 47	37 33	42·2	57 03	36 18	41·2	56 17	35 07	40·2	55 31	33 59	39·3	54 44	32 53	38·4	249	291
110	70	59 09	37 32	41·8	58 24	36 16	40·7	57 38	35 02	39·7	56 51	33 52	38·7	56 04	32 45	37·8	55 16	31 41	36·9	250	290
109	71	59 45	36 11	40·2	58 58	34 55	39·2	58 12	33 43	38·1	57 24	32 35	37·2	56 36	31 29	36·3	55 47	30 26	35·4	251	289
108	72	60 19	34 46	38·6	59 32	33 32	37·6	58 44	32 21	36·5	57 56	31 14	35·6	57 07	30 10	34·7	56 17	29 08	33·8	252	288
107	73	60 53	33 18	36·9	60 05	32 05	35·9	59 16	30 56	34·9	58 26	29 51	34·0	57 36	28 48	33·1	56 46	27 49	32·2	253	287
106	74	61 25	31 46	35·2	60 36	30 35	34·2	59 46	29 28	33·2	58 55	28 25	32·3	58 05	27 24	31·4	57 13	26 26	30·6	254	286
105	75	61 56	30 10	33·4	61 06	29 02	32·4	60 15	27 57	31·4	59 23	26 56	30·5	58 31	25 57	29·7	57 39	25 02	28·9	255	285
104	76	62 26	28 31	31·5	61 34	27 25	30·5	60 42	26 23	29·6	59 50	25 24	28·8	58 57	24 28	28·0	58 04	23 35	27·2	256	284
103	77	62 53	26 52	29·6	62 01	25 45	28·6	61 08	24 46	27·8	60 15	23 49	27·0	59 21	22 56	26·2	58 27	22 05	25·7	257	283
102	78	63 20	25 02	27·6	62 26	24 02	26·7	61 32	23 05	25·9	60 38	22 12	25·1	59 44	21 21	24·4	58 49	20 34	23·7	258	282
101	79	63 44	23 12	25·5	62 50	22 15	24·7	61 55	21 22	23·9	61 00	20 32	23·2	60 05	19 44	22·5	59 09	19 00	21·8	259	281
100	80	64 07	21 18	23·4	63 12	20 25	22·6	62 16	19 36	21·9	61 20	18 49	21·2	60 24	18 05	20·6	59 28	17 24	20·0	260	280
99	81	64 28	19 22	21·3	63 32	18 33	20·5	62 35	17 47	19·9	61 39	17 04	19·2	60 42	16 24	18·6	59 45	15 46	18·1	261	279
98	82	64 47	17 22	19·1	63 50	16 37	18·4	62 53	15 56	17·8	61 55	15 17	17·1	60 58	14 40	16·7	60 01	14 06	16·2	262	278
97	83	65 03	15 18	16·8	64 06	14 39	16·2	63 08	14 02	15·6	62 10	13 27	15·1	61 12	12 54	14·7	60 14	12 24	14·2	263	277
96	84	65 18	13 13	14·5	64 20	12 38	14·0	63 22	12 06	13·5	62 23	11 36	13·0	61 25	11 07	12·6	60 26	10 41	12·2	264	276
95	85	65 31	11 05	12·1	64 32	10 35	11·7	63 33	10 08	11·3	62 35	9 42	10·9	61 36	9 19	10·6	60 37	8 56	10·2	265	275
94	86	65 41	8 54	9·8	64 42	8 30	9·4	63 43	8 08	9·1	62 44	7 48	8·8	61 44	7 28	8·5	60 45	7 10	8·2	266	274
93	87	65 49	6 42	7·3	64 50	6 24	7·1	63 50	6 07	6·8	62 51	5 52	6·6	61 51	5 37	6·4	60 52	5 24	6·1	267	273
92	88	65 55	4 29	4·9	64 56	4 17	4·7	63 56	4 06	4·6	62 56	3 55	4·4	61 56	3 45	4·3	60 56	3 36	4·1	268	272
91	89	65 59	2 15	2·5	64 59	2 09	2·4	63 59	2 03	2·3	62 59	1 58	2·2	61 59	1 53	2·1	60 59	1 48	2·1	269	271
90	90	66 00	0 00	0·0	65 00	0 00	0·0	64 00	0 00	0·0	63 00	0 00	0·0	62 00	0 00	0·0	61 00	0 00	0·0	270	270

N. Lat.: for LHA > 180° ... $Z_n = Z$
for LHA < 180° ... $Z_n = 360° - Z$

S. Lat.: for LHA > 180° ... $Z_n = 180° - Z$
for LHA < 180° ... $Z_n = 180° + Z$

SIGHT REDUCTION TABLE

B: (−) for 90° < LHA < 270°
Dec:(−) for Lat. contrary name

Z₁: same sign as B
Z₂: (−) for F > 90°

LHA/F	Lat./A	30° A/H	30° B/P	30° Z₁/Z₂	31° A/H	31° B/P	31° Z₁/Z₂	32° A/H	32° B/P	32° Z₁/Z₂	33° A/H	33° B/P	33° Z₁/Z₂	34° A/H	34° B/P	34° Z₁/Z₂	35° A/H	35° B/P	35° Z₁/Z₂	Lat./A	LHA
0	180	0 00	60 00	90·0	0 00	59 00	90·0	0 00	58 00	90·0	0 00	57 00	90·0	0 00	56 00	90·0	0 00	55 00	90·0	180	360
1	179	0 52	60 00	89·5	0 51	59 00	89·5	0 51	58 00	89·5	0 50	57 00	89·5	0 50	56 00	89·5	0 49	55 00	89·4	181	359
2	178	1 44	59 59	89·0	1 43	58 59	89·0	1 42	57 59	88·9	1 41	56 59	88·9	1 39	55 59	88·9	1 38	54 59	88·9	182	358
3	177	2 36	59 58	88·5	2 34	58 58	88·5	2 33	57 58	88·4	2 31	56 58	88·4	2 29	55 58	88·3	2 27	54 58	88·3	183	357
4	176	3 28	59 56	88·0	3 26	58 56	88·0	3 23	57 56	87·9	3 21	56 56	87·8	3 19	55 56	87·8	3 17	54 56	87·7	184	356
5	175	4 20	59 54	87·5	4 17	58 54	87·4	4 14	57 54	87·3	4 12	56 54	87·3	4 09	55 54	87·2	4 06	54 54	87·1	185	355
6	174	5 12	59 52	87·0	5 08	58 52	86·9	5 05	57 52	86·8	5 02	56 51	86·7	4 58	55 51	86·6	4 55	54 51	86·6	186	354
7	173	6 04	59 49	86·5	6 00	58 49	86·4	5 56	57 48	86·3	5 52	56 48	86·2	5 48	55 48	86·1	5 44	54 48	86·0	187	353
8	172	6 55	59 45	86·0	6 51	58 45	85·9	6 47	57 45	85·7	6 42	56 45	85·6	6 38	55 44	85·5	6 33	54 44	85·4	188	352
9	171	7 47	59 42	85·5	7 42	58 41	85·3	7 37	57 41	85·2	7 32	56 40	85·1	7 27	55 40	84·9	7 22	54 40	84·8	189	351
10	170	8 39	59 37	85·0	8 34	58 37	84·8	8 28	57 36	84·7	8 22	56 36	84·5	8 17	55 36	84·4	8 11	54 35	84·2	190	350
11	169	9 31	59 32	84·4	9 25	58 32	84·3	9 19	57 31	84·1	9 13	56 31	84·0	9 06	55 30	83·8	9 00	54 30	83·6	191	349
12	168	10 22	59 27	83·9	10 16	58 26	83·8	10 09	57 26	83·6	10 03	56 25	83·4	9 56	55 25	83·2	9 48	54 24	83·0	192	348
13	167	11 14	59 21	83·4	11 07	58 20	83·2	11 00	57 20	83·0	10 52	56 19	82·8	10 45	55 18	82·6	10 37	54 18	82·5	193	347
14	166	12 06	59 15	82·9	11 58	58 14	82·7	11 50	57 13	82·5	11 42	56 12	82·3	11 34	55 12	82·1	11 26	54 11	81·9	194	346
15	165	12 57	59 08	82·4	12 49	58 07	82·1	12 41	57 06	81·9	12 32	56 05	81·7	12 23	55 04	81·5	12 14	54 04	81·3	195	345
16	164	13 49	59 01	81·8	13 40	57 59	81·6	13 31	56 58	81·4	13 22	55 56	81·1	13 13	54 57	80·9	13 03	53 56	80·7	196	344
17	163	14 40	58 53	81·3	14 31	57 51	81·1	14 21	56 50	80·8	14 12	55 49	80·5	14 02	54 48	80·3	13 51	53 47	80·1	197	343
18	162	15 31	58 44	80·8	15 22	57 43	80·5	15 12	56 42	80·2	15 01	55 40	80·0	14 51	54 39	79·7	14 40	53 38	79·4	198	342
19	161	16 23	58 35	80·2	16 12	57 34	79·9	16 02	56 32	79·7	15 51	55 31	79·4	15 40	54 30	79·1	15 28	53 29	78·8	199	341
20	160	17 14	58 26	79·7	17 03	57 24	79·4	16 52	56 23	79·1	16 40	55 21	78·8	16 28	54 20	78·5	16 16	53 19	78·2	200	340
21	159	18 05	58 16	79·1	17 54	57 14	78·8	17 42	56 12	78·5	17 29	55 11	78·2	17 17	54 09	77·9	17 04	53 08	77·6	201	339
22	158	18 56	58 05	78·6	18 44	57 03	78·2	18 31	56 01	77·9	18 19	55 00	77·6	18 06	53 58	77·3	17 52	52 56	77·0	202	338
23	157	19 47	57 54	78·0	19 34	56 52	77·7	19 21	55 50	77·3	19 08	54 48	77·0	18 54	53 46	76·6	18 40	52 44	76·3	203	337
24	156	20 37	57 42	77·4	20 24	56 40	77·1	20 11	55 38	76·7	19 57	54 36	76·4	19 42	53 34	76·0	19 28	52 32	75·7	204	336
25	155	21 28	57 30	76·9	21 14	56 27	76·5	21 00	55 25	76·1	20 46	54 23	75·7	20 31	53 21	75·4	20 15	52 19	75·0	205	335
26	154	22 19	57 17	76·3	22 04	56 14	75·9	21 49	55 12	75·5	21 34	54 09	75·1	21 19	53 07	74·7	21 03	52 05	74·4	206	334
27	153	23 09	57 03	75·7	22 54	56 00	75·3	22 39	54 57	74·9	22 23	53 55	74·5	22 07	52 52	74·1	21 50	51 50	73·7	207	333
28	152	23 59	56 49	75·1	23 44	55 46	74·7	23 28	54 43	74·3	23 11	53 40	73·8	22 54	52 37	73·4	22 37	51 35	73·0	208	332
29	151	24 50	56 34	74·5	24 33	55 31	74·1	24 17	54 27	73·6	23 59	53 24	73·2	23 42	52 22	72·8	23 24	51 19	72·4	209	331
30	150	25 40	56 19	73·9	25 23	55 15	73·4	25 05	54 11	73·0	24 48	53 08	72·5	24 29	52 05	72·1	24 11	51 03	71·7	210	330
31	149	26 29	56 02	73·3	26 12	54 58	72·8	25 54	53 54	72·3	25 35	52 51	71·9	25 17	51 48	71·4	24 57	50 45	71·0	211	329
32	148	27 19	55 45	72·6	27 01	54 41	72·2	26 42	53 37	71·7	26 23	52 33	71·2	26 04	51 30	70·7	25 44	50 27	70·3	212	328
33	147	28 09	55 27	72·0	27 50	54 23	71·5	27 31	53 19	71·0	27 11	52 15	70·5	26 50	51 12	70·0	26 30	50 08	69·6	213	327
34	146	28 58	55 09	71·4	28 38	54 04	70·8	28 19	53 00	70·3	27 58	51 56	69·8	27 37	50 52	69·3	27 16	49 49	68·8	214	326
35	145	29 47	54 49	70·7	29 27	53 44	70·2	29 06	52 40	69·6	28 45	51 36	69·1	28 24	50 32	68·6	28 01	49 29	68·1	215	325
36	144	30 36	54 29	70·0	30 15	53 24	69·5	29 54	52 19	68·9	29 32	51 15	68·4	29 10	50 11	67·9	28 47	49 07	67·4	216	324
37	143	31 25	54 08	69·4	31 03	53 03	68·8	30 41	51 58	68·2	30 19	50 53	67·7	29 56	49 49	67·2	29 32	48 45	66·6	217	323
38	142	32 13	53 46	68·7	31 51	52 40	68·1	31 28	51 35	67·5	31 05	50 30	66·9	30 41	49 26	66·4	30 17	48 23	65·9	218	322
39	141	33 02	53 23	68·0	32 39	52 17	67·4	32 15	51 12	66·8	31 51	50 07	66·2	31 27	49 03	65·6	31 02	47 59	65·1	219	321
40	140	33 50	53 00	67·2	33 26	51 54	66·6	33 02	50 48	66·0	32 37	49 43	65·4	32 12	48 38	64·9	31 46	47 34	64·3	220	320
41	139	34 37	52 35	66·5	34 13	51 29	65·9	33 48	50 23	65·3	33 23	49 17	64·7	32 57	48 13	64·1	32 30	47 09	63·5	221	319
42	138	35 25	52 09	65·8	35 00	51 03	65·1	34 34	49 56	64·5	34 08	48 51	63·9	33 42	47 46	63·2	33 14	46 42	62·7	222	318
43	137	36 12	51 43	65·0	35 46	50 36	64·3	35 20	49 29	63·7	34 53	48 25	63·1	34 26	47 19	62·5	33 58	46 15	61·9	223	317
44	136	36 59	51 15	64·2	36 33	50 08	63·6	36 06	49 01	62·9	35 38	47 59	62·3	35 10	46 51	61·6	34 41	45 46	61·0	224	316
45	135	37 46	50 46	63·4	37 19	49 39	62·7	36 51	48 32	62·1	36 22	47 26	61·4	35 53	46 21	60·8	35 24	45 17	60·2	225	315

Lat. / A	LHA/F	30° A/H	30° B/P	30° Z₁/Z₂	31° A/H	31° B/P	31° Z₁/Z₂	32° A/H	32° B/P	32° Z₁/Z₂	33° A/H	33° B/P	33° Z₁/Z₂	34° A/H	34° B/P	34° Z₁/Z₂	35° A/H	35° B/P	35° Z₁/Z₂	Lat. / A	LHA
45	135	37 46	50 46	63.4	37 19	49 39	62.7	36 51	48 32	62.1	36 22	47 26	61.4	35 53	46 21	60.8	35 24	45 17	60.2	225	315
46	134	38 32	50 16	62.6	38 04	49 08	61.9	37 36	48 02	61.2	37 06	46 56	60.6	36 37	45 51	59.9	36 06	44 46	59.3	226	314
47	133	39 18	49 45	61.8	38 49	48 37	61.1	38 20	47 30	60.4	37 50	46 24	59.7	37 19	45 19	59.1	36 48	44 15	58.4	227	313
48	132	40 04	49 13	61.0	39 34	48 05	60.2	39 04	46 58	59.5	38 33	45 51	58.9	38 02	44 46	58.2	37 30	43 42	57.5	228	312
49	131	40 49	48 39	60.1	40 19	47 31	59.4	39 48	46 24	58.6	39 16	45 18	57.9	38 44	44 12	57.2	38 11	43 08	56.6	229	311
50	130	41 34	48 04	59.2	41 03	46 56	58.5	40 31	45 49	57.7	39 59	44 42	57.0	39 26	43 37	56.3	38 52	42 33	55.6	230	310
51	129	42 18	47 28	58.3	41 46	46 20	57.5	41 14	45 12	56.8	40 41	44 06	56.1	40 07	43 01	55.4	39 32	41 57	54.7	231	309
52	128	43 02	46 50	57.4	42 29	45 42	56.6	41 56	44 34	55.9	41 22	43 28	55.1	40 47	42 23	54.4	40 12	41 19	53.7	232	308
53	127	43 46	46 11	56.4	43 12	45 03	55.6	42 38	43 55	54.9	42 03	42 49	54.1	41 28	41 44	53.4	40 52	40 41	52.7	233	307
54	126	44 29	45 31	55.5	43 54	44 22	54.7	43 19	43 15	53.9	42 44	42 09	53.1	42 07	41 04	52.4	41 30	40 01	51.7	234	306
55	125	45 11	44 49	54.5	44 36	43 40	53.7	44 00	42 33	52.9	43 24	41 27	52.1	42 46	40 23	51.4	42 09	39 19	50.7	235	305
56	124	45 53	44 05	53.5	45 17	42 57	52.6	44 40	41 50	51.8	44 04	40 44	51.1	43 25	39 40	50.3	42 46	38 37	49.6	236	304
57	123	46 35	43 20	52.4	45 58	42 11	51.6	45 20	41 05	50.8	44 42	39 59	50.0	44 03	38 55	49.3	43 24	37 53	48.5	237	303
58	122	47 16	42 33	51.3	46 38	41 25	50.5	45 59	40 18	49.7	45 20	39 13	48.9	44 40	38 09	48.2	44 00	37 07	47.5	238	302
59	121	47 56	41 44	50.2	47 17	40 36	49.4	46 38	39 30	48.6	45 58	38 25	47.8	45 17	37 22	47.1	44 36	36 20	46.3	239	301
60	120	48 35	40 54	49.1	47 56	39 46	48.3	47 16	38 40	47.5	46 35	37 36	46.7	45 53	36 33	45.9	45 11	35 32	45.2	240	300
61	119	49 14	40 01	47.9	48 34	38 54	47.1	47 53	37 48	46.3	47 11	36 45	45.5	46 29	35 43	44.7	45 46	34 42	44.0	241	299
62	118	49 53	39 07	46.8	49 11	38 00	45.9	48 29	36 55	45.1	47 46	35 52	44.3	47 03	34 50	43.6	46 19	33 50	42.8	242	298
63	117	50 30	38 11	45.5	49 48	37 04	44.7	49 05	36 00	43.9	48 21	34 57	43.1	47 37	33 57	42.3	46 53	32 57	41.6	243	297
64	116	51 07	37 13	44.3	50 23	36 07	43.4	49 40	35 03	42.6	48 55	34 01	41.8	48 10	33 01	41.1	47 25	32 03	40.4	244	296
65	115	51 43	36 12	43.0	50 58	35 06	42.2	50 14	34 04	41.3	49 28	33 03	40.6	48 43	32 04	39.8	47 56	31 07	39.1	245	295
66	114	52 18	35 10	41.7	51 33	34 06	40.8	50 47	33 04	40.0	50 01	32 04	39.3	49 14	31 05	38.5	48 27	30 09	37.8	246	294
67	113	52 52	34 05	40.3	52 06	33 02	39.5	51 19	32 01	38.7	50 32	31 02	37.9	49 44	30 05	37.2	48 56	29 10	36.5	247	293
68	112	53 25	32 59	38.9	52 38	31 56	38.1	51 50	30 57	37.3	51 02	29 59	36.6	50 14	29 03	35.8	49 25	28 09	35.2	248	292
69	111	53 57	31 50	37.5	53 09	30 49	36.7	52 21	29 50	35.9	51 32	28 53	35.2	50 43	27 59	34.5	49 53	27 06	33.8	249	291
70	110	54 28	30 39	36.1	53 39	29 39	35.2	52 50	28 42	34.5	52 00	27 46	33.8	51 10	26 53	33.1	50 20	26 02	32.4	250	290
71	109	54 58	29 25	34.6	54 08	28 27	33.8	53 18	27 31	33.0	52 28	26 38	32.3	51 37	25 46	31.6	50 46	24 56	31.0	251	289
72	108	55 27	28 09	33.0	54 37	27 13	32.2	53 46	26 19	31.5	52 54	25 27	30.8	52 03	24 37	30.2	51 10	23 49	29.5	252	288
73	107	55 55	26 51	31.4	55 03	25 57	30.7	54 12	25 04	30.0	53 19	24 14	29.3	52 27	23 26	28.7	51 34	22 40	28.1	253	287
74	106	56 21	25 31	29.8	55 29	24 39	29.1	54 36	23 48	28.4	53 43	23 00	27.8	52 50	22 14	27.1	51 57	21 29	26.6	254	286
75	105	56 46	24 09	28.2	55 53	23 18	27.5	55 00	22 30	26.8	54 06	21 44	26.2	53 12	21 00	25.6	52 18	20 17	25.0	255	285
76	104	57 10	22 44	26.5	56 16	21 56	25.8	55 22	21 10	25.2	54 28	20 26	24.6	53 33	19 44	24.0	52 38	19 04	23.5	256	284
77	103	57 33	21 17	24.8	56 38	20 31	24.1	55 43	19 48	23.5	54 48	19 06	23.0	53 53	18 27	22.4	52 57	17 49	21.9	257	283
78	102	57 54	19 48	23.0	56 59	19 05	22.4	56 03	18 24	21.9	55 07	17 45	21.3	54 11	17 08	20.8	53 15	16 32	20.3	258	282
79	101	58 13	18 17	21.2	57 17	17 37	20.7	56 21	16 59	20.1	55 25	16 22	19.6	54 28	15 48	19.2	53 31	15 15	18.7	259	281
80	100	58 32	16 44	19.4	57 35	16 07	18.9	56 38	15 32	18.4	55 41	14 58	17.9	54 44	14 26	17.5	53 47	13 56	17.1	260	280
81	99	58 48	15 10	17.6	57 51	14 36	17.1	56 53	14 03	16.6	55 56	13 33	16.2	54 58	13 03	15.8	54 00	12 36	15.4	261	279
82	98	59 03	13 33	15.7	58 05	13 02	15.3	57 07	12 33	14.9	56 09	12 06	14.5	55 11	11 40	14.1	54 13	11 14	13.8	262	278
83	97	59 16	11 55	13.7	58 18	11 28	13.4	57 19	11 02	13.0	56 21	10 38	12.7	55 22	10 14	12.4	54 24	9 52	12.1	263	277
84	96	59 28	10 16	11.9	58 29	9 52	11.5	57 30	9 30	11.2	56 31	9 09	10.9	55 32	8 49	10.6	54 33	8 29	10.4	264	276
85	95	59 37	8 35	9.9	58 38	8 15	9.6	57 39	7 56	9.4	56 40	7 39	9.1	55 41	7 22	8.9	54 41	7 06	8.7	265	275
86	94	59 46	6 53	8.0	58 46	6 37	7.7	57 47	6 22	7.5	56 47	6 08	7.3	55 48	5 54	7.1	54 48	5 41	7.0	266	274
87	93	59 52	5 11	6.0	58 52	4 59	5.8	57 52	4 47	5.6	56 53	4 36	5.5	55 53	4 26	5.3	54 53	4 16	5.2	267	273
88	92	59 56	3 28	4.0	58 57	3 19	3.9	57 57	3 12	3.8	56 57	3 05	3.7	55 57	2 58	3.6	54 57	2 51	3.5	268	272
89	91	59 59	1 44	2.0	58 59	1 40	1.9	57 59	1 36	1.9	56 59	1 32	1.8	55 59	1 29	1.8	54 59	1 26	1.7	269	271
90	90	60 00	0 00	0.0	59 00	0 00	0.0	58 00	0 00	0.0	57 00	0 00	0.0	56 00	0 00	0.0	55 00	0 00	0.0	270	270

N. Lat: for LHA > 180° ... $Z_n = Z$
for LHA < 180° ... $Z_n = 360° - Z$

S. Lat.: for LHA > 180° ... $Z_n = 180° - Z$
for LHA < 180° ... $Z_n = 180° + Z$

SIGHT REDUCTION TABLE

B: (−) for 90° < LHA < 270°
Dec:(−) for Lat. contrary name

Z₁: same sign as B
Z₂: (−) for F > 90°

Lat. / A (left, LHA/F) — Lat. / A (right, LHA)

LHA/F	36° A/H	36° B/P	36° Z_1/Z_2	37° A/H	37° B/P	37° Z_1/Z_2	38° A/H	38° B/P	38° Z_1/Z_2	39° A/H	39° B/P	39° Z_1/Z_2	40° A/H	40° B/P	40° Z_1/Z_2	41° A/H	41° B/P	41° Z_1/Z_2	LHA
0 / 180	0 00	54 00	90·0	0 00	53 00	90·0	0 00	52 00	90·0	0 00	51 00	90·0	0 00	50 00	90·0	0 00	49 00	90·0	180
1 / 179	0 49	54 00	89·4	0 48	53 00	89·4	0 47	52 00	89·4	0 47	51 00	89·4	0 46	50 00	89·4	0 45	49 00	89·3	181
2 / 178	1 37	53 59	88·8	1 36	52 59	88·8	1 35	51 59	88·8	1 33	50 59	88·7	1 32	49 59	88·7	1 31	48 59	88·7	182
3 / 177	2 26	53 58	88·2	2 24	52 58	88·2	2 22	51 58	88·2	2 20	50 58	88·1	2 18	49 58	88·1	2 16	48 58	88·0	183
4 / 176	3 14	53 56	87·6	3 12	52 56	87·6	3 09	51 56	87·6	3 06	50 56	87·5	3 04	49 56	87·4	3 01	48 56	87·4	184
5 / 175	4 03	53 54	87·1	3 59	52 54	87·1	3 56	51 54	87·0	3 53	50 54	86·9	3 50	49 54	86·8	3 46	48 54	86·7	185
6 / 174	4 51	53 51	86·5	4 47	52 51	86·5	4 43	51 51	86·4	4 40	50 51	86·2	4 36	49 51	86·1	4 31	48 51	86·1	186
7 / 173	5 39	53 48	85·9	5 35	52 48	85·8	5 31	51 48	85·8	5 26	50 47	85·5	5 22	49 47	85·5	5 17	48 47	85·5	187
8 / 172	6 28	53 44	85·3	6 23	52 44	85·3	6 18	51 44	85·1	6 13	50 44	84·9	6 07	49 43	84·8	6 02	48 43	84·7	188
9 / 171	7 16	53 40	84·7	7 11	52 39	84·7	7 05	51 39	84·6	6 59	50 39	84·3	6 53	49 39	84·2	6 47	48 39	84·1	189
10 / 170	8 05	53 35	84·1	7 58	52 35	84·1	7 52	51 34	84·0	7 45	50 34	83·7	7 39	49 34	83·5	7 32	48 34	83·4	190
11 / 169	8 53	53 30	83·5	8 46	52 29	83·5	8 39	51 29	83·3	8 32	50 29	83·0	8 24	49 29	82·9	8 17	48 28	82·7	191
12 / 168	9 41	53 24	82·9	9 33	52 23	82·9	9 26	51 23	82·7	9 18	50 23	82·4	9 10	49 23	82·2	9 02	48 22	82·1	192
13 / 167	10 29	53 17	82·3	10 21	52 17	82·3	10 13	51 17	82·1	10 04	50 16	81·7	9 55	49 16	81·6	9 46	48 16	81·4	193
14 / 166	11 17	53 10	81·7	11 08	52 10	81·7	10 59	51 10	81·5	10 50	50 09	81·1	10 41	49 09	80·9	10 31	48 09	80·7	194
15 / 165	12 05	53 03	81·0	11 56	52 02	81·1	11 46	51 02	80·8	11 36	50 02	80·4	11 26	49 01	80·2	11 16	48 01	80·0	195
16 / 164	12 53	52 55	80·4	12 43	51 54	80·4	12 33	50 54	80·2	12 22	49 53	79·8	12 11	48 53	79·6	12 00	47 53	79·3	196
17 / 163	13 41	52 46	79·8	13 30	51 46	79·8	13 19	50 45	79·6	13 08	49 45	79·1	12 57	48 44	78·9	12 45	47 44	78·7	197
18 / 162	14 29	52 37	79·2	14 17	51 37	79·2	14 06	50 36	78·9	13 54	49 35	78·4	13 42	48 35	78·2	13 29	47 34	78·0	198
19 / 161	15 16	52 28	78·6	15 04	51 27	78·6	14 52	50 26	78·3	14 39	49 25	77·8	14 27	48 25	77·5	14 13	47 24	77·3	199
20 / 160	16 04	52 17	77·9	15 51	51 16	77·9	15 38	50 16	77·6	15 25	49 15	77·1	15 11	48 14	76·8	14 58	47 14	76·6	200
21 / 159	16 51	52 07	77·3	16 38	51 05	77·3	16 24	50 05	77·0	16 10	49 04	76·4	15 56	48 03	76·1	15 42	47 03	75·9	201
22 / 158	17 39	51 55	76·6	17 24	50 54	76·6	17 10	49 53	76·3	16 56	48 52	75·7	16 41	47 51	75·4	16 25	46 51	75·2	202
23 / 157	18 26	51 43	76·0	18 11	50 42	76·0	17 56	49 41	75·7	17 41	48 40	75·0	17 25	47 39	74·7	17 09	46 38	74·4	203
24 / 156	19 13	51 30	75·3	18 57	50 29	75·3	18 42	49 28	75·0	18 26	48 27	74·3	18 09	47 26	74·0	17 53	46 25	73·7	204
25 / 155	20 00	51 17	74·7	19 44	50 15	74·7	19 27	49 14	74·3	19 10	48 13	73·6	18 53	47 12	73·3	18 36	46 12	73·0	205
26 / 154	20 46	51 03	74·0	20 30	50 01	74·0	20 13	49 00	73·6	19 55	47 59	72·9	19 37	46 58	72·6	19 19	45 57	72·3	206
27 / 153	21 33	50 48	73·3	21 15	49 47	73·3	20 58	48 45	73·0	20 40	47 44	72·2	20 21	46 43	71·9	20 02	45 42	71·5	207
28 / 152	22 19	50 33	72·6	22 01	49 31	72·6	21 43	48 30	72·3	21 24	47 28	71·5	21 04	46 28	71·1	20 45	45 27	70·8	208
29 / 151	23 06	50 17	72·0	22 47	49 15	72·0	22 28	48 14	71·6	22 08	47 12	70·8	21 48	46 11	70·4	21 28	45 11	70·0	209
30 / 150	23 52	50 00	71·3	23 32	48 58	71·3	23 12	47 57	70·8	22 52	46 55	70·0	22 31	45 54	69·6	22 10	44 54	69·3	210
31 / 149	24 37	49 43	70·5	24 17	48 41	70·5	23 57	47 39	70·1	23 36	46 38	69·3	23 14	45 37	68·9	22 52	44 36	68·5	211
32 / 148	25 23	49 25	69·8	25 02	48 23	69·8	24 41	47 21	69·4	24 19	46 19	68·5	23 57	45 18	68·1	23 34	44 17	67·7	212
33 / 147	26 09	49 06	69·1	25 47	48 04	69·1	25 25	47 02	68·7	25 02	46 01	67·8	24 40	45 00	67·3	24 16	43 58	66·9	213
34 / 146	26 54	48 46	68·4	26 32	47 44	68·4	26 09	46 42	67·9	25 45	45 41	67·0	25 22	44 39	66·6	24 58	43 39	66·1	214
35 / 145	27 39	48 26	67·6	27 16	47 23	67·6	26 52	46 21	67·1	26 28	45 20	66·2	26 04	44 19	65·8	25 39	43 18	65·3	215
36 / 144	28 24	48 04	66·9	28 00	47 02	66·9	27 36	46 00	66·4	27 11	44 58	65·4	26 46	43 57	65·0	26 20	42 57	64·5	216
37 / 143	29 08	47 42	66·1	28 44	46 40	66·1	28 19	45 38	65·6	27 53	44 36	64·6	27 27	43 35	64·2	27 01	42 34	63·7	217
38 / 142	29 52	47 19	65·3	29 27	46 17	65·3	29 01	45 15	64·8	28 35	44 13	63·8	28 08	43 12	63·3	27 41	42 12	62·9	218
39 / 141	30 36	46 56	64·5	30 10	45 53	64·5	29 44	44 51	64·0	29 17	43 49	63·0	28 49	42 48	62·5	28 21	41 48	62·0	219
40 / 140	31 20	46 31	63·7	30 53	45 28	63·7	30 26	44 26	63·2	29 58	43 25	62·2	29 30	42 24	61·7	29 01	41 23	61·2	220
41 / 139	32 03	46 05	62·9	31 36	45 03	62·9	31 08	44 01	62·4	30 39	42 59	61·3	30 10	41 58	60·8	29 41	40 58	60·3	221
42 / 138	32 46	45 39	62·1	32 18	44 36	62·1	31 49	43 34	61·5	31 20	42 33	60·5	30 50	41 32	59·9	30 20	40 32	59·4	222
43 / 137	33 29	45 11	61·3	33 00	44 09	61·5	32 30	43 07	60·7	32 00	42 05	59·6	31 30	41 05	59·1	30 59	40 04	58·5	223
44 / 136	34 12	44 43	60·4	33 42	43 40	60·7	33 11	42 38	59·8	32 40	41 37	58·7	32 09	40 36	58·2	31 37	39 36	57·6	224
45 / 135	34 55	44 13	59·6	34 23	43 11	59·8	33 52	42 09	59·0	33 20	41 08	57·8	32 48	40 07	57·3	32 15	39 08	56·7	225

Lat./A LHA/F		36° A/H	36° B/P	36° Z1/Z2	37° A/H	37° B/P	37° Z1/Z2	38° A/H	38° B/P	38° Z1/Z2	39° A/H	39° B/P	39° Z1/Z2	40° A/H	40° B/P	40° Z1/Z2	41° A/H	41° B/P	41° Z1/Z2	Lat./A LHA	
45	135	34 54	44 13	59·6	34 23	43 11	59·0	33 52	42 09	58·4	33 20	41 08	57·8	32 48	40 07	57·3	32 15	39 08	56·7	225	315
46	134	35 35	43 43	58·7	35 04	42 40	58·1	34 32	41 38	57·5	33 59	40 37	56·9	33 26	39 37	56·4	32 53	38 38	55·8	226	314
47	133	36 17	43 11	57·8	35 44	42 09	57·2	35 12	41 07	56·6	34 38	40 06	56·0	34 04	39 06	55·4	33 30	38 07	54·9	227	313
48	132	36 57	42 39	56·9	36 24	41 36	56·2	35 51	40 35	55·6	35 17	39 34	55·0	34 42	38 34	54·5	34 07	37 35	53·9	228	312
49	131	37 38	42 05	55·9	37 04	41 03	55·3	36 30	40 01	54·7	35 55	39 01	54·1	35 19	38 01	53·5	34 43	37 03	53·0	229	311
50	130	38 18	41 30	55·0	37 43	40 28	54·4	37 08	39 27	53·7	36 32	38 27	53·1	35 56	37 27	52·5	35 19	36 29	52·0	230	310
51	129	38 57	40 54	54·0	38 22	39 52	53·4	37 46	38 51	52·8	37 09	37 51	52·1	36 32	36 52	51·6	35 55	35 54	51·0	231	309
52	128	39 36	40 17	53·0	39 00	39 15	52·4	38 23	38 14	51·8	37 46	37 15	51·1	37 08	36 16	50·6	36 30	35 18	50·0	232	308
53	127	40 15	39 38	52·0	39 38	38 37	51·4	39 00	37 36	50·8	38 22	36 37	50·1	37 43	35 39	49·5	37 04	34 42	49·0	233	307
54	126	40 53	38 58	51·0	40 15	37 57	50·4	39 36	36 57	49·7	38 57	35 58	49·1	38 18	35 01	48·5	37 38	34 04	47·9	234	306
55	125	41 30	38 17	50·0	40 52	37 17	49·3	40 12	36 17	48·7	39 32	35 19	48·1	38 52	34 21	47·4	38 11	33 25	46·9	235	305
56	124	42 07	37 35	48·9	41 28	36 35	48·3	40 47	35 36	47·6	40 07	34 38	47·0	39 26	33 41	46·4	38 44	32 45	45·8	236	304
57	123	42 44	36 51	47·9	42 03	35 51	47·2	41 22	34 53	46·5	40 41	33 55	45·9	39 59	32 59	45·3	39 16	32 04	44·7	237	303
58	122	43 19	36 06	46·8	42 38	35 06	46·1	41 56	34 09	45·4	41 14	33 12	44·8	40 31	32 16	44·2	39 48	31 22	43·6	238	302
59	121	43 54	35 20	45·6	43 12	34 21	45·0	42 29	33 24	44·3	41 46	32 27	43·7	41 03	31 32	43·1	40 19	30 39	42·5	239	301
60	120	44 29	34 32	44·5	43 46	33 34	43·8	43 02	32 37	43·2	42 18	31 42	42·5	41 34	30 47	41·9	40 49	29 54	41·3	240	300
61	119	45 02	33 43	43·3	44 18	32 45	42·6	43 34	31 49	42·0	42 49	30 55	41·4	42 04	30 01	40·8	41 19	29 09	40·2	241	299
62	118	45 35	32 52	42·1	44 51	31 55	41·5	44 05	31 00	40·8	43 20	30 06	40·2	42 34	29 14	39·6	41 47	28 22	39·0	242	298
63	117	46 07	32 00	40·9	45 22	31 04	40·3	44 36	30 10	39·6	43 49	29 17	39·0	43 03	28 25	38·4	42 15	27 35	37·8	243	297
64	116	46 39	31 06	39·7	45 52	30 11	39·0	45 06	29 18	38·4	44 18	28 26	37·8	43 31	27 35	37·2	42 43	26 46	36·6	244	296
65	115	47 09	30 11	38·4	46 21	29 17	37·8	45 35	28 25	37·1	44 47	27 34	36·5	43 58	26 44	36·0	43 09	25 56	35·4	245	295
66	114	47 39	29 14	37·1	46 51	28 21	36·5	46 03	27 30	35·9	45 14	26 40	35·3	44 25	25 52	34·7	43 35	25 04	34·2	246	294
67	113	48 08	28 16	35·8	47 19	27 24	35·2	46 30	26 34	34·6	45 40	25 45	34·0	44 50	24 58	33·4	44 00	24 12	32·9	247	293
68	112	48 36	27 17	34·5	47 46	26 26	33·9	46 56	25 37	33·3	46 06	24 50	32·7	45 15	24 03	32·2	44 24	23 19	31·6	248	292
69	111	49 03	26 15	33·1	48 13	25 26	32·5	47 22	24 38	31·9	46 31	23 52	31·4	45 39	23 08	30·8	44 48	22 24	30·3	249	291
70	110	49 29	25 13	31·8	48 38	24 25	31·2	47 46	23 39	30·6	46 55	22 54	30·0	46 03	22 11	29·5	45 10	21 29	29·0	250	290
71	109	49 54	24 08	30·4	49 02	23 22	29·8	48 10	22 37	29·2	47 17	21 54	28·7	46 25	21 12	28·2	45 32	20 32	27·7	251	289
72	108	50 18	23 02	28·9	49 25	22 18	28·4	48 33	21 35	27·8	47 39	20 53	27·3	46 46	20 13	26·8	45 52	19 34	26·3	252	288
73	107	50 41	21 55	27·5	49 48	21 12	26·9	48 54	20 31	26·4	48 00	19 51	25·9	47 06	19 13	25·4	46 12	18 35	25·0	253	287
74	106	51 03	20 47	26·0	50 09	20 06	25·5	49 15	19 26	25·0	48 20	18 48	24·5	47 25	18 11	24·0	46 30	17 36	23·6	254	286
75	105	51 24	19 36	24·5	50 29	18 57	24·0	49 34	18 20	23·5	48 39	17 43	23·1	47 44	17 09	22·6	46 48	16 35	22·2	255	285
76	104	51 43	18 25	23·0	50 48	17 48	22·5	49 52	17 12	22·0	48 57	16 38	21·6	48 01	16 05	21·2	47 05	15 33	20·8	256	284
77	103	52 02	17 12	21·4	51 06	16 37	21·0	50 09	16 04	20·6	49 13	15 31	20·1	48 17	15 00	19·8	47 20	14 31	19·4	257	283
78	102	52 19	15 58	19·9	51 22	15 25	19·5	50 25	14 54	19·0	49 29	14 24	18·7	48 32	13 55	18·3	47 35	13 27	18·0	258	282
79	101	52 35	14 43	18·3	51 37	14 13	17·9	50 40	13 43	17·5	49 43	13 16	17·2	48 46	12 49	16·8	47 48	12 23	16·5	259	281
80	100	52 49	13 27	16·7	51 52	12 59	16·3	50 54	12 32	16·0	49 56	12 06	15·7	48 58	11 42	15·3	48 01	11 18	15·0	260	280
81	99	53 02	12 09	15·1	52 04	11 44	14·7	51 06	11 19	14·4	50 08	10 56	14·1	49 10	10 34	13·8	48 12	10 12	13·6	261	279
82	98	53 14	10 51	13·4	52 16	10 28	13·1	51 18	10 06	12·9	50 19	9 45	12·6	49 20	9 25	12·3	48 22	9 06	12·1	262	278
83	97	53 25	9 31	11·8	52 26	9 11	11·5	51 27	8 52	11·3	50 29	8 34	11·0	49 30	8 16	10·8	48 31	7 59	10·6	263	277
84	96	53 34	8 11	10·1	52 35	7 54	9·9	51 36	7 37	9·7	50 37	7 21	9·5	49 38	7 06	9·3	48 38	6 51	9·1	264	276
85	95	53 42	6 50	8·5	52 43	6 36	8·3	51 43	6 22	8·1	50 44	6 09	7·9	49 44	5 56	7·8	48 45	5 44	7·6	265	275
86	94	53 49	5 29	6·8	52 49	5 17	6·6	51 49	5 06	6·5	50 50	4 55	6·3	49 50	4 45	6·2	48 50	4 35	6·1	266	274
87	93	53 54	4 07	5·1	52 54	3 58	5·0	51 54	3 50	4·9	50 54	3 42	4·8	49 54	3 34	4·7	48 55	3 27	4·6	267	273
88	92	53 57	2 45	3·4	52 57	2 39	3·3	51 57	2 33	3·2	50 57	2 28	3·2	49 58	2 23	3·1	48 58	2 18	3·0	268	272
89	91	53 59	1 23	1·7	52 59	1 20	1·7	51 59	1 17	1·6	50 59	1 14	1·6	49 59	1 11	1·6	48 59	1 09	1·5	269	271
90	90	54 00	0 00	0·0	53 00	0 00	0·0	52 00	0 00	0·0	51 00	0 00	0·0	50 00	0 00	0·0	49 00	0 00	0·0	270	270

N. Lat: for LHA > 180° .... Zn = Z
        for LHA < 180° .... Zn = 360° − Z

S. Lat: for LHA > 180° .... Zn = 180° − Z
        for LHA < 180° .... Zn = 180° + Z

SIGHT REDUCTION TABLE

B: (−) for 90° < LHA < 270°
Dec:(−) for Lat. contrary name

Z₁: same sign as B
Z₂: (−) for F > 90°

Lat./A	42°			43°			44°			45°			46°			47°			Lat./A
LHA/F	A/H	B/P	Z_1/Z_2	A/H	B/P	Z_1/Z_2	A/H	B/P	Z_1/Z_2	A/H	B/P	Z_1/Z_2	A/H	B/P	Z_1/Z_2	A/H	B/P	Z_1/Z_2	LHA
0	0 00	48 00	90.0	0 00	47 00	90.0	0 00	46 00	90.0	0 00	45 00	90.0	0 00	44 00	90.0	0 00	43 00	90.0	180
1	0 45	48 00	89.3	0 44	47 00	89.3	0 43	46 00	89.3	0 42	45 00	89.3	0 42	44 00	89.3	0 41	43 00	89.3	181
2	1 29	47 59	88.7	1 28	46 59	88.6	1 26	45 59	88.6	1 25	44 59	88.6	1 23	43 59	88.6	1 22	42 59	88.5	182
3	2 14	47 58	88.0	2 12	46 58	88.0	2 09	45 58	88.0	2 07	44 58	87.9	2 05	43 58	87.9	2 03	42 58	87.8	183
4	2 58	47 56	87.3	2 55	46 56	87.3	2 53	45 56	87.3	2 50	44 56	87.2	2 47	43 56	87.2	2 44	42 56	87.1	184
5	3 43	47 53	86.6	3 39	46 53	86.6	3 36	45 53	86.5	3 32	44 53	86.5	3 28	43 53	86.4	3 24	42 53	86.3	185
6	4 27	47 51	86.0	4 23	46 51	85.9	4 19	45 51	85.8	4 14	44 51	85.7	4 10	43 51	85.7	4 05	42 51	85.6	186
7	5 12	47 47	85.3	5 07	46 47	85.2	5 02	45 47	85.2	4 57	44 47	85.0	4 52	43 47	85.0	4 46	42 47	84.9	187
8	5 56	47 43	84.6	5 51	46 43	84.5	5 45	45 43	84.4	5 39	44 43	84.3	5 33	43 43	84.2	5 27	42 43	84.1	188
9	6 41	47 39	84.0	6 34	46 39	83.8	6 28	45 39	83.7	6 21	44 39	83.6	6 14	43 39	83.5	6 07	42 39	83.4	189
10	7 25	47 34	83.3	7 18	46 34	83.1	7 11	45 34	83.0	7 03	44 34	82.9	6 56	43 34	82.8	6 48	42 34	82.7	190
11	8 09	47 28	82.6	8 01	46 28	82.4	7 53	45 28	82.3	7 45	44 28	82.2	7 37	43 28	82.0	7 29	42 28	81.9	191
12	8 53	47 22	81.9	8 45	46 22	81.8	8 36	45 22	81.6	8 27	44 22	81.5	8 18	43 22	81.3	8 09	42 22	81.2	192
13	9 37	47 16	81.2	9 28	46 15	81.1	9 19	45 15	80.9	9 09	44 15	80.7	8 59	43 15	80.6	8 49	42 16	80.4	193
14	10 21	47 08	80.5	10 11	46 08	80.3	10 01	45 08	80.2	9 51	44 08	80.0	9 40	43 08	79.8	9 30	42 08	79.7	194
15	11 05	47 01	79.8	10 55	46 00	79.6	10 44	45 00	79.5	10 33	44 00	79.3	10 21	43 00	79.1	10 10	42 01	78.9	195
16	11 49	46 52	79.1	11 38	45 52	78.9	11 26	44 52	78.7	11 14	43 52	78.5	11 02	42 52	78.3	10 50	41 52	78.2	196
17	12 33	46 43	78.4	12 21	45 43	78.2	12 08	44 43	78.0	11 56	43 43	77.8	11 43	42 43	77.6	11 30	41 44	77.4	197
18	13 17	46 34	77.7	13 04	45 34	77.5	12 51	44 34	77.3	12 37	43 34	77.1	12 24	42 34	76.8	12 10	41 34	76.6	198
19	14 00	46 24	77.0	13 46	45 24	76.8	13 33	44 24	76.5	13 19	43 24	76.3	13 04	42 24	76.1	12 50	41 24	75.9	199
20	14 44	46 13	76.3	14 29	45 13	76.1	14 15	44 13	75.8	14 00	43 13	75.6	13 45	42 13	75.3	13 29	41 14	75.1	200
21	15 27	46 02	75.6	15 12	45 02	75.3	14 56	44 02	75.1	14 41	43 02	74.8	14 25	42 02	74.6	14 09	41 03	74.3	201
22	16 10	45 50	74.9	15 54	44 50	74.6	15 38	43 50	74.3	15 22	42 50	74.1	15 05	41 50	73.8	14 48	40 51	73.5	202
23	16 53	45 38	74.1	16 36	44 38	73.9	16 19	43 38	73.6	16 02	42 38	73.3	15 45	41 38	73.0	15 27	40 39	72.8	203
24	17 36	45 25	73.4	17 18	44 25	73.1	17 01	43 25	72.8	16 43	42 25	72.5	16 25	41 25	72.2	16 06	40 26	72.0	204
25	18 18	45 11	72.7	18 00	44 11	72.4	17 42	43 11	72.1	17 23	42 11	71.8	17 04	41 12	71.5	16 45	40 12	71.2	205
26	19 01	44 57	71.9	18 42	43 57	71.6	18 23	42 57	71.3	18 03	41 57	71.0	17 44	40 57	70.7	17 24	39 58	70.4	206
27	19 43	44 42	71.2	19 24	43 42	70.8	19 04	42 42	70.5	18 43	41 42	70.2	18 23	40 43	69.9	18 02	39 43	69.6	207
28	20 25	44 26	70.4	20 05	43 26	70.1	19 44	42 26	69.7	19 23	41 27	69.4	19 02	40 27	69.1	18 40	39 28	68.8	208
29	21 07	44 10	69.6	20 46	43 10	69.3	20 25	42 10	68.9	20 03	41 10	68.6	19 41	40 11	68.3	19 18	39 12	67.9	209
30	21 49	43 53	68.9	21 27	42 53	68.5	21 05	41 53	68.1	20 42	40 54	67.8	20 19	39 54	67.4	19 56	38 55	67.1	210
31	22 30	43 35	68.1	22 08	42 35	67.7	21 45	41 36	67.3	21 21	40 36	67.0	20 58	39 37	66.6	20 34	38 38	66.3	211
32	23 11	43 17	67.3	22 48	42 17	66.9	22 24	41 17	66.5	22 00	40 18	66.2	21 36	39 19	65.8	21 11	38 20	65.4	212
33	23 53	42 58	66.5	23 28	41 58	66.1	23 04	40 58	65.7	22 39	39 59	65.3	22 14	39 00	65.0	21 48	38 02	64.6	213
34	24 33	42 38	65.7	24 08	41 38	65.3	23 43	40 39	64.9	23 17	39 40	64.5	22 51	38 41	64.1	22 25	37 42	63.7	214
35	25 14	42 18	64.9	24 48	41 18	64.5	24 22	40 18	64.1	23 56	39 19	63.7	23 29	38 21	63.3	23 02	37 23	62.9	215
36	25 54	41 56	64.1	25 28	40 57	63.6	25 01	39 57	63.2	24 34	38 58	62.8	24 06	38 00	62.4	23 38	37 02	62.0	216
37	26 34	41 34	63.2	26 07	40 35	62.8	25 39	39 35	62.4	25 11	38 38	61.9	24 43	37 38	61.5	24 14	36 41	61.1	217
38	27 13	41 11	62.4	26 46	40 12	61.9	26 17	39 13	61.5	25 48	38 14	61.1	25 19	37 16	60.7	24 50	36 19	60.3	218
39	27 53	40 48	61.5	27 24	39 48	61.1	26 55	38 50	60.6	26 25	37 51	60.2	25 55	36 53	59.8	25 25	35 56	59.4	219
40	28 32	40 23	60.7	28 02	39 24	60.2	27 32	38 25	59.8	27 02	37 27	59.3	26 31	36 30	58.9	26 00	35 32	58.5	220
41	29 11	39 59	59.8	28 40	38 59	59.3	28 10	38 01	58.9	27 38	37 03	58.4	27 07	36 05	58.0	26 35	35 08	57.6	221
42	29 49	39 32	58.9	29 18	38 33	58.4	28 46	37 37	58.0	28 14	36 38	57.5	27 42	35 40	57.1	27 09	34 43	56.6	222
43	30 27	39 05	58.0	29 55	38 06	57.5	29 23	37 08	57.1	28 50	36 11	56.6	28 17	35 14	56.1	27 43	34 18	55.7	223
44	31 05	38 37	57.1	30 32	37 39	56.6	29 59	36 41	56.1	29 25	35 44	55.7	28 51	34 47	55.2	28 17	33 51	54.8	224
45	31 42	38 09	56.2	31 08	37 10	55.7	30 34	36 13	55.2	30 00	35 16	54.7	29 25	34 20	54.3	28 50	33 24	53.8	225

S. Lat.: for LHA > 180° ... $Z_n = 180° - Z$
for LHA < 180° ... $Z_n = 180° + Z$

Lat./A LHA	Lat./A LHA	47° A/H	47° B/P	47° Z₁/Z₂	46° A/H	46° B/P	46° Z₁/Z₂	45° A/H	45° B/P	45° Z₁/Z₂	44° A/H	44° B/P	44° Z₁/Z₂	43° A/H	43° B/P	43° Z₁/Z₂	42° A/H	42° B/P	42° Z₁/Z₂	Lat./A Lat	Lat./A LHA/F
315	225	28 50	33 24	53·8	29 25	34 20	54·3	30 00	35 16	54·7	30 34	36 13	55·2	31 08	37 10	55·7	31 42	38 09	56·2	45	135
314	226	29 23	32 56	52·9	29 59	33 51	53·3	30 34	34 47	53·8	31 10	35 44	54·3	31 45	36 41	54·8	32 19	37 39	55·3	46	134
313	227	29 55	32 27	51·9	30 32	33 22	52·4	31 08	34 18	52·8	31 45	35 14	53·3	32 20	36 11	53·8	32 55	37 08	54·3	47	133
312	228	30 27	31 58	50·9	31 05	32 52	51·4	31 42	33 47	51·9	32 19	34 43	52·3	32 55	35 40	52·9	33 31	36 37	53·4	48	132
311	229	30 59	31 27	49·9	31 37	32 21	50·4	32 15	33 16	50·9	32 53	34 11	51·4	33 30	35 08	51·9	34 07	36 05	52·4	49	131
310	230	31 30	30 56	48·9	32 09	31 50	49·4	32 48	32 44	49·9	33 26	33 39	50·4	34 04	34 35	50·9	34 42	35 31	51·4	50	130
309	231	32 00	30 24	47·9	32 40	31 17	48·4	33 20	32 11	48·9	33 59	33 05	49·4	34 38	34 01	49·9	35 17	34 57	50·4	51	129
308	232	32 30	29 52	46·9	33 11	30 44	47·4	33 52	31 37	47·9	34 32	32 31	48·4	35 12	33 26	48·9	35 51	34 22	49·4	52	128
307	233	33 00	29 18	45·9	33 42	30 10	46·3	34 23	31 02	46·8	35 04	31 56	47·3	35 44	32 50	47·9	36 24	33 45	48·4	53	127
306	234	33 29	28 44	44·8	34 12	29 35	45·3	34 54	30 27	45·8	35 35	31 20	46·3	36 17	32 13	46·8	36 57	33 08	47·4	54	126
305	235	33 58	28 08	43·8	34 41	28 59	44·2	35 24	29 51	44·7	36 06	30 43	45·2	36 48	31 36	45·8	37 30	32 30	46·3	55	125
304	236	34 26	27 32	42·7	35 10	28 22	43·2	35 53	29 13	43·6	36 37	30 04	44·2	37 19	30 57	44·7	38 02	31 51	45·2	56	124
303	237	34 53	26 56	41·6	35 38	27 45	42·1	36 22	28 34	42·6	37 06	29 25	43·1	37 50	30 17	43·6	38 33	31 10	44·1	57	123
302	238	35 20	26 18	40·5	36 06	27 06	41·0	36 51	27 55	41·5	37 36	28 45	42·0	38 20	29 36	42·5	39 04	30 29	43·0	58	122
301	239	35 46	25 39	39·4	36 33	26 27	39·9	37 19	27 15	40·4	38 04	28 04	40·9	38 49	28 55	41·4	39 34	29 46	41·9	59	121
300	240	36 12	25 00	38·3	36 59	25 46	38·8	37 46	26 34	39·2	38 32	27 23	39·7	39 18	28 12	40·2	40 04	29 03	40·8	60	120
299	241	36 37	24 20	37·2	37 25	25 05	37·6	38 12	25 52	38·1	38 59	26 39	38·6	39 46	27 28	39·1	40 32	28 18	39·6	61	119
298	242	37 02	23 39	36·0	37 50	24 23	36·5	38 38	25 09	36·9	39 26	25 56	37·4	40 13	26 43	37·9	41 00	27 32	38·5	62	118
297	243	37 25	22 57	34·9	38 14	23 40	35·3	39 03	24 25	35·8	39 52	25 11	36·3	40 40	25 58	36·8	41 28	26 45	37·3	63	117
296	244	37 48	22 14	33·7	38 38	22 57	34·1	39 28	23 40	34·6	40 17	24 25	35·1	41 06	25 11	35·6	41 54	25 58	36·1	64	116
295	245	38 11	21 31	32·5	39 01	22 12	32·9	39 51	22 54	33·4	40 41	23 38	33·9	41 31	24 23	34·4	42 20	25 09	34·9	65	115
294	246	38 32	20 46	31·3	39 23	21 27	31·8	40 14	22 08	32·2	41 05	22 50	32·7	41 55	23 34	33·1	42 45	24 19	33·6	66	114
293	247	38 53	20 01	30·1	39 45	20 40	30·5	40 37	21 21	31·0	41 28	22 02	31·4	42 19	22 44	31·9	43 10	23 28	32·4	67	113
292	248	39 13	19 15	28·9	40 06	19 53	29·3	40 58	20 32	29·7	41 50	21 12	30·2	42 42	21 53	30·6	43 33	22 35	31·1	68	112
291	249	39 33	18 29	27·7	40 26	19 05	28·1	41 19	19 43	28·5	42 11	20 22	28·9	43 04	21 01	29·4	43 56	21 42	29·8	69	111
290	250	39 51	17 41	26·5	40 45	18 17	26·8	41 38	18 53	27·2	42 31	19 30	27·7	43 25	20 08	28·1	44 18	20 48	28·5	70	110
289	251	40 09	16 53	25·2	41 03	17 27	25·6	41 57	18 02	26·0	42 51	18 38	26·4	43 45	19 15	26·8	44 38	19 53	27·2	71	109
288	252	40 26	16 05	24·0	41 21	16 37	24·3	42 16	17 10	24·7	43 10	17 45	25·1	44 04	18 20	25·5	44 58	18 57	25·9	72	108
287	253	40 42	15 15	22·7	41 38	15 46	23·0	42 32	16 18	23·4	43 28	16 51	23·8	44 23	17 24	24·1	45 17	18 00	24·6	73	107
286	254	40 58	14 25	21·4	41 54	14 54	21·7	42 49	15 25	22·1	43 45	15 56	22·4	44 40	16 28	22·8	45 35	17 01	23·2	74	106
285	255	41 12	13 34	20·1	42 09	14 02	20·4	43 05	14 31	20·8	44 01	15 00	21·1	44 57	15 31	21·4	45 53	16 02	21·8	75	105
284	256	41 26	12 43	18·8	42 23	13 09	19·1	43 19	13 36	19·4	44 16	14 04	19·7	45 12	14 33	20·1	46 09	15 02	20·4	76	104
283	257	41 39	11 51	17·5	42 36	12 15	17·8	43 33	12 41	18·1	44 30	13 07	18·4	45 27	13 34	18·7	46 24	14 00	19·0	77	103
282	258	41 51	10 58	16·2	42 48	11 21	16·5	43 46	11 45	16·7	44 43	12 09	17·0	45 40	12 34	17·3	46 39	13 00	17·6	78	102
281	259	42 02	10 05	14·9	43 00	10 26	15·1	43 57	10 48	15·4	44 55	11 11	15·6	45 53	11 34	15·9	46 51	11 58	16·2	79	101
280	260	42 12	9 12	13·6	43 10	9 31	13·8	44 08	9 51	14·0	45 06	10 12	14·2	46 04	10 33	14·5	47 03	10 55	14·8	80	100
279	261	42 21	8 18	12·2	43 19	8 35	12·4	44 18	8 53	12·6	45 16	9 12	12·8	46 15	9 31	13·1	47 13	9 51	13·3	81	99
278	262	42 29	7 24	10·9	43 28	7 39	11·1	44 27	7 55	11·2	45 26	8 12	11·4	46 24	8 29	11·6	47 23	8 47	11·9	82	98
277	263	42 36	6 29	9·5	43 34	6 43	9·7	44 34	6 57	9·9	45 34	7 12	10·0	46 33	7 27	10·2	47 32	7 42	10·4	83	97
276	264	42 42	5 34	8·2	43 42	5 46	8·3	44 41	5 58	8·5	45 41	6 11	8·6	46 40	6 24	8·8	47 39	6 37	8·9	84	96
275	265	42 48	4 39	6·8	43 47	4 49	6·9	44 47	4 59	7·1	45 46	5 09	7·2	46 46	5 20	7·3	47 46	5 32	7·4	85	95
274	266	42 52	3 43	5·5	43 52	3 51	5·6	44 52	3 59	5·6	45 51	4 08	5·7	46 51	4 17	5·9	47 51	4 26	6·0	86	94
273	267	42 55	2 48	4·1	43 55	2 54	4·2	44 55	3 00	4·2	45 55	3 06	4·3	46 55	3 13	4·4	47 55	3 20	4·5	87	93
272	268	42 58	1 52	2·7	43 58	1 56	2·8	44 58	2 00	2·8	45 58	2 04	2·9	46 58	2 09	2·9	47 58	2 13	3·0	88	92
271	269	42 59	0 56	1·4	43 59	0 58	1·4	44 59	1 00	1·4	45 59	1 02	1·4	46 59	1 04	1·5	47 59	1 07	1·5	89	91
270	270	43 00	0 00	0·0	44 00	0 00	0·0	45 00	0 00	0·0	46 00	0 00	0·0	47 00	0 00	0·0	48 00	0 00	0·0	90	90

N. Lat.: for LHA > 180° ... $Z_n = Z$
for LHA < 180° ... $Z_n = 360° - Z$

SIGHT REDUCTION TABLE

B: (−) for 90° < LHA < 270°
Dec:(−) for Lat. contrary name

Z₁: same sign as B
Z₂: (−) for F > 90°

LHA	F	48° A/H	48° B/P	48° Z_1/Z_2	49° A/H	49° B/P	49° Z_1/Z_2	50° A/H	50° B/P	50° Z_1/Z_2	51° A/H	51° B/P	51° Z_1/Z_2	52° A/H	52° B/P	52° Z_1/Z_2	53° A/H	53° B/P	53° Z_1/Z_2	LHA	LHA
0	180	0 00	42 00	90.0	0 00	41 00	90.0	0 00	40 00	90.0	0 00	39 00	90.0	0 00	38 00	90.0	0 00	37 00	90.0	180	360
1	179	0 40	42 00	89.3	0 39	41 00	89.2	0 39	40 00	89.2	0 38	39 00	89.2	0 37	38 00	89.2	0 36	37 00	89.2	181	359
2	178	1 20	41 59	88.5	1 19	40 59	88.5	1 17	39 59	88.5	1 16	38 59	88.4	1 14	37 59	88.4	1 12	36 59	88.4	182	358
3	177	2 00	41 58	87.8	1 58	40 58	87.7	1 56	39 58	87.7	1 53	38 58	87.7	1 51	37 58	87.6	1 48	36 58	87.6	183	357
4	176	2 41	41 56	87.0	2 37	40 56	87.0	2 34	39 56	86.9	2 31	38 56	86.9	2 28	37 56	86.8	2 24	36 56	86.8	184	356
5	175	3 21	41 53	86.3	3 17	40 54	86.2	3 13	39 54	86.2	3 09	38 54	86.1	3 05	37 54	86.1	3 00	36 54	86.0	185	355
6	174	4 01	41 51	85.5	3 56	40 51	85.5	3 51	39 51	85.4	3 46	38 51	85.3	3 41	37 51	85.3	3 36	36 51	85.2	186	354
7	173	4 41	41 47	84.8	4 35	40 47	84.7	4 30	39 47	84.6	4 24	38 47	84.5	4 18	37 48	84.5	4 12	36 48	84.4	187	353
8	172	5 21	41 43	84.0	5 14	40 43	83.9	5 08	39 43	83.9	5 01	38 43	83.8	4 55	37 44	83.7	4 48	36 44	83.6	188	352
9	171	6 01	41 39	83.3	5 53	40 39	83.2	5 46	39 39	83.1	5 39	38 39	83.0	5 32	37 39	82.9	5 24	36 40	82.8	189	351
10	170	6 40	41 34	82.5	6 32	40 34	82.4	6 25	39 34	82.3	6 16	38 34	82.2	6 08	37 35	82.1	6 00	36 35	82.0	190	350
11	169	7 20	41 28	81.8	7 11	40 28	81.7	7 03	39 29	81.5	6 54	38 29	81.4	6 45	37 29	81.3	6 36	36 29	81.2	191	349
12	168	8 00	41 22	81.0	7 50	40 22	80.9	7 41	39 23	80.8	7 31	38 23	80.6	7 21	37 23	80.5	7 11	36 24	80.4	192	348
13	167	8 39	41 16	80.3	8 29	40 16	80.1	8 19	39 16	80.0	8 08	38 16	79.8	7 58	37 17	79.7	7 47	36 17	79.6	193	347
14	166	9 19	41 09	79.5	9 08	40 09	79.3	8 57	39 09	79.2	8 45	38 09	79.0	8 34	37 10	78.9	8 22	36 10	78.7	194	346
15	165	9 58	41 01	78.7	9 47	40 01	78.6	9 35	39 02	78.4	9 22	38 02	78.2	9 10	37 02	78.1	8 58	36 03	77.9	195	345
16	164	10 38	40 53	78.0	10 25	39 53	77.8	10 12	38 53	77.6	9 59	37 54	77.4	9 46	36 54	77.3	9 33	35 55	77.1	196	344
17	163	11 17	40 44	77.2	11 04	39 44	77.0	10 50	38 45	76.8	10 36	37 45	76.6	10 22	36 46	76.5	10 08	35 47	76.3	197	343
18	162	11 56	40 34	76.4	11 42	39 35	76.2	11 27	38 35	76.0	11 13	37 36	75.8	10 58	36 37	75.6	10 43	35 38	75.5	198	342
19	161	12 35	40 25	75.6	12 20	39 25	75.4	12 05	38 26	75.2	11 49	37 26	75.0	11 34	36 27	74.8	11 18	35 28	74.6	199	341
20	160	13 14	40 14	74.9	12 58	39 15	74.6	12 42	38 15	74.4	12 26	37 16	74.2	12 09	36 17	74.0	11 53	35 18	73.8	200	340
21	159	13 52	40 03	74.1	13 36	39 04	73.8	13 19	38 04	73.6	13 02	37 05	73.4	12 45	36 06	73.2	12 27	35 08	73.0	201	339
22	158	14 31	39 51	73.3	14 14	38 52	73.0	13 56	37 53	72.8	13 38	36 54	72.6	13 20	35 55	72.3	13 02	34 56	72.1	202	338
23	157	15 09	39 39	72.5	14 51	38 40	72.2	14 33	37 41	72.0	14 14	36 42	71.7	13 55	35 43	71.5	13 36	34 45	71.3	203	337
24	156	15 48	39 26	71.7	15 29	38 27	71.4	15 09	37 28	71.2	14 50	36 30	70.9	14 30	35 31	70.7	14 10	34 33	70.4	204	336
25	155	16 26	39 13	70.9	16 06	38 14	70.6	15 46	37 15	70.3	15 25	36 17	70.1	15 05	35 18	69.8	14 44	34 20	69.6	205	335
26	154	17 03	38 59	70.1	16 43	38 00	69.8	16 22	37 01	69.5	16 01	36 03	69.2	15 39	35 05	69.0	15 18	34 07	68.7	206	334
27	153	17 41	38 44	69.3	17 20	37 46	69.0	16 58	36 47	68.7	16 36	35 49	68.4	16 14	34 51	68.1	15 51	33 53	67.9	207	333
28	152	18 19	38 29	68.4	17 56	37 30	68.1	17 34	36 32	67.8	17 11	35 34	67.5	16 48	34 36	67.3	16 25	33 38	67.0	208	332
29	151	18 56	38 13	67.6	18 33	37 15	67.3	18 09	36 16	67.0	17 46	35 18	66.7	17 22	34 21	66.4	16 58	33 23	66.1	209	331
30	150	19 33	37 57	66.8	19 09	36 58	66.5	18 45	36 00	66.1	18 20	35 03	65.8	17 56	34 05	65.5	17 31	33 08	65.2	210	330
31	149	20 10	37 40	65.9	19 45	36 41	65.6	19 20	35 44	65.3	18 55	34 46	65.0	18 29	33 49	64.7	18 03	32 52	64.4	211	329
32	148	20 46	37 22	65.1	20 21	36 24	64.8	19 55	35 26	64.4	19 29	34 29	64.1	19 02	33 32	63.8	18 36	32 35	63.5	212	328
33	147	21 22	37 03	64.2	20 56	36 06	63.9	20 30	35 08	63.6	20 03	34 11	63.2	19 35	33 14	62.9	19 08	32 18	62.6	213	327
34	146	21 58	36 44	63.4	21 31	35 47	63.0	21 04	34 49	62.7	20 36	33 53	62.3	20 08	32 56	62.0	19 40	32 00	61.7	214	326
35	145	22 34	36 25	62.5	22 06	35 27	62.1	21 38	34 30	61.8	21 10	33 33	61.4	20 41	32 37	61.1	20 12	31 41	60.8	215	325
36	144	23 10	36 04	61.6	22 41	35 07	61.3	22 12	34 10	60.9	21 43	33 14	60.5	21 13	32 18	60.2	20 43	31 22	59.9	216	324
37	143	23 45	35 43	60.8	23 15	34 46	60.4	22 45	33 50	60.0	22 15	32 53	59.6	21 45	31 58	59.3	21 14	31 02	59.0	217	323
38	142	24 20	35 21	59.9	23 49	34 25	59.5	23 19	33 28	59.1	22 48	32 33	58.7	22 16	31 37	58.4	21 45	30 42	58.0	218	322
39	141	24 54	34 59	59.0	24 23	34 02	58.6	23 52	33 07	58.2	23 20	32 11	57.8	22 48	31 16	57.5	22 15	30 21	57.1	219	321
40	140	25 28	34 36	58.1	24 57	33 40	57.7	24 24	32 44	57.3	23 52	31 49	56.9	23 19	30 54	56.5	22 45	30 00	56.2	220	320
41	139	26 02	34 12	57.1	25 30	33 16	56.7	24 57	32 21	56.3	24 23	31 26	56.0	23 49	30 32	55.6	23 15	29 38	55.2	221	319
42	138	26 36	33 47	56.2	26 02	32 52	55.8	25 28	31 57	55.4	24 54	31 02	55.0	24 20	30 08	54.6	23 45	29 15	54.3	222	318
43	137	27 09	33 22	55.3	26 35	32 27	54.9	26 00	31 32	54.4	25 25	30 38	54.1	24 50	29 45	53.7	24 14	28 52	53.3	223	317
44	136	27 42	32 56	54.3	27 07	32 01	53.9	26 31	31 07	53.5	25 55	30 13	53.1	25 19	29 20	52.7	24 43	28 28	52.4	224	316
45	135	28 14	32 29	53.4	27 38	31 35	53.0	27 02	30 41	52.5	26 25	29 48	52.1	25 48	28 55	51.8	25 11	28 03	51.4	225	315

LHA	F	48° A/H	48° B/P	48° Z₁/Z₂	49° A/H	49° B/P	49° Z₁/Z₂	50° A/H	50° B/P	50° Z₁/Z₂	51° A/H	51° B/P	51° Z₁/Z₂	52° A/H	52° B/P	52° Z₁/Z₂	53° A/H	53° B/P	53° Z₁/Z₂	LHA
45	135	28 14	32 29	53.4	27 38	31 35	53.0	27 02	30 41	52.5	26 25	29 48	52.1	25 48	28 55	51.8	25 11	28 03	51.4	225 315
46	134	28 46	32 01	52.4	28 10	31 08	52.0	27 32	30 14	51.6	26 55	29 22	51.1	26 17	28 29	50.8	25 39	27 38	50.4	226 314
47	133	29 18	31 33	51.4	28 40	30 40	51.0	28 02	29 47	50.6	27 24	28 55	50.2	26 46	28 03	49.8	26 07	27 12	49.4	227 313
48	132	29 49	31 04	50.5	29 11	30 11	50.0	28 32	29 19	49.6	27 53	28 27	49.2	27 14	27 36	48.8	26 34	26 46	48.4	228 312
49	131	30 20	30 34	49.5	29 41	29 42	49.0	29 01	28 50	48.6	28 21	27 59	48.2	27 41	27 08	47.8	27 01	26 18	47.4	229 311
50	130	30 50	30 04	48.5	30 10	29 12	48.0	29 30	28 20	47.6	28 49	27 30	47.2	28 08	26 40	46.8	27 27	25 51	46.4	230 310
51	129	31 20	29 32	47.5	30 39	28 41	47.0	29 58	27 50	46.6	29 17	27 00	46.2	28 35	26 11	45.8	27 53	25 22	45.4	231 309
52	128	31 49	29 00	46.4	31 08	28 09	46.0	30 26	27 19	45.6	29 44	26 30	45.2	29 01	25 41	44.8	28 19	24 53	44.4	232 308
53	127	32 18	28 27	45.4	31 36	27 37	45.0	30 53	26 48	44.5	30 10	25 59	44.1	29 27	25 11	43.7	28 44	24 24	43.3	233 307
54	126	32 46	27 53	44.4	32 03	27 04	43.9	31 20	26 15	43.5	30 36	25 27	43.1	29 52	24 40	42.7	29 08	23 53	42.3	234 306
55	125	33 14	27 19	43.3	32 30	26 30	42.9	31 46	25 42	42.4	31 02	24 55	42.0	30 17	24 08	41.6	29 32	23 23	41.2	235 305
56	124	33 42	26 44	42.2	32 57	25 55	41.8	32 12	25 08	41.4	31 27	24 22	41.0	30 41	23 36	40.6	29 56	22 51	40.2	236 304
57	123	34 08	26 07	41.1	33 23	25 20	40.7	32 37	24 34	40.3	31 51	23 48	39.9	31 05	23 03	39.5	30 19	22 19	39.1	237 303
58	122	34 34	25 30	40.1	33 48	24 44	39.6	33 02	23 58	39.2	32 15	23 14	38.8	31 28	22 29	38.4	30 41	21 46	38.0	238 302
59	121	35 00	24 53	39.0	34 13	24 07	38.5	33 26	23 22	38.1	32 39	22 38	37.7	31 51	21 55	37.3	31 03	21 13	37.0	239 301
60	120	35 25	24 14	37.8	34 37	23 30	37.4	33 50	22 46	37.0	33 02	22 03	36.6	32 13	21 20	36.2	31 25	20 39	35.9	240 300
61	119	35 49	23 35	36.7	35 01	22 52	36.3	34 14	22 08	35.9	33 24	21 26	35.5	32 35	20 45	35.1	31 46	20 04	34.8	241 299
62	118	36 13	22 55	35.6	35 24	22 12	35.2	34 35	21 30	34.8	33 45	20 49	34.4	32 56	20 09	34.0	32 06	19 29	33.7	242 298
63	117	36 36	22 14	34.4	35 46	21 32	34.0	34 56	20 51	33.6	34 06	20 11	33.3	33 16	19 32	32.9	32 26	18 53	32.5	243 297
64	116	36 58	21 32	33.3	36 08	20 52	32.9	35 17	20 12	32.5	34 27	19 33	32.1	33 36	18 54	31.8	32 45	18 17	31.4	244 296
65	115	37 20	20 50	32.1	36 29	20 10	31.7	35 38	19 32	31.3	34 47	18 54	31.0	33 55	18 16	30.6	33 03	17 40	30.3	245 295
66	114	37 41	20 07	30.9	36 49	19 28	30.5	35 58	18 51	30.2	35 06	18 14	29.8	34 13	17 38	29.5	33 21	17 02	29.1	246 294
67	113	38 01	19 23	29.7	37 09	18 46	29.4	36 17	18 09	29.0	35 24	17 33	28.6	34 31	16 59	28.3	33 38	16 24	28.0	247 293
68	112	38 21	18 38	28.5	37 28	18 02	28.2	36 35	17 27	27.8	35 42	16 53	27.5	34 48	16 19	27.1	33 55	15 46	26.8	248 292
69	111	38 40	17 53	27.3	37 46	17 18	27.0	36 53	16 44	26.6	35 59	16 11	26.3	35 05	15 38	26.0	34 11	15 07	25.7	249 291
70	110	38 58	17 07	26.1	38 04	16 33	25.7	37 10	16 01	25.4	36 15	15 29	25.1	35 21	14 58	24.8	34 26	14 27	24.5	250 290
71	109	39 15	16 20	24.9	38 20	15 48	24.5	37 26	15 17	24.2	36 31	14 46	23.9	35 36	14 16	23.6	34 41	13 47	23.3	251 289
72	108	39 31	15 33	23.6	38 36	15 02	23.3	37 41	14 32	23.0	36 46	14 03	22.7	35 50	13 34	22.4	34 55	13 07	22.1	252 288
73	107	39 47	14 45	22.4	38 51	14 16	22.1	37 56	13 47	21.8	37 00	13 19	21.5	36 04	12 52	21.2	35 08	12 25	20.9	253 287
74	106	40 02	13 56	21.1	39 06	13 28	20.8	38 10	13 01	20.5	37 13	12 35	20.3	36 17	12 09	20.0	35 21	11 44	19.8	254 286
75	105	40 16	13 07	19.8	39 19	12 41	19.5	38 23	12 15	19.3	37 26	11 50	19.0	36 29	11 26	18.8	35 33	11 02	18.5	255 285
76	104	40 29	12 17	18.5	39 32	11 53	18.3	38 35	11 28	18.0	37 37	11 05	17.8	36 41	10 42	17.6	35 44	10 20	17.3	256 284
77	103	40 41	11 27	17.3	39 44	11 04	17.0	38 47	10 41	16.8	37 49	10 19	16.5	36 52	9 58	16.3	35 54	9 37	16.1	257 283
78	102	40 53	10 36	16.0	39 55	10 15	15.7	38 57	9 54	15.5	38 00	9 33	15.3	37 02	9 14	15.1	36 04	8 54	14.9	258 282
79	101	41 04	9 45	14.7	40 05	9 25	14.4	39 07	9 06	14.2	38 09	8 47	14.0	37 11	8 29	13.9	36 13	8 11	13.7	259 281
80	100	41 13	8 53	13.3	40 15	8 35	13.2	39 16	8 17	13.0	38 18	8 00	12.8	37 19	7 44	12.6	36 21	7 27	12.5	260 280
81	99	41 22	8 01	12.0	40 23	7 45	11.9	39 25	7 29	11.7	38 26	7 13	11.5	37 27	6 58	11.4	36 28	6 43	11.2	261 279
82	98	41 30	7 09	10.7	40 31	6 54	10.5	39 32	6 40	10.4	38 33	6 26	10.3	37 34	6 12	10.1	36 35	5 59	10.0	262 278
83	97	41 37	6 16	9.4	40 38	6 03	9.2	39 39	5 50	9.1	38 39	5 38	9.0	37 40	5 26	8.9	36 41	5 15	8.7	263 277
84	96	41 43	5 23	8.1	40 44	5 12	7.9	39 44	5 01	7.8	38 45	4 50	7.7	37 45	4 40	7.6	36 46	4 30	7.5	264 276
85	95	41 48	4 29	6.7	40 49	4 20	6.6	39 49	4 11	6.5	38 49	4 02	6.4	37 50	3 54	6.3	36 50	3 45	6.3	265 275
86	94	41 52	3 36	5.4	40 53	3 28	5.3	39 53	3 21	5.2	38 53	3 14	5.1	37 53	3 07	5.1	36 54	3 01	5.0	266 274
87	93	41 56	2 42	4.0	40 56	2 36	4.0	39 56	2 31	3.9	38 56	2 26	3.9	37 56	2 20	3.8	36 56	2 16	3.8	267 273
88	92	41 58	1 48	2.7	40 58	1 44	2.7	39 58	1 41	2.6	38 58	1 37	2.6	37 58	1 34	2.5	36 58	1 30	2.5	268 272
89	91	42 00	0 54	1.3	41 00	0 52	1.3	40 00	0 50	1.3	39 00	0 49	1.3	38 00	0 47	1.3	37 00	0 45	1.3	269 271
90	90	42 00	0 00	0.0	41 00	0 00	0.0	40 00	0 00	0.0	39 00	0 00	0.0	38 00	0 00	0.0	37 00	0 00	0.0	270 270

N. Lat: for LHA > 180° ... Zn = Z / for LHA < 180° ... Zn = 360° − Z

S. Lat: for LHA > 180° ... Zn = 180° − Z / for LHA < 180° ... Zn = 180° + Z

SIGHT REDUCTION TABLE

B: (−) for 90° < LHA < 270°
Dec:(−) for Lat. contrary name

Z₁: same sign as B
Z₂: (−) for F > 90°

Lat./A — LHA/F	54° A/H	54° B/P	54° Z_1/Z_2	55° A/H	55° B/P	55° Z_1/Z_2	56° A/H	56° B/P	56° Z_1/Z_2	57° A/H	57° B/P	57° Z_1/Z_2	58° A/H	58° B/P	58° Z_1/Z_2	59° A/H	59° B/P	59° Z_1/Z_2	Lat./A — LHA
0 / 180	0 00	36 00	90·0	0 00	35 00	90·0	0 00	34 00	90·0	0 00	33 00	90·0	0 00	32 00	90·0	0 00	31 00	90·0	180 / 360
1 / 179	0 35	36 00	89·2	0 34	35 00	89·2	0 34	34 00	89·2	0 33	33 00	89·2	0 32	32 00	89·2	0 31	31 00	89·1	181 / 359
2 / 178	1 11	35 59	88·4	1 09	34 59	88·4	1 07	33 59	88·3	1 05	32 59	88·3	1 04	31 59	88·3	1 02	30 59	88·3	182 / 358
3 / 177	1 46	35 58	87·6	1 43	34 58	87·5	1 41	33 58	87·5	1 38	32 58	87·5	1 35	31 58	87·5	1 33	30 58	87·4	183 / 357
4 / 176	2 21	35 56	86·8	2 18	34 56	86·7	2 14	33 56	86·7	2 11	32 56	86·6	2 07	31 56	86·6	2 04	30 56	86·6	184 / 356
5 / 175	2 56	35 54	86·0	2 52	34 54	85·9	2 48	33 54	85·9	2 43	32 54	85·8	2 39	31 54	85·8	2 34	30 54	85·7	185 / 355
6 / 174	3 31	35 51	85·1	3 26	34 51	85·1	3 21	33 51	85·0	3 16	32 51	85·0	3 11	31 52	84·9	3 05	30 52	84·9	186 / 354
7 / 173	4 06	35 48	84·3	4 00	34 48	84·3	3 54	33 48	84·2	3 48	32 48	84·1	3 42	31 48	84·1	3 36	30 49	84·0	187 / 353
8 / 172	4 42	35 44	83·5	4 35	34 44	83·4	4 28	33 44	83·4	4 21	32 45	83·3	4 14	31 45	83·3	4 07	30 45	83·1	188 / 352
9 / 171	5 17	35 40	82·7	5 09	34 40	82·6	5 01	33 40	82·5	4 53	32 41	82·4	4 45	31 41	82·4	4 37	30 41	82·3	189 / 351
10 / 170	5 51	35 35	81·9	5 43	34 35	81·8	5 34	33 36	81·7	5 26	32 36	81·6	5 17	31 36	81·5	5 08	30 37	81·4	190 / 350
11 / 169	6 26	35 30	81·1	6 17	34 30	81·0	6 08	33 31	80·8	5 58	32 31	80·7	5 48	31 31	80·6	5 38	30 32	80·5	191 / 349
12 / 168	7 01	35 24	80·2	6 51	34 24	80·1	6 41	33 25	80·0	6 30	32 25	79·9	6 20	31 26	79·8	6 09	30 27	79·7	192 / 348
13 / 167	7 36	35 18	79·4	7 25	34 18	79·3	7 14	33 19	79·2	7 02	32 19	79·0	6 51	31 20	78·9	6 39	30 21	78·8	193 / 347
14 / 166	8 11	35 11	78·6	7 59	34 12	78·5	7 46	33 12	78·3	7 34	32 13	78·2	7 22	31 14	78·1	7 09	30 15	77·9	194 / 346
15 / 165	8 45	35 04	77·8	8 32	34 04	77·6	8 19	33 05	77·5	8 06	32 06	77·3	7 53	31 07	77·2	7 40	30 08	77·1	195 / 345
16 / 164	9 19	34 56	76·9	9 06	33 57	76·8	8 52	32 58	76·6	8 38	31 58	76·5	8 24	31 00	76·3	8 10	30 01	76·2	196 / 344
17 / 163	9 54	34 47	76·1	9 39	33 48	75·9	9 25	32 49	75·8	9 10	31 50	75·6	8 55	30 52	75·5	8 40	29 53	75·3	197 / 343
18 / 162	10 28	34 39	75·3	10 13	33 40	75·1	9 57	32 41	74·9	9 41	31 42	74·8	9 25	30 43	74·6	9 09	29 45	74·4	198 / 342
19 / 161	11 02	34 29	74·4	10 46	33 30	74·2	10 29	32 32	74·1	10 13	31 33	73·9	9 56	30 35	73·7	9 39	29 36	73·6	199 / 341
20 / 160	11 36	34 19	73·6	11 19	33 21	73·4	11 02	32 22	73·2	10 44	31 24	73·0	10 27	30 25	72·8	10 09	29 27	72·7	200 / 340
21 / 159	12 10	34 09	72·7	11 52	33 10	72·5	11 34	32 12	72·3	11 15	31 14	72·2	10 57	30 15	72·0	10 38	29 17	71·8	201 / 339
22 / 158	12 43	33 58	71·9	12 24	33 00	71·7	12 06	32 01	71·5	11 46	31 03	71·3	11 27	30 05	71·1	11 07	29 07	70·9	202 / 338
23 / 157	13 17	33 46	71·0	12 57	32 48	70·8	12 37	31 50	70·6	12 17	30 52	70·4	11 57	29 54	70·2	11 37	28 57	70·0	203 / 337
24 / 156	13 50	33 34	70·2	13 29	32 36	70·0	13 09	31 38	69·7	12 48	30 41	69·5	12 27	29 43	69·3	12 06	28 46	69·1	204 / 336
25 / 155	14 23	33 22	69·3	14 02	32 24	69·1	13 40	31 26	68·9	13 18	30 29	68·6	12 56	29 31	68·4	12 34	28 34	68·2	205 / 335
26 / 154	14 56	33 09	68·5	14 34	32 11	68·2	14 11	31 14	68·0	13 49	30 16	67·8	13 26	29 19	67·5	13 03	28 22	67·3	206 / 334
27 / 153	15 29	32 55	67·6	15 06	31 58	67·3	14 42	31 00	67·1	14 19	30 03	66·9	13 55	29 06	66·6	13 31	28 10	66·4	207 / 333
28 / 152	16 01	32 41	66·7	15 37	31 44	66·5	15 13	30 47	66·2	14 49	29 50	66·0	14 24	28 53	65·7	14 00	27 57	65·5	208 / 332
29 / 151	16 33	32 26	65·8	16 09	31 29	65·6	15 44	30 32	65·3	15 19	29 36	65·1	14 53	28 39	64·8	14 28	27 43	64·6	209 / 331
30 / 150	17 05	32 11	65·0	16 40	31 14	64·7	16 14	30 17	64·4	15 48	29 21	64·2	15 22	28 25	63·9	14 55	27 29	63·7	210 / 330
31 / 149	17 37	31 55	64·1	17 11	30 58	63·8	16 44	30 02	63·5	16 17	29 06	63·3	15 50	28 10	63·0	15 23	27 15	62·7	211 / 329
32 / 148	18 09	31 38	63·2	17 42	30 42	62·9	17 14	29 46	62·6	16 47	28 51	62·3	16 19	27 55	62·1	15 50	27 00	61·8	212 / 328
33 / 147	18 40	31 21	62·3	18 12	30 25	62·0	17 44	29 30	61·7	17 15	28 34	61·4	16 47	27 39	61·2	16 17	26 45	60·9	213 / 327
34 / 146	19 11	31 04	61·4	18 42	30 08	61·1	18 13	29 13	60·8	17 44	28 18	60·5	17 14	27 23	60·2	16 44	26 29	60·0	214 / 326
35 / 145	19 42	30 46	60·5	19 12	29 50	60·2	18 42	28 55	59·9	18 12	28 01	59·6	17 42	27 06	59·3	17 11	26 12	59·0	215 / 325
36 / 144	20 13	30 27	59·6	19 42	29 32	59·2	19 11	28 37	59·0	18 40	27 43	58·6	18 09	26 49	58·4	17 37	25 55	58·1	216 / 324
37 / 143	20 43	30 07	58·7	20 12	29 13	58·3	19 40	28 19	58·0	19 08	27 25	57·7	18 36	26 31	57·4	18 03	25 38	57·1	217 / 323
38 / 142	21 13	29 48	57·7	20 41	28 53	57·4	20 08	27 59	57·1	19 35	27 06	56·8	19 02	26 13	56·5	18 29	25 20	56·2	218 / 322
39 / 141	21 43	29 27	56·8	21 10	28 33	56·4	20 36	27 40	56·2	20 03	26 47	55·8	19 29	25 54	55·5	18 55	25 02	55·2	219 / 321
40 / 140	22 12	29 06	55·8	21 38	28 13	55·5	21 04	27 20	55·2	20 30	26 27	54·9	19 55	25 35	54·6	19 20	24 43	54·3	220 / 320
41 / 139	22 41	28 44	54·9	22 06	27 51	54·5	21 31	26 59	54·3	20 56	26 07	53·9	20 21	25 15	53·6	19 45	24 24	53·3	221 / 319
42 / 138	23 10	28 22	53·9	22 34	27 29	53·6	21 58	26 37	53·3	21 22	25 46	52·9	20 46	24 55	52·6	20 10	24 04	52·3	222 / 318
43 / 137	23 38	27 59	53·0	23 02	27 07	52·6	22 25	26 15	52·3	21 48	25 24	52·0	21 11	24 34	51·7	20 34	23 43	51·4	223 / 317
44 / 136	24 06	27 36	52·0	23 29	26 44	51·7	22 51	25 53	51·4	22 14	25 02	51·0	21 36	24 12	50·7	20 58	23 23	50·4	224 / 316
45 / 135	24 34	27 11	51·0	23 56	26 20	50·7	23 17	25 30	50·4	22 39	24 40	50·0	22 00	23 50	49·7	21 21	23 01	49·4	225 / 315

Lat. / A	54°			55°			56°			57°			58°			59°			Lat. / A
LHA/F	A/H	B/P	Z_1/Z_2	A/H	B/P	Z_1/Z_2	A/H	B/P	Z_1/Z_2	A/H	B/P	Z_1/Z_2	A/H	B/P	Z_1/Z_2	A/H	B/P	Z_1/Z_2	LHA
45 / 135	24 34	27 11	51·0	23 56	26 20	50·7	23 17	25 30	50·3	22 39	24 40	50·0	22 00	23 50	49·7	21 21	23 01	49·4	225 / 315
46 / 134	25 01	26 47	50·0	24 22	25 56	49·7	23 43	25 06	49·4	23 04	24 17	49·0	22 24	23 28	48·7	21 45	22 39	48·4	226 / 314
47 / 133	25 28	26 22	49·1	24 48	25 32	48·7	24 08	24 42	48·4	23 28	23 53	48·0	22 48	23 05	47·7	22 08	22 17	47·4	227 / 313
48 / 132	25 54	25 56	48·1	25 14	25 06	47·7	24 33	24 17	47·4	23 53	23 29	47·0	23 11	22 41	46·7	22 32	21 54	46·4	228 / 312
49 / 131	26 20	25 29	47·1	25 39	24 40	46·7	24 58	23 52	46·4	24 16	23 05	46·0	23 34	22 17	45·7	22 52	21 31	45·4	229 / 311
50 / 130	26 46	25 02	46·0	26 04	24 14	45·7	25 22	23 26	45·3	24 40	22 39	45·0	23 57	21 53	44·7	23 14	21 07	44·4	230 / 310
51 / 129	27 11	24 34	45·0	26 28	23 47	44·7	25 45	23 00	44·3	25 02	22 14	44·0	24 19	21 28	43·7	23 36	20 43	43·4	231 / 309
52 / 128	27 36	24 06	44·0	26 52	23 19	43·6	26 09	22 33	43·3	25 25	21 48	43·0	24 41	21 03	42·7	23 57	20 18	42·3	232 / 308
53 / 127	28 00	23 37	43·0	27 16	22 51	42·6	26 32	22 05	42·3	25 47	21 21	41·9	25 02	20 37	41·6	24 17	19 53	41·3	233 / 307
54 / 126	28 24	23 07	41·9	27 39	22 22	41·6	26 54	21 38	41·2	26 09	20 54	40·9	25 23	20 10	40·6	24 37	19 27	40·3	234 / 306
55 / 125	28 47	22 37	40·9	28 01	21 53	40·5	27 16	21 09	40·2	26 30	20 26	39·9	25 44	19 43	39·5	24 57	19 01	39·2	235 / 305
56 / 124	29 10	22 07	39·8	28 24	21 23	39·5	27 37	20 40	39·1	26 50	19 57	38·8	26 04	19 16	38·5	25 17	18 34	38·2	236 / 304
57 / 123	29 32	21 35	38·8	28 45	20 52	38·4	27 58	20 10	38·1	27 11	19 29	37·8	26 23	18 48	37·4	25 35	18 07	37·1	237 / 303
58 / 122	29 54	21 03	37·7	29 06	20 21	37·3	28 19	19 40	37·0	27 31	18 59	36·7	26 42	18 19	36·4	25 54	17 40	36·1	238 / 302
59 / 121	30 15	20 31	36·6	29 27	19 50	36·3	28 38	19 09	35·9	27 50	18 30	35·6	27 01	17 50	35·3	26 12	17 12	35·0	239 / 301
60 / 120	30 36	19 58	35·5	29 47	19 18	35·1	28 58	18 38	34·9	28 09	17 59	34·5	27 19	17 21	34·2	26 29	16 43	34·0	240 / 300
61 / 119	30 56	19 24	34·4	30 07	18 45	34·1	29 17	18 06	33·8	28 27	17 29	33·5	27 37	16 51	33·2	26 46	16 14	32·9	241 / 299
62 / 118	31 16	18 50	33·3	30 26	18 12	33·0	29 35	17 34	32·7	28 45	16 57	32·4	27 54	16 21	32·1	27 03	15 45	31·8	242 / 298
63 / 117	31 35	18 15	32·2	30 44	17 38	31·9	29 53	17 02	31·6	29 02	16 26	31·3	28 10	15 50	31·0	27 19	15 15	30·7	243 / 297
64 / 116	31 53	17 40	31·1	31 02	17 04	30·8	30 10	16 28	30·5	29 19	15 53	30·2	28 27	15 19	29·9	27 35	14 45	29·6	244 / 296
65 / 115	32 11	17 04	30·0	31 19	16 29	29·7	30 27	15 55	29·4	29 35	15 21	29·1	28 42	14 48	28·8	27 50	14 15	28·5	245 / 295
66 / 114	32 28	16 28	28·8	31 36	15 54	28·5	30 43	15 20	28·2	29 51	14 48	28·0	28 57	14 16	27·7	28 04	13 44	27·4	246 / 294
67 / 113	32 45	15 51	27·7	31 52	15 18	27·4	30 59	14 46	27·1	30 05	14 14	26·8	29 12	13 43	26·6	28 18	13 13	26·3	247 / 293
68 / 112	33 01	15 14	26·5	32 08	14 42	26·3	31 14	14 11	26·0	30 20	13 40	25·7	29 26	13 10	25·5	28 31	12 41	25·2	248 / 292
69 / 111	33 17	14 36	25·4	32 23	14 05	25·1	31 28	13 35	24·8	30 34	13 06	24·6	29 39	12 37	24·4	28 44	12 09	24·1	249 / 291
70 / 110	33 32	13 57	24·2	32 37	13 28	24·0	31 42	12 59	23·7	30 47	12 31	23·5	29 52	12 04	23·2	28 57	11 37	23·0	250 / 290
71 / 109	33 46	13 18	23·1	32 51	12 51	22·8	31 55	12 23	22·6	31 00	11 56	22·3	30 04	11 30	22·1	29 09	11 04	21·9	251 / 289
72 / 108	33 59	12 39	21·9	33 04	12 13	21·6	32 08	11 46	21·4	31 12	11 21	21·2	30 16	10 56	21·0	29 20	10 31	20·8	252 / 288
73 / 107	34 12	12 00	20·7	33 16	11 34	20·5	32 20	11 09	20·2	31 23	10 45	20·0	30 27	10 21	19·8	29 30	9 58	19·6	253 / 287
74 / 106	34 24	11 19	19·5	33 28	10 55	19·3	32 31	10 32	19·1	31 34	10 09	18·9	30 37	9 46	18·7	29 41	9 24	18·5	254 / 286
75 / 105	34 36	10 39	18·3	33 39	10 16	18·1	32 42	9 54	17·9	31 44	9 32	17·7	30 47	9 11	17·5	29 50	8 50	17·4	255 / 285
76 / 104	34 46	9 58	17·1	33 49	9 37	16·9	32 52	9 16	16·7	31 54	8 56	16·6	30 57	8 36	16·4	29 59	8 16	16·2	256 / 284
77 / 103	34 56	9 17	15·9	33 59	8 57	15·7	33 01	8 38	15·6	32 03	8 19	15·4	31 05	8 00	15·2	30 07	7 42	15·1	257 / 283
78 / 102	35 06	8 35	14·7	34 08	8 17	14·5	33 10	7 59	14·4	32 11	7 41	14·2	31 13	7 24	14·1	30 15	7 07	13·9	258 / 282
79 / 101	35 14	7 54	13·5	34 16	7 37	13·3	33 18	7 20	13·2	32 21	7 04	13·0	31 21	6 48	12·9	30 22	6 32	12·8	259 / 281
80 / 100	35 22	7 11	12·3	34 24	6 56	12·1	33 25	6 41	12·0	32 26	6 26	11·9	31 27	6 12	11·7	30 29	5 57	11·6	260 / 280
81 / 99	35 29	6 29	11·1	34 30	6 15	10·9	33 32	6 01	10·8	32 33	5 48	10·7	31 34	5 35	10·6	30 35	5 22	10·5	261 / 279
82 / 98	35 36	5 46	9·9	34 37	5 34	9·7	33 37	5 22	9·6	32 38	5 10	9·5	31 39	4 58	9·4	30 40	4 47	9·3	262 / 278
83 / 97	35 41	5 04	8·6	34 42	4 53	8·5	33 43	4 42	8·4	32 43	4 32	8·3	31 44	4 21	8·2	30 45	4 11	8·2	263 / 277
84 / 96	35 46	4 21	7·4	34 47	4 11	7·3	33 47	4 02	7·2	32 48	3 53	7·1	31 48	3 44	7·1	30 49	3 36	7·0	264 / 276
85 / 95	35 51	3 37	6·2	34 51	3 30	6·1	33 51	3 22	6·0	32 52	3 14	6·0	31 52	3 07	5·9	30 52	3 00	5·8	265 / 275
86 / 94	35 54	2 54	4·9	34 54	2 48	4·9	33 54	2 42	4·8	32 55	2 36	4·8	31 55	2 30	4·7	30 55	2 24	4·7	266 / 274
87 / 93	35 57	2 11	3·7	34 57	2 06	3·7	33 57	2 01	3·6	32 57	1 57	3·6	31 57	1 52	3·5	30 57	1 48	3·5	267 / 273
88 / 92	35 58	1 27	2·5	34 59	1 24	2·4	33 59	1 21	2·4	32 59	1 18	2·4	31 59	1 15	2·3	30 59	1 12	2·3	268 / 272
89 / 91	36 00	0 44	1·2	35 00	0 42	1·2	34 00	0 40	1·2	33 00	0 39	1·2	32 00	0 37	1·2	31 00	0 36	1·2	269 / 271
90 / 90	36 00	0 00	0·0	35 00	0 00	0·0	34 00	0 00	0·0	33 00	0 00	0·0	32 00	0 00	0·0	31 00	0 00	0·0	270 / 270

N. Lat.: for LHA > 180° ... $Z_n = Z$
for LHA < 180° ... $Z_n = 360° - Z$

S. Lat.: for LHA > 180° ... $Z_n = 180° - Z$
for LHA < 180° ... $Z_n = 180° + Z$

SIGHT REDUCTION TABLE

B: (–) for 90° < LHA < 270°
Dec:(–) for Lat. contrary name

Z₁: same sign as B
Z₂: (–) for F > 90°

LHA/F		60°			61°			62°			63°			64°			65°			Lat. / A
Lat. / A		A/H	B/P	Z_1/Z_2	A/H	B/P	Z_1/Z_2	A/H	B/P	Z_1/Z_2	A/H	B/P	Z_1/Z_2	A/H	B/P	Z_1/Z_2	A/H	B/P	Z_1/Z_2	LHA
0	180	0 00	30 00	90·0	0 00	29 00	90·0	0 00	28 00	90·0	0 00	27 00	90·0	0 00	26 00	90·0	0 00	25 00	90·0	180 360
1	179	0 30	30 00	89·1	0 29	29 00	89·1	0 28	28 00	89·1	0 27	27 00	89·1	0 26	26 00	89·1	0 25	25 00	89·1	181 359
2	178	1 00	29 59	88·3	0 58	28 59	88·3	0 56	27 59	88·2	0 54	26 59	88·2	0 53	25 59	88·2	0 51	24 59	88·2	182 358
3	177	1 30	29 58	87·4	1 27	28 58	87·4	1 24	27 58	87·4	1 22	26 58	87·3	1 19	25 58	87·3	1 16	24 58	87·3	183 357
4	176	2 00	29 56	86·5	1 56	28 56	86·5	1 53	27 57	86·5	1 49	26 57	86·4	1 45	25 57	86·4	1 41	24 57	86·4	184 356
5	175	2 30	29 54	85·7	2 25	28 54	85·6	2 21	27 55	85·6	2 16	26 55	85·5	2 11	25 55	85·5	2 07	24 55	85·5	185 355
6	174	3 00	29 52	84·8	2 54	28 52	84·7	2 49	27 52	84·7	2 43	26 52	84·6	2 38	25 53	84·6	2 32	24 53	84·6	186 354
7	173	3 30	29 49	83·9	3 23	28 49	83·9	3 17	27 49	83·8	3 10	26 50	83·7	3 04	25 50	83·7	2 57	24 50	83·7	187 353
8	172	3 59	29 45	83·1	3 52	28 46	83·0	3 45	27 46	82·9	3 37	26 46	82·9	3 30	25 47	82·8	3 22	24 47	82·7	188 352
9	171	4 29	29 42	82·2	4 21	28 42	82·1	4 13	27 42	82·0	4 04	26 43	82·0	3 56	25 43	81·9	3 47	24 44	81·8	189 351
10	170	4 59	29 37	81·3	4 50	28 38	81·2	4 41	27 38	81·2	4 31	26 39	81·1	4 22	25 39	81·0	4 13	24 40	80·9	190 350
11	169	5 28	29 33	80·4	5 18	28 33	80·4	5 08	27 34	80·3	4 58	26 34	80·2	4 48	25 35	80·1	4 38	24 36	80·0	191 349
12	168	5 58	29 27	79·6	5 47	28 28	79·5	5 36	27 29	79·4	5 25	26 29	79·3	5 14	25 30	79·2	5 02	24 31	79·1	192 348
13	167	6 27	29 22	78·7	6 16	28 22	78·6	6 04	27 23	78·5	5 52	26 24	78·4	5 40	25 25	78·3	5 27	24 26	78·2	193 347
14	166	6 57	29 15	77·8	6 44	28 16	77·7	6 31	27 17	77·6	6 18	26 18	77·5	6 05	25 20	77·4	5 52	24 21	77·3	194 346
15	165	7 26	29 09	76·9	7 13	28 10	76·8	6 59	27 11	76·7	6 45	26 12	76·6	6 31	25 14	76·5	6 17	24 15	76·4	195 345
16	164	7 55	29 02	76·1	7 41	28 03	75·9	7 26	27 04	75·8	7 11	26 06	75·7	6 56	25 07	75·5	6 41	24 09	75·4	196 344
17	163	8 24	28 54	75·2	8 09	27 56	75·0	7 53	26 57	74·9	7 38	25 59	74·8	7 22	25 00	74·6	7 06	24 02	74·5	197 343
18	162	8 53	28 46	74·3	8 37	27 48	74·1	8 20	26 50	74·0	8 04	25 51	73·9	7 47	24 53	73·7	7 30	23 55	73·6	198 342
19	161	9 21	28 38	73·4	9 05	27 40	73·2	8 48	26 41	73·1	8 30	25 43	72·9	8 12	24 45	72·8	7 55	23 48	72·7	199 341
20	160	9 51	28 29	72·5	9 33	27 31	72·3	9 14	26 33	72·2	8 56	25 35	72·0	8 37	24 37	71·9	8 19	23 40	71·7	200 340
21	159	10 19	28 19	71·6	10 00	27 22	71·4	9 41	26 24	71·3	9 22	25 26	71·1	9 02	24 29	71·0	8 43	23 32	70·8	201 339
22	158	10 48	28 10	70·7	10 28	27 12	70·5	10 08	26 15	70·4	9 48	25 17	70·2	9 27	24 20	70·0	9 07	23 23	69·9	202 338
23	157	11 16	27 59	69·8	10 55	27 02	69·6	10 34	26 05	69·5	10 13	25 08	69·3	9 52	24 11	69·1	9 30	23 14	69·0	203 337
24	156	11 44	27 49	68·9	11 22	26 51	68·7	11 00	25 54	68·5	10 38	24 58	68·4	10 16	24 01	68·2	9 54	23 04	68·0	204 336
25	155	12 12	27 37	68·0	11 49	26 40	67·8	11 27	25 44	67·6	11 04	24 47	67·4	10 41	23 51	67·3	10 17	22 55	67·1	205 335
26	154	12 40	27 26	67·1	12 16	26 29	66·9	11 53	25 33	66·7	11 29	24 36	66·5	11 05	23 40	66·3	10 41	22 44	66·2	206 334
27	153	13 07	27 13	66·2	12 43	26 17	66·0	12 18	25 21	65·8	11 54	24 25	65·6	11 29	23 29	65·4	11 04	22 34	65·2	207 333
28	152	13 35	27 01	65·3	13 09	26 05	65·1	12 44	25 09	64·9	12 18	24 13	64·7	11 53	23 18	64·5	11 27	22 23	64·3	208 332
29	151	14 02	26 48	64·4	13 36	25 52	64·1	13 09	24 56	63·9	12 43	24 01	63·7	12 16	23 06	63·5	11 49	22 11	63·3	209 331
30	150	14 29	26 34	63·4	14 02	25 39	63·2	13 35	24 43	63·0	13 07	23 49	62·8	12 40	22 54	62·6	12 12	21 59	62·4	210 330
31	149	14 55	26 20	62·5	14 28	25 25	62·3	14 00	24 30	62·1	13 31	23 36	61·8	13 03	22 41	61·6	12 34	21 47	61·4	211 329
32	148	15 22	26 05	61·6	14 53	25 11	61·3	14 24	24 16	61·1	13 55	23 22	60·9	13 26	22 28	60·7	12 56	21 35	60·5	212 328
33	147	15 48	25 50	60·6	15 19	24 56	60·4	14 49	24 02	60·2	14 19	23 08	59·9	13 49	22 15	59·7	13 18	21 22	59·5	213 327
34	146	16 14	25 35	59·7	15 44	24 41	59·5	15 13	23 47	59·2	14 42	22 54	59·0	14 11	22 01	58·8	13 40	21 08	58·6	214 326
35	145	16 40	25 19	58·8	16 09	24 25	58·5	15 37	23 32	58·3	15 06	22 39	58·0	14 34	21 47	57·8	14 02	20 54	57·6	215 325
36	144	17 05	25 02	57·8	16 33	24 09	57·6	16 01	23 17	57·3	15 29	22 24	57·1	14 56	21 32	56·9	14 23	20 40	56·6	216 324
37	143	17 31	24 45	56·9	16 58	23 53	56·6	16 25	23 00	56·4	15 51	22 09	56·1	15 18	21 17	55·9	14 44	20 26	55·7	217 323
38	142	17 56	24 28	55·9	17 22	23 36	55·7	16 48	22 44	55·4	16 14	21 53	55·1	15 39	21 01	54·9	15 05	20 11	54·7	218 322
39	141	18 20	24 10	55·0	17 46	23 18	54·7	17 11	22 27	54·4	16 36	21 36	54·2	16 01	20 46	54·0	15 25	19 55	53·7	219 321
40	140	18 45	23 52	54·0	18 09	23 00	53·7	17 34	22 10	53·5	16 58	21 19	53·2	16 22	20 29	53·0	15 46	19 39	52·7	220 320
41	139	19 09	23 33	53·0	18 33	22 42	52·8	17 56	21 52	52·5	17 20	21 02	52·2	16 43	20 13	52·0	16 06	19 23	51·8	221 319
42	138	19 33	23 13	52·1	18 56	22 23	51·8	18 19	21 34	51·5	17 41	20 44	51·3	17 03	19 55	51·0	16 26	19 07	50·8	222 318
43	137	19 56	22 54	51·1	19 18	22 04	50·8	18 40	21 15	50·5	18 02	20 26	50·3	17 24	19 38	50·0	16 45	18 50	49·8	223 317
44	136	20 19	22 33	50·1	19 41	21 44	49·8	19 02	20 56	49·5	18 23	20 08	49·3	17 44	19 20	49·0	17 04	18 33	48·8	224 316
45	135	20 42	22 12	49·1	20 03	21 24	48·8	19 23	20 36	48·6	18 43	19 49	48·3	18 03	19 02	48·1	17 23	18 15	47·8	225 315

		60°			61°			62°			63°			64°			65°				
LHA/F	A	A/H	B/P	Z_1/Z_2	A/H	B/P	Z_1/Z_2	A/H	B/P	Z_1/Z_2	A/H	B/P	Z_1/Z_2	A/H	B/P	Z_1/Z_2	A/H	B/P	Z_1/Z_2	A	LHA
45	135	20 42	22 12	49·1	20 03	21 24	48·8	19 23	20 36	48·6	18 43	19 49	48·3	18 03	19 02	48·1	17 23	18 15	47·8	315	225
46	134	21 05	21 51	48·1	20 25	21 04	47·8	19 44	20 16	47·6	19 04	19 29	47·3	18 23	18 43	47·1	17 42	17 57	46·8	314	226
47	133	21 27	21 30	47·1	20 46	20 43	46·8	20 05	19 56	46·6	19 24	19 10	46·3	18 42	18 24	46·1	18 00	17 39	45·8	313	227
48	132	21 49	21 07	46·1	21 07	20 21	45·8	20 25	19 35	45·6	19 43	18 50	45·3	19 01	18 04	45·1	18 18	17 20	44·8	312	228
49	131	22 10	20 45	45·1	21 28	19 59	44·8	20 45	19 14	44·6	20 02	18 29	44·3	19 19	17 45	44·0	18 36	17 01	43·8	311	229
50	130	22 31	20 22	44·1	21 48	19 37	43·8	21 05	18 52	43·5	20 21	18 08	43·3	19 37	17 24	43·0	18 53	16 41	42·8	310	230
51	129	22 52	19 58	43·1	22 08	19 14	42·8	21 24	18 30	42·5	20 40	17 47	42·3	19 55	17 04	42·0	19 10	16 21	41·8	309	231
52	128	23 12	19 34	42·1	22 28	18 51	41·8	21 43	18 08	41·5	20 58	17 25	41·2	20 13	16 43	41·0	19 27	16 01	40·8	308	232
53	127	23 32	19 10	41·0	22 47	18 27	40·7	22 01	17 45	40·5	21 15	17 03	40·2	20 30	16 21	40·0	19 44	15 41	39·7	307	233
54	126	23 52	18 45	40·0	23 06	18 03	39·7	22 19	17 21	39·4	21 33	16 40	39·2	20 46	16 00	39·0	20 00	15 20	38·7	306	234
55	125	24 11	18 19	39·0	23 24	17 38	38·7	22 37	16 58	38·4	21 50	16 17	38·2	21 03	15 38	38·0	20 15	14 58	37·7	305	235
56	124	24 29	17 54	37·9	23 42	17 13	37·6	22 54	16 34	37·4	22 07	15 54	37·1	21 19	15 15	36·9	20 31	14 37	36·7	304	236
57	123	24 48	17 27	36·9	23 59	16 48	36·6	23 11	16 09	36·3	22 23	15 31	36·1	21 34	14 53	35·8	20 46	14 15	35·6	303	237
58	122	25 05	17 01	35·8	24 17	16 22	35·5	23 28	15 44	35·3	22 39	15 07	35·0	21 49	14 29	34·8	21 00	13 53	34·6	302	238
59	121	25 23	16 34	34·8	24 33	15 56	34·5	23 44	15 19	34·2	22 54	14 42	34·0	22 04	14 06	33·8	21 14	13 30	33·5	301	239
60	120	25 40	16 06	33·7	24 50	15 29	33·4	23 59	14 53	33·2	23 09	14 18	32·9	22 19	13 42	32·7	21 28	13 07	32·5	300	240
61	119	25 56	15 38	32·6	25 05	15 03	32·4	24 15	14 27	32·1	23 24	13 53	31·9	22 33	13 18	31·7	21 42	12 44	31·5	299	241
62	118	26 12	15 10	31·5	25 21	14 35	31·3	24 29	14 01	31·1	23 38	13 27	30·8	22 46	12 54	30·6	21 55	12 21	30·4	298	242
63	117	26 27	14 41	30·5	25 36	14 08	30·2	24 44	13 34	30·0	23 52	13 01	29·8	22 59	12 29	29·5	22 07	11 57	29·3	297	243
64	116	26 42	14 12	29·4	25 50	13 39	29·1	24 57	13 07	28·9	24 05	12 35	28·7	23 12	12 04	28·5	22 19	11 33	28·3	296	244
65	115	26 56	13 43	28·3	26 04	13 11	28·1	25 11	12 40	27·8	24 18	12 09	27·6	23 25	11 39	27·4	22 31	11 09	27·2	295	245
66	114	27 11	13 13	27·2	26 17	12 42	27·0	25 24	12 12	26·8	24 30	11 43	26·6	23 36	11 13	26·4	22 43	10 44	26·2	294	246
67	113	27 24	12 43	26·1	26 30	12 13	25·9	25 36	11 44	25·7	24 42	11 16	25·5	23 48	10 47	25·3	22 54	10 20	25·1	293	247
68	112	27 37	12 12	25·0	26 43	11 44	24·8	25 48	11 16	24·6	24 54	10 48	24·4	23 59	10 21	24·2	23 04	9 55	24·0	292	248
69	111	27 50	11 41	23·9	26 55	11 14	23·7	26 00	10 47	23·5	25 05	10 21	23·3	24 09	9 55	23·1	23 14	9 29	23·0	291	249
70	110	28 01	11 10	22·8	27 06	10 44	22·6	26 11	10 18	22·4	25 15	9 53	22·2	24 20	9 28	22·0	23 23	9 04	21·9	290	250
71	109	28 13	10 39	21·7	27 17	10 14	21·5	26 21	9 49	21·3	25 25	9 25	21·1	24 29	9 01	21·0	23 33	8 38	20·8	289	251
72	108	28 24	10 07	20·6	27 27	9 43	20·4	26 31	9 20	20·2	25 35	8 57	20·0	24 38	8 34	19·9	23 42	8 12	19·7	288	252
73	107	28 34	9 35	19·4	27 37	9 12	19·3	26 41	8 50	19·1	25 44	8 28	18·9	24 47	8 07	18·8	23 50	7 46	18·6	287	253
74	106	28 44	9 03	18·3	27 47	8 41	18·2	26 50	8 20	18·0	25 52	8 00	17·8	24 55	7 39	17·7	23 58	7 19	17·6	286	254
75	105	28 53	8 30	17·2	27 55	8 10	17·0	26 58	7 50	16·9	26 01	7 31	16·7	25 03	7 12	16·6	24 06	6 53	16·5	285	255
76	104	29 01	7 57	16·1	28 04	7 38	15·9	27 06	7 20	15·8	26 08	7 02	15·6	25 10	6 44	15·5	24 13	6 26	15·4	284	256
77	103	29 09	7 24	14·9	28 11	7 06	14·8	27 13	6 49	14·7	26 15	6 32	14·5	25 17	6 16	14·4	24 19	5 59	14·3	283	257
78	102	29 17	6 51	13·8	28 18	6 34	13·7	27 20	6 19	13·5	26 22	6 03	13·4	25 23	5 47	13·3	24 25	5 32	13·2	282	258
79	101	29 24	6 17	12·7	28 25	6 02	12·5	27 27	5 48	12·4	26 28	5 33	12·3	25 29	5 19	12·2	24 31	5 05	12·1	281	259
80	100	29 30	5 44	11·5	28 31	5 30	11·4	27 32	5 17	11·3	26 33	5 03	11·2	25 35	4 50	11·1	24 36	4 38	11·0	280	260
81	99	29 36	5 10	10·4	28 37	4 57	10·3	27 38	4 45	10·2	26 38	4 33	10·1	25 39	4 22	10·0	24 40	4 10	9·9	279	261
82	98	29 41	4 36	9·2	28 41	4 25	9·1	27 42	4 14	9·0	26 43	4 03	9·0	25 44	3 53	8·9	24 44	3 43	8·7	278	262
83	97	29 45	4 01	8·1	28 46	3 52	8·0	27 46	3 42	7·9	26 47	3 33	7·8	25 48	3 24	7·8	24 48	3 15	7·6	277	263
84	96	29 49	3 27	6·9	28 50	3 19	6·9	27 50	3 11	6·8	26 50	3 03	6·7	25 51	2 55	6·7	24 51	2 47	6·6	276	264
85	95	29 52	2 53	5·8	28 53	2 46	5·7	27 53	2 39	5·7	26 53	2 33	5·6	25 54	2 26	5·6	24 54	2 20	5·5	275	265
86	94	29 55	2 18	4·6	28 55	2 13	4·6	27 56	2 07	4·5	26 56	2 02	4·5	25 56	1 57	4·4	24 56	1 52	4·4	274	266
87	93	29 57	1 44	3·5	28 57	1 40	3·4	27 57	1 36	3·4	26 58	1 32	3·4	25 58	1 28	3·3	24 58	1 24	3·3	273	267
88	92	29 59	1 09	2·3	28 59	1 06	2·3	27 59	1 04	2·3	26 59	1 01	2·2	25 59	0 59	2·2	24 59	0 56	2·2	272	268
89	91	30 00	0 35	1·2	29 00	0 33	1·1	28 00	0 32	1·1	27 00	0 31	1·1	26 00	0 29	1·1	25 00	0 28	1·1	271	269
90	90	30 00	0 00	0·0	29 00	0 00	0·0	28 00	0 00	0·0	27 00	0 00	0·0	26 00	0 00	0·0	25 00	0 00	0·0	270	270

N. Lat.: for LHA > 180° ... $Z_n = Z$
       for LHA < 180° ... $Z_n = 360° - Z$

S. Lat.: for LHA > 180° ... $Z_n = 180° - Z$
      for LHA < 180° ... $Z_n = 180° + Z$

SIGHT REDUCTION TABLE

B: (−) for 90° < LHA < 270°
Dec:(−) for Lat. contrary name

Z₁: same sign as B
Z₂:(−) for F > 90°

LHA/F	66° A/H	66° B/P	66° Z₁/Z₂	67° A/H	67° B/P	67° Z₁/Z₂	68° A/H	68° B/P	68° Z₁/Z₂	69° A/H	69° B/P	69° Z₁/Z₂	70° A/H	70° B/P	70° Z₁/Z₂	71° A/H	71° B/P	71° Z₁/Z₂	LHA
0	0 00	24 00	90·0	0 00	23 00	90·0	0 00	22 00	90·0	0 00	21 00	90·0	0 00	20 00	90·0	0 00	19 00	90·0	180
1	0 24	24 00	89·1	0 23	23 00	89·1	0 22	22 00	89·1	0 22	21 00	89·1	0 21	20 00	89·1	0 20	19 00	89·1	181
2	0 49	23 59	88·2	0 47	22 59	88·2	0 45	21 59	88·1	0 43	20 59	88·1	0 41	19 59	88·1	0 39	18 59	88·1	182
3	1 13	23 58	87·3	1 10	22 58	87·2	1 07	21 58	87·2	1 04	20 58	87·2	1 02	19 58	87·2	0 59	18 59	87·2	183
4	1 38	23 57	86·3	1 34	22 57	86·3	1 30	21 57	86·3	1 26	20 57	86·3	1 22	19 57	86·2	1 18	18 57	86·2	184
5	2 02	23 55	85·4	1 57	22 55	85·4	1 52	21 55	85·4	1 47	20 56	85·3	1 42	19 56	85·3	1 38	18 56	85·3	185
6	2 26	23 53	84·5	2 20	22 53	84·5	2 15	21 53	84·4	2 09	20 54	84·4	2 03	19 54	84·4	1 57	18 54	84·3	186
7	2 50	23 50	83·6	2 44	22 50	83·6	2 37	21 51	83·5	2 30	20 51	83·5	2 23	19 52	83·4	2 16	18 52	83·4	187
8	3 15	23 48	82·7	3 07	22 48	82·6	2 59	21 48	82·6	2 52	20 49	82·5	2 44	19 49	82·5	2 36	18 50	82·4	188
9	3 39	23 44	81·8	3 30	22 45	81·7	3 22	21 45	81·6	3 13	20 46	81·6	3 04	19 46	81·6	2 55	18 47	81·5	189
10	4 03	23 41	80·8	3 53	22 41	80·8	3 44	21 42	80·7	3 34	20 42	80·7	3 24	19 43	80·6	3 14	18 44	80·5	190
11	4 27	23 36	79·9	4 17	22 37	79·9	4 06	21 38	79·8	3 55	20 39	79·6	3 45	19 40	79·6	3 34	18 41	79·6	191
12	4 51	23 32	79·0	4 40	22 33	78·9	4 28	21 34	78·9	4 16	20 35	78·7	4 05	19 36	78·7	3 53	18 37	78·6	192
13	5 15	23 27	78·1	5 03	22 28	78·0	4 50	21 29	77·9	4 37	20 30	77·8	4 25	19 32	77·7	4 12	18 33	77·7	193
14	5 39	23 22	77·2	5 25	22 23	77·1	5 12	21 24	77·0	4 58	20 26	76·9	4 45	19 27	76·8	4 31	18 28	76·7	194
15	6 03	23 16	76·2	5 48	22 18	76·1	5 34	21 19	76·0	5 19	20 21	75·9	5 05	19 22	75·8	4 50	18 24	75·8	195
16	6 26	23 10	75·3	6 11	22 12	75·2	5 56	21 13	75·1	5 40	20 15	75·0	5 25	19 17	74·9	5 09	18 19	74·8	196
17	6 50	23 04	74·4	6 34	22 06	74·3	6 17	21 08	74·2	6 01	20 09	74·1	5 44	19 11	74·0	5 28	18 14	73·9	197
18	7 13	22 57	73·5	6 56	21 59	73·3	6 39	21 01	73·2	6 21	20 03	73·1	6 04	19 06	73·0	5 46	18 08	72·9	198
19	7 37	22 50	72·5	7 19	21 52	72·4	7 00	20 54	72·3	6 42	19 57	72·2	6 24	18 59	72·0	6 05	18 02	72·0	199
20	8 00	22 42	71·6	7 41	21 45	71·5	7 22	20 47	71·4	7 03	19 50	71·2	6 43	18 53	71·1	6 24	17 56	71·0	200
21	8 23	22 34	70·7	8 03	21 37	70·5	7 43	20 40	70·4	7 23	19 43	70·3	7 02	18 46	70·2	6 42	17 49	70·1	201
22	8 46	22 26	69·7	8 25	21 29	69·6	8 04	20 32	69·5	7 43	19 35	69·3	7 22	18 39	69·2	7 00	17 42	69·1	202
23	9 09	22 17	68·8	8 47	21 21	68·7	8 25	20 24	68·5	8 03	19 28	68·4	7 41	18 31	68·3	7 19	17 35	68·1	203
24	9 31	22 08	67·9	9 09	21 12	67·7	8 46	20 16	67·6	8 23	19 19	67·4	8 00	18 24	67·3	7 37	17 28	67·2	204
25	9 54	21 58	66·9	9 30	21 03	66·8	9 07	20 07	66·6	8 43	19 11	66·3	8 19	18 15	66·2	7 55	17 20	66·2	205
26	10 16	21 49	66·0	9 52	20 53	65·8	9 27	19 57	65·5	9 02	19 02	65·5	8 37	18 07	65·4	8 12	17 12	65·2	206
27	10 38	21 38	65·0	10 13	20 43	64·9	9 48	19 48	64·7	9 22	18 53	64·6	8 56	17 58	64·4	8 30	17 03	64·3	207
28	11 00	21 28	64·1	10 34	20 33	63·9	10 08	19 38	63·8	9 41	18 43	63·6	9 14	17 49	63·5	8 48	16 55	63·3	208
29	11 22	21 17	63·1	10 55	20 22	63·0	10 28	19 28	62·8	10 00	18 34	62·6	9 33	17 39	62·5	9 05	16 46	62·3	209
30	11 44	21 05	62·2	11 16	20 11	62·0	10 48	19 17	61·8	10 19	18 23	61·7	9 51	17 30	61·5	9 22	16 36	61·4	210
31	12 06	20 53	61·2	11 37	20 00	61·1	11 07	19 06	60·9	10 38	18 13	60·7	10 09	17 20	60·5	9 39	16 27	60·4	211
32	12 27	20 41	60·3	11 57	19 48	60·1	11 27	18 55	59·9	10 57	18 02	59·7	10 27	17 09	59·6	9 56	16 17	59·4	212
33	12 48	20 29	59·3	12 17	19 36	59·1	11 46	18 43	58·8	11 15	17 51	58·8	10 44	16 58	58·6	10 13	16 06	58·4	213
34	13 09	20 16	58·4	12 37	19 23	58·2	12 06	18 31	58·0	11 34	17 39	57·8	11 02	16 47	57·6	10 29	15 56	57·5	214
35	13 29	20 02	57·4	12 57	19 10	57·2	12 24	18 19	57·0	11 52	17 27	56·8	11 19	16 36	56·7	10 46	15 45	56·5	215
36	13 50	19 49	56·4	13 17	18 57	56·2	12 43	18 06	56·0	12 10	17 15	55·9	11 36	16 24	55·7	11 02	15 34	55·5	216
37	14 10	19 34	55·5	13 36	18 44	55·3	13 02	17 53	55·1	12 27	17 03	54·9	11 53	16 12	54·7	11 18	15 23	54·5	217
38	14 30	19 20	54·5	13 55	18 30	54·3	13 20	17 40	54·1	12 45	16 50	53·9	12 09	16 00	53·7	11 34	15 11	53·5	218
39	14 50	19 05	53·5	14 14	18 15	53·3	13 38	17 26	53·1	13 02	16 37	52·9	12 26	15 48	52·6	11 49	14 59	52·6	219
40	15 09	18 50	52·5	14 33	18 01	52·3	13 56	17 12	52·1	13 19	16 23	51·9	12 42	15 35	51·6	12 05	14 47	51·6	220
41	15 29	18 34	51·5	14 51	17 46	51·3	14 14	16 57	51·1	13 36	16 09	50·9	12 58	15 22	50·6	12 20	14 34	50·6	221
42	15 48	18 18	50·6	15 09	17 30	50·3	14 31	16 43	50·1	13 52	15 55	49·9	13 14	15 08	49·8	12 35	14 21	49·6	222
43	16 06	18 02	49·6	15 27	17 15	49·4	14 48	16 28	49·2	14 09	15 41	49·0	13 29	14 54	48·8	12 50	14 08	48·6	223
44	16 25	17 46	48·6	15 45	16 59	48·4	15 05	16 12	48·2	14 25	15 26	48·0	13 45	14 40	47·8	13 04	13 55	47·6	224
45	16 43	17 29	47·6	16 02	16 42	47·4	15 22	15 57	47·2	14 41	15 11	47·0	14 00	14 26	46·8	13 19	13 41	46·6	225

Lat. / A — Lat. / A

LHA/F — LHA

B: (−) for 90° < LHA < 270° — for Lat. contrary name — for F > 90°

Lat./A LHA/F	A	66° A/H	66° B/P	66° Z₁/Z₂	67° A/H	67° B/P	67° Z₁/Z₂	68° A/H	68° B/P	68° Z₁/Z₂	69° A/H	69° B/P	69° Z₁/Z₂	70° A/H	70° B/P	70° Z₁/Z₂	71° A/H	71° B/P	71° Z₁/Z₂	A	Lat./A LHA
45	135	16 43	17 29	47·6	16 02	16 42	47·4	15 22	15 57	47·2	14 41	15 11	47·0	14 00	14 26	46·8	13 19	13 41	46·6	315	225
46	134	17 01	17 11	46·6	16 19	16 26	46·4	15 38	15 41	46·2	14 56	14 56	46·0	14 15	14 11	45·8	13 33	13 27	45·6	314	226
47	133	17 18	16 53	45·6	16 36	16 09	45·4	15 54	15 24	45·2	15 12	14 40	45·0	14 29	13 56	44·8	13 46	13 13	44·6	313	227
48	132	17 36	16 35	44·6	16 53	15 51	44·4	16 10	15 08	44·2	15 27	14 24	44·0	14 43	13 41	43·8	14 00	12 58	43·6	312	228
49	131	17 53	16 17	43·6	17 09	15 34	43·4	16 25	14 51	43·2	15 42	14 08	43·0	14 58	13 26	42·8	14 13	12 44	42·6	311	229
50	130	18 09	15 58	42·6	17 25	15 16	42·4	16 41	14 33	42·1	15 56	13 52	41·9	15 11	13 10	41·8	14 27	12 29	41·6	310	230
51	129	18 26	15 39	41·6	17 41	14 57	41·3	16 56	14 16	41·1	16 10	13 35	40·9	15 25	12 54	40·8	14 39	12 14	40·6	309	231
52	128	18 42	15 20	40·5	17 56	14 39	40·3	17 10	13 58	40·1	16 24	13 18	39·9	15 38	12 38	39·7	14 52	11 58	39·6	308	232
53	127	18 57	15 00	39·5	18 11	14 20	39·3	17 24	13 40	39·1	16 38	13 00	38·9	15 51	12 21	38·7	15 04	11 42	38·6	307	233
54	126	19 13	14 40	38·5	18 26	14 01	38·3	17 39	13 22	38·1	16 51	12 43	37·9	16 04	12 05	37·7	15 16	11 26	37·5	306	234
55	125	19 28	14 20	37·5	18 40	13 41	37·3	17 52	13 03	37·1	17 04	12 25	36·9	16 16	11 48	36·7	15 28	11 10	36·5	305	235
56	124	19 42	13 59	36·4	18 54	13 21	36·2	18 06	12 44	36·0	17 17	12 07	35·8	16 28	11 30	35·7	15 40	10 54	35·5	304	236
57	123	19 57	13 38	35·4	19 08	13 01	35·2	18 19	12 25	35·0	17 29	11 49	34·8	16 40	11 13	34·6	15 51	10 37	34·5	303	237
58	122	20 11	13 17	34·4	19 21	12 41	34·2	18 31	12 05	34·0	17 42	11 30	33·8	16 52	10 55	33·6	16 02	10 20	33·5	302	238
59	121	20 24	12 55	33·3	19 34	12 20	33·1	18 44	11 45	32·9	17 53	11 11	32·8	17 03	10 37	32·6	16 12	10 03	32·4	301	239
60	120	20 37	12 33	32·3	19 47	11 59	32·1	18 56	11 25	31·9	18 05	10 52	31·7	17 14	10 19	31·6	16 23	9 46	31·4	300	240
61	119	20 50	12 11	31·2	19 59	11 38	31·1	19 08	11 05	30·9	18 16	10 33	30·7	17 24	10 00	30·5	16 33	9 29	30·4	299	241
62	118	21 03	11 48	30·2	20 11	11 16	30·0	19 19	10 44	29·8	18 27	10 13	29·7	17 35	9 42	29·5	16 42	9 11	29·4	298	242
63	117	21 15	11 26	29·2	20 22	10 54	29·0	19 30	10 24	28·8	18 37	9 53	28·6	17 45	9 23	28·5	16 52	8 53	28·3	297	243
64	116	21 27	11 03	28·1	20 34	10 32	27·9	19 41	10 03	27·7	18 47	9 33	27·6	17 54	9 04	27·4	17 01	8 35	27·3	296	244
65	115	21 38	10 39	27·0	20 44	10 10	26·9	19 51	9 41	26·7	18 57	9 13	26·5	18 03	8 45	26·4	17 10	8 17	26·3	295	245
66	114	21 49	10 16	26·0	20 55	9 48	25·8	20 01	9 20	25·7	19 07	8 52	25·5	18 12	8 25	25·4	17 18	7 59	25·2	294	246
67	113	21 59	9 52	24·9	21 05	9 25	24·8	20 10	8 58	24·6	19 16	8 32	24·5	18 21	8 06	24·3	17 26	7 40	24·2	293	247
68	112	22 09	9 28	23·9	21 14	9 02	23·7	20 19	8 36	23·5	19 24	8 11	23·4	18 29	7 46	23·3	17 34	7 21	23·1	292	248
69	111	22 19	9 04	22·8	21 24	8 39	22·6	20 28	8 14	22·5	19 33	7 50	22·4	18 37	7 26	22·2	17 42	7 02	22·1	291	249
70	110	22 28	8 39	21·7	21 32	8 16	21·6	20 37	7 52	21·4	19 41	7 29	21·3	18 45	7 06	21·1	17 49	6 43	21·1	290	250
71	109	22 37	8 15	20·7	21 41	7 52	20·5	20 45	7 30	20·5	19 48	7 07	20·2	18 52	6 45	20·1	17 56	6 24	20·0	289	251
72	108	22 45	7 50	19·6	21 49	7 28	19·4	20 52	7 07	19·3	19 56	6 46	19·2	18 59	6 25	19·1	18 02	6 04	19·0	288	252
73	107	22 53	7 25	18·5	21 56	7 04	18·4	21 00	6 44	18·2	20 03	6 24	18·1	19 05	6 04	18·0	18 08	5 45	17·9	287	253
74	106	23 01	7 00	17·4	22 04	6 40	17·3	21 06	6 21	17·2	20 09	6 02	17·1	19 12	5 44	17·0	18 14	5 25	16·9	286	254
75	105	23 08	6 34	16·3	22 10	6 16	16·2	21 13	5 58	16·1	20 15	5 40	16·0	19 17	5 23	15·9	18 20	5 06	15·8	285	255
76	104	23 15	6 09	15·3	22 17	5 52	15·2	21 19	5 35	15·0	20 21	5 18	15·0	19 23	5 02	14·9	18 25	4 46	14·8	284	256
77	103	23 21	5 43	14·2	22 23	5 27	14·1	21 24	5 12	14·1	20 26	4 56	13·9	19 28	4 41	13·8	18 30	4 26	13·7	283	257
78	102	23 27	5 17	13·1	22 28	5 03	13·0	21 30	4 48	12·9	20 31	4 34	12·8	19 33	4 20	12·7	18 34	4 06	12·7	282	258
79	101	23 32	4 51	12·0	22 33	4 38	11·9	21 35	4 24	11·8	20 36	4 11	11·8	19 37	3 58	11·7	18 38	3 46	11·6	281	259
80	100	23 37	4 25	10·9	22 38	4 13	10·8	21 39	4 01	10·8	20 40	3 49	10·7	19 41	3 37	10·6	18 42	3 25	10·6	280	260
81	99	23 41	3 59	9·8	22 42	3 48	9·8	21 43	3 37	9·7	20 44	3 26	9·6	19 45	3 16	9·6	18 45	3 05	9·5	279	261
82	98	23 45	3 33	8·7	22 46	3 23	8·7	21 46	3 13	8·6	20 47	3 03	8·6	19 48	2 54	8·5	18 48	2 45	8·5	278	262
83	97	23 49	3 06	7·7	22 49	2 58	7·6	21 50	2 49	7·5	20 50	2 41	7·5	19 51	2 32	7·4	18 51	2 24	7·4	277	263
84	96	23 52	2 40	6·6	22 52	2 32	6·5	21 52	2 25	6·5	20 53	2 18	6·4	19 53	2 11	6·4	18 54	2 04	6·4	276	264
85	95	23 54	2 13	5·5	22 54	2 07	5·4	21 55	2 01	5·4	20 55	1 55	5·4	19 55	1 49	5·3	18 55	1 43	5·3	275	265
86	94	23 56	1 47	4·4	22 56	1 42	4·3	21 57	1 37	4·3	20 57	1 32	4·3	19 57	1 27	4·3	18 57	1 23	4·2	274	266
87	93	23 58	1 20	3·3	22 58	1 16	3·3	21 58	1 13	3·2	20 58	1 09	3·2	19 58	1 05	3·2	18 58	1 02	3·2	273	267
88	92	23 59	0 53	2·2	22 59	0 51	2·2	21 59	0 48	2·2	20 59	0 46	2·1	19 59	0 44	2·1	18 59	0 41	2·1	272	268
89	91	24 00	0 27	1·1	23 00	0 25	1·1	22 00	0 24	1·1	21 00	0 23	1·1	20 00	0 22	1·1	19 00	0 21	1·1	271	269
90	90	24 00	0 00	0·0	23 00	0 00	0·0	22 00	0 00	0·0	21 00	0 00	0·0	20 00	0 00	0·0	19 00	0 00	0·0	270	270

N. Lat: for LHA > 180°...Zₙ = Z / for LHA < 180°...Zₙ = 360° − Z

S. Lat: for LHA > 180°...Zₙ = 180° − Z / for LHA < 180°...Zₙ = 180° + Z

SIGHT REDUCTION TABLE

B: (−) for 90° < LHA < 270°
Dec:(−) for Lat. contrary name

Z₁: same sign as B
Z₂: (−) for F > 90°

LHA/F	°	72° A/H	72° B/P	72° Z₁/Z₂	73° A/H	73° B/P	73° Z₁/Z₂	74° A/H	74° B/P	74° Z₁/Z₂	75° A/H	75° B/P	75° Z₁/Z₂	76° A/H	76° B/P	76° Z₁/Z₂	77° A/H	77° B/P	77° Z₁/Z₂	Lat./A LHA	°
0	180	0 00	18 00	90·0	0 00	17 00	90·0	0 00	16 00	90·0	0 00	15 00	90·0	0 00	14 00	90·0	0 00	13 00	90·0	180	360
1	179	0 19	18 00	89·0	0 18	17 00	89·0	0 17	16 00	89·0	0 16	15 00	89·0	0 15	14 00	89·0	0 13	13 00	89·0	181	359
2	178	0 37	17 59	88·1	0 35	16 59	88·1	0 33	15 59	88·1	0 31	14 59	88·1	0 29	14 00	88·1	0 27	13 00	88·1	182	358
3	177	0 56	17 59	87·1	0 53	16 59	87·1	0 50	15 59	87·1	0 47	14 59	87·1	0 44	13 59	87·1	0 40	12 59	87·1	183	357
4	176	1 14	17 58	86·2	1 10	16 58	86·2	1 06	15 58	86·2	1 02	14 58	86·1	0 58	13 58	86·1	0 54	12 59	86·1	184	356
5	175	1 33	17 56	85·2	1 28	16 56	85·2	1 23	15 57	85·2	1 18	14 57	85·2	1 12	13 57	85·1	1 07	12 57	85·1	185	355
6	174	1 51	17 54	84·3	1 45	16 55	84·3	1 39	15 55	84·2	1 33	14 55	84·2	1 27	13 56	84·2	1 21	12 56	84·2	186	354
7	173	2 09	17 52	83·3	2 03	16 53	83·3	1 56	15 53	83·3	1 48	14 54	83·2	1 41	13 54	83·2	1 34	12 54	83·2	187	353
8	172	2 28	17 50	82·4	2 20	16 51	82·3	2 12	15 51	82·3	2 04	14 52	82·3	1 56	13 52	82·2	1 48	12 53	82·2	188	352
9	171	2 46	17 48	81·4	2 37	16 48	81·4	2 28	15 49	81·4	2 19	14 49	81·3	2 10	13 50	81·3	2 01	12 51	81·2	189	351
10	170	3 05	17 45	80·5	2 55	16 45	80·5	2 45	15 46	80·4	2 35	14 47	80·3	2 24	13 48	80·3	2 14	12 49	80·3	190	350
11	169	3 23	17 41	79·5	3 12	16 42	79·5	3 01	15 43	79·4	2 50	14 44	79·4	2 39	13 45	79·3	2 28	12 46	79·3	191	349
12	168	3 41	17 38	78·6	3 29	16 39	78·5	3 17	15 40	78·5	3 05	14 41	78·4	2 53	13 42	78·3	2 41	12 44	78·3	192	348
13	167	3 59	17 34	77·6	3 46	16 35	77·5	3 33	15 37	77·5	3 20	14 38	77·4	3 07	13 39	77·4	2 54	12 41	77·3	193	347
14	166	4 17	17 30	76·7	4 03	16 31	76·6	3 49	15 33	76·5	3 35	14 34	76·5	3 21	13 36	76·4	3 07	12 38	76·3	194	346
15	165	4 35	17 25	75·7	4 20	16 27	75·6	4 05	15 29	75·5	3 50	14 31	75·5	3 35	13 32	75·4	3 20	12 34	75·4	195	345
16	164	4 53	17 21	74·7	4 37	16 23	74·7	4 21	15 25	74·6	4 05	14 27	74·5	3 49	13 29	74·5	3 33	12 31	74·4	196	344
17	163	5 11	17 16	73·8	4 54	16 18	73·7	4 37	15 20	73·6	4 20	14 22	73·5	4 03	13 25	73·5	3 46	12 27	73·4	197	343
18	162	5 29	17 10	72·8	5 11	16 13	72·7	4 53	15 15	72·7	4 35	14 18	72·6	4 17	13 20	72·5	3 59	12 23	72·4	198	342
19	161	5 46	17 05	71·9	5 28	16 07	71·8	5 09	15 10	71·7	4 50	14 13	71·6	4 31	13 16	71·5	4 12	12 19	71·5	199	341
20	160	6 04	16 59	70·9	5 44	16 02	70·8	5 25	15 05	70·7	5 05	14 08	70·6	4 45	13 11	70·5	4 25	12 14	70·5	200	340
21	159	6 21	16 52	69·9	6 01	15 56	69·8	5 40	14 59	69·7	5 19	14 03	69·6	4 58	13 06	69·6	4 37	12 10	69·5	201	339
22	158	6 39	16 46	69·0	6 17	15 50	68·9	5 56	14 53	68·8	5 34	13 57	68·7	5 12	13 01	68·6	4 50	12 05	68·5	202	338
23	157	6 56	16 39	68·0	6 34	15 43	67·9	6 11	14 47	67·8	5 48	13 51	67·7	5 25	12 56	67·6	5 03	12 00	67·5	203	337
24	156	7 13	16 32	67·1	6 50	15 36	66·9	6 26	14 41	66·8	6 03	13 45	66·7	5 39	12 50	66·6	5 15	11 55	66·5	204	336
25	155	7 30	16 25	66·1	7 06	15 29	66·0	6 41	14 34	65·9	6 17	13 39	65·8	5 52	12 44	65·7	5 27	11 49	65·6	205	335
26	154	7 47	16 17	65·1	7 22	15 22	65·0	6 56	14 27	64·9	6 31	13 32	64·8	6 05	12 38	64·7	5 40	11 43	64·6	206	334
27	153	8 04	16 09	64·1	7 38	15 14	64·0	7 11	14 20	63·9	6 45	13 26	63·8	6 18	12 32	63·7	5 52	11 37	63·6	207	333
28	152	8 20	16 00	63·2	7 53	15 06	63·0	7 26	14 12	62·9	6 59	13 19	62·8	6 31	12 25	62·7	6 04	11 31	62·6	208	332
29	151	8 37	15 52	62·2	8 09	14 58	62·1	7 41	14 05	61·9	7 13	13 11	61·8	6 44	12 18	61·7	6 16	11 25	61·6	209	331
30	150	8 53	15 43	61·2	8 24	14 50	61·1	7 55	13 57	61·0	7 26	13 04	60·9	6 57	12 11	60·7	6 27	11 18	60·6	210	330
31	149	9 09	15 34	60·3	8 40	14 41	60·1	8 10	13 49	60·0	7 40	12 56	59·9	7 09	12 04	59·8	6 39	11 12	59·7	211	329
32	148	9 25	15 25	59·3	8 55	14 32	59·1	8 24	13 40	59·1	7 53	12 48	58·9	7 22	11 56	58·8	6 51	11 05	58·7	212	328
33	147	9 41	15 15	58·3	9 10	14 23	58·2	8 38	13 31	58·2	8 06	12 40	57·9	7 34	11 49	57·8	7 02	10 57	57·7	213	327
34	146	9 57	15 05	57·3	9 25	14 13	57·2	8 52	13 22	57·2	8 19	12 31	56·9	7 46	11 41	56·8	7 14	10 50	56·7	214	326
35	145	10 13	14 54	56·3	9 39	14 04	56·3	9 06	13 13	56·1	8 32	12 23	55·9	7 59	11 33	55·8	7 25	10 43	55·7	215	325
36	144	10 28	14 44	55·4	9 54	13 54	55·4	9 19	13 04	55·1	8 45	12 14	54·9	8 11	11 24	54·8	7 36	10 35	54·7	216	324
37	143	10 43	14 33	54·4	10 08	13 43	54·4	9 33	12 54	54·2	8 58	12 05	53·9	8 22	11 16	53·8	7 47	10 27	53·7	217	323
38	142	10 58	14 22	53·4	10 22	13 33	53·4	9 46	12 44	53·2	9 10	11 55	53·0	8 34	11 07	52·8	7 58	10 19	52·7	218	322
39	141	11 13	14 10	52·4	10 36	13 22	52·4	9 59	12 34	52·1	9 22	11 46	52·0	8 45	10 58	51·8	8 08	10 10	51·7	219	321
40	140	11 27	13 59	51·4	10 50	13 11	51·3	10 12	12 23	51·1	9 35	11 36	51·0	8 57	10 49	50·8	8 19	10 02	50·7	220	320
41	139	11 42	13 47	50·4	11 04	13 00	50·3	10 25	12 13	50·1	9 47	11 26	50·0	9 08	10 39	49·9	8 29	9 53	49·7	221	319
42	138	11 56	13 34	49·4	11 17	12 48	49·3	10 38	12 02	49·1	9 58	11 16	49·0	9 19	10 30	48·9	8 39	9 44	48·7	222	318
43	137	12 10	13 22	48·4	11 30	12 36	48·3	10 50	11 51	48·1	10 10	11 05	48·0	9 30	10 20	47·9	8 49	9 35	47·7	223	317
44	136	12 24	13 09	47·4	11 43	12 24	47·3	11 02	11 39	47·1	10 21	10 55	47·0	9 40	10 10	46·9	8 59	9 26	46·7	224	316
45	135	12 37	12 56	46·4	11 56	12 12	46·3	11 14	11 28	46·1	10 33	10 44	46·0	9 51	10 00	45·9	9 09	9 16	45·7	225	315

Lat./A (LHA)	LHA/F (F)	72° A/H	72° B/P	72° Z₁/Z₂	73° A/H	73° B/P	73° Z₁/Z₂	74° A/H	74° B/P	74° Z₁/Z₂	75° A/H	75° B/P	75° Z₁/Z₂	76° A/H	76° B/P	76° Z₁/Z₂	77° A/H	77° B/P	77° Z₁/Z₂	A	LHA
45	135	12 37	12 56	46·4	11 56	12 12	46·3	11 14	11 28	46·1	10 33	10 44	46·0	9 51	10 00	45·9	9 09	9 16	45·7	315	225
46	134	12 51	12 43	45·4	12 08	11 59	45·3	11 26	11 16	45·1	10 44	10 33	45·0	10 01	9 50	44·9	9 19	9 07	44·7	314	226
47	133	13 04	12 30	44·4	12 21	11 47	44·3	11 38	11 04	44·1	10 55	10 21	44·0	10 11	9 39	43·9	9 28	8 57	43·7	313	227
48	132	13 17	12 16	43·4	12 33	11 34	43·3	11 49	10 52	43·1	11 05	10 10	43·0	10 21	9 28	42·9	9 37	8 47	42·7	312	228
49	131	13 29	12 02	42·4	12 45	11 21	42·3	12 00	10 39	42·1	11 16	9 58	42·0	10 31	9 17	41·9	9 46	8 37	41·7	311	229
50	130	13 42	11 48	41·4	12 57	11 07	41·3	12 11	10 27	41·1	11 26	9 46	41·0	10 41	9 06	40·9	9 55	8 26	40·7	310	230
51	129	13 54	11 33	40·4	13 08	10 53	40·3	12 22	10 14	40·1	11 36	9 34	40·0	10 50	8 55	39·8	10 04	8 16	39·7	309	231
52	128	14 06	11 19	39·4	13 19	10 40	39·3	12 33	10 01	39·1	11 46	9 22	39·0	10 59	8 44	38·8	10 13	8 05	38·7	308	232
53	127	14 17	11 04	38·4	13 30	10 26	38·2	12 43	9 47	38·1	11 56	9 10	38·0	11 08	8 32	37·8	10 21	7 55	37·7	307	233
54	126	14 29	10 49	37·4	13 41	10 11	37·2	12 53	9 34	37·1	12 05	8 57	36·9	11 17	8 20	36·8	10 29	7 44	36·7	306	234
55	125	14 40	10 33	36·4	13 51	9 57	36·2	13 03	9 20	36·1	12 14	8 44	35·9	11 26	8 08	35·8	10 37	7 33	35·7	305	235
56	124	14 51	10 18	35·3	14 02	9 42	35·2	13 13	9 07	35·1	12 23	8 31	34·9	11 34	7 56	34·8	10 45	7 21	34·7	304	236
57	123	15 01	10 02	34·3	14 12	9 27	34·2	13 22	8 53	34·0	12 32	8 18	33·9	11 42	7 44	33·8	10 52	7 10	33·7	303	237
58	122	15 12	9 46	33·3	14 21	9 12	33·2	13 31	8 38	33·0	12 41	8 05	32·9	11 50	7 32	32·8	11 00	6 58	32·7	302	238
59	121	15 22	9 30	32·3	14 31	8 57	32·1	13 40	8 24	32·0	12 49	7 51	31·9	11 58	7 19	31·8	11 07	6 47	31·7	301	239
60	120	15 31	9 14	31·3	14 40	8 41	31·1	13 49	8 10	31·0	12 57	7 38	30·9	12 06	7 06	30·8	11 14	6 35	30·6	300	240
61	119	15 41	8 57	30·2	14 49	8 26	30·1	13 57	7 55	30·0	13 05	7 24	29·8	12 13	6 54	29·7	11 21	6 23	29·6	299	241
62	118	15 50	8 40	29·2	14 58	8 10	29·1	14 05	7 40	28·9	13 13	7 10	28·8	12 20	6 41	28·7	11 27	6 11	28·6	298	242
63	117	15 59	8 23	28·2	15 06	7 54	28·0	14 13	7 25	27·9	13 20	6 56	27·8	12 27	6 27	27·7	11 34	5 59	27·6	297	243
64	116	16 08	8 06	27·2	15 14	7 38	27·0	14 21	7 10	26·9	13 27	6 42	26·8	12 34	6 14	26·7	11 40	5 47	26·6	296	244
65	115	16 16	7 49	26·1	15 22	7 22	26·0	14 28	6 55	25·9	13 34	6 28	25·8	12 40	6 01	25·7	11 46	5 34	25·6	295	245
66	114	16 24	7 32	25·1	15 29	7 05	25·0	14 35	6 39	24·9	13 41	6 13	24·7	12 46	5 47	24·6	11 52	5 22	24·6	294	246
67	113	16 32	7 14	24·1	15 37	6 49	24·0	14 42	6 24	23·8	13 47	5 59	23·7	12 52	5 34	23·6	11 57	5 09	23·5	293	247
68	112	16 39	6 56	23·0	15 44	6 32	22·9	14 48	6 08	22·8	13 53	5 44	22·7	12 58	5 20	22·6	12 02	4 57	22·5	292	248
69	111	16 46	6 38	22·0	15 50	6 15	21·9	14 55	5 52	21·8	13 59	5 29	21·7	13 03	5 06	21·6	12 07	4 44	21·5	291	249
70	110	16 53	6 20	20·9	15 57	5 58	20·8	15 01	5 36	20·7	14 05	5 14	20·6	13 08	4 52	20·5	12 12	4 31	20·5	290	250
71	109	16 59	6 02	19·9	16 03	5 41	19·8	15 06	5 20	19·7	14 10	4 59	19·6	13 13	4 38	19·5	12 17	4 18	19·5	289	251
72	108	17 05	5 44	18·9	16 09	5 24	18·8	15 12	5 04	18·7	14 15	4 44	18·6	13 18	4 24	18·5	12 21	4 05	18·4	288	252
73	107	17 11	5 26	17·8	16 14	5 06	17·7	15 17	4 48	17·6	14 20	4 29	17·6	13 23	4 10	17·5	12 25	3 52	17·4	287	253
74	106	17 17	5 07	16·8	16 19	4 49	16·7	15 22	4 31	16·6	14 24	4 13	16·5	13 27	3 56	16·5	12 29	3 38	16·4	286	254
75	105	17 22	4 48	15·7	16 24	4 31	15·7	15 26	4 15	15·6	14 29	3 58	15·5	13 31	3 42	15·4	12 33	3 25	15·4	285	255
76	104	17 27	4 30	14·7	16 29	4 14	14·6	15 31	3 58	14·5	14 33	3 43	14·5	13 35	3 27	14·4	12 36	3 12	14·4	284	256
77	103	17 31	4 11	13·6	16 33	3 56	13·6	15 35	3 41	13·5	14 36	3 27	13·4	13 38	3 13	13·4	12 40	2 58	13·3	283	257
78	102	17 36	3 52	12·6	16 37	3 38	12·5	15 38	3 25	12·5	14 40	3 11	12·4	13 41	2 58	12·4	12 43	2 45	12·3	282	258
79	101	17 39	3 33	11·6	16 41	3 20	11·5	15 42	3 08	11·4	14 43	2 56	11·4	13 44	2 43	11·3	12 45	2 31	11·3	281	259
80	100	17 43	3 14	10·5	16 44	3 02	10·4	15 45	2 51	10·4	14 46	2 40	10·3	13 47	2 29	10·3	12 48	2 18	10·3	280	260
81	99	17 46	2 55	9·5	16 47	2 44	9·4	15 48	2 34	9·4	14 49	2 24	9·3	13 49	2 14	9·3	12 50	2 04	9·2	279	261
82	98	17 49	2 35	8·4	16 50	2 26	8·4	15 50	2 17	8·3	14 51	2 08	8·3	13 52	1 59	8·2	12 52	1 50	8·2	278	262
83	97	17 52	2 16	7·4	16 52	2 08	7·3	15 53	2 00	7·3	14 53	1 52	7·2	13 54	1 44	7·2	12 54	1 37	7·2	277	263
84	96	17 54	1 57	6·3	16 54	1 50	6·3	15 55	1 43	6·2	14 55	1 36	6·2	13 55	1 30	6·2	12 56	1 23	6·2	276	264
85	95	17 56	1 37	5·3	16 56	1 32	5·2	15 56	1 26	5·2	14 56	1 20	5·2	13 57	1 15	5·2	12 57	1 09	5·1	275	265
86	94	17 57	1 18	4·2	16 57	1 13	4·2	15 58	1 09	4·2	14 58	1 04	4·1	13 58	1 00	4·1	12 58	0 55	4·1	274	266
87	93	17 58	0 58	3·2	16 59	0 55	3·1	15 59	0 52	3·1	14 59	0 48	3·1	13 59	0 45	3·1	12 59	0 42	3·1	273	267
88	92	17 59	0 39	2·1	16 59	0 37	2·1	15 59	0 34	2·1	14 59	0 32	2·1	13 59	0 30	2·1	13 00	0 28	2·1	272	268
89	91	18 00	0 19	1·1	17 00	0 18	1·0	16 00	0 17	1·0	15 00	0 16	1·0	14 00	0 15	1·0	13 00	0 14	1·0	271	269
90	90	18 00	0 00	0·0	17 00	0 00	0·0	16 00	0 00	0·0	15 00	0 00	0·0	14 00	0 00	0·0	13 00	0 00	0·0	270	270

N. Lat.: for LHA > 180° ... $Z_n = Z$
for LHA < 180° ... $Z_n = 360° - Z$

S. Lat.: for LHA > 180° ... $Z_n = 180° - Z$
for LHA < 180° ... $Z_n = 180° + Z$

SIGHT REDUCTION TABLE

B: (−) for 90° < LHA < 270°
Dec:(−) for Lat. contrary name

Z1: same sign as B
Z2: (−) for F > 90°

Lat./A LHA/F	78° A/H	78° B/P	78° Z1/Z2	79° A/H	79° B/P	79° Z1/Z2	80° A/H	80° B/P	80° Z1/Z2	81° A/H	81° B/P	81° Z1/Z2	82° A/H	82° B/P	82° Z1/Z2	83° A/H	83° B/P	83° Z1/Z2	Lat./A LHA
0 180	0 00	12 00	90.0	0 00	11 00	90.0	0 00	10 00	90.0	0 00	9 00	90.0	0 00	8 00	90.0	0 00	7 00	90.0	180 360
1 179	0 12	12 00	89.0	0 11	11 00	89.0	0 10	10 00	89.0	0 09	9 00	89.0	0 08	8 00	89.0	0 07	7 00	89.0	181 359
2 178	0 25	12 00	88.0	0 23	11 00	88.0	0 21	10 00	88.0	0 19	9 00	88.0	0 17	8 00	88.0	0 15	7 00	88.0	182 358
3 177	0 37	11 59	87.1	0 34	10 59	87.1	0 31	9 59	87.0	0 28	8 59	87.0	0 25	7 59	87.0	0 22	6 59	87.0	183 357
4 176	0 50	11 58	86.1	0 46	10 58	86.1	0 42	9 59	86.1	0 38	8 59	86.0	0 33	7 59	86.0	0 29	6 59	86.0	184 356
5 175	1 02	11 57	85.1	0 57	10 58	85.1	0 52	9 58	85.1	0 47	8 58	85.1	0 42	7 58	85.1	0 37	6 58	85.0	185 355
6 174	1 15	11 56	84.1	1 09	10 56	84.1	1 02	9 57	84.1	0 56	8 57	84.1	0 50	7 57	84.1	0 44	6 58	84.1	186 354
7 173	1 27	11 55	83.2	1 20	10 55	83.1	1 13	9 56	83.1	1 06	8 56	83.1	0 58	7 56	83.1	0 51	6 57	83.1	187 353
8 172	1 39	11 53	82.2	1 31	10 54	82.2	1 23	9 54	82.1	1 15	8 55	82.1	1 07	7 55	82.1	0 58	6 56	82.1	188 352
9 171	1 52	11 51	81.2	1 43	10 52	81.2	1 33	9 53	81.1	1 24	8 53	81.1	1 15	7 54	81.1	1 06	6 55	81.1	189 351
10 170	2 04	11 49	80.2	1 54	10 50	80.2	1 44	9 51	80.1	1 33	8 52	80.1	1 23	7 53	80.1	1 13	6 54	80.1	190 350
11 169	2 16	11 47	79.2	2 05	10 48	79.2	1 54	9 49	79.2	1 43	8 50	79.1	1 31	7 51	79.1	1 20	6 52	79.1	191 349
12 168	2 29	11 45	78.3	2 16	10 46	78.2	2 04	9 47	78.2	1 52	8 48	78.1	1 39	7 50	78.1	1 27	6 51	78.1	192 348
13 167	2 41	11 42	77.3	2 28	10 43	77.2	2 14	9 45	77.2	2 01	8 46	77.2	1 48	7 48	77.1	1 34	6 49	77.1	193 347
14 166	2 53	11 39	76.3	2 39	10 41	76.2	2 24	9 43	76.2	2 10	8 44	76.2	1 56	7 46	76.2	1 41	6 48	76.1	194 346
15 165	3 05	11 36	75.3	2 50	10 38	75.3	2 35	9 40	75.2	2 19	8 42	75.2	2 04	7 44	75.2	1 48	6 46	75.1	195 345
16 164	3 17	11 33	74.3	3 01	10 35	74.3	2 45	9 37	74.2	2 28	8 39	74.2	2 12	7 42	74.2	1 56	6 44	74.1	196 344
17 163	3 29	11 29	73.4	3 12	10 32	73.3	2 55	9 34	73.2	2 37	8 37	73.2	2 20	7 39	73.2	2 03	6 42	73.1	197 343
18 162	3 41	11 26	72.4	3 23	10 28	72.3	3 05	9 31	72.3	2 46	8 34	72.2	2 28	7 37	72.2	2 09	6 40	72.1	198 342
19 161	3 53	11 22	71.4	3 34	10 25	71.4	3 14	9 28	71.3	2 55	8 31	71.2	2 36	7 34	71.2	2 16	6 37	71.1	199 341
20 160	4 05	11 18	70.4	3 45	10 21	70.4	3 24	9 24	70.3	3 04	8 28	70.2	2 44	7 31	70.2	2 23	6 35	70.1	200 340
21 159	4 16	11 13	69.4	3 55	10 17	69.4	3 34	9 21	69.3	3 13	8 25	69.2	2 52	7 28	69.2	2 30	6 32	69.1	201 339
22 158	4 28	11 09	68.4	4 06	10 13	68.4	3 44	9 17	68.3	3 22	8 21	68.2	3 00	7 25	68.2	2 37	6 30	68.1	202 338
23 157	4 40	11 04	67.5	4 17	10 09	67.4	3 53	9 13	67.3	3 30	8 18	67.3	3 07	7 22	67.2	2 44	6 27	67.2	203 337
24 156	4 51	10 59	66.5	4 27	10 04	66.4	4 03	9 09	66.3	3 39	8 14	66.3	3 15	7 19	66.2	2 50	6 24	66.2	204 336
25 155	5 02	10 54	65.5	4 38	9 59	65.4	4 13	9 05	65.3	3 47	8 10	65.3	3 22	7 16	65.2	2 57	6 21	65.2	205 335
26 154	5 14	10 49	64.5	4 48	9 55	64.4	4 22	9 00	64.3	3 56	8 06	64.3	3 30	7 12	64.2	3 04	6 18	64.2	206 334
27 153	5 25	10 43	63.5	4 58	9 50	63.5	4 31	8 56	63.4	4 04	8 02	63.3	3 37	7 08	63.2	3 10	6 15	63.2	207 333
28 152	5 36	10 38	62.5	5 08	9 44	62.5	4 41	8 51	62.4	4 13	7 58	62.3	3 45	7 04	62.2	3 17	6 11	62.2	208 332
29 151	5 47	10 32	61.5	5 18	9 39	61.5	4 50	8 46	61.4	4 21	7 53	61.3	3 52	7 00	61.2	3 23	6 08	61.2	209 331
30 150	5 58	10 26	60.5	5 28	9 33	60.5	4 59	8 41	60.4	4 29	7 49	60.3	3 59	6 56	60.2	3 30	6 04	60.2	210 330
31 149	6 09	10 20	59.6	5 38	9 28	59.5	5 08	8 36	59.4	4 37	7 44	59.3	4 07	6 52	59.2	3 36	6 00	59.2	211 329
32 148	6 20	10 13	58.6	5 48	9 22	58.5	5 17	8 30	58.4	4 45	7 39	58.3	4 14	6 48	58.2	3 42	5 57	58.2	212 328
33 147	6 30	10 06	57.6	5 58	9 16	57.5	5 26	8 25	57.4	4 53	7 34	57.3	4 21	6 43	57.3	3 48	5 53	57.2	213 327
34 146	6 41	10 00	56.6	6 08	9 09	56.6	5 34	8 19	56.4	5 01	7 29	56.3	4 28	6 39	56.2	3 54	5 49	56.2	214 326
35 145	6 51	9 53	55.6	6 17	9 03	55.6	5 43	8 13	55.4	5 09	7 24	55.4	4 35	6 34	55.2	4 00	5 45	55.2	215 325
36 144	7 01	9 45	54.6	6 26	8 56	54.6	5 51	8 07	54.4	5 17	7 18	54.3	4 42	6 29	54.2	4 06	5 40	54.2	216 324
37 143	7 11	9 38	53.6	6 36	8 49	53.6	6 00	8 01	53.4	5 24	7 13	53.3	4 48	6 24	53.2	4 12	5 36	53.2	217 323
38 142	7 21	9 31	52.6	6 45	8 43	52.6	6 08	7 55	52.4	5 32	7 07	52.3	4 55	6 19	52.2	4 18	5 32	52.2	218 322
39 141	7 31	9 23	51.6	6 54	8 35	51.6	6 16	7 48	51.4	5 39	7 01	51.3	5 01	6 14	51.2	4 24	5 27	51.2	219 321
40 140	7 41	9 15	50.6	7 03	8 28	50.6	6 25	7 42	50.4	5 46	6 55	50.3	5 08	6 09	50.2	4 30	5 22	50.2	220 320
41 139	7 50	9 07	49.6	7 11	8 21	49.6	6 32	7 35	49.4	5 53	6 49	49.4	5 14	6 03	49.2	4 35	5 18	49.2	221 319
42 138	8 00	8 59	48.6	7 20	8 13	48.6	6 40	7 28	48.4	6 01	6 43	48.4	5 21	5 58	48.2	4 41	5 13	48.2	222 318
43 137	8 09	8 50	47.6	7 29	8 05	47.6	6 48	7 21	47.4	6 07	6 36	47.4	5 27	5 52	47.2	4 46	5 08	47.2	223 317
44 136	8 18	8 42	46.6	7 37	7 58	46.6	6 56	7 14	46.4	6 14	6 30	46.4	5 33	5 46	46.2	4 51	5 03	46.2	224 316
45 135	8 27	8 33	45.6	7 45	7 50	45.6	7 03	7 06	45.4	6 21	6 23	45.4	5 39	5 41	45.2	4 57	4 58	45.2	225 315

Lat./A LHA/F		78° A/H	78° B/P	78° Z₁/Z₂	79° A/H	79° B/P	79° Z₁/Z₂	80° A/H	80° B/P	80° Z₁/Z₂	81° A/H	81° B/P	81° Z₁/Z₂	82° A/H	82° B/P	82° Z₁/Z₂	83° A/H	83° B/P	83° Z₁/Z₂	Lat./A LHA	
45	135	8 27	8 33	45·6	7 45	7 50	45·5	7 03	7 06	45·4	6 21	6 23	45·4	5 39	5 41	45·3	4 57	4 58	45·2	225	315
46	134	8 36	8 24	44·6	7 53	7 41	44·5	7 11	6 59	44·4	6 28	6 17	44·4	5 45	5 35	44·3	5 02	4 53	44·2	226	314
47	133	8 45	8 15	43·6	8 01	7 33	43·5	7 18	6 51	43·4	6 34	6 10	43·4	5 51	5 28	43·3	5 07	4 47	43·2	227	313
48	132	8 53	8 06	42·6	8 09	7 25	42·5	7 25	6 44	42·4	6 41	6 03	42·4	5 56	5 22	42·3	5 12	4 42	42·2	228	312
49	131	9 02	7 56	41·6	8 17	7 16	41·5	7 32	6 36	41·4	6 47	5 56	41·4	6 02	5 16	41·3	5 17	4 36	41·2	229	311
50	130	9 10	7 47	40·6	8 24	7 07	40·5	7 39	6 28	40·4	6 53	5 49	40·4	6 07	5 10	40·3	5 21	4 31	40·2	230	310
51	129	9 18	7 37	39·6	8 32	6 58	39·5	7 45	6 20	39·4	6 59	5 42	39·4	6 13	5 03	39·3	5 26	4 25	39·2	231	309
52	128	9 26	7 27	38·6	8 39	6 49	38·5	7 52	6 12	38·4	7 05	5 34	38·3	6 18	4 57	38·3	5 31	4 19	38·2	232	308
53	127	9 33	7 17	37·6	8 46	6 40	37·5	7 58	6 03	37·4	7 11	5 27	37·3	6 23	4 50	37·3	5 35	4 14	37·2	233	307
54	126	9 41	7 07	36·6	8 53	6 31	36·5	8 05	5 55	36·4	7 16	5 19	36·3	6 28	4 43	36·3	5 39	4 08	36·2	234	306
55	125	9 48	6 57	35·6	9 00	6 22	35·5	8 11	5 47	35·5	7 22	5 11	35·3	6 33	4 37	35·3	5 44	4 02	35·2	235	305
56	124	9 56	6 47	34·6	9 06	6 12	34·5	8 17	5 38	34·4	7 27	5 04	34·3	6 38	4 30	34·3	5 48	3 56	34·2	236	304
57	123	10 03	6 36	33·6	9 13	6 03	33·5	8 22	5 29	33·4	7 32	4 56	33·4	6 42	4 23	33·3	5 52	3 50	33·2	237	303
58	122	10 09	6 26	32·6	9 19	5 53	32·5	8 28	5 20	32·4	7 37	4 48	32·3	6 47	4 16	32·3	5 56	3 43	32·2	238	302
59	121	10 16	6 15	31·6	9 25	5 43	31·5	8 34	5 11	31·4	7 42	4 40	31·3	6 51	4 08	31·3	6 00	3 37	31·2	239	301
60	120	10 22	6 04	30·6	9 31	5 33	30·5	8 39	5 02	30·4	7 47	4 32	30·3	6 55	4 01	30·2	6 04	3 31	30·2	240	300
61	119	10 29	5 53	29·5	9 36	5 23	29·5	8 44	4 53	29·4	7 52	4 23	29·3	6 59	3 54	29·2	6 07	3 24	29·2	241	299
62	118	10 35	5 42	28·5	9 42	5 13	28·4	8 49	4 44	28·4	7 56	4 15	28·3	7 04	3 46	28·2	6 11	3 18	28·2	242	298
63	117	10 41	5 31	27·5	9 47	5 03	27·4	8 54	4 35	27·4	8 01	4 07	27·3	7 07	3 39	27·3	6 14	3 11	27·2	243	297
64	116	10 46	5 19	26·5	9 52	4 52	26·4	8 59	4 25	26·3	8 05	3 58	26·3	7 11	3 32	26·2	6 17	3 05	26·2	244	296
65	115	10 52	5 08	25·5	9 57	4 42	25·4	9 03	4 16	25·4	8 09	3 50	25·3	7 15	3 24	25·2	6 20	2 58	25·2	245	295
66	114	10 57	4 56	24·5	10 02	4 31	24·4	9 08	4 06	24·3	8 13	3 41	24·3	7 18	3 16	24·2	6 24	2 52	24·2	246	294
67	113	11 02	4 45	23·5	10 07	4 21	23·4	9 12	3 56	23·3	8 17	3 32	23·3	7 22	3 09	23·2	6 26	2 45	23·2	247	293
68	112	11 07	4 33	22·4	10 11	4 10	22·4	9 16	3 47	22·3	8 20	3 24	22·2	7 25	3 01	22·2	6 29	2 38	22·1	248	292
69	111	11 12	4 21	21·4	10 16	3 59	21·4	9 20	3 37	21·3	8 24	3 15	21·3	7 28	2 53	21·2	6 32	2 31	21·1	249	291
70	110	11 16	4 09	20·4	10 20	3 48	20·3	9 23	3 27	20·3	8 27	3 06	20·3	7 31	2 45	20·2	6 35	2 24	20·1	250	290
71	109	11 20	3 58	19·4	10 24	3 37	19·3	9 27	3 17	19·3	8 30	2 57	19·3	7 34	2 37	19·2	6 37	2 17	19·1	251	289
72	108	11 24	3 45	18·4	10 27	3 26	18·3	9 30	3 07	18·3	8 33	2 48	18·2	7 36	2 29	18·2	6 39	2 10	18·1	252	288
73	107	11 28	3 33	17·4	10 31	3 15	17·3	9 34	2 57	17·3	8 36	2 39	17·2	7 39	2 21	17·2	6 42	2 03	17·1	253	287
74	106	11 32	3 21	16·3	10 34	3 04	16·3	9 37	2 47	16·3	8 39	2 30	16·2	7 41	2 13	16·1	6 44	1 56	16·1	254	286
75	105	11 35	3 09	15·3	10 37	2 53	15·3	9 39	2 37	15·3	8 41	2 21	15·2	7 44	2 05	15·2	6 46	1 49	15·1	255	285
76	104	11 38	2 57	14·3	10 40	2 42	14·3	9 42	2 27	14·2	8 44	2 12	14·2	7 46	1 57	14·2	6 47	1 42	14·1	256	284
77	103	11 41	2 44	13·3	10 43	2 30	13·2	9 44	2 16	13·2	8 46	2 02	13·2	7 48	1 49	13·1	6 49	1 35	13·1	257	283
78	102	11 44	2 32	12·3	10 45	2 19	12·2	9 47	2 06	12·2	8 48	1 53	12·1	7 49	1 40	12·1	6 51	1 28	12·1	258	282
79	101	11 47	2 19	11·2	10 48	2 07	11·2	9 49	1 56	11·2	8 50	1 44	11·2	7 51	1 32	11·1	6 52	1 21	11·1	259	281
80	100	11 49	2 07	10·2	10 50	1 56	10·2	9 51	1 45	10·2	8 52	1 35	10·1	7 53	1 24	10·1	6 54	1 13	10·1	260	280
81	99	11 51	1 54	9·2	10 52	1 45	9·2	9 53	1 35	9·1	8 53	1 25	9·1	7 54	1 16	9·1	6 55	1 06	9·1	261	279
82	98	11 53	1 42	8·2	10 53	1 33	8·1	9 54	1 24	8·1	8 55	1 16	8·1	7 55	1 07	8·1	6 56	0 59	8·1	262	278
83	97	11 55	1 29	7·2	10 55	1 21	7·1	9 55	1 14	7·1	8 56	1 06	7·1	7 56	0 59	7·1	6 57	0 51	7·1	263	277
84	96	11 56	1 16	6·1	10 56	1 10	6·1	9 56	1 03	6·1	8 57	0 57	6·1	7 57	0 50	6·1	6 58	0 44	6·0	264	276
85	95	11 57	1 04	5·1	10 57	0 58	5·1	9 57	0 53	5·1	8 58	0 47	5·1	7 57	0 42	5·0	6 58	0 37	5·0	265	275
86	94	11 58	0 51	4·1	10 58	0 47	4·1	9 58	0 42	4·1	8 59	0 38	4·1	7 58	0 34	4·0	6 59	0 29	4·0	266	274
87	93	11 59	0 38	3·1	10 59	0 35	3·1	9 59	0 32	3·0	9 00	0 28	3·0	7 59	0 25	3·0	6 59	0 22	3·0	267	273
88	92	12 00	0 26	2·0	11 00	0 23	2·0	9 59	0 21	2·0	9 00	0 19	2·0	8 00	0 17	2·0	7 00	0 15	2·0	268	272
89	91	12 00	0 13	1·0	11 00	0 12	1·0	10 00	0 11	1·0	9 00	0 10	1·0	8 00	0 08	1·0	7 00	0 07	1·0	269	271
90	90	12 00	0 00	0·0	11 00	0 00	0·0	10 00	0 00	0·0	9 00	0 00	0·0	8 00	0 00	0·0	7 00	0 00	0·0	270	270

N. Lat.: for LHA > 180° ... $Z_n = Z$
for LHA < 180° ... $Z_n = 360° - Z$

S. Lat.: for LHA > 180° ... $Z_n = 180° - Z$
for LHA < 180° ... $Z_n = 180° + Z$

SIGHT REDUCTION TABLE

B: (−) for 90° < LHA < 270°
Dec:(−) for Lat. contrary name

Z₁: same sign as B
Z₂: (−) for F > 90°

Lat. / A		84°			85°			86°			87°			88°			89°			Lat. / A
LHA/F	A	A/H	B/P	Z_1/Z_2	A/H	B/P	Z_1/Z_2	A/H	B/P	Z_1/Z_2	A/H	B/P	Z_1/Z_2	A/H	B/P	Z_1/Z_2	A/H	B/P	Z_1/Z_2	LHA	
0	180	0 00	6 00	90·0	0 00	5 00	90·0	0 00	4 00	90·0	0 00	3 00	90·0	0 00	2 00	90·0	0 00	1 00	90·0	180	360
1	179	0 06	6 00	89·0	0 05	5 00	89·0	0 04	4 00	89·0	0 03	3 00	89·0	0 02	2 00	89·0	0 01	1 00	89·0	181	359
2	178	0 13	6 00	88·0	0 10	5 00	88·0	0 08	4 00	88·0	0 06	3 00	88·0	0 04	2 00	88·0	0 02	1 00	88·0	182	358
3	177	0 19	6 00	87·0	0 16	5 00	87·0	0 13	4 00	87·0	0 09	3 00	87·0	0 06	2 00	87·0	0 03	1 00	87·0	183	357
4	176	0 25	5 59	86·0	0 21	4 59	86·0	0 17	3 59	86·0	0 13	3 00	86·0	0 08	2 00	86·0	0 04	1 00	86·0	184	356
5	175	0 31	5 59	85·0	0 26	4 59	85·0	0 21	3 59	85·0	0 16	2 59	85·0	0 10	2 00	85·0	0 05	1 00	85·0	185	355
6	174	0 38	5 58	84·0	0 31	4 58	84·0	0 25	3 59	84·0	0 19	2 59	84·0	0 13	1 59	84·0	0 06	1 00	84·0	186	354
7	173	0 44	5 57	83·0	0 37	4 58	83·0	0 29	3 58	83·0	0 22	2 59	83·0	0 15	1 59	83·0	0 07	1 00	83·0	187	353
8	172	0 50	5 57	82·0	0 42	4 57	82·0	0 33	3 58	82·0	0 25	2 58	82·0	0 17	1 59	82·0	0 08	0 59	82·0	188	352
9	171	0 56	5 56	81·0	0 47	4 56	81·0	0 38	3 57	81·0	0 28	2 58	81·0	0 19	1 59	81·0	0 09	0 59	81·0	189	351
10	170	1 02	5 55	80·1	0 52	4 55	80·0	0 42	3 56	80·0	0 31	2 57	80·0	0 21	1 58	80·0	0 10	0 59	80·0	190	350
11	169	1 09	5 53	79·1	0 57	4 55	79·0	0 46	3 56	79·0	0 34	2 57	79·0	0 23	1 58	79·0	0 11	0 59	79·0	191	349
12	168	1 15	5 52	78·1	1 02	4 53	78·1	0 50	3 55	78·0	0 37	2 56	78·0	0 25	1 57	78·0	0 12	0 59	78·0	192	348
13	167	1 21	5 51	77·1	1 07	4 52	77·1	0 54	3 54	77·0	0 40	2 55	77·0	0 27	1 57	77·0	0 13	0 58	77·0	193	347
14	166	1 27	5 49	76·1	1 12	4 51	76·1	0 58	3 53	76·0	0 44	2 55	76·0	0 29	1 56	76·0	0 15	0 58	76·0	194	346
15	165	1 33	5 48	75·1	1 18	4 50	75·1	1 02	3 52	75·0	0 47	2 54	75·0	0 31	1 56	75·0	0 16	0 58	75·0	195	345
16	164	1 39	5 46	74·1	1 23	4 48	74·1	1 06	3 51	74·0	0 50	2 53	74·0	0 33	1 55	74·0	0 17	0 58	74·0	196	344
17	163	1 45	5 44	73·1	1 28	4 47	73·1	1 10	3 50	73·1	0 53	2 52	73·0	0 35	1 55	73·0	0 18	0 57	73·0	197	343
18	162	1 51	5 42	72·1	1 33	4 45	72·1	1 14	3 48	72·1	0 56	2 51	72·0	0 37	1 54	72·0	0 19	0 57	72·0	198	342
19	161	1 57	5 41	71·1	1 38	4 44	71·1	1 18	3 47	71·1	0 59	2 50	71·0	0 39	1 53	71·0	0 20	0 57	71·0	199	341
20	160	2 03	5 38	70·1	1 42	4 42	70·1	1 22	3 46	70·1	1 02	2 49	70·0	0 41	1 53	70·0	0 21	0 56	70·0	200	340
21	159	2 09	5 36	69·1	1 47	4 40	69·1	1 26	3 44	69·1	1 04	2 48	69·0	0 43	1 52	69·0	0 22	0 56	69·0	201	339
22	158	2 15	5 34	68·1	1 52	4 38	68·1	1 30	3 43	68·1	1 07	2 47	68·0	0 45	1 51	68·0	0 22	0 56	68·0	202	338
23	157	2 20	5 32	67·1	1 57	4 36	67·1	1 34	3 41	67·1	1 10	2 46	67·0	0 47	1 50	67·0	0 23	0 55	67·0	203	337
24	156	2 26	5 29	66·1	2 02	4 34	66·1	1 38	3 39	66·1	1 13	2 44	66·0	0 49	1 50	66·0	0 24	0 55	66·0	204	336
25	155	2 32	5 26	65·1	2 07	4 32	65·1	1 41	3 38	65·1	1 16	2 43	65·0	0 51	1 49	65·0	0 25	0 54	65·0	205	335
26	154	2 38	5 24	64·1	2 11	4 30	64·1	1 45	3 36	64·1	1 19	2 42	64·0	0 53	1 48	64·0	0 26	0 54	64·0	206	334
27	153	2 43	5 21	63·1	2 16	4 27	63·1	1 49	3 34	63·1	1 22	2 40	63·0	0 54	1 47	63·0	0 27	0 53	63·0	207	333
28	152	2 49	5 18	62·1	2 21	4 25	62·1	1 53	3 32	62·1	1 24	2 39	62·0	0 56	1 46	62·0	0 28	0 53	62·0	208	332
29	151	2 54	5 15	61·1	2 25	4 23	61·1	1 56	3 30	61·1	1 27	2 37	61·0	0 58	1 45	61·0	0 29	0 52	61·0	209	331
30	150	3 00	5 12	60·1	2 30	4 20	60·1	2 00	3 28	60·1	1 30	2 36	60·0	1 00	1 44	60·0	0 30	0 52	60·0	210	330
31	149	3 05	5 09	59·1	2 34	4 17	59·1	2 04	3 26	59·1	1 33	2 34	59·0	1 02	1 43	59·0	0 31	0 51	59·0	211	329
32	148	3 11	5 06	58·1	2 39	4 15	58·1	2 07	3 24	58·1	1 35	2 33	58·0	1 04	1 42	58·0	0 32	0 51	58·0	212	328
33	147	3 16	5 02	57·1	2 43	4 12	57·1	2 11	3 21	57·1	1 38	2 31	57·0	1 05	1 41	57·0	0 33	0 50	57·0	213	327
34	146	3 21	4 59	56·1	2 48	4 09	56·1	2 14	3 19	56·1	1 41	2 29	56·0	1 07	1 39	56·0	0 34	0 50	56·0	214	326
35	145	3 26	4 55	55·1	2 52	4 06	55·1	2 18	3 17	55·1	1 43	2 27	55·0	1 09	1 38	55·0	0 34	0 49	55·0	215	325
36	144	3 31	4 52	54·1	2 56	4 03	54·1	2 21	3 14	54·1	1 46	2 26	54·0	1 11	1 37	54·0	0 35	0 49	54·0	216	324
37	143	3 36	4 48	53·2	3 01	4 00	53·1	2 24	3 12	53·1	1 48	2 24	53·0	1 12	1 36	53·0	0 36	0 48	53·0	217	323
38	142	3 41	4 44	52·2	3 05	3 57	52·1	2 28	3 09	52·1	1 51	2 22	52·0	1 14	1 35	52·0	0 37	0 47	52·0	218	322
39	141	3 46	4 40	51·2	3 09	3 53	51·1	2 31	3 07	51·1	1 53	2 20	51·0	1 16	1 33	51·0	0 38	0 46	51·0	219	321
40	140	3 51	4 36	50·2	3 13	3 50	50·2	2 34	3 04	50·1	1 56	2 18	50·0	1 17	1 32	50·0	0 39	0 46	50·0	220	320
41	139	3 56	4 32	49·2	3 17	3 47	49·2	2 37	3 01	49·1	1 58	2 16	49·0	1 19	1 31	49·0	0 39	0 45	49·0	221	319
42	138	4 01	4 28	48·2	3 21	3 43	48·2	2 41	2 58	48·1	2 00	2 14	48·0	1 20	1 29	48·0	0 40	0 45	48·0	222	318
43	137	4 05	4 24	47·2	3 24	3 40	47·2	2 44	2 56	47·1	2 03	2 12	47·0	1 22	1 28	47·0	0 41	0 44	47·0	223	317
44	136	4 10	4 19	46·2	3 28	3 36	46·2	2 47	2 53	46·1	2 05	2 10	46·0	1 23	1 26	46·0	0 42	0 43	46·0	224	316
45	135	4 14	4 15	45·2	3 32	3 32	45·2	2 50	2 50	45·1	2 07	2 07	45·0	1 25	1 25	45·0	0 42	0 42	45·0	225	315

Upper section

A	LHA	89° Z_1/Z_2	89° B/P	89° A/H	88° Z_1/Z_2	88° B/P	88° A/H	87° Z_1/Z_2	87° B/P	87° A/H	A	LHA
315	225	45·0	0 42	0 42	45·0	1 25	1 25	45·0	2 07	2 07	315	225
314	226	44·0	0 42	0 43	44·0	1 24	1 26	44·0	2 05	2 09	314	226
313	227	43·0	0 41	0 44	43·0	1 22	1 28	43·0	2 03	2 12	313	227
312	228	42·0	0 40	0 45	42·0	1 20	1 29	42·0	2 01	2 14	312	228
311	229	41·0	0 40	0 45	41·0	1 19	1 31	41·0	1 58	2 16	311	229
310	230	40·0	0 39	0 46	40·0	1 17	1 32	40·0	1 56	2 18	310	230
309	231	39·0	0 38	0 47	39·0	1 16	1 33	39·0	1 53	2 20	309	231
308	232	38·0	0 37	0 47	38·0	1 14	1 35	38·0	1 51	2 22	308	232
307	233	37·0	0 36	0 48	37·0	1 12	1 36	37·0	1 48	2 24	307	233
306	234	36·0	0 35	0 49	36·0	1 11	1 37	36·0	1 46	2 26	306	234
305	235	35·0	0 34	0 49	35·0	1 09	1 38	35·0	1 43	2 27	305	235
304	236	34·0	0 34	0 50	34·0	1 07	1 39	34·0	1 41	2 29	304	236
303	237	33·0	0 33	0 50	33·0	1 05	1 41	33·0	1 38	2 31	303	237
302	238	32·0	0 32	0 51	32·0	1 04	1 42	32·0	1 35	2 33	302	238
301	239	31·0	0 31	0 51	31·0	1 02	1 43	31·0	1 33	2 34	301	239
300	240	30·0	0 30	0 52	30·0	1 00	1 44	30·0	1 30	2 36	300	240
299	241	29·0	0 29	0 52	29·0	0 58	1 45	29·0	1 27	2 37	299	241
298	242	28·0	0 28	0 53	28·0	0 56	1 46	28·0	1 25	2 39	298	242
297	243	27·0	0 27	0 53	27·0	0 54	1 47	27·0	1 22	2 40	297	243
296	244	26·0	0 26	0 54	26·0	0 53	1 48	26·0	1 19	2 42	296	244
295	245	25·0	0 25	0 54	25·0	0 51	1 49	25·0	1 16	2 43	295	245
294	246	24·0	0 24	0 55	24·0	0 49	1 50	24·0	1 13	2 44	294	246
293	247	23·0	0 23	0 55	23·0	0 47	1 51	23·0	1 10	2 46	293	247
292	248	22·0	0 22	0 56	22·0	0 45	1 52	22·0	1 07	2 47	292	248
291	249	21·0	0 22	0 56	21·0	0 43	1 52	21·0	1 05	2 48	291	249
290	250	20·0	0 21	0 56	20·0	0 41	1 53	20·0	1 02	2 49	290	250
289	251	19·0	0 20	0 57	19·0	0 39	1 53	19·0	0 59	2 50	289	251
288	252	18·0	0 19	0 57	18·0	0 37	1 54	18·0	0 56	2 51	288	252
287	253	17·0	0 18	0 57	17·0	0 35	1 55	17·0	0 53	2 52	287	253
286	254	16·0	0 17	0 58	16·0	0 33	1 55	16·0	0 50	2 53	286	254
285	255	15·0	0 16	0 58	15·0	0 31	1 56	15·0	0 47	2 54	285	255
284	256	14·0	0 15	0 58	14·0	0 29	1 56	14·0	0 44	2 55	284	256
283	257	13·0	0 14	0 59	13·0	0 27	1 57	13·0	0 41	2 56	283	257
282	258	12·0	0 13	0 59	12·0	0 25	1 57	12·0	0 37	2 56	282	258
281	259	11·0	0 12	0 59	11·0	0 23	1 58	11·0	0 34	2 57	281	259
280	260	10·0	0 11	0 59	10·0	0 21	1 58	10·0	0 31	2 57	280	260
279	261	9·0	0 09	0 59	9·0	0 19	1 58	9·0	0 28	2 58	279	261
278	262	8·0	0 08	0 59	8·0	0 17	1 59	8·0	0 25	2 58	278	262
277	263	7·0	0 07	1 00	7·0	0 15	1 59	7·0	0 22	2 59	277	263
276	264	6·0	0 06	1 00	6·0	0 13	1 59	6·0	0 19	2 59	276	264
275	265	5·0	0 05	1 00	5·0	0 10	1 59	5·0	0 16	2 59	275	265
274	266	4·0	0 04	1 00	4·0	0 08	2 00	4·0	0 13	3 00	274	266
273	267	3·0	0 03	1 00	3·0	0 06	2 00	3·0	0 09	3 00	273	267
272	268	2·0	0 02	1 00	2·0	0 04	2 00	2·0	0 06	3 00	272	268
271	269	1·0	0 01	1 00	1·0	0 02	2 00	1·0	0 03	3 00	271	269
270	270	0·0	0 00	1 00	0·0	0 00	2 00	0·0	0 00	3 00	270	270

S. Lat.: for LHA > 180° … $Z_n = 180° − Z$; for LHA < 180° … $Z_n = 180° + Z$

Lower section

LHA	F	84° A/H	84° B/P	84° Z_1/Z_2	85° A/H	85° B/P	85° Z_1/Z_2	86° A/H	86° B/P	86° Z_1/Z_2
45	135	4 14	4 15	45·2	3 32	3 32	45·1	2 50	2 50	45·1
46	134	4 19	4 11	44·2	3 36	3 29	44·1	2 53	2 47	44·1
47	133	4 23	4 06	43·2	3 39	3 25	43·1	2 55	2 44	43·1
48	132	4 27	4 01	42·2	3 43	3 21	42·1	2 58	2 41	42·1
49	131	4 31	3 57	41·2	3 46	3 17	41·1	3 01	2 38	41·1
50	130	4 36	3 52	40·2	3 50	3 13	40·1	3 04	2 34	40·1
51	129	4 40	3 47	39·2	3 53	3 09	39·1	3 06	2 31	39·1
52	128	4 43	3 42	38·2	3 56	3 05	38·1	3 09	2 28	38·1
53	127	4 47	3 37	37·2	3 59	3 01	37·1	3 12	2 25	37·1
54	126	4 51	3 32	36·1	4 03	2 57	36·1	3 14	2 21	36·1
55	125	4 55	3 27	35·1	4 06	2 52	35·1	3 17	2 18	35·1
56	124	4 58	3 22	34·1	4 09	2 48	34·1	3 19	2 14	34·1
57	123	5 02	3 17	33·1	4 12	2 44	33·1	3 21	2 11	33·1
58	122	5 05	3 11	32·1	4 14	2 39	32·1	3 23	2 07	32·1
59	121	5 08	3 06	31·1	4 17	2 35	31·1	3 26	2 04	31·1
60	120	5 12	3 00	30·1	4 20	2 30	30·1	3 28	2 00	30·1
61	119	5 15	2 55	29·1	4 22	2 26	29·1	3 30	1 56	29·1
62	118	5 18	2 49	28·1	4 25	2 21	28·1	3 32	1 53	28·1
63	117	5 21	2 44	27·1	4 27	2 16	27·1	3 34	1 49	27·1
64	116	5 23	2 38	26·1	4 30	2 12	26·1	3 36	1 45	26·1
65	115	5 26	2 33	25·1	4 32	2 07	25·1	3 37	1 42	25·1
66	114	5 29	2 27	24·1	4 34	2 02	24·1	3 39	1 38	24·1
67	113	5 31	2 21	23·1	4 36	1 57	23·1	3 41	1 34	23·1
68	112	5 34	2 15	22·1	4 38	1 53	22·1	3 42	1 30	22·1
69	111	5 36	2 09	21·1	4 40	1 48	21·1	3 44	1 26	21·1
70	110	5 38	2 04	20·1	4 42	1 43	20·1	3 46	1 22	20·1
71	109	5 40	1 58	19·1	4 44	1 38	19·1	3 47	1 18	19·1
72	108	5 42	1 52	18·1	4 45	1 33	18·1	3 48	1 14	18·1
73	107	5 44	1 46	17·1	4 47	1 28	17·1	3 49	1 10	17·1
74	106	5 46	1 40	16·1	4 48	1 23	16·1	3 51	1 06	16·1
75	105	5 48	1 33	15·1	4 50	1 18	15·1	3 52	1 02	15·1
76	104	5 49	1 27	14·1	4 51	1 13	14·1	3 53	0 58	14·1
77	103	5 51	1 21	13·1	4 52	1 08	13·0	3 54	0 54	13·1
78	102	5 52	1 15	12·1	4 53	1 03	12·0	3 55	0 50	12·1
79	101	5 53	1 09	11·1	4 54	0 57	11·0	3 56	0 46	11·1
80	100	5 55	1 03	10·1	4 55	0 52	10·0	3 56	0 42	10·0
81	99	5 56	0 57	9·0	4 56	0 47	9·0	3 57	0 38	9·0
82	98	5 56	0 50	8·0	4 57	0 42	8·0	3 58	0 33	8·0
83	97	5 57	0 44	7·0	4 58	0 37	7·0	3 58	0 29	7·0
84	96	5 58	0 38	6·0	4 58	0 31	6·0	3 59	0 25	6·0
85	95	5 59	0 31	5·0	4 59	0 26	5·0	3 59	0 21	5·0
86	94	5 59	0 25	4·0	4 59	0 21	4·0	3 59	0 17	4·0
87	93	6 00	0 19	3·0	5 00	0 16	3·0	4 00	0 13	3·0
88	92	6 00	0 13	2·0	5 00	0 10	2·0	4 00	0 08	2·0
89	91	6 00	0 06	1·0	5 00	0 05	1·0	4 00	0 04	1·0
90	90	6 00	0 00	0·0	5 00	0 00	0·0	4 00	0 00	0·0

N. Lat.: for LHA > 180° … $Z_n = Z$; for LHA < 180° … $Z_n = 360° − Z$

AUXILIARY TABLE

Sign for corr₂ for A'. →

Sign of corr₁ for F'. →   *Reverse* sign if $F > 90°$.

P°	F'+/−	$Z°$ / −A'/+A'	□/30	29/31	28/32	27/33	26/34	25/35	24/36	23/37	22/38	21/39	20/40	19/41	18/42	17/43	16/44	15/45	14/46	13/47	12/48	11/49	10/50	9/51	8/52	7/53	6/54	5/55	4/56	3/57	2/58	1/59
1	1/59	89	·	·	·	·	·	·	·	·	·	·	·	·	·	·	·	·	·	0	0	0	0	0	0	0	0	0	0	0	·	·
2	2/58	88	1	1	0	0	0	0	0	0	0	0	0	0	0	0	0	0	0	0	0	0	0	0	0	0	0	0	0	0	0	0
3	3/57	87	1	1	1	1	1	1	1	1	1	1	1	1	1	1	1	1	0	0	0	0	0	0	0	0	0	0	0	0	0	0
4	4/56	86	2	2	2	2	2	1	1	1	1	1	1	1	1	1	1	1	1	1	1	1	1	1	1	1	1	1	0	0	0	0
5	5/55	85	2	3	2	2	2	2	2	2	2	2	2	2	2	1	1	1	1	1	1	1	1	1	1	1	1	1	1	1	1	0
6	6/54	84	3	3	3	3	3	3	2	2	2	2	2	2	2	2	2	2	1	1	1	1	1	1	1	1	1	1	1	1	1	1
7	7/53	83	3	4	3	3	3	3	3	3	3	3	2	2	2	2	2	2	2	2	2	2	2	2	2	1	1	1	1	1	1	1
8	8/52	82	4	4	4	4	4	3	3	3	3	3	3	3	3	3	3	2	2	2	2	2	2	2	2	2	2	1	1	1	1	1
9	9/51	81	4	5	4	5	4	4	4	4	3	3	3	3	3	3	3	3	3	2	2	2	2	2	2	2	2	2	2	1	1	1
10	10/50	80	5	5	5	5	5	4	4	4	4	4	3	3	3	3	3	3	3	3	3	2	2	2	2	2	2	2	2	2	1	1
11	11/49	79	5	6	5	5	5	5	5	4	4	4	4	4	4	4	3	3	3	3	3	3	2	2	2	2	2	2	2	2	2	1
12	12/48	78	6	6	6	6	5	5	5	5	5	4	4	4	4	4	4	3	3	3	3	3	3	2	2	2	2	2	2	2	2	1
13	13/47	77	6	7	6	6	6	6	5	5	5	5	5	4	4	4	4	4	3	3	3	3	3	3	3	2	2	2	2	2	2	2
14	14/46	76	7	7	7	7	6	6	6	6	5	5	5	5	4	4	4	4	4	3	3	3	3	3	3	3	2	2	2	2	2	2
15	15/45	75	7	8	7	7	6	6	6	6	6	5	5	5	5	4	4	4	4	3	3	3	3	3	3	3	3	2	2	2	2	2
16	16/44	74	8	8	8	7	7	7	6	6	6	6	5	5	5	5	4	4	4	4	4	3	3	3	3	3	3	2	2	2	2	2
17	17/43	73	8	9	8	8	7	7	7	7	6	6	6	5	5	5	5	4	4	4	4	3	3	3	3	3	3	3	2	2	2	2
18	18/42	72	9	9	9	8	8	8	7	7	7	6	6	6	5	5	5	5	4	4	4	4	3	3	3	3	3	3	3	2	2	2
19	19/41	71	9	10	9	9	8	8	8	7	7	7	6	6	6	5	5	5	4	4	4	4	3	3	3	3	3	3	3	2	2	2
20	20/40	70	10	10	10	9	9	9	8	8	7	7	7	6	6	6	5	5	5	4	4	4	3	3	3	3	3	3	3	2	2	2
21	21/39	69	10	10	10	10	9	9	9	8	8	8	7	7	6	6	6	5	5	4	4	4	4	4	3	3	3	3	3	3	2	2
22	22/38	68	11	11	11	10	10	9	9	9	9	8	7	7	7	6	6	6	5	5	4	4	4	4	3	3	3	3	3	3	2	2
23	23/37	67	11	11	11	11	11	10	10	9	9	9	8	8	7	7	6	6	6	5	5	4	4	4	4	3	3	3	3	3	2	2
24	24/36	66	12	12	12	11	11	11	10	10	9	9	9	8	7	7	7	6	6	5	5	5	4	4	4	3	3	3	3	3	3	2
25	25/35	65	12	12	12	12	11	11	10	10	10	9	9	8	8	8	7	6	6	5	5	5	4	4	4	3	3	3	3	3	2	2
26	26/34	64	13	13	13	13	13	12	12	11	11	10	10	9	9	9	8	8	7	7	6	6	5	5	4	4	4	3	3	2	2	1
27	27/33	63	13	13	13	13	14	12	12	12	12	11	11	10	9	9	8	8	7	7	6	6	5	5	5	4	4	3	3	2	2	1
28	28/32	62	14	14	14	14	15	13	13	12	12	12	11	11	10	10	9	8	8	7	7	6	6	5	5	4	4	3	3	2	2	1
29	29/31	61	14	14	14	14	15	14	13	13	13	12	12	11	11	10	9	9	8	7	7	6	6	5	5	4	4	3	3	2	2	1
30	□/30	60	15	15	14	15	15	14	14	13	13	13	13	12	11	11	10	9	9	8	8	7	6	6	5	4	4	3	3	2	2	1
31		59	15	15	16	16	16	15	14	14	13	13	12	11	11	10	9	9	9	8	7	6	6	5	5	4	4	3	3	2	2	1
32		58	16	16	17	17	16	15	15	14	14	13	12	11	11	10	10	9	9	8	7	7	6	5	5	4	4	3	3	2	2	1
33		57	16	16	17	17	16	16	15	14	14	13	13	12	11	11	10	9	9	8	8	7	6	5	5	4	4	3	3	2	2	1
34		56	17	17	17	17	16	16	15	15	14	14	13	12	11	11	10	9	9	8	8	7	6	6	5	4	4	3	3	2	2	1
35		55	17	17	18	18	17	16	15	15	15	14	13	12	12	11	10	10	9	8	8	7	6	6	5	4	4	3	3	2	2	1
36		54	18	17	18	18	17	16	16	15	15	14	13	13	12	11	10	9	9	8	8	7	6	6	5	5	4	3	3	2	2	1
37		53	18	17	18	18	17	16	16	15	15	14	13	13	12	11	10	9	9	8	8	7	6	6	5	5	4	3	3	2	2	1
38		52	18	18	18	18	18	16	16	15	15	14	14	13	12	11	10	10	9	8	8	7	6	6	5	5	4	3	3	2	2	1
39		51	19	18	18	19	18	17	16	16	15	15	14	13	12	12	11	10	9	8	8	7	6	6	5	5	4	3	3	2	2	1
40		50	19	19	18	19	18	17	16	16	16	15	14	13	13	12	11	10	9	9	8	7	6	6	5	5	4	3	3	2	2	1

Top-right corner key: **− A' / + Z₂°**

Bottom-right note: For Z₂ < 10°, use 10°

Bottom-left note: For P > 80°, use 80°

F' + / − →	30 □	29 / 31	28 / 32	27 / 33	26 / 34	25 / 35	24 / 36	23 / 37	22 / 38	21 / 39	20 / 40	19 / 41	18 / 42	17 / 43	16 / 44	15 / 45	14 / 46	13 / 47	12 / 48	11 / 49	10 / 50	9 / 51	8 / 52	7 / 53	6 / 54	5 / 55	4 / 56	3 / 57	2 / 58	1 / 59	Z₂
P°	---	---	---	---	---	---	---	---	---	---	---	---	---	---	---	---	---	---	---	---	---	---	---	---	---	---	---	---	---	---	---
41	20	19	18	18	17	16	16	15	14	14	13	12	12	11	10	10	9	9	8	7	7	6	5	5	4	3	3	2	1	1	49
42	20	19	19	18	17	17	16	15	15	14	13	13	12	11	11	10	9	9	8	7	7	6	5	5	4	3	3	2	1	1	48
43	21	20	19	18	18	17	16	16	15	14	14	13	12	12	11	10	10	9	8	8	7	6	5	5	4	3	3	2	1	1	47
44	21	20	19	19	18	17	17	16	15	15	14	13	13	12	11	10	10	9	8	8	7	6	6	5	4	3	3	2	1	1	46
45	21	21	20	19	18	18	17	16	16	15	14	13	13	12	11	11	10	9	8	8	7	6	6	5	4	4	3	2	1	1	45
46	22	21	20	19	19	18	17	17	16	15	14	14	13	12	11	11	10	9	9	8	7	6	6	5	4	4	3	2	2	1	44
47	22	21	20	20	19	18	18	17	16	15	15	14	13	12	12	11	10	10	9	8	7	7	6	6	4	4	3	3	2	1	43
48	22	22	21	20	19	19	18	17	16	16	15	14	13	13	12	11	11	10	9	8	8	7	6	6	4	4	3	3	2	1	42
49	23	22	21	20	20	19	18	17	17	16	15	15	14	13	12	11	11	10	9	8	8	7	6	6	5	4	3	3	2	1	41
50	23	22	21	21	20	19	18	18	17	16	16	15	14	13	12	11	11	10	10	8	8	7	7	6	5	4	3	3	2	1	40
51	23	23	22	21	20	19	19	18	17	16	15	14	13	13	11	11	11	10	9	9	8	7	6	6	4	4	3	3	2	1	39
52	24	23	22	21	20	20	19	18	17	16	16	15	13	13	12	12	11	10	10	9	8	8	6	6	5	4	3	3	2	1	38
53	24	23	22	22	21	20	19	18	18	17	16	15	13	14	12	12	11	10	10	9	8	8	6	6	5	4	3	3	2	1	37
54	24	23	23	22	21	20	20	19	18	17	16	15	14	14	12	12	11	11	10	9	8	8	6	6	5	4	3	3	2	1	36
55	25	24	23	22	21	20	20	19	18	17	16	15	14	14	12	12	12	11	10	10	8	8	6	6	5	4	3	3	2	1	35
56	25	24	23	22	22	21	20	19	18	16	16	15	14	14	13	12	11	11	9	9	8	7	6	6	4	4	3	3	2	1	34
57	25	25	24	23	22	21	20	19	18	17	16	15	14	14	13	12	11	11	10	9	8	8	6	6	5	4	4	3	2	1	33
58	26	25	24	23	22	21	20	20	19	17	16	15	14	15	14	13	11	12	10	9	8	8	6	6	5	4	4	3	2	1	32
59	26	25	24	23	22	22	21	20	19	17	16	16	15	15	14	13	12	12	10	9	8	8	6	6	5	4	4	3	2	1	31
60	26	25	24	23	23	22	21	20	19	17	17	16	15	15	14	13	12	12	10	10	9	8	7	6	5	5	4	3	2	1	30
61	26	25	24	23	23	22	21	20	19	18	17	16	15	15	13	13	12	12	10	10	8	8	6	6	5	4	4	3	2	1	29
62	27	26	25	24	23	22	22	20	19	18	17	16	15	15	14	13	12	12	11	10	9	8	7	6	5	5	4	3	2	1	28
63	27	26	25	24	23	22	22	21	20	19	17	16	15	16	14	13	12	12	11	10	9	8	7	6	5	5	4	3	2	1	27
64	27	26	25	24	24	23	22	21	20	19	17	16	16	16	14	13	13	12	11	10	9	8	7	6	5	5	4	3	2	1	26
65	27	26	25	24	24	23	22	22	20	19	17	17	16	16	14	14	13	13	11	10	9	8	7	6	6	5	4	3	2	1	25
66	27	26	26	25	24	23	22	21	19	18	17	17	16	15	14	13	13	12	11	10	9	8	7	6	6	5	4	3	2	1	24
67	28	27	26	25	24	23	23	21	19	18	18	17	16	16	14	14	13	12	11	10	9	8	7	6	6	5	4	3	2	1	23
68	28	27	26	25	24	23	23	21	20	19	18	17	16	16	14	14	13	12	11	10	9	8	7	7	6	5	4	3	2	1	22
69	28	27	26	25	24	23	23	21	20	19	18	17	16	16	14	14	13	12	11	10	9	8	7	7	6	5	4	3	2	1	21
70	28	27	26	25	25	24	23	22	20	19	18	17	16	16	15	14	13	13	11	10	9	8	8	7	6	5	4	3	2	1	20
71	28	27	26	26	25	24	23	22	21	20	20	18	17	16	16	15	13	13	12	11	10	9	8	7	6	5	4	3	2	1	19
72	29	28	27	26	25	24	23	22	21	20	20	18	17	17	16	15	14	13	12	11	10	9	8	7	6	5	4	3	2	1	18
73	29	28	27	27	25	24	23	22	21	21	20	18	17	17	16	15	14	13	12	11	10	9	8	7	6	5	4	3	2	1	17
74	29	28	27	27	26	25	23	22	21	21	20	18	17	17	16	15	14	13	12	11	10	9	8	7	6	5	4	3	2	1	16
75	29	28	27	27	26	25	24	23	22	21	20	19	18	17	16	15	14	13	12	11	10	9	8	7	6	5	4	3	2	1	15
76	29	28	27	26	25	24	23	22	21	20	20	17	17	16	16	15	14	13	12	11	10	9	8	7	6	5	4	3	2	1	14
77	29	28	27	26	25	24	23	22	22	21	20	18	18	17	16	15	14	13	12	11	10	9	8	7	6	5	4	3	2	1	13
78	29	28	27	27	25	25	23	23	22	21	20	18	18	17	16	15	14	13	12	11	10	9	8	7	6	5	4	3	2	1	12
79	29	28	27	27	26	25	24	23	22	21	20	18	18	17	16	15	14	13	12	11	10	9	8	7	6	5	4	3	3	1	11
80	30	29	28	27	26	25	24	23	22	21	20	18	18	17	16	15	14	13	12	11	10	9	8	7	6	5	4	3	3	1	10

USE OF CONCISE SIGHT REDUCTION TABLES (continued)

4. *Example.* (b) Required the altitude and azimuth of *Vega* on 2018 July 29 at UT 04^h 50^m from the estimated position 152° west, 15° south.

1. Assumed latitude $Lat =$ 15° S
   From the almanac $GHA =$ 99° 54′
   Assumed longitude   151° 54′ W
   Local hour angle $LHA =$ 308

2. Reduction table, 1st entry
   $(Lat, LHA) = (15, 308)$ $A =$ 49   34 $A° = 50, A′ = 34$
                          $B = +66$ 29 $Z_1 = +71·7,$ $LHA > 270°$

3. From the almanac $Dec = -38$ 48   *Lat* and *Dec* contrary
   Sum $= B + Dec$ $F = +27$ 41 $F° = 28, F′ = 41$

4. Reduction table, 2nd entry
   $(A°, F°) = (50, 28)$ $H =$ 17   34 $P° = 37$
                                       $Z_2 = 67·8, Z_2° = 68$

5. Auxiliary table, 1st entry
   $(F′, P°) = (41, 37)$ $corr_1 =$ -11 $F < 90°, F′ > 29′$
   Sum   17   23

6. Auxiliary table, 2nd entry
   $(A′, Z_2°) = (34, 68)$ $corr_2 =$ $+10$ $A′ > 30′$

7. Sum = computed altitude $H_c = +17°$ 33′ $F > 0°$

8. Azimuth,   first component $Z_1 = +71·7$ same sign as B
            second component $Z_2 = +67·8$ $F < 90°, F > 0°$
   Sum = azimuth angle $Z =$ 139·5

   True azimuth $Z_n =$ 040°   S *Lat, LHA* > 180°

5. *Form for use with the Concise Sight Reduction Tables.* The form on the following page lays out the procedure explained on pages 284–285. Each step is shown, with notes and rules to ensure accuracy, rather than speed, throughout the calculation. The form is mainly intended for the calculation of star positions. It therefore includes the formation of the Greenwich hour of Aries (*GHA* Aries), and thus the Greenwich hour angle of the star (*GHA*) from its tabular sidereal hour angle (*SHA*). These calculations, included in step 1 of the form, can easily be replaced by the interpolation of *GHA* and *Dec* for the Sun, Moon or planets.

The form may be freely copied; however, acknowledgement of the source is requested.

Date & UT of observation			Body	Estimated Latitude & Longitude
	h m s			° ′ ° ′

Step	Calculate Altitude & Azimuth		Summary of Rules & Notes
Assumed latitude	$Lat =$ °		Nearest estimated latitude, integral number of degrees.
Assumed longitude	$Long =$ ° ′		Choose $Long$ so that LHA has integral number of degrees.
1. From the almanac:	$Dec =$ ° ′		Record the Dec for use in Step 3.
GHA Aries h	$=$ ° !		Needed if using SHA. Tabular value.
Increment m s	$=$ ° !		for minutes and seconds of time.
SHA	$SHA =$ ° !		
$GHA = GHA\ Aries + SHA$	$GHA =$ ° ′		Remove multiples of 360°.
Assumed longitude	$Long =$ ° ′		West longitudes are negative.
$LHA = GHA + Long$	$LHA =$ °		Remove multiples of 360°.
2. Reduction table, 1st entry $(Lat, LHA) = ($ °, °$)$ record A, B and Z_1.	$A =$ ° ′	$A° =$ °	nearest whole degree of A.
		$A' =$ ′	minutes part of A.
	$B =$ ° ′		B is minus if $90° < LHA < 270°$.
		$Z_1 =$ °	Z_1 has the same sign as B.
3. From step 1	$Dec =$ ° ′		Dec is minus if contrary to Lat.
$F = B + Dec$	$F =$ ° ′		Regard F as positive until step 7.
		$F° =$ °	nearest whole degree of F.
		$F' =$ ′	minutes part of F.
4. Reduction table, 2nd entry $(A°, F°) = ($ °, °$)$ record H, P and Z_2.	$H =$ ° ′	$P° =$ °	nearest whole degree of P.
		$Z_2 =$ °	
5. Auxiliary table, 1st entry $(F', P°) = ($ ′, °$)$ record $corr_1$	$corr_1 =$ ′		$corr_1$ is minus if $F < 90°$ & $F' > 29'$, or if $F > 90°$ & $F' < 30'$.
6. Auxiliary table, 2nd entry $(A', Z_2°) = ($ ′, °$)$ record $corr_2$	$corr_2 =$ ′		$Z_2°$ nearest whole degree of Z_2. $corr_2$ is minus if $A' < 30'$.
7. Calculated altitude $= H_C = H + corr_1 + corr_2$	$H_C =$ ° ′		H_C is minus if F is negative, and object is below the horizon.
8. Azimuth, 1st component	$Z_1 =$ °		Z_1 has the same sign as B.
2nd component	$Z_2 =$ °		Z_2 is minus if $F > 90°$. If F is negative, $Z_2 = 180° - Z_2$
$Z = Z_1 + Z_2$	$Z =$ °		Ignore the sign of Z.
		N Lat:	If $LHA > 180°$, $Z_n = Z$, or if $LHA < 180°$, $Z_n = 360° - Z$,
		S Lat:	If $LHA > 180°$, $Z_n = 180° - Z$, or if $LHA < 180°$, $Z_n = 180° + Z$.
True azimuth	$Z_n =$ °		©HMNAO

For use with *The Nautical Almanac's* Concise Sight Reduction Tables pages 284-318.

POLAR PHENOMENA

EXPLANATION

1. *Introduction.* The graphs on pages 322-325 give data concerning the rising and setting of the Sun and Moon and the duration of civil twilight for high latitudes. Graphs are given instead of tables for high latitudes because they give a clearer picture of the phenomena and of the attainable accuracy in any given case. In the regions of the graph that are difficult to read accurately, the phenomenon itself is generally uncertain.

2. *Semiduration of sunlight.* The graphs for the semiduration of sunlight (page 322) give for latitudes north of N 65° the number of hours from sunrise to meridian passage or from meridian passage to sunset. There is continuous daylight in an area marked "Sun above horizon", and no direct sunlight in an area marked "Sun below horizon". The figures near the top indicate, for several convenient dates, the local mean times of meridian passage; with the aid of the intermediate dots the LMT on any given day may be obtained to the nearest minute. The LMT of sunrise may be found by subtracting the semiduration from the time of meridian passage, and the time of sunset by adding. The equation of time is given by subtracting the time of meridian passage from noon.

Examples. (a) Estimate the time of sunrise and sunset on 2018 March 10 at latitude N 77°. The semiduration of sunlight (page 322) is about $5^h 00^m$. The time of meridian passage is $12^h 10^m$, and hence the LMT of sunrise is $07^h 10^m$, and of sunset $17^h 10^m$. (b) Estimate the dates, for the first half of 2018, when the Sun is continuously below and above the horizon at latitude N 80°. The semiduration of sunlight graph (page 322) indicates the Sun is continuously below the horizon until about February 21, and is continuously above the horizon after April 14.

3. *Duration of civil twilight.* The graphs for the duration of twilight (page 322) give the interval from the beginning of morning civil twilight (Sun 6° below the horizon) to the time of sunrise or from the time of sunset to the end of evening civil twilight. In a region marked "No twilight or sunlight", the Sun is continuously below the horizon by more than 6°. In a region marked "Continuous twilight or sunlight", the Sun never goes lower than 6° below the horizon.

Adjacent to a region marked "No twilight or sunlight" is a region in which the Sun is continuously below the horizon, but so near to the horizon during a portion of the day that there is twilight. This area is the shaded region. The value given by the graph in this shaded region is the interval from the beginning of morning twilight to meridian passage of the Sun, or from meridian passage to the end of evening twilight, the total duration of twilight being twice the value given by the graph. The border between this shaded region and the remainder of the graph indicates that the Sun only just rises at meridian passage at the date and latitude shown. The remainder of the graph gives the total duration of civil twilight.

Examples. (a) Estimate the time of the beginning of morning civil twilight at latitude N 77° on 2018 March 10. The duration of twilight (page 322) is about $1^h 35^m$. Applying this to the time of sunrise, $07^h 10^m$, found in the preceding example, the beginning of morning civil twilight is $05^h 35^m$ LMT. (b) Estimate, for the first half of 2018, the limiting dates of civil twilight and sunlight at latitude N 80°. The graphs (page 322) indicate there is no sunlight or twilight till about February 6, there is twilight but no sunlight from February 6 until February 21, sunlight and twilight till March 31, continuous twilight or sunlight till April 14, and then continuous sunlight. (c) Estimate the time of the beginning and end of civil twilight on 2018 February 14 at latitude N 80°. The graph (page 322) indicates there is no direct sunlight at this date and latitude, but three hours of twilight before and after meridian passage. Thus civil twilight begins at about 09^h and ends at about 15^h LMT.

4. *Semiduration of moonlight*   The graphs, for each month, for the semiduration of moonlight give for the Moon the same data as the graphs for the semiduration of sunlight give for the Sun. The scale near the top gives the LMT of meridian passage. In addition, the phase symbols are placed on the graphs to show the day on which each phase occurs. Since the times of meridian passage and the semiduration change more rapidly from day to day for the Moon than for the Sun, special care will be required in reading the graphs accurately.

For most purposes, in these high latitudes a rough idea of the time of moonrise or moonset is all that is required, and this may be obtained by a glance at the graph.

Example. Estimate the moon phase and the time of moonrise and moonset on 2018 February 7 at latitude N 70°. The phase is found from pages 323-325 to be near last quarter, and the Moon crosses the meridian at 06^h LMT. The semiduration of moonlight taken for the time of meridian passage is 4 hours, giving moonrise at 02^h LMT on February 7 and moonset at 10^h on February 7.

If greater accuracy is required, it is necessary to read the graph for the UT of each phenomenon at the desired meridian. The dates indicated on the graph are for 00^h UT, and intermediate values of the UT may be located by estimation.

Example. Required to improve the results obtained in the preceding example, assuming the observer to be in longitude W 90° (6^h) west.

The values found previously were:

		d	h			d	h
Time of meridian passage	2018 Feb.	7	06 LMT	=	Feb.	7	12 UT
Semiduration of moonlight			4				
Time of moonrise		Feb.	7	02 LMT	=	Feb.	7 08 UT
Time of moonset		Feb.	7	10 LMT	=	Feb.	7 16 UT

Returning to the graphs (pages 323-325) with these three values of the UT, the following results are obtained:

		d	h	m			d	h	m
Time of meridian passage	2018 Feb.	7	06	10 LMT	=	Feb.	7	12	10 UT
Semiduration for moonrise			03	50					
Time of moonrise		Feb.	7	02	20 LMT	=	Feb.	7	08	20 UT
Semiduration for moonset			03	40					
Time of moonset		Feb.	7	09	50 LMT	=	Feb.	7	15	50 UT

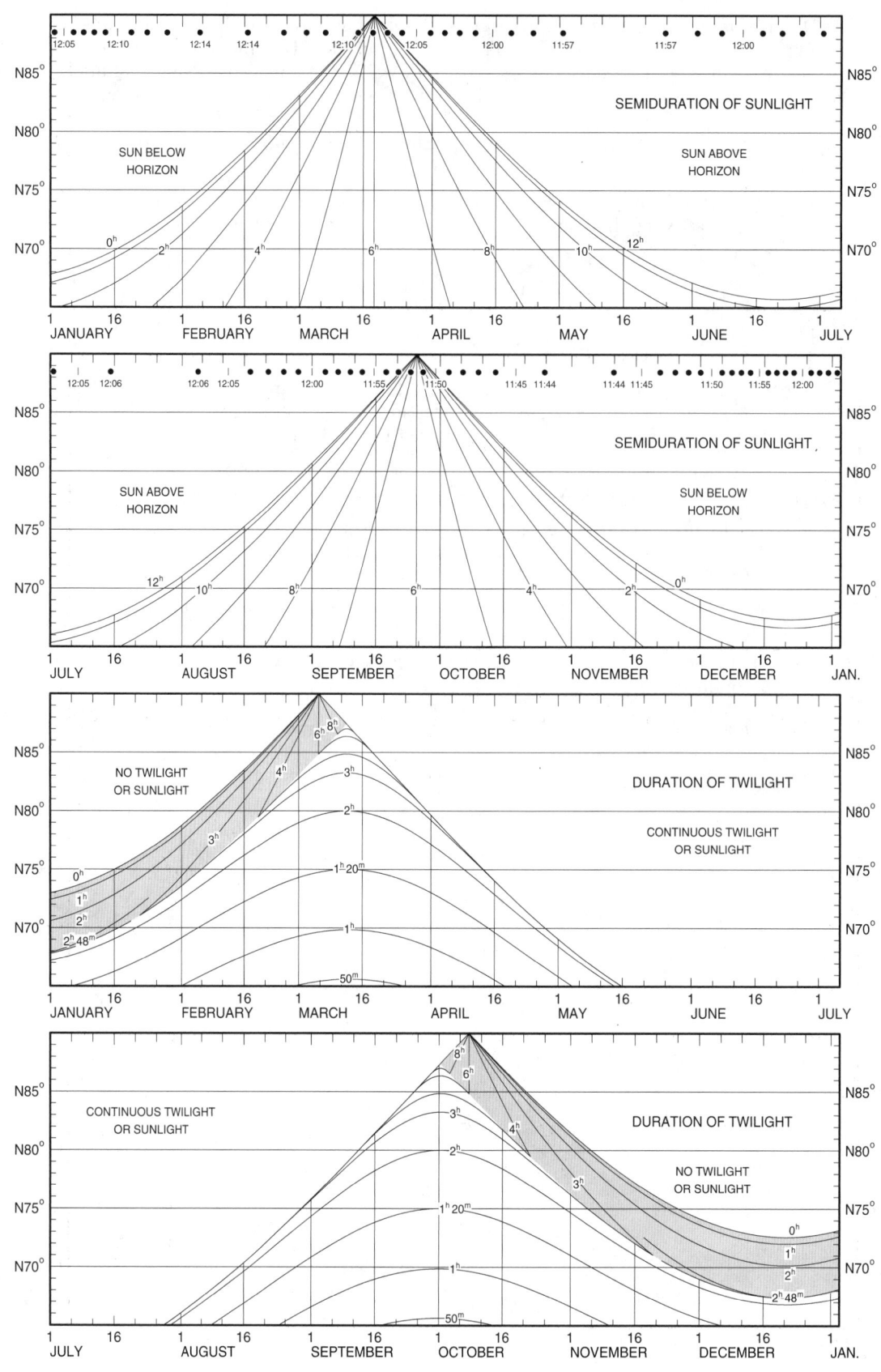

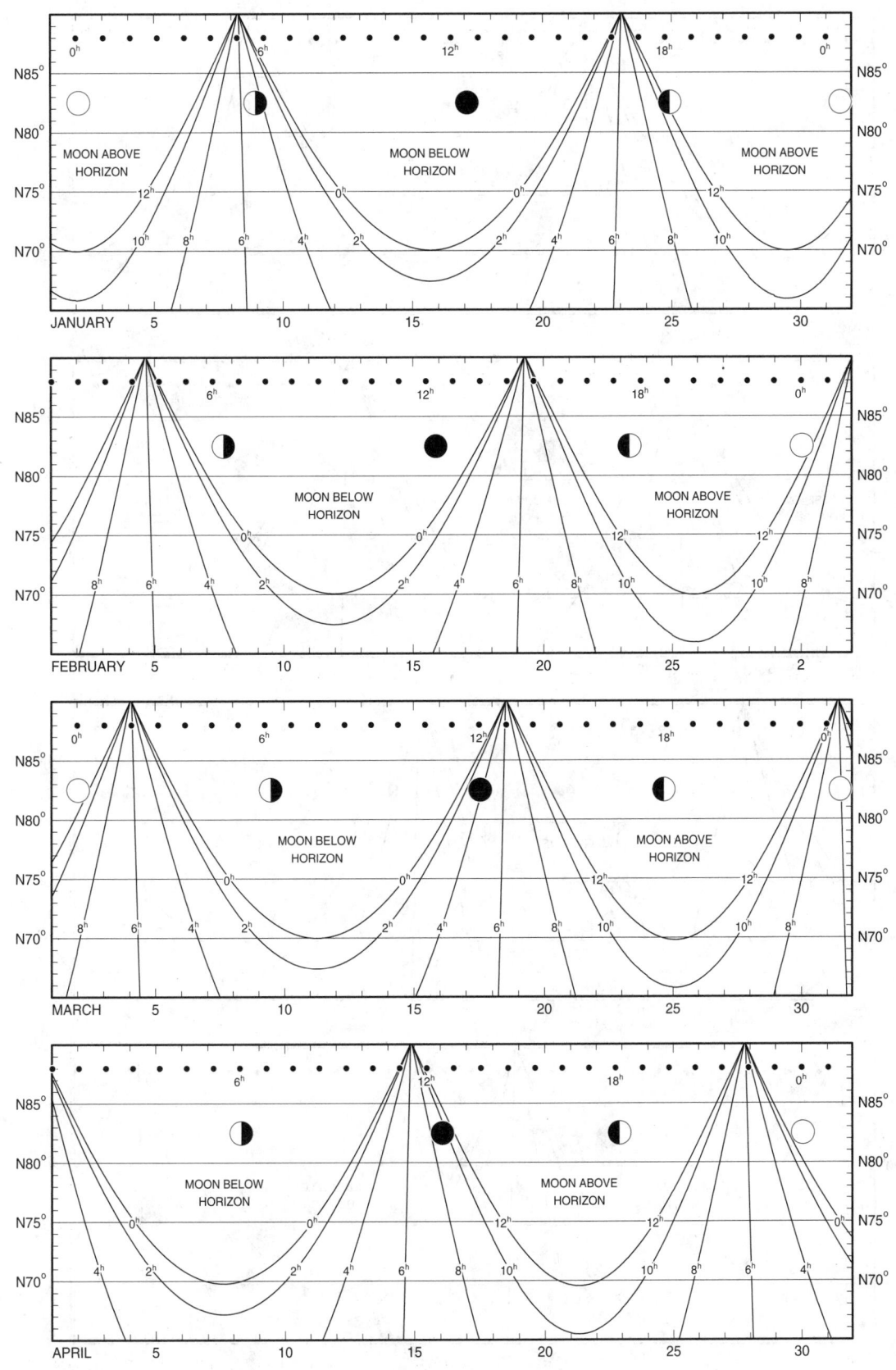

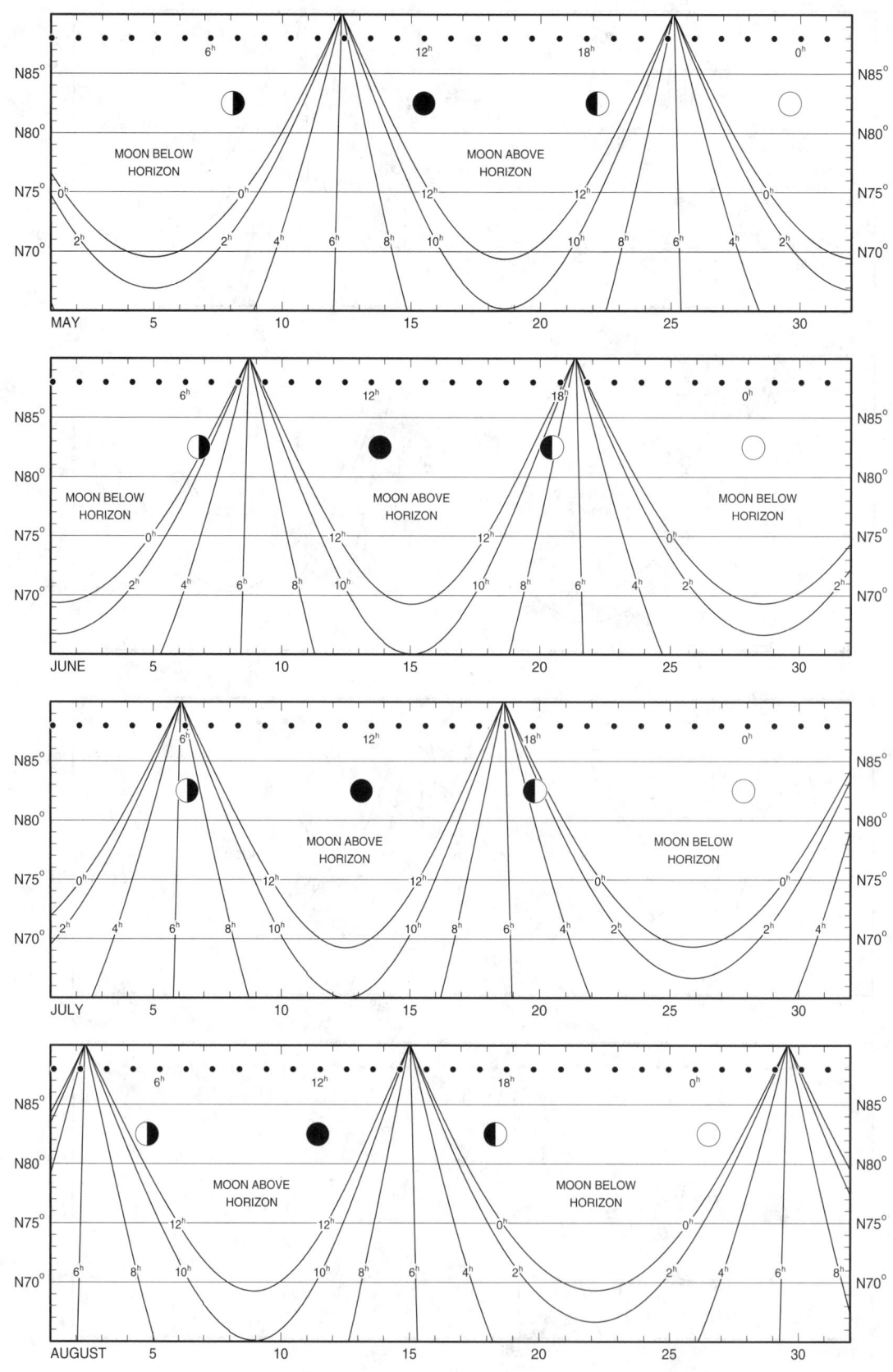

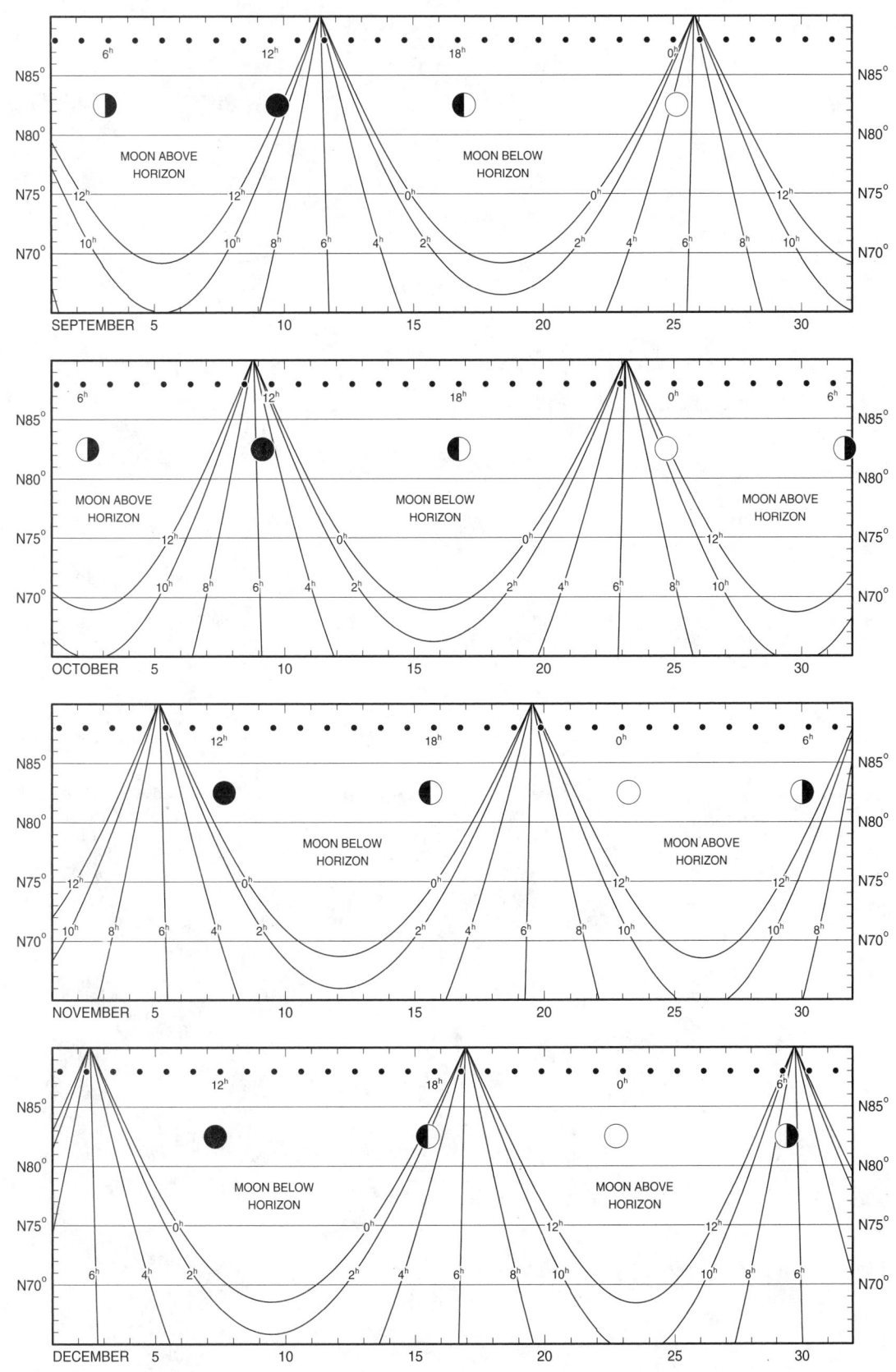

CONVERSION OF ARC TO TIME

0°–59°		60°–119°		120°–179°		180°–239°		240°–299°		300°–359°			0′.00	0′.25	0′.50	0′.75
°	h m	°	h m	°	h m	°	h m	°	h m	°	h m	′	m s	m s	m s	m s
0	0 00	60	4 00	120	8 00	180	12 00	240	16 00	300	20 00	0	0 00	0 01	0 02	0 03
1	0 04	61	4 04	121	8 04	181	12 04	241	16 04	301	20 04	1	0 04	0 05	0 06	0 07
2	0 08	62	4 08	122	8 08	182	12 08	242	16 08	302	20 08	2	0 08	0 09	0 10	0 11
3	0 12	63	4 12	123	8 12	183	12 12	243	16 12	303	20 12	3	0 12	0 13	0 14	0 15
4	0 16	64	4 16	124	8 16	184	12 16	244	16 16	304	20 16	4	0 16	0 17	0 18	0 19
5	0 20	65	4 20	125	8 20	185	12 20	245	16 20	305	20 20	5	0 20	0 21	0 22	0 23
6	0 24	66	4 24	126	8 24	186	12 24	246	16 24	306	20 24	6	0 24	0 25	0 26	0 27
7	0 28	67	4 28	127	8 28	187	12 28	247	16 28	307	20 28	7	0 28	0 29	0 30	0 31
8	0 32	68	4 32	128	8 32	188	12 32	248	16 32	308	20 32	8	0 32	0 33	0 34	0 35
9	0 36	69	4 36	129	8 36	189	12 36	249	16 36	309	20 36	9	0 36	0 37	0 38	0 39
10	0 40	70	4 40	130	8 40	190	12 40	250	16 40	310	20 40	10	0 40	0 41	0 42	0 43
11	0 44	71	4 44	131	8 44	191	12 44	251	16 44	311	20 44	11	0 44	0 45	0 46	0 47
12	0 48	72	4 48	132	8 48	192	12 48	252	16 48	312	20 48	12	0 48	0 49	0 50	0 51
13	0 52	73	4 52	133	8 52	193	12 52	253	16 52	313	20 52	13	0 52	0 53	0 54	0 55
14	0 56	74	4 56	134	8 56	194	12 56	254	16 56	314	20 56	14	0 56	0 57	0 58	0 59
15	1 00	75	5 00	135	9 00	195	13 00	255	17 00	315	21 00	15	1 00	1 01	1 02	1 03
16	1 04	76	5 04	136	9 04	196	13 04	256	17 04	316	21 04	16	1 04	1 05	1 06	1 07
17	1 08	77	5 08	137	9 08	197	13 08	257	17 08	317	21 08	17	1 08	1 09	1 10	1 11
18	1 12	78	5 12	138	9 12	198	13 12	258	17 12	318	21 12	18	1 12	1 13	1 14	1 15
19	1 16	79	5 16	139	9 16	199	13 16	259	17 16	319	21 16	19	1 16	1 17	1 18	1 19
20	1 20	80	5 20	140	9 20	200	13 20	260	17 20	320	21 20	20	1 20	1 21	1 22	1 23
21	1 24	81	5 24	141	9 24	201	13 24	261	17 24	321	21 24	21	1 24	1 25	1 26	1 27
22	1 28	82	5 28	142	9 28	202	13 28	262	17 28	322	21 28	22	1 28	1 29	1 30	1 31
23	1 32	83	5 32	143	9 32	203	13 32	263	17 32	323	21 32	23	1 32	1 33	1 34	1 35
24	1 36	84	5 36	144	9 36	204	13 36	264	17 36	324	21 36	24	1 36	1 37	1 38	1 39
25	1 40	85	5 40	145	9 40	205	13 40	265	17 40	325	21 40	25	1 40	1 41	1 42	1 43
26	1 44	86	5 44	146	9 44	206	13 44	266	17 44	326	21 44	26	1 44	1 45	1 46	1 47
27	1 48	87	5 48	147	9 48	207	13 48	267	17 48	327	21 48	27	1 48	1 49	1 50	1 51
28	1 52	88	5 52	148	9 52	208	13 52	268	17 52	328	21 52	28	1 52	1 53	1 54	1 55
29	1 56	89	5 56	149	9 56	209	13 56	269	17 56	329	21 56	29	1 56	1 57	1 58	1 59
30	2 00	90	6 00	150	10 00	210	14 00	270	18 00	330	22 00	30	2 00	2 01	2 02	2 03
31	2 04	91	6 04	151	10 04	211	14 04	271	18 04	331	22 04	31	2 04	2 05	2 06	2 07
32	2 08	92	6 08	152	10 08	212	14 08	272	18 08	332	22 08	32	2 08	2 09	2 10	2 11
33	2 12	93	6 12	153	10 12	213	14 12	273	18 12	333	22 12	33	2 12	2 13	2 14	2 15
34	2 16	94	6 16	154	10 16	214	14 16	274	18 16	334	22 16	34	2 16	2 17	2 18	2 19
35	2 20	95	6 20	155	10 20	215	14 20	275	18 20	335	22 20	35	2 20	2 21	2 22	2 23
36	2 24	96	6 24	156	10 24	216	14 24	276	18 24	336	22 24	36	2 24	2 25	2 26	2 27
37	2 28	97	6 28	157	10 28	217	14 28	277	18 28	337	22 28	37	2 28	2 29	2 30	2 31
38	2 32	98	6 32	158	10 32	218	14 32	278	18 32	338	22 32	38	2 32	2 33	2 34	2 35
39	2 36	99	6 36	159	10 36	219	14 36	279	18 36	339	22 36	39	2 36	2 37	2 38	2 39
40	2 40	100	6 40	160	10 40	220	14 40	280	18 40	340	22 40	40	2 40	2 41	2 42	2 43
41	2 44	101	6 44	161	10 44	221	14 44	281	18 44	341	22 44	41	2 44	2 45	2 46	2 47
42	2 48	102	6 48	162	10 48	222	14 48	282	18 48	342	22 48	42	2 48	2 49	2 50	2 51
43	2 52	103	6 52	163	10 52	223	14 52	283	18 52	343	22 52	43	2 52	2 53	2 54	2 55
44	2 56	104	6 56	164	10 56	224	14 56	284	18 56	344	22 56	44	2 56	2 57	2 58	2 59
45	3 00	105	7 00	165	11 00	225	15 00	285	19 00	345	23 00	45	3 00	3 01	3 02	3 03
46	3 04	106	7 04	166	11 04	226	15 04	286	19 04	346	23 04	46	3 04	3 05	3 06	3 07
47	3 08	107	7 08	167	11 08	227	15 08	287	19 08	347	23 08	47	3 08	3 09	3 10	3 11
48	3 12	108	7 12	168	11 12	228	15 12	288	19 12	348	23 12	48	3 12	3 13	3 14	3 15
49	3 16	109	7 16	169	11 16	229	15 16	289	19 16	349	23 16	49	3 16	3 17	3 18	3 19
50	3 20	110	7 20	170	11 20	230	15 20	290	19 20	350	23 20	50	3 20	3 21	3 22	3 23
51	3 24	111	7 24	171	11 24	231	15 24	291	19 24	351	23 24	51	3 24	3 25	3 26	3 27
52	3 28	112	7 28	172	11 28	232	15 28	292	19 28	352	23 28	52	3 28	3 29	3 30	3 31
53	3 32	113	7 32	173	11 32	233	15 32	293	19 32	353	23 32	53	3 32	3 33	3 34	3 35
54	3 36	114	7 36	174	11 36	234	15 36	294	19 36	354	23 36	54	3 36	3 37	3 38	3 39
55	3 40	115	7 40	175	11 40	235	15 40	295	19 40	355	23 40	55	3 40	3 41	3 42	3 43
56	3 44	116	7 44	176	11 44	236	15 44	296	19 44	356	23 44	56	3 44	3 45	3 46	3 47
57	3 48	117	7 48	177	11 48	237	15 48	297	19 48	357	23 48	57	3 48	3 49	3 50	3 51
58	3 52	118	7 52	178	11 52	238	15 52	298	19 52	358	23 52	58	3 52	3 53	3 54	3 55
59	3 56	119	7 56	179	11 56	239	15 56	299	19 56	359	23 56	59	3 56	3 57	3 58	3 59

The above table is for converting expressions in arc to their equivalent in time; its main use in this Almanac is for the conversion of longitude for application to LMT (*added* if *west*, *subtracted* if *east*) to give UT or vice versa, particularly in the case of sunrise, sunset, etc.

0ᵐ   INCREMENTS AND CORRECTIONS   1ᵐ

m 0	SUN PLANETS	ARIES	MOON	v or d Corrⁿ	v or d Corrⁿ	v or d Corrⁿ	m 1	SUN PLANETS	ARIES	MOON	v or d Corrⁿ	v or d Corrⁿ	v or d Corrⁿ
s	° ′	° ′	° ′	′ ′	′ ′	′ ′	s	° ′	° ′	° ′	′ ′	′ ′	′ ′
00	0 00·0	0 00·0	0 00·0	0·0 0·0	6·0 0·1	12·0 0·1	00	0 15·0	0 15·0	0 14·3	0·0 0·0	6·0 0·2	12·0 0·3
01	0 00·3	0 00·3	0 00·2	0·1 0·0	6·1 0·1	12·1 0·1	01	0 15·3	0 15·3	0 14·6	0·1 0·0	6·1 0·2	12·1 0·3
02	0 00·5	0 00·5	0 00·5	0·2 0·0	6·2 0·1	12·2 0·1	02	0 15·5	0 15·5	0 14·8	0·2 0·0	6·2 0·2	12·2 0·3
03	0 00·8	0 00·8	0 00·7	0·3 0·0	6·3 0·1	12·3 0·1	03	0 15·8	0 15·8	0 15·0	0·3 0·0	6·3 0·2	12·3 0·3
04	0 01·0	0 01·0	0 01·0	0·4 0·0	6·4 0·1	12·4 0·1	04	0 16·0	0 16·0	0 15·3	0·4 0·0	6·4 0·2	12·4 0·3
05	0 01·3	0 01·3	0 01·2	0·5 0·0	6·5 0·1	12·5 0·1	05	0 16·3	0 16·3	0 15·5	0·5 0·0	6·5 0·2	12·5 0·3
06	0 01·5	0 01·5	0 01·4	0·6 0·0	6·6 0·1	12·6 0·1	06	0 16·5	0 16·5	0 15·7	0·6 0·0	6·6 0·2	12·6 0·3
07	0 01·8	0 01·8	0 01·7	0·7 0·0	6·7 0·1	12·7 0·1	07	0 16·8	0 16·8	0 16·0	0·7 0·0	6·7 0·2	12·7 0·3
08	0 02·0	0 02·0	0 01·9	0·8 0·0	6·8 0·1	12·8 0·1	08	0 17·0	0 17·0	0 16·2	0·8 0·0	6·8 0·2	12·8 0·3
09	0 02·3	0 02·3	0 02·1	0·9 0·0	6·9 0·1	12·9 0·1	09	0 17·3	0 17·3	0 16·5	0·9 0·0	6·9 0·2	12·9 0·3
10	0 02·5	0 02·5	0 02·4	1·0 0·0	7·0 0·1	13·0 0·1	10	0 17·5	0 17·5	0 16·7	1·0 0·0	7·0 0·2	13·0 0·3
11	0 02·8	0 02·8	0 02·6	1·1 0·0	7·1 0·1	13·1 0·1	11	0 17·8	0 17·8	0 16·9	1·1 0·0	7·1 0·2	13·1 0·3
12	0 03·0	0 03·0	0 02·9	1·2 0·0	7·2 0·1	13·2 0·1	12	0 18·0	0 18·0	0 17·2	1·2 0·0	7·2 0·2	13·2 0·3
13	0 03·3	0 03·3	0 03·1	1·3 0·0	7·3 0·1	13·3 0·1	13	0 18·3	0 18·3	0 17·4	1·3 0·0	7·3 0·2	13·3 0·3
14	0 03·5	0 03·5	0 03·3	1·4 0·0	7·4 0·1	13·4 0·1	14	0 18·5	0 18·6	0 17·7	1·4 0·0	7·4 0·2	13·4 0·3
15	0 03·8	0 03·8	0 03·6	1·5 0·0	7·5 0·1	13·5 0·1	15	0 18·8	0 18·8	0 17·9	1·5 0·0	7·5 0·2	13·5 0·3
16	0 04·0	0 04·0	0 03·8	1·6 0·0	7·6 0·1	13·6 0·1	16	0 19·0	0 19·1	0 18·1	1·6 0·0	7·6 0·2	13·6 0·3
17	0 04·3	0 04·3	0 04·1	1·7 0·0	7·7 0·1	13·7 0·1	17	0 19·3	0 19·3	0 18·4	1·7 0·0	7·7 0·2	13·7 0·3
18	0 04·5	0 04·5	0 04·3	1·8 0·0	7·8 0·1	13·8 0·1	18	0 19·5	0 19·6	0 18·6	1·8 0·0	7·8 0·2	13·8 0·3
19	0 04·8	0 04·8	0 04·5	1·9 0·0	7·9 0·1	13·9 0·1	19	0 19·8	0 19·8	0 18·9	1·9 0·0	7·9 0·2	13·9 0·3
20	0 05·0	0 05·0	0 04·8	2·0 0·0	8·0 0·1	14·0 0·1	20	0 20·0	0 20·1	0 19·1	2·0 0·1	8·0 0·2	14·0 0·4
21	0 05·3	0 05·3	0 05·0	2·1 0·0	8·1 0·1	14·1 0·1	21	0 20·3	0 20·3	0 19·3	2·1 0·1	8·1 0·2	14·1 0·4
22	0 05·5	0 05·5	0 05·2	2·2 0·0	8·2 0·1	14·2 0·1	22	0 20·5	0 20·6	0 19·6	2·2 0·1	8·2 0·2	14·2 0·4
23	0 05·8	0 05·8	0 05·5	2·3 0·0	8·3 0·1	14·3 0·1	23	0 20·8	0 20·8	0 19·8	2·3 0·1	8·3 0·2	14·3 0·4
24	0 06·0	0 06·0	0 05·7	2·4 0·0	8·4 0·1	14·4 0·1	24	0 21·0	0 21·1	0 20·0	2·4 0·1	8·4 0·2	14·4 0·4
25	0 06·3	0 06·3	0 06·0	2·5 0·0	8·5 0·1	14·5 0·1	25	0 21·3	0 21·3	0 20·3	2·5 0·1	8·5 0·2	14·5 0·4
26	0 06·5	0 06·5	0 06·2	2·6 0·0	8·6 0·1	14·6 0·1	26	0 21·5	0 21·6	0 20·5	2·6 0·1	8·6 0·2	14·6 0·4
27	0 06·8	0 06·8	0 06·4	2·7 0·0	8·7 0·1	14·7 0·1	27	0 21·8	0 21·8	0 20·8	2·7 0·1	8·7 0·2	14·7 0·4
28	0 07·0	0 07·0	0 06·7	2·8 0·0	8·8 0·1	14·8 0·1	28	0 22·0	0 22·1	0 21·0	2·8 0·1	8·8 0·2	14·8 0·4
29	0 07·3	0 07·3	0 06·9	2·9 0·0	8·9 0·1	14·9 0·1	29	0 22·3	0 22·3	0 21·2	2·9 0·1	8·9 0·2	14·9 0·4
30	0 07·5	0 07·5	0 07·2	3·0 0·0	9·0 0·1	15·0 0·1	30	0 22·5	0 22·6	0 21·5	3·0 0·1	9·0 0·2	15·0 0·4
31	0 07·8	0 07·8	0 07·4	3·1 0·0	9·1 0·1	15·1 0·1	31	0 22·8	0 22·8	0 21·7	3·1 0·1	9·1 0·2	15·1 0·4
32	0 08·0	0 08·0	0 07·6	3·2 0·0	9·2 0·1	15·2 0·1	32	0 23·0	0 23·1	0 22·0	3·2 0·1	9·2 0·2	15·2 0·4
33	0 08·3	0 08·3	0 07·9	3·3 0·0	9·3 0·1	15·3 0·1	33	0 23·3	0 23·3	0 22·2	3·3 0·1	9·3 0·2	15·3 0·4
34	0 08·5	0 08·5	0 08·1	3·4 0·0	9·4 0·1	15·4 0·1	34	0 23·5	0 23·6	0 22·4	3·4 0·1	9·4 0·2	15·4 0·4
35	0 08·8	0 08·8	0 08·4	3·5 0·0	9·5 0·1	15·5 0·1	35	0 23·8	0 23·8	0 22·7	3·5 0·1	9·5 0·2	15·5 0·4
36	0 09·0	0 09·0	0 08·6	3·6 0·0	9·6 0·1	15·6 0·1	36	0 24·0	0 24·1	0 22·9	3·6 0·1	9·6 0·2	15·6 0·4
37	0 09·3	0 09·3	0 08·8	3·7 0·0	9·7 0·1	15·7 0·1	37	0 24·3	0 24·3	0 23·1	3·7 0·1	9·7 0·2	15·7 0·4
38	0 09·5	0 09·5	0 09·1	3·8 0·0	9·8 0·1	15·8 0·1	38	0 24·5	0 24·6	0 23·4	3·8 0·1	9·8 0·2	15·8 0·4
39	0 09·8	0 09·8	0 09·3	3·9 0·0	9·9 0·1	15·9 0·1	39	0 24·8	0 24·8	0 23·6	3·9 0·1	9·9 0·2	15·9 0·4
40	0 10·0	0 10·0	0 09·5	4·0 0·0	10·0 0·1	16·0 0·1	40	0 25·0	0 25·1	0 23·9	4·0 0·1	10·0 0·3	16·0 0·4
41	0 10·3	0 10·3	0 09·8	4·1 0·0	10·1 0·1	16·1 0·1	41	0 25·3	0 25·3	0 24·1	4·1 0·1	10·1 0·3	16·1 0·4
42	0 10·5	0 10·5	0 10·0	4·2 0·0	10·2 0·1	16·2 0·1	42	0 25·5	0 25·6	0 24·3	4·2 0·1	10·2 0·3	16·2 0·4
43	0 10·8	0 10·8	0 10·3	4·3 0·0	10·3 0·1	16·3 0·1	43	0 25·8	0 25·8	0 24·6	4·3 0·1	10·3 0·3	16·3 0·4
44	0 11·0	0 11·0	0 10·5	4·4 0·0	10·4 0·1	16·4 0·1	44	0 26·0	0 26·1	0 24·8	4·4 0·1	10·4 0·3	16·4 0·4
45	0 11·3	0 11·3	0 10·7	4·5 0·0	10·5 0·1	16·5 0·1	45	0 26·3	0 26·3	0 25·1	4·5 0·1	10·5 0·3	16·5 0·4
46	0 11·5	0 11·5	0 11·0	4·6 0·0	10·6 0·1	16·6 0·1	46	0 26·5	0 26·6	0 25·3	4·6 0·1	10·6 0·3	16·6 0·4
47	0 11·8	0 11·8	0 11·2	4·7 0·0	10·7 0·1	16·7 0·1	47	0 26·8	0 26·8	0 25·5	4·7 0·1	10·7 0·3	16·7 0·4
48	0 12·0	0 12·0	0 11·5	4·8 0·0	10·8 0·1	16·8 0·1	48	0 27·0	0 27·1	0 25·8	4·8 0·1	10·8 0·3	16·8 0·4
49	0 12·3	0 12·3	0 11·7	4·9 0·0	10·9 0·1	16·9 0·1	49	0 27·3	0 27·3	0 26·0	4·9 0·1	10·9 0·3	16·9 0·4
50	0 12·5	0 12·5	0 11·9	5·0 0·0	11·0 0·1	17·0 0·1	50	0 27·5	0 27·6	0 26·2	5·0 0·1	11·0 0·3	17·0 0·4
51	0 12·8	0 12·8	0 12·2	5·1 0·0	11·1 0·1	17·1 0·1	51	0 27·8	0 27·8	0 26·5	5·1 0·1	11·1 0·3	17·1 0·4
52	0 13·0	0 13·0	0 12·4	5·2 0·0	11·2 0·1	17·2 0·1	52	0 28·0	0 28·1	0 26·7	5·2 0·1	11·2 0·3	17·2 0·4
53	0 13·3	0 13·3	0 12·6	5·3 0·0	11·3 0·1	17·3 0·1	53	0 28·3	0 28·3	0 27·0	5·3 0·1	11·3 0·3	17·3 0·4
54	0 13·5	0 13·5	0 12·9	5·4 0·0	11·4 0·1	17·4 0·1	54	0 28·5	0 28·6	0 27·2	5·4 0·1	11·4 0·3	17·4 0·4
55	0 13·8	0 13·8	0 13·1	5·5 0·0	11·5 0·1	17·5 0·1	55	0 28·8	0 28·8	0 27·4	5·5 0·1	11·5 0·3	17·5 0·4
56	0 14·0	0 14·0	0 13·4	5·6 0·0	11·6 0·1	17·6 0·1	56	0 29·0	0 29·1	0 27·7	5·6 0·1	11·6 0·3	17·6 0·4
57	0 14·3	0 14·3	0 13·6	5·7 0·0	11·7 0·1	17·7 0·1	57	0 29·3	0 29·3	0 27·9	5·7 0·1	11·7 0·3	17·7 0·4
58	0 14·5	0 14·5	0 13·8	5·8 0·0	11·8 0·1	17·8 0·1	58	0 29·5	0 29·6	0 28·2	5·8 0·1	11·8 0·3	17·8 0·4
59	0 14·8	0 14·8	0 14·1	5·9 0·0	11·9 0·1	17·9 0·1	59	0 29·8	0 29·8	0 28·4	5·9 0·1	11·9 0·3	17·9 0·4
60	0 15·0	0 15·0	0 14·3	6·0 0·1	12·0 0·1	18·0 0·2	60	0 30·0	0 30·1	0 28·6	6·0 0·2	12·0 0·3	18·0 0·5

2 (m)	SUN PLANETS	ARIES	MOON	v or Corr^n d	v or Corr^n d	v or Corr^n d	3 (m)	SUN PLANETS	ARIES	MOON	v or Corr^n d	v or Corr^n d	v or Corr^n d
s	° ′	° ′	° ′	′ ′	′ ′	′ ′	s	° ′	° ′	° ′	′ ′	′ ′	′ ′
00	0 30·0	0 30·1	0 28·6	0·0 0·0	6·0 0·3	12·0 0·5	00	0 45·0	0 45·1	0 43·0	0·0 0·0	6·0 0·4	12·0 0·7
01	0 30·3	0 30·3	0 28·9	0·1 0·0	6·1 0·3	12·1 0·5	01	0 45·3	0 45·4	0 43·2	0·1 0·0	6·1 0·4	12·1 0·7
02	0 30·5	0 30·6	0 29·1	0·2 0·0	6·2 0·3	12·2 0·5	02	0 45·5	0 45·6	0 43·4	0·2 0·0	6·2 0·4	12·2 0·7
03	0 30·8	0 30·8	0 29·3	0·3 0·0	6·3 0·3	12·3 0·5	03	0 45·8	0 45·9	0 43·7	0·3 0·0	6·3 0·4	12·3 0·7
04	0 31·0	0 31·1	0 29·6	0·4 0·0	6·4 0·3	12·4 0·5	04	0 46·0	0 46·1	0 43·9	0·4 0·0	6·4 0·4	12·4 0·7
05	0 31·3	0 31·3	0 29·8	0·5 0·0	6·5 0·3	12·5 0·5	05	0 46·3	0 46·4	0 44·1	0·5 0·0	6·5 0·4	12·5 0·7
06	0 31·5	0 31·6	0 30·1	0·6 0·0	6·6 0·3	12·6 0·5	06	0 46·5	0 46·6	0 44·4	0·6 0·0	6·6 0·4	12·6 0·7
07	0 31·8	0 31·8	0 30·3	0·7 0·0	6·7 0·3	12·7 0·5	07	0 46·8	0 46·9	0 44·6	0·7 0·0	6·7 0·4	12·7 0·7
08	0 32·0	0 32·1	0 30·5	0·8 0·0	6·8 0·3	12·8 0·5	08	0 47·0	0 47·1	0 44·9	0·8 0·0	6·8 0·4	12·8 0·7
09	0 32·3	0 32·3	0 30·8	0·9 0·0	6·9 0·3	12·9 0·5	09	0 47·3	0 47·4	0 45·1	0·9 0·1	6·9 0·4	12·9 0·8
10	0 32·5	0 32·6	0 31·0	1·0 0·0	7·0 0·3	13·0 0·5	10	0 47·5	0 47·6	0 45·3	1·0 0·1	7·0 0·4	13·0 0·8
11	0 32·8	0 32·8	0 31·3	1·1 0·0	7·1 0·3	13·1 0·5	11	0 47·8	0 47·9	0 45·6	1·1 0·1	7·1 0·4	13·1 0·8
12	0 33·0	0 33·1	0 31·5	1·2 0·1	7·2 0·3	13·2 0·6	12	0 48·0	0 48·1	0 45·8	1·2 0·1	7·2 0·4	13·2 0·8
13	0 33·3	0 33·3	0 31·7	1·3 0·1	7·3 0·3	13·3 0·6	13	0 48·3	0 48·4	0 46·1	1·3 0·1	7·3 0·4	13·3 0·8
14	0 33·5	0 33·6	0 32·0	1·4 0·1	7·4 0·3	13·4 0·6	14	0 48·5	0 48·6	0 46·3	1·4 0·1	7·4 0·4	13·4 0·8
15	0 33·8	0 33·8	0 32·2	1·5 0·1	7·5 0·3	13·5 0·6	15	0 48·8	0 48·9	0 46·5	1·5 0·1	7·5 0·4	13·5 0·8
16	0 34·0	0 34·1	0 32·5	1·6 0·1	7·6 0·3	13·6 0·6	16	0 49·0	0 49·1	0 46·8	1·6 0·1	7·6 0·4	13·6 0·8
17	0 34·3	0 34·3	0 32·7	1·7 0·1	7·7 0·3	13·7 0·6	17	0 49·3	0 49·4	0 47·0	1·7 0·1	7·7 0·4	13·7 0·8
18	0 34·5	0 34·6	0 32·9	1·8 0·1	7·8 0·3	13·8 0·6	18	0 49·5	0 49·6	0 47·2	1·8 0·1	7·8 0·5	13·8 0·8
19	0 34·8	0 34·8	0 33·2	1·9 0·1	7·9 0·3	13·9 0·6	19	0 49·8	0 49·9	0 47·5	1·9 0·1	7·9 0·5	13·9 0·8
20	0 35·0	0 35·1	0 33·4	2·0 0·1	8·0 0·3	14·0 0·6	20	0 50·0	0 50·1	0 47·7	2·0 0·1	8·0 0·5	14·0 0·8
21	0 35·3	0 35·3	0 33·6	2·1 0·1	8·1 0·3	14·1 0·6	21	0 50·3	0 50·4	0 48·0	2·1 0·1	8·1 0·5	14·1 0·8
22	0 35·5	0 35·6	0 33·9	2·2 0·1	8·2 0·3	14·2 0·6	22	0 50·5	0 50·6	0 48·2	2·2 0·1	8·2 0·5	14·2 0·8
23	0 35·8	0 35·8	0 34·1	2·3 0·1	8·3 0·3	14·3 0·6	23	0 50·8	0 50·9	0 48·4	2·3 0·1	8·3 0·5	14·3 0·8
24	0 36·0	0 36·1	0 34·4	2·4 0·1	8·4 0·4	14·4 0·6	24	0 51·0	0 51·1	0 48·7	2·4 0·1	8·4 0·5	14·4 0·8
25	0 36·3	0 36·3	0 34·6	2·5 0·1	8·5 0·4	14·5 0·6	25	0 51·3	0 51·4	0 48·9	2·5 0·1	8·5 0·5	14·5 0·8
26	0 36·5	0 36·6	0 34·8	2·6 0·1	8·6 0·4	14·6 0·6	26	0 51·5	0 51·6	0 49·2	2·6 0·2	8·6 0·5	14·6 0·9
27	0 36·8	0 36·9	0 35·1	2·7 0·1	8·7 0·4	14·7 0·6	27	0 51·8	0 51·9	0 49·4	2·7 0·2	8·7 0·5	14·7 0·9
28	0 37·0	0 37·1	0 35·3	2·8 0·1	8·8 0·4	14·8 0·6	28	0 52·0	0 52·1	0 49·6	2·8 0·2	8·8 0·5	14·8 0·9
29	0 37·3	0 37·4	0 35·6	2·9 0·1	8·9 0·4	14·9 0·6	29	0 52·3	0 52·4	0 49·9	2·9 0·2	8·9 0·5	14·9 0·9
30	0 37·5	0 37·6	0 35·8	3·0 0·1	9·0 0·4	15·0 0·6	30	0 52·5	0 52·6	0 50·1	3·0 0·2	9·0 0·5	15·0 0·9
31	0 37·8	0 37·9	0 36·0	3·1 0·1	9·1 0·4	15·1 0·6	31	0 52·8	0 52·9	0 50·3	3·1 0·2	9·1 0·5	15·1 0·9
32	0 38·0	0 38·1	0 36·3	3·2 0·1	9·2 0·4	15·2 0·6	32	0 53·0	0 53·1	0 50·6	3·2 0·2	9·2 0·5	15·2 0·9
33	0 38·3	0 38·4	0 36·5	3·3 0·1	9·3 0·4	15·3 0·6	33	0 53·3	0 53·4	0 50·8	3·3 0·2	9·3 0·5	15·3 0·9
34	0 38·5	0 38·6	0 36·7	3·4 0·1	9·4 0·4	15·4 0·6	34	0 53·5	0 53·6	0 51·1	3·4 0·2	9·4 0·5	15·4 0·9
35	0 38·8	0 38·9	0 37·0	3·5 0·1	9·5 0·4	15·5 0·6	35	0 53·8	0 53·9	0 51·3	3·5 0·2	9·5 0·6	15·5 0·9
36	0 39·0	0 39·1	0 37·2	3·6 0·2	9·6 0·4	15·6 0·7	36	0 54·0	0 54·1	0 51·5	3·6 0·2	9·6 0·6	15·6 0·9
37	0 39·3	0 39·4	0 37·5	3·7 0·2	9·7 0·4	15·7 0·7	37	0 54·3	0 54·4	0 51·8	3·7 0·2	9·7 0·6	15·7 0·9
38	0 39·5	0 39·6	0 37·7	3·8 0·2	9·8 0·4	15·8 0·7	38	0 54·5	0 54·6	0 52·0	3·8 0·2	9·8 0·6	15·8 0·9
39	0 39·8	0 39·9	0 37·9	3·9 0·2	9·9 0·4	15·9 0·7	39	0 54·8	0 54·9	0 52·3	3·9 0·2	9·9 0·6	15·9 0·9
40	0 40·0	0 40·1	0 38·2	4·0 0·2	10·0 0·4	16·0 0·7	40	0 55·0	0 55·2	0 52·5	4·0 0·2	10·0 0·6	16·0 0·9
41	0 40·3	0 40·4	0 38·4	4·1 0·2	10·1 0·4	16·1 0·7	41	0 55·3	0 55·4	0 52·7	4·1 0·2	10·1 0·6	16·1 0·9
42	0 40·5	0 40·6	0 38·7	4·2 0·2	10·2 0·4	16·2 0·7	42	0 55·5	0 55·7	0 53·0	4·2 0·2	10·2 0·6	16·2 0·9
43	0 40·8	0 40·9	0 38·9	4·3 0·2	10·3 0·4	16·3 0·7	43	0 55·8	0 55·9	0 53·2	4·3 0·3	10·3 0·6	16·3 1·0
44	0 41·0	0 41·1	0 39·1	4·4 0·2	10·4 0·4	16·4 0·7	44	0 56·0	0 56·2	0 53·4	4·4 0·3	10·4 0·6	16·4 1·0
45	0 41·3	0 41·4	0 39·4	4·5 0·2	10·5 0·4	16·5 0·7	45	0 56·3	0 56·4	0 53·7	4·5 0·3	10·5 0·6	16·5 1·0
46	0 41·5	0 41·6	0 39·6	4·6 0·2	10·6 0·4	16·6 0·7	46	0 56·5	0 56·7	0 53·9	4·6 0·3	10·6 0·6	16·6 1·0
47	0 41·8	0 41·9	0 39·8	4·7 0·2	10·7 0·4	16·7 0·7	47	0 56·8	0 56·9	0 54·2	4·7 0·3	10·7 0·6	16·7 1·0
48	0 42·0	0 42·1	0 40·1	4·8 0·2	10·8 0·5	16·8 0·7	48	0 57·0	0 57·2	0 54·4	4·8 0·3	10·8 0·6	16·8 1·0
49	0 42·3	0 42·4	0 40·3	4·9 0·2	10·9 0·5	16·9 0·7	49	0 57·3	0 57·4	0 54·6	4·9 0·3	10·9 0·6	16·9 1·0
50	0 42·5	0 42·6	0 40·6	5·0 0·2	11·0 0·5	17·0 0·7	50	0 57·5	0 57·7	0 54·9	5·0 0·3	11·0 0·6	17·0 1·0
51	0 42·8	0 42·9	0 40·8	5·1 0·2	11·1 0·5	17·1 0·7	51	0 57·8	0 57·9	0 55·1	5·1 0·3	11·1 0·6	17·1 1·0
52	0 43·0	0 43·1	0 41·0	5·2 0·2	11·2 0·5	17·2 0·7	52	0 58·0	0 58·2	0 55·4	5·2 0·3	11·2 0·7	17·2 1·0
53	0 43·3	0 43·4	0 41·3	5·3 0·2	11·3 0·5	17·3 0·7	53	0 58·3	0 58·4	0 55·6	5·3 0·3	11·3 0·7	17·3 1·0
54	0 43·5	0 43·6	0 41·5	5·4 0·2	11·4 0·5	17·4 0·7	54	0 58·5	0 58·7	0 55·8	5·4 0·3	11·4 0·7	17·4 1·0
55	0 43·8	0 43·9	0 41·8	5·5 0·2	11·5 0·5	17·5 0·7	55	0 58·8	0 58·9	0 56·1	5·5 0·3	11·5 0·7	17·5 1·0
56	0 44·0	0 44·1	0 42·0	5·6 0·2	11·6 0·5	17·6 0·7	56	0 59·0	0 59·2	0 56·3	5·6 0·3	11·6 0·7	17·6 1·0
57	0 44·3	0 44·4	0 42·2	5·7 0·2	11·7 0·5	17·7 0·7	57	0 59·3	0 59·4	0 56·6	5·7 0·3	11·7 0·7	17·7 1·0
58	0 44·5	0 44·6	0 42·5	5·8 0·2	11·8 0·5	17·8 0·7	58	0 59·5	0 59·7	0 56·8	5·8 0·3	11·8 0·7	17·8 1·0
59	0 44·8	0 44·9	0 42·7	5·9 0·2	11·9 0·5	17·9 0·7	59	0 59·8	0 59·9	0 57·0	5·9 0·3	11·9 0·7	17·9 1·0
60	0 45·0	0 45·1	0 43·0	6·0 0·3	12·0 0·5	18·0 0·8	60	1 00·0	1 00·2	0 57·3	6·0 0·4	12·0 0·7	18·0 1·1

4 s	SUN PLANETS	ARIES	MOON	v or Corrⁿ d	v or Corrⁿ d	v or Corrⁿ d	5 s	SUN PLANETS	ARIES	MOON	v or Corrⁿ d	v or Corrⁿ d	v or Corrⁿ d
00	1 00·0	1 00·2	0 57·3	0·0 0·0	6·0 0·5	12·0 0·9	00	1 15·0	1 15·2	1 11·6	0·0 0·0	6·0 0·6	12·0 1·1
01	1 00·3	1 00·4	0 57·5	0·1 0·0	6·1 0·5	12·1 0·9	01	1 15·3	1 15·5	1 11·8	0·1 0·0	6·1 0·6	12·1 1·1
02	1 00·5	1 00·7	0 57·7	0·2 0·0	6·2 0·5	12·2 0·9	02	1 15·5	1 15·7	1 12·1	0·2 0·0	6·2 0·6	12·2 1·1
03	1 00·8	1 00·9	0 58·0	0·3 0·0	6·3 0·5	12·3 0·9	03	1 15·8	1 16·0	1 12·3	0·3 0·0	6·3 0·6	12·3 1·1
04	1 01·0	1 01·2	0 58·2	0·4 0·0	6·4 0·5	12·4 0·9	04	1 16·0	1 16·2	1 12·5	0·4 0·0	6·4 0·6	12·4 1·1
05	1 01·3	1 01·4	0 58·5	0·5 0·0	6·5 0·5	12·5 0·9	05	1 16·3	1 16·5	1 12·8	0·5 0·0	6·5 0·6	12·5 1·1
06	1 01·5	1 01·7	0 58·7	0·6 0·0	6·6 0·5	12·6 0·9	06	1 16·5	1 16·7	1 13·0	0·6 0·1	6·6 0·6	12·6 1·2
07	1 01·8	1 01·9	0 59·0	0·7 0·1	6·7 0·5	12·7 1·0	07	1 16·8	1 17·0	1 13·3	0·7 0·1	6·7 0·6	12·7 1·2
08	1 02·0	1 02·2	0 59·2	0·8 0·1	6·8 0·5	12·8 1·0	08	1 17·0	1 17·2	1 13·5	0·8 0·1	6·8 0·6	12·8 1·2
09	1 02·3	1 02·4	0 59·4	0·9 0·1	6·9 0·5	12·9 1·0	09	1 17·3	1 17·5	1 13·7	0·9 0·1	6·9 0·6	12·9 1·2
10	1 02·5	1 02·7	0 59·7	1·0 0·1	7·0 0·5	13·0 1·0	10	1 17·5	1 17·7	1 14·0	1·0 0·1	7·0 0·6	13·0 1·2
11	1 02·8	1 02·9	0 59·9	1·1 0·1	7·1 0·5	13·1 1·0	11	1 17·8	1 18·0	1 14·2	1·1 0·1	7·1 0·7	13·1 1·2
12	1 03·0	1 03·2	1 00·1	1·2 0·1	7·2 0·5	13·2 1·0	12	1 18·0	1 18·2	1 14·4	1·2 0·1	7·2 0·7	13·2 1·2
13	1 03·3	1 03·4	1 00·4	1·3 0·1	7·3 0·5	13·3 1·0	13	1 18·3	1 18·5	1 14·7	1·3 0·1	7·3 0·7	13·3 1·2
14	1 03·5	1 03·7	1 00·6	1·4 0·1	7·4 0·6	13·4 1·0	14	1 18·5	1 18·7	1 14·9	1·4 0·1	7·4 0·7	13·4 1·2
15	1 03·8	1 03·9	1 00·8	1·5 0·1	7·5 0·6	13·5 1·0	15	1 18·8	1 19·0	1 15·2	1·5 0·1	7·5 0·7	13·5 1·2
16	1 04·0	1 04·2	1 01·1	1·6 0·1	7·6 0·6	13·6 1·0	16	1 19·0	1 19·2	1 15·4	1·6 0·1	7·6 0·7	13·6 1·2
17	1 04·3	1 04·4	1 01·3	1·7 0·1	7·7 0·6	13·7 1·0	17	1 19·3	1 19·5	1 15·6	1·7 0·2	7·7 0·7	13·7 1·3
18	1 04·5	1 04·7	1 01·6	1·8 0·1	7·8 0·6	13·8 1·0	18	1 19·5	1 19·7	1 15·9	1·8 0·2	7·8 0·7	13·8 1·3
19	1 04·8	1 04·9	1 01·8	1·9 0·1	7·9 0·6	13·9 1·0	19	1 19·8	1 20·0	1 16·1	1·9 0·2	7·9 0·7	13·9 1·3
20	1 05·0	1 05·2	1 02·0	2·0 0·2	8·0 0·6	14·0 1·1	20	1 20·0	1 20·2	1 16·4	2·0 0·2	8·0 0·7	14·0 1·3
21	1 05·3	1 05·4	1 02·3	2·1 0·2	8·1 0·6	14·1 1·1	21	1 20·3	1 20·5	1 16·6	2·1 0·2	8·1 0·7	14·1 1·3
22	1 05·5	1 05·7	1 02·5	2·2 0·2	8·2 0·6	14·2 1·1	22	1 20·5	1 20·7	1 16·8	2·2 0·2	8·2 0·8	14·2 1·3
23	1 05·8	1 05·9	1 02·8	2·3 0·2	8·3 0·6	14·3 1·1	23	1 20·8	1 21·0	1 17·1	2·3 0·2	8·3 0·8	14·3 1·3
24	1 06·0	1 06·2	1 03·0	2·4 0·2	8·4 0·6	14·4 1·1	24	1 21·0	1 21·2	1 17·3	2·4 0·2	8·4 0·8	14·4 1·3
25	1 06·3	1 06·4	1 03·2	2·5 0·2	8·5 0·6	14·5 1·1	25	1 21·3	1 21·5	1 17·5	2·5 0·2	8·5 0·8	14·5 1·3
26	1 06·5	1 06·7	1 03·5	2·6 0·2	8·6 0·6	14·6 1·1	26	1 21·5	1 21·7	1 17·8	2·6 0·2	8·6 0·8	14·6 1·3
27	1 06·8	1 06·9	1 03·7	2·7 0·2	8·7 0·7	14·7 1·1	27	1 21·8	1 22·0	1 18·0	2·7 0·2	8·7 0·8	14·7 1·3
28	1 07·0	1 07·2	1 03·9	2·8 0·2	8·8 0·7	14·8 1·1	28	1 22·0	1 22·2	1 18·3	2·8 0·3	8·8 0·8	14·8 1·4
29	1 07·3	1 07·4	1 04·2	2·9 0·2	8·9 0·7	14·9 1·1	29	1 22·3	1 22·5	1 18·5	2·9 0·3	8·9 0·8	14·9 1·4
30	1 07·5	1 07·7	1 04·4	3·0 0·2	9·0 0·7	15·0 1·1	30	1 22·5	1 22·7	1 18·7	3·0 0·3	9·0 0·8	15·0 1·4
31	1 07·8	1 07·9	1 04·7	3·1 0·2	9·1 0·7	15·1 1·1	31	1 22·8	1 23·0	1 19·0	3·1 0·3	9·1 0·8	15·1 1·4
32	1 08·0	1 08·2	1 04·9	3·2 0·2	9·2 0·7	15·2 1·1	32	1 23·0	1 23·2	1 19·2	3·2 0·3	9·2 0·8	15·2 1·4
33	1 08·3	1 08·4	1 05·1	3·3 0·2	9·3 0·7	15·3 1·1	33	1 23·3	1 23·5	1 19·5	3·3 0·3	9·3 0·9	15·3 1·4
34	1 08·5	1 08·7	1 05·4	3·4 0·3	9·4 0·7	15·4 1·2	34	1 23·5	1 23·7	1 19·7	3·4 0·3	9·4 0·9	15·4 1·4
35	1 08·8	1 08·9	1 05·6	3·5 0·3	9·5 0·7	15·5 1·2	35	1 23·8	1 24·0	1 19·9	3·5 0·3	9·5 0·9	15·5 1·4
36	1 09·0	1 09·2	1 05·9	3·6 0·3	9·6 0·7	15·6 1·2	36	1 24·0	1 24·2	1 20·2	3·6 0·3	9·6 0·9	15·6 1·4
37	1 09·3	1 09·4	1 06·1	3·7 0·3	9·7 0·7	15·7 1·2	37	1 24·3	1 24·5	1 20·4	3·7 0·3	9·7 0·9	15·7 1·4
38	1 09·5	1 09·7	1 06·3	3·8 0·3	9·8 0·7	15·8 1·2	38	1 24·5	1 24·7	1 20·7	3·8 0·3	9·8 0·9	15·8 1·4
39	1 09·8	1 09·9	1 06·6	3·9 0·3	9·9 0·7	15·9 1·2	39	1 24·8	1 25·0	1 20·9	3·9 0·4	9·9 0·9	15·9 1·5
40	1 10·0	1 10·2	1 06·8	4·0 0·3	10·0 0·8	16·0 1·2	40	1 25·0	1 25·2	1 21·1	4·0 0·4	10·0 0·9	16·0 1·5
41	1 10·3	1 10·4	1 07·0	4·1 0·3	10·1 0·8	16·1 1·2	41	1 25·3	1 25·5	1 21·4	4·1 0·4	10·1 0·9	16·1 1·5
42	1 10·5	1 10·7	1 07·3	4·2 0·3	10·2 0·8	16·2 1·2	42	1 25·5	1 25·7	1 21·6	4·2 0·4	10·2 0·9	16·2 1·5
43	1 10·8	1 11·0	1 07·5	4·3 0·3	10·3 0·8	16·3 1·2	43	1 25·8	1 26·0	1 21·8	4·3 0·4	10·3 0·9	16·3 1·5
44	1 11·0	1 11·2	1 07·8	4·4 0·3	10·4 0·8	16·4 1·2	44	1 26·0	1 26·2	1 22·1	4·4 0·4	10·4 1·0	16·4 1·5
45	1 11·3	1 11·4	1 08·0	4·5 0·3	10·5 0·8	16·5 1·2	45	1 26·3	1 26·5	1 22·3	4·5 0·4	10·5 1·0	16·5 1·5
46	1 11·5	1 11·7	1 08·2	4·6 0·3	10·6 0·8	16·6 1·2	46	1 26·5	1 26·7	1 22·6	4·6 0·4	10·6 1·0	16·6 1·5
47	1 11·8	1 11·9	1 08·5	4·7 0·4	10·7 0·8	16·7 1·3	47	1 26·8	1 27·0	1 22·8	4·7 0·4	10·7 1·0	16·7 1·5
48	1 12·0	1 12·2	1 08·7	4·8 0·4	10·8 0·8	16·8 1·3	48	1 27·0	1 27·2	1 23·0	4·8 0·4	10·8 1·0	16·8 1·5
49	1 12·3	1 12·4	1 09·0	4·9 0·4	10·9 0·8	16·9 1·3	49	1 27·3	1 27·5	1 23·3	4·9 0·4	10·9 1·0	16·9 1·5
50	1 12·5	1 12·7	1 09·2	5·0 0·4	11·0 0·8	17·0 1·3	50	1 27·5	1 27·7	1 23·5	5·0 0·5	11·0 1·0	17·0 1·6
51	1 12·8	1 12·9	1 09·4	5·1 0·4	11·1 0·8	17·1 1·3	51	1 27·8	1 28·0	1 23·8	5·1 0·5	11·1 1·0	17·1 1·6
52	1 13·0	1 13·2	1 09·7	5·2 0·4	11·2 0·8	17·2 1·3	52	1 28·0	1 28·2	1 24·0	5·2 0·5	11·2 1·0	17·2 1·6
53	1 13·3	1 13·5	1 09·9	5·3 0·4	11·3 0·8	17·3 1·3	53	1 28·3	1 28·5	1 24·2	5·3 0·5	11·3 1·0	17·3 1·6
54	1 13·5	1 13·7	1 10·2	5·4 0·4	11·4 0·9	17·4 1·3	54	1 28·5	1 28·7	1 24·5	5·4 0·5	11·4 1·0	17·4 1·6
55	1 13·8	1 14·0	1 10·4	5·5 0·4	11·5 0·9	17·5 1·3	55	1 28·8	1 29·0	1 24·7	5·5 0·5	11·5 1·1	17·5 1·6
56	1 14·0	1 14·2	1 10·6	5·6 0·4	11·6 0·9	17·6 1·3	56	1 29·0	1 29·2	1 24·9	5·6 0·5	11·6 1·1	17·6 1·6
57	1 14·3	1 14·5	1 10·9	5·7 0·4	11·7 0·9	17·7 1·3	57	1 29·3	1 29·5	1 25·2	5·7 0·5	11·7 1·1	17·7 1·6
58	1 14·5	1 14·7	1 11·1	5·8 0·4	11·8 0·9	17·8 1·3	58	1 29·5	1 29·7	1 25·4	5·8 0·5	11·8 1·1	17·8 1·6
59	1 14·8	1 15·0	1 11·3	5·9 0·4	11·9 0·9	17·9 1·3	59	1 29·8	1 30·0	1 25·7	5·9 0·5	11·9 1·1	17·9 1·6
60	1 15·0	1 15·2	1 11·6	6·0 0·5	12·0 0·9	18·0 1·4	60	1 30·0	1 30·2	1 25·9	6·0 0·6	12·0 1·1	18·0 1·7

6ᵐ

6 s	SUN PLANETS	ARIES	MOON	v or d Corrⁿ	v or d Corrⁿ	v or d Corrⁿ
00	1 30·0	1 30·2	1 25·9	0·0 0·0	6·0 0·7	12·0 1·3
01	1 30·3	1 30·5	1 26·1	0·1 0·0	6·1 0·7	12·1 1·3
02	1 30·5	1 30·7	1 26·4	0·2 0·0	6·2 0·7	12·2 1·3
03	1 30·8	1 31·0	1 26·6	0·3 0·0	6·3 0·7	12·3 1·3
04	1 31·0	1 31·2	1 26·9	0·4 0·0	6·4 0·7	12·4 1·3
05	1 31·3	1 31·5	1 27·1	0·5 0·1	6·5 0·7	12·5 1·4
06	1 31·5	1 31·8	1 27·3	0·6 0·1	6·6 0·7	12·6 1·4
07	1 31·8	1 32·0	1 27·6	0·7 0·1	6·7 0·7	12·7 1·4
08	1 32·0	1 32·3	1 27·8	0·8 0·1	6·8 0·7	12·8 1·4
09	1 32·3	1 32·5	1 28·0	0·9 0·1	6·9 0·7	12·9 1·4
10	1 32·5	1 32·8	1 28·3	1·0 0·1	7·0 0·8	13·0 1·4
11	1 32·8	1 33·0	1 28·5	1·1 0·1	7·1 0·8	13·1 1·4
12	1 33·0	1 33·3	1 28·8	1·2 0·1	7·2 0·8	13·2 1·4
13	1 33·3	1 33·5	1 29·0	1·3 0·1	7·3 0·8	13·3 1·4
14	1 33·5	1 33·8	1 29·2	1·4 0·2	7·4 0·8	13·4 1·5
15	1 33·8	1 34·0	1 29·5	1·5 0·2	7·5 0·8	13·5 1·5
16	1 34·0	1 34·3	1 29·7	1·6 0·2	7·6 0·8	13·6 1·5
17	1 34·3	1 34·5	1 30·0	1·7 0·2	7·7 0·8	13·7 1·5
18	1 34·5	1 34·8	1 30·2	1·8 0·2	7·8 0·8	13·8 1·5
19	1 34·8	1 35·0	1 30·4	1·9 0·2	7·9 0·9	13·9 1·5
20	1 35·0	1 35·3	1 30·7	2·0 0·2	8·0 0·9	14·0 1·5
21	1 35·3	1 35·5	1 30·9	2·1 0·2	8·1 0·9	14·1 1·5
22	1 35·5	1 35·8	1 31·1	2·2 0·2	8·2 0·9	14·2 1·5
23	1 35·8	1 36·0	1 31·4	2·3 0·2	8·3 0·9	14·3 1·5
24	1 36·0	1 36·3	1 31·6	2·4 0·3	8·4 0·9	14·4 1·6
25	1 36·3	1 36·5	1 31·9	2·5 0·3	8·5 0·9	14·5 1·6
26	1 36·5	1 36·8	1 32·1	2·6 0·3	8·6 0·9	14·6 1·6
27	1 36·8	1 37·0	1 32·3	2·7 0·3	8·7 0·9	14·7 1·6
28	1 37·0	1 37·3	1 32·6	2·8 0·3	8·8 1·0	14·8 1·6
29	1 37·3	1 37·5	1 32·8	2·9 0·3	8·9 1·0	14·9 1·6
30	1 37·5	1 37·8	1 33·1	3·0 0·3	9·0 1·0	15·0 1·6
31	1 37·8	1 38·0	1 33·3	3·1 0·3	9·1 1·0	15·1 1·6
32	1 38·0	1 38·3	1 33·5	3·2 0·3	9·2 1·0	15·2 1·6
33	1 38·3	1 38·5	1 33·8	3·3 0·4	9·3 1·0	15·3 1·7
34	1 38·5	1 38·8	1 34·0	3·4 0·4	9·4 1·0	15·4 1·7
35	1 38·8	1 39·0	1 34·3	3·5 0·4	9·5 1·0	15·5 1·7
36	1 39·0	1 39·3	1 34·5	3·6 0·4	9·6 1·0	15·6 1·7
37	1 39·3	1 39·5	1 34·7	3·7 0·4	9·7 1·1	15·7 1·7
38	1 39·5	1 39·8	1 35·0	3·8 0·4	9·8 1·1	15·8 1·7
39	1 39·8	1 40·0	1 35·2	3·9 0·4	9·9 1·1	15·9 1·7
40	1 40·0	1 40·3	1 35·4	4·0 0·4	10·0 1·1	16·0 1·7
41	1 40·3	1 40·5	1 35·7	4·1 0·4	10·1 1·1	16·1 1·7
42	1 40·5	1 40·8	1 35·9	4·2 0·5	10·2 1·1	16·2 1·8
43	1 40·8	1 41·0	1 36·2	4·3 0·5	10·3 1·1	16·3 1·8
44	1 41·0	1 41·3	1 36·4	4·4 0·5	10·4 1·1	16·4 1·8
45	1 41·3	1 41·5	1 36·6	4·5 0·5	10·5 1·1	16·5 1·8
46	1 41·5	1 41·8	1 36·9	4·6 0·5	10·6 1·1	16·6 1·8
47	1 41·8	1 42·0	1 37·1	4·7 0·5	10·7 1·2	16·7 1·8
48	1 42·0	1 42·3	1 37·4	4·8 0·5	10·8 1·2	16·8 1·8
49	1 42·3	1 42·5	1 37·6	4·9 0·5	10·9 1·2	16·9 1·8
50	1 42·5	1 42·8	1 37·8	5·0 0·5	11·0 1·2	17·0 1·8
51	1 42·8	1 43·0	1 38·1	5·1 0·6	11·1 1·2	17·1 1·9
52	1 43·0	1 43·3	1 38·3	5·2 0·6	11·2 1·2	17·2 1·9
53	1 43·3	1 43·5	1 38·5	5·3 0·6	11·3 1·2	17·3 1·9
54	1 43·5	1 43·8	1 38·8	5·4 0·6	11·4 1·2	17·4 1·9
55	1 43·8	1 44·0	1 39·0	5·5 0·6	11·5 1·2	17·5 1·9
56	1 44·0	1 44·3	1 39·3	5·6 0·6	11·6 1·3	17·6 1·9
57	1 44·3	1 44·5	1 39·5	5·7 0·6	11·7 1·3	17·7 1·9
58	1 44·5	1 44·8	1 39·7	5·8 0·6	11·8 1·3	17·8 1·9
59	1 44·8	1 45·0	1 40·0	5·9 0·6	11·9 1·3	17·9 1·9
60	1 45·0	1 45·3	1 40·2	6·0 0·7	12·0 1·3	18·0 2·0

7ᵐ

7 s	SUN PLANETS	ARIES	MOON	v or d Corrⁿ	v or d Corrⁿ	v or d Corrⁿ
00	1 45·0	1 45·3	1 40·2	0·0 0·0	6·0 0·8	12·0 1·5
01	1 45·3	1 45·5	1 40·5	0·1 0·0	6·1 0·8	12·1 1·5
02	1 45·5	1 45·8	1 40·7	0·2 0·0	6·2 0·8	12·2 1·5
03	1 45·8	1 46·0	1 40·9	0·3 0·0	6·3 0·8	12·3 1·5
04	1 46·0	1 46·3	1 41·2	0·4 0·1	6·4 0·8	12·4 1·6
05	1 46·3	1 46·5	1 41·4	0·5 0·1	6·5 0·8	12·5 1·6
06	1 46·5	1 46·8	1 41·6	0·6 0·1	6·6 0·8	12·6 1·6
07	1 46·8	1 47·0	1 41·9	0·7 0·1	6·7 0·8	12·7 1·6
08	1 47·0	1 47·3	1 42·1	0·8 0·1	6·8 0·9	12·8 1·6
09	1 47·3	1 47·5	1 42·4	0·9 0·1	6·9 0·9	12·9 1·6
10	1 47·5	1 47·8	1 42·6	1·0 0·1	7·0 0·9	13·0 1·6
11	1 47·8	1 48·0	1 42·8	1·1 0·1	7·1 0·9	13·1 1·6
12	1 48·0	1 48·3	1 43·1	1·2 0·2	7·2 0·9	13·2 1·7
13	1 48·3	1 48·5	1 43·3	1·3 0·2	7·3 0·9	13·3 1·7
14	1 48·5	1 48·8	1 43·6	1·4 0·2	7·4 0·9	13·4 1·7
15	1 48·8	1 49·0	1 43·8	1·5 0·2	7·5 0·9	13·5 1·7
16	1 49·0	1 49·3	1 44·0	1·6 0·2	7·6 1·0	13·6 1·7
17	1 49·3	1 49·5	1 44·3	1·7 0·2	7·7 1·0	13·7 1·7
18	1 49·5	1 49·8	1 44·5	1·8 0·2	7·8 1·0	13·8 1·7
19	1 49·8	1 50·1	1 44·8	1·9 0·2	7·9 1·0	13·9 1·7
20	1 50·0	1 50·3	1 45·0	2·0 0·3	8·0 1·0	14·0 1·8
21	1 50·3	1 50·6	1 45·2	2·1 0·3	8·1 1·0	14·1 1·8
22	1 50·5	1 50·8	1 45·5	2·2 0·3	8·2 1·0	14·2 1·8
23	1 50·8	1 51·1	1 45·7	2·3 0·3	8·3 1·0	14·3 1·8
24	1 51·0	1 51·3	1 45·9	2·4 0·3	8·4 1·1	14·4 1·8
25	1 51·3	1 51·6	1 46·2	2·5 0·3	8·5 1·1	14·5 1·8
26	1 51·5	1 51·8	1 46·4	2·6 0·3	8·6 1·1	14·6 1·8
27	1 51·8	1 52·1	1 46·7	2·7 0·3	8·7 1·1	14·7 1·8
28	1 52·0	1 52·3	1 46·9	2·8 0·4	8·8 1·1	14·8 1·9
29	1 52·3	1 52·6	1 47·1	2·9 0·4	8·9 1·1	14·9 1·9
30	1 52·5	1 52·8	1 47·4	3·0 0·4	9·0 1·1	15·0 1·9
31	1 52·8	1 53·1	1 47·6	3·1 0·4	9·1 1·1	15·1 1·9
32	1 53·0	1 53·3	1 47·9	3·2 0·4	9·2 1·2	15·2 1·9
33	1 53·3	1 53·6	1 48·1	3·3 0·4	9·3 1·2	15·3 1·9
34	1 53·5	1 53·8	1 48·3	3·4 0·4	9·4 1·2	15·4 1·9
35	1 53·8	1 54·1	1 48·6	3·5 0·4	9·5 1·2	15·5 1·9
36	1 54·0	1 54·3	1 48·8	3·6 0·5	9·6 1·2	15·6 2·0
37	1 54·3	1 54·6	1 49·0	3·7 0·5	9·7 1·2	15·7 2·0
38	1 54·5	1 54·8	1 49·3	3·8 0·5	9·8 1·2	15·8 2·0
39	1 54·8	1 55·1	1 49·5	3·9 0·5	9·9 1·2	15·9 2·0
40	1 55·0	1 55·3	1 49·8	4·0 0·5	10·0 1·3	16·0 2·0
41	1 55·3	1 55·6	1 50·0	4·1 0·5	10·1 1·3	16·1 2·0
42	1 55·5	1 55·8	1 50·2	4·2 0·5	10·2 1·3	16·2 2·0
43	1 55·8	1 56·1	1 50·5	4·3 0·5	10·3 1·3	16·3 2·0
44	1 56·0	1 56·3	1 50·7	4·4 0·6	10·4 1·3	16·4 2·1
45	1 56·3	1 56·6	1 51·0	4·5 0·6	10·5 1·3	16·5 2·1
46	1 56·5	1 56·8	1 51·2	4·6 0·6	10·6 1·3	16·6 2·1
47	1 56·8	1 57·1	1 51·4	4·7 0·6	10·7 1·3	16·7 2·1
48	1 57·0	1 57·3	1 51·7	4·8 0·6	10·8 1·4	16·8 2·1
49	1 57·3	1 57·6	1 51·9	4·9 0·6	10·9 1·4	16·9 2·1
50	1 57·5	1 57·8	1 52·1	5·0 0·6	11·0 1·4	17·0 2·1
51	1 57·8	1 58·1	1 52·4	5·1 0·6	11·1 1·4	17·1 2·1
52	1 58·0	1 58·3	1 52·6	5·2 0·7	11·2 1·4	17·2 2·2
53	1 58·3	1 58·6	1 52·9	5·3 0·7	11·3 1·4	17·3 2·2
54	1 58·5	1 58·8	1 53·1	5·4 0·7	11·4 1·4	17·4 2·2
55	1 58·8	1 59·1	1 53·3	5·5 0·7	11·5 1·4	17·5 2·2
56	1 59·0	1 59·3	1 53·6	5·6 0·7	11·6 1·5	17·6 2·2
57	1 59·3	1 59·6	1 53·8	5·7 0·7	11·7 1·5	17·7 2·2
58	1 59·5	1 59·8	1 54·1	5·8 0·7	11·8 1·5	17·8 2·2
59	1 59·8	2 00·1	1 54·3	5·9 0·7	11·9 1·5	17·9 2·2
60	2 00·0	2 00·3	1 54·5	6·0 0·8	12·0 1·5	18·0 2·3

m 8	SUN PLANETS	ARIES	MOON	v or Corr^n d		v or Corr^n d		v or Corr^n d	
s	° ′	° ′	° ′	′	′	′	′	′	′
00	2 00·0	2 00·3	1 54·5	0·0	0·0	6·0	0·9	12·0	1·7
01	2 00·3	2 00·6	1 54·8	0·1	0·0	6·1	0·9	12·1	1·7
02	2 00·5	2 00·8	1 55·0	0·2	0·0	6·2	0·9	12·2	1·7
03	2 00·8	2 01·1	1 55·2	0·3	0·0	6·3	0·9	12·3	1·7
04	2 01·0	2 01·3	1 55·5	0·4	0·1	6·4	0·9	12·4	1·8
05	2 01·3	2 01·6	1 55·7	0·5	0·1	6·5	0·9	12·5	1·8
06	2 01·5	2 01·8	1 56·0	0·6	0·1	6·6	0·9	12·6	1·8
07	2 01·8	2 02·1	1 56·2	0·7	0·1	6·7	0·9	12·7	1·8
08	2 02·0	2 02·3	1 56·4	0·8	0·1	6·8	1·0	12·8	1·8
09	2 02·3	2 02·6	1 56·7	0·9	0·1	6·9	1·0	12·9	1·8
10	2 02·5	2 02·8	1 56·9	1·0	0·1	7·0	1·0	13·0	1·8
11	2 02·8	2 03·1	1 57·2	1·1	0·2	7·1	1·0	13·1	1·9
12	2 03·0	2 03·3	1 57·4	1·2	0·2	7·2	1·0	13·2	1·9
13	2 03·3	2 03·6	1 57·6	1·3	0·2	7·3	1·0	13·3	1·9
14	2 03·5	2 03·8	1 57·9	1·4	0·2	7·4	1·0	13·4	1·9
15	2 03·8	2 04·1	1 58·1	1·5	0·2	7·5	1·1	13·5	1·9
16	2 04·0	2 04·3	1 58·4	1·6	0·2	7·6	1·1	13·6	1·9
17	2 04·3	2 04·6	1 58·6	1·7	0·2	7·7	1·1	13·7	1·9
18	2 04·5	2 04·8	1 58·8	1·8	0·3	7·8	1·1	13·8	2·0
19	2 04·8	2 05·1	1 59·1	1·9	0·3	7·9	1·1	13·9	2·0
20	2 05·0	2 05·3	1 59·3	2·0	0·3	8·0	1·1	14·0	2·0
21	2 05·3	2 05·6	1 59·5	2·1	0·3	8·1	1·1	14·1	2·0
22	2 05·5	2 05·8	1 59·8	2·2	0·3	8·2	1·2	14·2	2·0
23	2 05·8	2 06·1	2 00·0	2·3	0·3	8·3	1·2	14·3	2·0
24	2 06·0	2 06·3	2 00·3	2·4	0·3	8·4	1·2	14·4	2·0
25	2 06·3	2 06·6	2 00·5	2·5	0·4	8·5	1·2	14·5	2·1
26	2 06·5	2 06·8	2 00·7	2·6	0·4	8·6	1·2	14·6	2·1
27	2 06·8	2 07·1	2 01·0	2·7	0·4	8·7	1·2	14·7	2·1
28	2 07·0	2 07·3	2 01·2	2·8	0·4	8·8	1·2	14·8	2·1
29	2 07·3	2 07·6	2 01·5	2·9	0·4	8·9	1·3	14·9	2·1
30	2 07·5	2 07·8	2 01·7	3·0	0·4	9·0	1·3	15·0	2·1
31	2 07·8	2 08·1	2 01·9	3·1	0·4	9·1	1·3	15·1	2·1
32	2 08·0	2 08·4	2 02·2	3·2	0·5	9·2	1·3	15·2	2·2
33	2 08·3	2 08·6	2 02·4	3·3	0·5	9·3	1·3	15·3	2·2
34	2 08·5	2 08·9	2 02·6	3·4	0·5	9·4	1·3	15·4	2·2
35	2 08·8	2 09·1	2 02·9	3·5	0·5	9·5	1·3	15·5	2·2
36	2 09·0	2 09·4	2 03·1	3·6	0·5	9·6	1·4	15·6	2·2
37	2 09·3	2 09·6	2 03·4	3·7	0·5	9·7	1·4	15·7	2·2
38	2 09·5	2 09·9	2 03·6	3·8	0·5	9·8	1·4	15·8	2·2
39	2 09·8	2 10·1	2 03·8	3·9	0·6	9·9	1·4	15·9	2·3
40	2 10·0	2 10·4	2 04·1	4·0	0·6	10·0	1·4	16·0	2·3
41	2 10·3	2 10·6	2 04·3	4·1	0·6	10·1	1·4	16·1	2·3
42	2 10·5	2 10·9	2 04·6	4·2	0·6	10·2	1·4	16·2	2·3
43	2 10·8	2 11·1	2 04·8	4·3	0·6	10·3	1·5	16·3	2·3
44	2 11·0	2 11·4	2 05·0	4·4	0·6	10·4	1·5	16·4	2·3
45	2 11·3	2 11·6	2 05·3	4·5	0·6	10·5	1·5	16·5	2·3
46	2 11·5	2 11·9	2 05·5	4·6	0·7	10·6	1·5	16·6	2·4
47	2 11·8	2 12·1	2 05·7	4·7	0·7	10·7	1·5	16·7	2·4
48	2 12·0	2 12·4	2 06·0	4·8	0·7	10·8	1·5	16·8	2·4
49	2 12·3	2 12·6	2 06·2	4·9	0·7	10·9	1·5	16·9	2·4
50	2 12·5	2 12·9	2 06·5	5·0	0·7	11·0	1·6	17·0	2·4
51	2 12·8	2 13·1	2 06·7	5·1	0·7	11·1	1·6	17·1	2·4
52	2 13·0	2 13·4	2 06·9	5·2	0·7	11·2	1·6	17·2	2·4
53	2 13·3	2 13·6	2 07·2	5·3	0·8	11·3	1·6	17·3	2·5
54	2 13·5	2 13·9	2 07·4	5·4	0·8	11·4	1·6	17·4	2·5
55	2 13·8	2 14·1	2 07·7	5·5	0·8	11·5	1·6	17·5	2·5
56	2 14·0	2 14·4	2 07·9	5·6	0·8	11·6	1·6	17·6	2·5
57	2 14·3	2 14·6	2 08·1	5·7	0·8	11·7	1·7	17·7	2·5
58	2 14·5	2 14·9	2 08·4	5·8	0·8	11·8	1·7	17·8	2·5
59	2 14·8	2 15·1	2 08·6	5·9	0·8	11·9	1·7	17·9	2·5
60	2 15·0	2 15·4	2 08·9	6·0	0·9	12·0	1·7	18·0	2·6

m 9	SUN PLANETS	ARIES	MOON	v or Corr^n d		v or Corr^n d		v or Corr^n d	
s	° ′	° ′	° ′	′	′	′	′	′	′
00	2 15·0	2 15·4	2 08·9	0·0	0·0	6·0	1·0	12·0	1·9
01	2 15·3	2 15·6	2 09·1	0·1	0·0	6·1	1·0	12·1	1·9
02	2 15·5	2 15·9	2 09·3	0·2	0·0	6·2	1·0	12·2	1·9
03	2 15·8	2 16·1	2 09·6	0·3	0·0	6·3	1·0	12·3	1·9
04	2 16·0	2 16·4	2 09·8	0·4	0·1	6·4	1·0	12·4	2·0
05	2 16·3	2 16·6	2 10·0	0·5	0·1	6·5	1·0	12·5	2·0
06	2 16·5	2 16·9	2 10·3	0·6	0·1	6·6	1·0	12·6	2·0
07	2 16·8	2 17·1	2 10·5	0·7	0·1	6·7	1·1	12·7	2·0
08	2 17·0	2 17·4	2 10·8	0·8	0·1	6·8	1·1	12·8	2·0
09	2 17·3	2 17·6	2 11·0	0·9	0·1	6·9	1·1	12·9	2·0
10	2 17·5	2 17·9	2 11·2	1·0	0·2	7·0	1·1	13·0	2·1
11	2 17·8	2 18·1	2 11·5	1·1	0·2	7·1	1·1	13·1	2·1
12	2 18·0	2 18·4	2 11·7	1·2	0·2	7·2	1·1	13·2	2·1
13	2 18·3	2 18·6	2 12·0	1·3	0·2	7·3	1·2	13·3	2·1
14	2 18·5	2 18·9	2 12·2	1·4	0·2	7·4	1·2	13·4	2·1
15	2 18·8	2 19·1	2 12·4	1·5	0·2	7·5	1·2	13·5	2·1
16	2 19·0	2 19·4	2 12·7	1·6	0·3	7·6	1·2	13·6	2·2
17	2 19·3	2 19·6	2 12·9	1·7	0·3	7·7	1·2	13·7	2·2
18	2 19·5	2 19·9	2 13·1	1·8	0·3	7·8	1·2	13·8	2·2
19	2 19·8	2 20·1	2 13·4	1·9	0·3	7·9	1·3	13·9	2·2
20	2 20·0	2 20·4	2 13·6	2·0	0·3	8·0	1·3	14·0	2·2
21	2 20·3	2 20·6	2 13·9	2·1	0·3	8·1	1·3	14·1	2·2
22	2 20·5	2 20·9	2 14·1	2·2	0·3	8·2	1·3	14·2	2·2
23	2 20·8	2 21·1	2 14·3	2·3	0·4	8·3	1·3	14·3	2·3
24	2 21·0	2 21·4	2 14·6	2·4	0·4	8·4	1·3	14·4	2·3
25	2 21·3	2 21·6	2 14·8	2·5	0·4	8·5	1·3	14·5	2·3
26	2 21·5	2 21·9	2 15·1	2·6	0·4	8·6	1·4	14·6	2·3
27	2 21·8	2 22·1	2 15·3	2·7	0·4	8·7	1·4	14·7	2·3
28	2 22·0	2 22·4	2 15·5	2·8	0·4	8·8	1·4	14·8	2·3
29	2 22·3	2 22·6	2 15·8	2·9	0·5	8·9	1·4	14·9	2·4
30	2 22·5	2 22·9	2 16·0	3·0	0·5	9·0	1·4	15·0	2·4
31	2 22·8	2 23·1	2 16·2	3·1	0·5	9·1	1·4	15·1	2·4
32	2 23·0	2 23·4	2 16·5	3·2	0·5	9·2	1·5	15·2	2·4
33	2 23·3	2 23·6	2 16·7	3·3	0·5	9·3	1·5	15·3	2·4
34	2 23·5	2 23·9	2 17·0	3·4	0·5	9·4	1·5	15·4	2·4
35	2 23·8	2 24·1	2 17·2	3·5	0·6	9·5	1·5	15·5	2·5
36	2 24·0	2 24·4	2 17·4	3·6	0·6	9·6	1·5	15·6	2·5
37	2 24·3	2 24·6	2 17·7	3·7	0·6	9·7	1·5	15·7	2·5
38	2 24·5	2 24·9	2 17·9	3·8	0·6	9·8	1·6	15·8	2·5
39	2 24·8	2 25·1	2 18·2	3·9	0·6	9·9	1·6	15·9	2·5
40	2 25·0	2 25·4	2 18·4	4·0	0·6	10·0	1·6	16·0	2·5
41	2 25·3	2 25·6	2 18·6	4·1	0·6	10·1	1·6	16·1	2·5
42	2 25·5	2 25·9	2 18·9	4·2	0·7	10·2	1·6	16·2	2·6
43	2 25·8	2 26·1	2 19·1	4·3	0·7	10·3	1·6	16·3	2·6
44	2 26·0	2 26·4	2 19·3	4·4	0·7	10·4	1·6	16·4	2·6
45	2 26·3	2 26·7	2 19·6	4·5	0·7	10·5	1·7	16·5	2·6
46	2 26·5	2 26·9	2 19·8	4·6	0·7	10·6	1·7	16·6	2·6
47	2 26·8	2 27·2	2 20·1	4·7	0·7	10·7	1·7	16·7	2·6
48	2 27·0	2 27·4	2 20·3	4·8	0·8	10·8	1·7	16·8	2·7
49	2 27·3	2 27·7	2 20·5	4·9	0·8	10·9	1·7	16·9	2·7
50	2 27·5	2 27·9	2 20·8	5·0	0·8	11·0	1·7	17·0	2·7
51	2 27·8	2 28·2	2 21·0	5·1	0·8	11·1	1·8	17·1	2·7
52	2 28·0	2 28·4	2 21·3	5·2	0·8	11·2	1·8	17·2	2·7
53	2 28·3	2 28·7	2 21·5	5·3	0·8	11·3	1·8	17·3	2·7
54	2 28·5	2 28·9	2 21·7	5·4	0·9	11·4	1·8	17·4	2·8
55	2 28·8	2 29·2	2 22·0	5·5	0·9	11·5	1·8	17·5	2·8
56	2 29·0	2 29·4	2 22·2	5·6	0·9	11·6	1·8	17·6	2·8
57	2 29·3	2 29·7	2 22·5	5·7	0·9	11·7	1·9	17·7	2·8
58	2 29·5	2 29·9	2 22·7	5·8	0·9	11·8	1·9	17·8	2·8
59	2 29·8	2 30·2	2 22·9	5·9	0·9	11·9	1·9	17·9	2·8
60	2 30·0	2 30·4	2 23·2	6·0	1·0	12·0	1·9	18·0	2·9

10	SUN PLANETS	ARIES	MOON	v or d	Corrⁿ	v or d	Corrⁿ	v or d	Corrⁿ
s	° ′	° ′	° ′	′	′	′	′	′	′
00	2 30.0	2 30.4	2 23.2	0.0	0.0	6.0	1.1	12.0	2.1
01	2 30.3	2 30.7	2 23.4	0.1	0.0	6.1	1.1	12.1	2.1
02	2 30.5	2 30.9	2 23.6	0.2	0.0	6.2	1.1	12.2	2.1
03	2 30.8	2 31.2	2 23.9	0.3	0.1	6.3	1.1	12.3	2.2
04	2 31.0	2 31.4	2 24.1	0.4	0.1	6.4	1.1	12.4	2.2
05	2 31.3	2 31.7	2 24.4	0.5	0.1	6.5	1.1	12.5	2.2
06	2 31.5	2 31.9	2 24.6	0.6	0.1	6.6	1.2	12.6	2.2
07	2 31.8	2 32.2	2 24.8	0.7	0.1	6.7	1.2	12.7	2.2
08	2 32.0	2 32.4	2 25.1	0.8	0.1	6.8	1.2	12.8	2.2
09	2 32.3	2 32.7	2 25.3	0.9	0.2	6.9	1.2	12.9	2.3
10	2 32.5	2 32.9	2 25.6	1.0	0.2	7.0	1.2	13.0	2.3
11	2 32.8	2 33.2	2 25.8	1.1	0.2	7.1	1.2	13.1	2.3
12	2 33.0	2 33.4	2 26.0	1.2	0.2	7.2	1.3	13.2	2.3
13	2 33.3	2 33.7	2 26.3	1.3	0.2	7.3	1.3	13.3	2.3
14	2 33.5	2 33.9	2 26.5	1.4	0.2	7.4	1.3	13.4	2.3
15	2 33.8	2 34.2	2 26.7	1.5	0.3	7.5	1.3	13.5	2.4
16	2 34.0	2 34.4	2 27.0	1.6	0.3	7.6	1.3	13.6	2.4
17	2 34.3	2 34.7	2 27.2	1.7	0.3	7.7	1.3	13.7	2.4
18	2 34.5	2 34.9	2 27.5	1.8	0.3	7.8	1.4	13.8	2.4
19	2 34.8	2 35.2	2 27.7	1.9	0.3	7.9	1.4	13.9	2.4
20	2 35.0	2 35.4	2 27.9	2.0	0.4	8.0	1.4	14.0	2.5
21	2 35.3	2 35.7	2 28.2	2.1	0.4	8.1	1.4	14.1	2.5
22	2 35.5	2 35.9	2 28.4	2.2	0.4	8.2	1.4	14.2	2.5
23	2 35.8	2 36.2	2 28.7	2.3	0.4	8.3	1.5	14.3	2.5
24	2 36.0	2 36.4	2 28.9	2.4	0.4	8.4	1.5	14.4	2.5
25	2 36.3	2 36.7	2 29.1	2.5	0.4	8.5	1.5	14.5	2.5
26	2 36.5	2 36.9	2 29.4	2.6	0.5	8.6	1.5	14.6	2.6
27	2 36.8	2 37.2	2 29.6	2.7	0.5	8.7	1.5	14.7	2.6
28	2 37.0	2 37.4	2 29.8	2.8	0.5	8.8	1.5	14.8	2.6
29	2 37.3	2 37.7	2 30.1	2.9	0.5	8.9	1.6	14.9	2.6
30	2 37.5	2 37.9	2 30.3	3.0	0.5	9.0	1.6	15.0	2.6
31	2 37.8	2 38.2	2 30.6	3.1	0.5	9.1	1.6	15.1	2.6
32	2 38.0	2 38.4	2 30.8	3.2	0.6	9.2	1.6	15.2	2.7
33	2 38.3	2 38.7	2 31.0	3.3	0.6	9.3	1.6	15.3	2.7
34	2 38.5	2 38.9	2 31.3	3.4	0.6	9.4	1.6	15.4	2.7
35	2 38.8	2 39.2	2 31.5	3.5	0.6	9.5	1.7	15.5	2.7
36	2 39.0	2 39.4	2 31.8	3.6	0.6	9.6	1.7	15.6	2.7
37	2 39.3	2 39.7	2 32.0	3.7	0.6	9.7	1.7	15.7	2.7
38	2 39.5	2 39.9	2 32.2	3.8	0.7	9.8	1.7	15.8	2.8
39	2 39.8	2 40.2	2 32.5	3.9	0.7	9.9	1.7	15.9	2.8
40	2 40.0	2 40.4	2 32.7	4.0	0.7	10.0	1.8	16.0	2.8
41	2 40.3	2 40.7	2 32.9	4.1	0.7	10.1	1.8	16.1	2.8
42	2 40.5	2 40.9	2 33.2	4.2	0.7	10.2	1.8	16.2	2.8
43	2 40.8	2 41.2	2 33.4	4.3	0.8	10.3	1.8	16.3	2.9
44	2 41.0	2 41.4	2 33.7	4.4	0.8	10.4	1.8	16.4	2.9
45	2 41.3	2 41.7	2 33.9	4.5	0.8	10.5	1.8	16.5	2.9
46	2 41.5	2 41.9	2 34.1	4.6	0.8	10.6	1.9	16.6	2.9
47	2 41.8	2 42.2	2 34.4	4.7	0.8	10.7	1.9	16.7	2.9
48	2 42.0	2 42.4	2 34.6	4.8	0.8	10.8	1.9	16.8	2.9
49	2 42.3	2 42.7	2 34.9	4.9	0.9	10.9	1.9	16.9	3.0
50	2 42.5	2 42.9	2 35.1	5.0	0.9	11.0	1.9	17.0	3.0
51	2 42.8	2 43.2	2 35.3	5.1	0.9	11.1	1.9	17.1	3.0
52	2 43.0	2 43.4	2 35.6	5.2	0.9	11.2	2.0	17.2	3.0
53	2 43.3	2 43.7	2 35.8	5.3	0.9	11.3	2.0	17.3	3.0
54	2 43.5	2 43.9	2 36.1	5.4	0.9	11.4	2.0	17.4	3.0
55	2 43.8	2 44.2	2 36.3	5.5	1.0	11.5	2.0	17.5	3.1
56	2 44.0	2 44.4	2 36.5	5.6	1.0	11.6	2.0	17.6	3.1
57	2 44.3	2 44.7	2 36.8	5.7	1.0	11.7	2.0	17.7	3.1
58	2 44.5	2 45.0	2 37.0	5.8	1.0	11.8	2.1	17.8	3.1
59	2 44.8	2 45.2	2 37.2	5.9	1.0	11.9	2.1	17.9	3.1
60	2 45.0	2 45.5	2 37.5	6.0	1.1	12.0	2.1	18.0	3.2

11	SUN PLANETS	ARIES	MOON	v or d	Corrⁿ	v or d	Corrⁿ	v or d	Corrⁿ
s	° ′	° ′	° ′	′	′	′	′	′	′
00	2 45.0	2 45.5	2 37.5	0.0	0.0	6.0	1.2	12.0	2.3
01	2 45.3	2 45.7	2 37.7	0.1	0.0	6.1	1.2	12.1	2.3
02	2 45.5	2 46.0	2 38.0	0.2	0.0	6.2	1.2	12.2	2.3
03	2 45.8	2 46.2	2 38.2	0.3	0.1	6.3	1.2	12.3	2.4
04	2 46.0	2 46.5	2 38.4	0.4	0.1	6.4	1.2	12.4	2.4
05	2 46.3	2 46.7	2 38.7	0.5	0.1	6.5	1.2	12.5	2.4
06	2 46.5	2 47.0	2 38.9	0.6	0.1	6.6	1.3	12.6	2.4
07	2 46.8	2 47.2	2 39.2	0.7	0.1	6.7	1.3	12.7	2.4
08	2 47.0	2 47.5	2 39.4	0.8	0.2	6.8	1.3	12.8	2.5
09	2 47.3	2 47.7	2 39.6	0.9	0.2	6.9	1.3	12.9	2.5
10	2 47.5	2 48.0	2 39.9	1.0	0.2	7.0	1.3	13.0	2.5
11	2 47.8	2 48.2	2 40.1	1.1	0.2	7.1	1.4	13.1	2.5
12	2 48.0	2 48.5	2 40.3	1.2	0.2	7.2	1.4	13.2	2.5
13	2 48.3	2 48.7	2 40.6	1.3	0.2	7.3	1.4	13.3	2.5
14	2 48.5	2 49.0	2 40.8	1.4	0.3	7.4	1.4	13.4	2.6
15	2 48.8	2 49.2	2 41.1	1.5	0.3	7.5	1.4	13.5	2.6
16	2 49.0	2 49.5	2 41.3	1.6	0.3	7.6	1.5	13.6	2.6
17	2 49.3	2 49.7	2 41.5	1.7	0.3	7.7	1.5	13.7	2.6
18	2 49.5	2 50.0	2 41.8	1.8	0.3	7.8	1.5	13.8	2.6
19	2 49.8	2 50.2	2 42.0	1.9	0.4	7.9	1.5	13.9	2.7
20	2 50.0	2 50.5	2 42.3	2.0	0.4	8.0	1.5	14.0	2.7
21	2 50.3	2 50.7	2 42.5	2.1	0.4	8.1	1.6	14.1	2.7
22	2 50.5	2 51.0	2 42.7	2.2	0.4	8.2	1.6	14.2	2.7
23	2 50.8	2 51.2	2 43.0	2.3	0.4	8.3	1.6	14.3	2.7
24	2 51.0	2 51.5	2 43.2	2.4	0.5	8.4	1.6	14.4	2.8
25	2 51.3	2 51.7	2 43.4	2.5	0.5	8.5	1.6	14.5	2.8
26	2 51.5	2 52.0	2 43.7	2.6	0.5	8.6	1.6	14.6	2.8
27	2 51.8	2 52.2	2 43.9	2.7	0.5	8.7	1.7	14.7	2.8
28	2 52.0	2 52.5	2 44.2	2.8	0.5	8.8	1.7	14.8	2.8
29	2 52.3	2 52.7	2 44.4	2.9	0.6	8.9	1.7	14.9	2.9
30	2 52.5	2 53.0	2 44.6	3.0	0.6	9.0	1.7	15.0	2.9
31	2 52.8	2 53.2	2 44.9	3.1	0.6	9.1	1.7	15.1	2.9
32	2 53.0	2 53.5	2 45.1	3.2	0.6	9.2	1.8	15.2	2.9
33	2 53.3	2 53.7	2 45.4	3.3	0.6	9.3	1.8	15.3	2.9
34	2 53.5	2 54.0	2 45.6	3.4	0.7	9.4	1.8	15.4	3.0
35	2 53.8	2 54.2	2 45.8	3.5	0.7	9.5	1.8	15.5	3.0
36	2 54.0	2 54.5	2 46.1	3.6	0.7	9.6	1.8	15.6	3.0
37	2 54.3	2 54.7	2 46.3	3.7	0.7	9.7	1.9	15.7	3.0
38	2 54.5	2 55.0	2 46.6	3.8	0.7	9.8	1.9	15.8	3.0
39	2 54.8	2 55.2	2 46.8	3.9	0.7	9.9	1.9	15.9	3.0
40	2 55.0	2 55.5	2 47.0	4.0	0.8	10.0	1.9	16.0	3.1
41	2 55.3	2 55.7	2 47.3	4.1	0.8	10.1	1.9	16.1	3.1
42	2 55.5	2 56.0	2 47.5	4.2	0.8	10.2	2.0	16.2	3.1
43	2 55.8	2 56.2	2 47.7	4.3	0.8	10.3	2.0	16.3	3.1
44	2 56.0	2 56.5	2 48.0	4.4	0.8	10.4	2.0	16.4	3.1
45	2 56.3	2 56.7	2 48.2	4.5	0.9	10.5	2.0	16.5	3.2
46	2 56.5	2 57.0	2 48.5	4.6	0.9	10.6	2.0	16.6	3.2
47	2 56.8	2 57.2	2 48.7	4.7	0.9	10.7	2.1	16.7	3.2
48	2 57.0	2 57.5	2 48.9	4.8	0.9	10.8	2.1	16.8	3.2
49	2 57.3	2 57.7	2 49.2	4.9	0.9	10.9	2.1	16.9	3.2
50	2 57.5	2 58.0	2 49.4	5.0	1.0	11.0	2.1	17.0	3.3
51	2 57.8	2 58.2	2 49.7	5.1	1.0	11.1	2.1	17.1	3.3
52	2 58.0	2 58.5	2 49.9	5.2	1.0	11.2	2.1	17.2	3.3
53	2 58.3	2 58.7	2 50.1	5.3	1.0	11.3	2.2	17.3	3.3
54	2 58.5	2 59.0	2 50.4	5.4	1.0	11.4	2.2	17.4	3.3
55	2 58.8	2 59.2	2 50.6	5.5	1.1	11.5	2.2	17.5	3.4
56	2 59.0	2 59.5	2 50.8	5.6	1.1	11.6	2.2	17.6	3.4
57	2 59.3	2 59.7	2 51.1	5.7	1.1	11.7	2.2	17.7	3.4
58	2 59.5	3 00.0	2 51.3	5.8	1.1	11.8	2.3	17.8	3.4
59	2 59.8	3 00.2	2 51.6	5.9	1.1	11.9	2.3	17.9	3.4
60	3 00.0	3 00.5	2 51.8	6.0	1.2	12.0	2.3	18.0	3.5

12ᵐ s	SUN PLANETS	ARIES	MOON	v or Corrⁿ d	v or Corrⁿ d	v or Corrⁿ d	13ᵐ s	SUN PLANETS	ARIES	MOON	v or Corrⁿ d	v or Corrⁿ d	v or Corrⁿ d
00	3 00·0	3 00·5	2 51·8	0·0 0·0	6·0 1·3	12·0 2·5	00	3 15·0	3 15·5	3 06·1	0·0 0·0	6·0 1·4	12·0 2·7
01	3 00·3	3 00·7	2 52·0	0·1 0·0	6·1 1·3	12·1 2·5	01	3 15·3	3 15·8	3 06·4	0·1 0·0	6·1 1·4	12·1 2·7
02	3 00·5	3 01·0	2 52·3	0·2 0·0	6·2 1·3	12·2 2·5	02	3 15·5	3 16·0	3 06·6	0·2 0·0	6·2 1·4	12·2 2·7
03	3 00·8	3 01·2	2 52·5	0·3 0·1	6·3 1·3	12·3 2·6	03	3 15·8	3 16·3	3 06·8	0·3 0·1	6·3 1·4	12·3 2·8
04	3 01·0	3 01·5	2 52·8	0·4 0·1	6·4 1·3	12·4 2·6	04	3 16·0	3 16·5	3 07·1	0·4 0·1	6·4 1·4	12·4 2·8
05	3 01·3	3 01·7	2 53·0	0·5 0·1	6·5 1·4	12·5 2·6	05	3 16·3	3 16·8	3 07·3	0·5 0·1	6·5 1·5	12·5 2·8
06	3 01·5	3 02·0	2 53·2	0·6 0·1	6·6 1·4	12·6 2·6	06	3 16·5	3 17·0	3 07·5	0·6 0·1	6·6 1·5	12·6 2·8
07	3 01·8	3 02·2	2 53·5	0·7 0·1	6·7 1·4	12·7 2·6	07	3 16·8	3 17·3	3 07·8	0·7 0·2	6·7 1·5	12·7 2·9
08	3 02·0	3 02·5	2 53·7	0·8 0·2	6·8 1·4	12·8 2·7	08	3 17·0	3 17·5	3 08·0	0·8 0·2	6·8 1·5	12·8 2·9
09	3 02·3	3 02·7	2 53·9	0·9 0·2	6·9 1·4	12·9 2·7	09	3 17·3	3 17·8	3 08·3	0·9 0·2	6·9 1·6	12·9 2·9
10	3 02·5	3 03·0	2 54·2	1·0 0·2	7·0 1·5	13·0 2·7	10	3 17·5	3 18·0	3 08·5	1·0 0·2	7·0 1·6	13·0 2·9
11	3 02·8	3 03·3	2 54·4	1·1 0·2	7·1 1·5	13·1 2·7	11	3 17·8	3 18·3	3 08·7	1·1 0·2	7·1 1·6	13·1 2·9
12	3 03·0	3 03·5	2 54·7	1·2 0·3	7·2 1·5	13·2 2·8	12	3 18·0	3 18·5	3 09·0	1·2 0·3	7·2 1·6	13·2 3·0
13	3 03·3	3 03·8	2 54·9	1·3 0·3	7·3 1·5	13·3 2·8	13	3 18·3	3 18·8	3 09·2	1·3 0·3	7·3 1·6	13·3 3·0
14	3 03·5	3 04·0	2 55·1	1·4 0·3	7·4 1·5	13·4 2·8	14	3 18·5	3 19·0	3 09·5	1·4 0·3	7·4 1·7	13·4 3·0
15	3 03·8	3 04·3	2 55·4	1·5 0·3	7·5 1·6	13·5 2·8	15	3 18·8	3 19·3	3 09·7	1·5 0·3	7·5 1·7	13·5 3·0
16	3 04·0	3 04·5	2 55·6	1·6 0·3	7·6 1·6	13·6 2·8	16	3 19·0	3 19·5	3 09·9	1·6 0·4	7·6 1·7	13·6 3·1
17	3 04·3	3 04·8	2 55·9	1·7 0·4	7·7 1·6	13·7 2·9	17	3 19·3	3 19·8	3 10·2	1·7 0·4	7·7 1·7	13·7 3·1
18	3 04·5	3 05·0	2 56·1	1·8 0·4	7·8 1·6	13·8 2·9	18	3 19·5	3 20·0	3 10·4	1·8 0·4	7·8 1·8	13·8 3·1
19	3 04·8	3 05·3	2 56·3	1·9 0·4	7·9 1·6	13·9 2·9	19	3 19·8	3 20·3	3 10·7	1·9 0·4	7·9 1·8	13·9 3·1
20	3 05·0	3 05·5	2 56·6	2·0 0·4	8·0 1·7	14·0 2·9	20	3 20·0	3 20·5	3 10·9	2·0 0·5	8·0 1·8	14·0 3·2
21	3 05·3	3 05·8	2 56·8	2·1 0·4	8·1 1·7	14·1 2·9	21	3 20·3	3 20·8	3 11·1	2·1 0·5	8·1 1·8	14·1 3·2
22	3 05·5	3 06·0	2 57·0	2·2 0·5	8·2 1·7	14·2 3·0	22	3 20·5	3 21·0	3 11·4	2·2 0·5	8·2 1·8	14·2 3·2
23	3 05·8	3 06·3	2 57·3	2·3 0·5	8·3 1·7	14·3 3·0	23	3 20·8	3 21·3	3 11·6	2·3 0·5	8·3 1·9	14·3 3·2
24	3 06·0	3 06·5	2 57·5	2·4 0·5	8·4 1·8	14·4 3·0	24	3 21·0	3 21·6	3 11·8	2·4 0·5	8·4 1·9	14·4 3·2
25	3 06·3	3 06·8	2 57·8	2·5 0·5	8·5 1·8	14·5 3·0	25	3 21·3	3 21·8	3 12·1	2·5 0·6	8·5 1·9	14·5 3·3
26	3 06·5	3 07·0	2 58·0	2·6 0·5	8·6 1·8	14·6 3·0	26	3 21·5	3 22·1	3 12·3	2·6 0·6	8·6 1·9	14·6 3·3
27	3 06·8	3 07·3	2 58·2	2·7 0·6	8·7 1·8	14·7 3·1	27	3 21·8	3 22·3	3 12·6	2·7 0·6	8·7 2·0	14·7 3·3
28	3 07·0	3 07·5	2 58·5	2·8 0·6	8·8 1·8	14·8 3·1	28	3 22·0	3 22·6	3 12·8	2·8 0·6	8·8 2·0	14·8 3·3
29	3 07·3	3 07·8	2 58·7	2·9 0·6	8·9 1·9	14·9 3·1	29	3 22·3	3 22·8	3 13·0	2·9 0·7	8·9 2·0	14·9 3·4
30	3 07·5	3 08·0	2 59·0	3·0 0·6	9·0 1·9	15·0 3·1	30	3 22·5	3 23·1	3 13·3	3·0 0·7	9·0 2·0	15·0 3·4
31	3 07·8	3 08·3	2 59·2	3·1 0·6	9·1 1·9	15·1 3·1	31	3 22·8	3 23·3	3 13·5	3·1 0·7	9·1 2·0	15·1 3·4
32	3 08·0	3 08·5	2 59·4	3·2 0·7	9·2 1·9	15·2 3·2	32	3 23·0	3 23·6	3 13·8	3·2 0·7	9·2 2·1	15·2 3·4
33	3 08·3	3 08·8	2 59·7	3·3 0·7	9·3 1·9	15·3 3·2	33	3 23·3	3 23·8	3 14·0	3·3 0·7	9·3 2·1	15·3 3·4
34	3 08·5	3 09·0	2 59·9	3·4 0·7	9·4 2·0	15·4 3·2	34	3 23·5	3 24·1	3 14·2	3·4 0·8	9·4 2·1	15·4 3·5
35	3 08·8	3 09·3	3 00·2	3·5 0·7	9·5 2·0	15·5 3·2	35	3 23·8	3 24·3	3 14·5	3·5 0·8	9·5 2·1	15·5 3·5
36	3 09·0	3 09·5	3 00·4	3·6 0·8	9·6 2·0	15·6 3·3	36	3 24·0	3 24·6	3 14·7	3·6 0·8	9·6 2·2	15·6 3·5
37	3 09·3	3 09·8	3 00·6	3·7 0·8	9·7 2·0	15·7 3·3	37	3 24·3	3 24·8	3 14·9	3·7 0·8	9·7 2·2	15·7 3·5
38	3 09·5	3 10·0	3 00·9	3·8 0·8	9·8 2·0	15·8 3·3	38	3 24·5	3 25·1	3 15·2	3·8 0·9	9·8 2·2	15·8 3·6
39	3 09·8	3 10·3	3 01·1	3·9 0·8	9·9 2·1	15·9 3·3	39	3 24·8	3 25·3	3 15·4	3·9 0·9	9·9 2·2	15·9 3·6
40	3 10·0	3 10·5	3 01·3	4·0 0·8	10·0 2·1	16·0 3·3	40	3 25·0	3 25·6	3 15·7	4·0 0·9	10·0 2·3	16·0 3·6
41	3 10·3	3 10·8	3 01·6	4·1 0·9	10·1 2·1	16·1 3·4	41	3 25·3	3 25·8	3 15·9	4·1 0·9	10·1 2·3	16·1 3·6
42	3 10·5	3 11·0	3 01·8	4·2 0·9	10·2 2·1	16·2 3·4	42	3 25·5	3 26·1	3 16·1	4·2 0·9	10·2 2·3	16·2 3·6
43	3 10·8	3 11·3	3 02·1	4·3 0·9	10·3 2·1	16·3 3·4	43	3 25·8	3 26·3	3 16·4	4·3 1·0	10·3 2·3	16·3 3·7
44	3 11·0	3 11·5	3 02·3	4·4 0·9	10·4 2·2	16·4 3·4	44	3 26·0	3 26·6	3 16·6	4·4 1·0	10·4 2·3	16·4 3·7
45	3 11·3	3 11·8	3 02·5	4·5 0·9	10·5 2·2	16·5 3·4	45	3 26·3	3 26·8	3 16·9	4·5 1·0	10·5 2·4	16·5 3·7
46	3 11·5	3 12·0	3 02·8	4·6 1·0	10·6 2·2	16·6 3·5	46	3 26·5	3 27·1	3 17·1	4·6 1·0	10·6 2·4	16·6 3·7
47	3 11·8	3 12·3	3 03·0	4·7 1·0	10·7 2·2	16·7 3·5	47	3 26·8	3 27·3	3 17·3	4·7 1·1	10·7 2·4	16·7 3·8
48	3 12·0	3 12·5	3 03·3	4·8 1·0	10·8 2·3	16·8 3·5	48	3 27·0	3 27·6	3 17·6	4·8 1·1	10·8 2·4	16·8 3·8
49	3 12·3	3 12·8	3 03·5	4·9 1·0	10·9 2·3	16·9 3·5	49	3 27·3	3 27·8	3 17·8	4·9 1·1	10·9 2·5	16·9 3·8
50	3 12·5	3 13·0	3 03·7	5·0 1·0	11·0 2·3	17·0 3·5	50	3 27·5	3 28·1	3 18·0	5·0 1·1	11·0 2·5	17·0 3·8
51	3 12·8	3 13·3	3 04·0	5·1 1·1	11·1 2·3	17·1 3·6	51	3 27·8	3 28·3	3 18·3	5·1 1·1	11·1 2·5	17·1 3·8
52	3 13·0	3 13·5	3 04·2	5·2 1·1	11·2 2·3	17·2 3·6	52	3 28·0	3 28·6	3 18·5	5·2 1·2	11·2 2·5	17·2 3·9
53	3 13·3	3 13·8	3 04·4	5·3 1·1	11·3 2·4	17·3 3·6	53	3 28·3	3 28·8	3 18·8	5·3 1·2	11·3 2·5	17·3 3·9
54	3 13·5	3 14·0	3 04·7	5·4 1·1	11·4 2·4	17·4 3·6	54	3 28·5	3 29·1	3 19·0	5·4 1·2	11·4 2·6	17·4 3·9
55	3 13·8	3 14·3	3 04·9	5·5 1·1	11·5 2·4	17·5 3·6	55	3 28·8	3 29·3	3 19·2	5·5 1·2	11·5 2·6	17·5 3·9
56	3 14·0	3 14·5	3 05·2	5·6 1·2	11·6 2·4	17·6 3·7	56	3 29·0	3 29·6	3 19·5	5·6 1·3	11·6 2·6	17·6 4·0
57	3 14·3	3 14·8	3 05·4	5·7 1·2	11·7 2·4	17·7 3·7	57	3 29·3	3 29·8	3 19·7	5·7 1·3	11·7 2·6	17·7 4·0
58	3 14·5	3 15·0	3 05·6	5·8 1·2	11·8 2·5	17·8 3·7	58	3 29·5	3 30·1	3 20·0	5·8 1·3	11·8 2·7	17·8 4·0
59	3 14·8	3 15·3	3 05·9	5·9 1·2	11·9 2·5	17·9 3·7	59	3 29·8	3 30·3	3 20·2	5·9 1·3	11·9 2·7	17·9 4·0
60	3 15·0	3 15·5	3 06·1	6·0 1·3	12·0 2·5	18·0 3·8	60	3 30·0	3 30·6	3 20·4	6·0 1·4	12·0 2·7	18·0 4·1

14 m	SUN PLANETS	ARIES	MOON	v or Corrⁿ d		v or Corrⁿ d		v or Corrⁿ d	
s	° ′	° ′	° ′	′	′	′	′	′	′
00	3 30·0	3 30·6	3 20·4	0·0	0·0	6·0	1·5	12·0	2·9
01	3 30·3	3 30·8	3 20·7	0·1	0·0	6·1	1·5	12·1	2·9
02	3 30·5	3 31·1	3 20·9	0·2	0·0	6·2	1·5	12·2	2·9
03	3 30·8	3 31·3	3 21·1	0·3	0·1	6·3	1·5	12·3	3·0
04	3 31·0	3 31·6	3 21·4	0·4	0·1	6·4	1·5	12·4	3·0
05	3 31·3	3 31·8	3 21·6	0·5	0·1	6·5	1·6	12·5	3·0
06	3 31·5	3 32·1	3 21·9	0·6	0·1	6·6	1·6	12·6	3·0
07	3 31·8	3 32·3	3 22·1	0·7	0·2	6·7	1·6	12·7	3·1
08	3 32·0	3 32·6	3 22·3	0·8	0·2	6·8	1·6	12·8	3·1
09	3 32·3	3 32·8	3 22·6	0·9	0·2	6·9	1·7	12·9	3·1
10	3 32·5	3 33·1	3 22·8	1·0	0·2	7·0	1·7	13·0	3·1
11	3 32·8	3 33·3	3 23·1	1·1	0·3	7·1	1·7	13·1	3·2
12	3 33·0	3 33·6	3 23·3	1·2	0·3	7·2	1·7	13·2	3·2
13	3 33·3	3 33·8	3 23·5	1·3	0·3	7·3	1·8	13·3	3·2
14	3 33·5	3 34·1	3 23·8	1·4	0·3	7·4	1·8	13·4	3·2
15	3 33·8	3 34·3	3 24·0	1·5	0·4	7·5	1·8	13·5	3·3
16	3 34·0	3 34·6	3 24·3	1·6	0·4	7·6	1·8	13·6	3·3
17	3 34·3	3 34·8	3 24·5	1·7	0·4	7·7	1·9	13·7	3·3
18	3 34·5	3 35·1	3 24·7	1·8	0·4	7·8	1·9	13·8	3·3
19	3 34·8	3 35·3	3 25·0	1·9	0·5	7·9	1·9	13·9	3·4
20	3 35·0	3 35·6	3 25·2	2·0	0·5	8·0	1·9	14·0	3·4
21	3 35·3	3 35·8	3 25·4	2·1	0·5	8·1	2·0	14·1	3·4
22	3 35·5	3 36·1	3 25·7	2·2	0·6	8·2	2·0	14·2	3·4
23	3 35·8	3 36·3	3 25·9	2·3	0·6	8·3	2·0	14·3	3·5
24	3 36·0	3 36·6	3 26·2	2·4	0·6	8·4	2·0	14·4	3·5
25	3 36·3	3 36·8	3 26·4	2·5	0·6	8·5	2·1	14·5	3·5
26	3 36·5	3 37·1	3 26·6	2·6	0·6	8·6	2·1	14·6	3·5
27	3 36·8	3 37·3	3 26·9	2·7	0·7	8·7	2·1	14·7	3·6
28	3 37·0	3 37·6	3 27·1	2·8	0·7	8·8	2·1	14·8	3·6
29	3 37·3	3 37·8	3 27·4	2·9	0·7	8·9	2·2	14·9	3·6
30	3 37·5	3 38·1	3 27·6	3·0	0·7	9·0	2·2	15·0	3·6
31	3 37·8	3 38·3	3 27·8	3·1	0·7	9·1	2·2	15·1	3·6
32	3 38·0	3 38·6	3 28·1	3·2	0·8	9·2	2·2	15·2	3·7
33	3 38·3	3 38·8	3 28·3	3·3	0·8	9·3	2·2	15·3	3·7
34	3 38·5	3 39·1	3 28·5	3·4	0·8	9·4	2·3	15·4	3·7
35	3 38·8	3 39·3	3 28·8	3·5	0·8	9·5	2·3	15·5	3·7
36	3 39·0	3 39·6	3 29·0	3·6	0·9	9·6	2·3	15·6	3·8
37	3 39·3	3 39·9	3 29·3	3·7	0·9	9·7	2·3	15·7	3·8
38	3 39·5	3 40·1	3 29·5	3·8	0·9	9·8	2·4	15·8	3·8
39	3 39·8	3 40·4	3 29·7	3·9	0·9	9·9	2·4	15·9	3·8
40	3 40·0	3 40·6	3 30·0	4·0	1·0	10·0	2·4	16·0	3·9
41	3 40·3	3 40·9	3 30·2	4·1	1·0	10·1	2·4	16·1	3·9
42	3 40·5	3 41·1	3 30·5	4·2	1·0	10·2	2·5	16·2	3·9
43	3 40·8	3 41·4	3 30·7	4·3	1·0	10·3	2·5	16·3	3·9
44	3 41·0	3 41·6	3 30·9	4·4	1·1	10·4	2·5	16·4	4·0
45	3 41·3	3 41·9	3 31·2	4·5	1·1	10·5	2·5	16·5	4·0
46	3 41·5	3 42·1	3 31·4	4·6	1·1	10·6	2·6	16·6	4·0
47	3 41·8	3 42·4	3 31·6	4·7	1·1	10·7	2·6	16·7	4·0
48	3 42·0	3 42·6	3 31·9	4·8	1·2	10·8	2·6	16·8	4·1
49	3 42·3	3 42·9	3 32·1	4·9	1·2	10·9	2·6	16·9	4·1
50	3 42·5	3 43·1	3 32·4	5·0	1·2	11·0	2·7	17·0	4·1
51	3 42·8	3 43·4	3 32·6	5·1	1·2	11·1	2·7	17·1	4·1
52	3 43·0	3 43·6	3 32·8	5·2	1·3	11·2	2·7	17·2	4·2
53	3 43·3	3 43·9	3 33·1	5·3	1·3	11·3	2·7	17·3	4·2
54	3 43·5	3 44·1	3 33·3	5·4	1·3	11·4	2·8	17·4	4·2
55	3 43·8	3 44·4	3 33·6	5·5	1·3	11·5	2·8	17·5	4·2
56	3 44·0	3 44·6	3 33·8	5·6	1·4	11·6	2·8	17·6	4·3
57	3 44·3	3 44·9	3 34·0	5·7	1·4	11·7	2·8	17·7	4·3
58	3 44·5	3 45·1	3 34·3	5·8	1·4	11·8	2·9	17·8	4·3
59	3 44·8	3 45·4	3 34·5	5·9	1·4	11·9	2·9	17·9	4·3
60	3 45·0	3 45·6	3 34·8	6·0	1·5	12·0	2·9	18·0	4·4

15 m	SUN PLANETS	ARIES	MOON	v or Corrⁿ d		v or Corrⁿ d		v or Corrⁿ d	
s	° ′	° ′	° ′	′	′	′	′	′	′
00	3 45·0	3 45·6	3 34·8	0·0	0·0	6·0	1·6	12·0	3·1
01	3 45·3	3 45·9	3 35·0	0·1	0·0	6·1	1·6	12·1	3·1
02	3 45·5	3 46·1	3 35·2	0·2	0·1	6·2	1·6	12·2	3·2
03	3 45·8	3 46·4	3 35·5	0·3	0·1	6·3	1·6	12·3	3·2
04	3 46·0	3 46·6	3 35·7	0·4	0·1	6·4	1·7	12·4	3·2
05	3 46·3	3 46·9	3 35·9	0·5	0·1	6·5	1·7	12·5	3·2
06	3 46·5	3 47·1	3 36·2	0·6	0·2	6·6	1·7	12·6	3·3
07	3 46·8	3 47·4	3 36·4	0·7	0·2	6·7	1·7	12·7	3·3
08	3 47·0	3 47·6	3 36·7	0·8	0·2	6·8	1·8	12·8	3·3
09	3 47·3	3 47·9	3 36·9	0·9	0·2	6·9	1·8	12·9	3·3
10	3 47·5	3 48·1	3 37·1	1·0	0·3	7·0	1·8	13·0	3·4
11	3 47·8	3 48·4	3 37·4	1·1	0·3	7·1	1·8	13·1	3·4
12	3 48·0	3 48·6	3 37·6	1·2	0·3	7·2	1·9	13·2	3·4
13	3 48·3	3 48·9	3 37·9	1·3	0·3	7·3	1·9	13·3	3·4
14	3 48·5	3 49·1	3 38·1	1·4	0·4	7·4	1·9	13·4	3·5
15	3 48·8	3 49·4	3 38·3	1·5	0·4	7·5	1·9	13·5	3·5
16	3 49·0	3 49·6	3 38·6	1·6	0·4	7·6	2·0	13·6	3·5
17	3 49·3	3 49·9	3 38·8	1·7	0·4	7·7	2·0	13·7	3·5
18	3 49·5	3 50·1	3 39·0	1·8	0·5	7·8	2·0	13·8	3·6
19	3 49·8	3 50·4	3 39·3	1·9	0·5	7·9	2·0	13·9	3·6
20	3 50·0	3 50·6	3 39·5	2·0	0·5	8·0	2·1	14·0	3·6
21	3 50·3	3 50·9	3 39·8	2·1	0·5	8·1	2·1	14·1	3·6
22	3 50·5	3 51·1	3 40·0	2·2	0·6	8·2	2·1	14·2	3·7
23	3 50·8	3 51·4	3 40·2	2·3	0·6	8·3	2·1	14·3	3·7
24	3 51·0	3 51·6	3 40·5	2·4	0·6	8·4	2·2	14·4	3·7
25	3 51·3	3 51·9	3 40·7	2·5	0·6	8·5	2·2	14·5	3·7
26	3 51·5	3 52·1	3 41·0	2·6	0·7	8·6	2·2	14·6	3·8
27	3 51·8	3 52·4	3 41·2	2·7	0·7	8·7	2·2	14·7	3·8
28	3 52·0	3 52·6	3 41·4	2·8	0·7	8·8	2·3	14·8	3·8
29	3 52·3	3 52·9	3 41·7	2·9	0·7	8·9	2·3	14·9	3·8
30	3 52·5	3 53·1	3 41·9	3·0	0·8	9·0	2·3	15·0	3·9
31	3 52·8	3 53·4	3 42·1	3·1	0·8	9·1	2·4	15·1	3·9
32	3 53·0	3 53·6	3 42·4	3·2	0·8	9·2	2·4	15·2	3·9
33	3 53·3	3 53·9	3 42·6	3·3	0·9	9·3	2·4	15·3	4·0
34	3 53·5	3 54·1	3 42·9	3·4	0·9	9·4	2·4	15·4	4·0
35	3 53·8	3 54·4	3 43·1	3·5	0·9	9·5	2·5	15·5	4·0
36	3 54·0	3 54·6	3 43·3	3·6	0·9	9·6	2·5	15·6	4·0
37	3 54·3	3 54·9	3 43·6	3·7	1·0	9·7	2·5	15·7	4·1
38	3 54·5	3 55·1	3 43·8	3·8	1·0	9·8	2·5	15·8	4·1
39	3 54·8	3 55·4	3 44·1	3·9	1·0	9·9	2·6	15·9	4·1
40	3 55·0	3 55·6	3 44·3	4·0	1·0	10·0	2·6	16·0	4·1
41	3 55·3	3 55·9	3 44·5	4·1	1·1	10·1	2·6	16·1	4·2
42	3 55·5	3 56·1	3 44·8	4·2	1·1	10·2	2·6	16·2	4·2
43	3 55·8	3 56·4	3 45·0	4·3	1·1	10·3	2·7	16·3	4·2
44	3 56·0	3 56·6	3 45·2	4·4	1·1	10·4	2·7	16·4	4·2
45	3 56·3	3 56·9	3 45·5	4·5	1·2	10·5	2·7	16·5	4·3
46	3 56·5	3 57·1	3 45·7	4·6	1·2	10·6	2·7	16·6	4·3
47	3 56·8	3 57·4	3 46·0	4·7	1·2	10·7	2·8	16·7	4·3
48	3 57·0	3 57·6	3 46·2	4·8	1·2	10·8	2·8	16·8	4·3
49	3 57·3	3 57·9	3 46·4	4·9	1·3	10·9	2·8	16·9	4·4
50	3 57·5	3 58·2	3 46·7	5·0	1·3	11·0	2·8	17·0	4·4
51	3 57·8	3 58·4	3 46·9	5·1	1·3	11·1	2·9	17·1	4·4
52	3 58·0	3 58·7	3 47·2	5·2	1·3	11·2	2·9	17·2	4·4
53	3 58·3	3 58·9	3 47·4	5·3	1·4	11·3	2·9	17·3	4·5
54	3 58·5	3 59·2	3 47·6	5·4	1·4	11·4	2·9	17·4	4·5
55	3 58·8	3 59·4	3 47·9	5·5	1·4	11·5	3·0	17·5	4·5
56	3 59·0	3 59·7	3 48·1	5·6	1·4	11·6	3·0	17·6	4·5
57	3 59·3	3 59·9	3 48·4	5·7	1·5	11·7	3·0	17·7	4·6
58	3 59·5	4 00·2	3 48·6	5·8	1·5	11·8	3·0	17·8	4·6
59	3 59·8	4 00·4	3 48·8	5·9	1·5	11·9	3·1	17·9	4·6
60	4 00·0	4 00·7	3 49·1	6·0	1·6	12·0	3·1	18·0	4·7

16 m/s	SUN PLANETS	ARIES	MOON	v or d Corrⁿ	v or d Corrⁿ	v or d Corrⁿ
s	° ′	° ′	° ′	′ ′	′ ′	′ ′
00	4 00·0	4 00·7	3 49·1	0·0 0·0	6·0 1·7	12·0 3·3
01	4 00·3	4 00·9	3 49·3	0·1 0·0	6·1 1·7	12·1 3·3
02	4 00·5	4 01·2	3 49·5	0·2 0·1	6·2 1·7	12·2 3·4
03	4 00·8	4 01·4	3 49·8	0·3 0·1	6·3 1·7	12·3 3·4
04	4 01·0	4 01·7	3 50·0	0·4 0·1	6·4 1·8	12·4 3·4
05	4 01·3	4 01·9	3 50·3	0·5 0·1	6·5 1·8	12·5 3·4
06	4 01·5	4 02·2	3 50·5	0·6 0·2	6·6 1·8	12·6 3·5
07	4 01·8	4 02·4	3 50·7	0·7 0·2	6·7 1·8	12·7 3·5
08	4 02·0	4 02·7	3 51·0	0·8 0·2	6·8 1·9	12·8 3·5
09	4 02·3	4 02·9	3 51·2	0·9 0·2	6·9 1·9	12·9 3·5
10	4 02·5	4 03·2	3 51·5	1·0 0·3	7·0 1·9	13·0 3·6
11	4 02·8	4 03·4	3 51·7	1·1 0·3	7·1 2·0	13·1 3·6
12	4 03·0	4 03·7	3 51·9	1·2 0·3	7·2 2·0	13·2 3·6
13	4 03·3	4 03·9	3 52·2	1·3 0·4	7·3 2·0	13·3 3·7
14	4 03·5	4 04·2	3 52·4	1·4 0·4	7·4 2·0	13·4 3·7
15	4 03·8	4 04·4	3 52·6	1·5 0·4	7·5 2·1	13·5 3·7
16	4 04·0	4 04·7	3 52·9	1·6 0·4	7·6 2·1	13·6 3·7
17	4 04·3	4 04·9	3 53·1	1·7 0·5	7·7 2·1	13·7 3·8
18	4 04·5	4 05·2	3 53·4	1·8 0·5	7·8 2·1	13·8 3·8
19	4 04·8	4 05·4	3 53·6	1·9 0·5	7·9 2·2	13·9 3·8
20	4 05·0	4 05·7	3 53·8	2·0 0·6	8·0 2·2	14·0 3·9
21	4 05·3	4 05·9	3 54·1	2·1 0·6	8·1 2·2	14·1 3·9
22	4 05·5	4 06·2	3 54·3	2·2 0·6	8·2 2·3	14·2 3·9
23	4 05·8	4 06·4	3 54·6	2·3 0·6	8·3 2·3	14·3 3·9
24	4 06·0	4 06·7	3 54·8	2·4 0·7	8·4 2·3	14·4 4·0
25	4 06·3	4 06·9	3 55·0	2·5 0·7	8·5 2·3	14·5 4·0
26	4 06·5	4 07·2	3 55·3	2·6 0·7	8·6 2·4	14·6 4·0
27	4 06·8	4 07·4	3 55·5	2·7 0·7	8·7 2·4	14·7 4·0
28	4 07·0	4 07·7	3 55·7	2·8 0·8	8·8 2·4	14·8 4·1
29	4 07·3	4 07·9	3 56·0	2·9 0·8	8·9 2·4	14·9 4·1
30	4 07·5	4 08·2	3 56·2	3·0 0·8	9·0 2·5	15·0 4·1
31	4 07·8	4 08·4	3 56·5	3·1 0·9	9·1 2·5	15·1 4·2
32	4 08·0	4 08·7	3 56·7	3·2 0·9	9·2 2·5	15·2 4·2
33	4 08·3	4 08·9	3 56·9	3·3 0·9	9·3 2·6	15·3 4·2
34	4 08·5	4 09·2	3 57·2	3·4 0·9	9·4 2·6	15·4 4·2
35	4 08·8	4 09·4	3 57·4	3·5 1·0	9·5 2·6	15·5 4·3
36	4 09·0	4 09·7	3 57·7	3·6 1·0	9·6 2·6	15·6 4·3
37	4 09·3	4 09·9	3 57·9	3·7 1·0	9·7 2·7	15·7 4·3
38	4 09·5	4 10·2	3 58·1	3·8 1·0	9·8 2·7	15·8 4·3
39	4 09·8	4 10·4	3 58·4	3·9 1·1	9·9 2·7	15·9 4·4
40	4 10·0	4 10·7	3 58·6	4·0 1·1	10·0 2·8	16·0 4·4
41	4 10·3	4 10·9	3 58·8	4·1 1·1	10·1 2·8	16·1 4·4
42	4 10·5	4 11·2	3 59·1	4·2 1·2	10·2 2·8	16·2 4·5
43	4 10·8	4 11·4	3 59·3	4·3 1·2	10·3 2·8	16·3 4·5
44	4 11·0	4 11·7	3 59·6	4·4 1·2	10·4 2·9	16·4 4·5
45	4 11·3	4 11·9	3 59·8	4·5 1·2	10·5 2·9	16·5 4·5
46	4 11·5	4 12·2	4 00·0	4·6 1·3	10·6 2·9	16·6 4·6
47	4 11·8	4 12·4	4 00·3	4·7 1·3	10·7 2·9	16·7 4·6
48	4 12·0	4 12·7	4 00·5	4·8 1·3	10·8 3·0	16·8 4·6
49	4 12·3	4 12·9	4 00·8	4·9 1·3	10·9 3·0	16·9 4·6
50	4 12·5	4 13·2	4 01·0	5·0 1·4	11·0 3·0	17·0 4·7
51	4 12·8	4 13·4	4 01·2	5·1 1·4	11·1 3·1	17·1 4·7
52	4 13·0	4 13·7	4 01·5	5·2 1·4	11·2 3·1	17·2 4·7
53	4 13·3	4 13·9	4 01·7	5·3 1·5	11·3 3·1	17·3 4·8
54	4 13·5	4 14·2	4 02·0	5·4 1·5	11·4 3·1	17·4 4·8
55	4 13·8	4 14·4	4 02·2	5·5 1·5	11·5 3·2	17·5 4·8
56	4 14·0	4 14·7	4 02·4	5·6 1·5	11·6 3·2	17·6 4·8
57	4 14·3	4 14·9	4 02·7	5·7 1·6	11·7 3·2	17·7 4·9
58	4 14·5	4 15·2	4 02·9	5·8 1·6	11·8 3·2	17·8 4·9
59	4 14·8	4 15·4	4 03·1	5·9 1·6	11·9 3·3	17·9 4·9
60	4 15·0	4 15·7	4 03·4	6·0 1·7	12·0 3·3	18·0 5·0

17 m/s	SUN PLANETS	ARIES	MOON	v or d Corrⁿ	v or d Corrⁿ	v or d Corrⁿ
s	° ′	° ′	° ′	′ ′	′ ′	′ ′
00	4 15·0	4 15·7	4 03·4	0·0 0·0	6·0 1·8	12·0 3·5
01	4 15·3	4 15·9	4 03·6	0·1 0·0	6·1 1·8	12·1 3·5
02	4 15·5	4 16·2	4 03·9	0·2 0·1	6·2 1·8	12·2 3·6
03	4 15·8	4 16·5	4 04·1	0·3 0·1	6·3 1·8	12·3 3·6
04	4 16·0	4 16·7	4 04·3	0·4 0·1	6·4 1·9	12·4 3·6
05	4 16·3	4 17·0	4 04·6	0·5 0·1	6·5 1·9	12·5 3·6
06	4 16·5	4 17·2	4 04·8	0·6 0·2	6·6 1·9	12·6 3·7
07	4 16·8	4 17·5	4 05·1	0·7 0·2	6·7 2·0	12·7 3·7
08	4 17·0	4 17·7	4 05·3	0·8 0·2	6·8 2·0	12·8 3·7
09	4 17·3	4 18·0	4 05·5	0·9 0·3	6·9 2·0	12·9 3·8
10	4 17·5	4 18·2	4 05·8	1·0 0·3	7·0 2·0	13·0 3·8
11	4 17·8	4 18·5	4 06·0	1·1 0·3	7·1 2·1	13·1 3·8
12	4 18·0	4 18·7	4 06·2	1·2 0·4	7·2 2·1	13·2 3·9
13	4 18·3	4 19·0	4 06·5	1·3 0·4	7·3 2·1	13·3 3·9
14	4 18·5	4 19·2	4 06·7	1·4 0·4	7·4 2·2	13·4 3·9
15	4 18·8	4 19·5	4 07·0	1·5 0·4	7·5 2·2	13·5 3·9
16	4 19·0	4 19·7	4 07·2	1·6 0·5	7·6 2·2	13·6 4·0
17	4 19·3	4 20·0	4 07·4	1·7 0·5	7·7 2·2	13·7 4·0
18	4 19·5	4 20·2	4 07·7	1·8 0·5	7·8 2·3	13·8 4·0
19	4 19·8	4 20·5	4 07·9	1·9 0·6	7·9 2·3	13·9 4·1
20	4 20·0	4 20·7	4 08·2	2·0 0·6	8·0 2·3	14·0 4·1
21	4 20·3	4 21·0	4 08·4	2·1 0·6	8·1 2·4	14·1 4·1
22	4 20·5	4 21·2	4 08·6	2·2 0·6	8·2 2·4	14·2 4·1
23	4 20·8	4 21·5	4 08·9	2·3 0·7	8·3 2·4	14·3 4·2
24	4 21·0	4 21·7	4 09·1	2·4 0·7	8·4 2·5	14·4 4·2
25	4 21·3	4 22·0	4 09·3	2·5 0·7	8·5 2·5	14·5 4·2
26	4 21·5	4 22·2	4 09·6	2·6 0·8	8·6 2·5	14·6 4·3
27	4 21·8	4 22·5	4 09·8	2·7 0·8	8·7 2·5	14·7 4·3
28	4 22·0	4 22·7	4 10·1	2·8 0·8	8·8 2·6	14·8 4·3
29	4 22·3	4 23·0	4 10·3	2·9 0·8	8·9 2·6	14·9 4·3
30	4 22·5	4 23·2	4 10·5	3·0 0·9	9·0 2·6	15·0 4·4
31	4 22·8	4 23·5	4 10·8	3·1 0·9	9·1 2·7	15·1 4·4
32	4 23·0	4 23·7	4 11·0	3·2 0·9	9·2 2·7	15·2 4·4
33	4 23·3	4 24·0	4 11·3	3·3 1·0	9·3 2·7	15·3 4·5
34	4 23·5	4 24·2	4 11·5	3·4 1·0	9·4 2·7	15·4 4·5
35	4 23·8	4 24·5	4 11·7	3·5 1·0	9·5 2·8	15·5 4·5
36	4 24·0	4 24·7	4 12·0	3·6 1·1	9·6 2·8	15·6 4·6
37	4 24·3	4 25·0	4 12·2	3·7 1·1	9·7 2·8	15·7 4·6
38	4 24·5	4 25·2	4 12·5	3·8 1·1	9·8 2·9	15·8 4·6
39	4 24·8	4 25·5	4 12·7	3·9 1·1	9·9 2·9	15·9 4·6
40	4 25·0	4 25·7	4 12·9	4·0 1·2	10·0 2·9	16·0 4·7
41	4 25·3	4 26·0	4 13·2	4·1 1·2	10·1 2·9	16·1 4·7
42	4 25·5	4 26·2	4 13·4	4·2 1·2	10·2 3·0	16·2 4·7
43	4 25·8	4 26·5	4 13·6	4·3 1·3	10·3 3·0	16·3 4·8
44	4 26·0	4 26·7	4 13·9	4·4 1·3	10·4 3·0	16·4 4·8
45	4 26·3	4 27·0	4 14·1	4·5 1·3	10·5 3·1	16·5 4·8
46	4 26·5	4 27·2	4 14·4	4·6 1·3	10·6 3·1	16·6 4·8
47	4 26·8	4 27·5	4 14·6	4·7 1·4	10·7 3·1	16·7 4·9
48	4 27·0	4 27·7	4 14·8	4·8 1·4	10·8 3·2	16·8 4·9
49	4 27·3	4 28·0	4 15·1	4·9 1·4	10·9 3·2	16·9 4·9
50	4 27·5	4 28·2	4 15·3	5·0 1·5	11·0 3·2	17·0 5·0
51	4 27·8	4 28·5	4 15·6	5·1 1·5	11·1 3·2	17·1 5·0
52	4 28·0	4 28·7	4 15·8	5·2 1·5	11·2 3·3	17·2 5·0
53	4 28·3	4 29·0	4 16·0	5·3 1·5	11·3 3·3	17·3 5·0
54	4 28·5	4 29·2	4 16·3	5·4 1·6	11·4 3·3	17·4 5·1
55	4 28·8	4 29·5	4 16·5	5·5 1·6	11·5 3·4	17·5 5·1
56	4 29·0	4 29·7	4 16·7	5·6 1·6	11·6 3·4	17·6 5·1
57	4 29·3	4 30·0	4 17·0	5·7 1·7	11·7 3·4	17·7 5·2
58	4 29·5	4 30·2	4 17·2	5·8 1·7	11·8 3·4	17·8 5·2
59	4 29·8	4 30·5	4 17·5	5·9 1·7	11·9 3·5	17·9 5·2
60	4 30·0	4 30·7	4 17·7	6·0 1·8	12·0 3·5	18·0 5·3

18ᵐ

18 (s)	SUN PLANETS	ARIES	MOON	v or d / Corrⁿ	v or d / Corrⁿ	v or d / Corrⁿ
	° ′	° ′	° ′	′ ′	′ ′	′ ′
00	4 30·0	4 30·7	4 17·7	0·0 0·0	6·0 1·9	12·0 3·7
01	4 30·3	4 31·0	4 17·9	0·1 0·0	6·1 1·9	12·1 3·7
02	4 30·5	4 31·2	4 18·2	0·2 0·1	6·2 1·9	12·2 3·8
03	4 30·8	4 31·5	4 18·4	0·3 0·1	6·3 1·9	12·3 3·8
04	4 31·0	4 31·7	4 18·7	0·4 0·1	6·4 2·0	12·4 3·8
05	4 31·3	4 32·0	4 18·9	0·5 0·2	6·5 2·0	12·5 3·9
06	4 31·5	4 32·2	4 19·1	0·6 0·2	6·6 2·0	12·6 3·9
07	4 31·8	4 32·5	4 19·4	0·7 0·2	6·7 2·1	12·7 3·9
08	4 32·0	4 32·7	4 19·6	0·8 0·2	6·8 2·1	12·8 3·9
09	4 32·3	4 33·0	4 19·8	0·9 0·3	6·9 2·1	12·9 4·0
10	4 32·5	4 33·2	4 20·1	1·0 0·3	7·0 2·2	13·0 4·0
11	4 32·8	4 33·5	4 20·3	1·1 0·3	7·1 2·2	13·1 4·0
12	4 33·0	4 33·7	4 20·6	1·2 0·4	7·2 2·2	13·2 4·1
13	4 33·3	4 34·0	4 20·8	1·3 0·4	7·3 2·3	13·3 4·1
14	4 33·5	4 34·2	4 21·0	1·4 0·4	7·4 2·3	13·4 4·1
15	4 33·8	4 34·5	4 21·3	1·5 0·5	7·5 2·3	13·5 4·2
16	4 34·0	4 34·8	4 21·5	1·6 0·5	7·6 2·3	13·6 4·2
17	4 34·3	4 35·0	4 21·8	1·7 0·5	7·7 2·4	13·7 4·2
18	4 34·5	4 35·3	4 22·0	1·8 0·6	7·8 2·4	13·8 4·3
19	4 34·8	4 35·5	4 22·2	1·9 0·6	7·9 2·4	13·9 4·3
20	4 35·0	4 35·8	4 22·5	2·0 0·6	8·0 2·5	14·0 4·3
21	4 35·3	4 36·0	4 22·7	2·1 0·6	8·1 2·5	14·1 4·3
22	4 35·5	4 36·3	4 22·9	2·2 0·7	8·2 2·5	14·2 4·4
23	4 35·8	4 36·5	4 23·2	2·3 0·7	8·3 2·6	14·3 4·4
24	4 36·0	4 36·8	4 23·4	2·4 0·7	8·4 2·6	14·4 4·4
25	4 36·3	4 37·0	4 23·7	2·5 0·8	8·5 2·6	14·5 4·5
26	4 36·5	4 37·3	4 23·9	2·6 0·8	8·6 2·7	14·6 4·5
27	4 36·8	4 37·5	4 24·1	2·7 0·8	8·7 2·7	14·7 4·5
28	4 37·0	4 37·8	4 24·4	2·8 0·9	8·8 2·7	14·8 4·6
29	4 37·3	4 38·0	4 24·6	2·9 0·9	8·9 2·7	14·9 4·6
30	4 37·5	4 38·3	4 24·9	3·0 0·9	9·0 2·8	15·0 4·6
31	4 37·8	4 38·5	4 25·1	3·1 1·0	9·1 2·8	15·1 4·7
32	4 38·0	4 38·8	4 25·3	3·2 1·0	9·2 2·8	15·2 4·7
33	4 38·3	4 39·0	4 25·6	3·3 1·0	9·3 2·9	15·3 4·7
34	4 38·5	4 39·3	4 25·8	3·4 1·0	9·4 2·9	15·4 4·7
35	4 38·8	4 39·5	4 26·1	3·5 1·1	9·5 2·9	15·5 4·8
36	4 39·0	4 39·8	4 26·3	3·6 1·1	9·6 3·0	15·6 4·8
37	4 39·3	4 40·0	4 26·5	3·7 1·1	9·7 3·0	15·7 4·8
38	4 39·5	4 40·3	4 26·8	3·8 1·2	9·8 3·0	15·8 4·9
39	4 39·8	4 40·5	4 27·0	3·9 1·2	9·9 3·1	15·9 4·9
40	4 40·0	4 40·8	4 27·2	4·0 1·2	10·0 3·1	16·0 4·9
41	4 40·3	4 41·0	4 27·5	4·1 1·3	10·1 3·1	16·1 5·0
42	4 40·5	4 41·3	4 27·7	4·2 1·3	10·2 3·1	16·2 5·0
43	4 40·8	4 41·5	4 28·0	4·3 1·3	10·3 3·2	16·3 5·0
44	4 41·0	4 41·8	4 28·2	4·4 1·4	10·4 3·2	16·4 5·1
45	4 41·3	4 42·0	4 28·4	4·5 1·4	10·5 3·2	16·5 5·1
46	4 41·5	4 42·3	4 28·7	4·6 1·4	10·6 3·3	16·6 5·1
47	4 41·8	4 42·5	4 28·9	4·7 1·4	10·7 3·3	16·7 5·1
48	4 42·0	4 42·8	4 29·2	4·8 1·5	10·8 3·3	16·8 5·2
49	4 42·3	4 43·0	4 29·4	4·9 1·5	10·9 3·4	16·9 5·2
50	4 42·5	4 43·3	4 29·6	5·0 1·5	11·0 3·4	17·0 5·2
51	4 42·8	4 43·5	4 29·9	5·1 1·6	11·1 3·4	17·1 5·3
52	4 43·0	4 43·8	4 30·1	5·2 1·6	11·2 3·5	17·2 5·3
53	4 43·3	4 44·0	4 30·3	5·3 1·6	11·3 3·5	17·3 5·3
54	4 43·5	4 44·3	4 30·6	5·4 1·7	11·4 3·5	17·4 5·4
55	4 43·8	4 44·5	4 30·8	5·5 1·7	11·5 3·5	17·5 5·4
56	4 44·0	4 44·8	4 31·1	5·6 1·7	11·6 3·6	17·6 5·4
57	4 44·3	4 45·0	4 31·3	5·7 1·8	11·7 3·6	17·7 5·5
58	4 44·5	4 45·3	4 31·5	5·8 1·8	11·8 3·6	17·8 5·5
59	4 44·8	4 45·5	4 31·8	5·9 1·8	11·9 3·7	17·9 5·5
60	4 45·0	4 45·8	4 32·0	6·0 1·9	12·0 3·7	18·0 5·6

19ᵐ

19 (s)	SUN PLANETS	ARIES	MOON	v or d / Corrⁿ	v or d / Corrⁿ	v or d / Corrⁿ
	° ′	° ′	° ′	′ ′	′ ′	′ ′
00	4 45·0	4 45·8	4 32·0	0·0 0·0	6·0 2·0	12·0 3·9
01	4 45·3	4 46·0	4 32·3	0·1 0·0	6·1 2·0	12·1 3·9
02	4 45·5	4 46·3	4 32·5	0·2 0·1	6·2 2·0	12·2 4·0
03	4 45·8	4 46·5	4 32·7	0·3 0·1	6·3 2·0	12·3 4·0
04	4 46·0	4 46·8	4 33·0	0·4 0·1	6·4 2·1	12·4 4·0
05	4 46·3	4 47·0	4 33·2	0·5 0·2	6·5 2·1	12·5 4·1
06	4 46·5	4 47·3	4 33·4	0·6 0·2	6·6 2·1	12·6 4·1
07	4 46·8	4 47·5	4 33·7	0·7 0·2	6·7 2·2	12·7 4·1
08	4 47·0	4 47·8	4 33·9	0·8 0·3	6·8 2·2	12·8 4·2
09	4 47·3	4 48·0	4 34·2	0·9 0·3	6·9 2·2	12·9 4·2
10	4 47·5	4 48·3	4 34·4	1·0 0·3	7·0 2·3	13·0 4·2
11	4 47·8	4 48·5	4 34·6	1·1 0·4	7·1 2·3	13·1 4·3
12	4 48·0	4 48·8	4 34·9	1·2 0·4	7·2 2·3	13·2 4·3
13	4 48·3	4 49·0	4 35·1	1·3 0·4	7·3 2·4	13·3 4·3
14	4 48·5	4 49·3	4 35·4	1·4 0·5	7·4 2·4	13·4 4·4
15	4 48·8	4 49·5	4 35·6	1·5 0·5	7·5 2·4	13·5 4·4
16	4 49·0	4 49·8	4 35·8	1·6 0·5	7·6 2·5	13·6 4·4
17	4 49·3	4 50·0	4 36·1	1·7 0·6	7·7 2·5	13·7 4·5
18	4 49·5	4 50·3	4 36·3	1·8 0·6	7·8 2·5	13·8 4·5
19	4 49·8	4 50·5	4 36·6	1·9 0·6	7·9 2·6	13·9 4·5
20	4 50·0	4 50·8	4 36·8	2·0 0·7	8·0 2·6	14·0 4·6
21	4 50·3	4 51·0	4 37·0	2·1 0·7	8·1 2·6	14·1 4·6
22	4 50·5	4 51·3	4 37·3	2·2 0·7	8·2 2·7	14·2 4·6
23	4 50·8	4 51·5	4 37·5	2·3 0·7	8·3 2·7	14·3 4·6
24	4 51·0	4 51·8	4 37·7	2·4 0·8	8·4 2·7	14·4 4·7
25	4 51·3	4 52·0	4 38·0	2·5 0·8	8·5 2·8	14·5 4·7
26	4 51·5	4 52·3	4 38·2	2·6 0·8	8·6 2·8	14·6 4·7
27	4 51·8	4 52·5	4 38·5	2·7 0·9	8·7 2·8	14·7 4·8
28	4 52·0	4 52·8	4 38·7	2·8 0·9	8·8 2·9	14·8 4·8
29	4 52·3	4 53·1	4 38·9	2·9 0·9	8·9 2·9	14·9 4·8
30	4 52·5	4 53·3	4 39·2	3·0 1·0	9·0 2·9	15·0 4·9
31	4 52·8	4 53·6	4 39·4	3·1 1·0	9·1 3·0	15·1 4·9
32	4 53·0	4 53·8	4 39·7	3·2 1·0	9·2 3·0	15·2 4·9
33	4 53·3	4 54·1	4 39·9	3·3 1·1	9·3 3·0	15·3 5·0
34	4 53·5	4 54·3	4 40·1	3·4 1·1	9·4 3·1	15·4 5·0
35	4 53·8	4 54·6	4 40·4	3·5 1·1	9·5 3·1	15·5 5·0
36	4 54·0	4 54·8	4 40·6	3·6 1·2	9·6 3·1	15·6 5·1
37	4 54·3	4 55·1	4 40·8	3·7 1·2	9·7 3·2	15·7 5·1
38	4 54·5	4 55·3	4 41·1	3·8 1·2	9·8 3·2	15·8 5·1
39	4 54·8	4 55·6	4 41·3	3·9 1·3	9·9 3·2	15·9 5·2
40	4 55·0	4 55·8	4 41·6	4·0 1·3	10·0 3·3	16·0 5·2
41	4 55·3	4 56·1	4 41·8	4·1 1·3	10·1 3·3	16·1 5·2
42	4 55·5	4 56·3	4 42·0	4·2 1·4	10·2 3·3	16·2 5·3
43	4 55·8	4 56·6	4 42·3	4·3 1·4	10·3 3·3	16·3 5·3
44	4 56·0	4 56·8	4 42·5	4·4 1·4	10·4 3·4	16·4 5·3
45	4 56·3	4 57·1	4 42·8	4·5 1·5	10·5 3·4	16·5 5·4
46	4 56·5	4 57·3	4 43·0	4·6 1·5	10·6 3·4	16·6 5·4
47	4 56·8	4 57·6	4 43·2	4·7 1·5	10·7 3·5	16·7 5·4
48	4 57·0	4 57·8	4 43·5	4·8 1·6	10·8 3·5	16·8 5·5
49	4 57·3	4 58·1	4 43·7	4·9 1·6	10·9 3·5	16·9 5·5
50	4 57·5	4 58·3	4 43·9	5·0 1·6	11·0 3·6	17·0 5·5
51	4 57·8	4 58·6	4 44·2	5·1 1·7	11·1 3·6	17·1 5·6
52	4 58·0	4 58·8	4 44·4	5·2 1·7	11·2 3·6	17·2 5·6
53	4 58·3	4 59·1	4 44·7	5·3 1·7	11·3 3·7	17·3 5·6
54	4 58·5	4 59·3	4 44·9	5·4 1·8	11·4 3·7	17·4 5·7
55	4 58·8	4 59·6	4 45·1	5·5 1·8	11·5 3·7	17·5 5·7
56	4 59·0	4 59·8	4 45·4	5·6 1·8	11·6 3·8	17·6 5·7
57	4 59·3	5 00·1	4 45·6	5·7 1·9	11·7 3·8	17·7 5·8
58	4 59·5	5 00·3	4 45·9	5·8 1·9	11·8 3·8	17·8 5·8
59	4 59·8	5 00·6	4 46·1	5·9 1·9	11·9 3·9	17·9 5·8
60	5 00·0	5 00·8	4 46·3	6·0 2·0	12·0 3·9	18·0 5·9

$\begin{array}{c}\text{m}\\20\end{array}$	SUN PLANETS	ARIES	MOON	$\begin{array}{c}v\\\text{or Corr}^n\\d\end{array}$		$\begin{array}{c}v\\\text{or Corr}^n\\d\end{array}$		$\begin{array}{c}v\\\text{or Corr}^n\\d\end{array}$	
s	° ′	° ′	° ′	′	′	′	′	′	′
00	5 00·0	5 00·8	4 46·3	0·0	0·0	6·0	2·1	12·0	4·1
01	5 00·3	5 01·1	4 46·6	0·1	0·0	6·1	2·1	12·1	4·1
02	5 00·5	5 01·3	4 46·8	0·2	0·1	6·2	2·1	12·2	4·2
03	5 00·8	5 01·6	4 47·0	0·3	0·1	6·3	2·2	12·3	4·2
04	5 01·0	5 01·8	4 47·3	0·4	0·1	6·4	2·2	12·4	4·2
05	5 01·3	5 02·1	4 47·5	0·5	0·2	6·5	2·2	12·5	4·3
06	5 01·5	5 02·3	4 47·8	0·6	0·2	6·6	2·3	12·6	4·3
07	5 01·8	5 02·6	4 48·0	0·7	0·2	6·7	2·3	12·7	4·3
08	5 02·0	5 02·8	4 48·2	0·8	0·3	6·8	2·3	12·8	4·4
09	5 02·3	5 03·1	4 48·5	0·9	0·3	6·9	2·4	12·9	4·4
10	5 02·5	5 03·3	4 48·7	1·0	0·3	7·0	2·4	13·0	4·4
11	5 02·8	5 03·6	4 49·0	1·1	0·4	7·1	2·4	13·1	4·5
12	5 03·0	5 03·8	4 49·2	1·2	0·4	7·2	2·5	13·2	4·5
13	5 03·3	5 04·1	4 49·4	1·3	0·4	7·3	2·5	13·3	4·5
14	5 03·5	5 04·3	4 49·7	1·4	0·5	7·4	2·5	13·4	4·6
15	5 03·8	5 04·6	4 49·9	1·5	0·5	7·5	2·6	13·5	4·6
16	5 04·0	5 04·8	4 50·2	1·6	0·5	7·6	2·6	13·6	4·6
17	5 04·3	5 05·1	4 50·4	1·7	0·6	7·7	2·6	13·7	4·7
18	5 04·5	5 05·3	4 50·6	1·8	0·6	7·8	2·7	13·8	4·7
19	5 04·8	5 05·6	4 50·9	1·9	0·6	7·9	2·7	13·9	4·7
20	5 05·0	5 05·8	4 51·1	2·0	0·7	8·0	2·7	14·0	4·8
21	5 05·3	5 06·1	4 51·3	2·1	0·7	8·1	2·8	14·1	4·8
22	5 05·5	5 06·3	4 51·6	2·2	0·8	8·2	2·8	14·2	4·9
23	5 05·8	5 06·6	4 51·8	2·3	0·8	8·3	2·8	14·3	4·9
24	5 06·0	5 06·8	4 52·1	2·4	0·8	8·4	2·9	14·4	4·9
25	5 06·3	5 07·1	4 52·3	2·5	0·9	8·5	2·9	14·5	5·0
26	5 06·5	5 07·3	4 52·5	2·6	0·9	8·6	2·9	14·6	5·0
27	5 06·8	5 07·6	4 52·8	2·7	0·9	8·7	3·0	14·7	5·0
28	5 07·0	5 07·8	4 53·0	2·8	1·0	8·8	3·0	14·8	5·1
29	5 07·3	5 08·1	4 53·3	2·9	1·0	8·9	3·0	14·9	5·1
30	5 07·5	5 08·3	4 53·5	3·0	1·0	9·0	3·1	15·0	5·1
31	5 07·8	5 08·6	4 53·7	3·1	1·1	9·1	3·1	15·1	5·2
32	5 08·0	5 08·8	4 54·0	3·2	1·1	9·2	3·1	15·2	5·2
33	5 08·3	5 09·1	4 54·2	3·3	1·1	9·3	3·2	15·3	5·2
34	5 08·5	5 09·3	4 54·4	3·4	1·2	9·4	3·2	15·4	5·3
35	5 08·8	5 09·6	4 54·7	3·5	1·2	9·5	3·2	15·5	5·3
36	5 09·0	5 09·8	4 54·9	3·6	1·2	9·6	3·3	15·6	5·3
37	5 09·3	5 10·1	4 55·2	3·7	1·3	9·7	3·3	15·7	5·4
38	5 09·5	5 10·3	4 55·4	3·8	1·3	9·8	3·3	15·8	5·4
39	5 09·8	5 10·6	4 55·6	3·9	1·3	9·9	3·4	15·9	5·4
40	5 10·0	5 10·8	4 55·9	4·0	1·4	10·0	3·4	16·0	5·5
41	5 10·3	5 11·1	4 56·1	4·1	1·4	10·1	3·5	16·1	5·5
42	5 10·5	5 11·4	4 56·4	4·2	1·4	10·2	3·5	16·2	5·5
43	5 10·8	5 11·6	4 56·6	4·3	1·5	10·3	3·5	16·3	5·6
44	5 11·0	5 11·9	4 56·8	4·4	1·5	10·4	3·6	16·4	5·6
45	5 11·3	5 12·1	4 57·1	4·5	1·5	10·5	3·6	16·5	5·6
46	5 11·5	5 12·4	4 57·3	4·6	1·6	10·6	3·6	16·6	5·7
47	5 11·8	5 12·6	4 57·5	4·7	1·6	10·7	3·7	16·7	5·7
48	5 12·0	5 12·9	4 57·8	4·8	1·6	10·8	3·7	16·8	5·7
49	5 12·3	5 13·1	4 58·0	4·9	1·7	10·9	3·7	16·9	5·8
50	5 12·5	5 13·4	4 58·3	5·0	1·7	11·0	3·8	17·0	5·8
51	5 12·8	5 13·6	4 58·5	5·1	1·7	11·1	3·8	17·1	5·8
52	5 13·0	5 13·9	4 58·7	5·2	1·8	11·2	3·8	17·2	5·9
53	5 13·3	5 14·1	4 59·0	5·3	1·8	11·3	3·9	17·3	5·9
54	5 13·5	5 14·4	4 59·2	5·4	1·8	11·4	3·9	17·4	5·9
55	5 13·8	5 14·6	4 59·5	5·5	1·9	11·5	3·9	17·5	6·0
56	5 14·0	5 14·9	4 59·7	5·6	1·9	11·6	4·0	17·6	6·0
57	5 14·3	5 15·1	4 59·9	5·7	1·9	11·7	4·0	17·7	6·0
58	5 14·5	5 15·4	5 00·2	5·8	2·0	11·8	4·0	17·8	6·1
59	5 14·8	5 15·6	5 00·4	5·9	2·0	11·9	4·1	17·9	6·1
60	5 15·0	5 15·9	5 00·7	6·0	2·1	12·0	4·1	18·0	6·2

$\begin{array}{c}\text{m}\\21\end{array}$	SUN PLANETS	ARIES	MOON	$\begin{array}{c}v\\\text{or Corr}^n\\d\end{array}$		$\begin{array}{c}v\\\text{or Corr}^n\\d\end{array}$		$\begin{array}{c}v\\\text{or Corr}^n\\d\end{array}$	
s	° ′	° ′	° ′	′	′	′	′	′	′
00	5 15·0	5 15·9	5 00·7	0·0	0·0	6·0	2·2	12·0	4·3
01	5 15·3	5 16·1	5 00·9	0·1	0·0	6·1	2·2	12·1	4·3
02	5 15·5	5 16·4	5 01·1	0·2	0·1	6·2	2·2	12·2	4·4
03	5 15·8	5 16·6	5 01·4	0·3	0·1	6·3	2·3	12·3	4·4
04	5 16·0	5 16·9	5 01·6	0·4	0·1	6·4	2·3	12·4	4·4
05	5 16·3	5 17·1	5 01·8	0·5	0·2	6·5	2·3	12·5	4·5
06	5 16·5	5 17·4	5 02·1	0·6	0·2	6·6	2·4	12·6	4·5
07	5 16·8	5 17·6	5 02·3	0·7	0·3	6·7	2·4	12·7	4·6
08	5 17·0	5 17·9	5 02·6	0·8	0·3	6·8	2·4	12·8	4·6
09	5 17·3	5 18·1	5 02·8	0·9	0·3	6·9	2·5	12·9	4·6
10	5 17·5	5 18·4	5 03·0	1·0	0·4	7·0	2·5	13·0	4·7
11	5 17·8	5 18·6	5 03·3	1·1	0·4	7·1	2·5	13·1	4·7
12	5 18·0	5 18·9	5 03·5	1·2	0·4	7·2	2·6	13·2	4·7
13	5 18·3	5 19·1	5 03·8	1·3	0·5	7·3	2·6	13·3	4·8
14	5 18·5	5 19·4	5 04·0	1·4	0·5	7·4	2·7	13·4	4·8
15	5 18·8	5 19·6	5 04·2	1·5	0·5	7·5	2·7	13·5	4·8
16	5 19·0	5 19·9	5 04·5	1·6	0·6	7·6	2·7	13·6	4·9
17	5 19·3	5 20·1	5 04·7	1·7	0·6	7·7	2·8	13·7	4·9
18	5 19·5	5 20·4	5 04·9	1·8	0·6	7·8	2·8	13·8	4·9
19	5 19·8	5 20·6	5 05·2	1·9	0·7	7·9	2·8	13·9	5·0
20	5 20·0	5 20·9	5 05·4	2·0	0·7	8·0	2·9	14·0	5·0
21	5 20·3	5 21·1	5 05·7	2·1	0·8	8·1	2·9	14·1	5·1
22	5 20·5	5 21·4	5 05·9	2·2	0·8	8·2	2·9	14·2	5·1
23	5 20·8	5 21·6	5 06·1	2·3	0·8	8·3	3·0	14·3	5·1
24	5 21·0	5 21·9	5 06·4	2·4	0·9	8·4	3·0	14·4	5·2
25	5 21·3	5 22·1	5 06·6	2·5	0·9	8·5	3·0	14·5	5·2
26	5 21·5	5 22·4	5 06·9	2·6	0·9	8·6	3·1	14·6	5·2
27	5 21·8	5 22·6	5 07·1	2·7	1·0	8·7	3·1	14·7	5·3
28	5 22·0	5 22·9	5 07·3	2·8	1·0	8·8	3·2	14·8	5·3
29	5 22·3	5 23·1	5 07·6	2·9	1·0	8·9	3·2	14·9	5·3
30	5 22·5	5 23·4	5 07·8	3·0	1·1	9·0	3·2	15·0	5·4
31	5 22·8	5 23·6	5 08·0	3·1	1·1	9·1	3·3	15·1	5·4
32	5 23·0	5 23·9	5 08·3	3·2	1·1	9·2	3·3	15·2	5·4
33	5 23·3	5 24·1	5 08·5	3·3	1·2	9·3	3·3	15·3	5·5
34	5 23·5	5 24·4	5 08·8	3·4	1·2	9·4	3·4	15·4	5·5
35	5 23·8	5 24·6	5 09·0	3·5	1·3	9·5	3·4	15·5	5·6
36	5 24·0	5 24·9	5 09·2	3·6	1·3	9·6	3·4	15·6	5·6
37	5 24·3	5 25·1	5 09·5	3·7	1·3	9·7	3·5	15·7	5·6
38	5 24·5	5 25·4	5 09·7	3·8	1·4	9·8	3·5	15·8	5·7
39	5 24·8	5 25·6	5 10·0	3·9	1·4	9·9	3·5	15·9	5·7
40	5 25·0	5 25·9	5 10·2	4·0	1·4	10·0	3·6	16·0	5·7
41	5 25·3	5 26·1	5 10·4	4·1	1·5	10·1	3·6	16·1	5·8
42	5 25·5	5 26·4	5 10·7	4·2	1·5	10·2	3·7	16·2	5·8
43	5 25·8	5 26·6	5 10·9	4·3	1·5	10·3	3·7	16·3	5·8
44	5 26·0	5 26·9	5 11·1	4·4	1·6	10·4	3·7	16·4	5·9
45	5 26·3	5 27·1	5 11·4	4·5	1·6	10·5	3·8	16·5	5·9
46	5 26·5	5 27·4	5 11·6	4·6	1·6	10·6	3·8	16·6	5·9
47	5 26·8	5 27·6	5 11·9	4·7	1·7	10·7	3·8	16·7	6·0
48	5 27·0	5 27·9	5 12·1	4·8	1·7	10·8	3·9	16·8	6·0
49	5 27·3	5 28·1	5 12·3	4·9	1·8	10·9	3·9	16·9	6·1
50	5 27·5	5 28·4	5 12·6	5·0	1·8	11·0	3·9	17·0	6·1
51	5 27·8	5 28·6	5 12·8	5·1	1·8	11·1	4·0	17·1	6·1
52	5 28·0	5 28·9	5 13·1	5·2	1·9	11·2	4·0	17·2	6·2
53	5 28·3	5 29·1	5 13·3	5·3	1·9	11·3	4·0	17·3	6·2
54	5 28·5	5 29·4	5 13·5	5·4	1·9	11·4	4·1	17·4	6·2
55	5 28·8	5 29·7	5 13·8	5·5	2·0	11·5	4·1	17·5	6·3
56	5 29·0	5 29·9	5 14·0	5·6	2·0	11·6	4·2	17·6	6·3
57	5 29·3	5 30·2	5 14·3	5·7	2·0	11·7	4·2	17·7	6·3
58	5 29·5	5 30·4	5 14·5	5·8	2·1	11·8	4·2	17·8	6·4
59	5 29·8	5 30·7	5 14·7	5·9	2·1	11·9	4·3	17·9	6·4
60	5 30·0	5 30·9	5 15·0	6·0	2·2	12·0	4·3	18·0	6·5

22ᵐ

22 s	SUN PLANETS	ARIES	MOON	v or Corrn d		v or Corrn d		v or Corrn d	
00	5 30.0	5 30.9	5 15.0	0.0	0.0	6.0	2.3	12.0	4.5
01	5 30.3	5 31.2	5 15.2	0.1	0.0	6.1	2.3	12.1	4.5
02	5 30.5	5 31.4	5 15.4	0.2	0.1	6.2	2.3	12.2	4.6
03	5 30.8	5 31.7	5 15.7	0.3	0.1	6.3	2.4	12.3	4.6
04	5 31.0	5 31.9	5 15.9	0.4	0.2	6.4	2.4	12.4	4.7
05	5 31.3	5 32.2	5 16.2	0.5	0.2	6.5	2.4	12.5	4.7
06	5 31.5	5 32.4	5 16.4	0.6	0.2	6.6	2.5	12.6	4.7
07	5 31.8	5 32.7	5 16.6	0.7	0.3	6.7	2.5	12.7	4.8
08	5 32.0	5 32.9	5 16.9	0.8	0.3	6.8	2.6	12.8	4.8
09	5 32.3	5 33.2	5 17.1	0.9	0.3	6.9	2.6	12.9	4.8
10	5 32.5	5 33.4	5 17.4	1.0	0.4	7.0	2.6	13.0	4.9
11	5 32.8	5 33.7	5 17.6	1.1	0.4	7.1	2.7	13.1	4.9
12	5 33.0	5 33.9	5 17.8	1.2	0.5	7.2	2.7	13.2	5.0
13	5 33.3	5 34.2	5 18.1	1.3	0.5	7.3	2.7	13.3	5.0
14	5 33.5	5 34.4	5 18.3	1.4	0.5	7.4	2.8	13.4	5.0
15	5 33.8	5 34.7	5 18.5	1.5	0.6	7.5	2.8	13.5	5.1
16	5 34.0	5 34.9	5 18.8	1.6	0.6	7.6	2.9	13.6	5.1
17	5 34.3	5 35.2	5 19.0	1.7	0.6	7.7	2.9	13.7	5.1
18	5 34.5	5 35.4	5 19.3	1.8	0.7	7.8	2.9	13.8	5.2
19	5 34.8	5 35.7	5 19.5	1.9	0.7	7.9	3.0	13.9	5.2
20	5 35.0	5 35.9	5 19.7	2.0	0.8	8.0	3.0	14.0	5.3
21	5 35.3	5 36.2	5 20.0	2.1	0.8	8.1	3.0	14.1	5.3
22	5 35.5	5 36.4	5 20.2	2.2	0.8	8.2	3.1	14.2	5.3
23	5 35.8	5 36.7	5 20.5	2.3	0.9	8.3	3.1	14.3	5.4
24	5 36.0	5 36.9	5 20.7	2.4	0.9	8.4	3.2	14.4	5.4
25	5 36.3	5 37.2	5 20.9	2.5	0.9	8.5	3.2	14.5	5.4
26	5 36.5	5 37.4	5 21.2	2.6	1.0	8.6	3.2	14.6	5.5
27	5 36.8	5 37.7	5 21.4	2.7	1.0	8.7	3.3	14.7	5.5
28	5 37.0	5 37.9	5 21.6	2.8	1.0	8.8	3.3	14.8	5.6
29	5 37.3	5 38.2	5 21.9	2.9	1.1	8.9	3.3	14.9	5.6
30	5 37.5	5 38.4	5 22.1	3.0	1.1	9.0	3.4	15.0	5.6
31	5 37.8	5 38.7	5 22.4	3.1	1.2	9.1	3.4	15.1	5.7
32	5 38.0	5 38.9	5 22.6	3.2	1.2	9.2	3.5	15.2	5.7
33	5 38.3	5 39.2	5 22.8	3.3	1.2	9.3	3.5	15.3	5.7
34	5 38.5	5 39.4	5 23.1	3.4	1.3	9.4	3.5	15.4	5.8
35	5 38.8	5 39.7	5 23.3	3.5	1.3	9.5	3.6	15.5	5.8
36	5 39.0	5 39.9	5 23.6	3.6	1.4	9.6	3.6	15.6	5.9
37	5 39.3	5 40.2	5 23.8	3.7	1.4	9.7	3.6	15.7	5.9
38	5 39.5	5 40.4	5 24.0	3.8	1.4	9.8	3.7	15.8	5.9
39	5 39.8	5 40.7	5 24.3	3.9	1.5	9.9	3.7	15.9	6.0
40	5 40.0	5 40.9	5 24.5	4.0	1.5	10.0	3.8	16.0	6.0
41	5 40.3	5 41.2	5 24.7	4.1	1.5	10.1	3.8	16.1	6.0
42	5 40.5	5 41.4	5 25.0	4.2	1.6	10.2	3.8	16.2	6.1
43	5 40.8	5 41.7	5 25.2	4.3	1.6	10.3	3.9	16.3	6.1
44	5 41.0	5 41.9	5 25.5	4.4	1.7	10.4	3.9	16.4	6.1
45	5 41.3	5 42.2	5 25.7	4.5	1.7	10.5	3.9	16.5	6.2
46	5 41.5	5 42.4	5 25.9	4.6	1.7	10.6	4.0	16.6	6.2
47	5 41.8	5 42.7	5 26.2	4.7	1.8	10.7	4.0	16.7	6.3
48	5 42.0	5 42.9	5 26.4	4.8	1.8	10.8	4.1	16.8	6.3
49	5 42.3	5 43.2	5 26.7	4.9	1.8	10.9	4.1	16.9	6.3
50	5 42.5	5 43.4	5 26.9	5.0	1.9	11.0	4.1	17.0	6.4
51	5 42.8	5 43.7	5 27.1	5.1	1.9	11.1	4.2	17.1	6.4
52	5 43.0	5 43.9	5 27.4	5.2	2.0	11.2	4.2	17.2	6.5
53	5 43.3	5 44.2	5 27.6	5.3	2.0	11.3	4.2	17.3	6.5
54	5 43.5	5 44.4	5 27.9	5.4	2.0	11.4	4.3	17.4	6.5
55	5 43.8	5 44.7	5 28.1	5.5	2.1	11.5	4.3	17.5	6.6
56	5 44.0	5 44.9	5 28.3	5.6	2.1	11.6	4.4	17.6	6.6
57	5 44.3	5 45.2	5 28.6	5.7	2.1	11.7	4.4	17.7	6.6
58	5 44.5	5 45.4	5 28.8	5.8	2.2	11.8	4.4	17.8	6.7
59	5 44.8	5 45.7	5 29.0	5.9	2.2	11.9	4.5	17.9	6.7
60	5 45.0	5 45.9	5 29.3	6.0	2.3	12.0	4.5	18.0	6.8

23ᵐ

23 s	SUN PLANETS	ARIES	MOON	v or Corrn d		v or Corrn d		v or Corrn d	
00	5 45.0	5 45.9	5 29.3	0.0	0.0	6.0	2.4	12.0	4.7
01	5 45.3	5 46.2	5 29.5	0.1	0.0	6.1	2.4	12.1	4.7
02	5 45.5	5 46.4	5 29.8	0.2	0.1	6.2	2.4	12.2	4.8
03	5 45.8	5 46.7	5 30.0	0.3	0.1	6.3	2.5	12.3	4.8
04	5 46.0	5 46.9	5 30.2	0.4	0.2	6.4	2.5	12.4	4.9
05	5 46.3	5 47.2	5 30.5	0.5	0.2	6.5	2.5	12.5	4.9
06	5 46.5	5 47.4	5 30.7	0.6	0.2	6.6	2.6	12.6	4.9
07	5 46.8	5 47.7	5 31.0	0.7	0.3	6.7	2.6	12.7	5.0
08	5 47.0	5 48.0	5 31.2	0.8	0.3	6.8	2.7	12.8	5.0
09	5 47.3	5 48.2	5 31.4	0.9	0.4	6.9	2.7	12.9	5.1
10	5 47.5	5 48.5	5 31.7	1.0	0.4	7.0	2.7	13.0	5.1
11	5 47.8	5 48.7	5 31.9	1.1	0.4	7.1	2.8	13.1	5.1
12	5 48.0	5 49.0	5 32.1	1.2	0.5	7.2	2.8	13.2	5.2
13	5 48.3	5 49.2	5 32.4	1.3	0.5	7.3	2.9	13.3	5.2
14	5 48.5	5 49.5	5 32.6	1.4	0.5	7.4	2.9	13.4	5.2
15	5 48.8	5 49.7	5 32.9	1.5	0.6	7.5	2.9	13.5	5.3
16	5 49.0	5 50.0	5 33.1	1.6	0.6	7.6	3.0	13.6	5.3
17	5 49.3	5 50.2	5 33.3	1.7	0.7	7.7	3.0	13.7	5.4
18	5 49.5	5 50.5	5 33.6	1.8	0.7	7.8	3.1	13.8	5.4
19	5 49.8	5 50.7	5 33.8	1.9	0.7	7.9	3.1	13.9	5.4
20	5 50.0	5 51.0	5 34.1	2.0	0.8	8.0	3.1	14.0	5.5
21	5 50.3	5 51.2	5 34.3	2.1	0.8	8.1	3.2	14.1	5.5
22	5 50.5	5 51.5	5 34.5	2.2	0.9	8.2	3.2	14.2	5.6
23	5 50.8	5 51.7	5 34.8	2.3	0.9	8.3	3.3	14.3	5.6
24	5 51.0	5 52.0	5 35.0	2.4	0.9	8.4	3.3	14.4	5.6
25	5 51.3	5 52.2	5 35.2	2.5	1.0	8.5	3.3	14.5	5.7
26	5 51.5	5 52.5	5 35.5	2.6	1.0	8.6	3.4	14.6	5.7
27	5 51.8	5 52.7	5 35.7	2.7	1.1	8.7	3.4	14.7	5.8
28	5 52.0	5 53.0	5 36.0	2.8	1.1	8.8	3.4	14.8	5.8
29	5 52.3	5 53.2	5 36.2	2.9	1.1	8.9	3.5	14.9	5.8
30	5 52.5	5 53.5	5 36.4	3.0	1.2	9.0	3.5	15.0	5.9
31	5 52.8	5 53.7	5 36.7	3.1	1.2	9.1	3.6	15.1	5.9
32	5 53.0	5 54.0	5 36.9	3.2	1.3	9.2	3.6	15.2	6.0
33	5 53.3	5 54.2	5 37.2	3.3	1.3	9.3	3.6	15.3	6.0
34	5 53.5	5 54.5	5 37.4	3.4	1.3	9.4	3.7	15.4	6.0
35	5 53.8	5 54.7	5 37.6	3.5	1.4	9.5	3.7	15.5	6.1
36	5 54.0	5 55.0	5 37.9	3.6	1.4	9.6	3.8	15.6	6.1
37	5 54.3	5 55.2	5 38.1	3.7	1.4	9.7	3.8	15.7	6.1
38	5 54.5	5 55.5	5 38.4	3.8	1.5	9.8	3.8	15.8	6.2
39	5 54.8	5 55.7	5 38.6	3.9	1.5	9.9	3.9	15.9	6.2
40	5 55.0	5 56.0	5 38.8	4.0	1.6	10.0	3.9	16.0	6.3
41	5 55.3	5 56.2	5 39.1	4.1	1.6	10.1	4.0	16.1	6.3
42	5 55.5	5 56.5	5 39.3	4.2	1.6	10.2	4.0	16.2	6.3
43	5 55.8	5 56.7	5 39.5	4.3	1.7	10.3	4.0	16.3	6.4
44	5 56.0	5 57.0	5 39.8	4.4	1.7	10.4	4.1	16.4	6.4
45	5 56.3	5 57.2	5 40.0	4.5	1.8	10.5	4.1	16.5	6.5
46	5 56.5	5 57.5	5 40.3	4.6	1.8	10.6	4.2	16.6	6.5
47	5 56.8	5 57.7	5 40.5	4.7	1.8	10.7	4.2	16.7	6.5
48	5 57.0	5 58.0	5 40.7	4.8	1.9	10.8	4.2	16.8	6.6
49	5 57.3	5 58.2	5 41.0	4.9	1.9	10.9	4.3	16.9	6.6
50	5 57.5	5 58.5	5 41.2	5.0	2.0	11.0	4.3	17.0	6.7
51	5 57.8	5 58.7	5 41.5	5.1	2.0	11.1	4.3	17.1	6.7
52	5 58.0	5 59.0	5 41.7	5.2	2.0	11.2	4.4	17.2	6.7
53	5 58.3	5 59.2	5 41.9	5.3	2.1	11.3	4.4	17.3	6.8
54	5 58.5	5 59.5	5 42.2	5.4	2.1	11.4	4.5	17.4	6.8
55	5 58.8	5 59.7	5 42.4	5.5	2.2	11.5	4.5	17.5	6.9
56	5 59.0	6 00.0	5 42.6	5.6	2.2	11.6	4.5	17.6	6.9
57	5 59.3	6 00.2	5 42.9	5.7	2.2	11.7	4.6	17.7	6.9
58	5 59.5	6 00.5	5 43.1	5.8	2.3	11.8	4.6	17.8	7.0
59	5 59.8	6 00.7	5 43.4	5.9	2.3	11.9	4.7	17.9	7.0
60	6 00.0	6 01.0	5 43.6	6.0	2.4	12.0	4.7	18.0	7.1

24^m	SUN PLANETS	ARIES	MOON	v or d Corr^n		v or d Corr^n		v or d Corr^n		25^m	SUN PLANETS	ARIES	MOON	v or d Corr^n		v or d Corr^n		v or d Corr^n	
s	° ′	° ′	° ′	′	′	′	′	′	′	s	° ′	° ′	° ′	′	′	′	′	′	′
00	6 00·0	6 01·0	5 43·6	0·0	0·0	6·0	2·5	12·0	4·9	00	6 15·0	6 16·0	5 57·9	0·0	0·0	6·0	2·6	12·0	5·1
01	6 00·3	6 01·2	5 43·8	0·1	0·0	6·1	2·5	12·1	4·9	01	6 15·3	6 16·3	5 58·2	0·1	0·0	6·1	2·6	12·1	5·1
02	6 00·5	6 01·5	5 44·1	0·2	0·1	6·2	2·5	12·2	5·0	02	6 15·5	6 16·5	5 58·4	0·2	0·1	6·2	2·6	12·2	5·2
03	6 00·8	6 01·7	5 44·3	0·3	0·1	6·3	2·6	12·3	5·0	03	6 15·8	6 16·8	5 58·6	0·3	0·1	6·3	2·7	12·3	5·2
04	6 01·0	6 02·0	5 44·6	0·4	0·2	6·4	2·6	12·4	5·1	04	6 16·0	6 17·0	5 58·9	0·4	0·2	6·4	2·7	12·4	5·3
05	6 01·3	6 02·2	5 44·8	0·5	0·2	6·5	2·7	12·5	5·1	05	6 16·3	6 17·3	5 59·1	0·5	0·2	6·5	2·8	12·5	5·3
06	6 01·5	6 02·5	5 45·0	0·6	0·2	6·6	2·7	12·6	5·1	06	6 16·5	6 17·5	5 59·3	0·6	0·3	6·6	2·8	12·6	5·4
07	6 01·8	6 02·7	5 45·3	0·7	0·3	6·7	2·7	12·7	5·2	07	6 16·8	6 17·8	5 59·6	0·7	0·3	6·7	2·8	12·7	5·4
08	6 02·0	6 03·0	5 45·5	0·8	0·3	6·8	2·8	12·8	5·2	08	6 17·0	6 18·0	5 59·8	0·8	0·3	6·8	2·9	12·8	5·4
09	6 02·3	6 03·2	5 45·7	0·9	0·4	6·9	2·8	12·9	5·3	09	6 17·3	6 18·3	6 00·1	0·9	0·4	6·9	2·9	12·9	5·5
10	6 02·5	6 03·5	5 46·0	1·0	0·4	7·0	2·9	13·0	5·3	10	6 17·5	6 18·5	6 00·3	1·0	0·4	7·0	3·0	13·0	5·5
11	6 02·8	6 03·7	5 46·2	1·1	0·4	7·1	2·9	13·1	5·3	11	6 17·8	6 18·8	6 00·5	1·1	0·5	7·1	3·0	13·1	5·6
12	6 03·0	6 04·0	5 46·5	1·2	0·5	7·2	2·9	13·2	5·4	12	6 18·0	6 19·0	6 00·8	1·2	0·5	7·2	3·1	13·2	5·6
13	6 03·3	6 04·2	5 46·7	1·3	0·5	7·3	3·0	13·3	5·4	13	6 18·3	6 19·3	6 01·0	1·3	0·6	7·3	3·1	13·3	5·7
14	6 03·5	6 04·5	5 46·9	1·4	0·6	7·4	3·0	13·4	5·5	14	6 18·5	6 19·5	6 01·3	1·4	0·6	7·4	3·1	13·4	5·7
15	6 03·8	6 04·7	5 47·2	1·5	0·6	7·5	3·1	13·5	5·5	15	6 18·8	6 19·8	6 01·5	1·5	0·6	7·5	3·2	13·5	5·7
16	6 04·0	6 05·0	5 47·4	1·6	0·7	7·6	3·1	13·6	5·6	16	6 19·0	6 20·0	6 01·7	1·6	0·7	7·6	3·2	13·6	5·8
17	6 04·3	6 05·2	5 47·7	1·7	0·7	7·7	3·1	13·7	5·6	17	6 19·3	6 20·3	6 02·0	1·7	0·7	7·7	3·3	13·7	5·8
18	6 04·5	6 05·5	5 47·9	1·8	0·7	7·8	3·2	13·8	5·6	18	6 19·5	6 20·5	6 02·2	1·8	0·8	7·8	3·3	13·8	5·9
19	6 04·8	6 05·7	5 48·1	1·9	0·8	7·9	3·2	13·9	5·7	19	6 19·8	6 20·8	6 02·5	1·9	0·8	7·9	3·4	13·9	5·9
20	6 05·0	6 06·0	5 48·4	2·0	0·8	8·0	3·3	14·0	5·7	20	6 20·0	6 21·0	6 02·7	2·0	0·9	8·0	3·4	14·0	6·0
21	6 05·3	6 06·3	5 48·6	2·1	0·9	8·1	3·3	14·1	5·8	21	6 20·3	6 21·3	6 02·9	2·1	0·9	8·1	3·4	14·1	6·0
22	6 05·5	6 06·5	5 48·8	2·2	0·9	8·2	3·3	14·2	5·8	22	6 20·5	6 21·5	6 03·2	2·2	0·9	8·2	3·5	14·2	6·0
23	6 05·8	6 06·8	5 49·1	2·3	0·9	8·3	3·4	14·3	5·8	23	6 20·8	6 21·8	6 03·4	2·3	1·0	8·3	3·5	14·3	6·1
24	6 06·0	6 07·0	5 49·3	2·4	1·0	8·4	3·4	14·4	5·9	24	6 21·0	6 22·0	6 03·6	2·4	1·0	8·4	3·6	14·4	6·1
25	6 06·3	6 07·3	5 49·6	2·5	1·0	8·5	3·5	14·5	5·9	25	6 21·3	6 22·3	6 03·9	2·5	1·1	8·5	3·6	14·5	6·2
26	6 06·5	6 07·5	5 49·8	2·6	1·1	8·6	3·5	14·6	6·0	26	6 21·5	6 22·5	6 04·1	2·6	1·1	8·6	3·7	14·6	6·2
27	6 06·8	6 07·8	5 50·0	2·7	1·1	8·7	3·6	14·7	6·0	27	6 21·8	6 22·8	6 04·4	2·7	1·1	8·7	3·7	14·7	6·2
28	6 07·0	6 08·0	5 50·3	2·8	1·1	8·8	3·6	14·8	6·0	28	6 22·0	6 23·0	6 04·6	2·8	1·2	8·8	3·7	14·8	6·3
29	6 07·3	6 08·3	5 50·5	2·9	1·2	8·9	3·6	14·9	6·1	29	6 22·3	6 23·3	6 04·8	2·9	1·2	8·9	3·8	14·9	6·3
30	6 07·5	6 08·5	5 50·8	3·0	1·2	9·0	3·7	15·0	6·1	30	6 22·5	6 23·5	6 05·1	3·0	1·3	9·0	3·8	15·0	6·4
31	6 07·8	6 08·8	5 51·0	3·1	1·3	9·1	3·7	15·1	6·2	31	6 22·8	6 23·8	6 05·3	3·1	1·3	9·1	3·9	15·1	6·4
32	6 08·0	6 09·0	5 51·2	3·2	1·3	9·2	3·8	15·2	6·2	32	6 23·0	6 24·0	6 05·6	3·2	1·4	9·2	3·9	15·2	6·5
33	6 08·3	6 09·3	5 51·5	3·3	1·3	9·3	3·8	15·3	6·2	33	6 23·3	6 24·3	6 05·8	3·3	1·4	9·3	4·0	15·3	6·5
34	6 08·5	6 09·5	5 51·7	3·4	1·4	9·4	3·8	15·4	6·3	34	6 23·5	6 24·5	6 06·0	3·4	1·4	9·4	4·0	15·4	6·5
35	6 08·8	6 09·8	5 52·0	3·5	1·4	9·5	3·9	15·5	6·3	35	6 23·8	6 24·8	6 06·3	3·5	1·5	9·5	4·0	15·5	6·6
36	6 09·0	6 10·0	5 52·2	3·6	1·5	9·6	3·9	15·6	6·4	36	6 24·0	6 25·1	6 06·5	3·6	1·5	9·6	4·1	15·6	6·6
37	6 09·3	6 10·3	5 52·4	3·7	1·5	9·7	4·0	15·7	6·4	37	6 24·3	6 25·3	6 06·7	3·7	1·6	9·7	4·1	15·7	6·7
38	6 09·5	6 10·5	5 52·7	3·8	1·6	9·8	4·0	15·8	6·5	38	6 24·5	6 25·6	6 07·0	3·8	1·6	9·8	4·2	15·8	6·7
39	6 09·8	6 10·8	5 52·9	3·9	1·6	9·9	4·0	15·9	6·5	39	6 24·8	6 25·8	6 07·2	3·9	1·7	9·9	4·2	15·9	6·8
40	6 10·0	6 11·0	5 53·1	4·0	1·6	10·0	4·1	16·0	6·5	40	6 25·0	6 26·1	6 07·5	4·0	1·7	10·0	4·3	16·0	6·8
41	6 10·3	6 11·3	5 53·4	4·1	1·7	10·1	4·1	16·1	6·6	41	6 25·3	6 26·3	6 07·7	4·1	1·7	10·1	4·3	16·1	6·8
42	6 10·5	6 11·5	5 53·6	4·2	1·7	10·2	4·2	16·2	6·6	42	6 25·5	6 26·6	6 07·9	4·2	1·8	10·2	4·3	16·2	6·9
43	6 10·8	6 11·8	5 53·9	4·3	1·8	10·3	4·2	16·3	6·7	43	6 25·8	6 26·8	6 08·2	4·3	1·8	10·3	4·4	16·3	6·9
44	6 11·0	6 12·0	5 54·1	4·4	1·8	10·4	4·2	16·4	6·7	44	6 26·0	6 27·1	6 08·4	4·4	1·9	10·4	4·4	16·4	7·0
45	6 11·3	6 12·3	5 54·3	4·5	1·8	10·5	4·3	16·5	6·7	45	6 26·3	6 27·3	6 08·7	4·5	1·9	10·5	4·5	16·5	7·0
46	6 11·5	6 12·5	5 54·6	4·6	1·9	10·6	4·3	16·6	6·8	46	6 26·5	6 27·6	6 08·9	4·6	2·0	10·6	4·5	16·6	7·1
47	6 11·8	6 12·8	5 54·8	4·7	1·9	10·7	4·4	16·7	6·8	47	6 26·8	6 27·8	6 09·1	4·7	2·0	10·7	4·5	16·7	7·1
48	6 12·0	6 13·0	5 55·1	4·8	2·0	10·8	4·4	16·8	6·9	48	6 27·0	6 28·1	6 09·4	4·8	2·0	10·8	4·6	16·8	7·1
49	6 12·3	6 13·3	5 55·3	4·9	2·0	10·9	4·5	16·9	6·9	49	6 27·3	6 28·3	6 09·6	4·9	2·1	10·9	4·6	16·9	7·2
50	6 12·5	6 13·5	5 55·5	5·0	2·0	11·0	4·5	17·0	6·9	50	6 27·5	6 28·6	6 09·8	5·0	2·1	11·0	4·7	17·0	7·2
51	6 12·8	6 13·8	5 55·8	5·1	2·1	11·1	4·5	17·1	7·0	51	6 27·8	6 28·8	6 10·1	5·1	2·2	11·1	4·7	17·1	7·3
52	6 13·0	6 14·0	5 56·0	5·2	2·1	11·2	4·6	17·2	7·0	52	6 28·0	6 29·1	6 10·3	5·2	2·2	11·2	4·8	17·2	7·3
53	6 13·3	6 14·3	5 56·2	5·3	2·2	11·3	4·6	17·3	7·1	53	6 28·3	6 29·3	6 10·6	5·3	2·3	11·3	4·8	17·3	7·4
54	6 13·5	6 14·5	5 56·5	5·4	2·2	11·4	4·7	17·4	7·1	54	6 28·5	6 29·6	6 10·8	5·4	2·3	11·4	4·8	17·4	7·4
55	6 13·8	6 14·8	5 56·7	5·5	2·2	11·5	4·7	17·5	7·1	55	6 28·8	6 29·8	6 11·0	5·5	2·3	11·5	4·9	17·5	7·4
56	6 14·0	6 15·0	5 57·0	5·6	2·3	11·6	4·7	17·6	7·2	56	6 29·0	6 30·1	6 11·3	5·6	2·4	11·6	4·9	17·6	7·5
57	6 14·3	6 15·3	5 57·2	5·7	2·3	11·7	4·8	17·7	7·2	57	6 29·3	6 30·3	6 11·5	5·7	2·4	11·7	5·0	17·7	7·5
58	6 14·5	6 15·5	5 57·4	5·8	2·4	11·8	4·8	17·8	7·3	58	6 29·5	6 30·6	6 11·8	5·8	2·5	11·8	5·0	17·8	7·6
59	6 14·8	6 15·8	5 57·7	5·9	2·4	11·9	4·9	17·9	7·3	59	6 29·8	6 30·8	6 12·0	5·9	2·5	11·9	5·1	17·9	7·6
60	6 15·0	6 16·0	5 57·9	6·0	2·5	12·0	4·9	18·0	7·4	60	6 30·0	6 31·1	6 12·2	6·0	2·6	12·0	5·1	18·0	7·7

26ᵐ

26	SUN PLANETS	ARIES	MOON	v or d	Corrⁿ	v or d	Corrⁿ	v or d	Corrⁿ
s	° ′	° ′	° ′	′	′	′	′	′	′
00	6 30·0	6 31·1	6 12·2	0·0	0·0	6·0	2·7	12·0	5·3
01	6 30·3	6 31·3	6 12·5	0·1	0·0	6·1	2·7	12·1	5·3
02	6 30·5	6 31·6	6 12·7	0·2	0·1	6·2	2·7	12·2	5·4
03	6 30·8	6 31·8	6 12·9	0·3	0·1	6·3	2·8	12·3	5·4
04	6 31·0	6 32·1	6 13·2	0·4	0·2	6·4	2·8	12·4	5·5
05	6 31·3	6 32·3	6 13·4	0·5	0·2	6·5	2·9	12·5	5·5
06	6 31·5	6 32·6	6 13·7	0·6	0·3	6·6	2·9	12·6	5·6
07	6 31·8	6 32·8	6 13·9	0·7	0·3	6·7	3·0	12·7	5·6
08	6 32·0	6 33·1	6 14·1	0·8	0·4	6·8	3·0	12·8	5·7
09	6 32·3	6 33·3	6 14·4	0·9	0·4	6·9	3·0	12·9	5·7
10	6 32·5	6 33·6	6 14·6	1·0	0·4	7·0	3·1	13·0	5·7
11	6 32·8	6 33·8	6 14·9	1·1	0·5	7·1	3·1	13·1	5·8
12	6 33·0	6 34·1	6 15·1	1·2	0·5	7·2	3·2	13·2	5·8
13	6 33·3	6 34·3	6 15·3	1·3	0·6	7·3	3·2	13·3	5·9
14	6 33·5	6 34·6	6 15·6	1·4	0·6	7·4	3·3	13·4	5·9
15	6 33·8	6 34·8	6 15·8	1·5	0·7	7·5	3·3	13·5	6·0
16	6 34·0	6 35·1	6 16·1	1·6	0·7	7·6	3·4	13·6	6·0
17	6 34·3	6 35·3	6 16·3	1·7	0·8	7·7	3·4	13·7	6·1
18	6 34·5	6 35·6	6 16·5	1·8	0·8	7·8	3·4	13·8	6·1
19	6 34·8	6 35·8	6 16·8	1·9	0·8	7·9	3·5	13·9	6·1
20	6 35·0	6 36·1	6 17·0	2·0	0·9	8·0	3·5	14·0	6·2
21	6 35·3	6 36·3	6 17·2	2·1	0·9	8·1	3·6	14·1	6·2
22	6 35·5	6 36·6	6 17·5	2·2	1·0	8·2	3·6	14·2	6·3
23	6 35·8	6 36·8	6 17·7	2·3	1·0	8·3	3·7	14·3	6·3
24	6 36·0	6 37·1	6 18·0	2·4	1·1	8·4	3·7	14·4	6·4
25	6 36·3	6 37·3	6 18·2	2·5	1·1	8·5	3·8	14·5	6·4
26	6 36·5	6 37·6	6 18·4	2·6	1·1	8·6	3·8	14·6	6·4
27	6 36·8	6 37·8	6 18·7	2·7	1·2	8·7	3·8	14·7	6·5
28	6 37·0	6 38·1	6 18·9	2·8	1·2	8·8	3·9	14·8	6·5
29	6 37·3	6 38·3	6 19·2	2·9	1·3	8·9	3·9	14·9	6·6
30	6 37·5	6 38·6	6 19·4	3·0	1·3	9·0	4·0	15·0	6·6
31	6 37·8	6 38·8	6 19·6	3·1	1·4	9·1	4·0	15·1	6·7
32	6 38·0	6 39·1	6 19·9	3·2	1·4	9·2	4·1	15·2	6·7
33	6 38·3	6 39·3	6 20·1	3·3	1·5	9·3	4·1	15·3	6·8
34	6 38·5	6 39·6	6 20·3	3·4	1·5	9·4	4·2	15·4	6·8
35	6 38·8	6 39·8	6 20·6	3·5	1·5	9·5	4·2	15·5	6·8
36	6 39·0	6 40·1	6 20·8	3·6	1·6	9·6	4·2	15·6	6·9
37	6 39·3	6 40·3	6 21·1	3·7	1·6	9·7	4·3	15·7	6·9
38	6 39·5	6 40·6	6 21·3	3·8	1·7	9·8	4·3	15·8	7·0
39	6 39·8	6 40·8	6 21·5	3·9	1·7	9·9	4·4	15·9	7·0
40	6 40·0	6 41·1	6 21·8	4·0	1·8	10·0	4·4	16·0	7·1
41	6 40·3	6 41·3	6 22·0	4·1	1·8	10·1	4·5	16·1	7·1
42	6 40·5	6 41·6	6 22·3	4·2	1·9	10·2	4·5	16·2	7·2
43	6 40·8	6 41·8	6 22·5	4·3	1·9	10·3	4·5	16·3	7·2
44	6 41·0	6 42·1	6 22·7	4·4	1·9	10·4	4·6	16·4	7·2
45	6 41·3	6 42·3	6 23·0	4·5	2·0	10·5	4·6	16·5	7·3
46	6 41·5	6 42·6	6 23·2	4·6	2·0	10·6	4·7	16·6	7·3
47	6 41·8	6 42·8	6 23·4	4·7	2·1	10·7	4·7	16·7	7·4
48	6 42·0	6 43·1	6 23·7	4·8	2·1	10·8	4·8	16·8	7·4
49	6 42·3	6 43·4	6 23·9	4·9	2·2	10·9	4·8	16·9	7·5
50	6 42·5	6 43·6	6 24·2	5·0	2·2	11·0	4·9	17·0	7·5
51	6 42·8	6 43·9	6 24·4	5·1	2·3	11·1	4·9	17·1	7·6
52	6 43·0	6 44·1	6 24·6	5·2	2·3	11·2	4·9	17·2	7·6
53	6 43·3	6 44·4	6 24·9	5·3	2·3	11·3	5·0	17·3	7·6
54	6 43·5	6 44·6	6 25·1	5·4	2·4	11·4	5·0	17·4	7·7
55	6 43·8	6 44·9	6 25·4	5·5	2·4	11·5	5·1	17·5	7·7
56	6 44·0	6 45·1	6 25·6	5·6	2·5	11·6	5·1	17·6	7·8
57	6 44·3	6 45·4	6 25·8	5·7	2·5	11·7	5·2	17·7	7·8
58	6 44·5	6 45·6	6 26·1	5·8	2·6	11·8	5·2	17·8	7·9
59	6 44·8	6 45·9	6 26·3	5·9	2·6	11·9	5·3	17·9	7·9
60	6 45·0	6 46·1	6 26·6	6·0	2·7	12·0	5·3	18·0	8·0

27ᵐ

27	SUN PLANETS	ARIES	MOON	v or d	Corrⁿ	v or d	Corrⁿ	v or d	Corrⁿ
s	° ′	° ′	° ′	′	′	′	′	′	′
00	6 45·0	6 46·1	6 26·6	0·0	0·0	6·0	2·8	12·0	5·5
01	6 45·3	6 46·4	6 26·8	0·1	0·0	6·1	2·8	12·1	5·5
02	6 45·5	6 46·6	6 27·0	0·2	0·1	6·2	2·8	12·2	5·6
03	6 45·8	6 46·9	6 27·3	0·3	0·1	6·3	2·9	12·3	5·6
04	6 46·0	6 47·1	6 27·5	0·4	0·2	6·4	2·9	12·4	5·7
05	6 46·3	6 47·4	6 27·7	0·5	0·2	6·5	3·0	12·5	5·7
06	6 46·5	6 47·6	6 28·0	0·6	0·3	6·6	3·0	12·6	5·8
07	6 46·8	6 47·9	6 28·2	0·7	0·3	6·7	3·1	12·7	5·8
08	6 47·0	6 48·1	6 28·5	0·8	0·4	6·8	3·1	12·8	5·9
09	6 47·3	6 48·4	6 28·7	0·9	0·4	6·9	3·2	12·9	5·9
10	6 47·5	6 48·6	6 28·9	1·0	0·5	7·0	3·2	13·0	6·0
11	6 47·8	6 48·9	6 29·2	1·1	0·5	7·1	3·3	13·1	6·0
12	6 48·0	6 49·1	6 29·4	1·2	0·6	7·2	3·3	13·2	6·1
13	6 48·3	6 49·4	6 29·7	1·3	0·6	7·3	3·3	13·3	6·1
14	6 48·5	6 49·6	6 29·9	1·4	0·6	7·4	3·4	13·4	6·1
15	6 48·8	6 49·9	6 30·1	1·5	0·7	7·5	3·4	13·5	6·2
16	6 49·0	6 50·1	6 30·4	1·6	0·7	7·6	3·5	13·6	6·2
17	6 49·3	6 50·4	6 30·6	1·7	0·8	7·7	3·5	13·7	6·3
18	6 49·5	6 50·6	6 30·8	1·8	0·8	7·8	3·6	13·8	6·3
19	6 49·8	6 50·9	6 31·1	1·9	0·9	7·9	3·6	13·9	6·4
20	6 50·0	6 51·1	6 31·3	2·0	0·9	8·0	3·7	14·0	6·4
21	6 50·3	6 51·4	6 31·6	2·1	1·0	8·1	3·7	14·1	6·5
22	6 50·5	6 51·6	6 31·8	2·2	1·0	8·2	3·8	14·2	6·5
23	6 50·8	6 51·9	6 32·0	2·3	1·1	8·3	3·8	14·3	6·6
24	6 51·0	6 52·1	6 32·3	2·4	1·1	8·4	3·9	14·4	6·6
25	6 51·3	6 52·4	6 32·5	2·5	1·1	8·5	3·9	14·5	6·6
26	6 51·5	6 52·6	6 32·8	2·6	1·2	8·6	3·9	14·6	6·7
27	6 51·8	6 52·9	6 33·0	2·7	1·2	8·7	4·0	14·7	6·7
28	6 52·0	6 53·1	6 33·2	2·8	1·3	8·8	4·0	14·8	6·8
29	6 52·3	6 53·4	6 33·5	2·9	1·3	8·9	4·1	14·9	6·8
30	6 52·5	6 53·6	6 33·7	3·0	1·4	9·0	4·1	15·0	6·9
31	6 52·8	6 53·9	6 33·9	3·1	1·4	9·1	4·2	15·1	6·9
32	6 53·0	6 54·1	6 34·2	3·2	1·5	9·2	4·2	15·2	7·0
33	6 53·3	6 54·4	6 34·4	3·3	1·5	9·3	4·3	15·3	7·0
34	6 53·5	6 54·6	6 34·7	3·4	1·6	9·4	4·3	15·4	7·1
35	6 53·8	6 54·9	6 34·9	3·5	1·6	9·5	4·4	15·5	7·1
36	6 54·0	6 55·1	6 35·1	3·6	1·7	9·6	4·4	15·6	7·2
37	6 54·3	6 55·4	6 35·4	3·7	1·7	9·7	4·4	15·7	7·2
38	6 54·5	6 55·6	6 35·6	3·8	1·7	9·8	4·5	15·8	7·2
39	6 54·8	6 55·9	6 35·9	3·9	1·8	9·9	4·5	15·9	7·3
40	6 55·0	6 56·1	6 36·1	4·0	1·8	10·0	4·6	16·0	7·3
41	6 55·3	6 56·4	6 36·3	4·1	1·9	10·1	4·6	16·1	7·4
42	6 55·5	6 56·6	6 36·6	4·2	1·9	10·2	4·7	16·2	7·4
43	6 55·8	6 56·9	6 36·8	4·3	2·0	10·3	4·7	16·3	7·5
44	6 56·0	6 57·1	6 37·0	4·4	2·0	10·4	4·8	16·4	7·5
45	6 56·3	6 57·4	6 37·3	4·5	2·1	10·5	4·8	16·5	7·6
46	6 56·5	6 57·6	6 37·5	4·6	2·1	10·6	4·9	16·6	7·6
47	6 56·8	6 57·9	6 37·8	4·7	2·2	10·7	4·9	16·7	7·7
48	6 57·0	6 58·1	6 38·0	4·8	2·2	10·8	5·0	16·8	7·7
49	6 57·3	6 58·4	6 38·2	4·9	2·2	10·9	5·0	16·9	7·7
50	6 57·5	6 58·6	6 38·5	5·0	2·3	11·0	5·0	17·0	7·8
51	6 57·8	6 58·9	6 38·7	5·1	2·3	11·1	5·1	17·1	7·8
52	6 58·0	6 59·1	6 39·0	5·2	2·4	11·2	5·1	17·2	7·9
53	6 58·3	6 59·4	6 39·2	5·3	2·4	11·3	5·2	17·3	7·9
54	6 58·5	6 59·6	6 39·4	5·4	2·5	11·4	5·2	17·4	8·0
55	6 58·8	6 59·9	6 39·7	5·5	2·5	11·5	5·3	17·5	8·0
56	6 59·0	7 00·1	6 39·9	5·6	2·6	11·6	5·3	17·6	8·1
57	6 59·3	7 00·4	6 40·2	5·7	2·6	11·7	5·4	17·7	8·1
58	6 59·5	7 00·6	6 40·4	5·8	2·7	11·8	5·4	17·8	8·2
59	6 59·8	7 00·9	6 40·6	5·9	2·7	11·9	5·5	17·9	8·2
60	7 00·0	7 01·1	6 40·9	6·0	2·8	12·0	5·5	18·0	8·3

28ᵐ

28 s	SUN PLANETS ° '	ARIES ° '	MOON ° '	v or d / Corrn '	v or d / Corrn '	v or d / Corrn '
00	7 00·0	7 01·1	6 40·9	0·0 0·0	6·0 2·9	12·0 5·7
01	7 00·3	7 01·4	6 41·1	0·1 0·0	6·1 2·9	12·1 5·7
02	7 00·5	7 01·7	6 41·3	0·2 0·1	6·2 2·9	12·2 5·8
03	7 00·8	7 01·9	6 41·6	0·3 0·1	6·3 3·0	12·3 5·8
04	7 01·0	7 02·2	6 41·8	0·4 0·2	6·4 3·0	12·4 5·9
05	7 01·3	7 02·4	6 42·1	0·5 0·2	6·5 3·1	12·5 5·9
06	7 01·5	7 02·7	6 42·3	0·6 0·3	6·6 3·1	12·6 6·0
07	7 01·8	7 02·9	6 42·5	0·7 0·3	6·7 3·2	12·7 6·0
08	7 02·0	7 03·2	6 42·8	0·8 0·4	6·8 3·2	12·8 6·1
09	7 02·3	7 03·4	6 43·0	0·9 0·4	6·9 3·3	12·9 6·1
10	7 02·5	7 03·7	6 43·3	1·0 0·5	7·0 3·3	13·0 6·2
11	7 02·8	7 03·9	6 43·5	1·1 0·5	7·1 3·4	13·1 6·2
12	7 03·0	7 04·2	6 43·7	1·2 0·6	7·2 3·4	13·2 6·3
13	7 03·3	7 04·4	6 44·0	1·3 0·6	7·3 3·5	13·3 6·3
14	7 03·5	7 04·7	6 44·2	1·4 0·7	7·4 3·5	13·4 6·4
15	7 03·8	7 04·9	6 44·4	1·5 0·7	7·5 3·6	13·5 6·4
16	7 04·0	7 05·2	6 44·7	1·6 0·8	7·6 3·6	13·6 6·5
17	7 04·3	7 05·4	6 44·9	1·7 0·8	7·7 3·7	13·7 6·5
18	7 04·5	7 05·7	6 45·2	1·8 0·9	7·8 3·7	13·8 6·6
19	7 04·8	7 05·9	6 45·4	1·9 0·9	7·9 3·8	13·9 6·6
20	7 05·0	7 06·2	6 45·6	2·0 1·0	8·0 3·8	14·0 6·7
21	7 05·3	7 06·4	6 45·9	2·1 1·0	8·1 3·8	14·1 6·7
22	7 05·5	7 06·7	6 46·1	2·2 1·0	8·2 3·9	14·2 6·7
23	7 05·8	7 06·9	6 46·4	2·3 1·1	8·3 3·9	14·3 6·8
24	7 06·0	7 07·2	6 46·6	2·4 1·1	8·4 4·0	14·4 6·8
25	7 06·3	7 07·4	6 46·8	2·5 1·2	8·5 4·0	14·5 6·9
26	7 06·5	7 07·7	6 47·1	2·6 1·2	8·6 4·1	14·6 6·9
27	7 06·8	7 07·9	6 47·3	2·7 1·3	8·7 4·1	14·7 7·0
28	7 07·0	7 08·2	6 47·5	2·8 1·3	8·8 4·2	14·8 7·0
29	7 07·3	7 08·4	6 47·8	2·9 1·4	8·9 4·2	14·9 7·1
30	7 07·5	7 08·7	6 48·0	3·0 1·4	9·0 4·3	15·0 7·1
31	7 07·8	7 08·9	6 48·3	3·1 1·5	9·1 4·3	15·1 7·2
32	7 08·0	7 09·2	6 48·5	3·2 1·5	9·2 4·4	15·2 7·2
33	7 08·3	7 09·4	6 48·7	3·3 1·6	9·3 4·4	15·3 7·3
34	7 08·5	7 09·7	6 49·0	3·4 1·6	9·4 4·5	15·4 7·3
35	7 08·8	7 09·9	6 49·2	3·5 1·7	9·5 4·5	15·5 7·4
36	7 09·0	7 10·2	6 49·5	3·6 1·7	9·6 4·6	15·6 7·4
37	7 09·3	7 10·4	6 49·7	3·7 1·8	9·7 4·6	15·7 7·5
38	7 09·5	7 10·7	6 49·9	3·8 1·8	9·8 4·7	15·8 7·5
39	7 09·8	7 10·9	6 50·2	3·9 1·9	9·9 4·7	15·9 7·6
40	7 10·0	7 11·2	6 50·4	4·0 1·9	10·0 4·8	16·0 7·6
41	7 10·3	7 11·4	6 50·6	4·1 1·9	10·1 4·8	16·1 7·6
42	7 10·5	7 11·7	6 50·9	4·2 2·0	10·2 4·8	16·2 7·7
43	7 10·8	7 11·9	6 51·1	4·3 2·0	10·3 4·9	16·3 7·7
44	7 11·0	7 12·2	6 51·4	4·4 2·1	10·4 4·9	16·4 7·8
45	7 11·3	7 12·4	6 51·6	4·5 2·1	10·5 5·0	16·5 7·8
46	7 11·5	7 12·7	6 51·8	4·6 2·2	10·6 5·0	16·6 7·9
47	7 11·8	7 12·9	6 52·1	4·7 2·2	10·7 5·1	16·7 7·9
48	7 12·0	7 13·2	6 52·3	4·8 2·3	10·8 5·1	16·8 8·0
49	7 12·3	7 13·4	6 52·6	4·9 2·3	10·9 5·2	16·9 8·0
50	7 12·5	7 13·7	6 52·8	5·0 2·4	11·0 5·2	17·0 8·1
51	7 12·8	7 13·9	6 53·0	5·1 2·4	11·1 5·3	17·1 8·1
52	7 13·0	7 14·2	6 53·3	5·2 2·5	11·2 5·3	17·2 8·2
53	7 13·3	7 14·4	6 53·5	5·3 2·5	11·3 5·4	17·3 8·2
54	7 13·5	7 14·7	6 53·8	5·4 2·6	11·4 5·4	17·4 8·3
55	7 13·8	7 14·9	6 54·0	5·5 2·6	11·5 5·5	17·5 8·3
56	7 14·0	7 15·2	6 54·2	5·6 2·7	11·6 5·5	17·6 8·4
57	7 14·3	7 15·4	6 54·5	5·7 2·7	11·7 5·6	17·7 8·4
58	7 14·5	7 15·7	6 54·7	5·8 2·8	11·8 5·6	17·8 8·5
59	7 14·8	7 15·9	6 54·9	5·9 2·8	11·9 5·7	17·9 8·5
60	7 15·0	7 16·2	6 55·2	6·0 2·9	12·0 5·7	18·0 8·6

29ᵐ

29 s	SUN PLANETS ° '	ARIES ° '	MOON ° '	v or d / Corrn '	v or d / Corrn '	v or d / Corrn '
00	7 15·0	7 16·2	6 55·2	0·0 0·0	6·0 3·0	12·0 5·9
01	7 15·3	7 16·4	6 55·4	0·1 0·0	6·1 3·0	12·1 5·9
02	7 15·5	7 16·7	6 55·7	0·2 0·1	6·2 3·0	12·2 6·0
03	7 15·8	7 16·9	6 55·9	0·3 0·1	6·3 3·1	12·3 6·0
04	7 16·0	7 17·2	6 56·1	0·4 0·2	6·4 3·1	12·4 6·1
05	7 16·3	7 17·4	6 56·4	0·5 0·2	6·5 3·2	12·5 6·1
06	7 16·5	7 17·7	6 56·6	0·6 0·3	6·6 3·2	12·6 6·2
07	7 16·8	7 17·9	6 56·9	0·7 0·3	6·7 3·3	12·7 6·2
08	7 17·0	7 18·2	6 57·1	0·8 0·4	6·8 3·3	12·8 6·3
09	7 17·3	7 18·4	6 57·3	0·9 0·4	6·9 3·4	12·9 6·3
10	7 17·5	7 18·7	6 57·6	1·0 0·5	7·0 3·4	13·0 6·4
11	7 17·8	7 18·9	6 57·8	1·1 0·5	7·1 3·5	13·1 6·4
12	7 18·0	7 19·2	6 58·0	1·2 0·6	7·2 3·5	13·2 6·5
13	7 18·3	7 19·4	6 58·3	1·3 0·6	7·3 3·6	13·3 6·5
14	7 18·5	7 19·7	6 58·5	1·4 0·7	7·4 3·6	13·4 6·5
15	7 18·8	7 20·0	6 58·8	1·5 0·7	7·5 3·7	13·5 6·6
16	7 19·0	7 20·2	6 59·0	1·6 0·8	7·6 3·7	13·6 6·7
17	7 19·3	7 20·5	6 59·2	1·7 0·8	7·7 3·8	13·7 6·7
18	7 19·5	7 20·7	6 59·5	1·8 0·9	7·8 3·8	13·8 6·8
19	7 19·8	7 21·0	6 59·7	1·9 0·9	7·9 3·9	13·9 6·8
20	7 20·0	7 21·2	7 00·0	2·0 1·0	8·0 3·9	14·0 6·9
21	7 20·3	7 21·5	7 00·2	2·1 1·0	8·1 4·0	14·1 6·9
22	7 20·5	7 21·7	7 00·4	2·2 1·1	8·2 4·0	14·2 7·0
23	7 20·8	7 22·0	7 00·7	2·3 1·1	8·3 4·1	14·3 7·0
24	7 21·0	7 22·2	7 00·9	2·4 1·2	8·4 4·1	14·4 7·1
25	7 21·3	7 22·5	7 01·1	2·5 1·2	8·5 4·2	14·5 7·1
26	7 21·5	7 22·7	7 01·4	2·6 1·3	8·6 4·2	14·6 7·2
27	7 21·8	7 23·0	7 01·6	2·7 1·3	8·7 4·3	14·7 7·2
28	7 22·0	7 23·2	7 01·9	2·8 1·4	8·8 4·3	14·8 7·3
29	7 22·3	7 23·5	7 02·1	2·9 1·4	8·9 4·4	14·9 7·3
30	7 22·5	7 23·7	7 02·3	3·0 1·5	9·0 4·4	15·0 7·4
31	7 22·8	7 24·0	7 02·6	3·1 1·5	9·1 4·5	15·1 7·4
32	7 23·0	7 24·2	7 02·8	3·2 1·6	9·2 4·5	15·2 7·5
33	7 23·3	7 24·5	7 03·1	3·3 1·6	9·3 4·6	15·3 7·5
34	7 23·5	7 24·7	7 03·3	3·4 1·7	9·4 4·6	15·4 7·6
35	7 23·8	7 25·0	7 03·5	3·5 1·7	9·5 4·7	15·5 7·6
36	7 24·0	7 25·2	7 03·8	3·6 1·8	9·6 4·7	15·6 7·7
37	7 24·3	7 25·5	7 04·0	3·7 1·8	9·7 4·8	15·7 7·7
38	7 24·5	7 25·7	7 04·3	3·8 1·9	9·8 4·8	15·8 7·8
39	7 24·8	7 26·0	7 04·5	3·9 1·9	9·9 4·9	15·9 7·8
40	7 25·0	7 26·2	7 04·7	4·0 2·0	10·0 4·9	16·0 7·9
41	7 25·3	7 26·5	7 05·0	4·1 2·0	10·1 5·0	16·1 7·9
42	7 25·5	7 26·7	7 05·2	4·2 2·1	10·2 5·0	16·2 8·0
43	7 25·8	7 27·0	7 05·4	4·3 2·1	10·3 5·1	16·3 8·0
44	7 26·0	7 27·2	7 05·7	4·4 2·2	10·4 5·1	16·4 8·1
45	7 26·3	7 27·5	7 05·9	4·5 2·2	10·5 5·2	16·5 8·1
46	7 26·5	7 27·7	7 06·2	4·6 2·3	10·6 5·2	16·6 8·2
47	7 26·8	7 28·0	7 06·4	4·7 2·3	10·7 5·3	16·7 8·2
48	7 27·0	7 28·2	7 06·6	4·8 2·4	10·8 5·3	16·8 8·3
49	7 27·3	7 28·5	7 06·9	4·9 2·4	10·9 5·4	16·9 8·3
50	7 27·5	7 28·7	7 07·1	5·0 2·5	11·0 5·4	17·0 8·4
51	7 27·8	7 29·0	7 07·4	5·1 2·5	11·1 5·5	17·1 8·4
52	7 28·0	7 29·2	7 07·6	5·2 2·6	11·2 5·5	17·2 8·5
53	7 28·3	7 29·5	7 07·8	5·3 2·6	11·3 5·6	17·3 8·5
54	7 28·5	7 29·7	7 08·1	5·4 2·7	11·4 5·6	17·4 8·6
55	7 28·8	7 30·0	7 08·3	5·5 2·7	11·5 5·7	17·5 8·6
56	7 29·0	7 30·2	7 08·5	5·6 2·8	11·6 5·7	17·6 8·7
57	7 29·3	7 30·5	7 08·8	5·7 2·8	11·7 5·8	17·7 8·7
58	7 29·5	7 30·7	7 09·0	5·8 2·9	11·8 5·8	17·8 8·8
59	7 29·8	7 31·0	7 09·3	5·9 2·9	11·9 5·9	17·9 8·8
60	7 30·0	7 31·2	7 09·5	6·0 3·0	12·0 5·9	18·0 8·9

30ᵐ

30 s	SUN PLANETS	ARIES	MOON	v or Corrⁿ d		v or Corrⁿ d		v or Corrⁿ d	
00	7 30·0	7 31·2	7 09·5	0·0	0·0	6·0	3·1	12·0	6·1
01	7 30·3	7 31·5	7 09·7	0·1	0·1	6·1	3·1	12·1	6·2
02	7 30·5	7 31·7	7 10·0	0·2	0·1	6·2	3·2	12·2	6·2
03	7 30·8	7 32·0	7 10·2	0·3	0·2	6·3	3·2	12·3	6·3
04	7 31·0	7 32·2	7 10·5	0·4	0·2	6·4	3·3	12·4	6·3
05	7 31·3	7 32·5	7 10·7	0·5	0·3	6·5	3·3	12·5	6·4
06	7 31·5	7 32·7	7 10·9	0·6	0·3	6·6	3·4	12·6	6·4
07	7 31·8	7 33·0	7 11·2	0·7	0·4	6·7	3·4	12·7	6·5
08	7 32·0	7 33·2	7 11·4	0·8	0·4	6·8	3·5	12·8	6·5
09	7 32·3	7 33·5	7 11·6	0·9	0·5	6·9	3·5	12·9	6·6
10	7 32·5	7 33·7	7 11·9	1·0	0·5	7·0	3·6	13·0	6·6
11	7 32·8	7 34·0	7 12·1	1·1	0·6	7·1	3·6	13·1	6·7
12	7 33·0	7 34·2	7 12·4	1·2	0·6	7·2	3·7	13·2	6·7
13	7 33·3	7 34·5	7 12·6	1·3	0·7	7·3	3·7	13·3	6·8
14	7 33·5	7 34·7	7 12·8	1·4	0·7	7·4	3·8	13·4	6·8
15	7 33·8	7 35·0	7 13·1	1·5	0·8	7·5	3·8	13·5	6·9
16	7 34·0	7 35·2	7 13·3	1·6	0·8	7·6	3·9	13·6	6·9
17	7 34·3	7 35·5	7 13·6	1·7	0·9	7·7	3·9	13·7	7·0
18	7 34·5	7 35·7	7 13·8	1·8	0·9	7·8	4·0	13·8	7·0
19	7 34·8	7 36·0	7 14·0	1·9	1·0	7·9	4·0	13·9	7·1
20	7 35·0	7 36·2	7 14·3	2·0	1·0	8·0	4·1	14·0	7·1
21	7 35·3	7 36·5	7 14·5	2·1	1·1	8·1	4·1	14·1	7·2
22	7 35·5	7 36·7	7 14·7	2·2	1·1	8·2	4·2	14·2	7·2
23	7 35·8	7 37·0	7 15·0	2·3	1·2	8·3	4·2	14·3	7·3
24	7 36·0	7 37·2	7 15·2	2·4	1·2	8·4	4·3	14·4	7·3
25	7 36·3	7 37·5	7 15·5	2·5	1·3	8·5	4·3	14·5	7·4
26	7 36·5	7 37·7	7 15·7	2·6	1·3	8·6	4·4	14·6	7·4
27	7 36·8	7 38·0	7 15·9	2·7	1·4	8·7	4·4	14·7	7·5
28	7 37·0	7 38·3	7 16·2	2·8	1·4	8·8	4·5	14·8	7·5
29	7 37·3	7 38·5	7 16·4	2·9	1·5	8·9	4·5	14·9	7·6
30	7 37·5	7 38·8	7 16·7	3·0	1·5	9·0	4·6	15·0	7·6
31	7 37·8	7 39·0	7 16·9	3·1	1·6	9·1	4·6	15·1	7·7
32	7 38·0	7 39·3	7 17·1	3·2	1·6	9·2	4·7	15·2	7·7
33	7 38·3	7 39·5	7 17·4	3·3	1·7	9·3	4·7	15·3	7·8
34	7 38·5	7 39·8	7 17·6	3·4	1·7	9·4	4·8	15·4	7·8
35	7 38·8	7 40·0	7 17·9	3·5	1·8	9·5	4·8	15·5	7·9
36	7 39·0	7 40·3	7 18·1	3·6	1·8	9·6	4·9	15·6	7·9
37	7 39·3	7 40·5	7 18·3	3·7	1·9	9·7	4·9	15·7	8·0
38	7 39·5	7 40·8	7 18·6	3·8	1·9	9·8	5·0	15·8	8·0
39	7 39·8	7 41·0	7 18·8	3·9	2·0	9·9	5·0	15·9	8·1
40	7 40·0	7 41·3	7 19·0	4·0	2·0	10·0	5·1	16·0	8·1
41	7 40·3	7 41·5	7 19·3	4·1	2·1	10·1	5·1	16·1	8·2
42	7 40·5	7 41·8	7 19·5	4·2	2·1	10·2	5·2	16·2	8·2
43	7 40·8	7 42·0	7 19·8	4·3	2·2	10·3	5·2	16·3	8·3
44	7 41·0	7 42·3	7 20·0	4·4	2·2	10·4	5·3	16·4	8·3
45	7 41·3	7 42·5	7 20·2	4·5	2·3	10·5	5·3	16·5	8·4
46	7 41·5	7 42·8	7 20·5	4·6	2·3	10·6	5·4	16·6	8·4
47	7 41·8	7 43·0	7 20·7	4·7	2·4	10·7	5·4	16·7	8·5
48	7 42·0	7 43·3	7 21·0	4·8	2·4	10·8	5·5	16·8	8·5
49	7 42·3	7 43·5	7 21·2	4·9	2·5	10·9	5·5	16·9	8·6
50	7 42·5	7 43·8	7 21·4	5·0	2·5	11·0	5·6	17·0	8·6
51	7 42·8	7 44·0	7 21·7	5·1	2·6	11·1	5·6	17·1	8·7
52	7 43·0	7 44·3	7 21·9	5·2	2·6	11·2	5·7	17·2	8·7
53	7 43·3	7 44·5	7 22·1	5·3	2·7	11·3	5·7	17·3	8·8
54	7 43·5	7 44·8	7 22·4	5·4	2·7	11·4	5·8	17·4	8·8
55	7 43·8	7 45·0	7 22·6	5·5	2·8	11·5	5·8	17·5	8·9
56	7 44·0	7 45·3	7 22·9	5·6	2·8	11·6	5·9	17·6	8·9
57	7 44·3	7 45·5	7 23·1	5·7	2·9	11·7	5·9	17·7	9·0
58	7 44·5	7 45·8	7 23·3	5·8	2·9	11·8	6·0	17·8	9·0
59	7 44·8	7 46·0	7 23·6	5·9	3·0	11·9	6·0	17·9	9·1
60	7 45·0	7 46·3	7 23·8	6·0	3·1	12·0	6·1	18·0	9·2

31ᵐ

31 s	SUN PLANETS	ARIES	MOON	v or Corrⁿ d		v or Corrⁿ d		v or Corrⁿ d	
00	7 45·0	7 46·3	7 23·8	0·0	0·0	6·0	3·2	12·0	6·3
01	7 45·3	7 46·5	7 24·1	0·1	0·1	6·1	3·2	12·1	6·4
02	7 45·5	7 46·8	7 24·3	0·2	0·1	6·2	3·3	12·2	6·4
03	7 45·8	7 47·0	7 24·5	0·3	0·2	6·3	3·3	12·3	6·5
04	7 46·0	7 47·3	7 24·8	0·4	0·2	6·4	3·4	12·4	6·5
05	7 46·3	7 47·5	7 25·0	0·5	0·3	6·5	3·4	12·5	6·6
06	7 46·5	7 47·8	7 25·2	0·6	0·3	6·6	3·5	12·6	6·6
07	7 46·8	7 48·0	7 25·5	0·7	0·4	6·7	3·5	12·7	6·7
08	7 47·0	7 48·3	7 25·7	0·8	0·4	6·8	3·6	12·8	6·7
09	7 47·3	7 48·5	7 26·0	0·9	0·5	6·9	3·6	12·9	6·8
10	7 47·5	7 48·8	7 26·2	1·0	0·5	7·0	3·7	13·0	6·8
11	7 47·8	7 49·0	7 26·4	1·1	0·6	7·1	3·7	13·1	6·9
12	7 48·0	7 49·3	7 26·7	1·2	0·6	7·2	3·8	13·2	6·9
13	7 48·3	7 49·5	7 26·9	1·3	0·7	7·3	3·8	13·3	7·0
14	7 48·5	7 49·8	7 27·2	1·4	0·7	7·4	3·9	13·4	7·0
15	7 48·8	7 50·0	7 27·4	1·5	0·8	7·5	3·9	13·5	7·1
16	7 49·0	7 50·3	7 27·6	1·6	0·8	7·6	4·0	13·6	7·1
17	7 49·3	7 50·5	7 27·9	1·7	0·9	7·7	4·0	13·7	7·2
18	7 49·5	7 50·8	7 28·1	1·8	0·9	7·8	4·1	13·8	7·2
19	7 49·8	7 51·0	7 28·4	1·9	1·0	7·9	4·1	13·9	7·3
20	7 50·0	7 51·3	7 28·6	2·0	1·1	8·0	4·2	14·0	7·4
21	7 50·3	7 51·5	7 28·8	2·1	1·1	8·1	4·3	14·1	7·4
22	7 50·5	7 51·8	7 29·1	2·2	1·2	8·2	4·3	14·2	7·5
23	7 50·8	7 52·0	7 29·3	2·3	1·2	8·3	4·4	14·3	7·5
24	7 51·0	7 52·3	7 29·5	2·4	1·3	8·4	4·4	14·4	7·6
25	7 51·3	7 52·5	7 29·8	2·5	1·3	8·5	4·5	14·5	7·6
26	7 51·5	7 52·8	7 30·0	2·6	1·4	8·6	4·5	14·6	7·7
27	7 51·8	7 53·0	7 30·3	2·7	1·4	8·7	4·6	14·7	7·7
28	7 52·0	7 53·3	7 30·5	2·8	1·5	8·8	4·6	14·8	7·8
29	7 52·3	7 53·5	7 30·7	2·9	1·5	8·9	4·7	14·9	7·8
30	7 52·5	7 53·8	7 31·0	3·0	1·6	9·0	4·7	15·0	7·9
31	7 52·8	7 54·0	7 31·2	3·1	1·6	9·1	4·8	15·1	7·9
32	7 53·0	7 54·3	7 31·5	3·2	1·7	9·2	4·8	15·2	8·0
33	7 53·3	7 54·5	7 31·7	3·3	1·7	9·3	4·9	15·3	8·0
34	7 53·5	7 54·8	7 31·9	3·4	1·8	9·4	4·9	15·4	8·1
35	7 53·8	7 55·0	7 32·2	3·5	1·8	9·5	5·0	15·5	8·1
36	7 54·0	7 55·3	7 32·4	3·6	1·9	9·6	5·0	15·6	8·2
37	7 54·3	7 55·5	7 32·6	3·7	1·9	9·7	5·1	15·7	8·2
38	7 54·5	7 55·8	7 32·9	3·8	2·0	9·8	5·1	15·8	8·3
39	7 54·8	7 56·0	7 33·1	3·9	2·0	9·9	5·2	15·9	8·3
40	7 55·0	7 56·3	7 33·4	4·0	2·1	10·0	5·3	16·0	8·4
41	7 55·3	7 56·6	7 33·6	4·1	2·2	10·1	5·3	16·1	8·5
42	7 55·5	7 56·8	7 33·8	4·2	2·2	10·2	5·4	16·2	8·5
43	7 55·8	7 57·1	7 34·1	4·3	2·3	10·3	5·4	16·3	8·6
44	7 56·0	7 57·3	7 34·3	4·4	2·3	10·4	5·5	16·4	8·6
45	7 56·3	7 57·6	7 34·6	4·5	2·4	10·5	5·5	16·5	8·7
46	7 56·5	7 57·8	7 34·8	4·6	2·4	10·6	5·6	16·6	8·7
47	7 56·8	7 58·1	7 35·0	4·7	2·5	10·7	5·6	16·7	8·8
48	7 57·0	7 58·3	7 35·3	4·8	2·5	10·8	5·7	16·8	8·8
49	7 57·3	7 58·6	7 35·5	4·9	2·6	10·9	5·7	16·9	8·9
50	7 57·5	7 58·8	7 35·7	5·0	2·6	11·0	5·8	17·0	8·9
51	7 57·8	7 59·1	7 36·0	5·1	2·7	11·1	5·8	17·1	9·0
52	7 58·0	7 59·3	7 36·2	5·2	2·7	11·2	5·9	17·2	9·0
53	7 58·3	7 59·6	7 36·5	5·3	2·8	11·3	5·9	17·3	9·1
54	7 58·5	7 59·8	7 36·7	5·4	2·8	11·4	6·0	17·4	9·1
55	7 58·8	8 00·1	7 36·9	5·5	2·9	11·5	6·0	17·5	9·2
56	7 59·0	8 00·3	7 37·2	5·6	2·9	11·6	6·1	17·6	9·2
57	7 59·3	8 00·6	7 37·4	5·7	3·0	11·7	6·1	17·7	9·3
58	7 59·5	8 00·8	7 37·7	5·8	3·0	11·8	6·2	17·8	9·3
59	7 59·8	8 01·1	7 37·9	5·9	3·1	11·9	6·2	17·9	9·4
60	8 00·0	8 01·3	7 38·1	6·0	3·2	12·0	6·3	18·0	9·5

32

m/s	SUN PLANETS	ARIES	MOON	v or Corrⁿ d		v or Corrⁿ d		v or Corrⁿ d	
s	° ′	° ′	° ′	′	′	′	′	′	′
00	8 00·0	8 01·3	7 38·1	0·0	0·0	6·0	3·3	12·0	6·5
01	8 00·3	8 01·6	7 38·4	0·1	0·1	6·1	3·3	12·1	6·6
02	8 00·5	8 01·8	7 38·6	0·2	0·1	6·2	3·4	12·2	6·6
03	8 00·8	8 02·1	7 38·8	0·3	0·2	6·3	3·4	12·3	6·7
04	8 01·0	8 02·3	7 39·1	0·4	0·2	6·4	3·5	12·4	6·7
05	8 01·3	8 02·6	7 39·3	0·5	0·3	6·5	3·5	12·5	6·8
06	8 01·5	8 02·8	7 39·6	0·6	0·3	6·6	3·6	12·6	6·8
07	8 01·8	8 03·1	7 39·8	0·7	0·4	6·7	3·6	12·7	6·9
08	8 02·0	8 03·3	7 40·0	0·8	0·4	6·8	3·7	12·8	6·9
09	8 02·3	8 03·6	7 40·3	0·9	0·5	6·9	3·7	12·9	7·0
10	8 02·5	8 03·8	7 40·5	1·0	0·5	7·0	3·8	13·0	7·0
11	8 02·8	8 04·1	7 40·8	1·1	0·6	7·1	3·8	13·1	7·1
12	8 03·0	8 04·3	7 41·0	1·2	0·7	7·2	3·9	13·2	7·2
13	8 03·3	8 04·6	7 41·2	1·3	0·7	7·3	4·0	13·3	7·2
14	8 03·5	8 04·8	7 41·5	1·4	0·8	7·4	4·0	13·4	7·3
15	8 03·8	8 05·1	7 41·7	1·5	0·8	7·5	4·1	13·5	7·3
16	8 04·0	8 05·3	7 42·0	1·6	0·9	7·6	4·1	13·6	7·4
17	8 04·3	8 05·6	7 42·2	1·7	0·9	7·7	4·2	13·7	7·4
18	8 04·5	8 05·8	7 42·4	1·8	1·0	7·8	4·2	13·8	7·5
19	8 04·8	8 06·1	7 42·7	1·9	1·0	7·9	4·3	13·9	7·5
20	8 05·0	8 06·3	7 42·9	2·0	1·1	8·0	4·3	14·0	7·6
21	8 05·3	8 06·6	7 43·1	2·1	1·1	8·1	4·4	14·1	7·6
22	8 05·5	8 06·8	7 43·4	2·2	1·2	8·2	4·4	14·2	7·7
23	8 05·8	8 07·1	7 43·6	2·3	1·2	8·3	4·5	14·3	7·7
24	8 06·0	8 07·3	7 43·9	2·4	1·3	8·4	4·6	14·4	7·8
25	8 06·3	8 07·6	7 44·1	2·5	1·4	8·5	4·6	14·5	7·9
26	8 06·5	8 07·8	7 44·3	2·6	1·4	8·6	4·7	14·6	7·9
27	8 06·8	8 08·1	7 44·6	2·7	1·5	8·7	4·7	14·7	8·0
28	8 07·0	8 08·3	7 44·8	2·8	1·5	8·8	4·8	14·8	8·0
29	8 07·3	8 08·6	7 45·1	2·9	1·6	8·9	4·8	14·9	8·1
30	8 07·5	8 08·8	7 45·3	3·0	1·6	9·0	4·9	15·0	8·1
31	8 07·8	8 09·1	7 45·5	3·1	1·7	9·1	4·9	15·1	8·2
32	8 08·0	8 09·3	7 45·8	3·2	1·7	9·2	5·0	15·2	8·2
33	8 08·3	8 09·6	7 46·0	3·3	1·8	9·3	5·0	15·3	8·3
34	8 08·5	8 09·8	7 46·2	3·4	1·8	9·4	5·1	15·4	8·3
35	8 08·8	8 10·1	7 46·5	3·5	1·9	9·5	5·1	15·5	8·4
36	8 09·0	8 10·3	7 46·7	3·6	2·0	9·6	5·2	15·6	8·5
37	8 09·3	8 10·6	7 47·0	3·7	2·0	9·7	5·3	15·7	8·5
38	8 09·5	8 10·8	7 47·2	3·8	2·1	9·8	5·3	15·8	8·6
39	8 09·8	8 11·1	7 47·4	3·9	2·1	9·9	5·4	15·9	8·6
40	8 10·0	8 11·3	7 47·7	4·0	2·2	10·0	5·4	16·0	8·7
41	8 10·3	8 11·6	7 47·9	4·1	2·2	10·1	5·5	16·1	8·7
42	8 10·5	8 11·8	7 48·2	4·2	2·3	10·2	5·5	16·2	8·8
43	8 10·8	8 12·1	7 48·4	4·3	2·3	10·3	5·6	16·3	8·8
44	8 11·0	8 12·3	7 48·6	4·4	2·4	10·4	5·6	16·4	8·9
45	8 11·3	8 12·6	7 48·9	4·5	2·4	10·5	5·7	16·5	8·9
46	8 11·5	8 12·8	7 49·1	4·6	2·5	10·6	5·7	16·6	9·0
47	8 11·8	8 13·1	7 49·3	4·7	2·5	10·7	5·8	16·7	9·0
48	8 12·0	8 13·3	7 49·6	4·8	2·6	10·8	5·9	16·8	9·1
49	8 12·3	8 13·6	7 49·8	4·9	2·7	10·9	5·9	16·9	9·2
50	8 12·5	8 13·8	7 50·1	5·0	2·7	11·0	6·0	17·0	9·2
51	8 12·8	8 14·1	7 50·3	5·1	2·8	11·1	6·0	17·1	9·3
52	8 13·0	8 14·3	7 50·5	5·2	2·8	11·2	6·1	17·2	9·3
53	8 13·3	8 14·6	7 50·8	5·3	2·9	11·3	6·1	17·3	9·4
54	8 13·5	8 14·9	7 51·0	5·4	2·9	11·4	6·2	17·4	9·4
55	8 13·8	8 15·1	7 51·3	5·5	3·0	11·5	6·2	17·5	9·5
56	8 14·0	8 15·4	7 51·5	5·6	3·0	11·6	6·3	17·6	9·5
57	8 14·3	8 15·6	7 51·7	5·7	3·1	11·7	6·3	17·7	9·6
58	8 14·5	8 15·9	7 52·0	5·8	3·1	11·8	6·4	17·8	9·6
59	8 14·8	8 16·1	7 52·2	5·9	3·2	11·9	6·4	17·9	9·7
60	8 15·0	8 16·4	7 52·5	6·0	3·3	12·0	6·5	18·0	9·8

33

m/s	SUN PLANETS	ARIES	MOON	v or Corrⁿ d		v or Corrⁿ d		v or Corrⁿ d	
s	° ′	° ′	° ′	′	′	′	′	′	′
00	8 15·0	8 16·4	7 52·5	0·0	0·0	6·0	3·4	12·0	6·7
01	8 15·3	8 16·6	7 52·7	0·1	0·1	6·1	3·4	12·1	6·8
02	8 15·5	8 16·9	7 52·9	0·2	0·1	6·2	3·5	12·2	6·8
03	8 15·8	8 17·1	7 53·2	0·3	0·2	6·3	3·5	12·3	6·9
04	8 16·0	8 17·4	7 53·4	0·4	0·2	6·4	3·6	12·4	6·9
05	8 16·3	8 17·6	7 53·6	0·5	0·3	6·5	3·6	12·5	7·0
06	8 16·5	8 17·9	7 53·9	0·6	0·3	6·6	3·7	12·6	7·0
07	8 16·8	8 18·1	7 54·1	0·7	0·4	6·7	3·7	12·7	7·1
08	8 17·0	8 18·4	7 54·4	0·8	0·4	6·8	3·8	12·8	7·1
09	8 17·3	8 18·6	7 54·6	0·9	0·5	6·9	3·9	12·9	7·2
10	8 17·5	8 18·9	7 54·8	1·0	0·6	7·0	3·9	13·0	7·3
11	8 17·8	8 19·1	7 55·1	1·1	0·6	7·1	4·0	13·1	7·3
12	8 18·0	8 19·4	7 55·3	1·2	0·7	7·2	4·0	13·2	7·4
13	8 18·3	8 19·6	7 55·5	1·3	0·7	7·3	4·1	13·3	7·4
14	8 18·5	8 19·9	7 55·8	1·4	0·8	7·4	4·1	13·4	7·5
15	8 18·8	8 20·1	7 56·0	1·5	0·8	7·5	4·2	13·5	7·5
16	8 19·0	8 20·4	7 56·3	1·6	0·9	7·6	4·2	13·6	7·6
17	8 19·3	8 20·6	7 56·5	1·7	0·9	7·7	4·3	13·7	7·6
18	8 19·5	8 20·9	7 56·7	1·8	1·0	7·8	4·4	13·8	7·7
19	8 19·8	8 21·1	7 57·0	1·9	1·1	7·9	4·4	13·9	7·7
20	8 20·0	8 21·4	7 57·2	2·0	1·1	8·0	4·5	14·0	7·8
21	8 20·3	8 21·6	7 57·5	2·1	1·2	8·1	4·5	14·1	7·9
22	8 20·5	8 21·9	7 57·7	2·2	1·2	8·2	4·6	14·2	7·9
23	8 20·8	8 22·1	7 57·9	2·3	1·3	8·3	4·6	14·3	8·0
24	8 21·0	8 22·4	7 58·2	2·4	1·3	8·4	4·7	14·4	8·0
25	8 21·3	8 22·6	7 58·4	2·5	1·4	8·5	4·7	14·5	8·1
26	8 21·5	8 22·9	7 58·7	2·6	1·5	8·6	4·8	14·6	8·2
27	8 21·8	8 23·1	7 58·9	2·7	1·5	8·7	4·9	14·7	8·2
28	8 22·0	8 23·4	7 59·1	2·8	1·6	8·8	4·9	14·8	8·3
29	8 22·3	8 23·6	7 59·4	2·9	1·6	8·9	5·0	14·9	8·3
30	8 22·5	8 23·9	7 59·6	3·0	1·7	9·0	5·0	15·0	8·4
31	8 22·8	8 24·1	7 59·8	3·1	1·7	9·1	5·1	15·1	8·4
32	8 23·0	8 24·4	8 00·1	3·2	1·8	9·2	5·1	15·2	8·5
33	8 23·3	8 24·6	8 00·3	3·3	1·8	9·3	5·2	15·3	8·5
34	8 23·5	8 24·9	8 00·6	3·4	1·9	9·4	5·2	15·4	8·6
35	8 23·8	8 25·1	8 00·8	3·5	2·0	9·5	5·3	15·5	8·7
36	8 24·0	8 25·4	8 01·0	3·6	2·0	9·6	5·4	15·6	8·7
37	8 24·3	8 25·6	8 01·3	3·7	2·1	9·7	5·4	15·7	8·8
38	8 24·5	8 25·9	8 01·5	3·8	2·1	9·8	5·5	15·8	8·8
39	8 24·8	8 26·1	8 01·8	3·9	2·2	9·9	5·5	15·9	8·9
40	8 25·0	8 26·4	8 02·0	4·0	2·2	10·0	5·6	16·0	8·9
41	8 25·3	8 26·6	8 02·2	4·1	2·3	10·1	5·6	16·1	9·0
42	8 25·5	8 26·9	8 02·5	4·2	2·3	10·2	5·7	16·2	9·0
43	8 25·8	8 27·1	8 02·7	4·3	2·4	10·3	5·8	16·3	9·1
44	8 26·0	8 27·4	8 02·9	4·4	2·5	10·4	5·8	16·4	9·2
45	8 26·3	8 27·6	8 03·2	4·5	2·5	10·5	5·9	16·5	9·2
46	8 26·5	8 27·9	8 03·4	4·6	2·6	10·6	5·9	16·6	9·3
47	8 26·8	8 28·1	8 03·7	4·7	2·6	10·7	6·0	16·7	9·3
48	8 27·0	8 28·4	8 03·9	4·8	2·7	10·8	6·0	16·8	9·4
49	8 27·3	8 28·6	8 04·1	4·9	2·7	10·9	6·1	16·9	9·4
50	8 27·5	8 28·9	8 04·4	5·0	2·8	11·0	6·1	17·0	9·5
51	8 27·8	8 29·1	8 04·6	5·1	2·8	11·1	6·2	17·1	9·5
52	8 28·0	8 29·4	8 04·9	5·2	2·9	11·2	6·3	17·2	9·6
53	8 28·3	8 29·6	8 05·1	5·3	3·0	11·3	6·3	17·3	9·7
54	8 28·5	8 29·9	8 05·3	5·4	3·0	11·4	6·4	17·4	9·7
55	8 28·8	8 30·1	8 05·6	5·5	3·1	11·5	6·4	17·5	9·8
56	8 29·0	8 30·4	8 05·8	5·6	3·1	11·6	6·5	17·6	9·8
57	8 29·3	8 30·6	8 06·1	5·7	3·2	11·7	6·5	17·7	9·9
58	8 29·5	8 30·9	8 06·3	5·8	3·2	11·8	6·6	17·8	9·9
59	8 29·8	8 31·1	8 06·5	5·9	3·3	11·9	6·6	17·9	10·0
60	8 30·0	8 31·4	8 06·8	6·0	3·4	12·0	6·7	18·0	10·1

34ᵐ	SUN PLANETS	ARIES	MOON	v or d Corrⁿ	v or d Corrⁿ	v or d Corrⁿ
s	° ′	° ′	° ′	′ ′	′ ′	′ ′
00	8 30·0	8 31·4	8 06·8	0·0 0·0	6·0 3·5	12·0 6·9
01	8 30·3	8 31·6	8 07·0	0·1 0·1	6·1 3·5	12·1 7·0
02	8 30·5	8 31·9	8 07·2	0·2 0·1	6·2 3·6	12·2 7·0
03	8 30·8	8 32·1	8 07·5	0·3 0·2	6·3 3·6	12·3 7·1
04	8 31·0	8 32·4	8 07·7	0·4 0·2	6·4 3·7	12·4 7·1
05	8 31·3	8 32·6	8 08·0	0·5 0·3	6·5 3·7	12·5 7·2
06	8 31·5	8 32·9	8 08·2	0·6 0·3	6·6 3·8	12·6 7·2
07	8 31·8	8 33·2	8 08·4	0·7 0·4	6·7 3·9	12·7 7·3
08	8 32·0	8 33·4	8 08·7	0·8 0·5	6·8 3·9	12·8 7·4
09	8 32·3	8 33·7	8 08·9	0·9 0·5	6·9 4·0	12·9 7·4
10	8 32·5	8 33·9	8 09·2	1·0 0·6	7·0 4·0	13·0 7·5
11	8 32·8	8 34·2	8 09·4	1·1 0·6	7·1 4·1	13·1 7·5
12	8 33·0	8 34·4	8 09·6	1·2 0·7	7·2 4·1	13·2 7·6
13	8 33·3	8 34·7	8 09·9	1·3 0·7	7·3 4·2	13·3 7·6
14	8 33·5	8 34·9	8 10·1	1·4 0·8	7·4 4·3	13·4 7·7
15	8 33·8	8 35·2	8 10·3	1·5 0·9	7·5 4·3	13·5 7·8
16	8 34·0	8 35·4	8 10·6	1·6 0·9	7·6 4·4	13·6 7·8
17	8 34·3	8 35·7	8 10·8	1·7 1·0	7·7 4·4	13·7 7·9
18	8 34·5	8 35·9	8 11·1	1·8 1·0	7·8 4·5	13·8 7·9
19	8 34·8	8 36·2	8 11·3	1·9 1·1	7·9 4·5	13·9 8·0
20	8 35·0	8 36·4	8 11·5	2·0 1·2	8·0 4·6	14·0 8·1
21	8 35·3	8 36·7	8 11·8	2·1 1·2	8·1 4·7	14·1 8·1
22	8 35·5	8 36·9	8 12·0	2·2 1·3	8·2 4·7	14·2 8·2
23	8 35·8	8 37·2	8 12·3	2·3 1·3	8·3 4·8	14·3 8·2
24	8 36·0	8 37·4	8 12·5	2·4 1·4	8·4 4·8	14·4 8·3
25	8 36·3	8 37·7	8 12·7	2·5 1·4	8·5 4·9	14·5 8·3
26	8 36·5	8 37·9	8 13·0	2·6 1·5	8·6 4·9	14·6 8·4
27	8 36·8	8 38·2	8 13·2	2·7 1·6	8·7 5·0	14·7 8·5
28	8 37·0	8 38·4	8 13·4	2·8 1·6	8·8 5·1	14·8 8·5
29	8 37·3	8 38·7	8 13·7	2·9 1·7	8·9 5·1	14·9 8·6
30	8 37·5	8 38·9	8 13·9	3·0 1·7	9·0 5·2	15·0 8·6
31	8 37·8	8 39·2	8 14·2	3·1 1·8	9·1 5·2	15·1 8·7
32	8 38·0	8 39·4	8 14·4	3·2 1·8	9·2 5·3	15·2 8·7
33	8 38·3	8 39·7	8 14·6	3·3 1·9	9·3 5·3	15·3 8·8
34	8 38·5	8 39·9	8 14·9	3·4 2·0	9·4 5·4	15·4 8·9
35	8 38·8	8 40·2	8 15·1	3·5 2·0	9·5 5·5	15·5 8·9
36	8 39·0	8 40·4	8 15·4	3·6 2·1	9·6 5·5	15·6 9·0
37	8 39·3	8 40·7	8 15·6	3·7 2·1	9·7 5·6	15·7 9·0
38	8 39·5	8 40·9	8 15·8	3·8 2·2	9·8 5·6	15·8 9·1
39	8 39·8	8 41·2	8 16·1	3·9 2·2	9·9 5·7	15·9 9·1
40	8 40·0	8 41·4	8 16·3	4·0 2·3	10·0 5·8	16·0 9·2
41	8 40·3	8 41·7	8 16·5	4·1 2·4	10·1 5·8	16·1 9·3
42	8 40·5	8 41·9	8 16·8	4·2 2·4	10·2 5·9	16·2 9·3
43	8 40·8	8 42·2	8 17·0	4·3 2·5	10·3 5·9	16·3 9·4
44	8 41·0	8 42·4	8 17·3	4·4 2·5	10·4 6·0	16·4 9·4
45	8 41·3	8 42·7	8 17·5	4·5 2·6	10·5 6·0	16·5 9·5
46	8 41·5	8 42·9	8 17·7	4·6 2·6	10·6 6·1	16·6 9·5
47	8 41·8	8 43·2	8 18·0	4·7 2·7	10·7 6·2	16·7 9·6
48	8 42·0	8 43·4	8 18·2	4·8 2·8	10·8 6·2	16·8 9·7
49	8 42·3	8 43·7	8 18·5	4·9 2·8	10·9 6·3	16·9 9·7
50	8 42·5	8 43·9	8 18·7	5·0 2·9	11·0 6·3	17·0 9·8
51	8 42·8	8 44·2	8 18·9	5·1 2·9	11·1 6·4	17·1 9·8
52	8 43·0	8 44·4	8 19·2	5·2 3·0	11·2 6·4	17·2 9·9
53	8 43·3	8 44·7	8 19·4	5·3 3·0	11·3 6·5	17·3 9·9
54	8 43·5	8 44·9	8 19·7	5·4 3·1	11·4 6·6	17·4 10·0
55	8 43·8	8 45·2	8 19·9	5·5 3·2	11·5 6·6	17·5 10·1
56	8 44·0	8 45·4	8 20·1	5·6 3·2	11·6 6·7	17·6 10·1
57	8 44·3	8 45·7	8 20·4	5·7 3·3	11·7 6·7	17·7 10·2
58	8 44·5	8 45·9	8 20·6	5·8 3·3	11·8 6·8	17·8 10·2
59	8 44·8	8 46·2	8 20·8	5·9 3·4	11·9 6·8	17·9 10·3
60	8 45·0	8 46·4	8 21·1	6·0 3·5	12·0 6·9	18·0 10·4

35ᵐ	SUN PLANETS	ARIES	MOON	v or d Corrⁿ	v or d Corrⁿ	v or d Corrⁿ
s	° ′	° ′	° ′	′ ′	′ ′	′ ′
00	8 45·0	8 46·4	8 21·1	0·0 0·0	6·0 3·6	12·0 7·1
01	8 45·3	8 46·7	8 21·3	0·1 0·1	6·1 3·6	12·1 7·2
02	8 45·5	8 46·9	8 21·6	0·2 0·1	6·2 3·7	12·2 7·2
03	8 45·8	8 47·2	8 21·8	0·3 0·2	6·3 3·7	12·3 7·3
04	8 46·0	8 47·4	8 22·0	0·4 0·2	6·4 3·8	12·4 7·3
05	8 46·3	8 47·7	8 22·3	0·5 0·3	6·5 3·8	12·5 7·4
06	8 46·5	8 47·9	8 22·5	0·6 0·4	6·6 3·9	12·6 7·5
07	8 46·8	8 48·2	8 22·8	0·7 0·4	6·7 4·0	12·7 7·5
08	8 47·0	8 48·4	8 23·0	0·8 0·5	6·8 4·0	12·8 7·6
09	8 47·3	8 48·7	8 23·2	0·9 0·5	6·9 4·1	12·9 7·6
10	8 47·5	8 48·9	8 23·5	1·0 0·6	7·0 4·1	13·0 7·7
11	8 47·8	8 49·2	8 23·7	1·1 0·7	7·1 4·2	13·1 7·8
12	8 48·0	8 49·4	8 23·9	1·2 0·7	7·2 4·3	13·2 7·8
13	8 48·3	8 49·7	8 24·2	1·3 0·8	7·3 4·3	13·3 7·9
14	8 48·5	8 49·9	8 24·4	1·4 0·8	7·4 4·4	13·4 7·9
15	8 48·8	8 50·2	8 24·7	1·5 0·9	7·5 4·4	13·5 8·0
16	8 49·0	8 50·4	8 24·9	1·6 0·9	7·6 4·5	13·6 8·0
17	8 49·3	8 50·7	8 25·1	1·7 1·0	7·7 4·6	13·7 8·1
18	8 49·5	8 50·9	8 25·4	1·8 1·1	7·8 4·6	13·8 8·2
19	8 49·8	8 51·2	8 25·6	1·9 1·1	7·9 4·7	13·9 8·2
20	8 50·0	8 51·5	8 25·9	2·0 1·2	8·0 4·7	14·0 8·3
21	8 50·3	8 51·7	8 26·1	2·1 1·2	8·1 4·8	14·1 8·3
22	8 50·5	8 52·0	8 26·3	2·2 1·3	8·2 4·9	14·2 8·4
23	8 50·8	8 52·2	8 26·6	2·3 1·4	8·3 4·9	14·3 8·5
24	8 51·0	8 52·5	8 26·8	2·4 1·4	8·4 5·0	14·4 8·5
25	8 51·3	8 52·7	8 27·0	2·5 1·5	8·5 5·0	14·5 8·6
26	8 51·5	8 53·0	8 27·3	2·6 1·5	8·6 5·1	14·6 8·6
27	8 51·8	8 53·2	8 27·5	2·7 1·6	8·7 5·1	14·7 8·7
28	8 52·0	8 53·5	8 27·8	2·8 1·7	8·8 5·2	14·8 8·8
29	8 52·3	8 53·7	8 28·0	2·9 1·7	8·9 5·3	14·9 8·8
30	8 52·5	8 54·0	8 28·2	3·0 1·8	9·0 5·3	15·0 8·9
31	8 52·8	8 54·2	8 28·5	3·1 1·8	9·1 5·4	15·1 8·9
32	8 53·0	8 54·5	8 28·7	3·2 1·9	9·2 5·4	15·2 9·0
33	8 53·3	8 54·7	8 29·0	3·3 2·0	9·3 5·5	15·3 9·1
34	8 53·5	8 55·0	8 29·2	3·4 2·0	9·4 5·6	15·4 9·1
35	8 53·8	8 55·2	8 29·4	3·5 2·1	9·5 5·6	15·5 9·2
36	8 54·0	8 55·5	8 29·7	3·6 2·1	9·6 5·7	15·6 9·2
37	8 54·3	8 55·7	8 29·9	3·7 2·2	9·7 5·7	15·7 9·3
38	8 54·5	8 56·0	8 30·2	3·8 2·2	9·8 5·8	15·8 9·3
39	8 54·8	8 56·2	8 30·4	3·9 2·3	9·9 5·9	15·9 9·4
40	8 55·0	8 56·5	8 30·6	4·0 2·4	10·0 5·9	16·0 9·5
41	8 55·3	8 56·7	8 30·9	4·1 2·4	10·1 6·0	16·1 9·5
42	8 55·5	8 57·0	8 31·1	4·2 2·5	10·2 6·0	16·2 9·6
43	8 55·8	8 57·2	8 31·3	4·3 2·5	10·3 6·1	16·3 9·6
44	8 56·0	8 57·5	8 31·6	4·4 2·6	10·4 6·2	16·4 9·7
45	8 56·3	8 57·7	8 31·8	4·5 2·7	10·5 6·2	16·5 9·8
46	8 56·5	8 58·0	8 32·1	4·6 2·7	10·6 6·3	16·6 9·8
47	8 56·8	8 58·2	8 32·3	4·7 2·8	10·7 6·3	16·7 9·9
48	8 57·0	8 58·5	8 32·5	4·8 2·8	10·8 6·4	16·8 9·9
49	8 57·3	8 58·7	8 32·8	4·9 2·9	10·9 6·4	16·9 10·0
50	8 57·5	8 59·0	8 33·0	5·0 3·0	11·0 6·5	17·0 10·1
51	8 57·8	8 59·2	8 33·3	5·1 3·0	11·1 6·6	17·1 10·1
52	8 58·0	8 59·5	8 33·5	5·2 3·1	11·2 6·6	17·2 10·2
53	8 58·3	8 59·7	8 33·7	5·3 3·1	11·3 6·7	17·3 10·2
54	8 58·5	9 00·0	8 34·0	5·4 3·2	11·4 6·7	17·4 10·3
55	8 58·8	9 00·2	8 34·2	5·5 3·3	11·5 6·8	17·5 10·4
56	8 59·0	9 00·5	8 34·4	5·6 3·3	11·6 6·9	17·6 10·4
57	8 59·3	9 00·7	8 34·7	5·7 3·4	11·7 6·9	17·7 10·5
58	8 59·5	9 01·0	8 34·9	5·8 3·4	11·8 7·0	17·8 10·5
59	8 59·8	9 01·2	8 35·2	5·9 3·5	11·9 7·0	17·9 10·6
60	9 00·0	9 01·5	8 35·4	6·0 3·6	12·0 7·1	18·0 10·7

36^m

s	SUN PLANETS	ARIES	MOON	v or d	Corrn	v or d	Corrn	v or d	Corrn
	° ′	° ′	° ′	′	′	′	′	′	′
00	9 00·0	9 01·5	8 35·4	0·0	0·0	6·0	3·7	12·0	7·3
01	9 00·3	9 01·7	8 35·6	0·1	0·1	6·1	3·7	12·1	7·4
02	9 00·5	9 02·0	8 35·9	0·2	0·1	6·2	3·8	12·2	7·4
03	9 00·8	9 02·2	8 36·1	0·3	0·2	6·3	3·8	12·3	7·5
04	9 01·0	9 02·5	8 36·4	0·4	0·2	6·4	3·9	12·4	7·5
05	9 01·3	9 02·7	8 36·6	0·5	0·3	6·5	4·0	12·5	7·6
06	9 01·5	9 03·0	8 36·8	0·6	0·4	6·6	4·0	12·6	7·7
07	9 01·8	9 03·2	8 37·1	0·7	0·4	6·7	4·1	12·7	7·7
08	9 02·0	9 03·5	8 37·3	0·8	0·5	6·8	4·1	12·8	7·8
09	9 02·3	9 03·7	8 37·5	0·9	0·5	6·9	4·2	12·9	7·8
10	9 02·5	9 04·0	8 37·8	1·0	0·6	7·0	4·3	13·0	7·9
11	9 02·8	9 04·2	8 38·0	1·1	0·7	7·1	4·3	13·1	8·0
12	9 03·0	9 04·5	8 38·3	1·2	0·7	7·2	4·4	13·2	8·0
13	9 03·3	9 04·7	8 38·5	1·3	0·8	7·3	4·4	13·3	8·1
14	9 03·5	9 05·0	8 38·7	1·4	0·9	7·4	4·5	13·4	8·2
15	9 03·8	9 05·2	8 39·0	1·5	0·9	7·5	4·6	13·5	8·2
16	9 04·0	9 05·5	8 39·2	1·6	1·0	7·6	4·6	13·6	8·3
17	9 04·3	9 05·7	8 39·5	1·7	1·0	7·7	4·7	13·7	8·3
18	9 04·5	9 06·0	8 39·7	1·8	1·1	7·8	4·7	13·8	8·4
19	9 04·8	9 06·2	8 39·9	1·9	1·2	7·9	4·8	13·9	8·5
20	9 05·0	9 06·5	8 40·2	2·0	1·2	8·0	4·9	14·0	8·5
21	9 05·3	9 06·7	8 40·4	2·1	1·3	8·1	4·9	14·1	8·6
22	9 05·5	9 07·0	8 40·6	2·2	1·3	8·2	5·0	14·2	8·6
23	9 05·8	9 07·2	8 40·9	2·3	1·4	8·3	5·0	14·3	8·7
24	9 06·0	9 07·5	8 41·1	2·4	1·5	8·4	5·1	14·4	8·8
25	9 06·3	9 07·7	8 41·4	2·5	1·5	8·5	5·2	14·5	8·8
26	9 06·5	9 08·0	8 41·6	2·6	1·6	8·6	5·2	14·6	8·9
27	9 06·8	9 08·2	8 41·8	2·7	1·6	8·7	5·3	14·7	8·9
28	9 07·0	9 08·5	8 42·1	2·8	1·7	8·8	5·3	14·8	9·0
29	9 07·3	9 08·7	8 42·3	2·9	1·8	8·9	5·4	14·9	9·1
30	9 07·5	9 09·0	8 42·6	3·0	1·8	9·0	5·5	15·0	9·1
31	9 07·8	9 09·2	8 42·8	3·1	1·9	9·1	5·5	15·1	9·2
32	9 08·0	9 09·5	8 43·0	3·2	1·9	9·2	5·6	15·2	9·2
33	9 08·3	9 09·8	8 43·3	3·3	2·0	9·3	5·7	15·3	9·3
34	9 08·5	9 10·0	8 43·5	3·4	2·1	9·4	5·7	15·4	9·4
35	9 08·8	9 10·3	8 43·8	3·5	2·1	9·5	5·8	15·5	9·4
36	9 09·0	9 10·5	8 44·0	3·6	2·2	9·6	5·8	15·6	9·5
37	9 09·3	9 10·8	8 44·2	3·7	2·3	9·7	5·9	15·7	9·6
38	9 09·5	9 11·0	8 44·5	3·8	2·3	9·8	6·0	15·8	9·6
39	9 09·8	9 11·3	8 44·7	3·9	2·4	9·9	6·0	15·9	9·7
40	9 10·0	9 11·5	8 44·9	4·0	2·4	10·0	6·1	16·0	9·7
41	9 10·3	9 11·8	8 45·2	4·1	2·5	10·1	6·1	16·1	9·8
42	9 10·5	9 12·0	8 45·4	4·2	2·6	10·2	6·2	16·2	9·9
43	9 10·8	9 12·3	8 45·7	4·3	2·6	10·3	6·3	16·3	9·9
44	9 11·0	9 12·5	8 45·9	4·4	2·7	10·4	6·3	16·4	10·0
45	9 11·3	9 12·8	8 46·1	4·5	2·7	10·5	6·4	16·5	10·0
46	9 11·5	9 13·0	8 46·4	4·6	2·8	10·6	6·4	16·6	10·1
47	9 11·8	9 13·3	8 46·6	4·7	2·9	10·7	6·5	16·7	10·2
48	9 12·0	9 13·5	8 46·9	4·8	2·9	10·8	6·6	16·8	10·2
49	9 12·3	9 13·8	8 47·1	4·9	3·0	10·9	6·6	16·9	10·3
50	9 12·5	9 14·0	8 47·3	5·0	3·0	11·0	6·7	17·0	10·3
51	9 12·8	9 14·3	8 47·6	5·1	3·1	11·1	6·8	17·1	10·4
52	9 13·0	9 14·5	8 47·8	5·2	3·2	11·2	6·8	17·2	10·5
53	9 13·3	9 14·8	8 48·0	5·3	3·2	11·3	6·9	17·3	10·5
54	9 13·5	9 15·0	8 48·3	5·4	3·3	11·4	6·9	17·4	10·6
55	9 13·8	9 15·3	8 48·5	5·5	3·3	11·5	7·0	17·5	10·6
56	9 14·0	9 15·5	8 48·8	5·6	3·4	11·6	7·1	17·6	10·7
57	9 14·3	9 15·8	8 49·0	5·7	3·5	11·7	7·1	17·7	10·8
58	9 14·5	9 16·0	8 49·2	5·8	3·5	11·8	7·2	17·8	10·8
59	9 14·8	9 16·3	8 49·5	5·9	3·6	11·9	7·2	17·9	10·9
60	9 15·0	9 16·5	8 49·7	6·0	3·7	12·0	7·3	18·0	11·0

37^m

s	SUN PLANETS	ARIES	MOON	v or d	Corrn	v or d	Corrn	v or d	Corrn
	° ′	° ′	° ′	′	′	′	′	′	′
00	9 15·0	9 16·5	8 49·7	0·0	0·0	6·0	3·8	12·0	7·5
01	9 15·3	9 16·8	8 50·0	0·1	0·1	6·1	3·8	12·1	7·6
02	9 15·5	9 17·0	8 50·2	0·2	0·1	6·2	3·9	12·2	7·6
03	9 15·8	9 17·3	8 50·4	0·3	0·2	6·3	3·9	12·3	7·7
04	9 16·0	9 17·5	8 50·7	0·4	0·3	6·4	4·0	12·4	7·8
05	9 16·3	9 17·8	8 50·9	0·5	0·3	6·5	4·1	12·5	7·8
06	9 16·5	9 18·0	8 51·1	0·6	0·4	6·6	4·1	12·6	7·9
07	9 16·8	9 18·3	8 51·4	0·7	0·4	6·7	4·2	12·7	7·9
08	9 17·0	9 18·5	8 51·6	0·8	0·5	6·8	4·3	12·8	8·0
09	9 17·3	9 18·8	8 51·9	0·9	0·6	6·9	4·3	12·9	8·1
10	9 17·5	9 19·0	8 52·1	1·0	0·6	7·0	4·4	13·0	8·1
11	9 17·8	9 19·3	8 52·3	1·1	0·7	7·1	4·4	13·1	8·2
12	9 18·0	9 19·5	8 52·6	1·2	0·8	7·2	4·5	13·2	8·3
13	9 18·3	9 19·8	8 52·8	1·3	0·8	7·3	4·6	13·3	8·3
14	9 18·5	9 20·0	8 53·1	1·4	0·9	7·4	4·6	13·4	8·4
15	9 18·8	9 20·3	8 53·3	1·5	0·9	7·5	4·7	13·5	8·4
16	9 19·0	9 20·5	8 53·5	1·6	1·0	7·6	4·8	13·6	8·5
17	9 19·3	9 20·8	8 53·8	1·7	1·1	7·7	4·8	13·7	8·6
18	9 19·5	9 21·0	8 54·0	1·8	1·1	7·8	4·9	13·8	8·6
19	9 19·8	9 21·3	8 54·3	1·9	1·2	7·9	4·9	13·9	8·7
20	9 20·0	9 21·5	8 54·5	2·0	1·3	8·0	5·0	14·0	8·8
21	9 20·3	9 21·8	8 54·7	2·1	1·3	8·1	5·1	14·1	8·8
22	9 20·5	9 22·0	8 55·0	2·2	1·4	8·2	5·1	14·2	8·9
23	9 20·8	9 22·3	8 55·2	2·3	1·4	8·3	5·2	14·3	8·9
24	9 21·0	9 22·5	8 55·4	2·4	1·5	8·4	5·3	14·4	9·0
25	9 21·3	9 22·8	8 55·7	2·5	1·6	8·5	5·3	14·5	9·1
26	9 21·5	9 23·0	8 55·9	2·6	1·6	8·6	5·4	14·6	9·1
27	9 21·8	9 23·3	8 56·2	2·7	1·7	8·7	5·4	14·7	9·2
28	9 22·0	9 23·5	8 56·4	2·8	1·8	8·8	5·5	14·8	9·3
29	9 22·3	9 23·8	8 56·6	2·9	1·8	8·9	5·6	14·9	9·3
30	9 22·5	9 24·0	8 56·9	3·0	1·9	9·0	5·6	15·0	9·4
31	9 22·8	9 24·3	8 57·1	3·1	1·9	9·1	5·7	15·1	9·4
32	9 23·0	9 24·5	8 57·4	3·2	2·0	9·2	5·8	15·2	9·5
33	9 23·3	9 24·8	8 57·6	3·3	2·1	9·3	5·8	15·3	9·6
34	9 23·5	9 25·0	8 57·8	3·4	2·1	9·4	5·9	15·4	9·6
35	9 23·8	9 25·3	8 58·1	3·5	2·2	9·5	5·9	15·5	9·7
36	9 24·0	9 25·5	8 58·3	3·6	2·3	9·6	6·0	15·6	9·8
37	9 24·3	9 25·8	8 58·5	3·7	2·3	9·7	6·1	15·7	9·8
38	9 24·5	9 26·0	8 58·8	3·8	2·4	9·8	6·1	15·8	9·9
39	9 24·8	9 26·3	8 59·0	3·9	2·4	9·9	6·2	15·9	9·9
40	9 25·0	9 26·5	8 59·3	4·0	2·5	10·0	6·3	16·0	10·0
41	9 25·3	9 26·8	8 59·5	4·1	2·6	10·1	6·3	16·1	10·1
42	9 25·5	9 27·0	8 59·7	4·2	2·6	10·2	6·4	16·2	10·1
43	9 25·8	9 27·3	9 00·0	4·3	2·7	10·3	6·4	16·3	10·2
44	9 26·0	9 27·5	9 00·2	4·4	2·8	10·4	6·5	16·4	10·3
45	9 26·3	9 27·8	9 00·5	4·5	2·8	10·5	6·6	16·5	10·3
46	9 26·5	9 28·1	9 00·7	4·6	2·9	10·6	6·6	16·6	10·4
47	9 26·8	9 28·3	9 00·9	4·7	2·9	10·7	6·7	16·7	10·4
48	9 27·0	9 28·6	9 01·2	4·8	3·0	10·8	6·8	16·8	10·5
49	9 27·3	9 28·8	9 01·4	4·9	3·1	10·9	6·8	16·9	10·6
50	9 27·5	9 29·1	9 01·6	5·0	3·1	11·0	6·9	17·0	10·6
51	9 27·8	9 29·3	9 01·9	5·1	3·2	11·1	6·9	17·1	10·7
52	9 28·0	9 29·6	9 02·1	5·2	3·3	11·2	7·0	17·2	10·8
53	9 28·3	9 29·8	9 02·4	5·3	3·3	11·3	7·1	17·3	10·8
54	9 28·5	9 30·1	9 02·6	5·4	3·4	11·4	7·1	17·4	10·9
55	9 28·8	9 30·3	9 02·8	5·5	3·4	11·5	7·2	17·5	10·9
56	9 29·0	9 30·6	9 03·1	5·6	3·5	11·6	7·3	17·6	11·0
57	9 29·3	9 30·8	9 03·3	5·7	3·6	11·7	7·3	17·7	11·1
58	9 29·5	9 31·1	9 03·6	5·8	3·6	11·8	7·4	17·8	11·1
59	9 29·8	9 31·3	9 03·8	5·9	3·7	11·9	7·4	17·9	11·2
60	9 30·0	9 31·6	9 04·0	6·0	3·8	12·0	7·5	18·0	11·3

38ᵐ

38ᵐ	SUN PLANETS	ARIES	MOON	v or d Corrⁿ		v or d Corrⁿ		v or d Corrⁿ	
s	° ′	° ′	° ′	′	′	′	′	′	′
00	9 30·0	9 31·6	9 04·0	0·0	0·0	6·0	3·9	12·0	7·7
01	9 30·3	9 31·8	9 04·3	0·1	0·1	6·1	3·9	12·1	7·8
02	9 30·5	9 32·1	9 04·5	0·2	0·1	6·2	4·0	12·2	7·8
03	9 30·8	9 32·3	9 04·7	0·3	0·2	6·3	4·0	12·3	7·9
04	9 31·0	9 32·6	9 05·0	0·4	0·3	6·4	4·1	12·4	8·0
05	9 31·3	9 32·8	9 05·2	0·5	0·3	6·5	4·2	12·5	8·0
06	9 31·5	9 33·1	9 05·5	0·6	0·4	6·6	4·2	12·6	8·1
07	9 31·8	9 33·3	9 05·7	0·7	0·4	6·7	4·3	12·7	8·1
08	9 32·0	9 33·6	9 05·9	0·8	0·5	6·8	4·4	12·8	8·2
09	9 32·3	9 33·8	9 06·2	0·9	0·6	6·9	4·4	12·9	8·3
10	9 32·5	9 34·1	9 06·4	1·0	0·6	7·0	4·5	13·0	8·3
11	9 32·8	9 34·3	9 06·7	1·1	0·7	7·1	4·6	13·1	8·4
12	9 33·0	9 34·6	9 06·9	1·2	0·8	7·2	4·6	13·2	8·5
13	9 33·3	9 34·8	9 07·1	1·3	0·8	7·3	4·7	13·3	8·5
14	9 33·5	9 35·1	9 07·4	1·4	0·9	7·4	4·7	13·4	8·6
15	9 33·8	9 35·3	9 07·6	1·5	1·0	7·5	4·8	13·5	8·7
16	9 34·0	9 35·6	9 07·9	1·6	1·0	7·6	4·9	13·6	8·7
17	9 34·3	9 35·8	9 08·1	1·7	1·1	7·7	4·9	13·7	8·8
18	9 34·5	9 36·1	9 08·3	1·8	1·2	7·8	5·0	13·8	8·9
19	9 34·8	9 36·3	9 08·6	1·9	1·2	7·9	5·1	13·9	8·9
20	9 35·0	9 36·6	9 08·8	2·0	1·3	8·0	5·1	14·0	9·0
21	9 35·3	9 36·8	9 09·0	2·1	1·3	8·1	5·2	14·1	9·0
22	9 35·5	9 37·1	9 09·3	2·2	1·4	8·2	5·3	14·2	9·1
23	9 35·8	9 37·3	9 09·5	2·3	1·5	8·3	5·3	14·3	9·2
24	9 36·0	9 37·6	9 09·8	2·4	1·5	8·4	5·4	14·4	9·2
25	9 36·3	9 37·8	9 10·0	2·5	1·6	8·5	5·5	14·5	9·3
26	9 36·5	9 38·1	9 10·2	2·6	1·7	8·6	5·5	14·6	9·4
27	9 36·8	9 38·3	9 10·5	2·7	1·7	8·7	5·6	14·7	9·4
28	9 37·0	9 38·6	9 10·7	2·8	1·8	8·8	5·6	14·8	9·5
29	9 37·3	9 38·8	9 11·0	2·9	1·9	8·9	5·7	14·9	9·6
30	9 37·5	9 39·1	9 11·2	3·0	1·9	9·0	5·8	15·0	9·6
31	9 37·8	9 39·3	9 11·4	3·1	2·0	9·1	5·8	15·1	9·7
32	9 38·0	9 39·6	9 11·7	3·2	2·1	9·2	5·9	15·2	9·8
33	9 38·3	9 39·8	9 11·9	3·3	2·1	9·3	6·0	15·3	9·8
34	9 38·5	9 40·1	9 12·1	3·4	2·2	9·4	6·0	15·4	9·9
35	9 38·8	9 40·3	9 12·4	3·5	2·2	9·5	6·1	15·5	9·9
36	9 39·0	9 40·6	9 12·6	3·6	2·3	9·6	6·2	15·6	10·0
37	9 39·3	9 40·8	9 12·9	3·7	2·4	9·7	6·2	15·7	10·1
38	9 39·5	9 41·1	9 13·1	3·8	2·4	9·8	6·3	15·8	10·1
39	9 39·8	9 41·3	9 13·3	3·9	2·5	9·9	6·4	15·9	10·2
40	9 40·0	9 41·6	9 13·6	4·0	2·6	10·0	6·4	16·0	10·3
41	9 40·3	9 41·8	9 13·8	4·1	2·6	10·1	6·5	16·1	10·3
42	9 40·5	9 42·1	9 14·1	4·2	2·7	10·2	6·5	16·2	10·4
43	9 40·8	9 42·3	9 14·3	4·3	2·8	10·3	6·6	16·3	10·5
44	9 41·0	9 42·6	9 14·5	4·4	2·8	10·4	6·7	16·4	10·5
45	9 41·3	9 42·8	9 14·8	4·5	2·9	10·5	6·7	16·5	10·6
46	9 41·5	9 43·1	9 15·0	4·6	3·0	10·6	6·8	16·6	10·7
47	9 41·8	9 43·3	9 15·2	4·7	3·0	10·7	6·9	16·7	10·7
48	9 42·0	9 43·6	9 15·5	4·8	3·1	10·8	6·9	16·8	10·8
49	9 42·3	9 43·8	9 15·7	4·9	3·1	10·9	7·0	16·9	10·8
50	9 42·5	9 44·1	9 16·0	5·0	3·2	11·0	7·1	17·0	10·9
51	9 42·8	9 44·3	9 16·2	5·1	3·3	11·1	7·1	17·1	11·0
52	9 43·0	9 44·6	9 16·4	5·2	3·3	11·2	7·2	17·2	11·0
53	9 43·3	9 44·8	9 16·7	5·3	3·4	11·3	7·3	17·3	11·1
54	9 43·5	9 45·1	9 16·9	5·4	3·5	11·4	7·3	17·4	11·2
55	9 43·8	9 45·3	9 17·2	5·5	3·5	11·5	7·4	17·5	11·2
56	9 44·0	9 45·6	9 17·4	5·6	3·6	11·6	7·4	17·6	11·3
57	9 44·3	9 45·8	9 17·6	5·7	3·7	11·7	7·5	17·7	11·4
58	9 44·5	9 46·1	9 17·9	5·8	3·7	11·8	7·6	17·8	11·4
59	9 44·8	9 46·4	9 18·1	5·9	3·8	11·9	7·6	17·9	11·5
60	9 45·0	9 46·6	9 18·4	6·0	3·9	12·0	7·7	18·0	11·6

39ᵐ

39ᵐ	SUN PLANETS	ARIES	MOON	v or d Corrⁿ		v or d Corrⁿ		v or d Corrⁿ	
s	° ′	° ′	° ′	′	′	′	′	′	′
00	9 45·0	9 46·6	9 18·4	0·0	0·0	6·0	4·0	12·0	7·9
01	9 45·3	9 46·9	9 18·6	0·1	0·1	6·1	4·0	12·1	8·0
02	9 45·5	9 47·1	9 18·8	0·2	0·1	6·2	4·1	12·2	8·0
03	9 45·8	9 47·4	9 19·1	0·3	0·2	6·3	4·1	12·3	8·1
04	9 46·0	9 47·6	9 19·3	0·4	0·3	6·4	4·2	12·4	8·2
05	9 46·3	9 47·9	9 19·5	0·5	0·3	6·5	4·3	12·5	8·2
06	9 46·5	9 48·1	9 19·8	0·6	0·4	6·6	4·3	12·6	8·3
07	9 46·8	9 48·4	9 20·0	0·7	0·5	6·7	4·4	12·7	8·4
08	9 47·0	9 48·6	9 20·3	0·8	0·5	6·8	4·5	12·8	8·4
09	9 47·3	9 48·9	9 20·5	0·9	0·6	6·9	4·5	12·9	8·5
10	9 47·5	9 49·1	9 20·7	1·0	0·7	7·0	4·6	13·0	8·6
11	9 47·8	9 49·4	9 21·0	1·1	0·7	7·1	4·7	13·1	8·6
12	9 48·0	9 49·6	9 21·2	1·2	0·8	7·2	4·7	13·2	8·7
13	9 48·3	9 49·9	9 21·5	1·3	0·9	7·3	4·8	13·3	8·8
14	9 48·5	9 50·1	9 21·7	1·4	0·9	7·4	4·9	13·4	8·8
15	9 48·8	9 50·4	9 21·9	1·5	1·0	7·5	4·9	13·5	8·9
16	9 49·0	9 50·6	9 22·2	1·6	1·1	7·6	5·0	13·6	9·0
17	9 49·3	9 50·9	9 22·4	1·7	1·1	7·7	5·1	13·7	9·0
18	9 49·5	9 51·1	9 22·6	1·8	1·2	7·8	5·1	13·8	9·1
19	9 49·8	9 51·4	9 22·9	1·9	1·3	7·9	5·2	13·9	9·2
20	9 50·0	9 51·6	9 23·1	2·0	1·3	8·0	5·3	14·0	9·2
21	9 50·3	9 51·9	9 23·4	2·1	1·4	8·1	5·3	14·1	9·3
22	9 50·5	9 52·1	9 23·6	2·2	1·4	8·2	5·4	14·2	9·3
23	9 50·8	9 52·4	9 23·8	2·3	1·5	8·3	5·5	14·3	9·4
24	9 51·0	9 52·6	9 24·1	2·4	1·6	8·4	5·5	14·4	9·5
25	9 51·3	9 52·9	9 24·3	2·5	1·6	8·5	5·6	14·5	9·5
26	9 51·5	9 53·1	9 24·6	2·6	1·7	8·6	5·7	14·6	9·6
27	9 51·8	9 53·4	9 24·8	2·7	1·8	8·7	5·7	14·7	9·7
28	9 52·0	9 53·6	9 25·0	2·8	1·8	8·8	5·8	14·8	9·7
29	9 52·3	9 53·9	9 25·3	2·9	1·9	8·9	5·9	14·9	9·8
30	9 52·5	9 54·1	9 25·5	3·0	2·0	9·0	5·9	15·0	9·9
31	9 52·8	9 54·4	9 25·7	3·1	2·0	9·1	6·0	15·1	9·9
32	9 53·0	9 54·6	9 26·0	3·2	2·1	9·2	6·1	15·2	10·0
33	9 53·3	9 54·9	9 26·2	3·3	2·2	9·3	6·1	15·3	10·1
34	9 53·5	9 55·1	9 26·5	3·4	2·2	9·4	6·2	15·4	10·1
35	9 53·8	9 55·4	9 26·7	3·5	2·3	9·5	6·3	15·5	10·2
36	9 54·0	9 55·6	9 26·9	3·6	2·4	9·6	6·3	15·6	10·3
37	9 54·3	9 55·9	9 27·2	3·7	2·4	9·7	6·4	15·7	10·3
38	9 54·5	9 56·1	9 27·4	3·8	2·5	9·8	6·5	15·8	10·4
39	9 54·8	9 56·4	9 27·7	3·9	2·6	9·9	6·5	15·9	10·5
40	9 55·0	9 56·6	9 27·9	4·0	2·6	10·0	6·6	16·0	10·5
41	9 55·3	9 56·9	9 28·1	4·1	2·7	10·1	6·6	16·1	10·6
42	9 55·5	9 57·1	9 28·4	4·2	2·8	10·2	6·7	16·2	10·7
43	9 55·8	9 57·4	9 28·6	4·3	2·8	10·3	6·8	16·3	10·7
44	9 56·0	9 57·6	9 28·8	4·4	2·9	10·4	6·8	16·4	10·8
45	9 56·3	9 57·9	9 29·1	4·5	3·0	10·5	6·9	16·5	10·9
46	9 56·5	9 58·1	9 29·3	4·6	3·0	10·6	7·0	16·6	10·9
47	9 56·8	9 58·4	9 29·6	4·7	3·1	10·7	7·0	16·7	11·0
48	9 57·0	9 58·6	9 29·8	4·8	3·2	10·8	7·1	16·8	11·1
49	9 57·3	9 58·9	9 30·0	4·9	3·2	10·9	7·2	16·9	11·1
50	9 57·5	9 59·1	9 30·3	5·0	3·3	11·0	7·2	17·0	11·2
51	9 57·8	9 59·4	9 30·5	5·1	3·4	11·1	7·3	17·1	11·3
52	9 58·0	9 59·6	9 30·8	5·2	3·4	11·2	7·4	17·2	11·3
53	9 58·3	9 59·9	9 31·0	5·3	3·5	11·3	7·4	17·3	11·4
54	9 58·5	10 00·1	9 31·2	5·4	3·6	11·4	7·5	17·4	11·5
55	9 58·8	10 00·4	9 31·5	5·5	3·6	11·5	7·6	17·5	11·5
56	9 59·0	10 00·6	9 31·7	5·6	3·7	11·6	7·6	17·6	11·6
57	9 59·3	10 00·9	9 32·0	5·7	3·8	11·7	7·7	17·7	11·7
58	9 59·5	10 01·1	9 32·2	5·8	3·8	11·8	7·8	17·8	11·7
59	9 59·8	10 01·4	9 32·4	5·9	3·9	11·9	7·8	17·9	11·8
60	10 00·0	10 01·6	9 32·7	6·0	4·0	12·0	7·9	18·0	11·9

40ᵐ

m 40 s	SUN PLANETS	ARIES	MOON	v or Corrⁿ d		v or Corrⁿ d		v or Corrⁿ d	
	° ′	° ′	° ′	′	′	′	′	′	′
00	10 00·0	10 01·6	9 32·7	0·0	0·0	6·0	4·1	12·0	8·1
01	10 00·3	10 01·9	9 32·9	0·1	0·1	6·1	4·1	12·1	8·2
02	10 00·5	10 02·1	9 33·1	0·2	0·1	6·2	4·2	12·2	8·2
03	10 00·8	10 02·4	9 33·4	0·3	0·2	6·3	4·3	12·3	8·3
04	10 01·0	10 02·6	9 33·6	0·4	0·3	6·4	4·3	12·4	8·4
05	10 01·3	10 02·9	9 33·9	0·5	0·3	6·5	4·4	12·5	8·4
06	10 01·5	10 03·1	9 34·1	0·6	0·4	6·6	4·5	12·6	8·5
07	10 01·8	10 03·4	9 34·3	0·7	0·5	6·7	4·5	12·7	8·6
08	10 02·0	10 03·6	9 34·6	0·8	0·5	6·8	4·6	12·8	8·6
09	10 02·3	10 03·9	9 34·8	0·9	0·6	6·9	4·7	12·9	8·7
10	10 02·5	10 04·1	9 35·1	1·0	0·7	7·0	4·7	13·0	8·8
11	10 02·8	10 04·4	9 35·3	1·1	0·7	7·1	4·8	13·1	8·8
12	10 03·0	10 04·7	9 35·5	1·2	0·8	7·2	4·9	13·2	8·9
13	10 03·3	10 04·9	9 35·8	1·3	0·9	7·3	4·9	13·3	9·0
14	10 03·5	10 05·2	9 36·0	1·4	0·9	7·4	5·0	13·4	9·0
15	10 03·8	10 05·4	9 36·2	1·5	1·0	7·5	5·1	13·5	9·1
16	10 04·0	10 05·7	9 36·5	1·6	1·1	7·6	5·1	13·6	9·2
17	10 04·3	10 05·9	9 36·7	1·7	1·1	7·7	5·2	13·7	9·2
18	10 04·5	10 06·2	9 37·0	1·8	1·2	7·8	5·3	13·8	9·3
19	10 04·8	10 06·4	9 37·2	1·9	1·3	7·9	5·3	13·9	9·4
20	10 05·0	10 06·7	9 37·4	2·0	1·4	8·0	5·4	14·0	9·5
21	10 05·3	10 06·9	9 37·7	2·1	1·4	8·1	5·5	14·1	9·5
22	10 05·5	10 07·2	9 37·9	2·2	1·5	8·2	5·5	14·2	9·6
23	10 05·8	10 07·4	9 38·2	2·3	1·6	8·3	5·6	14·3	9·7
24	10 06·0	10 07·7	9 38·4	2·4	1·6	8·4	5·7	14·4	9·7
25	10 06·3	10 07·9	9 38·6	2·5	1·7	8·5	5·7	14·5	9·8
26	10 06·5	10 08·2	9 38·9	2·6	1·8	8·6	5·8	14·6	9·9
27	10 06·8	10 08·4	9 39·1	2·7	1·8	8·7	5·9	14·7	9·9
28	10 07·0	10 08·7	9 39·3	2·8	1·9	8·8	5·9	14·8	10·0
29	10 07·3	10 08·9	9 39·6	2·9	2·0	8·9	6·0	14·9	10·1
30	10 07·5	10 09·2	9 39·8	3·0	2·0	9·0	6·1	15·0	10·1
31	10 07·8	10 09·4	9 40·1	3·1	2·1	9·1	6·1	15·1	10·2
32	10 08·0	10 09·7	9 40·3	3·2	2·2	9·2	6·2	15·2	10·3
33	10 08·3	10 09·9	9 40·5	3·3	2·2	9·3	6·3	15·3	10·3
34	10 08·5	10 10·2	9 40·8	3·4	2·3	9·4	6·3	15·4	10·4
35	10 08·8	10 10·4	9 41·0	3·5	2·4	9·5	6·4	15·5	10·5
36	10 09·0	10 10·7	9 41·3	3·6	2·4	9·6	6·5	15·6	10·5
37	10 09·3	10 10·9	9 41·5	3·7	2·5	9·7	6·5	15·7	10·6
38	10 09·5	10 11·2	9 41·7	3·8	2·6	9·8	6·6	15·8	10·7
39	10 09·8	10 11·4	9 42·0	3·9	2·6	9·9	6·7	15·9	10·7
40	10 10·0	10 11·7	9 42·2	4·0	2·7	10·0	6·8	16·0	10·8
41	10 10·3	10 11·9	9 42·4	4·1	2·8	10·1	6·8	16·1	10·9
42	10 10·5	10 12·2	9 42·7	4·2	2·8	10·2	6·9	16·2	10·9
43	10 10·8	10 12·4	9 42·9	4·3	2·9	10·3	7·0	16·3	11·0
44	10 11·0	10 12·7	9 43·2	4·4	3·0	10·4	7·0	16·4	11·1
45	10 11·3	10 12·9	9 43·4	4·5	3·0	10·5	7·1	16·5	11·1
46	10 11·5	10 13·2	9 43·6	4·6	3·1	10·6	7·2	16·6	11·2
47	10 11·8	10 13·4	9 43·9	4·7	3·2	10·7	7·2	16·7	11·3
48	10 12·0	10 13·7	9 44·1	4·8	3·2	10·8	7·3	16·8	11·3
49	10 12·3	10 13·9	9 44·4	4·9	3·3	10·9	7·4	16·9	11·4
50	10 12·5	10 14·2	9 44·6	5·0	3·4	11·0	7·4	17·0	11·5
51	10 12·8	10 14·4	9 44·8	5·1	3·4	11·1	7·5	17·1	11·5
52	10 13·0	10 14·7	9 45·1	5·2	3·5	11·2	7·6	17·2	11·6
53	10 13·3	10 14·9	9 45·3	5·3	3·6	11·3	7·6	17·3	11·7
54	10 13·5	10 15·2	9 45·6	5·4	3·6	11·4	7·7	17·4	11·7
55	10 13·8	10 15·4	9 45·8	5·5	3·7	11·5	7·8	17·5	11·8
56	10 14·0	10 15·7	9 46·0	5·6	3·8	11·6	7·8	17·6	11·9
57	10 14·3	10 15·9	9 46·3	5·7	3·8	11·7	7·9	17·7	11·9
58	10 14·5	10 16·2	9 46·5	5·8	3·9	11·8	8·0	17·8	12·0
59	10 14·8	10 16·4	9 46·7	5·9	4·0	11·9	8·0	17·9	12·1
60	10 15·0	10 16·7	9 47·0	6·0	4·1	12·0	8·1	18·0	12·2

41ᵐ

m 41 s	SUN PLANETS	ARIES	MOON	v or Corrⁿ d		v or Corrⁿ d		v or Corrⁿ d	
	° ′	° ′	° ′	′	′	′	′	′	′
00	10 15·0	10 16·7	9 47·0	0·0	0·0	6·0	4·2	12·0	8·3
01	10 15·3	10 16·9	9 47·2	0·1	0·1	6·1	4·2	12·1	8·4
02	10 15·5	10 17·2	9 47·5	0·2	0·1	6·2	4·3	12·2	8·4
03	10 15·8	10 17·4	9 47·7	0·3	0·2	6·3	4·4	12·3	8·5
04	10 16·0	10 17·7	9 47·9	0·4	0·3	6·4	4·4	12·4	8·6
05	10 16·3	10 17·9	9 48·2	0·5	0·3	6·5	4·5	12·5	8·6
06	10 16·5	10 18·2	9 48·4	0·6	0·4	6·6	4·6	12·6	8·7
07	10 16·8	10 18·4	9 48·7	0·7	0·5	6·7	4·6	12·7	8·8
08	10 17·0	10 18·7	9 48·9	0·8	0·6	6·8	4·7	12·8	8·9
09	10 17·3	10 18·9	9 49·1	0·9	0·6	6·9	4·8	12·9	8·9
10	10 17·5	10 19·2	9 49·4	1·0	0·7	7·0	4·8	13·0	9·0
11	10 17·8	10 19·4	9 49·6	1·1	0·8	7·1	4·9	13·1	9·1
12	10 18·0	10 19·7	9 49·8	1·2	0·8	7·2	5·0	13·2	9·1
13	10 18·3	10 19·9	9 50·1	1·3	0·9	7·3	5·0	13·3	9·2
14	10 18·5	10 20·2	9 50·3	1·4	1·0	7·4	5·1	13·4	9·3
15	10 18·8	10 20·4	9 50·6	1·5	1·0	7·5	5·2	13·5	9·3
16	10 19·0	10 20·7	9 50·8	1·6	1·1	7·6	5·3	13·6	9·4
17	10 19·3	10 20·9	9 51·0	1·7	1·2	7·7	5·3	13·7	9·5
18	10 19·5	10 21·2	9 51·3	1·8	1·2	7·8	5·4	13·8	9·5
19	10 19·8	10 21·4	9 51·5	1·9	1·3	7·9	5·5	13·9	9·6
20	10 20·0	10 21·7	9 51·8	2·0	1·4	8·0	5·5	14·0	9·7
21	10 20·3	10 21·9	9 52·0	2·1	1·5	8·1	5·6	14·1	9·8
22	10 20·5	10 22·2	9 52·2	2·2	1·5	8·2	5·7	14·2	9·8
23	10 20·8	10 22·4	9 52·5	2·3	1·6	8·3	5·7	14·3	9·9
24	10 21·0	10 22·7	9 52·7	2·4	1·7	8·4	5·8	14·4	10·0
25	10 21·3	10 23·0	9 52·9	2·5	1·7	8·5	5·9	14·5	10·0
26	10 21·5	10 23·2	9 53·2	2·6	1·8	8·6	5·9	14·6	10·1
27	10 21·8	10 23·5	9 53·4	2·7	1·9	8·7	6·0	14·7	10·2
28	10 22·0	10 23·7	9 53·7	2·8	1·9	8·8	6·1	14·8	10·2
29	10 22·3	10 24·0	9 53·9	2·9	2·0	8·9	6·2	14·9	10·3
30	10 22·5	10 24·2	9 54·1	3·0	2·1	9·0	6·2	15·0	10·4
31	10 22·8	10 24·5	9 54·4	3·1	2·1	9·1	6·3	15·1	10·4
32	10 23·0	10 24·7	9 54·6	3·2	2·2	9·2	6·4	15·2	10·5
33	10 23·3	10 25·0	9 54·9	3·3	2·3	9·3	6·4	15·3	10·6
34	10 23·5	10 25·2	9 55·1	3·4	2·4	9·4	6·5	15·4	10·7
35	10 23·8	10 25·5	9 55·3	3·5	2·4	9·5	6·6	15·5	10·7
36	10 24·0	10 25·7	9 55·6	3·6	2·5	9·6	6·6	15·6	10·8
37	10 24·3	10 26·0	9 55·8	3·7	2·6	9·7	6·7	15·7	10·9
38	10 24·5	10 26·2	9 56·1	3·8	2·6	9·8	6·7	15·8	10·9
39	10 24·8	10 26·5	9 56·3	3·9	2·7	9·9	6·8	15·9	11·0
40	10 25·0	10 26·7	9 56·5	4·0	2·8	10·0	6·9	16·0	11·1
41	10 25·3	10 27·0	9 56·8	4·1	2·8	10·1	7·0	16·1	11·1
42	10 25·5	10 27·2	9 57·0	4·2	2·9	10·2	7·1	16·2	11·2
43	10 25·8	10 27·5	9 57·2	4·3	3·0	10·3	7·1	16·3	11·3
44	10 26·0	10 27·7	9 57·5	4·4	3·0	10·4	7·2	16·4	11·3
45	10 26·3	10 28·0	9 57·7	4·5	3·1	10·5	7·3	16·5	11·4
46	10 26·5	10 28·2	9 58·0	4·6	3·2	10·6	7·3	16·6	11·5
47	10 26·8	10 28·5	9 58·2	4·7	3·3	10·7	7·4	16·7	11·6
48	10 27·0	10 28·7	9 58·4	4·8	3·3	10·8	7·5	16·8	11·6
49	10 27·3	10 29·0	9 58·7	4·9	3·4	10·9	7·5	16·9	11·7
50	10 27·5	10 29·2	9 58·9	5·0	3·5	11·0	7·6	17·0	11·8
51	10 27·8	10 29·5	9 59·2	5·1	3·5	11·1	7·7	17·1	11·8
52	10 28·0	10 29·7	9 59·4	5·2	3·6	11·2	7·7	17·2	11·9
53	10 28·3	10 30·0	9 59·6	5·3	3·7	11·3	7·8	17·3	12·0
54	10 28·5	10 30·2	9 59·9	5·4	3·7	11·4	7·9	17·4	12·0
55	10 28·8	10 30·5	10 00·1	5·5	3·8	11·5	8·0	17·5	12·1
56	10 29·0	10 30·7	10 00·3	5·6	3·9	11·6	8·0	17·6	12·2
57	10 29·3	10 31·0	10 00·6	5·7	3·9	11·7	8·1	17·7	12·2
58	10 29·5	10 31·2	10 00·8	5·8	4·0	11·8	8·2	17·8	12·3
59	10 29·8	10 31·5	10 01·1	5·9	4·1	11·9	8·2	17·9	12·4
60	10 30·0	10 31·7	10 01·3	6·0	4·2	12·0	8·3	18·0	12·5

42^m

^{m} 42 s	SUN PLANETS	ARIES	MOON	v or d	Corr^n	v or d	Corr^n	v or d	Corr^n
	° ′	° ′	° ′	′	′	′	′	′	′
00	10 30.0	10 31.7	10 01.3	0.0	0.0	6.0	4.3	12.0	8.5
01	10 30.3	10 32.0	10 01.5	0.1	0.1	6.1	4.3	12.1	8.6
02	10 30.5	10 32.2	10 01.8	0.2	0.1	6.2	4.4	12.2	8.6
03	10 30.8	10 32.5	10 02.0	0.3	0.2	6.3	4.5	12.3	8.7
04	10 31.0	10 32.7	10 02.3	0.4	0.3	6.4	4.5	12.4	8.8
05	10 31.3	10 33.0	10 02.5	0.5	0.4	6.5	4.6	12.5	8.9
06	10 31.5	10 33.2	10 02.7	0.6	0.4	6.6	4.7	12.6	8.9
07	10 31.8	10 33.5	10 03.0	0.7	0.5	6.7	4.7	12.7	9.0
08	10 32.0	10 33.7	10 03.2	0.8	0.6	6.8	4.8	12.8	9.1
09	10 32.3	10 34.0	10 03.4	0.9	0.6	6.9	4.9	12.9	9.1
10	10 32.5	10 34.2	10 03.7	1.0	0.7	7.0	5.0	13.0	9.2
11	10 32.8	10 34.5	10 03.9	1.1	0.8	7.1	5.0	13.1	9.3
12	10 33.0	10 34.7	10 04.2	1.2	0.9	7.2	5.1	13.2	9.4
13	10 33.3	10 35.0	10 04.4	1.3	0.9	7.3	5.2	13.3	9.4
14	10 33.5	10 35.2	10 04.6	1.4	1.0	7.4	5.2	13.4	9.5
15	10 33.8	10 35.5	10 04.9	1.5	1.1	7.5	5.3	13.5	9.6
16	10 34.0	10 35.7	10 05.1	1.6	1.1	7.6	5.4	13.6	9.6
17	10 34.3	10 36.0	10 05.4	1.7	1.2	7.7	5.5	13.7	9.7
18	10 34.5	10 36.2	10 05.6	1.8	1.3	7.8	5.5	13.8	9.8
19	10 34.8	10 36.5	10 05.8	1.9	1.3	7.9	5.6	13.9	9.8
20	10 35.0	10 36.7	10 06.1	2.0	1.4	8.0	5.7	14.0	9.9
21	10 35.3	10 37.0	10 06.3	2.1	1.5	8.1	5.7	14.1	10.0
22	10 35.5	10 37.2	10 06.5	2.2	1.6	8.2	5.8	14.2	10.1
23	10 35.8	10 37.5	10 06.8	2.3	1.6	8.3	5.9	14.3	10.1
24	10 36.0	10 37.7	10 07.0	2.4	1.7	8.4	6.0	14.4	10.2
25	10 36.3	10 38.0	10 07.3	2.5	1.8	8.5	6.0	14.5	10.3
26	10 36.5	10 38.2	10 07.5	2.6	1.8	8.6	6.1	14.6	10.3
27	10 36.8	10 38.5	10 07.7	2.7	1.9	8.7	6.2	14.7	10.4
28	10 37.0	10 38.7	10 08.0	2.8	2.0	8.8	6.2	14.8	10.5
29	10 37.3	10 39.0	10 08.2	2.9	2.1	8.9	6.3	14.9	10.6
30	10 37.5	10 39.2	10 08.5	3.0	2.1	9.0	6.4	15.0	10.6
31	10 37.8	10 39.5	10 08.7	3.1	2.2	9.1	6.4	15.1	10.7
32	10 38.0	10 39.7	10 08.9	3.2	2.3	9.2	6.5	15.2	10.8
33	10 38.3	10 40.0	10 09.2	3.3	2.3	9.3	6.6	15.3	10.8
34	10 38.5	10 40.2	10 09.4	3.4	2.4	9.4	6.7	15.4	10.9
35	10 38.8	10 40.5	10 09.7	3.5	2.5	9.5	6.7	15.5	11.0
36	10 39.0	10 40.7	10 09.9	3.6	2.6	9.6	6.8	15.6	11.1
37	10 39.3	10 41.0	10 10.1	3.7	2.6	9.7	6.9	15.7	11.1
38	10 39.5	10 41.3	10 10.4	3.8	2.7	9.8	6.9	15.8	11.2
39	10 39.8	10 41.5	10 10.6	3.9	2.8	9.9	7.0	15.9	11.3
40	10 40.0	10 41.8	10 10.8	4.0	2.8	10.0	7.1	16.0	11.3
41	10 40.3	10 42.0	10 11.1	4.1	2.9	10.1	7.2	16.1	11.4
42	10 40.5	10 42.3	10 11.3	4.2	3.0	10.2	7.2	16.2	11.5
43	10 40.8	10 42.5	10 11.6	4.3	3.0	10.3	7.3	16.3	11.5
44	10 41.0	10 42.8	10 11.8	4.4	3.1	10.4	7.4	16.4	11.6
45	10 41.3	10 43.0	10 12.0	4.5	3.2	10.5	7.4	16.5	11.7
46	10 41.5	10 43.3	10 12.3	4.6	3.3	10.6	7.5	16.6	11.8
47	10 41.8	10 43.5	10 12.5	4.7	3.3	10.7	7.6	16.7	11.8
48	10 42.0	10 43.8	10 12.8	4.8	3.4	10.8	7.7	16.8	11.9
49	10 42.3	10 44.0	10 13.0	4.9	3.5	10.9	7.7	16.9	12.0
50	10 42.5	10 44.3	10 13.2	5.0	3.5	11.0	7.8	17.0	12.0
51	10 42.8	10 44.5	10 13.5	5.1	3.6	11.1	7.9	17.1	12.1
52	10 43.0	10 44.8	10 13.7	5.2	3.7	11.2	7.9	17.2	12.2
53	10 43.3	10 45.0	10 13.9	5.3	3.8	11.3	8.0	17.3	12.3
54	10 43.5	10 45.3	10 14.2	5.4	3.8	11.4	8.1	17.4	12.3
55	10 43.8	10 45.5	10 14.4	5.5	3.9	11.5	8.1	17.5	12.4
56	10 44.0	10 45.8	10 14.7	5.6	4.0	11.6	8.2	17.6	12.5
57	10 44.3	10 46.0	10 14.9	5.7	4.0	11.7	8.3	17.7	12.5
58	10 44.5	10 46.3	10 15.1	5.8	4.1	11.8	8.4	17.8	12.6
59	10 44.8	10 46.5	10 15.4	5.9	4.2	11.9	8.4	17.9	12.7
60	10 45.0	10 46.8	10 15.6	6.0	4.3	12.0	8.5	18.0	12.8

43^m

^{m} 43 s	SUN PLANETS	ARIES	MOON	v or d	Corr^n	v or d	Corr^n	v or d	Corr^n
	° ′	° ′	° ′	′	′	′	′	′	′
00	10 45.0	10 46.8	10 15.6	0.0	0.0	6.0	4.4	12.0	8.7
01	10 45.3	10 47.0	10 15.9	0.1	0.1	6.1	4.4	12.1	8.8
02	10 45.5	10 47.3	10 16.1	0.2	0.1	6.2	4.5	12.2	8.8
03	10 45.8	10 47.5	10 16.3	0.3	0.2	6.3	4.6	12.3	8.9
04	10 46.0	10 47.8	10 16.6	0.4	0.3	6.4	4.6	12.4	9.0
05	10 46.3	10 48.0	10 16.8	0.5	0.4	6.5	4.7	12.5	9.1
06	10 46.5	10 48.3	10 17.0	0.6	0.4	6.6	4.8	12.6	9.1
07	10 46.8	10 48.5	10 17.3	0.7	0.5	6.7	4.9	12.7	9.2
08	10 47.0	10 48.8	10 17.5	0.8	0.6	6.8	4.9	12.8	9.3
09	10 47.3	10 49.0	10 17.8	0.9	0.7	6.9	5.0	12.9	9.4
10	10 47.5	10 49.3	10 18.0	1.0	0.7	7.0	5.1	13.0	9.4
11	10 47.8	10 49.5	10 18.2	1.1	0.8	7.1	5.1	13.1	9.5
12	10 48.0	10 49.8	10 18.5	1.2	0.9	7.2	5.2	13.2	9.6
13	10 48.3	10 50.0	10 18.7	1.3	0.9	7.3	5.3	13.3	9.6
14	10 48.5	10 50.3	10 19.0	1.4	1.0	7.4	5.4	13.4	9.7
15	10 48.8	10 50.5	10 19.2	1.5	1.1	7.5	5.4	13.5	9.8
16	10 49.0	10 50.8	10 19.4	1.6	1.2	7.6	5.5	13.6	9.9
17	10 49.3	10 51.0	10 19.7	1.7	1.2	7.7	5.6	13.7	9.9
18	10 49.5	10 51.3	10 19.9	1.8	1.3	7.8	5.7	13.8	10.0
19	10 49.8	10 51.5	10 20.2	1.9	1.4	7.9	5.7	13.9	10.1
20	10 50.0	10 51.8	10 20.4	2.0	1.5	8.0	5.8	14.0	10.2
21	10 50.3	10 52.0	10 20.6	2.1	1.5	8.1	5.9	14.1	10.2
22	10 50.5	10 52.3	10 20.9	2.2	1.6	8.2	5.9	14.2	10.3
23	10 50.8	10 52.5	10 21.1	2.3	1.7	8.3	6.0	14.3	10.4
24	10 51.0	10 52.8	10 21.3	2.4	1.7	8.4	6.1	14.4	10.4
25	10 51.3	10 53.0	10 21.6	2.5	1.8	8.5	6.2	14.5	10.5
26	10 51.5	10 53.3	10 21.8	2.6	1.9	8.6	6.2	14.6	10.6
27	10 51.8	10 53.5	10 22.1	2.7	2.0	8.7	6.3	14.7	10.7
28	10 52.0	10 53.8	10 22.3	2.8	2.0	8.8	6.4	14.8	10.7
29	10 52.3	10 54.0	10 22.5	2.9	2.1	8.9	6.5	14.9	10.8
30	10 52.5	10 54.3	10 22.8	3.0	2.2	9.0	6.5	15.0	10.9
31	10 52.8	10 54.5	10 23.0	3.1	2.2	9.1	6.6	15.1	10.9
32	10 53.0	10 54.8	10 23.3	3.2	2.3	9.2	6.7	15.2	11.0
33	10 53.3	10 55.0	10 23.5	3.3	2.4	9.3	6.7	15.3	11.1
34	10 53.5	10 55.3	10 23.7	3.4	2.5	9.4	6.8	15.4	11.2
35	10 53.8	10 55.5	10 24.0	3.5	2.5	9.5	6.9	15.5	11.2
36	10 54.0	10 55.8	10 24.2	3.6	2.6	9.6	7.0	15.6	11.3
37	10 54.3	10 56.0	10 24.4	3.7	2.7	9.7	7.0	15.7	11.4
38	10 54.5	10 56.3	10 24.7	3.8	2.8	9.8	7.1	15.8	11.5
39	10 54.8	10 56.5	10 24.9	3.9	2.8	9.9	7.2	15.9	11.5
40	10 55.0	10 56.8	10 25.2	4.0	2.9	10.0	7.3	16.0	11.6
41	10 55.3	10 57.0	10 25.4	4.1	3.0	10.1	7.3	16.1	11.7
42	10 55.5	10 57.3	10 25.6	4.2	3.0	10.2	7.4	16.2	11.7
43	10 55.8	10 57.5	10 25.9	4.3	3.1	10.3	7.5	16.3	11.8
44	10 56.0	10 57.8	10 26.1	4.4	3.2	10.4	7.5	16.4	11.9
45	10 56.3	10 58.0	10 26.4	4.5	3.3	10.5	7.6	16.5	12.0
46	10 56.5	10 58.3	10 26.6	4.6	3.3	10.6	7.7	16.6	12.0
47	10 56.8	10 58.5	10 26.8	4.7	3.4	10.7	7.8	16.7	12.1
48	10 57.0	10 58.8	10 27.1	4.8	3.5	10.8	7.8	16.8	12.2
49	10 57.3	10 59.0	10 27.3	4.9	3.6	10.9	7.9	16.9	12.3
50	10 57.5	10 59.3	10 27.5	5.0	3.6	11.0	8.0	17.0	12.3
51	10 57.8	10 59.6	10 27.8	5.1	3.7	11.1	8.0	17.1	12.4
52	10 58.0	10 59.8	10 28.0	5.2	3.8	11.2	8.1	17.2	12.5
53	10 58.3	11 00.1	10 28.3	5.3	3.8	11.3	8.2	17.3	12.5
54	10 58.5	11 00.3	10 28.5	5.4	3.9	11.4	8.3	17.4	12.6
55	10 58.8	11 00.6	10 28.7	5.5	4.0	11.5	8.3	17.5	12.7
56	10 59.0	11 00.8	10 29.0	5.6	4.1	11.6	8.4	17.6	12.8
57	10 59.3	11 01.1	10 29.2	5.7	4.1	11.7	8.5	17.7	12.8
58	10 59.5	11 01.3	10 29.5	5.8	4.2	11.8	8.6	17.8	12.9
59	10 59.8	11 01.6	10 29.7	5.9	4.3	11.9	8.6	17.9	13.0
60	11 00.0	11 01.8	10 29.9	6.0	4.4	12.0	8.7	18.0	13.1

44^m s	SUN PLANETS	ARIES	MOON	v or Corr^n d	v or Corr^n d	v or Corr^n d
	° ′	° ′	° ′	′ ′	′ ′	′ ′
00	11 00·0	11 01·8	10 29·9	0·0 0·0	6·0 4·5	12·0 8·9
01	11 00·3	11 02·1	10 30·2	0·1 0·1	6·1 4·5	12·1 9·0
02	11 00·5	11 02·3	10 30·4	0·2 0·1	6·2 4·6	12·2 9·0
03	11 00·8	11 02·6	10 30·6	0·3 0·2	6·3 4·7	12·3 9·1
04	11 01·0	11 02·8	10 30·9	0·4 0·3	6·4 4·7	12·4 9·2
05	11 01·3	11 03·1	10 31·1	0·5 0·4	6·5 4·8	12·5 9·3
06	11 01·5	11 03·3	10 31·4	0·6 0·4	6·6 4·9	12·6 9·3
07	11 01·8	11 03·6	10 31·6	0·7 0·5	6·7 5·0	12·7 9·4
08	11 02·0	11 03·8	10 31·8	0·8 0·6	6·8 5·0	12·8 9·5
09	11 02·3	11 04·1	10 32·1	0·9 0·7	6·9 5·1	12·9 9·6
10	11 02·5	11 04·3	10 32·3	1·0 0·7	7·0 5·2	13·0 9·6
11	11 02·8	11 04·6	10 32·6	1·1 0·8	7·1 5·3	13·1 9·7
12	11 03·0	11 04·8	10 32·8	1·2 0·9	7·2 5·3	13·2 9·8
13	11 03·3	11 05·1	10 33·0	1·3 1·0	7·3 5·4	13·3 9·9
14	11 03·5	11 05·3	10 33·3	1·4 1·0	7·4 5·5	13·4 9·9
15	11 03·8	11 05·6	10 33·5	1·5 1·1	7·5 5·6	13·5 10·0
16	11 04·0	11 05·8	10 33·8	1·6 1·2	7·6 5·6	13·6 10·1
17	11 04·3	11 06·1	10 34·0	1·7 1·3	7·7 5·7	13·7 10·2
18	11 04·5	11 06·3	10 34·2	1·8 1·3	7·8 5·8	13·8 10·2
19	11 04·8	11 06·6	10 34·5	1·9 1·4	7·9 5·9	13·9 10·3
20	11 05·0	11 06·8	10 34·7	2·0 1·5	8·0 5·9	14·0 10·4
21	11 05·3	11 07·1	10 34·9	2·1 1·6	8·1 6·0	14·1 10·5
22	11 05·5	11 07·3	10 35·2	2·2 1·6	8·2 6·1	14·2 10·5
23	11 05·8	11 07·6	10 35·4	2·3 1·7	8·3 6·2	14·3 10·6
24	11 06·0	11 07·8	10 35·7	2·4 1·8	8·4 6·2	14·4 10·7
25	11 06·3	11 08·1	10 35·9	2·5 1·9	8·5 6·3	14·5 10·8
26	11 06·5	11 08·3	10 36·1	2·6 1·9	8·6 6·4	14·6 10·8
27	11 06·8	11 08·6	10 36·4	2·7 2·0	8·7 6·5	14·7 10·9
28	11 07·0	11 08·8	10 36·6	2·8 2·1	8·8 6·5	14·8 11·0
29	11 07·3	11 09·1	10 36·9	2·9 2·2	8·9 6·6	14·9 11·1
30	11 07·5	11 09·3	10 37·1	3·0 2·2	9·0 6·7	15·0 11·1
31	11 07·8	11 09·6	10 37·3	3·1 2·3	9·1 6·7	15·1 11·2
32	11 08·0	11 09·8	10 37·6	3·2 2·4	9·2 6·8	15·2 11·3
33	11 08·3	11 10·1	10 37·8	3·3 2·4	9·3 6·9	15·3 11·3
34	11 08·5	11 10·3	10 38·0	3·4 2·5	9·4 7·0	15·4 11·4
35	11 08·8	11 10·6	10 38·3	3·5 2·6	9·5 7·0	15·5 11·5
36	11 09·0	11 10·8	10 38·5	3·6 2·7	9·6 7·1	15·6 11·6
37	11 09·3	11 11·1	10 38·8	3·7 2·7	9·7 7·2	15·7 11·6
38	11 09·5	11 11·3	10 39·0	3·8 2·8	9·8 7·3	15·8 11·7
39	11 09·8	11 11·6	10 39·2	3·9 2·9	9·9 7·3	15·9 11·8
40	11 10·0	11 11·8	10 39·5	4·0 3·0	10·0 7·4	16·0 11·9
41	11 10·3	11 12·1	10 39·7	4·1 3·0	10·1 7·5	16·1 11·9
42	11 10·5	11 12·3	10 40·0	4·2 3·1	10·2 7·6	16·2 12·0
43	11 10·8	11 12·6	10 40·2	4·3 3·2	10·3 7·6	16·3 12·1
44	11 11·0	11 12·8	10 40·4	4·4 3·3	10·4 7·7	16·4 12·2
45	11 11·3	11 13·1	10 40·7	4·5 3·3	10·5 7·8	16·5 12·2
46	11 11·5	11 13·3	10 40·9	4·6 3·4	10·6 7·9	16·6 12·3
47	11 11·8	11 13·6	10 41·1	4·7 3·5	10·7 7·9	16·7 12·4
48	11 12·0	11 13·8	10 41·4	4·8 3·6	10·8 8·0	16·8 12·5
49	11 12·3	11 14·1	10 41·6	4·9 3·6	10·9 8·1	16·9 12·5
50	11 12·5	11 14·3	10 41·9	5·0 3·7	11·0 8·2	17·0 12·6
51	11 12·8	11 14·6	10 42·1	5·1 3·8	11·1 8·2	17·1 12·7
52	11 13·0	11 14·8	10 42·3	5·2 3·9	11·2 8·3	17·2 12·8
53	11 13·3	11 15·1	10 42·6	5·3 3·9	11·3 8·4	17·3 12·8
54	11 13·5	11 15·3	10 42·8	5·4 4·0	11·4 8·5	17·4 12·9
55	11 13·8	11 15·6	10 43·1	5·5 4·1	11·5 8·5	17·5 13·0
56	11 14·0	11 15·8	10 43·3	5·6 4·2	11·6 8·6	17·6 13·1
57	11 14·3	11 16·1	10 43·5	5·7 4·2	11·7 8·7	17·7 13·1
58	11 14·5	11 16·3	10 43·8	5·8 4·3	11·8 8·8	17·8 13·2
59	11 14·8	11 16·6	10 44·0	5·9 4·4	11·9 8·8	17·9 13·3
60	11 15·0	11 16·8	10 44·3	6·0 4·5	12·0 8·9	18·0 13·4

45^m s	SUN PLANETS	ARIES	MOON	v or Corr^n d	v or Corr^n d	v or Corr^n d
	° ′	° ′	° ′	′ ′	′ ′	′ ′
00	11 15·0	11 16·8	10 44·3	0·0 0·0	6·0 4·6	12·0 9·1
01	11 15·3	11 17·1	10 44·5	0·1 0·1	6·1 4·6	12·1 9·2
02	11 15·5	11 17·3	10 44·7	0·2 0·2	6·2 4·7	12·2 9·3
03	11 15·8	11 17·6	10 45·0	0·3 0·2	6·3 4·8	12·3 9·3
04	11 16·0	11 17·9	10 45·2	0·4 0·3	6·4 4·9	12·4 9·4
05	11 16·3	11 18·1	10 45·4	0·5 0·4	6·5 4·9	12·5 9·5
06	11 16·5	11 18·4	10 45·7	0·6 0·5	6·6 5·0	12·6 9·6
07	11 16·8	11 18·6	10 45·9	0·7 0·5	6·7 5·1	12·7 9·6
08	11 17·0	11 18·9	10 46·2	0·8 0·6	6·8 5·2	12·8 9·7
09	11 17·3	11 19·1	10 46·4	0·9 0·7	6·9 5·2	12·9 9·8
10	11 17·5	11 19·4	10 46·6	1·0 0·8	7·0 5·3	13·0 9·9
11	11 17·8	11 19·6	10 46·9	1·1 0·8	7·1 5·4	13·1 9·9
12	11 18·0	11 19·9	10 47·1	1·2 0·9	7·2 5·5	13·2 10·0
13	11 18·3	11 20·1	10 47·4	1·3 1·0	7·3 5·5	13·3 10·1
14	11 18·5	11 20·4	10 47·6	1·4 1·1	7·4 5·6	13·4 10·2
15	11 18·8	11 20·6	10 47·8	1·5 1·1	7·5 5·7	13·5 10·2
16	11 19·0	11 20·9	10 48·1	1·6 1·2	7·6 5·8	13·6 10·3
17	11 19·3	11 21·1	10 48·3	1·7 1·3	7·7 5·8	13·7 10·4
18	11 19·5	11 21·4	10 48·5	1·8 1·4	7·8 5·9	13·8 10·5
19	11 19·8	11 21·6	10 48·8	1·9 1·4	7·9 6·0	13·9 10·5
20	11 20·0	11 21·9	10 49·0	2·0 1·5	8·0 6·1	14·0 10·6
21	11 20·3	11 22·1	10 49·3	2·1 1·6	8·1 6·1	14·1 10·7
22	11 20·5	11 22·4	10 49·5	2·2 1·7	8·2 6·2	14·2 10·8
23	11 20·8	11 22·6	10 49·7	2·3 1·7	8·3 6·3	14·3 10·8
24	11 21·0	11 22·9	10 50·0	2·4 1·8	8·4 6·4	14·4 10·9
25	11 21·3	11 23·1	10 50·2	2·5 1·9	8·5 6·4	14·5 11·0
26	11 21·5	11 23·4	10 50·5	2·6 2·0	8·6 6·5	14·6 11·1
27	11 21·8	11 23·6	10 50·7	2·7 2·0	8·7 6·6	14·7 11·1
28	11 22·0	11 23·9	10 50·9	2·8 2·1	8·8 6·7	14·8 11·2
29	11 22·3	11 24·1	10 51·2	2·9 2·2	8·9 6·7	14·9 11·3
30	11 22·5	11 24·4	10 51·4	3·0 2·3	9·0 6·8	15·0 11·4
31	11 22·8	11 24·6	10 51·6	3·1 2·4	9·1 6·9	15·1 11·5
32	11 23·0	11 24·9	10 51·9	3·2 2·4	9·2 7·0	15·2 11·5
33	11 23·3	11 25·1	10 52·1	3·3 2·5	9·3 7·1	15·3 11·6
34	11 23·5	11 25·4	10 52·4	3·4 2·6	9·4 7·1	15·4 11·7
35	11 23·8	11 25·6	10 52·6	3·5 2·7	9·5 7·2	15·5 11·8
36	11 24·0	11 25·9	10 52·8	3·6 2·7	9·6 7·3	15·6 11·8
37	11 24·3	11 26·1	10 53·1	3·7 2·8	9·7 7·4	15·7 11·9
38	11 24·5	11 26·4	10 53·3	3·8 2·9	9·8 7·4	15·8 12·0
39	11 24·8	11 26·6	10 53·6	3·9 3·0	9·9 7·5	15·9 12·1
40	11 25·0	11 26·9	10 53·8	4·0 3·0	10·0 7·6	16·0 12·1
41	11 25·3	11 27·1	10 54·0	4·1 3·1	10·1 7·7	16·1 12·2
42	11 25·5	11 27·4	10 54·3	4·2 3·2	10·2 7·7	16·2 12·3
43	11 25·8	11 27·6	10 54·5	4·3 3·3	10·3 7·8	16·3 12·4
44	11 26·0	11 27·9	10 54·7	4·4 3·3	10·4 7·9	16·4 12·4
45	11 26·3	11 28·1	10 55·0	4·5 3·4	10·5 8·0	16·5 12·5
46	11 26·5	11 28·4	10 55·2	4·6 3·5	10·6 8·0	16·6 12·6
47	11 26·8	11 28·6	10 55·5	4·7 3·6	10·7 8·1	16·7 12·7
48	11 27·0	11 28·9	10 55·7	4·8 3·6	10·8 8·2	16·8 12·7
49	11 27·3	11 29·1	10 55·9	4·9 3·7	10·9 8·3	16·9 12·8
50	11 27·5	11 29·4	10 56·2	5·0 3·8	11·0 8·3	17·0 12·9
51	11 27·8	11 29·6	10 56·4	5·1 3·9	11·1 8·4	17·1 13·0
52	11 28·0	11 29·9	10 56·7	5·2 3·9	11·2 8·5	17·2 13·0
53	11 28·3	11 30·1	10 56·9	5·3 4·0	11·3 8·6	17·3 13·1
54	11 28·5	11 30·4	10 57·1	5·4 4·1	11·4 8·6	17·4 13·2
55	11 28·8	11 30·6	10 57·4	5·5 4·2	11·5 8·7	17·5 13·3
56	11 29·0	11 30·9	10 57·6	5·6 4·2	11·6 8·8	17·6 13·3
57	11 29·3	11 31·1	10 57·9	5·7 4·3	11·7 8·9	17·7 13·4
58	11 29·5	11 31·4	10 58·1	5·8 4·4	11·8 8·9	17·8 13·5
59	11 29·8	11 31·6	10 58·3	5·9 4·5	11·9 9·0	17·9 13·6
60	11 30·0	11 31·9	10 58·6	6·0 4·6	12·0 9·1	18·0 13·7

INCREMENTS AND CORRECTIONS

46	SUN PLANETS	ARIES	MOON	v or Corrn d	v or Corrn d	v or Corrn d
s	° ′	° ′	° ′	′ ′	′ ′	′ ′
00	11 30·0	11 31·9	10 58·6	0·0 0·0	6·0 4·7	12·0 9·3
01	11 30·3	11 32·1	10 58·8	0·1 0·1	6·1 4·7	12·1 9·4
02	11 30·5	11 32·4	10 59·0	0·2 0·2	6·2 4·8	12·2 9·5
03	11 30·8	11 32·6	10 59·3	0·3 0·2	6·3 4·9	12·3 9·5
04	11 31·0	11 32·9	10 59·5	0·4 0·3	6·4 5·0	12·4 9·6
05	11 31·3	11 33·1	10 59·8	0·5 0·4	6·5 5·0	12·5 9·7
06	11 31·5	11 33·4	11 00·0	0·6 0·5	6·6 5·1	12·6 9·8
07	11 31·8	11 33·6	11 00·2	0·7 0·5	6·7 5·2	12·7 9·8
08	11 32·0	11 33·9	11 00·5	0·8 0·6	6·8 5·3	12·8 9·9
09	11 32·3	11 34·1	11 00·7	0·9 0·7	6·9 5·3	12·9 10·0
10	11 32·5	11 34·4	11 01·0	1·0 0·8	7·0 5·4	13·0 10·1
11	11 32·8	11 34·6	11 01·2	1·1 0·9	7·1 5·5	13·1 10·2
12	11 33·0	11 34·9	11 01·4	1·2 0·9	7·2 5·6	13·2 10·2
13	11 33·3	11 35·1	11 01·7	1·3 1·0	7·3 5·7	13·3 10·3
14	11 33·5	11 35·4	11 01·9	1·4 1·1	7·4 5·7	13·4 10·4
15	11 33·8	11 35·6	11 02·1	1·5 1·2	7·5 5·8	13·5 10·5
16	11 34·0	11 35·9	11 02·4	1·6 1·2	7·6 5·9	13·6 10·5
17	11 34·3	11 36·2	11 02·6	1·7 1·3	7·7 6·0	13·7 10·6
18	11 34·5	11 36·4	11 02·9	1·8 1·4	7·8 6·0	13·8 10·7
19	11 34·8	11 36·7	11 03·1	1·9 1·5	7·9 6·1	13·9 10·8
20	11 35·0	11 36·9	11 03·3	2·0 1·6	8·0 6·2	14·0 10·9
21	11 35·3	11 37·2	11 03·6	2·1 1·6	8·1 6·3	14·1 10·9
22	11 35·5	11 37·4	11 03·8	2·2 1·7	8·2 6·4	14·2 11·0
23	11 35·8	11 37·7	11 04·1	2·3 1·8	8·3 6·4	14·3 11·1
24	11 36·0	11 37·9	11 04·3	2·4 1·9	8·4 6·5	14·4 11·2
25	11 36·3	11 38·2	11 04·5	2·5 1·9	8·5 6·6	14·5 11·2
26	11 36·5	11 38·4	11 04·8	2·6 2·0	8·6 6·7	14·6 11·3
27	11 36·8	11 38·7	11 05·0	2·7 2·1	8·7 6·7	14·7 11·4
28	11 37·0	11 38·9	11 05·2	2·8 2·2	8·8 6·8	14·8 11·5
29	11 37·3	11 39·2	11 05·5	2·9 2·2	8·9 6·9	14·9 11·5
30	11 37·5	11 39·4	11 05·7	3·0 2·3	9·0 7·0	15·0 11·6
31	11 37·8	11 39·7	11 06·0	3·1 2·4	9·1 7·1	15·1 11·7
32	11 38·0	11 39·9	11 06·2	3·2 2·5	9·2 7·1	15·2 11·8
33	11 38·3	11 40·2	11 06·4	3·3 2·6	9·3 7·2	15·3 11·9
34	11 38·5	11 40·4	11 06·7	3·4 2·6	9·4 7·3	15·4 11·9
35	11 38·8	11 40·7	11 06·9	3·5 2·7	9·5 7·4	15·5 12·0
36	11 39·0	11 40·9	11 07·2	3·6 2·8	9·6 7·4	15·6 12·1
37	11 39·3	11 41·2	11 07·4	3·7 2·9	9·7 7·5	15·7 12·2
38	11 39·5	11 41·4	11 07·6	3·8 2·9	9·8 7·6	15·8 12·2
39	11 39·8	11 41·7	11 07·9	3·9 3·0	9·9 7·7	15·9 12·3
40	11 40·0	11 41·9	11 08·1	4·0 3·1	10·0 7·8	16·0 12·4
41	11 40·3	11 42·2	11 08·3	4·1 3·2	10·1 7·8	16·1 12·5
42	11 40·5	11 42·4	11 08·6	4·2 3·3	10·2 7·9	16·2 12·6
43	11 40·8	11 42·7	11 08·8	4·3 3·3	10·3 8·0	16·3 12·6
44	11 41·0	11 42·9	11 09·1	4·4 3·4	10·4 8·1	16·4 12·7
45	11 41·3	11 43·2	11 09·3	4·5 3·5	10·5 8·1	16·5 12·8
46	11 41·5	11 43·4	11 09·5	4·6 3·6	10·6 8·2	16·6 12·9
47	11 41·8	11 43·7	11 09·8	4·7 3·6	10·7 8·3	16·7 12·9
48	11 42·0	11 43·9	11 10·0	4·8 3·7	10·8 8·4	16·8 13·0
49	11 42·3	11 44·2	11 10·3	4·9 3·8	10·9 8·4	16·9 13·1
50	11 42·5	11 44·4	11 10·5	5·0 3·9	11·0 8·5	17·0 13·2
51	11 42·8	11 44·7	11 10·7	5·1 4·0	11·1 8·6	17·1 13·3
52	11 43·0	11 44·9	11 11·0	5·2 4·0	11·2 8·7	17·2 13·3
53	11 43·3	11 45·2	11 11·2	5·3 4·1	11·3 8·8	17·3 13·4
54	11 43·5	11 45·4	11 11·5	5·4 4·2	11·4 8·8	17·4 13·5
55	11 43·8	11 45·7	11 11·7	5·5 4·3	11·5 8·9	17·5 13·6
56	11 44·0	11 45·9	11 11·9	5·6 4·3	11·6 9·0	17·6 13·6
57	11 44·3	11 46·2	11 12·2	5·7 4·4	11·7 9·1	17·7 13·7
58	11 44·5	11 46·4	11 12·4	5·8 4·5	11·8 9·1	17·8 13·8
59	11 44·8	11 46·7	11 12·6	5·9 4·6	11·9 9·2	17·9 13·9
60	11 45·0	11 46·9	11 12·9	6·0 4·7	12·0 9·3	18·0 14·0

47	SUN PLANETS	ARIES	MOON	v or Corrn d	v or Corrn d	v or Corrn d
s	° ′	° ′	° ′	′ ′	′ ′	′ ′
00	11 45·0	11 46·9	11 12·9	0·0 0·0	6·0 4·8	12·0 9·5
01	11 45·3	11 47·2	11 13·1	0·1 0·1	6·1 4·8	12·1 9·6
02	11 45·5	11 47·4	11 13·4	0·2 0·2	6·2 4·9	12·2 9·7
03	11 45·8	11 47·7	11 13·6	0·3 0·2	6·3 5·0	12·3 9·7
04	11 46·0	11 47·9	11 13·8	0·4 0·3	6·4 5·1	12·4 9·8
05	11 46·3	11 48·2	11 14·1	0·5 0·4	6·5 5·1	12·5 9·9
06	11 46·5	11 48·4	11 14·3	0·6 0·5	6·6 5·2	12·6 10·0
07	11 46·8	11 48·7	11 14·6	0·7 0·6	6·7 5·3	12·7 10·1
08	11 47·0	11 48·9	11 14·8	0·8 0·6	6·8 5·4	12·8 10·1
09	11 47·3	11 49·2	11 15·0	0·9 0·7	6·9 5·5	12·9 10·2
10	11 47·5	11 49·4	11 15·3	1·0 0·8	7·0 5·5	13·0 10·3
11	11 47·8	11 49·7	11 15·5	1·1 0·9	7·1 5·6	13·1 10·4
12	11 48·0	11 49·9	11 15·7	1·2 1·0	7·2 5·7	13·2 10·5
13	11 48·3	11 50·2	11 16·0	1·3 1·0	7·3 5·8	13·3 10·5
14	11 48·5	11 50·4	11 16·2	1·4 1·1	7·4 5·9	13·4 10·6
15	11 48·8	11 50·7	11 16·5	1·5 1·2	7·5 5·9	13·5 10·7
16	11 49·0	11 50·9	11 16·7	1·6 1·3	7·6 6·0	13·6 10·8
17	11 49·3	11 51·2	11 16·9	1·7 1·3	7·7 6·1	13·7 10·8
18	11 49·5	11 51·4	11 17·2	1·8 1·4	7·8 6·2	13·8 10·9
19	11 49·8	11 51·7	11 17·4	1·9 1·5	7·9 6·3	13·9 11·0
20	11 50·0	11 51·9	11 17·7	2·0 1·6	8·0 6·3	14·0 11·1
21	11 50·3	11 52·2	11 17·9	2·1 1·7	8·1 6·4	14·1 11·2
22	11 50·5	11 52·4	11 18·1	2·2 1·7	8·2 6·5	14·2 11·2
23	11 50·8	11 52·7	11 18·4	2·3 1·8	8·3 6·6	14·3 11·3
24	11 51·0	11 52·9	11 18·6	2·4 1·9	8·4 6·7	14·4 11·4
25	11 51·3	11 53·2	11 18·8	2·5 2·0	8·5 6·7	14·5 11·5
26	11 51·5	11 53·4	11 19·1	2·6 2·1	8·6 6·8	14·6 11·6
27	11 51·8	11 53·7	11 19·3	2·7 2·1	8·7 6·9	14·7 11·6
28	11 52·0	11 53·9	11 19·6	2·8 2·2	8·8 7·0	14·8 11·7
29	11 52·3	11 54·2	11 19·8	2·9 2·3	8·9 7·0	14·9 11·8
30	11 52·5	11 54·5	11 20·0	3·0 2·4	9·0 7·1	15·0 11·9
31	11 52·8	11 54·7	11 20·3	3·1 2·5	9·1 7·2	15·1 12·0
32	11 53·0	11 55·0	11 20·5	3·2 2·5	9·2 7·3	15·2 12·0
33	11 53·3	11 55·2	11 20·8	3·3 2·6	9·3 7·4	15·3 12·1
34	11 53·5	11 55·5	11 21·0	3·4 2·7	9·4 7·4	15·4 12·2
35	11 53·8	11 55·7	11 21·2	3·5 2·8	9·5 7·5	15·5 12·3
36	11 54·0	11 56·0	11 21·5	3·6 2·9	9·6 7·6	15·6 12·4
37	11 54·3	11 56·2	11 21·7	3·7 2·9	9·7 7·7	15·7 12·4
38	11 54·5	11 56·5	11 22·0	3·8 3·0	9·8 7·8	15·8 12·5
39	11 54·8	11 56·7	11 22·2	3·9 3·1	9·9 7·8	15·9 12·6
40	11 55·0	11 57·0	11 22·4	4·0 3·2	10·0 7·9	16·0 12·7
41	11 55·3	11 57·2	11 22·7	4·1 3·2	10·1 8·0	16·1 12·7
42	11 55·5	11 57·5	11 22·9	4·2 3·3	10·2 8·1	16·2 12·8
43	11 55·8	11 57·7	11 23·1	4·3 3·4	10·3 8·2	16·3 12·9
44	11 56·0	11 58·0	11 23·4	4·4 3·5	10·4 8·2	16·4 13·0
45	11 56·3	11 58·2	11 23·6	4·5 3·6	10·5 8·3	16·5 13·1
46	11 56·5	11 58·5	11 23·9	4·6 3·6	10·6 8·4	16·6 13·1
47	11 56·8	11 58·7	11 24·1	4·7 3·7	10·7 8·5	16·7 13·2
48	11 57·0	11 59·0	11 24·3	4·8 3·8	10·8 8·6	16·8 13·3
49	11 57·3	11 59·2	11 24·6	4·9 3·9	10·9 8·6	16·9 13·4
50	11 57·5	11 59·5	11 24·8	5·0 4·0	11·0 8·7	17·0 13·5
51	11 57·8	11 59·7	11 25·1	5·1 4·0	11·1 8·8	17·1 13·5
52	11 58·0	12 00·0	11 25·3	5·2 4·1	11·2 8·9	17·2 13·6
53	11 58·3	12 00·2	11 25·5	5·3 4·2	11·3 8·9	17·3 13·7
54	11 58·5	12 00·5	11 25·8	5·4 4·3	11·4 9·0	17·4 13·8
55	11 58·8	12 00·7	11 26·0	5·5 4·4	11·5 9·1	17·5 13·9
56	11 59·0	12 01·0	11 26·2	5·6 4·4	11·6 9·2	17·6 13·9
57	11 59·3	12 01·2	11 26·5	5·7 4·5	11·7 9·3	17·7 14·0
58	11 59·5	12 01·5	11 26·7	5·8 4·6	11·8 9·3	17·8 14·1
59	11 59·8	12 01·7	11 27·0	5·9 4·7	11·9 9·4	17·9 14·2
60	12 00·0	12 02·0	11 27·2	6·0 4·8	12·0 9·5	18·0 14·3

48	SUN PLANETS	ARIES	MOON	v or d Corrⁿ	v or d Corrⁿ	v or d Corrⁿ
s	° ′	° ′	° ′	′ ′	′ ′	′ ′
00	12 00·0	12 02·0	11 27·2	0·0 0·0	6·0 4·9	12·0 9·7
01	12 00·3	12 02·2	11 27·4	0·1 0·1	6·1 4·9	12·1 9·8
02	12 00·5	12 02·5	11 27·7	0·2 0·2	6·2 5·0	12·2 9·9
03	12 00·8	12 02·7	11 27·9	0·3 0·2	6·3 5·1	12·3 9·9
04	12 01·0	12 03·0	11 28·2	0·4 0·3	6·4 5·2	12·4 10·0
05	12 01·3	12 03·2	11 28·4	0·5 0·4	6·5 5·3	12·5 10·1
06	12 01·5	12 03·5	11 28·6	0·6 0·5	6·6 5·3	12·6 10·2
07	12 01·8	12 03·7	11 28·9	0·7 0·6	6·7 5·4	12·7 10·3
08	12 02·0	12 04·0	11 29·1	0·8 0·6	6·8 5·5	12·8 10·3
09	12 02·3	12 04·2	11 29·3	0·9 0·7	6·9 5·6	12·9 10·4
10	12 02·5	12 04·5	11 29·6	1·0 0·8	7·0 5·7	13·0 10·5
11	12 02·8	12 04·7	11 29·8	1·1 0·9	7·1 5·7	13·1 10·6
12	12 03·0	12 05·0	11 30·1	1·2 1·0	7·2 5·8	13·2 10·7
13	12 03·3	12 05·2	11 30·3	1·3 1·1	7·3 5·9	13·3 10·8
14	12 03·5	12 05·5	11 30·5	1·4 1·1	7·4 6·0	13·4 10·8
15	12 03·8	12 05·7	11 30·8	1·5 1·2	7·5 6·1	13·5 10·9
16	12 04·0	12 06·0	11 31·0	1·6 1·3	7·6 6·1	13·6 11·0
17	12 04·3	12 06·2	11 31·3	1·7 1·4	7·7 6·2	13·7 11·1
18	12 04·5	12 06·5	11 31·5	1·8 1·5	7·8 6·3	13·8 11·2
19	12 04·8	12 06·7	11 31·7	1·9 1·5	7·9 6·4	13·9 11·2
20	12 05·0	12 07·0	11 32·0	2·0 1·6	8·0 6·5	14·0 11·3
21	12 05·3	12 07·2	11 32·2	2·1 1·7	8·1 6·5	14·1 11·4
22	12 05·5	12 07·5	11 32·4	2·2 1·8	8·2 6·6	14·2 11·5
23	12 05·8	12 07·7	11 32·7	2·3 1·9	8·3 6·7	14·3 11·6
24	12 06·0	12 08·0	11 32·9	2·4 1·9	8·4 6·8	14·4 11·6
25	12 06·3	12 08·2	11 33·2	2·5 2·0	8·5 6·9	14·5 11·7
26	12 06·5	12 08·5	11 33·4	2·6 2·1	8·6 7·0	14·6 11·8
27	12 06·8	12 08·7	11 33·6	2·7 2·2	8·7 7·0	14·7 11·9
28	12 07·0	12 09·0	11 33·9	2·8 2·3	8·8 7·1	14·8 12·0
29	12 07·3	12 09·2	11 34·1	2·9 2·3	8·9 7·2	14·9 12·0
30	12 07·5	12 09·5	11 34·4	3·0 2·4	9·0 7·3	15·0 12·1
31	12 07·8	12 09·7	11 34·6	3·1 2·5	9·1 7·4	15·1 12·2
32	12 08·0	12 10·0	11 34·8	3·2 2·6	9·2 7·4	15·2 12·3
33	12 08·3	12 10·2	11 35·1	3·3 2·7	9·3 7·5	15·3 12·4
34	12 08·5	12 10·5	11 35·3	3·4 2·7	9·4 7·6	15·4 12·4
35	12 08·8	12 10·7	11 35·6	3·5 2·8	9·5 7·7	15·5 12·5
36	12 09·0	12 11·0	11 35·8	3·6 2·9	9·6 7·8	15·6 12·6
37	12 09·3	12 11·2	11 36·0	3·7 3·0	9·7 7·8	15·7 12·7
38	12 09·5	12 11·5	11 36·3	3·8 3·1	9·8 7·9	15·8 12·8
39	12 09·8	12 11·7	11 36·5	3·9 3·2	9·9 8·0	15·9 12·9
40	12 10·0	12 12·0	11 36·7	4·0 3·2	10·0 8·1	16·0 12·9
41	12 10·3	12 12·2	11 37·0	4·1 3·3	10·1 8·2	16·1 13·0
42	12 10·5	12 12·5	11 37·2	4·2 3·4	10·2 8·2	16·2 13·1
43	12 10·8	12 12·8	11 37·5	4·3 3·5	10·3 8·3	16·3 13·2
44	12 11·0	12 13·0	11 37·7	4·4 3·6	10·4 8·4	16·4 13·3
45	12 11·3	12 13·3	11 37·9	4·5 3·6	10·5 8·5	16·5 13·3
46	12 11·5	12 13·5	11 38·2	4·6 3·7	10·6 8·6	16·6 13·4
47	12 11·8	12 13·8	11 38·4	4·7 3·8	10·7 8·6	16·7 13·5
48	12 12·0	12 14·0	11 38·7	4·8 3·9	10·8 8·7	16·8 13·6
49	12 12·3	12 14·3	11 38·9	4·9 4·0	10·9 8·8	16·9 13·7
50	12 12·5	12 14·5	11 39·1	5·0 4·0	11·0 8·9	17·0 13·7
51	12 12·8	12 14·8	11 39·4	5·1 4·1	11·1 9·0	17·1 13·8
52	12 13·0	12 15·0	11 39·6	5·2 4·2	11·2 9·1	17·2 13·9
53	12 13·3	12 15·3	11 39·8	5·3 4·3	11·3 9·1	17·3 14·0
54	12 13·5	12 15·5	11 40·1	5·4 4·4	11·4 9·2	17·4 14·1
55	12 13·8	12 15·8	11 40·3	5·5 4·4	11·5 9·3	17·5 14·1
56	12 14·0	12 16·0	11 40·6	5·6 4·5	11·6 9·4	17·6 14·2
57	12 14·3	12 16·3	11 40·8	5·7 4·6	11·7 9·5	17·7 14·3
58	12 14·5	12 16·5	11 41·0	5·8 4·7	11·8 9·5	17·8 14·4
59	12 14·8	12 16·8	11 41·3	5·9 4·8	11·9 9·6	17·9 14·5
60	12 15·0	12 17·0	11 41·5	6·0 4·9	12·0 9·7	18·0 14·6

49	SUN PLANETS	ARIES	MOON	v or d Corrⁿ	v or d Corrⁿ	v or d Corrⁿ
s	° ′	° ′	° ′	′ ′	′ ′	′ ′
00	12 15·0	12 17·0	11 41·5	0·0 0·0	6·0 5·0	12·0 9·9
01	12 15·3	12 17·3	11 41·8	0·1 0·1	6·1 5·0	12·1 10·0
02	12 15·5	12 17·5	11 42·0	0·2 0·2	6·2 5·1	12·2 10·1
03	12 15·8	12 17·8	11 42·2	0·3 0·2	6·3 5·2	12·3 10·1
04	12 16·0	12 18·0	11 42·5	0·4 0·3	6·4 5·3	12·4 10·2
05	12 16·3	12 18·3	11 42·7	0·5 0·4	6·5 5·4	12·5 10·3
06	12 16·5	12 18·5	11 42·9	0·6 0·5	6·6 5·4	12·6 10·4
07	12 16·8	12 18·8	11 43·2	0·7 0·6	6·7 5·5	12·7 10·5
08	12 17·0	12 19·0	11 43·4	0·8 0·7	6·8 5·6	12·8 10·6
09	12 17·3	12 19·3	11 43·7	0·9 0·7	6·9 5·7	12·9 10·6
10	12 17·5	12 19·5	11 43·9	1·0 0·8	7·0 5·8	13·0 10·7
11	12 17·8	12 19·8	11 44·1	1·1 0·9	7·1 5·9	13·1 10·8
12	12 18·0	12 20·0	11 44·4	1·2 1·0	7·2 5·9	13·2 10·9
13	12 18·3	12 20·3	11 44·6	1·3 1·1	7·3 6·0	13·3 11·0
14	12 18·5	12 20·5	11 44·9	1·4 1·2	7·4 6·1	13·4 11·1
15	12 18·8	12 20·8	11 45·1	1·5 1·2	7·5 6·2	13·5 11·1
16	12 19·0	12 21·0	11 45·3	1·6 1·3	7·6 6·3	13·6 11·2
17	12 19·3	12 21·3	11 45·6	1·7 1·4	7·7 6·4	13·7 11·3
18	12 19·5	12 21·5	11 45·8	1·8 1·5	7·8 6·4	13·8 11·4
19	12 19·8	12 21·8	11 46·1	1·9 1·6	7·9 6·5	13·9 11·5
20	12 20·0	12 22·0	11 46·3	2·0 1·7	8·0 6·6	14·0 11·6
21	12 20·3	12 22·3	11 46·5	2·1 1·7	8·1 6·7	14·1 11·6
22	12 20·5	12 22·5	11 46·8	2·2 1·8	8·2 6·8	14·2 11·7
23	12 20·8	12 22·8	11 47·0	2·3 1·9	8·3 6·8	14·3 11·8
24	12 21·0	12 23·0	11 47·2	2·4 2·0	8·4 6·9	14·4 11·9
25	12 21·3	12 23·3	11 47·5	2·5 2·1	8·5 7·0	14·5 12·0
26	12 21·5	12 23·5	11 47·7	2·6 2·1	8·6 7·1	14·6 12·0
27	12 21·8	12 23·8	11 48·0	2·7 2·2	8·7 7·2	14·7 12·1
28	12 22·0	12 24·0	11 48·2	2·8 2·3	8·8 7·3	14·8 12·2
29	12 22·3	12 24·3	11 48·4	2·9 2·4	8·9 7·3	14·9 12·3
30	12 22·5	12 24·5	11 48·7	3·0 2·5	9·0 7·4	15·0 12·4
31	12 22·8	12 24·8	11 48·9	3·1 2·6	9·1 7·5	15·1 12·5
32	12 23·0	12 25·0	11 49·2	3·2 2·6	9·2 7·6	15·2 12·5
33	12 23·3	12 25·3	11 49·4	3·3 2·7	9·3 7·7	15·3 12·6
34	12 23·5	12 25·5	11 49·6	3·4 2·8	9·4 7·8	15·4 12·7
35	12 23·8	12 25·8	11 49·9	3·5 2·9	9·5 7·8	15·5 12·8
36	12 24·0	12 26·0	11 50·1	3·6 3·0	9·6 7·9	15·6 12·9
37	12 24·3	12 26·3	11 50·3	3·7 3·1	9·7 8·0	15·7 13·0
38	12 24·5	12 26·5	11 50·6	3·8 3·1	9·8 8·1	15·8 13·0
39	12 24·8	12 26·8	11 50·8	3·9 3·2	9·9 8·2	15·9 13·1
40	12 25·0	12 27·0	11 51·1	4·0 3·3	10·0 8·3	16·0 13·2
41	12 25·3	12 27·3	11 51·3	4·1 3·4	10·1 8·3	16·1 13·3
42	12 25·5	12 27·5	11 51·5	4·2 3·5	10·2 8·4	16·2 13·4
43	12 25·8	12 27·8	11 51·8	4·3 3·5	10·3 8·5	16·3 13·4
44	12 26·0	12 28·0	11 52·0	4·4 3·6	10·4 8·6	16·4 13·5
45	12 26·3	12 28·3	11 52·3	4·5 3·7	10·5 8·7	16·5 13·6
46	12 26·5	12 28·5	11 52·5	4·6 3·8	10·6 8·7	16·6 13·7
47	12 26·8	12 28·8	11 52·7	4·7 3·9	10·7 8·8	16·7 13·8
48	12 27·0	12 29·0	11 53·0	4·8 4·0	10·8 8·9	16·8 13·9
49	12 27·3	12 29·3	11 53·2	4·9 4·0	10·9 9·0	16·9 13·9
50	12 27·5	12 29·5	11 53·4	5·0 4·1	11·0 9·1	17·0 14·0
51	12 27·8	12 29·8	11 53·7	5·1 4·2	11·1 9·2	17·1 14·1
52	12 28·0	12 30·0	11 53·9	5·2 4·3	11·2 9·2	17·2 14·2
53	12 28·3	12 30·3	11 54·2	5·3 4·4	11·3 9·3	17·3 14·3
54	12 28·5	12 30·5	11 54·4	5·4 4·5	11·4 9·4	17·4 14·4
55	12 28·8	12 30·8	11 54·6	5·5 4·5	11·5 9·5	17·5 14·4
56	12 29·0	12 31·1	11 54·9	5·6 4·6	11·6 9·6	17·6 14·5
57	12 29·3	12 31·3	11 55·1	5·7 4·7	11·7 9·7	17·7 14·6
58	12 29·5	12 31·6	11 55·4	5·8 4·8	11·8 9·7	17·8 14·7
59	12 29·8	12 31·8	11 55·6	5·9 4·9	11·9 9·8	17·9 14·8
60	12 30·0	12 32·1	11 55·8	6·0 5·0	12·0 9·9	18·0 14·9

50ᵐ

s	SUN PLANETS	ARIES	MOON	v or d	Corrⁿ	v or d	Corrⁿ	v or d	Corrⁿ
00	12 30.0	12 32.1	11 55.8	0.0	0.0	6.0	5.1	12.0	10.1
01	12 30.3	12 32.3	11 56.1	0.1	0.1	6.1	5.1	12.1	10.2
02	12 30.5	12 32.6	11 56.3	0.2	0.2	6.2	5.2	12.2	10.3
03	12 30.8	12 32.8	11 56.5	0.3	0.3	6.3	5.3	12.3	10.4
04	12 31.0	12 33.1	11 56.8	0.4	0.3	6.4	5.4	12.4	10.4
05	12 31.3	12 33.3	11 57.0	0.5	0.4	6.5	5.5	12.5	10.5
06	12 31.5	12 33.6	11 57.3	0.6	0.5	6.6	5.6	12.6	10.6
07	12 31.8	12 33.8	11 57.5	0.7	0.6	6.7	5.6	12.7	10.7
08	12 32.0	12 34.1	11 57.7	0.8	0.7	6.8	5.7	12.8	10.8
09	12 32.3	12 34.3	11 58.0	0.9	0.8	6.9	5.8	12.9	10.9
10	12 32.5	12 34.6	11 58.2	1.0	0.8	7.0	5.9	13.0	10.9
11	12 32.8	12 34.8	11 58.5	1.1	0.9	7.1	6.0	13.1	11.0
12	12 33.0	12 35.1	11 58.7	1.2	1.0	7.2	6.1	13.2	11.1
13	12 33.3	12 35.3	11 58.9	1.3	1.1	7.3	6.1	13.3	11.2
14	12 33.5	12 35.6	11 59.2	1.4	1.2	7.4	6.2	13.4	11.3
15	12 33.8	12 35.8	11 59.4	1.5	1.3	7.5	6.3	13.5	11.4
16	12 34.0	12 36.1	11 59.7	1.6	1.3	7.6	6.4	13.6	11.4
17	12 34.3	12 36.3	11 59.9	1.7	1.4	7.7	6.5	13.7	11.5
18	12 34.5	12 36.6	12 00.1	1.8	1.5	7.8	6.6	13.8	11.6
19	12 34.8	12 36.8	12 00.4	1.9	1.6	7.9	6.6	13.9	11.7
20	12 35.0	12 37.1	12 00.6	2.0	1.7	8.0	6.7	14.0	11.8
21	12 35.3	12 37.3	12 00.8	2.1	1.8	8.1	6.8	14.1	11.9
22	12 35.5	12 37.6	12 01.1	2.2	1.9	8.2	6.9	14.2	12.0
23	12 35.8	12 37.8	12 01.3	2.3	1.9	8.3	7.0	14.3	12.0
24	12 36.0	12 38.1	12 01.6	2.4	2.0	8.4	7.1	14.4	12.1
25	12 36.3	12 38.3	12 01.8	2.5	2.1	8.5	7.2	14.5	12.2
26	12 36.5	12 38.6	12 02.0	2.6	2.2	8.6	7.2	14.6	12.3
27	12 36.8	12 38.8	12 02.3	2.7	2.3	8.7	7.3	14.7	12.4
28	12 37.0	12 39.1	12 02.5	2.8	2.4	8.8	7.4	14.8	12.5
29	12 37.3	12 39.3	12 02.8	2.9	2.4	8.9	7.5	14.9	12.5
30	12 37.5	12 39.6	12 03.0	3.0	2.5	9.0	7.6	15.0	12.6
31	12 37.8	12 39.8	12 03.2	3.1	2.6	9.1	7.7	15.1	12.7
32	12 38.0	12 40.1	12 03.5	3.2	2.7	9.2	7.7	15.2	12.8
33	12 38.3	12 40.3	12 03.7	3.3	2.8	9.3	7.8	15.3	12.9
34	12 38.5	12 40.6	12 03.9	3.4	2.9	9.4	7.9	15.4	13.0
35	12 38.8	12 40.8	12 04.2	3.5	2.9	9.5	8.0	15.5	13.0
36	12 39.0	12 41.1	12 04.4	3.6	3.0	9.6	8.1	15.6	13.1
37	12 39.3	12 41.3	12 04.7	3.7	3.1	9.7	8.2	15.7	13.2
38	12 39.5	12 41.6	12 04.9	3.8	3.2	9.8	8.2	15.8	13.3
39	12 39.8	12 41.8	12 05.1	3.9	3.3	9.9	8.3	15.9	13.4
40	12 40.0	12 42.1	12 05.4	4.0	3.4	10.0	8.4	16.0	13.5
41	12 40.3	12 42.3	12 05.6	4.1	3.5	10.1	8.5	16.1	13.6
42	12 40.5	12 42.6	12 05.9	4.2	3.5	10.2	8.6	16.2	13.6
43	12 40.8	12 42.8	12 06.1	4.3	3.6	10.3	8.7	16.3	13.7
44	12 41.0	12 43.1	12 06.3	4.4	3.7	10.4	8.8	16.4	13.8
45	12 41.3	12 43.3	12 06.6	4.5	3.8	10.5	8.8	16.5	13.9
46	12 41.5	12 43.6	12 06.8	4.6	3.9	10.6	8.9	16.6	14.0
47	12 41.8	12 43.8	12 07.0	4.7	4.0	10.7	9.0	16.7	14.1
48	12 42.0	12 44.1	12 07.3	4.8	4.0	10.8	9.1	16.8	14.1
49	12 42.3	12 44.3	12 07.5	4.9	4.1	10.9	9.2	16.9	14.2
50	12 42.5	12 44.6	12 07.8	5.0	4.2	11.0	9.3	17.0	14.3
51	12 42.8	12 44.8	12 08.0	5.1	4.3	11.1	9.3	17.1	14.4
52	12 43.0	12 45.1	12 08.2	5.2	4.4	11.2	9.4	17.2	14.5
53	12 43.3	12 45.3	12 08.5	5.3	4.5	11.3	9.5	17.3	14.6
54	12 43.5	12 45.6	12 08.7	5.4	4.5	11.4	9.6	17.4	14.6
55	12 43.8	12 45.8	12 09.0	5.5	4.6	11.5	9.7	17.5	14.7
56	12 44.0	12 46.1	12 09.2	5.6	4.7	11.6	9.8	17.6	14.8
57	12 44.3	12 46.3	12 09.4	5.7	4.8	11.7	9.8	17.7	14.9
58	12 44.5	12 46.6	12 09.7	5.8	4.9	11.8	9.9	17.8	15.0
59	12 44.8	12 46.8	12 09.9	5.9	5.0	11.9	10.0	17.9	15.1
60	12 45.0	12 47.1	12 10.2	6.0	5.1	12.0	10.1	18.0	15.2

51ᵐ

s	SUN PLANETS	ARIES	MOON	v or d	Corrⁿ	v or d	Corrⁿ	v or d	Corrⁿ
00	12 45.0	12 47.1	12 10.2	0.0	0.0	6.0	5.2	12.0	10.3
01	12 45.3	12 47.3	12 10.4	0.1	0.1	6.1	5.2	12.1	10.4
02	12 45.5	12 47.6	12 10.6	0.2	0.2	6.2	5.3	12.2	10.5
03	12 45.8	12 47.8	12 10.9	0.3	0.3	6.3	5.4	12.3	10.6
04	12 46.0	12 48.1	12 11.1	0.4	0.3	6.4	5.5	12.4	10.6
05	12 46.3	12 48.3	12 11.3	0.5	0.4	6.5	5.6	12.5	10.7
06	12 46.5	12 48.6	12 11.6	0.6	0.5	6.6	5.7	12.6	10.8
07	12 46.8	12 48.8	12 11.8	0.7	0.6	6.7	5.8	12.7	10.9
08	12 47.0	12 49.1	12 12.1	0.8	0.7	6.8	5.8	12.8	11.0
09	12 47.3	12 49.4	12 12.3	0.9	0.8	6.9	5.9	12.9	11.1
10	12 47.5	12 49.6	12 12.5	1.0	0.9	7.0	6.0	13.0	11.2
11	12 47.8	12 49.9	12 12.8	1.1	0.9	7.1	6.1	13.1	11.2
12	12 48.0	12 50.1	12 13.0	1.2	1.0	7.2	6.2	13.2	11.3
13	12 48.3	12 50.4	12 13.3	1.3	1.1	7.3	6.3	13.3	11.4
14	12 48.5	12 50.6	12 13.5	1.4	1.2	7.4	6.4	13.4	11.5
15	12 48.8	12 50.9	12 13.7	1.5	1.3	7.5	6.4	13.5	11.6
16	12 49.0	12 51.1	12 14.0	1.6	1.4	7.6	6.5	13.6	11.7
17	12 49.3	12 51.4	12 14.2	1.7	1.5	7.7	6.6	13.7	11.8
18	12 49.5	12 51.6	12 14.4	1.8	1.5	7.8	6.7	13.8	11.8
19	12 49.8	12 51.9	12 14.7	1.9	1.6	7.9	6.8	13.9	11.9
20	12 50.0	12 52.1	12 14.9	2.0	1.7	8.0	6.9	14.0	12.0
21	12 50.3	12 52.4	12 15.2	2.1	1.8	8.1	7.0	14.1	12.1
22	12 50.5	12 52.6	12 15.4	2.2	1.9	8.2	7.0	14.2	12.2
23	12 50.8	12 52.9	12 15.6	2.3	2.0	8.3	7.1	14.3	12.3
24	12 51.0	12 53.1	12 15.9	2.4	2.1	8.4	7.2	14.4	12.4
25	12 51.3	12 53.4	12 16.1	2.5	2.1	8.5	7.3	14.5	12.4
26	12 51.5	12 53.6	12 16.4	2.6	2.2	8.6	7.4	14.6	12.5
27	12 51.8	12 53.9	12 16.6	2.7	2.3	8.7	7.5	14.7	12.6
28	12 52.0	12 54.1	12 16.8	2.8	2.4	8.8	7.6	14.8	12.7
29	12 52.3	12 54.4	12 17.1	2.9	2.5	8.9	7.6	14.9	12.8
30	12 52.5	12 54.6	12 17.3	3.0	2.6	9.0	7.7	15.0	12.9
31	12 52.8	12 54.9	12 17.5	3.1	2.7	9.1	7.8	15.1	13.0
32	12 53.0	12 55.1	12 17.8	3.2	2.7	9.2	7.9	15.2	13.0
33	12 53.3	12 55.4	12 18.0	3.3	2.8	9.3	8.0	15.3	13.1
34	12 53.5	12 55.6	12 18.3	3.4	2.9	9.4	8.1	15.4	13.2
35	12 53.8	12 55.9	12 18.5	3.5	3.0	9.5	8.2	15.5	13.3
36	12 54.0	12 56.1	12 18.7	3.6	3.1	9.6	8.2	15.6	13.4
37	12 54.3	12 56.4	12 19.0	3.7	3.2	9.7	8.3	15.7	13.5
38	12 54.5	12 56.6	12 19.2	3.8	3.3	9.8	8.4	15.8	13.6
39	12 54.8	12 56.9	12 19.5	3.9	3.3	9.9	8.5	15.9	13.6
40	12 55.0	12 57.1	12 19.7	4.0	3.4	10.0	8.6	16.0	13.7
41	12 55.3	12 57.4	12 19.9	4.1	3.5	10.1	8.7	16.1	13.8
42	12 55.5	12 57.6	12 20.2	4.2	3.6	10.2	8.8	16.2	13.9
43	12 55.8	12 57.9	12 20.4	4.3	3.7	10.3	8.8	16.3	14.0
44	12 56.0	12 58.1	12 20.6	4.4	3.8	10.4	8.9	16.4	14.1
45	12 56.3	12 58.4	12 20.9	4.5	3.9	10.5	9.0	16.5	14.2
46	12 56.5	12 58.6	12 21.1	4.6	3.9	10.6	9.1	16.6	14.2
47	12 56.8	12 58.9	12 21.4	4.7	4.0	10.7	9.2	16.7	14.3
48	12 57.0	12 59.1	12 21.6	4.8	4.1	10.8	9.3	16.8	14.4
49	12 57.3	12 59.4	12 21.8	4.9	4.2	10.9	9.4	16.9	14.5
50	12 57.5	12 59.6	12 22.1	5.0	4.3	11.0	9.4	17.0	14.6
51	12 57.8	12 59.9	12 22.3	5.1	4.4	11.1	9.5	17.1	14.7
52	12 58.0	13 00.1	12 22.6	5.2	4.5	11.2	9.6	17.2	14.8
53	12 58.3	13 00.4	12 22.8	5.3	4.5	11.3	9.7	17.3	14.8
54	12 58.5	13 00.6	12 23.0	5.4	4.6	11.4	9.8	17.4	14.9
55	12 58.8	13 00.9	12 23.3	5.5	4.7	11.5	9.9	17.5	15.0
56	12 59.0	13 01.1	12 23.5	5.6	4.8	11.6	10.0	17.6	15.1
57	12 59.3	13 01.4	12 23.8	5.7	4.9	11.7	10.0	17.7	15.2
58	12 59.5	13 01.6	12 24.0	5.8	5.0	11.8	10.1	17.8	15.3
59	12 59.8	13 01.9	12 24.2	5.9	5.1	11.9	10.2	17.9	15.4
60	13 00.0	13 02.1	12 24.5	6.0	5.2	12.0	10.3	18.0	15.5

52^m	SUN PLANETS	ARIES	MOON	v or d Corr^n	v or d Corr^n	v or d Corr^n
s	° ′	° ′	° ′	′ ′	′ ′	′ ′
00	13 00.0	13 02.1	12 24.5	0.0 0.0	6.0 5.3	12.0 10.5
01	13 00.3	13 02.4	12 24.7	0.1 0.1	6.1 5.3	12.1 10.6
02	13 00.5	13 02.6	12 24.9	0.2 0.2	6.2 5.4	12.2 10.7
03	13 00.8	13 02.9	12 25.2	0.3 0.3	6.3 5.5	12.3 10.8
04	13 01.0	13 03.1	12 25.4	0.4 0.4	6.4 5.6	12.4 10.9
05	13 01.3	13 03.4	12 25.7	0.5 0.4	6.5 5.7	12.5 10.9
06	13 01.5	13 03.6	12 25.9	0.6 0.5	6.6 5.8	12.6 11.0
07	13 01.8	13 03.9	12 26.1	0.7 0.6	6.7 5.9	12.7 11.1
08	13 02.0	13 04.1	12 26.4	0.8 0.7	6.8 6.0	12.8 11.2
09	13 02.3	13 04.4	12 26.6	0.9 0.8	6.9 6.0	12.9 11.3
10	13 02.5	13 04.6	12 26.9	1.0 0.9	7.0 6.1	13.0 11.4
11	13 02.8	13 04.9	12 27.1	1.1 1.0	7.1 6.2	13.1 11.5
12	13 03.0	13 05.1	12 27.3	1.2 1.1	7.2 6.3	13.2 11.6
13	13 03.3	13 05.4	12 27.6	1.3 1.1	7.3 6.4	13.3 11.6
14	13 03.5	13 05.6	12 27.8	1.4 1.2	7.4 6.5	13.4 11.7
15	13 03.8	13 05.9	12 28.0	1.5 1.3	7.5 6.6	13.5 11.8
16	13 04.0	13 06.1	12 28.3	1.6 1.4	7.6 6.7	13.6 11.9
17	13 04.3	13 06.4	12 28.5	1.7 1.5	7.7 6.7	13.7 12.0
18	13 04.5	13 06.6	12 28.8	1.8 1.6	7.8 6.8	13.8 12.1
19	13 04.8	13 06.9	12 29.0	1.9 1.7	7.9 6.9	13.9 12.2
20	13 05.0	13 07.1	12 29.2	2.0 1.8	8.0 7.0	14.0 12.3
21	13 05.3	13 07.4	12 29.5	2.1 1.8	8.1 7.1	14.1 12.3
22	13 05.5	13 07.7	12 29.7	2.2 1.9	8.2 7.2	14.2 12.4
23	13 05.8	13 07.9	12 30.0	2.3 2.0	8.3 7.3	14.3 12.5
24	13 06.0	13 08.2	12 30.2	2.4 2.1	8.4 7.4	14.4 12.6
25	13 06.3	13 08.4	12 30.4	2.5 2.2	8.5 7.4	14.5 12.7
26	13 06.5	13 08.7	12 30.7	2.6 2.3	8.6 7.5	14.6 12.8
27	13 06.8	13 08.9	12 30.9	2.7 2.4	8.7 7.6	14.7 12.9
28	13 07.0	13 09.2	12 31.1	2.8 2.5	8.8 7.7	14.8 13.0
29	13 07.3	13 09.4	12 31.4	2.9 2.5	8.9 7.8	14.9 13.0
30	13 07.5	13 09.7	12 31.6	3.0 2.6	9.0 7.9	15.0 13.1
31	13 07.8	13 09.9	12 31.9	3.1 2.7	9.1 8.0	15.1 13.2
32	13 08.0	13 10.2	12 32.1	3.2 2.8	9.2 8.0	15.2 13.3
33	13 08.3	13 10.4	12 32.3	3.3 2.9	9.3 8.1	15.3 13.4
34	13 08.5	13 10.7	12 32.6	3.4 3.0	9.4 8.2	15.4 13.5
35	13 08.8	13 10.9	12 32.8	3.5 3.1	9.5 8.3	15.5 13.6
36	13 09.0	13 11.2	12 33.1	3.6 3.2	9.6 8.4	15.6 13.7
37	13 09.3	13 11.4	12 33.3	3.7 3.2	9.7 8.5	15.7 13.7
38	13 09.5	13 11.7	12 33.5	3.8 3.3	9.8 8.6	15.8 13.8
39	13 09.8	13 11.9	12 33.8	3.9 3.4	9.9 8.7	15.9 13.9
40	13 10.0	13 12.2	12 34.0	4.0 3.5	10.0 8.8	16.0 14.0
41	13 10.3	13 12.4	12 34.2	4.1 3.6	10.1 8.8	16.1 14.1
42	13 10.5	13 12.7	12 34.5	4.2 3.7	10.2 8.9	16.2 14.2
43	13 10.8	13 12.9	12 34.7	4.3 3.8	10.3 9.0	16.3 14.3
44	13 11.0	13 13.2	12 35.0	4.4 3.9	10.4 9.1	16.4 14.3
45	13 11.3	13 13.4	12 35.2	4.5 3.9	10.5 9.2	16.5 14.4
46	13 11.5	13 13.7	12 35.4	4.6 4.0	10.6 9.3	16.6 14.5
47	13 11.8	13 13.9	12 35.7	4.7 4.1	10.7 9.4	16.7 14.6
48	13 12.0	13 14.2	12 35.9	4.8 4.2	10.8 9.5	16.8 14.7
49	13 12.3	13 14.4	12 36.2	4.9 4.3	10.9 9.5	16.9 14.8
50	13 12.5	13 14.7	12 36.4	5.0 4.4	11.0 9.6	17.0 14.9
51	13 12.8	13 14.9	12 36.6	5.1 4.5	11.1 9.7	17.1 15.0
52	13 13.0	13 15.2	12 36.9	5.2 4.6	11.2 9.8	17.2 15.1
53	13 13.3	13 15.4	12 37.1	5.3 4.6	11.3 9.9	17.3 15.1
54	13 13.5	13 15.7	12 37.4	5.4 4.7	11.4 10.0	17.4 15.2
55	13 13.8	13 15.9	12 37.6	5.5 4.8	11.5 10.1	17.5 15.3
56	13 14.0	13 16.2	12 37.8	5.6 4.9	11.6 10.2	17.6 15.4
57	13 14.3	13 16.4	12 38.1	5.7 5.0	11.7 10.2	17.7 15.5
58	13 14.5	13 16.7	12 38.3	5.8 5.1	11.8 10.3	17.8 15.6
59	13 14.8	13 16.9	12 38.5	5.9 5.2	11.9 10.4	17.9 15.7
60	13 15.0	13 17.2	12 38.8	6.0 5.3	12.0 10.5	18.0 15.8

53^m	SUN PLANETS	ARIES	MOON	v or d Corr^n	v or d Corr^n	v or d Corr^n
s	° ′	° ′	° ′	′ ′	′ ′	′ ′
00	13 15.0	13 17.2	12 38.8	0.0 0.0	6.0 5.4	12.0 10.7
01	13 15.3	13 17.4	12 39.0	0.1 0.1	6.1 5.4	12.1 10.8
02	13 15.5	13 17.7	12 39.3	0.2 0.2	6.2 5.5	12.2 10.9
03	13 15.8	13 17.9	12 39.5	0.3 0.3	6.3 5.6	12.3 11.0
04	13 16.0	13 18.2	12 39.7	0.4 0.4	6.4 5.7	12.4 11.1
05	13 16.3	13 18.4	12 40.0	0.5 0.4	6.5 5.8	12.5 11.1
06	13 16.5	13 18.7	12 40.2	0.6 0.5	6.6 5.9	12.6 11.2
07	13 16.8	13 18.9	12 40.5	0.7 0.6	6.7 6.0	12.7 11.3
08	13 17.0	13 19.2	12 40.7	0.8 0.7	6.8 6.1	12.8 11.4
09	13 17.3	13 19.4	12 40.9	0.9 0.8	6.9 6.2	12.9 11.5
10	13 17.5	13 19.7	12 41.2	1.0 0.9	7.0 6.2	13.0 11.6
11	13 17.8	13 19.9	12 41.4	1.1 1.0	7.1 6.3	13.1 11.7
12	13 18.0	13 20.2	12 41.6	1.2 1.1	7.2 6.4	13.2 11.8
13	13 18.3	13 20.4	12 41.9	1.3 1.2	7.3 6.5	13.3 11.9
14	13 18.5	13 20.7	12 42.1	1.4 1.2	7.4 6.6	13.4 11.9
15	13 18.8	13 20.9	12 42.4	1.5 1.3	7.5 6.7	13.5 12.0
16	13 19.0	13 21.2	12 42.6	1.6 1.4	7.6 6.8	13.6 12.1
17	13 19.3	13 21.4	12 42.8	1.7 1.5	7.7 6.9	13.7 12.2
18	13 19.5	13 21.7	12 43.1	1.8 1.6	7.8 7.0	13.8 12.3
19	13 19.8	13 21.9	12 43.3	1.9 1.7	7.9 7.0	13.9 12.4
20	13 20.0	13 22.2	12 43.6	2.0 1.8	8.0 7.1	14.0 12.5
21	13 20.3	13 22.4	12 43.8	2.1 1.9	8.1 7.2	14.1 12.6
22	13 20.5	13 22.7	12 44.0	2.2 2.0	8.2 7.3	14.2 12.7
23	13 20.8	13 22.9	12 44.3	2.3 2.1	8.3 7.4	14.3 12.8
24	13 21.0	13 23.2	12 44.5	2.4 2.1	8.4 7.5	14.4 12.8
25	13 21.3	13 23.4	12 44.7	2.5 2.2	8.5 7.6	14.5 12.9
26	13 21.5	13 23.7	12 45.0	2.6 2.3	8.6 7.7	14.6 13.0
27	13 21.8	13 23.9	12 45.2	2.7 2.4	8.7 7.8	14.7 13.1
28	13 22.0	13 24.2	12 45.5	2.8 2.5	8.8 7.8	14.8 13.2
29	13 22.3	13 24.4	12 45.7	2.9 2.6	8.9 7.9	14.9 13.3
30	13 22.5	13 24.7	12 45.9	3.0 2.7	9.0 8.0	15.0 13.4
31	13 22.8	13 24.9	12 46.2	3.1 2.8	9.1 8.1	15.1 13.5
32	13 23.0	13 25.2	12 46.4	3.2 2.9	9.2 8.2	15.2 13.6
33	13 23.3	13 25.4	12 46.7	3.3 2.9	9.3 8.3	15.3 13.6
34	13 23.5	13 25.7	12 46.9	3.4 3.0	9.4 8.4	15.4 13.7
35	13 23.8	13 26.0	12 47.1	3.5 3.1	9.5 8.5	15.5 13.8
36	13 24.0	13 26.2	12 47.4	3.6 3.2	9.6 8.6	15.6 13.9
37	13 24.3	13 26.5	12 47.6	3.7 3.3	9.7 8.6	15.7 14.0
38	13 24.5	13 26.7	12 47.9	3.8 3.4	9.8 8.7	15.8 14.1
39	13 24.8	13 27.0	12 48.1	3.9 3.5	9.9 8.8	15.9 14.2
40	13 25.0	13 27.2	12 48.3	4.0 3.6	10.0 8.9	16.0 14.3
41	13 25.3	13 27.5	12 48.6	4.1 3.7	10.1 9.0	16.1 14.4
42	13 25.5	13 27.7	12 48.8	4.2 3.7	10.2 9.1	16.2 14.4
43	13 25.8	13 28.0	12 49.0	4.3 3.8	10.3 9.2	16.3 14.5
44	13 26.0	13 28.2	12 49.3	4.4 3.9	10.4 9.3	16.4 14.6
45	13 26.3	13 28.5	12 49.5	4.5 4.0	10.5 9.4	16.5 14.7
46	13 26.5	13 28.7	12 49.8	4.6 4.1	10.6 9.5	16.6 14.8
47	13 26.8	13 29.0	12 50.0	4.7 4.2	10.7 9.5	16.7 14.9
48	13 27.0	13 29.2	12 50.2	4.8 4.3	10.8 9.6	16.8 15.0
49	13 27.3	13 29.5	12 50.5	4.9 4.4	10.9 9.7	16.9 15.1
50	13 27.5	13 29.7	12 50.7	5.0 4.5	11.0 9.8	17.0 15.2
51	13 27.8	13 30.0	12 51.0	5.1 4.5	11.1 9.9	17.1 15.2
52	13 28.0	13 30.2	12 51.2	5.2 4.6	11.2 10.0	17.2 15.3
53	13 28.3	13 30.5	12 51.4	5.3 4.7	11.3 10.1	17.3 15.4
54	13 28.5	13 30.7	12 51.7	5.4 4.8	11.4 10.2	17.4 15.5
55	13 28.8	13 31.0	12 51.9	5.5 4.9	11.5 10.3	17.5 15.6
56	13 29.0	13 31.2	12 52.1	5.6 5.0	11.6 10.3	17.6 15.7
57	13 29.3	13 31.5	12 52.4	5.7 5.1	11.7 10.4	17.7 15.8
58	13 29.5	13 31.7	12 52.6	5.8 5.2	11.8 10.5	17.8 15.9
59	13 29.8	13 32.0	12 52.9	5.9 5.3	11.9 10.6	17.9 16.0
60	13 30.0	13 32.2	12 53.1	6.0 5.4	12.0 10.7	18.0 16.1

54ᵐ	SUN PLANETS	ARIES	MOON	v or d Corrⁿ		v or d Corrⁿ		v or d Corrⁿ	
s	° ′	° ′	° ′	′	′	′	′	′	′
00	13 30·0	13 32·2	12 53·1	0·0	0·0	6·0	5·5	12·0	10·9
01	13 30·3	13 32·5	12 53·3	0·1	0·1	6·1	5·5	12·1	11·0
02	13 30·5	13 32·7	12 53·6	0·2	0·2	6·2	5·6	12·2	11·1
03	13 30·8	13 33·0	12 53·8	0·3	0·3	6·3	5·7	12·3	11·2
04	13 31·0	13 33·2	12 54·1	0·4	0·4	6·4	5·8	12·4	11·3
05	13 31·3	13 33·5	12 54·3	0·5	0·5	6·5	5·9	12·5	11·4
06	13 31·5	13 33·7	12 54·5	0·6	0·5	6·6	6·0	12·6	11·4
07	13 31·8	13 34·0	12 54·8	0·7	0·6	6·7	6·1	12·7	11·5
08	13 32·0	13 34·2	12 55·0	0·8	0·7	6·8	6·2	12·8	11·6
09	13 32·3	13 34·5	12 55·2	0·9	0·8	6·9	6·3	12·9	11·7
10	13 32·5	13 34·7	12 55·5	1·0	0·9	7·0	6·4	13·0	11·8
11	13 32·8	13 35·0	12 55·7	1·1	1·0	7·1	6·4	13·1	11·9
12	13 33·0	13 35·2	12 56·0	1·2	1·1	7·2	6·5	13·2	12·0
13	13 33·3	13 35·5	12 56·2	1·3	1·2	7·3	6·6	13·3	12·1
14	13 33·5	13 35·7	12 56·4	1·4	1·3	7·4	6·7	13·4	12·2
15	13 33·8	13 36·0	12 56·7	1·5	1·4	7·5	6·8	13·5	12·3
16	13 34·0	13 36·2	12 56·9	1·6	1·5	7·6	6·9	13·6	12·4
17	13 34·3	13 36·5	12 57·2	1·7	1·5	7·7	7·0	13·7	12·4
18	13 34·5	13 36·7	12 57·4	1·8	1·6	7·8	7·1	13·8	12·5
19	13 34·8	13 37·0	12 57·6	1·9	1·7	7·9	7·2	13·9	12·6
20	13 35·0	13 37·2	12 57·9	2·0	1·8	8·0	7·3	14·0	12·7
21	13 35·3	13 37·5	12 58·1	2·1	1·9	8·1	7·4	14·1	12·8
22	13 35·5	13 37·7	12 58·3	2·2	2·0	8·2	7·4	14·2	12·9
23	13 35·8	13 38·0	12 58·6	2·3	2·1	8·3	7·5	14·3	13·0
24	13 36·0	13 38·2	12 58·8	2·4	2·2	8·4	7·6	14·4	13·1
25	13 36·3	13 38·5	12 59·1	2·5	2·3	8·5	7·7	14·5	13·2
26	13 36·5	13 38·7	12 59·3	2·6	2·4	8·6	7·8	14·6	13·3
27	13 36·8	13 39·0	12 59·5	2·7	2·5	8·7	7·9	14·7	13·4
28	13 37·0	13 39·2	12 59·8	2·8	2·5	8·8	8·0	14·8	13·4
29	13 37·3	13 39·5	13 00·0	2·9	2·6	8·9	8·1	14·9	13·5
30	13 37·5	13 39·7	13 00·3	3·0	2·7	9·0	8·2	15·0	13·6
31	13 37·8	13 40·0	13 00·5	3·1	2·8	9·1	8·3	15·1	13·7
32	13 38·0	13 40·2	13 00·7	3·2	2·9	9·2	8·4	15·2	13·8
33	13 38·3	13 40·5	13 01·0	3·3	3·0	9·3	8·4	15·3	13·9
34	13 38·5	13 40·7	13 01·2	3·4	3·1	9·4	8·5	15·4	14·0
35	13 38·8	13 41·0	13 01·5	3·5	3·2	9·5	8·6	15·5	14·1
36	13 39·0	13 41·2	13 01·7	3·6	3·3	9·6	8·7	15·6	14·2
37	13 39·3	13 41·5	13 01·9	3·7	3·4	9·7	8·8	15·7	14·3
38	13 39·5	13 41·7	13 02·2	3·8	3·5	9·8	8·9	15·8	14·4
39	13 39·8	13 42·0	13 02·4	3·9	3·5	9·9	9·0	15·9	14·4
40	13 40·0	13 42·2	13 02·6	4·0	3·6	10·0	9·1	16·0	14·5
41	13 40·3	13 42·5	13 02·9	4·1	3·7	10·1	9·2	16·1	14·6
42	13 40·5	13 42·7	13 03·1	4·2	3·8	10·2	9·3	16·2	14·7
43	13 40·8	13 43·0	13 03·4	4·3	3·9	10·3	9·4	16·3	14·8
44	13 41·0	13 43·2	13 03·6	4·4	4·0	10·4	9·4	16·4	14·9
45	13 41·3	13 43·5	13 03·8	4·5	4·1	10·5	9·5	16·5	15·0
46	13 41·5	13 43·7	13 04·1	4·6	4·2	10·6	9·6	16·6	15·1
47	13 41·8	13 44·0	13 04·3	4·7	4·3	10·7	9·7	16·7	15·2
48	13 42·0	13 44·3	13 04·6	4·8	4·4	10·8	9·8	16·8	15·3
49	13 42·3	13 44·5	13 04·8	4·9	4·5	10·9	9·9	16·9	15·4
50	13 42·5	13 44·8	13 05·0	5·0	4·5	11·0	10·0	17·0	15·4
51	13 42·8	13 45·0	13 05·3	5·1	4·6	11·1	10·1	17·1	15·5
52	13 43·0	13 45·3	13 05·5	5·2	4·7	11·2	10·2	17·2	15·6
53	13 43·3	13 45·5	13 05·7	5·3	4·8	11·3	10·3	17·3	15·7
54	13 43·5	13 45·8	13 06·0	5·4	4·9	11·4	10·4	17·4	15·8
55	13 43·8	13 46·0	13 06·2	5·5	5·0	11·5	10·4	17·5	15·9
56	13 44·0	13 46·3	13 06·5	5·6	5·1	11·6	10·5	17·6	16·0
57	13 44·3	13 46·5	13 06·7	5·7	5·2	11·7	10·6	17·7	16·1
58	13 44·5	13 46·8	13 06·9	5·8	5·3	11·8	10·7	17·8	16·2
59	13 44·8	13 47·0	13 07·2	5·9	5·4	11·9	10·8	17·9	16·3
60	13 45·0	13 47·3	13 07·4	6·0	5·5	12·0	10·9	18·0	16·4

55ᵐ	SUN PLANETS	ARIES	MOON	v or d Corrⁿ		v or d Corrⁿ		v or d Corrⁿ	
s	° ′	° ′	° ′	′	′	′	′	′	′
00	13 45·0	13 47·3	13 07·4	0·0	0·0	6·0	5·6	12·0	11·1
01	13 45·3	13 47·5	13 07·7	0·1	0·1	6·1	5·6	12·1	11·2
02	13 45·5	13 47·8	13 07·9	0·2	0·2	6·2	5·7	12·2	11·3
03	13 45·8	13 48·0	13 08·1	0·3	0·3	6·3	5·8	12·3	11·4
04	13 46·0	13 48·3	13 08·4	0·4	0·4	6·4	5·9	12·4	11·5
05	13 46·3	13 48·5	13 08·6	0·5	0·5	6·5	6·0	12·5	11·6
06	13 46·5	13 48·8	13 08·8	0·6	0·6	6·6	6·1	12·6	11·7
07	13 46·8	13 49·0	13 09·1	0·7	0·6	6·7	6·2	12·7	11·7
08	13 47·0	13 49·3	13 09·3	0·8	0·7	6·8	6·3	12·8	11·8
09	13 47·3	13 49·5	13 09·6	0·9	0·8	6·9	6·4	12·9	11·9
10	13 47·5	13 49·8	13 09·8	1·0	0·9	7·0	6·5	13·0	12·0
11	13 47·8	13 50·0	13 10·0	1·1	1·0	7·1	6·6	13·1	12·1
12	13 48·0	13 50·3	13 10·3	1·2	1·1	7·2	6·7	13·2	12·2
13	13 48·3	13 50·5	13 10·5	1·3	1·2	7·3	6·8	13·3	12·3
14	13 48·5	13 50·8	13 10·8	1·4	1·3	7·4	6·8	13·4	12·4
15	13 48·8	13 51·0	13 11·0	1·5	1·4	7·5	6·9	13·5	12·5
16	13 49·0	13 51·3	13 11·2	1·6	1·5	7·6	7·0	13·6	12·6
17	13 49·3	13 51·5	13 11·5	1·7	1·6	7·7	7·1	13·7	12·7
18	13 49·5	13 51·8	13 11·7	1·8	1·7	7·8	7·2	13·8	12·8
19	13 49·8	13 52·0	13 12·0	1·9	1·8	7·9	7·3	13·9	12·9
20	13 50·0	13 52·3	13 12·2	2·0	1·9	8·0	7·4	14·0	13·0
21	13 50·3	13 52·5	13 12·4	2·1	1·9	8·1	7·5	14·1	13·0
22	13 50·5	13 52·8	13 12·7	2·2	2·0	8·2	7·6	14·2	13·1
23	13 50·8	13 53·0	13 12·9	2·3	2·1	8·3	7·7	14·3	13·2
24	13 51·0	13 53·3	13 13·1	2·4	2·2	8·4	7·8	14·4	13·3
25	13 51·3	13 53·5	13 13·4	2·5	2·3	8·5	7·9	14·5	13·4
26	13 51·5	13 53·8	13 13·6	2·6	2·4	8·6	8·0	14·6	13·5
27	13 51·8	13 54·0	13 13·9	2·7	2·5	8·7	8·0	14·7	13·6
28	13 52·0	13 54·3	13 14·1	2·8	2·6	8·8	8·1	14·8	13·7
29	13 52·3	13 54·5	13 14·3	2·9	2·7	8·9	8·2	14·9	13·8
30	13 52·5	13 54·8	13 14·6	3·0	2·8	9·0	8·3	15·0	13·9
31	13 52·8	13 55·0	13 14·8	3·1	2·9	9·1	8·4	15·1	14·0
32	13 53·0	13 55·3	13 15·1	3·2	3·0	9·2	8·5	15·2	14·1
33	13 53·3	13 55·5	13 15·3	3·3	3·1	9·3	8·6	15·3	14·2
34	13 53·5	13 55·8	13 15·5	3·4	3·1	9·4	8·7	15·4	14·2
35	13 53·8	13 56·0	13 15·8	3·5	3·2	9·5	8·8	15·5	14·3
36	13 54·0	13 56·3	13 16·0	3·6	3·3	9·6	8·9	15·6	14·4
37	13 54·3	13 56·5	13 16·2	3·7	3·4	9·7	9·0	15·7	14·5
38	13 54·5	13 56·8	13 16·5	3·8	3·5	9·8	9·1	15·8	14·6
39	13 54·8	13 57·0	13 16·7	3·9	3·6	9·9	9·2	15·9	14·7
40	13 55·0	13 57·3	13 17·0	4·0	3·7	10·0	9·3	16·0	14·8
41	13 55·3	13 57·5	13 17·2	4·1	3·8	10·1	9·3	16·1	14·9
42	13 55·5	13 57·8	13 17·4	4·2	3·9	10·2	9·4	16·2	15·0
43	13 55·8	13 58·0	13 17·7	4·3	4·0	10·3	9·5	16·3	15·1
44	13 56·0	13 58·3	13 17·9	4·4	4·1	10·4	9·6	16·4	15·2
45	13 56·3	13 58·5	13 18·2	4·5	4·2	10·5	9·7	16·5	15·3
46	13 56·5	13 58·8	13 18·4	4·6	4·3	10·6	9·8	16·6	15·4
47	13 56·8	13 59·0	13 18·6	4·7	4·3	10·7	9·9	16·7	15·4
48	13 57·0	13 59·3	13 18·9	4·8	4·4	10·8	10·0	16·8	15·5
49	13 57·3	13 59·5	13 19·1	4·9	4·5	10·9	10·1	16·9	15·6
50	13 57·5	13 59·8	13 19·3	5·0	4·6	11·0	10·2	17·0	15·7
51	13 57·8	14 00·0	13 19·6	5·1	4·7	11·1	10·3	17·1	15·8
52	13 58·0	14 00·3	13 19·8	5·2	4·8	11·2	10·4	17·2	15·9
53	13 58·3	14 00·5	13 20·1	5·3	4·9	11·3	10·5	17·3	16·0
54	13 58·5	14 00·8	13 20·3	5·4	5·0	11·4	10·5	17·4	16·1
55	13 58·8	14 01·0	13 20·5	5·5	5·1	11·5	10·6	17·5	16·2
56	13 59·0	14 01·3	13 20·8	5·6	5·2	11·6	10·7	17·6	16·3
57	13 59·3	14 01·5	13 21·0	5·7	5·3	11·7	10·8	17·7	16·4
58	13 59·5	14 01·8	13 21·3	5·8	5·4	11·8	10·9	17·8	16·5
59	13 59·8	14 02·0	13 21·5	5·9	5·5	11·9	11·0	17·9	16·6
60	14 00·0	14 02·3	13 21·7	6·0	5·6	12·0	11·1	18·0	16·7

56ᵐ	SUN PLANETS	ARIES	MOON	v or Corrⁿ d	v or Corrⁿ d	v or Corrⁿ d	57ᵐ	SUN PLANETS	ARIES	MOON	v or Corrⁿ d	v or Corrⁿ d	v or Corrⁿ d
s	° ′	° ′	° ′	′ ′	′ ′	′ ′	s	° ′	° ′	° ′	′ ′	′ ′	′ ′
00	14 00·0	14 02·3	13 21·7	0·0 0·0	6·0 5·7	12·0 11·3	00	14 15·0	14 17·3	13 36·1	0·0 0·0	6·0 5·8	12·0 11·5
01	14 00·3	14 02·6	13 22·0	0·1 0·1	6·1 5·7	12·1 11·4	01	14 15·3	14 17·6	13 36·3	0·1 0·1	6·1 5·8	12·1 11·6
02	14 00·5	14 02·8	13 22·2	0·2 0·2	6·2 5·8	12·2 11·5	02	14 15·5	14 17·8	13 36·5	0·2 0·2	6·2 5·9	12·2 11·7
03	14 00·8	14 03·1	13 22·4	0·3 0·3	6·3 5·9	12·3 11·6	03	14 15·8	14 18·1	13 36·8	0·3 0·3	6·3 6·0	12·3 11·8
04	14 01·0	14 03·3	13 22·7	0·4 0·4	6·4 6·0	12·4 11·7	04	14 16·0	14 18·3	13 37·0	0·4 0·4	6·4 6·1	12·4 11·9
05	14 01·3	14 03·6	13 22·9	0·5 0·5	6·5 6·1	12·5 11·8	05	14 16·3	14 18·6	13 37·2	0·5 0·5	6·5 6·2	12·5 12·0
06	14 01·5	14 03·8	13 23·2	0·6 0·6	6·6 6·2	12·6 11·9	06	14 16·5	14 18·8	13 37·5	0·6 0·6	6·6 6·3	12·6 12·1
07	14 01·8	14 04·1	13 23·4	0·7 0·7	6·7 6·3	12·7 12·0	07	14 16·8	14 19·1	13 37·7	0·7 0·7	6·7 6·4	12·7 12·2
08	14 02·0	14 04·3	13 23·6	0·8 0·8	6·8 6·4	12·8 12·1	08	14 17·0	14 19·3	13 38·0	0·8 0·8	6·8 6·5	12·8 12·3
09	14 02·3	14 04·6	13 23·9	0·9 0·9	6·9 6·5	12·9 12·1	09	14 17·3	14 19·6	13 38·2	0·9 0·9	6·9 6·6	12·9 12·4
10	14 02·5	14 04·8	13 24·1	1·0 0·9	7·0 6·6	13·0 12·2	10	14 17·5	14 19·8	13 38·4	1·0 1·0	7·0 6·7	13·0 12·5
11	14 02·8	14 05·1	13 24·4	1·1 1·0	7·1 6·7	13·1 12·3	11	14 17·8	14 20·1	13 38·7	1·1 1·1	7·1 6·8	13·1 12·6
12	14 03·0	14 05·3	13 24·6	1·2 1·1	7·2 6·8	13·2 12·4	12	14 18·0	14 20·3	13 38·9	1·2 1·2	7·2 6·9	13·2 12·7
13	14 03·3	14 05·6	13 24·8	1·3 1·2	7·3 6·9	13·3 12·5	13	14 18·3	14 20·6	13 39·2	1·3 1·2	7·3 7·0	13·3 12·7
14	14 03·5	14 05·8	13 25·1	1·4 1·3	7·4 7·0	13·4 12·6	14	14 18·5	14 20·9	13 39·4	1·4 1·3	7·4 7·1	13·4 12·8
15	14 03·8	14 06·1	13 25·3	1·5 1·4	7·5 7·1	13·5 12·7	15	14 18·8	14 21·1	13 39·6	1·5 1·4	7·5 7·2	13·5 12·9
16	14 04·0	14 06·3	13 25·6	1·6 1·5	7·6 7·2	13·6 12·8	16	14 19·0	14 21·4	13 39·9	1·6 1·5	7·6 7·3	13·6 13·0
17	14 04·3	14 06·6	13 25·8	1·7 1·6	7·7 7·3	13·7 12·9	17	14 19·3	14 21·6	13 40·1	1·7 1·6	7·7 7·4	13·7 13·1
18	14 04·5	14 06·8	13 26·0	1·8 1·7	7·8 7·3	13·8 13·0	18	14 19·5	14 21·9	13 40·3	1·8 1·7	7·8 7·5	13·8 13·2
19	14 04·8	14 07·1	13 26·3	1·9 1·8	7·9 7·4	13·9 13·1	19	14 19·8	14 22·1	13 40·6	1·9 1·8	7·9 7·6	13·9 13·3
20	14 05·0	14 07·3	13 26·5	2·0 1·9	8·0 7·5	14·0 13·2	20	14 20·0	14 22·4	13 40·8	2·0 1·9	8·0 7·7	14·0 13·4
21	14 05·3	14 07·6	13 26·7	2·1 2·0	8·1 7·6	14·1 13·3	21	14 20·3	14 22·6	13 41·1	2·1 2·0	8·1 7·8	14·1 13·5
22	14 05·5	14 07·8	13 27·0	2·2 2·1	8·2 7·7	14·2 13·4	22	14 20·5	14 22·9	13 41·3	2·2 2·1	8·2 7·9	14·2 13·6
23	14 05·8	14 08·1	13 27·2	2·3 2·2	8·3 7·8	14·3 13·5	23	14 20·8	14 23·1	13 41·5	2·3 2·2	8·3 8·0	14·3 13·7
24	14 06·0	14 08·3	13 27·5	2·4 2·3	8·4 7·9	14·4 13·6	24	14 21·0	14 23·4	13 41·8	2·4 2·3	8·4 8·1	14·4 13·8
25	14 06·3	14 08·6	13 27·7	2·5 2·4	8·5 8·0	14·5 13·7	25	14 21·3	14 23·6	13 42·0	2·5 2·4	8·5 8·1	14·5 13·9
26	14 06·5	14 08·8	13 27·9	2·6 2·4	8·6 8·1	14·6 13·7	26	14 21·5	14 23·9	13 42·3	2·6 2·5	8·6 8·2	14·6 14·0
27	14 06·8	14 09·1	13 28·2	2·7 2·5	8·7 8·2	14·7 13·8	27	14 21·8	14 24·1	13 42·5	2·7 2·6	8·7 8·3	14·7 14·1
28	14 07·0	14 09·3	13 28·4	2·8 2·6	8·8 8·3	14·8 13·9	28	14 22·0	14 24·4	13 42·7	2·8 2·7	8·8 8·4	14·8 14·2
29	14 07·3	14 09·6	13 28·7	2·9 2·7	8·9 8·4	14·9 14·0	29	14 22·3	14 24·6	13 43·0	2·9 2·8	8·9 8·5	14·9 14·3
30	14 07·5	14 09·8	13 28·9	3·0 2·8	9·0 8·5	15·0 14·1	30	14 22·5	14 24·9	13 43·2	3·0 2·9	9·0 8·6	15·0 14·4
31	14 07·8	14 10·1	13 29·1	3·1 2·9	9·1 8·6	15·1 14·2	31	14 22·8	14 25·1	13 43·4	3·1 3·0	9·1 8·7	15·1 14·5
32	14 08·0	14 10·3	13 29·4	3·2 3·0	9·2 8·7	15·2 14·3	32	14 23·0	14 25·4	13 43·7	3·2 3·1	9·2 8·8	15·2 14·6
33	14 08·3	14 10·6	13 29·6	3·3 3·1	9·3 8·8	15·3 14·4	33	14 23·3	14 25·6	13 43·9	3·3 3·2	9·3 8·9	15·3 14·7
34	14 08·5	14 10·8	13 29·8	3·4 3·2	9·4 8·9	15·4 14·5	34	14 23·5	14 25·9	13 44·2	3·4 3·3	9·4 9·0	15·4 14·8
35	14 08·8	14 11·1	13 30·1	3·5 3·3	9·5 8·9	15·5 14·6	35	14 23·8	14 26·1	13 44·4	3·5 3·4	9·5 9·1	15·5 14·9
36	14 09·0	14 11·3	13 30·3	3·6 3·4	9·6 9·0	15·6 14·7	36	14 24·0	14 26·4	13 44·6	3·6 3·5	9·6 9·2	15·6 15·0
37	14 09·3	14 11·6	13 30·6	3·7 3·5	9·7 9·1	15·7 14·8	37	14 24·3	14 26·6	13 44·9	3·7 3·5	9·7 9·3	15·7 15·0
38	14 09·5	14 11·8	13 30·8	3·8 3·6	9·8 9·2	15·8 14·9	38	14 24·5	14 26·9	13 45·1	3·8 3·6	9·8 9·4	15·8 15·1
39	14 09·8	14 12·1	13 31·0	3·9 3·7	9·9 9·3	15·9 15·0	39	14 24·8	14 27·1	13 45·4	3·9 3·7	9·9 9·5	15·9 15·2
40	14 10·0	14 12·3	13 31·3	4·0 3·8	10·0 9·4	16·0 15·1	40	14 25·0	14 27·4	13 45·6	4·0 3·8	10·0 9·6	16·0 15·3
41	14 10·3	14 12·6	13 31·5	4·1 3·9	10·1 9·5	16·1 15·2	41	14 25·3	14 27·6	13 45·8	4·1 3·9	10·1 9·7	16·1 15·4
42	14 10·5	14 12·8	13 31·8	4·2 4·0	10·2 9·6	16·2 15·3	42	14 25·5	14 27·9	13 46·1	4·2 4·0	10·2 9·8	16·2 15·5
43	14 10·8	14 13·1	13 32·0	4·3 4·0	10·3 9·7	16·3 15·3	43	14 25·8	14 28·1	13 46·3	4·3 4·1	10·3 9·9	16·3 15·6
44	14 11·0	14 13·3	13 32·2	4·4 4·1	10·4 9·8	16·4 15·4	44	14 26·0	14 28·4	13 46·5	4·4 4·2	10·4 10·0	16·4 15·7
45	14 11·3	14 13·6	13 32·5	4·5 4·2	10·5 9·9	16·5 15·5	45	14 26·3	14 28·6	13 46·8	4·5 4·3	10·5 10·1	16·5 15·8
46	14 11·5	14 13·8	13 32·7	4·6 4·3	10·6 10·0	16·6 15·6	46	14 26·5	14 28·9	13 47·0	4·6 4·4	10·6 10·2	16·6 15·9
47	14 11·8	14 14·1	13 32·9	4·7 4·4	10·7 10·1	16·7 15·7	47	14 26·8	14 29·1	13 47·3	4·7 4·5	10·7 10·3	16·7 16·0
48	14 12·0	14 14·3	13 33·2	4·8 4·5	10·8 10·2	16·8 15·8	48	14 27·0	14 29·4	13 47·5	4·8 4·6	10·8 10·4	16·8 16·1
49	14 12·3	14 14·6	13 33·4	4·9 4·6	10·9 10·3	16·9 15·9	49	14 27·3	14 29·6	13 47·7	4·9 4·7	10·9 10·4	16·9 16·2
50	14 12·5	14 14·8	13 33·7	5·0 4·7	11·0 10·4	17·0 16·0	50	14 27·5	14 29·9	13 48·0	5·0 4·8	11·0 10·5	17·0 16·3
51	14 12·8	14 15·1	13 33·9	5·1 4·8	11·1 10·5	17·1 16·1	51	14 27·8	14 30·1	13 48·2	5·1 4·9	11·1 10·6	17·1 16·4
52	14 13·0	14 15·3	13 34·1	5·2 4·9	11·2 10·5	17·2 16·2	52	14 28·0	14 30·4	13 48·5	5·2 5·0	11·2 10·7	17·2 16·5
53	14 13·3	14 15·6	13 34·4	5·3 5·0	11·3 10·6	17·3 16·3	53	14 28·3	14 30·6	13 48·7	5·3 5·1	11·3 10·8	17·3 16·6
54	14 13·5	14 15·8	13 34·6	5·4 5·1	11·4 10·7	17·4 16·4	54	14 28·5	14 30·9	13 48·9	5·4 5·2	11·4 10·9	17·4 16·7
55	14 13·8	14 16·1	13 34·9	5·5 5·2	11·5 10·8	17·5 16·5	55	14 28·8	14 31·1	13 49·2	5·5 5·3	11·5 11·0	17·5 16·8
56	14 14·0	14 16·3	13 35·1	5·6 5·3	11·6 10·9	17·6 16·6	56	14 29·0	14 31·4	13 49·4	5·6 5·4	11·6 11·1	17·6 16·9
57	14 14·3	14 16·6	13 35·3	5·7 5·4	11·7 11·0	17·7 16·7	57	14 29·3	14 31·6	13 49·7	5·7 5·5	11·7 11·2	17·7 17·0
58	14 14·5	14 16·8	13 35·6	5·8 5·5	11·8 11·1	17·8 16·8	58	14 29·5	14 31·9	13 49·9	5·8 5·6	11·8 11·3	17·8 17·1
59	14 14·8	14 17·1	13 35·8	5·9 5·6	11·9 11·2	17·9 16·9	59	14 29·8	14 32·1	13 50·1	5·9 5·7	11·9 11·4	17·9 17·2
60	14 15·0	14 17·3	13 36·1	6·0 5·7	12·0 11·3	18·0 17·0	60	14 30·0	14 32·4	13 50·4	6·0 5·8	12·0 11·5	18·0 17·3

58 m	SUN PLANETS	ARIES	MOON	v or Corrⁿ d		v or Corrⁿ d		v or Corrⁿ d		59 m	SUN PLANETS	ARIES	MOON	v or Corrⁿ d		v or Corrⁿ d		v or Corrⁿ d	
s	° ′	° ′	° ′	′	′	′	′	′	′	s	° ′	° ′	° ′	′	′	′	′	′	′
00	14 30·0	14 32·4	13 50·4	0·0	0·0	6·0	5·9	12·0	11·7	00	14 45·0	14 47·4	14 04·7	0·0	0·0	6·0	6·0	12·0	11·9
01	14 30·3	14 32·6	13 50·6	0·1	0·1	6·1	5·9	12·1	11·8	01	14 45·3	14 47·7	14 04·9	0·1	0·1	6·1	6·0	12·1	12·0
02	14 30·5	14 32·9	13 50·8	0·2	0·2	6·2	6·0	12·2	11·9	02	14 45·5	14 47·9	14 05·2	0·2	0·2	6·2	6·1	12·2	12·1
03	14 30·8	14 33·1	13 51·1	0·3	0·3	6·3	6·1	12·3	12·0	03	14 45·8	14 48·2	14 05·4	0·3	0·3	6·3	6·2	12·3	12·2
04	14 31·0	14 33·4	13 51·3	0·4	0·4	6·4	6·2	12·4	12·1	04	14 46·0	14 48·4	14 05·6	0·4	0·4	6·4	6·3	12·4	12·3
05	14 31·3	14 33·6	13 51·6	0·5	0·5	6·5	6·3	12·5	12·2	05	14 46·3	14 48·7	14 05·9	0·5	0·5	6·5	6·4	12·5	12·4
06	14 31·5	14 33·9	13 51·8	0·6	0·6	6·6	6·4	12·6	12·3	06	14 46·5	14 48·9	14 06·1	0·6	0·6	6·6	6·5	12·6	12·5
07	14 31·8	14 34·1	13 52·0	0·7	0·7	6·7	6·5	12·7	12·4	07	14 46·8	14 49·2	14 06·4	0·7	0·7	6·7	6·6	12·7	12·6
08	14 32·0	14 34·4	13 52·3	0·8	0·8	6·8	6·6	12·8	12·5	08	14 47·0	14 49·4	14 06·6	0·8	0·8	6·8	6·7	12·8	12·7
09	14 32·3	14 34·6	13 52·5	0·9	0·9	6·9	6·7	12·9	12·6	09	14 47·3	14 49·7	14 06·8	0·9	0·9	6·9	6·8	12·9	12·8
10	14 32·5	14 34·9	13 52·8	1·0	1·0	7·0	6·8	13·0	12·7	10	14 47·5	14 49·9	14 07·1	1·0	1·0	7·0	6·9	13·0	12·9
11	14 32·8	14 35·1	13 53·0	1·1	1·1	7·1	6·9	13·1	12·8	11	14 47·8	14 50·2	14 07·3	1·1	1·1	7·1	7·0	13·1	13·0
12	14 33·0	14 35·4	13 53·2	1·2	1·2	7·2	7·0	13·2	12·9	12	14 48·0	14 50·4	14 07·5	1·2	1·2	7·2	7·1	13·2	13·1
13	14 33·3	14 35·6	13 53·5	1·3	1·3	7·3	7·1	13·3	13·0	13	14 48·3	14 50·7	14 07·8	1·3	1·3	7·3	7·2	13·3	13·2
14	14 33·5	14 35·9	13 53·7	1·4	1·4	7·4	7·2	13·4	13·1	14	14 48·5	14 50·9	14 08·0	1·4	1·4	7·4	7·3	13·4	13·3
15	14 33·8	14 36·1	13 53·9	1·5	1·5	7·5	7·3	13·5	13·2	15	14 48·8	14 51·2	14 08·3	1·5	1·5	7·5	7·4	13·5	13·4
16	14 34·0	14 36·4	13 54·2	1·6	1·6	7·6	7·4	13·6	13·3	16	14 49·0	14 51·4	14 08·5	1·6	1·6	7·6	7·5	13·6	13·5
17	14 34·3	14 36·6	13 54·4	1·7	1·7	7·7	7·5	13·7	13·4	17	14 49·3	14 51·7	14 08·7	1·7	1·7	7·7	7·6	13·7	13·6
18	14 34·5	14 36·9	13 54·7	1·8	1·8	7·8	7·6	13·8	13·5	18	14 49·5	14 51·9	14 09·0	1·8	1·8	7·8	7·7	13·8	13·7
19	14 34·8	14 37·1	13 54·9	1·9	1·9	7·9	7·7	13·9	13·6	19	14 49·8	14 52·2	14 09·2	1·9	1·9	7·9	7·8	13·9	13·8
20	14 35·0	14 37·4	13 55·1	2·0	2·0	8·0	7·8	14·0	13·7	20	14 50·0	14 52·4	14 09·5	2·0	2·0	8·0	7·9	14·0	13·9
21	14 35·3	14 37·6	13 55·4	2·1	2·0	8·1	7·9	14·1	13·7	21	14 50·3	14 52·7	14 09·7	2·1	2·1	8·1	8·0	14·1	14·0
22	14 35·5	14 37·9	13 55·6	2·2	2·1	8·2	8·0	14·2	13·8	22	14 50·5	14 52·9	14 09·9	2·2	2·2	8·2	8·1	14·2	14·1
23	14 35·8	14 38·1	13 55·9	2·3	2·2	8·3	8·1	14·3	13·9	23	14 50·8	14 53·2	14 10·2	2·3	2·3	8·3	8·2	14·3	14·2
24	14 36·0	14 38·4	13 56·1	2·4	2·3	8·4	8·2	14·4	14·0	24	14 51·0	14 53·4	14 10·4	2·4	2·4	8·4	8·3	14·4	14·3
25	14 36·3	14 38·6	13 56·3	2·5	2·4	8·5	8·3	14·5	14·1	25	14 51·3	14 53·7	14 10·6	2·5	2·5	8·5	8·4	14·5	14·4
26	14 36·5	14 38·9	13 56·6	2·6	2·5	8·6	8·4	14·6	14·2	26	14 51·5	14 53·9	14 10·9	2·6	2·6	8·6	8·5	14·6	14·5
27	14 36·8	14 39·2	13 56·8	2·7	2·6	8·7	8·5	14·7	14·3	27	14 51·8	14 54·2	14 11·1	2·7	2·7	8·7	8·6	14·7	14·6
28	14 37·0	14 39·4	13 57·0	2·8	2·7	8·8	8·6	14·8	14·4	28	14 52·0	14 54·4	14 11·4	2·8	2·8	8·8	8·7	14·8	14·7
29	14 37·3	14 39·7	13 57·3	2·9	2·8	8·9	8·7	14·9	14·5	29	14 52·3	14 54·7	14 11·6	2·9	2·9	8·9	8·8	14·9	14·8
30	14 37·5	14 39·9	13 57·5	3·0	2·9	9·0	8·8	15·0	14·6	30	14 52·5	14 54·9	14 11·8	3·0	3·0	9·0	8·9	15·0	14·9
31	14 37·8	14 40·2	13 57·8	3·1	3·0	9·1	8·9	15·1	14·7	31	14 52·8	14 55·2	14 12·1	3·1	3·1	9·1	9·0	15·1	15·0
32	14 38·0	14 40·4	13 58·0	3·2	3·1	9·2	9·0	15·2	14·8	32	14 53·0	14 55·4	14 12·3	3·2	3·2	9·2	9·1	15·2	15·1
33	14 38·3	14 40·7	13 58·2	3·3	3·2	9·3	9·1	15·3	14·9	33	14 53·3	14 55·7	14 12·6	3·3	3·3	9·3	9·2	15·3	15·2
34	14 38·5	14 40·9	13 58·5	3·4	3·3	9·4	9·2	15·4	15·0	34	14 53·5	14 55·9	14 12·8	3·4	3·4	9·4	9·3	15·4	15·3
35	14 38·8	14 41·2	13 58·7	3·5	3·4	9·5	9·3	15·5	15·1	35	14 53·8	14 56·2	14 13·0	3·5	3·5	9·5	9·4	15·5	15·4
36	14 39·0	14 41·4	13 59·0	3·6	3·5	9·6	9·4	15·6	15·2	36	14 54·0	14 56·4	14 13·3	3·6	3·6	9·6	9·5	15·6	15·5
37	14 39·3	14 41·7	13 59·2	3·7	3·6	9·7	9·5	15·7	15·3	37	14 54·3	14 56·7	14 13·5	3·7	3·7	9·7	9·6	15·7	15·6
38	14 39·5	14 41·9	13 59·4	3·8	3·7	9·8	9·6	15·8	15·4	38	14 54·5	14 56·9	14 13·8	3·8	3·8	9·8	9·7	15·8	15·7
39	14 39·8	14 42·2	13 59·7	3·9	3·8	9·9	9·7	15·9	15·5	39	14 54·8	14 57·2	14 14·0	3·9	3·9	9·9	9·8	15·9	15·8
40	14 40·0	14 42·4	13 59·9	4·0	3·9	10·0	9·8	16·0	15·6	40	14 55·0	14 57·5	14 14·2	4·0	4·0	10·0	9·9	16·0	15·9
41	14 40·3	14 42·7	14 00·1	4·1	4·0	10·1	9·8	16·1	15·7	41	14 55·3	14 57·7	14 14·5	4·1	4·1	10·1	10·0	16·1	16·0
42	14 40·5	14 42·9	14 00·4	4·2	4·1	10·2	9·9	16·2	15·8	42	14 55·5	14 58·0	14 14·7	4·2	4·2	10·2	10·1	16·2	16·1
43	14 40·8	14 43·2	14 00·6	4·3	4·2	10·3	10·0	16·3	15·9	43	14 55·8	14 58·2	14 14·9	4·3	4·3	10·3	10·2	16·3	16·2
44	14 41·0	14 43·4	14 00·9	4·4	4·3	10·4	10·1	16·4	16·0	44	14 56·0	14 58·5	14 15·2	4·4	4·4	10·4	10·3	16·4	16·3
45	14 41·3	14 43·7	14 01·1	4·5	4·4	10·5	10·2	16·5	16·1	45	14 56·3	14 58·7	14 15·4	4·5	4·5	10·5	10·4	16·5	16·4
46	14 41·5	14 43·9	14 01·3	4·6	4·5	10·6	10·3	16·6	16·2	46	14 56·5	14 59·0	14 15·7	4·6	4·6	10·6	10·5	16·6	16·5
47	14 41·8	14 44·2	14 01·6	4·7	4·6	10·7	10·4	16·7	16·3	47	14 56·8	14 59·2	14 15·9	4·7	4·7	10·7	10·6	16·7	16·6
48	14 42·0	14 44·4	14 01·8	4·8	4·7	10·8	10·5	16·8	16·4	48	14 57·0	14 59·5	14 16·1	4·8	4·8	10·8	10·7	16·8	16·7
49	14 42·3	14 44·7	14 02·1	4·9	4·8	10·9	10·6	16·9	16·5	49	14 57·3	14 59·7	14 16·4	4·9	4·9	10·9	10·8	16·9	16·8
50	14 42·5	14 44·9	14 02·3	5·0	4·9	11·0	10·7	17·0	16·6	50	14 57·5	15 00·0	14 16·6	5·0	5·0	11·0	10·9	17·0	16·9
51	14 42·8	14 45·2	14 02·5	5·1	5·0	11·1	10·8	17·1	16·7	51	14 57·8	15 00·2	14 16·9	5·1	5·1	11·1	11·0	17·1	17·0
52	14 43·0	14 45·4	14 02·8	5·2	5·1	11·2	10·9	17·2	16·8	52	14 58·0	15 00·5	14 17·1	5·2	5·2	11·2	11·1	17·2	17·1
53	14 43·3	14 45·7	14 03·0	5·3	5·2	11·3	11·0	17·3	16·9	53	14 58·3	15 00·7	14 17·3	5·3	5·3	11·3	11·2	17·3	17·2
54	14 43·5	14 45·9	14 03·3	5·4	5·3	11·4	11·1	17·4	17·0	54	14 58·5	15 01·0	14 17·6	5·4	5·4	11·4	11·3	17·4	17·3
55	14 43·8	14 46·2	14 03·5	5·5	5·4	11·5	11·2	17·5	17·1	55	14 58·8	15 01·2	14 17·8	5·5	5·5	11·5	11·4	17·5	17·4
56	14 44·0	14 46·4	14 03·7	5·6	5·5	11·6	11·3	17·6	17·2	56	14 59·0	15 01·5	14 18·0	5·6	5·6	11·6	11·5	17·6	17·5
57	14 44·3	14 46·7	14 04·0	5·7	5·6	11·7	11·4	17·7	17·3	57	14 59·3	15 01·7	14 18·3	5·7	5·7	11·7	11·6	17·7	17·6
58	14 44·5	14 46·9	14 04·2	5·8	5·7	11·8	11·5	17·8	17·4	58	14 59·5	15 02·0	14 18·5	5·8	5·8	11·8	11·7	17·8	17·7
59	14 44·8	14 47·2	14 04·4	5·9	5·8	11·9	11·6	17·9	17·5	59	14 59·8	15 02·2	14 18·8	5·9	5·9	11·9	11·8	17·9	17·8
60	14 45·0	14 47·4	14 04·7	6·0	5·9	12·0	11·7	18·0	17·6	60	15 00·0	15 02·5	14 19·0	6·0	6·0	12·0	11·9	18·0	17·9

ALTITUDE CORRECTION TABLES 0°–35°— MOON

App. Alt.	0°–4° Corrn	5°–9° Corrn	10°–14° Corrn	15°–19° Corrn	20°–24° Corrn	25°–29° Corrn	30°–34° Corrn	App. Alt.
00	0° 34.5	5° 58.2	10° 62.1	15° 62.8	20° 62.2	25° 60.8	30° 58.9	00
10	36.5	58.5	62.2	62.8	62.2	60.8	58.8	10
20	38.3	58.7	62.2	62.8	62.1	60.7	58.8	20
30	40.0	58.9	62.3	62.8	62.1	60.7	58.7	30
40	41.5	59.1	62.3	62.8	62.0	60.6	58.6	40
50	42.9	59.3	62.4	62.7	62.0	60.6	58.5	50
00	1° 44.2	6° 59.5	11° 62.4	16° 62.7	21° 62.0	26° 60.5	31° 58.5	00
10	45.4	59.7	62.4	62.7	61.9	60.4	58.4	10
20	46.5	59.9	62.5	62.7	61.9	60.4	58.3	20
30	47.5	60.0	62.5	62.7	61.9	60.3	58.2	30
40	48.4	60.2	62.5	62.7	61.8	60.3	58.2	40
50	49.3	60.3	62.6	62.7	61.8	60.2	58.1	50
00	2° 50.1	7° 60.5	12° 62.6	17° 62.7	22° 61.7	27° 60.1	32° 58.0	00
10	50.8	60.6	62.6	62.6	61.7	60.1	57.9	10
20	51.5	60.7	62.6	62.6	61.6	60.0	57.8	20
30	52.2	60.9	62.7	62.6	61.6	59.9	57.8	30
40	52.8	61.0	62.7	62.6	61.6	59.9	57.7	40
50	53.4	61.1	62.7	62.6	61.5	59.8	57.6	50
00	3° 53.9	8° 61.2	13° 62.7	18° 62.5	23° 61.5	28° 59.7	33° 57.5	00
10	54.4	61.3	62.7	62.5	61.4	59.7	57.4	10
20	54.9	61.4	62.7	62.5	61.4	59.6	57.4	20
30	55.3	61.5	62.8	62.5	61.3	59.5	57.3	30
40	55.7	61.6	62.8	62.4	61.3	59.5	57.2	40
50	56.1	61.6	62.8	62.4	61.2	59.4	57.1	50
00	4° 56.4	9° 61.7	14° 62.8	19° 62.4	24° 61.2	29° 59.3	34° 57.0	00
10	56.8	61.8	62.8	62.4	61.1	59.3	56.9	10
20	57.1	61.9	62.8	62.3	61.1	59.2	56.9	20
30	57.4	61.9	62.8	62.3	61.0	59.1	56.8	30
40	57.7	62.0	62.8	62.3	61.0	59.1	56.7	40
50	58.0	62.1	62.8	62.2	60.9	59.0	56.6	50

HP	L U	L U	L U	L U	L U	L U	L U	HP
54.0	0.3 0.9	0.3 0.9	0.4 1.0	0.5 1.1	0.6 1.2	0.7 1.3	0.9 1.5	54.0
54.3	0.7 1.1	0.7 1.2	0.8 1.2	0.8 1.3	0.9 1.4	1.1 1.5	1.2 1.7	54.3
54.6	1.1 1.4	1.1 1.4	1.1 1.4	1.2 1.5	1.3 1.6	1.4 1.7	1.5 1.8	54.6
54.9	1.4 1.6	1.5 1.6	1.5 1.6	1.6 1.7	1.6 1.8	1.8 1.9	1.9 2.0	54.9
55.2	1.8 1.8	1.8 1.8	1.9 1.8	1.9 1.9	2.0 2.0	2.1 2.1	2.2 2.2	55.2
55.5	2.2 2.0	2.2 2.0	2.3 2.1	2.3 2.1	2.4 2.2	2.4 2.3	2.5 2.4	55.5
55.8	2.6 2.2	2.6 2.2	2.6 2.3	2.7 2.3	2.7 2.4	2.8 2.4	2.9 2.5	55.8
56.1	3.0 2.4	3.0 2.5	3.0 2.5	3.0 2.5	3.1 2.6	3.1 2.6	3.2 2.7	56.1
56.4	3.3 2.7	3.4 2.7	3.4 2.7	3.4 2.7	3.4 2.8	3.5 2.8	3.5 2.9	56.4
56.7	3.7 2.9	3.7 2.9	3.8 2.9	3.8 2.9	3.8 3.0	3.8 3.0	3.9 3.0	56.7
57.0	4.1 3.1	4.1 3.1	4.1 3.1	4.1 3.1	4.2 3.2	4.2 3.2	4.2 3.2	57.0
57.3	4.5 3.3	4.5 3.3	4.5 3.3	4.5 3.3	4.5 3.3	4.5 3.4	4.6 3.4	57.3
57.6	4.9 3.5	4.9 3.5	4.9 3.5	4.9 3.5	4.9 3.5	4.9 3.5	4.9 3.6	57.6
57.9	5.3 3.8	5.3 3.8	5.2 3.8	5.2 3.7	5.2 3.7	5.2 3.7	5.2 3.7	57.9
58.2	5.6 4.0	5.6 4.0	5.6 4.0	5.6 4.0	5.6 3.9	5.6 3.9	5.6 3.9	58.2
58.5	6.0 4.2	6.0 4.2	6.0 4.2	6.0 4.2	6.0 4.1	5.9 4.1	5.9 4.1	58.5
58.8	6.4 4.4	6.4 4.4	6.4 4.4	6.3 4.4	6.3 4.3	6.3 4.3	6.2 4.2	58.8
59.1	6.8 4.6	6.8 4.6	6.7 4.6	6.7 4.6	6.7 4.5	6.6 4.5	6.6 4.4	59.1
59.4	7.2 4.8	7.1 4.8	7.1 4.8	7.1 4.8	7.0 4.7	7.0 4.7	6.9 4.6	59.4
59.7	7.5 5.1	7.5 5.0	7.5 5.0	7.5 5.0	7.4 4.9	7.3 4.8	7.2 4.8	59.7
60.0	7.9 5.3	7.9 5.3	7.9 5.2	7.8 5.2	7.8 5.1	7.7 5.0	7.6 4.9	60.0
60.3	8.3 5.5	8.3 5.5	8.2 5.4	8.2 5.4	8.1 5.3	8.0 5.2	7.9 5.1	60.3
60.6	8.7 5.7	8.7 5.7	8.6 5.7	8.6 5.6	8.5 5.5	8.4 5.4	8.2 5.3	60.6
60.9	9.1 5.9	9.0 5.9	9.0 5.9	8.9 5.8	8.8 5.7	8.7 5.6	8.6 5.4	60.9
61.2	9.5 6.2	9.4 6.1	9.4 6.1	9.3 6.0	9.2 5.9	9.1 5.8	8.9 5.6	61.2
61.5	9.8 6.4	9.8 6.3	9.7 6.3	9.7 6.2	9.5 6.1	9.4 5.9	9.2 5.8	61.5

DIP

Ht. of Eye	Corrn	Ht. of Eye	Ht. of Eye	Corrn	Ht. of Eye
m		ft.	m		ft.
2.4	−2.8	8.0	9.5	−5.5	31.5
2.6	−2.9	8.6	9.9	−5.6	32.7
2.8	−3.0	9.2	10.3	−5.7	33.9
3.0	−3.1	9.8	10.6	−5.8	35.1
3.2	−3.2	10.5	11.0	−5.9	36.3
3.4	−3.3	11.2	11.4	−6.0	37.6
3.6	−3.4	11.9	11.8	−6.1	38.9
3.8	−3.5	12.6	12.2	−6.2	40.1
4.0	−3.6	13.3	12.6	−6.3	41.5
4.3	−3.7	14.1	13.0	−6.4	42.8
4.5	−3.8	14.9	13.4	−6.5	44.2
4.7	−3.9	15.7	13.8	−6.6	45.5
5.0	−4.0	16.5	14.2	−6.7	46.9
5.2	−4.1	17.4	14.7	−6.8	48.4
5.5	−4.2	18.3	15.1	−6.9	49.8
5.8	−4.3	19.1	15.5	−7.0	51.3
6.1	−4.4	20.1	16.0	−7.1	52.8
6.3	−4.5	21.0	16.5	−7.2	54.3
6.6	−4.6	22.0	16.9	−7.3	55.8
6.9	−4.7	22.9	17.4	−7.4	57.4
7.2	−4.8	23.9	17.9	−7.5	58.9
7.5	−4.9	24.9	18.4	−7.6	60.5
7.9	−5.0	26.0	18.8	−7.7	62.1
8.2	−5.1	27.1	19.3	−7.8	63.8
8.5	−5.2	28.1	19.8	−7.9	65.4
8.8	−5.3	29.2	20.4	−8.0	67.1
9.2	−5.4	30.4	20.9	−8.1	68.8
9.5		31.5	21.4		70.5

MOON CORRECTION TABLE

The correction is in two parts; the first correction is taken from the upper part of the table with argument apparent altitude, and the second from the lower part, with argument HP, in the same column as that from which the first correction was taken. Separate corrections are given in the lower part for lower (L) and upper(U) limbs. All corrections are to be **added** to apparent altitude, *but* 30′ *is to be subtracted from the altitude of the upper limb.*

For corrections for pressure and temperature see page A4.

For bubble sextant observations ignore dip, take the mean of upper and lower limb corrections and subtract 15′ from the altitude.

App. Alt. = Apparent altitude = Sextant altitude corrected for index error and dip.